THE OXFORD COMPANION TO THE DECORATIVE ARTS

EDITED BY

HAROLD OSBORNE

Oxford New York
OXFORD UNIVERSITY PRESS

Oxford University Press, Walton Street, Oxford OX2 6DP

Oxford New York Toronto
Petaling Jaya Singapore Hong Kong Tokyo
Delhi Bombay Calcutta Madras Karachi
Nairobi Dar es Salaam Cape Town
Melbourne Auckland

and associated companies in
Berlin Ibadan

Oxford is a trade mark of Oxford University Press

First published 1975
First issued as an Oxford University Press paperback,
with corrections, 1985
Reprinted 1985 (with corrections), 1986, 1988

British Library Cataloguing in Publication Data
The Oxford companion to the decorative arts.
—(Oxford paperbacks)
1. Art, Decorative—Dictionaries
2. Decoration and ornament—Dictionaries
I. Osborne, Harold
745'.03'21 NK28
ISBN 0–19–281863–5

Library of Congress Cataloging in Publication Data
The Oxford companion to the decorative arts.
(Oxford paperbacks)
Bibliography: p.
Includes index.
1.Decorative arts—Dictionaries
I. Osborne, Harold, 1905–
NK30093 1985 745'.03'21 84–19072
ISBN 0–19–281863–5 (pbk.)

Printed in Great Britain
at the University Printing House, Oxford
by David Stanford
Printer to the University

PREFACE

FOR reasons of space it was found necessary to confine *The Oxford Companion to Art* to what are known as the fine arts. The purpose of the present Companion is to provide a similar introduction to those arts which are made to serve a practical purpose but are nevertheless prized for the quality of their workmanship and the beauty of their appearance. The Companion includes major crafts whose origin goes back to prehistoric times such as leather-working, ceramics, textiles, costume, wood-working, metal-working, glass-making and so on; crafts which have arisen since the dawn of history such as bell-founding, paper-making, clock-making, typography, landscape gardening, photography; and specialised or luxury crafts such as arms and armour, enamels, lacquer, jewellery, toys, lace-making and embroidery. There is no single term which precisely and elegantly defines this field. The words 'practical' and 'useful' are both wider in their implications than is required. Following the French practice, the museums speak of the 'decorative arts' and this term has been adopted in the title of the Companion. It is in the field covered by the Companion that craftsmanship has made its most signal contribution to human progress and in some sectors the history of its achievement constitutes the archaeology of modern machine industry.

The distinction between the fine and the 'decorative' arts is ultimately a pragmatic one. It was unknown in antiquity and has been foreign to the outlook of most cultures other than our own. The very concept of fine art, with its aura of associated mystiques, arose late in the artistic history of the West, becoming established only in the course of the eighteenth century. Yet the distinction is now familiar and if a division has to be made, this one is both convenient and harmless so long as one recognizes that any classification which follows from it will be to some extent arbitrary. In *The Oxford Companion to Art* the expression 'fine art' was interpreted generously and some overlapping is inevitable. But the areas of overlap have been reduced to a minimum consistently with making each Companion independent and complete in itself.

Two of the most important border-line areas are occupied by architecture and ceramics and aspects of both were included in *The Oxford Companion to Art* for reasons explained in the Introduction to that work. Architecture, although not classified by Aristotle with the 'imitative' arts, has been traditionally one of the 'five arts' which were together regarded as 'arts of beauty' or fine arts. But with its related crafts of building and construction, quite apart from its multifarious decorative adjuncts, architecture forms so vast a theme that it could be treated in depth only by a separate Companion, and no attempt has been made to bring it within the scope of the present work. Ceramics is in a different position. It is here dealt with at some length as a fine craft in its own right rather than a manifestation of artistic style or evolving traditions of design. There are other border-line cases, such as bookbinding and typography, which together with other aspects of book production have been brought within the scope of the present Companion.

PREFACE

The word 'art', from the Latin *ars* or 'skill', is familiarly employed with both general and specific meanings in ordinary language. We speak of the 'art' of surgery, of fencing, of diplomacy, and so on. As a rough-and-ready guide it was decided in the first place to include in this Companion only arts or skills from whose exercise some enduring physical object is produced. Thus we exclude the arts of fencing and military tacts but include the making of arms and armour. As a border-line case we have included landscape gardening at periods when this and horticulture were reckoned among the aesthetic recreations. Among the arts which fall within our definition precedence has been given to those where delight in the design and appearance of the product has carried more weight than functional utility although both factors are usually present. Thus we have included decorative ironwork and costume, for example, but have excluded the crafts of the cooper, the wainwright, the shipbuilder and those connected with transport generally. The arts of stage design and the making of musical instruments belong rather to other Oxford Companions.

With these qualifications and necessary restrictions the idea of fine craftsmanship has been taken as the unifying concept and guiding thread of the book. To a certain extent this survey of craftsmanship breaks new ground. There have been studies and histories of the fine arts galore. There exist some general histories of technology. Comprehensive studies of particular crafts at various times and in different cultures attest a growing interest in the practical and decorative arts. But until now there has been no attempt to provide in one volume a general introduction to craftsmanship and its exercise on a world-wide basis.

Craftsmanship means more than technical virtuosity. It demands a profound understanding of materials and of the tools with which materials are fashioned. Most important of all it involves a genuine pride in the process of production itself, a pride which drives a man to make whatever things he makes as well as they can be made, even beyond what is required by the purpose they are designed to serve and beyond economic considerations of reward. This impulse, which lies at the roots of fine craftsmanship, is now recognized by anthropologists to have existed from the earliest stages of human activity. Graham Clark and Stuart Piggott, for example, in *Prehistoric Societies* (1965) find evidence in the Lower Palaeolithic age of what they call the 'cult of excellence, the determination to make things as perfect as they could be made, even if at a purely utilitarian level perfection might seem excessive . . .'. It is this impulse, almost a fixation, this cult of excellence, which through the centuries of prehistory and history led to the perpetuation of traditions of craftsmanship, the rich storehouses of know-how and skill. Gradually, in Western civilisation, more rapidly with some crafts and more slowly with others, the transmitted know-how and the inherited skills of the craftsmen have been converted into industrial science with articulate rules until, with something of a historical leap, we have reached the technological age of today, an age of predominantly machine production in which standardization ousts individuality and a premium is placed upon precision at the expense of personality. Over large areas of production the precision engineer and industrial designer have taken the place of the older craftsman while 'artist–craftsmen' survive in isolated pockets as a sentimental anachronism. At the same time the age-long 'cult of perfection' bids well to disappear. Often consumer goods are no longer made as well as they could be made, nor made to last as long as they could be made to last, but are deliberately adapted to the economics of the market. Not all factory products are designed to 'last for ever' but rather we live in an age when many goods are purposely given shorter lives or are cheaply and shoddily constructed in order that the demand for new ones may continue, when the fashion for novelty at all costs is fostered and when pride in individual workmanship is tending to disappear from our manufactories. It is against this background that the historical survey of craftsmanship was planned. By and large the story stops at the place where in each art developing craftsmanship surrenders to mass production. This is not necessarily the stage at which handicraft gives place to the machine. The distinction between tool and machine is after all a fine one and in certain areas some degree of craftsmanship has gone hand in hand with machine manufacture. Rather the distinction is connected with the ethics of mass production and the profit economy with consequent loss of the craftsman's pride in his work.

Although it is cast in the form of a one-volume encyclopedia, this work does not aspire to the detailed comprehensiveness of a conventional encyclopedia. Like the other Oxford Companions, it is conceived rather as a handbook whose purpose is to give introductory surveys over a very wide field. The articles are intended to furnish a preliminary insight into their subjects and together with the bibliographies (usually indicated by numerical references at the end of the article to a general bibliography) to serve as a guide for further study. The books listed in the bibliography have been selected so far as possible so as to include some which themselves contain comprehensive bibliographical information for each subject. The handbook is intended for the reader who wants a rapid and authoritative survey covering the main features of subjects other than those in which he has himself specialized. Besides its intrinsic interest to very many, a broadly conceived work of this sort has a place in the structure of contemporary scholarship because it does something to relieve the intellectual isolation which is one of the concomitants of increasing specialization and broadens the basis of communication between those working in different fields of knowledge.

The Companion includes both general articles on particular crafts and articles or groups of articles devoted to particular periods or cultures (ancient Egypt, Greek and Roman Antiquity, Africa, Pre-Columbian America, Russia and so on). Because appreciation of the practical and decorative arts, whether seen in museums or in private ownership, requires some understanding of the materials used and of the tools and techniques employed in working them, contributors have been encouraged to include descriptions of these materials, of their intrinsic qualities, their possibilities and their limitations, together with accounts of the tools and techniques of the craftsmen. There are also included some articles specifically devoted to particular techniques or materials (silk, copper and brass, pewter, weaving, ceramic techniques, and so on), something about prehistoric technologies and about the emergence in historical times of the main technologies of textiles, metallurgy and so on. These accounts, which are for the most part written by experts with practical experience of the crafts about which they write, provide a feature not often come by in the conventional histories. They are, however, conceived as ancillary to appreciation and not as an excursus into the history of technology for its own sake.

In addition to the main articles there are also short biographical accounts of outstanding craftsmen in the various fields and short entries on schools, styles and processes. But because practitioners of these arts have often been anonymous or have remained little more than names, less space proportionately is devoted to individual artists than to the practitioners of the fine arts in *The Oxford Companion to Art*.

Articles have been planned in somewhat greater detail in areas where information is less easily accessible to the ordinary reader. All the articles have been cross referenced by the use of small capitals for key words and names in the text.

In the planning of the articles and their layout the United States of America presented a special problem. It was necessary to decide whether to include a separate article or group of articles covering the development of the practical arts in the United States, as was done with China, Japan, Central Asia, Byzantium and the more exotic cultures mentioned already, or whether to treat the United States on the same lines as Britain and the European countries. The latter alternative seemed both logically and historically correct. During the early Colonial period the Americas imported their consumer products largely from Europe. As local manufactures were gradually established they too were at first largely dependent upon European immigrant craftsmen, who brought with them the traditional skills and stylistic preferences in which they had been trained. For these reasons fluctuations of style and fashion were reflected from Europe to America with only slight modifications at the beginning from indigenous traditions of craftsmanship. As time went on specifically American styles and techniques struck root and burgeoned, to very different degrees in the different arts and sometimes also in different parts of America. With the growth of autonomy and cultural assurance these specifically American innovations were increasingly reflected back to influence European taste and production in their turn. But always the practical and decorative arts of the Americas have remained closely related to the artistic traditions of Europe, constituting together with them what we call the culture of the Western world. Because of this affinity the arts of the Americas have been dealt with in the same manner as those of the European countries and Britain, where special features and developments associated with each country have been described according to their importance in the course of general articles on the particular arts. In some cases (e.g. furniture, costume, silver, glass) separate sections within the general articles have been devoted to America. In other cases the relevant information, including comparisons and accounts of interaction, are described in the body of the article itself as is done in the case of France, Germany, Spain, Italy, Britain and so on. It is hoped that this method will bring out most successfully the essential unity of Western culture in the decorative arts.

The economic prominence of the United States has been to a considerable extent bound up with technical advances in the production of durable consumer goods which in certain of the practical arts enabled it to take the lead in the passage from handicraft production or small-scale manufacture to factory mass production—almost, it might be said, a second Industrial Revolution. There comes a stage when the inherited skills and inarticulate know-how of the craftsman must be converted into rules and formulae of practical science to serve as the basis for machine production. Then new skills and a new aesthetic are evolved, while the new, synthetic materials, made to suit man's needs, demand new skills and technique for the realization of hitherto undreamed-of possibilities. It is at this point that the United States went into the van and it is in this field that it has continued to lead the world. The trade of horology is only one of a multifarious range of crafts in which the United States was prominent in developing the mass production of cheap and efficient commercial goods. But, as has been said, the primary theme of this Companion is to be found in those ageless traditions of craftsmanship whose slow formation provided the necessary background for the modern efflorescence of machine manufacture and so made possible our technological civilization even if they have been rendered to some extent obsolescent by it. The Companion carries the story up to this stage but does not attempt to trace in detail the early stages of modern technological progress.

H. OSBORNE

ACKNOWLEDGEMENTS

THE illustrations in this volume (the references below are to the page numbers) are reproduced by kind permission of the following: Rupert E. A. Abbs, 74 (13 c. bell, Canberra carillon); A.C.L. (Patrimoine des Musées Royaux des Beaux-Arts), Brussels, 111, 542 (casket); Staatliche Antikensammlungen, Munich, 443; Archives Photographiques, Paris, 756; The Art Institute of Chicago, 410, 741, 742, 743, 744, 745, 779; Museu Nacional de Arte Antiga, Lisbon, 352 (A, F); Ashmolean Museum, Oxford, 313, 316, 723, 738; B. T. Batsford Ltd., 816 (Estienne watch), 817 (Quare watch); G. Bell & Sons Ltd., 825; City Museum and Art Gallery, Birmingham, 314; Bodleian Library, Oxford, 264, 300, 322, 620, 797; Bowdoin College Museum of Art, Brunswick, Maine, 277; Bowes Museum, Barnard Castle, Co. Durham, 703; Brighton Art Gallery and Museums, 12; Trustees of the British Museum, 16, 17, 149, 213, 226, 228, 231, 244, 288, 312, 314 (rings), 437 (kylix), 544, 566, 724, 733, 816 (East watch); Cado Furniture (U.K.) Ltd., 378 (J); W. & R. Chambers and John Murray, 296 (child's diagram); City of Sheffield Museums, 289, 704; Museum of Classical Archaeology, Cambridge, 246; Cooper-Bridgeman Library, 727; Yolande Crowe, 151 (C); Danish National Museum, 723; Percival David Foundation of Chinese Art, London, 186 (vase, bowl), 191, 195, 196, 198, 199; Museum of Decorative Art, Copenhagen, 213; E. R. Delderfield, 462; Deutsches Ledermuseum, Offenbach, 542; Charles Eames, 378 (F); Embroiderers' Guild, London, 328 (child's dress), 329 (table cloth), 688; *Evening News*, London, 296 (war loan cartoon); Field Museum of Natural History, Chicago, 540; Museum of Fine Arts, Boston, Mass., 277; Syndics of the Fitzwilliam Museum, Cambridge, 585; Form International, 378 (D, E); The Gordon Fraser Gallery Ltd., 219; Free Library of Philadelphia, 635; David Garlick, 703 (A, C); Mrs. John Garlick, 703 (B); S. R. Gnamm, 378 (H); Keith Goddard, 627, 628; Collections of Greenfield Village and the Henry Ford Museum, Dearborn, Michigan, 372, 374 (A), 375; S. M. Groves, 589, 590; Calouste Gulbenkian Foundation, Lisbon, 149, 151, 765; Collection Haags Gemeentemuseum, The Hague, 149, 151; Trustees for Harvard University, 290; Hirmer Verlag, Munich, 87, 110 (A, C, D), 111 (ear-rings); R. F. Homer, 618, 619; Hull Museums, 698; Institut d'Ethnologie (Collection Musée de l'Homme), Paris, 273 (Inca costume), 807 (the Coya Chuquillanto), 820, 823; Musée de l'Impression sur Etoffes, Mulhouse, 280; M. E. Jones, 328 (apron); Keble College, Oxford, 739 (A); H. W. Keil, 362 (D, F); Collection K. Kellenberger, 226; K. Kemper, 24, 25, 26, 775, 776, 777; Heinz Edgar Kiewe, 328 (*broderie anglaise*); Kunsthistorisches Museum, Vienna, 128, 226; Kunstindustrimuseet, Oslo, 352 (B); Ronald A. Lee, 228 (A); Lips' Slotenfabrieken N.V., 551; University of Liverpool, 313; Arthur Lockwood, 295 (time chart, circular graph), 296 (computer diagram); Musée du Louvre, 111 (cliché Chuzeville), 593; Luton Museum and Art Gallery, 324, 325; Lutterworth Press, 423 (Greek Helmets); A. E. J. Mackett-Beeson, 159, 160, 161; Mansell Collection, 32, 247, 248, 250, 807 (Herod and Herodias); Metropolitan Museum of Art, New York, 213 (Gift of Mrs. John F. Seaman, 1925), 311, 323 (Rodger's Fund, 1923), 324 (Gift of Mrs. Thomas J. Watson, 1939), 372 (Joseph Pulitzer Bequest, 1940), 374 (B, Gift of Mrs. Gordon Dexter, 1943, C, Mrs. J. Insley Blair Bequest, 1952, F, Fletcher Fund, 1944, G, Gift of Mrs. Russell Sage, 1909); Museum of the City of New York, 374 (J); Trustees of the Museum of London, 546; Museum of Modern Art, New York, 378 (C, G); Réunion des Musées Nationaux, Paris, 593, 757, 761; National Museum of Ireland, Dublin, 540, 724; National Museum of Wales, Cardiff, 520, 689; National Portrait Gallery, London, 711 (C); Mrs. M. Neurath, 295 (isotype); The Observer Ltd., 296 (war loan cartoon); Österreichisches Museum für Angewandte Kunst, Vienna, 505; Phillips of Hitchin (Antiques), 362 (G), 363 (L); Phoenix

Assurance Company Ltd., 620; Mrs. Susan Picton, 642; John Pinches (Medallists) Ltd., 566 (The History of Man in Flight); Paul Popper Ltd., 9; Alain Presencer, 777; Presses Universitaires de France, Paris, 423 (vase paintings from J. Charbonneaux's *Les bronzes grecs*); Radio Times Hulton Picture Library, 63, 65; Rijksmuseum, Amsterdam, 287, 352 (C, G); Römisch-Germanisches Museum, Cologne, 435; Royal Ontario Museum, Toronto, 283, 284; Royal Scottish Museum, Edinburgh, 16, 312, 313 (Crown Copyright); St. Louis Art Museum, 741, 742, 743, 744; Science Museum, London, 227 (Crown Copyright), 654, 816 (oval verge watch—Crown Copyright), 828; Seal Studios, 74 (modern bell); Seattle Art Museum, 209; Smithsonian Institution, Washington, 607 (A); Sotheby & Company, 352 (H, J), 353 (K, N), 501 (swords), 731; Cyril Staal, 728, 730 (parcel-gilt cup), 732; Städtisches Museum, Braunschweig, 607 (B); Frank Staff, 635, 636, 637, 638; Textile Museum of the District of Columbia, Washington, 213; Thomas-Photos, Oxford, 258, 798 (Garamond), 799 (Aldus), 801; Times Newspapers Ltd., 168 (*ting, yu*); The Toledo Museum of Art, Toledo, Ohio, 277 (Gift of Florence Scott Libbey), 410 (aurene compote, Gift of Mrs. James A. Nicholson, 1966); Board of Trinity College, Dublin, 542 (budget); Victoria and Albert Museum, London, 71, 149, 150, 151, 152, 193, 214, 227, 228, 266, 282, 322 (Crown Copyright), 323, 325, 328 (Crown Copyright), 353 (M), 362 (A, B, C, H, J), 363 (K, M, N, O, P), 490, 498 (*inrō*) (Crown Copyright), 500, 501 (sword-guards), 505, 510, 521, 522, 523, 548, 581, 592, 607, 608, 660, 669 (Crown Copyright), 690, 691, 707, 710, 738, 758, 759, 762, 763, 766; Virginia Museum of Fine Arts, Richmond, 110; Wallace Collection, London, 228 (C—Crown Copyright), 352 (D, E—Crown Copyright), 353 (L—Crown Copyright); J. W. Waterer, 437 (Roman footwear), 539, 543 (all items), 544 (reliquary case), 545 (all items); E. W. Whitworth, 67 (Brandy), 831; Wine Label Circle, 67 (Burgundy); Henry Francis du Pont Winterthur Museum, Winterthur, Delaware, 372, 374 (D, E, H); G. B. Wood, 328 (chasuble); Worshipful Company of Goldsmiths, 730; Yorkshire Museum, York, 724.

LIST OF CONTRIBUTORS

Guy Atkins
Claude Blair
Iris Brooke
R. A. Brown
C. A. Burland
G. H. S. Bushnell
Edmund Capon
Harry Carter
P. L. Carter
Rollo Charles
L. J. Clarke
F. M. Collett
John Cooper
F. R. Cowell
Yolande Crowe
Robert Culff
E. R. Delderfield
Shirley S. DeVoe
W. A. W. Elloway
E. A. Entwisle
Arthur M. Feldman
Colin Franklin
David Garlick
Sylvia Groves
David A. Hanks
Mary Hillier
Henry Hodges
G. J. Hollister-Short
R. F. Homer
Dalu Jones
Mary Eirwen Jones
Edward T. Joy
John W. Keefe
John Kenworthy-Browne
Donald King
Peter Lazarus
Joan Liversidge
Arthur Lockwood
A. E. J. MacKett-Beeson
Ruari McLean
Victor Margrie
Enid Marx
Margaret Medley
R. W. Millard
Clifford Musgrave
Gillian Naylor
Erica O'Donnell
A. J. W. G. Ord-Hume
Harold Osborne
E. D. Phillips
Roger Powell
Alain Presencer
Mary Prior
Julia Raynsford
Tamara Talbot Rice
Carson I. A. Ritchie
L. R. Rogers
John Ruffle
Herwin Schaefer
Aaron Scharf
Frank Staff
Dorothy Stroud
Paul L. Taylor
G. L'Estrange Turner
M. L. Turner
R. F. Tylecote
R. J. Varney
F. A. B. Ward
John W. Waterer
Raymond Watkinson
James M. Wells
E. W. Whitworth
J. P. Wild
Geoffrey Wills
David Woodward
Louis Zara

NOTE

In order to refer the reader to other relevant articles, key terms or names occurring in the body of an article are set in small capitals. References to other articles bearing on the same subject are also set in small capitals when these occur at the end of an article or paragraph. The numbers at the end of an entry refer to the bibliography.

ABBREVIATIONS

Ass.	Association
B.M.	British Museum, London
Bodl.	Bodleian Library, Oxford
c.	century
c.	*circa*
Cath.	Cathedral
Coll.	Collection
ed.	edited, edition, editor
Found.	Foundation
Gal.	Gallery
Inst.	Institute
Lib.	Library
Mus.	Musée, Museo, Museum, etc.
Nat.	National
Samml.	Sammlung
St.	Saint
transl.	translation, translated
Univ.	University
V. & A. Mus.	Victoria and Albert Museum, London
vol.	volume

CONVERSION TABLE FOR WEIGHTS AND MEASURES

Note. The majority of the measurements in the Companion are given in metric units, and it has been thought desirable to include a list of approximate equivalents for the convenience of the reader.

Metric		*Imperial*
	LENGTH	
1 millimetre (mm)		0·04 inch
1 centimetre (cm)		0·39 inch
50 centimetres		19·68 inches
1 metre (m)		1·09 yards
50 metres		54·68 yards
1 kilometre (km)		0·62 mile
	AREA	
1 square centimetre (sq cm)		0·155 square inch
1 square metre (sq m)		1·196 square yards
1 hectare (ha)		2·47 acres
1 square kilometre (sq km)		0·39 square mile
	WEIGHT	
1 gramme (g)		0·04 ounce
100 grammes		3·53 ounces
1 kilogramme (kg)		2·20 pounds
1 metric tonne (1000 kg)	approximately	1 ton
	CAPACITY	
1 litre (l)		1·76 pints

A

AALTO, HUGO HENRIK ALVAR (1898–1976). Finnish architect who stood at the forefront of the modern movement in Scandinavia. In collaboration with Aino Marsio, whom he married in 1925, he originated the Artek furniture, first designed in 1928 for Paimio Sanatorium. His most characteristic furniture was constructed from continuous sheets of bent plywood in conjunction with solid wood supports. He applied to laminated wood the cantilever principle which was introduced by Marcel BREUER in his tubular metal furniture. See FURNITURE (MODERN).

ABBOTSFORD PERIOD. Term which came into use in the late 19th c. to denote heavy mock-Gothic FURNITURE made during the 1820s and 1830s. The term was derived from the name of Sir Walter Scott's house Abbotsford in Roxburghshire. Such furniture was sometimes made from fragments of medieval woodwork, panelling, etc. and often copied ecclesiastical designs. It was known at the time as 'monastic'. Nowadays it is also termed 'Baronial style'.

16, 24, 307.

ACANTHUS. A herbaceous plant (in English also called bear's-breech or brank-ursine) the formalized leaves of which were much used as an enrichment of MOULDINGS and surfaces and on capitals of the Corinthian and Composite Orders in Greek and Roman architecture. The type appears fully developed in the Erechtheum in the late 5th c. B.C. As a decorative motif it spread throughout the Greco-Roman world and it remained one of the commonest forms of ornamentation in many European styles. No symbolical significance appears to have been attached to the acanthus and its popularity seems to have rested on its decorative possibilities. There are several varieties of the plant, the most important being *Acanthus mollis*, with broad and rounded leaf tips, and *Acanthus spinosus*, with narrower leaves terminating in spines. Different styles are differentiated by their manner of treating the leaves. The Greek leaf has sharp edges and pointed tips, whereas in Roman ornament the tips are blunter and the curves bolder. The Byzantine and ROMANESQUE used a stiffer and more formalized design. GOTHIC returned to a more naturalistic (though not realistic) conception, early Gothic using rounded, bulbous forms and the later period preferring longer and narrower foliage. In the revival of classical forms at the Renaissance the acanthus was again perfected as an ornamental device with particular emphasis on the tendril. It was used in most subsequent styles and was carried to America and elsewhere wherever European influence penetrated.

In England the acanthus motif has been carved, inlaid or painted on furniture since the 16th c. Chairs and tables terminating in scrolls of acanthus leaves are sometimes described as having acanthus feet. The acanthus was particularly popular as an ornamental motif on furniture and as a frieze on plate *c.* 1670–90 and again during the Classical Revival *c.* 1770–1825.

ADAM, ROBERT (1728–92). Architect and furniture designer, second son of the Scottish architect, William Adam. After training under his father, he visited Italy in 1754 and returned in 1758 to set up an architectural practice in London with his three brothers. The part played by Adam in originating the NEO-CLASSICAL style is as yet unresolved; the *goût grec* (GREEK TASTE) was widespread in Paris in the late 1750s and this may have been the source of Adam's inspiration, though he himself paid only a brief visit to Paris in 1754. It is clear, however, that in the development of the style his was a highly individual interpretation applied to the whole field of decoration. He had many important clients, and the houses which he built or renovated in all parts of the country (see A. T. Bolton, *The Architecture of Robert and James Adam*, 2 vols., 1922) bear witness to his remarkable fertility of invention and his extensive vocabulary of classical decorative forms. These are displayed in *The Works in Architecture* which the firm began to publish in parts in 1773, and in the large collection of Adam's original drawings now in the Sir John Soane's Museum, London. These drawings are predominantly of wall furniture to match the decoration of his rooms and from *c.* 1772–3 essays in ETRUSCAN furniture, imitating the colour of Etruscan (more accurately, Greek) vases. It is now established that much of the rest of the furniture in Adam's houses was designed by cabinet-makers commissioned by the owners. These craftsmen, including LINNELL and CHIPPENDALE (the Elder), frequently used MARQUETRY on their furniture though Adam himself preferred gilded and painted decoration.

Adam's name has been widely identified with Neo-Classical developments in both interior decoration and a variety of crafts and his designs have been influential both in Britain and in the United States of America.

See FURNITURE (ENGLISH; AMERICAN).

348, 617.

ADAMS, ROBERT (active *c.* 1856–66). English gun-maker who designed a double-action revolver which rivalled the single-action COLT. As improved by a patent of Frederick Beaumont to allow separate cocking, the revolver was adopted by the British Army in 1856 and was also preferred by the East India Company. The Beaumont–Adams revolver was manufactured by the London Armoury Company.

ADZE. See WOOD-WORKING.

AELST, PIETER COECKE VAN. Flemish tapestry weaver active in Brussels in the 16th c. See TAPESTRY.

AFFLECK, THOMAS (d. 1795). American cabinet-maker. He was born in Aberdeen, Scotland, and after training in England went to Philadelphia in 1763, where he conducted a prosperous business as furniture manufacturer. He was expert in elaborately carved decoration and is often considered to be the finest exponent of the PHILADELPHIA CHIPPENDALE style. Examples of works attributed to him are in, among others, the Philadelphia Museum of Art, the Boston Museum of Fine Arts, and the Winterthur Museum, Delaware.

AFRICA

Before the Second World War crafts such as wood-carving, pottery, weaving and basketry were still a normal activity in most parts of Africa south of the Sahara. Graham Greene's *Journey without Maps* describes a typically busy scene in a remote village in north-eastern Liberia one afternoon during the mid 1930s. 'Five weavers were at work, each under his own little shelter of palm branches; a man was cutting leather sheaths for daggers; and in the smithy they were making blades, one man working a great leather bellows, another beating out the white-hot blade . . . In front of another hut two women were spinning a kind of top upon a plate, working the thread out of a mass of cotton. In a little enclosure a woman was boiling the leaves of a forest plant in a great cauldron to make a dark-blue dye . . . There seemed no end to the parade of industry.' Village crafts practised on this scale are no longer a common feature of everyday life, yet craftsmanship as such is more likely to survive in modern Africa than those forms of art which depend on a stable framework of religious beliefs and social institutions.

1. WOOD. Wood is the chief, though by no means the only, traditional medium for sculpture. Where religious sculpture and ordinary handicraft carving are practised side by side in the same community it is not always possible to draw a distinction between the work of the artist and that of the craftsman. But in some tribes the distinction is clear. Among the Bangwa of West Cameroun, for example, the carving of ritual and ceremonial objects such as masks, ancestor figures and royal stools is always done by professional artists, whereas domestic implements are manufactured by part-time craftsmen who make them for their own use as well as for sale in the market. Moreover the two types of object, religious and secular, differ in one other important respect. Ritual objects require medication by a ritual expert before they can be used, while purely domestic objects such as dishes or carved houseposts go into service straightaway. 'Medication', we read in a recent anthropological study of the Bangwa, 'gives the objects power: it makes a drum sound well, or a mask dance well . . . Objects which have been medicated are honoured and revered . . . They are regarded as beings and treated with exaggerated respect and are surrounded by taboos.' (Robert Brain and Adam Pollock, *Bangwa Funerary Sculpture*, 1971.)

The tools used by the traditional carver are simple and limited. The matchet is the commonest tool for felling the tree and cutting the block into shape. One or more adzes of different calibres serve for the more detailed work. At the final stage a small knife and sometimes a gouge or an awl may be needed. The surface can be smoothed with abrasive leaves or sandpaper.

The variety of household articles that are made from wood is enormous, ranging from wooden spoons, scoops and ladles to decoratively carved cups, weaving bobbins and cosmetic boxes to whole door-panels, bolts and houseposts sculpted with elaborate anthropomorphic, zoomorphic or geometrical designs. One of the most ubiquitous pieces of furniture in Africa is the low wooden stool used as a seat. It may be three-legged with a circular seat like our milking stool; or four-legged and rectangular, either with or without a base; or shaped like an hour-glass or cotton reel. Artistic elegance reaches its climax in the kneeling or standing caryatid stools of the north-eastern Luba in Zaïre (formerly the Belgian Congo). A typical stool of this kind shows a female figure with ornate hair-style and an intricate pattern of body scars, supporting the seat of the stool partly with the crown of her head and partly with the tips of her greatly elongated fingers. Caryatid stools and head-rests are also found in other parts of the continent. The Bamileke in Cameroun have chieftainly stools whose seat is supported by a whole circle of outward-facing figures. Other caryatid motifs from this region are leopards with human faces, baboons, spiders, buffaloes and elephants. Sometimes the whole surface of these stools and chairs is covered in coloured beads. According to Raymond Lecoq (*Les Bamiléké*, 1953) the Bamileke have a closed society whose members use a hierarchy of differently shaped stools to correspond with the various grades and ranks within the society. New members have to sit on the ground; those who have attained the lowest rank sit on a cylindrical stool resembling a drum with perforated sides; those of middle rank have stools that stand on three curved legs, the height of the stool differing according to two degrees of seniority; members in the top grades have rectangular seats made of bamboo; the chief sits either on a tall rectangular bamboo seat or on a stool decorated with the leopard emblem.

In addition to ceremonial stools many everyday objects are outstanding works of craftsmanship. They include food vessels, loom heddle pulleys, Ashanti dolls, roof-top ornaments, palm-wine cups, head-rests, bow-stands, musical instruments, etc. Illustrations of some of these may be found in *The Sculpture of Africa* by Eliosofon and Fagg.

2. IRON. Before discussing the uses made of iron, which is the commonest metal, it is necessary to say something about the character and status of the blacksmith in traditional African societies. Bohumil Holas, an expert on the art of the Ivory Coast, sums up the curiously ambivalent position of the blacksmith in west Africa as follows: 'The exceptional and permanent part which the blacksmith-priest plays in the community's religious and political life is due primarily to his power to extract minerals from the earth with impunity—by definition this is a dangerous proceeding because it entails being in close contact with the creatures who guard the riches of the underworld . . . This ambiguous situation naturally has many practical consequences. Every object leaving the blacksmith's hands has a sacred aura. This is true not only of agricultural tools (whose wooden handles are also made by the blacksmith) and knives and matchets, but even more so of protective amulets and ritual masks: the making of the latter is often (but not always) the prerogative of the blacksmith.' (*Craft and Culture in the Ivory Coast*, pp. 66–7.)

Another writer, Luc de Heusch, describes the smith's status, this time among the Tetela, a Bantu tribe, as 'respectable, but slightly odd'. The smith's power over fire and iron, comparable with the healer-magician's power over plants, places him outside the ordinary run of mankind. Among many of the Bantu, where fire is a royal symbol, the blacksmith is also the chief. By contrast, there are pastoral peoples among whom the smith is associated with evil and impurity.

The blacksmith's tools consist of hammers, chisels, tongs, anvil and bellows.

In agricultural tribes the smith makes implements for clearing the bush and tilling the soil: matchets, axes, bill-hooks, slashers, digging-spears and hoes; also knives of many kinds, as well as the tools needed by specialist craftsmen. The hunters and warriors of earlier days needed spears, arrows, daggers and swords. At a different level from these tools and weapons the smith might also be engaged in making a whole range of personal ornaments and dress accessories for his clients. In Uganda the following metal ornaments, amongst many others, were still worn in recent times: gorgets of up to 10 coils of wire; rings of beaten or coiled brass wire worn on the fingers and thumbs; heavy metal bangles as arm ornaments; metal anklets; chains which were sometimes worn below the knee; and various ritual ornaments, such as a set of bells worn on the thigh as part of the circumcision dress. These metal articles, together with others made of beads, leather, ivory, fibre and tortoise-shell, are illustrated in Margaret Trowell and K. P. Wachsmann, *Tribal Crafts of Uganda*, plates 52–5. It goes without saying that in Uganda, as elsewhere in Africa, imported jewellery is nowadays greatly on the increase.

3. BRONZE. In contrast with the blacksmith working alone at his forge the bronze-casters of Benin in Nigeria worked in a craft guild, living alongside each other in the same ward of the royal city. As metal craftsmen they were solely responsible to the *oba*, or divine ruler, and they held a special rank within the hierarchy of court officials. Benin bronze-casting by the *cire-perdue* process has a history going back to the 13th or 14th c., when—according to oral tradition—the technique was brought to the city by a master founder from the neighbouring kingdom of Ife. At Ife the casting of royal portrait heads in bronze had long been an established practice. How the technique originally reached Nigeria is unknown.

Benin 'bronze' varies from almost pure COPPER to brass. The peak period for the production of bronze objects, as regards sheer quantity, was the so-called 'middle' period of Benin art, dating from *c.* A.D. 1550 to 1700. In the 16th c. a large amount of metal became available to the Bini in the form of *manillas*, a trade currency consisting of horseshoe-shaped bars of solid copper or brass and used by European traders in exchange for commodities such as IVORY, palm oil, Benin cloth, Guinea pepper and slaves.

The large-scale discovery of Benin art in

Europe dates from 1897, when a British punitive expedition sacked and burnt most of the city of Benin. It is estimated that some 3,000 Benin art objects reached England at that time. They were mainly of bronze and ivory, though some were of iron and wood. A representative selection of these pieces stayed in Britain, but the bulk was put up for sale by the Foreign Office and acquired by ethnographic museums in Berlin, Stuttgart and Cologne. The most famous Benin casts are the memorial heads which stood on the royal ancestral altars and to which sacrifices were made. Of hardly less importance are the thousand or more surviving bronze plaques which once decorated the pillars of the palace. These plaques depict battles and other historical events as well as more purely anecdotal scenes from the life of the court. 'Benin art is essentially a court art; it is not an art of the people. Its principal functions are commemorative, ritual and ceremonial.' (W. and B. Forman and Philip Dark, *Benin Art*.) This description also applies to much of the typical art from other former African kingdoms.

In Benin city the blacksmiths lived in the same locality as the bronze-smiths but belonged to a different guild. The former produced weapons, domestic utensils and personal ornaments, whereas the bronze-smiths were mainly occupied with making ritual objects and symbols of prestige. They made the bronze staves and bells for the ancestral altars; the bronze cocks for the shrines of the queen mothers; and a large variety of different representations of the leopard motif, since the leopard represented the *oba*'s power. Thus a lidded bronze water vessel in the shape of a leopard was used for pouring water over the *oba*'s hands before a big ceremony and a bronze leopard mask, worn on the hip, formed part of the royal regalia. Serving merely as symbols of wealth and power, a magnificent pair of leopard figures, 71 centimetres high, now belongs to the Jos Museum in Nigeria. Other animals which figure in Benin iconography are elephants, rams, serpents and a variety of birds and fish.

Miniature in size but often of the highest artistic quality are the bronze or brass counterweights of the Baule (Ivory Coast) and Ashanti (Ghana). These weights, made by the *cire-perdue* process, seldom measure more than an inch or two in size. They were used for weighing gold-dust and nuggets of gold and they therefore had to conform to a very exact weight scale. For this reason it was sometimes necessary to graft a fragment of lead to the finished piece or to make a small indentation or hollow. The earliest weights are thought to be those that are geometrical in shape, e.g. spirals, squares, disks, lozenges, crosses, crescents and combinations of these and other symbolical or purely ornamental patterns. But the majority of weights are figurative, often alluding to a proverb as when a crocodile serves to illustrate the saying: 'When you are in the middle of the river, do not insult the crocodile.' The variety of creatures and objects depicted by the weights is so great as to defy classification. The animals include many kinds of snakes, birds, insects and fish, as well as chameleons, lizards, locusts, scorpions and larger beasts such as lions, leopards, antelopes and all kinds of domestic animals. The scenes involving people often display a keen sense of humour and a satirical power of observation. Inanimate objects are either taken from nature or they consist of everyday objects such as household utensils, furniture and musical instruments.

In the Ashanti capital of Kumasi, as was the case in Benin, the goldsmiths and other master craftsmen occupied a special quarter. The goldsmiths were not only responsible for manufacturing objects in gold, including the golden insignia for the ruler, but they also worked in bronze and made the bronze weights, scales, scoops and storage boxes that were the necessary accessories for the widespread trade in gold. Apart from their main commercial function the weights were sometimes used by story-tellers to illustrate a point or moral in the story, and they also served occasionally as dress ornaments and charms.

4. IVORY. The largest ivory carvings in Africa come from Benin. They consist of whole elephant tusks decorated in relief. The carvings on these tusks are of two kinds. In one the decoration forms an all-over pattern, depicting commemorative scenes not unlike those on the bronze plaques. The second type is much more restrained, consisting merely of several widely spaced bands of plaited or other abstract patterning. Both kinds of tusks served the same ritual function. They were displayed on the royal altars, surmounting the bronze portrait heads. These heads were hollow and had a large circular hole on top to accommodate the base of the tusk, so that the tusk sprouted out of the head like an incongruous column.

The kings of Benin had control over all the ivory in the kingdom and it seems likely that most of the ivory carvings were made exclusively for the royal household. The techniques of wood and ivory carving were so similar that the two types of craftsmen belonged to the same group in the guild quarter of Benin city. While the tusks, particularly when seen in their correct mounting, are by far the most spectacular ivory objects, there are others which show greater artistic subtlety. The British Museum owns a fine ivory staff nearly 1·5 metres long, which is made from two tusks fitted together. The staff is ringed in such a way as to imitate a bamboo rod. The top, elaborately decorated, is hollowed out to contain a rattle. It is known that this particular staff was owned by king Overami, who was deposed after the punitive raid of 1897. It was used for indicating victims for sacrifice. Amongst miscellaneous ivory objects from Benin there were instruments such as bells, horns and rattles, ivory swords, pendants, armlets and bracelets, cups, spoons and flywhisk handles, to name only a few. Apart from the authentic pieces mentioned there exists a whole range of so-called Afro-Portuguese ivories made to Portuguese orders.

Ivory work is not nearly as widespread in Africa as one might think. Outside the kingdoms of the Guinea Coast the two regions most notable for fine ivory carving are both situated in the Zaïre. The Pende, who live between the rivers Lutshima and Loange to the north of the Lunda Province of Angola, are famous for the small ivory amulets which men wore as pendants on a string round the neck. These pendants, known as *ikhoko*, are miniature replicas of a wooden mask to which curative powers were attributed. They are usually 5 centimetres long and triangular in shape. The reverse side is flat, but the front shows a face carved in high relief and displaying certain typical features which include: a high domed forehead; eyelids closed over salient eyeballs; arched eyebrows which form a continuous line but with a downward dip over the top of the nose; a triangular nose with inflated nostrils; everted lips; a sharply pointed chin; protruding ears. Some heads are shown wearing a three-pronged, starfish-shaped cap, which is the traditional head-dress of Pende chiefs. The finest ivories come from one small district, where the carving was done by artists who enjoyed high social esteem. They sometimes combined the functions of artist, blacksmith and chief. Their artistic skill was handed down from generation to generation. Pendants of lesser quality were also made of wood, bone, plant seeds and metal. The many different forms of Pende art are illustrated and described in a monograph by L. de Sousberghe, who spent several years on field research among the Pende during the 1950s.

The Lega, formerly known as Warega, live in the east of the Republic, between the river Lualaba and the northern end of Lake Tanganyika. Their most famous ivory carvings are small masks and figurines whose beauty is often enhanced by a deep reddish-brown patina. All Lega ivory objects were connected with the Bwami society, a hierarchical organization open to adult males. Until it was prohibited by a Belgian decree in 1947 the society was reckoned to include about 80% of all Lega men as members. There was also a women's branch. The Bwami society has been revived since Independence, but most of the ivory objects had by then already disappeared into art collections in Europe and America. The people themselves are reduced to using mass-produced substitutes for their ceremonies.

Ivory masks representing a human face were the exclusive attributes of the highest grade in the Bwami society. An interesting aspect of their usage is that they were seldom worn in front of the face—for which most of them were in any case too small. Instead they were displayed in a number of different and unexpected ways. They might be attached to the forehead or held against the chin; fixed to the side of the head or shoulders or worn on all four sides of the head or body in a double Janus pattern; or carried in the hand or trailed along by the beard, since many of the masks had a beard made of dried banana-leaf fibre. Or they might be deposited on the ground or tied to a special fence which served as a mask-rack during dances and instructional sessions.

Morphologically neither the statuettes nor the masks are sufficiently uniform to fit into any brief classification. According to a recent study by Nicolas de Kun ('L'Art Lega', *Africa-Tervuren*, xii, 1966, 3–4), there are some 20 to 30 different kinds of human statuettes. In size they vary from 4·5 to 20 centimetres, the largest known being 26 centimetres high. A common decorative motif on Lega ivory work is a pattern of small circles or dots within circles.

The Lega regarded ivory and elephant bone as having equal status. About one-quarter of their total production in these materials consists of spoons. These varied in style and size, a few having the handle shaped like a human body while in most cases it was perforated in a decorative geometrical pattern. These spoons were used within the Bwami society for the ritual consumption of pangolin meat. The other ivory objects, such as the numerous birds, animals and phalli, had a purely symbolical or didactic function.

5. POTTERY. In terms of basic technology there is no difference between African terracotta sculpture and the methods used in the production of pottery for everyday use, since African pots are traditionally built by hand without the aid of a wheel. Neither the potter's wheel nor the kiln is native to tropical Africa.

If we begin by discussing anthropomorphic sculpture and pottery, this is partly because complete examples of such work are known from an early period and partly because pottery incorporating human motifs tends to have a ritual function that sets it apart from the ordinary run of useful pots. Ancient terracotta sculptures in the form of human heads and whole figures are known from Nigeria. The earliest examples, belonging to the Nok culture in the northern region, are estimated to date from *c.* 250 B.C. After this there is a long historical gap before the Ife heads and body fragments which belong to the 11th or 12th c. A.D. Modern terracotta sculpture involving the human form is rather rare. The British Museum, which has published a fine exhibition catalogue of African pottery, owns a number of anthropomorphic cult pots from Nigeria and Ghana, but perhaps the most lifelike and certainly the most witty portrayal of the human face occurs on the 'singing' pots, with wide-open mouths, made by the Luba in the eastern Congo. Anthropomorphic funerary vases are found in the Ivory Coast and 'royal' pottery with ritual functions in some Central African kingdoms. In drawing a distinction between sacred and profane pottery we find that the production of the former is generally, though not quite always, the exclusive prerogative of men, whereas the production of pots for everyday use is overwhelmingly the task of women.

It is generally agreed that African pottery seldom achieves the same originality and elegance as two of the other major crafts, textiles and basketry. The modest quality of the pottery can be attributed partly to the archaic techniques employed and partly to the fact that pottery is the maid-of-all-work in the home. Pots, jars and earthenware saucepans are used for cooking, serving and storing food; for fetching and holding water; for holding milk and palm wine; for brewing and storing beer.

Here is a short outline of the various stages in the production of pottery. The newly dug clay is sun-dried, slaked and mixed with grit to the right consistency for building. No wheel is used and the tools are extremely simple, consisting of such readily available objects as corncobs, small blocks of wood, a scraper, a piece of wet rag or leather, a pebble for smoothing and polishing. Various methods are used in the manipulation of the clay. The first is to form it into a conical mass, which is scooped out from the top with the hand and shaped. At the final stage, when the pot is sufficiently dry, it is turned over and the base is completed. The second method is to roll the clay into long rings, which are built up in successive coils to form the body of the vessel. The potter stands in a bent posture, moving round and round the pot, moulding the clay with a rhythmical action of the fingers. The third method is to build the pot from 'bats' or flattened slabs of clay.

Before firing, while the pot is leather hard, the decoration is carried out in the following ways: by impressing with a roulette of carved wood or plaited fibre; by stamping with a corn-cob or other natural object; by incising the pattern with a finger-nail or the sharp edge of a shell or a knife; by adding bosses or ridges to the surface. Many pots are left undecorated or given only minimal embellishment.

The clay is open-fired and never glazed. The firing is done by placing a mound of pots on a layer of brushwood. Sometimes the pots are pre-heated to prevent cracking. The mound is then covered with grass and ignited. After firing, the pot may be burnished with a smooth pebble. Alternatively, while the pot is still hot, it may be given a dark lustre by dipping it in a vegetable decoction. Some of the best pots show a combination of several decorative techniques: moulded, impressed and incised work, with possibly a final addition of lustre or paint.

Calabashes are also very widely used with or without embellishments. The yellow surface is either left in its natural state or tinted red with a vegetable dye. Motifs are added by incision, occasionally by burning, or by removing the rind in such a way as to leave a raised pattern.

6. TEXTILES. The distribution map of the loom in sub-Saharan Africa has a curious pattern, with approximately half the total area showing a blank. The art of WEAVING is foreign to the whole of South Africa and the adjoining territories of Botswana, Rhodesia and Swaziland, as well as to most of the Sudan and its western neighbours, Chad and the Central African Republic. In the remaining area five main types of loom are used. The vertical mat loom, which is the most primitive, occurs in west-central Africa. The horizontal fixed heddle loom is indigenous to east Africa, including Madagascar. Elsewhere the most prevalent types are the horizontal narrow band loom of the Guinea Coast, going some way inland, and the pit treadle (or Hindu) loom found mainly among the Galla of Ethiopia and in the Somali Republic.

Weaving is known to have been a highly developed craft on the west coast and parts of the Congo since the 16th c. The fibres are raffia, cotton, imported SILK and combinations of these. Geometrical designs predominate, sometimes with symbolical meanings, but stylized human and animal shapes are also found. In woven as well as in printed textiles it is normal for a motif to be repeated along a whole band or panel of the cloth. Colours vary enormously so that at one extreme there is the monochrome pattern and EMBROIDERY on a natural raffia base, at the other the brilliant all-over blaze of colours of the Ghanaian *kente* cloths.

The range of dyeing techniques includes: stamp-printing and stencil-printing; rope tie and embroidered tie dyeing; resist dyeing either with starch paste or with mud; and the lengthy and complicated process used by the Bamana in Mali (see below).

The most famous raffia embroidery is the pile cloth produced by the Kuba at the confluence of the Sankuru and Kasai in the Republic of the Congo. The raffia is split into fine filaments and either bleached a pure white, left natural or dyed in a variety of colours. The weaving is done by men, the embroidery by women. The pile of the finished cloth is short, resembling the finest pile velvet.

Stamp-printing is seen at its best in the Ashanti *adinkira* cloths from Ghana. These are stamp-printed by means of small sections of calabash, each incised with a different motif. More than 50 of these motifs have been identified by name, e.g. 'castle', 'ram's horns', etc. As with the gold-weights from the same region, some figures allude to proverbs, others have historical, allegorical or magical implications.

Mordant dyeing has been brought to a very high degree of technical and artistic skill by the Bamana of west-central Mali. The cotton is grown locally and woven in lengths of up to 66 yards (60·35 m). The cloth is first dyed yellow and then the design is imposed with a spatula dipped in a specially matured mud; hence the name '*bokolanfini*' (mud cloth). The cloth has to be dipped and dried and over-painted several times. The design, which was originally black on a light background, emerges finally as white on a black background. The pattern consists of a large variety of abstract but meaningful symbols (see Imperato and Shamir, '*Bokolanfini*', *African Arts*, Summer 1970, pp. 32–41).

BARK CLOTH was at one time used for clothing and a variety of other purposes, such as the manufacture of masks. The bark is stripped off the tree in narrow bands, soaked in water and beaten out with a wooden mallet. This hammering almost trebles the width. A white or coloured pattern can be painted on the surface. Painted bark-cloth shirts are still worn by hunters in some parts of Africa.

7. BASKETRY. Basketry is the most basic and widespread craft in Africa. In practically every village there are ordinary men and women skilled in the art of making baskets and mats. Hence there is no need for professionals or specialists. The raw materials are everywhere abundantly available, whether in tropical forest, savanna and steppe, or swampland. The raffia and borassus palm (which also yields palm wine) are used, as well as many kinds of reeds, canes, bamboos, shrubs, grasses and cereal plants.

Baskets are either woven or coiled. Their shapes, patterns and sizes are as varied as the uses to which they are put. In Nigeria alone no fewer than 30 varieties of rectangular basket have been counted. In many Bantu languages each type of basket has its own name, but there is often no generic term for 'basket'. Some of the commonest uses for baskets are: as traps for fish, game and birds; as granaries; as cages for transporting livestock; and as containers for bringing cereals from the fields or for carrying these and other produce to and from market. In the homestead baskets serve for storing food and clothing, for sifting and winnowing, as food plates and dishes, and for drying foodstuffs in the sun. Some baskets are so closely woven and caulked that they are watertight.

Mats—rectangular, oval or round—are just as essential and ubiquitous. The two basic types are the reed mats (made by tying) and the plaited or woven fibre mats. Mats are used as beds, floor coverings and, when rolled, as head-loads for carrying all sorts of belongings on a journey. They also provide ceilings, screens and fences.

Baskets and mats are often embellished with coloured linear and geometrical designs, the most famous being the lidded dichroic Tutsi woven jars from Rwanda.

Home-made string and rope are used *inter alia* for such technical jobs as the manufacture of fish nets and hammocks and for fastening thatch to the framework of the roof.

8. PAINTING. Mural decorations on houses have long been traditional in many parts of Africa. Apart from ordinary domestic dwellings, they are found on palace walls, communal buildings and shrines.

A characteristic example of domestic wall painting is that of the Chokwe in north-eastern Angola. There the women decorate the walls of their houses during the dry season, from June to September, using mineral and vegetable pigments. Red, white and black are the most popular colours. The paint is applied with a stick which has been crushed at one end to make a crude kind of fibrous brush-head. The surface of the wall, being clay, receives no further preparatory treatment. The areas most commonly decorated are the exterior walls on each side of the entrance and the inside wall facing the door, which gets the best light. Motifs include geometrical and interlaced patterns; symbols of the sun, moon and stars; a repertory of real and mythological creatures; masks and masked dancers; trees, flowers and scenes from everyday life. The style of the painting is naïve and spontaneous, with no attempt at composition or perspective. The paintings on the outside walls are washed away as soon as the rains begin. The same fate normally befalls the painted mud sculptures and murals in the shrines of the Yoruba and neighbouring peoples of Nigeria. These shrines or *mbari* houses are half-open to the weather. This gives the painted gods and goddesses a duration of seldom more than a few seasons.

Apart from murals, painted decoration is carried out on some masks, pots and calabashes; on the human body; on bark cloth; and occasionally on cotton textiles.

9. BUILDING. It has justly been said that 'every man in an African society is an architect', and it is for this reason that folk-building in Africa must be counted as one of the crafts.

The most typical rural dwelling is the cone-on-cylinder hut or rondavel. At its simplest it is a circle of upright stakes topped by a conical thatched roof. The walls are wattle and mud. The interior is a single room with a few essential fittings such as a shelf where pots are kept and a rudimentary hearth. The hut is likely to be one of a cluster belonging to the same family; but in principle it is an all-purpose abode. In good weather the cooking is done either outside or in a cook-house, but when it is wet or cold the fire is lit inside the hut. The smoke escapes through the thatch. The standard rondavel has no windows. The height of the doorway varies from a mere 60 or 90 centimetres to the height of a normal person. Originally the door was a wattle screen, sometimes pivoted on two spikes, which could be barred from the inside. Later the halved door, as in European and Boer farmhouses, and the solid hinged door were introduced. As a variation upon the simplest rondavel, the roof can be extended over the doorway to form a porch or all the way round the house to make a verandah. If the verandah is wide and imposing, forked posts will be needed to support the eaves.

The rectangular type of hut has become popular in recent years. This kind of house has the advantage that it can be sub-divided into a living-room and bedroom. There are usually at least two windows, one on each side of the central door. Corrugated iron is often used for roofing.

Materials for building have to be gathered with care, since hard and straight posts are needed as uprights. The grass for thatching may have to be fetched during the rainy season, when the grass grows high, and stored until the weather is dry enough for building. The division of labour varies. Men carry out the heavy structural work, while women fetch and apply the clay to the walls and floor. The thatching is sometimes shared. If several huts are being built at the same time to form a compound, the task may be carried out on a communal basis.

It must be emphasized that the rondavel, of which there are many varieties, is only a single example of African rural architecture. In the introduction to a recent study of the dwellings in 16 different African countries the editor writes: 'Individual cultures have evolved forms as diverse as the great, arrow-head shaped houses of the Bamiliké in the Camerouns to the painted *kraals* of the N'Debele; from the demountable shelters of the pastoral Bantu to the mud cities of the Hausa states; from the troglodyte earth-caves of the Matmata to the "bomb" houses of the Massa.' (Paul Oliver in *Shelter in Africa*, 1971.)

10. MISCELLANEOUS. Making musical instruments is one of the most highly skilled crafts. Throughout Africa drums have the utmost importance. They are used for signalling, as status markers and for accompanying the dance. Xylophones are either played as solo instruments or grouped into large xylophone orchestras. At the opposite scale of size there is the little hand-piano, defined by Wachsmann as consisting of 'a set of thin lamellae set over a bridge on a sounding-board and plucked at the free ends'. It is held cupped in both hands and played on all occasions.

Beads, indigenous or imported, are not only made into bracelets and necklaces but in some tribes they are used for entirely covering chieftainly chairs and stools, masks and drums. LEATHER, often beautifully worked and ornamented, is made into furnishings (cushions, blankets), ceremonial wear, charms, saddles, satchels, shoes or sandals and boxes.

The art of body adornment, whether in the form of body-scarring, body-painting or elaborate coiffure, is still practised, particularly in areas remote from Western influence.

99, 189, 236, 270, 336, 403, 500, 507, 522, 638, 766, 781, 841, 842.

AGATE. See QUARTZ.

ALABASTER. Because the word 'alabaster' has come to be applied to two quite different substances it is useful to distinguish between them and explain that what was known as alabaster in classical antiquity was in fact onyx or stalagmitic marble. This alabaster used by the ancients, called 'Oriental' or calcareous alabaster in distinction from the modern or gypseous alabaster, is now sometimes known as 'Mexican onyx'. This substance is formed by the dripping of water from the roofs of caves. As the water percolates through the roof of a cavern in limestone rock it carries with it a portion of the calcareous material of the limestone. The drops falling on the floor of the cavern leave a deposit of calcite—the stalagmite—while a stalactite is also formed hanging down from the roof of the cavern. Carvings of gods made directly in the stalagmite occur in sacred caverns in China. More usually, however, onyx marble was simply quarried and worked elsewhere. The principal constituent of onyx marble is calcite, and it has a hardness of 3 on the MOHS SCALE. It can thus be readily worked, and when cut across it exhibits a beautiful pattern of concentric rings. Onyx marble is rarely white, because the water dripping through the cavern roof usually brings with it impurities, such as iron, which colour the calcite. Ancient alabaster is also deposited by the overflow from hot springs in volcanic regions. Important deposits occur in Arizona, at Yazapai, on the left bank of the Avon at Bristol, and at the quarries near Algiers from which much decorative stone was taken to embellish ancient Carthage. Ancient alabaster is harder than the modern variety, and it will stand weathering out of doors. It is also indissoluble in water. These qualities, and its highly decorative nature, caused it to be used for household objects and vessels of all sorts; in fact it became so popular for certain types of bottles and jars (of which the most curious was the lachrymatory or tear-bottle, found in ancient Roman tombs, which some archaeologists believe were intended to hold the tears of mourners) that the shapes of alabaster vessels were imitated by potters. Ancient alabaster was solid looking, shiny, translucent and slippery to the touch.

Alabaster carving appears very early in the history of civilization. At Warka, the biblical Erech, in a temple from the Protoliterate period (*c.* 3500–3000 B.C.) there was found an alabaster vase over three feet high with relief carvings depicting the festival of the god Tammuz (now in the British Museum). Fine alabaster busts from Sumer (now in the Louvre) go back as far as the 3rd millennium B.C. In EGYPT alabaster was used for sarcophagi (such as that of Seti I,

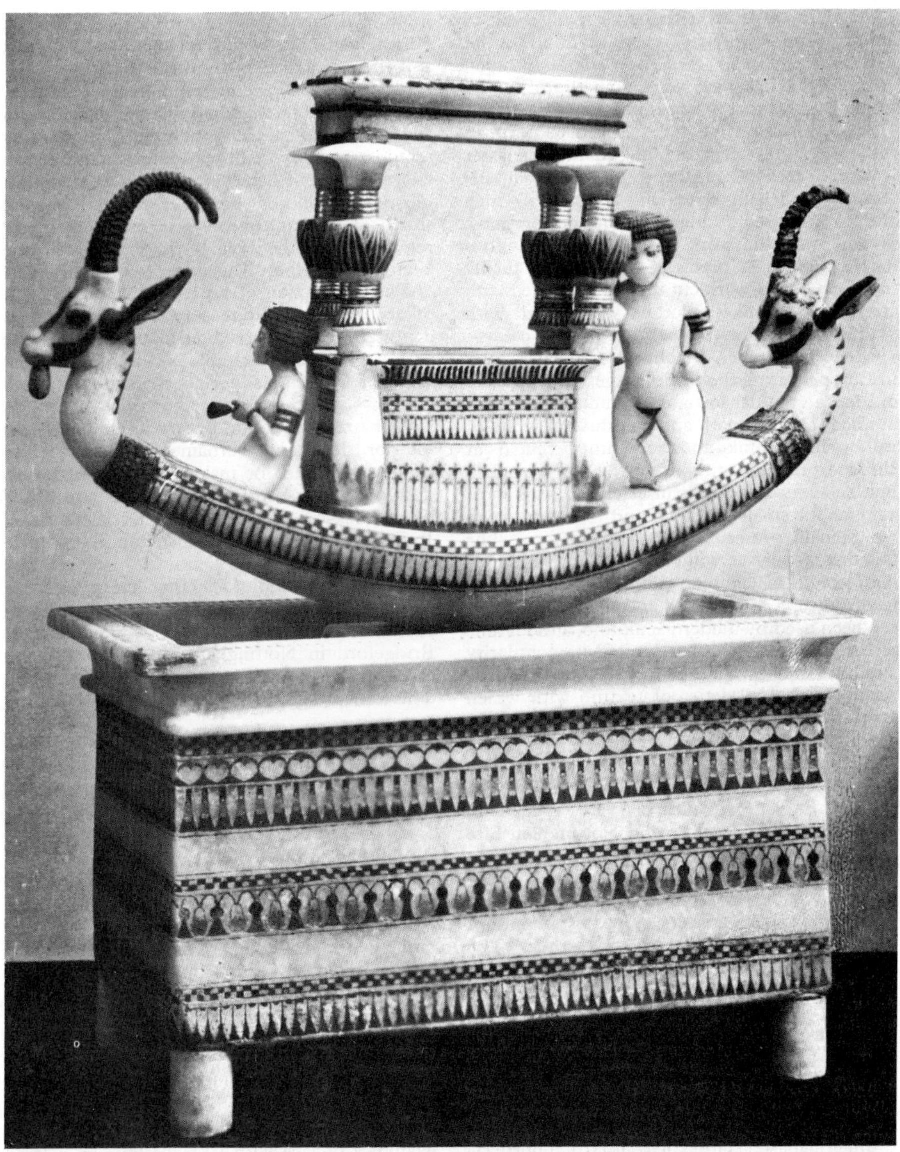

Ointment container in the form of a boat. A female figure holding a lotus flower is seated in the prow. In the stern a female dwarf is holding a pole, perhaps as guardian of the cabin, which is in the form of a shrine. The figure-head is a Syrian ibex with real horns. The boat stands on a pedestal. Alabaster inlaid with coloured glass paste, gold leaf and stones. From the tomb of Tutankhamun (Egyptian National Mus., Cairo, 14th c. B.C.)

d. 1304 B.C., now in the Sir John Soane's Museum, London), for lamps, canopic jars, toilet bottles and ointment containers. The tomb of Tutankhamun contained elaborate and beautiful alabaster objects, including a triple lamp in the form of three lotus flowers, an ointment container in the form of a boat with figure-head in the form of a Syrian ibex with real horns, an elaborate alabaster jar having two columns with lotus capitals supporting Bes's head and scenes on the sides showing dogs and lions hunting bulls and gazelles, and an elaborate chest whose four sides are incised with hieroglyphs stained with black pigment. The use of alabaster for statuary extends from ancient Egypt (head of Shepsekaf, 4th Dynasty, Mus. of Fine Arts, Boston) and through the history of Sumer, Babylonia and Assyria to Roman times.

'Modern alabaster' was occasionally used in antiquity as well. The reliefs of hunting and battle scenes which lined the walls of Assyrian palaces, for instance, were sometimes carved from alabaster and then painted.

Much alabaster has been carved in INDIA in the stone-cutting centres of the south. Alabaster is turned, carved and pierced to make up architectural models or boxes and containers which are characterized by many minute perforations. In sculpture the work is first outlined with a chisel, then more precisely defined, and finally has the detailed work cut in. It is polished with steel powder and a siliceous sand mixed with sealing wax.

Modern alabaster, which was used extensively in Europe during the Middle Ages, is a sulphate of lime, a granular form of gypsum. It is a fine-grained stone, smooth and translucent, white or yellowish or pink and sometimes veined or cloudy from impurities. It will take a high polish but it is very soft and bruises easily. It is most suitable for small sculpture and for work which will remain protected from the weather. The fact that its surface will paint without an underlying ground of gesso contributed to its popularity in the 14th c. for retables and tomb effigies. It has been used by modern sculptors, although its rather precious effect has limited its popularity and the smooth, polished surface offers little scope for the subtleties of texture with which some modern sculptors have been particularly concerned.

In the 14th and 15th centuries alabaster was quarried and carved chiefly in the Meuse valley and in England. Quarries were opened in Derbyshire, Staffordshire and Nottinghamshire and centres of carving sprang up also in Lincoln and York. About 1330 alabaster began to take the place of the harder stone or wood for tomb effigies and this became one of its most important uses until *c.* the middle of the 15th c. The earliest surviving alabaster effigy is at Hanbury, near the quarry of Tutbury in Staffordshire. One of the finest tomb effigies is that of Edward II in Gloucester Cathedral (*c.* 1331); other fine examples are those at Westminster Abbey of John of Eltham (d. 1334), second son of Edward II, and of the two young sons of Edward III (d. 1340).

Small alabaster statues of *weepers* (or mourners) became a feature of tombs of the nobility from *c.* 1290, an early instance being those on the tomb of John Eltham at Westminster Abbey. Alabaster was also used for making statuettes for placing on the altar, for relief retables and for other church ornaments. A flourishing school of carvers or 'alabastermen' soon achieved a Continental reputation and exported work widely, even as far as Italy, Spain and Russia. Their small alabaster statues were conceived in the round but usually had flat backs to stand against the altar, and were painted. Most of these were destroyed at the Reformation but a few remain in England, e.g. the three from Flawford church (now in the Nottingham Mus.) representing a *Virgin and Child*, *St. Peter* and a priestly donor; and there is a *Trinity* from the early 15th c. at Boston, Mass. Even more popular than free-standing figures were reliefs set in wooden frames and painted or gilded to be used as retables or reredoses. One of the earliest reredoses is an enormous set of panels ordered in 1372 for St. George's, Windsor; generally the reliefs were small. The best collection of extant alabaster retables is in the Hildeburgh bequest at the Victoria and Albert Museum.

The production of religious images was cut off abruptly by the Reformation but some tombs continued to be carved in alabaster until the 18th c. The latest example is believed to be the tomb of Rachel, Lady Pole, in Baxted, Suffolk (1725).

Alabaster has continued to be employed for interior decoration (ornamental slabs, balustrades, etc.) and for making toilet accessories, desk furniture, ornaments such as vases, ash-trays, clock-cases, etc., and commercial figurines. In Europe Florence has been an important centre of such alabaster work.

A particular kind of alabaster known as 'satin spar' consists of aggregates of finely fibrous crystals. It was at one time worked at East Bridgeford in Nottinghamshire for beads and other ornaments which were exported to America. This mineral shows a marked CHATOYANT quality.

ALB (Late Latin *alba*, white; sc. *tunica*). A full-length tunic of white linen worn by priests when officiating at religious ceremonies and sometimes by consecrated kings.

ALDUS. See MANUTIUS.

ALENÇON and ARGENTAN LACE. These laces evolved from the *point de France* (see LACE) made at the state factory established by Louis XIV's minister, Jean-Baptiste Colbert (1619–83), nearby. They were the most important and desirable of the French 18th-c. needlepoint laces. It is not, strictly speaking, possible to distinguish between the production of the two centres—indeed some laces were worked by specialists partly in one town, partly in the other—but it is customary to assign to Argentan examples of lace with large designs on a large hexagonal ground-mesh formed of tie-bars with a thread twined round them (the *bride tortillée*, at which the Argentan women are known to have excelled) or worked over them with buttonhole stitch, and to assign to Alençon those with a smaller, simple hexagonal mesh.

The technical skill and the variety of the open-work fillings give the floral patterns of the early and middle years of the century an extraordinary richness of effect. Later the designs were adapted to the increasing lightness of dress and became thinner and more scattered. The motifs continued to be outlined with raised threads thickly worked over with buttonhole stitches.

ALEXANDRITE. See CHRYSOBERYL.

ALGERIAN WARE. See EMBROIDERY (SPAIN AND PORTUGAL).

ALLEN PRESS. Founded by Lewis and Dorothy Allen in San Francisco as a private printing press in 1939, it produced several books of note during the 1940s including some on commission for the Book Club of California. After moving to France the Allens became enthusiastic converts to the French concept of the *livre de peintre*, in which the book is thought of as an instrument for the great artist to display his talent, as a portfolio in principle rather than as a book in the traditional manner. They have produced fine works in this style. In its general standards and the excellence of its artistic quality the Allen Press rivals the ASHENDENE in Britain and the CRANACH in Germany.

ALLIS. Family of United States cabinet-makers who worked in the Connecticut River Valley from the latter part of the 17th c. to the middle of the 18th c. The family was founded by WILLIAM Allis, who came to America on the third voyage of the *Mayflower*, landing at Boston on 1 July 1630. He was not himself a cabinet-maker but married a niece of Nicholas DISBROWE. His sons JOHN (1642–91) and SAMUEL (1647–91) were both cabinet-makers, as were John's sons ICHABOD (1675–1747) and JOHN (1682–?). The elder John Allis carried on business in partnership with Samuel BELDING and his brother and sons were taken into the firm. It is believed that many of the HADLEY CHESTS were made by the firm of Belding & Allis.

ALMORRATA or ALMORRATXA. A holy-water sprinkler of complex shape produced primarily in Catalonia during the 17th and 18th centuries. It had a tapering body on a pedestal base and water was poured from four hollow tubes.

ALTARE. See L'ALTARE.

AMBER. A fossil resin produced during the early Oligocene and late Eocine geological periods, *c.* 40 million years ago. At that time the climate and vegetation of northern Europe were similar to those of present-day Louisiana and California. Large forests abounded, made up of aloes, cinnamon, camellias, tulip trees, redwoods, camphors, together with the more common European species of today such as pines, oaks, poplars and walnuts. When large amounts of sap oozed from a diseased or damaged tree, so that insects and leaves became enwrapped in its sticky ooze, the whole mass, falling to the ground with the stricken tree, was embedded in a stratum known as the 'blue earth'—a sort of green-sand whose granules can often be seen adhering to raw amber—and fossilized, often changing colour in the process and becoming deeply cracked.

Although it might be possible to find amber wherever the Oligocene beds are exposed, as for example in Central America, where the Aztecs brought amber beads as a tribute to Montezuma, the commercial working of amber has been practically confined to the Samland peninsula on the Baltic coast of East Prussia and to the Chindwin river area of Burma. Other sources of amber are Sicily and Romania, but they are so much less important that when the Emperor Nero wanted amber to embellish the nets in the amphitheatre he sent a Roman knight to the Baltic, 1,600 kilometres away, rather than try to collect it in Sicily, only 500 kilometres away. Baltic amber is whisky-coloured, tawny and transparent, or osseous, yellow and opaque. Opacity in amber is caused by minute air bubbles trapped in the material. Sicilian amber can be either deep ruby, garnet-red, blue or even green. Romanian amber varies in colour between the normal yellow and red, brown or black. Burmese amber, in which most Chinese amber carvings are made, is either a transparent yellow or a fiery red. The Chinese seem to prefer the latter colour, and broken statues in Burmite, as Burmese amber is called, sometimes reveal that they have been stained red on the outside.

Amber is extremely soft and also very brittle. It can be charged with static electricity by rubbing it on the hair. Hence the Greek name for amber, *ēlektron*, has become our word for electricity. When charged it will pick up small pieces of paper. Opaque amber can be changed into clear by boiling it in oil. Its colour can also be changed by the same process, and it can be bent in the hot oil. Under pressure and with sufficient heat small pieces of amber can be fused into a large block. Because amber burns with an aromatic fragrance it was used as incense or even as fuel in parts of the world such as the Orkneys where its value was unknown.

In prehistoric times amber was probably worked with a flint scraper and polished with a piece of sheepskin, as was JET. In GREEK AND ROMAN ANTIQUITY it was shaped with a file and pumice stone, and polished with powdered gypsum. By imperial Roman times much amber was worked by means of edged tools and turned on the lathe. The Romans also used henna and kid suet to stain amber a deep red, and it may be questioned whether the fact that so many pieces of classical amber are of such a deep colour may not be due to this process as much as to natural discolouration. In modern times amber has been carved with gravers and files, sand-papered, and polished with tripoli in water followed by whiting. Because amber is such a brittle material the utmost care must be taken both during the process of working and in the polishing, when the amber is frequently laid aside in the belief that if it becomes too hot it will fly to pieces. Large works in amber have almost invariably been broken, sometimes more than once. A safe adhesive for the layman to apply to a broken amber is balsa cement.

To some extent the uses to which amber has been put have been dictated by the nature of the material and the beliefs which clustered round it. Thus whenever possible the craftsman has tried to keep intact the 'inclusions' of trapped insects or pine needles which are to be found in the raw material. These have held a fascination for the beholder from the time of Martial to that of Pope, who exclaimed:

Pretty in Amber to observe the forms
Of hairs and straw and dirt and grubs and worms.
The things we know, are neither rich nor rare,
But wonder how the devil they got there.

The very solid and lifelike appearance of the included insects may have led to the belief that they were preserved by the amber and this, together with its magnetic properties, caused it to be endowed with strong magical and medicinal virtues. For this reason it has been much used for amulets. Occasionally very large balls of amber may have been used as scrying glasses, while the amber cup which is preserved at Brighton may have owed its existence to the belief that amber would detect, or neutralize, the presence of poison. An extension of this belief, that amber could not carry infection, led to its being used as almost the sole material for the mouthpieces of pipes in the Middle East. Until comparatively recently many pipes made in Europe or America also had amber mouthpieces, although apart from its coolness amber has very little to recommend it for this purpose. It is so soft that it can be easily bitten through and so brittle that it breaks easily.

As it feels so cool to the hand it was commonly carried by Romans as a fingering piece. Because of the aromatic smell, which can be released by rubbing, the Emperor Heliogabalus had it crushed and spread on the ground under the porticoes of his palace. Its aromatic qualities made it a natural substance in which to make cosmetic pots and perfume bottles, while its coolness and agreeable tactile qualities caused it to be used for the handles of all sorts of implements. The Romans also made truffle knives from it, no doubt in the belief that it would impart its perfume to the truffles. Its transparency made the Chinese employ it for snuff-bottles, while the same quality caused it to be employed in the 17th c. for making magnifying glasses. The extremely rare and valuable nature of amber, which was reflected in the price that quite a small statue fetched in Roman times, higher than that of a good slave, has always meant that it was a favourite material for religious objects such as the rosaries carried by Muslims or the statues of Kwan Yin made by the Chinese. It has also been used for small carvings, reliefs, CHESS PIECES, toy figures, candelabra, cups and as an ornament for furniture and panelling.

Amber carving began in prehistoric times, and apart from beads fine animal statues were produced. In Italy carvings have survived in tombs dating from the early Iron Age. It was widely carved by the Etruscans and other Italian peoples.

Amber cup found in a barrow at Hove in 1857. (Brighton Art Gal. and Mus.)

Many Italic amber carvings are Greek in feeling if not in origin, but to adapt their work to a precious and difficult material the craftsmen often abandoned classical realism and spread the design over the surface of the lump of amber. During the tomb-robbing era amber beads were gathered by the bushel from Etruscan sepulchres. The British Museum has a fine collection of amber from classical Italian sites; the items exhibit the extraordinary colours only to be found in buried amber carvings. Amber was worked in the Minoan era, and it was widely used for fibulae and INLAYS. Homer describes Menelaus's palace as being decorated with amber. To the Romans amber was *the* luxury material. A statue of Augustus was carved entirely in amber, no doubt of blocks cemented together. Amber appears in both Celtic and Anglo-Saxon ecclesiastical art, but it is not until the medieval period that numbers of amber carvings, such as crucifixes and rosaries, begin to be mentioned. The golden age of amber carving in Europe came in the 17th c., when carvers such as Georg Scriba of Königsberg (active *c.* 1617) and Charles Marutus (active *c.* 1621) worked on plaques, flagons and tankards. Gottfried Turan of Danzig (active *c.* 1702) worked at the turn of the 18th c. on the panels for the Amber Room, originally intended for Frederick IV of Denmark, which was to find its way to Berlin and was eventually bought by Peter the Great and erected at Tsarskoye Selo near St. Petersburg (Leningrad). Turan was a member of the Amber Guild of Danzig, a body which, together with the continued patronage of the Electors of Brandenburg, did much to promote amber carving.

Amber carving can hardly be said to have a history in Europe after the 18th c. other than its use in JEWELLERY. In China on the other hand it continued to be a living craft down to our own day and works were not merely inspired by taste and skill but gave evidence of great daring and extreme virtuosity on the part of the carver, who cut opened-out and fretwork designs in this most fragile of all materials.

See GREEK AND ROMAN ANTIQUITY (JEWELLERY). 801, 913.

AMBRY. See AUMBRY.

AMELUNG, JOHN FREDERICK. Immigrant German who established the New Bremen Glass Manufactory in Maryland in 1748. See GLASS (AMERICA).

AMERINDIANS

A. NORTH AMERICAN INDIANS
B. MIDDLE CENTRAL AND SOUTH AMERICA (PRE-CONQUEST)

1. Ceramics
2. Textiles
3. Featherwork
4. Metalwork
5. Wood and stone carving
6. Arms and armour

A. NORTH AMERICAN INDIANS. The subcontinent extending from the Rio Grande to the Arctic Ocean is widely diversified in its ecology. The human inhabitants in Pre-Columbian times were few in numbers and widely separated, thus there was great diversity in material culture. The first reports by visiting Europeans indicate that apart from the Eskimo the level of clothing was minimal. Housing was only developed among the tribes of the Pacific Coast north of Oregon and in the Pueblo regions of the south-west U.S.A. Otherwise the agricultural peoples lived in bark-covered shelters with a slight framework of boughs, and those who were primarily hunters used the portable skin *tipi*. POTTERY seems to have had many separate areas of origin, but all of it was hand-coiled and none thrown on a POTTER'S WHEEL. Basketry was well developed everywhere and displays a great variety of techniques. There was no metal technology except cold-hammering of natural copper nodules found both in the Arctic Coppermine River region and in the natural copper region near Lake Superior. Transport was limited by the total ignorance of the wheel throughout the continent. In some areas much use was made of river transport by canoe, while back-packs, the *travois*, and the sledge (toboggan) were also used. The only animal used for transport was the dog. The horse was introduced only in the 16th c. from Spanish Mexico, and took two centuries to reach the region of the Great Lakes.

Water transport was surprisingly backward among American Indians. Only dug-out canoes and light frames covered with birch-bark or skin were used. All were paddled, none were equipped even with the simplest of sails. The Eskimo used the light skin-covered *kayak*, usually with a driftwood frame and a shell of seal-skin. It was usually a single-seat vessel, though in the Aleutians some were made to take two or three crew-men. The large open *umiaks* were similar in construction to the *kayak*, but were not decked. They were used for transporting possessions and for whale hunting.

In the eastern seaboard regions, the Great Lakes and eastern woodlands the birch-bark canoe with a very light wooden framing was used. This was sometimes large enough to carry six or eight men. It was easy to carry past rapids, easily repaired and quite remarkably flexible and tough. Its origins are not known but it was an important invention, facilitating contacts between tribes in the mountainous forest regions. The idea spread by way of the Great Lakes to some of the tribes of the Rocky Mountains region. In the Great Plains the bull-boat, a light coracle framework covered by a bison hide and circular in plan, was the only transport vessel. It was used for transporting family effects across rivers. A few Californian coastal tribes used dug-out canoes, and the peoples of the south-east had heavy dug-outs with a square stem and stern. The best American-Indian boats were those of the Pacific north-west. They were dug-outs, with carefully shaped stem and stern to make them speedy. Usually these boats were painted with totemic symbols. Used both in peace and in war, they sometimes ventured 160 kilometres out to sea. Some people have thought that the form of these splendid canoes was partially derived from the lines of Japanese fishing vessels which had visited those coasts.

The cultural level of the North American Indians varied from semi-nomadic hunting with seasonal movement following the game, or in the case of the Eskimos from summer hunting on land to winter hunting over the sea ice. At the other end of the scale were the Pueblo Indians concentrating on irrigated field cultivation with very little hunting. Technologically there was a range from a late Palaeolithic style of life to a developed Neolithic culture. In one area, the Pacific north-west coast, we have the example of a full Neolithic tool equipment used in a non-agricultural community.

Clothing was not related directly to levels of material culture. The Indians of Florida, agriculturists living in fixed settlements, went almost completely naked except for elaborate body paint and ornaments of shell, fibre and wood, while the Eskimo hunters had adapted to their circumstances by wearing fully tailored suits made from carefully selected furs. Many of the Plains Indians wore simple loin flaps for men and short leather skirts for women, though both sexes often went naked in the summer. The elaborate costume of shirt and leggings or long gown was evolved from contact with European fashions.

The art of WEAVING was not widespread. Much beautiful work was achieved by finger plaiting techniques which range from the ornamental leg-bands of the Iroquois to the Chilkat blankets of the Pacific north-west. Weaving on a simple back-strap loom appeared in the south-west with the spread of American cotton. It originated from Mexico and included both basketry and simple garments even in Pre-Columbian times. It appears that the efficient types of vertical loom used by Navajo and Pueblo weavers in recent times had their origin in culture contacts probably through Mexico with a Spanish textile tradition.

Throughout the continent there has been little emphasis on free-standing sculpture except on a very small scale. The tendency has been to decorate useful objects with linear design, sometimes in the form of low relief but more commonly with painted and incised decoration. The largest works of sculpture, the totemic carvings on houses and poles in the Pacific north-west, only developed on an important scale with the introduction of steel tools in the early 19th c. through the fur trade.

The equipment of tools was surprisingly similar throughout the continent. This was probably not due to the persistence of ancestral traditions but to similarities in need and in the available types of material. One notes for instance that all the tribes used some kind of hoe for breaking the ground. It is quite noticeably different from the digging-stick of the more highly civilized peoples of Mexico and the Andean region of South America. In the south-eastern U.S.A. the hoe was mostly made from the limb of a tree with part of the bole left and shaped to make the blade. In the middle Mississippi area the blade was a large flat stone very carefully flaked to the requisite shape, and in some other coastal areas it was made from the ground-down valve of a large clam shell. But always the hoe was made to a similar pattern. In maize-growing areas the broad blade was useful for gathering soil together to make the hillocks into which the maize grains were prodded either with the finger or by means of a piece of wood used as a dibble. An adze-like tool with the blade set transversely to the haft was very generally used throughout the continent. The Eskimos sometimes utilized driftwood of a suitable shape, to which they lashed a walrus tusk to make an efficient ice-pick. But because of the scarcity of wood they more frequently used the limb-bone of an animal, to which a bracket-top was lashed to provide a platform to which either a bone-pick or a polished stone adze-blade was attached. Scrapers were mounted with the bullnosed edge forwards in specially shaped hand-grips, which might be of wood or of walrus ivory.

Other, stone-bladed scrapers were used on the north-west Pacific coast, often for dressing skins as well as for smoothing wooden surfaces. The handles were of wood carved into a loop which would permit the use of two hands either in smoothing surfaces or in fleshing hides. Throughout the buffalo- (bison-) hunting area a leg-bone of bison was used to hold at one end a sharp flaked stone blade for cleaning flesh and hair from hides.

At a few very early sites in glacial moraines some very crudely flaked stone implements have been found in association with remains of burnt wood. They possibly represent an early human migration into America before the main waves of immigration occurred. Throughout the continent, however, the great majority of stone implements were flaked from siliceous stones. All show secondary flaking of high quality. In later times there can be observed an increase of very accurate pressure-flaking. The form of fastening to a stem varied with time, the development of a tang and barbs on projectile points becoming more important at later dates. Polished stone blades, adzes, axes, chisels and awls were evolved in all regions, though they are much more rare in the Great Plains where they served comparatively little purpose because of the lack of large timber or soft stones suitable for carving. The Eskimos had smooth chisels and sharpening stones of fine finish and made some use of adze blades for carving driftwood, walrus ivory and steatite.

Stone was carved among the Eskimos for oil dishes to serve as lamps and for cooking vessels. On the Pacific north-west harder stones were shaped into pestles and mortars, often decorated with relief masks of people and totemic animals. In the Plains and in many of the south-eastern areas of the U.S.A. stone tobacco-pipe bowls were made, often carved with human figures and the heads of birds and animals. The stone was shaped by abrasion and details scraped with stone-bladed knives. Boring was done by means of sticks or pieces of cane twirled between the palms of the hand with hard sand or other abrasives. Among the Eskimos the process of drilling was facilitated by the bow drill, in which a thong twisted once round the stem of the drill was attached to the two ends of a short bow of wood. A sawing motion of the bow turned the drill rapidly first in one direction and then in reverse. The top of the drill fitted into a smooth socket in a mouthpiece and the downward pressure was maintained by the head. By this means stone bowls could be hollowed by drilling a series of holes, which were then united by chipping away the intervening stone with a chisel.

Pottery was not made in the Arctic, mostly because the lack of fuel made it impossible to build a fire capable of producing a high enough temperature to fire the clay. There was no pottery in use on the Pacific north-west coast, nor among the forest peoples of Canada and Nova Scotia, but their needs were met by containers made of birch-bark and of hide. In the Great Plains pottery was scarce and primitive, but in the eastern U.S.A. pottery was made of grit-tempered clays and after coiling was decorated with simple patterns made with sticks or even with the finger-nail. The techniques resulted in wares very reminiscent of the early BRONZE AGE products of Europe. The highest quality of pottery in North America came from the *pueblos* of the south-west. Here the comparatively settled life allowed the development of specialist potters, although all women could make their own domestic utensils. The sand used as a tempering medium was collected from special areas often at considerable distances from the *pueblo*. Clay was coiled and curved sections of old broken pots were used as turn-tables to save time while the coils of clay were added in building up the body of the pot. The walls of the pots were thin and after being carefully shaped with scrapers were finished with burnishing stones. They were sometimes baked in closed ovens of adobe to produce a black ware from oxygen-reduced firing. In later times they were also fired in ovens heated with chopped grass, buffalo dung and leaves as fuel. While not constituting kilns with forced draught, these afforded a means of controlling the firing, and since the pots were usually baked singly there was more individuality in the products. But the basic styles and shapes were dictated by the social custom and collective taste of the community.

The impact of European settlement introduced much of importance to American Indian technology. In the east most tribes were driven from their homelands, and the bark-covered long-house of the Iroquois disappeared. In the south-east the wooden houses and villages survived until modern times, and the step to the modern timber-built bungalow was a small one. The transition from the portable skin *tipi* of the Plains Indians to the framed house has been slow, and some people live in houses but prefer to sleep in the old *tipi*. In spite of the diminution of numbers many Indian communities have flourished and in particular the nomadic Navajo have become settled communities. Both they and the Pueblo Indians have learned the arts of making silver jewellery of considerable beauty, though this has grown from the use of silver coinage as decoration and not from the development of a native metallurgy.

The most profound alteration has been in the development of clothing. The moccasin, loin cloth and apron of aboriginal times have given way to leather and later to cloth clothing. At first the tight skin leggings of the men seem to have had some relationship to the leggings of European sailors attached to a waist-belt. The jacket evolved from the finely dressed deerskin shirts adapted from the dress of the settlers in New England. The women only gradually adopted European fashions, and early pictures of Plains Indians show women wearing something like European EMPIRE-STYLE gowns with thin shoulder-straps shortly before the development of the long gown with a top very much like a Victorian tippet.

The introduction of clothing meant that much time was spent in preparing skins. They were stretched on a frame, thoroughly fleshed, and then animal brains and fat were worked thoroughly into the skin and scraped over. The process was sometimes repeated several times. The hides were then smoked over a low wood fire in a pit. The result was a fine soft LEATHER very nearly waterproof. Decoration of clothing was important. Earlier native decorations of belts and bands in porcupine-quill or moose-hair embroidery spread over the new garments. The old skin cloaks of men, decorated with shell beads like that attributed to Powhatan, were elaborated and decorated with paintings of the owners' exploits. Shell beads, which had a long tradition as decorations and which as *wampum* had been used as a means of communicating information, were replaced by imported European beads, though the designs often continued traditional tribal patterns. The head-dresses of men became more elaborate until many men of small social importance were wearing types

Argillite tobacco pipes representing the death of an Indian in an accident. (B.M., 1830–60)

Raven totem pole of Angyada. (Royal Scottish Mus., 1850–60)

NORTH AMERICAN INDIANS

A. Shirt of antelope skin with quill decoration. (Early 19th c.) Plains Indians

B. Masks worn at winter ceremonies. Haida Indians, Queen Charlotte's Islands. (B.M.)

C. Woman's basketry hat. Collected by Capt. James Cook. Nootka Sound. (B.M.)

D. Painted pottery storage jar. Pueblo Indians, Zuni, New Mexico. (B.M., *c.* 1890)

A

B

C

D

of head-dress once the prerogative of important chiefs.

One may say that the technology of the North American Indians was in general typical of Neolithic communities, and that it was elaborated and assumed greater brilliance of design in the Colonial period. It has now changed and American Indian basketry, silverwork, pottery and carvings in wood and steatite have been to some extent artificially encouraged and have in consequence adapted themselves to the tourist trade. Nevertheless Indian traditional custom has preserved some artefacts of ancient type for use by the native peoples themselves in their quest for a new unity impossible in the old days of intertribal strife.

B. MIDDLE, CENTRAL AND SOUTH AMERICA (PRE-CONQUEST)

I. CERAMICS. The use of fired clay to make vessels and other objects is world-wide, and most of the basic pottery-making processes are found in both the Old and the New Worlds. None of these processes is peculiar to the New World, which lacked the POTTER'S WHEEL. It also lacked hard products like PORCELAIN and STONEWARE, which need high temperatures for firing. GLAZE is exceptional, and was not used consciously to produce an impermeable surface. With these limitations the skill and artistry shown in New World ceramics bear comparison with any in the world. In addition to vessels pottery products include griddles for manioc, graters, stools, pot stands, figurines, roller stamps and flat stamps for body painting, musical instruments (drums, flutes, pan pipes, trumpets and rattles), spindle whorls and even pubic coverings for women.

There is little evidence as to the place of the potters in ancient communities. Modern examples from Mexico suggest that, so far from every woman making pots for her own household, there were villages which contained groups of potting families in which the man, his wife and the children took part in every process, from collecting the clay to firing, and traded the products over a comparatively wide area as well as to neighbouring markets. The bulk of the pottery produced in this way is utilitarian, for example cooking pots and storage jars, but there is a significant proportion of decorated vessels made and sold as toys or for religious purposes. Whether a pattern of this sort could account for the highly specialized ancient vessels, evolving rather rapidly and uniformly through time, of say Moche and Nasca on the Peruvian coast, is uncertain, but it may be suggested that, given the existence of potting communities, they had advanced specialists among them.

Materials. As in other parts of the world, the materials used were plastic clay and, where appropriate, tempering material such as crushed potsherds and rocks, sand, shell, volcanic ash and even vegetable fibres and siliceous material from the burnt bark of certain trees. The chief object of adding such materials is to encourage uniform drying of vessels before firing, so reducing flaws. There was a strong tendency to conservatism in the choice of tempering material for a given type of pottery, and this can assist in identifying widespread trade wares. In some areas the use of naturally sandy clays, shown by a marked lack of uniformity in grain size, rendered the addition of other material unnecessary, and another frequent natural constituent in areas rich in granite is flakes of mica.

Methods. Direct shaping from a lump of wet clay is difficult or impossible to demonstrate in archaeological material; but some tribes in lowland South America are known to have used it in historic times, so it was doubtless used by their ancestors. It is also used by the modern Maya of Yucatan.

The coiling method was used in many places. In many cases the coils were luted together with such skill that the tendency for the pots to break along their junctions, which is often the only indication that this method was employed, is not apparent. In times and places as far apart as the coast of Ecuador *c.* 2000 B.C. and the south-west of the United States *c.* A.D. 1000 coils were allowed to show deliberately on the necks of wide-mouthed jars; and in the south-west at about the same time grey-ware cooking pots were built of very fine coils composing the entire surface. The coils were corrugated by being pinched at varying intervals to diversify the surface, but the interior of the pot was smoothed. The corrugated surface presents a larger area to the fire than a smooth one, and it is said that this improves the efficiency of cooking.

Direct shaping and coiling are used alone and in combination by the modern Maya of Yucatan, whose conservatism suggests that they use the same techniques as their Pre-Columbian forefathers. Vessels are built or shaped on a cylindrical, saucer-like or square support of wood (*kabal*), which stands on a board on which it can be rotated by the feet. The *kabal* is not a wheel, since it has no axle, and the rotation is intermittent and generally slow, its chief function being to bring all parts of the mass of clay or vessel within easy reach of the potter's hands. In some villages it is rotated comparatively fast to form the rim of a pot, but even then at no more than about one-third of the velocity of a true wheel. Similar devices, all rotated by hand, are found sporadically in other parts of America, and the general conservatism of potters strongly suggests that all are of Pre-Columbian origin. There is no essential difference between the building up of a pot with a coil which encircles the vessel more than once and one with a series of rings each encircling it once or less, and in modern Yucatec potteries both may occur in a single vessel, depending on the diameter of the part being formed.

The paddle-and-anvil method of making pots was used in a limited area in the far north of the Peruvian coast, and the products have the appearance characteristic of this process in the Old World. Unlike the wooden paddles found in the Old World, the few surviving Peruvian examples are of pottery with impressed designs. When the pot had been shaped the surface was smoothed, after which the paddle was applied repeatedly so that the pattern covers the surface with some but not an excessive overlap. The interior has an undulating surface with slight depressions where the anvil has been placed.

One- and two-piece moulds, made of pottery, were widely used for figurines, and the material is very suitable since the wet clay shrinks as it dries and is therefore easy to detach from the mould. The casting process was particularly well developed on the north coast of Peru, and it was used in combination with coiling, stamping and hand modelling for making the complex forms of Moche and Chimù pottery, especially the stirrup-spouted bottle. In this the greater part of the body was cast in a two-piece mould, leaving an opening in the top into which the hand could be inserted to assist in joining the halves or to support the sides when applying a stamp for decoration, although in many cases the mould itself was designed to produce relief decoration. The vessel was closed by coiling. The stirrup spout was made separately, perhaps by wrapping sheets of clay around three rods and joining them, and was attached to the vessel with reinforcing coils at the junctions. When elaborate figure-subjects formed the body of the vessel, moulds of the appropriate shape were used but some details were modelled by hand.

Slip casting, in which a syrupy clay suspension is poured into a porous mould which absorbs water until the clay solidifies, is generally regarded as an exclusively European industrial process invented in the 18th c., but it seems to have been used for one purpose, for a limited period, in Peru long before. Between *c.* 600 B.C. and A.D. 400 pottery pan-pipes consisting of individual tubes stuck together with clay applied to the outside were made in the south and central coastal areas. The tubes are remarkably thin and uniform in bore, and microscopic examination shows that the interior may be left completely untouched, all features which could not have been produced in any other way. The process is not known to have been used for any other purpose, and it was forgotten when this sort of pan pipe ceased to be made.

Decoration. The earliest pottery found in most areas is unpainted, but it may show a wide variety of decorative processes such as polishing, incision, excision, brushing, application, stamping, rocker-stamping, cord-impression and punctation, most of which may be applied to restricted zones producing contrasts. At a slightly later stage comes painting with simple patterns in a limited range of colours, such as white on red, and red on buff, while the monochrome techniques continue. Later came more elaborate schemes, including polychromes. This was not a matter of simple progression but of preference, fashion and even possibly the availability of colouring matter. An instance is given by the finest pottery of the north and south coasts of Peru. The Moche wares of the north are skilfully and realistically modelled and painted, but the most frequent combination of colours is red and white, whereas the contemporary Nasca pottery of the south shows little interest in modelling and the painting is far more stylized, but up to eight colours were used.

A number of special techniques should be noted. The interest of the southern coastal people of Peru in colour is seen long before the potters learned how to produce a large range of colours in fired clay; for the Paracas pottery, which preceded Nasca (before *c.* 400 B.C.), was painted after firing with powdered minerals mixed with resin, producing most vivid lacquer-like reds, greens and yellows, which the dry conditions of the coast have allowed to survive in perfect condition. The same process was employed *c.* 2000 years ago on the coast of Ecuador, where its survival in the face of a much wetter climate is remarkable. Another process which can hardly be regarded as a true potter's technique is the coating of the surface of a finished pot with stucco, on which were painted elaborate designs in polychrome. This is found in the Classic Period, in the early centuries A.D., at Teotihuacan in central Mexico; but owing to the fragility of the stucco few examples have survived in good condition.

Negative painting is found in many parts of America from Peru to Mexico. In this process a design is painted on a fired light-coloured vessel with a slip-like mixture of clay, and when it is dry the whole vessel is smoked or coated with a water-soluble mixture which chars when heated, leaving a coating of carbon. The slip-paint is then easily removed, leaving the design in the colour of the vessel, commonly white, red or both, against a black ground. In some cases the black is somewhat fugitive, so the design may be indistinct. A good example of black negative painting on cream and red is the Tuncahuán style of highland Ecuador.

Two instances of the exceptional use of glaze may be given. In the south-west of the United States a red ware with simple decoration in black glaze spread from the Little Colorado valley to the Rio Grande drainage *c.* A.D. 1250. Here lead glazes, coloured with variable proportions of iron and manganese, were used to produce simple line decoration in black, green, brown or purple over red, buff or white slips, or to outline other colours. The glaze was used purely decoratively since it covers but a small proportion of the surface of any vessel on which it occurs. Its use continued until after the Spanish Conquest. Very different is PLUMBATE WARE, named from its appearance not its composition, belonging to the Toltec Period in Mexico (*c.* A.D. 900–1200). This has a slip rich in iron and aluminium, which when reduced in firing is hard, grey and vitrified. The vitrification is ascribed to the production by reduction of ferrous oxide, which is a violent flux, so this type of Plumbate owes its properties to the firing as well as to the composition of the clay in the slip. Plumbate ware was widely traded.

Firing. No Pre-Columbian kilns have been found, and until they are it must be assumed that firing was done on an open fire, as indeed it could have been. If the air can reach the pots freely during firing, they are normally oxidized and when there are sufficient iron compounds in the clay ferric oxide is formed, giving a red or brown colour. Smaller proportions of iron tend to produce cream or yellow colours. If the fire is smudged with leaves, grass or even earth towards the end of the process, grey or black pots may result, partly because the iron oxides tend to be reduced, producing a grey colour, and partly because the smoke may deposit carbon on the pottery or hinder carbon in the clay from burning out. At any rate potters in many parts of America showed a high degree of skill in controlling these processes.

2. TEXTILES. In most parts of America ancient textiles are only preserved sporadically and our knowledge of them is derived from rare finds in dry caves or in contact with copper salts, from impressions on pottery and representations on stone monuments or painted pottery. In addition to this a certain amount of information can be inferred with caution from the work of

modern weavers. The coast of Peru is a notable exception, since the dry climate has enabled textiles to survive in almost perfect condition, so most of our examples come from there.

Materials. The use of COTTON was widespread and examples are found from at least the south-west of the United States to Chile. The range of natural colours is considerable, including white, tan, dark brown and light grey; and these were fully utilized, at least in Peru. A number of bast fibres were also used, including a milkweed in Peru and aloe in Mexico. Besides these the Andean region had the wool of camelids, the domestic llama and alpaca and the wild guanaco and vicuña. The proportion of wool to cotton used on the coast, the only area where sufficient examples are preserved to give meaningful indications, tends to increase as time goes on, implying increased dependence on highland sources. The vicuña produces the finest wool but it is said to be more difficult to spin than alpaca wool, which can itself yield very fine threads. There are many cases of mixed fabrics, a simple example being tapestry with a cotton warp and a wool weft. This may have unfortunate consequences since the cotton may perish, leaving the wool unsupported.

Dyes. The textiles of the Peruvian coast are unrivalled in their range of colour, but a great deal remains to be done on the dyes and dyeing processes. A blue vegetable dye, indigo, was used as early as the pre-ceramic period, before 2000 B.C., and a red pigment was rubbed on to threads and finished cloth at the same time. Judging by the available resources, many vegetable dyes were used subsequently, but the wide range of colours on the superb textiles of Paracas, in the 1st millennium B.C., could have been produced by three dyes and mixtures of them (yellow to orange-brown, red and indigo) used in conjunction with the natural colours of cotton and wool. Red could have been derived from the cochineal insect or a root, and a purple obtained from a shell-fish appears to have been used also. Little is known about mordants, but 16th-c. sources suggest that alum was used. Compare COLOURS AND COLOURANTS.

Spinning. The Peruvians spun some of the finest yarns ever made, as can be illustrated by the TAPESTRIES. There is one of these which had an average of 327 wefts to the inch, rising in places to 500, as against a maximum of *c.* 85 in European tapestries of similar age, a remarkable difference even though they were designed for different purposes. Spinning was done with light, double-pointed spindles of wood and thorn fitted with small whorls of wood or pottery. The lower end of the spindle rested in a pottery bowl or a gourd to ensure smooth running. Modern Andean Indians use a falling spindle which is heavier, and in the highlands they spin as they walk to market. It is believed that this method originated in the highlands for spinning wool, and was spread to the coast in Inca times.

The direction of spinning varied, but when two threads were plied the direction was always reversed so that S-spun threads were always Z-plied and vice versa.

Looms. Most of the weaving in Peru and Mexico, and probably elsewhere, was done on a back-strap loom. Actual examples have been found in Peruvian graves, and there are pictures of them in Mexican codices. Illustrations of looms also occur in the Peruvian manuscript of Guaman Poma de Ayala (*c.* 1612). They were used to produce a wide variety of fabrics, some of which involved the use of at least three heddles. The vast majority of cloths consist of rectangular pieces from which most of the garments used could be made by sewing two or more lengths together in various ways. The cloth was never cut to shape, but it was possible to produce limited variations in shape during weaving by sloping the loom bars or by spreading the warp where it was desired to widen the cloth and inserting extra warps as required.

The maximum width which can be woven on a normal back-strap loom is governed by the weaver's reach and is *c.* 76 centimetres, and since cloths up to *c.* 5·5 metres wide and 26·5 metres long have been found at Paracas some other type of loom must have been used. There are Post-Conquest looms with the warp pegged out horizontally, or supported on a vertical frame, and it is known that back-strap looms operated by three weavers were used up to a generation ago; but it is not known what type of loom was actually used before the Conquest since there is no Pre-Conquest evidence for any of them.

Techniques. Many techniques required no loom, and among these were netting and varieties of plaiting used for such things as slings, bands and cords, and as in weaving (to quote one account) 'nearly every conceivable elaboration was developed beyond the dictates of necessity'. In pre-ceramic times, before the heddle loom was used, many fabrics were made by a technique of twining in which the warps are secured by pairs of wefts twined about them by hand, a process still used for making hammocks in northern Colombia. Highly stylized designs of birds, two-headed snakes and even human beings were produced by transposing warps in two colours in such a way that groups of a particular colour were brought to one face of the cloth. The introduction of the heddle, at about the same time as pottery, was accompanied by a variety of techniques, for some of which it was used and for some not. The final repertory included warp and weft stripes, warp and weft floats, tapestry, BROCADE, TWILL, double cloth, supplementary decorative wool wefts on plain-weave cotton cloth, gauze, and various types of open-work. A typical example of the last is a plain weave fabric with lozenge-shaped openings made by bunching groups of warps held by small bird motifs in tapestry. There were many other combinations, made possible by the flexibility of the simple loom and a readiness to drop any sort of mechanical aid and rely on the fingers. An example of this is given by patchwork or interlocking warp pattern, to which the key was given by finding an unfinished example. It is built up of coloured areas, typically rectangles and stepped bands, of plain weave, in which warps of one colour are everywhere crossed by wefts of the same. The warp was built up on taut scaffold wefts, which were subsequently removed and interlocked at colour changes, after which wefts of the appropriate colours were darned in. Very great skill was needed to maintain uniform tension. EMBROIDERY using many varieties of stitches has been found, particularly in the early south-coast cemeteries at Paracas, where the entire surface was covered with designs in wool on a cotton base. But embroidery became much less popular in later phases. Tie dyeing was used in at least two forms, *ikat* and *plangi*. The *ikat* examples are confined to rudimentary warp patterns in indigo. The *plangi* ones are equally simple—rings produced by tying bunches of cloth—but in some instances it was combined with a variety of the patchwork already described so that some squares were indigo and white, while others adjacent to them were either undyed or had the white rings dyed red after untying. In this case the different coloured constituents of warps and sometimes wefts were not interlocked, so that the squares fell apart when the scaffold threads were removed, but could be darned together after dyeing.

These are but a few samples to give some idea of the immense variety and complication which the Peruvian weavers could and had the wish to compass. What practical consideration, for instance, could lead to the production of triple and quadruple cloths? The unrivalled range of fibres must have encouraged these developments in Peru, but that the skill of the weavers there was not unique is shown by discoveries on the coast of Ecuador in recent years.

3. FEATHERWORK. The tropical area of America is inhabited by an abundance of brilliantly coloured birds, whose feathers are and have long been used to adorn human wearers by decorating garments such as shirts and mantles, making ornaments like armlets and diadems and even gluing them to the body, as was done during festivals of the Aztec feather-workers' guild. A few examples will be given from Mexico and Peru.

The graves of the dry coast of Peru have yielded hangings, sleeveless shirts and mantles which have a base of plain-weave cotton cloth to which the feathers are attached. Many of these were traded from the tropical lowlands east of the Andes. The feathers were hung in overlapping rows from cords sewn to the garment by bending the end of the quill into a hook which was tied down by a second cord. By arranging the feathers in patches of different colours intricate patterns were built up. Diadems were supported by light rings made from plaited reeds.

In Mexico flexible objects such as mantles were made by knotting feathers to a cloth background with aloe-fibre (maguey) thread, and some things such as fans by tying the feathers to a frame. Something of this kind is seen in the great series of classic Maya paintings, of about A.D. 800, in a temple at Bonampak, Chiapas. Here are chiefs wearing fantastic great headdresses with green quetzal-feather plumes, and, as if that was not enough, some of them wear even larger back-shields with a broad fringe of similar feathers. Elsewhere in the ceremonial series are men carrying what look like feather parasols, but their disposition suggests rather that they are a kind of banner. Parasols were carried over the Inca, his consort and some nobles to whom he granted the privilege as a sign of dignity, and the late 16th-c. writer Guaman Poma preserves a tradition that these were covered with feathers. A more complicated method of construction was used for rigid things like shields. For these a design was first painted on paper by an artist or scribe. A smooth aloe leaf was then covered with glue and carded cotton fibres were teased out into a film and applied to the glued surface. When it was dry more glue was applied so that it dried with a glossy surface. It was then peeled off and spread on the painted pattern, which was traced through. The film was then backed with coarse paper and a template of the object to be shown cut from it on a board. A second film of glued cotton was formed in the same way, and the design was outlined on it with the help of the template. This formed the base of the object. The feathers were then trimmed to shape with a copper, flint or obsidian blade and glued to the base in two layers by means of a bone blade. The first layer was of second-grade feathers, including some dyed ones, and the top one of carefully chosen feathers of the desired colours. The subjects were normally outlined in black feathers, but gold strips were used on the splendid Aztec shield in the Museum für Völkerkunde in Vienna. The feather-workers formed one of the most important guilds in Tenochtitlán, the Aztec capital, and all members of the families concerned took part, even children who prepared the glue. The craft survived the Conquest, and among the objects made shortly afterwards were some fine mitres, one of which is in Vienna. It did not die out until the 19th c. Examples of fine featherwork were shown in an exhibition of peasant crafts staged at Lima in the 1950s.

4. METALWORK. The earliest American metalworking known is that of the Old Copper culture of Lake Superior and the surrounding area. In this technique native copper was treated rather as a malleable stone than as a metal, and tools and weapons were beaten into shape. The copper was either collected as ingots on the surface of the ground or laboriously mined from outcrops with the use of fire, water, stone hammers made from boulders, and wooden levers and wedges. The objects made include spear-heads, harpoons,

fish-hooks and gorges, gouges, knives, chisels and adzes. Some of these followed stone prototypes, for example slate knife-blades. The process began at least as early as the 4th millennium B.C. but never developed into true metallurgy, and it was the only aboriginal metalwork which occurred over most of the United States apart from some few instances of copper working introduced into the south-west from Mexico.

Pre-Columbian metalwork elsewhere was practically confined to gold, silver and copper, with a minor use of lead, platinum and tin. It had a long history in the Central Andean area, Peru and Bolivia, where it began in the middle of the 1st millennium B.C. It flourished also in Ecuador, Colombia and the Isthmian area north to Costa Rica, beginning at much the same date although the dating is less reliable than it is in Peru. It is remarkable that it lagged far behind among the civilized peoples of Mexico, where it did not appear before *c.* A.D. 1000 and was used exclusively for ornaments.

The source of gold was almost entirely placer deposits, the beds of swift-flowing rivers; and the small amounts of platinum found, in Ecuador and Colombia, were similarly derived. The extent to which the smelting of the ores of copper and silver took place before the Spanish Conquest remains uncertain. High-grade copper ores, carbonates, oxides and even sulphides after roasting, could be reduced by heating with charcoal in the small pottery furnaces called *huairas* which have been found on hill slopes facing the prevailing wind in parts of highland Peru, Bolivia and Argentina. Their effectiveness was increased by heating the air outside the vents with charcoal and by blowing through copper tubes. The discovery of the bodies of two copper miners in a narrow mine shaft which had caved in on them, in northern Chile, accompanied by stone hammers and baskets filled with blue sand, the copper ore atacamite, is a demonstration of mining; but whether the ore was appreciated for its colour or obtained for smelting is uncertain. Perhaps the best evidence for smelting is the large quantity and widespread use of copper tools and ornaments, which are unlikely to have been obtained from the limited quantity of native copper available. Silver is found both native and as ores in Peru and Bolivia. It is probable that the smelting of the ores was accidental, and the discoverers may not have known what they were doing. In attempts to melt silver and remove earthy impurities it may have been heated with charcoal, and this could have caused the reduction of some ores which occurred naturally with the metal.

The keynote of metal working everywhere is great skill and ingenuity in the use of the simplest apparatus, in which respect it is similar to other crafts, especially weaving. Besides blow-pipes and charcoal the artificers had stone hammers, clay crucibles, and chisels, burins and punches of bronze and copper. Stone and pottery moulds were used for casting plain objects, such as copper axes, and are found in many places, for instance in a late Pre-Conquest setting on the coast of Ecuador. An elementary technique, which was employed on gold as early as the coastal Chavín period in Peru in the 1st millennium B.C., was simple hammering; and shaping by hammering over or into forms of stone or wood has also been found in many places, as is shown for instance by small stone relief carvings of birds, human beings or reptiles made for this purpose in the Chibcha region of Colombia. A preliminary stage in these processes was to hammer the metal into sheets. With silver and copper cold hammering causes greater hardness and brittleness, but this was countered by annealing. Copper masks produced by this process were made in the Chimù area of northern coastal Peru. Casting in open moulds has already been mentioned, but casting by the *cire-perdue* process was also commonly employed for elaborate forms and was used everywhere from Costa Rica to Peru. It spread to Mexico with other techniques at a late stage, and a detailed description of it in the 16th c. has been left by Bernadino de Sahagún. Soldering of gold was known, and soldered objects are found on the coast of Peru at least as early as the first quarter of the 1st millennium A.D. It was probably done by sticking the surfaces to be joined together with a mixture of gum and a powdered copper salt and then heating so that the gum charred and reduced the copper salt to copper. This combined with the gold to form an easily fusible alloy, which made the surfaces adhere. Objects made partly of gold and partly of silver, or of gold of two colours produced by alloys containing different amounts of silver, were made in Peru, Ecuador and Oaxaca, Mexico. They are believed to have been made by *cire-perdue* casting in two stages, a process easy to understand but needing almost incredible dexterity. A bronze Inca knife from Machu Picchu in Peru contained only 3% of tin but had a llama head on the end of the shank which was much richer in tin, and must have been cast round the shank. Metals and other substances were also joined mechanically; an object might be cast leaving hollows into which strips of metal were hammered, or stones such as TURQUOISE set. Combinations such as this may be pleasanter to our eyes than unrelieved gold.

Gilding, or the appearance of it, was attained in three ways. At the outset it must be said that there is no evidence whatever of mercury gilding. Alloys of gold and copper were heated with some kind of acid, probably a plant juice, which oxidized the copper on the surface. The oxide was removed so as to leave a concentration of gold, which was then burnished. Gold leaf could be applied to a copper object, a process which is illustrated by some nose rings found on the Ecuadorian coast. From the same country, the northern coastal province of Esmeraldas, come objects which have been gilded by running a molten gold–copper alloy containing not more than 20% of copper over the surface of a copper object heated with the blow-pipe on charcoal.

Of the rarer metals, platinum was used in ornaments, generally small, in Esmeraldas, Ecuador. The pure metal is not fusible at temperatures attainable by native smiths, but it has been shown (by Bergsøe) that grains of platinum, which are found in nature, when heated and hammered repeatedly with gold dust, a process known as 'sintering', will adhere together and eventually form a homogeneous mass since the gold will dissolve platinum and pass into it, forming small areas of alloys of lower melting-point than the pure metals. Tin was added to copper to make bronze but the exact process is uncertain. Cassiterite (tin stone) is common in Bolivia, and this could either have been smelted and the metal added to copper or ores of the two metals could have been smelted together. Bronze spread from Bolivia first to the coast of Peru and to north-western Argentina, and was carried further, notably to Ecuador, by the Inca in late Pre-Conquest times. In southern Peru, Bolivia and Argentina bronze with the greatest amount of tin was used in fairly complex castings for ornaments, whereas in Ecuador high-tin bronzes were used for axes, needles, knives and fish-hooks, where the hardness of such alloys was a desideratum. In the Chimù region of the north coast of Peru a native copper containing arsenic was used, and was considerably harder than ordinary copper. The hardness of both copper and bronze was considerably increased by cold hammering, and there is little doubt that this was realized and exploited. The use of lead was extremely rare; two nose-rings and some small ingots come from Esmeraldas, that home of rare metals and processes, and the Incas are said to have used it for inlays in wood. It is thought to have been obtained by heating the sulphide galena, which has a metallic appearance, on charcoal with a blow-pipe.

Many alloys apart from bronze were used. There was a considerable range of gold–copper ones, all called *tumbaga*, which are most frequently found in Colombia and seem to have spread from there to Central America and, to a lesser extent, to Ecuador and Peru. Some, but not all, of the objects of the Quimbaya gold style of the Cauca Valley, which are the finest in Colombia, are of *tumbaga*. These are mostly figures, flasks and close-fitting caps, and the alloy seems to have been appreciated for its reddish colour. There were also alloys of gold and silver or gold, silver and copper, some of which when cold hammered may be almost as hard as bronze. A copper–silver alloy was used on the south coast of Peru.

A word may be added on the appearance and the use of wire. Many of the flat *tumbaga* plaques of the Chibcha region of Colombia appear to have details added in wire, but actually they were made by the *cire-perdue* process. The regularity in thickness of the 'wires' seems to have been attained by extruding the wax in which they were modelled from some form of syringe. On the other hand some gold nose-ornaments made up of spirals and zig-zags from the Ecuadorian coast seem really to have been made of wire. It is suggested that this was hammered first into a bar and then forced, with heating, through an aperture or groove in a hard stone. Whatever the details, one of these needed 2·72 metres of wire for its manufacture, so this was no mean task.

5. WOOD AND STONE CARVING. The carving of wood, stone and indeed other materials such as bone and shell was subject to limitations imposed by the use in the main of stone tools, since there is no reason to believe in a dependence on tools of bronze and of alloys of comparable hardness although they may have been used occasionally. During the period before *c.* A.D. 1000 metals were simply not available in the Mexican area and they do not appear to have been used much for tools there even after that time. Hard igneous rocks and tough woods were used for many carvings everywhere, and the process of shaping them must have been excessively laborious.

In stone work it is probable that the desired form was outlined on a block of stone and the area outside it pounded and pecked with stone mauls, pulverizing the surface. When this was sufficiently reduced it could be smoothed and polished with sands of varying coarseness. Where possible advantage was taken of the natural shape of the stone, and of this the sculptures at San Agustín, Columbia, probably of the 1st millennium A.D., provide many examples. Here some statues were shaped from slabs, some from rectangular columns and some from cylindrical ones, and all these forms left their impress on the final result. The shaping process was assisted in some cases by the use of stones which were comparatively soft when quarried but hardened on exposure to the weather, like the volcanic tuff used at the Maya site of Copán, Honduras. The ability of the sculptors varied greatly from one area to another, but at least it can be said that each area had its own recognizable characteristics so that, for example, the work of San Agustín could not be confused with that of Tiahuanaco in Bolivia. Writers have never been lacking who have been so impressed with the fact of stone carving that they assume contacts between the areas where it is found with no support from chronology or specific resemblances; and so we find the figures of Sechín on the Peruvian coast compared with the *Danzantes* of Monte Alban, Oaxaca, Mexico, from which they are separated by thousands of miles and a considerable time, on no better grounds than that both are partly, though not entirely, outlined by grooves on a flat stone.

The sculpture of Middle America includes examples which show a competence and an elegance which are outstanding by any standards, particularly among the Maya and on the Gulf Coast, even though the human figures on the

Two-spouted embossed silver vessel with animal decoration. Nazca. (Kemper Coll.)

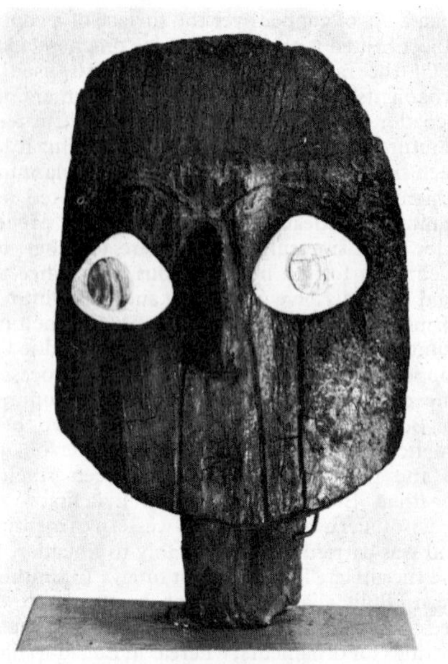

Wooden mummy head with cowrie-shell eyes. *c.* A.D. 1000. (Kemper Coll.)

Two Mochica portrait vessels depicting prisoners. (Kemper Coll.)

Silver and gold objects, including ceremonial Nazca crown, arm-bands and ear-plugs. (Kemper Coll.)

'Popper' for roasting maize. Mochica. (Kemper Coll.)

Double-bodied whistling jar. Chimù black ware. (Editor's Coll.)

Nazca painted vessel showing trophy heads. (Kemper Coll.)

Chimù black ware. (Kemper Coll.)

Detail of woven decoration. (Kemper Coll.)

Painted textile hanging. Paramonga. (Kemper Coll.)

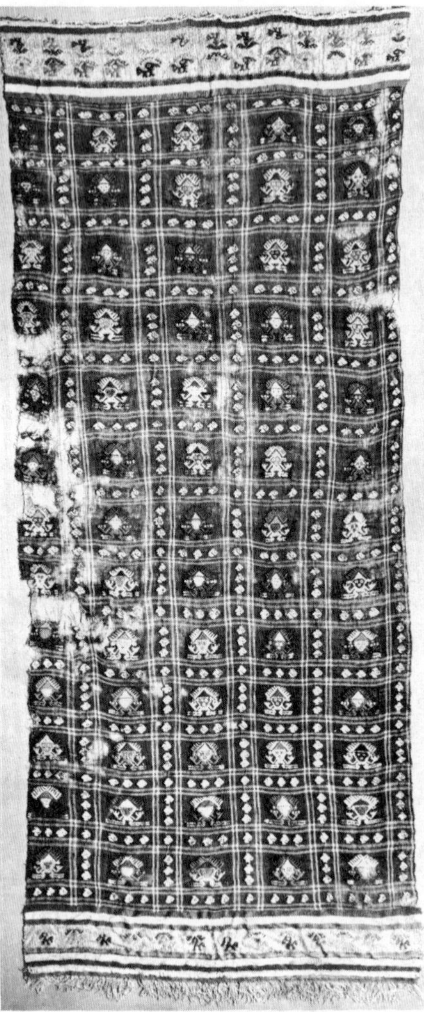

Finely woven mesh embroidered with multi-coloured figures. Chancay. (Kemper Coll.)

Maya stelae are partly enclosed in the stone. Some figures in this area were designed as architectural features. For example the great stiff Toltec warriors at Tula, which show minute details of dress, arms and equipment, were intended to support the roof of a temple, and they show it.

A few examples only will be used to indicate the range of capability in the rest of America. The figure work of the Central American countries is far cruder than that of the area north of them, but small objects like grinding stones (*metates*) in animal form may show considerable delicacy. Chavín, in northern Peru, attempts little work in the round but it excels in exceedingly complex designs in flat relief (i.e. relief in which the highest point of a sunken design is level with the surface of the block) on flat or gently curved surfaces, belonging to a period within 500 years on either side of 1000 B.C. From Chavín south-eastwards along the Andes carved stone statues and stelae of later date are found in several places. At their worst they are little more than shapeless to more or less conical stone blocks, with details to indicate a squatting figure with an over-large head worked on the surface in low relief. Best are the great statues of Tiahuanaco, which are basically columns of rectangular section with rounded corners on which limbs and details of costume are competently carved in low relief. These have considerable dignity. The famous monolithic doorway there is worked from a slab 305 × 308 centimetres. It has a central figure in low relief, and three rows of winged attendants in flat relief around him, and it seems that the Andean carvers were at their best in this type of work, as at Chavin.

The Incas produced virtually nothing in the way of monumental figure carving apart from a few quadrupeds and snakes in relief on the masonry at Cuzco, though they carved numerous miniature llamas and alpacas for fertility ceremonies with a great economy of line. By contrast they are famous for their masonry, in which large polygonal blocks of limestone or diorite are fitted together at the wall surface so precisely that a knife blade cannot be inserted between them. They also built regular masonry of rectangular blocks of lava, which could be flat but most frequently had the joints slightly recessed. The basic tools were stone hammers, preferably made of heavy ores such as haematite, but it is believed that sand and water were sometimes used to produce a smooth surface.

Small sculptures were rather a different matter from the larger ones. In these the process of carving the hardest stones was assisted by drilling holes with wood or bird-bone drills and by sawing with string, in both cases with abrasives, and results of great delicacy were achieved. The JADES of the Olmec of Mexico, and later those of the Maya, are among the finest examples.

Understanding and appreciation of the potentialities of wood-carving is hampered by the fact that in many areas wood is poorly preserved or not at all. As with stone-carving, tools were largely of stone and the many polished axes which are found must have played their part. Small, chunky ones with bruised butts were probably used as wedges for splitting wood. Animal teeth set in wooden handles are believed to have been used as gouges.

Some of the finest carvings are the two types of Aztec drum. The most notable of all is the great upright cylindrical war drum of Malinalco, which has elaborate low-relief carvings, including jaguars and eagles of a quality which recalls medieval heraldic design. There are also a number of horizontal tongued log drums, with highly competent low-relief carvings. At the other end of the scale comes the coast of Peru, where the greatest number of carvings are preserved by the dryness of the climate. They include many human figures, which demonstrate a stiffness and incompetence which is only partly excused by the fact that many of them were meant to be clothed. Some have shell inlay, and some details were painted red, which have been explained as an attempt to compensate for the lack of interesting form. Wooden staves and ceremonial tools of various kinds are crowned by rows of small figures and birds, and cut-out geometrical friezes. There are also boxes and bowls, often with incised designs, a process which lends itself better to the capabilities of the carvers than sculpture in the round, like the flat-relief stone carving.

6. ARMS AND ARMOUR. Both the Inca and the Aztec soldiers at the time of the Spanish Conquest were lightly equipped by European standards. Their body armour consisted of quilted cotton tunics which came down to the knees. For the climate and against Indian weapons these were superior to the European metal breastplates and they were often adopted by the Spanish from the Aztecs and the Inca. They protected their heads by quilted or wooden helmets or by caps of wickerwork; Aztec headgear was often more decorative than protective. The Inca soldiers hung on their backs round shields of chonta-palm framework covered with thick cotton cloth and carried on their left arm square or round shields made of thin boards covered with deerskin. At the back was a bar through which the hand could be thrust so that the shield hung from the wrist while the soldier grasped a halberd or mace in his hand. Both the Inca and the Aztec shields, particularly of the nobility, were often richly decorated with woven cloth or featherwork and might carry a clan device. In attacking a fortress they often made use of a large piece of coarse cloth capable of covering 50 or more men as some protection against stones and slings.

Their long-distance weapons were mainly the sling and the *bola*. The sling was made of hide, fibre or plaited llama wool with a finger loop at one end and a cradle for the missile in the middle.

The sling was also used for hunting and the early Spanish chroniclers bear witness to the surprising accuracy with which Inca troops could hurl from these weapons stones to the size of a duck's egg or larger. The sling was on average *c.* 60 cm in length, although war slings might be up to 2 metres. They were held doubled with both ends in one hand, one attached by fingers through the finger loop and the other free. They were then whirled round the head to give momentum and the loose end was released so that the stone was discharged from the cradle. The *bola* was primarily a hunting weapon of the mountain peoples, though it was also used in war. The instrument consisted of a number of stones or lumps of metal each fastened on to a thong and the ends of the thongs tied together. When whirled and discharged it would wrap round the enemy's legs or body and bring him down. Many varieties of bows and arrows were used by the forest peoples but the bow and arrow was not used by the highland peoples of the Andean region. In Central America the bow was a Toltec weapon. It was adopted by the Aztecs and used in the 10th c. with obsidian-tipped arrows. The spear-thrower is archaeologically very old in America. But by Inca times it had dropped out of use among the highlanders and neither javelins nor throwing spears were used, though they continued among the coastal Indians of Peru. Spear-throwers and obsidian-tipped javelins were very effectively used by the Aztecs.

Among the Inca soldiers the standard weapon for close-in fighting was a sword-shaped club (*macana*) made of hard chonta wood, double-edged, about 1·2 metres long. It was about 10 cm wide at the striking end, tapering towards the hilt, which was rounded and ended in a knob. Corresponding to this and still more formidable was the Aztec *maquahuitl*, toothed with sharp obsidian blades. In addition the Indians had a wide variety of spears, with fire-hardened wood or bronze points, and axes or halberds with stone or bronze heads. The halberds had an axe-head at one side and a single or double point at the other, or they might be fitted with a series of hooks. A characteristic weapon of the Inca was the 'star-headed mace', with a heavy bronze head shaped like a five-pointed star fitted on the end of a shaft some 3 to 4 ft (92 to 122 cm) long.

14, 58, 66, 90, 120, 121, 196, 210, 214, 216, 225, 271, 272, 331, 488, 539, 574, 721, 742, 763, 782, 932.

AMETHYST. The most important of the QUARTZ gemstones. It has been prized among the foremost gemstones since early antiquity and the fact that it is the only purple gemstone of note lent it a special significance in the centuries when purple was the royal colour. The amethyst was thought to protect the wearer from intoxication and from the 7th c. A.D. was importantly used as the gemstone in a bishop's ring. It was among the most expensive and appreciated of gemstones in the Middle Ages and through to the 19th c. Its depreciation in the 20th c. was partly consequent upon the flooding of the markets by South American mines. The finest amethysts used to come from Siberia. Now the main sources are Brazil and Uruguay; the term 'Siberian' refers to the rich purple colour which becomes red in artificial light. It is also found in India, Ceylon, Madagascar, Mexico, Persia and several regions of the U.S.A.

AMMAN, JOST (1539–91). Swiss wood engraver and illustrator. Born in Zürich, he worked for many years in Nuremberg and was one of the most prolific illustrators of his day. His wood engravings are valuable documents of contemporary life and his *Panoplia Omnium Artium* (1568) in particular contains a wealth of pictorial evidence on contemporary crafts and techniques. See also PLAYING CARDS.

ANDIRONS. See FIRE-DOGS.

ANDRÉ, JOHN. See SILHOUETTE.

ANIMAL STYLE (NOMAD). The expression 'Animal Style' has come to be used *par excellence* for a distinctive tradition of art in portable goods which was once spread, with local variations, among the mounted nomads of Europe and northern Asia right across the steppes from Hungary to the Gobi desert, and occasionally even beyond. The style was first studied in modern times when gold plaques representing animals were collected from western Siberia under Peter the Great of Russia, but it did not become well known until the barrows of south Russia began to be opened during the 18th c. and excavated more scientifically during the 19th c. Its origins are disputed and the whole subject is full of pitfalls.

In its fully developed form the Animal Style emerged first among the Scythian nomads of European physique and Iranian speech north of the Caucasus during the 6th c. B.C., but other forms arose not much later in west and central Siberia, in central Asia, and in Mongolia. It is agreed that no form of the developed style is as old as mounted nomadism itself. Mounted nomadism seems to have arisen about 1000 B.C. on the western half of the steppe-belt, perhaps again north of the Caucasus, and to have spread eastwards during the next centuries. The Animal Style was the creation of the western or Iranian stock of mounted nomads and declined as they were superseded by eastern peoples of Altaic speech and largely mongoloid physique. It left survivals and influences on other traditions of art in widely separated regions. Even among its originators it was not the only form of art, for they did sometimes represent the human form.

Known objects of the style come mainly from burials, but are obviously such as were used by the dead when they were alive. They were buried with much other gear and sometimes with the bodies of women, servants, and horses presumably intended to accompany their owners into the next world. From the modern excavator's point of view finds of animal figures can be classified according to two groups of materials, one durable such as bone, horn, bronze and gold, the other perishable such as textiles, felt, leather, wood, and in one case even the tattooed body of a chief. But the style in any one area varies little with the material.

In bone, horn, or boar's tusk and exceptionally in wood, plates, strips and pieces are found carved in the shapes of animals or birds of prey, or parts of these, particularly the head. Or again there are pieces covered with carvings in outline. In gold there are plaques and sheets for adorning harness, clothing, armour or weapons, including axe-handles, large plates for covering the nomad bow-cases and scabbards, torques, necklets, armlets and pendants. In bronze there are plaques, mirrors, cheek-pieces for bridles, ornamental pole-tops for standards, cauldrons and knives with ornamented handles, and mirrors with ornamented handles and backs. Flat surfaces of metal are worked in a technique that has the effect of low-relief or sometimes, particularly in Siberia, are made in open-work with empty spaces between figures; further west diadems are known in this style. Carving in the round occurs in some pole-tops, pendants and terminals of armlets and necklets. The textiles include rugs, hangings and saddle-cloths decorated with figures of animals and birds in felt appliqué, mostly in bright colours. Leatherwork in the same style and colouring is found both by itself and as appliqué ornament sewn to textiles or fastened to wood backing.

The metalwork has been found chiefly in the Scythian and Sarmatian tombs of south Russia and neighbouring countries, and is supplemented by scattered finds from Siberia, central Asia and Mongolia, many of them of unknown provenance. The textiles and other perishable objects come, with few exceptions, from the tombs of central Siberia and Mongolia. But this distribution of finds is due to the accidents of preservation. In the temperate west the perishable things have mouldered away while the metalwork has largely escaped plundering; in the harsher climate of the Altay permanent frost has preserved the perishable goods in tombs which were long ago plundered of their gold-work. Permanent damp deep underground has preserved the fabrics of Noin Ula in Mongolia, but once again most of the metal objects have been plundered. No doubt all such tombs of these nomads originally contained both durable and perishable objects. The great majority of the finds is now preserved in the Hermitage Museum at Leningrad. Their appearance is well known from publications.

1. GENERAL FEATURES AND SUGGESTED INTERPRETATION. In spite of variations some general remarks can be made on the Animal Style. Nearly every animal figure is at once recognizable, and even the monsters such as winged lions and eagle-griffins are of clearly defined types. But the figures of real animals are not naturalistic as they are in Greek, Assyrian or Chinese art. They are sometimes bent and folded upon themselves in a special manner, which in the best conveys an extreme tenseness and vitality. For example the stag, common in Scythian pieces, is shown with its legs drawn up and folded beneath it like those of a bird in flight and with its antlers laid along its back. Sometimes the legs are in standing position and the head is turned, so that the muzzle lies along the back and the antlers reach forward, which suggests hesitancy and listening. Sometimes forward movement is shown more accurately by the forelegs bent back and the hindlegs reaching backward as after a bound. But even the first pose is not one of rest. There are some extreme examples of the outstretched flying gallop in figures of griffins from Siberia. In contrast there are animals, which may be lions or panthers, bent into a ring—a pose nearly possible in real cats or weasels but here made absolute.

A subject which occurs rather rarely in the earliest Animal Style but grows commoner with time is the so-called animal combat, in which a lion, tiger, eagle or griffin pounces furiously upon a stag, elk, horse, hare, or other prey, biting and tearing it. Sometimes in Siberian work there is a more equal struggle, as between a tiger and a griffin or other monster. Nearly all these creatures are shown in profile, except that sometimes the head of the predator is depicted frontally making a bite. The attacked animals are often shown in a twisted pose with the hindlegs waving upwards. Another convention is the procession of beasts, shown on such objects as collars and diadems and borders of textiles. Animals rearing up in heraldic opposition are comparatively rare.

The folding and distortion may first have been adopted to fit all features on to a confined surface. But where there is room there is often another convention employed, that of carving small figures of other animals on the sides of larger figures, or again of making antlers or tails terminate in animal heads or forequarters. The style avoids smooth and featureless surfaces. One common feature of figures made in relief or in the round is the indication of rounded bodies or bunches of muscles by a bevelling technique of slanted surfaces that meet in a ridge along the line of greatest prominence. This is a natural way of working wood and appears notably in the wooden figures from the Altay.

Animal figures of this kind had evidently a deep meaning for the nomad artists. The animals represented are wild: formidable beasts or birds of prey, and game such as stags or elks and occasionally fish. The sheep and goats are wild kinds; the horses which appear are probably wild and so also are the yaks of some eastern pieces. The nomads did not represent the tame animals of their flocks and herds when they were practising the Animal Style. Some authorities have seen in the Animal Style a direct survival of the magical art of hunters, by which representations of the animals most hunted or dreaded could be used in rituals intended to control them. But such art is usually realistic rather than deliberately distorted. None the less, among both settled cultivators and nomadic herdsmen, hunting continued as a sport and as a training for war long after it had ceased to be needed for a livelihood, so that hunt animals remained a subject for art. From literary sources the nomads are known to have had a passion for hunting, as for war. Thus a close knowledge of animals continues to appear through the peculiar surface of the Animal Style. It has also been suggested that the animal figures were originally those of totems, animal ancestors and kin of the tribes that venerated them, and that the totems then developed into gods and spirits, the rulers of the world in which the nomads lived. These divine beings continued to be imagined in animal form. Animal art at this stage would embody a mythology that we cannot fully understand, and any borrowings from more civilized art would be made to serve this theriomorphic view of the world. Certainly such animal ancestors as the hind and the wolf appear later at the head of tribal genealogies among other nomads, for instance the Turks and Mongols. The animal figures would thus be emblems, some tribal, some cosmic. Such symbolical beasts are known in other arts, not least in the medieval heraldry of Europe.

2. ORIGIN, SPREAD AND VARIETIES. The question of the historical origins of the Animal Style is never likely to find a simple answer. The most that can be done is to trace some of its more important elements as they emerge. The first problem is to account for the combination of elements that created the earliest known form of the style at a particular place and time: north of the Caucasus and in south Russia from the 7th c. B.C. onwards.

Some authorities, notably Borovka and Minns, favoured a northern or north-eastern origin for the basis of the style, referring particularly to the very ancient tradition of working bone and horn among the hunting tribes of the Russian and Siberian forests. Rostovsteff was much impressed with its eastern affinities, comparing it with early Chinese art and suggesting an origin in central Asia between Iran and China. More recently the Karasuk culture of the Bronze Age in eastern Siberia, which has Chinese links, has been drawn into the discussion. Minns also allowed much influence on the south Russian style from Near Eastern traditions—Assyrian, Urartian, Anatolian and Iranian. This line of inquiry, further pressed by Tallgren, has yielded important results in the hands of Godard, Ghirshman, Sulimirski and others, who have used recent discoveries in north-western Iran. Schefold, a specialist in Greek Art, makes the Scythian style at all stages one more effect of archaic Greek art on that of surrounding peoples.

In the Pontic area the Animal Style is first represented by two small carvings in bone of an eagle's head and a curled animal from Temir Gora in the Taman Peninsula, dated about 650 B.C. But these are much later than the coming of the first Scythians, which has been connected by Sulimirski with the advance of the Timber Grave culture from the Volga to south Russia between 1000 and 900 B.C. Nothing is said of the Animal Style in connection with these earliest Scythians, even when some of them reach Transcaucasia in the next century. The developed Scythian style of such sites as Kelermes, Ul and Seven Brothers in the Kuban valley, and at Litoi in the Dnieper and Elisavetovskaya in the Don basin, is dated to the 6th c. by finds of Greek pottery along with the Scythian remains.

The elaborate gold-work in the Animal Style which appears at this date by the Kuban, Don and Dnieper has no forerunners north of the Caucasus. Among the weapons and gear in these tombs are some things which are not Scythian but Near Eastern: Assyrian, such as the gold sheath-plates from Kelermes and Litoi, decorated with monsters and genii, and rhyta with goats' heads from Seven Brothers; Median, using the older art of Urartu in Armenia, such as sword-hilts from Kelermes and Litoi. On a gold bowl from Kelermes are figures of ostriches, a lion, and goats in Assyrian style, but also a Scythian stag. South of the Caucasus a similar combination of Assyrian and Urartian monsters with Scythian stags, ibexes and small animals is found on a gold pectoral, an inlaid silver dish, gold sheathing, and other objects from the treasure of Ziwiye in Kurdistan, which is dated to the 7th c. and may have belonged to a Scythian or a Median chief.

That this contact with the Near East was not merely external or commercial is shown by Herodotus's account of the great Scythian irruption across the Caucasus some time before the fall of Assyria to the Medes, which is confirmed by Assyrian records and biblical references. Late in the 7th c. the Scythian horde from its base in Azerbaijan dominated a large area of the Near East for a generation or two before the Medes defeated it and drove it back across the Caucasus. During their stay in the Near East the Scythians picked up various features that then appear in the first developed Animal Style. When they left they are likely to have deported Oriental craftsmen, as the Mongols regularly did much later.

Arguing from this known contact of the

Scythians with the Assyrians and Medes, some scholars have claimed that the animal art of the horse-trappings, axe-heads and pin-heads of Luristan in the Zagros Mountains of western Iran contributed to the Scythian Animal Style. Though the horsemen of Luristan are reckoned to have been a rough Iranian people, Cimmerian or Median, and so akin to the Scythians, their style is visibly not the same as the Scythian and often makes use of the human figure as an essential part of designed groupings. There was also a vigorous tradition of metalwork with varieties of animal art in Transcaucasia, and earlier still Anatolian art makes much use of the stag and the boar, well-known subjects of Scythian art. Some contribution from all these sources is possible, but the threads were not gathered together until the Scythian invasion. Greek influence is apparent from an early date in the Scythian style, but it is at first only external. When it penetrated deeper, as in the late 6th and the 5th centuries along the coast of the Black Sea, it spoiled the style as no other influence had done, and in some pieces, such as the gold plate of the scabbard from Kul Oba in the Crimea, very nearly replaced it.

In the great barrows of the Dnieper valley the Scythian style persisted with Greek influence affecting it in varying strength, but to the north-west the original quality was either unaffected or, if there was change, the influence was usually not Greek. The bronze die, with stag and beasts of prey, from Garchinovo in Bulgaria and the gold stags from Tapioszentmarton and Zoldhalompuszta in Hungary show less vigorous versions of the Scythian style, in which the tradition was already failing. But the gold fish from Vettersfelde in Germany, bearing figures of other creatures and having its tail terminating in rams' heads of Greek appearance, is at least full of vigour. The Scythian style began to disappear during the 4th c. B.C.

East of the Scythians were kindred but distinct peoples, the Sarmatians beyond the Don and the Sakas of central Asia, but before their work is noticed, the Animal Styles of the Altay and of Minusinsk on the upper Yenisey deserve immediate mention. Though these regions are so distant from south Russia, the forms of the style found in them are more like the Scythian than anything yet known in the country lying between and are roughly contemporary with it. The Animal Style of the Maiemir and Pazyryk periods in the Altay is likely to have begun and ended somewhat later than the Scythian, for in its full growth it shows features in common with the Sarmatian style and among its remains are found also those of imports such as the famous carpet from the Achaemenid Empire of Persia and a tapestry from China of the age preceding the Han Dynasty. It may have arisen in the 5th c. and have lasted into the 3rd. In the valley of Pazyryk in the High Altay were found five great mounds, and near the village of Bashadar in the

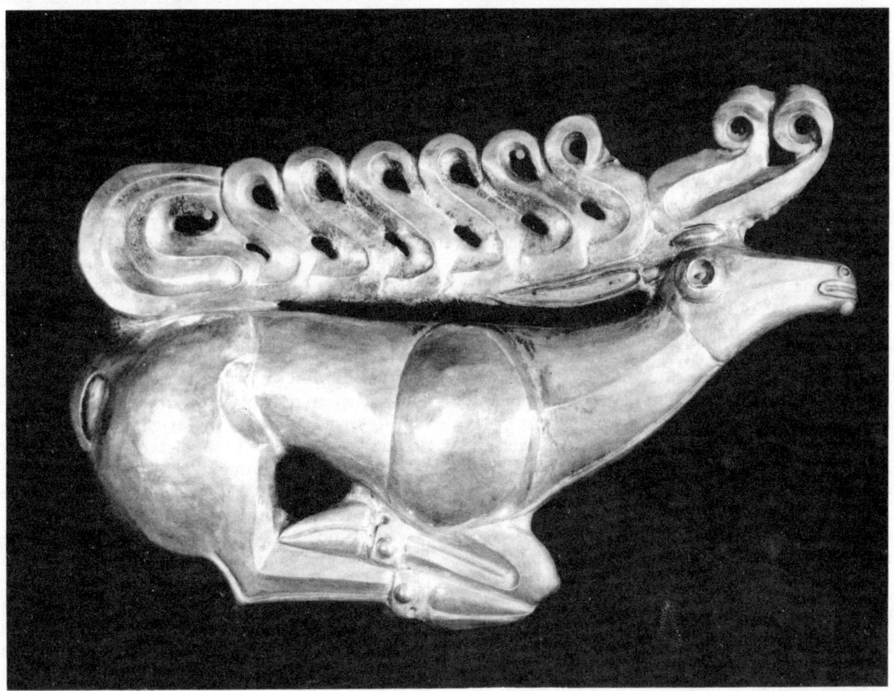

Gold stag from Kostromskaya in the Kuban valley. (Hermitage Mus., 7th–6th c. B.C.)

Bronze standard in shape of bird's head. From Ulski in the Kuban valley. (Hermitage Mus., 7th–6th c. B.C.)

central Altay two. The textiles, leatherwork and woodwork from Pazyryk show the same inspiration as known Scythian work in other materials, but in conditions which must have given it freer play. The extraordinary variety of bright colour, not all of it realistic for the animals shown, is specially noticeable in the textiles, felt and leather. Groups of animals are commoner than in the original Scythian style, and so are scenes of animal combat. The lines of composition are smoother and more flowing in the animal figures, which include the elks and tigers of the north-east as well as winged monsters. These appear also on the tattooed body of the chief from the second tomb. The procession of tigers on a coffin from Bashadar is in a style recalling Sarmatian work. In Minusinsk the corresponding culture of the Tagar period was likewise introduced by mounted nomads. They appear to have set the native bronze-workers to make pieces for them; the style of these is inferior and has been called 'underdog Scythian'. Minusinsk lies on the route of further diffusion to northern Mongolia.

Since the Pontic Scythians were always pressed from the east, they cannot have spread their style to the Altay and Minusinsk by conquest or migration. The only explanation must lie in peaceful intercourse, perhaps of very long standing. Herodotus mentions a Scythian trade route running far northward ultimately to a gold-bearing country, which should be the Altay and the gold-bearing sand of the Yenisey.

From unknown sites in the upper Ob basin of western Siberia come the famous gold plaques which were collected for Peter the Great. They show the Sarmatian version of the Animal Style, which is clearly influenced by the less nomad art of the Oxus Treasure from the north-eastern edge of the Achaemenid Empire, dated to the 5th and 4th centuries B.C. This mixed Median, Achaemenid and Saka art has beasts and birds of prey and griffins among its favourite subjects. Some of these are covered all over with cloisonné work, but later figures have only embossed reliefs or vestigial sockets for inlays of jewels. The Sarmatian plaques show the same succession of features through time. They represent a new development of the Animal Style, distinct from the Scythian and inspired by this later Iranian tradition, which spread with the Sarmatian migration westward through Kazakhstan and western Siberia until it reached south Russia. In this style the animal combat is fiercer and more dramatic than in any other. The style is also represented by many kinds of small ornament, by diadems and arm-bands with jewelled inlays from the Kuban and from the celebrated burial ground of Novocherkassk on the Don, and by other objects from south Russia or the Danube valley, notably bronze phalerae, disc-shaped horse-trappings, which show Greek influence and sometimes that of Parthian Iran.

Much further east, in the Ordos desert of north China and in neighbouring regions of the Gobi and of China, is the source of a scattered and vaguely defined group of objects, the Ordos bronzes. They do not represent a distinct and definite version of the Animal Style, but rather successive fashions carried eastwards through Zungaria by Sarmatian or other Iranian nomads. The styles were adopted by the largely Mongoloid nomads of the Gobi when they learned the techniques of mounted nomadism. The bronzes are very difficult to date, since some small pieces represent curled animals in Scythian style, some are pole-tops which might have been found in south Russia, and others are plaques which seem to be copies in bronze of well-known types of Siberian gold plaque. Others again show as marked a Chinese influence as some Scythian pieces do Greek. There should be a certain interval of time between the beginning of any south Russian or Siberian style and its reproduction in Ordos bronzes. Most of them should be dated to centuries immediately preceding or following the beginning of the Christian era, the period of Hsiung Nu domination on the steppe north of China, and of Han rule in China.

The tombs of Noin Ula in the basin of the Selenga near Lake Baikal, dated to the beginning of the Christian era, have yielded a few bronze plaques of the Ordos type and also a felt rug bordered with repeated scenes of combat between a yak and a lion and between a winged wolverine and an elk, very much in the Animal Style of Pazyryk. Further east there are traces of the style in Manchuria, Korea and Japan.

The Samartian style lasted in various forms between central Siberia and eastern Europe until a new age began with the advance of the Huns from eastern Asia in the 4th c. A.D. The Huns did not practise the Ordos styles, but something like them was known among their successors, the Avars. The influence of the Scythian style is apparent among the Celts, and of the Sarmatian style more strongly among the Germanic peoples, notably in the Vendel style which appeared in Sweden without known ancestry in the 7th c. A.D. A form of the Animal Style continued much longer in northern Tibet.

The end of the Animal Style, during the centuries after the Iranian nomad cultures disappeared from the steppes, was apparently brought about by the spread of Buddhism, Islam and Christianity, which destroyed the religious ideas embodied in it.

Information about the art of the mounted nomads has accumulated in bulk and in variety as excavations have continued through the 20th c. New discoveries are constantly being made not only in Central Asia and Siberia but even in the better explored territory of south Russia. New light might well be thrown by excavation of the rest of the 212 barrows of Noin Ula in Mongolia. Owing to this rapid growth of new excavated material bibliographical information has fallen rapidly out of date. Much of it is contained in works on the great regions which the Animal Style once covered. The specialist works to which reference is given necessarily deal largely with the relevant ethnology and geography; discussions of the aesthetic aspects of the Style are incidental and brief. Summaries of current Russian work are often to be found in Western journals of prehistory and archaeology.

See ASIA, CENTRAL; RUSSIA.

18, 665, 700, 702.

ANKH. Also called the Key of Life and Crux Ansata. In form it is a tau cross with a loop at the top. It was an ancient Egyptian symbol of life.

ANNEALING. See COPPER AND ITS ALLOYS.

ANTHEMION. Greek decorative motif based on stylized honeysuckle forms or palmette (date-palm) branches. The motif was frequently used during the 18th and early 19th centuries by classicizing designers as decoration for furniture, plate, etc.

'Anthemion back' is a modern term used to describe a type of chair which came into vogue in the last quarter of the 18th c. with pierced oval back and bars curving in the form of an anthemion pattern.

ANTHING, JOHANN FRIEDRICH (*c.* 1753–1805). Miniaturist and silhouettist, born at Gotha. He travelled extensively through Russia, making SILHOUETTE portraits of notable persons. He worked for the court and in 1784 did 12 heads of members of the Imperial Academy of Science at St. Petersburg (published in 1903 by the Archivist of the Academy). *A Conversation Piece* showing Paul I of Russia with the Empress and their two sons was shown at the Exhibition of Russian Art in London in June 1935. He was in London in 1789, where he made silhouettes of the Prince of Wales, Duke of York and Georgiana, Duchess of Devonshire. He visited Constantinople from Russia and was in Warsaw in 1795. 752.

ANTWERP LACE. A flourishing LACE-making industry grew up in Antwerp during the latter part of the 18th c. and Antwerp lace was widely exported, especially to Spanish America. It was characterized by designs of pots or vases, variously treated, with flowers springing up symmetrically from them. With its thick outlining thread and a ground mesh in the form of six-pointed stars it closely resembled CHANTILLY LACE.

ANTWERP-LOUVRE SCHOOL. The modern name given to the workshop, or group of workshops, responsible for a series of closely related embossed parade-armours and shields dating from the 3rd quarter of the 16th c. Many of these are associated with the French Court, and especially with Henri II (1547–59), as is a number of designs for armours belonging to the group—mostly in the Graphische Sammlung, Munich—which have been attributed with virtual certainty to Étienne Delaune (1518/19–1583). This association led to the pieces being ascribed to a theoretical French royal workshop, for which the name 'Louvre School' was coined. It was subsequently discovered that some armours and shields belonging to the group—now divided between the Livristkammar, Stockholm, the Castle of Skokloster, Sweden, and the Historisches Museum, Dresden—had been decorated in Antwerp for Eric XIV of Sweden during the period *c.* 1561–3 by a goldsmith named Eliseus Libaerts. It is uncertain whether all the armours in the group were made by Libaerts's workshop in Antwerp, whether the workshop was at some time situated or had a branch in Paris, or whether other workshops were involved. The possibility that some at least were produced in a French Court workshop cannot therefore be ruled out completely, so the undocumented pieces must, for the time being, be ascribed to either Antwerp or Paris. Examples can be seen in the Royal Collection, Windsor Castle; Wallace Collection; Musée de l'Armée, Paris; Kunsthistorisches Museum, Vienna; Metropolitan Museum, New York. See ARMS AND ARMOUR.

824.

ANTWERP TAPESTRIES. The weaving of TAPESTRIES was carried on in Antwerp from the 15th c. onwards, and during the 16th and 17th centuries the town was also the chief collecting point and mart for tapestries made in the other Flemish weaving centres. Among the principal workshops of the 17th c. in Antwerp were those of the families of Wouters and Van der Goten; signed sets by both are extant. Members of the Wouters family worked extensively for the English market. The town-mark of a pair of hands is sometimes found on Antwerp tapestries. 312.

APOSTLE SPOONS. Spoons with stems terminating in figures of the Apostles. The first reference to them is in a York will of 1494. The earliest known examples date from about the same period and the latest from the second half of the 17th c. A complete set usually but not always numbered 13 and included the figure of Christ. The actual Apostles vary in different sets; St. Paul often takes the place of one of them. Each Apostle bears his emblem and the Master an orb. In the 17th c. each figure wears a halo, often grotesquely large.

Apostle spoons are also found on the Continent, particularly in Holland and Germany, but not in complete sets. The latter were also extremely rare in England, partly because in the 16th and 17th centuries a silver spoon was a favourite christening gift. An Apostle spoon was regarded as particularly suitable if it represented the Saint whose name the child was to bear.

APPLIED WORK or APPLIQUÉ. A form of EMBROIDERY in which bold designs are produced by sewing shaped pieces of cloth or other material on to a contrasting ground. This technique, practised in ancient EGYPT and in medieval and Renaissance Europe, still remains in common use. The term is sometimes transferred to applied decoration in leatherwork, silverwork, etc.

APPRENTICE LOCKS. In the 17th and 18th centuries guild regulations in France and Germany, possibly elsewhere also, required apprentices to submit a finely worked LOCK AND KEY as a masterpiece. These locks were chiselled and engraved on the interior as well as the exterior and were not intended for use, but simply as displays of virtuosity in steel working. The French locks of the 17th c. with the front based on the façade of a Renaissance palace are the finest. Pattern books published in Paris by Mathurin Jousse and later by Jean BÉRAIN spread the French stylistic fashions widely.

AQUA FRESCA. Family of Italian gun-makers who worked at the village of Bargi, near Bologna. The earliest known member of the family is SEBASTANO, active in the 2nd half of the 17th c. Most famous member of the family was MATTEO (1651–1738), whose artistry was unsurpassed among Italian gunsmiths. He was an excellent steel chiseller and engraver and he concentrated on locks, rarely making his own barrels. He was also known for engraved steel SNUFF-BOXES. The family continued as gun-makers at Bargi, the last member being PIETRO ANTONIO (d. 1809).

AQUAMARINE. A blue variety of BERYL, originally known as 'blue beryl'. Slightly harder and more transparent than the EMERALD, it lacks the emerald's intensity of colour but unlike the emerald it can have brilliance if facet-cut. The crystals are in general larger than those of the emerald. Aquamarines are valued for blue colour rather than green and for clarity and freedom from flaws. The most common defect is a 'rain' of shining, needle-like crystalline lines. The finest aquamarines come from Brazil. Other sources are south-west Africa and Siberia.

AQUILATA. See EMBROIDERY (GERMANY AND THE LOW COUNTRIES).

ARABESQUE (French: Arabian). General term for a class of painted or low-relief surface ornament making use of leaves and branches in flowing lines with fancifully intertwined scroll work. The term is of very wide application in the decorative arts, being used to describe ornamental motifs in architectural and mural decoration, metalwork, WOODWORK, CERAMICS, BOOKBINDING, manuscript illumination, EMBROIDERY, TAPESTRY and so on. The type is of classical origin, being a characteristic feature of Hellenistic art in Asia Minor. It was adopted into Islamic art and from *c.* A.D. 1000 became one of the most ubiquitous features of Muslim decoration. In Islamic art the plant forms of the arabesque were rendered less naturalistically than in Hellenistic and Roman decoration, leaves and stems were reduced to formal patterns and the plant forms became schematic and remote from reality, preserving only the principle of the split leaf and the continuous stem. The ingenuity and imagination of the artist turned to devising complicated convolutions of symmetrically disposed pattern.

In Europe the term *rabeschi* was used in 16th-c. Italy to describe pilaster ornaments featuring ACANTHUS foliage. The French term '*arabesque*' was first applied in the latter part of the 17th c. to the GROTESQUES (*grotteschi*) of the Italian Renaissance, despite the classical origin of the latter. The characteristic development of the French arabesque combined bandwork deriving from the MORESQUE with decorative acanthus foliage or PALMETTES radiating from C-scrolls connected by short bars. It is a motif which appears to have been first exploited in embroidery and to have been developed in the garden design of Claude Mollet and Jacques Boyceau under Henry IV and Louis XIII. A fashion for painted arabesques in the Mannerist style with a central medallion combined with acanthus and other forms was introduced by

Simon Vouet (1590–1649) and was developed by Charles Lebrun (1619–90), notably in the interiors at Vaux and the Galerie d'Apollon at the Louvre. A novel feature of Lebrun's painted arabesques was the use of scrolls of flat bandwork joined by horizontal bars and contrasting with acanthus scrolls and palmette. Arabesques also figured largely in the tapestry designs of Lebrun and later of Noël Coypel (1628–1707), a pupil of Vouet. In contrast to the classicism of Charles Errard (1606–89) the more exuberant line of Lebrun was taken still further by Jean BÉRAIN, whose imaginative arabesques are considered to be one of the first intimations of a change of feeling that eventually blossomed into the ROCOCO in the hands of the ornamentalists Pierre LEPAUTRE and Claude AUDRAN. Lepautre transposed the forms of Bérain's painted arabesques from the flat to relief and thus transformed the arabesque from a flat panel filling to a carved frame.

ARCANUM. The secret formulae for the making of porcelain. They include kiln-construction as well as the composition and firing of bodies, glazes and colours. *Arcanist*: one who possessed these secrets.

ARGENTAN LACE. See ALENÇON AND ARGENTAN LACE.

ARKWRIGHT, RICHARD (1732–92). In early life a travelling barber of Preston, Lancashire, he became interested in mechanical problems and in 1769 took out a patent for a 'spinning-frame' which superseded the HARGREAVES spinning-jenny. It was capable of producing a yarn which could be used for warp as well as weft. In 1771 he established the first spinning-mill to be operated by water power. See COTTON AND COTTON PRINTING and WEAVING.

ARMADA CHESTS. Heavy iron or iron-bound coffers, unconnected with the Spanish Armada but manufactured in Germany, Flanders and Austria from the 16th to the 18th centuries. They had a dummy keyhole in the front and were secured by a lock on the underside of the lid, fastening it to the four sides by a system of bolts. These strong-boxes were exported in large numbers to England and elsewhere before the introduction of the modern safe.

ARMORIAL STYLE. Term used in the early 19th c. to describe Tudor timber-framed buildings decorated externally with heraldic motifs. In the 20th c. the term has been occasionally applied to furniture decorated with heraldic motifs during the ABBOTSFORD PERIOD.

ARMS AND ARMOUR

1. ARMOUR. Defensive armour has been used in most parts of the world since long before historical times. Its earliest form was probably a simple shield of wood, LEATHER or basket-work, which was later supplemented by helmets and body-defences made of the same materials or of bone, horn or padded cloth, of a kind used by many primitive peoples until quite recently. With the introduction of metal-working, however, more sophisticated societies developed armour of metal, at first of BRONZE and then of IRON AND STEEL, though at all times this was commonly accompanied by subsidiary defences of leather or padded cloth. Five main constructions were evolved: *lamellar*, consisting of small, approximately oblong, overlapping plates linked by an intricate system of continuous lacing; *scale*, consisting of small plates, usually leaf-shaped, arranged like roof-tiles and secured to a textile or leather garment; *mail*, a defence of interlinked rings, often incorrectly called *chain mail*; *plates* (or *coat-of-plates*), consisting of plates or hoops, overlapped and secured to a textile or leather lining or cover; *plate*, consisting mainly of large plates, most of which individually form a complete defence for some particular part of the body. Most forms of metal armour used from antiquity onwards fall into one of these categories, or a combination of several of them.

(*a*) *Ancient Times*. The earliest surviving examples of armour—dating from the 3rd millennium B.C.—appear to be the gold wig-shaped head-piece and the conical and rounded copper helmets excavated at Ur in Sumeria. The little evidence available from other sources suggests that they were worn in conjunction with only a cape or tunic, probably of quilted cloth, and a large shield. At approximately the same period, however, shirts made of copper, bronze or hide scales were already in use in Egypt. Some of these may have been true scale armour, but the most popular construction was probably the lamellar one, which is subsequently recorded all over the East—for example on the famous Assyrian reliefs in the British Museum—and survived there until the 19th c., notably in Japan. Mail too was probably used at an early date in the East, though it is first definitely recorded in Sarmatian graves of the 5th c. B.C.

The earliest surviving European armour recorded is a Mycenaean bronze panoply of the 15th c. B.C. from Dendra (Argolid), which consists of a complete defence for the torso made of horizontal hoops. Almost contemporary with this, and from the same cultural area, are a few conical helmets made of bronze or rows of boars' tusks applied to a leather cap, and large bronze figure-eight-shaped shields. At the same period a cuirass made of two solid bronze plates, covering the breast and back respectively and embossed to represent the body muscles, probably appeared in Greece, though the evidence for its general use before the 7th c. B.C. is scanty. From this last period it was widely adopted in Greece, accompanied by greaves—embossed to the shape of the legs—below the knees, a rounded helmet extending over the cheeks and equipped with a high horse-hair crest, and a large oval shield, again all of bronze. Similar cuirasses, probably based on Greek prototypes, appeared in central and southern Europe at the same time, though with other forms of helmet, conical or rounded and sometimes equipped with a triangular comb.

In addition to armour of solid plates the Greeks used the scale and lamellar constructions. All three were adopted by the Italic tribes, including the Etruscans and the Romans, though lamellar armour was probably chiefly used by the former. The classic Roman legionary equipment, which apparently developed in the 1st c. B.C., was the *lorica segmentata*, which consisted of a defence for the trunk made of transverse iron hoops and which was accompanied by large hooped shoulder-defences, a rounded helmet with deep cheek-pieces and a neck-guard, and a large rectangular wooden shield bowed towards the body. High-ranking officers wore solid bronze cuirasses embossed to represent the muscles of the trunk and often as well with elaborate decoration in relief. Armour decorated in a similar manner was also worn by gladiators. Mail too was known to the Romans at least as early as the 1st c. B.C., and during the later Empire was used for arming both horses and men of the heavy cavalry (*cataphractes*). At the same period a distinctive cavalry helmet was introduced, somewhat similar in form to that worn by the legionaries but with a solid mask protecting the face.

(*b*) *European Armour in the Middle Ages and Renaissance.* With the fall of the Roman Empire in the West body-armour made of solid plates apparently went out of general use, though it was probably never discarded completely. The patchy evidence available suggests that from *c.* the 6th c. A.D. the usual defensive equipment of those who could afford it was a shirt of mail (*hauberk* or *byrnie*), an iron helmet and a large oval or round shield of wood. Apart from an apparently short-lived survival among the Nordic peoples of a version of the Roman cavalry-helmet with a face-mask, the helmet used everywhere in Europe was now of conical form—derived from the East—with pendent cheek-pieces and sometimes a mail neck-guard. It remained in wide use until the 13th c., for most of this period to the exclusion of any other type. From some date prior to the 10th c. it was normally equipped with a down-projecting bar (*nasal*) over the nose.

The outlines of the development of medieval armour can only be traced clearly from the 11th c. onwards, when pictorial representations start to become common, while the vast majority of surviving specimens of armour date from after the middle of the 14th c. The key document at the beginning of this period is the BAYEUX TAPESTRY, executed after 1066 and probably before 1082, on which most warriors are shown wearing knee-length mail hauberks and conical nasal-helmets accompanied by kite-shaped shields. A few also wear mail hoods under their helmets and mail leggings (*hosen*). This equipment, which covered padded undergarments, survived with little variation until the early 14th c., though in the 12th c. mail hoods and *hosen* became general, while the sleeves of the hauberk were extended to form mittens over the hands. During the same period flat-topped and round-topped versions of the conical helmet appeared and at the end of the century the nasal was enlarged into a face-mask. In the early 13th c. the mask was extended round the back of the head so as to enclose it completely, so forming what is now usually called the *great helm.* This was to survive in warfare until the mid-14th c. and in the tournament until the 16th c. With the helm came the crest, a representation of the owner's device, made of coloured parchment or leather and mounted on its summit. In the 12th c. also appeared an open helmet like a broad-brimmed hat (*kettle-hat*), and a gown (now usually called the *surcoat*) covering the armour to below the knees but usually sleeveless. The wearer's heraldic arms were often depicted in colour on the gown—especially after the mid-13th c.—and on his shield. In the late 12th c. this last started to develop the characteristic modern 'heater' form, which it achieved in the 13th c. and retained until the shield was generally discarded in the West for mounted warfare early in the 15th c.

Though the equipment just described survived almost unchanged until the early 14th c., there is evidence to suggest that as early as the late 12th c. plate defences were being worn occasionally under the hauberk. The first appearance of plate on the illustrations that provide our main evidence at this date does not, however, occur until *c.* 1260, when small discs of metal or leather begin to be shown reinforcing the mail at the knees and elbows. In the last quarter of the 13th c. short sleeveless coats-of-plates (known simply as *the plates*), fastening up the back, began to come into general use together with gauntlets similarly constructed of metal plates riveted to a covering or lining. This plates construction was widely adopted in the early years of the 14th c. and was to remain the chief one for the defence of the trunk for nearly a century. With its general adoption came an increase in the reinforcement of the limbs until by *c.* 1340 they were entirely encased in gutter-shaped plates, articulated at the joints, though still worn over mail.

The 14th c. was a period of transition in which the armourers sought to develop the full potentialities of plate. The shape and articulation of the limb-defences were improved and they were made more compact, while the plates in the coat-of-plates tended to become larger and more shapely and after *c.* 1350 assumed a round-chested, wasp-waisted outline that was to be almost standard for the next fifty years. They were still normally held by rivets to a textile base, though now increasingly incorporating a solid breastplate, while a short, tight-fitting sleeveless gown (*jupon* or *coat-armour*), embroidered with the owner's coat-of-arms, was usually worn over them. A new helmet, the *basnet*, also appeared. It was conical in shape and fitted with a mail tippet (*aventail*), to protect the throat and neck, and a pointed visor. The visor was commonly made detachable so that the basnet could be worn under the great helm, though after *c.* 1350 this last tended to be relegated to the tournament field. From *c.* 1340 onwards inventories start to make a distinction between armour for the field and for the tournament, though it is not clear how the two differed at first. It can be assumed, however, that the tournament armour was more heavily reinforced, as was the case from the end of the 14th c. when it can first be identified clearly.

In the early years of the 15th c. the textiles that had covered and partly held the armour together began to be discarded. Henceforth armour was normally made of polished steel plates held together by riveted internal straps and sliding rivets, though the old plates construction survived for light body defences known as *brigandines*. By the second decade of the century armour had achieved the basic construction that it was to retain until it was finally discarded and henceforth changes were mainly in the details of form and decoration, on which contemporary styles of ornament and costume had considerable influence. A complete armour now consisted of solid breastplates and backplates (the *cuirass*) with a skirt of hoops, and articulated plates completely covering the limbs except for the backs of the thighs, all attached to each other or to the padded undergarment by straps and ties. The mail aventail on the basnet was replaced by plate and new helmet-forms appeared, of which the most important were: the Italian *barbuta*, a one-piece helmet that extended down over the cheeks; the *sallet*, shaped like a sou'wester with a fixed or movable visor worn with a separate chin-piece (*bevor*); the *armet*, which had hinged cheek-pieces, fastening at the chin and completely enclosing the face except for the eyes, and a movable visor; and, introduced at the end of the 15th c., the *close-helmet*, which resembled the armet except that the cheek-pieces were made in one and pivoted at the same points as the visor.

The left side of the armour was commonly more heavily reinforced than the right, because the lance—held against a bracket-shaped stop (the *rest*) on the right side of the breastplate—was couched across the horse's neck from right to left. These reinforcements were heavier on the special tournament armours that can be clearly identified for the first time *c.* 1400 because mobility was less important in the lists than in the field. In its most specialized form tournament armour was designed to give the protection and allow the movements necessary for a particular form of joust and so was equipped with a breastplate, left-arm defences and a helm of great weight—the last fastened down on the shoulders—but had only light defences, or none at all, elsewhere.

The 15th c. saw the emergence of the two great international areas of armour production, north Italy and south Germany, whose styles dominated Europe until the 17th c. Milan was the main Italian centre—though Brescia was also important—and the armourers there, among whom the members of the MISSAGLIA family were outstanding, evolved a style characterized by rounded smooth forms. The German centres, of which Augsburg and Nuremberg were the most important, produced armour under the influence of the High Gothic style that was angular, decorated with ripple-like FLUTING and cusping and with piercing along the edges, and of elegant elongated form. The greatest exponent of this style was Lorenz HELMSCHMIED of Augsburg (d. 1515), armourer to the Emperor Maximilian I.

In the closing years of the 15th c. a more international style began to develop. The Germans adopted the rounded Italian forms, while the Italians began to use a certain amount of fluting. During the period *c.* 1515–30 armours, especially in Germany, were often decorated with vertical flutes in the so-called 'Maximilian' style, while the general outline became much burlier than in the previous century. During the 1520s the breastplate, which had been markedly bulbous, became flatter and developed a medial ridge. By *c.* 1570 the peascod form, curving down to a blunt point at the bottom, had evolved and this remained in general use until the end of the century. During the whole of this period the close-helmet was normally worn with full armour, but the light-cavalry and infantry equipments were fitted with an open helmet with a peak and deep cheek-pieces (the *burgonet*), or alternatively in the case of the latter with a modified version of the old kettle-hat (the *morion*). From *c.* 1520 there was a tendency for the completely distinct tournament armour to be replaced by what was in effect a field armour with various reinforcing and alternative pieces by means of which it could be adapted to the requirements of the joust or of field service. These *garnitures*, which had first started to develop in late-15th-c. Germany, were sometimes of very great complexity during the period *c.* 1530–50. Thereafter they tended to become simpler.

Until the second half of the 15th c. the actual surfaces of armour, as opposed to the textile trimmings, were left largely undecorated, though they were occasionally painted, gilded or equipped with narrow ornamental borders of precious metal or brass. At this period, as already noted, the German armourers began to decorate the surfaces with fluting and the borders with cusping and piercing. At the end of the century a fashion started, apparently in Italy, for decorating the surfaces with etched and gilt designs and this became widespread in the early 16th c. Henceforth better-quality armours were commonly decorated in this way, the background to the etching sometimes being blackened instead of gilded.

Etched or engraved ornament did not interfere in any way with the functional properties of the armour, but other forms of ornament that appeared in the early 16th c. did. Surfaces were embossed and etched to imitate the puffed and slashed garments of the period, were DAMASCENED in gold and silver, or were entirely covered with damascened and gilt designs embossed in relief, the armour sometimes being also formed in imitation of an ancient Roman one. Armours decorated in this way were intended for parade only, symbols of the power and wealth of their owners, and their appearance was symptomatic of the beginning of the decline of armour as practical equipment. A number of distinguished artists, among them Dürer and the younger Holbein, and a host of minor ones, such as Jörg SORG and Daniel Hopfer of Augsburg, were responsible for the design and decoration of elaborate harnesses for the princes and nobles of the period. Some of these last founded their own court workshops, as did the Emperor Maximilian I (Innsbruck, 1504) and King Henry VIII (Greenwich, 1515), but the old centres of production in south Germany and north Italy still retained their supremacy. The greatest exponents of the art of embossing armour were the NEGROLI family of Milan in the second quarter of the 16th c. and the so-called ANTWERP–LOUVRE SCHOOL in its middle years. But fine work was produced by many other artist-armourers, among whom can be mentioned Bartolommeo CAMPI of Pesaro, Giorgio Ghisi of Mantua, Georg Sigman of Augsburg and Lucio Piccinino of Milan.

The use of elaborate parade-armours was, of course, confined to a small number of wealthy people on special occasions. Functional armour, both decorated and plain, continued to be worn throughout the 16th c., but there are signs that after *c.* 1550 increasing doubts began to be felt about its utility. New infantry tactics developed during the Italian wars of the late 15th and early 16th centuries, and new cavalry tactics made possible by the invention of the pistol *c.* 1530, made the heavily armoured man-at-arms obsolete, while improvements in the efficiency of fire-arms that took place during the 16th c. made it necessary to increase the weight of armour. From the last quarter of the century onwards there was a growing tendency to discard the defences for the arms and legs to counterbalance increased weight elsewhere, while at the same time a gradual decline in the artistic quality of armourers' work began. Complete armour still continued to be made for the tournament and parade until well into the 17th c., but by the outbreak of the Thirty Years War in 1618 even the heavy cavalry were being equipped with harnesses, often of great weight, that extended only to the knees. The heavy infantry, the pikemen, wore only a cuirass with two pendent plates protecting the thighs and an open helmet, and the musketeers only a helmet. Similar equipment was used during the English Civil Wars, though the cavalry soon reduced theirs to a cuirass worn over a coat of thick buff leather, a long gauntlet worn on the bridle-hand, and an open helmet with a barred face-defence. A modified version of this last equipment continued to be used by some heavy cavalry regiments on the Continent until the present century, and was revived for the English Household Cavalry after the Napoleonic Wars. These, however, were exceptional, and to all intents and purposes armour had gone out of practical use in Europe by *c.* 1700.

After the fall of the Roman Empire in the West, the practice of equipping horses with armour seems to have been discontinued. It was revived again in the 11th or 12th c., when horses were occasionally covered with mail trappers. From the 14th c. until the early 17th c. plate defences of similar construction to contemporary men's armour were in use. They did not cover the legs except in one or two very rare instances. Spurs were normally fitted with a simple spike until the early 14th c., when the modern rowel form, first recorded *c.* 1250, came into general use.

(*c*) *Later Eastern Armour.* Eastern armour was not subjected to the same changes of fashion as that used in the West, and the carefully shaped and articulated harness of complete plate was never made there. The ancient lamellar and scale armour was worn extensively in both the Near and Far East, including China and above all Japan, where lamellar reached its most elaborate form and survived until the 19th c. In the Islamic countries and India mail was widely employed and from at least as early as the 15th c. was the most popular form, surviving in some areas until the present century. It was commonly reinforced with small plates or else performed the function of holding a series of small plates together. The most common form of Eastern helmet was a rounded or conical cap of iron or steel, sometimes fitted with a mail neck- and face-defence. The Japanese, however, developed a form of helmet with a wide, flaring lamellar neck-guard and a half or full mask of plate that was normally embossed to represent a face. The Eastern shield was almost invariably circular and made of hide, steel, wood or basket-work. All this armour was frequently decorated, in the Islamic countries with gold and silver damascening and in Japan with LACQUER or elaborate encrustation in gold, silver or coloured metal.

2. ARMS

(*a*) *Swords.* The history of the sword begins in the BRONZE AGE, when the discovery of the art of casting bronze made possible the production of a weapon heavier and longer than the flint knife. The majority of these early swords were straight and double-edged with only a rudimentary guard for the hand; but in the Near East a sickle-shaped form (*khopesh*) developed, while the Greeks and Iberians sometimes used a curved, cleaver-like sword (*kopis* or *machaira*) resembling the modern Ghurka *kukri*. The decoration on these bronze swords was usually confined to a few incised geometrical designs and to carving or gold and silver overlays on their ivory, bone or wooden handles. A group of swords and daggers found at Mycenae and dating from the 16th c. B.C., however, have their blades inlaid with elaborate designs in gold, silver and NIELLO.

The earliest known iron swords date from the 3rd millennium B.C. and were found in Anatolia, but it was not until the 1st millennium that weapons of this type began to come into general use. The development of iron-working at first only altered the material from which the swords were made, and the forms remained basically unchanged: for example, the famous *gladius*, the short stabbing sword of the Roman legionary, which was probably adopted in the 3rd c. B.C., differed only slightly in form from many Bronze Age swords. The use of iron, however, made possible the manufacture of much longer swords, suitable for chariot or cavalry warfare, and these were already in use among the tribes around the Danube in the early Iron Age. During the later Iron Age the Celts developed a long, straight, two-edged sword that was subsequently adopted by the Romans as a cavalry weapon and from which the knightly sword of the Middle Ages was to evolve. The Celts were probably also responsible for introducing the *pattern-welding* technique (see IRON AND STEEL) for the manufacture of blades which remained in use until *c.* 1000. It involved the twisting together of bars of iron and steel and then hammer-welding them until they formed a homogeneous whole, so as to produce a blade that was both tough and resilient and which when polished had a characteristic watered surface-pattern.

The long, straight double-edged sword came into general use during the Migration Period, when it also developed a clearly defined cross-guard (*quillons*) for the hand and a *pommel* at the top of the handle to form a counter-balance for the weight of the blade. This pommel was at first formed as a short, straight cross-bar, rounded or bluntly pointed on top; but it subsequently developed a variety of shapes, triangular, lobated and towards the end of the 1st millennium A.D. circular and brazil-nut shaped. The blade was essentially a cutting one, broad and flat with a shallow central groove up each face and a rather blunt point. As the Middle Ages progressed the quillons tended to lengthen and were sometimes arched, while other forms of pommel appeared. From the late 13th c. onwards some swords were made with long grips that could be used with two hands if necessary (*hand-and-a-half swords*), while in the 14th c. the large two-hand sword appeared, though it was never widely used for other than ceremonial purposes. The early 14th c. also saw the appearance of a stiff, sharply tapering blade that could be used for thrusting, probably as a result of the general reintroduction of plate armour.

The simple cruciform sword remained the characteristic knightly weapon until the early 16th c. As early as the late 14th c., however, a small curved bar was occasionally fitted to the base of one quillon on the blade side to protect the forefinger when, as was common practice, it was hooked over the quillon to get a firmer grip. After the middle of the 15th c., especially in Spain, a corresponding bar was sometimes placed at the base of the other quillon. Towards the end of the century other guards, including side-rings and a curved bar to protect the knuckles, were occasionally added and these became usual after the first decade of the 16th c.

All the medieval swords described so far were essentially practical weapons, and any decoration that was applied to them rarely interfered with their functional qualities. It normally consisted of precious metal, precious stones or enamel applied to the hilt, the decoration of the blade being confined to engraved or inlaid inscriptions of copper or brass, often talismanic in character, or from the 2nd half of the 15th c. onwards etched and gilt ornament. The early years of the 16th c., however, saw the beginning of a change brought about by the general spread of a fashion, probably first adopted in Spain, of wearing a sword as a normal part of male civilian dress. This led to the development of a purely civilian sword, the *rapier*, which henceforth followed a separate, though parallel, line of evolution to that of the military sword. As the rapier was normally used without armour it developed a complex barred guard for the hand, while its wide adoption brought about a new demand for instruction in fencing, a science that had hitherto received comparatively little attention. For this reason the rapier came to be regarded as a sword used specifically for fencing, and from it descended all the swords designed for this purpose. Because it was worn regularly with everyday dress by gentlemen it soon came to be regarded as a badge of gentility, while for the same reason it was often elaborately decorated. Every technique known to the goldsmith and jeweller was used at one time or another for the decoration of rapiers, and on some of the most elaborate examples the ornament is so delicate as to render them almost useless for practical purposes and they can be regarded merely as a form of masculine JEWELLERY. Two popular types of decoration that did not interfere with the functional qualities of the weapon were gold and silver damascening and chiselling on the iron parts of the hilt. The art of the iron-chiseller in Europe probably reached its peak with the work of the so-called MUNICH SCHOOL in the late 16th and early 17th centuries.

Throughout the 16th c. the rapier was a long, rather clumsy weapon fitted with a barred hilt, and a slender, straight, double-edged blade that could be used for cutting as well as thrusting. It was normally used in conjunction with a *left-hand dagger*, decorated *en suite*, or a cloak wrapped round the left arm, both being used for parrying. In the early 17th c. with the development of new fencing techniques that involved the use of the sword for both attack and parry and rendered the left-hand dagger obsolete, the rapier became smaller and lighter. By the end of the century the guard had been reduced to two solid oval shells and a slender knuckle-bow, while the blade was henceforth usually of hollow triangular section and designed purely for thrusting. This form of rapier, the *small-sword*, remained the essential badge of a gentleman until almost the end of the 18th c., and in a debased form is still worn with formal Court dress in some countries. The decoration of the hilt of the small-sword in the 18th c. reached heights of elaboration that were exceeded only by contemporary SNUFF-BOXES.

In Spain and the Kingdom of Naples during the 17th c. and the first half of the 18th c. the old long rapier and dagger remained in regular use. The rapier was normally equipped with a bowl-shaped guard (*cup hilt*) and the dagger with a triangular plate covering the back of the hand, both often being elaborately pierced and chiselled.

The military sword was normally heavier than the rapier and had a broader blade. For much of the 16th c. it was fitted with a cross-guard with side-rings and sometimes a few bars round the base of the blade. In the 15th c., however, the Swiss had developed a short sword for infantry use on which the quillons were bent in the form of a letter S. In the early 16th c. both Swiss and German *Landsknechts* used a version of this sword with the quillons shaped as a figure-eight, to which bars protecting the back of the hand were subsequently added. It was probably from this that the basket-guard completely enclosing the hand in bars or solid plates evolved in the second half of the 16th c. At first used by the infantry, it was adopted in a variety of forms by the cavalry as well during the 2nd quarter of the 17th c., surviving with many modifications until the present day on swords with both straight and curved blades.

Swords with curved blades were not much used in Europe before the 16th c., though as early as the 13th c. a heavy, cleaver-like sword with a convex cutting-edge, the *falchion*, made its appearance. It remained in use until the 16th c., but from the 15th c. was normally curved. Also in the late 15th c. single-edged swords with curved blades of approximately equal width throughout their length were introduced. They were used mainly by civilians when travelling or hunting. Short swords of this form, as well as straight-bladed ones, have remained in use for hunting and for sea-service until the present day. In eastern Europe a long curved cavalry sword, the *sabre*, derived from the Orient, was used from at least as early as the 16th c. onwards. It was widely adopted in the West in the 18th c.

The manufacture of swords was carried on in many places in Europe, but as with armour the arms-centres of north Italy, notably Milan and Brescia, and of Germany, notably Passau and Solingen, were pre-eminent and carried on a large international trade. In the 16th and 17th centuries the blades of Toledo in Spain were held in high repute.

(*b*) *Later Eastern Swords*. The study of the history of Oriental swords, excluding those of JAPAN, has barely been extended beyond an ethnographical classification. The problem of dating is made difficult by the rarity of dated specimens and by the fact that Oriental hilts were normally fitted with only a simple guard, or even no guard at all, while the same forms remained in use for centuries. Though swords with straight blades were widely used in the East, it was the curved form that came to be most favoured there. The commonest type of Oriental curved blade was single-edged and rather narrow and tapered gradually to a point. Its origins are obscure, but it probably evolved first in central Asia among the Mongols, in the early years of the 1st millennium A.D. By at least as early as the 13th c. the curved sabre known as a *shamshir* (from which comes the word 'scimitar') was in use in Persia and it probably soon spread from there to both India and Turkey, and also to a number of eastern European countries, surviving until the present century. In its most characteristic form it had a simple cross-guard and a grip shaped rather like the butt of a pistol. Variants were used in Turkey (the *kilij*) and India (the *talwar*), of which the latter commonly had a disc-shaped pommel and a slender knuckle-guard. The finest blades were of steel made by the cementation process, which after it had been forged, polished and lightly etched had a distinctive watered pattern somewhat similar to that on European pattern-welded blades. This is often referred to as Damascus steel, though it was apparently made mainly in India and Persia. The blades and hilts of these swords were commonly decorated with gold DAMASCENING, the hilts sometimes also being ENAMELLED, set with precious stones or made of JADE or crystal.

In Japan—where until quite recently the sword had a semi-religious importance it never attained elsewhere—the most perfect sabre ever devised was produced. Its precursor was a sword with a straight, single-edged blade and an oval copper guard introduced by migrants from the mainland of Asia *c.* 2nd c. B.C., which may have originated from the same central-Asian prototype as the *shamshir*. By *c.* 8th c. A.D. the form of sword that was to persist with practically no alteration down to the present day in Japan had been evolved. This had a long wooden grip, bound with cord, a guard (*tsuba*) consisting of a flat oval or circular plate, and a slender, curved, single-edged blade. The last was made by a much refined version of the pattern-welding process in which bars of iron and steel, after being hammer-welded together, were repeatedly folded over and forged some fifteen or twenty times. This produced a metal, consisting of many thousands of layers of iron and steel, of great toughness and resilience which when skilfully polished had a distinctive 'wood-grain' pattern all over its surface. The beauty of a Japanese sword lies in the graceful form of the blade and in its surface pattern, and this part was rarely decorated. The *tsuba* and the metal mounts of the grip, especially in later periods, were often elaborately ornamented with designs pierced, engraved or encrusted in gold, silver or the many coloured alloys that were a speciality of the Japanese craftsmen. Three main types of sword, differing only in size and in the details of their mountings, were used: the *tachi*, a slung sword worn with armour; and a pair of swords (*daishō*), one long (*katana*) and the other short (*wakizashi*), which were carried thrust through the girdle of the civilian dress. See also JAPAN (SWORDS AND OTHER METALWORK). So many other forms of Oriental sword exist that it is impossible to discuss them all here. Reference must, however, be made to the Indian *pata*, a straight-bladed weapon with its hilt formed as an iron gauntlet, and the Sudanese *kaskara*, a straight-bladed cross-hilted sword that is often mistaken for a medieval European weapon.

(*c*) *Daggers*. Knives that would serve equally well as implements or arms first appeared in the late Stone Age, while what appear to be true daggers, designed primarily as weapons, were known in the Bronze Age. Both types have remained in use ever since in countless variations in all parts of the world.

It is broadly true to say that the earliest daggers were merely diminutive versions of contemporary straight, double-edged swords, like the Roman *parazonium*, while the all-purpose knife was a version of the domestic implement carried in a sheath. One distinctive form of the latter that can be mentioned was the *scramasax*, used in northern Europe from the Migration Period until the end of the 1st millennium A.D., which had a broad, single-edged blade formed in outline like a flattened triangle. It was sometimes made large enough to be regarded as a short sword. (See also CUTLERY.)

The dagger appears first to have been adopted as a regular part of military equipment in the 2nd half of the 13th c., when it is shown in illustrations worn on the right side to balance the sword on the left. Daggers of this period had broad, triangular blades, simple cross-guards, and wheel pommels, like the swords they accompanied. This form, often referred to as a *quillon dagger*, has remained in use, with variations, until modern times; but from the early 14th c. onwards a number of others were developed, among which the following can be mentioned:

1. The *rondel dagger* with the guard, and often the pommel also, formed as a disc. It was used from the 14th c. to the 16th c.

2. The *ballock knife* (modern *kidney dagger*) with a guard formed of two rounded lobes. Widely used from the 14th c. to the early 17th c., it was adapted in Scotland to produce the characteristic national dagger, the *dirk*, which still survives as an adjunct to Highland dress together with the diminutive stocking-knife (*sgian dubh*), though the latter was probably not adopted until the 18th c.

3. The *baselard*, a type of dagger—sometimes long enough to be classified as a short sword—which derives its name from the city of Basel, where it was apparently first made in the early 14th c. From this period until the late 15th c. it was widely used all over Europe, especially by civilians. It had a hilt formed like a letter 'I' and, usually, a straight blade. In Switzerland a short dagger—now often called the *Swiss dagger*—of similar form to the *baselard* survived until the early 17th c. Many examples have gilt-copper or brass scabbards cast and pierced with scenes, for which designs by a number of artists survive, among them Hans Holbein the Younger. For this reason they are sometimes called *Holbein daggers*.

4. The *cinquedea*. This name is now applied, on no very good authority, to a dagger or short sword with a wide triangular blade and very short down-sloped quillons that was worn by civilians in Italy in the late 15th and early 16th centuries. The blade is often elaborately etched with classical scenes and gilt.

5. The *ear-dagger*, a Spanish form, probably derived from a Moorish prototype, with its pommel formed of two discs set at an angle to each other like ears. It was used from the 14th c. to the late 16th c.

6. The *left-hand dagger* or *main-gauche*, usually a form of quillon dagger used in the left hand for parrying when fencing and made *en suite* with a companion rapier. The quillons were sometimes supplemented by a side-ring on the outside of the hand, and were often arched so that they could be used for entangling an opponent's blade. The type first appeared *c.* 1530 and remained in general use for about a century. In Spain and south Italy a special form with a triangular plate protecting the back of the hand was developed in the early 17th c. to accompany the cup-hilt rapier, surviving until the early 18th c.

7. The *stiletto*, a short dagger with a slender blade of stiff triangular section, used mainly in Italy in the 17th c.

8. The *bayonet*, a special type of dagger designed at first to be plugged into the muzzle of a gun to convert it into a spear. This form, which was probably introduced in the 2nd quarter of the 17th c., survived as a hunting arm in Spain until the 19th c. Elsewhere the bayonet was used mainly for military purposes and from the late 17th c. was normally equipped with a socket attachment that fitted round the muzzle of the gun, leaving it free for firing.

In the East the dagger was also made in a wide variety of forms, the majority with simple hilts and curved, knife-like blades sometimes reinforced at their points. Among the exceptions were the Indian *katar*, which had a triangular blade and a hilt formed like a letter 'H', the cross-bar serving as a grip, and the Malaysian *kris*, which had a double-edged blade, often made by a variant of the pattern-welding process and frequently with waved edges. In Japan the commonest dagger, the *tanto*, was a miniature version of the Japanese sword.

(*d*) *Staff Weapons*. To this category belong arms that comprise a wooden or metal shaft usually fitted with an offensive head. They fall into three categories, in which the basic types are the spear, the axe and the club—all of which have been used constantly since the Stone Age—though many staff weapons have characteristics of more than one type.

The spear has always retained the same fundamental shape, though the length of its staff and the size and outline of its head have varied considerably. The horseman's spear—later known as the *lance*—was commonly fitted with a circular hand-guard (*vamplate*) from the 14th c. to the early 17th c. Other special forms of spear were the *pike*, some 5·5 metres long and used from the 15th c. to the 17th c. by massed infantry to form a pallisade against cavalry, and the *partisan*, which had a long triangular blade with a pair of pointed lugs at its base. The latter still survives as the ceremonial arms of some state guards.

The true axe has always been of approximately similar shape to the modern implement, but in the later Middle Ages and the Renaissance in Europe a wide variety of axe-like weapons, many based on agricultural implements, were used. The commonest were the *halberd*, which had an axe-head of conventional form with a long spike above, and the *bill*, which resembled the agricultural implement of the same name.

The club started life as a simple tree-branch or wooden baton, but was subsequently often fitted with a spiked or flanged stone or metal head. This more elaborate form is usually referred to as a *mace*.

Oriental staff weapons fall into the same basic categories as in the West, but various forms of the spear were the ones most widely used. Among the latter was the Japanese *naginata*, which consisted of a curved, single-edged sword-blade mounted on a long haft.

(*e*) *Projectile Weapons*

The bow and crossbow. The bow has been used continuously everywhere in the world since the Stone Age. Though normally of wood, it has also been made of horn, a combination of horn, sinews and wood (*composite bow*), of metal and, in recent years, of fibreglass. The crossbow, which comprises a bow attached horizontally to the end of a stock (*tiller*), and is aimed like a gun, probably originated in China in the 1st millennium B.C. It was probably introduced into Europe from the East during the Roman Empire, and was used to some extent by the Romans, chiefly in the form of a large siege-engine. After the fall of Rome there is no evidence for the existence of crossbows in Europe until the 10th c. By 1139 its use had become so widespread that it was banned by the Second Lateran Council, held in that year, as a weapon unfit to be employed against Christians. Despite this the crossbow continued to be used widely, both in war and for sport, and has survived as a sporting-arm until the present day. The bows on all but the lightest examples were too strong to be drawn back by hand so various devices to do this were introduced. The earliest method was simply a hook attached by a rope to the girdle, so that bending could be effected by means of the leg muscles; but later examples were fitted with windlasses or levers. Most bows and crossbows shot arrows, but pellets were also used with some against small game.

Fire-arms. Incendiary missiles shot from bows or, like the Greek Fire of the Byzantines, blown from tubes have a long history. But the development of fire-arms as we know them today resulted from the discovery of gunpowder, an explosive composition of charcoal, saltpetre and sulphur. Though its origins are obscure, it seems probable that gunpowder was known in China as early as the 11th c. A.D. and that it was first used there for pyrotechnic weapons, including rockets. Fire-crackers made of gunpowder were recorded in Europe in the 13th c. by Roger Bacon of Oxford, and it was in Europe that the discovery that its explosive powers could be used to project a missile from a tube appears to have been made. The earliest definite evidence of the existence of guns occurs in two manuscripts, both of which are dated 1326. One relates to the purchase of guns by the commune of Florence and the other is a treatise on kingship by an English priest, Walter de Milemete, preserved in Christ Church Library, Oxford, which contains a picture of a vase-shaped cannon firing an arrow. After *c*. 1340 cannons came into widespread use in Europe, and by the end of the 14th c. they were firmly established. The earliest examples were cast in brass or bronze, but wrought iron was in use by the end of the 14th c., while cast-iron ordnance appeared in the 16th c. The finest cannons, however, continued to be cast in bronze and from the 15th c. to the 18th c. many splendidly decorated examples were made.

It is likely that small cannons that could be carried by a man (*hand-guns*) were made very shortly after the introduction of fire-arms, but the earliest definite evidence for their existence dates from the 3rd quarter of the 14th c. Like the larger field-cannons, they consisted basically of a tube, closed at the rear end and loaded from the muzzle with gunpowder and a ball. Ignition was by means of a piece of tinder or slow-match applied to a touch-hole drilled at right-angles to the powder-chamber. The hand-gun was attached to the end of a wooden or metal staff that could be tucked under the arm or rested on the ground when it was fired.

Early in the 15th c. the first mechanical lock, the *matchlock* appeared. At first this consisted of a pivoted lever with jaws at its upper end for the match, but in the 2nd half of the 15th c. a spring mechanism was introduced. At the same time the gun developed a stock, roughly resembling that of a modern rifle, that could be rested against the cheek when firing.

The matchlock remained in wide use in the armies of Europe until the late 17th c. Nevertheless it had many disadvantages, and at the beginning of the 16th c. a much improved ignition system, the *wheel-lock*, was invented, probably by Leonardo da Vinci. This utilized a spring-rotated wheel to strike an ignition spark from a piece of iron pyrites held in the jaws of a pivoted lever (the *cock*), and it made possible for the first time the manufacture of guns that could be carried ready for instant use indefinitely. The effect both on the development of fire-arms and on warfare was revolutionary. The pistol was invented and with it new cavalry tactics, while the upper classes now began to adopt fire-arms as their personal weapons both for war and for hunting. Henceforth, until the 19th c., the finest fire-arms were often elaborately ornamented, all the known decorative techniques being employed for this purpose, including engraving, etching, damascening and mounting in precious metals, inlaying, chiselling and enamelling. At the same time many efforts were made to improve their efficiency. One of these was the introduction of *rifling*, a series of spiral grooves inside the barrel which caused the projectile to spin in flight and so improved its accuracy. First recorded in the mid-16th c., it was adopted generally only in the 19th c.

Though the wheel-lock was complicated and expensive to manufacture, it remained in wide use until the mid-17th c. and survived on German sporting guns for a further hundred years. As early as *c.* 1540, however, a new form of lock, the *snaplock*, was invented, probably in Germany. This utilized a piece of flint held by a spring-actuated cock to strike the ignition sparks from a pivoted steel plate. Despite the fact that it was simpler and easier to make than the wheel-lock, it did not start to come into general use until after *c.* 1610, when an improved version, the *flintlock*, was invented, almost certainly in France. From *c.* 1650 until almost the middle of the 19th c. this form of lock was the one most widely used in Europe.

The era of modern fire-arms started in 1807 when a Scottish clergyman, Alexander Forsyth, patented an entirely new form of gun-lock in London. This, the *percussion lock*, utilized a chemical detonating compound, struck by a spring-actuated hammer, to ignite the charge of gunpowder in the barrel. Loose detonating-powder was used at first, but *c.* 1814 someone—probably the Alsatian-born London gun-maker Joseph EGG or the Anglo-American Joshua Shaw—hit on the idea of putting detonating compound in the bases of thimble-shaped metal caps. These were sold ready for use and were placed individually on a pierced nipple screwed into the breech of the gun and connecting to the powder-charge, where they were detonated by the hammer of the lock. After *c.* 1830 this form of percussion lock rapidly supplanted the flintlock in Europe, though the latter has remained in use in primitive societies.

From the 14th c. onwards attempts were made to produce breech-loading and repeating fire-arms, but with the exception of multi-barrelled arms none was successful before the 19th c. The invention of the percussion system, by simplifying ignition, made a new approach possible. In 1835 the American Samuel COLT patented the first successful revolver—probably based on much earlier unsuccessful models—and this was followed by a host of others all over the Western world. In 1812 the Swiss S. J. PAULY patented in France a breech-loading gun taking a paper cartridge with a reusable metal base recessed in the centre for detonating-powder. The invention was not commercially successful but it was the prototype from which the modern cartridge was developed and all modern breech-loading and repeating arms. These inventions brought about the end of gun-making as an art and, though finely decorated pieces continued to be made for wealthy individuals and for exhibition purposes, they were exceptional. Henceforth the majority of fire-arms were purely functional and fall outside the scope of this article.

Apart from making conventional fire-arms, gun-makers have, from certainly as early as the 15th c., occasionally produced arms that combined some other weapon with a gun or which employed more than one system of ignition. None of these appears to have achieved any real success.

Oriental fire-arms. Guns were in use in China as early as the 14th c., and in other parts of the Far East shortly afterwards. No technical development occurred there, however, and all the more advanced Oriental fire-arms were derived ultimately from Western prototypes. The matchlock was the most widely used mechanism, surviving in some areas until the present century, but various forms of snaplock were used in the Middle East, many of them imported from Europe.

Air- and gas-guns. The earliest form of air-gun is the simple blowpipe, which has a very long history and has remained in use in some primitive communities until the present day. The true air-gun, obtaining its power from a reservoir of compressed air, and the spring air-gun, in which a spring-operated piston discharges the projectile, both seem to have appeared first in Germany in the 16th c. The true air-gun was at first the more popular, and from the 17th c. to the 19th c. was produced in moderately large quantities, chiefly as a sporting and target weapon. Since the 2nd half of the 19th c. the spring variety has been widely used as a target gun.

The idea of using gas with a more powerful

rate of expansion than compressed air to discharge a projectile goes back to the steam-gun devised by Leonardo da Vinci, though probably never made. Other steam-guns were invented in the 19th c., but none was successful. In 1889, however, the Frenchman Paul Giffard patented a gun using liquid carbon dioxide as a propellant. His invention was not a commercial success, but his idea was revived in the present century and applied to target guns and pistols powered by ordinary soda-siphon bulbs.

Air-guns and gas-guns were normally similar in general design and decoration to contemporary fire-arms.

See also under AMERINDIANS; CHINA; GREEK AND ROMAN ANTIQUITY; JAPAN; etc.

68, 69, 72, 73, 74, 75, 82, 168, 197, 213, 234, 283, 284, 399, 405, 468, 469, 518, 622, 636, 661, 713, 714, 715, 745, 758, 761, 777, 778, 796, 818, 825, 838, 839, 887, 920, 935.

ARNOLD, JOHN (1736–99). English pioneer maker of CHRONOMETERS. He was apprenticed to his father, a watch-maker in Bodmin, Cornwall, in 1736 and worked there until *c.* 1760, when he moved to London. His great skill as a watch-maker was first noticed when in 1764 he presented to King George III an exceptionally small half-quarter repeating watch set in a ring. His main life-work was the improvement of marine chronometers and he produced them in considerable numbers. Harrison had shown in 1761 that it was possible to construct a timekeeper suitable for finding longitude at sea, and Arnold's contribution was to simplify the design so that chronometers could be manufactured in numbers. His inventions included the helical balance-spring and a form of detached escapement, both of which are incorporated in marine chronometers up to the present day. Arnold also made many fine precision watches, which were mechanically scaled-down versions of his marine chronometers. He was working in Devereux Court, Strand, London, from *c.* 1760 to 1776, when he moved to Adelphi Buildings, and in *c.* 1785 to 112 Cornhill. He also had a chronometer factory at Chigwell, Essex. From 1787 to his death in 1799 his son JOHN ROGER was in partnership with him, and the firm's products were signed 'Arnold & Son'.

ARRAS TAPESTRIES. These are first mentioned in 1313. Their pre-eminent reputation during the later Middle Ages is attested by the fact that the name of the town passed into several European languages as a generic term for tapestry hangings. But they were already overshadowed by the productions of Tournai when the capture of Arras and the dispersal of its inhabitants by Louis XI brought the industry to an end there in 1477. Subsequent attempts to re-establish it bore little fruit.

A number of tapestries have been ascribed to Arras looms. Those in Tournai Cathedral depicting the lives of SS. Piat and Eleuthère formerly bore the signature of Pierrot Feré of Arras and the date 1402. See TAPESTRY.

221.

ARRETINE WARE. A type of pottery which was very widespread in the Roman Empire. It has a red glossy surface which was obtained by dipping the pot in a suspension of illite clay and firing in an oxydizing kiln. The most famous centre of production in the 1st c. B.C. was Arretium (modern Arezzo), where a potter named Marcus Perennius Tigranus manufactured pottery of this type with relief decoration of high artistic quality (whence the name *terra sigillata*) suggestive of and perhaps influenced by repoussé metalwork. There were other centres both in Italy and in southern Gaul where this type of pottery was made, but the artistic quality is not in general considered to be equal to the products of Arretium. When fragments of Arretine ware were found in the 13th c. and onwards they aroused great enthusiasm among artists and humanists.

ART DÉCO. Name for the decorative arts of the 1920s and 1930s in Europe and America. *Art déco* was 'discovered' by the Paris Exposition Internationale des Arts Décoratifs et Industriels Modernes, which was underwritten by the French Government in 1925. The emphasis of the exhibition on individuality and fine workmanship was at the opposite extreme from the contemporary doctrines of the BAUHAUS and the prototypes for machine production which were the ideals of many of those behind the DEUTSCHER WERKBUND. It was successful for a while in reasserting the position of the French artist-craftsmen as arbiters of world taste in the practical arts. But the position of Paris was soon challenged from the United States, which then went into the lead though to a large extent changing the concept of *art déco* which had been created by the Paris exhibition.

Owing to a fund created in 1922 the Department of Decorative Arts in the Metropolitan Museum of Art, New York, was enabled to purchase examples of modern decorative art in Europe and America. The nucleus of a collection of outstanding individual pieces of contemporary craftsmanship was built up by the curator, Joseph Beck, between the years 1923 and 1925. In 1926 an exhibition of loan pieces from the Paris Exposition toured the museums of the U.S.A., being shown first by the Metropolitan Museum. Commerce was not slow to crowd its way in upon the band wagon and an exhibition of contemporary decorative art under the title 'Art in Trade' was staged by Macy's Department Store in 1927, to be followed by a number of others. In this way the standard of the original *art déco* was vulgarized and a debased form of it was popularized under the name of the style 'Moderne'. In 1929, however, the Metropolitan Museum held its own exhibition on the model of the Paris Exposition of 1925. The object of the exhibition was not only to show the best of what was being done but to encourage the creation of a new decorative style adapted to the needs of contemporary life. The exhibition was called 'The Architect and The Industrial Arts: An Exhibition of Contemporary American Design'. The over-all layout was planned by the Finnish-born architect Eliel Saarinen (1873–1950) and the exhibition displayed a series of interiors planned by architect-designers and largely stocked with objects manufactured by firms in close consultation with the designers.

A second exhibition of *art déco* was held by the Metropolitan Museum in 1934, in which the emphasis upon the general style and impression of an interior rather than upon the individual craft object was carried still further. Owing perhaps to the effects of the Depression emphasis was also given to materials and forms which could be easily and economically mass produced.

Characteristic of *art déco* was the vogue for the 'streamlined' style, which was hailed as the ultimate in modernity during the 1930s but within 20 years already seemed dated.

A revival of interest in *art déco* during the late 1960s and 1970s had an air of historicism analogous to the earlier enthusiasm for Victoriana, tempered perhaps by a touch of nostalgia.

49, 50, 380, 381.

ARTESONADO (from Spanish *artesón*, a wooden trough or panel). Type of wooden panelled or coffered ceilings of Moorish origin which were typical of the Mudéjar style in Spain. Sometimes flat but more often concave like an inverted trough, they were covered with endlessly repeating ornament in relief made by fitting together small wooden ribs either intersecting each other (*lacería*) or forming rows of polygonal coffers. The whole was painted in bright colours or gilded. Examples are to be seen in the chapter room of Toledo Cathedral, in convent churches such as San Clemente and Santa Paula in the old quarter of Seville and in the Alcazar. The type continued in Spanish America until well into the 17th c. See WOOD-WORKING.

ART NOUVEAU. *Art nouveau* was a deliberate attempt to create a new style in reaction from the academic historicism of the second half of the 19th c. It was primarily an art of ornament and its most typical manifestations occurred in the practical and decorative arts and in architecture, in *art mobilier*, graphic work and illustration. It was a complex, individualistic, dynamic and comparatively short-lived style, which flourished in Europe, and to a lesser extent in the United States of America, from *c.* 1890 to 1910. A revival of interest in the style occurred in the 1950s and was fostered by a series of exhibitions which included an Art Nouveau exhibition at Zürich in 1952, an exhibition of Victorian and Edwardian decorative arts at the Victoria and Albert Museum in the winter of 1952/3 and an exhibition of *art nouveau* at the Museum of Modern Art, New York, in 1960.

In its two-dimensional form *art nouveau* was essentially linear in character, deriving movement and plasticity from the use of sinuous, curved and undulating line. In applied design and architecture, however, *art nouveau* assumed within its national variations seemingly opposing characteristics, for while the organic flowing style was freely translated into three-dimensional form, a rigidly rectilinear, geometrical and abstract style also developed, especially in Scotland and Vienna, anticipating design solutions that are more characteristic of ART DÉCO and the so-called 'machine forms' of the early Modern Movement.

Although the style derived from many sources, Britain and JAPAN provided the formative influences. In Britain the art of William Blake, rediscovered in mid-century by the Pre-Raphaelites, had demonstrated the emotional and symbolic use of line—a concept that was latent in the work of many of the designers of the British ARTS AND CRAFTS MOVEMENT. The work of Walter CRANE for example, whose textiles and wallpapers were greatly admired on the Continent, shows all the characteristics of *art nouveau*. Furthermore Arts and Crafts ideology, formulated in the wake of the Gothic Revival, had stressed the unity of the arts and had demonstrated the ideal of the craftsman as artist. Following the precedent set by William MORRIS, British designers rejected academic systems of ornament and turned to nature for inspiration. Their individualistic interpretation of the tenets of truth to nature and truth to materials, together with their belief in the regenerative powers of craftsmanship, had contributed, towards the end of the century, to a renaissance of British practical art. But although a good deal of British design during the period from *c.* 1880 to 1900 can properly be described as an early stage of *art nouveau*—e.g. work by A. H. MACKMURDO's Century Guild, ASHBEE's Guild of Handicraft, by Walter Crane and Charles RICKETTS (1866–1931), etc.—the majority of British designers condemned *art nouveau* as decadent and bizarre. Walter Crane, for example, described it as a 'strange decorative disease' and the architect C. F. A. VOYSEY (1857–1941) maintained that the style was 'out of harmony with our national character and climate'. It was characteristic, therefore, of the Arts and Crafts morality of design, that work by Charles Rennie MACKINTOSH and Aubrey Beardsley (1872–98), which was both celebrated and influential on the Continent, should have been condemned by the majority of their contemporaries in Britain, and that the passion for Japanese work, which became so great a cult during the 1880s and 1890s, should also have been regarded with some suspicion by designers such as William Morris and Walter Crane.

Yet knowledge, appreciation and imitation of the Japanese achievement had been evident in

British and Continental art and design since the 1860s. In painting, illustration and textile design Japanese influence was apparent in the sophisticated and economic use of line and colour, the asymmetrical placing of the human figure and the articulation of forms within a two-dimensional rather than a three-dimensional plane. This may be seen in the work of Aubrey Beardsley and Toulouse-Lautrec (1864–1901). In three-dimensional design it was reflected in a preference for undecorated form and construction. The architect E. W. GODWIN's 'Anglo-Japanese' furniture, for example, first advertised in 1877, is light, taut and rectilinear, anticipating the work of Charles Rennie Mackintosh and Gerrit RIETVELD. In the same way Christopher Dresser (1834–1904), the British designer and theorist who had visited Japan on behalf of the British Government in 1876, designed asymmetrical, free-flowing glassware which is similar to work by Émile GALLÉ, while his metalware recalls early work by such BAUHAUS designers as Marianne Brandt and Wilhelm Wagenfeld.

During the 1890s an awareness of the British design achievement began to spread throughout the Continent, disseminated by displays organized by the Arts and Crafts Exhibition Society, and by the new magazine *Studio*, which was launched in 1893. The British, it seemed, by freeing themselves from historicism and academic restraint, and by proclaiming craftsmanship as an art, had set a standard which all Europe recognized and emulated. ('When English creations began to appear a cry of delight sounded throughout Europe. Its echo can still be heard in every country', wrote Samuel Bing in 1898, three years after he had opened his Galeries de l'Art Nouveau in Paris.) At the same time, however, the accompanying theory insisted that the design activity was as much a matter of ethics as of aesthetics, and although the social concern implicit in British attitudes contributed more to the development of the Modern Movement than to that of *art nouveau*, it stimulated several young painters in the 1890s to devote themselves to design and architecture: Richard Riemerschmid (1868–1957) and Peter BEHRENS in Germany, for example, and Henri Van de VELDE in Belgium.

Van de Velde was one of the most committed and articulate supporters of the new art and its morality. He trained as a painter in Paris, where he met Mallarmé, Verlaine and Debussy. In 1889, some four years after his return to Belgium, he joined Les Vingt, the *avant-garde* art group whose members included Ferdinand Knopff and James Ensor. At the age of 30, however, inspired by the example of William Morris, he abandoned painting in order to dedicate himself to architecture and the crafts—a reorientation that was also reflected in the activities of Les Vingt, which was reorganized in 1894 and renamed La Libre Esthétique to mark its concern for unity in all the arts.

During its 10 years of existence Les Vingt had promoted the work of such artists as Rodin, Whistler, Max Liebermann, van Gogh and Seurat, and the activities of this articulate *avant garde*, who were also preoccupied with symbolism in music and literature, no doubt contributed to the emergence in Brussels of the first clearly definable example of *art nouveau* in architecture. 'It remains a fact', writes Robert Schmutzler in his definitive study of *art nouveau*, 'that Continental High Art Nouveau found its first and most complete expression in the Maison Tassel, inasmuch as it combined architecture and decoration, structure and ornament, the two-dimensional and the three-dimensional, in other words the total work of art.' The Maison Tassel was designed by Victor HORTA in 1893. Horta, who was the son of a cobbler, had trained at the Académie des Beaux-Arts in Paris; on returning to Brussels in 1880 he became a pupil of Alphonse Balat at the Brussels Académie, where he was trained in strict classical disciplines, and his first houses were exercises in the traditional Neo-Renaissance style. Little is known of his activities between 1885 and 1892 when he was commissioned to design the Tassel House, but he emerged from this period of study and research to establish a new language of architecture. The total conception of the Maison Tassel was revolutionary and to Horta's contemporaries it seemed that in no detail was it derivative. The plan allowed for flexibility and variety in floor level; the iron framework was exposed, the cast-iron column in the entrance hall establishing with its questing, curving, plant-like tendrils the structural and decorative *leitmotif* for the house. The sources for so unprecedented a solution may, as many critics suggest, be found in the WALLPAPERS of the Century Guild and the graphic work of contemporary British illustrators such as Beardsley; Horta, nevertheless, was the first architect to translate these two-dimensional exercises into a three-dimensional form. Following the completion of the Tassel House, Horta undertook a series of commissions for private houses and public buildings in Brussels, among them the Hotel Solvay (1894), the Maison du Peuple (1895), the Hotel Aubecq (1899–1900) and the À L'Innovation department store (1901). All demonstrated his mastery of this new mode of formal expression and his ability to create and express a total unity of function, structure, space, form and decoration. After 1900 he abandoned *art nouveau* for a more sober and restrained style. His successors and imitators, however, of whom Paul Hankar (1859–1901) is among the most original, continued to work exuberantly in the style, making Brussels the capital of *art nouveau*.

Knowledge of the Belgian and particularly Horta's achievement contributed to the development of *art nouveau* in other European countries. In France Hector Guimard (1867–1942) had produced plans in a traditional Gothic-based style for the Castel Béranger in 1895 when he met Horta and visited the Tassel House. From then on he attempted, within the limitations of the original plan, to transform the Castel Béranger. He redesigned the entrance and entrance hall (the free-flowing ironwork of the entrance gate anticipates work by Gaudì), and he added balconies and decorative motifs in wrought iron. In 1899 this work gained an award for the most beautiful façade in Paris and initiated a whole series of commissions for Guimard—among them the Maison Canivet (1899) and the École Humbert de Romans (1901–2) in Paris, the Castel Henriette (1899–1900) in Sèvres and the Castel Orgeval near Morsang-sur-Orge (1905). Guimard's most celebrated achievement, however, remains the work he did for the Paris Métro in 1900. Difficult as it is to associate these sensuous, sinuous, sea-green structures with a modern means of mass transport, the Métro entrances nevertheless remain as emotive and integral a feature of the Paris townscape as the Eiffel Tower or the Arc de Triomphe.

Apart from Guimard, however, few French architects achieved that total fusion of structure and decoration that characterizes the best *art-nouveau* architecture. In applied design, however, there developed in NANCY a distinguished school of craftsmen. The most eminent of these was Émile Gallé, who had studied philosophy, drawing and botany and who had set up a workshop in Nancy, where his father produced luxury goods, in 1867. He began to concentrate on the design and production of glass in 1874, two years after he had been to London and had seen the collection of Japanese glassware in the Victoria and Albert Museum. He devised subtle techniques to achieve the form, quality and colour he required. The source of his inspiration was nature; he cultivated a large garden and, it is alleged, hung the following motto above his studio door: 'Our roots are in the depths of the woods—on the banks of the streams, in mosses.' At the same time, however, Gallé would have described himself as a symbolist; he called his glassware *verreries parlantes* and quotations from Mallarmé, Baudelaire, Poe and Maeterlinck were cut or engraved in his wares.

Gallé also produced some furniture—significantly enough his last work was a great bed with head- and foot-board decorated and shaped like the wings of a butterfly. Craftsmen contemporary with Gallé who were also working with him in Nancy include Louis Majorelle (1859–1929), Victor Prouvé (1858–1943) and Eugène Vallin (1856–1922). All worked in various media (Majorelle, for example, designed the iron stair-railings for the Galeries Lafayette in Paris); but they are probably best known for their furniture, which seemed sculpted rather than constructed and unlike the English Arts and Crafts furniture aspired to the plasticity of clay. The brothers Daum—Auguste (1853–1909) and Antonin (1864–1930)—were inspired by the work of Gallé to concentrate on glassware; they also worked in Nancy and achieved an international reputation.

A focal point for the sale and exhibition of international *art nouveau* in France was provided by Samuel Bing, who opened his Galeries de l'Art Nouveau in Paris in 1895. By the 1890s Bing was well known as an art dealer and critic, and as a collector of Japanese work. Earlier in the decade he had visited the United States on behalf of the French Government in order to study that country's decorative art and industry, and he returned with the intention of providing a forum for the best in contemporary art and design. He exhibited work by contemporary painters in his new gallery (including Bonnard, Denis and Vuillard from France, and Beardsley, Brangwyn, Crane and Mackintosh from England), and he also promoted designs by an international group of craftsmen whose work could be described as *art nouveau.*

Glassware by Gallé was represented there, as was that of Louis Comfort TIFFANY, whom Bing had met during his American visit. Tiffany, who was the son of the owner of the famous Fifth Avenue jewellery store, trained as a painter and after visiting Paris established himself in New York as an interior designer in 1879. Although in this capacity he had worked in stained glass, he did not begin to produce his famous *Favrile* glass until 1892–3, when he reorganized his company and renamed it The Tiffany Glass and Decorating Company. Like Gallé, Tiffany explored and extended the technique of glass production in order to achieve the subtle forms, colours, textures and transparencies he required. During the 1890s, when his inventiveness was at its peak, he designed glass which aspired to the sculptural qualities of frozen motion, and his work remains one of the finest achievements of *art nouveau.*

Just as Gallé and Tiffany had challenged and transcended traditional attitudes to shape and form within their chosen medium, their contemporary, René LALIQUE, who was also associated with Samuel Bing, designed jewellery that was totally alien to the accepted conventions in this field. Using semi-precious stones he created dynamic abstractions of plant and insect life, and by 1914 was considered the leading jeweller in Europe. (After the First World War he devoted most of his time to glass production.)

The supremacy of French *art nouveau* was demonstrated in the Paris Exhibition of 1900, and by that time most European countries were producing national variants of the style. In Scandinavia and Holland, however, the more sober humanism associated with the English Arts and Crafts reinterpretation of the vernacular provided the impetus for the renewal of the crafts, while in Germany *Jugendstil* was a brief and exuberant interlude which supplied the impetus for a reorientation towards industrial as opposed to craft design.

The search for new forms of expression in painting, architecture and the crafts came comparatively late to Germany. The magazine *Pan*, with contents similar to those of the British *Studio*, was founded in 1895, and the fact that five similar magazines were launched during the next two years marks the growing interest in art and decorative design. Three of these—*Jugend* (which gave its name to the style), *Kunst und Handwerk* and *Dekorative Kunst*—came from Munich, and the two others (*Deutsche Kunst und Dekoration* and *Kunst und Dekoration*) were published in Darmstadt, both centres for the German revival. The Grand Duke of Hesse had established his artists' colony on the Mathildenhöhe, near Darmstadt, in 1899, commissioning work from the Austrian J. M. Olbrich (1867–1908) as well as from C. R. Ashbee and M. H. Baillie-Scott. Two years earlier, in 1897, the Vereinigte Werkstätten für Kunst im Handwerk were founded in Munich, and by 1914 there were similar workshops in Dresden, Hellerau, Berlin and Hanover. The founder members of the Munich workshops included Hermann Obrist (1863–1927), Bernhard Pankok (1872–1943), Richard Riemerschmid (1868–1957) and Bruno Paul (1874–1954), while other artists working in Munich in the *Jugendstil* included Otto Eckmann (1865–1902), August Endell (1871–1921) and Peter Behrens. Obrist's 'whiplash' wall-hanging, produced in his embroidery studios in Munich 1892–4, and Endell's photographic studio Elvira, built in Munich 1897–8, are with justification included in every history of *art nouveau*. It is, however, significant that of the names listed at least three (Behrens, Riemerschmid and Paul) are associated with the Modern Movement and that from as early as 1904 several of the Werkstätten were experimenting with serial production, especially of furniture. Germany's determination to establish a European reputation for design and architecture was based on practical as well as aesthetic considerations, and was reflected in the various forms of cultural interchange which were encouraged there prior to the First World War. Hermann Muthesius, for example, spent seven years in London as an emissary of the Prussian Board of Trade, studying British architecture and design, and in 1901 Henri Van de Velde, at the height of his career as an *art-nouveau* artist, was lecturing in Germany and carrying out commissions such as the Habanna Companie cigar store, the Haby Hairdressing Salon, and the interiors of the Folkwang Museum at Hagen. Van de Velde's association with Weimar, where in 1906 he founded the school which later became the Bauhaus, dates from 1904, and in 1907 both he and Muthesius were founder members of that seminal organization, the DEUTSCHER WERKBUND. The formation of the Werkbund marks the end of *art nouveau* in Germany, for although Van de Velde and his sympathizers launched a spirited defence of the claims of the artist, programmes of reform were from then on directed towards the improvement of industrial rather than craft design.

Austria was the last country to embark on a programme of reform and renewal of its architecture and crafts; and although initially inspired by the ideals of the British Arts and Crafts Movement, the Vienna Workshops which were established by Josef HOFFMANN in 1903, produced work which with its obsessive geometry has more affinity with the modern and modernistic preoccupations of the 1920s than with turn-of-the-century plasticity. The impetus for Austria's *Sezession* came initially from the architect Otto Wagner (1841–1918), who was appointed professor at the Vienna Academy in 1894 and whose book *Moderne Architektur* called for new forms of architecture to 'correspond to new materials and the new requirements of our time'. Among his pupils at the Academy were Josef Hoffmann, J. F. Olbrich and Koloman Moser (1868–1918), who together with a group of radical painters led by Gustav Klimt (1862–1918) formed the *Wiener Sezession* in 1897. Olbrich designed their exhibition hall in 1898–9 and from then on the *Sezession* showed work by its own members as well as works by international artists. British work took pride of place in these displays (Ashbee's Guild of Handicraft was the model for the Vienna Workshops), but the artist whose achievements were most highly praised and imitated was Charles Rennie Mackintosh. Mackintosh in fact was more celebrated on the Continent than in Britain, his work representing the spirituality and unity of form and intent that Continental designers aspired to. Moreover there existed in Mackintosh's work a tension and duality that marks the transition from *art nouveau*, and the stark geometry of his later designs corresponds to the stylistic preoccupations of the Werkstätten which are epitomized by the work of Hoffmann.

Hoffmann was obsessed, to use his own words, by 'the pure square and use of black and white as dominant colours'. The silverware which he designed for the Werkstätten before 1914 is stark, simple and undecorated, anticipating the early metalware of the Bauhaus, while his furniture is almost Constructivist in inspiration and is stripped of all elements of *art nouveau*. His most remarkable achievement is the Palais Stoclet, which was built in Brussels 1905–11. This vast house, in spite of its use of rich materials (it is faced in gilt and marble and its dining-room is adorned with Klimt's famous mosaics), belongs to the Modern Movement, for here *art nouveau* is abandoned in favour of reinterpretation of classical forms.

It remained for a Spanish architect, Antoni Gaudí (1852–1926), to produce the most complete and personal demonstration of *art nouveau* in architecture. His work in Barcelona—the Casa Vicens (1878) the Palau Güell (1884–9), the Casa Battló and the Casa Milá (1905), and above all the church of the Sagrada Familia, which he began to work on in 1903—are demonstrations of a personal vision. Here the forms and rhythms defy their man-made origin. Gaudí's architecture, like his furniture, bears no relation to any recognizable precedent or convention; it is entirely individual, and as such demonstrates the potential as well as the limitations of *art nouveau*.

564, 693, 748, 852.

ARTS AND CRAFTS MOVEMENT. The Arts and Crafts Movement originated in Britain, where for more than 50 years before the formation of the Arts and Crafts Exhibition Society in 1888 designers, architects and theorists had deplored the aesthetic as well as the social effects of industrialization. The idea that mechanization dehumanized and so debased not only the quality of life but also that of art and craftsmanship was explored by several theorists in the first decades of the 19th c. It was John RUSKIN, however, who was to become the most eloquent and influential exponent of such opinions, and his theories were adopted as the corner-stone of 'Arts and Crafts' beliefs. Ruskin's championship of a craft as opposed to a machine aesthetic was most clearly expressed in 'On the nature of Gothic', a seminal chapter in the second volume of *The Stones of Venice* (1853). Here Ruskin was as much concerned with social reform as with art and architecture; he judged societies according to 'their influences on the life of the workman' and deemed the GOTHIC or early Christian style superior to all others since it was the least mechanistic, reflecting Christianity's tolerance of man's humanity and his imperfections. 'On the nature of Gothic' was read by William MORRIS when he was an undergraduate at Oxford, and in 1854 it was also distributed in pamphlet form to the students of F. D. Maurice's newly formed Working Men's College, where Ruskin was teaching. To these and to many other readers Ruskin's ideas had the appeal of total commitment to the ideal of a just society and to an aesthetic that would express the aspirations of such a society.

The Arts and Crafts aesthetic, therefore, was based on social and moral considerations. It was essentially anti-academic, celebrating the virtues of individualism and of the designer's right to experiment and explore to the full the possibilities of his materials. Nevertheless, the aim was not to create an *avante garde* but to reinstate the vernacular tradition, producing an 'art made by the people, and for the people, as a happiness to the maker and the user' (William Morris, *The Art of the People*, 1879).

Both as a theorist and in his practice as a designer William Morris was the greatest single influence on the Arts and Crafts Movement. He founded his firm, Morris, Marshall, Faulkner & Co., in 1861 soon after moving into The Red House, Upton, which had been built for him by Philip Webb. In its early stages the venture was essentially of Pre-Raphaelite inspiration, Dante Gabriel Rossetti, Ford Madox Brown and Edward Burne-Jones also being founders. At first the firm worked mainly for ecclesiastical clients, and at the outset stained glass formed the major part of its production. Furniture, glass, some metalware and tiles were also produced. But it was not until the 1870s (after some early experiments) that Morris began to concentrate on the designing of WALLPAPERS and fabrics. The wallpapers were hand-printed from wood blocks by Jeffrey & Co., but Morris found no similar commercial enterprise able to work to the standards he required for his textiles. He experimented with vegetable dyes, and his TAPESTRIES, weaves and prints (many of the latter are still sold today) were made by hand. Morris was inspired to set up his own printing press after hearing a talk given by Emery Walker to the Arts and Crafts Exhibition Society in 1888. Once again he scorned the commercial short cut; his paper was hand-made, his inks were imported from Hanover, and since he loathed the types that were commercially available he designed three faces for the press, based on 15th-c. types. Before he died he had issued over 50 titles, including the famous *Chaucer*, *The Nature of Gothic*, and an edition of his own *Earthly Paradise*. The Kelmscott achievement consolidated Morris's reputation both in Europe and in the United States; it stimulated the PRIVATE PRESS MOVEMENT, and contributed to the 20th-c. renaissance in commercial TYPOGRAPHY and book design in both continents.

Morris did not give his first public lecture (reprinted as *The Lesser Arts*) until 1877, and from that time he continued to write and lecture about his experience and convictions as a designer until the 1890s. These lectures (among the most well known are *The Art of the People*, *How we Live and How we might Live*, *The Aims of Art*, *Art and Socialism* and *A Factory as it Might Be*) reveal his passionate involvement with the growth of socialism in Britain and his conviction that a campaign for the renewal of art also involved political commitment to the Socialist cause.

Statements such as those of Morris, reinforced by the writings of Ruskin, together with the attempt, initially inspired by the Gothic Revival, to maintain or re-create the native or vernacular tradition in architecture and the practical arts inspired several architects to set up 'Guilds' providing craftwork for discerning clients. The first of these was the Century Guild, founded by the architect Arthur Heygate MACKMURDO in 1882; other founder members included Selwyn Image and Herbert Horne. Following the precedent set by Morris, the Guild produced furniture, textiles and metalwork. Mackmurdo anticipated Morris in one respect, however, in that he began experimenting with typography at an earlier date and the magazine *Hobby Horse*, carefully designed and printed, was first produced in 1884. Century Guild production is also remarkable for its latent ART NOUVEAU qualities: flame-like flowers, leaf and stem forms, appear on textiles and printed material as well as in the fretwork that embellished some of the furniture.

The Art Workers' Guild, which was also

founded in 1884, brought together the growing number of architect-craftsmen who needed a platform to air their views and compare experiences and who resented the indifference of the Royal Academy and the Institute of British Architects to their new ideals for the regeneration of design and architecture. Membership of the Guild (which was by election) carried considerable prestige, but several of its members were disappointed by its refusal to sponsor exhibitions. In 1888, therefore, the Arts and Crafts Exhibition Society was formed by a group of Guild members in order to promote the ideals of the craftsmen to a wider audience. The Society held its first exhibition in London in 1888; in 1891 it sponsored a display in Brussels, and throughout the 1890s British design and British design theory were admired and assimilated on the Continent, where they contributed to the ideology of *art nouveau* as well as to the social dogmas of the Modern Movement. Work by Morris and the Century Guild was exhibited in these Continental displays, as well as designs by C. R. ASHBEE, William De Morgan and Walter CRANE. The work of Walter Crane, who was a founder member of the Art Workers' Guild as well as of the Arts and Crafts Exhibition Society, was especially admired in Belgium, where Georges Lemmen wrote an important analysis of his work for the magazine *L'Art Nouveau* in 1891.

The greatest single influence on art education during this period, however, was W. R. LETHABY (1857–1931) who was appointed first principal of London's Central School of Arts and Crafts in 1896. Lethaby was a founder member of The Art Workers' Guild, and in 1890 had helped to set up a small firm, Kenton & Co., which aimed to produce furniture according to Arts and Crafts principles. This was a short-lived venture, but the younger members of the group he gathered together included Ernest GIMSON and the two BARNSLEY brothers, Edward and Sidney, who were to become the most influential of the Arts and Crafts furniture designers. They set up workshops in Gloucestershire, where they concentrated on the production of hand-made furniture. Some of these designs were *tours de force* with elaborate inlays; their most characteristic work, however, could be defined as 'cottage furniture', robust and deceptively simple, based on traditional solutions. The Daneway experiment inspired several similar ventures in the 1920s and 1930s, and it also stimulated a campaign, conducted mainly by Gordon RUSSELL and Ambrose HEAL, for better standards in mass production.

This attempt to extend craft values to the field of industrial design is characteristic of early 20th-c. design theory, and the impetus for so radical a change of emphasis came ironically enough from key members of the Arts and Crafts Movement. Lethaby, for example, gave his full support to the formation of the Design and Industries Association in 1914, and his essays of that period express a design philosophy similar to that of Walter Gropius when he founded the BAUHAUS. Similarly in 1911 C. R. Ashbee, who had devoted his career to the promotion of the craft ideal, declared in his book *Should we Stop Teaching Art?* that 'Modern civilisation rests on machinery, and no system for the endowment or encouragement or the teaching of art can be sound that does not recognise this'.

The failure of his Guild of Handicraft may have contributed to this change of attitude. There is little doubt, however, that Ashbee began to redefine his values after meeting Frank Lloyd WRIGHT in America. When Ashbee first met him (in 1900) Wright was just turned 30 and was working in Chicago, which was very much alive to the progress of the British Arts and Crafts Movement. Wright's lecture, significantly entitled *The Art and Craft of the Machine*, in which he defined the machine as 'the normal tool of our civilisation', was first delivered in Chicago in 1901. Although this text did not reach Europe for several years, its theme—that the machine could be controlled to fulfil the Arts and Crafts humanistic vision of design—was one that Ashbee discussed with Wright and one that was to be shared by Arts and Crafts designers throughout Europe.

In England, however, few designers were willing, or able, to make the transition from theory to practice, and although Arts and Crafts theory made a significant contribution to the ideology of the Modern Movement, the Movement's practical achievements are epitomized by the work of such individualists as William Morris, William De Morgan and Ernest Gimson, whose visions could never have been achieved by any other means than craft production.

See also ART NOUVEAU and PRIVATE PRESS MOVEMENT.

19, 621, 662.

ASH, GILBERT (1717–85). United States cabinet-maker who carried on business in New York. He is considered to be the most outstanding New York maker of furniture, particularly chairs, in the CHIPPENDALE style. He also carried on a business of manufacturing soap and candles and *c.* 1765 gave up his furniture business in favour of the latter. A set of chairs made for Sir William Johnson and attributed to Ash are distributed between the Winterthur Museum, Delaware, and Yale University Art Gallery, and chairs of the Van Rensselaer family attributed to him are in the Metropolitan Museum of Art, New York. THOMAS and WILLIAM Ash, who were making WINDSOR CHAIRS in New York during the last quarter of the 18th c., may have been his sons.

ASHBEE, CHARLES ROBERT (1863–1942). English architect and designer, who was a leading advocate of the principles which inspired the ARTS AND CRAFTS MOVEMENT. After reading history at Cambridge he began architectural training with G. F. Bodley (1827–1907), one of the first patrons of William MORRIS's firm. During this period he was living at Toynbee Hall, the pioneer university settlement, and he formed there a small evening class to study RUSKIN. This was the nucleus of his Guild of Handicrafts, which he founded in 1888 with three members and a capital of £50. The Guild flourished. True to Arts and Crafts principles its members were self-taught and their production—mainly silverware and furniture—found such a demand that Ashbee took premises at Essex House in the Mile End Road in 1890, at the same time opening a shop in Brook Street. The Guild's work soon became known in Europe and it exhibited with the Arts and Crafts Exhibition Society. Ashbee made the furniture (designed by Baillie Scott) for the Grand Duke of Hesse's palace at Darmstadt and Josef HOFFMANN's Wiener Werkstätten were largely inspired by the Guild. In 1898 Ashbee founded the Essex House Press, one of the many PRIVATE PRESSES inspired by William Morris's Kelmscott Press. In 1902 he moved his establishment to Chipping Campden in Gloucestershire, a move in keeping with Ruskinian idealism, and it was from this time that the fortunes of the Guild began to decline. This, together with his meeting with Frank Lloyd WRIGHT in 1900, may have contributed to the change in outlook which was expressed in the pamphlet *Should We Stop Teaching Art?* in 1911. In this new phase, abandoning his advocacy of the artist-craftsman, he argued that the machine is the vital instrument of contemporary civilization and that it is by the correct use of the machine that the ideals of the Arts and Crafts Movement are to be promoted. See also ART NOUVEAU.

ASHENDENE PRESS. A private printing press conducted from 1894 to 1935 by C. H. St. John Hornby, first at Ashendene, Herts., and from 1901 at Shelley House, Chelsea. Two new types, designed by Emery Walker, were specially cut for this press: 'Subiaco', used in Dante's *Inferno* (1902), based on the type employed by Sweynheim and Pannartz, the first printers in Italy, and 'Ptolemy', made for *Don Quixote* (1927), modelled upon the type used by F. Höller of Ulm for the 1482 edition of Ptolemy's *Geographia*. Among the artists connected with the press were Eric Gill and Graily Hewitt, who designed initial letters, and the illustrators Charles Gere (*Dante*, 1909) and Gwen Raverat (*Daphnis and Chloe*, 1933). See PRIVATE PRESS MOVEMENT.

134.

ASIA, CENTRAL. In ancient times the frontiers of major powers were generally recognized and respected, but those belonging to the various districts situated in western Turkestan, an area which is now divided between Russia and Afghanistan, were of only relative importance and did not hinder the passage of people or the interchange of goods and ideas. In the present context the term 'Central Asia' must therefore be expanded beyond its geographical and political limits to include three vast geographical zones rather than the four states which grew up within its boundaries. These three zones consist of central Asia proper, Siberia and, to the south, the whole of the great Eurasian plain, which, regardless of the mountain ranges that intersect it, stretches from the borders of China in the east across the steppe lands of the U.S.S.R. to include the Hungarian and Romanian sections of the central European plain. In the first millennium B.C. central Asia proper possessed an urban art formed in the cities belonging to such feudal states as Bactria (broadly speaking, present-day Afghanistan), Sogdia (which consisted of sections of present-day Uzbekistan and much of Tadzhikistan), Chorasmia (the Tashkent area) and Ferghana (parts of Uzbekistan), whilst the Eurasian plain was inhabited by nomads who practised an 'animal' art of an essentially decorative character which the Scythians of southern Russia succeeded in imbuing with quite remarkable beauty and vigour. See ANIMAL STYLE.

The Central Asian states owed their prosperity to the flourishing agriculture they had developed in the valleys and plains fertilized and watered by the great rivers which served as the spinal cord of each. Urbanization developed early in each of these states and with it the crafts. In the 6th c. B.C. Bactria and Sogdia were already so important that Darius referred to them in the great inscription cut by his orders on the face of the rock of Bisitun. In the 4th c. B.C. Alexander the Great was not content to conquer all four states but determined to assign a major role to them in the expansion of the trade which he planned to encourage between the Eastern and Western worlds. Merchants responding to the new opportunities he provided for them were quick to travel eastward in the wake of his conquering armies. In order to increase the West's trade with India Alexander founded the town of Alexandria-Kapisu (Begram) astride the chief caravan route linking India to the West. He wished it to serve both as his local capital and as a clearing-house for the goods being transported to and from India. Soon Indian religion, philosophy and artistic conventions began to flow into central Asia along with the goods which the caravans were conveying to the West, just as Western ideas and objects gradually travelled eastwards. The two civilizations, although basically very different, met and often blended at various points along these great caravan routes, but it was in Bactria that they actually fused to form a significant new style. The policy adopted by Alexander's Seleucid successors of sending back to Greece and Macedonia for artists and craftsmen did much to strengthen the influence which Hellenism had already started to exercise over the native craftsmen. Bactria's ultimate skill in merging the styles of Greece and Rome with her own is clearly to be seen in a sculptured frieze of musicians carved during the 1st c. A.D. to adorn a Buddhist monastery at Airtam, near Termez, on the Russian side of the Afghan frontier. This Westernized style had by then penetrated far beyond Bactria; by following other routes in addition to the Central Asian it had reached Taxila (Rawalpindi), Ghandara—a province in the lower Kabul valley—and Mathura in the Punjab, blending with Indian elements in order to serve Buddhism. In this way these new forms travelled northwards to Tibet, China and the oasis towns of the Tarim desert and then turned westwards into Central Asia to reach Bamyan in Afghanistan, whence certain Central Asian traits percolated back into eastern Turkestan.

Buddhism was the motive force of this latter style and its adoption of the Hindu institution of monasticism helped to disseminate it. The earliest figural sculptures of Buddha were produced in Gandhara and Mathura in the course of the 1st c. B.C.; but whereas Hellenistic influences prevailed in those modelled in Ghandara, Indian traits predominated in Mathura under the early Kushans (50 B.C.–A.D. 210). Ghandara sponsored the long-faced and long-nosed type of Buddha with his hair arranged in neat waves; it is known as the Apollo type. Several other versions of markedly Hellenistic character were also evolved, all of which penetrated to Kashmir and Turkestan to survive there till the 5th c. A.D. Mathura on the other hand favoured a straight-haired Buddha with features of Eastern type, the eyebrows extending in an unbroken curve along the base of the forehead and an enigmatic smile on the lips. The ear-lobes were elongated to proclaim his divinity, while his body was more flexibly rendered than in Ghandara, the whole treatment becoming softer and more sinuous. In Mathura Buddha soon began to be accompanied by a following of divinities portrayed in a similar style. In the minor arts of Central Asia the style is particularly well represented in IVORY carvings, especially those which have been excavated at Begram. They possess all the qualities of small-scale sculpture. On many of them nude or semi-nude women of Indian appearance assume the gracefully contorted poses associated with Indian monumental stone carvings of a somewhat later date. The Begram ivories date for the most part from the 1st to 4th centuries A.D., but women with similar, if attenuated, characteristics also appear on certain Bactrian silver ewers of Sassanian and post-Sassanian date. The latter are presented in a manner so similar to the Sassanian that originally the silver vessels were classified as Sassanian and it is only recently, partly owing to the better knowledge of Kushan art derived from sustained excavations, that the Indian characteristics of certain of these representations have been recognized and on the strength of this some of these silver vessels are now assigned to Bactria, at any rate by certain scholars.

Both on the ivories and on the silver vessels the women are often represented standing either in a niche or an alcove or beneath a garland or arch. These architectural features, possibly even the Indian stupas, reached Central Asia from the West and between the 5th and 7th centuries A.D. were widely used in Sogdia to decorate the exteriors of the rectangular clay ossuaries in use among the Zoroastrian communities. Sometimes the Western capitals were replaced in Sogdia by the ROSETTES which were extremely popular throughout Central Asia, where they often served to symbolize the sun. On the ossuaries figures were often placed under these arches, as in an interesting though damaged example found at Bia Naiman. Under Sassanian influence both the Indian versions of scenes of this type, as found in certain Begram ivories, and the Central Asian forms, as seen in the Bia Naiman ossuary, became simplified and in the process acquired a more Western elegance and sophistication.

Bactrian metal-workers were especially quick to respond to foreign influences. In the 4th and 5th centuries B.C., to judge by such examples as the cast-bronze lion-griffin and the gold armlets inlaid with coloured pastes from the Oxus Treasure in the British Museum, they were ready to work in the Scytho-Altaian style. But a series of silver dishes of a similar and slightly later date in the Hermitage Museum, Leningrad, display scenes drawn from Greek mythology and the tragedies of Euripides. They are executed in the Hellenistic style; others, although also worked in a Hellenistic style, feature Indian motifs such as elephants. Finally, during most of the first half of the 1st millennium A.D. the Kushan and Sassanian styles were to contend for supremacy throughout much of western Turkestan.

About 131 B.C. a formidable horde believed to have consisted of Yueh-Chi tribesmen supported by Hephthalite Huns, Sacae and Tokharian tribesmen swept the Greeks from Bactria and under the name of Kushans gained control of vast areas of Central Asia, capturing from the Parthians both a section of the Silk Road connecting China to Europe and part of India's western caravan route. In the 2nd c. A.D., when King Kanishka is thought to have lived and reigned, the Kushan empire also included Gandhara and Mathura. The sculptures and paintings of Bamyan represent the finest achievements of Kushan art in central Asia proper, yet Sassanian influence had established itself so firmly there that it even made itself felt in certain of Bamyan's Buddhist paintings. Indeed Sassanian influence became so strong throughout western Turkestan that it outlived the dynasty which created the Sassanian style in art by several centuries, surviving in certain districts almost to the end of the 1st millennium A.D. Not all the magnificent silver dishes in the Sassanian style belonging to the Hermitage Museum are to be assigned to Persia and the Sassanian age. Some are of considerably later date and were almost certainly produced in Bactria or Siberia, which also boasted a long tradition in working metals. A dish showing two warriors fighting on foot, with their broken and discarded weapons strewn around them, is almost certainly of Siberian origin. Some of the hunting scenes with slightly debased Sassanian designs are also unlikely to have been made in Persia; yet they follow Persian prototypes so closely that it is difficult to be absolutely certain of this.

The extent to which Sassanian customs affected the daily life of Central Asia's aristocracy can be seen in an exceptionally interesting series of wall-paintings, all of which were discovered in the 1940s in four major sites in western Turkestan. They survive on the walls of the feudal castle of Varaksha, situated a short distance to the north-west of Bukhara on soil which the desert has now reclaimed, at Pendzhikent, a city which grew up some 38 miles (60 km) to the east of Samarkand, Balalyk Tepe near Termez on the northern bank of the Amu Darya and Toprak Kala close to that river's mouth. Many of the paintings are of a secular character and all differ in almost every respect from the Buddhist paintings of Bamyan, although some occasionally link up with certain paintings in eastern Turkestan, more especially with those of Sorcuk and Kuca. Some of the earliest Central Asian works date from the 3rd and 4th centuries A.D. in contrast to those at Niya in eastern Turkestan, which date from the 2nd c. But they are too damaged to throw much light on the style and subject matter which then prevailed. The majority of the better preserved murals date from the 7th and early 8th centuries. They are of absorbing interest, ranging in subject from the religious to the secular, including battle and hunting scenes as well as state occasions and religious ceremonies. The work is accomplished, the style assured and fully formed with features which point to Sassanian Persia as their spring-board and others which must have served as a basis for the early Islamic school. It is sad that the opposition to figural art by the Arab invaders of Central Asia disrupted the development of this style. In a libation scene on the walls of a room in one of Pendzhikent's temples Sogdian notables are shown seated cross-legged in the Oriental manner, holding gold and silver vessels of Sassanian shapes; those held by the men have small, rounded bases, short stems and shallow bowls which are often fluted; those held by the women are taller and narrower. The men wear highly sophisticated, beautifully tailored three-quarter length tunics, which fit closely and are pulled in at the waist to give the wasp-shaped silhouette associated with Bahram Gur in some early Islamic miniatures. Some tunics have a single revers and closely resemble those in the mural paintings of Kizil and Kuca in eastern Turkestan. The crowns worn by certain figures are trimmed with ribbons, veils and bells, recalling the more elaborate versions which adorned the crowns of Persia's Sassanian rulers. Many of the garments are quite obviously made of contemporary stuffs. Some seem to depict textiles imported from Persia; but Sogdia was so noted at that time for its fabrics that the majority of the materials featured in the murals were probably of local make even when the motifs used by the native weavers had been obtained from Persia. At Balalyk Tepe a garment is made of a stuff which has as its repeat pattern a large tusked animal's head set within a circle in accordance with Sassanian tradition; the design closely resembles a fragment of an actual stuff found at Astana in eastern Turkestan and now in the National Museum, Delhi, which is dated to the 6th/7th c. At Varaksha a costume made of a textile, the main repeat motif of which shows a bird within a circle holding a streamer in its beak, probably presents a similarly close adaptation of a Sassanian textile motif even though no actual example of such a stuff has reached us. Other costumes, however, are made of fabrics for which we have as yet no parallels and these should therefore be regarded, at any rate for the present, as representations of Sogdian materials. Included in this group are an all-over pattern of diamond-shaped fish and another all-over design consisting of a quarter moon with balls suspended from it.

This group of Central Asian paintings seems to indicate that a love of painting and the ability to produce it were so widespread in western Turkestan from the opening centuries of our era that, to judge from a fragment of a painted wooden shield recovered from the site of the great feudal castle of Mug some 125 miles (200 km) east of Tashkent, a form of folk art had also developed. Mug originally stood on land rendered fertile by skilful irrigation; but as in all wars, when the victorious Arab armies reached the area early in the 8th c. agriculture suffered. The painstakingly maintained system of irrigation in use throughout western Turkestan broke down and the desert started to encroach again on these once carefully cultivated areas. It eventually engulfed the castle. A few years ago a shepherd happened to stumble across a basket filled with documents as he grazed his herds near the mound. He reported the find to the authorities. The documents were found to date from A.D. 717–19. Excavations followed, the ruins of a once magnificent castle were uncovered and a painted shield was also recovered from the site. Enough of it survives to show the figure of a wasp-waisted rider seated on a spirited, splendidly caparisoned horse; he wears a tunic of local cut and is armed with two daggers, a long sword, two bows and a quiver case. The style is a popular version of that seen in the more accomplished murals discovered at the four sites referred to above.

The sophistication of the inhabitants of western Turkestan encouraged artistry and the crafts, not least those of pottery and small-scale sculpture of the type which had been practised in the area from very ancient times. Zoroastrianism had many followers in the area and the craftsmen whose forbears had in antiquity produced clay statuettes of deities now used their skill on ossuaries and to make figurines of both nude and clothed women. Some of these doubtless represented the local goddess Anahita, just as some of the male statuettes depicted Syavush, the god of death and the rebirth of Spring, who figures prominently in some of the Pendzhikent paintings. Other statuettes show women wearing tiaras, hats or cloaks with hoods attached to them. Some wear straight, long-sleeved robes beneath sleeveless cloaks and hold a fruit as a symbol of fertility. At Tali-Barsu, in a southern suburb of Samarkand, figurines dating from the 3rd and 4th centuries A.D. include musicians, women flute-players, horsemen, various animals and the part-human, part-animal Iranian demi-god Shah Gopat. In the 7th and 8th centuries ALABASTER, terracotta and pottery statuettes were made in considerable quantity, some of the female ones displaying Indian traits. Indian influence is also evident in a carved wood statuette of a woman found at Pendzhikent.

Fine glazed and painted pottery does not seem to have been made in western Turkestan prior to the Arab invasion, while the elaborate and colourful tilework associated with the great mosques, seminaries and mausoleums of Samarkand and Bukhara dates from Mongol times, as do the earliest Islamic vessels decorated with animal, floral and geometrical motifs with fine script, often in Kufic characters, which contributes in no small measure to their beauty. At New Nisa some fine pottery was produced in the 15th c. with bird, animal and floral motifs predominating; but apart from the CARPETS and gold-thread EMBROIDERY for which Bukhara continued to be famed almost to the present day, the revival of the arts inaugurated by Tamerlane petered out in the 16th c.; and even when at its height it hardly rivalled the work being done in Sogdia and Chorasmia before the Arab invasion.

In the Eurasian plain creativity did not endure for as long as in the urban centres, largely disappearing with the passage of the Huns in the early centuries of our era. A number of important manifestations of artistry had occurred in Siberia in prehistoric times, some dating back as far as the 30th millennium B.C. The Neolithic, Bronze and Iron Ages were all productive of objects. Although metallurgy had become well established in certain areas, notably in the Minusinsk Basin, by the 3rd millennium B.C., it was with the rise of nomadism in the steppe lands and the wealth which certain of the tribal chieftains succeeded in amassing that the minor arts came into their own. It was thus, roughly speaking, between the 5th and 2nd centuries B.C. that the Siberians produced, under the impact of the Animal Art evolved by the Scythian nomads and those sharing their culture, a series of exceptionally interesting plaques and belt buckles, many of them cast in gold, many more in bronze, which will be discussed below.

From as early as the 1st millennium B.C. until about half-way through the following millennium the Eurasian nomads were so considerable a force that even great powers such as China and Persia had to take them into account. Indeed the nomads played no small part in shaping Central Asia's history. Numerous tribes roamed the great plain, transporting their women and children in ox-drawn covered wagons as they drove their herds ahead of them. They were often of different origins, but the majority followed a Scythian way of life and practised a Scythian type of art. It may be incorrect to describe their art as 'Scythian', but since the most recent excavations in Asiatic Russia have failed to provide it with a different origin it must continue to be known by that name, thanks to the discoveries made in the course of the 19th c. by archaeologists engaged in excavating the Scythian burials of southern Russia and the Kuban Basin in the Caucasus.

An offshoot of the Scythian Animal Style had been discovered in Siberia over a century earlier by the Russian settlers whom Peter the Great encouraged to seek a better life there. On arrival in Siberia some of the more adventurous newcomers had noted the region's numerous burial mounds, entered them and removed the more valuable of their contents—notably the cast gold and bronze plaques and buckles—which they proceeded to sell in the local markets. The Governor-General of Siberia acquired some of these objects and sent them to the Tsar with a report. Peter promptly gave orders for all tomb robbers to be punished and their finds confiscated and sent to him. His collection of gold plaques and buckles is now exhibited in the Hermitage alongside the gold objects excavated in southern Russia and is called after him. A chance find of a Scythian treasure—the Melgunov—during the reign of Catherine the Great was sent to the Empress and also now belongs to the Hermitage Museum. But the foundations of Scythian studies were laid only with the start of systematic excavations in the latter part of the 19th c.

Although the Scythians reached the Caucasus early in the 6th c. B.C. and some of their richest burials have been found in the Kuban Basin, it was in southern Russia, in the region lying between the rivers Don and Dnieper, that the most important branch, whom we know as the Royal Scyths, established a kingdom in the course of that century. Certain small groups of Scythians, probably single family units, penetrated soon afterwards into Pomerania and Lusatia, whilst some larger contingents moved into the Danubian plain. The bulk of the Scythians, however, remained concentrated in Royal Scythia until evicted from it by the Sarmatians, a tribe of similar Indo-Iranian stock, during the closing centuries of the millennium.

The climate of southern Russia is unsuited to the preservation of objects of a perishable nature if buried in the soil for any length of time. Those which have been recovered from the Scythian burials of southern Russia therefore consist almost entirely of articles made of metal, bone or wood, and occasionally of leather. Although most of the excavated burials had been plundered in antiquity, the number of gold articles found in them is astonishing. Some are in the form of personal adornments, but the majority consist of plaques intended to serve either as harness or as costume ornaments. They generally display animal designs although geometric and floral ones also appear and occasionally, under the impact of Greek influence, figural representations.

The finest and largest Scythian gold plaques measure some 30 centimetres in length and consist of a single animal which was probably intended to decorate the centre of a chieftain's shield. Like all the other plaques they clearly illustrate the Scythians' profound knowledge of the animals they were fond of portraying and testify both to their skill in working metals and to their artistic gifts. The animals are rendered naturalistically but at the same time they are sharply synthesized, with the result that their salient characteristics are instantly seen. To convey an impression of an animal's muscles, even when it is at rest, the goldsmiths working on the larger plaques skilfully inclined the metal in different directions so that the play of light as it falls on the different planes creates the ripple effect produced by muscles in movement. The technique may derive from wood carving, but it is supremely effective when used in metal especially when done with such sensitivity that at first sight the inclines pass almost unnoticed. The method was not used on the small stamped plaques intended to trim garments, many of which were not even chased; but the same understanding of drawing and superb graphic quality is found in all the works which the Scythians produced. This is especially evident in the portrayal of stags, the finest of those in a recumbent position being the 30 centimetre gold plaque of the 6th c. B.C. recovered from the Kostromskaya burial. The Scythians were so fascinated by decoration that they smothered their possessions in designs and often could not resist placing the representation of one animal in a vacant space on the body of another or using the extremity of one creature to turn it into that of another in what is known as a zoomorphic juncture.

The same absorption with animal design and the same love of decoration were displayed by nomads in the Asiatic section of the plain who followed a way of life similar to that of the Scythians and practised a similar type of art. The extent to which the culture and taste of these people corresponded with those of the Scythians was revealed by the remarkable excavations which Griaznov and Rudenko carried out in 1925–9 and 1947–50 on eight mounds at PAZYRYK, a cemetery situated on the western slopes of the Altay. The method of mound construction employed by the Pazyryk nomads together with the climatic conditions peculiar to the site resulted in the tomb chambers becoming quickly isolated from seasonal variations in temperature by a thick layer of ice. Thus the contents of the burials became deep frozen and were so well preserved that they have reached us almost in their original condition.

Like the Scythians the Pazyryk people believed in an after-life virtually identical with life on earth. They therefore tried to transform the tombs of their chieftains into exact equivalents of their earthly dwellings. The excavated burials had been rifled in antiquity so that little of intrinsic value was recovered from them; yet the variety and quantity of objects of a perishable nature which the excavators removed from the burials and succeeded in preserving are of inestimable value in enabling us to reconstruct the life not only of this group of nomads but, because of the similarity between the two types of art, also that of the Scyths proper. Like almost all the Scythian burials the Pazyryk ones were also horse burials, and the good condition in which the bodies were found at Pazyryk enabled the archaeologists to identify several breeds of horses and to preserve one body for inclusion among the Hermitage Museum's exhibits. Even more important was the recovery from one burial of the relatively well-preserved body of a man which had been tattooed with animal designs of Scythian character. It too is exhibited in the Hermitage Museum.

Whereas in the Scythian burials the bodies of the horses which had been killed in order to serve their master in his life beyond the grave were piled up round his grave chamber, the Pazyryk people constructed special burial chambers for the horses adjoining the north end of the human ones. The walls of these equine burials were draped with hangings and their trappings, including tail sheaths, saddles and saddle cloths, were placed in them. All the trappings had been adorned with plaques displaying animal forms, some of wood covered with gold foil, others of metal, and even the reins were often decorated with cut-outs of animals. In some cases a horse was provided with a head-dress terminating in a semi-mask; one head-dress found was in the form of a stag's head, another in that of a ram's head with a bird fixed between its horns. In the human burials clothing and furniture found in good condition compensated for the loss of valuable personal adornments. All the upper garments were smothered in decoration executed in strips of coloured furs, felt appliqué work or embroidery. In some cases even the soles of a pair of indoor bootees were decorated in this manner, as were all satchels and bags. Furnishings included a variety of cushions and turned or carved legs with detachable, tray-like oval tops. Many types of domestic utensils and tools were found. Weapons seemed to consist only of arrows, all of which had geometrical or linear designs painted on them.

From an artistic point of view the hangings worked in felt appliqué and the carved harness decorations are by far the most interesting of the finds. Although most of the saddle-cloths were decorated with geometrical forms, some of which foreshadow the designs found in far later carpets of nomadic make, a small number of hangings had figural representations and many featured combats between animals. One of the most interesting of the figural scenes appears as the repeat motif of a large hanging found in Tomb I, dating from early in the 5th c. B.C. It depicts an investiture or audience granted by a seated female divinity holding a tree of life in one hand as she receives an elegant, rather Parthian-looking rider seated on a spirited horse. Another more damaged hanging includes in its design a creature half-man, half-bird, whilst others display brightly coloured mythical creatures. Combat scenes between animals play an even more important part in the art of the Pazyryk people than in Scythian or even Siberian art of the same period and type. At Pazyryk the contests are so frenzied that often the hind quarters of the victim are so contorted as to become inverted. In Siberian plaques the plasticity is such that a single beast such as a panther is often shown curved into a circle; but the Siberian combat scenes are a trifle more sedate, the poses a little less unnatural than at Pazyryk, although the claws and teeth of the contestants are often more forcibly stressed. The Siberian beasts are often enclosed in a square or rectangular border and set against an open-work background. They are more illustrative in conception than the Pazyryk ones, which even when portraying imaginary creatures in completely unnatural poses convey a sharper impression of the heat of battle. Further to the east, in China's Ordos borderlands, where plaques of a comparable kind were made, the contours of the animals are rounder and their bodies rendered more flatly.

Lions with members of the reindeer and wild cat families occur with especial frequency in the art of the Pazyryk people. Animals of all species generally display dot-and-comma muscle markings. The variety, inventiveness and vitality of the designs are quite remarkable. Nevertheless certain chieftains were not satisfied with these local products and managed to acquire some very remarkable foreign ones. Among the more important Chinese imports are a section of a bronze mirror from the 5th c. B.C. and an almost perfectly preserved embroidered silk textile—the oldest Chinese embroidery so far known to us. The Persian objects consist of two fragments of patterned woven textiles from the 5th c. B.C., one strip displaying a procession of lions, the other a group of women gathered round an altar, and—most important of all—two fragments and one virtually complete pile wool knotted carpet also dating from the 5th c. B.C. The complete rug is the oldest in the world. It measures almost six feet (183 cm) square; its designs of geometrical, animal and figural character are arranged in concentric bands, the colours consisting chiefly of reds and ochres.

It was in the course of the 4th c. B.C. that the Huns started moving westward from the Ordos, where they had been living. They migrated at a steady pace and had entered Mongolia, where they set up their empire, by the 3rd c. B.C. The burial mounds of their dead mark their advance. Those which they constructed in the Zidsha valley lie in the same latitude as the Pazyryk burials and have undergone a similar process of congelation; yet so far the most exciting and richest of their burials are those which were excavated at Noin Ula, north of Ulan Bator, in 1924/5. Mound 6 contained the finest objects. Its contents reveal a fascinating and complex picture. They show that the chieftain buried in the tomb had established such close links with China that his treasured possessions included two fine LACQUER cups inscribed with the name of the Chinese craftsman who had made them, according to the inscription, on 5 September A.D. 13 for the Shahlin Palace. The dead man's body lay in a coffin of such neat and skilled workmanship that it too is thought to have been made by a Chinese carpenter. Yet the chieftain's cultural roots were firmly embedded in the world of the Eurasian nomads. His horse trappings were as lavishly ornamented as any of those discovered at Pazyryk although his saddle differed sharply from the appliqué-worked Pazyryk saddles, being made of leather threaded with red and black wool clipped to resemble velvet. His textiles of Central Asian character are no less interesting and arresting than the remarkable series of hangings found at Pazyryk. Among these a woven wool rug lined with thin leather must take pride of place. Its central design is in the form of a combat between a griffin and an elk of Scytho-Altaic appearance. Their bodies are outlined in cord and executed in purple, brown and white felt appliqué work and embroidery. Another less accomplished but equally fascinating rug simulates the splayed-out body of a double-headed tiger skin, the stripes being executed in black and white embroidery. The imported stuffs found in the tomb include some fragments of Parthian embroidery of a figural character. One shows a man's head which bears a slight physical resemblance to that of the rider in the Pazyryk hanging featuring an investiture scene; another depicts two elegantly dressed riders, their tunics recalling some of those in the mural paintings of western Turkestan, ambling across a countryside bathed in an idyllic atmosphere.

The Parthians set up their kingdom in Khurasan in the latter part of the 4th c. B.C. and quickly gained control of a vital section of the Silk Road and of the main caravan route linking India to the West. They grew rich from the heavy dues which they levied from caravans traversing their territory and the majority quickly became urbanized. It may have been partly owing to the pressure exercised on them by the migrating Huns, and partly owing to the tendency of all the central Asian tribes to move westward, that in *c.* 171 B.C. Mithridates I founded the town which is now known as Old Nisa to distinguish it from the later, neighbouring town of New Nisa, situated just south of Ashkhabad, in what is now Tadzhikistan, on the edge of the Karakorum desert. Mithridates intended it to become Parthia's capital, but it soon developed into more of a royal residence and necropolis than the kingdom's chief city. Excavations carried out on the site by Soviet archaeologists 1930–6 and from 1946 onwards have uncovered a number of ambitious buildings, many of which originally contained large clay statues of both men and women. The archaeologists were lucky to find the royal strong-room with many of its contents buried beneath the rubble of its roof and walls. They recovered from it a considerable number of statuettes in silver, cast bronze and clay, some representing local deities, others Greek gods, and others in the form of sphinxes or real or imaginary beasts. Bronze and iron weapons and burnished pottery were also found in considerable quantity. But the most spectacular finds consisted of a number of ivory rhytons, the majority terminating in the head and forequarters of one of the animal forms especially popular among the nomads such as a mountain goat or lion-griffin worked in the round. In sharp contrast to its terminal the top of one rhyton was encircled by a broad, frieze-like band displaying scenes of purely Hellenistic inspiration carved in high relief in a Central Asian version of the Hellenistic style. Another of the rhytons was adorned with PASTE inlay.

Paste inlay had been used by the Scythians from as early as the 6th c. B.C., as for example on the ear of the gold plaque in the form of a panther

HORSE TRAPPINGS

Section of open-work Siberian cast metal belt buckle of Scythian style. This example belongs to a small group which displays genre scenes conjectured to be illustrations of ancient epics. (Hermitage Mus., 6th–4th c. B.C.)

Carved wood bridle decoration from Pazyryk. 5th c. B.C. (Hermitage Mus.)

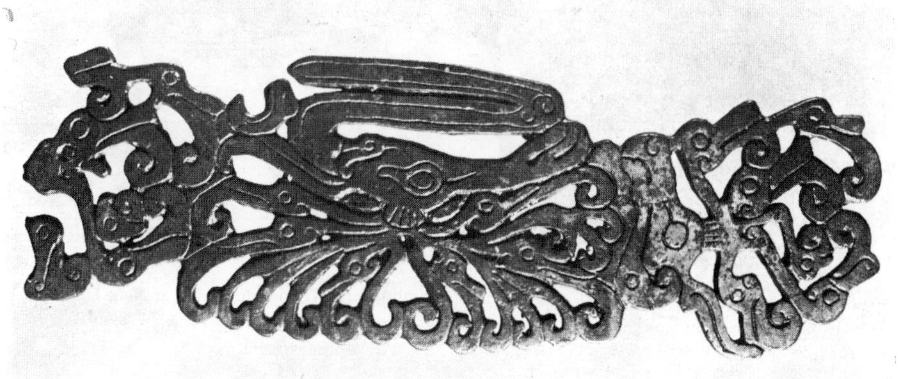

Bronze open-work belt buckle or horse's frontlet showing zoomorphic junctures. Kuban. 4th c. B.C. (Hermitage Mus.)

Parthian ivory rhyton from the site of Old Nisa. 2nd c. B.C. The terminal is in the Animal Style but the frieze decorating the upper section is Hellenistic. (*right*) Detail of frieze from foregoing. (Hermitage Mus.)

Embroideries from Hun burials at Noin Ula in outer Mongolia. 1st c. A.D. (Hermitage Mus.)

Bactrian silver dish. 6th–7th c. A.D. Opposite a representation of Silenus with a maenad is shown a Central Asian feasting or libation scene in which a man wearing a caftan with single revers is seated cross-legged holding a vessel of Sassanian shape. (Hermitage Mus.)

Reconstruction of terracotta ossuary found near Bia-Naiman, Sogdia. 5th–7th c. A.D. The pillars and capitals are of Western style, the pearls studding the arches are of Sassanian derivation and the borders of four-petalled flowers are in the local tradition. Life-size statues resembling the figures were used for interior decoration

Mural painting from Pianzhikent, showing a sacrificial scene. The painting shows vessels of Sassanian shape and illustrates the textile designs and styles of the garments

Textile design on costumes shown in murals of Balalyk Tepe

from the Kelermes burial; but the Scythians had always assigned a very subsidiary role to polychrome work. Siberian jewellers of the Scythian period had used it more extensively, as for example on the gold head-dress ornament of the 5th to 3rd c. B.C. in Peter the Great's collection showing a magnificent eagle-griffin grasping a wild boar in its claws. In its agony the victim has inverted its hind quarters in the manner which characterizes the Pazyryk combat scenes. The inlay, all of which has disappeared, originally decorated the eagle-griffin's breast, tail and upper wings. Inlay was also used by Ordos craftsmen, who produced plaques conforming to the Eurasian Animal Style such as that of a recumbent horse in the British Museum. It was only with the arrival of the Sarmatians in southern Russia, however, that inlay began to be used extensively to produce the colourful polychrome effects so sought after by these tribesmen.

Like the Scythians the Sarmatians were of Indo-European stock and spoke a related Iranian tongue. They followed a Scythian way of life, although they used a heavier type of cavalry in battle, equipping the horsemen with lances. The Sarmatians had begun to migrate westwards from Asia towards the middle of the 1st millennium B.C. and had reached the Volga in the early decades of the 5th c. B.C. By the 4th c. B.C. they had advanced to the Don. On crossing it they began to harass the Royal Scyths and managed in the course of the 3rd and 2nd centuries B.C. to evict them from their kingdom and push them into the Crimea. There the latter contrived to establish the state of Little Scythia. It proved short-lived, for by *c.* A.D. 100 the Sarmatians had succeeded in annihilating the Scythians. A couple of centuries or so later they in their turn suffered a similar fate at the hands of the Goths, but before that happened some groups had broken away from the main branch. While two of these, the Iasiges and the Roxolani, made their way into central Europe, certain Sarmatian units which had been incorporated into the Roman army found themselves stationed in Gaul whilst others were employed to mount guard over the wall which Hadrian had built along Britain's northern border.

Sarmatian studies date from early in the present century, when a start was made on the scientific examination of their burials, those situated in the region of the Volga being opened first. The field of research was then widened to include those in the Don district and it has since been extended further westward. The richest burials have proved to be the Khokhlach situated close to Novocherkassk, so that the finds from the wealthiest tomb have come to be known as the Novocherkassk Treasure. They came from a woman's burial, doubtless that of a queen, for Sarmatian women enjoyed equal rights with men and were expected to fight beside their men in battle before being permitted to marry. They are the Amazons of the Greeks. This woman's burial dates from the 1st c. B.C. One of several gold diadems recovered from it is especially impressive, if in rather a barbaric way. It consists of a gold band set with fine-quality Hellenistic gems; sharply contrasting with these is a series of stags executed in the round and set along the diadem's upper rim between trees of a distinctive artistic style. The stags are of the Scythian type, but they also resemble both the winged griffins carved in the round in wood and covered with gold foil of *c.* 400 B.C. which were found at Pazyryk; they are thought to have belonged to a necklace. The little gold griffin from the Oxus Treasure in the British Museum is of the same type. The Novocherkassk Treasure also contains a little gold bottle, a fine example of the type associated with the Sarmatians, which seldom exceed 9 centimetres in height and usually have a gold chain attached to them. The surface of this example is covered with stamped and chased animal designs of Scythian character.

Although the Sarmatians adopted the salient features of the Scythian Animal Style, they transformed it into something new by the extensive use which they made of polychrome effects. They achieved them alike by means of inset gems and coloured glass, by paste inlays and by champlevé and cloisonné ENAMEL. They also developed a liking for gold fringes and for open-work not unlike that which Siberian metalworkers of the same and earlier dates had been fond of producing.

Certain features of Sarmatian art such as the large beaked bird of Scytho-Siberian origin were eventually taken over by the Goths, who helped to disseminate them throughout western Europe. It was in this way that the Sarmatian style, itself a product of the styles evolved by the Eurasian nomads of the preceding millennium, played no small part in moulding those tried out during the Dark Ages in the applied arts of western and northern Europe.

18, 186, 274, 450, 578, 665, 700, 702, 725, 729, 809, 840, 931.

ASSISI WORK. See EMBROIDERY.

ASTERISM. Term in jewellery for the luminous star which may be seen in some RUBIES or SAPPHIRES when suitably cut in CABOCHON. Stones having this star are called 'star rubies' or 'star sapphires' or *asterias*. See JEWELLERY.

ASTRAGAL. A narrow MOULDING semicircular in section and often placed at the top or bottom of columns. A smaller version of the

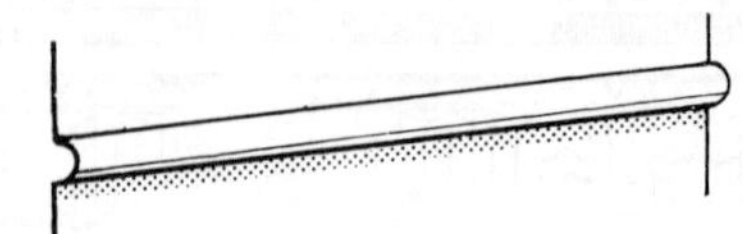

TORUS and the reverse of the SCOTIA. It is often decorated with an enrichment of BEAD-AND-REEL pattern.

ASTRALAGUS. See TOYS.

ASTRARIUM. Planetary clock. See DONDI.

ATHÉNIENNE. Ornate carved tripod stand in the style of bronzes from Herculaneum, a characteristic invention of the NEO-CLASSICAL movement in French furniture. See FURNITURE (EUROPEAN).

AUBUSSON TAPESTRIES AND CARPETS. Aubusson, a very ancient centre of tapestry weaving in France, was granted the title of Royal Manufactory in 1665. But its real importance began only in the second half of the 18th c. when great quantities of hangings and furniture coverings were woven there with pastoral and CHINOISERIE designs by OUDRY, BOUCHER and HUET. During the 19th c. skilful reproductions of earlier tapestries were made, and more recently Aubusson played a leading part in weaving the cartoons of such modern tapestry-designers as Jean Lurçat (1892–1966).

Aubusson has specialized in low-warp WEAVING. Its tapestries normally have a blue selvedge bearing the name of the town and the name or initials of the weaver. Floral patterned carpets woven by the tapestry process have also been extensively made at Aubusson. The patterns are generally in 18th-c. style but the majority of the carpets date from the 19th c. See TAPESTRY.

440, 491.

AUDRAN. Family of French painters and decorators, three of whom were named Claude. CLAUDE AUDRAN I, together with ERRARD and COYPEL, painted decorations for Versailles from 1661. CLAUDE AUDRAN II assisted in the decorations under Lebrun of the *Grands Appartements* of the king and queen at Versailles between 1671 and 1681. CLAUDE AUDRAN III (1658–1734) was one of the most prominent decorators in the last decade of the 17th c. and together with BÉRAIN originated the new decorative style in ARABESQUES and GROTESQUES which heralded the ROCOCO. In 1709 he painted the SINGERIES at Marly which was the first large example of this genre. He was curator at the Luxembourg and helped the painter Watteau (1684–1721), who worked as his assistant at Marly.

AUMBRY or AMBRY. Medieval term for an enclosed CUPBOARD or a storage niche enclosed by doors. The term remained in use chiefly for the enclosed wall aumbry near the altar in churches, in which sacramental vessels were kept.

AURICULAR STYLE. Also known as 'lobate style', in Germany as *Knorpelwerk* and in the Netherlands as *Ohrmuschel* or *Kwabornament*. A characteristic ornamental mode of early 17th-c. northern BAROQUE in which undulating, slithery and boneless forms occasionally carry a suggestion of the inside of an ear or of a conch shell. The style was used by Wendel Dietterlin of Strasbourg as early as 1598 and by Lucas Kilian of Augsburg for the frame of his portrait of Elias Holl (1619). In the Low Countries it was favoured by Hans VREDEMAN DE VRIES among others. Although the style extended to all the decorative arts, its most important development was in silverwork, where it was often combined with dolphins, sinuous nudes and rippling water. The heavily undulating lines of the auricular style were in fact particularly well adapted to suggest the fluid malleability of silver as a material. In silverwork the auricular style was developed most prominently by Paulus and later by Adam van VIANEN. Other Dutch silversmiths who adopted it were Thomas Bogaert and Jan Lutma. The style has a sensuous appeal which some connoisseurs regard as among the most astonishing achievements of virtuoso craftsmanship, although others find it distasteful. There was some revival of the style during the period of ROCOCO and again within the ambit of ART NOUVEAU.

AVENTURINE. A glass embodying gold glittering particles. It was an Egyptian invention and was revived at Murano, Venice, in the 15th c. See GLASS (HISTORY).

A variety of greenish QUARTZ speckled with scales of mica which was much used for bead jewellery in India.

B

BADIER, FLORIMOND (active 1630–60). French bookbinder who worked in the POINTILLÉ and mosaic styles. The profile man's head in dotted outline, which occurs on two of Badier's three known signed bindings, cannot be regarded as an exclusive personal device since it is found on a number of bindings from other workshops. A list of these is given by E. Dacier in an article 'Autour de Le Gascon et de Florimond Badier' in *Trésors des bibliothèques de France*, Vols. iii and iv (1930–3).

BAGNALL, BENJAMIN (1689–1740). American clock-maker. Born in England, he emigrated to Boston, Massachusetts, *c.* 1710 and was probably Boston's first clock-maker. His business, which included the manufacture of eight-day clocks, was carried on by his son SAMUEL until *c.* 1760.

BAKEWELL AND COMPANY (also referred to as Bakewell and Page) of Pittsburgh, Pennsylvania, was established in 1808 and is generally thought to have been the first American glass-house to produce cut GLASS commercially. It remained in operation until 1882, making some of the best clear cut and engraved glass of the 19th c. Until 1819 it was probably the sole United States manufacturer producing cut and engraved glass, and it also became a leader in the manufacture of plain and moulded tablewares and conventionally pressed types. The company made as well some of the best of the flasks depicting American historical subjects. With the Boston and Sandwich Glass Company of Cape Cod and the NEW ENGLAND GLASS COMPANY of East Cambridge, Massachusetts, Bakewell produced fine cut and engraved objects in the Early and Middle American Periods. The company maintained its reputation for this production in spite of several changes in name: 'Bakewell, Page, and Bakewell' in 1824 and later 'Bakewell, Pears, and Company'. The early cut products of the company closely followed the design of imported Anglo-Irish goods and identification is frequently difficult since its wares were also exported. The manufacture of pressed glass was started in 1825 and from that year until 1882 an extensive variety of practical and decorative wares was produced. In spite of its early reliance on the Anglo-Irish tradition of design the company gradually evolved indigenous Pittsburgh characteristics. See GLASS (AMERICA).

BALL CLAY. White clay from Devon and Dorset was so called in Staffordshire because it was transported in balls. The term is also used more generally for secondary clays which fire white or cream at a low or average temperature in contrast to the kaolins. See CLAY (MATERIAL).

BANDEROLE. A long flag or streamer with a cleft end or a ribbon-like scroll bearing a device. In architecture, a flat band with an inscription.

BANDHANA. Indian name for tie and dye work. See INDIA (TEXTILES).

BANDING. Term in cabinet-making for a decorative INLAID border of contrasting woods. It is called 'cross banding' when the wood is cut across the grain and 'straight banding' when it is cut with the grain. When the banding is composed of two strips of wood set at an angle to each other so as to form a HERRING-BONE pattern it is called 'herring-bone' or 'feather' banding. The latter was characteristic of English walnut furniture in the 2nd half of the 17th c.

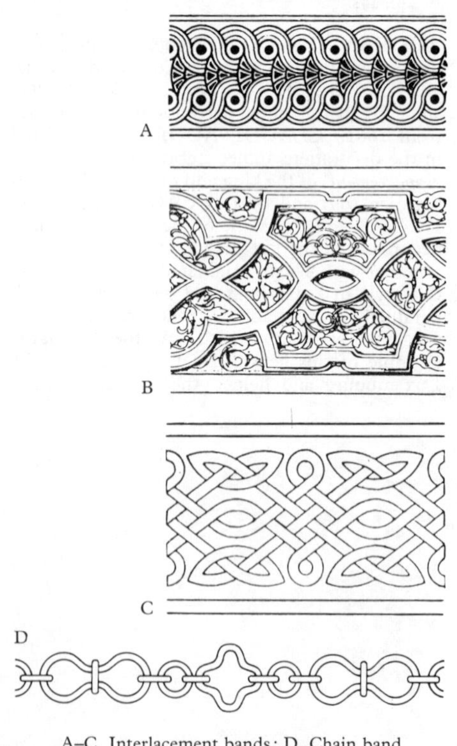

A–C. Interlacement bands; D. Chain band

BARK CLOTH. Of the materials which served mankind for clothing before the discovery of woven textiles the commonest were the pelts of animals (see LEATHERCRAFT) and bark cloth, or *tapa* (*tappa*) as it is often called from the Polynesian word for a cloth made from the bark of the paper mulberry. Bark cloth gives little protection against the cold and although there is evidence that it was once made by certain peoples of central Europe from the bark of lime trees, its main use has been confined to tropical and semi-tropical regions. There it has been very widespread indeed: central Africa, Japan, China, Southern and Central America (infrequent in North America), Polynesia, Indonesia and other tropical areas being the main centres. In some areas its production has persisted to a minor extent up to the present day. William T. Brigham writes that when he went to live in Hawaii in 1864 *kapa* (the Hawaiian name for bark cloth) was worn only in outlying districts and only the plainer forms were being made. Its antiquity in South America is attested by the fact that beaters for making bark cloth have been found at Huaca Prieta, Peru, in strata dating to the 3rd millennium B.C.

Bark cloth does not survive from remote antiquity, particularly in the moist and tropical regions where it was most in use. Our knowledge of its uses and the ways in which it was made derives mainly from accounts of 19th-c. travellers (the earliest account is perhaps one by the 16th-c. Italian explorer Antonio Pigaffetta, quoted by W. Naumann in the *C.I.B.A. Review*, xxxiii (1940)) and from collections of cloth and manufacturing tools made towards the end of the 19th c. One of the most extensive of these is in the Bernice P. Bishop Museum of Polynesian Ethnology and Natural History, Honolulu. The museum was founded in honour of the last member of the royal line of Kamehamela, from whom many of the examples of bark cloth come, in addition to examples collected by Captain Cook on his voyages to the South Seas. A curator of this museum, William T. Brigham, besides adding to the collection at the turn of the present century, published in 1911 what is now the standard work on the subject and in the museum catalogue lists and describes 8,270 pieces from Tahiti, Hawaii, Fiji, Tonga, Samoa, the New Hebrides, the Marshall and Solomon Islands, besides some from Africa and America. Other examples of bark cloth brought back to England by Captain Cook will be found in the Ethnographical Department of the British Museum. Information about bark cloth in the Pacific is fairly plentiful, but our knowledge of it in South America and central Africa is scanty by comparison, although in both these continents bark cloth is still being made.

The trees most commonly used for making bark cloth in the Pacific area belong to the mallow family. Commonest are the paper mulberry (*Broussonetia papyrifera*), the bread-fruit tree (*Artocarpus incisa*), the fig (*Ficus*) and some forms of hibiscus. In Japan and Java Kozo, of the mulberry family, is used. The Indians of North America used the bark of the birch, those of South America chiefly the banana tree (*Musa sapientum*), which was also used in Africa as well as the paper mulberry. Other trees and plants have been used, but the resulting cloth is usually of a coarser quality—although some of the bark cloth made in Uganda, although coarse, is soft and pliable with the texture of suede.

Bark cloth is made from the inner bark or bast of the tree. The methods are basically the same everywhere and are very similar to the techniques of paper-making.

In some places, e.g. Japan and Hawaii, the trees are specially cultivated for the purpose and are cut down when they are saplings about two years old. They are then about 2 m high and 2 cm or so in diameter. The tree often continues to produce shoots after being cut and these are cut in turn until the tree is too old to be of further use. The cloth made from the young saplings is finer and whiter than that made from older trees, which is often dark and cannot be beaten to such a degree of softness.

The bark is stripped off the tree lengthwise and taken in bundles to a stream, where it is left to soak in order to make it easier for the outer husk to be stripped off, leaving only the soft inner bast. In the Pacific Islands this operation is done by scraping off the outer bark with sharp shells; other methods are adopted elsewhere. After it has been separated the bast is again soaked until it reaches the point of fermentation, when it is at its most pliable. The long narrow strips are then paid out on the ground to allow the excess water to drain off and while it is still wet the beating starts. The bast is beaten on wooden boards, which are sometimes raised off the ground to

A Tongan woman at work on a length of 'tapa' cloth

render them more resilient. In Hawaii these boards are 6 to 9 m long and grooved to allow the excess water to run off. The first beat'ng is done with a heavy mallet, which flattens the fibres and increases the width of the bast. After this another beating process welds one strip to another so that the required length and width of cloth can be achieved. Some pieces of bark cloth are recorded to have been made as much as 200 metres long and several metres wide. William Brigham describes how a queen of Tonga had to roll herself into her state garment and roll herself out at the end of the ceremony. The usual size of Hawaiian cloth ranges from 9 to 15 metres in length and about 2½ metres in width. It is rarely that any form of adhesive is used to unite the pieces of beaten bast together. Bark cloth of the dimensions indicated is almost always produced by beating alone, which completely unites the fibres of the separate strips.

Throughout the process of beating the bast has to be kept very moist by constant sprinkling. When the required dimensions have been reached, it is washed to cleanse it and then beaten with variously grooved mallets to render it soft and pliable and to obtain the required surface texture. The texturing is done only after the cloth is already soft and pliable. By choice of an appropriate beater the bark cloth can be made to vary from a lace-like material to one like a heavy linen or cotton. Much of the bark cloth of Tahiti was as soft as silk and was worn by ladies as scarves and shawls. When a smooth surface is wanted the final beating is done with a very finely grooved mallet. Some cloth is ribbed like corduroy and some embossed with patterns. There is an endless variety. For blankets or floor mats several layers of cloth are welded together until the required thickness is achieved or sometimes they are made from old pieces of *tapa* pasted together.

The enormous variety of beaters used for making bark cloth in different parts of the world testifies to the ingenuity of primitive man within his technological competence. In Mexico the beaters are of grooved stone. Stones too are used in New Guinea and the Solomon Islands. In the Celebes they use stone beaters on which lines have been carved and which are fitted with rattan handles to make them more flexible in use. In the Admiralty Islands the beaters are bivalve shells, which are naturally grooved, and here too they are fitted with rattan handles. But for the greater part the beaters are of wood. Where the cloth is harsh and coarse the beaters are little more than primitive clubs. Where sophisticated varieties of cloth are made they are shaped and cut in an astonishing number of ways. William Brigham lists over 300 different types of Hawaiian beaters with carved designs, each with its descriptive title in Hawaiian. Many of them are four-sided with a different pattern on each side. The patterns are of course functional, for on them the quality and texture of the cloth depend.

In most countries the making of bark cloth is an occupation of women, often women of higher rank. In some countries it is a seasonal occupation in which everyone lends a hand. It is a noisy process, especially if the boards are raised from the ground so that they are resonant.

The decoration of bark cloth is virtually universal and the variety of methods and designs makes a fascinating study. Designs are often traditional to a region or even a caste.

In most of Africa the cloth is decorated by free-hand painting done with brushes made from grasses, as in Mangbetu in the Congo where what appear to be symbolic designs are drawn freely in repeat patterns. In Uganda the cloth is often brown as if dyed with catechu and black geometrical patterns are arranged in stripes, partly printed and partly painted in free-hand. Some of the garments have borders embroidered in raffia. In Ganda in central Africa black stamped decoration was a royal privilege while commoners wore a plain *tapa*. The stamps were cut from small pieces of calabash and each design had a symbolic significance. In Fiji, Samoa and Tahiti, where very sophisticated types of bark cloth were made, special techniques of decoration were evolved. In Hawaii, for example, little printing sticks were carved from bamboo, never more than about 5 centimetres long and about 1 centimetre wide, so that great skill and precision were needed to decorate large areas with repeat patterns. Sometimes the pattern was formed by the raised design on the stick; in others the pattern was printed in reverse, the stamp forming the background and the cut-away portions, which did not take up the colouring matter, serving to create light patterns in the natural colour of the *tapa*. Some of the small repeat patterns were made to serve as a textural background and large-scale designs were superimposed on them by free-hand painting in other colours or by lines forming stripes, checks or plaids. These lines were made with specially cut drawing tools. Decorating combs were also cut from hard wood or bamboo was split so as to form a multiple pen. Another technique used in Hawaii was to incorporate differently coloured particles in the making of the *tapa* or sometimes a semi-transparent cloth dyed a different colour and pierced with a lace-like pattern was pasted on to an under layer. A similar technique is used in Japan for the making of the finest decorative papers. See PAPERS, DECORATIVE.

In Fiji and Samoa a printing mat was made of bark cloth on to which had been attached the large ribs of leaves or woven grass cords in various patterns. These printing mats were used as a matrix; the bark cloth to be decorated was laid on them and colour was rubbed over so as to get an impression from the raised parts. Carved logs or the end of an old canoe were also used as printing matrixes from which rubbings were made much as brass rubbings are taken. In Fiji striped decoration was produced from rollers made from hardwood or bamboo. In the central Celebes bark cloth is embroidered both in order

Tongan men and women sewing twigs into designs on boards with which to print on the 'tapa' cloth

to strengthen it and for decorative effect. Sometimes small pieces of mica are stuck on to create a glittering effect. A form of appliqué is also used, large shapes of light bark cloth being applied on to a dark dyed background or the reverse.

The colourants used for printing and dyeing bark cloth were usually vegetable dyes, though some mineral and earth colours were used. Mordants appear also to have been used to render the colours fast. See COLOURS AND COLOURANTS.

Before the advent of woven textiles bark cloth was largely used for clothing. In Hawaii clothing consisted of a large loin-cloth, some 23 centimetres wide and 3 metres long, and a cloak above it. In Fiji a turban-like head-dress was also worn. In Hawaii, New Guinea and parts of Africa bark cloth is also used as a screen or to divide the enclosed dwelling into rooms and for decoration on porch or verandah. It is also sometimes used as a blanket and in many countries as a shroud for the dead. In many places, Hawaii and central Celebes for example, garments made of bark cloth were perfumed with sweet-smelling herbs or spices as the natural smell of felted bark-cloth is not pleasant.

In Japan bark cloth served a diversity of purposes. It was used for windows and as in parts of Africa and New Guinea for screens and room-dividers. The Japanese have also used it for making kites, for flags and for UMBRELLAS and raincoats—for which purposes it was finished with a water-repellent. In Java wax was used to make it waterproof and in the Pacific Islands it was sometimes glazed with oil or varnish. In New Amsterdam the glutinous juice of a herb served a similar purpose. In Hawaii, however, much of the cloth was so finely made that it could resist water without further finish.

Besides domestic uses bark cloth was also important for trading purposes and for honorific gifts. Chiefs and rulers would amass large stores kept in great rolls as a symbol and mark of their wealth.

102, 115, 171, 337, 484, 487, 531, 633, 726.

BARNSLEY, ERNEST ARTHUR (1863–1926) and SIDNEY (1865–1926). English artist-craftsmen and furniture designers, who in association with Ernest GIMSON produced well-designed furniture in the tradition of the ARTS AND CRAFTS MOVEMENT. The tradition is carried on by EDWARD Barnsley (1900–), son of Sidney, who set up business at Froxfield, Petersfield, Hampshire, in 1923. He introduced basic powered machines as his business expanded and from 1938 to 1965 he was adviser in woodwork design at Loughborough College for handicraft teachers.

BARONIAL STYLE. See ABBOTSFORD PERIOD.

BAROQUE. Stylistic term with both historical and descriptive connotations, whose primary application has been to the fine arts. Historically it refers to the period in European art from the late 16th c. until well into the 18th c., falling between Mannerism and ROCOCO. Descriptively, particularly when applied to the decorative arts, it carries the primary connotations of floridity, grandiloquence and exuberance in combination with an over-all attention to harmony and balance of forms.

BARRON, ROBERT. English locksmith who in 1778 took out a patent for a lock which combined two spring tumblers with the ward principle, thus bringing about a revolution in lock construction and anticipating the modern lever principle. See LOCKS AND KEYS and Illustration on p. 96.

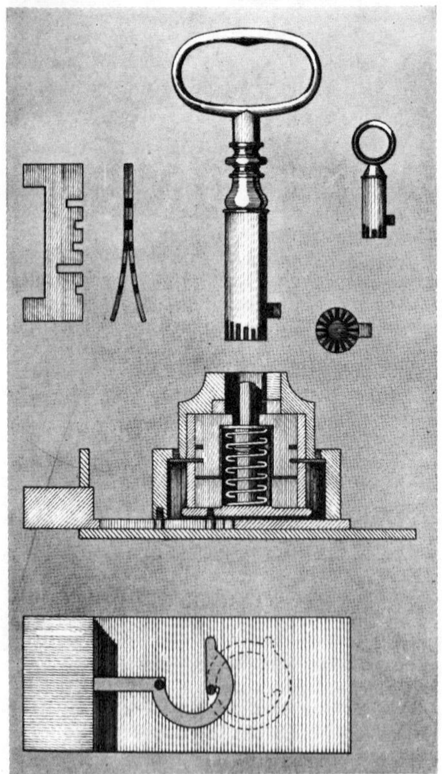

Joseph Bramah lock. (From V. J. M. Eras, *Locks and Keys throughout the Ages*)

BASALTES. An unglazed black STONEWARE produced by WEDGWOOD in the 1760s at Brick House, Burslem, and made by him the basis of his early ornamental ware. See CERAMICS.

BASKERVILLE, JOHN (1706–75). Born in Birmingham, he was the originator of the English tradition in fine printing. At first a writing master and cutter of lettering on tombstones, he made a fortune in JAPANNING and indulged a passion for printing and type-founding. His edition of Virgil, finished in 1757, made his reputation in Britain and abroad. His rounded roman letters with thin hair-strokes, his careful presswork, wide spacing, and hot-pressing of the sheets after printing gave his pages a lightness and a gloss that were admired by a generation addicted to copper-engraved lettering and ornament. His editions of the Latin classics, Milton's poems, his Books of Common Prayer and above all his folio Bible printed at Cambridge in 1763 are among the masterpieces of British book production. Baskerville's editions were, however, not remunerative, and when he tired of printing he failed to find a buyer for his equipment. His widow sold his type foundry to Beaumarchais, who used it for an edition of the works of Voltaire printed at Kehl in 1784–9.

abcdefghijklm
nopqrstuvwxyz
abcdefghijklmnop
qrstuvwxyz 30 pt. Baskerville

Modern reproductions of Baskerville's types are in great favour for bookwork. Philip Gaskell's *Baskerville* (1959: offset reprint, 1973) contains an Appendix of books printed in Baskerville type before 1775 by Robert Martin of Birmingham and at the Clarendon Press, Oxford. See TYPOGRAPHY.

291, 688.

BASKETRY. See AFRICA; AMERINDIANS; EGYPT, ANCIENT.

BASSE-TAILLE. See ENAMEL.

BATAILLE, NICOLAS. French tapestry-maker, active in Paris during the latter part of the 14th c. See TAPESTRY.

BATAVIAN WARE. A trade name for Chinese ceramic ware of the K'ang-hsi period (1662–1772) imported into Europe by the Dutch through their trading station at Batavia. The wares had a coffee-coloured or old gold glaze with white medallions decorated in underglaze blue or overglaze enamels. See CHINA (CERAMICS).

BATIK. An art of textile designing practised by the Toradja of central Celebes and in the islands of Java and Mandura. The design is produced by a negative dyeing method, being marked out in wax before the fabric is dipped so that the waxed portions do not take the dye but stand out in the original colour of the fabric. Originally the hot wax was applied to the fabric by a shaped strip of bamboo. The technique was improved by the invention in the 17th c. of the *tjanting*, a copper crucible with several spouts by which the wax could be applied in continuous lines of varying thickness.

The earliest batik patterns were monochrome, the design standing out against an indigo ground. From the 18th c. onwards multicoloured fabrics were produced by methods of dyeing introduced through Indian Muslims and cloths of very great beauty and rarity resulted. Many of the patterns depend on ancient traditional designs with symbolic meaning. In the so-called *Banji* pattern the design is built up organically from this basic motif. But the more usual form of design is achieved by means of symmetrical interplay of lines with design element incorporated into the pattern. Highly stylized intertwining flower and leaf patterns are also used. The social position of the owner was reflected by the beauty of the batik designs in the ceremonial and festive garments he wore and some of the ancient batiks are among the most superb examples of ornamental textile design that are known.

During the 19th and 20th centuries this traditional folk art has been progressively eliminated by economic contacts with the West and the importation of Western textiles. Attempts to commercialize the batik technique and to establish an indigenous mechanized weaving industry have led to a decline in craftsmanship while socio-political changes have undermined the significance of traditional patterns and iconography.

BATTERSEA ENAMELS. A factory for decorative ENAMELS was set up *c.* 1750 at York House, Battersea, by Sir Stephen Theodore Janssen, an Alderman of the City of London and Lord Mayor in 1754. The factory appears to have ceased production in 1756, when Sir Stephen became bankrupt.

The method chiefly used was by TRANSFER PRINTING from a copperplate engraving on to a background of smooth white enamel laid on a copper base. The transfer print was usually over-painted in delicately translucent colours. It is sometimes claimed that the technique of transfer printing was first practised at this factory or that it was introduced by Simon-François RAVENET, who engraved for the factory. Other engravers who worked there were Robert HANCOCK, John Hall (1739–97), John Brooks (d. *c.* 1760) and probably William Wynne Ryland (1732–83). The factory produced framed plaques with scenes or portraits and small objects such as SNUFF-BOXES, WINE LABELS, etc.

Wine label: Burgundy, Battersea (1753–6)

Brandy label, London or Birmingham (*c.* 1760)

An advertisement for the sale of Battersea enamels put out at the time of Janssen's bankruptcy lists them as follows: 'Beautiful enamels, coloured and uncoloured, of the new manufactory carried on at York House, Battersea, and never yet exhibited to public view, consisting of snuff-boxes of all sizes, of a great variety of patterns; of square and oval pictures of the Royal Family, history, and other pleasing subjects, very proper subjects for the cabinets of the curious; bottle tickets, with chains, for all sorts of liquors, and of different subjects; watch cases, tooth-pick cases, coat and sleeve buttons, crosses, and other curiosities, mostly mounted in metal, double gilt.'

The term 'Battersea enamel' may have originated with Horace Walpole, who used it in his description of Strawberry Hill. It came into use as a general term for English decorative enamels of the 18th and early 19th centuries. Enamels actually made at York House are relatively few in number and are prized collectors' pieces.

591.

BAUHAUS, THE. A design school in Germany, which existed from 1919 until 1933. In spite of its short life it represents the greatest single influence on design and design education in the 20th c. Its foundation in Weimar in 1919 actually represented an amalgamation of two older schools, an art academy and a school of arts and crafts, but owing to the hiatus of the First World War and the new ideas of its first Director, Walter Gropius, it really represented a new beginning of a radically new institution. Here according to the founding proclamation by Walter Gropius all the arts were to be brought together under the primacy of architecture; they were to be practised as crafts in the sense taught by William MORRIS, and to contribute to the *Gesamtkunstwerk*, the total work of art, the building and everything in it.

Gropius began with the remnants of an old staff and three new appointments: Johannes Itten, an art educator, the sculptor Gerhard Marcks and the painter Lyonel Feininger. Initially he felt that art and craft had grown apart and an organic unity of the two could not be taught by one person because people who combined artistic ability and the necessary technical know-how did not exist. The early scheme, therefore, was to have two teachers for each area, one an artist, the form master, and the other a craftsman or technician, the technical master, in the hope that they would convey to a generation of students a new organic approach, art and craft or art and technology as one. It is significant that Gropius deliberately did not use the term 'professor', but preferred 'master' for his teachers in order to emphasize the un-academic or anti-academic nature of the new school.

But before entering a specialized area such as weaving or metalwork all students passed through a preliminary course of six months, the so-called *Vorkurs*, and it was this course that was Itten's great contribution. In contrast to older schools, where the students were taught to look deferentially to the past, to see their models in the past and to copy, imitate or be inspired by the forms of the past, Itten's aim was to liberate the innate gifts and true capabilities of the students to create free from all association with, or reference to, the past. The core of the preliminary course was the exploration of, and experimentation with, materials and tools, to find and make use of their qualities and possibilities and to awaken in the students their intuitive responses and creative gifts.

In the first years at Weimar the methods of Itten were of the greatest importance for the Bauhaus. When a clear and organized programme did not as yet exist he used his extraordinary pedagogical capabilities to encourage, guide and help the young people who came to the new institution to develop and unfold their personalities. He was an adherent of Mazdaism, and his devotion to meditation, rhythmic exercises, fasts, dietary doctrines, the wearing of strange smocks and sandals, far from detracting from his influence in fact enhanced his standing with the students. In the extremely volatile, in fact revolutionary, atmosphere of the first post-war years in Germany the students were particularly responsive to this mixture of romanticism, intuition and mysticism.

Of necessity much was improvised in the first years. Gropius himself directed the woodworking shop; Gerhard Marcks was form master for the ceramics workshop. Feininger was at first not attached to any special workshop, but later headed the printing shop. In 1920 Gropius added new members to the staff: the painters Georg Muche, Oskar Schlemmer and Paul Klee. Muche became form master for the weaving workshop; Schlemmer was form master for sculpture, and after 1923 also for the Bauhaus stage; Klee was initially form master for stained glass, but also strongly influenced the weaving workshop and above all contributed fundamentally to the aesthetic and artistic education by his courses and lectures and by his own artistic output and personality. In 1922 the painter Wassily Kandinsky joined the staff and was made form master for mural painting.

Within a few years it became apparent that the initially intuitive, romantic and artistically expressionistic direction of the Bauhaus, with its emphasis on crafts and personal expression, was not to last. The modern world of industry, and new artistic influences such as Neo-Plasticism and Constructivism, began to make themselves felt. Gropius understood the new trend and moved in this direction himself, and inevitably a schism developed between him and Itten. It was contributed to and sharpened by Theo van Doesburg, the Dutch Constructivist, who resided in Weimar from 1921 until 1923 and continuously goaded and prodded the Bauhaus in the direction of rationality, clarity, structure and a conception of art which relied exclusively on abstract geometrical forms and the primary colours. In 1923 Itten left the Bauhaus and the Hungarian László Moholy-Nagy came in his stead to head the metal workshop and to give the preliminary course, the latter at the beginning with the help of Josef Albers, at that time a student. This was a crucial change. It meant turning from the crafts to the machine and industry, from a purely aesthetic and inherently ornamental approach to a functional and rational one, leading away from the earlier mysticism and romanticism.

Almost from its inception the Bauhaus was subject to political attacks from the conservative right which was especially strong in Weimar and the state of Thuringia, of which Weimar was the capital. In an atmosphere of particularly virulent attacks the Thuringian Government demanded in 1923 that Gropius give an account of his work and that of the school: thus Gropius was forced to present an exhibition of the accomplishments of the Bauhaus, which turned out to be a notable and memorable event. An experimental house was built for the exhibition and furnished completely with products designed and made at the Bauhaus with the exception of the china, which was already the product of collaboration with industry. The china was designed and developed in the Bauhaus workshop, but manufactured by the Volkstedt and by Berlin porcelain manufactures. In the school itself and its workshops murals, sculpture and stained glass were exhibited. The State Museum showed work by masters and journeymen done outside their school work: work by Gropius, Josef Albers, Herbert Bayer, Marcel BREUER, Lyonel Feininger, Johannes Itten, Wassily Kandinsky, Paul Klee, Gerhard Marcks, Oskar Schlemmer, and others, an extraordinary constellation. Gropius and his associate Adolf Meyer showed designs, drawings, photography and models of their architectural work. Schlemmer's *Triadic Ballet* was performed; musical performances included compositions by Hindemith, Busoni and Stravinsky, who came from Paris to Weimar for the event. The entire exhibition was recorded in *Staatliches Bauhaus in Weimar 1919–1923*, a documentation in book form, the cover designed by Herbert Bayer, the layout by Moholy-Nagy, with texts by Gropius, Klee, Kandinsky, Schlemmer and Moholy-Nagy. In a lecture Gropius proclaimed 'Art and Techniques, a new Unity', and thus set the new direction of the Bauhaus. The independent painters who had in part contributed directly as form masters remained as more general spiritual and creative influences while the workshops developed in the direction of industrial design. The dual system of form master and technical master began to bear fruit. Albers, Bayer, Breuer, Lindig, Stölzl, who had begun as students, had now acquired mastery of design and technique and soon formally joined the staff.

In spite of the success of the exhibition of 1923 and a following period of fruitful work and optimism, the Bauhaus was most seriously jeopardized in 1924 when a government of the right was elected in Thuringia and redoubled its attacks and threats on this unorthodox design school, leading at the end of the year to a declaration on the part of Gropius and the school's form masters that they would close the Bauhaus in Weimar rather than submit to crippling and degrading conditions. In a subsequent letter to the Government the whole Bauhaus community, students, apprentices and journeymen, declared their solidarity with this decision.

At the invitation of Dessau, a small manufacturing town *c.* 105 kilometres south-west of Berlin and within an easy train ride of the capital, the entire Bauhaus community moved there in 1925. Gropius himself designed a building to house all its activities, which has become not only a symbol of the Bauhaus and all it tried to achieve, but also a landmark of modern architecture in the 20th c. In Dessau both state and city administrations were sympathetic and the Bauhaus also received the enthusiastic support of at least some of the local intelligentsia. Here the new direction towards industry became set policy. The 'young masters' Albers, Bayer and Stölzl joined the older Gropius, Klee, Kandinsky, Moholy-Nagy, Muche and Schlemmer in a tremendously productive and successful activity, developing models for industry in furniture, metals, textiles, WALLPAPERS, printing and advertising. TYPOGRAPHY by Moholy-Nagy and Bayer, metalwork by Marianne Brandt and Wilhelm Wagenfeld, tubular metal furniture by Breuer, textiles by Gunta Stölzl and Otti Berger and the Bauhaus wallpapers have had lasting significance and value. Fourteen Bauhaus books set forth the ideas and philosophy of the group within the wider framework of the artistic thinking and working of Europe at the time.

Though the original Bauhaus manifesto of 1919 had declared architecture the ultimate goal and core of all artistic activity, architecture itself was not taught at the Bauhaus until 1927, when an architecture department was established and Hannes Meyer was called from Switzerland to head it. When political attacks were renewed and Gropius felt that all criticism aimed at him was in reality an effort to harm the Bauhaus, he resigned as Director to return to private practice as an architect and Hannes Meyer took over the Directorship in 1928. Breuer, Moholy-Nagy and Bayer left the Bauhaus with Gropius.

Gropius had created an institution that was of European and indeed world-wide importance in the short span given him and had done so under continuous difficulties of every kind, ideological internal discord, monetary stringencies and above all political harassment; he had shown himself a genius at compromising, at improvising, and yet leading a group of highly gifted people in collaboration towards a common goal of contributing to the creation of a new visual world. Hannes Meyer, who took over this heritage, was more matter-of-fact, colder, and above all politically and ideologically decidedly committed to a socialistic orientation of design and particularly architectural activity. Schlemmer wrote that with Gropius's going a bit of the aristocratic disappeared, that some of the *élan* left the Bauhaus.

The pendulum, which at the start of the Bauhaus had stood for the most individual, intuitive and artistic approach and had over the years found its way to a realization of the needs and realities of modern industrial society, swung to the extreme under the two-year directorship of Meyer, who systematized instruction, especially in the area of architecture and its subsidiary fields, and directed activity to socially significant and satisfying projects. This led on the one hand to renewed dedication and enthusiasm within the Bauhaus, but it also intensified the alienation of some of the most prominent original members such as Schlemmer, who left in 1929, and Kandinsky, who stood in opposition to Meyer.

The political development in Germany also, becoming ever more reactionary, was not favourable to the methods and aims of Meyer and it became necessary to dismiss him in 1930 in order to save the Bauhaus from internal and external collapse. The final Director was the noted architect Ludwig Mies van der Rohe, who brought back enforced calm to the Bauhaus by banishing political activity and concentrating on rigorous demands as to the quality of architectural training. With the help of Ludwig Hilberseimer, who had joined the architectural programme in 1928, he made an almost exclusively architectural school of the Bauhaus, relegating other artistic activities, which had played such a large part in the earlier years, far into the background. As a consequence Klee left in 1931.

In 1931 and 1932 the attacks of the National Socialists, who had gained a majority in the city council of Dessau, were intensified and they successfully demanded the closing of the Bauhaus in September 1932. Mies van der Rohe moved the institution to Berlin, where it was able to exist for another short period until it was closed down by police and storm-troopers in April 1933. The staff decided to disband and dissolve the Bauhaus on 19 July 1933.

Thus came to an end in almost pathetic submission to naked force an institution that had been a brilliantly creative experiment in the arts and design and which by the dissemination of its ideas through emigration of its members, mainly to America but also to other countries even as far away as Australia, was to exert in the following decades a decisive influence on educational methods in the fields of architecture and design all over the world. After a brief stay in England Gropius and Breuer took up residence at Harvard University, Gropius becoming chairman of the department of architecture there. Josef Albers took up his activities at Black Mountain College in North Carolina in 1933 and in 1950 became professor and chairman of the Fine Arts Department at Yale University. In 1937 Moholy-Nagy founded the New Bauhaus in Chicago, which successively became the School of Design and then in 1944 the Institute of Design of the Illinois Institute of Technology. This educational insemination by the *émigrés* was of the greatest consequence in changing and modernizing design training in America and elsewhere, while the professional work of Gropius and Breuer as architects, Bayer as graphic artist and TYPOGRAPHY designer, and that of other teachers and former Bauhaus students in other fields, played a large role in altering the practice and character of design. The Museum of Modern Art in New York first brought the Bauhaus to the attention of a wider American public by a historic exhibition in 1938. In conjunction with the exhibition the Museum published *Bauhaus 1919–28*, edited by Herbert Bayer and Ise and Walter Gropius, a classic publication which remained virtually the only informative book on the Bauhaus in English for 30 years, until the monumental publication in 1968 by the M.I.T. Press of Hans Maria Wingler's book *The Bauhaus*.

The brilliance of the artistic, aesthetic and pedagogical contribution that the Bauhaus made during the time that it functioned, and the profound effect it had throughout the world thereafter, are unquestionable; and yet this fact represents a kind of mystery. The more one delves into the details of the life and personalities, of events and activities, ideologies and conflicts, work and play at the Bauhaus, the more one is amazed and puzzled and increasingly aware that the essence is illusive, that the magic of the moment lay in the quality of the people and their interactions and collaborative contributions in ways which cannot be recorded. One is puzzled by the early emphasis on crafts when the fame of the Bauhaus rests on industrial design; one reads of meditation and rhythmic breathing exercises, of dietary, clothing, hair and behaviour fads that are the prototypes of latter-day hippies; one is astonished to read Schlemmer complaining repeatedly of the laziness and lack of accomplishment of the students. One also learns of the gay and splendid feasts, the kite-flying feast, the festival of lanterns, the metallic feast, the white feast, the feast of beards and noses. One reads of hunger and hardships among the students and their willingness to share and to help each other; one reads of the jazz band and the dances, the student magazine, and so many other aspects that are kaleidoscopic in their diversity and variety. Its programme was indefinite, actually only an idea, its achievement a fragment, an accomplishment left incomplete. How does it come to its fame? How did it become a legend?

Perhaps the most important reason is that the Bauhaus was an essential participant, a performer in the artistic drama of our time: having begun with an artistic and ideological heritage of pre-war values which included a veneration for William Morris, the solid work of the DEUTSCHER WERKBUND and the preliminary work of Henri van de VELDE in one of the parent institutions in Weimar, in the inter-war years it lived and acted out with its brilliant cast the change from Expressionism and Cubism to Constructivism and Functionalism, from artistic handicraft to industrial design and machine production. Pedagogically it contributed the key concept of the *Vorkurs*, the preliminary course, which again was pivotal, a turning from the methods and values of the past to the liberating freedom of exploration and experimentation in the forms of our time.

One of the most perceptive members of the Bauhaus, Oskar Schlemmer, wrote in March 1923: 'The Bauhaus is the seismograph of the international art scene', and in June 1923: 'Four years of Bauhaus are a piece of art history. But also history of our time, because the whole disjointedness of our people and of our time is reflected in it.' And Sigfried Giedion said of his visit to the Bauhaus on the occasion of its great exhibition and week of varied activities in 1923: 'I gazed into a world newly forming.' This participation in the creation of a new world at

Scenes from Bayeux Tapestry (with detail) showing death of king Harold. (V. & A. Mus.)

a critical point of change and inception constitutes the importance of the Bauhaus and has made it not only a legend but a lasting model—not for *what* it did, because that is time-bound, like a vintage motor-car, but for its spirit of openness, its eagerness to innovate and go new ways, and above all for its dedication and commitment.

52, 146, 215, 600, 923, 924.

BAUMHAUER, JOSEPH (d. 1772). French cabinet-maker of German origin. He used the business name 'Joseph'. About 1767 he was granted the title *ébéniste privilégé du roi.* He was noted for his commodes decorated with MARQUETRY and LACQUER panels in the Chinese style (see CHINESE TASTE), one of which is in the Victoria and Albert Museum.

BAVE. The thread spun by the silk-worm, consisting of two filaments called 'brins' cemented together by SERICIN. See SILK.

BAYEUX TAPESTRY. Most famous of all pieces of historical needlework, this is technically an EMBROIDERY not a TAPESTRY. Worked in two kinds of woollen thread on coarse linen, its dimensions are officially given as 70·34 metres long by 50 centimetres in width. Eight colours are used: three shades of blue, a bright and a dark green, buff yellow, red and grey. In 79 consecutive scenes, whose purport is elucidated by Latin inscriptions, the tapestry depicts the story of Harold, Earl of Wessex, during the years 1065–6 which culminates in the Battle of Hastings. Neither its date nor its place of origin is beyond doubt but there is evidence to suggest that it was embroidered within a few years of the Conquest, perhaps to the order of the Conqueror's brother, Bishop Odo of Bayeux, where the work still hangs. It was rediscovered by the French archaeologists M. Lancelot and Dom Bernard de Montfaucon early in the 18th c. and engravings were first published by the latter in *Monuments de la monarchie française* (1729–30). A comprehensive survey of the Bayeux Tapestry edited by Sir Frank Stenton was published by Phaidon Press in 1957 and a shorter work by Charles H. Gibbs-Smith in 1973, with summaries on the technique, reproduces many of the illustrations.

300, 558, 791.

BAZAN (1833–97). See JAPAN (NETSUKE).

BEAD. Term in joinery and cabinet-making for a small, plain MOULDING. It also denotes an enrichment ornamenting a moulding (e.g. an ASTRAGAL) in the form of a string of beads.

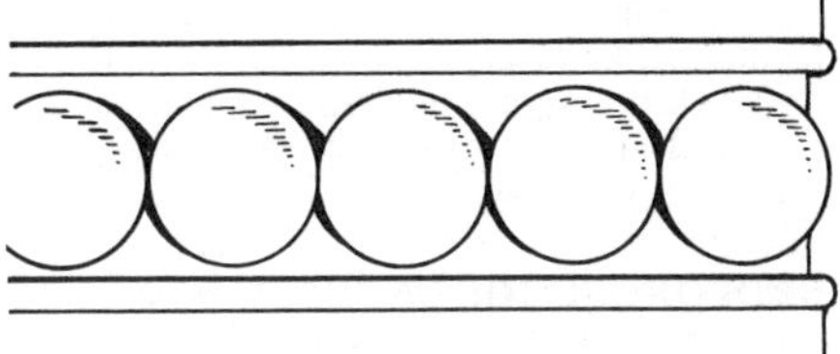

BEAD-AND-REEL. Ornamental motif of architectural origin, common as a decoration of furniture, silverware, etc. It consists of alternate circular elements (beads) and vertical oblongs

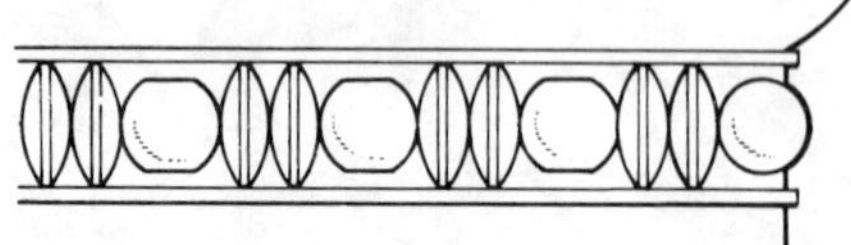

(reels). It was much used in the 16th and 17th centuries as a decorative border, e.g. on NONESUCH CHESTS, and it is commonly found as an enrichment of the ASTRAGAL.

BEADWORK. A type of NEEDLEWORK in which patterns are produced by sewing glass beads, sometimes diversified with seed PEARLS, CORAL, and other materials, to a textile or parchment ground. It was practised in Dynastic EGYPT and in medieval and Renaissance Europe. The Stuart embroiderers employed it for purses, biblical pictures and elaborate baskets, and it continued to be a popular decoration for a variety of small objects down to the 19th c. See also EMBROIDERY.

BEAUVAIS. The TAPESTRY manufactory of Beauvais was established under the patronage of Louis XIV in 1664. Under the directorship of Philippe Béhagle (1684–1704) a number of fine tapestries were woven, of which the best known is a set of GROTESQUES in the manner of BÉRAIN. From 1726 onwards successful designs were made for the factory by J. B. OUDRY, who in 1734 took over its direction; these include sets of La Fontaine's *Fables*, rural pastimes, hunts and other subjects. A set of 10 hangings with the story of *Don Quixote*, designed by Charles Natoire (1700–77), was begun in 1735. But the most successful of the designs woven at Beauvais were those supplied by BOUCHER between 1736 and 1755, which included the *Fêtes italiennes* (14 pieces), the story of *Psyche* (5 pieces), the Chinese Hangings (6 pieces), the *Loves of the Gods* (9 pieces), Operatic Scenes (5 pieces) and the *Noble Pastoral* (6 pieces). Among the many sets of hangings woven during the latter part of the 18th c. the most attractive is perhaps the set of *Pastorals with Blue Draperies*, begun in 1780, after designs by J. B. HUET. Besides the wall hangings Beauvais also produced furniture coverings, many of them designed by Boucher.

Despite various vicissitudes the factory has continued its activities down to the present. Its reputation, however, rests largely on its 18th-c. work, which so gracefully reflects the decorative taste of the period of Louis XV.

36.

BEDFORDSHIRE LACE. A bobbin LACE made in Bedfordshire, and closely resembling BUCKINGHAMSHIRE and LILLE. There is a tradition among lace-makers that the craft was established there by Catherine of Aragon, who was herself a skilled needlewoman and lace-maker. In the early part of the 19th c. a narrow lace edging known as 'baby lace' was in demand and *Regency point* with a mesh of plaited threads was made there. The hexagonal or six-pointed star ground-mesh was subsequently abandoned in favour of an independent trellis composed of the seed-like forms of MALTESE lace.

BEETHAM, ISABELLA *née* ROBINSON (b. 1744). English silhouettist, born at Sedgefield, Lancashire. In 1764 she eloped with Edward Beetham (properly Betham), an actor and inventor. With the assistance of the actor Samuel Foote she set up on her own account as a silhouettist, painting for the most part on card or glass. Her finest portraits were backed with plaster or, when painted on the back of convex glass, sometimes with wax. The hair and accessories were skilfully indicated by thinner use of pigment. She collaborated with her husband in the invention of new methods for gilding glass and made use of these to embellish her work. Mrs. Beetham has been regarded as one of the most proficient of silhouettists on glass, a perfectionist in detail and an adept at conveying a likeness.

BEGRAM. Modern name of the town Alexandria-Kapisu or Kapisha founded by Alexander the Great *c.* 60 kilometres north of Kabul straddling the caravan route to India. Alexander's policy to make the city a centre of cultural fusion between Greeks, Bactrians and Indians was pursued by the Seleucids and is reflected in the cosmopolitan character of the art. Excavations conducted in 1936 discovered a now famous treasure there. The most important of the finds are the Begram ivories, dating from the 1st to the 4th c. A.D., with pronounced Ghandara Indian characteristics. (See ASIA, CENTRAL.) There were also Chinese textiles and Greco-Roman objects, including Syrian glass, and Buddhist paintings showing a fusion of Indian and Sassanian styles.

BEHRENS, PETER (1868–1940). German architect and designer. Beginning as a painter, he came to architecture by way of an interest in the practical arts. From 1903 to 1907 he was head of the Düsseldorf School of Art. In 1907 he joined the firm of A.E.G. and designed both electrical equipment and packaging, posters, leaflets, etc. His design was in the Functionalist tradition and he set himself against the ART NOUVEAU principle of applying to machine production forms derived from handicrafts. He has been credited with originating the form of design specialization which is now known as 'Industrial Design'.

BEILBY, WILLIAM (1740–1819). English

ENAMELLER ON GLASS. He worked at Newcastle upon Tyne from *c.* 1762 to 1778, enamelling flint glass at first mainly with armorial devices but later with naturalistic birds, plants and landscapes in opaque white. His sister, MARY Beilby (1749–97), also enamelled on glass.

733.

BEKA (active latter part of the 12th c.). Master jeweller of Opiza and founder of the Opiza style. See GEORGIAN METALWORK.

BELDING (BELDEN), SAMUEL (*c.* 1633–1713). American cabinet-maker. He was born in Staffordshire and was brought to America by his parents *c.* 1640. In 1661 he came to Hadley in the Connecticut River Valley with John ALLIS, with whom he later formed a partnership under the title Belding & Allis. His son, SAMUEL (1657–*c.* 1737), carried on the partnership with Ichabod Allis after the death of their fathers. Many of the HADLEY CHESTS are attributed to this firm.

BELKEIN (BELKIN, BELLEKIN, BELKYN, BELLEQUIN). Dutch family of shell carvers, active in the 16th, 17th and early 18th centuries. See MOTHER OF PEARL and NAUTILUS SHELL.

BELLARMINES. Stoneware jugs or bottles decorated with a bearded mask at the base of the neck. They were so called after Cardinal Bellarmine, but in Germany they were called *Bartmannskrug*. Manufactured in Cologne in the first half of the 16th c., they were extensively exported to France and to England and the Netherlands. See CERAMICS (STONEWARE).

BELL-FOUNDING. The use of the bell as a musical instrument, an accessory to ritual, a plaything and a decorative adjunct to costume has been well nigh universal. Its origin must lie in the BRONZE AGE, when the superior resonance and tonal power of the cast-bronze disc over hammered copper would have become apparent. Probably the earliest type of bell was the saucer-shaped disc, although the hollow ball type is also of great antiquity. The latter type of bells were small in size, hollow balls of metal with a few holes here and there and a small metal ball rolling loose inside. The golden bells which adorned the ephod of Aaron (Exodus 39) were of this kind. They have changed little through the ages. Such bells were still hung as ornaments on the edges of capes and head-dresses in the Middle Ages, the cap and bells of the jester survived into the 17th c. and they have persisted as accessories to carnival costume and as children's appurtenances. Bells of this sort tuned in sets could once be heard on the music-hall stage.

While the hollow ball type of bell has remained virtually stationary through the ages, the saucer-shaped or basin-shaped bell has undergone vast and diverse development. It is from this type that the modern church bell evolved and the present article will be concerned with the craft of bell-casting in the West, although in fact the founding of bells and gongs was developed earlier in China and the Far East where they played an extremely important function in connection both with music and with religious rituals. In the *Exhibition of Archaeological Finds of the People's Republic of China* held at the Royal Academy, London, in 1973–4 there was shown a set of nine bronze bells tuned in scale (*pien chung*) recovered from the tomb of a Marquis of Ts'ai at Shou-hsien, excavated in 1965. The bells were without internal clapper but were intended to be hung and struck on nipples which line the sides. The tomb is dated to the first quarter of the 5th c. B.C. but it is stated that bells of this kind were made in China from the 10th c. B.C., when they appear in the ancient Chou homeland in the north-west.

The first stage in the development of the modern bell occurred when the basin-shaped bronze was inverted and fitted with a handle by which it could be held and rung with a clapper. As it increased in size and became too heavy to be rung by hand in this way, loops or 'ears' were cast on the head so that it could be suspended by them from a timber yoke and so struck with a hammer. While in the West the hanging bell was sounded by hitting it with an iron clapper or hammer, in the East a wooden beam is still frequently used instead. The beam is slung on a rope or chain from some support nearby and is worked after the manner of the old battering ram. Instead of an outside clapper, bells in the West came in the course of time to be fitted with an inside clapper which could be pulled against the side of the bell. This continues to be the usual method of sounding bells in eastern Europe and most of the enormous bells of Russia are sounded in this way. Later still gudgeons or axles running in plain brass bearings were fitted to the headstock or yoke across the top of the bell, the method favoured in Britain and western Europe. It produces the best possible tone and its potentialities came gradually to be exploited through the intricate art of change-ringing.

According to tradition bells were brought into use for the Christian Church some time during the 5th c. By the 7th and 8th centuries their use for church services had become fairly general. According to the 14th-c. or 15th-c. *History of Croyland*, formerly attributed to Ingulf, Abbot of Croyland Abbey (d. 1109), the Abbey had a ring of bells. About 945 the Abbot is said to have had one very large bell cast, which he called 'Guthlac' after St. Guthlac near whose tomb the Abbey was founded in the 8th c. His successor, Egelric the Elder (d. 984), is recorded to have added six more bells, two of which he called 'Bartholomew' and 'Betelin', two medium ones 'Turketil' and 'Tatwin' and two small ones 'Pega' and 'Bega'. Among other ecclesiastical bell-founders St. Dunstan is said to have been

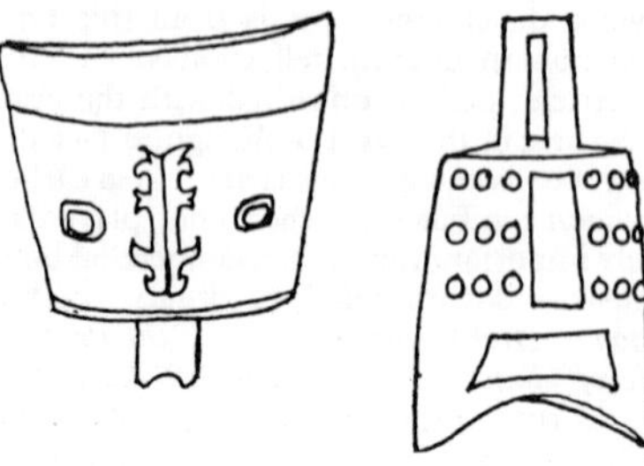

Shapes of ancient Chinese bronze bells

Thirteenth-c. bell. The bell is thickened at the 'sound-bow', where the clapper strikes fairly near the lip

Canberra carillon of 53 bells. Largest bell has diameter 218 cm, weight 1,562 kg. Note F♯

Modern bell on tuning machine. From Washington carillon. Diameter 264 cm, weight 11,000 kg. Note E♭

an expert metal-worker and to have cast a bell which for many years hung in Canterbury Cathedral. These early bells have long since disappeared. According to the campanologist Thomas North, the first Englishman known to have followed the trade of bell-founder was a certain Roger de Ropeford of Paignton, who in 1284 was commissioned to make four bells for the north tower of Exeter Cathedral. None of his bells, however, is known to survive.

Many of the earliest bells carried no marks or inscriptions at all, although some have a saint's name. Later an invocation to the saint or a line of ecclesiastical Latin was cast on the bell and sometimes the donor's name was added. Except in very rare instances neither the bell-founder's name nor the date of casting was given until towards the end of the 16th c. it began to be customary to record both on the bell. The earliest dated bell in England is at Claughton near Lancaster. With the exception of an initial cross, this bell bears no other inscription except the date in Roman letters: ANNO DOMINI MCCXCVI.

It was no doubt an instinctive feeling for tonal beauty that led the medieval bell-founders to experiment until they produced a bell which approximated to the present form. As the bell gradually became longer, various curvatures and variations of thickness were tried until in the 12th or 13th c. a contour not very different from the modern was reached. The outstanding feature of these bells was what is called the 'sound-bow' or thickened part where the clapper strikes fairly near the lip. The sound-bow, which is crucial to the development of the Western bell, is not found in bells of the Far East. It was not, however, until the 17th c. that bell-founders began to understand the problem of casting and tuning the harmonic bell, that is a bell having its subsidiary tones or 'harmonics' in true harmonic relation with its fundamental note. Marked progress in this direction was made in the course of the century, particularly by the brothers Francis and Peter HEMONY in the Netherlands. Their chief business was the founding of CARILLONS, their first carillon being made for the Wine House Tower at Zutfen in 1645. After the death of Francis in 1667 the business was carried on by Peter alone until 1678, when ill health compelled him to close the foundry. From this time the fortunes of the true harmonic bell declined until the late 19th c., when the art of bell-founding was revived in England with improved technical resources.

Like other musical instruments a bell sounds not only its main note but many others as well. These follow the natural rule of 'harmonics': e.g. if the fundamental note is a low C, the next harmonic is the C an octave above that, then the G a perfect fifth above that, then the C an octave above the former, and so on. A good bell should follow the rule of natural harmonics, but with one important difference. The bell sounds a minor third in addition, that is E♭ which is 2·4 times the frequency of the fundamental note and lies between the second C and the perfect fifth at G. It is this minor third which gives the bell its distinctive timbre. A bell made to sound a harmonic at a major third does not sound so well as one with a minor third. To produce bells of this sort was the problem which the British bell-founders at Loughborough set out to solve and the first set of scientifically tuned bells was installed in a church near Sheffield in 1896.

Having described the problems of the harmonic bell, it will be well to describe briefly the process of making and tuning a bell. The first operation is to make the inner mould or 'core', which is built up on a strong plate of cast iron. It is constructed of bricks jointed and coated with moulding-sand ground wet and mixed with other matter and it is shaped by means of a strickle, template or 'crook' as it is usually called in the trade: a board which revolves on pivots in the centre of the base-plate and is carefully cut away so that its inner form is the exact shape of the inside form of the bell. The second stage is the making of the 'cope', which is also done by a pivoting template or 'crook', this time cut to the shape of the outside of the bell. The moulder lines an iron case with the sand mixture, called 'loam', until the outer shape of the bell is fashioned. Both core and cope are finished by hand until the surfaces are smooth and they are then thoroughly dried in a core stove under a fairly low heat. Any inscription or decoration is impressed into the mould material of the cope so that it stands out in relief when the bell is cast. Finally the cope is placed over the core, care being taken that the two are concentric, and together they form the 'mould' for the bell. The melted bell metal is run into a ladle and poured into the mould until it is full.

Bell metal is a mixture of 13 parts of copper to 4 parts of tin. Although many other alloys have been tried, none has been found with a resonance equal to this. The metal must be run into the mould at the correct temperature, which varies according to the size of the bell. Small bells need a much higher temperature than large ones. The time taken for cooling after the bell is cast also varies with the size. Small bells can be taken from the mould the day after casting but larger ones need much longer than this. It may indeed be eight days or more before it is considered cool enough to be removed.

After it has been taken from the mould the bell must be tuned. The tuning machine is a vertical lathe so designed that a cutting tool can turn metal off the inside of the bell all round, and the bell is placed upon this mouth upwards. A bell is, of course, designed so that in theory its various thicknesses are such that it will come out from the mould 'in tune with itself', as it is said. In practice, however, this is rarely perfectly achieved and for this reason the use of the lathe is necessary. The bell is sounded on the tuning machine and the frequencies of the various harmonics are measured. It is then possible to calculate what modifications are necessary to bring it exactly into tune with the fundamental note. A mark is put on the inside of the bell and a light cut is taken. This process is carefully repeated until all the principal harmonics are in tune. In the case of the carillon particularly, extreme accuracy is necessary in the tuning and it is usual to tune a group of bells together, allowing them to stand until all the temperatures are the same before measuring the frequencies. For temperature also has an effect on the pitch of a bell, the hotter the temperature the lower the pitch, though fortunately all the harmonics move together with the pitch.

Just as with an organ the longer the pipe the deeper the note, so with a bell the bigger it is the deeper is its note and the more majestic and musical the sound. It is impossible to get a good sound out of a bell that is too thin and in effect the nature of the material dictates within fairly narrow limits what size a bell must be in order to produce a given note of good quality. The size of a bell is always spoken of in terms of the diameter, which is measured across its mouth. According to theory, for a bell to sound a low C, for instance, it will have a diameter of about 180 cm and weigh approximately 2 tonnes. The octave above will be half the diameter and approximately an eighth of the weight. Practice does not coincide exactly with the theoretical calculation, but it serves as a rough guide. In a peal of bells, for instance, the smaller, treble bells are made somewhat larger in diameter and therefore thicker and heavier than theory would dictate in order to get the correct note, the main reason being that up to a certain limit the weight of metal in a bell increases the power of the sound and this added weight therefore helps the smaller bells to be heard when they are sounded together with the large ones.

The most general use of sets of bells of this sort is for 'change ringing'. The set of bells is rung by means of wheels and ropes in full swing with one ringer to each bell. The usual number of bells is eight, but changes are also rung with 5, 6, 10 and 12 bells. 'Changes', as the conformations of sound are called, must obey two fundamental rules. First, no change must ever be repeated, and second, a bell may only move one place at a time. That is to say, if for instance a bell is ringing third in order, it may move to second or fourth place but no further. Change ringing appears to have had its origin in England about the same time as the beginning of the carillon in the Low Countries, or a very little later, about the beginning of the 17th c.

A carillon is a set of bells tuned to the chromatic scale so that music in two or more parts may be played upon them. The bells are hung stationary and are played either by a *carilloneur* or automatically. The smallest number of bells to which the term 'carillon' is correctly applied covers two chromatic octaves, i.e. 25 bells. A smaller set than this is correctly called a 'chime'. The number of bells in a carillon may extend to a range of four and a half chromatic octaves, which entails well over 50 bells. There is a great difference between the weights of the largest and smallest bells in such a carillon. When, for instance, in 1970 the Queen handed over to the Australian Government a carillon with a compass of four and a half octaves at Canberra, the largest bell weighed some 6 tonnes and the smallest about 9 kg. As has been said, the art of founding carillons fell into decline after the Hemonys. It was revived with the aid of modern scientific knowledge and technology towards the end of the 19th c. and musical carillons of extended compass are now made more successfully than before.

608, 867.

BELL-METAL. An alloy of copper and tin which has peculiar properties of resonance and from which bells are cast. See BELL-FOUNDING and BIDRIWARE.

BELTER, JOHN HENRY (1804–63). American cabinet-maker born and trained in Germany. He worked in New York City, where he became the pre-eminent furniture-maker during the years 1844–63. Much of the furniture he produced was of rosewood. The curved backs so characteristic of his chairs and sofas were achieved by means of a laminated construction which he invented. Carvings elaborate in the ROCOCO manner were another distinctive characteristic of his work. See FURNITURE (AMERICAN).

BENEMAN, GUILLAUME (d. after 1811). Principal cabinet-maker to the French Court during the last years of Louis XVI. A German by birth, he was admitted as master cabinet-maker in 1785. At this time RIESENER's high prices had cost him royal favour and Beneman received many commissions in his place. His work for the Court was carried out under the direction of the sculptor Jean Hauré, who was in charge of the Garde-Meuble.

BÉRAIN, JEAN (1640–1711). French decorator and designer. He was one of the most imaginative and influential of the designers during the last decades of the 17th c. and his ARABESQUES and GROTESQUES inaugurated a new movement which led towards the ROCOCO of the following century. His earliest official work consisted of 12 plates of ornament for Lebrun's Galerie d'Apollon at the Louvre. From *c.* 1670 he was employed occasionally as an engraver by the Bâtiments du roi. He was perhaps the most important artistic force in designing the elaborate stage settings, costumes and displays for the celebrations, out-of-door fêtes, ballet-operas, etc., given by Louis XIV. In the office of the Menus-Plaisirs he occupied the position of Dessinateur du roi from 1674 until his death. He took an important part in the Cabinet des Médailles (1682–4), for which he designed the famous Bureau du roi executed in MARQUETRY by OPPENORD.

He used Oriental motifs both in his designs

for court entertainments and in his arabesques, which were in the lighter style sometimes regarded as the first phase of Rococo; the style came into vogue shortly before 1700 and remained popular for the first quarter of the 18th c., continuing to be used for the decoration of faience (see CERAMICS, EARTHENWARE) at Moustiers and other provincial factories until the 1740s. He was one of the forerunners of French 18th-c. CHINOISERIE and he also seems to have begun the 18th-c. vogue for SINGERIES, though his monkey figures are as unmistakably denizens of the *Grand Siècle* as those of HUET and Watteau belong to the 18th c. His designs for furniture were widely copied not only in France but throughout the capitals of Europe.

BERGÈRE. French term for a form of upholstered armchair characterized by its closed arms and loose seat cushion. There were three principal types. One was closely related to the contemporary *fauteuil* but with a wider and deeper seat. The gondola-shaped *bergère*, or *bergère en gondole*, had an arched back in the form of a horseshoe and back and sides were upholstered as one unit. The *bergère confessionale* had a higher back and shallower wings, continuing the design of the earlier confessional chair. The *bergère* was perfected during the Louis XV period but all three types remained in vogue with characteristic modifications in style under Louis XVI and under the DIRECTOIRE and EMPIRE.

In England the term was adopted (also in the forms *burjair* or *bergier*) to denote upholstered armchairs with a long seat. From sometime before 1800 it was applied to a mahogany chair with back and sides of canework; sometimes the seat also was caned, having a loose cushion. These chairs became fashionable during the early decades of the 19th c. See FURNITURE (EUROPEAN).

BERLIN PORCELAIN. Berlin had two porcelain factories. Wegely's (1752–7), patronized by Frederick the Great, followed the styles of MEISSEN without much distinction. Gotzkowsky's, founded in 1761, became the Prussian royal factory two years later and continued into modern times. It had the benefit of painters and a modeller (F. E. Meyer) from Meissen. The cold white paste which is typical was adopted *c.* 1765, and during the best period (until 1786) was decorated with the characteristic scale-patterns and relief-mouldings of 'Potsdam Rococo'. The factory mark was a sceptre (from 1763).

BERLIN WOOLWORK. A type of *gros-point* EMBROIDERY which owes its name to the fact that in the early 19th c. the wools, canvasses and patterns used in it were distributed by Berlin firms. Towards the middle of the century, however, its vogue became very general. Elaborate needlework pictures of this type, usually with biblical or historical subjects, survive in considerable numbers but owing to their unimaginative execution they are little esteemed.

BEROVIERI. Muranese family of glass-makers to whom the discovery of Venetian CRISTALLO glass *c.* 1463 has been attributed. Angelo Berovieri has also been traditionally credited with the revival of the 13th-c. Islamic techniques of gilding and enamelling glass.

BERYL. A mineral species ($Be_3Al_2Si_6O_{18}$) to which several gemstones belong, including the EMERALD and AQUAMARINE. It crystallizes in hexagonal prisms and is harder than QUARTZ though softer than TOPAZ, 7½–8 on the MOHS SCALE. Under the Greek word *beryllos* antiquity recognized a number of stones which were distinguished by colour. It was Pliny who first suggested that the emerald was of the same species as the beryls. Today the golden beryl (the African variety of which is called 'helidore'), the orange beryl and the green beryl are sometimes cut as gems.

BESHKEN (latter 12th c.). Master jeweller of Opiza, known for the 'Beshken' Gospel cover. See GEORGIAN METALWORK.

BIBLE BOX. Nineteenth-c. term for rectangular boxes, usually of oak, which in the late 16th c. and throughout the 17th c. were made to hold the family Bible and important family documents. They had simple hinged lids, often sloping. Larger Bible boxes resembling miniature chests were made in the 17th and 18th centuries, chiefly in Wales where they sometimes surmounted a chest of drawers. Bible boxes were made during the early Colonial period in the United States and were often set on a stand—an idea which was the precursor of the HIGHBOY. See FURNITURE (AMERICAN).

BICCHERNA COVERS. Painted wooden covers made for tax account books used in the Biccherna and Gabella, the Exchequer and Tax Collector's offices respectively of the Commune of Siena. The earliest dated cover is 1258, the latest 1682. Each cover usually contains (1) an inscription recording the names and coats-of-arms of the treasury officials during the previous six months, and (2) a religious or secular painting. From the 14th to the 16th c. Biccherna covers were sometimes painted by leading Sienese artists, including Ambrogio Lorenzetti, Giovanni di Paolo, Beccafumi and Venturi Salimbeni. In modern times they have often been forged.

BIDRIWARE. A style of DAMASCENING believed to be named after the town of Bidar, India, where it is reputed to have been invented. The earliest known examples are from the 18th c. and the technique is used for hookah bases, surahis (ewers), charpoy legs (bed-legs), betel boxes and various domestic vessels. The metal used is BELL-METAL, an alloy of copper and tin, into which deep undercut grooves are carved following the final pattern. Silver wire is beaten into the grooves, where it is held firmly in place by the undercutting. The object is then polished and immersed in an acid which permanently blackens the whole surface. After a final polishing the silver line-decoration stands out from the smooth black surface.

612.

BIEDERMEIER. Term used to describe central European decorative arts, cabinet-work and interior decoration from *c.* 1820 to 1860 and sometimes also applied to German architecture and painting in the same period. The term is derived from the name Gottlieb Biedermeier, a fictional character from the journal *Fliegende Blätter* caricaturing middle-class vulgarity and Philistinism. The style tended to opulent tastelessness while even examples from the earlier years which displayed simplicity of design and ornament did not escape the commonplace. The cabinet-work has been aptly described as 'a potpourri of some of the features, but not always the best ones, of SHERATON, REGENCY, DIRECTOIRE and especially French EMPIRE minus the bronze appliqués'. There was a progressive taste for exaggerated curves and by 1840 ROCOCO influence was pronounced. Decorative supports to chairs and sofas were enriched with swans, griffins and dolphins and the carved detail was picked out in gilt in the manner of the French Empire. Realistically worked flowers and fruits came increasingly into vogue both in the carved decoration and in the textiles used for furniture coverings. Originating in Germany, the Biedermeier style spread among the *nouveaux riches* of England and elsewhere in Europe. See FURNITURE (EUROPEAN).

BILLET. MOULDING used in ROMANESQUE and GOTHIC architecture consisting of two or more bands of short raised cylinders or squares at

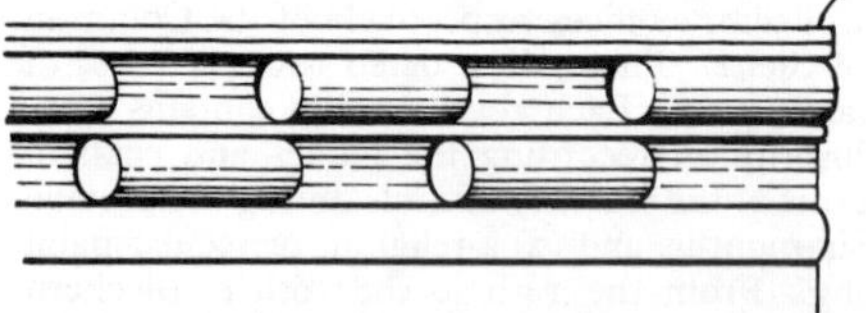

regular intervals. Similar decoration is found in silverware, etc. Also a term for a thumb-piece on a tankard, etc.

BINCHE LACE. A variety of VALENCIENNES distinguished by its predilection for decorative grounds such as *fond de neige* and by a more open texture in the solid parts of the pattern. Made during the 18th c. at Binche in Belgium and elsewhere, it was highly esteemed as a costume trimming.

BISCUIT. Term in ceramics for clay body fired or dried to a state in which it is not plastic but at which vitrification has not taken place and before glazing. See CERAMICS; CLAY; POTTERY TECHNIQUES.

BIZEN. One of the Six Ancient Kilns of Japan. The wares, thrown with a direct and apparently careless vigour, were fired for many days in wood kilns with no applied glaze, their quality and decoration depending upon the irregular partial glazing caused by the wood ash, the variations between oxidizing and reducing atmospheres and the degree of exposure to or protection from the fire caused by placing them within, against or on top of each other. See JAPAN.

BLACK LETTER. The English printer's name for a class of types reproducing Latin scripts of medieval origin written with a soft, broad, slanted nib producing broad main-strokes and fine hair-strokes, compressed letters and avoidance of curves, for which short oblique strokes were substituted. These scripts were evolved in western European countries during the 12th c. at much the same time as the GOTHIC style of architecture and by analogy the name 'gothic' is often used for them. Printing was invented while this style of writing prevailed, and except in Italy most early printers' types were modelled on it.

name for a class of types reproducing Latin

9 pt. German Fraktur

The names 'black letter' and 'gothic' are applied to many varieties of typefaces representing scripts of several degrees of formality and of different countries, such as textura, summa, bastarda, German FRAKTUR and Italian rotunda. The typical English black-letter type reproduced the French textura hand.

Black letter was displaced in British secular books towards the end of the 16th c., but some Bibles were set in it for another 40 years, books of the common law until late in the 18th c. and public general Acts of Parliament until 1793. See TYPOGRAPHY.

BLACKSMITH STYLE. A style of decorative wrought ironwork in which all the operations of fashioning are carried out at welding heat. The finest examples or ironwork in this style were produced in France prior to A.D. 1300. See IRON AND STEEL (DECORATIVE WROUGHT IRONWORK).

BLACKWORK. EMBROIDERY worked with a black thread, usually on white linen, was particularly fashionable for costume and furnishing in Tudor and early Stuart times, when it was not infrequently used in conjunction with embroidery in gold thread. It was not, as formerly supposed, identical with the embroidery known as Spanish work.

BLANC DE CHINE. Popular name of a type of Chinese pure white PORCELAIN of the Ming and Ch'ing periods. See CHINA (CERAMICS).

BLAZE. See FLOSS SILK.

BLONDE LACE. A LACE made from filmy, natural-coloured Chinese FLOSS SILK chiefly at Caen, Chantilly, Bayeux and Dieppe. Sometimes gold, silver or black thread was used and the work was occasionally decorated with pearls. A similar 'blonde' lace was made in Catalonia.

BLUE AND WHITE. Type name of Chinese decorated PORCELAINS of the Yüan and Ming periods. See CHINA (CERAMICS). The style and the name were adopted also in many European manufactures.

BOCCARO WARE. A Portuguese word originally applied to red EARTHENWARE of Mexico and afterwards to red STONEWARE imported from China. It was copied by BÖTTGER at MEISSEN. See CERAMICS (STONEWARE).

BODONI, GIAMBATTISTA (1740–1813). Printer, letter-cutter and type-founder, born at Saluzzo in Piedmont. He was apprenticed as a compositor at the press of the Sacra Congregatio de Propaganda Fide in Rome. He left there in 1766 and after working for a time as a type-founder was commissioned by the Duke of Parma in 1768 to set up a printing office for the Duchy, to which a type-foundry was soon added. Bodoni cut a series of typefaces in the manner of FOURNIER LE JEUNE and showed them in his first specimen-book of 1771. He then turned to Greek, Hebrew and exotic types, of which he cut a great many. His specimen of 1788 displays a second series of roman and italic types of a transitional kind under the influence of F.-A. Didot. In 1791 he printed Horace's poems in types of his third and latest design with unprecedented contrast of thick and thin strokes. This design combined with Bodoni's meticulous layout and impression was viewed throughout Europe as the height of typographical elegance and made him the supreme arbiter of taste in printing. After 1790 he printed books for customers abroad, including some for publishers in London. His style in TYPOGRAPHY remained dominant for half a century.

Bodoni's *Manuale tipografico*, published in 1818 by his widow, shows 285 of his latest typefaces and has a preface by him on the principles of his art. Altogether 667 faces of type were cut by him or under his supervision.

848, 857.

BOG OAK. Oak wood preserved in peat bogs in a black state, used from Elizabethan times for INLAY, etc. See WOOD-WORKING (SPECIAL TECHNIQUES).

BOKHARA (or BUKHARA) **RUGS.** See TURCOMAN RUGS.

BOLECTION. Term in architecture and cabinet-making for a MOULDING, usually OGEE in section, raised round a panel or generally a projection moulding serving to cover the joint between two members with different surface levels. The term is used also in the practical arts of furniture, silverwork, etc.

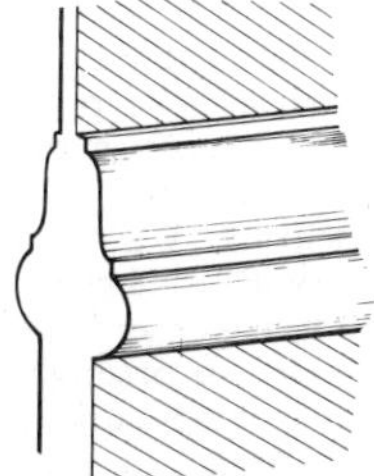

BONE CHINA. See CERAMICS; PORCELAIN.

BONGRACE. See COSTUME (TUDOR AND STUART).

BOOGE. The curved portion of a plate, etc., which joins the rim to the bottom. See PEWTER; CERAMICS; SILVER.

BOOKBINDING. I. TECHNIQUES. A bound book is a three-dimensional articulated whole, and its good or bad behaviour depends on the leaves, the structure and the cover being in scale and in sympathy with each other. Bookbinding is what is done to the leaves to keep them in order, to protect them, and make them easy or even pleasant to handle. It is very much more than the mere wrapping round them of a cover of some sort whether plain or sumptuous.

In the simplest form a pile of perhaps 25 leaves is folded in half and stitched or stapled along the fold, making a single-section binding. If the outer fold is rather more substantial than those it encloses, so much the better. Such a single-section booklet cannot conveniently have many more than 50 leaves, and even this number does not handle very comfortably in this form. So binding books with a greater number of leaves, such as are the stock-in-trade of the lending libraries, calls for more elaborate methods.

If we take the lending library as the starting-point, the first step up from the single-section booklet is probably not on the shelves at all but on a rack for periodicals or a table. Many glossy magazines are made up of numbers of folded sections piled on top of each other and united by staples passing right through the pile near the folds, from the first leaf to the last. Usually a decorative cover is wrapped round the whole and stuck to the backs of the folds. This is a degenerate version of what is basically the strongest form of bookbinding—the stabbed binding. But again it is unsuited for thick books or for permanent bindings, and it sheds its outer leaves while it grows out of date on the tables of waiting-rooms. None the less books specially designed for stabbed bindings, such as the *Encyclopaedia Britannica*, are long-lived and very well behaved.

Next up the ladder comes the contemporary paperback, now a very much more durable product than in its earlier days. It is again the result of a number of folded sections piled on each other, but with all the folds sheared away. A flexible adhesive is applied to the spine; that is to say to the inner edges of what is now a pile of single leaves. A stiffer paper cover is wrapped round the whole and stuck to the spine in the same way as the multi-sectioned periodical was covered. In fact this book itself may well be a periodical. Depending on the type of adhesive, the quality and character of the paper and the way it is directioned, this may be a surprisingly strong structure. But except by a comparatively costly treatment of the spine it cannot be provided with stiff boards and so it tends to become dog-eared, especially at the beginning and end.

Following the paperback comes the book with stiff boards. This too is a group of folded sections sewn along the folds like the first little booklet. But this time the thread passes from one section to the next outside the folds, linking each one to its neighbour. A fold of stronger paper is usually tipped to the inner edges of the first and last leaves of the text; the outer leaf of each of these folds becomes the paste-down inside the boards, while the inner ones become fly-leaves. The spine is usually lined with a light woven fabric which projects a little on each side to strengthen the joint between the text and the boards; in the finished book it can be recognized under the paste-down. The cover, of card with cloth or special paper covering, is made up in the flat separately from the text, and titled in the flat. The sewn text is then stuck inside it. When the book comes from the publishers there is almost invariably a dust-jacket carrying the title with graphic design of some sort together with advertising matter. Years ago such advertisement normally followed the text, being sewn and bound as part of the book.

These forms of binding are almost always the product of the machine. None of them is likely to be a collector's piece from the point of view of bookbinding; but all of them can be made by hand, and this introduction is concerned mainly with hand-binding.

When people speak of bookbinding as an art they are nearly always thinking of the elaborately decorated outer cover of gold-tooled leather; that is to say of bookbinding at the next higher level in the social scale. Indeed with many designers of hand-bound books the external appearance is almost the only consideration in mind. In some cases the display of craftsmanship in decorative design preponderates to such an extent that the book as an integrated whole tends to be disregarded.

The book in its present form has had a life of less than 2,000 years. When it first appeared it was in competition with the roll, which had served Egypt for 3,000 years or more. Although the roll was a book—its Latin name *volumen* gives us our word 'volume'—it obviously could not be bound; it was sometimes stored in cylindrical containers. The codex, from which the modern book is descended, was undoubtedly derived from wooden wax tablets (the Latin name *caudex* began life meaning a tree trunk) and from the parchment notebooks of the Romans. Its first use and development were associated with Christian literature, for which the change from roll to codex was virtually complete by the end of the 2nd c. A.D., though pagan writing retained the roll for some hundreds of years longer. What influenced the Christians in this innovation is a matter for speculation, but despite the lack of evidence one is tempted to picture a 1st-c. Christian frustrated by the difficulty of finding the reference he needed in a roll perhaps 9 metres long and hitting on the plan of folding it between the columns, thus producing a concertina-like 'codex' and almost achieving a book on the Chinese/Japanese pattern with doubled leaves folded on the fore-edge.

The earliest form of structure seems to have been a single-section book of perhaps 50 leaves stitched along the fold. It would have been awkward to handle, and no such complete book has come to light. Almost no codices exist in their original binding prior to the 7th c., so it is not possible to trace the structural development with certainty; but there may have been stabbed bindings. Early Coptic binding from Egypt seems to have been sewn much as machine-bound books are sewn today, each section being linked to its neighbour by stitches of the thread that united the leaves of the individual sections. It differed in that the sewing-thread also linked the text-leaves to the boards, and so in being covered, if covered at all, with the boards attached—unlike the publisher's case-binding. Some of the boards were made of stout folds of coarse PAPYRUS and were sewn in the same way as the sections, the two halves of the fold being stuck together after covering. Parchment and papyrus were both available in the 1st c.; and although local conditions may have influenced the choice of materials, there can be little doubt that while papyrus was well suited to rolls it was not satisfactory for codices. (See VELLUM AND PARCHMENT.) The basic structure persisted in the Mediterranean area, particularly for Greek texts, until at least the 16th c., and was certainly in use in Ethiopia well into the 20th c. The earliest binding believed to be European, the late-7th-c. or early-8th-c. Stonyhurst Gospel of St. John, follows the same pattern.

PAPER, although generally available in Europe in the 14th c., did not become the normal material for the leaves of books until the advent of printing from movable type in the 15th c. (See TYPOGRAPHY.) By then the techniques of book production were fairly firmly established. The scribe was supplied with separate quires of parchment, or possibly paper, which were often lightly stitched together. As he wrote he numbered the leaves on the recto, often in the lower right-hand corner, and also, or as an alternative, he would write a catchword (the first word on the following page) below the last word on each page. Sometimes he added his name at the end of the text with the date of completion and a prayer of thanksgiving. He usually left spaces for the insertion of coloured initials by another hand, a practice continued in the early years of printing. There was no title-page.

Compared with paper, vellum or parchment is enormously strong and the vellum-leaved book was a very tough structure indeed. It was sewn with thread so thick that it might well be described as string, passing round heavy cords or thongs stretched across the spine. The ends of these thongs or cords were laced through holes near the inner edges of wooden boards and held in place with wooden pegs which were cut off flush with the surfaces of the boards. Additional bands were added at head and tail by sewing round cords or thongs and tying them down to the leaves by stitching through the folds in the middle of each section. The ends of these head-bands and tail-bands were also laced into the boards. The whole was covered with leather and provided with clasps at the fore-edge, making a sort of press to keep the vellum flat when not in use.

When the leaves were made from the skins of animals (vellum or parchment) their dimensions had an overriding influence on the dimensions of the page. After it had been squared by cutting away the irregularities of projecting legs and neck, the skin of a sheep or calf when folded in half provided two large leaves, the animal's spine running horizontally across them. Cut down the fold and again folded in half the skin provided twice the number with the animal's spine running up and down. The process could not be repeated because a skin providing leaves pleasantly flexible if measuring 35 centimetres by 25 centimetres provides something much less so at 25 centimetres by 18 centimetres, and the leaves become intolerably stiff at 18 centimetres by 13 centimetres. Small books call for skins from small animals. Edward Johnston in his *Writing and Illuminating and Lettering* gave a simple test for arriving at optimum flexibility: if a piece of parchment or paper the size and shape of the chosen page is held vertically on a level table between two straight strips of wood, it should bend over of its own weight until the free edge touches the table. If it does not do this, it is too stiff.

With the introduction of printing there seems for a time to have been no clear recognition of the revolution involved. The typefaces imitated the writing of the scribes; spaces were still left for the insertion by hand of coloured initials, which were indicated by the lower-case impression of the letter required; there was still no title-page. But nearly all printed books were paper-leaved; and paper could be, and was, produced to accommodate any size of page without waste and of a substance to suit the page-area. The cost of books fell and mass production was on its way. In the last half of the 15th c. the paper-making industry, the type-founders and the book-binders managed somehow to cope with the production in Europe of some 30,000 separate titles while maintaining a high standard of quality. The editions were tiny compared with the present day but it was nevertheless an amazing achievement.

Bookbinders were at first dubious of the strength of paper, and in many early printed books strips of parchment cut from redundant manuscripts were used to reinforce the folds inside the quires (sometimes outside also) to prevent the sewing from tearing the paper. A system quickly developed whereby the first page of each section carried in the lower margin a letter of the Roman alphabet—the section signature—usually repeated with the addition of a numeral on the recto of each leaf up to the middle of the section, as Bii, Biii, etc. Pages were not numbered but each folio carried consecutive numbers, usually Roman, on the top outer corners of the rectos. Today these necessary guides to the binder remain in use, though numbers often replace the Roman alphabet and they may also appear on the outer folds, where when the quires are assembled they show in echelon as a quick check of the order. Pages have, of course, long been numbered, the rectos showing the odd numbers and the versos the evens. Title-pages soon made their appearance and quickly became the feature they remain today. The scribe's colophon survived in print and a register of the types used was often added to it. Later the information it contained was transferred to the title-page or to pages preceding it.

When a book is printed the pages are impressed on the opposite sides of a flat sheet in two operations. The flat sheet may receive 2, 4, 8, 16 or even 32 pages on each side, and it is the responsibility of the printers so to arrange the imposition that the pages are in the right order when the sheet is folded. An 8vo (octavo or eight-leaf) sheet imposed for hand-folding is illustrated below.

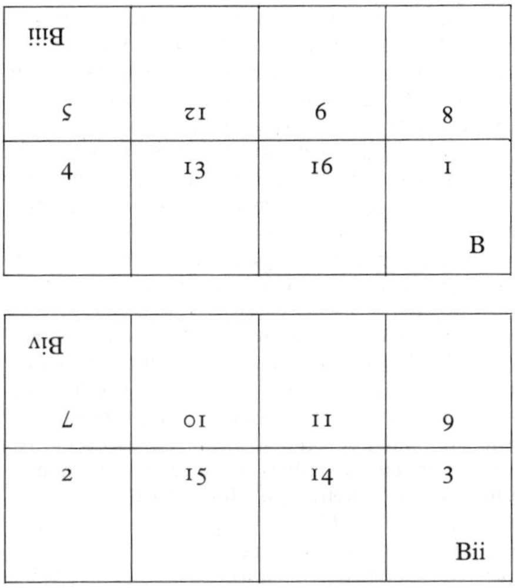

Biii 5	12	9	8
4	13	16	1 B

Biv 7	10	11	6
2	15	14	3 Bii

Because the sheets are now folded by machines which do not follow the sequence of hand-folding, the imposition is altered to suit the machine.

Today it is at the printing stage also that the behaviour of the finished book is very largely established for good or ill. The behaviour of the whole depends very much on the behaviour of the individual leaves. If they do not pass Edward Johnston's test, they are too stiff and the book tends to open like the ribs of a fan; if they pass it too easily, they may be too thin (a rare condition) and may collapse in vertical creases, particularly at the beginning and end. Stiffness in relation to the leaves of a book needs some qualification. Paper too stiff for a small 8vo volume would very likely be just right for a folio volume. Stiffness must be related to the page area, and Edward Johnston's test must be used with understanding. It will give reliable information only about hand-made paper in which the fibres are distributed equally in all directions. Nearly all books are now printed on machine-made paper, in which the fibres tend to lie parallel with the length of the endless ribbon of paper as it is formed. Because of this machine-made paper bends and folds more readily parallel with the direction of the fibres than across them. If a book is printed so that the machine direction of the paper runs up and down the page, it will open and lie open much more pleasantly than if it runs across it. With practice it is often possible to recognize the machine direction in the flat, but it is usually more easily shown by looking along the edges of a closed book. Often the edges show a slight wave or unevenness either on the fore-edge or on the edges at head and tail. If the waviness is on the fore-edge, the machine direction runs across the leaves—wrong; if it is at the head and tail, it runs up and down—right.

If the arrangement of the paper is the most important factor controlling good or bad behaviour, the next in importance is probably the number of leaves in each section. Other things being equal, a 4to (quarto) volume (one with four leaves to the quire) will open more pleasantly than a 16mo or a 32mo. With thicker sections there is a tendency for the book to open in chunks and for breakdown to occur between them—a tendency which is increased when the paper is too stiff. A similar breakdown is likely where a section of 'art' paper plates, or a section much thicker or thinner than the remainder, is interpolated.

Finally, there is the binding. To some extent every book presents the hand-binder with a different problem. When books were made by hand there was a close relationship between those choosing the material for the leaves, deciding their size and number, writing on them and illuminating them, and those responsible for their binding. At the beginning these may well have been one and the same person. Only very rarely is such a relationship possible today. With the introduction of printing from movable type the association began to break up, though judging from the many early printed books that have come down to us an understanding of each other's problems survived for many years.

Today few books are published that justify the special binding by hand of individual copies—the elaborate treatment aimed at the collector whether he is a monied bibliophile or some corporate body. And anyone with an urge to bind for himself books which for one reason or another have enduring attraction for him must search, or choose carefully, while having a serious look at the size and shape of the problem he is contemplating. A few days spent in a bindery are unlikely to reveal the full range of disasters waiting round the corner but will almost certainly show that a wide range of skills is demanded. In trade binderies it is customary for mending, sewing and head-banding to be done by women. The work of men is divided between forwarders and finishers. Forwarders glue, round and back, prepare and attach boards and cover; they may also wash, size and do other wet work. Finishers are responsible for gold- and blind-tooling, polishing and so on. An enthusiast working alone must master all these skills, and on occasion he must be something of a wood-worker and metal-worker as well. The designer and binder, if in the end he is to justify his activities, must produce something better behaved and better suited than what comes from the machine. Something made by hand is not on that account better than its machine-made counterpart—it may be very much worse. That the making may do something for the maker is another matter.

It is now not often that publishers are prepared to issue books in sheets or unbound quires; the book will have to be taken to pieces. Publishers, printers and their machines do not make things easy for the hand-binder but if a book behaves well in its publisher's case-binding, making it behave equally well when bound by hand will be that much easier. If it has a modern binding, there is likely to be difficulty in taking it to pieces without damage. Today's synthetic 'glues' are enormously stronger than traditional hide-glues and behave differently, and in the process of separating the sections the outer folds are likely to be torn and must be mended. New fly-leaves will be needed and they provide the first opportunity for judging the importance of keeping the parts of the whole compatible with each other and in scale. There is much to be said for giving them concealed linen joints and for sewing them on. The connection between covers and text is unavoidably liable to breakdown unless specially reinforced, because it has more work to do than any other part of the book and the boards swing on a narrow width of materials. The weakness was early realized and here also strips of redundant manuscript parchment are found reinforcing old books. Sewing on raised cords has an honourable tradition, but it is by no means always the best for all books. And it makes the job much more difficult for the inexperienced. If it is a medium-sized book, its spine will not need that sort of support. Sewing on tapes is associated with what are known as French joints, which provide a wider hinge for the boards and so allow leather to be left thicker without restricting their movement. Large, thick and heavy books need more support than can be given by tapes alone, and this is traditionally and effectively provided by sewing on cords, or double cords, of a thickness in scale with the size and weight of the book, perhaps in combination with special sewing. If the leaves are thick and stiff, it may be necessary to arrange that the book throws up like an old-style ledger so that the opening lies flat. This puts a great strain on the structure, which must be designed to stand up to it. This throw-up can be controlled if necessary by covering the cords completely with extra turns of the sewing thread, the strands lying in close contact as do the stones in the arch of a bridge—arch sewing. An early practice achieved the same effect with added solidity by using another system of sewing whereby at each double cord the thread picks up the sewing of the preceding section or even the preceding two or three sections.

The sewing-thread lying inside the folds of the sections makes this part of the book thicker than the remainder. This swelling is usefully accommodated by rounding and backing the spine; it helps to keep the book in shape while it stands on the shelf. But preceding this comparatively modern process of rounding and backing with a hammer (which is not altogether satisfactory), spines were rounded by lacing on the boards firmly and closing them on the leaves. Covering was done with the boards lying open on the bench, turning in the edges of the leather and again closing the boards. Both rounding and covering may have been combined in the same operation. Neither is possible with French joints, but with tight joints and strong boards both rounding and covering are simplified.

For hundreds of years it has been usual to achieve immediate solidity in books by gluing the spine and then pasting the cover to it directly. But the oldest known European binding had no adhesive on the spine and except for an unexplained break between the first and second sections, it is in quite surprisingly good order after more than 1,200 years. Adhesives break down and some of them are under more than a suspicion of causing damage to the folds of the sections; glue and its removal are certainly responsible for damage when books are taken to pieces. It is quite possible to produce a long-lived binding with almost no adhesives. For comparatively small books the answer may be a form of limp vellum binding. Important factors in its longevity are the lightness and suppleness of the cover, which is yet stiff enough to prevent the dog-earing suffered by the limp-covered paperback, and the fact that vellum is not subject to the deleterious effects of sulphur dioxide in city and industrial atmospheres. But vellum calls for skills and techniques not commonly available today and it does not lend itself, especially on a limp binding, to gold tooling, though there is some highly successful use of it on vellum in combination with pen work. At present it seems likely that leather will remain supreme in the field of collectors' pieces and other one-off special binding.

Modern leather for bookbinding is less liable to decay than it was in the 19th c. and the beginning of the 20th c. But although protective treatment enables it to stand up better to polluted atmospheres, it is unfortunately true that all vegetable-tanned leather succumbs to them eventually. There are grounds also for believing that the skins of domesticated animals are not as strong as once they were. Whatever the species, skins from very young animals are smaller and correspondingly tender compared with those from adults. Ideally, small skins should be used for small books and large skins for large ones—a counsel of perfection because skins tend towards a uniformity of area and thickness. It is the hair or grain side, or epidermis, that gives the surface of a well bound book its characteristically attractive appearance. But this outer layer is very thin and has little strength. To make a thick skin thin enough and flexible enough to cover a small duodecimo it would be necessary to pare away most of the tough corium layer, leaving something with not much more strength than paper.

MOROCCO, like so many materials, took its name from its place of origin; it is vegetable-tanned, and is properly a goatskin. It comes in a variety of guises, the best of them much used for binding small and medium-sized books. Levant morocco is a heavier skin with a beautiful bold grain. Many skins are over-stretched in manufacture to make flat what is not naturally so. Many can be improved in appearance and made easier to use by damping them very slightly and boarding them in all directions, inside and out; there will usually be a noticeable loss of footage. Calf provided much of the binders' leather in the past (it is the smell of rotting calf that novelists cannot resist when their characters find themselves within the confines of a stately library). It was probably made from the hides of more mature animals than is now normal practice. It is a smooth, rather tender material and little used in modern fine binding. The skins of calves and more mature animals are sometimes embossed with metal plates to imitate the skins of other animals—half a dozen crocodiles from one cow. Goatskins and sheepskins are similarly printed to give a more even over-all appearance which allows the use of what before being printed were the less attractive areas of the skins. Mineral tannages are less subject to decay but are difficult to use for bookbinding. White alum-tawed skins were much used in the 12th c. and later in

Germany. They have a very long life, and a few are used today; they are very suitable for the rebinding of valuable early books, for which rebinding should be necessary only very rarely. But they are white, and are less easy to use than morocco.

Leather is now to be had in a much wider range of colours than in the past. These colours can be produced by dyes or pigments or a combination of both. Pigments are sometimes used to hide blemishes in the skin, which may reappear in the process of covering or later when the pigment wears away. Undoubtedly good dyed skins are better looking than good pigmented skins, but they are comparatively scarce and so more expensive. But all vegetable-tanned skins fade or change colour with age because the whole thickness of the skin gradually becomes a reddish brown. The rate of change varies with the quality of the skin and with its environment; it is very much delayed by protection from light and from polluted atmospheres. The paler the colour and the further from the red band of the spectrum, the more will the change be apparent; reds, brown and black are safe, but natural (undyed) greens and blues are not. Heavy use of pigment hides the fading but the true character of the leather will be lost.

The decoration of books has a history almost as long as the book itself, and there are plenty of books surviving from the past from which to trace a reasonably clear genealogical tree showing its development from at least the 7th c. A tradition of leather decoration was ready to hand and the techniques developed for books range through the simple blind impression of metal TOOLS, the interlacing of contrasting material, the use of patterned excisions to show an underlying variant, bas-relief modelling, ink and paint, engraved rolls, and the decoration of large areas by impressing pictorially engraved panels, to the gold tooling and onlay still prevalent today. Church books not intended for liturgical use received on their upper covers carved IVORY panels or lavish encrustations of silver, gold and jewels. Metal clasps with metal bosses and corners for heavy books were much more than merely functional. See BOOK COVERS.

Once gold-leaf was adopted for book decoration its use spread rapidly to become by far the most popular medium in the form of gold tooling, often in combination with blind tooling and painted or onlaid (sometimes inlaid) colour. Although gold-leaf can be laid on a sticky surface, as in sign-writing or the decoration of ironwork or the cross and orb at the top of St. Paul's Cathedral, in bookbinding it is almost invariably impressed on the surface. At first, after marking a few guide-lines on the cover, the whole surface was treated with glaire (white of egg). When the glaire was dry it was lightly greased and covered with gold-leaf. The finisher then 'drew' his patterns by impressing heated tools in symmetrical arrangements. The hot tools 'fried' the egg-glaire and the gold-leaf stuck to it. The surplus gold was wiped off with an oily rag, from which it could be recovered later. It is now usual to prepare patterns on thin paper, which is then temporarily attached to the cover to be tooled; the tools are heated and worked through the paper, so leaving impressions in the leather. These are painted in with glaire, covered with gold-leaf and tooled as before. This ensures greater precision than the earlier free-hand treatment; it does not ensure that the result will be more attractive.

Gold-leaf has been available for thousands of years; that used by early EGYPTIANS was comparatively thick and could probably have been handled with the fingers. But the process of gold-beating has been developed to the degree that modern gold-leaf has a thickness or thinness of about 0·004 millimetres. A leaf of it held up to the light is semi-transparent and of a surprising greenish appearance. Bookbinders use what is known as loose gold. This comes in little single-section booklets of thin paper, treated to prevent sticking, interleaved with 25 leaves of gold, usually 82·55 mm by 82·55 mm. It is handled in draught-free surroundings with the aid of a gold-cushion, a gold-knife, a puff of breath and some good quality cotton-wool which has been wiped on a slightly greasy surface—often the face or hair of the finisher. See also GILDING.

The visual effect of gold on leather is at first surprising, very different from the effect of the black on white pattern from which it was transposed. The degree of surprise varies to some extent with the tone of the surface on which it is tooled. Gold tooling on vellum or on white leather, while often producing interesting texture, does not readily show its details in all lights, and titles in gold on vellum spines do not read easily. The size of tools that can be struck by hand is limited by the strength and skill of the finisher; such things as coats-of-arms call for a blocking- or arming-press.

2. HISTORICAL. The earliest books, being rolls, were unbound; they were stored in cylindrical containers. The codex, or book form as known today, was introduced early in the Christian era. It was bound in leather covers decorated with blind TOOLED designs of incised lines and pierced or APPLIQUÉ patterns. Egyptian skill in LEATHERCRAFT was carried by Muslim invaders of the 7th c. to Europe by way of North Africa, Sicily and Spain, and into the Islamic territories of the Near East. Islamic binding design was at first based on the austerely abstract styles of Coptic leatherwork, employing interlacing bands, knotwork, intricate geometrical ARABESQUES, and the various Arabic scripts. When artistic leadership of the Islamic world passed to Persia in the later Middle Ages new and more colourful decorative styles were evolved in the luxurious courts of the Timurid and Safavid dynasties. FILIGREE leather with gilded cut-paper work mounted on coloured

grounds, all-over patterns stamped from large metal blocks and miniature painting on PAPIER-MÂCHÉ boards under LACQUER varnish were among the various techniques adopted in the golden age of Islamic binding from the 15th to the 17th centuries.

In Christian Europe most of the early bindings were made by monastic craftsmen. Heavy wooden boards fitted with clasps were necessary to keep the vellum sheets, on which manuscripts were written, from buckling. Sumptuous book covers decorated with metalwork, sculptured IVORY panels, ENAMEL plaques, and jewellery were also made for church service-books; these belong to the arts of metalwork and sculpture rather than to bookbinding. Wooden covers painted with coats-of-arms and religious or secular subjects were used from the 13th to the 17th c. for the tax accounts books, used in the BICCHERNA and Gabella, the Exchequer and the Tax Collector's offices of the Commune of Siena.

But it was leather that became the principal material for bookbinding from the early Middle Ages onwards; the earliest known example is the Stonyhurst Gospel cover, which was taken from the coffin of St. Cuthbert (d. 687) at Durham in 1104 and is usually dated to the latter part of the 7th c. Two techniques were adopted for leather decoration: the incision of lines with a knife or a bone or wooden point, and the impression of cold metal tools and stamps in the dampened leather. CUIR CISELÉ bindings were executed mainly in Germany. Stamped decoration, which characterizes the so-called monastic bindings of the later Middle Ages, is represented by a small group of French and English ROMANESQUE bindings dating from the 12th c. and the more numerous French and Flemish examples of the 15th and early 16th centuries. The former are decorated with rows of repeated impressions from small, finely cut stamps depicting fabulous beasts, human figures and purely ornamental motifs such as ROSETTES and stars. The panel stamps in the second group are of larger dimensions and were impressed on the leather with a hand-press. The subjects of these engraved panel stamps were mainly religious and allegorical figures, the technique persisting in Germany until well into the 16th c. The mechanization of binding, made necessary by the increased circulation of books following the invention of printing in the middle of the 15th c., was also facilitated by the use of roll tools which produced a repeating pattern at one stroke.

The introduction of gold tooling in the 2nd half of the 15th c. marks the close of the medieval period of bookbinding. This technique, of Oriental origin, entered Italy at two points: first at Venice from the Near East *c.* 1640, and slightly later in the south at Naples, where it was probably introduced by Moorish leather-workers from Spain. Gold tooling emphasized and greatly increased the ornamental element in bookbinding in contrast to the more pictorial qualities displayed in blind-tooled panel stamps. It appealed also to the book collectors and bibliophiles, who regarded the panel stamp as an archaic survival of the Middle Ages inappropriate to the new learning. The individualism of Renaissance humanists found further expression in personal book-stamps, initials, ciphers and mottoes, as well as by the use of small intaglio portrait stamps simulating antique cameos, usually in blind though the sunk background is sometimes coloured. The best known are the so-called Canevari bindings made in Rome in the 1st half of the 16th c., probably for a member of the Farnese family. Gold tooling was exploited in north Italy, where the new technique was combined with Islamic decorative motifs which entered the European repertory through Venice, the centre of the book trade in Renaissance Italy.

Transplanted to France in the early 16th c., Italian styles were developed and perfected in bindings made for the French Court and other patrons, particularly the bibliophile and financier Jean GROLIER. The Grolier style consisted of interlacing ribbons, often coloured black or red, bearing a close resemblance to contemporary STRAPWORK ornament. Since the 16th c. there has been in France a constant succession of new styles and techniques which have been imitated throughout Europe. LYONNESE BINDINGS, so called because they often cover books printed in Lyon, were decorated with polychrome interlaced strapwork and arabesques, or with large centre and corner ornaments on a dotted ground. FANFARE BINDINGS have gold-tooled geometrical patterns enclosing naturalistic leaf sprays or winged volutes, FLEURONS and arabesques. The style was revived by Thouvenin in 1829 on a new binding made for a book entitled *Fanfares et corvées abbadesques des roule-bontemps* (1613); hence the name. For the *pointillé* work of Le Gascon and Florimond BADIER, executed *c.* 1622–57, dotted instead of outline tools were used, giving a brilliant filigree effect. DENTELLE BINDINGS decorated with wide, wavy borders, giving a lace-like effect, and mosaic bindings, in which coloured leathers were inlaid in massive scroll and floral shapes, were made by the PADELOUP, DEROME and MONNIER families in the 18th c. CATHEDRAL BINDINGS, popular *c.* 1815–40, were decorated usually in blind with a large stamp of a formalized cathedral façade or with smaller stamps reproducing windows or other motifs from GOTHIC architecture. Marius MICHEL led a reaction against the 19th-c. copying of earlier styles, introducing semi-naturalistic and 'illustrative' bindings related to the text of the book.

English bindings until the end of the 17th c. were copied from Continental models, being often made by foreign craftsmen working in Britain. (See WOTTON BINDINGS.) Embroidered bindings were popular in the early Stuart period, but the first truly national style was developed after the Restoration in the 'cottage' bindings decorated with a gilt or painted ornament in the form of a cottage roof or gable at the top and bottom of the central panel. During the 18th c. a number of distinctive bindings were produced in Dublin and Edinburgh as well as in London, where at the end of the century several decorative innovations were introduced by Roger PAYNE, one of the first binders to use straight-grained Morocco. He gave special attention to the spine, employing small, closely massed floral stamps, often in Pointillé. The firm of Edwards of Halifax, founded by William Edwards (1723–1808) and continued by his sons, used transparent vellum with paintings of allegorical figures or armorial bearings on the underside. They also popularized the so-called 'Etruscan' bindings in calf stained to imitate the terracotta shades of Greek and Etruscan vases (see ETRUSCAN STYLE) and topographical scenes painted on the fore-edges but concealed under gold so that they are visible only when the leaves of the book are splayed out.

Binding craft was profoundly affected in the 19th c. by new techniques introduced during the Industrial Revolution to meet the increased demand for books following educational and social reforms. Publishers' cheap cloth casings, prepared by machinery, largely superseded leather bindings made by hand in the traditional manner. A sharp distinction arose between 'fine' and 'trade' bindings, which has persisted to the present day though moderated by the revival of binding craft under the stimulus of William MORRIS. Since the First World War French designers and craftsmen, led by Pierre LEGRAIN, have refreshed bookbinding with new styles, often setting their titles in unconventional places.

153, 172, 226, 260, 313, 341, 392, 393, 394, 498, 540, 594, 595, 629, 850.

BOOK COVERS. This article concerns metal or IVORY coverings for books, as distinct from BOOKBINDING. Gold and precious stones adorned the covers of liturgical books as early as the 4th c., although the early Fathers disapproved of them. Few survive from before the time of Charlemagne. The earliest are those given by the Lombard queen Theolinda (d. 625) to the Basilica of St. John at Monza. A gem-studded gold cross divides the cover into four compartments, each laid with gold-leaf and set with an antique cameo, and the cross itself has a border of the glass-filled cloisonné that was used in the Germanic jewellery of the time. In a cover from Lindau (Pierpont Morgan Library, New York) the basic design of the cross is lavishly adorned with Irish-Saxon animal motifs as well as with ENAMELS, and a CLOISONNÉ ENAMEL decorates the Byzantine book covers (8th c.) at St. Mark's, Venice.

CAROLINGIAN and OTTONIAN book covers became immensely elaborate. That on the Codex Aureus from S. Emmeran (Munich) has REPOUSSÉ gold figures and richly set gems among delicate FILIGREE, and others incorporate ivory carvings—not necessarily contemporary but sometimes Byzantine or even antique—and enamels. For practical reasons the back was often either covered with plain cloth, VELLUM or LEATHER, or decorated with a sheet of silver openwork. Sometimes a simply bound book would be provided with an elaborate outer case. Many 13th-c. covers show the figure of Christ in Majesty, or the Crucifixion, in silver or silver-gilt, CHASED or in high relief, within a raised frame, which is often surrounded by filigree work enriched by naturalistic foliage. These were the precursors of the magnificent silver bindings of the High GOTHIC. The most popular covers for less ostentatious patronage during the late 12th c. and throughout the 13th c. were of Limoges champlevé enamel.

To judge by the few surviving examples enamelled and jewelled ornament was rarely employed during the later Middle Ages and silver alone became the usual medium. The most splendid of the late silver book covers is that made by the Aachen goldsmith Hans Reutlingen for the *Reichsevangeliar*, commissioned by the Emperor Maximilian and now in the Kunsthistorisches Museum, Vienna; but two detached book covers of comparable quality by a Bamberg goldsmith are in the British Museum (Waddesdon Bequest). These book covers with figure subjects embossed almost in the round, set with intricately pinnacled Gothic canopies, made no concessions to practical considerations. While France and Italy during the 16th c. were developing tooled and leather bindings the goldsmiths of Germany still received commissions for bindings of precious metal, though only for religious works. A group of 20 bindings, formerly in the University Library, Königsberg, made for Duke Albrecht of Brandenburg (1525–68) by various goldsmiths, were all of silver-gilt, and followed the layout of contemporary leather bindings, i.e. a rectangular panel in the middle and bosses or medallions in the corners. But instead of the tooled ornament of the leather bindings, they had etched or engraved designs of Oriental character or religious subjects copied from contemporary prints. The engraved ornament on some of these German bindings is of a quality which suggests the work of a professional engraver rather than of a goldsmith. During the 1st half of the 17th c. Dutch silver bindings engraved in the manner of J. T. de Bry were pre-eminent. The minute biblical subjects engraved on these bindings were appropriate for prayer books or the GIRDLE-BOOKS carried by ladies suspended by a chain from their girdles, but not for the big Missals used in Catholic churches. In Flanders and Italy a fashion arose for bindings coarsely embossed with figures of saints and florid BAROQUE scrollwork; and in the course of the 17th c. the taste for embossed book covers spread northwards, ousting the engraved covers even for small devotional works. During the 18th c. the finest bindings were produced in the south German cities of Augsburg and Nuremberg, where the art of embossing had been brought to the highest level by a number of goldsmith families (Telot, Biller, etc.). An individual type of silver book cover, made up of cast and pierced panels, was produced in Zürich, and the Venetian ambassadors or emissaries to foreign governments received their official instructions in pompously designed silver covers made by Venetian goldsmiths.

Gold and cloisonné enamel Gospel cover showing the Archangel Gabriel. (Treasury of St. Mark's Cathedral, Venice, 11th c.)

BOOK ILLUSTRATION. I. THE WOODCUT PERIOD, 15TH AND 16TH CENTURIES. Though the woodcut was known before the invention of printing with movable types, the early printer was slow to make use of it for book illustration. It was to the illuminator that he looked for decoration and illustration and the early printed book had great affinity with the illuminated manuscript. Margins, borders and title-pages were left blank for later illumination by hand as had been done in the manuscripts. The first books illustrated with woodcuts were printed at Bamberg by Albrecht Pfister from 1460 onwards. About 1470 Augsburg printers, notably Erhard Ratdolt, began to imitate in wood the elaborate borders of the illuminators, gradually extending them to surround the first page of text, which thereby became a title-page. During the latter part of the 15th c. illustrated book production spread throughout Germany, the chief centres being Augsburg, Ulm and Nuremberg, with Basle in Switzerland. The most famous books are the *Schatzbehalter* (Nuremberg, 1491) with about 100 illustrations, mostly of scriptural subjects; Hartmann Schedel's *Weltchronik* (called the Nuremberg Chronicle, 1493), a monumental undertaking with 645 separate woodcuts and 1,809 printed illustrations; Bernhard von Breydenbach's *Sanctae Peregrinationes* (1486); and an early topographical book with illustrations and maps by Erhard Reuwich. During the 16th c. Germany produced the famous series of illustrated books commissioned by the Emperor Maximilian called *Theuerdanck*.

The first Italian woodcut illustrations were crude line drawings in Turrecremata's *Meditationes* (Rome, 1467). Other notable Italian books are Valturius's *De Re Militari* (Verona, 1472) illustrated by Matteo dei Pasti, Aesop's *Fables* (Verona, 1479), the Venetian editions of classical authors, the Mallermi Bible (1490 and 1493), and the *Hypnerotomachia* (1499). The artistic perfection of the best woodcuts in Florentine books of the 15th c.—some attributed to pupils of Botticelli and Ghirlandaio and characterized by decorative borders—has rarely again been achieved. The *Savonarola* tracts and the *Rappresentazione* (1550–80), a popular series of miracle-plays, are typical. In the early 16th c. the chiaroscuro process, imported from Germany, was used in some Italian illustrated books.

In France early printed books, resembling Italian more than German work, had to compete with a fine tradition of manuscript books. The influence of the illuminator was especially noticeable in the innumerable editions of the *Horae*, or Books of Hours, printed until the middle of the 16th c. Every page is surrounded by an elaborate border generally made up of small pictures enclosed by intertwining foliage or other decorative framework. Some of the best of these books of private prayers were printed at Paris by Pigouchet. Lyon produced the *Mirourer de la rédemption* (1478), the earliest book with woodcuts, Terence's *Commoediae* (1493), and *La Grant Danse macabre* (1500). Toulouse, Abbeville and Rouen also produced illustrated books. Jean Du Pré produced the first illustrated book printed in Paris (1481), a missal, and also Boccaccio's *Les Cas et ruynes des nobles hommes et femmes* (1484). In the early 16th c., *manière criblée* was used in France as well as woodcut. Secular subjects (country and farming scenes) began to appear. The Gothic Book of Hours with its Germanic woodcuts and BLACK LETTER gave place to the new Renaissance form with classical motifs and ROMAN type.

In England woodcut illustration did not appear in any book until CAXTON used crude cuts in *Mirrour of the world* (*c.* 1481). Wynkyn de Worde, Caxton's successor, was more interested in illustration (his *Destruction of Jerusalem* has woodcut flower borders) and imported blocks from the Continent. None of the early illustrated books was of marked artistic merit and in none is observed the emergence of a characteristic national style. From 1521 onwards bordered title-pages became increasingly common in English books, though illustrations were not freely used. Foxe's *Book of Martyrs* (1563) was one of the most popular illustrated books of the time and John Day, who printed it, also brought out *A Book of Christian Prayers* (called Queen Elizabeth's Prayer-Book). It has a pictorial border to each page after the manner of the French *Horae* and is a curious revival.

During the 1st half of the 16th c. much fine woodcut book illustration was produced, notably by such important artists as Dürer, Burgkmair and Cranach. Theodore de Bry brought out his series of illustrated travel books; Holbein designed book decorations in the form of initial letters and borders characteristic of 16th-c. title-pages. There was little nationalism in printing. German printers worked in Italy, Caxton in the Netherlands; Latin was the universal language and pictures speak the same tongue everywhere so that the blocks could be freely interchanged between countries.

Though copper engraving was known, it was not generally used owing to the early printer's inability to overcome the technical difficulty of combining relief (letterpress) with intaglio (engraving) in one printing operation. Notable early attempts at engraved illustration are Caxton's *Recuyell of the Historyes of Troy* (1474–6), Ptolemy's *Cosmographia* (Bologna, 1477) and Bettini's *Monte Sancto di Dio* (Florence, 1477). The experience of 15th-c. printers with engraved illustrations began and ended in frustration and disappointment. But by the middle of the 16th c. the art of metal engraving began to assert itself. Copperplate engraving, which appealed to the artist-engraver as a more sympathetic vehicle for rendering half-tones and shadow, displaced the woodcut, which then practically disappeared for the next 200 years. Christopher PLANTIN, the last 16th-c. French printer of importance, helped to set a fashion of confining illustration to the title-page, a fashion which continued throughout the 17th and 18th centuries in France and elsewhere.

2. ENGRAVED ILLUSTRATION, 17TH CENTURY. During the 17th c., Italy and Germany lost their importance as centres of illustrated book production, but in the Netherlands Rubens designed title-pages and illustrations, training an influential group of engravers to translate his drawings into prints for book decoration. The De Passe family played an important role, particularly Crispin de Passe who designed the plates for Pluvinel's *Manège royal* (1623). The advent of copper-engraving resulted in a loss of the homogeneity between text and illustrations which is found in the woodcut books. Books were now 'adorn'd' rather than illustrated, with engravings printed on separate sheets of a finer paper than that used for the text and inserted between the leaves of the book or together at the end of the volume. The 17th c. was a 'scientific age' both generally and in book illustration. The artist was called upon to illustrate travel books, text-books on mathematics, astronomy, military strategy, fencing, gardening, etc. In France, where the majority of great book illustration was done, two traditions prevailed: the official classicist style of the Académie and the bizarre, visionary style of Callot (1592–1635). Emphasis was laid on the composition of the frontispiece (often an engraved portrait of the author) and ornamental title-page, sometimes allegorical but frequently in an architectural style with the title engraved on a pedestal or column or in a portico. The leading book illustrators were Leonard Gaultier and Claude Mellan. Mellan studied under Poussin and interpreted his designs for the *Virgil* (1641) and the Louvre Bible (1642). Philosophical systems were expounded in images and allegories, and mythology was much used. The depicting of great occasions and spectacles was developed, some of the best work being for theatre illustration and pomps. This was of two kinds: the 'official' or fêtes, entrées and receptions of the king, and the fantasies of the theatre showing costumes and stage machinery. This era also saw the rise of the periodical press. The early papers were usually called gazettes, the *Gazette de France* receiving the royal privilege in 1663.

3. ENGRAVED ILLUSTRATION, THE 18TH CENTURY. In 18th-c. France engraved illustration reached a high degree of taste and a technical virtuosity which has not been surpassed. The typical French illustrated book of this period is distinguished from its 17th-c. predecessor by the many pages decorated with vignettes and the frequently subordinate text which, serving much the same purpose as an opera libretto, was only a pretext for the artist to exercise his talents. Illustration became freer and more piquant, the plates for the many illustrated novels aspiring to a slightly erotic charm. Sometimes two sets of illustrations were provided, one decent and one indecent without descending to the pornographic. The period 1700–50, characterized by the absence of professional book illustrators, produced two masterpieces: Molière's *Œuvres* (1734) with illustrations designed by BOUCHER and offering a splendid panorama of Louis XV costumes, and *Fables de La Fontaine* (1755), for which OUDRY's 276 designs were done *c.* 1730. They were originally designed for BEAUVAIS tapestry and were adapted for book illustrations by Charles-Nicolas Cochin (1715–90). The period 1750–74 may be called the golden age of the great book illustrators—Cochin, Gravelot, Moreau-le-Jeune and others. Their many fine productions include Boccaccio's *Decameron* (1757), Ovid's *Metamorphoses* (1767) and the Fermiers Généraux edition of La Fontaine's *Fables* (1762). To the period of brilliant decline (1774–1800) belong works illustrated by Marillier and Prud'hon. Other important French illustrated books were the *Voyages pittoresques*, the gallery and sale catalogues with engraved plates and the *Almanachs*, of which Quevedo was the chief designer of decorations. These survived the Revolution to appear as the 'Keepsakes' of the first half of the 19th c.

4. THE MODERN PERIOD, 19TH AND 20TH CENTURIES. In France the Romantic and ornate school of engraving was ended by the Revolution. The next flash of genius is found in England in William Blake. His imaginative engravings for Young's *Night Thoughts* (1797) and the *Book of Job* (1825) are among his best work. He also illustrated Milton and Dante. Magnificent book illustrations were done by Turner for Rogers's *Italy* (1830) and Scott's *Prose Works* (1834–6). The Industrial Revolution produced a new reading public and a demand for larger editions than the expensive steel engraving process could provide. This process was replaced by wood engraving and lithography, which could withstand large printings. It became fashionable to collect engraved reproductions of paintings and drawings into book form, with or without text. Josi's *Collection d'imitations de dessins* and Bartolozzi's 81 plates for *Imitations of Original Drawings by Hans Holbein* are examples. The next step was the publication by contemporary artists of their own work; examples are Turner's *Liber Studiorum* and David Cox's coloured aquatints. The spate of books on topography and sport resulted in a transformation of ordinary commercial book illustration, aquatint becoming more popular than line engraving. Plates were hand-coloured and an enormous labour went into the books of tours (forerunners of today's *Baedekers*) issued by the Revd. Wm. Gilpin and Ackermann. Rowlandson worked for Ackermann and satirized Gilpin in his *Tours of Dr. Syntax*. In the 'Keepsakes' and *Almanachs* of the early 19th c. the picture is the *raison d'être* and the text (written afterwards) was the illustration, as in *The Book of Beauty* (1837). Great advances in colour printing were made and

George Baxter patented his new process in 1835. The rise of the illustrated magazines (*Punch* and the *Illustrated London News*) in the 1840s led to a steady debasement of wood engraving by hacks working to meet the enormous demand for illustrations. The Dalziel brothers' renderings in wood of the designs of Sir John Gilbert and Birket Foster were popular with mid-Victorians and the Tenniel illustrations for *Alice in Wonderland* are familiar to us today. Book illustration was, nevertheless, at a low ebb until the 1860s. Except for the illustrated children's books by CRANE, Randolph Caldecott and Kate Greenaway, the decade 1875–85 has been aptly called 'a no-man's land between woodcut and process'. The *English Illustrated Magazine* (1883) attempted to revive wood engraving and good work appeared in its earlier volumes.

Though no other country equalled England's output of illustrated books at this time, interesting work was done abroad, notably in France. Delacroix, an early exponent of lithography, illustrated Goethe's *Faust* (1827). Daumier, Gavarni and Doré were outstanding figures. Manet illustrated Edgar Allan Poe's *Poems* (1889) and Toulouse-Lautrec illustrated Renard's *Histoires naturelles* (1889).

William Morris's KELMSCOTT PRESS books with their medieval decorated woodcuts, the illustrated books from Lucien Pissarro's Eragny Press, and Charles RICKETTS's VALE PRESS were a protest against the prevailing vulgarity and the tyranny of the machine as well as a plea for integrity in taste and the nobility of craftsmanship. Notable book illustrators include Beardsley, who illustrated several works of Oscar Wilde in *The Yellow Book*; Arthur Rackham, who illustrated many presentation editions with three-colour work; Eric Gill; and Robert Gibbings.

In the 20th c. complete acceptance of the machine and the willing adoption of all that photography could contribute, along with a desire to teach the machine how to behave, inspired artists to design for the new processes and to experiment in many directions. Today more great artists have devoted themselves to the enrichment of literature than in any other period since the Middle Ages.

BOOK JACKETS. A book jacket, in the 3rd quarter of the 20th c., means a paper wrapper round a book with a design printed on the front and spine (and occasionally on the back as well) intended to identify and sell the book in competition with other books displayed for sale. It is a kind of packaging. From the point of view of the designer there is hardly any difference between designing a jacket and designing the cover of a paperback, since both are printed on paper; so as far as design is concerned what is said in this article about jackets will generally apply also to paperback covers.

The history of the book jacket is the history of book covering in paper. Books have been covered, and no doubt sold, in paper ever since paper was first used for books; but the book jacket proper emerged during the 19th c. step by step with the mechanization of printing and the development of publishing and bookselling as we recognize them today. A paper by G. Thomas Tanselle, 'Book-Jackets, Blurbs, and Bibliographers', read before The Bibliographical Society in London in 1970 and published with illustrations in *The Library*, 5th Ser., Vol. xxvi, No. 2, June 1971, lists and describes the earliest surviving actual book jackets, as far as they were known to the author when he wrote. The 'earliest known printed detachable paper covering for a book' (illustrated by a photograph) is for *The Keepsake*, published by Longmans in 1832; it is plainly typographical, within a border. The author notes that before this date, during the 1820s, several of the annuals (e.g. *The Forget Me Not* and *The Amulet*) were issued in four- or five-sided cardboard boxes with highly decorative printed paper sides. Some of these were even hand-coloured, e.g. *Friendships Offering* for 1825—this was a few years before the use of colour printing as a commercial process—and these detachable boxes are more direct precursors of the modern book jacket, because they were decoratively designed, than the bleak-looking detachable jackets that occur sporadically until the 1880s, when they came to be used more commonly by publishers. The first jacket bearing an illustration, shown by Mr. Tanselle, is for *The Vagabonds*, published by Lee and Shepard in Boston, Mass., in 1882; but the 'yellow back' style of binding, a picture printed in colours on yellow paper on boards, the exact counterpart of modern pictorial book jackets, was in use from the 1850s and flourished throughout the century. These were themselves preceded by highly decorative abstract designs, printed in colours and often very beautiful, used on both adult and children's books, bound in paper on boards, from at least the 1840s. That ornamental designs (which bore no relation to the contents of the book) preceded illustration on book covers is probably because the bookbinders were at first carrying on the tradition of tooling in gold on leather when they began to use cloth and paper for covering books.

Detachable jackets became more and more a normal part of a book during the 1890s. Mr. Tanselle makes the important point: 'most illustrated jackets of the nineties, however, merely repeat the binding, and the idea of producing a design specifically for a jacket was practically unknown before the turn of the century'. The word 'blurb', incidentally, describing the text on a jacket specially written to promote the book, seems to have been invented by the American humourist Gelett Burgess in 1907.

Designs apparently made specifically for book jackets by Peter BEHRENS and Toulouse-Lautrec before 1900 are illustrated in Kurt Weidemann's *Book Jackets and Record Sleeves* (1969); Aubrey Beardsley designed magazine and book covers, e.g. for *The Yellow Book* (1894), but does not seem to have designed a book jacket. After that, it became a normal activity for any artist to design book jackets and a temptation, not always resisted, to design a jacket which advertised himself rather than the book. But any artist of originality will produce work that proclaims itself to be by him and no other: it is his individuality that makes his work distinctive. This does not mean that a book jacket by such an artist will not do its job. It will proclaim its originator, certainly, to the few who recognize such things; but first and foremost, to the general public, or such of it as have eyes for these things, it will make the book stand out from the other books on the shelves, which is its function. That the visual character of the jacket should be in harmony with the literary character of the text, if this is possible (or that it should at the very least not clash with it), is the responsibility of the person choosing the designer, and is itself a creative function. Perhaps a more feasible aim is to try to design a jacket that will appeal to the sort of people most likely to buy the book.

The 'modern movement' in TYPOGRAPHY and design, which started chiefly in Germany in the 1920s, was reflected in book jackets by Theo van Doesburg, El Lissitzky, Jan Tschichold, L. MOHOLY-NAGY and John Heartfield, the two latter exploring new graphic uses of photography. This movement had little influence at the time in England. A break with tradition in book jacket design in England did occur when Stanley MORISON, then a director of the publishing firm of Victor Gollancz, introduced in 1929 his typographical jackets on yellow paper. It may have been the first time that a designer ever sat down, considered the specific problems of book jacket design and production in the then existing book trade, and produced a completely new idea. Morison decided that the potential buyer must be startled; but, better than that, he must be induced to start reading *on the jacket*, turn over to the flap, and then into the book itself. Morison made strident use of the newly designed Gill Sans type, various new bold faces imported from Germany, underlining with bold rules, black, red and magenta ink, and a special bright yellow paper—all in brutal contrast to the classical harmony and restraint of his typography inside the books themselves. The jackets, then revolutionary, were also successful, and a setback for those who at the time maintained that books could be sold only by pictorial jackets.

Morison's jackets not only sold individual books, they created a 'house style' which made Gollancz's books (falling usually into the two categories of best-selling fiction and left-wing politics) instantly recognizable. Two other publishers in that period also used a single artist to design a high proportion of their book jackets and thus create a house style: in New York, from 1926 or so, Alfred A. Knopf used W. A. DWIGGINS to design whole books, including jackets; and from the mid 1930s Jonathan Cape in London used Hans Tisdall. Both Dwiggins and Tisdall were a rare combination of artist and designer, and both were creative in the field of lettering (Tisdall had been a pupil of Anna Simons, the German pupil of Edward Johnston). Both produced jackets based on original lettering, with decoration or illustration from their own hands, which are among the finest examples of graphic art in the 20th c.

Of the other jackets produced in Britain in the 1st half of the century those most deserving of being called works of art in their own right were the autolithographic jackets of Barnett Freedman, usually for Faber & Faber but also for Cassell, Collins, John Murray and others; the strongly linear and witty designs of Edward Bawden, who as well as using autolithography cut many of his designs on linoleum; and the jackets of Rex Whistler, who did not design for any process but produced drawings or paintings for photographic reproduction which achieved an unsurpassed gaiety and elegance. Collectors of this period will also look for distinguished designs on jackets by John Piper, Lynton Lamb, Duncan Grant, Kenneth Rowntree, Graham Sutherland, Feliks Topolski, John Minton and Ronald Searle. Jackets by these artists were, basically, illustrative and drawn by the artists themselves. Stanley Morison's jackets represented another kind of design, which depended not on drawing but on the assembling of typographic material and in later hands perhaps the addition of visual material from the book. In the purely typographic style of jacket design those produced by the Curwen Press in London, under the direction of Oliver Simon from the 1930s until his death in 1956, are a notable artistic achievement. They were mostly designed for serious works of non-fiction which could not expect large sales, but some are so beautiful as to justify buying the book purely for the jacket.

Following more closely in Morison's tradition of hard-hitting salesmanship were the jackets designed by Robert Harling, who, having assimilated Morison's formula, was one of the first to see the eye-catching potential of 19th-c. poster types and whose jackets for Heinemann, Cobden-Sanderson, Constable and others before the war, and Peter Lunn and John Westhouse, Art & Technics and others after the war, were both commercially successful and aesthetically pleasing. They were also capable of being composed quickly—even in seconds—by a designer with vision and flair: in other words, they were a rational part of a production programme.

In the field of artist-designed jackets mention must be made of the 'New Naturalist' jackets designed by Clifford and Rosemary Ellis. This series of books was started by Collins in London shortly after the Second World War and new titles are still appearing. The Ellises have designed all the jackets—over eighty of them to date—and many connoisseurs would say that they are among the most satisfying designs of the whole period. It is an astonishing achievement to originate a style of jacket design which has continued to be valid for nearly a quarter of a century.

In the United States the two most gifted designers who made a major contribution to book jacket design in the mid-century were Alvin Lustig (1915–55) and Paul Rand (1916–); but the enormous financial rewards of the American advertising industry tended to take the most gifted designers away from the much less highly paid world of books. Genius returned to American book design, however, when Milton Glaser and Seymour Chwast graduated from Cooper Union Art School. The later Push Pin Studios, of which no member was born before 1929, was given the distinction of an exhibition in the Louvre in 1970, of which Henry Wolf wrote at the time: 'Push Pin is a Renaissance phenomenon coming home, for a time, to a Renaissance Palace.' Push Pin work may or may not be instantly recognizable; but if it is, it is because it is outstandingly brilliant, graphic and witty: it is an extraordinary phenomenon of a group of artists (twenty are shown in the photograph in *The Push Pin Style*, 1970) who have succeeded in establishing a style and imposing a high level of aesthetic performance on a sordidly commercial world without sacrificing a jot of individualism. In England today no comparable single group of artists engaged in book jacket and cover design exists, perhaps partly because there is not a comparable market for such designs (fees in New York for book jackets and cover designs are perhaps from four to at least twenty times greater than in London). But the standard of British book cover design is high. Penguin paperback covers are exceptionally good and worth watching as an index of contemporary taste, for designs are changed frequently and every trend is reflected. The most distinctive personal style is that of Alan Aldridge, witty, vulgar, voluptuous and highly visual.

Jackets using still photographs from films are usually boring, but a recent fashion has been the specially composed studio photograph, most often on the themes of sex or murder: these were often beautiful, highly dramatic and sensational at first, but became so frequent as to lack all novelty.

What sort of design does sell what kind of book? One answer is 'a kind that is not being used by one's competitors'. Another answer is 'any kind, provided it is distinguished'. Certainly a wealth of talent is being poured into the design of book covers today—more into the design of paperback covers than into detachable jackets, because they are produced in greater quantities, higher fees are paid for them, and a talented designer would rather design for the production run of tens of thousands of a paperback than the few thousand of the normal hard-back. A good selection of the best work of the 1960s in ten countries can be seen in Kurt Weidemann's *Book Jackets and Record Sleeves* (where they are shown reduced, in monochrome only, on shiny paper). But of course they can also be studied in the illustrated catalogues of various countries' annual book design competitions, of which those published by the American Institute of Graphic Arts are outstanding. Posters used to be called 'the poor man's art gallery', but since posters became almost exclusively photographic and boring it is perhaps book jackets and especially paperback covers that now fulfil this function: they are certainly among the most pleasing man-made articles to be seen in the world today.

BOOK LABELS. See BOOK-PLATES.

BOOK-PAPERS, DECORATED (German: Buntpapiere). Any type of decorated paper used in BOOKBINDING, either as a covering or as end-papers (see also MARBLING). Pattern papers, printed from wood blocks or stencils, became popular in Europe during the second half of the 17th c.; some of the finest, characterized by great variety and freedom of design, were produced in Italy by the Rizzi and Remondini families. Gilded paper with floral designs, known as 'Dutch floral' paper but actually south German, was widely used in the 18th c. A revival of interest in coloured papers accompanied the ART NOUVEAU movement in Germany at the end of the 19th c. In England interest in decorative and pictorial book-papers has been fostered in the 20th c. by PRIVATE PRESSES; the designs of Lucien Pissarro, RICKETTS, Walter CRANE and Lovat Fraser have been acclaimed. See also PAPERS, DECORATIVE.

537, 538.

BOOK-PLATES. The term 'book-plate' is applied to a label, usually pasted inside the front cover of a book, carrying the name or armorial bearings of the owner, or any other device indicating ownership, and sometimes the location of the book within a library. *Ex libris*, though not strictly confined to the movable label, is the most universally accepted equivalent in the non-English-speaking world, whilst in English it has come to be regarded as synonymous. In German the expression *Bibliothekzeichen* is also used. Some English writers prefer to reserve the term 'book-plate' to those labels which incorporate a pictorial element, using the word 'book label' for those of a purely inscriptional character.

Book-plates, which were first used in Germany towards the end of the 15th c., clearly developed from the ownership marks and inscriptions of earlier times. It is noticeable that in those countries where during the 16th c. wealthy bibliophiles preferred to use distinctive individual binding styles or armorial stamps in the form of *super libros* as indications of ownership, book-plates are not found until much later. Although several book-plates are to be found in most other European countries dating from the 2nd half of the 16th c., they cannot be said to have become common outside Germany until the early years of the 17th c. In England from the time of the Restoration until the present century book-plates were used almost universally by people having any pretensions whatsoever towards owning a library, and in North America they have been common since Colonial times.

Since book-plates originated and were intended as marks of ownership they retrospectively become of major bibliographical importance in establishing the provenance, or the pedigree of previous ownership, of any volume containing them. Of course by their nature they are removable and replaceable, and any such inquiry should proceed with the utmost caution. Nevertheless it is likely that much more damage has been done to the study of provenance by the wholesale removal of book-plates from the volumes to which they belong, for the benefit of collectors of these items, than by unscrupulous tampering with book-plate evidence undertaken to deceive the unwary collector.

An interest in book-plates as objects in themselves developed at about the same time in England and France during the mid 19th c. Poulet-Malassis's *Les Ex-libris français, depuis leur origine jusqu'à nos jours* appeared in 1875, to be followed in 1880 by *A Guide to the Study of Book-plates* by the Hon. J. Leicester Warren, later Lord de Tabley. Warren's *Guide* gave an enormous impetus to the collecting and study of book-plates. It not only provided carefully compiled lists of English and foreign book-plate engravers, but in the classification of styles in design, as can be seen from many surviving collections, it supplied a generation with a basis and a method of arrangement on which to build their collections. Warren's categories, such as Early Armorial, Jacobean, Chippendale and Festoon, have survived to this day as a generally accepted descriptive terminology.

By the end of the 19th c. most countries had their *ex libris* societies, which often issued their own journals and exchange lists. Moreover the habit grew up, particularly in the non-English-speaking countries, of producing book-plates merely for the purpose of supplying this exchange market, the original intention apparently having been forgotten in the general enthusiasm for collecting. This practice has never been wholly absent from foreign collecting, and as recently as the 1960s an Italian collector was reported as having in the region of 600 differently designed book-plates bearing his name. However, it was during the 'golden age' of book-plate collecting, from the publication of Warren's *Guide* in 1880 until the First World War, that the serious collectors provided many of what still remain standard works on the history of book-plates in various countries. More recent studies have tended towards presenting collections of book-plates designed by individual, and usually contemporary or recently deceased, artists.

Since the 16th c. and the examples by artists such as Joost AMMAN, Lucas Cranach, Albrecht Dürer and Hans Holbein, book-plates have provided many important artists with a medium in which to display their ability in relatively miniature design, and many lesser artists with regular commissions. Thus the collecting of book-plates designed by individual artists has always been popular and is often instructive. Among 18th-c. English book-plates many examples can be identified as the work of such masters as Bartolozzi, Bewick, Bickham, Cipriani, Gravelot, Hogarth, Pine and Vertue. The 2nd half of the 19th c. produced many designs by artists already involved in book work through their illustrations—J. D. Batten, R. Anning Bell, Randolph Caldecott, Walter CRANE, Kate Greenaway, James Guthrie, John Leighton, E. H. New, Charles RICKETTS and Gleeson White. The same trend continued in the 20th c. in the work of artists such as John Buckland-Wright, Robert Gibbings, Eric Gill, Stephen Gooden, Joan Hassall and Rex Whistler. In the 1960s there was a vogue for the inscriptional label, both typographic and calligraphic, perhaps best seen in the examples by Will Carter and Reynolds Stone. Leonard Baskin, the GRABHORNS, Rockwell Kent, Bruce ROGERS and D. B. UPDIKE are among the many fine American book designers and typographers producing book-plates in this century.

From the example of Hildebrand Brandenburg (*c.* 1470), until the middle of the 19th c. the majority of European book-plates, and a surprisingly large number of American ones, were heraldic in character. It is the student of family history and heraldry, therefore, who often has the most to gain from the study of book-plates; and conversely a certain amount of genealogical and heraldic expertise is necessary in dealing with any large collection owing to the large number of book-plates that carry nothing beyond the heraldic blazon. Even in the field of English book-plates such a large amount of material needs sub-dividing for the purpose of fruitful study, and the groupings adopted by Egerton Castle are possibly the most useful.

Group I. Early Armorial.
- *Style 1.* Tudoresque—covering the 16th and early 17th centuries.
- *Style 2.* Carolian—covering from *c.* 1625 to the Restoration.
- *Style 3.* Restoration—covering from the Restoration to the Hanoverian Succession.

Group II. Georgian.
- *Style 1.* Early (Warren's 'Jacobean', sometimes termed 'Grinling Gibbons').
- *Style 2.* Middle (Warren's 'Chippendale', sometimes termed 'Rococo').
- *Style 3.* Late (Warren's 'Festoon', sometimes termed 'Urn', 'Wreath and Ribbon' and 'Adams').

Group III. Modern Armorial.

This group covers the heraldic book-plates of the 19th c., which may be sub-divided by reference to the shield forms.

The possibilities of purely pictorial book-plate design are limitless; piles of books, library interiors, portraits, landscapes, seals, printers' marks, emblems, allegories and the erotic have all been regularly recurring themes throughout the history of these labels.

As mentioned earlier, many of the best works on book-plates date from the end of the 19th c. Particularly notable was the series published by George Bell, and edited by Gleeson White, all of which were very well illustrated and contained good listings and bibliographies. They included E. Castle, *English Book-plates*, 1893; C. D. Allen, *American Book-plates*, 1895; W. Hamilton, *French Book-plates*, 1893 and 1896; K. Emich, Count zu Leiningen-Westerburg, *German Book-plates*, 1901; and N. Labouchère. *Ladies' Book-plates*, 1895. The fullest listing of British and American book-plates remains E. R. J. Gambier Howe, *Catalogue of British and American Book Plates bequeathed to the Trustees of the British Museum by Sir Augustus Wollaston Franks*, 3 vols., 1903–4. Since the Franks Bequest the British Museum has acquired yet another very fine collection made by the late G. H. Viner, one of the more recent authorities on this subject, whose writings can profitably be consulted.

BOOK PRODUCTION. See BOOKBINDING; BOOK COVERS; BOOK ILLUSTRATION; BOOK JACKETS; BOOK-PAPERS, DECORATED; BOOK-PLATES; DIAGRAMS; FORE-EDGE PAINTING; PAPERS, DECORATIVE; PRINTERS' MARKS; PRIVATE PRESS MOVEMENT; TYPOGRAPHY; VELLUM AND PARCHMENT

226, 254, 302, 498, 517, 526, 561, 563, 626, 848, 855, 865.

BOSCOREALE. A village on the slopes of Mt. Vesuvius near Pompeii. Several country villas have been found there which were buried in the eruption of A.D. 79. The most famous of them, discovered in 1895, contained a treasure of over 100 pieces of silver plate, now in the Louvre, dating from the early Roman Empire and known as the Boscoreale Treasure.

BOSTON AND SANDWICH GLASS COMPANY. Although the Boston and Sandwich Glass Company was to become one of the largest and most important glass-houses of the 19th c., it opened on 4 July 1825 to an unfavourable beginning. Deming Jarves (1790–1869) founded the firm as the Sandwich Manufactory and had chosen the town of Sandwich on Cape Cod, Massachusetts, owing to its proximity to an inexhaustible supply of the sand required for the production of fine lead glass. But it was soon discovered that this local sand created a peculiar yellow hue in the glass. Since the Sandwich sand was unsatisfactory for manufacturing purposes, sand had to be imported from the Berkshire mountain range in western Massachusetts. In spite of this inauspicious opening the factory began to flourish, and the shrewd Jarves decided to expand. To do this he took in partners from Boston, and the original name was expanded to 'The Boston and Sandwich Glass Company'. Since Jarves had also been among the founders of THE NEW ENGLAND GLASS COMPANY in East Cambridge, it was inevitable that the production of the two houses should overlap. In fact while remaining competitors until 1888, both frequently had board members and distributing agents in common. The New England company also produced mould-blown and pressed glass, but the Sandwich company early assumed the lead in this production. So firmly associated with pressed lacy glass did the firm become that until recently all of these wares were frequently referred to by the generic term 'Sandwich glass'. It is now known that The New England Glass Company as well as the Bakewell firm of Pittsburgh, Pennsylvania, among others, also produced fine wares of this type.

The Boston and Sandwich Glass Company excelled in its coloured products and was as renowned for overlay cut wares as for engraved products. The factory produced a great variety of conventionally pressed 'pattern' glass, mercury glass and overshot types.

Among the notable men in American glass history who were associated with the company were Hiram Dillaway, the expert mould maker responsible for the handsome Sandwich patterns, and James Lloyd, the superb colourist of the firm. Mention should also be made of Mary Gregory in the decorating department, who became famous for figures of children in the Kate Greenaway style executed in white enamel on coloured glass, and of Nicholas Lutz, a famous blower who frequently made glass in elaborate threaded and other Venetian styles.

Like its rival in East Cambridge, the Boston and Sandwich Glass Company refused to lower the quality of its metal after the discovery of a new and cheaper soda-lime recipe in 1864 but continued the production of fine lead glass. Inevitably the result was a diminution of profits. In the face of threats of a strike for higher wages the factory closed in 1888. Various attempts were made to reopen the plant, but all failed after a short time. The most notable attempt was that of the Alton Manufacturing Company, which reopened the factory in 1907 and made a handsome glass in the ART NOUVEAU style. This was called 'Trevaise' and was an imitation of the glass of L. C. TIFFANY. It is today frequently sold as the product of the more famous maker. The Alton Manufacturing Company wound up in 1908, and the factory never reopened.

Nevertheless, before its closing in 1888 The Boston and Sandwich Glass Company was one of the giants in American glass-making and it produced some of the most important wares made in the country during the 19th c.

See GLASS (AMERICA).

BOSTON ROCKER. See ROCKING-CHAIR.

BÖTTGER, JOHANN FRIEDRICH (d.

1719). German alchemist who discovered the secret of true, hard-paste porcelain at MEISSEN in 1708–9. See CERAMICS; PORCELAIN.

BOUCHER, FRANÇOIS (1703–70). French painter in the ROCOCO style who best embodies the elegant superficiality of French life at the middle of the 18th c. He was described by de Goncourt as 'one of those men who typify the taste of a century, who express it, personify it, and incarnate it'. More than any other one man he was responsible for setting a fashion in interior decoration. From 1734 he supplied designs for the TAPESTRY hangings and furniture coverings manufactured at BEAUVAIS and his designs were also used at AUBUSSON. In 1755 he was appointed Director of the GOBELINS factory. Boucher mastered every branch of decorative and illustrative painting from colossal schemes of decoration for the royal châteaux of Versailles, Fontainebleau, Marly and Bellevue to stage settings for opera and designs for fans and slippers. He took in his stride the contemporary fashion for CHINOISERIES, making *tentures chinoises* for Beauvais tapestries in the late 1720s and the sets for Jean-Georges Noverre's ballet *Les Fêtes chinoises* in 1754. In his most characteristic paintings he turned the traditional mythological themes into wittily indecorous *scènes galantes* and his designs for the decorative arts were in a similar style. As a decorator he had a rich and varied talent, brilliance of execution and a light-hearted voluptuousness which suited the mood of his time, though it brought upon his head the execration of Diderot after French taste began to change in 1760.

BOULLE, ANDRÉ-CHARLES (1642–1732). The most celebrated French cabinet-maker working in the style of Louis XIV. Born in Paris of Swiss origin, he set up as a cabinet-maker in 1664. His ability was recognized by the king's adviser, Jean-Baptiste Colbert (1619–83), and he was given lodgings and workshops in the Louvre, where he made furniture for the king and nobility, receiving the title *premier ébéniste du roi*. Despite his very large earnings he was constantly in financial straits in consequence of his passion for collecting works of art and in 1720 he was ruined by a fire which destroyed his workshops, his stock and his collections. He nevertheless continued in business until the age of 82, when he was succeeded by four of his sons, JEAN-PHILIPPE (1680–1744), PIERRE-BENOIT (*c.* 1682–1741), ANDRÉ-CHARLES (1685–1745) and CHARLES-JOSEPH (1688–1754), who continued the business until the middle of the century.

Boulle was a talented craftsman in both wood and metal and a versatile designer. He collaborated closely with the designer Jean BÉRAIN, using decorative motifs based on classical antiquity combined with the insignia of the monarchy, allegorical emblems and GROTESQUES. He brought to perfection the then fashionable style of MARQUETRY in TORTOISESHELL, PEWTER and BRASS, using gilt bronze MOUNTS on an ebony ground. He was also a virtuoso of the elaborate marquetry in variously coloured woods which culminated in the 18th c.

Boulle's reputation was so high that his name has been given internationally (Boulle or Buhl) to the type of furniture in which his workshops specialized. His influence was felt in Germany through such craftsmen as H. D. Sommer, who worked in Künzelsau *c.* 1666–84 and specialized in fine inlays of tortoiseshell and MOTHER OF PEARL set in a pewter frame, Joseph Effner (1687–1768), a pupil of Boffrand, who worked at Schloss Schleissheim (1701–19), and the designs of François CUVILLIÈS.

354.

BOULSOVER, THOMAS (1704–88). A Sheffield cutler who *c.* 1742 invented the process of plating by fusing silver upon copper, which prepared the way for SHEFFIELD PLATE. After this discovery he began by manufacturing small articles such as buttons and SNUFF-BOXES, but it was a distant relative, Joseph HANCOCK, who was mainly responsible for exploiting the process commercially and by 1770 Boulsover was engaged in rolling plated copper for the industry. He later made improvements in the manufacture of saws.

BOULTON, MATTHEW (1728–1809). Industrialist who began as a Birmingham 'toy-maker' (manufacturer of small metal objects, étuis, SNUFF-BOXES, buckles, etc.). Later he combined the functions of manufacturer and merchant. In 1761 he established the firm of Boulton and Fothergill, which gradually extended its manufactures to include cut steel buckles and jewellery, CHATELAINES, etc., SHEFFIELD PLATE, silver and ORMOLU. He was the only manufacturer of ormolu in England and achieved a quality rivalling that of Parisian work. He turned out large numbers of mantelpiece garnitures of Derbyshire spar mounted with ormolu. As Joseph HANCOCK was mainly responsible for exploiting the commercial possibilities of Thomas BOULSOVER's discovery of Sheffield plating (see SHEFFIELD PLATE), Boulton developed the industry in Birmingham, where he obtained a monopoly for its manufacture and in his 'Soho' Manufactory there he produced articles of exceptional excellence. The Hon. Mrs. Montagu wrote to him as follows: 'I take greater pleasure in our victories over the French in the contention of arts than in arms; the achievements of Soho, instead of making orphans, make marriages and christenings. Your noble industry while elevating the public taste, provides new occupations for the poor, and enables them to bring their families up in comfort.' The ADAM brothers supplied designs for both his ormolu and his Sheffield plate, and the pattern books of his Birmingham factory are still preserved in the Birmingham public library. Boulton himself, an entrepreneur rather than an artist, showed great acumen in employing good designers, but his personal influence on design was probably slight. Much of his time was devoted to exploiting the possibilities of the newly invented steam-engine.

317.

BOURGEOYS, MARIN LE (*c.* 1550–1634). Gunsmith, scientific-instrument maker and painter. Born in Lisieux, Normandy, where he spent most of his life, he worked from 1598, or before, for Henri IV of France and then for Louis XIII. He is now best known as the probable inventor *c.* 610 of the flintlock gun-mechanism that was to be used in Europe to the almost complete exclusion of every other type from *c.* 1650 to *c.* 1830. He also invented an air-gun. Examples of his work are in the Hermitage, Leningrad, and the Musée de l'Armée, Paris. See ARMS AND ARMOUR.

578.

BOUTET, NICOLAS-NOËL (1761–1833). The last of the great artist-gunmakers. He worked at Versailles, first for Louis XVI and then from 1792 as technical director of the newly established state arms factory. While holding this office he made splendidly decorated swords and above all fire-arms, including many for the Emperor Napoleon I. After Waterloo Boutet set up in private business in Paris, where he remained until his death. Examples of his work can be seen in the Tower of London Armouries; Wallace Collection; Musée de l'Armée, Paris; Metropolitan Museum, New York; Glasgow Art Gallery and Museum. See ARMS AND ARMOUR.

BRACKET CLOCKS. This technical term is an unfortunate misnomer as it is usually applied to the wood-cased, spring-driven CLOCKS of the late 17th and 18th centuries, which were intended to stand on a table in the living-room or bedroom. Most of them are, in fact, provided with a handle or pair of handles to enable them to be carried from one room to another. Pioneer isolated examples of clocks of this type were made by Jobst Burgi, who was born in the Toggenburg valley in Switzerland but carried out his important work in Cassel and Prague. The type was, however, developed mainly in England from *c.* 1660 and spread to some extent into Holland, Germany and Austria. As with the contemporary LONG-CASE CLOCKS, the early bracket-clock cases of Edward EAST and others were of ebonized oak and of somewhat severe, architectural form. But design gradually became more free and in the hands of Thomas TOMPION, Joseph KNIBB and many other great makers of the period 1675 to 1750 it achieved a great but quiet beauty. As with long-case clocks, the square dials of the earlier period were replaced from *c.* 1710 with arched dials.

Bracket clocks are spring-driven pendulum clocks and many of them embody not only striking mechanisms but alarms and repeating mechanisms by means of which the hour, usually coupled with the quarter, can be sounded at will when a cord is pulled. It is thought that these clocks were taken into the bedroom at night and that the repeating mechanism was used as required. Bracket-clocks have a silvered hour-ring and beautifully shaped minute- and hour-hands, the latter usually pierced. Both front and rear doors are glazed, and the vertical back-plate of the clock movement is often profusely engraved with flowing designs.

BRAID. A woven fabric in the form of a band made of silk, cotton, wool, gold or silver thread. It is used primarily for trimming or binding. See EMBROIDERY (TECHNIQUES AND MATERIALS).

BRAMAH, JOSEPH (1749–1814). English locksmith noted for his inventions in lock construction. The Bramah Cylindrical Lock, patented in 1784, combined the principles of endwise pushing and turning of the key and won a world-wide reputation for security. The pipe of the key, which fits on a drill pin, has different-sized grooves corresponding to spring-loaded sliders in the lock mechanism, these in their turn having notches in different positions. When the key is inserted the notches in the sliders are made to coincide with projections of the ring and only then can the key be turned. Bramah also invented a hydrostatic press and mechanical improvements in liquid-pumping apparatus and in bank-note printing machines. See LOCKS AND KEYS and Illustration on p. 66.

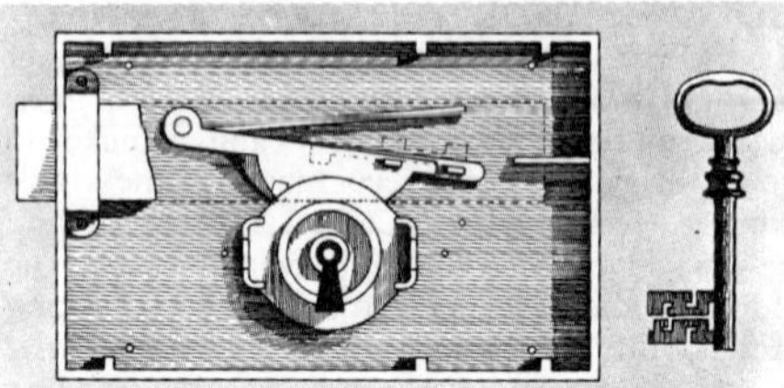

Robert Barron's lock. (From V. J. M. Eras, *Locks and Keys throughout the Ages*)

BRANDON. Centre of a traditional flint-knapping industry in Suffolk. During the 19th c. at Brandon the extraction of flint from bands occurring within the chalk continued throughout the year. The quarry pits are on average 9 m deep and although the galleries were never timbered, accidents were rare. Today flint is brought to the workshops by lorry from commercial chalk quarries, some of which are 50 kilometres distant. Once the quarried flint reaches the workshops there are four stages in the process of manufacture: drying, quartering, flaking and knapping. In the winter months the quarried flint is stacked around the workshop fireplace to dry but in the summer it is sun-dried.

The dry and warm flint nodule is then quartered with a flat-faced hammer some five pounds in weight to reduce it to a series of rectangular blocks averaging *c.* 15 centimetres square, although there is no strict regularity in size. The most skilful process is that of flaking, whereby a quartered block is reduced to a number of parallel-sided 'blades' by means of a hammer 680 g in weight. The residual cores from which the blades are struck are used as building flints. The final forming of the blades into gun-flints is done with a light, well-tempered steel hammer with a straight and narrow edge. Knapping hammers are often made from small flat files. Four is the usual number of flints produced from one blade and a good workman will produce 250 gun-flints in an hour. See also FLINT TOOLS.

774.

BRASS. In its modern sense 'brass' is an alloy of copper and zinc. Originally, however, the word was applied to the alloy of copper and tin which is now called 'bronze'. In Shakespeare and pre-Elizabethan writers, therefore, 'brass' and 'brazen' refer to bronze, not to what we know as 'brass'. The alloy now called 'brass' was first produced by mixing copper with zinc ore in the form of calamine (carbonate of zinc) and it was then given the name 'brass', which at that time was also the name of the alloy we now call 'bronze'. In a note to his translation of the *De Diversis Artibus* of THEOPHILUS (p. 125) C. R. Dodwell writes as follows: 'This sums up an important distinction in Theophilus's mind between bronze and brass. Nowadays, the distinction is one of ingredients but to Theophilus it was one of purpose. If metal is to be gilded, he refers to it by the appropriate Latin word *auricalcum*, which one would normally translate as "bronze". If it is not to be gilded, it is described as *aes* or "brass".'

The art of brass casting began in Britain in 1693, when a London merchant, John Lofting, was given a licence for casting thimbles; these had previously been imported from Holland. During the 18th c. brass was made by alloying copper with metallic zinc imported from China under the name TUTENAG. The smelting of zinc from the ore started in Europe *c.* 1730 and as metallic zinc became more plentiful the word 'brass' was reserved for this alloy while 'bronze' was used of the alloy of copper with tin formerly called 'brass'.

The hardness and the ductility of brass depend upon the proportion of zinc present in the alloy. Brass with less than 36% zinc is ductile when cold. For instance brass with 30% zinc is used for cartridge cases and is known as 'cartridge brass'. Brass with this or slightly higher zinc content was formerly used extensively for making the buttons of soldiers' uniforms because it could be pressed cold into dies and would take a clear impression while the operation of pressing increased its hardness so that the pattern was maintained. Above 36% zinc the brass becomes harder and stronger but has less plasticity at room temperature and is usually shaped by hot-rolling, etc. Domestic water taps, brass nuts, etc., are usually made from a 40–60% alloy.

During the ROMANESQUE period both brass and bronze were used for ecclesiastical and secular vessels: censers, candlesticks, etc. The most significant works in brass are a large Paschal candlestick at Léau (1483) by Renier van Thienen and baptismal fonts at Hal (1464). Bronze was chiefly used in the casting of statuary. A near-pure copper was little used except as the base for champlevé ENAMEL. The most important producer of brass in the Middle Ages was the Netherlands, with the main centre at Dinant—whence the term 'dinanderie', which came to be used of brass utensils in general, whatever their source. Brass exported from Holland to England in flat sheets was used for monumental brasses, until it became difficult to obtain after the destruction of Dinant in 1466.

For the most part brass has been an unassuming metal serving mainly for utensils in common domestic use without artistic pretensions. Exceptions are the SARACENIC BRASSWORK of Venice and the alms dishes which were made at Nuremberg and Augsburg from the 15th to the 18th c. The centres of the dishes were decorated with biblical subjects executed in relief by cold-pressing into a mould. As silver came into increasing use for ecclesiastic appurtenances brass came to be chiefly employed for the many-branched CHANDELIERS produced in the Netherlands and England. Fine chandeliers were made in Bristol—the earliest centre of zinc smelting—for West Country churches. From the middle of the 17th c. 'Surrey enamelling'—probably produced in London—was used to decorate HORSE BRASSES, sword hilts, stirrups, candlesticks and andirons. The colours were coarse and there was frequent discolouration from the firing. Similar enamelling was done in Holland and Germany. See also COPPER AND ITS ALLOYS.

914.

BREECH-LOADER. A general name for portable fire-arms which are loaded at the breech instead of the muzzle. It had always been recognized that the method of loading by ramming the charge with tamping into the barrel from the muzzle end had the disadvantage of clumsiness and slowness, rendering rapid fire virtually impossible. Early cannons had been loaded with powder and shot inserted at the breech and repeated attempts were made to apply this method to hand-guns. The difficulty to be overcome was a mechanical one of devising an opening in the breech which could be closed quickly after loading and which would be tight enough to prevent leakage of gases and flame which could cause loss of firing power and danger to the firer. (This was the defect for example of breech-loaders devised by Giuseppe Crespi of Milan in

1770 and William Thornton of the U.S.A. in 1811.) In the case of the rifle it was also necessary to ensure that the ball was a tight enough fit to rotate with the rifling.

Various attempts at an efficient breech-loading action were made through the 17th and 18th centuries. During the 3rd quarter of the 17th c. the Lorenzoni system, named after but probably not originated by Michele Lorenzoni (d. 1733) of Florence, came into use. It was based on a vertically revolving breech-block turned by a side lever and was adopted by gunmakers in a number of countries, among others by John Cookson of London in the 1680s. It was revived by H. W. Mortimer, Gunmaker to George III, towards the end of the 18th c. and it was advertised by a John Cookson of Boston, U.S.A., in the 1750s. This action was a considerable improvement on the Kalthoff system, for which the German gunmaker Peter KALTHOFF was given a monopoly by the Netherlands in 1641. His action made use of a sliding or vertically revolving breech-block attached to the trigger guard so that when the latter was rotated it loaded the chamber and cocked the lock. Another system of breech-loading, current in Germany at the end of the 16th c., made use of a screw plug at the top or the side of the chamber or the barrel; the plug was unscrewed and the gun was loaded through the hole. Guns of this type were made by a Munich gunsmith, Freiherr von Sprinzenstein, as early as 1593 and they continued to be made. The most important advance in the breech-loader was a mechanical improvement on this method invented by the Paris gunmaker Isaac de la Chaumette and approved by the Académie des Sciences in 1704. Chaumette designed a screw plug passing vertically through the breech and attached at its lower end to an extension of the trigger guard so that by moving the latter the plug could be withdrawn for loading and returned to position. The screw was cut deep so that one complete revolution of the guard was sufficient. This system was taken up by Paris gunmakers and was patented by Chaumette in England in 1721. It did not come into general use until a slight improvement, designed to prevent fouling on the screw, was patented by Captain Patrick Ferguson of the British army in 1776. A detachment of 100 men was equipped with the Ferguson rifle in the American War of Independence. But the system again was not further exploited although a number of rifles with Ferguson action were made for the East India Company and for private persons and the system was also applied to sporting guns. It was the Swiss gunmaker Johannes Samuel PAULY who, working in France, inaugurated the modern era of breech-loaders when he patented in 1812 a form of percussion action based on a firing pin which detonated a centrally inserted cartridge.

BREGUET, ABRAHAM LOUIS (1747–1823). Swiss watch-maker of eminence. He spent his early life in Neuchâtel, Switzerland, but moved to Paris in 1762 and passed the rest of his working life there, apart from the years 1791–5, during the Revolution, which he spent partly in Switzerland and partly in England. In 1807 he took his son LOUIS ANTOINE into partnership, after which date the work of his firm was signed 'Breguet et Fils'. The firm is still in existence with business premises in Paris. Breguet was a supreme craftsman and inventor in the field of precision WATCHES. In external form his watches were usually simple but of a refined design, and decoration was usually confined to the geometrical forms of engine-turning or matting. Internally they were of outstanding perfection and of a wide variety of design, many incorporating one or more of Breguet's own inventions. The latter include: the *tourbillon*, a device in which the whole escapement mechanism and balance-wheel rotate once a minute (in order to wipe out the so-called 'position errors' of the watch); the *parachute*, a spring end-bearing to prevent breakage of a vital shaft owing to shock; the *overcoil* balance-spring; and Breguet's successful forms of automatic winding, employed in his *montres perpetuelles*, and of the lever escapement and the temperature compensation curb for the balance-spring. Breguet also made simpler and cheaper watches, the so-called *souscription* watches, and at the other extreme watches and CLOCKS of great complication, including his *pendule sympathique* which was capable of automatically winding, correcting and regulating a watch entrusted to its care overnight.

BREUER, MARCEL (1902–). Hungarian-born German architect. In 1920 he joined the BAUHAUS as a student and by 1924 had become head of the furniture department there. He was an innovator in the designing of tubular metal furniture and together with Mies van der Rohe (1886–1969) he introduced the cantilever principle into the construction of the chair. His cantilevered tubular steel chair, designed in 1928 and manufactured by the THONET firm, has become a standard type for the commercial metal chair today. He also designed some of the first bent and moulded plywood furniture and some of the earliest chairs using aluminium structural frames. Breuer's designs were in the tradition of functionalism, with every element of the structure clearly expressed and articulated. In 1928 he left the Bauhaus and set up in practice as an architect and interior designer. See BAUHAUS; FURNITURE (MODERN); WOOD-WORKING.

BRIDE. Term in LACE-making and NEEDLEWORK for tie-bars or bridges of worked thread holding together the elements of an open-work pattern. These were sometimes themselves decorated with picots, dots, etc.

BRIGHT-CUT. A form of engraving on SILVER or other metal popular *c.* 1790. The metal is cut away with a bevel, lending a faceted and jewel-like sparkle to the surface.

BRILLIANT. Term used by jewellers and lapidaries for the cut of a DIAMOND or other transparent stone when it is faceted to secure maximum fire and brilliancy. The brilliant cut has 57 facets (or 58 if the base is cut with a CULET). The CROWN or upper surface has 33 facets: a large octagonal facet at the top (called the TABLE); 8 triangular star facets; 8 quadrilateral facets (4 templets and 4 quoins); and 16 other triangular facets. The base contains (apart from a culet) 24 facets: 8 pentagonal facets (of which 4 are called PAVILION facets and 4 quoins) and 16 triangular facets. The angles of the facets are designed to give maximum brilliance by causing the whole reflected light to come through the side facets of the crown and not through the table.

The American brilliant cut is a modification of the above, having a smaller table and additional facets around it, giving 66 facets in all (including table and culet). See JEWELLERY.

BRIN. The single filament of SILK bifilar thread as spun by the silk-worm. Two brins cemented together by SERICIN form the BAVE.

BRITANNIA METAL. An alloy akin to pewter. See PEWTER.

BRITANNIA STANDARD. See SILVER (ASSAYING AND HALL-MARKING).

BROCADE (formerly 'brocado' from Spanish *broca*, a boss). Like EMBROIDERY, brocade is a decorative overlay on cloth. It may resemble embroidery so closely that the two are difficult to distinguish; but the techniques are different. While embroidery is *added* to the cloth ground by means of a needle or needle-like implement, brocade is made during the WEAVING process by means of supplementary wefts which are brought to the surface when required by the pattern and hidden under the utilitarian weft when not so required. Therefore brocade must always follow the line of the weft, while embroidery may be stitched at any angle to it. Embroidery is typically taken right through the cloth to appear on the reverse, while brocade is hidden inside the cloth when not required by the pattern to show on the surface. In brocade the pattern is raised above the surface of the cloth and may be in gold or silver thread.

This fabric of raised figures may have been first manufactured in China. At first the word 'brocade' was applied only to materials of gold or silver threads or both in combination. Early accounts of brocades state that the cloths were 'broched' or embroidered upon coloured grounds. Later the word was applied to almost any material worked with metallic threads. Metallic tissues were manufactured in Venice, Florence and Genoa and also in Spain in the 16th c. Gradually silk was introduced into the fabrics, serving as ground for ornaments of gold or silver threads, for which the name was still retained. With time silk alone was used and the name 'brocade' was applied to any textile having a raised pattern woven into it. The term is also applied to cloth of gold and silver made in India.

BROCHÉ WORK. A type of EMBROIDERY which follows patterns woven into the material as in DAMASKS and furnishing fabrics. The fabrics usually have a wool base and filoselle silk is often used for the embroidery with four or more shades of one colour for the details of the design. Patterns are usually bold and floral and variety is given by the use of a large variety of stitches: stems and flowers are outlined in rope stitch, more delicate stitches are used for the petals and trellis is used as a filling stitch. French knots are prominent. Sometimes Japanese gold thread is used to give a pattern of over-stitching.

BRODERIE ANGLAISE. A type of WHITEWORK embroidery characterized by patterns composed of small holes edged with buttonhole stitches.

BRONZE. See COPPER AND ITS ALLOYS.

BRONZE AGE METALLURGY. What the archaeologists have been calling the Bronze Age for some time is in fact a complex period which starts with the use of pure COPPER. Copper is one of the few metals that occurs on the earth's crust in its true metallic state, and this 'native' copper must have always attracted the attention of the world's lithic societies, including the North American Indians (see AMERINDIANS). who have been using native copper for small implements since *c.* 3000 B.C.

It would appear that the Late Neolithic societies of the lower Danube soon learnt how to melt native copper and produce large copper castings for axe-heads to replace the earlier stone ones. Most of the native copper would be found in the vicinity of deposits of copper ore as it is associated with the weathered surface of such deposits. In this zone would be found blue-green oxide ores such as malachite and azurite, which would attract the attention of the Late Neolithic potter as a potential pigment for decoration. (See COLOURS AND COLOURANTS.) He would find, however, that it was not stable in the fire and under sufficiently reducing conditions might give rise to little blobs of metallic copper on the surface of his pots. He would at once recognize the similarity between this and the native copper that he had been casting for so long and would reproduce the accident under improved conditions in which the ore and the charcoal fuel were mixed. Thus the first smelting furnace and a true Copper Age would have arrived.

As the smelter used up the oxidized surface ores of his deposit he would find a rather different ore lower down, one containing arsenic or antimony which would give a stronger metal after hot and cold forging. He would learn to select such ores for the superior coppers that they produced and might learn to smelt the more difficult but far richer sulphide ores of the secondary enrichment zone, where a good deal of the copper dissolved at the surface had been deposited.

It is clear that Copper Age people living in areas where deposits of the rare tin-bearing minerals such as cassiterite occur must have obtained somewhere towards the end of the 3rd millennium B.C. a mixture of tin and copper ores. This was found to give an immensely superior copper in the cast state without the complex forging that is required to get the best out of the arsenical ores. In this way tin bronzes were discovered and very soon cassiterite would be sought and won from its alluvial deposits.

By this time the wealthy civilizations of the Near East, which had previously to depend on supplies of copper from the mountainous areas of Turkey, Iran and the Negev, would have developed the trade contacts which would allow them to exploit the discoveries of the Bronze Age people to the west of them. For tin ores do not seem to have been present in the Near East but were restricted to Italy, the Iberian peninsula, central France, Brittany, Cornwall, the Czecho-slovak–German border and Nigeria. Tin ores also occur in Malaysia, Thailand, China and South America, so these people could enter the Bronze Age with comparative ease.

By the middle of the 2nd millennium B.C. the true Bronze Age had spread right across Eurasia and casting techniques became much more sophisticated. The open stone mould which produced a rough shape that was finished by forging gave way to better two-part stone moulds and to clay and even bronze moulds. It was soon found that a certain amount of lead improved the fluidity of the bronze so that the liquid metal would fill the smallest detail. Techniques such as the lost wax (*cire-perdue*) process were probably developed about this time. Here the object would be modelled in beeswax and then 'invested' with the clay mould, which after drying could have the wax pattern removed by heating and the resulting cavity filled with metal. Church bells are still made by a technique that differs very little from this process. (See BELL-FOUNDING.) This, of course, is what the engineer calls a 'one-off' process and would only be justified for special art work. The more useful every-day things like axe-heads, swords, knives and so on would be made in large quantities with the more permanent stone or bronze moulds, from one pair of which 50 or more casts could be made. We have much evidence of the high level of technique of the Late Bronze Age smiths, one of whom, in Poland, travelled around with an oak sample-case to demonstrate the latest models; he would be prepared to take old scrap and make a new article of the latest type in exchange.

Unlike the smelter, the smith needed the minimum of equipment: usually a pair of bellows—an animal's skin would do—a tuyère or clay tube to protect the end of the bellows, a few stones, some crucibles, and charcoal. He probably made the crucibles himself out of suitable clays he found *en route*. Poorer quality clays tempered with chaff would do for the clay moulds. To lighten the load (on the donkey?) he would make one pair of stone moulds do for at least four different types of artefacts by cutting matrices on four sides and in some cases in the ends as well.

By the end of the Bronze Age, *c.* 500 B.C. in Britain, the output of the smiths was enormous to judge from the wealth of material from this period in our museums. Everybody would own at least one socketed axe for general chopping and carpentry. Most of the men would have large cast-bronze swords and the woodsman would have the heavier palstave. The rich would have sheet-bronze buckets and cauldrons and some, perhaps the priests, would have cast-bronze trumpets.

So much for Eurasia. About A.D. 500 people of the Mochica culture in Peru had got beyond the stage of casting native copper and were smelting copper on their own. The fact that people in South America went through the same sequence of metals—native, arsenical copper, finally reaching tin-bronze about the time of the arrival of Columbus—suggests that metallurgy was here an independent invention but motivated by the same circumstances as in Eurasia, i.e. the succession of minerals in a copper deposit. There would be no trouble in making the change to tin-bronze as tin ores occur in this area and are mined in Bolivia to this day.

In Africa, outside the north African littoral and EGYPT, the Bronze Age does not seem to have come until the arrival of the Portuguese. But a well-developed Iron Age had sprung up in Nigeria *c.* 300 B.C., which meant that bronze, when it came, was superfluous as far as weapons and implements were concerned and so was reserved for art forms.

3, 136, 163, 264, 265, 266, 269, 396, 769, 770, 845.

BROWN, LANCELOT, or 'CAPABILITY' (1716–83). Landscape gardener and architect, born at Kirkharle, Northumberland, of farming stock, who rose to be the leading practitioner of his time. He attended school at Cambo, and was subsequently employed on the estate of Sir William Loraine at Kirkharle, where he remained for *c.* 7 years. In 1739 he came south and after working for several months for Sir Richard Grenville at Wotton, Buckinghamshire, he moved to Stowe in the same county, which had what was then one of the finest although as yet uncompleted LANDSCAPE GARDENS in the country. Its owner Richard Temple, first Viscount Cobham, had already devoted 25 years and a large part of his fortune to transforming his house and grounds with the help of Sir John Vanbrugh, Bridgeman,

James Gibbs and William Kent. The latter's visits to the places for which he gave designs were, however, spasmodic and Cobham came to rely increasingly on Brown to see that his work was carried out. During the years from 1740 until Kent's death in 1748 Brown therefore had ample opportunity for studying his principles, and towards the end of the decade was himself being consulted by Cobham's neighbours on matters of garden design. At Wakefield he continued work begun for the Duke of Grafton by Kent, and *c.* 1748 he undertook the remodelling of the grounds at Warwick Castle which Horace Walpole was to describe as 'enchanting'. Writing to George Montagu on 22 July 1751 the latter went on to say: 'The view pleased me more than I can express, the river Avon tumbles down a cascade at the foot of it. It is well laid out by one Brown, who has set up on a few ideas of Kent and Mr. Southcote', the latter having been Kent's client at Woburn Farm, Surrey.

These 'ideas' assimilated by Brown were, however, to be strengthened in that decade by the publication of two books expressing theories closely concerned with landscape design. The first was William Hogarth's *Analysis of Beauty* (1753), in which the author maintained that a curving 'line of beauty' must be the most agreeable to the eye since when viewed from any angle it offered both movement and rhythm. Edmund Burke's *A Philosophical Enquiry into the Origin of our Ideas on the Sublime and Beautiful*, published in 1757, sought to define the ideal landscape through the various emotional or philosophical reactions to dimension, form, colour and texture.

Kent's death was followed by that of Lord Cobham in 1749 and Brown, now recognized as a competent designer, made plans to leave Stowe. By 1751 he had settled with his young wife and children in a house on the Mall at Hammersmith, from where his practice was conducted for the next 13 years. His employers were soon to find that he possessed qualities lacking in his predecessor, for unlike that charming, indolent genius with a gift for drawing but little practical knowledge, Brown had a thorough grounding in horticulture and the disposition of earth and water; thus he was prepared to tackle areas of far greater extent than Kent had ever envisaged. In 1751 he turned his attention to architecture as well as landscape, finding, as William Mason was later to recount, 'great difficulty . . . in forming a picturesque whole where the previous building had been ill-placed, or of improper dimensions'. The first product of this new venture was Croome, in Worcestershire, and in the next few years architecture as well as garden designs were involved at Burghley, Burton Constable and Corsham, where Brown added to an earlier house a magnificent picture gallery and other rooms. His house designs were usually Palladian, with occasional sorties into GOTHIC for decoration, as in the library at Corsham and various garden buildings.

By the early 1760s Brown had already been given the nickname of 'Capability' from his habit, it was said, of referring to the 'capabilities' of the places on which he was consulted. In 1764 he was appointed Surveyor to the Royal Gardens and Waters at Hampton Court and Richmond, moving into an official residence at the former. He did not in fact interfere with the formal gardens there, but supervised the planting in 1768 of the now famous Black Hamburg vine. At Richmond, in what was then the Old Park but is now part of Kew Gardens, he removed Merlin's Cave and other fantasies introduced by William Kent for Queen Caroline, and laid out the area near the river, which included the present rhododendron walk. In his private practice the great landscapes of this decade were Blenheim, Chatsworth, Castle Ashby, Longleat, Petworth, Ashburnham, Wimbledon, Compton Verney, Bowood and Milton Abbey.

While every commission produced its own physical conditions of which account had to be taken in preparing a design, the main elements with which Brown sought to create a scene of beauty and interest were sweeps of lawn stretching from the principal fronts of the house, with a ha-ha or sunk ditch to keep deer or cattle at a distance, flanked by plantations or shrubberies screening the offices and kitchen gardens. In the foreground would be a serpentine lake, its extremities concealed by trees, sometimes with a bridge to carry a drive or mask a difference in water levels. In the distance the higher ground would carry plantations of beech and oak, while groups of trees, often elm or chestnut, would be scattered in the foreground. Where earlier avenues were retained—and Brown did, in fact, incorporate several, as at Corsham, Wimpole, Castle Ashby and Blenheim—two or three trees would be removed at intervals on either side to open up cross views from different angles. Brown's critics who condemned the outlines of his 'clumps' of trees failed to realize that they would soften in time when the outer ring of quick-growing timber, which served as temporary protection, was in due course removed. This was a point appreciated by his successor Humphry REPTON, who defended Capability against the later attacks made on him by those protagonists of the 'picturesque', Richard Payne KNIGHT and Uvedale PRICE. Repton rightly pointed out that Brown and his patrons were planting for posterity as much as for their own pleasure, and that the initial appearance of 'the bare and the bald' was only a passing phase in the slow maturing of a well planned park.

As Brown did not venture into print, the surviving draft of a letter setting out his views is of particular interest. It was addressed in June 1775 to Thomas Dyer, who had consulted him on behalf of a friend in France eager to lay out a *jardin anglais*. 'I have made a Plan according to your desire, as well as I could from the survey and description you sent me, which I hope may be of use to the owner', Brown replied. 'In France they do not exactly comprehend our ideas on Gardening and Place-making which when rightly understood will supply all the elegance and all the comforts which Mankind wants in the Country and (I will add) if right, be exactly fit for the owner, the Poet and the Painter. To produce these effects there wants a good plan, good execution, a perfect knowledge of the country, and the objects in it, whether natural or artificial, and infinite delicacy in the planting, &c., so much Beauty depending on the size of the trees and the colour of their leaves to produce the effect of light and shade so very essential. . . .' In this last sentence Brown clearly echoes a passage in Burke's *Enquiry*, in which the latter emphasizes that variety of material is an essential and that it is by the use of such contrasting materials as the myrtle, vine and jasmine, which are as delicate and as beautiful as the oak, ash and elm are majestic, that a picturesque whole is created.

Brown's influence extended into almost every county of England. He is known to have prepared more than 200 designs, and even where he himself did not put them into execution they provided in most cases a basis for what was eventually carried out. Only one of his account books is known to have survived, but many of his drawings have come to light in recent years.

In 1770 Brown, by then aged 54 and increasingly afflicted by asthma, took as a young partner Henry Holland, the architect son of an old friend. In the previous year he had designed the carcass of a new house, Claremont, near Esher, for Lord Clive, a project which was to involve a considerable amount of work over the next few years, and for the completion of which Holland's help proved invaluable. Benham, Cadlands and Berrington were subsequent products of this very successful collaboration, which lasted until Brown's death in 1783 and which established Holland, who had by then married Brown's daughter Bridget, in his own distinguished career.

430, 804.

BROWN, WILLIAM HENRY. American cutter of silhouettes. See SILHOUETTE.

BRUNO, FRANCESCO. Carver of shell cameos at Trapani, Sicily. See SHELL CAMEOS.

BRUSSELS LACE. Name given to various types of LACE which were made principally in that city. An elaborate coverlet with many small figures in bobbin lace, presented to the Archduke Albert and the Archduchess Isabella in 1599, testifies to the proficiency of the Brussels lace-workers already in the 16th c. But it was not until the late 17th and 18th centuries that a characteristic local type of bobbin lace was developed, which was in common demand throughout Europe in the form of costume trimmings and pieces for ecclesiastical use under the misleading name POINT D'ANGLETERRE. Unlike MECHLIN or VALENCIENNES, this lace was made by specialist workers, of whom one made the individual motifs and a second the groundwork round them—generally in a hexagonal *réseau.* A third made the various kinds of open-work ornamental fillings, and so on. The conditions of labour became a reproach with awakened social consciousness: much of the work is said to have been done in underground workshops, which were kept deliberately damp in order to facilitate the manipulation of the thread. The floral designs were exceptionally elaborate and naturalistic, revealing great technical proficiency. They were characterized by ribbon-like outlines in slight relief. Lace continued to be made in this way during the 19th c., when it was closely imitated by the English HONITON. But it was to some extent supplanted by a cheaper article produced by the application of bobbin or needlepoint motifs to a machine-made net. During the latter part of the century Belgium achieved some prominence in the manufacture of machine net.

Brussels needlepoint lace from the 18th c. is relatively rare and resembles bobbin lace in its general effect. The fine, light Brussels needlepoint laces of the 19th c. are known as *point gaze*: patterns and grounds were done at the same time and the fabric was made in small sections. Needlepoint lace with bobbin-made groundmesh was also produced.

BRUSSELS TAPESTRIES. The beginnings of TAPESTRY weaving in Brussels are obscure, but by the middle of the 15th c. the industry was sufficiently developed for its products to be in demand at the Burgundian Court. By 1516, when Pope Leo X dispatched Raphael's cartoons of the Acts of the Apostles to the weaver Pieter van AELST, Brussels was already the chief European centre of tapestry weaving and its output of hangings during the next two and a half centuries was enormous.

It is probable that some of the splendid late GOTHIC hangings with religious subjects are the products of Brussels looms; but apart from the set of *Acts* just mentioned (Vatican) few Brussels tapestries are distinguishable with certainty before 1528, after which date they may be recognized by the presence of the town mark—a red shield flanked on either side by a letter 'B'. The industry was fostered by the Habsburgs, who employed their court painters Bernaert van Orley and Jan Vermeyen to design tapestries which were woven by members of the two great families of weavers in Brussels in the 16th and early 17th centuries, the Geubels and the Pannemakers.

Dynasties of weavers such as these, sometimes spanning several generations, were a characteristic feature of the Brussels industry. The families of Auwercx, de Vos, Le Clerc, Leyniers, Peemans, Raes, Reydams, Reymbouts, van den Hecke, van der Borght and van Leefdael all flourished in the 17th c. and numerous tapestries from their workshops, and from many others, are extant. This was the most productive period of the Brussels workshops. Though the establishment of royal manufactories abroad, such as those of Paris and MORTLAKE, drew off many of the best weavers and reduced the demand in Brussels for the most sumptuous class of work, the quality of the weaving remained extremely high. In design the rich but stiff late Renaissance style of the 2nd half of the 16th c. was replaced by an exuberant BAROQUE. Scenes from classical antiquity in the manner of Rubens were among the most popular subjects. The end of the 17th c. saw the introduction in Brussels of the so-called *tenières,* or Teniers tapestries, in which groups of small figures after, or in the manner of, Teniers (1610–90) are set against landscape backgrounds. These tapestries were widely imitated elsewhere.

Large numbers of tapestries continued to be made during the 18th c. in the workshops of the families of de Vos, Leyniers, van den Hecke and van der Borght. They lacked designers, however, comparable with those of the French factories and the demand for their work constantly diminished. The last looms ceased to operate before the close of the century.

312, 884.

BRUSTOLON, ANDREA (1662–1732). Venetian sculptor and carver who also made elaborately carved furniture in which sculpted figures in the round play an important part. His furniture can be seen in the Palazzo Rezzonico, Venice.

BUCCHERO WARE. Etruscan black pottery made before the introduction of the Greek black glaze technique. The pottery was made from iron-bearing clay, the black colour resulting from firing under reducing conditions and from carbon smudging. The term is also applied to the black ware of Pre-Columbian America, characteristic of Chimù.

BUCKINGHAMSHIRE LACE. The making of bobbin LACE was established as a domestic industry in Buckinghamshire in a small way in Tudor times. Children were taught the craft at an early age and would sing traditional 'tells' while throwing their bobbins to the rhythm. Main centres were Aylesbury, Great Marlow, Newport Pagnell, Hanslope, Stony Stratford and Olney. In the 19th c. Buckinghamshire lace had a ground-mesh of two threads twisted in a hexagonal or six-pointed star shape with unassuming patterns of floral sprays outlined in thicker thread, which made it reminiscent of the laces of MECHLIN or LILLE.

BULLA (Latin, boss or knob). A circular gold ornament which the early Etruscans wore as a pendant from a necklace. The *bulla* was adopted by the Romans and worn as an amulet against evil especially by children of nobles. When they reached maturity it was laid aside and dedicated to the Lares or tutelar deities of the home. *Bullae* of leather were hung round the necks of children of freedmen. See GREEK AND ROMAN ANTIQUITY (JEWELLERY).

BULLION. 1. Gold or silver wire twisted into thread or fringes made of such twists. See EMBROIDERY (TECHNIQUES).

2. A metal boss or convex ornament on BOOKBINDING, horse-trappings, etc.

BURNAP, DANIEL (1760–1838). American clock-maker who set up business in East Windsor, Connecticut, *c.* 1780. He is noted for his LONG-CASE clocks with brass works and faces of engraved silver, and chimes. He moved to Andover *c.* 1800.

BUSTELLI, FRANZ ANTON (1723–63). Of Italian-Swiss origin, born near Lugano in the Tessin, he was the outstanding modeller of porcelain figures at the NYMPHENBURG porcelain factory housed in one wing of the Nymphenburg palace, outside Munich. After J. J. KAENDLER at MEISSEN he was the most gifted of all the porcelain modellers in the German ROCOCO style.

BUSTLE. A pad or wire framework worn beneath a woman's skirt to make it stand out behind. The bustle superseded the CRINOLINE and came into fashion towards the end of the 1860s. See FARTHINGALE, BUSTLE, CRINOLINE.

BUTA. Local name of floral ornamental motifs used in Cashmere shawls. See SHAWLS.

BYSSUS SILK (also called MUSSEL SILK). Term denoting an exceedingly fine textile fibre and fabric of flax, known to classical antiquity; also the fine silky threads by which a Mediterranean species of mussel *Pinna nobilis* attaches itself to the sea bed or to rocks. With great skill these threads can be knitted into fabric so fine that a pair of gloves made from it were said to be contained in a walnut shell. Legend had it that this was the Golden Fleece which Jason sought. Whether any cloth was ever woven from this yarn is open to grave doubt on technical grounds. In ancient times, when the origin of silk itself was the subject of folklore, there may well have been confusion of thought.

BYZANTIUM

INTRODUCTION. Some civilizations have the gift of inspiring artists to transcend the existing standards of excellence to ever higher levels. Some towns seem at certain periods of economic and political power to endow their inhabitants with impeccable taste which transforms luxury goods into genuine *objets d'art*. Paris in the 19th c., Florence during the Renaissance, moulded the virtuosity of artists and the judgement of society. But none did it more thoroughly or over a longer period than Constantinople, the city chosen by Constantine the Great in A.D. 324 to replace Rome as the capital of his empire. It became the melting-pot in which the cultures of Greece and Rome were fused into a unique, wholly new civilization by Oriental prescience and Christian ideology. As such it was to reign supreme for a thousand years throughout its own territories and those of the Slavonic countries, and it was also to have a profound effect upon Christendom's response to and use of the arts. During the whole of that millennium Byzantine iconography and artistic ideas were reflected in a steady flow of works of art. Each of the empire's major regions shaped these concepts in accordance with its local tastes and traditions; but it was in Constantinople, with Salonica as a close runner up, that the style found its purest and most sophisticated expression with the greatest intensity of religious fervour. Since it is impossible to discuss local styles in a brief survey, it seems preferable to concentrate here on the works produced in Constantinople, a decision which can be justified on the grounds that throughout its existence the city remained the fountain-head of Byzantine art.

The birth of Byzantine art is not usually accepted as coinciding with the founding of Constantinople but rather with the age of Justinian the Great (527–65). The intervening centuries are regarded as the ones in which early Christian art became established and gradually developed into the Byzantine. Some scholars even assign the period of Justinian to the final phase of early Christian art so that certain works, for example the 6th-c. Homs vase in the Louvre, are claimed by both. Yet 6th-c. Byzantine art attained a higher degree of spirituality than that of the transition period and was in addition so refined, yet so vigorous, as to constitute something wholly new. The difference becomes evident if the fine 4th-c. silver-gilt amphora from Concesti, now in the Hermitage Museum, Leningrad, is compared with, say, the silver-gilt cross of *c.* 575 in the Vatican Museum, Rome.

Although Christianity was admittedly the most important thing in Byzantine life, the great scarcity of Byzantine objects of a secular nature nevertheless leaves us with a one-sided view of its art. So far only one humorous work has been discovered; it is the scene in the mosaic floor of the Great Palace of the Byzantine emperors at Constantinople in which a mule, feeling itself to have been overloaded, throws off both its load of faggots and its master, delivering a sharp kick on the latter's posterior as it looks back on him with a baleful, mulish eye. This single scene suffices to show that the Byzantines were close observers of nature and possessors of a sardonic type of wit. Several domestic articles such as the fork, which if not invented in Constantinople is believed to have first come into general use there, testify to the elegance and sophistication of its wealthier inhabitants. The only fork to survive is now in the Dumbarton Oaks Collection, Washington, together with its spoon. Both are assigned to the late 4th c. and may be of Sassanian make.

1. METALWORK. The finest metalwork, jewellery and textiles ranked as luxury wares. The most highly skilled of the craftsmen responsible for these things were therefore formed into imperial guilds and their workshops established within the precincts of the Great Palace. Specialists in the various techniques, such as those who produced the regalia and badges of office required by the civil servants or those who made the gold foundations needed by the cloisonné ENAMELLERS, were assigned to specific workshops. They were quick to surpass the universally renowned craftsmen of Antioch, so that even before Justinian's day Constantinople came to supplant Antioch as the main centre for the production of luxury wares.

In early Byzantine times so little SILVER was available that the small amount to reach the open market had a 10% tax imposed on it, whereas gold remained free. Most of the available silver was reserved for the emperor's personal use. Much of it was made into ornate vessels and dishes. Very occasionally the emperor would present one of these to a petty king or barbarian chieftain whom he wished to propitiate. From *c.* A.D. 350 each dish made in the imperial workshops was stamped either with the emperor's mark or with that of the responsible eparch, a practice which enables such objects to be assigned to a specific reign. Among the earliest stamped dishes is that made for Bishop Paternus bearing the mark of the Emperor Anastasius (491–518). Its centre is occupied by a splendid cross whilst its rim is decorated with repoussé (see EMBOSS) and chased animals in an idyllic setting, which are paralleled in certain objects from the Traprain Treasure in the National Museum of Antiquities, Edinburgh. Many of the dishes made for Justinian are decorated with similarly idyllic, almost Virgilian scenes, which accord in spirit with the rural scenes in the mosaic floor of the Great Palace. Other dishes display mythological scenes executed in a style based on the classical. A dish of the former type in the Hermitage Museum depicts a seated goatherd in idyllic surroundings. As he watches his flock, untroubled by a goat nibbling at a tree, his dog lies at his feet looking at him for any sign of command. Pastoral scenes such as this are among the most beautiful in Byzantine art, but the mythological often reflect a more earthy aspect of the Byzantine character. A Silenus on a damaged dish from the age of Justinian in the Dumbarton Oaks Collection is rendered in a vigorous style well suited to his voluptuous and virile character. A dish in the Hermitage Museum dating between 610 and 629 shows Atalanta and Meleager in a rural setting which includes a castle in its background; its style is reminiscent of the Hellenic. The same love of ancient Greek art pervades the scene of a Nereid seated on a sea monster which decorates a vase in the Hermitage Museum. A silver casserole of much the same date, also in the Hermitage Museum, displays a nude fisherman wearing a hat as he stands surrounded by fish, ducks and a scallop, but its style has more in common with the Roman than the Greek. A dish from the same period in the Metropolitan Museum, New York, showing David slaying a lion in an idyllic landscape is, however, rendered with classical purity; but its sense of movement, rhythmical lines and graphic quality point to links with the East.

Far more of the silver objects which survive from the Justinianic and later periods display religious than secular motifs. They include the Struma Paten in the Archaeological Museum, Istanbul (565–78), the silver-gilt Riha Paten of the same period at Dumbarton Oaks and the series of dishes associated with David (610–29) which are divided between the Nicosia Museum, the British Museum and the Metropolitan Museum, New York. In these the treatment of the designs is formal, severe and grand. Different again is a magnificent dish in the Archaeological Museum, Istanbul, which illustrates the Byzantine liking for personifications, a taste which led the silversmith who made it in the 6th c. to personify India by a splendid seated woman. She is surrounded in the lower half of the dish by a hawk, a human-headed dog, two lions each led by a woman, a cheetah and a turkey.

Silver was used throughout Byzantium's existence for various vessels, for chalices and for embossed and chased plaques to serve as icons, Gospel covers, liturgical vessels and devotional objects. The Marcian Library in Venice possesses several superb reliquaries and Gospel covers dating from the 10th, 11th and 12th centuries. The silver-gilt and enamelled icon of the 2nd half of the 10th c. in the Treasury of St. Mark's, Venice, with a bust of the Archangel Michael at its centre comes near to sculpture in the fine modelling of his face. Silver was also used for articles of personal adornment such as belt buckles, for strainers, for beautifully shaped spoons sometimes with an animal engraved on them, even for dividers. It was also used for some of the doors in the emperor's apartments in the Great Palace, but none has survived. The west and south bronze doors of the Sta Sophia in Constantinople dated to 838 may serve to represent work of that type. The decoration on the former consists of crosses worked in relief, while the latter are decorated with scrolls in high relief. There are several such doors in Italy and they doubtless inspired, for example, those of the Cathedral of St. Zeno at Verona.

Gold, often combined with silver-gilt, silver, gems, PEARLS and cloisonné enamels, was recognized as a more sumptuous metal than silver and was used by those able to afford it for religious appurtenances as well as for personal adornment. The designs were generally executed in repoussé work, but were sometimes stamped; engraving was also widely used, especially for inscriptions and for the monograms which were extremely popular in Byzantium. The most delicate work is found in the necklaces made up of tiny, beautifully shaped and worked sections, in the half-moon, open-work ear-rings with small globules attached to their lower rims and decorated with confronted or single birds of Eastern origin, rosettes or geometrical motifs. Another popular type of ear-ring had small jewelled fringes attached to a rectangular base. Bangles and finger-rings were more severe. The rounded bangles were plain but for their pear-shaped or rounded terminals, which were generally ornamented. Rings consisted either of a single stone or a bezel with a cross, an inscription or a complicated monogram engraved on it. Especial care was lavished on the marriage belts and rings, a groom's traditional gift to his bride on their wedding night. The belts were made up of a series of round discs, medallions or coins with two larger discs forming the clasp. The smaller discs were generally decorated with a stamped or chased mythological scene or figure, but the clasp showed Christ standing between the newly-weds in the act of joining their hands. Many of the discs had good wishes inscribed on them, the clasp's text usually consisting of the words 'From God: concord, grace, health'. The wedding-rings were plainer, consisting of a hoop with a round or octagonal bezel engraved with a marriage motif such as Christ, or a cross between the couple's busts and the word 'Concor' engraved on them. Medallions with religious scenes in repoussé or stamped and chased were popular; they were often arranged in three registers enclosed within a circle.

Of all the surviving secular works none evoke Byzantine court life better than the cloisonné ENAMELS from the crown of Constantine IX Monomachos (1042–55), now in the National Museum, Budapest, and thought to have been the crown of an *augusta* rather than of an empress.

Its shape is unknown, but it is unlikely to have been similar to that worn by the Empress Ariadne on the ivory plaque of *c.* 500 in the Bargello Museum, Florence, or to that of the Empress Zoe (1028–34) in the mural mosaic panel in the south gallery of the Sta Sophia. The enamelled panels are rounded at the top, fairly long and narrow in shape. Three represent the Empresses Zoe and Theodora and the Emperor Constantine IX, one is of a saint, the remainder of dancing girls in a garden setting. The girls' clothes are of great interest. In contrast to the robes worn by Justinian's wife Theodora in the wall mosaic in the Church of S. Vitale at Ravenna, to those in which later empresses appear and to those worn by women of the middle class, these seem to represent the dresses worn on private occasions in court circles rather than in the theatrical world. They consist of long wide skirts edged with embroidery and tunics differing in length and necklines but all fitting closely round the bust and waist before flaring out at the hips, either by being cut in the round or by means of triangular insertions (godets).

Like the silver panels the gold ones also served many purposes, some being used as icons and others made up into Gospel covers or reliquaries. The reliquary for a fragment of the True Cross dating from 960 and belonging to the Cathedral Treasury of Limburg owes its splendour to the lavish use of cloisonné enamels, as does the 10th-c. gold and cloisonné enamel reliquary in the Treasury of the Cathedral of Estergom, Hungary. The goldsmiths' fondness for adorning their beautifully executed designs with enamels is also clearly evident in works such as the BOOK COVER dated to between 866 and 912 in the Marcian Library where a central enamel of the crucified Christ is surrounded by medallions of saints and archangels, or in the 12th-c. silver-gilt covers in the same collection. The reliquary at Limburg is especially representative of Byzantium's love of fastidious opulence in the years of her greatest prosperity, years marked in the arts by a Golden Age as splendid as that which the country had enjoyed under Justinian. The reliquary also forcefully expresses the deep piety of Byzantium's religious arts. Each of its three sections aims at creating a slightly different form of beauty. On the lid an inscription is cut along the top, helping the artist gradually to transform the reliquary's rectangular shape into a square. The next stage is accomplished by means of a frame-like band of enamelled diamond designs, which is in its turn bordered at the top and bottom by a wide strip studded with enamel circles enclosing circles of CABOCHON jewels. There follows a narrow border made up of rectangular strips of repoussé goldwork and small enamel plaques displaying the busts of saints. The square central compartment which these borders help to form is filled with nine enamel plaques arranged in rows of three. On each plaque in the upper and lower rows stands a pair of Apostles at full length, whilst the centre row contains a five-figure *deesis* with the Virgin and the Archangel Michael standing on Christ's left instead of on His right as is customary and St. John paired with the Archangel Gabriel. Although the lid makes much use of enamels, it also displays to the full both the goldsmith's technical skills and his ability to use gems to good effect. In the interior the hollowed-out double cross designed to hold the relic divides the rectangle horizontally and perpendicularly, the space on either side being occupied with inscriptions and enamel representations of seraphs, archangels and angels. Here the texts and symmetrical layout strike a severe note. The back panel is still more restrained yet no less splendid, for it is filled with one of the finest decorative crosses ever devised.

The 12th-c. silver-gilt cross-shaped reliquary in the Treasury of Cosenza Cathedral portrays the crucified Christ in enamel at the centre of one side and Christ enthroned on the other, the arms on both faces being studded with medallions. Its quality is outstanding. Other fine small gold cloisonné enamels are to be found among the adornments of the *Pala d'Oro* in St. Mark's Cathedral. See also GEORGIAN METALWORK.

2. MINIATURE MOSAICS. Although there must be several hundred Byzantine enamels in existence to bear witness to the skill and artistry of their makers, the miniature mosaic icons are even rarer than the cloisonné enamel plaques and even more exquisite. Scarcely larger than a postcard, with cubes the size of a pin-head, notwithstanding their delicacy they possess a monumental quality which enables them to bear enlargement on a screen without loss. The 14th.-c. Annunciation in the Victoria and Albert Museum testifies to the inherent nobility and great beauty of these works. A more important example, also dating from the 14th c., belongs to the Treasury of Florence Cathedral. It presents the Twelve Feasts, most of them commemorating events from Christ's life.

3. GLASS. The glass mosaic tesserae used for both the large wall-panels and the small icons were manufactured in Constantinople, Salonica and possibly also some other major towns. Syrian glass-makers in addition to Roman must have helped to establish Byzantium's glass industry. By the 5th c. it was producing octagonal and rectangular panels for glazing, but these were still so small that they had to be mounted in stucco frames. Glass vessels of quality were probably being made in Constantinople at the same early date, but most of the surviving glass consists of the bases from some stemless vessels which were executed in the *fondo d'oro* technique, i.e. a gold design, usually a figural representation but sometimes an animal or geometrical motif, between two layers of glass. Most of these bases belong to the final phase of early Christian art rather than to the fully fledged Byzantine style, yet it is impossible not to mention the 4th-c.

example set in a cross of the 7th c. belonging to the Museo Civico, Brescia, portraying a mother, son and daughter all with astonishingly modern faces. Their name, Voyneri Kerami, is inscribed in Greek. A 6th-c. rouge-pot in the Cleveland Museum is made of fluted glass and its gold lid is decorated with a very delicately delineated vine-scroll. That the Byzantines knew the art of enamelling on glass is attested by the 11th-c. bowl in the Treasury of St. Mark's, Venice, where upon a background of roundels and scrolls larger roundels contain full-length mythological figures and some smaller figures in profile.

4. SEMI-PRECIOUS STONES AND MARBLES. Chalices and other vessels made of semi-precious stones such as jasper, onyx and ALABASTER or of beautifully veined marbles have survived in considerable numbers. The finest of these are set in gold, silver-gilt or silver, the metal sections being adorned with gems, pearls and cloisonné enamels. Surviving examples date from the 10th c. onwards. The Treasury of St. Mark's contains several very fine 11th-c. chalices, including one made of sardonyx set in silver and adorned with pearls and cloisonné enamels. In the way in which the stones and marbles are handled these objects are related to those produced in Western Europe during the BAROQUE and EMPIRE periods, all three groups appealing to tastes of a comparable kind.

5. BRONZE. For decorative purposes bronze was often combined with silver, as for example in a plaque in the Louvre where a hunting scene is delineated in inlayed silver (4th–5th c.). Mostly, however, bronze was used for the large altar crosses, censers, icons, lamps, weights and good quality bowls, jugs and goblets, cheaper versions of which were generally made of COPPER. Church lamps consisted of a plain or patterned horizontal hoop with the oil holders attached to its rim. (This type survived during the Middle Ages as the 'Corona', known also as 'rowell' or 'roelle', a forerunner of the CHANDELIER.) Domestic lamps at first copied Roman pottery lamps but quickly became more adventurous. Many were shaped like a foot, often with a griffin head as a handle and a cross surmounting the ankle; others depicted Peter and a companion fishing from a boat with a cross on its mast. The Virginia Museum has an almost unique variant on this theme. It dates from the 4th or 5th c. and Dr. Marvin Ross considers that the boat-shaped lamp illustrates a tale from the *Odyssey*. The bronze weights used in conjunction with balance pans also express the Byzantine liking for and knowledge of classical literature, for the majority are in the shape of the head and shoulders of women of Athenian appearance.

6. TEXTILES. It was during the 6th c. that woven patterned materials acquired Byzantine stylistic characteristics. Many of the designs consisted of floral arrangements or baskets of fruit not unlike those in the decorative mosaics on the arches of the Cathedral of Sta Sophia and in the borders of the *opus sectile* mosaic floor in the Great Palace at Constantinople. The Chi-Rho and other Christian symbols such as fish were also used by the weavers. Indeed fish designs must have retained their popularity throughout the centuries for the dead girl commemorated on the Cypriot mortuary icon of 1356 in the Phaneromeni Collection, Nicosia, is wearing a red brocade robe, clearly a real contemporary material, patterned with golden fish arranged in an almost cross-shaped design. The earliest piece of textile to survive is dated to the reign of the Emperor Heraclius (610–41) and is now at Liège; its decoration is of a geometrical character.

As in Caesar's Rome so in Constantine the Great's new capital SILK was the most coveted, most admired, rarest and most expensive of fabrics. It came from China along the silk caravan route in very small quantities. During two centuries the ceaseless efforts of the Byzantine emperors to increase its import either by direct trade along that route or by establishing new, complementary routes resulted in failure. Then in Justinian's day two Basileian missionaries, possibly acting under the emperor's orders, discovered the secret of silk-making and smuggled some silk-worm eggs out of China in their walking-sticks. As soon as the silk-worms were delivered to the emperor the silk industry was established and made an imperial monopoly. Looms were set up in the Great Palace, the Guild of Purple Dyers being established nearby in the fashionable Baths of Zeuxippus. The monograms of the emperor or of the responsible eparch were woven into the selvages of each completed length of silk. At first all the silk made in the imperial workshops was reserved for the emperor and his family. Later he used a very small number of lengths as gifts to certain foreign dignitaries, but strict control continued. As late as *c.* 970 Luitprand, Bishop of Cremona, was bitterly disappointed when the lengths he had bought whilst acting as Otto I's ambassador to the emperor were confiscated by the Customs on his homeward journey.

The finest Byzantine silks known to us date from the 8th c. up to the conquest of Constantinople in 1204. They include two splendid versions of the eagle motif, one preserved in the Treasury of Brixen Cathedral and the other in the Church of St. Eusèbe at Auxerre, both *c.* A.D. 1000. The choice of the eagle—the imperial crest—as their motif and of purple—the colour worn only by members of the imperial family—with flecks of gold as their colour scheme indicates that both fabrics were made for the emperor's personal use. Textiles such as these are masterpieces of their kind. They were so highly prized by the contemporary Western world that they were used there only for very special purposes. The fragments that survive had been shrouds for the most revered of the dead. The design on an 8th-c. silk in the Victoria and Albert Museum reveals a blend of Eastern and late Roman influences. It consists of a repeat motif arranged in wavy, horizontal bands depicting a gladiatorial combat between two confronted men each of whom wrestles with a lion. The same love of prowess underlies a silk with as its main repeat motif a lion hunt presented in a circle. It is of much the same date as the combat scene and is preserved in the Vatican Museum, but in it Sassanian influence dominates over the Roman. An 8th-c. silk in the Cluny Museum, Paris, although depicting an essentially Byzantine subject, namely a *quadriga* of the type used in the hippodrome races, and thus qualifying as a genre scene, also reflects Persian influence; for the *quadriga* is set in a circle which, like the four roundels linking it to its neighbours at the four points of the compass, is of Sassanian origin. Even an Annunciation, which may possibly date from as early as the 6th c., on a silk in the Vatican Museum is set in a floral circle and accompanied by other designs of Eastern origin. Persian influence retained its potency in the 11th c., when it led to the use of such Eastern features in the major motifs of repeat patterns as the winged griffin set in a circle and accompanied by fairly large diamonds studded with rosettes, in the silk belonging to the Treasury of Sens Cathedral. It is also apparent in a silk in the Treasury of Aachen Cathedral dating from *c.* 1000, where the centres of large circles contain a rather strange-looking elephant.

7. EMBROIDERY. Although there is a fair amount of indirect evidence to show that fine EMBROIDERY was done in Byzantium in early times, nothing of a secular nature is known to survive whilst the earliest surviving religious examples date from the 11th c. Yet a study of paintings indicates that much geometrical and floral embroidery was used for trimming on the more splendid robes. Records state that several halls in the Great Palace were hung with embroidered curtains, but their designs have not been described. It is sad that everything has perished and left no trace. Two 11th-c. panels that survive owe their preservation to their having been placed on the shroud of Philip of Swabia when he was buried at Speyer in 1208. They are now in Munich. One represents Christ and the other the Virgin, both depicted in a style closely related to that of the pictorial art. Two 14th-c. fragments of the Communion of the Apostles at Castel Arquato also follow the pictorial style of their day. It is the *epitaphios*, however, which owing to the loss of other types of embroidery is now most truly representative of the art in Byzantium. Amongst the finest portrayals of the dead Christ are that which Andronicos II Palaeologos (1282–1328) presented to the See of Ohrid and the one worked in Thessalonica during his reign, which is now in the Benaki Museum, Athens. The so-called 'Dalmatic of Charlemagne' in the Vatican Museum with the Transfiguration embroidered on one side and Christ among Angels on the other is of much the same date; yet it is the *epitaphios* which was especially admired in the Orthodox world. In the post-Byzantine period it is to these that embroiderers in all the Slavonic countries turned time and again for inspiration.

8. CARVING. The Byzantine genius for sculpture expressed itself with equal felicity in small-scale work whether in IVORY, in marble or on gems. Love of gladiatorial combats of much the same type as those depicted on the textiles, of men wrestling with lions or the hunting scene recorded on the Louvre's bronze and silver plaque were often included in the ivory diptychs commissioned by consuls to announce their nomination. Scenes of that type figure in the diptych of Flavius Areobindus (506) now in the Landesmuseum of Zürich, and in that of Flavius Anastasius (517) now in the Cabinet des Médailles, Paris. Each consular diptych embodies several ideas in its symbols and decorations; but at so early a date it is the classical elements which predominate in the manner of their presentation, dictating the architectural settings, the inclusion of heads shown in profile, even the shape of the consular thrones, although their features remain closer to the Roman tradition of portraiture. The same classical elements prevail in the diptych of Magnus (518), also in the Cabinet des Médailles. But it is the Roman influence which predominates in the later Magnus diptych of 525. The presence of these Helleno-Roman characteristics is hardly surprising in the diptychs, for when they were commissioned many of the consuls were of Roman descent. In 541 Justinian abolished the custom of commissioning diptychs of this type and soon after that the senior state appointments went to men of Greek extraction.

In the religious sphere the Byzantine style had almost crystallized by the 6th c. when the plaque of the Archangel Michael now in the British Museum was carved, for although it retains the architectural setting characteristic of the consular diptychs and notwithstanding the retention of the round Western type of face, the Archangel is clearly Byzantine in appearance. By the 9th c. the pure Byzantine style had become fully established. It can be seen on a fragmentary plaque in the W. R. Tyler Collection, Washington, of the Archangel Gabriel, whose robust build and sturdy, peasant-like face must have been fairly popular for a time, for it is also found on a 10th-c. Gospel cover of the enthroned Christ now in the Bodleian Library, Oxford.

The 10th c. is admirably represented by numerous panels, and more especially perhaps by the fragment in the Museum of Fine Arts, Moscow, of Christ crowning Constantine VII Porphyrogenitos (913–58) and the complete, less transcendental one in the Cabinet des Médailles of Christ crowning Romanos (959–63) and

Eudoxia. Many of the religious panels, diptychs and triptychs of the 11th and 10th centuries must represent the taste of the educated, prosperous citizens of Constantinople rather than that of the Court. On these the figures are often displayed full length and accompanied by medallions containing heads as well as by scrolls or geometrical decorations, and their backs are often adorned by a cross. An exceptionally beautiful cross appears on the back of the 10th-c. Harbaville triptych in the Louvre; it represents perhaps the pinnacle of achievement in this type of work in the 10th c. The cross rises from a wooded setting with an especially tall cypress tree growing on either side of it beneath a sky dotted with six-pointed stars. The Church disapproved of carvings in the round on grounds of idolatry, yet the Victoria and Albert Museum possesses an extremely beautiful and practically unique ivory statuette of a standing Virgin holding the Child in her arms, which dates from the 10th c.

The Veroli casket (V. & A. Mus.) was made in the 10th c. when interest in classical antiquity had once again revived. Caskets such as this were probably used as jewel cases. On it figural plaques are framed by narrow strips decorated with circles arranged in rows, each containing a rosette. The figural plaques are worked with consummate skill in a style which reverts to the classical tradition to depict scenes drawn from Greek mythology; they include the Rape of Europa, Europa with Mars and Venus, Bellerophon with Iphigenia, Bacchus, putti-like children, dogs and other animals. This casket ranks with the finest secular caskets that have survived, yet practically all of them reflect the refinement of court life. An 11th-c. example in the Cluny Museum illustrates a combat between mythical beings and so does another of much the same date in the Metropolitan Museum, New York. In this field also, however, the religious works greatly outnumber the secular. As in earlier centuries, some plaques were used to make pyxes and caskets—a plaque with scenes from the life of Joshua from one such casket is preserved in the Victoria and Albert Museum—but the majority are in the form of single panels or triptychs. A fine 10th-c. panel in the Berlin-Dahlem State Museum depicts the entry into Jerusalem with complete iconographic fidelity, but it conforms to the prevailing interest in Hellenism by giving all the figures the round Helleno-Roman type of head and by dressing the town's inhabitants in Hellenistic draperies. In addition the scene is set in a decorative archway which traces its descent back to archways such as that containing the figure of the Empress Ariadne on the ivory (*c.* 500) belonging to the Bargello Museum, Florence. Archways similar to that of the Entry into Jerusalem cannot have been uncommon in the 10th to 11th c. for a Nativity scene on an ivory triptych in the Louvre is framed by one and so is the scene of the Virgin's death on the ivory cover of Otto III's Gospels in the Bavarian State Library, Munich. The 11th-c. panel of the Forty Martyrs in the Berlin-Dahlem State Museum can be classed as a fine study of the nude, and as such is unusual. But it is as impossible to refer here to all the existing ivories as it is to convey verbally an adequate idea of their beauty. That they were from the start used for many purposes is evident from the fact that Bishop Maximian's throne was entirely made of carved ivory plaques. It dates from the middle of the 6th c. and is preserved in the Bishop's Palace at Ravenna.

It is difficult to establish precisely what type of craftsman produced the carved gems and the plaques made of semi-precious materials. The 11th-c. large rectangular icon of St. Eudoxia, now in the Archaeological Museum, Istanbul, executed in *opus sectile* with her face engraved on a piece of ivory could equally well have been made by a mosaicist, an ivory carver or a worker in marble; but it seems probable that the *opus sectile* floors and marble roundels with inlayed representations of hares, eagles, signs of the zodiac, Samson struggling with a lion and so on, found in the finest churches, were made by marble carvers. It seems reasonable to suppose that the religious scenes carved on plaques of such semi-precious materials as obsidian, jasper, serpentine, LAPIS LAZULI, porphyry, steatite and the like were worked by ivory carvers and that gems such as the AMETHYSTS with busts of Christ or the Virgin were cut by jewellers. The style of all such works closely corresponds to that of contemporary paintings and sculptures.

9. POTTERY. Very little is known about the earlier types of pottery made in Byzantium, but the few fragments that exist suggest that it was closely related to the unglazed Roman ware. The earliest glazed fragments that have so far been discovered were coated with a pale green lead glaze and designs of a religious, animal or essentially Byzantine geometrical character, as well as monograms, were engraved on them. In the 9th c. polychrome wares became fashionable, the many-coloured decorations being painted beneath a thin transparent glaze. In addition to the religious and geometrical decorations used on the *sgraffiato* wares others, largely animal, bird or floral, were added; they were often derived from those in use in the Islamic world, particularly Persia. Then, too, flat, curved and carefully shaped revetment plaques were made, chiefly for purposes of interior decoration. The majority were ornamented with geometrical motifs, roundels or rosettes. But some plaques must have been intended for use in churches, for examples have been found with figures of Christ or saints, whilst the Louvre possesses a fine, slightly damaged tile dating from *c.* 1000 on which appears the bust of the Virgin holding a medallion of Christ set within a circle. The Walters Art Gallery, Baltimore, owns one of similar date with a half-length figure of a saint holding a cross in his right hand. A large icon of Christ made up of tiles done in this technique was excavated at Preslav in Bulgaria. So

A

B

A. Silver dish depicting Silenus and a maenad. (Hermitage Mus., 610–29)

B. Lamp in the shape of a boat. Illustrating a scene from the *Odyssey*. (Virginia Mus., Richmond, 4th–5th c.)

C. Ivory plaque showing the Empress Ariadne in full regalia. (National Mus., Florence, *c.* 500)

D. Leaf of diptych illustrating the life of St. Paul. (National Mus., Florence, *c.* 500)

C

D

Woven silk from Münsterbilsen used for shroud of St. Landrade. The main repeat design is contained within a roundel of Sassanian derivation and shows a charioteer driving a *quadriga*. (Mus. Royaux d'Art et d'Histoire, Brussels)

Bronze plaque with hunting scene inlaid in silver. (Louvre, 4th–6th c.)

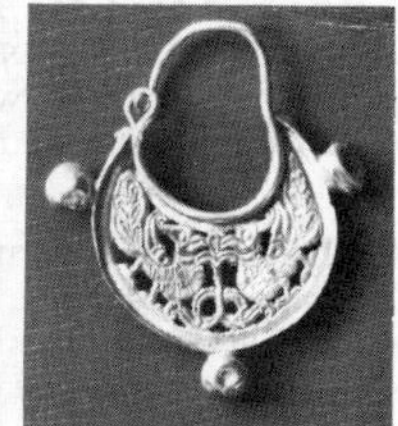

Gold ear-rings with designs featuring paired birds Oriental in origin. (Archaeological Mus., Istanbul, 6th–7th c.)

metropolitan is its style that it was assumed to be of Byzantine origin until it was found that the revetment plaques excavated at Preslav were of local make.

When the Byzantines reconquered Constantinople in 1264 the nation was impoverished, the capital had been ransacked, its treasures and relics dispersed. Its emperors were never again able to afford to eat off gold and silver plate, to erect mosaic panels on their walls, to import large quantities of ivory and precious stones from the East. Potters came forward to satisfy their love of beauty by producing vessels and dishes which, if not quite as fine as the Persian, nevertheless deserve to be regarded as notable works of art.

56, 185, 697, 698.

C

CABINET-MAKER. See CARPENTER, JOINER, CABINET-MAKER.

CABLE MOULDING. Term in ROMANESQUE and Norman architecture for a convex MOULDING with enrichment representing the twisted strands

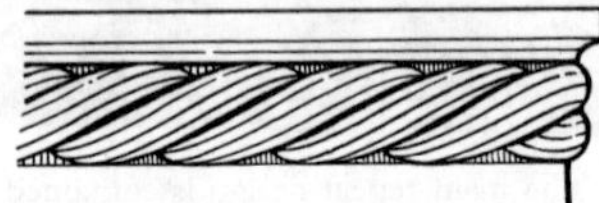

of a rope. This type of ornament is found in metalwork, furniture, etc. In the 18th c. the term 'cabling' was used for filling the fluting of a column up to the middle with a cable moulding.

CABLE STITCH. Also called 'rope stitch'. A stitch in EMBROIDERY which is technically a buttonhole stitch worked backwards and is used for outlining stems, flowers, etc.

CABOCHON. Term used by jewellers and lapidaries for a stone cut with the top surface domed and polished but without facets. The simple cabochon has domed top and flat base. The double cabochon has curved or domed surface top and bottom. When the curve above and below the plane formed by the edge of the GIRDLE is uniform these stones were often used as pendants or charms. Hollow cabochons are those in which the backs or undersides are concave. This form of cutting preceded BRILLIANT cut and is still used for opaque and sometimes for translucent stones. See JEWELLERY.

In cabinet-making and the decorative arts generally the term 'cabochon' is used for an ornament (e.g. on the knees of chair legs) in the form of a convex polished oval, usually surrounded by decorative carving.

776, 784, 921.

CABRIOLE. Term which came into use during the last quarter of the 18th c. to denote small stuffed armchairs and sofas. It is so used in HEPPLEWHITE's *The Cabinet-maker and Upholsterer's Guide* (1788) and SHERATON's *The Cabinet Dictionary* (1803). It was also current in America.

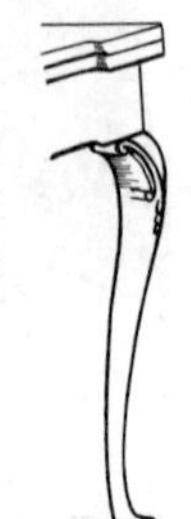

In the late 19th c. the term 'cabriole leg' became current to describe double curved legs with an outward-curving knee above and a concave curve below. This profile was used by the Greeks for some carved marble theatre seats. It was revived by Dutch and French furniture craftsmen in the late 17th c. and was introduced into England during the William and Mary period, remaining in fashion until the middle of the 18th c.

CAFFIERI. Family of sculptors, bronze-workers and decorators, of Italian origin, who worked in Paris under Louis XIV, XV and XVI. The best known are PHILIPPE I (1634–1716), who worked on the decoration of the Louvre under Charles Lebrun (1619–90), his son JACQUES (1678–1735), PHILIPPE II (1714–74), son of Jacques, and JEAN-JACQUES (1725–92), another son of Jacques, a sculptor of figures and portraits.

Jacques and his son Philippe II were considered the outstanding bronze-founders of the period of Louis XV and in turn held the title of Sculptor, Founder and Chaser to the King. The influence of MEISSONNIER was apparent in the work of both, but in their skill and decorative flair they were unique. Jacques was the most inventive worker in Rocaille bronzes (see ROCOCO) of his day. Both worked for the members of the royal family, the court and the aristocracy and were noted for their small ornaments such as clock cases, etc. Their chased and gilt-bronze furniture MOUNTS were held to be unrivalled in their day both for their decorative qualities and for their technical finish.

330.

CAGE-CUP. Also called *diatreton* or *vasa diatreta* from the Latin *diatretarii*, glass-cutters. Cage-cups are round-bottomed glass cups or bowls having the sides and base encased in a network of intricate and distinctive raised ornament. The surrounding 'cage' of ornament stands out from the body and is supported only by tiny and hardly visible struts. The most celebrated example of this type is the Lycurgus Cup (4th or 5th c. A.D.) now in the British Museum. Neither the origin of these cups nor the precise technique by which they were made is certain. Some historians believe that they were made by Syrians working in Rome, others that they came from Alexandria. Since some of these cups were found in graves in the Rhineland some historians have ascribed to them a Germanic origin, but see GREEK AND ROMAN ANTIQUITY (GLASS).

343, 344.

CAIRNGORM. See QUARTZ.

CALCEDONIO. A general term for GLASS made to resemble semi-precious stones such as onyx, agate, chalcedony, jasper and aventurine. A revival of an Alexandrian technique, the process was developed in Venice during the late 15th c. and after. This type of glass was later called *Schmelzglas* in Germany.

CALF. Leather made from calfskin. See BOOKBINDING and LEATHERCRAFT.

CALICO (also CALICUT). From the name of a city on the coast of Malabar, India. In the last quarter of the 16th c. the term was used of cotton cloth imported from the East. In Britain it is now used of plain white unprinted cotton cloth. In the U.S.A. it refers to a printed cotton cloth, coarser than muslin. See COTTON AND COTTON PRINTING.

CALOTYPE. An early photographic process for producing multiple prints from a single negative image. It was invented by an English scientist, William Henry Fox Talbot (1800–77), hence it was sometimes known as Talbotype. See PHOTOGRAPHY.

CAMBRIC. A fine white linen originally made at Cambray in Flanders. See WEAVING (FABRIC).

CAMEO. Engraved work on gemstones, GLASS, PASTE, CERAMICS or similar materials in which the surrounding ground is cut away so that the design stands up in relief above the surface. It is the opposite of INTAGLIO. See JEWELLERY and GREEK AND ROMAN ANTIQUITY (JEWELLERY).

More specifically, the term is often applied to a small relief carving cut in a banded or multi-coloured gemstone, such as an AGATE, in such a way as to exploit the effect of the different layers of colour.

See also SHELL CAMEOS.

784, 921.

CAMEO BINDINGS. Bookbindings with a central MEDALLION in low relief having the appearance of an antique CAMEO. They are produced from the impression of an INTAGLIO stamp direct into the leather and are usually in 'blind' (i.e. without GILDING), although the sunk background is sometimes coloured. They are also known as 'plaquette' bindings from their likeness to Italian metal relief plaquettes. The term is applied mainly to Italian RENAISSANCE bindings, the best known examples being the so-called Canevari bindings in MOROCCO leather made in Rome during the 1st half of the 16th c., which are decorated with a stamp of Helios in his chariot and Pegasus on Mount Helicon surrounded by the motto *ΟΡΘΩΣ ΚΑΙ ΜΗ ΛΟΞΙΩΣ* (straight and not crooked). Formerly attributed to the personal library of Demetrio Canevari (1559–1625), physician to Urban VII, these bindings are now thought to have been made for a member of the Farnese family, either Pier Luigi (1505–47) or his son Ottavio (d. 1588). A number bear the Farnese FLEUR-DE-LIS as part of the decoration. See BOOKBINDING (HISTORICAL).

393.

CAMEO GLASS. A glass-making technique first used in EGYPT. The upper of two superimposed layers of glass was ground away so as to leave a pattern standing up on a ground of contrasting colour, usually white on dark blue. The technique was developed in Italy in Roman times and a fine example is the 'Portland Vase' (B.M., 1st c. A.D.). See GLASS.

CAMPI, BARTOLOMMEO (*d.* 1573). Goldsmith, engraver, military engineer and armourer of Pesaro, Italy. From *c.* 1543 to *c.* 1554 he made amongst other things finely decorated arms for Guidobaldo II, Duke of Urbino. To this period belongs his one definitely identified work, a splendid parade-armour in the Roman style, made for Guidobaldo but later acquired, presumably as a gift, by Philip II of Spain. Now in the Armería Real, Madrid, it is signed and dated 1546. See ARMS AND ARMOUR.

CANAL BOAT DECORATION IN ENGLAND. The colourful decoration of the English canal boats is unlike that of other craft and is restricted to the boats of the network of narrow canals which were built in the Midlands in the late 18th and early 19th centuries. It was a folk art of the Industrial Revolution. To be appreciated fully the boats with their brilliant roses and castles must be seen against the grim industrial landscape of the Black Country, where they have a cheerful improbability, rather than on more idyllic stretches of waterway.

Though their painting is peculiar to them, it is far from being the boats' only decoration. A well-turned-out boat has much decorative ropework, brass outside and in, while ornamental china and white crochet work edged shelves and the frill surrounding the bed-place. The pattern is repeated in the cut-out edges of the fancy china plates which festoon the frill and crowd the walls, almost covering the roses and castles painted on them. The tiller of the butty is particularly handsome, with its ropework decoration of Turk's head and swan's neck. Even in the corrosive air of the Midlands bright brass gleams on the chimney, and inside the cabin there is still more.

The decoration of the boat increases as one moves back towards the cabin and the tiller. The painting of the bows is almost entirely functional, and much as that of other boats. Paint is used to outline the structure in such a way as to indicate the boat's width to oncoming traffic when it travels by night or passes through a tunnel. The cabin itself carries a large panel bearing the name of the owner and the boat's registration number. Early prints show such panels on Pickford's boats to have had a uniform design, but the detail is not clear. It is probable that each firm of carriers developed a distinctive name-panel. This panel is the work of the professional, and the only part of the boat's decoration subject to fashion. The fair-ground swagger of Edwardian lettering has too often given way to sans serif. Here as elsewhere the traditional colours are used: grounds are black, dark red, blue or green; lettering and moulding bright red, canary yellow and white. Strong primary colours are used to pick out geometrical patterns, which decorate a variety of areas: diamonds on masts, stripes on mop handles, circles on tillers and playing-card motifs on hatches. Often roses and daisies appear as an alternative. They occur also on separate panels. Inside the boat wood-graining replaces dark paint as a ground. Flowers are everywhere: over doors in rows, on stools and table-tops, wreathing water-cans and in tight posies on running blocks. Exuberant as they are, they are painted to a formula. In this they are unlike the castles which are used to decorate the important panel on the folding table and on the doors and side of the cabin. In these the painter is given a free hand. He may set his castle round with trees, lakes, bridges, mountains, swans, sunsets or boats as he chooses, and his castle may combine whatever architectural extravagance he fancies. The castle is his signature.

Canal boat decoration achieves the maximum effect with the minimum of skill, so making it possible for the boatman to decorate the boat himself. Choice of colour is limited, and the geometrical patterns require little more than a clean brush and a steady hand. The formula for painting the flowers has not changed in the 40 years since Camilla Doyle first described it in the *Burlington Magazine*. The same method was again described by Barbara Jones some 20 years later, and illiterate boatmen–painters use it still. Roses, for instance, are marked out first by discs of dark colour: dark red or even black for red roses, pink for white roses and ochre for yellow ones. A few dark petals are next flicked in. Then, using a fresh brush for each colour, petals are brushed in with light, bright colours. Everything is symmetrical, everything balanced. Some boatmen are adept; others do little more than touch up worn paintwork, leaving serious decoration to be done at the yard when the boat is overhauled. An employer may pay for the boat to be decorated to the boatman's taste.

The styles of different boatyards differ recognizably within the limits imposed by the boatmen's conservative taste. Work from the yard of Lee and Atkins, which flourished between the wars at Polesworth, is precise and rhythmic, highly stylized and elegant, and the colours are clear and cold. Altogether it has a classic hardness compared with the lushness of Braunston painting. Braunston work is very free and rich, the colour brilliant and perhaps a little soft. Names of early boatyard painters have in the main perished, but 20th-c. ones include Frank Jones and J. Allen of Leighton Buzzard, Ron Hough and Fred Nurser of Braunston, and George Tooley of Banbury. Among boatmen–painters T. Sibley, who works in the Polesworth style, is outstanding. A few yards specialized in the production of dippers and water-cans and other canal ware, and some boatmen too won a name for producing fine ware. The decoration of the can often included the name of the boatman, or a motto, and they were made to order. Such wares may be seen at the Waterways Museum at Stoke Bruern.

The origin of canal boat painting is still a matter for speculation. The first known description of it occurs in an article in *Household Words* for 1858, where it is described exactly as it is seen today. By this time railways were an effective rival to canals, and it would be surprising if the craft burgeoned in a time of decline. It must have originated earlier, possibly even at the end of the 18th c., passing unremarked because of the lack of interest among the educated at that time for working-class life and its pleasures. The boatman's castles, and the ogee arch of his bed-place, suggest a Gothic influence. The metalware too may owe something to a prevailing taste for the exotic and the Far East as filtered through by the East India Company. It was influenced in particular by the vogue for japan. The JAPANNING of metals was not limited to expensive wares, but extended to the cheapest and most utilitarian objects such as the boatmen used. The centres for the manufacture of cheap japan were Bilston and Wolverhampton, which lie in a network of waterways. Canal ware resembles japan in the nature of the goods treated and in that both cover easily corroded metal with an impermeable coating in one case of LACQUER and in the other of paint. Both laid a brilliant design on a dark ground and both applied a clear protective coat to the whole design. Canal ware is not fired as japan is, but otherwise it is a sort of 'do-it-yourself' japan. The cheapest early wares of Bilston and Wolverhampton have vanished, as cheap wares tend to when replacement is easy; but there is a distinct resemblance between canal ware and early American japanned wares. Many have regarded the 'foreign-looking' decoration of the boats as gipsy in origin, but boatmen resent any suggestion of gipsy ancestry for their art, and no solid evidence of it has been brought to light.

CANEVARI BINDINGS. See CAMEO BINDINGS.

CANTARO or CANTIR. A container for drinking-water with a globular body on a tall foot and a ring handle on top often surmounted by a stork or other bird. It was used as a communal drinking-vessel, supplying a thin stream of liquid without contact with the mouth. The type was produced mainly in Catalonia during the 17th and 18th centuries. Moorish influence in the designs was strong.

The 'cantar' was also a measure of capacity varying from 230 kg in Syria to 34 kg in Rome. The word *cántaro* is a general term in Spanish for a jug or wine measure.

CAQUETEUSE (French: *caqueter*, to chatter). A 'conversation' chair. A type of light, open-backed chair introduced into England from France in the latter part of the 16th c. See FURNITURE.

CARAT. A measure of weight used for precious stones (0·213 g) formerly $3\frac{1}{3}$ grains, (0·207 g) now $3\frac{1}{5}$ grains. Also a proportional measure for stating the fineness of gold, one carat being one 24th part. See GOLD AND SILVER.

CARBUNCLE. See GARNET.

CARDER, FREDERICK (1863–1963). One of the outstanding GLASS craftsmen of the 20th c., Frederick Carder was born in Staffordshire and early in life became a designer for the famed art glass works of Stevens and Williams. But through a series of complicated, and still controversial, events he emigrated to the United States and was instrumental in the founding of the famous Steuben Glass Works of Corning, New York, in 1903. Carder was the closest competitor of Louis Comfort TIFFANY in the production of fine coloured glass in an ART NOUVEAU and later in ART DÉCO vein. Probably the most famous of Carder's types was Aurene, a gold or blue iridescent glass of high quality. So close was it to the Tiffany type that Tiffany brought suit in 1913 for infringement of method, a case which he did not win. Carder also developed types which he called Verre de Soie, Calcite, Ivrene, Intarsia, Cintra and Cluthra. In his later years he experimented with sculptured pieces of the diatreta (see CAGE-CUP) type. Although he officially retired from the reorganized Corning Glass Works (of which Steuben was a division) in 1934, Carder continued his experiments with new types and forms of glass.

In addition to his celebrated coloured glass Carder was the developer in the *art déco* period of important decorative glass for architectural purposes. Some of the best of this architectural glass was installed at the Rockefeller Center in New York City. Widely hailed as a designer as well as a craftsman–inventor, Carder was a Fellow of the Society of Glass Technology, an honorary member of the American Ceramic Society and a member of the American Chemical Society. In 1925 he was appointed a member of the Hoover Commission as a representative for glass which was being shown at the Paris exhibition. He was also a member of the Advisory Committee of the Metropolitan Museum, New York, and a Fellow of the Royal Society of Arts in London. With Tiffany, Carder was one of the leading craftsmen–designers in glass of the present century, and is justly regarded as one of the most significant contributors to the *art nouveau* and *art déco* developments in America. See GLASS (AMERICA).

671.

CARDING. The process of cleansing wool, cotton or linen fibres by brushing. See WEAVING (THREAD).

CARILLON. A set of not less than 25 bells tuned to the notes of the chromatic scale over two octaves. See BELL-FOUNDING.

CARLIN, MARTIN (d. 1785). French cabinet-maker of German origin. He probably trained under OEBEN and became a master cabinet-maker in 1766. He worked principally for the *marchands-merciers* of Paris and it was doubtless for POIRIER and DAGUERRE that he produced his fine cabinet-pieces mounted with SÈVRES porcelain plaques. Carlin also used other materials, including LACQUER panels. Some of his early work, introducing MARQUETRY veneers, was inspired by the example of Oeben to whom he was related by marriage. The ORMOLU MOUNTS he used frequently included a distinctive design composed of swags of drapery.

738.

CAROLINGIAN. Term in the history of the fine and decorative arts for the art produced in the reigns of Charlemagne (768–814) and his successors until *c.* 900. The outstanding feature of this period was a revival of interest in Roman antiquity and inspiration was sought in the art of the Emperors Constantine and Theodosius. Works of the 6th and 7th centuries from BYZANTIUM served as models.

CARPENTER, JOINER, CABINET-MAKER. Throughout medieval Europe FURNITURE-making, like most other trades, was largely in the hands of craft guilds. In England the oldest London society concerned with WOODWORKING was that of the carpenters, whose history can be traced back to 1388 though they did not receive their charter until 1570. An offshoot from the carpenters was the company of joiners, who specialized in furniture as distinct from constructional woodwork. The two companies were periodically involved in disputes over questions of jurisdiction, and in 1632 the Court of Aldermen assigned to the joiners the exclusive right to manufacture bedsteads, framed chairs, tables and chests, and 'all sorts of Cabinets or Boxes duftalled, pynned or glued'. In fact by this award the joiners had gained in theory a virtual monopoly of all but the roughest furniture. But by that time the power of the guilds, in England as in the rest of Europe, had declined and they were not always able to enforce their rights. After the Restoration specialists in the new techniques of VENEERING and MARQUETRY, which were soon to be applied to most fine furniture, began to call themselves 'cabinet-makers' and gradually broke away from the joiners, as the joiners had broken away from the carpenters. In a well known passage the diarist John Evelyn (1620–1706) praised their skill, as well as that of the joiners and locksmiths, 'who from very vulgar and pitiful artists are now come to produce works as curious for the fitting and admirable for their Dexterity in Contriving as any we meet with abroad'. By *c.* 1750 the cabinet-makers had formed a separate society in London, and at the end of the century not only furniture-making, but also many kindred activities, such as upholstery, GILDING, carving, papering and decorating rooms, etc., were in their hands. It was not the custom for English cabinet-makers to 'sign' their furniture, though trade labels and other inscriptions occasionally occur. For this reason it is usually impossible to assign a piece of English furniture to a particular maker except in the comparatively rare cases where bills or other documentary evidence survives

In France, which in the 18th c. possessed the most important furniture-making industry in Europe, a parallel development may be observed. Furniture and constructional woodwork alike were originally the province of the *charpentiers* or carpenters, until the demand for goods of finer quality led to specialization. By the middle of the 15th c. furniture and other portable wooden wares had become the concern of the MENUISIER—a word derived from *menu*, 'small'. Towards the end of the 16th c. furniture decorated with marquetry and veneer gained popularity and the art of veneering in ebony was introduced into France from the Netherlands, particularly by the cabinet-maker Jean Macé, who was recalled by Marie de Médicis from Middelburg in the 1620s. The craftsmen in ebony veneering were members of the guild of *menuisiers* but were known as *menuisiers-ébénistes* or *menuisiers en ébène*. In the 17th c. the word *ébéniste* gradually became current, but it was not until 1743 that the term was officially recognized in the statutes of the company, where it was laid down that specialists in marquetry and veneering should be known as *menuisiers-ébénistes*, or simply *ébénistes*, without, however, forming a separate company. The trade was much more strictly organized than in England, and an *ordonnance* of 1741 required every *ébéniste* to stamp his manufactures with a distinguishing mark, the purpose of the rule being to ensure a high standard of craftsmanship and to facilitate the recognition of goods made by outsiders. Most of the stamps bear the name of the *ébéniste* or his initials, followed by the letters ME for *menuisier-ébéniste* (not *maître-ébéniste*). Thanks to this system the attribution of late 18th-c. furniture to individual makers is simpler and surer in France than elsewhere. The guilds were abolished during the Revolution, which meant that the trade of *ébéniste* was freed from the rules that had hitherto governed it, including that which required the maker to stamp his goods.

See ÉBÉNISTE.

231, 509, 520, 738.

CARPETS AND RUGS. These are, in general, stout, hard-wearing fabrics used as floor-coverings. Similar fabrics have, however, been used by Asiatic peoples for saddle-bags and various kinds of tent-furnishings, while in Europe they have often been employed as table-covers, as is shown in many paintings of the 16th and 17th centuries. In modern English usage the two terms are indicative of size, carpets being larger and rugs smaller pieces of the same type of fabric.

Carpets and rugs are made by a variety of techniques. A method favoured by the domestic needlewoman is that of working threads or other materials through the meshes of a coarse canvas, as in the needlework carpets popular in Europe from the 16th c. onwards, or in the HOOKED RUGS of America. Carpets can also be made by the TAPESTRY technique, as in AUBUSSON carpets or the KILIMS of western Asia. Another related technique used in western Asia is that of SUMAK. But the technique *par excellence*, used in the great majority of carpets which pretend to artistic merit, is that of knotted pile. This involves a warp stretched vertically between the two beams of a simple upright loom. Around the warp threads short lengths of yarn, generally wool but sometimes silk, are looped or knotted in such a way as to form a pile which stands perpendicular to the warp. The symmetrical Turkish knot (also called Ghiordes) in Asia Minor, etc., and the asymmetrical Persian knot, used chiefly in Persia, both encircle two warp threads; the single-warp knot, used chiefly in Spain, encircles one only, while the coarse Jufti knot encircles four. The work proceeds by making a row of knots horizontally from one side of the warp to the other, using variously dyed yarns as required by the design, then weaving plain weft threads through the warp to consolidate the

Saddle-cloth of coloured appliqué felts from Pazyryk. (Hermitage Mus., 5th c. B.C.) Certain later Caucasian and Anatolian carpet designs may have developed from nomadic work such as this

fabric, then making another row of variously coloured knots, and so on. Small rugs are generally made by a single weaver, wider carpets by several working side by side. The density of the knotting determines the fineness of the pattern; 5 knots per sq. cm suffice for angular, geometrical patterns, while 50 will permit smooth curves and more realistic rendering of naturalistic forms.

It has been suggested that the knotted-pile carpet, which may be regarded as an artificial imitation of an animal fleece, was first devised by the nomadic pastoral peoples of the cold Asiatic uplands. However this may be, it is certainly an invention of immemorial antiquity. The earliest extant example, found in a frozen tomb at PAZYRYK in Siberia and now in the Hermitage Museum, Leningrad, is a highly skilled production of *c.* the 5th or 4th c. B.C. Its pattern of ROSETTES, reminiscent of rugs depicted in the reliefs of Assyrian palaces, is surrounded by broad borders depicting a procession of stags and another of horsemen.

Oriental carpets with animal patterns are recorded in the literature of classical antiquity and fragmentary examples of late antique and medieval date have been found in central ASIA and EGYPT. From the 14th c. onwards, Italian and other paintings indicate that carpets from Asia Minor, often with repeating patterns of octagons containing animal motifs, were imported into Europe in considerable numbers; small rugs of this type are preserved in Berlin and Stockholm. Turkish and Egyptian carpets of the late 15th and early 16th centuries, with geometrical and interlace patterns, have survived in some numbers.

The most splendid of all extant carpets were made in Persia under the gorgeous dynasty of the Safavids (1502–1736). These are of various kinds, taking their names generally from some prominent motif—animal carpets, hunting carpets, garden carpets, vase carpets, medallion carpets and the miscalled Polish carpets rich with silk and gold. But all are alike in the saturated splendour of their colour, in the impeccable balance of their sinuously intricate designs and in their ornamental repertory of vegetable and animal forms which, though not in itself very extensive, nevertheless yields effects of infinite richness and variety. Individual variants of this style were developed in neighbouring Oriental empires. The Mogul carpets of India lean towards a more naturalistic rendering of plants and animals, while the court manufactory of the Ottoman sultans favoured a lusher vegetation and more fevered rhythms.

Meantime Asia Minor was producing other types of rugs, more angular in design and cruder in colour, many of which were exported to Europe. These are the Uşak (named from the assumed place of origin), Holbein (from their appearance in the works of that painter), Transylvanian (from the area where many have been found) and white-ground rugs.

Few of those early Oriental carpets are now to be seen outside museums, among which the collections in Berlin, London, New York, Paris and Vienna are especially rich. But the many sedentary and nomadic peoples inhabiting a broad zone of Asia from the Mediterranean to the Pacific have continued to make rugs down to the present day; and though their work has never again achieved the superlative quality of the aristocratic carpets of the 16th and 17th centuries, they have created much that is beautiful and a multitude of things that charm the eye. As a field for collector or connoisseur, however, these later rugs are full of pitfalls. There are many different types of rug—of which the more important are noted under separate headings—and there are also many rugs which belong to no specifiable type. The rugs of any one local type may vary greatly in quality, or their type-name may be applied to some inferior imitation made elsewhere. Again, rugs may be treated to give them a false appearance of age or quality. In order to achieve a discriminating appreciation of carpets and rugs it is wise to educate one's eye through the study of those in a good collection.

It must also be pointed out that since the middle of the 19th c. the character of Oriental rug-production has been undergoing a profound transformation. What was formerly an indigenous traditional art, designed for local use, has become to a great extent an organized industry supplying the Western market (on a smaller scale North African rug-production is similarly geared to French demand). The old skills of the dyer have yielded to chemical dyeing. Patterns are chosen and adapted to appeal to Western taste. The demand for cheap export goods has debased the quality of the fabrics. This does not mean that well-made rugs of good design are no longer seen. They are, it is true, hard to find, but they repay the search generously.

The history of carpet-making in the West can be briefly dealt with. The knotted-pile technique is not indigenous to Europe, and its laborious nature, together with the high cost of European labour, has hampered its development. That it was known in some localities in the Middle Ages is shown by its use in pictorial hangings of about 1200 A.D. at Quedlinburg; similar wall-carpets were still made in Germany in Renaissance times. It was also introduced into Spain at an early date, doubtless by the Moors. Surviving examples of Spanish carpets, assigned to the 14th and later centuries, derive their designs in part from Eastern rugs and in part from contemporary European embroidery and weaving.

Fifteenth-c. paintings indicate that Oriental rugs were widely known in western Europe by that date, though they remained articles of luxury, used more on tables than on floors, for another 200 years. By the 16th c. they were being successfully imitated, as for instance in a heraldic carpet dated 1570 (Earl of Verulam) and Ushak-type carpets dated 1584 and 1585 (Duke of Buccleuch), to name some of the earliest English examples. In France, the Savonnerie factory was founded in 1626. English taste in the 17th c. favoured floral designs, like those of contemporary English embroidery, both for large carpets and for 'turkey-work' upholstery. Floral patterns appear, too, in 17th-c. Polish rugs and in the shaggy peasant rugs made in Scandinavia down to recent times.

After a period of quiescence English carpet-making enjoyed a revival in the 2nd half of the 18th c., when some notable carpets were produced by, among others, Passavant at Exeter, Whitty at Axminster and Moore at Moorfields, the last-named specializing in designs for ADAM interiors. The hand-knotting of carpets, in small quantities, has continued in Europe and America down to the present day, in most cases for special purposes requiring fabrics of particular luxury, size or durability. Mention may be made of the series of carpets produced by William MORRIS at Hammersmith and later at Merton. Small rugs have been, and still are, knotted by amateurs on domestic looms, but such domestic effort has generally adopted the easier expedient of making pile-rugs by thrusting or pulling woollen tufts or scraps of cloth through a prepared canvas foundation; of this type are the hooked rugs which have acquired some value as antiques in the United States.

Since the later 18th c. the carpet industry of the West has been mainly concerned with carpets in which the pile is not knotted but woven. In the early 19th c. the manufacture of these was immensely forwarded by the introduction of the JACQUARD process of automatic pattern-weaving and the application of steam-power to the looms. Modern carpets of Axminster, Wilton, Brussels and other types (the names indicate the mode of weaving, not the place of manufacture), mass produced as they are at low cost, are indubitably a very great social benefit. There is cause for regret, if not for surprise, in the fact that their designs, whether reproducing an Oriental original or essaying some European idiom, old or new, compare unfavourably, in artistic individuality, with the creations of the rudest Asiatic mountaineer.

83, 159, 242, 243, 437, 440, 441, 471, 472, 490, 499, 705, 739, 755, 759, 823.

CARQUILLAT, FRANÇOIS. See STEVENGRAPHS.

CARRICKMACROSS LACE. A LACE made in Ireland during the 19th c. composed of motifs cut from cambric and applied to machine-made net.

CARTOGRAPHY. I. INTRODUCTION. Cartography has been defined as 'the art, science, and technology of making maps together with their study as scientific documents and works of art'. From the many possible approaches to the subject, the following summary outlines the development of cartography in broad chronological periods and within those divisions describes the maps in major groups according to function. The types of maps designed for these varied functions may be broadly identified as follows:

(*a*) *General reference maps* created to show the configuration and location of a large range of features on the earth's surface. In the early history of cartography these maps were largely of world, continental or regional extent, such as one finds in general atlases; but as the need grew for large-scale systematic coverage of whole countries the topographic map developed, fulfilling numerous functions from military and civil engineering to recreation.

(*b*) *Thematic maps* designed to show the distribution of specific types of information such as temperature, population density, geology, etc. This class of map characteristically employs special graphic devices developed by cartographers, such as the contour, the flow-line, etc.

(*c*) *Route or itinerary maps* constructed as an aid to the traveller wishing to travel from *A* to *B* by a particular route. Sea charts, road maps and air navigation charts fall into this category.

(*d*) *Property or cadastral maps* intended to define property boundaries and often designed for legal purposes.

Not all maps fit neatly into this classification as a number of separate functions are frequently incorporated in one map.

2. THE MAPS OF PRIMITIVE PEOPLES. The maps of primitive peoples recorded in the present or last century and those used by man in primeval times had much in common. They were fashioned simply, with the most readily available materials: stone, wood, bone, leather, bark, etc., and the medium governed the map form. Thus the North American Indians employed birch-bark, the Eskimos carved coastlines in wood or bone and the Marshall Islanders constructed frames of palm branches tied with threads of coconut fibre to represent patterns of wave movements. Shells were attached to indicate islands. An ancient Egyptian map, preserved in the Turin Museum, is drawn on PAPYRUS (*c.* 1200 B.C.). While the oldest maps which have survived are inscribed on clay tablets from the Babylonian era (a map of the Euphrates valley *c.* 3800 B.C. and a diagrammatic world map *c.* 500 B.C.), the art of map-making must have been practised long before, perhaps by drawing sketch maps in sand or on cave walls.

Another feature of primitive cartography is the preoccupation with immediate local problems, with an emphasis on itinerary and boundary maps of local surroundings rather than attempts at portraying concepts of the size and shape of the earth and the configuration of the continents.

The first recorded maps made in China, dating from *c.* 2000 B.C., appeared on copper or bronze vases, each with a representation of one of the nine provinces.

3. THE CLASSICAL PERIOD

(*a*) *General Maps.* The concept of the earth as a sphere, which may be traced back to Pythagoras (*c.* 500 B.C.), was essential to the impressive development of Greek cartography, culminating in the work of Claudius Ptolemy in the 2nd c. A.D. On the assumption that the earth was a sphere approximate latitude could be measured by observing the angle between the horizon and the pole-star. Observing the difference in latitude between Syene and Alexandria and the land distance between them measured with the aid of cadastral maps, Eratosthenes (*c.* 276–195 B.C.) was able to measure the circumference of the earth within a few hundred miles of the correct value, assuming as he did that the earth was a perfect sphere.

Since the earth was considered spherical, and since the most convenient form for maps was flat, the Greeks were faced by the theoretical problem of transforming a spherical surface to a plane without some kind of distortion. The method of objectively controlling this distortion is to use a map projection. While the Babylonian astronomers had been familiar with the theory of projections, it was not until the work of Marinos of Tyre (*c.* A.D. 100), known to us through the *Geographike Huphegesis* of Claudius Ptolemy, a 'Geographical Outline' for long a standard geographical textbook, that the use of projections for terrestrial cartography was set out in written form. Ptolemy's contribution was less that of an original scholar than a skilled compiler who was able to synthesize and communicate effectively the contribution of five centuries of Greek thinking on the subject of geography and cartography. In particular he stressed the importance of observing precise and accurate co-ordinates in defining the position of places and thus creating the framework of a world map. His *Geography*, unknown to western Europe during the Middle Ages, was revived in the 15th c. as the basis of Renaissance geography. It contains tables of the positions of all the principal places in the world as then known and was provided with maps. Some of these, which may be contemporary, have survived.

(*b*) *Route Maps.* While the Greek contribution to cartography lay more in the theoretical aspects of the world and regional map, Roman cartography was more adapted to the immediate needs of the Empire in the form of road maps and property surveys. The *itineraria scripta*, or written directions for travellers, became the *itineraria picta*, or diagrammatic itinerary maps, of which the outstanding example is the *Peutinger Tafel*, a 22 ft. × 1 ft. (*c.* 6·75 m × 30 cm) road map of the Roman Empire in which directions are generally ignored in order to condense this information into a portable rolled document. This map, originally made *c.* A.D. 250, is known to us through a copy dating from 1265.

(*c*) *Property Maps.* The Roman cadastral surveys were the work of a trained class of surveyors, known as *agrimensores*, who laid out a sophisticated rectangular grid system known as the *centuriatio*, which employed ingenious surveying instruments such as the *groma*, a device used for laying out right angles and straight lines.

The Romans were of course not alone in the employment of property surveys during classical times, for it is recorded that surveying methods were in use to reposition misplaced boundary stones in the Nile Valley, and the Greeks were no doubt capable of equally sophisticated surveying procedures.

4. THE MIDDLE AGES

(*a*) *General Maps.* Since the medieval Church adopted the Roman modes of thought in geography and cartography, it failed to capitalize on the work of Ptolemy and his predecessors. The medieval sources for the world map were literary rather than scientific, as the results illustrate, and since the maps were generally intended to reflect the teachings of the Church no attempt was made at geographical accuracy. The apparent lack of objectivity of the medieval world maps has led some to assume that the Middle Ages made no contribution to the development of cartography. This is far from the case. The local and regional general maps which appeared in the 13th c. are based on observation and measurement and were reflections of geographical fact designed for practical use.

(*b*) *Route Maps and Property Maps.* The most striking class of itinerary maps were the *portolan charts*, or compass charts, dating from the late 13th c. From the earliest known chart, the *Carte Pisane* (*c.* 1250–1300), to portolan charts of the 16th c., the method of construction appears to have been the same: they were compiled from bearings and rough distances from *A* to *B* gleaned from observation, written itineraries or other charts. The wind-roses and their rays commonly found on these charts appear to have been used for navigation purposes rather than in their construction, for they are usually added later and are rarely found in the same place on two charts.

The portolan charts provide an especially interesting example of the use of colour conventions in cartography. Not only was there meaning implied in the red and black names (it appears that red indicated harbour facilities), but in some groups of portolan charts certain colours were apparently reserved for certain islands: green for Sicily and Cyprus, red for Rhodes, etc. The significance of such conventions is not fully known, and deserves further study.

The apparent lack of geographical awareness reflected in the medieval world maps is also not evident in a number of medieval road maps, such as that of England constructed by Matthew Paris *c.* 1250, which usually follow the diagrammatic itinerary form. Likewise local surveys of estates, while not drawn with the aid of sophisticated surveying instruments, nevertheless attempt to show features in their correct relative position.

5. THE EARLY MODERN PERIOD (1450–1700). During this period the demand for maps was stimulated by a growing European awareness of land and its resources both abroad as colonies were sought and at home as 'nation' states were born. The resultant rise in map production called for greater sophistication in cartography as a useful art, made possible primarily by: (*a*) the adoption of the map compilation methods expounded by Claudius Ptolemy; (*b*) the rapid development of graphic printing processes; and (*c*) the appearance of more sophisticated surveying instruments and procedures.

(*a*) *Ptolemy.* While Ptolemy is better known for his influence on the Renaissance ideas of the configuration of the earth, his contribution to cartographic method was also considerable. In particular he insisted on the use of geographical co-ordinates in compiling maps, building the major structure of the map in the form of observed co-ordinates and filling in the detail within this structure. This was in distinct contrast to the method of compiling the portolan charts, which were apparently built up from observations of distance and direction, working from the part to the whole rather than vice versa. With the translation of Ptolemy's *Geography* into Latin *c.* 1406 and the printed editions with maps from 1477 onwards his influence reached far into the 16th c. and formed the basis of modern cartographic method.

(*b*) *Graphic Printing Processes.* The reproduction of graphic material consistently lagged behind improvements in printing with movable types. It was not until 1472, some 30 years after GUTENBERG had introduced a method of casting movable types, that the first known printed map in the Western world appeared. This was a simple woodcut world map printed by Günther Zainer in Augsburg. The woodcut enjoyed widespread use in the late 15th and early 16th centuries largely because it produced relief blocks that could be printed easily in the common printing press. Nevertheless for large, detailed work the woodcut proved generally to be too crude a technique. The *copperplate technique*, first used for maps in the Bologna edition of Ptolemy's *Geography* (1477), was to dominate map printing from *c.* 1550 to the end of this early modern period. The technique afforded considerable freedom to the engraver; with simple burin he could fashion both linework and lettering with unparalleled grace. Revision of maps was comparatively easy, by flattening out the old detail by burnishing or beating out, and hammering up the back of the plate to restore the flat printing surface so that new detail could be engraved in its place. As map plates passed from publisher to publisher whole sections of plates became changed, revealing an intriguing history of ownership.

The disadvantage of copperplates was that they required considerably more pressure in the press than wood blocks, and special stronger presses for the intaglio plates had to be developed such as that used by Francesco Rosselli at the beginning of the 16th c. In addition the technique was not well suited to the printing of maps in the text as two printings were necessary. Thus most of the copperplate maps appearing in books were tipped in on separate sheets, a procedure that added extra cost to an already expensive process. Nevertheless the copperplate technique held its own longer than any other single map-printing process and the copper engravers of the great 16th- and 17th-c. map-publishing houses of Italy, the Netherlands, France and Britain supplied Europe with fine atlases in what was probably the most flamboyant chapter in the history of commercial cartography.

(*c*) *Lettering on Printed Maps.* The problem of printing map lettering is one of the most pervasive in the history of cartography. Hand-lettering, carried to a high degree of excellence in the 16th and 17th centuries, has always suffered from the difficulty of finding enough craftsmen capable of sufficiently good work. For this reason very few maps are hand-lettered today. The alternative, type, has caused other problems. In the days of the woodcut ingenious methods of inserting foundry type or stereotype plates into the wood-block were devised to avoid the formidable task of cutting small letters backwards in the block by hand. The earliest known use of type on woodcut maps is in the *Rudimentum Noviciorum* (Lübeck, 1475). The earliest case so far proved of the use of stereotyping in map printing is in a world map of 1530 by Peter Apian. The technique may well go back to the late 15th c. Stereotyping was consistently used by the German cosmographers of the mid 16th c., culminating in the work of Philipp Apian in the *Bayerische Landtafeln* (1568), for which the majority of the wood-blocks are still preserved in the Bayerisches Nationalmuseum, Munich.

An interesting method of using foundry types in map printing was the *typometrie* of Wilhelm Haas (1741–1800) and others. Here the entire map was composed of movable type—lettering, linework and symbols—and these were locked together with spaces in between.

In the 19th c. the problem of combining type and linework on a lithographic stone or plate was particularly difficult, and attempts to overcome this are seen in the work of Eckstein (1861) with a type-transfer technique. Competitive map-printing techniques such as wax-engraving (1840–1950) derived much advantage from being highly adaptable to the use of type for the map lettering.

(*d*) *Surveying Techniques*. By the end of the 16th c. most surveying principles had been established. The astrolabe, which could be employed for measuring angles, had been in use since classical times, and was refined into the cross staff, or 'Jacob's staff', first described in Latin in 1342. This instrument developed into the back staff, which avoided the problem of the observer looking directly into the sun. From these crude beginnings developed the reflecting octant (Godfrey and Hadley, 1731).

The modern theodolite, capable of measuring both vertical and horizontal angles with a high degree of precision, has its roots in the *torquetum* of Regiomontanus (1475), the *polymetrum* of Waldseemüller (1512) and an instrument described by Digges (1571). The addition of telescopic sights to this and other surveying instruments in the 17th c. (Picard, 1669) resulted in a further increase in precision.

The development of the plane-table, first described by Foullon in 1551 and again by Digges in 1571, was especially important for local surveys. The basic value of the plane-table technique, whereby a third point could be fixed by observing from two known points, relied on the principle of triangulation, first explained by Gemma Frisius in 1533. The water level, which had been used since Roman times, was familiar in the 16th c. through its representation in Vitruvius' *De Architectura* (*c.* 27 B.C.), an edition of which by Sulpitius published in Rome in 1486 was followed by other editions and translations.

While the measurement of latitude could be accomplished with the astrolabe since classical times, the determination of longitude was a far more difficult task. Many astronomical methods had been suggested and used, but it was the principle of the precise timekeeper, or marine CHRONOMETER, which finally proved successful. The use of a timekeeper for the purpose was suggested by Johann Werner (1514) but it was left to John Harrison (1693–1776) to perfect a suitable instrument between 1729 and 1761.

(*e*) *General Maps*. The general-purpose regional, continental and world maps of this period reflect the improvements and innovations described above. With the development of map printing not only geographical conceptions and misconceptions but also cartographic techniques and conventions received a wider distribution, with the result that the cartographer's craft began to include a more involved task of evaluation and compilation of source material. The first cartographer to list his authorities, Abraham Ortelius (1527–98), deserves a particularly prominent place in the history of cartography for this reason. His general world atlas, the *Theatrum Orbis Terrarum* (1570), the forerunner of the modern world atlas, included maps compiled according to a particular format by the best authorities of the day.

The printing press also liberated the cartographer from the traditional forms of patronage. Famous in this regard is Francesco Rosselli (1447–1527), whose prosperity as a commercial cartographic publisher is revealed in the extant inventory of his stock published in 1527. As the 16th c. progressed the Italian map publishers grew in number and strength, reaching a peak in the work of Antoine Lafréry *c.* 1565–75. From Italy the centre of map production moved to the Netherlands, where the work of Mercator, Ortelius, Hondius, Blaeu, Jansson, and a large number of other well known cartographic publishers was of importance. By the 18th c. other centres had arisen in France, England and Germany.

The copperplate technique of engraving allowed the commercial publishers of this period to produce fine and decorative artefacts for their customers, many of whom were merchants and businessmen as well as the owners of fine libraries. No effort was spared to please the customer, as is evident from the elaborate CARTOUCHES (title pieces), small pictures of animals, ships, heraldic devices and so on. The craft of map-colouring arose in response to this demand, becoming an independent trade recognized by artists' guilds such as that of St. Luke at Antwerp. Ortelius himself started work as a map colourist before building his own cartographic publishing business.

In the 18th c. there was a distinct trend towards a more restrained use of colour and it began to be reserved for functional rather than decorative purposes. While the occasional map intended for presentation was still richly illuminated, the bulk of the commercial work of cartographers such as D'Anville, Moll, Senex or Delisle used colour sparingly, usually only to pick out boundaries.

As cartographic sophistication increased new projections were devised on which to plot the world maps of the day. While Ptolemy had discussed the question of projection in his *Geography*, it was not until the early 16th c. that a wide variety of projections with strict mathematical properties began to be employed for world maps. A pioneer in this field was Johann Werner, who in 1514 published an early equal-area cordiform (heart-shaped) projection of the world, a form that was adopted by many subsequent cartographers. In 1569 Gerhard Mercator (1512–94) published the world map on a projection which came to bear his name. While Mercator had developed the projection empirically, it was left to Edward Wright (*c.* 1558–1615) to work out the mathematical theory behind the projection and explain its properties in mathematical terms.

(*f*) *Route Maps.* The manuscript portolan charts soon found their printed equivalents in the first published sea atlases of the late 16th c., the *Spieghel der Zeevaert* (1584) and the *Thresoor der Zeefaert* (1592) of Waghenaer. These sea charts indicated depth soundings, anchorages and coastal landmarks to the mariner. In addition many profiles of the coastline in elevation were included in spare corners of the charts.

Road maps and itineraries were also produced to guide the traveller on land. Examples of these are the map of central Europe by Erhard Etzlaub (*c.* 1460–1532), showing pilgrimage routes to Rome, and a small German road map of the environs of Nuremberg, both of the late 15th and early 16th centuries. In the 17th c. strip maps based on measured distances such as those by Ogilby (1675) appeared as even more specialized forms of cartography.

(*g*) *Property Maps.* The improvement in surveying instruments and procedures helped to produce more precise local surveys of property which were commissioned by landowners for their own purpose. The profession of surveyor increased in strength and a number of important books on surveying method were published, of which that by Aaron Rathborne (1616) was the first comprehensive English textbook on the subject.

6. THE MODERN PERIOD (1700 to present day)

(*a*) *The Size and Shape of the Earth.* The growing interest in natural science exemplified in the formation of the Royal Society in 1660 and the Académie Royale des Sciences in 1666 led naturally to a desire to map the earth in a more systematic fashion than had been attempted in previous centuries. The 18th c. became a period of intense activity in cartography as nations became aware of the importance of national systematic topographic map series based on first-order geodetic triangulation. The basis of such work lay in a more accurate and precise knowledge of the size and shape of the earth. In 1669 Jean Picard measured a degree of latitude on the meridian of Paris and Jean-Dominique Cassini and his son Jacques continued to measure this meridian within France, finding erroneously that the length of a degree of latitude diminished towards the poles, or in other words that the earth was flattened at the Equator. Sir Isaac Newton's theoretical conclusion was the opposite of this. The case was settled when two French expeditions, one in Lapland under Maupertuis (1736/7) and one in Ecuador under La Condamine (1735–45), established that the earth was an oblate spheroid (flattened at the poles) and provided estimates for the length of a degree in various latitudes which were to form the basis of 18th-c. cartography. Measurements of meridians continued throughout the 19th c. to refine further the knowledge of the actual shape of the earth, and mathematically defined spheroids fitting this shape were developed by Delambre, Airy, Everest, Bessel, Clarke and others. It was realized early that a plumb-bob was deflected from its normal position (pointing to the centre of the earth) by gravity anomalies such as a large mountain mass, and that a theoretical body known as the *geoid* could be deduced, the surface of which was everywhere perpendicular to the direction of gravity. Since all observations are made on the geoid calculations are necessary to transfer these points to a mathematically defined spheroid, which in turn can be replotted on a chosen projection. Recently the use of satellites has established a more precise figure of the earth, revealing that the north and south hemispheres are not symmetrical.

(*b*) *Surveying Instruments.* The precise instruments needed to effect these rapid improvements in cartography in the 18th c. were supplied in large part by the London instrument-makers. The theodolite, the basic tool of topographic survey which could measure precisely angles both in azimuth (horizontally) and in elevation, could now be equipped with precisely divided scales engraved with a dividing engine developed by Jesse Ramsden (1766 and 1775). Thomas Wright and Jonathan Sisson replaced the open slotted sights by a telescope with cross hairs in the first half of the 18th c. For the measurement of altitude above a given datum, the Y-level, a cumbersome instrument with a long telescopic sight, was superseded by the Dumpy level (*c.* 1848). Such instruments made possible the canal surveys of the 18th c. and the railway building of the 19th c.; the surveying aneroid barometer was developed for portable use in areas of considerable relief. For the measurement of longitude, as an alternative to the method of taking lunar distances (which had become the standard technique in the 18th c.), John Harrison's fourth chronometer became the prototype for the marine chronometer in use from the beginning of the 19th c. to the present day. None of these instruments in the 18th and 19th centuries introduced any new principle: they were refinements on instruments proposed or developed in previous periods. It was not until the 20th c. that a number of revolutionary tools of surveying were systematically employed. One of these, air photography, had been used in an experimental way from balloons during the American Civil War (1861–5), but it was not until the 1920s that the technique became well known, and not until the Second World War that it became routine. Its impact on the speed of compiling and revising detail on large-scale systematic topographic surveys has been dramatic. For example, with its help about 1,000,000 sq. miles (2,600,000 sq. km.) of topographic mapping at the scale of 1:50,000 has been performed by the British Directorate of Overseas Surveys for emerging African nations since 1946.

The growth of the science of photogrammetry (measurement from photographs), has provided a strong theoretical base for this useful surveying tool.

Another major development was the invention of the radio, which could transmit time signals at noon from the Royal Observatory at Greenwich on the Prime Meridian (0° long.) as a check on a ship's own chronometer, set at Greenwich time, for the computation of the difference in longitude.

A significant change in surveying procedure has been the trend away from triangulation (measuring one side and two angles of a triangle) to trilateration (measuring all three sides of the triangle). This has been made possible by the development of extremely rapid and precise electronic methods of distance measurement since the late 1950s.

(*c*) *Drawing and Printing Techniques*. During this period there were also great advances in map-drawing and map-printing techniques. By the middle of the 19th c. the monopoly of copperplate engraving had been completely terminated. The first blow was undoubtedly dealt by lithography, invented by Alois SENEFELDER in 1796. Lithography was an extremely versatile medium which found favour with draughtsmen, who could use pen and ink on the stone or on paper transferred to the stone and could render a wide variety of tones with crayons or other grease-based media. Impressions could be pulled faster than copperplate prints. For these reasons among others lithography became an important medium for map reproduction by the second half of the 19th c. Nevertheless both copperplate engraving and lithography found it difficult to adapt to the steam presses of Koenig (1812, 1816 and 1817), which were designed for relief printing surfaces. In response to this need a large number of relief printing processes suitable for maps was developed, of which the most important was wax-engraving, employed primarily for the printing of commercial atlases in the United States from *c*. 1850 to 1950. These processes gave way to offset lithography, invented at the turn of the century by Ira Rubel and improved considerably between the World Wars.

The early application of photography to map reproduction is seen in the independent and contemporary efforts of Sir Henry James and J. W. Osborne. In 1859 the former had prints obtained from a process he called *photo-zincography*, which was adopted by the Ordnance Survey of Great Britain. Osborne, of the Survey Department of Victoria, Melbourne, recorded a similar process at about the same time, which he termed *photo-lithography*. In both techniques a positive photographic print of the original was prepared with greasy ink, and the print was transferred to zinc or stone for printing.

The use of photography enabled original ink drawings with 'stick-up' lettering to be reduced to any desired size and transferred to the printing plate. 'Stick-up' type was apparently introduced by the United States Geological Survey *c*. 1920 as a method in which names were printed on gummed paper and stuck to the manuscript. It was refined into the system in present use, in which type is photoset on transparent stripping film and stuck to the map manuscript with wax.

The Second World War gave a great impetus to the development of stable plastic drawing media and led to the method now used in all major cartographic establishments, i.e. scribing, in which a thin film of actinically opaque photosensitive material is removed from a plastic base with scribing tools of various sizes and shapes to make a direct negative from which contact positives may be made for reproduction.

(*d*) *Automatic Cartography*. Recent developments in cartography, the impact of which is likely to be far reaching, have included automatic draughting and type-placement equipment fed with streams of co-ordinates (x, y positions) stored on magnetic tape. These co-ordinates can be compiled from the required source material with equipment known as a digitizer, which translates positions into co-ordinates. Continuous lines may be automatically recorded with a special stylus as a series of points at small intervals along the line.

(*e*) *General Maps*. Based on the large number of accurately determined new positions on the earth's surface (109 in 1706, over 6,000 by 1817), supplied by refinements in surveying techniques, increased activity in exploration and the organization of systematic topographical surveys, the world map increased in accuracy, starting with the careful compilations of Guillaume Delisle (1675–1726) and J. B. Bourguignon d'Anville (1697–1782). Yet the actual techniques for plotting this new information in manuscript and then transferring it to the copperplate changed very little throughout the 17th and 18th centuries.

All scales of maps, from small-scale atlas maps to large-scale topographic maps, benefited from the 18th-c. development of geodesy. It probably would not be true to say that a completely new type of map was born with the 18th-c. topographic map, for this was a logical extension of the large- and medium-scale maps which had been produced in the 16th c.—for example, the 24-sheet map of Bavaria by Philipp Apian (1568) or that of Christopher Saxton for England (1579). Nevertheless the Cassini map of France in 182 sheets (completed under Cassini de Thury in 1793) was the first such map series based on precise triangulation, and was followed by similar national efforts in other countries. The British Ordnance Survey was founded in 1791 to continue work that William Roy had already started independently. Property maps and route maps also became based on the network of newly plotted positions and their production, especially in Britain, has become more integrated into the general mapping approach.

(*f*) *Thematic Cartography*. In response to a wide variety of new statistical information from the social and natural sciences, which became available in the late 18th and early 19th centuries, a new type of map, the thematic or special-purpose map, came into being. The thematic map is characterized by its specific function: to present cartographically a given theme, which may be altitude, temperature, geology, land use or other subjects. By 1855 almost all the basic devices for representing data on thematic maps had been introduced.

(*g*) *Cartographic Devices*. (i) *Choropleth*. In this technique an area symbol in the form of a tone or colour is applied to an administrative or statistical area according to the average values or absolute numbers observed for that area. It was introduced by Baron Charles Dupin in 1826.

(ii) *Dasymetric*. In this method the administrative or statistical area is subdivided into areas of degrees of likely incidence of the mapped phenomenon. These sub-areas are then mapped choroplethically. The best known early example of this technique was in the population density maps of Henry D. Harness to accompany the report of the Railway Commissioners for Ireland (1837), in which those areas unlikely to support population have been separated and symbolized accordingly. The result is that the original statistical areas do not show through the final map. The first use of the technique was probably in a small world map by George Poulett Scrope in 1833.

(iii) *Isarithmic*. This term is used to cover a number of techniques in which lines representing constant values (isarithms) are used. The development of the isarithm arose from two distinct beginnings. One was the concept of the isarithm as the intersection of the volume to be mapped and a plane parallel to a given datum. This is known as an isometric line. The idea may have occurred to Bruinss in a manuscript map of 1584. Numbered isometric lines are certainly found on a manuscript map by Ancellin (1697). Early printed instances are found in the maps of Cruquius (1729) and Buache (1737). All these examples are found in connection with showing the depth of the sea-bed (isobaths). Later the idea was adapted to show elevations on the land by du Carla (1782) and J. L. Dupain Triel (1791). By the 1820s the contour, as it was called, was a standard cartographic device, and it has remained so to the present day.

Another source of the isarithm was in the maps of equal magnetic variation, first appearing in published form in the maps of Edmund Halley (1701 and 1702). In this technique, while the lines represent constant values (in this case equal variation of the compass), no concept of a volume intersected by planes is involved.

The *isopleth*, a special kind of isarithm in which the lines represent constant quantities in the *areas* through which they pass (in contrast to the *points*), was suggested by Lalanne in 1845 and introduced by Ravn in a population density map of Denmark published in 1855.

(iv) *Relief shading*. The present system of depicting relief by shading this terrain as if lighted by a light source from the north-west has its roots in the crude hill drawing of the Middle Ages, which developed into crude hachuring in the 18th c. Early sophisticated printed relief shading, as in the work of J. F. W. Des Barres (*The Atlantic Neptune*, 1774–84), was done by 'engraving in the crayon manner', in which 'continuous' tones could be shown. With the invention of lithography *c*. 1796 graded tones began to appear on maps with increasing frequency, but their use for the representation of relief has recently become more sophisticated owing largely to the improvements in offset lithography, the development of the air brush, the refinement of the half-tone process and the increased interest in the theory of relief shading stimulated by the Second World War.

(v) *Flow-line*. This is a device that illustrates simultaneously the amount and the direction of a given phenomenon, in which a line shows the direction and the thickness of the line is proportional to the amount. It is now most commonly used in traffic maps to show the volume of traffic flow along particular routes. The idea was first set out by J. G. Lehmann (1765–1811) in the form of the hachure, in which the orientation of the line gave the direction of slope and its thickness was made proportional to the angle. The first use of the technique in its more conventional form to depict traffic flows appears to have been by Henry D. Harness in two traffic maps showing the number of passengers carried by public conveyances and the volume of freight traffic on the Irish canals and railways (1837).

(vi) *Graduated circle*. This is a symbol in which the area of a circle is drawn proportional to the amount of a phenomenon considered at a point. It appears to have been introduced by Henry D. Harness in the same work as the dasymetric and flow-line techniques, namely the atlas accompanying the final report of the Railway Commissioners for Ireland (1837).

Two production problems posed by thematic maps stand out as being of special significance: the representation of *tone* and *colour*. Before the invention of lithography graded tones were difficult to reproduce, but with the use of crayon subtle variations in tone were possible with the new technique. With the development of half-tone, arising from experiments begun in the 1870s, pencil or crayon drawings on paper could be transferred to the lithographic plate in reduced form, allowing the cartographer more flexibility.

The large number of categories characteristically shown on thematic maps called for more sophisticated ways of applying colour. Until the middle of the 19th c., when colour lithography was introduced, the printer had no means of applying flat colour to the map except by hand. There had been early experiments in colour map printing, but none of these proved very satisfactory. For extremely detailed colouring, such as is needed in geological maps, hand colouring is found extending into the 20th c., and the colouring task was of sufficient complexity to warrant the occasional acknowledgement of the map colourist.

8, 174, 536, 601, 837.

CARTOUCHE. Term with several meanings. In architecture it denotes a panel in the form of a scroll or sheet of paper with curling edges, which may bear an inscription. It may be a corbel, mutule or MODILLION. From the 17th c. it was also used generally to denote any ornament in the form of an Ionic scroll or volute. In metalwork and cabinet-making the term denotes a tablet, usually oval, with ornamented frame or scrolled ends and often containing an inscription, ornamental monogram, etc. In the 19th c. the term was used for oval figures in Egyptian hieroglyphics enclosing royal or divine names or titles. In printing, map-making, etc., the word often means a title-piece enclosed in a decorative frame.

CARTWRIGHT, EDMUND (1743–1823). A clergyman of Leicestershire who invented the first power loom and also a wool-combing machine. See WEAVING (FABRIC).

CARVER CHAIR. Term used in the United States of America for an early type of straight-backed, rush-seated chair with turned legs which rose above the level of the seat so as to support the arm spindles in front and at the back to serve as back posts terminating in ornamentally turned FINIALS. This type of chair is supposed to have been named after John Carver (*c.* 1575–1621) of Nottingham, the founder and first Governor of Plymouth Colony and one of the Pilgrim Fathers. See FURNITURE (AMERICAN).

In Britain the term is used for the elbow chair in a set of dining chairs.

67, 220, 645.

CASEMENT. Architectural term for a concave MOULDING such as SCOTIA or CAVETTO, used in door and window jambs, also frequent in late GOTHIC architecture. The term also means the swinging part of a window hinged to the upright side of the window frame.

CASHMERE. See SHAWLS.

CASLON, WILLIAM (1692–1766). The most famous of English type-founders. Born at Cradley, Worcestershire, he was apprenticed in London to a contractor to the Board of Ordnance for engraving marks on gun-locks. He followed this trade, and by 1719 was also cutting brass tools for BOOKBINDING. William Bowyer, the printer, admiring his brass letters, induced him to set up as a cutter of punches for type and as a type-founder, and lent him money. The first of Caslon's types was a Hebrew, finished *c.* 1722. In that year he undertook an Arabic for the Society for Promoting Christian Knowledge, and it was printed in 1725. By that time Caslon had also made a ROMAN and ITALIC for pica body. His *Specimen* of 1734 shows a comprehensive range of roman and italic faces and a number for BLACK LETTER, Greek, Hebrew and Oriental scripts.

Before 1742 Caslon had been joined in the business by his son, WILLIAM, a very skilful letter-cutter, and by the time of the latter's death in 1778 the Caslon type-foundry was extremely well equipped with type of all kinds. It went out of business in 1936.

Caslon was the first of the British type-founders who could offer type of his own cut and approximately uniform design to supply the needs of the printing trade. His roman and italic were modelled on the best Dutch work of the 17th c., and they soon superseded the miscellaneous collection, largely of foreign origin, previously in use in Britain. Large quantities of his types were exported to America and some to European countries. They went out of fashion *c.* 1800, but a taste for them revived 50 years later.

See TYPOGRAPHY.

610, 688.

CASSONE. A large clothes chest, which was often part of a wife's dowry. The Italian *cassoni* are among the most beautiful furniture of the Middle Ages and Renaissance. The earliest surviving examples, dating from the 15th c., are mostly decorated with painting and GILDING. The custom was to cover the wood with a thin skin of gesso, which might be either painted or carved with ornament in low relief. The repetitive conventional patterns at first employed recall the woven designs in medieval textiles. But as the 15th c. advanced the embossed decoration became bolder and freer, often taking the form of classical ARABESQUES and running scrolls of foliage, while artists such as Francesco di Stefano, called Pesellino (active Florence 1422–57), and

Francesco di Giorgio (Siena 1439–1502), among others, painted the front panels of *cassoni* with scenes from classical and biblical history or mythology. On marriage chests a favourite subject, rendered in low relief picked out in paint, was the betrothal ceremony, in which a procession of heralds, musicians and wedding guests bearing gifts, clad in brilliantly coloured late Gothic dress, advance over a flowery meadow towards the bride and groom.

In Florence and Siena the painted chest was one of the most delightful provinces of the narrative artist and Vasari, writing in the next century when the fashion had gone out, recalls nostalgically the day when 'even the foremost painters set themselves to do work of this kind and did not disdain, as many would now, to paint and gild such chattels'. Among the painters he had in mind were artists such as Uccello, Domenico Veneziano and Botticelli, whose panels, removed from their chests, are now framed like easel pictures in picture galleries. Other chests were decorated with carving or MARQUETRY.

In the 16th c. the love of solid architectural forms that characterizes the Italian Renaissance gradually transformed the design of the *cassone*. No longer a mere box with a flat lid, it acquired a massive, monumental aspect with a boldly profiled base, often supported on lion paws, a front framed between pilasters or caryatids and a coved top enriched like a classical cornice. The rectangular outline gave way to a rounded contour, a form first employed by Verrocchio in the bronze and porphyry sarcophagus which he made for the Medici brothers in 1472. Painted panels and delicate surface decoration in low relief were inappropriate to the new style and were superseded by carvings in solid walnut, to which the carver in imitation of the Roman sarcophagus sought to give a strong sculptural effect, often choosing as a theme for the frieze the heroic scenes of ancient history and mythology. Such chests often look like sarcophagi cast in bronze. The main centre of manufacture was Rome. In the 17th c. the *cassone* was displaced by the chest of drawers, the CUPBOARD, the cabinet and other more sophisticated and specialized types of furniture.

See also FURNITURE (EUROPEAN).

751.

CASTING. See COPPER AND ITS ALLOYS; see also IRON (CAST). An account of the techniques of casting statues by the *cire-perdue* (lost-wax) process will be found in *The Oxford Companion to Art*.

CATHEDRAL BINDINGS. Bookbindings decorated with a large stamp of a formalized cathedral façade, or with smaller stamps reproducing rose windows and other motifs from GOTHIC architecture. The decoration is usually in 'blind' (i.e. without GILDING) but on elaborate examples *appliqués* of coloured leathers were used to simulate mosaic or stained glass. Specially popular in France *c.* 1815–40, they were a minor manifestation of the Gothic Revival led by Viollet-le-Duc (1814–79) in France and by PUGIN in England. See BOOKBINDING.

CAUCASIAN RUGS. The product of various peoples inhabiting the mountainous tract between the Black and Caspian seas. The old cultural patterns of the region, of which rug-weaving was one expression, have in recent years been radically changed by Soviet Russian policy.

The charm of these rugs lies often in their abundant primitive vitality. The designs, often very naïve, rarely aspire beyond alignments or simple DIAPERS of geometrical figures (polygons, stars, crosses, stepped lozenges) and more or less conventionalized natural forms (flowers, Persian cones, quaint caricatures of animals and human beings) worked out in bright blues, reds, yellows and white. The pile is generally rather long, and tied with the Ghiordes or Turkish knot.

The rugs made in the northern and western parts of the area are for the most part frankly nomadic in character, with bold designs including a good deal of crude geometry and a very characteristic cross-shaped motif with flower-buds exploding from it. Of this group the Kazak rugs are the principal representatives. Nearly related to them are Cherkess, Gendje, Kutais and Tiflis rugs, of which the last two employ also cone and tree motifs.

The rugs of the south and east make use of a similar repertory of ornament but with greater refinement of taste. The geometrical elements are smaller and neater, and the floral and cone forms derived from Persia are much more in evidence. Shirvan and Daghestan rugs are the chief representatives of this group, which includes also Baku, and Chetchen, Derbend, Kabistan, Karabagh, Kuba, Lesghian, Seichur and Shusha rugs.

Of the pileless rugs of the area, SUMAK rugs stand alone by virtue of their peculiar technique but employ normal Caucasian ornament; Sile rugs, technically a variety of the Sumak, and the tapestry-woven Varna rugs display grotesque human and animal forms in striped or chequer patterns.

755.

CAVETTO. A convex MOULDING forming a quarter-circle in profile. It forms a prominent feature of the CORNICE in much case furniture.

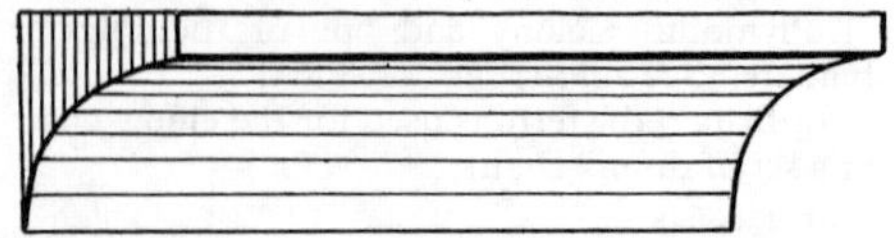

CAXTON, WILLIAM (*c.* 1422–*c.* 91). The first English printer. After serving an apprenticeship to a member of the Mercer's Company of London he was sent to the Company's subsidiary, the English Merchant Adventurers, at Bruges in 1441. He stayed in the Low Countries for 30 years and rose to be Governor of the English merchants there. The English-born Duchess of Burgundy encouraged him to translate into English the French legends of Trojan heroes, and he began this work in 1469. In 1470–1 he was in Cologne and there learned to print. He introduced the new art at Bruges, where he produced his *Recuyell of the Historyes of Troye*, the first book in English to be printed, and five other books before moving to England in 1476. At Westminster he set up his press and bookshop in the precincts of the Abbey. The earliest known piece of printing done in England, presumably by Caxton, is a letter of indulgence, of which the Public Record Office has a copy, dated by hand on 13 December 1476. In the following year he produced the first book to be printed in England, the *Dictes and Sayengis of the Philosophres*.

About 100 books, tracts and leaflets printed by Caxton are extant, among them liturgies, devotional works and grammars in Latin and Chaucer's poems and Malory's *Morte d'Arthur* in English. Particularly famous, because of their influence on the development of a standard form of written English, are his translations of French courtly romances and moral tales. He is believed to have died in 1491 or early in 1492. See TYPOGRAPHY.

71, 77, 175, 764.

CELADON. European term which refers imprecisely to Chinese and other PORCELAIN wares with a range of greyish-green glazes corresponding roughly to what the Chinese call *ch'ing* or *ts'ui* and the Japanese call *seiji*. It is conventionally restricted to Lung-chüan, northern Celadon and Yüeh (see CHINA, CERAMICS) and to Japanese and Korean wares with similar glazes, though in Japan and China Ju and Kuan would also be regarded as celadons. In his book *Chinese Celadon Wares* (1957) G. St. G. M. Gompertz proposes the following practical definition: 'Celadon may be held strictly to denote high-fired porcellanous wares with a felspathic glaze of characteristic bluish or greyish green tone derived from iron. From a technical point of view there is ground for including Chün ware among the celadons, for the colour of the glaze is now known to be attributable to iron and it is, of course, described as *ch'ing* in the Chinese literature. However, it is difficult to associate the intense blue of most Chün wares with the term celadon . . .'

The origin of the word is uncertain. It has been thought by some to derive from 'Céladon', a character in the stage version of an early 17th-c. pastoral romance *L'Astrée* by Honoré D'Urfé on account of the colour of his costume. Others have suggested that it is a corruption of Salah-ed-din or Saladin, an Egyptian Sultan who sent 40 pieces of this ware to the Sultan of Damascus in 1171.

CELLINI, BENVENUTO (1500–71). Florentine goldsmith and metal-worker who turned to large-scale sculpture. His autobiography, written in a racy vernacular, has been famous since the 18th c., when Goethe translated it, for its vivid picture of a Renaissance craftsman proud of his skill and independence, boastful, quarrelsome, superstitious and devoted to the great tradition embodied in Michelangelo. It has given him a wider reputation than could have come from his artistic work alone; but to modern eyes he also appears as one of the most important Mannerist sculptors.

His life can be roughly divided into three periods. From the first, spent mostly in Rome, nothing survives but some COINS and MEDALS and the impressions of two large seals. During the second (1540–5), which he spent in the service of Francis I of France, he created the famous salt-cellar of gold enriched with ENAMEL, exquisitely worked with two principal and many subsidiary figures. This (now in Vienna) is the most important piece of goldsmith's work that has survived from the Italian Renaissance. He also made for the king a large bronze relief, the *Nymph of Fontainebleau* (Louvre). The remainder of Cellini's life was passed in Florence in the service of Cosimo I. Here he cast the bronze *Perseus* (Loggia dei Lanzi, Florence, 1545–54) which, with the figures and reliefs of the pedestal, is reckoned his masterpiece. To this period also belong his marble sculptures, the *Apollo and Hyacinth* and *Narcissus* (both in the Bargello, Florence) and the *Crucifix* (Escorial).

Many goldsmiths' works have been attributed to him, but of these only the mounts of an agate vase in the British Museum may be by his hand. The influence of his technique is not obtrusive in his large sculpture, but appears strongly in the dry, precise chiselling of his two bronze busts, *Bindo Altoviti* (Gardner Mus., Boston, *c.* 1550) and *Cosimo I* (Bargello, Florence).

The manuscript of Cellini's autobiography disappeared during the 18th c. and was discovered in 1805. The source of the first printed edition (Naples, 1728) is not known. The *Life* was first translated into English by Thomas Nugent and since then there have been several English versions, including one by John Addington Symonds (1888).

CENNINI, CENNINO (*c.* 1370–*c.* 1440). Italian artist and writer. Born near Florence, he claims to have been a pupil of Agnolo Gaddi (*c.* 1345–96), who learnt from his father, Taddeo Gaddi (*d.* 1366), who in turn was a pupil of Giotto. No authenticated work by Cennino Cennini has survived and he is remembered for his craftsman's handbook *Il Libro dell'Arte* or *Trattado della Pittura*. This work stands between the

Salt-cellar by Benvenuto Cellini of gold, enamel and ivory. It was begun in Rome for Cardinal Ippolito d'Este and completed in Paris for Francis I. Charles IX gave it to the Archduke Ferdinand. The subject represents allegorically the production of salt by the interaction of sea (Neptune) and land. (Kunsthistorisches Mus., Vienna, 1540–3)

medieval and the modern periods in content and outlook. Cennini argues that painting has high merit in the scale of human occupations because it combines activity of the imagination with manual skill and he may have derived from the school of Giotto his precept that 'nature' is the artist's best master. In the main, however, the book is not a theoretical treatise but a practical manual for the apprentice and craftsman. He preserves the medieval precepts and technical formulae in the manner of THEOPHILUS but he was heir to the workshop tradition initiated by Giotto and his book is an invaluable source of information about the grinding of pigments, the making of brushes and pens, the preparation of grounds, plaster coating, tempera techniques, glass painting, casting, etc., with detailed instructions for procedure.

The earliest manuscript of his work is inscribed 1437 'in the debtors' prison in Florence', but this may be a posthumous copy of an earlier original.

92, 132.

CENTRAL ASIA. See ASIA, CENTRAL.

CERAMICS

1. INTRODUCTION. The potter shapes things in CLAY and then hardens them by heat. The craft is one of the oldest and most widely disseminated in the world. There are many different kinds of clay with different properties and many sources of heat, so the basic action is performed by different techniques with different results. Clay is used for architectural and industrial purposes as well as for the domestic ones of cooking, eating, pharmacy, etc. All of these uses are comprehended in the awkward word 'ceramics' or 'keramics', derived from the ancient Greek *κέραμος*, potter's clay. Architectural and industrial ceramics lie outside the scope of this article.

Clays are seldom found in a pure state, and need a great deal of refinement and manipulation before they can be used. Most clays also need to be mixed with FLUXES and other ingredients to give plasticity or stability, colour or whiteness or translucency. Few of the necessary ingredients are commonly found in one place. It is a modern potter's maxim that it is cheaper to take the clay to the coal than the coal to the clay.

The POTTER'S WHEEL is the basic tool of the trade. It was used in the Near East before 3000 B.C. (See PREHISTORIC TECHNOLOGY.) Our awareness of the impress on the wet spinning clay of two human hands is still an element of our enjoyment of a pot, and the human span is perhaps still an instinctive standard of scale. But clay vessels can be shaped by other means than by throwing on the wheel; by laborious hand-modelling in superimposed coils or round a solid core, or by moulding and casting; and hardened, unfired surfaces can be tooled and turned.

The shape imparted to the clay is made permanent by baking, or 'firing'. Common earthenware thus hardened remains porous. To prevent liquids permeating the ware, and to keep it cleaner, it has generally been found expedient to apply a GLAZE (see below).

The heat for firing the pottery must be controlled and sustained. The kiln was invented in the Middle East, some 6,000 years ago. For fuel primitive man used whatever came to hand. Wood has been the staple fuel for developed pottery, being supplanted by coal, gas, etc., only in the last two centuries. In general the greater the heat the more compact and tough is the 'body' of the ware. But firing is a very hazardous process unless it is perfectly understood and controlled, as every beginner knows. Small kiln-blemishes may perhaps be hidden, but fire, the potter's wild partner (to use Lane's phrase), must have destroyed almost as much as it has perfected, at any rate in terms of time, trouble and money. Baked clay cannot be re-formed; it can only be ground down. Nice adjustment of the fire of the kiln does, however, add to the resources of the potter: the effects on the ware of an 'oxidizing' flame, i.e. one burning fiercely, differ from those caused by a 'reducing' flame, i.e. one deprived of oxygen and giving off smoke.

The plasticity of clay invites the potter to modelling. This, the possibility of colouring clay and the colour-and-light effects inherent in even the simplest glaze arouse his decorative instincts and turn him willy-nilly into an artist. As a craftsman he is concerned with exploitation of his material and fitness for use; as an artist he is concerned too with aptness of decoration and such things as proportion, mass, rhythm and colour—the last being available to him in greater intensity and permanence than to most other artists. Like everybody else, he works within the artistic context of his own generation. Pottery reflects the art of its own age and often contributes conspicuously to it.

Its history therefore is written into the history of art, of social habits and of the movements of trade and fashion, as well as into the history of technology.

2. TECHNOLOGY

(*a*) *Ceramic Bodies.* Heat drives water from clay at temperatures between 450 °C. and 600 °C. Different clays can withstand different degrees of heat beyond this point, and some eventually vitrify; too much heat will melt them all.

(i) Earthenware. Tiles, flowerpots, etc., are fired at the relatively low temperature of 900 °C–1040 °C. Household earthenwares at temperatures up to 1200 °C. Earthenware clays do not vitrify, but remain porous and so require glazing for use. They fire to a wide variety of colours—black, red, brown and buff. Earthenware is the substance of primitive and peasant pottery, of most ancient, medieval and Near Eastern wares, and of most European painted pottery. Modern commercial white earthenware originated with refinements developed in Staffordshire in the 18th c.

(ii) Stoneware. This is fired at between 1200 °C. and 1280 °C., to the point of vitrification. Stoneware is non-porous and water-resistant: glazing is necessary merely for smoothness. The earliest known stonewares are Chinese, from the long centuries of the Chou Dynasty (10th to 3rd centuries B.C.). European stoneware is post-medieval and northern. Most stoneware clays fire to grey or buff, but fine red stonewares are also known. The Staffordshire revolution in the 18th c. produced a thin white stoneware and stoneware bodies which could be stained to simulate coloured stones.

(iii) Porcelain ('China'). This requires a kiln temperature of up to 1400 °C. It is distinguished by being white-bodied and translucent. It was evolved in CHINA from stoneware, between the times of the T'ang and Sung Dynasties (6th–13th centuries A.D.). Chinese porcelain—'true porcelain' or 'hard-paste' porcelain—is essentially made of two related minerals, china clay (kaolin) and the felspar china stone (*petuntse*). The formula was rediscovered at Dresden early in the 18th c. and remains the standard for Continental manufacturers. Modern Continental porcelain is actually 'harder' than Chinese. In the effort to reproduce the Chinese material European potters also invented various imitations, based mainly on the components of GLASS and firing at much lower temperatures (*c.* 1100 °C.)—'soft-paste' or 'frit' porcelains. 'Bone china', a hybrid body containing calcined ox bones, was developed in England *c.* 1800 and is still the standard British china. 'Parian' is a harder variety of it, invented in the middle of the 19th c. and mainly used for figures.

(*b*) *Glazes.* A glaze is a glossy coating, applied to the surface of the ware after shaping and fixed there by firing. Only glaze-compositions which combine chemically with components of the ware itself will adhere satisfactorily. The most widely used glazes have been the following:

Alkaline glazes, used in ancient EGYPT and elsewhere in the Middle East. These are virtually soda glass, i.e. sand fired with nitre or some other form of soda.

Lead glazes, made of sand fused with sulphide or oxide of lead. These were known to the Romans and in China from the time of the Han Dynasty (3rd c. B.C.–3rd c. A.D.) and have been very widely used in Europe from medieval times for earthenware and soft-paste porcelain.

Leadless glazes, substituting borax or some other flux in order to eliminate the deadly effect of working with lead compounds; developed in the 19th c.

Tin glazes are lead glazes made white and opaque by the addition of oxide of tin. The technique originated in the Middle East and spread into Europe mainly through Moorish Spain and Italy, wares so glazed being called successively maiolica, faience and delftware.

Salt glazes, used on stoneware and made by throwing salt into the kiln when the fire is hottest. This glaze adheres particularly closely to the ware, being more like a skin than a coat.

Felspathic glazes are used on hard-paste porcelain and on the Chinese porcellanous stonewares of the T'ang and Sung Dynasties. They have also been used on some English bone chinas. They are composed of china stone mixed with lime and other ingredients.

Wood-ash is used as a flux in glazes on Oriental stonewares.

Alkaline and lead glazes are particularly shiny and can be made perfectly transparent. All glazes can be coloured by staining, and certain combinations are possible, e.g. the application of a clear lead glaze over a tin glaze. Glazes are applied by dusting in powder form, or as liquids by spraying or dipping, to the raw, i.e. unfired, ware; or after an initial low-temperature 'biscuit' firing. If body and glaze expand and contract at different rates, the glaze will craze, i.e. split into a network of fine cracks. Chinese potters early learnt how to make a decorative virtue of this defect and to control it at will.

(*c*) *Decoration.* This can begin with the unfired clay itself, which can be modelled or moulded or tooled. Some stonewares and porcelains are hard enough after firing to be cut and polished like stones. Vessels can be made of variegated clays to resemble agate and other stones, and white clays can be stained. Liquefied clay, or SLIP, of a contrasting colour, or stained, can also be applied as decoration. Glazes also can be stained, crazed or otherwise exploited.

Fine relief work, or intricate shapes, can be achieved by pressing clay into moulds or by casting, that is by pouring slip into absorbent moulds. Ceramic figures are made either by direct modelling or by moulding or casting. European figures have almost all been made by the second or third method. Moulds are made from a dismembered master model and the separate parts, when moulded or cast, are joined together with slip. A single figure may have been formed by the joining of a dozen or more sections.

Painting in ochres and other earth colours has been practised since Neolithic times. Painting in colours derived from ores or metals began in China in T'ang times (7th–10th centuries A.D.). These are the 'high-temperature' colours, green from copper, blue from cobalt, purple from manganese and yellow from antimony: colours which require the full heat of the kiln for their development, and which can be used under or in a glaze. A colour-range virtually without limits is obtainable in 'low-temperature' colours: ENAMELS fluxed with lead, applied on top of a glaze after firing and themselves fired at much lower temperature or temperatures in a 'muffle' kiln. (See COLOURS AND COLOURANTS.)

Lustre is a fine coating of metal derived from an oxide or a sulphide (of gold, silver, copper or platinum) and applied on the glaze either as painting or as a ground-colour.

The soft, brownish GILDING of the 18th c. was applied as a paste made of gold leaf and honey and lightly fired. This could be chased and burnished. This method has been superseded by the use of an amalgam of gold and mercury, which is more economical but brassier and less attractive.

Transfer printing of line and stipple engravings was developed in England in the 18th c. and became of great commercial importance in the 19th c. Much mass-produced pictorial decoration is today applied by lithographic transfers: direct photographic printing has also been used.

3. EUROPEAN CERAMICS

(*a*) *Social History*. Medieval Europe probably found its chief uses for pottery in the kitchen and store-room, but the most numerous survivors are jugs and the fact that many were slip-decorated, or modelled with GROTESQUES, suggests that these at least were meant for the table. Being fragile, they were expendable. Those that exist today we owe to excavations and chance finds: little suggests that they were valued for anything other than their usefulness. Dissemination of certain distinctive wares proves that admiration for them could be widespread—for example, hard north-German pottery has been found in Sweden—but medieval wares were not handed down the generations as treasures, and our present recognition of their aesthetic qualities is hardly one generation old. Earlier ages thought them quaint, but coarse. Floor tiles inlaid with heraldic and other formal devices, and FIRE-BACKS similarly moulded, were more obviously artistic and meant to last.

About the medieval potters themselves we know next to nothing. Some were probably nomadic, moving around from place to place, as is suggested by the smallness of excavated kiln-sites. The manufacture of inlaid floor tiles seems to have been a monastic speciality, and the finding of sherds of hard, black-glazed earthenware on late-medieval monastic sites in the north of England has led to the association of this ware with the Cistercian order.

It was with the mastering of the new techniques of lead glaze and salt glaze in the 15th c. that pottery became decorative and moved up in the social scale. The big lustred dishes made in the 15th c. at Manises and Valencia in Spain were blazoned like flags with appropriate armorials and dispatched as royal presents all over Christendom. Drug jars were made for the monastic and aristocratic pharmacies which came into being as a result of the plagues of the Middle Ages. The potters of Beauvais made dishes moulded with the emblems of Christ's Passion, and these seem to have been intended for Church use. In the 16th c. we find the production of such highly exclusive wares as the mysterious Saint Porchaire earthenware made in Poitou, and the equally rare and even more famous Medici porcelain made in Florence for the Grand Duke—wares much too exalted for commerce. Finally, in the middle of the 16th c. we meet recognizable men such as the French master potter Bernard PALISSY, who was taken away from the entourage of the High Constable of France by the queen herself to make for her a pottery grotto in the Tuileries.

Such examples show the response in the Renaissance of the highest social classes to the potter's art, and its widespread adoption for daily needs will be the more easily imagined: dishes for the table, inkstands, decorative vases, stoves and so forth. Mention should also be made of the prevalence in Renaissance Italy of the *piatti di pompa*, display plates painted with historical and other figure compositions or—for use as love gifts—with the idealized portrait of a lovely girl or youth. These are the ancestors of the large family of wares intended chiefly for commemoration or propaganda. The highly developed skills of painting and potting reflected in objects such as all of these prompted also the creation of the virtuoso 'master pieces', dishes signed by the master painters Nicola Pellipario, Maestro Giorgio Andreoli (both working between 1510 and 1540) and others. Here too should be mentioned the stoneware bottles and jugs made on the Rhine and signed by the Mennickens and other potters in the next generation. Owners sometimes liked to mount them in silver, as they also mounted ostrich eggs, coconut shells, Chinese porcelain and other curiosities.

Porcelain and SILVER play a great part in the social history of European ceramics. As pottery made its way on to the table and into other forms of polite usage, it did so in competition with other materials—wood, LEATHER, PEWTER, and GLASS. Silver was always the most highly esteemed material, and vessels of clay have often been given the shape of metal, and specifically silver, prototypes. But it is sometimes necessary to melt silver for coinage, and this bodes well for the potter. A French edict of 1689, repeated in 1709, ordered the melting of all table vessels of silver and gold. Within a week all the upper classes of France were refurnishing their tables with faience and so great was the impulse given to the potters that many new works were established and there was a threat of fuel shortage; so the state had to step in and limit the expansion.

A new kind of prestige was given to pottery in the 17th and early 18th centuries by certain independent painters of note. These were the HAUSMALER, artists working in Augsburg, Nuremberg, Bohemia and elsewhere in Germany and the Empire, painting on enamels and glass as well as on faience and Chinese and European porcelain. Their style of painting is usually quite individual; their work (sometimes signed) includes some of the best ceramic painting of their time. Perhaps the most famous was Ignaz Bottengruber of Breslau (Wrocław) and Vienna, who worked in the early 18th c. Frederick van Frijtom of Delft (active 1658–92) was another artist whose work was famous in his own day.

The arrival of Oriental porcelain in Europe awoke not only the wish to reproduce it, but also the cult of collecting it. In the 18th c. this cult was sometimes taken to extreme lengths, particularly in Germany. A print of 1709 of the Porcelain Room in the Charlottenburg Palace in Berlin shows porcelain in massed display from the floor to the ceiling. The Elector of Saxony once traded a regiment of dragoons for eight enormous vases. The porcelain craze grew with the recognition of the possible financial rewards that a domestic porcelain factory might bring, and kings, princes and even bishops all over Europe turned themselves for a time into potters. MEISSEN, the royal factory near Dresden, used for a mark the crossed swords of Saxony. SÈVRES, the royal French factory, entwined two Ls for king Louis. This craze only began to die down in the 1770s, with the onset of NEO-CLASSICISM.

There had, however, been more sober reasons for the porcelain outburst. The East provided not only china, but China tea; and as tea, coffee and chocolate advanced in popularity in the new drawing-room culture of the 18th c., so did the material best suited for their service. In its artistic heyday European porcelain was not only a cult but also a growth industry, providing indeed an amazing variety of objects from equestrian statues and organ pipes to artificial flowers and false teeth. Its production was fostered on mercantilist principles. The aristocratic patrons protected their factories with the strongest fiscal fences that they could contrive. By the time that the *ancien régime* fell, the craft of the potter was—in England, France and Germany—fast becoming an industry: specialized, standardized, localized and recognized as a national asset. The social history of European ceramics from then on is a matter of labour relations at one end of the scale and the occasional knighthood and high civic office at the other.

Memories, however, that the industry had once been a craft and an art stirred in the middle of the 19th c. The cult of the hand-made pot began in the 1860s and 1870s with men like Théodore Deck in Paris and Henry Doulton in London. It was greatly forwarded by the English ARTS AND CRAFTS MOVEMENT, led by William MORRIS; by the excited discovery of early Chinese stonewares, newly revealed by excavation; and by the personal contact of Bernard Leach, the English potter, with the artist–potter tradition still precariously surviving into 20th-c. Japan. There is today a division in the world of ceramics between the pots of industry and the pots of the studio potter. The latter claim to be judged solely as works of art. Their appeal is to an educated and intellectual élite. But their quest for individuality and for refinement of form and decoration may also impress the minds of the designers of mass-produced wares, which may be admired for their technical perfection but hardly, perhaps, treasured.

(*b*) *Technical History*. The indigenous European pottery varies from soft earthenware at one extreme to hard stoneware at the other. When during the later Middle Ages isolated pieces of Chinese porcelain began to reach Europe they seemed to be made not of clay but of glass or some other substance. The new ideals of whiteness, translucency, delicacy and strength potently influenced the makers of fine pottery from then on, so that the traditions of the different materials blend. But in tracing the technical history of European ceramics it is convenient to deal with the broad categories of earthenware, stoneware and porcelain separately.

(i) Earthenware. Medieval Europe inherited its technology from the Dark Ages. The potter's wheel, lead glazing and the decorative use of slip had been known in the Roman Empire. They survived in a few places, to flourish again and become widespread. The stalwart jugs and pitchers of 13th-c. France and England were already wholly or partly dressed in rich lead glazes stained bright green by the use of copper oxides, or yellow or brown by those of iron. Italian potters, inspired by the more sophisticated wares of BYZANTIUM and the Islamic Near East (see below), had already begun to vary their surfaces by staining their glazes and engraving designs into them, and even to paint on a glaze made white and opaque by the use of tin-ashes.

These were two important developments. The former is the so-called *sgraffiato* (scratched) technique of engraving on to the surface of the pot through a slip overlay of a contrasting colour. This method of decoration was in wide use in the Byzantine Empire (doubtless its immediate source) and in northern Iran during the 11th and 12th centuries. It has been widely used in peasant pottery throughout Europe, but was also the vehicle for very distinguished decoration of figures, plant forms, etc., on dishes and bowls made at Bologna and elsewhere in Italy late in the 15th c., and at Beauvais (probably) early in the 16th c.

The other innovation was even more portentous. Fragments of primitive tin-glazed wares dating from the 11th to the 12th centuries have been found in Sicily and Apulia, and by the 14th c. the technique seems to have been widespread. Best known are the so-called Orvieto wares—a type actually made throughout Italy and beyond—which are decorated with bold, stylized paintings of plants, birds and beasts, in green or blue, with purple-brown outlines. These are the forerunners of the whole range of European painted pottery.

This green-and-purple style also took strong root in Spain, at Teruel and Paterna. But Spain in the 13th c. was still partly Moorish. Tin glaze had first been developed in Mesopotamia in the 9th c. and pottery painting had in the meanwhile blossomed into great splendour over wide areas of the Islamic world. Moorish potters at Malaga, in the 13th c., and later at Manises and elsewhere in Spain, created a painting style of the greatest boldness and richness.

The salient characteristic of this 'Hispano-Moresque' pottery painting was the use of lustre pigment. This too had been an Islamic invention, prompted no doubt by a religious injunction against the use of vessels of gold and silver. The golden lustre of Malaga was already famous in the 13th c. The painters in Spain applied it with brush or quill, and combined it with blue to form over-all designs of heraldry or heraldic beasts, scrolls, leaves and mock-Kufic inscriptions.

In the middle of the 15th c. Hispano-Moresque wares became very popular in Italy and were imitated there. Being imported by way of the island of Majorca they became known as Majorcan ware, maiolica. The word is already found in a document of 1454.

It has been said of maiolica that it is as representative of the Italian Renaissance as stained glass is of the Gothic world or carpet weaving of Islam. Its practice spread through Italy, the most important centres of production being Tuscany, Faenza and Deruta (15th c.), and Castel Durante, Caffaggiolo, Gubbio, Urbino and Venice (16th c.). These centres saw the heyday of maiolica: vessels nobly proportioned and gay with paintings which vary from the completely formal, through heraldry and commemorative portraiture to the illustration of classical or biblical stories. The painters developed the full use of high-temperature colours: those that could withstand, and would only develop under, the full heat of the glost or glazing kiln—brown-purple and black, blue, turquoise and green, orange and yellow (red was always elusive). The potters of Deruta and Gubbio, and sometimes those of Caffaggiolo too, added the further embellishment of lustre glazes. For protection the wares were fired in the glost kiln in clay boxes, or saggers: sometimes, and for further protection and enrichment, the painted surface was afterwards covered by a transparent lead glaze which required yet another firing.

In the 16th c. potters from Faenza carried the art of maiolica into France, Spain and the Netherlands, and from Antwerp it came into England. The name of the ware changed as a result to 'faience' or 'fayence': the word is found in France soon after 1600. Towards the middle of the 17th c. the Dutch faience industry became concentrated in Delft, whence in turn the English word 'delftware'. ('Gallipot' is another word borrowed from Holland, where it means a pot of the kind brought in in galleys, for example from Italy, i.e. tin-glazed earthenware.) But though 'faience' is basically synonymous with 'maiolica', by custom the former word is applied to objects made in the 17th c. and later, not the 16th c.

The 17th c. saw a great spreading of the art of faience. In France at Nevers, Rouen and Moustiers, in Switzerland and the Tyrol, in Germany at Hamburg, Hanau, Frankfurt, Nuremberg and Ansbach, and at Alcora in Spain; in all these places factories arose whose wares offered the widest and most accomplished diversity within the technique—and those named were only the leaders in each country. As well as in the current European artistic idioms of the day, these wares were often painted in the newly fashionable Chinese manner in underglaze, or in-glaze, blue. Technically the new ideal offered by Chinese porcelain also demanded improved methods of refining clay and thinner potting.

A new method of decoration became widespread in the middle years of the 18th c. This was the porcelain painter's technique of painting in 'low-temperature' pigments: vitreous enamels which, fired in an inner or muffle kiln, fused into the glaze at 700 °C.–900 °C. and offered an unlimited range of colours.

Painting on faience in these 'enamel colours', as they are also called, was first developed as a factory process by Paul Hannong at Strasbourg between 1745 and 1750. The new method quickly spread to other French factories, particularly those at Niderviller and Marseilles; all over Germany, being practised with great distinction at Höchst and Fulda; and to Sweden (Rörstrand and Marieburg) and elsewhere around the Baltic; becoming indeed everywhere the method of decoration of fashionable, as opposed to popular, faience.

The days of the faience industry were numbered, however. Fashion preferred porcelain. Economics favoured the new English creamwares, which carried all before them. Since *c.* 1800 faience has survived only as a peasant art, e.g. in Brittany, or to sustain the souvenir trade.

The oxides which provided the 'high-temperature' pigments for painting on tin glaze also provided the means of staining the lead glaze itself. This form of decoration, combined with the use of moulded relief, was widely used by the Germanic stove-makers, the HAFNER, in the 15th or 16th centuries. The richness of his glaze colours is the chief attraction of those few plates and dishes which because of their general excellence can be attributed to the hand of Bernard Palissy, and of the many which were made by his followers: and it is notable that here too one of the functions of colour was the enhancement of relief forms—snakes and other reptiles moulded, it is believed, from natural specimens. This kind of ornamentation sometimes also occurs on the slightly earlier Saint Porchaire earthenware—an ivory-coloured, very soft earthenware, more characteristically decorated with repeat patterns of scrolls and leaves very neatly painted in brown and black. The effect is very like printers' or bookbinders' decoration. Both these types of earthenware were frankly ornamental. Palissy-type wares, with mottled glazes, were continuously produced regionally in France for some two centuries: but they remained outside the mainstream of the development of useful pottery.

(ii) Stoneware. European stoneware is a German invention. Noticeably hard earthenwares began to predominate in Germany in the 12th c. True stoneware was first made towards the end of the 14th c., either at Dreihausen in Hesse or at Siegburg or the nearby Eiffel district in the Rhineland. Salt glaze seems to have been invented at about the same time as the ware itself.

The main centres of manufacture were Siegburg, Cologne and nearby Frechen, and Raeren. These centres all became established, and assumed great artistic importance, during the second half of the 16th c. They were succeeded by a group of factories in the Westerwald, at Höhr, Grenzau and Grenzhausen, to which many potters from Siegburg and Raeren migrated and which flourished particularly in the latter part of the 17th c. (after the 30 Years' War) and in the 18th c. Stoneware was also made at Dreihausen, as already mentioned, and at Kreussen in Franconia.

Colour is added to stoneware by thin washes of slip stained brown by iron, blue by cobalt or purple by manganese. A mottled brown glaze is characteristic of Cologne stoneware and earned for it the name of 'tigerware' in England. Blue and purple glazes seem to have been first developed at Raeren from *c.* 1587; they were the characteristic colours of the Westerwald potteries and remain characteristic of German souvenir stoneware to this day. Siegburg stonewares are generally off-white with a clear glaze.

These coloured slips were used to offset, or used in conjunction with, the relief decoration which is the typical embellishment of stoneware. The rugged material, and its exploitation by means of metal tools, are in clearest contrast to the softer southern maiolica with its sensuous white tin glaze which courts the paint brush. Equally distinct too are the vessels in which Rhenish stoneware found its characteristic expression: instead of the maiolica dishes and drug jars we find great jugs and tankards, bold in profile, crisp in detail and braggart in scale. Their decoration was cut or stamped or gouged, moulded or applied: leaves and flowers, lion masks and human masks, armorials and inscriptions, and panels and bands of relief figure compositions. Such vessels, highly personalized masterpieces by the master potters Jan Emens, Baldem Mennicken, Anno and Christian Knuetgen, etc., are today the pride of museums. The everyday products of the potteries were simpler pots for the tavern and table, the best known being the masked 'greybeard' or BELLARMINE bottles which found a wide market internationally. The manufacture of such 'Cologne ware' took root in England and in the Low Countries and northern France with far-reaching consequences described elsewhere. Meanwhile early in the 17th c. the stoneware potters at Kreussen, a family called Vest, had added a new technique in decorating their wares with enamel paints, an art they learnt from the glass painters. This practice was not widely followed—some very rare English examples are known, perhaps done by an independent painter early in the 18th c. It was of greater significance for the later German Hausmaler and porcelain painters.

Another important kind of stoneware was of direct Chinese inspiration. The cargoes of tea brought to Europe in the later 17th c. were accompanied by small red stoneware teapots, the so-called 'BOCCARO WARE', which were made at a place called Yi-hsing. (Boccaro is a Portuguese word, applied originally to scented red earthenware from Mexico.) It was found that these teapots made particularly good tea. It was also sensed that knowledge of the process of their manufacture might help towards a knowledge of how to make porcelain. At Delft one Lambert Cleffius announced that he was making such 'red teapots' in 1678. His work is not now known, but pieces of red stoneware made *c.* 1700 by rivals and successors, chiefly Lambert van Eenhorn and Arij de Milde, are preserved in Continental collections. Artistically these copy the Chinese closely. The technical achievement was important, and equally important was de Milde's contact with von Tschirnhausen and Johann Friedrich BÖTTGER, the inventors of Meissen porcelain. Böttger subsequently invented a very fine red stoneware, so hard that it could be cut and polished but also capable of being modelled and moulded: he even went a step further than the Chinese and provided it with a rich lead glaze on which he could apply gilding or painting in LACQUER-colours. This stoneware was first marketed at the Leipzig Fair of 1710, and was manufactured with great success until *c.* 1740, being imitated at Plaue, Ansbach and Bayreuth. Similar red stonewares were made in England.

Thereafter stoneware diminished in importance on the Continent. The Westerwald tradition continued. Elsewhere stoneware survived for humble utilitarian purposes or as a peasant craft, as at Beauvais and La Borne in France. The middle years of the 19th c., however, saw a renewal of its use for industrial tablewares, originating in France and England.

(iii) Porcelain. The first European-made porcelain remains the most exclusive, the artificial frit porcelain made at Florence for Francesco de' Medici between 1575 and 1587. The ware is white and translucent, with blue painting beneath the lead glaze. About 50 pieces are known.

The secret of true, hard-paste porcelain was

discovered at Meissen by von Tschirnhausen and Böttger in 1709, and the famous Meissen ('Dresden') factory was founded shortly afterwards. Despite strenuous efforts to guard it the secret, or *arcanum*, was quickly carried to Vienna, where a factory was started by C. I. Du Paquier in 1719, and thence to Venice, where another was started by F. & G. Vezzi, also in 1719. Meissen retained its technical primacy, however: unremitting efforts led to ever-increasing whiteness and consistency in the porcelain 'body'. By the 1720s a very full range of enamel colours had been developed by J. F. Höroldt, and by 1740 the general scale and scope of European porcelain sculpture had been established, principally by J. J. KAENDLER. Partial success was obtained in developing the much-desired underglaze-blue painting in the early 1720s; better results followed in 1732, though the wonderfully clear colour of the Chinese was never attained.

Böttger's discovery was due to systematic experiment. Later, European potters had the benefit of first-hand observations of the Chinese processes by the Jesuit missionary Père d'Entrecolles, observations published as letters in 1717 and 1724. Much helped by these, two independent discoveries of the hard-paste formula were made, one by the Russian Dmitri Vinogradov (*c.* 1748) the other by the Englishman William Cookworthy, who obtained his kaolin from America before finding it in Cornwall (1768). The fact, however, that the porcelain formula spread suddenly and rapidly across Europe in the 1750s was due to the enterprise of two men, J. J. Ringler and J. Benckgraff. Starting from Vienna they or their pupils carried and sold the formulae and the knowledge of the kiln construction far and wide. The establishment of major hard-paste factories at Höchst (1750), Fürstenberg (1753), Berlin (1752), Neudeck (later Nymphenburg) (1753), Frankenthal (1755) and Ludwigsburg (1756) indicated its progress across Germany before that country's big concentration of porcelain factories in Thuringia began to develop in the 1760s and 1770s. Factories abroad were started at Doccia in Italy in 1740, in Russia in 1758, Holland in 1759, Switzerland in 1763, Copenhagen in 1774 and Sweden in 1777: generally with the help of the Germans. The French potters of Sèvres, who had long known all about the precious *arcanum*, discovered after much search good French kaolin deposits at Limoges in 1768 and were thereafter able to supplement their own incomparable soft-paste with hard-paste, and in 1804 to turn to its use entirely. Numerous hard-paste factories sprang up in Paris and around Limoges from the end of the 18th c. Hard-paste porcelain, refined but basically unaltered since then, is still the normal chinaware of the Continent.

The history of soft-paste porcelain is less of a commercial success story, but rather longer. After the grand but short-lived beginnings in Florence, Europe's second effective porcelain was used for somewhat humbler wares which were made at Rouen, under the shadow of the faience industry, from 1673 to 1694. Very little has been identified, and probably little was made. Shortly afterwards—at an undetermined date between 1678 and 1693—another factory was started at St. Cloud, between Paris and Versailles. This lasted until 1766 and its products are well known. Other soft-paste factories were at Chantilly (*c.* 1725–*c.* 1800) and Mennecy (1748–1806). The French royal factory was founded at Vincennes in 1738. It was moved to Sèvres in 1756 and still flourishes, though long since making hard-paste not soft-paste porcelain. From 1743 very beautiful soft-paste was made at Capodimonte, outside Naples, at a factory which in 1759 was removed to Buen Retiro in Spain. Soft-paste porcelain was also made at Tournai in Belgium and experimentally elsewhere. Most of the English factories began by making some kind of soft-paste. It has also been made in Sweden and the U.S.A.

As mentioned elsewhere, these artificial porcelains were composed of fritted glass and other elements added to provide whiteness, opacity and plasticity. These elements varied. Kaolinic clay was used for Medici porcelain. The early French factories used chalk and lime. Sèvres used marl and alabaster, and sought plasticity by using soft soap. The composition of the English porcelains is discussed below.

The glazes used on hard-paste porcelains are felspathic. Soft-paste requires the softer lead glaze, and this adds a certain depth to enamel paints and staining minerals. The development of Sèvres was assiduously fostered by royal privileges at the expense of all other French porcelain factories. An outstanding result of this was the development of a series of very splendid ground-colours: dark blue in 1749, turquoise in 1752, yellow in 1753, apple-green in 1756, pink ('rose Pompadour') in 1757 and so on. These were imitated by all foreign competitors in the 18th c. as best they could (most successfully at Chelsea) but hardly matched before the 19th c.

Soft-paste porcelain is rather less plastic than hard-paste and therefore rather less useful for figure-modelling: the Germans could model figures of freer rhythm and gesture, and sharper detail, than the French. France's contribution to porcelain sculpture was the practice of leaving figures unglazed, in the so-called 'biscuit' state (*c.* 1753). The gain was questionable. Light-catching colour and glaze are a great enhancement of complex modelling. Soft-paste Sèvres is a particularly beautiful material, and the early biscuit figures, nymphs and children after BOUCHER and Falconet, were apt and charming. But the fashion spread everywhere, even among manufacturers of the colder-looking, less sympathetic hard-paste, and biscuit porcelain was reduced to a substitute for marble. The fact that 19th-c. English manufacturers should call their biscuit 'Parian' underlines the point. See also POTTERY TECHNIQUES.

(*c*) *Artistic History.* Three main elements require discussion here: (i) the interaction of cultures and the effects of trade; (ii) specific artistic sources; (iii) changes in international styles and fashions.

(i) The marked superiority of Chinese export wares prompted successive impulses of Oriental influence. Levantine traders brought Chinese porcelain (and their own imitations of it) to Venice and other Italian cities in the 16th c., and inspired blue-painted decoration on maiolica and on the famous Medici porcelain, which was termed *alla porcellana.* In the 17th c. Portuguese and Dutch ships brought in supplies of later Ming wares, which were widely imitated in the Peninsula and at Hamburg, Nevers, Savona and Delft. The apogee of these 17th-c. imitations was the copying at Delft and elsewhere—particularly at Delft's German offshoots —of the underglaze blue landscape and lotus decorations of the reign of the Emperor K'ang Hsi (1662–1722); and to this next wave of influence we also owe the acclimatization of what we now accept as normal vase shapes.

Underglaze blue is a form of decoration that is relatively easy to apply and cheap to produce. It was a staple of the Chinese export trade. The lasting success of 'blue and white' in Europe is a major artistic phenomenon. Which house does not possess a piece, to this day? Oriental blue and white was followed by the enamelled porcelains of the *famille verte* and *famille rose*, much copied at St. Cloud, Bow, Buen Retiro, etc.; and by the red stoneware copied in Holland, in Staffordshire and at Meissen.

Enthusiasm for Oriental ceramics meant collecting and copying. A wider, if generally superficial, interest in Chinese culture as a whole led to transient fashions for CHINOISERIES, decorative and fanciful depictions of life in what was almost another world. In porcelain this is virtually the monopoly of Meissen and much of the early achievement of Europe's premier factory is set within this delightful fashion. The transfer-printed WILLOW and allied patterns on English earthenware are a later manifestation of *chinoiserie.* By the middle of the 18th c. direct or indirect Chinese influence was probably at its widest; but Europe was now influencing China in return, since the dominant trading countries (England and France) controlled the taste of what Europe would buy and even imposed designs, shapes and colours on the Chinese themselves.

The debt to JAPAN was also great. The elegant KAKIEMON porcelains, with their sparing designs and beautifully balanced narrow range of colours, were popularized by Delft, Chantilly and Meissen, and through Meissen by Bow and other English factories; and the richer 'IMARI' porcelains were copied at Delft and, much later, by Vezzi's factory in Venice and in the early 19th c. by many English factories.

By the end of the 18th c. the long and glorious development of Chinese ceramics had apparently come to an end. Europe had caught up technically and, so far as could be judged, artistically. But there was more to come from the East. When Japan emerged from her long seclusion in the 1850s other wares, painted in an unfamiliar idiom, came to Europe's notice and, together with Japanese wood-block prints, lacquers, etc., inspired a cult of *japonnaiserie.* Enthusiasm for the cream, gold and brick-red 'satsuma' wares evaporated when it was realized that these did not represent true Japanese taste at all; but the appeal of delicately painted designs of cranes, bamboos, etc., became a distinct part of the general aesthetic of late 19th-c. 'art for art's sake' and of the ART NOUVEAU movement. Of even greater significance was the unearthing in China, from tombs disturbed by railway and road construction, of the unguessed-at wares of dynasties earlier than the Ming. Only in this century have systematic investigation and excavation begun to reveal the true magnitude of Chinese ceramic achievement, the distinct but comparable wares of Korea, and the wild sculpture of the vessels made for the Japanese tea-ceremony. These have all revealed to European potters whole new realms of artistic and aesthetic possibilities. The shapes and glazes produced by countless studio potters show the overwhelming impact of this new inheritance.

Stylistic links with the Near East have been fewer. From *c.* 1550 to *c.* 1700 there was a flourishing pottery centre at Iznik, in western Anatolia. Here were made jugs, plates, mugs, etc., of white earthenware which were painted with gay designs of scrolls, flowers (carnations, tulips, etc.) and sometimes of ships, in a novel mode of stylization and in strong rhythms and bright colours of turquoise, blue and brick-red. In ignorance of their true source these were long misnamed 'Rhodian' wares. Reflections of this most distinctive decoration are found on maiolica made at Padua (the so-called Candiana ware), on certain English delft blue-dash chargers of the 17th c., on Berlin faience of the 18th c. and on 'art pottery' vases and tiles made all over Europe at the end of the 19th c. A rare instance of pottery imported from the New World is the so-called 'boccaro' stoneware.

Such have been the artistic fruits of contacts between European and other cultures by trade. Within Europe itself cross-fertilization of artistic ideas has of course been prolific. As if by a law of nature the assimilation of a new technique meant the adoption of the artistic style of the source. Thus, for example, early Netherlandish maiolica reflects the styles of Faenza and Venice, English 17th-c. stoneware that of the Rhineland, and the early Continental creamwares those of Staffordshire and Leeds. Most European porcelain factories copied Meissen before they began to copy Sèvres. Wandering potters and artists took their styles from place to place, as for example the German porcelain modeller Feilner, who continued to make at Fürstenberg the masterly kind of figures which he had previously made at Höchst. Factories, and particularly porcelain factories, tried to protect themselves against this kind of thing; but copyright protection was unknown. A Sèvres model by Falconet could be copied, with greater or lesser skill, by half a dozen contemporary European porcelain factories. The famous Meissen group of the Tyrolean Dancers was copied by Chelsea, and even in China itself.

(ii) It must be remembered that influences and derivations from other art materials have always been present and often prevalent. The influence on ceramic sculpture of sculpture in marble, bronze and IVORY is an obvious example. The copying in clay of silver tablewares is another. In fact there is hardly any material—metal, stone, leather, plaster, jewellery, wood or fabric—of which potters at one time or another have not copied either the substance or the appearance.

Not all clay sculptures were copied from works pre-existing in another material. Many were original inventions; but many also derived from engravings. The engraver has always been the potter's friend. Printers' patterns and engraved ornament for bookbinders have been copied on pottery and porcelain (Saint Porchaire earthenware, Rouen faience, St. Cloud and early Vienna porcelain). The work of designers like Daniel MAROT and J.-A. MEISSONNIER, which provided the idiom for so much in the applied arts of the BAROQUE and ROCOCO periods, was used copiously (Delft, Meissen, etc.), as were such illustrative compendia as the publications of Stalker and Parker (1688), Robert Sayer (*The Ladies' Amusement*, *c.* 1760) and G. F. Riedel (1770). Such works were designed for decorators; but the potters have ranged further afield. Books of flowers, of costume and of travel were widely used. Maiolica, grandest of all painted pottery, carried copies of engravings after Raphael; the makers of the Staffordshire chimney ornaments, humblest of all ceramic figures, reproduced engravings from Victorian magazines and music covers; and such borrowings and adaptations have taken place at all times and in all categories in between. The transmuting of pictorial sources by the German 18th-c. figure modellers often shows inventiveness of the most admirable kind. Those derived from engravings of the actors of the Italian Comedy are among porcelain's greatest masterpieces, and Kaendler of Meissen and BUSTELLI of Nymphenburg must be ranked among the outstanding sculptors of their age.

(iii) The give and take between cultures, countries, factories and media took place within the broad contexts of the successive European styles which we call Renaissance, Baroque and so on. Not all of these terms can be applied with much precision to ceramics. The elements of proportion and space composition by which we characterize the architecture and painting of the Italian High Renaissance, for example, are hardly to be looked for in even the most splendid examples of contemporary maiolica (1500–80), and the pronounced emotionalism of the great Mannerist painters of the succeeding generation finds little reflection in the work of their humbler colleagues in the potteries. Nevertheless stylistic changes do occur which can be related to such larger movements. Contrast a painted dish of the early 16th c. with one made 100 years later: there will be differences in such matters as the balance between ornament and illustration, or the relationship of rim to centre, and these may well illustrate the difference in general artistic poise between the two ages. Pottery painters, like other designers, responded to the late Renaissance cult of elegant GROTESQUES, and at the same time as Palissy was decorating his weird dishes with casts of reptiles (*c.* 1550–80) architects were building new grottoes all over Europe and German silversmiths were publishing designs of similar snail-encumbered horrors. One can sometimes find 17th-c. wares fashioned into grandiose shapes or painted with scenes in a dizzy perspective which remind us of the histrionic ideals of the Baroque.

These styles, however, were mainly concerned with the fine arts. The succeeding styles were equally concerned with interior decoration, and here the link is much closer. The Rococo style (*c.* 1730–60) might indeed be said to have its perfect embodiment in porcelain, so aptly do the fragility, lightness, plasticity and brightness of the ceramic material embody the wit, elegance and caprice of the style. The formal characteristics of balance without symmetry, love of broken lines and complex rhythms, help to bring into recognition both the preceding static late-Baroque style and the succeeding Neo-Classicism, the reactionary simplicity of which (best exemplified in WEDGWOOD's stonewares) was both a return to basic sobriety and the first of the learned revivalist styles. There have been many since. Wedgwood's ideal of beauty was Hellenistic. A stricter and more ponderous classicism is purveyed by French EMPIRE porcelains of around 1800; a Rococo more florid than its original by French, English and German porcelains of the 1820s and 1830s. The 19th c., the age of eclecticism, saw the first of the International Exhibitions and also the foundation of the great museums, in which were garnered the ceramics of all ages and all countries available for study and available for imitation. And imitated they were. But style itself died of suffocation, and not even the earnest 20th-c. efforts of *art nouveau*, ART DÉCO, and the *Neue Sachlichkeit* have really brought it to life again.

4. BRITISH CERAMICS. The native pottery of Tudor England was common earthenware decorated with stained lead glazes and sometimes with trailed slip. About 1571 two Antwerp potters came to Lambeth by way of Norwich and started there the manufacture of maiolica. 'Delftware', as it came to be called, was made extensively at Lambeth and at other London potteries throughout the 17th and 18th centuries

and lingered on into the 19th c. It was also made in and around Bristol (Brislington and Wincanton) from the middle of the 17th c., at Liverpool from early in the 18th c. and at Dublin and Glasgow from the middle of the 18th c., though manufacture at the last two places was on a modest scale. It will be observed that all of these places are seaports. The essential tin had to be brought from Cornwall by sea.

Identification of the different places of origin of the delftwares rests on association pieces and on features of potting and painting, and is seldom easy. Some 16th-c. to 17th-c. jugs whose glaze is entirely covered with a mottled stain of blue, purple or brown are commonly associated with Malling in Kent, but were probably made in London. Their inspiration seems to have been imported Rhenish stoneware. In general, however, English delftware shows close affinity with Dutch maiolica and faience, though on the whole the English shapes are less suave, the glaze less white, the colour less clear and the brushwork less good than on Dutch faience at its best. Decoration was in the high-temperature colours of blue and manganese, green and yellow. It is worth noting that throughout the 17th c. and the first two decades of the 18th c. delftware was the only British earthenware that was white and was painted. The fact that it was clearly related to the Dutch wares, that the splendid faiences of Rouen and of southern and eastern France provoked so little imitation here, is no doubt due to the expansionist vigour of the Dutch and the extent of their carrying trade.

The objects principally made were drug-jars and pill-slabs for the pharmacy, wine-bottles, punch-bowls and posset-pots, commemorative or display dishes and, in the 18th c., tiles and tablewares, mostly plates. The decoration on early pieces tends to be heraldic or formal, and in in-glaze blue: coats of arms of livery companies, appropriate inscriptions on drug-jars and wine-bottles, and so on. But both early in the 17th c. and later the delftware potters delighted in producing great display dishes painted with views, fruit and flowers, representations of royal and other personages, or Adam and Eve, and these were in polychrome. From a characteristic style of decorating their rims they are sometimes known as 'blue dash chargers'. The freedom of their execution allies them with peasant pottery. In the middle of the 17th c. a wave of Chinese influence came in, however, and this both reinforced a general tendency (itself Chinese-inspired) to blue and white, and provided new and sophisticated styles of decoration, and henceforth Chinese patterns were never far to seek. The attraction of delftware is the painter's reponse, in simplicity of draughtsmanship and sureness of hand, to the demands of the absorbent glaze. Towards the end of the 18th c. delftware succumbed to cream-coloured earthenware and the old painters had to find new employment. One meets their familiar blue peonies and pagodas drawn with the same spirit, but with sadly restricted effect, on the new and less sympathetic ground. But the increased neatness of decoration which characterized all English pottery of the later 18th c. made itself apparent on delft too, and the old boldness with which Adam and Eve were drawn is lacking in trim depictions of the dawn of the space age with the ascent of Lunardi's balloon in 1784.

One pleasant peculiarity of London and Bristol potters of the mid century was the so-called *bianco sopra bianco*, the painting of opaque white scrolls and flowers on a bluish ground. The technique was possibly introduced from Rörstrand in Sweden. At Liverpool in the 1750s Sadler developed the technique of transfer printing designs on to delft tiles.

Stoneware was another import of the 17th c. The earliest recognizable maker was John Dwight of Fulham, whose first patent was taken out in 1671. This patent mentions porcelain and 'Cologne ware'. Examples of the output of his pottery are known, discovered on the site or traceable to Dwight's descendants. They consist in the main of small jugs and jars, and 'Bellarmine' wine-bottles such as were being imported from Germany. They do not include anything which would be called porcelain today, but consist of grey and white stonewares potted to great refinement (some semi-translucent) and showing considerable finesse of colouring and of decoration by the application of small stamped-out pads of clay. Dwight's most famous products, however, are life-size busts of King Charles II and Prince Rupert, and about a dozen small figures of his own daughter and of mythical characters. These were freely modelled with great mastery and are unique of their kind.

The making of grey or brown stoneware, salt glazed, spread elsewhere in London and to Staffordshire, Nottingham and Derby. Between 1693 and 1696 Dwight took legal action against his competitors for infringing his patents but failed to stop this growth. Washed with ferruginous slip beneath the salt glaze, these crisply potted wares assumed a lustrous brown colour. They were well suited for incised decoration or press-moulding and mugs, teapots and sauce-boats were made, as were double-walled jugs and jugs modelled as bears with shredded clay simulating the pelt. With the development of white stoneware in the 18th c. brown stoneware was virtually consigned to the ale-house and confined for a time to the form of bi-coloured brown mugs with applied figures of huntsmen or of topers copied from Hogarth. But this robust material came back into popularity in the 19th c., serving for toby jugs, flasks and pitchers moulded in high relief with vigorous Bacchic scenes after Rubens. Its artistic and sanitary developments were in the hands of Doulton. As a container for blacking, pastes, acids and ginger beer its day is hardly over yet.

Among Dwight's competitors were John and David Elers of Fulham, Dutchmen of German extraction, whom he accused of pirating his 'red theapotts'—unglazed red stoneware vessels like those being made at the time by Arij de Milde and others in Holland. The Elers transplanted their art into Staffordshire, where it became widespread in the 2nd half of the 18th c. This 'Elers ware' was at first decorated with small pseudo-Chinese ornaments stamped and applied to the surface or, after *c.* 1760, by the new technique of engine-turning. When in due course Wedgwood took up the medium he gave this Chinese-inspired Staffordshire ware a Greek or Egyptian decoration and the Italian name of *rosso antico*.

The basic and (by contrast) native tradition, however, was that of the potters in slip-decorated earthenware. It seems likely that the slipware potters relied for their daily bread on the production of utilitarian pottery, lead glazed and stained black or purple or yellow or green. Such everyday pottery tends to disappear. Excavated pieces help with dating, but unlocalized survivors are hard to place in time: this peasant pottery survived throughout the country for as long as peasantry itself. Its ceramic merits, which can be very considerable, are of the abstract sort. Similarly, slip decoration—the trailing of slip to form patterns, or incising patterns through slip in the manner elsewhere called *sgraffiato*—was very widespread. In the 17th c. it throve particularly in north Devon, at Wrotham in Kent, Harlow in Essex, in Derbyshire and in north Staffordshire. Most of the objects so decorated are containers for liquor—mugs, tygs and posset-pots, fuddling cups, puzzle jugs and big full-bellied harvest jugs—and they are often inscribed with bibulous legends occasionally rebuked by such terseness as 'Don't get Drunk'. The other main product was dishes, and slipware (especially Staffordshire slipware) became a vehicle for self-declared masterpieces: big formal heraldic or figure compositions in browns and yellows inscribed with the names of Thomas and Ralph Toft, Ralph Simpson and others. The slipware tradition still survives in the souvenir trade and in studio pottery. Its great days were at the end of the 17th c. and the beginning of the 18th c., when it showed (in the best pieces) uninhibited vigour and freedom of design.

The rise of the pottery industry in Staffordshire was due mainly to fortunate geological circumstances, coal and many different kinds of clay being there found side by side; and to its geographical situation, which afforded reasonable road and water-borne outlets to Liverpool and Hull and thence by sea to London and abroad.

The growth of technological skill on which Staffordshire's superiority was based can be studied in detail. A community of smallholders, part-time potters and part-time farmers, evolved from the 1st half of the 18th c. into a nexus of pottery towns with specialist firms and ancillary trades and services. The diversification of wares which took place in the early 18th c. was the product partly of the use of new raw materials and partly of improved techniques of sifting, throwing, turning and moulding. New colonial markets beckoned the potters and they were at pains to improve domestic communications in order to reach them. Alas for the foreign faience-makers, who were undersold, and for the Cornish tinmen, who had thriven on delft and on PEWTER.

The native slipware tradition had owed nothing to porcelain or any other foreign imports. The new redware made in Staffordshire by the Elers had shown what delicacy could be achieved by greater refinement of potting. The application of this new standard to the older tradition led, in earthenware, to the production of much more finely potted vessels, made of variegated clays to simulate agate, or marbled with variously stained glazes. The drab, high-fired stonewares were also found to be amenable to this new sophistication. The inescapable influence of porcelain brought the need for whiteness. The local pipeclay was suitable for decorative adjuncts but not for potting, but the addition of ground flints and of white clay from Dorset and Devon from the 1720s gave whiteness to the bodies of both earthenware and stoneware.

White salt-glazed stoneware was made in Staffordshire and elsewhere from the 1720s until the 1780s. Its heyday was from the 1740s to the 1760s, for both the quality and the quantity of the wares produced. The pottery was thin and admitted a remarkable sharpness of modelling: sharp enough to carry moulded inscriptions which remained legible and to enable the potters to slip-cast their vessels into intricate and bizarre shapes, too sharp perhaps for comfortable contact with cutlery. A *sgraffiato* form of decoration is known as 'scratch-blue' from the practice of filling engraved flower or bird forms with powdered cobalt (*c.* 1750). A much gayer result came from colouring the ware with slip stained deep blue or turquoise or pink, or from painting it with enamel paints. This last was embodied in Rococo floral or figure designs, or Chinese motives, often beautifully drawn and always of notably bright and clear colour. This work is said to have been started by two immigrant Dutch painters in Staffordshire; other painting is believed to have been applied abroad, in Holland itself. Salt-glazed stoneware also occasionally received printed decoration.

The figures made of this ware are naïve and particularly attractive. They are generally uncoloured (though enamelled figures are known, inspired perhaps by Chinese cloisonné work) and embellished with inlays of brown- or blue-stained clay. The most famous are the so-called 'pew groups', modelled groups of two or three figures standing or sitting against a wall. These can be dated to the 1730s or 1740s, and were perhaps all made by one artist. Later figures are copied or cast from porcelain originals and are for that reason attributed to William Littler of Longton Hall, who made both stoneware and porcelain.

Figures similar in character to the early salt-glazed figures, but made of lead-glazed earthenware of contrasting clays, are attributed to Thomas Astbury (1686–1743). Early figures whose colour is not in the clay but in the staining of the glaze are attributed to Thomas WHIELDON and Aaron Wood, the latter the founder of a famous line of Staffordshire potters. The glaze colours of these mid 18th-c. Staffordshire earthenwares are notable for their limpid richness. They are well seen on toby jugs, the cult for which arose now, and also on tablewares.

Lead-glazed earthenware and salt-glazed stoneware proceeded hand in hand. The same potters often made both, using sometimes the same moulds for both kinds of ware. From the two was developed the all-conquering creamware, a fine whitish earthenware body covered with a clear lead glaze. This was evolved in the 1720s but received its full development in the middle years of the century at the hands of Whieldon and Wedgwood.

Thomas Whieldon, of Fenton, was the key figure. He is less famous than Wedgwood, and his fame is popularly limited to creamware decorated with stained glazes and called 'tortoiseshell ware' or 'Whieldon ware'; but excavations on the sites of his factories show that he or his tenants made every type of earthenware and stoneware then known in the Potteries, and many of the leading potters of his own and the following generation became associated with him in one way or another. Aaron Wood, who cut moulds for figures, and Daniel and William Greatbach, modellers, worked for him. Josiah Spode, the founder of the famous firm of that name, was his apprentice. The young Wedgwood was his partner from 1754 to 1759.

Josiah WEDGWOOD was not only a highly proficient and inventive potter, quick to take advantage of industrial inventions; he was equally successful in management and labour relations, in market organization and in the anticipation and moulding of his customers' tastes. He quickly established himself as the dominant figure in the Potteries. Staffordshire potters had already moved forward to the establishment of regular trade outlets in London and other cities, and were exporting their wares to the Continent. Wedgwood's organizing talent greatly enhanced and enlarged the market; he contracted with decorating establishments far from Staffordshire—with John Sadler, the printer, at Liverpool and David Rhodes, the painter, at Leeds and London; he attracted workmen from abroad and he was in close working contact with such men as Robert ADAM, Flaxman the sculptor, Matthew BOULTON, and Vulliamy the clock-maker. Other eminent Staffordshire potters, Neale and Palmer, Turner, Meyer, the Woods and the Adams, shared in his establishment of Staffordshire's supremacy. But Wedgwood was the leader. His impact on the industry was epoch-making.

The range of his wares can only be summarized. He revived a brilliant green lead glaze which had not been used since Tudor times. He improved and refined the mottled glaze of marbled wares. In 1765 he produced a much improved creamware which, having secured a royal order, he christened 'Queen's Ware'. In 1775 china clay and china stone from Cornwall became available to Staffordshire potters, and *c.* 1779 Wedgwood produced his 'pearlware', which was whiter than creamware. As already said, he revived the use of red stoneware (*rosso antico*). He invented a fine black stoneware ('basaltes') *c.* 1767, and in 1774–5 the white stoneware which he stained blue (or green, mauve or yellow) and called 'Jasper'. These, with his cane-coloured ware, were ornamental in purpose, apt vehicles for the Neo-Classical style which he so successfully propagated. All were promptly reproduced by other potters everywhere. 'Jasperware' is still made today.

Of all of these the creamware and the pearlware were the most important commercially. Creamware was forthwith copied everywhere from Swansea to Newcastle: under the names of 'faience fine', 'Steingut', 'Engels porselein', 'terraglia inglese', etc., it invaded the Continent and within a generation drove the old faience off the market. A large part in this was played by the particularly fine creamwares of the Leeds factory. The countrywide adoption of pearlware was followed by a vast output of blue-printed decoration, England's second great onslaught on the world's markets.

In the crucial 1740s the first English porcelains appeared. Unlike most of their foreign contemporaries the English manufactures were private commercial undertakings, denied the support of a ruler's purse. This fact may possibly account for a certain bourgeois character in the wares of most of them. Even so English 18th-c. porcelain factories catered for purses of different depths. Many of them made figures and most of them made vases and other ornaments. In these products Chelsea was the most ambitious and the most accomplished. This factory's figures of the 'red anchor' period (1748–55 when the factory mark was an anchor painted in red) are among the loveliest in the whole range of European porcelain; its vases in the succeeding 'gold anchor' period were among the most richly decorated and fantastically modelled. These, clearly, were very expensive. Other factories emulated them with more or less success. But most also (though not Chelsea) produced much tableware decorated only in underglaze blue—cheaper articles for a middle-class market.

Most porcelains can be allotted fairly readily to one or other of the well-known factories, which moreover group themselves into technologically similar groups. Thus the London factories of Chelsea (founded *c.* 1744) and Bow (*c.* 1745), Longton Hall (Staffordshire, *c.* 1749) and Derby (*c.* 1750) made 'frit' porcelain. Lowestoft (1757) was an offshoot of Bow. Bow, and in time

Lowestoft, Chelsea and Derby, strengthened the porcelain body with calcined ox bones. In the west use of a body containing soapstone distinguishes a second family of factories dominated by that at Worcester (which had had its origins in Bristol in 1748) and including Caughley (*c.* 1772) and a group of obscure factories in Liverpool (mid 1750s). A third family of makers of true hard-paste porcelain consists of the Plymouth factory (1768), its successor at Bristol (1770) and Bristol's successor at New Hall in Staffordshire (1781).

Starting from Derby the painter and ARCANIST William Billingsley established short-lived factories or decorating establishments in the next generation at (among other places) Pinxton (1796), Swansea (1815) and Nantgarw (1813 and 1817), making at the last named a soft-paste porcelain which both in style and in translucency closely resembled soft-paste Sèvres. The leading porcelain makers of the early 19th c. were, however, John Rose of Coalport (from 1814) and Josiah Spode II of Stoke-on-Trent (from *c.* 1800). The latter is credited with the final formulation of the bone-china recipe, which has been the standard British table-porcelain ever since. These firms, and others such as Mintons (*c.* 1798), successfully industrialized what had hitherto been a very precarious calling. Of the earlier factories only those at Worcester and Derby were still in business by 1805. Porcelain had become no longer a luxury but a commodity, and the big Staffordshire firms saw to it that all modulations of style and fashion should be available to their customers over the widest possible price range. The costliest end of the trade was shared with other firms such as Chamberlains of Worcester (*c.* 1786) and the Rockingham factory (1826), and the other end by legions of small businesses in Staffordshire.

One element in the process of industrialization was the use of printed decoration. Isolated experiments in printing were made at Frankenthal in Germany and at Zürich in Switzerland in the 1750s and 1760s, but the main development took place in England. The transfer of designs printed on paper from copperplates, while those designs were still wet, was practised at the BATTERSEA ENAMEL factory *c.* 1753–6, and thereafter at Bow and Worcester. From the latter factory the technique was carried to Derby and to Caughley, and the Liverpool factories of both porcelain and earthenware. The early designs were printed on the glaze in black, blue or purple and were of little scenes of figures and landscapes or portraits of popular figures of the day such as King George III and his bride, or decorative arrangements of flowers, fruit and birds. They were often derived directly or indirectly from pattern books such as *The Ladies' Amusement* (*c.* 1760). Blue-printed ware became a staple product of the Worcester porcelain factory in the 1760s. Wedgwood was quick to exploit black printing on his creamware.

For a few years around 1800 the fashionable stipple-engraving was successfully applied to pottery and porcelain by the substitution for paper of pliable bats of solid gelatine ('bat printing').

These methods of on-glaze printing had required the application of a further protective glaze. The technique of printing direct on to the earthenware body, underglaze printing, was therefore a logical development. Underglaze printing began in the 1780s: mostly in blue, mostly of pseudo-Oriental scenes. The art clearly owed much to the new whiter earthenwares of which Wedgwood's pearlware was one. The vogue for this English 'blue and white' was enormous. It was intense until *c.* 1840, when printing in other colours such as green or pink challenged its popularity. And it is still alive today. It drew its decorative themes from China, Greco-Roman antiquity, romantic Italy, India, and (for patriotic Americans) the U.S.A. Cheap English blue-printed earthenware was exported to British colonies all over the world, to the gold prospectors in North America and to the young republics in South America. Its broken fragments adorn the temple walls of Bangkok.

The inventiveness of the Staffordshire potters brought other novelties: lustre colours derived from gold, silver and copper (from *c.* 1800) and used either for over-all decoration or for banding with 'resist' patterning; polychrome printing, mostly reproductive in character and used on pot-lids (*c.* 1850); a new marble-like body for figures, appropriately christened 'Parian' (*c.* 1840); and an almost limitless range of powerful ground-colours. The milestones of the potters' progress are the catalogues and surviving exhibits of the great successive International Exhibitions which took place in the 2nd half of the 19th c. The pace-makers were generally firms we have already met: Minton, Coalport and Copeland–Spode.

One new name emerges, that of a man from whom two most important new developments stem. Sir Henry Doulton was a second-generation stoneware potter of Lambeth. It was he who between the 1850s and 1870s pioneered the great 'sanitary revolution' of the age by providing the world with glazed stoneware baths, basins and drain-pipes—arguably one of the noblest of the ceramic achievements of the Victorian age. He also was one of the first to try to restore, in an industrial age, a potter's own artistic responsibility for his pot. The former lies outside the scope of this article. The history of the latter, from Doulton's first collaboration with the Lambeth School of Art, carries through to the modern artist-potter.

The English ceramic industry flourished so abundantly in the 19th c. because of the country's long start in industrialization. We can now recognize that industrialization produced its own folk art in the form of Staffordshire chimney ornaments, mass-produced earthenware figures of royalty, popular figures of literature, the stage, politics, etc., and animals. They were generally made in pairs and often plain-backed, for viewing from one side only. Their most characteristic colouring is orange and underglaze blue. Many seem to have been based on engravings. Their modelling is as simple as possible and generally owes nothing whatsoever to porcelain. Their decoration is as artless as their modelling, and as engaging.

5. MARKS. Marks have been added to pots by makers, workmen and artists for different reasons: to show the ownership or destination of the finished object or for identification for some domestic purpose within the factory, as well as for an indication of origin and sometimes of date. The Chinese indeed took the matter further, and decorated their wares with words or symbols of good wishes, as an alternative to the reign-mark of the ruling emperor—or of some other emperor ages dead, the wares of whose reign the potter admired or wished to emulate. The subject is therefore very complex. In Europe the use of a mark to denote the origin of a piece became general in the 18th c. It was never standardized, seldom enforced and marks were not effectively protected, so that abuse was easy. The famous crossed swords of Meissen and crossed Ls of Sèvres have been imitated and copied far and wide.

In the 18th c. the Sèvres marks included marks identifying the individual painters (as well as date-letters). Artists' signatures as such are rare until modern times.

6. IMITATIONS AND FAKES. Imitation being a normal commercial practice, little discredit attached to those early manufacturers who inflicted this compliment on their betters even to the extent of copying the latters' marks. The collecting of rarities or expensive wares from the past breeds true deceits. Genuine pieces may be given added decoration, or otherwise tampered with, to make them seem richer prizes; the marks on a less good piece may be removed and a costlier mark substituted; or downright copies may be made, to be sold as genuine. The collector who relies entirely on a factory mark as a badge of authenticity deserves what he gets. The detection of the more thoroughgoing forgeries demands much experience and discrimination. Lovers of soft-paste 18th-c. porcelain are particularly exposed to this nuisance, but forgeries of all collectable ceramics are known.

7. ISLAMIC CERAMICS

(*a*) *Background.* From the death of Muhammad in 732 the early stages of the Muslim conquest carried the new faith of the Prophet to the western limits of the Byzantine Empire and to the eastern provinces of the Sassanian state, from Spain to outer China. The first hereditary dynasty of the caliphs, the Ummayads (661–750), came from a background of partially settled south Arabian tribes; the town of Medina was their focal point. From this fairly important metropolis they moved the capital to Damascus. The empire grew in strength but one cannot speak yet of any radical transformation of the arts under them: the mosaics of the Dome of the Rock in Jerusalem and those of the Great Mosque in Damascus, for example, are signs of the blending of Sassanian and BYZANTINE motifs rather than an original style. By the time the Abbasids took over (750–1258) under Abul Abbas, a member of the family of the Prophet, the Arab empire had almost reached its zenith. Baghdad was now its capital, chiefly looking to the east. For a short time Samarra to the north took its place in the 9th c. The only surviving Ummayad fled to Spain and founded a small but flourishing state which lasted till 1031. It rivalled the most luxurious courts of the Mediterranean area.

The over-expanded Abbasid Empire soon had to relinquish its direct authority over its distant provinces, which only kept in touch through the mention of the caliph's name in the Friday prayer and through taxation. By the 10th c. the Samanids of Samarkand and Nishapur were virtually independent. The same went for the Ghaznavids (962–1186) and later the Ghorids of Afghanistan. At one stage the Buyids of Isfahan even reached as far as Baghdad. In fact the Abbasid rulers retained only the religious lead under the Turkish Seljuk sultans (1055–1256). Moving westwards from central Asia, the nomadic Seljuks also gained power as reliable mercenaries, adopted the Islamic faith and eventually became the overlords as far west as central Anatolia. The Seljuks of the Rum settled there and embellished their new capital, Konya. The so-called Great Seljuks never settled permanently in any one city. None the less each generation sponsored the local arts, adding new trends brought in from the Far East along the SILK route and across the oceans.

Meanwhile in Egypt the Berber Fatimids (969–1171) had taken over from the Tulunids and gathered for a time in Cairo the best craftsmen of the Muslim world. They too encouraged far-flung enterprises with China by the sea-routes. After the fall of Cairo to Saladin, the Kurdish Ayyubid, the Fatimid Empire broke up and local Berber dynasties ruled over North Africa in succession: the Beni Hammads (1007–1152) and the Almohads to the middle of the 13th c.

From the end of the 11th c. two small Christian groups started a new distribution of the arts from the eastern part of the Mediterranean. After the defeat of Byzantium at Manzikert (1071) in greater Armenia many Armenian families resettled in Cilicia, a key position in southern Turkey. On the other hand the intrusion of the Crusaders (1096–1270) as far as Palestine reinforced the activities of European traders, mainly Italian. Amongst other crafts they brought home what were for them unusual ceramics, *bacini*, some of which are still set in the walls of Italian and Greek churches.

Genghis Khan and his Mongol descendants

re-established some kind of unity across the Muslim world (1220–1353) after disrupting it completely. So did Timur (1353–1405) and his family, despite the effects of his first onslaught. It was under the *pax mongolica* that Marco Polo travelled to China. Several well known embassies were exchanged between western Europe, China and the Timurid Court.

Meanwhile the Ottoman Turks were laying the foundations of their vast empire despite the setback of Timur's victory at Ankara in 1402. By 1453 they had captured Constantinople from the last Byzantine emperor. Early in the 16th c. they finally defeated the Mamluks of Egypt (1261–1517). The Ottoman sultans usurped the religious attributes of the puppet caliph in Cairo and retained them till their final collapse in 1922.

The Persia of the Safavids (1502–1722) and later that of the Qajars (1794–1925) maintained fairly constant borders with the Ottoman Empire to the west and the Indian Mogul Empire to the east.

Early collectors of Islamic pottery concentrated on so-called Rhodes and Damascus wares, lustre plates and bowls and polychrome pieces easily available and pleasing to the European eye. Nobody was concerned with the decorative techniques or the quality and shaping of the clay. Only since the Second World War have chemical and spectographical methods of research come into their own. Through the analysis of these tests on shards and the added knowledge gained from scientific excavations a better understanding of the whole subject has slowly been possible.

The innovations of the Islamic potter lay not so much in the shaping of the clay but in the discovery of new techniques and means of decoration. Although the 'Hadith' or tradition did forbid all human representation as a sin against God's creation, more and more liberty was taken as the centuries went by. Furthermore the Koranic ban on the use of precious metal was compensated for by painting in lustre pigments to imitate silver and gold.

(*b*) *Early Mesopotamian and Egyptian Ceramics* (7th c. to 12th c. A.D.). It is hardly surprising that in early Islam the Nile, the Tigris and the Euphrates valleys should have harboured new pottery techniques in a very ancient local craft, since they presented the potter with ideal conditions in clay, water and combustibles. By the middle of the 8th c. the production of T'ang polychrome had come to a halt; none could have reached Mesopotamia. But it is quite possible that among the Chinese prisoners taken in Samarkand in 751 some might have been potters who introduced the technique of these yellow and green runny colours under a lead glaze. (See CHINA, CERAMICS.) According to a Persian historian the Governor of Khurasan gave Imperial China wares to the caliph Haroun-al-Raschid (786–809). These and other imported vessels would have been white and greyish stonewares and early porcelain pieces. Thus challenged, the Islamic potter was spurred into using a white surface finish. At first it was the usual white opaque traditional alkaline glaze and later a tin opacified lead glaze. Only COBALT blue with occasional green was used to depict simple motifs such as PALMETTES, leafy branches, palm trees, on flat plates with large rims or inside small bowls. Samples have been found in Iraq, Egypt and at Susa in Persia.

As for lustre painting, it is known as early as 772 on a glass beaker from Fostat, the early Cairo. When was lustre painting first applied to opaque tin glaze? In Egypt or in Mesopotamia? In any case it suggests a court luxury technique requiring extreme skill and patience. Early tiles like those of the mosque of Kairouan and large plates received a polychrome lustre decoration underlying crowded floral and geometrical patterns. In the later monochrome lustre these patterns were replaced by animal representations—birds, horses, camels—and some calligraphy. The signature of the Egyptian painter sometimes appears on the foot-ring. If he happened to be a Copt, he could depict priests, even Christ, or mythological themes which coincided with the classical revival in Byzantium. In many cases the subjects stand against a heavily filled background of closely packed strokes or circles with dots. Towards the end of the period monochrome lustre plates were also produced in Syria in a less sophisticated style.

Unglazed jars could have incised or moulded patterns: ACANTHUS, vine or ivy-leaf scrolls, even some early Arabic script. Occasionally they could be covered in the traditional blue-green alkaline glaze well known from the Parthian and Sassanian wares. Other fine relief ornaments on small shallow plates were delicately glazed dark green or brown.

(*c*) *Khurasan Wares* (10th c. to 13th c.). Under the rule of the Samanids (874–999) this area extended as far as Sistan to the south, Sari by the eastern shores of the Caspian and Transoxiana to the east. Most of the finds in these regions point to the same technique: to prevent the colours from running under the lead glaze a fine pipeclay was mixed with the pigments. As often happens in ceramic production the earliest pieces are the most handsome, as is illustrated by the calligraphic plates and large bowls found in Samarkand and Nishapur. In the darkest possible purple manganese colour Kufic writing offers wishes or religious advice. The more or less ornate Arabic characters stand out in one or two circles on a broad rim against a creamy white background; the reverse scheme can also be used. Sometimes the centre of the plate displays a long-beaked bird in the shape of some writing. The most common type of decoration is much less sophisticated but on the whole abstract: strapwork, foliation, radial imitations of unknown calligraphic panellings and densely packed 'peacock eyes' on bowls and plates. In the best examples purple or red slip replaces the white background. The patterns are picked out in orange, light green and yellow with a dark brown outline. All bodies are of fine pink clay. Only Nishapur potters seem to have depicted animals and people. Could it be due to the presence of non-Muslim people in this area of cross-roads, mainly Nestorians and Buddhists? Yellow is the dominant colour for hunting scenes and Bacchanalia. The Sari type of bowls and deeper plates depict much cruder animals, usually fish, and schematized flowers looking like clumsy blobs. Although less spectacular, the unglazed and unpainted wares offer a mine of original decoration in slip application, moulding or incising. Common motifs are ROSETTES, palmettes, lyras, plaited knots imitating belt clasps, and stylized goats, hares and birds. Some moulded tiles with animals, lions or gazelles, are glazed in green, blue or yellow.

Sometime during this period a new type of geometrical incised ware makes its first appearance with added streaks of yellow and green under a clear glaze. Sung incised decoration in the same spirit was well known in the 11th c. Some shards of this type were found in Samarra, which points to a much later occupation than was thought at first. In the earlier ware the lines and colour streaks blend admirably. Later the geometrical incisions became more casual and the yellows and greens took on duller shades. When Genghis Khan and his hordes invaded Khurasan and the adjoining areas they brought total destruction and the greater part of the local pottery production never recovered.

(*d*) *Azerbaijan Carved and Incised Wares and their Sequel* (from the 11th c.). As in the case of Khurasan examples, these incised wares were influenced by metal engraving techniques, either Sassanian or early Islamic. The potter scratches the pattern through a white slip to uncover parts of the body. With an added transparent lead glaze the pattern acquires a style of its own reminiscent in the best examples of Tzʿŭ-Chou ceramics produced in China under the northern Sung (960–1127). This technique, often called *sgraffiato*, was applied to the pottery production of a vast area. Its arbitrary sub-divisions only correspond to areas of commercial excavations such as Garrus or Amol or Aghkand. Contours of half-palmettes, ARABESQUES, imitation Kufic or simply geometrical patterns frame the centre part of the plates or bowls. Many kinds of large animals and birds sprawl there, often clumsily. A few human beings are represented, strangely square. Some animal-shaped jars and many plates have a clear green glaze finish which makes the carved parts appear almost black. In the special case of 'Lakabi' wares, which means 'painted', the colours were kept within the bounds of grooved or raised contours: simplified animals, eagles, a court scene, all gained in glamour through the application of vivid blues, greens, yellows and purples. Although reproduced in a simplified manner in Syria and in Egypt, the 'Lakabi' fashion does not seem to have lasted much beyond the 12th c. in Persia.

As for *sgraffiato* wares, they were soon to be made in neighbouring areas such as Georgia and greater Armenia, in now ruined towns such as Dvin and Ani. On the whole the incised patterns, often under a green glaze, became freer. With the drift of many families from that area to Cilicia, in particular after the Seljuk victory of Manzikert in 1071, *sgraffiato* wares reappear with a simplified line of decoration, often figural, on a pale creamy background. Monotonous sketchy birds and mounted knights fill the well of bowls and plates. Besides Cilicia, Crusaders' strongholds such as Cyprus, Corinth and Constantinople have yielded a number of them. On the Persian Gulf, too, a new style of *sgraffiato* has been observed since the excavations in Siraf. Here the incisions show up in a rough series of patterns under messy streaks of dull green, yellow or purple shades.

(*e*) *Persian and Anatolian Ceramics* (12th c., 13th c., 14th c.). The collapse of Fatimid Egypt and the ensuing upheavals led to the drift of many craftsmen to towns where suitable sponsors required them such as Rayy, Kashan, Isfahan or even Konya. The inscriptions on famous buildings recall the names of the great Seljuks, the Seljuks of the Rum, the triumphant Mongols and many minor rulers. For them the potters met the constant challenge of Chinese porcelain imports. They altered the composition of the clay body by making it very close to a glaze: thus body and glaze united much better. Attractive translucency, very fine walls and subtle carvings and mouldings made the white wares of this period the most delicate to feel and to look at.

Another technical innovation made possible a greater range of overglaze colour through a new style known as 'Minai'. Patterns were outlined in darkest black with very fine strokes of the brush, while the dresses of court scenes showed up in wine red. Other shades such as white, beige, purple green and light blue were painted either under or over the glaze. 'Minai' colours seem to have been in use only for a short time in the 13th c., on goblets, bowls, jugs and small tiles, usually with a white background. Later gold-leaf dots and diamonds brought interest to otherwise monotonous geometrical themes in opaque red, white and black on a rich lapis-blue field known as 'Lajvardina'. Bowls, jugs and tiles appear with this style of decoration.

As for monochrome lustre painting on ceramics, in its best examples it became a way of story-telling: court entertainments, hunting scenes, life in the open, fantastic animals and birds. No lustre pieces have so far been found made in Anatolia. Syria, and especially Persia, seem to have had the prerogative. But underglaze painting was a general practice over the whole area. The main impact was of black against white or turquoise for silhouette figures of impish characters of the shadow-play type.

Less successful motifs included clumsy animals entwined in vine scrolls. Blue could be used at the same time as black under a clear glaze on a white background for attractively striped bowls and jugs or to mark out up to eight panels on larger bowls and plates. These panels would be filled in with flowing motifs of winding water-weeds, scrolls or free arabesques. If the stripes did not meet in the centre of the plate, a loosely composed medallion would decorate it. Sometime in the 13th c. one can notice a freer use of the brush-stroke on ceramics of Gorgan and other provinces of eastern Persia, as in Hama and Raqqa in northern Syria. A rich consistency was given to usually smaller vessels through the medium of opaque thick glazes, chiefly turquoise, aubergine or cobalt blue. This glaze would run over moulded patterns of animals or geometrical shapes, or against carved designs reminiscent of T'ang Chinese wares. It gathered in thick blobs towards the foot-ring. This too used to happen in the T'ang stonewares of Yü-hsien in Honan.

Islamic potters never made a point of inventing new shapes. They might try to reproduce metal ones and concentrate on the visual impact. Nevertheless some new shapes appeared in the 13th c.: elongated jugs with double shells; long-necked bottles, some with the head of a cock, of Chinese origin; straight-sided beakers; squat jugs with a very thin spout. Small figurines stand in a group quite apart, totally unrelated to any Islamic tradition. They represent falcons, camels, horsemen, mother and child, harpies, with an opaque turquoise glaze or even lustre decoration.

Last but not least the challenge of wall decoration was now being met by the new use of 'kashi' tiles or by glazed mosaics on MIHRABS and large panels in mosques or on important cenotaphs. In many cases this replaced the less luxurious stucco or stone carvings. Large tiles could be flat or more often moulded to reproduce Koranic quotations in the Naskhi style of writing on a two-dimensional background of leaf-scrolls and flying birds. Other tiles, often smaller, could form patterns of stars and crosses, freely painted with animals, flowers, writing or scenes from some famous tale. The colour scheme varied from plain turquoise or black under a clear glaze as in Kubadabad, the Seljuk palace in Anatolia, or lapis-blue with added lustre, or just lustre painting on a white background. The famous lustre *mihrabs* range in date from 1205 to 1352. In the late 14th c. the lustre and lapis type of hexagonal tiles can be found as far apart as Bursa and Samarkand.

So-called faience mosaic decoration seems to have come into its own earlier in Anatolia, being less of a luxury. It was initiated by imported craftsmen from Persia. None the less the dazzling impact of the transition zone in the Karatay Medresse in Konya (1252) stresses the subtle indigenous use of the first three basic colours: dark blue, light blue and black. More colours were added in later centuries, including white, light brown, green and yellow. Again the mosaics can be found in western Turkey and eastern Khurasan.

Mention should be made of the range of Egyptian pottery under the Mamluks (1252–1517). One can recognize less inspired wares of the Persian types: underglazed painted bowls and pots in blue, black or green; rougher carved bowls usually with a rather heavy body. More interesting imitation of Chinese CELADON has been found in Egypt than in Persia at that time. The most typical of Mamluk wares are the high-footed bowls with *sgraffiato* design under a honey-coloured glaze in the well. They recall metalwares and depict well known blazons. Although very little lustre, if any, was made in Egypt following the burning of Fostat in 1169, after the fall of Raqqa to the Mongols (1259) Damascus seems to have been able to revive the art for a time. A new type of storage jar, the *albarello*, became a very popular container as far as western Europe. Broad calligraphy and emblems appear in relief under lustre decoration and blue glaze. The lustre colour ranges from a silvery tone to a brownish one. By the 14th c. Mediterranean Spain was reproducing this luxury production and many of the 'Hispano-moresque' large plates and jars display well known Islamic themes, not always fully understood.

(*f*) *The Fifteenth Century*. By the time of his death in 1505 Tamerlane had conquered most of western Asia. If his merciless wars halted the arts and cramped trade, his sons and grandsons soon renewed both. The monuments of Samarkand and Herat amongst others, and their faience mosaics and tiles, point to a vigorous revival in the field of decoration. Later in the century the 'blue' mosque in Tabriz (1465) indicates the prosperity of Azerbaijan and its famous city, an all-time favourite of many princes.

The whole area has always produced interesting ceramics, but scientific excavations have yet to be undertaken to locate the kilns. Throughout the 15th c. Persian paintings reproduced the fashionable 'blue and white' porcelain of the early Ming. Their fanciful bodies display a blend of LOTUSES, DRAGONS and cloud-bands with an almost Islamic sense of the arabesque. Few of these are known. As for imitations, one knows of one dated fragment of a spittoon (1444) made in Meshed. Some bowls with loose flowery arabesque show some Chinese influence.

To the same century Arthur Lane has attributed the early 'Kubachi' wares. This Caucasus town used to produce fire-arms, which were possibly traded further south for ceramics to decorate the walls of houses. So far no kilns have been located. Technically for the next 150 years their characteristics remained the same: a soft white body with an over-thin glaze likely to craze. On a plate dated 1468 the background is treated in black with incised white spirals; sprays fill the four panel-medallions, reserved in white. The whole decoration lies under a turquoise glaze. On later plates a bright yellow-green glaze replaces it, and finally after 1500 the 'blue and white' scheme reappears. When the Chinese potter started using cobalt blue under the Yüan Dynasty the mineral was actually imported from Persia. Might the first original 'blue and white' pieces have been exported to the Far East too? No final proof is yet available.

Our recovery of Egyptian production of the 15th c. is even poorer in complete pieces, but again many shards from Fostat allow some understanding of the patterns: figurative motifs, some of Chinese origin, supersede more and more the radiating panel style with its birds and flowers. Besides the 'blue and white', incised black under a turquoise glaze like the 'Kubachi' wares can be seen on a mosque lamp. Rougher bowls and plates are incised under a copper green glaze reminiscent of the Azerbaijan style.

From the end of the 14th c. Islamic pattern kept loosening up and this led to a freer style of decoration. The same thing can be noted on tile ornament. In Damascus (1423) hexagonal tiles 25·5 cm. across display rows of wind-blown flowers between rows of radiant stylized patterns. Other blue and white tiles in the mosque of Murad I (1435) display a great variety of flowers in a slightly more organized way. Triangular plain turquoise tiles fill in the gaps between them. Other tiles carry on the more traditional colour schemes: black under a turquoise glaze; or blue, turquoise and black under a transparent white glaze. This second colour combination could also be applied to the local 15th-c. wares: deep and shallow bowls and dishes with flanged rims known as 'Miletus' wares from early excavations in that town. In fact they were mostly made in Iznik (Nicaea). The reddish clay body is covered with a thin white slip and the patterns recall the radiating panel style of the 14th c. Some of their geometrical scrolls fill the background panels of early 'Hispano-moresque' plates and *albarelli*.

(*g*) *Ottoman Turkey* (from the 16th c. to the 20th c.). The triumph of Ottoman Turkish ceramics lies in the freshness of the colour combinations and the dynamic styles of the 16th and 17th centuries. It now seems reasonable to accept that Iznik was not the only place of production. Kütahya, further inland, also played a part. A blue and white ewer dated 1510 and a bottle dated 1529 have inscriptions naming Kütahya. This is not surprising since the colophon of an Armenian manuscript proves the existence of an Armenian church in that town as early as 1391. Among later documents the account books of the Suleymaniye mosque list tiles from Kütahya as well as from Iznik from 1550 to 1557.

As opposed to the red body of the 'Miletus' wares the new vessels and tiles had a very white one, heavily potted and covered in a very thin white wash of the same material. On this bright background, or on the early reserved white panels against a dark cobalt blue, the colour was applied and made to shine under a perfectly transparent lead glaze. The small class of 'Golden Horn' ceramics only lasted for a short time around the 1530s; their nearest visual parallels are to be found on formal signatures or tughra of the sultans. A mechanical series of fine light-blue scrolls covers the whole white surface of jugs and vast-footed bowls.

Once again in the early phase one must bear in mind the arrival of porcelain from the East to enhance the Sultan's collection. Inventories from the 'new Serai' start mentioning them from the turn of the century. Sixty-two pieces are included with the booty from the defeated Persians in Tabriz (1514). The present-day collection includes about 8,000 pieces of porcelain, with examples right up to the FAMILLE ROSE period. Early in the 16th c. the patterns of the regularly decorated bands and panels became flexible, the cobalt blue became lighter with some added touches of turquoise. The Chinese-inspired lotuses and cloud scrolls, once austere, adapted themselves to this new Ottoman style on dishes and standing bowls.

After copying for a time various Ming prototypes such as the well known bunches of grapes, the real Ottoman style comes into its own with an explosion of colours and flowers. A gradual introduction of new colours took place up to the 1550s: olive-green, purple and grey and finally the famous tomato-red. All flowers are now home-grown: the pointed-leaf tulips, the carnations, the bluebells, the hyacinths and various blossoms, some in clusters and others springing from vases. The cypress tree only appears at a later stage. Besides leaves and groups of three tulips at a time, the 'wave' pattern fills up the rather large rims of the plates. Sponsored European shapes such as tankards found their way back to Europe, and there received silver mounts. The dating of the mounts helps in the classification, as in the case of one specimen in Ham House, Surrey, with a London hallmark and date of 1592.

Undoubtedly the most original products were the vast tile panels found chiefly in mosques, tombs and palaces, those of Suleyman the Magnificent's (1520–66) court designers and such decoration as that in the Rustem Pasha Mosque (1561), the tombs of the Sultan and his wife Roxelan, the Piyale Mosque (1573). The glory of these tiles lies not only in their immense variety but in their extreme versatility despite the regular repetition of similar motifs.

Apart from a few cases like the imperial kiosk of the Yeni Mosque, finished in 1665, or certain special rooms in the Serai, the 17th c. was a period of general decline in ceramic production. By 1648 the historian Evliya Tchelebi noted nine potters' workshops in Iznik as opposed to 300 during the first 20 years of the century. An attempt was made to revive the industry in 1724 in the Tekfur Serai by the walls of Constantinople, but it was later replaced by a glass factory. Over the whole period the colour becomes duller, red changing to sallow brown, but a strong yellow appears and some motifs are outlined in black. Cobalt and green or turquoise and blue are the main combinations. A less imperial taste required new figurative subjects such as Mecca tiles and kiosks.

Greek sailors seem to have sponsored wares decorated with boats with lateen sails, human figures and even churches, to carry home. Some of these are dated in Armenian. They were first discovered on the island of Rhodes in the 19th c. and this fact led to the misnomer 'Rhodes ware'.

Other parts of the Ottoman Empire followed the fashions of the capital according to fluctuations in the economic situation. In Damascus Suleyman the Magnificent commissioned a mosque (1554–60). He also sponsored some restoration on the tilework of the Dome of the Rock from 1545. The local type of decoration on tilework or dishes favoured vases with large arabesques of flowers or cypress trees. Most colours are the same as the Iznik ones with a slight muddy quality to them and a tendency to run; the famous tomato-red never appears. The glazes are less pure and crack.

North Africa contributed also by the creation of tilework which is rather pleasant though not so inspired as the Damascene tiles. In the 16th c. Fez (Morocco) ceramics were decorated in polychrome patterns on a tin-glaze enamel. In the 19th c. Tunisian workshops came into their own showing a dual Syrian and Italian influence. Nowadays pleasantly decorated earthenware carries on the century-old tradition.

As for Kütahya, the picture is much clearer since the work of John Carswell. As Iznik declined only the Armenian production remained alive: besides the intriguing and naïve tiles for the Church of the Resurrection in Jerusalem (1719), depicting scenes from the Old and New Testaments, the potters excelled in the making of a variety of European shapes such as the early cups without handles, coffee cups with saucers, or else pilgrim flasks and even lemon squeezers, incense burners and 'eggs' with the six-winged angel decoration. After the earlier 'blue and white' period polychromy set in with fresh bright colours such as a gay yellow. A firm outline compensated for a rather slapdash placing of these colours. Nature still dominates the scene with the carnations, long saw-edged leaves and blobs at the end of stylized branches. Besides biblical scenes (Salome or St. Michael), one deep barber's plate contains an almost satirical fish. By the middle of the 18th c. the Kütahya production was going into decline.

From that time and for the next 150 years an original if not very glamorous peasant pottery springs from the town of Çanakkale on the Dardanelles. The body of the plates is the same as that of the earlier 'Miletus' wares: coarse red clay with a layer of white slip. Sometimes the pattern of clay slips is painted directly on the body. Purple and ochre dominate the colour scheme. A simplified repertory is carried on from the earlier Iznik and Kütahya ceramics. Flowers, fruit, sailing-boats, mosques and kiosks, giraffes, fish and birds decorate plates, ewers and jugs. Animal statuettes are also known.

The short-lived Eseri Istanbul porcelain factory could not compete profitably with European imports. The Sultan founded his own factory in 1893 and it survived until 1920 in the grounds of the Yildiz palace. It provided the Sultan with his own china and official gifts. A star and crescent mark was printed in green. Nowadays Turkish Kütahya produces a variety of wares and tiles which try to recapture the earlier and far more original creations.

(*h*) *Persian Ceramics* (from the 16th c.). Despite the vigorous work of classification done by Arthur Lane, the problem of organizing late Persian wares still remains considerable. European travellers, merchants, ambassadors and various East Indian companies, especially the Dutch ones, were the main links with the West beyond the solid wall of the Ottoman Empire. Travellers' journals and account books convey more about quantity than quality and decoration. The towns of Meshed and Kerman are regularly mentioned as the main centres of production. One wonders why Isfahan with its glut of tile decoration is not included. The capital of the Safavid Dynasty (1502–1722) was finally moved there in 1598, well away from the constant forays of the Ottomans in Azerbaijan. None the less the shrine to the Sufi founder of the dynasty in Ardebil received added embellishment at that time: the building of a new 'chini-khane' emphasized the value attached to its porcelain collection. In ceramics the Chinese influence lasted much longer in Persia than in Turkey, as did exchanges on all levels with Mogul India and further east. But original inspiration was slowly disappearing.

The previously mentioned 'blue and white' Kubachi wares of the 16th c. were not the only ones produced. They are known too from eastern towns in Persia, and ports like Gombroon (modern Bandar ʿAbbas) exported them. Both Meshed and Kerman (Maʿān) have holy shrines carefully redecorated under the Safavids. Once more the tiling can serve as a guide to the wares. The Friday mosque in Kerman, with a mihrab dated 1559, has two panels of blue and white tiles outside its main *iwan*. Each tile displays flowers and leaves recalling those of large jars, small plates and vases. These wares and a pilgrim flask (1523) show a more balanced feeling for decoration than the 17th-c. pieces produced, it seems, in much greater quantity for export in the Kraak style with a black outline. Black circular bands incised through to the white body often mark the rim or well of plates, as in the case of a poem inscribed in 1697. Chinese Wan-li (1573–1619) landscapes abound, as do dragons, huntsmen and deer, all distorted by careless copying. A certain type of bird becomes horribly fat-chested and in that state is even copied on Dutch tiles. In the early 1750s Dutch ledgers start mentioning the exports of Persian ceramics until the reopening of the Chinese kilns in 1683. Over 6,000 pieces were shipped in 1670 alone.

Shapes were more or less constant by now: large pilaw dishes, plates and bowls, long-necked bottles, cup-stands, sweetmeat dishes. In the 18th c. a general slackness set in. The cobalt blue is less well controlled, rough spur marks dig into the thicker ring bases. A 'tassel' marking, usually blue, appears on many foot-rings.

As for Meshed, it produced a very good-quality white body and its potting and decoration were superior to those of Kerman. The spacing of the design is far more graceful: cranes fly amongst Chinese flame symbols and in general the whole layout keeps closer to the Chinese original. An example is a *kalian* (water container for smoking), dated 1641, in the Victoria and Albert Museum. None the less some of these *kalians* have true Persian motifs such as a small lion or a duck. As in Kerman, later wares show pierced cross-decoration under a transparent glaze as late as 1809, and also GADROONING in plates. Here too Chinese character-marking is being imitated.

Undoubtedly other towns must have produced 'blue and white' and Arthur Lane suggested Yazd. Possibly Nain produced wares with incised patterns through a brown slip or with the body painted in light blue. One might add Shiraz to the list. Lane also suggests this town for the short revival of lustre wares in the late 17th and 18th centuries, basing his view on the deterioration of the style and the heavy potting. Typical forms are pear-shaped bottles with rather long necks and squat spittoons. Other wares recall those of western Europe in the early 18th c. such as small coffee cups or tulip vases. Glazes are transparent, but can also be tinted light or dark blue; the latter is often seen on the outsides of bowls or alternating with white strips on lobed bottles. The free designs of uninspired willows, leaves or iris plants do not add up to a style despite the lustre shining in brown or ruby tones. An odd example on a bottle is what looks like a large phoenix pursuing a herd of elephants in an underglaze opaque yellow colour. Three spur marks on the inside of the foot-ring point to an 18th-c. dating. The short-lived dynasty of the Zends (2nd half of the 18th c.), based in Shiraz, sponsored new mosques and tile decoration in graceful flower patterns. Why not lustre and other wares too?

As regards polychromy, it is useless to look for comparison with the vivid Iznik ceramics. In the 'Kubachi' series the colours are subdued under a yellowish cracked glaze and the iron red mixed with slip is rather brownish. The body is rather soft. Regardless of orthodoxy the Persian painter covered large plates (35 cm) with handsomely turbaned men. Women appear unveiled, which suggests courtesans. Both sexes have their faces framed by long hanging curls in the style which prevailed in the time of the Shah Abbas (1587–1629). Their busts are surrounded by flowing blobs of vegetation, some on long stalks. The rims of plates are filled with lackadaisical flowers. One plate is decorated with a full-length female dancer holding a tambourine. Other more usual themes are two confronted peacocks, or two cranes, a deer, a cock, a flying duck with a 'flame' motif, an extraordinary-looking harpy or just flowing branches. Four, six or ten flowery panels can busy the whole surface of a plate or the inside of a bowl.

Again the tiles are by far the most interesting. The early hexagonal ones depict various birds, flowers, an angel or a lion. On later ones the framing varies from corner-angle blue lines or filled-out triangles, to give the square tile a hexagon finish, to a star-shaped octagon, a mihrab or a multi-lobed frame. These pictures recall the busts on the plates. Now the left hand is sometimes visible, the men holding a flower, the women a fruit or a cup. Human types are more varied: women in ruffs, European sailors, a water-carrier with his pot. Several features are worth noting: the variety of materials of the garments, the recurrence of the dark 'flame' motif straight from the Chinese repertory, the scale pattern reminiscent of maiolica decoration around the 1530s and the Iznik fillings of the mid 1550s. Exceptionally, two large rectangular tiles depict two women preparing for the bath in a garden décor. The series of this supposedly north-western ceramic seems to be closed by a tomb-slab dated 1627.

The Kerman polychromy conveys a feeling of much greater freshness. As with the 'blue and white', the decoration gains in lightness through the addition of brown, ochre and also black lines with an enhancing red. This red is duller than the Iznik one, but on the white background it contrasts well with the blue strokes it underlines. It emphasizes patterns on tiles and becomes small carnations on bowls, *kalians* and very large plates. The blue 'tassel' mark appears on the foot-ring. Again this type of decoration must have been copied in the neighbouring provinces at least from the 17th c.

Isfahan, Shiraz and later Tehran were also famous for their polychrome tiles. It was a quick way of decorating huge surfaces of mosques, garden pavilions and baths. From the Safavid period onwards more and more yellow appears, leading up to the Qajar Dynasty (1786–1925) which moved the capital to Tehran. By that time one can almost talk about a surfeit of Victorian flowery decoration as seen inside and outside the Golestan Palace: large hunting scenes, series of gardens and pavilions. More graceful compositions were achieved on a white background under the Zends in Shiraz and the early Qajars in Kerman.

The competition of European porcelain in the 19th c. brought to an end the more sophisticated

A. Bowl painted in brown and yellow lustre. Mesopotamia. (B.M., 9th c.)

B. Bowl. Eastern Persia. (V. & A. Mus., 9th–10th c.)

C. Bowl. Persia. (Municipal Mus., The Hague, 11th–12th c.)

D. Pot from Raqqa. (Gulbenkian Foundation Mus., Lisbon, 12th c.)

A

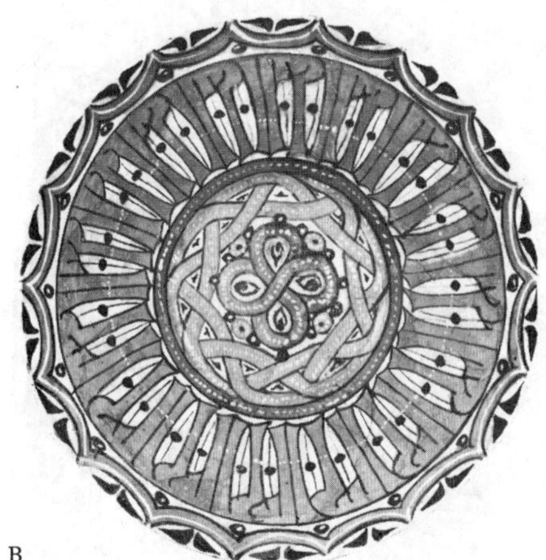

B

C

D

Wall tile from a *mihrab*. Persia. (V. & A. Mus., 13th c.)

A. Jug with relief ornament. Persia. (Municipal Mus., The Hague, 2nd half 12th c.)

B. Bowl. Persia (Rayy). (V. & A. Mus., 13th c.)

C. Hama plate. Syria. (Nat. Mus., Damascus, 14th c.)

D. Panel of twelve tiles. Turkey (Iznik). (Gulbenkian Foundation Mus., Lisbon, 16th–17th c.)

A

B

C

D

Dish. Persia (Kubachi). (V. & A. Mus., early 17th c.)

(*Right*) Ewer. Persia. (V. & A. Mus., 17th c.)

Persian production although various polychrome pieces still appear in the middle of the 19th c., judging by a large bowl (1851). Elegant human figures crowd a garden scene along with the inevitable clusters of flowers used as divisions as well to fill the gaps between the scenes on the outer part of the bowl.

One last polychrome ware worth mentioning is a peasant style produced to this day in Transoxiana. The slip decoration under a lead glaze recalls the much earlier Khurasan wares. The red body is the same. Some of these plates use an opaque tin glaze as a background for pale blue rosette patterns and stylized foliage.

Finally, among the monochrome ceramics, the imitations of Chinese celadons stand out. They were at their best under the Safavids with shades varying from pale green to grey. Gadrooning emphasizes the effective weight of large dishes. Smaller objects such as *kalians* and faceted bowls must have been made in Kerman. Some have patterns cut through the colour to show up the specially white body.

The standard opaque turquoise glaze covers the usual repertory of smaller wares such as plain and ribbed bowls, finely potted beakers, slightly incised plates, pourers and salvers. A small elephant figurine seems to be a rare piece.

Small moulded rosettes appear on many relief pieces, probably made chiefly in Isfahan. Their hard bodies are most suited for bottles and flasks, which are finally covered in a sharp green glaze. One can recognize the style of the Riza Abbasi school of painting in such relief scenes as a camel fight or a group of three musicians, a huntsman and a lion on a lead; or again in two flying bulls, known to exist in at least two examples. Smaller flasks and flat-sided containers have an amber glaze over conventional bouquet motifs. Clumsy-looking small tankards have moulded or cloisonné decoration under a turquoise or attractive light-blue glaze. Of all the monochrome pieces the most delicate remain the white ones, as in the 13th c. Translucent and thin-walled under a glassy transparent glaze, their finish enhances what would normally be banal shapes.

If a lot more research has still to be done in the field of later Persian ceramics, none at all has yet been done in Islamic India. All that has been noticed so far is the Persian-inspired decoration in glazed mosaics or tiles. These start appearing in India as early as the 15th c. in Gwalior and on the walls of the medresse of Bidar near Hyderabad dated 1472. In the 17th c. whole story-panels cover parts of the wall of Lahore fort; they depict vivid scenes of polo-playing or camel and elephant fights. Very little more is known about later Indian ceramics besides the day-to-day unglazed wares available in all market-places. In the Purana Qila in Delhi Khurasan and 'blue and white' exports from China have come to light. But this is a very meagre harvest for a whole continent and it is to be hoped that further excavations will yield more knowledge about local production of ceramics. Among the most useful recent studies of Islamic art is Géza Fehérvári's *Islamic Pottery. A Comprehensive Study based on the Barlow Collection*, published in 1973.

For techniques see POTTERY TECHNIQUES.

See also AFRICA (POTTERY): AMERINDIANS; BYZANTIUM (POTTERY); CHINA (CERAMICS); GREEK AND ROMAN ANTIQUITY; INDIA (TERRACOTTA FIGURINES); JAPAN (POTTERY AND PORCELAIN).

General: 87, 90, 137, 139, 140, 162, 170, 196, 206, 216, 217, 262, 263, 272, 308, 309, 401, 407, 408, 493, 495, 519, 657, 683, 685, 724, 756, 763.

Islamic Ceramics: 128, 237, 492, 494, 909.

CHALCEDONY. See QUARTZ.

CHAMPLEVÉ. See ENAMEL.

CHANDELIER. A term in general use from *c.* the middle of the 18th c. to denote branching lights hanging from a ceiling. The device is descended from the medieval candle beam or candylbeme, a pendant light with two or six flat wooden cross-pieces fitted with holders for candles at the ends of each arm, and from the 'corona', a suspended light used in churches and consisting of an iron hoop with spikes for candles or cups for oil fixed at intervals. By the middle of the 16th c. chandeliers had up to 24 branches and were made from gold or silver suspended by chains from the ceiling. In the 17th c. chandeliers were commonly of brass with crystal to add reflecting power. In the 18th c. floridly carved chandeliers in wood and gesso, often gilt, were the fashion, and designs for these were illustrated by CHIPPENDALE in his *Director*. From the early 16th c. Venice was famous for highly ornamented chandeliers of pincered and moulded GLASS and coloured glass flowers. The Spanish glass-house at La Granja was also celebrated for splendid chandeliers made of polygons of clear glass or decorated with faceted glass flowers. English chandeliers exploited the natural properties of the lead glass introduced by RAVENSCROFT. The earlier examples followed the pattern of the early 18th-c. brass chandeliers, having curved arms branching out from a tapering central shaft constructed of glass spheres of different sizes. Chandeliers gradually became more complex and their ornamentation more elaborate until during the REGENCY a cascade of hanging drops concealed the central shaft carrying a gilt metal ring set with candle-holders.

CHANGE-RINGING. See BELL-FOUNDING.

CHA-NO-YU. Japanese tea ceremony, associated with a taste for simplicity and rusticity in the decorative arts. A complete aesthetic centred upon this ceremony, and it has had certain distant echoes in the West. See JAPAN, particularly (POTTERY AND PORCELAIN).

CHANTILLY LACE. A bobbin LACE, generally of black or sometimes of white SILK, made during the 19th c. at Chantilly and other French towns, particularly Caen and Bayeux. The large, somewhat pompous floral patterns, very open in texture, were outlined with a heavier thread on a ground-mesh of six-pointed star form which derives its name, *fond chant*, from this type of lace. Veils and other large pieces were commonly made from Chantilly lace.

CHANTILLY PORCELAIN (1725–*c.* 1800). Soft-paste porcelain made in France, at first with a smooth, opaque white glaze containing tin oxide (like that of FAIENCE). The delightfully simple, lobed forms and sparing enamelled designs were both influenced by the Japanese KAKIEMON style. After *c.* 1750 the plainer SÈVRES styles were followed.

CHAPMAN, MOSES. American itinerant silhouettist of eastern Massachusetts, who made hollow-cut silhouette portraits by machine. See SILHOUETTE.

CHARLES, A. See SILHOUETTE.

CHASING. A technique of relief decoration on GOLD AND SILVER or other metal in which the design is raised by surface hammering. The term 'flat chasing' is used of surface decoration in low relief produced by hammering with small blunt tools. It was often used in conjunction with engraving. The term 'chase' is also used for finishing cast metalwork by filing or cutting away the roughnesses. Similar techniques are sometimes used with LEATHER. See also EMBOSS.

CHATELAINE. Decorative appendage worn at the waist with chains to support a pocket-watch, keys, étuis, thimbles, trinkets, etc. Gentlemen's chatelaines were longer and were worn suspended on each thigh so as to conceal the openings of the flap on the breeches. Besides watches they supported a variety of charms and seals and trinkets. Highly decorative chatelaines were fashionable in the 2nd half of the 18th c. Cut-steel chatelaines for gentlemen from the Birmingham factories of Matthew BOULTON and others were popular on the Continent in the 1780s. By the turn of the century chatelaines had become simpler in style, supporting only fob-seals, and watches were no longer worn in an exposed position. Chatelaines are now valued by collectors as objects of virtu.

CHATOYANT. Term in jewellery for the cat's-eye effect which is prized in some CHRYSOBERYLS and TOURMALINES. It is a single band of light which seems to live within a gemstone and which moves across the surface as the position of the stone is changed. See JEWELLERY.

784, 921.

CHENILLE (French, 'caterpillar'). 1. A velvety cord of silk and wool fibres round a central core of cotton or wire. It is used for trimming or bordering.

2. A type of needle used in embroidery, etc. See EMBROIDERY (TECHNIQUES).

CHESS PIECES. Since the game of chess originated somewhere perhaps on the banks of the Ganges and certainly many centuries ago it has spread throughout the world, surmounting barriers of language, nationality and creed. More than any other game or sport it has always attracted the skill of the craftsman. Many of the earliest sets were made to the order of kings and princes; others were made by craftsmen as a labour of love. In the Far East ornate, fanciful and exquisitely carved sets have for some centuries been made for the Western market; yet they have often lacked the individuality which has characterized the finest European pieces.

Interest in chess pieces was rare among private collectors until after the Second World War. Almost all the older sets are in museums or collections and it is rarely that a fine set made before the opening of the 18th c. comes into the market. Medieval chess-men are to be seen in most national museums and in the treasuries of a few churches. For the most part the pieces in these medieval sets bear scant resemblance to what they represent: kings and queens are roughly shaped blocks which represent thrones, bishops are cylinders with two projecting horns, knights are similar but with one projecting horn, the rooks are narrow tapering blocks with channels cut across their tops and pawns are simple conical shapes tapering from top to base with a small ball finial at the top. Such pieces are usually cut from walrus IVORY or wood. The most celebrated European pieces are the so-called Lewis chess-men. They were discovered in 1831 in an underground chamber at the head of the Bay of Uig on the west coast of the Isle of Lewis. They are carved from Morse ivory and their exact origin is unknown. They have been attributed to both Scotland and Scandinavia. They have been ascribed to the 12th c. but they may be much later. They are 78 in number and come from at least seven different sets. The British Museum has 67 and the remainder are in the National Museum, Edinburgh. The earliest authentic English chess piece is a 12th-c. walrus carving representing a mounted king; it is in the Salisbury museum. The most valuable chess set extant is a 14th-c. silver-mounted hardstone set known as the St. Louis in the Musée de Cluny. Many small wooden sets were made for actual play from *c.* the middle of the 15th c. Apart from their age they have no great value, but they do serve to illustrate the evolution of shapes.

1. ENGLAND. In the 1st half of the 19th c. English ivory and bone turners worked mainly in small one-man workshops in and around Birmingham and London and they were unable to compete with imported sets. The best were made by Charles Hastilow, one of whose finest sets with matching chess-board was shown at the Great Exhibition of 1851. In ceramics English chess-men more than held their own. Notable were the sets produced by WEDGWOOD in the second half of the 18th c. to designs by John Flaxman (1755–1826). Originally there were three different kings and three different queens, two types of bishop but only one type of knight and one type of rook. Charles Kemble, the brother of Sarah Siddons, sat as model for the kings and Mrs. Siddons herself sat for the queens. One type of bishop was a robed and mitred figure with one arm upraised and the other was a jester or French *fou.* The knights were mounted warriors, the rooks castellated towers with turret surmounts and the pawns were warriors in various postures. The sides were distinguished by different colours. Each piece in every set was marked 'WEDGWOOD' and in the original pieces Flaxman's mark will be found scratched in the paste. Unmarked but distinctive small military chess-men were produced at the beginning of the 19th c. at Castleford and in the 1st quarter of the century porcelain sets produced at Swinton under the Bramelds were finished in the distinctive apple green and periwinkle blue of Rockingham. In shape they resembled earlier German pieces. The Yorkshire Museum has a few unique pottery pieces which may be from Derby or Staffordshire and some time after 1842 the Minton factory produced a charming set in Parian ware. Each piece portrays a girl child. The sides are alike in form but the pieces of one side are coloured green and those of the other blue. Some pieces carry the Minton mark, others are unmarked. The designer George Tinworth at Doulton created a few sets in heavily glazed pottery in which every piece was a mouse, and each carries Tinworth's monogram. One side is finished in deep brown and the other in a light straw colour.

So far as can be ascertained no English silver sets were made before the 19th c., but a bust-type set by E. Fennel bears the silver mark for 1815. The two sides are not differentiated in shape but one side is gold plated.

Until the 1st quarter of the 19th c. playing sets varied markedly in shape and size. As the game became internationally competitive serious players began to be reluctant to play with an opponent's set because familiarity with shape and size was thought to constitute an advantage; therefore the need for a standardized set arose. This was provided by a set designed in 1835 by Nathaniel Cook, to which the British master Howard Staunton lent his name. This quickly won general acceptance and for over a century has remained standard throughout the world for serious chess. The design employs symbols in their plainest form: for the king a crown; for the queen a coronet; for the bishop a mitre; for the knight a horse's head (which was based on the Elgin Marbles); for the rook a castellated tower; and for the pawns circular discs surmounted by a ball. Each symbol was mounted on a plain turned stem rising from a heavy base. The king's side knights and rooks were marked with an impressed small crown so that they could be easily distinguished during play or when the game was being marked. The copyright of the design has remained the property of the firm John Jaques & Son Ltd.

2. FRANCE. The artistry of the many French turners who produced chess-men in and around Paris and Dieppe from *c.* the middle of the 18th c. was unrivalled. The more elaborate sets displayed a lively imagination, but simple playing sets of a very high quality were exported in large numbers. Of these the French St. George type was the most popular until it was superseded

by the Staunton set. A favourite theme of Dieppe craftsmen was Frenchmen against Africans. Of the superb ivory sets carved in Paris at the beginning of the 19th c. many featured the wars between France and England or France and Germany. From the second decade of the century Napoleon was commonly represented as king. There are some good sets featuring the Battle of Waterloo with Napoleon and Josephine as king and queen, Marshals Ney and Massena as bishops, French dragoons as knights and Napoleon's Old Guard as pawns. The opposing side shows The Duke and Duchess of Wellington, Lords Liverpool and Castlereagh, British dragoons and British grenadiers. One or two spectacular sets made about the same time have the Canadian campaign of 1759–60 as their theme. Many other battle scenes were featured.

Only one French silver set is known to exist. This carries the French silver mark for 1819 and is similar in design to many Austrian wooden sets of the same period.

Beautifully carved ivory sets of spiked chessmen were produced in the 18th c. for use on coaching journeys together with cushion boards embroidered with squares of alternating colours. Cruder bone-spiked sets were used at French watering-places with a board scratched out on the sand.

Delightful little pieces of the St. George type complete with matching tray-type boards were produced in FAIENCE at Rouen. They were well potted and heavily glazed in brilliant colours with a repeating pattern of fleurs-de-lis. A few high-quality porcelain sets were made at Sèvres with simple shapes finished in purple, brown and gold, each set with matching porcelain board.

3. GERMANY. Early German craftsmen, particularly those of Nuremberg and Augsburg, designed sets which for quality have rarely been surpassed. Attention was given to design, balance, historical association and over-all effect and historical details are meticulously exact. In this they differ from the contemporary French sets, in which more licence was allowed to the imagination. Exquisite wooden sets are sometimes mounted on silver plinths, which carry Nuremberg marks although the hardwood carvings may have been done elsewhere. Throughout the 19th c. thousands of wooden sets were carved from softwoods in the Tyrol and Black Forest, though they lack the quality and sophistication of the earlier German sets. In south Germany a few sets were carved from AMBER of differing colours, the pieces being set on silver mounts. In the 2nd quarter of the 18th c. a number of bust sets were cut from ivory and hardwoods. They are easy to identify because the eyes were made prominent by piercing and colouring the pupils; some wooden sets have the pupils burned in. Among the most interesting of all German sets are those featuring Reynard the Fox, carved to the designs of the Nazarene painter W. von Kaulbach (1805–74) and portraying Reynard in the roll of bishop with lion and lioness as king and queen and other animals for the remaining pieces. The few sets now known to exist were made in the late 18th c., but a slightly earlier example exists with monkey pawns and a similar set attributed to von Kaulbach himself is in the Bayerisches Nationalmuseum, Munich.

Early German sets often have the opposing sides carved from different materials. One important 18th-c. set, no doubt inspired by the Battle of Jarnac in 1569, portrays Catherine de Médicis and her followers in amber and the Huguenots under Condé in ivory.

The MEISSEN and FRANKENTHAL factories produced fine porcelain sets, the earliest Meissen sets being made in 1745 and a somewhat similar one reproduced in the 2nd half of the 19th c. Meissen continues to make good porcelain sets. Professor Max Esse of Berlin designed the modern marine set and other well known designers have been responsible for fine but less familiar types. The current frog set, designed by Struck, is well made and carefully finished in natural colours. At Frankenthal a delightful bust-type set was modelled by K. Linck in the 2nd half of the 18th c. It carries the maker's mark CT and is finished in soft colours. In 1806 the porcelain factory at Ludwigsburg, near Stuttgart, produced an important set figuring Heinrich der Löwe riding a lion as king with jesters mounted on asses as his bishops. Well potted chess-men in white and coloured porcelain were also made at Fürstenberg and Volkstedt.

Silversmiths working in Augsburg and Nuremberg produced more sets than were made elsewhere, but silver sets have always been expensive and have never enjoyed the popularity of well carved wood or ivory sets. The earliest recorded date of a silver set is 1700 and although a few sets have been ascribed to an earlier date, proof of this is lacking. An important silver set made in Königsberg is dated 1778 and features a battle between Roman and Moorish troops.

Cast-iron was used extensively for low-priced decorative sets and when the models for the moulds were the work of skilled craftsmen ornamental sets of distinction could be cast at little cost. The best cast-iron sets were made by Zimmermann of Hanau, near Frankfurt, where he produced no fewer than eight totally different designs. The most impressive were similar to a set presented by the American nation to the chess master Paul Morphy on his return from his European tour. Other Zimmermann sets in cast-iron portray famous battles, animals or the crafts. Original sets carry the maker's name and the place of manufacture stamped in the iron; cast-iron sets by other makers, who copied Zimmermann's models, do not carry marks.

4. ITALY. It has been said that several outstandingly beautiful sets were made by craftsmen of Milan and Florence during the 16th and 17th centuries, and inventories of the 15th and 16th centuries sometimes listed chess sets. But

if any of these exist, their whereabouts are not known. Late in the 18th c. some distinctive and beautifully made sets were carved from African ivory at Florence. The pieces on both sides are identical, depicting Roman emperors and empresses as kings and queens, Roman officials as bishops, while the knights are bridled horses' heads, the rooks castellated towers and the pawns well-turned simple stems terminating in acorn finials. The pieces of one side are dyed red or pale green. Glass chess-men made at Venice were usually based on earlier carved ivory pieces. Some were of solid glass; others were blown hollow and left with an opening at the base closed with a small cork so that coloured liquids could be poured into them. A more complex type was made from different coloured glasses fused together and overlaid in white. Towards the end of the 18th c. extremely fanciful sets were being made by Italian craftsmen with insects, birds, fish, etc., elaborated into fantastic motifs. In addition to these decorative and fanciful sets the glass-houses produced quantities of St. George type pieces from very hard glass with polished bases: they are in many colours, clear, pale and dark green, yellow, mauve and blue.

5. CENTRAL EUROPE. Fine hardwood sets were carved in Austria and Hungary and migratory craftsmen settled in other countries. They used many themes—animals, birds, tradesmen and peasantry—but there was no uniformity of style. Later, similar but much inferior sets were churned out from softwoods for the tourist trade. Double horses' heads were sometimes used for the knights in early playing sets of simple design but exquisite workmanship.

A few Austrian and Hungarian silver sets are known, but as they carry no mark it is impossible to be certain about their date or place of origin. Ornate silver sets are now made in Hungary with large pieces encrusted with semi-precious stones, some of the larger stones with intaglio engravings. The matching silver board is decorated with enamelled heraldic arms and emblems. Four silver horses act as supports for the corners of the board and are linked to emblems by silver chains.

A few Austro-Hungarian glass sets of the BIEDERMEIER period exist but they are rarely seen. The light side is made from uranium glass and the opposing side from glass containing gold oxide. The pieces are square in section, each terminating in a human head coloured in natural tints. Charming little porcelain sets were made in the Viennese Imperial China establishment towards the close of the 19th c., carefully painted in yellows and blacks with gold trim. An identical set was produced in 1926 and again in the post-war years.

In Bosnia and Herzegovina distinctive and unique little sets were made from bone and ivory. Kings, queens, bishops and pawns were represented by carved human heads mounted on pear-shaped stems rising from plain circular bases. Knights were the fore-parts of bridled horses and rooks pear-shaped castellated towers. In spite of poor workmanship the quaintness of these little sets exerted a strong appeal and they are eagerly sought by collectors. Most of them were made in the last quarter of the 18th c., but some may have been earlier and some possibly later.

Wood-carving reached its highest technical perfection in the last quarter of the 18th c., pear wood being used as well as hardwoods. The themes were highly imaginative and included battles, birds, animals, tradesmen and the crafts. Few early sets of this class have survived, but Bohemian sets sometimes come to light which compare favourably with anything of the kind produced elsewhere.

Until 1938 fine bust-type sets cast in heavy black and opaque glass were manufactured in Czechoslovakia. The craft was revived after the War and the old moulds were used to produce sets commercially. In Bulgaria and Romania cheap painted wooden sets were made in quantity until 1938, decorative but lacking in quality and finish. Swiss wood-carvers turned out quantities of cheap wooden sets during the last quarter of the 19th c. with the Bears of Berne as a theme. In general they are amusing but without special merit. But a few, and at least half-a-dozen ivory sets with the same theme, are of excellent quality.

6. NORTHERN EUROPE. The earliest Danish pieces, to be seen in the Nationalmuseet, Copenhagen, date from the 16th c. and are carved from walrus ivory. They were found in various places between 1841 and 1869. In the latter part of the 18th c. and the 19th c. Danish turners made quantities of playing sets for home use closely resembling contemporary French and German types. Dutch turners also produced simple playing sets in wood, bone and ivory from *c.* the middle of the 18th c. and they too resemble contemporary French and German playing sets. Although the design at first sight appears rather spindly by present standards, they are well balanced and were well suited to the small squares of early chess-boards and tables. Both Danish and Dutch silversmiths made small sets, Gustavus Adolphus and Ferdinand of Austria being the most popular themes. The skilled Flemish ivory carvers made but few chess sets but these of the highest quality. Virtue and Vice was the most popular theme. The majestic white king and queen were attended by church officials clasping closed bibles; the pawns were cherubs each holding a different emblem of love. The opposing king is Mephistopheles, who stands with his queen in a revealing robe. The bishops and knights are satyrs and the pawns imps armed with a club or stone. Several versions of the theme were used during the 1st quarter of the 19th c. and it is possible that the original was made *c.* the middle of the 18th c.

7. SPAIN. During the latter part of the 18th c.

Spanish craftsmen were occupied mainly with ecclesiastical work but at least one fairly large school devoted some time to chess-men. Some sets are simple, some very elaborate; but all have one feature in common: the main pieces are gallery or 'pulpit' mounted. Simple sets have plain symbols rising from ACANTHUS-leaf pulpits; elaborate ones have human figures on similar mounts. Usually the figures are ivory, while the mount is carved from bone.

8. RUSSIA. Legend has it that excellent chess pieces were carved by Russian craftsmen at a very early date, but almost all the Russian sets known were manufactured towards the end of the 18th c. Most of the Russian 18th-c. sets incorporate pieces which are replicas of those used in the original Indian game of *chatarunga*: Tsar (king); Ferz (counsellor); Slon (elephant); Kon (horse); Ladia (boat); and Pieshka (foot-soldier). Both walrus and mammoth ivory were used in the early sets.

Silver-mounted hardstone chess-men with matching boards were made by FABERGÉ to their usual standard of perfection. In the 20th c. porcelain propaganda sets of good quality were made in the old Imperial Porcelain Factory, now the Lomonosov Works. One side represents Communists and the other Capitalists.

9. ISLAM. Geometrical chess pieces have been used throughout the Muslim world for centuries. Some are very elaborate. A few examples have gold and silver wire spun over wooden formers; others are made from gold and silver with enamel overlay. Yemeni metal-workers still produce chess-men from woven copper and brass wire and the craft flourishes in Israel, where modern versions of much earlier sets are made from silver wire often with inlay of semi-precious stones. Small interesting geometrical sets have always been made by Turkish craftsmen of wood, brass, copper or pottery, and elaborate floral sets have been turned and carved from ivory.

10. PERSIA. Although many Persian pottery sets exist, none is earlier than the 18th c. They are simple in form, well potted and brilliantly enamelled in blue, green, yellow and red. Some sets are also finished with metallic lustre. Persian metal-workers cast and chased quantities of simple playing pieces and also made some striking sets from brass overlaid with enamels. Other elaborate Persian sets have pieces made from precious metals. Often the bases of one side are of gold with silver tops, while the opposing pieces have silver bases and gold tops. In addition the gold of the one side is inlaid with silver and the silver of the other is inlaid with gold.

11. FAR EAST. A modified version of *shatranj* (the medieval game of India) called *chit-tha-reen* was played in Burma from the beginning of the 17th c. Originally suitably marked cubes or discs were used but quite soon carved shapes came into fashion. Whereas in China and India craftsmen produced chess sets for export to the West, the Burmese cut chess-men in the form of figures simply for local demand and the few early sets which left the country were taken out by visitors who regarded them as a novelty. The earliest Burmese carved sets are of softwoods, but from the beginning of the 18th c. some excellent sets were cut in ivory. Later on hardstone sets which resemble Indian pieces were made from brown and smoky agate and by the 1st quarter of the 19th c. commercial sets were being turned and carved in quantity in and around Pagan. The best of these are not inferior to good Chinese work; others are poorly carved from inferior materials. Commercial Burmese sets are always cut from Indian ivory, whereas earlier sets made for local use were carved from Burmese ivory.

Both the Burmese and the Chinese games are variations of *shatranj* but the pieces used for them are quite different from each other and have different names and uses. Although it is sometimes claimed that the Chinese invented chess just over two thousand years ago during the Hansing campaign, *choke-choo-hong-ki*, the Chinese game, is, as has been said, a variation of *shatranj*. For the Chinese game circular engraved discs are used which are quite unsuitable for chess as we know it. The pieces are called Meng (king), Chekoy (general), Ratha (war chariot), Chein (elephant), Mhee (horse), Yein (foot-soldier) in the Burmese game, and Chong (king or general), Sou (prince or counsellor), Tchong (mandarin or elephant), Mai (horse), Tche (chariot), Pao (rocket boy or mortar) and Ping (pawn or foot-soldier) in the Chinese game.

Thousands of elaborately carved ivory chess sets were made in China for export. Almost all were carved from Indian ivory and all but those made around Macao bear a family resemblance. The best are quite perfect, the worst little better than rubbish since they are badly carved from the open end of the tusk. Four different types were made, each in several versions. But one type is superior to the others. The figures were boldly carved from solid ivory and each figure stands on a heavy octagonal carved base. Sets of this type are more robust than those mounted on concentric balls or rosettes. Those mounted on concentric balls are the most spectacular and certainly the most numerous. The Cantonese concentric ball has been used as a mount for chess-men since the 1st half of the 19th c. but the ball itself has been made for very much longer. There are no joints in the outer ball but each set of balls is cut from a solid block of ivory. The technique is slow and tedious but not too difficult for a skilled craftsman. A solid piece of ivory is turned to the right size on a lathe and the resulting ball is then drilled to its centre at equally spaced points with a hollow-ended taper drill. The craftsman then works through the taper holes and frees the second innermost ball. (The first was freed when the hollow-ended drill reached the centre point.) He then continues the process until all the balls are free and he has reached the outer one. The inner balls are then drilled with a suitable tool and the outer one carved to some elaborate design. Fine rosette-mounted sets incorporating European kings and queens were carved in French Indo-China. The rosette is merely a carved knop rising from a circular carved base and when they were so mounted the added height made small, unimportant pieces quite presentable.

Three main themes were used in Chinese sets destined for the Western markets: Chinese against Mongols; Chinese or Mongols against forces headed by an English or Portuguese king; Chinese or Mongolian forces against forces led by Napoleon. Apart from the kings and queens opposing sides are more or less alike. The most rare Chinese pieces are those made in the form of rats. Only a few are known to exist. They were carved in the 18th c. and were probably all the work of one skilled craftsman. Ruby and amber eye insertions give the rats a lifelike appearance and different postures heighten the effect. A few exceptional figure sets from CORAL, an extremely difficult material to handle, were made in the 19th c. Quantities of distinctive bust-type sets with European kings and queens on the white side were manufactured in and around the Portuguese settlement of Macao in the late 18th and early 19th centuries.

Shogi, Japanese chess, which is also considered to be a variant of *shatranj*, has been played for upwards of 700 years and has recently become popular in the United States, spreading from there to Europe. The pieces are all the same shape, elongated pentagonal tablets tapering from base to apex. They are identified by characters engraved on the obverse and pieces capable of promotion have their reverse faces engraved with promotion values. Since the end of the Second World War Japanese craftsmen have produced quantities of well made hardstone chess-men. Contrasting stones, such as jade, tiger eye, Brazilian rose quartz and African jade, are imported for the decoration and the finish of these sets equals that of the best early hardstone pieces.

Conventional wooden playing pieces have been made in Java for centuries. The Javanese game, called *chatur* and also of Indian origin, has pieces named Ratu (king), Pateh (queen or minister), two Prahu (rooks), two Mantri (bishops), two Jaran (knights) and eight Bidak (pawns). The game is played on a normal chess-board but in the original game the king was positioned on the left of the queen and in consequence opposing kings faced opposing queens or ministers. In the middle of the 19th c. very striking pieces were made from carved and painted bamboo. The main pieces were distorted representations of human beings with long protruding snouts and receding chins. Kings and bishops each had two pairs of eyes, one looking forward and the other backwards. Knights were horses' heads on human trunks and rooks elephants' heads on human trunks. The legs of each figure were in one plane; there was no left or right foot.

Although chess originated in India, no complete or incomplete sets for *chaturanga*, the earliest form of the game, exist and with few exceptions all decorative Indian pieces were made between the last quarter of the 18th c. and the 3rd quarter of the 19th c. It is known that decorative sets were made as early as 1686 but these were specially commissioned. Chess pieces made commercially for *c.* 180 years differ considerably in design, workmanship and material. The main theme has always been the rivalry between the Old East India Company and native rulers. Exquisite carved ivory sets with this theme will often portray a top-hatted white king together with top-hatted mounted bishops and knights. The majority of the 'John' type sets were made in and around Delhi. Similar sets, usually finished in polychrome, were made in Bengal and these generally incorporate boats as rooks. Large and small crudely carved but brightly coloured sets with the same theme were made in and around Madras while beautifully turned and carved Kashmir pieces often portrayed British and native foot-soldiers as pawns. Similar sets were cast from bronze and brass while one or two very small sets of the same type were made from gold with enamel finish and sometimes encrusted with jewels. Apart from the more elaborate figure sets great quantities of well-turned and well-carved playing sets were made from ivory, horn, sandalwood and shell. They usually have matching boards and backgammon sets housed in one case. India produced few hardstone sets though a very few simple and poorly finished sets were made in the 19th c. Excellent chess-men are still being made in India while at the same time cheap and worthless copies of earlier sets are being hacked out for the tourist trade.

In Ceylon the medieval game *shatranj* was played for many centuries but only functional pieces were made until the 19th c., when a few well-carved ivory and ebony sets were made in Colombo and the surrounding district. The kings represent Buddha and the queens his disciples in a state of Nirvana.

In Cambodia chess has been played with small, simple but well-made pieces for 500 years. The pieces are entirely functional. The kings, queens, bishops and rooks are simple pear-shaped turnings, the knights are well-carved horses' heads with the lower jaws resting on the necks and the pawns are small convex discs or shells. Almost always the queens are smaller than the other major pieces, a feature found only in Cambodian and early Siamese sets. The majority of sets attributed to Siam were carved in Burma. The only sets which can be authenticated as of early Siamese origin closely resemble those of Cambodia, small shell-like turned pieces with only the knight figurative. Chess-men which can be certainly attributed to Mongolia are most rare. They consist of carved and

Persian geometrical chess pieces (18th c.)

Pottery chess set by Wedgwood

Pawns and rook from Indian 'John' type chess set (*c.* 1790)

Italian piscatorial set. Ivory (*c.* 1800)

Chinese rosette-mounted chess-men. Made at Macao from Indian ivory for the Western market (*c.* 1800)

Spanish pulpit chess piece (last quarter 18th c.)

Cantonese chess set mounted on concentric balls. Made for the Western market with European king and queen (*c.* 1840)

Cast-iron chess set by Zimmermann of Hanau (*c.* 1850)

Staunton chess-men

painted wooden pieces featuring animals and birds with only the king representing a human figure.

12. MODERN. A constantly proliferating tourist trade has encouraged craftsmen in many countries to produce chess pieces. Authentic antique chess-men are very expensive and most collectors now look for modern sets which maintain a high standard of quality in craftsmanship.

About 20 different types of ivory chess-men can be purchased in Hong Kong. Japanese ivory sets resemble these, but Japanese hardstone sets leave little to be desired. The quality of Indian sets depends upon the cost; they range from fine bust-type sets to very poor reproductions of older types. In the Philippines a large local industry has been built up manufacturing chess sets from both hard and soft woods. In the Middle East and in Africa large quantities of wooden sets are made and in Egypt good carvers produce high quality ivory sets. Carved ebony and thornwood pieces are sold very cheaply in Tanzania and to meet the demands of Belgian settlers ivory workers of the Congo made good carved and turned pieces. Crude but very amusing little bronze chess-men are made in the Upper Volta region of Africa; they are poorly cast but brightly painted to cover the blemishes; and they reflect the vivid imagination of a primitive people. In the West Indies wooden chess pieces modelled on earlier French and German sets have been made for many years and in Haiti wooden sets based on European models have been manufactured since the 1st half of the 19th c. In Mexico there is a large output of crudely carved onyx sets which nevertheless represent good value in relation to their cost. In Ecuador a silver set is produced which in future years may become traditional. Almost all European countries have produced post-war sets. Poland and Spain make cheap but attractive sets of painted wood. Denmark, Austria, Hungary and Switzerland all make inferior versions of their earlier sets. All are now carved from softwood, but a few are worthy of a place in a modern collection.

Marble and synthetic marble pieces are prolific in many shapes and sizes but, like their plastic counterparts, apart from certain decorative qualities they have little merit. Dyed alabaster is sometimes used but it is too soft to be a good medium for the purpose. Possibly the most attractive post-war ceramic set is the porcelain one made in the Portuguese Vista Alegre factory. It is a bust-type set, portraying crusaders and Saracens, worthy of any collection. The majority of post-war Staunton type chess-men have been produced in France but a very superior version is being made in Japan.

528, 557, 590, 615, 902.

CHEVAL GLASS. See MIRRORS.

CHEVET. 1. Term in Christian church architecture for the east end of a church comprising the ambulatory, the apse and sometimes radiating chapels.

2. Term used by jewellers and lapidaries for an engraved gemstone in which the design or figures are cut in relief but so that the highest surfaces of the figures do not project above the surface of the stone. The method is analogous to the Egyptian form of relief carving known as coelanaglyphic.

784, 921.

CHEVRON. Term in heraldry for a shape like an inverted V, deriving from a pair of rafters which meet in this form. As an element in a repetitive zig-zag pattern it was used as an enrichment of MOULDINGS in ROMANESQUE and Norman architecture. In late 15th-c. and 16th-c. decoration the motif was carved or inlaid in wood, impressed in plasterwork, etc. When used on a moulding it was also known as dancette.

CHINA

1. Chinese chronology
2. Chinese craftsmanship
3. Bronzes
4. Mirrors
5. Weapons
6. Medieval bronzes
7. Ceramics
8. Glass
9. Cloisonné enamels
10. Canton enamels
11. Lacquer
12. Jade
13. Ivory
14. Rhinoceros horn
15. Gold and silver
16. Iron painting
17. Snuff-bottles
18. Textiles
19. Carpets
20. Costume

1. CHINESE CHRONOLOGY

Neolithic Period	? to 1765 or 1522 B.C.
Shang	
Traditional chronology	1766–1122
Revised chronology	1523–1028
Western Chou	
Traditional chronology	1122–772
Revised chronology	1028–772
Eastern Chou	771–256
Spring and Autumn era	772–481
Warring States era	480–221
Chʻin	221–206
Western (Former) Han	206 B.C.–A.D. 25
Eastern (Later) Han	A.D. 25–220
The Six Dynasties	221–581
The Three Kingdoms	221–280
Western and Eastern Chin	265–419
Period of Northern and Southern Dynasties	386–581
Northern Wei	386–535
Eastern Wei	534–550
Western Wei	535–557
Northern Chʻi	550–577
Northern Chou	557–581
Liu Sung	420–478
Southern Chʻi	479–502
Liang	502–556
Chʻên	557–581
Sui	581–618
Tʻang	618–906
The Five Dynasties	907–960
Liao	907–1125
Sung	960–1279
Northern Sung	960–1127
Southern Sung	1128–1279
Chin (Ju-chên or Golden Tartars)	1115–1234
Yüan (Mongols)	1260–1368
Ming	1368–1644
Hung-wu	1368–1398
Chien-wên	1399–1402
Yung-lo	1402–1424
Hsüan-tê	1426–1435
Chêng-tʻung	1436–1449
Ching-tʻai	1450–1457
Tʻien-shun	1457–1464
Chʻêng-hua	1465–1487
Hung-chih	1488–1505
Chêng-tê	1506–1521
Chia-ching	1522–1566
Lung-chʻing	1567–1572
Wan-li	1573–1619
Tʻai-chʻang	1620
Tʻien-chʻi	1621–1627
Chʻung-chêng	1628–1644
Chʻing	1644–1912
Shun-chih	1644–1661
Kʻang-hsi	1622–1722
Yung-chêng	1723–1735
Chʻien-lung	1736–1795
Chia-chʻing	1796–1821
Tao-kuang	1822–1851
Hsien-fêng	1852–1862
Tʻung-chih	1862–1875
Kuang-hsü	1875–1908
Hsüan-tʻung	1908–1912
Republic	1912–

2. CHINESE CRAFTSMANSHIP. The literature of the useful arts in China is singularly uneven both in the treatment of particular arts and in the breadth and depth of coverage, some arts being relatively well covered for all periods, others

barely considered and a few well documented for one period and not at all for another. In a sense this reflects the unevenness of the crafts themselves, for each craft seems to have achieved a peak in its own time and then diminished in importance, sometimes not to be revived in any way and sometimes to be redeveloped and achieve a new peak against a different background. From earliest times there have been in Chinese craftsmanship two outstanding features which cannot be ignored. The first is the phenomenal mastery of almost any material to which the artist turned his hand; and the second is that if there are more ways than one of creating an object, the Chinese craftsman invariably chooses the method which, to the European at least, seems to be the most difficult. These two points are remarkably well demonstrated in the ancient bronzes, which display an almost unparalleled control of the medium and are cast by the most difficult of all techniques, direct casting from piece-moulds; the *cire-perdue* technique was used for some objects, but the great mass of ancient bronzes were cast by the direct method with hand-cut piece-moulds mortised together round a central core. The much later archaistic bronzes of the Sung Dynasty and after, on which there has been very little work done, seem more commonly to have been made by the *cire-perdue* method.

Another craft, and one which in ancient times was confined to China, was JADE carving. This unresponsive medium, so laboriously worked in the early centuries, was not native to China but imported at great expense, and one wonders by what means the Chinese discovered how to work it and produce the marvellous objects that we regard as so peculiarly characteristic of China. Jade carving is a craft in which changes or developments in technique are virtually impossible. This is not true, however, of most other crafts. LACQUER for instance, while it is necessarily applied to a surface in the same way in any age, does allow of varied decorative treatments. Even the earliest examples dating back to the 6th c. B.C. indicate that not only was the technique of application to a surface thoroughly understood, but that the craftsmen were fully alive to the fact that the material could be coloured and used for painting; but it was a very long time before it was discovered that it could be used as a bed for inlay or carved into decorative patterns of great complexity.

A probable reason for such slow development of decorative technique was that originally lacquers were purely functional, being commonly used in wealthy households, as they still are in JAPAN, for the service of food and drink. It was only perhaps after ceramic wares had largely taken over this function in the majority of households that the lacquer craftsman was free to explore fully the decorative possibilities of the material. In CERAMICS a totally different situation existed. From Neolithic times onwards the potters were improving their techniques and expanding to the full the ingenuity which is perhaps most remarkably seen in the evolution of ceramics. Complex problems of construction, chemistry and firing seem to have been attacked with both zest and confidence, and solutions to many problems of the materials themselves and the techniques of handling were overcome in many cases at least a thousand years earlier than anywhere else. Indeed one of the greatest contributions to modern living must be attributed to the daring initiative of the Chinese potters, whose standards of craftsmanship at their best remain unsurpassed. So much is this the case that some things they succeeded in achieving have never yet been understood, Western science notwithstanding. Something like this can also be said of textiles, especially SILK WEAVING, in which the Chinese were both discoverers and inventors. To have discovered silk and learned already in Shang times to weave complex twills is an achievement almost without equal, and to have gone further and discovered the principle of the draw-loom, a most complicated piece of machinery, before the beginning of the Han Dynasty in 206 B.C. is one of the most astonishing advances in the whole history of technology. We need only look at the complicated gauzes woven by the Chinese that were discovered at Palmyra and which date from Han times, to appreciate the kind of impact Chinese textiles must have had on the Romans and their satellites in the Mediterranean area; it must have been much the same as that on Europe of the introduction of blue and white porcelain in the 17th c.

If the Chinese were great masters in bronze, jade, lacquer, ceramics and textiles, they were somewhat less accomplished in working in precious metals, even though they may dazzle the eye; the same could also be said about ENAMELLING and about their craftsmanship in GLASS, though here they achieved some very pleasing effects in the 18th c. A reason for their not attaining great heights in glass manufacture is simply that with ceramic materials to hand and craftsmen fully trained in this field, there was really no necessity to aim at mastery in this exacting craft.

Whatever material is treated the Chinese craftsman always has respect for it. He thoroughly understands its potentiality and its limitations; but if he feels a need to go beyond the limitations, he does not hesitate to do so, using all his ingenuity. The result of such excursions beyond the limits of the potential is that he advances the technology, and in the results he produces he generally achieves a balance between medium, form and surface ornamentation that temporarily deceives the beholder into thinking that the whole achievement is entirely appropriate. It is often necessary to look very closely indeed in order to discover the flaws; like looking into those IVORY balls, so intricate and marvellous in their complexity, one turning within another, that we do not notice the small errors where the knife has slipped. It is as true of 18th-c. craftsmanship as it is of the Shang bronze-casting. The total impression is what counts, the panache of the craftsman deceives the eye, while the hand slips more frequently than one is prepared in the first instance to believe. There are few objects that do not contain some evidence of the craftsman's error, but the total impression of perfection in form, proportion of parts to each other and to the whole, leave one with a sense of aesthetic honesty and conviction that forces one to accept the whole precisely as the Chinese artist-craftsman intended. It is this fact which points to the basic difference between the Chinese and the classical Greek approach to art and to the use of surface. The Chinese, almost arrogantly intuitive, work with a careless intensity and ingenuity that are the very opposite of the Greek analytical approach and the mathematical calculation of surface. The successful achievement of the Chinese result is perhaps also due in part to their preoccupation with linear rhythms, so that flowing lines in decoration are adapted instinctively to the forms, themselves frequently having flowing lines as a consequence of the quality of the material. This is probably more apparent in ceramics than in other arts, but remains largely true whatever the material that came to hand. Both material and surface are used harmonically to achieve a result that satisfies in an impression of counterpoint without a shadow of conflict or discord. The Greek approach, in which the material is subordinated to the competence of the designer and his disposal of the decorative elements according to a calculated assessment of the area of plain surface available, could not be more remote in terms of aesthetics from that of the Asiatic world, especially where man's greatest desire seems to have been, in China at least, to live in harmony with the universe while harnessing the resources to his use rather than bringing them under contol and making himself the absolute master.

The decorative themes in the earliest stages are those of an animal art, and it is interesting that floral elements do not enter the repertory until *c.* the 3rd or 4th c. B.C., and then they tend at first to be schematized flower-and-tree forms. The human figure begins to appear in Han times, but rarely as a dominant theme. This progression ultimately towards the human figure is common to all the arts. In a new medium, or in a new style through a particular period, this cycle is found repeatedly—in textiles, lacquer, ceramic decorations and metalwork—although after the end of the Han period, in the centuries during which Buddhism gained a firm hold, floral elements tend to become more commonly than animals the basis on which all else is constructed. The human figure always came as the final stage of development. Abstractions of all decorative elements occur at intervals, but geometrical patterns and abstractions that cannot be traced back to naturalistic origins are comparatively rare. Geometrical patterns are generally reserved for textiles, which lend themselves particularly well to this approach, and for lacquers, where the intractability of the knife has to be taken into consideration. In the decoration of a surface as a whole the craftsman tends to use the surface rather than fill it. This is in marked contrast, for instance, to the traditions of Islamic art, where intricate mathematical division and filling of surface gives a total enrichment in colour and texture. It is not that the Chinese are not capable of this; but they prefer, except when they are subject to heavy outside pressure, to give free reign to their inventive use of linear rhythms. Even when the whole surface is filled with decorative elements it is found that the design is based on a freedom of line. In the literature relating to design and decoration there has not so far been made available any systematic study of the Chinese approach to these aspects of the arts, and one can only glean what one can from amidst a great mass of general writing or from specialist works dealing with only a single art.

As in most cultures, the arts of China have flowered best in periods either of groping unrest or of great prosperity. Thus in the Bronze Age, under a royal and military autocracy during the Shang period, the bronze masters, financed and kept at work by the aristocracy of the period, were in a sense free to exploit the material, just as were the contemporary jade carvers. Both materials were symbols of wealth and prestige and thus destined for the best artistic expression of the age. In the middle and later centuries of the Chou Dynasty, when social changes had set in which resulted in a gradual shift of power from the king to the princes and then imperceptibly to the ministers, another flowering in the bronze arts took place with an almost entirely new expression; the craftsmanship was often of a very high order, but showed distinguishable differences from one part of China to another, as might be expected in a country which by middle Chou times had broken up into a number of virtually independent states, some of which would be open to influences from the northern borderlands and others exposed to influences from the south.

After the unification of China by the short-lived Chʻin, the Han Dynasty consolidated the newly won unity and the divergent character of the arts began to coalesce into a new and more unified style. This in spite of the fact that certain centres such as Chêngtu in Ssŭ-chʻüan and Chang-sha in Hunan, both producing lacquer, displayed distinctive differences. In bronzes, which by this time had ceased to be ritualistic, MIRRORS formed the main output, such vessels as were produced being either almost undecorated, or finely inlaid in gold or silver, or perhaps gilt. Many of the best mirrors were made directly under imperial patronage and the silk woven during this time was also executed very largely under the supervision of the court, which employed craftsmen directly in factories set up for the purpose. In ceramics alone it seems unlikely that the ruling class had any direct control. This is simply explained by the fact that kilns would naturally come into existence wherever the raw materials might be available to supply local needs. The only area where there may have been some kind of patronage of an aristocratic kind from late Han times on was probably in northern Chekiang, where high-quality STONEWARES were manufactured in considerable quantities.

After the collapse of the Han empire, during the centuries between A.D. 221 and the reunification of China in A.D. 580 by the Sui Dynasty, developments in the applied arts are very difficult to follow. This is partly due to the great destruction of property during this long period of internecine strife and partly because much of the creative energy was directed towards Buddhist sculpture in stone and gilt bronze. By Sui times and the following T'ang Dynasty in A.D. 618 Chinese society had undergone a profound change. Although there remained imperial patronage of the crafts, a new and relatively powerful middle class and merchant class had emerged. At the same time commercial contacts with INDIA, Persia and the central ASIAN states had been established and were fairly flourishing. There was also a lively sea trade with South East Asia and Indonesia, in which the Arabs played an essential part. As a result crafts and craftsmanship became more popular and the centres more widespread, although there seems little doubt that the best craftsmanship and the most important centres were located in the metropolitan areas of Ch'ang-an and Lo-yang, the two capital cities in the north. Subject as China was at this period to many outside influences, it is only natural that foreign forms and decorative motifs should have been accepted into the craftsman's repertory. Besides these new techniques were also learned. The Chinese craftsman, whatever the medium in which he worked, was always willing to accept and adapt anything new that caught his imagination. In this respect the T'ang period marks one of the great peaks in craftsmanship in SILVER, decorative bronze, textiles, WOOD-WORKING and ceramics. There has so far been no systematic survey in a European language of the development of the arts of this golden age, although the Japanese have begun this work on the basis of the great wealth of material available to them in the Shōsōin, the imperial repository at Nara, which was dedicated and virtually sealed in the 8th c. Much material is available in museums, but information on it has to be culled from a large number of articles scattered through periodicals slanted towards art and the Orient, not all of them easily accessible. Gold and silver alone have been treated separately by Dr. Bo Gyllensvärd in *Chinese Gold and Silver in the Carl Kempe Collection* (Stockholm, 1953) and in his *T'ang Gold and Silver* (Stockholm, 1957).

After the end of the T'ang Dynasty the picture of Chinese crafts and craftsmanship changes again and the bulk of what survives from the Sung Dynasty (960–1279) and the Mongol Yüan Dynasty (1265–1368) is largely confined to ceramics with the addition of a small amount of lacquer and silver. The ceramics have been fairly well covered in the available literature, partly because of the aesthetic attraction of the wares and partly because of the development of many new types of wares and their wider distribution in the two periods. The numerous recorded kilns and the imperial, popular and foreign patronage to which they became subject, largely through commercial channels, have made the study of the material appreciably easier than for earlier times. Moreover the great collections that were built up outside China, particularly in Europe, from the late 17th c. onwards have made the availability and popularity of ceramics for first-hand study a stimulus to writers. Stephen Bushell, writing at the end of the 19th c., left us with two important works, *Oriental Ceramic Art* (New York, 1899) and his translation of Chu Yen's *T'ao-shuo* (*Description of Chinese Pottery and Porcelain*, Oxford, 1910), which have served as starting-points of no mean value. And since then there has been a long stream of works, articles in periodicals as well as books, on this subject. On both lacquer and silver there is still much work to be done before a literature can be expected to become generally available.

Once the Ming period (1368–1644) is reached the situation is rather different, for we are almost in modern times. The unity of the arts and the standards of craftsmanship attained are remarkable, especially during the 15th c., when the imperial court exerted strong control. At the beginning of the century, in the Yung-lo period (1402–21), a number of imperial factories were set up to produce objects of fine quality in both materials and craftsmanship for imperial use. It is probably in these workshops that all the really fine Ming lacquers, cloisonné enamels and work in rhinoceros horn originated. Soochow, which had always been an important centre for silk-weaving, increased its production with the establishment of a special workshop under the supervision of the Board of Public Works. The main centre for the production of ceramics was now in the vicinity of Ching-tê Chên in the province of Kiangsi, on which the manufacture of porcelain was now almost exclusively concentrated. Contrary to the general belief, there was no imperial factory as such at this period, but a degree of control was exerted through taxation and through a system of sub-contracting orders for wares for the palace, orders for such wares being sent down from the palace through the Board of Public Works and the local tax offices. The ceramic industry, for such it had now become, was largely financed by syndicates of merchants, and high standards of craftsmanship were not only expected but were also undoubtedly achieved.

The same system of controlling the crafts was

continued in the Ch'ing Dynasty from 1644 until the Revolution in 1912, with one difference. This was the creation at Ching-tê Chên itself, under the direct control of the palace, of an imperial kiln which operated under the supervision of an imperially appointed superintendent. This means that from the late 17th c. all the crafts in some degree came under the direct control of the palace and were subject to imperial patronage, perhaps for the first time since the Shang Dynasty, 3,000 years earlier. The effect of this was an extreme emphasis on technical skill. An absolute perfection in execution was required, whatever the medium. The result of this requirement was not always very happy; but the craftsmen, now servants of the emperor in the fullest sense, achieved a mastery, particularly in small objects, in most media that can rarely be equalled. Jade-carving came into its own once more; textile-weaving, especially the type known as *k'o-ssŭ*, which is really TAPESTRY, attained a perfection and often a complication that leaves the impression of unbelievable wealth and a total disregard of time.

It is perhaps this sense that time was unimportant which makes the Chinese crafts and standards of craftsmanship so impressive. The time element can indeed have had little importance in such things as silk tapestry-weaving, lacquer and jade-carving, all three notoriously slow. But there is also a sense of timelessness in the forms and decorations of all the arts, which often makes them seem as modern—or contemporary—now as they were at the time of their creation.

3. BRONZES. China is probably unique in having had a bronze culture that sprang directly out of the Neolithic civilization without an intervening Chalcolithic Age, however abbreviated. The continuity is tenuous but discernible, especially in the central plain of north China where the Bronze Age attained its finest expression. Archaeological studies and excavations from *c.* 1950 by the Chinese themselves have clarified many outstanding problems and suggested solutions to some of them. For instance in the years before the Second World War it seemed as though the bronze art was already fully matured when it was first revealed to us in the excavations at An-yang, the site of the last Shang capital, and that it had no antecedents; there seemed to be no primitive stage that could be so defined, when the technological skill was uncertain and the forms and decorations ill-defined or unfinished. Thus neither Karlgren in *Yin and Chou in Chinese Bronzes* (Stockholm, 1935) nor W. P. Yetts in *Catalogue of the Chinese Bronzes and Jades in the George Eumorfopoulos Collection* (London, 1929–32) and *The Cull Bronzes* (London, 1939) was able to establish any chronological group of material earlier than that which is now termed Shang III, from the An-yang period, that is from *c.* 1300 B.C., to the fall of the dynasty in *c.* 1027 B.C. Since 1947 the excavations at Chêng-chou, 193 kilometres south of An-yang, have changed the position radically and the date of the Bronze Age has been pushed firmly back to *c.* 1500 B.C. Two distinctively earlier stages, which have been identified on the basis of stratification, have been uncovered at Chêng-chou, with a third, later one that can be connected with the earliest stratum at An-yang. A summary of the new finds and the relationship of these to An-yang is given by Chêng Tê-k'un in *Archaeology in China*, Vol. i, *Shang China* (Cambridge, 1959) and by William Watson in both *Ancient Chinese Bronzes* (London, 1962) and *China before the Han Dynasty* (London, 1961).

The bronze objects produced during the whole period from the middle of the Shang Dynasty to the end of the Bronze Age, conventionally dated to 206 B.C., may be divided into four groups: (1) vessels, which are almost without exception ritual objects; (2) bells and weapons; (3) mirrors; and finally (4) fittings for chariots and horses. The decorative styles can be divided into seven chronological groups: (1) Early Shang, not very clearly defined; (2) Middle Shang and (3) Late Shang, which includes material common to both the last period at Chêng-chou and the whole of the An-yang production; (4) Early Chou; (5) Middle Chou and (6) Late Chou, a somewhat uncertain group; and finally (7) the Huai style group. This is the grouping used in modern Chinese studies summarized by Chêng Tê-k'un. Max Loehr in *Ritual Vessels of Bronze Age China* (New York, 1968) proposed a scheme distinguishing five stylistic phases for the whole Shang period. This scheme was the development of a conception formulated in an article published in 1953, 'The Bronze styles of the An-yang period' in *Archives of the Chinese Art Society of America*, Vol. vii. For the Chou period Loehr makes closer distinctions than the ones employed by the Chinese; he distinguishes Early, Middle and Late Western Chou and Early and Late Eastern Chou, the last being roughly equivalent to the Huai style.

The bronze vessels can be divided into two main classes: (*a*) food vessels; (*b*) wine and water vessels. These comprise in all 22 (Yetts) or 23 (Watson) classes of vessel. Watson points out that in one or two instances two vessels of different names may be fundamentally the same vessel which has undergone some modification in form and so later in Chinese history has been thought to be of a different class altogether. As most of the names by which the vessels are now known were attached to them in the Sung period (A.D. 960–1279), a time when antiquarian studies first came into their own, some confusion is not surprising, and it is not always certain that the names attached to particular forms are the real ones.

(*a*) *Food Vessels* can be divided into those for

the preparation of food and those for holding or serving it. Vessels belonging to the first group are:

TING. A round or rectangular vessel on three or four legs, with two loop handles at the rim or rising from the outside just below the edge. Common to all stylistic periods, it derives ultimately from a pottery tripod prototype of northern Honan, which is found in both Yang-shao and Lung-shan Neolithic cultures. In form and decoration it changes noticeably from one period to another, the most striking change occurring *c.* 900 B.C., when CABRIOLE legs replaced the earlier columnar type. From *c.* 600 B.C. most examples have lids.

LI. A vessel with three hollow legs, a form not known outside China. It is based on a pottery prototype associated with the Lung-shan culture of north-east China. The true form is confined to Shang, but the name is also given to a similar tripod of Middle (or Late Western) Chou times, in which the line of the bottom between adjacent legs forms a continuous arch.

HSIEN or YEN. This resembles two vessels such as a *li*-tripod with a basin on the top. It is in fact a sort of steamer with a grill partition between the lower and upper parts. Found in all stylistic periods down to the Han period, some of those made in Middle Chou were rectangular.

Belonging to the second group are:

KUEI. A circular vessel on a ring foot, with two or, more rarely, four handles; one small group has none. It is sometimes provided with a lid. A few stand on massive cubic plinths. Late examples may stand on three rather small feet. It is common to all stylistic periods, but less frequent in the Huai period.

HSÜ and FU. A rectangular vessel with rounded corners and with handles on the short sides only. It has a cover with four cumbersome projections, which when removed from the vessel and reversed resembles an additional dish. Restricted to the Middle Chou period, it is really an elongated *kuei*. The *fu* is similar, but the two parts of the vessels are identical and reversible.

TUI. This is a nearly spherical version of the *fu*, with three ornamental projections on each part which serve as feet. It seems to have become current in the late 6th c. and continued until the 4th c. B.C.

TOU. A wide bowl on a high spreading foot, deriving ultimately from a Neolithic form found in the pottery of the Lung-shan culture. By *c.* 500 B.C. the shape had changed to a hemispherical bowl with ring handles, with a hemispherical cover similarly adorned, standing on a tall slender stem with wide spreading foot. It continued until the 3rd c. B.C.

(*b*) *Wine Vessels* can similarly be divided into those for holding liquids and those for either pouring or drinking. To the first group belong:

FANG-I. A rectangular vessel, tall in the body, usually described as a wine vessel but not certainly used as such. It is surmounted by a lid of hipped roof shape, with a knob repeating this form on a small scale. Generally richly ornamented, it is one of the more eccentric vessels of the late Shang. It was discontinued shortly after the beginning of Chou.

YU. A wine bucket with a swing handle and full belly. It is usually oval in horizontal cross-section, has a domed cover surmounted by a knob on a short column, and has a handle attached across the narrow axis in the earlier examples. Later the handles were changed to fit across the wide axis. The type only begins in late Shang. A more slender form survived into early Chou, during which some strange zoomorphic examples occur.

TSʻUN. A generic term for ritual vessels, but generally applied now to a vase with thickened mid-section, wide flaring mouth and spreading foot, or with a ring foot like that on the chih (see below). Shang and Early Chou periods.

HU. A wine storage vessel of tall pear shape, with two handles at the base of the neck. It is common to all stylistic periods, the earliest ones being elliptical and with cylindrical fittings at the sides to take a rope handle instead of having the more common ring handles. About 900 B.C. a big-bellied type of circular cross-section replaced the older elliptical form; later a type with square section was introduced; and later still a number of variants such as the flattened type, and an asymmetrical type known as a gourd *hu*

LEI. Either a wine or a water vessel, circular or rectangular in horizontal section. Usually high shouldered, the body tapers to the base or foot. Rectangular examples have a lid resembling a hipped roof. There are two ring handles on the sides of the vessel at its widest point, and a third low down on the body between the two side handles. Datable from Shang to Middle Chou.

KUANG. A vessel shaped like a sauce-boat with a wide spout. The body is usually elliptical and raised on a foot-ring; the handle at the back may be elaborate and the cover, generally overhanging the spout, is ornamented with an animal head. The inside of the vessel may be divided into two compartments, a front one and a back one, with a ladle which fitted in at the back. Because of this arrangement the vessel is sometimes referred to as a wine mixer. The decoration is frequently of the elaborate kind found in the late Shang period, and the dating seems to be confined to late Shang and Early Chou.

Bronze ritual *ting* from Chêng-chou, Honan. Ht. 19 cm. (Shang Dynasty, 16th–15th c. B.C.)

Bronze ritual wine vessel *lei* from Chêng-chou, Honan. Ht. 25 cm. (Shang Dynasty, 16th–15th c. B.C.)

Bronze ritual wine vessel *lei*. Ht. 46·1 cm. (Western Chou Dynasty, *c.* 900 B.C.)

Bronze ritual wine bucket *yu* from T'un-hsi, Anhui. Ht. 23·5 cm. (Western Chou Dynasty, 11th–10th c. B.C.)

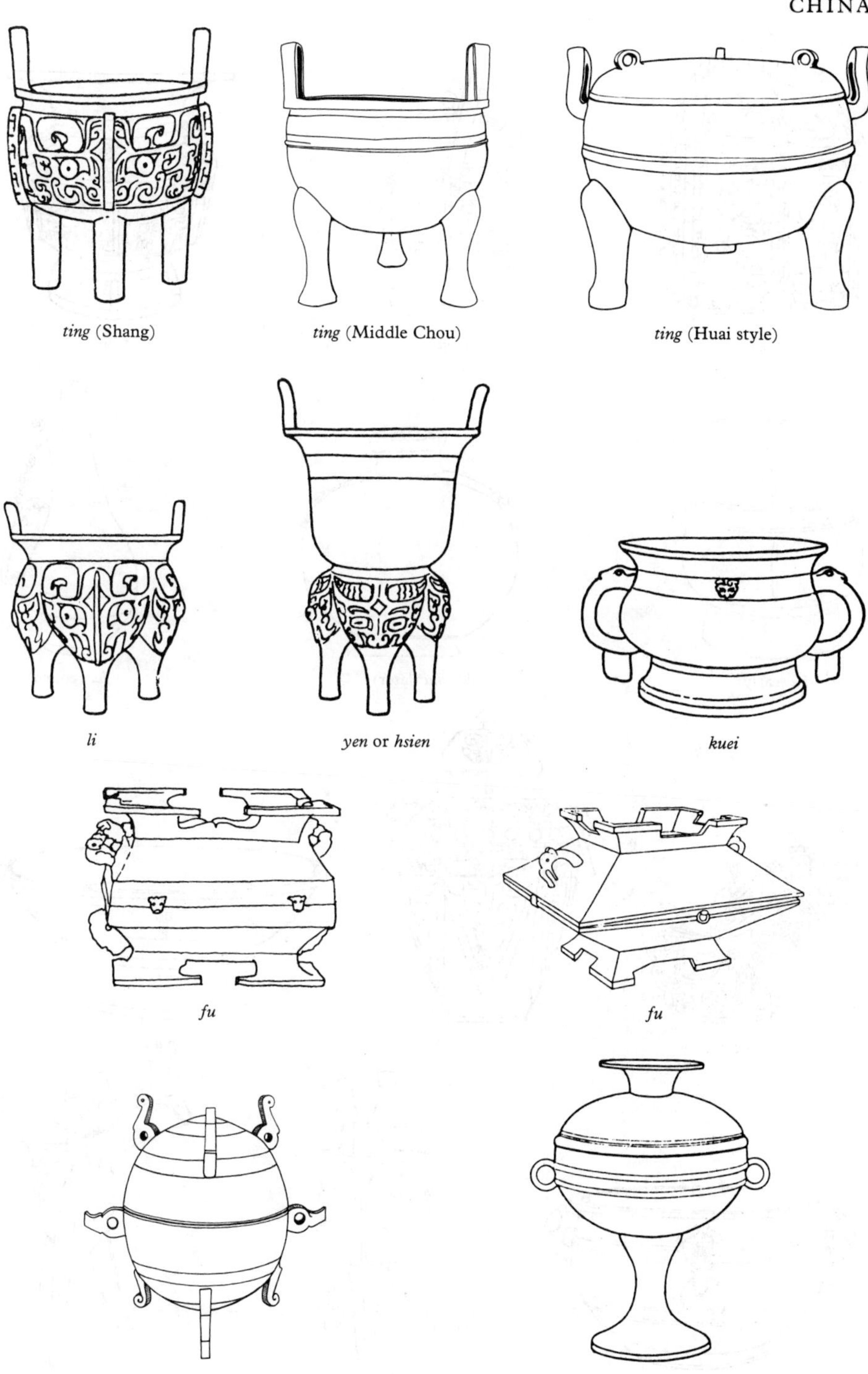

CHINESE BRONZES: Food vessels

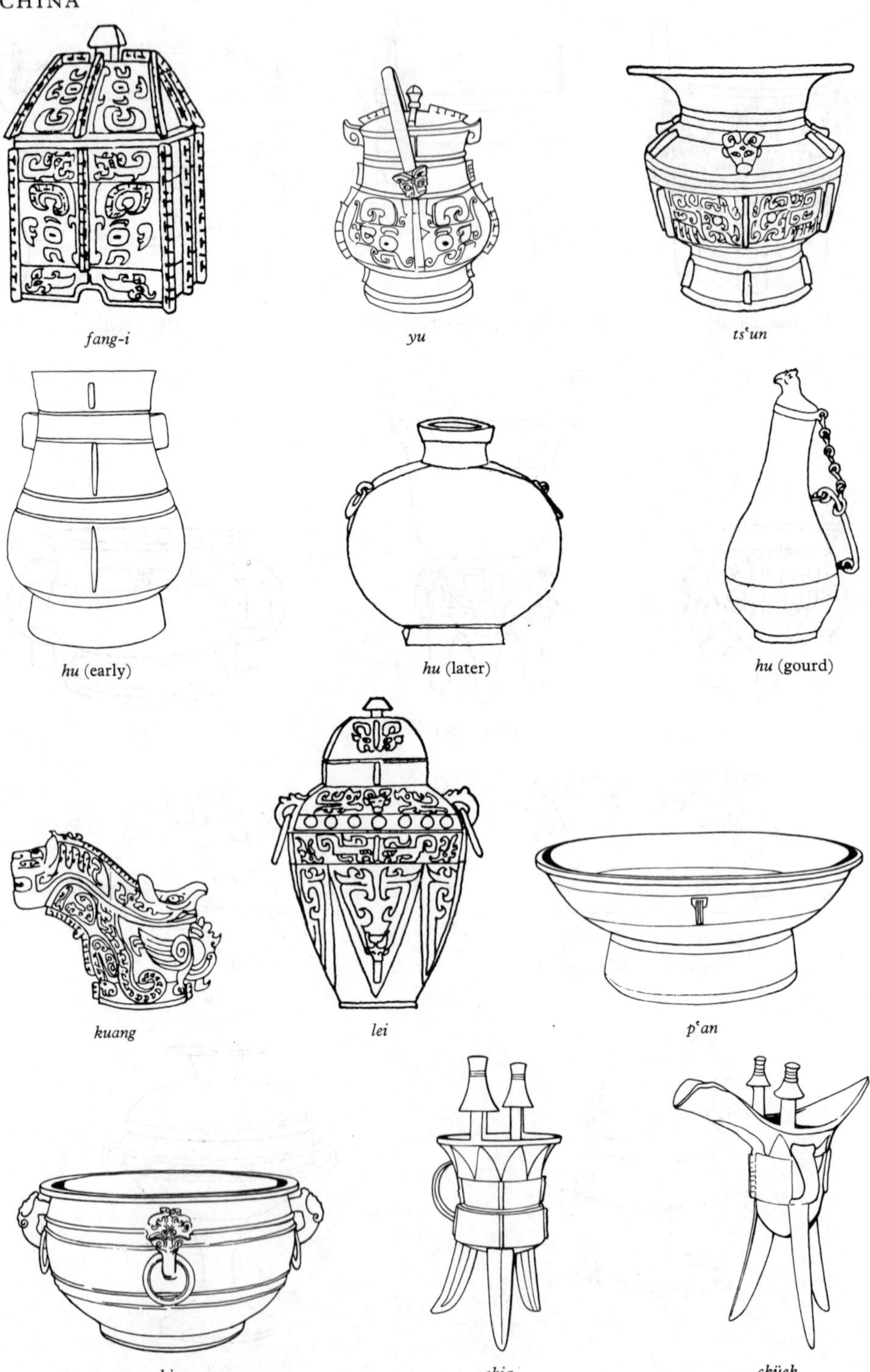

CHINESE BRONZES: Wine and water vessels

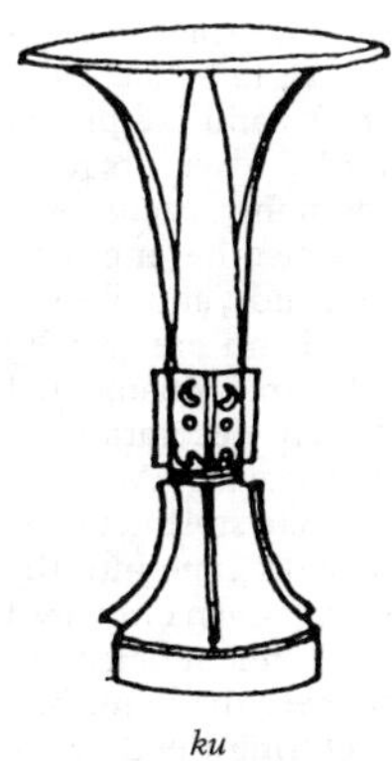

ku

pʻou

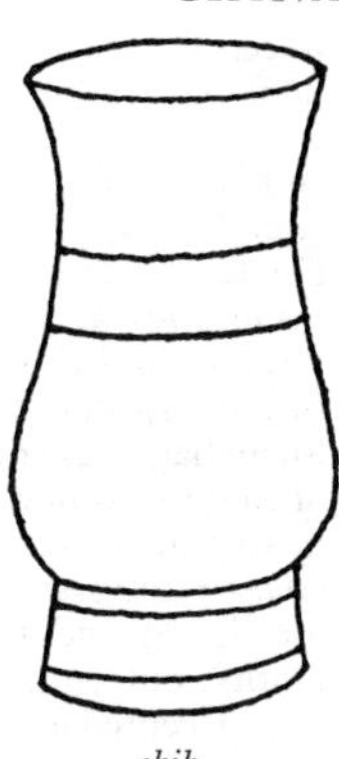

chih

CHINESE BRONZES: Wine and water vessels

YI. This is another sauce-boat type of vessel, but differs from the *kuang* in the earliest examples in that the body is raised on four legs and is not provided with a cover. The earliest occurrence of the type seems to be late 8th or early 7th c. B.C., and it ceases at the end of the 5th c. or a little later. While it is described as a wine vessel, it is often found in association with the *pʻan*, which was used for water, and so it may also have been used as a water vessel, perhaps for ritual ablutions.

PʻAN. A round shallow basin, which in the earliest examples stands on a ring foot. Some of the earliest examples lack the side handles which are a constant feature of the later ones. The type appears first in late Shang times and continues into the late 8th or early 7th c. B.C. Late examples may stand on three small feet attached to the lower edge of the ring foot.

HO. A wine kettle on three or four legs, the body often being lobed and close in form to the *li* in early examples. The spout is straight and tubular and the cover is attached to the handle at the back by two or three chain links. Developed in late Shang, it persists intermittently to the end of the Bronze Age, changing its form *c.* the 5th c., when it assumed a rounder body, the legs becoming of the cabriole type and the handle being moved from the back to become an elegant arch over the top of the cover; the spout ceases to be straight tubular and becomes instead an S-curve.

CHIEN. A deep circular basin with two or four handles fitted with rings. It was apparently used for a variety of purposes such as an ice container, a food container and as a vessel for washing in. Most examples date from the 5th c.

(*c*) *Bells*, used either singly or in chimes, are known from Shang times onward. The earliest seem all to have been used singly for both ceremonial and ritual purposes. These are of two main types: one relatively small and somewhat resembling a Swiss cow-bell has a loop handle and a clapper; and the other, fitted with a socket, was intended to be mounted open end upwards on a wooden shaft. The first type is named *ling* and the second *chêng* within the generic name of *chung*. In later Chou times bells made to hang alone were often of large size, and because they were clapperless they were struck with a special hammer. Chimes of bells of a similar clapperless type have been excavated, and from these examples it is clear that sets were hung from a stout wooden frame, which was coated and painted with LACQUER. Complete sets of 13 in graded sizes providing a musical scale have been found. They are elliptical in section, narrowing towards the flat top, on which there is a more or less elaborate loop. The two surfaces of the long sides of the ellipse are divided into three main panels on each side, with a deep decorated panel across the lower parts. The central panel in the upper part narrows towards the top and is either plain or carries an inscription. The two panels on either side are ornamented with three rows of three bosses each, alternating with three narrow bands either plain or decorated. They occur in this form from *c.* the middle of Chou and continue well into the period of the Huai style in the 3rd c. B.C. The later examples are most elaborately decorated, even the bosses being modelled as coiled serpents, or toads, with fine detail.

(*d*) *Decoration.* The decoration of Chinese archaic bronzes is both complex and varied, not only in its elements but also in the combinations used on a particular surface. But however varied it may be in detail and complex in arrangement, it remains a type of decoration predominantly based on animal forms, of which the most outstanding are the tiger and the DRAGON. A dominant feature deriving either from the tiger or the buffalo is the *tʻao-tʻieh*, or monster mask with prominent eyeballs and gaping jaw. The classification of decorative elements and studies of the iconography have been attempted by a number of specialists, of whom W. P. Yetts and Bernhard Karlgren were the first among a series of European specialists to work in this difficult area.

Recently important and constructive contributions have been made by Max Loehr in *Ritual Vessels of Bronze Age Chira* (New York, 1968) and William Watson in *Ancient Chinese Bronzes* (London, 1962), while other specialists in the Far East such as Seiichi Mizuno in Japan in his *Inshū seido-ki to gyoku* (*Bronzes and Jades of Ancient China*) and Jung Kêng in *Shang Chou i-chʻi tʻung-kʻao* (*Shang and Chou Bronze Studies*, Shanghai, 1941) present the schemes and datings of those who have taken part in the excavations in that area. Karlgren in his *Yin and Chou in Chinese Bronzes* (Stockholm, 1935) enumerated for Shang and Early Chou a list of 22 basic motifs, but while his nomenclature has largely been accepted for the purposes of bronze description, there are aspects of his classification and chronology with which experts disagree.

The stylistic changes in bronze decoration, as in the early stages in any of the applied arts, are not easily dated within narrow limits. It is even more difficult in China than in most parts of the world because the area comprehended is so much more extensive at this stage in cultural development, and it is consequently subject to regional and tribal variations within a given period as well as to influences from outside the immediate confines of what is known and normally understood by the term 'China' proper. Nevertheless there are certain general rules that are adhered to throughout the Bronze Age, especially with regard to laying out the decoration over the surface.

In the earliest stages so far known, Shang I and Shang II, decoration is confined to a narrow figured band in sharp relief, and only sometimes extends to a large area. The *tʻao-tʻieh* normally occurs at least twice in such a band in a setting of scrolling and hooked linear relief patterning, the outer limits of the band being defined by small circles or by spirals resembling key-fret. From this early simple banded treatment it is not surprising to find that the division of surface into a series of bands or zones was a natural development. Sometimes the elements found in one band or zone appear quite unrelated to those in adjacent bands on the same vessel. The general practice is to have a wide central band or zone supported by a series of narrow bands, the central one almost invariably being dominated by the *tʻao-tʻieh* mask, sometimes feline in character, sometimes bovine, and occasionally an indeterminate mixture; but the same motif may also occur in more than one band and with varying degrees of ferocity. Geometrical designs are limited both in variety and in frequency, and like the purely animal designs are confined to bands of varying width, in only a relatively few instances achieving a major role in the decoration. Large birds in a dominating role are also fairly uncommon, even in Early Chou; they are generally reserved for *yu* wine buckets, some of which were also made in the form of addorsed owls, and *tsʻun* wine vases, among which there are also examples made in the shapes of animals. When birds play a major part in surface decoration they are usually of a long-tailed, crested variety with prominent eyeballs, and are placed in confrontation. Small birds, *kʻuei* dragons, cicadas and snakes very commonly occur processionally on either side of some other motif on one or other of the subsidiary bands, and like the dominant motifs of the main band are usually placed against a fine-squared spiral-ornamented or textured ground. The rich decoration of Shang III, mainly associated with An-yang finds, to which this more elaborate style belongs, continued at its height for a short time into the Chou period. But the Chou craftsmen only used the style as a basis for the development of a more Baroque treatment, which has been distinguished by the name 'Early Chou'. During the dynasty new influences became operative and the basic style taken over from Shang began to change from one of relative naturalism and great vigour to a more highly schematized and abstract one, in which the weight of the main elements was increased against a ground that was now plain instead of intricately textured with spirals. Broad bands of heavy, solidly outlined ornament, perhaps better suited to quick production, became the accepted mode. And with it there inevitably came an adjustment in the contours of some of the vessels, the total elimination of a few of the more eccentric ones that had originated in Shang and the introduction of a few new ones, some of which on detailed analysis are revealed as revolutionary conceptions of earlier forms—such as for instance the *yi*, with its low-slung body and broad-banded ornament below the rim, which turns out to be a reinterpretation of the abandoned Shang form *kuang*, a much more elaborate vessel. Animal forms which had played so large a part in the Shang repertory are now largely dispensed with and animal decorative elements, which had been dominant, are relegated to a purely superficial supporting role with the new scale bands, overlapping scales and 'wavy band' taking over in their place.

The 'wavy band' made its appearance without antecedents and has been traced to the state of Sung in the late 9th c., where it is found on a number of well known vessels. At the same time interlacing elements begin to appear, and these seem to be due to influences from the north-west and come in with barbarian penetrations which forced the Chou court eastwards to Loyang. The incursions of the barbarian tribes continued and the interlacing elements introduced at this time stimulated a change in direction, which may be seen in a number of vessels found in Honan. These date between *c.* 800 B.C. and the middle to end of the 7th c. The later vessels of this series have elegant interlacing elements, mainly dragons, and are reduced in scale. At first the elements were in relief with animal eyes standing out strongly; but gradually the relief was reduced along with the scale until ornament becomes in these last pieces a simple enrichment of surface that

tʻao-tʻieh

kuei dragons

Cicada

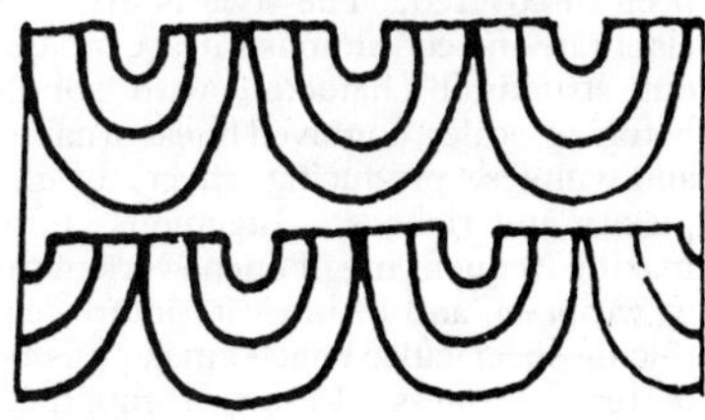

Overlapping scales

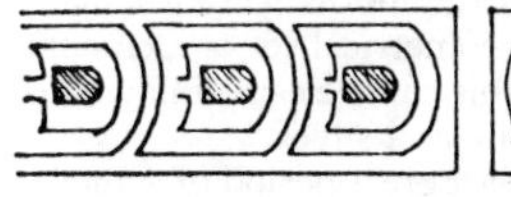

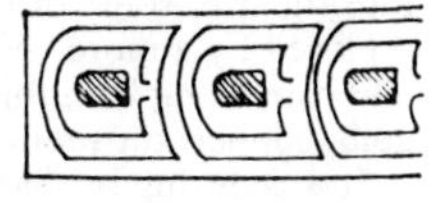

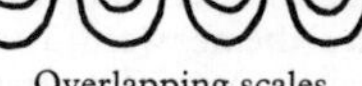

Scale bands

Wavy bands

Huai style

CHINESE BRONZES: Decoration

looks forward to the new exuberance of the Huai style.

Further north in the southern part of Shansi, *c.* the middle of the 6th c. and confined to the northern bank of the Yellow River, another style of distinctive character emerged briefly, in which interlacing elements are also found. The style is associated with the hoard found in 1923 at Li-yü. The refined patterning of repeating spirals and granulation, a forerunner of the Huai 'hook and volute' style, is particularly notable, as is also the very high quality of the casting and the use of freely modelled naturalistic ducks and buffaloes. Eastwards a variant of the style is found in Hopei in bronzes displaying hunting scenes, which perhaps recall the style of the more northerly areas outside the limits of China. The productions of Hopei are related both to the Li-yü and to the Huai style of Chʻu state in the south.

The Huai style had begun to emerge with the rapid development of bronze-casting in the southern and reputedly barbarous state of Chʻu, which occupied the territory on both sides of the Yangtse river and spread northwards into the Huai valley, where most of the earliest finds were made. Here the frequency of the finds suggests local manufacture, but no foundry has yet been discovered. The style is distinguished by elaborate and continuous surface ornament without structural character, with spirals, spurs, hatching, scales, engraved linear ornament, hooks and volutes, producing effects of great complexity and richness. Ingenious craftsmanship making frequent use of open-work in the handles of weapons, and of intricate interlacement producing spectacular effects, make this period one of real greatness. Lasting through the 5th c. into the 4th, some of the motifs were gradually replaced by a more geometrical set of elements, and coinciding with this change came inlaying in gold, copper, turquoise and silver.

It was during this last great period of achievement in bronze-casting and decoration that a gradual secularization began and that bronze mirrors, displaying on their backs a great diversity of decoration, began to appear. These ornamented mirrors had their own development and form a subject in their own right.

4. MIRRORS. Bronze MIRRORS seem already to have appeared in China in the 8th or 7th c. B.C., but little is known of them, the earliest datable ones being attributable only to *c.* 500 B.C. From that time on they remained a constant feature until at least the Sung period in the 12th and 13th centuries A.D., a very few others being known as late as the 15th c., in the Ming Dynasty. Chinese mirrors differ fundamentally from those in the ancient European tradition in that they are thin discs with ornament cast in low relief on the back, and instead of a handle jutting from the edge they are provided with a simple loop at the centre for the passage of a cord or ribbon by which they could be suspended from the belt; no engraved ornament is ever found. From the decorative point of view they form a valuable body of reference material on the history of Chinese ornament as well as, in the case of the earlier ones, of the mythology. From very early times they were credited with all kinds of magical powers and so find frequent mention in the ancient literature of the pre-Han period. Among the most important magical powers attributed to them was that of storing up the light of the sun, so that when a mirror was buried with a dead man the light from it could guide the deceased through the underworld. Largely on account of this belief the surviving body of material is unusually large, and it is rare to find an early tomb without its complement of mirrors.

A number of studies of mirrors have been published over the years, not all of equal value. Bernhard Karlgren in 'Huai and Han' in *Bulletin of the Museum of Far Eastern Antiquities*, xiii (Stockholm, 1941), made the first systematic study of these objects from their earliest appearance until about the middle of the Han period in the 1st c. A.D. This constitutes a useful starting-point for the study of the earlier types, which would seem to have had their origins in two different areas, one in the Loyang region of north-western Honan and the other in the vicinity of Shou Hsien in the Huai river valley in modern Anhui. Material later than the Han period has barely been touched, although there is a considerable body of it, including a reasonably large number of dated examples.

The earliest mirror backs are dominated by hook and volute, and writhing animal motifs; birds and elaborate scrolling patterns were added in the late 4th c. B.C., and the first inscribed mirrors date from the very end of the 3rd or beginning of the 2nd c. B.C., at the beginning of the Han Dynasty. During the Han period mirrors became heavier than formerly and the narrow concave rim is replaced by a wide thick rim with the addition of ornament, often in several bands, while the reflecting face is made convex. During this period mythological scenes and cosmological themes were introduced. These fall into two main groups. The first includes such Taoist themes as 'HSI WANG MU' and 'huang kung wang' and inscriptions relating to the heavens and the magical properties of mirrors; and the second, more purely cosmological in intention, includes what are called the TLV group and its variants. The TLV type is so called on account of the shapes resembling these letters that play a dominant role in the designs. One series of this type has the animals of the quadrant included in the decoration, and with them are very often birds and *hsien* ('fairies') disposed processionally round the central knob. During the Six Dynasties period Taoist and cosmological themes remained dominant, and the mirrors continued to be thick and heavy. A change comes in the Tʻang period, when additional shapes were introduced, a complete change in decorative style occurred and inscriptions were eliminated. Lobed mirrors are among those

Bronze monster mask from Yi-hsien, Hopei. Total length 45 cm. (Warring States, 5th c. B.C.)

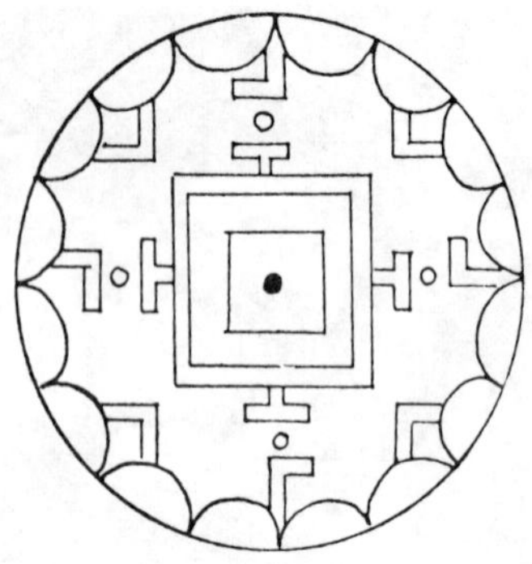

TLV cosmic type mirrors

introduced and so too are foliated ones, and there is a small number of square ones. Some can hardly have been intended for practical use since they measure only *c.* 5 centimetres in diameter; it seems likely that these were intended as charms to ward off evil spirits. Most measure some 15 cm or more in diameter. The decoration includes birds, flowers, animals, hunting scenes, DRAGONS and PHOENIXES and in at least one case landscape. Much of the decoration has symbolic intention: two mandarin ducks or two parrots, for instance, carry the blessing for a happy marriage. The treatment of the cast relief is robust and vigorous with the elaborate detail of the earlier periods completely suppressed. In order to satisfy a demand for greater enrichment the use of gold or silver or silver-gilt plates worked in repoussé with traced detail was introduced, the plates being bedded down on the back with LACQUER as an adhesive. Another type introduced at this time was ornamented in the technique best known by its Japanese name *heidatsu*, which consists of thin sheets of gold and silver with engraved details, usually birds and flower elements, embedded in a thick base of black lacquer applied to the mirror back. Even more elaborate is the insetting of engraved MOTHER OF PEARL and AMBER into a lacquered ground. This rather extravagant treatment seems to date from the middle years of the T'ang Dynasty in the 8th c. and some of the best preserved examples are those in the Shōsōin repository at Nara in Japan. After the end of the T'ang Dynasty the number of mirrors surviving is rather small and there is a marked deterioration in quality, most being thin and unimaginatively treated as to decoration. Little is known of these later stages and there is almost no literature, even on the T'ang tradition, for which there is a great corpus of material.

5. WEAPONS. These are numerous and include all those that one would normally expect such as knives, daggers, swords, spears, arrows and axes, as well as a type of halberd or dagger axe quite unlike any found elsewhere. The literature is considerable, but widely scattered through learned journals. The most recent and useful work, however, is Max Loehr's *Chinese Bronze Age Weapons* (Ann Arbor, 1956), where a comprehensive bibliography will be found.

(*a*) *Axes*. Three types of axe were current during the Bronze Age: the socketed, the ring hafted and the tanged.

(i) Socketed type. The blade was variable in width, either narrow at the base and slightly flaring to the edge and with three horizontal ribs, or rounded or oval. Any of these three variants might have a jutting back projection.

(ii) Ring hafted type. The blade may be narrow, oblong or flaring to a broad arc at the cutting edge with an ornamented ring and base. A variant of the type has a pointed blade, sometimes slightly downward drooping, strengthened with a median rib. This variant is an intermediate type between the true axe and the weapon peculiar to China, the *ko* or dagger axe.

(iii) Tanged axes. These are broad at the base, where the piece is hafted by a slightly narrower tang. The blade widens to a broad or even semicircular arc edge. Many are richly ornamented, especially those of the Shang period, and some may have a large circular perforation or ornamental aperture in the centre.

(*b*) *Dagger Axes*. There were two methods of hafting these: (i) The tang or shafting plate was inserted through a slot in a wooden shaft and then secured with thongs lashed through narrow oblong slots at the base of the blade and round the shaft; (ii) The shaft was forced through a slightly tapered ring. Both types occur in Shang times, but the second type is rare in the succeeding Chou period.

The blade shapes are of four main kinds:

(i) Broad triangular blade with tang, called *k'uei*. The blade is generally symmetrical with a strong central rib and a round perforation near the base. It is not a common type. Decoration may be found on the tang and in some cases on the blade as well; some are encrusted with turquoise. Loehr regards the type as specifically Shang.

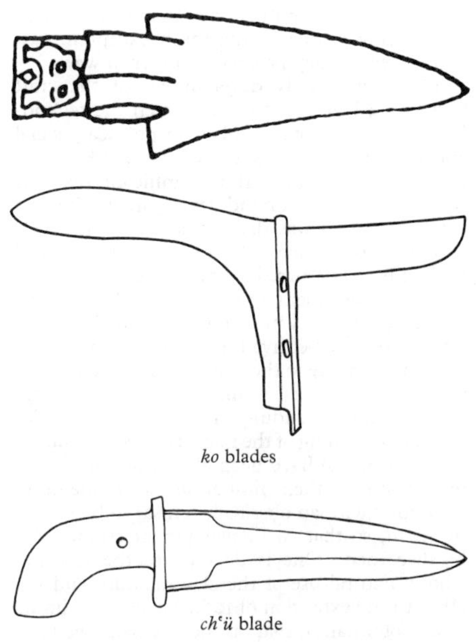

ko blades

chʻü blade

(ii) Slender blade with tang, called *ko*. A varied group often with shafting lugs and a tang, or *nei*, that may curve downwards where it projects at the back. There is no central rib. As time passed the blade took on a rounder, fuller and even drooping contour. Decoration is similar to that of the broad triangular type. Examples have been found at An-yang, the Shang site, and at Hsin-tsʻun, the Early Chou site.

(iii) Slender blades with shafting rings, called *chʻü*. The blade is fairly commonly strengthened with a central rib; it may often be slightly curving and have a drooping tang. It is related to the Type (ii) axe and dates from late Shang to Early Chou.

(iv) Slender blade with descending edge, called *ko*. This unusual weapon combines a horizontal and vertical blade mounted with a shafting plate or tang and with slots for lashing to the shaft. Unique to China, it persists from Shang into Han.

(*c*) *Knives and Daggers*. Knives in Shang and Chou times were generally simply curved or sinuously curved in outline with a single edge and thickened back or spine, and a ring handle. Related to these are the knives with animal-headed handles, which have affiliations with those of the Eurasian steppe cultures, especially those of Karasuk and Ordos. (See ASIA, CENTRAL.) Alfred Salmony in *Sino-Siberian Art* (Paris, 1933) was the first scholar to discuss some of the problems relating to these knives and the short, straight-bladed daggers, but more recent work by Loehr and others has now superseded this.

(*d*) *Swords*. These weapons do not appear in their fully developed form at a very early date. The earliest examples had a leaf-shaped blade and were tanged. These appeared *c*. the beginning of the 1st millennium B.C. and are atypical. Later there developed a sword with hollow hilt and a strong median rib the length of the blade cast in a single piece. This elegant and well-balanced type appeared in its fully developed form *c*. 500 B.C., and became standard until bronze began to be replaced by iron. All the bronze swords are double edged, unlike most of the iron ones which replaced them; these were long, narrow and thickened slightly up the back, with a ring replacing the more usual pommel stud. The Chinese weapon is unusual in that it has no guard and a purely vestigial cross-piece often made of JADE with ornament in low relief; a few are inlaid in gold.

(*e*) *Spears*. No really primitive weapons survive although they can be traced back to *c*. the 13th c. at An-yang. All examples are socketed and are basically leaf-shaped. There is a great variety ranging from a simple slender leaf shape, with tapering socket reaching almost to the tip and with two small lugs at each side of the end for additional attachment, to a rather large-bladed type with the blade edge extending down to the base of the socket. Late examples have no loops for additional security of attachment, but may have an ornamental loop at the base of the central rib for a tassel or pennant. The most comprehensive study of these and a discussion of the dating problems are included in Max Loehr, *Chinese Bronze Age Weapons*.

6. MEDIEVAL BRONZES. The appearance of illustrated catalogues of collections of ancient bronzes such as Lü Ta-lin's *Kʻao-ku tu* (*Pictures for the Study of Antiquity*) in 1092 and *Hsüan-ho Po-ku tʻu-lu* (*Album of Antiquities of the Hsüan-ho Emperor*) early in the 12th c. stimulated both scholarly interest and the skill of the contemporary bronze-caster. Copies began to be made, some of which were more faithful to the woodcut illustration than others. The *Hsüan-ho Po-ku tʻu-lu* only survives in editions based on that of the period 1308–11, which in turn was printed from a manuscript version to which it is possible that later, archaistic material was added. For this reason the distinctions between Sung and Yüan bronzes based on illustrations of archaic or fake archaic vessels are likely to be speculative. Ming and Chʻing examples, however, are more easily distinguished since large additions, 8% or more, of zinc were made to the alloy. The problems relating to these bronzes have so far been largely neglected and only two or three articles are concerned with them. The most generally useful introduction is William Watson's 'Bronze, iron and pewter', an essay forming Chapter III in R. Soame Jenyns and William Watson, *Chinese Art: The Minor Arts. Gold, Silver and Bronze*, etc. (London, 1963), and the same author's 'Sung Bronzes' in *Transactions of the Oriental Ceramic Society*, xxxii, 1959–60. More specific problems are dealt with by Robert Poor in 'Evolution of a secular vessel

type', *Oriental Art*, xiv, 1968, and Aschwin Lippe, 'Two archaistic bronzes of the Ming Dynasty', *Archives of the Chinese Art Society of America*, xi, 1957.

The Southern Sung period was one during which antiquarianism flourished and archaic forms were much in favour in ceramics. The bronzes, which were usually inlaid in gold and silver, looked back not to Shang but to the later bronzes of the 4th c. B.C. in the Chou Huai style. But the treatment in the detail of the inlay designs serves to distinguish them from the originals, being less geometricized and often more florid, as the two large vases in the Victoria and Albert Museum collection indicate.

Three groups of Ming bronzes can be distinguished. First there are the smoothly finished large heavy pieces, often with fine silver inlay or inscriptions in Arabic; second there are the rather small pieces, also with silver and sometimes gold inlay and with parts of the decoration in relief, the decoration following the basic designs of the Shang bronzes with *t'ao-t'ieh* fairly closely; and third there is a group of wholly original vessels, none very large, but of fine workmanship with decoration having parallels in other contemporary arts. This last group constitutes the output of a craftsman Hu Wên-ming, who inscribed and dated many of his pieces and who on the basis of these is thought to have been active from at least 1583 to 1613. His finest work includes delicate casting in relief and the use of well executed parcel gilding.

In the Ch'ing Dynasty many copies of the Ming type in the first group were made, but there are others which reintroduce a form of decoration having its origin in the 15th c. Others were slavish attempts to imitate ancient bronzes, but without order or feeling for design.

7. CERAMICS

(*a*) *Introduction*. It is perhaps inevitable that of all Chinese arts the ceramics should be both the best known and the most widely appreciated. The unequalled resources of raw materials in almost every province meant that it became as natural for the Chinese to use pottery for vessels from earliest times in an unbroken tradition until now, as for wood, pewter or silver to be used in other countries. Fundamentally more important even than the materials was the Chinese skill in achieving controlled high temperatures in the furnaces, a skill developed largely as a result of their ability to smelt bronze and cast it by ceramic piece-moulding techniques. It was this skill too that made possible the early development of STONEWARES and high-fired felspathic GLAZES. Also interesting is the fact that the high-fired glazes were in use long before the low-fired lead glazes, the reverse of what occurred in Europe and other parts of the world. It was only at about the time of Alexander the Great in the 4th c. B.C. that lead glazes appeared in China, to be widely used for tomb furniture and figures in the Han Dynasty while the high-fired stonewares were reserved for daily domestic use and were rarely buried in the tomb except in east China, where they became a universal ware.

The slow, steady development of the craft followed a logical pattern in which the technological advances were linked to political, social and economic changes as well as to the artistic climate of each age. It is significant that the two periods of most rapid development, the first when porcelain was discovered in T'ang times and the second when COBALT blue was introduced in the 14th c., occurred at or just after times when foreign involvement in China, mainly in terms of trade, was at its most intense, and the maintenance of an inventive line of development is in no small part due to the stimulus provided by the needs of the overseas market and not to any intrinsic understanding of the materials. Yet the understanding of the materials was profound. There seems to have been almost an instinctive perception of their limitations as a medium, combined with an obstinate refusal to be bound by them, so that two development strands can be discerned. One is devoted to the full and wholly natural use of the clay medium and the other to the extension of it far beyond the limits of its potential, so that on the one hand we have the exquisite forms and proportions of the natural thrown or simple moulded object, and at the other extreme we have those alarming constructions which appear at first sight ludicrously alien to clay yet perfectly appropriate to some other material. The two aspects are apparent from earliest Neolithic times right down to the present day.

The literature available is fairly plentiful but rather uneven, and much of it out of date, while pre-Han material has to be sought in archaeological journals most of which are only available in Chinese. Among the older books which are still valuable in spite of many shortcomings are Stephen Bushell's *Oriental Ceramic Art* (1899) and R. L. Hobson's *Chinese Pottery and Porcelain* (1915) in two volumes. Although in many respects they are rather obviously out of date, they include much material not available elsewhere. Bushell is particularly valuable on Ch'ing material, while Hobson's judgements have far more often been proved right than wrong. Apart from these there are few really up-to-date books giving a comprehensive picture of the evolution of Chinese ceramics, and reference has to be made to monographs on different aspects or periods and to catalogues of collections.

(*b*) *Materials—Clays*

(i) EARTHENWARE bodies, which are variable in colour and texture, are generally very plastic. These contain the clays, usually red or buff, without which the making of pottery could hardly have begun. These clays are very widely distributed in China and were used in all periods. The bodies fire satisfactorily at temperatures between *c.* 800 °C. and 1,100 °C. and are used for vessels in an unglazed or a glazed state, glazing imparting impermeability to vessels intended for liquids although for cooking-pots a degree of impermeability can be attained without it.

(ii) STONEWARE bodies, which are also variable in texture and usually buff in colour, less commonly red, are less plastic than earthenware clays. They also are widely distributed in China. On firing they mature and become impermeable in the range between 1,200 °C. and 1,300 °C. This type of body is the most widely used in China and has the advantage of relatively good plasticity combined with impermeability.

(iii) Porcelain, or rather porcelain-producing clays, are very rarely found outcropping in nature, for the name 'porcelain' is given to the end-product, which is white, vitrified and translucent. The body is usually artificially constituted of kaolin, a relatively aplastic material largely free of metallic oxides other than alumina and silica, and a refractory China stone. Chinese kaolins appear to be more plastic in character than those used in Europe. The material vitrifies from 1,280 °C. (Seger cone 9) upwards. If used alone, an impracticability, kaolin would require a temperature of 1,770 °C. The resources of kaolin are less widespread in China than stoneware clays. The purest form, used for the true porcelain that first reached Europe in the 17th c., seems to be that from the province of Kiangsi, but less pure deposits are found in Chekiang and Fukien in the south and in Hopei and probably Honan in the north.

(iv) *Hua-shih* is a natural white-firing body from the province of Kiangsi, which when used alone has a somewhat variable character. This only came into use in the 18th c. and is probably a pegmatite. It may be absolutely opaque or relatively translucent. Objects made exclusively of this material are termed Chinese 'soft-paste', a term not to be confused with the European type, which is an artificially constituted body made up from clay and glass frit, a practice to which the Chinese do not appear to have resorted. The firing temperature is not precisely known, but seems to have been mainly in the stoneware range.

Glazes

(i) Lead glazes are those fluxed with lead. These glazes in China may be colourless or stained with metallic oxides such as those of copper, iron or cobalt. They are always transparent and may be used either monochromatically or for polychrome effects. They are low-firing or 'soft' glazes and are used on earthenware bodies that fire not higher than 1,150 °C. They may also be used on a stoneware or porcelain body provided the body has been fired first in the unglazed state to the appropriate maturing temperature. Finally, by slight variation in constitution, they can also be used for decoration over a porcelain glaze; they are then termed 'overglaze enamels'.

(ii) Ash glazes are those fluxed with the natural potash and lime obtained by burning different types of wood, straw or brushwood foliage. The actual range of composition of these glazes varies widely with the type of tree, season and geographical locale. The firing temperature of this type of glaze is high in the stoneware and porcelain range. Wood-ash is known to constitute an important element in stoneware and porcelain glazes from *c.* the T'ang period onwards, but may very well have been widely used at an early stage in ceramic development. More will perhaps be known about the Chinese use of these glazes when it becomes possible to undertake systematic analyses.

(iii) Felspathic glazes are those fluxed with potash, lime and soda, all three of which are constituents in varying proportions of felspar. Chinese felspathic glazes are of the predominantly potash/lime variety. These glazes, termed 'hard' glazes, may be either transparent or opaque when used on a stoneware body, but are usually transparent when used on a porcelain body. In order to mature they require temperatures in excess of 1,200 °C.

(*c*) *Techniques*

(i) Construction. In the past the Chinese have used all the pre-industrial means known except slip casting. They used the pad and beater and coil-building methods in Neolithic times, and by the late Neolithic period they were not only using a turn-table for finishing pots but also throwing on the wheel. From very early times they were familiar with the process of luting parts together. It is not clear how early moulding processes were introduced but small moulded ornaments were being sprigged to vessels at least as early as the middle of the 3rd c. B.C. and had become common practice as part of the making of tomb figurines by the beginning of the T'ang Dynasty in the early 7th c. A.D., if not earlier. Except for a small group of tomb vessels produced in mid T'ang times, however, moulds for complete vessels do not seem to have been introduced until *c.* A.D. 1100, in the north in the first instance. Later, in both the north and the south, moulding techniques were elaborated until they became very generally used. See POTTERY TECHNIQUES.

(ii) Decoration. The earliest decoration, and the simplest, was that of cord markings, which became gradually more refined, and specific designs were often used. Small stamps were also used from an early date. On smooth surfaces incising and scoring of the damp body was common, while carving in the green-hard state was later developed. Semi-smooth surfaces were sometimes burnished in horizontal bands or simple designs executed with a special tool. Reliefs, either modelled or moulded, were applied, the former from quite early times and the latter from at least the 3rd c. A.D. Painting in coloured slips on earthenware goes back to Neolithic times, but it seems to have disappeared. When painting occurs later in the Warring States era, in the 4th or 3rd c. B.C., it is executed in unfired pigments. Much later underglaze painting in black or dark-brown slips on a white slip ground was introduced on stonewares probably in late T'ang times, while *sgraffiato* decoration and the complex use of slips were introduced in the Sung period. Polychrome effects with lead glazes and wax resists were also employed from T'ang times and special transmutations with copper and iron in felspathic glazes were used in Sung times. This was followed by underglaze painting in cobalt blue, copper red and iron oxide on a porcelain body in the Yüan period. The final stage in painting with metallic oxides came in overglaze enamelling. By the end of the 14th c. all the pre-industrial decorative techniques with the exception of LUSTRE and tin-glazing, which were never attempted, had been mastered. (See POTTERY TECHNIQUES and CERAMICS.)

(iii) Distribution of kilns. The kilns of China are as widely distributed as the natural resources, but it is convenient to consider them in three groups. In the north the major kilns are in Hopei, Honan, Shansi, Shensi, Shantung, Anhui and Kiangsu and in Neolithic times there were centres in Kansu. In the eastern group are those of Chekiang and Fukien, while in the southern group are Kiangsi, Hunan and Kuangtung with a few minor kilns in Ssŭ-ch'üan and Yünnan.

(iv) Kiln types. It has been shown from excavations that in Neolithic times a simple up-draught kiln was used. This was round in plan with a series of circular or elliptical vents in the floor for the passage of the flame from the fire-pit below and a little to one side of the perimeter.

The best known types of kiln are those of the Sung period revealed by excavations undertaken from *c.* 1950. The northern type was a down-draught kiln of 'horseshoe' shape; this is the Chinese name. It is roughly semicircular in plan with the chimney-stack behind a massive diameter wall at the base of which is a series of vents to lead the smoke and flames out through a chimney. At the opposite side, in the centre of the arc, was a firebox with a deep ash-pit below a grating. Separating the firebox from the main chamber a bag wall of light construction had to be built to about two-thirds of the height of the kiln each time it had been stacked with wares. The roof of the kiln was domed and the outer wall was heavily constructed and sunk into the ground so that the whole floor area was about 2 m below ground level. As the firebox lay just inside the whole semicircular construction it could easily be shut off by doors or clamps. The kiln was thus basically a reduction kiln and it is noteworthy that nearly all wares of the Sung period were fired with a reducing cycle. The eastern kilns, also intended for reducing cycles, were of a similar type but differently laid out. This type, known as the 'dragon' kiln, was inclined on a hillside and consisted of a series of small chambers set one slightly above the other up the slope with spy-holes on one side of each chamber and fire doors at the base of the chain and at intervals on the other side, opposite the spy-hole. The last type, that of the southern group, was the so-called 'beehive' kiln used in Kiangsi at Ching-tê chên. This was a near-equivalent to the English bottle kiln, and is illustrated with descriptions in a number of albums now in libraries in Paris, London and Lund.

(*d*) *Neolithic Pottery*. The Neolithic potteries of north China can be divided conveniently into two main types. One was produced in Honan, southern Shansi and Shensi, with an extension in Kansu, while the other was an eastern tradition found in the coastal region from southern Manchuria southwards through Shantung to as far as northern Chekiang, which to the west overlapped in Honan with the central and western type. The central and western type is known by the Neolithic culture name Yang-shao after the type-site of that name in the province of Honan, discovered in 1922 by J. Gunnar Andersson (*Children of the Yellow Earth*, 1934). The north-eastern and eastern coastal type takes its name from Lung-shan in Shantung on the edge of the central plain, the type-site having been discovered at Chêng-tzŭ Yai in 1931 and systematically excavated by the Chinese; the culture with which it is associated is also named the Black Pottery culture. The dating of both cultures remains uncertain and they were ultimately replaced by the Shang bronze culture, in which elements of both to some extent survived, features of the Lung-shan culture, which at An-yang overlie those of Yang-shao, being the more persistent.

(i) Yang-shao pottery. Since Andersson's discovery of the important type-site many other burial and habitation sites have been found, and of these Pan-p'o Ts'un near Si-an in Shensi has proved the most important (W. Watson, *China before the Han Dynasty*, London, 1961). The pottery is of two main types: (1) a coarse grey earthenware; (2) a fine-grained reddish earthenware. The former is a rough household ware, mainly hand-made with pad and beater technique and with corded decoration. The shapes include tripods, rough jars and bag-shaped pots everted at the rim. The second was a superior ware comprising basins with flattened or in-turned rim and either flat or rounded base, globular urns and ewers. These appear to have been constructed by the coiling method and have been carefully smoothed, often even showing traces of knife trimming near the base. There were also tripod bowls and a tall amphora form with narrow neck and pointed base. The finest wares are well smoothed and burnished, with painting in black or black and maroon or brown slip according to the locality, with geometrical or simple schematic designs of fish and the human face, or with bold coiling designs. On some sites white slip is also used and this gives a more spectacular effect to the decoration. Material from the western extension of this culture in

Kansu is slightly different in character. Here urns with narrow neck and swelling body are painted only on the upper part, black and red or brown in zones or panels of distinctive character, often including a dog-tooth element named by Andersson 'death pattern' because his finds of this type were from burial sites.

(ii) Lung-shan pottery. The culture which produced this pottery was located in the east, overlapping the Yang-shao on the central plain; it was different in many respects from that of Yang-shao, not least in the wider variety of forms. It included in common with Yang-shao a rough grey pottery which is difficult to distinguish in the central plain from that of the more westerly culture because of similarity of form, method of construction and corded decoration. In the more southerly extension of the Lung-shan culture the common grey ware is to some extent replaced by a brown type. The finest products of the culture were the black pottery wares, which give it its alternative name. The forms include handled cups, bowls, deep goblets either straight-sided or sloping or vertical at the sides, with an angularity of contour not often found when dissociated from metalwork. These vessels were often wheel-made and turned, the finished articles not infrequently being as thin as three millimetres. The surface was smooth, often burnished, and might be decorated with simple incised geometrical designs. On the type-site no metal was found but some vessels, particularly a *chüeh* form with a yellowish-brown body, were found that link them with the Bronze Age development of the central plain in Shang times. Some of the commoner and coarser types were also found to overlap with and in some cases overlie Yang-shao material at An-yang in Honan, the first Shang Bronze Age site to be systematically excavated.

(iii) South-eastern Neolithic pottery. So far as is known at present the Neolithic culture of the more southerly regions of China is distinctively different from and probably later than that of the north. The pottery here is brownish, superior in quality and fairly hard. Pieces are relatively thin and decorated with squared spirals, stamped designs, impressed cords, matting and shells. Some examples are coated with slip and others are painted black with simple geometrical designs. Both the wheel and simple moulds were used, but most pieces were hand-made. The development in the south generally lags behind that of the north and may include elements taken over from it. But the published material even in Chinese is limited, with T'an-shih Shan in Fukien as the only site so far to have been properly reported.

(*e*) *Shang Pottery*. Most published material for this, the first historical period, is based on the finds made in the systematic excavation of the last Shang capital, An-yang in Honan, between 1929 and 1936. Only a little has been included from work carried out at Chêng-chou *c*. 160 kilometres away, where excavation began in 1947. Chêng-chou is an earlier site than An-yang, but its latest stratum is about contemporary with the earliest stratum at An-yang. Both W. Watson (*China before the Han Dynasty*) and Chêng Tê-k'un (*Archaeology of China*, Vol. ii, *Shang*) cover the period as far as it is known. Four main types of pottery are recorded for the whole period from *c*. 1500 to 1027 B.C.

(i) Coarse grey pottery with cord impressions continues the Neolithic tradition. It was evidently intended for household use, and was employed for cooking and general purposes. Much of it was hand-made, but some was finished by turning on the wheel. The forms are simple and functional, while the decorations, mainly of impressed cords and simple geometrical designs, follow on naturally from the earlier tradition.

(ii) Dark-grey pottery, close in texture and heavy in structure, is characterized by a tendency to follow forms already common in bronze. In many cases, indeed, it was probably intended as a cheap substitute for bronze as a burial ware, the *chüeh*, *kuei* and *ts'un* forms being relatively common. The decoration consisted of simple incised geometrical designs on a carefully smoothed surface and was occasionally supplemented with simple modelled elements luted to the surface. Many of these pieces were finished if not made on the wheel.

(iii) White pottery must be regarded as the most sophisticated. It is kaolinic in character and variable in texture. The forms for the most part closely resemble the contemporary bronzes, especially those of the An-yang period in the last 250 years of Shang. In decoration, which is carved, the motifs also reflect the influence of the bronze art. The craftsmanship is of a remarkably high standard, the *t'ao-t'ieh* masks and the squared spirals so characteristic of the style being cut with great precision. The type disappears abruptly on the fall of the dynasty *c*. 1027 B.C.

(iv) Glazed stoneware. Little is known of this type and few examples are at present recorded. Some, such as the bowl with flared rim in the Nelson Gallery of Art in Kansas, is hand-made and patterned with a beater, and other pieces, such as the jar in the Royal Ontario Museum in Toronto, are made on the wheel, exceptionally well finished and virtually undecorated, but with a few parts, such as shoulder lugs, luted on before glazing. The body is fine-textured and grey, showing a tendency to scorch brown where exposed, and the glaze is a thin olive-grey or olive-brown.

(*f*) *Chou and Warring States Pottery*. The centuries following the Chou conquest *c*. 1027 B.C. are remarkable for the poverty of the pottery, as though the whole creative energy had been diverted to bronze. Four groups of potteries can, however, be distinguished.

(i) A rough grey type which perpetuates the earlier Neolithic and Shang pottery.

(ii) A dark-grey type, the forms of which adhere closely to the bronzes, with burnished or incised decoration, a tradition already established in Shang.

(iii) A grey stoneware with brown or olive-green glaze and with incised and impressed matting decoration, which appears to be a continuation of the Shang tradition. Little more is known about this type than about the Shang production and it may have died out or only continued intermittently. Such pieces as are recorded are nearly related in form to metalwork.

(iv) Towards the end of Chou, in the Warring States era, 5th–3rd centuries B.C., a red earthenware was introduced. This had a coarse, rather soft body and the forms, like the dark-grey earthenware and the grey stoneware, resembled those of the bronzes. One type of decoration was unusual in that glass insets were apparently pressed into the soft clay. A jar in the Nelson Gallery in Kansas is decorated in this way. The other decorative treatment appears to have been the use of moulded bands of intricate designs imitating those of the contemporary Huai style bronzes. It is on this type of earthenware that lead glazes were used for the first time. A fine example of this new type is in the Nelson Gallery of Art in Kansas; it has a surprisingly well-preserved brownish-green glaze.

(*g*) *Southern Chinese Wares of the Warring States Era*. In the regions to the south and south-east of the north China plain, where the Chou cultural elements are less easily identified, a different series of cultural traits developed, the expression of which may be discerned in lacquer work as well as in pottery from the tomb finds associated with the state of Chʻu, particularly in the vicinity of Chʻang-sha in the province of Hunan. It is at present believed that a fine quality pale-brown glazed stoneware was made in this area, the forms of which find no parallel among those of the north. There are jars with globular body, raised splaying foot-ring and an upstanding collar round the mouth with narrow slots through it at regular intervals alternating with finely incised rectilinear ornament. Some specimens have slightly domed covers and one piece, in the Chicago Art Institute, has a gilt bronze MOUNT on the rim of the collar. Other sophisticated stonewares of the eastern regions include jars and vessels nearer in form to late Chou bronzes but decorated with wavy lines combed into the still soft body and with roughly gouged vertical grooving. Among unglazed jars are some handsome examples with carefully impressed decorations, and some of these have a light-buff slip dressing.

(*h*) *Han Pottery and Stoneware*. The ceramic production of this long period is more varied than that of any of the preceding centuries. The output can be broadly divided into earthenware, either thrown on the wheel or modelled, and stoneware, thrown on the wheel and sometimes with additional elements luted on.

(i) Earthenware can be classified in various ways but the primary factor is the type of body. One type is soft, heavy, fairly fine textured and grey, continuing the older Chou tradition but with decoration painted on in unfired pigments. The thrown forms closely resemble those of the contemporary bronzes, especially vases, and the decoration is organized in bands with elements similar to those on the inlaid bronzes. These vessels appear to have been intended as burial ware and have come mainly from cemetery sites in the vicinity of Chʻang-an and Loyang in the Yellow River and north China plain area. The modelled forms include a wide range of objects also intended as tomb furniture. Houses, gateways with towers, farm buildings and cooking stoves, and figures of men and animals are among the commonest objects. Some have painted decoration, others have moulded elements forming an integral part of the object. Among miscellaneous unglazed grey wares of the period is a very large series of impressed or moulded tomb bricks. Some are simple rectangular bricks for lining the tomb chamber, decorated with impressed scrolling or geometrical patterns or with chariots and horses; others are more consciously pictorial with impressed patterns made up of a limited number of motifs, sometimes the same one repeated, sometimes two or three combined in various ways to make simple scenes of the hunt or a stroll in the country. The best known series, now in the Royal Ontario Museum, combines a goose in flight, a leaping stag, a dog and a huntsman in various ways on large rectangular or triangular surfaces. In some series of this kind details may be picked out in unfired pigments. A second type of body is hard reddish earthenware either thrown, moulded or modelled, and covered with a lead glaze, which is most often coloured green but may be a warm amber brown. The green glaze, which is fairly thick and soft, deteriorates in burial and acquires an attractive silvery iridescence. The variety of forms is greater and includes figures engaged in a number of different occupations and a wide range of household equipment which provides the historian with an invaluable social document. There are also incense burners with mountain-shaped covers often ornamented with lively hunting scenes in moulded relief. These lead-glazed wares were apparently discontinued after the fall of the Han Dynasty in the 3rd c. A.D.

(ii) Stonewares are almost all grey bodied and greenish glazed, the body tending to burn brown where exposed in the firing. They were made over a wide area in the eastern half of the country, reaching from Kwangtung in the south to Kiangsu and Anhui in the north, and have been found in excavations in Hunan in the south and at Kalgan north of the Great Wall. Three classes have been distinguished by Hochstadter ('Pottery and stonewares of Shang, Chou and Han', *Bulletin of the Museum of Far Eastern*

Antiquities, xxiv, Stockholm, 1952), of which ultimately the most persistent, and the important immediate precursor of the Chekiang CELADONS, was the Yüeh type, among which various models are found in addition to the handsome vase and jar shapes common to the whole range. Decoration when incised on vase and jar forms is usually confined to the upper part of the vessel. Stamped decoration, which is more often found on the southern wares, may cover the whole vessel.

(*i*) *Six Dynasties Period.* The long period of disruption between the fall of Han in A.D. 220 and the reunification of China under Sui in A.D. 580, to which this name is conveniently applied, is only gradually yielding to a more precise pattern in terms of types and chronology. Grey earthenware painted in unfired pigments continued for burial purposes, but the lead-glazed wares seem to have died out. The stonewares of celadon type with a grey body now begin to achieve dominance and are the main product of Chekiang, the most important kiln sites being found in the northern part of the province in the area from Tê-chʻing, north of Hang-chou, to Shao-hsing to the east, with a southward extension to Wên-chou on the coast. The wares from the northern part of the province are usually included under the name Yüeh, or in modern Chinese terminology 'green wares', and a useful preliminary study has been made by M. Tregear ('Early Chinese Green Wares', *Oriental Art*, xiii, 1967, 29–35).

The forms of vessels now begin to be liberated from the heavier and rather sombre bronze shapes. Wide-mouthed jars with swelling body that narrows to the base, ewers of nearly globular form with cylindrical neck and small cock's-headed spout rising from high on the shoulder opposite a simple strap handle, small water pots and water droppers and small models—human figures, birds and animals—became popular in these Yüeh stonewares. For decoration stamping and impressing with DIAPER bands were common and in many cases vessels were further embellished with small moulded or modelled reliefs of animal heads or seated figures of the Buddha, sprigged directly to the body before glazing. A more ambitious but only temporary innovation was the addition of excess iron oxide spots that burned brown or black against the olive-green glaze. Towards the end of this confused period, in the 6th c., some massive and handsome covered jars make their appearance, and these are often decorated with carved patterns of lotus petals. Some may be Yüeh, but others seem to come from other kilns of which we have as yet no certain knowledge.

Further inland and to the south in Hunan there may have been a somewhat similar, more provincial production, but this is still uncertain. In the north, in Honan, there seems to have been a variant type with a brownish-green glaze, but little is certainly known of this as yet.

(*j*) *Sui and Tʻang.* The period from the end of the 6th c. to the beginning of the 10th c. is particularly rich and varied, including as it does earthenware, stoneware and the first of the porcelains.

(i) Earthenware is either grey or pinkish white, the latter being more common and persistent. It is used almost exclusively for tomb wares, vessels and figures of men, women and animals being almost equally common. Moulding plays a prominent part in the construction and the unglazed pieces are frequently coated with a white slip to provide a suitable surface for painting in unfired pigments. The reintroduction of lead glazing (which presents an unsolved problem) and its use on these objects and figures either monochromatically or for polychrome effects lends them great variety and splendour, particularly in the 8th c. when production seems to have been at its height. The forms of the vessels fall into two clearly defined groups, the first of which is fundamentally Chinese. These include a large series of jars, often with domed covers, characterized by extreme simplicity and robust strength, and bowls and cups. The second group constitutes an alien intrusion and is based almost entirely on metalwork. It includes elaborate ewers with relief decoration, offering trays on three short legs with die-stamped patterns, stem-cups and amphorae, all of which can be traced immediately to Persian and central Asian origins, and some of which can ultimately be identified in forms associated with the Greco-Roman world in the Mediterranean area. A few survive into the 9th c. in a hard white earthenware but most cease fairly abruptly soon after the middle of the 8th c. when China was convulsed by the devastating An Lu-shan rebellion.

(ii) Stonewares of this period deserve more attention than they have hitherto received. They are varied in both quality and texture of body and in glaze colour, an indication of wide distribution of kilns and activity over a long period. In the north there is now evidence of production at three centres which achieved great importance in the 11th c. Yao-chou in Shensi, *c.* 70 miles (112 km.) north of Chʻang-an, the capital, produced good-quality black-glazed stoneware that included ewers, jars and bowls. There was also a stoneware dressed with white slip painted in black under a transparent glaze, and some greenish-glazed wares which were the precursors of the Northern Celadon of this area in Sung times. Yü-hsien in Honan was making a greyish or brownish stoneware with a grey glaze or a blackish glaze with smoky grey suffusions; these wares were mainly ewers and vases, some of which were gourd-shaped and fitted with lugs just below the mouth rim. Ting-chou in Hopei was also making a superior stoneware with greyish-white body.

In the east Yüeh ware continued and developed at kilns around Shao-hsing and Yü-hsien in northern Chekiang. The best known kiln is Shang-lin Hu. The output from these northern

Chekiang kilns was destined not only for the home market but also for South East Asia, India and the Muslim world of Persia and Egypt. Bowls, basins and dishes were made in large quantities, with carved and incised decoration of DRAGONS, PHOENIXES, flowers, birds, butterflies and ribbons, and scrolling motifs. For the home market there is evidence of a production of ovoid vases, jars and urns with long necks, widening and flanged at the mouth to take a lid; these might be decorated with applied relief as well as with the more usual carved and incised motifs.

South and west from Chekiang, in the area around Chʻang-sha in Hunan, a provincial type of celadon, resembling Yüeh in some respects, was produced; but the kiln area of Wa-chʻa pʻing, just south of Chʻang-sha, is best known for a ware that was grey in body with transparent brownish glaze and green, white, blue and dark-brown decorations which are probably abstracted from floral motifs. Bowls and head-rests seem to have been fairly common.

(iii) Porcelain. The date of the discovery of this material in the form known to us today remains uncertain; it was to have far-reaching effects on the ceramics of the rest of the world. That it can be dated broadly to the Tʻang period is sure; but where it was first developed still remains in doubt, although the provinces of Hopei and Kiangsi would seem the most likely with a greater degree of probability in favour of Kiangsi. The discovery and early development of this vitrified translucent body would seem to belong to the 2nd half of the Tʻang Dynasty and the earliest examples, such as those found at Samarra, were first discussed by E. Herzfeld (*Die Ausgrabungen von Samarra*, Berlin, 1927). Other pieces found or identified in recent years generally prove to be small in size, simple in form and virtually undecorated. The most common form was probably a shallow bowl, often thickened at the rim, almost straight-sided and with a wide low foot-ring and a small dab of glaze in the base; the inside of the bowl was frequently dressed with slip, which tended to increase the whiteness of the body under the transparent or slightly cold bluish-tinted glaze, as though the piece had been dipped in skimmed milk. Chinese traditions hold that these were produced in Hsing-chou in southern Hopei, but there is no kiln evidence to confirm this. Although some pieces with these features have been found in the Ting-chou kiln area further north, there are no specific grounds for supposing a northern origin for porcelain for other high-quality pieces have come from Kiangsi, including the famous phoenix-head ewer from Chi-chou in the southern part of the province, now in the British Museum, which is likely to be of early 10th-c. date. This remarkable piece with its elaborately carved decoration, and a recently identified companion piece of similar date, now in Japan, indicate a different tradition. Thus the problem of both date and locale remains open and further excavation will be necessary before it can be resolved. The literature on the subject in the meantime remains scanty and widely scattered in Chinese, Japanese and European languages.

(*k*) *Sung Stoneware and Porcelain*. The Sung period has been named the classic age in the ceramic history of China largely owing to the esteem in which the wares have always been held by the Chinese themselves. In terms of variety the richness of the era was remarkable and it was even richer in technical development than the Tʻang had been. This was partly due to the influence exerted, albeit indirectly, by the Liao people in the north, whose ceramic tradition was inherited directly from the Tʻang. Evidence of this influence is first to be discerned in the northern area. It is indeed convenient to divide the production into northern and southern areas of China, even though this may involve some dislocation in the previously accepted view of dating and attributions on a dynastic basis. The named kilns in all areas of China are more numerous than they were even in *c.* 1950, and it is usual in modern Chinese literature to name the kiln, if this is known, or to refer to particular pieces as of the type of such and such a kiln. For present purposes it is simplest to use the type names, especially for the northern wares, although some specific kilns will be noted. Thus Ting, and perhaps Ju, which only came from one locality, remain firm as both are justified by tradition. Chün, Northern Celadon and Tzʻŭ-chou are now to be regarded as type names, in each of which there is considerable variation since the types were produced at a great number of kilns some of which made a wider variety of wares than was formerly appreciated. In the south the variety of types was less numerous and the kiln areas are well known in most cases. It should be emphasized that during the Sung period as a whole the concentration was on stoneware and porcelain to the virtual exclusion of earthenware.

(i) Ting. The kilns making this ware were discovered in 1941 by Professor Fujio Koyama following leads in the contemporary Chinese literature. They are situated in the mountains in the province of Hopei about 56 kilometres north-west of modern Ting Hsien. The find was briefly reported by James Marshall Plumer in *Archives of the Chinese Art Society of America*, iii, 1948–9. The sites were also visited by Dr. Chʻên Wan-li, the Chinese specialist, in 1947 and by Fêng Hsien-ming, whose report in Chinese was published in 1959. Then in 1961 and 1962 a trial excavation was undertaken, the report of which appeared in *Kʻao-ku* in 1965; this has been published in summary translation in the Oriental Ceramic Society's *Chinese Translations*, No. 4, 'Investigation of the Ting ware kiln site at Chien-tzʻŭ Tsʻun in Hopei'. Both the Japanese and the Chinese reports are inaccurate as regards dating, partly owing to the curtailed nature of the visits paid in 1941 and

1947, and also to the superficial character of the trial digging on this very extensive site. The wares found fall into four main groups. The first is predominant in Sung, Chin and early Yüan times; this is white-bodied with a transparent ivory-toned glaze. The second includes white-bodied wares with either a soft dark-brown glaze or a black glaze; the latter is extremely rare. The third group, also rare, is a white type with underglaze brown (iron) painted decoration. The fourth group includes an uncertainly dated series of wares with coloured glazes fluxed with lead, about which little is at present known. The greater part of the production was given over to bowls, plates and basins, with a small number of vases. In construction the wheel was used, but bowls with moulded decoration were often made by beating the clay over a mould set up on a turn-table, while plates were made by means of the fast wheel and template, a technique known as 'jolleying'. The decorative motifs in the carved and incised wares include floral scrolls and sprays, LOTUS, pomegranate and peony being popular, ducks and water-weed, fish and dragons. The designs are generally rather open and well spaced, executed with remarkable fluency and an apparently unfailing sense of compositional balance. In the wares decorated from stoneware moulds, carved intaglio, the vocabulary was enlarged to include phoenixes, a wider range of floral motifs, birds, animals, landscape and children. Firing of the white-bodied wares was at a high temperature and bowls, plates and basins were normally fired on the mouth-rim, a position which reduced the danger of warping the thin body but which also involved a need to conceal the unglazed rim; this was done by binding the edge with thin brassy alloy. The glaze on bowls, plates, basins and dishes, except on the black and the brown glazed wares, covers the base and the foot-ring. A curious feature of the bowls is what the Chinese refer to as 'tear-stain marks', which are thickened areas in the glaze running down on one side of the vessel outside towards the foot-ring. The carved and incised wares are the earliest, and these continue through the whole period of activity from the early or middle 11th c. until some time in the 13th c. Moulded decoration was introduced *c.* the end of the 11th c., the beating method being used. It does not seem to be until after the end of the Northern Sung Dynasty, in 1127, that the fast-wheel and template technique was introduced, but even then the beating method continued alongside the more mechanical technique. The chronology of Ting has been systematically studied from the stylistic point of view by Jan Wirgin in *Sung Ceramic Designs* (Stockholm, 1970). The earlier work on Ting, 'Hsing-yao and Ting-yao' (*Bulletin of the Museum for Far Eastern Antiquities*, xxv, Stockholm, 1953), by G. Lindberg was based on certain misunderstandings, but is useful for its wealth of illustration.

(ii) Chün. The chief kiln centres were in Honan, at Lin-ju Hsien and at Yü-hsien, but other minor kilns seem to have been scattered over a wide area. The body is classified as a stoneware, but the firing temperature did not always reach the stoneware range. In colour and texture the body is variable; it may be fine grained and pale grey or it may be buff or brown. Some very late pieces have an almost black body, which may be fine grained or rather coarse. The glaze is opalescent lavender-blue, often rather thick with a tendency to collect in a welt round the lower part of a vessel. One special variety of glaze is green; this is rather a dark colour, thickly applied and semi-opaque and thus not easily confused with the green of Northern Celadon. It is only the lavender-blue type of glaze coloured by the natural iron in the glaze material that is suffused with crimson or crimson-purple derived from copper. Decoration is largely confined to these suffusions, which sometimes occur in the semblance of patterning. On rather late pieces there may be additional ornament and this usually takes the form of applied reliefs sprigged to the body before glazing. The shapes include a wide range of bowls, dishes, plates, saucers, vases, cups, flower-pots, bulb bowls, tripod incense burners and a small number of head-rests. The wheel was used for hand-throwing cups, bowls and vases, but the fast wheel and template were introduced in the 12th c. for the manufacture of plates with flattened rim. Bulb-bowls and flowerpots, which occur late in the evolution of the ware, were made by twin and complex moulding techniques. Many bulb-bowls and flowerpots are impressed on the base with numbers, running from one to ten, indicating the size in a series associated with a particular design. Some Chün was BISCUIT fired and some was fired green. The glaze was fired under reducing conditions and the fuel used was either wood or coal. According to the reports of the excavations at Yü-hsien the best-quality wares were fired with wood and the less good pieces with coal; evidence of both fuels has been found in the ash and clinker in the old fireboxes of the kilns so far excavated. There may have been more than one layer of glaze used even on those pieces that are free of crimson; it seems to have been common to apply more than one layer on those pieces displaying suffusions. The earliest material does not include any with copper-crimson or purple; this probably does not begin until early in the 12th c., but the evidence is rather uncertain. The first pieces had suffusions of an uncontrolled character and only later in the 12th c. was there any attempt at patterning. By the late 13th c. a few examples of carefully predetermined designs were produced, such as the head-rest in the Metropolitan Museum of Art, New York, with the character *shên* ('head-rest') roughly painted on it in copper red. Most of the bulb-bowls and flowerpots seem to form a special group differing in body and glaze from the rest. These are likely to be late, beginning almost certainly in the latter part of the 13th c.

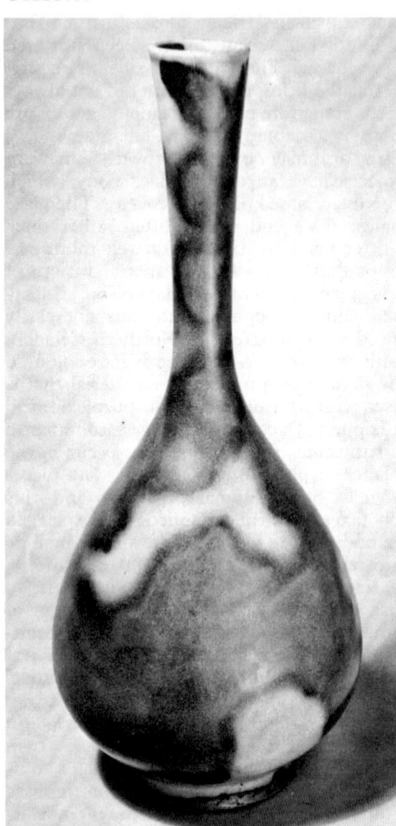

Chün vase with purple suffusions on a lavender blue ground. Ht. 29·1 cm. (Sung Dynasty, 12th c. A.D.)

Chün head-rest with the character *shên* (head-rest) inscribed in copper oxide, burning purple on a bluish ground. W. *c.* 30·5 cm. (Yüan Dynasty, early 14th c.) (Met. Mus., New York)

Ju ware bowl with lavender grey-blue glaze with a fine crackle. D. 16·7 cm. (Early 12th c.)

and continuing perhaps into the 15th c., early in the Ming Dynasty. The glaze on these is almost invariably deep crimson-purple on the outside and rather grey blue or whitish inside. Only a very few pieces fail to display any crimson or purple, and only a small number are wholly stained with this colour. Activity at some kilns continued into the Ming Dynasty, and the ultimate ancestry can be traced back into the stoneware of late T'ang times. Technically Chün is one of the most puzzling wares and one on which systematic research needs to be undertaken.

(iii) Ju. The rarest ceramic ware of the Sung period. Its early history is very uncertain but that it came to an end in A.D. 1127, when the Sung court fled south under the attack of the Chin or Golden Tartars, there is no doubt whatever. No kiln site has ever been discovered and the identification of the ware is dependent on Chinese sources investigated by Sir Percival David and expounded by him in his 'Commentary on Ju ware' (*Transactions of the Oriental Ceramic Society*, 1937). The kiln is believed to have been in the precincts of the Sung Palace at K'ai-fêng in Honan, but the possibility of finding the site now is extremely remote owing to repeated flooding in the area. The ware itself is related to Northern Celadon and to Chün and seems to stem from both, perhaps at Lin-ju Hsien where both these wares were produced; the name 'Ju' alone suggests this. At the present time there are only thirty surviving recorded pieces; they are listed by Gompertz in *Chinese Celadon Wares* (London, 1958) with the whereabouts of each piece. Although there are so few specimens, they are uniform in body, glaze and form characteristics. The body is classified as a stoneware fired at a relatively low temperature. The colour of the body is pale buff and it is fine in texture; the glaze is a slightly variable, semi-opaque grey-blue with a fine crackle which is almost certainly accidental but nevertheless attractive. The shapes adopted are generally simple and related to metalwork, though it is unwise to be dogmatic with only thirty specimens from which to draw conclusions. Only two are decorated, both with the same impressed ornament in an elliptically shaped saucer. In construction they are either wheel-made or carefully fashioned, with or without moulds, and superbly finished. The glaze, stained with less than 3% iron oxide, is thick and fired in a reducing atmosphere. All pieces are glazed over the whole surface and spurs have been used in firing; the marks of these are small, white and narrowly elliptical, being described by the Chinese as 'sesamum seed marks'. There are usually three or five of them; the only exceptions are on the narcissus bowls, which are large, wide elliptical vessels, and these have six, one at each end and two each along the longer sides. In terms of chronology it seems unlikely that the ware was made for more than 25 or 30 years and the antecedents in the 11th c. remain somewhat uncertain, the dated ring of A.D. 1107 on which the original chronology is based being a wholly unreliable document.

(iv) Northern Celadon. This is now one of the best-attested wares of North China with two identified kilns which have been subjected to archaeological investigation, one at Yao-chou in Shensi, about 112 kilometres north of Ch'ang-an (Si-an) in Shensi, and the other at Lin-ju Hsien in western Honan. The Yao-chou site has been fairly systematically studied, but so far only preliminary investigation has been undertaken at Lin-ju Hsien. The ware, deriving from a late T'ang stoneware tradition, reached its apogee in the early 12th c., after which it began to undergo changes indicating decline and it ultimately disappeared some time probably in the late 13th c., after the Mongol conquest. The stoneware body is compact, grey in colour, with only a slight tendency to burn brown when exposed in the firing. The glaze, coloured with an iron oxide, is generally transparent and either olive-green or olive-brown depending on the degree of reduction in the firing. Early pieces are usually glossy but late ones may be matt, dull and fairly opaque in the glaze. Very late pieces may be a pronounced muddy brown, indicating a total failure in reduction. The shapes include, in the early period of activity in the Northern Sung period, high-shouldered ewers with trumpet mouth, some with relief decoration luted on round the base of the neck, and some curious lampstands as well as the common range of bowls and dishes. There are also some deep bowls with low-domed covers and a small number of elegant vases. In the later period, from the early 12th c., bowls and dishes became predominant. The decoration was carved or incised in the early pieces, but moulding was introduced in the late 11th or early 12th c. and gradually this became the more popular type. The wheel was used for the carved wares, but moulded pieces were constructed with a turn-table and bat. There does not at present seem to be any evidence in this ware of the use of the fast wheel and template in the making of moulded pieces. The decorative motifs were mainly floral, the peony and the lotus being the most common; fish and waves, lotus ponds and ducks appear, as do cranes, butterflies, and in the later stages children. Floral motifs may be arranged as scrolls or as sprays. In some of the later bowls when flower sprays are used they may be set out in six panels on the inside with a single central motif. The outside of a bowl, whether carved or moulded, may be decorated with carved lotus petals or with straight-sliced knife cuts. Towards the end of the activity of the Yao-chou kilns it was not uncommon for the wares to be stacked one bowl inside another, and this led to the practice of leaving an unglazed ring at the centre so that, though unsightly, the bowls did not stick together in the firing. Although the basic floral motifs are common to both major kiln sites, they vary in detail and differ somewhat in style. The differences are not always easy to define, and without the published reports from which many examples can be identified it is often difficult to decide at which kiln a particular piece was made.

(v) Tzʻŭ-Chou. A widely and justly popular type, Tzʻŭ-chou was made at a very large number of kilns in north China from *c.* the end of the 10th c. The ware takes its name from the kilns in the prefecture of Tzʻŭ-chou, now Tzʻŭ-hsien, in the province of Hopei. The other main centres of production were Mi-hsien, Yü-hsien and Hsiu-wu in Honan, but there were probably other kilns in both Honan and Hopei which have not yet been located, as well as in Shansi. A stoneware in body, it varies widely in colour and texture, grey or whitish and buff being the most common colours; but dark brown and very dark charcoal grey are also known especially among the later wares, which continue into the 14th c. and even later. The glaze is transparent, only occasionally creamy, and either colourless or green in the early pieces, turquoise being added late in the development, perhaps in the 14th c. One group described as Tzʻŭ-chou is deep brown or black glazed. Also associated with the type name are the earliest examples of overglazed enamel wares; the earliest recorded date of this type is 1201, inscribed on a bowl in the Tokyo National Museum. The forms are those common to the northern tradition, including as they do a variety of bowls, basins, jars, vases, ewers and round boxes; but there are also many head-rests and the vase form known by the name *mei-pʻing* ('prunus vase') with high shoulders, small neck and mouth and a tall tapering body; there is also an unusual 'truncated' form of this, consisting only of the upper half. Toys and small figures are also known, especially the latter, among the polychrome enamelled wares of the 13th c. and later. The decoration is technically the most varied of any ware. It includes carving and incising, *sgraffiato* with either one or two slips, glaze cutting, slip painting, impressing, moulding, roller patterning (rouletting) and polychrome overglaze enamelling. The decorative motifs are as varied as the techniques, including a full range of floral elements, birds, animals, figures, landscapes, fish, waves and water-weeds, basket-work patterns, impressed diapers and scrolling elements. Both decorative techniques and elements are so varied and the wares so diverse that it is convenient to divide them into groups not on the basis of the kiln sites, but on that of the technique employed.

(1) *Carving and incising through slip.* This type of decoration is found throughout the development. One of the earliest kilns, Mi-hsien in eastern Honan, seems to have been using it in the early 11th c., and head-rests of bean shape have come from the site, with a white slip cut through to a reddish-stained body or to a greyish body, the background to the main design often being ring-matted, thus taking over into ceramics a technique used extensively in silver-working to throw up the design in sharp contrast on the smooth metallic surface. Not all pieces were executed in this way. Many were produced with a *sgraffiato* striated ground, and others had the white background cut away altogether. When the background was completely cut away the body naturally showed up even more strongly as dark grey or brown against the whitish slip of the decoration. Most kilns produced this type of ware and it is sometimes possible to identify vessels with specific kilns on the basis of the material found on the sites. Such identifications are based on treatment of detail and perhaps less definable qualities such as glaze-tone and body-colour. But the common style of the wares and the influence of one kiln upon another makes positive identification difficult.

(2) *Glaze cutting* represents a departure from normal ceramic techniques of decoration. It is one which produced striking effects since the glaze used was almost always dark brown or black. The grey or buff stoneware body was covered with the dark glaze, often fairly thickly, and then this while still damp was incised or cut away in the same manner as a slip. In the firing, owing to the viscous nature of the glaze, the incised lines remained to reveal traces of the light body, and the areas scraped free of glaze similarly displayed the light grey or buff of the body. The technique was largely reserved for big pieces such as wine-jars and large bottles of pear shape with flared and trumpet mouths. The designs were usually bold and worked out in large-scale bands round the body. The technique seems to have been introduced only in the late 12th or 13th c. and it continued until at least the end of the Yüan period in the late 14th c.

(3) *Slip-painting.* The underglaze slip-painting in black or dark brown is usually carried out on a white slip-dressed body under the common transparent colourless glaze; but some kilns, especially those further north, used a transparent deep emerald-green glaze as well. The designs were either free-flowing over the whole surface without regard for contour or confined to a series of zones or bands. Some of the truncated *mei-pʻing* vases were painted with a few stiff flower sprays with petal bands confining them from above round the shoulder and below round the base. Dishes and bowls were frequently painted with abstract floral designs confined by a broad and a narrow band of black round the rim. A few bowls carry inscriptions, either single characters or short poems confined in the same way. Head-rests are more varied. The flat top surface, and in the rectangular examples the sides as well, lent themselves to a more painterly treatment, but even in these the scenes are often confined by ogival panels. One of the main centres for the production of head-rests was at Tzʻŭ-hsien in Hopei, where the Chang Company (Chang-chia) had its kilns. These were in operation from *c.* the middle of the 11th c. until perhaps as late as the middle of the 14th c., many

of the head-rests being impressed with the company's seal and some also with a date. There is a small amount of literature on this type of production and a considerable range of illustrative material. See R. T. Paine, 'Chinese ceramic pillows . . .', *Far Eastern Ceramic Bulletin*, 1960, Vol. xii, Nos. 1–2, and H. E. Fernald, 'Chinese mortuary pillows . . .', in the same journal, 1952, Vol. iv, No. 1.

(4) *Painted and incised.* This group is less numerous than the preceding ones, but there is nevertheless a fair amount of material. Jars and vases of various kinds, as well as head-rests, may be decorated in this way. The body, dressed with white slip, is painted with designs in black or in some cases brown slip, through which details are incised only as far as the underlying white layer. Sometimes the incising is bold and broad, but it may also be remarkably delicate and is sometimes executed with combing tools. The effect in either case is bold and aesthetically satisfying. The technique was probably used at a number of kilns, but the best-known examples are those from the Yü-hsien kilns in north central Honan. They persist well into the Yüan period, that is into the 14th c.

(5) *Roller patterning*, or rouletting, seems to have been confined largely to deep cylindrical bowls and jars with shallow-domed covers. The normal practice was to roll the decoration on through a black slip to a white one. Most examples of this type are to be found in Japanese collections and the Japanese attribute them to the Hsiu-wu kilns in northern Honan, but the evidence for this is uncertain.

(6) *Moulding* was not often used and seems to have been reserved for head-rests made by the Chang Company in Tzʿŭ-hsien and by related kilns in this area. The head-rests are generally rectangular and the surface decoration simulates basketwork. Most are covered with a brown glaze varying as to tone according to the thickness of the glaze. From Yü-hsien came a different type of moulding. From these kilns came a number of head-rests in the form of reclining lions and tigers, some of them plain white and some painted in black on white.

(7) *Overglaze enamelling* was introduced towards the end of the 11th c. and the earliest dated piece is that of A.D. 1201 in Tokyo National Museum. The technique is found most commonly in bowls and small figures; by the 14th c. wine-jars were also being treated in this way. The body, as with other types in the Tzʿŭ-chou group, was dressed with white slip and then transparently glazed, and the piece fired to a temperature in the stoneware range. After that designs of lotus, birds or fish, as well as other motifs, mainly floral, were painted over the glaze in iron-red and copper-green, with the addition on some types of a bright antimony-yellow, the designs being confined by a series of two or three red rings varying in width. The pieces were then fired in a muffle kiln to the much lower temperature of *c.* 800 °C. suitable for lead silicate enamels. In the late 13th c. or early 14th c. black and brown were added to the palette.

(vi) Northern Black Wares. These are stonewares, some of which are now known to have been produced at kilns whose main output was of Tzʿŭ-chou type. They form a body of popular wares distinct from the Ju wares and the best of the Northern Celadon and Chün. The body-colour varies from white to grey and shades of buff and brown, and white bodies may sometimes be stained black on the exposed surfaces round the foot. A wide range of forms was made with bowls, pear-shaped vases and stocky jars among the most common. The glaze, generally thick, is a deep blackish brown or dense black, and may display rust-brown streaks, or there may be 'oil-spot' effects which indicate a precipitation of metallic iron in the course of the firing. Among the later pieces of the 13th and 14th centuries there is a large number of vases and jars with blackish-brown glaze and rust-brown decoration, often of birds in flight, painted in so cursive a style in some cases as to be barely recognizable. Both 'oil-spot' and rust-brown decoration is achieved by a double-glazing technique using about 10% iron oxide and the introduction of a period of reduction in the course of firing. At the present time there is no literature available on this interesting group apart from what has been included in the older general histories. Now that it can be shown to be closely related to Tzʿŭ-chou types, it is possible that a classification of the wares as well as serious study may be undertaken.

(*l*) *Liao Pottery.* The Liao Dynasty, which held part of Inner Mongolia, Manchuria and part of north China, although an alien intrusion into the Chinese cultural field, yet has to be considered since it was from Tʿang China that both the metal-working and the ceramic traditions were inherited, to flow back with beneficial effects. Little is known of the chronology, but the types of ceramic wares are clearly distinguished one from another, some of the kiln sites are known and a few of them have also been subjected to preliminary investigation.

(i) Earthenware with monochrome glaze. The Liao earthenwares have a body fired to very near the maximum temperature of 1,050 °C. The ware is very hard, reddish or reddish brown in colour, often rather coarse and covered with a white slip that hardly ever reaches the base. The glazes are transparent, colourless or warm amber-brown or green, and are fluxed with lead. Some of the colourless pieces may have lightly incised decoration with pale washy green touches. The vessels include jars, spittoons, ewers, and vases of inverted pear shape with a long neck expanding towards the mouth or with a long cylindrical neck terminating in a bird's head. Decoration is generally incised, but there are a few moulded pieces and pieces with sprigged reliefs. Floral and leaf motifs are the most common.

(ii) Earthenware with polychrome glazes. This type constitutes a large and important group, less because of the inheritance from T'ang polychromy than because of the manufacturing techniques employed and the shapes adopted. It was in this type of rather high-fired earthenware with lead glazes that moulding seems first to have been employed on a fairly large scale. The forms adopted by the Liao potters are admirably adapted and are peculiar to the culture. Plates, flanged saucers and small dishes, all with decoration included in the mould, were made by this method. The outlines desired being irregular, the wheel-throwing method of construction was ruled out; so pottery moulds of the required shape had to be made, incorporating into the surface floral sprays, wave patterns and fish, all cut in intaglio. After the clay mould was fired, the vessel could then be roughly shaped and beaten over the mould with a small bat. Thereafter it was fired and then glazed with the different-coloured glazes and fired a second time; or if it was well dried, it could be appropriately glazed and then fired in a single process. Whichever method was adopted at this stage, the way was opened to mass production. Most of the Liao pieces produced in this way were small and they present a gay appearance on the most immediately visible surface, but are somewhat rough underneath.

(iii) Porcelain. Most of the wares made of this material are small, rather thin and light in weight. Some are well finished with a neat footring; others are rough on the underside, sometimes with a little grit adhering to the foot, and in most cases the glaze is thin, in a few cases quite exceptionally thin. The saucers and small bowls, which make up the bulk of the production, are shallow with lobed or foliated rims. The best pieces were often scratched on the base with the characters *kuan* or *hsin kuan*, 'official' and 'new official'. These are believed to have been the Liao imperial ware. Jars and vases, which are in a minority, were sometimes nearer to stoneware on account of the roughness and impurity of the body. These were stouter in construction than the bowls and were sometimes spotted with abstract or floral patterns in iron oxide, which fired brown. It is possible that some of these porcelains and porcellanous wares were produced in Hopei during and just after the time when in the early 11th c. the Liao overran Ting-chou and the kilns in that area.

(iv) Lung-ch'üan celadon of central and southern Chekiang is the natural heir to the Yüeh of the northern end of the province and to the long tradition of carved and incised wares. The kilns associated with the name of Lung-ch'üan are exceptionally numerous and spread out over a wide area of the province from Li-shui, in the centre of the province on the confluence of the Ta and Fêng rivers, southwards up the Ta valley, past Lung-ch'üan to kilns lying in the mountains at the extreme northern end of Fukien. According to Fujio Koyama, the Japanese specialist, there are over 1,000 kilns recorded in the province, and according to Ch'ên Wan-li, the Chinese authority on celadon, there were at least 150 kilns operating in the Ta valley alone in the 13th c. In G. St. G. M. Gompertz, *Chinese Celadon Wares* (London, 1958), Japanese views are clearly placed alongside those of European scholars.

The body of the ware, which is often thick and heavy, varies between a stoneware of fine quality and a porcellanous ware; that is it may be dull grey in body or almost white, and when the latter it may, if thin enough, be fairly well vitrified and slightly translucent as the result of high firing. The most nearly white body shows only very slight traces of buff or brown burning on the exposed parts. The glaze, which is generally opaque and thick, varies between olive-green and a subtle smoky grey-blue. It is only late in the development that a change occurs and a translucent glaze begins to replace the earlier opaque one. The forms are more varied than in the northern wares and owe much to the interest of Chinese scholars in the archaic bronzes on the one hand and to the introduction of Near Eastern metal and glass forms on the other, while between these two extremes the traditional bowls and saucers continue with unabated vigour. Among the forms associated with the archaic bronzes are the *kuei*, *ts'un*, *ku* and *li*, and later on *ting* forms. Those related to the Near Eastern traditions are ewers, bowls with small foot and in-turned rim, and dishes with rounded well and flattened rim either straight or foliated at the edge. Many of these dishes are massive and clearly of a type made for export; in fact very few have been found in China and in any case they served little purpose in that country. As decoration there was initially a continuation of the incising and carving that had been common in Yüeh, but after the arrival of the Sung court at Hang-chou in A.D. 1128, with the consequent transfer of patronage to the Chekiang kilns, the improved quality of the wares and the emphasis on an opaque almost jade-like glaze, the decoration became somewhat restrained. Bowls might be carved with lotus petals on the outside and reliefs were occasionally applied directly to the body, but most of the bowls, saucers and dishes were left devoid of ornament, the beauty of form and glaze evidently being regarded as sufficient to satisfy the most exacting aesthete. It was probably *c.* the middle of the 13th c. that the more elaborate decoration began, along with increased use of applied reliefs under the glaze; the usual motifs were the peony or pomegranate scrolls on vases and jars, but with twin fish or dragons in the bottom of basins and dishes. After the Mongol invasion of south China in the middle of the 13th c. the elaboration in decoration began to increase, coming to a peak in the 14th c. with bold and even ornate carving of vases, of which the great vase in the Percival David Foundation of Chinese Art, dated 1327, is a supreme example.

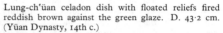

Lung-chʻüan celadon vase with carved decoration and an inscription dating the vessel to 1327 in the Yüan Dynasty. Ht. 70·2 cm

Lung-chʻüan celadon dish with floated reliefs fired reddish brown against the green glaze. D. 43·2 cm. (Yüan Dynasty, 14th c.)

During this period also the application of reliefs directly to the body was common, but a new and unexpected variant on this technique was to 'float' a raw clay relief on the glaze so that it burnt bright rust-brown against the grey-green celadon glaze, a technique that could only be successful on a piece fired with the decorated surface in the horizontal plane in the kiln. For vertical surfaces a wax resist technique was instituted and examples of this are also to be found in the 14th c. on a number of octagonal vases and stem cups. The kiln producing this latter type appears not to have employed the 'floating' technique, which was associated with a quite different kiln. Towards the end of the 14th c. and in the early 15th c. the scale of individual pieces increased and some massive jars and vases with moulded scenes from drama and legend made their appearance alongside equally massive basins. At the same time carved decorations such as floral scrolls and bunches of lotus and water-weeds tied with ribbons came into favour; but the style differed from that of the early part of the century in being much lighter, more cursive and more akin to the painted decorations of the blue and white porcelains from the neighbouring province of Kiangsi.

One variant decorative technique which had only limited popularity was that known as spotted celadon, or *tobi-seiji*, as the Japanese term it. This consisted of spotting the glaze with dabs of excess iron oxide which burnt deep blackish brown in the firing against the soft green. The spots are disposed sparingly over the surface, sometimes in a loosely organized pattern and sometimes in a purely random manner. A very few pieces have copper-red spots or copper combined with iron-brown; one such piece is a spouted bowl in the Fujita Museum in Osaka, Japan. The technique was an innovation of the 14th c. and survived only briefly into the early 15th c.

(v) Chi-chou ware from the province of Kiangsi is a varied and popular type that may be identified by the alternative names of Chi-an or Kian ware, or Yung-ho ware. The kilns, which lie north of the city of Chi-chou and are in fact located at Yung-ho, seem to have come into operation in late Tʻang times or at some time in the 10th c. and continued to function until some time in the 14th c. in the Yüan period, when there was a major drift of labour northwards to Ching-tê Chên, then beginning to emerge as the principal centre for the manufacture of high-quality porcelain.

Among the earliest ware was a stout white porcelain with a slightly greenish or bluish glaze not unlike *ch'ing-pai* (see below), of which the finest example, of the 10th c., is the phoenix-head ewer, with richly carved floral decoration round the ovoid body, now in the British Museum. In recent years a number of such ewers have come to light in Indonesia, South East Asia and the Philippines. Later, in the Sung Dynasty, the region became well known for a type of ware with a dark mottled glaze, mainly bowls, with deep brown or black paper-cut decorations of flowers and birds. A variant of this was what is called 'leaf *temmoku*': bowls with a dark brown or black glaze ornamented with a pale, golden-brown leaf shape. There were also bowls with 'tortoiseshell' effects produced by splashing a transparent yellowish glaze over a dark brown one. All these three types have a coarse grey or bright brown stoneware body with a rather carelessly finished foot.

A pale, creamy, sandy stoneware, or high-fired earthenware, made its appearance during the Sung Dynasty. This was covered with a transparent glaze, sometimes over a moulded and sometimes over a wheel-thrown body. The glaze was often soft and many pieces, especially those with a similar but harder glaze, might have the glaze cut away in floral designs to the body. Boxes, jars and vases of this kind with either a transparent colourless glaze or a dark, blackish brown glaze were not uncommon. Finally there was a pale honey-coloured stoneware body of rather close fine texture, which was painted in iron-brown and covered with a thin colourless glaze. The shapes of this type are very diverse and the decorations varied; they include floral designs, some of them complex, and waves and ogival panels enclosing floral or other elements. This last type continued into the 14th c. A preliminary study of the production of the area has been made by Jan Wirgin in 'Some ceramic wares from Chi-chou', *Bulletin of the Museum of Far Eastern Antiquities*, XXXIV, Stockholm, 1962, based on a recent Chinese publication.

(vi) Chien is a dark-bodied stoneware which in its most common form is covered with a black glaze streaked with brown and metallic blue-black in 'hare's fur' effects. There are variants with rust-brown or pale yellowish brown glazes. The forms are almost exclusively bowls with straight conical or slightly rounded sides, restricted towards the mouth-rim. Most bowls are about 10–12·5 centimetres in diameter, but a few, with a flared instead of the restricted rim, are much larger; the biggest one on record, in the Percival David Foundation of Chinese Art in London, is 26·7 centimetres. Each bowl was fired in its own saggar with a fire-clay button supporting it under the small foot. As the glaze tended to run down the sides during the firing, pieces were glazed only to about half-way down the outside. Even with this precaution the glaze nearly always congeals in a thick welt just above the foot-ring. The kiln site at Chien-yang in Fukien was discovered by James Marshall Plumer in 1935, and was reported by him in a brief note in *Ostasiatische Zeitschrift*, Vol. 21, 1935, pp. 193 ff. Great quantities of sherds, kiln wasters and kiln furniture were found, but little material that would help to date the kiln production more closely than to the Sung period as a whole. The ware became very popular among the Japanese, who refer to it as *temmoku* after the hill T'ien-mu shan near Hang-chou, the capital of the Southern Sung Dynasty.

(vii) Ch'ing-pai, a pure white porcelain of deceptively fragile appearance with transparent, slightly bluish, or more rarely greenish, glaze was a major product of the kilns in the province of Kiangsi, especially those in the vicinity of Jao-chou at the northern end of the province. The name 'ch'ing-pai' first occurs in Chinese literature at the beginning of the 13th c. and it is preferable to use it instead of the dealers' term *ying-ch'ing* ('shadow blue'), which was probably only introduced in the 18th c. The origins of the ware may go back into the late T'ang Dynasty in the 9th c. and it continued until it was transformed or modified in the 14th c. into the *Shu-fu* on the one hand and the basic material for blue and white on the other. It was a popular ware, but one of extremely variable quality, the best being comparable to the finest Ting, the northern white ware, and the worst being coarse and heavy like stoneware besides being dull and poor in the colour of the glaze. The earlier pieces, mainly bowls, saucers and ewers, were ornamented with carved floral decorations; but later moulding was adopted, probably as the result of the introduction of this technique from the Ting kilns in the north. Soon after this the practice of firing bowls upside down on the rim was also adopted, almost certainly as the result of the same northern influence. The decorative motifs are similar to those employed in Ting: lotus scrolls, phoenixes, dragons and a variety of floral elements, and in later examples children sporting among flowers. The common artistic climate is likely to account largely for the similarity of the motifs and also for their organization on the surface. In the latter part of the 13th c., especially after the collapse of the Southern Sung Dynasty, changes set in with new forms such as the pear-shaped vase with narrow neck expanding to an everted lip, known as the *yü-hu ch'un-p'ing*, and there was a sudden increase in the popularity of some shapes such as the high-shouldered *mei-p'ing*. Carved decoration of a bolder, heavier style than formerly was introduced and the surfaces were broken up into a series of well-defined bands. Some of the pieces, notably the pear-shaped vases, may be exceptionally light in weight, while the *mei-p'ing* are generally the

Ch'ing-pai porcelain figure of a Bodhisattva decorated with beaded reliefs. Ht. 22·9 cm. (Yüan Dynasty, early 14th c.)

reverse, being stoutly constructed and heavy—facts which suggest that the forms were specialities of particular kilns. The final stage before the disappearance of the ware was the unexpected introduction of relief elements such as beading and the use of moulded floral elements which were plugged to the body of a vessel with small knobs of clay. These occur mainly *c.* A.D. 1300 and in the succeeding 30 years. The recent discovery of figures of Bodhisattvas ornamented with strings of beads, one of which, in the Nelson Gallery in Kansas City, is dated to 1298 or 1299, enables us to pinpoint this unusual development, which also coincides with a change in the character of the glaze. The latter becomes less transparent and slightly bluer in tone, and leads on into the blue and white and the *Shu-fu* of the Yüan Dynasty. The only literature dealing with the problems of *ch'ing-pai*, and there are many, is included in the work by Jan Wirgin, *Sung Ceramic Designs* (Stockholm, 1970), but he does not carry his study beyond the end of the Sung period to any appreciable extent. On the beaded Bodhisattva figures John Ayers's 'Buddhist Porcelain Figures of the Yüan Dynasty' (*Victoria and Albert Museum Year Book*, 1969) will be found a valuable contribution on a specialized aspect.

As a popular ware it was widely exported throughout its history and finds have been made in Indonesia and the Philippines, most of those from the latter being later in date than those from Indonesia. The Philippines finds are rather different in character and include many very small pieces such as jarlets, small figures and brush washers often with brown or red or blue spots. The publication of Leandro and Cecile Locsin's *Oriental Ceramics from the Philippines* (Tokyo and Rutland, Vermont, 1967), provides an interesting record of this later exported material.

(*m*) *Yüan or Mongol Period.* During this short period of 134 years in north China and a bare 90 years in the south Chinese ceramics underwent a remarkable transformation that affected both form and decoration. It was also a period during which the production began not only to be concentrated on one type of body, porcelain, but also in two relatively small areas of south China, one in Kiangsi and the other in Chekiang. After the fall of the Sung Dynasty in the years between 1269 and 1279 the potters of these two areas were released from the exacting requirements of a sophisticated court and were free to follow their inclination and respond to the stimulus of foreign influences. The 14th c. especially is remarkable for innovations and freedom of invention. Experimentalist attitudes are discernible in almost every ceramic ware of this century. The sizes of vessels seem suddenly to increase, contours become strongly, robustly curved and decoration in red and blue and brown as well as in bright enamel colours suddenly breaks through the sombre restraint and elegant refinement to which one had become accustomed in the Sung tradition. A new direction was now taken which was to have revolutionary effects on the ceramic development in Japan, Korea, Islam and Europe, although the age began quietly enough with the continuance of such wares as *ch'ing-pai* and Lung-ch'üan celadon, both of which were gradually changed in character, becoming rougher and heavier. Chün also continued and like Tz'ŭ-chou changed, but the change was much more a transformation from a local hand-made ware to a solid, mechanically produced range. Ting and the Northern Celadons died out and the north, except for a few Tz'ŭ-chou and Chün centres, lost its importance in ceramic production in face of the increasing tendency of the southern kilns towards industrialization. Kilns ceased gradually to be privately owned and began to be financed by syndicates of merchants, many of them aiming at satisfying the overseas markets and consequently introducing ideas from abroad, which the potters in their new-found freedom were glad to accept and adapt, responding with the production of the most revolutionary ware of all, the underglaze blue-painted porcelains of Jaochou. The wares to be considered individually during this period number only three, all products of the Jao-chou kilns, the history of the Lung-chʻüan celadons having already been dealt with above. The three wares are Shu-fu, the blue and white and the monochrome blues and reds.

(i) Shu-fu. This ware, developed from the Sung tradition of *chʻing-pai* ware, is a stoutly made, fairly heavy porcelain produced in the vicinity of Ching-tê Chên a short distance from Jao-chou, the chief marketing city in the region. The glaze of this type differs from that of *chʻing-pai* in being slightly opaque, relatively thick and often matt, but it retains its affinity with its precursor in being slightly tinged with blue, giving a faint skimmed-milk impression to the eye. The main output was of bowls with moulded decoration round the inside consisting of formalized lotus scrolls or of geese in flight among clouds. In the centre of some pieces a double *vajra*, or Buddhist thunderbolt, may also be moulded. Late pieces sometimes have incised lotus panels round the outside just above the foot and an undulating combed pattern below the rim. The foot-ring itself is thick and there is a tendency for the unglazed base to display a marked convexity, even in some cases rising to a pronounced peak. The ware takes its name from the characters *shu* and *fu*, applied in slip and facing each other across the inside of the bowl; the characters are often added over the decoration, and always before glazing. The combination of characters has been interpreted as meaning 'Privy Council' and tradition has it that the ware was imperial and for the use of the Mongol rulers. There is at present no secure evidence that this was the case, but the tradition has been traced back to the antiquarian's handbook *Ko-ku yao-lun* by Tsʻao Chao, published in 1388. The author refers in this work to the wares of Jao-chou, mentioning 'imperial paste', and follows this with a reference to Ting, the Sung ware from north China. He then changes his subject and comments on the wares with Shu-fu characters and concludes by saying simply that they were of very high quality. The type, whether truly intended for the court in the Yüan period or not, continued into the early years of the Ming Dynasty at the end of the 14th c., and was certainly the logical antecedent to the early 15th-c. white porcelains.

(ii) Blue and white porcelain, which made its appearance in the 1st half of the 14th c., has been well studied and there is a wide range of literature on the subject. The most important publications for the period are J. A. Pope, *Fourteenth century Blue and White in Topkapi Sarayi Muzesi, Istanbul* (Washington, revised edn., 1970), the same author's *Chinese Porcelains from the Ardebil Shrine* (Washington, 1952), and Sir Harry Garner, *Oriental Blue and White* (London, 3rd edn., 1970). All three works include useful references to articles in journals.

In the past there has been a persistent tendency to believe that blue and white began in the Sung Dynasty, but there is no evidence to give substance to this. It now seems clear that the introduction of COBALT blue occurred as the result of the freedom accorded to foreign merchants to place orders for overseas requirements at the superior centres of Chinese production. All the cobalt blue used in China in the 14th c. was imported, almost certainly by the sea route from the Persian Gulf round the south of India, through the Malacca Straits and up the east coast of Vietnam to the ports on the south-east and east coast of China, where Islamic communities flourished. The rapid development of the ware occurred very largely under the stimulus provided by these foreign merchants, and nearly all the best was made to satisfy the overseas demand. The large dishes with flattened foliated rims, the faceted vases and ewers, were forms alien to the Chinese repertory, while the elaborate decoration that enriched these pieces was disagreeable to Chinese taste. The fact that very few examples of this kind have been recovered from Chinese soil tends to reinforce the view that the type was developed to please foreign taste even more than the fact that the largest collections are to be found in Persia, Turkey and Indonesia. Moreover the opinion expressed so pungently by Tsʻao Chao in his *Ko-ku yao-lun* of 1388 that blue and white was regarded as 'very vulgar' lends credence to this view. Nevertheless some of the production was intended for the home market; but the domestic requirement was for smaller pieces, such as elegant pear-shaped bottle vases of a kind already popular in *chʻing-pai*, and stem cups suitable for the family altar, while the existence of a few elaborately decorated pieces such as the David Vases of A.D. 1351, in the Percival David Foundation in London, made for a local temple in south China, perhaps indicates that popular taste in the south was ahead of that of the sophisticated scholar and aristocratic class.

The most popular decorations were those of purely Chinese origin, the ubiquitous lotus scroll, the peony and chrysanthemum, animals, both fabulous such as the dragon, phoenix and kylin, and birds such as ducks and pheasants, as well as fishes and insects. As border patterns, fillers and dividing bands there were wave patterns, classical scrolls and diaper bands of various kinds together with the curious element the 'petal panel', which might enclose a lotus spray, an auspicious emblem or a simple curlicue. The surfaces of vases were generally divided into a series of bands or panels, and these were organized so that the central band of some width enclosed a scene from a drama or a peony scroll of large size to dominate the narrower supporting bands above and below, which enclosed a series of wholly unrelated elements. A similar treatment was accorded to dishes, in which a rather freely painted central theme of fish among water-weed, a lotus pond or an animal or bird among foliage, for instance, would be surrounded in the well by a floral scroll and on the

Blue and white vases, known as the David Vases, dated by a dedicatory inscription to 1351. Ht. 63·6 cm

rim by a wave pattern or diaper band, or in later examples by a classical scroll. The tendency during the century was to organize more tightly and carefully. Early pieces show a carelessness in the organization of surface that speaks of a free and experimental approach to design; but as time passed, as interest was stimulated and skill increased, the designs became more symmetrical and more controlled by a logical division of surface until great mathematical precision in organization was achieved. The cobalt blue used was generally strong and often brilliant, although it was inclined to burn blackish in places where it oxidized on coming through the glaze, for the practice was to paint the pigment directly on to the body. If the application was too concentrated, the excess would push upwards and outwards from the body in the firing along with the natural gases given off by the body and would be deposited on the surface. Although this is technically a fault, it often enhances the total effect. Because cobalt blue is a very strong pigment it also tends to contaminate a surrounding area so that the unpainted parts acquire a slightly bluish cast, an effect that is not easily overcome and only finally disappeared at the end of the 17th c. The apogee of Yüan blue and white was attained in the period from *c.* 1350 to *c.* 1365, when changes set in that laid the foundations for the fresh developments in the Ming Dynasty under a newly won imperial patronage.

(iii) Monochromes. The use of monochrome glazes on porcelain was expanded in the Yüan period to include, alongside the celadons, a plain cobalt blue, a plain copper red and on rare occasions a blackish brown. The vessels on which these were used are dishes and bowls with rounded sides, usually with an everted rim, and stem cups with hollow stems. The inside surface carries moulded decoration of five-clawed dragons among clouds, though there are a few instances of other decorations; on late 14th-c. examples there are often three lightly incised cloud forms in the central area. The bases of both dishes and bowls were left free of glaze and burned reddish brown, often being disfigured by scaly ferruginous impurities. The blue glazes are always a good clean colour, but the copper reds are generally dull and rather muddy.

(*n*) *Ming*. The Ming Dynasty, which established its first capital in Nanking in 1368, continued the transformation begun in the early 14th c. and matured a new style in the 15th c. Porcelain as we define it in Europe was now the material predominantly used and only at a few provincial centres did stoneware hold its own. Of earthenware, except for glazed roof-tiles and figures, there was virtually none. Colour and decoration were exploited to the full and the overseas market flourished, the new colourful wares of China evidently making a wide appeal. For the first time Europeans became acquainted with Chinese porcelain, the Portuguese reaching China in 1516 and from then on taking a place that first rivalled and then surpassed that of the Arabs in the local trade of eastern Asia; they were followed early in the 17th c. by the Dutch and British. For the first time the Chinese court sent specific orders for porcelains, requiring their decoration in accordance with designs supplied from the capital, and for the first time wares were marked with the reign periods of Chinese emperors, and there are also numerous inscribed and dated pieces. The scale of production was enormous and must have astonished the European merchants, who pounced on the wares with an eagerness and enthusiasm that was to be amply rewarded in the course of succeeding centuries. The available literature for the period is considerable with J. A. Pope, *Chinese Porcelains from the Ardebil Shrine* (Washington, 1956), Soame Jenyns, *Ming Pottery and Porcelain* (London, 1953) and Sir Harry Garner, *Oriental Blue and White* (London, 3rd edn., 1970), leading the field and with Sections 3 and 5 of *Illustrated Catalogue of Chinese Porcelains in the Percival David Foundation of Chinese Art* (London, 1963 and 1968) supplementing these and covering certain aspects not considered elsewhere. In addition there are numerous articles in journals such as *Oriental Art*, *Archives of Asian Art* and *Transactions of the Oriental Ceramic Society*.

The wares of the Ming Dynasty fall into a number of easily defined categories with (i) blue and white as the most important, followed by (ii) polychrome wares of the *tou-tsʻai*, *wu-tsʻai san-tsʻai* and *fa-hua* classes, (iii) monochromes and (iv) white wares of Ching-tê Chên and of Tê-hua.

(i) Blue and white. The literature is voluminous, and postwar publications such as those of Pope, Garner and the Percival David Foundation of Chinese Art are well up to date. The importation of cobalt became slightly intermittent from *c.* the middle of the 15th c. and deficiencies were made up from the discovery and purification of a native cobalt ore whose chief impurity was manganese, a dulling agent in glass. During the 15th c. pieces were painted with imported blue or with native blue or with a mixture of the two. In the 16th c. native blue gained in importance, but the different types of blue can only be distinguished on a fired piece by means of chemical or spectroscopic tests. The forms were the common ones already accepted into the repertory, but a few figures appear in the latter part of the dynasty. Floral scrolls and

Blue and white porcelain flask. Ht. 30·8 cm. (Ming Dynasty, early 15th c.)

sprays of flowers and fruit were popular all through but men and children, landscapes and scenes from dramas and novels re-entered the repertory of decoration in the 16th c. after having disappeared for a century or more. The first true export wares for European customers appeared at the same time, with badly written inscriptions in Latin or with the arms of Portugal.

(ii) Polychrome wares are divisible into four classes:

(1) *Tou-ts'ai*: the most sophisticated class, for which M. Medley gives the translation 'dovetailed colours' in the introduction to *Illustrated Catalogue of Ming Polychrome Porcelains in the Percival David Foundation of Chinese Art* (Section 5 of the *Catalogue*, London, 1968). These begin in the late 15th c. but fade out through most of the 16th c., to be revived at the beginning of the 18th c. in the Ch'ing Dynasty. In this class the outlines to the decoration are carried out in underglaze blue and the other colours are fired on after the porcelain has been glazed and fired once already.

(2) *Wu-ts'ai*: polychrome ware of a popular kind in which the decorative elements are outlined in either red or black over the glaze. This class also appears in the late 15th c., but continues without a break. One variant was made with the addition of gilt floral scrolls, mainly for the Japanese market in the 16th c., and this is usually known by its Japanese name *kinrande*, 'gold brocaded' ware.

(3) *San-ts'ai*, or *Ming san-ts'ai*, is a different technique from the previous two. In this the porcelain is fired in the unglazed state and then the lead silicate glazes, or 'enamels', are painted directly on to the biscuit body and fired at a relatively low temperature. The effect is warmer than in the other two classes and the designs differ, a warm golden yellow being common as a background in place of the cold white of the porcelain glaze. Combined with yellow was a bright emerald green and later turquoise, aubergine purple, black and a neutral glaze were added. In early examples of the 16th c. the designs and some details were incised before firing, but later the outlines were painted in black.

(4) *Fa-hua*: an artificial term coined in England, for which the Japanese have provided Chinese characters. The term is applied to a ware produced by the same biscuit technique as *san-ts'ai*. It differs, however, in largeness of size and scale and in the use of a differently balanced palette, dark cobalt blue or brilliant turquoise usually providing the background colour. The main outlines of the decoration and some of the details are made by the application of threads of clay to the surface, and the colours are confined within the outlines in a manner similar to cloisonné enamelling; occasionally small details may be incised. Most pieces are large, especially in the early period of the late 15th and early 16th centuries. Massive wine-jars and drum-shaped garden seats are common and, as Chinese sources say, are 'dazzling to the eye'.

All these types were made at Ching-tê Chên and in the vicinity of this great centre in Kiangsi, but *wu-ts'ai* was also made at other centres further east and south-east, such as that made in the extreme south of Fukien, which came to be known as 'Swatow' ware after the name of the port from which it was exported during the 16th and 17th centuries. This type is bold and spontaneous, owing little to the central tradition, and is dominated by lavish use of red, green and turquoise. Most of the Swatow wares found their way overseas.

(iii) Monochromes. The Yüan blue and red monochromes continued into the early Ming, but gradually the preference for plain surfaces resulted in the disappearance of moulded relief decorations of dragons and clouds. The blue remained a good colour, while the copper red, dull in the Yüan, became brilliant in the 15th c., failed early in the 16th c. and was abandoned for monochrome use by the end of the 1st quarter of that century. It was replaced by a monochrome iron red of a somewhat fierce orange hue. A clear yellow was introduced about the middle of the 15th c. and continued through to the end of the dynasty. In the Chia-ching period (1522–66) an overglaze green enamel derived from copper was introduced and this too continued through to the end of the dynasty. A group of pieces of both iron red and copper green were often decorated in gilt with floral scrolls, and these were mainly for the Japanese market. This type is known as *kinrande*, 'gold brocaded'. The other colours used, but less commonly, were a brilliant turquoise blue and a celadon-type glaze used on a porcelain body of perfect whiteness. At the same time the true celadon from Chekiang with its grey body continued in production for both the home and the overseas markets.

(iv) White wares. Plain white porcelain seems not to have been as popular in the Ming period as the coloured wares, but some pieces of fine quality were produced in the 15th c. with both incised and moulded decoration, many of them of the kind termed *an-hua*, 'secret decoration', which is so fine as only to be visible in strong transmitted light. Such pieces, highly valued, have often been associated with the reign of Yung-lo (1402–21), but the validity of the attributions to this period is a matter of dispute even when there is a reign mark inscribed in the bottom. The white wares are all bowls, dishes, stem cups and ewers when they have come from Ching-tê Chên, but the white wares from Tê-hua in Fukien, distinguished by a different body, are of another kind. Visually the body has a lard-like quality and the facture is more glassy than that of the Kiangsi porcelain from Ching-tê Chên. The early history of the wares and of the development of the kiln area is at present obscure, but by the end of the Ming period the region had become famous for its pure white or soft ivory-toned figures of Kuan-yin, the goddess

Tê-hua, or *blanc de Chine*, figure of Bodhidharma. Ht. 26·5 cm. (17th c.)

of mercy, Kuan-ti, god of war, Bodhidharma, the reputed founder of Zen Buddhism, and the Buddha. There were also bowls and incense burners in the forms of archaic bronzes. The ware is popularly known as *blanc de Chine* and the only literature available at present is P. J. Donnelly, *Blanc de Chine* (London, 1970), where some of the problems of the early history of the kilns are discussed. The Chinese have undertaken some preliminary investigations in the area, but the results are meagre and inconclusive, although they indicate that some form of pure white porcelain was being produced as early as sometime in the Sung Dynasty. The height of prosperity was achieved in the region during the 17th and 18th centuries, mainly in the Ch'ing Dynasty.

(*o*) *The Transitional Style.* The name is given to a large body of material datable to the period between the death of the Emperor Wan-li of Ming in 1619 and the appointment of a superintendent of the newly established Imperial Kiln by the Emperor K'ang-hsi of Ch'ing *c.* 1680, following a rigorous inquiry into the state of the industry. In the course of the 17th c. the production of the government kilns deteriorated, the quality became very poor, and much of the best in both blue and white and polychrome was made by the privately owned kilns. It is to this privately financed ware that the name 'Transitional Style' has been attached as a description of a very characteristic type. While the forms and decorations retain certain elements of Ming at its most mature, there is a largeness of scale, and a freedom and boldness that distinguish the wares from the central tradition. In some respects the 17th c. resembles the Yüan interlude in the 14th c., when experiment became the password to success in establishing a new tradition. The forms in some cases undergo revolutionary changes, vases particularly becoming large and often more massive. New forms were introduced, such as the tall cylindrical vase with a constricted neck, for which there appear to be no logical antecedents. Decoration frees itself from the restrictions of bands and flows freely over the whole surface. Landscapes, scenes from dramas and novels, and flower sprays are common themes, handled with boldness and complete assurance. It is a period when many interesting and unusual pieces were produced, often of exceptionally fine quality. The only special treatment accorded the period is Soame Jenyns's 'The Wares of the Transitional Period between the Ming and the Ch'ing 1620–1683', *Archives of the Chinese Art Society of America*, ix, 1955.

(*p*) *Ch'ing.* The last dynastic period in the development of Chinese ceramics is marked by a high standard of craftsmanship on the one hand and by a certain disregard for purity of form on the other. The meticulous perfection of execution far exceeds anything previously recorded and the quality of body and glaze is unequalled. In invention the efforts of the potters were for the first time deliberately directed towards glazes, and the early 18th c. is remarkable for the introduction of a series of entirely new glazes and glaze effects. At the same time Europe made her sole contribution to Chinese ceramic history by the introduction of the tin-glaze enamel that is immortalized in the delicate opaque pink colours called *famille rose*, which made possible a new approach to decoration resulting in an almost miniature style of painting that at its best is unsurpassed even by Dresden or SÈVRES and at its worst is either meretricious or sloppy.

The export trade to Europe reached its apogee in the late 17th c. and the 1st half of the 18th c.; it thereafter began to decline, partly because the wares began to be replaced by those of Europe and partly because the novelty of Oriental wonders was wearing off. Blue and white, which for so long had held a dominant position, began to decline in the early 18th c. as polychrome and monochrome gained greater favour. In the 19th c. there was a general decline both in quality of material and in craftsmanship consequent upon internal disruption and economic pressures, some of which were due indirectly to Europe's industrial revolution. Even so, right up to modern times the Chinese potter could still achieve miracles and remained within a narrow field a great master. It is, however, noticeable that the best work of this final period is seen in small pieces made under imperial patronage.

The literature on the ceramics of the Ch'ing period is extensive, the subject having been covered by most specialists in the field at one time or another. Soame Jenyns's *Later Chinese Porcelain* (London, 3rd edn., 1965) is one of the more recent contributions, but Stephen Bushell's *Oriental Ceramic Art* (New York, 1897) and R. L. Hobson's publications such as *Chinese Pottery and Porcelain*, ii (London, 1915) and *Later Ceramic Wares of China* (London, 1925) are still valuable reference works. W. B. Honey's *Guide to Later Chinese Porcelain* (London, 1927) is also useful as an introduction to the collections in the Victoria and Albert Museum. In addition to these there are innumerable articles in periodicals and in journals of learned societies.

The blue and white so generally popular in Ming times continued to find favour in the K'ang-hsi period (1662–1722), especially in Europe, but after that declined. Much of what was made for Europe was made to order, patterns of forms and often decorations as well being sent out from Holland and England. The export trade is interestingly discussed by T. Volker in *Porcelain and the Dutch East India Company* (Leiden, 1954).

Polychrome wares can be divided into three main groups, of which the earliest is the *famille verte* characterized by the constant use of a translucent green enamel. The name was coined by A. Jacquemart and E. Le Blant, *Histoire de la porcelaine* (Paris, 1862), and, with its variants *famille noire* and *famille jaune*, is a convenient means of referring to an easily identifiable type. A sub-group of *famille verte* is formed by those pieces on which the enamels have been applied directly to the biscuit instead of over the glaze. This 'enamel on biscuit' type gives a softer and slightly warmer effect because the use of white is kept to a minimum. Next in time came the *famille rose*, introduced from Europe in the 1720s; the colour is derived from colloidal gold. The problems of the group and its evolution have been discussed by Sir Harry Garner in 'The

Porcelain flask decorated in overglaze polychrome enamels of the *famille rose* group. Ht. 29·4 cm. (Ch'ing Dynasty, Yung-chêng period, 1723–35)

Origins of *Famille Rose*', *Transactions of the Oriental Ceramic Society*, xxxvii (1967–8, 1968–9). The third group is that called *Ku Yüeh Hsüan*, which is a highly sophisticated and refined form of *famille rose*. All pieces are small and the decorations specially designed for the surface. On the base of each piece is a mark in overglaze blue enamel enclosed in a double square.

Monochromes. It was in the exploitation and deliberate experiment in the constitution and management of glaze that the Ch'ing potters achieved their greatest successes. Copper red was reintroduced and developed with the 'peach bloom' effect as the most remarkable. Different tones of blue, turquoise, yellow and green were common, as too was the iron red (*rouge de fer*). In the 18th c. with the introduction of the opaque rose the way was open for other colours also to be made opaque, and yellow, green, red and turquoise were treated in this way. More ambitious was the range of lustrous browns varying from pale *café au lait* brown to a deep glossy tone. Finally, there was also admirable double glazing with iron oxides, which produced the 'tea dust' and 'iron rust' types, and with cobalt and copper, which produced 'robin's egg' effects.

White wares are divisible into three groups. First there were the plain white porcelains from Ching-tê Chên, which followed the common style of the period. Second there were the so-called Chinese 'soft paste' wares from other kilns in the vicinity of Ching-tê Chên. It should be pointed out that Chinese 'soft paste' is in fact a natural white firing earthenware, which is variable as regards translucency, and should not be confused with European soft-paste, an artificially constituted body composed of plastic clay and well ground glass frit. Many of the Chinese soft-paste pieces are miniatures. They are unusually light in weight and include a large number of archaistic bronze forms with only a little lightly incised decoration, but there are a few complicated moulded pieces.

The third group consists of the products of the Tê-hua kilns in the province of Fukien, which are known as *blanc de Chine*. Ceramic sculpture here and at this time, especially in the late 17th c. and early 18th c., achieves its finest expression in figures of Kuan-yin, Bodhidharma and the Buddha. Bowls, cups and incense burners were also made; these are generally sturdy in build and heavy. Few pieces are marked in such a way as to help in dating, but unusual in this ware is the fact that the names of some of the potters, especially those making figures, are recorded both in the contemporary literature and in the impressed marks found on the backs of some of their figures. Not only this, but the approximate period of the activity of some is also known.

Provincial kilns. Two provincial kilns have achieved wide repute. One is that of I-hsing, which is famous for its brown stoneware teapots so many of which came to Europe during the 18th c. in the tea-chests and which were a source of inspiration to J. F. BÖTTGER in his ceramic research. The other was in Kuang-tung near Canton, where a dark reddish-brown stoneware covered with a dark smoky-blue glaze reminiscent of *Chün* was made and became a valued general-purpose household ware. It is still being made, and is commonly imitated in Japan for flower and *bonsai* pots, as well as for large storage crocks. Early examples are handsome in form and often pleasing in glaze colour and texture, but gradually refinement diminished. No extensive studies have so far been made of either of these wares.

8. GLASS. The literature on this subject is extremely limited despite the relatively large quantity of material. A recent summary is that by Soame Jenyns, 'Glass and painting on glass', which forms Chapter II in Soame Jenyns and William Watson, *Chinese Art : The Minor Arts II* (London, 1965). The literary sources are noted at the end of the chapter.

The earliest Chinese glass, of the 4th c. B.C., is mainly in the form of eye-beads in direct imitation of the Western type familiar in the Roman Near East. Many of the Chinese examples, however, differ in having a very high barium content, an element unknown except as a trace element in Western glass until the 19th c. The earliest recorded mention of glass in Chinese literature occurs in the 5th c. A.D., when in A.D. 435 it is recorded that Western travellers brought this skill to China. There are in fact some pieces of Han glass pre-dating this; these are mainly small sword-fittings recovered from tombs located in the region of Loyang in Honan. The earliest date of blown glass in China is not known, and of the available material of this type none has so far been dated earlier than late Ming. In the late 17th and 18th centuries the output became varied and can be divided into a number of groups: (i) transparent glass—often crizzled; (ii) opaque glass with carved decoration; (iii) vessels made in two colours, one forming the body of the vessel and the other colour partly overlying it; and both colours may be carved. These three groups include many forms held in common with ceramics. (iv) Opaque milky glass with polychrome lead silicate enamel decoration fired on in *Ku-yüeh Hsüan* style. See above, p. 199.

9. CLOISONNÉ ENAMELS. The earliest reference to cloisonné enamelling in China is to be found in a work on antiquities for scholars and collectors called *Ko-ku yao-lun* by Ts'ao Chên and first published in 1388. It is described in a short section entitled *Ta-shih yao*, 'Arabian ware'. The author comments that it is also called *Kuei-kuo yao*, 'Ware of the devil's country'. Both names immediately convey to the reader the fact that the technique came from abroad, while the date of the text makes it clear that it was currently practised. Unfortunately no properly authenticated examples can at present be dated earlier than some time in the 1st half of the 15th c., by which time the Chinese had achieved notable mastery. The history of cloisonné in China and a discussion of the technique as practised there is available in *Chinese and Japanese Cloisonné Enamels* (London, 1962) by Sir Harry Garner.

The body of Chinese cloisonné, on which the ENAMELS (glass pastes) were applied, was either of copper or an alloy of copper with other metals such as tin, zinc and lead. The earliest body used by the Chinese was cast bronze with a fairly high proportion of zinc. This means that the early pieces tend to be rather heavy; but very late pieces are also heavy, usually, however, because of clumsy workmanship and ungainly forms. In the early 16th c. the Chinese built up the base from sheet copper so that the vessels became appreciably lighter in weight. The wires, which had to be soldered on to the base, were made of bronze in Ming times, and it was not until the Ch'ing Dynasty that copper came universally to be used for both the base and the wires forming the *cloisons*, or cells. There is one small group of gold-based pieces with gold wires, which form a special type in the 18th c. At first the bronze wires had to be beaten from ingots, a laborious process involving constant annealing, which if not carried out properly resulted in splitting, a defect often seen on earlier pieces especially when the gilding has worn off. It was not until the early 17th c. that the technique of wire drawing was introduced into China and in the 2nd half of the century copper wires drawn through dies replaced the bronze ones. In fixing the wires to the body solder was used, somewhat lavishly in the early stages, but this was modified as time went on; then in the late 17th c. or early 18th c. an adhesive was brought in that burnt up in the process of firing the enamels, so that everything was held in place by the strength of the enamels themselves. The two methods of fixing seem to have been used alongside each other. The drawback to using an adhesive in place of solder is that a break in the enamel may result in a large part of the decoration breaking away from the base.

The colour schemes employed vary considerably, but within certain limits they can be sorted out into a number of chronological groups. It is, however, difficult to establish a precise chronological order within a given group, or to determine with any degree of accuracy the dates at which changes took place, for there is inevitably some overlapping. The early 15th-c. colours are simple with a bright turquoise blue generally used for the background. Other colours include a dark green, sometimes approaching black, a brilliant cobalt blue, red, yellow and white. Towards the end of the century a semi-translucent aubergine purple was added to the palette. At about the same time the first 'mixed' colour, known as 'Ming pink', was introduced. This was achieved by mixing ground-up red and white frits; as the grinding was coarse these did not completely fuse in the firing and particles of each can be clearly distinguished in the *cloisons*. The pink derived from gold, a true rose pink, did not appear until the 18th c. At the very end of the 15th c. or the beginning of the 16th c. yellow and green were 'mixed' to produce a pale green. In the early 16th c. a turquoise green and semi-translucent brown were introduced, and during the same century further new colours were arrived at by mixing, sometimes as many as three different ones being used together. At the same time the cobalt blue lost some of its brilliance and was more sparingly used. In some instances two different colours were used alongside each other, not mixed, a practice derived from the West; this is easily seen as there is a distinct line where one colour fades into another.

A certain number of pieces carry reign marks and if these occur as part of the decoration, they can be accepted. If on the other hand they appear on the base plate, which is normally gilt, they should be regarded with caution. The most popular mark so used is that of Ching-tʻai (1450–7), which invariably appears on the base. This has not so far been proved in any instance to be genuinely the date of the object. Garner finds that the mark was not used before the 17th c., and he deals comprehensively with what he calls the Ching-tʻai 'myth' in *Chinese and Japanese Cloisonné Enamels*.

The forms of the vessels are similar to those in the repertories of ceramics and metalwork, though there is a strong predilection for archaistic bronze forms such as the *kuei*, *tʻsun*, *ku* and *ting*. The decoration of these forms until the 18th c., however, is rarely of the kind associated with the originals of Shang or early Chou times; indeed, before the 18th c. there is only one piece, at present dated to the 1st half of the 15th c., which reflects at all faithfully the ancient decorative style (Garner, Pl. 21B). It is much more usual for such pieces to be decorated with lotus scrolls. Other motifs such as fruiting sprays and dragons among clouds are also fairly commonly found in the 15th c., and at that time the large scale of the designs and their organization on the surface were such that the wires supporting the enamels were spaced so that it was not necessary to introduce additional curls of wire to hold the background in place. In the 16th c., when the scale became smaller and there was a larger expanse of background, it became essential to add extra curls of wire in order to support the larger blank areas. During the 16th c. animals were introduced along with a small number of pleasing landscape scenes in which herons and ducks figure. There are also from this century a small number of plates decorated with romantic scenes of men and women gathered on terraces, a type of design seen also in lacquer and porcelain of the same period. Only in the 17th c. does true landscape occur. This is not so aesthetically satisfactory as the bolder style employing a smaller number of elements on a large scale, although when well handled the landscape can be attractive. In the 18th and 19th centuries the most successful pieces are generally small with the designs carefully organized in bands and panels. In the course of the 18th c. incense burners especially in the form of birds, ducks and cranes became popular. Animals are also found either as incense burners or as purely ornamental objects. To this repertory were finally added figures of small children and dwarfs, sometimes acting as supports for more massive objects, sometimes free-standing. One object of unusual form found in metalwork, jade and lacquer and finally in cloisonné enamel is the strange sceptre known as the *ju-i* sceptre, an emblem of authority and good wishes. An admirable one of the Chʻien-lung period is illustrated by Garner (Pl. 69B); it is ornamented with *shou* characters conveying a wish for long life.

The quality of the craftsmanship in the Chʻien-lung period is exceptionally high, especially in the smaller pieces, but after the end of the 18th c. the standards began to decline, the forms often becoming cumbersome and the enamels less fresh in colour, less well applied and frequently disfigured by pits in the surface.

10. CANTON ENAMELS. This is the name given to Chinese enamelling on a copper base. Technically it stems from Limoges enamelling, but the colour range is considerably greater, including as it does the rose pink derived from gold. The ground colour is generally an opaque enamel, commonly white, above which the other colours are painted and then fired on. The resulting

surface is smooth and the best examples are finely painted and delicately coloured. The date of the introduction of the technique is not precisely known, but it seems to have been towards the end of the K'ang-hsi period in the early part of the 18th c. The problem is intimately related to the development of what in ceramics is known as *famille rose* and is discussed in the only authoritative paper on the subject, 'The Origins of *Famille Rose*' (*Transactions of the Oriental Ceramic Society*, xxxvii, 1967–9) by Sir Harry Garner. It is apparent that the development of Canton enamelling was both later and slower than was previously supposed and much work remains to be done in this area. The problem is slightly complicated by the fact that the Chinese terms *yang-ts'ai* 'foreign colours' and *yang-tz'u* 'foreign porcelain' are applied indiscriminately to both Canton enamelling on metal and to the *famille rose* type of enamelling on porcelain. This is less surprising than it seems, as this type of painting with opaque colours was initially done in the same factory and similar designs may be found on both metal and porcelain.

11. LACQUER. The word is derived from the Hindustani *lakh*, which is a hard varnish processed from the gummy deposit of the insect *Tachardia lacca*. It is the basis of 'resin lac' or 'shellac', and it is the substance used by European craftsmen in the 16th c. and onwards when they imitated Chinese and Japanese lacquer work. Chinese as well as Japanese and Korean lacquer is a different substance and is possessed of quite different qualities, the most important of which is extreme durability. Chinese lacquer is the purified sap of the shrubby tree *Rhus vernicifera*, native to the southern and western provinces of China. When processed it can be applied to almost any surface and can be artificially coloured. It is most commonly applied in thin layers to a wooden or basket-work carcass, which it makes impermeable; it can also be applied to a fabric base with similar results. Its application to the desired surface is in thin or relatively thin layers, each of which is dried in a damp atmosphere before the next is added. Most pieces have at least two layers of single or varying colours. The final layer has to be polished and then it may either be left as a plain lustrous surface or it may be decorated in any of a number of ways, as by painting, incising, carving or inlaying. In carving a single colour may be used, or by introducing layers of different colours at various stages in preparation the carving may be executed so as to make use of the variety of colours in the different strata.

In China lacquer was employed purely for utilitarian purposes in the first instance; but the introduction of decoration on its surface, which soon followed, foreshadowed an ultimate interest in its decorative value and use. It was not, however, until *c.* the 14th c., nearly 2,000 years after its first use, that it began to be exploited for its purely decorative appeal, and it was only in the 18th c. that it was used almost exclusively for this purpose. So far there has been no really comprehensive work published on the subject, the first attempt in this direction being Edward F. Strange's *Chinese Lacquer* (London, 1926), which is mainly concerned with the later material from *c.* the 17th c. onwards. The next important essay was Soame Jenyns's paper 'Chinese Lacquer' in *Transactions of the Oriental Ceramic Society*, xvii, 1939–40. The author here deals with much earlier material from the Sung Dynasty onwards, with a brief reference to the earliest material as it was then known and with a short note on the material itself and the technique of its use. Since this last article Sir Harry Garner has published three papers on aspects of Ming lacquers, and these systematic studies open the way for a more serious examination of the whole development of the craft. The first contribution was 'Guri Lacquer of the Ming Dynasty' in *Transactions of the Oriental Ceramic Society*, xxxi, 1957–9, followed by 'Diaper Backgrounds on Chinese Carved Lacquer', *Ars Orientalis*, vi, 1966, and 'A Group of Chinese Lacquers with Basketry Panels', *Archives of Asian Art*, xx, 1966–7.

The earliest surviving example of lacquer ware dates from *c.* the middle of the 7th c. B.C. This is a fragmentary piece in the shape of a bronze *tou*, found in tomb 1704 at Shang ts'un ling (Report for 1959); and from that time on until the end of the Han Dynasty at the beginning of the 3rd c. A.D. black lacquered surfaces were generally decorated with paintings in different-coloured lacquers—red, blue, yellow and white being those normally used. Some of the yellows are nearer to orange and the black is often not a true colour, tending as it frequently does to brown. Bowls, basins and cups were common, the cups usually elliptical in shape with ears jutting out along the longer arcs. There was also an unusual tall cylindrical vessel with gilt bronze base and cabriole feet, fitted at the mouth-rim, or just below, with a ring handle surmounted by a curved thumb-piece. This type of vessel was decorated in bands of geometrical or scrolling motifs, or sometimes with friezes of hunters and animals, or with processional scenes. Even in designs that appear superficially geometrical and abstract animal forms are at this time often the ultimate source, and the heads of animals often occur as terminal elements in a decoration. By the Han period the use of lacquer was widespread. Stands for chimes of bells and the outer casings of coffins painted with lacquer had been common for some time; but with the Han period toilet requisites and boxes are found covered with lacquer and painted with elaborate and lively designs, and in addition there is furniture such as tables and toilet stands somewhat resembling the Victorian shaving stand. An example of this type is illustrated in the toilet scene of the 'Admonitions' scroll in the British Museum. Pieces such as these have been found in excavations over a wide area, not only in China but also in places as far apart as Korea in the east and

Begram in Afghanistan in the west, where China had commercial contacts in the first imperial age. The most important finds of lacquer outside China have been in Korea, where the Chinese had a well-established colony with senior officials as administrators. At Lo-lang (in the vicinity of modern Seoul), for instance, fine-quality lacquers were found by the Japanese in the years between the wars, and have been subsequently well published in the Government General of Korea archaeological reports. The dated inscriptions on a number of the pieces found here and on others later found in Inner Mongolia have been of great value because they have included not only the names of craftsmen and indications of the roles they played in the creation of the object, but also the names of the places where the pieces were made. W. Willetts in *Foundations of Chinese Art* (London, 1965) discusses some of these pieces and the main centres of manufacture in the vicinity of Chêng-tu in the western province of Ssŭ-chʻüan. Finds in China proper have been mainly in Hunan, which was also a region where lacquer was produced, and in other areas south of the Yangtze river.

The discovery of tombs in the region of Chang-sha since 1950 has resulted in a much improved understanding and appreciation of the lacquers from this region, many examples of which have been published in Chinese archaeological reports. The style differs in being slightly more florid than that associated with the material known to have come from Ssŭ-chʻüan. The range of shapes is also much greater. Among the more unusual ones are stands for musical instruments and some very spectacular painted shields, one of which was in a remarkably good state of preservation. Apart from these there was a varied selection of bowls, basins, dishes, two types of eared cups, and trays. At about this time protective lacquer covering was being added to tables and it is possible to speak of this period as marking the beginning of lacquered furniture.

After the end of the Han Dynasty we lose track of lacquer for some centuries and it is not until the Tʻang Dynasty that it becomes possible once more to identify objects. But the context is now different and the use to which the material is put also differs. While it is still used for many small objects, it is now found more generally associated with furniture and it is from this period that we are able to date the first lacquered armchairs, generally plain with gilt metal fittings and ornament or with painted decoration. There were two other quite unusual uses to which lacquer was put during this dynasty. It is found as what is called 'dry lacquer', that is it is built up with cloth round a rough core, subsequently removed, to form sculptures, mainly Buddhist in intention. The figure of the Buddha in meditation, in the Metropolitan Museum of Art, New York, with its painted and gilt surface, is an outstanding example of this technique. The other way in which lacquer is used is as a bed on a bronze base, or even on leather, for the insetting of gold and silver foil, AMBER or MOTHER OF PEARL. On bronze it occurs mainly on mirror backs or on boxes, of which some of the finest examples are those in the Shōsōin (Imperial Repository) at Nara in Japan. On leather it may be used in the same way; but it may also be found on 'plates' of leather, used as a hardening agent, for armour. Examples of this kind have been found in some of the ruined garrison posts on the northwestern frontier of China with central Asia, and have been published by Sir Aurel Stein in *Serindia* (London, 1921) and *Innermost Asia* (London, 1928).

During the Sung and Yüan Dynasties lacquer is once more found on utilitarian objects such as cups, cup-stands, bowls and boxes. These are generally extremely simple and wholly lacking in decoration. Dark brown, black and red, each used monochromatically, seem to have been the common colours. Cups and bowls have come from a number of Sung tombs in recent years, especially from tombs in the provinces of Kiangsu and Anhui. The forms used have close parallels with contemporary ceramics, especially those of the Southern Sung period. Whether or not the next step forward actually occurred in Sung or Yüan times is at present uncertain. There is a tradition that the carving of lacquer occurred as early as the Tʻang Dynasty, but at present no firm evidence justifies such an assumption. The first evidence of carving cannot at the moment be dated earlier than some time in the latter half of the Sung Dynasty, and it is probably of the type described as *guri*, a Japanese term meaning 'in whorls'. This style is characterized by cutting a slanting V-line through a series of layers of different-coloured lacquers so that the multicoloured layering shows up in the scrolling design. In order to achieve this effect the total number of layers has to be substantially increased, with the result that the weight of the object is mainly in the lacquer itself rather than in the carcass, usually of light wood, to which the material has been applied.

At about the same time, either in the Sung or in early Yüan, another new technique was introduced, so far only found on such objects as *Sutra* boxes. This was the incising of a complex series of designs, some geometrical and some naturalistic representations of birds and clouds or of human figures, and the incisions then gilt, a technique named by the Chinese *chʻiang-chin*, for which there is no English equivalent. As with the forms of the simple vessels of Sung times, these pieces reflect contemporary designs in their decoration. The forms were mainly those common to such media as ceramics and metalwork. From the 14th c. onwards it is not difficult to discern close relationships between one medium and another, not only in form but also in the decoration, and the reason probably lies in the increased patronage of the court and the growing commercial interest.

During the 14th c., when the interest in lacquer was growing, carved lacquers evidently became

Carved red lacquer dish with peonies. D. 16·7 cm. (Ming Dynasty, early 15th c.)

well known and in the literature references are made to outstanding masters; Chang Chʻêng, Yang Mao and the more recently identified Master Hu. Mention of these master craftsmen is made in the nearly contemporary collector's handbook *Ko-ku yao-lun*, and the names of Chang and Mao particularly have been associated with the highest standards; the two names are often found incised with a fine point into the base of top-quality 15th-c. carved pieces. The date at which these names were incised on the objects must of course remain open to suspicion, since they could have been added at any time and are thus not evidence of authenticity. What is of interest, however, is that the style and quality of the pieces to which they are added are such as to indicate that only the very best 15th-c. pieces could qualify for this flattering addition. In the 15th c. trays and boxes, and a few vases with decorations of the flowers of the seasons and of birds and dragons, became exceptionally popular. Most are in plain red lacquer, often with traces of a yellow ground, a few are black with similar traces of a red ground and towards the end of the century red and yellow are found, in some pieces with additions of green. The yellow colour is rather a dull ochre tone when used in quantity. Landscape scenes and scenes of sages on terraces with trees and water gained especial favour as the century neared its end. The style of the carving is smooth and rounded with very refined detail and the total effect is visually soft, much at variance with the later, 16th-c. style with its crisper, sharper carving, when terrace scenes and buildings became more common. Dragons, which occur in some 15th-c. pieces, have a more sinuous flowing contour and a smoother, more rhythmic line in the body than is found in the 16th c., when the rhythms became sharper, more nervous and jerky. The flowers of the seasons continued to be in demand in the 16th c., but they played a less important role, being confined as a rule to panels subordinated to the main field and often spaced out on DIAPER grounds.

Most of the more complicated scenes in carved lacquers include areas in which repeating diapers of various kinds are used; those for water, for instance, differ from those employed to depict the sky or the paved terrace of a mansion. These diaper patterns themselves can, within limits, be dated and a close study of them was made by Sir Harry Garner in the well illustrated article 'Diaper Backgrounds on Chinese Carved Lacquer' (*Ars Orientalis*, vi, 1966). This is an important article since it establishes the groundwork for successful dating of Ming lacquers. In Chʻing times, however, it is less the diaper patterns than the iconography that tends to be the guide. The hard-edged cutting and sharp jerky rhythms persist but the linear quality breaks through in the late 17th-c. and 18th-c. examples. Many of the pieces are heavy, with the weight of innumerable layers of lacquer, and the carving is deeper and more intricate than formerly. Extreme complexity of design and decorative detail and a certain denial of the integrity of form characterizes the 18th c., when reverence for technique overcame respect for good form. It is not unusual to find forms more suited to other media being employed as a vehicle for a display of technical virtuosity.

Incising and inlaying of lacquer is another new technique, probably introduced in the late 14th c. or early 15th c. This consists of cutting out a design in depth in a red or a brown ground and then inlaying these areas with lacquers of other colours, the line of contact between two colours and incised details of various elements being gilt. This is really a highly sophisticated development from the earlier 14th-c. technique of *chʻiang-chin*, mentioned above. The types of object on which this technique is used are mainly dishes and bowls, although a few fairly large pieces such as writing-boxes and small chests are known. The decorative themes are generally dragons, birds and floral motifs, including the emblems of Buddhism and Taoism. The development of the style of drawing follows closely that found in other media employing similar motifs, such as the painted porcelains either in blue and white or in polychrome enamel. This inlaid type of lacquer maintained the popularity established, especially in the 16th c., well on into the 18th c., when unlike the contemporary carved lacquers they remained simple in form, though they sometimes became very much larger in scale, some really massive boxes and basins being produced under imperial patronage.

Lac burgauté. A technique evolved, so far as we know, in the 16th c., it perhaps had its ultimate ancestry going back to the Tʻang Dynasty, when gold and silver were inset in a bed of lacquer on mirror backs. In the 16th c. the use of mother of pearl for its decorative effect was exploited in this way on trays, dishes and boxes. While the decorations executed in this time-consuming technique of insetting, often with minute fragments of shell, were once more floral, landscapes and scenes with sages and buildings were also regarded as appropriate subjects. The shell, inset into the still soft lacquer, was pressed firmly and evenly into place, and when the material was thoroughly dried and hardened the surface was polished so that the shell lay flush with the surface, producing—particularly in the very refined 18th-c. examples—subtle colour variations as the shifting light caught the shell. The Ming examples, in many ways relatively simple, make use of large pieces of shell and there are often details lightly engraved on them. The Chʻing Dynasty specimens are generally smaller in size, and this is certainly true of the finest-quality pieces, with very minute pieces of shell laboriously inlaid in complex designs and often with pearl-inlaid diaper grounds of extreme delicacy. It is rare to find any large specimens in this technique, but there are a very few really large screens of twelve folds, very elaborately treated, which date from the early years of the 18th c. when imperial patronage in the Chʻing Dynasty was at its height.

Coromandel lacquer. The name is given to a type of lacquer ware, mainly furniture, which was exported from China and transhipped for the European merchants on the Coromandel coast of India. Technically it differs hardly if at all from what used to be called Bantam work, a term now obsolete. Originally the technique stemmed from the practice of coating semi-hardwood furniture with a protective series of lacquer layers as a defence against insect attack and was very much a southern Chinese practice. Such lacquered furniture was often simply painted or gilt, but about the 17th c. craftsmen, perhaps attracted by carved lacquer but unwilling to spend any great length of time painting on innumerable coats of lacquer for this treatment, began to carve designs through the polished coating directly to the wood below, which was then covered with a thin layer of gesso or plaster and subsequently painted in coloured or gold lacquer and left unpolished. Quicker to execute than carved lacquer, lighter in weight and cheaper, it was a technique quite well suited for the purpose. The type became popular among the Chinese and a large number of pieces of furniture were treated in this way. Twelvefold screens and large chests and cupboards were ornamented in this for wealthy patrons in the late 17th c. and probably about this time were seen by foreign traders, who were attracted by the undoubted splendour of these handsome objects. As a result much second-rate furniture and panels decorated in this way found their way overseas. It became not uncommon in the 18th c., for instance, for panels to be exported in bulk and then on arrival in Europe to be cut up and used in whatever way was thought desirable. Even picture and mirror frames were made from such panels, with a disregard for the design as a whole that would have struck the Chinese craftsman dumb with horror and would have been regarded as an act of sacrilege such as could only be committed by the Western barbarians.

See also LACQUER AND JAPANNING.

CHINA

12. JADE. In Chinese the term *yü* applies to a large variety of gemstones worked by the lapidary as well as to the two materials nephrite and jadeite which truly qualify for the blanket term. These two materials are not as a rule distinguishable in their finished state, although chemically and in crystalline structure they are quite different. Both materials are very hard and extremely tough, but paradoxically they are also brittle and can easily shatter. Both are commercially useless stones which the Chinese used for ritual decorative purposes at least as early as Neolithic times. Neither is believed to have been native to China but they had to be imported from the Khotanese and Yarkand regions of central Asia, and southern Siberia, and from the 18th c. jadeite came from Burma. It was admired and revered by the Chinese on account of its hardness and its texture and in early times, partly perhaps because of its high cost, it was not only a mark of wealth but was also considered appropriate for ritual and ceremonial use. But the mystique which engulfs jade in the Chinese mind appears almost incomprehensible to the Occidental. The reverence accorded the material stemmed partly from the belief that it had a supernatural origin and the capacity, also supernatural, to control the constellations and the world of nature. It was also due to the very hardness and textural quality of the stone; the smoothness and gloss were likened to benevolence, the compact strength seemed like intelligence, its angularity without sharpness was an analogue of righteousness—all qualities especially associated with the *Chün-tzū* or superior man. It was admired, too, for its coolness to the touch and for the prolonged musical note it emits when a thin piece is struck like a gong. Confucius expatiates on its qualities at some length, likening them to those of the true incorruptible gentleman.

The material as it survives falls into two main groups, the first from earliest times until the Han Dynasty (206 B.C.–A.D. 220) and the second from Ming times onwards. The long period from Han to Ming is represented by relatively little material, most of it impossible to date except on ill-defined stylistic grounds. A large part of the first group is ritual and ceremonial in intention with small pieces for decorative uses, while the bulk of the second group is predominantly ornamental and decorative. The literature relevant to both groups has been exhaustively covered by S. Howard Hansford in *Chinese Jade Carving* (London, 1950) and *Chinese Carved Jade* (London, 1968) and close studies of the early material have been made by Alfred Salmony in *Carved Jade of Ancient China* (Berkeley, 1938) and in *Archaic Chinese Jades in the Sonnenschein Collection* (Chicago, 1952).

The ritual and ceremonial jades include some deriving from stone tools such as axes and adzes, and others in the forms of sceptres pointed at the end and with a central spine; these are usually designated by the term *kuei*, the primary meaning

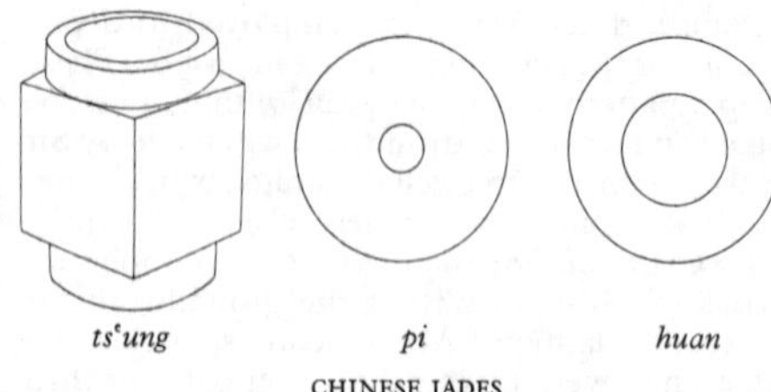

CHINESE JADES

of which is a flat tool, sceptre or baton carried as a mark of office. Among the later Shang jades are some described as dagger axes, but these seem to be a variant form of the *kuei*. The other important ritual jade object is the *ts'ung*, which is a tube within a rectangle. In addition there are annular discs of various kinds, of which the most important are the *pi* with only a small hole in the centre and the *huan* with a much larger aperture.

Among the decorative pieces are numerous thin flat plaques in the form of birds, animals and fish with only lightly worked details which spring from a common style best seen in the bronze art. In Chou times the material was more often worked in the round, and flat worked dragons and decorative plaques were frequently incorporated in cast bronze; this is most often seen in belt hooks, of which there are a number of fine elaborate examples with gilt metal against which the pale jade stands out in marked decorative contrast. By Han times whole belt hooks and sword fittings were being made of this intractable material, and purely decorative pieces became much larger and more often modelled in the round, lions and winged tigers as well as figures being not uncommon. The decorative style is, all through this early period, closely related to that of the dominant art of the time, the bronze art.

The standard of craftsmanship is very high despite what must have been a fairly limited range of tools and of abrasive sands, for jade has to be cut with diamond or ground down by means of abrasive sands, a slow and hence costly process. By the Ming period rotary tools were in common use and these undoubtedly speeded up production and made larger and more elaborate pieces economically possible and even desirable: animals in the round, brush pots with elaborate landscapes as a setting for romantic scenes and groups of immortals, vases with covers and ring handles all incorporated in a single piece of masterly carving, bowls, dishes and ornaments including elements making up a rebus for the aspiring scholar. The almost inexhaustible repertory of symbolic elements was translated into visual three-dimensional terms with what seems unbelievable mastery of the material. The literature for the craft in these later stages has to be sought in that of legend and romance and of the styles in contemporary painting, illustrated books and ceramic decoration.

On account of the nature of the material the

dating of the earlier group is relatively easier, because of the archaeological work since *c.* 1930, than that of the later group and those pieces which seem to lie between the two for which there is no archaeological evidence. Of necessity the craft itself was so little subject to changes in technique that little can be gained from this aspect and Hansford's discussion of the technique remains the standard one.

See also JADE.

13. IVORY. The Chinese use of IVORY dates back to the Shang Dynasty, when the elephant was still a familiar animal in north China though no longer indigenous to that region. The many small ivory carvings among the finds at An-yang show that the artistic style as revealed in the bronzes is reflected in ivory, while at Chêng-chou, more recently, an ivory beaker, probably the largest piece of early date so far found, is fairly faithful to the form of a cast-bronze *chih* beaker. Between Shang and T'ang there is virtually no material surviving, although ivory was probably in use on a limited scale throughout the intervening centuries. In T'ang times, when imports from South East Asia and India increased, ivory was much used for inlaying furniture and musical instruments as well as for making rulers, a number of which, stained red or green and delicately engraved, survive in the Shōsōin Collection in Nara, Japan, and are datable to the 8th c. From this time ivory continued to be imported for making inlay, small seals and combs. Small figures carved in the round began to make their appearance in the Sung and were fairly frequently produced in Ming Dynasties, though often with a painted lacquer coating. The Sung and Ming figures are difficult to date with any precision as there is only style on which to base an assessment. The Ch'ing figures are usually easily distinguished from earlier ones but again, since style is the only criterion, dating within the period is problematic. In Ch'ing times carved panels and engraved and painted boxes, as well as intricately carved wrist-rests, became common. There is very little literature, but Soame Jenyns, 'Chinese Carvings in Elephant Ivory', *Transactions of the Oriental Ceramic Society*, xxvii (1951–2), and S. E. Lucas, *Catalogue of the Sassoon Chinese Ivories* (3 vols., London, 1950), may be consulted. On the early history and the beliefs associated with the material B. Laufer, *Ivory in China* (Chicago, 1925), is valuable.

14. RHINOCEROS HORN. The rhinoceros, like the elephant, was in very ancient times native to China and it is clear from a number of late Shang or early Chou bronze vessels and fittings that the northern Chinese were sufficiently familiar with its appearance to depict it realistically. How early the carving of the horns began is very uncertain, but the belief in the magical properties of the material can be established from the literature as having already been strong by the 4th c. A.D. The Chinese held it at that time to be prophylactic and to have special anti-poisonous qualities; later it came to be regarded as an aphrodisiac. It is largely on account of these beliefs that the Chinese demand for the horns has led to the destruction of the animal almost to the point of total extinction; for not only did they use horn of the Asiatic species, but from Ming times onward the horn of the African species was also in demand.

The earliest carvings are belt plaques, pendants, knife handles and a simple cup in the Shōsōin Collection at Nara; and these are attributable to the 8th c. Thereafter cups are known that have been attributed to Sung and a very few to early Ming. The earliest precisely dated examples are of the Wan-li period and up to this time the cups were extremely simple. Even one dated 1580 in the Museum voor Land en Volkenkunde, Rotterdam, is exceptionally simple; but another of the same date in a French collection is carved with decoration resembling that of the archaic bronzes. A figure of Kuan-yin seated on a rock, dated 1599, is a fine example of a departure from the usual practice of making cups.

Cups were imported into Europe from the late 16th c. and probably some of the earliest are to be found in the Kunsthistorisches Museum, Vienna, which houses the Habsburg Collection. Slightly later in England the name of John Tradescant the Elder, who died in 1632, is associated with a pleasantly carved cup presented by Elias Ashmole to Oxford University in 1683, which is now in the Ashmolean Museum, Oxford, and is datable within fairly narrow limits in the opinion of Soame Jenyns, the only expert to have written on this intriguing subject in 'The Chinese Rhinoceros and Chinese Carving in Rhinoceros Horn' (*Transactions of the Oriental Ceramic Society*, xxix, 1954–5). Most pieces that survive date from the 18th c. and 19th c. and the exceptionally long horns carved in complicated open-work with Taoist themes are almost all from the 18th c. or later.

15. GOLD AND SILVER. Precious metals do not play the same part in the arts and crafts of China as they do in Europe and other parts of Asia, and the enormous value set on gold in the West has been replaced in China to a large extent by the value and the mystique ascribed in the first instance to bronze and later to jade. Even SILVER, although honoured, admired and thought desirable from time to time, was very largely overshadowed and replaced for practical purposes by lacquer and porcelain. At least part of this difference in use and attitude can be accounted for by the easy availability of lacquer and ceramic clays and the relatively more difficult acquisition of gold and silver from the earth by panning and mining. Mining was always reluctantly undertaken by the Chinese since it was thought to disturb the spirits not only of the earth but also those of the ancestors on their way through the

underworld; an additional reason was that it was believed to disturb the equilibrium of the DRAGON and force him to ascend to the skies and bring rains at unwelcome seasons. This has meant that although both metals were used from early times for decorative purposes, mainly for inlay and plating or gilding, they were rarely used for the manufacture of complete objects until about Han times. The proportion of vessels and other objects made in precious metals in China has thus remained remarkably small as compared with those of earthenware and lacquer, and the statements made by Bo Gyllensvärd in *Gold and Silver in the Carl Kempe Collection* (Stockholm, 1953) on this aspect have remained fundamentally unchanged despite the results of archaeological work in subsequent years. It is in chronology that Gyllensvärd's work now requires revision in certain respects, especially with regard to the T'ang material ('T'ang Gold and Silver' in *Bulletin of the Museum of Far Eastern Antiquities*, xxix, Stockholm, 1957).

The use of thin sheet gold with tooled detail, inlaying, and gilding seems to have been, if not common, at least well known by late Chou times, as inlaid and gilt bronzes of the period show; but GRANULATION techniques, which were not known until at least the Han period, were introduced from the West, as later still was tracing, which seems to have appeared only when silver assumed greater importance. Casting of gold and silver was practised, as one might expect in a country where the casting of bronze was a highly developed technique, but this is less appropriate to the materials than beating. There are a few really good cast-gold pieces surviving, but all are small and none can be dated earlier than *c.* the 4th c. B.C. One of the largest and best pieces, and also most characteristic of the period, is the gold dagger hilt in the British Museum, evidently cast by the *cire-perdue* method. After the end of the Han Dynasty cast gold is extremely rare, and when it occurs it is confined to rather smaller pieces such as handles of cups, which are soldered on to the main body of the beaten object. Granulation, which was introduced during the Han period when the Chinese Empire expanded across central Asia to the Persian frontier, was practised to a limited extent and mainly on small ornamental plaques and miniature vessels, of which there are a few, the best probably being the small flask with spatula less than 5 centimetres high in the Nelson Gallery of Art, Kansas. The casting of silver also seems largely to have been discontinued after the Han period, although some Ch'ing Dynasty pieces are known.

Silver was more widely used than gold but was often gilt or parcel gilt even in Han times. The great age of silver-working, with or without gilding, was the T'ang Dynasty, when the Chinese achieved a second imperial era of great magnificence. A very large body of material dating from the late 7th c. to the end of T'ang has survived, much of it of fine quality and manifesting strong influences from the western side of central Asia in both form and decoration. It was a period when foreign merchants and craftsmen settled in China and brought with them new techniques as well as new forms and decorations. It was at this time or a little before that the practice of ring-punching the backgrounds was introduced in combination with traced designs. Among the alien forms introduced the best known is the stem cup, a form ultimately of Mediterranean origin, which had for a long while been used in Persia and a little to the north-east on the borders of central Asia. The Chinese treatment of the form was often elaborate and most examples are richly decorated with small traced flowers, animals, birds and hunting scenes against a ring-punched ground. If the cup was not lobed, it was usually fitted with a plain liner soldered in round the rim in order to conceal the marks of the tracing and punching, which would otherwise be clearly visible on the inner wall of the beaten metal. The stems were soldered on, sometimes in such a way as to cut off a little of the decoration round the bottom, indicating that this was done after the whole design had been completed. Soldering was often rather poorly done and not much effort was made to conceal it. Moreover pieces were sometimes constructed in surprising ways, soldering lines appearing in unusual and apparently illogical places in relation to the form of the object. As usual the Chinese craftsman was more interested in the total effect than in the details.

In the T'ang Dynasty there are three stylistically discernible groups, for which recent archaeological work now provides a limited amount of confirmatory evidence. The first group, which includes almost all the stem cups and small cups with handles and the greater part of the most richly ornamented material, can be dated from *c.* A.D. 700 to *c.* A.D. 756. The second group, not quite so rich, includes the more truly Chinese forms and is less fine in craftsmanship; it is also in this group that repoussé seems to gain greater favour, being employed as a decorative technique noticeably more often. This group seems to begin shortly after the end of the An Lu-shan rebellion and the Tibetan invasions of A.D. 763 and continues until about the end of the 1st quarter of the 9th c. The third group continues what was now a declining tradition into the 10th c., when it was transmitted to the Liao kingdom in the north and there revived against a new and different cultural background. The period as a whole requires much study, the only published work at present being Gyllensvärd's 'T'ang Gold and Silver', a pioneer work, which provides a starting-point but which was completed before the reports of Chinese excavations of T'ang sites began to become available.

Sung material is limited and often poor in craftsmanship. Interest does not appear to have been very strong, but this may be because the growing ceramic industry to some extent diverted educated taste from the more costly material. In any case it has to be remembered that silver

Silver bowl with traced and gilt decoration. T'ang Dynasty, 1st half 8th c. (Seattle Art Mus., Washington)

and gold could all too easily be melted down and used again. Whether or not this did happen it is not possible to discover. Yüan silver, as we know it from the few hoards that have come to light since *c.* 1940, is very different in character, some of it being rather plain. Pear-shaped vases, simple bowls of various sizes, round and rectangular plates with shaped corners and spouted bowls, all of fairly thin beaten silver, are recorded from a tomb dated 1333 in the province of Anhui, and this find represents the plain type. The only really distinguished pieces belong to two groups. One, in the Nelson Gallery of Art in Kansas, includes some fine lobed and fluted cups with traced decoration and splendid censers for use in Buddhist ceremonies. The other group, excavated from a tomb in the province of Kiangsu, includes some magnificent lobed boxes. One, in a series of tiers which fit into one another, is decorated with phoenixes and with fine traced or engraved flowers of the twelve months arranged in a series of medallions; another with an elaborate repoussé decoration of birds and flowers on the lid. The reports of this and other finds are all in Chinese, and so far there has been no publication in a European language covering any of the late Sung and Yüan finds other than Watson's essay in *Chinese Art: The Minor Arts: Gold, Silver, Bronze, etc.* (London, 1963), by R. Soame Jenyns and William Watson.

In the Ming Dynasty working in precious metal was revived, perhaps as the result of renewed imperial patronage. An important and somewhat spectacular group of gold vessels, inset with semi-precious and precious stones, is that associated with the name of the Emperor Hsüan-tê (1426–35), from whose tomb they are supposed to have come. This is not a well attested attribution, but there is no doubt of the quality of the craftsmanship or of an early 15th-c. date. In this group are basins and a ewer now in the Philadelphia Museum of Art, a covered globular jar in the Freer Gallery of Art, Washington, and a large ornate jewelled plaque in the British Museum. All are decorated with rampant dragons of typical 15th-c. style with powerful coiling bodies and wide-spreading claws. A more recent find, this time very well attested if not yet well published, was in the Wan-li emperor's tomb of 1620 outside Peking; here were found an elegant open-work gold head-dress and some vessels of fine quality, which included a remarkable ewer on a tall spreading foot. Open-work gold and silver-gilt filigree were evidently popular among the very rich and princely households, and a number of head-dresses survive from the Ming period that are lavishly adorned with filigree elements. The same taste seems to have continued into the Ch'ing Dynasty and examples are known in both gold and silver, as well as silver gilt, and all are embellished with delicate phoenixes, dragons and floral elements mounted with kingfisher feathers, rose and colourless ROCK-CRYSTAL and freshwater pearls, each element being attached to the open-work frame with short wires so that when the wearer moved the ornaments danced. This tradition in jewellery persisted right up to the end of the Empire in 1911. But alongside it there also continued on a diminished scale the older treatment of the metals that had begun in the T'ang Dynasty, the beating of metal in the form of bowls, cups, small boxes for vermilion seal paste and cosmetics, with traced decoration.

16. IRON PAINTING. The forging of iron to make decorative open-work panels of 'pictures'. This craft is recorded in the late 17th c., when the names of two craftsmen from Anhui are noticed. One, Liang Ying-fêng, signed and dated some of his pieces, but the other, T'ang P'êng (called T'ien-ch'ih), is only known by name. Although the craft has continued into the present century, it is not possible to date the panels at all closely. The subject matter was mainly landscapes, bamboo and rocks, and the 'Flowers of the Four Seasons' making up sets of four panels. Of these last both the British Museum and the Victoria and Albert Museum have sets. There is no literature except in Chinese.

17. SNUFF-BOTTLES. It is generally believed that tobacco was introduced into China towards the end of the 16th c., but on the basis of present knowledge it was probably not taken as snuff before the middle of the 17th c. Although there are a few snuff-bottles of 17th-c. date, mainly of BRASS, it was not until the 2nd quarter of the 18th c. that these bottles, predominantly for aristocratic use, began to be made in significant numbers. The materials used include: (i) jade and other stones such as crystal, agate and semi-precious stones such as aquamarine, beryl, lapis lazuli and malachite; (ii) porcelain, either monochrome or decorated; (iii) glass, plain or carved in monochrome or polychrome, or painted on the inside; (iv) other materials such as lacquer, ivory, horn, coral and wood. Although there is this great variety of material, it is glass which has been most popular. The 'inside painted' type, discussed by Schuyler Cammann in 'Chinese Inside-painted Snuff-bottles', *Harvard Journal of Asiatic Studies*, xx, 1957, appears not to have begun until the last quarter of the 19th c. While snuff-bottles have always interested collectors, it is only since *c.* 1950 that they have been the subject of serious study. Soame Jenyns's essay 'Snuff Bottle', forming Chapter V of Soame Jenyns and William Watson's *Chinese Art: The Minor Arts II* (London, 1965), is a useful introduction, and L. S. Perry, *Chinese Snuff Bottles* (Rutland, Vermont and Tokyo, 1960), offers a more detailed, collector's approach. Research in this field promises much in the future.

18. TEXTILES. Although archaeology has yet to provide all the answers concerning the origins of spun textiles, it seems doubtful at present that the technique of spinning SILK originated in the Far East. There is no doubt, however, that China attained, and maintained, a position as perhaps the leading centre of the silk industry from a very early age.

In China the earliest indications of a textile industry are provided by some minute fragments encrusted into buried bronzes of the Shang Dynasty (*c.* 1600–1027 B.C.). Apart from establishing the existence of woven silks at this time, investigations into the nature of these fragments have shown that the Shang people practised a true sericulture. Scientific analysis has proved the threads to be reeled silk of the *Bombyx mori*, the principal 'domesticated' silk-producing moth.

So far as the weave is concerned the fragments, and the impressions left in the bronze, suggest that it was a simple tabby weave, but in three variant forms. The characteristic feature of these earliest Chinese weaves, which sets the pattern for later and especially for Han-period developments, is the importance of the warp threads. In one variation of these Shang weaves the warps outnumber the wefts approximately two to one, in another the warps only marginally outnumber the wefts and in the third, where the warps and wefts do not interlace regularly, the warp threads pass over three or more wefts. Thus it was the warps which produced the pattern, a feature which both characterizes early Chinese WEAVING techniques and distinguishes them from the fundamentally weft-patterned Western silks.

This principle is clearly illustrated in a number of fragments dating from the Han period (206 B.C.–A.D. 220), excavated from sites in Chinese Turkestan. On the evidence of these excavated pieces two principal weaving techniques were employed: DAMASK and polychrome weaves. The former, a simple method whereby the pattern in a single-coloured textile is achieved by selected warp threads passing over more than one thread in the opposite direction, is a logical development of the earliest Shang weaves. In his analysis of pieces excavated at Noin-ula (in Northern Mongolia), however, Rudenko shows that one fragment was in fact weft-patterned; thus although warp-patterned fabrics certainly predominate, it was not an exclusive weave.

The more complex polychrome weave represents a development of the damask, employing as it does coloured warps which produce a design that appears readable on both sides. The fact that it is the warps which are coloured emphasizes the importance of those threads in the definition and formation of pattern. The different courses followed by these threads permitted greater flexibility in design and the representation of figurative and naturalistic patterns.

These designs, embodying combinations of geometrical motifs derived from designs decorating earlier bronze vessels with semi-naturalistic bird and beast motifs, are representative of Han decorative art. In particular these patterns may be associated with those on contemporary lacquers. The Han period was a turning-point in the history of ornament in Chinese art. The bronze tradition dominated the pre-Han repertory of decorative motifs, but all this was changed with the admission of Western-inspired naturalistic designs late in the pre-Christian era, and nowhere are these fresh ideas better expressed than in these woven silks. That these fragmentary survivals of a rich and highly developed industry should have been recovered from central Asian sites is significant, for they are evidence of the considerable trade in the export of Han silks from China to the West to which literary references allude. It was along these same routes through Kansu province, Sinkiang and the Tarim river basin that Western decorative ideas were transported to China.

Of these sites, that excavated by Sir Aurel Stein in 1914 at Lou-lan in the dry wind-swept desert to the north of Lop-nor in Chinese Turkestan has produced the most varied and representative examples. Similar pieces with scrolling beast forms, in a style closely related to the ornament of late Chou (*c.* 5th–4th c. B.C.) inlaid bronzes, have more recently (in 1960) been found in the Min-feng district of Sinkiang. Another Han textile, excavated from Noin Ula by Kozlov in 1924–5, which employs silk warp threads, these producing the pattern, on a linen weft (preserved in the Hermitage Museum), is indicative of the developments and experiments that occurred in textile technique at this time.

The earliest surviving examples of Chinese EMBROIDERY also date from the Han period, and once again it is the cemetery sites of Chinese Turkestan which provide the evidence. Strangely unrelated in both style and ornament to the woven pieces, these fragmentary examples display what appear to be strong central Asian influences. (See ASIA, CENTRAL.) The largest piece is of green silk, embroidered with animal and flower motifs in a disintegrated over-all pattern, which contrasts with the essential formalism of the woven designs. This example, others from the Noinula site and some still more recently excavated in the Huai-an district of Shansi province are executed entirely in chain stitches, suggesting the close relationship between embroidery and drawing or painting designs. Some of the Noin-ula pieces also employ the 'French knot' (Peking stitch) and the subsequently ubiquitous satin stitch.

As in the Bronze Age Chou Dynasty (1027–221 B.C.), there is little surviving evidence of the textile industry of the Six Dynasties period (220 B.C.–A.D. 581). Isolated finds, however, confirm the existence of a continuing Han tradition. From T'u Lu-fan, also in Sinkiang, has come a polychrome weave fragment ornamented with lions amid a formalized animal scroll of typical Han type, woven in shades of green, gold and red on a blue ground. It is typical of the earlier Han woven silks in colour, weave and design.

Surviving embroideries of this period are similarly rare. A few fragments were excavated in 1965 from a Northern Wei (386–535) cave at the Buddhist cave temples of Tun-huang in Kansu on the ancient trade route to the West and well outside metropolitan China. Although as yet inadequately published, these fragments appear to be executed entirely in chain stitches with Peking knots, illustrating their dependence upon earlier Han techniques. The designs, Buddhist figures with embroidered inscriptions, are more ambitious than the more ornamental Han types.

In addition to these surviving examples we have literary references which testify to the developed state of the textile industry in China at this time. For example in 560 the second Emperor of the Northern Chou Dynasty (557–81) was '. . . pleased to have fashioned on behalf of the late Emperor one *woven* icon of Vairocana with two Bodhisattvas, twenty-six feet high . . .', and again the Emperor Wu Ti of the same dynasty '. . . had fashioned on behalf of His Imperial Majesty a *brocaded* icon of Śākyamuni, sixteen feet high . . .'. Perhaps the most striking aspect of these references is the enormous size of the commissions. A 26 ft. (8 m) high woven hanging clearly suggests a highly developed textile industry as well as indicating that perhaps such workshops were under state control.

T'ang Dynasty (618–906). Our knowledge and understanding of pre-T'ang textiles rests on the isolated examples which have come to light through archaeological work. Sufficient to suggest that the silk industry in China had attained a high degree of sophistication as early as the pre-Christian era, they are none the less insufficient to provide us with a continuing and coherent picture. From the T'ang period the quantity of surviving material is sufficient to give a much clearer idea of the extent, in both technique and ornament, of the textile industry. Fortunately excavated material, most of which again comes from the sites along the ancient silk route in Chinese Turkestan, is supplemented by pieces preserved in the Imperial Treasury of the Shōsōin at Nara in Japan.

The polychrome weave examples illustrate one of the characteristic features of Tʻang art: the Sassanian-inspired decorative style. In place of the geometrical and bird and animal patterned fabrics of the Han period we are here confronted with a predominance of repetitive medallion-ornamented silks embodying such characteristic Sassanian motifs as confronted winged beasts, birds or lions. The medallion is delineated by a pearl border or perhaps a floral scroll, these often incorporating a vine-leaf pattern. Alternatively the design may be less rigid and based on an over-all pattern of floral medallions, with infilling naturalistic motifs comprising floral, bird and animal subjects. Another favourite Sassanian theme, widely adopted on Tʻang textiles, is the hunting scene with huntsman mounted on his steed at full pace and turning backwards to face his prey. This particular theme, in medallion form enclosed by a pearl border, is represented on the famous fragment of a banner, formerly in the Hōryūji temple at Nara and now in the Imperial Household Museum, Tokyo.

A large number of similarly inspired woven fragments, recovered by Sir Aurel Stein from the 'Thousand Buddha Cave' (Chʻien-fo-tʻung) at Tun-huang, illustrate the wide variety of decorative patterns employed on these textiles. Although of Sassanian inspiration, there is no doubt about the Chinese character of the interpretation of the designs on these fragments of banners, coats and shoes. Examples from the Stein expeditions are preserved in the British Museum and the Victoria and Albert Museum.

Similar influences are detectable in the designs applied to Tʻang resist-dyed textiles (mainly silks), a technique which on the evidence of surviving material first appeared in China during the 6th to 7th centuries. Apart from the considerable quantities recovered by Stein at Tun-huang, which generally featured floral motifs and medallions of types associated with the woven fragments, pieces preserved in the Shōsōin show a refreshingly informal approach to design. Outstanding are the panels, probably from a screen, featuring an elephant and bird beneath a tree, interspersed with naturalistic elements such as flowers, plants and tufts of grass. Not being restricted to the common medallion form there is a breadth to these designs which perhaps indicates the freedom permitted by the particular technique. Closer to the Sassanian-inspired woven ideal is the rampant lion within a floral medallion printed on a fragment found in Chinese Turkestan and preserved in the Fogg Museum, Boston.

To complete the picture of an expanding and experimenting industry during the Tʻang era, examples of embroidery displaying a new range of stitch techniques have survived. The most outstanding example is the half life-size picture of Śākyamuni Buddha, recovered by Stein from Tun-huang and now in the British Museum, which is executed in satin and chain stitches. New techniques introduced during the Tʻang included embroidery with metal threads, in which the gold and silver threads were laid on the silk and then tacked down with couching silks.

Sung Dynasty (960–1279). Much of our knowledge of Han and Tʻang textiles was obtained from examples excavated from sites along the ancient trade routes through central Asia. The more introverted Sung court was less concerned with commercial associations with the West than with the re-establishment of traditional Confucian ideals. Also Buddhism was on the wane in China and the flow of monks and followers along these routes lessened considerably. Thus these arid cemetery sites fell into disuse. For evidence of the textile industry in China at this time we have to look, therefore, at remnants preserved principally in China and Japan, and above all at the mounts supporting old Sung or earlier paintings.

A distinct change in the character of the decoration is the outstanding feature of Sung textiles, for no longer do Western-inspired motifs predominate. The few woven brocades which have survived are ornamented with floral patterns—peonies, lotus, camelia—of the types which characterize Sung ceramic design. Such elements also feature in Sung embroideries, although the largest surviving body of such material suggests that they were inspired directly by paintings. This was to become in the later Ming and Chʻing periods a familiar occurrence, the embroiderers copying the more typically Chinese compositions such as landscapes, bird and flower paintings. The satin stitch was almost exclusively employed on Sung embroideries and the couched gold and silver thread largely abandoned.

The most significant development in textile technique during the Sung Dynasty was that of *kʻo-ssŭ*, literally 'cut silk' but in fact silk TAPESTRY. Woven in the same way as European GOBELIN tapestries, this fine technique was to become one of the major achievements of the Chinese silk industry and there are endless references in Chinese literature to the fineness and beauty of *kʻo-ssŭ*. Small floral figured fragments retrieved by Stein and le Coq from central Asian sites suggest that the technique was a Tʻang innovation, although it has subsequently been suggested that these are not of Chinese but Uighur origin. These are supplemented by fragments, preserved in the Kyōōgokuk-ji, Kyoto, of a priest's robe of *kʻo-ssŭ*, and reputedly of 9th-c. date. Although there can be no doubt as to the nature of the technique, the comparative fineness of the weave and the informal fluent naturalistic designs in a thoroughly Chinese style contrast with the formalized Western-inspired designs which characterize

Embroidered picture of Sākyamuni Buddha from the 'Cave of a Thousand Buddhas'. Tun-huang. (Recovered by Sir Aurel Stein.) Ht. 244 cm. T'ang Dynasty, 618–906. (B.M.)

Fragment of woven silk from the 'Cave of a Thousand Buddhas'. Tun-huang. (Recovered by Sir Aurel Stein.) T'ang Dynasty, 618–906. (B.M.)

Fragment of *k'o-ssŭ* (silk tapestry). 21·95 cm × 34·29 cm. Sung Dynasty, 10th–12th c. (Textile Mus. of the District of Columbia, Washington)

K'o-ssŭ panel with phoenixes amid peony, magnolia and cherry trees. 299 cm × 208 cm. K'ang-hsi period, 1622–1722. (Met. Mus. of Art, New York)

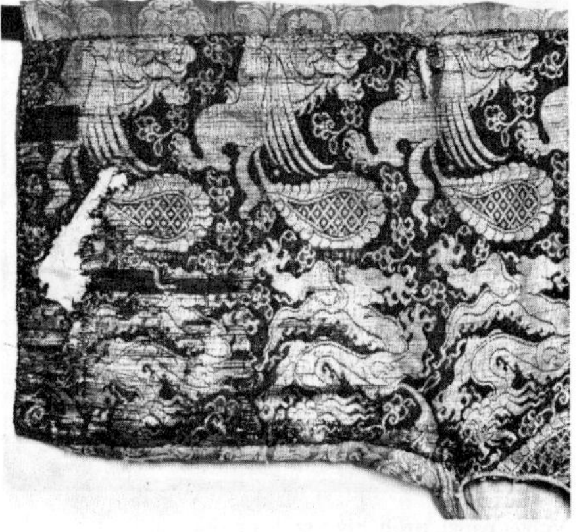

Sleeve of a dalmatic brocaded with 'strap-gold' on a red ground. Yüan Dynasty, 14th c. (Kunstindustrimus., Copenhagen)

Velvet panel, probably a table or altar cloth. 160·02 cm × 50·80 cm. (V. & A. Mus., 18th c.)

Empress's dragon robe embroidered with coloured silks, gold thread, seed pearls and coral beads on yellow silk. Ht. 144·78 cm. (V. & A. Mus., 19th c.)

K'o-ssŭ panel with mandarin ducks amid lotus plants and landscape. 60·06 cm × 39·37 cm. Ming Dynasty, 15th *c.* (V. & A. Mus.)

T'ang textile design. Also the first appearance of the word *k'o-ssŭ* in literary texts is in the Sung and it is from that period that a number of fragments survive which clearly illustrate the technique. A group of pieces ornamented in similar style with floral motifs, birds and rabbits represent the main body of material. The palmettes form floral patterns and surprised but immobile birds are clearly inspired by the incised ornament decorating T'ang three-coloured earthenware dishes. When compared with the extreme refinement of later Ming and early Ch'ing *k'o-ssŭ* the relative coarseness of these weaves suggests that the technique was still in the early stages of development. Somewhat finer is the peony-ornamented piece attached to the mount of the famous Ku K'ai-chih scroll in the British Museum. The colours of this *k'o-ssŭ*, principally shades of blue, green and yellow, complement the purples, blues and yellows of the former group.

Yüan (1279–1368) and *Ming* (1368–1644) *Dynasties.* The advent of the Mongol Yüan Dynasty re-established the considerable trade links between China and the West. Indeed many of the surviving Yüan textiles have been preserved in Western ecclesiastical institutions, where they were imported for use as vestments. This resurgence of trade also witnessed the re-adoption of Western, principally Islamic, ornament.

Yüan embroidery seems to be virtually unknown, and the majority of surviving pieces are woven as brocades where the wefts 'float' on the reverse side, selvedge to selvedge, except where they are required to form the pattern on the positive side. Much Yüan weaving also used 'strap-gold', strips of leather with one gilt side, although these were soon replaced with gilt paper strips. The strong Islamic flavour to the designs of these brocades is illustrated in the portion of a dalmatic preserved in the Kunstindustrimuseum, Copenhagen. More characteristically Chinese are the patterns embodying *shou* (long life) symbols with cloud scrolls, ornamenting silk damasks which were found in the Near East and Egypt in particular. By association with other excavated material these textiles may be dated to the 14th c.

Early in the Ming period trade with the West declined and it was not until the middle of the 16th c. that activities recommenced. From that time on Chinese textiles were imported into Europe in ever increasing quantities. Late Ming brocades and damasks were widely used in European ecclesiastical establishments for vestments and it has been noted that late in the 17th c. even Russian flags were made from Chinese damasks. The export silks also display changing decorative attitudes and we see both typical Chinese subjects such as the eight Taoist Immortals, cranes and phoenixes as well as designs clearly inspired by European ideals.

K'o-ssŭ always maintained a totally Chinese character and in the Ming period a distinctive '*k'o-ssŭ* style' evolved. Technically the process was improved and the weave made noticeably finer. At the same time designs became more complex and the undertakings more ambitious. In the *Ko Ku Yao Lun*, an early Ming chronicle on the arts and connoisseurship, there is a reference to 'a dance-carpet (of *k'o-ssŭ*) over three metres wide, evenly and tightly woven and very thick'. However, generally it seems that the loom widths for *k'o-ssŭ* were comparatively modest, usually less than 61 centimetres. The patterns on Ming *k'o-ssŭ* are varied and colourful, but always utterly in the Chinese taste. Landscapes were popular subjects, perhaps inspired by contemporary or earlier paintings. Another favourite theme was birds, usually the phoenix or mandarin duck, amid highly stylized cloud and landscape forms.

In general Ming embroidery also reflects a conscientiously Chinese culture. In place of the Sassanian-inspired floral scrolls and medallions of T'ang embroidery those which survive from the Ming display traditional Chinese themes.

Many fragments of larger hangings, possibly originally screen panels or hanging scrolls in imitation of paintings, are preserved in Western collections. These again adopt Chinese themes; those based on paintings are generally traditional landscape scenes whilst those possibly from screens are often embroidered with common mythological subjects: the Taoist Immortals, cranes, phoenixes and the symbolism of longevity and prosperity. Buddhist embroideries which, on the basis of literary references and the large hanging in the British Museum, had formed an important category of earlier (T'ang and pre-T'ang) embroidered material, do not survive from the Yüan and Ming periods. Perhaps this is evidence of the declining fortunes of the faith in China.

Embroidery techniques clearly developed considerably during the Ming period and a group of mandarin squares, or badges of rank worn by the mandarins on their outer coats (*p'u-fu*), have been preserved and illustrate the wide range of stitches and threads used at that time.

Gold thread, produced by winding strips of gold-leaf around a fine silk thread, secured by couching silks, was widely used on these squares particularly for the principal motif—in such cases the bird or animal representative of the rank (civil and military respectively). The satin stitch remained the fundamental embroidery process, but was supplemented by the 'long and short' stitch, which provided shading, the stem stitch for definition and a kind of 'surface' satin stitch employing floats of floss silk. This last technique was often subsequently couched, sometimes in a criss-cross pattern, to provide large areas of the same colour with a convincing, but textured, evenness. Another innovation was 'padding', whereby certain prominent elements such as the eyes of the principal motif were padded with pieces of cloth and subsequently embroidered with satin stitches.

Ch'ing Dynasty (1644–1911). The enormous amount of material surviving from the Ch'ing Dynasty, albeit most of it from the 19th c., provides us with a comprehensive picture of the wide-ranging textile industry which existed in China during this period. The established weaving techniques, polychrome or twill weaves, damasks and brocades, all continued and to these was added velvet weaving. This technique was probably introduced late in the Ming Dynasty although no surviving examples can assuredly be ascribed to such a date. Many of the earliest extant Chinese velvets now preserved in Western collections are comparatively short runners, 130–150 centimetres long and *c.* 16 centimetres in width, which were almost certainly table- or altar-cloths. These again retain characteristically Chinese décor, mainly floral scrolls of peony, lotus and chrysanthemum. The sumptuous blues and reds which predominate reflect the richness and sophistication of the technique. Later in the dynasty, in the 19th c., the definition of the pattern was obtained by cutting away the pile, leaving just the design in relief. These cut velvets were widely used on later 19th-c. ladies' robes and jackets.

Chinese decorative style also dominated *k'o-ssŭ* during the Ch'ing period. Continuing without interruption from the preceding Ming Dynasty these tapestry-woven silks were produced in ever increasing quantities, but retained their exclusive character. Early Ch'ing *k'o-ssŭ* illustrates typical themes: phoenixes in landscape settings, dragons, floral patterns and mythological scenes and figures. The technique seems to have reached its apogee early in the Ch'ien Lung period at the beginning of the 18th c. At this time the occasional introduction of gold thread as the background gave added richness to an already highly sophisticated weave.

From *c.* the middle of the 18th c. a slight decline in the quality of the finish is detectable. The smallest details, hitherto always woven into the over-all pattern, were then painted in. Although many later 18th-c. *k'o-ssŭ* panels continued to be entirely woven, on some examples the detail such as foliage and facial features on figures, was painted in. As the over-all quality deteriorated in the 19th c. so the amount of painting increased. The weave became coarser and the colours poorer. Many small panels modelled on those for table screens are preserved in the West and these use a sombre grey background to landscape scenes with figures, usually on horseback, illustrating subjects from popular legends. In such pieces, produced in quantity, all the quality and sophistication of late Ming and early Ch'ing *k'o-ssŭ* is lost. A glance at the reverse side shows just how much of the detail is painted in.

Perhaps the widest variety of style and ornament in Ch'ing textiles is to be seen in the embroideries. The majority of European commissions also appear to have been for embroidered material, and certainly most of the textiles which were made clearly to European or Western tastes were embroidered. In Western museums and private collections are preserved examples of the whole enormous range of embroidered hangings, screen panels, hanging scrolls and above all costume and costume accessories. The range of stitches and techniques exceeds those of the Ming: couched gold thread, satin, stem, long and short stitches and Peking knots. Early in the 19th c. there developed the custom of further embellishing embroideries with seed pearls, coral beads and bird feathers (principally the peacock). As innovation became of greater concern than quality more eccentric devices were employed to catch the eye, such as exaggerated padding, varieties of metal threads and metal or glass beads and discs.

Small knots, the precursor of the Peking stitch, were first encountered on some Han fragments from Noin Ula. The technique subsequently disappeared from the embroidery repertory until it intermittently appeared in Ming and early Ch'ing embroideries. But it was not until the 18th c. that this stitch came to be widely used. The distinctive appearance of Peking knot embroideries, permitting dense and well-defined areas of colour with a variable texture, gave rise to much legend concerning its execution: that it was so fine it caused blindness and that it was banned by Imperial edict—hence the term 'forbidden stitch' often applied to it. No edict containing such a proscription has ever come to light, however.

Silk gauze was also widely used in addition to silk and satin as the base material for embroidery. As the stitches are obliged to follow the course of the weave a distinctive, rather squared, appearance is obtained. The principal stitch employed in embroideries on gauze was the tent stitch, consisting of horizontal lines of very small stitches climbing diagonally across the gauze at the point where warp and weft interlace.

The Development of the Industry. The earliest pictorial representations of the textile industry in China are provided by stone reliefs, of Han date, depicting figures at work on draw-looms and at spinning-wheels. The consistency of the loom width of woven Han silks, *c.* 50 cm, leads us to believe that these early polychrome weaves were produced in state-controlled factories. Literary references imply that the basic plain silk was collected from the population as tribute.

The same kind of state control over the silk industry existed during the T'ang and Sung Dynasties, and again the consistency in loom width and in the decorative patterns suggests this. There is little information available, however, concerning the organization of the industry at that time or the location of the main workshops.

Literary records of the Ming period provide us with a clearer picture of the textile industry in China from the 14th to the 17th centuries, particularly with regard to silk. The *T'ien-kung k'ai-wu*, a text on basic industries, states, for example, that the Ming Imperial Weaving

Factories were in Hangchou (Chekiang province), Suchou and Nanking (both in Kiangsu). The draw-looms evidently increased in size and capacity, as the author of the same text describes one used in the making of brocades for dragon robes as being 4·5 metres high. Accuracy in dyeing was also demanded by the Imperial court, for the varying shades of the yellow of their robes denoted rank.

The principal yellow dyes were obtained from the sumac tree, the gardenia and the Amur cork tree; the principal red dyes from the safflower (a type of thistle), sapan wood and the madder plant; the blue dyes from types of indigo plants, mainly the 'Dyers' Knotweed' which grew in Manchuria and parts of north China. These dyes were also used during the succeeding Chʻing period until the introduction of chemical (aniline) dyes in the early 1860s.

Although under foreign, Manchu, rule, the silk industry during the Chʻing period continued to be organized in the traditional Chinese manner. The Imperial Weaving and Dyeing Office was situated in Peking and controlled the factories in the southern coastal provinces. As the demand for export silks increased so did the number of factories, inevitably outside state control. It was this situation together with a weakening Imperial House which resulted in the eventual breakdown of state control and the making of official dragon-figured silks, mainly for robes, in private workshops.

For native consumption cotton was by far the most important product, grown principally in the Yangtze and Yellow river basins. In the north and the far west wool was produced as early as the Han period. In Mongolia both camel and sheep wool was made, whilst in the west it was obtained from sheep. Fragments of wool pile carpets were recovered by Stein from the central Asian sites which betray strong Western influences in the decorative patterns. Woollen products, however, never acquired the kind of state and imperial patronage which fostered the silk industry in China. Both wool and cotton were evidently considered to be lowly utilitarian products suited to the inhabitants of those areas where they were most readily available—far away from the metropolitan centres.

19. CARPETS. With their ornamental repertory of flowers, butterflies, mythical beasts, frets, waves and symbolic characters and their soft harmonies of yellow, blue, apricot and rose, the carpets of China give expression to Chinese decorative taste in an unusual medium. Of various sizes and types—one variety is designed to enwrap architectural columns—they are usually coarsely knotted with the Sena knot, sometimes in silk. A technical procedure peculiar to them is that of clipping the pile on the outlines of the pattern motifs in order to give them smoother contours and an effect of slight relief. A few rugs have been doubtfully assigned to the Ming period, but most are of comparatively recent date. Similar rugs are made in adjacent territories and westwards to the extreme boundaries of Tibet and Sinkiang, where, as Kashgar, Tarkand and Samarkand rugs, they show a slight admixture of Persian and Turcoman elements. See also CARPETS AND RUGS.

20. COSTUME. Clothing has been the most important use of textiles, though late Chou documents are known to have been written with ink and brush on silk after drafts had first been composed on wooden or bamboo slips. Later silk was extensively used for painting and for mounting paintings, while brocades provided the precious material for sutra covers, book-cases, and boxes for *objets d'art*. Silk tapestries were used for festooning chariots, making flags and banners and internally decorating residences of the rich with hangings, framed folding screens and cosy wrappings.

The basic Chinese costume seems to have been established by the 6th c. B.C., and consisted of a two-piece outfit: a long belted tunic topped by a jacket. The design was the same for all classes and both sexes, but the materials, colours and the refinements of detail varied considerably in accordance with the wearer's social position. Dresses of various grades of court officials were already strictly controlled by Han sumptuary laws. A sizeable stock of silk robes was required for court and ceremonial functions, for which most men wore additional outer garments of mystic colours and symbolic patterns. The ceremonial garments (robe and skirt) made for the imperial sacrifices were decorated with the Twelve Symbols (the first six painted on the robe and the other six embroidered on the skirt in the traditional style). These are sacred symbols that go back to antiquity and are first described in the late Chou *Book of History* (*Shu-ching*). The Twelve Symbols, some of which occur alone in other media than textiles, are: Sun, Moon, Constellation, Mountains, Dragon, Pheasant, Bronze Sacrificial Cups, Water-Weed, Grain, Fire, Axe and the *Fu* symbol. Sun, Moon and Constellation were symbols of enlightenment and Heaven, the Mountains of protection and earth. The Dragon was symbolic of adaptability on account of the transformations of which it is capable. The Pheasant was symbolic of literary refinement and the two together represented animals and birds, or animate nature. The pair of Bronze Sacrificial Cups symbolized filial piety, the Water-Weed purity, Grain ability to feed the people, and Fire brilliance: these four with the Mountains represented the Five Elements (*wu hsing*): Metal, Water, Fire, Wood and Earth. The Axe represented the power to punish, and the *Fu* symbol the power to judge. These symbols were often executed in textiles in the five primary colours (*wu sê*)—blue, yellow, red, white and black—and corresponded to the Five Elements, Seasons and Directions. Only the emperor was entitled to display all twelve, the last two being his special emblems of authority.

When all twelve symbols appear on robes they assume cosmic significance and give a symbolic interpretation of the Universe (e.g. the 12-symbol imperial robes of the Chʻing period). The Ming and Chʻing official robes were further embellished with 'Mandarin squares', badges of rank which were first used decoratively in Tʻang times. The Ming squares were broad and made in one piece, generally from *kʻo-ssŭ*, while the Manchus, who were content with embroidery, used them in pairs back and front, splitting the front panel down the centre to fit their open riding jackets. Official regulations prescribed bird motifs (symbolizing literary elegance) for civilian officials, and animals (suggesting fierce courage) for the military. Though the magnificent woven and embroidered garments vanished with the fall of the Manchu Dynasty, their counterparts may still be seen today in the traditional Chinese theatre.

References to the essential literature are given in the body of the text. The reader may find the following references to the Bibliography also of interest. General: 119, 254, 257, 288, 290, 460, 586, 689, 810, 812. Ceramics: 31, 289, 315, 323, 448, 449, 673, 925, 930. Lacquer: 370, 543, 779, 800. Jade: 340, 341, 353, 635, 652, 938. Textiles: 11, 122, 123, 238, 293, 294, 611, 678, 767, 768, 814.

The Connoisseur for January 1975 has up-to-date information about recent discoveries in China.

CHINESE TASTE. Chinese wares, notably SILK, PORCELAIN and LACQUER, have long fascinated Europeans as luxury articles. They have been imported from Roman times and attempts to reproduce or to copy them go back at least as far as the early centuries of the Christian era. A fragment of textile decorated with a design in Han style (206 B.C.–A.D. 220) was found at Dura Europos (3rd c. A.D.). Certain motifs such as DRAGONS, PHOENIXES, peacocks used in BYZANTINE times were of Chinese origin; phoenixes of Chinese derivation occur in illuminated manuscripts of the 10th c. and on an 11th-c. ivory casket in the Cathedral Treasury at Troyes. During the Middle Ages contact with China by way of the interior of Asia was always maintained and through travellers' stories 'Cathay' acquired a romantic and legendary aura. Christopher Columbus sailed with the object of coming by sea to the Kingdom of Cathay with its fabulous riches, about which he had learned from Marco Polo's account of his travels in the territories of the Grand Khan, and when he landed in America Columbus believed he had come to a land contiguous with China. After the discovery of the sea route round Africa and the first landing of the Portuguese on Chinese soil in 1515 trade with the Far East expanded. During the 16th c. the bulk of the China trade was in the hands of the Portuguese. In the 17th c. the East Asiatic market was controlled by the Dutch and the Dutch East India Company operated with enormous success, increasing the volume of imports to meet a rapidly growing demand. In the 2nd half of the same century the English also were moving their trade from the Near East to India and China and in the 18th c. the English East India Company displaced the Dutch in the van of the Far Eastern trade. By comparison the trade of the French Compagnie des Indes Orientales, founded by Colbert in 1664, was insignificant and the greater part of her Chinese imports reached France by way of Holland.

Besides spices, etc. this trade consisted largely of luxury goods such as silks, porcelain, CHINTZES, lacquer, which came either direct from China or through Indian ports. By the 2nd half of the 17th c. these things were becoming an accepted adjunct to fashionable living and were exercising an important influence on European taste in interior decoration, furniture styles, ceramics and many of the other arts. The fashion for the 'Chinese Cabinet' particularly in the Netherlands is illustrated in the designs of Daniel Marot (1663–1752) showing lacquer panels lining the walls and serried rows of Chinese porcelain surrounding doors and chimney-piece. Inevitably attempts were made to copy the Chinese wares. JAPANNING strove to render the effect of lacquer, the tin-glazed earthenware of DELFT copied the late Ming blue and white porcelain and the eventual discovery of a hard-paste porcelain at MEISSEN in the early years of the 18th c. crowned a deliberate attempt to reproduce the qualities of Chinese porcelain. Even more pervasive in its influence upon taste was the vogue for Chinese decorative motifs, which led to the curious phenomenon of CHINOISERIE, a European style in the arts and crafts which reflected a romantic and fanciful notion of the Chinese. This in turn reacted upon Oriental production and in both India and China during the 18th and 19th centuries goods were manufactured specially for the Western market with designs adapted specifically for the Western idea of a romanticized Orient. (See also INDIA (TEXTILES); COTTON AND COTTON PRINTING.) It even happened that goods designed by Indian craftsmen for the Western 'China fashion' were exported from India to China as a novelty and Chinese craftsmen then began to produce goods for the European market with designs based upon these models.

Although the French were later than the Portuguese, Dutch, English and Spanish in entering the Chinese trade, Chinese motifs were an important if minor feature of French ROCOCO and French designers and craftsmen helped to spread the vogue for *chinoiserie* throughout Europe. Chinese porcelains and *objets d'art* were already being collected in France in the time of Mazarin and according to the description by La Fontaine in 1668 Chinese textiles adorned the Appartement du Roi at Versailles. The

Claydon House, Buckinghamshire, a property of the National Trust. Chinese room, alcove

Trianon de Porcelaine built by Louis le Vau (1612–70) in the park at Versailles (1670) became the prototype of Chinese pagodas, kiosks, etc. throughout Europe and the Chinese figures introduced by BÉRAIN into his ARABESQUES had widespread ramifications. The 'Chinese' panels painted by Jean-Antoine Watteau *c.* 1709 for the Cabinet du Roi in the Château de la Muette were engraved under the title *Figures chinoises et tartares* and the titles, if not the small prominence given to the figures in his designs for engraved arabesques, *Empereur chinois* and *Divinité chinoise*, witness the existence of a Chinese vogue. A more original concept of the gay and voluptuous Orient imbued the TAPESTRY designs of François BOUCHER and his décor for Noverre's ballet *Les Fêtes chinoises*, drawings for which were engraved and published as *Livre des chinois*, as also his easel paintings such as *The Chinese Lovers* and *Chinese Fishing Party* (1742). A number of designers and decorators of the Rococo by their pattern-books, engravings and executed works spread the fashion for *chinoiserie* widely outside the boundaries of France. We may instance the *chinoiseries* of Christophe Huet (d. 1759) at the Château of Champs in Brie, the lacquer panels of De Cotte's designs for the Chambre du lit pour les bains at Bonn (1717) and designs by OPPENORD, Boffrand (1667–1754), Jacques de Lajour (1686–1761) and others. The vogue for *chinoiseries* was carried to Germany by François CUVILLIÈS and the prints and designs of Jean Baptiste Pillement (1727–1808) were popular in several countries. Many of his designs were included in *The Ladies' Amusement* (1760), which was a source-book for engravings by Simon François RAVENET, Robert HANCOCK and other designers for TRANSFER PRINTING on BATTERSEA ENAMELS and English blue and white china.

Although in general the NEO-CLASSICAL movement which predominated in the latter part of the 18th c. was unfavourable to the fancifulness of *chinoiserie*, Chinese taste nevertheless held its own in England in architecture and interior decoration as a romantic and exotic relief from Classical severity until in the REGENCY it had become a recognized constituent of what was known as the Picturesque. Among his pattern-books for domestic architecture William HALFPENNY published *Rural Architecture in the Chinese Taste* (1750–2) and *Chinese and Gothic Architecture Properly Ornamented* (1752), both of which were much used by provincial craftsmen. CHIPPENDALE's *Director* (1754) contained illustrations of both Chinese and Gothic styles, and a bedstead from Badminton is an excellent example of his Chinese manner (V. & A. Mus.). In France the furniture of M. Carlin (d. 1785) and other ÉBÉNISTES was frequently embellished by panels of Oriental lacquer. In Germany David Roentgen (1743–1807) was fond of depicting Chinese scenes in MARQUETRY. In Regency England Chinese interiors were included in such guides to taste as Thomas HOPE's *Household Furniture and Interior Decoration* (1807) and George Smith's *Collection of Designs for Household Furniture and Interior Decoration* (1808) and his *The Cabinet-maker and Upholsterer's Guide* (1828). Two engravings of the Prince Regent's Chinese Room at Carlton House were included in SHERATON's *The Cabinet-maker's and Upholsterer's Drawing Book* (1791–4). The fashion for imported hand-painted WALLPAPERS depicting flowering shrubs with birds and scenes from Chinese life lasted through the 2nd half of the 18th and early 19th centuries. *Chinoiseries* such as the well known WILLOW PATTERN were a favourite feature of English transfer-painted blue and white porcelain.

The most serious attempt at an introduction of a Chinese style was made by Sir William Chambers (1723–96), who as a young man travelled to China in the service of the Swedish East India Company and again in later life went to the Far East as architect to the king. His ideas were embodied in *Designs of Chinese Buildings, Furniture, etc.* (1757) and *Essay on Oriental Gardening* (1772). The outstanding instances of a Chinese revival at this time were the interior decoration of the Royal Pavilion at Brighton and Chambers's Chinese Garden at Kew. The latter was the first Chinese garden in Europe and set a fashion, which in France became popular from 1760 as the 'Chinese-English' style. The pagoda at Kew was copied at Het Loo in Holland, by the Chinese tower in the Englischer Garten at Munich and on an estate of the Duc de Choiseul at Chanteloup on the Loire. In Germany the Chinese garden came into fashion somewhat later than in France. Chiefly responsible for its introduction was the landscape gardener F. L. Sekell, who was sent by Max Josef IV in 1773 to study the new style of garden-craft under Chambers. The most ambitious example was the 'Chinese village' of Moulang established by the Landgrave of Kassel beside the lake in the grounds of the Schloss Wilhelmshöhe. In Germany too the Chinese garden was made the theme of a special aesthetic philosophy of its own: in a work *On Chinese Gardens* (1773) Ludwig A. Unzer treats them as the model of garden art and C. S. E. Hirschfeld, Professor of Aesthetics at Kiel, in a discussion of the art of gardens (*Theorie der Gartenkunst*, 1779–85) said: 'Of all the gardens of all the different parts of the world, none has excited more attention than the Chinese, or that which has been so charmingly described as such.' An Encyclopedia completed in 1787 had as its object 'to promote the progress of Garden-craft, since everyone knows that the English garden is only an imitation of the Chinese'. But in England reaction had already set in. William Mason had published his poem *The English Garden* in 1767 and Humphrey REPTON stood forth as the champion of a natural simplicity in landscape gardening against the affectation of the Chinese style.

160, 412, 460, 618, 689.

CHINOISERIE. The term *chinoiserie* refers to something more specific than the general spread of CHINESE TASTE in many countries of Europe from the 2nd half of the 17th c. to the early 19th c. as a result of the expansion of Chinese and Far Eastern trade. It is not properly applied to deliberate attempts to reproduce Chinese goods, such as JAPANNING, the blue and white earthenware of Delft and the hard-paste porcelain of MEISSEN. It is often used to refer to the inclusion in European art works of Chinese or pseudo-Chinese decorative motifs such as the Chinese dragons of Bernard Toro (1672–1731) and Gabriel-Germain Boffrand (1667–1754), the Chinese figures of BÉRAIN and François BOUCHER and the SINGERIES of Christophe HUET, Claude AUDRAN III, Claude Gillot (1673–1732) and Gilles-Marie OPPENORD. These motifs were popular during the ROCOCO and RÉGENCE periods in interior decoration and over a wide field of decorative arts even when the work of art in its general style had little or nothing that was Chinese about it. But perhaps the term *chinoiserie* is most appropriately applied to a style in European arts and crafts that reflects the fanciful notions of China which from the Middle Ages have been fostered by travellers' tales and a rather imperfect knowledge of imported textiles, porcelain and *objets d'art*. The romantic concepts of an idealized 'Cathay' have varied from age to age, often bearing so little resemblance to the real thing that the European taste for Chinese goods, made effective through merchants and importers, influenced the Chinese craftsmen who were manufacturing for the Western market and caused them to adapt their designs specially for this taste.

The prevalence of *chinoiserie* in the decorative arts was associated with a literary interest in the Far East and books published during the 17th c., mainly in Holland, created a halo of mystery and legend while their illustrations provided a source of 'Chinese' ornamental motifs. Illustrated descriptions of Dutch embassies to China such as Nieuhoff's *Embassy to the Emperor of China* (1655) and that of J. de Kayser in 1665 were copied by French engravers. A *Novus Atlas Sinensis de Martino Martini*, published in Vienna in 1655, had a wide circulation and influenced Athanasius Kircher's *China monumentis qua sacris qua profanis illustrata* (1667), which was translated into French and remained for decades the favourite authority of enthusiasts for the Chinese. Based very largely upon such sources engravers such as Matthias Beilter in Holland and Valentin Sezenius in Denmark produced patterns of Oriental designs for decorative artists and the same sources were used by the great French designers of the Rococo period.

160, 412.

CHINTZ. The word was originally 'chints', plural of Hindi *chīnt* (vernacular *chīte*), a vari-coloured cloth. This transliteration was treated as a singular with the plural 'chintzes'. It was originally applied to the painted CALICOES imported from India. The term is currently used for cotton cloths fast-dyed in a number of colours and usually glazed. The Portuguese term was *pintado*, meaning a painted or coloured or spotted cloth. This word was adopted into English from the early 18th c. The French term *indienne* was applied both to imported chintzes and to home-printed calicoes.

The Indian chintz is the result of many elaborate stages of resist-dyeing, mordant painting, plain painting, dyeing and much washing and bleaching.

See COTTON AND COTTON PRINTING; INDIA (TEXTILES).

CHIPPENDALE, THOMAS THE ELDER (1718–79). English cabinet-maker and furniture designer, born at Otley, Yorkshire. He set up in business in London and in 1753 or 1754 moved to 60 St. Martin's Lane, where he went into partnership with James Rannie (d. 1766). In 1771 he took Thomas Haig as partner, and the firm was styled Chippendale, Haig & Co. He became a member of the Society of Arts in 1760. In 1754 he published a pattern-book: *The Gentleman and Cabinet-maker's Director, being a Collection of the most Elegant and Useful Designs of Household Furniture in the most Fashionable Taste* (2nd edn. 1755, 3rd edn. with additional plates, 1759–62). Credit for the *Director* designs was at one time given to M. LOCK and H. COPLAND (see F. Kimball and E. Donnell, 'Creators of the Chippendale Style', *Metropolitan Museum Studies*, May and Nov. 1929), but recent research and close study of the drawings confirm Chippendale's main responsibility. The practice of publishing furniture designs was known in Europe from *c.* 1550, but Chippendale's seems to have been the first work on such a grand scale and the first to be entirely devoted to furniture design. The 1st and 2nd editions had 160 plates and the 3rd had 200, mainly in ROCOCO taste but with designs for two subsidiary styles, Chinese (see CHINESE TASTE) and GOTHIC. It is to this pattern-book that Chippendale owes his great reputation as the originator of the version of the English Rococo which goes by his name. It does not now appear that he was outstanding as a practical craftsman or carver among his gifted contemporaries. Rather he was an organizer with a fine sense of business acumen. During his closing years (1770–9) he produced MARQUETRY and inlaid pieces in the NEO-CLASSICAL style of Robert ADAM, and this may well represent his best work.

As a stylistic term current in the late 19th and 20th centuries, 'Chippendale' describes English furniture made during the 1750s and 1760s broadly in the Rococo style. Although business accounts of the firm exist, it has proved difficult to identify pieces made in Chippendale's shop and to distinguish them from the work of contemporaries. Authenticated furniture at Nostell Priory, Yorkshire, from 1766 to 1770, includes pieces in Rococo style. Furniture at Harewood House, Yorkshire, *c.* 1772, represents his later style and there is growing proof that he himself (and not Adam) designed much of the furniture in Adam's houses, as at Harewood and Mersham-le-Hatch, Kent. Increasing documentary evidence reveals that Chippendale had an extensive and influential clientele, though he never received a royal appointment.

His eldest son, THOMAS CHIPPENDALE THE YOUNGER (1749–1822), was a partner in the firm of Chippendale & Haig, 1779–96, in succession to his father. The firm was made bankrupt in 1804 but was reopened and a second shop was established at 57 Haymarket in 1814. In 1821 the premises were moved to 42 Jermyn Street. The firm remained active and retained its reputation for high-quality workmanship. The younger Chippendale supplied furniture to Harewood House (1796–7) and to Stourhead (1795–1820). He was a member of the Society of Arts and exhibited paintings at the Royal Academy (1784–1801). He published a small *Book of Designs*, a copy of which is preserved in the Victoria & Albert Museum. His furniture provides excellent examples of restrained REGENCY taste of a high standard.

See also FURNITURE (ENGLISH; AMERICAN).

252, 361, 477, 814.

CHRÉTIEN, G. L. (1754–1811). French musician and silhouettist. He invented a portrait-cutting machine called the *physionotrace*, the original drawing for which is preserved in the Bibliothèque nationale, Paris. With this he made a large number of silhouette portraits, sometimes engraving them after cutting. See SILHOUETTE.

CHRONOMETER. The definition of this term varies in the different countries of Europe. In the United Kingdom it refers to a timekeeper specifically designed for use in a ship for finding longitude; such an instrument almost invariably employs a special detent escapement named the 'chronometer escapement' and in the U.K. a 'chronometer watch' is a watch which embodies this escapement, not often used in watches. On the Continent the term 'chronometer' is applied to any highly accurate portable timekeeper.

CHRYSOBERYL. A gemstone which in classical antiquity was named as if it were a yellow BERYL. It is now known to be a different stone, an aluminate of glucinum, related chemically to the SPINEL and structurally to the PERIDOT. It has a hardness index of 8½ on the MOHS SCALE.

Two varieties of chrysoberyl are especially prized. The rare 'alexandrite' was discovered in the 19th c. in the Urals on the birthday of the Tsar Alexander II, for whom it was named. By daylight it is bluish green and in artificial light it changes colour to an orange red. Also among the highly prized chrysoberyls is 'cat's-eye', which used to be called 'cymophane'. When the stone is highly polished its CHATOYANT quality is very distinct. It is harder, heavier and finer than 'cat's-eye' QUARTZ.

784, 921.

CHRYSOPRASE. See QUARTZ.

CHUBB, JEREMIAH, CHARLES and JOHN. English lock-makers who together invented and patented (1824, 1833, 1846, 1847) locks on the lever principle which proved the most successful mechanism for the construction of a lock that can be operated only by the corresponding key. They also incorporated the 'detector' design, whereby in case of attempts to open the lock by a false key or a picklock the lever nearest the lock bolt functions to block the mechanism so that when the true key is inserted it must be turned in the reverse direction to unblock the mechanism before it can operate. Although many improvements have been made since the original invention, the lever principle remains basic for this kind of lock. See LOCKS AND KEYS.

CINQUEFOIL. See FOIL.

CITRINE. See QUARTZ.

CLASSICAL. The term 'classical', which is widely used of all the arts, has historical, descriptive and evaluative connotations. In the evaluative or qualitative sense a work is said to be 'classical' as being an excellent or typical example of a specific style or period. From the 1st c. A.D. the adjective *classicus* (lit. 'belonging to a *classis* or division of the Roman people') acquired the meaning 'of the highest class', 'superior', 'authoritative'. Thus Aulus Gellius (2nd c. A.D.) wrote: 'classicus adsiduusque aliquis scriptor, non proletarius.' Among its other significations the word 'classical' has tended to retain implications of excellence. From the turn of the 18th c. and the beginning of the 19th c. 'classical' began to be used in a descriptive sense with reference to the restrained and balanced style of Greek and Roman literature and art and indicated a formal and orderly style as opposed to the more emotional and effusive manner favoured by the Romantic movement. In its historical sense 'classical' has referred primarily to the art and literature of Greek and Roman antiquity generally. Since the latter part of the 19th c. art historians have applied the word more specifically to Greek art produced in the period between the Persian wars (481–479 B.C.) and the death of Alexander the Great (323 B.C.), distinguishing the art of this period from that of the earlier 'Archaic' and the later 'Hellenistic' periods. The use of 'classical' in this restricted sense also tended to carry with it implications that the art of this period was of outstanding excellence, that it displayed most typically the characteristics of order and balance and that it should be regarded as a standard by which the art of other periods could be judged.

CLAUDET, ANTOINE FRANÇOIS JEAN, F.R.S. (1797–1867). French-born photographer, who in 1827 set up as a glass importer in London. In 1839 he bought from Louis Jacques Mandé Daguerre the licence to practise the DAGUERREOTYPE process in Britain and in the Great Exhibition of 1851 he won the Council Medal for his daguerreotypes. He was himself a fertile inventor and improver of photographic processes. In 1840–1 he invented a method of accelerating the daguerreotype process by rendering the plate more sensitive with a combination of chlorine and iodine vapour and in 1841 he patented the first photographic darkroom light. In 1843 he took out a patent for a method of photo-etching by an electrotype process based on methods originated by the French physicist Hippolyte Fizeau. In 1848 he perfected a photographometer which was the prototype of the light meter and in 1848–9 he invented instruments for measuring the chemical focus of achromatic lenses and for measuring the speed of a lens. He made stereoscopic photographs of the royal family and in 1853 he was appointed Photographer-in-Ordinary to Queen Victoria. See also PHOTOGRAPHY.

297, 627.

CLAY. In its ubiquity no less than the variety of purposes which it serves clay has been one of the most useful of all substances in the technological progress of mankind. Because of its permanence objects fashioned from clay provide a major part of our information about early civilizations, while the fragility of some clay artefacts—such as CERAMICS—has led to their constant renewal and so enables archaeologists to trace the evolution of manners and customs and styles step by step from the discarded shards which remain in refuse tips.

1. USES. As a building material clay has been most widely used in the form of bricks and tiles. Sun-dried bricks have been found at the site of Jericho from the 8th millennium B.C. before pottery was made, and the Mesopotamian civilizations of Uruk, Eridu, Ur, etc. built with sun-dried bricks sometimes with an outer casing of burned brickwork. The Indus cultures of Mohenjo-daro and Harappa made invariable use of burnt brick in the 3rd millennium B.C. In Pre-Columbian America semi-subterranean houses began to be lined with sun-dried bricks, or adobe, instead of cobble-stones as in the Formative Period (*c.* 1250–850 B.C.) and adobe became the most general material of building, as it still is today in the native villages of many regions. In Europe the art of building with burnt bricks seems to have started with the Etruscans (Arretium). It was adopted by the Romans in the 1st c. B.C. and spread throughout the empire. The craft was lost in Europe with the collapse of the Roman empire and was reintroduced from the Near East by way of Flanders possibly in the 12th c. A.D. Building bricks were first known in England as 'Flanders tiles' and the word 'brick' did not come into common use until Tudor times. The processes of manufacture were regulated by Act of Parliament in 1477, when decorative bricklaying was popular. The craft was introduced into the U.S.A. *c.* 1600 and early examples of American brickwork are to be found at Richmond.

Clay tiles have been almost as widely used as bricks for building purposes. They have been used for roofs or floors, as decorative facing, and structurally. Roofing tiles are of three basic types. The Greeks from the 7th c. B.C. used a curved tile with a semicircular section overlapping the joints. This style has remained general in the Mediterranean area and a similar form was known in China from the Han Dynasty. Plain flat tiles have been used in central Europe, including Britain. Pantiles, transversely curved in an OGEE shape so that the overlap is part of the tile itself, are used in Japan and in Scandinavia. In the later Middle Ages, as towns increased in size, clay tiles were made compulsory for roofing in many places (A.D. 1212 in London) because of the danger of fire from wooden or thatch roofs.

The Roman use of concrete as a building material was made possible by a Greek invention of adding clay to limestone while it was being burnt to make mortar. The Romans also used clay tiles structurally in their characteristic concrete vaults. Clay tiles were laid over a wooden framework with smaller tiles overlapping the joints and some of the latter were stood on edge to prevent the concrete running down the curvature. Hollow fired-clay boxes and hollow earthenware jars were set into the concrete vaults to reduce the absolute weight. Similar rectangular hollow clay blocks were set in the walls to conduct hot air from under-floor central-heating systems.

The decorative use of glazed tiles to face indoor stoves, etc. (Russia, Poland, Germany, Scandinavia, the Low Countries) and the outside of buildings (Islam, Spain, Portugal, Central and South America) is an interesting craft.

Among the structural uses of clay mention must also be made of its employment for water and sewage systems by all advanced civilizations from those of the Indus Valley to modern salt-glazed pipes and fittings.

Among the primary uses of clay are included CERAMICS, which is the subject of a separate article, and its employment as a medium of artistic expression in the making of terracotta figures of all sorts and for the modelling of figures subsequently to be cast in bronze or other metals.

Clay tablets and cylinders were used by many early peoples for perpetuating writing and seals, and on these are enshrined the earliest written records of the human race.

In addition to these primary uses clay has other, secondary ones as an essential adjunct to various industries and crafts. Special heat-resistant clays called 'refractory clays' or 'fire-clays' are necessary to line the kilns in which ceramics are fired and furnaces of all kinds must be lined with a coating of refractory bricks. The iron and steel and oil industries, the gas and coke industry, and many others today are dependent upon refractory clays. Refractory clay is also used for making sparking-plugs for internal combustion engines. (For the special requirements of rocket and nuclear mechanics other substances, such as silicon carbide, or nitride and boron nitride are being developed.) The other important field in which modern technology requires special heat-resistant clays is in the electrical industry for the production of porcelain insulators.

To complete the story it should be mentioned that besides its many uses as an independent substance, clay as a filling or glazing material serves as an ingredient in many technologies, such as paper-making, linoleum, cheap textiles, insecticides and many others.

2. MATERIAL. Clay results from the decomposition by weathering of felspar, one of the three elements resulting from the breakdown of granitic and basaltic rock. It is made up of silica and alumina in composition with water and exists in two forms, known as primary and secondary clays. Primary clay, also called 'kaolin' and 'china clay', is mined in the original beds where it was formed in the absence of air. It is found in the Pyrenees, Limoges, central Europe (Saxony, Poland, Czechoslovakia, the Ukraine), the southern United States, China, south-west England and Brittany. Kaolin is white in appearance and insufficiently plastic for the purpose of the potter unless it is mixed with other materials. Chinese kaolin had greater plasticity than European and when mixed with a related felspathic rock (*petuntse*), which also served as a glaze, it formed the basis of the 'true' or 'hard-paste' porcelain. Secondary clays are those which have been carried by the action of rivers and waters away from the original beds and have acquired admixtures of various other minerals and colouring matters such as iron oxides. They form one of the principal ingredients of the earth's surface and occur everywhere except in deserts, coral islands and regions of mud such as the valley of the Mississippi. Secondary clays which have acquired little colouring matter and which therefore fire white or cream are called 'ball' clays. In general secondary clays require a certain amount of processing to remove impurities before they are suitable to be used in ceramics; often they are too slimy to hold a modelled shape and have to be mixed with other materials (including ground-up fired clay, or 'grog') to reduce their plasticity before being used by the potter. The very great differences in the quality, consistency and colour of secondary clays, and the different methods of processing them for use, are largely responsible for the characteristic qualities of the world's ceramic bodies.

Clay has a structure of minute flat hexagonal crystals, which slide about on each other like pieces of glass when lubricated by water. It is this which gives it its plasticity. In its natural state clay is usually composed of crystalline particles of vastly different sizes. This is particularly likely in primary clays since the natural processes by which secondary clays have been washed down tend to produce some degree of equalization as the larger particles are progressively deposited as sediment. Most clays, however, require 'levigation' before being used for finer work: this consists of a number of washings with sedimentation down a series of tubs, which has the effect of removing the particles of larger grain as well as foreign substances embedded in the clay. In modern china manufacture—and also of course in many other clay techniques—two or more kinds of clay are mixed and some substance such as calcined flint or chert is added. This process is called 'blunging' and is now done in a power-driven blunging machine. In essence the process consists of mixing the clays with water to the consistency of cream (called 'slip' at this stage) and then churning the liquids thoroughly together. Small particles of foreign matter are sieved out and iron particles, which might discolour the clay during firing, are removed with a magnet. After the surplus water has been forced out the clay must undergo a further process of 'slapping' or 'wedging' before it is ready for use. This consists of prolonged kneading and manipulation in order to eliminate air bubbles and secure uniform plasticity and regularity of grain, without which the clay might crack or burst in firing. This process was done with the feet in ancient Egypt; it was still done by hand in 19th-c. English china factories, each pile of clay being worked over several times a week for some three months. It is now done in a machine called a pug-mill—like a giant mincing-machine—from which the clay is extruded under pressure in an endless roll, which is cut up into slabs. In the United States a method of dry mixing is popular: impurities such as particles of sand and pyrites are removed by air flotation and the dry clay is shipped to the potteries in sealed bags.

Clay contains water both in solution and in chemical combination. Properly prepared clay, sufficiently moist, can be moulded into a required shape whether it be a pot in the craft of ceramics or a tile for building purposes. But if allowed to dry, the clay crumbles and the shape is lost. For this reason sculptors who model figures in clay for subsequent casting or firing keep the clay moist by covering it with damp cloths or by spraying. The shape is rendered permanent by firing in a kiln (or sometimes by sun-drying in the case of bricks). The effect of firing, after much of the water in solution has been dried out, is to drive out the water in chemical composition, leaving the clay form hard, permanent and no longer plastic. This stage is called 'biscuit'. When fired to the biscuit state clay bodies can be decorated, cut or incised, or covered with glaze. At higher temperatures clays vitrify, becoming impervious to liquid, and at a still higher temperature they collapse into slag. Since with many clays the gap between the temperature at which the clay vitrifies and the temperature of collapse is small, it is a common practice, after the pot has been fired to the biscuit state, to cover it with glaze which fuses with it and vitrifies at a lower temperature than that at which the clay itself would melt. The techniques involved are very complicated and form the essence of the craft of ceramics.

CLEMENT, WILLIAM (1633–1704). A leading English maker of fine LONG-CASE CLOCKS and a possible inventor of the anchor escapement. Clement was born in Rotherhithe, Surrey. At first an anchorsmith and blacksmith, he came to London and took up clock-making in 1671, his first products being TURRET CLOCKS. But he soon turned to long-case clocks and produced many fine examples, most of which employed the anchor escapement and his screw regulation of the pendulum, and many used the long $1\frac{1}{4}$-second pendulum which he favoured. He entered the Clockmakers' Company in 1677 and became its Master in 1694.

CLOCKS. Timekeepers represent an extremely interesting and intimate collaboration between craftsmanship and applied science. The skill of the craftsman was essential for the purpose of producing a mechanical device which would satisfy the requirements of accurate timekeeping and yet remain within the compass of convenience. The ingenuity of craftsmen contributed largely to the development of clocks and watches by a series of inventions improving the efficiency and reliability of the mechanism while having regard to practical convenience. On the other side of the picture, clocks came to be regarded as articles of fine furniture and watches as articles of personal jewellery so that both offered appropriate fields for the development of craftsmanship in over-all design and in decorative ornament.

The first mechanical clocks were the great structures of iron wheels mounted in open-work frames of forged iron which were set in the bell-towers of churches, abbeys or civic buildings and sounded the hours. These are known as turret clocks. They were driven by weights suspended inside the towers, and the ropes from which the weights hung were wound round wooden drums linked by a ratchet mechanism with the first toothed wheel of the clock movement. The earliest records of such clocks go back to the late 13th c. in Europe, but the earliest example that has survived is the clock of Salisbury Cathedral, which has been restored and is now in working condition in the nave of that cathedral. It has both going and striking trains, and there is strong evidence that it dates from 1386. The earliest clock with quarter chimes is that of Rouen, dating from 1389; and the Wells Cathedral clock of 1392, whose movement is now in the Science Museum, London, also chimes the quarters.

The earliest domestic clocks were similar structures on a smaller scale, with the wheel-work mounted in an iron cage resting on a stand or wall-bracket with driving weights hanging and the bell or bells mounted above, usually within a spire or dome-shaped frame. The time-keeping controller of these early clocks before the invention of the pendulum clock in the middle of the 17th c. was sadly lacking in regularity, and they were therefore inaccurate timekeepers. The main types of clocks are dealt with under their separate headings. See BRACKET CLOCKS, GOTHIC CLOCKS, LANTERN CLOCKS, LONG-CASE CLOCKS, MANTEL CLOCKS, SKELETON CLOCKS, TABLE CLOCKS. WATCHES are also dealt with under a separate heading, as are CHRONOMETERS. The following paragraphs serve merely to give a general account of the types and development of clocks, linking together the separate articles on this subject.

The Gothic style of domestic weight-driven clock persisted all over Europe until the end of the 16th c. In England and France it gave way in the 17th c. to the rather more refined lantern clock, of somewhat similar type but made of BRASS. The most important development in the design of clocks and their cases came in the same century with the introduction of the long-case clock, which stood on the floor, the movement being mounted on a tall wooden case inside which hung the weights. There was a wooden hood to protect the movement from dust.

Spring-driven clocks originated during the 2nd half of the 15th c. They were at first encased wholly in metal, and it was not until *c.* 1660, with the introduction of the pendulum, that wood-cased spring-driven clocks became the standard form. These clocks, termed 'bracket' clocks in spite of the fact that they were most usually placed on a table, quickly reached in England a high standard of excellence and this standard was maintained with variations of style up to the end of the 18th c. In France the typical spring-driven clock of the period of the English bracket clock was the 'mantel' clock, with a much more ornate case. In Germany and Austria spring-driven clocks were made during the same period in a great variety of forms.

The evolution of the domestic clock as a handsome piece of furniture almost reached its end by the year 1800, after which there was a decline of artistic standards with occasional revivals of earlier styles. In the U.S.A., however, some attractive new styles appeared, including the 'shelf' and 'banjo' types.

Clocks as precision timekeepers for scientific or observatory purposes continued to make great progress. Whereas in the early 18th c. a long-case clock specially designed for accuracy would have an error of a few seconds a day, the Dent clock made for Greenwich Observatory in 1872, the most accurate all-mechanical clock ever made, varied by only about one-hundredth of a second a day. Modern electrical timekeeping devices, which are outside the scope of this

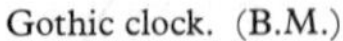
Gothic clock. (B.M.)

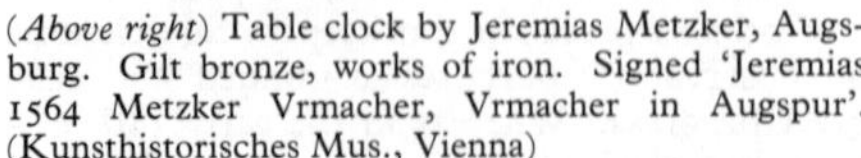
(*Above right*) Table clock by Jeremias Metzker, Augsburg. Gilt bronze, works of iron. Signed 'Jeremias 1564 Metzker Vrmacher, Vrmacher in Augspur'. (Kunsthistorisches Mus., Vienna)

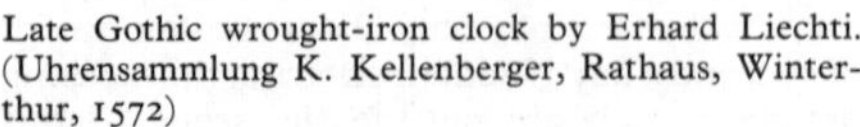
Late Gothic wrought-iron clock by Erhard Liechti. (Uhrensammlung K. Kellenberger, Rathaus, Winterthur, 1572)

Mantel clock by Gaudron, Paris. (V. & A. Mus., 1677)

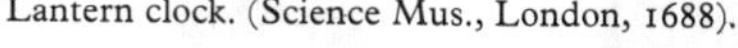

(*Below left*) Bracket clock by Martin, London. (V. & A. Mus., *c.* 1695)

Lantern clock. (Science Mus., London, 1688).

Long-case clocks by: A. Joseph Knibb; B. Mansell Bennett (V. & A. Mus., *c.* 1700); C. Thomas Tompion (Wallace Coll.); D. George Graham (B.M.)

article, have achieved an immense improvement over this, their errors being less than one thousand millionth part of a second in a day, equivalent to an error of one second in 30,000 years.

Biographical notes of the following U.S.A. clock-makers will be found under BAGNALL, BURNUP, JEROME, RITTENHOUSE, TABER, TERRY and WILLARD.

40, 106, 177, 458, 535, 869.

CLOISONNÉ. See ENAMEL.

CLOSE PLATING. A process of covering an article with silver foil by the use of tin as a solder. See SHEFFIELD PLATE, OLD.

COBALT. Cobalt oxide is a powerful blue colourant which has been used for CERAMICS and GLASS from prehistoric times. It has been found in blue glass from Eridu dated *c.* 2000 B.C. The use of cobalt spread from the Near East to Europe, where it provided the essential blue pigment for Roman glass, Celtic ENAMELS and BYZANTINE mosaics, etc. It provided the main blue colouring matter in Islamic pottery and glazes. In antiquity the main source of cobalt was Persia and from the 14th c. Persian cobalt was exported to CHINA for use in the decoration of PORCELAIN.

Among the blue pigments cobalt has the advantage that it will stand up to the high temperatures required for glass-making and porcelain-firing. But because of its intensity it requires careful processing in order to produce a satisfactory pigment and the necessary know-how has not always been present. The cobalt ore must be calcined and fritted with sand to produce zaffre, the basic 'cobalt blue' colouring matter. Zaffre is then fused with potassium carbonate to make smalt, a form of dark-blue glass which when pulverized and levigated in water is sold commercially as a blue pigment.

Powdered zaffre and smalt were the essential colouring matter used in the manufacture of English blue and white china both for underglaze painting (or TRANSFER PRINTING) and for tinting the glaze to imitate the appearance of imported Chinese porcelain. These materials were imported from Saxony, the chief European source of supply. Cobalt ore exists in Cornwall but owing to lack of technical knowledge in the manufacture of zaffre and smalt a satisfactory pigment was not produced from native ores until early in the 10th c.

See also COLOURS AND COLOURANTS.

COBB, JOHN (d. 1778). English cabinet-maker and upholsterer of St. Martin's Lane, who worked in partnership with William VILE until the latter's retirement in 1765, when he carried on the business. He was patronized by George III and by the nobility. Furniture made by the firm remains in the Royal Collection at Buckingham Palace, and other houses supplied include The Vyne, Came House, Strawberry Hill and Corsham. There is a personal description of Cobb in *Nollekens and his Times* (1828) by J. T. Smith, who ridicules him for his pride and pomposity. His later furniture, of high quality, is in NEO-CLASSICAL style and decorated with MARQUETRY. He left property and £20,000.

COGGESHALL LACE. A LACE made at Coggeshall, Essex, during the 19th c., consisting of either bobbin or machine net on which designs were worked in chain stitch.

COINS. There have been many books written for coin collectors and coins have been extensively studied both for their ancillary value to history and for their artistic beauty as a special branch of relief sculpture. This article offers an introduction to the craft of coin-making and its bearing upon these interests.

The art of coining is over 2,500 years old and during this time an immense amount and variety of work has been produced. A great many coins have survived and are preserved in collections, many of them public, in almost every part of the world. The study of coins, together with the closely related study of MEDALS, is the concern of the science of numismatics.

Coins are of inestimable value to the archaeologist and historian. They provide evidence for the spread of cultures and empires and for the dates of important events; they provide portraits of historically important people whose features would otherwise be completely unknown; they are stamped with a vast profusion of symbolic devices which are of great interest to the iconographer; and they are a valuable record of the development of artistic styles. Because their function is to be exchanged, and because they are so easily carried from place to place, they have contributed greatly to the dissemination of visual ideas and their influence has been out of all proportion to their size. In addition to all this many coins are valuable in themselves as miniature works of art.

No certain date can be given for the invention of coinage. It is likely that the first coins as we know them were produced in Lydia in Asia Minor in the 7th or 8th c. B.C., but it is possible that even earlier forms of coinage were produced in China and India. The practice of coining spread from Lydia to the rest of the Greek world, then to Rome and the Roman Empire, and then to medieval Europe. Nowadays coins are an accepted medium of exchange in all civilized countries.

A coin usually has a design in relief on both sides. The numismatic terms for the sides of coins are the *obverse*, which is the side bearing the principal design, usually a head; and the *reverse*, which is the back, or tail. The relief designs themselves are usually referred to as *types*.

The earliest coins were stamped with a device or figure on only one side, but *c.* 566 B.C. the ruler of Athens, Pisistratus, had coins produced with a type on both sides. On the reverse he put an owl, the symbol of Athens, and on the obverse the head of Athene, the patron goddess of the city. Since then almost all coins have been imprinted with a head on their obverse and on the reverse a symbolic device of some kind related to the city or state for which they were produced. Greeks in other cities put representations of other gods—Dionysus, Aphrodite, Apollo, Hermes, etc.—on the obverse of their coins. From the representation of gods it was only a short step to imprinting coins with the head of a reigning monarch. At first these heads were merely symbolic images, but early in the Hellenistic age actual portraits began to appear in various parts of the Persian and Greek worlds. The value of coins as instruments of propaganda was exploited by the Romans in their use of devices and legends of political significance.

In order to appreciate the design of coins it is necessary to know something of the ways in which they were and are made and something of the constraints which are imposed on the coin artist by the processes of manufacture and the functions which coins are required to fulfil.

The process of producing coins by striking has not changed in principle since they were first made. It is true a few coins have been produced by casting, that is by pouring molten metal into a mould, and by other processes; but these were nowhere near as successful as striking and are of little significance. For striking a coin two main things are required: a plain metal disc, known as a *blank* or *flan*, and a pair of dies, one for the obverse and one for the reverse, into which the coin types have been carved in intaglio. The blank, heated to make it more plastic, is placed between the two dies. Then by means of a hammer blow on the upper die, or by some kind of mechanical pressure, the metal of the blank is squeezed into the intaglio designs on the dies.

Until the 16th c. A.D. all coins were manufactured by hand. Then machinery invented in Italy primarily to facilitate the production of medals was adapted for minting coins. The machines included a rolling-mill for producing an even thickness of metal, a cutting press for producing regular standardized blanks and a screw press to provide a more controllable and accurate means of striking than hammering. Nowadays, of course, the processes are carried out at a high speed by automated minting machinery.

The process of striking, however it is done, imposes severe limitations on the kind of relief which can be achieved on a coin. First of all it limits the degree of projection of the forms. To attempt to force metal into a too deeply hollowed-out die would be to court failure, particularly in hammered coins. And secondly, because the die has to be withdrawn from the imprinted coin, there can be no undercutting; the forms of the relief must meet the background at an open angle.

One of the main requirements of modern coinage is that every coin in an issue shall be identical in shape, size and weight. When coins were first made in precious metals it was most important for them to be identical in weight, since this affected their real value. The blanks were therefore carefully adjusted to the right weight. Size and shape, however, which were very difficult to control, were not as critical as weight and they varied a good deal. Striking coins by hand was a somewhat hit or miss procedure. To start with the coin blank was not a perfect shape and the punch into which the upper die was cut would often not be placed in the exact centre of the blank when it was struck with the hammer. Moreover the blank would spread out unevenly under the force of the blow. As a result of all this ancient coins are much more irregular than modern ones. The roughness and irregularity of hand-made coins laid them open to 'clipping' and forgery, both of which, in spite of severe penalties, were rife in the Middle Ages. Clipped coins are those which have had small quantities of metal removed from their edges. This, of course, lessened the value of the coins, which depended on the weight of metal in them. The regularity of the shape of machine-produced coins and the introduction of the milled or grained edge made clipping virtually impossible and forgery more difficult and costly.

Another important requirement of modern coins is that they should stack easily into neat, secure piles. This is one reason why they have a raised rim of even height all round their perimeter and why their relief designs are flat, even, and level with the rim. We should not forget too that the coins of today have to suffer the indignity of being put into slot machines, which is another reason why they must be perfectly alike and of an even thickness. No such requirements restricted the modelling on ancient coins and the relief on them tends to be somewhat bolder, more rounded, and altogether more irregular.

From an aesthetic point of view the most important aspect of coinage is the design and execution of the reliefs on its two sides. Until recent times these designs were carved in intaglio directly into the face of a metal die by a coin engraver. This was difficult work. Not only is the material hard and intractable and the scale of work almost impossibly small, but the whole design has to be cut as a negative form and in reverse. Even with a positive model as a pattern and the possibility of taking pressings constantly in some plastic material as a check on the progress of the work, it still calls for a high degree of skill. The majority of coin engravers were simply craftsmen who more or less competently produced something which was merely useful; but some were artists of the first quality, who were able to use the processes of coining as a means of producing superb miniature works of relief sculpture. Fine coins have been produced in many parts of the world but it seems to be universally acknowledged by those who are interested in coins as works of art that not only did the ancient Greek world invent coinage as we know it but that it also produced coins whose beauty has never been equalled, let alone surpassed. Some of these Greek coin artists even signed their work, thus enabling us to assign a few masterpieces of coinage to such artists as Cimon, Euaenetus, Theodotus, Polycrates, Heracleidas and Eucleidas. Many of the finest Greek coins were produced in Syracuse.

One of the coin artist's main problems is to treat the forms of his low reliefs in a manner which is suitable to the small scale of a coin. Reducing the complex planes and details of a human head or, say, the complexities of a chariot drawn by a team of four horses to the scale of a circular field which is little more than 2·5 centimetres in diameter is a difficult exercise in simplification. It is not just a matter of deciding what to omit but also one of breadth of modelling, and the fusion of small planes and details into a bold and expressive image. In many ancient coins the quality of modelling is perfectly adapted to the scale of the coin. This is no doubt due largely to the fact that the artists themselves worked directly on the dies at the scale of the coins. A comparable breadth of modelling is difficult to achieve on modern coins. There are many reasons for this, but the main one is that the coin types are no longer cut directly into the dies. The modern practice is to model the relief several times larger than the coin will be and then to produce an electrotype cast from it. This electrotype copy is then mounted on a reducing machine, which works on the principle of a PANTOGRAPH and reproduces the design at coin size on a steel block. This reduced copy serves as a master punch from which a series of working dies may be produced. While such a process avoids the strain of working on a minute scale and allows greater accuracy, it tends to encourage the inclusion of too much detail and a lack of breadth in the modelling.

One of the last coin types to be directly engraved by the artist himself was the well known *St. George and the Dragon* by Benedetto Pistrucci. It was executed in 1817 and has been used repeatedly on British coins for nearly 150 years. It is a fine relief, full of energy, highly plastic, and well adapted to a circular field.

Coins are not works of art which are put in a frame or mounted on a pedestal to be merely

Syracuse decadrachma. Obverse: a quadriga; reverse: Arethusa. (B.M., *c.* 410 B.C.)

George III crown by Pistrucci. (B.M., 1820)

Aureus of Roman Emperor Claudius. Obverse: triumphal arch symbolizing conquest of Britain; reverse: head of Claudius. (B.M., A.D. 46)

U.S.A. gold ten-dollar piece. (B.M., 1893)

looked at. They are carried about in purses and pockets and, above all, they are handled. Their tactile qualities are therefore an important aspect of their design. The bold, organic modelling of many hand-produced coins is extremely pleasing to the sense of touch. The tactility of coins may be improved by a certain amount of wear and ageing. Because coins are handled and slid across counters and table-tops the high points of their surfaces, their sharp edges, ridges and other prominences are softened and then rubbed smooth. Ultimately, of course, the whole type can disappear. Ageing can also improve the visual qualities of coins. When they are used and exposed most coins change their colour in ways that are an improvement on their freshly minted appearance. The uppermost layers of their reliefs are polished bright while the areas around the outlines of the forms and the hollower parts of the modelling become dull and oxidized. These effects are particularly attractive on old copper coins. The contrast of rich dark-brown recessed surfaces with shining metallic high-points on a Victorian penny provides a well known instance. Old silver coins, too, acquire in time a certain softness of surface and subtle colour differences. It must be said, however, that collectors prefer to have a coin in 'mint condition'.

The heads on coins may be regarded as examples of the art of portraiture and there are many which convey a convincing and lively impression of the character of a living person. Many Roman and Hellenistic coins, for example, do this brilliantly. But, of course, the images of rulers on coins are usually required to be more idealized than even the general run of royal portraits and they are often mere stereotypes of imperial power or vacant generalizations. The heads on a number of Byzantine and Sassanid coins are rendered in a non-naturalistic manner as a rich pattern of vigorous ridges and bosses. There are few, if any, outstanding works of art among mechanically produced coins. This is not so much the fault of the artists as of the way in which they are required to work in order to satisfy the requirements of modern methods of coin production and the standards of precision and mechanical perfection which are now universal. In the circumstances it is surprising that some artists can produce even moderately good work.

33, 127, 219, 281, 287, 391, 553, 580, 619, 675, 687, 691.

COLMAN FAMILY. See HELMSCHMIED FAMILY.

COLOGNE WORK. See EMBROIDERY (GERMANY AND THE LOW COUNTRIES).

COLONIAL GEORGIAN. Term used to denote a style in architecture, interior decoration, furniture, etc. which prevailed in America during the period, roughly corresponding with Middle GEORGIAN, from *c.* the accession of George I until the Declaration of Independence. Colonial Georgian was more than a reflection of English Georgian. American architects and craftsmen developed the Classical and Palladian idiom into a distinct national style.

COLOURS AND COLOURANTS. A colour other than its own may be given to an object by a limited number of processes: a paint may be applied to the surface; the object may be dyed or stained; the surface may be coloured by causing a chemical change in its constituents; or in the case of a vitreous material a metallic chemical element may be diffused throughout it. All these methods of colouring artefacts were practised from antiquity, and many from the very remote past.

Paints are composed of two major ingredients: one, the pigment, is material in the form of a fine powder that gives both colour and opacity to the paint; the other, the medium, binds the powder and makes it adhere to the surface to which it is applied. Thus in common speech paints are frequently classified either by reference to the pigment, as when one speaks of a 'lead' paint, in which the pigment is a compound of lead, or by naming the type of medium, as with 'oil paints' in which the medium is a drying oil. By contrast dyes and stains are normally materials which are soluble in water, or less commonly in an organic solvent such as alcohol, and which are absorbed by the material which is to be coloured. Furthermore in application dyes enter into some form of chemical combination with the material being coloured for if they did not do so, they would be easily removed by washing. In the case of GLASSES, GLAZES and ENAMELS, which are chemically all closely related vitreous materials, colour is provided for by mixing into them when molten small quantities of other substances, usually the common ores of metals. It is the metallic chemical elements dispersed throughout glasses that give them their colour. A number of processes have been used for colouring metallic objects, which depend upon chemical change. Thus one of the ingredients of an alloy may be removed by chemical solution, a process referred to as *mise en couleur*; or the whole surface may be converted into a new compound, often resembling a naturally formed product of corrosion, which is usually called a patina. Equally the same type of chemical change may be induced on the surface of materials of organic origin, as for example when the surface of wood is darkened by the application of strong oxidizing agents.

1. PIGMENTS AND PAINTS. The earliest pigments known to have been used by man were the naturally occurring earths, of which the ores of iron were the most common. Hence the cave paintings of south-western Europe of the later Palaeolithic period were executed largely by the use of limonite and haematite, which gave varying shades of yellow and red, and magnetite, which provided a dark brown or black. There is, however, some evidence from burials that even before this period these iron compounds were in use as pigments, perhaps as paints for decorating the body. During the subsequent Neolithic period the blue and green ores of COPPER, azurite and malachite, were added to the palette. Their use, of course, depended upon availability, for the ores of copper are far less widespread than those of iron, and at present it is impossible to say with certainty when and where exactly they began to be employed. As mining and trading activities became increasingly developed during the Copper and Bronze ages, so a limited number of relatively rare ores began to be exploited as colourants. Undoubtedly the rarest of these was LAPIS LAZULI, a blue, semi-precious stone often used in the manner of a gemstone. In the form of powder lapis lazuli gave a rich blue pigment. In the same way the sulphide ore of mercury, cinnabar, was crushed to provide vermilion, while the sulphide ores of arsenic, realgar and orpiment gave vivid shades of yellow and orange. The sources of lapis lazuli, cinnabar and realgar and their earliest periods of use as pigments remain obscure and the subject of much debate, but certainly by the beginning of the first millennium B.C. all were known, although they were not in widespread use, both in China and the Middle East. From this time onwards very few new naturally occurring minerals were added as pigments to the artist's palette; and such additions that were made were rather a matter of degree than of kind. Thus the ambers and siennas of the late Middle Ages that could be calcined, or 'burnt', to give redder shades, are merely specific types of the ferruginous earths that had been in use since the Palaeolithic period.

The first millennium B.C. saw in the Middle East the introduction of a new type of mineral pigment, namely one that was deliberately synthesized. Metallic lead, which had been long in use for many purposes, was calcined to provide a yellow pigment, litharge, a paler yellow than any hitherto available. If heated to a higher temperature, litharge gave a brilliant red, red lead or minium, which was commonly used as a substitute for the rare and expensive cinnabar vermilion. A blue-green pigment, verdigris, was made by dissolving copper or its ores in vinegar, a by-product of wine-making. Other pigments were, apparently, the by-products of glass and glaze manufacture. A turquoise blue pigment known as Egyptian frit, for example, was made by fusing quartz and lime with a small addition of an ore of copper, a process very similar to the production of the so-called 'Egyptian faience'. Similarly the ores of lead and antimony were mixed and fused to provide the deep yellow of lead antimonate, Naples yellow. Primarily used as a colourant for the glazed façades of Mesopotamian palaces, blocks of Naples yellow have been recovered from archaeological excavations such as those at Babylon; and although the evidence is very slender, the material was presumably also used as a pigment. The same must be said of a blue glass-like material, smalt, made by fusing small quantities of COBALT ores with a soda glass. Smalt gave the rich, pure blue so typical of later glazed blue and white ceramics, and like Naples yellow was used primarily as a colourant for glazes. Although its use as a pigment seems probable during the period, that it was in fact used in this way remains the subject of investigation.

During the first millennium B.C. a wide range or pigments was being derived from a source completely different from that so far considered. Many dyestuffs then commonly in use could be mixed directly with the media to give paints: other dyestuffs needed first to be combined with a white inert base to provide a pigment, or lake. The nature of dyestuffs and their use as lakes will be discussed more conveniently later, but in the meantime it should be noticed that these materials very considerably increased the range of colours that could be used in paints.

Apart from dyestuffs and lakes few new pigments were exploited during the long period from classical antiquity to the 18th c., but with the development of applied chemistry there slowly evolved a new interest in the possibilities of creating synthetic pigments. Prussian blue was discovered early in the 18th c.; Scheele's green, cobalt green and barium yellow in the last two decades. Then in the 19th c. there followed a spate of new pigments. Ultramarine, a synthetic form of lapis lazuli, chrome red, chrome yellow, cobalt blue and emerald green were all first synthesized within the period of the Napoleonic wars. By the middle of the century antimony vermilion, cobalt yellow and lithol red had been discovered, and by the end of the century cobalt violet, manganese violet, para red and cadmium red were all in common use. Thus in a little less than two centuries the total number of pigments from inorganic sources had been virtually doubled, while the range of colours made possible by mixing pigments was enormously increased, especially in the ranges of reds and greens. Equally, as will be seen later, a vast range of lakes became available as a result of the newly developing synthetic dyestuff industry. Taken together, the new pigments and dyestuffs created a situation in which it became possible to make a paint of almost any tone and shade required, a situation very different from that at the close of the 17th c.

It is very difficult to say anything precise about early paint media, largely because, being of organic origin, they have become destroyed or so altered with age that they can no longer be identified. To judge by the practices of primitive craftsmen today, animal fats were probably the first media to be used; but albumen, derived from eggs or blood, milk, and some of the more easily obtained water-soluble gums extracted from plants may also have been employed. With the development of cooking in the Neolithic period, especially casserole cooking, there seems little doubt that sizes, made by the prolonged boiling of hoof, sinew and skin, and starch pastes, which could be obtained from cereal or root staples, began to be used as painting media. Apart from these materials there is some evidence that during the first millennium B.C. plant resins, insoluble in water but soluble in a number of fairly easily extracted oils, were used in the making of paints. Resins and waxes, however, could be used as media in quite a different manner since, once mixed with the pigment, they could be applied in the hot, molten state to the surface to be coloured. Thus resins and waxes used as media gave a wide range of techniques of application from straightforward brush painting to the manipulation of Chinese LACQUERS and the encaustic decoration of, for example, late Egyptian sarcophagi. Exactly when the so-called drying oils began to be used as media is uncertain. Linseed oil may be taken as the most typical of this class in that on exposure it gradually forms a gel and finally becomes a solid elastic film. Its use by the 12th c. in Europe is certain, but before this a lack of analyses and inadequate texts leave room for considerable doubt.

2. DYES AND DYESTUFFS. Our knowledge of early dyestuffs is even less complete than our knowledge of pigments for the very simple reason that very few have survived the rigours of time; and even when one comes to the period of classical antiquity descriptions of dyestuffs are frequently so inadequate that it is impossible to be certain exactly what was intended. Added to this difficulty the majority of ancient dyes belong to a limited number of closely related chemical groups, with the result that analysis of samples from the past often proves to be unrewarding. Very little of use can, therefore, be said about dyestuffs before the Greek and Roman periods.

Although the majority of dyes used in antiquity were derived from the plant kingdom, some of the earliest known to have been prepared were extracted from insects or their secretions. Hence the three red dyes, kermes, cochineal and lac, all chemically anthraquinone derivatives, were obtained from different species of the *coccus* family. The kermes insect is indigenous to the Mediterranean area and is believed to have been in use during the Neolithic period; the cochineal insect is recorded as having provided a red dye in Armenia early in the first millennium B.C.; while the lac insect, native to India and South East Asia, provided through its secretion, shellac, a source of red dye that was in all probability in use in the Neolithic period. Although known in

Egypt in Roman times, lac was not imported into the Western world in any quantity until after the period of Arab expansion. Thus kermes and to a lesser extent cochineal were the common dyes of this group known in the West during classical antiquity. Dyed on to an alumina base they gave crimson lakes.

During the first millennium B.C. a number of red dyes were also extracted from plants. Undoubtedly the most important of these were madder and henna, both plants indigenous to the eastern Mediterranean and both being under cultivation in Egypt and the Levant by the Roman period. Both dyes were used in the preparation of lakes, madder especially. A third red dye known to have been prepared from the middle of the first millennium B.C. onwards was fucus, or as it is known today, litmus. It was extracted from a species of seaweed, and although the main recorded centre of production was Cyprus, it was probably manufactured widely throughout the eastern Mediterranean.

In India and South East Asia the main sources of red dyes derived from the plant kingdom appear to have been brazil and dragon's blood. The first of these was extracted from the wood of a tree of the *caesalpina* family, the second from the resin of the rattan palm. When these dyestuffs began to be exploited is quite unknown, but in view of the great age of dyeing techniques in India one must assume it was well before the first millennium B.C. Neither appears to be recorded in Greek or Latin texts.

The main blue dyes of antiquity were woad and indigo, in which the principal colouring ingredient is the same, indigotin; but whereas the woad plant is indigenous to eastern Europe and the Balkans, indigo is native to India. Thus while there is evidence that woad was being cultivated in many parts of the Middle East by the beginning of the first millennium B.C., there is nothing to suggest that indigo was being imported to the West before the late Roman period, when it was brought to Egypt as an item of trade.

Undoubtedly the most singular of all the dyes known in antiquity was purple obtained from a shellfish of the *murex* family. This mollusc is found widely throughout the Mediterranean, and heaps of discarded shells, a clear indication of the extraction of purple, are recorded from Greece and the Adriatic coast, Tobruk, Djerba and Syracuse. The main centre of production, however, was the Levant coast, particularly the city of Tyre. The yield from the individual mollusc is extremely small and Friedländer, who established its composition at the very end of the 19th c., obtained only 1·4 grammes of pure dye from 12,000 specimens of *murex*. The cost of the dye must have been prohibitive, so that there is a sound economic reason why in Roman times it was reserved for the emperor. A cheaper substitute was found by mixing red and blue dyes, while there seems little doubt that purple itself was frequently adulterated to make it go further. Chemically speaking, purple is a bromo derivative of indigotin.

A wide range of yellow dyes was available in antiquity, all of which were derived from the plant kingdom and all of which belong to the flavone group of chemical compounds. In Europe the major sources of yellow dye appear to have been saffron, obtained from the flowers of the autumn crocus, which is known to have been cultivated in south-west Anatolia and Sicily, weld (*Reseda* sp.) and the dyer's broom. In the Middle East a similar range of yellow dyes was obtained from Persian berries (*Rhamnus* sp.), sumach (*Rhus* sp.) and the root of the kurkum plant (*Curcuma* sp.). Safflower (*Carthamus* sp.) is known to have been under cultivation in Egypt and Mesopotamia, but was probably of Indian origin. It gave either deep-yellow or red dyes according to its treatment, and was hitherto used to colour British government red tape. Specifically of Indian origin was the dye cutch, the generic name of yellow dye obtained from at least three distinct families of plants indigenous to India and South East Asia. Little is known about their origins, but it may be assumed that both safflower and cutch were in common use in India before the first millennium B.C. There is far less certainty about the dye known as Indian yellow, a product of Bengal, obtained by the evaporation of the urine of cattle which had been fed on the leaves of the mango.

While this list of yellow dyes possibly represents the major sources of the better dyes, it is very far from comprehensive. About a hundred flavone dyes have been isolated from different plants, and an equally wide range of sources may have been used in antiquity. Thus barberry, birch, bracken, camomile, dog's mercury, gorse, marsh marigold, nettle, onion and ragwort, to mention only a few, could all have produced adequate yellow dyes.

Very few plants produce satisfactory green or black dyestuffs so that in antiquity as a general rule greens were obtained by overdyeing in yellow and blue, while blacks of a kind were the result of overdyeing in dark red and blue. But oak galls, the over-ripe husks of walnuts and the myrtle were used as sources of very dark dyes that if used in sufficient concentration, gave adequate blacks.

The Middle Ages saw the introduction of very few new dyes but a wide traffic in those already known, at first as a result of Arab sea-going trade to India and the Far East and later as an outcome of Venetian and Genoan activities. Exceptions must be made, however, for two green dyes that appeared, apparently, for the first time during the medieval period. Sap green, obtained from the berries of the buckthorn, and iris green, extracted from the leaves of that plant, were used on medieval manuscripts in Europe and, with less certainty, for dyeing textiles. Even the discovery of the New World brought few new dyes, although the dyestuffs used there were themselves different. Cochineal and brazil were known to the Amerindians of Mexico and South America. Haematin, extracted from the Central American logwood tree, and flavine from the North American quercitron, very similar in chemical composition to the red and yellow dyes brazil and sumach, were known in the Old World from antiquity.

The manufacture of synthetic dyes began more than a century later than that of synthetic pigments with the discovery by Perkin, in 1856, of mauve while he was attempting to synthesize quinine. Three years later Verguin discovered magenta, and the effect of these two completely new colours on Late Victorian taste is a matter of record. The following quarter-century was to see an explosion in this field. In 1859, the same year that saw the discovery of magenta, Griess synthesized aniline yellow, the first of the azo-dyes, at that time manufactured from coal-tar fractions. By 1885 thousands of azo-compounds had been patented in western Europe as dyes, although only a few were in production. Meanwhile alizarin, the colouring matter in madder, and indigo had both been synthesized, and their production costs totally undercut those of imported natural dyestuffs. By 1914 about a thousand azo-dyes were in regular production. The number today is certainly more than double this figure.

Many natural fibres do not combine adequately with all dyestuffs, no sufficiently strong chemical link being formed to prevent them from becoming fugitive, and this is more commonly the case with plant fibres, such as cotton and linen, than with the animal fibres such as wool and silk. Normally a chemical link has to be provided, a mordant, which is a material that will combine equally with fibre and dye. In antiquity the sulphates of aluminium and iron were the materials commonly used as mordants, although today compounds of chromium and tin are also employed. Tannins, either deliberately added or present as impurities in the dye-bath, would often perform the same function. Hence cutch and sumach, both of which dyestuffs contained considerable quantities of tannins, required no mordants in application. Iron salts present in the dye-bath, however, had the effect of darkening the dye. This could be put to practical use when a black was required, but elsewhere it was objectionable. Natural sources of pure alum were, therefore, of the utmost importance in the ancient world. Whether the Arabs learnt to purify alum from the Indians, following their occupation of the Punjab, or whether they evolved the process themselves, is unknown; but for a large part of the Middle Ages the Arabs, and later also the Byzantines, had a virtual monopoly in this commodity. Following the early Ottoman conquests Europe was deprived of alum, but a source was found at Tolfa. These deposits lay within papal territory and the Papacy attempted to create a monopoly in alum, but it was found impossible to enforce. Even so the threat stimulated a search for other sources, and by the mid 16th c. alum was being produced widely throughout Europe.

3. VITREOUS COLOURS. Glass-like substances are usually coloured by the presence of metallic ions dispersed throughout them, the ions normally entering the molten glass through the addition of metallic oxides. The metals most commonly used for this purpose are iron, copper, cobalt, manganese and chromium, but the colours they give may depend either upon the valence of the ion or upon the fluxes present in the glass. Hence iron will colour a glass amber or green depending upon whether it is in the ferric or ferrous state, a situation clearly illustrated by bottles used for beers and wines today, in which the precise colour of the glass is often immaterial. On the other hand copper ions in the presence of alkaline fluxes give glasses a turquoise colour while in the presence of lead the colour is a leaf green.

The earliest of the vitreous materials, 'Egyptian faience', was either left uncoloured or was made turquoise by the addition of copper. First appearing in the fourth millennium B.C., this remained the only colour in use until early in the second millennium B.C., when craftsmen in Mesopotamia, Egypt and Crete began to experiment with new colourants. Manganese ores, if used in sufficient quantity, gave a black used for outlining or linear designs, while if used at lower concentrations they gave a purple colour; iron or antimony mixed with lead provided an amber and a brilliant yellow; copper mixed with lead gave a leaf green, while limited quantities of cobalt were employed to make royal blue. There was also a limited use of copper in the reduced, cuprous state that gave a blood-red glass, and colourless 'faience' was sometimes made white and opaque by the addition of lime. This range of colourants is to be seen not only in the brilliant 'faience' decorations of the palaces of Akhenaten and the later Assyrian and Babylonian rulers, but also in glass vessels, especially in Egypt during the early first millennium B.C.

Briefly, several centuries before the expansion of Greece and Rome all but a few of the common glass colourants were known, if not in wide use. In the centuries to follow advances in the techniques of colouring vitreous materials were made not so much in the discovery of new colourants as in the art of controlling those already in use. Hence chromium, which can give a wide range of colours from browns to greens but which is very difficult to manipulate, was never used with regularity before its adoption as a colourant by Chinese overglaze enamellers.

In so far as glazes are concerned, only four of these colourants can be used at high temperatures—cobalt, copper, iron and manganese. Thus wherever underglaze colouring was the means of decoration employed the craftsman's palette was confined to these four high-temperature colours and mixtures thereof. While this gave a fairly wide range of possibilities in the colours from yellow to purple, it left a very real deficiency in the reds and oranges. Hence until the development of overglaze enamels, reds could only be produced by one of two means: one could use a thick layer of red-firing clay, Armenian bole, under the clear glaze, or one could use reduced copper as a true colourant. This in turn meant that copper could be used either as the sole colourant or in combination only with those colourants unaffected by reduction firing, namely cobalt and manganese. It is against these limitations that one must view the achievements of early craftsmen.

Chemically altered surfaces. Various techniques were used in antiquity to change the surface colour of metallic objects, and by the time of Greek and Roman dominance there is a small body of written evidence which shows the nature of the processes used. Prior to this period there is some indication that similar techniques were already in use in Mesopotamia, and in Egypt before the end of the second millennium B.C. Unfortunately, however, the objects that have survived have suffered considerable corrosive changes during the past two or three millennia, so that they can only rarely be used to confirm the precise nature of the processes.

Broadly speaking, the processes were either additive or subtractive. Thus an alloy of gold, silver and copper might be heated in a crucible containing common salt and brick dust, as recorded by Pliny. The result was the surface enrichment of the alloy owing to the removal from the surface of both silver and copper. Such a treatment would have made the alloy appear to be of pure gold. The same effect could have been achieved by prolonged soaking in a number of organic acids which would dissolve the silver and copper at the surface, a process which, incidentally, is known to have been used by the Aztecs at the time of the Spanish conquest.

A red- or rose-coloured gold manufactured by the Egyptians has been the subject of much research, and it would seem that this was made first by fusing gold with iron pyrites, or 'fool's gold', both of which have similar melting-points. The resulting alloy, after shaping, was then oxidized to provide at the surface an admixture of gold and haematite, the latter tinting the surface red. Silver, on the other hand, was sometimes made to simulate gold by treating the surface with orpiment, which gave the metal a very thin yellow film.

By contrast copper alloys were not infrequently darkened by rubbing the surface with materials containing sulphur, amongst which were the yolks of eggs. The film of copper sulphide so formed allowed the surface to be brought to a high, even polish and it is not therefore surprising that this technique was often used to prepare the reflecting surfaces of MIRRORS. The same process, however, equally simulated the effect of tarnishing with age and may at times have been employed to give an object an air of antiquity. More commonly, however, techniques of patination were aimed at providing a green surface. The principal agents used for this kind of work were common salt and acetic acid (in the form of vinegar), which gave the chlorides and acetate of copper respectively as alteration products on the surface of the metal. Patinas of this nature were produced extensively by the Chinese, but to what degree they were used in the West is a matter of speculation.

The fact that mercury readily forms amalgams with other metals and can easily be volatilized by heating allowed the gilding and silvering of baser metals. Thus a silver amalgam might be applied to the surface of a bronze object, and after heating to remove the mercury the object would present a silvered surface. Equally goldleaf, laid down on a copper surface that had been rubbed with mercury, would, after heating to volatilize the mercury, be found to adhere strongly to the base.

It will be noticed that most of the processes discussed above were aimed at making a metallic object appear to be of rather greater value than in fact it was and it is perfectly obvious from early written sources that this was the intention and that the practitioners were well aware that their products were counterfeit. The same methods of colouring metals were in use throughout the Middle Ages and Renaissance. But the attitude of scholars to the nature of the processes seems to have changed, and the belief became firmly rooted that it was possible, if only one knew how, to transmute baser into more noble metals. Mercury, arsenic and sulphur, the main agents of these colouring processes, were endowed with almost mystical properties, and from this branch of the applied arts more than any other developed the whole dogma of medieval alchemy. The true nature of these changes was understood only after the nature of chemical change had been propounded by Dalton.

Materials other than metals, as for example wood, ivory and stone, were most commonly coloured in antiquity by the use of dyes. Thus ivory might be stained green to imitate jade or wood might be dyed black to counterfeit ebony. The use of chemical agents to alter the nature of surfaces appears to have been far less common. There are, however, a few records showing that quartz, for instance, was heated in various concoctions so that the surface would absorb colourants that imitated precious stones such as emerald and sapphire. See also GREEK AND ROMAN ANTIQUITY (PIGMENTS).

59, 143, 145, 298, 299, 396, 503, 565, 654.

COLT, SAMUEL (1814–62). Inventor and firearms-manufacturer of Hartford, Connecticut, where he spent most of his life. He is chiefly known for his invention of the first successful revolving pistol. This was first patented in England in December 1835 and was a muzzle-loading percussion weapon with a hand-rotated cylinder. After various setbacks Colt was able to establish his own factory at Hartford in 1848, which was immensely successful. The majority of his products were utilitarian, but a few arms made for presentation purposes were elaborately engraved and encrusted with figures and scenes in gold. Examples of Colt fire-arms can be seen in most major collections of 19th-c. arms. See ARMS AND ARMOUR.

74, 761, 920.

COLUMBINE CUP. A tall silver standing cup the form of which was based on the flower of that name. It was prescribed in Nuremberg during the 16th c. and later as the masterpiece to be completed by apprentices, the earliest reference dating from 1531. The usual attribution of the original columbine cup design to Wenzel JAMNITZER (b. 1508) does not carry complete conviction. The completed cups remained the property of the guild and were not therefore marked. There are two examples in the Victoria and Albert Museum, one in the British Museum.

COMINAZZO FAMILY. A famous family of gun-barrel makers of Gardone, in the Val Trompia, north of Brescia, north Italy. They are first recorded in the 2nd half of the 16th c. and were still active in the early 19th c. The most famous member was ANGELO LAZARINO COMINAZZO, from whom the diarist John Evelyn purchased a carbine in Brescia in 1646. He appears to have been the first to sign his barrels *Lazarino Cominazzo*, though this signature was also used by later members of the family and was also widely copied by other makers. Examples of the work of the family are in the Tower of London Armouries; Victoria and Albert Museum; Wallace Collection; Musée de l'Armée, Paris; Metropolitan Museum, New York. See ARMS AND ARMOUR.

283, 284.

CONEY, JOHN (1655/6–1722) of Boston. One of the best of America's early silversmiths, whose work spanned three stylistic periods. Both he and Jeremiah Dummer served their apprenticeship with Hull and Sanderson. Like most American silversmiths of the period he was a highly respected citizen, to whom coins could be entrusted for reshaping into useful objects. Evidence for this is seen in the fact that he was elected Constable in 1688 and afterwards held other offices. The quantity of silver that Coney made suggests he may have had a large number of apprentices.

CONGÉ. Term in architecture or furniture design for an OVOLO or CAVETTO MOULDING.

CONNECTICUT CHEST. Name given to regional chests made in the Connecticut river valley of New England in the last quarter of the 17th c. They were MULE CHESTS with panels and drawer fronts carved with tulip and sunflower ornament based on English Jacobean chests and presses of the early 17th c. and they were sometimes decorated with split balusters applied to the verticals. See FURNITURE (AMERICAN).

CONSOLE. See MODILLION.

CONSOLE TABLE. 'Console' is an architectural term for a projecting ornamental bracket such as supports the upper members of a cornice. The term 'console table' was applied to a table fixed to a wall and supported by legs at the front or by ornamental brackets such as an eagle or intertwined dolphins. The console table was introduced into England from France and became fashionable in the early part of the 18th c.

CONSULAT STYLE. See DIRECTOIRE.

COPLAND, HENRY. English furniture designer. His name appears on trade cards as early as 1738. He published *A New Book of Ornaments* (1746) with early examples of ROCOCO ornament in England, and another book in 1752, with the same title, in partnership with Matthias LOCK. Both he and Lock appear to have been employed by Thomas CHIPPENDALE the Elder, but claims that they were responsible for most of the *Director*'s plates are now discounted on grounds of insufficient evidence. Copland emerges as a pioneer of the English Rococo furniture style.

COPPER AND ITS ALLOYS. Copper, being extremely resistant to corrosion, can be found in the earth's crust as native metal, i.e. in a relatively pure metallic state, as well as in the form of ores where it is in chemical combination with other elements. One of the earliest metals to be used, it was probably discovered as a native metal, its attractive colour and the ease with which it could be hammered into useful shapes making it of interest and value to early civilizations. The exact way in which copper metallurgy developed is uncertain but evidence would suggest that three major steps followed the initial shaping of the native metal by hammering. These were the smelting of copper from its ores, the development of casting techniques and the deliberate mixing of copper with other metals, in particular tin and zinc, to form a range of useful alloys.

It is probable that copper-working originated in the Middle East in centres around the valleys of the Tigris and the Euphrates somewhere between 5000 and 4500 B.C. A copper spearhead was discovered at Ur below the clay deposit of the Great Flood and excavations of the Royal Graves *c.* 3200 B.C. have revealed copper bowls, buckets, ribbed trays and other vessels. In Pre-Dynastic EGYPT copper was used for the manufacture of axes, adzes and boring tools as well as for weapons. Smelted copper is extremely malleable and will deform easily when it is cold forged. As it is worked, however, it gradually hardens, becomes brittle, and it will ultimately crack if working continues. This condition, known as work-hardening, can be relieved and the metal restored to its initial malleability by the process of annealing, i.e. the heating of the metal to a full red and then cooling it. Knowledge of this process would be essential to the working of the far less malleable native coppers that were initially available and it would appear to have been understood shortly after 5000 B.C. Close upon the discovery of annealing came the realization that copper would shape more easily hot than cold, a fact supported by metallurgical examinations that indicate hot working in some early artefacts.

It is probable that the melting of copper was preceded by the discovery of the technique for smelting copper from oxidized copper ores. This process would require temperatures above the melting-point of pure copper, 1,083 °C., and a reducing atmosphere. Suitable conditions were attainable in early pottery kilns but only rarely in open camp fires. It seems likely that the technique for reducing oxidized copper ores was discovered in the pottery kilns from observation of the behaviour of glazes that included copper oxide as one of their ingredients. Sulphide ores were smelted at a later period, either by using an initial roasting to convert the sulphide to an oxide and then smelting as before or by smelting the ore direct to give copper sulphide and slag and then oxidizing the copper sulphide to give metallic copper. The discovery of annealing and hot working would have eased the work involved in the shaping of copper. Then the discovery of smelting led to the realization that copper could be cast, a technique that still further eased the problems of shaping and permitted the manufacture of new forms.

The second millennium B.C. saw a change from copper to bronze, an alloy of copper and tin. (See also BRONZE AGE METALLURGY.) It is possible that early bronzes were obtained by smelting the naturally occurring mixed ores of copper and tin such as those found in Cornwall, although it seems more likely that they were often obtained by smelting a mixture of copper and tin ores made up by the smelter. The next stage in the production of bronze was to heat metallic copper, tin oxide and charcoal together, the charcoal reducing the tin oxide to metallic tin. The final process that permitted a more accurate control of the alloy was to smelt tin and copper separately and then to melt metallic tin and metallic copper together in the required proportions. This final stage was attained *c.* 1500 B.C. The greater fluidity of bronze over copper as a casting metal and the fact that bronze is *c.* 70% stronger than copper and will become twice as hard when hammered, account for the growth in popularity of the new metal. To obtain these advantages the alloy needs to contain between 9% and 10% tin. Bronzes of this composition appear *c.* 1700 B.C.

Copper can also be combined with zinc to form the alloy that today is called BRASS. Originally the word was applied to the alloy of copper and tin already referred to above as 'bronze'.

It was *c.* A.D. 1730, when copper/zinc alloys were more common, that the two alloys were clearly differentiated and 'bronze' was used of copper/tin alloys, and 'brass' of copper/zinc alloys. Prior to Roman times the introduction of zinc into copper was carried out by the smelting of copper and zinc ores together. During the Roman period and until the 18th c. brass was produced by the calamine method. This process consisted of heating together a mixture of metallic copper, charcoal and calamine (zinc carbonate) to a temperature high enough to melt the copper (1,083 °C.). Hot charcoal reduces the calamine to zinc, which vapourizes at this temperature. But if a reducing atmosphere is maintained in the crucible, oxidation of the zinc vapour is restricted and an appreciable percentage is dissolved into the molten copper. By regulating the proportions of copper and calamine in the crucible a range of alloys could be produced having different properties and colours. Common brass, generally used for castings, has *c.* 70% copper and 30% zinc; hot-working brasses have *c.* 60% copper and 40% zinc; cold-working brasses have *c.* 80% copper and 20% zinc. The last alloy has the name 'Dutch metal', is a golden yellow colour which simulates gold in imitation jewellery and can be made into thin sheets and foil.

Many alloys of copper share with GOLD AND SILVER the property of malleability. This has enabled them to be cold worked in sheet form from the earliest of times. Initially the sheet metal would have had to be hammered from the cake of metal obtained from the smelting-furnace. This would first be roughly flattened whilst hot by blows from a large hammer or by pressure from the end of a small tree trunk. The flattened mass would then be further reduced in thickness by hammering with a straight *pêne* hammer. Partially worked cakes discovered in Ireland suggest the hammer could have been similar to the socketed celt of the Bronze Age. Parallel rows of blows on one face of the cake would stretch the metal in a direction at right angles to the hammer *pêne*. Similar rows of blows on the reverse side but placed at 90° to the first rows of blows would stretch the metal in a direction normal to the original direction. The thickness of sheets making up early cauldrons is sometimes only 0·25 mm, a tribute to the skill of these metal-workers. The advent of water-power enabled cast slabs to be 'battered' into sheets under tilt hammers of various kinds. In the 16th c. brass was cast between heavy stones standing on end to produce flat ingots of *c.* 30 kg weight. These slabs were battered into plates after being annealed in a coal and charcoal fire. After an initial reduction in thickness the plates were cut into smaller pieces, often discs, by bench-mounted or larger water-powered shears. Several of the smaller pieces were then stacked together and the battering continued until pieces of the required size and thickness were obtained. The rolling of sheet was introduced in the 17th c. but the battery process continued until the late 18th c., when mechanical presses were introduced. The construction of large lathes in the 19th c. made possible the machining of accurate cast iron rolls that could produce the sheets of even thickness necessary for the successful employment of presses to stamp and raise patterns in brass sheets and to manufacture pressed brass hollow-ware.

In antiquity copper which had first been hammered into sheets was further fashioned into bowls, dishes and cauldrons as well as portions of statues. Subsequently gold and then silver were worked in similar ways and as knowledge of these more precious metals grew, copper and its alloys were used less for ornaments and more and more for useful objects. Depending upon the form of the final object, malleable sheet metal can be hand-shaped by one of several processes with a hammer or a mallet, while the work is supported either on a shaped wooden block or on a leather bag full of sand or on an anvil of a suitable shape called a 'stake'. Low, shallow forms are obtained by hollowing or sinking. Hollowing involves the hammering or malleting of a metal disc, using a depression carved into a block of wood or a leather bag of sand as a support. Shaping takes place on the inside of the form, the point of impact of the hammer on the work being in advance of the point where the metal touches the hollow in the wooden block. Each blow stretches the metal into the depression, and as this stretching tends to thin the metal the depth of hollowed work is limited. Larger forms are hollowed on a sandbag by means of a mallet with an egg-shaped head, the hollow into which the metal is stretched being formed in the sand by the action of the mallet. An 18th-c. illustration shows very large bowls being hollowed into a dished block by a water-powered hammer. Sinking is also a hollowing process but one in which it is only the centre portion of the disc that is sunk and which leaves a flat rim on the final form as in plates, trays and salvers. A circle is first marked on the disc to define the limit of the sinking. The end grain of a hardwood block is marked with an arc of the same radius as the disc. Two pegs are inserted in this arc to ensure that when the circumference of the disc is pressed against them the point where the disc is to be depressed comes directly over the edge of the wooden block. The disc is then held horizontally against the vertical pegs and is lightly struck with an oval hammer at the point directly above the edge of the wooden block. By rotating the disc a fraction between each blow a hammered circle is produced and the centre is depressed about 4 mm. The rim is trued on a flat block and the process repeated with intermittent annealing until a sufficient depth has been reached. Large work that is too heavy to be supported by hand may

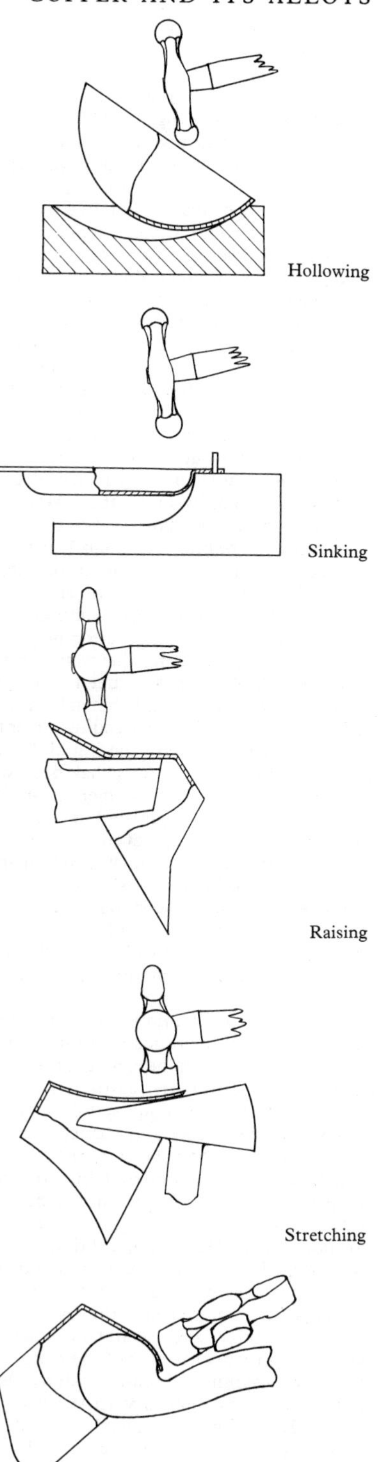

be supported over the block by means of cords and a pulley.

Deeper forms than those possible by hollowing can be raised. Raised forms are worked externally, commencing at the base on the underside of the work and continuing to the edge, by a contracting operation on a stake which produces the height of the form by raising its rim. This operation may be carried out on a ball or domed stake with a wedge-shaped mallet or by using a stake curved across its breadth with a radius of *c.* 40 mm, on to which the metal is contracted by a hammer with a rectangular face and with all sharp edges and corners removed. As this is a contraction process there is no stretching with its subsequent thinning of the metal, so tall forms can be produced. Raising was the shaping process of the medieval craftsman and is the basis of all modern hammered work. The mechanical equivalent to raising is spinning. Here the metal is shaped by a firm pressure whilst it is rotating rapidly in a lathe. Artefacts from the early Iron Age show marks that might be attributed to spinning although if it was in fact in use as early as this, the technique would probably have been used as a finishing operation after initial shaping with the hammer.

Once raised, forms can be further shaped by stretching or contracting the metal. Stretching will take place when the metal is compressed between the hammer and the stake and is thus thinned with resultant spreading. Contracting involves the reduction of the initial diameter by compression. When a form has been obtained with the mallet or the hammer its surface will be uneven. These blemishes are removed by planishing, which is the even and regular hammering of the surface against a well fitting stake with a light and highly polished hammer. When suitable stakes for planishing cannot be found the vessel may be filled with a mixture of two parts pitch and one part plaster of Paris or with molten lead and the final planishing carried out on these fillings.

Alongside the techniques of hammered work there developed the processes of casting, copper being cast by the Sumerians *c.* 3000 B.C. It is most likely that the first castings were made in open sand or earth moulds, followed by open moulds of baked clay and shaped stone. Early practice seems to have been to cast rough forms, which were then hammered into the required shapes. Later in the Bronze Age two-part moulds of clay, stone and even cast bronze were introduced. Perfect castings of thin blades could be obtained by heating the clay moulds to a red heat before pouring the metal. When hollow castings were required, as in the case of a socketed spear-head, clay cores would be placed in the mould to obstruct the flow of the metal and produce the required hollow. Many Egyptian statues were cast hollow with the help of sand cores. Bronze pins or chaplets were used to locate the large core and to prevent it touching the sides of the mould. A technique for producing intricate castings that originated *c.* 2500 B.C. and which is still being used today is the 'lost wax' process. A core model is built that roughly resembles the finished article. This is then covered with several layers of wax, upon which the exact surface details are worked. The system necessary for running the metal is then added and the whole assembly encased in a suitable mould material. Initially clay, this has now been replaced with an investment plaster. The wax is melted out, then the mould is heated to a red heat and the metal poured in. A fuller account of the *cire-perdue* process as used for casting statues will be found in *The Oxford Companion to Art* under BRONZE SCULPTURE.

By the middle of the 14th c. the industries involving brass- and bronze-founding had subdivided into specialist groups. Brass pots and small cauldrons were being cast in loam moulds that were formed by strickling in a manner similar to BELL-FOUNDING. Handles and feet made from wax were added to the strickled pattern and melted out of the mould before the metal was poured. Bells and cannon were cast in bronze, whilst 'latoners' worked brass into many domestic forms. In his book *Pirotechnia* (1540) the Italian metallurgist Vannoccio Biringuccio describes the mass production of harness buckles, cups, belt buckles, chain links, thimbles and window fastenings. Composite patterns were made from brass or tin that consisted of 20 or more of the article required together with the complete pouring and venting system for the mould. These were moulded in lute or clay moulding composition, which was then baked firm and assembled into stacks of about 20 sections. The completed stacks were again baked and poured in one pour to give over 400 articles per stack.

Although many articles can be shaped from a single sheet or cast in a single piece, it was soon necessary to fabricate items from a number of parts. As copper and its alloys will not pressure-weld with the same facility as iron, their joining presents a different problem. Initial joints would be mechanical with edges folded and hammered together or overlapped and riveted with portions of thin rod specifically produced for this purpose. In antiquity the problem facing the metal-worker was the production of suitable holes for the rivets. These would have to be punched with bronze or later with carburized iron punches in the absence of suitable drills. But as the knowledge of metals grew, soldering techniques were developed. Soldering unites metallic components by means of a metal or metallic alloy that has a lower melting temperature than the metals to be joined. Fluxes are necessary to prevent oxidation so that the molten solder may alloy with the surfaces to be joined and thus unite them. 'Soft' solders melt below red heat, are usually tin/lead alloys and can be applied with a soldering iron, whilst 'hard' solders melt above red heat and require a greater heat source. Initially copper was soldered with silver or an alloy of copper and silver. The Romans developed soldering techniques which used tin/lead alloys and high zinc-content brasses to join copper and bronze. Resin was used as a flux and soft-soldered joints made with a soldering-iron. Hard-soldered joints were made by heating the pieces to be joined by placing them on a bed of glowing charcoal and blowing the area adjacent to the joint with a blow-pipe. Another technique was developed in antiquity for more massive joints such as the repair of swords or parts of statues. The broken parts were assembled together and surrounded by a clay mould. This was then heated in a fire and molten bronze was poured through the mould to fuse the edges together and supply additional metal to the joint.

See also BRASS; BRONZE AGE METALLURGY; PREHISTORIC TECHNOLOGY.

3, 163, 264, 269, 333, 396, 845, 914.

CORAL. Coral is a marine gem composed of aragonite, a substance largely built up of calcium carbonate and formed by the secretion of sea-water by the coral polyp, a marine creature which lives in colonies. Although there are many kinds of corals, which are produced by various polyps, hydroids and algae, only one of them, precious coral, is of interest to craftsmen. This is a compact and homogenous material, quite unlike the other corals, which are spongy, porous and rock-like in their formation. It has a hardness of only 3–4 on the MOHS SCALE, so that it can readily be filed and carved to shape, and then polished to a brilliant finish. The principal species of corals which contribute to coral carving are: *Corallium rubrum*, which is the most familiar, and which occurs in the Mediterranean and various other localities, notably the Fiji Islands; *Corallium Japonicum Kish*, *Corallium secundum Dana*, *Corallium elatius Ridl* and *Corallium konojoi Kish*, all of which are found in the Japanese archipelago; *Corallium Johnsoni* from the Canary Islands; and *Corallium Lubrani* from Cape Verde in Africa. American readers may be fortunate enough to discover varieties of precious coral which have not been worked hitherto. A blue and yellow coral were both fished at one time, but now never come on the market. But coral propagates itself so easily that it is unlikely that any species has become completely extinct. Modern colours range from white to a deep red; brown and black corals come from coral bushes which have died and been fished subsequently.

A coral colony is a tree-like growth which roots itself to a spot on the sea bed, below five fathoms in depth. Coral bushes will attach themselves to any hard substance offering purchase, even a skull. Shakespeare was in line with these facts when he wrote:

> Full fathom five thy father lies,
> Of his bones are coral made.

The coral polyps inhabit the outer coat of the coral bush. This is a thin, friable covering, called *sarcosoma* by marine biologists, and on its surface blister-like holes appear. Through these the coral polyps, which if magnified would resemble sea anemones, thrust their heads to eat. Underneath this friable and thin outer covering the structure of precious coral is composed of myriads of fine hard rods like the strands of a cable. These corded structures have to be ground away in order to shape coral, and even after it is finished there are often small pitted indentations in a polished piece. These marks should be looked for as a test for authenticity, and coral should be tested for hardness. If a drop of sulphuric acid is poured on a piece of coral, it should effervesce.

Not merely the colour, but the shape of any coral bush will depend on its species, and where it grows. Coral off the North African coast grows straight upright with occasional branches pushing out, and shows bright rather than dark colours; coral which grows off Sardinia, on the other hand, has a low bushy habit and exhibits a really dark red colour. The Japanese corals are very different from the Mediterranean ones. They are much thicker and heavier, while the branches strike out to the right or to the left, and not in all directions. The stem of a Japanese coral bush, in fact, is easily converted into a figure statue. Moreover various seas in the Japanese archipelago produce different colours of coral; the sea of Hoki produces a white coral, the sea of Tosa a vermilion one. Because Japanese coral is harder, more compact, more weighty, and because it attains a larger size than Mediterranean coral, it is much more suitable for figure carving and it has been employed for this purpose even by Italian carvers since the end of the 19th c. Just as the Chinese prefer a more speckled TORTOISESHELL to the blonde which is the fashionable shade in Europe, so the Chinese and Japanese have different preferences for the colours of coral. The pink Formosan coral has always been popular, and it is to be found as far apart as Tibet and Mongolia. Another Oriental coral, that of India, has been famous since Roman times.

Until recently coral was fished by dragging a weighted drogue hung with bags of netting along the sea bed, so that it entangled the coral branches in the meshes. It was then brought to the surface by hauling in the cable with a windlass aboard the *corallina* or fishing-boat. The modern coral fisher often goes to the bottom with skin-diving equipment, a net on a handle, and an adze with which to chip off coral bushes. This is a big improvement on the old method, which was such hard work that a Neapolitan proverb said that only a thief or a murderer deserved to become a coral fisher. Nevertheless coral is still won with some danger as well as difficulty and this factor has helped to contribute to its mystique. Another contributory factor is its colour, generally red, which has caused it to be associated with blood and in particular with the blood shed by infants while teething. From the 16th c. down to Victorian times babies were given coral branches with gold or silver bells to bite on to help them cut their teeth. The mystery concerning the origin of coral (only in the 18th c. was it recognized to be an animal and not a plant), its brilliant and generally unfading colours, the fact that a natural piece of coral can be found in almost any shape—all this helped to make coral the substance *par excellence* for amulets. Its softness, which meant that it could be worked by very primitive methods, brought it early into the range of artistic materials. A Neolithic image made in partly shaped raw coral has been found in the Grótta dei Piccioni in Bolignano, Chieti, Italy. Probably it was worked by being abraded with a flat stone rubber, pierced and cut with sharp pointed and edged stone splinters, and finally polished with sand. By Carthaginian times amulets were being carved in the form of statuettes completely in the round. These would involve the use of a metal-edged tool. The kind of methods in use in Naples today probably date back to the 16th c., if not the Middle Ages. Raw coral is sorted into different sizes, then cloven into short lengths by being filed with a triangular file, sawn half-way through with a double-edged cleaver, and severed with a pair of heavy clippers. At this stage most coral goes to the *bucatrice* or 'drill women', Neapolitan housewives who are usually resident at Torre del Greco. They fix the coral on a stand and then drill through it with a bow-drill, a very primitive-looking instrument, which, however, enables them to 'feel' the coral as it is being drilled and determine whether the hole is being bored properly. Once drilled, the blanks for beads are strung on steel wires stretched across a wooden bench, and a sandstone block is pushed to and fro over them to give a first shaping. Now they are filed and ground into the required contour on a grooved grindstone, against which they are held by a needle pushed into a piece of wood. Next comes a bath in a solution of hydrogen peroxide, which is supposed to heighten the colour, and finally they are polished by being shaken in cylindrical drums filled with pumice powder, and at a subsequent stage with calcined deer's horns to which soapsuds have been added. Coral can be shaped with the bow-drill, or by gravers and files.

The sizes and shapes in which coral is obtainable have had an important influence in determining the objects made from it. Only the finest pieces of Japanese coral will serve as raw material for a statuette. Some Japanese coral comes to Europe, but the choicest pieces are probably kept for the home market. Because large pieces of coral are rare, much work has always been done with the tiny sprigs or twiglets at the ends of the branches. These can simply be bored as beads for JEWELLERY, but great ingenuity has been shown in using them also as a form of mosaic or encrustation in massed decorations. While the larger sections served for statuettes, vases and snuff-bottles, or for Second Grade mandarin's buttons, smaller pieces were made into handles for utensils such as spoons or knobs for the lids of boxes or developed as whole coral trees combined with a statuette of St. Sebastian or Actaeon in some other precious material. Coral was worked up into crucifixes, credences, CHESS PIECES, etc., sawn into slabs so as to serve for small reliefs, used to encrust altar frontals, employed as a decorative element on weapons and armour, and made into beads for church embroidery.

As has been said, the history of coral carving extends from the Stone Age, whence come numerous finds in the Upper Palaeolithic levels at Wildscheuer in Germany and other localities, to our own day, when the 'School of Coral' at Torre del Greco, Naples, endeavours not merely to keep the art of coral jewellery alive but to revitalize figure-carving, mosaic and all the sculptural arts. Coral was employed for jewellery in Sumer and ancient EGYPT, where a Red Sea species known as *Tubipora musica* was brought into use. The ancient Britons were great amateurs of coral. Pliny tells us that the Gauls were so fond of coral from India that there was more of it to be found in Gaul than in the land which produced it. Giovanni Tescioni, the world authority on coral, lays emphasis on the Battersea shield in the British Museum. But it would appear that this is correctly described as being decorated with red glass, not coral. There can be no doubt that the Witham shield of the same period is decorated with coral, however. The British Museum also has one of the best Roman coral statuettes, that of Jove Serapis in the Towneley Collection. Coral necklaces have been found in the catacombs, while in BYZANTIUM coral began its long career as a decorative material for religious objects. A crucifix now in the Vatican attests to its popularity in the Byzantine Empire. Throughout the Middle Ages coral was popular for amulets and rosaries, reliquaries, madonnas and other ecclesiastical appurtenances. But the apogee of coral-carving came in the 17th and 18th centuries. The names of one or two of the carvers have survived such as that of Franco Alfieri (active during the 17th c.). Usually, however, the best works, such as the splendid vases, credences and monstrances where coral mosaic is combined with goldsmith's work, are unsigned. Trapani in Sicily and Naples were the great centres of coral working though the German goldsmiths often incorporated coral into their statues. In Italy the output of the 17th and early 18th centuries really deserves the epithet 'The Coral Renaissance' which Tescioni has applied to it. Coral carving never achieved greater heights of skill than during the BAROQUE period in Italy with creations such as the incredible *presepio* of coral, gilded bronze and ENAMEL in the San Marino Museum at Naples. The decline was not long delayed, however, and by the 19th c. it is a relief to turn to the coral carvings of the

Orient. A coral branch is one of the Seven Legendary Treasures of Nippon, and it is perhaps in Japan that the best work is still being done. In China the choice of coral for the button worn by Second Grade mandarins, who stood next to the Princes of the Blood, indicates the taste for this material. Many fine carvings were made during the 19th c., principally in the shape of snuff-bottles, vases and figures. Tibet and Nepal were centres of quite distinctive styles of coral carving. In the West commercial coral-working has little to recommend it and the future of the ancient art of coral carving, if it has a future, rests with the amateurs.

822.

CORNELIAN. See QUARTZ.

CORNICE. Architectural term for a horizontal projecting MOULDING which crowns a building, particularly the uppermost member of an entablature. Also the ornamental moulding running round the walls of a room, such as a picture moulding or the projection within which curtains are hung.

COROMANDEL LACQUER. See CHINA (LACQUER) and LACQUER AND JAPANNING.

COSTUME

1. Greek and Roman antiquity.
2. Byzantium.
3. Medieval Europe.
4. Tudor and Stuart.
5. Eighteenth to twentieth centuries, Europe.
6. Indians of the Inca Empire.
7. Colonial North America.

See also: CHINA (COSTUME) and INDIA (COSTUME)

1. GREEK AND ROMAN ANTIQUITY. No more than a few deteriorated scraps of Greek garments have survived and our knowledge of Greek dress therefore depends on literary references and on depictions in the visual arts. Of the latter the vase painters were generally both skilful and exact in their representation of costume, although allowance must be made for the fact that photographic reproductions of drawings on a curved surface may be misleading in the general impression they create. The sculpture also supplies valuable data particularly in the earlier periods before an interest in drapery for its own sake led to a certain exuberance and exaggeration of effect.

Like the costume of ancient Egypt and Mesopotamia and in contrast with that of the Persians and Scythians, Greek dress depended upon hanging or draping rather than upon fitting. There was relatively little change in basic pattern from the Archaic to the Roman period and throughout these centuries the costume was characterized by simplicity of conception with attention devoted primarily to elegance of line revealing the structure and movements of the body. The natural proportions of the body were not concealed or distorted by a multiplicity of garments or by a display of irrelevant ornament, but the function of dress was always to drape the form with dignity and elegance. There was an instinctive avoidance of anything exaggerated or grotesque.

The main garments were two, which the Greeks themselves referred to as *endymata* and *periblemata*, inner and outer garments. The main endyma was the *chiton*, which was common to both sexes. It existed in two styles, the Doric and the Ionic, though in the course of time they were to some extent merged in a common Greek style. According to Herodotus the Doric chiton was universally worn until the 6th c. It was a simple woollen shift consisting of an oblong piece of material (or two pieces sewn together at one side up to the breast) whose dimensions depended on the height of the wearer; the width was about twice the distance from elbow to elbow with arms outstretched and its length was about 46 centimetres more than the height from shoulder to ground. It was draped so as to fall to the feet and allow the top to hang in a graceful fold or lappet across the chest and down perhaps to the waist. The turn-over or lappet, called *diploidion* or *epomis*, was fastened by clasps at each shoulder. The chiton was sleeveless and might be fastened at the waist by a girdle. The Ionian style was associated with the Greeks of Asia Minor and with the Athenians. It was made of linen, sometimes so thin as to be transparent, and was more ample than the Doric chiton, made from a longer piece of material. The armholes were usually but not always at the top instead of the sides and it was fastened along the top edge by a row of pins or brooches running from neck to wrist. Sometimes it was fastened with a double girdle, below the breasts and at the hips, so as to form a bulging fold called a *kolpos*. In order to release the arms and give greater freedom of movement the Ionic chiton was sometimes fastened with a cord looped in front over the armpits and tied between the shoulder-blades at the back. Homer applies the epithet *helkechitones* (wearers of long trailing chitons) to the Ionians, among whom the Athenians were numbered. Thucydides, near the beginning of *The Peloponnesian War*, says that 'it was no long time' since the old men at Athens had abandoned the Ionian linen chiton, and it is clear from Aristophanes (*Knights* 1330; *Clouds* 984) that

Doric chiton with dagger-like pins. From a toilet box (B.M.)

Ionic chiton and himation. Bronze statuette (B.M.)

the longer chiton was already outmoded at the time of the Peloponnesian War.

Older men wore the chiton to the feet as the women's chiton. But younger men and manual workers often wore it only to mid thigh in order to allow greater freedom of movement. There were two styles: the *amphimaschalos* had two armholes and covered both shoulders; the other, the *heteromaschalos* worn mainly by athletes and workers, had only one armhole and left the right arm and shoulder uncovered. It was also called *exomis* and could serve as an outer garment or *himation* also. It was the usual dress of the working classes and slaves. In the *Lysistrata* of Aristophanes the Chorus of old men for comic effect wear the exomis (line 662).

It seems that the chiton was usually worn next to the skin without any under-garment, although the literature speaks of a *chitonion* (in the case of women) and *chitoniskos* (of men). The chitonion was an under-shift below the chiton, but how general was its use we do not know. In the *Adoniazusae* of Theocritus Praxagora wears a chitonion while washing herself and afterwards puts on the upper endyma or chiton. So too Athenaeus (xiii. 590) tells us that the famous courtesan Phryne wore a chitonion next the skin and it was this which in a well known incident the orator Hyperides snatched away to reveal her naked breasts at the conclusion of his speech in her defence. The male chitoniskos on the contrary was not an under-garment. The word simply refers to a short chiton. When, for example, in Plato's *Hippias Minor* Socrates enumerates the articles of Hippias's wardrobe he mentions sandals, girdle, himation and chitoniskos, but no third garment. Women might also wear a band around the breasts (called *tainia*, *mitra* or *apodesmos*) under the chiton or a body band (*perizoma*) around the stomach. This is not to be confused with the girdle or *zōnē*.

The main outer garment or periblema was the himation, which was the Greek antecedent of the Roman toga. It was common to both sexes; indeed a wife could wear her husband's himation. The himation was a large square piece of cloth. Properly worn it was first thrown over the left shoulder, then brought round the back to the right side, over or below the right arm, and then thrown over the left arm, where it was fastened with a clasp. Great attention was paid to its proper adjustment and it was a mark of good breeding to wear the himation with dignified and elegant folds, whereas to wear it draped untidily or from the wrong side was a sign of bad breeding or clottishness. (Plato, *Theaetetus* 175, says that it is a mark of the *aneleutheros* and *apaideutos*—ill-bred and uneducated—to wind the himation the wrong way; and Aristophanes, *Birds* 1565, says the same of the barbarian.) In early times the himation was worn to the ground, as Quintilian says (*Instit. Orat.* xi. 3. 143: 'togas veteres ad calceos usque demittebant ut Graeci pallium' ('of old they wore their togas to the heels as the Greeks the pallium'). Later this was regarded as a sign of pride and luxuriousness (Demosthenes, *De Falsa Leg.* 422; Lucian, *Amor.* 3). But to wear it above the knee was thought unbecoming (Theophrastus, *Char.* 4, says it is the sign of the yokel to wear it above the knee). The Spartans, however, and those who aped their customs wore a short, coarse outer mantle called *tribon* (Plato, *Protagoras* 342). The boys at Sparta were allowed a chiton until their twelfth year but thereafter the tribon was the sole article of dress winter and summer alike. In Athens the youths on becoming *ephebos* at the age of 18 wore a short cloak called the *chlamys*. The chlamys was properly a short riding cloak of Thessalian or Macedonian origin and it was used on journeys or by messengers. When it came into vogue in Greece is uncertain, but according to the lexicographer Pollux it was mentioned by the poetess Sappho (latter 7th c.). The female himation was usually named *ampechone*, though it differed in no essentials from the male garment, and the diminutive *ampechonion* may refer to a smaller version thrown over the shoulders in the manner of a shawl.

The himation often had a decorative border and sometimes a fringe of tassels or some small weight of beads attached to the corners so that in movement the weight swung away from the body and emphasized the pattern and the lie of the folds. It sometimes hung in pleats to the feet. On women the long pleated himation was often called a *peplos*, a word which appears not to have denoted any separate garment but which is used more particularly with reference to female attire (*Odyssey* xviii. 292; Xenophon, *Cyropaedia* v. 1. 6). When used of male attire it is usually with reference to the long Persian dresses (e.g. Aeschylus, *Persae* 468, 1030). The word 'peplos' was also used specifically of the embroidered robe which was carried in procession at the Panathenaic festival of Athens.

The materials of Greek dress were mainly wool and linen. After the Ionian linen chiton had gone out of fashion for men wool was the sole material. The most celebrated wool came from Miletus (Aristophanes, *Lysistrata* 729; Strabo xii. 7. 6). In winter a thicker and coarser weave was used for the himation, which was then called *chlaina* (Aristophanes, *Birds* 714, says that the appearance of the swallow indicated the time to buy the chlaina). The lighter summer garment was called *theristria* (Theocritus xv. 69) and the *chlanis* was also probably a light summer cloak. For women's garments, in addition to wool and linen, the ancients speak of *byssos*, which was a vegetable fibre though it is not certain precisely what was meant. Herodotus uses the word of the wrappings of Egyptian mummies (ii. 86), which were of flax, and of material for bandages (vii. 181). Pollux says that it was a form of linen (vii. 76) and Plutarch appears to agree (*De Pythiae Orac.* 4) but Philostratus (*Vit. Apollon.* ii. 20) says it grew from a tree. It seems likely that by 'byssos' cotton was sometimes meant and that thicker forms of cotton were confused with linen. Byssos was usually white like cotton, but a yellow kind was also known, which grew around Elis and was exceptionally expensive. But it appears unlikely that cotton was used for complete garments until after the Classical period in Greece. The manufacture of SILK from the *bombyx* is described by Aristotle (*Hist. Anim.* v. 17) and his description was repeated by Pliny (*Nat. Hist.* vi. 17. 20 and xi. 22. 23). Silk was imported both in the manufactured state (*serika*) and in cocoons (*metaxa*), which were unwound and processed chiefly in the island of Cos. But this was at a later period and the diaphanous garments mentioned in the Classical period (e.g. Aristophanes, *Lysistrata* 48) were made of a specially fine byssos or of *amorgos*, a fine fabric of flax which took its name from the island Amorgos where it was chiefly grown. Furs were not used on account of the mildness of the climate. Leather chitons are mentioned by

Pollux (vii. 70) and in the time of Pausanias (2nd c. A.D.) the poor people of Phocis and Euboea wore chitons of hogs' hides.

In regard to colour, white or yellowish white was regarded as the most respectable for a discreet woman of the upper classes, but bright colours were still much used particularly among women. Pollux (vii. 55) draws a distinction between the colours worn by men and those which were confined to women. For men he mentions blue-purple (*halourgis*), red-purple (*porphyris*), red (*phoinikis*) and frog-green (*batrachis*). A dark-coloured chiton (*phaios*, perhaps from a brown undyed wool) is also mentioned for academicians (Athenaeus xii. 544). The women's colours given by Pollux are saffron (*krokotos*), olive-green (*omphakinon*, the colour of unripe grapes), apple-green (*melinon*), light blue (*aerinos*, mist coloured, from light blue to light grey) and grey (*killios*, donkey grey). He also mentions the purple stripe (*paralourgis*).

The chiton was commonly decorated by coloured borders, called *pezae*, around the bottom, the hole for the neck or the edge of the diploidion. These might either be woven into the material or sewn on so as to be renewable. Double vertical stripes appear where the two sides of the chiton are sewn together, sometimes running the whole length and sometimes only on the diploidion. Similar sleeve ornaments also occur. The himation had similar ornamentation. The decorative fringes and tassels, whose purpose was also functional, have been mentioned. Sometimes the garment was decorated with an all-over pattern of embroidered flowers or stars (Plato, *Republic* viii. 557, mentions the *poikilon himation*, *pasin anthesi pepoikilmenon*, 'dappled with all flowers'; and Homer, *Iliad* v. 735, etc., uses 'poikilos' as an epithet of 'peplos').

Footwear was of many kinds and the vocabulary is both large and indefinite. It was customary for Greeks to go barefoot indoors and to put on footwear (*pedila*) when going out (*Iliad* xi. 44; *Odyssey* xvii. 2; Plato, *Republic* ii. 372). But many people of simple habits went abroad unshod except for special or ceremonial occasions (Plato, *Symposium* 220; Xenophon, *Memorabilia* i. 6. 2; Plutarch, *Phocian* 4). In Sparta this was compulsory for younger people by law (Plato, *Laws*, i. 633; Xenophon, *De Republ. Laced.* ii. 3). Footwear was of two types, the sandal and a true shoe, with many intermediate forms. The true sandal, bound underneath the foot, was called *hypodema*. The Greek word *sandalion* referred to a transitional form which had a thong across the toes and a small upper leather, called *zygon*, partially covering the foot (Aristophanes, *Lysistrata* 416). The thong passed between the big and second toe and was fastened by a leaf-shaped clasp to two side straps and then to a back strap. These straps were sometimes extended in a crossed pattern to cover the lower part of the calf. The *krepis*, from which the

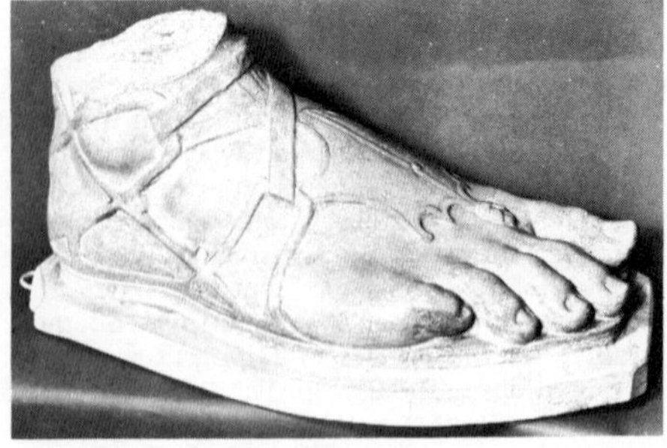

Foot of the Hermes of Praxiteles showing the type of thick-soled sandal called crepida. (Mus. of Classical Archaeology, Cambridge)

Romans derived the word *crepida*, was a kind of half-shoe with a thicker sole than the sandal. The *embades* and *Lakonikae* were full shoes, last-made, worn only by men (Aristophanes, *Knights* 872, *Wasps* 1157, *Ecclesiazusae* 47, 314, 345, 507). *Blautae* were finer and more elegant shoes worn on special occasions; they were worn by Socrates when he went to dine with Agathon (Plato, *Symposium* 174). The *cothurnus* (as distinct from the high shoe of the tragic actor) was a common form of footwear worn by both men and women and suited to either foot. There were also various kinds of women's shoe, of which Aristophanes mentions the *Persica*, which covered the whole foot. Shoes were commonly made of leather but sometimes of felt, and felt socks could be worn inside shoes or sandals. Soles were sometimes thickened with cork and men's shoes for hard wear might be strengthened with nails. Mention is made of sandals ornamented with embroidery or gold and the habit is castigated by Clement of Alexandria (*Paed.* ii. 11). Well-fitting footwear was considered a mark of good breeding and the contrary a sign of boorishness (Plato, *Protagoras* 322, *Phaedo* 64, *Hippias Major* 294; Theophrastus, *Char.* 4).

Great attention was devoted to the dressing of the hair and in hair-style the Athenians differed from the Spartans, who followed the old Dorian custom of allowing the hair to grow long. Spartan boys wore their hair short and first let it grow on reaching the age of manhood. In Athens, however, the boys had long hair and the cutting of the hair was part of the maturity ritual of the ephebos, when locks might be dedicated to a deity. Men grew the hair longer again but kept it carefully trimmed. The barbers' shops were social centres and were described by Theophrastus as 'wineless symposia'. Barbers also trimmed the beard and manicured the nails. A variety of hair-styles for men is apparent from pictorial representations and sculpture of the Classical age. Perhaps the most general was for the front hair to be curled in a tightly set and oiled cluster of bubble curls and waved over the top and back as if it were plaited wet and allowed to dry. The hair was bound with a fillet. The

Charioteer of Delphi

Charioteer of Delphi (*c.* 470 B.C.) has his hair elaborately curled at the sides and held together by a wide fillet, which also holds the back hair rolled over it. Beards were trimmed to a point and might also be curled. Shaving the beard was brought into fashion by Alexander the Great, though the practice was not unknown before.

Greek women wore their hair in free-flowing locks or in a series of tight plaits or bound up in a chignon behind. In the 5th c. they drew back their waved hair and bound it in a knot behind. But later, in the Hellenistic period, styles became more elaborate and varied. The hair was held by kerchiefs, snoods or nets. The nets, worn night and day like the Roman *reticulum*, were very fine, made sometimes of gold threads or yellow byssos, and were called *kekryphalos*. The snoods (*sakkoi*) were made more stoutly, sometimes covering the whole head and sometimes open at the back so that the hair hung out behind. The kerchief (*mitra*), often worked in a pattern, covered either the entire head or a part of it. A low forehead was considered a mark of beauty and therefore the hair was brought well down over it in front. A sling-shaped band, called a *sphendone*, was also worn, broad over the forehead and tapering at the sides. It was sometimes made of metal or gilded leather.

Ladies wore no hat but for protection against the sun used a sunshade (*skiadeion*). Men also went ordinarily hatless but for journeys, hunting or the theatre wore types of hat which were also in general use among artisans, fishermen and farm labourers. These were of two main kinds, the brimless 'helmet' type called *kynē* or the close-fitting felt cap called *pilos*. The *petasos* was a flat felt hat with a round broad brim. It was of Thessalonian origin and was a distinguishing mark of the ephebos together with the chlamys. The epheboi on the Parthenon wear a petasos with brim bent downwards and four arched cuts forming four corners one of which extends over the forehead. Hermes is usually represented in a winged petasos. The Romans wore a similar hat in the country or when travelling but in the city it was worn only at the theatre. The *pilos*, Latin *pilleus*, was a round, close-fitting felt cap with very narrow brim, which was the ordinary wear of fishermen, sailors and artisans but worn by the upper classes only in the country. In Rome it was worn by the whole people at the *Saturnalia* and by freedmen as a symbol of their status. The *kausia*, of Macedonian origin, was a flat broad-rimmed felt hat which differed from the petasos in having a higher crown flat on top. It was adopted by sailors and fishermen at Rome and in the imperial period was worn at the theatre as a protection from the sun by the upper classes.

Roman women of the Augustan age wore a costume very similar to that of the Greek women but with the addition of an under-tunic (*tunica interior*) as a regular garment. The *tunica interior* was sleeveless and was worn with a brassière (*strophium*). Over it, corresponding to the Greek chiton, was worn the *stola*, a longer tunic with sleeves and with a broad flounce sewn on the bottom which half covered the feet when the stola was girded up into folds below the breast. Above this, worn only out of doors, was the *palla* corresponding to the Greek himation. There were many ways of draping the palla according to taste. It usually began hanging down from the left shoulder, passed across the back towards the right and ended hanging over the left arm. It might or might not be drawn over the head and could pass over or under the right shoulder. There were a number of variations on this basic costume; for example, the stola might be sleeveless and be cut to reveal elbow-length sleeves on the *tunica interior*. The stola of the Roman matron had a narrow border called *instita* at the bottom or as a special sign of honour a gold border.

Roman men wore a *tunica* with or without sleeves and with armholes at the sides. The plebeian, working-class tunic was knee length and girded at the waist. The right arm could be withdrawn, leaving the right shoulder bare and the arm free. But longer tunics were worn and the *tunica talaris* came down to the ankles. The usual tunic was of plain wool or linen. It might be decorated by a stripe (*clavus*) down the centre front and back or by two stripes down each side —the distinguishing feature of the Roman knights. The *tunica palmata*, worn by Roman emperors and later by consuls, was embroidered in gold all over on a purple ground. The *colobium* was a tunic with shortened sleeves worn by free-born citizens. It was later adopted by Christian deacons before the dalmatic.

The most distinctive feature of Roman dress was the *toga*. It was the outer garment *de rigueur* for respectable citizens on all public occasions, forbidden to foreigners and exiles. It was formed from a piece of woollen fabric shaped like the arc of a circle, in length something more than three times the height of the wearer and at its greatest depth about twice his height. It might be decorated with a stripe along the straight edge. The manner of draping was complex and became ever more complicated as time went on. In the Augustan age it was as follows. The cloth was first folded lengthwise, not down the centre but so that one fold was thicker than the other. It was then bunched together and thrown over the left shoulder so that one-third hung down in front to the feet and the other two-thirds remained behind. The latter part was then brought round under the right arm, opened so as to cover the whole of the right side from armpit to calf, and then gathered and thrown again over the left shoulder from front to back, covering the greater part of the left arm. The semicircular over-fold was allowed to droop into a pocket, called the *sinus*, which could either be used as a receptacle or lifted to cover the head. Finally the third of the cloth which, thrown over the left shoulder from the back first hung down in front to the feet, was lifted up off the ground to give a hanging loop known as the *umbo* or boss. The *toga virilis*, the ordinary formal dress of a Roman citizen, was made of natural coloured wool undecorated. The toga of the senator had a broad purple stripe in front, the *latus clavus*, that of the knights two narrow stripes, *angustus clavus*. The *toga praetexta* had a purple or scarlet stripe along the straight edge; it was worn by curule magistrates and censors, by youths until they attained manhood, and by unmarried girls. Candidates for public office wore the *toga candida*, a new toga whitened with chalk and undecorated. The *toga trabea*, with scarlet stripes and a purple hem, was worn by augurs. The *toga picta*, embroidered with gold stars on purple, was worn by a general celebrating his triumph, by a magistrate who was giving public games and in imperial times by a consul when entering on office and by the emperor

Detail from precinct walls of the Ara Pacis, Rome, showing figures wearing the toga

on festal occasions. A dark toga, the *toga pulla*, was worn by the working classes or for mourning or by an accused person. In the 6th c. a simpler form of toga had been the dress of men and women alike. But by imperial times the toga was not worn by women except courtesans.

The toga was the distinctive garb of peace. In addition there were various types of military cloak: the red *abolla* worn by officers in the army and by philosophers; the *paludamentum* which was put on symbolically by a Roman general when he was leaving the city for a campaign; and the *sagum*, a thick woollen cloak fastened at the neck with a clasp and worn by the rank and file. The *paenula* was a semicircular woollen cloak fastened up the front and sometimes with a hood attached, which was worn by men and women on journeys, by country people instead of a toga and by slaves. The *lacerna* was a rectangular cape worn over the toga as an additional wrap.

For jewellery see GREEK AND ROMAN ANTIQUITY (JEWELLERY).

2. BYZANTIUM. What little we know about Byzantine costume is derived from murals, mosaics, ivories and illuminated manuscripts, in all of which the artists were as a rule more interested to portray decoration and patterns than details of the actual garments. The representations chiefly depict rulers, nobility, high ecclesiastics, or saints and martyrs costumed in the manner of these. From the little we know it is nevertheless clear that Byzantine styles influenced court costume in most countries of Europe during the Middle Ages.

The main principle of Byzantine costume as we know it was a continued simplicity of construction combined with ever increasing magnificence in sumptuous materials and ornamentation. From the 3rd to the 6th c. the toga gradually went out of use except for ceremonial occasions and the basic garment for men was a simple, T-shaped tunic (*tunica*), which was worn of varying lengths to the knee or to the ankle. This gradually increased in width, both in the sleeves and in the body, until it developed into the loose, wide-sleeved garment known as the *dalmatic* (from Dalmatia, where it was a national dress). Above this was worn a wide *colobium* and for dignified wear a *pallium* draped as a wrap. With women the stola gradually fell into disuse from *c.* the 3rd c. and was succeeded by the *colobium*. Above this was worn a *palla* bound at the waist by a jewelled belt. The *colobium* or the *dalmatic* was decorated with embroidered or jewelled stripes, a survival of the Roman *clavi*. A few examples may illustrate the ensemble.

A 6th-c. mosaic at the church of S. Vitale, Ravenna, shows the Emperor Justinian and his wife, Theodora. He is dressed in a white knee-length tunic embroidered in gold and above it a semicircular purple cloak lined with red (called *paludamentum*). Upon it is the richly embroidered panel (*tablion*) which remained a feature of court dress from the 5th c. to the 11th c. (and was worn by empresses also from the 8th c. to the 11th c.). He has purple hose and red shoes decorated with pearls. Theodora has a white, gold-embroidered tunica similar to that of Justinian with the exception that it falls to the ankles. Above it she wears a semicircular purple cloak lined with blue and embroidered in gold; at the hem the embroidery depicts the adoration of the Magi. She has a jewelled collar (*superhumeral*) and under the crown a head-dress of Asiatic style.

A mosaic in the church of S. Apollinare Nuovo at Ravenna shows a procession of 22 virgin martyrs offering their crowns to the Virgin. They are dressed in long tunics with jewelled cuffs, over which is the *colobium* decorated with *clavi* in the form of floral bands. Above this is draped a *palla* about a metre wide by about three metres long, whose jewelled panel hangs down in front. In a mosaic from the 1st half of the 7th c. in her Basilica at Rome St. Agnes is represented between the popes Honorius and Symmachus. The saint is dressed in a tight-sleeved tunic and above it a *colobium* or *dalmatic* with three-quarter-length sleeves and jewelled *clavi*. Two embroidered medallions (*segmentae*) appear below the knees. Above the *dalmatic* is worn a long jewelled band, which appears to be the prototype of the ecclesiastical *omophorion* of the Orthodox Church or the *pallium* of the Roman Church. In the 10th c. a short over-tunic with or without sleeves became fashionable for women's dress. An example may be seen in a 10th-c. textile at Bamberg Cathedral representing a western princess paying homage to the Emperor Nicephoros Phocas.

Many of the Church vestments originated from Byzantine court dress. The long, tight-sleeved white tunic became the *alb*, the outer tunic with its wider sleeves became the ecclesiastical *dalmatic*, which was cut in the fashion of what was later known as the *surplice*. The *pallium*, which in Roman times was a cloak, had become by the 8th c. a long band of white linen which encircled the shoulders and hung down before and behind to the base of the chasuble. In the Western Church it was also made of lamb's wool, was *c.* three fingers wide and was embroidered with four crosses before and behind. The cope was descended from the outer cloak or *paenula*, which belonged to the transition period between Roman and Byzantine. The *stola* survived as the *stole*, a narrow strip of silk or linen with embroidered ends which was worn round the shoulders hanging down to below the knees under the dalmatic.

3. MEDIEVAL EUROPE. It would be both misleading and confusing to describe the various parts of dress worn during the Middle Ages by their contemporary names. Such names were coined from various languages and dialects; nor did the names given to a garment in one decade necessarily mean the same thing in the next. Almost as soon as a term had become familiar to describe some new garment the garment in

The Empress Theodora with attendants, from the Church of S. Vitale, Ravenna (*c*. A.D. 547)

question changed or disappeared and the old name was used for something different. In the 14th and 15th centuries particularly this is one of the major problems for the student of costume. For instance the words used to describe a short body-covering garment, with or without sleeves, could be taken from a dozen different sources. In English 'doublet', 'gipon', 'jupon', 'jacket', 'jack', 'gambesons' or 'pourpoints' were all used to describe something that fitted from shoulder to waist, some longer than others, sometimes of leather, sometimes quilted or padded, some with skirts and some without. An outer gown of more lavish cut could be a super-tunic, surcote, robe, coat, mantle, houpelande, cotehardie, cloak or gown. All of these names and many others appear from time to time in the descriptive writings of the Middle Ages; none of them can be attached to one particular style or cut for any length of time, though the gambesons and pourpoints were originally padded protective garments worn under armour and later used to give a fashionable silhouette to a tight-fitting jacket worn over them. Thus for the sake of clarity this summary does not, on the whole, attempt to include fluctuations of fashion descriptions. The intention is rather to give a clear picture of costume from the 11th c. until the spread of printing helped to stabilize nomenclature.

The costume worn in England at the time of the Norman Conquest differed very little from anywhere else in Europe. Indeed there had been little change since the time of the Romans and the only distinguishing features between rich and poor were in the length and decoration of tunic and super-tunic. Those in authority wore long gowns and the artisan or labourer wore his as short as he chose, covering his legs with ankle-length trousers bound at the knee with leather thongs or with a footless sock called 'hose'. Before the turn of the century, however, the trousers or leg coverings were sometimes cut off at the knee or the hose worn longer and tied to a belt at the waist. The idea of the shortened trousers did not appear to have been so universal as that of the long hose though they were worn for some years by soldiers and those who found the tunic skirts inconvenient. The hose had no foot in normal circumstances, a boot of soft leather being worn over the bare foot. These boots were cut to cover the ankle and fastened either at the side or in front. They often had a decorative edge at the top.

About the only types of head covering in use during the 11th c. were either a hood or some variety of the Phrygian cap, which could be either decorated or plain. Decoration tended to be in bands of embroidery on most of the garments of the wealthy and they wore a linen shirt beneath the tunic. In England such luxury was reserved for those who could afford to buy the fabrics imported from across the Channel. Wool was the basic fabric of the time. Linen and SILK both had to be imported at a fairly high price and distinguished the households where luxury was an accepted privilege. Cotton was rare in Europe until the 16th c. See COTTON AND COTTON PRINTING.

The tunic normally had very long sleeves, tight at the wrist and then pushed up the arm, forming a concertina-like series of rucks from wrist to elbow. Over this was worn a super-tunic perhaps with short, elbow-length sleeves. The super-tunic, decorated and cut with a fuller skirt, was often a sign of social eminence, though simple versions were worn for warmth by ordinary people in the winter. It could be of any length that suited the wearer and his needs. Cloaks were worn for their decorative quality or the dignity that they gave on special occasions. Based on the form of a half-circle, they could serve as a covering, a blanket, or just as an extra garment in case of inclement weather.

Except among the aristocracy women's dress was devoid of extravagance. Their tunics fitted from the neck to the ground, an all-covering garment. They could, of course, have an under-garment of silk or linen, but normal wear in the Anglo-Saxon or Norman world was no more than two garments over a shift or body-garment: a long tunic, then perhaps a super-tunic in cold weather, and a cloak for out-of-doors. The Christian requirement for a woman to cover her head persisted until *c.* the end of the 11th c., when the Crusades and the impact of new ideas from Islamic countries caused a change.

The whole of the 12th c. was influenced by the contact with Jerusalem and the various countries through which the crusaders had to travel. New fabrics, new designs and an interest in hair-dressing were the first noticeable signs that a change in traditional costume had begun and by *c.* 1130 women's clothes had taken on a completely new silhouette. No longer was the figure hidden in cumbersome draperies. It was displayed or even accentuated by some form of tight-lacing at the waist and garments were cut to fit tightly from shoulder to hip, from where they flared out into a series of folds at the feet. Hair was not only visible once more but worn in two or four long plaits, which were ornamented with bands and added to with false hair or long funnels at the extremities decorated with beads, tassels or precious stones, according to wealth and status. Normally parted in the middle and held in place with a band or coronet on the brow, it received more attention than at any time since imperial Rome.

The vogue for elongation extended to practically every item of the costume, particularly to such things as girdles, sleeves and trains. The girdles were worn round the waist crossed over and knotted in the front, falling loosely over the hips, and were decorated with knots and tassels. Sleeves, particularly, received every possible attention to give a sense of luxury and trailing glory. They could be bell-shaped with such wide openings that on occasion they were actually fastened in a great knot to keep them from trailing on the ground. They could be tightly fitting from shoulder to elbow, where a tippet, or strip of contrasting material, was attached around the arm and hung down a couple of feet or more. At times the sleeve developed a wide lip just below the elbow and was turned back in a wide cuff, stiffened and lined with some contrasting fabric. Contemporary moralistic drawings show devils riding on the trains of some of these gowns and the craze for knots in trailing sleeves or trains is satirized by such devils wearing their tails knotted too. These were the excessive fashions peculiar to the 12th and early 13th centuries. Such garments could not be made in homespun and their richer material proclaimed the status of the wearer.

No such drastic change took place with the men's garments, and though sleeves of the super-tunic were often bell-shaped too, revealing a tight long sleeve underneath, and the skirts of tunics flared more fully than before, the basic garments remained unchanged. The accent on the hair was as noticeable with the well-dressed man as with his wife. The hair was elaborately curled and often worn down to the shoulders; beards, if worn, received no less attention and were parted, curled and arranged to dignify in much the same manner as the Assyrians of old. Tabards or sleeveless tunics, called surcotes, were sometimes added and the skirts of the super-tunic were frequently split up the sides to show off more of the garment worn underneath or to give an extra edge which could be decorated. Semicircular cloaks of varying length were worn by both sexes either fastened on one shoulder or held in place with a pair of decorative discs and a long cord tied across the chest.

The worker still retained the full trousers tucked into his hose, sometimes cut short but often calf-length and bagged out so that they gave an effect of loose knee-breeches pushed up above the knee. In pictures of men working in the fields at this time few of them wear any sort of shirt or tunic, but it is very clear that their legs were covered and that the breeches were of varying lengths.

The well-dressed man wore his hose decorated with a variety of patterns. Probably these were knitted, for the patterns appear in stripes going round the legs and add colour and interest when the skirts of his garments are short. Pointed-toed shoes and ankle-length boots were also decorated in many ways from punched leather holes to bands of decorative gilded leather or embroideries.

It was during the 12th c. that particoloured and two-coloured garments first made their appearance and these continued to be worn, often as a uniform, until the end of the 15th c. The fashion may have originated because it was impossible to buy the right length of one material, or perhaps because the new figure-fitting style required that the fabric be cut on the cross, which necessitated a seam down the front and back as well as at the sides. Whatever the reason the fashion persisted and was normally worn with hose cut from the same fabric as the tunic or surcote but their colours contrasting with the colours above. Thus if the right side of the tunic were red and the left green, the right leg would be green and the left one red.

The 13th c. continued to follow in the traditional lines but a special feature derived from interest in adapting the silhouette of the crusader to normal domestic requirements. Basically this silhouette could be traced to the surcote or tabard, which had been originally devised to protect the armour both from the heat of the sun and from rusting during rain storms. It was a loose tunic with wide openings under the arms, possibly lacing at the sides from the waist downwards, normally covering the knees but belted at the waist with the long sword-belt. Sometimes it was split in the front from the waist downwards, sometimes left open at one or both sides. The ladies found such a garment an attractive asset to enhance their long gowns and, made in a variety of materials, this sleeveless over-dress with various modifications and exaggerations continued to be worn until the close of the 15th c. One modification was the attachment of a sleeve at the back of the armhole only so that it could be left to hang down behind when not needed for warmth or when one wanted the arm free. Such a sleeve was the inspiration of the false sleeve of a later date whose function was purely decorative. The sleeve could be a fitted one or a wide hanging folded panel similar to the sleeve in a Japanese kimono, and it could be knotted at will. It appeared on both women's and men's garments.

A particularly interesting head-dress of the period can be traced to its inspiration from the crusaders' chain-mail head covering, normally held in place with a small coronet or fillet round the forehead and worn over a coif (a tight-fitting bonnet with a strap under the chin). Women devised a head covering which gave much the same impression. Their long hair was tucked up into a net, termed a crespin, and a band of linen was worn under the chin fastening on top of the head (barbette) and finished off with a fillet or coronet. Sometimes a veil was worn over this, sometimes the fillet was made like a hat with a flat crown and a variety of different sorts of decoration to the taste of the wearer. The fashion was peculiar to the century and was succeeded by the wimple of the 14th c. for those who wished to cover their necks and frame their faces.

The figure-fitting gowns of the 12th and early 13th centuries were succeeded by a general interest in a flowing, unrestricted outline without sleeves and without any sort of visible belt or girdle; this fashion was partly due to interest in the idea of the surcote open at the sides, which was normally worn over a kirtle or contrasting under-dress. The under-dress was girdled and carried the domestic trifles necessary to the lady of the house, such as keys, purse, etc. It was a simple matter to pull these out when necessary but they were not exposed. Later the gowns were made with slits at the side-front if the sides themselves were closed. This was the forerunner of a pocket and was a universal fashion for both sexes during the 14th c.

Probably the most spectacular innovation in the habits of the men was the introduction of a long, loose gown with hanging sleeves that often had two vents for the arms, one at the side and another at the bottom. This was the model for the scholar's gown and normally marked the man of learning rather than the man of action. Such gowns were made to fasten in the front and sometimes had a deep shoulder-cape or hood or both. They differed from the habit of a priest or friar in that the robes worn by ecclesiastics did not open down the front and were tied at the waist with a girdle.

Hoods were also becoming an essential part of dress for the winter months before the close of the 13th c. Already the interest in points was developing, points on the tops of caps, points to the hoods and points to the toes of the shoes—a fashion which became more and more exaggerated throughout the 14th c. till we find its climax of absurdity in the Court of Richard II, when sumptuary laws had to be enforced against toes projecting as much as 46 cm.

Shaped, quilted and padded doublets were worn under the armour if a buff or leather garment was not worn. During the 14th c. these gambesons or pourpoints, as they were called, were frequently adapted for civil wear and started a fashion in tightly fitting jerkins with buttons all down the front. The terms 'jacket', 'jerkin' and 'doublet' all refer to a short, fitting garment. A doublet was at that time without sleeves.

Once more numerous changes in costume took place at the turn of the century and the shape of things to come began to be visible *c.* 1320. It was a century of excess in both extremes; described by Chaucer in *The Persones Tale* as 'outragious array of clothing . . . precious clothing is culpable for derthe of it, and for his softnesse, and for his strangenesse and disguising, and for superfluitee or for the inordinat scantnesse of it . . .' The ravages of the Black Death did little to stem excess and both brasses and tomb figures bear witness to the rich variety of costumes that were worn by the wealthy in the 14th c. The new craze for a tightly fitting garment meant that buttons came into use as never before. Sleeves fitted from elbow to knuckles, funnelling out over the hand and done up with small buttons frequently to the elbow. Collars, following the same tendency, rose to the ears and buttoned to the chin. To exaggerate the tight effect of the jerkin a belt was worn around the hips, not at the waist; the waistline was already nipped in as closely as possible and this fashion was followed by both men and women whenever a belt was visible. Some of these belts were richly decorated with jewels or engraved metallic plaques which were linked together or decorated a leather surface.

Long, tightly fitting hose were tied with points (short leather thongs) to a waist-length, sleeveless doublet worn under the jerkin. A fashion for cutting the hems or edges of every garment in a series of decorative patterns such as leaves or scallops was symptomatic of the elongated phase, and few borders of the men's garments were free from this sort of decoration—normally called 'dagging', 'jagging' or by some heraldic term to suggest the actual form the decoration took.

Hoods had now become the typical feature of men's head-dress and throughout the 14th and 15th centuries their evolution from a simple head and neck covering to an extremely decorative hat took place in a dozen different shapes. At the beginning of the 14th c. the hood was little more than a cowl with a gorget over the shoulders, a protection in all weathers for head, ears and throat which fitted snugly over the shoulders. Gradually the point of the cowl became elongated and eventually developed into a pipe-like appendage that might be over a metre long; this was called a 'liripipe' and could be worn with the extremity tucked into the belt, serving as a purse or even a cosh in emergency. It could also be wound round the head and padded into a sort of brim. The edge of the gorget, following the tendency of the age, was dagged and often lined with a contrasting colour. Sometime towards the end of the 1st quarter of the century the aperture, which had originally been made for the face, was put on the head. The liripipe was wound about the head and the gorget with its ornamental edge, now on the top of the head, could be arranged as a coxcomb or draped about the face to form a hat of quite extraordinary versatility. At the same time it was a really useful head covering when occasion demanded. During the closing years of the century the arrangement became a gimmick and the most fantastic head-gear, derived from this fairly simple expedient, led to brimmed hats, coxcomb decorations and an enlarged form of liripipe, cut and decorated to fall over the shoulder, which had no contact with the original hood at all. Funnel-shaped sleeves, tight from shoulder to elbow with a wide opening falling over the forearm, were also worn by both men and women. These showed a tight sleeve from the garment which was worn underneath. Tippets hanging from the elbow were once more a decoration, particularly worn by women. They were usually embroidered and lined and could fall almost to the ground.

The majority of ladies still wore three main garments—first a shift of linen or even of silk; then the tightly fitting kirtle or under-gown, which was laced down the back as tightly as possible so that there were no folds or loose fabric except in the skirts which flared out from the hips; over this a surcote, which more often than not was sleeveless. One of the most typical styles of this over-dress was that with the sides cut away in a deep curve to show the kirtle beneath from shoulder to hip, where the belt could be easily seen and was readily accessible. This sideless garment was the elaborate extension of the sleeveless gown of the previous century and remained in use in varying forms until the 1480s. Sometimes the cut-away front and back of this surcote were only a few inches wide and the front appeared as if it were held in place by the row of ornamental buttons that usually adorned the front.

Typical hairdressing of the century was based on various arrangements of plaits. These were worn doubled up over the ears, across the head or rolled into a snood, or snoods, of gold mesh, one over each ear. By far the most popular style for such an arrangement appeared to be combined with a small coronet with a wire or metal appendage which came down over the cheeks. The hair was then parted in two and doubled back in heavy plaits, which were laced or wound on to this face-framing device. The back of the hair might be covered by a small veil or left uncovered at will. During the first few years of the 14th c. the wimple or chin veil was worn by the majority of married women, young girls wearing their hair often uncovered. Throughout the next century or more the wimple remained the favourite head-dress for the more sedate. It was at once becoming and less revealing than the more complicated hair arrangements. An interesting type of head veil with goffered layers of frills stitched across the front and framing the face was first worn *c.* 1360; probably the style was exaggerated and eventually developed into the heavily frilled head-dress so typical of the closing years of the century which completely framed the face, leaving only the chin free, with a 10-centimetre layer of tightly goffered frills.

It was a century of excess in fashionable extravagances and culminated with the courts of Richard II and Anne of Bohemia, who is generally reputed to have introduced the fantastic head-dresses which characterize the ladies of the 15th c. Before this time practically all women's head-dresses had been inspired either as a covering for the hair or as a means of drawing attention to its beauty and abundance; now the trend was to cover completely any possibility of seeing the hair. So numerous were the varieties of head-dress introduced during the closing years of the 14th c. and indeed throughout the entire 15th c. that it becomes an impossibility to enumerate them. It was an age of fantasy and the lady who devised a new method of adorning her head, whether it were with a flowerpot or with a pair of horns, pads or boxes, or a new variety of the steeple or henin, was at once the envy of all. Nor indeed was the absurdity of exaggerated head covering exclusively the prerogative of the ladies, for the huge Burgundian beavers and gigantic domed hats from the courts of Italy were probably as often seen as the converted hoods with their coxcomb or mantling.

The early years of Richard II's reign also witnessed the introduction of a vast new gown called a 'houpelande'. Circular in cut, with gigantic hanging and trailing sleeves dagged and punched with holes through which the lining showed, these gowns were worn by both sexes. Belted low at the hips when worn by the men and high under the breasts when worn by women, they were condemned by the critics of superfluity. If it were not for Chaucer's comments already referred to it might be difficult to date the houpelande in England, for there are few illustrations before *c.* 1420, when it suddenly became the typical robe engraved on contemporary brasses. It was, however, mentioned in France by Froissart as early as 1385 as a large, all-enveloping garment. Another absurd excess of the time was the wearing of bells: bells on belts, on the toes of shoes, on the ends of hoods and on bands strung across the chest.

The 15th c., then, saw the full flowering of extravagance in courtly costume with extremes both in brevity and in trailing magnificence, a never-ending succession of competitive fashions introduced from one European court or another. The sequence of such fashions is hard to follow for there were a great many barbaric and exotic deviations, but it is fairly safe to say that the ladies at least tended to wear only two kinds of over-dress for some half a century. One of these was the sideless surcote which gave the effect of a very low waist and the other was that devised originally from the houpelande with its low neckline and very high waist. Both of these were worn over a tightly fitting kirtle and both were worn very full and usually trailing on the ground. The sleeves of the houpelande were nearly always bell-shaped, falling back to reveal the tight sleeve beneath or gathered in at the wrist like a gigantic bag. The other surcote had no sleeves and always revealed a great deal of the kirtle at the sides. That the cut of these garments varied considerably is evident, but the general effect remained fairly constant. It was not until the middle of the century that the waistline once more reverted to its natural place.

Width of shoulder was the newest feature in men's clothes at the beginning of the 15th c. This effect could be achieved by various means such as a rolled puff at the top of the arm, a decorative epaulette, a padded, gathered upper sleeve or a leg-of-mutton sleeve tight at the wrist and gathered full on the shoulder. Sleeves were at this time more varied than they had ever been previously and false sleeves, hanging sleeves and those tied on at the shoulder were the vogue.

A short circular garment, split at the sides like a tabard, made its appearance in a number of different guises. This could be worn with or without a belt or sometimes belted at the front only so that the back fell like a cloak behind. It could have hanging 'wings' or sleeves. It could be lined with fur or the back half only could be so lined. It was worn of any length. One excellent example can be seen in Van Eyck's painting *Arnolfini and his wife* (N.G., London 1434), where Arnolfini is wearing a knee-length, fur-edged version.

Aristocratic English lady wearing houpelande and head-dress in the fashion of the early 15th c.

One of the more noticeable features of costume during the first half of the 15th c. was the wealth of colour and design. This may be explained first by the fashion for heraldry and the romantic significance of such things as mantling and heraldic colours and devices on gold and silver, secondly by the importation of fabrics woven with designs characteristic of the south, where such things as pineapples and pomegranates, acanthus leaves and variegated vegetation gave the wearer a fascinating and romantic contact with an exotic world of strange plants and fruits. Despite political upheavals, wars and civil wars, the 15th c. was a time of comparative luxury, when the wealthy merchant classes as well as the yeoman farmers lived well and were warmly clad. The merchants were often the most extravagantly dressed, for their foreign contacts gave an interesting variety to their choice. Italian merchants with their distant contacts continued to bring into London a rich variety of luxurious woven fabrics, fine silks, velvets and damasks, which had a ready market amongst the wealthy. But English fashions were beginning to follow their own lines, which tended to rely to a great extent on wool. The costumes of 15th-c. Italy, pictured by the artists of the Renaissance, were strangely unlike those worn in the north. There was, for example, no barrier to ladies wearing their hair showing; in fact Italian ladies of the aristocracy went to considerable trouble to display their flowing locks and though the forehead was revealed, and a high forehead considered a mark of beauty, the back hair was often dyed, frizzed, piled up and added to in order to form a gigantic head covering which was held in place with transparent nets or strings of pearls or even draped or plaited into the head-dress itself. This led to the extraordinary idea of wearing a pair of horns on the back of the head with the hair drawn through them and falling into two separate streamers of waving locks down the back of the gown. In Italy a feminine head-dress was a method of drawing attention to the hair whilst in England, France and Holland the bare forehead was so fashionable that it was shaved or plucked to accentuate the bulge above the brow and any vestige of hair was completely hidden under the head-dress.

Nor did the Italian Renaissance styles in dress favour the heavy houpelande or the cut-away surcote which was such a feature of ladies' fashions in the north. Their gowns were fitted tightly from the shoulder to a high waistline, laced either at the back or the front. Sleeves were of various designs and often quite separate from the gown itself. The skirts of the gown were immensely full, cut so that they flared, as well as being gathered from the fitted top and swept out into enormous trains. Sometimes the sleeves were also shaped so that they almost vied with the train itself in fullness and decoration. Fine silks, samite and cloth of gold and silver distinguished these wealthy and elegant ladies. Florentine, Venetian and Roman fashions all differed slightly and every state produced artists who pictured these luxurious women with a maximum of jewellery and clad in gowns of brilliant colours and rich design, sweeping like peacocks across the canvas or walls they decorated. The men were no less gorgeous, and fine embroideries and exotic weaving appear on their elegantly cut and flared garments, the richness of the multiple folds of their minute skirts contrasting with the skin-fitting luxury of their embroidered, striped, or particoloured hose, their sweeping sleeves hanging like wings or cloaks from shoulder to below the hems of their garments, their hair long, waved and shining. Later these fashions were adopted by the aristocrats in other countries of Europe. Certainly the high waist and tightly fitting bodice and the men's fashions followed closely the lead of Italy, though England never developed the strange and decorative hairdressing of the Italian Renaissance.

4. TUDOR AND STUART. An inventory of the clothing required by a smartly clad young man towards the end of the 15th c. would give prominence to the elegance of his shirt, the brevity of his doublet and the variegated decoration of his hose. That he also wore a short gown with huge sleeves and favoured wide-toed buskins or short boots may be seen from the paintings of Carpaccio and Bellini and is attested by references in morality plays.

The beginning of a change from the fluted pleats, flared skirts and sweeping gowns of the Middle Ages, which veiled or disclosed the gaily coloured leg, began to show itself not only in the decoration but also in the more complex make-up of the hose. These had been made skin-fitting for some considerable time and experiment in their decoration seems to have reached its zenith during the 1490s. The tailored cod-piece had already become a necessity when the hose were as closely fitting as a ballet dancer's tights. It was but a short step to the invention of linings and to the vogue for displaying them through carefully arranged slits or cuts or 'slashings' as they were later called. Decorative bands were sewn round the tops of the legs to hold these linings in place and from such beginnings developed the 'trunk-hose' of a later date. This fashion went on developing—particularly in Germany—until the hose literally hung down in ribbons and the linings could be seen through cuts and slashes in a different pattern on each leg. The Swiss Guards' uniform still carries an intimation of its original form in the early years of the 16th c.

It was also at some time during the closing years of the 15th c. that the square yoked gown began to replace almost every other outer garment worn by men. The interest in pleating, more particularly cartridge pleating, and gathering on to such a yoke supplanted the circular or semicircular garments that had been the fashion for so many years. These new gowns could be knee-length or down to the ankle, their sleeve either hanging or a bag-sleeve. Fur linings sometimes added bulk to the already bulky garment and the silhouette of one such knee-length gown is familiar in portraits of Henry VIII.

A year or two after the beginning of the 16th c. a pleated skirt attached to the doublet and called 'bases' started to cover up the hose. These bases may possibly have been derived from the knee-length skirts or tassets on the armour of the Roman emperors. Decoration consisting of bands of velvet was popular for some 20 years or more; these were sewn at intervals in two or three rows on the skirts of the coats as well as on the bases and are peculiarly characteristic of early Tudor costume in England. Caps of wool or velvet were worn throughout the first two Tudor reigns and came to be known later as the Tudor bonnet. They were worn over a coif of matching fabric for over a century by the elderly and by both doctors and scholars. The Tudor bonnet varied in size but normally the brim was a little wider than the crown, which was soft like a cloth cap, and the whole could be flattened when not worn.

The greatest change that took place in Henry VIII's reign was the rising neckline of the shirt and the gradual lowering of the waist of the doublet. During the whole of Henry VII's reign the shirt had been worn low at the neck, a peculiarity of the time that does not seem to have occurred again in the history of men's costume. The 'partlet strip', or first separate collar round the throat, appeared between 1520 and 1530. Much the same effect could be achieved by drawing the string at the top of the shirt tightly round the throat so as to form a frill or ruffle. In England at least a characteristic squareness in shape prevailed throughout the first half of the century.

A radical change from the medieval style took place in women's clothes also during the 1480s and by the turn of the century the high-waisted, tightly fitting bodice, cut square across the breast, had replaced the older fashions. This square neck opening or straight line across the chest could reveal either a low or high neck of the shift underneath, which might be almost transparent. Skirts were full and hung softly to the ground, where they often developed into a train behind; these could be pinned up to the waist and a variety of tucked-up skirts can be seen in the pictured domestic scenes of the time. In England the hair remained covered and the development of the French hood to the gable or kennel head-dress became an absorbing interest for ladies of fashion.

When it first appears in illuminated manuscripts and portraits *c.* 1475, the French hood was extremely simple, made from a strip of material, usually black velvet, about one metre in length and some 38 centimetres or more wide. This was normally lined, folded in half, sewn up the back to form a peak, but probably left open at the bottom. It could be worn over a conical head-dress or on its own. For further freedom the sides were cut up almost to the ear, the front was turned back from the face and the edge decorated. As the hood developed into a more ornate form the turned-back sides were doubled back, stiffened, decorated with goldsmiths' work and jewels and eventually stitched back over a gable-shaped framework; the back of the hood was opened and a stiffened square inserted to hold the gable shape in place. Here we have the head-dress depicted in the portraits of both Elizabeth of York, wife of Henry VII, and Catherine of Aragon. Such a head-dress with a variety of different arrangements of the side lappets and hanging back continued to be worn until the end of Henry VIII's reign. There is a charming set of sketches by Holbein (Windsor Castle) showing just how this style developed during his lifetime. Like so many fashions in the past the names lost their original meaning and the term 'French hood' came eventually to be used for a variety of head-dress with a black veil behind. But in Henry VIII's State Papers, 1548, there is a record of his allowing Catherine Howard after her imprisonment and before her execution 'six French hoods with edgings of goldsmiths' work but without pearl or diamond'. This shows that the term 'French hood' was at that time still used for the complicated head-dresses peculiar to the age.

Another head-dress of the time was 'the coif with a circlet about it full of rich stones' which was worn by Anne Boleyn for her coronation. This is the head-dress worn by both Mary I and the Princess Elizabeth in early portraits. A variety of bonnets, caps and hoods were also worn during the 1st half of the 16th c.

Exactly when the farthingale first made its appearance is very difficult to discover. It is first depicted in two Spanish paintings some time in the 1460s, one attributed to Francisco Gallegos (*Beheading of John the Baptist*, Prado, Madrid), the other by an unknown artist (Muntadas Coll., Barcelona). It is possible that Catherine of Aragon brought the fashion with her from Spain at the beginning of the century for state occasions but there is no concrete evidence of the farthingale in use in England until the first adult portraits of Mary I. Known as the 'Spanish farthingale', this hooped skirt was eminently suitable to display the rich DAMASKS and finely worked embroideries so typical of the middle of the century. The gown itself was tightly fitted over a corset from shoulder to waist with a point in front, the skirts flared and gathered at the waist and left open in front to display an underskirt of a different design. Sleeves were various but during the 1540s and early 1550s tended to follow a curious tendency which included two separate cuffs, if they can be termed such. The sleeve from shoulder to about half-way down the upper arm was tight-fitting and made from the same material as the gown. From this short sleeve depended another made of some contrasting material, bell-shaped and falling open to mid forearm. Under this a separate cuff of rich and very much stiffened material, again contrasting in design, was fastened with pins or jewels at intervals from wrist to elbow. This cuff was shaped so as to be tight at the wrist and very wide at the elbow and was cut and slashed to show the embroidered sleeve of the shift beneath, which was worn with a ruffle or frill showing at the wrist. Generally the bodice remained square cut until the beginning of Elizabeth I's reign, but more often than not the neckline finished with a yoke of velvet rather than the shift alone; partlet strips might be worn by both sexes.

From the middle of the 1550s a great change began to take place in the manner of dress in England, perhaps partly as a result of the brief visit of Philip of Spain. Characteristic of the change were the ruffle, the long-waisted doublet with a hip-length peplum, the trunk-hose divided into upper-stocks and nether-stocks, which eventually developed into the separate breeches of the next decade, cloaks and hats with a high crown, and shoes with pointed toes once again fitting the shape of a normal foot. All these ideas were new and all of them developed during the following decade into the typical clothing of the gentleman in the early years of Elizabeth I's reign. Perhaps there has never been quite so much variety in men's fashions as there was during the last half of the 16th c. But a sort of standardized simplification of dress for the ordinary man was based on all the items here mentioned as being of Spanish origin. The elderly still clung to their ankle-length robes and these we can still see on the many tombs of the time. But cloaks had come to stay as a dashing and decorative adjunct to costume and there was great variety in their shapes and sizes, from a very short circular one to the knee length. Gored and shaped on the shoulders, this could be lined with fur or shag (contemporary rough wool made to look like fur), decorated with guards and worn with or without a collar.

Hats, having once more taken precedence over the homely cap or bonnet, developed in a dozen different ways, with large and small brims, tall and flat crowns made from velvet or felt decorated with hatbands of jewels and precious stones, with feathers and brooches. The variety was infinite.

The ruffle grew in size as experiments in starch progressed and this strange habit of neck ornament continued to expand into the vast cartwheels of starched and laced lawn propped up with a support at the back of the neck called a supertasse. It is mentioned in Stubbs's *The Anatomie of Abuses* (1583). 'The women use great ruffs or neckerchers of holland, lawn, cambric, and such cloth as the greatest thread shall not be so big as the least hair there is, and lest they should fall down they are smeared and starched with starch; after that dried with great diligence, stroaked, patted, and rubbed very nicely; and so applied to their goodly necks and, withal, underpropped with supertasses . . .' Such monstrous ruffles were worn by both men and women; but persons of more modest tastes preferred a collar which stood up at the back and was worn open in the front.

From *c.* 1560 breeches and/or the trunk-hose began to assume enormous proportions and although there was great variety in their cut, the common practice was to stuff them with horsehair, bran, wool or even rags in order to give them the bombast effect that was to become so much a part of Elizabethan fashion. Venetians, which were a sort of knee-breeches, much padded on the hips and tapering to the knee, where they finished with a cuff, were first seen in England during the early years of the 1670s. They continued in use until well into James I's reign and became the normal breeches worn with the extraordinary fashion of a 'Peasecod Belly' doublet. This strange fashion grew from the first short-waisted, armorial doublet padded down the front. The padding gradually became more and more pronounced until it assumed the proportions of a gigantic hooked nose from the neck to well below the stomach, with buttons down the front. An example of this fashion survives in the traditional figure of Punch.

Leg coverings were also very various during the last quarter of the century. Trunk-hose, as brief as possible in the trunk, stuck out like pumpkins around the hips, accentuating the length of leg until the new style came in of trunk-hose with canions, a thigh-fitting appendage to the pumpkin worn tucked into hose which reached up to mid-thigh. Sometimes these garments were stiffened into a drum-shaped framework and vied in width with the ladies' skirts. Open breeches, resembling very long shorts reaching just below the knees, made their appearance during the last decade of the century, as did the really baggy ones, full at the top and bottom and tightly gartered at the knees, which later appear as typical of the time of James I. Sleeves held in place on the shoulders with something resembling an epaulette, or a roll of material or a huge puff, were characteristic of the time. These could be tight-fitting, loose and padded or padded tightly so that their bombast shape vied in distortion with the doublets and hose.

Throughout this half-century the fashion for slashing garments persisted. Slashing could consist of multiple minute cuts arranged in rows or patterns or of long cuts in the fabric to 'draw out' the linings underneath, as indeed the majority of the trunk-hose did.

Few of the women's clothes escaped decorations and the embroideries, particularly floral designs, were much more varied than those of the men. The split skirt worn over a contrasting underskirt was worn throughout Elizabeth's reign, but there were also plain skirts which went all round. Fashions depended mainly on the shape of the farthingale itself. This varied from its original form, which had been rather like a bell, to an immense cone and from that to the French farthingale, a sort of cartwheel worn tipped forward at the hips so that the skirts over it had to be considerably longer at the back in order to give an even hem. It appeared first in England during the late 1570s. Before its introduction a rather charming over-dress had been adopted for use over the Spanish hoops. This consisted of a bell-shaped gown with short padded sleeves like balloons on the shoulders. The gown was flared gently from shoulder to the ground and was decorated with bands of velvet

Elizabethan lady (formerly described as portrait of Queen Elizabeth I). Anonymous. She is wearing a white satin dress embroidered in gold, red and blue; with gauze streamers behind the arms; standing lace ruff; a long rope of pearls and pearl necklace. (Bodl.)

or embroideries. Its shape, however, made it impossible to wear over the larger hoops of the French farthingale and it was not much seen after the 1570s.

With the advent of hats for men came an equally multifarious fashion in hats and headdresses for women. Tiny velvet caps were worn over small embroidered bonnets; a type of cap wired to cover the back of the head framed the puffed-up sides of the hair and, coming down over the forehead in a tongue or point, was the forerunner of what we now call the 'Mary Stuart' cap. A flat stiffened veil worn on the top of the head and projecting over the forehead was worn over the bonnet and referred to as the 'bongrace'—a much used word in the 16th c. to describe any sort of head covering which might protect the forehead from the sun.

It was during the last 20 years of the century that shoes began to have heels. First the heel was merely a thickening of the leather layers at the back. Gradually this turned into a separate heel and by the end of the century both men and women wore heels up to 5 centimetres high. Women also favoured high cork-soled overshoes, termed 'pantoffles', and some still to be seen in museums show that they assumed amazing heights. The idea was to keep the skirts from touching the mire of the streets; their exaggeration was a whim of fashion.

Whenever the gigantic French farthingale was worn the stomacher was made long and pointed, possibly to accentuate the smallness of the waist or at least to give the illusion of a tapering body concealed beneath the hoop. This fashion reached its most exaggerated form during the 1590s, when it developed into a false stomacher and was worn at an angle away from the main bodice of the dress. It was then an entirely separate structure, stiffened with horn, much decorated after the fashion of the dress proper and attached to the neck opening, which was cut square and low on the bosom. The bottom point rested on the rim of the farthingale and probably helped to keep it at the required angle. The best example of this fashion exists in the painting attributed to Robert Peake of *Queen Elizabeth's Progress* (1600; Sherborne Castle) where the Queen has her right hand concealed behind the false stomacher. It was an absurdity of fashion which lasted a comparatively short time and was probably reserved for occasions when the wearer was not called upon for active movement. The French farthingales of James I's Court were nothing like so monstrous as those of Elizabeth's time and the waistline began to rise again as the skirts diminished in size. A padded roll worn round the hips and a stiffened hem to the skirts gave much the same outline in lesser degree for those who were not prepared to adopt the more exaggerated fashions in hoops.

The 1st quarter of the 17th c. saw little change from the closing decade of the 16th, but some modifications in the shape and size of garments took place and ladies' necks and even their breasts were frequently visible above a deeply curved *décolleté* corsage. Ruffles of finest lace and high curving lace collars framing the head and shoulders were characteristic of the time, as was an increasing fashion in high-piled hair sweeping back from a high forehead, puffed out at the sides, decorated with jewels and small ornaments and framed by the lace edge of a cap worn at the back of the head. Early Stuart portraiture produces an overwhelming impression of delicate lace—lace in gold and silver even on such things as shoe ornaments and garters, snowy white or rich cream lace on collars, cuffs, ruffles, kerchiefs, bonnets and borders. Embroidery too was worn wherever possible, from the clocks on the hose and shoes to the nightcaps and bonnets.

It was not until after 1625 that any major change in silhouette began to be noticeable. But the farthingales and huge breeches seemed to collapse almost as soon as James I died. The new French fashions, probably introduced by the young queen Henrietta Maria, favoured a classical softness and a sweeping freedom which had been unknown throughout the 16th c. Bombast and bones were discarded, a high waist favoured. Soft fabrics such as spot muslins and transparent lawns, and fine silks and satins, took the place of the stiffened velvets, heavy brocades and damasks which had been so popular for so many years. Ribbons and unstarched lace, paler and more subtle and delicate colours succeeded the rather harsh brilliance of an earlier decade. Most noticeable of all was the studied nonchalance of the new styles of hairdressing for both men and women, for men had begun to let their hair grow into lovelocks as soon as the ruffles had been exchanged for collars and following the style of the French court, they now puffed and curled their hair into a frizzed frame for the face and decorated the lovelocks with bows of ribbon. But this fashion was of short duration because of an increasing interest in growing the hair as long as possible so that it could be cunningly spread out over the shoulder on a Van Dyck collar. Beards and moustaches fitted into this new picture of a man and are typical of the Cavalier.

Most of the doublets at this time were high-waisted with tassets or flaps tied to the waist with points or bows of ribbon. The sleeves were cut in a variety of ways so that the shirt could be seen. Fashion demanded that fine linen, embroidered and laced, should be displayed and this remained one of the major marks of elegance in both sexes well into the 18th c. Fine embroideries adorned the backs of gloves and gauntlets, shoes and hose, sword-belts and boot-hose, and the new cut of the clothes emphasized these refinements instead of merging them in a welter of detail as in earlier fashions. Even the breeches were made so that the sides could be left open for several centimetres above the garter so as to show off the fine white linings underneath, and some of the doublets were buttoned down the

Typical Cavalier costume after the French fashion with lovelocks, Van Dyck collar, mock coat, split doublet with tassets, boot-hose and bucket-topped boots (*c.* 1627)

back as well as the front so that they too could be undone to show the shirt.

Decorative boots first came in as a fashionable excess of the Cavalier. But with an almost endless variety in cuffs at the knee, they understandably earned the name of 'bucket-tops', while the spurs were attached with a giant butterfly of leather across the instep. It was also considered necessary to wear fine linen boot-hose with the lace edge falling down over the tops of the boots.

Before 1640 knee-length open breeches supplanted the baggy type. These were the forerunners of the fantastic petticoat-breeches so popular at the courts in France and Holland during the time of Commonwealth in England. They were also worn in England during the 1650s but were less extravagant than those at Louis XV's Court. Samuel Pepys mentions wearing them in 1659 (5 Jan.). 'This morning I rose, put on my suit with great skirts, having not lately worn any other clothes but them . . .' Under these great skirts were worn baggy linings drawn in above the knee. During the 1640s, however, they were not great skirts but resembled loose shorts decorated with bunches of ribbon at hem and hips. A new style of doublet was worn with these petticoat-breeches, short and loose and finishing at the waist. It quickly became known as the 'Jackanapes' coat; but in spite of ridicule the fashion persisted until well after the Restoration. It seems to have originated in a desire to show even more of the shirt than previously. With the breeches worn well down on the hips the shirt could be puffed out round the waist and the coat cut just as short as the wearer chose. Sleeves continued to be split or cut short so that the very full shirt sleeve and laced cuff could be seen.

From 1625 to 1640 practically all ladies wore a high waist; from then on it started to descend again. The high-waisted gown was usually cut very low at the neck and a collar of fine lace or lawn decorated with a lace edge was always worn. This covered the shoulders and back but finished just below the collar-bone, where it was attached to the stomacher. These stomachers were of varying length with the point coming well down over the skirts of the garment and curving out from the high waistline. The line of the top of the stomacher made the deeply cut corsage square. Should a lady prefer to cover her neck, there was a fashion for wearing yet another collar over the first one or a sort of lace square folded and pinned at the throat so that the impression was as if the wearer had two or more collars. Sleeves puffed and beribboned, slashed and laced, were similar to those worn by the men. They were also becoming much shorter so that some 15 centimetres of forearm was visible. This fashion naturally heralded the introduction of long gloves and muffs in winter. The fashion for wearing two skirts or petticoats persisted; the top one, attached to the bodice and called a petticoat-bodice, was worn open in the front and the other, called a petticoat, was worn underneath. The variety of tucked-up skirts and skirts bunched or draped at the back, tied with ribbons or held in place with pins, was a charming feature of the time. It was not only useful to keep the over-dress clean when walking in the streets, but it could be vastly entertaining for the wearer to experiment with different effects even to the wearing of an apron in front and completely covering the under-petticoat. Long aprons of fine lawn or net with an edging of lace were an essential part of every lady's wardrobe, as were veils to protect the face from frost and sunburn. The veils were worn directly on the hair without a hat of any sort. Hats were not worn much by the women, but hoods and masks and veils were all considered necessary. Little lacy bonnets with lappets over the ears were worn by those who had not the abundance of curly locks prescribed by fashion. The Puritan caps were made on similar lines but from plain linen or without lace.

The Puritan movement aimed at eliminating excess and it is in the 1640s that we can see how the basic costume of the time, stripped of its lace, ribbon and fine fabrics, appeared in sensible form. In *The School for Husbands* Molière has Sganarelle say: 'In spite of the fashions, I'll have a brim to my hat, under which my head may find a convenient shelter; a large, long doublet, buttoned close as it ought to be, that it may keep my stomach warm to digest well; a pair of breeches made exactly to fit my thighs, and shoes wherein my feet may not be tortured; such as our forefathers wore . . .' Unfortunately Puritan costume was imposed without adequate concessions to the frailties of human nature, for within a year of Cromwell's rule those in authority and their wives and daughters were mostly clothed with a richness almost exceeding that of the defeated Royalists. The miniature of Cromwell's daughter, wife of Ireton (V. & A. Mus.), shows us a lady with curled hair and ribbon-tied lovelocks, her dress right off the shoulders and held up with strings of jewels, her corsage decked with pearls of great size drawing attention to the very low-cut gown.

The Restoration brought an unprecedented inrush of Continental fashions along with new patterns of behaviour and foreign affectations: pet monkeys and parrots; little black boys dressed in turbans to hold up the trailing skirts of courtly gowns; spices, snuff and perfumes from the East Indies; gowns of Oriental or Indian stuffs, and a hundred elegancies all requiring special attire, such as those worn for coffee and tea gatherings. From France came the new idea of men wearing wigs rather than their own hair. In his diary for 3 November 1663 Samuel Pepys records that his own hair was cut off to make another periwig and that he paid £3 for a new one. This fashion continued for more than a century and every ten years or so saw a new vogue in wigs. For the rest of the century they tended to increase in size and lost any semblance to human hair. By the 1690s they were monstrous and divided into three separate bunches of curls at the bottom with two horns standing up from the forehead. They were also powdered with gold-dust or powder of some other colour to increase their thickness as well as to carry some new type of perfume. These were known as 'full-bottom' wigs.

With the growing popularity of the wig, collars also changed: first a band at the back of the neck with two wide flaps in the front, then a cravat of lace tied under the chin with a bunch of ribbons. As the wigs fell over the shoulders in front there was no longer a need for the wide shoulder collar which once had acted as a background for natural hair.

Within a year or so of the Restoration the cassock coat, of Persian cut, with a long waistcoat almost to the knees, became fashionable among the less frivolous. For several years the cassock, or 'tunique and vest' as Pepys called it, and the petticoat-breeches and 'jackanapes' coat were both to be seen at the same time. But the new fashion prevailed and the petticoat-breeches had been abandoned in favour of long coats by *c.* 1670. Boot-hose were worn without boots as a sort of decorative covering for the legs, and the breeches continued to be decorated with ribbons at the knee well into the 1680s.

The story of the coat's development is an interesting one, for from its introduction during the 1670s it went through various phases until it emerged as the frock-coat of the early 20th c. To begin with these long coats with large pockets were cut fairly straight and the side and centre back seams were left open from the waist down so that the sword could be worn underneath with its hilt easily accessible on the left hip and also so that the skirts could be folded back when riding. At this time a sash was often worn over the coat. Gradually the back became more shaped to the body and the side vents moved further towards the centre back seam; then these vents developed pleats, which sprang from the side seam well below the shaping for the waist. With this the full-skirted, low-waisted coat, later to become typical of the 18th c., had arrived. Decoration was at seams, round armholes, on the cuffs and pockets, and more particularly at buttonholes. Buttons on vest and tunic, cuffs and pockets, kept the button-makers busy for another century or more.

For several years after the long coat had become an accepted fashion experiment in the shaping of breeches continued, but as they could not really be seen much below the knee-length coat they soon developed into knee-breeches, worn fairly loose and just covering the knee. The ribbons and other more complicated decorations were gradually discarded until the 1690s, when the hose were pulled up over the knee and developed a roll just above the knee-cap.

The Restoration ladies appeared at Court in the latest fashions from Paris, which included once again an exaggeratedly elongated stomacher. Now, however, it fitted close to the body and was part of a stiffly boned bodice cut extremely low at the neck, so low that it was often actually off the shoulders. It was the mode to wear a very deep lace collar round the shoulders, sometimes almost down to the elbow where a puffed sleeve appeared from beneath and ended in a lacy cascade half-way down the forearm. Trailing skirts, which could of course still be pinned up when necessary, created new folds and falls at the back. When the skirts were worn trailing it was an extravagance of the time to employ the services of a little black slave to walk behind and hold the train.

Styles in hairdressing continued for some ten years to favour the little curls arranged both on the forehead and at the back of the neck; the side hair was puffed or tied with bunches of ribbon and curls were worn at the sides. These were often false and did not indeed have to match the owner's hair. Hair at the back was plaited or tied up away from the neck.

Shoes with long pointed toes, cut square at the tips, were worn by everyone. These normally had bows of ribbon on the toes and the ladies' shoes were nearly always embroidered.

About 1670 a new fashion in corseting came in together with new modes of deportment. The stays were made to fit snugly over the back right up to the low neckline. It is still possible to see from contemporary portraits that ladies' shoulders pulled away from their gowns when they leaned forward. The stays pushed up the breasts and forced the waist itself into compliance with the demands of fashion.

Hoods and bonnets were both popular, though hats were rarely worn by fashionable ladies except with riding clothes. Little lacy caps with bows of ribbon in the front were worn over a tightly curled coiffure during the 1670s and eventually developed into the extraordinary head-dress which included layers of upstanding frills, bows of ribbon, wire and a bonnet with long streamers. Each item of this strange head-dress had a French name: the term 'pinner' was used for the frill in front and the whole arrangement was called a 'commode'. No self-respecting lady could be seen abroad without her head dressed in this manner after *c.* 1685. Veils and scarves, as well as hoods, had to be of considerable size to cover these head-dresses and it is possible that men dressed their wigs so high in order not to be dwarfed by the ladies.

This was the age of PATCHES and curls. Patches of different shapes and sizes were used to set off a dimple or draw attention to a pretty mouth or eye, to hide a smallpox scar or cover some other blemish.

The deep shoulder collar disappeared during the 1670s and the tighter stays produced a new silhouette, which concentrated even more on the bustle shape of the skirts tucked up behind and the very low neckline, which was so revealing of the breasts that often a little lacy frill was tucked into the bodice for modesty. A pad or bustle was first introduced *c.* 1690 and a tendency to stiffen the petticoats and hold out the skirts of the gowns still further led to the introduction of the first quilted petticoats. Ornament took on a new formality at this time. Spots, stripes and strapwork designs or designs reminiscent of iron-work took the place of floral decoration. Such designs often included deep fringe and tassels.

During the closing years of the 17th c. a lady's silhouette much resembled that of the Victorian bustle of the 1870s; the main difference lay not so much in the costume as in the head-dress. These towered some 30 to 45 centimetres above the face, a smother of stiffly formal frills and ribbons, nodding as the ladies walked beside their gallants. The latter tiptoed on their high-heeled shoes with long flaps or tongues reaching half-way up their shins; their coats cut with very low waists and full pleats behind; their immense cravats vying with the lacy, ribboned confections on their ladies' heads; their huge periwigs; their gigantic muffs fastened at the waist with a decorative belt; their swords of fine workmanship swinging from a sword-belt which in its turn carried fringe and ribbons. Both gallants and ladies wore patches and powder, flaunted perfume from decorated gloves and mouchoirs.

5. EIGHTEENTH TO TWENTIETH CENTURIES. One of the most spectacular innovations in the history of English costume might have been seen in the streets of London during the year 1709. This was the exaggerated hooped petticoat. If we are to believe the writers of the day, its circumference was something over 5 metres and Addison in *The Tatler* of 5 June 1710 even gives it as around 7 m. Certainly the early illustrations give the impression that it was both unwieldy and destructive; and it became a general target for criticism and abuse. But these gigantic hoops did not remain long in favour and a flattened hoop, wide at the sides only, made its appearance in 1714. For the next half-century fashion was occupied with experiments in hoops of all sizes and shapes and museums have varied collections of them made from wire, whalebone and horsehair woven into springy, resilient pads. Hoops made from wicker and wood and even hinged metal were rarer, but examples can still be found. Polly in *The Beggar's Opera* (1728) had to purchase 'hoops and stays' for the exorbitant sum of 14 guineas.

Lady wearing the new hinged hoop (to make sitting down easier) and gentleman with wide skirted coat, tricorn hat and knee-breeches (*c.* 1750)

With the appearance of the hooped petticoat the tall head-dress disappeared and a minute bonnet took its place. The hair was tucked away neatly and a fine forehead was of more account than a multitude of curls. The *Spectator* of 1711 makes the following comment on the new silhouette: 'At present the whole sex is in a manner dwarfed and shrunk into a race of beauties that seem almost another species. I remember several ladies who were once near seven foot high that at present want some inches of five.'

Stays of intricate pattern, laced both front and back, varied very little for the first three-quarters of the century. They were incredibly stiffly boned all over and had an extra stiffening in front which held the body rigid from waist to breasts; because of this pressure they tended to force up the breasts so that throughout this period the more modest covered their necks and shoulders with a fichu or 'necklace'. The 'necklace' was made from lace and had no connection with the strings of beads that the term denotes today. Full dress demanded the low bare neck with various lacy devices to give originality. Lace was still of very great importance and value; few ladies or gentlemen throughout the 18th c. were to be seen without ruffles at wrist and throat.

The fabrics used during the century were on the whole very light in weight; silks and taffetas, cut velvets of almost transparent weave, satins and fine printed linens were the most popular throughout the reign of the hooped petticoat.

There was a basic gown peculiar to the 18th c. after the side hoops had replaced the circular hoop and though this changed in effect several times, it retained certain qualities of construction that could serve equally well from 1714 to 1780. Its form was that of an over-dress with tightly fitting bodice and skirts open in the front to display a petticoat to match or a fine quilted one or an embroidered full-length apron. The back was shaped so that a centre panel, folded and stitched from neck to waist, contained sufficient material to flare out from waist to hem in unrestricted pleats. The front of the gown fastened over a stomacher or folded across the stays; the skirts were pleated in wide pleats from the back panel to the front opening and often cut away in a deep curve to show off as much of the petticoat as possible. There was a placket hole over each hip through which a lady could both adjust her hoops and get at her pockets, which were tied round the waist over the petticoat and under the gown. Sometimes the skirts were tucked up by the simple process of pulling the hem through the placket hole; sometimes they were arranged in a more careful manner by a strong thread made in a large loop sewn on the inside of the waist, which was brought round the skirts and fastened on to minute buttons sewn on either side of the loose back panel. Thus the 'bunched-up' effect seen in so many paintings of the mid 18th c. was achieved.

The 'sac'-backed gown was in a sense a natural development from the panel form. It was a particularly elegant style that fitted the body in front and hung away in deep pleats from shoulder to hem at the back; two widths of material were folded into the back to form a graceful train, although the sides of the gown could accommodate hoops of any size. With full dress the sides were pleated in a variety of ways so that they could accommodate the largest possible side hoops.

As long as the large hoops remained in fashion a vast variety of little waistcoats with elbow-length sleeves, full-skirted jackets and laced bodices were worn. These were just as useful with or without a hoop and for informal wear could be worn over a quilted petticoat. Undress was of great importance to a lady of fashion for it was possible thus to discard both hoops and stays.

As the hoop was the most noticeable innovation for the ladies of the 18th c. so was the white wig for the gentlemen, and it also appeared during the first decade of the century. Presumably the fashion for the immense full-bottomed wig died hard with the older generation, for as late as 1730 we still see portraits of elderly gentlemen wearing them. John Gay tells us: 'The full-bottom formally combed all before denotes the lawyer and the politician; the smart tie-wig with the black ribbon shows a man of fierceness of temper; and he that burdens himself with a superfluity of white hair which flows down his back and mantles in waving curles over the shoulders, is generally observed to be less curious in the furniture of the inward recesses of his skull.' Within some five years of the introduction of the small wig a dozen or more styles came into vogue and barbers vied with each other to produce new fashions each more fantastic than the last. Many of these were drawn by Bernard Lens in 1725–6 (V. & A. Mus.) and from this date to the end of the century powdered wigs were still worn. The style may have been connected with the NEO-CLASSICAL vogue.

As ladies' skirts expanded in size the elegant gentleman's skirts took on a competing outline. Small springs and even foxes' tails were put under the pleats at the sides of the coats so that the skirts almost assumed the quality of the skirts of a ballet-dancer. The waistcoats were sometimes worn with long sleeves, the cuff turned back over the wide cuff of the coat; they were worn indoors and without the coat for informal occasions as the coats were both fragile and costly. One can say the same of the wigs, for this was the time when nightcaps and turbans took the place of the wig in the privacy of the home. By 1740 the now tightly fitting knee-breeches were brought down over the knee and fastened either with a buckle or with buttons just below the knee. And almost as soon as this fashion was introduced the waistcoats lost their sleeves and gradually began to get shorter, a process that continued year by year until the 1780s, when they barely reached the waist. Characteristic of the first half-century was the dependence on the waistcoat to cover the shirt. The coat itself rarely had functional buttons, for these would have damaged the swing and cut of the garment. Coats were made to be left open and display the elegant features of an even more decorative waistcoat; neither did these coats have collars, for the neckcloth or cravat had to be displayed to the best advantage.

Country gentlemen and people of modest means followed the fashion only as far as suited their pockets. There were of course a great many sensible woollen fabrics to be had and the frock-coat which could button up in front was a useful top coat for all occasions, whilst the waistcoat remained the normal wear for servants and workmen.

It was in 1754 that we find the first reference to 'a gown worn without hoops which was made for them' and from that date followed an enchanting variety of experiments with the skirts of the gowns and new gowns made to give something of the same effect. But for full dress gowns continued to have hoops until the 19th c.

Two ladies in the dress of 1778. (Bodl. print)

Throughout the 1750s there was an increasing vogue for the pastoral: the milkmaid hat, the tucked-up petticoats, tiny aprons and fichus, bonnets and mobs. The mob-cap itself was a bonnet which fitted the back of the head and carried elegant little frills round the face. It was not yet the grotesque affair worn over the frizzed hair of the 1790s. During the 1760s the hair style began to rise. Little pads and rolls were put on the top of the head and the hair was dressed over them; bonnets were now of a different shape and tied under the chin with a lacy frill. Slowly the hair rose, and as it was often necessary to introduce false hair to achieve the fashionable height powder was introduced for ladies as well as gentlemen. By the 1770s fantastic heights had been reached and wire frames, padding and endless false curls went to the construction of a lady's 'head'. This was the time when caricaturists portrayed the court ladies wearing ships in full sail upon their heads, coaches and horses, windmills and other improbable decorations, held in place by a multitude of ribbons, laces, feathers and jewels. It was an absurdity of fashion that

High dressed lady's hair, powdered and arranged over a wire frame with feather decoration. Stitched pleating in the back of the gown and skirts pulled up with cords and fastened with buttons at the back, a method of draping which came into fashion in the 18th c. after hoops were discarded (*c.* 1772)

lasted little more than a decade, but it has made an enduring impression on the history of hairdressing. The stories of mice making nests within the structure, of ladies sleeping upright so that their hair would be unspoiled for the next day's functions are too numerous to ignore.

The 1770s and 1780s were the years that saw the most extravagant styles in men's wear. The calculated elegance of the time depended almost entirely upon a skin-tight effect for men and an overwhelming superfluity of draperies, frills, ribbons and ostentatious decoration for women.

The traditional 18th-c. coat had by 1775 shrunk to a very scanty covering for back and arms. The vest or waistcoat was of the utmost importance and delicate embroideries lavishly decorated the front. Coats were made with tightly fitting sleeves and a small cuff; the buttons and buttonholes were not intended to be anything but a decorative excuse for embroideries. The tails—or what had been the skirts—were cut right back and two pleats only were now set close together in the centre of the back. These were finished with two buttons, a survival of what had once been the functional buttons on which a horseman fastened back his skirts when riding.

In order to compete to some extent with the towering height of the ladies' hairdressing, a new style of wig with a built-up puff in front and a long turned-back tail behind, tied low down at the back of the neck, was worn for a few years. Collars on coats, their purpose to elongate the neck, were introduced during the 1760s.

The most exaggerated fashion was considered to be Italian in origin, for the dandies of the day were called 'Macaronis'. With high-heeled shoes, high wigs, minute hats, striped stockings, and waistcoats, these elegants minced their uncomfortable way with the assistance of long silver-topped walking-sticks.

For a few years before the French Revolution some of the more ROCOCO women's fashions filtered from the French court into England. The so-called negligent hairdressing depicted by Gainsborough and Lawrence, Joshua Reynolds, Rowlandson and Romney displays a mass of curled and frizzed hair standing out from the head and falling over the shoulders in profusion, powdered and dimmed with backcombing. At the same time the waist-length stays gave way to a much shortened version which forced the breasts even higher than before and made it always necessary for ladies to muffle themselves in fichus and shawls.

FASHION PLATES, which were beginning to appear in both France and England, have an exaggeratedly pigeon-breasted appearance and the ladies wear gigantic hats or huge mob-caps; they totter on minute feet with high heels, trailing yards of diaphanous material behind them. A sort of bustle effect is also discernible, for their gowns were cut with a great deal of material gathered into the high waist at the back and little jackets flared out behind well above the waist.

After a renewed phase of experiment in the 1790s fashion settled down to a new 'classical' simplicity. The scanty attire of the ladies in particular would have seemed outrageous to the older generations. High-waisted, devoid of stays, the dress clung in simple folds from neck to ankle. Gone were the petticoats, high heels and frizzed hair. It was even the extreme of fashion to wear one's hair cut short to the ears and arranged in curls round the head. White was the right colour for all day dresses in the summer, fine white lawn possibly with some delicate spot pattern. As the white wigs had been considered classical, so were the white gowns; and the tendency to mimic statuary was carried so far that some ladies wore buckskin under-garments and damped the folds of their gowns so that they clung to the body. Men's knee-breeches began to disappear in favour of pantaloons at the same time. First they wore elongated breeches clinging tightly to the legs and usually made from buckskin; then these descended to below the calf and boots became a general fashion—short boots, long boots, decorative boots with tassels for ballroom wear. The 'Wellington' and the 'hessian' boot ousted the buckled shoe of a decade before. Coats cut away in front and with long tails behind, high-waisted, double or single breasted, showed the full length of the skin-tight pantaloons from waist to ankle. So tight were they that in polite society the ultra-fastidious were compelled to stand or merely lift a foot straight up and place it on a convenient resting-place. It was not possible to sit down without damaging the correct beauty of a creaseless line. Such was the dependence on a 'fine leg' that false calves were introduced, and the extravagances of fashion also insisted on immensely high collars and cravats which came right up on to the cheeks. The tricorne hat, which had been worn for 100 years, was replaced by a tall or 'top' hat and the wig, which had been worn for 150 years, was at last discarded.

Mob-cap of exaggerated dimensions as worn over high dressed hair (*c.* 1790)

Practically every aspect of the 18th-c. fashions had vanished and what we now call 'REGENCY' fashions were well established by the turn of the century. A hundred little garments such as

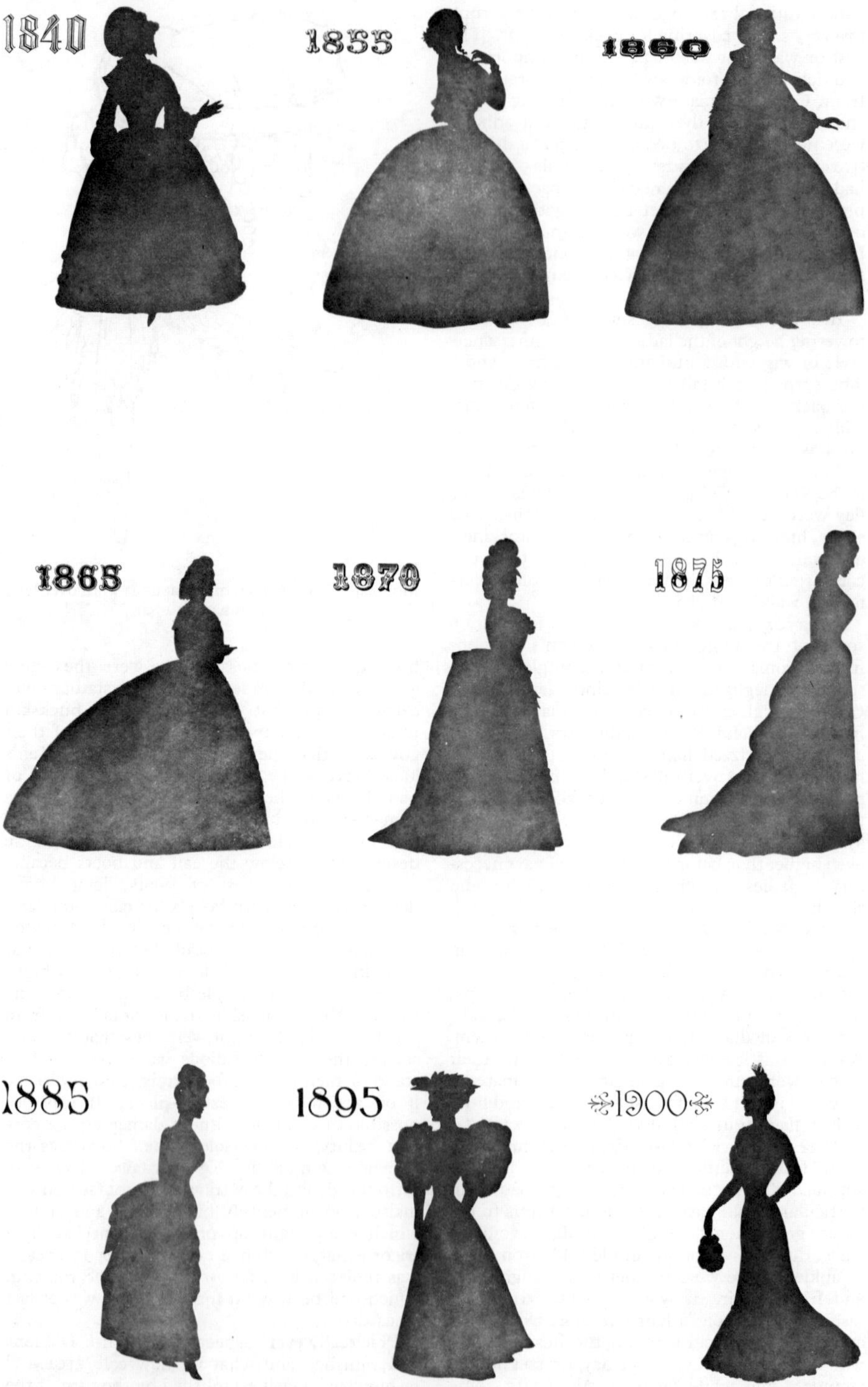

1840

1855

1860

1865

1870

1875

The female silhouette in 19th-c. fashions from *The Fashionable Lady in the 19th Century*. (V. & A. Mus., 1960)

tippets and sashes, peignoirs and pelerines, tuckers and spencers, pelisses, shawls and scarves went with the simple dresses of the early years of the 19th c. Lacy bonnets, nightcaps and turbans were worn indoors and large bonnets, muffs and gloves all helped to contribute a measure of variety to the simplicity of the long straight dress. Slowly, towards 1825, dresses began to get fuller, the shoulders wider, the waistline lower, until the skirts, now showing the ankle, were once more supported by a variety of petticoats and the shoulders accentuated by the use of little pillows. By 1830 a new and absurd silhouette had arrived. Women were once more tightly laced; wasp-waisted with a petticoat made of a bouncy fabric called 'crinoline'; sleeves so large that they were actually termed 'imbécile'; hairdressing for full-dress occasions now piled up on the top of the head in a variety of knots, plaits and loops tied and decorated with ribbons, feathers, flowers and other gewgaws. Hats and bonnets, dress caps, turbans and what were then called berets, all lavishly decorated with flowers, fruit and feathers, were worn during the daytime.

Men's clothes also developed into a wide-hipped, wide-shouldered, tight-waisted version of the original long trousers and cut-away coat. By 1830, though the elderly still clung to the subdued fashions of the 18th c., the young man-about-town wore stays, pads on his hips to give the now fairly loose trousers a peg-top shape, straps under the foot to keep them trim, a coat with sleeves padded and gathered at the shoulders, wide lapels to his coat, a short gay waistcoat, highly coloured cravat and an immensely tall top hat. Often his coat was both full and long, sometimes even with a fur collar, but tightly waisted and full skirted whatever the length. These were the fashions immediately preceding the reign of Victoria and much of the exaggerated shaping began to disappear during the 1840s, though the

Evening gown of French silk called *soie de Pompadour*, with cushions in the sleeves and swansdown tippet. According to a contemporary description the hair is 'parted on the forehead and disposed partly in a plaited band which forms a diadem round the summit of the head and partly in a full knot placed quite behind. A cluster of ringlets issues from the knot, which is transpierced by a pearl arrow. The braid is also entwined with pearls, a single row of which are brought low over the forehead' (*c.* 1832)

English country squire in frock coat, top hat and top boots (*c.* 1820)

skirts continued to get larger and larger until the final introduction of the 'crinoline' frame in the 1850s. This was a vast structure of tapes and wire hoops which could collapse gently when ladies sat down and successfully held out the numerous petticoats to the desired width.

The wraps and scarves of the 1830s were succeeded by an even greater variety of garments to cover the upper part of the body. It was rarely necessary to add to the covering of the lower part for already there were many layers, usually including a red flannel petticoat worn next to the drawers and pantelettes (legs like sleeves from knee to ankle). Although the cashmere SHAWL continued to be a prized possession, these new shoulder coverings were generally worn. Contemporary names included the casaweck, mantelet, visite and a host of new ones coined each year to add interest to the fashion plates which now appeared in every women's magazine. Bonnets, now much less ostentatious, were worn on the back of the head and showed a neat coiffure with a centre parting. All married ladies wore bonnets or 'caps' indoors, tiny confections of lace and ribbon which were supposedly the sign of respectability. Large straw hats were worn in the summer.

As the crinoline grew larger and larger the sleeves of the gown also expanded at the bottom. Huge bell-shaped openings had to be filled with a false sleeve of lace or fine embroidered net from wrist to elbow. The year 1860 saw the circular crinoline in its most exaggerated form. By 1861 fashion tended to emphasize the back until many of the skirts had a train and stood out more at the back than anywhere else. By 1866 an extra series of smaller hoops had been added behind and two years later the gigantic crinoline hoops had been discarded and the bustle had arrived—still at first with a hooped frame but a much smaller one with a series of hoops at the back superimposed on the smaller structure.

Check, plaid and striped materials were something new during the 1840s—possibly the fashion was connected with the Queen's love for Balmoral and things Scottish. Gentlemen were quick to follow the trend and trousers of such materials were much in demand until the 1880s. The development of men's fashions now proceeded at a leisurely pace. The tall and chimney-pot hats disappeared; the top hat became the normal wear for everyone until the introduction of various sporting hats during the 1860s. The most noticeable innovation of this decade was the new sack-coat—possibly the forerunner of the lounge suit of the 20th c., the first coat to be

Short lace and satin mantle worn over a full crinoline. Bonnet with an eye-veil on a drawstring so that the face can be concealed at will (*c.* 1854)

Lowered top hat, Dundreary moustache, new style of velvet coat bound with braid and having only the top button fastened, plaid trousers without crease (*c.* 1869)

worn without any sort of tails or skirt. It was made with only three buttons, of which the top one only was fastened, a new conception of freedom and nonchalance in dress which set the caricaturists a new problem to satirize the elegant gentleman of the day. With his loose, uncreased trousers, casual loose coat, tie and collar, it was his Dundreary whiskers and perhaps a monocle that proclaimed him a 'nut'. Hats and caps took on new variety. A flat tweed cap with a turned-up brim first appeared during the 1860s, as did a shortened version of the top hat. From this time until the end of the century the deer-stalker hat, the hard straw hat, the bowler and eventually the cloth cap all made their appearance for casual wear, although the top hat continued to be *de rigueur* for formal dress.

The waistcoat, once the most decorative item in any man's wardrobe, ceased to be anything more than part of a suit almost as soon as the sack-coat came in, though occasionally it might be a decorative addition to a cut-away coat. Morning coats were worn with a grey waistcoat.

Colours throughout Queen Victoria's reign tended to be influenced by the predominant etiquette of black and white; white and pale pastel shades for young ladies, black for the older generations because of the social necessity to wear mourning after the death of even the most remote relations. Mourning could after the first year or so be relieved by half-mourning, which included white, mauve and grey with perhaps some slight relief of a red trimming. Although bright colours occasionally appeared in fashionable crowds, they were on the whole considered 'racy' by most respectable people; it was more convenient and economic to stick to the subdued tones prescribed by convention.

When the bustle replaced the crinoline the whole silhouette changed. The hair was let down, falling in ringlets from a knot of curls at the back of the head. Hats of varying shapes, mostly absurdly small, began to replace the bonnet, which had also become minute. The stays or corsets assumed a shape which fitted well down over the hips, laced extremely tightly to accentuate the hour-glass curve. Skirts in layers of draperies of different materials, arranged to accentuate the bustle, occupied the attention of fashionable dressmakers. Many of these dresses had long sweeping trains or layers of frills trailing out behind. The bustle as a structure, worn at the back only, had two distinct phases—the first was that of the 1870s following directly after the discarded crinoline; then after a few years' experiment at the end of the decade came the second phase, that of the 1880s when no actual structure was used. Of the two the first had a great deal of charm because of its floating quality; the second very little, because it was over-accentuated, jerking the bosom and bottom into an S-shape tilted so that an upright line drawn through it formed the tiny waist. With the second bustle fashion demanded that the hair should be pulled up on to the top and front of the head, where it was arranged as high as possible. Hats were taller and perched well on top of the piled-up hair; a high collar was worn on all day dresses. The low, off-the-shoulder line continued to be worn for evening dress but some sort of ruffle or lacy neck decoration was normal, as were black velvet ribbons.

The last decade of the 19th c. witnessed some memorable changes—the bustle was discarded, the waist became if possible even smaller to match the boned necks of lace that every lady wore, skirts were full and flaring out behind, shoulders once more almost as wide as those of the 1830s, hats of unwieldy proportions, often held in place with veils. A dozen different gowns for different functions were advertised in every journal of fashion. The mode now included the breeches

Dress of white *broderie anglaise* with high boned collar; long-handled sunshade with onyx grip; small reticule in right hand; straw hat decorated with lace and flowers under the brim (*c.* 1900)

bicycling suit, the motoring dust coat, the correct ensemble for shooting, hunting and fishing, tennis and golf; the morning gown, the tea gown, the matinée gown and many others. It was in this context of 'appropriate costume' that the blouse and skirt made its début, held neatly in place by a belt which buckled in front.

While the wide sleeves were fashionable until about 1900, capes of all sorts were to be seen, mostly short with high upstanding collars.

It is difficult to appreciate the changes that took place in the clothing worn by gentlemen immediately before or just after the turn of the century because when we look at the drawings of the time there seems to be little that is remarkable in the cut and line of their clothes. What was remarkable at the time was the new informality of dress for, although the frock-coat and the morning suit were worn for formal occasions, there was a continuous trend towards appropriate informal attire. Knee-breeches and stockings, spats and gaiters for sports, white flannel trousers for cricket and tennis, lounge suits, Norfolk suits, shooting jackets, blazers, motoring coats, the caped coats now so reminiscent of Sherlock Holmes, cloth caps, soft tweed ones, bowler hats, felt hats, hard hats and soft hats, straw boaters and panama hats all made their appearance before the end of the 19th c.

Life moved less quickly then than it does today. The same well-bred, decorous styles might appear over and over again without comment or loss of prestige. Two outstanding alterations which are worth recording during the years immediately preceding the First World War were first the abandonment of tight-lacing and trailing skirts for women and second the new effect of well-tailored trousers with a pressed crease down the front of the leg.

Experiments in high waists and princess gowns, gowns without emphatic waistline, shorter skirts, tighter skirts, even skirts split at the ankle to give more freedom in movement, all appeared between 1910 and 1914, and by the beginning of that year an advertisement warned the fashionable world that: 'Every lady of fashion in Europe and America now knows it. The waist and hips are gone, the back is flat, the figure lithe, sinuous and normal. Everything tends towards perfect, natural youthfulness.'

The First World War was responsible for the final abandonment of trailing garments except for the elegance of extremely formal occasions. It was also responsible for short hair cut off just below the lobe of the ears and called 'bobbed' or 'clubbed'—a style which began with children and gradually spread to their mothers and aunts. Neat tailored suits, slightly masculine in cut with skirts just below the calf, first made their appearance at this time. Such skirts were worn either tight or flared.

The fashions that had sufficed during the war years were, on the whole, reasonably useful—skirts full enough and short enough to make movement and travel comfortable. The only real incongruity was the still vast size and shape of hats. The year 1920 heralded a new barrel-like contour with clothes swathed round the body in a variety of ungainly arrangements, often held in place with a belt round the widest part of the hips. The proof that one was fashion-conscious and adaptable to this new art in dress lay in the ability to wear a Spanish shawl as an evening dress with no other garment visible, or to drape a loose coat and hold it in place without fastening. Five years of experiment with Red Indian, Spanish, Egyptian and Chinese ideas preceded the short knee-length skirt, Eton crop, slave bangles and long cigarette-holders of 1925 to 1930. During this time the passion for sports had helped to introduce the Fair Isle sweater and the brief tennis dress. It was in the early 1920s that a prelude to the first mini-skirts suggested such diverse experiments as the handkerchief skirts with their dangling squares of ninon or georgette, skirts daringly short in front with almost a train at the back and other ingenious inventions to break the monotony of outline. Also during these years came new shapes in hats that tended to cover the eyebrows or even the eyes. From 1925 onwards hats became almost optional. It was no longer necessary to wear a hat when the hair was cut short and almost stuck into position with the newer styles of waving. Hats were reserved for amusement or formality, such occasions as weddings, Ascot, etc.

Full evening dress demanded a minimum of material and a maximum of bare back, shoulders and arms. Beads and fringes, bits of transparent floating drapery, costume jewellery, long earrings and strings of beads were the ornaments adopted to show off the slinky contours of the now weight-conscious lady. Stockings of pinkish silk, called 'flesh-colour', were finished at the top with lisle or some thicker substance to hold the pressure of suspenders. Informal dress now included the pyjama suit or lounge pyjamas, full in the leg and with a long Chinese-style top. During the 1930s these developed into a one-piece garment frequently worn for informal evening occasions.

Though the war years had made so many alterations to the habits of life, the full impact of change in men's clothes was not really discernible until the 1920s, when the tailored suit with turn-up trousers, wide lapels and a soft shirt with changeable collars suddenly became a uniform for the man-about-town. Before the war there had been few businessmen who dared to appear at their office without formal morning dress. Bowler hats and soft felt hats called 'trilbys' were now considered possible alternatives to a top hat. Freedom from restriction introduced the Fair Isle sweater for men as well as for women and children. Pull-overs and polo-necked sweaters, plus-fours and Oxford bags were all introduced before the end of the 1920s. The plus-fours were incredibly baggy and wide, falling over the stockings to within some 15 centimetres of the ankle. Oxford bags, favoured by the young, had extremely wide legs, being something over 76 centimetres at the bottom, their flapping shapes contrasting with the short flapping skirts of their partners when dancing the Charleston. Coats and trousers were rarely made from similar materials for informal wear; the sports jacket and 'flannel bags' were being worn in every walk of life. Sports shirts with collars attached, made from various coloured fabrics, began to be worn even for business occasions. The stiff collar which had been worn for well over a century became outdated. Full evening dress and occasions that demand morning suits long remained the sole outposts of such civilized inconveniences.

Colours of the 1920s were both garish and shimmering. The brilliant Cubist and geometrical shapes that were used to ornament both day and evening clothes vied in colour with the Fair Isle knitting patterns. Shiny silks and rayons, bead dresses and gold or silver lamé glittered at every evening function.

Hesitating between long and short, the evening gowns of 1930 suddenly took the plunge and descended evenly to the ground. The picture dress had once more come back into vogue, but with a difference. This time it was cut draping rather than hanging straight and the fullness was reserved so that a swirl of fabric sprang out from the knees to the feet. This shape was achieved by cutting the main part of the garment on the cross so that it clung tightly to the body with the lower part cut circular so that a complete circle of material was used for the added fullness at the bottom. The principle was elegant and for some five or six years the general idea was experimented with and improved upon. These few years witnessed the incredible ingenuity of the fashionable dress-designer, who worked on a principle entirely governed by pulling and patting materials into the desired clinging lines; tucks and darts governed the hang of individual garments so that it was difficult if not impossible to make a good copy. They hung and clung to the body, and the day dresses descended inch by inch to just below the calf. It was a short period of dressiness—picture dresses to the ground, wide shoulders and huge hats for garden-parties and daytime functions; draped dresses and hats of felt dragged and pulled into a draped effect for undress occasions. Before the end of the 1930s skirts were full again and up to the knees. This time, however, the waist was in the normal place and an emphasis on the hem showed a tendency towards lacy frills. Men's clothes had settled into a traditional outfit which included the lounge suit, dinner jacket, tails and sports clothes. Trousers were still very wide and a turn-up at the hem was normal.

It is difficult to place the responsibility for change entirely on wars, but there is no doubt that in Europe the Second World War imposed so many restrictions that there was little hope of altering clothes until 1949, when rationing was at last abandoned. Parcels for Britain contained such an assortment of American styles for the young that the war years witnessed the introduction of a hundred new ideas for youth. Jeans and lumber-jackets, cowboy shirts and check or plaid coats, snow-suits, sneakers, bobby-socks, engine-drivers' caps, caps with earpieces. It was little wonder that youth in the 1950s saw no reason to follow any prewar traditions in clothing.

One peculiarity of women's styles at this time was the continued fashion for sophisticated hairdressing: shoulder-length or piled up on top of the head, Mozart and Pompadour styles, anything that might defeat the eclipse of feminine individuality.

Utility garments curtailed the use of fabrics. Men's 'civvy' suits having no turn-ups and the leg much narrower, no waistcoats, no tails to shirts, socks of a minimum length. All such restrictions pertained to the 'demob' suits handed out at the close of hostilities.

In 1947 Dior's 'New Look' came in in France, and the first long dresses to within some 18 cm of the ankle began to arrive in England. After almost 10 years of knee-length dresses and skirts of minimum width the fashion was welcomed once again, particularly the ballet-length full skirt for cocktail and semi-evening occasions to take the place of the antiquated picture frocks left over from the 1930s. Tight-waisted with high, stand-up collars, full or draped skirts, flaring peplums, strapless evening gowns, elaborately dressed hair or the new urchin cut were typical features of the early 1950s. Skirts were getting shorter towards the end of the decade. In 1957 the stiletto heel began its damaging career: at first both elegant and graceful after the clumsiness of the platform sole, but later to develop into the grotesquely long-toed shoe which gave the impression of incredibly large feet.

Fashion shifted during the late 1950s into a series of new ideas for the young. 'Teddy-boy' suits, winkle-picker shoes, the 'Zute suit' were the first of these experiments and since that time there has hardly been a year without its change, from the leather suit studded with brass to the elegantly frilled shirts made from saris. Long hair for men began to come into general use with this new freedom from convention, at first a student craze which developed into a fashion. Girls started to wear their hair long and straight at much the same time as the beginning of the mini-skirt and knee-length boots in 1966. The mini-skirt slowly progressed up the thigh until in 1969 it could get no shorter and the maxi arrived as a counter-interest. In 1971 any length was permissible, mini, maxi or midi and the uniformity of dress which had developed during the last years of the 1960s was once more broken. Among the multifarious affectations and experiments of the young has been the free revival of fashions from the past.

6. INDIANS OF THE INCA EMPIRE. Our knowledge of dress in the Inca Empire of Pre-Columbian Peru is derived from incidental

descriptions in the writings of the chroniclers, from the excellent drawings with which Guaman Poma de Ayala illustrated his *Nueva Coronica* and from actual garments or remnants found in burials. Many of the early Spanish chroniclers remarked on the numerous regional variations of costume, particularly head-dress, among the Andean Indians at the time of the Conquest. Local habits of dress were strongly supported by tradition and were retained even when a man moved from one locality to another, so that by his dress it was possible to tell a man's origin. Describing Cuzco as he saw it, Cieza de Léon said: 'The city was full of strangers from all parts, Indians of Chile and Pasto, Cañaris, Chachapoyas, Huanocos, Collas, and men of all the tribes in the provinces, each living apart in the quarters assigned by the governors of the city. They all retained the costume of their fathers and went about after the manner of their native land; and even when one hundred thousand men were assembled together, the country of each Indian was easily known by the peculiar head-dress which distinguished him.' In aetiological myths these local differences were ascribed to the origin of the race, when after the destruction of the first breed of giants in a deluge the Creator God fashioned the present races of men with the appropriate costume for each district. Under the Inca administration, probably in the time of Pachacuti Inca Yupanqui, these local differentiations of dress were perpetuated by decree and made compulsory. Acosta notes: 'We see great diversitie amongest the provinces especially in the attire of their head, . . . They had a straight and inviolable law, that no man might change the fashion of the garments of his province, although hee went to live in another.'

In addition to these local variations within the central area of the Inca Empire there were larger differences between the Quechua highlanders of Peru on the one hand and the southern, Aymara, highlanders who dwelt on what is now the Bolivian Altiplano, and again between the highlanders and those who lived in the warmer coastal valleys, called Yungas. In general the coastal Indians wore cotton and the highlanders wore garments woven from the wool of the llama or alpaca, sometimes quilted with cotton. There were two types of woollen material: a coarser grade (*awasca*) worn by the common people and a finer grade (*cumpi*) made for the nobility. The latter might be richly embroidered (*tocapu*) or woven with tapestry designs. The natives of the tropical eastern valleys of the Cordillera and the fringes of the Amazonian forest dressed differently again. Their clothing was much scantier and consisted of either cotton or barkcloth or raffia.

The body garments of the Quechua Indians who formed the central core of the empire consisted of a brief breech-clout, a tunic and a cloak. The breech-clout (*wara*) was made of ordinary unpatterned *awasca*, was passed between the legs and was held up by a narrow belt. It was assumed by the Inca boys at puberty as part of an elaborate maturity ceremonial. The tunic (*uncu*; called by the Spanish, *camiseta*) was sleeveless and consisted of a piece of woven material *c.* 170 centimetres long, which was doubled over and allowed to hang down back and front with a slit for the head. It was not tailored but was sewn together at the sides with holes at the top for the arms to pass through. When worn it came down to mid-thigh. Cobo says: 'Over the *guaras* they wear a garment without sleeves or collar, which they call *uncu* and we call *camiseta* since it has the cut of our *camisetas*; each garment is individually woven, for they do not weave long pieces of stuff like us and cut out the garments from them. The material from which they make this *camiseta* is like a length of finely woven wool fabric (*jergueta*); it is three and a half palms in width and two *varas* in length. In the weave itself they leave the neck open so that it is unnecessary to cut; nothing else is necessary than to fold it over and sew the sides with the same thread as that from which it is woven as one sews a sack, leaving on each side at the top sufficient space for the arms to go through. They usually come down to the knees or three or four fingers above.' The *uncu* was often elaborately decorated in stripes or with a chequered pattern. The decoration was most commonly at the neck and in the form of a chequered band of embroidery at the waist: above and below the garment might be of different colours. In the coastal districts the tunic was of cotton and often had sleeves. The cloak (*yacolla*) was a rectangular piece of cloth about 180 by 90 centimetres in size, made by sewing two loom-widths of material together up the middle. It was worn above the *uncu*, thrown loosely over the shoulders and was usually of a contrasting colour. In the dance or during exercise the two ends were fastened over the left shoulder so as to leave the right arm free. Hung over the left shoulder below the cloak but above the tunic they carried a woven bag for coca or other small objects, such as is still worn by the highland Indians today.

For footwear both men and women were shod with a sandal (*usuta*) made of untanned skin from the neck of the llama. It consisted only of a sole, which was cut rather shorter than the length of the foot in order that the toes might grip the ground when a man was walking up hill. The soles were bound to the foot from heel to instep with gaily coloured woollen bands which were wound crossed around the ankles and over the top of the foot. *Usutas* were also made of cotton or wool or were plaited from aloe fibre (agave). The Collas of the southern Altiplano wore a kind of moccasin which covered the toes and sides of the feet. Fringed leg bands were worn by the Inca below the knees and at the ankles.

As has been said, the head-dresses were particularly subject to regional variation. Acosta

Inca garment with short sleeves and neck opening. Woven with Tihuanacu step pattern decoration at bottom and sleeves. (Kemper Coll.)

Chimū garment with short sleeves and neck opening. Woven with pattern of birds and below a band with human figures. (Kemper Coll.)

Inca costume of a marriageable woman at the time of the Inca Empire from *Nueva Coronica* of Guaman Poma de Ayala, p. 223

writes: 'In some places they carried a long piece of cloth which went often about, in some places a large piece of cloth which went but once about, in some parts as it were little mortars or hattes, in some places as it were high and round bonets and some like the bottome of sacks, with a thousand other differences.' The normal headgear of the Quechua Indians was the *llautu*, a woollen fillet of about a finger's breadth which was wound two or three times round the head or which might be wound round repeatedly to form a kind of crown. Different colours and styles of wearing the *llautu* were used for various ceremonial occasions or as symbols of rank or as a distinguishing feature of this or that tribe. The Aymara of the southern highlands wore a characteristic cap (*chuco*) which might be flat or shaped like a truncated cone. Knitted woollen hats, pointed and with flaps over the ears, were also worn as a protection against the cold winds.

The women wore a full-length dress (*acsu*) bound at the waist by an ornamental belt (*chumpi*) and over it a long mantle (*lliclla*), described as follows: 'The women wear what they call *acsos* in the manner of *yacollas*, made of their native wool [i.e. llama or alpaca wool]. They wear these next to the skin and they come from the shoulders to the instep. They fasten them at the shoulders with large silver pins which they call *topos*, with broad round tops, or some are of copper. Above they wear a mantle which they call *lliquilla*, which covers them from the shoulders to the knees and these they fasten at the breast with a *topo* of the same workmanship' (*Relación geográfica*). He adds: 'On the head they wear a kerchief, which they call *uincha*, and they gird themselves with a large girdle and then with a narrow one encircling the body several times, which they call *chumbe*. And their footwear is similar to that of the men.' The dress, which was also called *anacu*, was of the same width throughout its length. It had no sleeves and no hole for the neck, but was wound round the body from the arms down and the ends were drawn over the shoulders and fastened with pins. The *lliclla*, which came down to the knees, was of fine material, usually square, and would be beautifully decorated. The sash (*chumbi*), which was wound several times round the waist, would be of richly decorated tapestry-woven material and above it the women sometimes wore a second multicoloured girdle. The hair was worn long with a gaily decorated fillet, 6 or 7 cm wide, binding it on the head. The women of the nobility wore instead a kerchief or mantilla, called *ñañaca* or *iñaca*, which was a piece of *cumbi* folded so that one corner rested on the forehead and the other at the back, leaving the hair free at the sides. Some of the Aymara women wore their hair in plaits without head-dress and those of La Paz are said to have worn a lock of rolled hair adorned with pearls on the right side of the forehead.

The Inca men wore their hair cut short as a distinctive feature and different Inca tribes (*ayllus*) wore it cut in a different fashion. The children's hair was cut for the first time at two years of age in the ceremony of naming and was cut in the final distinctive fashion at the *rutuchiku* ceremony which formed part of the maturity rites by which they were initiated into manhood.

The most distinctive adornments of the Inca peoples were 'ear-plugs', which were worn not as hanging ear-rings but enclosed within holes pierced in the ear-lobes. They varied in size and material according to tribe and privilege from the round plaques of gold or silver some 15 cm in diameter worn by the Inca royalty, distending the ear-lobes to extraordinary proportions—for which reason they were called by the Spaniards *orejones*—to mere wisps of wool or splinters of reed. Garcilaso describes the custom as follows: 'Besides having their hair cut short they had their ears pierced in the place where women are accustomed to pierce them for ear-rings; but they increased the size of the hole artificially to extraordinary size, unbelievable to anyone who had not seen them, for it seems impossible that the small amount of flesh that there is beneath the ear should be extended so as to be able to contain an ear-plug of the size and shape of the stopper of a jar: for like stoppers were the plugs which they set in those loops which they made of their ears. And if they happened to break these loops, they measured a good quarter of a *vara* [21 centimetres] in length and half a finger in thickness . . . The Inca granted his people another privilege in that they were commanded to pierce their ears. But there was a limitation on the size of the hole, which was not to exceed half that of the Inca. And each tribe and province wore different things as ear-stoppers. To some, such as the nation called Mayu and Sancu, he granted as their emblem to wear a wisp of straw in their ears of the thickness of the little finger. Others he commanded to wear a tuft of white wool, which was to stick out on both sides of the ear as far as the length of the first joint of the thumb; these were the people called Poques. The nations of the Muina, Huaruc, Chillqui he commanded to wear ear-stoppers made of the common reed which the Indians call *tutura*. The people of Rimactampu and their neighbours he commanded to wear them made of a wood which is called *maguey* in the Isles of Barvolento and chuchau in the language of Peru: when the bark is removed the pith is soft, spongy and light. . . . They were called ear-plugs (*orejeras*) and not ear-rings because they did not hang from the ears but were framed round by the hole like the stopper in the mouth of a jar.'

The ears of the Inca nobility were bored as part of the maturity rites and the size of the hole was gradually enlarged by inserting larger and larger plaques. If in later life the enormously extended lobe broke or tore, this was regarded as a sign of ill omen and the unfortunate man was debarred from participating in religious ceremonies. According to Guaman Poma such persons were customarily sent from Cuzco to some administrative office in the provinces.

The men also wore gold arm-bands, which were open up the side to allow them to be fitted over the forearm, and necklaces of pierced stones. A characteristic adornment was *chaquiri*, fine and beautifully wrought gold sequins. The jewellery of the women consisted of the pins (*topu*) with which they fastened their cloaks, and necklaces of shells.

Among the insignia of the reigning Inca the most distinctive was the *masca paycha*, or 'fringe', which was worn suspended from the *llautu* over the forehead. It was of scarlet wool hanging from a number of small gold tubes. Pedro Pizarro describes the *masca paycha* worn by Atahualpa as follows: 'On his forehead he had a fringe as broad as a hand, fastened to the fillet. It was of scarlet wool, evenly parted and this wool was very finely wound in the middle round two small gold tubes. The wool was first woven, but twined from the tubes downwards and that is what fell over the forehead. The fringe came down over the eyes, was the length of a finger and covered the whole forehead.' The conferring of the *masca paycha* symbolized the assumption of royal dignity and power like the crowning of a king in European ceremonial. As a symbol of granting powers of life and death the reigning Inca would give to certain high officials a replica of the *masca paycha*, which, however, they were not entitled to wear but carried before them on a lance. The *llautu* itself was of a distinctive colour, usually red, about the thickness of a finger, and was wound four or five times round the head. Above it, on a short rod, rose a tuft surmounted by three feathers of the *coraquenque* bird. The whole ensemble was referred to by the Spanish as the *borla*.

After the Conquest many of the more picturesque elements of native culture rapidly decayed and certain features of Spanish dress ousted the local customs. The Spanish greed for gold and silver caused their use for bodily adornment to be discontinued and the finer types of cloth ceased to be woven or worn. The influence of the Church caused short trousers to be introduced in lieu of the *wara* for men and at some time during the Colonial period the women took to wearing skirts.

The two most characteristic changes were the introduction of the *poncho* and the shortened *lliclla*. The poncho is a square piece of material (or sometimes two rectangular pieces sewn together) with an opening for the head in the direction of the length. It is worn loosely over the shoulders, coming down usually to the knees, and is neither girt nor sewn at the sides. Its origin is obscure, but it has remained until the present day the most characteristic garment of the highland Indians. The women's *lliclla* has been shortened into an oblong piece of material which is tied in front of the chest and allowed to hang behind the shoulder in the form of a pouch in which the baby is carried. The characteristic 'bowler hats' which form a striking feature of the costume of the chola women today came in about a century and a half ago.

7. COLONIAL NORTH AMERICA. The early settlers in what is now the United States of America arrived with the ideas and habits of dress which prevailed in their countries of origin, often indeed bringing their actual wardrobes and spares with them. This made for a high degree of regionalism, which was heightened by differences of religion that were often reflected in

Modern Indian costume. (Aymara)

Modern Indian costume. (Quechua)

the manner of dress; and although differences were to some extent modified and ironed out by common needs of life and climatic conditions, and as time went on by the influence of European fashions on the dress of the more well-to-do, nevertheless a measure of regionalism persisted well into the period of Independence. Although English customs prevailed on the whole except for isolated pockets, to be modified by French fashions in the 18th c., there was still a vast difference in the early years between regions such as Massachusetts and New England, where Puritan ideas of sobriety and simplicity prevailed, and the more wealthy tobacco-growing south, which favoured Cavalier flamboyance and display. Changes of fashion too were brought in by successive waves of arrival. Salem planters of 1628 wore long hose or breeches, but by 1635 long hose were out of fashion with the New Hampshire arrivals. Even so late as the early years of the 19th c. German settlers in Pennsylvania, Ohio and Iowa, with their strong religious convictions, continued to wear sunbonnets and ankle-length skirts oblivious of the progress of fashion elsewhere.

In general warmth, strength and durability were the desiderata in the early years. Doublets and jerkins were often of leather or the longer 'cassock' was of strong cloth or canvas; shoes were heavy and caps were warm. The early hunters and trappers wore buckskin tunics tanned and softened with animal brains—an Indian technique—and hanging thongs served the practical purpose of tying up their game. For shoes they wore the moccasin and their hats were often made from fur. Otherwise spinning and weaving were cottage industries and some use was made of homespun materials for everyday working costume. But there were few sheep in America until after *c.* 1660 and little local manufacture of textiles until the late 17th c., while the manufacture of cotton and linen made little headway until the end of the 18th c. Imported fabrics were controlled and most clothes other than rough workaday wear had to be ordered, mainly from London. The difficulty and expense of renewal put additional emphasis on durability and wardrobes were often handed down in the family or bequeathed. Indeed it is from inventories in wills as well as from surviving orders and invoices with London supplying houses that much of our information is derived about the habits of dress that prevailed in this period.

With the building up of wealth, however, a taste for luxury in dress soon made its appearance and in the larger towns at any rate people became almost excessively fashion-conscious. As often happens in new and isolated communities, dress was not only a badge of rank and a stamp of social distinction but a mark of self-respect. Where difficulties are excessive, to dress well and in the reigning fashion acquires importance incumbent to a man's dignity and estate. Even so thrifty an economist as Benjamin Franklin sent back from France white cloaks and plumes, silk négligés, satin cardinals, paste shoe-buckles to his womenfolk so that they should not 'dress with singularity'. From boyhood George Washington showed a proper concern for dress and was minute in his specifications that both he and his family should be richly and appropriately dressed in the latest fashion. The following is a list of garments ordered from England for his step-daughter at the age of four:

8 pairs kid mitts
4 ,, gloves
2 ,, silk shoes
4 ,, Calamanco shoes
4 ,, leather pumps
6 ,, fine thread stockings
4 ,, worsted stockings
2 Caps
2 pairs ruffles
2 tuckers, bibs, and aprons if Fashionable
2 Fans
2 Masks
2 bonnets
1 Cloth Cloak
1 Stiffened Coat of Fashionable silk made to pack-thread stays
6 yards ribbons
2 Necklaces
1 Pair Silver Sleeve Buttons with Stones
6 Pocket Handkerchiefs

In the 1620s John Pory, Secretary of the Virginia colony, wrote: 'Our cowkeeper here of James citty on Sundays goes accoutred all in ffreshe fflaminge silke, and a wife of one that had in England professed the blacke arte not of a Scholler but of a Collier weares her rough bever hatt with a faire perle hatband, and a silken sute thereto correspondent.' By the middle of the century luxury of dress had increased in most of the larger cities and was becoming the butt of satirists and earning the reprobation of moralists. Writing of the extravagance of New York, the Chevalier de Crèvecœur said: 'If there is a town on the American continent where English luxury displays its follies it is in New York . . . In the dress of the women you will see the most brilliant silks, gauzes, hats and borrowed hair.' Philadelphia was notorious for luxury and display. The élite of Boston were likened to the extravagances of a European court. The daughters of General Huntington of Norwich, Connecticut, were sent to a finishing school in Boston with the regulation complement of 12 silk gowns, but the chaperon wrote that they must have another gown of 'recently imported rich fabric' in order to dress in accordance with their rank and station. Sumptuary laws were passed from time to time in various states, usually prohibiting extravagances of fashion and costly accessories to those whose income did not exceed a certain figure. Although these laws were rarely enforced and seem to have been little effective, their specific prohibitions do serve to indicate the tendencies which it was felt necessary to hold in check. Typical was a provision in Massachusetts prohibiting to those with an estate under

John Smibert, *Mrs. Nathaniel Cunningham.* (Toledo Mus. of Art, Toledo, Ohio, *c.* 1733)

Robert Feke, *James Bowdoin II.* (Bowdoin College Mus. of Art, Brunswick, Maine, 1748)

John Greenwood, *The Greenwood-Lee Family.* (Mus. of Fine Arts, Boston, *c.* 1747)

£200 the wearing of gold or silver thread lace, all kinds of cut-works, embroideries or needle-work in the form of caps, bands or rails, gold and silver girdles, hatbands, belts, ruffs or beaver hats, knots of ribbon, broad shoulder-bands, silk roses, double ruffs or capes, gold and silver buttons, silk points, silk and tiffany hoods and scarfs. In the Puritan areas, where the taste for fine dress also penetrated, the fashion for slashed wear and for bustles met with particular opposition.

It is against this picture of regional difference and constant change that the following account of 'usual' costume must be read.

Men wore breeches full at the knee and waist, doublet and jerkin or the longer cassock, a loose cloak or mandillion lined with cotton or silk, and a strong coat of buff leather tied at the waist by a sash. The doublet, which might also be worn by women and children, was surmounted by a high stiff collar. Boots of buff leather with turned-down tops, called French falls, were superseded *c.* 1660 by the Jack boot of shiny black leather. About the same time the coat, vest, cravat, sash garters and buckle shoes also came in and *c.* 1690 breeches began to be fitted to the shape of the leg. The high steeple hat was worn by both men and women in Puritan communities. By the end of the century this had been replaced by the tricorne hat and periwigs, lace or linen ruffles, skirted coats and tight breeches had come in.

Women wore short, strong gowns, full skirts, homespun petticoats and long aprons of white linen. Separate or detached sleeves were worn, especially by the women of Dutch origin with whom a pair of sleeves trimmed with lace was a normal article of attire. The double-puffed 'virago' sleeve, full at elbow and shoulder and drawn in at intervals by ribbons was popular. The 'slytting' or slashing of sleeves was considered an idle vanity at the time of the Pilgrim Fathers and in Massachusetts sleeves with more than one slash or sleeves more than half an ell wide were forbidden to both men and women. Linen cuffs had to be worn with short sleeves 'whereby the nakedness of the arm may be discovered'. Sometimes too a partlet or neckerchief was worn and it might be full like a shirt and extend under the bodice. Hoods were worn throughout the period. The so-called French hood was fur lined and loosely tied under the chin. But hoods were also made of lighter materials, of silk or of gauze, such as the 'love-hoods' of New York. Hoods of camlet are also mentioned. The popular riding-hoods were often fitted with a deep cape, sometimes with armholes and sometimes richly embroidered.

With the growth of luxury in the 2nd half of the 17th c. and the early 18th c. women's dress became more and more subject to the vagaries of European fashions. Elegant aprons trimmed with lace or of embroidered lawn became an essential fashionable adjunct to ladies' costume as they were in England under Queen Anne. Sample aprons were sent from England to be copied. An advertisement is quoted from the *New England Weekly Journal* of 1739: 'Beautiful Gold and Silver Brocade Apron.' The bustle was fashionable until *c.* 1710, when it was succeeded by the hoop. Embroidered or hand-painted white linen and cotton gowns were a feature of American fashionable costume that came in about the middle of the 18th c. Examples are preserved in the Metropolitan Museum, New York. Their cut varied from decade to decade, following in general that of the wide skirts which were worn over the pannier-like hoops of the petticoat, but they were of lighter material than the heavy brocades, cut velvets or stiff taffetas which were common in Europe.

American costume became increasingly elegant through the 1st half of the 18th c. Women affected the long-waisted, pointed bodice, low necks with square or rounded line, full skirt, tight sleeves with ruffles at the elbow and brocade slippers. Hoods became more colourful. The cardinal, a scarlet hooded cloak, was the vogue. The Polonese, a light open gown worn looped at the sides and trailing behind came in during the 2nd half of the century. The calash was fashionable from *c.* 1765 for the rest of the century and indeed was worn up to the middle of the 19th c. This was a large head-dress made of thin green silk shirred on lengths of rattan or whalebone drawn in at the neck; it could be extended over the face or drawn out by ribbons and bridles or it could be gathered into a mass at the back of the head. This enormous shade was worn over the high pompadour hair-styles which also became fashionable. By the middle of the century both men's and women's caps had blossomed into a bewildering variety of forms. Among the most popular were the women's mob-caps familiar from portraits of Martha Washington. They were large baggy caps of white lace or lawn with floppy frills or ruffles and lappets or streamers (i.e. mobs), which were crossed under the chin and tied at the back with the ends left floating. For men the waistcoat became shorter, the coat was cut back at the sides and after *c.* 1760 breeches were buttoned at the knee. The opening of the East India trade brought to America an influx of Indian and Chinese stuffs, which also had their influence on the elaboration of costume.

By the middle of the century high fashion was fully established and America followed closely behind European, mainly Parisian, modes. The first jointed fashion dolls reached New England in the 1750s. These dolls, dressed in Paris, were the precursors of the FASHION PLATE and were equipped to the last meticulous detail with every accoutrement of the latest mode, including frills, necklaces, ruffles, bows, buckles, even to the stays and hooped petticoats. Their arrival made possible the birth of *haute couture.* They were followed at the end of the century by fashion plates and women's magazines.

2, 12, 25, 30, 62, 85, 93, 96, 112, 121, 169, 178, 179, 181, 182, 183, 192, 224, 339, 352, 364, 379, 469, 504, 655, 669, 681, 775, 904, 905, 906, 918.

COTSWOLD SCHOOL. School of 20th-c. furniture design founded by the brothers Sidney and Ernest BARNSLEY and Ernest GIMSON. See FURNITURE (ENGLISH).

COTTAGE BINDINGS. A kind of bookbinding which had a vogue in the late 17th and early 18th centuries, so named because the most characteristic feature of its decoration was a gilt or painted roof or gable at the top or bottom of the cover. See BOOKBINDING (HISTORICAL).

COTTE, ROBERT DE (1656–1735). French architect and decorator. He was given the rank of architect in the Bâtiments du Roi in 1685 and was made a member of the Académie in 1687. When Jules-Hardouin Mansart (1646–1708), whose brother-in-law he was, was appointed Surintendant des Bâtiments in 1699 De Cotte was made his second in command with the title Architecte Ordinaire. He also became Director of the Academy of Architecture and of the GOBELINS factory. On the death of Mansart he succeeded him as chief architect. He worked with Mansart on the Place Vendôme and the chapel at Versailles. His personal works included numerous houses in Paris and the provinces (Hôtel d'Estrées). He was also responsible in Paris for the façade of Saint-Roch and the decoration of the choir of Notre-Dame and in the provinces for the episcopal palaces at Strasbourg and Verdun, and the Place Bellecour at Lyon. Outside France he supplied designs for the Elector of Bavaria, the Elector of Cologne at Bonn, Victor-Amadeus II of Savoy, Philip V of Spain and others. In decorative style he was a pioneer of the ROCOCO.

COTTON AND COTTON PRINTING. The word 'cotton' is a transliteration of the Arabic *qutn*. Cotton is obtained from the fibrous substance which encases the seeds of several trees of the genus *Gossypium*. It has been used in the wild state and has also been cultivated from remote antiquity in various regions of Asia and America. In order to be usable for textile production the lint, or seed hairs, must first be separated from the seeds, a process known as 'ginning'. The earliest known mechanical gin was used in India. It was replaced in the U.S.A. by a saw-type gin invented by Eli Whiting in 1794 and improved by Hogden Homes in 1796. The ginned cotton is then 'carded', a process by which impurities are removed, and is next 'combed' in order to separate the shorter fibres. Only then is it in a suitable state for spinning into yarns from which fabrics can be woven. See TEXTILE MANUFACTURE IN ANTIQUITY.

Cotton yarns were found at Mohenjo-Daro as early as 3000 B.C. and there is mention of cotton in the *Rig-Veda*, *c.* 1500 B.C. Herodotus in the 5th c. B.C. mentions cotton as an unusual product of a 'wool-bearing tree' in India and speaks of the hand-plucking of the lint from the seeds, the carding and spinning into yarn. But in antiquity the cultivation of cotton in the Western world was confined to Egypt and the Sudan, though some Indian cotton may have been imported in Roman times. (See GREEK AND ROMAN ANTIQUITY, TEXTILE MANUFACTURE.) In the New World cotton was found in the earliest agricultural, pre-ceramic cultures of coastal Peru. Spinning into yarns for making nets, traps, etc. preceded weaving. Cotton, believed to have been an Asiatic–American hybrid, was cultivated and spun in many regions of South and Central America and it was used both for fabrics and for padding and quilting garments by the Pre-Conquest cultures of the Andean region. The natives of Yucatan presented cotton garments to Hernando Cortés and the Mexicans wore cotton when the Spanish colonized Vera Cruz.

During the Middle Ages cotton wool, fibre and yarn reached western Europe through Spain and the maritime towns of Italy from the eastern Mediterranean, but it was not until the 12th c. that it began to be grown in Spain and Sicily. Cotton wool was used for padding QUILTS and cotton candle-wicks burned without smell. Small items of cotton such as ribbons, gloves and bonnets became available in the major medieval trade markets. Generally the yarn was mixed with linen to form a composite textile called FUSTIAN, which was used for linings and shirts. It was also woven with SILK, as in Italy for *bombasine* and in France for *bourras*, a rough grey cloth which came into use in the 16th c. About the same time plain white cotton also began to be woven in western Europe.

But throughout the Middle Ages cotton was an exotic material around which legend and story accumulated. It was partly the desire to increase direct imports of cotton which served as a stimulus for exploration of the Far East and in 1498 Vasco da Gama brought back *pintados* or calicoes and opened up the route for direct trade with India. (See INDIA, TEXTILES.) The great attraction of these ornate cottons, pintados or CHINTZES, besides their novelty, lay in their fast dyes and durability. A century later the Spanish blockade stimulated Dutch and English merchants to trade directly with the East and the rival East India companies were formed early in the 17th c. The French company came into existence in 1664; other companies such as the Swedish one followed in the 18th c. With the aristocracy and the courts leading the fashion, pintados and chintzes became the craze in the 2nd half of the 17th c. and there were never enough to satisfy the demand. Just as imported blue and white porcelain from China influenced European ceramics production, so too the chintzes were imitated, mostly on imported cotton fabrics. These substitute chintzes also worked out cheaper and came within reach of a wider public. One of the first factories to be recorded was founded near Amsterdam in 1671. By 1689 Jeremias Neuhofer was copying exotic patterns in Augsburg. William Sherwin of West Ham had patented his 'new way for printing broad calico' by 1676. He had grasped the possibility of printing the mordant and then dyeing the piece in madder.

The wool, linen and silk manufacturers soon felt threatened by the immediate success of the calico printers and used their influence to have the trade and the East India Company's imports forbidden by Acts of Parliament in 1700 and 1721. The Manchester Act of 1736 allowed fustian printing as long as it had a linen warp. The British ban on the printing of cotton cloths was finally removed in 1774 although taxes were still heavy. The ban in France started as early as 1686, first on the importation and then on the imitation of Oriental fabrics, and it lasted until 1759, except for Marseilles. Block printing in this free port must have started *c.* 1648. Soon Armenian craftsmen were at work with their own techniques and by 1733 the town had as many as 24 workshops producing *indiennes* (printed calicos or chintzes) for the so-called export trade. Other Armenians settled in Genoa. As a result contraband thrived during the ban. Among the Huguenot émigrés who fled French territory after the revocation of the Edict of Nantes in 1685 many were calico printers and taking with them their trade secrets and specialized know-how they settled elsewhere in Europe on the banks of rivers suitable for bleaching, founding businesses in Berlin (1686), Geneva (1688), Neuchâtel (1707) and in other parts of Prussia (1741).

As soon as the ban was removed Christophe Philippe OBERKAMPF started the manufacture of printed cottons at Jouy between Paris and Versailles. The success of the TOILES DE JOUY, as

Toile de Jouy. *Les Travaux de la Manufacture* by Jean-Baptiste Huet. (Musée de l'Impression sur Étoffes, Mulhouse, 1783)

they were known, was rapid and their popularity for both furnishings and clothing remained such that after Oberkampf's death in 1815 the factory continued in operation until 1843, although from the first he was the moving spirit.

Copper-plate printing replaced block printing in 1781 and roller printing followed shortly after. Christophe HUET, Jean-Baptiste PILLEMENT and the engraver, J.-P. Le Bas designed delicate subjects in harmony with the ROCOCO and later the NEO-CLASSICAL fashions: CHINOISERIES, antiquities, pastoral and village scenes, Napoleonic episodes, games and sports. Jouy's flowers, floral bands, *camaïeux* and stripes were all the vogue. Louis XVI and Napoleon I both honoured Oberkampf, which is more than can be said of any other of the many French calico printers who started in business soon after the end of the ban. Paris, Rouen, Bordeaux with the Beautiran factory, Marseilles and Provence all had their *indienneurs*. As in the case of Nantes, the émigré Protestant dyers and engravers such as Gorgerat and Petitpierre were returning from Switzerland and Germany. The home market did not absorb the bulk of the production from these factories, but from the mid 18th c. they produced quantities of cheaper printed cottons for the slave trade. Simple catchy patterns decorated these cloths: lions and elephants, palanquins, palm trees and dragons, and natives dancing. After the abolition of slavery this production continued as standard trade goods for the French colonies.

In countries without prohibition, such as Holland, Germany and Switzerland, calico printing expanded rapidly in the 18th c. There were centres in Geneva, Neuchâtel, Berne, Aargau, Basle and Zürich. The free city of Mulhouse in Alsace linked France to the rest of Europe. Through sheer hard work and perseverance Koecklin and other printers started factories in the 1740s, well ahead of France. By 1788 there were 40 of them.

Like the secret of porcelain after 1710, the technique of fast-dyeing spread rapidly through Europe. Austria and Poland had their factories and by the end of the century Russian sponsors set up several factories organized by Swiss or German specialists. In the same way Speich, from the canton of Glarus, settled in Genoa in 1789. He printed *mezzari*, elegant cotton voiles with central flowery patterns, some details of which recalled Oriental inspiration such as minarets, tamarisk trees, red monkeys and white elephants. He brought back to life the fashion of the *pezzotto*, a 15th-c. creation. Originally it was a white rectangular scarf lighter to wear than a *mezzaro*. Now it was made with flowery branch patterns and was chiefly worn by young girls. In Spain also two English printers set up a factory in Avila in 1787, producing printed cottons with the usual patterns of large Indian-style flowers or more natural blooms in fairly tight compositions.

As for the history of British chintz, this came into its own during the planning of two exhibitions, in Manchester (1955) and in London (1960). Up to then many of the printed calico fragments had been attributed to Jouy. As happened in France, the ban would have delayed the development of calico printing in England had it not been for a striking series of mechanical discoveries which made the British manufacturers the leaders in their field.

In Ireland Francis Nixon used for the first time in 1752 an engraved copper plate (6 ft. × 2 ft.) (182 × 61 cm) to print with fast colours. Four years later he came to England and joined Amyand in Surrey, to whom he had sold his secret. Very soon other manufactories were started up: Robert Jones's factory at Old Ford, Poplar, is well known for its attractive pastoral scene of 1761, as is Collins's of Hertfordshire for its Chinese pattern of 1766, and Talwin and Foster at Bromley Hall on the Lea for floral and bird designs, sports and various pastimes and varieties of so-called pillar prints. In Scotland printed linen dates back to the 17th c. By 1758 copper plates were used in Edinburgh, by 1770 in Glasgow. Through their academies and societies both towns encouraged the arts and fostered original creations in many fields such as calico printing. Factories began to move out of the towns and settled in the valleys such as the Leven. Several of their pattern-books have been recovered, containing Indian shawl designs with the 'pine cone' device from fine copper-pinned blocks and delicate patterns such as light sprigs and sprays and ribbon-tied posies.

In 1769 ARKWRIGHT patented the spinning frame and Bell invented cylinder printing. The use of power looms initiated by CARTWRIGHT in the mid 1780s accelerated production but led to less polished creations. This may explain the return to block printing for high-quality chintzes from the turn of the century. At that time the floral chintz with a dark ground was at the height of fashion, as were the 'drab' designs, done only in yellows and greens, created chiefly by Daniel Goddard. In the latter part of the century the NEO-CLASSICAL revival was reflected by a number of outstanding designers in cotton, using WEDGWOOD's 'rosso antico', classical monuments or such subjects as the Battle of the Nile. Nevertheless they could not fully break away from the traditional Indian influence, especially in furniture chintzes. They also imitated Chinese wallpapers, such as the pink one in the Brighton Pavilion, producing designs of large flowering branches or smaller sprays, imbricated segments building up into a hillock, and Kashmir SHAWL patterns.

With the rise of commercial upholsterers a new link appeared between the calico printer and the furniture maker. The printers moved out of London and by the beginning of the 19th c. had settled mainly in Lancashire. In the 1820s there was a short return to the fine monochrome roller printing as seen in patterns of Gothic ruins and farm buildings or the famous reproductions of

Cotton textile plate-printed in red. Inscribed 'R.I. & Co. Old Ford 1761' and 'R. Jones 1761'. The pastoral scene is taken from an etching by Nicholas Berchem dated 1752; the peacock and poultry from an engraving by Josephus Sympson, published in London 1740, after the painting by Marmaduke Cradock; the stag and dog from plate 18 of *Animals of Various Species accurately drawn by Francis Barlow.* (V. & A. Mus.)

Audubon's *Birds of America* (1827–8). With the growth of industrialization craftsmanship was submerged by mass production and only a few enlightened designers such as William MORRIS rescued the craft from banality. Morris founded his own firm and produced his own designs such as the 'tulip and willow' pattern for wood-blocks. Early in the 20th c. the OMEGA WORKSHOPS carried on the work started by Morris and produced geometrical and abstract designs for cotton textiles.

In America most printed textiles were imported up to 1782 through a well organized ordering system. One of the heroes of the War of Independence was John Hewson, the calico printer, who had come to Philadelphia from England in 1774. Before him short-lived attempts had been made by German and Dutch printers. After the war Mrs. Washington, the wife of the President, is recorded as having paraded Hewson's calicoes, establishing for them a vogue. Manufactories soon sprang up in Rhode Island, Massachusetts, and Pennsylvania, where power machinery was used from 1788. The next year Beverly, Mass., had the first American cotton mill. Cylinder printing started in 1803, power looms in 1814. Samples of early American printed fabrics are very scarce: examples of designs are President Zachary Taylor on horseback and episodes of the Mexican war. During the 1812 war cotton printing increased in importance. The mill and its surrounding village became 'a symbol of New England's industrial importance'.

PRE-CONQUEST AMERICA. Cotton was cultivated by Pre-Columbian American Indians and knowledge of cotton techniques was spread to many tribes chiefly by the Caribs and Guaraní. Wild cotton was also collected, ginned and spun by many tribes, including the Aymara, Bororo, and the peoples of the river Pilcomayo. Cotton yarns were spun by means of spindles, all of which had whorls to steady the revolving movement. There were two methods of spinning. The so-called Andean drop-spindle was held vertically and given a twirl with the fingers of the right hand. The highland tribes still spin by this method while walking. It was practised by the Incas and was widely disseminated by them. A perhaps older method, called 'Bororo', uses a slender spindle which is held and rotated horizontally. Many spindles of this type have been recovered from pre-Inca burials in the coastal districts of Peru. The method is still practised in eastern Bolivia and Ecuador.

BLOCK-PRINTING. The origin of block-printing is still a matter of uncertainty, but Indian craftsmen may have been the first to use wood-blocks for this purpose. Strabo (*c.* 64 B.C.–A.D. 19) mentioned printed textiles imported from India. In China a very complicated technique of block-printing was practised from the 6th c. but it was used on cotton yarns only from the Sung Dynasty (960–1278). Up to then the cotton plant served only a decorative purpose. From China the planting and the techniques passed over to Japan, where after the 17th c. a large variety of printed motifs was developed in a more suggestive and abstract manner than the large flower motifs on the chintzes imported from India.

In Europe the Italian Cennino CENNINI gave

Palampore. India, Coromandel coast, northern region. Made for the European market. The design is influenced by Chinese embroidery on wallpaper and bears the United East India Company stamp. (Royal Ontario Mus., Toronto, 2nd quarter 18th c.)

Hanging of painted and dyed cotton. India, Coromandel coast, southern region. Made for the European market. The design is an adaptation of a decorative composition by Jean Bérain. (Royal Ontario Mus., Toronto, early 18th c.)

a detailed description of the technique as practised *c.* 1372. It was applied in the Rhineland and the Tyrol to altar covers and ecclesiastical vestments to replace the more costly BROCADES. The technique had come into its own by the 15th c.: Charles VIII of France offered a printed cloth from Reims to the Ottoman Sultan Bayazid II. By 1582, under another sultan, Murad III, printing blocks were being used in Constantinople, as depicted in a miniature made during his reign. Evlia Tchelebi, the Ottoman traveller, counted up to 100 printers in the guilds parade of 1634: on the whole they were Armenians from the eastern part of Turkey, Persians and Indians. They practised the mordant technique. The 17th-c. French diamond merchant and traveller Jean-Baptiste Tavernier judged the local Persian production so poor that it could not be exported. During the 19th c. many examples appeared on the European market. Another 17th-c. traveller, Chardin, mentioned printed designs in gold and silver but in no other colour since it was better done in India. The justice of this can be well appreciated if one examines fragments of Indian cottons from possibly 12th-c. tombs in Egypt. Tavernier also noticed enterprising Armenian block-printers in Isfahan. This very active community produced printed textiles for its own use —elaborate church fabrics and cloths for book-bindings—from the 14th c. On the whole red was the dominant colour, indigo being used sparingly.

Until the mordant and resist-dye techniques were fully understood in Europe the locally printed and painted fabrics could not stand up to hard wear. The printer's black ink and the oil-mixed pigments decayed very fast. When the first imported chintzes arrived from western India they were mainly made into quilting or hangings. But soon the production of southern India took precedence. The early painted patterns reflected the styles of the local potentates, the Persianized Islamic court of Golconda and that of the Hindu rulers. Back in Europe the poorer classes made do with these patterns, but fashionable society had specific patterns adapted to their own taste. Drawings were sent out to the factories of the Coromandel coast, which produced lengths suitable for clothing, for furnishing whole bedrooms, and for wall-hangings or the palampores with vertical flowering branches or dense arabesques. See INDIA, TEXTILES.

The interpretation of the patterns produced by the local craftsmen led to surprising results when unravelled by J. Irwin in 1970, such as the flowering tree design with its blend of Persian, Indian, Chinese, CHINOISERIE and European elements. Other hangings reflect the differences between the French taste with a certain gracefulness characteristic of Jean BÉRAIN and the ROCOCO and the English taste with its greater ebullience. In Holland an outer gown called *wentke* worn by the women of Hindeloopen was cut out of various chintzes and passed down from generation to generation. Examples of gilded chintzes still exist in Dutch collections.

62, 70, 433, 716, 861, 866.

COUCHING. A technique used in embroidery and other forms of needlework. A gold thread or other material is laid flat upon the surface of the fabric and is fastened in place by fine stitches of another thread. See EMBROIDERY (TYPES).

COURT CUPBOARD. Contemporary term to describe a three-tiered open CUPBOARD or sideboard for displaying plate which came into vogue in the latter part of the 16th c. The term is sometimes confused with the larger PRESS CUPBOARD and by the 18th c. court cupboards were called 'buffets'. See FURNITURE (ENGLISH).

CRACKLE GLASS. A type of decorative Venetian GLASS evolved during the 16th c., in which the surface, or part of the surface, is covered with an irregular multiplicity of tiny cracks. Two techniques have been suggested for its production: (1) that after blowing and while still hot the vessel was plunged into cold water so that innumerable hair cracks were formed on the surface and that it was then reheated; (2) that while still soft the vessel was marvered on to a bed of splintered glass and then reheated so that the small slivers fused with the body of the vessel. This type was also called 'ice glass' because of its likeness to broken ice.

CRANACH PRESS. A private printing press set up by Count Harry Kessler at Weimar, Germany, in 1913. He had the help of Edward Johnston and Emery Walker of the DOVES PRESS in designing the type and the assistance of compositors from the Doves Press also. Production was interrupted by the First World War but was resumed in the 1920s. The outstanding works of the Cranach Press were the *Eclogues* of Virgil (German edition in 1926, English edition in 1927), for which Maillol made the woodcuts; and *Hamlet*, printed in a BLACK LETTER typeface designed by Johnston and with woodcuts by Gordon Craig. In 1931 the Press produced an edition of *Canticum canticorum* with wood engravings by Eric Gill. See PRIVATE PRESS MOVEMENT.

131, 134, 277.

CRANE, WALTER (1845–1915). English illustrator and designer. Best remembered today as an illustrator of children's books, he was also a painter and he designed textiles, WALLPAPERS and CERAMICS. His work was exhibited in the U.S.A. as well as in Europe and in Britain he achieved some prestige as a writer and educationist. His books include *Line and Form* (1900), *Ideals in Art* (1905), *An Artist's Reminiscences* (1907) and *William Morris to Whistler* (1911). He began his teaching career in 1893, when he was appointed Director of Design at Manchester Municipal School of Art; he became Art Director of Reading University College in 1896 and was Principal of The Royal College of Art for one year in 1898, when he introduced Art Workers' Guild members and methods to the College. He was influential in the ARTS AND CRAFTS MOVEMENT, being a founder-member of the Art Workers' Guild as well as of the Arts and Crafts Exhibition Society, and influential also in the spread of ART NOUVEAU. In Belgium, where his work was particularly admired, an analysis by Georges Lemmen appeared in the magazine *L'Art nouveau* in 1891. See also ARTS AND CRAFTS MOVEMENT and ART NOUVEAU.

CRÊPE-DE-CHINE. A soft, more or less lustrous crape fabric originally produced with a raw SILK warp and filling yarns of hard-twisted raw silk thread.

CRESSENT, CHARLES (1685–1768). French sculptor, bronze worker and cabinet-maker. He became *ébéniste* to the Regent in 1719, after his marriage with the widow of the cabinet-maker Joseph Poitu and his work is closely identified with the RÉGENCE style. He made his own gilt-bronze MOUNTS, inspired by the designs of BÉRAIN, Robert de COTTE, Gillot and even the painter Watteau (1684–1721). There is little doubt that the characteristic Louis XV commode of bombé form, supported on four legs of CABRIOLE shape, in which the gilt-bronze mounts perform a significant decorative function, owes its inception to Cressent. He exerted considerable influence in his lifetime and numbered several foreign princes among his clients.

738.

CRESTING. Term in architecture for a decorated finishing which surmounts a wall screen or roof. In metalware and ceramics it denotes ornamentation, often foliate, which runs along the top of horizontal members.

CREWEL. Thin worsted yarn used in EMBROIDERY and TAPESTRY.

CREWEL WORK. EMBROIDERY in coloured worsteds (crewels), worked generally on white sheeting. Though used also for costume and other purposes, it is best exemplified by the English bed-hangings of the late 17th and early 18th centuries. These usually have tree designs, with bold curling leaves and exotic flowers, inspired by the painted and embroidered hangings then being imported from INDIA. Solid fillings give strength and durability to the work. Chain stitch, stem stitch, herring-bone, buttonhole stitch and satin stitch are usual.

Crewel work became characteristic of Britain and established itself in the United States, where its popularity continued through the 19th c. Mrs. Washington embroidered 12 chair cushions in crewel work; on coarse canvas cloth she worked a design of shells in brown and yellow wools with highlights flecked with gold and coloured silks.

CRINOLINE. A stiff material made of horsehair and cotton or linen thread, formerly used for skirts or linings. Petticoats made of this material worn under the skirt in order to distend it came into fashion *c.* 1830. The term is also applied to the hoop-petticoat of the middle of the 19th c. See FARTHINGALE, BUSTLE, CRINOLINE.

CRISTALLO. Name given to the decolourized glass produced in Venice from early in the 16th c. It was so named because of its likeness to ROCK-CRYSTAL. See GLASS (VENICE).

CRIZZLING. Term used in glass-making. A roughening of the surface due to a fine network of cracks. The word may be a diminutive of 'craze' as used of pottery.

CROCHET. A kind of knitting or LACE-making done with a single, hooked needle. Either cotton or wool thread is generally used. The basis of crochet work is the chain, from which a variety of stitches and patterns are built up.

Filet crochet consists of a groundwork of square mesh, each square being formed of two chain stitches with a triple stitch at each end. Filet crochet work may be darned with a pattern in a manner similar to darned netting or the old LACIS technique.

In *Irish* crochet double crochet is worked closely over padding of linen thread to form the motifs of the pattern. Sometimes the motifs are worked separately and then formed into a whole by means of a network called the *filling*. There are two classes of Irish crochet work. The heavy GUIPURE kind of lace is worked on a foundation which has the design stamped on it. The lighter *bébé* lace is worked into a pattern of squares, hexagons or octagons which are joined together without a foundation.

See NEEDLEWORK.

CROCKET. Akin to CRESTING. Term in Gothic architecture and medieval times for ornament on metalwork, etc., usually in the form of buds or curled leaves decorating the inclined sides of pinnacles, finials, etc. or projecting at regular intervals from the angles of spires, canopies, gables, etc.

English crewel work. The piece may have been cut from matching wall-hangings or from bed-curtains. It is worked in coloured wools on a cotton twill ground. The design of exotic foliage may have been inspired by Indian chintzes. (Rijksmus., Amsterdam, late 17th c. or early 18th c.)

CROMPTON, SAMUEL (1735–1827). Cotton worker of Bolton, Lancashire, who invented the spinning mule. See WEAVING (THREAD).

CROWN. Term used by jewellers and lapidaries for the upper portions of a cut gemstone comprising the part above the GIRDLE, i.e. the flat TABLE and the planes or facets cut at the sides of it.

See JEWELLERY.

784.

CRYSTALLO-CERAMIE. A fashion of embedding small ceramic portraits or figurines in clear glass for use in decorating small bowls, paper-weights, etc. The process originated in France towards the end of the 18th c. and was introduced into England by Apsley Pellatt (1719–1863), owner of a glass-house in Southwark, *c.* 1820. Pellatt's productions were also known as 'Sulphides' and he obtained a patent for their manufacture in 1831. His firm continued their production until the middle of the century.

CUIR BOUILLI. (French, 'boiled leather'.) The traditional term for moulded leather. See LEATHERCRAFT.

CUIR CISELÉ. A technique of cut LEATHER decoration in which designs are incised in outline with sharp pointed tools and then opened and deepened with blunter tools. In the later Middle Ages the technique was applied to BOOKBINDING, particularly in south Germany. In distinction from stamped decoration with engraved TOOLS the design, usually a pictorial motif, was cut free-hand on the leather. Each binding thus decorated is an individual piece of work.

88.

CULET. Term used by jewellers and lapidaries for the small plane surface on the back portion, or PAVILION, of a faceted gemstone parallel to the large facet on the top surface or TABLE. Its purpose was often to prevent the stone from chipping when being set.

See JEWELLERY.

CUPBOARD. Originally, in the 14th and 15th centuries, a 'board' or table for storing or displaying cups and drinking-vessels. In the 16th c. cupboards were open shelves on which plate, etc. was displayed. From the latter part of the 16th c. 'cupboard' has been a generic term for a receptacle fitted with shelves and enclosed by doors. See FURNITURE (ENGLISH). See also: AUMBRY; COURT CUPBOARD; LIVERY CUPBOARD; PRESS CUPBOARD.

CUPELLATION. A process of separating copper from its natural alloys or of separating silver from argentiferous lead. See GOLD AND SILVER and SILVER (ASSAYING AND HALLMARKING).

CUTLERY. There is no easy answer to the question when artisans began to use bladed tools as distinct from tools for piercing, scraping, chopping, hacking and rasping. The advanced Palaeolithic peoples, who occupied parts of Europe and south-west Asia in the late Upper Pleistocene age (*c.* 35,000–10,000 B.C.), first made primary use of flint blades in place of flakes, developing the bladed flint for working antler, bone and ivory. The Gravettian culture has left a variety of narrow 'penknife' bladed flints, including various microlithic backed bladelets. From Pavlov in Gravettian territory also come handled spoons and ladles which were no doubt used for eating. Stone knives have also been found in the hill-sites of the Palaeoindians of North America. Just as the medieval soldier used his dagger for skinning, dividing and spearing meat, so in the ages of stone tools the functions of dagger and knife must certainly have coincided. It is not until Neolithic times that a tool corresponding to the modern conception of a knife can be traced. Obsidian knives with a cutting blade and blunt back have been reported from Kenya and slate knives from the Arctic peoples. Obsidian blades may have been used for shaving in or before Mycenaean times. In ancient EGYPT and elsewhere stone knives, often set in decorated holders, served a sacerdotal function for sacrifices. It is not to be supposed that in prehistoric times knives were designed for the purpose of eating food.

With the advent of metallurgy in the course of the Neolithic period bronze, and later iron, knives and razors were made. Bronze razors have been found in burials over a large part of central and western Europe and in the British Isles. They had a thin, flat blade, sometimes with a decorative finish, and later ones often had a split or 'bifid' blade. Some have tangs to accommodate handles, others are made with a hole for pinning into flint or bone scales. The bronze blades were cast and then hammered into shape. It seems to have been the custom to bury a man's razor with him together with his sword.

We may assume that from the time that men began to boil their food by putting heated stones into containers of water they used suitably shaped shells to do duty as spoons. As has been said, stone spoons or scoops, perhaps for extracting marrow, have survived from the Upper Pleistocene age. Clay spoons and scoops are known from the Neolithic age and curious bone spoons of Roman origin with perforated bowl have been found in Britain. The ancient Egyptians used elegantly shaped metal spoons about the size of a teaspoon, often with a spike at the end of the handle presumably for the purpose of extracting snails or shellfish from the shell. Inscribed silver spoons of Roman origin were found at MILDENHALL and in the SUTTON HOO hoard, and copper spoons were common in Saxon times for kitchen use. Spoons were not articles of tableware during the Middle Ages. When they first came into use for eating they were made of PEWTER or of BRITANNIA METAL and indeed pewter spoons did not wholly disappear from use in England until late in the 19th c. Desert spoons were not made before the 20th c.

In the Andean region of South America 'spoons' with pointed handles were made from local silver, often with finely engraved bowl and decorated handle, from the years after the Conquest through Colonial times. These were copied from the spoons brought in by the Spanish *conquistadores* but were used by the indigenous population not for eating but as decorative pins for fastening their shawls.

Small scissors of the flexible type, corresponding to modern hand sheep shears, have been found in bronze and larger ones of iron. The Romans seem to have been the first to make iron scissors of a modern pattern. They also produced the first clasp (shutting) knives. Roman general-purpose knives were often scimitar shaped and sometimes had tangs to which were fastened bone scales to form a handle. The tombstone of a cutler from the 1st c. A.D. shows a cutlery stall with knives similar to a present-day butcher's knife, sickles, pruning knives, etc. In Roman times too it was not unusual for the name of the maker (or the owner) to be engraved on a knife.

The typical Anglo-Saxon knife was the *scramasax*, which like the later American Bowie was carried at the belt and combined the functions of dagger and knife. It was sometimes DAMASCENED and inlaid with inscriptions and the owner's name. A broad-bladed type, probably

Anglo-Saxon scramasax. (B.M.)

Roman cutler's shop from the tombstone of L. Cornelius Atimetus. Knives and sickles hang from the shelves in the background. L. Cornelius Atimetus is depicted on the right dressed only in a tunic. He is offering a knife to a customer dressed in a toga. (Vatican Mus.)

used for carving meat, was sometimes inscribed with the text of graces to be said at meals. Table utensils other than the pointed knife or dagger were not in use during the early Middle Ages. A writer on etiquette in the 15th c. says that it was not good manners to seize one's meat with both hands; it should be taken up and conveyed to the mouth with three fingers only and not too much at once. The custom of eating with the fingers (as for example in Morocco today) made it necessary to wash the hands before and after meals and explains the large numbers of ewers and basins dating from medieval times. In the late 15th or early 16th c. the points of knives began to be rounded, which meant that the knife could no longer be used to spear food and transfer it to the mouth. This coincides with the introduction of forks about the same time into general use. Although table knives, distinct from the general-purpose dagger-knife, were not in use until the close of the Middle Ages, serving knives were known. In princely houses of the later medieval period the squire carver carried a set of knives contained in a CUIR BOUILLI case for cutting bread and meat and a large serving dish or *présentoir*. Sometimes the set contained a fork as well, but used only for purposes of carving. Fine sets with silver handles enamelled with the arms of Burgundian nobility are in the Wallace Collection, London.

Forks first came into general use in Constantinople in the course of the 4th c. A.D. and a spoon and fork from there are preserved in the Dumbarton Oaks Collection, Washington. Forks were not table utensils in western Europe during the Middle Ages and even in the 15th and 16th centuries they were generally used only for sweetmeats and fruit. Meat forks for use at table first came into fashion in Italy, where the fastidiousness of the better classes found it repugnant that meat in the common dish should be grasped in the fingers by each diner in turn while he hacked off a piece for himself with his knife. Thomas Coryat, an English traveller to Italy in 1608, writes as follows: 'I observed a custome in all those Italian Cities and Townes through the which I passed, that is not used in any other country that I saw in my travels, neither doe I thinke that any other nation of Christendome doth use it, but only Italy. The Italian and also most strangers that are commorant in Italy, doe alwaies at their meales use a little forke when they cut their meat. For while with their knife which they hold in one hand they cut their meate out of the dish, they fasten their forke which they hold in their other hand upon the same dish, so that whatsoever he be that sitting in the company of any others at meale, should unadvisedly touch the dish of meate with his fingers from which all at the table doe cut, he will give occasion of offence unto the company, as having transgressed the lawes of good manners, in so much that for his error he shall be at the least brow-beaten, if not reprehended in wordes. This forme of feeding I understand is generally used in all places of Italy, their forkes being for the most part made of yron or steele, and some of silver, but those are used only by Gentlemen. The reason of this their curiosity is, because the Italian cannot by any means indure to have his dish touched with fingers, seeing all mens fingers are not alike cleane' (*Coryat's Crudities*). The earliest known English fork for individual table use is a two-prong silver fork with a London hallmark of 1632 (V. & A. Mus.).

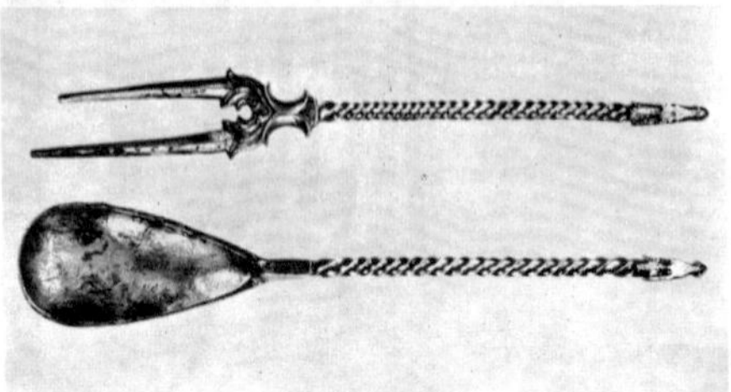

Silver spoon (24·3 cm) and fork (24 cm) with Hellenistic acanthus leaf forming base of each prong. (Dumbarton Oaks Coll., 4th–5th c.)

As men of the nobility were accustomed to carry a knife at the belt, so ladies carried knives for domestic uses attached to the girdle. During the 16th c. and in the 1st half of the 17th c. there was a custom to present brides with knives contained in an embroidered bag with strings to be suspended from the girdle. These 'wedding knives' were particularly popular in England and Holland, often finely wrought and decorated, and examples survive bearing the dagger mark of the Cutlers' Company. The handles are made from a variety of exotic materials such as AMBER, IVORY, rare woods, etc., and they are often inscribed with the name of the bride and the date of the wedding. In Holland a characteristic form of wedding knife was evolved with handle of silver (or, rarely, gold) embellished with minute engravings of religious subjects after designs by Johann Theodor de Bry and Michel Leblon. Some of the finest are attributed to Abraham van den Hecken.

Until the latter part of the 17th c. knives and forks for table use were individual possessions and were made in pairs (at first two knives, later a knife and fork). As long as they were designed for individual ownership they were given decorative treatment. When in the 18th c. they began to be made in sets of a dozen or more for household use, they became standardized—though for a time travelling sets continued to be artistically made to individual design.

In France, while some of the most artistic knives were made in Paris, the centre of the cutlery industry from the 13th c. onwards has been at Thiers. Thiers was exporting to Italy, Spain and the Netherlands by the 14th c. and towards the end of the 15th c. exports to Spain expanded as a result of orders for the New World. Fine combination daggers and knives were produced in the main centres of metalwork such as Toledo, Madrid, Seville and Barcelona in Spain, Florence, Rome and Milan in Italy. In Germany the centre of the cutlery industry was at Augsburg, where the forging of blades was controlled by regulation in 1346. In Austria a cutlery craft was established by the beginning of the 15th c. with its main centre at Steyr. Solingen in Prussia is reputed to have started cutlery making in the 12th c. with craftsmen from Damascus, making at first fine quality swords, and became in the course of time the main competitor to Sheffield in England. There were three separate guilds in the 15th c. and a separate Finishers' and Knife Makers' Guild was established in 1571. The London cutlers were associated into a guild by the middle of the 12th c. divided into three sections: blade-makers, cutlers and hafters (assemblers and finishers) and sheath-makers. The earliest documentary evidence for Sheffield cutlery dates from the reign of Edward I (1272–1307). Chaucer mentions 'A Schefeld thwytel' (i.e. whittle, an all-purpose knife used also for eating). Records of the Cutlers' Company of Hallamshire (of which district Sheffield was the centre) can be taken back to 1565, when the craft is already mentioned as 'ancient' and there are references to 'damasking, inlaying and studding' of knives. Thaxted, Essex, was a centre of the cutlery craft from the middle of the 13th c. and in the reign of Edward II (1307–27) trade fairs were held there on the feast of St. Lawrence, the patron saint of the cutlers. Cutlery continued to be practised there in a small way until the 17th c. In the U.S.A. knives and cutlery were at first imported mainly from Sheffield and local manufacture started early in the 19th c. The first manufacturers, mainly in Connecticut, based their designs on Sheffield models and employed craftsmen from Sheffield. The most notable American innovation was the Bowie knife, a combined hunting knife, dagger, throwing knife and all-purpose implement. These knives were named after James Bowie (1799–1836), who was born in Kentucky and died in the defence of Alamo. The Bowie knife, designed by Bowie for the special needs of the frontiersmen, was a descendant of the Saxon scramasax and the Sheffield whittle. It was made in the first instance by Sheffield firms and gained a world-wide reputation as a fighting implement. In the Second World War it was a side-arm of the Unites States Army and Navy.

384, 650.

CUVILLIÈS, FRANÇOIS THE ELDER (1695–1768). A Walloon by birth Cuvilliès was appointed Court Dwarf at the Munich Court of Max Emanuel of Bavaria in 1706. He was sent to learn architectural design in Paris between 1720 and 1724 and upon his return to Munich became the leading architect to Karl Albrecht of Bavaria. He published numerous extremely lively sets of designs for furniture in an advanced ROCOCO style and was responsible for many enchanting Rococo interiors at Nymphenburg, Schleissheim and in the Residenz at Munich, all palaces of the ruling house of Bavaria.

CYMA RECTA. See OGEE.

CYMA REVERSA. See OGEE.

D

DAGUERRE, DOMINIQUE. A Parisian MARCHAND-MERCIER who succeeded to Simon-Philippe POIRIER's business in 1778. It is uncertain whether he himself was a practising cabinet-maker but he employed other craftsmen to carry out important commissions. His English clients, to whom he sold large quantities of Louis XVI furniture, included the Prince of Wales, Lord Spencer and the Duke of Northumberland.

738, 880.

DAGUERREOTYPE. An early photographic process in which the image was produced on a silvered copper plate sensitized by iodine. It was invented by a French artist, Louis Jacques Mandé Daguerre (1789–1851). See PHOTOGRAPHY.

297, 475, 627.

DAMASCENING. Term somewhat loosely used in the literature of the arts and not to be confused with the manufacture of 'Damascus' steel or pattern-welded blades. It is correctly applied to the process of decorating iron with flat ornament in precious metal. The surface of the iron is first roughened with a file so as to give purchase to the gold or silver, which is hammered on and then cut to the desired pattern. According to the gauge of the gold or silver wire used damascened ornament can be varied in scale. The technique was practised in Europe during the Dark Ages, particularly on weapons, but lapsed and was only reintroduced early in the 16th c. through Italian, probably Venetian, contact with the Near East. Even when it had been fully mastered by the Italian goldsmiths its Oriental origin was not forgotten. ARABESQUE designs of Oriental inspiration are almost as important as Renaissance elements in Italian damascening. In the Near East damascening had been mainly used on arms and armour, and the Italian goldsmiths applied it at first to weapons also. Subsequently it was used on a great variety of iron articles, even tables and chairs, for which its minute scale made it unsuitable.

There must have been goldsmiths capable of working in this technique in many north Italian cities. Benvenuto CELLINI, for instance, relates in his *Autobiography* that he had mastered it. Nearly all the extant examples, in particular the caskets, are attributed to Milanese workshops, which during the second half of the 16th c. also turned out embossed and damascened sheets or strips which were sold to CABINET-MAKERS for the embellishment of furniture, etc. The later Italian damascening shows the inevitable defects of routine production, but the earlier examples, such as the stirrups of the Emperor Charles V (V. & A. Mus.) by Bartolommeo CAMPI of Pesaro, equal the best Near Eastern work.

Damascening was also practised in Germany and France, possibly by immigrant Italian craftsmen, but on a much smaller scale. There was a school of immigrant 'damaskers' in London during the late 16th and early 17th centuries, but they concentrated on decorating knife-hafts and sword and dagger hilts.

See IRON AND STEEL; ARMS AND ARMOUR.

DAMASK. A rich SILK fabric with elaborate figures and designs woven into it; originally made at Damascus. Also twilled linen or cotton fabric woven with designs which show up with opposite reflections of light from the surface. Unlike BROCADE the patterns are not raised from the surface.

DANCETTE. See CHEVRON.

DARBY, ABRAHAM (1678–1717). English metallurgist. He went to Holland probably in 1704, studied the Dutch techniques for casting bronze cooking-pots and tried unsuccessfully to persuade them to cast pots in iron from sand moulds. In 1707 he took out a patent for casting iron-bellied pots in sand. This provided a marketable product for iron produced by the coke smelting process, which he developed *c.* 1709. His son, also named ABRAHAM Darby (1711–63), who managed the foundry 1738–63, further developed this process and is credited with successfully producing a refineable iron *c.* 1750. See IRON AND STEEL.

DARLY, MATTHEW (d. *c.* 1780). English designer and engraver. In 1750–1 he published *A New Book of Chinese, Gothic and Modern Chairs*, the first book in English to be specifically devoted to chairs. In 1754 he published together with George Edwards *A New Book of Chinese Designs*, and in 1770 *The Compleat Architect*. He engraved many of the plates in CHIPPENDALE's *Director* and in *The Universal System of Household Furniture* published by the cabinet-makers William Ince and John Mayhew between 1759 and 1762 in rivalry with the *Director*.

251, 303, 304, 461.

DECK, THÉODORE. A practical potter who did much to revive the cult for the hand-made decorative pot in the latter part of the 19th c. He set himself up in Paris in 1856 as a maker of decorative EARTHENWARE and from 1887 until his death in 1891 he was art director at SÈVRES.

DECORATIVE IRONWORK. See IRON AND STEEL.

DELANOIS or LANOIX, LOUIS (1731–92). French cabinet-maker who specialized in chair-making. He became a master in 1761 and was soon afterwards employed by Madame du Barry on furniture for her apartments at Fontainebleau, and for her celebrated Pavilion of Louveciennes. He amassed a considerable fortune but was ruined by the Revolution. His work illustrates the transition from the *Rocaille* to the NEO-CLASSICAL styles. See ROCOCO.

738.

DELFTWARE. See CERAMICS.

DEME. See JAPAN (NETSUKE).

DENTELLE BINDINGS. Bookbindings decorated with wide, wavy borders giving a lace-like effect often described as *à la dentelle*. The term is usually applied to the bindings produced by PADELOUP, DEROME-le-Jeune, Douceur, Dubuisson and other French binders during the 18th c., although the style originated in the repeating pattern used as edging for the narrow borders on 17th-c. FANFARE and POINTILLÉ bindings. On small books the dentelle design was produced by individual tools; for larger bindings engraved stamps and corner-pieces were used. Pierre-Paul Dubuisson (active 1746–62) specialized in the production of almanacks decorated with all-over designs stamped from single bronze plaques. See BOOKBINDING (HISTORICAL).

594.

DERBY PORCELAIN. The factory, founded *c.* 1750 and managed from 1756 by William Duesbury, was prolific in 'soft-paste' table wares and figure models, at first in deliberate emulation of MEISSEN and Chelsea. 'Patch-marks' on the base help to identify the figures, which from the 'Chelsea–Derby' period (1770–84) onwards were often made in unglazed 'biscuit': a SÈVRES fashion was also reflected in the decoration of useful wares. Fine landscape painting marks many late 18th-c. wares. About 1784 the crowned 'D' mark was adopted, and continued until the factory was closed down in 1848.

DEROME. French family of BOOKBINDERS active for three generations and contemporary with the PADELOUP and the MONNIER families. Both JACQUES-ANTHOINE (1696–1760) and his third son, NICOLAS-DENIS (1731–88), executed mosaic bindings but the reputation of the latter rests chiefly on his DENTELLE bindings. His TOOLINGS are finer than Padeloup's and frequently include in the borders a small bird motif which, though not exclusive to Derome-le-Jeune, is one of his distinguishing marks. Towards the end of his life he abandoned dentelles for a more sober style of narrow, straight borders and adopted English cross-grained blue MOROCCO in preference to the crimson morocco commonly used in France. See BOOKBINDING (HISTORICAL).

594.

DEUTSCHER WERKBUND. An organization founded in 1907 at the instigation of the German architect Hermann Muthesius (1861–1927), partly under the influence of the doctrines of William MORRIS, with the expressed objects of improving the aesthetic standard of engineering construction and the artistic quality of product design. With Muthesius were associated such architects as Hans Poelzig (1869–1936), Josef HOFFMANN and Henri Van de VELDE. Great emphasis was laid on the quality of workmanship and unlike many of the followers of Morris, the theorists of the Werkbund came fully to terms with the machine, welcoming it as a means to the mass production of high-quality goods with an aesthetic of their own. In 1914 the Werkbund held an important exhibition of industrial art at Cologne and in 1927 an exhibition, which included a housing exhibition, at Stuttgart. In 1930 it was appointed by the German Government to organize the German section in the Paris International Exhibition. This was dedicated to housing and the industrial arts and was planned by Walter GROPIUS with the assistance of three colleagues from the BAUHAUS, Marcel BREUER, Herman Bayer and László Moholy-Nagy. The Werkbund was disbanded with the advent of National Socialism in the 1930s. On its model an Austrian Werkbund was formed in 1910 and a Swiss Werkbund in 1913. It was a model for the British Design and Industries Association formed in 1915.

DHOTI. See INDIA (COSTUME).

DIAGRAMS. Diagrams are the visual method of explaining, interpreting and analysing information by means of points, lines, areas and other geometrical forms and symbols. Through diagrams quantitative information can be shown in a simple and effective way which makes possible easy comparison of values, trends and relationships. Diagrams have advantages over a textual or tabular form of presentation. Visual methods make a strong impact on the attention of the reader. Relationships shown in a diagram can be more clearly seen and remembered. A diagram is a visual shorthand for something which could take a page of text. Familiar information shown in an original way can stimulate thinking as well as aid understanding.

The appearance of a diagram is influenced by several factors working on the information to be communicated. Appearance also depends on the context in which it is being used—whether it is for a newspaper, a magazine, a book, or for television. For example, a diagram in a television documentary can only appear on the screen for a short time. It must make its impact and be understood rapidly in that time. Wording is kept to the minimum, and the message must be clear and simple. Another factor influencing appearance is the person who is going to look at the diagram. The diagram in an academic journal can obviously be more complex than that in a children's book. A still further, and by no means unimportant, influence on the diagram is fashion. This will determine the kind of lettering used, the design and drawing of the diagram itself.

There are two kinds of diagram: statistical diagrams, which give information about and comparison of quantities; and explanatory diagrams, which elucidate, give information about or explain particular things, their modes of operation and so on (technological, anatomical, etc.). Both statistical and explanatory diagrams can be superimposed on MAPS.

Statistical diagrams as we know them began with William Playfair (1759–1823). He created techniques for showing and analysing statistical data and developed such ways as the bar graph, circular graph, divided circle. His most important book, *The Commercial and Political Atlas*, was published in 1786.

The other important pioneer of diagrammatic technique was Otto Neurath (d. 1945). His aim was to give information visually so that it would be understood by all people irrespective of linguistic and cultural barriers. To do this he devised an internationally acceptable picture language called 'Isotype' (International System Of Typographic Picture Education). An isotype is a symbol to be used as part of a picture diagram. The best example of this means of explanation is *Modern Man in the Making* by Otto Neurath, published in 1939.

Statistical information can be shown in various ways and according to the nature of the figures different methods will be used. Some methods are best suited to show relationships, others show areas; some can deal with numerous items and some can only deal with one at a time. The following are the main types of statistical diagrams:

Graphs show how the changes in one quantity are related to changes in another quantity. They are widely used to show such things as temperature, unemployment, share prices. The one quantity (temperature, number of workers, price) is related to another quantity (time). The first is called the dependent variable; it changes irregularly and represents quantitative or percentage values. The second is called the independent variable and changes regularly, as for instance a series of equal time divisions.

The divided or compound line graph shows the value of both the total and its parts by a series of lines on the same diagram. The area beneath the main graph line can be divided into any number of parts. But it is not easy to follow increase or decrease in all the parts of this kind of graph.

The logarithmic graph shows the rate of increase as well as the amount. The scale on this kind of graph appears distorted. The vertical scale is unevenly spaced; the spacing accords with the logarithmic factor and is not a linear progression. This graph is particularly useful when it is desired to illustrate production where comparison of the rate of increase is more important than the actual amount.

Circular graphs show figures which recur regularly, e.g. rainfall or temperature figures, and these can be plotted on a circular graph. Where a weekly or yearly cycle takes place the normal line or bar graph may be a disadvantage as the left- and right-hand edges break continuity. There are variations of the circular graph, the wind rose and circular bar graph being the most common.

The scatter graph is a specialist diagram and derives from the 'scatter' of dots plotted on the graph. These dots are not joined as in the line graph but the information is interpreted from the pattern which the scatter suggests.

The bar (column) graph is similar to the line graph. It is drawn from a series of values plotted against two axes. Instead of being joined by a line, the values are represented by vertical bars. Each bar is usually kept separate from its neighbour. The bar graph emphasizes the actual quantities while the single-line graph shows more clearly the rise and fall of the values of one item. The bars can be set vertically or horizontally—a most important advantage for the placing of lettering for easy reading.

A *histogram* is similar to the bar graph. This usually shows percentages while the bar graph gives absolute quantities. The histogram usually has no spacing between columns since there is no definite break in the series.

The divided (compound) bar graph shows divisions of the bars so that parts as well as the total are compared.

The population pyramid is the method of showing the sex and age structure of a population. The pyramid is made up of horizontal bars representing population in age groups, male on one side and female on the other side of a vertical line. Information is read by comparing the shape of one pyramid with that of another as well as from the length of the bars.

Block diagrams represent statistical information by means of a square or 'block'. This sort of diagram best shows information related to its nature, i.e. area or volume.

The divided rectangle can simply be a rectangle divided into parts. More common is the comparison of several rectangles of the same size divided on a percentage basis.

The divided circle (pie or cake graph) uses a circle divided into parts as in cutting up a cake. Each section is in proportion to the value it represents. The diagram is difficult to plot though tables and special graph paper can be used. It is also difficult to read, since comparison of small sections of a circle is not easy. The divided rectangle is probably a more useful means of comparison.

The pictorial graph is an adaptation of the bar graph and is used to give the same kind of information. It aims to overcome the lack of appeal of the bar chart by actually representing the subject. The application of pictorial techniques to presenting information was pioneered by Otto Neurath.

Diagrams are used to explain e.g. how an engine works, stages in a manufacturing process, the structure of an organization, the relation of a series of events. These diagrams do not usually make quantitative statements but some can be adapted to do so.

The main problem of explanatory diagrams is reducing complex information to the essential without distortion. A power station, a three-dimensional object, tall and covering a huge area, has to be reduced to two dimensions and half a page. These diagrams are devised in ways varying from a representational approach to a near-abstract one. Factors already mentioned influence the style: amount of information to be shown, audience, size to be used, etc.

The flow chart shows successive movements through a process from beginning to completion. The simplest type of flow chart is typographical and resembles the organization chart with arrows indicating direction of flow. A more complex one is that which shows the manufacturing process, depicting each stage and the machinery involved. The problem is simplification of a complex operation so that the principle is clear. The lines or arrows can be coded to show the different stages, and by varying the thickness of the flow line quantitative information can be given.

The organization chart shows the inter-relations, the responsibilities and the authority of various units of an organization. The units may be officials or departments of a government or sections of a business. The names of units may be enclosed in boxes or circles which are then joined by a line that shows the delegation of responsibility or authority. The diagram can be typographical or pictorial.

The family tree is a special kind of organization chart. Usually designed to show the genealogy of one person, it can be adapted to show relationships outside the human family—language, energy sources, evolution.

Time charts show information related to a

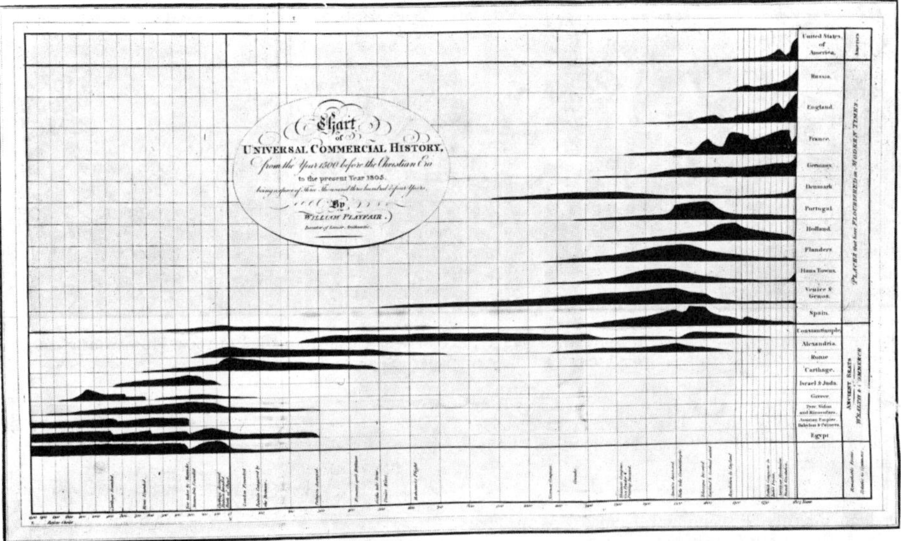

Time chart. The horizontal scale goes from 1500 B.C. to A.D. 1805. Various civilizations and their importance are shown on the vertical scale, starting with Egypt and ending with the United States of America. From William Playfair, *An Inquiry into the Permanent Causes of the Decline and Fall of Powerful and Wealthy Nations* (1805)

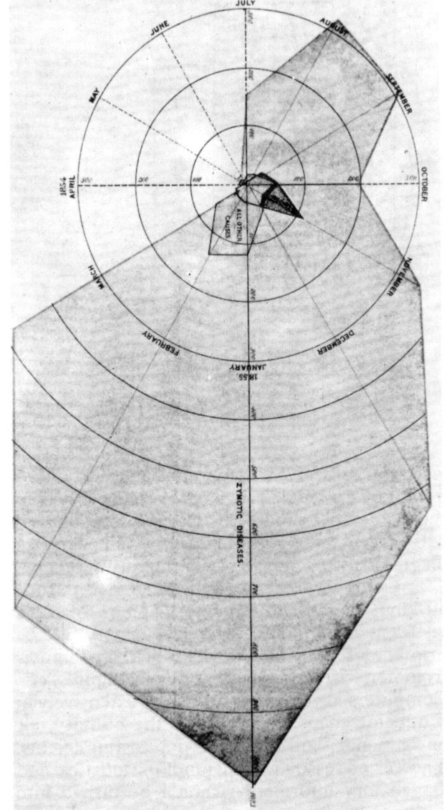

Circular graph used by Florence Nightingale to show the mortality rate in Army hospitals in the East for each month from April 1854 to March 1855. Cause of death (wounds, zymotic diseases, other causes) is colour coded

Isotype. A diagram which uses symbols to facilitate immediate understanding of the information. This example comes from *Modern Man in the Making* (1939) by Otto Neurath, who pioneered this form of diagram

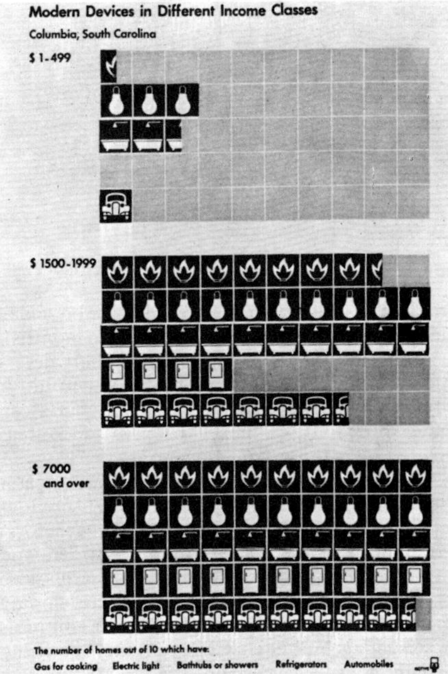

Bar graph used in *The Observer* to show the average price of War Loan from 1948 to 1969. Humorously embellished to attract the newspaper reader to the article

Diagram drawn by a child showing the villages from where the children in a class come. From *Pictorial Representation*, one of the books in the Nuffield Mathematics Project

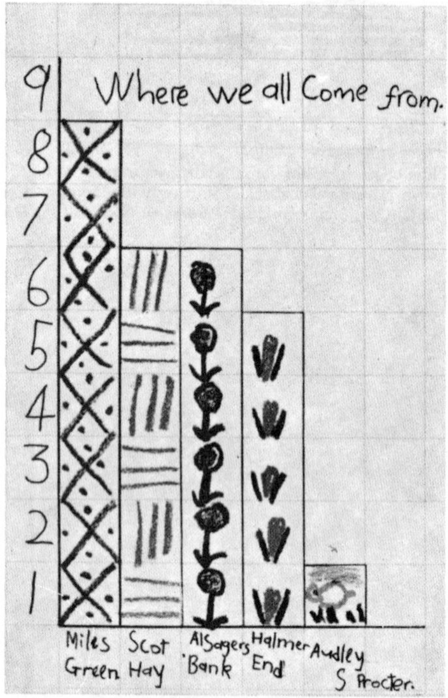

Diagram produced by computer. Isometric perspective view of the neutron distribution in a reactor

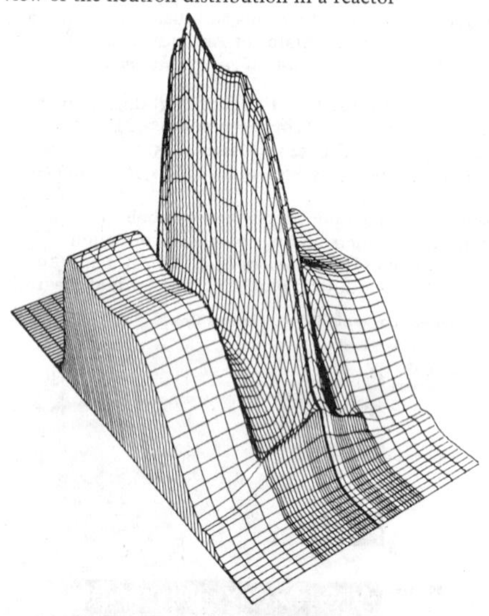

time-scale. The period covered may be a day (divided into hours), a year (divided into months), recorded history. The aim of each chart determines the information plotted. Quantitative information can be included. Time charts can show spheres of influence or give land areas covered by empires or civilizations.

The 'information explosion' will mean greater use of diagrammatic explanation. Future developments could be influenced by three factors:

1. Children are being taught to understand information through diagrams. Research into teaching methods has resulted in developing imaginative approaches with particular emphasis on visual techniques. Children are becoming visually as well as verbally literate. Such projects as Nuffield Mathematics have introduced to children a whole range of diagrams that help them to understand statistical information and will give them a vocabulary for understanding diagrams they come across in the future.

2. Computers are being programmed to turn all kinds of information into diagram form. A visual image which can be understood may be printed out after interpretation by the computer from non-visual impulses or signals, figures, etc. Computers have already been used extensively in producing maps, especially in the military, air navigational and weather forecasting fields. There is no reason why all kinds of statistical and explanatory information cannot be turned into a variety of diagram forms by the computer.

3. Developments in printing and marketing will result in even cheaper printing and more extensive use of full colour for books and magazines. Large editions bring the unit cost down and at the moment this is being achieved in various ways. International co-productions mean that publishers in several countries share the costs and make possible a printing that in total is very large. Part-works are books that by being sold in weekly instalments on magazine stands at low prices get a large circulation. Mail order techniques of selling books specially devised for the mass market achieve sales far above conventional bookselling methods. These ways of expanding sales and thus print orders make the use of full colour as well as specially devised diagrammatic explanation economic.

But in spite of this the full potential of diagrams is not understood or used to advantage by the communications industry. In the newspapers the approach has been conventional and limited with perhaps only *The Sunday Times* making the effort to produce an arresting and informative diagrammatic explanation of a news event. Among magazines the *Scientific American* has not been bettered in the traditional approach. English magazines follow, but rarely use visual explanation for its own sake. In part-works there is a new field for diagrammatic explanation but it has not often reached the imaginative and wide-ranging solutions to statistical presentation used in the *History of the 20th Century*. In publishing, co-produced books and books designed for the mass market have had the most scope and firms such as Time-Life, Readers Digest and Mitchell Beazley pay particular attention to diagrams.

61, 601.

DIAMOND. Diamond consists of pure carbon crystallized in regular octahedrons or related forms and is the hardest substance known. It includes the transparent gemstone which is supreme among all other gemstones for fire and brilliance. The great majority of diamond found, however, is *bort*, the translucent to opaque industrial diamond or imperfectly crystallized masses or crystal fragments which are useless as gems and serve industrial purposes only. Other varieties with only industrial uses are *ballas* and *carbonado*.

Diamond was known to antiquity but was often confused with other stones such as ROCK CRYSTAL and colourless TOPAZ or BERYL. The Greek word *adamas* (unconquerable), from which 'diamond' derives, referred to the hardest metal known (probably steel) and to certain forms of corundum. It was used by Theophrastus (*c.* 371–*c.* 287 B.C.) probably of gem diamonds, which in antiquity were known to come from India. Pliny called the diamond 'the most valuable of gems known only to kings' and other writers mention its origin from Indian rivers.

Until it is facet cut the latent fire and brilliance of the diamond are not in evidence and it is a rather uninteresting stone visually. It was valued in the past for its rarity and for the very hardness which made its cutting as a BRILLIANT impossible by the methods then available. The Indians, to whom the true diamond was known from well before the Christian era, first developed the art of polishing and faceting it by the use of diamond dust as an abrasive. But they faceted only for the purpose of removing or concealing flaws and the typical Indian 'point cut' did little more in principle than define and polish the facets of the stone's natural octahedron shape. The 'table cut', also practised by the Indians, went little beyond this except that the top and bottom points of the octahedron were ground flat to give a TABLE and CULET. Geometrical cutting for brilliance began in the 16th c. and is usually attributed to the Venetian jeweller Vincento Peruzzi, although it too may have originated in India. From the early ROSE cut developed the brilliant cut and from that time the supremacy of the diamond among gemstones was assured.

Until the 18th c. Borneo and India, particularly Hyderabad, were the most important sources of diamonds. In 1725 the Minas Gerais of Brazil were discovered and exploited by the Portuguese, taking the lead in world production from *c.* 1740 until the discovery of the South African diamond mines in the 19th c. The discovery of the first diamond by the Orange River in 1867 led to the Kimberley diamond rush and the supremacy of South Africa in the diamond trade. Under the impetus of Cecil Rhodes production was centralized in the De Beers company of 1873. At the end of the 19th c. the Diamond Syndicate was formed with the object of controlling the supply of gem diamonds to the market and stabilizing the relations between supply and demand. Further centralization was achieved with the formation of the Diamond Producers' Association in 1933 and the Diamond Trading Company in 1934, by which virtually worldwide control of the diamond industry was secured. Africa in all produces about 97% of the world output of diamonds.

HISTORIC DIAMONDS. Although large stones are not recorded before *c.* A.D. 1000, most of the famous stones in the past have come from the Indian mines. The following are some which have acquired fame or notoriety.

The *Orloff*, a rose-cut diamond of 199·6 carats, is said to have been stolen from the eye of a god in a Brahmin temple at Trichinopoly. It was bought by Prince Orloff in Amsterdam in 1744 and presented by him to Catherine the Great. It was mounted in the sceptre of the Romanovs and is now in the diamond treasury of the U.S.S.R.

The *Koh-i-Noor* (mountain of light) was taken in 1304 from the Raja of Malwa by the Sultan Ala-ed-din. Later it adorned the Peacock Throne of the Shah Jahan, builder of the Taj Mahal. It eventually came into the possession of the British East India Company, by whom it was presented to Queen Victoria in 1862. It then weighed 191 carats and it was recut in London into a brilliant weighing 108 carats. It was the central stone in the crown made in 1937 for the coronation of Queen Elizabeth II and is part of the British Crown Jewels.

The *Great Mogul.* This legendary stone is thought to have been discovered in the Golconda mines *c.* 1650 and is reputed to have weighed 787 carats uncut. It was described by the French diamond merchant and traveller Jean-Baptiste Tavernier, who saw it in 1665, as rose cut. It was subsequently lost from sight and some experts have thought that the Orloff or the Koh-i-Noor may have derived from it.

The *Shah* is an engraved and polished but uncut yellowish diamond of 88·7 carats. It is engraved with the name of the Muslim prince who was its first owner in 1591, with an inscription of 1641 which identifies it as belonging to the Shah Jahan and with an inscription which places it in the possession of the Shah of Persia in 1824. In 1829 it passed into the possession of the Russians as reparation for the murder of a Russian ambassador in Teheran and it is now in the diamond treasury of the U.S.S.R.

The *Akbar Shah*, a diamond of 116 carats, was engraved with the names of the Shah Akbar in 1650 and Shah Jahan in 1661. It was brought to London in 1866 and recut as a brilliant of 71·7 carats, then sold to the ruler of Baroda.

The *Hope*, a blue diamond of 44·5 carats, was given in 1958 to the Smithsonian Institute by Harry Winston to start a diamond collection. It is thought perhaps to have been part of a stone of 112·5 carats which was sold to Louis XIV of France by Tavernier, cut to 68 carats, and stolen in 1792.

The *Pitt*, a diamond of 410 carats, was found in the Partial mines *c.* 1701 and was bought by Thomas Pitt, grandfather of William Pitt, Earl of Chatham, at that time Governor of Madras. It was cut to a stone of 140·5 carats and sold to the Duke of Orleans in 1717. It was stolen in 1792 along with the Hope, but was recovered and is now in the Louvre.

The *Florentine* is a pale yellow diamond of 137 carats which was part of the Austrian crown jewels. It was seized by the Germans in 1938 but was returned to Austria after the Second World War and is now in the Schatzkammer, Vienna.

Two notable stones have come from the Brazilian mines: the *Star of the South*, found in 1853, a diamond of 261·9 carats, which was cut to a brilliant of 128·8 carats and sold to the ruler of Baroda; and the *President Vargas*, found in 1938, which weighed 726·6 carats. It was purchased by a U.S.A. jeweller and cut into 29 gemstones.

Since the mines of South Africa were worked the largest diamonds have come from there. The most famous is the *Cullinan*, a diamond of 3,106 metric carats found in Transvaal in 1905. It was presented to King Edward VII of England, and was cut in Amsterdam into 9 main gemstones, the four largest of which form part of the British Crown Jewels. Other outstanding stones are: the *Jonker*, found in 1934, 726 carats rough, cut into 12 stones; the *Jubilee*, 650·8 carats, cut to 245·3 carats; the *Excelsior*, 995·2 carats rough, cut into 21 stones; the *Victoria*, 469 carats rough, cut to 184·5 carats; the *Tiffany*, a yellow diamond of 128·7 carats cut.

SYNTHETIC DIAMONDS. Claims to have made diamonds by a synthetic process were put forward in 1880 by J. B. Hannay and in 1890 by Henri Moissan. But the first fully authenticated claim was that made in 1955 by the General Electric company of Schenectady, N.Y. In 1960 General Electric began making industrial diamonds on a large scale at prices comparable to those of natural industrial diamonds and of comparable quality. Since that time industrial diamonds have also been produced by synthetic processes in other laboratories.

7, 51, 209, 776, 784, 797, 921.

DIAPER (through Old French *diapre* from Byzantine Greek *diaspros*). In its primary sense this term denotes a fabric with a monochromatic woven pattern which shows up by means of opposing textures causing different reflections from the surface.

In the language of ornament the term denotes an over-all pattern (such as that of a wallpaper)

capable of indefinite extension in any direction, the elements of the design admitting of uninterrupted repetition. The elements may be either geometrical or representational or a combination of the two. Diaper patterns may be either polyaxial or biaxial (or a combination of both). Polyaxial diapers are constructed on a symmetrical square or triangular network (e.g. ordinary graph paper) with expansion regularly in all four directions. Biaxial diaper patterns expand in one, usually a vertical, direction while extension horizontally is secured by juxtaposition of pattern elements either simply or in reversal. Oblique expansion is possible but rare.

The opposite of diaper pattern is 'panel' ornament, in which the decorative motif is discontinuous and fits into a definite, bounded space.

DIATRETA (Latin, pierced or filigree work). See CAGE-CUP; GLASS (ROMAN EMPIRE).

DIDOT. Family of publishers, printers and type-founders working in Paris over the years 1758 to 1876. They were scholars and men of letters as well as technicians and designers. Their severe NEO-CLASSICAL style of typography and layout was dominant throughout continental European book production for a century and a half. FRANÇOIS Didot, bookseller, who died in 1758, left two sons, FRANÇOIS-AMBROISE (1730–1804) and PIERRE-FRANÇOIS (1732–93 or 95). They both printed fine books and had type-foundries of their own. F.-A. Didot designed some large types of considerable merit in the years 1781–5, introduced the making of wove paper to France and reformed the scale of sizes of type by relating it to the standard French foot. His scale was not affected by the adoption of the metric system and is now universally used in Continental type-founding. Pierre-François, known as Didot-le-Jeune, acquired a paper-mill at Essonne.

PIERRE, called Didot *fils aîné*, the elder son of François-Ambroise, designed for his press types which carried the 19th-c. taste for plainness and precision to the extreme. His younger brother, FIRMIN (1764–1836), became the most famous of the family, both as printer and as type-founder. His austere and superbly finished types and imitations of them were normally used in French printing for a hundred years. He developed a method of stereotyping which enabled him to turn out large editions of standard works at low prices. HENRI (1765–1852), second son of Pierre-François, excelled at cutting punches for type. At an advanced age, variously given as 66 and 71, he cut the smallest type ever made, the *Microscopique* (2½ points). His younger brother, DIDOT ST. LEGER, took charge of the mill at Essonne and promoted his foreman's invention of a machine for making paper. It was perfected in 1816 and is essentially the one now used by all paper-makers.

DINANDERIE (from the Belgian town Dinant, formerly Dinand). A general name for kitchen utensils made of brass. See BRASS.

DIRECTOIRE. A transitional style in French taste between the NEO-CLASSICISM of Louis XVI and the EMPIRE, covering roughly the decade 1793–1804. The name refers to the Directorate which was established in 1795 and overthrown when Napoleon formed the Consulate in 1804. As a stylistic term 'Directoire' is applied to the useful arts of furniture, textiles, costume, etc. rather than the field of the fine arts. No interiors have survived from the Directoire period, but contemporary fashion prints provide a guide to dress styles: a loose, lightly draped, semi-classical arrangement worn without corset or substructure. The 'Grecian' vogue is well illustrated in Jacques Louis David's well known portrait *Madame Récamier* (1800). In cabinet-making, while much of the furniture during this period was designed in the Louis XVI style, the more distinctive note was struck by pieces more or less faithfully copied from Greco-Roman models from Pompeii and Herculaneum and a fashion for the 'Greek' prevailed. (See GREEK TASTE.) Characteristic of the Directoire were the 'Greek' chair, or KLISMOS, with concave or rolled-over back, STOOLS of curule form with X-shaped supports, bronze tripods on the ancient Roman model and bedsteads with triangular pediments. These were featured in collections of designs for furniture from *c.* 1790. Decoration embodied Revolutionary emblems and civic symbols such as the Phrygian bonnet or cap of Liberty, the pike of Freedom, the fasces which symbolized strength through union, clasped hands as an emblem of Fraternity, the oak as a symbol of social virtues, and so on. Antique Greek ornamental motifs were also in vogue. Largely instrumental in establishing the Directoire designs in cabinet-making was Georges JACOB (1739–1814) working under the inspiration of the Neo-Classical painter Jacques Louis David (1748–1825). As a result of Napoleon's campaigns in 1798–9 EGYPTIAN TASTE in ornament also prevailed in this period, its main protagonist being Baron Dominique Vivant de Denon (1747–1825). The latter part of the Directoire period, i.e. 1799–*c.* 1804, is sometimes distinguished as the 'Consulat' style. See also FURNITURE (EUROPEAN).

DISBROWE, NICHOLAS (1612–83). American cabinet-maker, born in England, at Maldon, Essex. He went to Hartford, Connecticut, *c.* 1636 and conducted a cabinet-making business there. A carved oak chest which he made *c.* 1680 for Mary Allyn, daughter of the Secretary of the Colony, is the earliest piece of American furniture inscribed with the maker's name. It is profusely carved with an undulating pattern of vines and tulips. Other chests attributed to Disbrowe are at Yale University Art Gallery, the Metropolitan Museum of Art, New York, and the Rhode Island School of Design. They are MULE CHESTS and have stylistic affinities with the so-called CONNECTICUT CHESTS such as that made by Peter Blin of Wethersfield (Brooklyn Mus., 1675–1700) and the HADLEY CHESTS. An oak chair at the Wesleyan University, Middletown, Connecticut, is also attributed to Disbrowe.

DOLLS. See TOYS.

67, 84, 220, 235, 252, 278, 301, 383, 630, 645, 899.

DONDI, GIOVANNI DE' (1318–89). Italian designer and horologist. Son of a physician, he was born in Chioggia, Italy, and moved with his family to Padua in 1349. Giovanni was also a physician, and *c.* 1350 was appointed Professor of Medicine at the University of Padua. From 1370 onwards he became involved in affairs of State, and in 1382 he transferred to Pavia, where he came under the patronage and friendship of the Visconti. He died in Milan. His chief title to fame derives from the astrarium or planetary clock which he designed and constructed over

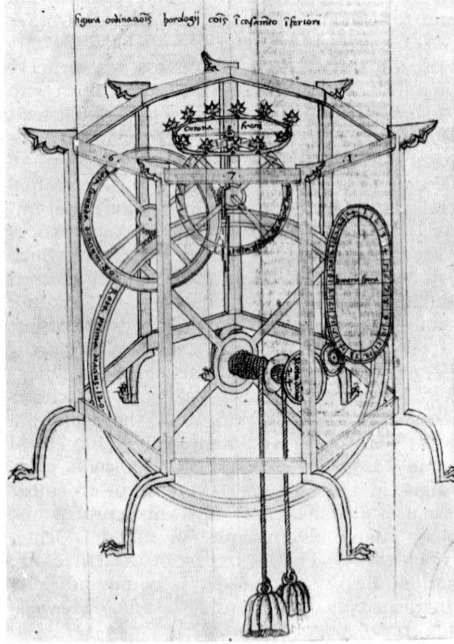

Design for the Astrarium

the years 1348–64. He described its construction in great detail in a manuscript work *Tractatus astrarii* of which several near-contemporary copies survive.

The astrarium consisted of a set of seven dials mounted upon and driven by a weight-driven mechanical clockwork supported in a frame of seven bronze columns. Each dial showed the position and movement in the heavens of one of the seven then known planets, viz. sun, moon, Mars, Jupiter, Saturn, Venus and Mercury. The motions were shown in great detail according to the Ptolemaic theory with allowance for their inclined and elliptic orbits, which necessitated the use of most elaborate mechanical contrivances including rotating and sliding links and even elliptical gear-wheels. Additional dials showed the position of the moon's nodes for predicting eclipses, and the times of sunrise and sunset throughout the year. An annual calendar showed saints' days and other holy days, the length of daylight each day, and the date of the movable feasts of the ecclesiastical year. This masterpiece was made almost wholly of bronze, whereas iron was the material usually employed for early mechanical clocks. The astrarium far exceeded in complexity anything made before it, and nothing comparable was made for nearly 200 years afterwards. Its eventual fate is still not known with certainty; all we know is that either the astrarium itself or a 16th-c. copy was destroyed by fire in Spain in 1809 during the Peninsular War. Modern reconstructions have been made with the aid of Dondi's own very detailed instructions in the manuscripts.

106.

DOVES PRESS. A private printing press founded in 1900 at Hammersmith, London, by the bookbinder T. J. Cobden-Sanderson and the printer Emery Walker. Of the 51 titles produced the most important was the Bible (1903–5) in five volumes. The type was based upon the ROMAN letter of Nicolas Jenson. It was thrown into the Thames by Cobden-Sanderson when the Press was closed down in 1916. See PRIVATE PRESS MOVEMENT.

131, 134, 277.

DRAGON (Greek *drakōn*, snake). A huge, scaly, snake-like monster often resembling the crocodile or alligator, sometimes winged and sometimes (especially in medieval Christian iconography) fire-breathing, which plays a number of different roles in European and Asiatic mythologies and is a frequent motif in the decorative arts of many nations. The view has sometimes been advanced that the dragon represents a fusion between the serpent and obscure racial memories of extinct dinosaurians or winged lizards whose fossilized remains are from time to time unearthed; but such ideas must remain in the realm of speculation. It is interesting that among some African tribes the crocodile figure represents the fertility of the waters.

In the Edfu cosmogonical myth of ancient Egypt the dragon was the enemy-snake, who was defeated in battle by the sun-god Horus, the Falcon. It was the symbol of Apopis, the realm of darkness, who was vanquished by Ra. In the ancient Middle East and in Hebrew mythology it was generally the emblem of evil. In Akkadian seals the fire-spitting dragon draws the chariot of the storm-god and dragons symbolize the raging of the storm. A relief from Nimrud shows the weather-god with thunderbolt pursuing a snarling winged dragon. And the Chaldean goddess Tiamat, symbolizing primeval chaos, was identified with a four-legged dragon with wings and scales. In Greek mythology the symbolism of the dragon was ambivalent. Snakes were guardians of shrines and of treasure. The snake was an attribute of Asclepius, the god of healing (perhaps because the sloughing of the skin was taken as a sign of rejuvenescence) and entwined serpents decorated the staff (*kērukeion*, *caduceus*) of Hermes. (The single serpent of Asclepius was perpetuated as the emblem of the

Royal Army Medical Corps and the coiled serpents of Hermes, regarded as the patron of commerce, appear on the bronze entrance doors of the Bank of England.) Winged dragons drew the chariots of Medea and Triptolemus, and in the myth of the foundation of Thebes Cadmus was ordered by Athene to sow the dragon's teeth, from which sprang up armed warriors. Cadmus and his wife Harmonia at the end of their lives were turned into serpents and carried to Elysium. The Hydra, a fearsome dragon, offspring of Typhon and Echidna, was a poisonous many-headed water-snake and when one of its heads was cut off others grew in its place. It was destroyed by Heracles.

The dragon of the Apocalypse had seven heads and ten horns and was identified with the Devil (Rev. 12: 3, 9). In medieval Christianity the dragon was symbolic of sin and paganism and is represented in art as being slain by St. George or St. Michael. Similarly in Norse mythology the dragon is slain by the hero—Beowulf, Arthur, Tristram, Lancelot. Yet as an emblem the dragon has symbolized heroism and strength in Western tradition. Agamemnon in the *Iliad* bore a three-headed snake on his shield as well as the head of Medusa. In the time of the Emperor Trajan the serpent (*draco*) was adopted by the Romans from the Dacians as the standard of a cohort and the purple dragon later became an imperial ensign. In the Middle Ages the Draco was carried as a banner in Rogation processions. Norse warriors had snakes emblazoned on their shields and carved dragons' heads on the prows of their ships. The dragon was the ensign of Anglo-Saxon kings and of Norman dukes. Richard I used it as a standard on the First Crusade and it remained a battle standard of the English kings. In the 20th c. it was incorporated into the armorial bearings of the Prince of Wales.

The dragon motif is one of the commonest and most ancient in the decorative arts of CHINA, where the depth and range of its symbolic significance gave it an importance which it never assumed in the West. Stylized dragons in an abundance of forms appear on pre-Han bronzes from the close of the 2nd millennium B.C. onwards and in historical times the dragon was ubiquitous in TEXTILE designs, EMBROIDERY, METALWORK, JADES, LACQUER, POTTERY, etc. and was also a recognized genre in pictorial art. Tradition tells of dragon paintings in the Han era, and the court painter Ts'ao Pu-hsing in the 3rd c. A.D. is reputed to have specialized in dragons. Apart from a mural of a winged dragon in a Korean tomb of the 6th c. A.D., the earliest dragon painting to have survived is probably the handscroll of 'The Nine Dragons' (Mus. of Fine Arts, Boston), dated A.D. 1244, by Ch'en Jung, the most famous of the dragon painters. A large number of offshoots of the dragon were traditionally ascribed special characteristics rendering them suitable for decorating particular objects, as for example: the tops of bells and gongs (*P'u-lao*); screws of musical instruments (*Ch'iu-niu*); sword-hilts (*Yai-tzu*); beams of bridges (*Chih-wen*); door-handles (*Chiao-t'u*); food vessels (*T'ao-t'ieh*); and so on.

The dragon of China was not the horrendous monster of medieval Western imagination but 'a benevolent and generally auspicious creature, bringer of rain and emblem of the Emperor' (Michael Sullivan, *A Short History of Chinese Art*).

1. As a fabulous beast the Dragon was chief of the scaly beings, one of the four classes into which Chinese mythology divided all living creatures. He could transform himself, render himself visible or invisible at will and was capable of diminishing and increasing in size. The dragon symbolized the active principle of *yin* in contrast to the female or dark principle. Because of his *yin* aspect he could rise up from the deep into the skies and produce clouds on which he would ride. The dragon often appeared as a protector of the righteous, particularly the defenceless. He was an emblem of vigilance and guardian of treasures.

In representation the Chinese dragon was a composite creature which assumed many forms in different contexts. The antiquarian Wang Fu analyses it as follows (*c.* A.D. 1123): 'It has nine resemblances or forms, viz.: the head of a camel, the horns of a deer, eyes of a rabbit, ears of a cow, neck of a snake, belly of a frog, scales of a carp, claws of a hawk, and palm of a tiger. There is a ridge of scales along its back, eighty-one in number; the scales on its throat lie towards the head, and those on the head are disposed like the ridges in a chain of mountains. On each side of its mouth are whiskers, and a beard hangs under its chin, where also is placed a bright pearl. . . . Its breath proceeds from the mouth like a cloud, being sometimes changed into water at other times into fire; its voice is like the jingling of copper pans. There are several varieties: some are horned and others hornless, some are scaleless, most are wingless.' The 'nine authenticating marks', which are valid only for the scaly dragon, are given as follows by Henry Doré (*Researches into Chinese Superstitions*, v): 1. Horns of a deer; 2. Head of a camel; 3. Demon's eyes; 4. Neck of a snake; 5. Tortoise's viscera; 6. Hawk's claws; 7. Palms of a tiger; 8. Cow's ears (i.e. deaf); 9. Hears through the horns.

2. As a deity the dragon was associated with rain and fertility, with the return of nature's energies at the spring and the renewal of productive forces. Prayers were offered using models of dragons in different colours according to a traditionally established pattern.

The dragon played an important part in the iconography of Chinese and Japanese Buddhism, dragons being used in place of the Indian Naga, or serpent spirits, the many-headed cobras. The dragon also replaced the Hindu deity Indra, associated with thunder and the storm. For the Taoists the dragon might stand for the principle of Tao itself, and its sudden appearance might symbolize the vision of truth.

Since the Han dynasty the dragon was the emblem of imperial power and authority. The Emperor sat in state upon the Dragon Throne and the Order of the Dragon in a number of grades was conferred as a mark of imperial favour. Dragon robes, decorated with the dragon and the Twelve Symbols, were a royal prerogative from the 13th c. onwards. Hornless dragons came in Ming times to be placed on tombs of high officials.

The emblem of the dragon was the pearl of potentiality or 'night-shining' pearl. The theme of the dragon pursuing the pearl has been explained in a number of ways, Werner's explanation in *Dictionary of Chinese Mythology* being perhaps the most convincing. The pearl was believed to be the sun and because for the dragon to swallow the sun was an impossible feat it became customary to paint this design on the screen outside a magistrate's office, the idea being that for an official to deal unjustly was as impossible as for the dragon to swallow the sun.

This wealth of symbolism, mythological, metaphysical and social, gives a density of significance to the dragon as a decorative element in the Orient which it lacks in the Western arts.

DRAW-LOOM. See WEAVING.

DRAWN WORK. Needlework made by drawing threads out of a woven fabric and embroidering over the remaining threads so as to produce an open-work pattern. Generally worked in white thread on a white ground, it has been in common use since medieval times for personal linen, bed-furniture, table-covers and the like.

DRESDEN CHINA. See MEISSEN.

DUBOIS, JACQUES (1693–1763). French cabinet-maker, who was admitted by the guild as a master in 1742. He did much work in LACQUER and represents a culmination of the ROCOCO fantasy, often enriching his furniture with female subjects in the manner of the sculptor Étienne-Maurice Falconet (1716–91). His business was carried on after his death by his second son RENÉ (1757–98), who became a master in 1755 and worked as cabinet-maker for Marie Antoinette. His most famous piece is a black lacquer commode in Chinese style (see CHINESE TASTE) made by request for the marriage of Marie Antoinette. There is in the Wallace Collection a writing table and filing cabinet lacquered with green VERNIS MARTIN bearing the stamp of I. Dubois, probably that of René rather than Jacques as both used the same stamp. These pieces are believed to have belonged to Catherine II of Russia, to whom they were perhaps presented by Louis XV.

305, 358, 738.

DUCERCEAU, JACQUES ANDROUET (*c.* 1510–84). French architect and ornamental designer whose numerous designs for furniture, among other things, had a powerful influence on French Renaissance work.

DUTCH LACE. A name given to a bobbin LACE made, perhaps in Brabant, in the late 17th and early 18th centuries. Technically similar to VALENCIENNES, it is much heavier in design and denser in texture.

DUTCH METAL. A malleable alloy of copper and zinc, which beaten into thin leaves is used as an imitation of gold-leaf. See COPPER AND ITS ALLOYS.

DWIGGINS, WILLIAM ADDISON (1880–1956). American typographer, who was born in Martinsville, Ohio, and studied lettering under GOUDY in Chicago. He was interested in book design and founded the Society of Calligraphers, of which he and his cousin Sieveling were the only members. He was acting Director of the Harvard University Press for a short period during the First World War and from 1923 was influential in forming the house style of Alfred A. Knopf in book production. He also designed de luxe editions for George Macy's Limited Editions Club, founded in 1929. He designed 11 type faces for Linotype, of which two, Electra and Caledonia, are much used in American book printing. He also had a strong influence on BOOKBINDING and jacket designing.

DYEING. See COLOURS AND COLOURANTS.

59, 70, 145, 565, 716.

E

EARNSHAW, THOMAS (1749–1829). British maker of CHRONOMETERS and WATCHES. Earnshaw was born in Ashton-under-Lyne, Lancashire, and his career was in many ways parallel with that of John ARNOLD. He was a pioneer in the manufacture of chronometers and of precision watches, and two of his inventions have continued unchanged as features of chronometers up to the present day: the spring detent escapement, a vital factor in the precision of time-keeping, and his method of making and assembling the 'compensation balance', which makes the time-keeping very nearly independent of variations of the air temperature. There was great rivalry between him and Arnold. Earnshaw's work was equal to that of Arnold in all technical aspects, though his watches lacked some of the visual appeal of Arnold's.

EARTHENWARE. Wares made with CLAYS fired at temperatures *c.* 800 °C. to *c.* 1200 °C. At these temperatures the body does not vitrify but remains slightly porous. See CERAMICS (STONEWARE) and POTTERY TECHNIQUES.

EAST, EDWARD (1602–97). East was one of the band of English pioneers in the making of wood-cased CLOCKS during the 17th c. and was also a maker of WATCHES of the highest quality, perhaps the first great English watch-maker. He was born at Southill, Bedfordshire, was a founder member of the Clockmakers' Company in 1631 and was its Master in 1645 and 1652. He was made Chief Clockmaker to Charles I and Keeper of the Privy Clocks in 1662. His clocks cover mainly the early years of the pendulum in England, 1660–70, and their cases were mainly in the 'architectural' style of the period.

EASTLAKE, CHARLES LOCK (1836–1906). English architect and furniture designer. He was nephew of the painter Sir Charles Lock Eastlake (1793–1865), who was Commissioner for the 1851 Exhibition and Director of the National Gallery from 1855 until his death. The nephew was not a practising craftsman but his designs were executed by professional cabinet-makers. He was an ardent exponent of medievalism. His book *Hints on Household Taste in Furniture, Upholstery and other Details*, published in 1868, won immediate popularity in both England and America and started a vogue for furniture in what came to be known as the 'Eastlake Style'. In this work Eastlake deplores the fashionable furniture in the French mode and advocates a return to simplicity and practicality. His own designs were based on medieval English and Jacobean forms. He was Secretary of the Royal Institute of British Architects (1866–77) and Keeper of the National Gallery (1878–98). See FURNITURE (ENGLISH; AMERICAN).

ÉBÉNISTE; ÉBÉNISME (French). Anglicized as EBONIST. The art of VENEERING in ebony was introduced into France from the Netherlands in the 1620s when the French cabinet-maker Jean Macé was recalled from Middelburg by Marie de Médicis. The craftsmen in ebony veneering were members of the Guild of *menuisiers* or joiners, which in 1743 took the new title Corporation de Menuisiers-Ébénistes. Furniture in ebony veneering became so popular in the second half of the 17th c. and the 18th c. that the term *menuisiers en ébène*, later shortened to *ébénistes*, came to denote skilled craftsmen of luxury furniture or cabinet-makers. See CARPENTER, JOINER, CABINET-MAKER.

509, 520.

ECHINUS (Greek: sea-urchin). An OVOLO MOULDING.

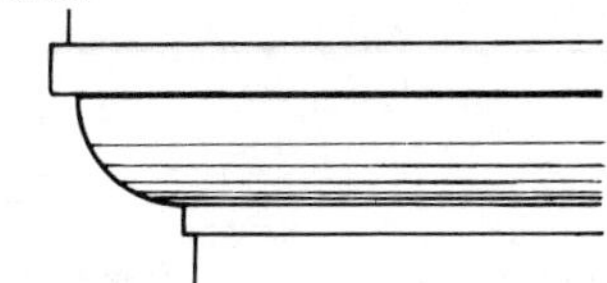

EDKINS, MICHAEL (1734–1811). English ENAMELLER ON GLASS. He worked at Bristol from *c.* 1762 to 1811 enamelling on opaque milk-white or blue glass usually with birds or figural scenes.

EDOUART, AUGUSTIN AMANT CONSTANT FIDÈLE (1789–1861). Silhouettist. Born at Dunkirk, he emigrated to England in 1814 and at first made a living doing portraits of animals and human beings in human hair and wax, some of which were exhibited in the Royal Academy. In 1826 he began as a silhouettist, setting up first at Bath. He used the method of freehand cutting in black paper, which he cut double so that he had one copy for the sitter and one for record. He avoided touching up with paint but indicated the whites of collars, handkerchiefs, etc., by the method known as 'slashing'—that is snipping away the black paper so that the white mount showed through from beneath.

He visited Oxford, Cambridge and Cheltenham, with a London season in 1829. In 1830 he opened up business in Edinburgh, where he was invited to the Palace of Holyrood to make silhouettes of the exile king Charles X of France and his family and entourage. The collection of 78 portraits is now in the Bibliothèque nationale, Paris. After short visits to Glasgow and Perth he then went to Ireland, spending about one year in Dublin where he made some 6,000 portraits. While in Ireland he wrote a semi-autobiographical work, *A Treatise on Silhouette Likenesses*, which was published in Cork in 1835. After a tour of the Midlands he sailed for America in 1839, where he was an immediate success and worked energetically for the next ten years. Some account of his American portraits, which constitute an invaluable social record, may be found in *Ancestors in Silhouette* (1921) by E. Nevill Jackson. On his return to France in 1849 with complete files of his 200,000 portraits, the duplicates of which he kept, his ship was wrecked and all but some 9,000 were lost. He was befriended by a Guernsey family, with whom he left the surviving silhouettes, and then settled in Guines, France, where he died.

Edouart had greater facility than any other freehand cut-out silhouettist and may justly be regarded as the most accomplished of all silhouette artists. He had an aptitude for catching a likeness, a pose, a gesture, or a suggestion in pure outline which was equalled by no other.

227, 374, 434, 436, 514, 533, 926.

EDWARDS OF HALIFAX. See BOOKBINDING.

342.

EGG, DURS (1745–1834). Swiss gun-maker who set up business in London in 1772 and became Royal Gun-maker. He was prominent in an age of great gun-makers and became famous for the quality of his double-barrelled shot guns and for his flintlock duelling pistols. JOSEPH EGG, his nephew, was also a gunsmith of eminence. He made a new form of pocket pistol without a 'turn off' barrel but with mainspring on the outside of the lockplate and in the double-barrelled variety he used a patented sear which enabled the barrels to be discharged successively by two pulls on a single trigger. He was also among those who claimed to have invented the copper percussion cap.

EGG-AND-DART. Ornamental motif often found as an enrichment on an OVOLO or ASTRAGAL MOULDING. It consists of alternate circular and dart-like forms. It is also called 'egg-and-tongue', 'egg-and-anchor'.

EGG-AND-TONGUE. See EGG-AND-DART.

EGYPT, ANCIENT

INTRODUCTION. The Neolithic and earlier cultures of Ancient Egypt are usually described as Pre-Dynastic since the historical or Pharaonic period is generally still divided into the 30 dynasties of the historian Manetho. These are grouped into three major periods, viz. the Old Kingdom (Dynasties III–VI; *c.* 2686–2181 B.C.), the Middle Kingdom (Dynasties XI–XII; *c.* 2133–1786 B.C.) and the New Kingdom (Dynasties XVIII–XXI; *c.* 1567–1070 B.C.). The later dynasties of the 1st millennium saw much foreign influence, particularly Hellenistic, culminating in Alexander's conquest in 332 B.C.

Two factors have combined to preserve for us more objects of the practical and decorative arts from Ancient Egypt than from any comparable ancient civilization. The nature of their beliefs about the after-life prompted the Egyptians to bury many possessions with the dead and the aridity of the climate meant that a high proportion of these have been preserved more or less intact. We are also fortunate in the numerous wall-paintings in tombs with scenes that illustrate the methods and techniques of production and the conditions which prevailed in the workshops.

Both the quality of the design and the high level of technical ability revealed in their products account for the high prestige in which the craftsmen of Ancient Egypt have been held, although both design and technical skill are likely to have been as high in, for instance, Mesopotamia, where conditions have not usually favoured survival. For all their skill, however, the Egyptian craftsmen do not seem to have been distinguished by a willingness to experiment with new techniques or materials beyond the desire to perfect what had already been achieved. In the Old Kingdom the crafts were probably fairly strictly supervised by the priests of Ptah, traditional patron of craftsmen, whose temple at Memphis seems to have incorporated a large craft school, and thus there were religious sanctions against deviation from the accepted canon. The less stable conditions of western Asia, however, seem to have thrown up major technical innovations, which eventually appeared in Egypt also; e.g. glazing and the use of copper in the Pre-Dynastic (or prehistoric) periods and the use of bronze and the vertical loom *c.* 1600 B.C. Egypt's involvement in external affairs increased in the XVIIIth Dynasty and later led to more interchange of skills as workers moved, willingly or as captives, between different countries. Even so some discoveries were not exploited, such as the working of iron, known amongst the Hittites *c.* 1350 B.C. and in Palestine *c.* 1000 B.C. (see 1 Sam. 13: 19–22) but not undertaken on a large scale in Dynastic Egypt.

In the view of the ancient writers the craftsman was a member of a lowly class whose work often involved unpleasant smells, excessive heat and even some personal danger, and he was considered much inferior to the scribes who pestered him with continual instruction and demands. The tomb scenes show the craftsmen active in the workshops attached to the temples or nobles' estates and it is evident that this was the customary way in which labour was organized, especially when dealing with valuable materials. These workshops were controlled by high-ranking temple staff such as Puyemre and Nesamun (both Second Prophet of Amun, under Tuthmosis III, Dynasty XVIII, and Ramesses IX, Dynasty XX, respectively) but there is no evidence that they had any practical skill. Distinguished craftsmen who reached supervisory grades, such as the Chief of Sculptors and High Priest of Amun in Sma Behdet, Ya (mid-XXVIIIth Dynasty) and the Royal Scribe Minmose (under Tuthmosis III), who supervised several temple building projects, seem occasionally to have been rewarded with priestly titles, but not always in the main cult temples and the posts may have been sinecures. The humbler crafts such as basket-making and pottery may also have been undertaken by self-employed specialists if not by housewives.

Surviving documents from the village of Deir el Medineh illustrate how the life of the craftsmen was regulated. This was the home of the workers employed in the construction, decorating and equipping of the royal tombs at Thebes in the New Kingdom and similar regulations probably held good in the earlier villages at Kahun and Amarna. Housing was provided on a standard plan and services such as the water-supply arranged for the whole community. The workers were divided into two teams, and records were kept of their absenteeism along with the excuse. Work diaries recorded the progress of each job and the causes of delays. The issue of tools was strictly supervised and they were weighed on issue and return, for bronze was valuable. Although life seems to have been strictly regimented in the close confines of this hot, dusty village on the edge of the desert, the workers were proud of their status and the records show several sons succeeding their fathers in their trade. They enjoyed some privileges, such as a village council for settling disputes, and when their shift had its alternate fortnight at home they could hire out their skill to the rich or work on their own tombs near the village. They even organized strikes and protest marches when their rations fell into arrears in the XXth Dynasty.

1. WOOD-WORKING. Although wooden objects survive well in the Upper Egyptian climate, it is not favourable to the growth of many trees and the material available for WOOD-WORKING was very poor. Acacia, sidder, sycamore-fig and tamarisk are the principal native woods but they seldom yield long clean planks and for most of his bigger jobs the craftsman had to rely on imported timber, of which the most important was cedar brought in large quantities from Lebanon. Other woods of western Asia, such as box, were used, but ebony seems to have been the only wood imported from Africa.

Wood-working developed with the increased use of copper tools in the early Dynastic period. Several examples survive from the Old Kingdom onwards and include chisels, awls, axes and adzes. The bow-drill using a copper bit is shown in Old Kingdom scenes. Hammers were often rough club-shaped pieces of wood but the bell shape still used by stonemasons is shown in the New Kingdom tomb scenes. Saws were set so that the cut was made on the pulling stroke and for rip-sawing a plank would be lashed to an upright post and sawn vertically. Planes were not used until Roman times and the use of the lathe is generally discounted—some XVIIIth Dynasty work appears to show signs of turning, but the craft is never illustrated.

Scarcity of material taught the Egyptian craftsmen many tricks of economy. Knots were cut out and patched; irregular planks were roughly smoothed and fitted together with pegs or lashings, and battens. Deficiencies could be made good with generous applications of plaster. The jigsaw effect of the use of short timbers is sometimes seen in tomb paintings of small boats and in actual examples of cheaper coffins. Long planks for shipbuilding were sometimes made up by joining two lengths with scarf joints held by dovetail wedges. Another economizing device was to work with a framework of rails and stiles filled in with veneered panels. An early but rare example of plywood is found in the IIIrd Dynasty.

In construction work the common varieties of mitres, mortise and tenon and dovetails are all found. In the Old Kingdom joints were frequently lashed with leather, string or copper bands. Wooden pegs were later used and bronze nails are found in the XVIIIth Dynasty. These were often made a decorative feature and capped with gold. Hinges of copper were used from the XVIIIth Dynasty onwards, but most lids were arranged to slide. They were secured by lashings round two ornate knobs, for LOCKS were practically unknown although some coffins were locked by irreversible tumbling devices.

Wood was used in the production of furniture, particularly boxes and chests, for chairs, stools and tables could be constructed in reed-work, a fact reflected in the design of many early pieces featuring bent-wood struts. Chairs were occasionally quite low, with seats less than 30 centimetres from the ground. In the New Kingdom beds were sometimes shaped by cutting the stretchers from bent timbers and by the same technique chair and stool seats were made deeply concave to take large cushions. Chairs and beds often had legs in the form of lions' legs and bedheads were sometimes ornamented with lions' heads. In the New Kingdom folding stools with leather seats and legs terminating in carved ducks' heads are found. Wood-carving was also practised for the making of wooden statuary, which followed the forms and canons of stone carving, and for smaller wooden items such as cosmetic equipment. Fine boxwood spoons in the shape of birds, trussed animals or swimming girls were popular.

The fine woodwork was seldom left unadorned. Some of the New Kingdom pieces are profusely ornamented with faience and ivory inlay. Veneered work was another way of disguising inferior timber, and the carcase of some pieces, like the XVIIIth Dynasty shrines of Tutankhamun, were covered with gesso, modelled and gilded.

The taste of the earlier periods was plain and elegant but none the less opulent. Perhaps the finest examples are the equipment of the IVth Dynasty Queen Hetepheres. In her tomb was found a fine carrying-chair of cedar wood, the poles of which are decorated with gold-covered palm-frond finials and the frame encased in gold. The panels of the chair are left in plain cedar wood except for a strip of ebony finely inlaid with her title in gold hieroglyphs. Her bed and chair are similarly gold-sheathed and stand under a canopy supported on a collapsible framework, again gold-covered. The uprights are socketed into copper-sheathed mortises and lashed together through copper staples.

Boat-building of course employed many carpenters and the arrival of the chariot in the XVIIIth Dynasty led to the development of the wheelwright's craft. A light but strong structure was essential for a chariot and the bent-wood frame was often used lashed and panelled with leatherwork, although for the more sumptuous state chariots wooden panels were used, covered with modelled and gilded gesso.

2. IVORY. Ivory was a valued material for small fine carvings and inlay work. Hippopotamus ivory was restricted almost entirely to the making of amuletic wands which provided magical protection against snake-bite, but elephant ivory was imported in quantity from the Sudan and in the New Kingdom from Syria. It was used for combs, small containers, jewellery and figurines in the late Neolithic period and later from Hierakonpolis there are some very fine human figurines and animal gaming pieces. The New Kingdom ivory was used for many purposes —fan and mirror handles, scribal palettes, cosmetic containers, gaming pieces—and it was often carved in relief in the style of the famous Syrian school for inlay into wooden caskets. Bone was used for similar purposes if there was case for economy.

3. PLASTER AND CARTONNAGE. The poor quality of native wood often resulted in rough surfaces and imperfect joints, which could be hidden by a thin coat of plaster that made a fine smooth surface for painting. On wooden statuary the finer details could often be added by modelling on a thin coat of plaster.

The plaster was sometimes reinforced with a layer of linen and it soon became apparent to the Egyptians that two or three layers of linen coated with plaster could be moulded into any shape desired and would hold it when dry. This so-called 'cartonnage' became a popular material for coffin cases since these often followed the contours of the body. The head-piece in particular could be modelled and then painted and gilded so as to produce a fair copy of the much more expensive gold masks.

4. GLASS AND GLAZES. The manufacturing of GLASS is a fairly simple process but requires accuracy in measuring the proportions of the ingredients and close control over the firing and cooling process. The ancient glass-makers had perforce to rely on their experience and instinct, and some of their accidents may have led them on to new developments. Most of the new techniques, and indeed the original discovery of the process, seem to have taken place in Mesopotamia, but Egyptian glass-workers have produced many fine masterpieces in this material.

The earliest form of glass in Egypt (dating from *c.* 4000 B.C.) is as a blue or green GLAZE on beads. It is basically silica, usually in the form of sand, and an alkaline substance such as potash or natron. Copper oxides, present as impurities in the sand, gave it its green colour and it was prized as a substitute for TURQUOISE—valued for its magical properties. Without a tin or lead content the glaze contracts on cooling and it would not adhere to clay which did not contain silica (i.e. silicon dioxide, in addition to the silicates normally present in clay). Glazed pottery is therefore quite unknown in Dynastic Egypt. But the glaze does adhere well to steatite (hydrated magnesium silicate), which is easily carved and hardens when heated. This was the ideal material for beads and amulets and was extremely popular.

Soon after the glazed steatite beads we find beads of faience. This term as it is used in Egyptological literature has nothing to do with the glazed pottery of Faenza but describes an artificial composition of powdered quartz mixed to a paste with an alkaline binding agent such as natron in solution. The paste can be modelled, moulded or thrown on a wheel and hardens on firing although its texture varies according to the composition and degree of firing. The body is white but the surface could be coloured with powdered glazes painted on before firing, which also gave it a fine smooth surface. It is possible that a coloured glazing material mixed with the body would 'travel' to the surface during firing, producing the same effect. A similar synthetic substance is Egyptian blue, which is coloured throughout by the presence of copper calcium tetra-silicate.

The early use of faience was for beads and small amulets, but small statuettes date from *c.* 3000 B.C. and it was extensively used to make the tiles which decorate some of the underground chambers of the IIIrd Dynasty Step Pyramid. In the Middle Kingdom vessels were made of faience and many small model animals were produced, including a number of hippopotami charmingly painted with LOTUS flowers. The products of the New Kingdom and later are outstanding for the wide variety of colours and the delicacy of their modelling.

About 1550 B.C. glass itself was introduced into Egypt, perhaps owing to a mistake in the proportions of silica and the alkali when making faience or more likely as one of the western Asiatic inventions that found their way to Egypt at this time. Glass vessels were made on a core of mud, on which the body of the vessel was built up and decorated while still soft with threads of coloured glass which were then smoothed down to form an even surface. Zig-zag decorations were also popular, formed by dragging a pointed tool through the coloured threads.

At the end of the New Kingdom glass-making was abandoned in favour of faience and it was not revived until the 6th c. B.C. Techniques of glass-blowing and the large-scale production of clear glass were not established until the Hellenistic period.

Although shades of green and blue were the most popular colours, experiment showed that other colours could be achieved by adding various oxides—cobalt for a deep blue, iron for yellow and red and tin for white. In the New Kingdom there was much experiment with new materials and some very fine results were achieved. Glass and faience were extensively used for cosmetic containers, gaming sets, funerary statuettes (*ushabtis*) and jewellery. Painted and inlaid tiles were popular architectural ornaments in palaces and temples and composite statuettes often had some distinctive feature such as the Blue or Red Crown added in the appropriate coloured glass or faience. Glass shapes were also inlaid in wood to decorate shrines and caskets and in metal as a substitute for precious stones in jewellery. The latter were usually cut or moulded separately and cemented or clasped in position in the cloison, but at least one piece of Tutankhamun's jewellery appears to show evidence of powdered glass being fired in position in the cloison, which, if it is correct, demonstrates the earliest known example of the ENAMELLER's art.

5. STONE-WORKING. The Egyptians were competent metal-workers and fine wood-workers but they had a particular flair for stone-working and cut the hardest stones with such precision that they are often credited with having developed techniques now lost. There is no evidence that they possessed a secret process for tempering copper or that they used diamonds or other stones set in a cutting edge, but it is clear that they were familiar with the potential of their material and were very skilled in working it.

Limestone and sandstone were the common building stones, and can be worked with copper tools; but much harder stones, such as basalt, granite, diorite and quartzite, were often used at various periods for statuary, coffins and vessels. These stones could be pounded roughly into shape by using mauls of another stone such as dolerite. Surfaces could be polished with abrasives such as quartz-sand and much work was done with a drill operating a crescent-shaped flint bit or, on the harder stones, a metal bit and abrasive. The discovery of a number of drill cores shows that a hollow tubular bit was often used to reduce the amount of material to be abraded, but none of these survive. The pressure of these drills could be increased by weighting them with a bag of stones, but it is not clear how upward pressure was applied to hollow out the interior of a stone vessel under its shoulder. We would also like to know more about how the Egyptians achieved the sharp outline for hieroglyphic inscriptions in the hardest stones and the precise and clean-cut internal rectangles in quartzite sarcophagi.

The first use of stone was for axes, arrowheads and knives in the Pre-Dynastic period. There are Palaeolithic hand-axes in brown chert made in the same forms as the early European types, but the Egyptian industry seems to have been unaffected by later developments elsewhere and developed its own particularly delicate forms of tools. In the late Pre-Dynastic period the art of forming an evenly rippled surface on a chert flake was at its highest. Regular rows of minute teeth about a millimetre across could be formed on a blade in similar manner by pressing with a bone point. Towards the end of the Pre-Dynastic period this skill was extended to the making of slate cosmetic palettes, often with the outline of animals, small figures and stone vessels, mostly bowls and dishes. The first two or three Dynasties saw the stone-worker's art at its peak. Particularly notable are a series of dishes in slate and greywacke (often described as schist) where these easily fractured stones have been carved into the most remarkable forms, suggesting metal prototypes, with very thin walls, twisted and curved and deeply undercut.

Larger bowls and dishes are also found in great number at this time. Although they are made in stones like diorite, brecchia and porphyry, they too are finely finished and usually exactly symmetrical. Cosmetic oils and ointments throughout the Dynastic period were kept in small jars of fine stone, usually calcite (calcium carbonate, often wrongly described as ALABASTER, calcium sulphate). The translucent veining that occurs in this stone is often cleverly used to enhance the appearance.

Semi-precious stones occur in quantities in the deserts on either side of the Nile Valley and were widely used in jewellery and for inlay work. The eyes of some statues, for instance, are made more lifelike by quartz and rock-crystal insets, but unlike Mesopotamian practice these prized stones were seldom used in seal manufacture. Engraved gemstones are not common before the Hellenistic period and most SCARAB seals were made of soft steatite, hardened by firing, with a coat of glaze.

6. METAL-WORKING. COPPER ores are found in the eastern Desert, Nubia and Sinai but were almost completely worked out by the New Kingdom. After this copper was imported from Cyprus and other foreign sources. Bronze was probably imported from western Asia, whence it was introduced in the middle of the 2nd millennium and iron long remained an 'industrial secret' of the Hittites and their contacts (see 1 Sam. 13: 19–22). A few artefacts found their way to Egypt, for instance the iron dagger in the tomb of Tutankhamun, but the metal was not widely used there until Roman times.

Copper working began on a small scale in the late Pre-Dynastic period. Smelting was done in small furnaces and the resulting ingot, small and brittle, was broken up and the pieces hammered into the required shape. The ingot was sometimes re-melted in a crucible and rough casting in open moulds of stone or pottery could be undertaken. In the Old Kingdom the need for annealing to reduce the brittleness caused by prolonged hammering was understood. Bowls and ewers could be raised by this method and there exist from the VIth Dynasty statues of sheet metal hammered over a wooden core. The spouts of the ewers and other joints were sometimes riveted and soldering is also found in objects from the tomb of Queen Hetepheres. There is evidence for casting in a closed mould in the Middle Kingdom and a New Kingdom tomb-painting shows a big multi-spouted mould in which a large casting of a door-leaf is undertaken. These paintings also show the use of bellows, but the Old Kingdom scenes only show blowpipes.

Bronze working was practised with the same techniques, and in the first millennium B.C., when the metal was widely used for the manufacture of figurines, it was usual to economize by making them hollow, using the *cire perdue* process, with the wax built upon a core of sandy material that is usually left *in situ* in the finished object. Some of these figurines are decorated with inlaid designs in silver or gold and there are occasional examples of gold plating.

Copper and bronze were used extensively for tools and weapons and for the equipment of temples: offering stands, incense burners, vessels, bells and rattles and above all large numbers of votive figurines of various deities are common. Even so these were valuable metals and poorer households long continued to use stone knives. Other economies were practised such as providing small model metal tools or even pottery or wood replicas as burial equipment.

GOLD was obtained from the Eastern Desert and the Sudan; it often had a high silver content and the alloy ELECTRUM (gold with 20% silver) occurred naturally and was long regarded as a separate metal. Native sources of SILVER had a high gold content, up to 40%, and it was not until the New Kingdom that a more refined silver was imported in quantity from western Asia.

The techniques of copper and bronze working could be applied to these metals. Repoussé and chased work was also undertaken and when both processes were applied together very high reliefs were obtainable. Thin sheet gold was also hammered, rubbed or stamped into dies to make amulets. In small jobs a wood panel might be overlaid with thin gold sheet, which was worked in repoussé then laid flat, face down, and the hollows filled with plaster. This plaster fill supported the raised areas of the gold when the sheet was stuck on to the surface of the wood.

Soldering was done with a silver–gold alloy and the technique of colloidal gold soldering using a gold–copper alloy was also practised. A copper compound mixed with a gum was used to stick the parts in place; and as the job was heated the compound reduced first to metallic copper, then at 878 °C. alloyed with the gold surface to make a welded joint. In the absence of copper gold does not melt until it reaches 1063 °C., so the main part of the job remained unaffected.

Soldering was necessary for a number of processes. Wire was probably made by cutting thin strips from sheet metal and soldering them end to end, or in the New Kingdom by soldering beads together and rolling them smooth. Small round beads or granules were soldered in patterns on to a larger sheet and cloisonné work was also popular in jewellery-making. The cloisons were formed by strips of metal soldered on edge on a base plate.

Gold was widely used in the production of jewellery and for fine vessels, hammered into elaborate forms and often decorated by low repoussé or by tracing usually with a floral design or a hieroglyphic inscription. Several fine

XVIIIth Dynasty examples exist and even in the politically weak and unstable later dynasties of the 1st millennium the art of the gold- and silversmiths was maintained.

Silver, at one time rarer and more highly prized than gold, became increasingly available. Several fine vessels in both metals were recovered from a hoard at Tell Basta (Dynasty XX) and a particularly noteworthy piece of silverwork is the coffin with falcon-shaped head of the XXIInd Dynasty ruler Sheshonq, discovered at Tanis.

Discussion of metal-working is seriously hampered by the fact that much of the evidence has long ago been melted down. This particularly applies to the larger pieces, which posed the greatest problems in their manufacture. The records speak, for instance, of an electrum statue made in the Old Kingdom (probably plated like the copper ones) and the New Kingdom tomb-paintings show large silver vessels, apparently 60–90 cm high, being finished.

7. JEWELLERY. Jewellery in Ancient Egypt served a number of purposes besides the obvious one of adornment. It often had a religious function—either as protective amulets or as part of the regalia of a king or high official. This had an important effect both on the design, for hieroglyphs and divine symbols had to be incorporated, and on the materials, for the colour of the stones had magical significance—green for growth, red for flesh and blue to protect against the evil eye, and so on. Gold was seldom used alone and when it was its plainness was usually ornamented by GRANULATION or filigree designs.

Many gemstones are to be found in the desert around the Nile Valley: CORNELIAN, JASPER, ROCK-CRYSTAL, AGATE, AMETHYST, CHALCEDONY, CHRYSOPRASE, felspar, GARNET, NEPHRITE all occur in Egypt or close to its southern boundary in ancient Nubia. Turquoise was popular but involved a difficult journey and mining in Sinai and LAPIS LAZULI had to be imported from as far away as Afghanistan. It is likely that faience and coloured glazes were developed as substitutes for these stones.

The popularity of different types and styles of jewellery varied from period to period. On the whole the Old and Middle Kingdom work was more restrained than the New Kingdom pieces, the design was simpler and the stones were of one or two colours only; but in the New Kingdom there was a fashion for heavily encrusted jewellery with large stones and many colours in one piece. Such ostentation perhaps reflects the *nouveau riche* origin of many of the richer New Kingdom families and the increased wealth of Egypt as a result of her imperial status at that time.

At all times pectorals were popular, especially as regalia; the design is often built around symbols of the king and incorporates his cartouche. Funeral pectoral plaques showed Osiris and other inhabitants of the Afterworld and had a strongly ritualistic purpose. Broad bead collars and diadems or fillets, based often on wreaths of flowers, were another type popular at all periods; but ear-rings and ear-studs and signet rings only became popular in the New Kingdom. Bracelets and anklets were often heavy, made of beadwork or of two semi-circular hinged plates with ingenious sliding clasps.

Beads of faience were widely used, carefully threaded to make multi-coloured designs on the bracelets and necklaces. Cylindrical beads are most common, but in the New Kingdom they are sometimes shaped as flower petals, fruits or hieroglyphs. Mats of coloured beads were sometimes made up to form a mask for a mummy and bead nets were often laid over mummies in the later periods.

8. DRESS AND TEXTILES. Most Egyptians dressed in white linen—men wore a skirt or kilt and women a tight-fitting sheath dress. Workmen are often shown naked in the Old Kingdom and usually preferred a short loin-cloth. The upper classes sometimes wore a long, loose cloak of light linen and in the New Kingdom the taste for luxury expressed itself in longer, fuller skirts and more voluminous cloaks, intricately pleated.

Spinning and WEAVING were highly developed crafts in Egypt. By the beginning of the Dynastic period (*c.* 3000 B.C.) all the variants of plain or tabby weaving known today were being exploited although the linen weave with single threads alternating was the commonest. The best linen was made from better quality flax than occurs in Egypt today and dentages of 65 warp threads to the centimetre with 50 wefts to the centimetre are known; some of the Tutankhamun fabrics had 112 × 32 threads to the centimetre.

After retting and beating to separate the bast fibres they were loosely twisted into roves and wound into balls. The balls were placed in heavy buckets and the roves passed through a ring in the bucket which helped to maintain tension. No distaff was used and the thread was spun on a spindle usually weighted with a wood, stone or pottery whorl. In the Pre-Dynastic period and occasionally later the threads were used doubled for added strength.

The earliest looms were horizontal, the warp being wound on two beams each supported on a pair of pegs driven into the ground. Models from the XIIth Dynasty tomb of Meketré show how the warp was set up on pegs driven into a convenient wall and then transferred to the loom, where alternate threads were lashed to a rod-heddle, which was raised to make the shed or space through which the bobbin carrying the weft was passed. On the return stroke the other threads were lifted by a shed rod. These two rods replaced the reed, in the absence of which the warp threads are occasionally rather irregular. About 1600 B.C. the vertical loom was introduced, which enabled the weaver to come closer to his work. In Egypt the two beams were still used fastened on an upright frame, unlike most other countries where the bottom beam was replaced by a row of weights. At the same time men replaced women at this work.

The introduction of the vertical loom coincided with the introduction of new types of weaving, probably also derived from western Asia. TAPESTRY weave was popular, as was also the warp-faced weave used for braids. Some of the more complicated patterns required several heddles but might have been made on a ground loom with paired warp threads in two colours, the weaver selecting only the colour needed for the pattern while the other floated at the back.

COTTON was not used in any quantity before the Hellenistic period and wool seems to have been subject to a taboo of some kind. Herodotus records that it was forbidden for use in religious ceremonies or in burials. Few specimens survive from the Old and Middle Kingdoms although it was widely used in the Christian period.

The decoration of some Pre-Dynastic pots shows how they were carried in a string net. From Dynastic times there are illustrations of these nets in tomb scenes and there is a particularly noteworthy example extant of very fine MACRAMÉ work from the Middle Kingdom.

Quantities of textiles were found in the cemeteries of Antinoopolis and Achmin and other cities dating from the late Roman period until after the Arab conquest. They are usually described as Coptic, a term best reserved for the language and distinctively Christian aspects of Egyptian culture in the 1st millennium A.D. In fact the earliest examples show Hellenistic influences both in the subjects and in their treatment, and recognizably Christian subjects do not occur before the 7th c. The designs are worked in coloured wool, usually in tapestry weave and mostly in the form of bands at the neck and cuff and roundels on the shoulders. The earliest designs, mostly in purple wool on white linen, are inhabited borders and geometrical designs based on animal and plant forms; but later more colours were used and human figures introduced.

9. POTTERY. The craft of the potter was practised widely in Egypt but seldom with any great finesse. When more attractive alternatives such as stone, metal and glass were available, pottery was a poor man's substitute for small containers, or was used only for very large containers.

Pottery is first found in the Nile Valley in the early Neolithic cultures of the 5th millennium, where it is hand-made. A slow wheel was introduced about the end of the 4th millennium but it was probably no more than a pivoted disc that the potter moved round with one hand (see POTTER'S WHEEL). This type of wheel, sometimes turned by an assistant, is still shown in the tomb scenes of the New Kingdom, and the fast foot-turned wheel was not in use much before the end of the Dynastic period. The earliest illustration of a kiln is of a tall narrow type in a Vth Dynasty tomb, but the controlled firing of earlier pots suggests such kilns were well established by then.

The clay normally used was the ordinary river clay found throughout the Nile Valley. This fires to a brown or red colour, but a finer calcareous clay, firing to a grey or buff colour, was used in Dynastic times for finer ware. This is found in the region of Qena, still an important centre of the pottery industry. Blackening could be achieved by exposure to smoke during firing and a fine red colour, ideally produced by good firing, could be simulated by a red ochre wash or SLIP or simply by burnishing the brown clay.

The principal use of pottery was of course for making general-purpose containers. Some of the finest of these were made in the late Pre-Dynastic period and include a variety of bowls and vases in a fine, highly burnished red ware, often with a shiny blackened top.

Decorated pottery was also produced just after this period with interesting painted designs of ships, trees and animals. Thereafter the pottery was generally uninspired and utilitarian except for the large painted jars of the Amarna Period (mid-XVIIIth Dynasty), which have big floral patterns in light blue picked out in red and black, and some fine palace wares also of the XVIIIth Dynasty.

A few Pre-Dynastic pots have animals modelled on the rim or in high relief on the walls and during the New Kingdom there was a short phase when vases were modelled in the form of seated figures. Solid modelling in clay was also practised and from the late Neolithic period there are model figurines, usually of steatopygous women with their arms raised in dancing postures. Model animals are also known. In Dynastic times there are figures of naked women thought to be intended as concubines for the dead and clay statuettes representing enemies who could be magically destroyed by rituals. Model houses were also provided for the dead, especially in the Middle Kingdom, and other items of funeral paraphernalia, including even coffins, were sometimes made in pottery especially for poorer burials.

10. BASKETRY AND MATTING. Baskets were usually made from the fronds of date or dom-palms but reed, halfa-grass and straw were also used. Bundles of fibres were coiled round in a spiral and each row was sewn to the one below by a strip of the same fibres. Several varieties of stitching were practised and the sewing strips were occasionally coloured so that a geometrical pattern was formed. The coil began with a simple snail centre but in the Middle Kingdom the four-cross centre was introduced from Nubia, though it never became popular in the north. Staked or randed baskets are unknown.

Some baskets were very finely made with intricate patterns for use as work-baskets or containers for fine materials, but large rounded baskets were also made in great quantities as general-purpose containers and even pressed into service as coffins for the poor.

Matting was also used for wrapping the dead and as well as being a floor covering could be used as a light door or wall and even as the basis for a roof. The same fibres were used as in basketry and were placed side by side in bundles, sometimes plaited and then knotted or laced together with a thread. In other examples the bundles were woven together on a loom in plain or twill patterns.

Some bags were made of fine matting rather than basket-work techniques and there are also boxes made of the tough outer rind of papyrus.

11. LEATHER. Leather was extensively used from the earliest times. Skins were used for clothing in Pre-Dynastic times and tanned specimens are known from *c.* 4500 B.C. Goat and

Wooden model of a weaving shop illustrating preparation of roves (*left*), spinning (*centre*), setting up warp on wall (*right*) and use of the horizontal loom (*top and bottom*). From Thebes. Middle Kingdom. 93 × 45 cm and 25 cm high. (Met. Mus., New York)

Wall painting from the tomb of the Vizier Rekhmiré at Thebes, illustrating metal-workers manœuvring a crucible over the kiln and pouring into a multi-spouted mould. From N. de G. Davies, *The Tomb of Rekh-Mi-Re at Thebes* (1943), Vol. II, Plate LII

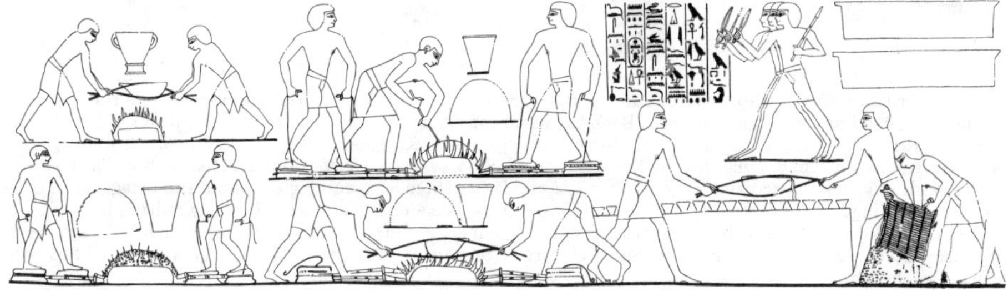

Coil basket originally containing a set of carpenter's tools. Thebes. New Kingdom. 30·48 cm high. (B.M.)

Toilet box of the lady Tutu. Cedar wood with ebony inlay on internal divisions. The contents include: pair of leather sandals, pumice stone, comb, kohl containers and stick for application, calcite and pottery vessels of unguents, etc. Thebes. New Kingdom. 35·56 cm high. (B.M.)

Chair of hard local timber. Square seat frame with woven seat (restored), short back continuous with rear legs and angle-pieces holding back rigidly to seat. Back has panel consisting of three wide and two narrower stiles. There are two rails each connecting two front and two rear legs. New Kingdom. (Royal Scottish Mus., Edinburgh.) Wooden stool with semicircular seat hollowed above, slightly cambered below and covered with a thin layer of white gesso now discoloured and worn away in places. It has three legs, curving outwards and octagonal in section. New Kingdom. (Royal Scottish Mus., Edinburgh.) Wooden stool frame. It has cylindrical legs waisted at lower half and decorated with concentric rings. Rails connect each leg with its fellows about half-way up. Seat is square and curved deeply downwards from each corner (restored with leather). New Kingdom. (Royal Scottish Mus., Edinburgh)

Ivory statuette of a queen or consort of a god. New Kingdom. (Royal Scottish Mus., Edinburgh)

Painted pottery from Abydos. New Kingdom

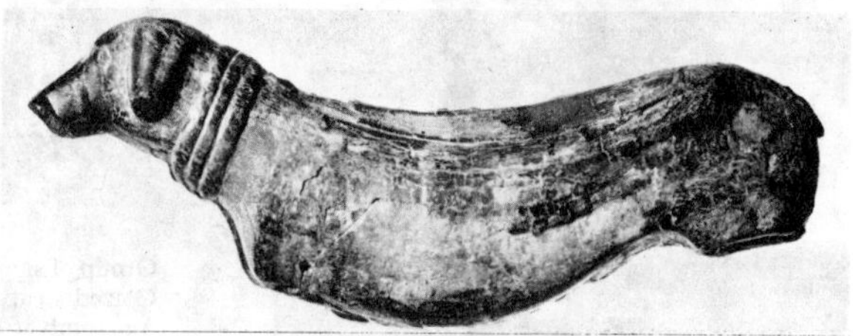

Ivory figure of dog. From Hierakopolis. Probably 1st/2nd Dynasties. (Ashmolean Mus., Oxford)

Ivory figure of a lion. From Hierakopolis. Probably 1st/2nd Dynasties. (Ashmolean Mus., Oxford)

Hippocampus. Painted green, red and yellow cartonnage. Probably decoration of a coffin. Provenance unknown. Late Period. (School of Archaeology and Oriental Studies, University of Liverpool)

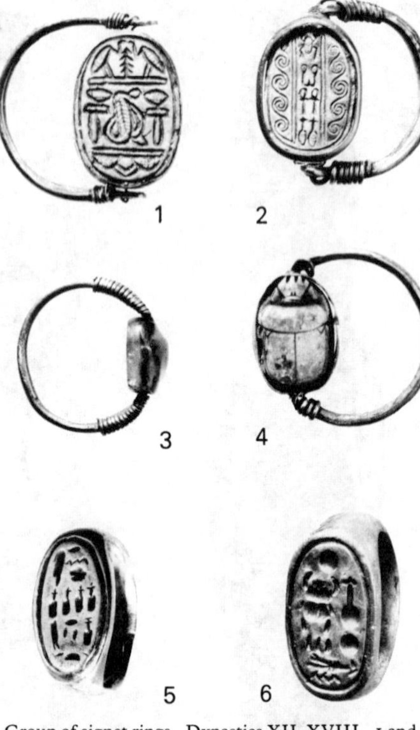

Group of signet rings. Dynasties XII–XVIII. 1 and 2. Glazed steatite scarabs. Excavated in Middle Bronze Age tomb at Jericho. 3. Amethyst scarab, gold mount. 4. Faience scarab, gold mount. 5. Gold ring inscribed with name of Queen Nefertiti, wife of Akhenaten. 6. Silver ring inscribed with name of Akhenaten

Solid cast-bronze figure of Osiris. Excavated at Sakkara. Actual size. (Birmingham City Mus., *c.* 2nd c. B.C.)

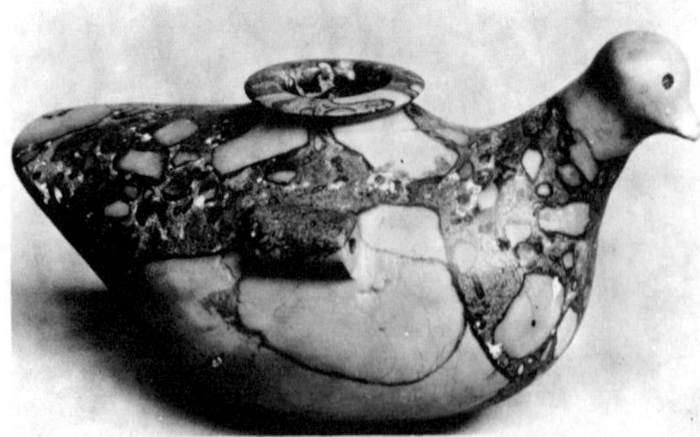

Red breccia vase in the form of a pigeon or dove. Late Pre-Dynastic period–early Dynastic period. Length 19 cm. (B.M., *c.* 3000 B.C.)

Glass vessel in the form of a fish, coloured blue, white and yellow. From Amarna. XVIII Dynasty. Length 14 cm. (B.M., *c.* 1370 B.C.)

cow skins are the principal ones that have been identified, and the tomb scenes show that the methods and tools of the leather-worker have changed very little in the course of time. Acacia pods were a convenient source of tannin. From the colours in which model shields are depicted it seems that the hair was often left in place—perhaps for added strength—but for other articles the leather was dyed or painted.

Until the heavier weapons of the New Kingdom thick raw hide could be used for armour. It provided protection without undue impediment and, as well as its use on shields, was strong enough to make the sides and floors of chariots. Quivers, mirror- and fan-cases and bags were made in coloured leather, sewn with leather thongs. Pieces of leather and interwoven thongs were used to make seats for chairs and stools or were stretched on a bed frame. Thongs of leather were used for lashings and made up into ropes. Fine leather was occasionally used as a writing material and for the rare examples of gloves and ritual braces that survive. Leather nets were worn as loin-cloths by workmen and finer-meshed specimens exist which were used in some religious ceremonies. These are slit at very close intervals, each slit about 1 cm long, so as to produce a very fine-meshed lattice. Pierced leather skirts or kilts ornamented with beads and fringing are also found in Pre-Dynastic graves.

Sandals were an obvious use for leather. They consisted of a single piece forming the sole, to which a thong was attached that went round the heel over the instep and through the sole between the first and second toes. This was stitched or knotted in place, though it has been suggested that some specimens were glued.

CONCLUSION. Unlike the distinctive statuary, reliefs and tomb-paintings, the craftwork is not always immediately recognizable as Egyptian; yet it shares some of the characteristics of the fine arts as well as having a charm and beauty of its own. The design is usually simple and functional and the more adventurous pieces show deep understanding of the material and confidence in the worker's own skill.

The ornamentation is also functional. It is based on a sort of simple heraldry—e.g. the intertwining LOTUS and PAPYRUS on a royal throne symbolize the union of the two kingdoms of Upper and Lower Egypt—or even more simply on the symmetrical arrangement of a single line of carefully inscribed hieroglyphs recording the owner's name and titles. Even the ornate decoration of the New Kingdom jewellery may be justified by its purpose, albeit a magical or ritualistic one.

It is unfortunate that these smaller masterpieces of the Egyptian craftsmen often pass unnoticed, overshadowed by the monumental building projects or ignored in favour of the esoteric funeral practices, for they are equally worthy memorials of a sophisticated and artistic people.

4, 350, 355, 466, 544, 596, 708, 730.

EGYPTIAN TASTE. From the middle of the 18th c. scholars and connoisseurs began to interest themselves in ancient EGYPT and in 1769 Giovanni Battista Piranesi (1720–78) published a number of designs of Egyptian ornament in his *Diverse maniere di adornare i cammini*. But this specialized interest did not affect popular fashion until Napoleon's Egyptian campaign in 1798 made it topical and stimulated the taste for eclectic exoticism which prevailed in France during the DIRECTOIRE and early EMPIRE periods. The fashion was helped by Dominique-Vivant Denon, an archaeologist and engraver who accompanied Napoleon in his campaign as head of the archaeological expedition to Egypt and was later director of the Musée Napoléon in the Louvre. His lavishly illustrated *Voyage dans la Basse- et Haute-Égypte* was published in 1802 both in Paris and in London and provided artists and designers with a large repertory of ready-made ornament—Egyptian mummy-cases and idols, cats, hawks, sphinxes, winged globes, obelisks, hieroglyphics, etc. Egyptian heads, sphinxes, and the rest, were incorporated into the design of tables, chairs, cupboards and so on, either carved as the termination of pilasters and other supports or made in metal and applied. The *lit en bateau* or bed in the shape of a gondola (thought to be an Egyptian motif) was particularly popular. Egyptian motifs were introduced into the furniture made for Napoleon's private suite at the Tuileries and a set of Egyptian furniture was made for Denon himself by the famous cabinet-maker Georges JACOB.

In England the vogue reached its height in the years between 1805 and 1815.

Furniture in the Egyptian taste was illustrated in SHERATON's *Cabinet-maker, Upholsterer and General Artists' Encyclopaedia*, which was issued in parts between 1804 and 1806. Thomas Chippendale the younger (1749–1822) made Egyptian furniture for Stourhead in Wiltshire in 1804–5. Thomas HOPE had studied architecture in Egypt as well as Greece, Turkey and Syria and his *Household Furniture and Interior Decoration*, published in 1807, included examples of Egyptian furniture decoration and interiors. In the following year the London cabinet-maker George Smith published *A Collection of Designs for Household Furniture and Interior Decoration*, in which he claimed to interpret the spirit of antiquity from the best examples of Egyptian, Greek and Roman styles. His knowledge of the Egyptian was taken at second-hand from Denon and was often misapplied, but none the less appealed to the public fancy. Thus Egyptian models contributed one of the strands of exoticism which were accommodated within the

Egyptian room from Thomas Hope, *Household Furniture and Interior Decoration* (1807)

picturesque ideal of the REGENCY. The grandiose and melodramatic painter John Martin (1789–1854), whose engravings had considerable influence in France, regarded Egypt as a particular inspiration for the 'sublime'. In architecture the Egyptian style made less headway. An 'Egyptian Hall' at the Mansion House was decorated by Sir Robert Smirke (1780–1867). P. F. Robinson, author of *Village Architecture*, was responsible for the Egyptian Hall in Piccadilly. J. Foulston, author of *Public Buildings Erected in the West of England as designed by J.F.* (1838), built an Egyptian Library at Plymouth (*c.* 1824). But these were little more than curiosities. C. A. Busby seems to have expressed the general feeling when he said in *Designs for Villas and Country Houses* (1808) that 'of all the vanities which a sickly fashion has produced, the Egyptian style in modern architecture is the most absurd'.

In Italy Egyptian motifs were introduced with other elements of the French Empire style. Largely under Napoleonic patronage, sphinxes, Egyptian heads and caryatids, lion-paw feet, crocodile decoration and the rest were popularized by French cabinet-makers and the fashion was adopted by Italian craftsmen in both furniture and textiles.

305, 618, 686.

ELECTRUM. .Native argentiferous gold containing from 20% to 50% of silver. The word is also applied to alloys of gold and silver deliberately produced and is sometimes used of an alloy of copper, zinc and nickel.

The Greek word ἤλεκτρον and the Latin '*electrum*' meant 'AMBER'. In a secondary sense they were applied to a gold and silver alloy which resembled amber in colour. According to Pliny the electrum of antiquity contained one part of silver to five parts of gold, but this is unlikely to have been a very constant ratio. Electrum was used for jewellery by the ancient Egyptians and electrum jewellery was found in excavations at the site of Troy. Homer describes the palace of Menelaus as resplendent with gold and electrum and silver and ivory (*Odyssey* iv. 71 ff.).

ELZEVIER (ELSEVIER). Family of booksellers, publishers and printers in Holland during the 17th c. The first of them, LOUIS, a Protestant refugee from the Spanish Netherlands, settled at Leiden in 1580 and began a bookselling business. Of his six sons two carried on his firm, two set up as booksellers at Utrecht and The Hague, and another, ISAAC, opened a printing office at Leiden in 1617.

In 1626 the booksellers BONAVENTURE and ABRAHAM bought Isaac's business and succeeded him as printers to the University. In their time (until 1652) the firm was at the height of its fame. It printed learned books, many by the Leiden professors, and the classics of French literature, which sold widely throughout Europe. The well printed pocket editions of the Elzeviers were eagerly collected—and, it is now thought, overrated—by 19th-c. bibliophiles.

DANIEL Elzevier left Leiden for Amsterdam in 1655 and became a learned bookseller, publisher and printer of international repute. He died in 1680. The parent house was carried on by JOHANNES Elzevier until 1661, and lingered in a declining state until the last of the firm, ABRAHAM II, died in 1712.

193, 912.

EMBOSS. A technique of producing a design in relief by hammering the reverse side of a ductile material such as gold, silver or copper. Embossed work is also commonly referred to as repoussé. In embossed work the design is first drawn on the surface of the plate and then transferred through to the back by pressure with a tracing tool. Thus prepared the plate is set face downwards in asphalt or supported on a block of pitch or wood and the portions of the design that are to be raised are hammered down into the resilient asphalt with punches and a light hammer which has a springy haft. When all the portions of the design to be raised have been set down, the plate is lifted from the asphalt, turned over, and set once again in asphalt. The relief of the pattern is further increased by setting down portions of the background of the plate from the front. Hollow-ware can be embossed by the use of a snarling iron. This is a piece of steel which has one end shaped to enable it to produce the required pattern and bent upwards at right angles to the bar. The opposite end of the bar is bent downwards and may be held in a vice or driven into a block of wood. The shaped end is inserted into the neck of the vessel that is to be embossed and a sharp blow at a point near where the snarling iron is secured causes the patterned end to strike the inside of the vessel. The pattern is rough-worked in this manner and then completed by filling the vessel with asphalt and working over the outside surface with CHASING tools. The process of chasing is accomplished by the use of punches that have been so shaped on their face that they will give a particular raised form when struck with a hammer. With skill designs such as scrolls and leaves can be produced. Chasing is also used further to work or finish the surface of an ornamented casting.

Embossing techniques are also used on a variety of non-metallic materials such for example as LEATHER and PAPER.

EMBROIDERY. 1. TECHNIQUES AND MATERIALS. Embroidery is the ornamentation of textiles with decorative stitchery. This is done by a needle of suitable size and thickness threaded with silk, cotton, wool or other thread. The ornamentation may be guided by the eye; it may be done on drawn threads or on marked patterns, on a suitable material or a collection of materials. Designs may be embroidered by means of counted threads or by checked paper.

Many kinds of material have been used as the ground. Among the more usual are linen, coarse or fine, velvet, leather, cambric, muslin and silk. Materials of man-made fibre (nylon net, chiffon, organza, dacron lawn, rayon substitutes, etc.) are also used. The threads used for the stitchery are also very various and part of the embroiderer's skill consists in the exploitation of different textures and thicknesses of thread. A thick crewel wool is specially prepared for coarse work, and tapestry wool, which is twice as thick as crewel wool, is extensively used. Raw or spun silk is often seen in old embroideries, especially for representing flowers. Arrasene is a thick thread of wool and silk, giving an effect of luxuriousness. It resembles CHENILLE in appearance and is generally used where a thick outline or broad effect is sought. Bobbin silk is popular, and strands can be withdrawn to work in the required thickness. Filoselle is a less glossy silk and is sometimes used instead of bobbin silk for the sake of economy. Stranded silk or stranded cotton can be unravelled any number of strands to give the required thickness.

Gold and silver thread was used extensively in old and precious embroidery. For the sake of economy, metal-wound thread, called 'purl' or 'purling', used to be laid on the surface only of the foundation material and secured in place by fine silk stitching. Bullion, a thread made of twisted gold or silver wire, was also used. It was often worked by what is known as the 'Burgundian lazur' process, in which the metallic threads are laid along the lines of the design and secured in position by silk threads. In this technique variation of light and dark was obtained by inserting the silk stitches more closely or further apart as required. Another substitute available since the Second World War is lurex, a flat-sided, untarnishable metallic thread available in a variety of colours.

Braids and other kinds of trimmings may also be couched to the foundation material, replacing on occasion the embroidery stitch. Braids used in medieval embroidery were often of gold or silver. Tudor and Stuart embroideries continued the use of braids and by careful stitchery on the braid itself the craftsman succeeded unobtrusively in getting it to lie flat.

Other objects which have been used as applied decoration are cords and fringes, beads, sequins, spangles and paillettes, PEARLS and other precious stones. Feathers have played a role of major importance in certain styles of Oriental and Pre-Columbian American embroidery. (See AMERINDIANS.) Coins and small metallic ornaments have been used, and even such strange substances as the skins of snakes, the integuments of insects and nails or claws of animals have been employed with effect.

Needles are used to carry the thread and work the stitches. Bone and gold needles have been found in Neolithic tumuli. Bronze and wooden needles have been used. In early periods fine work was even done by improvised needles made from twisted wire. Modern needles are of steel. Embroidery needles are designed according to their function, varying in thickness and length, size of eye and type of point. Whereas in ordinary dressmaking, where the greater part of the stitchery is concealed, an all-purpose needle is possible, in embroidery the stitchery constitutes the art and it is essential to have the proper needle for each purpose. Among the main types of embroidery needles are: crewel (fine-pointed, medium length, long-eyed but with the eye end little thicker than the tip); tapestry needles (short, blunt, with a long eye suitable for thick threads); chenille (short, fine-pointed); bodkins (long, blunt, with a large eye and sometimes bent at the point); bead needle (long, fine, sharp, with long but narrow eye).

Frames were used to secure the fabric and keep the material taut for working and for tracing the outline of the design on it. Larger pieces of fabric are usually set in a square frame made of parallel bars kept apart by means of wooden screws. Smaller embroideries are secured to a circular or tambour frame, of Chinese origin. Towards the end of the Middle Ages frames were largely abandoned and at the Renaissance a variety of new stitches came into use calling for deftness and freedom in the manipulation of the cloth. Tambour frames or 'hoops' are, however, still recommended to amateur embroiderers.

Before working an embroidery the design is transferred to the material. Such designs, called 'cartoons', were either done by the embroiderer himself or commissioned, as were TAPESTRY designs, from an artist. The outlines of the cartoon were pricked on to a sheet of paper, which was then laid on the fabric and powdered charcoal or other such substance, called POUNCE, was rubbed over this so that through the pricked holes it marked the outline on the fabric. The outline design would then be fixed by Chinese white or Indian ink. This technique was described by the Italian Pagnino in *Il Burato Libro de' Recami* in 1527 and had changed little by the time that Charles-Germain de St. Aubin wrote *L'Art du brodeur* in 1770. Today 'transfers' can be purchased by amateur embroiderers and stamped directly on to the fabric.

Shading can be introduced in embroidery by the use of ombré silks or more artistically by varying the stitchery. By means of split stitches, feather stitches and others, and by the use of variegated thread, broken masses are given light and shade. Stitches may be varied in size, as with a leaf form, and the base of a leaf may be worked in darker shades than the top. Tonal variation can be obtained by means of the light shining on fabrics and threads and the effect can be enhanced by stitches running in different directions worked with a shiny thread. The effect of relief can be given by the use of raised stitches such as knots and this can be enhanced by the use of padding. A judicious selection of colours in combination often enhances the impression of naturalistic shading and relief. Sometimes with embroidered pictures, as in French Renaissance work, for instance, paint was also used for toning.

Machine embroidery has increased in scope and popularity since it was introduced during the Industrial Revolution. Perhaps the earliest embroidery machine was that exhibited at the French Industrial Exhibition of 1854 by M. Hellman of Mulhouse. Up to 140 needles fitted with eyes in their middles and with points at either end rotated on to material conveyed on a movable carriage or frame. The machine was held under strict control both of velocity and of direction. It was patented in England and many improvements were introduced. There are now three types of domestic electric embroidery machines. The straight stitch machine gives only the basic machine stitch. The swing needle machine can work a zig-zag or satin stitch and gives a thicker line than the straight stitch machine. The automatic machine is capable of both straight stitch and zig-zag work and has in addition a number of built-in stitch patterns.

TAPESTRY is defined as a technique of embroidery on bare warps, the pattern being formed by the weft. It is dealt with in a separate article.

2. STITCHES. Embroidery stitches are very many and they represent the development of embroidery through the ages. Although there are more than 300 named embroidery stitches, they fall into four (or according to some authorities three) basic types.

(*a*) Flat stitches include all stitches which lie on the surface of the fabric without being looped or knotted or linked. Their fundamental purpose is to lay a certain amount of embroidery thread on the surface of the fabric. They derive from the simple *running stitch* and *darning stitch* used in ordinary needlework but in embroidery they are worked with more precision and regularity. All stitches are of equal length and are spaced at regular intervals. In the running stitch the space between each two stitches is equal to the length of the stitches; darning stitches are longer and the spaces between stitches are smaller. These give rise to the *outline stitch* and the *stem stitch*, which are alike in technique except that the stem stitch or back stitch is worked upwards and the outline stitch downwards, the thread being swung to the left. These stitches are used for working fine lines in the design such as thin outlines, lines on hands and faces, stems, tendrils, etc.

An area is said to be worked in *satin stitch* when it is embroidered with flat stitchery laid so closely together that each thread touches the one beside it. When worked perfectly, with exact precision, the effect is as of woven satin. The beauty of the finest Chinese embroidery is largely a result of the perfection with which satin stitch is used. Satin stitch is very widely used for embroidering small areas such as flowers, leaves and broad stems. Stitches may be either straight or slightly slanting to fit in with the design.

The variety of flat stitch known as *cross stitch* is worked by a number of methods and is one of the most widely used of all embroidery stitches. Most countries of eastern and central Europe developed a characteristic style of cross stitch. The American Pennsylvania Dutch embroideries used it with attractive boldness. The Victorian SAMPLER relied almost exclusively on this stitch. It is used in counted thread embroidery. Sometimes the background is worked in cross stitch and the design appears in the plain material. Cross stitch is always square and this encourages geometrical patterns and accounts for its often quaint and stylized charm.

Herring-bone is a flat stitch where the stitches are made alternately from side to side, being placed at an acute angle to each other. *Roumanian stitch* is essentially a herring-bone but has a small holding stitch to anchor each long angular stitch in the centre. It may be worked openly or set close together to form a solid filling. These stitches can be used for border motifs or as filling stitches and are popular for leaves and stems.

(*b*) *Linked* or *chain stitches* form a second group. To make a simple chain stitch the thread is drawn through the fabric at the desired point, the needle is then inserted immediately beside the point of emergence and its point is then brought out a short distance away and the thread is wound round its tip before drawing it out again. The looped thread should lie snugly on the surface. Of this basic pattern there are many varieties. The chain stitch is one of the easiest and fastest to work. It is, however, capable of very beautiful effects and can suggest subtle shading and modelling by the direction of the stitch. Many exquisite old embroideries, including ancient English altar cloths, are worked entirely or mainly in this stitch. It is also the easiest stitch in machine embroidery.

A twisted chain or *condorcet stitch* resembles the simple chain stitch with the difference that each fresh stitch starts from the left-hand side of the previous one instead of from the middle. In the *zig-zag chain* the stitches are set in a zig-zag line and the needle pierces the end of each loop as it enters the material to form the next link. One of the most popular varieties of chain stitch is the *fly stitch*, or *Lazy Daisy* as it is called in America. In this stitch each loop in the chain is pulled down and held by a small stitch. Arranged in a circle, such stitching gives the appearance of a flower.

(*c*) The *buttonhole* and *blanket stitches* are identical in formation and differ only in that buttonhole stitches are set close together to form a solid line whereas blanket stitches are spaced to give a more open effect. To make this stitch the needle is inserted and emerges from the fabric a short distance away; before it is drawn all the way through the thread is looped around the point of the needle. The most common embroidery stitch in this group is the *feather stitch*, which is a buttonhole stitch with the stitches worked at an angle to left and to right alternately. Feather stitch gives a suggestion of lightness and can become a delicate tracery over the surface; or it can be used as a line stitch or for borders. It is much used for delicate decoration of children's clothing or as part of the ornamental stitchery which embellishes smocking. Another variety is the *rope stitch*, which is technically a buttonhole stitch worked backwards. It is used for making curved stems, scrolled borders and ARABESQUES.

(*d*) *Knot stitches* form the fourth type. The main varieties are the *French knot*, the *bullion stitch*, the *coral stitch* (which is a series of simple knots connected with each other on the surface of the fabric) and the *double knot stitch*, sometimes called the *German knot*. Knot stitches are chiefly used to accent points in the design, as for example the centres of flowers or berries or an emphatic raised outline.

In addition to these basic types it may be useful to mention a few of the commoner canvas stitches. *Hungarian stitch* is in effect a satin stitch worked vertically to varied lengths so as to create a diamond or chequered pattern. The same stitch worked diagonally is known as the *mosaic*. The *tent stitch* is actually half a cross stitch and is worked on canvas with wool. For the finer work the double strands of the canvas are separated and the stitch is worked diagonally over a single mesh. This style of work is known as *petit point*. *Holbein stitch* is a double running stitch, which is used to outline a design, often in contrasting colour, in Assisi work (see below). Like Assisi work it appears alike on both sides of the fabric. *Florentine stitch* is a straight upright stitch used as a filling stitch for working stepped patterns known as Florentine work. Upright stitches of regular length are worked in a slanting series. *Gobelin stitch* is a slanting stitch covering two weft threads and used to cover largish areas of canvas.

3. TYPES OF EMBROIDERY. Beyond the general division into white and coloured embroidery no satisfactory classification has been found. Classification by stitchery is not feasible because a very large number of embroideries use a variety of stitches according to the effect desired. Classification by techniques has the advantage that there usually exists a close bond between technique and material, especially in traditional styles of folk embroidery. A comprehensive classification in detail is not here attempted.

(*a*) Flat mass or surface embroideries are contrasted with appliqué QUILTING and other forms of raised or padded embroidery. The simplest form is outline embroidery, where a pattern, design or picture is worked in outline on the foundation material. A variety of stitches may be used, such as stem, rope, chain, coral and cable. A common technique for this purpose is couching. The main thread is laid on the surface in the required position and is then fastened down by a finer thread with a plain stitch such as satin, darning or cross stitch.

In open-work embroidery open areas are achieved either by hemstitching with the drawing of threads from the foundation fabric or by cutting away the background fabric, buttonholing the edges and filling or partially filling the openings with various kinds of needle weaving. The most popular and perhaps the most beautiful type of cut-out work is *broderie anglaise*, which is done entirely in round, oval or leaf-shaped eyelets and is finished with buttonhole stitch. It is worked in white on white with an occasional accent in satin stitch motif. *Broderie anglaise* appeared in its finest form during the 18th and 19th centuries, being used on sleeves, caps, baby clothes, household linens, etc.

When cut-out areas are large the work may be strengthened by *laddering*. As the edges of the cut are buttonholed the thread is carried over at specific points to the opposite side and secured there by a tiny stitch, being then buttonholed back over the connecting thread. In *Richelieu* and *Venetian* ladderwork designs are usually stylized, with conventional leaves or flowers linked by *brides* or buttonholed bars. In Venetian work the background to the design is cut away completely, while in Richelieu it is only cut away in parts.

Hedebo is a style of embroidery originating in Denmark which combines open-work achieved by drawing threads from the foundation fabric and whipping them into squares with surface embroidery worked in chain stitch. It is graceful in design and notoriously strong. *Hardanger*, a Norwegian style, also employs cut-out, drawn-thread and surface embroidery. The patterns are geometrical and heavy in line, being suitable for aprons and household linen. It lacks the flexibility of hedebo, being controlled by thread count.

Assisi is an embroidery style of traditional Italian origin. The pattern, outlined in black or contrasting colours with a double running or Holbein stitch, is left blank and the background is worked over in cross stitch. The stitchery shows identical on both sides of the fabric, which is therefore reversible.

Shadow embroidery, sometimes called *Etruscan,* is worked on the reverse side of a thin fabric, giving a shadowy effect on the right side. Two methods are used. In one method double back stitching on the reverse side makes the area worked slightly opaque and the surface design is outlined in tiny stitches that touch each other. In the other method the design is formed by applying cut pieces of the same material outlined with pin stitches, which show on the surface as a double line of tiny holes or openings.

Berlin work, called *Zephyrs* in the U.S.A., is a form of wool embroidery on canvas which had a considerable vogue in Victorian times. It received this name because some of the most popular patterns were published from 1810 onwards by the house of Wittich, a Berlin printseller. A variety of stitches was used and the designs were often based on well known paintings.

(*b*) *Appliqué* is a general term for types of embroidery where a design is cut out in pieces of material which are *applied* to the foundation fabric by embroidery stitches. Sometimes the applied pieces are pre-embroidered.

In *inlaid appliqué* the designs are cut out of two pieces of fabric, either similar or contrasting, and the pieces of one are inserted into the spaces cut in the other. *Onlaid appliqué* is made by cutting out patterns and designs in one material and sewing them with a solid outline on to the foundation fabric. In the later Middle Ages western Europe lagged somewhat behind in the creation of rich materials and appliqué work enjoyed a vogue as a means to simulate sumptuous effects. After a period of neglect appliqué work has been revived and is used particularly where bold decorative effects are sought. It is a popular method of decorating children's linens, table linens, towels, curtains and even rugs. Where weight and bulk are required the appliqué material may be padded, as in quilting, solid raised stitchery can be used or articles such as seeds, etc., may be sewn on the work.

Patchwork is made from scraps and oddments of different materials. These may be of irregular shapes sewn together and this is known as *crazy patchwork. Appliqué patchwork* is made of scraps cut into different shapes—squares, oblongs, hexagons, etc.—by means of a template and then mounted on to a foundation fabric such as unbleached calico. Interesting designs are created by bringing into play contrasts of colour and material. In some American styles of patchwork the foundation material shows between the patches to form part of the design.

Stumpwork is a form of raised and padded embroidery which had its origin in Italy but became a characteristic feature of picture embroidery in Stuart England.

In addition to pearls, sequins, etc., seeds were used for embroidery on velvet or faced cloth. Melon seeds were used for the petals of flowers and hollyhock seeds for the leaves. Stalks were worked in light brown silk.

Smocking is a process of gathering the material into decorative folds or pleats, which are then caught together with various combinations of fancy stitches. Traditional smocking was usually done with threads matching the fabric but today use is often made of contrasting colours. Three traditional stitches used in smocking with stem stitch are rope, basket and chevron. Today the most popular form is honeycomb smocking. The stitching is done on the right side and is worked from left to right.

SAMPLERS were originally samples or pattern books of different stitches, usually worked by children or beginners. They are treated in a separate article.

4. HISTORY. The art of embroidery is coeval with the weaving of fabrics. It has been prac-

tised in all ages and in almost all parts of the world. Primitive forms of embroidery together with gold needles have been found in European tumuli from the Neolithic period. In the Far East it was established from a very early time and was regarded as an honoured art, being practised by men and women of all classes from prince to peasant. The Chinese have the highest reputation for exquisite workmanship, working mainly in silk, with the designs outlined in gold thread. See CHINA (TEXTILES).

The earliest embroideries that have been found are those on mummy cloths from Egypt. Both surviving specimens and the indications in mural paintings evidence the high level of craftsmanship. Herodotus describes a corselet of King Amasis: 'It was of linen, ornamented with numerous figures of animals worked in gold and cotton.' The Hebrews learnt embroidery from the Egyptians. The hangings of the tabernacle and the priest's vestments were elaborately embroidered (Ex. 26: 36; 28: 39; etc.). Josephus gives an account of the embroidered veil presented by Herod to the Temple in 19 B.C.

Both the Greeks and the Romans in classical antiquity were impressed by the opulence of embroidery in the Middle East, perhaps by contrast with the greater austerity of their own costumes. Homer mentions embroiderers brought from Sidon to Troy and speaks of a mantle worn by Odysseus embroidered with hunting scenes. Virgil in the *Aeneid* describes a magnificent decorated robe presented by Aeneas to Cleanthes. Embroidered garments and cloths were regarded by the Romans as luxury articles and were usually imported. In the later Empire, when luxury became excessive, sumptuary legislation was passed restricting the use of richer embroideries and Diodorus Siculus may have been reflecting the atmosphere of his own day when he wrote that the Locrian legislator Zaleucus in the 7th c. B.C. prohibited the wearing of embroidered robes by courtesans.

There was some indigenous embroidery tradition in western Europe. Pliny, writing of the 'barbaric' Gauls, testifies that they were 'skilful in embroidering carpets, in making felt with wool'. But in Christian Europe the main embroidery tradition during the early Middle Ages was carried by Byzantium. Unfortunately, no Byzantine embroidery earlier than the 11th c. survives. (See BYZANTIUM.) In the later Middle Ages the craftsmanship which had flourished at Byzantium spread to Rome and the West, a process which was furthered by the influence of the Crusades. Both in eastern and western Europe embroidery enjoyed a special prestige owing to its use for decorating ecclesiastical vestments and appurtenances. Lavishly embroidered copes in particular were greatly prized. The Syon cope (V. & A. Mus.) is an excellent example of ecclesiastical embroidery at its best. It is 9 ft. 7 in. (nearly 3 m.) long and 4 ft. 8 in. (nearly 2·50 m.) wide, made of linen and embroidered in coloured silks and gold and silver thread with scenes from the life of Christ. Embroidery also had secular importance for the costumes of the noble and the rich and for domestic furnishings. As from the 11th c. to the 14th c. the standard of luxury increased in Europe, so lavish embroidery came into ever growing demand. Ladies of the aristocracy embroidered with the aid of skilled needlewomen and guilds flourished in many countries. In his *Book of Crafts* Étienne Boileau, provost of Paris merchants from 1258 to 1268, gives eminence to embroiderers and embroidery designers among the craftsmen working in the textile trades. So extravagant became the style of richly embroidered costume that the Plantagenet kings were compelled to pass sumptuary laws regulating dress. The French set the acknowledged standard of elegance and Froissart records that the French nobles who went against the Turks in 1396 under the Duke of Burgundy were 'so richly dressed in their emblazoned surcoats that they looked like little kings'. As the accessories to dress grew more elaborate these too afforded scope for embroidery and display. A custom prevailed of wearing bands after the manner of phylacteries and these were intricately embroidered with the figures of protecting saints and the signs of the zodiac. Both men and women carried bags at their girdles for holding books of devotion and other personal requirements; these were often embroidered with personal devices or coats of arms. They were of sufficient value to figure in inventories and wills. Gloves were also worn both for their utilitarian value in hawking or to protect the hands when wearing chain mail and for their symbolic and ceremonial significance. In the later Middle Ages it was a favourite occupation of ladies to embroider gloves with silk and gold threads.

With the growth of luxury embroidery was used to an increasing degree on domestic textiles and furnishings. It was a custom for large and draughty rooms to be partitioned by hanging sets of embroidered curtains—called *salles*—and these were changed according to the season, each set being embroidered appropriately. Furniture coverings were also embroidered—known generally by the French term *courtepointerie*—and bed-curtains, counterpanes, canopies, etc., were elaborately worked. Great store was set on opulent textiles and collections are often mentioned in inventories. The furnishings of Queen Joan of Burgundy included some embroidered with 321 parrots and the King's arms and another with 561 butterflies and the Queen's arms, all worked in fine gold.

Christian iconography inevitably dominated the design of ecclesiastical embroidery—though even here there was some Oriental influence in and through Byzantine work. Christian motifs were also included in embroidery designed for secular use, sometimes in combination with astrological devices such as the signs of the zodiac and with purely traditional decorative patterns.

(*Above*) Silk embroidered roundels. Coptic. Depicting the Last Supper. With borders of floral and geometrical motifs. Features are in black silk firmly drawn to the back of the work. (V. & A. Mus., 8th–9th c.)

Embroidered binding traditionally ascribed to Queen Elizabeth I. Given by her to Catherine Parr as a New Year's gift, covering *The Mirroir of the synneful soule*. Worked with gold and silver wire purl in plaited braid stitched on a ground of blue corded silk. (Bodl., 1544)

Orphrey from the back of a chasuble. Flemish. Panel embroidered with blue, red and green silk and gold thread. Satin stitch, couching and split stitch for faces. (V. & A. Mus., 1st half of 16th c.)

Woman's jacket in fine white linen embroidered in silver-gilt thread. English. (Met. Mus., New York, late 16th or early 17th c.)

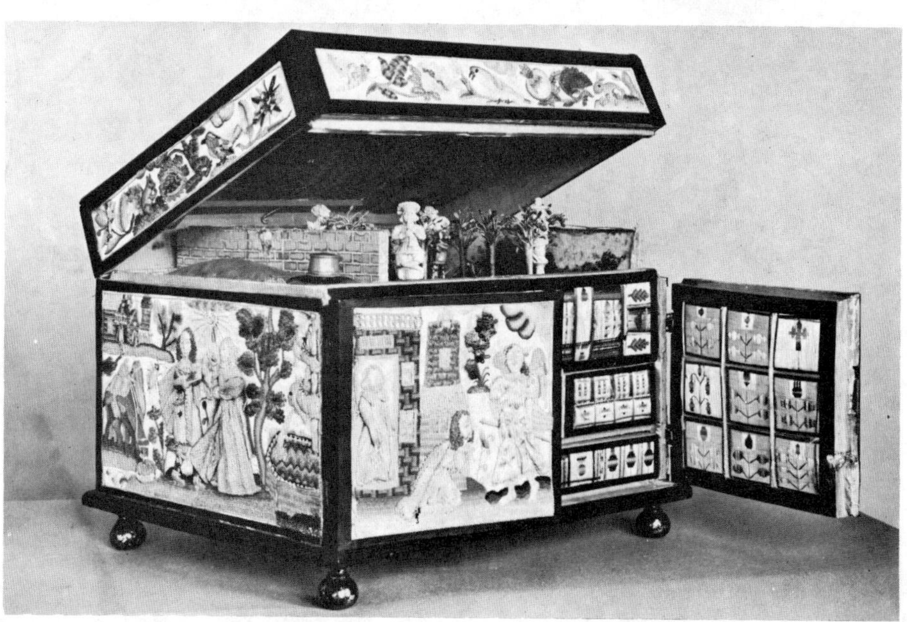

Casket with embroidered panels on wooden base. English. Figures in Stuart costume against background of contemporary furniture. Stumpwork is a feature. (V. & A. Mus., 17th c.)

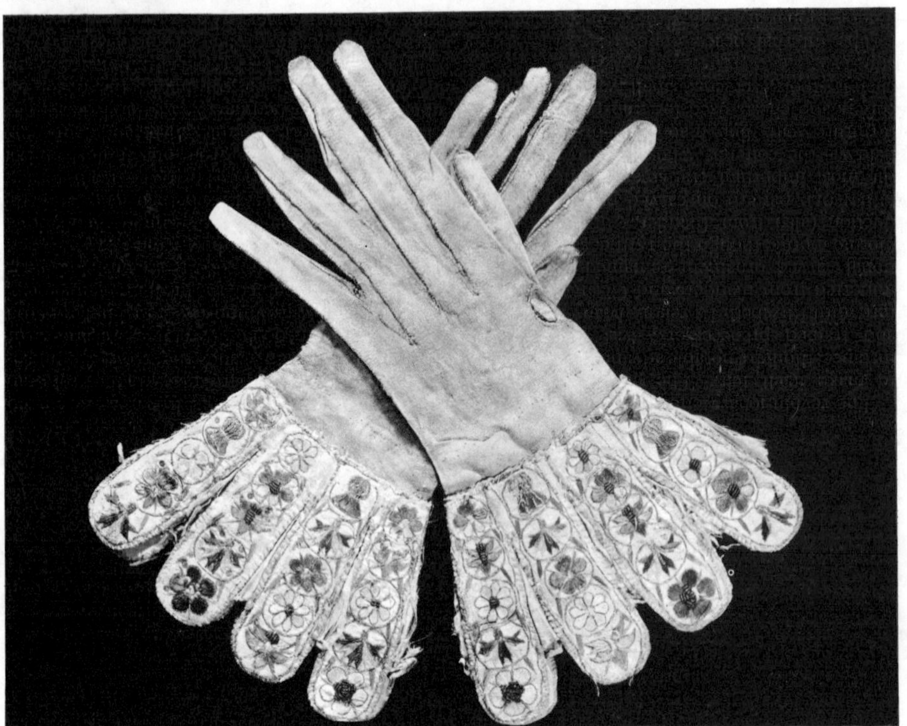

Pair of lady's gloves with gauntlets. French. Panels embroidered with flower and leaf motifs in red, blue, green, yellow and brown silks and metal thread on soft leather. (Luton Mus. and Art Gal., 17th c.)

Basket embroidered in beadwork. English. (Met. Mus., New York, 18th c.)

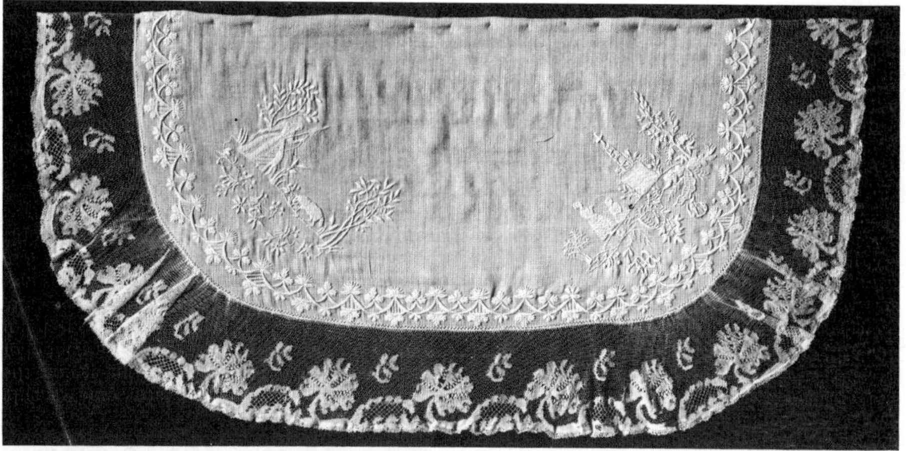

Handkerchief with whitework centre showing spinster in left corner and mourners in right corner. Borders embroidered with open-work stitches. Probably French. (Luton Mus. and Art Gal., late 19th c.)

Child's christening robe. English. White muslin with panels embroidered in white open-work. (V. & A. Mus., 19th c.)

With the growth of chivalry in the later Middle Ages, partly associated with the Crusades, heraldry provided a second major inspiration and the influence of heraldic symbolism and devices was so pervasive that it can be detected in embroidery motifs which have persisted to this day. Of special interest is the embroidery of banners or *oriflammes* and pennons carried by knights at tournaments or sometimes by ladies acting as umpires. These had to be worked in such a way that the design was equally visible on both sides, which led to a form of embroidery known as *à deux endroits.* Indeed from the language of heraldry embroidery borrowed a number of terms and a specific technical vocabulary, such as: *opus plumarium* (feather stitch or feather work); *opus pulvinarium* (the 'powderings' of heraldic devices); *opus consutum* (a kind of patchwork appliqué); *damier* (cross hatching); *damassé* (damasked). Heraldic embroidery was also prominent on military costume and particularly on the jupons which were worn over armour. (See ARMS AND ARMOUR.) A replica of the surcoat of the Black Prince embroidered with the royal arms on a ground of red and blue velvet may be seen above his tomb at Canterbury Cathedral.

During the 15th c. embroidery suffered an eclipse and the subsequent history on a national basis reflects the vicissitudes of national circumstance, the persistence of various folk traditions, and above all the vitality of the craft on a domestic basis. This history can be dealt with here only in a very summary manner.

(*a*) *England.* There is evidence that embroidery was practised in England from the early Middle Ages. St. Etheldreda, first abbess of a convent at Ely, was an embroiderer. Emma, daughter of the Norman duke Richard Sanspeur and wife successively of Ethelred the Unready and Canute, was renowned as an ecclesiastical embroiderer. Edith, daughter of Earl Godwin and wife of Edward the Confessor, embroidered the mantle which the king wore at his coronation and was described by William of Malmesbury as a 'perfect mistress of her needle'. St. Dunstan (924–88), Archbishop of Canterbury designed embroideries to be worked by noble ladies. Matilda, queen of William the Conqueror, was famed as an embroiderer and the BAYEUX TAPESTRY has been associated rightly or wrongly with her name. This work is technically an embroidery not a tapestry. Although its historical interest is great, the workmanship is not highly skilled and does not represent the best of its time. In the 13th and 14th centuries, however, English embroidery achieved international fame for the quality of its workmanship and design under the name OPUS ANGLICANUM. It was at its best in ecclesiastical work and was favoured by a succession of Popes, so that the inventories of the papal treasury afford one of the most valuable sources of information about this work.

Opus anglicanum is usually divided into three periods according to the design and workmanship. The first period, *c.* 1250–*c.* 1275, is characterized by figures of saints and representations of biblical events enclosed in MEDALLIONS surrounded by garlands and arranged in concentric circles. Only fragments survive from this period. In the next period, *c.* 1275–*c.* 1325, there is greater freedom of design and scenes are enclosed in ROMANESQUE QUATREFOILS, sometimes interlaced. The finest examples of this work are the Syon cope already mentioned and the Daroca cope (Mus. Arqueológico, Madrid). The last period, *c.* 1325 to the end of the century, is regarded as the best. Designs are represented under GOTHIC arches and scenes are separated by architectural columns or enlaced ribbons or stems. Characteristic features are animals realistically portrayed, abundance of birds, foliage and flowers, cherubs on wheels and angels with gaily coloured wings. Stitchery is outstanding for its fineness and evenness. Colours are arbitrary rather than realistic but remarkable effects of relief are obtained by means of stitchery only. The term *façon d'Angleterre*, sometimes applied to embroidery in the literature of the time, may refer to high-quality embroidery executed on the Continent in the manner of *opus anglicanum.*

Despite a general decline in the art of embroidery in the 15th c., canons of good taste and craftsmanship were carried on in the religious houses until their dissolution in 1536. The recrudescence of pomp and magnificence in the Tudor period is attested by accounts of the Field of the Cloth of Gold and by portraits and records of the period. Catherine of Aragon was devoted to embroidery and may have been instrumental in introducing a vogue for 'Spanish work', which lasted well into the Stuart period. At this time too there emerged a type of embroidery called 'paned work', in which effects were produced not only by stitchery but by the blending of different materials in contrasting panels. A hanging which dates from the reign of Edward VI has panels in ivory damask and crimson embroidered with gold and a trailing stem design in brown silk cord (V. & A. Mus.). In the time of Queen Elizabeth I there was a fine efflorescence of English embroidery. The Queen herself was addicted to embroidery and although more has been attributed to her than can be fully accredited, her love of dress certainly encouraged the art. Both Mary Tudor and Mary Queen of Scots were fond of embroidery and were themselves performers. In Elizabeth's time, too, embroidery ceased to be a prerogative of the professional and the nobility and spread to the wealthy and leisured merchant classes. In 1561 Elizabeth granted a charter to the Broders' Company, and embroiderers' guilds did much to foster the craft. New fabrics and silks were imported from the Levant and during the reign of Mary steel needles came into general use instead of the wire ones which had hitherto been used. The introduction of printed books had some influence on embroidery designs and also encouraged a vogue for embroidered bindings. Since velvet does not lend itself readily to stitchery a fashion arose among Elizabethan embroiderers for a style of appliqué in which designs were cut out of silk or linen, embroidered and applied to a foundation of velvet, producing a result which compared with the rich brocades that were then popular. Curtains and hangings worked in this way are preserved at Penshurst and at Oxburgh Hall, Norfolk.

Floral decoration came to a peak in Elizabethan embroidery and remained in vogue during the 17th c. While the general designs were formal, flowers and fruit were portrayed realistically, the wild strawberry being a favourite. The woodcuts of Gerard's *Herbal*, which first appeared in 1597, were used as embroiderers' models and others followed, such as Simpson's *Flowers, Fruits, Birds and Beasts* and the famous *The Schole House of the Needle* by Richard Shoreleyker in 1624, and a popular work by John Taylor, the Water Poet, entitled *The Needles Excellency: A new book wherein are divers admirable works wrought with the needle for the pleasure and profit.* Spanish work retained its popularity especially among those who favoured a more sober style in dress than was the fashion of the Cavalier period. Appliqué also continued its vogue and developed into the stumpwork which is characteristic of embroidered pictures in the Stuart period. Embroidered BOOKBINDINGS continued in favour until the close of the reign of Charles II, when leather and cloth bindings became more general. Relief embroidery was also much used for the decoration of caskets, trays and trinket boxes.

Through the 18th c. embroidery made little headway as an independent art although design was affected to a minor extent by the prevalent fashions such as ROCOCO and CHINOISERIE. The East India Company made available decorative linens, cottons and CHINTZES from the East, which took the place of velvets and brocades, and a special material with a linen warp and cotton weft was used for embroidery in coloured worsteds. The decline continued through the 19th c. and Victorian taste delighted in wool crewel work, BERLIN WOOLWORK and pictures on canvas. Miss Linwood's *Pictures in Worsted* and other similar models were esteemed as works of art and inspired an avalanche of tasteless and crudely coloured amateur work. The embroidering of braces and boots, screens and footstools became an accomplishment of young ladies. Despite the influence of William MORRIS and the efforts from 1872 of the Royal School of Needlework, it was not until after the Second World War that a new feeling for design made itself apparent.

(*b*) *Italy and France.* In the 12th c. a textile industry flourished in Sicily under Saracen influence. The workshops of Palermo attained an international reputation for velvets and brocades and for embroidered hangings. Particularly popular was a form of appliqué work known as Saracenic cut cloth in which a pattern was cut in one fabric and stitched to another with polychrome silk threads. These skills spread to the mainland, where from the 11th and 12th centuries the influence of Byzantine craftsmen was also felt. It was in the 15th c., however, that Italian embroidery rose to prominence under the impetus of patronage from the Medicis and other princely families and from successive Popes. Linen embroidery was exceptionally fine. Much of it was in open-work. Threads were drawn from the foundation linen until the fabric resembled fine gauze and a pattern was darned on with a coarse linen thread. By the end of the century and through the 16th c. Italian embroidery was famous throughout Europe for its meticulous detail and technical proficiency. Prominent artists such as Raphael, Cosimo Tura and Dosso Dossi were commissioned to make designs for embroidery and embroiderers emulated the painters in the attention they paid to the blending of colours and effects of light and shade. Italy was the chief source of pattern-books for embroidery and LACE in most countries of Europe. Milan supplied needles and Lucca gold threads.

During the 17th c. the influence of the East was strong. Furnishing materials were embroidered with large all-over floral patterns in floss silk; gold thread was couched with silks and used in basket stitch with gold wire. Replicas were made in embroidery of the woven patterns of the East. In the 18th c. floss silks were used in conjunction with paper for a special type of embroidery known as *colifichet.* The technique was used for making pictures which showed two surfaces simultaneously and the finished article was mounted between two sheets of glass.

In France there was an efflorescence of embroidery together with mosaic and mural painting in connection with Romanesque building at the beginning of the 12th c. Along with murals and stained glass it was executed in bright colours and was used to embellish the bare walls in church or castle. With the higher standard of personal comfort embroidery became of increasing importance for articles of personal wear and use. In the 13th c. France had an international reputation for embroidered pouches and forels or covers for books. The chief centre of manufacture was Caen. But as elsewhere in Europe, embroidery continued to be devoted primarily to church decorations and to ecclesiastical vestments and accessories. Through the 14th c. design followed the general development of Gothic style and was influenced by architectural decoration (altar frontal in the Mus. St. Raymond, Toulouse; altar frontal at St. Martin's, Liège). Through the 14th and 15th centuries French embroidered mitres, copes, gloves, mittens and other accessories were unsurpassed in Europe. A famous set of embroideries, made by Pierre du Vaillant, a painter and embroiderer of Avignon, was given by René d'Anjou to the cathedral at Angers.

In the Renaissance period embroidery, like the other arts, came under the influence of Italian styles with the influx of Italian craftsmen after the overthrow of Naples by Charles VIII in 1494. Prominent artists making designs for embroideries included Raphael, who was commissioned by Francis I (Mus. Cluny). From this time embroidery pictures were popular and great attention was paid to the naturalistic blending of colours, particularly for human flesh. Pattern-books were many, among the most popular being one by Pierre Quinty (1527). Catherine de Médicis was a skilled embroiderer and instructed Mary Queen of Scots in the art. With the growth of domestic luxury and extravagance in costume the prestige and demand for fine embroidery increased. The court of Henry III was particularly notable in this respect and a further impetus to heraldic embroidery was given by his formation of the Order of the Holy Spirit in 1578. The reign of Louis XIV marks an era of magnificence and greatness in the history of France and Versailles became the centre of luxury and taste throughout Europe. Louis XIV was a keen patron of embroidery and had a number of professional embroiderers in his personal household. Artists employed for the GOBELINS tapestry factory also made pictures and designs for the royal embroideries. Madame de Maintenon taught embroidery in a college which she established at St. Cyr, where girls of noble blood were engaged in making embroidered hangings for Fontainebleau. With the passing of the great period of French classicism and the growing influence of Chinese and Indian trends during the Rococo period Paris continued to be the centre of sartorial taste and costume embroidery maintained its prestige. Floss and spun silks were used and designs were accentuated by beads, spangles and silk-wrapped gimp or chenille. All women's garments were embroidered and cambrics or muslins were favoured. Louis XV was himself an embroiderer and boasted of his skill. Despite the loss of textile craftsmen consequent to the Revocation of the Edict of Nantes in 1685 France continued to be the most important European centre for the manufacture of embroidered furnishings. The silk industry was centred at Lyon, linen at Lille, Cambrai and Valenciennes. Royal patronage for embroidery continued under Louis XVI and Marie-Antoinette embroidered hangings in canvas work for the Louvre.

The Revolution not only interrupted this French tradition of fine embroidery but brought

Child's dress with front, sleeves and cuffs embroidered on white ground. Designed from traditional peasant embroidery. Czechoslovakia (20th c.)

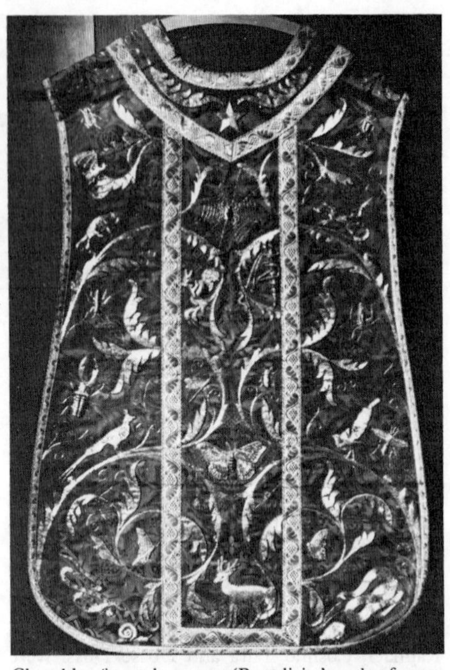

Chasuble of a set known as 'Benedicite' made of green Kirkstall brocade. Worked in Japanese gold thread, couched down with different coloured silks to give light and shade to the many birds, fishes and insects. (York Minster, early 1920s)

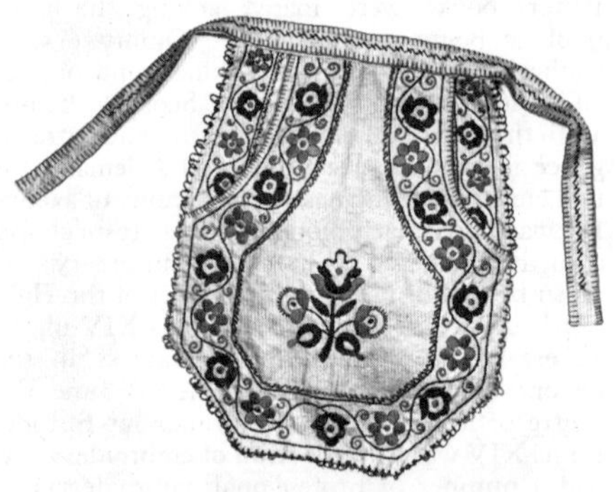

Conventional design in red and black. Spain (20th c.)

Broderie anglaise on linen. County Armagh, Northern Ireland (*c.* 1906)

Panel in modern style incorporating designs prevalent in medieval times. Extensive use of appliqué work. Britain. (V. & A. Mus., 20th c.)

in its train ruthless destruction. Old embroideries were systematically unpicked for the sake of the metallic thread, and *parfilage* as it was called (in England it was known as 'drizzling) became a patriotic occupation. Both embroidery and lace were patronized by Napoleon in the attempt to revive French crafts, but these losses could not be made good and although the fashion for embroidery became more democratic, the native industry did not compete with imported Oriental embroideries. Finally with the coming of the machine age the old techniques and craftsmanship underwent a period of decline.

Corner of table cloth. South Africa (20th c.)

Free machine embroidery. Pittsburgh, U.S.A. (20th c.)

(*c*) *Spain and Portugal.* The Moorish influence in Spain was particularly strong in the art of embroidery and after their expulsion from Spain in the 16th c. the Moors established in Algeria a style of embroidery, mainly door-curtains and head-shawls, which became popular in Europe as 'Algerian ware'. Spanish embroidery was also influenced in design by the fine Pre-Conquest embroideries brought to Spain from Peru. At the Renaissance and after 'Spanish work' was popular in most countries of Europe. As has been said, it was thought to have been introduced into England by Catherine of Aragon. As black outline embroidery on white it had its origin in Moorish styles. It developed into over-all pattern in black, making much use of climbing tendrils carrying leaves and flowers. Fillings were sometimes of red silk in the form of diapering lines, and gold and silver threads were sometimes couched alongside scroll patterns in what was known as 'Spanish stitch'. In Spain itself, besides rich ecclesiastical work, embroidered pictures after paintings by Murillo and other artists were fashionable. Examples may be seen in the Musée Cluny, Paris. A speciality of Spain was drawn work in designs akin to lace, and embroidery on fine nettings and muslins reached a high level of skill, particularly in Andalusia. The usual colours were black on white or black and red with touches of blue and yellow. In Castile a special style in blue and honey-coloured threads was known by the general term *toallas.*

In Portugal embroidery was mainly an aristocratic craft. Influences were similar to those in Spain but Portugal was more affected by Oriental designs and motifs of DRAGONS, butterflies and exotic birds and flowers played a larger role. A special technique was developed in Portugal whereby the front surface was covered with silk and the reverse showed the design in outline. There has been in addition a regional peasant tradition in polychrome embroidery with designs including both geometrical patterns and indigenous animal and plant forms.

(*d*) *Germany and the Low Countries.* In Germany traditions of aristocratic and peasant embroidery existed side by side from the early Middle Ages. Charlemagne's court encouraged embroidery and set the example. Byzantine influences on both design and fabrics were prominent. The eagle motif was so general that the embroideries of Charlemagne's court were known as *aquilata.* An example is a cope presented by Charlemagne to the cathedral of Metz. Judith, mother of Charles the Bold, embroidered a baptismal mantle for King Harold of Denmark, her godson. Adelais, wife of Hugh Capet, was a skilled embroiderer, as also was Queen Gisela, sister of Henry II and wife of St. Stephen I of Hungary. She set up an embroidery workshop, where according to tradition originated the *point de Hongrie* or Hungarian Stitch (see above). An outstanding example of this embroidery tradition is a cope of the emperor Henry II preserved in the cathedral treasury of Bamberg. It is done mainly in couched work on a silk foundation and in design displays a characteristic blending of western and Byzantine influences. From this reign also comes a celebrated German state chasuble known as the cloak of Queen Kunigunde.

Linen embroidery combined with low warp weaving became popular in the later Middle Ages and was known as Cologne work. Embroidery on linen woven on high warp looms and used mainly for orphreys was centred in the Rhineland and continued to be popular until the Renaissance. The Victoria and Albert Museum has an example of Cologne work with figures woven into the fabric and details emphasized by embroidery. A fine example from the 14th c. is an altar frontal from Sarnen now in the Industrie- und Gewerbemuseum at St. Gallen. In the 15th c. Germany was known as the chief source of wool embroideries for furnishings and wall hangings. Lüneburg and Wienhausen were specially famous centres for this work. In the 15th and 16th centuries a style of embroidery in coloured linen thread with designs akin to needlepoint lace was favoured by German craftsmen.

Peasant embroidery which owed little to foreign influences flourished in Germany from the time of Charlemagne. It was worked mainly on linen with silk or wool. A cope in this style may be seen in the Vienna Art Museum and examples are in collections at Hanover, Brunswick, Halberstadt and Erfurt.

In the 19th c. Germany was the source of a type of embroidery known as Berlin Woolwork which had a vogue in most European countries and in America. It was stitched in soft wool from Saxony sheep on soft canvas and was used for embroidery pictures and for domestic furnishings.

(*e*) *Modern Embroidery*. The traditions of aristocratic embroidery have not survived changing social conditions in the 20th c. and folk traditions have continued only sporadically. Survivals and revivals have turned embroidery into an amateur craft as a more or less conscious foil to machine work. Conditions have not favoured the meticulous training and the expenditure necessary for the finest craftsmanship, and emphasis has been rather on design. CREWEL WORK and various forms of applied work have been popular with amateur embroiderers though some advantage has been taken of new opportunities and techniques offered by man-made fibres and other new materials. Modernistic design has spread to embroidery while traditional motifs have also been revived in numerous commercial pattern-books and educational publications. The cost of fine hand embroidery prohibits its production on a large scale as in the past.

See also APPLIED WORK, BAYEUX TAPESTRY, BEADWORK, BERLIN WOOLWORK, BLACKWORK, BRODERIE ANGLAISE, BYZANTIUM, CREWEL WORK, DRAWN WORK, GROS POINT, LINWOOD, OPUS ANGLICANUM, OUDENARDE TAPESTRIES, PATCHWORK, PETIT POINT, RUSSIA (EMBROIDERY), SHELDON TAPESTRIES, SMOCKING, SOHO TAPESTRIES, STUMPWORK, WHITEWORK. See also CHINA (TEXTILES) and INDIA (TEXTILES).

5, 22, 56, 89, 130, 142, 157, 212, 238, 300, 402, 421, 422, 456, 457, 470, 479, 558, 598, 607, 707, 708, 750, 779, 791, 826, 896.

EMERALD. A green variety of BERYL which has been valued as a gemstone since the 3rd millennium B.C. In antiquity it was mined in Upper Egypt from *c.* 1700 B.C. and also in India. The Cleopatra mines near Aswam, which were worked during the Roman Empire, were lost from sight until rediscovered in 1818. Today the finest emeralds come from Colombia, whose mines were worked before the Conquest and were rediscovered by the Spanish in 1588. Other major sources are southern Africa, Brazil and since 1830 the Urals.

Emeralds have a hardness index of 7½ on the MOHS SCALE. They are valued for intensity of colour, transparency, size and freedom from flaws. They are in abundant supply but large unflawed emeralds are extremely scarce. The flaws of emeralds may, however, be both beautiful and fascinating in themselves and are referred to as their 'jardin'. In antiquity emeralds were lightly polished and either drilled lengthwise to be worn as beads or notched so as to be hung, a practice which has persisted in India and the Near East. In the West, however, they are facet cut with a view to displaying the depth of colour to best advantage.

Emeralds have been ascribed talismanic, prophylactic and curative powers. Perhaps owing to their colour they were thought to cure bad eyesight, and the famous emerald carried by the Emperor Nero may have been credited with such power. They have been believed to cure dysentery, to act as a protection against epilepsy, to assist in childbirth, to repel evil spirits, to ensure the chastity of the wearer and have been regarded as a symbol of immortality.

A method of synthesizing emeralds was discovered in 1930 and since 1946 synthetic emeralds of good quality have been made in the U.S.A. by a secret process. Both natural and synthetic emeralds retain their colour in artificial light, but the inclusions in synthetic emeralds have a distinctive quality.

The most famous historical emeralds are the 453 emeralds totalling 1,500 carats which were confiscated from the Incas and used in the construction of the Crown of the Andes dedicated by the Spanish citizens of Popayán in 1599.

92.

EMPIRE STYLE. The term is applied primarily to a style of furniture and interior decoration which started in Paris after the French Revolution and spread through Europe. The name is derived from the First Empire (1804–14) but the style continued in a more or less desultory fashion until a form of Gothic revival came into vogue *c.* 1830. It corresponds to the REGENCY STYLE in England. Its origin was largely due to the architects Charles PERCIER and Pierre-François-Léonard FONTAINE, who decorated the state apartments of the First Consul. Interiors designed by them survive at Fontainebleau, Compiègne and Malmaison. Their new style, which rapidly became internationally fashionable, was set out in *Recueil de décorations intérieures* (1801 and 1812). Basically the style is NEO-CLASSICAL but with an increment of archaeological interest and an attempt to copy what was known of ancient furniture and decorative motifs. There was also an affectation of Egyptian motifs, owing no doubt to interest inspired by Napoleon's Egyptian campaigns. The period saw the creation in furniture of the chaise-longue, the *lit – bateau* and the *psyché* or long free-standing looking-glass. In women's dress the Empire style coincided with a distinctive high-waisted fashion embellished with dazzling embroidery.

The art work under the Second Empire (1852–70) was largely derivative in style and when 'Empire' is used as a stylistic term in art history it is to the earlier period that it refers.

See also FURNITURE (EUROPEAN).

320, 358.

ENAMEL. Today the word 'enamel' is loosely used of any glossy protective covering such as durable paint or varnish applied to the surface of objects made from metal, wood, etc., as for example the lining of cooking vessels. In its original and stricter sense enamel is GLASS or vitreous paste fused to a prepared surface, usually of metal though ceramic substances possessing a higher fusing point than glass can also be enamelled. 'Enamelling' is the art of decorating surfaces in this way and in the language of jewellery and the decorative arts 'enamels' are objects so decorated. The word derives from the Old French *esmail* or *esmal* first used in the 13th c. and itself derived, through the 12th-c. plural *esmauz*, from the medieval Latin *smaltum*.

Though easily fractured, like glass, enamel is extremely durable and gives great brilliance of colour, especially when used in its translucent form against a ground of precious metal. Many of the most attractive goldsmith's works of all time have owed their beauty to enamelled enrichment. But although metal-working and glass-making are among the oldest of crafts, their combination in enamelling presents peculiar technical problems in causing the two different substances to fuse together. For this reason enamels are often particularly fragile and many of the oldest examples of enamelling may have disintegrated. There are five main types of enamelling: cloisonné, champlevé, *basse-taille* or translucent, encrusted and painted. Satisfactory English equivalents for the French terms do not exist.

In cloisonné enamelling cells, or cloisons, are built up on a thin sheet of metal by attaching metal wire or fine strips of metal fixed edgewise. These cells are filled with finely powdered glass paste, which is then fused to the metal in a furnace. As the enamel shrinks on melting and cools with a concave surface, more has to be poured in and the process repeated. Finally the surface is levelled and the whole is smoothed and polished. Neither the place nor the period when cloisonné enamelling originated is known with certainty, but the process may well have come as a development of the even earlier jeweller's technique practised in Mesopotamia by the middle of the 3rd millennium B.C., in which coloured stones were set in cells formed by soldering thin strips of metal edgeways on a back plate. It was an obvious step to replace the stones with enamel and so avoid the tedious process of cutting them to shape. Although champlevé is the easier technique, cloisonné enamelling was practised earlier and this may well have been because it is more suitable to gold and more economic of the metal. The EGYPTIANS may have used a form of enamelling on earthenware as early as the XIth Dynasty, but seem not to have done enamelling on metal until considerably later. The earliest known enamels are articles of jewellery from Mycenaean Greece in cobalt-blue and green enamel from *c.* the 13th c. B.C. The finest piece is a gold sceptre with a spherical knob surmounted by two hawks (Nicosia Mus., Cyprus). A very small amount of blue and white enamelling appears on Greek gold jewellery from the 6th to the 3rd c. B.C. There is also some evidence of enamel together with various other forms of inlaid work at Kuban in the Caucasus and this polychrome decorative tradition was carried by the Sarmatians into western Europe as far as Spain and southern England from the 2nd c. It has been conjectured that enamelling in France and Germany may derive from this source.

Cloisonné enamelling first appears as a major art in Europe in the BYZANTINE empire, the earliest examples dating from the 6th c. Very little of the earlier Byzantine enamel has survived, much having been destroyed in the course of the Iconoclastic disputes of the 8th c. The conclusion of these disputes in 842 was followed by a great revival which lasted into the 11th c. Enamel held a special appeal for the Byzantine love of brilliance and luxury and the Byzantine enamels are of great magnificence. Gold was used for both the ground and the framework of the cells, giving added brilliance to the enamel colours. Two forms of cloisonné enamel were employed. In the earlier the whole surface of the gold plaque to be enamelled was covered with enamel (Beresford-Mope cross, V. & A. Mus.); in the other process part of the surface of the plaque was recessed and in the field thus created the cells were built up. When the process was completed the enamelled surface was polished level with the surrounding gold border. The greatest monuments of Byzantine enamelling in western Europe are the Reliquary of the Holy Cross (Cathedral Treasury, Limburg) and the golden altar front of St. Mark's, Venice (Pala d'oro), which contains 83 enamelled panels of Byzantine origin. There are also a number of BOOK COVERS in western Europe set with Byzantine enamels; some of these were doubtless imported, others may have been loot brought back from the Fourth Crusade.

Cloisonné enamelling was soon copied in western Europe, where it was probably introduced by Greek goldsmiths (cross in the Sancta Sanctorum chapel of the Vatican). But the process of constructing cells of gold and inlaying them with cut glass or GARNETS had been most skilfully practised and brought to a high degree of elaboration by the goldsmiths of the Anglo-Saxon and northern Germanic peoples (SUTTON HOO treasure). Cloisonné enamel played a most important part in the goldsmith's art of the CAROLINGIAN and OTTONIAN eras, when it was used as an alternative to or in combination with precious stones. The earliest examples are probably of Italian workmanship (Beresford-Mope cross, which may date from the 8th c.), but the most ambitious cloisonné enamelled work of the early Middle Ages, the altar frontal of S. Ambrogio, Milan (the Paliotto), signed and dated Wolvinius in the year 835, is the work of a German artist. In the Ottonian period workshops seem to have existed in the German monasteries, in particular at Trier, Essen, Regensburg and Reichenau; but knowledge of the technique spread as far as England (the Alfred Jewel in the Ashmolean Mus. and the Soltikoff Cross in the V. & A. Mus.). A list of early ROMANESQUE objects enriched with cloisonné enamel would comprise nearly all the major goldsmith's work of the period, including the crowns of St. Stephen and of Constantine Monomachos in Budapest, the regalia and vestments of the Holy Roman Empire in Vienna, and many chalices, book covers and portable altars.

In champlevé the design to be enamelled is cut out of the thickness of the metal ground and glass powder is placed in the resulting cavities. After firing the enamelled surface is smoothed level with the metal and polished. While the Romans made little, if any, use of enamel, the process was certainly employed by many of the peoples they conquered. Amongst the latter were the Britons, who had achieved great skill before the Roman conquest (Battersea Reach shield in the B.M.), and numerous domestic objects decorated with champlevé enamel dating from the Roman period have been excavated in England. Provincial Roman and the subsequent Celtic enamels were produced on a bronze base. The incursions of invading peoples drove the Celtic enamellers westwards to Ireland, where the art of champlevé enamelling enjoyed a late flowering.

During the Middle Ages champlevé had occasionally been used to supplement the effect of cloisonné in western Europe but in the 12th c. it began to predominate. Towards the end of the 11th c. champlevé enamelling on copper had sprung up almost simultaneously in various countries and it continued to be produced on an increasingly commercial scale, although still as a fine craft, until the beginning of the 14th c.

The source of this efflorescence about the time that stained glass was beginning to be manufactured on a large scale is a matter of conjecture. Some authorities have maintained that this type of enamelling spread to Europe from western Asia by way of Spain. There is a legend of doubtful authenticity that it was first taught to German craftsmen by Byzantine goldsmiths who came in the train of the Byzantine princess Theophano when she married Otto II in 973. Others have thought that it was a development from the polychrome style of decoration carried to western Europe by the Sarmatians. There is no certainty.

The champlevé technique had the advantage that a greater degree of expression could be achieved than had been possible when the design had to be built up from cells. Though figure subjects were rendered in cloisonné, their treatment had been extremely formalized. Instead of gold a copper ground was now used, an inexpensive material that made possible the production of pieces of monumental proportions. As the copper ground discoloured when the enamel was fired, it was necessary to use opaque colours. These, while lacking the brilliance of translucent colours, did not fuse so easily and it was therefore possible to combine several colours within one cavity, giving an effect of shading and colour gradation. Champlevé enamels were produced in three main regions, first in the towns on the Rhine and the Meuse, secondly in the French city of Limoges and thirdly in Spain. The Mosan enamels are readily identifiable but the distinction between those of Limoges and Spain is less clear. It is not possible to determine which of these centres was the first to exploit the possibilities of the technique, but the fact that Abbot Suger of St. Denis brought enamellers from Lorraine to work on a large cross in honour of his patron saint, consecrated in 1147, indicates that the northern enamels were widely known at an early date. The Mosan enamels were of very high quality, and the drawing of the figures carved in the copper plate reveals a superb sense of line. The names of several Mosan goldsmith-enamellers are known. GODEFROID DE CLAIR of Huy on the Meuse is generally regarded as the author of the finest of early examples, his greatest work being the Heribert shrine at Cologne which has twelve large roundels on the roof enamelled with scenes from the life of the Saint. Of the later artists, working about the end of the 12th and beginning of the 13th c., NICOLAS OF VERDUN, master of the triptych altar at Klosterneuburg and of the shrine of the Three Kings at Cologne, is outstanding. The finer productions of the Mosan enamellers rank among the major achievements of Romanesque art. The enamel plaques do not, however, always play a leading part in Mosan goldsmiths' work; in some of the shrines the figure subjects are rendered in high relief and enamel is confined to a minor decorative role (the shrine of the Three Kings, Cathedral Treasury, Cologne, or the Eltenberg Reliquary, V. & A. Mus.). The design of Mosan figure subjects was derived from contemporary manuscripts, and it is by reference to manuscripts of the Winchester School that the few known examples of English 12th-c. champlevé enamel have been identified. The most important examples hitherto accepted as English are two ciboria (the Warwick ciborium and the Balfour ciborium, both in the V. & A. Mus.).

While Mosan enamelling was gradually crowded out by other techniques of goldsmiths' ornament without, however, suffering any marked decline in quality, the history of Limoges enamel shows a steady decline as mass-production methods were adopted to deal with the great demand from all over western Europe. The earlier Limoges, dating from the first half of the 12th c., is timid in design, the enamel being confined to roundels. By the second half of the century exquisitely drawn figures in coloured enamels against a VERMICULATED ground were produced, the most splendid example being the sepulchral monument of Geoffrey Plantagenet at Le Mans, from the third quarter of the 12th c. In the 13th c. the practice was reversed. Instead of the figures being coloured against a gilt ground, the ground was cut away and enamelled and the figures merely engraved and gilded. Though some Limoges enamels may have been produced in monastic workshops, in particular those of the Abbeys of St. Martial and Grandmont, the scale and variety of production were such as to predicate large-scale manufacture in several workshops. In the 13th c., as had also been the case in the Mosan shops, figures were rendered in relief, but at Limoges these were hammered into moulds instead of being worked up by hand. Limoges did not produce great spectacular pieces such as the shrines made by Mosan goldsmiths and enamellers, but manufactured smaller pieces which were within the reach of parish churches as well as the great abbeys. Amongst their most popular lines were crucifix figures of various sizes, book covers, small chasses, candlesticks, and even secular objects such as horse-bits, caskets and gemel-rings. Coffers mounted with a large number of plaques were also made, but few survive. Production continued throughout the 13th c. and the most imposing example in England, the enamelled effigy of William de Valence in Westminster Abbey, dates from the first decade of the 14th c. Damage caused by a fire made necessary the repair of the Klosterneuburg altar in the year 1322 and the skill with which this was done has led to the recognition of a school of enamelling in Vienna in the first half of the 14th c. to which a small number of champlevé enamelled pieces of high quality have been attributed.

While the Romanesque goldsmiths had worked with opaque enamels, their successors found the brilliance of translucent enamels better suited to match the delicate architectural structure of Gothic goldsmiths' work. Silver or, rarely, gold was used instead of copper. A further refinement was achieved by the Gothic enamellers in that they sculptured their designs in the thickness of the plaque, so that when enamelled the highest parts of the relief were pale in colour while the lower parts showed darker, thus providing graduated effects of light and shade. The technique, called *basse-taille*, probably originated in Italy towards the close of the 13th c. and the earliest examples are Italian. But in the 14th c. it quickly spread over western Europe and was freely used in the decoration of chalices, crosses, diptychs, and other objects of religious use as well as for domestic plate and jewellery. The earliest surviving example, a chalice in the Franciscan monastery at Assisi, is signed by a Sienese goldsmith and Siena remained the centre of such enamelling in Italy. Its chief monuments are the Reliquary of Orvieto Cathedral of 1338, and the great silver altars of Pistoia and Florence.

An important school of goldsmith-enamellers grew up in Paris but it is no longer generally accepted that the small enamelled plaques which are found mounted on ecclesiastical and domestic vessels made elsewhere were exported from France. The finest surviving example of French 14th-c. *basse-taille* enamelling is the Royal Gold Cup in the British Museum, probably identical with one described in the Inventory of King Charles VI's treasure of 1391. This piece is an almost solitary survivor of the numberless superb pieces of goldsmith's work referred to in 14th-c. inventories. The art of *basse-taille* enamelling spread so widely that it is impossible to separate with any certainty the productions of different schools. A group of small diptychs have been identified as English and to the same group may be added the gold triptych formerly belonging to Mary, Queen of Scots (Stonyhurst College). Enamelling of exceptionally fine quality was achieved by the 14th-c. goldsmiths of Stockholm, to whom a series of richly enamelled chalices and patens in Swedish churches are attributed. The Basle Münsterschatz contains many 14th-c. enamelled pieces and allows us to recognize Basle as another centre of the art.

On the earlier pieces the figures are reversed and only the background enamelled. Subsequently the whole surface of the plaque was enamelled with the exception of the faces of the figures, the lines of modelling of which were filled with opaque enamel. Translucent enamel is extremely fragile and very few medieval pieces survive in pristine condition. The most famous English example for instance, the so-called King

John's cup of King's Lynn Corporation, from the late 14th c., is much restored.

In the 15th c. the next technique, that of encrusted enamel (*émail en ronde bosse*), was introduced. In the Middle Ages translucent enamel could only be used on more or less flat surfaces; when applied to a small figure it flaked off. This effect did not apply to opaque colours painted on a slightly roughened surface and there exists a small group of 15th-c. gold reliquaries with numerous figures so enamelled, mostly in white and blue. Most of these are the work of Paris goldsmiths, and constitute some of the most sumptuous examples of the goldsmith's craft in existence. The type is represented in England by the Reliquary of the Holy Thorn (Waddesdon Bequest, B.M.) from the Geistliche Schatzkammer, Vienna. Every resource of the goldsmith's art was lavished on this and the similar pieces, of which the most famous is the 'Goldene Rössel' in the Pilgrimage Church of Altötting, Bavaria. This same type of encrusted enamel is also found on jewellery, and continued to be used until the 17th c.; the Burgundian betrothal jewel in the Kunsthistorisches Museum, Vienna, is the most attractive of the few surviving medieval jewels in this technique. Painted enamel proper was also introduced during the 15th c. In this technique repeated firings were necessary as the colours fused at different temperatures. The object decorated had also to be enamelled on both sides. Gold, silver or copper could be used as a ground and the process was less exacting altogether than that of translucent enamel. Painted enamels appeared about the middle of the century in Italy, France and the Netherlands. Particularly attractive were the enamelled drinking vessels produced by Netherlandish goldsmiths for the Burgundian Court (the Monkey Cup, Metropolitan Mus., New York). These, usually executed in grisaille, display a sophistication of taste typical of late Gothic art. They were the work of a few individual masters; but at Limoges an important workshop was already in existence by the third quarter of the 16th c. The early technique of these Limoges masters was not far removed from that of the translucent enamels, since over a ground enamelled brown the contours of the design were drawn in black enamel and the figures then filled in with translucent colours.

In grisaille of the kind also called *camaïeu*, instead of using a carved ground, the enamel was applied with a spatula to a flat ground on which was traced a design. In this style white enamel paste was superimposed on a ground of black or dark blue enamel paste and then the outlines of the design were carved down with the spatula to the level of the dark ground in the manner of CAMEO carving. In grisaille the whole surface was covered with a layer of enamel not subdivided into cells and it thus paved the way for true painted enamels, in which coloured designs in enamel were painted on to a smooth white enamel ground which had been previously fired on to a metal plaque. Unlike earlier techniques of enamelling this style has more affinity with the art of the miniature painter than with the goldsmith's craft. The work was generally confined to miniature portraiture and the decoration of watches, etc. The origin of painted enamels is usually attributed to Jean Toutin (1578–1644) of Blois *c.* 1630, although none of his work survives. He founded a school at Blois and enamels are known by his sons and by a pupil, Jean Pettitot. The Blois school influenced the style of Limoges, as painted decoration came increasingly to be added to the typical grisaille. It also had an important influence on the painted enamels of China. Painted enamel passed to southern Germany, where the 'Hausmaler' had developed the craft of painting enamel on pottery by 1680, and thence to Hungary, where it was practised by Bertalan Weigl, a goldsmith of Banskà Stiavnica, now in Czechoslovakia. Its greatest exponent was János Szilassy (*c.* 1715–82) of Löcse (now Levoča, Czechoslovakia).

A variant of cloisonné called FILIGREE enamel can be traced back to Venetian goldsmiths of the 13th c. From there it spread to northern Italy and thence to Spain. In this technique the design, usually of floral motifs, was worked in silver wire soldered to a silver base. The powdered enamel was put into the spaces formed by the wire and when it had contracted slightly after fusing, the outlines of the wire showed above the surface of the enamel. The method was carried to Hungary towards the end of the 14th c. and developed there in a distinctive manner for some 150 years. The characteristic features of Hungarian filigree enamel were that it was usually done on small plates which were subsequently attached to the object to be decorated and the enamel covered the whole surface of the plate, not merely the spaces within the twisted wire design. It relied in the main on flowers and foliated scroll motifs, particularly the three-petal tulip, the carnation and the pomegranate. The technique was also practised in Prague, Vienna, Poland and spread to Russia as a folk art. It was used chiefly for the decoration of goblets and chalices and in the 17th c. also for some secular objects. Examples of Hungarian filigree are the Nyitra Evangelistary (Esztergom Cath., *c.* 1370), in which the silver cover is decorated at the corners with four quadrifoliate medallions of dark blue and red filigree enamel, a reliquary bust of King Ladislav (Györ Cath., *c.* 1405), in which filigree enamel is used on the robes, the Suky chalice (Esztergom Cath., *c.* 1440) and a similar viaticum casket (Hungarian Nat. Mus., Budapest, dated 1451) and belts excavated at Calchis (B.M., early 15th c.). A chalice made for Dénes Széchy, Cardinal Archbishop of Esztergom 1440–60 (Esztergom Cath.) and the Tamás Bakócz chalice (Hungarian Nat. Mus.) have the distinctive feature that small globules of gilded silver are soldered to the filigree wire.

Transylvanian enamel, which became fairly

popular *c*. the middle of the 16th c. and which was used mainly for jewellery and secular objects, is regarded as a variant of Hungarian filigree. Its distinctive feature is the outlining of the designs by a silver frame instead of filigree wire. The details of the design were often overpainted or emphasized with dots or fine lines of a contrasting colour. An early example of the method is the head-dress made for István Báthory, King of Poland 1576–86 (Czartorisky Mus., Cracow).

See also BATTERSEA ENAMELS; CHINA (CLOISONNÉ ENAMEL; CANTON ENAMELS); GEORGIAN METALWORK.

9, 47, 100, 180, 292, 572.

ENAMELLING ON GLASS. The art of enamelling on glass consists of painting it with vitreous colours—that is metallic pigments compounded with glassy matter—which melt and adhere to the glass when fired in a 'muffle' kiln at a temperature lower than that required to melt the glass itself. Gilding is often used to supplement enamel colours, and this is fixed in a second firing.

Enamelling on glass was practised in Roman times, and was brought to a high degree of perfection in the Islamic countries of the Near East in the 13th and 14th centuries, after which it declined. It was revived, or rediscovered, at Venice in the second half of the 15th c., traditionally by a member of the Barovieri family. The earliest known example of this work—a goblet of blue glass—dates, according to a credible tradition, from 1465, and is decorated with the Flight into Egypt. Most of the earliest work is done on translucent coloured glass of dark tone (usually green, blue or manganese-purple) in rather thick opaque enamels. The decorative themes are more usually secular than religious—allegorical triumphs, homage to Venus, allegories of Love, grotesques, etc.—and are probably based on contemporary woodcut and NIELLO designs. Accompanying the figural decoration were formal borders of enamel dots, usually laid on a zone of gilding which was itself often incised with a point in a series of scalloped lines to form a scale pattern. The figural painting scarcely survived the turn of the century, but the formal designs of gilding and enamel dots continued in favour, often as a setting for armorial representations enamelled to the order of princely or noble patrons. Armorial glasses were often also made for German customers, frequently in shapes adapted to German tastes. It is often difficult to distinguish between these export glasses and those made and enamelled in Germany itself from about the middle of the 16th c. Enamelled glass began to go out of fashion in Italy during the 2nd quarter of the century, but its popularity persisted in Germany for a further 200 years.

During the 17th c. German enamelling became stereotyped within a limited range of subjects. The shape of glass most frequently decorated was the cylindrical beaker—often very large—known as *Humpen*. These beakers, usually of brownish, yellowish, or greenish glass, were painted with thick opaque enamel colours which formed a gay and unsophisticated harmony. Frequently gilding, in conjunction with dots of enamel, was used for border designs in the earlier Venetian tradition. The most favoured types included: the *Reichsadlerhumpen* (Imperial Eagle *Humpen*), on which was enamelled the imperial double-headed eagle with the figure of Christ crucified, or an orb, on its breast and the coats-of-arms of the hierarchy of the Empire displayed on its wings; and the *Kurfürstenhumpen* (Electors' *Humpen*), one variant showing the emperor sitting amidst his electors with the three spiritual lords on his right and the four temporal lords on his left, the other variant showing the eight potentates on horseback, arranged in two superimposed rows. Other subjects were provided by the Old and New Testaments, while allegorical figures such as the Eight Virtues, the Four Seasons, and the Ages of Man were much favoured. The enamelling of these glasses is the stereotyped work of artisans rather than the work of original artists, but their very naïvety as well as their gay colour schemes give them a certain charm of their own. During the 18th c. the level of technical proficiency declined and the tumblers and spirit flasks (the commonest forms) produced can only be reckoned as works of peasant art.

In marked contrast to this crude work is a class of glasses painted in Nuremberg mainly during the third quarter of the 17th c. Enamelled chiefly in black or sepia (*Schwarzlotmalerei*) with occasional use of red or, even more rarely, of other translucent enamels, these glasses derive from the work of the stained-glass craftsmen. The most notable figure, and the founder, of this Nuremberg school—Johann SCHAPER—had himself been a painter of stained glass. Most of his glasses, which were usually of the typical Nuremberg form of a small beaker on three ball-feet, are painted with delicate landscapes and architecture and a considerable amount of the detail is incised with a fine point through the black enamel to the clear glass. The majority of Schaper's dated pieces were painted in the 1660s. None of his followers—of whom J. L. Faber, Hermann Benkert (1652–81), Johann Keyll and Abraham Helmhack are the most noteworthy—equalled him in skill. Somewhat later (*c*. 1675) Johann Anton Carli of Andernach (d. 1682), painted in schwarzlot a fine goblet bearing a view of Andernach and a beautifully rendered hunting scene. Other glasses with views of Rhineland towns may perhaps be connected with Carli's work rather than with Nuremberg.

Schwarzlot painting, often heightened with touches of gold, was practised in Bohemia and Silesia at the beginning of the 18th c. and drew on the current fashionable sources of design—mainly ARABESQUES and STRAPWORK derived from engravings in the style of BÉRAIN, or CHINOISERIES, *putti*, etc., in the manner of Paul Decker. Two members of the Preissler family—Daniel (1636–1733) and his son Ignaz—are known to have done this work, but no existing pieces can be certainly attributed to either.

The importance of enamelling on clear colourless glass declined in Germany during the 18th c. but there, as in many other countries, opaque-white glass simulating PORCELAIN was painted in enamel colours to heighten the illusion. In Venice, with its long tradition of making opaque glass-metals, there was a considerable production of this imitation porcelain, two families in particular—the Miotti and the Bertolini—being engaged in its manufacture during the first half of the century. In England many centres produced it, but only one artist is known by name, Michael EDKINS. Enamelling on transparent colourless glass was also practised in both England and Venice during the second half of the 18th c. In England members of the BEILBY family decorated decanters and wineglasses with enamelling of a high artistic order, mainly in white. In Venice Osvaldo Brussa and his son Angelo, towards the end of the century, enamelled tumblers and decanters, sometimes in white and sometimes in colours, in a rather crude style.

In the early 19th c. there was in Germany a revival of interest in enamelled glass, perhaps partly as a result of the growing contemporary taste for stained glass in windows. The enamelling of this period, furthermore, exchanged the opaque enamels of the previous century for transparent colours—among them the grisaille (black or grey) and 'yellow stain' of the stained-glass artist. Amongst the best enamellers of this period were Samuel Mohn (1762–1815) of Dresden and his son Gottlob Samuel (1789–1825), who migrated to Vienna in 1811. The Mohns had a number of followers, of whom the most able was Anton Kothgasser (1769–1851). These artists specialized in views and scenes in the Romantic spirit of the period.

During the second half of the 19th c. enamelling ceased to play an important part in the decoration of glass, although the French artists Joseph Brocard, Émile GALLÉ and Eugène Rousseau (1827–91) made considerable use of it. In the 20th c. it has been revived to good effect, even if on a limited scale, in Germany and Czechoslovakia, the glass technical School at Zwiesel in Bavaria producing especially distinguished results mostly from designs by Bruno Mauder, who taught there from 1910.

409, 465.

ENGRÊLURE. Narrow edgings attached to a flounce or border in LACE or NEEDLEWORK for the purpose of strengthening, as when the lace was sewn on to a garment.

ERAGNY PRESS. A private printing press established by Lucien Pissarro in 1894 at Bedford Park, London, and transferred to Hammersmith in 1903. It was named after the Normandy village where Pissarro lived before coming to England. From 1894 to 1903 the Eragny books were printed in the 'Vale' type designed by Charles RICKETTS. After 1903 the 'Brook' type, designed by Pissarro himself, was used. Characteristic of Eragny books, many of which were issued in small format, were coloured frontispieces, woodcuts, initials and decoration designed by Pissarro and executed by himself and his wife. The press closed down in 1914. See also PRIVATE PRESS MOVEMENT.

131, 134, 277.

ESSEX HOUSE PRESS. A private printing press founded in 1898 by C. R. ASHBEE and the Guild of Handicrafts to continue the traditions of William MORRIS'S KELMSCOTT PRESS. The ink, paper and vellum were the same as those used in the Kelmscott books, though a special watermark was employed and experiments made in printing on grey paper with various colours. Ashbee employed Walter CRANE and other artists of note to illustrate his publications. In 1902 the press was transferred from Essex House, Mile End Road, to Chipping Campden, Gloucestershire. Eighty-four titles were issued before the press closed down in 1909. See also PRIVATE PRESS MOVEMENT.

131, 134, 277.

ESTIENNE, ROBERT (1503–59). The foremost learned publisher and printer of the French Renaissance working in Paris. He is remembered especially for his critical editions of the scriptures in Latin, Greek and Hebrew, and for his *Thesaurus linguae latinae*, the first scientific dictionary of classical Latin. He also printed fine and accurate editions of Greek and Latin classics. He began in 1530 to use the types of GARAMOND and was the first to add small capitals to his founts of ROMAN type. Appointed Royal Printer for Greek in 1540, he persuaded Francis I to commission Garamond to cut his beautiful Greek types. His division of the text in numbered verses in his Greek New Testament of 1551 led to the adoption of this practice in complete Bibles. Trouble with the censors about heterodox expressions in the notes and summaries ended with a ban on the sale of Estienne's Bibles in 1548 and led to his removal to Geneva in 1550, where he printed among other things works by Calvin.

Among scholars he and his learned son Henri were known by the Latin form of their name, 'Stephanus', and older English writers often refer to them as 'Stephens'.

17.

ETCHED DECORATION OF ARMOUR. The art of biting a design into metal with acid was known in the 13th c., but the earliest extant piece of armour decorated in this way is a late 15th-c. Italian breastplate in the Imperial

Armoury, Vienna, said to have belonged to Bartolommeo Colleoni (1399–1475). The decoration is executed in a light, free line against a closely hatched ground, characteristic of Italian etching down to *c.* 1530. After this date the line tends to become harder and the etching deeper, finally degenerating at the end of the century into the so-called 'Pisan' style, characterised by an excess of confused and meaningless ornament.

In Germany etched armour appears at the beginning of the 16th c., a link with etched prints on paper being provided by the Augsburg artist Daniel Hopfer. The style is different from the Italian, being deeper and more precise, while the background usually consists of raised dots. As in Italy there was a general degeneration in quality at the end of the 16th c.

At all times the etching was usually gilded or brought into relief by blackening the background.

ETRURIA. .Mention of Etrurian crafts will be found in the articles on GREEK AND ROMAN ANTIQUITY.

ETRUSCAN TASTE. A fashion in interior decoration and furnishing which formed part of the 18th-c. Classical Revival (see NEO-CLASSICISM), stimulated by excavations at Pompeii, Herculaneum and Paestum between 1738 and 1756 and popularized by such illustrated works as *Recueil d'antiquités égyptiennes, étrusques, grecques, romaines et gauloises* by the antiquarian Comte Claude-Philippe de Caylus (1692–1765). From *c.* 1780 furniture painted in the 'Etruscan' style became increasingly popular in England. The style is particularly associated with the name of Robert ADAM, who designed painted furniture for an Etruscan Room at Osterley Park and for Derby House and Cumberland House. The main feature of the style was the use of contrasting colours of black, white and terracotta, based on murals and vase paintings found at Pompeii, at Herculaneum and in Rome. These were believed to date from *c.* the 9th c. B.C. and to belong to the Etruscans, who were thought of as forerunners of the Romans: they are now known to be provincial Greek or Roman. An 'Etruscan' dinner service made at the Royal Neapolitan Porcelain Factory, 1785–7, contains plates painted with different antique vases and other vessels modelled on ancient pottery and silverware.

In France the Etruscan taste was fashionable in the late Louis XVI and DIRECTOIRE periods. In 1787 Georges JACOB, the leading cabinet-maker of the day, made a chair for the Queen's dairy at Rambouillet claimed to be designed in the Etruscan manner *(du genre étrusque)* by the painter Hubert Robert (1733–1808). Interest in the antique maintained itself under the Directoire and was fostered by the architects Charles PERCIER and Pierre-François-Léonard Fontaine, who had studied the originals in Italy. The interior designs of J.-D. Dugourc in a Neo-Pompeian manner attracted the attention of wealthy patrons and the Jacob brothers were among many makers who produced furniture in a so-called Etruscan style.

In England the 'Etruscan taste' was one of the elements which was taken up into the eclectic fashion of 19th-c. REGENCY.

160, 305, 618, 686.

EVE, NICOLAS and CLOVIS. French BOOKBINDERS and publishers, who successively held the post of Royal Binder between 1578 and 1634, Clovis probably being Nicolas's son or nephew. Nicolas executed for Henry III a series of bindings covering the Statutes of the Order of the Holy Spirit, decorated with the royal arms and with corner-pieces containing a dove, device of the Order, cut by Philippe Damphrie, engraver to the Royal Mint, upon a field sprinkled with FLEUR-DE-LIS. A similar pattern, often of crowned H's or L's instead of fleurs-de-lis, was adopted by Clovis Eve on bindings made for Henry IV and Louis XIII. Although the Eves are often credited with FANFARE bindings, which became fashionable in their day, it is doubtful whether they invented them or even did much work in this style. See BOOKBINDING.

594.

EX LIBRIS. See BOOK-PLATES.

F

FABERGÉ. The firm of Fabergé, jewellers and goldsmiths of St. Petersburg, was first established in 1842, but did not begin to achieve an international reputation until Peter Carl Fabergé took over control in 1870. Under his business management the firm, in which several other members of the family were employed, soon became the most fashionable house for jewellery in Europe, a position which was maintained until the outbreak of the First World War. The firm specialized in useful objects such as cigarette cases, bell-pushes, etc., which were produced in a style derived from Parisian 18th-c. goldsmiths' work. A very high level of craftsmanship was achieved; the most original productions were miniature figures of animals and peasant types carved in hardstone, but on the whole the Fabergé creations were artistically sterile.

41, 723.

FACIO DE DUILLIER, NICOLAS (1664–1753). Swiss watchmaker from Basle, who spent almost all his working life in England. He was the first to use pierced jewels as bearings for watches. The hardness of the jewels greatly reduces friction with a consequent improvement in the performance of the watch.

154, 458.

FAÇON D'ALTARE. See L'ALTARE.

FAÇON DE VENISE. A European style of glass which emerged largely under the influence of emigrant craftsmen from Venice. See GLASS (VENICE).

FAIENCE. See CERAMICS.

FAMILLE VERTE. FAMILLE ROSE. Names for successive types of tin-glaze enamel decoration of Chinese PORCELAIN of the Ch'ing period. Both types had considerable influence on European ceramics manufacture. In *famille verte* a translucent green enamel is supported by strong yellow, purplish blue and brick red. The colours of *famille rose* are softer, more varied and often mixed with white. They are dominated by a delicate opaque rose-pink, a colour also used on Chinese ENAMELS and enamels of European origin. See CHINA (CERAMICS) and CERAMICS.

FANFARE BINDINGS. A decorative style of BOOKBINDING adopted by Parisian binders in the late 16th and early 17th centuries, doubtfully associated with Nicolas and Clovis EVE, royal binders between 1578 and 1634. The STRAPWORK ornament used on GROLIER and MAIOLI BINDINGS was reduced to a geometrical pattern of interlacing ribbons often forming oval and circular compartments based on the figure 8. The blank spaces were then decorated with naturalistic olive, bay or laurel sprays and a profusion of small toolings such as winged volutes, FLEURONS, and coils of ARABESQUES of a type already common in other applied arts. The epithet 'fanfare' dates from 1829, when the French Restoration binder Thouvenin revived the style on a binding made by him for a book entitled *Fanfares et Corvées abbadesques des Roule-Bontemps* (1613), belonging to the bibliophile Charles Nodier.

394.

FARTHINGALE, BUSTLE, CRINOLINE. The costume of the ancient Greeks (see GREEK AND ROMAN ANTIQUITY) and to some extent also that of INDIA was *draped* and was designed to display with elegance the natural conformations of the body in movement and in rest. Very commonly, however, both primitive and sophisticated costume has had as its object to emphasize or conceal, to modify or to distort, certain features of the human form. One thinks of course immediately of those features which are regarded as evidential of masculine prowess or feminine attractiveness; but such vagaries as artificially heightened footwear, phantastic hair-styles and concealing uniforms of all kinds come into the general category. Of all the distorting parodies of the human frame none has been stranger than the European and American fashion which started with the farthingale and carried through to the crinoline.

The farthingale, also written 'vardingale' and 'verdingale', first appeared in France during the reign of Henry II and in England in the reign of Edward VI. At first it consisted of a kind of padded bolster worn round the hips beneath the skirt. By the end of the 16th c. it had become a framework of whale-bone hoops extending the skirt round the hips so that the wearer seemed to be standing within a kind of cartwheel. Thus began the mode of the 'hoop' or hooped petticoat. Stiff and ungainly as it was, the hoop did serve to relieve the heavy weight of the skirts, which would otherwise have depended from the waist. The hooped farthingale went out of fashion in England in the reign of Charles I. But it persisted on the Continent and it was reintroduced to England by Catherine of Braganza from Spain in the reign of Charles II.

During the reign of Queen Anne it was constantly ridiculed, among others by Addison in *The Spectator*. The fashion came to America *c.* the beginning of the 18th c. and despite condemnation by the moralists—in 1722 the *New England Courant* sold a pamphlet entitled *Hoop-Pettycoats Arraigned and Condemned by the Light of Nature and Laws of God*—hoops continued in vogue. Hooped and quilted petticoats were imported and petticoats consigned from England had to be ample enough to accommodate hoops of whalebone or cane. The sizes and shapes of hoops varied regionally and from decade to decade. In 1748 the *Boston Independent Advertiser* carried an advertisement for 'Fine Newest Fashion Hoop Petticoats from 3 yards to 5 yards made with fine Long Bone'. In the 1720s dome-shaped 'bell hoops', very large at the base, were worn. During the 1750s, 'fly hoops' and the pyramidal 'fan hoops' came in, while during the second half of the century the cumbersome 'pocket hoop' was worn with pannier-like humps extending anything up to half a metre horizontally from each hip so that from the side the hips looked comparatively slender but when seen from the front they appeared enormous. In England the hoop went out of fashion except for Court dress *c.* 1780 and it was banished from Court dress by George IV in 1820. In France the Classical mode banished hoops from the court of Josephine but the respite was no more than temporary.

The bustle, a pad or wire framework worn under the skirt to make it stand out behind, was in vogue during the 1st decade of the 18th c. and again from the middle 1770s until the end of the century. From the middle 1780s the skirt was trained supported over a bustle behind. During the first decades of the 19th c. skirts continued to become more voluminous and the bustle took the form of a protuberant cushion or a tier of stiff frills. From *c.* 1815 bustles in the form of large rolls stuffed with horse-hair (French, *crin*) and tied as high as possible under the back of the skirt gave rise to the fashionable 'Grecian bend'. In 1830 Mary Russell Mitford wrote in *Our Village*: 'A waist like a wasp, a magnificent bustle.' By the middle of the century the dome-like appearance of skirts made to extend over ever larger bustles was enhanced by petticoats stiffened with crinoline, a material made from horse-hair and wool.

The crinoline itself, which appeared in the 1850s, was an enormous cage of cane and metal and whalebone and became so cumbersome that a lady could not sit down without adjusting it on supports and special furniture was made to accommodate its wearer. Despite satire and ridicule the fashion spread to all ranks of society; crinolines were worn by servants and working girls and even by children. In the middle 1860s it became somewhat lower in the front but even larger behind and it was not until the end of the 1860s that the fashion showed signs of disappearing. In 1869 a newspaper report of Paris fashions ran: 'A few weeks ago ladies who could afford to wear nine or ten flounced muslin petticoats discontinued their crinolines; of course this made but very slight difference in the circumference either at the bottom or top of the skirt, as all these petticoats were so gored as to be quite plain on the hips. The weather is so warm that so great a weight of skirts would be unbearable; therefore, at the present moment, under thin dresses, one thick petticoat and two thin ones are worn over a small crinoline, under thick skirts two petticoats, the one next the cage being always white. There are two forms of crinoline worn—one round and rather short for out-of-door dresses when looped up; the other rather larger and with a train, for indoor dress or when the skirt is allowed to rest on the ground.' (Quoted by James Laver in *Clothes*, 1952.) When the crinoline went out in the 1870s the spare material at the back of women's dresses was gathered up and bunched into the characteristic bustle of that period.

See also COSTUME.

85, 93, 96, 111, 178, 224.

FASHION PLATES. Women's magazines have carried fashion plates from the last quarter of the 18th c. These were engraved and often hand-coloured. They have considerable historical interest as illustrating the evolution of COSTUME. They have also been valued by collectors both for their artistic merit and for rarity.

Perhaps the earliest magazine with costume plates was the *Gallerie des Modes et des Costumes Français* (1778–87). Other early French magazines were: *Magazin des Modes Nouvelles, Françaises et Anglaises* (commenced 1786); *Le Beau Monde* (1806); *Le Petit Courrier des Dames* (1822–68), which merged in 1868 with *Le Journal des Demoiselles* (commenced 1833); *Le Follet Courrier des Salons* (1829–99), which also sold in England; *La Mode* (1829–32); *Journal des Dames* (commenced 1834); *Les Modes Parisiennes* (1843–75); *Le Moniteur de la Mode* (1843–92); *Le Magazin des Demoiselles* (1844–93); *La Mode Illustrée* (commenced 1869); *La Revue de la Mode* (1872–88).

In England *The Ladies' Magazine* (1770–1828) had fashion plates. The earliest journal devoted to fashion was *The Gallery of Fashion* (1794–1803) with plates by van Heideloff. Other 19th-c. magazines of fashion with plates were: *La Belle Assemblée* (1806–69), which had plates either in colour or at a lower price in black and white; *Townsend's Selection of Parisian Costumes* (1823–88); *The World of Fashion* (1824–38); *The Ladies' Cabinet* (1832–70); *The Ladies' Gazette of Fashion* (1842–94); *The Englishwoman's Domestic Magazine* (1852–77); *Myra's Journal of Dress and Fashion* (1875–93); *The Queen* (1861–). The fashion plates for these magazines were often imported from France.

In America the main 19th-c. fashion journals

were: *Godey's Ladies' Book* (Philadelphia, 1830–98); *Graham's American Monthly Magazine of Literature, Art and Fashion* (1824–58).

Prominent among the artists who designed fashion plates are: David JULES; Nicolaus van HEIDELOFF; Anaïs TOUDOUZE; and the caricaturist Garvani (Sulpice Paul Chevalier, 1804–66), who designed plates for *La Mode*.

364, 404, 504.

FEATHER PATTERN. See HERRING-BONE.

FEDERAL STYLE. Term used to denote the transitional phase of the Classical Revival in the U.S.A. between *c.* 1790 and *c.* 1820. Based on the work of Robert and James ADAM, it reached America primarily through their publications and those of James Paine (*c.* 1716–89), the two volumes of whose *Plans, Elevations and Sections of Noblemen's and Gentlemen's Houses* were published in 1767 and 1783. The architectural style is characterized by slender proportions, flat surfaces, thin mouldings and small but delicate ornament. Notable features are the elliptical fanlight and the free-standing colossal portico. Walls were generally of brick, with their flatness emphasized by crisply defined openings. Windows were frequently framed by shallow wall arches. In the interiors the graceful elliptical rooms and circular flying staircases reflect the curvilinear quality of the decorative features. The purest examples of the style are found in the work of the New England architects Charles Bulfinch (1763–1844) and Samuel McIntire (1757–1811).

In furniture it corresponded initially with the work of designers such as HEPPLEWHITE, Thomas Shearer and SHERATON combined with French influences from the early years of the 19th c. But far from being derivative, it developed into an identifiable national style which, with the growing influence of French DIRECTOIRE taste from the 1820s, merged into the American Empire style. The Federal style was evolved by American cabinet-makers of Baltimore, Boston, Salem, Philadelphia and New York.

See FURNITURE (AMERICAN).

645.

FELLETIN TAPESTRIES. Felletin, a centre of tapestry weaving since the Middle Ages, received the title of Royal Manufactory in 1727. Its 18th-c. tapestries may be distinguished from those of the neighbouring town of AUBUSSON by their rather coarser quality and by the presence of a brown selvedge with the mark M.R.D.F. (Manufacture royale de Felletin). In recent years it has been associated with Aubusson in weaving many cartoons by the modern school of tapestry designers.

FESTOON. Ornament representing a garland of fruit or flowers suspended from both ends in

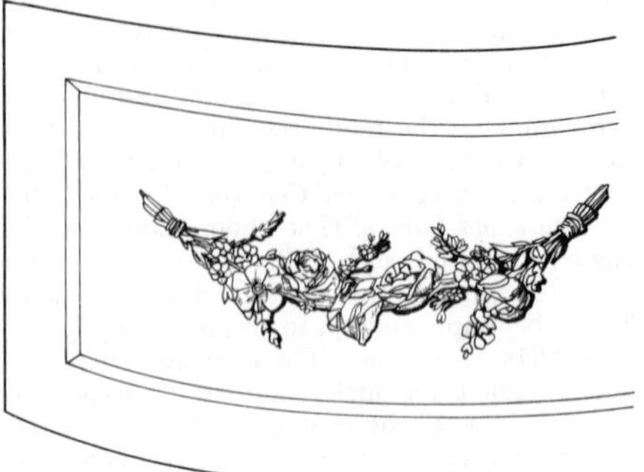

a loop and hanging in a curve. Common architectural term from the early 17th c. A common ornament on plate in the 16th c. and during the NEO-CLASSICAL revival. Also called 'swag'.

FIELD, JOHN (1771–1841). English silhouettist and painter in water-colour. He was trained by John MIERS and was taken into partnership by him some time after setting up business in London. After the death of John Miers Field carried on the business in partnership with his son, William Miers, until 1830. In 1831 he was appointed Profilist to Queen Adelaide and H.R.H. the Princess Augusta. From 1800 to 1836 he exhibited at the Royal Academy monochrome landscapes painted on plaster. Field's work was proficient and meticulous. He was a pioneer in the style of 'bronzing' and in emphasizing the highlights with touches of gold. His superb craftsmanship is evidenced in his miniature work on ivory for rings and jewellery. He is also known, however, to have done some larger scenic pieces.

374, 533, 926.

FILIGREE (from Latin *filum* 'thread' and *granum* 'grain'). Ornamental work of fine wire, twisted and plaited and soldered into a design. The wire is usually gold or silver, but in late Roman times bronze was also used. There were then two techniques, used mainly for JEWELLERY: in the one the wire was soldered on to a backing of sheet metal, and in the other, practised especially in the Christian East, the design was openwork, unsupported. Filigree on a solid backing remained popular in the Dark Ages and in Anglo-Saxon jewellery of the 7th and 8th centuries (e.g. the SUTTON HOO treasure) it achieved an astonishing delicacy. Carolingian and Ottonian metal-workers first exploited its full decorative possibilities, not only in jewellery but on BOOK COVERS and reliquaries and other ecclesiastical objects, combining with the filigree precious stones, CAMEOS, INTAGLIOS, IVORIES and enamels. In the 13th c. it continued to be produced in Germany and Italy, where the wire used was thicker and the scrolls larger and tighter. Filigree retained its abstract character throughout the early Middle Ages, but in France *c.* 1200–30 HUGO D'OIGNIES and his circle began to enrich it with naturalistic shapes such as vine-leaves in punched sheet metal, and this practice led to an elaboration of ornament which cannot be called filigree.

Another type of filigree work is believed to have originated in Venice in the 13th or 14th c., whence it spread westwards across northern Italy as far as Spain and northwards to Hungary and eastern Europe. In this technique the filigree was enriched with enamel, the twisted silver wire being soldered to a sheet-silver base to form cloisons for the application of polychrome enamel. The Italian goldsmiths used this form of decoration sparingly, as on a famous reliquary of the Santa Croce in the cathedral of Padua. In Italy this technique did not survive the Renaissance, but in eastern Europe it has been practised in a degenerate form until almost modern times. See also ENAMEL.

Possibly connected with the Hungarian school of filigree, possibly an independent development, was the south German filigree of the 17th c. Caskets, small boxes, cases for toilet implements, etc., were produced. The process of manufacture differed in that the cloisons were composed, not of twisted silver wire, but of flat strip which was bent and soldered together to form panels of geometrical or foliate design. Only a few of the cloisons were enamelled; the remainder were left blank, showing the silver ground below. The caskets, etc., in this technique are all very similar and were probably produced in one workshop, believed to have been in the city of Nuremberg.

While in the early Middle Ages filigree had been used to enrich vessels or reliquaries of exceptional splendour, in the post-medieval period it was definitely a product of the lower end of the goldsmiths' trade. During the 16th c. large caskets and dishes, painfully built up from innumerable pieces of wire, were thought worthy of inclusion in the typical princely *Kunstkammer*. But the art of filigree soon declined, surviving as little more than a peasant craft for jewel caskets, bookbindings, cases for toilet implements, buttons and cheap jewellery. Trivial objects of this nature were made all over Europe and it is practically impossible to identify their source. The craft still lingers on as an appendage of the tourist trade in Tuscany and in Norway.

FILLET. Term in architecture and decorative art for a narrow flat raised band separating two MOULDINGS or running down a shaft or along an

arch or between the FLUTES of a column. It is also a term for the top member of a CORNICE, otherwise called 'listel'. In BOOKBINDING it is a plain line impressed on the cover of a book.

FILOSELLE. See EMBROIDERY (TECHNIQUES AND MATERIALS).

FINIAL. Term in architecture and the decorative arts for an ornament, such as a foliated FLEUR-DE-LIS, placed upon a roof, pediment or gable or in the four corners of a tower. In cabinet-making it is an ornament such as a vase with drapery placed at the intersection of stretchers, on cabinets, fire-screens, the back uprights of chairs, pew ends, etc. They sometimes consist of a knob, called a *pommel*, sometimes of clustered foliage, flowers or fruit or even of a human or animal figure.

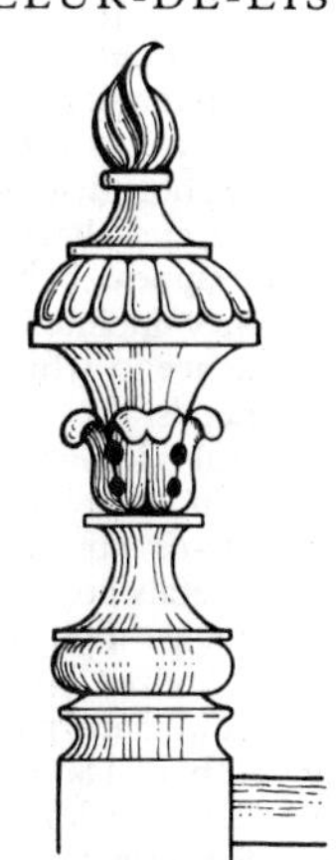

FIRE-BACK. The rectangular panel of cast-iron set vertically at the back of the hearth to protect the brickwork from heat. From the 15th to the 17th c. fire-backs constituted one of the main productions of the Sussex ironmasters. The most effective designs were heraldic, the royal arms being particularly favoured; their presence does not indicate that a fire-back was made for a royal residence. Outside England fire-backs were produced in Flanders, France and Germany, but were less important than the iron stove-plates which were cast from finely carved wood models. See IRON AND STEEL (CAST IRON).

FIRE-DOGS (ANDIRONS). Metal brackets used in pairs to support logs burning in the hearth. During the Middle Ages they were usually of wrought or cast IRON, but few have survived. In the 16th c. more imposing examples were made: in England and Flanders of cast brass (examples at Knole, Kent); in Italy of wrought iron, and towards the end of the century of bronze. Some of the last, of baluster form surmounted by a human figure, rank high amongst Renaissance bronzes. Early fire-dogs are often very tall, the front part reaching half-way up to the mantelpiece. Brass or iron with brass knobs were the usual materials, though the Sussex ironfounders cast them in iron. Later in the 17th c. fire-dogs were made lower but more magnificent, the finest being of embossed silver surmounted by a flaming urn. Small pairs of fire-dogs, known as 'creepers', were placed between the large ones to support shorter logs. During the 18th c. fire-dogs were replaced by the less ornamental grate in which coal could be burnt.

FLASH. See HORSE-BRASSES.

FLEUR-DE-LIS (French, lily flower). A stylized emblem widely used both as a heraldic device and in ornament. (The naturalistic lily is not called *fleur-de-lis* in heraldry but *lis de jardin*.) The device consists of three formalized petals, the centre one standing upright and those on the left and right side of it inclined away from it. The petals are bound by a band a short distance above the bottom and their lower extremities appear below the band, similarly inclined. A form of the device in which the feet of the petals are replaced by a pedestal is known as *fleur-de-lis coupé* and there are other variations, such as the *fleur-de-lis florencé* in which the heads of the three petals are divided like flowers.

A device of this sort, whether or not originating as the stylization of petals of a flower, is widespread in many parts of the world. The *fleur-de-lis* proper has acquired great importance in Western heraldry and ornament owing to its association with the French royal arms.

FLEURON. A flower-shaped ornament. The motif is used in architecture, furniture, metalwork, printing, on coins, etc.

FLINT TOOLS. The ability to fashion tools to a set and regular pattern distinguishes man from other social animals. A hunter and gatherer for at least two million years, it is only in archaeologically recent time, during the past few thousand years, that man has lived in permanent settlements using a technology based on raw materials other than stone. The importance of stone is perhaps over-emphasized in the archaeological record as less durable materials such as bone, horn or wood are rarely preserved. Nevertheless the ability to fashion stone tools by flaking or chipping is the seed from which all modern technology has developed.

Early man used a wide range of stones from which to fashion his tools. Flint, obsidian, CHALCEDONY, chert and other fine-grained rocks with a conchoidal fracture were preferred, but coarse-grained and intractable rocks such as quartzite and other crystalline igneous forms were also used.

To produce tools to a set and regular pattern care must be taken to control the technique of flaking. The earliest recognizable technique is that of direct percussion, in which a hammer stone is used to remove *flakes* from a *core*. Either the core or the resultant flakes may be used as tools. A refinement of the direct percussion technique is the use of a soft rather than a hard hammer, for example one of bone rather than stone, which enables flatter, thinner flakes to be removed and thus a straighter cutting edge to be produced on the core tool. Flakes can also be removed from the core by the anvil technique, in which the core itself is struck against a large stone or anvil. This method is used for the production of flake tools and the resultant core is a waste product. A major technological innovation was the development of indirect percussion techniques, in which an intermediate punch is placed between the hammer and the core that is being worked. The punch makes possible greater precision of flaking and concentrates the force of the hammer blow at a particular point, thus enabling long thin flakes or *blades* to be consistently produced. A development of the indirect percussion technique is that of pressure flaking, whereby a punch of pencil-like proportions is used to push very fine and thin blades or flakes from the core tool without the use of a hammer.

Present evidence points to eastern Africa as the area where tool-making first developed. The earliest indisputable artefacts occur on occupation sites at Olduvai Gorge in Tanzania. Intimately associated with hominid remains are both core and flake tools typified by the *Oldowan* choppers, unmodified flakes and polyhedral cores. Oldowan tools also occur at Koobi Fora in Kenya and at Ain Hanech in Morocco. Somewhat more recent are the Oldowan tools from Vallonet in southern France.

The rich series of sites at Olduvai Gorge provide a stratified sequence of industries from the Oldowan complex to the *Acheulean*, which contains carefully prepared bifacial *hand-axes* and formalized flake tools. Acheulean industries are widespread in Africa, Europe and south-west Asia. In both Oldowan and the early Acheulean assemblages the core tools are as important as the flake tools, but as the Acheulean develops the flake tools become increasingly important and dominate in the succeeding *prepared core* industries. The diagnostic feature of these industries is the careful preparation of the shape of the flake or flakes prior to removal from the core. The resultant *disc* cores and *Levallois* cores are waste products, the detached flakes being used as tools with or without secondary working.

Prepared core industries are widespread in Africa, Europe and Asia and give the first clear indication of regional specialization in the archaeological record.

Regional specialization becomes very marked amongst the supervening *blade industries*, which contain highly specialized tool types of limited distribution and in the later phases become *microlithic* in character. Microlithic industries in western Europe were contemporary with the earliest farming communities; in parts of Africa and in Australia they continued in widespread use until the Christian era. Despite the rapid progress of technology during the past 100 years the craft of flaking stone still continues in places as far apart as Turkey, Ethiopia, southern Africa, the Far East and eastern England, where at BRANDON in Suffolk an active trade producing gun flints for export still flourishes. The antiquity of the Brandon industry is not in doubt but it remains to be shown that the modern workshops are a direct and uninterrupted continuation of a prehistoric tradition. It is likely that the other survivals are directly descended from prehistoric antecedents. See also PREHISTORIC TECHNOLOGY.

266, 396, 769, 774.

FLOSS SILK (also called BLAZE). A low-grade SILK from the outer part of the cocoon or serving as a scaffold to support the cocoon. The term is also used for soft silk yarn without twist, used for EMBROIDERY and for electrical insulation.

FLUTING. Term in classical architecture for vertical channels of rounded section cut for decorative effect in the shafts of columns or pilasters. In metalwork such channels are often

embossed on plate. In cabinet-making they were in use from the 16th c. but are particularly characteristic of the last quarter of the 18th c., when they were succeeded by REEDING.

FLUX. Term in CERAMICS for alkaline substances present in CLAY and necessary to bring about fusing and vitrification. The term is also used for substances which are added to clays or GLAZES in order to bring about fusion at lower temperatures. See also POTTERY TECHNIQUES.

FLY TERRET (also called SWINGER). See HORSE-BRASSES.

FOIL. Term in architecture for the lobe or leaf-shaped form between the cusps of a window or

arch. The compounds trefoil, quatrefoil, cinquefoil, multifoil, however, denote ornamental patterns in architecture and the decorative arts with their outlines so divided by cusps as to give them the appearance of radiating leaflets or petals. The term is also used for a thin sheet of metal placed under a precious stone to increase its brilliancy or under some other substance to give it the appearance of a precious stone. See JEWELLERY.

FOLIATE AND STRAPWORK. See LAUB- UND BANDELWERK.

FONDO D'ORO. A technique of decorative GLASS in which a design in gold was enclosed between two layers of clear glass. See BYZANTIUM (GLASS). See also ZWISCHENGOLDGLAS.

FONTAINE, PIERRE-FRANÇOIS LÉONARD. See PERCIER.

FORE-EDGE PAINTING. The practice of painting a design on the front or outer edge and occasionally the top edge of a book. 'The edge is fanned out and tied between boards, and whilst in that position some landscape or other scene, either taken from the book or appropriate to the subject of it, is painted on the fore-edge, and when quite dry it is gilt on the flat in the usual manner. The colours used must be more of a stain than a body colour, and the edges should be scraped first.' (J. W. Zaehnsdorf, *Art of Bookbinding*, 1890.) Fore-edge painting can only be done successfully when the paper is thin and of good quality. Very little, if any, of the design can be seen beneath the GILDING while the book is closed. See BOOKBINDING.

FORKS. See CUTLERY.

FOURNIER. French family of printers and type-founders. The most important in the history of TYPOGRAPHY is PIERRE-SIMON (1712–68) called *le Jeune* to distinguish him from his elder brother JEAN-PIERRE. After working under his brother at the Le Bé type-foundry, he set up his own type-foundry in Paris in 1736 and in 1737 published a 'Table of type sizes', which was the first attempt to codify and standardize type measurements. His specimen book *Modèles des Caractères de l'Imprimerie* (1742) influenced BODONI. He is chiefly known, however, for his introduction of the ROCOCO style of ornament into typography, converting the then fashionable engraved decorations into letterpress material. Before his death he printed two volumes of his *Manuel typographique*.

FRAKTUR. So-called GOTHIC black-letter type face which developed from the black-letter script used for liturgical manuscripts and called *textura*. These Gothic type faces were replaced by the ROMAN except in Germany, where they remained in use well into the 20th c. See TYPOGRAPHY.

FRAMES. Any painting, drawing or print is visualized by the artist as having limits of height and width; these are in part governed by the medium on which it is executed and in part by the artist's own conception. A large fresco is contained by the architectural features of the wall or ceiling on which it is painted, just as a miniature is restricted by the available area of a piece of ivory. An applied frame assists both artist and onlooker by helping to focus the eye, while at the same time it can enhance and protect the work. The following brief remarks are necessarily little more than generalizations in view of the individual relationship between each picture and its frame. Much depends on the taste of the owner and on the taste, skill and experience of the craftsman, so that each task of framing demands to be treated on its merits.

1. OIL-PAINTINGS. While picture frames were known in ancient times, their usage at the present day dates from the Renaissance. Some surviving Italian religious paintings retain their original framings, which take the form of small-scale reproductions of the buildings for which the works were intended. In some instances the frame with its complex pattern of woodwork tends to overshadow the painting or paintings it surrounds. The panels of many predellas are, for example, semi-hidden in a profusion of lancet-shaped mouldings, crockets and pendent tracery all glittering with burnished gold-leaf. Alternatively the panel on which a picture was painted might sometimes be made in one with a simple moulded edge forming a rim about it, so that it was little different in appearance from a removable frame. Other paintings were given frames composed of narrow carved and gilt mouldings divided by a band of carved gesso or painted decoration.

The 16th c. saw the making of small-sized frames for table-MIRRORS, which were sometimes of rare and costly materials. Carved wood and cast metal were also employed for the same purpose. It was in the succeeding century that artists, who had previously worked mainly for the Church, began to look increasingly to the domestic interior and the home. As the demand for painting became universal, styles in framing followed the changing fashions of taste and in each country the design of picture frames fluctuated together with the styles of interior decoration and other furnishings. In addition the collecting of paintings old and new stimulated the interest in framing. Charles I was prominent among English collectors, the early death in 1612 of his elder brother, Prince Henry, making him heir to the nucleus of a collection to which he added with discernment. A painter named Richard Greenbury was allowed payment in 1630–1 'for carving and painting one great frame for the Souldier at length by Titian'. The same man was also responsible for similar work in connection with other pictures which he had executed himself or commissioned from others on behalf of the Queen, Henrietta Maria. About the same time commenced the long popularity of frames veneered with ebony finished in wave-like mouldings. They were backed with oak or softwood and sometimes the black wood was relieved with panels of brown or restained TORTOISESHELL. Frames of these types were revived, especially for the display of Netherlandish cabinet pictures, during the 19th c., when the ebony was often replaced by cheap JAPANNED finishes. These cabinet pictures were often framed in carved and gilt frames at the time they were painted, and they are not infrequently depicted in such frames in the backgrounds of interiors by artists such as de Hoogh and Vermeer. The decoration of the frames embodied the auricular patterns popularized by members of the van VIANEN family of silversmiths, whose work influenced design in many media not only in their native Holland but further afield.

By the second half of the 17th c., at any rate in England, standard patterns for fabricating in required sizes were available. Evidence of this is forthcoming from Samuel Pepys, who spent a busy day going from craftsman to craftsman on 30 April 1669 and noted: 'Thence to the frame-maker's, one Norris, in Long Acre, who showed me several forms of frames, which were pretty, in little bits of mouldings, to choose patterns by.' In contrast to these ready-made designs there was the highly individual work of Grinling GIBBONS, whose agile chisel was exercised on wood picture frames as well as architectural ornaments. More frames are attributed to him than he is likely to have made, although he lived to the age of 72. Some of the frames by Gibbons and his imitators, as well as other frames of about the same date, may have been intended at the time for mirror-glass, and it is seldom possible to be certain of their original use.

A proportion of the frames made from *c.* 1680 onwards were oval to conform with a fashion for canvasses of that form. As a compromise, probably in order to save paying the higher cost otherwise involved, a portrait was sometimes executed within a painted or 'feigned' oval on a conventional rectangular canvas for framing in the latter shape. Successive styles of design were followed during the course of the 18th c., the earlier straight-sided mouldings being elaborated to embrace shaped corners and centre ornaments at the top and bottom. These additions meant that each frame had to be individually carved, as shaped pieces precluded manufacture in ready-made lengths. As earlier it was not uncommon to surmount the frame holding a royal portrait by a crown, so it later became fashionable to place carved military and other trophies over appropriate subjects.

Both Thomas CHIPPENDALE and Thomas JOHNSON published designs for frames in the ROCOCO style, and there are records of numerous examples supplied by the former. These two men, and others, also designed chimney-pieces with integral overmantel picture frames. A drawing of one by John LINNELL is in the Victoria and Albert Museum, while the marble chimney-piece and gilt wood overmantel executed from it, which incorporates both mirror-glass and a picture, is at Osterley Park, Middlesex. Frame-making was a specialist activity and only the larger cabinet-makers included it in their ordinary business. Most of them sub-contracted orders to one of the numerous carvers and gilders who did only that work. They included such men as Richard Fletcher, with premises at The Golden Head, Watling Street, London, *c.* 1770, who not only announced that he made and sold plain and gilt frames but added 'pictures carefully Clean'd, & broken Paintings Mended'. At about the same date in America, Garrat Noel, next door to the Merchants' Coffee House, New York, proudly offered for sale 'a Great Variety of the most elegant Pictures, framed and glazed in America, which in Neatness of Workmanship, equal any imported from England, and will be Sold at a much lower Price'.

The ensuing NEO-CLASSICAL style saw changes in the design of frames as well as in materials used for their making. ADAM's favourite garlands of husks, for example, were too fragile in carved wood, so it was more usual to mould them from a composition backed by wire. Gradually composition or plaster began to oust carving, for it was considerably quicker and cheaper to model or press-mould a putty-like material than to carve wood with a chisel. PAPIER MÂCHÉ was also sometimes employed in the same manner.

In the early 19th c. the plain rectangular lines of a century before were again in fashion. The deeply moulded curves were occupied at the edges by ribbons and ACANTHUS leaves, either carved or more often made from composition. Use of the latter steadily increased despite the fact that although it remains deceptive for a long time, it eventually develops cracks that betray it. Confirmation of its employment can be easily determined by the ease with which it bends the end of a pin. A further revival of about the same period was the oval, a shape favoured by Sir Thomas Lawrence and some of his contemporaries. In this instance the shaped rectangular frame was given integral inner corners, or spandrels, so that the finished article had a conventional squarish outline but a curved opening. The reign of Queen Victoria saw numerous styles come and go, but almost all were based on those of the previous century with composition substituted for hand-carving. There were, however, attempts to break away from the past. James McNeill Whistler designed and decorated frames suited to his paintings, and some of his French contemporaries did the same.

In the 20th c. many experiments have been made to accommodate picture to frame and frame to room. Some artists, among them notably John Singer Sargent, placed their work in antique frames. These were often re-gilded, painted or stripped to the bare wood and left in a worn or 'distressed' state, thus dramatically contrasting old and new. Others used only a very narrow plain moulding to mark the outer confines of their canvasses, and these and similar innovations continue to be tried. Possibly the most effective change of recent decades has been the removal of the protective sheet of glass which was once considered indispensable for any canvas on public display, and during the 19th c. often within the home. The use of glass necessitated the incorporation between glass and picture of a shallow moulding ('slip', 'mount' or 'insert') to prevent the two surfaces from coming into contact, and sometimes to provide a link in colour and texture.

2. WATER-COLOURS AND DRAWINGS. The comparatively delicate appearance of the majority of water-colours and drawings has demanded a different treatment as regards framing from the generally more robust painting in oils. In most instances the frame is both simple and narrow, often gilt, and the subject is bordered by a mount (in the U.S.A. called 'mat') to complement or contrast with it. Glazing is indispensable for protection from dirt in the atmosphere or from casual handling. For some decades around 1900 it was common for the mount to be of gilded card, but this fashion has been abandoned in favour of a reversion to the earlier custom of using a slightly tinted or white card. On this the opening is bordered by hand-drawn lines in ink or pencil with intervening narrow bands of pale colour: the so-called 'wash mount'. The opening within which the painting is displayed is often cut with a bevel, and occasionally is of thick card similarly angled and completely covered in paper. The latter may be tinted and formed with rough or smooth surface according to circumstances.

3. PRINTS. For the same reasons both black and white and coloured prints of all periods require special treatment for display. In the 18th c. the ebonized pearwood frame with a narrow carved and gilt inner moulding (the 'Hogarth' frame) was the most popular, especially for uncoloured engravings. It was followed by the wider frame veneered with bird's-eye maple and fitted with a gilt inner slip. A common practice in the late 18th c. and early 19th c. was to border the covering glass with VERRE ÉGLOMISÉ.

In modern times a very narrow simple black frame of JAPANNED wood usually encloses a print which—in contrast to past practice when it was cut close to the plate mark—is surrounded by an area of white mount. Lithographs, many of which are strongly coloured, are often given bolder framing with a wide area of carved wood and a coarsely textured mount.

4. MINIATURES AND SILHOUETTES. Miniatures of the late 16th c. and early 17th c. were often kept in cases of gold richly ornamented with patterns in ENAMEL and inset with semi-precious stones. Designs for them by French artists were engraved and doubtless circulated in many countries (see J. Evans, *A History of Jewellery*, second edn., 1970, pp. 126–8, plates 103–6).

During the 18th c., when the art of miniature-painting had numerous practitioners and demand for their work was at its height, the case most often took the form of a simple gold rim holding convex glasses at back and front. The latter enclosed the portrait, while at the back was arranged some of the hair of the sitter.

The SILHOUETTE gradually ousted the more costly miniature, and from *c.* 1760 to 1790 was usually framed in an oval. This was made either of moulded ebonized pearwood or of stamped brass backed with pine. By the 1790s a more or less standard rival frame had made its appearance and soon became universally popular. It was a rectangular frame of shining japanned papier mâché, with a gilt metal border round the opening and a gilt metal stamped ornament at the top holding a ring for suspension.

246, 372, 373.

FRANCE, WILLIAM (d. before 1774). English cabinet-maker and upholsterer. He succeeded William VILE as cabinet-maker to the Crown in 1764, and between 1768 and 1771, with Thomas CHIPPENDALE the Elder, he supplied furniture to the first Lord Mansfield at Kenwood, some of it after designs by Robert ADAM. A reading-stand made for the Kenwood library is in the Victoria and Albert Museum. The firm France and Beckwith continued in business until early in the 19th c.

231, 251, 361, 411.

FRANKENTHAL PORCELAIN (1755–99). Paul-Antoine Hannong, an Alsatian, had been making porcelain at Strasbourg, but when Vincennes (SÈVRES) obtained a monopoly he migrated to Frankenthal in the Palatinate and obtained a privilege from the Elector. The French influence persists in the table wares; but some notable individual figures were modelled by J. W. Lanz, Johann Friedrich Lück, Konrad Linck, K. G. Lück and, from 1779, by Johann Peter Melchior.

FRET. A type of decorative pattern composed of a continuous interlace of straight lines intersecting at right angles. It was derived from

classical Greek architecture and was particularly characteristic of the NEO-CLASSICAL revival. It is also called 'key pattern' and 'meander'. The term is also used for carved or moulded ornament consisting of straight lines in relief (particularly on ceilings).

FRISON. See KNUB.

FRIT. Term in GLASS-making for the materials from which glass is made after they have been calcined or partly fired. In CERAMICS or ENAMEL it refers to a ground glass used for GLAZES or enamels that have been formed by melting the ingredients and then cooling them rapidly. This process converts water-soluble materials into insoluble glass that can be evenly suspended in water to form a glaze. Early glazes were often made from marble (calcium carbonate), sand and soda, similar ingredients to those used to make one form of glass. Copper oxide or other materials would be added to give the colour. See POTTERY TECHNIQUES.

FROMANTEEL, AHASUERUS. Member of a family of clock-makers of Dutch or Flemish origin. A pioneer maker of LONG-CASE CLOCKS, who came to London from Norwich as a young man in 1629, was a member of the Blacksmiths' Company in 1630 and of the Clockmakers' Company (founded 1631) from 1632 to 1656. He sent his son JOHANNES to The Hague from September 1657 to May 1658 to receive instruction in the making of pendulum clocks from Samuel Coster, who was making them there according to Huygens's invention of 1656, and from 1658 onwards Ahasuerus Fromanteel began the construction of pendulum clocks in England. The earliest surviving example is spring-driven and dated 1658. The first weight-driven example dates from *c.* 1659/60. From this date to *c.* 1670 the Fromanteels established the first standard design of long-case clocks with their tall slim cases of oak veneered with ebony and hoods of architectural form with Corinthian columns at the sides and triangular pediment. The Fromanteels also made sprint TABLE or BRACKET CLOCKS and hanging wall-clocks.

40.

FROTHINGHAM, BENJAMIN, JR. (1734–1809). American cabinet-maker and furniture designer. Born in Boston, Mass., he learned his trade from his father and was established in Charlestown, Mass., by 1756. He is noted for his block-front furniture, which compares favourably with that of the GODDARD–Townsend group of Newport, Rhode Island; but his designs are simpler and rounder than those of the Newport group. He made reverse serpentine-front chests and desks, though some of his later work was in the HEPPLEWHITE style. Some distinguishing characteristics of his work are the shaping of the top drawer front, a delicate ogival bracket foot and FINIALS shaped like corkscrew flames rising from an urn. See FURNITURE (AMERICAN).

FURNITURE

1. European.
2. English.
3. American.
4. Modern.

For furniture in antiquity see EGYPT and GREEK AND ROMAN ANTIQUITY.

1. EUROPEAN.

(*a*) *The Middle Ages.* Furniture from before 1400 is too rare to allow of a comprehensive account. The styles determining early European furniture were, in brief: the refined BYZANTINE in the east; the vigorous Scandinavian from the north; and in central and western Europe the ROMANESQUE, tinged with the fading memory of ancient Rome. Although ordinary citizens may have been content with tables, benches and chests of the simplest carpentry, one cannot assume that palaces and courts did not own pieces of quality. There is evidence on carvings and in illuminated manuscripts that throughout the CAROLINGIAN period there were carved thrones and folding stools based on types used in imperial Rome. Formerly the prerogative of emperors and governors, they were now used by kings, bishops and judges. There survive some 12th-c. CUPBOARDS and chests, generally of a sturdy plank construction, the sides and the corners (if reinforced) projecting as feet. A late 12th-c. tympanum at Chartres shows a Nativity scene with a bed the structural members of which are carved with open arcading of some elegance. Such carved decoration as survives on furniture was either geometrical or, by the 12th c., architectural with round arches, columns and roundels.

The new style in the 13th c. was the courtly GOTHIC, which originated in France. It expressed a new humanism in which chivalry played a great part. At Cluny there is a chest of *c.* 1300 the front of which is carved in low relief with armoured knights standing formally like saints under a traceried arcade. Secular furniture probably made a progress similar to that of church furniture, of which there survives a quantity of choir stalls, vestment chests, cupboards and money chests. But there are important differences between court and church styles. The life of the nobility was lived between many castles, and anything of value was carried round with the retinue. Consequently if furniture could not be taken away, it was unlikely to become a craftsman's piece. Cupboards and chests would either take to pieces or be made in sections and serve as trunks and crates for transporting goods on wagons. Up to the 17th c. and sometimes later much furniture remained portable in this way.

Textiles were of the greatest importance to interior furnishing until they were displaced to some extent by cabinet-making. The richness of a room depended principally on the TAPESTRIES, VELVETS, SILKS, EMBROIDERIES and carpets which draped the walls, beds, tables and chairs. In the Middle Ages these were costly things and before they were manufactured in France, northern Italy and Spain they were generally imported from the East through trading centres such as Venice, Genoa and Santiago.

For the 15th c. there is surer evidence of style, not only from the greater quantity of surviving pieces but from the paintings by Flemish and other artists. The Gothic style became 'International'. But the best work was associated with the royal and ducal courts: Paris, Burgundy, Barcelona, southern Germany; and trading centres rose up, particularly in Flanders, where at Antwerp the arts were produced on a commercial basis. As for construction, planks were used for chests and stools, sometimes nailed together, sometimes with projecting tenons secured by loose pegs; or benches of open construction were 'joined' by the tenon and mortise method. Joined PANELLING had been developed by 1400, probably in Flanders, which greatly helped the lighter construction and appearance of chests, food and credence cupboards, desks and beds. Paintings often show a bed with a panelled head-board rising to support a hood or with a complete tester resting on a head-board and carved columns at the foot. Curtains were used on beds and benches to reduce draughts, and benches and chairs were high and provided with footstools or foot-boards to avoid the cold floors. During the 15th c. the Flemish had invented LINENFOLD decoration on panels, which was clearly a stylized imitation of curtaining. It became more popular at the beginning of the next century. Otherwise carvings remained chiefly architectural and tracery, either pierced or carved in relief, followed the flamboyant style. Chests often had applied buttresses separating the tracery panels. In the north oak was used, for which elm was a cheaper and less durable substitute. In the south walnut was preferred, and there was a variety of materials available, including fruitwoods and cypress. The most highly developed furniture in the Gothic style was probably in south Germany, where large cupboards had flat surfaces VENEERED with figured ashwood.

Spain is a special case because European influences combined with a Moorish legacy. The Hispano-Moresque style with its mosaic-like patterns and geometrical intricacy can still be detected there as late as 1700. European and Saracenic forces combined in Spain to produce a national style that is both elaborate and well balanced. The typical Spanish piece, the VARGUEÑO cabinet on an arcaded stand or chest, with a florid gilt gesso and ivory front, developed in the 16th c.

(*b*) *The Renaissance.* Italy had never fully

accepted northern Gothic, and before the Renaissance her furniture was generally of plain construction, painted rather than carved. As Renaissance ideals spread from Florence to Mantua, Urbino, Milan, Venice and elsewhere, furniture in the ducal courts took on its characteristic refinements. Most typical of Italian is the CASSONE or clothes chest, often a luxurious piece and often part of a dowry. There were three basic methods of construction. It could be made of planks, covered with parchment or carved gesso and gilded or painted; and the painted sections might be by celebrated artists such as Pesellino or Francesco di Giorgio. Or it could be panelled, but not like the joinery-work of the north. Tuscan panelling, with its fine mouldings and mitred corners, is remarkably similar to ancient Roman work which we now know from Herculaneum. The third type of *cassone* was made of wood, generally walnut, thick enough to take carving of some depth, with mouldings, gadroons (see GADROONING), etc., and figures or sirens at the corners. When carved with a large mythological scene the *cassone* really became sculptor's work. In seat furniture the 'Savonarola cross' chair is a traditional folding stool, the high back fixed by means of a panel of wood or leather. Meanwhile stools, chairs, benches and tall candlestands developed from the basic plank construction but were shaped into vases, panels or scrolls and carved with classical details in relief. As the Renaissance developed into Mannerism the carvings became convoluted with inventive scroll-work, CARTOUCHES and sirens or nymphs, generally based on artists' engravings. But a more sober style also continued, with solid well-proportioned construction making much use of Vitruvian columns and pilasters. The Tuscan tables, cupboards and buffets are generally in these forms.

Eastern fabrics, Genoese velvet and Lucchese silk made interiors in Italy seem very opulent to northern visitors. The usual furniture material was walnut, which when carved and polished could take on an appearance not unlike bronze; it might be wholly or partly gilded. But the number of woods available, as demonstrated by INTARSIA work, is amazing. In the *studiolo* of the Ducal Palace at Urbino (1470s) nearly 30 different kinds have been identified. In this room the *intarsia* or MARQUETRY gives a remarkably detailed illusion in *trompe-l'œil* perspective of built-in bookshelves, cupboards and writing desks, together with books and musical instruments. Each nail and dovetail is precisely shown.

Northern countries adopted Renaissance detail soon after 1500, and used it on their traditional chests and buffets. In France the productions of the Loire and Dijon showed great refinement, and the conventional ACANTHUS, candelabra, *putti* and profile heads can be as delicate as anything in Florence or Urbino. In 1550 Jacques Androuet du Cerceau, engraver and architectural theorist, published patterns for furniture which set the style of French Mannerism. This was based on the Italian style as interpreted at Fontainebleau, and made much use of solid carving with GROTESQUE figures and demon masks. Hugues Sambin published another collection of designs in Dijon in 1572. French furniture was carefully designed and seldom became ponderous. The French dresser of *c.* 1560 was a buffet cupboard in two stages, with slender colonnettes and low-relief panels carved in the style of Jean Goujon (*c.* 1510–68). Nearly always of walnut, these dressers incorporated panels of dusky veined marbles. In the south of Germany and Switzerland national styles continued which also used Italian decoration on rather ponderous traditional forms. Peter FLÖTNER, the outstanding designer in Augsburg and Nuremberg, also published patterns of Renaissance ornament. Here also the craftsmen mastered the *intarsia* technique, and perspectives and scenes of ruins were inlaid on buffets, chests and cabinets more often than had been the case in Italy. *Intarsia* spread further north, where it became reduced to simple and adventitious patterns of marquetry and inlay.

In Holland Hans Vredeman de VRIES published pattern-books *c.* 1580. They included furniture in which the subtle erudition of Italian Mannerism had turned into something finite, harsh and bulky. With his rectangular forms and mouldings, ponderous scrolls, intrusive and rather crude carving, and strapwork that seems to be based on iron rather than on leather, de Vries set the decorative style for the Protestant world. Calvinist Switzerland allied itself stylistically with Holland rather than with south Germany. In Scandinavia Dutch ornament was half accepted, but used with courtly refinement. But in northern Germany heaviness and bulk were completely the vogue. Rectangular buffets, COURT CUPBOARDS, tables and wardrobes, already massive in shape, stagger under a profusion of overripe fruits and hideously carved caryatids. Table legs and bed-posts were generally extremely bulbous. In the Protestant north oak was the accepted material for furniture, to which the Dutch would very often add decorative raised panels of ebony and occasionally of other woods.

(*c*) *Craftsmanship and the Baroque*. Craftsmanship in southern Germany was at its best in Augsburg and Nuremberg, which had become commercial manufacturing centres rivalling Antwerp. Besides their famous SILVER and metalwork they specialized in collectors' cabinets designed with a multitude of small drawers for coins and gems. During the late 16th c. cabinets were made with exquisite mouldings, carvings, *intarsia* panels, PIETRE DURE, ivory and silver, and themselves became articles of virtu. The Bohemian town of Eger also developed its own style in cabinets, the panels of which were carved in low relief with religious scenes after engravings, in cedar or boxwood with fruitwood or ebony mouldings and enrichments. Antwerp followed international styles rather than forming one of its own but was also famous for its cabinets, which had to be submitted to the guild by its members. These works were ruled to be of a plain design. They were made of many different materials and marquetry of flowers developed by the second quarter of the century. Brightly coloured composition might be included, and also mother of pearl. Netherlandish cabinets again were often painted on the drawer-fronts and the interiors of the doors with biblical or mythological scenes or with scenes from contemporary life. There is a more common type of 17th-c. cabinet, veneered with red TORTOISESHELL and ebony mouldings and with gilt-bronze appliqués. With a more or less ostentatious front composed of architectural details, columns, scrolls and statuettes, it is not always easy to tell whether such a piece is from Holland, Germany, Spain or Italy.

In Florence the Grand Duke Ferdinand de' Medici founded the Opificio delle Pietre Dure in 1599, establishing as Florentine a technique that really originated in Milan. Panels of *pietre dure* were collected all over Europe to be made up into cabinets. These panels were of birds, flowers or fruit, either in realistic relief or smooth and planar. More notable are the table tops, often of great size, smoothed and highly polished and inlaid with a fantastic amount of detail in LAPIS LAZULI, jasper, sardonyx, AGATE and other highly coloured hardstones. The brilliance of the Florentine works was never surpassed, although they were sometimes imitated in less expensive materials such as marble. Besides panels for cabinets and cupboards, bold clusters of hardstone fruits were sometimes incorporated in Florentine furniture, as on a *prie-dieu* designed by the sculptor Giovanni Battista Foggini and completed in 1706.

The BAROQUE taste was born in Rome, where a succession of nepotistic popes, the Borghese, Barberini, Pamphili, Ludovisi and others, had palaces built for their families. These contained state rooms that were intended for show rather than for use. In the Palazzo Colonna there still exist side-tables of the sumptuous kind made for these houses. Richly carved with a profusion of naked figures, tritons and *putti*, with scrolls, foliage and shells, all made from softwood and gilded, these Baroque creations really fall within the field of sculpture. As furniture such work was quite without precedent. Outside Rome, in Bologna, Genoa, Venice and Turin, the Baroque style was taken up and traditions of virtuoso wood-carving were established. At Genoa the work was particularly elaborate, and gilded scrolling leaves might fill an entire wall of a room, setting off a diminutive throne or looking-glass. Few names of the designers are known, but there is a famous table and pier glass by the Genoese sculptor Domenico Parodi, *c.* 1690–1710. In this rather late example the *putti* are playful, and the earnest conviction of the Baroque is already giving way to ROCOCO tendencies. Magnificent as such gilded furniture may appear, it is often of poor construction and the workmanship and art of the joiner has all but disappeared before the sculptor. Such, however, is not the case with the finest of this carved furniture, namely the Venetian pieces made by Andrea Brustolon for the Venier family, 1684–96. Here the workmanship is impeccable throughout. Made of boxwood and ebony, the chairs, tables and plant stands with gnarled tree stumps, dragons and athletic negro slaves were influential in England during the 18th c. Architects are known to have designed certain showpieces, and Carlo Fontana's cabinet (1678–80) in the Palazzo Colonna, Rome, has a fine architectural front with ivory carvings. It rests on a stand realistically carved with bowed Atlas figures.

German Baroque furniture emerged along rather predictable lines. The materials used in the south were chiefly oak, elm, walnut and ash, and cupboards were loaded with scrolls, caryatid figures, mouldings and obelisks. In the south panel mouldings were varied in shape, while the northern contours tended to be more austere and rectangular. The courts of Sweden and Prussia followed the styles of Holland and then of France, and the petty princes of the empire were doing the same by the end of the century. More than any other country outside France, Holland formed a national style. Among her rich merchants carved oak became outmoded, although large wardrobes and mirrors using raised panels in ebony borders were made until *c.* 1700. The Dutch exploited the woods found along their trade routes, particularly in the East Indies. Padouk was for chairs; kingwood and acacia were used in veneers, especially for patterns in oyster PARQUETRY. Marquetry was elaborated into pictures of flowers in vases, like the Dutch paintings, and Philippus van Santwijk in The Hague and Jan van Mekeren in Amsterdam are the best known craftsmen in the style. Marquetry and veneered furniture took on a new outline, simpler and more austere, relieved by the richness and fine grain of the woods employed. Then when Daniel MAROT came to Holland from France after 1685 he established a new Baroque style. A typical 'Marot' chair has a high shaped back carved with scrolls and is very unlike its French contemporary. A simpler style of chair that emanated from Holland, carved with lobed scrolls, a rather stiff leaf form and often cherub heads, spread over northern Europe including England.

In the 17th c. Oriental LACQUER, like PORCELAIN, was a rare curiosity. Traders like the Dutch could obtain Japanese or Chinese cabinets and set them upon carved stands; and screens or boards of lacquer were incorporated into furniture and wall decoration. The alternative to buying these costly items was to imitate them at home; and most countries set up workshops for lacquer. Although the Italian or German product had only a faint resemblance to the genuine imported article, it was still suitable for cupboards and cabinets and harpsichord cases.

Such things were made in Paris and Venice, and Gerard Dagly in 1687 set up a workshop in Berlin for the Elector of Prussia.

(*d*) *French Furniture 1600–1660.* The 17th c. in France is treated separately here because of the rather special and authoritative nature of Louis XIV furniture. The French style is characterized by good proportion, clear design, restraint in ornament, and generally by an aristocratic refinement. To these must be added workmanship of a very high order. Excessive ornament obscuring the construction lines is alien to the French logical and academic taste.

In 1606, when craftsmanship in Paris was at a low level, Henry IV set up workshops in the Louvre and attracted craftsmen from Flanders and Italy. During the next 50 years the French learnt the crafts themselves and eventually surpassed their masters. France under Henry IV had a period of stability, reflected in the many new *hôtels* and châteaux built in and around Paris. Interiors of rooms, however richly they were decorated, still preserved until 1650 archaic features like beamed ceilings and joined panelling. Walls were often hung with TAPESTRY. The French bourgeois interior can be well studied in engravings by Abraham Bosse (1602–76). As for the courts, there is little pictorial record but inventories such as those of Mazarin (1653) and Anne of Austria (1666) show that Italian furniture, paintings and sculpture were still very much sought after by collectors.

The most characteristic display piece was the cabinet, of which many were imported. An emerging French style, however, was already apparent, marking the beginning of cabinet-making (*ébénisterie*) (see CARPENTER, JOINER, CABINET-MAKER), and the Louis XIII cabinet is veneered with ebony thick enough to take carving in low relief, within moulded geometrical borders. About 1640 a new style grew up combining Flemish and Italian techniques, and cabinets were veneered in marquetry with rich floral or ARABESQUE patterns, set off by exotic woods, PEWTER, silver, *pietre dure* from Florence, etc. The French buffet persisted, made generally of walnut. As for joinery (MENUISERIE) there were low-back chairs as in Holland and England. The high-back chair appears to have developed at court. Of comparatively simple design, it was well proportioned and the turning of the legs and stretchers was finer and sharper than in neighbouring countries. The chief decoration whether of chairs or beds was in their upholstery; and a plain framework of a bed would usually be quite hidden under the velvet, silk or linen hangings, bordered with braid, fringes and tassels.

(*e*) *Louis XIV, 1660–1700.* With the personal rule of Louis XIV, and the virtual imprisonment of the aristocracy at Versailles, French furniture became almost a fine art. Bourgeois and provincial furniture, when it can be identified at all with certainty, is unimportant. Colbert, the First Minister, arranged for the glory of the Sun King to be reflected in the splendour of all French arts and crafts; and once Bernini's unsuccessful visit to Paris in 1665 was over and forgotten, Colbert placed all artistic matters under the Académie Royale. The arts of France no longer bowed to the authority of Italy.

The essentials of the Louis XIV style were largely determined before 1665 in two houses, the Hôtel de Lambert in Paris (1650–60) and Vaux le Vicomte (1658–64). The architect of both was Louis Le Vau (1612–70), and the interior designer Charles Lebrun (1619–90). After 1665 Lebrun designed the complete interiors for the Louvre and Versailles, with all architectural features, furniture, carpets and tapestries. Called the 'dictator of the arts', he became director of the GOBELINS factory, which in 1667 was named officially *Manufacture Royale des meubles de la Couronne.* Here everything relating to furniture was made regardless of expense: marquetry, mosaic, tapestry, joinery, bronze and ORMOLU, and MIRRORS. Many of the craftsmen came from Italy or Flanders and became naturalized at the Gobelins, where they were looked after and pensioned by the state.

Louis XIV furniture is sumptuously opulent, but also academic and classical, and rigidly symmetrical. The most recognizable technique is known as 'Boulle' after its presumed inventor André-Charles BOULLE. This consists of marquetry (on an oak casework) of brass and tortoiseshell. When sheets of these materials were sawn together into the patterns, the resulting design could be made up either with a brass design on tortoiseshell ground (*première partie*) or with tortoiseshell design on brass (*contre-partie*). So a pair of chests could be made, one being the reverse or 'negative' of the other. In Boulle's early work the materials used in the marquetry were very numerous and included pewter, ivory, horn (often stained blue) and naturalistic floral designs in exotic woods imitating those of Antwerp. By 1685 Boulle work was generally confined to stylized foliage or arabesques in brass, pewter and brown or red tortoiseshell within ebony borders. The MOUNTS of ormolu, which developed from protective metal corners, became elaborately decorative, and were the product of a specialized craft. The sunburst or Apollo mask, crossed L's and dolphins were all royal devices suitable for ormolu appliqués in the centres of panels; while for borders, etc., ormolu was lavishly applied in ACANTHUS leaves, strapwork, PATERAE or cupids, all derived from classical sources.

So long as the life of fashion was spent in public at court important furniture was confined to those pieces intended for state rooms. In 1682 the *Galerie des Glaces* at Versailles had tables, stands and *jardinières* of silver, but they were all melted down to pay for the wars in 1689 and 1709. Certain new types of furniture were evolved. The cabinet, although occasionally made for special reasons (for instance to hold the jewellery of a royal mistress), became obsolete as also did the chest (*coffre*). The cupboard (*armoire*), which could be either a high or a low wardrobe, took its place and during the 1690s the chest of drawers (*commode*) was in use. Writing tables were of two sorts: the large *bureau plat* was heavy and solid, and suitable for official work. The *bureau Mazarin* was a knee-hole table raised on scrolled legs and with drawers on either side and sometimes pigeon-holes above. Tables were normally carved with conventional acanthus, strapwork and other scrolled devices. Lebrun often designed *menuiserie* with mythological figures which derived from the Italian Baroque: *putti*, caryatids and mermaids. The same style was applied to brackets, candlestands (*guéridons*) and chairs, all of which were classed as *menuiserie*. These were normally carved in oak, either gilded or silvered, or polished in natural wood.

Seats at court were objects of dispute. Only the king might sit in an armchair (*fauteuil*), or even a chair without arms (*chaise*). Courtiers argued and flattered for the privilege of a stool (*tabouret*) in public. Folding stools (*pliants*) were reserved for duchesses. At home, of course, there were upholstered armchairs and wing chairs for relaxation. Generally these had high upholstered backs, and the arm supports and legs would be scrolled and finely carved. Straight stretchers gave way to scrolled X-shapes *c.* 1690, and shortly afterwards the structure and carving became lighter in form.

(*f*) *Régence and Louis XV, 1700–1765*. In 1699 Louis XIV was aware that fashions at Versailles were too serious and joyless for his grandchildren and their generation. It was the time when the tyranny of the Académie was beginning to relax in the fields of painting and sculpture. In interior decoration the light arabesque patterns designed by Jean BÉRAIN, with little Italian Comedy figures and SINGERIES, were adapted to Boulle furniture, and developed into the decorative schemes of Watteau and PILLEMENT. On the death of Louis XIV in 1715 Versailles was abandoned for 20 years, and a gayer style of living ensued in Paris around the court of the Regent. A movement towards ease and comfort showed itself in the more supple appearance of chairs and settees, and in the lighter colours of upholstery and décor generally. When Louis XV returned to Versailles in 1735 he presided over his court with the minimum of formality. Meanwhile the bourgeois were also demanding furniture, and were supplied by the newly established dealers or MARCHANDS-MERCIERS.

If society was relaxing its standards of behaviour, the high standards of craftsmanship were certainly not lowered. Paris furniture-making until 1791 was ruled by the guilds surviving from the Middle Ages, and every craft was strictly controlled and separated. A single chair might have to be worked in turn by the joiner, carver, gilder or polisher, and upholsterer, each of whom exercised a distinct craft. Other guilds related to furniture-making included those of cabinet-makers, bronze-casters, glaziers and so on. In 1743 the guild ruled that each maker (*menuisier* or *ébéniste*) should stamp his work with his name, and that it should be stamped also JME (*juré des menuisiers-ébénistes*) to show that it had been passed by the guild for standard of workmanship and design.

The first generation of Rococo designers included Bérain and the architect Robert de COTTE. During the régence Gilles-Marie OPPENORD, a Dutchman by birth, designed interiors with panelling to be carved with *rocaille* work; Juste-Aurèle MEISSONNIER designed ormolu pieces in a violently asymmetrical style of scrollwork; and Nicolas PINEAU also rejected classical forms in favour of the Rococo scrolls, shells and 'auricular work'. Rococo in France reached its climax *c.* 1730–5, after which logic prevailed and design became subject again to rules of proportion. The typical Louis XV chair is made up of a continuous undulating curve, apparently informal, but actually of a severely controlled and disciplined shape.

New materials and techniques were used. By 1720 veneers were in light, richly toned kingwood, purplewood and tulipwood. In order to cover the three-dimensional curve of a *bombé* commode the sheet of veneer was quartered or divided into smaller, carefully matched sections. The direction of the grain in French parquetry is always an important part of its decoration. Marquetry in woods was revived after 1740, at first consisting merely of trailing flowers inlaid in the veneer. Marble tops of tables and commodes had interesting colours and figuring. Ormolu mounts under such renowned makers as CAFFIERI and CRESSENT might cover the whole surface of a commode in a decorative pattern.

Oriental lacquer in panels, which had been both used and imitated during the previous century, became very popular, and could be incorporated into commodes and cupboards. The French imitation was called VERNIS MARTIN. *Vernis* could be made with pale grounds, which were more suitable for boudoirs than black or scarlet, and very often it was painted with European rather than Oriental flowers.

After 1700 the commode became the luxury piece of furniture. The *commode en tombeau* was the early form, having three drawers reaching almost to the ground. The *commode Cressent* came later, with two drawers and raised on slender curved legs. As an extension of the commode corner cupboards (*encoignures*) were made in matching pairs. The *bureau plat* persisted, with a serpentine top and cabriole legs. A *secrétaire en pente* (or *à dos d'âne*), like the English fall-front bureau, is somewhat uncommon. From *c.* 1750 the *secrétaire à abattant* or upright *secrétaire* was very commonly made. There were ingenious kinds of gaming and music tables, a little work table or *chiffonnier*, and for dressing the *poudreuse* was little more than a large vanity case on legs. The *coiffeuse* was larger,

A

B

C

D

E

F

G

H

J

K

L

M

A. Portuguese carved ceremonial chair, traditionally known as the throne of Don Alfonso V. (Mus. Nacional de Arte Antiga, Lisbon, *c.* 1470)

B. French *chaise caqueteuse*. Île de France. (Kunstindustrimus., Oslo, *c.* 1550)

C. Rosewood chair with pierced strapwork and carved finials. North Netherlands. (Rijksmus., Amsterdam, early 17th c.)

D. Italian carved walnut chair with inlaid back-rail. (Wallace Coll., 17th c.)

E. Louis XIV carved walnut armchair with cane back and seat, a type which was imitated in England and the Netherlands. (Wallace Coll.)

F. Portuguese walnut chair with tooled leather seat and back. (Mus. Nacional de Arte Antiga, Lisbon, late 17th c.)

G. Dutch walnut chair with marquetry panels. (Rijksmus., Amsterdam, early 18th c.)

H. French Régence walnut armchair with caned back and seat (*c.* 1730)

J. Louis XV *bergère à oreilles* or wing chair (also called *en confessional*) (*c.* 1740)

K. Louis XV walnut *bergère* with needlework upholstery (*c.* 1750)

N

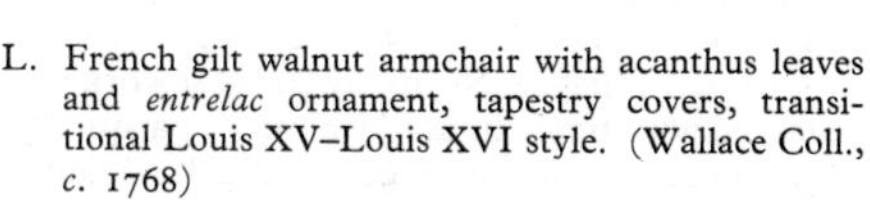

L. French gilt walnut armchair with acanthus leaves and *entrelac* ornament, tapestry covers, transitional Louis XV–Louis XVI style. (Wallace Coll., *c.* 1768)

M. Louis XVI *bergère* by Georges Jacob with fleur-de-lis upholstery. (V. & A. Mus., *c.* 1780–5)

N. French mahogany armchair with silk upholstery (*c.* 1820)

being a dressing table with compartments and a mirror under three rising flaps.

French social life was ruled by women and the conventions of polite conversation, and the innumerable chairs reflect this. There were basically two sorts of chair: the *siège meuble*, which was large and stood against the wall as part of the essential design of the room; and the smaller *siège courant* which a servant would bring up on request. *Fauteuils* had their arms set back to accommodate hooped dresses. By *c.* 1740 there were two types: the *fauteuil à la reine*, favoured by Queen Marie Leczynska, with a flat back; and the *fauteuil en cabriolet* with a more comfortable-looking curved back. The *bergère*, a relaxing tub-chair with upholstered arms and cushions, came after 1725. The *marquise* was a small settee or wide chair (i.e. a 'love seat'). Lounging became popular among both sexes, and the sofa (*canapé*) developed in

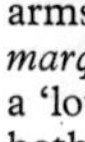

many varieties. One of these was the *duchesse*, which is a day-bed or *chaise longue*. Beds themselves were given carved frames soon after 1700, and these also occurred in many shapes.

Cupboards (*armoires*) were made carved in solid wood, both in Paris and in the provinces. Liège became famous for the high quality of its carved oak furniture. Much provincial furniture has survived, such as chests of drawers, small tables, and ladder-back chairs with rush seats. All these may be seen in paintings by Chardin and Greuze. The better pieces were of walnut or fruitwood, the inferior ones of elm.

(*g*) *Rococo outside France*. The political and intellectual tempers of different countries were expressed in the furniture of the 18th c. more than in that of any other time. France was now the cultural dictator of Europe; but although French influence can generally be seen in countries ruled by a court, its extent should not be exaggerated. Local traditions remained strong in all countries, and particularly so in Spain and Portugal. There are also inconsistent but unmistakable signs of English influence, chiefly in those countries connected with Britain by trade. Thus early 18th-c. CLOCKS of Scandinavia are often of the English type, as are many JAPANNED bureau-bookcases in Italy. QUEEN ANNE and CHIPPENDALE features are to be seen on Spanish chairs. George III chairs were closely imitated in Denmark, and HEPPLEWHITE shield-backs are not uncommon in Naples.

Rococo became the spirit of the age. But Protestant countries in the north, notably Holland, opposed its excesses and continued faithful to their thrifty traditions. The Dutch cabinets generally became large and serpentine, but lacked invention. The bureau-bookcase or bureau-cabinet was almost unknown in France and Spain, but occurs nearly everywhere else (including Italy). Generally speaking it was a Germanic piece, and examples abound with highly inventive *bombé* and contrasting curves, while the shaped and broken cornices sprouted with carved foliage. Normally the casework was veneered with finely figured walnut or parquetry, while more expensive pieces would have landscapes or inlaid strapwork. In Prussia and Scandinavia these pieces could be enormous and heavily mounted with ormolu.

One of the enduring Italian traditions was for fine carving, and all through the century there were displays of considerable virtuosity in gilded softwood. In the great palaces of Turin, Genoa and Bologna this was used for the panelling, side tables, *torchères*, chairs, mirror FRAMES in state rooms. The Rococo everywhere left behind the serious and erudite mood of the Baroque, and the Italian decorative arts became more hedonistic than in either France or Germany. From *c*. 1730 the Rococo was at its height, and its repertory of ornament was used with considerable freedom. Side tables and mirrors became lighter and gayer, the curves, flowers and dancing cherubs all ascending through space as though defying the force of gravity. In the gallery of a great house the serpentine curves on chairs and long settees would continue in the decoration of the walls, with mirrors framed by interlaced scrolling, with candle sconces and brackets, and a cornice whose ornaments would continue in the painted ceiling. Carved furniture took on fantastic shapes that often look affected to northern observers. As for cabinet-work, marquetry in general formed bolder and more highly stylized patterns than were usual in France, and the choice of woods was somewhat more limited in colouring and contrast. Meanwhile for smaller rooms functional furniture of simpler form was made in native woods, generally walnut, and often with a finely figured veneer.

Italian regional styles are important and fairly easily distinguished. Piedmont had recently become a little kingdom of great political importance and its courtly furniture, although consciously based on the French, tended to be heavy and architectural. The palaces of Turin were built by the architect Filippo Juvarra (1678–1736), who also designed some of the furniture and interior decoration. The sumptuous rooms of the Palazzo Madama are possibly unequalled in Italy. The furniture matches the decorations rich with carved or gilded wood, mirror panelling and Oriental lacquer. Marquetry was magnificently carried out by the court cabinet-maker Pietro PIFFETTI, whose astonishing work was veneered with exotic Oriental woods, etched ivory, mother of pearl, steel, silver, hardstones, and sometimes had ormolu mounts by Francesco Ladatte. Lombardy, under Habsburg rule, was less courtly than Piedmont, but the exuberance of its style can be appreciated from the Tiepolo room of the Palazzo Clerici in Milan. A characteristic Lombard piece is a settee in which the arms have apparently been lowered to incline outwards at a low angle. The Venetian was the most distinctive of all Italian Rococo styles, and became almost outrageous in its *joie de vivre*. The carved gilded furniture of Antonio Corradini (1668–1752) at the Ca' Rezzonico, like that of Domenico Parodi (1668–1740) in Genoa, is really sculptor's work. Venetian tables and *bombé* commodes had exaggerated contours, swelling wide at the top and tapering to a narrow base. Painted or japanned in bright red, green or white with CHINOISERIES or flowers, they seem slightly dulled today because the varnish has darkened with age. Genoa was a rich trading port, and its Royal Palace contains many examples of delicacy in carving. Florence, where there was no ducal court after 1737, became by comparison sober and made little contribution to the Rococo. Enrico Hugford, Abbot of Vallombrosa, and his pupil Lamberto Cristiano Gori perfected a technique using *scagliola* pastes as paints in imitation of *pietre dure*, which was used for table tops and also for wall pictures. Roman furniture was rich but did not run to excess: the Gallery in the Palazzo Doria Pamphili has gilded tables and cartouche-shaped chairs of Rococo form but almost classical proportions. The furniture of Naples is more eccentric, for here the Baroque was slow to die and the carving, instead of appearing weightless, became top-heavy. Yet Neapolitan furniture shows a more interesting regional character than that of either Rome or Florence.

National styles in Germany varied even more than those of Italy because the Germans were less bound by their own traditions and more open to outside influences. The general picture of German Rococo is complicated. Along the Rhineland French or Belgian taste prevailed. In other courts, including Vienna, the furniture was based on Paris or Italian fashions. Certain princes, however, were bolder and more original. Fine furniture was expensive, and could only be obtained where money could be raised or extorted. Only a few of the centres can be mentioned here.

Mainz was well known for large cupboards and two-tier cabinets. The boldly moulded Baroque details became fanciful, and the shaped case-work was inlaid with strapwork or marquetry in a variety of different woods. In Franconia the palaces at Würzburg, Bamberg and Bayreuth gave employment for the cabinet-makers, among whom were the SPINDLER brothers. In Bavaria *c.* 1700 the Elector Maximilian Emmanuel had followed the French example in having Boulle-type furniture made. Josef Effner (1687–1745), the court architect in 1724, also strongly favoured French styles. Jean François de CUVILLIÈS returned in 1724 from four years' study in Paris and worked with Effner on the Residenz in Munich and at Nymphenburg. Here the Rococo reached a sensitive balance between French sophistication and German ambition. The carved and gilded commodes, chairs and console tables, like the panelled and mirrored rooms they occupy, are highly decorated, carrying French Rococo to an extreme of virtuosity without either heaviness or vulgarity. In Prussia Frederick the Great furnished new palaces at Charlottenburg, Potsdam and Sans-Souci, attracting talent and craftsmen from all over Germany. The outstanding designers were Johann August NAHL (who had worked in Italy and Paris), the HOPPENHAUPT brothers Johann Michael and Johann Christian, and Johann Melchior KAMBLI. Frederickian Rococo is somewhat heavy compared with Bavarian, but is vigorous and forceful with bold sweeping curves and profuse, deep carving. Frederick II was conservative by taste, and he clung to his Rococo style after it had become outmoded elsewhere.

Abraham ROENTGEN, who set up his workshop at Neuwied in 1750, illustrates the international character of German Rococo. He had learnt his trade in Holland and England, and although his works (of which the mechanical card tables are best known in England) are predominantly north German in character, they include motifs borrowed from other countries.

The remaining countries of northern Europe evolved different combinations of foreign styles. In Sweden many currents of taste mingled, based on English, Dutch and German styles. The typical Swedish commode, with exaggerated shoulders and widely splayed feet, seems derived from the Prussian style of the Hoppenhaupts. On the other hand the court aped French fashions and sent its artists and designers to study in Paris. Swedish imitations of the Louis XV style, for instance by Dahlin, seem closer to the true French spirit than those of any other country. In Poland, too, French fashions were closely followed. Russia during the 18th c. was fast adapting herself to the Western way of life; her Rococo was predominantly German in character, but the forms were somewhat more cumbersome.

(*h*) *Neo-Classicism in France.* The Louis XVI style was partly a reaction against the hedonism of Rococo, implying a return to the classical discipline of Louis XIV, and partly the result of a new appreciation of the antique deriving from popular interest in excavations at Herculaneum and Pompeii. In 1754 the engraver Charles-Nicolas Cochin pleaded for a return to the 'good taste of the preceding century'. His studies in Italy with the Marquis de Marigny and the architect Jacques-Germain Soufflot (1713–80) date from 1749 to 1751; and the first attempts to realize the antique idea in Neo-Classical interiors date from the 1750s. During this decade the ruins of Greece were studied (rather over-hastily) by the architect Leroy, and intellectual Paris paid lip-service to what they confusingly called the *goût grec.* This 'GREEK TASTE' was not specifically Greek. In furniture it is represented by severe and massive pieces with rectilinear lines and mounted with heavy laurel swags, classical mouldings and bold key-pattern in ormolu. The first known pieces in the style, a *bureau plat* and a *cartonnier* now at Chantilly, were designed in 1756. It is significant that until recently they were thought to be of the Louis XIV period.

The *goût grec* was intellectual, ponderous and severe, ill suited to the salons and sophisticated feminine society of Paris. The Louis XVI style (properly so called) came in later, and was preceded by the 'Transitional' (*c.* 1760–5 to 1770–5). In Transitional *menuiserie* the grace of Louis XV curves was modified by angles, classical mouldings and rosettes. Transitional *ébénisterie* is more common, and included commodes of rectangular shape but set on cabriole legs. The Bureau du Roi at Versailles (1760–9) by OEBEN and RIESENER was the most important piece to be made in this style. The plane surfaces provided space for marquetry, which underwent a revival.

Louis XVI furniture came into general fashion during the 1770s. It is characterized by linear shapes, flat surfaces decorated with lacquer, parquetry or marquetry of the very finest quality, and its corners are protected by ormolu cast in classical forms. Ormolu was also used to ornament friezes, and craftsmen such as Pierre GOUTHIÈRE and Thomire could achieve work of the utmost delicacy, cast in leaf scrolls, flower swags, goats and *putti*; or classical mouldings, guilloche and wave-pattern. In spite of the use of classical details, however, it is misleading to speak of Louis XVI furniture as 'architectural'. The French were too logical to confuse the arts of furniture and architecture.

The fashion at first was for marquetry (landscapes and perspectives can show German influence) or parquetry. Oeben used cube-parquetry and his successor Riesener and others developed lozenge or trellis patterns looking like elegant DIAPERS, made from woods of the finest grain carefully chosen with subtly contrasting and matching colours. Pearwood was often scorched to imply shading or volume on details like rosettes, or was stained green. During the 1780s there was a vogue for English fashions, and MAHOGANY veneer was used in large sheets. This generally lacked any pronounced flame figure and its fine grain or burr and its colour were enhanced by ormolu borders and plaques; the final effect therefore was very unlike English mahogany furniture. Satinwood was used more rarely. During the 1780s mahogany came in for single chairs with solid carved backs, again in the English style. The lyre-back was a favourite, both in gilded wood and in mahogany.

Boulle furniture closely imitating the Louis XIV style was revived; but for their more intimate rooms the ladies required something of greater delicacy. WEISWEILER provided this in his upright cabinets and writing tables, which have herm caryatids in ormolu, or slender columns inset at the corners, graceful supports and interlaced stretchers. Weisweiler's furniture seems a French interpretation of two styles, namely Pompeian decoration and the English Neo-Classicism of Robert ADAM. Another fashion, generally associated with the *ébéniste* Martin CARLIN, was to mount writing cabinets and tea tables with plaques of SÈVRES porcelain painted with sprays of flowers in variously coloured borders. Such work does not appear to have been attractive to the Crown, but was popular among the affluent middle classes; and Carlin's work is known to have been distributed through the *marchands-merciers*.

Marie-Antoinette's personal influence over design may not have been very extensive, although she had taste and could choose her architects and designers well. She appreciated the best quality, but did not like affectation. Her Egyptian seat furniture made by Georges JACOB for Saint-Cloud (*c.* 1784) was a great novelty. For state apartments she preferred sensible and solid-looking pieces by makers such as Riesener and Beneman. She liked light-coloured grounds for rooms and panelling; and she seems to have been largely responsible for the profusion of natural, unstylized flowers which appeared in every material: marquetry, carving, *vernis* and ormolu, woven into Lyon silk hangings or painted on silk upholstery. Flowers were often shown ribboned and tasselled, which reflected the art of the upholsterer (*tapissier*).

Most types of *menuiserie* continued with little change from the previous years, but chairs looked more solid with their rectangular or circular seats and the frames appeared wider with their classical mouldings. The cartouche-shaped back developed into the medallion back, which Madame du Barry had at Louveciennes by 1771. The most famous maker of chairs was Georges Jacob, whose house Jacob Frères, and from 1803 Jacob-Desmalter, continued working until 1849. New furniture forms included an ATHÉNIENNE or carved tripod stand derived from bronze examples on altars found at Herculaneum. Eight different uses were specified for this article, including a work-table, a candle or plant stand, a fish-bowl stand, a brazier, etc. Thus it was a classical form of *guéridon* or circular stand.

New forms of *ébénisterie* included the glazed display cupboard (*vitrine*) and plant stand (*jardinière*). The *bureau plat* never lost popularity, and the upright *secrétaire* (*secrétaire à abattant*) became universal. The cylindrical writing-table (*bureau à cylindre*) was more practical for serious work, while the *bonheur du jour* was a small cabinet of little use for anything more than a lady's scribbling. Several different kinds of commode, large and small, were specified. The *commode à vantaux* had two or three doors concealing shelves or drawers. The semicircular commode is nowadays known as a *demi-lune*. There was a great increase in mechanical furniture, particularly as regards reading, work and dressing-tables, and most small *tables ambulantes* were fitted with drawers containing pen trays, hinged reading stands or mirrors. Other types of furniture new to France included the dining table (which was not yet universal), dumb waiter (*serviteur fidèle*) and sideboard (*console desserte*); neither of the last two much resembled their English prototypes. Generally Louis XVI furniture, when not ceremonious, reflected a growing taste for informality. This does not mean, however, that the French demands in intelligence or manners were at all relaxed. The pre-Revolutionary society of Paris was in many ways the most cultivated that modern Europe has known; and its furniture was without doubt the most refined and sophisticated that has ever been produced.

DIRECTOIRE furniture (*c.* 1790–1800), made for a society impoverished by the Revolution, shows that craftsmanship and sophistication were not dependent only on vast expenditure. Colour schemes and upholstery remained light and gay; but the expensive work of veneering, marquetry and ormolu were avoided. There was a thinning down of structure and chairs in particular became light, slender and streamlined. One result of this economy was the 'gondola chair'; another was the panel-back chair, based on the ancient Greek KLISMOS. A new use of classical and 'Etruscan' details reflected the moralistic attempt to revive the supposed manners and virtues of the ancient Roman Republic. Animals were now carved in solid wood, generally beech, and formed the arms and legs of chairs. The painter Jacques-Louis David (1748–1825) had anticipated this archaeological style in his paintings *Brutus* and *Paris and Helen* of 1789, and had ordered Jacob to base the style of his furniture on some of his own drawings made at Naples.

With the abolition of the guilds in 1791 certain rules were also abolished, such as the distinction between *menuisiers* and *ébénistes* and the compulsory vetting and stamping of furniture.

It was during the Consulat and Empire (*c.* 1800–14) that French furniture lost some of its finesse. Napoleon saw himself as a new Caesar, and chose the monumental style of Imperial Rome; and he was obeyed implicitly by his architects, PERCIER and FONTAINE, who became the new dictators of fashion. Empire furniture was primarily for display and prestige; its forms and decorations were invariably classical, and the style itself became amazingly uniform, even lacking in personality. An Empire commode, table or pianoforte is well proportioned, but of massive shape without mouldings or projections. Even drawer handles and key plates were often omitted. The favourite veneer was mahogany, now imported in quantity from the West Indies; it was chosen for its curl and flame figure (the same quality which had been exploited by the English 60 years before). Well-figured native woods were also used after *c.* 1810, including burr-yew and the lighter-coloured beech, ash and elm. Applied ormolu mounts became common once more, but they were no longer functional. Instead of protecting the corners they were designed (often by artists of repute) as classical gods and goddesses or as musical instruments, stylized laurel wreaths, palmettes or vines. Gilt-bronze plaques therefore took over the previous decorative function of marquetry.

Chairs became solid classical thrones, large, rigid and uncomfortable. Their legs and arms were sometimes carved with Egyptian figures and sphinxes (referring to the Egyptian campaign of 1798–9), dog or lion legs, or swans (from Joséphine's coat of arms). The previous variety of furniture was much reduced. A favourite seat was the *méridienne* or *chaise longue* with two raised ends and a back. This showed to advantage a reclining lady dressed *à l'antique*, as David had painted Madame Récamier in 1800. The newly invented *psyche* was a cheval looking-glass; and the boat-shaped bed (*lit en gondole* or *en bateau*) was one of the happy inventions of the period. In personalities like the Empress Joséphine there remained some of the sophistication and refinement of the 18th c. and at her Château de Malmaison there are pieces of delicacy, such as work and dressing tables, *athéniennes* and *jardinières*.

During the Restoration (1815–30) furniture-makers continued the methods and techniques of the Empire for some years. About 1824 light-coloured woods were used very widely, and they were chosen so that the figuring and colour made subtle and delicate contrasts. Other woods might be bleached (*bois clair*). Furniture shapes remained simple, the harsh rigid lines of the Empire were considerably softened and the corners rounded. Ormolu plaques went once more out of fashion. Among the royal family the Duchess de Berry showed artistic taste and has left her name to a new type of classical inlay in dark, contrasting rosewood; but otherwise the court and aristocracy had clearly lost either their interest or their confidence. Although Restoration furniture is distinctive and fine in craftsmanship, it has unmistakable bourgeois tendencies.

(*i*) *Neo-Classicism outside France.* Since the Rococo style survived into the 1780s in many parts of Europe, the spread of the new Classicism was neither immediate nor uniform. The Italian style was still dominated by the carving tradition. In Rome Giovanni Battista Piranesi published (1769) designs for fireplaces and furniture (*Diverse Maniere d'adornare i Camini*). Overloaded and impractical as they may seem, their importance should not be underrated as their influence can be detected as far away as Spain and Russia. Actual documented examples of Roman furniture are rare, but the famous gilded side-table (*c.* 1769, now at Minneapolis) is a piece actually designed by Piranesi. In Rome there were splendid new interiors, as in the Palazzo Chigi (1765) and the Villa Borghese (*c.* 1780); and at the Villa Borghese can be seen several carved and painted side-tables and some gilded chairs, all of a fine and original design. Neapolitan furniture of the 1780s is characterized by a new lightness of form and novelty in design. Much of it is painted and partly gilded. Chairs often have unmistakable English features such as open shield-backs; and these occur elsewhere in Italy, as in Florence and Venice.

In northern Italy marquetry (*intarsia*) was revived. The outstanding maker was Giuseppe Maggiolini of Milan, who often worked to designs by Andrea Appiani and Levati. He is known to have used 85 different kinds of wood in 1795, none of which he ever stained artificially. The patterns are bold, with contrasted panels of GROTESQUES, foliage, profile busts and landscapes; but although the final effect is handsome, it often seems stereotyped. Revelli of Turin worked in marquetry with rather more artistic freedom. Piedmont followed the French fashions closely, and the chairs can be very close to Paris models. Most Turin furniture, however, was more lavish in its carving than was ever the case in France; and the commodes with their drawer-fronts carved in relief with scrolling foliage are quite unlike French veneered commodes. Giuseppe Maria Bonzanigo was the leading craftsman, and a most delicate carver in wood. The usual practice in Italy was to paint and gild these pieces, or to japan them with flowers.

Rococo was still prevalent in Spain when the Neapolitan Matias Gasparini became director of the Royal Workshops in 1769, and the Gasparini Room (1770–80) in the Royal Palace in Madrid was completely in the old style. Neo-Classical furniture thereafter was of a predominantly Italian character, but showed greater richness both in design and in materials. Gasparini's chairs were veneered or worked with fine marquetry as nowhere else in Europe; or they had intricately carved and gilded backs in very inventive patterns or surprisingly stilted shapes. Piranesi's spirit can be seen in chair designs, and in the profusion of ornament on writing-tables and commodes even after 1800. Piranesi's influence was strong also in Russia through Catherine the Great's court architect Charles Cameron (1740–1812); and it can be seen in the profusely carved side-tables and mirrors, as well as in much of the steel furniture that was made up to 1796 in the State Arsenal at TULA.

All central and northern courts, however, followed French fashions to some degree; and the French *marchands-merciers* exported furniture, thus diffusing the sophisticated Paris fashions. The most famous German cabinet-maker, David Roentgen (son of Abraham), rivalled the Paris *ébénistes* to the extent that they persuaded him to become a *maître* of their guild in 1780. He sold works to Louis XVI and to royalty all over Europe, and is best known for his own special technique in pictorial marquetry, often made after paintings by J. Zick, and also for his ingenious mechanical furniture. The Swedish court was consciously modelled on that of Paris, especially under King Gustavus III (1771–92), and the latest refinements of Louis XVI furniture were eagerly copied. Georg HAUPT was Sweden's most famous cabinet-maker, who returned from Paris and London in 1769.

Under Napoleon France established a hegemony of decorative style, partly owing to the success of Percier and Fontaine's pattern-book and partly owing to the extension of Napoleonic patronage in the wake of political domination. Some of the Empire furniture in Holland, Madrid, Milan and Naples is thought to have been sent out from Paris; but much of it was made locally, although many of the gilt-bronze plaques may have been obtained from France. In Florence Giovanni Socchi is known for furniture in the Pitti Palace which he made for Elisa Baciocchi, Grand Duchess of Tuscany, and which includes some unique cupboards in the form of drums and a pair of oval folding writing-tables. In spite of the levelling influence of Napoleonic uniformity, however, local and national characteristics are apparent, most of all perhaps in Vienna and Spain, where clearly the 18th-c. traditions and principles of design were still strong. The Royal Palace in Madrid has a quantity of Empire furniture in which a rather restricted repertory of ornament is used lavishly and with great invention.

In Turin the magnificence of the Empire style increased right up to 1840. Pelagio Pelagi furnished the Palace with rooms in which the imperial taste, intensified and overloaded, comes dangerously near to being a vulgar display of opulence; and late Neo-Classical ensembles exist elsewhere in Italy, as in the Palace of Caserta near Naples. A complete contrast to these is provided by the Prussian architect Karl Friedrich Schinkel, who from 1800 designed furniture in an informal, free classical or 'Greek' style which anticipated Restoration fashions. His achievement was not only original and contemporary, but simple and unpretentious. The chairs, tables and beds were generally in light figured native woods such as beech, ash, pear or cherry. There is an easy transition from Schinkel to the interesting and ingenious furniture inventions of post-Napoleonic Germany, with their bold and fantastic shapes; and thence to the BIEDERMEIER style. Josef Danhauser, whose factory flourished from 1804 to 1830, was the most important manufacturer. *Biedermeier*, as its name implies, provided functional and convenient furniture for the German and Austrian middle classes. The forms and decorations were still based in Neo-Classicism, but angles were smoothed and the shapes swollen out, showing invention and novelty. Native woods, especially cherry and ash, and the deep upholstered sofas and chairs, all contributed cosiness. *Biedermeier* corresponds to French Restoration and marks the end of a long unbroken tradition of furniture design and manufacture. The old methods were abruptly to change in the coming age.

(*j*) *Romanticism and the Industrial Age.* After 1820 Paris remained the principal centre of culture in Europe; and it is best first to consider the French styles as hitherto because they closely correspond to the currents of taste in most other countries. There is at present more information available about French fashions than about fashions elsewhere.

The July monarchy and Second Empire (*c.* 1830–70) were pervaded by Romanticism and the revival of ancient or exotic styles. The period was characterized by the emergence of a new, large and affluent middle class demanding quantities of furniture convenient for moderate-scale living and rented apartments. In this period too the influence of new machines and methods of mass production made itself felt. By 1830 Romantic styles in furniture were already taking shape and the cabinet-makers who worked with traditional methods for individual patrons found they could no longer compete. Alphonse Jacob-Desmalter (see Georges JACOB) retired in 1849. An eclectic style emerged which is very uneven and not pleasing to modern taste. It can be seen best in sideboards, upright pianos and writing cabinets, generally in mahogany, walnut or ebony. The uprights are turned or given spiral twist and the panels are filled with fretwork or inlaid with rather meagre foliate scrolls. Small 'occasional' chairs with caned seats, and the ebonized frames inlaid with mother of pearl and gilt, were novelties in the 1840s.

The new methods of manufacture ensured convenience, cheapness and above all novelty. The first style to be revived was the Gothic, known as the 'Cathedral' or 'Troubadour' style. Pointed arches had appeared tentatively on Restoration chairs during the 1820s; but by 1830 furniture appeared whole-heartedly and profusely traceried, cusped and crocketted. Sets of Gothic chairs were also cast in iron. They had no similarity to genuine medieval furniture which, strangely, was as yet almost unknown. Decoration was borrowed from cathedral and church architecture. But the vogue withered rather quickly and was followed by ephemeral attempts to establish Chinese, Assyrian, Persian and Egyptian styles. All these were possible because of new publications by professional designers, who plundered exotic architecture for repertories of ornaments and decorations. Aimée Chenavard's *Nouveau Recueil d'ornements* (1833–5) was an enormous collection of such details which any commercial manufacturer could select and combine at will. The results tended to be overcrowded.

One of the more enduring revivals was for Renaissance furniture involving much carving in oak and walnut. Although of rather melancholy aspect, this revival was scholarly and lasted until the end of the century. Michel Liénard carried out a great deal of research among the French châteaux and their decorations during the 1840s. In 1866 he published an encyclopedic work on ornament, which was very much used in the industrial applied arts.

The best known of the revivals was that for Louis XV and Louis XVI furniture. Under the July monarchy Louis XV was popular; and since furniture design was not yet quite a dead art, the result was not pure pastiche. Dark-coloured native woods were used, burr-walnut and sycamore being popular, serpentine curves were somewhat pronounced and cabriole legs made sturdy. Inlay and marquetry were lavish, sometimes overpowering. The decorative effect of such pieces is reduced by the starved appearance of bandings and mouldings, which generally betray their machine technique, and by the poor quality of machine-made gilt-bronze mounts. Louis-Philippe 'Louis' developed a liking for porcelain plaques, which were boldly painted with flowers, with classical and romantic landscapes, or with Louis XV himself and his court ladies and set off with gaudy turquoise borders and much raised gilding. The result had little in common with the exquisite works of Carlin.

The Louis XV revival intensified during the Second Empire, when it departed so much from the 18th-c. prototype that it is best called 'Rococo'. Even English Chippendale had a short revival. The Great Exhibition of 1851 in London, followed by the Universal Exhibitions held in Paris in 1855 and 1867, encouraged lavish displays of machine carving in mahogany, walnut or gilded softwood. The resulting magnificence was to the taste of the court. The revival of Louis XIV furniture is associated with the Second Empire, and resulted in huge quantities of mass-produced Boulle tables and cabinets. In these marquetry of gaudy brass and red tortoiseshell lies with panels of hardstones in smoothly finished, inert-looking ebony borders. Generally workmanship declined as time went on, and gilt metal mounts and borders could be of lamentable quality. Unfortunately the Empress Eugénie had little appreciation for fine craftsmanship. About 1865 she developed a romantic interest in Marie-Antoinette and brought out from store genuine pieces of the Louis XVI period. But the 19th c. did not exist on sophistication and refinement alone, and the drawing rooms of the Second Empire filled up with vitrines, dwarf cabinets and numerous occasional tables and chairs arranged in 'circles' for conversations.

Seat furniture expressed the true spirit of the age; and the over-all impression of a drawing room was chiefly conveyed by its buttoned plush upholstery and deep fringes. The supple contours of Louis XV armchairs were modified by their stout carved or veneered frames set on castors. New forms of seating were designed to show off the ballooning crinoline dresses. Settees called *confidentes* were made in daring shapes; chairs came in low, wide serpentine frames; and even STOOLS and pouffes were made to look comfortable. A pouffe could be large and circular, with a raised conical back support at its centre. A surprising and delightful invention was a stool carved like enormous knotted and tasselled ropes. Some examples of these stools are at the Empress's Château de Compiègne.

There were, indeed, craftsmen almost as efficient technically as those of the 18th c., but generally they had no outlet other than making copies or pastiches of Louis XV and Louis XVI furniture. The best known of these makers are Paul Sormani and Henri Dasson. Marquetry was finely imitated and matched; and ormolu mounts were either remodelled with ancient techniques, or cast direct from the 18th-c. work. The copy of the *Bureau du Roi* in the Wallace Collection is an example of this class of furniture.

The sequence of styles outside France was not very different. The Gothic and Renaissance revivals in Germany were long-lived, reaching a climax in the castles of Ludwig II. The Rococo of the 1850s was welcome everywhere, particularly in the conservative court of Vienna. Spain, Holland and Sweden all had their Gothic, Renaissance and Rococo vogues, through which, none the less, national characteristics are sometimes apparent. But the indigenous styles were not always able to survive in the machine age and traditional craftsmanship was given little encouragement in the international exhibitions. In Russia the revival of the Louis styles was particularly sumptuous, and the court taste gave them an unexpected dignity. A Russian speciality was veneering 'Louis XV' chairs and tables with MALACHITE mounted with gilt metal. These presentation pieces can be found in various places. A suite was received at Chatsworth in 1844; others are at Aranjuez and the Pitti Palace in Florence.

In Italy the tradition for pictorial marquetry remained strong, but the choice of woods was restricted and their grain somewhat coarse. A style of cabinet work of ebony or walnut inlaid with Mannerist patterns in ivory was cleverly imitated in England by the firm of GILLOW. Another novelty was mirrors overlaid with carved scales of ivory. After the *Risorgimento* there was another Romantic style of decoration in Italy, the 'Dantesque', which copied late medieval and early Renaissance furniture, looking back to the greatest period of Italian history. The result of all this was that the European interior became overloaded and eclectic, and by the 1880s magpie collections of works of art dating from all periods produced internationally a 'High Victorian' atmosphere.

2. ENGLISH. Very little of the furniture made in England before 1500 has survived, but there is sufficient documentary and pictorial evidence to show that its main characteristics, at least until the 15th c., were portability and adaptability. It was designed to lead a nomadic existence and spent much of its time in the baggage trains of its wealthy owners, the king and his court and the feudal magnates, on their periodic progresses through their territories. Like other household goods furniture ranked as 'movables', a concept which still survives in the word for 'furniture' current in many European languages (e.g. French, *meubles*). The pieces subject to this kind of usage were made by the CARPENTER and were inevitably rough and clumsy. Oak was the most widely used timber. As such pieces were comparatively scarce, they were wherever possible put to more than one use. Chests, for instance, which were among the more important articles as they were the repositories of family treasure and valuables, were also used as seats, tables and beds. Even within the palace, castle or manor house where the furniture was temporarily deposited it retained its mobile character. The communal life of a large medieval household was centred in the great hall. Tables (or 'boards' as they were originally called, the term denoting any flat surface of wood, as in the modern 'board of directors', 'notice board', etc.) were usually planks placed on trestles for meals and then dismantled when the hall was cleared. Meals were taken by the family on the dais at one end of the hall while retainers sat 'below the salt' in the body of the hall on tripod STOOLS or benches. These were the commonest seats and were stored against the walls when the meal was over. Settles, benches with arms and usually backs, had a more permanent setting against the wall. The chair was a rare piece and a symbol of authority reserved for the head of the household. Its grandest form was the canopied chair of state, seen in the throne in royal palaces (the Coronation Chair in Westminster Abbey, made *c.* 1300, is the most famous example), and in the bishop's seat in his cathedral, which takes its name from *cathedra*, the Greek word for 'chair' or 'throne'. The ancient symbolism of the chair has never been entirely lost; it is evident today in the Speaker's chair in the House of Commons, to which all members of Parliament, who sit on benches, pay deference, and in many other examples, such as the respect accorded to the chairman at committee meetings. Medieval CUPBOARDS were literally cup-boards or side tables for utensils and food. An enclosed structure or compartment was usually known as an AUMBRY. The bed was the costliest piece and treasured as a family heirloom because of its rich hangings, which covered the wooden framework and hung down from a canopy attached by cords to the ceiling. All available evidence indicates that medieval furniture was brightly painted both to protect the wood and to add colour to the interior.

After *c.* 1540 developments in domestic life encouraged the use of more static ('dormant') furniture. One can detect here the influence of the rising merchant class, especially those engaged in the lucrative wool trade, and of the craft guilds. While the old feudal aristocracy was killing itself off in the long Wars of the Roses (1455–85) large areas of the country, untouched by war, grew prosperous. Increasing emphasis was laid on domestic comfort. A great advance in constructional methods was marked by the introduction of the PANEL and frame, a technique which reached England from Flanders. Previously oak had had the disadvantage of splitting, owing to incomplete seasoning, when nailed or pegged. Now oak panels were fitted into grooves worked on the inner surface of frames, which were secured by the mortise and tenon joint, the tenon, or projecting member, fitting into the mortise or socket and being fastened by pegs. Not only did this give panels a certain freedom of movement which curtailed splitting, but it also ensured much more careful design and workmanship, for the number of panels required had to be calculated beforehand and the joints had to be skilfully constructed. A new class of furniture craftsmen, the joiners, now became responsible for joined (or 'joint') work, including chests, chairs, doors and wall panelling. The panel-back chair (which was also panelled beneath the arms and seat) was to establish for two centuries the standard pattern of the chair with back of square or rectangular shape. Joined construction was also found on the standing table, the 'table dormant' of the kind which Chaucer describes as permanently set up in the Franklin's hall.

The revolutionary effect of joinery took time to make itself felt. The panelled chest, for instance, though a notable advance on its boarded and framed predecessors, was comparatively rare until Elizabeth I's reign. Many chests were imported from Flanders and Germany. Traditional carved ornament remained, particularly Gothic motifs, though the 15th c. saw the introduction (also from Flanders) of the so-called LINENFOLD pattern on carved panels. By 1500 the most important craftsman in the furniture field was the 'cofferer', whose skill lay in covering furniture with fine materials—first of all the coffers and chests used for transport, then later chairs, stools, screens, small writing cabinets, etc.

The internal peace imposed by the strong Tudor monarchy (1485–1603) encouraged the building of houses primarily for comfort and not defence. Gunpowder had in any case made the castle obsolete. A new class of landowners, created by the Tudors through the sale of monastic lands which became available after the dissolution of the monasteries (1536 and 1539), was intent on exploiting its territories to the full, and during the long reign of Elizabeth I (1559–1603) many large 'prodigy' houses were built of H or half-H form, surrounded by gardens and rearranged internally to include a great chamber, long gallery, private family dining-room and numerous separate rooms. All these needed furnishing, often with touches of luxury. Richly upholstered chairs, for instance, probably of foreign make, were found with more refined types of panel-backs as well as new types such as the CAQUETEUSE, a lighter, open-framed chair with a single panel in the back. In the dining-room the draw table, with two extendible leaves which could double its length when required, came into use after 1550, and in addition to stools and benches there was now the back stool, a chair without arms but with a half-upholstered back. The COURT CUPBOARD, an open, three-tiered side table for displaying the family plate, was seen in larger households, and various types of enclosed cupboards, such as the LIVERY CUPBOARD (with perforated doors, for use as a food store) and PRESS CUPBOARD were in use.

English furniture, however, fell far below the standard of the best Continental examples, and progress was hampered by lack of direct contact with Italy, the home of the Renaissance. Henry VIII had indeed shown interest in the Classical Revival and had invited Italian craftsmen to England. Early Tudor furniture occasionally reveals some attempts at classical decoration, notably in the ROMAYNE work of carved profile heads in medallions on panels, but such influences were imperfectly understood and were freely and incongruously mixed with Gothic, linenfold and other traditional motifs. The tenuous links with Italy were broken *c.* 1530 at the Reformation, and for the rest of the century English decorative forms were mainly influenced by the flamboyant version of the Renaissance current in northern Europe, particularly in the Protestant areas of Germany and the Low Countries. Printed pattern-books of architectural and furniture designs were imported into England from these areas and copied, the most influential being the furniture designs of the Flemish designer, Vredeman de VRIES, published in 1580.

Florid ornament clearly suited the national exuberance of the Elizabethan era, and the methods of decoration borrowed from foreign sources included the grotesque 'bulbs' on the legs and supports of tables, beds and court cupboards, inlaid chequered and floral designs of coloured woods set just below the decorated surface (to a depth of about 3 millimetres), and STRAPWORK, or low relief carving in geometrical and ARABESQUE forms. The 'Great Bed of Ware' (*c.* 1590), now in the Victoria & Albert Museum, is probably the most famous example of the more garish manifestation of these enrichments. The typical panel-back chair of *c.* 1600 had inlaid decoration in the back, and carved 'head' and 'ear' pieces. By this date the panels beneath the arms and seat were being discarded and the front legs and arm supports were usually turned in attractive forms.

Until *c.* 1660 oak remained the principal fashionable wood and Tudor types of furniture and decoration continued in general under the early Stuarts. Progress towards emulating the best Continental standards remained, however, disappointingly slow. Charles I, the greatest patron of the arts that had ever occupied the English throne, had made determined attempts to bring England into the full current of Renaissance culture. His magnificent collection of paintings, the introduction of Palladian architecture to England by the royal architect, Inigo Jones, the patronage of Rubens and van Dyck at the English court—all these promised a new age in English artistic life. But Charles's schemes were wrecked by the Civil War and the 11 years (1649–60) of austere Puritan rule under Cromwell were not conducive to improvement in the arts and crafts. There were, nevertheless, signs that more furniture was coming into use. The worst excesses of Tudor decoration were toned down; more graceful turned decoration, for instance, replaced the 'bulbs', and carved ornament included more classical motifs. Fixed upholstery became a regular feature of seat furniture, particularly in the form of needlework in coloured wools on a canvas base. Varieties of small tables, some of the gate-leg type, stood about the house. By 1650 a form of chest of drawers was established. The survival from this period of vernacular types of chairs, such as the turned (or 'thrown') chair, the stick-back (today called the WINDSOR CHAIR) and the Yorkshire–Derbyshire chair, which had an open arcaded or broadly hooped back, indicates wider employment of furniture in yeomen's houses as well as the development of country and regional styles.

Perhaps the most important turning-point in

A

B

C

D

E

F

G

H

J

K

L

M

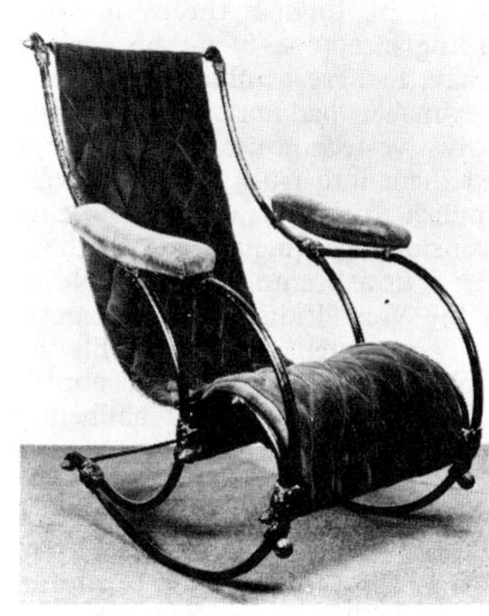

N

O

P

A. Armchair ('box-chair'). Oak, the panels carved in relief with Renaissance ornament and linenfold. (V. & A. Mus., 2nd quarter 16th c.) B. Armchair (*caqueteuse* or conversation chair). Carved oak. An English version of a French type. Colyton, South Devon. (V. & A. Mus., 2nd quarter 16th c.) C. Armchair (so-called 'Glastonbury' type). Carved oak. A Gothic example said to have come from Glastonbury Abbey, it is now in the Bishop's Palace at Wells. (V. & A. Mus., early 17th c., possibly with later carving.) D. Back stool. Oak with leather upholstery, spiral turned legs and stretchers (mid 17th c.). E. William and Mary chair, japanned black and gold (*c.* 1690). F. Walnut armchair, curvilinear type, with cabriole legs and claw-and-ball feet (*c.* 1720). G. Wing armchair. Mahogany, with cabriole legs and claw-and-ball feet, *c.* 1740. H. Armchair. Carved mahogany, the seat upholstered in needlework of coloured silks and wools. Closely similar to a design dated 1753 in Chippendale's *Director*, 1st edn., 1754, plate xii (3) and probably made by his firm. J. Armchair. Turned and carved yew. 'Windsor' type, in the 'Gothick' taste. (V. & A. Mus., mid 18th c.) K. Armchair. Carved mahogany with metal strings, modern upholstery. John Linnell and Robert Adam had used the classical lyre as a splat in furniture design by then, but this chair could well have been made under the influence of François Hervé, who worked for Henry Holland at Carlton House (*c.* 1775). L. Shield-back armchair. Mahogany, tapered legs in Neo-Classical taste. Hepplewhite style, *c.* 1775. M. Chair. Beech, japanned black and gilded with brass enrichments. Caned seat. (V. & A. Mus., *c.* 1810.) N. Victorian rocking chair. (V. & A. Mus., 19th c.) O. Papier-mâché balloon-back chair. (V. & A. Mus., *c.* 1850.) P. Chair. Oak with upholstered seat. Design by C. R. Mackintosh and exhibited at the Vienna *Sezession* Exhibition, 1900. (V. & A. Mus.)

English furniture history occurred in 1660, the date of Charles II's restoration to the throne. Close links were forged with the most up-to-date developments abroad, especially with those of France, which under Louis XIV was becoming the cultural centre of Europe. Holland, where the new French techniques were mastered, supplied England with trained craftsmen to teach English apprentices. Throwing off Puritan austerity and enjoying the benefits of rising national prosperity through trade, industry and colonization, the landowning and merchant classes eagerly followed the example of Charles II and his luxury-loving court, and sought the latest styles and decorative methods. The Great Fire of London in 1666 provided an unforeseen opportunity to rebuild and refurnish a large area of the City. In the new types of houses, brick-built, well lit by large sash windows and with the rooms brightly painted inside, the old-fashioned oak furniture was too dark and clumsy. A revolutionary change occurred with the advent of VENEERING, for which walnut, warm in tone and finely figured, became the most fashionable wood. Veneering, the gluing of thin saw-cut sheets of wood to flush surfaces, and its allied techniques of MARQUETRY (floral and arabesque patterns, built up with varieties of coloured woods) and PARQUETRY (geometrical designs composed of oval 'oyster pieces' cut mainly from the branches of walnut, olive and laburnum trees) required new constructional methods which superseded those of the joiner. Hence the emergence of the cabinet-maker, the creator of the prestige piece, the cabinet, on which all these fresh skills were lavished. Another form of fashionable decoration was LACQUER from the Far East. Lacquered furniture was imported by the East India Company for the well-to-do, or English craftsmen bought lacquered pieces such as screens to divide and apply to their own furniture. The attractively bright and durable colours of lacquer encouraged home-made substitutes, but the resulting material, known as JAPAN, never matched the brilliance of the original. Stalker and Parker's manual of 1688, *A Treatise of Japanning*, encouraged enthusiastic amateurs to decorate their own furniture, and in 1701, following petitions by professional japanners, Parliament raised crippling tariffs on imported lacquer. This left the home market practically free for English japanners and fostered a widespread interest in CHINOISERIES, which had an important influence on English furniture.

For a time it was customary to follow the Continental fashion of placing cabinets (which contained valuable collections of small articles or 'curiosities') on stands, a method adopted for other types of case furniture such as chests of drawers and writing cabinets. The latter, like their French prototypes from which they acquired the name of SCRUTOIRES, had a large fall-front for writing. Later in the century these stands were replaced by chests of drawers to form a stronger base, thus producing, among other pieces, the double chest of drawers, the 'chest-on-chest', now known as the TALLBOY. But the large fall-front of the scrutoire proved unwieldy and the bureau, with a sloping top and convenient space behind for papers, gradually took its place.

In the later Stuart period many skilled Huguenot craftsmen fled from France to England after the Revocation of the Edict of Nantes in 1685. Some are known to have worked at the English court in the latest techniques of gilt gesso and Boulle decoration. The latter, derived from the inlay of brass and tortoiseshell perfected by Louis XIV's cabinet-maker, A.-C. BOULLE, was the inspiration of the arabesque and SEAWEED MARQUETRY produced by English craftsmen. Huguenot SILK weavers also introduced their craft to England, with beneficial improvements in various types of upholstery materials. Outstanding among Huguenot designers was Daniel MAROT, who had fled to Holland and served the Dutch court. After William III of Holland came to the English throne in 1689 Marot visited England (1694–8) and his designs are known to have had great influence. By 1700 English cabinet-makers had not only assimilated the most progressive techniques in Europe but had translated them into truly national forms. Moreover English furniture was now being exported in considerable quantities throughout Europe, to the Turkish empire and to North America and the West Indies. These exports were principally unpretentious and utilitarian in character, obviously highly regarded abroad for their sound craftsmanship and eminently suited for middle-class homes.

For some time after 1660 the 'politer way of living' which, in the words of the diarist John Evelyn, was introduced by the Restoration, encouraged elaborate decoration of furniture. This is characteristically seen in the tall-backed Carolean chairs with their spiral turned uprights, the exuberant carving on their cresting, on the frames of the back panels of imported cane and on their front stretchers, and the scrolled legs, arms and arm supports. During the reign of William and Mary (1689–1702) much of this fanciful ornament was discarded. Graceful baluster-turned uprights and front legs, and upholstered backs or backs with fillings of upright balusters or, under Marot's influence, of pierced and carved work, all gave chairs a dignified appearance. Careful attention was paid to upholstery of wing armchairs designed for comfort with their ear-pieces to exclude draughts and their well-padded backs and arms.

The assertion of good taste is visibly recorded in the walnut furniture of Queen Anne's reign (1702–14), which achieved a stately dignity and marked this as one of the great periods of English craftsmanship. The curvilinear chair with hooped back, which is often associated exclusively with Queen Anne but which was made mainly after 1720, marked a totally new conception in chair design. The central support of the back, a solid splat, was usually shaped in vase or urn forms and was concave at shoulder level for the sitter's comfort (hence the contemporary name of 'bended back' for these chairs). The rounded seat was supported on cabriole legs which curved down from a sturdy knee-piece to slender ankles and to feet of club, hoof or claw-and-ball form which no longer required the use of stretchers. In this new era of curvilinear chair construction England took a leading part. Chests of drawers and bureaux acquired the forms which are still familiar. For their bases bracket feet were widely adopted after 1700 in place of their former ball or bun feet. It was a period which persistently sought good proportions in its furniture, exemplified in the development of such composite pieces as the bureau-cabinet and bureau-bookcase, with looking-glass plates on their doors and their cornices surmounted by graceful arched domes or broken pediments. The *Diary* of Samuel Pepys (July, 1666) makes the first recorded reference to a domestic bookcase in England, and this piece of furniture developed rapidly in a country where a good library was considered a necessary part of every gentleman's home. Further notable achievements were in CLOCK-making, in which England again played a leading role. With the introduction of the pendulum and the anchor escapement (reflecting the growing interest in science of the age of the Royal Society and Sir Isaac Newton) clock movements attained improved accuracy and both the LONG-CASE ('grandfather') clock and the smaller, portable TABLE ('BRACKET') clock were given cases of great beauty by the case-makers.

Looking-glasses came into wider use when the manufacture of MIRROR glass was started in England at Vauxhall shortly after 1660, though it remained an expensive commodity even when it had no longer to be imported. Mirrors added further brightness to interiors when set as pier glasses on the wall between windows, and an attractive arrangement popular at this time was the 'table, glass and stands', i.e. a side table standing beneath a pier glass and flanked by a pair of candlestands. Varieties of small tables multiplied. The first tables specifically designed for card playing appeared in William and Mary's reign; they had folding tops so as to serve as side tables when not in use for cards. Sets of gate-legged tables—usually sets of three, one rectangular and two semicircular—were opened and put together to form a dining-table. After the meal they could be closed and used as side tables. Dressing-tables were also popular, either the knee-hole kind with pedestals or a table with drawers on short cabriole legs.

Hampton Court Palace still contains outstanding examples of furniture made in England in this so-called 'walnut period'. They include John Pelletier's carved and gilt stands, Richard Roberts's walnut curvilinear chairs, John GUMLEY's carved and gilt mirrors, and other gesso pieces by Gumley's partner, James MOORE. Examples of Gerreit JENSEN's arabesque marquetry are in Windsor Castle. All these pieces were made between 1690 and 1720. The Victoria and Albert Museum has notable examples of marquetry and of japanned and walnut pieces of this period. Chatsworth is perhaps supreme among the great houses which were furnished at the time.

The GEORGIAN period, from 1714 to 1830, has been justly acclaimed as the 'Golden Age' of English furniture. The secret of its success cannot simply be attributed to excellent craftsmanship, rich patrons and fine materials, for all three features can be found at other times, for instance in the Victorian period. It is rather to be found in a unique combination of these factors. At the time when the classical Renaissance blossomed in England taste was governed by the cultured upper classes whose education was thoroughly grounded in a study of the classics and also had a strong practical side, completed by the Grand Tour abroad to view the principal sites of antiquity and of the Renaissance. All this gave a competent working knowledge of architecture, painting, sculpture and interior decoration. Recent research is making it abundantly clear that furniture craftsmen did not merely execute designs given to them by their patrons and architects but were trained to design and make furniture independently, if the need arose, although their work was still in perfect conformity with the decorative schemes of the house in which they were engaged. There was plenty of scope for talent, for the age encouraged experiment and new styles were eagerly accepted—some, such as the BAROQUE and NEO-CLASSICAL, being variations of the classical theme, while others, such as the ROCOCO, GOTHIC and Chinese were in antithesis to it. Rising national prosperity allowed the richer classes to indulge their tastes.

Georgian craftsmen found their ideal medium in MAHOGANY. This wood began to affect furniture design after 1725, when timbers from British colonies in America were freed from their former heavy import duties, and by 1750 it had superseded walnut for fashionable furniture. Its metallic strength encouraged further bold changes in design; in, for example, the slender supports for tables, in daring splatwork on chair backs, and in fine, crisp carved decoration. It could equally well be used as a veneer, and some of its figures—curls, feathers, mottles, fiddle-back, etc.—added great beauty to furniture. It provided wide planks for cupboard doors and table tops, achieved a beautiful patina in use and unlike walnut was strongly resistant to worm. The earliest variety of mahogany in favour was 'Spanish wood' from the West Indies, particularly from San Domingo and Jamaica, close-grained, dark and heavy, and very suitable for carving. Later, supplies came from Honduras and Cuba, lighter in weight and colour and providing, in the Cuban variety, fine figures.

FURNITURE

The early Georgian period saw the emergence of the first English architect to include furniture as an essential part of his decorative schemes. This was William KENT (1685–1748), a very versatile designer who under the guidance of his patron, the Earl of Burlington, revived the Palladian style for the exteriors of his buildings and for the interiors, in complete contrast, designed rich and massive Baroque furniture. He made great use of monumental pieces, gilt or in mahogany 'parcel' (i.e. partially) gilt, adorned with a profusion of carved masks, lion heads, SWAGS, shells and ACANTHUS, best typified in his gigantic side tables and in the newly fashionable CONSOLE TABLES of French inspiration, supported on two brackets or on a spread eagle. Pedestals, pier glasses, bookcases, chests and grand gilded chairs all featured in this Kentian decoration in one form or another. But though this Baroque phase is of interest and Kent's furniture fitted perfectly (as at Holkham and Houghton, two of his best-known houses) into its surroundings, it was alien to the English tradition. It was the conception of an architect and not of a cabinet-maker, and was soon regarded, in the words of Horace Walpole, as 'often immeasurably ponderous'. Outside the circles in which he worked Kent's designs seem to have influenced an architectural treatment of case furniture. But in general the remarkable qualities of mahogany encouraged a return to carved ornament and a gradual abandonment of veneering. Prominent carved motifs were lions' paws and masks on cabriole legs—hence the term 'lion period' sometimes applied to the 1730s and 1740s. Other common motifs were acanthus, shells, satyr masks, cabochons and eagle heads.

The mid 18th c. is inseparably coupled with the name of Thomas CHIPPENDALE (1718–79), the most famous of all English cabinet-makers. He still remains a somewhat shadowy figure in spite of the rapidly increasing information which modern research is revealing about him. Born in Yorkshire, he migrated to London and established a flourishing business in St. Martin's Lane, the most fashionable centre of London cabinet-making. He had many wealthy patrons yet never achieved a royal appointment, a distinction which went to a number of talented contemporaries, including Benjamin GOODISON, William VILE (d. 1767), John Bradburn and William FRANCE. Chippendale achieved fame through the publication of his *Gentleman and Cabinet-Maker's Director* in 1754 (republished in 1755 and, enlarged, in 1762). With perceptive business acumen he saw the reaction against Classicism which had begun in France, and to which the name of ROCOCO has been given, and in the *Director* he translated this new style into anglicized versions for the benefit of craftsmen and prospective patrons. The unique character of the *Director*—the first pattern-book to be entirely devoted to furniture and the first to be published by a cabinet-maker—made Chippendale's name widely known and has bequeathed it as a very convenient label for the mid-century taste. Rococo ornament was based on C and S scrolls, often employed asymmetrically, and on furniture it could be admirably executed by delicate carving in mahogany. *Director* chairs in this form have a 'cupid's bow' cresting rail, curved uprights, finely carved and pierced splats, and cabriole legs ending in 'French scroll' or 'knurl' feet, the former outward- and the latter inward-curving. In case furniture curved and serpentine forms characterize the style. The *Director* also added designs in two subsidiary fashions, the Gothic and the Chinese, the former influenced by Horace Walpole's Gothic villa at Strawberry Hill, the latter taking advantage of a renewed interest in CHINOISERIES. Both these styles merged easily into the Rococo, the Gothic in the form of carved crockets, pointed arches and pinnacles, etc., the Chinese in the form of Oriental motifs—mandarins, bells, long-necked birds, temples, etc.—mingled with asymmetrical scrolls, as is perhaps best illustrated in gilded mirror frames. But Chinese ornament also included, in contrast, 'railings' or geometrical frets, which were used as tiny galleries on tea (or 'china') tables, or in low relief ('card cut') on the legs of chairs and tables. Tea furniture, in the development of which the English were pioneers, consisted of charming small portable pieces such as tea-caddy stands and urn stands, as well as tables, and one version of the latter, the 'pillar and claw' with a circular top supported on a column and tripod feet, was particularly fashionable.

Assignment of English furniture to particular makers is a difficult task as they rarely signed or stamped their work. As the *Director* was intended to be a guide to craftsmen, a great deal of furniture based on Chippendale's designs was made, yet very little in this style can be traced directly to his own workshop (where, it must be noted, he superintended production and did not actually make furniture himself). Documentary evidence, however, proves that Chippendale was responsible for the furnishing of Nostell Priory, Yorkshire, where his most celebrated piece in *Director* taste (though a late example) is the superbly carved library table supplied in 1767 for £72. 10*s*. Yet the best furniture in Rococo style was undoubtedly produced by Chippendale's near neighbour in St. Martin's Lane, William Vile, whose pieces, authenticated by the royal accounts, have perhaps the finest carvings ever seen on English furniture and rank among the supreme achievements of English craftsmanship. They include the bureau-cabinet and jewel cabinet (1761) and bookcase (1762) supplied to Queen Charlotte, and a medal cabinet altered for George III in 1761. An end cabinet from this last piece is now in the Victoria and Albert Museum.

In the late 1760s the Rococo went out of fashion in favour of a revived Classicism (NEO-CLASSICISM): first Robert ADAM's light and delicate interpretation, which obviously owed much to the Rococo; and then, after *c.* 1790, a stricter archaeological version based on actual models of classical antiquity, in the phase known as the REGENCY.

Contrary to long-held belief it is uncertain how far Adam himself was the originator of the style that goes by his name. There is evidence, not yet entirely conclusive, that France may have been first in this field. What is certain is that Adam, a Scottish architect who had travelled extensively abroad before beginning his professional career in London with his three brothers in 1758, gradually developed a highly individual approach and united architecture, decoration and furnishings into a close-knit unity of a kind never seen before, and one that marks a brilliant phase in English craftsmanship. Adam employed an extensive vocabulary of classical ornament—PATERAE, festoons of husks, ANTHEMION, rams' heads, medallions, vases, etc.—delicately applied to furniture in varied forms—painted, carved and in marquetry. Marquetry underwent a remarkable revival at this time after half a century of disuse. There was a general return to light-coloured woods, especially satinwood, but effective use was also made of bright ORMOLU mounts on a background of mahogany.

It has been traditionally held that Adam himself designed all the furniture which fits so readily into his interiors, as at Osterley, Syon House, Kedleston, Harewood House, Saltram and elsewhere. The great collection of Adam drawings in the Sir John Soane's Museum, London, includes designs for furniture, and where there is no design for a piece which stands in an Adam house and is obviously part of the general decorative scheme it has been assumed that the architect sent the design to cabinet-makers to execute and that it was never returned. Recent evidence, however, brings these assumptions seriously into question. Adam's drawings show that he was responsible mainly for furniture that stood against the wall—sideboards, side tables, mirrors, pedestals, stands, and some chairs—as these completed his decoration of the room. They included some notable compositions, particularly of matching mirrors and side tables or of side tables flanked by a pair of pedestals and urns—the forerunners of modern sideboards. But apart from these pieces the furniture in Adam's rooms was designed separately by cabinet-makers who were commissioned by the owners, though no doubt much of their work was carried out in discussion with the architect. In sum, it is reasonable, when an Adam drawing for a piece of furniture is lacking, to credit the design to the cabinet-maker. Chippendale, for instance, can be held responsible for designing and producing much of the furniture in Adam houses, and indeed his best work was done in Neo-Classical taste and not in his own *Director* style. Harewood House contains some of his masterpieces, among which the famous 'Diana and Minerva' commode, supplied in 1773 at a cost of £86, is the most celebrated. In at least one case, Appuldurcombe Park, Isle of Wight, Chippendale is known to have furnished completely with Neo-Classical furniture a house with which Adam had no connection whatever. Other craftsmen, such as John LINNELL at Osterley and John COBB at Corsham, carried out their own designs in Neo-Classical style.

The Adam era also ushered in another attractive phase of chair design. Round and oval backs became fashionable, and variations of these shapes produced some fascinating forms—heart, kidney and above all shield, a particularly delightful contribution. The legs of chairs, as indeed of furniture generally, tended to be straight (of round or square section) and tapered. It is the achievement of George HEPPLEWHITE that the gracefulness of the Neo-Classical style was transmitted into furniture for middle-class homes. Hepplewhite's life is wrapped in obscurity. He kept a shop in unfashionable Cripplegate, London, and his designs, which were not original and did not claim to be so, were published by his widow in 1788, two years after his death, in a pattern-book entitled *The Cabinet-Maker and Upholsterer's Guide* (reissued in 1789 and 1794). The elegant and well-proportioned furniture of all types illustrated in the *Guide* reflects the general taste of the last quarter of the century, and faithfully fulfils its noble aim, declared in the preface to the 1794 edition, 'to unite elegance and utility and blend the useful with the agreeable'. Among Hepplewhite's chair designs his variations on the shield-back are especially well known, perhaps the most famous being that incorporating the Prince of Wales's feathers which, like the classical motifs of vases, draperies, husks, etc., on other chairs, he popularized but did not originate. Other typical Hepplewhite pieces are the small sideboard with bow front, the attractive PEMBROKE TABLE (introduced *c.* 1765) with serpentine, rectangular or semicircular flaps, the chest of drawers with serpentine or bow front, and JAPANNED furniture intended mainly for bedrooms. Legs followed, in general, the Neo-Classical fashion of straight tapered form on plinth (or spade) feet, but some case furniture (e.g. chests of drawers) had outward-curving feet and a curved apron-piece at the bottom of the frame. When the same preface of 1794 also declared that 'English taste and workmanship have, of late years, been much sought for by surrounding nations', it was paying a well-deserved tribute to the superb standard of English furniture design and the wide esteem in which it was held throughout Europe, from Norway and Denmark in the north to Spain and Portugal in the south and to Russia and Poland in the east. In all these countries English furniture was imported, copied and adapted.

The trend towards lightness of design which had been evident since 1760 reached its peak in the designs of Thomas SHERATON's *Cabinet-Maker and Upholsterer's Drawing Book*, published in parts between 1791 and 1794. Sheraton did not even own a workshop and died in poverty. No furniture by him (or for that matter by Hepplewhite) has ever been identified. But the name 'Sheraton' is fittingly applied to some of the most delicate furniture made in England, displaying in its simplicity of line and decoration a masterly compactness and, often, portability. The population explosion of the late 18th c. put an unprecedented strain upon living space in cities, above all in London, and compact, multi-purpose furniture, invaluable for saving space, was in great demand. Hence the range of small pieces in the *Drawing Book* such as portable bookcases and tables which could be used for a number of functions—writing, reading, needlework, games, toilet, etc.—as well as larger pieces with ingeniously fitted interiors. Sheraton was keenly aware of the current interest in mechanical devices of all kinds which had been aroused by the Industrial Revolution and applied gadgets to some of his furniture to save space and increase its versatility. The 'Harlequin Pembroke Table', for instance, incorporated a mechanism which, if the owner wished, could cause a nest of small drawers equipped with writing materials to rise above its surface. Chairs followed the prevailing trend by generally adopting square backs, their lightness emphasized by cane seats, tapered legs and upward-sweeping arms. Economy of line and of decoration was to a large extent conditioned by economy of material, itself imposed by war-time stringency. The long French wars (1793–1815) curtailed the expensive methods of carving and marquetry in favour of painted and japanned decoration (for which native beech was ideal) or simple line-inlay ('stringing') in ebonized wood or the more durable brass.

Sheraton's designs mark the transition between Adam's Neo-Classicism and the archaeological interpretation of the Regency, a term which in the context of the decorative arts overlaps the political Regency of the Prince of Wales, 1811–20. Sheraton's later works, the *Cabinet Dictionary* of 1803 and an unfinished *Encyclopaedia* of 1804–6, show increasing awareness of the new approach, but the last book presents designs of such fantasy as to suggest a deranged mind. Since the middle of the 18th c. excavations in Italy and Greece had provided a growing body of accurate information on the furniture of antiquity, and in 1798 Napoleon's campaign in Egypt considerably increased interest in and knowledge of Egyptian antiquities. French *ébénistes* had already begun to produce furniture closely based on classical models and in 1783 the new style reached England when the Prince of Wales (the future George IV) came of age and furnished Carlton House, his official residence, with the latest French furniture. The Prince and his Whig friends adopted a marked pro-French policy in defiance of the Tory anti-French sentiments of George III. Carlton House inspired the building or modernization of a number of great Whig houses, outstanding among which is Southill, rebuilt for Samuel Whitbread in 1795, much of the interior furnishing in each case being carried out by French craftsmen under the direction of the Prince's gifted architect Henry Holland, a strong exponent of the new classical forms. Between the French Revolution in 1789 and the outbreak of war in 1793 more of the latest French furniture reached England, either bought in France at sales of aristocratic homes or brought over by émigrés.

Exactitude based on scholarship was at first the keynote of the new interpretation after 1800 and was clearly formulated in Thomas HOPE's *Household Furniture and Interior Decoration* (1807), in which the author, a rich connoisseur who had travelled widely in search of authentic material, illustrated furniture designed for his own home. In general Regency furniture of this kind favoured straight lines, unbroken surfaces and low height. Dark glossy woods with striped figure, such as rosewood, amboyna, zebra wood, calamander and selected mahogany, were used as a foil for bright metal ornaments—lions' heads, anthemion, acanthus, and the more novel Egyptian motifs of winged sphinxes, lotus, etc.—and brass trellis work, galleries, paw feet and columns. Typical pieces of this phase are low square bookcases with brass trellis doors backed by silk hangings, chiffoniers (low cupboards with bookshelves), sofa tables with rectangular tops and two end-flaps, round tables on pillar-and-claw or pedestal bases, Carlton House tables with nests of drawers on top at the back and sides, and circular mirrors. The 'Grecian' couch was very fashionable, as were 'Grecian' chairs based on the classical KLISMOS with shoulder-board, curved ('sabre') legs and boldly swept arms. One light version, the Trafalgar chair, had a cane seat and square back of Sheraton type with turned top-rail and sometimes with rope decoration which, like the anchor and dolphin, symbolized Nelson's naval victories.

Though much Regency furniture was characterized by good proportions and fine craftsmanship in the best English tradition, in its later stages, when it was popularized through commercial production (a tendency which Hope in 1807 had already perceived and criticized), it showed signs of degeneration. George SMITH's pattern-book of 1808, *Designs for Household Furniture and Interior Decoration*, lacks Hope's precise scholarship and mixes styles in an incongruous manner. By the time of George IV's death in 1830 it was abundantly clear that the long reign of classical decoration was over. It would be a mistake, however, to take the traditional view of dismissing the Victorian period (1837–1901) as one of unrelieved and cataclysmic decline in standards of taste. The considerable research that is going on into the history of Victorian furniture has very considerably modified this opinion. Against the background of the Industrial Revolution, which saw economic and social changes of unprecedented magnitude and rapidity, three aspects are worth studying: the general commercial production of furniture, the endeavours of pioneer designers to relate furniture intimately to the new age and the development of vernacular furniture. The last is now understood to have been one of the sources of the 'modern' movement in furniture.

Commercial manufacture of furniture expanded enormously to meet the needs of the continually rising population. More English people than ever before had the opportunity and means to furnish a home of their own. This home was the focal point of family life and its prime feature was comfort, for which industry could provide the necessary materials and which the working classes could justifiably claim as a reward for their skill and toil. Factory-produced upholstery fabrics, for instance, were available at low prices; hence the deep-sprung covering on so much early- and mid-Victorian seating furniture, hiding the former elegant outlines. In this respect commercial production hastened the decline in standards of design. The Great Exhibition of 1851 encouraged the process, for the temptation for manufacturers to over-decorate their exhibits was too strong—though their elaborate furniture pictured in the Exhibition catalogues can no longer be taken as typical (as it once was) of all contemporary furniture.

With Classicism in decline the void was filled with revivals of historical styles. In 1833 J. C. LOUDON's *Encyclopaedia of Cottage, Farm and Villa Architecture and Furniture* named the four prevailing styles as Grecian (the last fling of Classicism), Gothic, Elizabethan and Louis Quatorze. Two of these harked back to earlier English history and were considered, according to the current theory of 'association of ideas', to reflect the sturdiness of the national character. The Louis Quatorze revival was a further indication of the traditional admiration for France, where the recent Bourbon restoration had resuscitated *ancien régime* styles. Historical revivals, which were largely misunderstood even by their most skilled exponents, were enthusiastically taken up by commercial manufacturers. Decorative details such as turned members, fretwork and strapwork were cheap to produce and thus helped to perpetuate the debased ornament on so much Victorian furniture. A love of show, unfettered by ingrained standards of taste, was perhaps inevitable in the conditions of the 19th c., which in this respect as in others has affinities with the Tudor period.

Until the 1890s reforming designers of the period worked entirely within the framework of historical revivals. The merit of their work lies in their true understanding of the past and of its applicability, suitably modified, to the changing scene, above all with reference to traditional craftsmanship. A. W. N. PUGIN, for example, designed Gothic furniture in which ornament was an integral part of the design and not merely trimmings added to current forms; he also openly revealed constructional methods such as the pegs securing joints, recognizing construction as fundamentally attractive in itself and not something to be hidden, however skilfully, as had been cabinet-making practice for two centuries.

The most celebrated reformer was William MORRIS, who founded his firm (subsequently Morris & Co.) in 1861 to combat the ugliness of commercial production. As well as expensive ('state') furniture for rich clients the firm made, mainly through its chief designer, Philip WEBB, much simple, workaday furniture in which revealed honest construction was an integral part of the design. About 1865 the firm began to produce cheap chairs with beech frames and rush seats based on a traditional Sussex type and these had a great success. Interesting Gothic furniture, revealing understanding and sensitivity, was designed in the 1860s and 1870s by Bruce James Talbert (1838–81) and William Burges (1827–81), and Charles Locke EASTLAKE popularized simple and practical furniture, based on medieval and Jacobean forms, in his *Hints on Household Taste* (1868), which had wide sales in America as well as in England. The architect E. W. Godwin (1833–86), who at first designed furniture in the Neo-Jacobean style, was greatly influenced after *c.* 1867 by Japanese art and ingeniously adapted the style to light and delicate furniture with slender supports, much of it in ebonized woods.

With the foundation of the Century Guild by A. H. MACKMURDO in 1882 there began a remarkable revival of craftsmanship through the ARTS AND CRAFTS MOVEMENT, in which Morris's influence was potently felt. Groups of craftsmen and designers combined to revive hand skill and good design with a strong sense of social reform, and to make their work known through exhibitions. Much 18th-c. furniture served as models for the Movement, but one of its most enduring aspects was the resurgence of traditional cottage furniture through the Cotswold School. From *c.* 1890 onwards came ART NOUVEAU, which drew inspiration from the sinuous waving forms in nature and was thus the only Victorian style which was not based on a historical precedent. In spite of its name the new movement was regarded abroad as owing much of its inception to England, particularly through the furniture designs of C. F. A. VOYSEY, who, though adopting such characteristic mannerisms as the upward continuation of structural members into free-standing columns (e.g. of chair uprights above their cresting), large hinges and other metal fitments, and use of the heart motif, did so with masterly control of simple and elegant lines in plain oak.

In the present century leadership of the Modern Movement has passed to Scandinavian and German industrial designers, particularly the latter, whose BAUHAUS furniture (1919–33) based on mechanized production and the use of new materials has set the standard of creative design in Europe and America. The reluctance of English designers to face the problem of machine production largely explains their loss of leadership. Recently, however, the validity of the Bauhaus approach to modern furniture design is being questioned as insufficiently heedful of national traditions. There is now active reappraisal of the 19th c. in terms of vernacular functionalism. The 'almost timeless maturity' (to use Sigfried Giedion's phrase) of English furniture of the Hepplewhite–Sheraton era has by no means disappeared. Sheraton's pioneer designs incorporating mechanical devices in compact furniture were part of a very interesting phase between 1800 and 1850, when English designers were in the forefront in allying cabinet-making of great skill with precision engineering in the production of 'patent furniture', a current term for mechanical furniture whether officially patented or not. In general the wide range of convertible pieces of this phase stressed utilitarian functional forms until they succumbed to the elaboration engendered by the Great Exhibition.

Vernacular furniture, with its intuitive adaptation to function, sturdily survived the Victorian period. The WINDSOR CHAIR, for example, the making of which was centred in High Wycombe, showed both an amazing vitality and a remarkable variety of forms. The trade card of Edwin Skull, a High Wycombe manufacturer, *c.* 1870, illustrates well over 100 different types of Windsor and other traditional chairs adapted for every possible occasion. The fostering of simple, useful and graceful furniture of vernacular tradition by Morris and Co. was continued by the Cotswold School. Here the dominant figure was the architect Ernest GIMSON who, under Morris's direct inspiration, went to the Cotswolds in 1893 with two brothers, Sidney and Ernest BARNSLEY, and set up a workshop near Cirencester. Having mastered the craft of chair-making from a rural craftsman, Gimson devoted his life to designing elegant furniture in the best traditions of English rural craftsmanship. Until 1914 his furniture, which displayed a wonderful feeling for materials and never confused tradition with imitation, was much admired abroad, more so in fact than at home. His personal influence can be seen today in the number of small shops specializing in fine, mainly hand-made furniture, notably that of Edward Barnsley, the son of Sidney Barnsley.

The importance of the significant Victorian trends outlined above is emphasized by the careers of the two most prominent designers of the 20th c., Sir Ambrose HEAL (1872–1959) and Sir Gordon RUSSELL (1892–). Both men were reared in the Arts and Crafts Movement, both added machine production to handicraft, and both have designed in full awareness of vernacular tradition. As early as 1898 Heal's first Plain Oak Furniture catalogue illustrated good, well-designed and low-priced furniture of the kind which the firm continues to make. Russell's approach to design, expressed in his conviction that 'the English tradition has always been to use the most suitable materials available in a straightforward downright way', shows the relevancy, even for a modern mechanized woodworking industry, of a study of English furniture from its origins.

3. AMERICAN. The history of furniture in North America is intrinsically bound up with the transplantation of European culture and traditions to its shores. Seventeenth-c. American furniture, far from being in a singular and consistent style, emerged from the tastes of many lands. The predominant colonizers were the English, who settled both in New England and in the south. The Dutch colonized the Hudson valley and Swedish and German settlements existed in Pennsylvania. Since there was little intercommunication among these earliest settlements, interplay of ideas and craft techniques was slight. Most of the furniture as well as changes in taste and style came directly from the mother countries. For the most part too the Colonial methods of house construction as well as the crafts were rooted in medieval tradition. Furniture was scarce in 17th-c. America and few pieces remain. The articles in most frequent use were stools, benches, small tables, and some chest-and-drawer combinations. The earliest indigenous furniture that has been preserved was made in New England by anonymous craftsmen, who based themselves on medieval traditions with utilitarian concerns predominant. Much of it was devoid of ornament, massive, rectangular and boxy. Turning was the most common form of decorative treatment. This enabled the craftsmen to elaborate the forms of legs, back-posts, stretchers and rungs. Late in the 17th c. turnings of the balluster type were introduced as well as melon, disc and spool turnings. In addition to turned decoration there was some shallow carving of leaves, rosettes and geometrical patterns.

Chairs with straight back-posts and rush seats were very common throughout the early Colonial period. When greater refinement was sought an adjustment in the turnings was made. The Carver chair, named after the first Governor of Plymouth, is an example of a type of quality chair of the period. But by the end of the 17th c. American craftsmen were copying the elaborate court style originating from England. The lighter and simpler pieces of the earlier part of the century were replaced by heavier, WAINSCOTED furniture. Renaissance and, later, BAROQUE decorative motifs were used. Carving tended to emphasize the structural elements. The Restoration style which emanated from Flanders and France was essentially Baroque and considerably lighter in design. Furniture such as this was at first rare in the colonies; but as wealth increased, first in the south and later in New England, the taste for opulence encouraged its production. Following English prototypes, two-tiered cupboards with carving and turned decoration were made. Chests and storage boxes were among the newer pieces of useful furniture. In America these chests were often named after the area from which they came—two examples are the Hartford chests of CONNECTICUT and the HADLEY CHESTS of Massachusetts. Common also in this period was the BIBLE BOX. Designed to hold the family bible and important papers, it had a simple hinged top and was often placed on a stand.

American Colonial furniture styles were marked by simplicity and functionality while still remaining within the ambit of European and primarily English prototypes. Space was at a premium and many of the pieces of furniture combined several functions (e.g. chair-tables) and others could fold up to save space (e.g. drop-leaf, butterfly and gate-legged tables). Thus from the earliest times American furniture bore an individual stamp which, far from being always provincial, sometimes represented an advance on English models. A variety of both soft- and hardwoods was available to the colonial craftsmen. Pine was readily available, as were oak, birch, maple and hickory. Towards the end of the 17th c. walnut became popular when it was realized that its fine grain was suitable for elaborate carving and turning.

By the 18th c. there was an established merchant class on the eastern coast. Finer houses and finer interior appointments were more common. Further commercial development accelerated the exchange of stylistic ideas and modified styles originating from Holland, Spain, Italy and China also came to America. New wealth on both sides of the ocean was displayed in stately homes with refined and elaborate furnishings. The demand for comfort and elegance led to new furniture design. The rural arts and crafts of the previous century were transformed into a culture which was now urban in character. In America the new enlarged houses contained several rooms, including a central hall, two parlours and a separate dining-room. One of the parlours was usually for formal use, containing sofa, chairs, mirror, several small tables, and possibly a desk. The other was for the family and contained a day-bed, chairs, pine tables, and perhaps a cradle. Other specific furniture was needed for the dining-room and bedroom. Furniture-making in the 18th c. was one of the first trades in which the American craftsmen could both match, and free themselves from dependence on, their English counterparts. The settlers of the previous century had of necessity to be adept at a variety of skills. In contrast the 18th c. was an age of specialization. The cabinet-maker was now able to devote himself full time to his trade.

As oak was the wood most suitable for 17th-c. furniture, so walnut was best adapted for the styles of WILLIAM AND MARY and QUEEN ANNE. The close graining of walnut made it ideal for carving and the cutting of VENEERS. Other woods used were the fruit woods such as peach, apple and cherry. Veneering was only one of the innovations employed with William and Mary furniture. Carving became bolder. Vigorously carved Baroque details were incorporated into the still rectilinear shapes. The Spanish foot, resembling a semi-flexed fist resting on knuckles, was a notable sophistication away from the turned legs common to the earlier period.

For America the William and Mary style was significant because it introduced many new furniture forms—the high chest of drawers on a stand (commonly called the 'highboy'), the LOWBOY, the day-bed, the slope-top or slant-top desk, the upholstered easy chair, and additionally several types of functional tables. It should be remembered that pattern-books were scarce and that from the beginning the American craftsmen took the fundamental furniture forms and from them developed an indigenous style. Chairs of this period are very characteristic in that they no longer implied formality but were in common use throughout the house. There were also sofas and settees. One of the most notable innovations of the period was the upholstered armchair. The storage chests of the earlier period also underwent a considerable change. There were still chests of drawers but the drawers were veneered, the divisions on the front were accentuated by mouldings, and the whole piece now rested on ball or turnip feet. A further practical innovation was the raising of the chest on a framework of legs and stretchers, from which resulted the earliest form of true high-chest. In America this is most commonly called the 'highboy'. This form lost favour in England after the Queen Anne period, but remained popular in America throughout the years 1700–80. The finest American William and Mary highboys exhibit beautiful use of burl and crotch walnut veneering while others were lacquered black and decorated with colour in a Chinese manner. Another piece of furniture which developed in this period was the desk with the slanted or sloping top. This was essentially a chest of drawers, but topped with an additional section containing small drawers, pigeon-holes and a writing surface. Occasionally a cupboard with panelled doors was added on top of the desk, creating another form called the SECRETARY. Import of ceramics increased the demand for yet other new furniture forms. Corner cupboards as well as several varieties of tables were used to fulfil this need.

By 1725 the fundamental Baroque character of the William and Mary style was being merged with the more sophisticated Queen Anne forms, which had lost the stiffness of earlier times. A distinct elegance emerged. Although American Queen Anne models were based on English styles, they were simpler than their counterparts. Whereas English furniture relied on carving and gilding for decoration, American pieces were plainer and relied more on symmetry and proportion. American furniture craftsmen always had a respect for the natural qualities of the wood. The most important element in Queen Anne

William and Mary high chest with bolection moulding. (Greenfield Village and Henry Ford Mus., Dearborn, Mich., 1700–20)

(*Below left*) Japanese Queen Anne highboy of maple and white pine. Boston. (Met. Mus., New York, *c.* 1735)

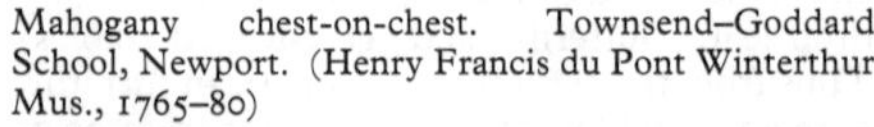

Mahogany chest-on-chest. Townsend–Goddard School, Newport. (Henry Francis du Pont Winterthur Mus., 1765–80)

designs was the CYMA curve, the use of which went beyond decoration and was incorporated into the structure itself. The cyma curve is ubiquitous—on legs, on seats and backs of chairs, on table aprons and on the scroll tops of highboys. During the Queen Anne period marked variations of style both regional and national developed. Regional differences can be noted in the carving of the feet, the secondary woods used, the shape of chair seats, construction methods, finials on case pieces, and over-all form and proportion.

Because 18th-c. chairs required a variety of skills—upholsterer, joiner, carver, turner—the American Queen Anne style is epitomized in the chair. It alone is fully capable of reflecting Colonial tastes of the period. American Queen Anne chairs are usually smaller than those of England. They possess an organic unity which makes use of both bold outline and a subtle interplay of curves. New England chairs had square seats, were tall and usually had stretchers connecting the legs. The pad foot was most commonly used. New York chairs were broad and heavy with a thick and pointed foot. The stiles (back-posts) had hitched reversing of curves which matched the vase splats. Carving on New York chairs had strong Dutch characteristics. A most important centre was Philadelphia, the largest colonial city in America. It was there that the Queen Anne chair achieved its greatest refinement. The straight line was completely eliminated. The square seat was replaced by the horseshoe or 'compass' seat, which was in keeping with the curved splats and stiles. The elimination of stretchers gave the chair a continuous undulating line. Another Philadelphia characteristic was the stump rear legs with trifid or drake feet. The Philadelphia arm-chair shows an integrated blending of the arm with the back of the seat. A chair innovation of the period was the corner or 'roundabout' chair with its back curving around two sides and with a corner pointing to the front.

No discussion of American furniture of this period would be complete without mentioning the WINDSOR CHAIR. Brought from England in the early 1700s, established by 1736, the Windsor chair remained popular with all classes throughout the colonies. Simple, utilitarian, made of common available woods, the Windsor achieved a lean elegance combining lightness with strength. The chairs were frequently painted black or green, with coloured lines for added decoration. Like other styles brought to America, the Windsor chair was also modified, new forms emerging unknown in the land of its origin.

The cabriole leg adapted well to the popular highboy. The flat-topped highboys of the William and Mary period became more elaborate in the Queen Anne period with the scroll top and bonnet-top pediments above the cornice. The drop-leaf table with cabriole legs replaced the gate-legged table. As tea-drinking became fashionable in America it gave rise to a variety of tea-tables, some with marble tops. This use of a heat-resistant surface on a table can be considered as a forerunner of the sideboard.

The lasting popularity of the Queen Anne style cannot be wholly attributed to a provincial lag. It is evident that the Colonial cabinet-maker as well as his client preferred the style. In fact American Queen Anne furniture long continued as a rival to the styles which followed.

Thomas CHIPPENDALE's *The Gentleman and Cabinet-Maker's Director* was published in 1754 but its influence was not fully felt in the Colonies until 1760. It is by his name, however, that the American furniture of the ROCOCO phase is known. As has been said, the Queen Anne which had won quick acceptance among American patrons and cabinet-makers was slow in yielding to the new style, whose designs brought an infusion not only of French and Gothic forms, but of Oriental decorative elements and CHINOISERIE. The curvilinear construction of the Queen Anne was still in evidence, but there was now a tendency towards greater magnificence. Florid decorations replaced the simple lines and light proportions of the earlier style. The yoke-back of Queen Anne chairs began to be replaced by the low, broad 'cupid's-bow' back. The simple Dutch foot became webbed, anticipating the highly ornamental forms of the Rococo. Although Chippendale's book was an important influence, there were certain forms not illustrated in the *Director* which persisted in the Colonies, such as the ball-and-claw foot. A flourishing trade with the West Indies helped develop the vogue for imported mahogany, and as walnut was the hallmark of Queen Anne furniture so mahogany became that of the Chippendale period. Being hard and sturdy along with its warm red-brown colour, mahogany was particularly suited to the new styles.

The Chippendale influence on chair designs was particularly marked. The chairs were larger, more imposing and more elaborately carved. Instead of the continuous flowing curves of the Queen Anne, C and S scrolls became characteristic. Straight lines (on seats) and curves intermingle, providing a very animated variety of line movement. The front and sides of the seat are straight and the backs generally rectangular. The back splat is pierced and elaborated with ribbon-like interlacing forms. The vigorously formed cabriole legs terminate in a ball-and-claw foot.

The types of furniture did not change radically from those of the Queen Anne period, however. Tea-tables, folding card-tables and tripod pedestals were still popular, but the legs were profusely carved. The high pier-table used in dining-rooms and halls came into its own in this period. Their tops were of marble and the carving on the legs and front apron was most elaborate. Chests of drawers began to be made with bracket feet, which were additionally carved. An innovation was the block-front chest, which appears to have originated with the GODDARD and TOWNSEND

A B C

D E F

G H J

A. Carver-type maple armchair. New England. (Greenfield Village and Henry Ford Mus., Dearborn, Mich., 1640–60)

B. William and Mary caned maple side-chair. (Met. Mus., New York, 1710–30)

C. Ebonized maple armchair. American Queen Anne style with piercing and cresting in the manner of John Gaines II of Portsmouth, New Hampshire. (Met. Mus., New York, 1700–25)

D. Walnut side chair. Regional American Queen Anne style. Probably Newport. With cresting and shell ornament on the knees. (Henry Francis du Pont Winterthur Mus., 1740–50)

E. Sample chair, possibly by Benjamin Randolph. Design of back from Chippendale's *Director*. (Greenfield Village and Henry Ford Mus., Dearborn, Mich., 1760–75)

F. Chippendale-style armchair with Marlboro' leg. Boston. (Met. Mus., New York, 1765–70)

G. Martha Washington mahogany armchair. (Met. Mus., New York, *c.* 1790)

H. Graduated slat-back chair. New Jersey. (Henry Francis du Pont Winterthur Mus., 1800–30)

J. Mahogany side-chair, by Duncan Phyfe with Roman curule or X-base. (Mus. of the City of New York, *c.* 1810–20)

K. Cast-iron garden seat with decoration of scrolling vine-leaves and grapes. Stamped E. T. Barnum, Detroit, Michigan. (Greenfield Village and Henry Ford Mus., Dearborn, Mich., *c.* 1880)

K

families of Newport, Rhode Island. Instead of plain straight fronts a characteristic fashion of the mid 18th c. was to divide the front of a commode or tall bureau-bookcase into three vertical 'blocks', of which the middle one was usually recessed while the lateral ones were given a slight projection. These chests were usually undecorated except for a shell motif, which was carved alternately concave and convex. Particularly popular in America were the matching highboy and lowboy. These along with the chest-on-chest were made in the new Chippendale style, though there were really no close parallels in English furniture. Other forms of furniture also underwent elaboration and change. The four-poster canopy bed with hangings of wool, linen and damask became fashionable. The bed-posts were ornate with fluting and carved decoration. The simple 'wag' wall-clock developed into the tall-case clock. Mirrors were larger and had complex frames, which were additionally carved, gilded or painted. In general the forms of architectural enrichments were scaled down to furniture proportions and were used without any vestige of structural significance. In particular, versions of the broken pediment and small quarter-round columns on the corners of chests and highboys continued to be used.

The elaborate French influence was most successful in Philadelphia, where the highboy epitomized the Rococo in America. William SAVERY, a Philadelphia cabinet-maker, worked within the Chippendale mode to create a uniquely American highboy. His highboys as well as others from Philadelphia have a subtle refinement of design and vigorous surface carving effectively unifies and animates them. Asymmetrical foliate patterns were applied across the skirt and across the pedimental area below the broken-arch pediment. Shell-like carvings decorated the central drawers top and bottom. Finials in flame form flank the pediment and the central finial is the Rococo scroll device known as a CABOCHON. A CARTOUCHE was also used. Though American Chippendale furniture is more restrained than the name implies, the style lasted well beyond the Revolutionary period.

Although the American Revolution delayed the impact of the early archaeological publications of the NEO-CLASSICAL period on American furniture design, the impact of Classicism was all the greater during the years 1780 to 1790 when the time was right to receive it. The scholarly Classical Revival merged well with the new ideals of government and was an appropriate expression of the young Republic.

It was the mid 18th-c. designs of Robert ADAM which provided the foundation of the Classical Revival in post-Revolutionary America. England had already met the need for popular versions of Adam's designs. A simplified approach to the classical mode emerged in the designs and works of George HEPPLEWHITE and Thomas SHERATON. Each of these men, like Chippendale before them, published handbooks of designs for furniture and interior decoration. Hepplewhite and Sheraton replaced the richly carved ornament of Adam with classical motifs in surface inlay.

The style of Adam, Sheraton and Hepplewhite filtered into America well in advance of their published works. As the American Rococo spirit was seen in the use of eccentric curvilinear movement, so the new style expressed a spirit of Classicism by means of straight lines, minimal carving and the contrast of colour among veneered and inlay woods. Restraint and a touch of formality replaced the vigour of Georgian furniture. The art of inlay flourished in many of the larger American cities and reached a peak in Baltimore, where the quality and skill achieved in this technique were unsurpassed. Classical decorative motifs such as urns and swags, as also indigenous American patriotic motifs (e.g. eagles), were very popular. This new style provided a genuine expression for the feelings of a new nation.

Innovations of the period included the TAMBOUR desk, which was occasionally topped with a bookcase. The bookcase also emerged as a separate piece of furniture. A great variety of tables came into vogue, including extension tables in several parts which could be assembled to seat large groups. The long sideboard for use in the dining-room was one of the most convenient of the newer pieces of furniture. The various arrangement of drawers and cupboards allowed for considerable storage of linen and silver. The finest American craftsmen of the period working in this idiom were Samuel MCINTYRE and John SEYMOUR in New England. In New York the early Classical styles were best evidenced in the works of Duncan PHYFE.

The EMPIRE style of Napoleon had already reached America by the third decade of the 19th c. New furniture forms were adopted for 19th-c. needs, incorporating Roman, Greek and Egyptian motifs. Where there was no archaeological precedent, substitutions were devised such as bookcases designed to suggest temple façades, couches modelled after Roman beds, and console units inspired by ancient altars. The incorporation of Classical forms such as columns and caryatids, combinations of marble and brass, of ORMOLU with wood, and the use of composite animal forms (sphinxes, hairy claw feet and eagle heads) were all incorporated within the Empire style. Archaeological information was often misunderstood. Pompeiian delicacy yielded to Greco-Egyptian solidity. A major characteristic of the American Empire style was the increased weight of all the parts. The delicate proportions current at the turn of the century were replaced by heavier and more massive furniture. Chair railings were virtually eliminated so as to leave an unbroken expanse of wall that provided a severe background to set off objects in the rooms, and this more monumental furniture in turn required larger and more imposing interiors.

Even the Classical work of Duncan Phyfe took a new turn after 1825. He and Charles H. LANNUIER working in New York remained the outstanding American furniture designers of the period.

Two divergent trends away from the Empire and the various revivals became evident during the early part of the century—the HITCHCOCK chair and the furniture of the Shakers. The Hitchcock chair was based on former Sheraton models and was mass produced. From as early as 1818 items were sent by the thousand throughout the country.

The SHAKERS, a religious sect, retained the uncomplicated forms of the 18th c. in their furniture. They made simple tables, Windsor chairs and various plain chests. They retained the traditional furniture forms and improved upon them, making more comfortable and efficient household items.

American furniture design of the Victorian period is a composite, adapted from earlier styles. Through a constant striving for novelty combined with elegance Victorian furniture styles were always in a state of flux. The great international exhibitions in London, Paris, Vienna, Philadelphia and Chicago stepped up the international diffusion of ideas in furniture design and played their part in contributing to the battle of styles during the second half of the 19th c. in America. Even after 1850 American Victorian furniture design still reflected an interest in the Empire mode. Though the handicraft tradition existed, several small factories had initiated the rudimentary beginnings of mass production. Industrialization and specialization in their turn influenced changes in some of the traditional furniture forms. By 1840 there were several manufacturers with 'hundred men' shops. The furniture designs were created by the shop-owner, while skilled and semi-skilled workers produced the goods. Many factory pieces combined machined parts with hand-finishing.

By 1850 interior decoration and furniture design reflected the increased popularity of the Gothic Revival. But its influence on furniture design was less important because of the lack of genuine models. The only authentic pieces to copy were altars and choir-stalls. Machined parts such as ribbed patterns, trefoils and pointed arches were virtually grafted on to existing furniture forms of the mid 19th c. Bookcases especially lent themselves to this Gothic idiom. But the interest in medievalism which was associated with the Gothic Revival indirectly stimulated a later revival in handicrafts.

French aristocratic styles remained popular throughout much of the 19th c. Elegance was achieved by combining marble with gilding and textures of silk and satin. Colour was as omnipresent as pattern. American Victorian furniture in this mode contrasted with the 18th-c. style it was trying to emulate. Frames for upholstered pieces were thin with long and narrow legs. The cabriole leg so well utilized in the

18th c. lost its organic strength. Only the works of John BELTER in New York emerged as a potent force. In them a genuine merging of the historic, the machined, and the handicrafted came to realization.

All the major furniture types persisted during the Victorian period. New pieces included the OTTOMAN, the Lazy Susan Table, and the wardrobe. The preference for weight and complexity reached its height in the 1870s. Also in the 1870s and 1880s designers following the *Hints on Household Taste* of Charles Locke EASTLAKE turned the trend away from the French aristocratic styles towards the craftsmanship traditions of the Middle Ages and the Renaissance. Function and honest construction were the new values sought instead of elaboration.

The styles of the 1880s and 1890s fell under academic influences such as that of the École des Beaux-Arts. Authentic period interiors were desired rather than an indiscriminate mixing of styles. Between 1890 and 1910 a 'craftsman' movement emerged as a reaction against eclecticism.

There was little progressive furniture design in the years immediately following the First World War and a stagnant traditionalism dominated furniture production during the 1920s and 1930s. The popularity of the Baroque and Rococo receded and interest in simpler historical styles—Early American, Shaker, Windsor, and French Provincial—was revived.

In Europe at this time a spirit of experimentation existed. Heavy geometric interpretations were emerging from Germany. The Scandinavians were experimenting with plywood and curvilinear forms, seeking to break up mechanical regularity. A small amount of American furniture reflected these modes prior to the Second World War.

Contemporary furniture is international, having no geographic boundaries. Modern industrial methods and materials contribute much to this end. Roughly three categories have emerged in contemporary American furniture design—furniture with the machined look; furniture with the handicrafted look; and furniture with the biomorphic sculptural look. Specific pieces of furniture need not conform entirely to any one of these categories.

4. MODERN. Modern furniture in the 20th c. brings to mind a multiplicity of images: stark, cool, bent tubular steel furniture; the most refined sculptural forms in handicrafted woods as well as in moulded plywood; fantasy shapes in hard plastics; no-shapes in soft plastics; and many others. The common underlying principle is a search for functional form, comfortable, useful, economical, in the various materials and techniques available today. Historical styles, decoration and personal expression have been almost universally avoided and the emphasis has been put on pure formal values that are often related to or derived from the larger artistic movements of our time. The best modern furniture, though it may be of extreme elegance and costliness and though it may show evidence of a high level of sensitivity and ingenuity on the part of the designer, yet also has a curiously anonymous, timeless and universal quality, one in which individual self-expression is almost totally suppressed in favour of a refined understatement that allows for diversity within conformity to basic aesthetic and technical requirements.

Modern furniture so defined is not entirely a product of the 20th c.; it has its earlier sources and antecedents. One source is English furniture of the late 18th c. and the early 19th c., which achieved a peculiar blend of the practical and the useful with the utmost refinement of form through the discipline of the NEO-CLASSICAL style. It became influential on the Continent as the *style anglais*, and its impact was felt most strongly in northern Europe. There are lines of descent to modern furniture, such as the fine Danish furniture of the 1930s onwards, that go back directly to this model of noble simplicity and functional directness. For example the Danes established the so-called Royal Furniture Store House in Copenhagen at the beginning of the 19th c. It was state-supported and was stocked with fine English furniture to supply local cabinet-makers with high-quality designs and examples of professional craftsmanship, and was instrumental in establishing traditions in Denmark which came to their finest flowering towards the middle of the 20th c., when they were coupled with the gifts of the most sensitive designers.

Another root lies in vernacular furniture, especially two important types of chairs, the ladderback and the WINDSOR, both going back into the 18th c. Vernacular furniture, though often rustic and rude, also achieved refinement and a quality of form in the 19th c. which make it timelessly modern. The furniture of the SHAKER sect in America is derived from traditional forms but simplified, pared down, provided with ingenious functional details and at the same time purified in form and proportions to express the spirituality of its makers.

A similar example of timeless form is the Chiavari chair from Italy, a ladderback which was produced throughout the 19th c. and is still made in almost the identical form as an eminently acceptable, inexpensive modern chair. The Sussex chairs produced by the William MORRIS firm from the 1860s on, and also the furniture produced by representatives of the ARTS AND CRAFTS MOVEMENT and the COTSWOLD SCHOOL of Ernest GIMSON and the BARNSLEYS, of George Walton and Ambrose HEAL in England, and Gustav Stickley, Elbert Hubbard, the Greene brothers and the early Frank Lloyd WRIGHT in America, are of this same vernacular derivation and have the timeless functional quality in common.

The most interesting example of anticipatory

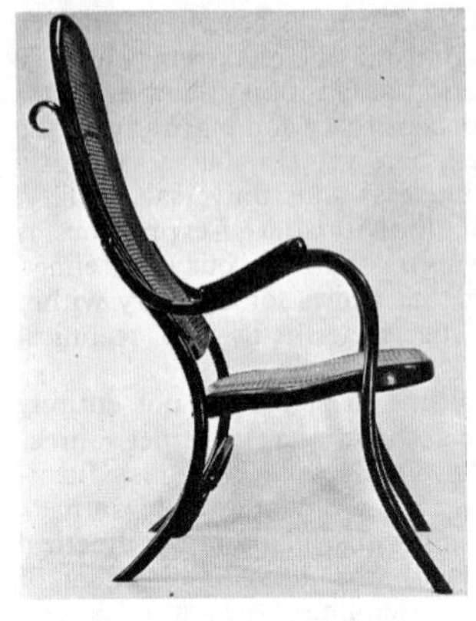

A

B

C

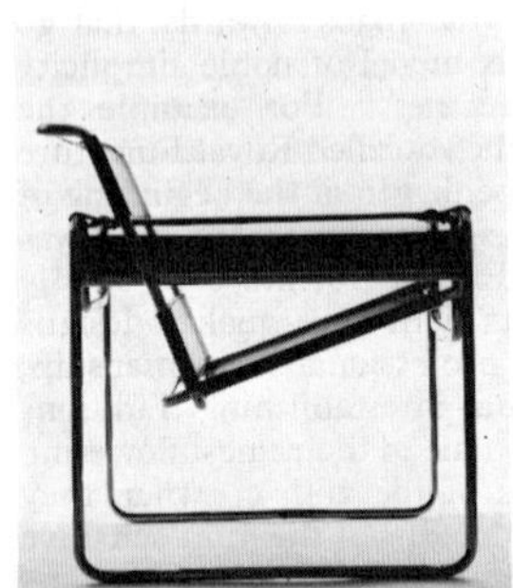

D

E

F

G

H

J

modern is one in which a new technique is applied to the traditional material, wood. This is the bentwood furniture of the German-Austrian Michael THONET—simple, sturdy, eminently useful and inexpensive, its modern form has been in continuous production since the 1850s and 1860s.

Not only is such early modern furniture in many cases still in production and use, but its qualities of simplicity, usefulness and economy are cited as exemplary at critical points in the development of modern furniture in the 20th c. by writers, critics and designers, such as Adolf Loos and Le Corbusier.

Generally one thinks of the ART NOUVEAU at the turn of the century as the first expression of modern design. But if we define 'modern' as rational design of pure form based on function, quality of material and workmanship, emphasizing social purpose by economy of production, then the artistically expressive and highly ornamental designs of the *art nouveau*, designed and made for individual wealthy clients, are hardly in this category. Furniture designs by Henri van de VELDE, Charles Rennie MACKINTOSH, or Émile GALLÉ are personal aesthetic statements of artists, not pieces of furniture with their function and their economic feasibility primarily in mind. Above all *art-nouveau* furniture was a momentary phenomenon, an often bright and brilliant one, but ephemeral and with no future before it. It was a flower, not a seed. On the other hand the German architect Richard Riemerschmid designed a chair in 1899 which does have the quality we call modern, a simple, serviceable armchair, sensibly and sensitively designed to give comfort and grace with a minimum of structure and bulk and no extraneous decoration or emotional pathos. Significantly it also was still in production in 1970, and as modern then as it was at the turn of the century. Though many talked and wrote of the necessity to design handsome furniture to be made for the many by industry, Riemerschmid in 1904 was one of the first actually to do this. This furniture was not to be constructed and joined by craftsmen in the traditional way, but was actually produced in a factory and its design deliberately took this into account. Members were not joined but overlapped and were nailed together without any attempt to hide this fact and simulate other, older or more expensive ways of constructing furniture.

Modern furniture in the 20th c. runs essentially in two parallel streams: one which sees itself as part of a tradition and seeks its inspiration in models from the past that are timeless and congruent with the aesthetic and artistic aspirations of our own time, or which makes them so by restatement in new terms; and the other, more innovative, explorative, which seeks to find its solutions in materials and techniques that are new and more specifically of our time, resulting in forms that are necessarily also often new and different, often also more explicitly in tune with the larger artistic movements of the age. The best from both streams can be set side by side and we will recognize their difference in inspiration and technique, but also their essential harmony and their common ground. The one is more technically orientated, the other more humanistically inclined, without either excluding the preference of the other.

If we discuss first the types more organically connected with tradition, there are those that represent that tradition itself, such as the Chiavari chair and the Windsor chair, still being made in their modest, anonymously functional modern forms as they were made throughout the 19th c. Then there are the versions of these same chairs designed by modern architect-designers, such as the Gio Ponti or E. Rambaldi version of the Chiavari chair, Hans Wegner's Windsor chair made by Johannes Hansen in Denmark, and also the American George Nakashima's handmade chairs, which are refined versions of simple, sturdy, vernacular Windsor forms.

But this tradition becomes more interesting when it is based on more sophisticated forms, such as the classical English furniture of the late 18th c. or Chinese, Greek or Egyptian furniture, and when it either refines and reformulates these models into the modern idiom or is inspired by them to create new forms which yet have the unassertive timeless qualities that make them part of the same tradition. For this, of course, we look primarily to Scandinavia, from where the finest furniture within this humanistic tradition of craftsmanship and design has come in this century. Its pioneer is the Dane Kaare Klint, who did his first furniture designs even before the First World War. In 1924 he was

(*Opposite*) A. Michael Thonet fireside armchair, first produced in the late 1860s. B. Michael Thonet low-backed desk chair, first produced *c.* 1870. This is the chair admired and used by Le Corbusier in the 1920s and 1930s. C. Frank Lloyd Wright armchair. Pine with upholstery. (Mus. of Modern Art, New York, 1904.) D. Marcel Breuer tubular steel and canvas chair, 1925, used by Wassily Kandinsky. Manufactured again since *c.* 1967. E. Mies van der Rohe 'Barcelona' chair, designed for the German Pavilion, International Exhibition, Barcelona, 1929. Manufactured again since 1948. F. Charles and Ray Eames two-piece moulded plywood chair (1946). G. Frank Lloyd Wright straight chair. Wood with separate upholstered pillow. (Mus. of Modern Art, New York, 1957.) H. Modern version of the Chiavari chair, designed by E. Rambaldi and manufactured by G. B. Maragone in Chiavari, Italy. (Neue Samml., Staatl. Mus. für Angewandte Kunst, Munich.) J. Steen Østergaard armchair 291. Nylon reinforced with fibreglass, injection moulded in one single operation, with removable seat cushion in moulded polyurethane foam mounted on a plywood disc (1970)

appointed to the newly established professorship for furniture design at the Academy of Fine Arts in Copenhagen and was thus able to exert an influence on future developments in the field. Klint was not interested in finding new technical solutions with new materials—something not very feasible in any case in a country not highly industrialized—nor was he interested in an exciting design for its own sake. He wanted to design good, comfortable and useful furniture. For this he looked to classical solutions in the past and restated them in terms of his own time, basing rational proportions and measurements on research into practical everyday needs and usage. Table and chair heights, drawer and shelf sizes, were standardized at the optimum of convenience and comfort. The excellence of later Danish furniture owes much to the pioneering activity of Kaare Klint, who died in 1954.

Two other Scandinavian figures must be mentioned for their contributions in the inter-war period. Both used wood in new ways and with new techniques. Karl Bruno Mathsson in Sweden used bent laminated wood particularly for chair frames to create fluid curved shapes of extraordinary grace and litheness. Seating may be of webbing made of a paper compound or more luxurious upholstered pads. His tables are supported by legs that open like petals at the top to widen their support and add stability, both visually and actually.

In Finland Alvar AALTO, one of the greatest and most prolific furniture designers of modern times, used solid wood, laminated wood and combinations of the two. His supports for tables, desks, chairs and stools are of solid wood which separates at the knee into laminated curves that run either part way under seat, table or chest, or connect horizontally for strength and stability with the opposite leg. He used bent laminated strips to create cantilevered frames or sled-like curved frames in which a curved laminated sheet combining seat and back in one piece is suspended. Both Mathsson's and Aalto's more advanced techniques and unusual forms occupy an intermediary position between the usually more tradition-orientated Scandinavians and the designers of central Europe with their passion for experimentation and new forms. It is interesting to note that the bentwood forms of these two designers are like an echo of the 19th-c. bentwood forms of Thonet, but they are sparser, less playful than Thonet's—the difference between 19th-c. and 20th-c. modern.

Tradition, disciplined training and inspiration came to fruition in Denmark after the Second World War and brought an astonishing richness of the most refined designs and the highest level of craftsmanship. Finn Juhl, Hans Wegner, Peder Moos, Ole Wanscher, Børge Mogensen are names which represent the finest in Danish furniture, and indeed in the world. Their furniture is largely hand-made; but it is not the product of a single craftsman who designs and also executes his own designs, but rather of a collaboration between the designer—usually an architect—and a cabinet-maker. And *his* contribution is surely also noteworthy, so that we should be aware, for example, that Hans Wegner's designs are made by Johannes Hansen, or Finn Juhl's by Niels Vodder. In fact the establishment in 1927 of a highly selective annual exhibition of the best Danish furniture in Copenhagen by the Copenhagen Cabinet-Makers' Guild is an important reason for the high quality of Danish furniture. Though the workshops are equipped with power-driven tools, much of the work is of necessity done with age-old tools to achieve the highest standards of craftsmanship in forms that are subtly sculptural and details that are decorative but the result of structure and function. These masterpieces of furniture are made in small quantities and are therefore very expensive, so expensive that they are sadly inaccessible to the kind of people to whose life-style they seem most suitable. More mechanized, industrial production is the answer to this and it is not neglected in Scandinavia.

The more technologically orientated strain of modern furniture has its 19th-c. forerunners in the Thonet bentwood furniture already mentioned and also in the metal furniture that has been astonishingly popular, beginning with designs in LOUDON's *Encyclopedia of Cottage, Farm, and Villa Architecture and Furniture* (1833) and somewhat later the metal rockers, office chairs and of course the beautiful garden furniture that is still used in France in much the same forms that were common in the 19th c. At the turn of the century, when *art nouveau* reigned supreme, there were some designers who reacted against it or ignored it altogether. In Vienna the architect Adolf Loos designed some furniture which is sturdy and sensible without any trace of the prevalent fashion. But he was influential mainly through his writings, in which he insisted again and again that modern furniture was not necessarily of new design, that the modern was simply the best that could be done within good, common-sense traditions and that it was this which would be lasting while the fashionably new—meaning by that the *art nouveau*—would soon be old-fashioned and rejected by everyone. His plea for sensible, functional furniture and his particular passion against ornamentation of any kind had a profound effect on the next decades. As mentioned above, Richard Riemerschmid in Germany designed just such a chair, a reasonable, handsome chair that is not outside good traditions but is also of validity for the future.

In a tangential way Frank Lloyd Wright was also a key figure at this time. Wright designed furniture for many of his houses, most often as part of the design of a particular house and an integral part of it, often literally part of it as built-in structural details. Such furniture cannot be transferred to a different environment but is an individualized solution, which is opposed to a fundamental tendency of our time to seek more generally applicable solutions. Yet at the beginning of his career, in the 1890s and in the first decade of the 20th c., Wright designed some furniture that contributed to the mainstream of design. For his own house he designed chairs that were indebted to the Arts and Crafts Movement, but had a sturdy structural quality that is altogether singular. In 1904 he designed chairs that wilfully exploit their angular structure, with the addition of slanted backs that startle by contrast with the rigidly upright frames and in the case of the side-chairs reach down almost to the floor. For the Larkin Building in Buffalo he designed related chairs of metal with wooden seats.

There is a curious link between these relatively few early seminal pieces by Wright and the beginnings of new developments in furniture design in Europe in the years immediately after the First World War. Wright's work was published in Germany by Wasmuth in 1910 and 1911, and the Dutch architect Robert van't Hoff, who had travelled in America just prior to the War and had become acquainted with the work of Wright, returned and built two houses in Holland very much in Wright's style. The Dutch furniture-maker and later architect Gerrit RIETVELD arrived at furniture designs in those years that are radically different from anything that had gone before. It was as though he took the parts of furniture—rails, stiles and panels—and did not join them but composed them side by side as separate entities that remained so and were merely attached to each other. The piece of furniture became a relationship of straight lines and geometric planes with interstices between them. This lent a hovering quality which was emphasized by the extended cantilevered surfaces of his pieces, and the result was curiously Wrightian. Indeed in 1918 he was asked to design furniture for the Wrightian houses that van't Hoff had built, and did so apparently to full satisfaction.

Like many other modern artists and designers, Rietveld sought to give his work justification and wider implications by theories and philosophy. He was one of a group of Dutch architects, designers and artists who called themselves Neo-Plasticists and explained their theories in the magazine *de Stijl*, a name which has since been applied to the group itself. Their ideal was based on the abstract elementary rectangular forms, using only the primary colours of red, blue and yellow, and to these forms and colours they gave spiritual and philosophical connotations. They believed that by abstraction and simplification art and design would achieve a universal harmony and appeal, and would help to transform an individualistic, materialistic society into a spiritual, idealistic and socialistic one. Their social consciousness made them embrace the machine, standardization, and the new, clear, hard, industrially produced materials in the hope that more people would be able to benefit. These social ideals and the emphasis on clarity and honesty of construction, lightness and cleanness of form, were the legacies of the de Stijl group to the modern style. Their furniture designs are like primitive archetypes which are the starting-point of all changes and accretions of the next decades. Their ideas and aspirations were in tune with the deepest hopes of the turbulent, revolutionary times immediately after the First World War and were thus influential either directly or indirectly.

The basic ideas of the de Stijl group were fruitfully adopted and incorporated in the teaching of a new design school in Germany, the BAUHAUS, which became the most potent centre for the creation and dissemination of the modern style. Under the leadership of its first director, Walter Gropius, it revolutionized the training of designers by stressing experimentation, searching, probing, with the aim of solving functional problems, rather than designing to models and preconceived standards. The students were taught to seek solutions which resulted from the materials and techniques employed and satisfied the functional requirements of each task. It was here that Marcel BREUER began his career as designer and architect, first as student, then as teacher. His first student efforts, as well as those of others, in furniture design in wood have a marked resemblance to the work of Rietveld in Holland. Breuer here first experimented in making furniture of curved metal tubing, in the exuberance of fresh experimentation unknowingly taking up an area already well explored in the 19th c. His first tubular metal chair also echoed Rietveld's wooden furniture in its structure, its angular and parallel forms; but Breuer used new and lighter materials, gleaming chrome for the frame and canvas to give resilience to the weight-bearing surfaces. One continuous piece of bent tubular steel formed the basic frame, and front and back were connected by runners along the floor on both sides in place of conventional legs.

This chair was the first of many pieces of furniture in which metal was used by preference for its combination of lightness with strength, which permitted greater freedom in design and favoured the pursuit of one of the basic tenets of modern industrial production as seen at that time: to do more with less material and to reduce the processes of production. The use of metal tubing led to the cantilever chair, which discards the traditional four legs, cantilevering the seat from the two front supports, thus giving resilience and comfort without the weight and multiplicity of parts needed in traditional joinery.

This kind of experimentation in new materials and methods, with an element of social doctrine underlying it, led to numerous fine solutions, many of which are either being manufactured again because of their timelessly modern character or have become the progenitors of countless derivatives. Breuer himself designed a number of pieces of furniture during the 1920s, including a tubular metal cantilevered chair, which have remained classics. Mies van der Rohe designed a handsome cantilever chair of tubular metal in which the front support was given a sweeping, semicircular form. His most celebrated chair, however, is the Barcelona chair designed in 1929 for the German pavilion, also designed by him, at the International Exhibition held in Barcelona. It is perhaps the most beautiful of all modern chairs. In profile it consists of two crossing curves of polished steel bars, the single curve of the back crossing the reverse curve of the seat to form an expressive linear pattern. The seat is of leather straps supporting welted leather-covered cushions. Meticulous in its proportions and details, the chair is a product of modern technology and impeccable craftsmanship resulting in matchless elegance. It is perhaps worth comparing this superb example of the innovative technically orientated design, which nevertheless needs craftsmanship to achieve its perfection, with the classic modern chairs of Hans Wegner or Finn Juhl. The Danes design essentially for traditional materials, construction and workmanship and achieve furniture which has a very fine human quality, is modest, unassertive and ideally suited to the life-style of a cultivated middle class. This is true also of the furniture of Aalto and Mathsson, though it employs more advanced techniques. Mies's Barcelona chair is aristocratic, demanding and elegant, and it is no wonder that its use today is by and large restricted to the very rich and to company offices, institutions and banks.

In France during the 1920s Le Corbusier and his circle made significant furniture contributions. In collaboration with his associate Charlotte Perriand, Le Corbusier designed metal furniture which is closely related to that produced in Germany, but in some respects he went further. His furniture does not seem so experimental and was not meant to be; in the late 1920s he could already draw on the experiences of others. Though his furniture is unmistakably his own and bears the mark of his personality, it was his intention, in line with the aspirations of the time, to design anonymous furniture—equipment, as he called it, to serve general purposes. He reduced all furniture to three categories—chairs, tables and open or enclosed shelves for storage—and proceeded to design standard forms for each category: a multi-use table, standardized sectional cabinets, open and closed chairs for various purposes, working, relaxing, a *chaise longue*, an easy chair, a pivotal working chair, and a *fauteuil*—and then never concerned himself with the problem again. This equipment was meant to be used in any of his architectural settings and contribute to the architectonic effect; but it was not intended to be artistic, it was not to make emotional demands as an 'artistic' object. It was to be integrated in the setting, to be a commonplace, part of the 'machine for living'. In seeking the generally applicable form, in de-emphasizing the individual or artistic form and in applying advanced technical materials and methods, Le Corbusier was sharing the concerns of most Continental architects and drew on ideas and attitudes that had been developing since the turn of the century.

All these promising achievements came to an end in the 1930s first in Germany through the repressive measures of the National Socialist regime, which would not tolerate modern architecture and design, and a few years later through the outbreak of the Second World War. By emigrating the most prominent and creative of the German designers spread new attitudes and approaches practically around the globe. Breuer left Germany to design first in Paris, where he won a design competition for aluminium furniture. His designs exploit the lightness, strength and resilience of this material as he had earlier made use of the properties of steel tubing. In 1935 he went to England and designed bentwood furniture for the London firm of Isokon. Employing the same material and technique this furniture inevitably has some relation to Aalto's, though it is more direct in its use of the properties involved. A reclining chair rests on runners, parts of which divide and rise to form supports and arm-rests. In a set of stacking tables of bent plywood a single sheet is bent into a U-shape to form table and supports in one piece, a solution more radical than any of Aalto's in the economy of material and technique.

After its contribution to the beginnings of modern design in the form of the Arts and Crafts Movement, Britain had remained backward in furniture design until the developments on the Continent at last penetrated through publications and exhibitions. Some notable designs were then produced by Serge Chermayeff, Wells Coates and Betty Joel. But England was receptive of the new and adopted it rather than creating it. The same must be said of America in the inter-war decades. Richard Neutra, Howe and Lescaze, Kem Webber and others worked in the new idiom, but they did not make significant new contributions of their own.

The U.S.A. was to come into its own immediately after the Second World War, but the beginnings lay in an experiment just before the War. In 1940 the Museum of Modern Art in New York inaugurated a competition for 'Organic Design in Home Furnishings', in which two young architects, Eero Saarinen and Charles Eames, won the first prize for seating and other living-room furniture. While sectional cases of standardized shapes which could be used with great versatility had ample antecedents in the work of Breuer, Gropius, Le Corbusier and the Scandinavians, their chair designs were revolutionary for they united seat, back and arm-rests in a single shell form made of veneer and glue laminated in a cast-iron mould. This shell form was mounted on a base, either metal or wood, that could take a variety of forms. This was a great step forward in the reduction of the industrial process for the making of a chair and was to have immense consequences after the War, for the War made it impossible to exploit this new idea immediately.

In 1946 Eames produced the first of a long line of notable and innovative designs, a chair composed of two pieces of plywood moulded in multiple curves to fit the body comfortably and shock-mounted by means of thick rubber discs on to a spider-thin frame of chrome rods. This design and all his later ones were manufactured by the Hermann Miller Furniture Company. This firm had helped him in his early experiments and became one of America's leading manufacturers of modern furniture in the post-war decades.

In 1948 the Museum of Modern Art sponsored an 'International Competition for Low Cost Furniture', in which Eames again won a prize, this time for a moulded plastic and fibreglass shell chair which was actually a fulfilment of the ideas developed by Eames and Saarinen in their prize-winning design of the 1940 competition.

In the same years Eames developed storage units of a few standardized parts, all of them taken from stock industrial production, vertical aluminium angles with diagonal bracings of round metal rods, plywood for shelves to which coloured formica panels and drawers could be added, all of which were assembled with a fine feeling for scale and colour to produce a gay, light series of storage pieces intended, again, not as ponderous objects of art but for easy maintenance and visual and practical enjoyment. In the same spirit he designed a series of folding tables, a screen of moulded plywood, and more recently chairs of wire mesh, aluminium furniture and very luxurious lounging chairs with embracing curved forms of bent plywood veneered with rosewood, covered with foam rubber upholstery and black leather cushions filled with down, and set on a metal swivel base.

Soon after the War Eero Saarinen in turn introduced his version of the pre-war design experiment in the so-called 'womb' chair. It is a large shell of fibreglass and resins covered with foam rubber padding and fabric and mounted on a cradle of metal rods. A few years later he produced his pedestal chair, a startling and elegant shape composed of a shell of plastic and fibreglass mounted on a single weighted aluminium pedestal.

The ideas of Eames as well as those of Saarinen have been imitated, adapted, restated all over the world where furniture is made and have in fact become common property and a kind of vernacular of design. Wherever designers have sought advanced technical solutions they have taken moulded plywood and plastic shells and used them in ways that are inevitably reminiscent in some measure of Eames and Saarinen; it is part of the logic of modern industrial production. It is true of the Scandinavians who abandoned the perfection and costliness of handicraft production to design a more social product, designers like Arne Jacobsen, Verner Panton, Peter Hvidt and O. Mölgaard Nielsen. Their furniture is designed for industrial mass production with visual qualities that are imaginative and pleasing and at the same time practical and economical, making use of plywood and plastics in increasing measure.

In all these designs involving moulded plywood and plastics the aim has been to reduce the number of parts and minimize manufacturing processes. Clearly the ultimate is the one-piece object made in one single production process. Rietveld experimented with the idea in metal in the late 1920s; Breuer achieved it with his little Isokon plywood table in 1935; in the late 1940s Eames produced a child's chair of moulded plywood all in one piece; and in 1947 Mies van der Rohe made drawings for two different versions of large armchairs to be made in one piece of plastic. The Dane Verner Panton designed a wonderfully fluent high-backed S-shaped one-piece bent plywood chair for Thonet in 1955.

In plastics the first one-piece table was designed by Walter Papst in Germany in 1959; the first one-piece plastic chair was designed and patented by the American R. G. Reineman in 1960. The German Georg Leowald designed a plastic armchair of one piece in 1963, and H. Bätzner a chair very similar to that of Reineman in 1966. During the 1960s plastic furniture became a commonplace with the ever-growing use of plastics in all areas of our lives. This has created a new aesthetic of furniture design, an aesthetic no longer based on construction (which had in fact been breaking down since the first designs of Eames) but on casting, moulding, shaping. It has resulted in very fluid, curved and often daring forms or, if use is made of plastic foam, in soft sculptural forms. Finally, vinyl and other plastics can be used as flexible envelopes and filled with balls of polystyrene plastic or blown up with air, in the latter case producing deflatable, temporary furniture.

By the end of the 1960s plastic furniture was in the forefront of development everywhere; it was being made wherever industry was sufficiently developed to produce it: in America, in almost every European country and in Japan. It provided the sensation at every furniture mart and exhibition and was much publicized in the home furnishing magazines as the newest and most chic. While many of the designs for plastic furniture were beyond contempt and many were purely experimental, there were even then some quite admirable shapes and forms. Verner Panton designed several excellent one-piece plastic chairs, one of which in particular gives one the impression of a soaring bird; his compatriot Steen Østergaard designed a handsome stacking chair that combines elegance with practicality. There were benches, desks, tables, beds, all made in one piece reinforced polyester plastic.

Soft polyurethane foam covered with fabric was also being experimented with more and more, often in forms that invite their combination into 'furniture landscapes', such as a design by Sebastian Matta, or another by Andreas Hansen of Copenhagen. Others are formed like sculpture, some assuming Arp-like shapes in which one may lounge or sit, such as those designed by Luigi Colani, a very imaginative and gifted German designer of Italian descent, who also designed beautiful outdoor furniture of reinforced polyester. The strength of this material in relation to its bulk is so great that extremely thin surfaces can be shaped, and in the hands of the right designer they can assume graceful, lilting forms that are a delight. Yet in 1970 the use of this material was still in its infancy and no one could foresee what radically different forms of furniture it would lead to.

16, 24, 42, 67, 86, 160, 165, 220, 230, 231, 232, 233, 244, 250, 301, 303, 304, 305, 307, 320, 347, 348, 349, 354, 357, 358, 361, 385, 411, 414, 429, 459, 461, 462, 477, 496, 509, 515, 516, 527, 529, 534, 585, 589, 602, 617, 618, 645, 646, 662, 684, 703, 738, 743, 746, 751, 757, 790, 815, 816, 864, 868, 880, 923.

FUSTIAN (from Fostat, a suburb of Cairo from where the material first came). The term originally meant a coarse cloth with a weft of cotton thread and a warp of flax. In the later Middle Ages it appeared at fairs throughout Europe. Provins, France, is known to have had its own fustian looms as early as 1163 and Florence about the same time. In 13th-c. Spain the *fustaneros* were already organized in a guild. From *c.* 1320 until the end of the 15th c. most fustians were bleached but not dyed. From Ulm and other towns in southern Germany, for instance, such fustians were sent to Lübeck, Antwerp, Calais, Italy and Switzerland. By *c.* the middle of the 16th c. Dutch emigrants had settled first in Norwich and then in Lancashire and brought with them the traditions of Flemish fustian which was so admired by the English in the 15th c. From *c.* 1620 English manufactories were themselves exporting to the Continent. After the middle of the 17th c. fustian underwent a recession as printed CALICOES stole the market, but after the Manchester Act of 1736 it enjoyed a short revival.

The term 'fustian' is now used of a thick cotton cloth with a short nap or pile, usually dyed a dark colour. See COTTON AND COTTON PRINTING.

G

GADROON. Term in architecture, the decorative arts and COSTUME for a type of ornament consisting of a pattern of convex curves or arcs

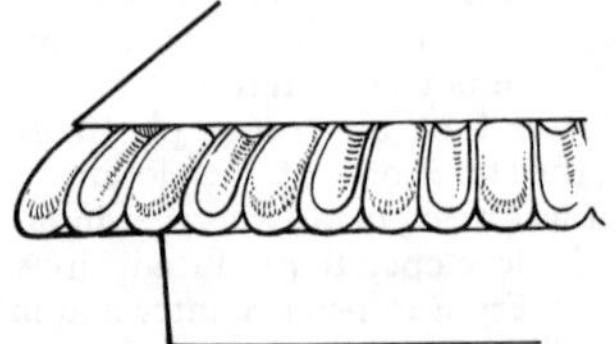

joined at their extremities. In metalware it was frequently applied to edging. In cabinet-making it was popular from the early 16th c. to the middle of the 17th c. as a decoration on oak and again *c.* the middle of the 18th c., when gadrooned metal edging was sometimes applied. Gadrooning was also called lobing or knurling (nulling).

GAINES, JOHN (1677–*c.* 1750). Chair-maker of Ipswich, Massachusetts. His son THOMAS carried on business with him and their account books are preserved at the Winterthur Museum, Delaware. Another son, JOHN (1704–43), learned his father's trade and opened his own shop at Portsmouth in 1724. Four side-chairs attributed to him by family tradition are in the ownership of his descendants. On the basis of similarities of style chairs in the Winterthur Museum, Delaware, and the Metropolitan Museum of Art, New York, are attributed to him, as also is a maple armchair in the same museum. He is also thought to have made or designed a type of staircase baluster characteristic of Portsmouth houses of the period. He had a son, GEORGE (1736–1808), who became the most prominent cabinet-maker of his day in Portsmouth. See FURNITURE (AMERICAN).

67, 220.

GALLATIN, ALBERT. American glass manufacturer who founded the New Geneva Glassworks in western Pennsylvania in 1797 and began the tradition of American glass produced at Pittsburgh and the Ohio centres. See GLASS (AMERICA).

GALLÉ, ÉMILE (1846–1904). French glassmaker and furniture designer, who through his writings and his works became one of the leading figures of the ART NOUVEAU movement in France. He opposed the revival of historical styles without subscribing to the functionalist theories of the 'modern' movement or to the social doctrines of the ARTS AND CRAFTS MOVEMENT, but rather he sought novel decorative patterns from the organic forms of nature. His interest in botany coincided with his position as the leading exponent of the French 'floral' style of decorative adornment. In cabinet-making he inaugurated a revival of MARQUETRY. In glass-making he experimented with opaque and semi-translucent glass and won international recognition for his moulded and coloured glass with floral effects in the *art nouveau* style. He was instrumental in founding the NANCY SCHOOL, of which he was the first President. See also GLASS (EUROPEAN), and ART NOUVEAU.

GARAMOND, CLAUDE (d. 1561). The most celebrated of French letter-cutters for type-founding. His early life is obscure; the first types identifiable as his appear in the printing of Robert ESTIENNE in 1530. There is a tradition that he had guidance from Geofroi TORY in the best design of ROMAN letters, and it is probable that Estienne taught him to admire the roman of Aldus MANUTIUS and to reproduce it in a somewhat lighter and more gracious form. Unlike Aldus, Garamond had to provide this style of letter in the variety of sizes to which French printers were accustomed by this time. His fame rests principally on Greek type of three sizes commissioned by King Francis I and cut in 1541–9, rendering the copying hand of the king's Cretan scribe Angelos Vergetios. From *c.* 1550 Garamond cut his roman type faces anew. He also made a small ITALIC copying that of Aldus and a large one of more modern fashion, besides a Hebrew and a small BLACK LETTER. A collection of matrices for the type faces attributed to Garamond in the inventories of Christopher Plantin exists at the Museum Plantin-Moretus at Antwerp, and the *Specimen* of Conrad Berner (Frankfurt, 1592) shows a range of roman faces attributed to him by that type-founder.

Garamond's roman types with the italics of Robert Granjon prevailed in French printing until late in the 18th c. and were extensively used in the Low Countries and for Latin books in Germany. His romans and greeks were copied by other type-founders. See TYPOGRAPHY.

54, 505.

GARDENS. See LANDSCAPE GARDENING.

GARDNER, FRANCIS. Russian of Scottish descent, who established a china and PORCELAIN factory at Verbilki, near Moscow. See RUSSIA.

GARNET. A large and varied family of vitreous minerals, with a hardness index ranging from $6\frac{1}{2}$ to $7\frac{1}{2}$ on the MOHS SCALE and a glossy or near adamantine lustre, members of which have been employed as gemstones since the Bronze Age. Garnets were used in jewellery by the ancient EGYPTIANS, by the Greeks, the Romans and the Celtic peoples. They have been used for CAMEOS and INTAGLIOS and were cut into slivers for decorative inlays. The name is thought to derive from the Latin *granatus* and to indicate a supposed likeness of the crystals either in colour or in the shape to the seeds of the pomegranate. Garnets are oxides of aluminium with other metals such as iron, magnesium, calcium, etc., in combination, the colour depending on the composition. The almandine is an oxide of aluminium with iron and some magnesium in combination; when the magnesium preponderates over the iron we have the pyrope garnet. There are many other variant types.

The *almandine* garnet has a deep purplish red or amethyst violet colour. Cut as a high CABOCHON it was probably the 'carbuncle' which was greatly prized in the ancient world, by the Anglo-Saxons and throughout the Middle Ages. It sometimes shows a four-rayed star. See ASTERISM.

The *pyrope* (fire-eyed) is a deep warm red, which when ROSE cut was much used in 19th-c. jewellery.

The brownish red *cinnamon stone* or *hessonite* is translucent and can be facet cut. It has sometimes been known as *jacinth*, an old name of the ZIRCON.

The transparent green *demantoid* has been found in the Urals since *c.* 1860. It has a characteristic flaw like tufts of hair, which is due to the inclusion of fine asbestos fibres. The demantoid garnet has brilliance second only to that of the DIAMOND, but is very rarely found in crystals of more than three grains. When sherry yellow the same stone is known as *topazlite*. *Grossularite*, an opaque or semi-opaque green garnet, is found in South Africa and is sometimes called Transvaal jade. It may be speckled with black.

776, 784, 921.

GAUDREAU (or GAUDREAUX), ANTOINE-ROBERT (*c.* 1680–1751). French cabinet-maker to Louis XV. He was employed on the interior decoration of the Bibliothèque Royale and in the Tuileries in Paris and some time after 1726 was attached to the service of the Garde-Meuble de la Couronne. Two of his best known works are a celebrated medal-cabinet made for Louis XV in 1738 and now in the Cabinet Intérieur at Versailles, and an elaborate veneered commode, probably adapted from a design attributed to the brothers SLODTZ, delivered in 1739 for use in the apartments of Louis XV at Versailles and now in the Wallace Collection.

738, 880.

GAUFFERING. Term in BOOKBINDING for the decoration of previously gilded book edges by heated TOOLS similar to those used on the covers. The technique was introduced in the 16th c. French binders used pointed tools to make designs picked out in dots. On German books the edges were often gauffered and painted with coats of arms and allegorical figures.

GAULETTE, JEAN. See MOTHER OF PEARL.

GENOESE LACE. Genoa, with Milan, was a leading centre for the manufacture of bobbin LACE in Italy. The name 'Genoese lace' was given to a bobbin lace of somewhat coarse texture made, supposedly at Genoa, mainly during the first half of the 17th c. It was in demand as collar lace. Its geometrical designs were composed of narrow tape-like bands and characteristic small 'wheat-grain' motifs. A flat bobbin-made braid was sometimes worked into it.

GEORGIAN. A general descriptive term loosely applied to various styles in English architecture, decoration, FURNITURE, SILVER, etc., from the accession of George I (1714) to the death of George IV (1830). The term 'Early Georgian' is used of the period from *c.* 1714 to the 1730s. 'Middle Georgian' (covering the 1740s and 1750s) and 'Late Georgian' (from the 1760s to *c.* 1830) are infrequently used, the movements in style and taste during these years being separately designated (ADAM style, ROCOCO, GREEK TASTE, NEO-CLASSICISM, GOTHIC REVIVAL, ETRUSCAN TASTE, EGYPTIAN TASTE, etc., and in furniture CHIPPENDALE, HEPPLEWHITE, SHERATON, etc.). The latter part of 'Late Georgian' is known as REGENCY. Stylistically the period had little uniformity. So far as over-all characterization is possible, its salient features were respect for competent craftsmanship and a predilection for a classical system of design and proportion flexible enough to accommodate phases as different as CHINOISERIE and Pompeian. Today the term 'Georgian' is also current as a trade description to designate objects manufactured in a vaguely 18th-c. manner without reference to date.

In architecture the Georgian style begins with a revival of Palladianism under the influence of Lord Burlington (1694–1753) and Colen Campbell (d. 1729), who published the first volume of *Vitruvius Britannicus* in 1715 and whose Wanstead House in Essex (1715–22) became a model for the English Palladian country house. Interior design and decoration tended to be more elaborate than the exteriors, which in Early Georgian domestic architecture retained something of the unpretentious functional simplicity of the QUEEN ANNE style. In the smaller houses wood panelling was extensively used, its surface being covered by painting or graining. The panels were recessed in the manner introduced by Inigo Jones (1593–1652) and the shelved recesses framed with pilasters were a distinctive feature of the Early Georgian. After the middle of the century the vogue for WALLPAPER or walls hung with silk gained popularity and by the end of the century wood panelling was virtually obsolete. The vogue in American Colonial interiors took the same course, taste being influenced largely by English handbooks of architecture, interior decoration and furniture design. In contrast the interiors of the large Palladian mansions had as their keynote formal elegance and Italianate grandeur rather than comfort or homeliness. Venetian windows were introduced and stuccoed walls ornamented by Italian craftsmen became the rule. The *stuccatori* introduced the garland and the scroll as decorative motifs as well as relief-moulded masks and figures. From the middle of the century rapidly changing fashions in design and ornamentation reflected influences from the Rococo, Gothic, *chinoiserie* and Greek. In the first half of the century the prominent figure in interior decoration and furniture design was William KENT, whose *Designs of Inigo Jones* was published in 1727 with the financial assistance of Lord Burlington. In the second half of the century taste in decorative design was dominated by the ADAM brothers and their followers, Joseph Bonomi and Samuel and James Wyatt.

86, 231, 233.

GEORGIAN METALWORK. (This article deals with the metalwork of ancient Georgia, not with the Georgian period in Britain.) Georgia, one of the 15 republics of the U.S.S.R., is situated in western Transcaucasia. It stretches from Russia's borders in the north to those of Armenia in the south and from the shores of the Black Sea in the west to the borders of the republic of Azerbaidjan in the east. Its history is a long and chequered one, periods of great artistic achievements alternating with years verging on stagnation, periods of military glory and political independence with decades of subordination. Few branches of its minor arts, least of all those of a secular nature, have survived the numerous vicissitudes which Georgia has endured since Romans and Achaemenids first fought to gain control of it. Metalwork has proved the one notable exception, owing its preservation in ancient times to its durable nature, in Christian times largely to the protection which the Church was able to extend to objects of a religious nature. As a result most of the metalwork which survives from pre-Christian times is secular in character whilst much that dates from *c.* the 5th to *c.* the 18th c. is religious in content.

Metallurgy developed in Georgia at so early a date that the ancient Greeks associated Colchis with the land of the Golden Fleece whilst the medieval world regarded it as the industry's place of origin. In reality Georgia shares the latter distinction with such regions as the Minusinsk Basin in eastern Kazakhstan, north-eastern Persia and Anatolia. (See PREHISTORIC TECHNOLOGY.) From the start its metal-workers were willing to take the achievements of these neighbouring regions into account when evolving their own tastes and styles. The princely burials of Maikop are among the oldest and richest of Georgia's numerous prehistoric sites. Situated in the Kuban Basin and dating from *c.* 2300 B.C., they are noted for their copper tools, which include shaft-hole axes, for a series of bronze animal figurines, chiefly of bulls, and for several silver vessels, the most important of which carries a very remarkable incised design. A mountain range is depicted on its upper rim with two rivers descending from it to spread out in different directions along the vessel's sides before disgorging near its base into a lake or enclosed sea. Some scholars identify the mountain range with the Caucasian range as seen from the north-west and the two rivers as the Terek and the Kuban; if their assumption is correct, the scene must rank as one of man's earliest attempts at portraying a landscape. It is enlivened here by the inclusion of a bull, a Przhevalsky horse and a lion with a bird perched on its back. They advance in single file in one direction whilst another bull walks away from them; below them a wild boar, a panther and two antelopes walk round the lake. Although processions of animals such as these are especially associated with the ancient Orient, they were adopted by those nomads of the 1st millennium B.C. who belonged to the cultural world of the Scythians and were featured by them in their own arts.

It is as impossible to establish the racial origin of the chieftains who were buried in the Maikop mounds as it is to establish that of the people who were buried in the Trialeti cemetery, where the graves range in date from the Obsidian Period through the Neolithic and Bronze Ages to the end of the Copper Age. The cemetery is situated 110 kilometres or so to the south of Tbilisi in what is one of Georgia's oldest cultural centres. The metal objects recovered from its Copper Age burials show the adoption of techniques which were to remain in use in Georgia throughout the centuries. They include a gold goblet dating from 1800 to 1700 B.C. decorated with bands, some of them curved, formed of strips of fine filigree. They were attached to its surface by a method of cold soldering the secret of which is now lost to us. The bands are studded with TURQUOISES, still today a very popular stone in Georgia, and other gems mounted in circlets. Pieces of jewellery which date from the 5th c. B.C. and form part of the Akhalgori treasure, notably ear-rings, are also lavishly adorned with filigree and with slightly larger granules as well as with stones in CABOCHON mounts and metal bosses.

A silver goblet from Kurk Tash, near Trialeti, dating from the middle of the 2nd millennium B.C. resembles the gold Trialeti one in shape. Its more important decorations are, however, disposed in two frieze-like bands. The upper and wider of the two contains a procession of animal-headed human beings advancing from left to right, bearing offerings to a seated deity. In the lower bands stags and does walk in single file in the opposite direction from the tribute-bearers. Instead of being incised like the scene on the Maikop vessel these decorations are EMBOSSED and chased, techniques at which Georgia's jewellers were later to excel. A comparable procession, this time of birds, occupies the widest band on a splendid gold disc, possibly a horse's breastplate, belonging to the Akhalgori treasure; it displays certain affinities with the Scythian silver disc of a slightly earlier date belonging to the Sakkiz treasure. The Georgian disc contains a circle of bosses simulating cabochon jewels—a form of decoration which may well have served as a prototype for the Sassanian pearl-studded circlets—whilst its centre is marked by a variant of the rosette which was so popular at the time among the sun-worshipping nomads of central ASIA. Finer versions of this rosette appear on the pendants to the gold head-dress from the same treasure. There they are combined with figures of horses which, although Achaemenid in conception, have the added vitality found in the animal art of the Scythian world. (See ANIMAL STYLE.) PASTE inlays adorn other objects belonging to the Akhalgori treasure. They foreshadow the love for polychrome effects which the Georgians were to express in their religious art by means of glass, stone and paste inlays and by champlevé, painted and above all cloisonné ENAMELS. The burials at the mouth of the Armazisk dating from the 2nd to 3rd c. A.D. are among the earliest Georgian sites that have provided examples of cloisonné enamels and multicoloured jewellery. Among the more important objects found there is a belt made of gold rectangular sections adorned with a semi-transparent, greyish-white paste, true enamels, stone and glass.

No doubt these early examples of the goldsmith's art reflect the taste of a wealthy and sophisticated class, whilst the contemporary bronze and iron objects worked in a very different style by craftsmen living in the northern foothills of the Caucasian range probably represent the taste of the poorer sections of the pagan population. Much of this metalwork was recovered from the burials of Kumbulta, Faskau and Kamunta and ranges in date from 1200 B.C. to A.D. 500. It represents a culture known as the Koban after the site where it was first identified. From *c.* the middle of the 5th c. B.C. square or near-square bronze or iron belt-buckles become numerous. Their central decoration usually depicts either a stag of strongly Scythian appearance or a horse of the Hellenistic type shown in profile and accompanied by one or two smaller animals such as dogs. The latter are placed either between the legs of the larger animal or above its back, all the creatures appearing against an open-work background the idea for which may have originated in Siberia. They are framed by borders, the corners of which contain bosses whilst the bands are decorated either with lines simulating filigree or with patterns which were derived either from textiles or from earlier pieces of metalwork such as the bronze belt from Trialeti dating *c.* 1200 B.C., in which the border most probably also copies that of a textile.

Georgia was as greatly coveted by the Persians as it was first by the Romans, then by the Byzantines. The imprint of these cultures is clearly evident in Georgian art, but the adoption of Christianity in the first half of the 4th c. put a term to the influence both of the contemporary Sassanian empire and of Rome. Henceforth Georgian artists looked to BYZANTIUM, the most vital centre of Christian art; but although they followed Byzantium's precepts they proceeded from the start to develop a distinct and truly national style. From a very early date they excelled at building superb churches in carefully dressed stone, at adorning them with tiled and mosaic floors, carved altar rails, sculptured capitals, religious plaques, and eventually also with mural paintings. They were especially noteworthy for the development of very complicated geometrical ground-plans which contrasted sharply with the simple basilical plan adopted in the West in early Christian times.

The figural sculptures probably helped to encourage the gold- and silversmiths to perfect a form of icon which is especially characteristic of Georgia. Although generally made of silver, which was sometimes partly gilt, it is also found in gold, copper, copper-gilt and lead. Whatever the metal, a thin sheet of it was laid on resin, pitch or tar and the main features of the design, such as the heads, bodies and clothes of the figures were beaten out from behind in varying degrees of relief and filled with a red substance to prevent the raised parts from sinking. The face of the sheet was then finished off by chasing, the completed panel being used either as an icon or to form a BOOK COVER, to face a cross or to make up a reliquary. The idea and technique may well have originated with the gold-foil decorations with which the Scythian nomads of southern Russia encased their harness ornaments, sword sheaths and the like during the greater part of the 1st millennium B.C. Much of the quality of the Georgian plaques depends upon the chasing and the degree and variations of the relief work.

The earliest example of this type of Georgian metalwork is a silver-gilt fragment showing St. Gregory the Illuminator, originally part of a reliquary. The wording of the inscription and the style of its lettering assign it to the 5th c. The sculptural quality attained in such works can be appreciated in the silver-gilt disc (6th–7th c.) showing St. Mamas seated astride a lion, holding a cross in his right hand and raising the left in a gesture of supplication. Although his head and shoulders are shown three-quarter face, the lower part of his body and that of the lion are rendered in profile. Persian influence is reflected in the treatment of the lion's head and mane and in the leaf-shaped terminal to its tail; but its teeth and claws are more in line with work of the Scythian school. In contrast St. Mamas's elongated face with its strongly marked eyes and nose derive from the Christian world, as do his robes even though their rhythmical folds differ in shape and treatment from the Byzantine. The saint's halo, robe and cross together with the lion's mane, claws, teeth and eye are gilt whilst the remainder of their bodies and the entire background remain silver. The touches of gold seen against the silver and the depth of the relief work provide an interplay of light which intensifies the sense of movement created by the pose of the lion's feet.

The art developed and gained in sculptural quality, reaching its peak in the 11th and 12th centuries. In the 11th c. it remained customary for the human figures to appear against plain backgrounds, although the height of the relief was increased. Faces were made to look young and handsome; well modelled draperies concealed bodies which had acquired weight and vividly conveyed a sense of movement. Much of the best work, however, dates from the 12th c. —the century of Queen Tamara's reign, when the country's foremost poet, Shota Rustaveli, lived and wrote his masterpiece, *The Man in the Panther's Skin.* Although many fine panels must have been produced in most of the larger monasteries, three main centres grew up round Opiza, Tbeti and Gelati. Opiza had in the past already developed into a vital centre of culture, and led by two master jewellers it was now once again to take the lead. Beshken was probably the older of the two craftsmen and seemingly also rather the less adventurous. He is known by one work, the Beshken Gospel cover, which he signed. It suffices to ensure his reputation. He lived in the latter part of the 12th c., as did Beka, the founder of the Opiza style. Beka was more of an individualist and appears to have loved decoration for its own sake; for whilst Beshken's Gospel cover retains the plain background which had become traditional, confining the decoration to its S-shaped corner pieces, Beka's backgrounds are filled with designs consisting of a FLEUR-DE-LIS, a diamond or a lozenge formed either by an ACANTHUS leaf or by the two-lobed leaf used at the time by the Seljuks of Rum in their stone sculptures. Beka's works include an icon of Christ assigned to between 1184 and 1193, the cover of the Tskarostavsk Gospel dated 1193 and the Tselkinik Gospel of the same date, now unfortunately lost. The Tbeti school is best represented by the unsigned 12th-c. Gospel cover of that name whilst the Gelati school is seen at its best in the unsigned Gospel cover made for David Narin (1243–93). The sculptor Assat is also known to us by name because he signed the superb silver cross which he made for the Curopolate David.

Religious art retained its importance and its high standards in the 15th c. A superb cross of the period in the Georgian Museum of Arts, Tbilisi, is signed by Mamas and attests to the

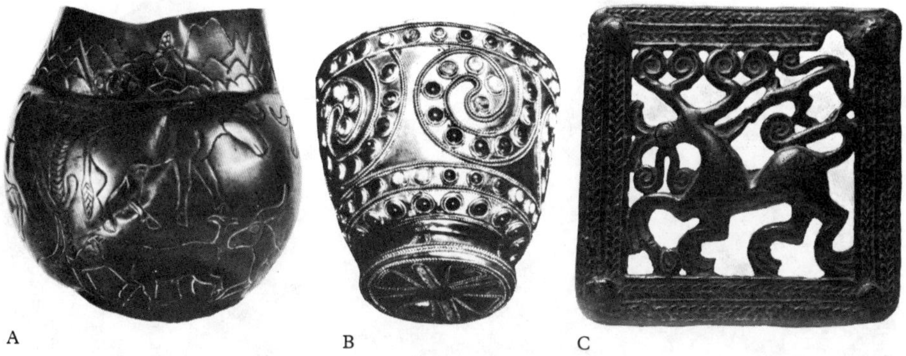

A. Silver bowl from Maicop. A mountain range is engraved on the neck. A bull, displaying certain Anatolian stylistic characteristics, stands near a river with a procession of animals below. (Georgia State Mus., 3rd millennium B.C.)

B. Gold goblet from Trialeti with coloured stones and filigree decoration. (Georgia State Mus., 2nd millenium B.C.)

C. Bronze Koban buckle with marked Scythian features, particularly in the use of a zoomorphic juncture to form a dog-like creature from the main animal's antler. The open-work suggests Siberian influence. Hellenistic period. (Georgia State Mus.)

Gold head-dress terminals from the Akhalgori Treasure, displaying Achaemenid influence. (Georgia State Mus., 6th c. B.C.)

Fragment of a chased silver icon of the *deesis* by Beka Opisari. Showing John the Baptist. From Anchiskhati. (Georgia State Mus., A.D. 1184–93)

Copper plaque showing God the Almighty and the Son. (Hermitage Mus., 11th–12th c.)

Silver fragment showing a group of worshippers. (Hermitage Mus., 11th–12th c.)

excellence of his craftsmanship. In the 16th c., however, the Perso-Turkish wars were largely fought on Georgian territory and they interfered with all cultural activities. Jewellers of the period show no less skill, yet they contented themselves with working in the styles which had flourished between the 12th c. and their own rather than evolving anything new; although they now often filled their backgrounds with arabesques. In western Georgia, however, plain backgrounds were retained, although studs simulating cabochon jewels were often included in them. Throughout the country the human figure underwent elongation, the slant of the shoulders was accentuated and the folds of draperies, although more rigid, were often curved. A sense of movement and conviction was retained, yet the workmanship began to decline. The arrival of Catholic missionaries in the 17th and 18th centuries opened the way to easel painting and the naturalistic Italianate style, which did much to hasten the lowering of standards. In the 19th c., when Pepu Meunargi (d. 1857) was the subject of general admiration, the style became Russianized and declined still more. But secular works had by then become more important than the religious. Many were admirably designed and worked, weapons being often exquisitely ornamented with NIELLO. Sumptuous silver or gold horse-trappings were also elaborately worked and often adorned with Islamic crescents and small bells. Snuff-boxes and cigarette-cases were decorated either with niello or with enamels, as were spoons and other articles of tableware. FILIGREE continued to play an important part in the decoration of jewellery.

The Georgian love of polychrome effects can be traced back to the Akhalgori treasure. It was manifested in the enamels. At first the cloisonné technique was more common but an icon of the Archangels Gabriel and Michael executed in the champlevé technique shows that this form of enamelling was known to the Georgians in the 13th and 14th centuries. The icon has been lost in recent years and since it is the only recorded example of this technique from that date its disappearance is to be especially regretted. Cloisonné enamelling, although the most difficult of all techniques, had been fully mastered by the Georgians at any rate by the 9th c., but they used a cold soldering method for securing the little gold partitions to a copper rather than to a gold ground. Like their Byzantine prototypes the enamels are religious as well as decorative in character and take the form of medallions or plaques. They are larger and a trifle heavier than the Byzantine ones which they so closely resemble. Their flesh tints also differ slightly from the Byzantine, and their colour range is wider and brighter, clearer also than the examples from Kiev. The differences in the colours probably resulted from the nature of the pastes. By and large Georgian enamels are less accomplished than the Byzantine, the firing rarely being quite as good, but their plaques often include more figures than do the Byzantine examples. The heads and hands are larger and they are more expressive. The earlier examples are distinguished by their green backgrounds, and although some scholars assign these to the 9th c., others consider that the halo and adornments on the icon of the Virgin of Kobi, which bears an inscription referring to Leo III, King of Abkazia (957–67), are the earliest enamels to survive together with three fragments of the Khakhuli triptych. Enamels of the first half of the 12th c.; which were made by Asan of Tchkondidi for Simon Tchkondideli (Martvili), indicate that a centre of production may have existed at Martvili. The finest work, however, is to be seen in the three delicate pinky-lilac sections forming the face and hands of the Virgin. They originally belonged to a *deesis* scene and were made in the 10th c. They were reused in the 12th c. to depict the Virgin occupying the centre of the main panel of the Khakhuli triptych. The triptych is of gold and is adorned with over 100 figural and decorative cloisonné enamel plaques, some of Byzantine origin, others of local make and with 32 of a later date. Like the cabochon jewels and small crosses which complete the triptych's decorations, these plaques and medallions are set in pearl surrounds against a background of delicately chased and embossed scrolls enhanced here and there by exquisite filigree work. The design of the whole is carefully balanced, the workmanship superb, yet the three fragments which succeed in portraying the Virgin are so expressive that they dominate the triptych whilst blending with it. Were Georgian metalwork known to us by only this one work, its reputation would be assured; but the many masterpieces whose quality is so well represented in the Khakhuli triptych form a rich school of a distinctive character.

9, 496.

GERMAN SILVER. An alloy of nickel–copper with zinc based upon imported PAKTONG. This became possible to manufacture only after nickel was available in sufficient quantities and at commercial prices. It was first manufactured on a commercial scale *c.* 1824 in Berlin and in Saxony (under the name Argentan or Neusilber). A similar alloy was first made in England by Henry Merry of Birmingham *c.* 1830 and was sold under the name 'Merry's Plate'. From *c.* 1840 German silver has been very extensively used as a base for electro-plating. The French name for this alloy is '*maillechort*' and the Italian name '*pachfong*'.

GHANTA. Ritual prayer-bell which symbolized the 'doctrine' in Lamaistic Buddhism and was associated with the VAJRA, which symbolized the 'method'. The bell was shaped like a *stupa* and the handle was often in the form of a *vajra*. The bell was cast from a bronze alloy to which some silver was added and this gave to the bell its clear and resonant note.

GIBBONS, GRINLING (1648–1721). Wood-carver, probably born in Rotterdam and trained in Holland. He came to England *c.* 1663, where he was taken up by Hugh May (1622–84), Sir Peter Lely (1618–80) and John Evelyn (see *Diary*, 18 Jan. 1671). He was introduced *c.* 1670 to the King and to Sir Christopher Wren (1632–1723), and was employed by the latter on decorations at Hampton Court, on the choir stalls and organ case at St. Paul's and on the archbishop's throne at Canterbury. In 1714 he was made master carver to King George I. Gibbons was unsurpassed in his day for naturalistic decorative carving of fruits, flowers, shells, strung together in garlands and festoons, with small animals, cherubs' heads, etc. His virtuosity in wood was not equalled in marble or bronze and George Vertue (1684–1756) said of him: 'He was a most excellent carver in wood, he was neither well skill'd or practized in Marble or Brass for which works he employd the best artists he coud procure.' About 1684 he took as partner Artus Quellin III, who is thought to have been responsible for some of the figure sculpture attributed to Gibbons. Among private houses Petworth and Belton contain good examples of his work. His carving adorns many colleges and churches, including Trinity College, Oxford, and Trinity College, Cambridge, St. James's church in Piccadilly, St. George's Chapel at Windsor Castle, although much of the work attributed to him has been shown to have been done by other wood-carvers influenced by his style. His work is notable for its minute detail, its naturalism and its delicacy and grace. Horace Walpole said of him: 'There is no instance of a man before Gibbons who gave to wood the loose and airy lightness of flowers, and chained together the various productions of the elements with the free disorder natural to each species' (*Anecdotes of Painting in England*). He was the main representative in England of the Continental tradition of classical BAROQUE as opposed to that of Bernini (1598–1680).

324.

GILDING. Because of its great malleability gold can be beaten into extremely thin sheets, which may be applied to other surfaces (see GOLD AND SILVER). Gold has been used to embellish wood and other surfaces from very ancient times throughout the Near and Far East, in China and Japan, Egypt and ancient Greece and Rome. Exquisite gilding was done by the Pre-Columbian civilizations of southern and Central America (see AMERINDIANS). In BYZANTINE times it was very extensively used for architectural enrichment and decoration, and in painting for backgrounds and haloes and the decoration of robes and accessories. In medieval western Europe also much use was made of gold for the illumination of manuscripts, BOOKBINDING, FURNITURE, etc., and for many types of painting including murals. It was also used to enrich architecture and sculpture, particularly in churches, and a number of Italian CASSONI of the 15th and 16th centuries were gilt. Towards the end of the 17th c. the love of splendour which characterized the BAROQUE led to an increased use of gilding, and elaborately carved tables, picture FRAMES and mirror frames, cabinet-stands and chairs were often entirely or partly covered with gold. The fashion declined somewhat towards the middle of the 18th c. but revived in a more restrained way with the NEO-CLASSICAL style.

Gilding consists of the application of thin sheets of gold to a surface. Technical accounts of gilding such as those of THEOPHILUS, Cennino CENNINI, John Stalker and George Parker in their treatise on *Japanning and Gilding* (1688) and SHERATON in his *Cabinet Dictionary* indicate that methods have varied little over the years. When gold is beaten into thin sheets it is known as 'foil' in the thicker form and as 'leaf' when it is very thin. Cennini says that 145 leaves can be beaten from one ducat although he does not advise more than 100—that is, enough leaf to cover an area of six to seven square metres. The leaf is applied with the help of an adhesive called a 'mordant' and there are two distinct processes, oil gilding and water gilding. The former is simpler and more durable and was therefore recommended for most kinds of furniture by Sheraton. But the gold cannot be burnished. Water gilding can be burnished but the process is more laborious and the gilding is more fragile, being particularly vulnerable to damp.

In both methods the gilder first prepares a very hard and smooth ground of gesso laid on in successive coats. The next step is to apply the mordant, which 'bites' into the gold leaf and causes it to adhere. In oil gilding the mordant is dried linseed oil, which is naturally sticky. In water gilding it was customary to use a pigment, usually a reddish earth colour called Armenian bole or gilder's red clay, which has to be wetted before it will grip. The red bole gives the translucent gold leaf a richer glow. The gold is laid on in small rectangular leaves and the gilded surface is then rubbed with a pad to give it a matt finish.

Water gilding can then be burnished by being rubbed with a hard object (garnets, agates, topazes, emeralds were recommended) shaped like a dog's tooth (Cennini recommended the use of an actual tooth). This increases its smoothness and reflecting power so that it picks up the shadows as well as the lights and looks more brilliant and darker than an unburnished surface. An important feature of gilding was 'tooling' in order to obtain a patterned surface. Lines were incised around the areas of gold leaf and incised patterns were tooled on the gold itself. The effect of tooling was to provide textural variation instead of the flat glitter of gold while at the same time the play of light on the broken surface enhanced its brilliance and luminosity.

GILLOW. English firm of furniture-makers and upholsterers, founded in 1695 by ROBERT Gillow at Lancaster. His son, RICHARD, was trained as an architect and designed the Customs House of Lancaster. He became a partner in the firm in 1757 and in 1761 a London branch was opened in what is now Oxford Street. Furniture was sent to London and exported abroad, to the West Indies and elsewhere, in considerable quantities. The records of the firm, which is now represented by Waring & Gillow Ltd., go back to 1731 and are preserved in the Victoria Library. The Victoria and Albert Museum has a sofa made by Gillows in 1805. Most of the firm's furniture was stamped with their name after 1820. They remained prominent in the 19th c. and supplied furniture for the new Houses of Parliament, the Law Courts, St. Pancras Hotel, etc. The family home, Leighton Hall, Lancashire, is open to the public and has a comprehensive range of the firm's furniture.

GIMSON, ERNEST (1864–1919). English architect and craftsman in furniture, metalwork, plaster and embroidery. He was trained at Leicester Art School. In 1884 he met William MORRIS and came under his influence; he later came into contact with Philip WEBB and leaders of the ARTS AND CRAFTS MOVEMENT. He came to London in 1886 and met Sidney and Ernest BARNSLEY. With them and W. R. LETHABY in 1890 he formed 'Kenton & Co.', furniture designers and makers, and then in 1893 moved to Gloucestershire, all three finally settling at Sapperton, where they had workshops. Gimson, who designed and did not make furniture, had a masterly understanding of craft processes and respect for materials, and he made a considerable contribution to the emergence of a recognizable early-20th-c. style. A permanent exhibition of his work can be seen at the Leicester Museum and Art Gallery. See FURNITURE (MODERN).

521.

GIRDLE. Term used by jewellers and lapidaries for the edge of a cut gemstone where it is of maximum width, which divides the CROWN from the base and determines the shape of the stone. See JEWELLERY.

784.

GIRDLE-BOOKS. In the 16th and 17th centuries the small devotional books carried at the belt by the wives of the very rich had covers of gold enriched with ENAMELS and jewels. The best known of these is the Girdle-book of Queen Elizabeth I (B.M.) but other examples exist, mostly connected by tradition with a reigning queen. The most beautiful is that made for Princess Augusta of Denmark in 1617, probably by Corvinianus Saur, the Danish Court Jeweller. It is of heavy sheet gold decorated with champlevé translucent enamels (Rosenburg Palace, Copenhagen).

GLASS

See also PREHISTORIC TECHNOLOGY; EGYPT, ANCIENT (Glass and Glazes); GREEK AND ROMAN ANTIQUITY (Glass); CHINA (Glass)

1. MATERIAL AND TECHNIQUES. Glass is known amongst its workers as 'the metal' and until about the beginning of the Christian era the forms moulded in glass mainly followed those of metallic objects or earthenware. This branch of glass-making has continued throughout the centuries until today. The other branch, which gives glass its unique quality in art, stems from the invention of blowing in the 1st c. B.C. The inflation of the molten 'metal' by human breath, followed by cutting, pincering and other rapidly executed decorations, results in the glass becoming, as W. B. Honey wrote in his magisterial work *Glass* (1940) 'the pattern of a gesture'. Thus the ephemeral beauty of a moment's inspiration and skill is caught for ever, or for a time limited only by the fragility of the delicate material.

(*a*) *Material.* Glass is an artificial compound made by fusion of a silica with an alkaline flux in a furnace. These are the essentials; but in order to obtain different qualities, for instance toughness or shine, extra ingredients are incorporated.

The three main silicates used are sand or QUARTZ or flints. The two main alkali fluxes are soda-ash or potash.

The choice is usually determined by the place of manufacture. Thus soda-ash was used by the EGYPTIANS, Romans and Syrians, since it was obtained from soda-bearing marine plants found on Mediterranean shores. Potash, or brushwood ash, is the alkali of German, Bohemian and English glass. For similar reasons Venetian glass depended on the silica of white quartz pebbles obtained from the bed of the Trevire river. Powdered flint was used in England when English glass-makers broke free from the Venetian monopolies and began making their own characteristic metal in the late 17th c. and the import of quartz from Venice was discontinued. In present-day commercial glass both potash and soda (extracted from common salt) are used.

The most important addition to the silica–alkali fundamentals of glass was lead. This had been added from early times; it is mentioned in the 12th c. as an ingredient of the artificial PASTE gems made by the Jews. Its widest use, however, was in English glass of the late 17th c. and the 1st half of the 18th c. English glass of that period is distinguished by its peculiar brilliance and fire, since light is dispersed through it at a high rate. It is naturally heavy owing to the weight of lead, softer in outline and more resonant than the earlier 'crystal' glass. Like many successful innovations the use of lead was almost accidental, in so far as George RAVENSCROFT was experimenting (*c.* 1675) to cure the 'crizzling' or fine net of interior cracks caused by an excess of alkali. This excess was itself caused by the use of English flint in place of Venetian quartz. By the addition of lead Ravenscroft produced a glass of lustre and shine which took it quite out of the class of 'crystal-type' glass hitherto considered to be the finest.

Early glass, up to the 15th c., was always coloured faintly green or brown owing to the presence of iron in the silicas. Where this was considered unacceptable the glass was decorated or deliberately coloured in a deeper tone. In the 15th c., or perhaps somewhat earlier, Venetian glass-makers discovered that oxide of manganese would decolourize and clarify their glass, making it colourless and transparent. (A compound of arsenic or nickel will have the same effect.) This clarification was the basis for the vast success of Venetian glass during the Renaissance period, since the resulting metal was comparable with ROCK-CRYSTAL, a treasured and prized substance throughout the centuries. Hence the name of *cristallo* for Venetian glass. The modern use of the word 'crystal' for glass lacks precise meaning and generally signifies hand-blown, good-quality glass as opposed to commercial mass-produced mould-blown ware. In 18th-c. France '*cristal*' signified glass made in the English manner. In Germany and Bohemia the word indicated an attempt to make a glass like rock-crystal, but with lime as an additive and not lead. This hard, slightly grey material in fact resembled rock-crystal more closely than the English lead glass but lacked the latter's 'oily' brilliance. 'Crystal glass' can therefore have several meanings according to time and place. In sum, it can mean: Venetian colourless glass; German or Bohemian rock-crystal-like ware; English-type lustrous, shadowy glass; or, finally, modern high-class products.

The ingredients having been weighed and combined in the crucible, a fire-clay pot usually about 1 to 1·25 metres high, they are melted by the furnace for up to 48 hours, impurities being skimmed off. Imperfectly fused glass is full of bubbles and undissolved particles. Obviously the fuels used vary according to time and place. Huge quantities of wood fuel were used by early glass-makers, causing them to move about in forest land, much as the potters did and for precisely the same reason. Centres such as Venice depended on sea transport to bring fuel. Coal was first used in England in the 17th c. In recent years oil, gas and electricity have of course replaced wood and coal. The glass having been fused, it is then almost fluid, ductile and sticky, that is it will adhere to an iron rod. As it stiffens rapidly it can be cut, twisted or blown. A thread of glass can be drawn up from a lump (called the paraison) to form a tube nine metres long or more and only three mm in diameter. (In this way clinical thermometers are made.) Repeated return to the furnace will renew the plasticity as long as required, and restores the 'fire-polish' or brilliant fused surface peculiar to glass.

Certain early glass centres used ingots of ready fused glass made elsewhere, which they simply heated to form the desired articles. Generally, however, glass-houses handled the complete process.

All glass, whether made by hand or machine, must be 'annealed', that is slowly cooled in a warm oven or chamber. This strengthens the material, which has been strained by shaping and rapid cooling and reheating. If not annealed, it would be brittle. Modern specially toughened glass is treated at this stage, sometimes by plunging it in boiling oil.

(*b*) *Techniques.* There are basically two techniques, as there are basically two ingredients, in glass-making with local variations and specialities. These techniques are *moulding* and *blowing*. But the earliest use of glass, other than as a GLAZE on earthenware beads, was for making 'core-wound' pots. This technique meant winding the 'worm' of glass, while still molten, round a core of sand and clay. Repeated heatings enabled the worm or thread to be pressed together to form a solid wall or to be inlaid with threads of differing colours. Handles were then separately applied, surface irregularities were smoothed down by abrasives and a limited amount of fire-polish was achieved by a final heating. The sand or clay core was finally scraped out.

Moulding, as carried out up to the invention of blowing, was a simple pressing of the metal over a shaped mould, probably of the same sandy clay as was used for core-wound vessels. Alternatively, the mould was carved with a pattern in relief. An important version of this was the mosaic-glass technique, originally Egyptian and adapted to Roman design. Varicoloured glass rods were lightly fused together to form one thick rod. This was then extended to the required length and thinness. When hard it was sliced laterally, so that each slice had the coloured pattern on it. The slices were then laid side by side in a mould and fused sufficiently so that they adhered to each other. These bowls, being translucent, exceeded in beauty the jasper, agate or sardonyx (see QUARTZ) vessels which had inspired them. Cameo glass, made of two layers of different coloured glass, was another imitation of stone.

It will be clear that this manner of treating glass showed that it was conceived as an alternative or substitute for coloured stones or gemstones. Its ductility when heated was only exploited in order to fashion objects more easily than by carving them from hard or brittle materials. This attitude to glass has continued throughout the centuries, particularly in Germany and in certain phases of modern design. It has consistently been deprecated by those (including Ruskin) who claim that such an approach ignores the true character and beauty of glass, which can only be seen in blown objects.

It seems probable that the invention of blowing glass through a hollow rod may have arisen from the use of concave rather than convex moulds. The metal had for long been picked up on rods. The use of a hollow one may have been accidental. At first, about the beginning of the Christian era, blown vessels bear the mark of the mould into which they have been projected. A very rapid development took place, however, and during the 1st c. A.D. a large variety of bottles and containers for perfumes, oils, liquids, even cinerary urns, were made at various places in the Roman Empire, notably Alexandria.

The true 'pattern of a gesture' method, however, developed in Syria and the Near East during the 14th and 15th centuries with the swan-necked decanters and flasks and reached its apogee in the fantastic forms blown at Venice and by Venetian craftsmen working elsewhere. This kind of technical *tour de force* continues particularly at Murano. But glass-blowers were not necessarily distracted into fantasy; the sober taste of the early 18th c. in England, for example, produced the gloriously simple shapes, not metallic and not derivative from SILVER forms, which arise purely from the craftsman's skill at revealing the special qualities inherent in the material of glass—the play of light, the fugitive shadows and refractions, the soft yet clear outline and the fluidity which is so apt for the compass of wine.

The method and tools for blowing glass have continued almost unchanged. The required lump of molten glass having been taken up on the iron rod, the blower will either sit on a chair with long parallel arms, rolling the rod rhythmically back and forth while the bubble of glass rolls on a marble table (the marver) beside him, or if the work is small, will stand to it. The bubble having been rotated into a cylindrical shape, can then be blown. Still attached to the rod, it can next be swung about to elongate it, cut, pincered and otherwise manipulated. During this time it will be repeatedly reheated and re-rolled. It can then be decorated with threads of glass wound round ('trailing'), small decorative bosses ('prunts'), and handles and other extra pieces can be attached. Drinking glasses can either have their feet drawn out from the main body and folded under, or the feet can be attached separately. The mark of the 'puntil' or blowing-tube can frequently be seen under a glass foot, more or less well smoothed off.

Mould-blown glass. Modern glass produced for commercial purposes, milk bottles, electric light bulbs, etc., is power-blown by electricity into metal moulds. Sometimes the pressing principle is used, and after the glass has been blown into the mould a plunger is driven in, forcing it into the extremities. This is much used for cheap imitations of cut glass. The machinery for these techniques was largely developed in the United States of America.

(*c*) *Decoration*. Decoration of glass is either integral, that is arising during the making of the object, or external and applied afterwards.

The various shapings possible during the blowing process have already been referred to and will be further described under the following sections of this article. The insertion of coloured strands or of air bubbles is also done while the glass is ductile. The Venetian *latticino* ware, for instance, or the English 'air-twist' stem glasses, are examples which have great fascination for the collector or observer. The underlying principle, however, is very simple: whatever coloured rods or bubbles of air are introduced into the paraison or lump of glass at the outset will retain the same relation to each other however far the paraison is extended. In the case of *latticino* the paraison is twisted and spun so that what was a small ball of glass, on to which the various white threads were carefully picked up, becomes a flat dish with a fine network of white lines. Similarly a glass bubble in a stem can be drawn out a little to form a 'tear' or extended spirally into an air-twist. The principle is simple, but the manual skill required to control the paraison at this stage is exceptionally great and accounts for the respect in which these complex pieces are held.

'Flashing' or colouring is the taking up of a coloured metallic oxide mixed with a glassy frit or flux on to the paraison, so that a layer of colour adheres to the colourless ground. This method is used to produce stained glass for windows. In glass vessels this flashing can be cut through to make a pattern of coloured-on-clear, or vice versa, as is common in 19th-c. and 20th-c. Bohemian and English glass.

When applied externally to the finished object colour is in the same form, a metallic oxide mixed with a glassy flux. It is then powdered and applied with a brush in an oily medium. The painting when heated in a muffle (mild) kiln adheres to the softened surface of the vessel, the medium vaporizing away. This mild firing may have to be repeated for each colour according to the chemical structure of the different oxides. Red or ruby glass is derived from gold and was therefore considered specially valuable. These metallic oxide paints are the same as those used on PORCELAIN. The colours are not easy to control and require a chemist for their composition. There is no question, as in oil painting, of mixing tones at will.

(*d*) *Engraving*

(i) *Wheel-engraving and cutting*. Since the cutting of rock-crystal and other gemstones on a lapidary's wheel was already well established in Roman times, particularly in CAMEOS, this method of decoration was obviously applicable to glass in so far as glass was regarded as an essentially dense and hard material. Consequently throughout the centuries, wherever glass has been formed in shapes similar to silver or stone, it has been cut or engraved. Two examples are the work inspired in the medieval Near East by the carvers of rock-crystal and in 16th-c. Prague and elsewhere by the armourers and metal-engravers.

In the 2nd half of the 18th c. and the 19th c., primarily in England, engraved decorations on blown glass were widely used. The main reason for this was the taste for more decoration after *c.* 1745. During this period the splendid refractions of facet-cut English-type glass were increasingly appreciated and facet-cutting (using the cutting-wheel to slice the surface of the vessel rather than to incise a picture) became the main mode of decoration in the 19th c. This was also rewarding to the makers, since it was very much easier and therefore cheaper than fine pictorial engraving, also of course done on the wheel.

The 'wheel' is a grindstone, using small discs of metal, usually copper, in various sizes and turned by water or electric power. An abrasive stream of emery or sand and water is fed through it and as the vessel is held to the wheel the pattern or picture is ground into the surface. The engraving is then either polished or left matt. Like blowing, the essential process is simple to describe but requires a dexterity very rarely seen in the present century. Pictorial engraving was particularly developed in Germany and also in Holland. English undecorated vessels were sent to Holland to be engraved, particularly for the Dutch speciality of stipple-engraving, or pricking the glass surface with dots.

(ii) *Diamond-point engraving*. This is a free-hand technique of simply scratching the surface with a diamond held in a pen-like holder. It has been practised throughout the history of glass, but particularly from the 16th to the 18th centuries by amateurs. Diamond-point inscriptions and decorations were frequently done on older pieces of glass and are not necessarily contemporary with the making of the vessel.

(iii) *Etching*. A modern development (though the process was known in the 17th c.) is etching of glass with hydrofluoric acid. This is widely used for producing textured 'frosted' glass and for pictorial decoration of large surfaces in architectural glass. It is an application of the 'resist' technique, where the blank parts of the design are coated with wax or other protection and the acid then bites the uncovered surfaces. In their turn parts of the bitten design can then be blocked out and the etching deepened in certain areas by further immersion in the acid.

Sand-blasting is a variation of this. A stream of sand or powdered iron or flint is projected at the sheet of glass, parts of which are protected by a metal stencil or by a wax or rubber resist. This technique is generally used for large surfaces, but can be done on mass-produced drinking or eating wares.

The standard by which quality in glass may be judged is the same as that which applies to all the decorative arts. Does the decoration obscure either the form or the function of the object? In so far as it does, the object is badly designed. It may none the less be of exceptional rarity or historical interest; or it may exhibit a phenomenal technical skill. Yet it remains true that if a bowl is so encrusted with decoration that its shape is imperceptible or if a wineglass is impossible to drink from, then, however interesting, it lacks quality as an object of decorative art.

A criterion which has often been applied to glass is that of truth to the material. This is the basis for the criticism of glass which is treated as if it were metal or stone. If this argument is pushed to its extreme, engraving on glass would be precluded. Since facet-cutting and certain types of engraving undoubtedly serve to enhance the light-transmitting and light-refracting quality of glass which makes it different from all other material, it would be a pity to exclude them. The general principle is surely valid, however, and provides a sound basis for the formation of taste.

2. ANTIQUITY

(*a*) *Ancient Egypt.* It is not known precisely when the Egyptians, probably through experimenting with ceramic glazes, produced glass. (See also PREHISTORIC TECHNOLOGY.) Glass beads were being made by the middle of the 3rd millennium B.C., but vessels are not certainly known to have been made until 1,000 years later, and even these were small. They were produced by covering a removable core with viscous glass and decorating the resultant form by means of parallel glass threads of contrasting colours laid on in zig-zags and festoons and then pressed in flush with the surface. Egypt remained the main centre of glass-making until Hellenistic times, and the products of Greece, Assyria and Syria were mostly copied from the Egyptians, though glass engraving may have been a speciality of western Asia. Although by the 1st c. B.C. rival glass industries had sprung up in other countries, Egypt—and Alexandria in particular—was still pre-eminent in many branches.

The first of these—MOSAIC GLASS—had already been foreshadowed in dynastic times. Glass rods were built up into composite canes with a pattern in cross-section like Brighton rock. Sections from these canes could then be fused into sheets, which when re-heated could in turn be formed in clay moulds to give open vessels such as bowls or dishes. The patterns were usually fairly simple (scrolls, concentric circles, etc.) but the more elaborate examples include representational subjects such as flowers (*millefiori*) or butterflies. These vessels could also be made of variegated glass imitating gemstones, and sometimes they enclosed glittering gold particles ('aventurine' glass). The pieces were usually finished by wheel-polishing.

The second great Egyptian school of glass decoration was that of the cutters and engravers. Although simple engraving on glass was known in the 18th Dynasty (15th–14th c. B.C.), the work of the Hellenistic period seems to have derived from the lapidary's art, for the pieces were cut from a solid block or a roughly moulded form. Later shallow oval facets were cut, either in overlapping rows or in simple repetitive designs. Vessels of exceptional luxury were occasionally engraved with designs, such as repeated LOTUS buds or flowers, left in relief by grinding away the ground.

A related technique was that of grinding away the upper of two superimposed layers of glass to leave a design standing on a ground of contrasting colour, usually white on dark blue ('cameo' glass). This technique was taken up and developed in Italy, where probably the Portland Vase (British Museum, 1st c. A.D.) was produced, the outstanding example of the technique.

ENAMEL painting also appears to have been invented in Egypt, as well as the technique by which a leaf of gold, etched with a coloured design, was sandwiched between two fused layers of glass somewhat in the manner of VERRE ÉGLOMISÉ.

(*b*) *Syria.* It was probably the Syrians who invented glass-blowing, the fundamental technique of the art, *c.* the end of the 1st c. B.C. It appears to have been at first intimately connected with mould-blowing, a process by which patterns were produced in relief by blowing the metal into a two-part mould. Later, however, glass blowing developed into an art in its own right, vessels of varying size and almost any shape being produced by blowing alone. With this unfettered manipulation of the form itself went a free use of threads and blobs of plastic glass for decoration. The ductile but quickly cooling Syrian soda metal encouraged the emergence of a school of craftsmanship in which fantasy and a light touch were at a premium.

(*c*) *Roman Empire.* Although the new method of blown glass answered innumerable everyday and commercial needs, nevertheless the extension and consolidation of the Roman Empire helped the industry to flourish and expand as never before. Glass-workers showed themselves willing to migrate so as to be nearer their markets and this diffusion combined with the unifying influence of the Roman rule to produce a distinctive style in glass, which might in some places be 'provincial' but was everywhere recognizably Roman. The first blending apparently took place in Italy in the 1st c. A.D., for not only did the Syrian craftsmen migrate with their mould-blowing technique, but Egyptian skills were also transplanted. Glass-cutting and the gold-leaf technique were certainly practised in Italy at this time. As cutters the Italians surpassed their teachers in virtuosity. On their famous CAGE-CUPS or *diatreta* network designs and inscriptions were left standing completely free of their ground except for an occasional supporting strut.

The industrial lead soon passed, however, from Italy to Gaul and thence to the Germanic border provinces, of which Cologne was the most important glass centre. In this area glass of a generally Syrian type was made, but engraving too was practised and even included representation of figural themes. A speciality was the 'snake-thread' glasses (*Schlangenfadengläser*)—flasks and goblets decorated with ribbons, usually of coloured glass, TRAILED on in fantastic patterns and notched with a transverse ribbed effect.

The break-up of the Roman Empire affected glass-making differently in different provinces. In the north the Barbarian invasions changed glass-making from a fairly centralized industry into a scattering of glass-houses isolated in the forests which supplied them with fuel. Here simple forms were made in an impure greenish or yellowish material with no more decoration than a trailing of glass threads. Virtuosity, however, was later displayed in the fantastic 'claw-beakers' (*Rüsselbecher*), which were decorated with two superimposed rows of hollow trunk-like protrusions curved down and rejoined to the wall of the vessel. In the east, however, urban life continued and the glass tradition was carried on unbroken into Islamic times. Syria appears to have remained the chief centre and still favoured plastic decoration, which until the coming of Islam was often fantastically elaborate. In Egypt the art declined after the Roman period, only rough vessels being made in an impure metal. In Byzantium the status of glass-making is obscure though to judge from the glass brought back by Crusaders to Venice in 1204, and from the fact that glass-cutters were distinguished by law from glass-blowers, expensive cut glass was favoured there.

(*d*) *Islam.* In the middle decades of the 7th c. the whole of the Near East was overrun by the Arabs. Despite factions between rival dynasties a political unity was achieved comparable with that of the Roman Empire. Similar conditions produced similar results and in glass-making an Islamic style evolved which was scarcely less uniform than the Roman. Syria and Egypt were still the most important centres, but under the Abbasid dynasty from the middle of the 8th c. glass-making flourished in Mesopotamia also. The Syrian industry seems to have retained its predilection for applied and trailed decoration but was probably responsible also for a renaissance of mould-blown ornament, usually of simple DIAPER patterns or vertical ribs. The Egyptians made innovations and revived old techniques. Within the glass-house itself they evolved a method of impressing decoration either by stamping on applied pads or by gripping the upright walls of cylindrical bowls between the jaws of a tool like a pair of tongs so as to produce designs of stylized lettering, flowers, animals, etc. They also discovered a new means of decorating glass once it had cooled by painting it with metallic 'lustre' and used various stains of like character to produce splendid chromatic effects, of which unfortunately no intact example survives. It was probably the Egyptians too who revived *millefiori* glass and gilding, which had both flourished in Roman times. They reintroduced the ancient fern and feather patterns made by incorporating white threads in a dark body. Cutting and engraving too were probably practised in Egypt, although Mesopotamia seems to have been the chief centre for these. There not only were the facet-cutting and boss-cutting familiar from Sassanian times continued, but there arose a splendid school of linear engraving on colourless glass and probably also a school of engraving in high relief with birds and spirited animals finely rendered in outline with notched cordons. Recent finds make it probable that such work was also done in Persia.

The crowning achievement of the Islamic world in this art was its enamelled and gilt glass. From Syria—probably the cities of Raqqa, Damascus and Aleppo—came a great series of drinking beakers, bottles, mosque lamps and other objects, decorated with inscriptions, figural subjects and ARABESQUES in enamel colours (mainly blue, red and opaque white) on a ground of gilding. These enamelled glasses of the 13th and 14th centuries are among the most sumptuous ever produced. In Europe they were treasured as rarities, mounted as reliquaries in precious metal settings and preserved in church treasuries or jealously guarded as family heirlooms in specially made leather cases.

Syria was overrun and Damascus destroyed by Timur in 1400. The art of glass thereafter declined in the Islamic countries, although enamelled glass of poorer quality was still made, probably in Egypt, during the early part of the 15th c. By the 2nd half of the century, however, even the sultans of Egypt were supplied with glass from Murano.

3. EUROPE

(*a*) *Venice.* Although Venice had long been in contact with the Near East and was the heir to its glory in the art of glass, there is no clear evidence that it was directly indebted for the type of glass which made it famous as the greatest of all glass-making centres. The Venetian enamelled glass of the late 15th c. differs in many respects from the Syrian of the 14th and according to Venetian tradition it was first made by a member of the famous glass-making family of Barovieri. The earlier Venetian glass, known only from paintings, seems to have consisted only of plain tumblers and spherical flasks on low feet. To these forms new ones were added in the 15th c., many of them apparently inspired by contemporary metalwork just as the enamelled decoration echoed the painting of the time. Characteristically, as Italians of the Renaissance, the Venetians seem to have been keenly aware of the achievements of classical antiquity. Not only did they reproduce the Roman 'mosaic' and *millefiori* glass and the material made of blended opaque colours in imitation of natural stones (*calcedonio*, sometimes miscalled *Schmelzglas*), but they seem even to have copied such typical Roman shapes as for instance the bowl with external vertical ribs. They also reproduced the aventurine glass of Egypt.

Although Venice was renowned for coloured glass, probably evolved to serve its enormous trade in beads, it was the colourless glass which was most coveted abroad. The art of decolourizing glass by the use of manganese dioxide was lost in Europe during the Dark Ages and its revival in Venice produced a metal which contemporaries compared with rock-crystal and therefore called *cristallo*. The Venetian glass nevertheless frequently had a slight brownish or greyish tint very sympathetic to the modern eye. With this material, which could be worked very thin and demanded great speed and dexterity, the Venetian craftsmen of the 1st half of the 16th c. produced forms of great beauty—simple and sober at first, then more elaborate and inclining to fantasy, until in the 17th c. stems and handles were wrought into complex writhing forms often of a flame-like vivacity. The plain *cristallo* was early diversified in other ways. Already in the 1st half of the 16th c. threads of opaque white glass (*latticinio* or *latticino*) had begun to be used for decoration. This became progressively more complex with the introduction of canes containing spirally twisted opaque white threads embedded in clear glass, until finally the whole surface might be enmeshed in a lacy white pattern (*vitro di trina*, lace glass). A crackled surface could be produced on plain glass vessels by dipping them whilst hot into water or by rolling them on a bed of glass fragments ('ice glass'). *Cristallo* was also found suitable for engraving with the diamond-point, which produced spidery opaque lines effective in the rendering of delicate lacy patterns.

There is no doubt that glass was made in the Venetian Republic before the year 1292, but it is in that year that the glass-houses were established on the island of Murano, where many still continue. The Doge and the ruling Court of Venice were extremely jealous of the secrets of the glass trade and so all glass-workers became virtual prisoners of the State, whilst enjoying privileges which verged on those of the nobility. The trade was organized into a highly elaborate guild system, and for a glass craftsman to flee the country carried the death penalty. In some cases the Doge's arm was long and glass-masters who had fled the Republic were found murdered abroad by hired assassins.

Venetian glass was very similar to Roman glass in its consistency. It is the type commonly known as 'soda glass' and was made from soda-ash, which was obtained mainly from the Near East or Spain, and lime in the form of powdered marble and white pebbles from the river Po. The early Venetian glass was both utilitarian and simple in design, but by the 15th c. it had begun to be strongly influenced by the ideas of the Renaissance, particularly the shapes of contemporary silverware. At the same time the art of colouring glass was being discovered and together with the enamel work of the time it reflected the magnificence and splendour of Renaissance Italy at the end of the 15th c.

By the beginning of the 16th c. glass was being worked in blue, purple and green, and by far the most important in opaque white. This early opaque white glass was certainly used by Antonio di San Simone in 1470, for the first recorded experiment in the making of European PORCELAIN. But it is the use of enamel decoration during this period which is the highlight of Venetian glass, although there were many other types produced, particularly in imitation of gemstones, a craft practised by the Jews in Palestine for making PASTE jewellery from very early times. The use of enamel on glass was an Islamic technique learnt from the Near East and Syria. In most cases a dark, solid, coloured background of glass was used to display medallions and scenes which were painted in fusible enamel and fired in a small oven. This technique stems from the 13th c. and was probably developed from the use of enamel on metal, for which the Venetian Republic was already famous.

It is the Venetian glass of the 16th c. that is by far the most important and decorative. It became a great luxury sought after by every well-to-do family throughout Europe. Important glass objects, some of them merely decorative, were used as centre-pieces on tables in place of silver and gold. By the middle of the century the technical skill of the Venetian glass-workers had not only shown remarkable development but had achieved a character and distinctive style of its own rather than copying the designs and patterns of the metal-workers. This does not mean to say that the Venetian glass-works were entirely confined to ornate luxury goods. There were four main categories of glass-maker and almost certainly the lowest category of all, that is to say the bead-makers or *paternostreri*, *margaritai* or *perlai*, contributed more to the success of Venetian glass financially than any of the others. As their name implies, they were the makers of rosaries and small beads, one of the most ancient of all the crafts. The other three groups were the makers of window-glass and vessels, known as *fioleri* and *verieri*, the *cristallai* who made optical glass and last of all the mirror-glass makers, who were known as *specchiai*.

Venetian glass was so fragile that it did not lend itself to any form of engraving other than the finest use of diamond-point, and even this decoration was very rare indeed. On the other hand the Venetians perfected the art of moulding the most complicated and elaborate shapes, such as the hollow-blown lion-mask on the stems of 15th-c., 16th-c. and 17th-c. glasses. They developed many other skills in decorated glass, particularly that of *latticinio* or *vitro di trina* where the glass had incorporated into its body a coloured or opaque thread in the most complex form. These glasses were very popular in the 16th and early 17th centuries. Another form of decoration developed at this period was that of 'crackle glass' or 'ice glass', where the whole body of the article appears to be fragmented.

By the beginning of the 17th c. glass-houses in the style of Venice had been well established in most of the large Italian states, but mainly at Bologna, Ferrara and Genoa. The unrelenting restrictions of the Venetian authorities forced many a younger son to flee from the island of Murano to other parts of Europe, particularly to Normandy, Spain, Bohemia and most important of all to the Low Countries around Antwerp and Liège. The spread of knowledge of how to make glass in the Venetian style or FAÇON DE VENISE led to a decline in the European dominance of the Venetian glass industry, which coincided with a general decline in the influence of Venice on the economy of Europe. Throughout the 16th c. more and more glass-houses were being founded without the aid of Venetian craftsmen, and by the middle of the 17th c. the Venetian glass trade was at a very low ebb as the new glass-houses in many countries began to establish national styles. While there is no doubt that up to this time Venetian ideas, styles and methods of production were of paramount importance, the decline from the middle of the 17th c. was as spectacular as the rise had been in the 15th and 16th centuries. As it is very difficult to find Venetian glass which can be definitely dated before the middle of the 15th c., it is equally difficult to find glass which can be definitely attributed to Venice made after the 1st quarter of the 18th c.

(*b*) *Russia*. Very little glass was produced in Russia until the middle of the 17th c. when a Swedish artilleryman, Elias Koyet, received permission from the Tsar to start a factory near Moscow. In 1668 another factory was founded at Izmaylovo near the Summer Palace of the Tsar and here Venetian glass-blowers were employed. Very early in the 18th c. a glass-works was established at Sparrow Hills, just outside Moscow. The first craftsmen and glass-masters here were English, but these were later replaced by Russians whom they had trained. Almost the entire production of the Russian glass-houses during this early period was taken up by the court and the aristocracy; but under Peter the Great the Russian glass industry advanced swiftly, particularly with regard to the manufacture of glass panels, chandeliers, lustres, girondoles and candelabra. In 1714 the Tsar decided that the Sparrow Hills glass-works should be moved to Yamburg (Kingisepp) and also to Zhabino. Both these small towns were on the banks of the River Luga and very close to the new capital St. Petersburg (Leningrad). By the middle of the 18th c. the Yamburg factory had changed its name to The St. Petersburg Crystal Factory and controlled a large department store on the Nevsky Prospect. Probably the most successful of the Russian glass-makers was Thoma Maltzev, who opened a glass-house in 1760 and worked principally for Catherine the Great, whilst the other great glass-works, the Nazya Factory, was controlled by Prince Potemkin. In both cases the glass was made almost exclusively for the royal household and the great noble houses. At this time the glass itself was of only mediocre quality in comparison with that of other European countries; but under the great glazier Bakhnetev, who developed not only crystal glass but also the creamy-white OPALINE glass peculiar to Russia, the quality of the glass reached a very high standard. Bakhnetev, together with a chemist and scholar by the name of Lomonosov, also developed the art of *smalta* (thick coloured glass) from which were produced medallions, brooches and particularly fine mosaics. In 1765 Lomonosov was elected a member of the Academy of Science at Bologna for his 'distinguished work in the field of glass'. By the end of the 18th c. the milky-white opaline glass was much sought after for decoration and was used in the form of medallions set in clear glass on almost every type of glassware from goblets and cups to carafes, plates and commemorative plaques.

Despite the law of 1744 which required all factories to impress and mark their products, there are very few pieces of glass which are signed and dated. Those that are marked come from the last quarter of the 18th c. But with the discovery of opaline glass, which could be decorated with all forms of enamel and lent itself to inscriptions, many more pieces were both signed and dated.

The finest period of Russian glass extends over the last quarter of the 18th c. and the 1st quarter of the 19th c., when glass was manufactured in every hue and the Russian diamond-cut glass was of very high quality. The decoration of glass and porcelain was very similar and in 1792 the State Glass Factory was amalgamated with the State Porcelain Factory; but from 1825 onwards we know of very little glass being made there. The Maltzev glass-works ceased to produce luxury goods and concentrated on mass-produced domestic glassware, but the Bakhnetev works continued to produce some exceptionally fine art glass and does so still under the name of the 'Krasniy Gigant' glass-works. See also RUSSIA.

(*c*) *Bohemia and Germany*. Whilst the brilliant art of glass-making flourished in the Near East glass-makers in northern Europe concentrated on coloured glass for church windows, treating glass vessels as only secondary. Yet some traditions of craftsmanship did survive and in the later Middle Ages a distinctive Germanic style emerged over the whole area from the Baltic in the north to the lands bordering on the Venetian Republic in the south. This glass falls into two main categories.

(i) First comes the simple medieval utilitarian glassware, exemplified in the *Passglas* and *Humpen*, which were no more than large cylindrical vessels to be passed round from hand to hand. To this category also belonged the *Krautstrunk* and *Nuppenbecher*, both of which were shorter beakers usually decorated with small applied raspberry prunts and made of the most crude type of *Waldglas*. This *Waldglas* was pale green in colour and was manufactured in almost every German principality and state. Its quality was poor and the colour derived from iron impurities present in the silica and soda from which it was made. Into the same category falls the most common of all European glasses, the *Roemer*, which has persisted from the 15th c. up to the present day. The bowl is the shape of an orange with its top cut off and it is set upon a small waist with applied raspberry prunts and a hollow-spun foot. This type of glass can still be found in most German restaurants. The centres of glass production were many and varied: Bohemia itself, Silesia, Moravia, Thuringia, Saxony, Franconia, Tyrol, Hesse and Carinthia all manufactured glass in the 15th and 16th centuries. The great northern glass-houses of Hanover, Brandenburg, Brunswick and even Potsdam did not really come into their own until the 17th and 18th centuries.

(ii) Into the second category fall the high-quality glass of Bohemia and the superb decorations in the form of enamel work and engraving that can be traced to two or three major innovations. It is interesting to note that with the exception of the early *Krautstrunk* and *Passglas* there is very little everyday glass to be found from these areas, but what decorated early European glass is still extant is of the 'grand' quality, designed and made for the luxury market created by the great patrons of the arts, often by large landowners seeking to increase their income by founding glass-houses on their estates, or for the monasteries and town councils.

In the early 15th and 16th centuries Bohemia was famous for its ROCK-CRYSTAL vessels and the rareness of this, together with the development of the Venetian *cristallo*, led to such important lapidaries as Caspar LEHMANN developing the art of cutting and engraving on glass. Lehmann was the official jeweller to the court of Rudolf II at Prague and many of his great works in rock-crystal (*Böhmisches Bergkristall*) are in the style of Italian Renaissance works. Lehmann tried to develop the art of cutting Venetian *cristallo* in the same manner as he carved rock-crystal but the consistency of the metal used in the Venetian glass was far too brittle; this led to the development of a strong potash-lime glass, which came into its own in the last quarter of the 17th c. The art of engraving on glass was not Lehmann's alone, and after his death he was followed by a senior assistant, Georg SCHWANHARDT. Schwanhardt moved to Nuremberg because of the upheaval caused by the Thirty Years War, and it is here in Nuremberg that a great tradition of glass-cutting and polishing was begun. Schwanhardt had two sons, Georg and Heinrich, and it is the latter who is supposed to have discovered the use of hydrofluoric acid for etching glass, a process which after his day fell into disuse for a century or more. These two were followed by Hans Schmidt and Hermann Schwinger (1640–83). Probably the last of the great Nuremberg engravers was Georg Killinger, who worked from the last quarter of the 17th c. until his death in 1726. The Nuremberg engraved glass of this period is of exceptionally high quality, but it too was made for a 'grand' purpose rather than as everyday domestic ware. Up until the time of Killinger the glass-engravers used the lapidary's tools, mainly small wheels driven by hand, and diamond-point etching, but early in the 18th c. both water power and the foot-treadle began to be used by glass-engravers.

As the craftsmen moved further afield it is to Silesia that we look for really high-quality engraved glass. Indeed it became so refined that two distinct schools arose: the *Hochschnitt*, which was engraving in high relief, and the *Tiefschnitt* or intaglio type of engraving. All the fine floweriness of the ROCOCO period is apparent in glasses of this time, although later it got a trifle out of hand. Over-elaborate scrolls and garlands, known as LAUB- UND BANDELWERK, developed to such an extent that the glasses became far too heavy; bowls and stems were out of proportion with the foot and in many cases the whole surface of the bowl was obscured by engraving.

During the 18th c. a number of great glass-houses were established in north Germany. Of these one of the most important was the Lauenstein Glass-House, which came under patronage of the Palatinate of Hanover. Many of the Lauenstein glasses are almost English in design. It is supposed that George I sent English craftsmen to Lauenstein and that Lauenstein indeed was the first German glass-house to introduce lead glass of similar formula to that inaugurated by Ravenscroft. Unfortunately the German chemists were not as successful as their English counterparts and much of the glass of this period from Lauenstein, as well as that of Potsdam and Kassel, suffered from 'glass disease'. This defect was brought about by the incorrect amount of chemicals being mixed into the batch when the metal was prepared for blowing, and meant that in course of time the glass became crizzled and almost opaque. Some of the Lauenstein glasses are marked on the base with a rampant lion, but these are few and far between.

It is from north Germany, particularly Potsdam, that the first important coloured glass emanated. By the beginning of the 18th c. deep blue and green glass of rare quality was being produced, but it is for the development of red glass, particularly the 'gold-ruby' (*Goldrubinglas*) discovered by Johann KUNCKEL, that Potsdam is most famous. This red has the rare quality of being both exceptionally dark in certain lights and yet translucent and bright as red ink in others. Its colour was perfected by the addition of gold, gold coins being dropped into the mix when the batch of metal had reached a certain temperature. Many other glass-makers tried to imitate 'gold-ruby' glass by the addition of other materials, particularly copper, but with little or no success. Unfortunately Kunckel's experiments were too expensive for his patron, the Elector Frederick of Brandenburg, who was to become Frederick I. Kunckel was asked to account for his experiments and Frederick was so horrified at the expense that he demanded repayment and in consequence Kunckel died a disillusioned pauper in 1703.

One of the earliest forms of glass decoration from the 15th c. onwards was the addition of simple enamel-work pictures. These are not only colourful and attractive but often give us a glimpse of history which might so easily have been lost. Large *Humpen* and *Passglas* vessels are decorated with varied scenes ranging from marriages on wedding goblets to business contracts. These include such glasses as *Reichsadler Humpen*, which show the hierarchy of the Holy Roman Empire and its various noble houses. There were also smaller straight-sided beakers often decorated with applied enamels to show an event and its date. From these highly decorative, charming, but crude works with their cold enamel paintwork evolved one of the finest forms of enamelling technique, that known as SCHWARZLOT. This was developed by a Nuremberg craftsman, Johann SCHAPER, in the middle of the 17th c. A mixture of copper oxide and glass was fused to the surface of the vessels, which turned black on a second firing. Some of Schaper's work, particularly his portraiture, is of a quality unsurpassed by any SILHOUETTE miniaturist of the period. Of all German glass it is probably the *Schwarzlot* glasses which come nearest to good taste.

A further technique, which was developed in Austria at Gutenbrunn by Joseph Mildner (1763–1808), was that of *Zwischengoldglas*, in which small double-walled beakers were decorated in the style of VERRE ÉGLOMISÉ by the insertion of miniature portraits or scenes in gold leaf between two walls. Most *Zwischengoldglas* is in the form of simple beakers with straight sides decorated with hunting and religious scenes. The edge of the beaker is folded over and a joint usually shows just below the rim. Mildner is also known for his medallions and silhouette engraving on glass.

At the same time as Mildner was working on *Zwischengoldglas* Samuel Mohn (1762–1815) was working with enamels in Dresden. His son Gottlob moved to Vienna, where together with Anton Kothgasser (1769–1851) he produced some of the most beautifully enamelled glasses with a wide variety of scenes and other forms of decoration. Both Kothgasser and Mohn favoured a very simple glass, a plain beaker flared at the rim with a cut cog-wheel base, called a *Ranftbecher*.

Bohemian coloured glass continued to develop throughout the 19th c. particularly in such glass as 'Hyalith', made in imitation of natural stone. This was usually completely opaque and either deep purple or black. One of the most interesting developments was that of Frederick Egermann, who produced a glass called 'Lithyalin', which had the texture, colour and consistency of marble and was often veined and multicoloured. Another form of glass which was produced in Germany in large quantities during the 18th and 19th centuries was *Milchglas*, a white translucent glass which if held up to the light has a fiery-red colour. Its opaqueness was due to the addition of arsenic and tin oxide. It was not, however, of the same quality or consistency as opaline Bristol. The decoration on all these glasses tended to be cold gilding or cold enamel work of poor quality which was not fired on to the glass and therefore tended to rub or chip.

By the middle of the 19th c., the Bohemian glass-works were by far the most important in the world. Probably one of the greatest names of the period was Dominic Biemann, whose miniature portrait-engraving on glass is unique. By the end of the century the *Jugendstil* (see ART NOUVEAU) movement had its followers in the glass industry. Amongst these the most famous must be Lobmeyr of Vienna, who brought together probably all that was best in the German and Czech *art-nouveau* movement and together with Loetz and Moser produced some of the finest ornamental glass of the period. For the first time, instead of being leaders in design, they were content to adopt both the style and the designs of the American Louis Comfort TIFFANY. Loetz in particular was famous for his peacock hues and iridescent colours.

(*d*) *Spain*. Although glass is known to have been made in Spain since the Roman occupation, very little of consequence has emanated from there. Certainly a national style was developed far later than in almost any other European country owing mainly to the strength of Moorish and Venetian influences. Such Spanish glass as remains from the period prior to the mid 18th c. is of rather poor quality. The metal is soda glass, very bubbly and not at all clear, and the designs tend to be crude. The enamel work is attractive, as instead of the more elaborate Venetian fired enamel the Spanish craftsmen tended to apply trails of opaque white cords, which add to the delicacy of the finished product. The Moorish influence is most prominent in the pincer work to be found on the typical Spanish vessels known as *cantaros* and *porrones*. These pieces are attributed to Granada and to Catalonia.

The most important glass-works was that of the Royal Factory at La Granja, the only major factory to produce glass of quality comparable to that of other European glass-houses. Although it was founded in 1728, it is only from the last quarter of the 18th c. that any quantity of really fine crystal glass was produced there. The typical form of decoration was for the body to be engraved with continuous floral swags and other patterns, which were then gilded. La Granja also produced some coloured glass and milk-white opaque glass but in contrast to Bohemian and German work the enamel decoration usually consisted only of simple floral patterns.

(*e*) *France*. It is strange that, although glass was produced in France from Roman times, a country with so fine a tradition of craftsmanship should have produced so little of note until the 19th c. From time to time glass-makers were imported from Italy; but these were no more than temporary installations.

The most noteworthy achievement in the glass industry during the 17th and early 18th centuries was the establishment of a plate-glass casting-works, which led to a virtual monopoly in the manufacture of MIRRORS and to the development of mould-blown glass by Bernard Perror of Orléans, who was certainly using anthracite as a fuel as early as 1665. Although his style was for the most part based on the Venetian, he did produce some charming objects in glass, including small scent bottles shaped as FLEURS-DE-LIS.

Another interesting, if not very significant, type of glassware was that known as *verre de Nevers*. Manufactured in the region of Nevers, it consisted of small figures representing a wide variety of subjects from classical or religious themes to comedy scenes and animal shapes. Multicoloured glass was trailed on to copper wire threads and the intricately detailed figures, which are rarely more than 7–10 cm high, have a characteristic charm.

Yet in the 18th c. there was virtually no French glass of really high quality. Drinking-glasses were crude both in design and in composition. The metal, made with soda and lime, was bubbly; the colour tended to be hazy and was not nearly so clear as the English lead crystal glass. In the early part of the century the majority of glass-manufacturers were Huguenots living in the northern part of France. Glass-making was considered a trade suitable for the impoverished aristocracy and many of the Huguenot families bore the title 'Gentilhommes verriers'. When religious persecution forced them into exile many of these families took refuge in the Low Countries or in England, where they either joined existing glass-houses or set up their own small establishments producing mainly window-glass. In England they came to be known as 'Lorrainers' and to this day 'Lorraine' is a fairly common surname in the West Country.

In the late 18th c. and early 19th c. the drain upon the French economy of the Napoleonic wars was great and it was not until after the fall of Napoleon that the great glass-houses of the 19th c. were set up. The two most important of these were St. Louis and Baccarat, both in the Vosges mountains where there was a plentiful supply of timber for the furnaces and good silicate sand for the manufacture of the metal. A third glass-house of importance was set up at Clichy-en-Garonne, near Paris. The rivalry of the Venetian glass-houses, which had been a serious danger to French industry towards the end of the 18th c., was broken when in 1806 Napoleon dissolved the Guild of Murano glass-makers by decree. Yet French glass manufacture remained in the doldrums until *c.* the middle of the 1840s, when some coloured glass paperweights made by revived Venetian glass-houses under the Austro-Hungarian Empire were bought by a French commercial attaché at a Trade Fair in Vienna and sent to Paris, where they reached the saleroom of Launey Hautin. These were taken to Baccarat and St. Louis, where they became the models which stimulated the great period of development in French luxury glass—paperweights, decorative sulphide beakers, ewers and claret jugs, fanciful and decorative wares in every shape and form.

The fine paperweights emanating from the glass-houses of Baccarat, St. Louis and Clichy were the cornerstone of the glass industry for which France is remembered now. These paperweights came in three different sizes: miniature under 5 cm, average between 5 and 10 cm and the magnum weights which were over 10 cm in diameter. Baccarat dated several of their weights from 1846 to 1849 and sometimes put a small 'B' beside the date. They are the easiest of the French paperweights to identify, having many small 'trade marks'. Typical were the silhouettes set into canes, broad arrows and whorls, as well as stardust clusters and honeycomb moulding; but in addition Baccarat produced mushrooms, snakes, butterflies and flower weights in profuse variety. The St. Louis weights are also distinctive. Their colours are far softer than those of Clichy or Baccarat, and for some years they were also dated, sometimes with the initials 'S.L.' preceding the date. St. Louis also was famous for its flowers, mushrooms, salamanders and snakes, but it is the fruit weights set on *latticinio* baskets and the hollow-blown crown weights for which it is most famous. The Clichy weights were very different. The colours were bright and gay but it is rare to find Clichy flowers. Probably the most distinctive features of Clichy weights were their swirls and colour grounds. Only occasionally did Clichy mark their weights with an initial 'C'. The most famous of their 'trade marks' was a very small rose, which came in many colours and varieties but is quite distinctive.

As fashions die, so the fashion for paperweights died after some 40 years and it was left to several remarkable individual talents of the *art-nouveau* period to perfect the achievement in French glass. Most prominent were Émile GALLÉ, the Daum brothers of Nancy and René LALIQUE. Chinese and Japanese influences in the manufacture of cameo glassware in this period were considerable. And it was apparent not only in cameo work, but also in the fusion of enamel on glass and in the general character of design and decoration. These artists all signed their work and Gallé tended to vary his signature as his ideas developed. At one stage he incorporated the *croix de Lorraine* into his work. After his death his glass manufactory was carried on until the beginning of the First World War, producing work under his signature but with a small star placed in front of his name. The Daum brothers of Nancy followed in the style of Gallé and they too used the *croix de Lorraine*. Their naturalistic enamel work particularly is famous. Probably the best known of all was René Lalique. His early success as a jeweller is not nearly so generally known as his commercial success as a maker of glass. Lalique was fascinated by the mystic colour of moonstones and it is this cloudy pale blue opalescence for which his glass is renowned. Some of his original works, which were almost entirely geometrical in design and style, are rare and beautiful; but the commercial success of his glass led to mass production, particularly of toilet ware for the firm of Coty. Most of the early Lalique glass was signed with diamond-point and numbered, but later on the signature tended to be stamped into the mould and after Lalique's death in 1945 the initial 'R' was omitted. Lalique was also an innovator in the use of glass for architecture.

The great houses of St. Louis and Baccarat have been revived and are producing paper-weights and fine glass of almost the same excellence as in the 19th c.

(*f*) *England*. A desire for durability and a taste for plainness created in the 17th c. a demand for glasses of sober form, whether supplied by the English glass-houses or imported from Venice. Concurrently, the nascent spirit of scientific research combined with the contemporary economic theory of 'mercantilism' to instigate researches in glass technology. These researches, deputed by the London Company of Glass-Sellers to George RAVENSCROFT, were probably intended to substitute native materials for the imported *barilla* (ash of marine plants) used as a flux, and the Ticino pebbles used as silica. Eventually, in 1675, Ravenscroft introduced oxide of lead as a flux, with revolutionary effect. The new glass was solid, heavy and less fragile than the Venetian, and it diffused light with a brilliance enhanced by the darkness of its shadows. The new material, more sluggish to work, called forth a new manner, from which Venetian tricks of style were progressively discarded. The form *par excellence* in which this new style emerged was the drinking-glass. It had a plain foot, normally a funnel-shaped bowl, and a stem compiled of bulbous and pear-shaped knops in all kinds of combinations. The proportions of these parts, their simplicity, and the quality of their metal constitute the crowning glory of English glass-making.

The plain English manner of the late 17th c. and early 18th c., which accorded so well with the elegance and simplicity of the Queen Anne style, was modified as the 18th c. approached its mid-point. The glasses became smaller and their stems lighter. If taste now favoured lightness, an Excise Act of 1745 made it imperative for glass. This levied a duty on glass by weight, and the immediate effect was to reduce the size of glasses, and probably also the quantities of lead oxide used. By way of compensation glasses began to be decorated. The knop containing air-bubbles, which had been a feature of some of the lighter baluster glasses, was drawn out and twisted into a stem containing a multiple spiral of air-lines. These were later superseded by threads of opaque-white glass in the old Venetian *latticinio* technique, and sometimes coloured glass also was used. Engraving, practised sporadically in England since the 17th c., mostly by immigrant Germans, became much commoner. Between 1762 and *c.* 1780 enamelling was used on clear glass with distinction by the BEILBY family of Newcastle upon Tyne, and by their imitators; and gilding, though never properly understood in England as in Germany, was sometimes attempted. English glass, mainly from Newcastle upon Tyne, was greatly in demand in the Netherlands for the flourishing school of wheel-engraving in the German manner as well as the indigenous school of engraving with the diamond-point.

The most significant development in England, however, was the spread of cut decoration. English glass-metal, with its diffractive qualities, was peculiarly suited to cutting. The earliest existing pieces appear to date from *c.* 1730. The cutting was mainly confined to brims and feet, which were scalloped and notched, and to the thicker parts of a glass such as the stem, which might be fluted or cut into a honeycomb of flat diamonds. This flat, sliced cutting—the main patterns of which were diamonds in low relief, crescents or triangles—was congenial to the ROCOCO taste and continued throughout the 3rd quarter of the 18th c., with increasing elaboration. It then gave way before a more austere cutting in keeping with the plainer shapes of English NEO-CLASSICISM. At the end of the century the forms of vessels became heavier and the lighter style of cutting was largely superseded by a system in which long parallel horizontal furrows, vertical fluting and diamonds in appreciable relief played the main part. These relief diamonds continued as the main stock-in-trade of the English cutter throughout the REGENCY period, and culminated in the 'prickly monstrosities' of the Great Exhibition of 1851.

The latter part of the 19th c. in England witnessed a revulsion from the idea of cut crystal, but under Ruskin's influence it took the form of a reversion to a style which emphasized the plastic qualities of glass. In this movement the firm of James Powell & Sons played a leading part. Cut crystal, however, continued to be the stock-in-trade of the glass-houses of the

Midlands and the two traditions have to some extent merged in the simplicity of the style which characterized the 2nd quarter of the 20th c.

(*g*) *Netherlands.* Until the coming of Venetian influence in the 1st half of the 16th c. little or no glass of distinction was made in the Low Countries apart from the crude green or brownish WALDGLAS. The most common type in this early period was the *Roemer*, a beaker with base formed of a trailed thread and a thick stem decorated with raspberry PRUNTS. The type has persisted to this day and such glasses may be seen in restaurants along the Rhine to Rotterdam. The prunts, or applied bosses, now function as ornament but up to the 17th c. they had a utilitarian function, permitting the glass to be held firmly in the hand without slipping.

Talented craftsmen from Venice and L'Altare began to migrate to the Low Countries early in the 16th c. They had nothing to sell but their craft and this they sold to the highest bidder, settling in the rich towns. Despite rivalry between Flemish and Dutch factions, Spanish domination and fierce nationalistic and religious differences, economic growth and a prosperous middle class based on the wool trade created conditions favourable to the formation of a flourishing glass industry. By the middle of the century glass-houses had been established in Antwerp and Liège. Despite some influence from German workers recruited mainly from the Grand Duchy of Hesse, the predominant fashion was created by the Italian craftsmen working in the Italian manner and there emerged the style known as '*façon de Venise*', so similar to Venetian work that it is often impossible to distinguish pieces made by Italian craftsmen locally from those imported from Venice.

As the 17th c. progressed other centres sprang up at Louvain, Brussels, Dordrecht, Middelburg and Amsterdam and by the middle of the century most towns of any size had their own glass-works. There were glass-houses of note at The Hague, Rotterdam, Maastricht, Leiden, Delft and elsewhere. The persistence of Italian influence is evidenced by the names of glass-masters from Antwerp, such as Pasqueti, Gridolphie and Mongarda. Glass in the *façon de Venise* continued to be produced with most of the styles and techniques of Venice represented: *latticino*, lion masks, turquoise pincer work, GADROONING and collaring, trailed work and moulded wings were all to be found. Nevertheless a more sober local style began to emerge and more simple and economic designs gradually superseded the garish enamels and fanciful work of Murano. In particular the art of glass engraving was carried to its highest perfection and by the 18th c. the Low Countries, and especially Holland, had achieved a reputation for the finest engraved glass. This included diamond engravings, at first largely an amateur craft, professional wheel engraving whose technique was perhaps derived from Germany, and diamond stippling engraving. Fine engraving demands glass of high quality and this led to strong links being developed between the glass-houses of Newcastle upon Tyne and the artist engravers of Holland. Before the middle of the 18th c. the Newcastle glass-houses were exporting quantities of English lead glass to Holland for engraving. Political ties established by William of Orange with England and cemented by the marriage of Princess Anne with William IV of Holland furthered the growth of export trade from England to the Low Countries.

Among the most celebrated of the Netherlandish engravers on glass were the Heemskerk family and it is believed that this work may have been developed in the first place as a family hobby. Willem Jacobsz van HEEMSKERK was noted particularly for his lettering and curlicues. Two amateur women engravers working in this early style may be mentioned: Anna Roemers Visscher (1583–1651) and her sister, Maria Tesselschade Roemers Visscher (1595–1649). Both specialized in flowers, fruit and insects with copperplate inscriptions. Outstanding later were Frans GREENWOOD, whose earliest known signed piece is dated 1720, Jacob SANG, whose earliest known signed piece is dated 1737, and David WOLFF, who used only English glasses. These three men developed the craft of diamond stipple engraving to its highest level. The design is made up of minute dots stabbed into the glass with a diamond-point set in a small hammer, and observed under a magnifying glass the impression is much like that of an enlarged newspaper photograph. Subjects ranged from armorial wedding goblets to conversation pieces and country scenes and they were observed in such detail as to be reminiscent of a copperplate engraving. This was an esoteric craft and few others have excelled in it.

Throughout the 18th c. the Netherlandish glass-houses endeavoured to make lead glass and although by the end of the century some success had been achieved, the glass was not of the highest quality and the Netherlands is remembered rather for the earlier *façon de Venise* glassware and for the engraving on imported English glass. Dutch glass is lighter in texture and inferior in quality to the finest English lead glass. The advent of mass production led to the closure of nearly all the glass-houses in Holland with the exception of the Royal Dutch Glass-house at Leerdam.

(*h*) *Norway.* Virtually the only glass-house of consequence in Norway was established at Nøstetangen south-west of Oslo in 1741 under the patronage of Christian VI of Denmark and Norway. The craftsmen were mainly from Germany and produced glass of a German type. In 1753 the industry was enlarged and an Englishman, James Keith from Newcastle upon Tyne, was employed. He produced lead crystal instead of German soda glass and, although some of the German forms were retained, under his direction glass was produced which is today almost indistinguishable from English glass of the same period.

Following a decline in the industry the Nøstetangen glass-house was closed in 1777 and production was moved to the Hurdels Verk, where similar types of glass were made with a preference for coloured wares from *c.* 1780. In 1809 the Hurdels Verk was closed and a new glass-house was opened at Gjovik. This in turn was killed by the advent of mass production and closed in 1847.

Engraving reached a high standard of proficiency under the direction of the German engraver, Heinrich Gottlieb Kohler, who was brought in from Copenhagen as artistic director *c.* 1780 and his pupil Villas Vintner. Few glasses by either of these men are known today.

4. ISLAMIC GLASS AND ROCK-CRYSTAL. Despite a comprehensive study, *Mittelalterliche Gläser*, published by C. J. Lamm in 1929, and a number of specialized articles on particular objects our knowledge of Islamic glass and ROCK-CRYSTAL remains fragmentary and still awaits integration into the general context of Islamic craftsmanship. Attribution and dating present unusual difficulties partly because it is hard to establish the sources of raw materials by technological analysis since these are common to widely separated regions and partly because most objects in public and private collections have not come from properly stratified digs or in some cases even from known sites. The purpose of the present article is therefore to give some indication of what can be reliably known from the information available.

The earliest reliably dated glass objects to come from the Middle East after the advent of Islam are glass weights and vessel stamps. Because of the difficulty of tampering with them they were officially issued to check coins and other commodities in accordance with a practice already established by Byzantine officials in Pre-Islamic times. They bear the names of caliphs and high officials and sometimes even the date of their manufacture, whilst their weights are uniform and accurate. They thus not only provide evidence of a high degree of technological sophistication, but together with contemporary literary sources indicate how widespread and how differentiated was the use of glass as early as Umayyad times (A.D. 661–750). It seems that these weights were made principally in Egypt and Syria, both of which countries had a very ancient tradition of glass-making. That glass was not only a luxury article but was in common use in Egypt is confirmed by later literary sources. A Persian traveller, Nāṣr-i Khusraw, who visited Egypt in the 11th c., noted that Egyptian grocers and druggists gave away the glass containers for their merchandise. He also mentions the existence of several glass-houses in Cairo and Tyre. Literary sources, however, are not entirely reliable because it is often unclear whether they refer to glass or rock-crystal. These had common techniques and styles and the same craftsmen probably worked in both materials.

Attempts to date some early Islamic objects in glass and rock-crystal are supported by the records of various European treasuries where they were kept. They were brought over by crusaders and pilgrims or as diplomatic gifts and their origin was forgotten; but preciously mounted as reliquaries they assumed in the West a new function, often religious but sometimes magical as well. These entries, and the fact that three rock-crystal pieces actually bear the names of two Fatimid caliphs and a general of the Fatimid court, help in defining a certain style of glass and rock-crystal cutting which was very popular from the 9th c. to the 11th c. in the Near East. Although Basra and Baghdad are mentioned in the sources as centres for clear and cut glass and rock-crystal, the main workshops must have been centred around Cairo and the Fatimid court (A.D. 969–1171).

Much discussion has been devoted to the question whether or not Persia could have maintained an alternative centre of production. Glass vessels have been found in Iran in old Islamic towns but little is known about Persian glass and rock-crystal. The beautiful Sassanian vessels, and the early Islamic ones that resemble them, are more likely to have been made not in Persia but in Syria or Mesopotamia, where the capitals of both the Sassanian (A.D. 226–641) and the ʿAbbāsid (A.D. 750–1258) empires were situated. These vessels are decorated mostly with very distinctive cut abstract patterns: facets or large roundels and grooves. If their inscription has been correctly read, there is a group of mould-blown glass vessels of the 9th or 10th c. actually made in Baghdad. Some 10th-c. engraved and cut glasses have also been found in Tunisia, but they are inferior in technique and seem to be provincial copies of Egyptian work. The decoration of all these hand-cut or wheel-cut vessels is stylized and shows variations of the ancient motifs of running animals and confronting birds separated by a 'Tree of Life'. There is possibly a slight progression from a more naturalistic treatment in the direction of greater emphasis on abstract and decorative values. Ultimately fantastic animals are merged with floral design and both blend in elaborate patterns which anticipate the 'Hedwig' glass decoration of the 11th and 12th centuries.

Hedwig glass, mainly beakers, takes its name from St. Hedwig (d. 1243), patron saint of Silesia, to whom one beaker of this group, now in the Schlesisches Museum, Breslau (Wrocław), is supposed to have belonged. Miraculous powers in confinements were attributed to another such beaker, which later belonged to Martin Luther. Hedwig glasses are made from thick metal which usually has a brown or yellowish hue. The decoration is achieved by cutting away the background, leaving the design of incised heraldic animals in relief. The beakers are squat and straight-sided, with a top wider than the base. Almost certainly they were made in Egypt. Nevertheless, attributions on stylistic grounds alone tend to be unreliable because of the over-all uniformity of decorative motifs with itinerant craftsmen travelling far afield but drawing from common cultural traditions. In this respect it seems that Jewish workmen contributed considerably to the diffusion of a common style in glass-cutting by retaining the predominance in the trade which they had acquired in Pre-Islamic times, particularly in the Syrian ports.

The ultimate achievement of the Hellenistic glass-making tradition is found in Egypt, where excavations in Fostat have produced one of the earliest pieces of Islamic glass. It is a lustre-glass goblet bearing the name of a governor of Egypt in A.D. 772–3. This find is crucial for establishing the origins of the lustre technique as applied not only to glass but to pottery. That the decoration and the technique of lustred glass—glass, that is, that has a lustrous metallic film—one akin to those used in contemporary pottery, is proved by the similarity of signatures found on Fatimid glass fragments and shards. (See CERAMICS, ISLAMIC.) The implication is that skilled Fatimid potters would also decorate glass vessels. A glass ingot factory has also been found; the ingots were ground to make frits for pottery.

Egypt too had an ancient tradition of gilding on clear glass. It is possible that émigré Egyptian craftsmen brought this technique to Syria, where it developed into one of the highest achievements of Islamic craftsmanship from the 12th to the 14th centuries. The relationship between some Byzantine glasses and 12th-c. Seljuk gilt glass is not yet clear, but it must be linked with the emigration of Egyptian craftsmen not only to Islamic centres but possibly also to Byzantine ones such as Corinth, where there have recently been important finds of gilt glassware related by their decoration to Islamic examples.

Glass enamelling and gilding were perfected in Aleppo in the 13th c. and in Damascus in the 14th c. under the patronage of Mamluk dynasties. A whole range of blown-glass vessels was decorated with this technique; the most sumptuous ones are long-necked bottles and mosque lamps. These are more easily datable as they often bear the coats of arms of various sultans and emirs. One of the most remarkable groups was made for a dynasty of Yemeni emirs, the Rasulids, great patrons of art (A.D. 1228–1442). The craft was brought to an abrupt halt in 1400 with Timur's invasion of Syria and the subsequent dispersal and deportation of its craftsmen. Syria had already experienced a Mongol invasion in the 13th c., but it seems to have disrupted mainly the production of glass-factories in Aleppo. Apparently it was then that Aleppo craftsmen moved to Damascus. Mongol and ultimately Chinese influences were fostered also by peaceful means. Commercial exchanges took place between Syria, Egypt and China and it may well be that special orders for Chinese clients were made in Damascus. It is significant that beautiful Islamic enamelled and gilt pieces were in fact acquired in China.

In the earlier Syrian pieces the emphasis is on the whole on calligraphic decoration with restrained arabesques, whilst later greater prominence tends to be given to colour contrasts, while in the Chinese style cloud-bands, long-tailed phoenixes, animals and flowers cover the whole surface. This is particularly true in objects designed for secular use. A favoured inscription on the neck of the lamps was a quotation from Sura 24 of the Koran, vv. 36 ff.: 'God is the light of heaven and earth. His light is like a niche in which is a lamp, the lamp encased in glass, the glass like a glittering star. . . .' In a group apart stands the 'Syro-Frankish' gilt and enamelled glass, apparently made in one workshop in the Latin states by a certain 'Magister Aldrevandini', which is a rather debased version of the Muslim products.

The decline of Syrian glass-making contributed to the rise of the Venetian glass industry, and Venetian glass was being exported to Syria at the end of the 15th c. and soon afterwards to Istanbul. There is a Venetian document of 1569 stating the number of pieces to be specially made to Ottoman specifications as laid down by the Grand Vizier. The measure of how highly regarded such glasses were is given by the fact that the order includes lamps to be put in newly built mosques and lamps for the Grand Vizier's own seraglio. These lamps, mostly made in the *latticino* technique, were then over-painted in Turkey by local artists with designs common to contemporary Turkish textiles and pottery, thus initiating a practice which has been commonly followed down to the 20th c. not only in Turkey but in Persia and India as well. Dutch canister bottles too were painted in Persia and in India with figures copied from contemporary miniatures and tiles.

It was not only Venice that exported glass to the East. German and English cut glass were also exported from the 17th c. onwards. There were also local glass workshops, however, in the Islamic world. Their production is documented by miniatures and travellers' descriptions. But it seems that in Turkey at least they specialized in work connected with circular window-panes and with the very characteristic window grilles which were closed by coloured glass cut to shape and inserted in a stucco frame, at first in abstract patterns and then in floral designs.

Europeans travelling in Persia in the 17th c. did not seem to think highly of the glass made in great quantity in Isfahan and especially in Shiraz, but this may be the result of an inability to appreciate Eastern taste and of the great advances made by that time in European glass techniques. Safavid (A.D. 1502–1736) coloured glass rose-water sprinklers and ewers have characteristic elongated shapes with exaggerated necks. Some are gold-washed all over in a manner apparently peculiar to Persian glass at different times. But mostly they are plain with graceful spiral twists and sometimes with applied spun threads, which follow the lines of the body, using glass for its own inherent qualities rather than imitating metal or pottery shapes as had been done previously.

In the 16th c. Persian glass was exported to India, where it may have influenced local production. Some beautiful glass, however, 'hookah' bowls in particular, was made locally in India during later Mogul times. The bowls, in clear coloured glass, are decorated in a restrained manner with symmetrical floral patterns very much in the taste of contemporary metalwork and textiles. Some are set with jewels or enamelled in imitation of jewel settings.

The revival of glass-making in Safavid Persia and the glass production of Ottoman Turkey and Mogul India certainly seem to have been originated by Europeans or to have been based on imported European prototypes. But this fact need not exclude this later glass from its place in the development of Islamic glass craftsmanship; for the decoration was transformed by the local artists according to their own traditions, with the result that these objects are ultimately part of the Islamic glass tradition.

5. AMERICA. A growing interest in the glass produced in what is now the United States has led to the establishment of a widely accepted chronology for the history of American glass. As originally proposed in Dorothy Daniel's important book, *American Cut and Engraved Glass* (1950), a sound understanding of American glass is best reached by dividing its production into the four following periods: (1) Early Period, 1739–1830; (2) Middle Period, 1830–80; (3) Brilliant Period, 1880–1915; (4) Modern Period, 1915– . As is the case with all such broad divisions, these can only be regarded as general guide-lines intended for scholarly convenience. The styles always overlapped and the divisions should, therefore, never be regarded as absolutes.

The making of glass in the Colonies began at Jamestown, Virginia, in 1608, a year after the arrival of the first settlers. The London company hoped to establish a successful industry, for England was importing its finest drinking vessels and other table wares from the Continent, and the fledgling English manufacture of glass was hampered by dwindling forest preserves, whose wood was crucial to the firing of the furnaces. Jamestown appeared to possess all the necessary raw materials, but the exigencies of frontier life caused attention to be turned to agriculture. The first Jamestown furnaces never produced anything beyond beads, bottles and perhaps some crude drinking vessels. These articles were presumably based upon English designs and began the tradition of borrowing styles and techniques which has persisted in the manufacture of glass in America until the present day.

After the establishment of a second glass-making venture at Jamestown in 1622 and its demise shortly afterwards the next glass-house was opened in Salem, Massachusetts, *c.* 1641. Like its southern predecessor, the experiment met with no great success and produced only window or crown glass and spirits bottles. From *c.* 1650 to 1674 New Amsterdam (now New York City) had two glass-houses in operation, and it is thought that these produced the usual window and bottle glass as well as tablewares, which indubitably imitated Low Country types and forms. It is extremely unlikely, however, that the New Amsterdam manufactories produced any of the wheel-engraved or diamond-point-engraved glass traditionally associated with the Netherlands during the 17th c. The only other early glass-making enterprise is believed to have been at Philadelphia, Pennsylvania; it was founded in 1683. Almost nothing is known of the glass it produced.

Very little is known about the small quantities of glass produced by these first American enterprises, and the historian must proceed to the year 1739, when a prosperous German immigrant businessman, Caspar Wistar, opened a glass factory in southern New Jersey. Wistar had previously been involved in the business world of Philadelphia and must have realized a potential market in a country whose inhabitants were, for glass, entirely dependent on imports. The Wistar factory became the first successful manufacturer of glass in the Colonies and remained in operation for *c.* 40 years. Since Wistar had no practical knowledge of glass-making when he founded his factory, he was forced to seek trained men from Europe; existing documents indicate that he brought glass-workers from Germany and Holland. Although there are very few objects which can be attributed definitely to the Wistar glass-house, it is known that the usual wine and spirit bottles were produced as well as table and decorative wares; these followed the forms and decoration of German or Dutch peasant glass. The tradition begun by the Wistar workmen and those of a factory opened in 1781 at nearby Glassboro, New Jersey, is today referred to as 'South Jersey'.

The glass produced in this area (and in this style) was most frequently free-blown and formed into pitchers, bowls, candlesticks and vases of simple, bold lines. The favoured colours in the metal were light aquamarine, green, amber and brown. A high proportion of South Jersey glass was decorated by superimposed bands of glass which were crimped, pinched, trailed or quilled. Frequently swirled and looped effects were created by the use of an opaque white, blue or red glass. These decorative techniques were applied to forms derived from the Anglo-Irish glass-making tradition. One important—and totally original—decorative technique emerged from the South Jersey tradition, however, and this was the 'lily-pad' motif. This decorative method involved tooling and pulling the metal into a form which resembled a water-lily stem and pad; it is a handsome device, and a uniquely American contribution to the history of glass-making. The tradition begun in South Jersey was of crucial importance for the entire history of glass in America, for the forms and decorations used there followed the path of civilization. South Jersey types spread to New Hampshire and Upper New York state (notably at Redwood and Redford) and were made there as late as 1850. The tradition was, in fact, the longest-lived one in American glass-making.

Perhaps the most famous of the early American glass-manufacturers was Henry William Stiegel, sometimes referred to as 'Baron' Stiegel (1729–85). Like Wistar, Stiegel was a German immigrant who was engaged in another profession before turning to the production of glass. In 1763 he opened his first factory at Elizabeth Furnace, Pennsylvania. This Manheim factory was the first of two. The primary significance of the Stiegel factories was that for a brief 11 years they produced elegant and sophisticated table glass, equal to that then being imported from England and the Continent.

The Stiegel glass-houses produced expanded mould-blown (or pattern-moulded) wares, wheel-engraved and enamelled glass. The last of these was based upon the type of peasant glass produced since the 17th c. in Bohemia, Switzerland and Germany. The decorative devices used were of the sort referred to today in the United States as 'Pennsylvania Dutch'. Stiegel was the first American manufacturer of glass to establish rigid quality controls and to insist on a standardized production; in this sense he was the first truly commercial glass-maker in the country. Stiegel also advertised extensively and had agents in the major colonial cities. In spite of his astute practices in some aspects of his business, however, he over-extended himself with the construction of the second facility at Manheim in 1768, when the disrupting influence of the American Revolution was gathering force. His personal life-style had become increasingly elaborate and aped the fashions of Continental nobility. All of these circumstances contributed to his financial ruin, and on 5 May 1774 the Stiegel furnaces at Manheim were closed. Although Stiegel died 11 years later in poverty, the brief years of his glass-making activity were of enormous importance for American glass history. With the closing of the Manheim factories the English and Continental workers hired by him sought work elsewhere, taking with them the skills and high standards insisted upon by their autocratic former employer. The importance of this broadened Stiegel influence cannot be too strongly emphasized.

The third major American glass-maker of the 18th c. was also a German, John Frederick Amelung, who established his New Bremen Glass Manufactory near Frederick, Maryland, in 1784. The factory was unique for America in several respects. It was financed by foreign capital, and the standard of its production was high enough to inaugurate an entirely new level of design and decoration in American glass. The New Bremen factory closely imitated fashionable European forms, and the engraved decoration of the factory's presentation pieces was in an opulent late Rococo style. Also produced were pattern-moulded wares in the Stiegel vein as well as decanters and drinking glasses with cut and engraved decoration. The Amelung factory closed just 10 years after its founding, but during that time produced glass of excellent design and superb execution. Important Amelung examples are today among the greatest rarities in American glass.

Glass factories were, quite naturally, established along the expanding frontier. In 1797 Albert Gallatin founded his New Geneva Glass-works in western Pennsylvania; this was the first glass-house west of the Allegheny Mountains, then the outer limit of any settlement. The wares produced by the Gallatin factory tended to be simple and somewhat crude and revealed their German heritage. The Gallatin factory opened the way for other glass-houses, and began the tradition of mid-western glass produced in Pittsburgh, Pennsylvania, and the Ohio centres of Zanesville, Mantua, Ravenna and Kent. Pittsburgh became a centre for fine cut and engraved table and decorative wares, its BAKEWELL AND COMPANY producing the first commercial cut glass in America (1808). The early Ohio wares were of a simpler variety, characterized by bold shapes, as in the celebrated 'chestnut' bottles, and a pronounced ribbing. The great period of Ohio glass of this type extended approximately from 1815 to 1835.

Of prime importance in the history of American glass was the founding of the NEW ENGLAND GLASS COMPANY in East Cambridge, Massachusetts, in 1818. This factory became, until its closing in 1888, one of the glass-making giants of the century and produced an enormous variety of wares of international importance. The factory early became prominent in its use of pressed glass, and its free-blown objects represented a high point in American craft and design. The great competitor of the New England Glass Company was a Cape Cod firm, the BOSTON AND SANDWICH GLASS COMPANY, founded in 1825. Although until recently the name 'Sandwich Glass' was applied chiefly to almost all pressed glass of the lacy type, it is now known that the firm early produced outstanding blown three-mould glass as well as cut and engraved and conventionally pressed types. It was, however, pre-eminent in the development of pressing techniques. Like its chief rival, the Boston and Sandwich Glass Company produced wares of great quality until its demise in 1888–9.

With the passage of the Baldwin Act in 1830 the Early American Period of American glass manufacture ended. This Act can be credited with the establishment of glass-making as an industry of national importance, for it required the collection of port duties and a high tariff, both of which severely limited imports. The restriction on imports made the production of fine tableware profitable and by 1840 there are thought to have been at least 81 glass-houses in operation. Since this manufacturing independence was accompanied by rapidly expanding national prosperity, a great demand for glass objects arose. This Middle Period of American glass history is generally considered to have lasted until *c.* 1880.

During the Middle Period engraving, fine line-cutting, coloured cased and flashed wares, as well as flute- or panel-cutting became fashionable. The major New England glass-houses and those in the Philadelphia and Pittsburgh areas produced cut lead glass of extremely high quality at this time. Bohemian-style glass gained popularity *c.* 1845 in America and replaced the chaste Anglo-Irish stylistic tradition of cut designs with opulent colour and more typically Victorian decoration. Most fashionable were wares cased, flashed, or stained in red and engraved with scenes of the hunt and trophies of game or musical instruments. Bohemian-style items were also made with cobalt blue, green and yellow. It was pressed glass, however, which was the popular favourite of the Middle Period since it required little hand-finishing and was therefore considerably less expensive. Press-moulding, evolved in the 1820s, was the unique American contribution to the techniques of glass-making. A mass of glass was pressed by a plunger into a patterned mould. Used at first for open shapes such as dishes and bowls, it was later extended to the manufacture of goblets, cream-jugs, etc. It made possible the economic production of wares, both in clear and in coloured glass, with lavish over-all patterning in keeping with the taste of the mid 19th c. With improved moulds a virtually unlimited variety of patterns was available, and the glass companies were thus able to meet the vast public demand for novelty of form and design. So popular did these pressed types become that their competition threatened to end the manufacture of the more expensive blown, cut and engraved wares. In 1864 William Leighton of the Hobbs–Brockunier Company of Wheeling, West Virginia, developed a new type of soda-lime glass, which was as clear as expensive lead glass but was far less expensive to produce. This invention was of enormous importance to the entire industry and permitted pressed wares to imitate even more closely fine lead glass. Most American glass-houses quickly adopted this new soda-lime type, impinging increasingly on those manufactories, such as the New England Glass Company and the Boston and Sandwich Company, which continued their lead glass production. This threat to the fine glass producers caused them to create cut items whose appearance could not be imitated by pressing techniques: flutes, fans, cross-hatching and diamond motifs continued to be fashionable but were used in greater profusion than previously. Talented engravers such as Henry Fillebrown and Louis Vaupel produced objects of spirited and spectacular detail. But rising costs of production and the disruptions of the Civil War did little to promote a taste for expensive tableware and decorative objects. By 1870 the luxury glass trade had been severely hampered by pressed wares, and the panic of 1873 forced the closing of many of the remaining cutting houses. By the time of the celebrated Philadelphia Centennial Exhibition in 1876 the leading glass manufacturers realized the necessity of a vigorous campaign to revive the failing market. Important firms such as Christian Dorflinger of White Mills, Pennsylvania, Gillender and Sons of Philadelphia, the New England, Mount Washington, and Boston and Sandwich glass companies, presented elaborate exhibits which attracted great critical and public acclaim. The exhibited glass bore deeper cuttings and more elaborate patterns than those customarily seen and began an unprecedented popularity for cut glass. By 1880 this interest had become sufficiently influential to introduce a new taste, which is today referred to as the 'Brilliant Period'.

American glass of the Brilliant Period was characterized by metal of considerable weight and was characteristically covered by deep cutting of hob-stars, rosettes and pinwheels. Cut glass of this type differed from that of the Middle Period in that its decoration was of primary importance and was not merely regarded as a means of enhancing form. Leading firms in the United States producing these wares were the LIBBEY GLASS COMPANY of Toledo, Ohio (successor to the former New England Glass Company), the Dorflinger Glass Company, the Majesty Cut Glass Company of Elmira, New York, T. G. Hawkes and Company and the Egginton Rich Cut Glass Company of Corning, New York, among others. This typically late-Victorian cut glass remained the popular favourite until *c.* 1915, although fine pieces in this taste were produced as late as the mid 1920s. Although the aesthetic value of some Brilliant Period cut and engraved glass is controversial today, it should be emphasized that the metal itself was generally of extremely high quality and was definitely the equal of, if not actually better than, analogous European wares.

Contemporaneous with the vogue for these cut and engraved types was a taste for 'art glass'. Art glass may be regarded as the logical outcome of the American demand for novelty during the 19th c. and was characterized by elaborate form and exotic finish. Complex shaded colour effects, elaborate enamelling, as well as casing, crimping, mould-blowing, engraving and metal mounts were typical of American art glasses. This glass was intended chiefly for decorative

Steuben 'Aurene Compote'. Free blown metallized glass, fumed gold iridescence with purple tones on stem and foot. (Toledo, Ohio, Mus., early 20th c.)

'Bottle Boogie.' Free blown clear glass with incised lines; surface brown, yellow, black. By Joel Philip Myers. (Toledo, Ohio, Mus., 1968)

Steuben Vase. Designed by Paul Manship. (The Art Institute of Chicago, 1940)

American glass water-pitcher, probably 'South Jersey' glass. (The Art Institute of Chicago, 1833–42)

purposes, the majority of pieces functioning as cabinet objects. Important types of art glass were Amberina, Agata and Pomona of the New England Glass Company; Satin Glass, Crown Milano, Burmese and Royal Flemish by the Mount Washington Glass Company; and the Peachblow of Wheeling, West Virginia's Hobbs–Brockunier Company, which imitated Chinese PORCELAIN. Numerous smaller firms such as the Smith Brothers of New Bedford, Massachusetts, the C. F. Monroe Company of Meriden, Connecticut and Dalzell, Gilmore & Leighton of Finday, Ohio, produced interesting types of art glass. While much American art glass is of aesthetic importance in the history of 19th-c. decorative arts, it must be admitted that a considerable quantity did not exhibit superior form and that decoration was not always of the highest quality. The excesses of the art glass types, as well as the increasing elaboration and expense of cut glass, led to a new sympathy for objects in the ART-NOUVEAU style, the tenets of which were in direct opposition to the prevailing Brilliant Period aesthetic.

The *art-nouveau* movement in the field of glass sought to replace the high colour and ornate outlines of art glass with objects of sinuous and refined form, soft colour and elegant finish. Decoration was largely derived from floral and vegetable motifs; a brilliant eclecticism prevailed, with elements from ancient Egyptian, Chinese, Japanese and Persian art combined. Surfaces were frequently iridescent in imitation of the nacreous deposits seen on ancient glass which has been buried. The movement was an intellectual one, and the objects produced by it were understood with greater difficulty by the American public. But although the style had originally been appreciated by a small group of *avant-garde* craftsmen, designers and artists, it soon became widely acclaimed. *Art-nouveau* glass became prestigious and a symbol of modernity. The great genius of the style in the United States was Louis Comfort TIFFANY, whose Tiffany Glass Company produced a spectacular array of forms and finishes. Tiffany designs were influential on an international scale and affected glass-workers in France, Germany, Austria and Czechoslovakia. In America too his famous blown 'Favrile' glass was widely imitated. A significant imitator of Tiffany design and technique was the Quezal Art Glass and Decorating Company of Brooklyn, New York. The most successful competitor to the famed Tiffany products was the 'Aurene' iridescent glass developed by Frederick CARDER for the Steuben Glass Works in Corning, New York, and first produced in 1904. *Art-nouveau* design was a major force in American glass production from *c.* 1895 until 1915, although its waning influence continued until *c.* 1925 as seen in the products of such firms as the Vineland (New Jersey) Flint Glass Works of Victor Durand (1870–1931). It should be stressed, however, that *art-nouveau* glass, with its evanescent colour and lyrical elegance, was originally favoured simultaneously with the heavy opulence of Brilliant Period cut glass.

The years following the First World War were marked by severe change. Dress and social customs underwent radical modifications, as did taste in glass. With the decline in demand for the Victorian art glass, cut glass and *art-nouveau* glass, a new period in the history of American glass, the Modern, may be said to emerge. The dominant influence in the design of this period has been that of Functionalism. Originally a European concept formulated by the German BAUHAUS group and the French architect–designer Le Corbusier, Functionalism required that form should follow function. Form must be simple, outlines stark and surfaces plain. If decoration were employed, it should be based upon strict geometrical relationships. With the acceptance of Functionalist theory American glass became truly international and was influenced by a variety of design sources. The ART-DÉCO objects shown by René LALIQUE at the 1925 Paris exposition and the heavy, limpid designs in clear glass produced by such celebrated Scandinavian houses as Orrefors and Kosta were among the most significant of these influences.

Most notable among the American firms working in the new style was the Steuben Glass Works, which in the 1920s continued to produce a line of coloured glass. This was designed by Frederick Carder, but employed simplified forms reflecting the tenets of Functionalism. In 1933 the company began to produce a heavy transparent metal which was frequently decorated with wheel-engraving inspired by contemporary subject matter. The architect John Monteith Gates (1905–) and the sculptor Sidney Waugh (1904–) supervised the design department in producing designs of a Functionalist–*art-déco* type. The Steuben works continues to produce objects in a related style today. Less well known but also influential was A. Douglas Nash (1880–1940), whose family had been vital in the operation of the Tiffany works at Corona, Long Island. Tiffany signed over his interests in the works to the A. Douglas Nash Corporation in 1919, and glass of the Tiffany type was produced until 1928 with some significant, more contemporary variations. With the closing of the Corona works, however, Nash was commissioned by the Libbey Glass Company of Toledo, Ohio, to design a new luxury series. The elaborate Nash line specialized in spectacular surface effects, elegant contrasts of colour and simple, bold outlines. The Depression, however, effectively put a stop to this production in 1935. The following year the company, then a division of the Owens-Illinois Glass Company, hired Edwin W. Fuerst (1903–) to design a new 'Modern American' series. The new designs were introduced in 1939–40 and were intended to compete with the luxury market monopolized in the United States by Steuben. Objects in the series were of a heavy brilliant transparent metal, and the simple bold designs were influenced strongly by Functionalist thought and contemporary Scandinavian glass styles. Owing to the war effort this significant production was discontinued in 1945. The Second World War did not, however, generally produce any radical changes in glass design as had been the case with the First World War. As aptly pointed out by Ada Polak in her important book, *Modern Glass* (1962), Functionalist concepts simply provided a basis for new related developments which can best be described as 'Neo-Functionalism'. Glass produced in this period continued to be influenced by Scandinavian design. Although the Steuben factory remained the most important industrial maker of fine glass, good decorative glass was produced by such houses as the Blenko Glass Company of West Virginia.

The most important and influential events in the history of recent American glass, however, took place in 1962 with the organization of a glass-working seminar at The Toledo Museum of Art, Toledo, Ohio. By bringing together interested glass craftsmen the seminar was able to prove that glass could be blown and worked in the small individual studio. Led by Dominick LABINO and Harvey K. LITTLETON, the experimentation began a renaissance in contemporary hand-worked glass. The most significant result of the original seminar and its subsequent sessions was the re-establishment of the designer and blower as the same person. This had, of course, early been the case in glass-making, but the development of the large glass-house had as early as the late 18th c. divided the functions of designer and draftsmen. Re-uniting these roles, the seminars created a new sculptural approach to glass as a medium. In the 1970s *c.* 15 university courses in glass craftsmanship were being taught in the United States and England, while individuals in those countries as well as Italy and Germany had been influenced by the new tenets of design and technique. Some of the notable American craftsmen working in the new manner were C. Fritz Dreisbach (1941–), Joel Philip Myers (1934–) and Marvin Lipofsky (1938–).

The history of glass production in the United States has been one of important contributions to a national aesthetic expression as well as to the international history of the medium. With the emergence of the country as a leader in contemporary glass craftsmanship these important influences will, no doubt, continue to contribute to the history of glass.

53, 63, 114, 187, 195, 273, 343, 344, 409, 410, 465, 473, 482, 483, 511, 512, 513, 549, 554, 555, 569, 623, 656, 671, 693, 694, 695, 747, 753, 830, 872, 877, 893, 910, 911, 915, 916.

GLAZE. Fired to a temperature of approximately 1250 °C. with variations according to the type, CLAY vitrifies and becomes impermeable to liquids. But the margin between vitrifaction and melting or collapse is sometimes small and kiln temperatures in the past were seldom completely under control. Therefore in order to avoid excessive wastage vessels were made watertight at lower temperatures by coating them with a vitreous surface known as a 'glaze'. The glaze also imparts to the vessel a glossy smooth surface easily cleaned and opens up to the potter an infinite repertory of decorative possibilities.

Glazes are of similar composition to clay but with the addition of a *fluxing agent*—such as lead, soda, potassium, borax, calcium—which has the property of causing the glaze to melt and adhere to the surface of the vessel at a lower temperature. Silica is added in the form of silver sand, ground flint or quartz. Glaze is normally applied to the BISCUIT in liquid form after the latter has been ornamented and perhaps painted; the porous biscuit absorbs liquid from the glaze and the vessel is then fired to the temperature at which the glaze vitrifies.

There are several main families of glazes:

Lead glaze. Lead oxide (litharge) and lead carbonate are among the easiest and have been among the most widespread glazes. They can be sprinkled on the surface in powder form and fuse at a relatively low temperature of *c.* 800 °C. They give a rich metallic surface and combine with other metallic oxides to produce a fine range of colours, copper producing brilliant leaf-green and iron a variety of yellow and brown hues. Lead-glazed pottery with moulded decoration akin to ARRETINE WARE was made in Asia Minor at the end of the 1st c. B.C. and in the 1st c. A.D. The technique spread to Italy and thence to Gaul, where by the middle of the century Vichy and St-Rémy-en-Rollat were centres of its manufacture. From *c.* 200 A.D. it was made in the Rhineland and in Britain it was produced at Holt in Denbighshire. After the collapse of the Roman empire the technique was kept alive in Byzantium and lead glazing remained one of the most popular methods of pottery manufacture in Europe until the 18th c. In the 19th c. its use was restricted by law owing to the discovery of the dangers of lead poisoning attendant on the use of the material in its raw state. It is therefore now subjected to a process called 'fritting'. The lead oxide is combined with silica and the compound is ground to a powder called a 'frit'.

Tin glaze. Tin glaze is composed of a vitreous lead glaze made opaque by the addition of tin oxide. After firing it produces a dense white surface which conceals any colour in the underlying clay and forms a background for painted decoration. Owing to the high temperature of fusing metallic pigments are used. Tin-glaze techniques were known in the ancient Near East and were established in Mesopotamia by the 9th c. A.D. They were carried by the Moors to Spain and from there spread to the rest of Europe. Tin-glazed pottery is called *Maiolica* in Italy, *faïence* in France and *Fayence* in Germany. Between the 13th and the 17th centuries lustre colours were painted over the tin glaze after firing and in the 18th c. ENAMEL colours were sometimes similarly used. A fairly comprehensive account of tin-glaze pottery styles may be found in Alan Conger Smith, *Tin-Glaze Pottery in Europe and the Islamic World. The Traditions of 1000 Years in Maiolica, Faience, Delftware* (1973).

Salt glaze. Salt glaze is used with STONEWARE, which is heated to a high temperature in an open kiln. Salt is thrown into the kiln and on volatilizing causes the soda to combine with the silica in the clay vessel to form a glassy surface. The technique began in the Rhineland during the 14th c. It was introduced into England in the 1670s by John Dwight. It is now used for sanitary ware, etc. But in the 1930s the technique was adapted by French artist-potters such as Paul Beyer to artistic purposes.

Felspathic glaze. Felspathic glazes are non-vitreous, made from powdered felspathic rock (see PETUNTSE). They were used with hard PORCELAIN and are thin and hard in appearance. They were usually fired in one operation with the body of the vessel but were sometimes put on for a second firing and a fluxing agent was used to reduce the temperature of fusing. The latter type of glaze is called by the Chinese 'chicken skin'.

There have been evolved a very great variety of techniques for decorating pottery by, through or on glazes. Some of these are described in the articles CERAMICS and POTTERY TECHNIQUES.

GLOMY, JEAN-BAPTISTE (d. 1786). See VERRE ÉGLOMISÉ.

GOBELINS. The most famous of all TAPESTRY manufactories, it derives its name from the 15th-c. scarlet-dyers Jean and Philibert Gobelin, whose works were situated on the Bièvre, a small stream in Paris. In or near these buildings the Flemish tapestry weavers De Comans and De la Planche, summoned by Henri IV, set up their looms at the beginning of the 17th c. and it was here that Louis XIV reorganized the tapestry weavers of Paris in 1662. The factory of the Gobelins, with Colbert as superintendent and Charles Lebrun (1619–90) as artistic director, commanding a galaxy of designers which included Van der Meulen, Noel Coypel, Monnoyer and many others, now entered on a brilliant period. Among the notable tapestries woven were the *History of the King* (14 pieces), *History of Alexander* (11 pieces), *Royal Palaces* (12 pieces), *Elements* (4 pieces) and *Seasons* (4 pieces), as well as numerous reproductions of 16th-c. designs. All were of superb quality. The principal weavers of the late 17th and early 18th centuries were the families of Jans and Lefebure.

The grand style and strong simple colouring of Lebrun yielded gradually in the 18th c. to ROCOCO grace of design and soft hues in an enormous variety of delicate shades, a transformation which owed much to the influence of OUDRY and BOUCHER, successively inspectors of the works (1733–70). The tapestries of this period, besides Oudry's *Hunts of Louis XV* and Boucher's *Tentures de François Boucher*, include the *Story of Don Quixote* (28 pieces) by Charles-Antoine Coypel (1696–1751), and the *Stories of Esther* (7 pieces) and *Jason* (7 pieces) by Jean-François de Troy (1679–1752). The best known weavers of the 18th c. at the Gobelins were the Scot, James Neilson, and the families of Audran and Cozette.

The Revolutionary period was unproductive, but numbers of large tapestries, many of them with historical subjects, were woven during the 19th and early 20th centuries. The Gobelins continues in production. See also TAPESTRY.

442, 451, 828, 891.

GODDARD. United States family of cabinet-makers established at Newport, Rhode Island, who with the TOWNSEND family constituted one of the outstanding groups of American furniture-makers during the 18th and 19th centuries. Both families were Quakers. They worked closely together and there was intermarriage between them. They are variously known as the 'Newport' or the 'Rhode Island' group.

The Goddard family was established in Newport by DANIEL Goddard (d. 1764), described as a housewright. His two sons, JOHN (1723–85) and JAMES (1727–?) were both cabinet-makers. Both married daughters of Job Townsend. John was born at Dartmouth, Mass., apprenticed to Job and Christopher Townsend, who were established in business at Easton's Point, and set up business on his own account some time after his marriage in 1746. Three of his sons became cabinet-makers. TOWNSEND (1750–90) set up his own business during his father's lifetime. STEPHEN (1764–1804) and THOMAS (1765–1858) carried on their father's business after his death. Stephen's son JOHN (1789–1843) also had a furniture-making business in Newport.

The Newport furniture is noted for the excellent quality of its design and workmanship. The most outstanding contribution was the block-front shell-curved chest. Examples may be seen in the Boston Museum of Fine Arts, the Winterthur Museum, Delaware and the Metropolitan Museum of Art, New York. Extensive records are preserved by the Newport Historical Society and the Rhode Island Historical Society at Providence.

220, 645.

GODDARD FOOT. A type of bracket foot favoured by the Newport group of American cabinet-makers (see GODDARD) and typical of much of their work.

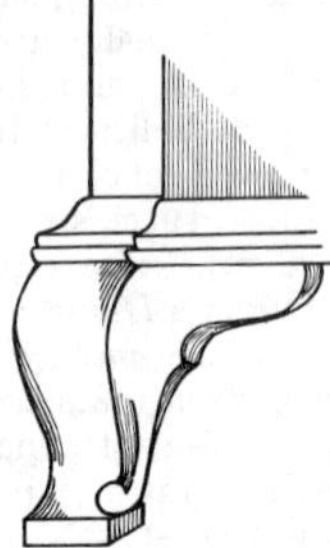

GODEFROID DE CLAIR. The leading Mosan goldsmith–enameller during the 3rd quarter of the 12th c. Born at Huy, he was probably trained in the workshop of RENIER OF HUY and subsequently worked in Germany at the courts of the Emperors Lothar (d. 1137) and Conrad (d. 1152). In 1174 he became a canon in the monastery of Neufmonstier near Huy. Two shrines only, those of St. Domitian and St. Mangold, both made for Huy, are documented as his work, but a formidable quantity of pieces of high quality have been attributed to Godefroid or his workshop. Amongst his early works the most important are the Head Reliquary of Alexander, ordered in 1155 by Abbot Wibald of Stavelot (Musée de Cinquantenaire, Brussels) and the St. Martin Madelinus shrine at Visé. The main work of his middle period, and altogether his greatest surviving achievement, is the Heribert shrine at Cologne. This piece, with its wealth of figure ornament in gilt bronze and brilliant ENAMEL enrichment, shows ROMANESQUE art at its most expressive and set the fashion for monumental shrines of architectural design for over 100 years. His later works include the St. Servatius shrine at Maastricht, the documented shrines at Huy and the Arm Reliquary of Charlemagne from Aachen (Louvre). His main contribution to Romanesque art of the Meuse valley lies in his development of the art of champlevé enamelling. See also ENAMEL.

GODWIN, EDWARD WILLIAM (1833–86). English architect and furniture designer. He was born and trained in Bristol and came to London in 1865. He designed the White House in Tite Street, Chelsea, for the artist Whistler. As an architect he was an exponent of medievalism and as a furniture designer worked in the fashionable Neo-Jacobean style. But from *c.* 1867 he succumbed to the enthusiasm for Japanese taste and produced designs, some in conjunction with Whistler, for light and graceful cabinet work in this style, mainly in ebonized wood. He was partly responsible for the popular fashion for bamboo and wicker furniture. In the Victoria and Albert Museum are his many notebooks and a selection of his pieces, including a sideboard in ebonized wood with silver-plated fittings and panels of embossed leather, which illustrates his own description of 'the grouping of solid and void'. From 1868 onwards Godwin was widely engaged as a professional designer.

GOLD AND SILVER. Classed as a noble metal because of its permanence and durability when in contact with air, acids and weathering influences, gold can be melted and re-melted without loss of weight and will hold a polish over a long period without tarnishing. Though it is too soft for tools and weapons, its permanence and colour led to its use for COINS and JEWELLERY and thus its ultimate association with wealth. Along with COPPER gold is one of the earliest metals to be known as it is inevitably found as native metal in its metallic state. By 5000 B.C. primitive jewellery was being made from semi-precious stones and small gold nuggets were also being collected along with the stones. Initial sources of the metal were nuggets found in the alluvial deposits of sand, gravel and grit occurring on the beds of ancient streams. As these were depleted it became necessary to separate out the much finer grains or 'dust' from the sand by a washing process. For this purpose fleeces were used, the particles of gold adhering to the hairs whilst the lighter sand was washed away by running water. In this technique may probably be found the origin of the legend of the Golden Fleece. Mining for gold had commenced before 3000 B.C. to utilize deposits that existed as veins in minerals such as quartz. The EGYPTIANS crushed the quarried material, first with stone hammers and then with rubbing-mills. The powdered material was washed through sieves of copper wire on to inclined tables, where most of the remaining waste was washed away. The final washing to remove the finest waste was carried out in large flat dishes. It was the Greeks who discovered the liquid metal, mercury, but it was the Romans who made use of the fact that it forms a ready amalgam with gold to devise a technique for the removal of the gold from the minerals in which it was embedded. The gold was then extracted from the amalgam by evaporating off the mercury, which could be reclaimed and re-used. Until *c.* A.D. 1850, however, the major supplies of gold were obtained from the washing of gravels and alluvial deposits although the application of the amalgamation process of antiquity did make the working of some less rich deposits profitable. The 19th c. saw the invention of a cyaniding process, in which gold is dissolved from crushed minerals by a weak alkaline cyanide solution and is then precipitated out by treating the solution with metallic zinc.

Natural gold is rarely more than 80% pure gold, being usually alloyed in varying proportions with silver and also to some extent with copper. Base metals such as copper could be removed from these natural alloys by a process known as CUPELLATION, but the removal of silver requires a more complex procedure that is unlikely to have occurred before Roman times. The noble metals of the early metal-workers were thus a range of gold/silver alloys, which included ELECTRUM, the whitish coloured alloy which contains more than 40% silver. Initially a natural alloy, electrum was later deliberately produced as it was found that it could be made to imitate purer gold by dissolving out the surface silver with acid. Silver was eventually separated from gold by mixing granulated gold/silver alloys together with salt and clay and bringing the mixture to a red heat. The silver chloride formed is held in the clay whilst the gold remains unaffected. The clay containing the silver chloride is mixed with lead and the silver reclaimed in a cupellation hearth. Further techniques for separating silver from gold were developed by the medieval alchemists. These processes included heating the molten alloys with sulphur to produce a silver sulphide from which the silver was extracted and the dissolving of silver from the gold with nitric acid.

Pure gold is too soft to be used on its own and must therefore be hardened by the intentional addition of alloying elements such as silver, copper, zinc, cadmium and nickel. The quantities of these elements must be balanced to maintain the desired colour of the alloy. The quality of the alloy is given by a CARAT system of classification, the term 'carat' indicating a twenty-fourth part. For example, 24 carat gold is pure gold, 18 carat gold has 18 parts of gold to six parts of alloying elements. Hallmarked gold carries in many instances a figure to indicate the percentage of gold in the alloy. For example, 9 carat gold has 37·5% gold so '0·375' will often be found stamped alongside the carat mark. Nine carat gold is the lowest grade permitted to carry an English hallmark.

The term 'noble' is also at times given to silver, which like gold and copper is found in the metallic state although less frequently and usually in pieces too small to be usable on their own. The metal occurs as a chloride ore that can be readily smelted, in lead ores such as argentiferous galena and alloyed with native gold. The richest source of silver has been argentiferous galena and thus its production has been closely linked to the production of lead. Galena, a sulphide ore, can be easily reduced to lead. Further heating oxidizes the lead to a powder, leaving behind any metallic silver present in the ore. Production of silver by this technique became viable in the 3rd millennium B.C. with the introduction of cupellation, a process that involves the oxidation of lead to litharge. The litharge dissolves any base metals that are present and is itself absorbed into quantities of bone ash in the fire, leaving unaltered any metallic silver. This technique can be used to remove silver from base metals by heating them with lead but will not remove silver from gold. Techniques employed in post-Roman times for separating silver from gold have been mentioned earlier.

Early metal-workers were familiar with all the techniques necessary for shaping and ornamenting the copper alloys, gold and silver. These techniques were not developed on one particular metal for the malleability and ductility of these metals, together with the ease with which they could be cast, meant that the processes applicable to one were by and large applicable to the others as well. Gold, however, has exceptional malleability, which enables the skilled craftsman to beat it into the finest foil by hammering it between hides, and the Egyptians were capable of producing a gold foil that was only 0·005 mm in thickness. Similar techniques were practised by the advanced civilizations of South and Central America in Pre-Columbian times. See AMERINDIANS (SOUTH AND CENTRAL). The characteristic malleability of gold was utilized in the construction of gold torques in the BRONZE AGE. Thin gold sheet was rolled around rods to make delicate tubes the edges of which were soldered together. To give the tubes the requisite strength they were filled with wax or resin around an iron core. Other hollow objects made from thin sheet gold were sometimes filled with lead.

By 3000 B.C. gold was used to give a more attractive appearance to inferior materials. At first gold sheet and then the finer gold leaf was used to cover articles of copper, bronze, bitumen, wood and stone. The malleable gold was accurately worked to the contours of the object and where necessary held in place by pins or with an adhesive such as the albumen from egg whites. The cladding of inferior metals by hammering on thin gold sheet was practised in the Middle Ages and today an adaptation of the process is continued in rolled gold. Here thin gold veneers are affixed to a base metal and the laminate so formed is rolled to give a thin sheet of base metal covered with a film of gold. Base metals were also clad in silver. In 1742 a Sheffield cutler, Thomas BOULSOVER, invented a process for fixing a veneer of silver to copper, brass or other base metals. This consisted of binding a thin silver plate to a thicker and larger plate of the base metal with iron binding wire. The edges were fluxed with borax and the two sheets sweated together in a red-hot furnace. The composite sheet thus formed was then rolled to the required thickness. The finished material is known as SHEFFIELD PLATE. The discovery of mercury made other silvering and GILDING techniques possible. Copper and bronze articles were rubbed with mercury and then silvered or gilt by the application of the appropriate amalgam of silver or gold. This form of silvering was used in Greek and Roman times for the silvering of bronze mirrors. Another ancient process was to clean the bronze article in hot vinegar, rub it with mercury whilst it was still hot and then tool gold leaf on to the surface. When it had been finally covered the article was heated to evaporate off the mercury and make the gold adhere permanently. In the 18th and 19th centuries ORMOLU ornaments were produced by a very similar technique.

Hollowed forms in gold and silver were produced by techniques of hollowing and raising similar to those employed in the working of COPPER AND ITS ALLOYS. The higher value placed on work in the more precious metals often led to greater enrichment and decoration. One of the earliest techniques employed was that of EMBOSSING, where designs were raised in relief from the reverse side of the article. Surfaces may also be decorated by lines cut or incised into the surface of the metal. This technique is known as *engraving* and is executed with a tool known as a burin, with small gouges or with needles. Another process is *inlaying*, where the decoration is undercut with a sharp instrument and the material to be inlaid is forced into the cut. Weapons were often inlaid with intricate patterns of gold and silver wires. A common inlay material used from early times is NIELLO, a black powder produced by first melting together three parts of silver, two parts of copper, and one part of lead and then adding sulphur. The resulting material is powdered with a file. The article to be decorated is first engraved and then fluxed. The niello powder is sprinkled over the engraved areas and heated until it melts into the engraving. Any excess can be scraped off so as to leave a bold black pattern. Gold and silver are also decorated with ENAMELS.

Being extremely ductile, gold and silver can both be easily formed into wires. Round wire was first produced from thin strips of metal which were hammered as round as possible and then rolled between flat surfaces. Later both round wires and wires of other section were produced by being drawn through holes in a steel plate known as a wortle plate. Today the goldsmith still uses this ancient technique to make the varied wires that he requires. Wires may be used in the production of jewellery and also as decoration and surface enrichment, the various elements of a piece of work being assembled by soldering. Good soldering and the use of copper as a solder for gold are evidenced in the construction of Bronze Age torques. Hard soldering utilizes metals which melt at temperatures above red heat but which are lower than the melting temperature of the metal being joined. As gold and silver were found together as natural alloys of varied composition, the fact that a range of melting temperatures can be obtained by varying the percentages of the metals in the alloy could have been discovered through observations made when melting native metal. Gold can also be pressure welded at room temperatures owing to its freedom from oxides and some early work employs this technique. The use of copper/silver alloys for joining silver work was also developed. Pure tin was, occasionally, used for joining silver and there are also examples of the use of tin/lead alloys in early work. This is a bad practice for lead solders will lead to the corrosion of silver and if silver is heated in contact with lead, it will be damaged.

1, 3, 34, 100, 264, 269, 396, 670, 813, 845.

GOLDEN COCKEREL PRESS. A private printing press founded in 1920 at Waltham St. Lawrence, Berkshire, by Harold Taylor, taken over by Robert Gibbings in 1924 and transferred to Staple Inn, London. From 1936 it was directed by Christopher Sandford and Owen Rutter. Under Gibbings's influence illustration received equal emphasis with typography. The Four Gospels (1931), the press's outstanding production, which has been compared with the KELMSCOTT Chaucer and the DOVES Bible, contains wood engravings by Eric Gill, who also designed the special 'Golden Cockerel' type. The books issued by this press have been described in a bibliography *Chaunticleer* (1936) and its successor *Pertelote* (1943). See also PRIVATE PRESS MOVEMENT.

131, 134, 277.

GOLDEN HORN. Pottery consisting mainly of large dishes and standing bowls and attributed to the second Iznik (Nicaea) period (A.D. 1525–55). They are painted with scroll patterns and small flowers in light blue on a white ground and covered with a transparent glaze. They were named 'Golden Horn' because they were once thought to have been made in the Golden Horn district of Istanbul. See CERAMICS, ISLAMIC.

GONORD, FRANÇOIS (active second half of 18th c.). French copper-engraver and silhouettist. Gonord used and perhaps improved the *physionotrace* of CHRÉTIEN and seems to have been the first to use a PANTOGRAPH for reducing silhouettes. In 1799 he published portraits of the members of the French Consulate cut with the *physionotrace*. He worked in Paris and Vienna. See SILHOUETTE.

GOODISON, BENJAMIN (d. 1767). English cabinet-maker working in London between 1725 and 1767. He supplied furniture to the royal palaces, Longford Castle, Holkham and Deene Park, among others. Among the best examples of his work are a set of herm-shaped stands at Hampton Court Palace, two day-beds and ten stools at Longford Castle and a gilt mirror in the Victoria and Albert Museum.

GOTHIC. Term in the history and criticism of architecture and the fine arts which was originally coined by Italian artists of the Renaissance to denote the type of medieval architecture which they condemned as barbaric (implying thereby that it was the architecture of the Gothic tribes who had destroyed the classical art of the Roman empire). In England the word 'Gothick' was often used by 17th-c. and 18th-c. writers with the sense of 'tasteless' or 'bizarre', but with the Romantic interest in medievalism the term lost its derogatory overtones and a vogue for its stylistic features was renewed in the Gothic Revival. The application of the term 'Gothic' was extended from its more precise architectural connotation to the ornament, sculpture and painting of the period in which Gothic architecture was prevalent. It is also applied to the decorative arts in a descriptive sense. If architecture is taken as the standard for determining the Gothic period, it lasted some 400 years from *c.* 1140 to after the middle of the 16th c. It succeeded the ROMANESQUE and was the second of the great international medieval styles of Western Europe.

GOTHIC CLOCKS. These are weight-driven domestic CLOCKS made almost wholly of iron, and they may be regarded as small-scale versions of the iron TURRET or tower clocks which preceded them. The wheelwork is mounted in an open-work lantern-like frame with posts at each corner and it is surmounted by a spire consisting of four curved straps, below which the bell is mounted and which has a FINIAL above. There are also often finials above each corner-post of the frame. These posts carry GOTHIC mouldings and the straps have additional ornaments of Gothic type.

Gothic clocks were made mainly in Germany, Austria and Switzerland in the 15th and 16th centuries. They require to be mounted on a bracket projecting from a wall with their driving weights hanging down below.

106, 458, 535.

GOUDY, FREDERIC W. (1865–1947). Most prolific of American type-designers. Born in Bloomington, Illinois, he moved to Chicago in 1890 and founded the Camelot Press and later, in 1903, the Village Press. With some reputation as a free-lance type-designer he began in 1908 an association with the Lanston Monotype Company, which lasted almost until his death. Much of his best work, done for this Company, was inspired by an enthusiasm for Roman inscriptions. Besides a number of books of type design and lettering, he edited the journals *Typographica* and *Ars Typographica*. See TYPOGRAPHY.

GOUTHIÈRE, PIERRE (1732–1813/14). Prominent French chaser and gilder of metalwork. He became a *Maître Doreur* in 1758. He was noted for the great variety of his work, particularly gilt bronze MOUNTS. He was employed by the Court and made the bronze fitments for Madame du Barry's château at Louveciennes. His work was renowned in his day for the quality of its artistry and craftsmanship. He collaborated with Jean-Antoine Houdon (1741–1828) and others in making the famous jewel cabinet of the Dauphine Marie Antoinette, given to her by Louis XV. His success was so great that he embarked upon the purchase of two luxurious town houses but this extravagance brought him to bankruptcy in 1788 and he died a pauper. In spite of his fame his known works are rare, a clock in the Wallace Collection being one of his few signed works.

717.

GRABHORN, EDWIN and ROBERT. Brothers. Born in Indiana, they set up a private printing press in San Francisco in 1919 and quickly won a high reputation for the originality of their work in the best traditions of the PRIVATE PRESS MOVEMENT. They produced books on commission for the Book Club of California and also for private publication. With their influence on later private printers such as Adrian Wilson and Sherwood Grover they may be said to have been among the originators of the national private press movement in the U.S.A.

GRAHAM, GEORGE (1674–1751). British horologist who made important contributions in the field of CLOCK-, WATCH-, and scientific instrument-making, both as a scientist and inventor and as a practical craftsman. He was born in rural Cumberland late in 1673 or the first half of 1674 (the date cannot be fixed more precisely than this) and was apprenticed to the clock-maker Henry Aske in London in 1688. In 1695 he became a free clock-maker and entered Thomas TOMPION's workshops. Here he remained until Tompion's death in 1713, being a partner from 1710 onwards and succeeding to his business after his death. He was elected a Fellow of the Royal Society of London in 1721 and Master of the Clockmakers' Company in 1722. Graham's principal claim to fame lies in three inventions: the dead-beat escapement for clocks, *c.* 1715; the cylinder escapement for watches, *c.* 1725; and the mercury temperature-compensating pendulum for clocks, with which he had been experimenting from *c.* 1717 but which he described to the Royal Society in 1726. As a working maker of clocks and watches his output was not very large; but his products were of the highest perfection mechanically and although he was inclined to eschew ornamentation, his cases and dials for both clocks and watches have the utmost dignity and quiet taste. Graham was also a noted maker of other types of scientific instruments, mainly for astronomy, and his works include an 8-foot (2·43-m) mural quadrant made for Halley in 1725; a 24-foot (7·32-m) zenith sector; a 12½-foot (3·80-m) telescope; and a transit instrument. He is buried in Westminster Abbey beside his former master and partner, Thomas Tompion.

GRANULATION. A method of working decorative GOLD, or less often silver, so that the metal forms into tiny spheres which create a granulated surface. In antiquity the method was used by the Minoans and granulated gold was among the jewellery found at Troy and elsewhere in the Aegean. The technique was carried to greatest perfection by the Etruscans.

(See GREEK AND ROMAN ANTIQUITY, JEWELLERY.) It was also used in Celtic jewellery. Granulation in jewellery was practised by craftsmen of the Italian Renaissance though the technique was on the whole less accomplished than that of the Etruscans. During the 19th c. there was again a vogue for granulated gold, often finely done, in the settings of semi-precious jewellery. Particularly noteworthy were the Italian jewellers Fortunato Castellani and his sons, who sought to revive the techniques of the ancient Greeks and Etruscans.

GREEK AND ROMAN ANTIQUITY

See also COSTUME (GREEK AND ROMAN ANTIQUITY)

1. TEXTILE MANUFACTURE. The five main stages in modern textile manufacture (the growing of raw materials; preparation of fibres; spinning; weaving; dyeing and finishing) can be conveniently taken as the basis of an account of the Greco-Roman textile industry. In antiquity dyeing took place before spinning; otherwise the sequence is correct.

(*a*) *Raw Materials.* Greek and Roman sheep were small with short-stapled brown fleeces. By A.D. 100 selective breeding had given rise to a race of fine-woolled white sheep, but they were probably not in a majority anywhere. Some curiosities are recorded, too, such as the Arab fat-tailed sheep, but they were only of local interest. Linen took second place to wool, and much of it was supplied by Syria and EGYPT under Greek, then Roman, domination. Here flax was an important crop. Some flax, however, was grown in the Rhone and Po deltas and other fertile river valleys. In the north its primary use was for household goods—only in the east was it an everyday clothing fabric. Hemp was utilized for rope and sailcloth, rarely for clothing. Its culture was restricted for that reason. Cotton-growing was confined to Egypt and the Sudan, but some Bahreini and Indian cotton may have been imported. Outside Egypt it is not often found, but Roman writers use ambiguous terminology and so we may underestimate its importance. SILK was an import until the Byzantine period, and came as yarn or woven cloth from China and northern India. The trade along the Asian silk routes flourished throughout the Roman period.

(*b*) *Preparation of Fibres.* Greek and Roman sheep were shorn in early summer with shears closely resembling modern ones. Only fine-woolled sheep were washed first. Foreign bodies in the fleece were usually picked out by hand. To obtain a longer staple the Romans sometimes combed their wool on flat iron wool-combs mounted on posts. In Egypt wool was beaten with rods to make it fluffy and to loosen the dirt. Harvested flax was retted, broken, scutched and hackled in the age-old manner described by Pliny (A.D. 24–79). The hackle was a board set with iron spikes through which the fibres were drawn. Hemp, which gives a tougher fibre, was prepared in a similar way. We learn that its final treatment could be left for winter evenings. As to the more exotic fibres, no ancient writer describes the preparation of cotton but we know from Aristotle how the Coan wild silk cocoons were unreeled before the moths emerged.

(*c*) *Spinning.* Spinning was a basic task for every Greek and Roman woman. The operation of spinning became second nature to her, and the quality of yarn produced was generally high. In classical times the 'suspended spindle' method of spinning (whereby the spindle, while rotating, hung down on a length of new-spun thread) was normal and there is little evidence of any other. For soft, frail yarns, however, the spindle could be rotated with its lower end resting on a saucer. Spindles with whorls of bone or pottery usually had plain tips, but the Greeks sometimes put a hook at the top on which to knot the yarn. Distaffs could be simple forked sticks or, at their most elaborate, carved rods of JET. Long distaffs to be tucked into the waist-band had apparently not yet evolved. In the western Roman provinces spindles were rotated clockwise, in the eastern anti-clockwise. There are few exceptions to this rule, for conservatism prevailed.

(*d*) *Weaving.* A surprising amount of woven material still survives from the classical period. Much of it has been found on the periphery of the Greco-Roman world, where peculiar climatic conditions (such as the deserts of Egypt, the bogs of north Europe) preserve textiles. Few pieces are imposing in themselves, but technical analysis of several hundred fragments can be revealing.

Vase paintings and references in literature indicate that the Greeks wove on a warp-weighted vertical loom. Loom-weights are among the commonest finds on Greek settlement sites. During the Republican period the Romans too were content with this loom, but later they came into contact with new forms of loom as their empire expanded. The two-beam vertical loom, often used for TAPESTRY weaving, was known in Rome from the 1st c. A.D., but the warp-weighted loom was never supplanted. In the east new types of loom were developed for weaving complex patterns. They were probably horizontal, but may not have been so advanced as the draw-loom of medieval times. Tablet-weaving and bandloom-weaving are both attested by archaeological remains in the Roman provinces. The earliest known Roman knitting with two needles comes from Dura-Europos on the Euphrates (3rd c. A.D.) and some fabrics in Sprang-technique (plaited netting) occur in both the eastern and western provinces. Tapestry weaving in GOBELIN technique, sometimes with elaborate figured designs, was practised in Classical Greece and was later a speciality of the eastern provinces of the Roman Empire. Large quantities of linen cloth decorated with tapestry-woven panels of wool are found in late Roman graves in Egypt.

Even in the late Roman period separate technical traditions, many centuries old, can be discerned in the eastern and western parts of the Greco-Roman world. Advances in textile technology seem to have been made on the fringes of the Mediterranean basin, not in its centre.

(*e*) *Dyeing and Finishing*. Dyeing and finishing in classical antiquity required considerable capital outlay on plant and equipment. They were specialized industries and evidence for them is scarce outside the towns.

Vats and boilers were the main equipment of the dyer. He handled principally unspun wool and had at his disposal an astonishingly wide range of animal, vegetable and mineral dyes. Most of his recipes, however, were based on plant dyes, and gave colours in the blue–purple–red range. The most sought-after dye was the purple obtained from a whelk of the *murex* family. Piece-dyeing was not common, but there is some evidence for resist-dyeing and printing in Roman Egypt.

The fuller cleaned and finished wool cloth, using a variety of tubs and tanks. The numerous fulleries uncovered in Pompeii show that business was brisk. Pompeian wall-paintings depict the treading of cloth in water containing a detergent to clean and shrink it, the raising of the nap, and the bleaching of cloth. The nap was cropped with huge shears and the cloth finally pressed in a screw-press. See also TEXTILE MANUFACTURE IN ANTIQUITY; NEEDLEWORK; WEAVING; SILK.

267, 400.

2. PIGMENTS. In remote antiquity the use of colour probably began with primitive man applying paint to his person in order to make himself more fearsome in war, more impressive on religious occasions or more attractive to primitive woman, and such incentives led to the gradual development of the knowledge of sources for pigments and dyes. In course of time these were also applied to pottery, wood, stone, bone and ivory, textiles and metals, and used to decorate buildings and objects of all kinds from the Palaeolithic cave-painters onwards.

The first dyes were made from fruit, berries, leaves or crushed flowers, from the roots of certain plants or from bark. Pigments are normally dry coloured powders used for painting, the earliest example being the red ochre which was often scattered over the bones of prehistoric man. Pliny (A.D. 23/4–79; *Naturalis Historia* xxxv) is our chief source for knowledge of the colours used in antiquity. Other evidence comes from Dioscurides (1st c. A.D.) and Vitruvius (*c.* 50–26 B.C.). Chemists find a certain confusion in their accounts.

Red seems to have been the favourite colour, and discoveries of both pigments and paintings at Pompeii and Herculaneum show a wide range from dark, almost purple, or brown shades, through rose to pink and orange. Ochres are natural earth-colours stained by iron oxides. Pliny terms the red *rubrica* or *sinopis* after the Pontic city of Sinope, where he says it was first found. The best kind, however, came from caves in Cappadocia or on Lemnos. Other sources include Egypt, the Balearic Islands and Africa. African red seems to have been the brightest and it was recommended for wall-painting. Some *rubrica* also occurred in mines. Red lead or minium came from the silver–lead mines in Spain and was prepared by smelting lead and dross together and then grinding and heating the resulting litharge. Cinnabar or red mercuric sulphide obtained from sulphur and mercury, haematite and orpiment (sulphide of arsenic), which produced a brown shade, were other sources of red pigments. Vitruvius mentions that yellow ochre burnt and then quenched with vinegar turned purple, but if it was burnt without the vinegar the result was merely brown. Analysis done on the pigments found in Pompeian shops shows that, like the famous dye, purple was also made from the juice of the *murex*. This occurs all round the Mediterranean coast and was trapped, mussels being used as bait.

Blue, usually called '*caeruleum*', was less easy to produce. LAPIS LAZULI is a doubtful possibility since the methods by which it can be successfully used did not develop until later. In Egypt azurite, basic copper carbonate obtained from Sinai, was used in early times, but was later replaced by an artificial compound known as 'Egyptian blue'. Vitruvius describes this as being manufactured in Alexandria. Sand and soda were ground together and sprinkled with ground-up copper, made into balls and allowed to dry. The mixture was then put in pottery jars and baked in a furnace. The particles had to be fairly coarse to get the best results. Later another factory for this process was started at Puteoli. This pigment could only be used with a binding agent, as the lime in a wall newly plastered for fresco painting would destroy it.

Yellow was an easier colour, mostly the result of natural iron oxides, ochres or limonite. Pliny tells us that the best was Attic at two *denarii* a pound; cheaper qualities came from elsewhere in Greece, Italy and Gaul. Polygnotus and Micon, adds Pliny, were the first to use Attic ochre (*Nat. Hist.* xxxiii. 158–63). Orpiment was another source. Red and yellow ochres mixed together could also produce browns.

Powdered MALACHITE was one source of green and came from Cyprus, Arcadia, Macedonia and Spain. An artificial variety was made from copper salts obtained by evaporation from mine-washings. The colour of both could be improved by treatment with alum and vegetable dyes. A cheaper imitation was made from the green celadonite earth known to exist naturally at Verona and in parts of France, Germany, Cyprus and Britain (Cornwall). Vitruvius remarks that the best quality came from Smyrna.

Soot was the chief source of black and was acquired in various ways. Vitruvius advises a furnace with outlets into a marble-faced vaulted room. Wood and resin were then burnt and the resulting soot scraped up. Simpler methods included the burning of pine branches or wine lees. Grey was obtained from soot mixed with gypsum, charcoal or ochre. Chalk was the chief ingredient for white pigments but china clay and burnt gypsum were also used. White lead was obtained from Rhodes, Corinth and Pompeii and was also manufactured by heating lead shavings over a pan of vinegar or pickling them in vinegar, scraping the fragments, heating the scrapings, washing until all impurities were eliminated, and then allowing the residue to dry and making it into tablets. Chalk was also used with other pigments to obtain lighter shades: with red, for example, to obtain pink.

Most of the pigments mentioned above have been found in the ruins of the shops of the Pompeian pigment sellers, and analysed. There is scope, however, for much more scientific investigation of pigments from other sites. A report on material from two Swiss sites, Munzingen and Holstein, mentions the identification of Egyptian blue and a red made from haematite. It also sheds light on the vexed question how far Roman mural painters used fresco technique in the accepted sense. Students of such wall-paintings have often noticed a difference in quality between the background colouring and the details painted on it, but the layers of paint are thin and do not seem to penetrate the wall-plaster beneath. Now it appears that in some cases the Roman work can be accurately termed fresco, but it does differ from later work of this nature. Vitruvius describes how the walls should be built up with layers of sandy mortar and marble dust, and then the colours laid on the damp plaster. Until recently this proviso of the dampness of the plaster has been a problem, suggesting that small portions of wall would have to be damped just ahead of the painter's progress. It has now been realized, however, that a wall of Vitruvian type would take some time to dry out, and the very porous texture of the coarse-grained plaster below the pigment layer would result in a hard and durable finish, with the pigment firmly tied to the plaster.

The Swiss sites mentioned above produced both fresco and painting employing a binding agent, and surface examination suggests that the same is true of several Romano-British sites. So far the nature of this binding agent is uncertain, but milk or egg, both mentioned by Pliny, seem likely possibilities. Certain pigments, including purple and blue, and also orpiment and white lead, were not compatible with lime and so could not be used for fresco. Pigments blended with wax were used for encaustic painting, a process of Egyptian origin later adopted by Greek and Roman artists especially for portrait painting. See also COLOURS AND COLOURANTS.

28, 266, 299, 503.

3. METALWORK. Ever since men came to realize the superiority of metals over wood or stone for weapons and tools the role of the smith has been an important one and with the growing complexities of civilization the value of the metal-worker has steadily increased. In Mycenaean and Homeric Greece the mining of the ores and the production of finished objects might still be done by the same individual. In Classical Greece distinctions began to arise, and by Roman times the miner, the worker who turned the ore into metal ready for use so that it could be transported in convenient blocks or ingots to the rural and urban markets, and the craftsman who produced the completed product and often sold it to the customer, are clearly differentiated.

The earliest metal objects were made of bronze (see BRONZE AGE METALLURGY), and for this copper brought from the Cyclades, Euboea and Cyprus was used at first. By the 1st millennium B.C., however, the Phoenicians and Carthaginians were bringing in copper and lead from Spain and British tin from Cornwall, and this traffic continued under the Romans. In some cases the long sea voyage from Britain was replaced by land travel across France, Switzerland and Italy, and this accounts for the appearance in these countries of fine Greek bronzes. Under the Romans river transport was extensively used, barges travelling down the Rhône to the port of Arles and to Narbonne.

Classical Greece obtained SILVER and lead from Thrace and Macedonia, and also from the mines at Laurion at the southern end of the Athenian peninsula. Aegean gold seems to have been one source of the wealth of the Minoan and Mycenaean civilizations, and its use continued until the Roman period. By then many of these early mines seem to have been worked out, and Roman gold came largely from north-western Spain. One British gold-mine was worked at Dolaucothi (Carmarthenshire), and other sources included Carinthia, Hungary, Transylvania and Nubia. Lead was also worked and exported by the Romans in Britain. Some lead was also worked in Brittany and the Rhineland. With the development of Spanish sources the British tin trade declined, but Cornish tin became important again from the 3rd c. as the Spanish tin-mines began to run down. Iron is widespread, so most areas used their own local supplies; but iron from Carinthia in the province of Noricum was famous. The use of zinc combined with copper to produce BRASS seems to have been a Roman discovery of the late 1st c. B.C.

In the time of the Roman Republic mines had been contracted out to private individuals or companies but under the Empire they were usually imperial property controlled by procurators, financial officers reporting directly to the emperor. The mining was sometimes done by gangs of slaves or convicts; but more often areas were leased out either to small lessees, working under procuratorial control on a percentage basis, or to wealthy *conductores* who might rent whole mines for 50% of the profit and run them independently. There was no central ministry of mines in Rome so efficiency varied, especially as workers with technical knowledge were scarce. The large number of foreign mining terms identified suggest that extensive use was made of local knowledge. Features of similarity in the Spanish mines have led scholars to believe that something in the nature of a mining school may have existed at Rio Tinto.

Two inscriptions found near Aljustrel, Portugal, from the silver- and copper-mining area at Vipasca preserve many of the details of mine tenure and operation in the 2nd c. A.D. They also list regulations made by the procurator for the control of various amenities used by the miners, among them baths and the shops of barbers, fullers and shoemakers. Safety precautions relating to the proper maintenance of reinforcement and pit props and to drainage are also included, with penalties for their neglect. Lamps, ladders, iron wedges and other tools, and evidence for large wheels used for raising buckets and even for the Archimedean screw, have been found in several Roman mines. The investigation of a few carefully chosen sites could shed much light on the rather neglected subject of ancient mining.

The mined ore was often processed into ingots at the mines and occasionally craftsmen also worked near the source of supply. Usually, however, the metal seems to have been transported to the towns, where workshops have been found ranging in size from small factories to the one-man business with one or two assistants in a building which also served as shop and living quarters. Some craftsmen seem to have travelled extensively wherever their services were in demand, and the skill of Greek gold- and silversmiths was well known from the 7th c. B.C. onwards. Lists of plate show that important temples accumulated vast treasures made in Corinth, Chios, Rhodes and other centres. By Hellenistic times the number of craftsmen in some places led to the development of silversmiths' quarters, while the various kings employed their own court artists and craftsmen. Greece, Syria, Asia Minor, Egypt and southern Italy all had important workshops for bronze and silver vessels by this period, among them Alexandria, Corinth, Samos, Athens and Cumae.

In remote antiquity silver was a rarer metal than gold since it had to be obtained by mining whereas gold was gained from alluvial deposits by simple washing. It may have been the Phoenicians who first brought silver into general use and silver objects mentioned in Homer often have Sidonian associations. The main sources of silver in Classical Greece were Bactriana, Colchis, Lydia, Thrace and Laurion until 413 B.C. In the western Mediterranean Spain was the most important source, though silver also came from Gaul and Britain. Silver was less extensively used than gold for jewellery, chiefly for producing especially luxurious examples of items which were ordinarily made from bronze. Its commonest use was for plate accumulated by the very wealthy.

Diodorus (*c.* 40 B.C.) describes how iron from Elba was shipped to Puteoli and made there into tools and armour, and the products of a factory making bronze vessels at Capua have been found as far afield as Germany, Scotland and Scandinavia. Bronze statuary and furniture for the adornment of houses at Pompeii and Herculaneum were also made at Capua. In the provinces Aquileia was famous for ironwork made of Norican iron, and at Aquincum (near Budapest) a bronze-worker's shop was found in the market-place. Foundry moulds, trial casts, bronze and iron slag and bronze objects are known from other shops in the province of Pannonia, including sites at Brigetio and Emona. In France bronze vessels distributed over a wide area were made at Lyon. At Gressenich, near Aachen, Germany, brass was made from local supplies of zinc and used for vessels such as the Hemmoor buckets which in the 2nd c. A.D. were great favourites with the 'barbarians' outside the Roman frontiers. Silverware was made at Rome, Capua, Aquileia and many other large towns.

Inscriptions found all over the Roman empire testify to the importance of the *collegia fabrorum* or guilds of smiths. By this time, too, metalworking was growing more specialized, so as well as the *fabri ferrarii* known from Lyon we also find in Asia Minor nail-smiths at Hierapolis and makers of metal beds at Tralles. Factories producing silver plate in Rome included polishers and gilders among their employees, and Pliny comments (*Nat. Hist.* xxxiii. 139) on how Roman fashions changed with varying demands for plate made at the factories of Clodius, Furnius and Gratius. Individual craftsmen at Rome worked beside the Via Sacra, where Nero allocated to them numerous shops, and wealthy men often had their own silversmiths as well as servants to clean and look after their plate.

Museum collections all over the world provide evidence for the labours of the ancient miners and craftsmen. Bronze was used for a far greater variety of objects than it is today; bronze MIRRORS, for instance, with polished discs for

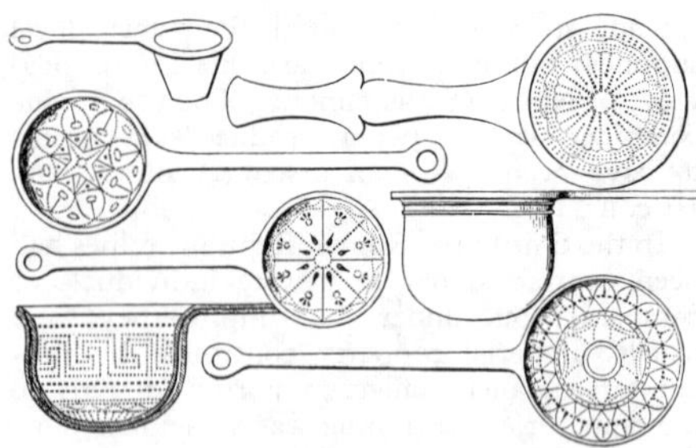

Roman cooking utensils. From J. A. Overbeck, *Pompeji* (1884)

reflection were made in Greece from the 6th c. B.C. Later a thin sheet of silver was attached to the disc to improve the reflection. Bronze combs, toilet implements including tweezers, nail-cleaners and ear-scoops, and surgical instruments have all been found. Strigils used in the baths might be of iron, bronze or silver and occasionally blades used as razors are also discovered. Silver and bronze spoons and iron knives with bronze or bone handles are not uncommon. (See CUTLERY.)

The Greeks made very fine large bronze vessels for holding wine and water and these were often richly ornamented. Vessels of a similar type were also used by the Etruscans and Romans, but they gradually became less decorative. Greek *paterae* with shallow bowls often had handles with anthropomorphic stems until the 5th c. B.C., when simpler handles became fashionable. A design with a fluted cylindrical stem ending in the head of a dog or ram continued to be made by the Romans. The saucepan type of *patera* with deeper bowl had a flat handle ending in a loop and sometimes decorated in relief. *Paterae* were used for serving wine and for pouring libations. Those of Roman date were made at Alexandria, Capua and in the provinces. Roman bronze cauldrons, often carefully patched in antiquity, are sometimes discovered, and also small cooking-pots with lids, baking tins and long-handled frying-pans used with iron grids and tripods for cooking over charcoal fires. Silver and bronze long-handled wine-strainers with holes arranged in decorative patterns are known from Hellenistic times onwards.

Greek silver treasure from the 5th c. B.C. onwards includes perfume bottles, drinking cups and bowls, some of them ornamented with Scythian scenes, made at Panticapaeum by Greek artists. The repertory of types grew steadily until imports of Spanish silver and the booty captured in war led to an abundance of silver plate in Rome, increasing from the 3rd c. B.C. onwards. Most families of any consequence possessed a complete table service as well as showpieces for display, and the hoards of over 100 items from the Campanian villas of Boscoreale and the Casa del Menandro are well known. Drinking cups, often richly decorated with EMBOSSED reliefs or chased or engraved ornament, were the most popular type. The making of statuettes of bronze or silver, often votive offerings, was an important branch of metal-working, as well as the production of bronze busts and statues. A Greek vase from the 5th c. B.C. shows the casting of a statue with the furnace on the left, and on the right the newly cast statue about to have the head attached. On the other side another statue is being finished off. Various tools also appear.

At the other end of the scale from these luxury objects are the numerous workaday iron tools. Tombstones from Aquileia and Ostia show the Roman blacksmith at work with hammer, tongs and anvil, his furnace close at hand and his wares, including a lock, a spearhead, saws, hatchets, shears and surgical instruments, etc., hung up around him. A grave relief in the Vatican Museum depicts a cutler's shop with various sizes of sickles, knives and wool-combs arranged in neat rows. Large hoards of ironwork found in Germany and Britain also contain harness and wagon fittings, and agricultural items such as scythes, hoes, spades and ploughshares.

4. ARMS AND ARMOUR. Evidence for the types of arms and armour used at various periods is provided by sculpture, vase painting, richly furnished tombs, votive offerings, and material recovered from military sites and battlefields. Their development was dictated by the materials available, the methods of combat, whether by individual champions or by groups of warriors in disciplined formations, and the terrain. In Archaic and Classical Greece the characteristic soldiers were the hoplites, heavily armed infantry who fought in lines eight deep. They were recruited from the citizens of the Greek city-states who could afford the necessary equipment.

The hoplite wore a helmet, body armour and greaves. From *c.* the 8th c. to the 5th c. B.C., with a few later examples, the helmet might be of Corinthian type, invented at Corinth and made from a single sheet of bronze. It covered the whole head including the ears, cheekpieces came round to either side of the mouth and chin, and another piece between the eyes protected the nose. At the back the base curved upwards to

Detail of Greek vase painting illustrating the casting of a statue. (Staatliche Mus., Berlin)

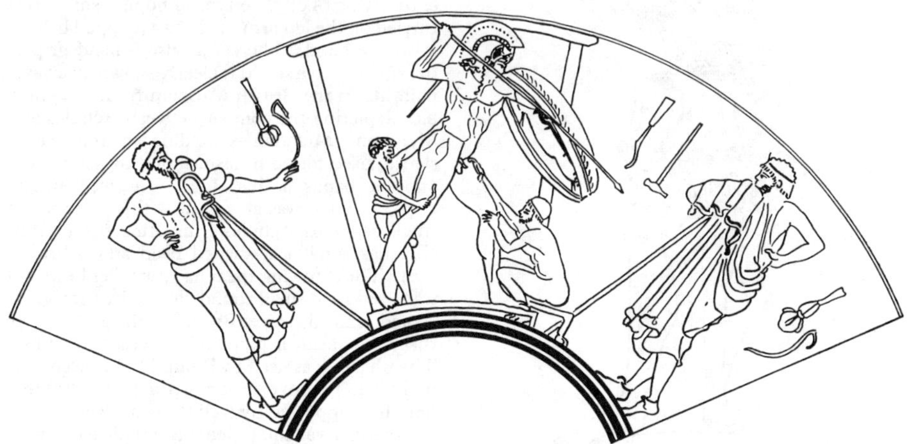

Detail of Greek vase painting illustrating the polishing of a bronze statue (Staatliche Mus., Berlin)

Greek helmets from 5th c. B.C. Attic red-figure vases. From R. E. Oakeshott, *The Archaeology of Weapons* (1960)

provide a neck-guard. Rows of holes along the edges indicate that a felt or leather lining was kept in place. Crests of horse-hair were attached in various ways, some helmets having small pegs on top for this purpose. Decoration consisted of engraved designs or even silver inlay, and some cheekpieces have EMBOSSED reliefs of a ram's head or other motif. The other characteristic Greek helmet is the Attic type, used from the 6th c. B.C. onwards, a cap which left the ears uncovered

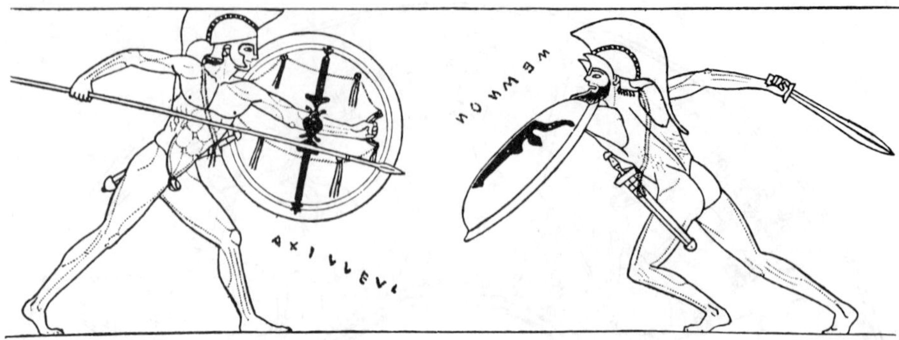

Detail from a 5th-c. B.C. vase painting depicting the combat between Achilles and Memnon and showing the Classical Greek weapons. Fig. 93 from *British Museum Guide to Exhibition illustrating Greek and Roman Life* (1920)

Greek soldier putting on his cuirass. From a vase painting by the painter Duris. Fig. 78 from *British Museum Guide to Exhibition illustrating Greek and Roman Life* (1920)

but to which neck-, cheek- and nosepieces could be attached. The cheekpieces were sometimes hinged, and the helmet ornamented in relief.

Two bronze plates roughly shaped to fit back and chest, and fastened together on the shoulders and the sides, were the earliest type of Greek body armour. This type spread to Italy and appears later among the Etruscans and Romans. It was clumsy and not comfortable in hot weather, so it was soon replaced by a leather foundation to which small bronze plates were attached with wire. An example is clearly shown on a red-figure vase by the painter Duris (510–465 B.C.), depicting a soldier dressing. Greaves shaped out of thin bronze protected the legs, and were padded at the ankles to prevent chafing. Gorgon's heads in relief decorate the knees.

Round or oval shields of wood or leather were used by the Greeks, plated with bronze from *c.* the 7th c. B.C. The typical hoplite shield was carried on the left arm, which was slipped behind a bronze band. There was also a hand-grip at the rim. Such a shield is clearly shown on a vase-painting in the British Museum from the 5th c. B.C. depicting the combat between Achilles and Memnon. Memnon is welding an iron-bladed sword, used for both slashing and thrusting, and another hangs at his side. A curved single-edged weapon was also used at this period, and small daggers. Achilles's thrusting spear probably has a flat leaf-shaped head and a bronze butt. The throwing spear had a smaller head and was used with small round shields by the lightly armed skirmishers. By the 4th c. B.C. the thrusting spear or pike had increased in length. The phalanx, as used by Philip II of Macedonia, included infantry using spears of different lengths, supported by well trained cavalry.

Etruscan war equipment had much in common with Greek. Contemporary with both was much magnificent armour among the barbarians. In Romania fine examples of Thraco-Getic art included 5th-c. gold helmets shaped like pointed caps found at Coţofeneşti and Băiceni, and the 4th-c. Agighiol tomb in northern Dobrudja included a partially gilded silver helmet, its forehead ornamented with two eyes in relief while riders appear on the cheekpieces. Two silver greaves decorated with the heads of Amazons come from this tomb.

In western Europe the arms and armour of the aristocracy were decorated in the manner of Celtic geometrical art inspired by Greek influences. Examples include the late 4th-c. or early 3rd-c. cap-like helmet of embossed bronze from Amfreville, France. A sheet of gold-leaf was hammered over the bronze and the elaborate decoration included studs of ENAMELLING. By the end of the 2nd c. and in the 1st c. B.C.

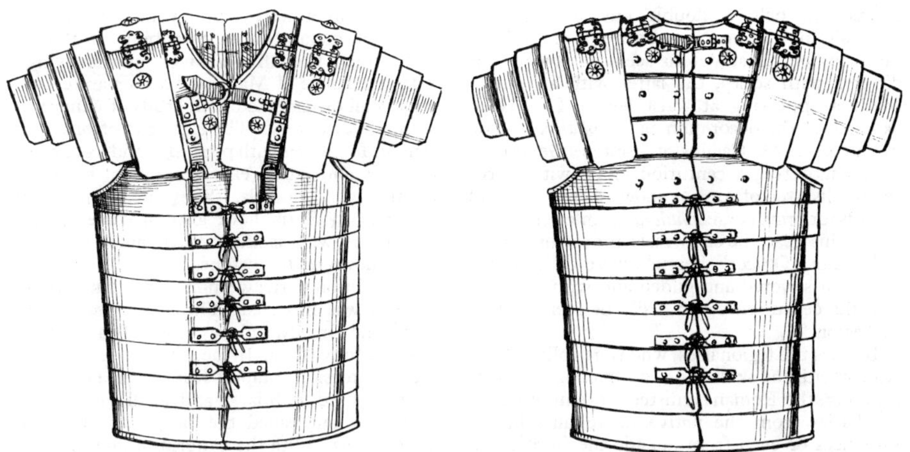

Front and back view of a reconstruction by H. Russell Robinson and C. M. Daniels of a 1st-c. A.D. *lorica segmentata* found in 1964 in the Agricolan fort at Corbridge on Tyne

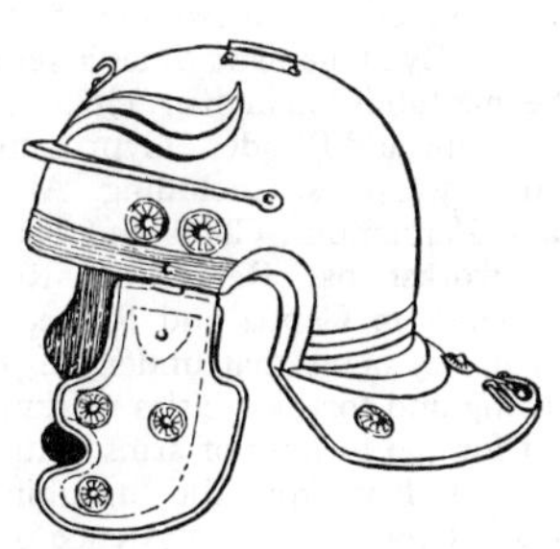

Roman legionary helmet of late 1st c. A.D. Fig. 19 from G. Webster, *The Roman Imperial Army* (1969)

long iron swords were in use, their scabbards decorated with fine incised ornament. Oval leather or wooden shields were decorated in relief with bronze bosses and terminal roundels. Arms of this period are shown on the triumphal arch depicting the battles of the Gauls and the Romans at Orange, while Dacian equipment of later date appears on Trajan's column.

The earliest Roman armies were equipped in much the same way as the Greeks, but with the development of the legionary formations new techniques emerged. The spear or *pilum* developed into a carefully balanced javelin, forged with soft iron behind the point so that it bent on impact and could not be thrown back. One javelin could pierce and lock together several of the enemy's overlapping shields, so that they had to be thrown away. Thrusting spears or pikes were also used against cavalry. For fighting at close quarters the *gladius*, a short double-edged sword, was carried in a scabbard often decorated with bronze plates. A fine example from the early part of the 1st c. A.D., perhaps a sword of honour, was found in the Rhine at Mainz and is now in the British Museum. Its blade is 53 cm in length. The wooden scabbard is covered with thin silver-gilt plate with reliefs in gilt-bronze including a scene showing the Emperor Tiberius receiving the victorious Germanicus in A.D. 17. Four attached loops indicate where the scabbard was hooked on to the sword-belt of leather, probably with more metal plates and buckles. The dagger (*pugio*) was used as a knife for many purposes or for fighting if the sword was lost. Legionary shields were curved to fit the body and were made of thin pieces of plywood covered with leather. The centre was hollowed out to provide a hand-grip protected by a metal boss. The rim had bronze or iron bindings. Various decorations, such as the thunderbolts visible on Trajan's column, in bronze, silver or gold, often painted, helped to identify different units.

Over woollen tunics, and in cold climates knee-length leather breeches, the legionaries wore body armour of leather jerkins with metal shoulder-pieces and either interlocking rings or small scales sewn on in overlapping rows. Both types appear on the column of Marcus Aurelius, and so does the *lorica segmentata*, a complicated arrangement of metal strips and plates laced and buckled into place, which is shown more clearly on Trajan's column. A scarf prevented chafing at the neck. From a wide belt was suspended a dagger, and in front a kind of apron or sporran of leather thongs with metal plates attached gave extra protection. Bronze helmets were lined with an iron skull cap, which in the late 1st c. had a projection sloping downwards at the back to protect the neck, ear-pieces, and on top an attachment for the plume.

Several tombstones from the middle of the 1st c. A.D. depict splendidly clad centurions. M. Favonius Facilis at Colchester wears a leather or mail corselet with metal shoulder-pieces, a splendid belt, a double kilt and greaves. T. Calidius Severus at Carnuntum and Q. Sertorius Festus at Verona seem to have jerkins covered with scales, the latter with a head of Medusa appearing at waist level. This is an example of the decoration called *phalerae*. The memorial to M. Caelius at Xanten (Germany), commemorating a centurion killed with Varus in the disaster of A.D. 9, shows a fine series of awards for bravery: six *phalerae*, armlets, torques, and on his head the oak wreath for saving a comrade's life. Officer's helmets were of legionary type, but silvered and gilded and with crests so that the centurion could easily be identified by his legion.

Besides the legionaries, who were fully trained Roman citizens skilled in road-making and fort-building, the Romans enlisted large numbers of auxiliaries from the native inhabitants in the provinces or even from outside the frontiers of the empire. These were used for reconnaisance and did much of the fighting, using their own native weapons. Many had the *spatha*, a long straight two-edged sword ending in a point. Some examples found in Scandinavian bogs or in rampart material from the fort at South Shields, Northumberland, are pattern-welded, forged from steel rods twisted together and then beaten out. One example from South Shields was decorated near the hilt in gilt-bronze inlay with a figure of Mars and an eagle between two standards.

In addition to the *spatha* the auxiliary cavalryman often used a spear or lance with a long narrow blade, and units from the eastern provinces included archers with bows of composite type. Vegetius (4th c. A.D.) also mentions the cross-bow and Trajan's column portrays the Sarmatians fighting the Romans with weapons of this type. Slingers had lead bullets of a kind already used by the Greeks. Protective clothing was often of leather, but the Sarmatian cavalry are shown with both themselves and their horses covered with scale armour from neck to knee. This armour reappears with the *catafractarii*—soldiers as weighed down with armour as were the medieval knights.

For festive occasions and tournaments the army presented a colourful picture, and in A.D. 136 the historian Arrian described them in all the glory of their gay clothing, crests, pennons and shining metal. The auxiliaries in particular seem to have kept special light-weight helmets for such occasions, usually of bronze but sometimes of iron or even silver. Decorated with scenes in relief or engraving, they might have separated cheekpieces or visor-masks which completely covered the wearer's face so that he appeared like some young hero, often with elaborately curled hair. Some helmets with face-masks may have been actual portraits. They are found all over the empire, but especially in the north and west. Eleven examples are known from Britain, three of them from the Scottish fort at Newstead. Seven face-masks and one helmet-bonnet were found with a remarkable hoard of metalwork at Straubing in Bavaria. With them were five greaves, one showing a splendid figure of Mars, and six separate knee-guards all ornamented with heads of Minerva—a unique discovery. The eight chamfrons, face-armour for horses with pierced roundels covering the eyes and more relief decoration, have only fragmentary parallels. Sites including Dura-Europos in Syria have also produced horse-armour as well as the normal horse-trappings often shown on tombstones.

In addition to the weapons already mentioned artillery was also used. The catapult started life under the Greeks, and was originally a large bow mounted on a stand. In the 4th c. B.C. it developed into the torsion catapult firing iron darts. The Romans used both large and small varieties and also a variant called the *onager* which hurled large stones. With the battering-ram these were mainly siege-weapons.

Evidence about the workshops making arms is scanty. Greece may have learnt to make iron swords from armourers in Cyprus, and other skills may have emanated from central Europe and the East. By Hellenistic times arsenals seem to have been established in many cities, including Cyzicus, Sinope and Rhodes. Cyprus continued to produce weapons, including Alexander's sword, and Pergamum, Chios and Samos may have had workshops. Republican Rome had smiths at work in Capua and Rome. Tacitus (*Histories* ii. 82) notes that under Vespasian in all the strong and fortified cities workmen were appointed for the forging of arms. An inscription on a chamfron from the Straubing hoard reminds us of the possible existence of private workshops for the elaborately decorated armour. By the time of Diocletian all imperial arms were made in state factories. At the end of the 4th c. 15 of these are known in the east, some making a variety of weapons, others specializing. Antioch, for example, made weapons, including shields, and also heavy cavalry armour. Of the 20 factories in the west, six were in Italy, five in Illyricum and nine in Gaul. Shields, swords and armour were made at Trier, bows at Ticinum, breast-plates at Mantua and various arms at Salona in Yugoslavia.

See also ARMS AND ARMOUR.

5. JEWELLERY. The origins of many articles of adornment are to be found in the ancient civilizations of EGYPT and the Near East, whence they spread to the Aegean area, reaching Bronze Age Crete *c.* 2400 B.C. Gold, easily worked and unaffected by corrosion, is the favourite material at all periods and has survived best. Silver objects were more perishable and so are less frequent; and humbler materials, including bronze, IRON, bone and GLASS also occur. Much jewellery has been recovered from tombs and from hoards buried in unsettled times, but stray finds due to ancient carelessness are not uncommon in excavations. Sometimes painting and sculpture also

depict jewellery, particularly necklaces, rings and brooches.

In Greece a period of fine gold work began *c.* 800 B.C., centred at first on Knossos, Corinth and Athens, and then spreading to the Greek Islands and Asia Minor. It followed several centuries of poverty after the collapse of the Mycenaean civilization, and was probably inspired by an influx of craftsmen from Phoenicia. Ear-rings, diadems, finger-rings and the safety-pin type of brooches called *fibulae*, decorated in various ways, are among the more common discoveries. This was succeeded by another period from *c.* 600 to *c.* 475 B.C. when gold was scarce, and the bronze and silver objects worn instead have rarely survived.

In addition to metalwork glass and AMBER were used for beads and seal-stones, and continued with varying degrees of popularity until Roman times or even later. The art of making glass beads was probably learnt from Egypt. In one method small tubes of glass were cut into short lengths and polished. Otherwise moulds could be used. A wide range of colours occurs, several being sometimes used together. The eye-bead, decorated with contrasting spots, spread over much of Europe and the Near East between *c.* 550 B.C. and A.D. 400, and was also regarded as an amulet against the evil eye. Amber first appears in shaft graves at Mycenae. The chief source of supply was the Baltic, and from the late Bronze Age onwards an important trade route developed from Jutland to the Adriatic. In Greece it was not so popular as elsewhere in Mediterranean Europe, but in Italy it remained a favourite. Amber was believed to have healing and magical powers, so it was also used for amulets as well as for decorative inlays.

The finest Greek jewellery belongs to the Classical period of 475 to 330 B.C., examples also coming from Cyprus, Thrace and southern Italy. The wreaths worn by victors at the games, or by the wealthy at parties or in processions, sometimes survive in tombs. Made of gold, silver, gilded wood or bronze, they imitate actual wreaths of myrtle or olive. Strips of gold decorated with embossed ROSETTES or PALMETTES belonged to diadems or they were soldered on to leather backing. More elaborate types showing figure scenes have also been found. The more common types of ear-ring include spirals with the thin end passing through the ear and the other end ornamented with an animal or human head, and boat-shaped ones, sometimes with large rosettes or short pendant chains ending in birds or cockle-shells. There were also disc-shaped ear-studs.

Necklaces of melon or egg-shaped golden beads had pendants of palmettes or animal heads. An example from Nymphaeum, now in the Ashmolean Museum (4th c. B.C.), with double palmette dividers has tiny egg and larger acorn pendants, and a fine necklace of the same date from Tarentum is similar but more elaborate, with human heads of varying size instead of eggs and acorns. Bracelets consisting of a large ring left incomplete so as to admit the wrist began during the preceding period and continued in vogue for a very long time. The ends were decorated with animal heads. A fine 4th-c. pair from Kul-Oba, however, are of twisted gold completed with the fore-parts of sphinxes and with the gap closed by a fastening between the two pairs of front paws. Spiral snake bracelets, another long-lived type, are also found. Pins of gold or bronze with heads of various shapes, including pine-cones, hearts, bees and even Ionic capitals, were worn in pairs, one on each shoulder, sometimes linked by a chain. *Fibulae* were rare in Greece but occur in neighbouring areas and in Italy, where brooches have a long history of development from the Bronze Age into Etruscan times.

The ring has a long history and several varieties were in use by Mycenaean times. They were made from two pieces of sheet metal, one the hoop with the lining of the bezel and the other the bezel, moulded or decorated with engraving and fixed on top. Signet rings with various devices and bezels inlaid with glass or such stones as AMETHYST or cornelian are also found. By the time of Archaic and Classical

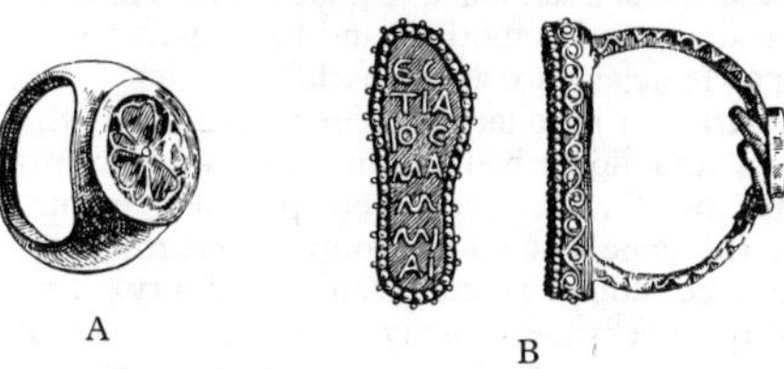

Second-c. B.C. finger-rings from Artjukhov's barrow. Figs. 28 and 29 from R. A. Higgins, *Greek and Roman Jewellery* (1961). A. With circular bezel inlaid with glass. B. Bezel of sandal shape inscribed in Greek 'Hestiaios to his mother'. At the back garnet inlaid in a Heracles knot

Greece rings were frequently set with stones which imitated the Egyptian scarab beetle. These often swivel to reveal a flat lower surface carved with a device used as a seal. New techniques including the use of a cutting wheel and a drill made it possible to engrave hard stones such as cornelian, and from the 6th c. B.C. onwards we find the great schools of Classical Greek gem-engraving developing. Young athletes and some mythical personages were favourite subjects. Gradually the swivel device disappeared and the motif was engraved on the upper side of the fixed gem, often convex. Inscribed gold betrothal rings are known from the 4th c. B.C.

Loot from Alexander's conquests and the exploitation of the Macedonian gold-mines led to more abundant gold jewellery in Hellenistic times. The motifs reflect influences from Egypt and western Asia, and the Greek Eros was also popular. Jewellery seems to have been made at a number of centres, including Antioch and

Alexandria, and a goldsmith's hoard found at Geljub, Egypt, dating from the 2nd c. B.C., included a number of bronze punches and cores for hammering out sheet gold. A characteristic of this period is the increasing use of colour in the form of inlays of glass, ENAMEL or gemstones.

Temple inventories found at Delos dating from 279 B.C. list wreaths of ivy, laurel, oak, vine, etc., usually of gold foil, diadems, necklaces and other objects. A lady of the 2nd c. might wear a triangular diadem, disc ear-rings with pendants studded with GARNETS, a gold chain necklace with tiny enamelled rosettes and pendants of small jars or spear-heads, circular brooches, finger-rings and bracelets. Ear-rings could also take the form of hoops, one end tapering to a point, which was thrust through the ear-lobe and fastened by a loop attached to the larger end, which had a decorative finial, often an animal's head. Later beads were also threaded on to the hoop. In addition to strip and chain necklace a type consisting of bezel-set stones now appears and goes on well into the Roman period. Rings were usually set with plain or engraved gems, garnet and TOPAZ being new additions to the repertory. Portraits of rulers or deities began to be worn. Other rings have circular bezels inlaid with glass. One bezel in the shape of a sandalled foot is inscribed in Greek 'Hestiaios to his mother' and has a garnet inlaid in a Heracles knot at the back.

Etruscan jewellery appeared in the late 8th c. B.C., and flourished at the same time as pre-Hellenic Greek. Both were probably inspired by the same Phoenician sources, but the Etruscans developed greater technical ability. Their early work is noteworthy for fine GRANULATION, a process in which minute grains of gold are arranged in patterns and soldered on to a background with copper carbonate mixed with water and fish glue. Workshops may have existed at Latium and Vetulonia. The earliest phases of this jewellery included spiral hair-ornaments, ear-rings and necklaces with various pendants including the circular gold BULLA, an ornament which the Romans eventually adopted as an amulet which was worn in particular by free-born children for protection against evil. *Fibulae* were popular and some splendid gold and silver examples have survived, including the leech or boat brooch with an arched, thickened bow. A fine gold brooch from Vulci has the bow above the hinge decorated with granulation, and then continuing as a slender bar above the long pin. Along the bar marches a procession of tiny gold animals. Greek jewellery types also appeared increasingly with motifs presumably brought by Greek craftsmen. A recession of some kind may have caused a scarcity of jewellery in the 5th c., but after 400 B.C. there was a renaissance. Granulation was little used, being replaced by embossed decoration, and wreaths, ear-rings, *bullae*, bracelets and rings predominated. Finger-rings had become increasingly important from the 6th c. as craftsmen from eastern Greece took their skill in gem-engraving to Italy. Workshops in Etruria produced scarab-rings and gems engraved with scenes sometimes showing more than one individual. Small boys carrying their masters' bathing oils and strigils, or squatting down waiting for them, are often found. Some of these slaves are Negroes. With the development in Etruria of a round-headed drill some figure work eventually deteriorated, tending to consist of large blobs; but attendant details, such as the feathers in the popular scenes with winged creatures, were still carefully worked. Scarab-rings continued longer than in Greece, and some are contemporary with Hellenistic jewellery. Otherwise, after 250 B.C. Etruria was strongly influenced by Hellenistic fashions.

Early Roman ornaments resembled contemporary Greek and Etruscan ones. During the Republic ostentatious display was prevented by law, but under the emperors the jeweller came into his own. EMERALDS from new Egyptian mines, PEARLS, AQUAMARINES, SAPPHIRES and sometimes uncut DIAMONDS now appeared, while the old techniques of granulation and FILIGREE almost vanished. Decoration was chiselled on plain surfaces, but in the later Empire from *c.* A.D. 200 the gold might be cut into a fine fretwork known as *opus interrasile*. Contemporary silversmiths favoured engraved designs filled in with NIELLO. Amber rings, and also small amber pots, distaffs and knife handles, and lumps of amber carved into *objets d'art* were also popular in Roman times. In Britain and Germany JET beads, hairpins, rings and pendants were sometimes used, probably Whitby jet worked at York and exported to the Rhineland in a finished or semi-finished state.

Busts in relief, some of them perhaps portraits, decorated the jet pendants, and portraits occur not infrequently carved on gems. According to Pliny (*Nat. Hist.* xxxiii. 12) Claudius gave permission for the wearing of rings bearing his portrait; but there are also earlier examples, notably a beautiful banded agate in shades of yellow, brown and red carved with a bust of Augustus. The CAMEO, first developed in Hellenistic times, now becomes popular. To obtain the desired effect the weathered surface of a pebble or gem, lighter in colour than the stone it protects, is carved in relief, while the rest of the stone provides a darker background. Imperial portraits again occur, and the subjects for all types of ring with relief decoration include deities, mythological figure-scenes, animals and imaginary monsters. In the 2nd c. A.D. coins of the reigning Emperors were also set in rings.

Although under the Republic and the early Empire gold rings were a sign of rank worn only by certain people, these restrictions soon disappeared and both men and women often wore several. The hoop varied in thickness and was sometimes engraved, bezels tended to be oval rather than the circular type customary in Hellenistic times, and shapes of shoulders varied. Double rings for two fingers are one of the later developments. As well as gold and silver, bronze and iron rings are found, some of them with a small key attached. These may also have been worn round the neck as pendants. The key may have unlocked a *dactyliotheca* or cabinet of rings mentioned in literature of the 1st c. B.C. or the jewel-boxes which appear on women's tombstones.

The diadem is rarely found in Roman times and wreaths are rare, very stylized and chiefly known from south Russian tombs of the first two centuries A.D. and from mummy portraits. Elaborate hair-styles were emphasized by hair-pins with ornamental heads of gold, silver, ivory, jet or bone, carved into busts, small figures, pine-cones, etc. Other pins had heads consisting of a single pearl or gold bead. Hoop ear-rings continued in fashion, sometimes suspended from a long hook. In the 1st c. A.D. a ball of gold or a cluster of glass beads or pearls hanging from an S-shaped hook is found at Pompeii and at sites in the eastern provinces. This was replaced in the 2nd c. by pendants sometimes suspended on chains from a bezel-set stone, a type also found in the west.

Among the most decorative necklaces are those made up of a variety of stones or glass in bezel settings. Simpler chains, sometimes with wheel- or crescent-shaped pendants, are also found. Coins too were turned into pendants. Bead necklaces, including the typical blue-green melon beads, are frequent. Bracelets also included the chain and pendant types, but snake bracelets seem to have gone out of fashion in Italy in the 1st c. A.D. The slip-on bracelet with serpents' heads at the open ends still occurs, but sometimes it has a fastening decorated with a bezel-cut gem. In the provinces bronze bracelets were common and include a slender type made of twisted wire. By the 4th c. broader wrist-bands carved with intricate open-work patterns had appeared.

Brooches and *fibulae* are chiefly found in the western Empire, mostly developed from Celtic prototypes. Occasional gold and silver examples survive, but the majority are of bronze. In the 2nd c. in particular they tend to be decorated with enamel—fish, insects such as ladybirds, and small animals being favourite subjects—as well as with polychrome discs. In fact polychrome decoration for all jewellery increased steadily in popularity throughout the Roman period. Rings set with stones or glass of several colours all round the hoops are a late 3rd-c. and 4th-c. development.

Evidence for the goldsmith's craft is limited to occasional inscriptions and such rare and notable discoveries as the painted Cupids playing goldsmiths on the walls of the House of the Vettii at Pompeii. In the early Empire Alexandria, Antioch and Rome itself were important production centres and their work was probably exported. Craftsmen in other cities may have worked more for local markets. The making of simpler items such as *fibulae* was sometimes included among villa activities as at Anthe, Belgium. Another such centre was at Nornour, one of the Scilly Isles.

See also JEWELLERY.

78, 79, 80, 104, 155, 375, 376, 801.

6. WOOD-WORKING AND TOOLS. Timber played an important part in the life of the ancient world. Its many uses included building, transport by carriage, wagon or ship, and shafts or handles for weapons and tools. Few tools survive from ancient Greece, but from the Roman period they are more plentiful. Carpenters at work, or

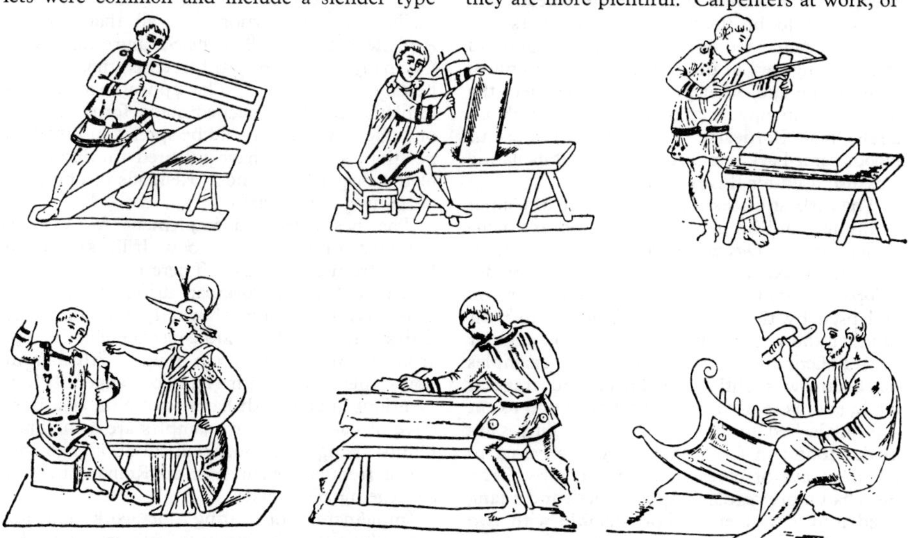

Roman carpenters at work. From a painted glass fragment. Fig. 234 from C. Singer *et al.* (eds.), *History of Technology*, Vol. II (1956)

shown with items of their equipment, appear on Roman tombstones and wall-paintings. These tools bear enough superficial resemblance to their modern counterparts to allow them to be identified, but the expert can find evidence of development and material for closer dating in many details of their design and construction. Tools consist of two essential elements, the handle and the blade, and the methods by which these two were fixed together is one source of chronological information.

Timber used by the early civilizations of the Near East and Greece was only obtainable from certain areas. Often it had to be imported, so for furniture and smaller articles it was used with economy. Flaws were disguised by veneers or paint. Items in the accounts surviving from the erection of the temple of Asklepios at Epidaurus in the 4th c. B.C. give details of the contracts drawn up for the woodwork. The materials include silver fir from Corinth and cypress probably from Crete. Beams six to nine metres long were transported in wagons, probably three to a load. The first building seems to have been a workshop and for this elm, nettle-tree wood and box were used, perhaps obtainable locally. Cypress and box were used for ceiling coffers in the temple, cypress and elm for the doors, and box for mouldings and door-hinges. Treaties were made between different cities for the sale of wood and the employment of carpenters. Craftsmen were one of a city's assets and in an emergency might be needed at home to build fortifications.

Rome was far better off for timber supplies. Oak, fir, beech, holly, lime and yew were all used, and in addition certain imported woods such as Syrian cedar and citrus wood from Africa. Gaul was particularly well endowed with forests, and lumber could be floated down the rivers and shipped from Mediterranean ports. Guilds of workers engaged in the timber trade are known from Rome and other places—among them the *lignarii*, who appear moving a tree-trunk on a relief from Bordeaux. Veneering with precious woods came back into fashion, and metal-plating was also used for this purpose.

The earliest Greek metal tools were of copper or bronze, and bronze axes and adzes are mentioned in the *Odyssey*. Double axes or tools combining axe and adze blades had also developed, and all these types were copied in iron and used by the Romans, who added to their number the axe-hammer. The saw is another very ancient tool. The early bronze examples had a narrow, slightly curved blade and irregular teeth, and were used with a pulling action to cut a beam lashed to an upright post. Tiny saw-blades found in Crete may have been used to cut the teeth of bone or wooden combs. Iron saws had more regularly spaced teeth and a tang fixed into a wooden or horn handle with two rivets. A well-preserved example comes from the Glastonbury lake village (Somerset) of *c*. 200 B.C.

The Romans introduced several improvements, including the important one of setting the teeth so that they projected right and left alternately. Pliny (*Nat. Hist*. xvi. 83) mentions this, although he does not entirely understand its advantages. Saws with teeth of this type could be pushed as well as pulled and they have straight handles; the wood could be placed on a stool and kept in position by the carpenter's knee or hand. The next problem was finding a means to use a longer blade without buckling. One method was to extend the handle along the top of the blade, but the more popular solution was to fix the blade in some form of frame. A type found in Egypt has a piece of wood bent like a bow for the frame, each of the ends being attached to one end of an iron saw blade. This type of tool may have been developed in Greece. Much more common is the blade fixed into two wooden uprights connected by a cross-bar. Above this was another cross-bar or a cord tied to the uprights and tightened with a toggle-stick, although this is a detail often omitted by artists. This tool could also be used as a double saw. The timber is placed across a sawing horse or, for double sawing, one craftsman might stand on a plank raised on trestles. The frame-saw was made in various sizes.

There is a tradition that the plane was a Greek invention but there is no real evidence for this as the earliest examples known come from Pompeii. Pliny, however, writing in the 1st c. A.D., seems well acquainted with this tool. Planes also were made in varying sizes and their details differ. The majority consisted of a narrow blade wedged at an angle so that it protruded through the iron sole of a box-like body. Wood was used for the body, but as time went on much of this tended to be replaced by iron and normally the iron portions are all that survive. A plane lost in a well at the Saalburg fort, West Germany, however, still retains most of its beechwood handles. The appearance of this implement, which needed some form of table on which the wood could be spread and fixed in position, seems to have inspired the invention of the carpenter's bench. Remains of one were also found at the Saalburg.

The best recorded implement for making holes in timber is the bow-drill, known in Egypt from *c*. 2700 B.C. There is a representation of a Roman workman using one but the artist has mistakenly shown him holding the drill stock round the middle instead of at the top. Iron spoon-bits are often found, either from bow-drills or used with a handle as augers. Pliny mentions augers with handles of elm, ash, box, olive or oak, and bone examples are sometimes found. Tanged and socketed chisels and gouges are of frequent occurrence on Roman sites, as also the mortise chisel.

Implements for setting out work and for measurement are favourite subjects for the tombstones of Roman carpenters. The marks of the points of bronze dividers are sometimes visible, and these were used for transferring measurements from rulers as well as for drawing circles. The rulers show the Roman foot of *c.* 39·5 centimetres divided into four *palmi* or 12 *unciae*. Folding rules of bronze also survive. Several types of set-square are depicted, and also a level consisting of three pieces of wood joined together to make an 'A' with a plumb-bob suspended by a line from the top corner. This type is first found in Egypt in the 14th c. B.C. Evidence for tool-bags is lacking, but leather bags or baskets are a possibility and a bucket out of the Saalburg well contained an assortment of axes and chisels.

Hellenistic or Roman woodwork surviving from Panticapaeum in the Crimea includes boxes with sliding lids. At Pompeii and Herculaneum doors, panelled and trellised partitions and staircases have been found, as well as furniture. Pliny (*Nat. Hist.* xvi. 82) mentions panelled doors made in the Greek, Campanian or Sicilian styles, and recommends fir as the best material. The Herculaneum survivals may be of Campanian type. How did they differ from the others? Was there another style in Roman Egypt, which has produced panelled cupboard doors similar to the one visible in the Simpelveld sarcophagus, now in the Leiden Museum? One from Abusir dating from the 2nd c. A.D. is in the Berlin Museum. Another example of later date from the Fayûm is at the City Museum, Bristol. They show that the craftsmen who constructed them must have had a variety of implements, including about six different types of plane, in their tool-kits. See also WOOD-WORKING.

117, 118, 318, 770.

7. FURNITURE. Remains of ancient furniture before the Roman period are practically nonexistent, and they remain rare for many centuries thereafter. Occasionally wooden fragments are preserved in especially damp or dry conditions or metal objects such as couch-rests, folding-stools or tripods turn up in hoards or burials. The chief exceptions are the couches and tables found at Herculaneum and Pompeii. Otherwise we must either look back at earlier finds of furniture from the Near East and EGYPT or rely on pictorial evidence from paintings and sculptured reliefs and statues. Furniture so depicted is apt to be shown in use with the details of chairs or couches obscured by the persons or draperies of the occupants. Despite such limitations, however, much can be learnt from the lively scenes portrayed on Greek vases or in Roman funerary reliefs. Some assistance is also obtainable from literary evidence, particularly on the subject of materials. Timber was naturally the favourite, but bronze, iron and stone played a part. Glue was used by both Greeks and Romans and according to Pliny (*Nat. Hist.* xvi. 226) only woods which could take glue easily were acceptable. Other fastenings included wooden dowels or tenons and metal hinges. Beech was a favourite material and, like ash, especially suitable for couch-frames as was cypress for articles liable to hard usage such as chests. Oak, willow, fir, cedar and holly are also mentioned. Varieties of maple were prized for their grain and colour, and cheaper timber was often veneered with more decorative woods or metal, TORTOISESHELL or bone. Cheaper furniture might be painted to imitate such veneers. Cedar was imported from Crete, Syria or Africa; but the most prized wood was citron from north-west Africa, which was so popular that the supply became exhausted. Cicero is said to have given a million sesterces for a citron table.

Greek interests tended to lie outside the home, so at first houses were sparsely furnished for sleeping and eating, with simple stools and beds with wooden frames standing on four legs and filled in with a network of cords or leather thongs. Such beds continued in use for the poorer people and one appears in a painting from the Catacomb of St. Callixtus. Beds, however, soon increased in importance, especially since from *c.* the 6th c. B.C. it became customary to use them also as couches and to recline on them at banquets. Egyptian influence is obvious in the early Greek couches with animal legs, but the vertical Egyptian foot-board and separate head-rest were not adopted. From the 8th c. onwards couches with carved or painted rectangular supports with cut-out incisions halfway down became popular, and these seem to have been a Greek innovation. Sometimes they flared out at the head into decorative finials which could be used to support a pillow. Decorative motifs included the PALMETTE and volute. The best work dates from the 5th c. Turned legs, also a result of Egyptian influence encouraged perhaps by the invention of the lathe, survived with varying degrees of popularity well into the Roman period. Decorated with a variety of mouldings, they had various degrees of elaboration and sometimes became dangerously slender above flaring feet.

Turned legs, sometimes joined by stretchers, were also used for the *diphros*, a backless STOOL. Simple forms of this appear on the Parthenon frieze, while lower stools with undecorated legs were used by workmen. Other seats consisted of rectangular boxes, the sides painted with geometrical motifs or figures, and these were sometimes wide enough to support several people. The folding stool (*diphros okladias*), another Egyptian legacy, with two pairs of animal legs ending in hooves or claw feet, was popular and is frequently depicted on 6th-c. and 5th-c. black-figure vases.

At the opposite extreme to the stool was the throne, reserved for deities, rulers and important dignitaries. As with couches, the throne occurs with legs ending in animal feet or with turned or rectangular legs. Greek examples of the first variety found in the 6th and the 1st half of the 5th centuries B.C., however, had improved on the Egyptian prototypes by adding arm-rails and decorative finials such as gracefully carved birds to the backs. Human figures might help to support the seat or lions rampage along the stretcher-bars. The thrones with turned or rectangular legs might also have stretcher-bars, arm-rails and low backs. Elaborate and delightful decoration is a feature of these thrones. Sphinxes support arm-rails and animal heads appear with backs of varying height. Homer mentions gold inlay, silver studs and many colours; the Parthenon accounts list items with backs inlaid with ivory; and other writers, including Pausanias, mention precious stones, painted animals and wrought images.

To the Greeks we owe the most graceful chair ever invented, the KLISMOS. It had a seat filled in with plaited thongs, stood on curving legs, and the back was constructed of three uprights fitted on to a curved board at shoulder height. Comfortable and easily portable, it occurs in many intimate scenes on vase paintings. Undecorated, it reached the height of elegance in the 5th c. It remained popular until the Roman period, but in later examples the curves had become excessive and the back-board clumsy.

Rectangular foot-stools, sometimes with inlaid sides or resting on claw feet, are frequently represented especially along with couches and thrones. Standing in front of many couches are also the small individual light tables, one for each diner. The tops were round on three bandy animal legs, or oblong with two legs at one end and a third in the middle of the other end. Four-legged rectangular tables also occur, usually with stretcher-bars, and some of them were obviously work-tables.

Vase paintings show that the Greeks tended to hang their possessions up on the wall or put them on shelves, so furniture for storage never acquired great importance. Chests of all sizes for clothing and valuables are known, however, with curved, flat or gabled covers, and examples used as coffins survive from the 4th c. B.C. in southern Russia. The best set of illustrations for the furniture of this period is to be found on an Apulian volute *krater* by the 'Darius painter', now in the Museo Nazionale, Naples. It shows the emperor Darius and his councillors.

By Hellenistic times deities and important theatre-goers were provided with thrones having stone seats, often solid blocks of stone with rounded or rectangular backs. Simpler forms are known from earlier times, but from the 3rd c. B.C. the bases tended to be carved with animal legs or foreparts in relief. Late Hellenistic examples survive from the theatres at Delos, Priene, etc. A number of such thrones of varying dates from the theatre at Athens include the throne of the priest of Dionysos Eleutherios with reliefs inside the back, on the arms and across the front of the seat depicting satyrs, Erotes with fighting cocks and Orientals battling with monsters. Also of Hellenistic date is a new and larger table, which was used out of doors and perhaps functioned rather as a sideboard. It consisted of a rectangular slab of stone or possibly wood resting on two transverse stone supports, often elaborately carved with ACANTHUS foliage. The cupboard with wooden doors and shelves was also probably a development of this period, used to house statuettes or the book-rolls of the growing libraries.

Greek ideas on furnishing had spread to Etruria by the 6th c. B.C. The pieces tended to be very massive and are well illustrated in the tombs at Tarquinia (paintings) and Cerveteri (carvings). A comfortable chair with a barrel-shaped base and a back curving round to form arms may have been a native invention. It survives in bronze or stone, but may also have been made in wood or wickerwork. A circular coffer (*cista*) of wood or bronze was another development, and the bronze survivals are engraved with lively scenes and stand on low feet.

Rome at first carried on earlier traditions such as couches with elaborate head-rests and foot-rests decorated with inlays and finials of Erotes, heads of mules, swans or even elephants. Their rails were also inlaid and the turned legs were sheathed in bronze. This is the type found in the bedrooms of Pompeii and Herculaneum, and they could be objects of great luxury. By the end of the 1st c. A.D., however, the elaborate head-rests tended to disappear, being often replaced by a high back and sides the front edges of which were sometimes decorated with dolphins. The spread of Roman civilization is well shown by the occurrence of such couches on tombstones and sarcophagi from all over the empire. With them as part of the funeral banquet scene frequently appears the small bandy-legged table, sometimes plain but more often having its three legs decorated with animal heads and ending in claw feet. Actual tables from Pompeii and Herculaneum include a heavier marble variety with lion or panther heads rising out of a band of acanthus foliage. A Pompeian bronze table has the heads and foreparts of dogs apparently climbing up it, and one of wood from Herculaneum has lion–griffin heads with outstretched tongues, the band of acanthus being here replaced by fluting. In southern Britain Dorset craftsmen seem to have been acquainted with all these motifs as is evidenced by a number of table-legs made of Kimmeridge shale, a kind of oily slate, which have survived. The griffin with its outstretched tongue is the favourite, but on several examples this motif is combined with part of a second animal (? dog) climbing up, perhaps to attack it—an interesting development. Tables standing on a single leg decorated with animal heads are sometimes found in Italy and elsewhere, and sturdy work-tables and benches of wood also appear on reliefs and wall-paintings. At Pompeii and Herculaneum there survive examples of the rectangular slab on carved stone supports. The fine carvings now include griffins as well as foliate motifs.

Thrones with turned or rectangular legs with cut-out incisions continued in use, as did the throne with solid sides though now with a back of varying height. The Etruscan armchair with curved back and sides became popular. Though they were usually of wood, some reliefs show that they were also made of wickerwork, the pattern of the weave varying. Two full-scale stone models with very low arms found in a 2nd-c. tomb at Weiden, near Cologne, are unoccupied and so provide evidence of the existence of a seat-cushion. Reliefs depicting the wooden chairs show that some of them had bases with panelled sides. One suspects that this comfortable chair was speedily adopted in the provinces. The *cathedra*, a clumsier variant of the *klismos*, does not seem to have been so widespread outside Italy. Stools of *diphros* type continued in use, and actual wooden legs have been found in Egypt. On some Gallic reliefs clerks sit on box-like seats or wickerwork tuffets or panelled chairs at substantial wooden counters. Folding chairs remained great favourites. A heavier type with curved legs was adopted as the *sella curulis* of the magistrate, but it was also used more generally. Examples of the straight-legged folding stool have survived and include one from Ostia plated in silver, and stools with several pairs of legs appear on reliefs. Several iron stools have been preserved from sites in Britain, Belgium, Bulgaria, etc., and these have one seat-bar divided in half, each piece being supported by a bracket. The reason for this is obscure. Romans sat on such stools with one bar under the thighs and the other at the back. One or more cushions were customary, and possibly the split seat-bar prevented the front bar cutting into the sitter's legs. Small bronze sandalled feet have been discovered which may have decorated folding stools or collapsible tripods which supported trays or bowls. These were usually of bronze and often elaborately decorated with human or animal heads, but a beautiful silver example, and also a three-legged table, survive in the HILDESHEIM TREASURE dated to the early 1st c. A.D.

Footstools, chests—often sheathed in iron—and even a wooden cradle on rockers from Herculaneum are other articles of furniture in use at this period. The Romans also had shelves and a variety of CUPBOARDS for use as bookcases, wardrobes or *lararia* for the household gods.

In addition to the couches, tables, etc., the soft furnishings must not be forgotten, although as textiles are so perishable some imagination is needed to recreate ancient interiors and we lean heavily on the literary evidence. The Homeric heroes seem to have had pillows, bed-coverlets and skin rugs. Fabrics of wool or linen with decorations of woven designs, EMBROIDERY or even paint occur in Greco-Roman antiquity, and an inscribed list of furnishings belonging to Alcibiades and his associates includes mattresses and stuffing for both mattresses and pillows, as well as rush mats. Decorative draperies were also spread over couches and chairs for daytime use, and some couches had valances. Mattresses tended to increase in thickness and with their decorative covers are a noticeable feature of such Roman reliefs as the monument of the Haterii (1st c. A.D.). Stuffing for both mattresses and pillows was of wool or down, while poorer people might use straw or leaves. Curtains hung from wood or metal curtain-rings sometimes replaced partition walls in houses or even cupboard doors. Table-cloths appear on Gallo-Roman reliefs. All these textiles were gaily coloured, and furniture might be painted, veneered or decorated with inlays including multicoloured glass. When placed in rooms with elaborate wall-paintings and polychrome mosaics they must have presented a brilliant spectacle, preserved for us by such scenes as the Pompeian painting of Venus and Mars from the House of Marcus Lucretius Fronto. Here we see purple, scarlet or green coverlets, others striped in scarlet and yellow, and some embellished with a gold fringe.

358, 534.

8. GLASS. Recent research suggests that glass-making originated in western Asia about the middle of the 3rd millennium B.C. The few examples of such early date which survive mostly consist of beads or small heads, obviously rare and precious objects. By 1500 B.C. glass vessels were appearing in Mesopotamia and north Syria, and soon after they are found in EGYPT. By 1200 B.C. there may have been workshops in Cyprus and the Aegean, but the disasters which mark the end of the Bronze Age led to a decline in glass-making.

Glass is produced by heating silica, lime and soda in a crucible until they fuse together into a liquid of high viscosity. In the Late Bronze Age four methods were used for making vessels. In one the methods of the stone-cutter were employed to grind and polish a shape made out of a lump of glass. In a second glass rods of various colours were cut up and the pieces fixed with an adhesive over a core. The result was placed in an outer mould and heated until the pieces fused, producing mosaic glass. Or powdered glass was placed between the outer and inner moulds, a method which could also be used for statuettes and other objects. The most popular process, however, for small narrow-mouthed vessels made use of a core of sand or mud and straw fixed to a metal rod. This core was dipped in molten glass, the outer surface smoothed, and threads or blobs of coloured glass were often added for decoration. Handles and footstands were added as required, the core was removed and the rim attached. Materials used to colour glass included oxides of copper, iron and manganese.

The next important period of glass-making begins in Mesopotamia and on the Syrian coast in the 9th c. B.C. The same techniques continued, but the glass made in a mould was now clear instead of opaque and might have ground or polished decoration. A fine omphalos bowl from a grave at Gordion dated to the 8th c. B.C. has a cut pattern of fluting or petals, copying contemporary metal bowls, and this type also occurs in 5th-c. and 4th-c. contexts. By this time glass-making was probably also being carried on in Crete and the Aegean, possible sources for the green or yellow moulded vessels of this period. The core technique also continued in use for handled bottles and jugs, and examples dating from the 5th c. have been found in Etruria. Discoveries of other vessels suggest that the industry may have started in northern Italy as early as the 8th c.

By the late 4th c. B.C. glass was being made in Syria and on Rhodes and Cyprus. In the 3rd c. an important type of moulded bowls in green, blue, wine-coloured or almost colourless glass from Syria were being widely exported to many Hellenistic regions in the eastern Mediterranean. By the 1st c. B.C. these bowls were decorated with external horizontal ribbing, the precursors of the pillar-moulded bowl which was widespread in Italy and western Europe a century later. The Syrian techniques spread to Egypt, where no glass had been made since the Bronze Age, and glass-houses were set up in Alexandria soon after the city's foundation in 352 B.C. These produced fine cast, cut and polished vessels of various shapes and colours, some of which occur at sites in Greece. A late 3rd-c. burial at Canosa, Italy, contained ten glass vessels including two shallow dishes, one painted and gilded on the exterior and the other a mosaic; a deep-blue bowl; and a cup with winged handles on a tall footstand. A deep bowl was decorated with wheel-cut grooves and petal designs, and had a band of almond-shaped raised bosses outside the lip. Another bowl was moulded in two layers fitting over one another; between the layers is a highly complicated design based on the ACANTHUS and cut out in gold leaf. This bowl and the mosaic were both Alexandrian work. All these glasses are in the British Museum. Workers from Syria and Egypt must soon have set up glass-houses elsewhere, and their products went as far afield as southern Russia. In Italy the industry grew noticeably from the 3rd c. B.C. onwards, using Hellenistic techniques which were probably brought by Alexandrian craftsmen to Campania.

Towards the end of the 1st c. B.C. glass blowing was developed, possibly by Syrian or Phoenician workers who realized that it was easier to maintain an even flow of molten glass into a mould by inflation than by pouring. A lump of molten glass was picked up with the end of an iron blowpipe, slightly inflated, and shaped either in a mould with tools or on a flat surface. Then it was re-heated and blown into its final shape. This process enabled a much wider range of vessels to be made, often in thinner, clearer glass and at much greater speed. Early in the 1st c. A.D. glass-blowers had set up factories in Italy, and there were Alexandrian workmen at the mouth of the Volturnus and Syrians in Rome itself. Pliny (*Nat. Hist.* xxxvi. 195) mentions that the industry had spread to Gaul and Spain. The great Syrian glass-maker who signed his cups 'Ennion' seems to have set up subsidiary factories, one of them perhaps at Aquilea, and such Syrian-type glass was widely exported and has been found in Germany and Britain. By the middle of the 1st c. glass was being made in the Rhône valley, and recent investigation has shown that glass-houses at Cologne may date from this time. Similar developments took place as far east as Parthia and the Crimea.

Roman glass-makers gradually developed a wide range of types and a considerable repertory of ornament. In addition to blown glass, mosaic glass was developed into the MILLEFIORI wares which had a wide distribution in the 1st c. A.D., and moulded vessels with lathe-cut decoration which may have been an earlier Alexandrian invention. Cameo glasses, in which a design was cut through a surface layer of white fused on to a darker ground, were found at Pompeii, and the PORTLAND VASE is a famous example of this technique, which is said to have inspired Josiah WEDGWOOD. Colourless glass also became fashionable and was extensively produced at Cologne until the 3rd c., when coloured wares returned to favour. Mould-blown wares might depict elaborate scenes like the circus cup from Colchester, which shows a chariot race and includes the names of the participants. A flask from Cyprus takes the form of a curly-headed youth, and a two-handled flask blown in a bipartite mould resembles a bivalve shell with neck and handles added. Elegant flagons with slender necks and tooled spiral ribbing round the body, more stalwart jugs with ribbed handles and many small perfume flasks are other 1st-c. types.

After the 1st c. there seem to have been frequent contacts between the glass-houses of the east and west, partly through exports but much more through Syrian and Egyptian craftsmen migrating to Gaul and the Rhineland. Glass-making gradually spread north from southern France. An inscription of *c.* A.D. 200 from Lyon mentions a Carthaginian glass-worker, Julius Alexander. In the 2nd c. sturdy green bottles of square or hexagonal shape with one or two handles were being made in the Amiens–Abbeville area. These were often used as cremation urns. Smaller, more elegant jugs in green or blue were also made and sometimes decorated with medallions attached at the base of the handle. A pale-blue example from Litlington, Cambridgeshire, has a mask of Medusa at this place. By the 3rd c. factories in the same area or further east may have made the barrel jugs (*barillets*) with horizontal ribbing, sometimes signed 'Felix' or 'Frontinus'.

Further east still, probably in Belgium, flasks fashioned to look like bunches of grapes were produced. Dull-looking objects at first sight, when lit up they glow realistically in purple or green. They may have been made around Namur, and were perhaps inspired by Syrian prototypes. Trail ornament, threads of glass trailed round a vessel in a variety of patterns, may have originated in Syria and there the threads are usually the same colour as the vessel they adorn. In the Seine–Rhine area, however, especially at Cologne, this trail or snake-thread decoration is usually multicoloured. There it was popular from *c.* A.D. 200 for over a century.

In the 2nd and 3rd centuries the Egyptians were producing glasses with wheel-engraving and facet-cutting to depict mythological scenes. Some of these were imported into western Europe perhaps by Egyptian craftsmen, who continued to develop these techniques in Italy and the Rhineland. In the early 4th c. a number of bowls with free-hand flint-engraved decoration were made at Cologne. Two found their way to Britain, one depicting a Bacchic scene with dancers (Dorchester Mus.) and the other a lively hare hunt (Ashmolean Mus., Oxford). A similar type of hunting scene was found at Bonn and a chariot race appears on a bowl from Cologne, which also has a head of the sun god as a centre-piece.

Another late development is the CAGE-CUP or *diatreta* made from a thick hollow blank of glass from which a pattern was ground until it stood out like a delicate tracery around the cup. Sometimes this cage is a different colour from the cup it encloses and beautiful examples can be seen in the Museums at Cologne and Trier. Other cups have figure decoration in high relief instead of the cage; one now in Venice has a frieze of huntsmen and a silver-gilt handle. The cup in the British Museum showing the death of Lycurgus is cut similarly. Of opaque

Diatreta from the burials of the villa at Cologne-Braunsfeld. (Römisch-Germanisches Mus., Cologne)

green glass, it glows red when lit up, a characteristic it shares with the Belgian grape-flasks. The distribution of cage-cups in the Rhineland, and the fragments of them found in Britain and some of the eastern European provinces, may indicate an Italian centre, perhaps at Aquileia, with a possible subsidiary at Cologne. Also of Italian origin may be a group of 3rd-c. or 4th-c. vessels with gilded decoration between two layers of glass, descendants of the earlier find in the grave at Canosa. The majority of them have been found in the Roman Catacombs. These also occur in Rhenish graves.

Ancient glass preserved through the centuries, usually in graves, is one of the most beautiful legacies from the past, and no mere description can do it justice. Its variety is so great that it can only be fully appreciated by detailed surveys combined with the study of such outstanding collections as those of the British Museum, the Römisch-Germanisches Museum, Cologne, the Maison Curtius, Liège, or the Corning Museum of Glass, to mention but a few. Other uses for glass include the manufacture of window-panes, known in Italy from the 1st c. onwards. The glass-houses making them in Rome were in trouble in the 3rd c. when the smoke from their furnaces led to their removal to a special quarter. (See WINDOW-GLASS.) Glass MIRRORS backed with tin or lead, replacing the earlier polished metal and occasional black glass varieties, seem to date from the Roman period. Glass *tesserae* were also used for mosaics, particularly for walls. Several survive lining fountain niches at Pompeii and Herculaneum. Decorative glass inlays, and jewellery ornamented with lumps of glass instead of precious stones, also occur.

See also GLASS.

114, 268, 343, 344.

9. LEATHER. By Greek times the processing of the hides of larger animals and the skins of smaller ones and their treatment was well understood. For tanning tannic acid, usually made from oak bark or oak-galls, was the chief agent. The hide was stretched out and worked with a blunt tool until it was supple. A stiff leather could also be made by soaking in alum. This was called in Latin *aluta* and was often dyed gay colours. Sinews and thongs were used to stitch the pieces together.

In ancient Greece clothes and boots made from pelts with the fur worn inside were gradually relegated to shepherds and other country folk; they were also worn by Roman slaves and tended to become somewhat malodorous. In Homer's day shields, etc. were already of leather (see ARMS AND ARMOUR) as well as caps, clothes, wine-skins, bed-covers, bags and other small containers. Boots and shoes often had goatskin uppers and soles of cow-hide or wood. Hides were imported into Greece from the Black Sea, Cyrenaica, Sicily and Asia Minor. Like the maker of fish-sauce, the tanner was not popular with his neighbours. He was often relegated to a special quarter and is the butt of some of Aristophanes's jokes. Even so the tanners were well-to-do and formed some of the oldest and most powerful of the craftsmen's guilds.

Excavations have so far revealed few traces of Greek tanneries. More is known of Roman establishments, including a converted house at Pompeii. The hides arrived in bundles of 10 and were worked in the former atrium. Pits in a room behind were used for tanning, and the tannic acid was prepared in the peristyle. In the atrium many implements were found, including the characteristic knife with a blade in the shape of a half-moon, and awls. M. Vesonius Primus, the probable owner of this tannery, may have supplied all the small leather-workers' shops in Pompeii. In Britain a small provincial tannery attached at one period to the villa at Lullingstone, Kent, produced evidence for more than 30 boots and sandals, and a large piece of leather.

The Romans were the first to distinguish the furrier from the currier, and there is evidence from Republican times for guilds of both, and also saddle, tent, shield, breast-plate, wine-skin or water-skin and thong makers. Hides formed part of the taxation in kind imposed on Illyria, Gaul, Spain, Britain and the Alpine provinces, and were ear-marked for the needs of the army. Fine leather and furs came from the Near East and from further north.

Pieces of leather, usually calfskin, from tents of the three sizes depicted on Trajan's column survive from military sites such as the forts at Valkenburg, Holland, Birdoswald, England, and Newstead, Scotland, and scholars have differentiated between at least six types of stitches used in sewing the pieces together. Valkenburg also produced interesting examples of the high-peaked military saddle which appears on so many tombstones. The horses were gaily caparisoned, their harness straps and bridles being of dyed leather. Clothing from various sites is usually fragmentary with evidence of careful patching, but a pair of 'bikini' briefs laced up on each hip were found in a London rubbish pit. Similar garments are worn by girls on a mosaic floor from the late villa at Piazza Armerina, Sicily. Julius Caesar noted the skin-covered British boats and the leather sails of the Veneti.

The most prevalent survivals of the ancient leather-workers' activities are footwear. A number of different types of sandals, as well as various forms of protective leggings, were made in Classical Greece as well as low shoes worn by soldiers and shoes with soles reaching 7·5 cm in height worn by actors. A well-known painted amphora of the 6th c. B.C. in the Museum of Fine Arts, Boston, shows a customer standing on the cobbler's bench having a sole cut out round his foot. The cobbler holds a half-moon knife, and lasts and various leather articles are hung up behind him.

Greek fashions were introduced into Italy by the Etruscans and the Romans took to shoemaking in a big way. Factories were developed to supply the army with footwear, which had soles of two or usually three layers of rawhide fixed together with hob-nails, and uppers of open-work straps which laced up so as to leave the toes uncovered. Some of these found at the Swiss legionary fortress of Vindonissa were of goatskin or calfskin. The characteristic sandals consisted of a leather sole held to the foot by a thong passing between the first and second toes and looped round the ankle. These were sufficient for warm climates, but even in Rome more substantial uppers soon developed. There were uppers with cut-out decoration, sometimes threaded with thongs which tied round the leg, and the *calceus*, a bootee in which an upper of leather or cloth covered the foot, was correct outdoor wear with the toga. Later *calcei* were replaced by *gallicae*, shoes of Gallic origin, hob-nailed, with soles of one layer for men or double-soled for farm-workers. These appear in Diocletian's *Edict of Prices* as costing between 60 and 80 *denarii*. Women's shoes found in French graves include goatskin slippers, wool-lined shoes leaving the heel bare, and sandal types with uppers. Wooden clogs were also worn. Women's shoes tend to be made of the softest leathers in bright colours. Men's shoes in general tended to be black, but the Roman aristocracy sported them in yellow, red and green. Purple was the imperial prerogative. Cobbler's shops are not infrequently depicted, the best example perhaps being the Reims rèlief with the workman astride his bench making a shoe, his tools on a rack above, and a basket of shoes on the ground near him. His own shoes seem to have double soles. Actual Roman iron lasts are also sometimes found.

See also LEATHERCRAFT.

10. MUSICAL INSTRUMENTS. The Greeks considered that music was of divine origin and associated with it such mythological characters as Olympus, Apollo and Orpheus. In actual fact it was probably part of a heritage of prehistoric magic, substantially affected by influences from EGYPT, Babylon and Palestine absorbed through Asia Minor and Crete. Its importance for soothing the sick was also realized from early times and stressed particularly by Aristotle and later by Quintilian and Athenaeus. Music was an essential adjunct of the drama.

In Homeric times the Greeks were already singing about the exploits of heroes, and Achilles himself passed his time in his tent with similar songs accompanied on the lyre while from inside Troy came the sounds of the *aulos* and *syrinx*. A dirge was sung at the funeral of Patroclus. Chiron, the wise centaur, is reputed to have included lessons on the lyre in his curriculum, and musical proficiency by heroes and aristocrats was not considered unseemly. In the 7th and early 6th centuries B.C. Sparta seems to have been the centre for music and poetry, and Plutarch mentions the poet Terpander who specialized in poems sung as solos to the accom-

From 6th-c. B.C. kylix showing a shoemaker cutting leather (restored). On the wall hang a half-moon knife, shoes and a hammer, etc. (B.M.)

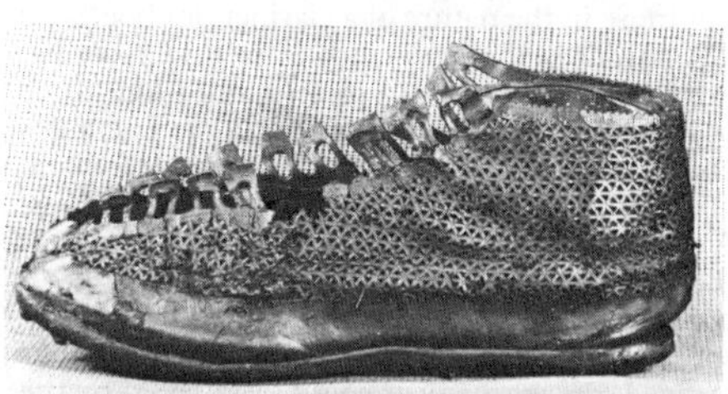

Roman shoe of vegetable-tanned hide. The upper is decorated with cut-out triangles and a series of loops through some of which laces are passed. (Guildhall Mus., London, 2nd c. A.D.)

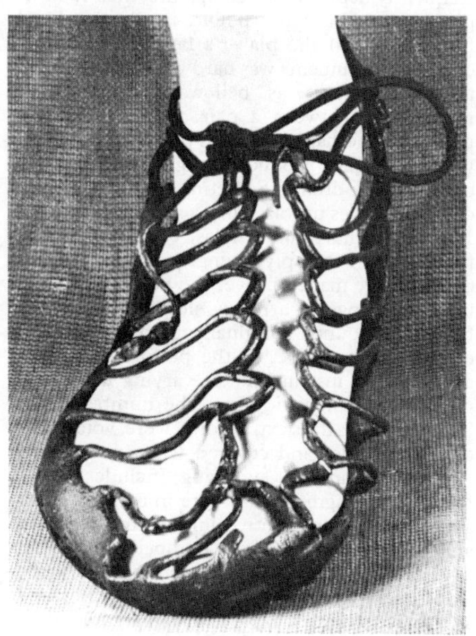

Upper from a pair of Roman women's *sicyonia*, cut from a single piece of vegetable-tanned hide. The cuts are edge-tooled. The lace has a 'spear' point. (Mus. of Leathercraft, 2nd c. A.D.)

paniment of the *cithara*. Musical competitions and choral singing and dancing became a feature of Spartan religious festivals. Later Plato emphasized the importance of music in education and character formation. Certain types of music encouraged bravery, others were effeminate. A youth who could not take his place as singer and dancer with a choir was not well educated. The 5th c. seems to have been the golden age of Greek music. It was disrupted by the troubles at the end of the century, after which musicians were less interested in the old accepted forms and popular music of a more ephemeral nature developed.

In the 4th c. Aristotle still regarded music as important for character building and relaxation. The connection of music with philosophy and mathematics, which goes back to Pythagoras, became increasingly important and the intervals of the scale led to much discussion, continued in the work of Aristotle's contemporary Aristoxenos and in that of Ptolemy in the 2nd c. A.D. Greek melody was based on tetrachords, a group of three or four notes fitted into the interval of a fourth. The last note of the tetrachord could be repeated as the first note of the next to give a succession of seven notes, or a second tetrachord could follow on at an interval of a tone and then the two would give eight notes and form an octave. Within the tetrachord the position of the semitones varied, and these variations were known as modes, which were given regional names: Dorian, Phrygian, Lydian, etc. Finer gradations than the semitone were also used. Choice of mode made a melody sad, effeminate or manly. The theoretical aspects of Greek music need detailed study and are not yet fully understood.

In addition to the literary allusions from about twenty sources, mostly connected with philosophy, acoustics or mathematics rather than practical musical matters, about a dozen musical fragments survive from the Greco-Roman period. These are mostly written on parchment or papyrus in a notation based on the letters of the Greek alphabet which gives few clues as to exact tonality or rhythm. The oral tradition in music-making was strong and long-lived, and the oldest recorded document is a papyrus fragment of the 5th c. B.C., one of the songs of the chorus in Euripides's *Orestes*. Another papyrus fragment, probably from an unknown tragedy of *c*. 250 B.C., is preserved in the Cairo Museum. At Delphi parts of two hymns to Apollo survive, inscribed in stone on the walls of the Athenian treasury. One may have been composed by a prize-winner at the Pythian festival, as it seems to be written in an archaic, academic style. The second hymn describes Apollo's arrival at Delphi, and concludes with a prayer for the Roman

Empire. Both probably date from the middle of the 2nd c. B.C. A song engraved on a column at Tralles, Asia Minor, may be of the same period.

Other fragments were written in the Roman period in the 2nd c. A.D. but may in fact record the work or at least the traditions of earlier times. In Berlin are five fragments of papyrus comprising four lines of a paean on Ajax's suicide, two scraps of instrumental music, half a line from a lyric and 12 lines from another paean said to be in the Hellenistic manner. From Athens come two portions of a hymn to the Muses, and hymns to Nemesis and the Sun which may have been written by Mesomedes in the reign of Hadrian. The list is completed by part of a 3rd-c. hymn from Oxyrhynchus.

Harmony and counterpoint in the modern sense are absent at this early date. The choirs sang in unison or, in the case of mixed choirs, at the interval of an octave. Some elaboration might be permitted in instrumental accompaniments, which could be at the interval of a fourth, fifth or octave, or consist of extra notes to the beat used by the main melodic line. In singing the poetic metre of the lyric shaped the rhythm and the word accents the pitch, producing a very flexible effect. Speeds were moderate and steady, and sudden changes of tempo were disliked. In drama the spoken dialogue was enlivened with vocal solos, often alternating with the choruses.

A vase painting in the Staatliche Antikensammlungen und Glyptothek, Munich, dating to the end of the 5th c. B.C., shows three girls playing the harp, cithara and lyre. This trio represents the most important Greek stringed instruments. The lyre, associated with Apollo, is a more primitive type than the cithara, and was constructed of a tortoise-shell or a wooden bowl covered with skin as a sound-box. From this spring two slender curving arms or horns joined by a cross-bar. The strings, first of hemp and later of gut, were stretched over a bridge between the sound-box and the cross-bar, and kept in place with rolls of greasy skin. The instrument was held slanting or even horizontally away from the player. The earliest lyres, of 9th-c. date, seem to have had three or four strings, but the number gradually increased to 10 or 12 in the 5th c. and after. The instrument was mostly used by beginners and amateurs, and was played with the left hand.

Homer hardly discriminates between the lyre and cithara, but from the 9th c. the cithara appears as a larger wooden instrument with a broader sound-box and more substantial sidepieces, which also helped to amplify the sound. The same number of strings were secured in similar fashion to those of the lyre. The instrument was played with a plectrum by the right hand and with the fingers of the left. The right hand may have swept across the strings in a glissando, while the left hand plucked out the melody or damped or altered the pitch of certain strings. The cithara was held horizontally and sometimes supported by a strap. It was a concert instrument played by professionals who attracted considerable followings and by the Roman period some of them were highly paid for their performances. The crude method of securing the strings with skin was replaced by various devices, some perhaps more like pegs, and one which shifted the entire cross-bar to tighten the strings.

The earliest reference to the harp dates from the 5th c. B.C. Of Oriental origin, it was not as popular as the other stringed instruments. It had 20 strings arranged in 10 pairs tuned in octaves, and sometimes a front pillar. A small boat-shaped example appears on a Roman wall-painting from Stabiae, being idly plucked by a woman who also holds a small cithara. The lute was also rare among the Greeks but more popular with the Romans. It had a small body, a long neck marked out in frets, and up to eight strings passing over a bridge and secured like those of the cithara. It was played with a plectrum.

The major item among the wind instruments was, of course, the aulos. This was not a flute but more in the nature of a clarinet or oboe, with a sonorous, exciting sound. The first recorded virtuoso was Sacadas, prize-winner on three occasions at Sparta in the 6th c. B.C. The aulos consisted of a cylindrical tube of reed, wood, bone, ivory or even metal, built up in sections. A connecting link fitted over one end of this with the conical detachable mouthpiece, usually of bone, inserted into it. It was played with either a single or a double reed. Early auloi have only four or five holes, as many as could be covered by the fingers of one hand. Experiments have shown that more than one note could be obtained from each hole by the method of altering the air-pressure known as over-blowing. Auloi are frequently depicted played in pairs, their mouthpieces stuck through two holes in a leather band fastened round the player's head. Performing on these instruments was hard work as the player used his cheeks as bellows. The musical relationship between a pair of instruments is uncertain; perhaps one aulos played the melody while the other produced long sustained notes or acted as a drone. Sometimes the end of one of a pair curves upwards like a shepherd's crook. Later auloi have more holes, even as many as fifteen. As the supply of fingers ran out various devices were made to cover the holes not in use, including rings or a rotary sleeve which could be turned round. Originally each aulos could only play one mode, so the performer needed a number of instruments of varying mode and pitch. By Hellenistic times the number could be reduced as the extra holes were voiced for different modes and covered when not in use. Actual instruments surviving include a pair found with fragments of a lyre in a 5th-c. tomb at Athens, a bronze votive aulos from Pergamon and two pairs of auloi from Pompeii.

Greek literature and vase paintings show the aulos accompanying singing and dancing and as a solo instrument capable of remarkable feats.

For his prize-winning performance at the Delphic games of 586 B.C. Sacadas is recorded as playing double auloi in a dramatic composition of five movements describing Apollo's battle with the Python, a formidable she-dragon which guarded Delphi. A prelude was followed by the preliminary skirmish, the actual contest, the victory and the Python's death, a piercing harmonic representing its expiring breath.

The Romans inherited from the Etruscans a reed pipe called the *tibia* and this was employed for recreation, festivals and on all occasions of importance. It usually appears on reliefs depicting sacrifices, its music being used to drown any sounds of ill omen which might invalidate the ceremony. It was soon so strongly influenced by the aulos that the two became indistinguishable. To obtain the bass part a special form of tibia was used with a reed inserted into a mouthpiece placed in the side of the instrument. The upper end of the tube was closed. Examples surviving in the British Museum show that each had two groups of three holes. This instrument was more in the nature of a bassoon and may have been a Roman invention. The true cross-flute seems to have been unknown to the Greeks but one was found in an Etruscan tomb of the 2nd c. B.C., the Sepolcro dei Volumni at Perugia. Of more ancient origin was the syrinx or pan-pipes, consisting of up to seven reeds of varying lengths tied together and played like a vertical flute or flageolet, the air being blown across the edges so that no separate reed was necessary. The syrinx was particularly associated with country folk or Dionysiac feasts, and actual Roman examples of bronze, wood and pottery have survived. A set found at Alise-Sainte-Reine, near Dijon, France, has eight tubes drilled through a piece of box-wood. An Alexandrian figurine of the 1st c. B.C. shows a man playing a syrinx with a long hollow cane connecting it to skin bellows which he is working with his foot and compressing with his arms. This may be an early form of the bagpipes known from Roman times. Usually these were played by country folk or low-class musicians, but according to Suetonius the emperor Nero was a performer. The syrinx and bagpipes also have a place as the ancestors of the *hydraulis*, the water-organ invented by Ctesibius of Alexandria in the 3rd c. B.C. and mentioned by Vitruvius and other writers, including Cicero, who considered an organ recital the highest pleasure. A row of pipes (graduated auloi) was set over the holes in a bronze plate covering a wind-chest. Two attendants pumped air into a chamber which contained an inverted bell immersed in water. The balance between the water pressure and the incoming air forced the air up into the wind-chest. Under each pipe was a box with a sliding top with a hole. The keys of a keyboard each pushed in a slide and caused the relevant pipe to sound. Representations of this organ in terracotta and mosaic are known in the Roman period. An example from Carthage in the 2nd c. A.D. shows an organist standing on a pedestal pressing down the keys of an organ with 18 or 19 pipes, and the figures of the blowers appear with an organ depicted on a gem. Actual fragments have been found at Pompeii and Saalburg, but the most exciting survival is the organ from Aquincum (Budapest). It stood on the first floor of the building belonging to the *collegium centonariorum*, a guild connected with textile workers who also acted as the town fire-brigade although in spite of this their hall was burnt down in the 2nd half of the 3rd c. Although the leather bellows and wooden parts of the instrument were destroyed, enough bronze pipes and other fittings survived to permit a reconstruction. It had 52 pipes of varying size in four rows of 13, and four stops. The pipes were bound together by a strap decorated at each end with silver medallions of Eros. The water-chamber is missing as by this time some organs were purely pneumatic. An inscribed bronze tablet attached to the Aquincum organ records that it was presented in A.D. 228 by Gaius Julius Victorinus, a member of the city council and chairman of the fire-brigade.

Other musical instruments were developed for such military purposes as signalling. The Greeks used the *salpinx*, a form of short trumpet mentioned by Homer. Representations of early date show a mouth-band similar to that used by the aulos players. The salpinx grew into the Roman *tuba*, a straight trumpet of bronze, iron or wood, built up with cylindrical sections fitting into each other. The end expanded into a bell and the mouthpiece was conical. It was up to 1·20 m in length, and the length of tube and type of mouthpiece determined the pitch and quality of the sound. The bronze mouthpieces belonging to tubas sometimes survive. The tuba needed vigorous blowing. In the army it was used to signal attack or retreat or to call a halt and to mark the times for changing the guard.

A curved form of trumpet, probably of Etruscan origin, is the *lituus*, and actual Roman examples of it survive in Germany. The best is one found in the Rhine at Düsseldorf, and now in the Saalburg Museum. It is in the key of A with a range of six notes, and may have been used by the auxiliaries for the signals rendered by the legionaries on the tuba. It may be related to the *carnyx* used by the Celts, but the latter had a fierce dragon's head instead of the bell-shaped mouth. Good examples of the carnyx occur in the battle-scenes on the Triumphal Arch at Orange.

Sometimes, instead of being straight, the tuba might be curved into the shape of the letter G. Then it was known as the *cornu*. Bronze remains have been found at Pompeii, but the cornu may originally have been of horn. A wooden cross-bar joined the two sections of the curve. The player held this in his left hand and rested it on his shoulder. The bell-mouth of the cornu was then above his head, facing the direction in which he was marching. One Pompeian example had a tube 3·30 metres long and was tuned in G minor with a range of 17 notes. It may have sounded rather like a modern French horn.

A small curved trumpet which appears on a Mainz tombstone may be the *bucina*, an instrument described but not certainly illustrated. Originally probably made of horn, it seems to have belonged to the countryside. Less powerful than the others, its army use may have been confined to non-tactical signals such as guard-changing. It had, however, the privilege of playing the *classicum*, the salute for the commander-in-chief and other dignitaries.

Percussion instruments such as small drums, tambourines, cymbals, castanets and clappers should not be forgotten. Cymbals played an important part in rituals connected with Dionysus and Cybele, and the *sistrum*, an elaborate rattle, is associated with the worship of Isis. An actual example survives in Switzerland at Vidy.

Greek music teaching was mainly oral and largely by example, the pupil watching and listening to the master. Several vase paintings show such lessons, as do wall-paintings of the Roman period, when the pupils are often girls. A relief found in southern Italy and now in Munich is exceptional. It portrays the master with a lyre and the pupil singing from something written down on a scroll he holds in his hands. Was this music or perhaps just the words of a lyric? At Arles the cithara, lute and organ carved on the sarcophagus of Julia Tyrannia suggest that this was the coffin of an accomplished musician.

Roman concern for clear speech and declamation led to music of an increasingly rhythmic nature being included in education, and contemporary interest in music at this period is probably underestimated. Besides the light music which might enliven the evening after dinner, and the place held by music on religious occasions, orchestras and bands were further developed. When an emperor returned to Rome there was music to greet him, and triumphs were marked by the sound of the tuba. Seneca complains of strident music on the lake at Baiae. Titus sang, Hadrian was a good cithara player, and Nero's activities as singer, instrumentalist and composer are notorious. In the theatre the popular mimes and pantomimes were accompanied by one or more auloi or citharae, panpipes, drums and cymbals, while singers also took part. In some cases theatre orchestras reached such proportions that Seneca declared there were more performers than members of the audience. In the amphitheatre the aulos, the tuba and the cornu were joined by the organ, and they are depicted on mosaics of gladiatorial scenes found at the villas at Zliten in north Africa and Nennig in Germany.

11. TOYS AND GAMES. A set of small Greek painted jugs in the British Museum show scenes of child life in the 5th c. B.C., beginning with a baby kicking his legs through the holes in a turret-shaped high-chair and waving a rattle. The latter probably consisted of discs and rings fixed at the end of a long handle. An alternative would be hinged pieces of wood rattled or clapped together. The small jugs were probably children's gifts to mark the festival of Dionysus. Two such jugs are actually depicted in other scenes from the same series depicting two small boys. One sits on the ground with his jug beside him and holds the pole of a little two-wheeled go-cart complete with a small platform. He is stretching out his hand for a bunch of grapes held out to him by another boy who comes along hauling his cart with his jug on its platform. Pictures of such small carts or hobby-horses are not uncommon, and by Roman times they had developed into small chariots in which a child could stand and drive a team of goats, dogs or even other small children.

Toys on wheels which could be pulled along by a string sometimes survive, and a terracotta example from Athens in the 4th c. A.D. consists of a sturdy horse mounted on four stalwart wheels. Two more such toys from Cologne also have miniature riders. Terracotta animals used as playthings include a wide range of horses, deer, cows, goats, rams, pigs, lions, tortoises, birds and the occasional dolphin. Nibbling mice were favourites, and a small bronze mouse from a Roman grave at York seems more likely to have comforted a child than to have represented religious associations with the underworld. This, of course, is the problem with many of these models. When are they votive offerings and when are they merely toys? Probably it is not necessary to draw too fine a distinction as on reaching adolescence boys might dedicate their toys in a temple of Apollo or Hermes, and girls on the eve of marriage did the same in the temples of Artemis, Aphrodite, Athena or Demeter. Roman girls followed this custom too, first to honour the Lares and later when making a dedication to Venus.

The dog is associated with healing, and canine models are often offerings at healing centres. Several bronze ones come from the Romano-British temple of Lydney, Gloucestershire. But it is difficult to believe that these models, which include a wide range of breeds large and small, are all religious. Representations of live dogs, birds and other creatures frequently appear on children's tombstones, showing that they were cherished as pets. There are other terracottas too, including Greek examples of an old woman on a mule or a donkey with a fish on its back. Some clay animals have been baked with pebbles inside them which rattle. Larger Roman models include a stag and a ram with movable heads found at Kreuznach, Germany.

The history of dolls begins in EGYPT, and several Egyptian rag dolls survive. The oldest examples from Greece are four Boeotian terracottas with long necks and tiny arms, but movable legs attached with wires. They have dresses painted with birds and geometrical motifs.

Some dolls from the 6th c. B.C. have movable arms, and by the middle of the 5th c. legs were attached at the knees. Some of these dolls hold cymbals. No dresses are depicted, so presumably they were clothed by their owners. By the 4th c. legs were hollow, made with knee-joints, and were more carefully inserted instead of dangling loosely on wires. Some dolls have holes in their heads through which strings may have passed to move the limbs puppet-fashion. Early Hellenistic dolls seem to have been modelled on dancing girls with pleated skirts.

Wooden dolls include one 30 cm high with jointed shoulders, hips, elbows and knees, found in the coffin of a 14-year-old girl in Rome. Bone was another material used and the earliest bone doll known is dated to the 3rd c. B.C. Many crudely shaped examples, sometimes with missing limbs which may originally have been of cloth or leather, have been found in the Roman catacombs. A 2nd-c. IVORY doll from a catacomb grave, now in the Vatican Museum, has limbs secured with small pins and the remains of a dress with traces of gold thread. Of much the same date is another ivory doll with articulated limbs found outside Rome with the mummy of an eight-year-old girl. Some attempt to depict contemporary hair-styles is found with dolls of most periods.

The burial of the eight-year-old girl at Rome included miniature pots and a doll's wine service, and similar discoveries are known from other graves. From Athens in the 4th c. B.C. comes a terracotta girl-doll seated in a chair and holding a dove. Beside her are model shoes, a spinning implement and a bowl on a tall stand which may be a marriage-bowl. This may have been the burial of a young bride.

Toys used by older children include balls, hoops and bronze or terracotta tops. Roman reliefs and wall-paintings at Herculaneum show us games of hide-and-seek, blind man's buff, leap-frog or a game in which one child carries another on his shoulders, and the occasional fight. Marbles and nuts were used for other games, and girls in particular played with knuckle-bones thrown up in the air and caught on the back of the hand. Terracotta or stone games-boards, small bone, glass or terracotta counters, and dice, are evidence for early forms of backgammon and draughts, and a war-game called *ludus latrunculorum* was probably played by both children and their elders.

12. GREEK CERAMICS

(*a*) *Technique.* No account survives of the processes used by Attic potters, but recent research has found a practicable solution to the more difficult problems. The principles involved are first that oxides of iron (which are present in most Greek clays) give a red or black colour according as they are exposed during firing to an oxidizing or reducing atmosphere, and secondly that if the particles of clay are fine enough, they will have a sheen. Clay of this fineness cannot be prepared by simple washing; but if such chemicals as potash are added, there is a 'peptic' effect which breaks up the larger coagulations of particles that remain, and the further addition of a 'protective colloid' (as for instance urine) prevents new coagulations. It seems likely then that the Attic practice was roughly as follows. The potter threw his pot, whole or in sections; then he let it dry to a leathery hardness; and next he proceeded to assemble, trim and paint it. In painting he first gave the surface a thin coating of dilute 'peptized' clay which quickly dried on. Next, with or without the aid of preliminary sketches, he painted in the areas which were to be black, using as his pigment a denser solution of the 'peptized' clay; if further detail was wanted—incision, or purple or white paint—it was added at this time. The pot was now ready to be put in the kiln and fired. Since the maximum temperature of firing was *c.* 950 °C., there was no danger of fusion or running, and so pots could be stacked in direct contact with each other. The firing was done in three stages. At first the atmosphere was oxidizing so that the iron oxides became red, the denser 'peptized' parts being naturally deeper in tone. Next, by sealing up the kiln, and perhaps using damp fuel or water, a reducing atmosphere was obtained and the iron oxides turned to grey and black. Lastly, an oxidizing atmosphere was restored and the change back to red begun, but since the denser 'peptized' clay was less pervious or had sintered its reoxidation was retarded or prevented: so in the period when it was not reoxidized and still remained black, but the rest of the pot was reoxidized and so had turned brownish red, the firing was stopped. These tricky processes were most completely mastered in Attica in the 6th c. to the 4th c. B.C., but they were practised with more or less success on most good Greek pottery. See also POTTERY TECHNIQUES.

(*b*) *Decoration.* Painted Greek pottery, of which very much survives, engaged good and even great artists till the 5th c. B.C. But its technique and decorative principles are now strange. The Greeks did not use glaze, though they obtained a smooth sheen by a method (lately rediscovered) of refining their clay. In shapes they had a liking for sharp definition of the parts, realizing that the potter's wheel permits turnery. The decoration, which depends on line—painted or engraved—for its detail, was imposed on the pot with due regard to the shape, and did not until very late pretend to pictorial depth.

By the late 11th c. B.C. the Mycenaean style had become degenerate. Now there was a sudden reformation, aiming at sharper definition of shape and ornament. Free-hand spirals, for instance, were replaced by sets of circles and semicircles drawn with compasses. The decoration was simple and sparing, and soon it became usual to fill in the undecorated areas with dark paint. This *Proto-Geometric* style began at Athens, but quickly spread throughout Greek lands. At the end of the 10th c. the *Geometric* style proper made shapes tauter and decoration more precise. Of its ornaments, constructed still of straight lines and circles, the most characteristic is the key meander, large and lightly hatched, often running round the pot like a belt. Again Athens initiated and most other Greek districts followed. In the 8th c. a richer taste multiplied the bands of decoration over most of the surface of the pot and added the human figure, adapted to Geometric rules of construction.

The *Orientalizing* style, which appeared in the late 8th c. at Corinth and soon elsewhere, replaced the Geometric ornaments by LOTUS flowers, palmettes, volutes and a varied fauna mostly culled from Syria. More significant were the enlargement of the main field and the evolution of the human figures which sometimes occupied it. The strictly Orientalizing style, with its groups or files of lions, bulls, boars, goats, etc., soon became decoratively conventional, and interest turned to human or mythological scenes. The painted terracotta metopes from Thermon show the Corinthian concept of the human figure about 630 B.C., though the technique of vase painting was different. Geometric vase-painters had been content with silhouette, which some of the Greek Orientalizing schools enlivened by drawing the heads in outline. But Corinth quickly preferred the so-called 'black-figure' technique of incising —that is, engraving—details on a full silhouette, with dashes of accessory colour, first purple and then also white. The steady competence of the Corinthian workshops encouraged wide export

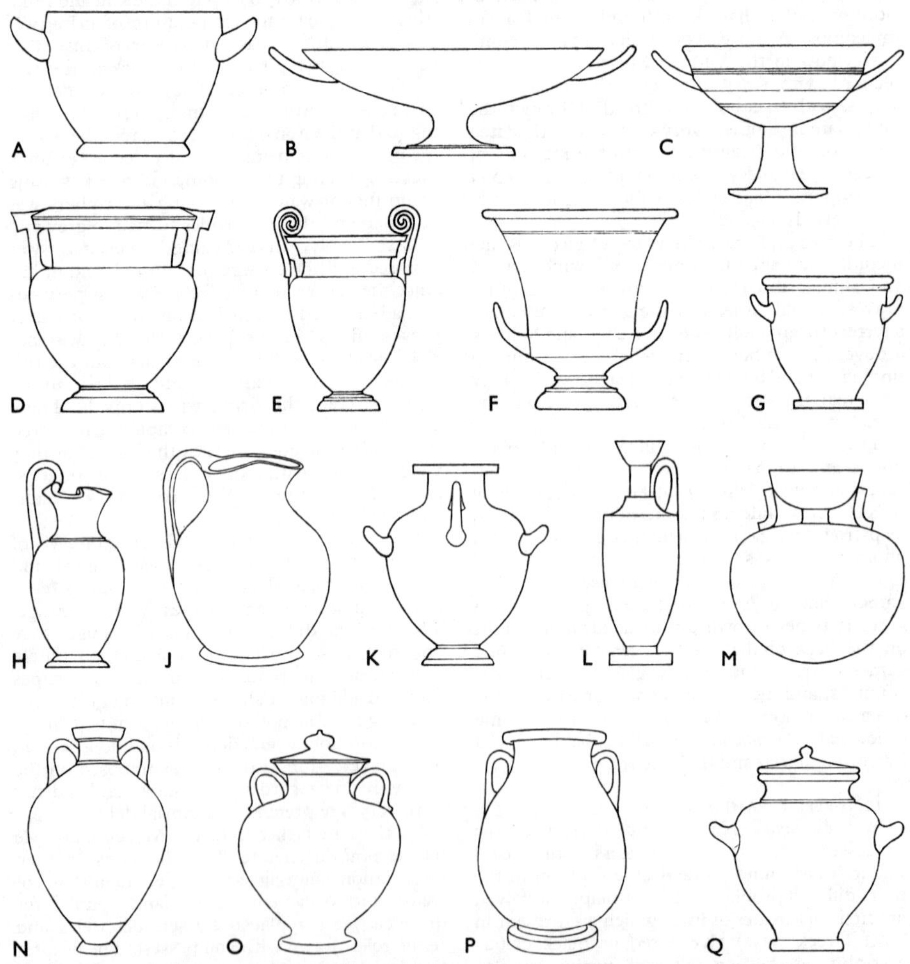

Drinking cups: A. *skyphos*; B. *kylix*, continuous curve shape; C. *kylix*, offset lip shape. Bowls for mixing wine and water: D. *column krater*; E. *volute krater*; F. *calyx krater*; G. *bell krater*. Wine jugs: H. *oinochoe*; J. *oinochoe* (*chous*). Water jar: K. *hydria* (*kalpis*). Oil flasks: L. *lekythos*; M. *aryballos*. Storage jars: N. *amphora* (*panathenaic*); O. *neck amphora*; P. *pelike*. Wine or water container: Q. *stamnos*

and imitation until, in the early 6th c., they succumbed to their Attic rivals, who after two generations of erratic grandeur had around 630 B.C. accepted the black-figure discipline. At Corinth Orientalizing animals remained the staple decoration; Athens in the 2nd quarter of the 6th c. put its faith in human figures, and its well made products with their improved orange-brown clay and black paint set the standard for other Greek schools. The mature Attic black-figure style has a precise vigour and elegance, but the technique was not suited to express quiet moods; and though this was achieved by Execias, its greatest master, it is not surprising that one of his pupils introduced the 'red-figure' technique.

Meanwhile the other Greek schools, which had shown a promising diversity in the 7th c., were more or less exhausted. The fitful skill of Crete soon flickered out. The showy clumsiness of 'Melian', which in the Cyclades had followed several small groups of pleasant mannerists, expired in the early 6th c. Laconian, naïvely sturdy, lasted a generation longer. The Greeks of the eastern Aegean maintained a costive Orientalizing style, which at the end of the 7th c. disastrously adopted the black-figure technique of Corinth; though in the 6th c. eastern Greek workshops occasionally showed originality, they could not withstand the Attic invasion. Boeotia and Etruria, which for long retained some degree of clumsy stylistic independence, were still producing painted pottery, but now it was in awkward imitation of black-figure Attic.

The red-figure technique was a draughtsman's technique. The figures were sketched in outline, details drawn in thin lines of paint and the background filled in with black. The lines used for details were of two kinds—the 'relief line', which stands up like a wire thread, and a flush line, varying in density of colour from black to a golden brown. So far views of figures had been fairly strictly in profile, except that the chest might be frontal. Just before 500 B.C., as in relief sculpture and painting proper, new views of body and limbs were mastered, though the three-quarter head was not accepted till the later 5th c. Expression too of face and gesture grew subtler, and action was no longer essential. In the early 5th c. the red-figure style reached its perfection, if by that is meant the combination of skill and art. The next generation vainly followed picture-painters in the representation of spatial depth or else lost heart, and though respectable work in a mildly Classical style continued into the 4th c. and technical ability was misapplied in more elaborate confections, vase painting sank to a minor art. In Athens the end came around 325 B.C.; a little later in south Italy, where the red-figure style had been transplanted in the later 5th c.

Besides red-figure there was in Athens the 'white-ground' style, best known from the grave *lekythoi* of the 2nd half of the 5th c. These *lekythoi* have a tall cylindrical body, on which is the main field of decoration; it is covered with a white slip. The drawing is often softer than in red-figure, and a wide range of colours is used for drapery. The earlier *lekythoi* show a

Detail from vase painting showing pottery making, including a kiln being fired. (Staatliche Antikensammlungen, Munich)

melancholy grace in their scenes of domestic life or farewell; the later, with a few exceptions are less competent and more emotional.

The principal shapes of Greek painted pottery served constant functions; their variations from one time and place to another were mainly in proportions and finish. The finest period is from the mid 6th c. to the mid 5th c. at Athens. The current names of shapes, though mostly Greek, are not always applied correctly.

2, 42, 104, 114, 117, 118, 136, 263, 264, 267, 343, 358, 375, 376, 385, 481, 503, 534, 550, 623, 624, 631, 684, 703, 719, 777, 778, 802, 887, 889.

GREEK TASTE. The serious study of Greek architecture and design was one feature of the NEO-CLASSICAL movement which spread through most of Europe in the second half of the 18th c. The French architect Jacques-Germain Soufflot (1713–80) was measuring and drawing buildings at Paestum in 1750 and from 1751 to 1755 James Stuart and Nicholas Revett, sponsored by the Society of Dilettanti, were measuring and drawing at Athens in preparation for *The Antiquities of Athens.* From 1764 to 1766 Revett made another expedition, again sponsored by the Society of Dilettanti, to measure and draw the antiquities of Asia Minor and the results of this were published under the title *The Antiquities of Ionia.* Leroy's *Ruines des plus beaux monuments de la Grèce* appeared in 1758 and in 1764 J. J. Winckelmann's *Geschichte der Kunst* for the

Greek Room, from Thomas Hope, *Household Furniture and Interior Decoration* (1807)

first time maintained the absolute superiority of Greek art, encapsulating the spirit of the antique in his phrase 'noble simplicity and calm grandeur'. There followed a long controversy on the respective merits of Greek and Roman architecture and design with Piranesi as the chief proponent of the Roman 'dignity and amplitude'.

Greek taste, *le goût grec*, was, however, both in France and in England, also a superficial fashion in decoration, furniture, bibelots, costume, etc. often with very little at all to do with historical Greek styles. In his *Correspondance littéraire*, May 1763, Baron Grimm remarked that 'all Paris is *à la grecque*'. 'Our ladies have their hair done *à la grecque*, our *petits-maîtres* would be ashamed to carry a snuff-box that was not *à la grecque*.' In costume the mode was caricatured in E.-A. Petitot's *Mascarade à la grecque* (1771). Remarking on the attempt in architecture to return to the good taste of the preceding century, Charles-Nicholas Cochin said: 'And as everything has to be given a nickname in Paris, this was called architecture *à la grecque*, and soon even lace and ribbons were being made *à la grecque*; it remained good taste only in the hands of a small number of people and became a folly in the hands of the rest.' An English impression is given in a letter written by Horace Walpole to Mann, 9 April 1764, in which he says that the French 'believe they make discoveries when they adopt what we have had these twenty years. For instance, they begin to see beauties in the antique—everything must be *à la grecque*.' The absurdities of fashion did not discount the seriousness with which the study of classical antiquity was pursued, although it is a matter of surprise today to realize how very little from pre-Hellenistic Greece was actually known even to Winckelmann. The 'Greek-style' drawings and decorations by Flaxman, Asmus Jakob Carstens and others were based upon vase-paintings found in Italian sites.

See also FURNITURE (EUROPEAN).

244, 414.

GREENWICH ARMOURY. The only outstanding English armour-making workshop, established by Henry VIII at Greenwich Palace. Its origins are probably to be found in two small workshops set up at Greenwich in 1511, of which one was staffed by Milanese and the other by armourers from Brussels. The main workshop was, however, founded in 1515 and staffed with a group of 'Almayns', that is Germans and Flemings, whence it was usually referred to as the 'Almayn Armory'. It remained in existence until the outbreak of the Civil War in 1642, though when it was finally closed few if any aliens appear to have been employed there. The most important of the Master Workmen who successively controlled it were Erasmus Kyrkenar, *c.* 1525–67; John Kelt, 1567–77; Jacob Halder, 1577–1607; and William Pickering, 1607–18.

The Almayn Armory was a private one, making armour for the king's own person and members of his household, though privileged persons could purchase a suit there on production of a royal warrant. The output of the shop was far smaller than that of the great Continental centres, though the quality of work was always of the highest. The key to the identification of the Greenwich style is an album of line and wash designs—now in the Victoria and Albert Museum—for armours made in the workshop for various Elizabethan notables, whose names appear on them. Two of the drawings bear the name 'Jacobe'—whence it is commonly called the *Jacobe Album*—which can be identified with virtual certainty as that of the German Jacob Halder, Master Workman from 1577 to 1607. Some of the actual armours can be identified, the majority in the Tower of London Armouries and the Metropolitan Museum of Art, New York. See ARMS AND ARMOUR.

75, 197, 213.

GREENWOOD, FRANS (1680–1761). Dutch engraver on GLASS to whom is usually attributed the invention of the technique of diamond-point stipple engraving. Born at Rotterdam, perhaps of English parents, he worked in Dordrecht from 1726. His earliest known signed work, dated 1720, is a wine-glass decorated with line engraving showing figures from Italian Comedy. Signed examples of his stipple engravings are dated between 1722 and 1755. See GLASS (NETHERLANDS).

GREETINGS CARDS. See POSTAL COMMUNICATIONS, PICTORIAL.

GRIFFIN (GRYPHON). A fabulous beast with the body of a lion and the head and wings of an eagle. In Greek legend (Herodotus, Pliny) the griffins were guardians of the gold in Scythia. Representations of griffins were common in ancient Assyrian and Greek art. They are a familiar motif in European decorative art and in heraldry. (The griffin is the badge of the Society of Gray's Inn.) The device appears in

The Griffin of the Honourable Society of Gray's Inn

Tenniel's illustrations of the Gryphon for *Alice in Wonderland*.

901.

GROLIER, JEAN (1479–1565). French bibliophile and financier, son of Étienne Grolier of Lyon, whom he succeeded as treasurer of the Duchy of Milan (1510–20) during the French occupation. By his marriage in 1520 with Isabelle-Anne Briçonnet, Grolier allied himself with one of the most influential banking families in France. After leaving Italy for Paris in 1521 he held various offices connected with the administration of the royal revenues, becoming Treasurer-General of Finance in 1547, a post he held until his death. It is primarily as a bibliophile that Grolier is remembered. His library, of which nearly 600 volumes survive out of a probable total of 3,000, contained the finest examples of Renaissance printing and BOOKBINDING. Grolier set the fashion in France for gold-tooled luxury bindings in the Italian style and popularized the practice of stamping book covers with names and mottoes as a mark of ownership. His motto 'Portio mea, domine, sit in terra viventium' and the formula 'Io. Grolieri et amicorum' are commonly found stamped in gold on his bindings.

With the exception of a small group of Italian bindings dating from *c.* 1510–20, decorated with MEDALLIONS of classical scenes imitating metal plaquettes, most of Grolier's bindings were made in Paris after he finally settled there in 1530. It was formerly thought that these bindings were Italian, but a French, probably Parisian, origin is now generally accepted; they are in smooth CALF in place of the fine-grained MOROCCO commonly employed by Italian binders at this time. The early bindings had simple STRAPWORK designs, often an interlacing rectangle and lozenge with FLEURON decoration, but after 1550 these developed into elaborate patterns of curvilinear ribbons and ARABESQUES. In these later bindings the strap or ribbon work was often emphasized by colour, usually black or red, and the leaves of the arabesques hatched with parallel lines. The identity of the binders who worked for Grolier is unknown. He patronized several binderies, one of which employed TOOLS and designs similar to those used by Étienne Roffet, royal binder between 1539 and 1547.

260, 540.

GROPIUS, WALTER (1883–1969). See BAUHAUS.

GROS POINT. Or cross stitch, is a cross-shaped EMBROIDERY stitch, much used since the 16th c. for such objects as carpets, chair coverings, needlework pictures and SAMPLERS. See also NEEDLEWORK.

GROTESQUE (Italian *grotteschi*). A type of mural decoration, painted, carved or moulded in stucco, which in the early 16th c. spread from Italy to most countries in Europe. It was characterized by the use of floral motifs, animal and human figures, masks, etc. copied from the ornament found in Roman buildings (called *grotte*) such as the Domus Aurea of Nero excavated *c.* 1500, the whole being imaginatively combined into fanciful and playful schemes. One of the earliest examples of 'grotesque' ornament can be found in the frieze in Carlo Crivelli's *Annunciation* (N.G., London, 1486). In 1502 Pintoricchio was commissioned to decorate the ceiling vaults of the Cathedral Library, Siena, in this style and Signorelli's decorations for Orvieto Cathedral (1499–1504) made even more extravagant use of it. In the earlier phase the decorations were usually arranged in narrow vertical panels with branching scrolls symmetrical about a central stem as in the decorations for the Loggie of the Vatican by Raphael and Giovanni da Udine (1517–19). The Roman Mannerists applied the style to broader surfaces, sometimes with disjointed bands or opposed scrolls as in the grotesque suite of Jacques Androuet Ducerceau (1556). The grotesque style was distinguished by its disintegration of natural forms and the redistribution of the parts in accordance with the fantasy of the artist.

From the later 17th c. this kind of decoration was called ARABESQUE in France and in elaboration of the earlier arabesques by BÉRAIN and Claude Audran III (1658–1734) it became a characteristic feature of the ROCOCO, though it lost much of its initial connection with the Roman motifs. The individual motifs of the *grotteschi* were brought in again by classicists such as Giovanni Battista Piranesi (1720–78) and Robert ADAM in the context of the NEO-CLASSICAL movement and became an occasional feature in all the decorative arts. But the distinctive fanciful combinations of the Renaissance grotesques were not revived.

In France the word 'grotesque' was applied to literature and even to people fairly early in the 17th c. and in 1694 it was defined by the *Dictionnaire de l'Académie françoise* as 'Bizarre, fantastique, extravagant, capricieux'. This extended sense of the word, which became current also in England after the Restoration, with its connotations of the ridiculous, absurd and unnatural, carried implications of disapproval for the Age of Reason and by the time Neo-Classicism was in vogue both the word and the style had acquired a pejorative sense. It was synonymous with the excessive, the preposterous and reprehensible. Hogarth, for instance, describes caricature as 'that intermediate species of subject which may be placed between the sublime and the grotesque'. During the Gothic Revival and in certain phases of the Romantic movement the grotesque again came into repute though not in its original connotation. Ruskin's treatment of the grotesque had the effect of establishing it as a respectable genre of art both in decoration and more widely, although he was unwilling to allow the decorative grotesque a place in the higher branches of art. Of the original grotesque 'which first developed itself among the enervated Romans' he speaks only with disdain. For him the 'true grotesque' was that which revealed an insight into the dreadfulness of nature.

Thus the word 'grotesque', originating as a technical term designating a late Roman type of decoration and a Renaissance decorative style based upon it, came to imply whatever is incongruous with the accepted norm whether in life or in art.

467.

GUÉRARD, NICOLAS. French engraver and designer who published a pattern-book for firearms entitled *Diverses Pièces d'Arquebuserie.* The designs date from *c.* 1715–20 and while using elements from Jean BÉRAIN, they belong to the elegant RÉGENCE style. The pattern-book had a wide popularity among makers of luxury firearms throughout Europe, being extensively used at the Russian TULA works among others. It was reissued by Johann Weigel in Nuremberg.

GUÉRIDON. French term of uncertain derivation denoting a decorative candle stand such as was used in France from *c.* the middle of the 17th c. The original type had a circular top and a central standard, often in the form of a Moor, or, as the taste for exoticism increased, of a negress or Indian. In the Louis XV and Louis XVI periods guéridons became small movable tables which were made in various forms with great delicacy of MARQUETRY and ORMOLU. Towards the end of the 18th c. a guéridon in the form of an antique tripod came into fashion.

The guéridon with Moor or Blackamoor standard was introduced into England from Italy and Holland in the second half of the 17th c.

GUEUSE (French: female beggar). A kind of LACE worked loosely in thick thread.

GUILLOCHE. Sometimes called 'Interlacement Band', this is a mode of ornament in the form of two or more bands or strings interlaced or plaited over each other so as to repeat the same figure in a continued series (such as interlaced circles) by the spiral return of the bands and usually symmetrical about a longitudinal axis. The principle is that the interlacing broad lines shall pass over and under one another alternately. Guilloche ornament has been very widely used in architecture, textiles, pottery, for the decoration of manuscripts, picture frames, mouldings, etc. It is found in most styles and periods, though more common or varied in some than in others. In antiquity the interlacing lines were often distinguished from each other by colour, or in raised ornament were fluted or channelled. In Celtic, Anglo-Saxon and early Scandinavian art the guilloche was the most conspicuous form of ornament and often achieved very complicated interlacings with the special feature that the same band appears in different colours in different sections of a continuous band of ornament. In the Middle Ages the guilloche was most popular with BYZANTINE and ROMANESQUE and the angular band was added to the forms used in antiquity. In Islamic and particularly in Moorish decoration the guilloche was extensively used, often in a special style in which the bands are straight rather than curved, bending at angles of either 90° or 135°. A very great elaboration of the guilloche took place at the Renaissance, based chiefly on elements taken from medieval, Moorish and classical models.

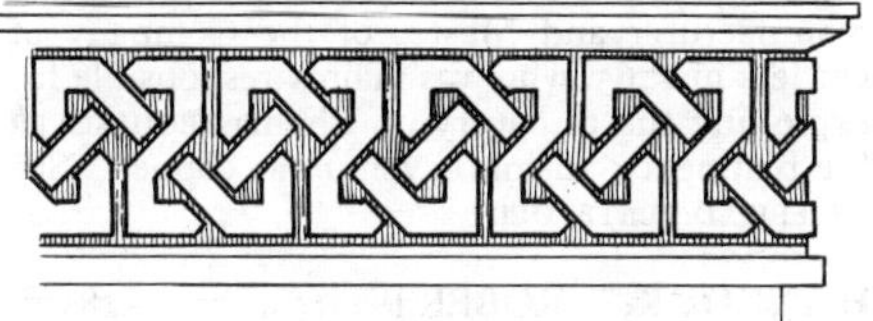

Guilloche ornament was used on furniture throughout the 16th, 17th and 18th centuries.

GUIMARD, HECTOR (1867–1942). French architect and designer who is considered to have been the most eminent French exponent of *art nouveau.* In his building he was influenced by the Belgian architect HORTA. He is most widely known for his imaginative and original entrances to the Paris Métro. See also ART NOUVEAU.

GUIPURE LACE. A kind of LACE in which the flowers of the pattern are joined by coarse stitches or threads without any ground at all. It was made with twisted SILK and *cartisane,* a narrow strip of VELLUM or PARCHMENT covered with silk or metallic threads.

GUMLEY, JOHN (d. 1729). English cabinet-maker and looking-glass manufacturer. He set up business in the Strand in 1694, was cabinet-maker to George I and in 1705 set up his looking-glass manufactory at Lambeth. He was in partnership with the cabinet-maker James MOORE from 1714 until the latter's death in 1726, and with the looking-glass maker William Turing from 1721. In a detailed description of his workshop Richard Steele declared that 'it is not in the power of any Potentate in Europe to have so beautiful a mirror as he may purchase here for a trifle' (*The Lover,* 13 May 1715). MIRRORS by Gumley can be seen at Hampton Court (one is marked with his name on a gilt slip) and Chatsworth. He left a large fortune and his daughter married the Earl of Bath.

231.

GUTENBERG, JOHANN (d. *c.* 1468). The inventor of typographical printing, he was born of a patrician family at Mainz and after a victory of the popular faction in the city was banished and moved in 1428 to Strasbourg. There he gave lessons in jeweller's work and formed a partnership for making metal badges for pilgrims. In 1438 he agreed to teach three others an art with which he had been experimenting in secret, involving a press and goldsmith's work 'in connection with printing'. He was back in Mainz by 1448, and in 1450 he borrowed a large sum of money from a goldsmith, Johann Fust, to finance a 'work of books'. From an account taken in 1455 for the purposes of a lawsuit against him by Fust it appears that Gutenberg had pledged his stock and apparatus to Fust as security for the loan and that Fust was claiming to take possession of them; but the outcome of the suit is not known. In 1465 Gutenberg was granted, or bought, an annuity from the revenues of the archbishopric of Mainz. In 1468 the equipment for printing of the deceased Gutenberg belonged to a lawyer, Conrad Humery, at Mainz.

Nothing is known to have been printed by Gutenberg. The first piece of printing to give the name of its printer, the Mainz Psalter dated in 1457, was printed by Fust and Peter Schoeffer. According to the *Cologne Chronicle* of 1499, printing began at Mainz in 1450 and the first book printed was a Bible. The so-called '42-line Bible', finished in or before 1456, which is without date or name of place or printer, is generally assumed to be wholly or partly the work of Gutenberg for lack of evidence that anyone else was printing when it must have been begun. On somewhat fanciful grounds he has also been credited with the Mainz edition of the *Catholicon* of 1460.

The invention, and the perfecting of it in so short a time, is one of the most remarkable in human history, there being no convincing reason to believe that the inventor had guidance from techniques practised earlier in Europe or in the Far East. It involved a press of an elaborate kind with moving parts adapted for inking and the accurate register of type and paper, an ink which adhered to metal, a suitable alloy for type-metal, and (what distinguishes this from earlier printing in the Far East) a mould to which interchangeable matrices to form the faces of letters could be fastened and which would cast letters of different widths. See TYPOGRAPHY.

204, 253, 731.

H

HADLEY CHEST. A group of regional chests made in the Connecticut River Valley at Hadley and Hatfield *c.* 1675–*c.* 1740. They are without applied decoration but are ornamented with flat carving of entwined leaves and flowers which covers the entire front surface of the chest. Many of these chests are attributed to the partnership of BELDING and ALLIS. See FURNITURE (AMERICAN).

HAFNER. Stove-makers in Germany and the Alpine lands who produced a variety of lead-glazed or tin-glazed pottery wares in Renaissance times, as well as stove tiles and architectural ornaments. Nuremberg, Salzburg and Winterthur were prominent centres of the craft.

HALFPENNY, WILLIAM and JOHN. Father and son, active mid 18th c. English architects and designers. *New Designs for Chinese Temples, Garden Seats, etc.*, published in parts between 1750 and 1752, is the earliest known English book of designs in the so-called CHINESE TASTE. It contained a few designs for chairs. It was followed in 1752 by *Rural Architecture in the Chinese Taste* and *Chinese and Gothic Architecture.*

HALLMARK. See PEWTER (MARKS) and SILVER (ASSAYING AND HALLMARKING).

HAMMER, VICTOR (1882–1967). Born in Vienna and trained as an architect, he was a typical artist–craftsman in many fields with a particular interest in calligraphy and printing. He began printing in Florence during the early 1920s and in 1931 his Stamperia del Santuccio published Milton's *Samson Agonistes.* He subsequently moved to Alsace and Austria and in 1939, upon the Nazi occupation of Austria, he set up in the U.S.A. He continued to produce books under the imprint of the Stamperia del Santuccio but also between 1941 and 1949 used the imprint of Wells College Press of Aurora, New York. From 1945 with his son, JACOB, he produced books in similar style from the Hammer Press and after 1945 from the Anvil Press in Lexington, Kentucky, where he also had considerable influence during the 1950s on the work of Joseph C. Graves at the Gravesend Press. See also PRIVATE PRESS MOVEMENT.

HANCOCK, JOSEPH (1711–91). Sheffield manufacturer and Master of the Company of Cutlers in 1765, who was mainly responsible for exploiting the discovery of Thomas BOULSOVER for plating by fusing silver upon copper. See SHEFFIELD PLATE, OLD.

HANCOCK, ROBERT (*c.* 1731–1817). Engraver who probably worked together with

Simon François RAVENET at the enamels factory of Sir Stephen Theodore Janssen at York House, Battersea (see BATTERSEA ENAMELS). When the Battersea factory closed in 1756 he went with Ravenet to the china factory at Bow. Shortly afterwards (in 1756 or early 1757) he was working at the Worcester Porcelain Company's factory, where he introduced the method of decoration by TRANSFER PRINTING from designs engraved on copper plates. In 1774 he sold his part share in the Worcester factory and until *c.* 1780 he was in partnership with Thomas Turner at the Salopian china factory at Caughley.

43, 161.

HANIWA. Japanese pottery grave-figures. See JAPAN (POTTERY AND PORCELAIN).

HARACHE, PIERRE (d. 1700). Huguenot goldsmith and silversmith working in London from *c.* 1695. He was succeeded by his son, of the same name.

HARGREAVES, JAMES (1720–78). Lancashire mechanic who invented the spinning-jenny, a labour-saving device which prepared the way for the Industrial Revolution. See WEAVING.

HARQUEBUS (ARQUEBUS: HACKBUSH: HACKBUT). From the German *Hakenbüchse*, a hook gun. In the course of the 14th c., as the craft of the gunmakers improved, barrels of hand guns were made longer and the charge of gunpowder stronger. As a result the recoil was more forceful. In order, therefore, to cushion the recoil and also to relieve the firer of part of the weight, hand guns were often cast with a hook attached to the underside of the barrel which could be fastened to a suitable support such as a wall or parapet or stand. This is almost certainly the origin of the term rather than the model of matchlock musket which was introduced *c.* the middle of the 16th c. with a butt curving downwards so that it could be held under the arms and supported against the chest while firing. The word 'harquebus' or 'arquebus' nevertheless became a general term in the 16th c. for portable firearms of all kinds.

HARRINGTON, SARAH. English silhouettist, popular in the last quarter of the 18th c. She obtained a patent for a machine with which to make hollow-cut silhouette portraits. She also cut free-hand silhouettes and painted on silk. In 1782 she exhibited silhouette portraits on silk of Admiral Lord Howe and Lord Shelburne. The WEDGWOOD medallion portrait of the authoress Maria Edgeworth was taken from a silhouette portrait by Mrs. Harrington. See SILHOUETTE.

HARRISON, JOHN (1693–1776). The first man to make a timekeeper or CHRONOMETER which would keep time at sea sufficiently accurately to enable a ship to find its longitude. He was born at Foulby, Wragby, near Wakefield, Yorkshire, his father being at the time an estate carpenter at Nostell Priory. The family moved to Barrow-on-Humber, Lincolnshire, when he was three years old, and he began his working career as a carpenter. In 1713 he made a LONG-CASE CLOCK with a movement almost entirely of wood, which is now in the Museum of the Clockworkers' Company, Guildhall, London, and in 1715 and 1717 two similar clocks, which also survive. He wrote in 1730 a manuscript on the 'gridiron' temperature-compensating pendulum which he and his younger brother JAMES had applied to two precision clocks made *c.* 1726. This and GRAHAM's mercury pendulum of the same date were the first temperature-compensating devices of any kind.

Harrison became fired with the idea of winning the £20,000 prize offered by the British government in 1713 for a timekeeper which would be accurate enough at sea to enable a ship to find its longitude. His first marine timekeeper, a large machine completed in 1735, was highly successful on a short voyage, and he proceeded to build a second in 1739 soon after he removed to London, a third in 1757 and a fourth in 1761. After a long series of trials and conflict with the government Harrison, with the support of King George III, eventually won the full award in 1773. The fourth timekeeper, on which the award was based, was a superb piece of craftsmanship in every way. Externally it took the form of a large and handsome WATCH, and internally it embodied the utmost refinement of mechanical perfection coupled with inventive genius.

106, 458, 535.

HAUPT, GEORG (1741–84). Swedish cabinet-maker. He was in Paris between 1764 and 1768, where he is thought to have worked under RIESENER. He then came to London, where he worked for a year before returning to Stockholm in 1769. He was there appointed cabinet-maker to the Court and was responsible for bringing the Louis XVI style of furniture to Sweden. There is a commode signed by him in the Victoria and Albert Museum.

HAUSMALER. Independent ENAMEL-painters working chiefly in Bavaria, Silesia and Bohemia, at first chiefly on glass and silver but later also on faience and PORCELAIN. They obtained ceramic wares 'in the white' (not always with the manufacturer's approval), painted them with designs which were often of fine quality, fired them, and sold them as their own. The variety of wares and styles employed make *Hausmalerei* a fascinating if somewhat problematic study. At Nuremberg after *c.* 1660 Johann SCHAPER, Abraham Helmhack and the monogrammist 'W. R.' decorated Frankfurt and Hanau faience with landscape and mythological subjects predominantly in black monochrome

(Schwarzlot), later using full colour. At Augsburg the Seuter family and J. Aufenwerth painted much early MEISSEN porcelain, especially with gilt CHINOISERIES in monochrome. Ignaz Bottengruber, of Breslau and Vienna (*c.* 1720–35), was perhaps the finest of the Hausmaler; J. F. Metzsch of Bayreuth, and the prolific F. F. Mayer of Pressnitz (*c.* 1745–70), employed porcelain from China as well as from the Meissen, Vienna and other factories. See also CERAMICS.

HEAL, SIR AMBROSE (1872–1959). English artist–craftsman and designer, and chairman from 1913 of the family business in Tottenham Court Road, London, until his retirement in 1953. He served his apprenticeship in cabinet-making and won a silver medal at the Paris Exhibition, 1900, for a bedroom suite. This was in the full tradition of the ARTS AND CRAFTS MOVEMENT. When Heal entered the firm in 1893 his direction of design policy resulted in the production of simply designed furniture, exemplified in the Plain Oak Furniture catalogue of 1898, which was destined to have considerable influence in the first quarter of the 20th c. By turning also to machine production Heal established his reputation as a pioneer of the Modern Movement in English furniture. He was knighted in 1933. See FURNITURE (MODERN).

HEDEBO. See EMBROIDERY (TYPES).

HEEMSKERK. Dutch family of amateur diamond-engravers on GLASS. WILLEM JACOBSZ van Heemskerk of Leiden (1613–92) took up the craft professionally and signed examples of his work are fairly numerous in museums. See GLASS (NETHERLANDS).

HEIDELOFF, NICOLAUS INNOCENTIUS WILHELM CLEMENS VAN (1761–1837). Born in Stuttgart, he worked in Paris as a miniaturist and fled to England during the Revolution, where he worked for the publisher Ackermann. He made FASHION PLATES for *The Gallery of Fashion*, some of which are reproduced in *Gallery of Fashion, 1790–1822* (1949), by Sacheverell Sitwell and Doris Langley Moore. From 1815 until his death Heideloff was a director of the Mauritshuis in The Hague.

364, 404, 504.

HELMSCHMIED FAMILY. Family of armourers who were active in Augsburg in the 15th and 16th centuries. Outstanding members were: LORENZ, who among other things made a complete set of armour for the Archduke Maximilian in 1480; KOLOMON, who was active in the first half of the 16th c.; and DESIDERIUS, who among others worked for Philip II of Spain. Jörg SORG worked as an engraver in the Helmschmied workshops and married into the family.

HEMMING-BIRD. Needlework clamp. See NEEDLEWORK.

HEMONY, FRANCIS and PETER. Brothers. Netherlandish bell-founders and pioneers in the casting of the 'harmonic' bell. Their main business was the founding of CARILLONS. Francis Hemony died in 1667 and the foundry was continued in operation by Peter until 1678. See BELL-FOUNDING.

HEPPLEWHITE, GEORGE (d. 1786). English cabinet-maker and furniture designer. He was an apprentice to GILLOW of Lancaster and came to London, where he set up a shop in Cripplegate. Little is known of him and no furniture by him or his firm has ever been identified. In 1788, two years after his death, his widow, Alice, who continued the business, published a book of nearly 300 designs 'from drawings by A. Hepplewhite and Co., Cabinet-Makers' with the title *The Cabinet-Maker and Upholsterer's Guide* (2nd ed., 1789, 3rd ed., 1794). The designs reflect the light and elegant furniture fashionable in the last quarter of the 18th c., but how far Hepplewhite was personally responsible for them has not been determined. The preface to the *Guide* does not claim originality; the pattern-book may be regarded as vernacular interpretation of ADAM's NEO-CLASSICISM. *The Cabinet-Makers' London Book of Prices* (1788) has 10 designs inscribed 'Heppelwhite' or 'Hepplewhite'. See FURNITURE (ENGLISH).

361, 617.

HEPPLEWHITE STYLE. Name popularly given to furniture in the NEO-CLASSICAL style of Robert ADAM, as represented by the designs in George HEPPLEWHITE's *The Cabinet-Maker and Upholsterer's Guide* (1788). The style was not originated by Hepplewhite although it bears his name, but represents the classical mode in furniture which prevailed during the last quarter of the 18th c. It is characterized by the use of MARLBORO' legs, shield-backed chairs and a restrained application of classical ornament.

HERRING-BONE. An ornamental pattern resembling the bones of a herring. In architecture it is applied particularly to masonry or paving in which the units are set obliquely in alternate rows so as to form a zig-zag pattern. In cabinet-making it refers to a type of BANDING producing a similar effect of pattern. It is also known as feather pattern. In embroidery and knitting it names a particular stitch. See EMBROIDERY and NEEDLEWORK.

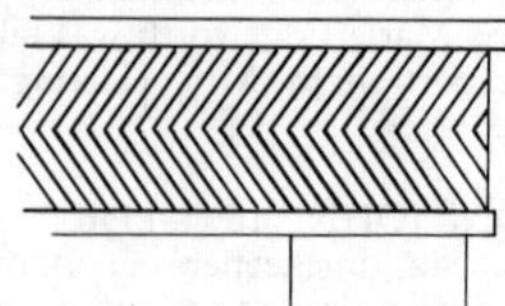

HEWSON, JOHN. Early American calico-printer. See COTTON AND COTTON PRINTING.

HIGHBOY. American term, originating in the 18th c., for a high chest or chest-on-chest, usually raised on legs. The term was an equivalent of the English TALLBOY. See FURNITURE (AMERICAN).

HILDESHEIM TREASURE. A collection of Roman SILVER plate found at Hildesheim near Hanover in 1868 and now in Berlin. It consists of a number of EMBOSSED drinking-bowls and a large mixing-bowl with floral relief resembling that of the Ara Pacis. The treasure is assigned to the Augustan Age and may have been booty from the camp of Quintilius Varus in the Teutoburger Wald (A.D. 9).

HILL, DAVID OCTAVIUS (1802–70). Scottish landscape painter in the Romantic picturesque manner, who exhibited at the Royal Scottish Academy and was its secretary 1830–69. He took up the then new art of lithography and his *Sketches of Scenery in Perthshire drawn from Nature & on Stone* was one of the first lithographic works in Britain. He also illustrated the Blackie edition of the works of James Hogg (The Ettrick Shepherd). In collaboration with the photographer Robert Adamson he gained a European reputation for photographic portraits by the calotype process. See PHOTOGRAPHY.

HITCHCOCK, LAMBERT (1795–1852). American cabinet-maker and chair manufacturer. Born in Cheshire, Connecticut, of English descent, he set up a factory at Barkhamsted in western Connecticut *c.* 1818. At first he made chair parts, which were shipped to Charleston and as far west as Chicago. Business flourished and *c.* 1826 he built a factory for the construction of complete chairs. The business went into bankruptcy in 1829 but recovered and was continued in partnership with a former employee, Arba Alford, under the title 'Hitchcock, Alford & Co.' until 1843, when Hitchcock opened an independent factory in Unionville.

The Hitchcock chair was an early example of mass production and conformed to a few standard types. It was a small open-back chair with wide horizontal back-rest and crest-rail. The seats were at first of rush, later of cane or plank. The uprights were flat in front to allow painted decoration and were continuous with rounded rear legs. The rounded front legs were often reeded and splayed. The legs were connected by a turned and shaped stretcher in front, two plain round stretchers at each side and one at the back. The Hitchcock chairs were usually painted black over a coat of red and were decorated with painted or stencilled designs of leaves, flowers and fruit on the back splat, on the top rail and often on the uprights. The narrow marginal lines and the turnings of the legs were often picked out in gilt.

67, 645.

HOFFMANN, JOSEF (1870–1956). Austrian architect and designer who studied under Otto Wagner (1841–1918) and developed the latter's rationalist theories of construction. He was greatly interested in the design of craft objects and from 1899 taught in the Vienna School of Applied Arts. Together with Koloman Moser (1860–1936) he set up the *Wiener Werkstätten* and in 1897 he was one of the group of artists who founded the *Wiener Sezession.* Influenced by the Glasgow School of Charles Rennie MACKINTOSH and by the Belgian ART NOUVEAU, he was perhaps the most influential figure in the late florescence of the 'new art' in Austria. He continued to move with the times and in the early years of the present century he co-operated with the new *avant garde* which with the painter Gustav Klimt (1862–1918) formed the *Kunstschau*, called the 'Secession from the Secession'.

HOLLIE POINT. A very fine Needlepoint LACE with pattern formed by rows of tiny holes. It was popular in England for insertions into baby clothes during the 17th and 18th centuries.

HONITON LACE. A Bobbin LACE made principally in and around Honiton, Devonshire, in the 18th and 19th centuries. It won popularity at the Great Exhibition of 1851 and was patronized by Queen Victoria. The black silk lace of the district had a considerable demand. Floral ornaments of sprays and springs, bold in scale, often with a thicker thread giving slight relief to one side, were made separately and then linked together by needle or bobbin. In design and technique it closely resembled the contemporary *duchesse* lace of Brussels, though the thread was generally less fine. The seed-like forms of MALTESE lace were also sometimes used. Honiton lace was made in both large and small pieces and the industry extended over an area from Exmouth to Torbay.

HOOKED RUGS. See RUGS, AMERICAN.

HOPE, THOMAS (1769–1831). Connoisseur, architect, furniture designer and author. The son of John Hope, banker and merchant of Amsterdam, he studied architecture and travelled widely as a young man through the Mediterranean area. He came to London when the French occupied Holland in 1794. He designed the interior decoration and furniture of his London house in Duchess Street, Cavendish Square, and of his Surrey home, Deepdene, in both of which he kept his large collection of antique sculpture and vases. His *Household Furniture and Interior Decoration* (1807) illustrates his designs at Duchess Street. These show a scholarly adaptation of antique classical (including Egyptian) elements to furniture and reflect the meticulous archaeological approach of the early REGENCY style. A circular table (monopodium) of mahogany inlaid with ebony and silver, designed by Hope for Deepdene and corresponding with Plate 39 in *Household Furniture*, is now in the Victoria and Albert Museum.

HOPPENHAUPT, JOHANN MICHAEL (1709–*c.* 1755) and JOHANN CHRISTIAN (d. *c.* 1785). Brothers, German carvers and cabinet-makers. They worked in Berlin between 1740 and 1755 and under the direction of Johann August NAHL (1710–85) were active originators of the Frederickan ROCOCO style in furniture and decoration. They had an important share in designing and executing the decoration of Frederick the Great's Castle at Berlin and his palaces of Potsdam and Sans-Souci. They succeeded Nahl in his post of Director of Ornaments at Berlin. Their work was particularly noted for the masterly way in which they contrasted plain surfaces with MARQUETRY and combined ornament with form. The designs of Johann Michael were published 1751–5.

HORSE-BRASSES. In Victorian and Edwardian times it was almost impossible to walk through London or indeed any other large British town without seeing cart-horses bedecked with horse-brasses and other ornaments on the harness. These were usually the property of the carman himself, not of the horse's owner. Carmen were proud of them and kept them well polished. They were handed down from father to son so that many were quite old.

Roughly speaking all brasses are based on three patterns: crescents, heart shapes and the disc or sun design. They were originally worn to ward off the evil eye, horses for some reason being considered to be particularly susceptible to its effects so that from very early times they had to be protected by amulets. It was the first glance only of the evil eye which did the mischief, and as the polished brasses glittered brilliantly and swayed and swung with the movement of the horse the evil eye was attracted first by them. They acted as a lightning conductor and distracted the evil eye from both the horse and its driver.

One of the most popular designs among carters was that known as a 'flash' and was simply a plain, very highly polished circle of brass. It was easy to clean and very decorative. This may have been a relic of primitive sun worship.

We read about horse and camel amulets in the Bible. Both the Egyptians and the Romans used them on the harnesses of their chariots. It has sometimes been stated that they came to western Europe with the Crusaders or with the gipsies from Spain, etc.; but in actual fact their general use dates from *c.* 1860, when they became very popular. It is known, however, that as early as 1715 Henry Carver and Walter Tupper, who ran a brass foundry in Birmingham, were making what they described as 'Horse Furniture and Amulets'. These were made from sheet metal by chisel, hammer and punch and very few are now in existence. Later brasses were cast and finished off with a file.

Some authorities claim that the use of horse-brasses started in the West Country, and this may well be true as one of the first brass foundries was established at Bristol and some of the oldest specimens of horse-brasses have been found in the West Country. Horse harness, which probably included horse-brasses, was taken round the country by travelling salesmen and sold mainly at horse fairs. This may account for the fact that no brasses were ever made or even sold in any quantity by country saddlers until recent times. Pride of ownership and the desire to mark valued horses without resorting to branding helped to bring brasses into general use. A driver liked his horses to look smart and be conspicuous. As their use spread both in the cities and in the country owners began to ask for designs in keeping with their trade. Thus we find barrels for the brewers, the sheaf of wheat for the millers, the wheel for the coach-builders, the churn for dairymen, and of course the engines for the railway transport horses. The emblems are numerous, but nearly all are inserted in a sun or moon shape or with the lower portion of the brass thickened to form a crescent. Commemorative brasses, generally very ugly, were also popular and a large number of designs were made to commemorate the 1887 Jubilee of Queen Victoria, and later the 1897 Diamond Jubilee. Furthermore we have brasses commemorating the Boer War, Lord Baden Powell, Lord Roberts, Disraeli (surrounded by primroses), Gladstone, and all the kings and queens since Queen Victoria. Many carmen also decorated their horses with brasses incorporating the sign of their favourite inn. The Royal Society for the Prevention of Cruelty to Animals had two designs: one the Shield which has been given at the Cart-horse Parade in Regent's Park since 1896 and at the Van-horse Parade since 1907, and the other a circular design which was given in commercial horse classes at country shows. As entries at the various Regent's Park parades averaged about 750 before 1914, there are still many of these brasses to be found.

A set of brasses as worn by a cart-horse properly dressed for a show included a face-piece hanging over the forehead (which should always be a sun design), two brasses behind the ears, three brasses at each side of the runners at the shoulders and from six to ten brasses hanging down the front and affixed to the martingale (i.e. the strap hanging from the horse girth between the forelegs). In addition hearts, diamonds and other shaped pieces of metal were inserted in the harness at haphazard where space allowed. Sometimes there were also nose-plates and name-plates. Above the head was a small ornament called a flyer or swinger, or fly terret, usually a replica in miniature of the larger brasses. Brushes were also mounted on the fly terret, usually of red, white or blue hair, though sometimes small bells were used instead. Only a really hefty cart-horse could bear the weight of three to four kg of brass on its head and shoulders.

Estimates of the number of different designs range from 1,500 to 3,000. The writer has personally handled nearly 1,000 different designs or variations, different edgings, etc. One firm alone before the First World War could supply 400 different patterns.

How is it possible to distinguish the genuine old horse-brass from the many modern replicas made in order to meet the requirements of collectors, for decorating hotels, etc.? Frankly, this is difficult in some cases, though the majority of modern ones can be easily detected by the bright condition of the back and by the roughness and lack of finish typical of mass-produced articles. If the intersections have not been filed clean, the brass is almost certainly modern. The older brasses, which are desired by collectors, can usually be recognized by their weight and by the smoothness and softness that can only be produced by constant wear and cleaning. Wear can be detected particularly on the loop, which should be worn down by constant rubbing against the strap which holds it. The foot of the brass should also show evident signs of wear; and though the worn loop can be reproduced, it is not so easy to imitate the signs of wear at the foot. Collectors therefore look for this softness and smoothness resulting from wear and for the beautiful velvety patina which comes only from constant cleaning and which is lost if the brass is lacquered.

A horse-brass cast from a pattern comes out rough and needs to be finished by sand-blasting and filing. Modern replicas are made in the same way as the old brasses but the designs are often inferior and odd pieces of metal redundant to the design are left. All old designs had a knob or slight protuberance on either side of the back so that the brass could be gripped in a vice for finishing. Some modern replicas reproduce these knobs but they are made of soft metal and are flimsy by comparison with the older ones. Nevertheless some of the modern designs are well made and designs such as the King Rufus Stirrup, first made in 1946, the Winston Churchill brass, and the Signs of the Zodiac, deserve a place in a collection.

As cart-horses became lighter to suit the conditions of modern traffic the use of full sets of harness decoration went out of fashion and it has become rare to see a heavy horse with a complete set of brasses.

420.

HORTA, VICTOR (1861–1947). Belgian architect and designer. Although his chief importance lay in the influence he had on the Modern Movement in architecture, he created an original vocabulary of ornament which made him a leading figure in European ART NOUVEAU.

HORTICULTURE. See LANDSCAPE GARDENING.

HSI WANG MU. Taoist decorative motif, Queen Mother of the West, said in legend to be formed of the pure Quintessence of the Western Air. Her residence, in which she is attended by genii and JADE maidens, was in the K'un-lun Mountains, the Taoist equivalent of the Buddhist Mount Sumeru. She is said to have been visited by Mu Wang, King Mu of the Chou dynasty, who was received by her on the shore of the Yao-ch'ih, or Jasper Lake. She is also said, because of having been born of the Western Air, to be the passive *yin* principle in contradistinction to Mu Kung, also called Tung Wang Kung, King of the East, who was formed of the Eastern Air and representative of the active *yang* principle.

HUET, CHRISTOPHE (d. 1759). French painter and designer in the ROCOCO style. He belongs to the tradition of decorative designers stemming from BÉRAIN and AUDRAN. There are 10 paintings of Oriental subjects at Chantilly executed for the Duke of Bourbon and signed and dated 1735. Huet has been credited with the *Grande Singerie* and the *Petite Singerie* at Chantilly and the CHINOISERIES at the Château de Champs in Brie have also been attributed to him. He painted the ARABESQUES of the *Cabinet des Singes* in the Hôtel Rohan (1749–52). He also did designs for TAPESTRY and carpets for AUBUSSON and probably elsewhere.

HUGO D'OIGNIES. A lay brother of the Augustinian Order, probably trained in the school of NICOLAS OF VERDUN, who worked as a goldsmith from 1187 to 1228. He was one of four brothers from the monastery of Walcourt who founded a priory at Oignies near Namur, which was dedicated in 1204. Most of his work, including three signed pieces, a BOOK COVER, a chalice and paten, and a reliquary for the rib of St. Peter dated 1204, are in the convent of Notre-Dame de Namur. In England a reliquary cross in the Victoria and Albert Museum and a bronze gilt crozier in the British Museum are attributed to him. His work is characteristic of the change-over from the heavy ROMANESQUE to the delicacy of GOTHIC art. Instead of ENAMEL his usual materials were silver, often enriched with gilding, NIELLO, ROCK-CRYSTAL and FILIGREE. The last was particularly important, and took the form of naturalistic vine-scrolls inhabited by animals and even human figures.

HUSK. Ornamental motif consisting of elements resembling a husk of wheat used in repeating or diminishing pattern. It was a favourite with ADAM and HEPPLEWHITE furniture and was characteristic of NEO-CLASSICAL taste in the 2nd half of the 18th c.

I

ICE GLASS. Alternative name for CRACKLE GLASS.

IKKAN (19th c.). Japanese *netsuke* carver of Nagoya. He worked mainly in wood and specialized in finely finished animals. His rats were particularly famous. See JAPAN (NETSUKE).

IMARI. JAPANese PORCELAIN wares made at Arita for the European export trade. They made use of red and gilding over a purplish-blue underglaze. They were popular in Europe during the vogue for the Oriental in the 18th c. and were copied at DELFT in Holland, at Ansbach in Germany and elsewhere. See CERAMICS.

INCUNABULA, THE (Latin, 'swaddling-clothes'). The name given to the period in the history of printing before 1501 and often used, less accurately, for books printed during that time. See TYPOGRAPHY.

INDIA

1. Textiles.
2. Carpets.
3. Costume.
4. Jewellery.
5. Terracotta figurines.

1. TEXTILES. Weaving and embroidery are known to be of great antiquity in India although no actual examples survive which are earlier than the 17th c. A.D. Cotton was cultivated by Indus Valley peoples from 2400 B.C. and on at least one figurine dated to this period a shawl is represented, the pattern being carved in low relief and strongly suggesting embroidery. After the end of the Indus Valley civilization, *c.* 1500 B.C., there is no direct evidence for textile production until the 2nd c. A.D., but from then on sculptured figures are often represented wearing textiles. During the 1st c. A.D. Indian muslins had become famous in Rome under such names as '*venti textiles*' (woven winds), which translates exactly the technical name of a special type of muslin woven in Dacca until modern times. Visual evidence is to be found in the cave temples of Ajanta, especially in those caves attributable to the 6th c. A.D., where various textile techniques can be identified in the painted murals, including woven patterns, tie-and-dye printing and double-tied dyeing, where the warp and weft threads are dyed separately before weaving.

Apart from carpets no textiles are known to survive from before the arrival of the Portuguese, the Dutch and the British in India during the time of the Mogul Empire (early 17th c.). These early voyages were undertaken mainly in order to obtain spices directly from source and so avoid the heavy costs incidental to obtaining them from middlemen on the Middle East trade routes. But for the British merchants in the 16th c. there was an even more important purpose, and this was to sell English cloth to Asia. The staple industry of England in the 16th c. was the weaving and dyeing of woollen cloth, much of which was exported to the continent of Europe. But as the European market was greatly reduced in consequence of wars and unrest outlets had to be found elsewhere. It was thought at first that the climate of China and Japan would make them suitable markets for the sale of the heavy English woollens. But it was soon found impracticable to reach and develop these markets and except as novelties the woollens found little sale in India. The Spice Islands of the Indonesian archipelago would only purchase specially produced export goods from India, which had to be purchased with gold. Thus bullion was exported from England and used to purchase cloth in India for sale in the Spice Islands in exchange for spices for England. Incidentally to this trade a number of large hangings were brought back to England from India in the late 16th and early 17th centuries as an experiment. The fashion caught on and in the second half of the 17th c. they were increasingly imported into Europe as trade goods by the Portuguese, Dutch, British and French East India Companies. Most of these hangings and bedspreads were coloured by the wax-resist method, in which the outline of the design was first stencilled and pounced with charcoal, then painted over with a black edge. The areas of the cloth to be kept free from dye were painted with wax, which was removed with boiling water after the whole cloth had been immersed in the dye. Some of the final colours were painted on by hand. The designs themselves were often Indian adaptations of designs sent out from Europe. French and Dutch designs were particularly in demand in the later years of the 17th c. Thus the Indian CHINTZES which are often thought to have had so important an influence on European fashions were largely in fact an Indian version of European patterns. (See COTTON AND COTTON PRINTING.) Some of the hangings were embroidered, mainly in chain stitch, and these share with the painted cloths the flowering tree or vase and flowers type of design.

The earliest surviving embroideries, made for the Mogul court rather than for the export trade, are of the Jehangir period (1605–27) and are tent hangings, some of brocaded velvet and others worked in silks or silver-gilt and gilt threads on a woven cotton ground. These are products of the court workshops (*kharkhanahs*), which had been set up under Akbar (1556–1605) for all the arts, and both Persian and Hindu craftsmen were employed in them. The products of this co-operation eventually gave rise to the Mogul style, a synthesis of the Persian and Hindu elements.

The famous shawls of Kashmir, prized by the Moguls as princely gifts, were not a product of the court workshops; the industry certainly pre-dated the Mogul Empire, though it is not known for certain when it originated. An account of the manufacture, trade with the West and European imitations will be found in the article SHAWLS.

Tie-and-dye work, or *bandhana*, is known to have been practised in India since the 6th c. A.D. With this technique portions of cloth to be patterned are tied tightly with waxed thread or scraps of cloth before dipping into a dye vat. By the use of different tying combinations many different patterns can be obtained, usually consisting of spots or small circles. A variation of this occurs in patterns of transverse bands or zig-zags of different colours, produced by tying the cloth in folds before it is dipped in the dye. This kind of patterning is particularly associated with long lengths of muslin used for turbans.

Allied to *bandhana* in its use of tie-and-dye is the technique of double-resist dyeing, in which the warp and the weft are dyed separately by the tie-and-dye process before weaving. This is an extraordinarily laborious and skilful process. A special effect characteristic of this method is a slight merging together of adjacent colours in the pattern. The best known textiles made by this technique are the Patola marriage *saris* from Gujarat, whose patterns are either all-over geometrical designs or with borders containing birds and animals or even human figures.

Embroidery has always been an outstanding village art in India and it is almost always carried out by the women. The styles are strictly local and can be classified on a regional basis. Among the most traditional are the *phulkari* dam-stitch embroideries of the Punjab, which are worked upon a coarse cotton cloth often of English origin. The ground is dyed a shade of earth brown or deep blue, tending sometimes to black. The embroidery is usually in yellow floss silk but sometimes white and green cotton threads are also used. The cloth is always worked from the reverse side, the patterns being regulated by counting the threads. The patterns preserve some of the geometrical designs from the cave paintings of Ajanta. Sometimes pieces of convex mirror-glass are fixed into them by button-hole stitching.

The chain-stitch embroideries of Cutch and Kathiawar represent another distinct regional style. The ground cloth is usually silk or satin, dyed dark blue, yellow or red. The pattern is worked in chain stitch and also often includes pieces of mirror. A characteristic design is of alternating rows of peacocks and floral sprigs though human figures are sometimes introduced.

2. CARPETS. During the 17th c. Indian carpets rivalled the contemporary carpets of Persia, differing from them chiefly in the more naturalistic or pictorial treatment of the flowers, men and animals which figure in the designs. Numbers of these carpets were conveyed to England by the British East India Company. Later rugs, with few exceptions, fall far below this level. In the 19th c. the Indian carpet industry, always burdened with poor wool and an unfavourable climate, was forced to compete with carpets made in the gaols. Only commercial carpets of low quality, with designs of every conceivable kind worked in a long dull woollen pile, now reached the West. The Sena knot was normally used. Cotton tapestry-woven carpets, called *daris*, were also made. See also CARPETS AND RUGS.

3. COSTUME

(*a*) *National Costume*. Dress for both men and women in the Indian subcontinent remained essentially unchanged in any major particular from the 16th c. until the country was divided into India and Pakistan in 1947. Differences in clothing during this period basically reflected differences of religion and social class although there has always been some variation according to region and climate. Even today the national costume of the two countries shows the difference of religious belief although India is a secular state.

Since independence the national dress for women in India is the *sari*, worn with a short close-fitting bodice or blouse, called *choli*, and this costume with minor variations has been worn by Hindu ladies of the upper classes for *c.* 300 years. The modern *sari* is basically a piece of cloth 5·5 metres or so in length and from 1 to 1·5 metres in width with the main pattern across one end. It is normally worn by winding it around the lower part of the body 3 or 4 times, tucking at the waist and sometimes knotting at the front to keep it in place. The loose end is then thrown over the shoulder or sometimes brought over the head like a shawl to hang down in front of the body. Often only sufficient free cloth is left to drape over the shoulder, in which case the end hangs down the back. Modern *saris* are wrapped anti-clockwise and therefore the left shoulder is always covered by the draping. This one length of cloth can be a perfectly modest garment in itself and in some regions of India has been the only garment worn, especially by the poor; but normally it is worn with a *choli*. Sometimes the midriff is left bare although often it is completely covered by the folds of the *sari* itself. Outdoor footwear is usually a light sandal or open-back slipper, sometimes with a turned-up toe.

Men tend to wear Western clothing for formal occasions, trousers and high-buttoned short coat over a shirt of Western type and closed shoes. As head-gear the military-style cap as used by Mahatma Gandhi and Pandit Nehru is worn. Much more common, however, as everyday dress throughout most of India is the traditional *dhoti*. This is a piece of cloth about 4·5 metres long and about 1·2 metres wide, usually made of muslin or light cotton, which is draped round the lower part of the body and tied or pleated at the waist; sometimes the loose end is drawn between the legs and tucked in at the back. Many men, especially the poor, wear the *lungi*, which is a smaller version of the *dhoti* worn around the waist and often allowed to hang down to the ankles or sometimes doubled up and tucked in at the waist to leave freedom of movement for the legs while working. Over the *dhoti* or *lungi* is usually worn a shirt-like garment which can be buttoned to the neck but which does not have a collar.

(*b*) *History*. Clothing in early India at least from 1500 B.C. onwards was not very different in idea from the dress of modern times. It was based as now upon lengths of cloth which were draped round the body rather than shaped and was thus similar to costumes worn by most ancient peoples in hot climates. The lengths of cloth were fastened with belts or pins at the waist and often looped over the shoulders. This type of costume formed the basis of clothing for both sexes and is still the foundation of modern Indian dress.

Sewn garments were comparatively rare though not unknown and there are many illustrations of women wearing jackets and bodices. With the invasions from central Asia between 100 B.C. and A.D. 100 trousers were introduced. Variations in dress between the north and the south seem to have been due to climate as much as fashion. Both in medieval Kashmir, and throughout most of the rest of the sub-continent, shirts and trousers seem to have been quite common; but the material used for these garments reflects the differences in climate, wool or padded or quilted cotton being worn in the northern winters and diaphanous silks and muslins in the tropical regions of the south.

Turbans were the most popular head-gear for men, sometimes fastened in elaborate patterns. Women are also sometimes shown in sculpture wearing elaborate head-gear, but the majority appear to have been bare-headed with a large bun at the nape of the neck, though elaborate jewellery was often worn.

Footwear was either not worn at all or consisted of a light sandal to protect the feet from the hot ground. In the northern mountains boots were often worn in winter.

From *c*. the 8th c. onwards India was invaded by various Muslim groups who established ruling dynasties. The Muslim conquerors remained aloof as a ruling class, sometimes persecuting but more often tolerating the practices of the conquered Hindus, who largely retained their traditional dress. At all times there were Hindu chiefs ruling in outlying parts of India, who paid tribute to their Muslim overlords. This often meant a trip to the Muslim court, where Persian dress was worn. Sometimes Persian fashions were adopted by these rulers, spreading the influences to their own domains but modified according to taste. Within the Muslim territories Hindu and Muslim came to live side by side distinguished from each other by dress and habits, though well-to-do Hindu families often adopted the system of strict 'purdah' from the Muslims and made their womenfolk veil themselves in public. This borrowing was probably made for strictly practical reasons at first, since Muslim rulers would sometimes take for the royal harem any attractive female seen unveiled in public.

The Hindu kingdoms in the far south retained their independence far longer. One or two were never conquered by the Muslims and as a result became relatively isolated from the rest of the peninsula. South Indian costumes were thus able to retain their 'classical' flavour and even today are much closer to the costume depicted in medieval temples than those of the northern regions.

In the 16th and 17th centuries the Mogul emperors were for a comparatively short time able to unify politically practically the whole of north India and much of the Deccan. Under the Emperor Akbar (1556–1606) a conscious fusing of Hindu and Muslim culture was attempted. Akbar himself married Hindu princesses, who brought their traditional wardrobes with them to the Mogul court, and his courtiers were not discouraged from marrying Hindu wives. Many Hindu rajahs of vassal states were taken into the imperial service without insistence upon their conversion to Islam. Many of these adopted Mogul court dress, sometimes with some modification, and Muslim courtiers were also not discouraged from adopting some of the fashions of their Hindu colleagues.

Akbar's great-grandson, Aurangzeb (1659–1707), orthodox and fanatical, reversed this policy and encouraged discrimination against non-believers both at court and throughout the empire. The Hindu rajahs retired to their chiefdoms and many of them rebelled against the emperor. The resulting lack of contact encouraged regional variation in dress once again though many aspects of Mogul costume continued in vogue among the Hindu ruling classes.

The 18th c. saw a revival of Hindu political power as the Mogul empire gradually disintegrated, but these upheavals did not produce a parallel cultural revival. The century did, however, see the establishment of the Sikhs as a powerful religious and political group. Originally founded in the 16th c., persecution in the 18th c. welded them together in opposition as

A

B

C

D

E

F

BRIDAL COSTUMES

A. Gujarat, western India, a silk *choli* heavily embroidered in gold and silver, a *sari* wrapped in the Gujarati style and kept in place with a kind of cummerbund, and over the head a *dopatta* with tie-and-dye printing. B. Lucknow, Uttar Pradesh, a *choli* of embroidered muslin beneath a *sari* of similar material heavily embroidered in gold and silver. C. Orissa, a *choli* beneath a plain *sari* with a border woven in gold and silver thread. D. Rajasthan, a *choli* and *sari* with embroidery and tie-and-dye decoration. The ornate nose-ring is becoming less common. E. Banjari costume from Rajasthan. The Banjaris were originally a tribe of gypsies. Rajasthan costume does not often include the *sari*, here a *choli* and skirt are worn with a long robe worn over the head and draped down to the feet. Everyday costume would be less ornate and the long robe much shorter, perhaps not even reaching the waist. The costume is embroidered and set with mirror glass. F. Madras. This dress is a rather ornate version of the typical dress of south India. A brief *choli* beneath a rich *sari* with borders and ends woven in gold or silver thread

a martial brotherhood with special customs and distinctive dress, who built near the end of the century an important kingdom in the Punjab.

These events tended to inhibit cultural interchange and habits of costume became regional for all classes. Among the lower classes in particular, they being least affected by any kind of change, costume was always more regional in style and is still so today.

(*c*) *Regional Costume.* Although politically united, with a style of dress which is described as 'national', India is still in many ways a collection of individual states each with its own tradition in costume. To a casual observer it can appear that there is both a sameness of dress in different parts of India and at the same time a bewildering variety of costume to be seen in any particular place. This is because superimposed upon regional variation there are also social differences in the way people dress. For instance although the *sari* is considered to be the most Indian of all garments, there are millions of women in India who would never normally wear one. There are also tribal peoples in various parts of the country whose modes of dress would hardly be recognized as having any relationship with the costume of other Indians at all. Regional costume is less adopted by the upper classes and the rich, who have greater freedom of movement, than by the poor and the highly orthodox, who are not in the habit of travelling outside their region.

There is a general tendency for Muslim women to wear some form of trousers and for Hindu women to wear the *sari* or the skirt. The *sari* becomes more the normal dress the farther south and east one travels and these are the areas in which Muslim penetration has been least, with the exception of East Bengal. In the centre of the peninsula, formerly the Muslim state of Hyderabad, both the *sari* and trousers are found.

Men's dress on the other hand tends to vary more in accordance with occupation than by area though there are exceptions. Farmers and traders tend to be more traditional in their dress and to wear the *dhoti*. Many farm-workers wear the smaller *lungi* when working in the fields as it leaves the legs more freedom of movement. The turban should always be worn by a Sikh and it is also common throughout the Punjab and Rajasthan and although some people are found wearing turbans all over India, they are much more common among the farmers of Mysore and Madras and the boatmen of Kerala. The wearing of tight trousers or pyjamas is only common in the Punjab and in Rajasthan, and in Rajasthan the *jama* is sometimes worn. This is a long dress-like coat of muslin with long tightish sleeves and the front is tied under the armpit. It derives directly from Mogul costume.

Women's dress varies more by region. In the Himalayas, especially in Kashmir, a Muslim area, many women wear a shirt-like dress over wide trousers gathered at the ankle, though until recently this costume was almost always completely covered by the *burkha* when out of doors. The *burkha* is a tent-like garment enveloping the whole body, and is fitted with an embroidered lattice-window to enable the wearer to see and breathe. Sometimes an enormous shawl is used for the same purpose. In the Punjab a shirt-like dress over trousers is also worn, but here the trousers often cling closely to the legs. A shawl is worn over the head and around the shoulders and this is often of muslin. In Rajasthan people wear an ankle-length skirt and the short blouse or *choli* and over them a shawl, usually of cotton. A similar costume is worn in Kathiwar and Madhya Bharat. In the Ganges basin from Uttar Pradesh to west Bengal white *saris* with a narrow, coloured border are popular. The end of the *sari* is often drawn over the head like a shawl. The *sari* is also worn in central India. But a little farther south, in the parts of Maharasthra and Andhra Pradesh which were formerly the Muslim state of Hyderabad, many women wear the tight trousers of the Punjab, but the shirt-like dress is usually longer than in the north. In south India proper, the states of Anhra, Mysore, Madras and Kerala, the *sari* is almost always worn. It is a fuller and glossier garment than in the north and often almost completely conceals the *choli*. The head is usually left bare and the hair is either plaited or tied back in a bun over the nape of the neck.

4. JEWELLERY. The custom of ornamenting the human body has been practised from the earliest times and is probably therefore the oldest of the arts. Ornaments can be fashioned from all kinds of materials, from plants and pebbles to gold and precious gems, but the term 'JEWELLERY' implies the use of gemstones and in this sense the earliest evidence of jewellery in India dates from *c.* 2500 B.C. when the Indus Valley civilization flourished in what is now western Pakistan and parts of Gujarat and Rajasthan in India. Figurines have been discovered from the remains of city sites in this region which clearly show lavish ornament. Excavations have also brought to light evidence of workshops where beads were fashioned in precious and semi-precious stones, and some of these beads are known to have been exported to Mesopotamia.

The basic styles of traditional Indian jewellery were established during the classical period of Indian history from *c.* the beginning of the Christian era up to the end of the 12th c. Few pieces remain from this period but evidence of jewellery styles has been drawn from the sculptured figures which survive on temples, especially those in central and southern India. Many of these figures are shown wearing lavish jewellery which has been carved in great detail, and often much of the frieze and pillar decoration of the temple buildings is also in the form of jewellery. The style of these ornaments bears a strong resemblance to many of the pieces worn in modern times. Both men and women of this period wore a profusion of jewellery, and the accomplishments of cultured citizens included the ability to recognize and judge the quality of gemstones and to distinguish real gold from imitation. These styles remained popular for centuries, even after the Muslims established kingdoms in northern India at the end of the 12th c. The eventual establishment of the Mogul dynasty in the 16th and 17th centuries brought into India styles which were strongly Persian in character and though there was at first little exchange on a cultural level, the most famous of the Mogul emperors, Akbar, an exact contemporary of Queen Elizabeth I of England, sought to encourage a deliberate synthesis of Persian and Hindu cultural styles. He married Hindu princesses who brought their jewellery with them to the Mogul court and he established court workshops for all the crafts, where Hindu and Muslim craftsmen worked together. The lavish court life of the Moguls encouraged the patronage of jewellers and goldsmiths and as a result magnificent articles of jewellery were produced. The technique of ENAMELLING was developed in India at this time, probably also as an imported craft from Persia.

Few actual examples of jewellery, however, have survived which are earlier than the 18th c. since fashions changed and it was the custom to remake old pieces in more modern styles. These changes were also encouraged by the Indian custom of carrying the family funds in the form of jewellery worn by the womenfolk, to be sold back to the jewellers in time of need. Evidence of jewellery styles has therefore to be obtained from secondary sources. Sculpture has already been referred to as such a source, and others are mural paintings, miniatures and literary sources including accounts by travellers to India from other countries.

For the European, at least from Roman times onwards, India has been famous as a source of jewels and spices. For medieval Europe India was the fabulous land of riches, and the British Crown Jewels contain at least one Indian diamond, the famous Koh-i-Noor, which probably originated in Golconda, where the most renowned Indian mines were situated. These mines, and most of the others in India, are now worked out, although recent surveys have located new areas for exploration. In the past EMERALDS, RUBIES, SAPPHIRES and PEARLS, in addition to DIAMONDS, have been obtained from Indian sources.

The traditional Indian craftsman has been primarily concerned to create a total effect in an ornament and has not been involved with the creation of fire and sparkle in individual stones. The art of cutting and polishing scientifically, whilst known and understood, has not been developed to the same extent as in Europe. A piece of Indian jewellery will often include flawed stones if they are otherwise suitable in shape and colour. Really prized gems were usually set into turban ornaments or used as pendants to necklaces. Those in royal collections were often engraved with the name of the owner. A common method of setting in India has been to bed stones in a hard resin of lac which is contained in a kind of trough of gold. The gems are backed with silver foil to improve their lustre. The reverse of the piece was often finely CHASED and was sometimes enamelled, especially in the case of very important pieces. Enamelling came to be a highly specialized skill in India and all the main colours could be obtained by a skilled craftsman. The method used was champlevé, where the metal is hollowed out and the enamel is fired into the depressions so as to leave a thin gold line separating the segments of colour. Translucent enamels were invariably used and the best pieces were manufactured in Jaipur. Traditionally the jeweller worked at the house of the customer, using materials supplied by him, usually old pieces which were no longer in fashion. In this way the client was theoretically able to oversee the work as it progressed and could also ensure that he was not being cheated. This is still the normal system in many parts of India, but in the larger cities ornaments are now often ready-made and are purchased from shops.

Styles of ornament varied from region to region and in all areas there were different styles for men and women. At the courts of rulers jewellery was worn lavishly by both sexes, but elsewhere women wore many more ornaments than the men. Regional differences were such that it was usually possible to identify the region and sometimes even the caste of an individual purely by the ornaments worn in conjunction with costume styles, and this is still true in many areas today. But there is a growing section of the community, especially in the large cities, who no longer wear the great quantity of ornaments which were once obligatory and who prefer modern products which do not fall within the traditional classifications although they are often still based upon the traditional forms.

In shape and design traditional ornaments often either directly reproduce, or are very closely based upon, natural forms: flowers, seeds, nuts, leaves, etc. This type of pattern can be traced back from evidence in painting and sculpture to pre-medieval times. Indeed there exist today in India tribal groups some of whom still make and wear ornaments made of grasses, leaves, seeds and stones.

A vast majority of the ordinary people could never afford more than one or two pieces of jewellery in GOLD or SILVER, and in fact there are prohibitions against the wearing of precious metals by some of the lower castes. There have also been prohibitions against the wearing of precious metals on certain parts of the body and many caste groups are forbidden to wear gold ornaments below the waist. A high proportion of ornaments worn in India are therefore manufactured of brass, copper or white metal and most of the villagers throughout India wear only ornaments of this type.

5. TERRACOTTA FIGURINES. These are found almost all over India and are sold at fairs and festivals. Sometimes they are used as objects of village worship and plaques of terracotta have been used to decorate the walls of village temples, particularly in Bengal and Bihar. Their history can be traced back to the terracotta TOYS of the Indus Valley culture (2500–1500 B.C.). The technique followed has been very much the same throughout history wherever suitable clay has been available. The modeller makes an original sculpted figurine in fine clay, from which a mould or moulds are taken. From such moulds casts are made in finely prepared clay. As these are drying, fine detail is worked in with chisels and they are then smoothed ready for firing. After firing the mould joins are smoothed out and the piece is ready. Sometimes the finished pieces are painted and occasionally glazed and fired in the kiln.

23, 27, 48, 62, 234, 314, 335, 432, 433, 486, 612, 897.

INDIENNE (French). See CHINTZ and COTTON AND COTTON PRINTING.

INLAY. A decorative technique in wood- or metal-working, in which a substance of a different kind is embedded in a solid support so that its surface is more or less continuous with that of the matrix. See WOOD-WORKING (SPECIAL TECHNIQUES).

INN SIGNS. When the Roman cities of Pompeii and Herculaneum were excavated it was found that most of the shops displayed a sign indicating the nature of the business. They bore little resemblance to signs as we know them. In the main they were plaques of stone or terracotta carved in relief, and were inset at the sides of the open shop fronts. The nature of the business was clearly delineated: a goat was the sign of a dairy, a schoolmaster thrashing a boy indicated a school and among the most frequent was the sign of the wine shop, a display of vine leaves or the bush always associated with Bacchus.

There is little doubt that the custom was introduced into Britain during the Roman occupation, and the idea quickly gained popularity. But there were few ale-houses outside the cities until the 14th c., when pilgrimages to religious shrines involved more people in travel. What had been goat- and mule-paths gradually evolved into rough tracks and beside them ale-houses and very primitive inns, where travellers provided their own food and slept communally, came into being. Several inns along the old Pilgrim's Way to Canterbury owe their foundation to the pilgrimages to the tomb of Thomas à Becket.

Hostels for pilgrims were also set up by the various religious orders. Signs associated with the individual orders were displayed outside so that they could be easily identified, for even the illiterate could recognize a picture-sign. The *Bull*, still a very popular sign, was in the first place derived from La Bulle (Latin, *bulla*) the seal of a collegiate body or monastery. Some of these original hostels remain, including the *New Inn*, Gloucester; the *George*, Norton St. Philip (Somerset) and Winchcombe (Gloucestershire); *Olde Bell*, Hurley (Berkshire) and many more. Signs stemming from religion are numerous and popular still. They include the *Star* (Star of Bethlehem); *Seven Stars* (representing the seven-starred celestial crown of the Virgin Mary); *Anchor* (Hope as an anchor of the soul, Heb. 6: 19); *Ship* (reference to the Ark); *Lamb and Flag* (Holy Lamb with nimbus and banner); *Cross Keys* (St. Peter); and *Lion and Lamb* (reference to Proverbs). All had their signboards with a descriptive picture.

The system which had commenced as charitable monastic hostels gradually became a thriving commercial business, until in consequence of the Dissolution of the Monasteries what had been religious hostels became secular premises, and the inn took the first important step towards the form we know today. Tradesmen took over the old idea of the sign and by the 15th and 16th centuries city streets abounded in colourful and imaginative signs. Some of them are today housed in the Guildhall Museum, London. Most of the earlier examples were carved on stone, as had been those in Roman cities, or were made up of tiles or consisted of replicas such as a leather bottle displayed outside the premises.

From the 14th c. ale-houses and inns came under strict surveillance by the authorities, and were compelled by law to display a sign. Their number was strictly limited even so, and when the population of England and Wales was only five million some 13,000 premises were licensed. The increased competition caused publicans to vie with each other in displaying larger and more ostentatious signs. Many were mounted on posts which obstructed the footway and at one period the height of an 'ale stake' was limited to 7 ft. (2·13 m). Then there appeared massive structures known as gallows or beam signs which spanned the roadway until in the mid 17th c. they reached such a size as to become dangerous and accidents to pedestrians were frequent. An Act of Parliament then decreed that no signboards should hang across the street but all were to be fixed to some part of the house. Today there are less than a dozen surviving examples of the gallows sign spanning a street: *The Magpie*, Stoneham (Suffolk); *Fox and Hounds*, Barley (Hertfordshire); *Green Man and Black's Head*, Ashbourne (Derbyshire) and less elaborate but ancient ones, *Ye Old Starre*, York, and *The Swan*, Stroud (Gloucestershire). Another elaborate type of sign was sometimes made of wrought iron and was the work of master craftsmen. That at *The Ship*, Mere (Wiltshire), is an excellent 18th-c. example.

Until street numbering was brought in, and it was not adopted in Britain until 1805, it was a complicated business to give directions or an address and the nearest signboard proved a boon—'. . . hard by the *Swan and Eaglet*', etc. was the regular form. This practice continued well into the 19th c. and new streets were often named after nearby taverns. Typical is Half Moon Street, Piccadilly, London. Even in 1839, when the Croydon railway was opened, many of its stations were named after popular inns on the route, including New Cross, Dartmouth Arms and Anerley Arms.

Signboards of more modest size, either fixed or swinging and bearing a picture, became popular towards the end of the 18th c., and inn signs have remained largely in that form ever since.

The drift away from religious signs accelerated after the Dissolution of the Monasteries in the 16th c., and royal signs as a compliment to the monarchs became popular. This is the explanation of many of the animals and some other symbols on signs. Lions have been identified on armorial bearings of British kings since the Conquest and figured on the badges of William I, William II and Henry I (blue lion) and most of the monarchs up to the present day. Edward III used as a badge the rising sun. There were swans and antelopes (Henry VI); Edward IV had the black dragon, black bull, greyhound, falcon and white lion. The queens of Henry VIII each had their coats-of-arms and from them came the *Eagle*, *Griffin*, *Black Lion*, etc. The Hanoverians brought the white horse into prominence and the kings of Scotland the unicorn. Over and above these there was the *Crown*, of which there are about 1,000 in Britain today, and the *King's Arms*. In the latter case it is often possible to note which king's arms they are, thus getting a clue as to the date of the inn. There were also houses named after specific kings, queens and princesses from Ethelbert the Saxon up to the reigning monarch.

Inns also took their signs from the heraldic devices or coats-of-arms of the landed aristocracy as a tribute to the overlord, and much duplication was caused owing to the extensive estates of some of them. When old soldiers or retainers entered civilian life and set up as innkeepers they were often proud to adopt the armorial bearings of their former overlords as their own business sign. The *Eagle and Child* from the arms of the Earls of Derby is an instance, and the *Devonshire Arms* is to be found in Devon, Derbyshire, Yorkshire and elsewhere.

In the Middle Ages churchwardens were often responsible for brewing beer for social or revenue-raising events at the church, and parishes sometimes had their own brew-house. Such places later became inns and the *Church House* is even now in some places to be found situated next to the church.

The great advances that came with the coaching era and the consequent improvement of highways, together with the growth of the middle classes, brought into being a new type of inn. Now more and more people travelled as a matter of course, and they needed inns at which to stay at the end of every stage. These coaching inns became larger and more efficient. One coach- and inn-owner in London possessed 1,500 horses and 60 coaches, while the *Bull and Mouth*, St. Martins-le-Grand, had underground stables to accommodate 700 horses. The new inn signs were associated with the coaches or the inns. Many coaches lent their names to the inns they patronized, as for instance the *Quicksilver Mail*, *Flying Bull* and *Gloucester Flying Machine*, all of which are still in being and have excellent signs. The new highway system and the days of the horse encouraged further signs—*Horse and Groom*, *Toll Gate*, *Turnpike House*, *Postboy* and, most popular of all, *Coach and Horses*.

There seem to have been relatively few waterside inns bearing a name or sign until the canals became an integral part of the transport system, at about the time of the Industrial Revolution. The canals, like the coach roads, called for stages and so inns began to spring up at regular intervals along the routes. These bore the names of the canal services, as the *Paddington Packet*, or the canal names, as the *Grand Junction*. The *Ship and Shovel* was named after the custom of shovelling grain into canal boats.

The innkeeper, adept at turning circumstances to his advantage, saw possibilities in the craftsmen's guilds and soon set up signs to attract the men of certain trades. Hundreds of these names and signs exist today. Many of the trades have died out but the names remain to form part of Britain's industrial history: basket-makers, brick-setters, dowel-turners, lathe-cleavers, draymen, printers' devils, slubbers, well-diggers, whitesmiths, etc. mostly followed by the word 'Arms', though the guild or society's arms only rarely appeared on the sign. There are still some to be found, such as the rare *Plaisterers Arms*, Winchcombe (Gloucestershire), as well as many *Carpenters' Arms*. Naturally the country districts had their own loyalties, and inns named after tools and aspects of agriculture became numerous.

Perhaps the most interesting of all are the signs which honour or commemorate popular or illustrious people. There are soldiers, sailors, politicians, saints, philanthropists, sportsmen, explorers and even fictional heroes such as Sherlock Holmes, and it is a tribute to the strength of tradition that so many remain. Soldiers and sailors are the most popular, with Nelson and Wellington in the van. Politicians of the 18th c. are numerous and typical of keeping this feeling up to date is the portrait on the sign of the *Pride of the Valley*, Churt (Surrey), where Lloyd George lived, and the name of *Winston Churchill* in different parts of the country.

As the coaching era brought new names, so did the railways in the mid 19th c. Hundreds of inns sprang up bearing such names as *Railway*, *Station* or *Great Western* and other company names. That period is now in decline but nostalgia over the passing of steam has brought about many new signs to take the place of the sombre *Railway Arms*. In this group are *Puffing*

Billy, *Royal Scot* and *Golden Arrow*. As modes of travel have changed inn signs have kept pace. There are many aircraft signs relating to early machines and some which became famous in the war: the *Canopus*, Rochester (Kent); *Wayfarer*, Bristol; *Wellington*, Hastings (Sussex) and even the *Air Hostess*, London Airport. Space travel signs include *Man in Space*, Stoke-on-Trent (Staffordshire); *Other Side of the Moon*, Nottingham; *Full Moon*, *Spotted Cow* and many others.

The meaning of many signs is obscure, but usually these obscurities are due to a combination of two names when the licence of one had lapsed. The practice has produced such examples as *Railway and Linnet* or *Swan and Railway*. Some names have come down to us through the Englishman's inability to pronounce foreign words, or perhaps his sheer contrariness. *Bull and Mouth* is derived from 'Boulogne Mouth', the mouth of Boulogne harbour, following the capture of the town by Henry VIII in 1544. *God Encompasses Us* was a popular religious sign but with usage it became *Goat and Compasses*.

Inns and their signs have even influenced the English language, for such everyday expressions as 'a Cock and Bull story', 'Hobson's choice', 'a good wine needs no bush', all found their origins in this terrain.

Many signs have their origin in past history and often industrial history can be traced by inn signs. There are *Miners' Arms* in remote villages which recall a long-past mining boom. Many signs identify historical events, as the numerous inns named *Rose and Crown* in approval of the marriage of Henry VII to Elizabeth, which ended the Wars of the Roses. The sign of the *Royal Oak* is a colourful reminder of Charles II and his escape after the battle of Worcester, and the *Rose Revived* is an allusion to the Restoration. Great events in more recent centuries are recalled by *Crystal Palace* and *Glasshouse*, both reminders of the Great Exhibition of 1851.

In the last 200 years the sign language has become widespread. There are more than 1,000 bird signs, hundreds of animals in all kinds of attitudes and with a variety of often strange companions.

Crafts and guilds were identified on inn signs. *Plaisterers Arms*, Winchcombe (Glos.)

The *New Inn*, Gloucester. One of the few remaining galleried inns of the pilgrim days

Inns gave their names to the coaches. 'The Quicksilver Mail' ran from London to Cornwall

Railway signs become nostalgic

Race-horses flourish, particularly in the North Country. There are signs recalling local legends, fairy tales, literary associations and even giants.

At first the signs were painted by anyone who could wield a brush, sometimes as repayment for board and lodging. Many a *faux pas* resulted, some of which were amusing. A classic example is the *Black Prince*, named in compliment to the hero of Crécy. An ignorant artist, commissioned to repaint the almost obliterated sign, painted an Indian chief. The *Swan with two necks* was really *Swan with two nicks* (the markings on swans signifying ownership of the Dyers and Vintners Company). Famous artists have, however, made their contribution, including William Hogarth, who was responsible for the famous *Man with the load of Mischief*. Sir Godfrey Kneller and George Moreland are known to have painted an occasional sign. David Cox's *Royal Oak* at Bettws-y-coed (Caernarvonshire) is now behind glass inside the inn.

Today the painting of signboards is recognized as a craft; the subjects are no longer left to the artist's imagination and great pains are taken to ensure complete accuracy. Few breweries employ their own staff for the purpose as the work is usually put out to specialists in the field. Every type of material is used, including stone, wood, iron, steel, copper and glass. The great difficulty has always been the effect of weather on painted signs, which required continual renovation. A process which simplifies this task has now been evolved. The outline of the artist's original work is enlarged and then engraved on a metal sheet, which is painted in accordance with the original. When the sign needs repainting—and this occurs at a point varying between three and five years—the work can then be carried out by a comparatively unskilled painter following the colour guide and the easily traced lines on the metal. In recent years most brewery companies have realized the interest aroused by a good sign, both as a tourist attraction and as maintaining a tradition. The numbers of signs vary considerably in different parts of Britain. The midlands, south and west abound in good signs, but they are more sparse in the north although there is a gradual increase in numbers.

For centuries the British people have cherished their local inn. They are delighted when somebody or something they admire is perpetuated in what has been called the nation's open-air art gallery. Often despite the brewers' decision to change a name they have been forced by public opinion to desist. A case in point was the portrait of Nelson on the sign of *The Hero*, Burnham Overy (Norfolk). The suggested change was from Nelson to Guy Gibson, V.C., of the 'dam buster' squadron of the Second World War. The sign still portrays Nelson. New houses, however, keep up with the times. The lone voyages of Sir Francis Chichester and Sir Alec Rose have already been recorded.

The inn sign has remained by and large an English institution. Britain is the only country in which signs still flourish on any scale. There are some 70,000 pubs in Britain and a high proportion have a sign. Many old signs are purchased and shipped to America to adorn restaurants and the American tourist loves the British signs, but the custom is not general in the United States. Recently some 'British Pubs' have been opened on the Continent, but otherwise hostelry signs there are few and far between.

200, 201.

INRŌ. Among the articles of personal necessity which the Japanese carried suspended from the belt (see NETSUKE) were the case containing brush and ink tablet, the pipe-case and the *inrō* ('seal case'). These last were boxes intended at first for seals but later used for medicines and sundry other objects. They were usually of LACQUERED wood, sometimes inlaid with IVORY, MOTHER OF PEARL, etc. They were made with anything from one to five compartments. Like the *netsuke*, the decoration of the *inrō* was a miniature art. It was also described in the *Sōken Kishō* (1781) and its development paralleled that of the *netsuke*. Artists began increasingly to sign their work in the first half of the 19th c. The variety of subjects was similar to that of the *netsuke*, though since the decoration of the *inrō* was by painting or inlay more scope was possible for landscape and scenes. The *inrō* differed from the *netsuke* also in that it called for the highly skilled craft of lacquer work. See JAPAN.

439.

INTAGLIO. Engraved or incised work on gemstones, GLASS, CERAMICS or similar materials in which the design is sunk beneath the surface of the material. It is the opposite of CAMEO. An 'intaglio' often means an engraved gem in which figures or other devices are carved into the stone so that when pressed upon a plastic material it produces a likeness in relief. The intaglio is the most ancient form of engraved gems, the earliest known being the Babylonian cylinder seals dating from *c.* 4000 B.C., which were rolled upon damp clay and the impression baked to leave a durable record. See also GREEK AND ROMAN ANTIQUITY and JEWELLERY.

INTAGLIO PRINTING. A technique of making prints from an engraved plate when the print is taken from ink rubbed into the incised lines after the surface of the plate has been wiped clean.

INTARSIA. From *c.* the 15th c. *tarsia* was the Italian term for inlay work of all kinds, including marquetry. Alongside this noun there was also the verb *intarsiare* and practitioners of the craft were known as *intarsiatori*. During the 19th c. the terms *intarsio* and *intarsia* seem to have come into use. Modern Italian has preferred the masculine form, but in English writing the feminine *intarsia* has prevalied. In common with current practice in English the form *intarsia* has been adopted in this *Companion*. A kind of geometrical *intarsia* on CASSONI was popular in

Venice in the 15th c. Florence was renowned for *intarsia* representing pictorial scenes, architectural perspectives, still lifes, etc. on wall panels, panels of cassoni, cupboards, wardrobes, etc. The vogue remained popular in the 16th c.

Intarsia was also used by the cabinet-makers of the important south German centres of Augsburg and Nuremberg. Italian designs were introduced by the Nuremberg carver Peter Flötner (d. 1546) and the painter Lorenz Stoer published a collection of woodcut designs for *intarsia* panels which were popular among Augsburg craftsmen. Italian Renaissance influences spread to France in the 16th c. and among them *intarsia*. Among the 22 Italian craftsmen taken to France by Charles VIII after the capture of Naples in 1495 were two expert craftsmen of *intarsia*, Domenico da Cortona and Bernado da Brescia. Through the 16th c. Italian influence on French furniture was felt primarily through the introduction of colour by means of *intarsia*. See also MARQUETRY, FURNITURE (EUROPEAN) and WOOD-WORKING.

IRON AND STEEL

1. Production.
2. Processing.
3. Cast iron.
4. Decorative wrought ironwork.
5. The work of the forge.
6. Iron-chiselling.
7. Iron jewellery.

1. PRODUCTION. Except in the form of meteoric fragments iron does not occur as a native metal and although these small pieces were highly prized and worked up as ornaments from as early as the beginning of the 3rd millennium B.C., the earliest man-made iron dates from *c.* 2800 B.C. But iron did not become important as a metal until ways had been found both of producing it on a relatively large scale and of giving it a hardness superior to that of bronze, that is of converting it into steel. This was probably an achievement of the Hittites *c.* 1400 B.C. The area where this occurred is thought to have lain about the River Halys in Anatolia, whence in course of time the technique was diffused both east and west through Eurasia, reaching China at about the same time as Europe (the 1st half of the 1st millennium B.C.). Subsequent development in these two regions did not proceed at an equal pace, however, and it was not until the close of the 14th c. A.D. that European iron-workers began to draw level with the Chinese in the various ways of handling iron in its three states: cast iron, steel and wrought iron. It is helpful to think of these three substances in this order since steel is an intermediate product having between 0·5% and 1·5% of carbon as compared with the 2% to 5% carbon of cast iron and the 0·01% of wrought iron. The amount of carbon present determines the qualities of each of these materials and prescribes not only the uses to which they may be put but equally the manner in which they must be handled.

In Europe iron was produced by the direct method for nearly two and a half millennia, from *c.* 1000 B.C. to *c.* A.D. 1400. The term 'direct method' indicates a sequence of operations by means of which iron ore is converted into wrought iron or steel without the metal ever having melted. The ore, washed or roasted, broken into small fragments and mixed with charcoal, was reduced to a pasty condition in the furnace at a temperature too low, *c.* 1200 °C., for liquation to occur. Opinion varies as to whether cast iron could or could not have been produced at will in the various types, shaft or bowl form, of furnace known to have existed. Certainly fragments of cast iron of pre-Roman date have been discovered, but they were evidently discarded as waste. It might well be prudent, therefore, to conclude that care at least was taken to see that furnace temperatures were delicately controlled and kept below the level at which fusion would take place. This was necessary because then and for long afterwards no means were known by which cast iron could be decarburized so as to produce either steel or wrought iron. Nor apparently was it appreciated that the iron if liquefied might be cast into useful shapes. It is only at the close of the 14th c. A.D. that there is for the first time in Europe conclusive evidence of iron being cast (into cannon).

The first furnaces, usually little more than hollows in the ground lined with clay and supplied with a blast from foot- or hand-operated bellows, produced only limited quantities—about a kilo—of iron at a time. The metal gradually separating from the ore sank to the bottom of the bowl and formed a pasty lump, much intermixed with slag, known as a 'bloom'. The iron was refined by repeated hammerings, which served to expel most but not all of this foreign matter. Because of the smallness of the pieces produced it was usually necessary to amalgamate by welding a number of these lumps into more serviceable masses. The product might be either wrought iron or natural steel, the latter resulting if the ore contained traces of manganese. A second means of producing steel, by surface-carburization or case-hardening, was known and involved subjecting wrought iron to prolonged heating in glowing charcoal. These procedures as well as the technique of quenching and probably that of tempering, by means of which the quality of the steel might be improved, were all known in pre-Roman times.

Until the 11th c. A.D. there was little change except that furnaces tended to grow rather larger and to yield larger pieces of iron. About this time the technique of making high quality pattern-welded steel, which since the 5th c. A.D. had been used to fabricate swords of great beauty and serviceability, seems to have been lost or discontinued. Their surfaces, etched and polished, reveal a finely developed interwoven texture, the outcome of repeatedly piling, twisting and drawing out the metal so as to produce, not indeed a homogeneous steel, but one in which steely iron, soft iron and slag were evenly distributed. Such even distribution was essential since otherwise slag intrusions, always present in the metal, were likely to form planes of weakness along which fractures might occur. (See also ARMS AND ARMOUR.) During the same century a dramatic change began to take place in the basic industries of Europe. Muscle-power began to be replaced by water-power. The water-wheel had been known in Europe for 1000 years and during that time had been exploited only for the grinding of grain. By the addition of cams to its axle it was now enabled to provide power for a wide variety of operations. There is little doubt that at iron furnaces the stamps, bellows and hammers now began to be mechanically powered, and certainly by the 12th c. A.D. the generalization of this process was well under way, the leading role being taken by monasteries of the Cistercian order. Production, no longer tied to the frail capacities of human muscle and sinew, made dramatic strides. Whereas a medieval furnace without water-power might have produced three tonnes of iron a year, one with water-powered belows could achieve something like 25 tonnes and if the hammer were powered similarly, 45 tonnes, although it is important to remember that the actual production process was still the ancient one in all its essentials.

Towards the end of the 14th c., however, this too began to change. From the 1380s and 1390s it is evident that iron was being liquefied and cast into cannon and shot and then, slightly later, into pots, frying pans and stoves. For long this change was held to be the result of a slow process of internal evolution in European iron technology, but increasingly it begins to appear that the stimulus leading to these new procedures, if not the actual technique employed, was ultimately of Chinese origin, reaching the West through Persia or the Khanate of the Golden Horde, or again possibly through both since evidence of such influences comes from the territories of Venice and from Sweden. Almost simultaneously blast-furnaces producing cast iron cannon appear in Germany (Frankfurt, 1390), France (Dijon, 1409), and Italy (Brescia, 1429). If after long ages the European iron-masters had stumbled independently on the potentialities of cast iron, one would not expect perhaps that a whole range of new and sophisticated procedures should have become standard practice almost simultaneously; yet such was the case. Alongside the old mechanized bowl-furnaces producing iron by the direct method there now appeared blast-furnaces, much greater in height, producing liquid iron not simply in the form of castings but as pig-iron destined for conversion into wrought iron and steel. The technique for converting pig-iron into wrought iron involved the use of one or two more associated furnaces: the finery hearth and the chafery. The temperature of the finery hearth, to which the pig-iron was first taken, was sufficiently high to melt the pig but too low to melt wrought iron, with the result that as the carbon was burnt from it the liquefying pig would re-congeal into a plastic condition and gather at the bottom of the hearth in exactly the condition of the bloom long familiar in European practice. The bloom would then be twice lifted to the surface and broken up before being consolidated under the hammer. This done, it would be left to 'soak' for an hour in the bottom of the hearth before being hammered out into an ancony. It would be given its final bar form either at the same hearth, in the German one-hearth process, or at a second hearth, the chafery, if the Walloon two-hearth process was employed. In Styria it was the practice to break up the pig initially before using the two-hearth process. As for more sophisticated methods of shaping the refined wrought iron than subjecting it to the hammer, Leonardo da Vinci had already projected in some detail the water-driven machinery that would be needed for rolling and profiling iron bars. The first actual slitting and rolling mill that we know of, at Nuremberg in 1539, produced, however, only nail iron and wire, and in fact construction of plant on the scale Leonardo had envisaged lay far in the future.

To return to the subject of refining, it is significant that the first reference to an *affineur de fer* is as early as 1402, so that there is reason to think that the conversion technique described above was coeval with the appearance of the blast-furnace itself. It ought perhaps to be mentioned here that alongside the blast-furnace, capable even in its early forms of producing something approaching 200 tonnes a year, there persisted in use not only the old bowl-furnace but also an intermediate type which could be converted quite easily from bloom to pig production as market conditions warranted: the terms *Blauofen* and *Stuckofen* denoted these two forms. The blast-furnace, however, possessed such great advantages that except in isolated localities it steadily ousted the others, which were unable to compete with it in terms either of output or extraction rate from the ore or economy in the use of fuel. England, backward in metallurgy, adopted the blast-furnace only tardily. The first, at Newbridge in Sussex, was built in 1496 and its adoption outside Sussex began only in the 2nd half of the 16th c. As for the conformation of the blast-furnace it can only be said here that Hassenfratz in his *La Sidérotechnie* (1812) was able to distinguish nine major types in use during the 17th and 18th centuries. What distinguished all of them from the bowl type was their height: whereas the bowl-furnace probably never exceeded one and a half or two metres, the blast-furnace was commonly over six metres and might exceptionally reach over 10 metres, the limit in each case being set by the capacity of the charcoal fuel to resist, without being crushed, the load of ore and flux with which it was mixed and which it had to sustain as the mixture made its slow descent down the shaft.

At the same time that wrought-iron manufacture was undergoing transformation so too was that of steel. Reference has been made to the possibility that new techniques were entering both northern and southern Europe from Asia at the close of the 14th c. and colour is lent to such an assumption by the fact that new and distinctly different ways of making steel emerged about this time north and south of the Alps. In the south the steel produced was characteristically of the Bergamasque or co-fusion type. Co-fusion steel—the coinage is Joseph Needham's—was made by binding together thin sheets of wrought iron and immersing them in a bath of liquid cast iron. Complete fusion did not, however, take place since the temperature employed was below that of the melting point of wrought iron. Some of the carbon in the cast iron was absorbed by the plates, which became steeled on their surfaces so that the resulting product was rather like a sandwich of cast iron, steel and wrought iron and was in every way identical with Chinese and central Indian 'wootz' steel of this type. North of the Alps the mazeage process predominated, a forerunner of Bessemer's, in which discs of hot cast iron were hammered under a cold blast in order to decarburize them. At the finish the carbon content of the disc would rise from zero at the centre to the high figures characteristic of cast iron on the periphery.

Both methods tended to be displaced from the end of the 16th c. onwards by yet another process, that of cementation, although whether steel of this sort grew to be preferred because it was cheaper or because it was of better quality is hard to say. The earliest description, in Della Porta's *Magia Naturalis* (1588), is soon followed by the name of one of the first developers of the technique, Johann Nussbaum, in 1601. To make steel in this way bars of best-quality wrought iron were placed in boxes of fire-clay and tightly packed with charcoal. The boxes, closely sealed, were then put in the hearth for varying periods. Nussbaum's contribution was to place such boxes in a reverberatory furnace so that an even heat enveloped them on all sides; and whereas Porta thought an hour sufficient time, Nussbaum permitted them to glow for three days and nights. This was sufficient time for a skin of steel perhaps as much as six millimetres in thickness to have formed round the still unaltered cores of the bars. 'Blister steel' was the English term for this product and referred to the characteristic appearance presented by the bars as they were taken from their 'coffins', as the chests were called. To produce a more even distribution of the steely areas a technique was used similar to that employed centuries before in the manufacture of the pattern-welded swords already referred to. 'Shear steel', as such forged steel was called, was used for cutlery, and double shear, in which the piling and drawing out was performed a second time, was the best quality available in Europe and served for precision uses such as watch-springs and surgical tools. It may be noted that coal fuel instead of charcoal was used in the production of cementation steel. This was possible since the iron was safely sealed up in its boxes and was in any case secluded by the reverberatory furnace's construction from all contact with the burning coal, which nearly always contained substances injurious to iron. Yet such steel, however carefully prepared, was not homogeneous since intrusions of slag and silica would inevitably be present in unfused metal, to say nothing of unaltered soft iron. This was why Moxon in his *Mechanik Exercises* (1678) and Réaumur in his *L'Art d'Adoucir le Fer Fondu* (1722) had both stated that wootz or DAMASCENE steel was the finest in the world and to be preferred to all others, although it was virtually unobtainable in Europe and presented such novel difficulties to European smiths that they were quite unable to work it successfully. It is interesting to note the unanimity of Porta, Moxon and Réaumur on this point. 'Too much heat makes it crumble, and cold it is stubborn', remarked Porta, to which Moxon was to add: 'It is the most difficult of any steel to work at the forge, for you shall scarce be able to strike upon a bloodheat but it will redsear' (crack and crumble). In 1722 Réaumur, having with great difficulty obtained a cake of wootz, was disappointed to find 'no artisan in Paris who succeeded in forging a tool out of it. It withstood the fire hardly better than cast iron.' Wootz was in fact, except in its central Indian form, a homogeneous steel, whether produced in the manner of Mysore or in that of Hyderabad. The product of complete fusion in closed clay crucibles and entirely free of foreign matter, it required great skill in the smith who forged it. The extreme beauty of the surface textures which skilful cross-working served to reveal and magnify long excited the admiration of Europeans who, accustomed only to the somewhat similar but much inferior effects produced by pattern-welding, were long baffled by its secrets. Only in 1821 was Bréant able to demonstrate conclusively that damascene-patterning was chemically and not mechanically produced. Curiously enough an Englishman, Benjamin Huntsman, either by chance or through intuition, began in 1742 to produce a European variety of crucible steel which closely resembled wootz in its working properties. Jars in his *Voyages Métallurgiques* (1774–81), reporting on English metallurgical progress to the French government, remarked that it ran like sand under the hammer, words which recall the difficulty Moxon had described in the working of imported wootz. It could of course be forged but only at very low temperatures. Once the special disciplines its working required were understood, its superb quality amply repaid the pains of the careful smith.

Ever since the 16th c. the English had taken the lead in seeking to substitute coal and coke for charcoal fuel in a wide variety of industrial processes. The reasons were economic: coal was more plentiful and cheaper in England than anywhere else in Europe. The effort met with much success except in iron smelting. Although coal had been used since medieval times in smiths' forges in both England and Europe, since the sulphur and phosphorus that coal usually contained did no harm to already formed iron, attempts to use it in blast-furnaces and fineries resulted only in iron that was hot or cold short, that is brittle iron that would crack at the first attempt to work it hot or cold. The first breakthrough came with Abraham Darby's successful use of coke in a blast-furnace at Coalbrookdale, Shropshire, in 1709. Either by chance or by design he used a coal unusually free from these injurious elements. His purpose was limited. He did not attempt, as far as we know, to refine coke-fired pig into bar-iron since he was interested only in producing liquid metal for casting cooking-pots. Little notice was taken of his achievement and there were few other experiments with coke before the 1750s when, for reasons which remain as obscure as the earlier neglect, ironmasters began to use coke in increasing numbers. There are certain clues, however: the change almost certainly owed something to the new cylinder-blower, patented in 1757 by Isaac Wilkinson, which made possible a much fiercer blast than the old cuneate type of bellows had been capable of. Steam-driven water-returning engines and ultimately steam-driven blowers working quite independently of water-power were certainly involved also. So rapid was the change that after 1775 no new charcoal-fired blast-furnace was built in England. An increasing quantity of cast-iron goods not unnaturally resulted from the growing use of coke since at this stage no satisfactory technique had been devised for refining coke-pig into good quality wrought iron. The quality of cast iron, however, was constantly being improved. If they were to be operated satisfactorily, coke-fired blast-furnaces needed to be run at higher temperatures than had been customary when charcoal was the fuel. The liquid iron was consequently rendered much less viscous than previously and could therefore be led into much more delicate shapes and patterns. Notable victims of this growing expertise were the smiths producing decorative wrought ironwork. Decorative cast iron was much cheaper, even if aesthetically speaking it left much to be desired, and tended all over Europe to drive the smiths from the field. In the matter of learning how to convert coke-pig into bar-iron some progress had been made by the middle of the century. About 1748 Abraham Darby the Younger had managed to produce a grade good enough for nail manufacture though one still quite unfit for normal forge work. In the 2nd half of the century experimenters were not lacking, for success would quite clearly have revolutionary effects. The Government and the ironmasters realized this no less clearly than the Swedish government, whose blast-furnaces supplied England with bar-iron. England, chronically short of this and having to import something approaching 70% of the supplies its forges required, would at one blow be freed from the danger of having its supplies cut off in wartime at the very moment when they would be most urgently needed. The Cranage brothers failed in their efforts at Coalbrookdale in 1766. Jesson and Wright's patent process of 1774 was capable of refining coke-pig into good bar-iron but was too slow and costly to represent more than a very limited success. In 1783 the efforts of Onions, another Coalbrookdale worker, came to nothing. Success was finally achieved by Sir Henry Cort at Fontley in Hampshire. His patents of 1783 and 1784 for rolling and puddling iron marked the final stage of a sustained effort to free the iron industry in Britain in all its branches from dependence on charcoal fuel. Steam-power at the same time was freeing the industry from its dependence on falling water to activate its bellows and hammers and rollers. The entire ecology of the industry was in future to depend on the location of coal and iron ore fields.

Cort's process was rapidly taken up, in the first instance by the great Welsh ironmasters. When the patent royalty of ten shillings (50p) a ton ceased to be enforced after 1789 a further boost was given to its employment and although like all new methods it was not without its teething troubles and was subject to continual small improvements, figures for British iron production show its impact clearly enough. By the end of the century output had quadrupled and at something like 250,000 tonnes was near to equalling the combined production of the rest of Europe. By 1835 over 1,000,000 tonnes were being produced annually.

As for the process itself, the first step was to place the coke-pig in a reverberatory furnace. A raw coal fire, separated by a shallow bridge from the sand bed on which the pig-iron was placed, was prevented from supplying, under strong draft, more than its heat to the iron. As the iron melted it was vigorously stirred with rods so as to expose all parts of it to the flames. As this process of burning off the carbon neared its end, the iron began to thicken since the heat of the furnace, while great enough to liquefy cast iron, was below the melting point of wrought iron, which was of course what the mass was now on the point of becoming. The iron, once it reached a pasty state, or as Cort termed it 'had come to nature', was gathered up in lumps weighing about 45 kg and roughly consolidated under a hammer. Then instead of being refined further in this way, as if in the two-hearth process, the rough blocks were fed between rollers which forcibly expelled the slag. Twenty tonnes of iron could be rolled a day as against the one tonne a day refinable under the hammer.

During the first half of the 19th c. small

improvements at all stages of the production process greatly cheapened the cost of both cast and wrought iron and probably had as great an effect cumulatively as more striking innovations. An example of the latter was the hot blast introduced by Neilsen in 1829. Great economies in fuel resulted and even bigger savings were realized as blast temperatures were progressively raised. Puddling practice was similarly revolutionized from 1830 when the sand bed of the reverberatory furnace, extraordinarily wasteful of pig-iron, began to be replaced by one made from cinders and hammer scale. With the new lining virtually none of the pig was wasted. Europe and the United States were slow to adopt English methods. In the U.S.A. puddling became general by the 1840s, the use of coke in the blast furnaces by the 1850s. In Europe Prussia most closely followed this pattern, coke-pig production first equalling that of charcoal-pig in 1856; but France, Sweden and Russia changed over much more slowly. Scarcely, however, had the new methods become established than they were rendered obsolete by the emergence of the Bessemer and Siemens–Martin processes. The Iron Age was ending, the coming age would be the age of steel.

2. PROCESSING. Wrought iron was the first ferrous metal to be produced, at first directly from the ores and later by decarburizing cast iron. Malleable, ductile and with a fibrous structure, wrought iron softens at temperatures *c.* 1000 °C. and melts completely at 1500 °C. The reduced iron drips through the fire and collects at the bottom of the furnace in a sponge-like mass which before it can be converted into useful artefacts must be re-heated to *c.* 1350 °C. so that the spongy texture can be consolidated by welding under a hammer. This also squeezes some of the slag out of the bloom. Blooms averaged between 20 and 25 kg and took *c.* 100 kg of charcoal to produce.

The development of furnaces capable of higher temperatures produced an iron with much higher carbon content; but too brittle to be forged, this iron had to be refined into wrought iron. The indirect process, i.e. ore to pig-iron to wrought iron, involved an additional furnace with an oxidizing atmosphere in which unwanted impurities in the pig were oxidized away. The various forms of indirect process made possible the production of larger blooms.

As wrought iron must be forged hot if it is to be shaped easily, tongs are required to hold the work. These developed from the tweezer-like tongs which were used to hold the crucibles of the bronze-founder. By 500 B.C. hinged tongs, very similar to those seen today, were in fairly common use. In the first instance the small blooms produced would be worked directly into artefacts. Larger articles such as swords were made from flattened strips that were piled together and welded into a single mass. Small pieces of iron could be worked with the hammers of the bronze-smiths. Early anvils were flat stones. Later anvils were made from cast bronze and, by Roman times, from iron shaped by hammering and built up by welding. Hammers were first made from bronze and then from iron, although Agricola (Georg Bauer, 1494–1555) shows wooden mallets being used to consolidate the spongy iron into a solid mass. The development of water-power permitted larger forgings to be made, by means of lift, tilt and helve hammers. This form of power-hammer persisted in one form or another until their limited capacity led to the invention of the steam-hammer by James Nasmyth in 1839. This hammer enabled the paddle shafts of the early steamships to be forged. For small, repetitive work such as nail-making an 'oliver' hammer was developed. This was a foot-operated hammer in which a rope from a springy pole was passed around a cylinder pivoted horizontally in a frame. The hammer protruded from the cylinder and the blow was struck by pressure of the foot in a loop at the end of the rope. The spring of the pole returned the hammer, leaving the smith's hands free to manipulate the tools and the work.

The advent of the water-powered hammer enabled workers in iron to obtain their raw material in rough bar-form. Sheet material for the production of armour would also be drawn out under the hammer and finished on small anvils or stakes with hand hammers. Rolling and slitting mills developed during the 16th c. but were only used to finish bars produced under the hammer. Rolling mills were not strong enough to produce rolled bars or sheet iron directly until the middle of the 18th c. Iron wire was made by hand-forging until the 10th c., after which the wire was drawn through a series of graded holes in a draw-plate or wortle-plate. To do this the wire-drawer sat on a swing, the plate being firmly fixed in a log of wood. Kicking back off the log, he used the momentum of his body to assist in pulling the wire through the plate. As he swung back towards the plate he was able to take a new grip with his tongs further up the wire. For wires of heavier section the tongs were attached by a strap to a crank operated by a water-wheel, which provided the additional power required.

The forging of iron has changed little in its essentials since Roman times. When iron in its malleable state is struck a square blow with the flat pein of a hammer the metal tends to spread in all directions. To control this spread the smith can strike a directional blow that not only flattens the metal but also forces it to move in the required direction. If a cross-pein hammer is used, the metal will tend to move at right angles to the pein. To reduce the section of a square or rectangular bar the bar is worked between fullers, which act as the cross-pein hammer, indenting the bar and causing it to be squeezed longitudinally rather than across its width. The marks of the fullers can be removed with a flat-pein hammer or with either a flatter or a set-hammer. Round sections such as may be found

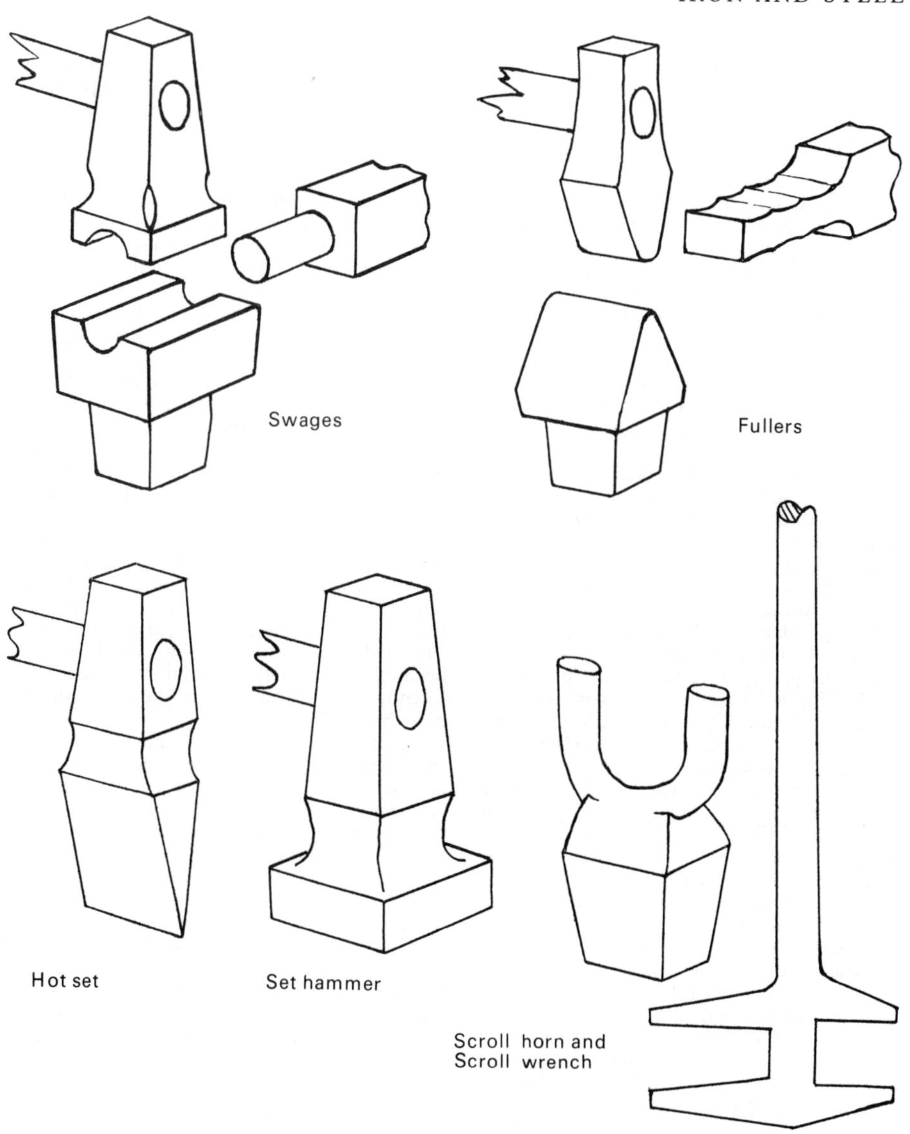

IRON-WORKING TOOLS

as spills on the ends of gate-bars are first drawn down square, then octagonal and finally round, the final operation being performed between swages. This sequence is necessary to prevent the end of the bar hollowing and splitting as it is drawn down.

To thicken (jump up or upset) a bar the heat must be confined to the section required to be thickened by cooling the other portions of the bar. This is to minimize unwanted bending. Short bars are then struck axially on their ends with a hammer, whilst larger bars may be bounced on the anvil-face or on an iron block set in the floor. Larger swellings may be produced on a bar by first jumping up the bar and then welding a collar round the area where the swelling is required and the swellings may be given more decorative forms by finishing them between specially shaped swages. Jumping up can be a tedious operation and is avoided when possible. It is often easier to obtain a similar result by drawing down the ends of a bar of larger section to match the original section and then joining the sections by fire-welding. The thickened heel at the hanging end of the bottom bar of a gate is often formed in this way.

Angles are more difficult to forge than curves as the metal tends to thin at the corner of a sharp external angle. This can be overcome by first upsetting (thickening) the bar in the region of the bend. To complete a right angle it is necessary to keep the angle at not less than 100° until the corner is forged. When making a ring or a curve the metal is always struck just clear of the anvil or former to prevent it being trapped by the blow and thinned.

Holes in smith's work are punched rather than drilled through the hot metal. Tapered punches of the required section are driven into the hot metal until a small black mark can be seen on the reverse side of the bar. The bar is then turned over and the punch driven through from the back. As virtually no metal is removed by this process, the cross-section of the area of the bar around the punched hole remains the same as that of the original bar. The hole is finished to size with a parallel drift and the swelling produced around the hole is forged with a fuller and swage to produce the characteristic blockings seen where one member of a forged gate passes through another.

Cutting is done with handled tools called sets, with chisels and gouges or with an anvil-tool called a hardie, on which the metal is placed and struck with a hammer. In decorative work special chisels and gouges are forged to cut any special curves. Cutting can be done when the metal is hot or cold. Hot tools are not hardened and have a 30° cutting angle as opposed to the 60° angle on cold tools. The practice of splitting sections of bars to produce decorative features by bending and shaping the cut portions is more evident in the work of German smiths. Work cut or split from the parent bar with a set or chisel shows a bold, bevelled edge that results from the direct cutting of the material. Chisels may also be used to cut simple line- or DIAPER-patterns into the faces of bars.

The traditional method of joining iron at the forge is by fire-welding. This operation is carried out at 1350 °C., at which temperature the surface of the iron is oxidized. Flakes of oxide continually break off the surface of the iron, giving the characteristic spark and leaving the surface clean. If two pieces of iron in this state are brought into intimate contact and hammered, the crystalline structure of the metal at its surface breaks down. New crystals form across the joint and unite the iron inseparably. For this operation to be successful the fire must be clean and free from slag and this is ensured by fluxing both the metal and the fire with silver sand. The continual oxidation of the iron during the welding process greatly reduces the size of the bar and, to compensate for this wasting, the parts to be joined are jumped up to increase their size. The joint is then scarfed, i.e. shaped so that its surfaces are convex, to ensure that any slag trapped in the joint is squeezed outwards from the centre of the joint. This form of welding has been practised from the earliest times, an early example being the iron head-rest of Tutankhamun (*c.* 1350 B.C.). It is the complete mastery of this technique that makes possible the flowing scrollwork in decorative ironwork, in which a series of scrolls are assembled in stages by welding. Scrolls may also be assembled by clipping. Clips are bands of iron bent around a suitably sized former. When the scrolls have been bunched together the clip is opened, dropped on to them and then squeezed shut. If this is done hot, the clip shrinks tightly on to the scrolls as it cools. In the 18th c. clips were made from separate pieces and assembled around the scrolls by riveting. The two parts of the St. Swithin's grille at Winchester Cathedral demonstrate the different visual qualities of clipped and welded scrollwork. Iron can also be joined by brazing. This process involves heating the iron to a red heat, fluxing with borax to remove oxides and then melting a brass spelter into the joint as the joining medium. Before the advent of gas torches parts to be brazed would be laid on a bed of glowing charcoal and the joint raised to the required temperature by the application of local blast through a blowpipe. Larger work was surrounded by clay after borax and brass had been placed around the joint and the whole assembly was then heated in the fire until the brass had melted.

Decorative scrolls may be formed by first rolling the end of the bar over the edge of the anvil and then tapping back the curve with the hammer. Once started, the scroll is continued by placing the bar between the scroll horns held in the anvil and pulling the bar into shape with the forks of the scroll wrench. The elaborate mask and leaf work of the 18th-c. smiths would be formed either by placing sheet iron on to a block of pitch to which sulphur had been added to make the pitch less brittle or by laying the iron on a block of lead. The mask or leaf could then be worked from the back with chisels and punches to obtain the required relief. In the better work the leaves are welded into the scroll work, an operation requiring much skill owing to the differing thicknesses of metal involved. Twisted bars are made by heating the bar, holding one end in a vice and twisting the other with a suitable wrench. More elaborate twists can be made by chiselling grooves in the faces of the bar, forging the corners or making up a composite bar by welding together bars of different sections.

So far iron has been treated as a malleable metal that is worked under the hammer. The production of iron as a liquid metal gave rise to other possibilities. During the 15th c. the techniques necessary for casting iron were developed and in the 16th c. an important cannon-founding industry was established in southern England. An early use for cast iron was for FIRE-BACKS. These were moulded on the foundry floor in a bed of cinders topped with sand and crushed

A. Clip as initially forged
B. Clip opened to enable it to be fixed around scrolls in clipped work

SEQUENCE FOR WELDING SCROLLWORK

charcoal. The mould into which the metal was poured was made by running a roller along wooden rails so that about half the roller sank into the sand, rolling a firm bed about 5 to 7·5 cm deep. The surface of the mould was decorated by impressing into it everyday articles such as daggers, keys and ropes. As skill grew these were replaced by elaborate carvings and crests. The early use of moulding boxes is described by Vannoccio Biringuccio (1480–1539), who also details the composition of loams and sands for casting.

It is most probable that it was the desire for cannon that gave impetus to the use of iron as a casting metal. In the first instance cannon were cast in bronze or brass or constructed from wrought-iron bars bound round with iron bands. Moulds for casting iron cannon were constructed from loam and the cannon were cast in pits at the mouth of the furnace, for unlike the BELL FOUNDERS the iron founders tended to work directly from the smelting furnaces. The cannon mould was made from a number of parts. The bore was formed by a core produced by winding a straw rope around a bar, coating it with loam and then strickling the core round by supporting it on trestles and rotating it against a flat board. The outside form of the cannon was constructed in a similar manner. A tapered wooden pole replaced the bar on the trestle and was bound with straw and coated with loam, but the flat board was replaced by one cut to the outline of the cannon. When the form was complete trunnions were added separately. The loam pattern was then coated with charcoal as a separating agent and completely covered with loam. The pattern with its loam jacket was securely strapped with iron bars and the whole mass was dried by rotating it slowly over a fire. When all was completely dry the pole which carried the pattern was shaken to break up the pattern, which could then be extracted piecemeal, leaving inside the reinforcing cage a mould of the desired cannon. A breech mould and a pouring head were then constructed and the whole mould, together with the core for the bore, was assembled vertically in a pit in front of the furnace and held in place by sand consolidated around the mould as it was assembled. As many as four cannon might be cast in a single tapping of the furnace.

Abraham Darby developed a technique for sand-casting cooking-pots in 1707. Other castings produced at this time were cast rolls and domestic items such as grates, smoothing irons, door-frames, weights, baking plates and pestles and mortars. Later in the century came the finely detailed Coalbrookdale plates. The most notable achievement of this ironworks is the cast-iron bridge across the Severn at Ironbridge, near Coalbrookdale, in Shropshire. Erected in 1779, it is still standing and has a single span of 30 metres. Its members were cast in sand. The casting techniques developed for cannon also made possible the casting of cylinders for steam engines. The 19th c. saw an increased application of this material and its use in railings and gates was a contributory factor to the decline of wrought work in this field.

Wrought iron is malleable and tough, cast iron hard but brittle. A metal that will cut other metals needs to be both tough and hard. Such a metal is steel. Today steels contain a variety of alloying elements to produce the qualities that are required, but in simple steels the hardness values are approximately proportional to the amount of carbon that the steel contains. Steels may be produced by adding carbon to wrought iron or by reducing the carbon content of cast iron. Today the carbon content of a steel is adjusted whilst it is in the molten state but early iron-workers were unable to melt wrought iron. For them the only practical method of carburizing the iron was to heat it in close association with carbonaceous material and allow the carbon to be absorbed from the surface. Today this process is known as case-hardening and it produces a skin of high-carbon steel on a low-carbon material. The constant heating of a bloom in a charcoal fire would carburize its surface and when the ore used to produce the iron was an iron carbonate containing some manganese a steel was more easily produced. Smelting at lower temperatures for a longer period of time would also increase the amount of surface carburization. René Antoine Ferchault de Réaumur (1638–1757) describes how the surface of a bloom would be cut away to be used as steel. In early times a prized steel known as 'wootz' was produced in the Hyderabad district of INDIA by heating lumps of wrought iron together with wood and leaves in a crucible at a high temperature. This resulted in steel cakes about 1 kg in weight and about 12·5 cm in diameter. In medieval times iron files were carburized by packing them in contact with leather and bone. Steel was produced by immersing spongy iron blooms in molten cast iron until they became sufficiently carburized. Surface-carburization does not produce a homogeneous steel as there must be more carbon near the surface. Attempts were made to overcome this by piling together carburized bars, welding them into a solid mass and drawing out this mass into new bars. Eventually Benjamin Huntsman, a Sheffield watch-maker, in 1740 developed a crucible process by which carburized bars could be melted and recast to produce a homogeneous material known as cast steel.

Greek and Roman smiths were able to handle steel quite well and knew how to control its physical properties by heating and quenching to harden, by gently reheating after hardening to temper or regulate hardness and by heating and cooling slowly to soften or anneal. Steel was important in sword-making and interesting variations were made on the technique of welding carburized strips together to produce a more homogeneous material. The bars from which the sword was to be made were first twisted, either over their length or intermittently, before they were assembled with other bars and pack-welded together. The resultant blade after forging and etching by natural processes or by immersion in acidic liquids showed complex rune-like patterns on its surface. More delicate patterning was produced on damascene blades that were forged from cakes of wootz. Opinion varies as to the exact technique employed to produce this patterning, but it would appear probable that this was a further refinement of pattern-welding.

The hardening qualities of steel naturally improved the tools used by craftsmen. Planes, chisels and saws became available to the woodworker whilst files, saws, chisels, drills, punches and graving tools became available to the metalworker. The improved ability to cut and shape iron with steel tools shows in the change in the character of architectural ironwork in the 15th c. and in the delicate work of the LOCKSMITHS, gunsmiths and instrument-makers. A hundred and fifty years ago it was wrought iron that was the most important of the ferrous metals. Steel was an expensive material used for swords, tools and springs. Today the improved steel-making techniques that have developed from the Bessemer and Siemens–Martin processes in the mid 19th c. make steel the most common of metals.

3. CAST IRON. The history of cast-iron production begins in China, where as early as the 6th c. B.C. the art of liquefying iron and casting it into moulds had been mastered. The earliest dated pieces are iron cauldrons from *c.* 512 B.C. It is probable that shortly after this time cast-iron ploughshares were being produced and thereafter the record is one of steadily widening application in which ultimately the use of the material for structural purposes proceeded *pari passu* with the production of ornamental objects. The culmination of this development was reached in the Sung dynasty, although before this cast iron had been used for pillars in structural work at Canton *c.* A.D. 950 and for the casting in A.D. 953 of the Great Lion of Tsangchou, 6 m high and 5·4 m long, which is still standing amid the fields 80 km to the south of Tientsin. The most astonishing achievement in cast iron of the Sung dynasty is the pagoda erected in A.D. 1061, 21 m and 13 storeys high and weighing some 53 tonnes, situated near Tangyang in Hupei province. At least four centuries of development preceded this work since a number of much smaller structures, which are known to have been set up during the 7th c. A.D., were reported by Ennin, a Japanese Buddhist monk, during his travels in China from A.D. 838 to A.D. 847. Huge bells and statues of Buddha as well as pillars for bridges were also cast in iron during Sung times.

It is thought likely by many historians of technology that the beginning of cast-iron production in Europe came in response to knowledge reaching the West that in Cathay liquid iron was used to produce useful articles. Whether or not there was direct dissemination of techniques remains uncertain. In any case cast-iron cannon began to be produced in China in the 2nd half of the 14th c. (the earliest dated piece was cast in the year 1356). The first documentary evidence of cast iron in Europe relates to the activities of a gun-founder, Merckiln Gast, at Frankfurt in 1536. Thereafter notices become common. Wessell in Germany possessed a cannon in 1400, cast-iron cannon were being made at Dijon in 1409, by 1415 Breisgau had an iron-founder, while in 1442 prices of cast-iron frying pans were being quoted in Brescia. Cast-iron cannon had three prime virtues: cheapness, ease of fabrication and resistance to fatigue. Their great drawback was that even on the eve of their supersession in the 1860s the gun-founders were still handicapped by their inability to control the properties of the metal with precision, although by then disintegration of ordnance during firing was not the danger that it had been in the previous century. Towards 1450 cannon-balls of cast iron were replacing stone shot and by the 2nd half of the century the material was beginning to be exploited for more peaceful uses. From this time began the production of bells, water-pipes, ovens, cauldrons, fire-backs and stove-plates. The production of cast iron began in England in the 1490s, and by the 1540s a wide range of articles was being made.

The cast-iron ordnance of the mid 16th c. had evolved away from the large calibre mortar type towards more elegant tapering forms such as the culverin weighing about two tonnes and firing a 8 kg shot. Little surface decoration was employed. Fire-backs, coming into ever greater use as wall fireplaces with chimneys displaced the old central hearths, were at first decorated in a simple but effective manner. The mould boards were plain so that the sand bed would simply be flattened and compressed on application. The mould would then often have pressed into it whatever objects chanced to be at hand. Fire-backs of rather greater sophistication would have patterns impressed upon the mould from previously prepared carved wooden stamps. As wooden mould boards complete with intricate carved designs came into use in Europe generally, such simple patterns gave way to more ambitious schemes. One of the earliest dated German examples, of 1512, has an interlacing vine pattern; but only slightly later come biblical scenes (Sheba astonished at the splendour of Solomon), coats of arms and allegorical subjects. The range of subjects was extended again by the 17th c., when genre scenes, often of much charm, came into fashion. An example is a well known English fire-back representing a forge master surrounded by his equipment and bearing the legend 'Richard Lenard Founder at Bred Fournis 1636'.

During the 2nd half of the 17th c., at a time when European smiths working with wrought iron were producing some of the finest decorative ensembles ever achieved in that material, cast iron, an unlikely and indeed one would have thought an uncouth competitor, began to gain prominence. This had as much to do with the increasing skill of the mould-board designers and foundry masters as with the high cost of fine wrought ironwork. Almost as an accepted thing rather than a novelty Charles Augustin d'Aviler in his *Cours d'Architecture* of 1691, among designs for wrought-iron balconies and railings, shows '*balustres fondus*' and a '*balcon de fer fondu*', while later editions have the designs up-dated but with cast iron still figuring in some of them as a cheap alternative to repoussé work '*ornements de tôle refendue et relevée ou de métal fondu*'. Likewise by 1700 a London foundry was advertising balconies of cast iron. The enclosing railings of St. Paul's Cathedral, London, erected in 1714, appear to be the oldest known example of decorative cast ironwork. Other examples of its early use in England occur in 1719 at Chirk Castle, Denbighshire, *c.* 1726 at St. Martin-in-the-Fields, London, and in 1730 at the Senate House, Cambridge, all of which might serve as a basis for Isaac Ware's reflection in his *Complete Body of Architecture* (1756) that cast iron is 'serviceable to the builder and a vast expense is saved in many cases by using it; in rails and balusters it makes a rich and massy appearance when it has cost very little, and when wrought iron much less substantial would come to a vast sum'. Less often quoted is the caveat which follows: 'on the other hand, there is a neatness and finished look in wrought iron that will never be seen in the cast, and it bears accidents vastly better.'

In France similarly, although no such early examples of its actual employment are known, cast iron had probably come into fairly common use soon after d'Aviler's time since otherwise it would be difficult to account for the pains taken by R. A. F. de Réaumur to find some way of improving its appearance when it was used in place of decorative wrought ironwork. Beginning work in 1716, Réaumur published his *L'Art d'adoucir le fer fondu ou de faire des ouvrages de fer fondu aussi finis que de fer forgé* in 1722. A further work on the treatment of large castings, *Le Nouvel Art*, was written in 1726 but published only in 1762. Commenting on the cost of wrought ironwork, he reflects that other metals than iron are easily dressed after being cast and that his method for softening cast-iron objects so that they can be similarly treated will result in a material 'of no great beauty' becoming capable of being given as beautiful a finish as if the objects were of wrought iron or steel. Réaumur did in fact develop a fully fledged method of annealing cast iron (i.e. decarburizing its superficial layers) in the presence of various compounds, preferably of charcoal and bone-ash. Treated in this way the skin of a casting became wrought iron and so was easily filed and chased. He knew that some success had been achieved in this direction in France *c.* 1700 and was encouraged by it to proceed. His informants had made it clear, however, that chance had played a large part in the process. Réaumur had been anticipated in England as well. Prince Rupert, whether or not his claim had substance, declared in Patent No. 161 of 1 December 1670 that he could soften 'cast or melt iron so that it may be filed and wrought as forged iron is'. As far as is known, however, Rupert's methods died with him, and it was Réaumur's which were adopted in England, commented on (rather ignorantly) by Henry Horne in his *Essays Concerning Iron and Steel* (1773), noted by a French traveller, Baradelle, towards the close of the century and thus reintroduced into France, where they had been neglected since 1724 when a manufactory set up at Cosne the year before by Marie Henri de Béthune for the production of malleable cast iron on Réaumur's principles was shut down for good. *Le Nouvel Art* was in fact written, in 1726, in the light of the experience Réaumur had gained at Cosne.

Despite the rather tantalizing obscurity of the process there can be little doubt about the progress that decorative cast ironwork was making at the expense of decorative wrought ironwork in the 1st half of the 18th c., the triumphs of TIJOU, Lamour and OEGG and many other talented smiths notwithstanding. The NEO-CLASSICAL style, ousting ROCOCO and BAROQUE all over Europe in the 2nd half of the century, lowered the barriers against cast iron largely because it put a premium on qualities which, while they might with infinite labour be obtained at the forge, were far more in keeping with what could most easily be achieved in the foundry. Architects and designers were not slow to take advantage of the situation so that even in France decorative smiths were remorselessly driven out of existence by the unequal struggle. In England the decorative smiths' battle for survival had been lost long before that and the selling up of the Worshipful Company's Hall in 1785 set the seal on the decline. The growing use of cheap coke fuel, first in Britain, and the growing expertise of founders everywhere in Europe sharpened the competition by lowering the price of decorative cast iron at the same time as its quality was improving. A builder's price-book published in London in 1805 quoted cast iron at 14 shillings to 18 shillings a hundredweight as against 75 shillings to 131 shillings for ornamental wrought ironwork, 'the prices allowed by the most eminent surveyors in London'. In France the pattern-book of the foundry-master André, published at much the same time, shows the range of castings that could be offered from the smallest screen-work to life-size iron statuary. It was, however, in Germany at this time that artistic cast ironwork was being most fully developed. Sculptural casting (*vollplastische Güsse*) had its beginnings in 1784 at Lauchhammer, which produced an outstanding series of works of this sort. The Royal Prussian foundries in Gleiwitz, Berlin and Sayn followed this lead and adopted artistic casting, first at Gleiwitz in 1800, then at Berlin in 1804 and at Sayn in 1815 when it came under Prussian control. Gleiwitz was the most prolific of the three in the variety of its production. Outstanding are the medallions, many executed to the designs of Leonhard Posch. Among the best of these are portrait-busts of Schiller and Goethe. It was here also that the manufacture of cast-iron jewellery began, based on the designs of Johann Geiss, who by 1830 had begun to manufacture on his own account. Work of this sort was later taken up in Berlin and Sayn. New Year cards of iron were also produced.

Outside Prussia the Royal Württemberg foundry at Wasseralfingen produced panels of charming genre scenes to the designs of the sculptors Georg Weitbrecht and Christian Plock. In Austria–Hungary the Komárov ironworks produced jewellery to the designs of the Prague goldsmith Jan Richter and like the Prussian foundries made decorative plaques and statuary. Similar work was done by the foundries at Nizbor and Nový Jáchymov.

Aesthetically, however, all was not well; or, to be quite fair, all was not to be well. The decorative style of the period, as has been mentioned, accorded well with the capacity of cast iron. Since these were qualities which wrought iron could not yield, there was at this time no question of one material imitating the other. W. R. Lethaby (1857–1931) remarked of cast iron that the pattern should be what a comparatively coarse granular material can encompass without any feeling being aroused that it had fallen short of what was expected of it. The plate, plain or pierced, was the primary fact, a panel of equally distributed substance and one avoiding foliage, which must always appear feeble and coarse. One of the examples of cast iron from this period, conforming exactly to Lethaby's rule, is the panel work to the Castle Bridge (*Schlossbrücke*), Berlin, designed and built by Karl Friedrich Schinkel in 1822–4. Strongly outlined panels with a frieze of Greek key fret each enclose a pair of sea-horses supporting a trident. By degrees this capacity to control the material, which means to recognize its limitations, was lost and the florid vulgarity of later 19th-c. cast ironwork was already well in evidence by the mid century. Style-mongering inevitably led to a situation in which cast iron was made to do that for which it was unfitted, and infinitely skilful pattern making merely ensured that the process of vulgarization would be thoroughgoing. A contemporary critic could remark in 1892 that 'casting in iron has been so abased and abused that it is difficult to believe that the metal has anything to offer to the arts.' Cast-iron furniture, chimney-pieces, gates and railings all bear witness to the abrupt departure of sense and taste. Pugin's condemnation of 1843 is eloquent evidence of what was happening, and not only in England: 'The fender is a sort of embattled parapet with a lodge gate at each end; the end of a poker is a sharp pointed finial; and at the summit of the tongs is a saint. . . . But this is nothing when compared to what we see continually produced from those inexhaustible mines of bad taste, Birmingham and Sheffield.' There was in fact no limit to such falsification and the very tractability of cast iron, its chief virtue, rapidly became its vice.

The use of cast iron as a structural material,

however, shows clearly enough that when utility alone was in point the same age could achieve effects of considerable beauty and economy. From the first great cast-iron structure, the Coalbrookdale bridge of 1779, and the iron-framed mills of the north, to the iron and glass palm-houses and conservatories and train-sheds of the 19th c., to say nothing of the Crystal Palace of 1851, the plastic qualities of the material were exploited sensibly and in ways which were to mark a revolution in Western architecture. Cast iron made possible a definitive escape from the weight-bearing wall. From this time the wall could become not an exoskeleton but a skin, largely of glass, a curtain to exclude the weather.

4. DECORATIVE WROUGHT IRONWORK. Iron has always been valued chiefly for its usefulness as a material for tools and weapons, but examples of its decorative use occur right from the beginning of the Iron Age. Spiral brooches appeared in Greece *c.* 1000 B.C., at a time when the metal was still valuable enough to be kept in royal treasuries. By *c.* 900 B.C. it was already in common use for tools and indeed the Homeric poems frequently allude to it. The episode in the *Odyssey* when the hot stake is plunged into Polyphemus's eye provides the earliest evidence for the technique of hardening iron by quenching, Homer likening the sizzling noise as the giant is blinded to the sound of hot iron being thrust into water. To this period also belong the earliest large-scale decorative works that have survived: an iron lightstand nearly 2 metres in height supported by 3 feet of zoomorphic form has been found at Priene, and at Argos a pair of FIRE-DOGS 1·3 metres long in the form of stylized ships form part of the burial goods of a warrior's tomb. A similar pair was found in a tomb of *c.* 700 B.C. in Cyprus. Iron spits commonly occur in burials of the Archaic period in Greece and later in Etruscan tombs, while the use of fire-dogs in Celtic burials towards the end of the millennium illustrates the geographical extension of the concept of the other-worldly feast, all these objects symbolizing what has been called 'the hospitable hearth for the feast beyond the grave'.

The distribution of Celtic fire-dogs of the standardized ox-headed type, either single-headed or double-headed, extends from Wales in the north-west to Bohemia and Styria in the east. The Capel Garmon fire-dog (*c.* 50 B.C.) from Denbighshire, North Wales, now in the National Museum of Wales, is perhaps the finest of these. The Germanic peoples, who made a cult of weapon-smithery, also appreciated the artistic potentialities of iron, as is evidenced by the Royal Standard found at SUTTON HOO, and the many elaborately forged Anglo-Saxon shield-bosses. Among the Celtic peoples something of the feeling survived and St. Patrick's bell (5th *c.* A.D.), now in the National Museum, Dublin, is perhaps the best known example of the quadrangular form of iron bell developed in Ireland in the early Middle Ages, a type which spread later as far as Switzerland. All these early examples notwithstanding, it only begins to be possible to write a connected account of the stylistic changes that occurred in decorative wrought iron and of the technical developments that accompanied them from *c.* the middle of the 11th c. The earliest surviving European work from approximately this time is English. On the doors of two churches, at Stillingfleet (Yorkshire) and Staplehurst (Kent), are elaborate crescent-shaped hinges with snake-head terminals accompanied by numerous subsidiary pieces of iron fashioned to represent human figures, ships, fish and SWASTIKAS. It has recently been argued that these forms are neither arbitrary nor vaguely propitiatory but symbolic representations of *Ragnarok*, the Nordic Day of Judgement, and that they were executed for patrons, possibly Danish. The presence of pagan symbolism in a Christian context would be by no means without parallel. It is interesting that at Staplehurst the smith used a triangular punch on the larger straps in order to throw up the DIAPER ornament in high relief. Such a technique foreshadows the much more sophisticated methods used in the 12th and 13th centuries in England and France, and rather later further to the east, to produce profiled straps and stamped flowers of great delicacy. From England, where its vogue was continuous from the 11th c. onwards, the fashion for decorative ironwork spread into France—or so the fact that all the earliest French work involves crescent-shaped forms would seem to indicate. Slightly later the crescent appears in Hungary, Sweden, Spain, Germany and Poland. One piece of Swedish work, that at Versås in Vestergotland, possibly from the 12th c. and rather like the earlier English ones, draws on Nordic mythology and portrays Sigurd slaying the serpent Fafnir. It is the earliest signed work, bearing a runic inscription in iron: *Asmutr karthi dyrr* ('Asmund made the door'). Fragments of symbolic work also survive at Eisdorf in Germany, but their isolation makes it unlikely that they belong to the Anglo-Scandinavian group of symbolic designs.

It is certain that by the end of the 12th c. the fashion for decorative ironwork in the form of more or less elaborate hinge-work had, with the exception of Italy, spread to all Christian countries. With the passage of time other forms besides the crescent began to be developed. Horizontal bands, from which sprang subsidiary ornament often in the form of volutes, evolved by degrees into ever richer forms, eventually becoming the predominant type. Foliated crosses were also frequently employed, while at the opposite ends of Europe petal-form arrangements at Beaulieu in England and at Czerwinsk in Poland illustrate how blacksmiths evolved naïve but charming designs drawn no doubt from the repertories of folk art. Amidst the wealth of 12th-c. forms there is a noticeable tendency to finish the terminals of straps and bars with roughly fashioned flowers or leaves, which were executed with increasing refinement through the 13th c. This, however, is to run too far ahead and leaves the beginnings of the second great class of decorative work, that of screens, unaccounted for. Many churches possessing relics often housed in costly reliquaries desired at once to protect them and to leave them visible to pilgrims. The need for a defensive yet transparent structure, fencing off shrine or apse or chancel, led to the construction of iron screens. The earliest documentary evidence and what is probably the oldest surviving example of such work come from England. The screen made to protect the shrine of St. Swithin in Winchester Cathedral, only portions of which remain, is perhaps as early as 1093 and illustrates the simple but beautiful form that such work at first took. A framework of iron bars of square section, one of the most difficult forms to produce at the anvil, is filled with C-shaped scrolls gathered in clusters and secured by collars at their mid-points and where they touch the framework or each other. A manuscript drawing of Canterbury Cathedral from *c.* 1140 showing a similar sort of screen or gate securing the entry to the cloister is again the earliest closely datable evidence for this sort of work that has so far been discovered.

Screens showing in some cases greater inventiveness of scrollwork and also a keener eye for aesthetic effects, but in other cases conforming more closely to the St. Swithin type, may be seen in France at Conques, S. Aventin and Le Puy and in Spain at Pamplona and Palencia. In the 13th c. screens of more sophisticated design began to be produced. The most beautiful example, composed of intricately clustered C-shaped scrolls, is one made for Ourscamp Abbey early in the century and now preserved in Rouen Museum. It is exceptional, however, in that it shows no advance technically over the earlier examples although an increasing degree of refinement began to characterize both screens and hinge-work during the course of the 13th c., especially in France. This growing refinement resulted from methods for fabricating more finely profiled bars and leaf-work, methods which had been slowly developing over a long period. The sequence of changes seems to follow on logically from the early use of chisels and punches on hot iron to produce linear designs of simple form such as CHEVRONS and lozenges or even, as at Staplehurst, primitive three-dimensional effects. Everything did not depend, however, on the accuracy with which the blows of the chisel were delivered. The metal displaced by the use of broad punches would produce swellings in the unstruck areas. The next step, the object of which was to control the whole surface of the metal being worked, was to cut the negative of the desired profile in a block of soft iron. This block when steeled would serve as a die or matrix for the iron which was to be hammered into it at welding heat. If both sides of the piece were to be thus moulded, a top matrix would be added to the bottom one and the bar would be passed by stages between them, taking up the design in its passage far more precisely than would have been possible if hand and eye had worked alone without such aid. A further refinement was to cut additional matrices, open only at one end, for the easy multiplication of terminal ornaments. The preferred forms were ROSETTES, grape-clusters and variously-lobed vine leaves. Stamped ornament was widely used in central France and the screens at Rouen, Sens and Noyon are decorated in this way in addition to many beautiful fragments preserved in museums. Their delicately stamped leaves and channelled stems leave no doubt that French smiths of that period were unrivalled in the use of stamps.

Besides France only England has stamped screenwork of the 13th c. One piece from Chichester, now in the Victoria and Albert Museum and interesting for the variety of its scrollwork, has some rather crude disc-like terminals. The other is the Eleanor grille in Westminster Abbey. Finished in 1294, it is the work of one Thomas de Leightone, for which he received £13. This is the first screenwork in Europe whose date is fixed by documentary evidence.

Thirteenth-c. hinge-work likewise took on increasingly rich forms. The horizontal scrolled strap was the most favoured form and the techniques of profiling and stamping used in screenwork were deployed here also to produce channelled stems and leaves. The 13th c. has been termed the century of the Great Hinge for no other reason than that the hinges and the ornament which sprang from them would frequently quite mask the timbers of the door to which they were attached. The greatest work of this kind is that on the Porte Sainte Anne, Notre-Dame, Paris. Two out of the three double doors at the western front of the cathedral are covered with ornament, each of the doors being hung from three hinges between which are further horizontal bands of decoration. (The third door was completed in the 19th c. by Boulanger.) The volutes, richly decorated with vine leaves, shelter a variety of exotic animals and recall the inhabited scrolls of medieval illuminated manuscripts. Work of a similar but simpler character exists at St. Paul's Cathedral, Liège, while in England a number of such works at St. George's Chapel, Windsor, at Eaton Bray, Leighton Buzzard, Turvey and Merton College, Oxford, are probably also to be ascribed to Thomas de Leightone. All are richly decorated with stamped ornament of great delicacy. Both in France and in England this type of work came to an abrupt end in the 14th c., but further north and east, in Flanders, Germany and Poland, hinge-work, scrolled and stamped, continued to be produced up to the 17th c. In Germany a peculiar thistle-ornament appeared in place of the hitherto almost universally used vine leaf. Everywhere ancient designs such as the crescent lingered on alongside the newer ones. Examples of such late work in what is known as the 'Blacksmith style', that is work in which all the operations are carried out at welding heat, exist in great numbers. Notable works are those at Notre Dame, Hal (early 15th c.), Erfurt Cathedral (15th c.) and Krolowka (late 16th c.). The first has scrolled and profiled volutes finished with stamped ornament, the second is of similar character, while the third exhibits the Tree of Life pattern. Minor work undertaken by blacksmiths from the 12th c. onwards consisted of ornamental bands for chests and coffers, by which their poor construction was supplemented. Windows too were sometimes protected with severe grids of horizontal and vertical bars.

About 1300 the 'Blacksmith style' with its developed technique and elaborate decorative forms fell abruptly out of favour in England and France. At first glance the 'Locksmith style' which took its place would appear to indicate so complete a discontinuity that to search for its antecedents in the previous techniques might well seem hopeless. Whereas formerly iron had been modelled exclusively at welding heat, such operations were now largely reserved for the preliminary stages, such as the production of bars and sheets, where they were indispensable. Afterwards the iron was worked much as if it were a species of very hard wood. Chisels and saws played a large part in the preparation of ornament while the old techniques of securing pieces by means of welding and the use of collars were frequently discarded in favour of methods taken over from the joiner; the use of halving joints, tenons and mortices, and pins now became general. Not less different was the visual appearance of work in the 'Locksmith style', abstract geometrical ornament or severe trellis work replacing the old flowing forms. Despite appearances, however, its origins may be traced back to the early 12th c. and the new style can be seen as a late outcome of the complex of cultural changes that were then beginning to affect Europe. The artistic culture of the Christian West was still in a primitive state of development compared with that of Islam, whose arts and sciences became henceforth the yardsticks against which Europe measured its progress. Even 150 years later Roger Bacon could conclude that there was little hope of converting the Arabs until the Christians had equalled their achievements. Parallel with the zeal of Europeans to master and incorporate Arab learning into Western scholarship went a deep admiration for Islamic decorative styles, knowledge of both entering Europe through two main channels, Spain and Sicily. In addition certain Italian cities such as Venice were by reason of their extensive trading connections with the Islamic lands well placed to become familiar with the new ideas.

As early as the 1130s simple geometrical ornament begins to make its appearance in ironwork, followed in the 13th c. by rather more intricate figures and the first essays in pierced sheetwork. It would seem in fact that a certain inertia carried the 'Blacksmith style' forward to its culmination in such work as that at Notre-Dame, Paris, and Westminster Abbey even while at the same time the steady infiltration of new motifs was cumulatively making such work unfashionable. Although it has been customary to use the term 'Locksmith style' to describe the new mode, there is little satisfaction in employing so undistinguishing and restrictive a term. It has sometimes been called 'Gothic' but this too would be misleading; for although its appearance is directly related to the change from ROMANESQUE to GOTHIC in architectural styles, its sources are plainly to be found in Islam.

In England the earliest work in the new style, the choir gates at Canterbury Cathedral (*c.* 1300), display a rich repeating pattern of hexagons and trefoils, the bars being halved where they cross. The screen at St. Alban's Abbey, probably of similar date, is of trellis work with alternating panels of diamonds and squares. At this period appears the first decorative ironwork in Italy. Screens at St. Anastasia, Verona, and St. Mark's, Venice, are each made up of panels of sheet iron pierced with geometrical ornament let into grooved frameworks. The finest screen of this type, at Santa Maria Novella, Florence, was constructed *c.* 1360. Similar work was produced also in France and Bohemia. By the 15th c. 'Locksmith work' of a more ambitious character was being attempted in respect of intricacy of design and there was a tendency for work whether large or small to reproduce the features of the Decorated and Flamboyant architectural styles then in vogue. By this time the style had spread into Flanders and Germany, while in Spain it acquired an altogether distinctive character. In England two major works, the Henry V screen of 1431 in Westminster Abbey and the Edward IV screen of 1483 in St. George's Chapel, Windsor, exemplify the architectural phase of 'Locksmith work'. In the former case two tiers of quatrefoils are surmounted by decorated Gothic tracery, while in the latter, perhaps the finest work of this kind in Europe, two towers nearly 2·7 metres high flank gates of half that height, the whole work being a perfect rendering of Flamboyant architectural detail much of it chiselled out of solid iron. Geometrical work appeared in France also after 1300, but it is exquisite miniature work of filed and chiselled iron that constitutes the great glory of French 'Locksmith work'. From this time small-scale work of extreme beauty and distinction in the form of rich casings for locks began to be produced, taking on something of the character of jewellery. Just as large screens took over the features of contemporary architecture, so too did much of this smaller work. Carved from the solid, *pris dans la masse*, lock-cases often exhibit astonishingly detailed architectural ensembles complete with figures beneath canopied niches. Such work, moreover, would seem to have been regarded as within the capacity of any competent French smith, since when Charles VI reviewed the privileges of the iron-workers in 1411, Article 17 of the modified *Statuts des Serruriers* required every apprentice desiring to become a master to produce a masterpiece lock and key. (See also LOCKS AND KEYS and APPRENTICE LOCKS.) Other works made in this style were tabernacles and CLOCKS. 'Locksmith work' continued fashionable in the 16th c. but from the time of Francis I (1515–47) the Renaissance style in repoussé work was beginning to challenge it.

German work of the 14th and 15th centuries presents a complicated picture with 'Blacksmith' and 'Locksmith' work flourishing side by side and even exchanging decorative forms and techniques. One finds, for instance, doors completely sheathed in sheet iron with a superimposed, geometrically arranged grid of bands in which all the work has been executed at welding heat. The sheet iron is often decorated with stamped ornament, but may equally well take the pierced geometrical forms of 'Locksmith work'. Magnificent work of this character was produced *c.* 1450 at Erfurt Cathedral. It was popular also in Austria, a fine 15th-c. example being that at the Priory of Bruck, and in Poland, where the sacristy door (*c.* 1450) of Sandomierz Cathedral shows a rather coarser workmanship. Trellis work was produced in Germany in the 14th c. but screens employing Gothic tracery in their design were rare, the two finest examples being from the 15th c. That at St. Ulric's in Augsburg (1470), displays Flamboyant forms but, reflecting again the fusion of techniques that has been noticed, is joined by means of welds and collars. The other, the screen to Bishop Ernst's Chapel in Magdeburg Cathedral (1498), is a thoroughgoing piece of 'Locksmith work' in which the joining techniques are as characteristic as the design. Much small work was also produced in Germany, as the numerous surviving door-fittings and lock-cases testify, but it does not approach French work either in complexity of ornament or in delicacy of execution. Two Austrian works deserve mention, a door at the Maria Stiegenkirche, Vienna, and a tabernacle screen from Ottoburg, now in the Victoria and Albert Museum, both with decorated tracery.

Italy, as mentioned above, produced ironwork ornamented in the geometrical style, and there too it was followed by more ambitious work conceived in architectural terms. The earliest and most beautiful piece is the screen at Santa Croce, Florence (1371), the gate of which consists of two tiers of Gothic tracery. A good deal of this work, however, was forge work such as the twisted bars used in the gate and the quatrefoils fashioned in bar iron rather than cut from sheet. Both these features became common all over Europe in the 15th c. Other important Italian works, the Scaligeri screens in Verona, those in the Palazzo Pubblico of Siena, and that at Santa Trinità, Florence, are notable examples of richly developed quatrefoil decoration. They show the Italian flair for this sort of ornament as well as their equally marked liking for lavish sheet-iron flower and foliage work. Spanish work of this period, unlike earlier work which had followed Anglo-French models, developed very special characteristics which persisted unaltered through the 16th and 17th centuries. When the scroll type of screen was abandoned the Spanish adopted, from the first, screens composed of closely spaced vertical bars strengthened at intervals by horizontals, architectural forms finding expression in the OGEE curves of the gates and in the tracery of the CRESTING. The form of these screens warrants further examination. As in much of central Europe, blacksmith work continued to play a large part, perhaps the larger part, in the preparation of work. The bars alone involved tremendous labour at the anvil and often they were subsequently twisted and made to alternate with plain bars, both of which were frequently split in mid-course and fashioned into lozenges and a variety of other forms. Such decoration served to soften the severe lines of the verticals, as did the pierced sheet-iron ornament with which the horizontals were often enriched. Also characteristically Spanish was the scale upon which such screens began to be planned, resulting in the 16th c. in enormous work of 12 to 13 metres in height. By then, however, the gradual reception of Renaissance motifs into their design led to horizontal bands of repoussé figure work replacing pierced sheet iron of Gothic design. Parallel changes occurred in the rich cresting with which nearly all screens were finished. Notable examples of Gothic screens are those in the cloister of Barcelona Cathedral and those at San Pablo, Palencia, and in the Capilla de Santa Ana at Burgos, all of the 15th c.

Except in Spain the application of classical motifs to ironwork proceeded slowly, and it would not be too much to say that what is for convenience described as Renaissance work in most cases warrants the name for no better reason than that it was produced during the period when the classical Renaissance was manifest in the other arts. At this time decorative ironwork declined in popularity through much of Europe, partly no doubt because more precious metals began to be preferred and iron had in any case no place in the Vitruvian canon, partly perhaps because it was too strongly identified with the Gothic style. It is an interesting fact that in Spain and Germany, where 15th-c. smithwork had not surrendered itself so completely as elsewhere to Gothic forms, the following century, far from being a period of eclipse, was one of intense activity and one in which their finest works were achieved. Elsewhere, in Italy, France and England, the period was one in which little notable large-scale work was achieved. Italian 16th-c. ironwork is almost non-existent except for a few quatrefoil screens and the art only began to revive during the 17th c., when particularly in Venice new and sophisticated forms began to be evolved. But unlike a parallel and contemporary development in France, it did not form part of a larger complex of changes and resulted only in pleasant but undeniably minor work. Finer pieces earlier in the century are almost always heavily indebted to Spanish and German models and later to those coming from France. During the 16th c. French smiths for long continued to produce 'Locksmith work', although Italian influence had some impact on the court style from the time of Francis I. It is curious to observe also that although this court work was at first decorated with repoussé ornament, the old 'Locksmith' method of working was so strongly entrenched that it was able to resist the fashion for sheet-metal ornament even when Renaissance forms were universally adopted later in the century. But of large work there was none. In England too screenwork was abandoned for something like 150 years. Tomb railings, surviving in some numbers and betraying traces of Renaissance feeling in the 17th c., establish a thread of continuity between the last great 'Locksmith work' and the first premonitions of the Baroque style. Such works, often carefully executed, seem to indicate that a lack of patrons rather than a lack of skill held back the smiths from larger work.

German smiths of the 15th c., working often in the 'Blacksmith style' even when employing Gothic ornament, conserved both their skills and their capacity for design so that once the grip of the Gothic taste was broken they were poised, so to speak, for further activity. During the first half of the 16th c., moreover, talented designers such as Dürer and Solis were providing models of ARABESQUES, knot work and calligraphic interlace; these were seized on by German smiths and remained the fundamental elements of their style until towards the end of the 17th c. the impact of French Baroque work caused them to be abandoned. The dominant features are the use of inter-threaded round bars to produce panels of graceful spirals and even more intricate work in which the central area of calligraphic interlace is built up from rods which begin and end their passage through the maze from the spiral scrolls which surround it. The flowers of open coil work with which the terminals of scrolls are decorated are no less distinctive in character. The earliest mature work in this style appeared *c.* 1550 in Dresden but the best work is somewhat later. What is perhaps the finest example, the screen surrounding the tomb of the Emperor Maximilian in the Franciscan Church at Innsbruck, was completed in 1573 by Jorg Schmidhammer of Prague, working to the design of Paul Trabel. It has 20 panels of delicate interlace finished with a variety of leaf forms and a top rail of *amorini* in repoussé work amid further scroll work. The gate to the Silver Chapel in the same church, made by Hans Beck in 1588, also displays fine workmanship. Hans Mezger, another outstanding smith of the period, made the screen to the Fugger Chapel in St. Ulric's Church, Augsburg, *c.* 1580, which like Schmidhammer's is of great lightness and inventiveness. Large numbers of such screens and window grills were made in the 16th and 17th centuries and spread far beyond the borders of Germany. The appearance of such work in northern Italy, Denmark, Poland and Hungary is an indication of the popularity of the style. Besides screens and gates there are staircase-railings, as in the library stairs of St. Mary's Church, Wrocław (Breslau) (1661), well-covers as at Neisse, Silesia (1668), and fanlights, as in the grating (*c.* 1608) preserved in the Pomorskie Museum, Danzig. There remains, however, to be noted another category of work, equally widely distributed. These are the perspective screens. It is, however, unclear how far the German smiths were responsible for the design as opposed to the execution of illusionistic work. The earliest such screen is that closing the choir in Lucerne Cathedral, made by Johann Reifell, who was the city smith of Constance, during the years 1641–4. A slightly later example was one made by Vincent Nussbaumer von Aegeri, a monk, for the monastery of Maria-Einsiedeln *c.* 1684. Prague has two such screens both *c.* 1650, one in the Italian Chapel, the other in the Collegium Clementinum. Indeed *trompe-l'œil* screens were very popular, and a list of examples could be greatly expanded. One in Augsburg of 1712 still shows typical Renaissance spiral work, but here the fashion was already being carried over into the Baroque style. Constance Cathedral has one from *c.* 1710, while that at the Abbey of Weingarten (*c.* 1735) might be regarded as the culmination of all such efforts were it not that, magnificent as it is, a Rococo choir screen (1756) at the Abbey of Zweifalten eclipses it.

Spanish screens of the Gothic period were largely constructed by 'Blacksmith' methods supplemented in most cases by no more than a light cosmetic garnish of 'Locksmith' work. By contrast Renaissance ornament enters fully into the great work of the 16th c. The panels of vertical bars were no longer simply passed through undecorated horizontal rails but were set between pilasters enriched with classically styled repoussé work in the so-called Plateresque manner. The horizontals dividing the tiers of vertical bars received equally rich ornament, the sumptuousness of such work being brought into a final balance by rich crestings of arabesques often enfolding figure work or medallions. The square bars, plain or twisted, of the Gothic period were evidently felt by some smiths to be inadequate to support such splendour and in many 16th-c. works they were replaced by moulded and spindled balusters often embellished with chiselled or repoussé ornament. Very many such screens were made in the 16th c. and they certainly exceeded both in size and in splendour anything hitherto achieved in iron. The choir screen at Seville Cathedral, made by Sancho Muñez of Cuenca in 1519, has pillars lavishly decorated with repoussé work terminating in Corinthian capitals. The twisted bars, spindled balusters and cresting of figures and acanthus scrollwork are of equal magnificence. The screen to the Capilla Mayor, the eastern end of the choir, in the same cathedral, made between 1518 and 1533, is the masterpiece of Francisco de Salamanca and deploys the whole Plateresque repertory with brilliant effect. In the cresting the entombment of Christ is represented. Perhaps the finest of all such screens is that to the Royal Chapel at Granada Cathedral, made between 1520 and 1530 by Master Bartolomeo, a sculptor as well as a smith. Rich with repoussé work, it has three tiers of twisted bars, the bottom ones of split work, divided by two massive friezes, the whole surmounted by a cresting of candelabra linked by arabesques whose interspaces contain ten scenes from the life of Christ. The great period of Spanish decorative work came to an end *c*. 1600, and later work is unremarkable. Besides screens much other work was undertaken and was equally ornate in character. Window-grills, pulpits and tomb-railings were sometimes of extravagant splendour. Small-scale work of great delicacy in the form of iron plates and locks was used to decorate VARGUEÑO cabinets, while caskets and coffers wholly of iron were also made.

The earliest Baroque ironwork in France during the reign of Louis XIII was influenced by the sumptuous Flemish forms then in vogue. The smiths working in the new style restricted themselves from the outset to antique forms of ornament, while the architecturally conceived frameworks were similarly based on classical models. The course was now set that was to result during the next 100 years in a series of works of great nobility not only in France but in most of Europe as well. Two features characterized the Baroque style of ironwork and gave it its dignity and beauty. The first was an inevitable result of the architectural nature of the style and made itself felt in the strong emphasis given to the vertical and horizontal members enclosing the panels of which the work was composed. Furthermore the sharply defined zones which thus resulted were themselves proportionally related to one another. The second element, which served to relieve what would otherwise have been overly severe, was provided by a rich variety of scroll forms with which the panels were filled out. This was, as it were, their negative function; but they played in addition an active role, their exuberant and flowing lines providing the plasticity and energy which informs all Baroque art. But the smiths of the French Baroque, desiring above all else to achieve balance, clarity and controlled energy, could not leave the matter there. Scroll forms, except in slighter and more delicate work, were rarely relied upon exclusively, and this again for two main reasons. First, they could not by themselves compete with the more massive bars which formed their framework unless elements of mass—focuses for the eye to rest on—were introduced into the purely linear patterns that they produced. Accordingly repoussé work in the form of acanthus leaves, husks, grotesque masks, scallops and rosettes were introduced to redress the imbalance. At the same time their second function both as absorbers and as nodes of energy was fulfilled as they brought the swirling movement of the scrolls to momentary rest. In gates a number of similar devices were used to retard the violent effect of movement which large regions of vertical bars would otherwise have given to the work. So too the collars used to connect bars and scrolls performed a valuable role in this respect and compel the observation that they had been exploited long before for this property, both in the scrollwork of the 'Blacksmith' period, where they were functionally indispensable, and later in 'Locksmith work' to relieve the monotony of endlessly repeating quatrefoils. In a similar way a variety of classical forms—lyres, terms, rouleaux, arabesques and interlaces—served as fillings for friezes and pilasters.

If these were the means by which the forms and energies of Baroque ironwork were governed and brought into balance, nevertheless they were not achieved at once. The style in its fully developed form coincides with the reign of Louis XIV (1643–1715) and owed an enormous debt to the outstandingly gifted architects and designers who came to prominence during this period. Jean Lepautre, beginning work in 1645, was the most prolific of these and many of his engraved designs were intended as models for ironwork. Equally influential at a rather later stage was the work of Jean BÉRAIN and his son, whose designs for ironwork exhibit the grace and charm that was to characterize French work towards the end of the century. Jean Marot, whose ironwork designs are excessively dense, represents a further aspect of the Baroque influential in the 1650s, and one from which a certain Flemish ponderousness had not yet been refined. Despite a certain tension between stylistic trends, one can say that the ironwork actually produced achieved its peak of gravity and nobility in the middle years of the reign and was certainly moving by the 1690s to work of a more graceful character. The latter represents a transition separating the sombre earlier Baroque from the voluptuousness and exuberance of the Rococo.

Here one must notice the wider scope which was being opened to the smiths by the changes taking place in France towards 1660. The nobility were beginning to forsake their fortified strongholds in favour of châteaux built on open plans and surrounded on all sides, not by ditches and counterscarps, but by elaborate formal gardens. (See LANDSCAPE GARDENING.) The interiors of such châteaux required large numbers of balconies, staircase-railings and elaborate iron doors, which like all interior pieces had to be more finely fashioned than external work because they were to be seen at close quarters. Outside the house the forecourt was protected by a screen and gates, transparent yet defensive, fulfilling a similar function to that of the church screens. For the first time iron was being used externally on the grandest scale. Nor was this all.

The formal gardens also required many gates to close the diminishing perspectives of avenues and to mark off and at the same time reveal the untamed country which lay beyond them. Much still survives of the work done for these houses: for example, the screens and gates at Meudon designed by Mansart and those of the palace of St. Cloud by Gittard. The nobility followed the example of the king, who at Versailles spent enormous sums from 1664 to 1680 on ironwork made for him by the most talented smiths in France. Delobel made the iron gates for the *Escalier du roi* and the window balconies, Baron did work in the library and Godignon and Dezeutres for the screen to the *Cour d'honneur*. Other ironwork was done for the Trianon at Fontainebleau, for the Palais-Royal and for the Bibliothèque. The most superb work of the period was, however, that made for the Château de Maison near Poissy *c.* 1658. Two gates from there are now preserved in the Louvre and are of exquisite craftsmanship. They are from the hand of an unknown smith working, it is thought, to the designs of Jean Marot. They were said by Réaumur, in his *L'Art d'adoucir le fer fondu* (1722), to have cost 69,000 *écus*.

Outside France the Baroque style made its greatest impact in England and Germany. In England the sudden and splendid revival of ironwork is often associated with the succession of William and Mary (1689–1702), and this is largely correct since it was under their patronage that much of the best work was produced. It is, moreover, hard to point to anything done before 1689 that might indicate an already developing taste for Baroque ironwork. The only work which can be definitely dated close to this time, the gates at Ham House, Surrey (1673–5), while plainly a premonition of the Baroque, cannot be regarded as anything more. The engravings of country houses in such works as Robert Plot's *Natural History of Staffordshire* (1686), show only very simple railings. In fact it seems fair to regard the flowering of the style as a direct result of the important commissions given to one man, Jean TIJOU. He is first heard of at Chatsworth, Derbyshire, early in 1688, but in 1689 he was already in London and working on a great screen to enclose Queen Mary's garden at Hampton Court. Completed in 1690 at a cost of £775, it is one of the masterpieces of the Baroque style. By 1695 he was making screens and gates for St. Paul's Cathedral, and shortly afterwards was executing work for a number of aristocratic patrons. Most of the designs appearing in his *New Booke of Drawings* (1693) were carried out; but it is significant of the state of the art in England that whereas this was the first such design-book, innumerable works of this sort had been appearing in France since 1615.

A number of English smiths, most likely trained by Tijou, produced work in the Baroque manner. John Gardon, who worked with Tijou at Chatsworth in 1688–9, seems to have been the first of these. The Duke's gates at Chatsworth are probably his and also the work at Castle Howard, Yorkshire. William Edney's gates of 1710 in St. Mary Redcliffe, Bristol, make it appear likely that he too worked with Tijou. But the Baroque style in the specific French manner was undergoing modification even during the period of Tijou's activity (1688–1712). Reaction set in quite rapidly against these heavy forms and a lighter, plainer style of ironwork resulted, the first example of which seems to be the gate and screen made in 1711 for New College, Oxford, by Thomas Robinson. This sober English Baroque persisted until the middle of the century and gave way finally not to Rococo but to Neo-Classical forms and to pieces of a curiously hybrid character, half-Baroque with Chinese or Gothic embellishments. English Baroque work, despite its relative plainness, is often of great beauty. The work of John Warren at Clare College, Cambridge (1715) and at Powis Castle (*c.* 1725) and that of Robert Bakewell at Okeover (1736–45) and at the Radcliffe Camera, Oxford (1744–6) is evidence of this. Their work was in fact an exercise in reducing Baroque to its plainest terms with few concessions to the rich origins from which it sprang; yet it was saved from sterility by an elegance coming from a precise control of proportion.

The Baroque, or to use the German term, *Laub- und Bandelwerk* ('foliate and strapwork'), entered Germany at much the same time as England, but ran a very different course. The still flourishing Renaissance style did not at once disappear. Furthermore it was a later and less oppressive Baroque which formed the model for German smiths, whereas Tijou's designs belonged to the idiom of the 1670s and 1680s. The first German Baroque work, no longer surviving, was a choir screen made in 1688–90 by Hans Rieger for the church of Obermarchthal in Bavaria and displayed a mixture of Baroque and Renaissance forms. But within a very few years Baroque work purely French in spirit was being produced. The screen in the Holy Cross Church, Augsburg, a screen in Graz Cathedral of extraordinary delicacy, the door to St. Emmeran's Church, Regensburg, which might have come straight from a page of Jean Bérain and work in the University at Wrocław (Breslau) are good examples of how completely the style had been accepted. Certain other work, however, was already displaying in the 1720s an exuberance of form that was quite un-French; and although still employing symmetrical forms, was manifestly on the point of escaping altogether from the tight control of authentic Baroque. Such were the gates and screens made for the palaces of Prince Eugène of Austria at Schloss Belvedere, Vienna, and at Schlosshof on the Marchfeld. The overthrows of the gates, swollen to gigantic size, plainly prefigure the Rococo and it can hardly be a coincidence that Johann Georg Oegg, later to be the master smith of Rococo ironwork in Germany, was until 1733 working for Prince Eugène at the palace smithy in Vienna.

IRON AND STEEL

Surpassing even the collaborative efforts of the architects, designers and smiths who had developed the Baroque style of ironwork in France together with their successors during the RÉGENCE and the early years of the reign of Louis XV—notably MEISSONNIER and OPPENORD—carried further that gradual movement towards Rococo lightness. The style they created *c.* 1715–30 was, architecturally, a Baroque one into which a new vigour, a restless undulating movement, had been injected. No less important was their use of the highly expressive rocaille ornament, whose abstract forms seem sometimes like shells, or like froth or flames. The main exponents of the style all produced designs for iron, whose very nature as a material was consonant with the demands made upon it. Its plasticity at welding heat permitted the smiths unrestricted freedom to guide it into the supple and sinuous forms that were required. Never did their prestige as artists stand higher, so perfectly did they catch the spirit of the new style. Jean LAMOUR, the greatest smith of the Rococo in France put the point admirably in the *Préliminaire apologétique* to his *Receuil des Ouvrages*: 'Elle (la serrurerie) est susceptible de toutes les formes. Elle a, quand elle le veut, l'énergie de la peinture et de la sculpture, la hardiesse de l'architecture et toujours la solidité. Tout ce qui sort de ses mains devient monument.' Lamour's masterpieces were made between 1751 and 1759 in Nancy under the patronage of King Stanislas Lesczinsky and were all that he claimed. In France itself an enormous quantity of work was made for the Church, notable examples of which are the choir screens at Bourges and Amiens, the work of Pérès and Vivarais respectively, both to the designs of SLODTZ. Much work was done also for aristocratic patrons. Neslé made gates and screens for the château of Arnouville, later taken to Vaux de Cernay; Franque made similar work for the Marquis d'Argenson at Neuilly. Other fine gates, the work of unknown smiths, are to be seen at the châteaux of Bagatelle and Dampierre.

Italian Rococo work of some distinction is to be seen in Mantua Cathedral, where the screen to the Cappella della Confraternità dei Fabbri is a delightful work with touches of CHINOISERIE. At Milan, in Sant'Ambrogio, the choir screen illustrates the almost insensible movement from Baroque to Rococo, while a further example in Bologna, the screen in S. Petronio, of richly undulating form, retains in its panels vertical bars of Spanish type. In Austria and Germany Rococo ironwork received its extreme and most brilliant forms. Reference has already been made to work produced for the royal palaces in Austria, which in the 1720s was already taking on an exuberance that foreshadowed the Rococo and that there is no denying the virtuosity of design which marked the Rococo style itself and the extreme technical skill of the smiths who worked in it. Johann Georg Oegg, the most celebrated of them, was active between the years 1733 and 1767, for the whole of which time he was chief smith at Würzburg to a succession of Prince-Bishops. His work for them resulted in some of the finest gates and screens ever produced in Germany. But other contemporary smiths, although less well known, produced work of great brilliance. Two, Köbst and Müller, working to the designs of François CUVILLIÈS at Schloss Brühl, the palace of the Elector of Cologne, made railings, balconies and a great lantern of much refinement which were put in place in 1743. Again Peter Schoch's gate to the Jesuit Church in Mannheim (*c.* 1750) and Marcus Gattinger's choir screen for Würzburg Cathedral (1749) and another for the Abbey of Amorbach 48 km to the west, set up in 1750, suggest that Oegg had a number of peers. Yet it was Joseph Büssel of Rankweil who, working for five years on a choir screen for the Abbey of Zweifalten, set up in 1756 the ultimate statement of exploding perspective in iron. Although imposing works on the grandest scale claim first notice, the Rococo was a style that found ready acceptance at all levels of society in Germany. Modest works such as sign-brackets, door-hinges, window-grilles, grave-crosses and candlesticks, survive as evidence of this. Such small work reproduces the swirling lines and the deeply veined and twisted leaf-work of the greater pieces.

The change from the freedom of the Rococo to the restrained and, for ironwork, constrictive forms of the Neo-Classical style began even in the heyday of the Rococo. Work of this character began to appear in France between 1745 and 1750 and during the next 20 years became a dominant style. The taste for elegant precision, straight lines and regular forms such as the Greek key, was unfavourable to ironwork, and although a number of pieces were made, large works such as screens and gates become unusual, the bulk of the surviving work being slighter productions such as railings and balconies. The earliest examples of Neo-Classical work come from Paris: railings in St. Roch and St. Germain l'Auxerrois both *c.* 1750, the work of Doré and Deumier respectively, show the rigidity of the style. The leading features were minimal leaf work and that of a size and type more suited to castings than repoussé work, together with the passion for the sharp angles of Greek frets relieved only by the undulating Vitruvian fret employed as a frieze for the panels. Later work is not always quite so uncompromisingly hostile to the forms most natural to iron. The railings of the Grand Trianon are formed of large S-scrolls with acanthus-leaf enrichment while those at the École militaire are extremely beautiful Vitruvian scrolls with acanthus leaves and rosettes filling out the panels. But it became increasingly the fashion to restrict smith-work to the producton of the scrolls and rails and to employ cast brass for foliage work. In such a way Gamain embellished the railings for the Petit Trianon (*c.* 1768), as did Gabriel those for the Château de Compiègne. Two gates in Paris, those at the École militaire and at the Palais de Justice, show that smiths such as Gabriel and Bigonnet were equal to the severe demands that large-scale work in the Neo-Classical taste imposed upon them; but the fact remains that cast iron was soon substituted for handiwork. Its use had of course been proposed before. Charles d'Aviler as early as 1691 had shown balusters and balconies of cast iron in his designs, and Réaumur in 1722 set out methods by which its appearance, 'of no great beauty' as he rightly says, might be improved. At this period, however, it made little impact except where cheapness was the main consideration or where it was aesthetically unobjectionable. Such considerations largely lost their force in the Neo-Classical style, which in this sense was itself responsible for the decline which wrought ironwork now suffered. In addition technical improvements in the production of cast iron served both to improve its quality and greatly to reduce its price. It has in fact been suggested that the excessively lean character which wrought ironwork assumed at the turn of the century was the result of smiths' deliberately simplifying their style in order to keep down costs in the face of the constantly falling price of ornamental cast ironwork. If this was so, then they were merely hastening their own demise.

Outside France Robert ADAM took the leading role in popularizing the style in England; and although there it took on an altogether gayer air, the consequences were no less fatal to smithwork. The small, jewel-like ornaments which were required for railings and fanlights were more easily supplied by the founder than the smith. The latter was confined to the fashioning of the bars and rails and since these were of simple form it was not long before they too were replaced by castings. What must be the last work made in defiance of the ruling taste was the splendid Chinese gate at Portway House, Warminster, *c.* 1765. In Germany, Italy and Poland, where Rococo, or in the case of Poland Baroque, forms long remained in favour, Neo-Classical work appeared only in the closing years of the century. A screen at Schloss Veitshochheim shows clearly the attenuated forms which were to deliver the craft into the hands of founders, while a similar poverty is visible in work of the 1790s in Warsaw, notably the gate to the Archbishop's Palace. In Italy alone a gate in the Cathedral of Arezzo, *c.* 1785, in the ETRUSCAN TASTE, exhibits vitality and inventiveness in the face of what had rapidly become for wrought ironwork a withering and then a killing style. Unhappily cast iron from its beginning was also dead, able to counterfeit wrought iron only when distance, lending it some charm, smudged the details. Yet so completely did it become established that it proved difficult to dislodge even when a change of taste brought forms into vogue that were eminently suited to wrought iron.

So low had wrought iron's fortunes sunk by the middle of the 19th c. that even in France few craftsmen in iron besides shoeing smiths were to be found. The revival of the art there owed much to the architect Eugène Viollet-Le-Duc, who set up a smithy at Chapelle Saint Denis when as part of his restoration of Notre-Dame, Paris, it was necessary in the 1850s to repair the 13th-c. hinge-work of the Porte Sainte Anne. This work, as well as the fashioning of new hinges for the central door, was undertaken by Boulanger, who in addition trained the men who would ensure the future survival of the craft. In England likewise the Norfolk Gates for Sandringham and a number of other works displayed in 1862 at the International Exhibition indicated that an attempt was being made to revive the craft there also. Such ventures are to be seen as part of a larger revolt against what Ruskin in his *Seven Lamps of Architecture* (1849) had called 'operative deceit', that is the substitution of cast or machine work for what had formerly been produced by hand.

From the 1860s onwards architects in England and France were regularly including designs for gates and screens in their commissions and thus provided work for the revived craft guilds and artistic smiths who now began to appear. It was from this time also that a similar revival started in Germany. By the 1880s and 1890s, when historians of decorative wrought ironwork such as Havard in France, Meyer in Germany and Starkie Gardner in England were writing, it really seemed to them that the revival was solidly based, and in so far as the repertory of techniques had been securely repossessed they were right. Yet on a larger view, and with the advantage of hindsight, they were over-optimistic. Most of the work undertaken from their day to this has been period design, drawing more or less heavily on historical styles, and absorption with pastiche, whatever its proximate causes, would seem to be symptomatic of sterility rather than vigour. Ironwork which has sought to find its place in contemporary architecture has had to adapt to an unpropitious milieu of unadorned shapes and surfaces and hence has either had to assume such forms itself or else travel another road altogether and, in the form of quasi-sculptural set pieces, seek through the rough textures and vigorous shapes naturally belonging to wrought iron to exploit such settings. A feeling for qualities of this sort would also serve to explain why sculptors have sometimes turned to working in iron and why interior decorators have frequently made use of it. Altogether they offer grounds for believing that the craft of working a material of such immense aesthetic potential will continue to survive.

5. THE WORK OF THE FORGE. It would be an unenviable task to attempt to write of the working of iron and its decorative use without employing the terms of art that properly belong to each. The purpose of the section which follows is to serve as a guide to these terms and also to indicate something of the technique of the blacksmith, from which of course they are inseparable. Forge

work, as Henri Havard remarked long ago in his *La Serrurerie*, is particularly interesting in that nothing is done mechanically or by chance; indeed the smith works under a special constraint, peculiar to his craft, which ensures that this shall be so. Except when rendered plastic by heat, wrought iron is a stubborn material and if the smith were not able to fashion it rapidly and precisely in the brief interval before the iron grows cold again after being taken from the fire, his work would be painful and protracted indeed. So it is that the indispensable tools were and are the hammer and the anvil since although cold working of the metal has played a part, and at some periods a large part, in the working of iron, the essence of the blacksmith's art is to fashion the metal while it is hot. The conduct of the fire, the positioning of the pieces of iron to be worked in the fire so that they heat evenly and without burning, their withdrawal at the correct temperature for the operation in hand, are matters of crucial importance. The shaping of the metal is for the most part performed when it has attained a bright yellow colour. In this condition the piece can be lengthened or widened, its cross-section reduced or 'drawn down' by hammering. In this way one would produce, for instance, the spear-point of a vertical bar in a railing, or the diminishing section of a bar that is to be scrolled and finished with some delicate terminal. Its cross-sectional area can be increased by heating the portion it is desired to thicken. The end of the bar is then struck axially on the anvil so as to cause the iron to swell at that point where the heat has made it momentarily plastic. This is what the blacksmith would call 'jumping up' the iron. This operation might be performed to thicken the metal preparatory to giving it some ornamental shape, as a preliminary to joining it to some other piece by welding, for providing a sufficiency of metal for making a bend with a square corner, or in order to make the piece substantial enough for a hole to be driven through it. As will be evident, these operations of 'thinning down' and 'thickening up' the metal are commonly a preliminary to further operations in which other tools come into play. Swages or matrices, for instance, are tools having in negative form the profile it is desired to give the metal. If only one side of the metal is to be thus profiled, a bottom swage is secured in the anvil, which has a hole in it, called the 'hardie hole', expressly designed to receive the shank of such a piece. The metal is laid on the swage and is either struck directly with the hammer or is held in place with a flatter which controls the whole upper surface of the metal. In this case the flatter itself receives the blow. A top swage is used in conjunction with a bottom swage when a complete profile rather than a half-profile is desired. In either case the smith would have needed an assistant to help him with such tools unless the forge contained an oliver, that is a treadle-operated hammer which left the hands free. The strap work of door-hinges is typical of a situation where only half-profile work would be necessary. A free-standing screen, on the other hand, able to be seen from all sides, might well receive complete profiling.

Fullers by contrast work in exactly the opposite way. They have convex profiles and make depressions in the metal when hammered into them. Just as with swages, so one can have top and bottom fullers. Historically their use, as also the use of chisels and punches, seems to have preceded that of swages in producing surface decoration. Scrolls of various forms could be, and doubtless very often were, formed free-hand by hammering the metal into a curve round the tapering end, or bick, of the anvil. More commonly a scroll fork, with two stout prongs, is fixed in the hardie hole, the heated end of the bar is placed between them and then pulled into a curving shape by means of a double-pronged tool called a scroll wrench. As the scroll develops its accuracy is gauged against the line of a scroll previously drawn in chalk on a piece of sheet metal acting as a template. Since considerable numbers of scrolls of the same dimensions are invariably required in large works with repeating patterns, this care is frequently bestowed only on a master or false scroll. The curves of the false scroll subsequently serve to guide the curves of the bars bent around it. Yet in practice the matter was scarcely ever quite as simple as this. It has to be borne in mind that the scroll was often made to diminish in cross-sectional area towards its centre if it contained many turns. The bar, in other words, would have been drawn down towards its end before it began to be scrolled. Not to have done this would have led to a considerable visual loss since a scroll formed from a bar of uniform thickness would inevitably have too dense a centre when it was scrolled simply because the space between the turns would progressively diminish. Nor were the inner terminals of scrolls left unadorned, for a whole repertory of scroll end-forms lay at the disposition of the smith. Although simple enumeration of the types would scarcely be helpful, it has to be said that in the total aesthetic effect of the work they play an important part. Some forms are light and graceful, others bold and vigorous, selection depending always on the visual effect it is desired to achieve. Interior work, necessarily seen at closer range and protected from the weather, would require highly finished and delicate forms inappropriate to forecourt railings, gates and so forth. These needed rather to be bold and simple if they were not to be lost in their surroundings. The paint which would be needed to protect them from rust would in any case have obscured finely chased work. Much the same might be said of twist work. Here bars of various profiles, whether square or round, used singly or in clusters, would be heated along the portion to be worked and given as tight or as loose a twist as was demanded for the visual effect of the ensemble.

Except for relatively simple designs the work,

whatever its particular form or function, has to be built up from a number of pieces of metal which before this stage have already received their forms. The heart of blacksmith work resides, in short, in the techniques of fire-welding, of joining the parts. If a bright yellow heat suffices for the operations already mentioned, nothing but white heat is sufficient for welding. At this temperature two pieces of metal, if properly prepared, will fuse together completely and, if the work is done with skill, leave no irregularity behind to reveal where they were joined. Where slighter pieces are to be joined small wisps of iron called 'collars' are often employed. The hot iron is wrapped round the pieces to be secured and as it cools it contracts and grips them tightly together. Nor need collars be plain. If previously profiled by means of swages, or on a swage block which has a large number of channels in its surface, they too can have an aesthetic as well as a functional role.

Cold working, although one might regard it as an intrusive element in the blacksmith's art, demands attention because, especially during the 'Locksmith' phase of decorative ironwork lasting from *c.* the 14th c. to the 17th c., it came to play a major part in the elaboration of ensembles based upon designs that were often purely architectural in inspiration. The flowing lines into which hot iron can so naturally be guided had but a small part to play here. It has been said elsewhere that iron during that period was treated very much as if it were a very hard wood, and it was indeed worked with tools previously seen only in the hands of carpenters and joiners. Piece was joined to piece not by welds and collars but by means of halving joints or mortices and tenons. Pins and rivets, cotter pins and screws, completed the revolution in technique. Large-scale works of this sort, and indeed even small pieces, required prodigies of application, so that besides being extremely costly each example seems really to be in the nature of a *tour de force*.

There remains to be mentioned, as a part of the cold working of iron, the art of repoussé work. It played a large part in Spanish Renaissance work and thereafter spread with the French Baroque style into northern and eastern Europe. In the finest work of this sort the profile of the piece to be worked was first cut out from a paper pattern pasted upon a thin sheet of metal. The piece so shaped was then placed face downwards on a bed of pitch and was hammered into the low relief that the design required, following the pattern already marked out upon the metal. The final sharpening of the lines was then executed by means of chasing tools on the face of the metal. In the 18th c. some smiths preferred to make such leaf or shell or grotesque work on the anvil, subsequently fire-welding it to the scrolls it was to embelish. Short-cuts were resorted to as well, however, and flimsy work of insufficient gauge for welding would often be set into a recess cut in the scroll and, secured there with pins, would all too easily fall prey to rust. Where repoussé work in deep relief is required, sheet metal of thicker gauge is heated and beaten out over a ring.

Until the mid 18th c. mechanization had not directly affected the work of the blacksmith, and even where methods such as have been described were developed to speed up his work everything still depended on his hand and eye. About this time, however, Chopitel, a Parisian *maître serrurier*, set up a water-driven rolling mill to produce hot rolled steel and wrought-iron bars of various profiles for use in window-frames and hand-rails, a procedure designed to replace the laborious hand-swaging of such pieces. A report on the invention was submitted to the Académie des sciences in 1752 and by 1753 profiled bars from Chopitel's works at Essonne were being offered for sale from a warehouse in Paris. In 1765 Chopitel's mill was illustrated in Diderot and d'Alembert's *Encyclopédie*. The next year the idea was adopted, although for more utilitarian purposes, in England and presumably this and other ventures of the same sort provided the cue for Henry Cort's experiments in rolling puddled lumps of iron free of slag by means of profiled rolls. In the 19th c. steam-driven planing machines, cutting the metal cold, replaced rolling mills and were used not only for profiling but for cutting chamfers and producing perfectly finished surfaces generally. By this stage, however, we are plainly entering the realm of engineering even if we have not left that of art.

6. IRON-CHISELLING. This is improperly called steel-chiselling, as steel is too hard for the purpose. During the second half of the 16th c. the fashion for chiselled and gilt furniture and for swords and fire-arms brought into play the craft of the 'steel-chisellers'. Some of the hilts chiselled by the craftsmen attached to the Saxon and Bavarian courts are of a quality that could only have been achieved by a trained MEDAL die-cutter. The greatest names amongst 16th-c. craftsmen were Othmar Wetter (worked first at Munich and subsequently at Dresden), Emanuel Sadeler, who held the court appointment to the Duke of Bavaria, and his younger brother, Daniel, who after working for the Emperor Rudolf II in Prague returned to Munich to enter the service of the Bavarian court. Most of the 17th-c. craftsmen are anonymous, with the exception of Gottfried LEYGEBE, who worked at Nuremberg and subsequently Berlin.

The 18th-c. fashion for small-swords with finely chiselled hilts brought a revival to the trade, and the Parisian craftsmen of the time were capable of chiselling iron with a precision and delicacy that rivalled the achievements of the goldsmith working in precious metal.

At Brescia in northern Italy and in the surrounding valleys a remarkable school of 'steel-chisellers' was at work during the 17th c. They decorated chiefly gun furniture but also produced SNUFF-BOXES and trinkets. Unlike most artists of western Europe they did not draw their designs from the usual source of printed pattern-books, but kept consistently to a form of foliate ornament that was probably derived from local folk art. Another local school was active in Naples during the 17th and 18th centuries; their finest productions are to be found in cup-hilts for rapiers and in gun-locks. During the mid 19th c. the art was revived with considerable success in particular by the French-born Antoine Vechte.

7. IRON JEWELLERY.

(*a*) *Woodstock Cut Steelwork.* A traditional local industry in cut steelwork is associated with the small town of Woodstock, near Oxford, and may go back to Elizabethan times, for there is a mention of 'Woodstock work' in *Certaine Satyres* of John Marston in 1598. Little or nothing is known about it, however, until *c.* the middle of the 18th c., by which time Woodstock work had achieved international prestige for fine craftsmanship. In 1742 Horace Walpole sent a box of Woodstock steel wares to Horace Mann, British Consul at Florence, for use as presents and their quality is praised by others at this time. They were valued for their high polish, their fine hand-workmanship, the intricacy of the cut-out ornament and because the various articles could be dismantled for cleaning. Such articles as scissors, buckles, watch-chairs, CHATELAINES, sword hilts, etc. are mentioned.

About the middle of the century or slightly later Woodstock turned to the making of steel jewellery such as necklaces, bracelets, brooches, etc. The method of manufacture is interesting. Thin sheets of brass or even tin were cut into the required shape and were then thickly covered with cut-steel studs not inset in claws like MARCASITES but each fastened to the base-plate by a minute rivet. The base-plate was usually made with a number of sections held together by metal girders but able to be disassembled by the wearer. At a time when the DIAMOND was paramount in jewellery colour was relatively unimportant, and highly polished steel has glitter. Since all the light is reflected from the surface it has not, of course, any of the fire or brilliance of a diamond; but in compensation for this it does not require the highly accurate cutting of a gemstone and the studs were often cut with very many facets to increase the sparkle of reflected light, and many studs were packed closely together.

The demand for cut-steel 'toys' became so great in the second half of the century that that far-seeing industrialist Matthew BOULTON took up their manufacture and Birmingham became the centre of a prolific trade. Cut steel was exported to the Low Countries, Russia, Germany, Spain, Italy and France. In France the vogue for cut-steel jewellery received a fillip when in 1759 the well-to-do were asked to hand in their jewels to replenish the Treasury, and further by the period of financial stringency at the end of the Napoleonic wars. Napoleon presented his bride Marie Louise with a cut-steel parure. About the middle of the century an exclusive store, *Au Petit Dunkerque*, was opened in Paris by M. Granchez, jeweller to Marie Antoinette, where steel goods were said to be more expensive than gold. The manufacture of cut-steel jewellery began in France during the first two decades of the 19th c., the most prominent makers being the firm of Frichot.

(*b*) *Berlin Iron Jewellery.* Berlin iron jewellery received this name from its manufacture among other things by the Royal Berlin Factory, opened in 1804, but iron jewellery may have been made in France as early as the last decade of the 18th c. and was made in Silesia before Berlin. The range of articles was wide, including besides personal jewellery (though chatelaines were not made) such articles as eye-glass frames, watch-keys, clavichord-keys, tatting shuttles and tinder-boxes. The peak of production was at the period of the War of Liberation (1813–15), when the wealthy were pressed to give up their jewels in aid of the national cause and were given iron tokens in exchange. A special feature of the Berlin Factory were the *Neujahrplaketten* (New Year Reliefs), which were popular as New Year gifts between *c.* 1808 and 1848.

Unlike the cut-steel jewellery, Berlin iron jewellery did not copy the styles of contemporary gemstone jewellery. The craft was probably a development from the ornamental ironwork which had been produced during the 17th and 18th centuries probably by armourers as the demand for decorated armour declined. Except for the very fine 'spider' wire-work, the main skill lay in the making and designing of moulds from which the articles were cast.

The most comprehensive collection of cut-steel and Berlin iron jewellery is in the St. Laurent Museum, Rouen.

3, 32, 152, 258, 264, 269, 276, 333, 350, 397, 398, 480, 489, 530, 532, 732, 765, 845, 860, 940.

ISLAMIC GARDENS. See LANDSCAPE GARDENING (ISLAMIC).

ISLE OF WIGHT LACE. LACE made in the Isle of Wight during the 19th c., consisting of machine-made net on which designs are EMBROIDERED with the needle. The patterns, which include various kinds of open-work fillings, are outlined with a doubled thread.

ITALIC. Italic type derives from a script of the early Italian humanists. It was more quickly written than the roman and was characterized by narrow letters closely spaced and adapted for an easy passage of the pen from letter to letter, also normally by a forward inclination of the strokes. The first type of the kind was cut by Francesco Griffo of Bologna for ALDUS, who used it from 1501 onwards for the texts of learned books in small formats. A more elaborate cursive hand was developed from the same humanistic script by scribes in the Papal chancery and taught by Italian writing masters of the 16th c. (whence the name 'italic', distinguishing it from the gothic hands). The first of many typefaces rendering it was used in a writing manual by Ludovico degli Arrighi in 1523.

In France italics less closely modelled on writing and more nearly resembling ROMAN type, but preserving the slope and other features common to the Aldine and Roman chancery styles, were introduced by Simon de Colines in 1528–36. Parisian punch-cutters in the middle of the century refined the design, and Robert Granjon (1513–89) by the end of his life had cut a range of italics in a style that has been normal since that time.

Early italics had upright capital letters. Inclined capitals were first made at Vienna in 1532 and were generally used after *c.* 1560. The italics of the early 16th c. were intended for setting texts. After that they began to be used to distinguish parts of books other than the text, such as prefaces, commendatory verses, headings, quoted matter, and for decorative effect. About 1550–60 an Antwerp type-founder, François Guyot, was offering roman founts with italics suitable for use with them. To do so has been the normal practice of type-founders since *c.* 1600. See TYPOGRAPHY.

IVORY. Histories of ivory-carving usually make but slight reference to its practical uses but ever since the Stone Age primitive peoples have valued it for its utilitarian as well as its decorative possibilities. It was an important element in the equipment of the early hunter and has been pressed into use for both weapons and tools. In later times it has been used to make the swivel-catches which released crossbow bolts, for the verniers of marine sextants, for piano-keys and even for false teeth. Ivory-carving as a branch of fine art is dealt with in an article IVORIES in the *Oxford Companion to Art*; the present article deals with the uses of ivory in the field of craftsmanship.

Although ivory is usually taken to refer to the tusks of elephants, the teeth of various mammals and even of one reptile, the crocodile, have been pressed into use for the purposes of carving at one time or another. All teeth are composed of three substances: osteo-dentine, which forms the root; dentine, which forms the body of the tooth; and enamel, which crowns it and sometimes protects the sides as well. For the purposes of the practical carver there is no distinction between the first two substances. Tusks can be carved right down to the root. Enamel, however, is really quite a distinct substance from ivory. Sometimes it is sufficiently soft to be carved along with the dentine which forms the central part of the tooth, as is the case with an elephant's tusk for example. At other times it is so hard that it must be removed before carving can be done. This is the case with hippopotamus teeth, which are covered on their outer surfaces with a layer of enamel which is about the same hardness as JADE and must be the hardest substance produced by any animal. If ivory is merely the interior of a tooth, would any teeth serve to produce ivory? A very wide variety of teeth have at one time or another been used for this purpose. They include those of the elephant seal, the rhinoceros, the boar, the warthog, the hippopotamus and of course man himself. But there are practical limitations on carving just any kind of teeth as ivory. Those of the dolphin, for example, would yield just as good ivory as those of the closely related sperm whale, but in such small quantities that it would be impracticable ever to make use of them. Strictly speaking every kind of ivory is different and sometimes this difference is very marked. A section through a walrus tooth shows a central core of hard bone which is quite distinct from the ivory which surrounds it and pieces of walrus tooth, however small, are unlikely to be mistaken for any other kind of ivory because the central core will be visible at both ends. It is more difficult, however, to tell at a glance what kind of ivory an object is made from if it is taken from one of the larger tusks. But different ivories display different colours under ultra-violet light. Soft African elephant shows purple and white, hard African elephant white with some ringing, stale African soft is white with brown marks where stained. Indian elephant is much whiter than African, with purple buff streaks. Siamese elephant is purple and white with onion-skin ringing; hippopotamus is bluish white; mammoth is a yellow white which does not give much light, with pronounced rings; sperm whale is white, blue and buff; walrus buff and white with the bone core showing up in a 'bird's eye' effect; warthog bluish, buff and pink; and narwhal buff and white. Yet the ultra-violet reaction of an ivory is not a certain test of its provenance or even its authenticity. Colour is a comparative factor, while ivory may have been subjected to staining in the ground. Ivory should be tested for hardness and should be slightly softer than bone. A piece of soft ivory can be scratched by stone of hardness 2 on the MOHS SCALE. Ivory does not burn but will char black. Many tusks are 'striated', that is they show alternate white and darker lines like fat and lean bacon. Some ivory, however, such as that used for piano-keys, has no markings of this sort.

Ivory is organic and hygroscopic. It will warp and split easily if exposed to extremes of temperature. The writer once left a block of Siamese ivory on his desk overnight and the warmth from the central heating caused it to crack spirally. This of course is what has happened to mammoth tusks which have been long buried in the earth and ice. Ivory should be kept at a cold but constant temperature. The store-rooms for ivory in a warehouse are below ground and unheated. Extremes of moisture or dryness are equally unsuitable.

Historically the most important sources for

ivory are the enormous beds of fossil mammoth tusks which begin in Alaska and stretch into Siberia. In Escholz Bay, on the American side of the Bering Straits, 'the cliffs are said to be either ice, or partly coated with ice; and on the top of them, embedded in and partly coated by the boggy or sandy soil, are numberless bones [of mammoths], the whole island having a charnel-house smell'. Although the American deposits provided some of the ivory which was carved in Europe, much more was obtained on the Russian side. The mammoth, a gigantic proto-elephant which died out *c.* 3,000,000 years ago, had tusks 5 m long which could weigh up to 225 kg. Although much mammoth ivory was split and decayed, some tusks might be in pristine condition—some mammoths had remained preserved so well in the icy wastes of Siberia that starving hunters made a meal from them. The Bear Islands and the New Siberian Islands were favourite collecting places for mammoth ivory, much of which was gathered by convicts. Between 1825 and 1831 about 2,000 *poods* or 35,000 kg of mammoth ivory was sold in one market alone, Yakutsk. Long before the Russians took Siberia in the 17th c. the Eskimos, Lapps, Koryaks, Yakuts, Lamuts and Tunguses had exploited its ivory. The Chinese also came to buy ivory. 'We may read about the digging vole of the north', wrote the Chinese emperor Kang Hsi (1661–1721). 'Far in the north, in the land of the Russians, these rats, as large as elephants, live in the ground. When air or sunlight touches them, they die immediately . . . Their teeth are like those of elephants, and the people of the north make vessels, combs, knife handles, and other articles out of them.'

From ancient EGYPTIAN times the elephant has been another important source of ivory. There are two principal kinds of African ivory. The 'soft-tusked' African elephant has long, curving, fat tusks. The 'hard' variety of tusks are straight and much narrower than the soft ones. There is in fact not much difference in the hardness, but a good deal in the amount of ivory obtained from each. India produces its own breed of elephants, but since Roman times at least African ivory has been bought by Indian traders for import, either, as it is said, because it works up better or because the Indian elephant is domesticated and so less likely to be killed for its tusks. Ceylon has its own elephants but they are usually tuskless, and elephants are also to be found in other Asiatic countries such as Siam, which is thought to produce the finest of all ivories.

Africa, long the most important source of ivory, still holds this position, although the doubling in price of African ivory during the 1960s and the appearance in ivory warehouses of baby-elephant tusks—a result of the cropping policy followed by most African states—indicates that the supply is not inexhaustible.

Much of the elephant ivory which has been imported from Africa bears traces of its treatment before shipping. Many tusks are coloured a warm chocolate brown because they have been stored in the roof of an African hut exposed to smoke. Others are 'stale', that is pitted with a mesh of cracks running deep into the tusk from the outside. Stale ivory may have been collected dead. In spite of the legend of the elephants' graveyard where all the great pachyderms were supposed to go when they knew they were going to die, four-fifths of the ivory sold during the 19th c. was picked up in the bush. Slaves were marched to the coast from the interior, the men carrying tusks, the women the smaller 'scrivelloes'.

Next to the mammoth and the elephant the hippopotamus has probably provided most ivory for the craftsman. *Hippopotamus amphibius* has a dozen teeth large enough to carve, but only the large upper and large lower teeth are really important, because the others have 'shakes' or cracks in them and are often rather yellow besides. The French explorer Chambonneau pointed out as early as the 17th c. that the ivory of the hippopotamus was finer than that of the elephant and very suitable for making carvings. ('Deux textes sur le Sénégal (1673–1677)', edited by Carson I. A. Ritchie, *Bulletin de l'Institut fondamental d'Afrique Noire*, tome xxx, série B, no. 1, Janvier 1968, p. 330.) The larger hippopotamus tusks offer difficulties to the carver, however, because their outside curve is sheathed in extremely hard enamel which can only be removed with a grindstone. Moreover hippopotamus ivory is slightly harder than elephant ivory, and it comes in a rather awkward shape and size. Although hippopotamus teeth, or 'sea horse' teeth as they were picturesquely termed, were expensive in the 19th c. when they were sought for by dentists as a raw material for false teeth, they are now considerably cheaper than elephant ivory.

The walrus provides two tusks, which may weigh as much as 5–6 kg. Only the outside of the tooth is ivory, however. The core is a hard osteo-dentine, dark and unsightly when cut across but eagerly sought throughout history for the hilts of weapons and for drinking cups, because it was believed that it could enable the possessor to resist the effects of poison and to be cured of any wounds he received in battle. Nowadays the walrus is all but extinct, and Eskimos are forced to carve imported elephant ivory.

No animal is more productive of ivory than the whale. There may be thirty teeth on the lower jaw of a sperm whale and something can be made from them all. Whales' teeth are either pointed and sharp or ground to peg tops by long use. A layer of dentine, or perhaps of differently coloured ivory, surrounds the central core of the tooth, which is yellow. The outside is much whiter.

Ivory has earned its place as one of the most favoured of all craft materials by the combination of special qualities which it enjoys. First of all it feels 'natural' and 'sympathetic' to the touch. It offers a great variety of colour, from luminous white to a dead-leaf brown. It is no more difficult to carve than most sculptural materials. Certainly it is much easier to saw and file than to cut with chisels or gravers; but on the other hand it is a very tough material and almost impossible to splinter or split unless it is left near a heater of some sort. Workmen in ivory warehouses walk across the tusks as though they were logs of wood. It is easy to polish and keep clean, it can be worked in very small sizes—hence its popularity with miniature artists—can be painted and gilded, or even made translucent. It is relatively flexible, so that it can be bent slightly or formed into articles which require considerable play, such as riding whips.

Many different methods have been employed to work ivory. In prehistoric times it was scraped with a flint knife and also engraved with an Eskimo style—a tool which continued in use in the Arctic until the 19th c. It consisted of a splinter of quartz set in the end of a pen-shaped wooden peg. By means of the style Neolithic craftsmen produced masterly engravings on pieces of mammoth tusk, and afterwards emphasized the lines by darkening them with pigment as in SCRIMSHAW. Assyrian ivories must have been roughly shaped with a saw, which has left characteristic slanting marks, and use of a straight graver may be also deduced from the fact that some curved lines take a straight course when they were not intended to. The faces of some ivories from Syrian sites have scratches suggesting that they were cleaned up with a sharp knife. Others show intersecting planes, suggesting that the carver blocked out the contours with a chisel. Early Syrian ivories also have holes of regular width—clear evidence that they have been bored with a metal drill or auger.

The tool-kit of a contemporary Indian ivory-carver includes saw, knives, chisels, files, scrapers, which leave a bevelled surface, and gravers. No doubt these tools bear considerable resemblance to those used in antiquity.

A good deal is known about the tools and methods of the ivory-carvers of Dieppe in the 19th c. They probably resemble closely the tools used as far back as the 16th c. Ivory-carvers tend to hand down their tools to some chosen successor. The workshop of a Dieppe carver has been reconstructed by M. Pierre Bazin, curator of the Dieppe Museum, with the help of local knowledge, and from this one may see the way in which a Dieppe ivory was carved. Starting from the pattern-book which every carver kept, with the large glass bottle called a *boule de verre* used to condense the flame of a candle and throw it on the work, the bench or *établi* with a half-circle cut into it for the carver's body, and in the centre of the circle a sawing pin called a *cheville* or *taquet*, the equipment is complete. The carver used saws to cut his ivory into pieces, which he would then hold firm in a hand-vice or *main* while he filed them with knife-shaped rasps called *grêles* or *écouanes*. Gouges and chisels were also used. Designs were pricked through the pattern by a method akin to POUNCING and plaster models were also used as a guide. Fine work was cut with five differently shaped burins, and delicate work was done by means of a twist drill with a weighted shaft and a pierced bow which enabled the craftsman to work the drill with one hand simply by pressing it up and down. Similar types of drills are used by jewellers to pierce beads. With this relatively simple tool the carver did all the very elaborate piercings or *mosaïque* which are so characteristic of Dieppe carvings. He would make a single hole and then four others round it in the form of a quincunx.

Different substances have probably been employed at different times to polish ivory. Nowadays it is polished by sandpaper, or rather flour paper, followed by an application of powdered pumice. A final polish is given with putty powder (oxide of tin) or jeweller's rouge. Sometimes a proprietory soap powder is used for this purpose. Ivory is a substance which polishes very easily because the animal matter contained in it can be released by the heat of rubbing and serve as a polish. Many ivory-carvings were not polished but have acquired a polish by constant handling.

The principal uses of ivory apart from figural carving as a fine art include CHESS-men, furniture accessories of all sorts (the Erbach carvers made ivory tables, and Queen Victoria's carriage on the royal train had ivory door-knobs), musical instruments (the best piano-keys are still veneered with ivory by craftsmen who keep their methods of work a closely guarded secret and are supposed to sharpen their saws twice a day so as to ensure a clean cut), buttons (Belleteste, a 19th-c. Dieppe carver, is said to have made his fortune carving shirt buttons), jewellery, such as that made by Theodor Mayer (1860–1929), boxes, tea caddies, fans and many other articles. The principal commercial products today, besides veneers for piano-keys, are the backs of hairbrushes.

The principal schools of craftsmanship have been in RUSSIA, Dieppe, Erbach and the prison camps of England during the Napoleonic wars, where American prisoners perfected the ivory model.

Russian ivory-carving has never received the recognition that it deserves. The *Encyclopaedia Britannica* is silent on the subject and little has been written about it even in Russian. Yet from the 10th to the 15th centuries Russia developed a highly individual school of carving. So influential was it that the Chinese may have derived from it their concentric ivory balls, the Dieppe artist his *mosaïque* or pierced work and the American scrimshoner his olive-branch decoration, which appears painted on Russian walrus-ivory boxes of the 17th c. before it is found inscribed on sperm whale teeth. Many diverse influences undoubtedly flowed into Russian carving, from Byzantium and also from the Arctic, where the Yakuts of Siberia probably originated the *mosaïque* or pierced style of decoration later to be used with such effect by Russian carvers. Ivory workshops flourished in Archangel and Kholmogory, and the people of these

Carved and gilt ivory fan, painted by E. Moreau. French, shown at the Paris Exhibition of 1867. (V. & A. Mus.)

towns took orders from Moscow or came themselves to work at the Armoury Chamber Workshops in the Kremlin. After 1703, when St. Petersburg was founded, northern carvers worked there as well, often alongside foreign artists. Trade figures from Archangel reveal considerable exports to Europe and in 1822 there is specific mention of the export of carved ivories. It is by such exports that the influence of the Russian school may have spread. The material in which the Russian craftsmen worked was usually walrus ivory or mammoth tusks. Their most successful products were the wonderfully fretted, painted and engraved boxes, secretaires and *toilettes*, which have survived in considerable numbers. The carvers, who were apparently free craftsmen, also made chess-men, combs, walking sticks, needle-cases and boxes, besides other purely artistic works such as portraits and vases. O. K. Dudin was at work in the 1770s carving beer flagons. N. S. Vereshchagin at the end of the 18th c. was carving superb vases, which are technical as well as artistic triumphs. Russian ivory-carving continued throughout the 19th c. and beyond and there is still a colony of ivory carvers at Lomonosov, in Kholmogory.

Although the Russian school still has vitality, the same cannot be said for Dieppe, where the carvers are no more than a handful struggling in the face of competition from Hong Kong, rising costs of ivory, and the disappearance of a rich clientele who were prepared to pay high prices for the best workmanship. Dieppe ivory-carving, established during the 16th c., received its first major blow with the revocation of the Edict of Nantes in 1685, as many of the ivory-carvers were Huguenots. In 1694 an Anglo-Dutch fleet bombarded the town, wreaking further havoc. In 1740 a local historian, the Abbé Guibert, wrote: 'These costly products . . . have had a chequered career. There are still some shops where one can find good workmanship, but the small outlet for sales, and consequently the modesty of the workman's rewards, makes it difficult to find skilled craftsmen, who are becoming scarcer, and who, in spite of that, are not any better paid.' Towards the end of the 18th c. Dieppe craftsmen had begun to use a lot of bone—mostly sheep—in their work. Then came the Revolution. By 1791 the two ivory-carvers and six ivory-sculptors of Dieppe were ruined. They had made their living by carving religious ivories such as crucifixes, and trifles such as *navettes* (spindles) for aristocratic ladies. Ivory-carving languished throughout the Napoleonic wars in spite of attempts by the Emperor to popularize Dieppe ivories by buying a model ship—which was one of the most favoured of all the Dieppe products. The return of peace brought an upsurge in business. Many men of Dieppe were released from British prison camps, where they had made their fortunes by selling ivory and bone ships and other knick-knacks to their captors. The duchesse de Berry made the little sea-port famous by her summer holidays there. Best of all many English tourists stopped there on their way to the Continent, and bought what the Dieppois had to sell.

In order to please the clientele of seaside visitors who watched the ivory-carvers at work through their shop windows the Dieppe craftsmen evolved a special repertory of carvings. They included genre-figures of the fishermen of the suburb of Le Pollet, which often swung round on one foot toy-fashion, miniature games of all sorts, low reliefs, and snuff-boxes and other articles carved in *mosaïque* (the local name for work which was pierced with many decorative openings and adorned with swags, garlands and other decorations). The craft ran in families such as the Colettes, who are still represented in the town. Much of the best work of Dieppe, such as that of Pierre Graillon, belongs to fine art rather than to the useful arts, but the work of the most talented sculptors was not widely appreciated. Dieppe carving was at its most successful while it was a local folk art, inspired by the innate Norman genius for design. By 1870 the great days of Dieppe were over. The Prussians occupied the town, and by the time they had departed, taking with them the motif of the Dieppe rose, which became the famous Erbach rose, the wealthy international visitors who bought the ivory carvers' wares had begun to go further afield.

The decline of Dieppe saw the rise of Erbach, a small town in the Rhineland. Count Francis I of Erbach-Erbach (b. 1754) was a *philosophe* who had travelled in France and whose hobby was ivory turning. He brought from the nearby town of Michelstadt his teacher, Johann Tobias Arzt, and set up a guild of ivory-carvers in his own principality. From the first the guild aimed at producing useful as well as artistic ivories. Count Francis set the example by making billiard balls and a chess set, which are still preserved in the Palace. The Erbach school first made its name by the production of ivory jewellery during the BIEDERMEIER period, and this jewellery often embodies the two principal Erbach designs, the rose (which has been already mentioned as an importation from Dieppe), and the stag. Other objects such as fans, furniture, low reliefs and statues were also made. Erbach is the most flourishing ivory centre in Europe and an account of the carvers still at work there may be found in *Elfenbein in Plastik, Schmuck und Gerät* by Hans Werner Hegemann and *Travaux d'Artistes et Artisans allemands*, Musée de Genève, 1961, by Hegemann and Kurt Degen.

Apart from scrimshaw American ivory-carving has never received attention, yet during the early years of the 19th c. unknown American prisoners at various camps in England, particularly Forton and Portchester castle, built ivory and bone model ships which were equal to anything which the professional Dieppe ivory-carvers could do and which have been eagerly acquired by British collectors under the impression they were of French workmanship. Although the Americans had to travel in a few months a road which the Dieppe carvers had taken hundreds of years to traverse, they were able to equal if not excel the French masters under whom they studied in the prison camps, as is proved by the fact that no one has ever been able to sort out the American from the French models.

In England the so-called 'Voyez' work, that of Charles Cockle Lucas and the lathe work of Holtzapfel call for mention. Stephany and Dresch, together with Hager and Hess, were apparently German workers living in England. Their work is very similar and is often described collectively as 'Voyez' ivories. They made box tops of various sizes, all with open-work and cut into a silhouette design of incredible delicacy representing marine landscapes or country scenes. Stephany and Dresch were exhibiting ivory-carvings at the Royal Academy from 1791 to 1803, and in 1800 they are referred to as 'Sculptors in Miniature to their Majesties'. Charles Cockle Lucas (1800–83) progressed from carving ivory knife-handles to making exhibition ivories, some of which were on view during the Great Exhibition of 1851. Ivory boxes by Mr. Garrett of Ipswich and chess-men by Staight were also on view. Benjamin Cheverton (1794?–1876) invented a machine for making small copies of full-size busts or plaques and many of his copies were in ivory. Cheverton must have worked over his busts with sculptor's tools after they had been cut mechanically, as no marks of the reducing machine can be seen even under a magnifying glass. Perhaps the biggest influence on craft ivories during the 19th c., however, was Charles Holtzapfel, who in 1847 published a book entitled *Turning and Mechanical Manipulation*. He demonstrated the most ingenious ivories which were made by an ordinary lathe, or one with the special appliances which he had added to it. Although the ARTS AND CRAFTS MOVEMENT once more turned craftsmen's minds towards useful ivories, generally speaking the rest of the 19th and the 20th centuries have been with a few exceptions devoted to artistic ivories.

J

JACINTH. See GARNET and ZIRCON.

JACOB, GEORGES (1739–1814). French cabinet-maker and founder of a celebrated family business. Jacob was born of peasant stock at Cheny in Burgundy. He went to Paris at the age of 16 and is thought to have served his apprenticeship under Louis Delanois, becoming a master in 1765. Like Delanois he specialized in chair-making and became the most outstanding French 18th-c. craftsman in this field. He greatly admired antiquity and made pieces in the austere classical style for the studio of the painter Jacques Louis David (1748–1825) to the artist's own designs. He gradually introduced NEO-CLASSICAL features into his own work and the general form of the Louis XVI chair owes much to Jacob's innovations. By the 1780s his work was already providing a foretaste of the EMPIRE style. He was, perhaps, the first French craftsman to use mahogany for chair-making and in doing so was accepting an English tradition which was new to French taste. He also adopted the lyre-back from the repertory of English late 18th-c. design. His output was immense and he received many royal commissions. In 1796 he handed over his factory to his sons, GEORGES and FRANÇOIS-HONORÉ. Under the name he adopted of JACOB-DESMALTER, the latter became the leading cabinet-maker under the Empire and a favourite of Napoleon. The firm was carried on under the name of Jacob Frères until the death of Georges in 1803, when its title was changed to Jacob-Desmalter et Cie. From 1825 to 1847 the business was directed by GEORGES-ALPHONSE, the son of François-Honoré. Working in conjunction with the architect-designers PERCIER and Fontaine and François-Joseph Bélanger (1745–1818), the Jacob-Desmalters were the most fashionable cabinet-makers in France during the Empire period.

509, 515, 516, 738.

JACOBE ALBUM. See GREENWICH ARMOURY.

JACQUARD LOOM. See WEAVING.

JADE. 1. MATERIAL. Jade is the generic term for two unrelated compact minerals which, most favoured today in their opaque green colours, are among the hardest and toughest stones on earth. In cultures as widely separated as the Chinese and the Aztec they were held in higher esteem than any other precious substance, yet neither appeared in European literature until after the discovery of America. Nephrite, the first, has been described as 'the true jade' because it was prized in China from the 3rd millennium B.C. for tools, weapons and important grave goods. We now know that nephrite was used for tools during the Stone Age in both Europe and Siberia. Jadeite, the second mineral, is by far the rarer stone, comprising less than 10% of all the jade ever found. The Olmecs and the Mayas worked it in Central Mexico from *c.* 1500 B.C., but it did not come into China (from Burma) until *c.* A.D. 1780. The New World jadeite was received in Europe after 1519 as a totally new material. The Bronze Age axes of jadeite, later found in Britain, France, Spain, Portugal and Germany, have been traced to no mineral source anywhere.

'*Chalchihuitl*' was the Nahuatl word for the rare green jewels that Montezuma gave to Cortes, declaring that each splendid bit was worth two loads of gold. Such loot was sent home by the Conquistadores. Hundreds of green stones were acquired as soon as the invaders learned that the mineral was valued as a cure for colic. The Spaniards called it *piedra de la ijade* (stone for the flank or the colic) or *piedra de los riñones* (stone for the kidneys). Sir Walter Raleigh, introducing 'spleene stones' to England, called them *piedras hijadas* (1595). The French turned feminine *l'ejade* to masculine *le jade*; in English it became *jade*.

Like the gold and the emeralds of the Americas the jades disappeared so completely in trade or in princely collections that men could later disbelieve that jade had ever existed in the New World. When sea trade with China opened in the mid 17th c. and nephrites reached Europe, they too were accepted as a new mineral. The jade artefacts from the habitations of prehistoric Swiss lake-dwellers were considered earlier imports; Europe was believed to harbour no deposits. Yet the legend of the colic stone persisted, and in 1789 A. G. Werner drew upon the Latin *lapis nephriticus* (stone for the kidney) to name it 'nephrite'. With the jade of America forgotten, nephrite was the only jade until new loot appeared from the sacking of the Summer Palace in Peking in 1860. A. A. Damour, who had been studying Oriental jades since 1846, discovered, when he examined an emerald-green carving newly arrived in Paris, that it was not Werner's nephrite. In 1863 he named the new species 'jadeite'. Then, analysing *chalchihuitl* received from Spain, he found that the Mexican mineral too was jadeite. 'Jade' remained the umbrella name for both these unusual minerals.

Nephrite and jadeite are chain-silicates, nephrite a silicate of calcium and magnesium, jadeite a silicate of sodium and aluminium. Nephrite has some iron content and water and traces of other elements. Jadeite has replacements in varying amounts of calcium, magnesium and iron.

Nephrite, a fine-grained tremolite-actinolite, belongs to the amphibole group. Some long-fibred actinolites provide excellent asbestos. Nephrite, however, is the result of a felting process during high-stress rock movements when masses of short fibres, already twisted and tangled, were sheared, re-crystallized and compacted under enormous pressures. The product is the remarkably tough, almost unbreakable nephrite. Jadeite was formed under high pressure so deep in the earth that even in upheavals it seldom worked up to where it could be taken in ordinary mining; hence its rarity. Jadeite is never in fibres but in aggregates of short, granular crystals so tightly interlocked, as in a mosaic, that they are seldom visible except under magnification. Nephrite is the tougher, for the felted mass offers greater resistance to a breaking force; jadeite is the harder (jadeite: 6·5–7 MOHS SCALE; nephrite: 6–6·5). Jadeite fractures more easily and is also denser or heavier (jadeite: spec. gr. 3·30–3·36; nephrite: spec. gr. 2·9–3·01). Neither can be scratched by an ordinary steel penknife. Jadeite, however, being harder, can scratch nephrite. When polished jadeite has a shiny or glossy appearance; a polished nephrite looks oily or even soapy. Hardness and specific gravity tests are not always reliable; in doubtful instances only the X-ray diffraction powder test is conclusive.

Although jade is popularly synonymous with some shade of green, both jades occur in many colours: white and grey to green, brown and yellow to red, mauve and blue to black. The intense colours are peculiar to jadeite, which displays an extraordinary range; the subdued colours occur in nephrite. The costly 'kingfisher green' or *fei-ts'ui*, which rivals the emerald, appears in jadeite. All colour distinctions are caused by minute quantities of different iron compounds, chromium, manganese and possibly nickel, titanium and vanadium.

The majority of all jade is opaque and unimpressive. Boulders of even colour for carving are scarce, those of translucent material suitable for jewellery are very rare. While nephrite is abundant compared to jadeite, in good colour it too is uncommon. Surprising is the fact that nephrite seems never to have come from the original Eighteen Provinces of the Middle Kingdom (China); to date no deposits have been reported. The enormous volume of nephrite the Chinese required came from the Khotan and Yarkand areas in Eastern Turkestan, now Sinkiang.

To the Chinese nephrite was *yü*, a name they applied to all hard stones, but only nephrite was venerated in their sacred rituals. Upon it they conferred virtues that endowed it with every conceivable excellence. Long after jade had ceased to have practical use it remained an unparalleled cultural asset, without peer for status and ornamentation, from toggles to vases, carved 'mountains', and even books of jade.

Nephrite from the Lake Baikal region in Siberia was identified by the Russians *c.* 1850, but the Chinese seem to have used it earlier, perhaps in the 18th c. and certainly in the 19th c. The colour of boiled spinach sparsely flecked with black chromite, it was less popular with the Chinese than the Yarkand type. New Zealand nephrite was probably unknown in China before the 20th c. but the scarce, clear apple-green type called *kaburangi* has a charm of its own.

From their arrival in New Zealand in the 14th c. the Maoris worked the South Island *pounamu* for tools, for weapons such as the prized *mere* war-club, for talismans such as the *hei-tiki* pendant, and for ornaments and toggles.

From prehistoric times the Eskimos of Alaska fished cobbles of nephrite from the Shungnak Creek and Kobuk River below Jade Mountain and used them for adzes, hoe-blades, knives and amulets. In Canada the Salish, Tlingit and Haidan Indians of British Columbia fashioned cutting tools, from small chisel-edges to large war-picks, of Fraser River nephrite.

Today nephrite seems to be available from every continent. In 1884 it was rediscovered in Europe at Jordansmühl, Silesia. Recently deposits were uncovered in south-east Switzerland and in the Apennines. Africa affords a dark green nephrite, like the Siberian material, from Mashaba, Rhodesia (1960). In South America Brazil has deposits somewhere in the Amazon River valley and large reserves in the Bahia district. In Asia Taiwan produces a medium-dark green. In the South Pacific, New Caledonia and New Guinea (Papua) are known to have deposits, while a site 480 km west of Adelaide in South Australia produces a dark green variety like New Zealand's nephrite (1965). The largest reserves may be in the United States. The first natural deposit of jade in the western hemisphere was discovered north of the Arctic Circle in Alaska in 1883 on Jade Mountain, to which the Eskimos had drawn attention. This asbestos-rich area could supply vast quantities if weather and transportation permitted. Some translucent Alaskan nephrite was exported to China.

The first to recognize the jades in the United States may have been the Chinese coolies who came to labour in the gold fields. After a jade 'craze' swept the world in 1919, active prospecting revealed many American finds, and nephrite has been worked since that time in home workshops, especially in the western states. Wyoming, where nephrite was discovered *c.* 1930, enjoyed a 'Jade Rush' in 1944, with tonnes mined or picked from the surface and a 198 kilogramme mass of gem material recovered. California, Utah, Washington and Wisconsin also have offered nephrite, but Wyoming has been the best producer with California second. Offshore, at Jade Cove in the Monterey area, a 1,270 kilogramme boulder of gem nephrite was brought up by scuba divers (1963). From the Fraser River area in British Columbia a steady production appears year after year.

An extraordinary communal achievement is the striking clock constructed entirely of jade over 7 years by 28 members of the San Francisco Gem and Mineral Society. At completion, in 1962, 12,000 man-hours had been consumed and more than $10,000 expended for jades, tools and abrasives. The clock strikes the hours with clear bell-tones on a gong of black Wyoming nephrite. Bearings are of Chatham-cultured emeralds, aquamarines and morganites, the pendulum bob and weights of California jadeite, most of the working parts of Wyoming nephrite. Colours included are apple-green, grey, black, white-and-green mottled and snowflake nephrite, plus light green-with-lavender jadeite from Burma. A relatively small percentage of jadeite is also present in the clock. For there are no major sources of jadeite except in the Myitkyina district of Upper Burma, which supplies the best greens and whites and also, infrequently, the rare 'kingfisher green', egg-yolk yellow, tomato red and, reportedly, even sapphire blue. It was jadeite from these remote quarries that the Ch'ien-lung emperor also accepted as *yü*.

Jadeite in minor quantities has been taken from San Benito County, California (1936), and from Wisconsin and Washington. It is known to exist in the Celebes (1947). It has been reported in the Apennines. A find of lichen-green was made in Guatemala (1952) near Manzanal. When a deposit was discovered in the Kotaki District of Japan (1953) the government acted to protect it as a 'national treasure'.

From where did the Olmecs, Mixtecs, Aztecs,

Toltecs and Mayas obtain the *chalchihuitl* for priestly use and votive offerings? We simply do not know. Jadeite had been worked in Mexico for 2,000 years before Cortes, yet except for the one minor find in Guatemala the natural provenance of green or blue jadeite, even of the lesser mixes of albite-jadeite and diopside-jadeite, so often used by the Olmecs for large masks and figures, remains hidden. The majority of the jades now displayed in museums were dredged from the sacred 'cenotes' where hundreds of plaques, tubes, beads and figurines had been flung for sacrifice. Other jades turn up often enough to encourage a continued search. Somewhere there must exist a deposit of blue jade with veins of the emerald-green that is so tantalizing in the best celts, pendants and figurines from the Linea Vieja in Costa Rica.

2. TECHNIQUE. Jade is not carved—it is too hard to be carved—but ground. Jade craftsmanship depends today, as it did at the dawn of history, more on the application of abrasives than on the hardness of tools. The abrasive is the all-important working element, close control together with unlimited patience (and experience) determining the quality of the product.

The San Francisco jade-clock workers employed the most advanced technology: a diamond-saw for rough cutting, diamond-impregnated precision-tools for drilling, sanding on a drum-sander and polishing with tin oxide. Certain operations were speeded by the new tools; the finishing still demanded countless hours of slow and careful hand-work.

The Neolithic jade-worker had neither metals nor the wheel to help him. He shaped his jade tools from cobbles that he found preformed in contours he desired. He pecked and tapped, and perhaps flaked and hammered, with pieces of quartz or garnet, which are harder than nephrite. For sharpening tool-edges he ground determinedly against hard sandstone. When he found a preformed shape of bird, beast or human being he released it from the stone by rubbing with wet sand to abrade and smooth and then pressed with hard gourds to bring up a polish.

To slice jade, however, for uses beyond the original shapes called for greater ingenuity. The earliest jade-workers of China cut slabs less than two millimetres thick by pulling back and forth across the stone with a toothless saw on which an abrasive, such as fine wet sand, was carried. Not the strong vine or thin slate or taut cord, but the abrasive, did the cutting. The technique of 'string-sawing' was effective in Costa Rica. The Indians of British Columbia cut jade boulders with sharp slabs of sandstone or thin slabs of hard wood. A thin spar of jade would cut another jade as diamond cuts diamond; but such a procedure apparently was not used, although tools, drill-points and gravers of jadeite and reamers and polishers of chloromelanite, an iron-rich jadeite, have been found in Guatemalan sites.

Holes could be drilled with tubular splinters of bone, reed, flint, bamboo or even a stick with abrasive applied to the point. The Maoris drilled with a flint at the end of a split stick fixed in a cord-drill; the Mayas used a pump-drill. Tiny fragments of jade would drill holes; the Aztecs and Mayas sometimes used crushed jade for abrasive. In China bronze cutting-edges and bronze-tipped drills became available early, but Aztec and Mayan workers, with no metal harder than copper, sawed jade mosaic-plates less than half a millimetre thick. In China the coming of iron eventually lightened the burden, but iron did not appear in middle America. It is doubtful if the early Chinese craftsman knew either crushed corundum or the diamond drill-point. Neither was essential; the jade masterpieces of the late Eastern Chou Period (770–256 B.C.) and of the Olmecs (880 B.C.–A.D. 600) were created when the distance between jade and its artisan was still minimal.

The Eskimos and Maoris created pieces of limited scope either because they had not lived with jade long enough to subdue it or because their meagre cultures demanded too little of them. The Chou craftsman was permitted no limitations. His bamboos fortified with abrasives cut holes, slots and channels, loose-linked parts, and hollowed tubes and vessels. Lathe-type rotary cutting and grinding tools and new abrasive compounds were welcome, but the basic mastery had preceded the innovations.

The Chinese triumph in jade is distinguished by incredible subtlety of design, in ritual objects with complex, rice-grain patterns, in plaques and buckles laced and scrolled with heraldic creatures, in belt-hooks and scabbard-hilts and vases up which DRAGONS clamber. The middle American achievement is marked by the even more astonishing vigour of the bold Olmec and Aztec figures, as well as those Mayan portrait-plaques that radiate serene confidence in a well-ordered cosmos. Only the Moguls of India, who in the 16th and 17th centuries produced vessels of unbelievable thinness and translucence, obviously by use of corundum and probably the diamond point, made any new contribution to the art of jade grinding. Shah Jahan's nephrite cup with ibex-headed handle is a high-water mark of their artistry. The Imperial workshops in Peking founded an 'Indian school' to rival the Moguls, but the encrusting of jade with precious stones, gold and enamels they left to India's jewellers. In the gem-adorned bibelots of jade the walls are thicker to support the jewels, the delightful eggshell-thinness perforce abandoned. Thick or thin, the Mogul confections are in a class apart.

Every desirable jade that has appeared in trade has probably been copied innumerable times, often with great skill. This is especially true of Chinese jades, which were deliberately reproduced in homage to earlier dynasties. The Maori *hei-tiki* have been copied widely. Similar precautions must be uttered on Middle American jades unless their provenance can be clearly established.

To the expert perfection of style often bespeaks authenticity; but where a piece cannot be traced to an excavation close examination is absolutely essential. The evidence of high-speed tools and modern polishing may be disguised, but they cannot be entirely eradicated. To the connoisseur who has been trained to bow before the spiritual quality of the great jades, the physical impressiveness of the new is not enough. Yet jade of fine colour and noble design, whether ageless or new work, remains commanding and will always have a place among the most desired of man's possessions.

In 1968 the important Man Ch'eng tombs were excavated in the district of Hopei. In addition to many other jade objects, mostly of a ritual or ceremonial nature, there were found the bodies of Prince Liu Sheng and his wife, Princess Tou Wan, of the Han Dynasty, both bodies completely encased in suits of jade. Liu Sheng's suit was made of 2,690 and Tou Wan's of 2,160 pieces of finely carved jade sewn together with gold and silver thread. The suits were made in twelve sections finished with piping of silk-wound iron wire round the edges and fastened flexibly together with gold wire when fitted to the corpse. The funeral suit of Princess Tou Wan formed the star exhibit at the Exhibition of Archaeological Finds of the People's Republic of China held at the Royal Academy, London, in 1973–4. In *Princes of Jade* by Edmund Capon and William Macquitty (published to commemorate the Exhibition) it is estimated that with the tools then available it would have taken an expert jadesmith of the Han Dynasty ten years to make one such suit. These suits together with the many other jade ceremonial objects found in tombs testify to the virtue and power ascribed to jade in early Chinese mythology.

See also CHINA (JADE).

55, 125, 210, 225, 271, 340, 342, 353, 635, 652, 917, 938.

JAMNITZER, WENZEL (1508–85). The leading goldsmith of his day in Nuremberg, he was the protagonist of Mannerism in this art and is believed to have originated the fashion, which prevailed in German work, of casting from nature figures of lizards, beetles, frogs, etc. ('*alle Thier auf Erden*'). Amongst surviving works decorated by him in this manner are basins in the Louvre and in Dubrovnik Cathedral. He made many objects for the Habsburg emperors and other princes, but most of them are lost and the only relics of his famous '*Lustbrunnen*' (a table-fountain made for Rudolf II) are the bronze supporting figures which he cast from models by J. C. von der Schardt. He was also a maker of scientific instruments. His large workshop employed other members of his family, the most distinguished being CHRISTIAN and HANS. His grandson, CHRISTOPH (1563–1618), was also among the leading goldsmiths of his day.

JANVIER, ANTIDE (1751–1835). French clockmaker, who spent his early years in Besançon but moved to Paris in 1807. He is well known as a maker of fine TABLE and MANTEL CLOCKS in the EMPIRE style. Their movements are of the finest workmanship and include many extra features such as elaborate calendar gearing, but their outstanding feature is the beauty of the ENAMEL dials on which this information is displayed and indicated by a group of hands. A fine selection of his work may be seen in the Conservatoire des Arts et Métiers, Paris.

JAPAN

1. Historical background.
2. *Netsuke.*
3. Lacquer.
4. *Inrō.*
5. Swords and other metalwork.
6. Pottery and porcelain.
7. Paper.
8. Japanese and Korean textiles.

1. HISTORICAL BACKGROUND. In the Ancient World the Isles of Japan stood, rather like Australasia, on the rim of the map. They occupied a singular position of isolation which was subject only to influences from the mainland of CHINA and Korea. The Japanese both borrowed and copied Chinese forms and they worked with many of the materials common to both countries; but they finally evolved uniquely Japanese and nationalistic decorative arts in the fields of LACQUER, POTTERY, textiles, sculpture, painting and metalwork.

Ethnographically, it is uncertain how the people of Japan originated. The aborigines, the *Ainu*, are looked upon as a separate race and to this day preserve folk traditions quite distinct from the major part of the country. The authority of the divine rulers of the Japanese was founded on legend, since the emperors are by tradition descended from the Sun Goddess, whereas the original religion, Shintoism, was based on nature worship and the importance of the seasonal succession of seed time and harvest. The love of nature has in fact been integral to Japanese arts through the ages and there is no nation in the world which has represented natural forms more diversely or more beautifully.

Before discussing these art forms it is necessary to establish certain periods of Japanese history important to their evolution, since they were from earliest times so influenced by the political, military and religious progression of events.

The *Pre-Buddhist Period*, extending from Neolithic times up to the introduction of Buddhism in the 6th c. A.D. saw the birth of the arts in Japan, but has mainly an archaeological interest.

The *Asuka Period* (mid 6th to mid 7th c.) was so called because the capital of Japan was situated at Asuka, Nara Province, and was especially notable for the official introduction of the Buddhist religion (A.D. 538) by way of Korea, and the consequent spread of Chinese styles in painting, sculpture and all the decorative arts. The new religion was patronized by the Imperial House and encouraged by such a gifted protagonist as Prince Shōtoku, regent for the Empress Suikō (592–628). Large monasteries were built and the techniques of metal-forging and inlay made great advances in the interest of image- and shrine-making.

Nara Period (710–794). A new capital city was set up at Nara in 710, imitating Chinese ideals both in government and in architectural style. Until 793 Japan was dominated by the influence of China, then at one of its cultural peaks under the T'ang Dynasty. In 756 the treasured collection of the Emperor Shōmu, some 3,000 objects, was presented to the Tōdaiji temple in Nara. It was then lodged in a building called the Shōsōin. Fire and earthquake have destroyed many famous repositories of early treasures, but despite all the vicissitudes which have beset Japan the Shōsōin has by some miracle survived and provides an invaluable commentary on the art products of that period, the majority being of Chinese origin or influence.

Heian Period (794–1185). The capital was moved to Kyoto (early name Heian) in 794. During the next three centuries there was a gradual development of classical Japanese art and the emergence of a characteristically national style. It was a period of great courtly beauty and luxury. In *The Tale of Genji* by Lady Murasaki (written in the 10th c.) we get some concept of the way of life and of the elegant and elaborate taste of court officials. The great beauty of the wooden sculpture and ritualistic Buddhist objects was accompanied by important advances in the secular arts: decoration of household furnishings, sliding doors, folding screens and the introduction of the *makie* technique notable in lacquer production. The *yamato-e* (nationalistic painting style of old Japan) scrolls, dating from this period, give some idea of the beauty and variety of the costume, picturing poetic scenes from the famous Genji story and other literary works.

Kamakura Period (1185–1334). A series of civil wars between independent military leaders led to the setting up in 1185 of a military government at Kamakura, 354 km east of Kyoto, by Yoritomo of the Genji family. The pattern of military rule in a feudal regime with overlords and attendant Samurai, noble supporters, was to continue until the 19th c. Swords and armour obviously assumed great importance and this was an age of virile taste dictated by the warlords and their rival factions. Zen Buddhism, introduced from China, influenced the decorative arts since its simplicity and directness appealed to the military classes. The Kamakura period lasted until 1334, when the political centre once more returned to Kyoto at Muromachi under the Ashikaga family.

Muromachi Period (1334–1573). The arts became more sophisticated and with the vogue for the tea ceremony (*cha-no-yu*), which stressed beauty and simplicity, even rusticity, a great impetus was given to ceramics and metalwork (tea bowls, tea kettles, etc.) used in the performance. This was one of the most important periods in Japanese art and in it Zen ink-painting and calligraphy reached their height.

Momoyama Period (1573–1614). This period is named after the magnificent palace built for Hideyoshi, a great general, who at this time managed to unify Japan and introduce a spell of progress and prosperity in which the arts flourished and fine palaces were built, decorated and embellished in luxurious style. Korean potters were brought back by Hideyoshi after a campaign in that country, and kilns were established which produced fine PORCELAIN and pottery. Lavish costume encouraged new methods of weaving textiles. Hideyoshi himself was a great patron of the tea and incense ceremonies and it was under his rule that the Portuguese were encouraged to trade and the Jesuits allowed to introduce Christianity. Two Japanese missions visited Europe, and the Dutch, Portuguese and for a short time the English had trading commissions. It is fruitless to speculate on what might have happened if Japan had been converted to Christianity; but although Christian motifs do appear as decoration on art objects, the religion soon became suspect for political reasons and on Hideyoshi's death all foreigners were expelled, Christianity was banned and Japan was once again almost completely secluded from the outside world.

Edo Period (1615–1867). Under the Tokugawa regime a military government strictly feudalistic in nature was maintained at Edo (the old name for Tokyo) and a long peaceful period very propitious to the arts lasted until the Meiji restoration of 1868. The merchant class now began to gain ascendancy. The Kabuki theatre of historical dramas became extremely popular and inspired woodcuts depicting the favourite actors of the day and splendidly illustrating the costumes. *Ukiyo-e*, the art of the everyday or 'passing world', depicted characters from every walk of life, including the girls from the 'gay quarter', the dandies, the shops and inns and the teeming crowds at festival time or entering a theatre. The Edo period saw the rise of a luxury-loving society with both noblemen and wealthy merchants sponsoring craftsmen. Affluence led to a great increase in the volume and variety of the decorative arts and many of the greatest names in pottery, lacquer, textiles, metalwork and *netsuke*—not to mention the fine arts of painting and print-making—were established during these 250 years.

Meiji Period (1868–1911). The move to modernize Japan resulted in the Meiji restoration of 1868, when progressive Japanese saw the need to reform the old feudal system, abolish the power of the Samurai, reinstate the Emperor and introduce government on democratic Western lines. During the Meiji period many fine examples of earlier decorative arts were sold to European and American collections, but at the same time a popular vogue in Europe for furnishing *à la Japonaise* encouraged the production of goods made to Western taste: enormous vases which might hold peacock feathers or pampas-grass, ornate screens and cabinets with intricate inlay, realistic figure groups carved in ivory, fragile over-pretty tea-sets and luridly patterned textiles.

The modern Japanese are faced with many of the same problems that beset the Western world. Inevitably the old arts are dying and in fact many of the wares being made in traditional styles are now more curiosities than necessities. Japan has one of the most swiftly progressing economies of the world and their old skills and talents for design have put them in the forefront of modern industrial design. One of the most endearing gestures of the Japanese Government has been to designate certain surviving craftsmen 'living National Treasures' because of the traditional skills they preserve. But when these men and women die even state patronage may not be sufficient to save their crafts. The Japanese craftsman possessed a unique sense of design and a special aptitude for balancing differing or contrasting textures: base with precious metal as instanced by a gold inlay on an iron *tsuba*; ceramic and mother-of-pearl glistening inset on smooth pure black lacquer; brilliant decorative lacquer panels setting off the natural wood surfaces of musical instruments. In books and textiles, and especially in modern architecture, Japanese qualities of design have been accepted and exploited everywhere so that they no longer seem to us as exotic as at their first impact. The use of space to emphasize design was a powerful precept early hit upon by the painters and lacquerers of Japan, as was the technique (now common in photography) of throwing back a scene into the distance by intruding some stark subject directly in the foreground.

There seems no explanation for the unerring sense of pattern and *mise-en-page* shown by the Japanese in all their arts. They inherited many of the methods and ploys of the Chinese but they are usually at their most telling the further they depart from them. The Japanese themselves, in assessing the best of their own work, place special emphasis on the identification of the craftsman with his materials. There is a refined sensitivity, a concept of the practically untranslatable *mono no aware*, 'the sorrow at the heart of things', which conveys beauty with underlying poetry.

Whilst it is possible to generalize on certain methods of design common to all the decorative arts of Japan, it is necessary to itemize the objects themselves since they were so often associated with a way of life fundamentally Japanese and without a parallel in the West.

2. NETSUKE. The traditional costume of Japan lacked pockets and the outer garment, the loose *kimono*, was held in place by the *obi*—a wide sash for women but for men a comparatively narrow belt. For fastening things at this belt a small toggle or *netsuke* was often used. As indicated by its derivation (literally *ne*—root, *tsuke*—to fasten), the *netsuke* was no doubt originally a purely practical object such as a natural node of wood or a small gourd; but with the Japanese flair for improving on nature and making the useful beautiful it came in time to have almost unlimited variety and to be made from every sort of material.

The things carried—suspended from the *netsuke* by cords passing behind the *obi*—included pipe-cases (tobacco was introduced by the Portuguese explorers in the 16th c.) tobacco-pouch and ash tray, *yabate* (writing set), flint and steel or money-purse and *inrō* (seal box or medicine chest). Some of the earliest *netsuke* were made from Chinese seals through which a hole had been bored. Rare examples showed a Christian theme and others were functional in their use: a silver ash tray embedded in a carved ivory conch shell, a little compass mounted in a *manjū* (bun-shaped) wooden case or a tiny perfume container made of a lacquered gourd.

The best of photographs are inadequate to convey the especial three-dimensional charm of these miniature sculptures. A *netsuke* should be seen and handled. The appeal and artistry may lie in the material used (every sort of wood, ivory, metal, hardstone and also natural objects such as nuts or gourds) or in the subject represented. Above all the *netsuke* had to fit into a smooth over-all shape so it should not snag the fine material against which it constantly rubbed. This influenced design so that the legs, ears and tail of an animal, for example, had to be depicted without sharp protruding edges and it was often shown recumbent. With age both wood and ivory acquire a beautiful patina and outlines are softened by the constant burnishing. The *kagamibuta* (mirror-lid), as the name suggests, was a variation of the *manjū* type with an inserted metal disc inlaid or engraved. The work was often signed by a specialist metal-worker.

The twin cords which held together *inrō* and *netsuke* were loosened or tightened by a bead called *ojime*, which might be of natural hardstone but was also often carved or lacquered *en suite*. Between *netsuke*, *ojime* and *inrō*, in fact, there usually existed some intimate connection in subject or pattern. Now amongst collectors the three are often displayed separately, but in Japan there was a subtle participation between the beholder and the artist. A literary allusion or reference to ritual, omen or legend would not pass unnoticed, just as the reader of a *haiku*, the seventeen-syllable poem of Japan, understands both what is written and what is left unsaid: the elusive *rapport* between writer and reader. The allusions in *netsuke* and *inrō* are a never-failing source of entertainment to the Western collector, who for verification must delve into a huge repertory of elaborate legends and characters

Inrō in lacquer with *netsuke* and *ojime*

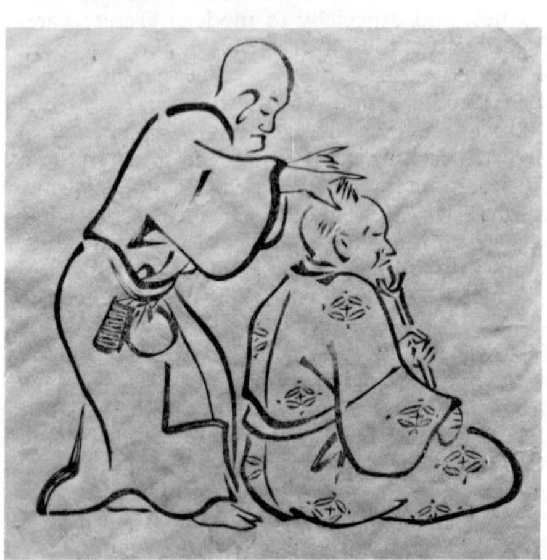

Book illustrations demonstrating the manner in which *netsuke*, *inrō* and pouch were worn at the belt. (*Left*) Woodcut reproduction of an early 17th c. painting from *Koto Shu* 'Curios' (1815) showing a Samurai with two swords and his attendant. (*Above*) Painting by Meiyo Kokan from *Rusei Soga* (1724) showing a masseur at work

in some such work as *Japanese Legends* by H. L. Joly; *Koji Hoten* by V. F. Weber or *Pointers and Clues* by W. H. Edmunds.

Although not a great deal is known about most of the individual carvers, many of the *netsuke* are signed and so by assembling collections it has been possible to establish criteria of their work, the sort of materials they favoured and their individual styles and favourite subjects. Much research has been done to establish schools of carving by virtue of resemblances or a family name in common. Originally craftsmen in some other art form perhaps made *netsuke* as a sort of side-line or even as a hobby. The famed Deme family, who were pre-eminent in the making of masks, excelled also in carving miniature mask *netsuke* (17th–18th centuries). It is thought that the makers of musical instruments used scrap ivory for miniature works and certainly some early *netsuke*, usually unsigned, favour patterns which conform to a triangular shape such as might belong to a piece of waste ivory. A favourite subject was the 'foreigner' holding a dog or cockerel, evidencing native interest in the costumes and customs of the Dutch and Portuguese traders. Certainly by the Edo period there were specialist carvers. A Japanese book published in 1781, *Sōken Kishō*, dealt among other matters of connoisseurship with master *netsuke*-carvers famous at that time. Fifty-four were mentioned and a few examples of their work shown, with just enough information to tantalize the present-day collector avid for facts. Foremost among them was Yoshimura Shūzan of Osaka, a notable painter also, who carved in soft *hinoki* wood and decorated his work with bright colours over a sort of gesso base. In fact he reproduced in miniature the type of statuary of figurines and gods used in temples, but as he never signed his pieces it has been difficult to establish genuine Shūzans from later copies in his style. Tomotada of Kyoto worked in ivory and his reputation was such that he was already being imitated in his own day. He specialized in animals, particularly recumbent oxen, but genuine works are much harder to discover than those bearing a forged signature. Many known carvers are associated with a special type of work: MASANAO of Kyoto (18th c.), famed for animals in wood and ivory; Kōkei of Ise (18th c.), who loved to depict the animals of the Zodiac (in Japan each year has a Zodiacal symbol which has lucky significance); Toyomasa of Tamba (1773–1856), who used inlaid eyes of translucent tortoise-shell and often carved legendary beasts; Ikkan of Nagoya (18th c.), whose speciality was rats and the sleeping *shōjō* (red-haired drunken imp); Bazan (1833–97), who achieved realistic rotten pears, sometimes with an attendant wasp, and whose works were signed in relief.

The early masters are usually marked by a free, broad style of carving but in the 19th c. the work became progressively more detailed and precious. One of the most original artists, Ohara Mitsuhiro (1810–75), introduced a very individualistic style of streamlined carvings of botanical subjects and birds. In fact the finest *netsuke* were miniature masterpieces made with loving care and taking time, sometimes months, to finish. Such carvings are beautiful from any angle, well balanced, bringing out the best from the material and proclaiming something of the personality of the artist who made them. Ryūsa (18th c.) perfected a means of decorating the turned *manjū*-shaped *netsuke* by cutting and perforating the material in intricate designs of flowers and birds. This made a lighter object and was widely copied. His name was adopted to describe the type. Shibayama (18th c.) also gave his name to a distinctive style, setting a fashion for carvings encrusted with inlay of shell, pearl, hard stone, etc. to create a rich design such as a caparisoned elephant. Hakuryū excelled at tigers, Horaku at bats. Kokusai (b. 1835) was a specialist in the use of stag's antler as a cheaper, but difficult material. His *netsuke* often show a sly humour and it is not surprising to learn he was at one time a professional jester. One of the most famous artists, the versatile Kaigyokusai Masatsuga (1813–92) was self-taught and highly original; he used only the best materials and has the distinction of being possibly the most sought after artist by modern collectors. He made much use of ivory and his *netsuke* are sometimes made to open and show intricate carving within. A *meiji* artist, he had many pupils and excelled also at *okimono* carving ('alcove carving' of larger groups).

Most of the *netsuke* carvers worked in the cities and their work was bought by the dandies, the merchants and the Samurai of Tokyo or Kyoto. Provincial schools existed such as Sessai of Echizen (1821–80) and the famous family of Iwami province founded by Tomiharu (1723–1811). He and his followers carved outstanding *netsuke* in wood and ivory but also used such unusual maritime materials as *umimatsu* (fossil coral), *umoregi* (fossil wood), whale tooth, etc. Often their work was inscribed and signed with minute carved characters and the detail was rendered with exquisite care. Mainly naturalistic subjects and still lifes were favoured.

These miracles of carving were only a few centimetres in size and they depicted every imaginable theme. Artists showed enormous resource when they set out to charm or amuse or frighten or merely to illustrate an old fable. The Japanese had a great fear of the supernatural and believed that spirits returned to haunt the scene of their earthly life. Much of their art reflects a capacity for frightening themselves to death. No nation has more excelled at inventing terrifying monsters and phantoms or telling horrendous legends. Perhaps this is connected with the physical nature of a country that before industrialization was full of dark pine forests, rushing cascades, mountains and earth tremors, hot springs, swirling mists and storms. Both lucky and unlucky creatures provided favourite subjects for design and the Japanese

Lacquer document box with sprays of fern and butterflies in gold *makie* on black ground. (V. & A. Mus., late 14th c.)

seem to have had a special predilection for the miniature, setting themselves the task of reducing a design to the dimensions suitable for a *netsuke*, *inrō* or an ornament of sword furniture.

3. LACQUER. If originally the art of lacquering was acquired from the Chinese (see CHINA, LACQUER), the Japanese made of it something singularly their own. The pupil outstripped the teacher, and it may be remembered that European lacquer was called JAPANNING. The process in the East is different, however. Lacquer was known from very early times. The raw material is a latex from *Rhus vernicifera*, a plant indigenous to Japan (perhaps originally introduced from China). The tree dies after it is tapped at about five years old so a constant succession needs to be grown. The lacquer can be used as a varnish for making objects watertight or, with repeated applications and polishing, for building up decorative surfaces. After application on a suitably prepared surface—cloth, leather, paper, wood or pottery—it is essential for it to dry slowly in a moist atmosphere to achieve the fine hard surface impervious to water or acid. Repeated layers need to be applied by the same method so it is a long, slow process.

As with other Japanese art forms it is necessary to master a whole vocabulary of descriptive terms to cover the various techniques and surfaces of decoration as well as the manifold objects decorated. Lacquer can be coloured by the addition of various chemicals and the favourites in Japan were red, by addition of cinnabar, and deep black by mixing with iron acetate. Blue, yellow, green, purple, brown and white lacquer were less common. The art of *makie* (literally 'sprinkled picture') was the secret of the great advance in the Japanese decorative lacquer wares. The technique allows a design to be built up by alternate applications of lacquer and sprayed metallic dustings, thereby achieving most beautiful effects. An early example of *makie* lacquer is in the Shōsōin but the technique is not thought to have been generally employed until the 9th c. A.D. Other forms of sophisticated decoration included sprinkling coarser grades of metal powders, various types of inlay, carving the surface (*kamakura-bori*), and actually adding to the surface by raised designs (*taka makie*) or high relief (*shishiai makie*), using an additional paste to build up the design.

All manner of useful and decorative ware was made, though it should be remembered that the Japanese believe a thing is beautiful only if it is for a purpose, which helps to explain how widespread in everyday life were their decorative arts. Lacquer was used for larger pieces of furniture: cabinets, tables, *kimono* stands, arm rests, bowls, trays, picnic boxes, writing cases (*suzuri-bako*) and for many toilet wares such as mirror-stands and cosmetic boxes (*tebako*) and for the decorative pins and combs which the Japanese lady used in dressing her hair. In the *Genji* story Prince Genji inspects a present sent to a lady of his choice consisting of comb-boxes, scrap-boxes, cases for incense jars. 'He picked up at random one of the comb-boxes; it was a work of fascinating elegance and delicacy, decorated with flowers. In the very centre of one petal was an inscription. He read the poem.'

4. INRŌ. Pre-eminent among the works of art achieved by the lacquer masters is the *inrō*. The first use of a small wooden box for containing a man's personal seal and ink pad may have originated in China but the principle of wearing a cunningly tiered portable box with small close-fitting compartments was essentially Japanese. The earliest *inrō* were probably cut from natural wood and the cords which held them to a toggle (*netsuke*) at the belt passed through metal ringlets. But this early type developed into a far more sophisticated article which was fashionable with a class of men who were able to patronize the best artist–craftsmen to make *inrō* in competitive variety both for personal wear and as gifts. The earliest seem to date from the Momoyama period and display patterns and designs of a subdued, refined nature. In the Edo period they became lavish and even ostentatious. Great lacquer families arose, like the generations of metal-workers who made sword furniture, and making *inrō* was possibly often team-work. Specialist joiners would make the actual case and other craftsmen would give the preliminary coatings of lacquer up to the stage where an expert artist would take over to finish the design. Some of the famous families were Kajikawa (17th–19th centuries); Kōami School (15th–19th centuries); Kōetsu-Kōrin (16th–20th centuries). Individual genius was displayed by

an artist such as RITSUŌ in using pewter and ceramic inlays and sometimes elaborating on the natural wood surface so the grain might provide part of the decorative effect. His work was often copied and forged. A later artist, also a painter, was Shibata Zeshin (d. 1891), who was trained under the Koma family and combined great technical skill with originality. The Victoria and Albert Museum has a set of *inrō* made by him in 1865, *The Twelve Months*, with a different shape and a suitable seasonal design for each *inrō*.

The Japanese above all assimilated natural forms. They appreciated the asymmetry of the stars, the distribution of leaves on a tree or the random pattern of fallen petals, spiders' webs, snails' trails, the spoors of animals or the track of birds' feet. 'All things counter, original, spare, strange . . .' Even the most haphazard effect of worm-holes in rotted wood or the bruised patch on fruit aroused their artistic sensibility. They used the keenest observation to reproduce tiny insects, shells, the natural pose of an animal, and they were masters of atmosphere, conveying the beauty of the moment when the moon looks through a veil of cloud or a fish ripples the surface of sunlit water. They especially enjoyed the sort of trick mastery of depicting paper as leather, making leather resemble lacquer, or lacquer imitate a metallic or wooden surface. It was almost an artistic joke, a virtuosity understood by those subtle enough to appreciate their work.

5. SWORDS AND OTHER METALWORK. Sword-making in Japan was the most revered of all the crafts and the process almost amounted to a religious ritual. Consequently the art is one of the most adequately recorded from early times. Only a few exponents of the mysteries of forging a fine sword remain today, and early blades still need to be returned to Japan for expert treatment if they have deteriorated from neglect. The earliest documented blades date from the Nara period, but the impetus given to the craft by civil wars of the late Heian period led to the foundation of several famous schools of sword-making. The peak was probably in the late 14th-c. Muromachi period.

The Japanese sword blade is famed on account of its very special qualities and the skill with which individual smiths forged it. Unlike the European blades, which are evenly tempered throughout, it had an edge of great hardness backed by softer metal to ensure toughness and to allow it to give rather than snap when a blow was struck. It is estimated that as many as 5,000,000 blades may have been made and very many smiths are recorded who passed on their secret processes within the family and jealously guarded their techniques through generations.

Workmanship on sword mountings was originally directed to the need for protecting the blade and shielding the user from danger. Later two swords were evolved, one for use in battle (*tachi*) and the other for decorative and ceremonial purposes (*katana*). After the Heian period there was a clear distinction between the two types.

The component parts of the Japanese sword were the blade with *tang*, which bears the sword-smith's signature and date; the hilt (*tsuka*) made of wood overlaid with fish skin and bound with silk braid which binds on the *kashira* or pommel; the *menuki*, a pair of metal ornaments marking the hilt peg and assisting the grip on the hilt; the *fuchi*, a colar linking hilt to blade; and the

Sword-guards (*tsuba*) from left to right: eagle with brass incrustation on iron (*c.* 1700); iron with gold overlay Hosokawa badges. Signed Harumitsu of Higo (*c.* 1800); *sentoku* (a yellow alloy) with gold and silver inlay of rice fields by moonlight in the style of Hirata Hikozo; iron with gold overlay of nightingale in a plum tree. Signed Hayashi (*c.* 1800)

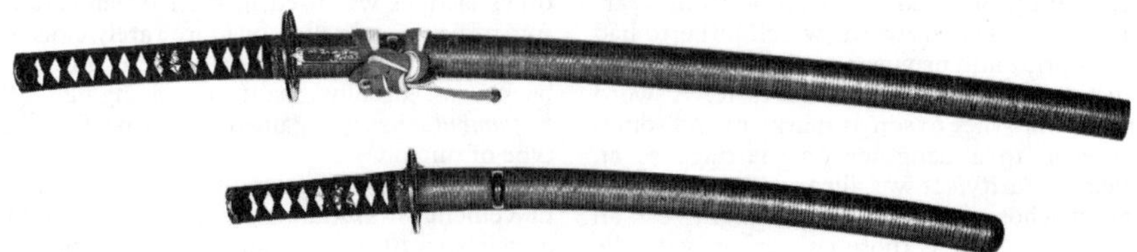

Pair of Samurai swords: *daishō* (the great and the small); *katana* (long sword) and *wakizashi* (short sword). Signed Musashi Kami Fujiwara Morimichi. Scabbard of black and brown lacquer with alternate stripes and decorated with sprinkled *aogai* (mother of pearl); *tsuba* by Soten. Lengths 70 cm, and 47 cm (late 16th c.)

tsuba or guard, held in place by the pair of metal washers. Twin holes in the *tsuba* or sword-guard were made to house a small dagger (*kozuka*) and a sort of skewer or bodkin (*kōgai*). These are held in the body of the wooden scabbard but have decorative heads. As may be seen, there is ample scope for decoration in a highly ornamental manner. Originally the *tsuba* were forged by the swordsmiths themselves and simple designs of beaten iron (Ashikaga period) were the forerunners of the later specialist *tsuba*-makers with more ornate patterns. It is said that specialization began with the Gotō school from the 15th c. In the Edo period especially very beautiful decorative work appeared as this 'Samurai' art was fostered by each Lord of a Province. The Gotō school excelled in high-relief design with precious metals. The Myōchin family of armourers worked chiefly in thin metal but there was great variety in their work with pieces engraved, perforated or inlaid. In addition, as a sort of *tour de force*, they produced articulated animals and snakes, dragons, etc. from many little separate sections linked and riveted together. The Shoami family were early established in Kyoto but branches spread throughout Japan. The *tsuba* was usually roundish or oval, but this family experimented with different shapes—square, geometrical, or resembling petals. Styles and designs were influenced by the fashions of the period and both to some extent followed schools of painting. With the popularity of the *Ukiyo-e* style of painting in the 18th c. coloured inlays were much used. Beautiful alloys such as *shibuichi* (silver and copper) and *shakudō* (gold and copper) were used with great effect. Conforming to the prescribed shape and small dimensions of the sword fittings, much of the work was nothing short of miraculous. (See also ARMS AND ARMOUR.)

On 5th May, the traditional Boys' Festival day, costumed dolls representing famous warriors and heroes with helmet, armour and horses clad in war paraphernalia, all in miniature, were displayed in houses where the family had a son. Vases of irises, whose blade-like leaves are thought to resemble swords, were arranged to remind the child that 'the sword is the soul of the Samurai' and it was once the custom for a boy to have a bath in hot iris water to instil in him physical courage, just as he learnt tradition from the pageantry. In 1877 the government prohibited the Samurai from wearing in public the two swords which hitherto had been his pride and privilege and at the same time the distinctive mark of his martial caste. A sword passed from father to son as heirloom and sometimes even to a daughter on marriage as an emblem of purity. It was always regarded as the friend at whose thrust its owner might seek an honourable death, as those conversant with the Japanese theatre will know. Often the plot of a drama ends with *seppuku* or *harakiri* suicide. The Samurai at the end of the 19th c. were so impoverished that they were even forced to sell their treasured swords and many fine blades at that period found their way to Europe.

Though the Samurai are long disbanded, something of their proud history is perpetuated in the *mon* or family badges which have played an important part in the decorative art of Japan since the Kamakura period when many of the influential clans created a crest to decorate their banners and armour. In decoration the *mon* was usually displayed in a roundel and, as happened with heraldic devices in the West, in the course of time the *mon* ceased to be restricted to aristocratic warrior families. Flower and bird motifs were popular, as also were geometrical designs, which sometimes had a legendary purport. Some very simple designs were reminiscent of patterns doodled in a school notebook with a pair of compasses, others were highly sophisticated. They were used widely on every sort of ware: metal, lacquer, textiles and paper. The sixteen-petalled chrysanthemum, the imperial crest of the emperor and that of the empress, the leaves and flower of the Paulownia, were especially popular. In coloured woodcuts showing actors it is often possible to identify an actor from the *mon* design stencilled on his kimono as his personal crest. Mostly the designs were traditional and anonymous, but a few were conceived by such artists as Hokusai (1760–1849) and various lists of them were published.

Other workers in metals were not perhaps so esteemed as the swordsmiths and armourers, but there existed fine artisans in every type of craft. The Dutch traveller Kaempfer (1692) noted artistic flower arrangements and commented on its being 'as much an art in this country to range flowerpots in proper order as it is in Europe to carve or lay the table. Sometimes there is instead of a flowerpot a perfuming pot of excellent workmanship cast in brass or copper, resembling a crane, lion, dragon or other strange animal.'

The Japanese MIRROR was made of polished bronze with one side for reflection and a design on the reverse. It was the general practice to decorate this surface with auspicious patterns, symbols of longevity such as the tortoise or the pine-tree. Mirrors have always been held in superstitious regard by primitive peoples. Very early examples of Japanese mirrors have been found by excavating lakes where they were originally tossed as religious offerings. Sometimes lacquer was used in their ornamentation, sometimes metal relief, or more rarely cloisonné enamel. A perforated knob at the centre of the back was usually made for hanging. The *kagamibuta netsuke* gained its name from this type of mirror.

In the Kamakura period there emerged a new movement in Buddhism which involved faith in relics and thus brought about a demand for reliquaries. Examples still survive in some old monasteries and they were reputed to contain sacred relics of the Buddha and consequently were lavishly decorated with cut metal and lacquered wood. Another survival of Buddhist ritual is represented in the Shōsōin treasure-house: rich floral baskets served as containers for lotus flowers during worship and were ornamented with delicate arabesques and open-work.

6. POTTERY AND PORCELAIN. The most highly developed craft of the primitive civilization of the Japanese islanders in Neolithic times was a crude hand-moulded and lightly fired monochrome pottery. Decorated often by means of impressions from woven string or matting (as well as other natural objects such as sticks and shells), it was called JŌMON, literally 'rope-pattern', which gave the name to the period, roughly the 3rd and 2nd centuries B.C. and possibly earlier. This gave place to the Yayoi period, lasting until the 3rd c. A.D., called after a style of pottery examples of which were first found at Yayoi-cho near Tokyo in 1884. As well as wheel-turned pottery utensils, interesting tomb-burial finds have been made of *Haniwa* or grave-guardians, pottery effigies of figures and animals thought to represent the original human sacrifice which took place at burial rites. Many of these are highly individualistic in style and they are a valuable reference to costume and accoutrements of the period. Glazed ware was developed throughout the 5th to the 13th centuries in places where natural clay was found. The glaze was quite often formed by the natural ash during the firing process but later variations of artificial high-temperature glazes date from the Heian period onwards. During the Kamakura and Muromachī periods there were kilns at Seto, Tokoname, Shigaraki, Tamba, Echizen and BIZEN. These are known as 'the six old Kilns of Japan'. They are especially famous for wares produced for the tea ceremony and consequently revered.

The aesthetics of the Japanese tea ceremony, *cha-no-yu*, had a profound effect on the decorative arts. Introduced with Zen philosophy, it associated meditation with the presence of beautiful and simple art forms and the habit of regarding them in a reverent spirit. With the tea ceremony was associated the attendant art of flower arrangement and the setting up of a single painting or example of fine calligraphy in the *tokonoma* (a niche set aside in the tea-house expressly for this purpose). In the 15th c. the priest Shūkō, adviser to the Shogun Ashikaga Yoshimasa, actually laid down set rules for the performance of the tea ceremony and formulated procedure and utensils. From this time on it was necessary that the wares should appeal aesthetically to the touch as well as in appearance and this produced a demand for the 'rustic' type of pottery so prized by the great tea masters, made at kilns such as Seto, Iga, Shino, Oribe. Some tea bowls were turned on the wheel, some shaped by hand with no attempt at uniformity and even with deliberately added irregularities. The glaze sometimes only partially covered the bowl, leaving some of the surface exposed. The method produced a type of ware which is perhaps aesthetically an acquired taste but is nevertheless completely satisfying to the enthusiast. Early examples are greatly valued in modern Japan. One of the most famous varieties, RAKU, is so called since the great general Hideyoshi presented a seal with the character *Raku* (Joy) honouring a potter called Jokei, whose descendants each used the name. Made in Kyoto since the Momoyama period, the early ware had a characteristic lustrous thick black glaze.

Ogata KENZAN, a painter as well as a potter, made soft-texture pottery resembling *Raku* ware but he decorated it as well with simple but masterly designs. Many amateurs imitated this type of ware. A revered historic piece which is cracked is sometimes healed with gold lacquer which adds to rather than detracts from its value.

The secrets of porcelain making, which had been jealously guarded, were introduced to Japan when one of Hideyoshi's generals brought back potters captured in Korea and established them in Satsuma province. This gave its name to a type of ware which had a soft warm creamy ground of ivory-like lustre with a crackled glaze adorned in later periods with a wealth of gold and colour. Other porcelain potteries were set up when deposits of kaolin were found in Japan. *Arita* ware was exported from the port of Imari: this was basically underglaze blue design on white ground, but colours were sometimes added in overglaze to hide discrepancies when the blue had blurred. 'Kakiemon' was a name bestowed on a potter called Sakaida who had pleased his overlord with a model of twin persimmon (*kaki*: persimmon) and he then perfected the distinctive palette of soft red, yellow, blue and turquoise green which is characteristic of *Kakiemon* wares. *Kakiemon* became popular in the West and the style was copied in Europe by many manufacturers in the 18th c. But the *Kakiemon* designs were purely Japanese in style and often portrayed Japanese scenes, whereas the *Kutani* porcelain made by Kyoto potters in the 17th c. was very ornate and derived from the late Ming wares of China. By the end of the 19th c. the Japanese ceramic industry was seduced in competition with the West into producing too vulgarly ornate vases and other tourist pieces. But thanks to the gospel preached by Bernard Leach and his followers in modern times there has been an increasing interest in the work and thought of some of the early masters.

7. PAPER. Japanese hand-made papers are unique. Nowadays they are increasingly rare and produced only in remote areas by traditional methods which cannot be imitated by machinery. Paper played a large part in the old Japanese way of life. Apart from the fine papers for painting or woodblock printing and many decorative papers for calligraphy and scroll mounting, a specially stout and tough type was used for screens and *fusuma* (sliding doors), affording

an excellent surface for gold-leaf and brush work and the opportunity for some of the best large decorative compositions.

For domestic uses paper, steeped in oil, became as tough and waterproof as leather and was used as fabric for UMBRELLAS, parasols, hats, etc. Finer grades did duty for glass in sliding doors and windows, less transparent than glass but more impervious to cold. Beautiful WALL-PAPERS and screen backings, handkerchiefs as flimsy as gossamer, myriad toys from PAPIER MÂCHÉ or folded paper (*origami*), gift wrappings and lanterns, fans and shadow shows, all relied on the variety of a large output of paper. Since it was used for making intricate stencils, paper also played an important part in the design of textiles. See also PAPERS, DECORATIVE.

8. JAPANESE AND KOREAN TEXTILES

(*a*) *Japan.* Until the admission of Chinese and Korean weavers to Japan, possibly as early as the 4th c. during the turbulent years after the break-up of the Han empire, there is little evidence of a developed textile industry there. Tradition holds that the 5th c. was the date when Chinese and Korean craftsmen first ventured to Japan and that these contacts developed rapidly when in the first half of the 6th c. the Buddhist faith was transmitted to Japan, again from China through Korea. Prior to these contacts Japanese civilization had developed independent of outside influences under the Jōmon (before *c.* 200 B.C.), Yayoi (*c.* 200 B.C.–A.D. 200) and early 'Tumulus' periods (3rd–6th centuries). There is no doubt that the principles of WEAVING were known to the Japanese at that time, for pottery figures of the Jōmon period illustrate men and women dressed in figured cloths. These were probably woven from twisted yarns of bark and stalk fibres. Such primitive features were characteristic of the Japanese textile industry before the influx of Chinese and Korean craftsmen with their superior techniques and developed sense of ornament and style.

During the centuries of close commercial and cultural contact with China, first overland through Korea and later (from the 8th c.) through direct sea trade, the Japanese SILK industry was virtually indistinguishable from its Chinese counterpart. The flow of Chinese craftsmen, particularly weavers, into Japan naturally led to common techniques and decorative styles. Indeed there is some doubt about many of the fragments preserved in the Shōsōin in Nara, which are generally thought to be Chinese but which could have been produced in Japan either by Chinese weavers or at least under Chinese supervision.

Many of the earliest surviving Japanese textiles were made in the service of the Buddhist religion and these also reflect their Chinese ancestry. The most famous is a small fragment dating from the 7th c. and embroidered with a scene from the Western Paradise of Amida, which both stylistically and technically is dependent upon Chinese prototypes. Woven fragments of the 7th and 8th centuries have formal compartmentalized patterns, often featuring confronting beasts of the type so familiar to Sassanian-inspired Chinese polychrome silks of the T'ang dynasty. Resist-dyeing techniques were also practised in Japan at this time, these too probably inherited from China. A rare example, preserved in the Victoria and Albert Museum, ornamented with a stencilled pattern consisting of the eight-spoked Buddhist emblem, the wheel of the law (*rimbō*), which symbolized the teaching of the Buddha, is generally attributed to the Nara period. The deep red of the design is on a contrasting white-figured DAMASK, the latter closely resembling early T'ang Chinese damask silks.

Three principal dyeing techniques were used in Japan at this time: *rōkechi*, like BATIK, where the areas not to be coloured are covered with a wax-resist; *kōkechi* or binding the cloth with thread so that when dipped into the dye the bound yarns remain uncoloured; and *kyōkechi*, in which the cloth is pressed between wooden boards carved with designs so that the pattern stands out in relief and compresses the fabric to exclude the dye and thus produces an uncoloured area of design. Whereas in China these dyeing techniques appear to have fallen into comparative disuse after the T'ang period except for native cotton products, in Japan they continued and were considerably developed. The importance of the dyeing tradition in Japan is illustrated by the few examples surviving from the Heian and Kamakura periods. In the Kyōōgokoku-ji in Kyoto is preserved a costume for the *bugaku* ballet and attributed to the Kamakura period. It is ornamented with a printed pattern of lions within an arabesque medallion of a type clearly inspired by Chinese-Sassanian decorative style.

No doubt silk-weaving continued in medieval Japan but there is little evidence of it in surviving material. Chinese woven silks, however, continued to be imported and were obviously highly prized, for they have been preserved, mainly as mounts for scroll paintings and as tea-ceremony bags.

Among the decrees issued in the Kamakura period was one limiting the width of woven fabrics to a maximum of 37 cm. This must have had a restricting effect upon the industry and possibly led to an even greater dependence upon Chinese imports. In the 14th c., however, the introduction of the Nōh theatre provided a much-needed impulse to the Japanese textile industry to produce new fabrics with vital designs of native inspiration. The challenge was certainly accepted, as is evidenced by the many examples (mainly of the 18th and 19th centuries) of Nōh costume preserved in Western museums with striking, boldly conceived designs of highly coloured floral patterns often on semi-abstract backgrounds. The 15th and 16th centuries were significant periods in the development of a textile tradition independent of China, and the part played by the demands of the Nōh theatre was

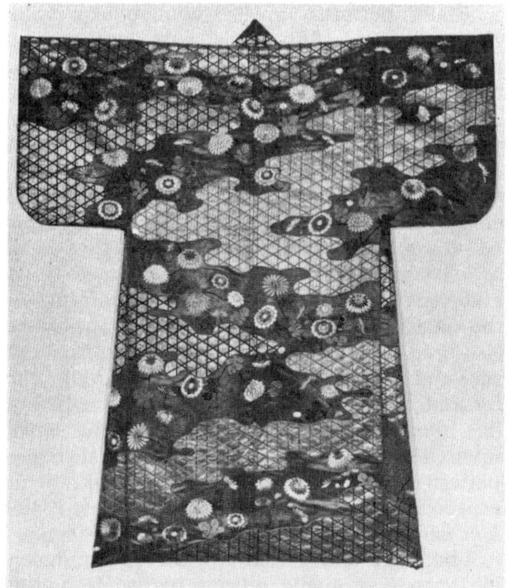

Embroidered *Nōh* robe, floral motifs on a brick-red ground with gold background. (Österreichisches Mus. für Angewandte Kunst, Vienna, 17th c.)

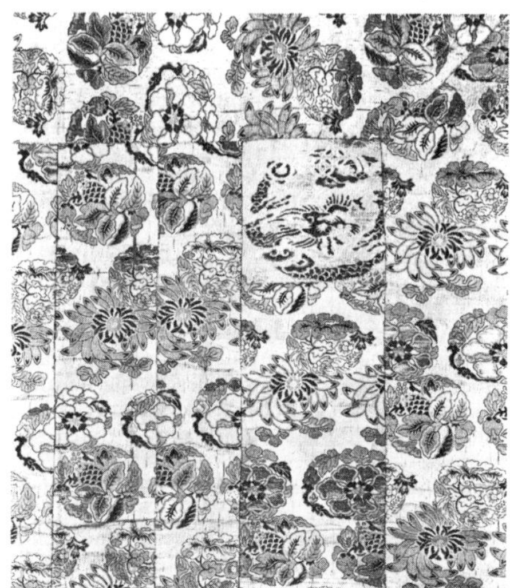

Part of a Buddhist priest's robe or *kesa*, brocaded on a pale cream silk ground. (V. & A. Mus., 18th c.)

Detail of a stencilled and drawn resist-dyed cotton cover (*nori-zome*). (V. & A. Mus., 19th c.)

Detail of a *kasuri* with tiger and bamboo design 'reserved' on a dark-blue cotton ground. (V. & A. Mus., 19th c.)

considerable. Although few pieces of this date survive, at least in the West, a fine example in the Österreichisches Museum für Angewandte Kunst, Vienna, is representative of the tradition. With the advent of the Edo period under the Tokugawa regime a more feudal type of society was established and virtually all foreign trade was prohibited. In spite of these restrictions, and possibly even spurred on by the need for self-reliance, the textile and particularly the silk industry continued to flourish and developed a still more characteristically Japanese tradition. Woven silks of the 17th and 18th centuries were rich with gold thread and gilt paper in predominantly floral, above all chrysanthemum, figured brocades. Again the Nōh theatre inspired designers and weavers to new achievements, and the demands of the Buddhist religion similarly stimulated the industry. The *kesa*, or priest's robe, was generally ornamented with broad floral, bird or animal patterns, often in an over-all medallion form that is perhaps less characteristically Japanese but is still representative of an independently developing style. Geometrical motifs, hexagonal DIAPERS, zig-zag or chevron patterns and broad chequer designs were widely used on these later woven silks, usually brocades, and distinguish them from their Chinese counterparts. The concept of a formal abstract design as a background to naturalistic motifs is strikingly evident in Japanese silks of the Edo period, and indeed also in contemporary lacquers. Often this concept is applied in an unusual and peculiarly Japanese manner by embroidering the naturalistic motifs on a patterned background, sometimes a brocade but more usually a printed silk base.

Another large category of later Japanese textiles which have been preserved in Western collections, and which also give an indication to the variety of techniques employed, is that of the *fukusa* or gift cover. These covers, usually about 46 to 61 centimetres square, were used to wrap presents but did not form part of the gift as it was customary to return them to the donor. The majority are brocades, though both embroidered and *k'o-ssŭ* examples survive. They employ traditional Japanese designs: birds, fishes, mythological scenes, landscapes and flowers, particularly chrysanthemums, and plants associated with river life.

Japanese *k'o-ssŭ*, or *tsuzure-ori*, was generally coarser than Chinese silk TAPESTRY, from which it was certainly derived. Also it did not enjoy the same patronage or attain the same high level of sophistication as the Chinese *k'o-ssŭ*. As if acknowledging the debt to China, the designs used in Japanese silk tapestry were less Japanese and more Chinese in character.

Probably the most developed aspect of the Japanese textile industry was the resist-dyeing tradition. Originally imported from China in the 7th c. it developed continuously from that time and with the introduction of cotton in the 16th c. became widespread as a kind of cottage industry. In particular the southern islands of Kyūshū, Okinawa and the Ryūkyūs became known for their dyed and printed fabrics. Two principal methods were employed: resist dyeing of the yarns before weaving and resist dyeing of the completed fabric, principally cotton. Of the former the *kasuri* was the most common: in this lengths of yarn were bound at certain predetermined points to prevent absorption of the dye and then woven. Blue was by far the most popular colour and the essentially geometrical patterns were regular and bold.

Greater decorative scope was permitted in the resist dyeing of the completed fabric. The principal method used was to apply a resist paste to the areas of design so that after dyeing the pattern would be left in reserve on the coloured ground. The paste was either applied by stencil (*katagami*) or by a free-hand drawing method. The latter permitted great freedom of expression to the designer. The resist paste was applied through a tube, usually made from bamboo, and held by the designer in the same way as a crayon. As the industry developed so did the technical variations, and often combinations of resist dyeing and direct printing were used. The term *yuzen* implies combination, and these fabrics employed both stencil resist dyeing for the overall design and direct printing for the detail over-colours. Sometimes a third process was involved: free-hand drawing-in or painting of the final touches. Tie-dyeing techniques were also used on completed fabrics, both cotton and silk, and Kyoto became and remains today the centre for this tradition. Fabrics ornamented in this manner are characterized by the small squared motifs which in turn comprise larger patterns. It was widely used on silk, being especially suited to soft materials, and many later *kimonos* were made from such tie-dyed silks.

The large and varied resist-dyeing industry in Japan continually reflects native decorative traditions, except for the earliest examples when Chinese styles dominated the textile industry. Once the tradition had become established the products were generally for local consumption and so were never influenced by outside styles or the demands of foreign markets. It is, therefore, these unique and varied products of localized printing and dyeing workshops which provide us with the purest reflection of native taste and style in the Japanese textile industry.

(*b*) *Korea*. The significance of the Korean peninsula in the transmission of Chinese cultural elements to Japan has been noted. Korean culture itself remained continuously indebted to China and never attained the independence eventually achieved by Japan. Korea was never totally absorbed into the Chinese sphere of influence, however, and its art and culture illustrate its derivative yet distinctive nature. At the beginning of the Christian era Korea was under Han Chinese rule. Lacquers retrieved from Lo-lang are totally Chinese in character, but the small fragments of yellow silk recovered during these excavations tell us nothing of the textile industry in Korea at that time. Indeed it is possible that these silks were of Chinese origin. In the 3rd c. Korea obtained independence as a result of the fall of the Han empire. Although no textiles of Korean origin have survived, it is assumed that some kind of industry existed, probably on the same state-controlled lines as that of Han China. Literary references describe the export of silks from Korea to Japan in the 6th, 7th and 8th centuries; but in view of the position of Korea as both a cultural and a commercial intermediary between China and Japan it is always possible that these were really T'ang Chinese silks which we know from the examples in Nara to have been exported. At this time the Buddhist religion was firmly established in Korea and must have required silks for vestments and banners. Once again, however, no such pieces survive, although we may surmise that they were totally Chinese in character. Another indication of the existence and the nature of a textile industry in Korea at that time is provided by fragments of clothing, woven with gold thread, from a tomb in Paekche kingdom (*c.* A.D. 313 to 663), which controlled the south-west of the peninsula.

One of the earliest indications of an independently developing textile tradition emerging in Korea is suggested by the incised ornament on earthenware tiles from the kingdom of Silla (5th to 6th c.). These are ornamented with rigid geometrical patterns, often concentric semicircles, of a type which appear consistently on later Korean embroideries. The earliest surviving Korean textiles adopt motifs from the common Chinese decorative repertory of dragons, cranes, Buddhist figures and symbols of longevity and prosperity. The robes too were in the Chinese style. The interpretation was, however, distinctive. In many instances the formalization of naturalistic elements into a rigid pattern was stronger in Korea than it was in China, particularly with textiles. Few woven textiles have survived, which suggests that it was the art of embroidery which was the principal textile technique.

Embroideries dating from the 17th and 18th centuries reveal a highly developed art, although both the techniques employed and the ornament were clearly based on Chinese prototypes. For example screen panels were embroidered with landscape, hunting and palace or pavillion scenes. Some items of official Court costume illustrate the familiar dependence upon Chinese patterns, but again with a distinctive interpretation. The over-all style of the dragon robe was adopted and the waves around the hem were in Korea embroidered in a series of tight formalized concentric circles, the clouds in a slightly eccentric but rigid form which is in contrast to the more fluent Chinese designs. Literary records concerning dragon and phoenix robes, both adopted from China, go back as far as the 11th c. in Korea and in succeeding centuries Korean costume remained constantly indebted to the Chinese style. In the Ming period dragon-figured robes were presented to the Koreans, such events no doubt stimulating native production. The custom of presenting robes and silks to the Koreans continued under the later Chʻing dynasty, and these too must have served as models for the Korean silk industry.

The distinctive appearance of Korean embroidery was obtained by their highly individual form of COUCHING. Silk and linen threads were laid in parallel on the base material, following the lines of the prescribed design, and they were subsequently embroidered over with silks, generally a silk cord. The effect is one of a tight but confident and well-defined design, given greater expression through the depth provided by the silk or linen laid threads. With so little material to judge by it is these highly stylized embroideries which characterize and distinguish Korean textiles from those of her more illustrious neighbours.

30, 234, 255, 288, 370, 382, 405, 439, 446, 447, 463, 464, 573, 597, 613, 620, 632, 637, 690, 704, 714, 715, 735, 792, 798, 833, 835, 853, 862, 936, 937.

JAPANNING. The genuine Oriental LACQUER which became so popular during the 2nd half of the 17th c. was both expensive and difficult to obtain. The publication in England in 1688 by John Stalker and George Parker of their book of recipes and engraved designs, *A Treatise of Japanning and Varnishing*, made possible the development on a considerable scale of a European substitute. This form of lacquer, known as japanning, used a groundwork of white, yellow, blue and green in addition to the more sombre black and red of the imported panels. It consisted, not of the genuine lac, but of a hard film which was built up by the application of many coats of a varnish composed of shellac dissolved in spirit. Eventually this was polished with a powder made from rotten-stone or decomposed siliceous limestone, sometimes called 'tripoli powder' after its country of origin. Decoration was raised in gold or silver, and was usually Oriental in style and subject matter.

Venetian imitation lacquer became well known during the 2nd half of the 17th c. and in France japanning was practised during the reign of Louis XIV at the GOBELINS, where it attained a high standard of excellence under the guidance of Le Moyne. But the ablest exponent of the craft in Europe was probably Gerhard Dagly of Liège, who worked in the Prussian Court in Berlin for over 20 years until the death of Frederick III in 1713. Lacquer writing cabinets were a particular feature of Saxony, where Martin Schnell was appointed to the Electoral Court at Dresden in 1710. His furniture for the Japanese Palace at Dresden included gilt copper on a red enamel. Japanned furniture developed in America rather more slowly than in Europe. Although a few pieces date from *c.* 1700, it was not until 1740 that it became well established in the Massachusetts–Connecticut area, with Boston as its principal centre. The Winterthur Museum, Delaware, possesses a particularly fine high chest in maple and pine from the Boston workshops of John Pimm, the painting of which in imitation of Oriental lacquer is attributed to Thomas Johnson. An unusually hard transparent varnish was developed *c.* 1740 in France by a family of craftsmen named Martin. Under the name of VERNIS MARTIN, it was used as a high-quality substitute for lacquer by, among others, Roger Vandercruse, RISEN BURGH and WEISWEILER.

In Europe the mid 18th c. saw the beginning of a decline in the quality of japanned work, which at its best was only a substitute for the genuine article. Being capable of considerable abuse, it was at its worst little better than varnished oil paint. In England, where it had rarely attained the standard of the best Continental work, japanning became a fashionable social pastime which, together with the worst Italian *lacca* of the period applied to badly constructed furniture, helped to establish for the craft a general reputation for shoddiness which it did not altogether deserve. About the middle of the 19th c. there was a revival in France of dark japanned furniture decorated with gay floral designs in bright colours. Japanning was also used to protect and decorate the surface of PAPIER-MÂCHÉ furniture, which at that time enjoyed considerable popularity in England, France and America; indeed in one of the main centres of the trade in England, at Birmingham, japanning and *papier mâché* were spoken of synonymously. Many small wares were produced during the second half of the century, especially jewel cabinets, tea-trays, letter-racks and boxes of all kinds, which however modest and inexpensive they were originally have come to possess a special charm of their own today.

790.

JARGOON. See ZIRCON.

JASPER. See QUARTZ.

JASPER WARE. See CERAMICS.

JENSEN, GEORG (1866–1935). Danish silversmith, whose work in Copenhagen exemplified the ideals of the ARTS AND CRAFTS MOVEMENT and C. R. ASHBEE, with emphasis upon quality of material and workmanship. During the 1920s he made some concessions to ART DÉCO style, but his international reputation depended rather upon the unelaborated elegance of his designs and the craftsmanlike appearance of his work. His almost matt hammered finish, his short-bladed knives and round-bowled spoons were widely imitated and in its own sphere his work was typical of the standards which prevailed during the first half of the 20th c.

JENSEN, GERREIT (anglicized as JOHNSON, GARRETT). Of Dutch or Flemish origin, he was 'Glasse-seller' and cabinet-maker to the Royal Household *c.* 1680–1715. He specialized in furniture decorated with MARQUETRY and JAPANNING and was probably the first cabinet-maker in England to work in the BOULLE techniques. There are examples of his work at Boughton House, Windsor Castle and Kensington Palace.

JEROME, CHAUNCEY (1793–1860). American clockmaker of Bristol, Connecticut, where he established a factory for clock cases and movements *c.* 1821, and worked in partnership with his brother, NOBLE, until *c.* 1840. He initiated the mass production of wheels and the clocks manufactured by his firm Jerome & Co. of New Haven were sold widely in the U.S.A. and in Britain. In 1855 the firm became The New Haven Clock Company. Chauncey Jerome published *A History of the American Clock Business* in 1860.

JET. The gem which is peculiarly associated with Great Britain. It is flotsam from the prehistoric seas which washed over the mud to be laid down as the lias shale 70 million years ago. Pressure and chemical action have turned jet, which was originally driftwood from pines of the *araucaria* or monkey-puzzle tree family, into a soft compact substance with a browny-black outer skin, which when broken shatters into a conchoidal fracture revealing a glossy black interior. Jet can usually be distinguished from similar substances, such as black glass, by its lightness, its softness and the fact that it will burn with a greenish flame when exposed to an open light and go on burning when removed, leaving a charred deposit like the end of a match. Jet is not a unified substance but has lines of alum, and sometimes also harder substances such as iron pyrites or the lias shale, running through it where the original piece of driftwood has cracked. The lines of the growth rings of the

Jensen 'Acorn' silver tableware. Designed by Johan Rohde. (1916)

Jensen 'Cypress' silver tableware. Designed by Tias Eckhoff. (1953)

tree from which it came can often be observed. Jet can be divided into a hard and a soft variety, the former found in the lower lias beds, the latter in those which are more recent. In spite of the name there is no appreciable difference of hardness between the two kinds of jet, but the soft variety is much more difficult to work because it is more fragile and wears and breaks much more easily. The best work is done in the hard variety and both the Whitby craftsmen and the guildsmen of Renaissance Spain demanded hard jet for their finest carvings. Jet is carved easily provided allowance is made for its fragility, and it readily takes a brilliant polish which surpasses that of black glass or obsidian. The fact that it is found in limited quantities, which occur in the form of irregular masses or pebbles, and the drawback that parts of any piece of jet are likely to be unusable because of the lines of harder inclusions or 'spar' running through it, together with the careful handling which such fragile material demands, have meant that articles made of jet are always expensive.

For practical purposes jet production is confined to Whitby in Yorkshire, where quantities are gathered on the beach. In the past it was mined at Villaviciosa, Spain, Württemberg, Germany, and in the Aude in France. Although jet is found in many localities in North America, and occurs in indigenous carvings from localities as far apart as Pueblo Bonito in New Mexico and Ipiutak in Alaska, it does not appear to have been widely used by white Americans, though Pennsylvanian anthracite has been used as a substitute.

In Iron Age times jet was worked in England by being scraped and then polished with the scrapings mixed with oil and spread on a piece of sheepskin. The ancient Britons also drilled through pieces of jet to pierce them for stringing, but their drills could not have been very long as it is noticeable that they preferred to drill diagonally through the edges of a flat plaque rather than directly through it. Jet was known to the Romans and was presumably worked by them with the same kind of tools they would use to fashion AMBER. It was known to them as *gagates*, from the river of that name in Sicily where according to Pliny it was believed to have been first found. By the Middle Ages crosses and beads were being made with a knife, file and rubbing stone, and jet ornaments continued to be made in this way in England until, shortly after 1800, first a lathe and then other pieces of machinery such as grindstones and polishing boards began to be used at Whitby. Emery, rotten-stone, jeweller's rouge and lamp-black were used to achieve a final polish, while Victorian amateur lapidaries polished it with charcoal powder and soft soap.

Like amber, which it resembles, for example in the aromatic fragrance which it exudes while being sawn, jet has been carved from prehistoric times. Its early and continued employment has been due as much to the occult properties with which it was invested as to its real qualities. St. Isidore, writing in the 6th c., sums up the beliefs of earlier writers such as Aristotle and Pliny by declaring that jet is a sovereign amulet for diseases of the eyes, will drive away serpents, destroy demons and test virginity. It is not surprising that jet came to be accounted an effective amulet for all diseases of the eye, as a highly polished piece looks like the iris of a healthy eye. By a natural transition, it soon came to be regarded as an equally effective prophylactic against 'fascination', or the evil eye.

Because of its amuletic properties much of the carving made in jet has consisted of personal ornaments. These include toggles for fastening garments, beads, rings, amulets and pendants. In medieval times statues of saints were carved from jet, as were paxes and crucifixes. By the reign of Queen Victoria card-cases, paper-knives, busts, seals and a wide variety of other ornaments were being made from it. It was also used for inlaying in ALABASTER.

More jet was carved in prehistoric Britain than is made up today. It is found in Iron Age burials as far away as Argyllshire. It went on being worked throughout the Roman period, and the Anglo-Saxon poet Caedmon refers to it in his *Translation on Jewels*. Throughout the Middle Ages jet rosaries and other ornaments continued to be made in Whitby for sale to pilgrims. After the Reformation jet-carving languished, although it did not die out entirely.

Meanwhile in Spain jet had become an almost universal amulet against the evil eye. The Arab writer Benbuclaris (active 1085–1109) says that children in Spain wore a piece of jet around their necks. Although the form of the amulet was at first unimportant, by the 13th c. it had become standardized as the *higa* or fist, with the fingers clenched in a protective gesture. Though this amulet was probably an Arab importation from North Africa, where it had been known since Carthaginian times, it was adopted by Christian Spain, and soon became one of the fairings bought by the pilgrims to the shrine of Santiago de Compostela. The pilgrim trade throve particularly in the 16th c. and other kinds of carvings made in large numbers included figures of Santiago, either in his warlike guise of *Matamoros* routing the Moors on horseback, or dressed in pilgrim's hat and weeds and carrying a pilgrim's staff with a rosary or a book. Sometimes two much smaller figures of *orantes* are praying at his feet. Cockle-shells, rosaries, crucifixes, paxes and other religious carvings were made. By the 15th c. the craftsmen were strongly organized into guilds, all of which were at first in Santiago de Compostela. Each guild had its own shop, where all sales had to be made, and governed its members by strict regulations, such as those of the Santa Maria guild in 1443. The kind of jet to be employed, the form the decoration was to take, and other matters were carefully prescribed. The names of more than 157 jet carvers are known, extending from 1402

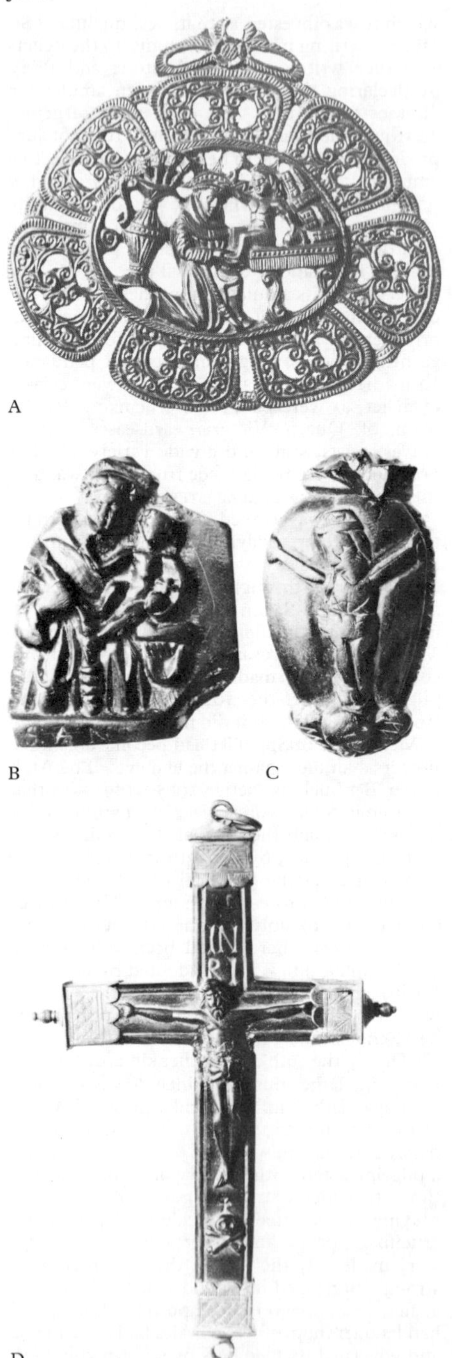

A

B C

D

A and B. St. Anthony of Padua (probably 17th c.) C. Christ on the Cross and the head of the Virgin (probably 17th c.) D. Crucifix. Jet with silver mounts (18th c.). All Spanish from Santiago de Compostela (V. & A. Mus.)

to 1800. It is to the existence of these guilds that we owe some of the finest pieces, the 'master works' which apprentices had to make to obtain their mastership. These include intricately worked boxes with rounded tops and carved open-work designs which are not merely extremely effective but technically very difficult to make. By the end of the 16th c. jet-working had spread to the province of Compostela, and even to the valleys of the Asturias. As the craft became more widely distributed, the fine touch which had characterized the jet carver up till the middle of the 16th c. began to disappear. Carvings became coarse and repetitious, and the wars of religion in the 17th c. sounded the knell of the jet carver by diminishing the flow of pilgrims. It was in vain that the guilds tried to decentralize the craft, carrying it to Gijon, Villaviciosa and other places. The old shops disappeared and pedlars now attended the provincial fairs, selling not merely the usual pilgrim's wares but gewgaws for country folk, head-dresses and collets. By the 18th c. jet-carving was in the final stage of its decline. It had reverted to the production of *higa* amulets and nothing else.

In Whitby jet-carving began a period of expansion during the first decade of the 19th c. Two entrepreneurs, Robert Jefferson and John Carter, were encouraged by a naval pensioner, Captain Tremlett, to start a jet-turning industry. The venture flourished, helped by periods of mourning for celebrities such as the Duke of Wellington and Prince Albert. Fourteen hundred hands were employed at the start of the 1870s, and orders for jet ornaments poured in from all parts of Europe and America. The Queen of Bavaria wore a jet cable-guard, and Whitby jet could be bought in many shops in Regent Street. But the very popularity of Whitby jet led to its decline. Work became more and more stereotyped, its quality deteriorated and workmanship became shoddy. No systematic art training was given to the workmen, who had to rely on designs imported from elsewhere such as the 'classic features of Victor Emmanuel' which as a visitor to Whitby complained, stared at him from the bottom of an alabaster card tray. To satisfy the demand the workers began to use soft jet, either mined locally or imported from Spain. This soon splintered and wore away, giving the product a bad name. As anyone could become a jet carver without having to serve an apprenticeship, the market was soon flooded with under-priced and worthless articles. Soon imitations of jet in vulcanite and black glass disillusioned patrons still further. By 1884 the industry had declined to about a quarter of its former size and now there are only two jet works in operation. Soon the art will have disappeared completely.

JEWELLERY. The urge to adorn and beautify the person by painting, scarifying or tattooing the body, and still more by attaching decorative materials to it, has made itself felt among practically all sections of human society for as far back as it is possible to penetrate into the distant origins of the race. Before the discovery of the New World by the Spanish the ancient Inca peoples of Peru used to pierce the ear-lobes of the youths at puberty and extend them to enormous proportions by inserting plaques of gold or other materials according to rank and privilege. Other races have embedded decorative materials into the lower lip or pierced the septum of the nose for the insertion of a horizontal bar of metal, bone or wood. The variations of adornment by a sort of quasi-mutilation have been infinite and what has seemed to one people to be beautification has appeared to others barbaric or merely grotesque. No less ubiquitous has been the custom to seek personal embellishment by hanging objects, from flowers to elaborately wrought artefacts, from various parts of the body. Indeed it has been claimed that the impulse to carry objects hanging about the body for the sake of adornment is instinctive even to the higher apes (Wolfgang Köhler, *The Mentality of Apes*, 1926, ch. 2). It seems, nevertheless, that Neanderthal man in the Middle Palaeolithic period was as devoid of any impulse to adornment as of any form of plastic or decorative art, for the burials have not yielded even pierced animal teeth, the commonest form of decorative beads worn by pre-agricultural hunting communities. But from the Advanced Palaeolithic period onwards hunters have used adornments of perforated animal teeth, shells, stone discs and certainly of other, more perishable materials. Russian excavations at Sungir, north-east of Moscow, have shown that Gravettian hunters wore ornaments sewn on to skin clothing. Bodily ornaments are shown in the rock paintings of the Spanish Levant and anklets and armlets are worn by figures in frescoes from the Pastoralist period at Tassili in the Sahara. Pierced AMBER beads and other objects of personal adornment have been recovered among the mobiliary art from the Maglemosian culture of the Baltic. It is this fundamental and quite general impulse to adorn the body with hanging or removable artefacts which lies at the root of the craft which we call jewellery. The variety of materials which have been pressed into service is infinite. In Tibet and Nepal even human bones and skulls have been utilized for ritualistic and personal jewellery.

The term 'jewellery' refers primarily to artefacts fashioned from precious metals, gemstones or ENAMELS designed to be suspended from some part of the human body for the sake of adornment. In a secondary sense the term is now also applied to ceremonial, liturgical, heraldic or other articles made from precious metals and gemstones, such as seals, MEDALS, BOOK COVERS, chalices, emblems of office, etc. We are concerned in this article with jewellery designed as personal adornment. The strength of the impulse which brought jewellery into being and which has supported it through the ages is attested by the fact that the most precious materials known in any age have been devoted to its manufacture and the utmost resources of skilled craftsmanship have been employed to work the most intractable substances and to reveal the latent beauties of the hardest stones. Yet the urge to self-adornment seems to express a need which lies deeper than mere human vanity. Jewellery has been linked with the desire to transform and heighten the impact of the wearer's personality, the quasi-magical aura which reflects a man's dignity and standing among his fellows, and perhaps for this reason talismanic and occult powers have generally been ascribed to gemstones. An extensive and ancient magical lore is interwoven with the history of the gemstone.

As may be gathered from these introductory remarks, the subject of jewellery is so vast and so multifarious that it would not be profitable to attempt to cover the whole field in the cursory way which would alone be possible within the confines of a single article. Sections on jewellery will be found in the articles dealing with GREEK AND ROMAN ANTIQUITY, ancient EGYPT, INDIA, and something is said about jewellery in the articles on CHINA. Relevant material will also be found in articles on the working of substances such as AMBER, JADE, JET, MOTHER OF PEARL, etc. Something also is said in the articles on SILVER and ENAMEL. Further, the interest in jewellery is closely linked to the study of fashion in costume and references to jewellery will be found in the articles on COSTUME. The present article will be devoted to gemstones and their working.

The jewellers of the advanced Chaldean civilization, as evidenced for example by excavations at Ur in Mesopotamia, had achieved great technical skill in the working of silver and gold. They made extensive use of LAPIS LAZULI. In the near-contemporary civilizations of the Indus valley metals were rare but use was made of stones such as cornelians, agate, jasper, steatite, jade and lapis lazuli for decorative beads and belts, etc. By the Egyptian Middle Kingdom the craft of the jeweller had reached a very high level of skill. The stones used included AMETHYST, onyx, lapis lazuli, TURQUOISE, ROCK-CRYSTAL, GARNET, mother of pearl, chalcedony, jasper, as well as porphyry, cornelian, basalt and haematite. Stones were carried by Phoenician merchants to Greece and later to Rome and by the 4th and 3rd centuries cornelians, turquoise, garnets and malachites were used and stones such as chalcedony and rock-crystal were fairly common. Amber, which had been known and worked from Mesolithic times, also became popular in this period. The Etruscans carried the art of GRANULATED goldwork to a high perfection and some of their work in this technique has seldom been equalled. Roman jewellery combined techniques inherited from the Etruscans and the Greeks and later, under the Empire, Celtic and Germanic influences. These last resulted in a fashion for heavy gold ornaments set with garnets and other coloured stones. Under the Roman Empire too gemstones began to be valued for their own sake as well as for their contribution to jewellery and it was at this time that the gem assumed the importance which it has never lost. Finally, the Romans turned their skill in GLASS-making to the manufacture of PASTE and created a form of popular paste jewellery akin to the 'costume jewellery' of today. PEARLS also, derived mainly from the Red Sea, assumed in Roman times the importance they have since maintained.

The craft of engraving gems reached its highest technical and artistic level in the hands of the Greeks of classical antiquity. The superb quality of their work served as an inspiration for Italian craftsmen of the Renaissance and has never been surpassed. The art is ultimately descended from the Mesopotamian cylinder seal, which was well developed by the 4th millennium B.C. and was perfected by the Sumerians *c.* 2700 B.C. The cylinder seal, originally of clay but later of marble, QUARTZ, rock-crystal or haematite, was a roll pierced down the middle and engraved on the outside so that the design could be impressed. The Egyptians cut seals, including the scarabs, in semi-precious stones such as cornelian or agate or often in FAIENCE. Like the Mesopotamian cylinder seals the Egyptian engraved gems had a functional purpose for identification as well as sometimes an amuletic or magical one. It was in the hands of the Minoans that these originally functional objects became works of art, perfected by the Greek craftsmen from the 6th c. B.C. onwards. The early engraved gems, until the Hellenistic period, were all INTAGLIOS: that is, the stone was cut so that the design lay below the level of the surrounding surface. This is the natural form of cutting when the stone is considered in its function as a seal to impress a signature or identifying mark. In the Hellenistic period stones began to be cut with the design standing out in relief, that is as CAMEOS. The designs included mythological subjects, scenes from everyday life and in the later period portraits. They reflect the artistic styles of the period in which they were made. These seals might also be worn in rings or otherwise as personal adornment.

To serve for an engraved seal a stone must be hard and durable, not liable to fissure. TOPAZ, garnet, amethyst and cornelian as well as rock-crystal, which had been used since Sumerian times, were among the stones preferred. A perfect stone in the modern sense of being homogeneous was not needed and a layered structure with variations of colour, such as the agate and sardonyx, challenged the craftsmen to put these variations to effective use by bringing them up at different levels of the design. When a suitable stone had been chosen it was first ground to the required over-all shape with a flat top, or table, on which to engrave. The stone was then fixed in a gemstick and cut with a bow-drill or a cutting wheel, a mixture of oil and fine SAPPHIRE dust being used as abrasive. The Romans probably knew also the use of diamond dust. Modern techniques are in principle the same, though with the addition of the electrically driven wheel and the dentist's drill.

During the Middle Ages the art of cutting intaglios and cameos declined, to be revived at the time of the Italian Renaissance with the new enthusiasm for classical antiquity. Engraved gems were at that time regarded as one of the more important manifestations of classical art and Italian craftsmen developed considerable skill in copying them and in cutting designs in the classical fashion. In the 17th c. interest turned from engraving to facet cutting, but a temporary revival of engraving took place during the 18th c. in France. The engraved gem must, however, be regarded as a craft of classical antiquity *par excellence*.

The very different craft of cutting cameos by hand tools in mollusc shells was practised in Italy since the 15th c. and has been very popular as a cheap form of jewellery since the 18th c. These SHELL CAMEOS are, however, of very variable quality and are not to be confused with the engraved gemstone.

The cutter and shaper of gemstones is called a 'lapidary' and the science of stones is now often referred to as 'gemmology'. Even when we allow for the mystique which has so often surrounded early technologies, the craft of the lapidary has been unusually secretive and it is only recently that the skills and knowledge have become available more generally. The scientific study of gems is also so recent that a new word has been coined to name it. This is partly because the fields of specialized knowledge upon which it is based—in mineralogy, crystallography, etc.—have become sciences only in our own time, but also undoubtedly because of the penumbra of superstition and credulity which has persistently attached to man's dealings with precious stones. In antiquity Theophrastus (*c.* 371–287 B.C.), the successor of Aristotle as the head of the Peripatetic school of philosophy, wrote a treatise *On Stones* which has the clear-headed outlook of a mineralogist. In his encyclopaedic *Naturalis Historia* Pliny the Elder (A.D. 23/24–79) assembled in Bks. xxiii–xxxvii a comprehensive summary of what was known about mineralogy including gemstones, fact and superstition, in his day. But through the Middle Ages and afterwards the whole subject of gems was obscured by the perpetuation of ancient superstitions in conjunction with astrology, alchemy and the medical doctrine of 'humours'. From the time of Pliny lapidaries were more concerned with the supposed talismanic and curative powers of stones than with their mineralogical properties. Francis Bacon (1561–1626) introduced an air of common sense unusual for the time when in his *Sylva Sylvarum*, sect. 960, he wrote: 'There be many things that work upon the spirits of man by secret sympathy and antipathy: the virtues of precious stones worn, have been anciently and generally received, and curiously assigned to work several effects. So much is true; that stones have in them fine spirits, as appeareth by their splendour; and therefore they may work by consent upon the spirits of men, to comfort and exhilarate them. Those that are the best, for that effect, are the diamond, the emerald, the hyacinth oriental, and the gold stone, which is the yellow topaz. As for their particular properties, there is no credit to be given to them.' But in 1609 Anselmus de Boot, physician to the Holy Roman Emperor Rudolf II, wrote *De Lapidibus et Gemmis*, a tract which has been described as 'of perhaps greater interest to historians than mineralogists, as he gave the cures-by-stones which were still in current use; also the "true meanings" of stones, as well as their temperature and sex'. In 1658, however, Sir Thomas Browne says in his *Pseudodoxia Epidemica* (Bk. II, ch. 3) of de Boot's work that 'his Discourse is consonant unto Experience and Reason'.

One of the superstitions which has had unusual powers of survival is the astrologically derived belief in 'birthstones', which seems to have spread from Poland in the 16th c. although the custom of wearing natal stones did not become general until the 18th c. The association of stones with particular months is based mainly on colour and has been linked with the list of symbolic stones in the High Priest's Breastplate given in Exodus, 28 (other priests also besides the Jewish have had regalia of astrologically symbolic jewels) and the foundation stones of the New Jerusalem given in The Revelation of St. John the Divine, 21 : 19–20. In 1937 the National Association of Goldsmiths in Great Britain established a list of birthstones which has been followed in other Commonwealth countries and in the U.S.A. The list is as follows:

Month	*Colour*	*Stone*
January	dark red	garnet
February	purple	amethyst
March	pale blue	aquamarine or bloodstone
April	colourless	diamond or rock-crystal
May	bright green	emerald or chrysoprase
June	cream	pearl or moon-stone
July	red	ruby or cornelian or onyx
August	pale green	peridot or sar-donyx
September	deep blue	sapphire or lapis lazuli
October	variegated	opal
November	yellow	topaz
December	sky blue	turquoise

The modern classification of jewellery stones into 'precious' and 'semi-precious' has little foundation other than fashion and price and the general term 'gemstone' is to be preferred. The qualities for which individual stones are valued are more precise. For purposes of jewellery *beauty* comes high in the list and since gemstones began to be prized for their own sakes rather than merely as ingredients in a setting in Imperial Roman times beauty has been increasingly important. The beauty of a gemstone depends on the characteristics of colour, brilliance, lustre and fire. Of these colour is the loosest and the most difficult to pinpoint. The colour of most gemstones derives from impurities, which may be evenly distributed throughout a stone or unevenly distributed so as to produce variations in shade or tone or intensity. As a general rule, though with some exceptions, a stone of intense colour with evenly distributed pigmentation giving uniform shade and tone is most highly valued. Brilliance is a function of transparency, which is measured by a stone's power to transmit light rather than the ability to see through it. Stones are classified as transparent (DIAMOND, sapphire, rock-crystal), translucent (CHRYSOBERYL, jade, amber) and opaque (malachite, turquoise). Lustre is the surface quality of a stone and is most important with translucent and opaque varieties. The various qualities of lustre are described with some precision in the language of the lapidary. There is, for example, the adamantine lustre of the diamond, the vitreous lustre of the EMERALD, the greasy lustre of the OPAL and lapis lazuli, which seem to have a metallic or oily sheen, the silky lustre of malachite and some chrysoberyl, the milky or pearly lustre exemplified in the pearl, and so on. Fire is a quality which is brought out by cutting and faceting. It is the power of a stone as it were to concentrate light and give it forth in many-coloured flashing sparks. The well-cut diamond has this quality *par excellence*; the emerald, sapphire and RUBY, though they may have brilliance, do not have fire.

Second to beauty among the qualities for which gemstones are valued comes durability, which is largely a function of hardness. Hardness is defined as the ability of a stone to scratch other stones or to resist scratching. It is now measured by the MOHS SCALE, originated by the Austrian Friedrich Mohs in 1822, by which stones are graded from 1 to 10. The scale is odd in that the steps in the degrees of hardness are not evenly graded. There is, for example, a greater difference between 10 (where the diamond stands alone) and 9 (the corundum family, including ruby and sapphire) than between 9 and 1. The chrysoberyls come between 9 and 8; the BERYLS, including the AQUAMARINE and emerald, are approximately 8; the quartz family with ZIRCONS and TOURMALINES are 7. Most gemstones used for jewellery lie between 5 and 9 on the scale. Hardness, however, is only one aspect of durability. In addition consideration must be given to a stone's liability to crack, fracture or otherwise to flaw in use. When, for example, the Spanish Conquistadores discovered the emerald mines of Colombia in 1588 they put the stones to the test of the hammer, ignorantly shattering innumerable of the finest fragile emeralds.

The market value of stones is also dictated by rarity and by the fluctuating dictates of fashion. Rarity is a complicated thing, which may apply to certain types of a stone only and may depend either on absolute scarcity or on political or artificially created commercial reasons. Perfect blue and green diamonds are absolutely scarce, as are the large black opals from Australia. Green garnets are more valuable than the far commoner rose-red garnets. Large Kashmir blue sapphires are scarce indeed, as are pigeon-blood rubies and large unflawed emeralds. Valuation by scarcity and fashion demands the specialized knowledge of the practical expert in the trade.

Although stones are in general prized for their homogeneity both of structure and of pigmentation and for their freedom from irregularities and flaws, some irregularities are valued for their own sake. For example the presence of minute needles of titanium ore (rutile) can create a perfect star in a suitably cut ruby or sapphire, a phenomenon known as 'ASTERISM'. The cloudy blue sapphires of Ceylon, which form a luminous star when CABOCHON cut and seen in a suitable light, are particularly prized. The perfect, unflawed emerald of any size is rare indeed, but the 'flaws' can be a beauty in themselves and are commonly known as the emerald's 'jardin'. The CHATOYANT (cat's eye) quality of undulating lustre is possessed by some chrysoberyls and by some felspars and quartzes; it is caused by the presence of some substance such as asbestos fibre in minute quantities. It is akin to the 'zoning' which may be seen in tourmalines, a streak of light which duplicates the effects of a cat's eye. The peculiar vanishing lustre called 'schiller' seen in stones such as moonstones, when the crystalline structure forms in thin layers, is due to the passage of light from one layer to another layer of different optical character.

The art of the lapidary is to reveal the latent beauty hidden in the uncut stone. He does this by shaping, cutting and polishing, having due consideration for the nature of the material, its crystalline structure and the idiosyncracies of the individual stone upon which he is working. He is also expected to produce the largest possible gem consistent with the removal of flaws and irregularities which constitute blemishes. The extent of the transformation which he effects may be appreciated by comparing lumps of uncut gemstones, as sometimes displayed in the windows of jewellers' shops, with the BRILLIANT cut gem which emerges from them. At the Renaissance and through to the 18th c. and after it was customary for lapidaries to 'back' jewels with coloured and reflecting foil to aid their brilliance and colour. Recipes for different foils are given in the *Trattati* of CELLINI. Nowadays the lapidary eschews this practice and relies solely upon the choice of a stone and the effectiveness of the cut.

Before describing the several types of cut and the methods of cutting it will be well to give the main terms that are in use for the parts of a jewel. The widest part of the stone, which determines its shape and divides the upper from the lower parts of a faceted stone, is called the *girdle*. The part above this is the *crown* and the part below it the *pavilion*. The flat plane on top of the crown, which corresponds to the flat surface for engraving in engraved gems, is the *table* and if the stone is cut with a flat plane at the bottom, this is called the *culet*. The planes cut at angles on the sides of the crown and the pavilion are called *facets*. Their function is to obtain the maximum concentration of light reflected from the back facets through the stone and emerging at the front. In order to achieve this the angles of all the facets must be planned and worked with minute accuracy. In a well-cut faceted stone the total volume of light entering through the table would be twice totally reflected by the back facets, to emerge at the crown so that the stone seems to have a silvered back.

The earliest type of cut, used almost exclusively in antiquity and until the 17th c. and still used for opaque and for some translucent stones, was the *cabochon*. The simple cabochon is in the form of a dome resting upon a flat base, the girdle or widest part being at the base. It consists of little more than smoothing away irregularities and roughnesses, allowing the stone to retain its original shape. The double cabochon has a rounded base so that the completed stone is egg-shaped. The hollow cabochon is ground with a concave base whose purpose is to permit the insertion of foil to improve the stone's colour. When a cabochon is cut with a flat surface on top of the dome it is called a *table cut*.

Until the 15th c. the diamond was considered to be too hard to be cut and its use was restricted for this reason. Until it is cut and polished a diamond is relatively uninteresting in appearance and it is since the discovery of faceted cutting that its brilliance has been revealed and it has become the most highly valued of all gemstones. During the 15th and early 16th centuries the diamond was still cut in a pyramidical shape known as the 'diamond point' or '*point naïve*', sometimes ground with a flat table but otherwise virtually the octahedron of the diamond crystal with its natural faces ground to regularity and polished. The possibility of facet-cutting the diamond was discovered by the Indian lapidaries in antiquity but was used by them only to remove flaws and irregularities, not to produce fire and brilliance. The origin of geometrical cutting has been attributed to Louis de Berquem of Bruges in the 15th c. and alternatively to the Venetian jeweller Vincenzo Peruzzi in the 16th c. The modern ROSE CUT is attributed to Cardinal Mazarin (1602–61) although it is probable that

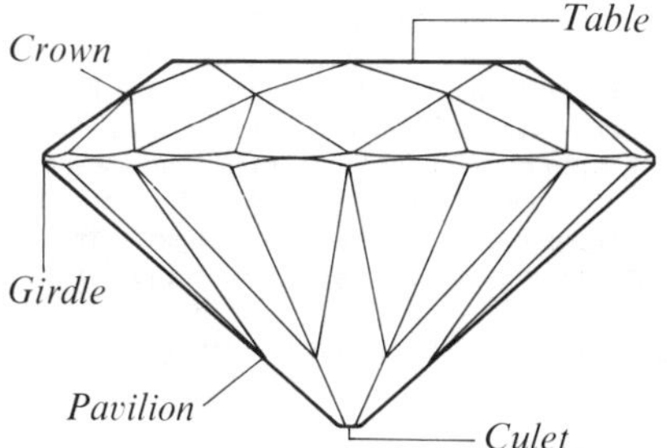

Principal parts of a cut gemstone

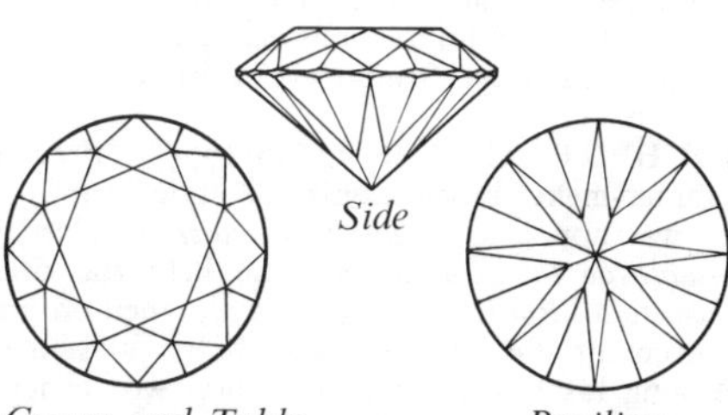

Brilliant cut

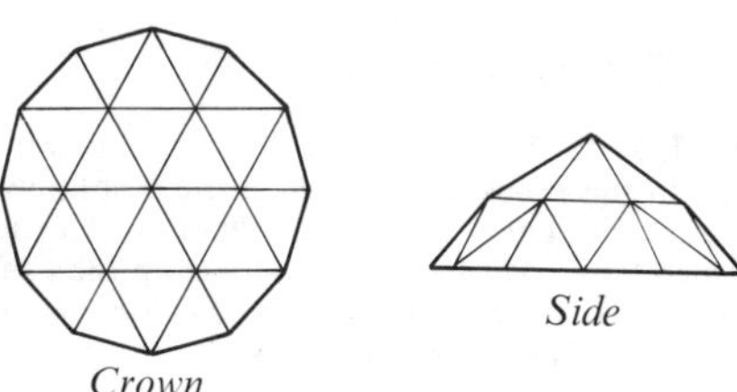

Rose cut

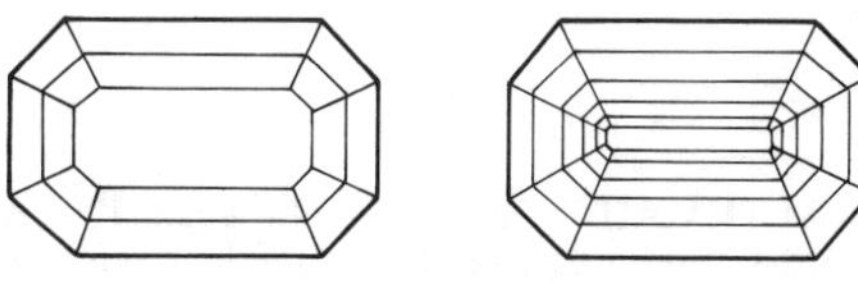
Step cut

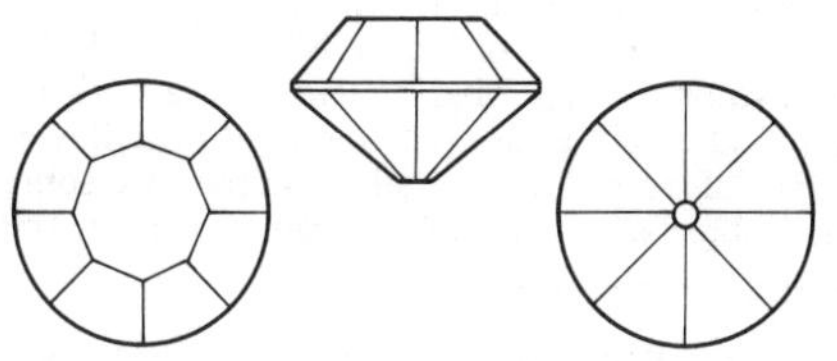
Single, or eight cut

it too originated in India and was merely sponsored by Mazarin. From this time faceting of all gems became more skilled. The varieties of the step cut and the brilliant cut were developed and jewellery became more and more an excuse for displaying the beauty and fire and brilliance of the individual stone.

The *table* cut was widely used in most countries of Europe during the 16th c. for diamonds as well as coloured stones. The large table was often framed with a bevelled edge or a ring of small facets. The *rose* cut is a logical variant of the table cut, the table being replaced by a ring of six triangular facets coming to a point at the top with a further eighteen facets cut on the crown. The pavilion was often dispensed with so that the stone had a flat base. The *step* cut, sometimes called the *emerald* cut or *trap* cut, is much used with coloured stones where the display of the colour is the prime consideration. The crown is cut with facets running horizontally round the edge in inclined planes so that the table is ringed with sloping steps leading down to the girdle. The pavilion may also be cut in three or sometimes four steps leading down to an oblong culet. The *brilliant* cut is ideal for the diamond, where the maximum brilliance and fire are required, and has been chiefly responsible for the pre-eminence which the diamond has assumed in jewellery. In its usual form it consists of 33 facets on the crown and 25 on the pavilion including the culet. The table is a regular octagon and is the largest of the facets. The brilliant cut enables a transparent stone to be cut with the least loss of weight while making the most of its optical properties. There are many varieties of these basic types of cut. In the mixed cut, for instance, where both brilliance and colour are aimed at, the crown is brilliant cut and the pavilion step cut. It is popular for sapphires. The *scissors* cut or *cross* cut is a modified form of the brilliant sometimes used for square stones.

The work of the lapidary consists of three basic processes: shaping, cutting and polishing. First comes cleavage, in which the stone is caused to fracture or split in such a way as to remove flawed portions and obtain the largest possible perfect stone. An intimate knowledge of the structure and sometimes a prolonged study of the individual stone is necessary in order to bring about a split along a predetermined cleavage line. Nowadays stones, even diamonds, can also be sawn. In 1885 the use of a lathe with a diamond-cutting tool was introduced. Now a phosphor-bronze wheel charged with diamond dust is used to saw the stone and induce cleavage. After cleavage the stone is blocked out into the required shape by abrasion to remove irregularities. After shaping the stone is cut, which is the most delicate operation of all and the one requiring most skill. Methods have changed little since remote antiquity. The shaped stone is embedded with a cement in a depression at the end of a gem-stick, called a 'dopt', leaving exposed only the section which is required to be ground away. It is then ground on horizontal iron wheels called 'skaifs' with oil and abrasive. Finally the cut stone must be polished to remove its 'skin' and reveal the brilliance. This is done by burnishing against a revolving buff of leather or wood charged with a polishing agent such as an oxide of cerium, chromium or tin. A method of mass polishing is also practised in which stones are put in a revolving barrel filled with rough stones, abrasive material and water.

Gemstones belong to a limited range of mineral species. Among the quartzes are amethyst, rock-crystal, citrine and cairngorm, while a large number of the gems most familiar to the ancient world, such as agate, jasper, chalcedony, bloodstone, sardonyx, onyx, chrysoprase, also belong to a quartz family. From the felspars come the moonstone, amazonite and orthoclase. The mineral species beryl, a silicate of aluminium, includes the emerald and aquamarine as well as the beryl and chrysoberyl. The mineral species corundum includes the sapphire and the ruby as well as the 'oriental' topaz, emerald and amethyst. Zircon is a silicate of zirconium and garnet and tourmaline are mineral species. The fuller characterization of gemstones belongs to the science of mineralogy. But some account of the stones which have been most important in the history of jewellery is given in separate articles.

See also GREEK AND ROMAN ANTIQUITY (JEWELLERY); INDIA (JEWELLERY); IRON AND STEEL (IRON JEWELLERY); EGYPT (JEWELLERY).

4, 37, 51, 78, 79, 80, 97, 116, 155, 245, 246, 248, 261, 296, 322, 375, 417, 527, 609, 737, 776, 784, 797, 908, 919, 921.

JOHNSON, THOMAS. English carver, gilder and designer, established in business in London from *c.* 1755. His designs were the most characteristic and distinguished version of English ROCOCO. He published *Twelve Girandoles* in 1755 and *One Hundred and Fifty New Designs* in parts between 1756 and 1758. The latter was a pattern-book for carvers' pieces, frames, candlestands, candelabra, tables and lanterns.

JOINER. See CARPENTER, JOINER, CABINET-MAKER.

JŌMON (Japanese, 'ropework'). Japanese monochrome earthenware pottery from the prehistoric period. The vessels are of distinctive shape and are made by the 'coiling' process. They are decorated with elaborate patterns of ropework or by impressions made from woven string or matting. See JAPAN (POTTERY).

JOUBERT, GILLES (1689–1775). French cabinet-maker in the Louis XV style. In 1758 he was appointed *ébéniste ordinaire du Garde-meuble de la Couronne* and he held the title *ébéniste du Roi* from 1763 to 1774, when on his retirement he was succeeded by RIESENER. Among his best known works are two corner-cupboards (*encoigneurs*) made in 1755 to accompany GAUDREAU's medal cabinet for the king's private apartments at Versailles. They are now in the Bibliothèque nationale, Paris.

JOUY. See TOILES DE JOUY.

JULES, DAVID (1808–92). Book illustrator who in the 1860s became one of the best known French designers of FASHION PLATES. He designed for *Le Moniteur de la Mode* from 1843 and his plates were used in *The Englishwoman's Domestic Magazine* in the 1860s.

K

KAENDLER, JOHANN JOACHIM (1706–75). Modeller and sculptor mainly in ceramics. He worked at MEISSEN from 1731 until his death and influenced the production of the factory throughout its history. He was virtually the creator of the European porcelain figure. See CERAMICS (EUROPEAN).

KAKIEMON. Family of potters from Arita, Japan, credited with having introduced (*c.* 1650) the technique of overglaze enamels on porcelain. The name was applied to a type of ware whose characteristic asymmetrical designs became popular in Europe in the 18th c. and were copied at MEISSEN, CHELSEA and elsewhere. See JAPAN (POTTERY AND PORCELAIN).

KALTEMAIL (German: 'cold enamel'). A hard-setting LACQUER, less durable than true ENAMEL but used as a substitute for it in the 16th and 17th centuries. Besides being cheaper it was suitable for surfaces which could be damaged by the heat of firing or which were too large to be placed in the kiln. The polychrome decoration on the armour of Prince Nicholas Radziwil (Kunsthistorisches Mus., Vienna, mid 16th c.) is in Kaltemail, as are the colours on the flower finials of some 16th-c. silver cups. In some large objects, such as mirror frames, it takes the place of translucent enamel.

KALTHOFF. Family of gunmakers of Solingen. The best known was PETER (d. 1672), who worked in the service of Frederick III and Christian V from 1646 until his death and in 1641 was given a monopoly by the States General of the Netherlands for the manufacture of breech-loading guns. His brother MATTHIAS was also active in Copenhagen from 1660 to *c.* 1680. The brothers made magazine rifles which were supplied to the Danish army and were known for their repeaters. They devised a complicated and ingenious system with a box breech which moved horizontally when the trigger-guard was rotated, loading the gun from two magazines in the butt.

CASPAR Kalthoff, another member of the Solingen family, came to England in 1654 and worked there until his death in 1664 under the patronage of the Earl of Worcester.

KAMBLI, JOHANN MELCHIOR (1718–83). German cabinet-maker and craftsman of Swiss origin. He went to Potsdam in 1746 as a sculptor but became one of the outstanding artists and designers of the German ROCOCO. In 1752 he was given royal privilege to set up a workshop for ORMOLU MOUNTS and he made much splendid furniture for the Sans-Souci and other palaces of Frederick the Great. He was particularly famous for his decoration of the 'Bronzezimmer' in the Berlin palace (1754–5).

KARCHER, NICOLAS and HANS. Flemish tapestry weavers in Italy in the 16th c. See TAPESTRY.

KASHMIR. See SHAWLS.

KEITH, JAMES. English glass-worker who left Newcastle upon Tyne in 1755 and joined the Norwegian glass-house at Nöstetangen, which had been opened in 1741 under the patronage of Christian VI king of Norway and Denmark. Keith was responsible for the introduction there of the English lead GLASS in place of German soda glass. When the Nöstetangen factory closed in 1777 Keith joined the Hurdals Verk, to which production had been transferred. Keith retired in 1787 but various of his descendants have figured in Scandinavian glass production under such surnames as Kith, Keth, etc.

KELMSCOTT PRESS. A private printing press founded in 1891 by William MORRIS in Hammersmith, London, and named after his house in the Cotswolds. The Press was continued by trustees for two years after Morris's death to complete books upon which substantial work had been done. It closed in 1898. Morris's purpose in founding the Press was to bring about a reform in printing based upon the types of early printed books and to exemplify his philosophy of craftsmanship in the field of BOOK PRODUCTION. He designed three types for the Press. The 'Golden' type, designed for *The Golden Legend*, was based on the ROMAN letter of Nicolas Jensen (1470). The 'Troy', a BLACK-LETTER type, was designed in 1891 and used for the reprint of CAXTON's translation *The Recuyell of the Historyes of Troye*, published in 1782. The 'Chaucer' used for the double-columned *Chaucer*, the most important production of the Press, was a smaller version of the 'Troy'. In the seven years of its existence the Kelmscott Press issued 55 titles in a total of 65 volumes. It was the most important single influence in the PRIVATE PRESS MOVEMENT.

131, 134, 277, 366, 551.

KENT, WILLIAM (1685–1748). English architect, furniture designer, painter and landscape gardener. He was the first English architect to include furniture as an integral part of his interior decoration and was the greatest exponent of English BAROQUE furniture. His is the classic GEORGIAN example of close relationship between architect and discerning patron, in this case Lord Burlington, who first met Kent as a young art student in Rome. Through Burlington's patronage Kent became a master designer: 'he was not only consulted for furniture, as frames of pictures, glasses, tables and chairs, etc., but for plate, for a barge, for a cradle' (Horace Walpole, *Anecdotes of Painting*). He was responsible for a number of Palladian houses for Burlington and his circle and completed the interiors with large-scale furniture of florid but controlled vitality, lavishly ornamented but perfectly congruent with its setting. Surviving pieces from his designs are at Houghton, Holkham, Raynham, Rousham and Wilton. John Vardy's *Some Designs of Mr. Inigo Jones and Mr. William Kent* (1744), includes examples of Kent's furniture. See also LANDSCAPE GARDENING.

459.

KENZAN, OGATA (1663–1743). Japanese potter, whose work owed much to the Zen painting tradition and to the decorative school of Koetsu, to which his brother Kōrin belonged. He also made *inrō* of porcelain. See JAPAN (POTTERY AND PORCELAIN).

KILIM (KHILIM, GILIM, GHILIM, GILEEM, etc.). Transliteration of a Turkish word. Pile-less rugs woven in western Asia by the TAPESTRY process so that the fabric is alike on both sides. Such rugs made in Persia and central Asia are called *Palas*. Anatolian kilims are sometimes called *Karamanis* after the Turkish province Karaman where kilims are made. It is characteristic of the kilim technique that open spaces between warp threads are left where changes of colours are made. Turkey, the Caucasus, Persia and Turkestan all produce kilims in patterns resembling those of the local pile rugs.

Kilims are used for floor coverings, to place over reed matting on benches, for awnings over wagons, for packing bales and so on. They are generally between 40 and 168 centimetres wide and between 3·5 and 5·0 metres long. Smaller rugs are also made for various uses, such as travelling prayer rugs. In Turkey it was a custom for a bride to present her future husband with a kilim—called *kis-kilim*—woven by herself as a sample of her skill. See also CARPETS AND RUGS.

83, 159, 211, 242, 437, 471, 490.

KLISMOS. Chair which was used in Greece from the 6th c. B.C. It had a plaited seat standing on concave curved legs which flared outwards. The back was formed of three uprights with a curved board at shoulder level. It was comfortable and John Gloag says of it that it was 'the first chair that allowed people to sit freely in a relaxed, natural position'. The beauty of its lines, particularly in the 5th c. has been frequently remarked. The klismos was the most characteristic model in the French DIRECTOIRE and English REGENCY styles. It was also adopted in the American EMPIRE style from *c.* 1810. See also GREEK AND ROMAN ANTIQUITY (FURNITURE).

KNIBB, JOSEPH (1640–1711). Joseph Knibb is known as the English clock-maker who attained the highest perfection in the imaginative design and construction of wooden LONG-CASE and BRACKET CLOCKS and he was probably the inventor of three of the most widely used clock escapements, though he himself made no claim for these inventions and published nothing. Born at Claydon, Oxfordshire, he was probably apprenticed to his cousin, SAMUEL Knibb, from 1655 to 1662. About this latter year he set up in business in Oxford itself, and in 1670 he moved to London and became a freeman of the Clockmakers' Company. He retired in 1697 to Hanslope. His superb long clock cases were mainly of walnut veneer (on oak) or of olive wood, with floral MARQUETRY panels or with geometrical PARQUETRY, and his bracket clock cases were mounted with silver. No furniture of the period exceeds these clock cases in quality of workmanship. On the mechanical side he strove to improve the time-keeping of pendulum clocks by the invention of better escapements. The TURRET CLOCK made for Wadham College, Oxford, in 1669 is almost certainly his work and is the earliest known clock with an anchor escapement, presumably Knibb's own invention. The forerunner of this escapement may have been the 'pendulum crossbeat' with which he was experimenting for domestic clocks in 1668; and he also invented the simple 'tic-tac' escapement for bracket clocks.

106.

KNIGHT, RICHARD PAYNE (1750–1824). Equally distinguished as an antiquary, a collector and an aesthetician of the Picturesque, his name in that controversial field was linked with that of his Herefordshire neighbour, Uvedale PRICE of Foxley. In their background the two men had much in common, both enjoying inherited wealth, opportunities for extensive travel and when at home a passion for fox-hunting. Both followed the usual course by which young men of means then entered Parliament, and both devoted much time to improving their estates. Temperamentally, however, they diverged, Price combining his intellectual qualities with the pursuits of a country gentleman happy in his family life, whereas underlying Knight's flair and brilliance lay a restless disposition and a tendency to depression for which his early years were probably responsible.

Born in 1750, Richard was the elder child of the Revd. Thomas Knight, who had married Ursula Nash late in life. Their second son, Thomas Andrew, did not arrive until 1759 and as Richard's health kept him from school for several years he led a somewhat solitary existence, in which he developed a phenomenal capacity for reading. The death of his father in 1764 brought him the Downton estate at 14, the same age at which Price had inherited Foxley. Three years later Knight set out for Italy, remaining abroad until he had attained his majority.

It was while he was still in Rome that the young man appears first to have given serious thought to building a new house at Downton, plans being obtained in his absence from T. F. Pritchard of Shrewsbury, who had already worked at Croft Castle for one of Knight's uncles. On his return, however, Knight drew up his own designs for the house, although as an amateur he may well have relied to some extent on Pritchard's help over practical details. By the end of 1774 the carcase was progressing and the stone cornice for the octagonal tower was already cut. This imposing tower at the south-west angle, with another of circular form at the north-west and a square 'keep' in the centre of the south front, combined to give Downton its uniquely irregular outline on a lofty site above the rocky course of the river Teme. In devising this essentially picturesque silhouette, Knight was, on the evidence of his *Analytical Inquiry into the Principles of Taste* (1805), inspired not by the medieval castles of England but by the defensive buildings which frequently appear in the paintings of Claude and Poussin. An equally remarkable feature of Downton was the contrast of its 'Gothic' exterior with the severe Classicism adopted for its principal rooms. On this duality Knight also touches in the *Analytical Inquiry*, recollecting that it was then 'more than thirty years since the author . . . ventured to build a house, ornamented with what are called Gothic towers and battlements without, and with Grecian ceilings, columns, and entablatures within; and though his example has not been much followed, he has every reason to congratulate himself upon the success of the experiment; he having, at once, the advantage of a picturesque object, and of an elegant and convenient dwelling; though less perfect in both respects than if he had executed it at a maturer age'.

Knight was, in fact, unduly modest in thinking that it had 'not been much followed', for Downton had from the outset a profound influence among subscribers to the picturesque ideal, and particularly on the architect John Nash, in whose subsequent 'castles' it had a distinct echo.

As soon as Downton was approaching completion Knight set out in 1777 on a second Continental tour, which was to take him to Sicily in company with Charles Gore and the German landscape painter Philipp Hackert. A diary kept by Knight, and describing their various excursions, was later included by Goethe in his biography of Hackert. A third journey to Italy was made early in the 1780s, and it was in the course of this that Knight stayed in Naples and there heard from Sir William Hamilton, then British Minister, of the latter's discovery of a pagan fertility cult still practised at Isernia in Abruzzo. This cult, thinly disguised as a Christian festival of St. Cosmo, was described by Hamilton in a communication to the Society of Dilettanti in May 1784, but two years later Knight, now back in England, published an illustrated account, based on Sir William's but with additional material gathered from D'Hancarville, under the title of *The Worship of Priapus lately existing in Isernia*. The book was immediately attacked by prudish reviewers, whereupon Knight bought up and destroyed as many copies as possible.

His next venture into print, although on the most innocent of subjects, was again to involve Knight in controversy. His interest in picturesque scenery, particularly in its application to the surroundings of a house, had been stimulated by the work in progress at Downton. Here the outline and situation of the house provided all those dramatic and colourful qualities admired by such friends as the Revd. William Gilpin and Uvedale Price, who was in process of collecting material for his *Essay on the Picturesque*. With characteristic enthusiasm Knight decided to produce his own literary contribution and in a few weeks completed a didactic poem entitled *The Landscape* dedicated to Price and embodying many of the principles which they shared. Both their works were published in 1794. In his poem Knight advised his readers to seek 'the true ingredients of the painter's grace' and to 'bid the verdant Landscape rise, / To please the fancy and delight the eyes / With secret skill and counterfeit neglect.' To illustrate his thesis he included two plates from drawings by Thomas Hearn. The first showed a Palladian mansion in an 'unpicturesque' setting, with groups of trees and a serpentine stream in a smooth expanse of lawn as condemned by the poet. The second depicted a 'picturesque' rendering of the same subject, the house having undergone a Jacobean transformation while the stream threaded through a rocky course and the trees rose from tangled undergrowth. Today the former illustration is as likely to appeal as is that which Knight intended should arouse our admiration; but to those who shared his ideals it was the second plate, suggesting the 'gloom which native thickets shed' and the stream 'with moss and fern o'ergrown', which proved the unassailable superiority of the *picturesque*.

In the second edition of *The Landscape* Knight included a minor criticism of one of Uvedale Price's theories, to which the latter made reply in his *Dialogue . . . on the Character of the Picturesque* (1801). To this Knight in turn took exception, and on these trivial issues the long friendship of the two Herefordshire squires was to founder. Knight made one more contribution to the aesthetics of the Picturesque with his *Analytical Inquiry* of 1805, but after this his interest in the subject seems to have waned, and he became increasingly preoccupied with classical studies and with his collections of bronzes, gems and drawings. In 1809 he handed over Downton to his brother, Thomas Andrew Knight the distinguished horticulturist, and thereafter spent most of his time at his London house in Soho Square. In collaboration with his friend Charles Townley he prepared for publication in 1809 a work entitled *Specimens from Ancient Sculpture*, in which 23 of the pieces illustrated were from his own collection. He contributed to *Archaeologia*, the *Edinburgh Review*, Young's *Annals of Agriculture* and other publications, and wrote various papers on classical Greece and its language. He served as Vice-President of the Society of Antiquaries, and as a member of the so-called 'Committee of Taste' formed to report on models for public monuments. Knight was not afraid on occasion to take a stand contrary to general opinion, of which a notable example was his lack of enthusiasm for the Elgin marbles. Asked to give evidence before a Select Committee, he strongly opposed the proposal that these should be purchased for the nation.

In spite of his wide circle of acquaintances Knight remained a somewhat solitary figure, subject to increasing periods of depression. His death on 28 April 1824 was ascribed to an apoplectic seizure, but some years later Samuel Rogers confided to a friend that Knight put an end to his life by taking poison. Many of his finest gems and drawings, including 273 drawings by Claude, were left to the British Museum, and were then said to be worth £50,000.

428, 584, 663, 727.

KNITTING. See NEEDLEWORK.

KNIVES. See CUTLERY.

KNOTTED PILE. The most general technique used in the making of Oriental carpets. See CARPETS AND RUGS and WEAVING (PILE WEAVING).

KNUB (also called FRISON). A form of waste from the outer layers of the cocoon, a by-product of the process of reeling raw SILK from the cocoons.

KŌKEI. See JAPAN (NETSUKE).

KOKUSAI. See JAPAN (NETSUKE).

KRAUSE, JAKOB (1531/2–85). German bookbinder, chiefly active in Dresden where he introduced gold tooling and designs based on French–Italian models. Between 1566 and 1585 he was Court Binder to the Elector Friedrich-August. Many of Krause's richly gilded bindings contain portrait stamps and initials of the electoral family, with elaborately painted and GAUFFERED book-edges.

754.

KUNCKEL, JOHANN (probably 1630–1703). German chemist and GLASS technologist whose work culminated in the production of a massive, clear glass metal which prompted comparison with ROCK-CRYSTAL and provided an ideal medium for engraving, permitting a greater depth of incision than had been possible before. He was also known for his invention of a ruby gold glass (*Goldrubinglas*). In 1669 Kunckel was appointed director of the Elector of Brandenburg's glass-houses at Potsdam.

L

LABINO, DOMINICK (1910–). One of the leading American craftsmen promoting the resurgence of interest in contemporary hand-crafted glass. Together with Harvey K. LITTLETON he developed the first seminar on the subject at the Toledo Museum of Art in 1962. This and subsequent seminars were to prove that glass could be blown and successfully crafted in the small individual studio. Labino designed the first furnace and developed the glass for those initial experiments.

Formerly vice-president for research at the Johns–Manville Fiber Glass Corporation, Labino is today considered one of the leading American artists working in glass. He has won national acclaim, has influenced other noted glass craftsmen, has aided in the establishment of glass-making classes at various universities and has written *Visual Art in Glass*. In addition he is Honorary Curator of Glass at the famed glass collections of the Toledo Museum.

The prime interests of Labino are in colour and its influence upon form; he has continued experiments in relation to these interests at his studio in Grand Rapids, Ohio. His glass is notable for its refinement of colour, the quality of the metal and its beauty of finish. Examples of his work are in the Toledo Museum of Art, the Art Institute of Chicago and the Cincinnati Art Museum, among others. See GLASS (AMERICA).

LACE. 1. TECHNIQUE. One of a number of techniques whereby threads are twisted or knotted together to form a delicate, open-work fabric in which a solid pattern stands out against a net-like background. Analogous fabrics were made in Bronze Age Denmark and in Pre-Columbian America; and in both Europe and America similar effects were produced during the Middle Ages and after by EMBROIDERY on open-meshed net fabrics, a technique known as LACIS or *lacez*. What is regarded as true lace, however, cannot be traced further back than 16th-c. Venice, though it may possibly have been introduced there from the East.

Lace may be made from many kinds of thread, including cotton and silk; but the most usual is fine white linen. There are two main types of lace, made by different techniques. They are Bobbin or Pillow lace and Needlepoint lace.

Bobbin or Pillow lace (sometimes also known as Bone lace) is made on a round or oval pillow, which is held on the knees of the lace-maker or placed on an elevated frame. The pattern is drawn on a piece of parchment, which is then stretched on to the pillow and pins inserted following the design. A thread is looped round each pin and then wound round a bone or wooden

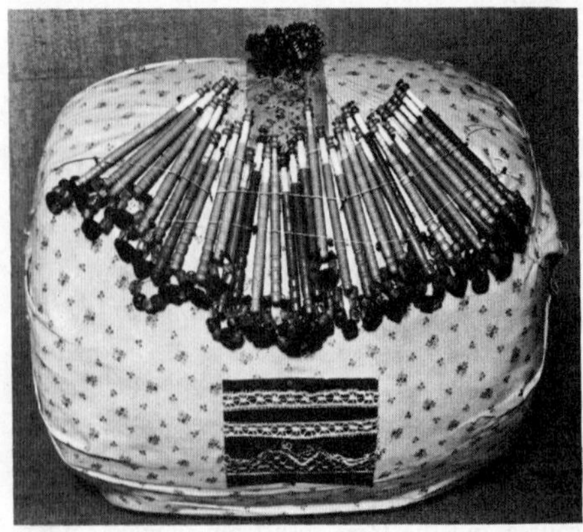

Lace-making pillow with bobbins

bobbin, being held in position by a groove. A separate bobbin is used for each thread and they may be as many as 200 in number. To help the lace-maker distinguish between them they are often decorated differently or weighted with coloured beads. For it is by the skilful manipulation of the bobbins, which are thrown and twisted around the pins, that the groundwork of the fabric is formed. The pattern is sometimes worked by interweaving a thicker thread than those used for the ground. The old bone or wooden bobbins used for making Pillow lace, often decorated and inscribed, and also the decorative spangles, have become of interest to collectors since the craft has virtually died out.

Needlepoint lace was known as *point à l'aiguille* in France and as *punto in aco* in Italy. In origin it is a special kind of NEEDLEWORK or open-work embroidery which has freed itself from the ground on which conventional embroidery is worked and has become self-supporting. In 16th-c. examples its evolution can be traced from modest beginnings as a decorative filling for small holes cut in the fabric (cut work) to the ambitious 'spider work' (*opus araneum*) and RETICELLAS in which all but a few supporting threads of the original fabric have been drawn or cut away, until eventually it launches itself into space beyond the margins of the original cloth as unsupported scallops of *punto in aria*.

These two kinds of lace differ in character. The airy delicacy of Bobbin lace made it especially suitable for the adornment of personal linen, while the sculptural richness of Needlepoint fitted it for ecclesiastical and ceremonial uses. Yet since the primary purpose of both was the same—as accessories of costume: collars, cuffs, caps, flounces and the like—each constantly emulated the effects of the other and their history can be summarized together.

In addition to the extensive nomenclature of stitches, most of which were common to needlework and embroidery, the craft of lace-making developed a large technical vocabulary of its own, taken mainly from the French. The following basic terms may be of interest. The fabric ground was called *entoilage* and the pattern *toilé*. Alternative names for the ground were: *treille*, *fond* or *champ*. Different types of network ground had their own names, such as: *réseau*, wire, Brussels, trolly, *fond clair*, *fond double*. The holes cut in open-work techniques were joined by *brides* or tie-bars. A raised cord used to introduce high relief mainly into Needlepoint lace was called a *cordonnet*. The outer edge of the lace was the *couronne* and the narrow edging which served as a border and as a strengthening when the lace was sewn to a garment was called *engrêlure*.

Collar of Needlepoint lace. *Gros point de Venise*. (V. & A. Mus., 17th c.)

2. HISTORY. From the late Middle Ages down to the 19th c. much more abundant use was made of lace for both male and female COSTUME than is usual today and in most countries of Europe lace and embroidery were in constant demand with the well-to-do. The laces of the 16th and early 17th centuries were characterized generally by a linear and wiry treatment of their designs, which were partly geometrical and partly composed of the neat scrolls and urns which were characteristic of Renaissance ornament. Much of the Needlepoint lace of the period is commonly called 'Venetian lace', while the Bobbin lace is apt to be known as 'Genoese'; but in fact similar laces, based to a large extent on the Venetian pattern-books which circulated in large numbers, were being made throughout western Europe by the latter half of the 16th c. Venetian lace was used at the coronation of King Richard III and Venetian laces were a treasured possession of Elizabeth I. Among other Italian centres of lace-making Milan was at one time noted for PASSEMENTS, the island of Palestrina made laces suitable for household furnishings and Albiesola, near Savona, made a black lace which attracted notice at the coronation of Napoleon I.

From the 15th c. Flanders lace rapidly achieved prominence because of the fine quality of Flemish linen thread and the quality of the workmanship. The Flemish lace schools had an international reputation and Flemish craftsmen carried the techniques to France and England.

In the Baroque laces of the middle of the 17th c. the small rhythmic effects of the preceding period were abandoned in favour of a vague, conventionalized floral ornament whose broad sweeping scrolls grew so densely that brides were wholly or partly dispensed with. Fine examples of this type are to be found among the Flemish and Milanese laces, but the technical mastery of the period is best seen in Venetian lace with its varied filling-patterns and effects of high relief.

Towards the end of the 17th c. Italian supremacy disappeared and the lead in Needlepoint passed to France. As leaders of fashion and

Jabot of Needlepoint lace. *Point de France.* (V. & A. Mus., end 17th c.)

elegance the French had been important consumers of lace. In the 16th c. a main centre of lace-making existed at Le Puy and the craft had been fostered by Henry of Navarre. But it was not until Colbert under Louis XIV set up his state factory at Lonray near ALENÇON and Argentan that French Needlepoint lace under the general name of *point de France* established its reputation. Flemish lace-makers were brought in to teach their craft in France. But the French lace was at first an imitation of the Venetian. The grounds had regular meshes decorated with tiny picots or loops. Gradually the meshes became smaller, the *petit réseau* or small-mesh style was evolved, and in the next century characteristic local styles such as those of Alençon and Argentan were developed. French Bobbin lace, although it never equalled the prestige of Needlepoint, was none the less widely popular. It seems to have been a traditional folk craft with centres at Le Puy, Dieppe, Bayeux and Caen, featuring in local costume, particularly head-dresses, and with patterns traditional to each locality.

Simultaneously with the rise to prominence of French lace the Low Countries also developed an astonishing variety of local styles in Bobbin lace of high quality. In all these styles the floral forms gradually became lighter and more elegant; they were no longer linked by irregular brides but displayed on a regular *réseau* or ground mesh. Many of these types persisted into the 19th c. alongside other newer ones, some of which—such as LILLE, TONDER, BUCKINGHAMSHIRE and BEDFORDSHIRE laces—were small and unpretentious borders, while others—such as CHANTILLY, HONITON and MALTESE—were more ambitious, but generally heavy and elaborate in design.

In Britain lace was particularly lavishly employed during the Tudor and Stuart periods both for costume and for domestic articles such as towels, cushions and bed linen. Sumptuary laws were countered by a flourishing business

Shawl of Buckinghamshire Bobbin lace. (V. & A. Mus., first half 19th c.)

in smuggling. Bobbin lace from the Low Countries was the most popular and this eventually established itself as a local craft in a number of centres. According to a tradition kept alive by lace-makers, Catherine of Aragon taught the craft to the peasants while living at Ampthill and so laid the foundation of the Bedfordshire pillow lace industry. Towards the end of the 17th c. districts in Northamptonshire, Bedfordshire and Buckinghamshire were emerging as centres. In the Isle of Wight, the Isle of Man and Devonshire traditional patterns are believed to derive from the influence of smuggled lace.

Spanish lace had a high reputation, rivalling in its own sphere that of the Netherlands. The term *point d'Espagne* was used with special reference to the rich laces made in Spain from gold or silver thread. The former was devoted mainly to ecclesiastical vestments and appurtenances, the latter for court and ceremonial dress. A highly prized lace from Spain was the *punto di Spagna frisado en oro*, which was of fine texture with motifs outlined in gold thread bearing picots and designs decorated in polychrome silk. Spanish Needlepoint lace was more closely worked than Italian and Moorish influence was apparent in the designs. Lace in which Moorish influence was strong was known as *Morisco*. *Point de Milan*, despite its name, was a Spanish lace with motifs massed together on a groundwork of open-mesh squares. The

Flounce of Pillow lace. Maltese. (V. & A. Mus., early 19th c.)

motifs ranged from elaborate scrolls and geometrical patterns to floral designs and national emblems. BLONDE LACE was made in Catalonia and used for the mantilla. There was also a demand for this from America.

In Portugal Needlepoint lace was chiefly made, although in the 18th c. Lisbon was renowned for a coarse white Bobbin lace and Bobbin lace from Peniche, near Lisbon, was in demand in the 19th c. Madeira lace, resembling Torchon, with pattern reminiscent of early Greek or Maltese designs, also won a high reputation.

Lace was made in the Scandinavian countries mainly as a domestic industry, fostered by the religious houses, and was used in national costume. There was a fairly active lace industry in Germany in the 16th c. with Berlin as a main centre and a lace school was established at Annaberg. The industry depended largely on refugee craftsmen from France and the Netherlands in the ensuing century. During the 19th c. lace-making flourished in Saxony and a so-called 'caterpillar lace' from Munich, made from a strong web, was popular for durability.

Fine laces, exquisite in workmanship and design, were made in the Aegean Islands, Sicily, Sardinia, Morocco, the Barbary states and Turkey. By the 17th c. characteristic English Needlepoint laces were being made, one remarkable for its naturalistic rendering of flowers and biblical scenes and another using the more modest HOLLIE POINT. Sometimes the *réseau* was bobbin-made and the threads attached to the open edges of the *toilé*, following the pattern. Sometimes in Bobbin lace the flowers of the pattern were finely worked with Needlepoint filling. Flowers and leaves were often worked in high relief achieved not by the use of a coarser thread but by plaiting and twisting bobbins.

During the 19th c. much substitute lace was made by means of hand embroidery on machine-made net (CARRICKMACROSS; COGGESHALL; ISLE OF WIGHT; LIMERICK). Changed economic conditions in the 20th c. and a general decline in appreciation of handicraft products led to the virtual supersession of hand-made lace by laces made wholly by machinery. In scattered localities the craft survives or is revived by craft guilds, but contemporary lace-making does not aspire beyond the reproduction of the simpler types of old lace.

For lace-making in Russia see RUSSIA (LACE).

3. IDENTIFICATION. Although a very large number of localities developed their own characteristic and recognizable styles of lace-making, there was continual interchange of techniques among them and alongside traditional patterns, whose influence was strongest where lace-making was a domestic industry, many pattern-books circulated internationally. For this reason it is not always easy to identify the source of particular examples of lace. The following general principles may therefore be of interest. They do not, of course, serve as an alternative to expert knowledge.

The main categories of lace may be recognized in general terms by the fact that in Bobbin lace the groundwork or *réseau* has threads which are twisted or plaited. In Needlepoint lace the *réseau* is of untwisted threads usually in a variety of buttonhole stitching. The *réseau* of machine-made lace is stiffer and less resilient and the mesh has a precision and regularity which are lacking in hand-made lace. In some laces there is a combination of techniques: in particular the *réseau* may be Bobbin-made and the pattern done in Needlepoint. Needlepoint lace does not easily unravel because of the knots in the *réseau*. The threads of Bobbin lace will unravel, though not easily because of the twisting. The threads of machine-made lace will unravel continuously. Some indication of date may be given by the number of joinings in the threads. Threads with very few joinings date usually from the 19th c.

The date can also be gathered in a rough and ready way from the type of pattern. As has been said, in the 16th c. geometrical designs were most prevalent and floral designs, when they occurred, were treated with angularity. In the 17th c. patterns became more ambitious and almost obliterated the background. Scrolls, urns, etc. were joined by brides. The fashion in brides also changed. From being quite plain, in the course of the 16th c. they came to carry loops or dots, sometimes a double loop, and in the 17th c. a star motif was often used on a bride. Rough dating is also possible from the style in the *couronne* and *engrêlure*. Very early lace usually has an angular edging; during the 16th c. a softer finish was often given by scalloping; in the later 17th c. it became fashionable for the scalloping to be ornamented with a dot or a star; and in the 18th c. a small scallop was often alternated with a larger one. Dating by *engrêlure* is less reliable because these were less durable than the flounce and were often renewed. The earliest *engrêlures* consisted simply of cross-bars and old hand-made *engrêlures* were usually of flax thread. In machine-made lace cotton thread was used. It must be remembered, however, that changes and developments in both techniques and styles of design which are given in the histories represent general tendencies only; in individual work, influenced perhaps by a family tradition through the generations, and in isolated localities, types of pattern, methods of treatment and techniques often persisted long after a general change had taken place.

435, 581, 651, 677, 870, 929.

LACIS. A technique of NEEDLEWORK akin to LACE-making, which was widely practised in Europe during the Middle Ages and after. The method consists of darning a pattern into a fine net. Patterns were angular and often coarse but could achieve delicacy if the net was sufficiently fine. When the work was done on net with wide, square meshes and fine thread it was known as *opus araneum* or spider work. During the

Middle Ages and Renaissance coloured silks and gold thread were introduced to enhance the pattern, but later examples are generally in white only.

LACQUER AND JAPANNING. (The following article brings together material from the sections on lacquer under CHINA and JAPAN and the article on JAPANNING.) Lacquer is the sap of a tree, *Rhus vernicifera*, which from very early times has been used in China and Japan to overlay objects made of wood and other materials with a hard smooth skin, lustrous and extremely durable. Bowls, boxes and other utensils were usually made of very thin pinewood, over which the lacquer, purified by straining and heating, was laid on in a series of coats, sometimes as many as twenty, each one being allowed to dry and harden before the next was applied. The final surface, ground smooth with a whetstone and highly polished, was decorated by an artist who had at his disposal a number of processes. One of the commonest was a form of low relief built up in successive layers of lacquer, the details being afterwards picked out in colours. Another method, at which the Chinese excelled, was to carve the surface with a knife. Encrustations of shell, MOTHER OF PEARL, CORAL and metal were also employed and subtle effects were obtained, especially in Japan, where from the 8th c. onwards a native technique was developed, called *makie*, of sprinkling the surface with flaked or powdered gold, silver and copper. The ground was usually coloured black or red, but other colours such as green, yellow and brown are also found. Landscapes, flowers, birds and animals were favourite subjects, but conventional and emblematic motifs were also used, particularly in China. Japanese lacquer tends to be more highly finished than Chinese. 'Coromandel lacquer', so called because it was exported to Europe by way of the Coromandel coast of India, is made only in China. It is made by overlaying a wood frame with a layer of lacquer composition in which the design is cut out in INTAGLIO and painted, a process which produces a brilliantly decorative effect suitable for screens and cabinets.

The art of lacquering originated in China. Among the most ancient specimens known are a bowl and a jar of paper-thin lacquer in the Victoria and Albert Museum which date from the Han Dynasty. Lacquer of the T'ang Dynasty is represented by a number of 8th-c. examples in the Japanese Imperial Repository, known as the Shōsōin. During the Sung Dynasty most of the types of lacquer known today were being produced according to an account written in 1387 by a scholar named Tsao Ch'ao. But examples of such early lacquer are exceedingly rare and it is not until the Ming Dynasty that they become more common. Relatively large quantities have survived from the times of the Ch'ing Emperors. An important factory for making carved lacquer was founded within the royal palace at Peking by the Emperor K'ang Hsi in 1680 and was still producing under Chien Lung (1736–95), whose throne of red 'Peking lacquer' is in the Victoria and Albert Museum.

Lacquering was introduced into Japan from China before the Heian Period. Dry lacquer (*kaushitsu*) became very popular in the 8th c. for Buddhist statues, either hollow or moulded on a wooden core. This technique is said to have originated in China; but no Chinese examples have survived, whereas in Japan many excellent works have been preserved which rank among the finest Buddhist sculptures found in that country. The art of lacquering attained its highest peak of development under the Togugawa Shoguns in the 17th, 18th and early 19th centuries. During this period a great school of lacquer artists existed at Tokyo, where the Koma family held the appointment of court lacquerers for eleven generations. The Kajikawa family was also celebrated for its lacquer wares throughout this period, while Kōrin (1661–1716) and Ritsuō (1663–1747) were pre-eminent as individual artists. A characteristic Japanese object made in lacquer during these years is the *inrō*, a miniature medicine-case consisting of as many as five compartments, which was worn on the girdle. The craft survives in wares made at Kamakura and called *Kamakura-bori*.

From *c.* 1600 consignments of lacquer screens, chests and cabinets began to reach Europe mainly through the Dutch East India Company, which specialized in such wares and enjoyed a monopoly of trade with Japan. As with PORCELAIN, attempts were soon made to imitate them. The kind of decoration employed is suggested by an entry in an inventory of the Earl of Northampton's furniture taken in 1614, which reads: 'one small table of China Worke in gold and colours with flies and women . . .' An example of Charles I's reign is the cabinet painted with Oriental figures and arabesques in gold on a black ground in the Victoria and Albert Museum. But it was not until the 2nd half of the century that the fashion took firm hold and a flourishing trade in imitations began. In England the process known as japanning, and described in *A Treatise of Japanning and Varnishing* (1688) by John Stalker and George Parker, was to cover the wood with a skin of gesso, thus forming a hard, smooth ground, over which a coat of varnish, black or coloured, was laid on with a brush. Detailed instructions are given for applying raised and painted decoration, for which the authors provide a number of engraved patterns made up of flowers and birds, pagodas, rocky landscapes and figures in pseudo-Oriental costumes. Many of the motifs employed by the japanner were garnered from the illustrated travel books that appeared in the latter half of the century.

Great quantities of japanned ware were also produced in France, Germany and Holland. Among the most successful artists were Gérard and Jacques Dagly, of German origin, who obtained a patent for their process in Paris in 1713. To them are attributed a number of cabinets in which the japanning, of exceptionally fine quality, comes deceptively close to Oriental lacquer. A little later Robert Martin with his three brothers founded a factory in Paris for making a special kind of lacquer which they called VERNIS MARTIN. As a rule it is not difficult to recognize the European imitations, for apart from the gesso ground the surface is not so lustrous and the drawing portrays a conscious *naïveté* and lacks the accomplished fluency of the Oriental artist.

The taste for lacquer continued in Europe intermittently all through the 18th c. In the ROCOCO period Parisian cabinet-makers were fond of framing panels of real or imitation Japanese lacquer in the fronts of commodes, and the custom was continued by certain *ébénistes* of the NEO-CLASSICAL revival, notably by Martin CARLIN. In England furniture made in the CHINESE TASTE under the influence of designers such as CHIPPENDALE, or G. Edwards and E. Darly, was often japanned. After *c.* 1770 the quality of European japanning declined seriously and there is little to distinguish it from ordinary painting.

370, 460, 543, 613, 790, 798, 799, 800, 835.

LAJOUE, JAQUES DE (1686–1761). French painter, designer and ornamentalist. He is named by Jacques-François Blondel (1705–74) with PINEAU and MEISSONNIER as one of the three 'inventors' of the PITTORESQUE phase of French ROCOCO. Lajoue designed nothing actually for construction. But the fancifulness of his asymmetrical motifs and his *rocaille* fountains and canopies and trellises outdid those of Meissonnier and had a considerable influence in their day. His fantasies were taken up in particular by CUVILLIÈS.

LAKES. A variant of 'lac', from the Hindustani 'lakh', a resinous encrustation produced on certain trees by the insect *Cocus lacca* and used in the East as a scarlet dye. Originally the term was used for a reddish dye obtained from lac. Now 'lake' is used for a class of pigments obtained by combining a colouring matter with metallic oxide or earth. It is often qualified by a colour epithet such as 'scarlet', 'madder', etc. See COLOURS AND COLOURANTS.

LALIQUE, RENÉ (1860–1945). French jeweller and glass-maker. See GLASS (FRANCE). See also ART NOUVEAU.

L'ALTARE. A hamlet near Genoa, the centre of a GLASS industry which developed alongside that of Venice and Murano on such closely similar lines that the products of the two centres are often indistinguishable. The industry was founded by emigrant glass-workers from Normandy and Picardy in the 9th c. and from time to time craftsmen from Venice found their way to the glass-houses of L'Altare. The workers of Altare were never subject to the same severe restrictions as those of Venice and for that reason they made their influence felt in Europe somewhat earlier. But although contemporary records speak of a *façon de Venise* and a *façon d'Altare*, the two influences and styles are virtually indistinguishable. In so far as there was a difference, GADROONING, applied work and FINIALS are more commonly associated with Altare.

LAMBREQUIN. A scarf or other piece of material worn over a helmet as a covering. In interior decoration a term used in the U.S.A. for drapery, with the lower edge scalloped, hanging from the top of a door or window or bed or mantelshelf. In ceramics it is a term for an ornament of solid colour with the lower edge jagged or scalloped; a pendant ornament of 'vandyke' pattern.

LAMERIE, PAUL (DE) (1688–1751). English silversmith of Huguenot descent. He was born at 's Hertogenbosch, Holland, and his parents, religious refugees who at that time spelt their name 'de la Marie', came to England *c.* 1691. In 1703 he was apprenticed to the Huguenot goldsmith Pierre or Peter PLATEL and in 1712, having completed his apprenticeship, he was made free of the Goldsmiths' Company and set up business on his own. In 1716 he was appointed goldsmith to the King and in 1717 was admitted to the Livery of the Goldsmiths' Company, of which he became a member of the governing body in 1731. His long and prosperous career brought him the highest reputation among London goldsmiths and silversmiths of the 18th c. At the beginning of his career he worked both in the plain, undecorated style which had become established during the reign of Queen Anne and also in the more elaborate Huguenot style with GADROONING, cut-card work and heavy cast ornament. He was among the first to introduce the asymmetrical ROCOCO style to England and during the 1730s and 1740s developed an individual version of that style which, unlike the more Continental work of Charles Kandler, always retained something of English feeling.

Like others of his contemporaries in England, Lamerie not only worked to commission but also kept a large stock of—usually simpler and more traditional—work for sale to the casual buyer. He was thus one of the pioneers in the practice which led to the gradual industrialization of the silversmith's trade.

668.

LAMOUR, JEAN-BAPTISTE (1698–1771). French smith born in Nancy and son of JEAN Lamour, who since 1684 had held the position of city smith there. From 1712 he was serving an apprenticeship as a smith in Metz, making two journeys to Paris to perfect himself in his craft. On his father's death in 1719 he was appointed city smith in his place, and returned to Nancy the following year. His work there was for many years of a utilitarian character and his name would scarcely now be known but for ornamental work commissioned by Stanislas Lesczinsky, Duke of Lorraine, from 1735. This gave Lamour his opportunity and from 1751 he began his major commissions in Nancy itself. The Place royale, now the Place Stanislas, was enclosed with a series of gates and screens of great size and magnificence, so that when Lamour published his *Receuil des ouvrages* in 1767 he could justly claim that his work in the Place royale did not show 'cette maigreur ordinaire des ouvrages de ce genre'. By 1759 he had also completed the superb staircase rail for the Hôtel de Ville, sparing no effort, as he tells us in the *Receuil*, to see that it gave the effect of 'bronze giselé et recherché avec exactitude'. On the death of Stanislas in 1766 Nancy lost its privileged position and the works abruptly ceased. What may be Lamour's last work, exquisite balconies for his houses at 32 rue Notre Dame and at 5 rue St. Thiebault, probably belong to this period and reveal no less than the large public works his mastery of the ROCOCO style. His work inevitably invites comparison with that by his contemporary OEGG at Würzburg and reveals the different character of Rococo in France and Germany. The *rocaille* ornament of Lamour's work, rich as it was, was still subordinated to the architectural framework and it was this restraint which gave his work its refinement and dignity. Oegg was able to achieve his greater vigour at the expense of these qualities. See also IRON AND STEEL (DECORATIVE WROUGHT IRONWORK).

LANDSCAPE GARDENING

1. Europe. 2. England. 3. Islamic.

1. EUROPE. Landscape gardening, the art of laying out grounds so as to produce the effect of natural scenery, was not generally recognized as a necessary or useful art much before the middle of the 18th c., and then first in England. Gardening for pleasure began during the late Middle Ages but was not fully developed until the 16th c. Then also great efforts were soon made to improve the appearance of the enclosed land beyond the confines of the garden.

Italy. One of the first such landscaped parks was that added to the gardens of the renowned Villa Lante at Bagnia, designed by Giacomo da Vignola (1507–73). An engraving by G. Laurie (1584–1637) shows its many avenues of trees, trellises, basins, fountains, cascades and a labyrinth. It antedated the better known work of eminent French designers of large gardens and grounds, whom it may directly or indirectly have inspired. Other large Italian gardens, designed by architects, were usually carefully planned on formal, geometrical lines with avenues of cypress or pine trees, often on several levels. They stimulated many visitors to wish to beautify their own living-space.

France. With larger resources, more space and usually on less difficult, hilly sites, French kings and aristocrats expanded and varied the early Italian examples. By the end of the 16th c. Bernard PALISSY said: 'There are more than four thousand noble houses in France.' Royal domains, Fontainebleau, Saint-Germain-en-Laye, the Luxembourg Gardens in Paris, were among the greater show-places. They and the lesser estates of the nobility which they inspired were large parks rather than grounds landscaped to resemble natural scenery. John Evelyn in 1644 described Richelieu's vast estate at Ruelle as 'containing vineyards, cornfields, meadows, groves, whereof one is of perennial greenes, and walkes of vast lengths'. Famous gardeners, Boyceau de la Barauderie, Jacques Mollet, Claude his son and André his grandson, inspired by the architect Dupérac (?1525–1604) pioneered the specific French style of garden which André le Nôtre (1613–1700) carried to its greatest development at Vaux-le-Vicomte, Versailles, Chantilly, Dampierre and elsewhere. The principles of this classical French layout were set out in André Mollet's *Le Jardin de Plaisir*. From a large, bare semicircular or square piece of ground in front of the house long radial avenues in 'goose-claw' pattern of lime or elm trees should stretch away to the boundary of the estate. At the back of the house parterres set out in embroidery patterns, free of trees or fences, should provide an intriguing design to be viewed from the windows. Beyond them were to lie lawns, shrubberies, flower-beds and long alleys with tall hedges carefully trimmed, enhanced with fountains and statues or sometimes at their far end with a large painted landscape on canvas protected from the weather. So far away were the boundaries of these sumptuous, well-ordered plantings that they were beyond the range of easy vision, which would be fully absorbed by the magnificent, carefully arranged scenery in the midst of which the house was placed. More than a garden, these grounds were so many formal, ordered parkscapes. Magnificent, architecturally designed, geometrical, they were as much an intellectual as an artistic achievement, and excited the wonder and admiration of Europe. Royalty, Electors, Dukes and Counts were stirred to employ gardeners trained in the style of the Mollets and Le Nôtre, to repeat this French formal style in their own lands. In Spain the gardens at Aranjuez and La Granja were created for Philip V; in Italy his son Charles II of Naples had a splendid garden at Caserta. In Portugal there was the garden at Queluz. Versailles stimulated Peter the Great at Peterhof and the Esterhazys in Hungary. At Herrenhausen in Hanover the Electress Sophia, who died a few months before she should have succeeded Queen Anne in England, created a fine garden with the help of the philosopher Leibniz. Her daughter-in-law, Caroline of Ansbach, the most intelligent and worthy of all the Hanoverian Queens of England, caught there the enthusiasm for gardening which she was later to reveal at Richmond and Kensington.

The 'English Garden'. All these great gardens and formalized parklands followed the French style, which seemed so perfect, so rationally correct in every way, that no better alternative for their sites could easily be imagined. In Great Britain also it prevailed until the 18th c., when the first murmurs of dissent began to be heard. In an essay of 1625 Francis Bacon described a formal garden but at the same time he wanted two or three mounts, one of more than 9 m high 'to look abroad into the fields' as though the fair and open face of nature was an Englishman's birthright. By the early 18th c. this note was increasingly heard. Until then wild nature was rarely regarded as having marked aesthetic quality. Popular writers such as Addison (1672–1719) and poets such as Pope (1688–1744), Dyer (1699–1758) and Shenstone (1714–63) aided gardeners such as Batty Langley (*New Principles of Gardening*, 1728) and Switzer (*Iconographia Rustica*, 1718) to attack the formal French precedents. William KENT (1684–1748) and above all, Lancelot 'Capability' BROWN effected the revolution in garden design by creating the new taste for landscape gardening proper. Brown destroyed all traces of formal design, walls, fences, flower-beds, box hedges, alleys, avenues and garden furniture in general, leaving the house in the middle of vast expanses of grassland. To break the monotony he planted clumps of trees at what he thought aesthetically pleasing points and diverted streams or rivers wherever he could to form a large lake or a river with a subtly curving course between smooth grassy banks, the 'serpentine line of beauty' popularized by Hogarth (1697–1764). A belt of trees round the estate screened it from the public. Like many striking novelties in art, the 'English Garden' caught public fancy. It was a change that provoked much writing about aesthetics in general and 'the picturesque' in particular. Thomas Whately's *Observations on Modern Gardening* (1770) was translated into French and it also influenced many landowners in Germany. Continued in England but later modified by Humphry REPTON, Brown's revolution was gradually worked out, becoming already somewhat old-fashioned by the time of J. C. LOUDON.

The English Style in France. On the Continent English and Scottish gardeners were employed to replace many a formal garden by a landscaped scene in the English manner. Diderot vaunted the merits of the new English garden in the *Encyclopédie* (1751–72). It found an early convert in Catherine II of Russia, who told Voltaire in 1772: 'I have a passion for gardens in the English style, the curved lines, the gentle slopes, the ponds pretending to be lakes. . . . I spurn straight lines . . .' Like many imitations, the 'English Garden' was rarely copied with great success. In England, where much of the land had, as Brown said, 'capabilities' for improvement on his lines, the new idea was not uniformly successful. In the Netherlands and other flat lands large estates lacked such 'capabilities'. There the formal, classical French layout better suited the lie of the land at least where private gardens were concerned.

Among French enthusiasts for the new 'English' style was the Marquis de Girardin, friend and patron of Rousseau who had celebrated the charm of a 'romantic' garden in *La Nouvelle Héloïse*. His gardens of Ermenonville, which he described in 1788, were devised with great skill and were thought to seem wild and natural except that, after the Romantic formula, they were provided with imitations of a Doric temple, a mill, cottages and other fakes. Rousseau's tomb on an island of poplar trees in the middle of the lake perpetuates the renown of Girardin's achievement. Philippe l'Égalité after 1774 overdid the practice of building sham antiques and picturesque ruins in his large Parc Monceau, once like Kensington Gardens in London beyond the confines of the city but now the resort of children and nursemaids and well within Paris, where its 'English' character remains to contrast with the more formal, traditional style of other Parisian gardens except the Bois de Boulogne. The charms of Morfontaine (1770) and Méréville, near Rambouillet (1784), are more sober. A Scottish gardener planted out the garden of Bagatelle in the Bois de Boulogne in 1777 for the Comte d'Artois, making use of 'movements of the ground to vary the perspective and form many beautiful landscapes'. It also had 'curiosities': a Chinese pavilion, statues, rocks, Muhammad's tomb and a Chinese bridge. Sir William Chambers had stimulated interest in Chinese gardens by his *Dissertation on Oriental Gardening* (1772), which had been at once translated into French. Marie Antoinette refused to allow her 'English Garden' at the Trianon in Versailles to be cluttered up in such a way, determined to preserve the character of her Hameau by the lake. Despite such efforts, J. C. Loudon said in 1834 that he had never seen a single good example of 'the natural or English style of landscape gardening in France'.

The great achievement of the Second Empire was the reshaping of much of Paris by Baron Hausmann between 1853 and 1870. After the disasters of 1870–1 many French landowners began to revive the traditional, classical style of Le Nôtre which seems to accord with the

Cartesian spirit of France. At Voisins, Condé-sur-Iton, Villandry and elsewhere architects such as Henri and Achille Duchêne, A. Laprade, André and Paul Véra restored many a formal garden and park to its original splendour. André le Nôtre's Versailles, still the most famous, was largely restored in modern times with American aid. Today the strong urge to live in a garden suburb outside Paris is providing a stimulating challenge to many landscape gardeners.

The Netherlands. In comparison with the vast estates of many a French aristocrat those of the Netherlands were relatively small but, as Repton found, they were as well kept as the ledgers of the rich Dutch merchants. Where in earlier times larger estates existed they were not elaborate. Evelyn, who saw the park of the Prince of Orange in 1641, said that it had 'nothing more remarkable than the delicious walks planted with lime trees'. When William III became King of England he and Queen Mary had the grounds of their new palace at Kensington laid out on the model of those at his favourite palace, the Loo. In modern times a new enthusiasm for landscaped public parks has been evident in Holland. In 1928 Het Amsterdamse Bos, or forest park, expanded a site of 285 hectares to 900 hectares at a cost of 18 million guilders. In 1970 it covered 1,200 hectares and further increase is thought likely to continue. It includes long cycleways, a riding-school and ornamental water.

Germany. 'The singular and deplorable Gallomania that pervaded Germany from prince to peasant' was lamented by C. C. L. Hirschfeld in the five volumes of his *Theorie der Gartenkunst* published simultaneously in French and German between 1779 and 1785. Instead he praised the 'happy changes made in England' in landscape gardening, quoting from Whately and other English books. They accorded well with the Romantic spirit evidenced in the writings of Novalis (1773–1801), A. W. Schlegel (1767–1845) and others, particularly Goethe. A surviving 'English Garden' from this period is that in Munich, designed by Louis Seckell and Count Rumford in 1789. There were others, such as those of Frankfurt praised by J. C. Loudon in 1834. No German aristocrat excelled Count, later Prince, Hermann Pückler-Muskau, an ardent visionary Romantic. Encouraged by Goethe, he began in 1811 at prodigious labour and expense to construct a huge landscaped parkland on his unpromising estate about 160 kilometres south-east of Berlin. His woods, rivers, lakes, meadows and flowers drew visitors from far and wide. Princes, Dukes and Duchesses sought his help. Others could read his *Hints on Landscape Gardening* (1835). Believing that 'art is the noblest thing in life', he thought that his creations at Muskau and his second astonishing achievement at his estate at Branitz in 1846 would cause his name 'to be mentioned for centuries with honour and love'.

Public works rather than private patrons now provide landscape gardeners in Germany with their greatest challenge, as landscaping is applied to industrial slag-heaps, motorways, canal tow-paths and town parks. Cologne's Green Belt of parkland was developed between 1905 and 1924, largely by the architect Fritz Enke. Others are the Rhein Park at Cologne, the Westfalen Park of Dortmund, the parks of Karlsruhe and the Schlossgarten in the middle of Stuttgart. Landscape gardening has become a highly specialized profession in Germany, where 18 months practical work is required as a preliminary to a four-year academic course. Many visitors have opportunities along the great new motorways to relish the pleasant effects of a harmonious co-operation between highway engineers and landscape gardeners so that the best use is made of earthworks and drainage courses to enhance rather than to diminish the beauty of the countryside by suitably placed screens of trees carefully selected for their varied foliage. At convenient intervals, often where there is a good viewpoint, a small space is provided where about a dozen cars at a time can pull in off the road for a pause or a picnic. Landscape gardening, created for the wealthy, now serves a vast and growing population, fostering and satisfying a new awareness of the aesthetic value of the countryside as well as conserving and enhancing natural beauty.

2. ENGLAND. 'Landscape Gardening' is a term which Humphry REPTON, the last of its three great British exponents, claimed to have introduced. He adopted it as a replacement for what had previously been called 'English Gardening', 'Modern Gardening', or sometimes 'Place-making', and he explained that he considered Landscape Gardening as 'most proper because the art can only be advanced and perfected by the united powers of the *landscape painter* and the *practical gardener*. The former must conceive a plan which the latter may be able to execute; for though a painter may represent a beautiful landscape on his canvass, and even surpass Nature by the combination of her choicest materials, yet the luxuriant imagination of the painter must be subjected to the gardener's practical knowledge in planting, digging and moving earth' (Introduction to *Sketches and Hints on Landscape Gardening*, 1795). While the pedant might point out a contradiction in Repton's description, since 'garden' derives from 'gard' or 'yard', an enclosed space, while 'landscape' embraces all that the eye can see at a glance, the phrase quickly passed into general usage as denoting the phenomenon which waxed and waned between the accession of George I and the last years of George III. There were, of course, signs and portents before 1714 and echoes after 1820; but it was during the intervening years that the cult of the landscape garden transformed a large part of the English countryside,

and thereby gave it much of the beauty which we take for granted today.

Up to the end of the 17th c. gardens in Britain were, generally speaking, enclosed areas, those of any size being divided with geometrical precision into terraces and parterres with small beds, usually edged with box and often containing not only flowers but pebbles, sand or even iron filings. There would probably be a bowling-alley, a pool or long canal, and hedges of clipped yew. Almost certainly the whole would be bounded by a high wall, within which the pleasaunce offered a retreat from unkempt, sometimes hostile, conditions prevailing beyond, for it has been estimated that more than half the countryside of that time was forest, heath, scrub or bog. Roads were often little more than cart tracks, overgrown in summer or deep in mud during the winter months, and making travelling hazardous. In the villages church, mansion and cottages usually huddled together as they had done from medieval times, and only in rare instances was a house of importance to be found in that isolated grandeur which in the following century came to be considered a desirable setting.

After the Restoration Charles II endeavoured to emulate the French monarch for whom Le Nôtre was transforming the surroundings of Versailles. There a vast acreage was laid out in a network of alleys, intersecting at *rond-points* and enlivened by statuary, while countless fountains cascaded into stone basins or canals. Louis XIV's employment of a sizeable part of his army for digging or transplanting several thousand fully grown trees was, however, something beyond the means of King Charles; yet at Hampton Court and St. James's Park he achieved in a remarkably short time two notable examples of formality on a grand scale. Samuel Pepys, who had watched the work at the latter in progress, noted 'the making a river through the Park', and was by 1668 able to enjoy walking along paths laid with 'the best gravell in the world'. He added that: 'Our business here being ayre, this is the best way, only with a little mixture of statues, or pots, which may be handsome.'

With the accession of William and Mary formality became even more rigid as those who sought to display their allegiance to the new regime took their models from Holland instead of France, pleaching their limes and fashioning their yews into the weird and wonderful shapes which were to become a butt for satire in the next generation. The accounts given by Celia Fiennes, that intrepid traveller who rode from one great house to another at the end of the century, confirm the similarity apparent in each, with 'rows of trees paled in gravel walks, fine cut hedges, flower-pots on walls, terraces, statues, fountains, basins, grass squares and exact, uniform plots'. And further evidence is provided by the delineations of Johannes Kip and Leonard Knyff.

There were, however, writers in the 2nd half of the 17th c. in whose works can be detected a growing discontent with this extreme formality. Sir William Temple, having retired from public life to Moor Park, Surrey, wrote of the charms of garden design as practised by the Chinese, 'without any order or disposition of parts, the successful effect of such scenes being termed "sharawadgi"' (*Upon the Gardens of Epicurus*, 1685). A painting of Temple's own garden, however, shows it to have been of the formal kind, while his friend Sir Thomas Browne, in whose *Garden of Cyrus* (1658) are passages praising the natural garden, nevertheless advocated the quincunx, or geometrical arrangement of trees in a network formation. 'What looks better than quincunx layout which is in line whichever way you look?' he asked. In short, despite their wide knowledge and love of gardening, the idea of naturalism held by these writers bore little resemblance to that which emerged after the turn of the century.

The concept of a garden devised as a succession of picturesque views grew out of artistic and philosophical ideals, but it was strongly reinforced by coincidence with a number of social and practical factors which also emerged early in the 18th c. The ascendancy of the Whig party, with a hierarchy composed of wealthy landowners anxious to assert their position by a display of palatial houses and grounds, new Acts for the inclosure of commons, advanced methods of husbandry and reclamation, better roads and lighter vehicles, all contributed to the new outlook in which 'improvement' became a counterpart of landscaping, while for the latter the temperate English climate provided ideal conditions for the essential media of trees, grass and water. To these concomitants was added the all-important revival of interest in Palladian architecture under the aegis of the Earls of Burlington and Pembroke, for whom the settings of houses were to become as important as the buildings themselves.

During the first years of the new century discontent with the old formality became increasingly outspoken, and several influential writers turned the thoughts of their readers towards adopting a freedom more in tune with current liberal philosophy and applying poetic and artistic concepts to their gardening activities. Sir John Vanbrugh, submitting a report to the Duchess of Marlborough on 11 June 1709, pressed for the retention of part of Old Woodstock Manor, and gave his view that 'were the inclosure filled with Trees (principally Fine Yews and Hollys) Promiscuously set to grow up in a Wild Thicket so that all the Building left . . . might appear in Two Risings amongst 'em, it would make one of the Most Agreeable Objects that the best of Landskip Painters can invent' (*Reasons for Preserving Part of the Old Manor*). Two years later the Whig philosopher Anthony Ashley Cooper, third Earl of Shaftesbury, expressed in his *Characteristics of Men, Manners, Opinions, Times* (1711) the view that 'rude Rocks, the mossy Caverns, the irregular unwrought Grottos, and broken falls of Waters . . . as representing Nature more, will be the more engaging and appear with a Magnificence beyond the formal mockery of princely Gardens'. In the same year Shaftesbury retired to Italy for his health, but his appreciation of nature continued to be upheld by Joseph Addison in the *Spectator* and subsequently by Richard Steele in the *Guardian*. Addison, deploring the 'mark of scissors upon every plant and bush', extolled the beauty of an unclipped tree 'in all its luxuriancy and diffusion of boughs and branches' (*Spectator*, no. 414, 25 June 1712). He also claimed to have adopted a 'natural' design for his own small estate at Bilton. How much of it was actually carried out cannot now be proved, but in his own words it had irregular plantations watered by a winding rill. 'My compositions in gardening', he explained, 'are altogether after the Pindaric manner and run into the beautiful wildness of nature' (*Spectator*, no. 477, 6 Sept. 1772). Elsewhere he advised others to follow this course: 'Why may not a whole Estate be thrown into a kind of garden by frequent Plantations? . . . If the *natural* embroidery of the meadows were helped and improved by some small additions of *Art* . . . a man might make a pretty *Landskape* of his own possessions.' A year later Stephen Switzer, a professional gardener and hydraulic engineer, advocated in his *Nobelman's, Gentleman's and Gardener's Recreation* (which was enlarged and reprinted in 1718 as *Iconographia Rustica*) that 'all the adjacent country be laid open to view', and that gardens should not be bounded with high walls 'by which the eye is as it were imprisoned and the feet fettered in the midst of the extensive charms of nature'.

At this point the advice which was being proffered seems suddenly to have taken hold; and while the long tradition of axial layout did not die overnight, the artificiality and the boundaries began to come down, allowing walks and rides to extend far into the adjoining countryside, while gravel gave way to turf and canals to meandering streams. In the proliferation of the new ideas there can be little doubt that a considerable part was played by the Kit Cat Club, that select coterie which assembled regularly to dine and exchange views in Jacob Tonson's rooms at Barn Elms. Since its members included on the one hand such advocates of a natural scene as Vanbrugh, Addison, Steele and Pope, and on the other many of the wealthiest landowners of the day, it is not surprising that the latter were soon influenced by the enthusiasm of the former. From 1715 the Dukes of Newcastle and Grafton, Lord Carlisle and Lord Cobham, Lord Scarborough, Sir Robert Walpole and General Dormer, all of whom were Kit Cat members, embarked on the transformation of their estates and set a fashion among their neighbours.

Of the early, or transitional, landscapes which have survived Cirencester Park, laid out by Lord Bathurst in frequent consultation with his friend Pope, is outstanding, as are the grounds of Studley Royal, which incorporate the ruins of Fountains Abbey, and the parks at Castle Howard and Bramham. These show how much had already been achieved before the fully fledged landscape emerged at the end of the 1720s when William Kent, Lord Burlington's protégé, assumed the joint role of architect and landscape gardener. Kent's earlier years had been given mainly to painting, in which he achieved only moderate success. A long period of study abroad had, however, given him a wide knowledge of the great landscape painters of the preceding century, and it was this which was to prove of value in his new venture, enabling him to visualize the setting of a house, and the views from its windows, as a series of pastoral scenes such as Claude and Salvator Rosa might have captured on canvas. He was, as Horace Walpole wrote later, 'painter enough to taste the charms of landscape, bold and opinionative enough to dare and to dictate, and born with a genius to strike out a great system from the twilight of imperfect essays' (*On Modern Gardening*, printed in *Anecdotes of Painting*, 1785). Kent, in fact, crystallized in his designs the ideal Claudian scene, although through a lack of practical experience they tended to lack extent and depth. His first garden work was for his patron, Lord Burlington, at Chiswick *c.* 1728, but other important commissions came quickly and in 1734 Sir Thomas Robinson wrote to his father-in-law, Lord Carlisle, that the gardens of Carlton House, Claremont and Stowe were full of labourers carrying out Kent's designs (Sir Thomas Robinson to the 4th Earl of Carlisle, R.C.H. MSS. Carlisle). Holkham and Esher Place were also in hand, and were followed by Badminton, Euston and Rousham. It was from Kent that two talented amateurs, the Hon. Charles Hamilton and Philip Southcote, derived inspiration for designing their own grounds at Pain's Hill and Woburn in Surrey, while Henry Hoare, the creator of Stourhead, must also have owed much to him, as must Lord Lyttleton at Hagley, and the poet William Shenstone at the Leasowes.

Many of the larger landowners were now planting in terms of 250 to 300 hectares with the result that a perceptible change was already taking place in the appearance of the countryside. Moreover a new dimension was added to the social life of the well-to-do, for a sizeable estate embellished with viewpoints, temples, rustic seats and inscribed urns invited perambulation either on foot or even by chaise along the turfed rides with which most were bounded. Even without the acquaintance of an owner production of a visiting card would often admit an interested visitor, and tours of houses and gardens became an increasingly popular diversion. In 1739 Francis Hare, Bishop of Chichester, wrote to his son: 'I promised your mamma to make a ramble with her of a few days to see some fine seats', and went on to describe their visits to Canons, Moor Park, Cranford, Dawley, Caversham and Richmond, where they were shown Merlin's Cave, recently completed for Queen Caroline to Kent's design (Francis Hare, Bishop of Chichester to his son Francis Naylor (Hare), R.C.H. MSS. Buckinghamshire, etc. 1895).

It was in the course of a somewhat similar country-house tour 13 years later that Horace Walpole made the first recorded comment on an early work of Lancelot BROWN, who was soon to become the most renowned of all landscape gardeners. 'Capability', as he later became known from his habit of referring to the capabilities of the places on which he was consulted, had recently laid out the grounds of Warwick Castle, which Walpole described in a letter to George Montagu as 'well laid out by one Brown who has set up on a few ideas of Kent . . .' (Horace Walpole to George Montagu, 22 July 1751. *Letters*, ed. P. Toynbee 1903–25). More than ten years spent in Lord Cobham's employment at Stowe had given Brown ample opportunity to assimilate Kent's theories, which he was to maintain but which he strengthened with his practical knowledge of horticulture. He was also to be influenced by two books which appeared soon after he had established his own practice. Hogarth's *Analysis of Beauty*, published in 1735, with its emphasis on the merits of the serpentine line—the 'line of beauty', as he termed it—and Burke's *A Philosophical Inquiry into the Origin of our Ideas of the Sublime and Beautiful* (1757), setting out the importance of variety in shape and colour, made an impact on landscaping aesthetics in general and on the development of Brown's mature style in particular. Of this style, with its broad, sweeping outlines, serpentine water and carefully planned contrasts, one of the outstanding characteristics was a grandeur of scale which carried Brown's works far beyond the limited acreage of Kent's designs and involved changes in terrain which the latter could never have undertaken. For over three decades he dominated the landscape scene with a practice which extended from Northumberland to Devon and which provided a model for those who made their own Elysian scenes.

Meanwhile the praises of nature as revealed in the landscape garden were sung by Dyer and Shenstone, Whitehead, Mason and countless other poets, while guide-books appeared for the more important gardens and a number of volumes were published on practical aspects of landscaping. One of the most notable of the latter was the Revd. William Hanbury's *Complete Body of Planting and Gardening* (1770), which illustrates the remarkably wide range of material which was by then available in the way of trees and shrubs. In the same year Thomas Whately produced the first edition of his *Observations on Modern Gardening*, which contained in its Introduction a useful summary of current principles as well as detailed descriptions of several of the finest gardens. Horace Walpole's essay with almost the same title, *On Modern Gardening*, was penned a few months later and in fact makes reference to Whately's book, but was not published until 1785, when it appeared as part of his *Anecdotes of Painting*. Walpole digressed on the history as well as on the recent development of his subject, and paid due tribute to William Kent—although he admitted that the latter's landscapes lacked greatness, largely owing to the 'novelty of his art'. He considered it fortunate that Kent had been succeeded by that 'very able master' Brown, by whose hand the landscape garden had arrived at its then happy state. 'How rich, how gay, how picturesque the face of the country!' he exclaimed. 'Every journey is made through a succession of pictures; and even where taste is wanting in the spot improved, the general view is embellished by variety. If no relapse to barbarism, formality, and seclusion is made, what landscapes will dignify every quarter of our island when the daily plantations that we are making have attained venerable maturity.'

Brown had in fact died two years before Walpole's essay was published, and another three were to pass before Humphry REPTON established himself as a landscape designer of consequence. Repton adopted Brown's tenets in general, but expanded them with theories of his own which he set out in a series of publications as well as in practice. While he was enjoying the first successes of his enterprise, however, the hitherto peaceful progress of his art was to be rudely shattered. The point at issue involved the nature of the word 'picturesque', which had previously been used in an adjectival sense, but was now elevated to a noun with a definite article and specific implications, over the precise interpretation of which writers argued and friendships were broken. No longer was it considered sufficient to compose a landscape in broad terms of lawn, lake and plantations, as Brown had done or Kent before him. The pundits now required—at least in their writings—that each design should produce subtleties of texture and colouring, strong contrasts of light and shade and appealing incident of a kind that would be suitable for a painter to emulate on canvas. Thus instead of the classical subjects of Claude and Salvator providing the models for the early and mid 18th-c. garden, the new ideal, its protagonists asserted, should reverse the process and provide subjects for the artist, in whose pictures water must no longer be shown as a lucid reflection of the sky but fretting its way over a rocky course, while the worthy peasant with his shaggy donkey and rustic cot replaced the nymphs and sheep of the Arcadian scene. The origins of this change in outlook are complex, but it was in a large measure due to the writings of the Revd. William Gilpin, a schoolmaster cleric who was a brother of the painter Sawrey Gilpin and himself an able draughtsman with a deep love of natural scenery.

Early in the 1770s William Gilpin 'discovered' the natural beauties of the river Wye as it flowed through Herefordshire, and by his *Observations on the River Wye*, published in 1782, popularized it to such an extent that several boats were made available to convey eager visitors along its course. The main purpose of this and several later essays was, however, to analyse the principles of picturesque beauty in general, somewhat on the lines of Burke's *Inquiry* nearly 30 years earlier. In 1792 Gilpin published three essays in one volume, entitled respectively 'Picturesque Beauty', 'Picturesque Travel', and 'Sketching Landscape'. In the first he set out his view that Beauty, by itself, was usually associated with the smooth and neat, in short the placid scenes achieved by Brown, whereas Picturesque Beauty implied roughness of texture and ruggedness in delineation. As an artist himself he found these latter qualities the more appealing. Garden scenes, he maintained, 'are never *picturesque*. They want the bold roughness of nature. A principal beauty in our *gardens*, as Mr. Walpole justly observes, is the smoothness of the turf; but in a *picture*, this becomes a dead and uniform spot; incapable of light and shade.' In spite of his preference, however, Gilpin was a gentle character with a liberal outlook, so that he could appreciate the man-made landscapes of Fonthill, Longleat—which he found noble—and Stourhead, being 'much pleased' with the latter, which he thought showed 'greatness in the design'. He must therefore have been more than a little surprised by the animosity which suddenly developed among garden enthusiasts and which came to a head in 1794 following the publication of works by his two friends, Richard Payne KNIGHT of Downton, and Uvedale PRICE of Foxley. Unlike Gilpin these two Herefordshire squires were men of strong opinions, and both Knight's didactic poem *The Landscape*, and Price's *Essay on the Picturesque* castigated the earlier landscape school in general and Brown in particular. Even Repton, with whom both had previously been on good terms, came in for a scathing comment by Price, to which he was able to reply in a footnote hastily inserted in his own book *Sketches and Hints on Landscape Gardening*, which was about to go to press at the beginning of 1795. In this he maintained that while he fully appreciated many of the qualities extolled by the new theorists, commonsense must prevail; and that while mouldering abbeys and the antiquated cottage with its chimney smothered with ivy may be eminently appealing to the painter, 'in whatever relates to man, propriety and convenience are not less objects of good taste than picturesque effect'. In 1801 Knight took offence at a comment in one of Price's later publications published in that year, *A Dialogue on the Distinct Characters of the Picturesque and Beautiful*, resulting in yet another estrangement and amazing the onlookers of this philosophical battle by the heat and bitterness which it generated. To Daniel Malthus, Price and Knight appeared 'more like Luther and Calvin than a couple of west country gentlemen talking of gravel walks and syringas', while Shelley, in a letter to Thomas Love Peacock, likened them to 'ill-trained beagles . . . snarling at each other when they could not catch the hare' (Percy Bysshe Shelley to Thomas Love Peacock, 21 Mar. 1821). Horace Walpole, who, as might be expected, remained a firm supporter of the old school, seems not to have read *The Landscape* until two years after its publication, by which time he was just on eighty. Intensely irritated by what he considered an 'insolent and self conceited Poem . . . by a trumpery prosaic poetaster', he besought William Mason to compose a reply in defence of Brown. But the latter, no doubt feeling that he had expressed his views well enough in his *English Garden*, published in the previous decade, now decided to keep silent. A vituperative poem *Addressed to Richard Payne Knight Esq.* had, however, already appeared anonymously, but probably came from the pen of John Matthews of Belmont, a house which has now gone but stood in landscaped grounds on the outskirts of Hereford. This 'doggerel ode' was in turn attacked by Knight in a second edition of *The Landscape*.

For Peacock and several other writers the cult of the picturesque offered a topic for gentle satire, and in *Headlong Hall* Marmaduke Milestone and Sir Patrick O'Prism represent the opposing schools of thought while Squire Headlong nearly liquidates several of his guests in his hurry to blow up an outcrop of rock and thereby make his grounds more in keeping with current ideas. Jane Austen's knowledge of the arguments is revealed by several passages in her books. In *Mansfield Park* she not only mentions Repton by name but makes her characters discuss at length the improvement of Sotherton and Thornton Lacey; while in *Sense and Sensibility* Marianne Dashwood and Edward Ferrers air their divergent views, Marianne opining that 'everybody pretends to feel and tries to describe it [the landscape] with the taste and elegance of him who first defined what picturesque beauty was'. Edward, however, comes down firmly on the side of the Brownian school by replying that he likes a fine prospect but 'not on picturesque principles. I do not like crooked, twisted, blasted trees. I admire them much more if they are tall, straight and flourishing. I am not fond of nettles or thistles or heath blossoms.'

In spite of the vast number of words and strong feelings expended on it, the cult of the picturesque was to remain almost entirely a literary manifestation and had comparatively little practical application. Payne Knight created his own ideal in the natural contours of Downton, but in general few owners were endowed with the overhanging crags, swiftly flowing streams, gnarled oaks and tortuous paths which supporters of the new aesthetic admired. In the less dramatic situations prevailing in many counties Repton's brand of landscaping, with gentle undulations, luxuriant plantations and smooth lawns, enlivened where possible with deer or cattle, sufficed for the taste of their owners, and long after the dust created by Price and Knight had settled, he was busily engaged with commissions. Ill health following an accident eventually brought his practice to a close, and during his last years as an invalid he became conscious of a decline which was affecting the landscape movement as a whole. The advent of the Industrial Revolution with its attendant changes in social and economic conditions was unpropitious for the continuance of a leisurely art. In his last book, *Fragments on the Theory and Practice of Landscape Gardening*, published in 1816, Repton noted the recent tendency to shut out the public. 'Formerly', he wrote, 'I can recollect the art being complimented as likely to extend its influence till all England would become one landscape garden; and it was then the pride of a country gentleman to show the beauties of his place to the public, as at Audley End, Shardeloes, and many other celebrated parks through which public roads were purposely made to pass and the views displayed by means of sunk fences.' The new class of owner was not interested in such things. Much occupied with business and with little time to spare, he asked for quick results and found more pleasure in an acre or two of lawn studded with laurels, monkey puzzles and beds containing a bright display of annuals.

James Claudius LOUDON, who was born in 1783, showed an early interest in the landscape, but proved to have no real aptitude for it and eventually made his name by his botanical studies in the 1820s and his architectural encyclopedias of the following decade. A few echoes of the landscape-gardening tradition can be traced in such development projects as Decimus Burton's Calverley Park at Tunbridge Wells (1828) and Charles Barry's uncompleted scheme for Queen's Park, Brighton (*c.* 1829), while a late instance appeared, most surprisingly, from the hand of that arch-Victorian Joseph Paxton at Birkenhead Park (*c.* 1851).

Towards the end of the 19th c. William Robinson and Gertrude Jekyll fostered a revival of naturalism in the garden with the planting of bulbs in drifts rather than beds and groups of flowering shrubs in dells and woodland walks, which could be said to echo the past. The great landscape garden, however, was made up of far more than informality in planting, and neither the social conditions nor the genius which brought it to life in the 18th c. are likely ever to occur again.

3. ISLAMIC. Like nearly all nomads Muhammad's first followers, the desert Arabs, knew nothing of horticulture or pleasure gardens. But Islamic religious fervour did not involve an asceticism in rejection of earthly and sensual enjoyments such as was imposed by early Christianity; so the impetuous Arabs, as they burst in upon the Middle East, were able to learn from the lands they conquered in a way that Christians could not when they in turn fought Islam. If the gardens of Alexandria mentioned by Strabo survived into Byzantine times, they seem to have made no impression upon the Arabs who destroyed the city in A.D. 641. But in Persia the results of their conquest were very much more fruitful. When Al-Mansur (?712–75), second Abbassid Caliph, established Baghdad on the Tigris (762) he added a garden of Persian inspiration to his Palace of Eternity which was said to rival the promised Paradise gardens of the Koran. The Persians had a garden tradition of great antiquity. They were encouraged by the religion of Zoroaster to plough, sow, irrigate and plant trees—activities thought demeaning to an Arab nomad. Iran had many areas abounding in an immense variety of splendid wild flowers with a scented glory that was to make the fortune of many European gardens—jonquils, hyacinths, lilies-of-the-valley, daffodils, marigolds, gillyflowers, red ranunculi, iris, delphiniums and others. Above all there were roses of great fertility and powerful scent. It was a land of contrasts where the arid treeless steppes of the Iranian plateau with its winter cold made the wealth of spring flowers in the mountain valleys all the more enchanting. Such plants were sought and collected to grace the gardens in which the Persians sought a private, enclosed retreat from the cares of the world and the heat and burdens of their days. Life could be tragic in such a land situated on the cross-roads between East and West. Despite fierce conflicts with Turks and Arabs, and the horrors of invasion by the savage Mongols, traditional garden art survived to carry forward into many lands their garden form of great antiquity, the wide right-angled cross said to represent the Four Quarters of the Universe separated by four great rivers. This ancient symbolism appeared also on the CARPETS of Persia that brought a vivid memory of a summer garden into the homes. A most famous carpet in this manner, depicting every beautiful sweet-scented flower and adorned with precious stones, was the vast Winter carpet *c.* 17 m square of King Chosroes I (531–79), the great Sassanid warrior. Cherished by his successors, it fell as booty to the invading Arabs, whereupon Caliph Omar had it cut up in 637 so that he could give pieces of it as reward to his warriors. No carpet earlier than the 17th c. has survived, but literary sources, miniature paintings and archaeological discoveries confirm the antiquity and the persistence of the flower-garden pattern in their design.

Every Persian garden had a fine pool of water as its central feature. A large garden might have more than one. Often raised above the level of the ground, these pools had to be kept full to the brim and therefore the edges had to be uniformly level. A subterranean channel, the

Quanat line, brought the water, often from the foot of a mountain. Shade from the fierce rays of the sun was essential, so trees were indispensable—planes, oaks, elms, maples, willows, pines and cypresses were the chief. Fruit trees, prized for their blossoms quite as much as for their summer fruits, were general also. They included cherry, almond, apricot, peach, plum, fig, orange, lemon, lime, quince, pistachio, pomegranate and filbert. Lilac, myrtle and other flowering shrubs were also planted. Much pleasure was derived in Islamic gardens from the play of reflected light and the leaves mirrored in the pool. Miniature paintings from the 15th c. onwards depict flowers glowing brightly under the shade of trees and along the cruciform watercourses. Characteristic of Islamic gardens was the practice of sinking flower-beds below the level of the paths so that visitors seemed to be walking on a splendid coloured carpet while the view of other features was not obstructed by vegetation. As in other civilizations, flowers accompanied festive merry-making, feasting and rejoicing. Tulips, pinks, carnations, jasmine and roses were very generally planted. Probably climatic conditions accounted for the general absence of grass lawns.

Natural beauty was augmented by physical means. Coloured glazed tiles had from time immemorial been used in the art of western Asia. As adornments to walls and patios they heightened the colour and attraction of the garden scene, particularly in the strong sunlight of a Persian summer. Shelter from the heat and glare of the sun was essential, so the shade provided by trees was supplemented by garden pavilions or 'kiosks', a word of Turkish origin. Such kiosks have been credited to Mongol invaders whose Far Eastern origin would have made them familiar with the Chinese way of life in which lake pavilions and garden kiosks were general. Some Persian pavilions of the wealthy were large and nobly designed. Another seeming link with China was the poetry of Persian garden names, such as 'Garden of the Nightingale', 'Garden of Heart's Ease', 'Garden of the Glory of the World'.

As in ancient Persia, gardens were enlivened by decorative birds—swans, pelicans, pheasants, ducks, pigeons and others—while the larger ones held deer as in the old royal 'paradise' hunting parks. All these many aids to pleasurable sensation satisfied not a desire for beauty alone but also an underlying poetical feeling and mystic fervour, thus blending religious and aesthetic considerations. Generations of Persian poets celebrated flowers and gardens in a manner recalling the spirit in which Herrick and Wordsworth later wrote in England. From such a fountain-head of feeling for garden arts the followers of Islam spread the cult of gardens to other parts of the empire. Other cultural interests were notably developed by the more intellectually alert Arabic-speaking peoples subject to Islamic rule just as peoples of western Europe had learned Latin and honoured the gods of Rome. Berbers, Christians, Jews and Byzantine minorities were among them. In Spain Islamic civilization brought an immensely fertilizing cultural influence from the East. Córdoba, founded in 750, began within two or three generations to rival the magnificence of Baghdad. Before its capture by Christians in 1034, after which it swiftly declined, three centuries of peaceful co-operation between Berbers (Moors), Jews and Christians had, it was alleged with evident exaggeration, created 200,000 houses, 600 mosques, 900 baths and 50,000 gardens in and around the city. Of them all, including a university and public and private libraries, nothing remains save the vast mosque and the tradition of glazed and coloured tiles and small fountains preserved in many a Spanish patio. Refugees from Córdoba, Seville, Valencia and other Islamic centres fled to Kamatta or Granada in its mountain valley until it also was eventually captured in 1492. Among the scanty remains of Islamic civilization still to be seen are the palace of Alhambra and the Generalife on the hill above. Often regarded, like the Palace Garden at Seville, as the creation of Islamic Moorish designers, they have been pronounced to be modern, planned in the Renaissance style followed by Le Nôtre, and completely foreign to the Muslim style. Investigations after a fire in 1958 revealed the original design of the Islamic garden in the Patio de la Acequia, but it was obliterated once more by a modern garden. A Moorish water-staircase above it is all that remains. Reporting this in 1968, J. Dickie stated that one informal Islamic garden had survived between Granada and Motril (*Journal of the School of Oriental Studies*, xxxi, 1968, 237–48).

Arabic literature, despite its repeated invocation of flowers and gardens, is almost silent about the nature of the vanished Islamic gardens. Dickie reported two passages only, of the 11th and 14th centuries. Among references to the 52 commonest flowers he met with jasmine, violet, mauve stock, pheasant-eye narcissus, wallflower, rose, lily, iris, water-lily, marguerite, poppy, lavender, carnation, thyme, mint, saffron. Flowering trees and shrubs included almond, pomegranate, myrtle, laurel, pear, plum, mulberry, medlar, quince, apple, fig, cherry, vine. Islamic Moors have been credited with introducing some of these; but most were known in Roman times, although some may have disappeared during the Dark Ages. Apricots, bananas, spinach, artichokes, rice, sugar-cane and the silk-worm were probably due to Islamic influence. But whatever the extent and variety of Islamic gardens may once have been in Spain, their creation by the infidel and their ministration to sensuous, worldly enjoyment doomed them in Christian Spain even supposing that the invading Christians had possessed sufficient skill to maintain them together with the irrigation and terracing upon which many of them depended. How diametrically opposed Islamic and Christian ideas were may be seen in the funereal gloom of the Escorial (1562–84).

Islamic gardens, lost to Europe, were soon carried to the East, where they were splendidly magnified and perpetuated by the Islamic rulers of northern India beginning with Zehir-ed-Din Muhammad Barbur, who invaded Hindustan in 1524. He was a Muslim Turk from Afghan, regarded by the Indians as a Mogul. He and his descendants until the end of the 17th c. created gardens that survived, despite neglect, far better than the Islamic gardens of Spain. His *Memoirs* testify to his enthusiasm for flowers, trees and gardens. He had already made a great garden near Kabul and he vaunted the garden joys of Samarkand. Dismayed by the lack of anything similar in Hindustan, he set about remedying the defect with a large *charbagh*, a garden with the fourfold Persian symbolism, which included a pool and a great well, at Agra in 1526. *Bagh*, the Persian word for garden, was adopted in India, where early Sanskrit had no word for the pleasure garden it denotes. He and his chief followers created many more gardens by the Jumna river, bringing gardeners and plants from Afghanistan. Mogul gardens begun by Barbur had their greatest development under his successors Akbar (1556–1605), Jahangir (1605–27) and Shah Jahan (1627–58). Despite conspiracies, violence, rebellions and war, Mogul art, architecture and literature also flourished. In the glorious valley of Kashmir, annexed in 1586, a new stimulus was given to the desire for scenic beauty and exotic plants. Jahangir's wife, Nur Jahan ('Light of the World'), did more for gardens in Hindustan than Jahangir would have achieved alone. For her daughter-in-law, Mumtaz Mahal, their son Shah Jahan created the Taj Mahal, one of the wonders of the world, whose architectural magnificence dwarfs the noble garden beside which it was set out on the banks of the Jumna. With him, a fanatical Muslim, Islamic cultural inspiration began to flag. This decline was swift under his feeble successors. In 1761 Clive stepped in to rescue the land from further invasion and anarchy, whereafter the great Mogul gardens slowly decayed.

7, 8, 35, 147, 151, 207, 237, 275, 332, 387, 389, 427, 430, 431, 438, 542, 566, 568, 628, 804, 805, 806, 811, 903.

LANGLEY, BATTY (1696–1751). English architect and designer, author of some 20 architectural books which were for the most part manuals for country builders and artisans. With his brother Thomas (b. 1702), an engraver, he set up a school of architectural drawing in Soho *c.* 1740. In the same year he published *The City and Country Builder's and Workman's Treasury of Designs*, which contained 400 plates, many of them for furniture, some of which were closely based on plates by French designers such as BÉRAIN and MAROT. He is best known as an exponent of the GOTHIC taste. In *Gothic Architecture Restored and Improved* (1741) he formalized KENT's Neo-Gothic into five Orders, which were condemned by Horace Walpole. His book *The Builder's Director or Bench-Mate*, which contained many details of Gothic ornament and buildings, had a considerable circulation among country builders and craftsmen, serving to spread the knowledge of Gothic ornament among them.

LANNUIER, CHARLES-HONORÉ (1779–1819). French cabinet-maker who emigrated to the U.S.A. in 1803 and was active in New York from then until his death. He worked in the French DIRECTOIRE and EMPIRE styles and was influential in establishing the American Empire Style. His furniture was characterized by the use of metal MOUNTS imported from France.

LANTERN CLOCKS. These were the English and French successors of the GOTHIC CLOCK and were popular throughout the 17th c. In form they are generally similar to the Gothic clock but they are made almost wholly of brass and the Gothic mouldings and decorations have disappeared. The time-keeping, as with Gothic clocks, was at first controlled by a wheel foliot, but after the invention of the pendulum in 1656 most later examples were designed for pendulum control, and many earlier examples were converted. In spite of the improved time-keeping given by the pendulum, very few were provided with an additional minute-hand.

LAPIS LAZULI. A complex mineral which was prized as a gemstone in the ancient world and was the original source of the colour ultramarine. (See COLOURS AND COLOURANTS.) From the 4th millennium B.C. it was used in jewellery by the Sumerians, the ancient Egyptians, the Assyrians and the Greeks. The Greek 'sappheiros' and the 'sapphire' of the Old Testament were probably lapis lazuli. It was mined in antiquity in the Badakhshan region of Afghanistan. Modern sources are also in Siberia and Chile.

Lapis lazuli is often speckled with grains of iron pyrites, which have sometimes been mistaken for gold (Pliny, Marco Polo). It sometimes has inclusions of hornblende and augite, which make it difficult to work. Pieces of deep uniform blue are preferred and these are not common. Lapis lazuli has been used for beads, stones and seals for rings and brooches and for decorative inlay; larger pieces have been carved into bowls and vases, handles for cutlery, and so on. Some of the furniture in the tomb of Tutankhamun contains inlay and mosaic of lapis lazuli. By order of Catherine II of Russia the walls of a room in one of the Tsar's palaces were covered with slabs of lapis lazuli and AMBER.

LASALLE, PHILIPPE DE (1723–1803). SILK-designer and technician, the creator of the most splendid of the furnishing silks woven at Lyon during the 2nd half of the 18th c. His compositions of flower garlands, ribbons, musical instruments and birds are gay yet dignified, naturalistic yet exquisitely artificial. After enjoying the patronage of Louis XV, Louis XVI, Catherine the Great, the Court of Spain and the exiled King of Poland, he was ruined by the French Revolution and retired into obscurity.

LATTICINO GLASS. A development of LATTIMO GLASS where threads of opaque milky white glass were alternated with clear glass. When the pattern formed a fairly simple network design this was known as *vitro de trina*. When the pattern was more complex, creating a lacy effect, it was known as *vitro a reticelli.*

LATTIMO GLASS. An opaque or semi-opaque milky white glass made in Murano, Venice, from *c.* 1500 and akin to the German MILCHGLAS. It was often used as a background for enamel painting. Towards the end of the 17th c. it was often exploited as a substitute for Chinese PORCELAIN. Two families particularly associated with this type of glass were the Miottis and the Bertolinis.

LAUB- UND BANDELWERK (German: foliate and strapwork). Term for an ornamental motif representing the last phase of BAROQUE ACANTHUS-leaf pattern, in which the foliage becomes more delicate and is interspersed with interlacing straps. Introduced by Jean BÉRAIN and Daniel MAROT towards the end of the 17th c., it gained considerable currency among designers during the 1st quarter of the 18th c. It was also known as *Régence.*

LEADWORK. Lead is easily mined and manipulated and almost endlessly durable, but so soft that its uses to the craftsman are very limited. Its obvious practical applications—for roofs, cisterns, pipes, and coffins—were well known to the Romans. Ever since the Roman occupation lead has been mined in Britain and exported, and it is probable that during the Middle Ages it was more widely used there for architectural decoration than in any other European country. Spires and roofs were covered with strips of lead in striking herring-bone patterns. But the most interesting use of the metal was for baptismal fonts, which were produced in large numbers during the 12th and early 13th centuries. In design they are much like the stone fonts of the 12th c., with ornamental foliage or with figures under an arcade of round-headed arches. Some of them are striking examples of ROMANESQUE art, e.g. those at Dorchester and Walton-on-the-Hill, and several in Gloucestershire which are cast from the same mould. Lead fonts continued to be made as late as the 15th c., but they did not again achieve the same high standard.

As has been said, the extreme softness of lead has always limited the number of uses to which it could be put. In Germany the most interesting development of the 16th c. was the use of lead for plaquettes. These were produced by artists such as Peter FLÖTNER and Hans JAMNITZER from models carved in boxwood or Solnhofer stone or modelled in wax. Moulds were taken from the models and from these lead casts were made and sold to goldsmiths throughout western Europe. For this purpose lead had the advantage that a perfect impression could be obtained by casting and no after-chiselling was required. The lead plaquettes were employed as models for embossed decoration and their circulation accounts for the exact repetition of subjects by goldsmiths in widely separated cities. The most complete collection of lead goldsmiths' models, other than plaquettes, is preserved in the Amerbachisches Kunstkabinett, Historisches Museum, Basle. In England rain-water pipe heads of lead have been a prominent feature of country houses since the 15th c. Those of the 16th c. were ornamented with rather unimaginative GOTHIC tracery and with decorative ciphers, but in the following century they became important features of architectural ornament, bearing the coat-of-arms of the owner of the house often, as may still be seen in the Oxford colleges, picked out in colour. At the same time lead rain-water cisterns were to be found in most country houses, though few now remain in their original position at the foot of rain-water pipes. Their ornament is almost invariably in the form of STRAPWORK of Jacobean character, and remained unchanged until well into the 18th c.

During the 17th c. lead was increasingly used as a material for garden sculpture, and lead figures were produced by sculptors such as Adriaen de Vries and Hubert Gerhard as well as by anonymous craftsmen whose work was less than mediocre. In England the leading artist–craftsmen in the production of garden statuary and vases were the two John Van Nos, father and son, active during the latter part of the 17th and the early decades of the 18th c. The fashion for lead vases for garden ornaments persisted throughout the 18th c. and examples of every form of vase or urn from BAROQUE to NEO-CLASSICAL are to be found in country houses. In Germany and Austria artists of the calibre of Andreas Schlüter and Balthasar Moll designed monumental lead coffins for members of the houses of Brandenburg and Habsburg respectively. These still survive and rank as the most ambitious works of art in lead.

LEATHERCRAFT. Some knowledge of what leather is and what properties it can be made to possess is essential to the understanding of what can be done with it and to an appreciation of the craftsmanship involved in its products. Leather is a man-made material, yet it is made from an organic substance—the skin of a once living creature—which is without parallel in nature or artifice. In its natural state the pelt of a dead animal is virtually useless, liable to rapid putrefaction if it remains wet, and a hard, horny, intractable substance if dried out. In prehistoric times men discovered how to isolate the essential fabric from the tripartite structure of the skin, to preserve this from decay and to impart to it a still increasing range of properties. Leather of a primitive kind was among man's first manufactures after the earliest Palaeolithic stone tools and implements which made it possible.

Leather has a sensuous appeal of its own. Its nature is to be strong yet flexible, though in varying degrees. According to the manner in which it has been made it can be as firm (but still slightly supple) as sole leather for heavy-duty boots or it can be as mellow and clinging as the softest velvet and suitable for use as clothing. Because of the nature of its fibrous structure it is amenable to a wide range of manipulative processes, of which one of the most remarkable is its capacity to be moulded into intricate shapes and to set permanently in them.

Leather is made from the middle layer of the hide (of larger beasts) or skin (of smaller ones), which is called the *corium*. First the hides or skins are soaked in lime and water, which loosens the hair or wool so that it can be easily scraped off and also brings the *corium* into a condition which makes it readily receptive of the processes which follow. Next the outer layer is scraped off. This is the epidermal system, hair follicles, fat and sweat glands, hair erector muscles and blood vessels. Finally the adipose tissue, by which the skin was attached to the flesh of the animal, is cut away. The *corium* which remains is a wonderful texture of microscopic collagen fibrils which are grouped together into fine fibres and these in turn into bundles of some 25 to 50 fibres each. These fibre bundles are woven together in every direction and are enveloped with a fine, filamentous network called the reticular tissue. It is this complex fibrous structure which, when isolated, is turned into leather by any of several processes which are collectively though loosely called tanning. Tanning consists, basically, in protecting the *corium* against corruption and imparting to it, by a variety of means covered by the term 'dressing', characteristics from which it derives its ultimate properties, such as strength, flexibility, plasticity and resistance to water, without sacrificing its breathing capacity.

The *corium* can be protected from putrefaction by any of three basic and very ancient methods or by a combination of two of them: (1) by steeping in solutions containing tannin, the name given to a group of astringent substances present in varying degrees in barks, leaves and nuts and possessing the property of combining with the gelatin in hide substance (collagen fibres); (2) by steeping in solutions of certain mineral salts, of which alum was the first to be used; (3) by impregnation with fish or marine animal oils, which under heat and pressure develop products that effectively protect the fibres. The three methods produce leathers of quite different character. The first process is called vegetable tannage, the second mineral tannage or 'tawing' and the third oil tannage, known formerly as 'chamoising' from the fact that it was mainly used on chamois skins to produce washable leathers for clothing, gloves and pouches. These three processes are still the basis of tanning. But all three have been extensively developed, particularly in recent years, and important advances have been made with combination tannages by means of which the characteristics of two different processes can be combined to impart to the leather special properties which have enormously widened its uses. Such uses are primarily industrial and therefore outside the scope of this article; for example, the use of pliable, water-resistant leather for footwear uppers, the leather diaphragms which measure gas in meters and last many years without attention, and protective gloves made from leathers specially developed to resist acid or heat. The principal leathers employed in fields which offer scope for craftsmanship are vegetable tanned. They include:

HIDE LEATHERS

Sole bends (i.e. the half of a back): firm, dry

Photomicrograph section of vegetable-tanned sole leather (cattle hide) showing the fibrous structure (mag. × 15)

dressed leather of fine quality, compacted by hammering or rolling, without surface finish.

Harness or strap backs (i.e. the main part of the hide after removal of the belly and shoulder): dressed with grease (curried) to render them strong and supple.

Bag or case leathers: made from split hides (i.e. reduced in substance to *c.* 1·5 to 2 mm) dry dressed (with some exceptions), the surface being coloured by dyeing or staining and either made smooth and glossy by plating (i.e. pressing by machine with a heated, highly polished metal plate) or embossed with an artificial grain, of which there are many varieties.

Upholstery hide: soft dressed, 'boarded' leather, today almost always coloured by a film of pigmented nitro-cellulose with a suitable grain. (The process of boarding consists of folding the leather grain to grain and rolling it in two directions with a cork-covered board. An analogous process is now done by machines.)

SKIN LEATHERS

Calf: a soft, fine-grain leather finished in a great variety of colours and surface grains.

Modelling calf: a fine-quality leather without any kind of surface finish or colouring.

Morocco leather: goatskin tanned with sumach, the natural grain being brought up to a characteristic pebbly surface by boarding or alternatively a long grain produced by boarding but only in one direction. The surface is coloured by a variety of different methods.

Mineral-tanned leathers and other leathers produced by a combination of mineral and vegetable tanning are principally used for footwear uppers, women's handbags, soft washable clothing and for certain industrial purposes. The ancient alum-'tawed' leathers, once so largely used for gloves and pouches, have been supplanted by white washable leathers made by modern processes employing salts of zirconium or formaldehyde, and apart from their use for women's gloves are outside the scope of this article. Chamoised or oil-dressed leathers are now largely limited to the so-called 'shammy' leather, made from the under split of sheep or lamb skins and used for gloves or for cleaning windows or cars.

These, then, are in outline the principal methods by which leather is produced from animal pelts. The following sections are devoted to the various ways in which leathers can be manipulated, utilized and ornamented.

CUTTING. In the first place the would-be worker in leather needs to become familiar with the physical properties of the leather or leathers he is to use, their superficial appearance, their 'feel' and their degree of pliability and stretch. Leathers will normally stretch more from side to side, across the pelt, than from neck to tail. And this feature is more noticeable in *skins* of small animals (e.g. sheep, goat and pig) than in *hides* of large animals (such as cattle, horse or buffalo). Skins intended for gloves are so dressed that they possess what glove-makers call 'run', i.e. the leather stretches when pulled but does not spring back when the pull ceases, and also the property that the stretch in one direction is eliminated when the leather is pulled in the opposite direction. It is important too to realize that the best part of a hide or skin is the back and the weakest is the softer and thinner belly, while the shoulder usually provides leather of good quality but apt to be marked, often conspicuously, by creases resulting from the movement of head and neck of the animal when alive. These and other natural features such as barbed-wire scratches, growth marks and healed holes left by warbles from the gad-fly larvae, affect the manner in which a hide or skin is cut. The requirements of cutting are also, of course, influenced by the nature of the object to be made and the nature of its component parts. For instance the main body of a document case or certain kinds of bags and pouches should be cut from the best part, i.e. the back, whereas gussets, which have to be folded and will frequently flex, need to be of thinner and softer leather. Thus cutting up a hide or skin is an art in itself. In addition to weak places, scars and flesh cuts, both hides and skins may vary in colour or grain and must be examined on both sides so that what is cut may not only be economical of the material but also suitable for the use for which it is intended. It must also be taken into consideration that no matter what care the leather producer has taken to equalize the product, its thickness will almost certainly vary to some extent from one part to another, so that the final adjustment to the requirements will have to be made by splitting or skiving. Splitting can be done only by machine, even if only a small hand-splitter. Skiving was originally accomplished only by a highly skilled hand operation, but is now chiefly done with small power-driven machines.

There are many different kinds of leather-cutting knives, both general-purpose knives and knives which have been gradually evolved for particular needs. The most ancient, descended from an ancient Egyptian knife *c.* 1500 B.C., is the half-moon knife with its several variants.

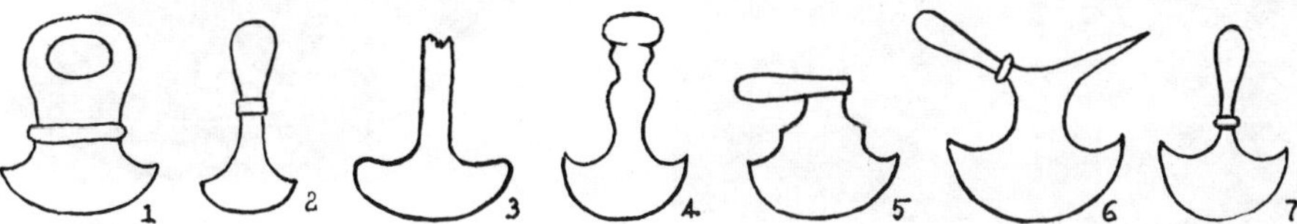

Various forms of half-moon knife: 1 and 2, Egyptian; 3, Iron Age, from La Tène; 4, Pompeian; 5 and 6, medieval European; 7, modern

Why this particular form was evolved is something of a mystery. It cannot be said to fulfil any one specific purpose with distinction, although in skilled hands by gradually moving from one end of its curved cutting edge to the other (e.g. when cutting a long strap from heavy hide) a consistently sharp edge can be brought into play, whilst its broad flat surface held vertically serves as a useful directional guide. This knife is used without a straight edge of wood or metal such as is sometimes employed along with a small knife, but it follows a guiding line marked on the surface of the leather with a blunt awl. Some workers also use it as a skiving knife, holding the blade more or less horizontally. It is certainly not a tool for the amateur. But perhaps the cutting knife in most general use is the American 'clicking knife', which may have derived its name from the sound it makes as the cutter releases it with a turn of the wrist when cutting on a wooden bed. The handle is in two parts that screw together tightening a pair of jaws on to the blade, which is a flat piece of steel about 9 mm wide carried in a slot right through the handle. The cutting edge is on a hollow curve ground out on one side of the blade near the top so as to leave a sharp point, and this business end can be made to protrude from the jaws to whatever length the cutter requires. Many a simple knife has been made from a strip of suitable steel, about 2·5 cm wide, with a cutting edge ground at 45 degrees at one end, the opposite end having a strip of leather wound round it to form a hand-grip.

Not all cutting serves merely a utilitarian purpose. From very early times cutting has been used as a means of decoration and sometimes decorative and useful functions have been combined. A remarkable example of this comes from ancient Egypt *c.* 1500 B.C., namely gazelle skins cut into a fine network with an uncut border round the edges. The skins were thin and soft and at this period the knives can only have been of copper, which required constant hammering to keep the edges sharp. One slip and the whole skin would have been ruined, for it would have been impossible to join broken strands. The purpose of this leather netting is unknown. In murals men—generally sailors or men in some way connected with boats—are shown wearing these nettings as loin-cloths, but the use of such delicate and costly objects for this purpose seems curious. Also astonishing were the Roman *sicyonia* (see p. 437), or shoes of Sicyon, designed for women but worn also by foppish men. These had open-work uppers attached to a clumsy sole formed of three pieces of thick hide joined together with hob-nails such as was also used for sandals. The delicate open-work is beautifully cut without regard to economy of time or material (the pieces cut out could have been of little use for anything else) and all the cut edges have been edge-tooled, i.e. given a tiny bevel. No less remarkable is a pierced shoe from the same period, in which the tiny triangular holes are not, as might be thought, punched out with a metal tool but are painstakingly and individually cut out, perhaps with a knife specially designed for the job. The perfection of this cutting is a *tour de force*. Examples of decorative cutting also come from Ireland *c.* the beginning of the Christian era. A shoe is decorated in an astonishing manner by means of incised lines, some in parallel, cut down to about half the thickness of the leather, which causes the cuts to open and become conspicuous. Other fine examples of leathercraft survive from the early Christian period in Ireland, including budgets or satchels for religious manuscripts, and probably all this work was monastic in origin (see J. W. Waterer, *Medieval Archaeology*, xii, 1968). Such fine handwork is found only in early leathercraft. The practice of piercing leather for practical purposes (ventilation) as well as for

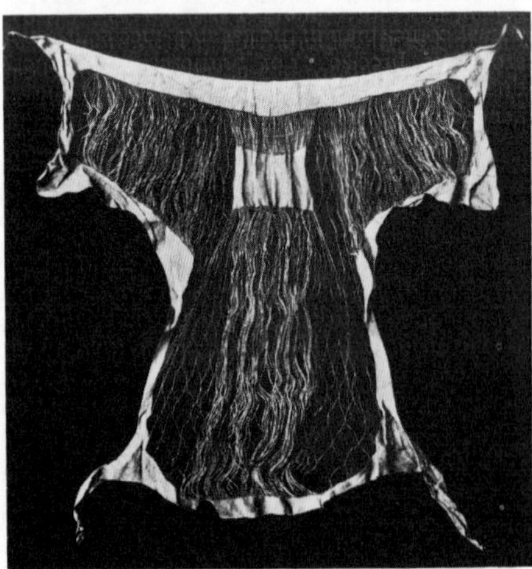

Egyptian network of gazelle skin. (Field Mus. of Natural History, Chicago)

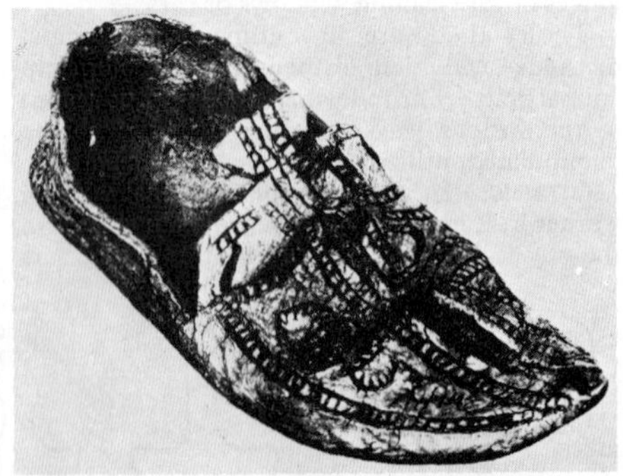

Irish shoe from a single piece of cattle hide with ornament cut to about half the thickness of the leather. Early Christian period. (Nat. Mus. of Ireland)

decoration continued through the medieval period and probably without a break into modern times, but it was mostly done with iron punches.

SKIVING. This operation consists in thinning down or reducing the substance of the leather from the flesh side and serves many purposes. It may be done to thin down a piece of leather all over its area or simply at one place or to form a chamfer with a feather edge for a scarfe joint or a turned edge. There are several kinds of skiving knives (or the half-moon knife described above may be used). For most work a broad blade is used with a bevel to the cutting edge on the upper surface only. Good skiving consists in cutting away successive exceedingly thin slices until the desired effect has been achieved.

EDGE FINISHING. If desired, the edges of some kinds of leather objects can be protected by chamfering them to a feather edge and then turning them over on to the back, where they are stuck down. But with leather of good quality this is not necessary. In cut-edge work the raw edges are treated with a mixture of glue-water and dye and well rubbed up. A final application of wax and the edge will withstand a great deal of rough wear. In addition to treatment of the edges modern leather-workers prefer to crease a line or lines near to the edge with a heated creasing iron.

ASSEMBLING. When leather goods consist of a number of parts which have to be assembled and joined together this may be done by a number of different methods, of which the principal ones are sticking, stitching and riveting.

There are various techniques which employ sticking. If the object to which leather is to be applied has a rigid base, as for example a wooden box, the leather is cut in pieces of the exact size required. The covering would start at the inside back, be brought over the back edge, down the outside back, underneath and across the base, up the front, over the front edge and a little way inside. Sufficient margin would be allowed at the sides for the leather to be taken over all the side edges and stuck down for *c.* 1 centimetre. The lid would be similarly covered and then the ends of both body and lid would be covered with separate pieces of leather, which would overlap the turns and so make an inconspicuous joint. The traditional adhesive for box covering is hot animal glue, as for most leather spread on a flat surface.

SEWING. Bags and pouches of many different kinds are sewn together. They are usually sewn inside out and afterwards turned so that no raw edges are visible; and they often have a piping which strengthens the seam and improves the appearance. Most joining of this kind is now done by machine sewing.

The first needles were of bone, the eye laboriously bored through with thin flakes of flint, and these were an enormous advance on the previous practice of joining pieces of leather or fur skin by threading sinews or laces of untanned hide through a series of slots cut out with a flint awl. Right up to modern times the finest stitching—in which shoemakers took such pride and which saddlers employed for some of the decorative parts of their work—was done not with steel needles but by means of a hog's bristle worked into the end of a thread with wax. One may imagine the difficulty of what is called blind stabbing as the craftsman tries with this delicate instrument to penetrate a tiny, invisible hole made from the outside of a boot with an awl little bigger than a needle.

Machine-made sewing thread in a variety of thicknesses and colours, and wound into cops, is relatively modern. In earlier times leather-workers made their own thread from hemp or flax yarn, twisting the required number of 'cords' by rolling them with the hand over a leather apron with constant applications of beeswax. Even at its best thread made in this way is less uniform than machine-made thread, but the wax with which it is impregnated preserves it longer and causes it to grip the material tenaciously.

Much stitching of leather is done double-handed, i.e. a length of waxed thread has a needle at both ends and both needles are pushed through holes made by an awl from opposite sides. When well done this kind of stitching looks approximately the same from all sides. Leather which is so thick that it cannot satisfactorily be overlapped often has the edges butted together (as in the Cromwellian buff coats) and is sewn from one side with stitches that go down to about half the thickness and then turn upwards to the same side from which they entered. This is called butt closing and when well done has a beautiful appearance.

QUILTING was widely used in saddlery, and occasionally in other forms of leatherwork, from the 17th c. to the late 19th c.: it was ornamental as well as functional, especially in making a comfortable seat that was both firm and yielding, the most flexible leather being doeskin or pigskin backed with serge and stuffed with wool.

RIVETING is primarily used for industrial work and military equipment where great strength is required and although good riveting demands considerable skill and can in certain circumstances have a beauty of its own, it strikes most people as a rather clumsy way of joining two pieces of leather together when more refined methods are available.

MOULDING. From very early times leather objects have also been shaped by moulding, and indeed some moulded articles survive from prehistoric times. It may seem strange that leather, which is essentially a flexible material, can be so manipulated that the resultant object is almost as hard as if it were made of wood and that in favourable conditions it will remain permanently in its set form. Examples of such leather objects are armour, great tankards and drinking-vessels, bottles and buckets. These are the very antithesis of articles which rely for their character and purpose on the suppleness of leather; and yet both result from the same essential characteristic, its fibrous structure. From medieval times the traditional term for moulded leather has been *cuir bouilli* (French, boiled leather), although in point of fact no leather made in medieval times could be boiled. This has created a mystique that has obscured its true nature. Actually the process is quite simple and has been employed without a break from as far back as we can discern up to the present day. It can be used only with vegetable-tanned leather and it consists in soaking the leather (of any thickness) in cold water until it is thoroughly saturated and then laying it aside until all surplus water has drained off. The leather is then in a highly plastic condition and can be modelled into quite extraordinary shapes over formers, in moulds of plaster, wood or brass, or in the case of, say, a flask by hand over a filling of wet sand or clay. If the surface is to be ornamented by tooling, stamping or punching (as for example in BOOKBINDING), it must be done at this stage whilst the leather is still damp (if need be, it can be kept damp for a considerable time by repeated wetting). When the work is completed the object is set in a warm place to dry gradually, still supported by its mould, former or filling, which can be removed later. Only a moderate heat is to be used because the higher the temperature the harder will the leather set until it becomes brittle. By this simple process, in medieval times and later, were made jugs (bombards), flagons, flasks and bottles, mugs and blackjacks, sheaths, buckets, armour, helmets, crests, bookbindings, box-like containers of every conceivable shape and size and a great variety of decorative devices. Objects designed to hold liquids were lined with pitch or resin to prevent the liquid soaking into the flesh side and gradually softening the leather again. From the 17th c. drinking-vessels were often fitted with a liner of PEWTER or SILVER and given silver ornaments outside. Modern uses of the same basic process include saddle seats, cigar cases, trunk corners, pump cups and washers. Finally, the process was used for Spanish wall-hangings which were embossed with intricate designs, certain details of which stood up several centimetres from the surface, and then painted.

Occasionally medieval objects come to light which appear at first sight to be made of *cuir bouilli* but which are notably harder—for example, knife cases. These are made of rawhide (not leather), which can be moulded and decorated only when wet—in which state it is very soft and pliable. So far as is known this technique was limited to Italy and France and examples are very rare. But it was also utilized from prehistoric to modern times in Libya, where it is known as *tandu*. It has sometimes been thought that the material was softened by boiling. But this is manifestly incorrect as in merely hot water it is quickly dissolved, making size or glue. In fact the wetting must have been done with great care in cold water and the work

Budget of the Book of Armagh (back) with hand-tooling. Irish. (Trinity College, Dublin, 11th or 12th c.)

Detail of the tooling (modelling, incising and punching) of a *cuir boulli* container for a two-handled cup; the decoration, in part coloured red and white, includes the von Rican arms. Prague. (Deutsches Ledermus., Offenbach, 1376–8)

Wood casket covered with pieces of calf leather. Ornament embossed from flesh side and finished from grain side with incising and punching. Flemish. (Mus. Royaux des Beaux-Arts de Belgique, Brussels, 14th c.)

Model travel case. 'The Ziperior.' Designed by John W. Waterer. (Mus. of Leathercraft)

Missal case of *cuir bouilli* decorated with modelling, incising and stamping and with the legend *Par faite joie*. French. (Mus. of Leathercraft, 15th c.)

carried out fairly quickly before the hide started to harden again. The surface was coloured brown, so that it is difficult to tell it from leather at a casual glance.

A delicate form of modelling in the round was employed for decorative sprays and swags of foliage, flowers, fruits and sometimes birds, which originally were gilded or silvered and used to embellish elaborate MIRROR FRAMES and the like. This technique is believed to have originated in Spain, in the 16th or 17th c., but spread to Britain during the 18th c. where, usually devoid of silver or gilt, it seems to have been utilized as a simulation of wood carving. During the 19th c. it became a genteel occupation for ladies, adding to the modelling strips of folded leather which were woven into tortuous patterns. Many examples of this work are still extant, including decorated mirror and picture frames, brackets and baskets of fruit. The modelling was done by hand with calf leather, damped, shaped, veined and supported by wires.

Quiver of rawhide shaped and ornamented by modelling and punching while wet. Florentine. (Mus. of Leathercraft, 15th c.)

Mirror frame of natural calf moulded with flowers and foliage. Labelled 'Made by Mrs. Whitworth Turner, late Miss Stubbs, of Ripon, Yorkshire, in 1859'. (Mus. of Leathercraft)

Forepart of shoe decorated by cut-out work combined with modelling. Found in London, probably French. (B.M., 15th c.)

Another kind of moulding is known by craftsmen as built-up work. This normally consisted in making a former, usually of wood, the exact size and shape of the interior of the object to be constructed. Over the former was first placed the lining (paper or thin textile) and over this were pasted successive layers of very fine leather finishing with the exterior covering, the overlap joints being feather-edged so that they could hardly be detected. In some cases a crease-line was made over the joints so that they were quite invisible. Such objects were limited to shapes from which the former could be withdrawn when they were dry. The term has been extended to include small boxes, usually made of some kind of board such as strawboard, which were then covered with thin leather with overlap joints.

LAMINATING. For certain purposes, mainly special industrial uses, leather of the sole bend type is built up into solid blocks by sticking layers together with PVA adhesive and drying them under heavy pressure. Such blocks can be turned on a lathe. This process has also been used for making domestic objects such as holders for glass ash-trays, and at least one sculptor has produced carvings in which the lines made by the layers were exploited. Lathes are also employed for making certain kinds of pump cups, the leather in this case being stiffened by impregnating it (stuffing) with molten wax.

DRAPING. The property of draping gracefully is one of the important attributes of modern leathers made specially for clothing. Advantage has effectively been taken of this for making curtains. For this purpose the leather must have been made by a combination tannage, usually chrome followed by vegetable tanning. This will ensure long life, resistance to rot caused by sulphur dioxide and will render the leather impervious to attacks by pests. Leather is heavier than most textiles and when used for curtains care needs to be taken to ensure that it is adequately supported by strong and durable fittings.

ORNAMENTATION. Of the many ways in which the surface of leather can be ornamented the best known today are gold and blind tooling as used for bookbindings. This involves the use of patterned brass tools, which are heated. The design may be lightly traced on the surface of the leather and is then lightly impressed with the heated tools. Glaire (white of egg) or gold size is then applied to the parts to be gilded. Gold leaf (no easy material to handle) is then put on the surface and the design is gone over a second time with the heated tools. The gold adheres to the prepared surface under heat and pressure, and superfluous gold may be brushed away. Cut-out work has already been mentioned. Inlay and appliqué, as other EMBROIDERY techniques, follow the same pattern as with other materials. But a little must be said about the technique of tooling smooth-surfaced leather (calf or cowhide) as it was practised in a great deal of medieval work. The main processes were: (1) incising with sharp or blunt tools; (2) punching, used usually to give a texture to the background of incised designs, and for which a variety of small iron punches were used; (3) modelling in low relief with a small tool sometimes called a spade, which in fact depressed the background leaving the important features apparently in relief; (4) EMBOSSING, which is done from the flesh side with a ball tool, the leather being damped; and (5) carving, which is

Reliquary case. Limewood covered with thick calf leather; freehand incised decoration with Virgin and Child against floral background. French. (Mus. of Leathercraft, 15th c.)

done from the grain side with a special knife that can be inserted more or less horizontally and partially raises up a thin layer until the form—say, a leaf—appears to lie on the surface. The last technique is not found in ancient work but all the others are, sometimes alone and sometimes in combination. To the elaborate tooling both colour and gilding were often added in medieval times, though more often than not this has worn off. In a few recorded cases coloured dyes appear to have been used, usually with some paint (often tempera) added; but this is now very faded. The use of coloured dyes in combination with incised work on the natural modelling calf was very popular among amateurs during the first quarter of the present century. The only process which still survives among professional leather-workers is that known as creasing, which consists of running one or more straight lines with a heated iron around, say, the lid of a case sometimes with a decorative device in the corners. It is still an almost invariable practice to crease the edges of straps, saddle flaps and so on.

An attractive form of ornamentation sometimes found from the 16th to the 18th centuries in both Italy and Spain is that known as scorching. The precise manner in which this was done is not known, but its effect was to create patterns, often very beautiful, by momentary contact under pressure with heated metal. The leather used was sheepskin of light biscuit colour and the contrast between this and the brown scorched pattern was striking. Finally, ornament is sometimes provided by bright metal fittings, which may either be purely decorative—as corners, feet, swags and elaborate handles in ORMOLU on Georgian caskets—or primarily functional—as well-designed locks or lock-escutcheons, hinges, attachments for leather handles and name-plates.

Plaiting (or braiding) is a decorative use of leather and sometimes of rawhide, which in skilled hands can be wholly delightful. It was once widespread, probably too much so, and it is still regularly used for handles of whips and quirts.

Craftsmanship comes from an attitude of mind. The true craftsman strives always after perfection in the control of his materials and tools, to the point where his imagination points

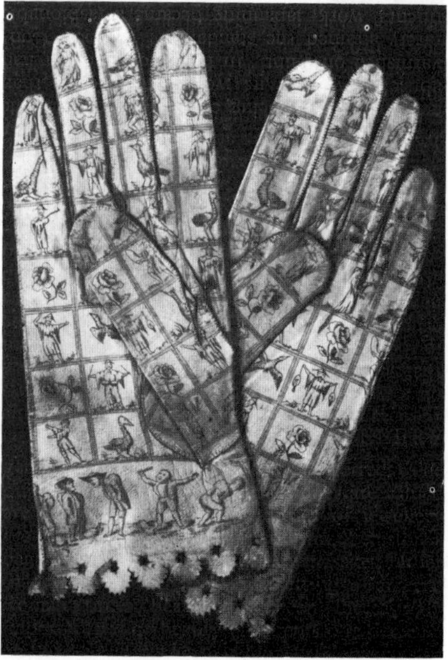

Woman's yellow kid gloves with design printed from copper plate. (Mus. of Leathercraft, *c.* 1800)

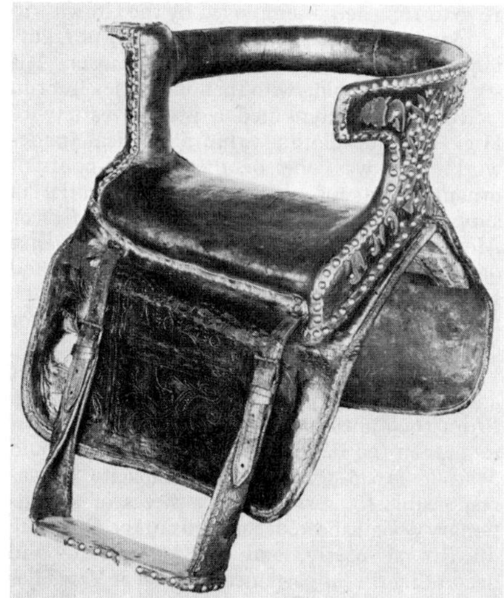

Woman's side-saddle with ornament of incised design and brass nails. (Mus. of Leathercraft, 1828)

Hand-quilted 'Somerset' saddle of soft-dressed cow-hide. (Mus. of Leathercraft, first half 19th c.)

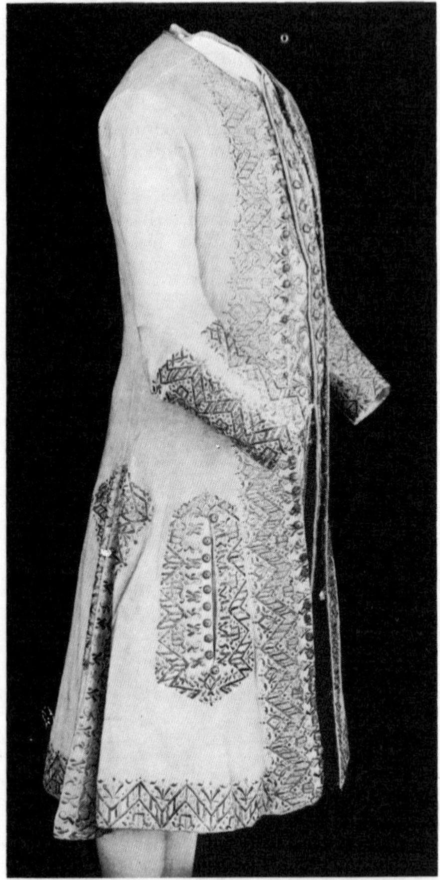

Man's buff leather coat with embroidery in silver wire. English. (London Mus., 18th c.)

the way to beauty of form, detail and ornamentation that in its appropriateness and moderation enhances the essential beauty of the object. The craftsman in leather starts with the inestimable advantage of having a material lovely to see and to handle and a great tradition both to maintain and to build on in the future.

See also GREEK AND ROMAN ANTIQUITY (LEATHER) and BOOKBINDING.

26, 88, 285, 327, 524, 550, 873, 874, 875, 876, 882.

LEGRAIN, PIERRE (1888–1929). French bookbinder, originator of a modern style in binding design. A CABINET-MAKER by training, Legrain began designing book covers for the collector Jacques Doucet in 1917–19. His use of motifs from Cubist and Abstract painting, combined with an unconventional placing of the title and the author's name, often at the bottom of the spine or cover, were an abrupt departure from the floral and illustrative binding practised during the previous 30 years by the Marius MICHEL school. Another innovation was his use of all-over designs extending to both front and back cover and ignoring the classical proportions of the book. Legrain's use of new materials such as metal and IVORY inlays and his experiments with inlaid leathers of contrasting colours, have been continued by his successors in the modern Parisian school, notably Paul Bonet and Rose Adler. See BOOKBINDING.

LEHMANN, CASPAR (1570–1622). German lapidary, official jeweller to the Court of Rudolf II at Prague. He was noted for his works in ROCK-CRYSTAL and inaugurated the art of cutting GLASS of the Venetian CRISTALLO type in the manner of rock-crystal, a technique which led to the production of a stronger potash-lime glass.

LEIGHTON, WILLIAM. Glass craftsman of the Hobbs–Brockunier Company of Wheeling, West Virginia, who in 1864 developed a new type of soda-lime glass. See GLASS (AMERICA).

LELEU, JEAN-FRANÇOIS (1729–1807). French cabinet-maker and a pupil of J. F. OEBEN. He was made master of the guild in 1764 and until his retirement in 1792 did much work for the court and principally for the Prince de Condé. His work represents the evolution of French taste from ROCOCO to NEO-CLASSICAL elegance.

LEPAUTRE, JEAN (1618–82). French engraver and ornamentalist, brother of the architect ANTOINE (1621–81). He engraved drawings of BAROQUE ornamental motifs made by his master Adam Philippon in Rome (issued in 1645). After engraving over some years for painters he produced a large quantity of original designs and motifs, from 1657 to *c.* 1670. From 1670 to 1680 he was employed by the Crown and in 1677 he was elected to the Academy of Painting and Sculpture as *dessinateur et graveur*. His style was in keeping with that of Charles Lebrun (1619–90) and combined a prolific variety of High Baroque motifs within a classical framework. He was one of the most important ornamentalists of his time and influential in supporting the work of Lebrun. His *Livre de Miroirs* and *Tables de Guéridons* had an influence on furniture design in the Netherlands and England. He produced more than 2,000 prints, from which about 10 suites were intended for goldsmiths and silversmiths.

PIERRE (*c.* 1648–1716). French engraver and interior decorator, son of the foregoing. From 1699 until his death he was *dessinateur et graveur* in the Bâtiments under Jules-Hardouin Mansart (1646–1708). In this capacity he was responsible for new chimney-pieces of revolutionary design and redecorations to the Chambre du Roi at Marly, and for remodelling and decorating the Appartement du Roi at Versailles and at Trianon. He was also concerned with designs for the altar of Notre-Dame de Paris and the choir of the cathedral of Orléans.

Lepautre made much use of the arabesque forms of BÉRAIN, incorporating them into the moulded outlines of panels and frames. But he was a designer of considerable originality and contributed to the advanced ideas in interior decoration which prevailed during the concluding years of Louis XIV, anticipating stylistic changes which came to fruition under Louis XV. Fiske Kimball writes in *The Creation of the Rococo* (1964): 'The essential creative act in the genesis of the ROCOCO was performed by Pierre Lepautre on his appointment in 1600 as *Dessinateur* in the *Bâtiments*, in designing changes at Marly. Taking elements of the painted arabesque of Bérain, he transposed it from the flat to relief, from a panel-filling to a frame, superseding the rigid geometry of assemblage.'

LETHABY, WILLIAM RICHARD (1857–1931). British architect and theorist who was associated with the formation of the Art Workers' Guild and the Design and Industries Association. See ARTS AND CRAFTS MOVEMENT.

LEVASSEUR, ÉTIENNE (1721–98). French cabinet-maker, admitted master in 1767. He was trained by one of the sons of BOULLE and specialized in copying and repairing pieces in the Boulle manner. One of the first cabinet-makers to use mahogany, he provided mahogany cabinet-furniture for the aunts of Louis XVI, Mesdames Adélaïde and Victoire, at the Château de Bellevue.

LEYGEBE, GOTTFRIED (1630–83). Iron-chiseller, medallist and die-engraver. Born in Freistad, Silesia, he moved to Nuremberg *c.* 1645, where he worked first, probably as an apprentice, for a swordsmith. He was presumably employed chiefly in the decoration of sword-hilts and a sword with an iron hilt signed by him, decorated with figures sculptured in high relief, is in the Victoria and Albert Museum. Other chiselled iron sword-hilts have been attributed to him on no very certain grounds. He is best known for three equestrian statuettes sculptured in iron (Rosenborg Castle, Denmark; Grünes Gewölbe, Dresden; Staatliche Sammlungen, Berlin) and a series of plaques and medallions. Much of his identified surviving work dates from after his appointment as *Münzschneider* (coin-die engraver) to the Elector of Brandenburg in 1668, when he moved to Berlin, remaining there until his death. See ARMS AND ARMOUR and IRON AND STEEL (IRON-CHISELLING).

109.

LIBAERTS, ELISEUS. See ANTWERP-LOUVRE SCHOOL.

LIBBEY GLASS COMPANY, THE. The successor to the celebrated NEW ENGLAND GLASS COMPANY of East Cambridge, Massachusetts. When that house was forced to draw its furnaces in 1888, the owner, Edward Drummond Libbey, brought the company to Toledo, Ohio, where natural gas was available as an inexpensive and abundant fuel. After a series of modifications in name the firm became The Libbey Glass Company in February 1892. During the early years in Toledo the company went in perpetual danger of bankruptcy; the World's Columbian Exposition of 1893 in Chicago, Illinois, however, changed its prospects. At considerable financial risk Edward Libbey erected an elaborate pavilion to house a furnace and a display of cut glass. This display caught the public imagination, and with the help of shrewd publicity devices it established The Libbey Glass Company as one of the most prominent Brilliant Period cutting houses in the United States. Popular during the Brilliant Period were heavily mitre-cut wares of great refractive qualities as well as formal engraved types. When the popularity of these designs waned the company made *svelte* tablewares in the ART DÉCO manner, and in the 1930s hired A. Douglas Nash (1885–1940) to design a luxury line of CHASED, cut and engraved wares. This series was so expensive, however, that its production was terminated in 1935 during the Depression.

In 1936 The Libbey Glass Company became a division of the Owens-Illinois Glass Company and employed Edwin W. Fuerst (1903–) to design a new 'Modern American' series; this was to be of a fine transparent crystal not unlike that produced by the Steuben Glass Works of Corning, New York. Simplicity of form was emphasized with occasional light-cut or engraved decoration. 'Modern American' was first presented in late 1939 and released publicly in 1940. The line was among the most beautiful produced in America at the period, but production was stopped because of the war effort *c.* 1945 and never resumed.

The Libbey Glass Company is now a division of Owens-Illinois Incorporated and produces commercial tablewares. But it is the heir to a 154-year tradition of glass-making in America. See GLASS (AMERICA).

LIECHTI FAMILY (*c.* 1500–1810). The Liechti family of Winterthur, Switzerland, were makers of TURRET CLOCKS and clocks for the home over a period of three centuries, and their clocks, made wholly of iron, are remarkable for the attractiveness and appeal of their design. A representative collection of their products may be seen in the Rathaus and in the Heimatsmuseum in Winterthur. LAURENZ, who died in 1545, made in 1529 a turret clock for the Käfigtor, Winterthur, now preserved and displayed in the Heimatsmuseum. Its gaily painted astronomical dial shows the position in the heavens of the sun and moon, and the moon's nodes (whose position determines eclipses). The gearing behind this dial is the earliest known example of an epicyclic gearing, a device much used in later engineering. Laurenz's son ERHARD turned his attention to domestic clocks of the GOTHIC type, with an open-work iron frame, a painted iron dial with a moon-phase indicator above the hour-ring, and the bell mounted within an open spire culminating in a finial. These and later clocks by the Liechti family are noteworthy for the rich and gay ornamentation of the spire with tendrils, scrolls and carnations, and for the bright and attractive patterns of their painted dial-plates, which relieve the otherwise rather sombre appearance of the Gothic type of clock. Many of them bear dates and the initials of the maker. The tradition was carried on by Erhard's sons ULRICH and ANDREAS, by the four sons of Andreas, and by four further generations, the last member of the family being HANS HEINRICH (d. 1810). With a single exception the clocks made by the Liechti family were all driven by suspended weights.

LIGNEREUX, MARTIN-ÉLOY (1750/1–1809). French *marchand-mercier* who was associated with Dominique DAGUERRE from the middle of the reign of Louis XVI. He took over Daguerre's business in 1793. He made furniture as well as being a dealer and his success helped to make it possible for the furniture traditions of the 18th c. to be carried into the 19th c.

LILLE LACE. A Bobbin LACE much resembling MECHLIN but distinguished from it by the simpler construction of the hexagonal ground-mesh and the prevalence of square dots in the design. It was much used for narrow trimmings in the late 18th and early 19th centuries and was sometimes referred to as a PASSEMENT.

LIMERICK LACE. LACE made during the 19th c. in Ireland, where the craft was introduced from COGGESHALL. Bobbin or machine-made net is stretched on a tambour frame and the designs are traced in Irish lace thread through the meshes in ordinary CROCHET chain-stitch by means of a sewing needle. Stitches are made on the design with a hooked or tambour needle in order to introduce relief. Shawls, wedding-veils and the like are commonly made in this way.

LINENFOLD. Nineteenth-c. term for a decorative pattern carved on wall panelling and panels of furniture such as presses, chests, chairs, chimney-pieces, etc. It was so named because of its resemblance to linen arranged in stylized vertical folds. The pattern apparently originated with Flemish craftsmen and spread with local variations to France, Germany and England in the late 15th c. It was one of the few GOTHIC wood-working motifs which had not an architectural prototype.

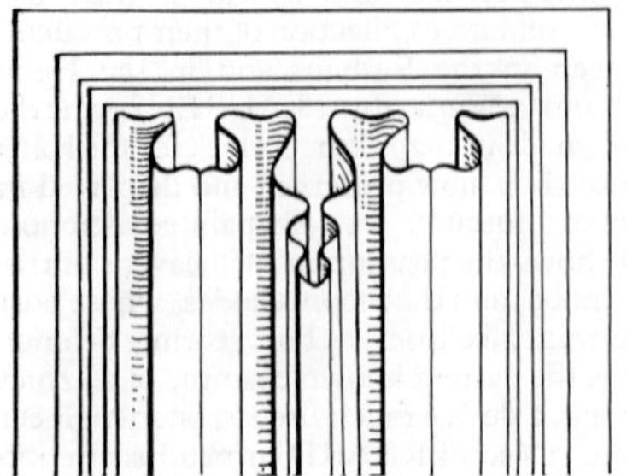

LINNELL, WILLIAM (*c.* 1708–63) and JOHN (*c.* 1737–96), his son and successor. English furniture-makers and upholsterers at 28 Berkeley Square, London. Surviving bills show that the firm worked for Sir Richard Hoare at Barn Elms (1739–53) and for William Drake of Shardeloes (1763–8). The drawings of John Linnell preserved in the Victoria and Albert Museum reveal

Drawing by John Linnell for chimney-piece with integral over-mantel picture frame. (V. & A. Mus.)

that he had many distinguished clients and exemplify the transition from ROCOCO to NEO-CLASSICAL and then to the early REGENCY style in English furniture design. He can be credited with the design of the Library and Breakfast Room furniture at Osterley, and of the famous Chinese Bedroom furniture (including the bed now in the Victoria and Albert Museum) formerly at Badminton and for long attributed to CHIPPENDALE.

356.

LINWOOD, MARY (1755–1854). Widely known for her EMBROIDERY pictures in coloured wools, which during her lifetime fetched enormous prices. Her exhibition of 100 needlework pictures after various masters—she copied among others Raphael, Dolci, Maratta, Gainsborough, Reynolds, Opie and Morland—was shown in London in 1798, and subsequently in many provincial towns. See also NEEDLEWORK.

LIPS, JACOBUS (1848–1921). Born in Rotterdam and apprenticed to his father's smithy, he took over a workshop in Dordrecht for the manufacture of safes, etc. and later founded the Lips Safe and Lock Manufacturing Company of international repute. Carried on by the three sons of the founder, this Company has been responsible for many improvements in the designing of security locks and safes. The Lips Collection of LOCKS AND KEYS is famous.

LITTLETON, HARVEY K. (1922–). American glass-maker responsible with Dominick LABINO for leadership of the United States in contemporary hand-worked glass craftsmanship. This has been due to the 1962 seminar on the subject held at the Toledo Museum of Art, which brought interested artists together and established that glass could be successfully worked at the small studio furnace. Originally trained as a potter, Littleton first proposed the idea of the Toledo seminar on glass as an expressive medium. He and Dominick Labino worked out details of this seminar, the successful outcome of which has been the establishment of some 15 university courses in glass craftsmanship in the United States and Britain. Professor Littleton now teaches the subject at the University of Wisconsin.

Examples of work by Littleton may be seen in the Toledo Museum of Art and the Elvehjem Art Center, Madison, Wisconsin.

See GLASS (AMERICA).

LIVERY CUPBOARD. Term which came into use *c.* the middle of the 16th c. for an open two-tiered cupboard, similar to a COURT CUPBOARD and used for food and drink. The livery cupboard seems to have superseded the AUMBRY. See FURNITURE (ENGLISH).

LOBING. See GADROONING.

LOCK, MATTHIAS. English carver and furniture designer who was a pioneer of the ROCOCO style in England. He was in business *c.* 1746 near Long Acre, London, and also in partnership with Henry COPLAND in Tottenham Court Road. Between 1740 and 1746 he produced a number of pattern-books and plates of ornamental motifs for carvers and other craftsmen. He also published a number of books of designs in collaboration with Copland, including *A New Book of Ornaments, Chimneys, Sconces, Tables, etc.*, 1752. From these books it was at one time inferred that they were employed by Thomas CHIPPENDALE for the designs in his *Director* and that they were thus primarily responsible for the style known as 'Chippendale'. But this latter view is no longer accepted. Lock's later works contain the earliest known published designs in NEO-CLASSICAL style. These are *A New Book of Ornaments, consisting of Tables, Chimnies, Sconces, Clock Cases, etc.*, 1768; *A New Book of Foliage*, 1769; *A New Book of Pier Frames*, 1769. A portfolio of his drawings (done 1740–65) is preserved in the Victoria and Albert Museum.

LOCKS AND KEYS. The earliest outline of a door fastening is the sealed bolt which appears in the ancient Egyptian script as the hieroglyph for the sound-value 's'. Since the Egyptian alphabet was adopted *c.* 3100 B.C. (First Dynasty) the sealed bolt must have been a familiar object long before that. The simple bolt of wood that slides freely to bar a door was probably known from earliest predynastic times. Sealing the bolt was an innovation in security for two new elements extended the effectiveness of the simple bolt: a cord wedged in a groove cut across the top and wound around, and a dab of sealing material, mud or wax, impressed on the ends of the cord to harden and make fast all the units. Any attempt to withdraw the bolt broke the seal.

The next advance was the invention of the ingenious key. Cord and sealing material were not needed. The bolt, no longer grooved, was hollowed at one end with a shallow socket drilled in its top to receive a thick pin or peg which dropped from a holding bar. As the pin dropped it secured the bolt, that is kept it from moving. Many pins could be introduced, each to fall, or tumble, from its own weight into the proper holes. As these tumblers fell the bolt locked, to be freed only when the pins were lifted. That lifting action was effected by the key, a rod or stick which carried on its far end the precise number of pins to match the tumblers. With the pins up the key was thrust into the hollow bolt until the pins reached the fallen tumblers. Pressure on the handle raised the pins to lift the tumblers up and out of their holes. Now the key could move the freed bolt back and forth, and the door could be opened.

What has been described is the complicated operation of the pin tumbler lock. The same basic principle was employed by Linus YALE, Senior, in 1857 when he patented his five-pin tumbler padlock, and the same idea miniaturized was used by his son, Linus Yale, Junior, when he produced the cylinder lock which, with its small flat key, became the most versatile lock ever known.

Pliny the Elder (A.D. 23/4–79) declared in his *Naturalis Historia* that the key was invented by Theodorus of Samos in the 6th c. B.C. Eustathius (12th c. A.D.) attributed it to the Spartans. Literary and physical evidence refute both authors. For Homer described in the *Odyssey* (Bk. xxi) how Penelope used a crooked key of bronze with an ivory handle to shoot back the doorbolts to Ulysses's treasure chamber. Furthermore in the excavations at Khorsabad for the palace of Sargon II of Persia (722–705 B.C.) there was found a gate closed by a heavy wooden lock that could only be opened by a key so huge that one man could hardly carry it. Sargon's contemporary Isaiah (22: 22) describes the key of the House of David as so large that it was laid on a man's shoulder. Pictorial evidence from Egypt also disposes of Pliny's statement. A low-relief on a column at the great temple at Karnak (1567–1085 B.C.) shows a long sickle-shaped key that worked one of the large locks, while from nearby Luxor have come similar keys of wood, a number with iron pins, some ornamented with precious metals. Clearly huge locks and large keys, both of wood, were available in Egypt from the 2nd millennium B.C., i.e. 4,000 years ago.

Today locks are mounted either on the outside of the door or within the material frame with only the keyhole face exposed. The early Egyptian locks, however, were mounted on the inside of the door. Keyholes were not invented until the Roman period. Egyptian doors therefore had sizeable holes through which an arm could enter to insert the key directly into the bolt. Under such conditions it was essential that the keys be large and their handles long and bent so that pressing down would lift the tumblers. Only with the invention of the keyhole could the lock be fastened on the outside and the key become a straight implement. The handle could be formed into a graceful bow or circle; the middle part, called the stem or shank, could be as long or as short as the locksmith pleased, the working end or bit as complicated as the mechanism required.

Wood limited the efficiency of the lock, for the pressure as the key made contact inside the lock abraded both devices. All-metal locks and keys, first of bronze, later of iron, were introduced by the Romans; some Roman locks have parts made of both metals. The affluent Romans, prizing intimacy, considered locks and keys a household necessity. Accordingly their craftsmen were stimulated to make efficient improvements and to conserve the metal they reduced the sizes of both locks and keys. More important, they designed the parts to fit closely, the central principle in the best modern lock-making. For smoother operation they also introduced the spring to press the pins into the bolt. Finally they invented the wards, which are fixed projections inside the lock to impede the turning of any key which lacks corresponding slots, or steps, in its bit. These wards or little fins placed around the keyhole were the chief advance in security until the 18th-c. British inventions.

The portable padlock—which is not affixed to a door but hangs by its shackle from a staple—was apparently preferred by the Romans to the larger, more permanent lock, and was in demand for chests and strong-boxes and for the chains and fetters of slaves. Another Roman innovation was the small key that ended in a ring to be worn on the finger. Many ring-keys, obviously for the élite, have been found with bezels inset with fine INTAGLIOS of CORNELIAN or JASPER.

As iron and steel became familiar metals locks came into more general use in the cities, but the wooden lock was not yet replaced by the all-metal one. As late as the 10th c., when Alfred the Great is said to have introduced the all-metal lock to England, stout oaken locks continued to be popular, especially in rural areas. Indeed in northern Scandinavia and the Alpine regions, in North and tropical Africa, in the Near East and in Oceania, wooden locks are still in use.

Whether of wood or metal, the elements of the lock were now housed in a case. Elaborate efforts continued to be made to multiply the number of wards or impediments inside so that the lock would reject alien keys. Keyholes were often concealed by special covers and even by additional locks over the keyholes. As the exteriors of the cases came to be adorned, the keys too became ornate, the bits reflecting the more complicated wards, the bows shaped into a variety of designs.

The keys of the medieval period in Europe, from the 6th to the 10th and 11th centuries, are difficult to attribute unless they are accompanied by their locks, which usually display the reigning style of a period. Merovingian keys (*c.* 500–750), coarser in design than those that went before, reveal a sharp decline in craftsmanship. Carolingian keys (*c.* 750–960) have for the most part bow shapes like a bishop's mitre or some other ecclesiastical motif, with—a point to remember in identification—the distance between bow and bit greatly reduced. Gothic keys (*c.* 1150–1400) are often diamond-shaped or in the form of a lozenge, the ladder-steps in their bits indicating that they were contrived to clear many wards around the keyholes. Early Gothic door-locks, with their impressive exteriors, were at first constructed with horizontal keyholes. The change to the vertical keyhole apparently came later for aesthetic reasons.

From the 15th c. the locksmith began to enjoy a unique position. A master locksmith (a title first conferred in Germany in 1411) was a craftsman of great technical versatility and a master of the techniques of ornament. In command of his iron, he could shape any kind of scrolling, including animal and vegetable forms copied from illuminated manuscripts. In the later Gothic period he also employed calligraphic ornamentation. See also IRON AND STEEL (DECORATIVE WROUGHT IRONWORK). Great locksmiths often travelled from court to court to create locks and keys for royalty and for affluent merchants.

At the Renaissance the locksmith was freed from his dependence on the forge. The simple vigour of the best Gothic work was replaced by an astonishing virtuosity as the metal was manipulated cold. File, cold chisel and steel saw-blade were his chief tools. No longer compelled to work swiftly while the metal was hot,

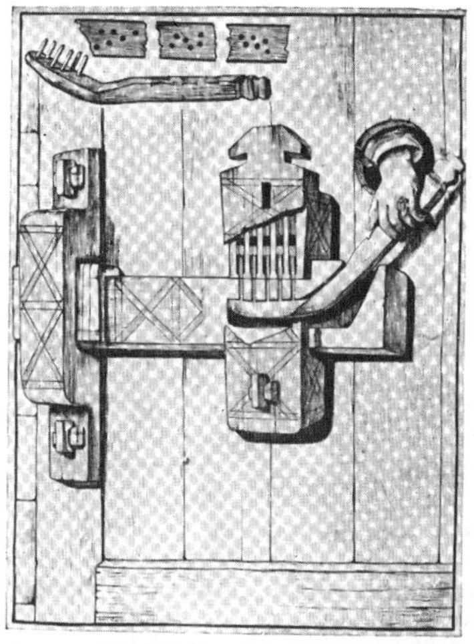

A

B

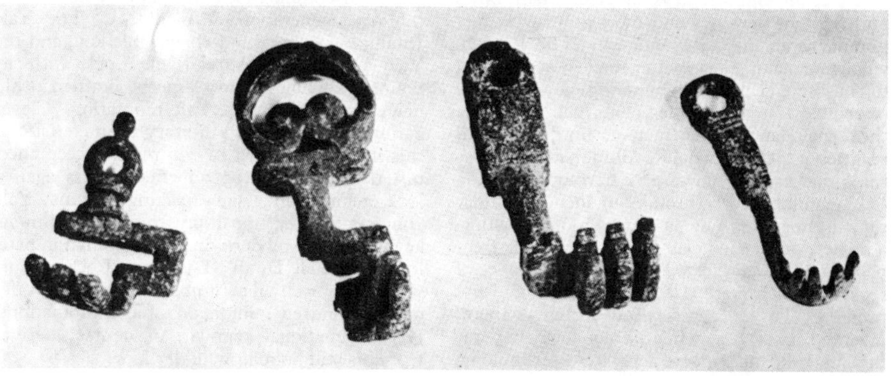

C

D

A. Ancient Egyptian lock. From Vincent J. M. Eras, *Locks and Keys Throughout the Ages* (1957)

B. Egyptian lock dismantled. (Lips Coll.)

C. Oldest known Roman and Greek keys. (Lips Coll.)

D. Arab carrying keys on his shoulder. From Vincent J. M. Eras, *Locks and Keys Throughout the Ages* (1957)

he was able at a slower pace to create infinitely finer detail. The bow of the Renaissance key suddenly became the stage for a new, three-dimensional plastic expression produced entirely at the bench. The best examples are the *clefs de chef-d'œuvre*, or masterpiece keys, of the French masters (1550–1650). (See also APPRENTICE LOCKS.) The locksmith, to prove himself worthy of guild membership, had to produce a sample of his best workmanship and skill. The bows of such keys, often in the form of inverted pyramids over rounded devices, were enriched with spirals, ARABESQUES and traceries borrowed from the most elaborate architectural enrichments. The shanks were short, the bits proportionately large, with steps in series like the teeth in a comb. The French locksmiths were acknowledged to be the greatest masters, the Germans next, the Italians third. Spanish craftsmen excelled in locks for the popular VARGUEÑO chests and in heavy padlocks.

In the early 18th c. French and English locksmiths competed in the market-place. The light and elegant English keys of steel, their bows crowned with ciphers and monograms, became popular even on the Continent. The French, who were making keys with bronze bows, turned to chasing, gilding and engraving. In a century of refined taste both sides continued to pursue the ornate and the attractive, until the hard realities of the Industrial Revolution made everything that had preceded seem frivolous.

A genuine break-through in lock ingenuity came in England in the last quarter of the 18th c. The new propertied class, affronted by the free-booting of skilled picklocks, wanted assurance of security which mere size and ornament did not provide. To meet this need Robert BARRON invented in 1778 a twin-tumbler lock that was the first advance in modern lock technology. His new construction introduced various cuts in the bit of the key to correspond with two-spring tumblers which checked the bolt. The Barron lock was surpassed by Joseph BRAMAH, who devised an improvement with a system of sliders inside the mechanism. Barron had depended on the traditional rotating movement of the key; Bramah used endway pushing as well as revolving motion. The Bramah lock was the first since the Romans to be operated by a small key that could be carried unobtrusively or pocketed. In 1811 Bramah, with a scheme for manufacturing separate parts in quantities, started the first lock-making industry, indeed one of the first assembly-line efforts. Justly proud of his lock, he offered 200 guineas to anyone who could pick it. That challenge galvanized rival inventors. In 1818 the brothers Charles and Jeremiah CHUBB patented their Detector Lock; others, including Cotterill in 1846, improved upon it. In 1851 an overseas competitor, the American Alfred C. Hobbs, with his kit of lock-picking tools opened both a Bramah and a Chubb lock at the Crystal Palace in London. Hobbs ultimately won the 200 guineas prize by also picking a Bramah padlock. The contributions of Bramah and the Chubbs, however, were revolutionary to lock-making and needed no apology. Besides in 1854 Hobbs's own patent Protector lock was successfully picked by one of Chubb's craftsmen. The competition, vexing for the manufacturers, did encourage more ingenious lock construction. Strong-boxes had to be made safe, and for the huge safes of bankers new engineering had to be supplied. Innovations included intricate watch movements to prevent a lock from being opened except at a pre-set hour.

American expertise entered the lock industry with A. C. Hobbs, but many other inventors won acclaim. Among them Solomon Andrews in 1836 invented a lock in which the position of the tumblers could be changed, with movable bits that could be shifted easily on the key to correspond to new positions. The two Linus Yales, father and son, were the first Americans to make truly outstanding contributions. They took the Egyptian lock, added to it something of the ingenuity of the Bramah lock, and created a family of complex locks to baffle, if not defeat, the new generation of picklocks. The Yale Infallible Lock, with a changeable key, and the Yale Double Treasury Bank Lock with its double keyholes and superb craftsmanship helped to establish the Yale reputation. Clever naming of the locks, a literary characteristic of this industry, helped to win public acceptance, but their fame rested on effectiveness against lock-picking and safe-cracking. Linus Yale Junior made the transition from the traditional key lock to the modern dial or combination bank lock. His Yale Double Dial Bank Lock with its stack of four circular tumblers was said to offer over a hundred million possible combinations. His international renown, of course, derives from his still popular cylinder lock.

Superb improvements in lock technology have been made since by other masters, including the Dutch Lips firm's patented cylinder lock, which resists drilling, and James Sargent's greatly improved time-lock for bank vault use, which employed magnets to control various parts and foil unlocking procedures.

'Secret' locks have included multiple bolts, hidden keyholes and devices that register the number of times a lock is opened. Originally it was the padlock that lent itself to a multiplicity of rings or dials with a great number of combinations. Indeed the combination lock that employed letters or ciphers was known in the 17th c. Today the most intricate and efficient combination locks are used for large bank vaults, utilizing also electrical current and motors and electronic barriers.

Varieties of locks for different purposes are almost endless: mortise locks, flush locks, rim locks, locks that are knob-operated, locks that are lever-handled, front-door locks with latch and dead bolt, master-keyed locks all controlled by a grand master key, and finally huge vault doors with imposing dials and steel bolts, of unusual weights and thicknesses and, notably, auxiliary alarm devices.

As most lock-makers will testify, the terms 'police lock' and 'burglar-proof' lock merely indicate great strength of parts engineered to close tolerances, or devices adjacent to the lock or door to deter the burglar. Paradoxically perhaps, it is nevertheless true that every locking device, however impressive, demands constant vigilance, especially now that the thermo-lance has been devised to burn through steel walls in a matter of minutes.

The locksmith's specialized terminology is complicated and the following nomenclature, although not complete, will be of use to those studying the subject of locks and keys.

KEYS. Most keys consist of three parts: the *bow*, a ring or hoop by which it is held; the *stem* or *shank* between the bow and the bit; and the *bit* or *beard* or *blade*, which projects from the shank at the opposite end from the bow. The bit is cut away or notched so as to allow the wards of the lock to pass through it (called a *warded* key) or with a series of notches and projections (also called *bits* or *steps*) which serve to raise the levers of the lock when the key is turned. A key with bittings or steps on both sides of the shank is called a *double-bitted* key.

A *pipe* or *barrel* key is a key with a flat bit and a round shaft with a hole in its end made to fit over a drill pin in the lock. A *corrugated* key is a key made from sheet metal with corrugations in the bit or shaft, such as is used to operate a cylinder lock. Such a key is called *paracentric* when the corrugations reach nearly to the central thickness of the bit in order to prevent the picking of the lock by a flat strip such as a knife-blade. A *master* key is a key made to actuate a series of locks, each of which is actuated by a different key (called a *servant* key) or by the master key. A *skeleton* key is a key in which the bit is cut away as much as possible to avoid obstructions in the lock but with enough left to move the bolt or actuate the levers. A *control* key is one used to readjust a combination lock.

LOCKS. The following terms refer to some of the main parts of a lock. The *case* is the exterior part or box into which the action and mechanism are built. The *bolt* is the sliding piece which by the action of the key is made to shoot out of the lock case and fit into a socket or staple in the door-frame, etc. It may be square or round in section. A *dead bolt* is one which is moved both inwards and outwards by the key. *Wards* are fixed projections designed to prevent a key from entering or turning unless it is grooved to coincide with them. Such protective devices are also more generally named *guards*. *Levers* are modelled projections in the lock which obstruct the movement of the bolt unless simultaneously lifted by the steps of a suitable key. These are also referred to as *tumblers*, particularly in the U.S.A. The *cylinder* is a short cylindrical plug which in some forms of lock contains the keyhole and mechanism, providing the security. Slots in the levers, through which the bolt stump passes when it is shot, are called *gatings*.

A *mortise* lock is one fitted into a cavity cut in the edge of a door. A *knob* lock is a lock having a spring bolt which can be withdrawn by a knob and a dead bolt which is moved by a key. A *cylinder* lock is a lock in which keyhole and lever mechanism are contained in a cylinder or cylinders separate from the lock case. A *combination* lock is a keyless lock with changeable tumblers operated by a rotating dial on the face of the door.

241, 276, 415, 939.

LOCKSMITH STYLE. A style of decorative wrought ironwork which succeeded the BLACKSMITH STYLE *c.* 1300 in France and England. Technically, methods analogous to wood-working techniques were used after the preliminary production of bars and sheets. Stylistically, design was strongly influenced by the geometrical motifs of Islamic countries. See IRON AND STEEL (DECORATIVE WROUGHT IRONWORK).

LONG-CASE CLOCKS. A type of CLOCK pioneered in Europe by a few isolated examples but developed in England in the 17th c. as a clock for the home. In an English long-case clock the movement is supported on a tall wooden case inside which hang the driving weights and, in all but the very early examples, the long pendulum of one or one and a quarter seconds beat. The movement rests on a *seat-board* and is protected by a hood with glazed front door and usually with glazed side panels. The whole hood can be either lifted upwards (as in some early examples) or slid forward and lifted away to give access to the mechanism if required. The case is normally provided with a hinged front door to give access to the pendulum and weights. This door is sometimes provided with a bull's eye through which the swinging pendulum can be seen. The hoods of the earlier long-case clocks (1660–70) were of a dignified but somewhat formal character. After 1670 the design became more relaxed, and the pediment was replaced by mouldings or cresting. About 1710 the broken or break-arch form of dial appeared, and this became the standard for the rest of the 18th c. The dial was usually of brass, with an applied, silvered chapter-ring and applied spandrels in the corners. The centre was usually matted, occasionally engraved. The case and hood of the early long-case clocks were usually of oak veneered with ebony. Later a great variety of woods was used, including walnut and mulberry, and MARQUETRY designs were employed to great effect. In the 2nd half of the 18th c. MAHOGANY was introduced and designs became more severe again. Long-case clocks were also made in Holland and in other parts of Europe. The Dutch long-case clocks resemble in many ways their English counterparts. In the earlier examples, with square dials, the cresting tended to be more elaborate than with English clocks. Later these clocks were often very large and splendidly exuberant in form, with swelling bases and tall, arched hoods surmounted by tall statuettes. English long-case clocks made in London and the larger provincial centres were almost invariably given hour-hands and minute-hands, and their dials were graduated in hours and minutes; they were wound through holes in the dial and ran for eight days at a single winding. Country-made long-case clocks, on the other hand, more usually had only a single hour-hand. A single weight hung from an endless cord served to drive both going and striking trains and they ran for only a maximum of 30 hours at a winding.

LOOMS. See TEXTILE MANUFACTURE IN ANTIQUITY and WEAVING.

LORRAINE LACE. Sometimes called 'Saint Michel' laces, these were similar to the lace of LILLE. Floral patterns, usually in white, were appliquéd on to the *réseau*.

LOTUS. The Greek word 'lotus' was applied to a variety of different plants. The plant which provided the food of forgetfulness for the fabulous lotus-eaters (*Odyssey* ix. 90 ff.) has sometimes been identified with the jujube tree (*Zizyphus lotus*) or north Africa. The Egyptian white and blue water-lily was called by the Greeks *nymphaea* ('sacred to the nymphs') and has the botanical name *Nymphaea lotus*. It was this which provided the prototype for the 'lotus' decoration of Egypt, Mesopotamia and the Mediterranean countries. The leaves, which float on the surface of the water each on a separate stalk, are almost circular, about a foot in diameter, and have a cleft almost to the centre. The bud is enclosed by four sepals, three of which are visible from any of four points of view (one full face and two in profile). As the flower opens out the sepals curl down, leaving the blossom and petals separate from them. The ovary has a bright yellow saucer-like stigma, from which stamens like petals diverge. These features, particularly the cleft leaf and the triple spike of the sepals, form the basis of decorative lotus motifs, both naturalistic and stylized, which derive from Egypt. The 'red lotus' of India and China is a different plant, the *Nelumbium speciosum*. (The *Nelumbia*, from the Sinhalese *nelumbu*, are a genus of water-beans.) It provides the basis of Indian and Asiatic 'lotus' decoration and imagery. The leaves, which are carried to a height of several feet above the water, are bell-shaped and without cleft. The bud is enclosed by a ring of overlapping sepals, which do not present the three-spike appearance of the Egyptian *Nymphaea*. The petals are broad and when it is fully open the flower has the appearance of a blown tulip. Herodotus (*c.* 480–*c.* 425 B.C.) mentions a 'rose-like' water-lily growing in Egypt (Bk. ii, ch. 92); but the *Nelumbium* did not provide an ornamental motif in Egyptian decorative art.

The water-lily was used by the Egyptians for ritualistic offerings to the gods as early as 3000 B.C. In Egyptian mythology it was associated particularly with the sun-god Horus: the morning sun was pictured as rising from a lotus flower and the sun returned into the lotus at night. The dead were pictured as being reborn into the future life in divine form from the flowers of the lotus. As associated with Isis the lotus symbolized fecundity. (Curiously, the lily of the Virgin in Christian iconography is descended from this motif.) The Hawk of Horus and the Solar Disc are represented as supported by a lotus flower and Isis–Hathor is pictured among lotus flowers or crowned with a lotus diadem. The lotus, together with the papyrus motif, was ubiquitous in Egyptian decorative art. It was prominent in mortuary representations. Spoons, knives, toilet boxes and other domestic utensils were commonly ornamented with the flower. Capitals of architectural columns were shaped in the form of a lotus bud or the open flower. The lotus was the most common element in decorative borders and over-all patterns. The trilobe lotus bud with a semicircle of radiating petals formed the basis of the Egyptian PALMETTE, and from the stigma the ROSETTE motif was developed.

From Egypt the lotus motif was carried to Mesopotamia, where it appears on seals as an offering to the gods and is incorporated in representations of the Assyrian 'Sacred Tree'. The lotus motif formed the basis of what used to be called the 'Phoenician palmette' and Phoenician lotus capitals were prototypes of the Greek Ionic Order. The Greeks made extensive use of a stylized lotus motif both in ceramic decoration and in the enrichment of architecture, developing it into the ANTHEMION and the EGG AND DART pattern. The Romans used these motifs, combining Etruscan and Near Eastern forms with the Greek. At various levels of stylization the lotus patterns descended by way of BYZANTINE, ROMANESQUE and GOTHIC to the Renaissance and are still in use although their origin and source are for the most part forgotten.

In Hindu mythology the lotus is associated with the god Brahma who according to one legend sprang from a lotus which grew out of the navel of Vishnu while he slumbered upon the primeval waters supported by the serpent Sasha. The lotus is also the symbol of Lakshmi, goddess of Fortune and wife of Vishnu, and she is normally shown holding a lotus in one of her hands. She is also often portrayed standing or seated on a lotus throne. Lakshmi herself is most probably derived from the earth-mother goddess of ancient times. Her ancient role of Sarasvati was both Lady of the Lotus Ponds and the divine personification of the river Sarasvati.

In traditional Indian iconography the eight-petalled lotus was both a metaphysical and cosmic symbol and also a stock emblem of male and female beauty in the erotic literature. In later times (17th c. onwards) the association of the lotus with male and female beauty was carried on in the miniature paintings of northern India, especially in Rajasthan and the Himalayan foothills. The influence of its very ancient metaphysical significance is traced in the incorporation of the lotus pediment into the structure of the stupa and in the octagonál radiation of the Japanese pagoda. Taken over into Buddhist thought, it symbolized the purity of the essential nature of all beings unsmirched by immersion into the sphere of *samsara* or world-process. It also stood for the pure being of *nirvana* in contrast with the world of illusion. At the same time it retained its earlier cosmic significance, the stalk representing the *axis mundi* from which the universe unfolds in all directions. From the time of Asoka (*c.* 274 B.C.) the conventionalized lotus was a feature of Buddhist ornament and it came to be associated with representations of the Wheel of Doctrine. From the Gandhara period sacred figures of the Buddha were often depicted seated on a lotus throne, which was emblematic of the Buddha in his capacity of spiritual leader of the world and the embodiment of Absolute Being. It was associated particularly with figures of the preaching Buddha. Throughout Buddhist countries the lotus was also an attribute of the Bodhisattva Padmapani ('he who holds the lotus'), an epithet of Avalokiteshvara, who is represented as holding a lotus bloom or seated upon a lotus. The faithful are represented as being reborn from lotus flowers into the visionary 'Pure Land' of the Buddha and the lotus emblem is especially associated with Avalokiteshvara in his capacity of guide to the way of salvation, leading souls into the Pure Land (*Sukhavati*). The *Saddharma-Pundarika* ('The Lotus of Good Doctrine') was translated into Chinese (*c.* 4th c. A.D.) and became one of the most fertile sources of themes for Chinese Buddhist art.

The *Nelumbo nucifera*, described as the 'Indian' or 'Sacred' lotus, was native to China and was cultivated for food and for medicinal and cosmetic purposes. With the introduction of Buddhism into China the Indian-Buddhist lotus symbolism was also adopted. By Sung times, however, i.e. from *c.* the end of the 10th c., much of its specific Buddhist association had been shed, although much of its symbolic meaning had been adopted and adapted, gradually becoming absorbed into new and typically Chinese conceptions. From the 11th c. the lotus has been the symbol of the perfect man and the uncorrupted official and in the series of the Flowers of the Twelve Months and Four Seasons it is associated with summer. Among Taoists the lotus plant was prized as an attribute of Ho Hsien-ku, one of the Eight Taoist Immortals. The seed pod has generally the rather obvious associations with fertility and numerous offspring. Lotus flowers came to be much used ornamentally in Chinese pictorial art and in a rather more stylized form for decorative patterns in embroidery, carpets and even ceramics. But the lotus never became so ubiquitous an ornamental motif in Chinese decoration as it was in Egypt and the Mediterranean countries.

LOUDON, JOHN CLAUDIUS (1783–1843). So far as LANDSCAPE GARDENING is concerned Loudon was not on the same plane as the three great leaders of the movement who preceded him, 'Capability' BROWN, Humphry REPTON and Uvedale PRICE; but he played a minor role with some success, invented what he termed the 'gardenesque' form of layout, and made a considerable contribution to horticulture in general by his practical experiments, to which he devoted several publications in the first two decades of the 19th c. More influential, however, were the encyclopedias and magazines which he edited later in his career and which swayed Victorian architectural taste, although not always with the best results.

The son of a successful farmer, Loudon was born at Cambustay in Lanarkshire on 8 April 1783. After attending school in Edinburgh he went to work at the age of 15 with the Scottish landscape gardener John Mawer of Easter Dalry, and after the latter's death continued with a Mr. Dickson of Leith. He also put in some spare-time study with the Professor of Agriculture at Edinburgh University, Dr. Coventry, and made himself familiar with current 'Picturesque' theories through the writings of Gilpin, Payne KNIGHT and Uvedale Price, by whose *Essay* he was profoundly influenced. In 1803 Loudon moved to London, where he set up in practice, receiving commissions to plant, drain or otherwise improve 'several noblemen's and gentlemen's' estates. In 1804 he produced his first book, *Observations on the . . . Theory and Practice of Landscape Gardening*, which not only borrowed extensively from Repton's publications but bore a title which was in part identical with the latter's work of 1803. This debt, however, he can be said to have repaid many years later by editing a useful complete edition of Repton's gardening books in 1840.

Other books followed, including a treatise on *Laying out Farms and Farm Buildings in the Scotch Style, adapted to England* (1811), which brought Loudon to the notice of General Stratton of Tew Park, Oxfordshire. The outcome was that he moved to Tew and there initiated one of the most enterprising schemes of his life, the establishment of an agricultural college intended for potential landed proprietors, agents and others with similar interests. The experiment, however, did not succeed and the college closed two years later, leaving a gap in facilities for agricultural education until the founding of the Royal Agricultural College at Cirencester in 1840. Loudon had by now learnt to develop ideas of his own, and an increasing number of publications flowed from his pen on subjects ranging from the use of paper roofing, with which he had experimented at Tew Lodge, to designs for curvilinear hothouses, the latter being supported by wrought-iron framing of a kind which was later to be developed by Joseph Paxton at Chatsworth and for the Crystal Palace.

From *c.* 1820 Loudon suffered from increasing ill health, as a result of which his right arm became useless and eventually had to be amputated. In spite of this he continued to work with remarkable fortitude, concentrating on a steady output of publications. Among the more important titles of this period were the *Encyclopaedia of Gardening*, first published in 1822, followed by the *Encyclopaedia of Agriculture* (1825) and the *Gardener's Magazine*, a quarterly established in 1826. His range of interests now widened to include houses and decoration, and in 1830 he initiated what was probably his most influential work, the *Encyclopaedia of Cottage, Farm and Villa Architecture and Furniture*, a compilation which reappeared with additions in 1842, and again in 1846. For it Loudon assembled designs from a number of young architects, including Charles Barry, W. H. Leeds and some with less talent such as Edward Buckton Lamb, whose exuberant essays in a variety of styles were to provoke acid comments from A. W. PUGIN and other critics. Discrimination, however, was not Loudon's strong point, and convinced that the publication of these designs, together with his own observations as to their appropriate application, would meet a growing demand as middle- and lower-class housing reached a crescendo, he widened the scope of the supplement and subsequently that of the *Encyclopaedia*'s successor, *The Architectural Magazine*, by including designs for public houses, schools and even railway stations, while illustrations of furniture ranged from a square piano with projecting keys to bar fittings and beds.

There can be no doubt that by publishing these designs Loudon encouraged the artisans of Victorian England to proliferate a vast amount that was mediocre if not utterly tasteless, but it would be unjust to let them obscure the merits of his earlier horticultural and botanical writings. In 1823 he designed the interesting semi-detached house in Porchester Terrace, Bayswater, of which one half, numbered 3 and surviving, was to be his home for the rest of his life. On 14 September 1830 he married Jane Webb, the authoress of an imaginative novel entitled *The Mummy: a Tale of the Twenty-second Century*, which had appeared anonymously two years earlier and aroused considerable interest. She proved an ideal wife, sharing her husband's interests, acting as his amanuensis, and absorbing so much knowledge from him that she was later to produce her own very successful *Ladies' Companion to the Flower Garden* (1841) and the *Lady's Country Companion* (1845), as well as many other books on botany and natural history.

306, 416.

LOUVRE SCHOOL. See ANTWERP-LOUVRE SCHOOL.

824.

LOWBOY. American term for a small dressing-table or shallow chest with drawers mounted on four, or sometimes six, turned legs with stretchers. It appeared in the late 17th c. After *c.* 1730 it often had four drawers and was set on CABRIOLE legs to form a sort of table, the apron or lower edge usually being cut out in an undulating line. A chest of drawers placed on top of the lowboy converted it into a HIGHBOY and the two types of furniture were sometimes made to go together in sets. The lowboy was an elegant piece of furniture intended primarily for ladies and was among the most distinctive and popular pieces during the 18th c. in the U.S.A. See FURNITURE (AMERICAN).

LUCET. Implement used for making cords or laces. See NEEDLEWORK.

LUNETTE. Term in architecture for a semi-circular opening, for example a tympanum or the area between the lintel of a doorway and the

arch above it. In cabinet-making the term refers to any fan-shaped decoration such as was frequently found carved on oak furniture or painted or INLAID in late 18th-c. furniture.

LYONNESE BINDINGS. Mid 16th-c. French bookbindings decorated with polychrome interlaced strapwork or with large centre and corner ornaments on a dotted ground; so called because they often cover books printed in Lyon. The decoration is usually impressed by a panel stamp, a labour-saving device giving the effect of the elaborately tooled designs on bindings of the type made for GROLIER. See BOOKBINDING (HISTORICAL).

M

MCINTIRE, SAMUEL (1757–1811). American cabinet-maker, carver, designer, architect and musician, born at Salem, Massachusetts. He designed many of the most beautiful houses of New England in the FEDERAL style. His forte was the carving of mantels, cornices, stairways and window- and door-trims. A frequent identifying motif is the horn of plenty and the basket of fruit. His designs for interior woodwork were influenced by ADAM. His furniture was in a delicate NEO-CLASSICAL style deriving from SHERATON and HEPPLEWHITE. It was usually of MAHOGANY, shield-backed, with plain tapered legs and finely carved.

67.

MACKINTOSH, CHARLES RENNIE (1868–1928). Scottish architect and designer who as leader of the Glasgow School was one of the precursors of British and European *art nouveau.* In his domestic architecture particularly, and in the design of his building for the Glasgow School of Art, he opposed the current historicism and anticipated the rational functionalism of the Modern Movement. His furniture design and interior decoration, often done in collaboration with Margaret Macdonald (1865–1933), whom he married in 1900, had a mannered grace combined with functionalist austerity which became a keynote of the new art. His influence on the *avant garde* in Europe was very great, particularly in Germany and Austria, so much so that the advanced style of the early 20th c. was sometimes known as 'Mackintoshismus'. In December 1895 he participated in the opening exhibition of the *Maison de l'Art Nouveau* in Paris. His style of interior decoration was most spectacularly displayed in the furniture and decorations he designed for the four Cranston tearooms in Glasgow *c.* 1897–1912. This became known on the Continent through reproductions in *The Studio* in 1897 and in 1898 he exhibited a suite of furniture in Munich. In a competition for the design of a connoisseur's house organized by the *Zeitschrift für Innendekoration* of Darmstadt in 1901 he was awarded second prize and in 1902 he laid out the Scottish section of the Turin exhibition. He had considerable influence on the Austrian architects Josef HOFFMANN and Joseph Maria Olbrich (1867–1908) and in 1900 he exhibited with the Vienna SEZESSION, some of whose members later went to Glasgow to study his buildings there. His work was exhibited in Budapest, Munich, Dresden, Venice, Vienna and Moscow, attracting the enthusiasm of the *avant garde.* In 1914 he settled in London and did work as a designer of fabrics, book covers and furniture. See ART NOUVEAU and FURNITURE (MODERN).

564, 748.

MACKMURDO, ARTHUR H. (1851–1942). Scottish architect and designer who set up in London in 1875, came under the influence of William MORRIS and became one of the pioneers of the ARTS AND CRAFTS MOVEMENT. During the 1880s he was in advance of his time in domestic design and his influence was strongly felt on the Continent, especially by van de VELDE and the founders of the DEUTSCHER WERKBUND. In 1880 he founded the Century Guild, a group of artist–craftsmen which included Selwyn Image (1849–1930) and William de Morgan (1832–1911). In 1884, with Herbert Horne, he started the magazine *The Hobby Horse,* which was the focus of the new art movement for many years. It aroused William Morris's interest in printing and was one of the influences which led him to found the KELMSCOTT PRESS.

MACRAMÉ. Knotted work and in particular a trimming or fringe of knotted threads. See NEEDLEWORK.

MAGGIOLINI, GIUSEPPE. Outstanding Italian cabinet-maker of Milan in the 18th c. when Milan was the most famous centre of MARQUETRY. Maggiolini signed a number of cabinets and commodes decorated with marquetry in the NEO-CLASSICAL style and his name is used in the antique trade to describe most such pieces made in Italy.

MAGNUS (mid 17th c.). Dutch family of BOOKBINDERS active in Amsterdam. As successful imitators of contemporary French POINTILLÉ BINDINGS they have been credited with most of the fine Dutch bindings of the period. MAGNUSZ HENDRIKSZ (1610–74) and his son HENDRIK MAGNUSZ (1639–*c.* 1686) were employed by the publishing house of ELZEVIER, the latter being commissioned in 1679 to bind copies of Heinsius's 1676 edition of Virgil for presentation to Louis XIV and the Dauphin. The '*pointillé*' FLEURONS and floral TOOLINGS massed inside rectangular roll-borders, which were characteristic of Magnus bindings, influenced English bookbinding design after the Restoration. Magnus bindings may sometimes be distinguished from their French prototypes by the presence of bird motifs in the borders.

MAHOGANY. A heavy and durable hardwood, which seasons to a rich red-brown. It began to be used extensively for FURNITURE in the early GEORGIAN period and gave rise to what is sometimes referred to as the 'Mahogany Period'. Although this wood had been known and admired since it was first observed by the carpenter on Sir Walter Raleigh's ship during a voyage to South America in 1595, its general use for furniture began in the 1720s, at first largely owing to a scarcity of walnut. It was originally imported mainly from San Domingo, Cuba and Puerto Rico. Jamaica became a major source of supply, and the wood was also known as 'Jamaica wood'. In the U.S.A. it was in use from the 1730s and it was typical for the CHIPPENDALE style. See FURNITURE and WOOD-WORKING.

MAIOLI BINDINGS. A group of over 90 16th-c. bindings, probably made in Paris, stamped with the name 'Thos. Maioli' and the mottoes *Inmichi mei mea mihi non me michi* ('My enemies may rob me of my possessions but not of my soul') and *Ingratis servire nephas* ('One should not help the ungrateful'). Though Maioli's nationality is disputed, he has been identified by G. D. Hobson (*Maioli and others*, 1927) with Thomas Mahieu, probably of Italian origin, who was secretary to Catherine de Médicis (1549–60) and one of Jean GROLIER's successors as Treasurer of France. Active as a book collector 1530–65, he was still alive in 1575. Maioli's bindings, though mostly later than those made for Grolier, display similar ARABESQUES and flowing STRAPWORK designs. On some of the plainer bindings the leather has been rubbed with gold to produce a powdered effect.

393.

MAIOLICA. See CERAMICS.

682.

MAKIE (Japanese, sprinkled picture). A Japanese technique of decorative lacquer work. See JAPAN (LACQUER).

MALACHITE. A bright green mineral, basically copper carbonate, which is found in very many copper-mining areas. It has a hardness of 3·5 to 4 on the MOHS SCALE. It does not crystallize well and for that reason has not been used as a gemstone, but over the years it has had a considerable vogue as a decorative material for *objets d'art*. The best variety comes from the U.S.S.R., where it has been particularly popular as an ornamental stone.

MALTESE LACE. The LACE of Malta was a product of the enterprise of Lady Hamilton Chichester, who introduced Genoese lace-workers into Malta in 1833. Shawls and veils as well as narrow trimmings were made—often of silk, both black and white—in which the old patterns of the GENOESE bobbin lace with their liberal use of seed-like forms were adapted to 19th-c. taste. This lace was subsequently imitated both in France and in England.

435, 651.

MANTEL CLOCKS. A type of CLOCK associated mainly with France and Switzerland and designed, as its name implies, to stand on a broad mantelpiece. The earliest examples, the so-called '*religieuses*' of France, were of architectural form and had some links with the Dutch 'Haagse' clocks; but later in the reign of Louis XIV the design grew a little more free and culminated in the flowing curves and applied ORMOLU work of the Louis XV period. Considerable use was also made of BOULLE work. Mantel clocks of the Louis XIV and Louis XV periods are spring-driven pendulum clocks, the pendulum being often visible through the glass front of the case below the ENAMEL dial. They are usually designed to be not only wound but regulated from the front, and a very small hole into which a key can be inserted for this purpose can usually be seen just above the XII-hour figures. An offshoot from the Louis XIV and Louis XV styles was the somewhat simpler 'Neuchâtel' type developed in Switzerland, which persists to the present day. The reign of Louis XVI was a period of great variety in the type of clock-cases. The case, in fact, developed almost into an independent art form of itself, with the clock dial merely one element in the design and not even particularly prominent. The case was no longer specially suitable for a mantelpiece, but could be seen to advantage in a variety of situations.

106, 458, 535.

MANTON, JOSEPH (1766–1835). Regarded by many as the greatest English gun-maker. Born at Grantham in Lincolnshire, in 1781 he set up in business in London, where he remained until his death, making a great name for himself for the manufacture of all types of fire-arms but especially fine-quality sporting-guns. The development of the classic English shotgun, decorated austerely but beautifully proportioned and superbly made, owes much to Manton. Examples of his work are in the Tower of London Armouries; Glasgow Art Gallery and Museum. See ARMS AND ARMOUR.

622.

MANUTIUS, ALDUS (1449–1515). Italian scholar and printer, who opened an academy in Venice for the study of Greek, and in 1489 began to equip a press with Greek and Latin types. He printed the first editions of many of the classics as well as works by Erasmus and other contemporary humanists and his own Latin grammars. After his death his publishing and printing firm was carried on by his father-in-law and then by his son and grandson until 1597.

Aldus had an enduring influence on European TYPOGRAPHY. His Greek type faces reproduced a current accented script with hundreds of ligatured letters and abbreviations, so that in one of them there were 1,400 characters. Such was his prestige that Greek types of this kind were normally used until *c.* 1800. The ROMAN type cut for Aldus and used first in his edition of Pietro Bembo's *De Aetna* in 1495 served as a pattern for the great school of Parisian type-founders of the following century, and a modern reproduction of it is in great favour. Lastly, Aldus had the first ITALIC made for the texts of his series of cheap pocket editions of the Latin classics, begun in 1501. His types were cut for him by Francesco Griffo of Bologna, who deserves much of the credit for them.

679, 692.

MARBLING. The process of colouring paper in conventional imitation of marble. Prepared colours, dropped on to the surface of a bath of size, are drawn or 'combed' into veined patterns which are transferred to a sheet of paper laid on the floating colours. This technique, almost certainly of Persian origin, was introduced into Europe from Turkey at the end of the 16th c. Marbled papers were manufactured in France during the 17th c. by the Le Breton family and used for lining and end-papers by Mace Ruette, Le Gascon and other French BOOKBINDERS; the practice of marbling book-edges was introduced by Dutch binders *c.* 1675. See PAPERS, DECORATIVE.

538.

MARCASITE. A crystallized form of iron pyrites which was used for costume jewellery in the 18th and 19th centuries when the vogue for PASTE was at its height. The crystals are small, hard and do not transmit light so that it is impossible to imitate the effects of gemstones with them. But when faceted by hand and carefully set they reflect light from the surfaces with a metallic glitter which can be in its own way effective. A craft of hand-cutting and setting marcasite was built up chiefly in France and Switzerland and still persists to a minor degree. When the workmanship is good marcasite jewellery has a certain charm of its own and is not to be confused with cheap mass-produced imitations.

MARCHANDS-MERCIERS. Strictly speaking 18th-c. and 19th-c. French furniture-dealers, in practice they were the equivalent of the modern interior decorator, purveying furniture, porcelain, gilt bronzes and luxury fittings of various kinds to their clients. They had considerable influence on contemporary taste and many of the leading Parisian cabinet-makers and chair-makers worked exclusively for them. Simon-Philippe POIRIER, Dominique DAGUERRE and Martin-Éloy LIGNEREUX were *marchands-merciers*.

520.

MARKWART (Spanish MACUARTE). Family of gunsmiths from Augsburg. They were employed by Charles V and the two brothers SIMON and PETER, sons of Bartolomäus Markwart, were brought by Charles V to Madrid *c.* 1530. The Spanish gunmaker Alonso Martinez de Espinar mentions this in his treatise *Arte de Ballesteria y Monteria* (1644), describing them as 'very great craftsmen in the making of barrels and wheel-locks' and as the best craftsmen that the Emperor found in Germany. He says that they also worked both for Philip II and for Philip III. The Markwart family all used the sickle as their mark.

Simon Markwart had a son also called SIMON, who in Isidro Soler's *Compendio Historico de los Arcabuceros de Madrid* (1795) is described as gunmaker to Philip II and Philip III and is credited with the invention of the 'Spanish snap-lock', the type which was later known as the miquelet. It is thought that this may have consisted in a modification of the Italian type of snap-lock with certain additional features.

MARLBORO' LEG. Term used in cabinet-making during the 2nd half of the 18th c. for a tapering leg of square section.

MAROT, DANIEL (1663–1752). French architect, furniture designer and engraver. He was a Huguenot who left France for Holland a year before the Revocation of the Edict of Nantes (1685) and entered the service of the Stadtholder, later William III of England. As William's court architect Marot visited England 1694–8 and was probably consulted on the furnishing and interior decoration of Hampton Court Palace, where he is known to have planned the gardens. Engraved designs by Marot (a collected edition, *Œuvres du Sieur D. Marot, Architecte de Guillaume III, roy de la Grande Bretagne*, was published in Holland in 1702) were widely influential in England. His designs of furniture were of a decorative BAROQUE character derived from the latest style at Louis XIV's court, set against complete schemes of interior decoration. The latter included a room in CHINESE TASTE. There are examples of elaborate beds based on his designs, and chairs of *c.* 1690–1700 with completely carved and pierced backs are described as 'in the style of Daniel Marot'.

MARQUETRY. A process used in cabinet-making for decorating a surface with patterns composed of small pieces of differently coloured woods, IVORY, metal, TORTOISESHELL, MOTHER OF PEARL or other materials. There are two types of marquetry. The simpler method, sometimes called 'inlaying', is to chisel out shallow cavities in the surface of the wood and insert the decorative materials into them. The more complicated process, commonly employed in the 17th and 18th centuries, consists in fitting the various pieces of decorative material together into a thin sheet, which is then glued like a VENEER to the surface to be decorated. The usual method of cutting the pattern was to fasten tightly together two or more sheets of wood, brass, tortoiseshell, etc., as required, with a sheet of paper on top marked out with the design. The craftsman then cut along the lines of the design with a fine fretsaw, after which the parts cut out of the top sheet could be exactly fitted into the lower sheet and vice versa, so that there resulted two sets of marquetry for every two sheets of material employed.

Marquetry was used in ancient EGYPT and in GREEK AND ROMAN ANTIQUITY. In western Europe it was first extensively practised in Italy during the 15th c. under the name *tarsia* (later and in Mod. Ital. *intarsio*). In the earlier part of the century *tarsia* composed of simple chequerwork or interlaced geometrical patterns was popular in Venice on CASSONI. Later in the century Florence became renowned for pictorial *tarsia* decorating wall panelling, chests, cupboards, wardrobes and other furniture. The subject matter was elaborated to include landscape, architectural perspectives, still lifes, etc., and the *intarsiatore* strove to imitate the themes of the painters as closely as possible, often working from cartoons by eminent artists such as Botticelli (1444–1512) and Piero della Francesca (1410/20–92). They were particularly fond of still life and, aided by the new rules of perspective, they often succeeded in obtaining remarkably illusionistic effects. A favourite subject for *trompe-l'œil* was the half-open cupboard door revealing a collection of books, instruments and other objects haphazardly arranged, as in the marquetry wall-panelling of the Palazzo Ducale at Urbino. In northern Italy there was a special variety of *tarsia* known as *alla certosina* from its supposed association with the Charterhouse monasteries. It was derived from Arabic models and was executed with small pieces of bone, ivory or wood inlaid in abstract geometrical patterns.

In the 16th c. *tarsia* was also practised by the cabinet-makers of the important south German centres of Augsburg and Nuremberg. Italianate designs were introduced by the Nuremberg carver Peter Flötner and the painter Lorenz Stoer published a collection of woodcut designs for *tarsia* panels in his book *Geometria und Perspectiva* (1567), which were popular with Augsburg craftsmen. From Germany the craft spread to the Netherlands and England, where simple inlaid floral ornament and pictures of fanciful buildings were used to decorate the fronts of chests and the headboards of beds in Elizabethan and Jacobean furniture. During the 16th c. *tarsia* also spread to France along with other influences of the Italian Renaissance. Among the 22 craftsmen taken to France by Charles VIII after the capture of Naples in 1495 two were expert craftsmen in *tarsia*, namely Domenico da Cortona and Bernardo da Brescia. Through the 16th c. Italian influence on French furniture was felt primarily through the introduction of colour by means of *tarsia*.

During the 17th c., as the practice of veneering became more prevalent, the more complicated technique of marquetry was developed first in the Low Countries and then in France. (See CARPENTER, JOINER, CABINET-MAKER.) The most famous practitioner during the 2nd half of the century was BOULLE. Compositions of flowers and birds, executed in coloured woods and reminiscent of the paintings of artists such as Jean-Baptiste Monnoyer (1634–99), were popular in France and Holland and the vogue spread to England after the Restoration. Towards the end of the century, under the influence of designers such as BÉRAIN, fanciful GROTESQUES based on Renaissance prototypes became a common theme, particularly in France, where they were adapted to treatment in brass and tortoiseshell as in the manner of Boulle.

The techniques of Boulle were not adopted in England except perhaps by Gerreit JENSEN. Floral marquetry was popular in the time of Charles II, while ARABESQUES and abstract forms of ornament such as SEAWEED or ENDIVE were fashionable in the William and Mary style. During the first half of the 18th c. marquetry went out of fashion in England, but in France the technique was carried to its highest perfection by the 18th-c. craftsmen. Vases of flowers, trophies of arms, musical instruments, landscapes and classical ruins, ROCOCO phantasies and still life compositions, were all rendered with brilliant naturalism by the *ébénistes* such as J.-F. OEBEN and J.-H. RIESENER, while the German David ROENTGEN went even further in the virtuosity of his imitations of painted pictures. In England marquetry came back into favour during the last quarter of the century, but the designs were largely those of the NEO-CLASSICAL type and the style popularized by the ADAM brothers. Marquetry was also a feature among others of furniture made in the U.S.A. in the FEDERAL and EMPIRE styles.

529.

MARTHA WASHINGTON. Name given in the U.S.A. to a type of inlaid and upholstered open armchair, with high back, which was first manufactured in New Hampshire in the first decade of the 19th c.

MASAMUNE, GORŌ NYŪDŌ (1264–1343), of Sagami. Generally regarded as the greatest of all the Japanese bladesmiths. He made a comprehensive study of the techniques of all the best masters of his time and founded an important school of swordsmiths. Examples of his work are in the Victoria and Albert Museum and the Metropolitan Museum, New York.

MASANAO. Eighteenth-c. Japanese *netsuke* carver of Kyoto, mentioned in the *Sōken Kishō*. He was founder of a famous school of ivory-carving. There were several other *netsuke* carvers of the same name, pre-eminent among them being Masanao of Yamada (1815–90), who carved mainly animals in wood. See JAPAN (NETSUKE).

MASATSUGU, KAIGYOKUSAI. See JAPAN (NETSUKE).

MEANDER. See FRET.

MECHANICAL MUSICAL INSTRUMENTS. The history of mechanical music and its instruments exhibits its close dependence on craftsmanship and precision engineering, a reliance only to be equalled in its parent art form, horology. From their earliest beginning instruments of mechanical music have displayed technological standards equal to the highest pertaining in their time. When, for example, the clockwork spinet was devised during the 1st half of the 16th c., the techniques used for the transcription of contemporary music by means of pins set in a wooden barrel required their placing to be determined with the utmost accuracy. The slightest error in the positioning of a pin would show up at once as a faulty musical performance. Aside from the precision of manufacture of the musical part of these diminutive table-top spinets, the motive power was provided by a fusée-wound clockwork spring motor made to the highest contemporary engineering standards. As a mechanism the need for perfection was met and then the whole was embellished by the artistry of the cabinet-maker. Decoration in the form of chased filigree brasswork, exquisite casework enhanced by valuable metals and minerals, panelling and painting, all combined to produce an instrument which not only performed faultlessly but which could also take its place as a work of decorative art. That several of these instruments survive today in playing order after *c.* 400 years is a daunting indictment of many later and less durable craft products.

Craftsmanship did not cease with performance and decoration but extended to durability, which was achieved without any heaviness or ugliness. It was an outcome of a highly developed sensitivity of the craftsman to the characteristics of his materials. Many of the church and chamber barrel organs made during the 18th and 19th centuries, for example, have remained in playing order. This is not necessarily to imply that they have continued in perfect condition without subsequent attention, but the bellows often remain airtight and pallet chests and soundboards remain serviceable, witnessing to their careful manufacture from selected well-seasoned materials.

Although it represents but one aspect of mechanical musical instruments, in the 110 years or thereabouts of its life the cylinder musical box is not only a fascinating example of craftsmanship in itself but illustrates also the shift of emphasis in artistry which occurred in the later years of the 19th c. The invention of the tuned steel comb, itself demanding the best available steel and the most delicate workmanship to evoke from it a musical sound, prepared the way for the manufacture of a new type of instrument which, although incapable of reproducing the sound of any other, more familiar one, could generate a new and captivating sound within the limits of which music might be rendered. The earliest musical movements of this type were made by clock- and watch-makers and these craftsmen at once appreciated the potential of the musical box. Hand-made musical movements of the early part of the 19th c. frequently played operatic, traditional and sacred music and provided the public with pre-recorded music in their homes. Finely cut musical combs—some so fine that a cigarette paper might only just be inserted between the teeth—and brass cylinders containing many thousands of minute steel pins formed the salient parts of musical movements which required for their manufacturers not only artisans of the highest quality, to whom the tools and teachings of the watch-makers' trade were second nature, but ones possessing a thorough command of musical knowledge. To them the *arpeggio* and the embellishment of a musical phrase were inseparably associated with the dividing head, the lathe and the ability to drill a hole a few thousandths of a centimetre in diameter to within even finer limits of a pre-ordained position.

In the beginning musical boxes were almost always incorporated as part of a larger whole, sometimes with complex automata but more usually with a clock. By *c.* 1805 the musical box materialized as an instrument in its own right. Here was something which could be sold on its merits as an interpreter of music rather than as an adjunct to some other mechanism. It comes as something of a surprise, then, to find that the majority of these very early musical boxes, whilst of undoubted quality when viewed in the light of contemporary technology, were offered for sale in the plainest of wooden cases. Oak or walnut and sometimes fruitwoods were used, but the accoutrements were of the simplest possible kind. Some employed wire hasps and staples as hinges for the lid whilst the simple scythe-shaped fly catch was used to secure it. The control levers for the mechanism protruded through the end of the case.

With the completion of the first quarter of the 19th c. the basic cylinder musical-box movement had developed into a style of component layout and function which was to remain fundamentally unaltered throughout its life. The manufacture was still organized along the lines of a cottage industry and this mode rapidly developed craftsmen of the best quality. The nature of their work and the physical separation of the workers did, however, prevent many of them from ever seeing the finished object of their labours. Whereas the first movements were almost exclusively the work of scattered watch-makers in the Swiss Jura, certain centres soon developed—La Chaux-de-Fonds, Le Locle, Ste-Croix and, in the Vallée de Joux, Le Pont, Le Brassus and Yverdon. The setting up of centres in Geneva itself coupled with the foundation of a concerted export trade led to the realization that the musical-box case itself should assume a decorative appearance as well as its functional purpose. The popularity of MARQUETRY and PARQUETRY led to the treatment of the wooden case as a vehicle for inlays of rare woods, brass (sometimes silver and occasionally pewter), mother of pearl, enamels and very occasionally miniature paintings in reverse on glass.

From *c.* 1835 to *c.* 1845 musical boxes reached a quality seldom equalled in later years. The techniques of cylinder-pinning—the actual setting of the musical programme into the mechanism—had become so advanced that whereas originally movements had only played 3 or 4 airs (Nicole produced some truly astounding three-overture boxes), 6 or even 8 tunes could now be set on one cylinder. The cylinder shifted laterally a distance equal to a fraction more than the thickness of a cylinder pin between each tune, thereby allowing the pins for 5 other (or in the case of an 8-tune box, 7 other) circumferential rows of pins to pass between the accurately-ground tips of the musical comb teeth. The precision needed to achieve this left no room for error since the minutest sideways variation would result in the playing of two tunes together as the comb teeth engaged in two rows of pins. Exquisite case-inlays representing complex designs executed in many different woods characterized the period.

A shortcoming of the cylinder musical box was that it would only play the tunes which were pinned to its cylinder. Numerous attempts were made to overcome this defect, often displaying extraordinary ingenuity and manufacturing skill. Amédée Paillard of the Ste-Croix family, which established the first musical-box manufactury proper, devised the so-called 'revolver' movement by which 6 cylinders each playing up to 8 tunes could be mounted between the flanges of 2 large hoop-like wheels within the musical movement. The indexing of the whole assembly would bring a fresh cylinder into play and, at the completion of its programme or at the will of the listener, the cylinder could be 'discarded' and another rotated into place. The sheer technique needed to produce such a remarkable mechanism is to be admired even more when one considers the types of machine tools available and the need to work either by daylight or by oil-lamp. Naturally a mechanism of this type was enormously expensive and it never really became a commercial proposition. Its inventor went on to develop a musical box which would play interchangeable cylinders, spare ones being kept in a drawer in the special table supplied with the box.

Soon many of the larger makers were producing this type of instrument and extra cylinders could be purchased as and when needed. Even more complex movements were to be produced, among them the *Plérodiénique* type in which two cylinders of equal length and diameter were mounted end to end on a common shaft and arranged to telescope into a central collar. Each cylinder was pinned with part of the same melody and was arranged in the mechanism so that one made its lateral shift to bring another, adjacent circumferential row of pins into line with the comb teeth, slightly ahead of the change of the other. The result was a musical box which could play a relatively long piece of music without a break since whilst one cylinder advanced in silence the other still played. Because contemporary engineering was producing remarkable mechanisms in many other fields, wonders of precision such as this were treated as commonplace when new.

The decline of the cylinder box, brought about by the arrival of the disc-playing instrument whose repertory could be up-dated for a few pence, was hastened by the phonograph and the cylinder box was finally forgotten in the turmoil of the First World War. With this came a general lowering of standards. Mass-production of musical movements quickly eradicated the stand made by the craftsmen builders and the wooden casework deteriorated to the point where poor-quality timber blinded by red lead and then artificially grained superseded even veneered wood. Lids, however, remained veneered and inlaid, although the delicacy of the craft had been lost. Finally perfection of the lithographed colour transfer, which could imitate the appearance of a complete inlaid lid, deprived the box of its last vestige of artistry.

Meanwhile production of the disc-playing musical box had got under way in 1890. Here was a totally different mechanism which called for a large case. For the smaller, table-top models, cases resembling caskets were made, the larger ones heavily corniced and embellished with mouldings and a central lid inlay. The larger instruments, some of which stood over two metres high, permitted the use of an architectural approach including the free use of turned columns, pediments, galleries and finials combining with carving, cornice and fret. Although mass-produced, these marked the treatment of the musical box as a free-standing article of furniture.

The architectural design of the instruments of mechanical music reached its zenith in the orchestrion organs and piano orchestrions of the 1920s and 1930s, whilst the ROCOCO style was exploited by the Parisian show-organ manufacturers such as Gavioli, Gaudin and Marenghi. The subtleties of pneumatic action, which reached its climax with the reproducing player pianos in the years between the World Wars, demonstrated infinite skill and ingenuity.

It is a sad reflection both on the achievements of the craftsmen who built mechanical musical instruments in the past and on the standards of today that many of the skills evinced in their work are lost and those that remain are generally considered to be uneconomical in modern conditions.

112, 140, 148, 188, 644, 817, 885.

MECHLIN LACE. Name given to a bobbin LACE made at Mechlin (Malines) and other Flemish towns (Antwerp, Lier, Turnhout) in the 18th and 19th centuries. Pattern and ground-mesh were worked in one piece as in VALENCIENNES, but Mechlin is readily distinguished from the latter by the presence of a thick glossy thread outlining the motifs. The ground was commonly hexagonal, but was often varied with decorative effects such as *fond de neige*. Patterns included flowers, sprigs and leaves. The graceful, elegant designs together with their ingenious use of ornamental nets vie with those of BRUSSELS and ALENÇON and in the 18th c. it was graced with the title *la reine des dentelles*. It was also sometimes named *point de Malines*, incorrectly because it was not a needlepoint lace, and because of its likeness to EMBROIDERY it has also been called *broderie de Malines*. It was much in demand in England during the REGENCY and experienced a vogue in France during the First Empire. Light and gossamer, Mechlin lace was much used as an edging for muslin gowns and for frills.

435, 651.

MEDALS. The medal did not make its appearance until the 15th c. Often regarded as a creation of Renaissance painters and sculptors, it was actually an inspired re-invention in Italy of the commemorative medallion of the late Roman emperors; as such, it was one of the more tangible fruits of the classical revival which took place in the Quattrocento.

Unlike the medallions, which were struck from dies in GOLD or SILVER, the best medals were cast of BRONZE; silver was used later in Germany. The medallions had been the privilege of rulers and celebrated events of state; medals were vehicles for individual glorification. Any person of means could trumpet forth his achievements, or merely satisfy a whim, by commissioning a medal with his effigy. All medals except those produced at the Vatican were private, social rather than official documents. The medal in Italy was essentially humanistic, an instrument for the glorification of man; religious sentiments did not appear until the German medallists.

In the late 14th c. an unusual series of medals by northern French or Burgundian artists had been struck in gold and silver to the order of Jean, duc de Berry. All known examples are bronze casts of the originals, which are lost, but the vigorous execution speaks of the extraordinary skill of the unknown craftsmen who designed them. One has a remarkable equestrian portrait of Constantine the Great, another a powerful bust of the Emperor Heraclius with a dynamic design of a horse-drawn chariot on the reverse. At their time these medals seem to have exerted no influence, and so they can only be regarded as precursors of the medallic art form in a historical sense.

The choice of bronze for the Renaissance medal was not due to chance. Bronze COINAGE had ended in the 6th c. and was not renewed except sporadically. As a utilitarian metal, however, bronze had no rival. It was easily worked, was highly durable, and yielded agreeably to patination, as the Greek and Roman bronzes testified. (See COPPER AND ITS ALLOYS.) Italy had long supported a bronze-casting industry. In Florence the sculptor Donatello (1386–1466) and his followers, notably Bertoldo di Giovanni (*c*. 1420–91) and Andrea del Verrocchio (*c*. 1435–88), cast statuettes and spirited small figures in bronze. A steady flow of utilitarian objects—ornamented mortars, candlesticks and bowls—came from the foundries in Padua and Venice. Commercially it was a natural step from these to small reliefs, plaquettes, pendants and badges. Countless plaquettes, many of considerable artistic merit, were cast as paxes, the tablets presented at the Mass. These were decorated on one side and the reverses left blank. The medal, however, had relief illustration or a legend on the reverse, an addition borrowed from coinage, so that both sides of the planchet were used. The private, even intimate, nature of the medal further dictated that it had to be of a size convenient to be held in the hand and admired. Thus from its beginning the medal was restricted to a diameter of between 5 and 12 cm, and was rarely as large as 16 or 18 cm.

What suddenly inspired the re-creation of the medal is not clear, but there is no dispute that the supreme master in this field was Antonio Pisano of Verona, known as PISANELLO. Already known as a painter of portraits and of animals, he raised his signature boldly 'Pisani Pictoris' on his medals. If he served a trial period in modelling and casting, there is no record of any earlier bronze work. His very first issue was a masterpiece. In 1438, when the Emperor of Constantinople, John VIII Paleologue, visited the Pope and the Council of Ferrara, Pisanello designed and executed a bronze medal showing on the obverse a great profile of the Emperor wearing a curious high-peaked hat and on the reverse a representation of him riding past a wayside cross with a mounted page behind him. The new medium of the medal unleashed in Pisanello a rare creative vigour. He modelled the features of the Emperor, the curled locks over the collar and even the bulge of the shoulder with a depth of relief that broke with the flat stylization to which portraits on metal had been confined since the time of the Roman coiners. He triumphed over the spatial limitation (103 millimetres), yet did not miniaturize. The bust rises in an open field of space while near the rim, running the entire circumference except at the peak of the hat, there is a full legend with the Emperor's official title in Greek—each letter and accent nobly in proportion and yet the whole subordinated to the strong profile.

This fine achievement inspired others to adopt the new form and influenced an entire generation of coin-engravers. For the next 16 years, Pisanello produced one splendid portrait medal after another, bequeathing to posterity a remarkable gallery of Renaissance notables in bronze.

The quality of the sinister is directly stated in his spare portrait of the despot Sigismondo Malatesta. The essence of the purposeful is expressed in his lean, tight-lipped profile of the Marquis of Mantua, Ludovico III Gonzaga. His Don Iñigo d'Avalos, perhaps his most beautiful creation, presents the Grand Chamberlain of Naples in a draped hat of marvellous modelling. The elongate bust of his Cecilia Gonzaga captures all feminine sweetness. Nor did imagination fail him when he composed his reverses. Frequently he used his beloved horses, but men in armour, eagles, angels and mythological figures or heraldic devices saved his work from the monotony to which later medallists so often succumbed in the designing of reverses. That he was not without humour and subtlety is shown in the reverse for his marriage medal of Leonello d'Este, Marquess of Ferrara, where a little Cupid teaches the lion, obviously a personification of the subject, to sing.

The best medals by his contemporaries fall short of this excellence. Costanzo of Ferrara's medal of Sultan Muhammad II, made *c.* 1481, is a superior portrait, although on the reverse the mount on which the sovereign rides is a poor, plodding beast. Yet compare it to the portrait of the same Sultan by the sculptor Bertoldo di Giovanni and the vigour of Costanzo's characterization becomes apparent. Matteo dei Pasti (1441–68), also of Verona, created a series of fine bronze portraits, and his Sigismondo Malatesta, made a year after Pisanello's, deserves particular acclaim. The reverse, showing the great castle at Rimini, is superb. Pasti's portrait of Malatesta's wife, Isotta degli Atti da Rimini, while not as fine as Pisanello's delicate Cecilia Gonzaga, is nevertheless unusually attractive; the elephant on the reverse is ungainly but not impossible. The capable Sperandio of Mantua (*c.* 1425–1504), achieved facility in the new medium with portraits that are harshly frank—e.g. those of the merchant Bartolommeo Pendaglia and Giovanni II Bentivoglio of Bologna—and some that are surprisingly forbidding. But his reverses lack spirit: often they are over-crowded and the lettering is weak. The Venetian Giovanni Boldu (active 1454–73) extended the range to antique themes, but his portraits are over-idealized. Niccolò Fiorentino (1430–1514), however, displayed greater versatility. The design of his tortured half-length figure of Savonarola clasping a large cross on which hangs the crucified Christ summons at once the whole fevered world of the preacher's fanaticism. His powerful medal of Charles VIII of France is a model portrait of that invader. His Lorenzo the Magnificent (Lorenzo de' Medici) presents a grave and thoughtful Medici prince, and his bust of the lady Giovanna Albizzi, with its reverse displaying the three nude Graces, radiates a quiet serenity.

Until the next century Italian artists had the medal largely to themselves. Any list of the masters who signed their works (many, regrettably, did not) must include Laurana, Pomedelli, Caradossa, Cattaneo, Guacialotti, Cristoforo di Geremia, Francesco da Sangallo, that excellent portrayer of fashionable ladies Pastorino da Siena, the prolific Leone Leoni, and Antonio Abondio, who exerted a strong influence on the course of medallic art in central Europe.

There were no important changes of technique in Italy. Each side of the medal was modelled in wax on a separate flat base. The bases were removed and the sides, fitted back to back, were impressed in suitable moulding material, either a paste of very fine ashes or a mixture of moistened ground chalk. After this material had hardened the negative impressions were pulled away, to permit removal of the wax positives. Now the negative moulds were joined again and the molten bronze was poured in. When cooled, the mould was separated to release the medal, which was now complete except for finishing touches. It is believed that most artists first poured a cast in LEAD both as a trial proof and to save for future moulds since the wax impression was fragile. Such lead proofs may be thought of as the real 'originals'. After seeing his lead proof the artist could improve on the wax models if he chose. This procedure was not, strictly speaking, the *cire-perdue* method, which was used for statues and reliefs with models made in clay, from which a wax replica was cast.

We have no way of knowing how many times any artist cast a single work; probably not many because some minor shrinkage resulted with each new cast. That is why dimensions of cast medals do vary. The cast of 103 millimetres of the Paleologue medal, for instance, may be presumed to be earlier than the one that is 101 millimetres or that which is 98 millimetres.

The cooled medal was a raw bright disc with rough edges and perhaps minor surface flaws. The edges were smoothed with a file, while the surface might be burnished or matured with GILDING or colour by heating in oil or coating with lacquer or varnish. For the final polish wax was applied. The portrait medal was less expensive than a portrait painting, which no doubt increased its popularity, and it permitted the casting of a few copies for friends, colleagues, patrons or followers.

The first to encourage the art in Germany may have been the Archduke Maximilian of Austria, later Emperor, for whose marriage to Marie of Burgundy the Italian Candida cast a medal as early as 1477. Medal-casting by native artists, however, did not come until the end of the century. The Germans excelled at working in miniature, in jewellery and goldsmith's work, and in the striking of 'show-thalers'. Already proficient as carvers of wood and stone, they did not need to model in clay or wax. The most appealing German medal portraits still extant are the wood and stone originals from which the moulding negatives were made. The German achievement has often been under-rated because the Italian finesse in refining and ennobling their subjects came closer to the classical models which were the taste of the High Renaissance. German realism, without this restraint, made a virtue of stressing stark, often uncomfortable truth.

Hans Schwarz (1492–after 1535) of Augsburg, who deserves acknowledgement as the first German master, provides excellent examples. His powerful portrait of Kunz von der Rosen (d. 1519) shows a tempestuous Imperial Councillor's bearded head jutting out of the medal (64 millimetres), as if to snap a reprimand at some courtier. His Magdalena Schlauderspacher (1519) is a simple rendering of a homely woman. His Lucia Dorer (1522), dominated by hat and coiffed hairdress, renders to the life a determined, haughty female. His Georg Schlauderspacher, bearded son of Magdalena with upturned nose and half-smile, is amiably smug. Georg's sister Ursula Imhoff appears in a sympathetic portrait, with broad hat, braided hair and necklace, that makes no effort to conceal the plainness of the seventeen-year-old. Friedrich Hagenauer's enormous bellied Christoph von Nellenburg in profile would have been shown by the Italians only with massive head; the German artist insists on the bulk too, and with it creates an almost grotesque half-figure. On the other hand a later master, Joachim Deschler, also employing bulk for his Hieronymus Parmgartner (1553), turned the full-lipped churchwarden into a full-face portrait and made him coarse and almost foolishly friendly. Hagenauer's medals of the humanist Philipp Melanchthon, however, and of others, are distinguished for more conventional portraiture. In Nuremberg the leading master was Matthes Gebel (active 1523–74). His Albrecht Dürer (1528) is a superb portrait of the great artist leaning forward as if to listen to the music of the spheres. Gebel's Felizitas Löffelholz, with long braids and wide-eyed look, is an uncommonly charming picture of a 15-year-old girl. Here, as German medallists were wont to do, the bust is extended to the rim of the disc in order to gain relief and support a more life-like volume. Dürer himself made a strong medal (1521) of the youthful Emperor Charles V, with the eyes cold and the Burgundian chin thrust out. Yet Dürer's medal of his own father shines with filial tenderness. The roll of German masters includes Christoph Weiditz (before 1523–60), whose clean reserved portraits of Hernán Cortés, Othmar Widenmann and Hieronymus Tucher have great merit. Also distinguished are Martin Schaffner (1478–1546?), whose Christina Beltzinger is outstanding, Hans Kels (1529–65), the extremely able Hans Daucher (active 1515–29), who rivals Hans Schwarz for vigorous delineation, Peter FLÖTNER, Hans Boesterer, Ludwig Neufahrer and, of course, Valentin Maler (active 1563–93), who was highly successful with slightly averted full-face portraits. One of the most popular medallists, and the finest for minor details and CHASING on the finished metal, was Hans Reinhart the Elder (active 1539–81). His *chef-d'œuvre* is probably the great Holy Trinity medal he made for Maurice of Saxony. It is of silver, however, and a triumph rather of the goldsmith's zeal for minutiae than of portraiture.

German medallists often cast in silver. Their reverses, unless these were graced with second portraits as on husband-and-wife medals, were uniformly commonplace. The coats of arms are pedestrian except to the student of heraldry, and the legends are often unimpressive.

French rulers long employed expert Italian medallists such as Pietro da Milano, Francesco Laurana and Giovanni di Candida. Occasionally native artists were commissioned, as for example Nicolas Leclerc and Jean de Saint-Priest (1500) for the superb medal of Louis XII and Anne of Brittany, or the great sculptor Germain Pilon (1537–90) for medals of Henri II and Henri III and Catherine de Médicis. But not until the advent of Guillaume Dupré (*c.* 1576–1643) did France produce a great native medallist.

Dupré's astonishing virtuosity overshadows the work of all other French medallists. His models may have been Italian, but he brought to them a uniquely Gallic quality. His early masterpiece (1601), with jugated busts of Henry IV and Marie de Médicis presents the King in cuirass, but it gives a very human expression to the eyes and bearded lips; and the Queen, elevated slightly behind him by the height of her hairdress, wears a benign smile. Dupré's portrait of the Duke of Mantua (1612), one of his largest medals (163 millimetres), though formalized with armour, great ruffed collar and curled hair, depicts a sober and troubled man, who died the year he came to power. The placing of the collar at a curved diagonal as if to divide head from body is an extraordinary feat of design. His portrait (1618) of Pierre Jeannin (190 millimetres), the King's Superintendent of Finance, depicts a hulking, elderly figure but the draping of the gown and the arched brow are handled in a manner to make the man appear more worldly-wise than he may have been. Dupré never lacked for ingenuity. His medal of Marie de Médicis, made 21 years after the portrait with her husband, shows her as an ageing woman with extra chin, plumpish neck, depressions under the eyes and queenly decolletage. A great fan-like sweep of regal lace collar takes the gaze from such harsh details to the larger fluted heart design.

France, of course, had many fine medallists, among them Jean Warin (*c.* 1604–72), who made an excellent portrait medal of Cardinal Richelieu.

Antonio Pisano (Pisanello), *John VIII Paleologue.* (B.M., 1438)

Niccolò Fiorentino, *Giovanna Albizzi.* (B.M., 1490)

Matthes Gebel, *Albrecht Dürer.* (B.M., 1528)

Hans Reinhart the Elder, *Holy Trinity* made for Maurice of Saxony. (B.M., 1544)

Peter Flötner, *Raimund Fugger* of Augsburg. (B.M., 1527)

Guillaume Dupré, *Henry IV* and *Marie de Médicis.* (B.M., 1601)

(*All above reproduced third actual size*)

A

'The History of Man in Flight.'
Commemorative medals. The Royal Air Force Museum (1972)

A. Leonardo da Vinci—First scientific studies of flight. B. De Rozier and D'Arlande—First manned flight. C. Lilienthal—Glider pioneer. D. R.A.F. Fighter Command—The Battle of Britain. E. Armstrong and Aldrin—First men on the moon

(*Reproduced half actual size*)

B

C

D

E

But the equal of Dupré did not appear. Great medallists did not appear in the Netherlands either, except for the Fleming Jacob Jonghelinck (1531–1606) and perhaps Steven van Herwijk (active 1557–65). Quentin Metsys, the painter (*c.* 1460–1530), cast an extraordinary portrait of Erasmus, but it seems to have been his only medal. Van Herwijk made a superb medal of Henry VII, and the Italians Leone Leoni, Jacopo da Trezzo and Poggini cast superior medals of other rulers and dignitaries in England. There were no native medallists in England until the 17th c. with Thomas Simon, George Bowers and Thomas Rawlins.

The introduction in Augsburg of a die-stamping machine in 1550 signalled the death of the cast medal. Already artists had found the cutting of INTAGLIO dies for their medals more economical than relief modelling. From the steel dies many examples could be struck, each the same size, each equally sharp; indeed the lines were cleaner than in the cast. Dürer's medal of Charles V had been struck. In Italy, France and England, as in Germany, every coin-engraver felt encouraged now to create medals. The influence of the machine was eventually to foster a voluminous production in every land. Inevitably the mediocre triumphed, but it would be unfair to imply that the medal ceased to be an art because no Pisanellos, Schwarzes and Duprés appeared. The dedicated masters who struck superb medals decade after decade demonstrated that in the hands of the gifted craftsman the die could be utilized as powerfully as the cast.

The medal became a device for the commemoration of history and was proliferated to cover countless subjects, with series to celebrate architecture, medicine, science, exploration and aviation as well as topics of only trivial interest. Through the issuing of orders and decorations to celebrate campaigns and victories, and to honour service and valour, the medal also became an instrument of the state. In passing it should be noted that while the medal was utilized to promote religion, it was also sometime a vehicle for virulent hate-propaganda, as with the infamous 'Jew' medals of the 17th and 18th centuries.

In 1839, the reducing machine invented by Contamin, from a device of Houlot (1766), made its appearance in Paris and suddenly brought about a radical change in the activities of medallists everywhere. No longer did the artist need to work to exact size; he could make a large-scale model of his work and leave it to a mechanical PANTOGRAPH to reduce to the precise facsimile required for the die and the subsequent striking. Jacques Wiener of Belgium is believed to have been the last medallist in the 19th c. to cut his steel dies with his own hands.

Recent years have seen so extraordinary a revival of interest in medallic art that, looking back, one may be inclined to say that the medal, dormant as an art form for decades, has suddenly been roused. During a century of progressive movements in painting and sculpture the art of the medal seemed to stagnate. All at once, as exhibition after exhibition sponsored by the progressive Fédération Internationale de la Médaille (F.I.D.E.M.) has been held, the works of new experimenters from every land have been brought to notice. The boldest, having turned their backs on the past, in many instances have even returned to the cast. They have introduced irregular shapes, altered surfaces, invited new patinas and inlays, and employed repoussés, appliqués and combinations of all these. The bust naturally remains the most popular subject but full-face has been attempted, as well as massed figures and negative impressions. Even the techniques of the great JAPANESE metal masters of the *tsuba* have been borrowed to advantage. Continued experimentations have brought startling results. Many would appear crude to the old masters, but the new vigour and daring would surely excite their curiosity.

33, 65, 378, 552, 619, 900.

MEISSEN (sometimes called 'Dresden' in England). The first European manufacture of hard-paste PORCELAIN was established in 1710 at Meissen, near Dresden, by Frederick Augustus (the Strong), Elector of Saxony. He had employed an alchemist J. F. BÖTTGER to make experiments and the factory's early productions resemble Böttger's already famous red stonewares, their forms and simple relief mouldings being either Orientally inspired or borrowed from contemporary silverwork. Under J. G. Höroldt's artistic directorship (from 1720) Meissen perfected its characteristic brilliant white paste and glaze and its enamel colours; it was he who introduced the graceful styles on which the factory's reputation largely rests. The painted decoration often copied the Japanese KAKIEMON, and the so-called *indische Blumen* were taken from the Chinese FAMILLE VERTE. To these were added European scenes—landscapes, harbours, and groups of figures often set in panels on coloured grounds. Some blue and white was also made.

Augustus was fond of figure models, and many masterpieces were modelled by J. J. KAENDLER, who worked at Meissen from 1731 to 1775. His influence also extended to elaborately moulded table wares, such as the famous 'Swan Service' for Count Brühl, and monumental table decorations which replaced those formerly made in sugar or wax.

About 1740 a lighter, ROCOCO style spread from France, and the Oriental subjects were replaced by European flowers (*deutsche Blumen*), fruit, birds and insects, or 'Watteau' figure-scenes set more freely within coloured and patterned grounds. Kaendler's work remained superb until his death in 1775. But from 1756 the Seven Years War was disastrous for Meissen and the initiative was lost to SÈVRES and the new German establishments. Count Marcolini, who directed Meissen from 1774 to 1814, restored it to prosperity but not to artistic independence, for it now followed the style of miniature painting developed in Sèvres and Vienna. The factory's later wares have mostly been revivals of former designs. Marks: the well known 'crossed swords', first used in 1724, continues in various forms. See CERAMICS.

407.

MEISSONNIER, JUSTE-AURÈLE (1695–1750). French designer and decorator, born at Turin. He began as a designer for gold and silverwork and in 1724 was appointed *Orfèvre du Roi* at the GOBELINS. In 1726 he was appointed *Dessinateur de la Chambre et du Cabinet du Roi*, a post which had formerly been occupied by BÉRAIN and which Meissonnier held until his death. He was ambitious to make his name in architecture but few of his architectural projects were executed. It was in his designs for silverware and by his cultivation of asymmetrical design in ornament that he was one of the main originators of the final and most fanciful phase of the ROCOCO which went by the name of PITTORESQUE. His engraved works were published by Huquier.

MENNECY PORCELAIN. Founded in Paris in 1735, this manufacture was moved to Mennecy in 1748 and in 1773 to Bourg-la-Reine (where it soon declined). Its wares were of soft-paste, with brilliant, 'wet' glaze, and enamelling of flower sprays, etc. employing a characteristic rose-pink. Some charming figure-groups were also made.

MENUISIER. The rigid guild system which prevailed in France during the 18th c. differentiated the several crafts which contributed to cabinet-making and made of each piece of furniture a collective work. The piece was conceived and signed by the *menuisier*, or joiner, who cut and shaped it in solid wood, carved the mouldings, etc. Relief decoration was the prerogative of the carvers' guild. The painter or gilder supplied colour as desired. The piece was then finally waxed and polished by the *menuisier*. See also CARPENTER, JOINER, CABINET-MAKER.

520.

MEZZARO. See COTTON AND COTTON PRINTING.

MICHEL, HENRI-FRANÇOIS-VICTOR, known as MARIUS Michel (1846–1925). French bookbinder, leader of the reaction against excessive copying of earlier styles which characterized French binding in the mid 19th c. With his father, MARIUS Michel, also a binder and GILDER, he set up a workshop in Paris in 1876, where new principles of design were realized. Inspired in part by William MORRIS, Michel based his designs on naturalistic flowers placed within a FILLET framework or freely disposed as bouquets, with which the title or some other emblematic allusion was often combined. He also used mosaic INLAYS and gave careful attention to the colours of his leathers, relating both to the décor and the contents of the book whenever appropriate. Michel, who was much patronized by collectors of contemporary de luxe editions, also wrote several works on the history of bookbinding: *La Reliure française* (1880) remains a standard work. See BOOKBINDING (HISTORICAL).

MIERS, JOHN (1756–1821). English silhouettist born at Leeds, where he set up business as a 'Profilist', charging 2*s*. 6*d*. (12½p) for a 'shade' neatly framed, and 2*s*. (10p) for a second copy. He worked mainly on plaster but also painted on card, and he was an expert in contrasting the dead black rendering of the face with smoky, translucent grey (without admixture of white pigment) for the hair, lace, shirt frills, muslins, etc. In 1783 he visited Newcastle upon Tyne, advertising 'a perfect Likeness in an elegant gilt Frame and glass at 5*s*. (25p) each, or reduced upon ivory for Rings, Pins, or Bracelets at the same price'. He was in Liverpool in 1785 and in 1786 took a studio in Edinburgh, where among others he did several silhouette portraits of Robert Burns (Nat. Portrait Gal., Edinburgh). In 1788, now a recognized profile painter, he moved to London and opened up business in the Strand, taking into partnership John FIELD. Miers is often considered the most accomplished of the English silhouettists. His son WILLIAM carried on the business after his father's death in partnership with John Field until 1830, when the partnership was dissolved and he continued to trade as a Frame-Maker and Naturalist.

MIGEON. French family of cabinet-makers, father, son and grandson all named PIERRE. The most celebrated was the second Pierre (1701–58), who worked for Louis XV and Madame de Pompadour in a restrained ROCOCO style, often continuing to use the geometrical MARQUETRY of the RÉGENCE. He specialized in small pieces.

MIHRAB. Term in Islamic architecture for a commemorative niche related either to the person of the *imam* (devotional leader) or to the place where the Prophet stood while leading prayers. Rather simple in early Islam, the *mihrab* became from *c*. the 10th c. a focal point for the decoration of the mosque. It also became a favourite motif in the decorative designs on tombstones, prayer rugs, etc. See also CERAMICS (ISLAMIC).

MILANESE LACE. Name given to two types of bobbin LACE supposedly made in Milan. The earlier, dating mainly from the middle of the 17th c., has imposing BAROQUE floral scrolls with individual motifs linked by BRIDES (which were dispensed with if the design was sufficiently dense). The other, made in the late 17th and early 18th centuries, had designs composed of thin, tape-like scrolls on a regular ground-mesh, which was commonly diamond-stamped but varied somewhat in form.

MILCHGLAS. An opaque white glass produced by Johann KUNCKEL at Potsdam in competition with the porcelain of MEISSEN. See also OPALINE.

MILDENHALL TREASURE. A hoard of Roman SILVER plate found *c.* 1942 at Mildenhall, Suffolk, and acquired by the British Museum in 1946. The hoard consists of 34 pieces, the most important of which is a dish 60·5 cm in diameter with naturalistic relief ornament and incised detail depicting the triumph of Bacchus over Hercules. The pieces also include a dish and bowl ornamented in NIELLO, five ladles with dolphin handles and eight spoons of which three have Christian inscriptions and may have been intended as christening spoons. The workmanship of most of these pieces is of a high standard and most are ascribed to various periods in the 4th c. A.D. It is thought that they may have been hidden on the eve of evacuation before the advancing Barbarian invasion.

Near Mildenhall there have also been found Saxon cruciform brooches dated to the 4th c.

98.

MILDNER, JOHANN JOSEPH (*c.* 1763–1808). One of the earliest Bohemian craftsmen producing decorative glassware in the NEO-CLASSICAL style. He worked at Gutenbrunn in Austria. Much of his work employed the ZWISCHENGOLDGLAS technique but instead of completely clothing the vessel with an outer wall of glass he used only shaped panels and borders. See GLASS.

MILETUS WARE. Pottery consisting mainly of deep or shallow bowls and dishes of a reddish clay body covered in a thin white ground slip and painted in blue, black and green in geometrical patterns, thick radiating lines and plant motifs. It was called 'Miletus' because pieces of this type were first found in excavations at this town; but they are now thought to have been made at Iznik (the ancient Nicaea) from the middle of the 14th c. to the end of the 15th c. See CERAMICS (ISLAMIC).

MILLEFIORI (a thousand flowers). A glass-making technique in which glass rods of different colours and lengths are fused together and the mass is then cut transversely into sections, which may be bored for beads or embedded for decorative effect in transparent colourless glass. The technique was known to the Egyptians from *c.* 1500 B.C. and was developed by the Romans. It was much used by the Venetian glass-workers and was revived for making Victorian paper-weights, etc. The technique reached its supreme decorative refinement in the French paper-weights made at Baccarat and Clichy. See GLASS.

MINAI (enamel). A ceramics technique of over-glaze painting usually in blue, green, brown, black, dull red, gold and white, the colours being fixed by a second firing. See CERAMICS (ISLAMIC).

MINIATURE CASES. The making of leather-covered cases, which had previously been used for small painted portraits, developed into a new craft from *c.* 1839 when, chiefly in the U.S.A., they began to be used for DAGUERREOTYPES. Through the 1840s case-making blossomed into a rapidly expanding industry and small case factories were scattered throughout Connecticut. From 1852 thermoplastic cases began to supersede those of leather. They were the invention of Samuel Peck of New Haven, Connecticut, and were the first plastic products to be patented and mass produced in America. Case-making declined in the 1860s, when the use of paper and cheaper methods of photography caused the conventional photograph album to take the place of the miniature case.

Miniature cases claim to be objects of art because their embossed covers were made from dies cut by artist-engravers, whose designs reflected the artistic preferences of the American public. It has been stated by their historians that: 'Their rich heritage of designs, both in leather and plastic, boasts a greater variety than any other 19th-c. craft. Although many patterns may have been merely faithful copies from contemporary art sources, most designs demonstrate a freshness and originality totally unexpected from this short-lived art form.'

706.

MIRECOURT LACE. A LACE made at and around Le Puy consisting of hand-made patterns of flowers and sprigs attached to a machine-made net. At first emulating LILLE LACE, it later copied that of BRUSSELS and had for a time some considerable vogue.

435, 651.

MIRRORS. 1. INTRODUCTION. The mirror has possessed a ritual significance for many races at different periods. Its property of reflecting was considered to be magical and it was employed, for instance, for divining by the ancient Greeks. Mirrors are commonly found in graves, and various theories have been advanced to account for their presence there. Primitive man is said to have considered both his shadow and his reflected image as representing his soul. Illness meant a possibility of the soul escaping from within the body, and this led to a widespread and enduring custom of covering any mirror in a sick-room. For a similar reason mirrors in a house wherein rested a deceased person were covered in the period between death and burial.

MIRRORS

From the Middle Ages travellers and adventurers have profited by the interest in mirrors shown by primitive peoples, and gifts of pieces of polished metal or silvered glass could gain concessions where other means failed. The Great Chamberlain's accounts record that Queen Anne bestowed '. . . one Cask of round Eye'd Hatchets, One Cask of Looking Glass[s] . . .' on 'y[e] Indians' in America in 1708. Explorers in Africa, too, carried supplies of similar gifts, and many 18th-c. and 19th-c. carved wood fetishes were embellished with small squares of bright mirror-glass or reflecting metal to increase their magical powers.

The ancient EGYPTIANS, Chinese (see CHINA, MIRRORS) and Greeks all used polished bronze mirrors, and there are extant examples of Greek mirrors from the 5th–4th centuries B.C., which were copied in turn by the Etruscans and Romans. The mirrors take the form of a disc bearing on one side an incised or repoussé pattern and on the other a polished surface. They were conveniently fitted with a decorative handle, often of a high artistic standard, and in later specimens this terminated in a base to form a stand. Some of the mirrors were double-sided, concave and convex for enlarging or diminishing the image. An alternative type comprised two circular plates hinged to fold and protect the reflecting surface. In addition to mirrors of bronze there survive examples made of silver and others partly plated with silver.

Seneca (*c.* 4 B.C.–A.D. 65) noted that large wall-mirrors were in existence in his lifetime. Possibly they were known at an earlier date, because it is recorded that the Athenian orator Demosthenes (383–322 B.C.) had the habit of practising his speeches before a mirror. The Romans spread copies of their own manufactures to the lands they conquered and locally-made bronze mirrors have been found in England and elsewhere. English graves dating from Roman as well as from Saxon times have yielded examples.

Metal mirrors continued to enjoy popularity in the Middle Ages, perhaps because they were well-nigh unbreakable and if given a true surface and a high polish were superior to any silvered glass then obtainable. The latter is recorded in a French document of the mid 13th c., and by 1373 a guild of mirror-makers was centred on Nuremberg, Germany. Occasionally use was made also of ROCK-CRYSTAL, cut, ground and silvered in the same manner as glass. It was, however, expensive because of the rarity of large unblemished pieces and the amount of labour required to work it.

At about the same date some of the tribes of Central America were employing another natural material, obsidian, a glass-like product of volcanic activity, which gives a sombre reflection from its polished surface. Surviving hand-mirrors from the same region were made from glittering flakes of iron pyrites, which were framed in slate and acted as reflectors. Other mirrors were made by them from solid lumps of pyrites, and one extant specimen is of marcasite ground to give a magnified image. Such objects almost certainly had a ritual rather than a practical purpose, playing a part in the religious observances of the Mayas and Aztecs.

In addition to polished bronze and silver Europeans living in the Middle Ages also made use of 'steel'. This was not the familiar metal of today, but is less confusingly referred to by its alternative name of 'speculum'. (See COPPER AND ITS ALLOYS.) It is a hard, silvery-looking alloy of tin and copper with the addition of arsenic and other ingredients to remove discolouration. Speculum takes a high polish, tends to tarnish slowly and was usually cast in pieces of small size which were ground flat on one side.

2. MIRROR GLASS. The use of GLASS for mirrors remained comparatively rare until the middle of the 16th c. Then in 1564 the Venetian mirror-makers formed themselves into a corporation and before long had succeeded in introducing their products throughout Europe. Hitherto mirrors had been only small in size and limited in use, but the glass workers of Murano were able to make them suitable for playing a part in schemes of interior decoration. Their glass plates were made in an ingenious but skilful manner by what is known as the 'Lorraine' or 'broad' process. For this the blowpipe was used to gather metal from the furnace, and a succession of inflations and re-heatings produced a large bubble which was manipulated until it became elongated. When sufficiently large it was laid down, both ends were sheared off and a slit made along its length so that the semi-molten tube could be rolled open to form a flat sheet. The glass was carefully cooled (annealed) and then polished to make the surfaces as true as possible. The size of a plate made by the 'broad' process was limited by the dexterity of the craftsman and the difficulty of making the resulting sheet an even thickness throughout. The larger the bubble the greater became the difficulties and it was found in practice that something like 125 cm × 90 cm was about the maximum that could be satisfactorily achieved.

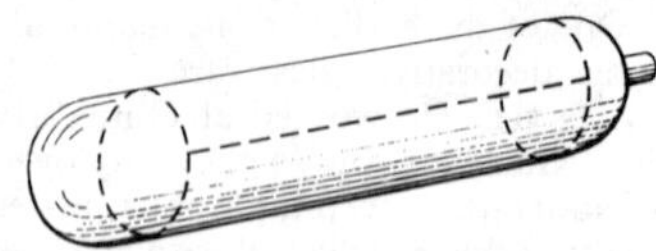

'Lorraine' or 'broad' method of manufacturing plate-glass. After the ends have been sheared off the cylinder of glass is slit longitudinally and opened out flat, annealed, polished and silvered

Silvering, or 'foiling' as it was usually termed, was the final process. Mercury was poured on to a large sheet of tinfoil, the plate of glass was carefully laid upon it while care was taken to exclude any dust, and the surplus mercury was drained off over a period of days.

Despite attempts by the Venetian authorities to maintain their monopoly by preventing the craftsmen from leaving, some did succeed in emigrating and carried their skills with them. In this way glass-making techniques spread to Germany, the Netherlands, France and England (see GLASS, including plate-glass and mirror-glass). In England in the early 17th c. imports were prohibited and Sir Robert Mansell was granted a monopoly of plate-glass making. His success cannot be gauged as no examples of his products have been identified and documentary evidence is largely confined to his own statement in 1624 that he employed at least 500 people on this work. By the mid 1650s Mansell had died and the importation of Venetian glass was resumed. Then in 1663 the second Duke of Buckingham established a plate-glass manufactory at Vauxhall, of which the products have become legendary. The term 'Vauxhall glass' has for long been used to describe any old-looking mirror although no existing example can be traced with certainty to that source.

A notable technical advance came just before the close of the century when a Frenchman, Bernard Perrot, devised a method of casting large plates of glass of over-all even thickness. The process was exploited by Louis-Lucas de Nehou at Touraville, Normandy, and later at Saint Gobain in Picardy. Casting on a small scale had been known to the Romans, who are thought to have used hollowed out stones for the purpose. In the modern version an iron bed with adjustable sides was employed, and on to this was poured the hot metal. The cooled glass was then carefully removed for annealing and eventual silvering.

In succeeding years there grew a demand in England for plates of larger size than could be obtained locally, and they were therefore imported from France. By the 1770s they were being sent to London in quantity despite a protective duty which made their high cost even higher. There is good evidence that much of the glass was being smuggled and it is now known that many of the handsome large plates of mirror-glass in some of the greatest mansions in the country came to England in this manner. The trade was an organized one, the buyers were often aware of what was occurring and although the matter was discussed in Parliament and investigated by a committee, no decisive action was taken. In 1773, however, a group of Englishmen decided they would manufacture by the French method in their own country and established the British Cast Plate Glass Company at Ravenhead, St. Helens, Lancashire. The first successful large sheet of mirror-glass made there

Casting plate-glass. The molten metal has been poured on to the table from the square container. The end of the table is being adjusted by the man on the right while the two men on the left spread the metal with a roller. From the *Encyclopédie* of Diderot and D'Alembert (1765)

is still to be seen at Osterley Park, Middlesex, where it was placed in Mrs. Child's bedroom in 1776. From then onwards the French, who were increasingly preoccupied with political troubles, gradually ceased to supply the English market, and after early difficulties had been overcome good quantities of reliable plate were obtained from the works at St. Helens. In the present century the original company was absorbed by Pilkington Brothers, who remain today among the foremost suppliers of plate glass in the world.

Like blown glass, cast glass plates required grinding and polishing, and sometimes also bevelling. This was a particularly arduous and noisy process, and an Englishman, Dr. Martin Lister, described it after he had seen and heard it in France (*A Journey to Paris in the Year 1698*, London, 1699). Lister wrote that 600 men were then being employed at it. They used sandstone and then iron ore (haematite), both in finely powdered form, which were rubbed on by hand and made a very loud and unpleasant noise 'which cannot be endured to one that is not used to it'. Bevelling, i.e. angling the outer inch or so of the edges of a plate, was a refinement that was often a matter of personal taste on the part of designer or buyer. At certain periods such a finish was more fashionable than at others, and during the decades either side of 1700 it was at the height of its popularity. The bevelling executed at that period was a gentle curve instead of the sharp angle common in the present century. The former type of bevelling has been assumed to be a hallmark of genuinely old Vauxhall glass, but it has not proved to be beyond the skill of modern craftsmen to imitate it with success. The same thing applies also to the blue-grey tint noticeable in much old mirror-glass, which has also been counterfeited sufficiently well to deceive the unsuspecting.

Silvering, which has been described above, continued to be executed with mercury and tin-foil until *c.* the middle of the 19th c. Then in 1835 the German chemist Justus von Liebig discovered a method of depositing a thin layer of pure silver on the surface of glass, and in due course his process ousted the earlier one. An example treated by the newer method is usually recognizable by the back being painted with red lead or paint, whereas the mercury-tin amalgam was left in its natural state. In appearance this somewhat resembles aluminium paint, and the latter has sometimes been used to disguise the Liebig-silvered plate.

3. FRAMED MIRRORS. Apart from those of classical times mentioned above the earliest surviving framed mirrors date from the Middle Ages. Neither glass nor metal could be produced satisfactorily in large pieces for the purpose, so the majority of mirrors made prior to *c.* 1550 had a reflecting surface measuring no more than a few square centimetres. They were framed so as to be suspended from a belt or girdle, or to stand on a dressing-table.

A French fashion of the late 14th to early 15th centuries was for a mirror to be carried about the person, and extant examples are enclosed in cases of carved ivory. They may be seen in the principal museums of many countries, and there can be no doubt that their pleasing designs and the high quality of their workmanship have ensured their preservation (Raymond Koechlin, *Les Ivoires gothiques français*, 2 vols., 1924). The framed mirrors are flat, measure an average of 10 cm or so square, and are of irregular shape with neatly contrived corner ornaments projecting from a central roundel. It is this last feature on which the craftsmen of the time expended their skill, depicting fanciful romantic subjects such as groups of knights skirmishing with ladies in the Castle of Love or a lady and a knight playing chess for stakes of the knight's life against the lady's virtue. There is some uncertainty how these French mirrors were originally used. Some examples match in both size and style of ornament so as to suggest that a complete mirror was in two parts, of which one contained the glass or metal and the other formed a protective cover for it. In that event they would have been held together in some way either by a metal hinge or by a fabric tie, but signs of such joining are very rarely apparent. Holes have often been bored in the cases, but usually at a later date and for mounting them on BOOK COVERS or for similar reasons.

Surviving standing mirrors are few, but they are mentioned in contemporary documents so that their appearance can be visualized. Probably the most sumptuous to be seen now is that of Marie de Médicis, consort of Henri IV of France; it is in the Louvre (illustrated in colour in S. Roche, *Mirrors*, 1957). The frame is of architectural design with side columns and a pediment, made of gilt copper and enamelled gold inset with large and small emeralds and chalcedony, some of the latter carved in cameo portraits, and it features two busts carved in GARNET.

The custom of hanging a mirror on one of the walls of a room dates from the mid 16th c. By then mirrors were less rare, and it had become fashionable for them to be used for interior decoration as well as on the toilet table. Paul Hentzner, who visited England in 1598, wrote of a mirror at Hampton Court, framed 'with columns and little images of alabaster', which he saw in the hall presumably displayed on a wall (*Paul Hentzner's Travels in England*, ed. H. Walpole, 1757). The same informant also observed a more extravagant use of the material, which indicates that good supplies of it were available to those who could afford its cost. He wrote of seeing in the same palace 'two bathing-rooms, ceiled and wainscoted with looking-glass'. Hentzner's employment of the term 'looking-glass' would probably conform with modern usage. In common with other writers of his time and later, he reserved 'mirror' for a plate of polished metal. When 'steel' is specified, however, it is uncertain now whether speculum or actual polished steel is intended. 'Crystal' was occasionally used as an alternative for 'glass', or could refer to rock-crystal.

More representative of the time if less extravagant in appearance were metal-plate mirrors in carved wood frames. The latter were again architectural in conception, usually made of walnut or boxwood, and were sometimes provided with a sliding door or a curtain to preserve the reflector from scratches and tarnishing. They were alternatively placed in frames of cast iron or bronze finished with gilding. By the middle years of the 17th c. plates of silvered glass averaging some 60 centimetres by 50 centimetres were being made in quantity in Venice and in smaller numbers elsewhere. Their value in furnishing a room by apparently increasing its size and by amplifying the light began to be appreciated. Frames were designed so that they complemented and echoed the prevailing decorative style and at the same time set off the glass to the best possible advantage.

In England *c.* 1675 frames were mostly of plain design, the favourite being the so-called 'cushion' shape: these were almost square and composed of a wide convex moulding, the top having an applied shaped cresting. The basic oak was veneered with OYSTERING of walnut or exotic timbers or with fragments of Oriental LACQUER. In a few instances the wood framework was overlaid with embossed silver and formed a suite with a matching table and a pair of candlestands. (Examples at Windsor Castle, Knole, Kent, and the Metropolitan Museum of Art, New York.) A taste for carved and gilded wood developed at about the same date in France and Italy. Frames roughly conforming in outline to the 'cushion' type were fashionable, and to increase the area of glass and heighten the contrast between gold and silver the principal plate was further bordered with strips of glass. The border was either plain silvered, cut with simple patterns or decorated on the back in gold and colours (VERRE ÉGLOMISÉ). The last was most popular in France and was practised to a lesser extent in England and the Netherlands.

In England the wall spaces between windows, known as piers, were often selected for the hanging of mirrors, and a tall narrow glass is referred to as a 'pier-glass'. Many of the late 17th-c. and early 18th-c. examples were composed of two plates of glass arranged one above the other and bordered by narrow strips of cut and bevelled glass so that no woodwork was visible. A similar technique was employed in Venice, where square mirror-plates were bordered with straight and shaped pieces of glass and the cresting was likewise a mosaic. Both coloured and clear glass were skilfully arranged to form a pattern. The Venetian craftsmen also engraved designs on the reverse of the plate so that when it was silvered the work remained matt against the surrounding bright mirror.

In France, while frames for mirrors were not uncommon, it was also the custom to incorporate looking-glass in the wood panelling of a room or even, as had been noted at an earlier date by Hentzner, to line all four walls with mirror. A few such rooms were to be seen in London by *c.* 1670. But the most important and enduring of such rooms was that completed in 1684, when Jules-Hardouin Mansart (1646–1708) created for Louis XIV the *Galerie des Glaces* at Versailles. This vast room contains 17 tall arched windows faced by matching shaped spaces lined with a total of 306 plates of mirror-glass set in gilt-bronze mouldings. Both the palace and the style of its interior decoration were imitated far and wide; not least in Germany, where several of the principalities became proud possessors of 'mirror-salons'. From the early 18th c. it became customary for the fireplace, normally the focal point of a room, to have a mirror above the mantelpiece. In France it was framed in sympathy with the general decorative scheme and a plate of mirror-glass replaced a plain panel of wood. Elsewhere in a room similar panels would be enclosed within carved borders, and the designs of P.-A. OPPENORD and Nicolas PINEAU show the styles current in the years 1730–50. English homes seldom adhered to such a rigid decorative scheme, and the overmantel glass was often much less imposing than those on the Continent. The most common type made between 1720 and 1730 took the form of a narrow frame of carved gilt gesso on pinewood measuring some 2 metres in length and 45 centimetres in height and enclosing three plates of glass. The centre plate was usually larger than the other two and all the edges were bevelled so that where they abutted the junction was less obvious. Mirror-glass was employed in many of the wall-lights, known also as sconces or girandoles, fashionable from the late 17th c. The glass was framed in the style adopted for looking-glasses, and it provided a reflector for the one or more candles supported in arms before it.

Toilet-glasses, for use at the dressing-tables, were continually in demand. Late 17th-c. examples were framed in wood, silver, needlework or in imitation of imported lacquer. They were usually supported on a simple standing frame, within which the glass could be adjusted for angle, or with a strut at the back. The silver mirrors formed part of a toilet set in which all pieces were made to match, including covered boxes, brush-backs, etc. From early in the 18th c. such mirrors were raised on a box base fitted with small drawers, the mirror swinging between upright side-struts rising from the top of the base. The bases were veneered with walnut or JAPANNED. A few surviving specimens are larger than the average and are raised on tall legged stands so that they are in effect mirrors and dressing-tables in one. With the introduction of mahogany there was little change in the general style of such glasses. The box base remained a firm favourite, but the mirror itself was framed in an oval or a shield shape and the base was given a bowed or serpentine front. Large dressing-glasses for a full length reflection, known as 'Cheval Glasses' or 'Horse Dressing Glasses', became popular late in the 18th c., and Thomas SHERATON printed designs for some in his *Drawing Book* (1791–4).

Newspaper advertisements of 1700 announced that the Vauxhall glass-house would supply 'rough plates from the smallest size to those of six feet in length'; but the latter would have been costly rarities. The majority of surviving mirrors made in England during the first decades of the 18th c. measure on average 60 by 50 centimetres. Most larger ones would have been imported, but in the absence of documentary evidence there is no way of determining the precise origin of a sheet of plate glass. In spite of the handicap of restricted size—or perhaps on account of it—English frame-makers succeeded in producing attractive looking-glasses. In the earlier decades of the 18th c. the frames were invariably of carved and gilt gesso on wood, but later the gold was contrasted with walnut veneer. Carving was composed of ACANTHUS leaves, EGG-AND-DART MOULDING and scallop shells, the CRESTING often in the form of an eagle with outstretched wings. This last motif was often used on frames exported to America, where dealers in New York and other cities advertised the arrival of fresh consignments from London as well as from Germany and France. Gilders and other craftsmen emigrated across the Atlantic as soon as it became possible for them to gain a living there. From the late 1730s onwards newspapers printed offers to make and repair looking-glass frames and to polish or re-polish plates. A few documented American glasses survive from the 18th c., some of them known to have been continuously in the possession of a single family. Others bear makers' labels, which show that mirrors made in America often followed a style some decades behind the fashion in London.

Soon after 1740 the ROCOCO style began to make its appearance in England, and perhaps on no other pieces of furniture did it have a greater effect than on mirror-frames. The foremost designers, Matthias LOCK, Thomas CHIPPENDALE and Thomas JOHNSON, blended the various elements of the style and created English versions of Continental originals. A score of years later came the NEO-CLASSICAL style, with its urns, husks, griffins and other ornaments borrowed from Pompeii and Herculaneum. In England Robert ADAM made a number of designs for looking-glass frames as well as for a mirror-lined room (for Northumberland House, Strand, now in the Victoria and Albert Museum), in which he employed metal and PAPIER MÂCHÉ in conjunction with wood. His imitators were numerous, for not only did Lock and Chippendale make essays in the style but there were plenty of designers among Adam's contemporaries and juniors. The more correctly classical REGENCY is best remembered by its convex mirrors. Many small wall-mirrors survive from this time, the majority of them tall and narrow and topped by a small oblong panel of *verre églomisé* or a back-painted picture in colours. Their gilt framework is usually of small significance, consisting of little more than simple mouldings and perhaps a Corinthian-capped column at either side. Overmantel mirrors of the period repeat these features, except that they are greater in width than in height. During the remainder of the 19th c. changes were rung on the past. Up to 1880 there were numerous versions of Rococo, many with little more than a passing resemblance to earlier examples but some of them deceptively close in spirit. The Adam revival of the 1880s saw a brief return to Neo-Classical frames, and the ensuing ART NOUVEAU swept away the old in favour of whip-lash curves and embossed copper and pewter mounts. From the 1920s or 1930s there has been a succession of styles for mirror-frames. Above all new materials have been developed and it has been possible to obtain glass of any size at a comparatively reasonable price so that designers have never before been so unrestricted.

4. CONVEX MIRRORS. Circular convex glasses, in the words of Thomas Sheraton (1803), 'strengthen the colour and take off the coarseness of objects by contracting them'. They had been made in Nuremberg from the 15th c. and are occasionally depicted in manuscripts of that time. Jan van Eyck's painting of Giovanni Arnolfini and Giovanna Cenami (Nat. Gal., London, 1434) shows a framed convex glass behind the couple, and in it their backs are reflected in miniature.

Such glasses enjoyed popularity in the 18th c., when they were being made in France and perhaps also in England. Designs for framed convex mirrors were given by William Ince and John Mayhew in their *Universal System of Household Furniture* (*c.* 1762). By the early years of the 19th c. the British Cast Plate Glass Company was making convexes and a particular type of frame became standard. It consists of a deeply curved gilt wood moulding in which a series of gilt balls are fixed at equal intervals, while between this and the glass there is a narrow ebonized ring. The whole is usually surmounted by an eagle holding in its beak a chain from which a ball is suspended, and at the base there is a series of leaves from which spring a pair of arms with candle-holders. See also CHINA (MIRRORS) and JAPAN.

718, 916.

MISE EN COULEUR. See COLOURS AND COLOURANTS.

MISERICORD. Term in Christian church architecture for a corbel, enriched with carving, placed on the lower side of the seat of a choir stall. The seat is hinged so that it can be raised and the corbel then provides a means of support for the occupant when standing. Such a device was necessary on account of the physical strain imposed upon the priests by the length of the medieval church services. Choir seats which could be raised in this manner existed in France and Germany in the 12th c., although no complete stalls from this period survive. Misericords, since they were seldom seen, did not necessarily conform to the decorative or didactic schemes of the choir stalls to which they belonged. It is unusual to find a series carved to a single pattern or theme and sacred subjects do not preponderate. The finest are in cathedrals but parishioners' gifts enabled many parish churches to have choir stalls with carved misericords. In England the earliest surviving examples date from the 13th c. (Exeter Cathedral). These are of a simple kind in which the corbel has straight or convex sides and the carving beneath is in high relief, representing perhaps a single animal or figure, and is not connected with the overhanging corbel shelf. In the 14th c. more complicated subjects were introduced, the carving began to be treated more naturalistically and was linked to and clearly supported the corbel shelf, which was polygonal in shape (Beverley Minster). Scenes from domestic life, medieval romances such as Tristan and Iseult (Lincoln Cathedral), jousting (Worcester Cathedral), animals parodying human activities (Bristol Cathedral), grotesque scenes and fantastic creatures (Norwich Cathedral) are included in a repertory common to European GOTHIC. The practice of carving misericords continued into the 17th c. in England (Lincoln College, Oxford) but gradually died out as RENAISSANCE principles gained dominance.

MISSAGLIA FAMILY (properly NEGRONI DA ELLO DETTO MISSAGLIA) of Milan. The most celebrated of the 15th-c. Italian armourers, operating an extensive international trade. The most important members were PIETRO (d. before 1429), his son TOMASO (d. 1452) and his grandson ANTONIO (d. 1496), all successively heads of the large family workshop. Examples of their work are in the Kunsthistorisches Museum, Vienna; Metropolitan Museum, New York; Wallace Collection, London; Tower of London Armouries. See ARMS AND ARMOUR.

MITSUHIRO, OHARA. See JAPAN (NETSUKE).

MODILLION. Term in architecture for a small projecting bracket such as were in classical architecture often placed in series as decoration below the uppermost member of the CORNICE in Corinthian, Composite and Roman Ionic orders. The term is also used in connection with furniture of an architectural character. It is also known as *mutule* or *console* in the decorative arts.

MOHOLY-NAGY, LÁSZLÓ (1895–1946). Hungarian-born painter and designer. After studying law and then painting in Hungary, he was influenced in 1919 by the Russian Suprematist painter Kasimir Malevich (1878–1935) and by Lissitsky (1890–1947), becoming a convert to Constructivist techniques in the use of transparent and semi-transparent film or plastic material for the organization of space. From 1923 to 1928 he taught at the BAUHAUS with Gropius and experimented with the various new techniques in this field which he described as 'photograms' or painting with light. After two years in London, where he began his series of coloured constructs in translucent materials which he called 'space modulators', he settled in the U.S.A. in 1937 and founded a school which he called the 'New Bauhaus' in Chicago. He exercised an important influence in introducing Constructivist techniques in the U.S.A. and in spreading the doctrines of the Bauhaus in architecture, interior decoration and the decorative arts.

MOHS SCALE. A method of assessing and classifying the relative hardness of minerals originated by the Austrian mineralogist Friedrich Mohs (1773–1839) in 1812 and now in standard use. Ten minerals are used to create an artificial scale of reference and the hardness of any mineral is tested according to whether a point of one mineral will scratch a smooth surface of another or be scratched by it. The ten minerals used to create the scale are: (1) Talc; (2) Gypsum; (3) Calcite; (4) Fluorite; (5) Apatite; (6) Felspar; (7) Quartz; (8) Topaz; (9) Corundum; (10) Diamond. The steps in the scale are not regular, the difference between diamond and corundum, for example, being greater than the rest of the scale. But the scale has been found useful for practical purposes. In general gemstones are considered to be of a hardness from 5 upwards, though some substances valued in jewellery, such as PEARL and CORAL, are softer than this.

MOLITOR, BERNARD (d. 1819). German cabinet-maker who moved to Paris and became a master in 1787. His cabinet-pieces illustrate the late Louis XVI style in their simple, formal lines, restrained MOUNTS and frequent use of mahogany veneers. Such features provided a foretaste of the DIRECTOIRE style.

MON. Japanese designs which served as family crests in the manner of coats-of-arms in the West. See JAPAN.

MONNIER or **LEMONNIER.** French BOOKBINDING family. LOUIS-FRANÇOIS Monnier became a master-binder in 1737, and his son

JEAN-CHARLES (d. 1782) was binder to the Duke of Orleans. The Monniers excelled in the production of inlaid mosaic bindings, in which large pieces of citron-yellow, red and green leather are combined in massive scroll and floral shapes incorporating birds and figures in the CHINOISERIE fashion. The exuberant, sometimes coarse designs, resembling MARQUETRY rather than mosaic work, have a BAROQUE flavour in marked contrast to the ROCOCO intricacy of DENTELLE BINDINGS made during the reign of Louis XV. A number are signed 'Monnier' without initials. See BOOKBINDING (HISTORICAL).

MOORE, JAMES (*c.* 1670–1726). English cabinet-maker. He was in the royal service from *c.* 1708 to 1726, and partner from 1714 of John GUMLEY. He specialized in gilt gesso furniture and incised his name on some of his pieces (e.g. at Hampton Court and Buckingham Palace). MIRRORS, sconces and a silver table are among his surviving pieces at Erthig, Denbighshire. He had many important clients and was associated with William KENT at Kensington Palace.

MORESQUE. Bandwork or galloon patterns of Islamic origin used particularly in EMBROIDERY and LACE during the latter part of the 16th c. and the early 17th c. An anonymous *Passements de moresques* dated 1563 contains patterns of continuous bands with interlace, lozenges, trefoil, etc. combined with scrollwork. A similar type of pattern with scrolled bands in connection with ACANTHUS leaves appeared in the designs of Paul Androuet DUCERCEAU for embroideries and textiles. The *moresque* was one of the elements which contributed to the characteristic French development of the ARABESQUE.

The term is also used more generally to describe any characteristic Moorish or Arabian ornamental design, and in the 18th c. was sometimes applied to arabesque decoration.

MORISON, STANLEY (1889–1967). British typographer and author, who developed the historical study of printing type on foundations laid by William Blades, T. B. Reed, T. L. De Vinne, and D. B. UPDIKE and applied his knowledge in the production of typefaces for mechanical composition. As typographical adviser to The Monotype Corporation, Ltd he was responsible for the making of many of the types now commonly used by British printers, some of them—Aldine Bembo, Poliphilus, Ehrhardt, Fournier, Bell—revivals of old designs, others—Perpetua, Gill Sanserif, Goudy Modern, Lutetia—from designs by living artists. He thus took the leading part in providing book and commercial printers with a repertory of good typefaces in succession to a very limited choice, largely of poor or ephemeral design, previously available.

The history and styles of English newspapers was one of his main interests. Commissioned in 1929 to refashion the printing of *The Times*, he produced the Times Roman text type and a range of related bold, semi-bold and heading types, which, introduced in 1932, met with almost universal approval and amounted to the first conscious attempt at making a modern daily newspaper visually a harmonious whole, legible, orderly and sightly. These types, adapted for setting by Linotype and Monotype machines (see TYPOGRAPHY), were later put at the disposal of the printing trade in general.

Morison's scholarly research in the history of epigraphy, calligraphy, printing and typography is contained in a long series of his articles in periodicals, *The Fleuron* (of which he was co-founder in 1923), the *Penrose Annual*, the *Monotype Recorder*, etc., and in his many books. His essay on 'The First Principles of Typography' has been translated into several languages. He was a contributor to the *Encyclopaedia Britannica* and a member of its editorial board.

Morison was essentially self-educated, having been obliged to leave school at the age of 15 in order to help to support his family. Soon afterwards he was converted to Roman Catholicism, a position which colours much of his historical writing and gave him a lifelong interest in liturgy and ecclesiology. He acknowledged great help and encouragement in his early life from Wilfrid Meynell, the Roman Catholic publisher, and from his son Francis (later Sir Francis Meynell). Morison combined his religious views with an extreme liberalism, for a time with Marxism. His conscientious objection to military service and war work led to imprisonment in 1916–18. In later life he was strongly attracted to the power that is exercised through journalism. His post as typographical adviser to *The Times* developed into a confidential relationship with R. M. Barrington-Ward, the Editor. He wrote much of the *History of The Times* and was editor of *The Times Literary Supplement* in 1945–7. He became a close friend of Lord Beaverbrook.

The University of Cambridge, to whose Press he was Typographical Consultant from 1925, made him a Doctor of Letters *honoris causa* in 1950, and he was similarly honoured by the University of Birmingham and by two universities in America. He was a Fellow of the British Academy and a Royal Designer for Industry. The Bibliographical Society and the American Institute of Graphic Arts awarded him their gold medals.

45.

MOROCCO. Leather made originally in Morocco and the Barbary States from goatskins tanned with sumac. The term is also applied to other leathers made in imitation of this. It is used largely in BOOKBINDING and for other purposes requiring a fine, soft leather. See LEATHERCRAFT.

MORRIS, WILLIAM (1834–96). The main inspiration of the ARTS AND CRAFTS MOVEMENT, an original poet, re-creator also of epic poems of the past, writer of prose romances, one a classic of socialist literature; one of the founders of British Socialism, lecturer on the arts, the finest pattern-designer of his day; reviver of several ancient crafts; founder of the Society for the Protection of Ancient Buildings, medievalist turned Marxist, this 'poetic upholsterer' as he quite properly termed himself in a moment of rage, was 'an artist and literary man pretty well known throughout Europe'. He was in the dock in a London police court charged with causing a disturbance on the occasion of the prosecution of a fellow-Socialist speaker. On another occasion he declined the Chair of Poetry at his own university of Oxford, doubting the value of attempting to teach 'the wholly incommunicable art of poetry'. When he died, in 1896, his doctor said it was simply 'of being William Morris, and doing more work than any ten men'.

One consequence of his leadership in the Arts and Crafts Movement has been that many marginal ideas, by no means his, are attributed to him, and we are presented with images, ranging from the romantic dreamer to the cranky buffoon, so remote from reality as to be not even caricatures. Precisely because he was so multifarious, nothing is easier than to choose one's Morris and treat him as romantic poet, craftsman, designer, conservationist, printer or socialist, pointing to his remarkable achievements and decisive influence in the field of our fancy or our prejudice. But we must accept him whole, and the only way to study him is historically, as a man attuned to his times, growing with them to the end of his days, each new phase of work and personality stemming from and containing what went before. The simple view of Morris is the most misleading, and the essential curve of his life was plotted in a succinct phrase by E. P. Thompson in the title of his indispensable book, *William Morris: Romantic to Revolutionary*. The young romantic poet, the disciple of Rossetti, the successful designer, the master craftsman, the socialist propagandist, are all one man: his politics were about art, his art led him to politics.

Mere cult accounts of Morris, now that so much serious study of the 19th c. has been made, will no longer do. It is only as he is seen quite inseparably from the busy and prolific world of Victorian architecture, design, literature and politics, that the reality of his central position can be grasped. This lay not so much in any uniqueness of most of the things he did, but in being Morris and doing all that many others did, better, with greater insight, with larger understanding and with the strong impress of his own style and imagination.

Full and vivid accounts of Morris's Walthamstow childhood, his schooling at the newly founded Marlborough, his life at Oxford, the founding of friendships, his absorption in art and poetry and the revelation to him, through his circle of friends from Birmingham, of the life of a modern industrial town; his first poems and prose romances; *The Oxford and Cambridge Magazine*, which he financed for a year; his growing passion for architecture and his short year in Street's office; the liberating influence and inspiration, for himself and Burne-Jones, of Rossetti and the two years spent under that influence in painting; the meeting in 1857 with Jane Burden; the publication of his *Defence of Guenevere*; his marriage in 1859 and the building of Red House, planned with Philip Webb, in 1859–60—all this was given long ago by J. W. Mackail and Georgiana Burne-Jones in books which can now be supplemented or corrected but not, within their scope, bettered. This article attempts an assessment of Morris's mature achievement, noting only what a dream-like foreshadowing of it is to be seen in the years between his going to Oxford and the founding, in April 1861, as a result of the furnishing and decoration of Red House to their own designs and largely by their own hands, of 'the Firm'—Morris, Marshall, Faulkner and Co.

On the slender capital of £1 a head from each of the seven, and a loan of £100 from Morris's mother, this artists' co-operative set out on its course, ready to undertake a revolution in design, in church and domestic furnishing, painting, jewellery, embroidery—'a bunch of amateurs who are going to teach us our trade', as they were described by an old hand in 1866 to Lewis F. Day, just beginning his own career in the same field. The success of the Firm was from the start specially identified with Morris, though Rossetti's was the best known name and his too were many of the valuable connections which brought commissions. When its award-winning goods were shown in the Exhibition of 1862 it was already being referred to as Morris and Co., though this was not its legal style until 1874–5, when Morris bought out the rest. Co-operative though it was in spirit, for 10 years virtually all its capital was contributed by Morris; it is doubtful whether any of the rest put in more than the initial £1. From the beginning he was the one who managed and coordinated, Faulkner keeping the accounts. When Warrington Taylor from 1865, then George Wardle from 1870, undertook the business management, Morris worked rather as artistic director, who in addition to his own always put into production the designs of his friends.

From the mid 1870s dates Morris's extension of the Firm's work, above all in woven and printed fabrics, WALLPAPERS, carpets and TAPESTRY; his first political activity, his first public lectures on art, his founding of the Society for the Protection of Ancient Buildings, his finest poem, *Sigurd*. The 1880s saw the development of the Merton works, the Honorary Fellowship of his old College, his joining of the Social Democratic Federation at almost the same moment—the beginning of over a decade of socialist activity; his influential participation in the work of the Art Workers' Guild and the Arts and

Crafts Exhibition Society. During all this time he acted as an adviser to the South Kensington Museum and as examiner to the School of Design. The last six years of his life saw the founding of the KELMSCOTT PRESS, his absorption in type-design, TYPOGRAPHY, and BOOK PRODUCTION, which was to have an immediate and a lasting effect on printing, first in a very active PRIVATE PRESS movement, and then in the trade. These years too saw the publication of his prose romances; but from 1858, the year of the publication of *The Defence of Guenevere*, he had published steadily, poetry and prose.

It was as a writer that he first made any name. Respect for the author of *The Life and Death of Jason* helped to establish the work of the designer. But his influence was not greatest in this field; it was as a designer and a theorist that he had his following, among whom LETHABY, ASHBEE, Selwyn Image and Walter CRANE are perhaps the most notable, carrying his work into this century.

Morris designed some furniture in the Red Lion Square days, but after the setting up of the Firm he seems to have left this to Webb. He designed stained glass, but never meddled with blown GLASS, as Webb did. It seems to have come about quite naturally that he concentrated on the field in which he became such a master, that of continuous pattern design and flat ornament. It is a field which is as conspicuously medieval as the Gothic architecture in which he was educated. The enrichment of surfaces in every material, but especially the patterning of textiles, is one of the great achievements of the Middle Ages, and one of the attractions of pattern design to Morris must have been the extent to which its evolution escaped the dominance of either Greece or Rome. The thread of its growth runs from ancient EGYPT to BYZANTIUM, with offshoots to Persia and India, returning to enrich the European product through the silk mills of Sicily, the velvet looms of Bruges and Genoa.

It was Lewis F. Day, in the Easter *Art Annual* for 1899—the first published monograph on Morris, valuable because Day was a fellow-designer and often a collaborator—who first pointed out the close relation between changes of style in Morris's designs and the fabrics he studied; often these were textiles bought for the South Kensington Museum on his advice. The theme was taken up in the 1950s by Peter Floud. By researches in the Patent Office and elsewhere, identifying the dated designs registered with the Board of Trade, he demonstrated in detail the truth of Day's observation. Yet Morris made original designs, not copies or imitations; no one would mistake his fabrics for medieval. His grounding in Gothic as well as his own rational mind gave him a strong bent towards formal order. In the lecture 'On Pattern Designing', given first at the Working-Men's College, he says that the repeats of a pattern should not be hidden; their geometrical structure not only orders the disposition of form and colour, but is itself an indispensable pattern element, not to be suppressed without loss of vitality. Too much ingenuity in disguising the repeat leads to vagueness, which in everything he abhorred. With such a bias nothing would have been easier than for Morris to become a very rigid and imitative designer. But the apparent diversion of his two years as a painter was of enormous service to him, compelling him to seek in nature the material for his patterns. He learned from Rossetti how barren was the imitation of historic forms, from Ruskin and the Pre-Raphaelite painters how fruitful the ultimate source of living nature, and this he extended from the area of form to that of colour. He treats colour very differently from his contemporaries, who, captivated by the demonstrable scientific order of the spectrum, easily reduced colour-relations to a mechanical level. Morris refers us to the typical relations of colour in nature and makes this, not the laboratory experiment, the basis of colour in design. He aimed in his pattern-making at an element of reference of a subtle kind. If he created a bower-like quality, as so often he did, this gave his CHINTZ and wallpaper references to natural growth, to the movement of man and animal: references, too, to such poetry as Chaucer's—to another art, and another age, enriched the material. It was this effect, reached by so few others, that he meant by postulating imagination with beauty and order as the three essential elements in pattern-making. It has been said, slightingly, that his patterns were like poems, his poems like tapestries; as if this were both defect and accident. For Morris it was neither, but the triumph of his art.

His notion of beauty—which he would never discuss as an abstraction—was very much bound up with the feel of making, the use of the tool, the handling of the material—much more than with the elegant refinement of form. He had a frank preference for the rough and strong over the sweet and subtle—which by no means barred the latter qualities from much of his work, verbal or visual: witness the coarse earthenware Flemish cup from which he preferred to drink, the robust semi-circular chair he designed when he began to weave, his thanking God for anything so strong as an onion. To his mature mind the extreme refinement of craft which would smooth away every tool-mark was itself the mark of the mechanical, the timid: of the slave mind, not the mind of the free man. And by freedom he certainly meant not just a state of physical and social liberty, but freedom of the mind, the conscious life of the imagination.

Morris wrote out his lectures carefully, though they were not always given in quite the same form. He said, writing to Charles Rowley, 'I have only one subject: Art and Labour.' On this subject he addressed scores of audiences of every kind. He aimed at the utmost simplicity and clarity in expression, as in the actual practice of design. Nothing is easier than to be deceived by this into thinking Morris's thought unsophisticated: it is very far from that. There is a concreteness in his language and thought which, combined with his sense of history, his rationality, made Marxism when he came to it more than merely acceptable. The moral concern of his romantic youth, too, became quite naturally political in his middle age. Nothing about him is clearer than this development; yet, as much because of his highly personal language as for any other reason, nothing more easily evades his readers. His prose style is deceptively plain. In the late romances, certainly, it uses archaisms for special effects; yet in general they do not impede his clarity. The basis of his style is twofold: to get rid of any word not Anglo-Saxon in its root so as to keep within the understanding of the simplest, and the desire to be as physically real as possible—in a word, to keep up the metaphorical use of language. This was not easy even in the telling of a tale. In talking of art or social order it was much harder. All theory tends to the making of abstract vocabularies: yet behind every abstract term there lies some ultimate sensory and emotional experience for which the term was at first a metaphor. It was Morris's constant endeavour to carry on all discussion, as well as all poetry and tale-telling, in material and metaphorical terms. This is what underlies his 'simple' language; this, and his wish to make himself clear to all, not simply to professionals. He had no patience with mere jargon: his last coherent words were: 'I want to get mumbo-jumbo out of the world.' It was as poet, as artist, as craftsman, not as aesthetician, that he found his way to his philosophy of art. We must pursue his meaning as energetically as he did himself, not expect to lean on the crutches of a conventional vocabulary. If the unsophistication of the working man made some of Morris's ideas difficult to grasp, the professionally educated might well be deluded into thinking they had understood, where they had read without penetration an apparently innocent pattern of ordinary words. For Morris no abstraction was worth discussing that did not spring from and enhance material fact. Not least of his gifts was his power to restore the unity of abstract and concrete, and it was to this end that he made his 'simple' language.

Speaking of fabric printing, for example, in which he achieved the most sumptuous effects, he said: 'There is nothing for it but the trouble and simplicity of the earlier craft, if you are to have any beauty in cloth printing at all. And if not, why should we trouble to have a pattern of any sort on our cotton cloths? I for one am dead against it, unless the pattern is really beautiful: it is so very worthless if it is not' (*Lecture on Dyeing*, 1884). The same concept underlies his ideas on the printing of books. 'Whatever the subject of a book may be, and however bare it may be of decoration, it can still be a work of art, if the type be good, and attention paid to its general arrangement. A book quite unornamented can look actually and positively beautiful if it be, so to say, architecturally good. First, the pages must be clear and easy to read: which they can hardly be unless, Secondly, the type is well designed; and Thirdly, whether the margins be big or small, they must be in due proportion to the page of letter.'

Morris was a designer before he was a craftsman; and when he joined the Social Democratic Federation he described himself as such, though by then he had already made himself master of many crafts: wood-engraving, embroidery, dyeing, weaving. It gave him immense satisfaction to fashion with his hands. But it was with a twofold object that he undertook craft after craft: on the one hand, the more fully to understand how to design for each; and on the other to have the most complete control of standards of quality not only in his own workshops but in those trade shops to which he put out work. Embroidery and carving he had begun in Street's office; but dyeing, weaving, carpet-knotting, belong to the days when, in Queen Square, he began to move into the textile field. It was having some hangings returned because their colours had not been fast that determined him never to use the then new and unreliable aniline colours, and to master the ancient dyeing craft himself.

This gave him valuable insight into fundamentals of design, gave him the control he wanted. But it gave him other insights no less important, for which his discipleship of Ruskin and his friendship with Madox Brown had prepared him: a deep regard for work as a positive good, a necessity of pleasure as well as of mere subsistence; a deep regard too for the life of the workman. It helped in his development of a mature philosophy of art, extending beyond consideration of the work of art as such to the place of art in the social order; and it modified very considerably his earliest romantic notions on the subject. During the 1880s, in his lectures, we see also the important change in his view of the machine. Morris is usually described as a mere machine hater. And this in his Ruskinian youth, far from the world of industry, he was; but not in his mature thought. He was highly critical, not of machinery, but of the uses to which it was put, a criticism partly technical and wholly social. There is no book or even a single lecture by him on this—which indicates that he was not at all obsessed with it. But from two or three of his lectures and from *News from Nowhere*, which embodies his full thought on the matter, it is possible to give his views in his own words, which resolved themselves very quickly in the early 1880s. In the lecture 'How we live and how we might live'—first published in *Commonweal*—he says: 'If the necessary reasonable work be of a mechanical kind, I must be helped to do it by a machine, not to cheapen my labour, but so that as little time as possible may be spent on it, and that I may be able to think of other things while I am tending the machine . . . The last claim I should make for my work is that the places I worked in, factories or workshops, should be pleasant, just as the fields where our most necessary work is done are pleasant. Believe me there is nothing in the world to prevent this being done, save the necessity to make profits on all wares: in other words, the wares are cheapened at the expense of people being forced to work in crowded, unwholesome, noisy squalid dens; that is to say, they are cheapened at the expense of the workman's life. Before I leave this subject of the surroundings of life, I wish to meet a possible objection. I have spoken of machinery being used freely for releasing people from the more mechanical and repulsive part of necessary labour: and I know that to some people, people of the artistic turn of mind, machinery is particularly distasteful, and they will be apt to say to you that you will never get your surroundings pleasant as long as you are surrounded by machinery. I don't quite admit that: it is the allowing machines to be our masters and not our servants that so injures the beauty of life nowadays.'

There has from the mid 20th c. been a marked revival of interest in Morris's designs for wallpaper and printed fabrics, and his work in these fields is more widely seen and more seriously regarded than it was earlier in the century. But it must be recognized that this revival has its fashionable and ephemeral side. The trades which promote this fashion do so without feeling or discrimination—especially as to colour, the element most easily distorted—or historical sense, cheerfully confounding Morris, Rossetti, Beardsley and others in one psychedelic welter. But the fact that old inhibitions about 19th-c. art have been dissolved by serious historical study as well as by the romantic discoveries of the young (a more important element than it has ever been) means that the work of Morris and his fellows can be enjoyed, used and reassessed in a more than merely fashionable way; and we may fairly believe that a serious evaluation of that work, based once more on living with it, will give it a permanent place in our regard.

Yet welcome as this revaluation of the actual products is, it is ultimately the less important side of Morris's significance for us—as in the end it was for his contemporaries. To declare boldly that Morris was the finest decorator of his day is only to concur in the judgement of those contemporaries and so to realize the basis of his authority among them. This visible demonstration of power was necessary to the exercise of that leadership which Morris accepted but never sought. But it was not just as a fine designer that he won such regard, nor even as the example of a type lost since Renaissance times—the artist-craftsman—which so defines the Arts and Crafts Movement. In the end, though practice gave him his authority, it was as the man of ideas, the theorist of the movement which he had so largely made, as the exponent of far-reaching ideas on the nature and function of art as a signal and necessary human activity, that he was important to his fellow-Victorians, and it is in this sense that he continues to be of importance for the future even more than for the present.

101, 131, 199, 366, 367, 551, 827, 878.

MORTLAKE. English tapestry works inaugurated by King James I at Mortlake in 1619 on the model of that established in Paris by Henri IV a few years earlier. Under the directorship of Sir Francis Crane (1619–36) a team of highly skilled Flemish weavers was assembled at Mortlake and some of the finest of all 17th-c. tapestries were made there for Charles I, who took a very active interest in the work, and for various members of his court. The Civil War depressed the industry and it never regained its initial prosperity, though tapestries continued to be woven in small numbers under the direction of Sir Sackville Crow (1661–7) and subsequently of Lady Harvey, down to 1703.

Francis Clein, a native of Mecklenburg and former court-painter of Christian IV of Denmark, was artistic director of the factory until his death in 1658. He contributed the designs for the set of *Horses* (8 pieces) and for the *Story of Hero and Leander*, of which there is a magnificent set, rich with gold, in the Swedish Royal Collection. But for the most part Mortlake relied on earlier designs such as the *Triumph of Caesar* by Mantegna, the *Acts of the Apostles* by Raphael (Charles I purchased the Raphael cartoons, now in the Victoria and Albert Museum, especially for the use of the Mortlake factory), the *Playing Boys* by Giulio Romano and the 16th-c. Flemish designs of the *Twelve Months* and the *Story of Vulcan and Venus*.

Several of these designs were also woven towards the end of the 17th c. by a number of former Mortlake weavers who had broken away from the parent factory and set up their looms elsewhere, though they continued in some cases to utilize the Mortlake mark of a red cross on a white shield. Among these new independent establishments were those of Thomas and Francis Poyntz at Hatton Garden, John and William Benood at Lambeth and Stephen de May. See also TAPESTRY.

MOSAIC GLASS. A decorative glass invented and made in Egypt. It was made by first building up glass rods into composite canes with a pattern in cross-section. These canes were then sectioned and the pieces fused into sheets which were reheated and formed in moulds. See also MILLEFIORI.

MOTHER OF PEARL. The animal equivalent of the mineral aragonite. A mixture of calcite and calcium carbonate, it is deposited on the outside of the mantle or skin which surrounds the body of certain molluscs. The special properties of mother of pearl do not come from its composition—aragonite has none of the sheeny lustre which is associated with pearl-shell—but from the arrangement of its layers.

Carving by Jean Gaulette. French. (V. & A. Mus., 17th c.)

German religious medallion. (V. & A. Mus., 15th c.)

Chinese scratch-carved card marker made for the European market. (18th c.)

It is built up on the mantle in a continuous succession of prismatic folds which reflect back light like a series of tiny mirrors. Sir David Brewster demonstrated in 1830 that mother of pearl owes its iridescence to this layer arrangement by making a cast from a pearl-shell which demonstrated the same glassy lustre as the shell. In spite of attempts to reproduce the layers in steel and to imitate mother of pearl in other ways, however, no satisfactory substitute for pearl-shell has been discovered. Real shell will fluoresce blue when exposed to artificial light (aragonite is one of the more important fluorescent minerals) and it will effervesce when dipped in acid. Perhaps the famous story about Cleopatra and the pearl which she dissolved in wine to impress Antony has been misunderstood. A pearl dropped in transparent but acid wine would effervesce sufficiently to demonstrate its genuineness, and thus its suitability as a gift. William Dampier, the American buccaneer, declared many years ago that 'the inside of the shell is more glorious than the pearl itself'. (In fact there is no difference between the composition of mother of pearl and PEARLS; indeed the latter are sometimes found completely embedded in a layer of mother of pearl or protruding from the side of an oyster as a blister pearl.) The prismatic effect of nacre runs right through the layer of mother of pearl which extends from the inside of a pearl-shell valve to the hard, brown and horny layer of *conchyolin* which constitutes the outside of the shell. It cannot be destroyed by grinding or cutting. Although all nacre is equally iridescent, however, this iridescence is not permanent. It can be, and frequently is, destroyed by exposure to sunlight. The shell then becomes 'blind', to use a trade term. The lustre disappears completely, or at best can only faintly be glimpsed by tilting the shell sideways against the sun. Shell dealers are well aware of this property of 'mop', as it is known in the trade, and will only buy 'blind' shell if it is thick enough to split so as to reveal the iridescence of the newly exposed faces in the middle. This peculiarity of shell has not always been noticed by museum officials, who often display mother-of-pearl carvings in unshaded daylight.

Nacre is produced by a wide variety of shells, of which the most important are the pearl oyster, the NAUTILUS, the red abalone, the most famous of all American iridescent shells, and many varieties employed in the Far East. Less important species include those found in European waters: the edible mussel, the swan mussel and the pearl mussel. The pearl oyster is the most important, not merely because of its wide distribution, but because it provides a really thick layer of material, *c.* 2 centimetres thick. The sea in which it is fished determines the colour of mother of pearl. White mop is characteristic of Australian waters, but even within the Australian range it is possible to distinguish between shells from Darwin and those from the Arafura Sea. White mop also comes from

Celebes, Borneo, Macassar and Arawe Island. As the shell beds get nearer to the equator the 'gold lip' makes its appearance. This is a warm, amber-coloured tone, spreading inwards from the edge of the shell. The waters of Mergui and the Malay peninsula produce a colourful shell, while those of Tahiti and the Cook Islands yield a black or smoky-looking shell known as 'black lip'. Black lip, incidentally, is a kind of mother of pearl likely to be familiar because many shirt buttons are made from it. The Red Sea and the Persian Gulf produce poor and small meleagrinas, in which nevertheless important carvings were made during Sumerian and Babylonian times. Although all types of shell have been used at one time or another (golden lip features in some Chinese export carvings to Europe, for instance), white has always been the most popular with carvers. To be usable shell must be in good condition. Pearl oysters are attacked by boring parasites and once they have reached their optimum size for carvings—about a pound and a half—they become so riddled as to be rejected by the manufacturers of pearl buttons and are sold to the religious craftsmen of Bethlehem and other towns of the Holy Land, who prefer defective Australian shell from which to make their medallions and rosaries.

The shell carver has a twofold task. First he must remove the hard horny outer layer of conchyolin without damaging the inner layer of nacre and then he must carve the mother of pearl, polish it and condition it so as to bring out the full iridescence. Different methods have been evolved at different times and in different parts of the world. Primitive peoples suspended iridescent shells in a bonfire of green leaves. The smoke, which contained pyroligneous acid, helped to remove the outer layer, which was then scraped off by hand. The shells were polished and boiled in tea to enhance their iridescence. In the Far East shells were ground down by hand with a stone rubber. Because it took so long to grind off the conchyolin only a few pearl-shells could be processed a day, and mother of pearl was correspondingly expensive. It was consequently employed in a very economical way by being used in very thin slices. Some Chinese shells, such as the window-pane oyster, gave a thin section anyway. In the West the removal of the conchyolin was carried out easily by the use of a grindstone revolving in a water-filled trough. In the East the pearl-shell was carved by hand, but the Western, particularly the Italian, carver adopted the daring and reprehensible expedient of dissolving away part of the mother of pearl in an acid bath, after the areas of the carving which were to stand out had been coated in wax. This saved wear and tear on chisels and scorpers, but even after the resulting carving had been bathed in water, some acid would remain, to yellow the nacre and reduce its iridescence. All traces of the carver's tools were now removed with scrapers and finally the carving was polished with a linen rag dipped in emery powder, while specially shaped sticks cut from lime wood and dipped in emery were forced into crevices where the rag could not penetrate. Next the work was polished with the finest powdered tripoli, and finally tripoli powder and sulphuric acid, well mixed together, were applied to the design on the end of a cork. Care had to be taken not to make the mixture too strong or else the acid would penetrate the nacre. In the Far East polishing was done with abrasives.

Mother of pearl has been very widely employed by craftsmen to make inlay for statuary and jewellery, for low reliefs, to ornament pillars and walls and to enhance furniture and musical instruments. It is one of the materials which continue from the ancient Near East to modern times, when it can still be found on gaming boards, furniture and weapons, just as in Sumerian and Babylonian times. In Europe it began to be used from the 14th c. in small carvings, often religious, medallions, crucifixes, cameos, inlay for furniture and other articles. In the Far East iridescent shells formed an important decoration for LACQUER articles. Iridescent shell was the only component which the lacquerer knew would remain untarnished and unaltered, so it is not surprising that it was widely employed. Nacre was also used as an inlay directly into wood, and was used to produce card markers for the European market, as well as to make NETSUKES in Japan and mandarin's buttons of the sixth grade in China.

The origin of shell carving goes back to prehistoric times. The 'Pearlies', London costermongers whose coats used to be decorated with innumerable pearl buttons, are sometimes traced back to the Thames-side dwellers who co-operated with the Roman invaders and were allowed to retain their distinctive shell ornaments. The first important shell carvings were made in the first half of the 3rd millennium B.C., when mother of pearl was used as mosaic inlay on the famous 'Standard of Ur' and other Sumerian articles. In his book *Sumer* (1960) André Parrot has rightly praised the imaginative effect and technical proficiency of these carvings, though he is mistaken in the belief that the material from which they are made is so extremely brittle that it cannot be retouched. The Near East remained a focus for shell carving. Nacre was used for inlay in Islamic Egypt, and in Palestine religious articles such as crucifixes, medallions and rosaries were carved in nacre and were brought to Europe by pilgrims. Often olive wood was used in conjunction with mother of pearl. The religious carvers of today, many of whom are resident in Bethlehem, produce a similar kind of carving. For hundreds of years they formed the customary souvenir of Jerusalem which pilgrims would buy outside the Church of the Holy Sepulchre.

In Europe mother of pearl first became important in the 14th c., when German craftsmen carved it into medallions of religious subjects which were sometimes worn, but more often decorated church furniture. Many of the designs were taken from contemporary engravings, or the woodcuts which they resemble in their coarseness.

German goldsmiths of the Renaissance made gold-mounted cups and bowls from small plates of mother of pearl fixed to a wooden core, or mounted whole nautilus or turbo shells as elaborate cups. These shells were sometimes engraved, or etched with acid to leave patterns in relief. Elias Geyer (active 1485–1546) and the JAMNITZER family amongst others practised this art. More widespread was the carving of cameos, often leaving the dark outer layer of shell in imitation of SARDONYX; the designs of these were sometimes taken from medals or plaquettes, and portraits in mother of pearl remained popular into the 18th c. In the 17th c. Holland, controlling the sources of mother of pearl, developed the art of engraving it, with artists such as the BELKEINS, who combined engraving with carving. The peasant scenes of Teniers and the putti of Duquesnoy provided popular subjects. Paris was the centre of the 18th-c. trade in SNUFF-BOXES, fans and étuis, for which mother of pearl proved so well suited, and there were many skilful artists working in it.

Nacre carving had been very much of an art till the 17th c.; thereafter it became an important industry in Italy and England. The Italians even fabricated textiles entirely decorated with mother-of-pearl sequins. In England Birmingham was the centre of the pearl-shell industry. Nacre was carved into knife handles and many other products. The price of shell fluctuated violently during the 19th c., and much shell which had depreciated in price was buried to get rid of it. In 1878 a shell merchant suggested that Birmingham Town Hall should be torn down and the foundations dug up for the vast mounds of shell they contained, remarking: 'It would almost pay, at present prices.' Large amounts of shell were incorporated as decoration in lacquer and JAPANNED articles produced in England. Today mother of pearl is mostly used for making pearl buttons; these are made by machinery and hardly qualify as craftsmanship.

In the Far East Chinese carvers made the famous 'scratch carvings', many of them for card markers for the European market. In Japan pearl-shell entered very largely into the best output of the lacquerers, such as Kōrin (1658–1716).

MOULDINGS. Architectural term for contours given to projecting members, or for continuous decorative bands leading from one surface to another or serving to give linear emphasis to a surface. In the decorative arts the term is applied to contour-bands defining surfaces, e.g. in cabinet-making or metalwork, whether by carving or by incising or by the application of prepared bands in relief. Mouldings are often ornamented, such ornamentation being called 'enrichment'. They are named and classified by reference to their own contours in section and by reference to the ornamental pattern with which they are 'enriched'. Most but not all of the mouldings used in Western cabinet-making and metalwork had architectural prototypes. Exceptions are bead and butt, bead and flush, bead and quirk, which originated in joinery. For types of moulding see: ASTRAGAL, BILLET, BOLECTION, CASEMENT, CAVETTO, CONGÉ, CORNICE, ECHINUS, FILLET, OGEE, OVOLO, SCOTIA, TORUS, WAVE.

MOUNTS. A comprehensive term in cabinet-making for metal adjuncts to furniture such as handles, hinges or locks; for metal edges or guards used to protect angles or prominent parts of furniture; and for the bronze or brass gilt decoration used in ORMOLU and other styles of 18th-c. furniture.

The term is also used for the card surround which it is customary to set round water-colours, drawings, lithographs, etc. inside the frame. See FRAMES.

MULE CHEST. Modern term for a chest with a plinth base in which are two or three drawers. Such chests were introduced in England in the late 16th c.

MUNICH SCHOOL. Name given to a group of iron-chisellers who worked on the decoration of fine quality arms, chiefly for the Munich Court, from the late 16th c. to the late 17th c. The first name associated with the school is that of Ottmar Wetter (d. 1598), who is recorded in Munich during the period 1583–9, moving to Dresden in 1589. He was succeeded as Court *Eisenarbeiter* (worker in iron) in 1594 by the Antwerp master Emmanuel Sadeler (d. 1610), who on his death was succeeded by his younger brother Daniel (d. *c.* 1632), who had previously worked for the Emperor Rudolf II at Prague. After Daniel's death, the workshop was continued by Caspar Spät (d. 1691), who had apparently been trained by the Sadelers.

The products of the School consist chiefly of sword-hilts and fire-arm mounts chiselled in relief with scenes and foliage, usually coloured blue against a gold ground. Examples are in the Victoria and Albert Museum; Wallace Collection, London; British Museum; Bayerisches Nationalmuseum, Munich; Metropolitan Museum, New York; Kunsthistorisches Museum, Vienna. See ARMS AND ARMOUR and IRON AND STEEL (IRON CHISELLING).

MUSICAL BOXES. See MECHANICAL MUSICAL INSTRUMENTS.

MUSSEL SILK. See BYSSUS SILK.

MUTULE. See MODILLION.

MYERS, MYER (1723–95) of New York. A leading American silversmith of Dutch descent and Jewish faith, Myers served as chairman of the 'Gold and Silver Smiths' Society' in 1786. His most famous ecclesiastical pieces were commissioned by the Synagogue in Newport, Rhode Island. During the Revolution Myers supported the revolutionary cause, and when British troops overtook New York he took refuge first in Connecticut and later in Philadelphia. His work throughout the 2nd half of the 18th c. reflected the changing styles from ROCOCO to NEO-CLASSICAL. The high quality of his craftsmanship brought him many commissions, and his work can be seen today in many American museums.

MYŌCHIN FAMILY. The most famous family of Japanese armourers. They first rose to eminence in the early 16th c. and remained at the head of their craft until the middle of the 19th c. As well as armour they produced a variety of decorative objects in iron and steel, including a remarkable series of figures of animals and birds. Examples of their work are in the Victoria and Albert Museum; Tower of London Armouries; Metropolitan Museum, New York.

715.

N

NACRE. See MOTHER OF PEARL.

NAHL, JOHANN AUGUST (1710–85). German carver and designer and one of the leading exponents of German ROCOCO under Frederick the Great. He had travelled in France and Italy and in 1735 was working at the Palais Rohan in Strasbourg. He was invited to Berlin by Georg Wenzeslaus Knobelsdorff, Superintendant of the palaces of Frederick the Great, and in 1741 was made *Directeur des Ornements*. In 1746 he left Potsdam and worked in Kassel. His most celebrated work was the Golden Gallery in the palace at Charlottenburg. With the HOPPENHAUPT brothers Nahl was the most important formative influence in German ROCOCO.

NANCY SCHOOL. A group of French decorative artists who formed themselves into a 'school' *c.* 1890 on the initiative of Émile GALLÉ, a native of Nancy. The group consisted of: Victor Prouvé (1858–1943), painter, engraver and modeller, who worked many years for Gallé, whom he suceeded as President of the group and director of the École des Beaux-Arts, Nancy; the brothers Paul Daum (1888–1944) and Michel Daum (1900–), glass-makers; the decorative artist Louis Majorelle (1859–1926); and a potter, Georges Hoentschel. In the years around the turn of the century the group had considerable influence in France and more widely in propagating a version of the ART NOUVEAU ideas unconnected with theories of functionalism or socialism. They set themselves in opposition to the current pastiche of revived historical styles and advocated a new and original manner in the decorative arts derived from the rhythmical forms of organic nature. Their views were propagated in a review *Art et industrie* under the editorship of G. Grouthière-Vernolle.

NARIN, DAVID (1243–93). Jeweller and metal-worker of Gelati. See GEORGIAN METAL-WORK.

NAUTILUS SHELL. In the Pacific and Indian oceans are shoals of a gregarious bottom-feeding octopus called the Pearly or Chambered Nautilus. *Nautilus pompilus* lives at the very mouth of its shell, and even this it shares with parasitic crustacea. The rest is 'camerated' or sealed off into compartments of diminishing size, so that when it is cut open it reveals a section like a watch spring which has unwound. The sealed chambers made the nautilus a special shell from the carver's point of view; they reduced its holding capacity, so as to make it a suitable size for a wine goblet, and provided the workman with a maze of little boxes which he could open, wholly or in part, to astonish his patron. The outer shell of the nautilus is covered with handsome yellow and orange stripes, which can easily be scraped away to reveal the shimmering iridescent layer of nacre beneath. See MOTHER OF PEARL.

The nautilus was caught with basket traps baited with boiled crayfish and was dried for food. By the 16th c., if not earlier, the Chinese had begun to carve the shell, cutting away the outer layer to produce a design in relief against the nacre, as in a Ming Dynasty shell in a 16th-c. Continental mounting in the Waddesdon Collection in the British Museum, or engraving the shell with a scratch-carved design in which no pigment was added to the engraved lines, as in an example in the Fitzwilliam Museum, Cam-

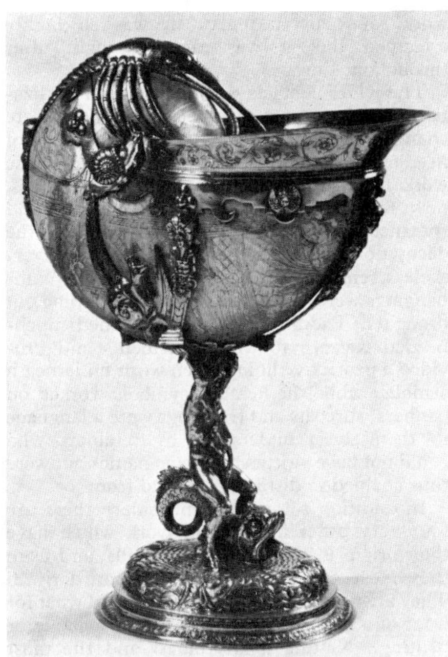

Nautilus-shell cup. The mount is London goldsmith's work, *c.* 1585–6. The shell is scratch-carved and is Chinese Ming work, roughly contemporary with the mount. (Fitzwilliam Mus., Cambridge)

bridge, which appears to be a Ming carving roughly contemporary with its mount, made by a London goldsmith *c.* 1585.

By 1609 Amboyna, where many nautili were caught, had become one of the corner-stones of the Dutch East Indian Trading Company. The Dutch adopted the carving methods which the Chinese had used and developed others for themselves. If the shell was to be burnished but left plain, it was steeped in some kind of acid for ten or twelve days, for example in fermented rice, vinegar or water in which some vine leaves had rotted. Then the outer coating was scoured off, beginning with the thickest part of the shell. The stripped shell was then polished with diluted alcohol (*sterk water*) until the beautiful lustre of the mother of pearl appeared, after which it was rinsed in soapy water to clean it. If the outer crust of the shell was to be cut into open-work patterns so as to display a contrast between it and the iridescent layer of mother of pearl below, the designs were painted on the shell in beeswax mixed with turpentine and black pigment. Then the unpainted parts were wiped over with a rag dipped in alcohol tied to a wooden pin. This process corroded away the outer crust, and the edges of the design were finally tidied up with a small graver. The wax coating was then removed. The designs used are described by a contemporary as: 'lying on top like loose work', and indeed some of them seem to be related to the EMBROIDERY designs of the 17th c. If the shell was to be ornamented by pierced work, with decorative openings cut into the walls of the chambers, the parts of the shell which were occupied by sealed chambers were cut open. In the inner curl of the shell a visored helmet, crest and helmet cloth were often cut. The effect is beautifully described by the American poet Oliver Wendell Holmes, who wrote:

Wrecked is the ship of pearl
And every chambered cell
Where its dim dreaming life was wont to dwell
As the frail tenant shaped his growing shell
Before thee lies revealed
Its irised ceiling rent, its sunless crypt unsealed.

If a shell was to be decorated with blind engraving in the Chinese manner, the lines were simply cut in with a graver such as those used for cutting copper-engraving plates. If a black line-engraving was wanted, the lines were then rubbed with powdered coal mixed with wax or oil. Direct relief sculpture on a nautilus shell is extremely difficult, owing to the fragile nature of the shell, which is as thin as cartridge paper. Sometimes heads would be cut in relief with a graver, but it was much more usual for relief carving to be applied to the boss on the shell, which is thicker.

Nautilus shells were almost invariably worked for drinking vessels. They were carved in a functional, not an ornamental way. This can be seen from the fact that the flaring lip of the nautilus (one of the most ornamental features of the natural shell) is cut away to leave a straight edge, which is usually lined with precious metal so as to make a more convenient drinking surface. Retaining the flared lip would have resulted in some of the liquor in the cup being spilled as it was raised to the mouth.

Nautilus shell was such a rare and precious material that if a shell did get broken while being engraved, the pieces would be made up into SNUFF-BOX lids, pictures and the other small items for which mother of pearl was ordinarily used.

The art of nautilus-shell carving had its heyday in Holland during the 17th c. Fine work began with Jérémie Belquin, a religious refugee who made ornamental plaques for gun stocks, and who moved from Metz to Amsterdam during the 16th c. He was succeeded by his son Jean, born *c.* 1597, and his grandson Cornelis Bellekin carried on the tradition of fine shell-carving into the 18th c. Although only the Belkeins (as their name is usually spelt) signed their work, other shell-engravers were active in the 17th c., and they include Jochem Kuhne, Roeners and Evans. There were other workers, whose names we do not know.

With the death of Cornelis Belkein (before 1711) the great age of the nautilus shell comes to an end. His successors, such as Jan Bernard Barckhuysen (1684–1760), Christian Konsé, born in Frankfurt (1700) and Cornelis la Motte, born in Schoonhaven (1749), had lost the light touch and delicacy of fancy which had characterized the famous Belkeins, such as Claes, Jan and Cornelis. Eighteenth-c. engravers tended to copy published prints for their subjects. Some nautilus shells were mounted plain. There is a good Polish example, dated 1770, in the British Museum.

By the 19th c. the nautilus shell was merely a curiosity. A humble working man named Wood entered a nautilus shell, carved with the Apotheosis of Nelson, in the Great Exhibition of 1851. Two magnificent and unpublished nautilus shells in the vaults of the National Maritime Museum, one of the 'Great Britain' and the other of the 'Great Eastern' steamships, associated with the late 1850s, may also be by Wood, the last nautilus carver of whom any notice was taken.

709.

NEEDLEWORK. In the early Stone Age, when sewing was confined to the stitching together of the hides of animals, the tough skins were pierced with a sharply pointed tool, probably of flint, and a length of sinew attached to a thorn or slender bone was passed through the holes. As time progressed the invention of woven cloth made it possible to combine these two operations: needles having an eye at one end came into use, fashioned from wood, bone, ivory or shell or hammered out of various metals, while spun thread took the place of sinew. Unlike fur or skin, woven material will fray along the cut edges unless the loose ends of the threads are firmly secured. With the introduction of textiles, therefore, the 'seam' and the 'hem' became all-important. Eventually, to disguise these long lines of stitching, further stitches of different lengths and colours were added to form simple patterns. It was in this manner that surface-EMBROIDERY gradually evolved. Its purpose in these early centuries was not, however, solely to decorate: the ornamental stitching on a seam was employed to give extra strength where the fabric was joined; when elaborately worked over the hem of a garment was less liable to rub or tear.

It is clear from the alabaster sculptures of Mesopotamia and adjacent countries that embroidery had reached a very high standard many centuries before the Christian era. The influence of the Middle East is apparent in the needlework of the early Christian church, where ecclesiastical robes, glittering with gold thread, and the rich silks of Byzantium, were worked by dedicated women who had learned their art as part of their general education in the convents. Athelfleda, wife of Brithnod, a Northumberland chief of the 7th c., recorded the daring deeds of her husband with her needle, and was the head of a race of skilled embroiderers. When in the 11th c. the Normans conquered Britain they found vestments and hangings in cathedrals, churches and palaces. By the 12th and 13th centuries English work, or OPUS ANGLICANUM, was so highly esteemed that it was eagerly sought after throughout Europe.

The wider contacts with the Saracen civilization during the Crusades heralded a complete change in the traditional styles and patterns of needlework. The ladies of noble houses, whose work had formerly ornamented the churches, now found their inspiration in chivalry and romance and turned their attention to the decoration of their homes. Embroidery, nevertheless, remained predominantly practical. Wall-hangings were a virtual necessity for keeping out draughts. Padding and quilting added much-needed warmth to winter garments and provided a protective lining when worn underneath armour; while the heraldic symbols worked on banners, surcoats and trappings were a language in themselves, understood by retainers who could not have written their own names but were thus enabled to distinguish friend from foe.

In addition to surface-embroidery there are four very different types of work which have their origin in simple domestic skills, and from these most other kinds of needlework are derived. They are netting, knitting, knotting and what for want of a better term may be called twisting or plaiting. Netting is the oldest and the most essential. The fisherman, the sailor, the farmer, the fowler and the hunter all required nets for their different occupations: and the housewife needed them for penning in her poultry and protecting her fruit trees from the ravages of birds. The tools used were at first extremely simple. For a shuttle all that was required was a strip of wood having a V-shaped cut at either end; another short piece of wood formed the gauge. Later, when it was realized that net could be used for decorative purposes, netting needles were fashioned from iron, steel or bone; they were similar to the shuttles, though much finer, and were wound in the same manner with thread, having an open 'eye' at either end. Net-work, that is the darning or embroidery of net, was probably introduced into Europe from the Orient by returning Crusaders in the 11th and 12th centuries: veils of gold and silver mesh interwoven with coloured silks had from very early times formed part of the traditionally gorgeous raiment of the East. During the two succeeding centuries it was known in the West as *opus araneum* (spiderwork) but in the 15th c. it was superseded by white net-work in which both the background and the embroidery were composed of linen thread. Whitework was much in demand at this period, mainly for the ornamentation of the linen underclothing which was gradually supplanting the heavy and often unwashable garments of earlier years. Strips of fine-gauge mesh were therefore mounted in light wire frames to be embroidered for use as insertions and edgings. It was known as filet lace or LACIS. Eventually it was found that a similar effect could be obtained by withdrawing or cutting away some of the threads from linen, thus leaving a network of loosened threads that could be buttonholed over, or clustered together with a looped stitch. It was in this way that the type of needle-made LACE that we now know as RETICELLA work developed, the name being derived from the Italian *rete*, a net. And this led in due course to the making of needlepoint lace, in which buttonhole stitching was used to build up the design on a framework of tacking stitches outlining the pattern on a strip of parchment. As the lace had been made by adding stitch to stitch, without any background of fabric, it was named, very aptly, *punto in aria*: literally 'stitch in air'.

Knitting, which is closely allied to netting, has a very different history. From examples that have been found in Coptic tombs it is clear that in the East extremely fine knitting was a well-established art in the 4th and 5th centuries. The Arabs, who were expert knitters, used the process for making CARPETS and wall-hangings, and it was probably the Arab traders, travelling from country to country, who first taught the people of the Mediterranean lands to knit, the knowledge of the craft spreading gradually through Spain and Italy to the West. Evidence suggests that in these early days the thread was held in the left hand and that the needles were hooked at one end like modern crochet-hooks: but by the Middle Ages straight pointed needles had come into general use. Peg- or ring-knitting (more familiar today as 'corking') was employed for making simple objects such as caps or pockets. In the 15th c. 'capknytting' was a recognized occupation for which a licence had to be obtained. On the other hand knitted stockings had not yet come into use; hose still consisted of pieces of cloth shaped and sewn together. The young King Edward VI is known to have received a formal present of a pair of knitted silk stockings, obtained most probably from Italy. Stow tells us that the first pair of worsted stockings to be knitted in England were made in Queen Elizabeth I's reign, copied by a man from a pair that he had seen in an Italian merchant's shop.

Knotting and twisting threads to form cords and braids is an age-old occupation which had many necessary domestic uses; but it was in the Eastern countries, where the making of textiles originated, that it first emerged as a decorative art. The weaver, on removing his work from the loom, found at each end of the fabric he had woven a fringe formed by the unused extremities of the warp threads. Unwilling to cut off, and so waste, his precious yarn, he soon devised a method of plaiting and tying the loose threads into deep borders that were not only ornamental but added length and weight to carpets, shawls, towels, window blinds and other household objects. So effective was this work that in the course of time it developed into a craft independent of weaving. A horizontal thread was stretched taut across a pillow and a series of vertical threads knotted on to it so that they hung down in front of the worker. It was called macrami work, the term being derived from the Turkish word *magrama*, a towel; in modern times it is more familiar as macramé.

It was nevertheless realized that the close knotting made the trimmings stiff and unyielding and therefore quite unsuitable for the decoration of soft and delicate fabrics. Moreover when one was making a narrow border or insertion the continual knotting of short threads into a horizontal heading was extremely tedious. Eventually it was discovered that these difficulties could be overcome if the strip of trimming, instead of being worked horizontally from left to right, was worked vertically, the threads now running through the length instead of the width of the strip. These threads, which might be many yards long, were wound on to bobbins, the loose ends having been attached to pins stuck in the pillow. Knotting had been dispensed with, so that with the use of the finest thread trimmings and edgings of the utmost softness and delicacy could be made.

Thus originated bobbin lace, which became a formidable rival of needlepoint lace. The two kinds of work are nevertheless quite distinct. Pillow or bobbin lace is composed of twisted threads. Needlepoint lace is derived from surface-embroidery and is made with a needle.

With the period of comparative peace and prosperity ushered in by the reign of Henry VII a new era was dawning in the history of English needlework. This was the age of great houses, which were being built throughout the countryside: the fashion for luxurious living set by Henry VIII and his court had spread to the wealthier classes in general. And a similar situation pertained on the Continent. To furnish these houses, and to dress their occupants in the style considered appropriate to their surroundings, resident embroiderers were needed, more particularly gold embroiderers. It is significant that when, in 1651, the Broderers Company was revived and received its Charter from Elizabeth I it was the broche and the spool of thread of the gold-worker that appeared on the arms. The broche is a wooden tool similar to a bobbin but mounted on a handle; it is used by the embroiderer for laying gold. The metal thread is wound on to the centre of the implement and the end passed through a deep cleft at the point. Once this loose end has been attached to the work the thread can be unwound and laid in position without coming into contact with the hands, a matter of importance where gold and silver are concerned.

Pattern-books concerned specifically with needlework were being printed in Germany in the early 1520s. A few years later a number of elegant parchment-covered booklets were published in Italy, with patterns for embroidery and lace. They were costly to produce and were little known outside the exclusive coterie of queens, princesses and other ladies of noble rank to whom they were dedicated. Their titles are as flowery and extravagant as the language of their long prefaces extolling the virtues of their patrons. As printing developed books intended for a wider public made their appearance, and by the beginning of the 17th c. Federico Vinciolo's famous designs for lace and embroidery were as well known in Paris and London as they were in Venice. Shorleyker's *A Schole-house for the Needle* (1624), was extremely popular in England and Boler's *The Needle's Excellency* had reached several editions by 1630. Whitney's *A Choice of Emblemes*, a book of designs intended for craftsmen in general, was also much consulted: the pattern used in making a delicate lace ruffle might equally well be found DAMASCENED on to a sword blade or a suit of armour.

It is significant that many of the trimmings and accessories mentioned in the domestic accounts of the period are listed as 'boughten goods'. Needlework in its various branches was becoming an important industry. It was the almost insatiable demand for lace, with which the garments of both men and women were loaded, that brought into existence the village lace schools, where children were instructed at a very early age in the art of twisting collars, cuffs, edgings and insertions. To own a well-furnished pillow and pincushion was the ambition of many a young girl. The bobbins, usually of bone or wood, carefully carved and sometimes decorated with beads and brass wire, were often the gift of an admirer, and were pricked with a name or perhaps a phrase such as 'Kiss me quick' or 'Don't tell Mother'; some might have the name of the village added. There were also historical and topical bobbins, recording notable events. Each district had its distinctive tools and pillows, suited to the type of lace being made, and each family its SAMPLER of patterns which was handed down from one generation to another.

Knitting, still largely a masculine occupation, was also becoming an important and organized industry. A man was required to serve an apprenticeship of six years before submitting his masterpiece to entitle him to full membership of his guild. A carpet by a master knitter might contain as many as 12 colours, while shirts and coats of silk and metal threads, patterned with fruits and flowers in purl and other raised stitches, rivalled those made from the richest BROCADES. In the wool-producing districts the cottage knitters made warm and useful garments from their homespun yarn, and to them rapidity was of primary concern. It was this necessity for speed that led to the invention of the knitting sheath. This was an implement worn on the right hip, tucked into the belt or apron string. Its purpose was to support the needle usually held in the right hand. At the top end of the sheath a hole was bored, approximately 2·5 centimetres in depth, and in this the needle was inserted, leaving the fingers of the right hand completely free so that they could be held immediately over the points of the needles, where they took over and manipulated the working thread much more quickly than was possible with the older method. Most knitting sheaths in England are made of wood, and as they were often given as love tokens may bear a date and initials. Continental examples are frequently fashioned from silver and have a ring attached through which a cord or ribbon could be threaded; others are made from IVORY, AMBER, PORCELAIN, shagreen or maybe of boxwood intricately carved.

The growth in the number of professional embroiderers, and the expansion of the cottage industries, in no way diminished the interest or the importance of the work done by those in more affluent circumstances. Even by the 18th c. so few things could be bought ready-made that there was ample opportunity for any woman of leisure to exercise her skills. She would most probably spin her own sewing thread on a small, specially designed table-wheel of bronze and ivory, for the linen yarn obtainable from the village spinsters was apt to be coarse and uneven. It required great care and delicacy of touch to produce a fine, smooth thread; indeed, so difficult was it to procure such a yarn that the packmen who called at the doors of large houses with pins, needles, ribbons and all kinds of haberdashery, were only too glad to barter their wares for the sewing thread spun by the lady of the house.

Purse-making was an important branch of domestic needlework; metal frames and fastenings were extremely costly and for most people quite unobtainable. Small bags, knitted, netted or worked in buttonhole stitch over moulds of wood or metal, were in continual demand by both men and women. The bases of these purses were often beaded, not merely for ornamentation but to support the weight of the coins. In the absence of metal fastenings many garments were drawn-up or laced-up by means of cords, which again had to be made in the home, usually with a small lyre-shaped implement known as a lucet that may still occasionally be found in an old work-box; while for the softer piping cords and the braids used for upholstery quite different tools would be required. Another most important accessory was the needlework clamp, of wood, ivory or metal, used by the seamstress to fix a piece of material firmly to the table so that she could hold it taut with one hand while stitching with the other. The most ingenious type of clamp was the hemming-bird, an invention of early Georgian days, fitted with a spring beneath the body and so devised that the material when inserted in the bird's beak could be gripped and firmly held there. Special clamps were also made for netting, having a knob or hook over which the foundation loop could be slipped. Wool-winding clamps, of a somewhat different construction, were made in pairs.

It was probably the Dutch, through their close contacts with the English Court in the 17th c., who introduced knotting with a shuttle into

Ivory decorated needlework and netting clamps (18th and 19th c.)

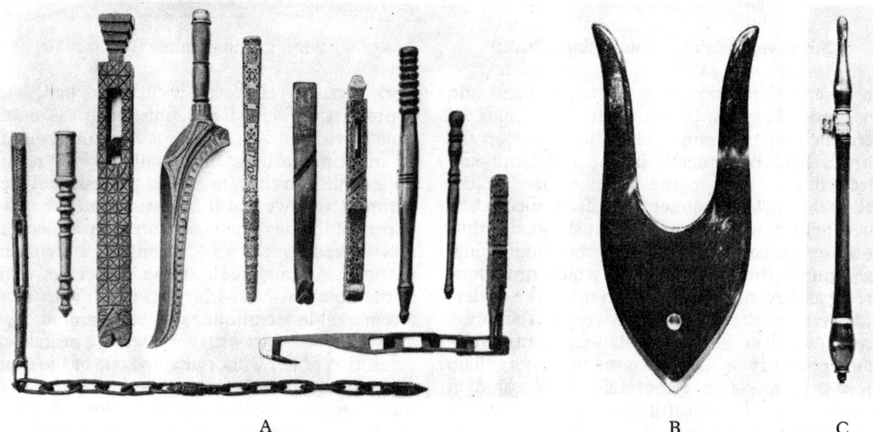

A B C

A. Wooden knitting sheaths (18th and early 19th c.) B. Lucet of tortoiseshell (18th c.) C. Gold-mounted tambour hook. The top and base unscrew and spare hooks are in the handle (18th c.)

Britain, for Holland at this time had extensive trading relations with the East, and the Chinese made frequent use of knotted lines in their embroidery. The thread required was first wound on to the shuttle, and by means of this a series of picots or knots were made in it at close intervals so that it formed a narrow trimming bearing some resemblance to a string of beads. Afterwards it was COUCHED down in patterns with fine stitching on to linen doublets, hangings and counterpanes. The shuttles were generally 2·5–5 centimetres in width and about 10–15 centimetres long, and were often exquisitely made of silver, cut-steel, ivory or tortoiseshell. The Day Book of Lazare Duvaux contains several references to knotting shuttles bought for Madame de Pompadour, the most elaborate of gold with enamelled branches hung with cherries formed of cornelians, and costing 550 livres. At the sale of the Duc de Lorraine's possessions in 1781 no less than 17 knotting shuttles were listed, some of them of the very finest craftsmanship.

In Italy knotting developed somewhat differently: it was not employed in surface-decoration but as a method of making lace-like collars and trimmings. The shuttles were much smaller, and the white thread was knotted into rings or 'eyes', whence its name *occhi*. These rings had afterwards to be joined together by tying or stitching, and being made up of so many bits and pieces the work, when introduced into England, was called tatting. As time progressed the invention of more advanced techniques made it possible to join the various motifs while working the pattern, while the addition of small purls or picots made at intervals on the outer edges of the rings gave the finished product a lighter and more delicate appearance, which it still retains at the present day.

In letters and diaries of the Georgian period there are many references to tambour-work, so called because in the East, where it originated, the fabric to be decorated was stretched tightly on a frame resembling a tambour or drum. The implement employed was a fine metal hook with a sharp point, which was screwed into a handle of bone, ivory or mother of pearl. It was held

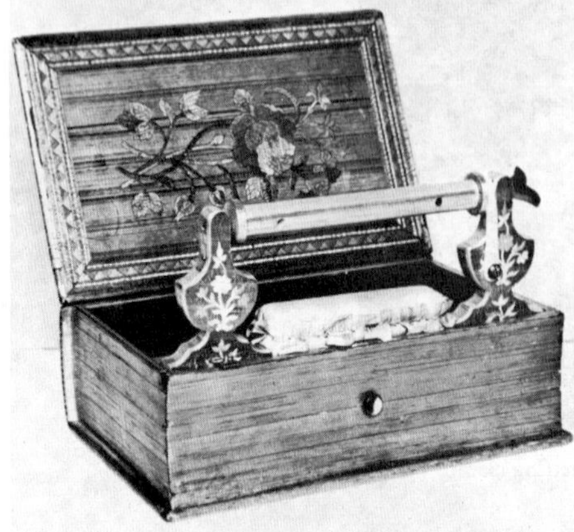

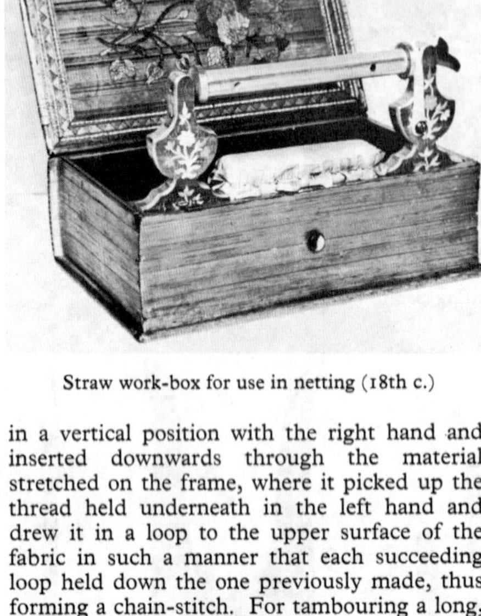

Straw work-box for use in netting (18th c.)

Tortoiseshell knotting shuttle with inlay of silver and coloured golds. French (18th c.)

Silver knotting shuttle (18th c.)

in a vertical position with the right hand and inserted downwards through the material stretched on the frame, where it picked up the thread held underneath in the left hand and drew it in a loop to the upper surface of the fabric in such a manner that each succeeding loop held down the one previously made, thus forming a chain-stitch. For tambouring a long, continuous thread is required which must flow freely and evenly as it is drawn up to the underside of the work; a fashionable woman, therefore, would wear at her waist an ornamental reel-holder of ivory or silver hanging by a short chain from a clasp, often elaborately ornamented in keeping with the graceful dresses of the period. Meanwhile in France the work, which was known there as CROCHET (having taken its name from the hook rather than the frame), was undergoing a gradual change. Instead of being employed for surface-embroidery, the hook was now used for making a series of chain-stitches looped into one another in such a manner that they formed complete and independent edgings and insertions that could be utilized in the same way as lace. This method of working, to which the French gave the appropriate name of '*crochet en air*', is the crochet that we know today. It was developed and popularized in Britain in the early 19th c. by a Mlle Riego, the daughter of a French nobleman who had fled to England at the time of the Revolution, but there is little doubt that in a simpler form it was known in many parts of Europe in the 16th c., particularly in the wool-producing areas, where shepherds and their families made garments for themselves with the aid of hooks which they whittled down from odd pieces of bone or wood. It is significant that Mlle Riego in the first of her instruction booklets refers to the work as 'Shepherd's knitting'.

The Georgian era was the age of the decorative sampler, no longer a record of patterns but an educational exercise for children from four years upwards. It was also the age of the needlework picture. However undistinguished, such a production served a definite purpose at the time at which it was made, for a coloured picture of any kind to hang on a wall was not readily obtainable. In the late 18th c. professional male embroiderers were still advertising in the newspapers of the day, but their number was decreasing. Needlework was becoming a feminine pastime. Among the most notable needlewomen of the time was Miss Mary LINWOOD who, using a remarkable technique, sought to imitate well-known works of art with her needle; a permanent exhibition of her work remained one of the sights of London until the early years of Queen Victoria's reign. Before the invention of colour printing a picture prepared for working on canvas was necessarily costly, for it had to be painted and squared up entirely by hand; but in 1804 a German print-seller devised a method of producing patterns in quantity which could be coloured without employing skilled labour. BERLIN WOOLWORK became a craze, and it is by the mats, footstools and firescreens which once cluttered Victorian drawing-rooms that the age is apt to be remembered, while much that is of interest has been obscured. It should not be forgotten that the traditional craft of smocking reached its peak in the first half of the 19th c.

The attempt to link needlework once more with the world of art was begun by William MORRIS in the 1850s, and in 1872 the Royal School of Art Needlework came into existence. This led to the foundation of a number of schools of embroidery and work-societies, both in Europe and in America, which in the years ahead did much to raise the standard of needlework as a whole. By the 1890s the influence of the ART NOUVEAU movement was the dominant feature in design.

The half-century disrupted by two World Wars was a period of conservation: in an increasingly mechanized age the need for practising, and so preserving, traditional skills which might otherwise have been forgotten seemed paramount. This interest in basic materials and techniques still persists; but since *c.* 1950 an experimental trend has emerged. The modern needlewoman, discarding the more orthodox approach, uses the sewing machine, and the wealth of man-made fibres and fabrics that scientific invention has made available, to express the manners, moods and perplexities of the times.

5, 10, 212, 329, 421, 435, 470, 598, 651, 677, 929.

NÈGRE, CHARLES (1820–79). French painter and photographer. He was a pupil of Ingres and Delaroche and was among the more prominent of the artists who used photography as a basis for painting. In the 1850s he was known for excellent half-tone photographs executed by the CALOTYPE process. See PHOTOGRAPHY.

NEGROLI FAMILY (properly BARINI DETTI NEGROLI) of Milan. The most famous 16th-c. family of Italian armourers. Renowned especially for the making of elaborately embossed parade-armours, often DAMASCENED with gold and silver, which show a mastery of material combined with restraint in the use of ornament that has never been equalled in this field. Some 22 members of the family are recorded, but their fame is due chiefly to the work of one member, FILIPPO (recorded 1531–51), who signed a number of surviving pieces, including an important group made for the Emperor Charles V, now in the Armería Real, Madrid. His signature is sometimes accompanied by the words '*et fratres*', which presumably refer to some, or all, of his brothers, Giovanni Battista, Alessandro and Francesco, of whom the last is known to have worked as a gilder and damascener. The only other member of the family whose work can be identified is Filippo's second cousin, GIOVANNI PAOLO (recorded 1525–61), whose signature occurs on an embossed and etched breastplate of *c.* 1545 in the Metropolitan Museum, New York. He probably worked for a time at the court of Francis I of France. Important works are in the Armería Real, Madrid; Kunsthistorisches Museum, Vienna; Tower of London Armouries; Metropolitan Museum, New York. See ARMS AND ARMOUR.

82, 325.

NEGRONI. See MISSAGLIA FAMILY.

NEO-CLASSICISM. An aesthetic movement and artistic style which spread through Europe and America in the second half of the 18th c., combining reaction from the ROCOCO with a new interest in Greek and Roman antiquity. The latter went hand in hand with archaeological enthusiasm excited by excavations carried out at Herculaneum, Paestum and Pompeii in the years 1738–56 and was popularized by a number of finely illustrated volumes devoted to the archaeological finds and to the decorative arts and architecture of antiquity. The best known of these were: *Recueil d'antiquités égyptiennes, étrusques, grecques, romaines et gauloises* (1752–67) by comte Claude-Philippe Caylus (1692–1765), *Vedute di Roma* (1750), *Magnificenza di Roma* (1751) and *Antichità romane* (1756) by Giovanni Battista Piranesi (1720–78), *The Antiquities of Athens measured and delineated by James Stuart, F.R.S. and F.S.A., and Nicholas Revett, Painters and Architects* (1st volume 1762, 2nd 1788–9, 3rd 1795 and supplements in 1816 and 1830), *Antiquities of Ionia*, published in two volumes (1769–97) by the Society of Dilettanti with illustrations by Nicholas Revett (1720–1804) and *The Works in Architecture of Robert and James Adam* (1st volume 1773, 2nd 1779, 3rd 1822). Neo-Classicism was a movement which extended over both the fine arts, including architecture, and the practical and decorative arts under a variety of more particular names. In France it permeated what are known as the Louis XVI style, the RÉGENCE, the DIRECTOIRE and the EMPIRE. In England it was reflected in the ADAM style, HEPPLEWHITE and SHERATON in furniture, and it constituted one of the main elements of the REGENCY. The main theorists of the movement were J. J. Winckelmann (1717–68) in Germany and in France Antoine Quatremère de Quincy, whose book *An Essay on the Nature and Means of Imitation in the Fine Arts* was published in English in 1837. Its chief initiator in painting was A. R. Mengs (1728–79), who influenced such artists as Benjamin West (1738–1820) from America, Gavin Hamilton (1723–98) of Scotland and (through Joseph-Marie Vien) Jacques-Louis David (1748–1825) in France. Among sculptors whose work was of wide general influence were Antonio Canova (1757–1822) and Bertel Thorwaldsen (1768–1884) who worked in Rome, Jean-Baptiste Pigalle (1714–85) and Jean-Antoine Houdon (1741–1828) in France and John Flaxman (1755–1826) in England. Neo-Classicism differs from previous classical revivals and renascences in Europe by the fact that it was more than a recrudescence of interest in surviving Classical traditions, expressing itself in the deliberate and conscious attempt to discover and imitate antique models as the basis for a universal criterion of good taste. In the decorative and applied arts it was often largely a matter of fashion.

In England the Society of Dilettanti was formed in 1732 to promote excavation and the study of Greek antiquities. English artists and patrons of the arts visited the archaeological sites and brought back examples of sculpture, pottery and decoration. Investigation of the antique was encouraged for its own sake and because from a better knowledge of antique models it was hoped to discover the foundations of a universal good taste. The most important figure during the early years of the movement was Robert ADAM, who returned in 1758 after four years in Italy and was appointed architect to George III. An antiquary as well as an architect and designer, Adam maintained that 'the domestic architecture of the Greeks and Romans was entirely distinct from that of their temples', and criticized the Palladian school for having confused the two. Instead of the massive orders of Palladianism he favoured a system of decoration in low relief without structural significance and based largely on painted and stucco ornament such as had been found at Pompeii. He repudiated the asymmetry of ROCOCO, substituting for it a strict axial symmetry, and he relied mainly on motifs of classical origin such as medallions, TROPHIES, urns, PATERAE, tripods, masks, etc. A large repertory of such classical motifs became current wherever the principles of Neo-Classicism penetrated and were somewhat monotonously applied to furniture, pottery, textiles, plate and interior decoration. In his designs for furniture Adam also introduced the simple, rectilinear forms which in the 1770s and 1780s were popular through much of Europe. His was a predominant influence on Hepplewhite and later on Sheraton, both of which styles reflected the Neo-Classical taste in English furniture design. Neo-Classical designing in the other industrial arts followed closely upon architecture, interior decoration and furniture and the new style was fairly established by 1770. The great period of Neo-Classical taste in CERAMICS, silverware, etc. extended from *c.* 1770 to 1820 and at no other period was the influence of classical design and decoration so pervasive. In ceramics Josiah WEDGWOOD took the lead, producing in his new 'basaltes' ware a simple and elegantly sober pottery admirably adapted to the Neo-Classical interior. Among others Wedgwood employed Flaxman for his classical designs. Robert Adam designed for Matthew BOULTON, a pioneer in SHEFFIELD PLATE, and some of his designs for silverware are preserved in the Sir John Soane's Museum, London (a prize cup for the Richmond races, 1770, a cup and a candlestick for the Duke of Roxburghe, 1775, and two soup tureens for the Duke of Northumberland, 1779). The architect Henry Holland (1745–1806), a precursor of the Regency style, also made designs for furniture and interior fittings, notably at Southill in Bedfordshire, which he rebuilt in 1795. In the early years of the 19th c. Neo-Classicism in England received an added boost from the reflex influence of the French *Directoire*.

'Dancing nymph' plaque in basaltes ware with integral fluted frame border and red background. One of a series known as the 'Herculaneum Nymphs' produced by Wedgwood from the Marquess of Lansdowne's reliefs made after frescoes discovered at Pompeii in 1748. (Lady Lever Art Gal., Port Sunlight, 1770–80)

In France the advent of Neo-Classicism represented a reaction from the frivolities of Rococo and a nostalgia for the Grand Style of Louis XIV and the Classicism of Poussin in painting. Important among the pioneers in architecture—with which, particularly in France, taste in interior decoration is inevitably linked—were Ange-Jacques Gabriel (1698–1782), who built the Place de la Concorde in 1754 and whose Petit Trianon at Versailles was regarded as the most perfect example of 'Attic' in French architecture, and Jacques-Germain Soufflot (1713–80), who came to Paris in 1755 as Surveyor of Works and was instrumental in introducing the new Classicism into plans for reconstructing Paris. In applied art Neo-Classicism covers the periods of Louis XVI, the *Régence*, the *Directoire* and the *Empire*. In its aspect of a revolution in taste Neo-Classicism was symbolized by a work of the architect Jacques-François Blondel (1705–74), *De la distribution des maisons de plaisance* (1737–8), in which he derided the asymmetrical style of the Rococo, and his *Cours d'architecture* (1771–8), in which he condemned the works of people like MEISSONNIER, OPPENORD and CUVILLIÈS as a 'frivolous genre' and 'une singularité, une bizarrerie, permise tout au plus dans les ameublemens, les porcelains, les bronzes, etc.' So too in an article entitled 'Supplication aux orfèvres' (1754) Charles-Nicolas Cochin the younger (1715–90) attacked the Rococo love of scrolls and curves, pleading for a return to classical simplicity and grandeur. Yet Cochin was no indiscriminate enthusiast for the antique and had no admiration for the new discoveries at Herculaneum, treating only the small decorative objects with less severity. In its other aspect the Classical Revival in France was associated with a change in social outlook and a desire to restore the 'ancient Roman' virtues into civic life. This aspect of the movement found its most typical expression in the paintings of Jacques-Louis David, who through the cabinet-maker Georges JACOB, the archaeologist baron Dominique Vivant de Denon and others exerted a pervasive influence upon taste.

In France the new Classicism found expression

Jacques-Louis David, *Mme Récamier*. The portrait represents French Neo-Classical ideals of costume. The subject reclines on a *chaise-longue*, beside which stands an *athénienne*. (Louvre)

largely in the spheres of interior decoration and furniture styles. Among the leading representatives of the Louis XVI style were the German cabinet-makers Jean-Henri RIESENER, David ROENTGEN and Guillaume BENEMAN, the French-born Martin CARLIN and the metal-workers Pierre Gouthière (1740–1806) and Pierre-Philippe Thomire. The creators of the French *Empire* style were the architects and designers Pierre-François FONTAINE (1762–1853) and Charles PERCIER (1764–1838), who studied in Rome and on their return to France attracted the attention of David, who presented them to Napoleon. Both were fervent admirers of Greek and Roman ideals and they succeeded in blending harmoniously the prevailing Neo-Classical conception of the simplicity of the antique with the imperial grandeur of the Napoleonic era. In the Preface to their *Recueil de décorations intérieures* (1812), a book which had an important influence on taste and design in both France and England, they set forth the aesthetic doctrines which they believed to underlie the Empire style.

13, 20, 349, 414, 617, 815.

NEPHRITE. See JADE.

NETSUKE. Japanese national dress had no pockets and articles of personal necessity were carried on a cord attached to the belt by means of a toggle. The toggle was called *netsuke* ('end attachment'). *Netsuke* were made from a large variety of materials. In the early period *netsuke* made in Tokyo, Kyoto and Osaka were frequently of IVORY, including marine-tooth ivory. But many kinds of wood were also used and many other materials, such as JET, CORAL, JADE, AMBER, crystal, PORCELAIN, TORTOISESHELL and horn. *Netsuke* were carved in a very large variety of forms: birds, animals, insects, reptiles, fishes, plants, flowers, fruits; they were in the form of emblems, historical, mythological and legendary figures, masks and objects from the drama, tools, utensils and everyday objects. The miscellany of subjects is endless. The Japanese genius has had a special inclination for art in miniature and the *netsuke*, together with the INRŌ, offered a fertile field for miniaturization.

In early times *netsuke* were not valued and little or nothing is known about them. The earliest account of them is in the *Sōken Kishō*, which was published in 1781. This book gives the name of some 50 carvers of *netsuke* and illustrates their work, giving some idea of the form of *netsuke* prevalent at the time. It appears that some were imported from China and it has sometimes been thought that the *netsuke* may have originated there. Towards the end of the 18th c. more artists took up *netsuke*-carving and many began to sign their work. There have been over 2,000 *netsuke* carvers who have signed their work and a very large number of other craftsmen who worked anonymously. The great age of the *netsuke* was the first half of the 19th c., design tending to become generally more naturalistic and more intricate. From 1868, when European dress began to be worn in Japan, *netsuke* were made for export to Europe and quality declined. Many spurious pieces were turned out for Western collectors signed with the names of the better known *netsuke* artists.

Netsuke were commonly made with two holes (*himotoshi*, cord passage) at the back through which the cord was passed. Mask *netsuke* were generally made in this way. Some *netsuke* called *sashi* or *obi-hasami* were long in shape and were intended to be secured between the belt and the dress: these had the hole for the cord at the top. Others were rounded in shape with a spindle in the middle which was pierced for the cord: these were called *manjū*. In other cases the form of the object itself provided holes through which the cord could be passed. See also JAPAN (NETSUKE).

690, 735.

NETTING. See NEEDLEWORK.

NET-WORK. See NEEDLEWORK.

NEW ENGLAND GLASS COMPANY, THE. Founded in 1818, The New England Glass Company of East Cambridge, Massachusetts, was one of the international glass giants of the 19th c. Although until recently less well known than the BOSTON AND SANDWICH GLASS COMPANY of Cape Cod, The New England Glass Company was responsible for some of the most important technological innovations and developments in fine glass production of the century. The first agent, or general manager, of the firm was Deming Jarves (1790–1856), a Boston businessman who controlled the American monopoly on the production of the red lead essential to the making of fine tablewares. Jarves was also an important experimenter in the pressing and colouring of glass and in new methods of manufacture. Many of his techniques for the pressing of glass were adopted by European as well as by American glass-houses. The early years of the company were marked by great financial success due to skilful management and standards which produced glass equal in quality to much European material. By 1865 The New England employed about 500 men and boys and was soon to establish specialized departments of cutting, engraving, pressing, enamelling and gilding. Almost all of the wares made at East Cambridge were of fine flint or lead glass, but the development in 1864 in West Virginia of a less costly soda-lime glass ushered in a new period of diminished prosperity. Although almost all the contemporary glass-houses switched to the production of the cheaper variety of glass, The New England refused to lower the standard of its metal, with the result of sharply curtailed profits. The fourth and last agent of the company was William L. Libbey, who took office in 1870. Libbey continued to produce the fine metal for which the company was famed. His son, Edward Drummond Libbey, took control of the company in 1883 and operated it until 1888, when strikes and rising costs forced him to close the East Cambridge plant and move to Toledo, Ohio, where in 1892 The New England Glass Company became the equally celebrated Libbey Glass Company. From its earliest days The New England had produced fine free-blown wares, and its Middle Period (1830–80) engraved objects were among the highest achievements in the American decorative arts. In the latter part of the century the company produced superbly designed and executed cut glass as well as a variety of art glass developed by Joseph Locke (1846–1936). The most famous of Locke's patents for the company was that for Amberina, a red-shaded glass. But Pomona, Wild Rose, Agata, and Maize were also types of art glass produced by the company. These are widely collected today in the United States.

The seventy-year history of The New England Glass Company was one of the most distinguished in the history of American glass, and its wares were among the finest produced in the country. See GLASS (AMERICA).

NICOLAS OF VERDUN (active late 12th c.–early 13th c.). Goldsmith, enameller and metalworker. He is considered the last of the great ROMANESQUE goldsmiths. He was a pupil of GODEFROID DE CLAIR and owed much to Frederick of Cologne. His own style, particularly in his modelling of figures, displays a movement towards greater realism and the more sensitive feeling for the human form which was a characteristic of GOTHIC art.

He is known by two signed masterpieces: an ENAMELLED pulpit frontal made for Klosterneuburg, near Vienna (completed in 1181, damaged in 1320, and then remodelled into its present triptych-altar form) and the Shrine of St. Mary for Tournai Cathedral (1205). The former has 51 arcaded arches and is enamelled with parallel scenes from the Old and New Testaments. The Shrine of St. Mary is an edifice constructed at two levels in gold and silver with 1,500 stones and four finials of ROCK-CRYSTAL. In the long sides the arcades have six prophets in the lower stage and six Apostles in the upper. At one end is Isaiah between the Flagellation and the Crucifixion and at the other end the Virgin stands between the Three Kings and the Baptism, with Christ enthroned above. Among smaller works attributed to him the chalice of the church of St. Nicolas, Berlin, is considered to be of great beauty. Mention may also be made of the Trivulzio candlestick in Milan Cathedral and four small figures of prophets in the Ashmolean Museum, Oxford.

NIELLO (medieval Latin *nigello*, *neello*, black).

A dark composition of metallic alloys which was used for inlaying engraved designs on polished silver, gold or other metals. Hence the term is used of ornamental metalwork decorated by this method. The alloy consisted of copper, silver and lead, to which had been added sulphur while the metal was in fluid form. When cold the composition was reduced to a powder. In making niello work a decorative pattern was first engraved on polished metal. This was then brushed over with a solution of borax, and the powdered composition rubbed into the design. When the metal was heated the alloy fused and filled the engraved lines of the design. After cooling it was scraped off the surface so as to leave only the filling of the incised pattern. Silver was the preferred metal for niello because of the contrast offered between the light silver and the dark composition filling. In the early Christian period religious symbols and inscriptions on church plate were executed in niello. Subsequently it was popular in BYZANTIUM from the 6th to the 11th centuries for the enrichment of jewellery, small reliquaries and pendant crosses, as well as for domestic plate. It was also used in the West. From the early pagan period until the 11th c. it was a common feature of Anglo-Saxon jewellery. Such important pieces as the Tassilo chalice at Kremsmünster, Austria, (8th c.), King Ethelwulf's ring in the British Museum (9th c.) and the Fuller disc-brooch in the British Museum (9th c.) indicate the variety of its uses.

In the ROMANESQUE period the more colourful ENAMELS were preferred to the somewhat subdued effect of niello decoration but in the 13th c. the GOTHIC jewellers and silversmiths turned again to niello, especially for emphasizing the engraved ornament on rings.

It was popular in Germany and Bohemia during the 15th c., but the most ambitious and elaborate niello was created by Italian craftsmen about the middle of that century, when such things as cups and paxes with greater surface area were ornamented with graphic subjects. It was at this time that the goldsmith Maso Finiguerra (d. 1464) first took paper proofs from his niellos, thus initiating the niello print. After the Renaissance we find a black composition, not true niello, being used by Dutch engravers as a background filling during the great period of Dutch silver-engraving from the late 16th c. to the mid 17th c.

Niello techniques have been cultivated in many parts of the world where decorative metalwork has been practised. It has been used, for example, in India and in Islamic countries. It was native to South Russia and the Caucasus. A form of niello was also practised at TULA for decorating snuff-boxes, etc. and was known as 'Tula metal' or sometimes popularly as 'platina', although platinum was not used.

NONESUCH (or NONSUCH) **CHEST.** Modern term for chests with inlaid designs representing formal architectural views made in England, probably under Flemish influence, in the late 16th c. and early 17th c. The name originates from a 19th-c. belief that the designs represented Henry VIII's Palace of Nonesuch at Cheam, Surrey.

NONESUCH PRESS. A publishing firm founded in 1923 in London by Sir Francis Meynell, Vera Mendel and David Garnett for the production of books characterized by 'significance of subject, beauty of format, and moderation of price'. The books were printed at various presses, as well as a few at the Nonesuch, with the aim of extending the standards of book design already achieved in a more limited field by the Private Presses. Although typographical excellence was the primary aim, many Nonesuch books were remarkable also for their illustrations. Among the artists employed were Stephen Gooden (*Anacreon*, 1923), E. McKnight Kauffer (Burton's *Anatomy of Melancholy*, 1926) and Paul Nash (*Genesis*, 1929). The first hundred books issued by the press are described in the *Nonesuch Centenary* (1936).

In 1938 the controlling interest in the Nonesuch Press was sold but after the war an arrangement was reached whereby the existing Nonesuch titles were transferred to the Heritage Press, New York, and Sir Francis Meynell obtained sole use of the Nonesuch Press imprint for subsequent publications. See also PRIVATE PRESS MOVEMENT.

NORTHAMPTONSHIRE LACE. A bobbin lace made during the 19th c. in Northamptonshire with an elaborate ground and largely geometrical patterns. A speciality was lace made from thread of yak wool. Lace made with a thick thread or *cordonnet* to emphasize the design was known as 'trolly lace'.

NOVOCHERKASSK TREASURE. Name given to the objects found in a female Sarmatian burial at Khoklach near Novocherkassk, *c.* 1st c. B.C. See ASIA, CENTRAL.

NULLING. See GADROONING.

O

OBERKAMPF, CHRISTOPHE-PHILIPPE (d. 1815). From 1686 until 1759 edicts were issued in France prohibiting first the importation and then the imitation of Oriental fabrics. As soon as the ban was removed Oberkampf opened up his cotton-printing factory at Jouy, between Paris and Versailles, in 1759. He was born in Baden, trained as a dyer with his father and had learnt the other skills of a calico printer in Switzerland. He spent a short time with the Koecklin firm at Mulhouse. He no doubt chose Jouy for his venture on account of the abundant clear water and broad banks of the Bièvre, for its suitably temperate climate and its easy accessibility. Oberkampf was not only an excellent craftsman but a good man of business and the fame of the *toiles de Jouy* was assured from the first. They were used for both furnishings and clothing and were among the most popular of the printed fabrics in the new Orientalizing style. The factory continued after Oberkampf's death until 1843. See also COTTON AND COTTON PRINTING and TOILES DE JOUY.

OBI. In Japanese costume the sash which held in place the loose kimono and to which the *netsuke* was affixed. See JAPAN (NETSUKE).

OBRISSET, JOHN (active *c.* 1705–28). Huguenot of Dieppe, thought to be a son of an IVORY carver, who emigrated to England in 1686 and specialized in impressed designs in horn and TORTOISESHELL, a technique in which he had few followers. Thirty-three signed works are known and about a dozen are credibly attributed to him on stylistic grounds. He made snuff-boxes and plaques. He is best known for his portraits, including royal portraits (Charles I, James II, Queen Anne), but there are a dozen designs illustrating biblical or mythological themes and a well known impress representing the arms of Sir Francis Drake.

667.

OCCHI. Italian knotting. See NEEDLEWORK.

OEBEN, JEAN-FRANÇOIS (*c.* 1720–63). French cabinet-maker of German origin. He was trained by Charles-Joseph BOULLE, whom he succeeded as *ébéniste du Roi* in 1754. He exercised a determinant influence on the transitional style from ROCOCO towards NEO-CLASSICISM and through his workshop assistants J.-H. RIESENER and J.-F. LELEU he handed on the traditions of 18th-c. craftsmanship. From *c.* 1745 he was extensively patronized by Madame de Pompadour and he made furniture for her apartments at Versailles, Marly and Fontainebleau. In 1760 he was commissioned to produce the celebrated *bureau du Roi* (now in the Louvre), which was finished by Riesener. It is thought that the *bureau du Roi Stanislas* (Wallace Coll.), although signed only by Riesener, was probably designed by Oeben. A skilled mechanic and metal-worker, he owed much of his fame to his pieces with mechanical fitments which could fulfil a number of functions.

OEGG, JOHANN GEORG. German smith born at Silz *c.* 30 kilometres from Innsbruck. He was trained at Linz by his uncle, PETER Oegg, and in the 1720s was employed as a journeyman in the palace smithy of Prince Eugene of Austria, which supplied the many gates, screens and railings for the palaces then being erected in and around the city. In 1733 he entered the service of Bishop Friedrich Karl von Schönborn as palace smith (*Hofschlosser*) and with 25 journeymen and apprentices supplied the gates and screens for the *Residenzschloss*, then being built by the architect Johann Balthasar Neumann (1687–1753). Much of Oegg's work in the Rococo style survives and in its exuberance and vitality no less than its technical skill it is among the finest decorative wrought ironwork ever made in Germany. His first large work was the screen for the Schönborn chapel in Würzburg Cathedral (1734–5). The great curving screen to the *cour d'honneur*, consisting of eight ornamental panels on each side of a central pair of gates, followed and took five years to make (1736–41). This was Oegg's greatest work, but it was taken down and presumably destroyed in 1821, being now known only from an engraving by J. B. Gutwein. The screens and gates for the *Hofpromenade* (1746–9) remain, as do the garden gates opening on to the *Residenzplatz* and the *Rennweg*. Oegg retired in 1767 and was succeeded by his son, JOHANN ANTON.

See also IRON AND STEEL (DECORATIVE WROUGHT IRONWORK).

OGEE. A MOULDING whose section is made up of two contrary curves. The moulding with concave curve above and convex below is called *cyma recta*; that with convex above and concave below is called *cyma reversa*.

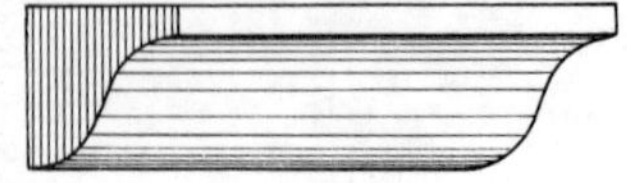

OIGNIES, HUGO. See HUGO D'OIGNIES.

OJIME. In traditional Japanese costume the bead by which the cords binding together *inrō* and *netsuke* were loosened or tightened. See JAPAN (NETSUKE).

OMEGA WORKSHOPS. An undertaking with certain analogies to the firm of William MORRIS, founded by Roger Fry (1866–1934) in 1913. The enterprise was the outcome of views about the functions of art in society developed by Fry partly perhaps under the influence of Veblen's *Theory of the Leisure Class.* It was an attempt to produce works of domestic utility into whose designing had gone the skill and taste of the best artists and thus to convert the new sensibility of modern art into a social force and by applying the decorative qualities of Post-Impressionist art in the production of articles of use to elevate the general taste. The Workshops produced or designed pottery, furniture, fabrics, rugs, embroidery, block-printing, etc. and Fry believed that through the pleasure which he and his colleagues took in the production of these objects a sense of the joy of artistic creation would be communicated to their users. Among his associates in this venture were Vanessa Bell and Duncan Grant. The Workshops were closed in 1919 partly for financial reasons and partly owing to a lack of enthusiasm in the associates, who were artists rather than practical craftsmen.

ONYX. See QUARTZ.

OPAL. A non-crystalline form of hydrous silica somewhat resembling QUARTZ, certain varieties of which are valued as gemstones. It has a hardness index of 5½ to 6½ on the MOHS SCALE. The characteristic play of colour is caused by interference as reflected light passes from one layer to another of the material: it is the same effect as that seen in a soap bubble or an oil slick on water. Opals came in the past mainly from India and Hungary. Today the most important sources are Queensland and New South Wales. The much-prized black opal, first discovered in 1905, comes only from Lightning Ridge on the borders of New South Wales and Queensland. The 'fire opal', which comes from Mexico, is orange-red or yellow. It is the only opal which can be cut as a brilliant.

By the Romans the opal was valued next to the EMERALD. It continued to be valued through the Middle Ages, when it was thought to have powers to predict disaster and to cure ophthalmia. It was much used in late Victorian jewellery. More recently it gradually acquired the reputation of being an unlucky stone and its popularity has dwindled.

OPALINE or OPAL GLASS. In the 17th c. 'opaline' or 'opal glass' was used of any opaque GLASS, such for example as the opaque coloured glass invented by Johann KUNCKEL as well as his transparent glasses. The term is now used chiefly for opaque white glass such as that which was called MILCHGLAS in Germany. Opaque glass, often enamelled, was popular in France in the 1st half of the 18th c. and was there called *opaline.* It was made both in white and in apple green in the 19th c. and was frequently painted on a gilt ground. A characteristic ornament was a coiled snake. In England opaque white glass, known as opal glass, was made at Bristol from before 1800 but the period of its greatest vogue was *c.* the middle of the 19th c. Its texture was softer and it was creamier than the French *opaline.* A distinctive creamy-white opaline was developed by the Russian glass-maker Bakhnetev.

OPPENORD, GILLES-MARIE (1672–1742). French designer and interior decorator in the ROCOCO style. He was the son of a Dutch-born cabinet-maker, JEAN Oppenord (1639–1715), who was naturalized in 1679 and received the title *ébéniste du Roi.* Gilles-Marie was trained in the ateliers of the Louvre, where his father had lodgings from 1684, and went to Rome in 1692 as a protégé of the *surintendant,* the Marquis de Villacerf. There he concentrated his interest on the Italian BAROQUE and accumulated in his notebooks a large repertory of ornamental motifs and forms. Returning to Paris in 1699, he studied native French traditions of decoration and also the new trends exemplified by such designers as BÉRAIN, LEPAUTRE and AUDRAN. Oppenord's early work, mainly ecclesiastical, was strongly reminiscent of the Baroque but already showed a fertile originality of ornamental detail. He came into his own under the Regency, when he was employed by the duc d'Orléans, and with François-Antoine Vassé became one of the most important formative influences in the RÉGENCE style. The chief outlet for his artistic activity was provided by the remodelling and redecoration of the Palais-Royal, but nothing now survives of his work there. During this period he also designed for the Hôtel Assy a salon which is now occupied by the Archives Nationales.

Oppenord's reputation has rested rather on his designs than his executed works. Some 2,000 of these were bought after the artist's death by the engraver Huquier and published in collections known as the *Petit, Moyen* and *Grand Oppenord.* Three of his sketch-books also survive (Berlin, Stockholm, Lyon).

OPUS ANGLICANUM (English work). Term internationally applied in the late 13th and 14th centuries to the English embroidery of that period and all other embroidery in similar style. It was among the most sumptuous and delicate NEEDLEWORK ever made. The surviving ecclesiastical vestments of this kind display small figures or religious scenes, comparable in style with East Anglian manuscript illumination, framed by foliaged scrolls or in geometrical or architectural compartments; these designs are worked in coloured silks in fine regular split stitch, generally on backgrounds of couched gold thread. The Vatican inventories of 1295 contain well over 100 references to such work, while vestments of *opus anglicanum* donated by Pope Nicholas IV to the cathedral of Ascoli Piceno (1295), by Boniface VIII to that of Anagni (*c.* 1300), by Clement V to that of Saint-Bertrand-de-Comminges (1309) and by Pius II to that of Pienza (1462) may still be seen in those towns. Among museum collections, that of the Victoria and Albert Museum, which includes the well known Syon cope, is the most comprehensive. See EMBROIDERY (ENGLAND).

OPUS ARANEUM (i.e. spider-work). See NEEDLEWORK and LACE and LACIS.

ORIENTAL CARPETS. See CARPETS AND RUGS.

ORMOLU (French: *or moulu*, the gold-leaf used for gilding metals). Term used in Britain and America, not in France, from the late 18th c. to describe the gilt bronze of which 18th-c. furniture MOUNTS and decorative metalwork in the French fashion were made. Its manufacture was not confined to France, but craftsmen elsewhere never achieved the French elegance of design and perfection of finish. True ormolu should be distinguished from the cheaper types of bronze which were cast, finished, and LACQUERED (*mis en couleur d'or*) in the founder's workshop. The former, after being cast in the foundry, was passed to the *ciseleur-doreur*, where it was finely chiselled and fire-gilt. The quality of ormolu objects depends on the amount of work put into them by the *ciseleur-doreur*, and the finest were hardly less expensive than similar articles in precious metal. The most characteristic productions were candlesticks and wall-sconces, chandeliers, clock-cases, FIRE-DOGS, table-centres, and mounts for PORCELAIN and furniture. It was not till the 2nd half of the 18th c. that the most exquisite work was produced; the earlier ormolu is vigorous but lacks the perfect finish of the Louis XVI pieces. Quality of design and execution remained very high during the French Empire but there was a rapid decline in standards during the 19th c., when cheap reproductions of earlier styles were mass produced.

Outside France the bronze founders who produced ormolu have remained anonymous, with the exception of the firm of BOULTON and Fothergill, whose Soho factory outside Birmingham enjoyed great success during the 1760s and 1770s. Many of the French artists in this medium hold a prominent place in the history of French decorative art, e.g. Charles CRESSENT, Pierre GOUTHIÈRE, and the CAFFIERI family. See also FURNITURE (EUROPEAN).

ORREFORS. Swedish glass-house celebrated for the technical quality of its products in clear, simple colours and for the restrained moderation of their forms in keeping with the 'modern' movement in taste.

OTTOMAN. A long upholstered seat of Turkish origin which was introduced into England in the late 18th c. and is illustrated by SHERATON and Thomas HOPE. Circular and octagonal ottomans were introduced *c.* the middle of the 19th c. Ottomans of all sorts became popular in America from *c.* 1840. In France the *ottomane* came into vogue with other *turqueries* in the time of Louis XV.

OTTONIAN. Term in the history of the fine and decorative arts for a distinctive style which began to develop, primarily in Germany, by the end of the 1st millennium A.D. Although named after the Ottonian emperors (919–1024), it actually extended further into the 11th c. The style represented an amalgam of a revival of CAROLINGIAN art, a renewed interest in early Christian art and a strong influence from contemporary BYZANTINE art with an admixture of certain northern traditions. Outstanding examples of the Ottonian style are the bronzes of Hildesheim Cathedral and the large gold altar frontals of Henry II (Musée Cluny, Paris). Important workshops of IVORY-carving were at Echternach (Moselle) and on the island of Reichenau in Lake Constance. The period is also important for stylistic developments in the art of manuscript illumination.

OUDENARDE TAPESTRIES. Oudenarde in Belgium was an important and very productive centre of tapestry-weaving from the 15th to the 18th centuries. It is best known for its landscape tapestries carried out almost entirely in blues, greens and yellows. The town-mark is a pair of spectacles, alone or attached to a shield.

OUDRY, JEAN-BAPTISTE (1686–1755). French painter, pupil of Nicolas de Largillière (1656–1746), a historical painter who worked with Charles Lebrun (1639–90) at Versailles. Oudry first made his name as a painter of still lifes and animals but later became interested in landscape and his *Chasses de Louis XV* (Fontainebleau), made for TAPESTRY design, have been called 'the finest evocation of natural scenery in 18th-century France'. He was also known for his illustrations of La Fontaine. But his chief renown rested upon his designs for the BEAUVAIS tapestry works, of which he was made Director in 1734.

OVOLO. A wide convex MOULDING whose profile in section is a quarter-circle or a quarter-ellipse receding from the vertical downwards. In Classical architecture it was used below the abacus of a Doric capital. It was frequently

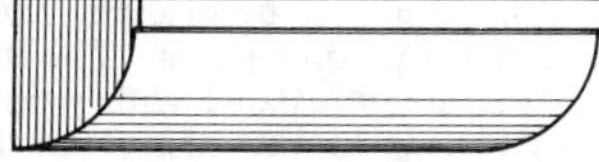

decorated with enrichment of EGG-AND-DART pattern. It was also known as ECHINUS and in cabinet-making and plate as 'quarter round'. See also CONGÉ.

OYSTERING. A type of VENEER popular in England after the Restoration and in the William and Mary period. The veneer was made from small oval slices cut transversely, at an oblique angle to the length, from the roots or smaller boughs of walnut, olive, laburnum, cedar, etc. so that the full decorative effect of the grain was obtained. These pieces were joined together to form a sheet of veneer, which was called 'oyster-shell veneer' because it resembled the oyster shell in effect. Oystering was used for borders, for the fronts of drawers and for complete panels. It remained popular until the 18th c., when it was superseded by 'burr walnut' veneering. See also WOOD-WORKING.

P

PADELOUP. French bookbinding family active in the 17th and 18th centuries. ANTOINE-MICHEL (1685–1758), known as le Jeune, succeeded Antoine Boyet as Royal Binder in 1733. He produced signed mosaic bindings in variously coloured leathers, but is best known for his DENTELLE BINDINGS, which were widely imitated throughout the 18th c. He specialized in the binding of fête books in large formats with engraved illustrations by Audran, Cochin and others, and was one of the first binders to sign his work with a printed ticket inside the book cover. See BOOKBINDING (HISTORICAL).

PAINTS AND PIGMENTS. See COLOURS AND COLOURANTS.

PAISLEY. See SHAWLS.

PAKTONG (Chinese *pai-t'ung*, white copper). An alloy made by combining nickel–copper with zinc, or TUTENAG. It was described by Libavius in *De Natura Metallorum* (1597) as *aeș album*, i.e. white bronze. Paktong was white, resembling silver, sometimes with a slight yellowish tinge according to the proportions of the component metals. It is hard and tough, not easily corroded, and gives out a bell-like note when struck. It was not imported by the East India Company but is supposed to have been brought in by officers in the Company's service as a 'private' import from Canton, where it was manufactured. Articles made from paktong and retailed to the public in England were mistakenly described as 'tutenag'. A similar alloy was made in the West only after nickel had been isolated in sufficient quantities for commercial purposes. It was first produced by Edward Thomason of Birmingham in 1823. Some years later it was produced in Germany and introduced into England with the name 'GERMAN SILVER'.

Paktong was used in England mainly for decorative candlesticks (V. & A. Mus.) from *c.* the middle of the 19th c. These are rare and have sometimes been silver plated. A few fire-grates and fenders of Paktong in the style of Robert ADAM are also known.

PALAMPORE. A kind of CHINTZ bed-cover formerly imported from India. See COTTON AND COTTON PRINTING.

PALISSY, BERNARD (*c.* 1510–*c.* 1590). French master potter, born near Agen. He first worked as an artist in stained glass and established himself at Saintes as a potter *c.* 1542, where he achieved a high reputation. He was patronized in 1555 by the High Constable de Montmorency and was brought to Paris in 1566 by Catherine de Médicis. Palissy was outstanding for the fineness of his wares and for his mastery of rich polychrome glaze colours. His dishes and bowls were ornamented with snakes, lizards, frogs, fish, foliage, etc. cast from the life and for this type of ware he was given the title 'inventor of the king's rustic pottery'. He also worked from casts taken from SILVER and PEWTER dishes. Wares of the type for which he was famous continued to be produced regionally in France for some two centuries after his death. See CERAMICS.

PALMETTE. Ornamental motif consisting of an odd number of leaves, naturalistically rendered or conventionalized, radiating out like the fingers of a hand. The central leaf is the largest and the leaves diminish in size on each side of it. The tips of the leaves lie on a regular curve and their lower ends are disconnected, springing from a tongue-shaped leaf, conventionalized floral stigma, etc. The palmette was used in Egyptian decoration, where it was sometimes constructed

from LOTUS elements. It was common in Mesopotamian ornament and in Mycenaean and proto-Greek. The palmette is a particularly characteristic feature of Greek classical ornament, both as free ornament and in bands for border decoration or the enrichment of cornices, etc. When used in a band the palmette is usually combined with scrolls or spirals connecting the elements.

PANEL. Term used in architecture, furniture and other decorative arts for any surface sunk within a framework. The term 'panel painting' is sometimes used in distinction from 'mural painting' for a painting done on movable board, in a similar sense to 'easel painting'.

Stone panelling was much used in GOTHIC interiors as for example in the English Perpendicular style, where the design of the window tracery of a church might be carried down the wall below in a series of panels. Panelling in wood, the fitting of thin sheets into frames so that they do not warp or split, had a considerable vogue in the 15th c., and the introduction of joined panelling at the beginning of the century lightened the construction of chests, cupboards, beds, etc. Wood panelling for interiors was particularly popular in northern Europe, where a draught-proof house was desirable, and reached a peak of elaboration in the traceried panels of late medieval northern Germany and the Low Countries. The LINENFOLD pattern was invented in Flanders during the 15th c., a stylized imitation of curtaining, and appeared in England late in the century. Full panelling persisted in small rectangular and richly decorated panels through the reign of Henry VIII, when it was accompanied by Renaissance motifs such as profile heads set in wreaths. In the time of Elizabeth I the panels were plainer or ornamented with chip carving. In the earlier panelling the horizontal rails 'ran through' the uprights. The next step was to *return* the mouldings, i.e. to make them turn the corner round each panel, but the frame was still cut in the old way with the returned corner carved on the rail. The diagonal mitred joint came at the end of the 16th c.

Fielded, or raised panels and BOLECTION moulded panels, with the moulding projecting beyond the face of the framing, appeared in the 17th c. and the size of the panels was considerably increased. This was made possible by the import of new woods: Norway oak, more tractable than British; pine, at first unpainted and used for its colour; and figured hardwoods that could be laid in thin sheets. In the early 18th c. oak was replaced largely by deal and thereafter the painted panel predominated. The BAROQUE panel and the ROCOCO panel with painting or ARABESQUES belong to the history of interior decoration when the arts of painting, carving and architecture were united in the formation of one unified artistic whole. National styles developed in France, Italy and Germany with mutual influences and interaction.

PANEL ORNAMENT. See DIAPER.

PANTIN. See TOYS.

PANTIN, SIMON. Huguenot goldsmith and silversmith who worked in London 1699–1728.

PANTOGRAPH. See SILHOUETTE and MEDALS.

PAPER. Paper has been commonly prepared from pulped vegetable fibres, often extracted from cotton or linen rags. The pulp is shaken in a sieve, technically known as the 'mould', to drain away the moisture and the solid sheet which remains is removed, pressed and dried. It is then sized to give a non-absorbent surface. Paper made in this way is known as 'laid', and when held against the light shows transparent marks called 'chain-lines' (thick) and 'wire-lines' (thin) where the pulp has rested on the wire mesh of the mould. WATERMARKS are produced in a similar manner. 'Woven' paper, made in a mould of closely woven brass wires, has a smooth surface without chain-lines. It was used for the BASKERVILLE *Virgil* (1757) and was adapted to machine processes early in the 19th c. Until the invention of the paper machine by Nicholas-Louis Robert in 1798 all paper was made by hand. For special purposes, such as the printing of *de luxe* editions, hand-made paper is still produced.

The earliest form of paper was PAPYRUS, thought to have been invented by Egyptians *c.* the middle of the 3rd millennium B.C. and made from strips of a native sedge laid crosswise in several layers and soaked and pressed together. It was extensively used for writing in GREEK AND ROMAN ANTIQUITY. Dressed animal skins were also used for writing in classical antiquity, especially at Pergamum (whence comes the word 'parchment') from the 2nd c. B.C. VELLUM was used for writing and also for BOOKBINDING in late classical antiquity and by the early Christian monks. Paper in the modern sense was first made by the Chinese, probably as early as the 2nd c. A.D. By the end of the 8th c. the process was known to the Arabs, who introduced the use of paper into Spain *c.* A.D. 950. The earliest surviving European paper document is Sicilian and dated 1109. Paper-mills are first mentioned in Spain at Jativa (1150), in Italy at Fabiano (1276), in France near Troyes (1348), in Germany at Nuremberg (1390). The first paper-mill in England was started by John Tate at Hertford in 1495. The more general use of paper in Europe instead of vellum followed the invention of printing with movable types *c.* the middle of the 15th c. (See TYPOGRAPHY.) The use of paper for drawing, as an alternative to parchment, is mentioned in CENNINI's *Treatise on Painting* (early 14th c.), where it is described as *carta bambagina.* Coloured paper dates from the late 15th c., the earliest being the famous *carta azzurra,* or blue-toned paper, manufactured at Venice.

See also PAPIER MÂCHÉ and PAPERS, DECORATIVE.

PAPERS, DECORATIVE. Decorative or pattern papers have been produced in many countries of Europe since Renaissance times. The early European pattern papers were chiefly associated with books, either as binding or as end-papers. They were also used as lining papers.

In the East, pattern papers are far older. They may well date as far back as A.D. 105, when the idea of forming a sheet of paper from wood is credited to a Chinese court official. Paper then started to be made in quantity by macerating in water vegetable matter such as the bark of the mulberry, rags or even old fishing nets. This matter was then beaten to a pulp, the pulp was passed through a mould and the water shaken out, so as to produce a sheet of paper.

The knowledge of paper-making spread very slowly from China, first to Korea in the 7th c. and from there to Japan. Later it spread westwards to the Near East and from there to Europe. See PAPIER MÂCHÉ.

It was in the 15th c. that paper began to be in general use for writing, gradually replacing the use of vellum. After GUTENBERG's invention of printing from movable type in 1450 books came into ever more frequent use and binding was a necessity for their protection. It is largely through the craft of BOOKBINDING that the development of European pattern papers can be traced. There was a great variety of methods for decorating the protective end-papers of calf bindings, including woodcut prints, embossing, MARBLING and paste papers. The designs reflect the tastes and fashions of their periods, as do the colours used.

The art of marbling is thought to have come to Europe from the Middle East, having been learnt by the monks at the time of the Crusades. Marbled papers are sometimes referred to as 'Turkish' paper, the Turks having had a reputation for producing fine marbled designs. Marbling is done by laying a sheet of paper on to a trough containing a gelatinous liquid such as size or gum, on to which colour is dropped. A moiré effect can be obtained by gently shaking the trough as the paper is laid on the colour. The colours used may be either oil or water-colour. The decorative quality comes about from the ways in which the colours are caused to spread. Effects are often gained by combing the colours with a tool and many of the combed patterns are named and can be repeated by skilled craftsmen. Nevertheless each sheet is individually made, so that no two sheets are absolutely identical. Mrs. Rosamond B. Loring, an American authority, herself a skilled craftsman, says that marbled papers were greatly valued by collectors in the 17th c., when some beautiful patterns were produced. At least from the 18th c. onwards binders sometimes also marbled the fore-edges of books. There are artist–craftsmen making fine marbled papers today, both in Europe and in America. A delightful and unusual 20th-c. Turkish paper may be seen in the print room of the Victoria and Albert Museum with a design of tulips marbled on paper.

Paste papers, sometimes confused with marbled papers, are patterned by a different technique. In this case the paste is mixed with powdered colour and is then brushed directly on to dampened paper. The pattern is made whilst the coloured paste is wet by drawing with a tool, brush, stylo, comb or even with the finger. Alternatively patterns can be made by laying the pasted surfaces of two sheets together; then gently rubbing them on the back, and pulling them apart. This results in a distinctive textural quality, such as that which can be also obtained when wood-blocks are printed with paste colour. Between 1760 and 1825 a German sect called the Herrnhut Brotherhood set up a sister house where a large quantity of paste-paper pattern papers were produced. These sheets were sold throughout Germany by the running stationers. They were much sought after by the binders, the designs being so notable that the name Herrnhut became synonymous for paste pattern papers. The paste-paper technique has been most interestingly developed by a 20th-c. Italian artist, Ugo Zovetti, and there is a small collection of his designs in the Print Room of the Victoria and Albert Museum. The designs are the outcome of a mixed technique of wax and paste, printed lithographically. The technique was also taken up and adapted by some Surrealist artists for the production of 'automatic' or unplanned results.

Block-printed designs done by hand form by far the largest group of the older European pattern papers. There is a vast variety in the types of patterns, and each country has its distinctive styles and fashions. They were not only used as covers and end-papers for books but also as lining papers for chests, caskets and boxes, and for wrapping. Indeed the printers often used the same blocks for several different purposes. Some of the pattern papers that have survived will have been travellers' samples or trial prints for CHINTZ. Textile printers sometimes printed on paper when there was a hold-up in the delivery of cloth and since paper was expensive, sometimes a discarded or a censored text would be overprinted with a pattern. Censored books would be ordered to be 'damasked'. These sheets could then be sold to merchants for resale as lining papers for chests and boxes. Some of the wood-blocks were even used as ginger-bread moulds. Because the import duty on pattern papers was heavy in England, some came from the Continent as wrappings on toys and other small objects. The binders bought the wrapping papers, which they smoothed and then used as end-papers.

The earliest surviving English pattern papers date from the mid 16th c. and were printed on small sheets. Some had decorative designs which did not fill the entire sheet but left wide margins of plain paper on all sides. The early designs were rather coarsely cut wood-blocks in a manner which resembles that of the illustrated Herbals and chap-books of the time. In the Print Room of the Victoria and Albert Museum there is an early example of an English paper which was used to line an oak chest. It is a Tudor rose design printed in black monochrome and is dated 1550. Another, printed in scarlet on a grey ground, has a 'Dodo', possibly taken from a bestiary, enclosed in a circle; the date is 1609. It was used as a cover for a churchwarden's account book. Another, also used in a churchwarden's account book, has a design printed in black on a grey paper; the date is 1614 or 1615. The size of these sheets is approximately 30 cm by 40 cm. An 18th-c. paper was found lining a chest in St. Paul's Cathedral. It has a design of flowers printed in *gouache* colours of green, grey, black and white. These English designs are typical of their kind, unsuitable as WALLPAPERS because the sheets cannot easily be pasted together to form a continuous repeating pattern without a great deal of cutting and waste. They were intended for binding. Some have borders, some have stripes, and in the 18th c. some were printed with spotted piqué backgrounds. These last were probably printed from wood-blocks intended for calico printing.

Italian designs, many of which date back to the Renaissance, have often been reprinted or reproduced. A collection of old Italian blocks was reproduced in the 20th c. by a Florentine firm employing craftsmen from one of the leather shops of Florence. Earlier, in 1814, an Italian, Giuseppe Rizzi of Varese, reprinted a number of early Renaissance papers and issued a sample brochure. An Italian book, published in Venice in 1812, has a charming binding of a little lozenge-shaped spot pattern printed in pink.

French pattern papers were printed by the 'Dominotiers', the name given to the guild that was engaged in printing *imagerie*, and who also did marbling. Indeed they took their name from the hooded cloaks or dominoes, worn by the Italian marblers, whence the name '*dominoterie*' for coloured papers. They started as early as the 14th c., but few early examples of their printing or wood-blocks have survived. They printed many things, from fables, Bible pictures, stories of horror and adventure, PLAYING CARDS and other games, as well as decorative papers used by the binders and also by the poorer people to decorate their walls. The works of the printers of *imagerie* are now greatly valued and collected, and many books have been published about those in the different districts in France. Enough of the pattern papers printed in the 18th c. remain to give a good idea of their great charm and variety. They included, for example, figured and coloured papers, flowers, sprigs and sprays, spots, stripes and all-over patterns, some with figurative subjects, the cries of Paris, a sheet of scenes illustrating a child's story. The printing blocks were cut from pear wood and the sheets were sold in the streets by the running stationers. The French marbled and veined papers have a very distinctive character.

Embossing was another form of decorative patterning, from the 17th c. to the middle of the 19th c. Embossed patterns were made from metal plates, and later from small engraved rollers which were pressed into the dampened paper. It is likely that at times bookbinders' punches were also used. Some of the embossed designs follow closely the styles of the calf bindings. The paper was sometimes tinted before embossing; sometimes it was coloured by stencils or by hand, before or after the embossed design was applied. Many of the sheets were laid with a foil of gold, copper or silver. In some cases colours were stencilled over the emboss on gold, a case of gilding the gingerbread. The Dutch were famous for the embossed covers used on chap-books and embossed papers are sometimes referred to as 'Dutch' papers. In fact, however, embossed papers are thought to have originated in Venice. Certainly many fine embossed designs can be found on Italian books of the 17th and 18th centuries, chiefly on the smaller publications such as books of poems, legal treatises and pamphlets. In Germany, France, Portugal, England and other European countries embossed designs were also made. The earlier types of design were ROCOCO, with scroll-like figures and vignettes following closely the fashions of the silk BROCADES. There are also star patterns, frets and classical heads, also little scenes, armorial bearings and indeed a great diversity of subjects.

The embossed patterns of the 19th c. made in England had a quite different character. They were mass produced from roller printing and they fall roughly into two categories. Firstly pretty, rather ornate borders. These were used for writing-papers and envelopes, with the expansion of the postal services. They were also used on invitation cards, Valentines and later for Christmas cards and scraps. (See POSTAL COMMUNICATIONS, PICTORIAL.) Then there was a large group of embossed textures, simulating such things as basket-work, sharkskin, crocodile. There is a 19th-c. pattern-book in the Print Room at the Victoria and Albert Museum entitled *A Pattern Book of Fancy Papers, gold borders, ovals and circles, Chinese paper, and screen handles.* A foreword explaining the contents describes the papers as: Splashed and figured (this appears to mean all-over patterns); Gold and Silver Chinese (these are foil papers on a coloured ground); Improved Cypress (this is a type of water marbling); Tortoiseshell (another form of marbling); Plain and grained Morocco; Embossed papers, mainly Honeycomb (a very heavy emboss of honeycomb pattern); Antique Wicker (another heavy emboss); Hair-plait, Stormont, Shagreen, Seed and Wave, Mother of pearl or Silver figured; Flower and Post papers of various colours, matt and burnished gold, Silver Moss and Sea Weed. The great majority of papers in this little sample book were clearly intended for the purpose of making up boxes or as wrappings and not, as at an earlier date, for bookbinding or end-papers.

The pattern papers of the East have different functions from those of the West, which have been so largely associated with books. Books in China and Japan in ancient times took the form of scrolls. Even today Japanese books are bound in a different manner from those of the West. On the other hand paper is used for a much greater variety of purposes, many of which—particularly in Japan—lend themselves to the use of decorative paper. For example interior paper screens are used in Japan for dividing rooms; paper is used for lampshades, fans, umbrellas, and even for clothing. Raincoats are made of a certain type of specially tough paper. These papers are decorated in a great number of different ways. They are made, many of them even today, by hand. The Japanese have developed the craft of paper-making, which came originally from China, to a fine art.

The very process of paper-making by hand imparts certain aesthetic qualities. First, in the material chosen for the pulp. In the West the pulp for the hand-made papers was made from linen rag. This is where Japanese paper-making is fundamentally different. The pulp used in Japanese papers is of a vegetable, mucilaginous matter called in Japan 'neri', a plant of which there are two species. The 'neri' is soaked in water and beaten and pressed to extract the glue; it is then mixed in a vat with other vegetable fibres, chief of which are *kozo*, *gampi* and *mitsumata*, *kozo* being the one in most frequent use. But every fibre has its own particular qualities. *Gampi* paper is reputed to have noble qualities, *kozo* to be strong and masculine and *mitsumata* to form a feminine and elegant sheet. In Japanese papers one often finds that the textural qualities are enhanced by extraneous substances added to the pulp in the course of manufacture. These additions may sometimes take the form of different fibres, contrasting with the main pulp—shiny, dull, thin, flat, rough—or they may form strands of a different colour. Some papers are spattered with particles of gold or silver dusted on to the pulp; others have leaves or even butterflies incorporated into the sheet. Stencils are used in Japan for patterning papers, often in several colours for small all-over designs. Another method is a form of tie-dyeing by means of folding so that the pigment only reaches the creased parts of the paper, which is unsized, so that the colours spread in a distinctive manner. The most exotic and interesting pattern papers made anywhere today are the Japanese lace papers. These lace-like patterns are produced by using a form of stencil which is made of a thin metal sheet on which a pattern has been pierced or cut. This sheet is placed on the mould after a thin coat of pulp has formed; then the mould is subjected to an intense spray of water, which washes away all but the finest filament of pulp from the parts of the mould where there are holes in the metal plate. The resulting pattern is sometimes transparent on semi-transparent paper or, if a pattern is made on a thicker pulp, it resembles more the sort of figuring associated with watermarks on Western hand-made papers. But the watermarks of the West were made purely for the functional purpose of identification, not as pattern papers.

In China, Persia and India beautiful foil pattern papers were made, many of them to serve as frames for manuscript paintings. Today in Britain pattern papers have largely become associated with wrapping papers, as books are seldom bound, but cased. The designs are mass produced and the majority reproduced by photolithography. Japan is one of the few places where the old techniques for making pattern papers in quantities still exist and even develop with fresh experimentation; though they are expensive, so long as there are the craftsmen to make these lovely individual sheets there will be a market for them. See bibliography on p. 865.

PAPER-WEIGHTS. See GLASS (FRANCE).

PAPIER MÂCHÉ. Useful and decorative articles made of papier mâché have been produced the world over from early in the Christian era and are still being made today. Some articles were made of pulp and others of laminated paper, but both are classed as papier mâché. While the basic materials have remained the same through the centuries, the form and decoration of the products have varied from age to age and from country to country.

Although the origin of the term 'papier mâché' is uncertain, it seems probable that it began to be used in England in the 17th c. and not as one would suppose in France. The *Oxford English Dictionary* notes that: 'Although composed of French words, it is not recognized in French dictionaries.' The use of the words, no doubt, came about as follows. In 17th-c. England paper pulp was called 'chewed paper'. The French word for 'chew' is *mâcher*; so with many French émigrés employed in the English industry at that time 'chewed paper' became 'papier mâché' or, as is was sometimes mis-spelled in the 18th c., 'papier machine' and 'papier mâchée'.

The art of moulding pulp and pasteboard was an outgrowth of the invention of paper-making by the Chinese. Known examples of their LACQUERED papier mâché are a war helmet and lacquered pot-lids, the latter attributed to the Han Dynasty, *c.* A.D. 206. There exist as well specimens of thick pasteboard made in Tibet at a remote period. The Oriental papier-mâché objects are generally classified as lacquer ware, no distinction being made between the wood-based and paper-based articles, and expert examination is often required to determine the basic material.

Historians do not agree upon the date of the invention of paper-making by the Chinese but it is believed they were making paper before the beginning of the Christian era. Credit is given to a Chinese court official named Tsʻai Lun for discovering in A.D. 105 that paper could be made from wood—a fact known to the wasp, which makes its paper nests from wood. The Chinese made paper from silk rags, hemp waste, fish-nets, raw fibres from the mulberry bark and bamboo. The Chinese also originated the processes of loading, sizing (using starch) and coating paper. The Japanese began to make paper *c.* A.D. 610, over 500 years after Tsʻai Lun conceived the art in China. The Japanese gained their first knowledge of paper from Korea, then a part of China, when in the 7th c. Korean Buddhist monks brought manuscripts to Japan.

From China the knowledge of paper-making spread to the Middle East when in A.D. 751 the Arabs, who then occupied Samarkand, were attacked by the Chinese. The Arabs were the victors and took among their prisoners some skilled paper-makers, who in time taught their captors the art. The knowledge then spread through the Arab dominions. The Arabs employed skilled Persian workmen who, having no mulberries, resorted to flax that grew in abundance in Khurasan, a Persian province under Arab rule. Eventually it became necessary to use rags and vegetable fibres as well as flax. Paper-making then spread from Samarkand to Damascus and by A.D. 1100 had reached Morocco. The Spanish, who were the first to have a paper-mill in Europe, learned from the Moors. Eventually mills were established in France and in 1189 in the Netherlands. The first mill in Italy was built in 1276 and was considered superior to any other at that time. According to William Caxton there was a paper-mill in England at Stevenage, Herts., *c.* 1495. Paper and blotting-paper appear to have been early products in England, but in the 17th c. French paper was imported by the book trade. From *The Annals of Bristol in the Seventeenth Century* (1900) by John Latimer we learn that a certain Thomas Thomas, a bookseller, on 23 January 1667, successfully petitioned the Privy Council to grant booksellers a licence to operate two small vessels for the importation of paper from Normandy. The same authority records that French emigrant paper-makers opened mills in England in 1690.

In the same year William Rittenhouse, a Mennonite minister, brought the paper industry to the American colonies. He built a mill about 8 km north of Philadelphia, where *c.* 1,200 reams of paper, made from homespun and woven linen rags, were produced in a year. From that time other mills were established in the colonies until by the 1st quarter of the 19th c. paper-making had become a full grown industry. Benjamin Franklin, the American printer, had helped in this growth for he took such great interest in paper-mills that he started 18 of them.

Paper-making was a slow and costly process in the early days, so paper was not in common use for a long time. Briefly the process was to put rags and clear water into stone mortars, then beat or pound them with pestles or mallets operated by hand (later by water-power) into a pulp. The pulp was then placed in a mould frame and dried. Because of this prolonged hand-labour paper was re-used whenever possible. Shopkeepers wrapped their merchandise in old manuscripts, music scores and other used papers. Scrap paper was saved and mashed into pulp, which could then be moulded into a variety of articles. The only mention of collecting waste paper for this purpose appears in *Nuit de Paris* by Restif de la Bretonne (1734–1806), in which he describes the work of the billboard strippers of Paris as follows: 'He pulls posters off the bill-boards at street corners and that provides for all his needs . . . He sells the single ones to the grocer for three sous a pound; those stuck one on top of the other he sells to the cardboard maker; and whatever is absolutely filthy and ruined he collects in his little room and keeps himself warm with it during the winter.' For all this work the stripper earned from 12 to 15 sous a day.

For the method of making papier mâché, whether of pulp or of laminated paper, we must rely on English references. Descriptions of methods used in other countries are non-existent or scanty. In any case the early methods used elsewhere must have been similar to those of the English artisans who were working with pulp before 1750. Until the end of the 18th c. English production was mainly the work of individuals making small quantities of pulp products such as gilded wall-brackets, sconces and ornamental MIRRORS. Robert Boyle (1627–91) in *Uses of Natural Things* wrote that one should soak a convenient quantity of whitish paper, then mash it in hot water. J. Peele, whose information came chiefly from a manuscript of the great Mr. Boyle, wrote in *A New and Curious Method of Japanning* (1732): 'In *Japan* the people have a method of making Bowls, Plates and other Vessels from Paper and sometimes Sawdust . . . [and] these Vessels are in great Esteem among us.' Peele's instructions were to take slips of brown paper and 'boil them in Common Water and mash it with a stick while it boils. When it almost becomes a paste, take it from the Water and beat it well in a mortar til reduced to a pulp. Then make a strong Gum-Water with Gum-Arabick and Water, a quantity sufficient to cover your Paper-paste an inch. Put these together in a glazed Pipkin and let boil, stirring well til impregnated with the Gum. Put into mould.' In the late 18th c. the English manufacturers mashed the pulp in large vats with steam-power but later on paper companies supplied the industry with ready-made pulp, a convenience for the moulders and blank-makers. Pulp was also formed into slabs of pasteboard by first steam-kneading the mixture and then pressing it through rollers to form sheets of uniform thickness. This board was then dried at a slow temperature. A 19th-c. pulp producer named George Iles, a machinist by trade, made a plastic pulp of coloured silks which he used for moulding inkstands and picture frames.

As has been said, panels of laminated paper were made at an early date in the Far East; but in 1772 Henry Clay of Birmingham received a patent for an improved heat-resistant paper-board. It was capable of being handled like wood and could be stove-dried without fear of warping. This panel was made of about ten sheets of unsized paper glued and layered on a metal core or mould. Each sheet had to be carefully smoothed each time by pressing it with a trowel-like tool to remove all air-bubbles. Women and girls seated at tables cut the paper to the right size and passed it along to the paster, also a woman. The work required skill and patience. When all the paper was pasted and all the edges trimmed even with the mould, it was drenched in linseed oil to make it waterproof. The panel was then dried at a temperature of 38 °C. A plane with a serrated blade, set upright in the block rather than on a slant as in a wood-working tool, was used to smooth and finish the panel.

In 1847 the Birmingham firm of Jennens & Bettridge took out a patent for applying steam to soften the panel and make it pliable. It could then be pressed or moulded into any form. If left hard and firm, the panel was as tough as plywood and could be worked with carpenter's tools. Any number of paper sheets could be used but a thicker panel required longer drying. When the die press or stamping machine was introduced in the 19th c. a thick panel was necessary to endure the pressure of the machine. The die press could stamp out a tray form in one operation. A thick panel was also needed for prefabricated houses. George Bielefeld of London, an inventor and manufacturer, introduced paper panels that measured 1·8 by 2·5 metres and were 127 mm thick. These tough and soundproof panels, said to be more durable for painting than canvas, were moulded on a skeleton support of wood. They were used for bulkheads and cabin partitions in some of the fine steamers of the day as well as for cottages. In 1846 Bielefeld received a patent for making moulds and dies used in the manufacture of all types of imitation plaster ornament, all of which were presented in the beautifully rendered plates of his catalogue of 1850. In 1853 he built a patented waterproof paper village for a man named Seymour, who was planning to set the buildings up in Australia.

Making a building of papier mâché was not a new idea, for in 1793 a church of that material was erected near Bergen, Norway, and it survived for 37 years before it was demolished. There was also a man in London named Lewis Charles Ducrest, who in 1788 patented a process for 'making paper for building houses, shops, boats and all kinds of wheeled carriages, Sedan chairs, tables, etc.' Ducrest's houses were to be formed of rooms piled up like boxes and put together with iron bolts, pre-dating the contemporary design of 'Habitat '67' by Moshe Sofdie for Expo '67 at Montreal. In the 18th c. the firm of Jackson & Son of London made architectural ornaments for interiors—such things as cornices, ceiling ornaments and wall motifs—that were imitations of the more costly real plasterwork so much in vogue in fine English houses. George Jackson began as a carver of wooden moulds for Robert ADAM in 1765. This firm, which is still in business, has thousands of the original moulds still available.

The idea of imitating carved plaster by moulded papier mâché seems to have originated with the English quite early in the 18th c. That their work was admired by the French is evident in the following paragraph written in 1778 and published in the Bielefeld catalogue in 1850. 'The English cast in cardboard the ceiling ornaments that we make in plaster; they are more durable; break off with difficulty, or if they do break off the danger is of no account and the repair is less expensive.'

In England the paper first used for papier mâché was described as 'whited brown' or 'brown', but later grey was used. This 'making paper', as it was called, was made from linen rags and was unsized so that it would readily absorb the paste. This also shortened the drying time. Each sheet measured 4 × 3 ft. (122 × 91·5 cm.) and was dried once before it was pressed and packaged in the legal quantities. Each bundle weighed either 28 or 56 pounds. A band or strip of pink paper was wrapped around each bundle to indicate that the tax of 3*d*. a pound had been paid. Narrow cardboard strips called 'button boards' were another convenience for the trade. Each strip was wide enough to stamp out a string of buttons, which were then coated with japan varnish and ornamented with paint and mother of pearl. Every English mill had to be licensed for operation and was subject to an annual fee. The rules in *Instructions for the Officers Who Survey Paper Makers*, issued in 1842, stated that the paper manufacturers were not to use any material in pasteboard except paper on which full duties had been charged and which had not been used for any other purpose. This of course ensured that more paper would be made and used, thus providing the government with more revenue. An excise officer was stationed at every mill to weigh, label and number the paper, requirements that were considered by the mill owners to be a 'burden and an oppressive yoke'. These regulations, they complained, caused delays and hindrances because of the constant surveillance of their books and works by the government men.

The hand-turned moulds on which the articles were formed were of hard wood and had a hole in the centre through which any excess water and paste could drain away. For raised figures on the surface of an object an INTAGLIO design was cut into the mould. These were called 'hollow' or 'sunk' moulds and were patented by William Brindley of Twickenham. Later some moulds were made of metal and all moulds whether of wood or metal had to be greased to permit easy removal of the dried article. Certain pieces of furniture had parts made of moulded panel, such as pedestals, table-tops and chair-backs. Others were made entirely of panel and still others were of panel combined with wood or iron. The English industry outdistanced all other countries in the variety, quality and quantity of their papier-mâché products. The peak years of their production were those of the mid-Victorian period and it is those mass-produced, painted and pearled JAPANNED wares that are best known today. Produced mainly for export, their products were shipped to Spain, Portugal, North and South America and India.

Indian papier-mâché products were envelope cases, paper-knives, boxes, bowls and candlesticks produced in the Kashmiri Valley. Pencil boxes were a popular article made in the 18th and 19th centuries. These boxes were meant to hold the fine camel's-hair paint-brushes then called 'pencils'. At the Institute of Paper Chemistry at Appleton, Wisconsin, there is a Persian–Kashmiri pencil box that had been made and used as a coffin for a mummified falcon, the favourite bird of a Persian nobleman. Lacquered caskets, mirror bowls and boxes, were other Persian–Kashmiri products. Native artists painted the dull grey articles with designs believed to be Florentine in character and to have come overland at the time of the building of the Taj Mahal in the 17th c. The Italian influence is evident in many Eastern designs of that period.

The Italians, we are told, learned to make papier mâché by way of the Venetian trade when the 'Queen of the Adriatic' was at the height of her maritime importance. Their papier-mâché products have not, so far, been identified.

The best known German wares are the much prized papier-mâché SNUFF-BOXES made by George Sigmund Stobwasser (b. 1740). His factory was established in Brunswick in 1763 under the auspices of the Duke. Frederick the Great, a Francophile, admired the French boxes made from the billboard strippers' scavengings and as a result he established a factory in Berlin in 1765. Other papier-mâché industries arose later in several other areas of Germany. An unusual German product, made in 1883, was a watch made entirely of paper by a Dresden watch-maker. It was claimed to be as serviceable as any timepiece made from the customary metals.

It was not until 1830 that Russian lacquered papier-mâché wares were made, by the English method. This work was first practised in the village of Fedoskino, near Moscow, by peasant workmen who were pioneers in folk-art painting on papier mâché. The most successful factory was maintained by the Lukutin family, whose boxes, chests and trays were marked with a double eagle within an oval. After the Revolution, *c.* 1922, unemployed ikon painters of Mstera and Palekh found employment in these factories. From then the products were marked 'Made in the Soviet Union'.

Among the many English artisans who settled in the American colonies were several who made papier mâché. The *New York General Advertiser* mentions three located in New York City. They were Nicholas Bernard, who in 1769 was making 'papier machine' for ceilings; a London-trained carver and gilder named Munshall, who in the same year was making 'paper ornaments for ceilings and staircases in the present mode'; and John Keating, who made paper and pasteboard and sold waste paper. Ceiling ornaments were also available in Philadelphia. When Mrs. Franklin was redecorating her home Benjamin, then sojourning in London, advised her in a letter to have 'papier mâché musical figures' tacked to the ceiling of one room. George Washington, however, ordered ceiling ornaments for two rooms from his London factor. Interest in imitation plaster ornament continued into the 19th c. in the United States, for F. R. DePlanque of Philadelphia published a small catalogue in 1855 in which were drawings of arms and armament for use in the interiors of buildings. It was not until 1850 that japanned papier mâché in the English style was made in any quantity in America. The Litchfield Manufacturing Company (1850–4), of Litchfield, Connecticut, first made card trays, face fans and daguerreotype cases, which were sold along with imported English-made papier-mâché goods. This company used English-trained japanners, who taught local girls to paint and varnish their products. In 1852 they concentrated solely on clock-cases made of paper panel, which they supplied to many Connecticut clock companies. An economic slump ended this firm as well as several of the clock companies they supplied. The Wadhams Manufacturing Company was located in Torrington, not far from Litchfield. From 1851 to 1861, in an old button shop on their premises, they produced lap desks, folios, game boards, card and daguerreotype cases and stair-rods. Some of their products were plain black with neat borders of broken pearl shell. This company ended its production of papier mâché in 1861, the first year of the American Civil War.

Small souvenirs in the late 19th c. were made from the pulp of retired U.S. bank-notes and currency. On 23 June 1874 an Act of Congress made it possible to have such bills destroyed by maceration. A solution of soda, ash and lime was added to the pulp to destroy the identity of the currency. This mixture was moulded into

Mirror case of papier mâché, lacquered and gilt. Persian. (V. & A. Mus., *c.* 1770–80)

Mirror case of papier mâché, lacquered and in colours. Persian. (V. & A. Mus.)

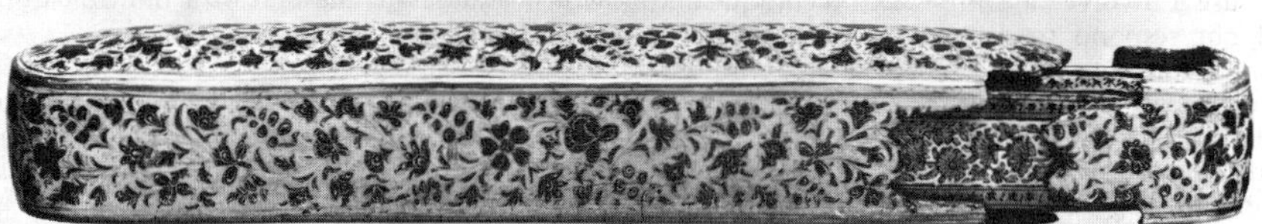

Indian papier-mâché pencil box. (V. & A. Mus., 18th–19th c.)

A

B

A. Head of Abraham Lincoln moulded in papier mâché made from the pulp of mashed withdrawn currency. (Smithsonian Inst., Washington D.C.) B. *Stobwasser* boxes of papier mâché. (Städtisches Mus., Braunschweig, 18th and 19th c.)

Chair with moulded papier-mâché panel, japanned, painted and pearled. (V. & A. Mus.)

busts of prominent Americans and replicas of national monuments, which were then sold to the public. These ten-cm-high souvenirs were not lacquered but were left in the grey, raw pulp. The usual procedure, however, in any country was to coat the dull forms with a finish and further to enhance it with a painted decoration. The Oriental countries used lacquer, but this medium was not practical in the West because it involved a complicated technique and did not respond to dry heat. It hardened in about 4 hours in a damp atmosphere at a temperature of *c.* 21 °C. There was also the problem of the acute dermatitis this member of the sumac family caused in some people. Therefore European and English artists sought a hard varnish not only for papier mâché but for general use. In England, the varnish, whether clear or black, was termed 'Japan' after the country whose lacquer wares were considered superior to any other and which the English hoped to equal with their pseudo-lacquer. French varnished or 'lacquered' articles are called VERNIS MARTIN, now a generic term, after the Martin brothers, the famous 18th-c. Parisian *vernisseurs*.

MOTHER OF PEARL, long used in the East for decorative work, enhanced the painted and gilded papier-mâché articles and was especially popular in the Victorian period.

Papier mâché has been a useful medium for centuries because of its malleability, its low cost and its lightness. For these reasons there is an interest today in the material for theatrical properties, costume jewellery, kindergarten craft work and for mercantile display items as well. Old newspapers provide a suitable basic material for the amateur.

PAPYRUS. A writing material prepared from the stem of the marsh plant of the same name, growing in antiquity principally in EGYPT and now in the Sudan. It was used in Egypt from the 3rd millennium B.C. onwards and was the standard writing material in ancient Greece and throughout the Roman Empire. From the 4th c. A.D. onwards it was increasingly replaced by PARCHMENT though it continued to be used, for example in the papal chancery, until the 10th c. It was used from the earliest times to take paint as well as ink; illustrated papyri survive from the Middle and New Kingdoms (Egypt) and there are a few fragmentary examples of illuminated classical texts as well as, for example, weavers' patterns.

Papyrus was also used in Egypt to make light boats, mats and other plaited articles. The flower of the papyrus was a favourite ornamental motif in Egyptian decorative art and appears also in the ornamental repertory of Greece and the Middle East. The motif came again into vogue at the time of the Classical Revival and the REGENCY. See EGYPTIAN TASTE and NEO-CLASSICISM.

PARAISON. Term in glass-making for the lump of fused glass metal of treacly consistency which adheres to the end of a blowing-iron in the crucible.

PARCHMENT. See VELLUM. The word 'parchment' derives from the Latin *pergamena* (sc. *charta*), 'Pergamene writing sheet'. Pliny, *Nat. Hist.* xiii. 11 (A.D. *c.* 23–79), quoting Varro (116–27 B.C.), mistakenly claims that parchment (or vellum) was discovered by Eumenes II (197–159 B.C.) of Pergamum after the Ptolemies had banned the export of PAPYRUS from Egypt in an attempt to prevent the growth of the Pergamene library.

PARIAN. A variety of unglazed or biscuit porcelain of soft or hard paste, developed in England in the 1840s, and mainly used for figures.

PARQUETRY. Term for INLAY or MARQUETRY in different-coloured woods when the elements are regularly shaped and put together so as to form a geometrical pattern or mosaic. See WOOD-WORKING.

PARTHIAN ARTS AND CRAFTSMANSHIP. See ASIA, CENTRAL and ANIMAL STYLE.

PASSEMENT. General term for BRAIDS,

gimps and LACES made in a variety of threads. Braid or passement lace was made by tacking thick braid on to a piece of linen or strong paper on which a pattern had been traced. The spaces were then filled with *barettes*, or bars, composed of four or five threads stretched across and overset with buttonhole stitch. In the middle of each bar was a *picot*, formed by a small loop of thread which, after being filled in with buttonhole stitch, was drawn up tightly and the bar then continued as before. Upon passing from one bar to the next a few invisible stitches on the edge of the braid were used instead of breaking off the thread. After the bars had been completed the backing was removed.

PASTE (Italian, *pasta*, pastry). A material, usually GLASS, used as a substitute for a gemstone in jewellery. Paste jewellery is of great antiquity, though it is probable that in the past, before the distinction was current between precious and semi-precious stones, paste was regarded as an alternative rather than a substitute. In ancient EGYPT it was common for FAIENCE to be used for the same purposes and for similar effects as gemstones in jewellery. Roman jewellers took advantage of the glass-making skills to develop an extensive technique of paste. Paste was also used in conjunction with semi-precious stones in Anglo-Saxon jewellery and Italian jewellers at the Renaissance made some use of glass. The great period of paste jewellery was, however, in the 2nd half of the 18th c., when the value of precious stones had been established and glass was deliberately used as a substitute to imitate the effects of certain stones. In particular lead glass to a formula said to have been invented by a Viennese jeweller Josef Strass was used as a substitute for DIAMONDS. Vast quantities of paste jewellery were produced at this time and considerable amounts have survived. The paste was often of good quality and the cutting and setting might involve no less skilled workmanship than jewellery made from genuine stones. Such paste jewellery has a beauty and charm which endear it to connoisseurs.

While imitation of the more valuable gemstones was the primary purpose of this jewellery, craftsmen also developed certain effects which were peculiar to paste itself. So Joan Evans writes in *A History of Jewellery 1100–1870*: 'The function of paste had primarily been to imitate diamonds cheaply; but it was not long before the jewellers created *genres* of paste that had little relation with real stones. Aventurine paste in brown was apt to be even brighter than its natural prototype, and was soon made . . . with a bright blue base on which its golden flecks made a brilliant effect. In France, again, and to a lesser degree in England, opal paste was produced, of a pinkish milky kind that derived a novel beauty from the rose-coloured foil over which it was set. It is not in the least like opals, but it is quite charming.' For Egyptian paste see POTTERY TECHNIQUES.

PASTEBOARD. See PAPIER MÂCHÉ.

PASTE PAPERS. See PAPERS, DECORATIVE.

PATCH BOXES. Small boxes used by ladies for carrying their PATCHES, now treasured by collectors and connoisseurs. They were ordinarily round or oval, 4 or 5 cm in diameter, made of TORTOISESHELL or silver or BATTERSEA ENAMEL on brass or sometimes china medallions set in silver gilt. They were usually fitted with a mirror or polished steel disc inside the lid so that the lady could see to adjust her patches. They were sometimes decorated with a French beauty or a shepherdess or festoons of flowers, but more often with a moral verse or posy.

PATCHES. The custom of wearing small facial patches of soft leather was affected by the ancient Romans. The patches simulated moles, which were regarded as a mark of beauty. In European fashion history the custom seems to have originated with the court ladies of Venice *c.* the middle of the 16th c. From Italy it spread throughout fashionable Europe towards the end of the century. Its heyday was in the 3 or 4 decades spanning the middle of the 17th c. but patches—called *mouches* (flies) in France—continued to be worn through the early decades of the 18th c. Patches were cut from black velvet or taffeta or black silk and were attached on the face, throat or breasts with mastic. They were carried by ladies in tiny decorative and jewelled PATCH BOXES. Although the usual form was a small circular black spot, they were on occasion cut in elaborate and fanciful shapes. The satirical *Anthropometamorphosis of John Bulwer* (1650) contains the words: 'Our ladies have lately entertained a vaine custom of spotting their faces out of an affectation of a mole, to set off their beauty, such as Venus had; and it is well if one black patch will serve to make their faces remarkable, for some fill their visages full of them, varied into all manner of shapes.' The accompanying engraving shows a woman with a crescent-shaped patch under each eye, a five-point star on one cheek, a circular spot on the point of the chin and a coach and horses on her forehead. Patches were also affected by men. Another satirical work, *Lady's Privilege* (1640), advises a young gallant that a spot or two will 'make your face more amorous and appear more gracious in your mistress' eye'. A woodcut in the 'Roxburghe' *Ballads* shows a milliner with patched face offering to customers a fan and a mask.

Patches were worn by fashionable ladies of Boston, Philadelphia and New York in the 2nd half of the 18th c.

PATCHWORK. The sewing together of shaped pieces of various fabrics so as to form a cloth mosaic. This simple and economical method of producing patterned textiles is both ancient and widespread. In Renaissance times, using silks and velvets as its raw materials, it was a sumptuous element in ecclesiastical and secular decoration. From the 18th c. onwards patchwork QUILTS—their kaleidoscopic patterns formed from innumerable, regularly shaped scraps of printed cotton—have been an interesting feature of popular culture. Of comparable non-European work, the Resht rugs of Persia are the most familiar example. See EMBROIDERY (TYPES).

PATERAE. In classical architecture a flat, circular or oval ornament, which was itself often decorated with ROSETTE, ACANTHUS, etc., carved, painted or INLAID on furniture. Paterae were a part of the repertory of classical ornamental motifs popular in the NEO-CLASSICAL style which prevailed in the 2nd half of the 18th c. In the early part of the 19th c. paterae cast in brass were applied to furniture.

PAULY, SAMUEL JOHANNES (1766–?). Swiss gunmaker, born at Vechigen, near Bern. He came to Paris in the early years of the 19th c. and in 1812 obtained a patent for a breech-loading mechanism employing percussion ignition. The breech was opened by means of a hinged lever and it was loaded with a rechargeable brass shell, which was detonated by a firing pin. He employed the Prussian Johann Nikolaus von Dreyse, who later invented the 'needle gun', which was adopted by the Prussian army in 1848. Although Pauly's invention was strongly recommended to Napoleon by the Société pour l'Encouragement de l'Industrie Nationale, it was not widely exploited by the gun trade and in 1814 he came to England, where he took out a patent for a breech-loading mechanism which detonated the fulminate in the cartridge by means of compressed air.

PAVILION. In architecture an ornamental, lightly constructed building such as a summer-house in a garden or a building for players and spectators attached to a sports ground.

Term used by jewellers and lapidaries for the underside of a faceted gemstone, the portion below the GIRDLE, which in a BRILLIANT consists of small facets drawing to a point at the tip. See JEWELLERY.

PAYNE, ROGER (1739–97). English bookbinder who opened a bindery (1766) in Leicester Square, London, employing his brother THOMAS and David Wier. Though widely patronized by wealthy bibliophiles, he died in poverty. Payne was an exquisite craftsman, cutting his own TOOLS. He chose his leathers with care, preferring straight-grained MOROCCO, which he was one of the first binders to use. He also gave special attention to the spine, employing small, closely massed floral stamps, often in POINTILLÉ. His designs were widely imitated in France and England, particularly by the early 19th-c. binders Lewis and Herring. See BOOKBINDING (HISTORICAL).

PAZYRYK. A cemetery on the western slopes of the Altay which was excavated by M. P. Griaznov and S. I. Rudenko in the years 1925–9 and 1947–50. It yielded rich finds of craft objects decorated in the ANIMAL STYLE. The nomadic people to whom the cemetery belonged are also known as 'Pazyryk'. See ASIA, CENTRAL.

PEALE, CHARLES WILLSON and his son REMBRANDT. American artists and silhouettists. See SILHOUETTE.

PEARL. An organic, non-crystalline gemstone which occurs as a concretion within the epithelium of certain molluscs. The so-called 'pearl oyster' is not of the same family as the edible oyster; the concretions of the latter are usually dark purple or black, without lustre, and are not true pearls. The substance of the pearl consists of nacre (MOTHER OF PEARL), the same substance as the shell of the mollusc, and it is formed when shell-building cells are deposited in layers round some foreign body which has penetrated the mantle of the living mollusc. If the penetration is deep, a cyst is first formed around the foreign body and the pearl is formed within the cyst, usually globular or pear-shaped. When the cyst is formed in muscular or other tissue which obstructs its free growth the shape of the pearl may be irregular. These oddly shaped pearls are known as 'Baroque' pearls; they were popular with Renaissance jewellers. When penetration is shallow the sac may become attached to the shell and the pearl is then a half-sphere flat on one side. These are called 'blister' pearls. Pearls weighing less than 0·016 gramme are called 'seed' pearls.

Pearls are among the softest of gemstones, having an index of only $3\frac{1}{2}$ to 4 on the MOHS SCALE. They are valued for their soft translucent iridescence and for the depth of their lustre, which is called the 'orient' and is the result of light being broken up as it encounters the thin layers of nacre from which the substance of the pearl is built up. Being organic, pearls gradually lose their quality or 'die' with age and they are damaged by acids, even by the minute quantities of acid contained in exudations from the human skin. It is considered that an average pearl necklace should have a luminous life of from 150 to 200 years.

The high value placed upon pearls dates from great antiquity. They were used for jewellery by the ancient Egyptians and in the ancient Middle East; they feature in archaic Greek and Etruscan jewellery and they were prized by the Romans. They were known and loved in India from before 1500 B.C. and pearl jewellery has been found in graves of the Aztec and Toltec cultures of Central America. In Europe Oriental pearls were little known until the late Middle Ages when trade with the Far East developed, but since that time their popularity has continued without diminution.

The most highly valued 'Oriental' pearls are

fished in the Persian Gulf and off the Island of Bahrain. They are also obtained in the Bay of Bengal, the coastal waters of East Africa and off the Celebes and the islands of the South Pacific. Caribbean pearls are larger than the 'Oriental' ones but are considered less fine. Pearls with a dark metallic sheen as well as white pearls are found in the Gulf of Mexico and the Gulf of California. In the time of the Ptolemies pearls were also fished in the Red Sea. Freshwater pearls have been known in China since before 2000 B.C. and are still obtained in the Mississippi and elsewhere in the U.S.A. and in certain parts of central Europe.

Cultured pearls are those which are caused to grow artificially by introducing some foreign body into the shell of a freshwater mussel. Pearls, chiefly blister pearls, have been obtained in this way in China since the 13th c. A.D. But the method of producing complete pearls by culture was first perfected in Japan and the Japanese industry of cultured pearls has flourished since 1890.

PEFFENHAUSER, ANTON (1525–1603) of Augsburg. The last of the great German armourers, he worked extensively for the German princes and for members of the Court of Phillip II of Spain. Examples of his work are in the Tower of London Armouries; Wallace Collection; Kunsthistorisches Museum, Vienna; Historisches Museum, Dresden; Metropolitan Museum, New York. See ARMS AND ARMOUR.

PELICAN. According to legend the pelican nourishes its young on its own blood, making a wound in its breast. According to the version given by Epiphanius, Bishop of Constantia, in his *Physiologus* (1588) the mother bird kills her young with the strength of her love and the male bird after three days brings them to life with blood from its side. Since the 13th c. the pelican has been employed on seals, in illuminated manuscripts, ecclesiastical sculpture, etc. as a symbol of the redemption of man by Christ. In 1516 it was adopted as a device by Corpus Christi College, Oxford, and by Corpus Christi, Cambridge, in 1570. It is the emblem of the State of Louisiana.

Woodcut from Albertus Magnus, *Hortus Sanitatis* (1491)

PEMBROKE TABLE. Name current in the latter part of the 18th c. for a small, light table with extensible flaps and drawers below the top which was introduced by HEPPLEWHITE *c.* 1765 and illustrated by SHERATON in his *Cabinet-Maker and Upholsterer's Drawing Book*. Pembroke tables with a characteristic lyre pattern in the side supports were designed by Duncan PHYFE in America and also by Thomas Elfe (1719–75) of Charleston, South Carolina. The type had become very popular in the U.S.A. by the end of the 18th c. and continued to be made in many centres.

PENTIMENTO. As a painting ages it sometimes happens that in the course of time the paint becomes somewhat transparent. It may then be possible in some paintings to see the original lines and marks which the artist has over-painted as he changed his mind in the course of his work. These first stages of the work are called *pentimenti* (Italian, repentances) because the painter 'repented' and changed his mind. Art historians have made use of *pentimenti* as indications of the psychology and methods of working of artists in a way analogous to that in which literary and musical historians make use of the corrections in the original manuscripts of poems or musical compositions.

PERCIER, CHARLES (1764–1838) and **FONTAINE,** PIERRE-FRANÇOIS-LÉONARD (1762–1853). Parisian architects who worked together between 1794 and 1814. They published in 1801 their *Recueil de décorations intérieurs*, a set of engraved designs for interiors and furniture which proved of enormous influence in the development of the EMPIRE style.

PERIDOT. A form of olivine prized since antiquity as a gemstone. It has a hardness index of 6½ to 7 on the MOHS SCALE and ranges in colour from golden or cool lettuce green to dark olive green. Although the mineral olivine is common, gem crystals of sufficient size for the purposes of jewellery are rare. Originally limited to the island of Zeberged in the Red Sea, where mines were worked from the 2nd millennium B.C., it is now found also in Upper Burma and Brazil and is worked by the Navajo Indians of Arizona. In the ancient world the peridot was prized as a gemstone along with the EMERALD, carbuncle

(GARNET) and LAPIS LAZULI. The 'topaz' of antiquity was very often a peridot. The green peridot was brought to Europe in quantities by the crusaders and was often mistaken for emerald.

PERSIAN RUGS. In recent times, though they lack the vigorous fecundity of design which characterized their predecessors of the Safavid period, Persian rugs nevertheless retain a grace and refinement which distinguish them from all other Oriental rugs. Their soft rich tones are broken up in small floral designs—the commonest are the Herati, Mina Khani, Guli Hinnai (henna-blossom) and cone patterns—which sometimes occupy the entire field and are sometimes disposed in and around elegant medallions. The Ghiordes knot is quite commonly used in western districts but a fine Sena knotting predominates. A considerable number of silk rugs are made, particularly at Tabriz, Kashan and Kerman.

To distinguish between the various types of Persian rugs requires practice, since similar designs are used throughout the area. From the middle of the 19th c. onwards some contamination of designs has also resulted from the large commercial production, much of it directed by Western firms.

Many of these commercial carpets are of excellent quality, as for instance those of Tabriz with their graceful medallion designs. In the same north-western district Herez, Gorevan, Serapi and Bakhshayesh rugs have medallion patterns of more angular character, while Karabagh rugs incline towards Caucasian geometry. Further south Bijar, Suj Bulak, Kurdistan and Mosul rugs are made, heavy fabrics of varied design but favouring the Mina Khani pattern. The central area produces many types—Sena rugs with very minute designs, Hamadan rugs with a great deal of natural camel-hair, Ferahan rugs, usually with the Herati pattern, Serabend rugs with all-over cone designs, Kashan and Saruk rugs with curvilinear medallions, the less well-defined Bakhtiaris and Joshagans, and the various commercial types of Kermanshahs, Sultanabads and Muskabads. In the south hexagonal and lozenge-shaped medallions give Shiraz rugs a characteristic angularity, while the neighbouring Niris and Afshar rugs have the cone patterns. The finely woven Kerman rugs of the south-east are notable for very naturalistic floral motifs, elaborate medallion designs and picture rugs with figure subjects. Khurasan, Meshed and Herat rugs in eastern Persia utilize all the main types of Persian design.

KILIMS are also made in Persia. See also CARPETS AND RUGS.

PETIT POINT. Also called tent stitch, is an EMBROIDERY stitch lying diagonally to the threads of the canvas foundation. It has been much used since the 16th c. for needlework pictures, chair seats and the like, especially where a more detailed effect than that of gros point is desired. See also EMBROIDERY (STITCHES).

PETRONEL. A long-barrelled pistol or carbine which was manufactured in Germany and France during the 3rd quarter of the 16th c. with a distinctive shape of stock with a downward curving butt cut off diagonally at the end. The word 'petronel' has usually been derived from the French *poitrine* on the assumption that the weapon was fired from the chest. But it has been pointed out that a butt so shaped is not adapted to be fired from the chest and it is suggested that the petronel was a two-purpose weapon: it could either be fired from one hand as a long-barrelled horse pistol or the butt could be steadied against the upper arm while both hands held the weapon to take aim.

PETUNTSE. French version of *pai-tun-tzŭ* or china clay, a felspathic rock which was an essential element in the making of true or 'hard-paste' porcelain. A felspathic glaze is also made from this material, by fluxing with lime and potash, which is comparable to the 'hard-paste' porcelain body. See CHINA, CERAMICS and PORCELAIN.

PEWTER. 1. MATERIAL AND TECHNIQUE. Pewter is an alloy consisting mainly of tin, with a small proportion of lead or copper or both. From at least the middle of the 14th c. two qualities of metal were recognized in England: 'fine' or 'plate' metal consisting of tin and copper in the proportions of about 97 parts of the former to 3 parts of the latter; and a cheaper 'ley' or 'lay' metal in which the tin was alloyed with up to 20% of lead. Fine metal, being harder and stronger, was used for plates, dishes and articles requiring a degree of rigidity, the so-called 'sad-ware'. Ley metal was used for flagons, tankards, measures and similar vessels, where the shape of the object gave it a degree of strength. Sometime *c.* 1600 a third alloy, 'trifle', was permitted by the Pewterers' Company and this contained equal parts of fine metal and ley metal, that is 1 to 2% of copper and up to 10% of lead. Similar alloys were used by European pewterers, though more frequently lead appears to have been the only alloying metal. Because of inadequate assaying methods, and the custom of recovering and remelting old pewter ware, the composition of actual pieces of old pewter is variable and uncertain within the limits given above.

With the passage of time the control of the Pewterers' Company and the similar guilds in provincial centres waned, and standards ceased to be observed. Cheapness encouraged the addition of lead, giving a soft dull alloy. In the 18th c. antimony was added to confer hardness and brilliance. Bismuth, or 'tin-glass', was another additive used from quite early times to give the metal better working qualities.

The expressions 'tin' and 'pewter' were used indiscriminately both in England and on the Continent to describe pewter alloys. It is most unlikely that pure tin was ever used for fabrication purposes, though some early spoons contain as much as 96% tin. Britannia metal springs directly from the later 18th-c. pewter alloys containing antimony, and does not differ essentially from them in composition. The distinction lies more in the method of fabrication than in the metal. Britannia alloys are spun, stamped or rolled, and articles are thin and light in construction. Pewter is cast and turned, and in addition it may be hammered to compact and strengthen it.

Pewter is a low-melting alloy and can be readily cast into complex shapes in moulds of plaster, stone or bronze. Multi-section bronze moulds for making pewter utensils survive in some quantity from the late 17th and 18th centuries. Indeed some 18th-c. bronze moulds are still in use for making reproduction pewter, and at least one early 19th-c. pewterer in England was casting broad-rimmed plates in moulds some 150 years old. Such moulds represented a major investment for a pewterer and were sometimes owned communally for hiring out to individual craftsmen as required. In Europe, and also probably in England, moulds carved from 'tuff', a soft volcanic stone, were in use in the early 16th c. Roman limestone moulds for pewter dishes have been excavated.

The roughly cast article, assembled from its pieces by soldering, was finished by turning, scraping and burnishing. In England the Pewterers' Company required that the ware also be hammered to compact and harden it, and the serried rows of hammer marks still visible on the underside of the booge of many plates give evidence of the considerable dexterity of the 'hammerman'. But despite the edicts of the Company some of its members failed to comply with this requirement, and its archives from time to time record the seizure of unhammered articles. On the Continent hammering was less frequently practised.

An interesting technique was used for turning pewter plates and dishes. A plate was fixed by means of solder on to the face-plate of the lathe, and its outer surface turned. A second plate was then attached to the first with three blobs of solder at the circumference; this was then similarly turned, and the process was repeated to give a stack of plates each turned on one face. The stack was then reversed in the lathe and the undersides turned, the solder being removed at the end of each operation to free each finished plate in turn. In Britain it is usual to find the seams of multi-section vessels running round the body. On the Continent seams customarily ran vertically. Handles may be attached by soldering, but solid handles were commonly cast directly on to the body and so became welded to it.

2. HISTORY. Roman pewter made from Spanish and later from Cornish tin, with added lead, first appeared in the mid 3rd c. A.D. and some 200 examples of plates, bowls, ewers and jugs survive in museum collections. The most recent major find, uncovered in 1968 during gravel excavation at Appleford, Berks., consisted of 22 pieces from the 4th c. Plates followed pottery styles and a characteristic feature is the presence of one or more cast foot-rings, which are not found on later pewter. Apart from a few isolated references to pewter for ecclesiastical purposes, such as the permission given by the Synod of Rouen in 1074 and the Council of Winchester in 1076 for pewter vessels to be used in churches too poor to afford silver, and the survival of a few sepulchral chalices and patens from the graves of 13th-c. clerics, there is a complete gap in our knowledge of British and Continental pewter from Roman times to the 14th c.

In 1348 the first ordinances were promulgated for the regulation of pewtering in London. They reflect a highly developed craft even at that date, and it is in them that the first standards for metal are laid down. As early as 1350 John de Hiltone, 'peautrer', was summoned before the mayor and aldermen for making vessels 'the greater part of the metal of which was lead', and the vessels were forfeited and sold.

The Worshipful Company of Pewterers received their first charter from Edward IV in 1473 and for two and a half centuries sought with some measure of success to control the craft throughout much of England. They had power of search and seizure of inferior-quality goods and they required each member to have a distinctive mark, or 'touch', so that objects could be attributed to the maker in case of failure to meet standards of quality or manufacture. Similar guilds were established in provincial towns. York in 1445, Norwich in 1449, Bristol in 1456 were among them. In Scotland, Edinburgh had its Guild of Hammermen in 1496, followed by St. Andrews in 1539 and Perth in 1546. Dublin had a Guild of Smiths in 1556. In European towns and cities, such as Bruges, Paris and Augsburg, the craft was organized in the 14th c. and by 1500 pewter was made in many centres in France, Germany and the Low Countries.

British settlers introduced the craft into the American colonies in the 17th c. and one Richard Graves had a pewtering shop in Salem, Mass., in 1635. Even by 1700, however, there were probably fewer than a dozen practising craftsmen in America. This was undoubtedly due to legislation introduced at the behest of the Pewterers' Company which made the export of raw tin difficult or uneconomic through tariffs and bans. The only metal with which the colonial pewterers could work was that which they obtained by melting down old imported pewter ware. Enormous quantities of pewter were shipped from England. A bill of lading of 1693 for a cargo of pewter from London to Boston, packed in hogsheads, includes tankards, porringers, candlesticks, chamber-pots, spoons, basins and wine measures. Before 1700 some £4,000 worth of pewter was shipped annually to America; by 1760 the figure reached £38,000, about 350 tons, per annum. The collection of discarded utensils for recasting was well organized and some half to two-thirds of the new price was paid for old plates taken in part exchange for new. Some of those who established themselves in Boston, Philadelphia and New York were emigrant members of the London Company, such as Simon Edgell and William Cox of London and Philadelphia, and William Digg(e)s of London and New York. Others were from the provinces: Samuel Carter of Bristol and Boston, and Lawrence Langworthy of Exeter and Newport.

3. MARKS. A statute of 1503 required 'that the makers of such (pewter) wares shall mark the same wares with several marks of their own to the intent that the makers of such wares shall avow the same', and further that 'all and every such wares . . . not marked in the form aforesaid . . . shall be forfeited'. An inventory of the Pewterers' Company in 1550 refers to 'a table of pewter with every man's mark thereon'. Unfortunately this 'table', or 'touch plate', together with any others prior to 1666, perished in the Great Fire of London and we have no record of the marks of this early period. In 1667 the Company 'paid for a plate to strike the touches on . . . 8*s*', and this plate survives as well as four later ones. Together they provide a record of some 1,071 touches covering the period *c.* 1640 to *c.* 1840, the earlier ones being restrikes by pewterers who lived through the Fire. Two touch-plates of the Edinburgh Guild of Hammermen also survive, covering the period from *c.* 1600 to 1764, with 143 touches.

Many London pewterers seem, however, not to have struck their touches on the London touch-plates, and there is no record of large numbers of provincial pewterers. The standard work *Old Pewter, its Makers and Marks*, by H. H. Cotterell lists some 6,000 pewterers known to him in 1929.

Marks prior to *c.* 1660 are simple circular or oval punches frequently containing only initials, sometimes with a simple device. Later they become larger, incorporating the full name of the pewterer in labels above and below an oval or shield-shaped device which may be flanked by palm leaves. Some are dated, but the date is either that of the first striking of the touch or the date of one of the edicts of the Company requiring touches to be reregistered. Thus a marked piece may have been made at any time in the working life of the owner of the mark.

As well as the maker's personal touch other secondary marks are found. Chief among these are the so-called 'Hall Marks', found in England from *c.* 1630 to 1720 or later, and also found on American and European pewter. Originally struck on the face of plates and dishes, they are later found on the back. Frank imitations of silver marks, they were clearly intended to give to the casual observer of an array of pewter the impression that it was silver rather than the humbler base metal. A source of embarrassment to the Company, which never sanctioned their use, they were the cause of continual complaint from the Goldsmiths' Company.

From the end of the 17th c., in England, an 'X' surmounted by a crown was used as a mark of quality, approved by the Pewterers' Company for use on metal of a particular composition. Later it became debased in use and by the 19th c. was meaningless. Additional marks such as the 'rose-and-crown' and labels bearing legends such as 'LONDON' and 'SUPERFINE HARD METAL' are found. The 'LONDON' mark appears on much Continental pewter and on some American, an indication of the esteem in which English pewter was held abroad. Despite the hold of the Company over the craft, much pewter remained unmarked. While there is perhaps less interest in a piece which cannot be attributed to a maker, the quality of much unmarked ware is in no way inferior to that of marked pewter.

4. USES. Pewter ware was essentially utilitarian and simple in concept, but nevertheless pleasing in proportion and style. For three centuries it was the common table and kitchen ware of the yeoman, the merchant and the middle class. Harrison in his *Description of England*, written *c.* 1577, says that tin and lead are common here 'whereby my contriemen doo reape no small commoditie, but especiallie our pewterers, who in time past imploied the use of pewter onlie upon dishes, pots, and a few other trifles for service, where-as now they are grown unto such exquisit cunning, that they can in manner imitate by infusion anie forme or fashion of cup, dish, salt, bowle or goblet, which is made by goldsmiths' craft, though they be never so curious, exquisite and artificiallie forged. Such furniture of household of this mettall as we commonlie call by the name of vessell, is sold usuallie by the garnish, which dooth conteine twelve platters, twelve dishes, twelve saucers, and those are either of silver fashion, or else with brode or narrow brims, and bought by the pound, which is now valued at six or seven pence, or peradventure at eight pence. Of porringers, pots and other like I speake not, albeit that in the making of all these things there is such exquisit diligence used, I meane for the mixture of the mettall and true making of this commoditie (by reason of the sharpe laws provided in that behalf) as the like is not to be found in anie other trade.

'In some places beyond the sea a garnish of good flat English pewter, of an ordinarie making, is esteemed almost so pretious, as the like number of vessells that are made of fine silver, and in a manner no less desired among the great estates, whose workmen are nothing so skillful in that trade as ours, neither their metall so good, nor plentie so great, as we have here in England.'

Of pewter of this period practically none survives owing to the practice of remelting old metal. Consideration of British pewter before *c.* 1600 rests mainly on the evidence of excavated pieces. Of these spoons form the bulk, having been lost under floors and in drains and cesspits. Styles of pewter spoons can be followed from *c.* 1300, through the period which concerns us here, and on for another 200 years, and closely follow the styles of contemporary silver. The very early leaf-shaped bowl gave place for a short period to a round one, and then to the characteristic fig-shaped one which predominated for some two centuries, from *c.* 1450 to 1650. Stems originally slender, and round or diamond in section, became hexagonal, and by 1650 somewhat flattened. Knops abound in many forms: ball, acorn, diamond, hexagon, seal and baluster, and some incorporating human or animal symbolism, the maidenhead, the apostle, the wild man and the lion sejant. Spoons apart, Tudor domestic pewter is represented by a few plates and dishes, a handful of porringers and an equally small number of measures. A few chalices, patens, cruets and one or two flagons complete the remaining evidence. Mention should, however, be made of pilgrims' badges, and many of these made in pewter have been dredged from the Thames.

On such slender evidence dating can only be conjectural except where excavated material is found in a well defined context. From *c.* 1600 onwards we are on much firmer ground; a few dated pieces exist, records of purchases of identifiable church pewter survive, and marks become attributable from the middle of the 17th c. onwards.

Although in general British pewter was not decorated, it is curious that the earliest datable coherent group of British pewter, made between *c.* 1600 and *c.* 1620, should be heavily decorated with relief-cast motifs. A dozen or so extant pieces include several wine cups and beakers, a footed plate, a candlestick, a small plate and a wine taster. Several have the date '1616' incorporated in the design, for what reason is quite unknown, and one has a contemporary inscription including this date. Decoration is based on running vine and rose designs. Such relief-cast decoration was not uncommon on Continental pewter of the mid 16th c. and a number of German plates, known as *Apostelteller* and *Kaiserteller*, cast with religious or classical motifs, have survived. In France jugs and plates cast with Briot-inspired designs were made in the 2nd half of the 16th c. Reaching its highest excellence in the mid 17th c., pewter sought on the one hand to imitate silver and on the other evolved its own characteristic forms and usages in areas where there was no silver prototype. The appeal of the pewter of this period lies in its dignified proportions, simple shapes and mellow lustre. Decoration was restrained or absent, and functional considerations were supreme in the designer's mind. Where similar objects were made in silver and in pewter the style of the latter closely followed the silver counterpart. Spoons, plates, chargers, salts, tankards, flagons, porringers and candlesticks are found in essentially identical forms in both metals. The limitations imposed on pewter by its softness and low melting-point precluded its use for a few applications such as cooking vessels, but on the other hand its cheapness and toughness made it ideally suited to a range of tavern vessels, measures, pots and tankards of a characteristic shape which have no counterpart in the precious metals.

It is perhaps convenient here to consider the main stream of British pewter from the early 17th c. to the mid 18th c., when it was rapidly being replaced by cheap pottery, in three categories: Ecclesiastical pewter, Domestic pewter and Tavern pewter.

Ecclesiastical Pewter. Among the earliest surviving pewter relics are the shallow-bowled pewter sepulchral chalices which have been found from time to time in the graves of 12th-c. and 13th-c. clerics. It is not clear whether these vessels were actually used for the celebration of the mass, or whether they were 'tokens' made solely for interment with the priest. It should be noted, however, that William de Blois, Bishop of Worcester in 1229, ruled that two chalices were to be provided for every church, one for the mass to be of silver and one of tin for burial with the priest. Whether the poorer churches could afford the former seems doubtful and we have seen that the Synod of Rouen in 1074 permitted pewter for sacramental use. A few medieval patens, cruets and pyxes have also been found. Not until *c.* 1600 does a connected series of ecclesiastical pewter survive in England. Flagons of pewter appear to have been generally introduced following the Canons of 1603 which permitted pewter vessels to be used for sacramental wine. These earlier flagons were tall, tapering, straight-sided vessels of heavy construction, with knopped bun lids and plain sweeping handles surmounted by massive upright thumb-pieces or purchases. As the century wore on the 'beefeater' style with its spreading base and characteristic cover was adopted, followed at the close of the century by the plain flat-lidded Stuart type with a range of ornamental thumb-pieces. From *c.* 1700 dome-lidded flagons with knopped covers and flared, skirted bases, later with double curved handles, predominated. A few local styles are found, such as that originating in York with an acorn-shaped body and elegant knop to its domed lid. Irish flagons of the latter half of the 18th c. have a body reminiscent of the beefeater, with an even wider base and a large, boldly curved handle. In Scotland the 18th c. produced a plain, slightly tapering flagon with a quite flat or slightly convex lid, and often a slightly incurving contour to the body, which was encircled by a bold single fillet round the centre. By no means all pewter flagons were used in churches. Many were undoubtedly for domestic use and unless they are inscribed or of known provenance, the original use can only be conjectured. Alms-dishes of pewter, sometimes inscribed and sometimes decorated with punched or repoussé work, are found and a few bear in the centre a brass boss enamelled with a coat-of-arms. Similarly TAZZAS, or footed plates for church use, can be identified from inscriptions or designs. Font bowls and christening bowls were also made in pewter, the latter apparently particularly in Scotland. Early chalices in pewter are rare, since there was reluctance to use base metal for holding consecrated wine, but such as there are follow the forms found in silver. Communion cups, however, particularly in Scotland, are plentiful.

Church plate of pewter, in styles based on English and Continental prototypes, was made in the American colonial settlements during the 18th and early 19th centuries.

Domestic Pewter. Pewter vessels, the poor man's silver, dominated the English household scene for some 250 years. Their use began with the rise of the moneyed middle class in the 15th c. and continued until they were ousted by cheap pottery in the mid 18th c. Inventories show that even the humble yeomen owned a few prized pieces of pewter, a spoon or two, a bowl and a few dishes, and perhaps a candlestick. The huge households of the noble families owned it by the ton. The Earl of Northumberland in 1512 'hired' 100 dozen pewter vessels to last his household one year. (The reference to hiring is obscure; perhaps they were traded in for remelting at the end of the year.) At the other end of the scale William Windle, a Warwickshire yeoman, died in 1612 possessed of 'x pewter dishes or platters, x sawcers, ii salts, a counterfiet [i.e. wrought] dish and a candlestick' valued at 12*s*.

In the New World in 1640 Bertha Cartwright of Salem, Mass., bequeathed '3 platters, a salt cellar, six spoons, and a porringer'. Five years earlier Sarah Dillingham of Ipswich, Mass., had died leaving 40½ pounds of pewter valued at £2. 4*s*.

It is perhaps pewter plates which survive in the largest quantity. An extant record of the Pewterers' Company for 1438 sets out a classified table of pewter ware and lists 12 types of flatware ranging from 'chargeours of the largest size' weighing 7 lb. each to 'small sawcers weighing 5¼ ozs. only'. This list was supplemented from time to time; but despite the detailed record we are on uncertain ground in attempting to date early plates and dishes and not until the early to mid 17th c. can we establish a certain chronology. Most desirable in workmanship and form are undoubtedly the beautifully proportioned broad-rimmed chargers made from *c.* 1650 to *c.* 1680 in sizes commonly from 15 to 20 in. (38–50·8 cm) in diameter but exceptionally up to 24 or 27 in. (61 or 68·5 cm). Indeed a unique set of six of 36 in. (91·5 cm) across is known. Frequently found with coats-of-arms engraved on the rim, the English broad-rimmed charger represents one of the pewterer's finest achievements. Overlapping in period with the broad-rimmed style is the reeded-edge plate, originally with broadish rims but from *c.* 1670 onwards with normally proportioned rims, and also with very narrow rims scarcely wider than the REEDING. Originally incised on the lathe, the reeding was later cast proud of the surface. By the early years of the 18th c. the single-reeded plate appeared, to be superseded by the mid century by the plain rim, which was made well into the 19th c. for use as platters in eating houses. Fancy scalloped or wavy-edged plates had a short vogue in the mid 18th c. in imitation no doubt of the current silver fashion, and oval, octagonal and decagonal plates were also made in small numbers. The hollow hot-water plate, the interior of which was filled with heated water to keep the food warm, is a typical pewter style which does not seem to be found in silver.

English plates from which food was eaten, as opposed to serving plates and voiders, were commonly 9 to 10 in. (22·8–25·4 cm) in diameter, as were the Continental ones. In America a slightly smaller 8-in. (20·3 cm) plate was the fashion, most usually with a single reeded rim. This style of rim was made in America well on into the 19th c., over a century after the style had become obsolete in Britain. Garnishes of plates, comprising a dozen each of several sizes, were the common stock of the 17th-c. and 18th-c. pewterers. [Strictly the term 'plate' is applied to those of a size from which food was eaten; the larger sizes were dishes, up to some 18 in. (45·7 cm) in diameter, and above this the term 'charger' is properly used.]

Our knowledge of early drinking-vessels derives solely from records which as early as 1482 describe 'tanggard potts', and in 1595 beakers. Of the vessels themselves few survive from before the Restoration, when the flat-lidded tankard closely copying its silver counterpart was popular. Again, as with the broad-rimmed dish, the flat-lid tankard shows the pewterer's craft at its best. The plain drum, often with a slight entasis, was sometimes decorated with 'wriggle-work' designs of symbolic or commemorative significance, as for example portraits of William III and William and Mary. The ornate thumb-pieces of these tankards with their profusion of design make a study on their own. By the 1690s the lid had become domed, and from *c.* 1700 the drum was encircled with a reeding about a third of the way up. The elaborate thumb-pieces of the earlier styles gradually gave way to the simple 'chair-back' pattern. The tulip shape became popular *c.* 1730, but by 1800 the design had become debased and tankards of this later period are best considered tavern pewter rather than domestic.

The single-eared shallow porringer with booged bowl is a characteristic pewter shape for containing semi-liquid food. As with the thumb-pieces of tankards, the ears of porringers are of many forms and include cast dolphin and coronet ears as well as the more usual perforated 'English'-pattern ear. The porringer had died out in Britain by soon after 1700 but remained in use much later on the Continent, and also in America. American porringers in traditional English style were made in quantity well on into the 19th c. In Scotland the porringer as such does not seem to have been made, and its place was taken by the quaich, a small bowl with two lug ears, which, however, is very rarely encountered.

Salts and spoons in styles closely following silver complete the range of tableware. The slip-top spoon, commoner in pewter than in silver, gave way in the mid 17th c. to the Puritan spoon with the 'modern' egg-shaped bowl, and by way of trifid ends and shield tops to the spoon shapes current today. Commemorative spoons with portraits of William and Mary, Queen Anne, William III, and George III and Charlotte cast on the stem form an interesting group of pewter souvenirs of coronations and royal events. Forks were not made in pewter as the metal was too soft for the purpose.

Pewter candlesticks are recorded from the 15th c., though the earliest surviving does not date before *c.* 1620. Much more vulnerable than those of brass or silver on account of the low melting-point of the alloy, comparatively few have survived from before *c.* 1800. Those of the Restoration period with octagonal bases and centrally placed drip-pans are found with both plain and knopped columns, and are fine examples of pewter craft at its best. Curiously very few pewter candlesticks are found from *c.* 1700 until the latter half of the century. No doubt better and cheaper BRASS, made in England from the end of the 17th c., led to its use instead of pewter. Candle moulds of pewter enabled the housewife to make her own candles and tapers. To complete the range of domestic pewter mention should be made of beakers and wine cups, two-handled 'loving-cups', inkstands, pepper, spice and pounce pots, snuff-boxes, tobacco jars and chamber-pots, all following closely the design of the contemporary silverware.

Decoration on domestic pewter is uncommon, but from *c.* 1660 until *c.* 1720 there was a vogue for 'wriggled-work' decoration on tankards and plates. As a soft metal pewter is not well suited to the fine lines of the engraver, and instead a bolder engraving technique was used in which the design is executed in a zig-zag pattern formed by rocking a narrow chisel-shaped tool from side to side as the design was traced out. Perhaps the finest examples of wriggled decoration are also the earliest, a magnificent series of broad-rimmed chargers wriggled all over with the royal arms and supporters with floral motifs on the rim, commemorative of either the Restoration itself, or more probably (from the date 1662 which some of them bear) of the marriage of the restored monarch to Catherine of Braganza.

At a lesser level a wide range of designs is found. Some, with William and Mary, commemorate another royal occasion; others with flowers and conventional ornament are purely decorative; but an interesting series with symbolic beasts and birds clearly served for wedding and christening gifts. The peacock and peahen with the initials of the bride and bridegroom are typical. A single peacock plate engraved on the back 'William Brook's, born July ye 26th 1717' commemorates another family occasion. Bold in concept, but usually naïve to the point of crudeness in execution, the wriggled designs on pewter are reminiscent of the motifs found on early English SLIPWARE pottery. From a comparison of a number of plates with identical designs it is apparent that at least in the later part of the period transfers were used to ensure uniformity, and some makers who specialized in wriggled domestic plates must have employed teams of engravers to work for them.

From the first decades of the 18th c. pewter began to feel keen competition from pottery. The Pewterers' Company complained in 1710 that trade is 'now reduced to a very deplorable condicion in this Kingdom and in fforeign parts'. In the face of this competition the day-to-day use of pewter in the home waned and died.

Tavern pewter. It is in the field of cheap durable tavern pots and measures that pewter became a unique material in its own right. Silver was too expensive, pottery too fragile for these hard-worked vessels. From the 16th c. almost to the present day pewter reigned supreme.

Characteristic of this form of pewter, and unique to Britain, is the baluster wine measure. Deriving their shape from the medieval baluster jug and the leathern black-jack, the earliest surviving examples date from before 1600. From then until the latter years of the 18th c. countless thousands of baluster measures were used in inns up and down the country in sizes from half a gill to a gallon. Originally they were rather tall and slender with simple wedge or ball-and-wedge thumb-pieces on the lid. There later developed three main styles in a chronological sequence: the 'hammerhead', current from before 1600 until *c.* 1670; the 'bud', so called from the design of the thumb-piece, current until perhaps 1730; and the 'double volute' with its thumb-piece resembling the Prince of Wales's feathers and FLEUR-DE-LIS attachment to the lid, which carried on until the end of the century. In Scotland the same baluster shape was made but with a rim under the lid to locate it in the neck of the measure, a practical feature never found on the English types. These Scottish measures are comparatively late, and were made well on into the 1st half of the 19th c. Though they are customarily lidded to prevent spillage between the cellar and the table, a number of lidless baluster measures were made in the earlier period and from *c.* 1800 manufacture of lidded measures ceased. As the 19th c. moved on the baluster-shaped lidless measure became squatter and finally passed into the familiar Victorian pot-bellied measure of the type still made today. In the Victorian period the straight-sided dual-purpose measure and tankard evolved as more convenient for drinking from than the pot-bellied variety. Straight-sided measures are found in a limited range of sizes—half-pint,

English spoons: Dog-nose (*c.* 1730); Trifid (*c.* 1700); Trifid (*c.* 1670); Slip-top (*c.* 1650); Acorn (*c.* 1550); Horned head-dress (*c.* 1500); Baluster (*c.* 1550)

Beefeater flagon with twin-cusp thumb-piece (*c.* 1650)

Pint and half-pint baluster measures with bud thumb-pieces and triple reeded plate (*c.* 1680)

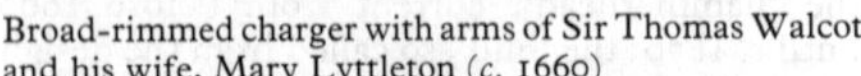

Broad-rimmed charger with arms of Sir Thomas Walcot and his wife, Mary Lyttleton (*c.* 1660)

Scottish lidless pot-bellied measure (*c.* 1680) and plate with wriggled peacock design, dated 1717

Flagon with chair-back thumb-piece and double-curved handle (*c.* 1730)

Flat-lidded tankard with wriggled portraits of William and Mary (*c.* 1688)

Coronet ear porringer (*c.* 1690)

Set of Irish haystack measures ranging from half-gill to gallon (early 19th c.)

pint and quart—while the pot-bellied shapes are found in a long range, from as small as a sixth of a gill to a gallon. Whereas baluster measures usually conform to the old pre-Imperial standard, the Queen Anne Wine Gallon, the later forms are Imperial, a standard introduced in 1824.

Tavern pots, that is drinking-vessels as opposed to measures, are rare but are extant from the late 17th c. At that time they were of tall elegant shape, straight-sided and tapering, lidless, and usually with two bands or FILLETS round the drum. Often they are inscribed with the name of the tavern, and may have an inscription such as 'If sold, stole'. It appears that it was the custom of the innkeeper, when selling ale or wine to be taken away, to loan drinking-pots with it, so that the cautionary inscription may have had a real purpose. About 1700 pots were made with an elegant GADROONED pattern cast on the lower third of the body, and a rare variant, cup-shaped, is also found with this decoration. In the 1st half of the 18th c. pots were rather squatter and some have only one fillet round the drum. Again these are rare.

Characteristic forms of measures were made in, and for use in, the Channel Islands in sizes corresponding to the local standards. These have tall bulging bodies with flat heart-shaped lids, and the Continental twin-acorn thumb-piece. Sometimes they are without lids. In Scotland the 'tappit hen', a tall, waisted measure with tapering cylindrical lower section and deep cylindrical collar, surmounted by a domed lid, was the characteristic form from *c.* 1700 until after 1800. Properly 'tappit hen' is the name of the capacity, a Scots pint or 3 English pints, and smaller measures should be referred to as the 'chopin' ($1\frac{1}{2}$ English pints) and the 'mutchkin'

($\frac{3}{4}$ of an English pint), but a long range of sizes were made both in Scottish and English measures, and 'tappit hen' is a useful descriptive name for the type as a whole. An earlier Scottish measure, the pot-bellied measure, was made as early as 1650 and both this and the tappit-hen types are also found in lidless varieties. The lidless tappit hen is particularly associated with Aberdeen.

Irish forms include the 'haystack' measure of double conical form, and later a group of lidless and handleless baluster measures in a limited range of sizes. Local English forms of 19th-c. measure abound. Worth particular notice is the West Country style of squat measure with short spouted neck, identical in shape to the more frequently seen copper measures, and the 'waisted' form of Victorian measure associated with Norfolk and Suffolk.

Medical and Miscellaneous. Mention should perhaps be made of the range of medical requisites made in pewter during the 18th and early 19th centuries. Bleeding-bowls in the form of graduated eared dishes, pap-boats, feeding-bottles, syringes and clysters, inhalers and 'Mr. Gibson's Physic Spoon'. This last was an ingenious device for the forcible administration of nauseous medicines to an unwilling recipient, invented about 1825.

Miscellaneous objects include dog-whistles, buckles and buttons, chimney ornaments, pipe-stoppers, communion tokens issued by Scottish churches as 'admission tickets' for those wishing to take Holy Communion, MEDALS and COINS. Pewter farthings and halfpennies were minted by James II and numerous 17th-c. and 18th-c. pewter tokens were issued by tradesmen. Pewter teapots, in contrast to Britannia metal ones, are scarce. Food bottles and wine cans of Continental manufacture are found in a variety of forms and periods. Finally it should not be overlooked that 'tin' organ pipes are in fact made from a low grade, lead-rich pewter alloy known as pipe metal.

5. MUSEUMS. Fine collections of pewter are to be seen at the Victoria and Albert Museum and the Guildhall Museum, London, the Kelvin Museum, Glasgow, and by prior arrangement at Pewterers' Hall, London. Abroad the Boymans Museum, Rotterdam, the Rijksmuseum, Amsterdam, the Metropolitan Museum of Art, New York and the Art Gallery of New South Wales, Sydney, have collections, the last strong in English pewter.

PEZOTTO. See COTTON AND COTTON PRINTING.

PHILADELPHIA CHIPPENDALE. A regional variation of the CHIPPENDALE style which was produced in the flourishing furniture industry at Philadelphia during the 2nd half of the 18th c. by cabinet-makers such as Thomas AFFLECK and Benjamin RANDOLPH, who worked from copies of Chippendale's *Director*. The style was robust and masculine, with luxurious carved ornament.

PHOENIX. A fabulous bird, the only one of its kind, which after living for 500 or 600 years burnt itself on a funeral pyre and arose as a young bird from its own ashes. The legend was known to classical antiquity and is reported in various forms by Herodotus, Pliny, Tacitus and other writers. Pliny's description of the bird (*Naturalis Historia* x. 2) tallies fairly closely with the golden eagle of the Far East. In ancient Egypt the

Decorated initial from Alexander Gottlieb Baumgarten, *de ordine in audiendis philosophicis per triennium academicum.* (Bodl., 1738)

Phoenix adopted as its emblem by the Phoenix Assurance Company in 1782 (symbolizing new life arising from the ashes)

phoenix was a symbol of the sun, which arises anew every morning. In Rome it became the symbol of the imperial apotheosis and it was adopted by the early Christians as a symbol of resurrection. An elegiac poem of 170 lines *De ave phoenice*, a medley of pagan and Christian elements, is attributed to the Christian convert Lactantius (? A.D. 250–317). The phoenix appears as a device in the catacombs and later in mosaics and illuminated manuscripts throughout the Middle Ages. In modern times it was adopted as its emblem by the Phoenix Assurance Company.

PHOTOGRAPHY. The photographer today has at his disposal a large number of technical means by which he may control or manipulate his medium. No less than the painter in his craft the photographer can literally speaking render works expressive. Though photography may predominantly be employed in a documentary way, to record rather than to interpret the external world, in one degree or another much photographic imagery is a product of conscious choice, deliberate control and the application of special techniques.

The manipulative side of photography has a history which begins in 1839 with the announcement of the discovery itself. There were at first two main processes from which to choose: the DAGUERREOTYPE and the calotype. They involved two distinctly different techniques and produced two distinctly different kinds of image. The image of the daguerreotype, made on a silvered copper plate, was a single and unique one. It was characterized by its fugitive quality when turned into the light and by the fine detail in the definition of forms. Conversely, the calotype was a negative process by which an unlimited number of prints could be produced. Because the negative was made on sensitized paper, waxed or oiled to render it translucent, the fibrous quality of the material inevitably acted upon the print, imparting to it soft contours and a sense of atmospheric light. Apart from the cheaper cost and greater ease with which a calotype could be made, and the advantage of taking multiple copies from one negative, it was often used by photographers in preference to the daguerreotype because of its 'artistic' effect. Notable among these photographers were David Octavius HILL and Charles NÈGRE. Both of them were known equally well as painters.

Choice, too, could be exercised in the use of lenses to accommodate diverse aesthetic tastes. The standardized excellence of lens manufacture inhibited the control of the image. Photographers therefore devised modifications for this purpose, or even means for counteracting the effects of excessive regularity. Imperfect lenses are known to have been deliberately employed in the early 1850s to alter the focus not just in depth but in the same lateral plane. Even the effect of spherical aberration, normally considered a serious fault in lenses, was sought as a means of diffusing the focus. Antoine CLAUDET in London later used pieces of ground glass intervening between the lens and the subject, and between the lens and the plate, to obtain a 'harmonious effect'. Fox TALBOT is believed to have suppressed undue optical sharpness in any one plane by interposing one or more sheets of paper between the negative and the print to be made. In the 1860s, to create 'harmony and artistic effect in photographic portraits', Claudet placed the lens in a movable tube, much as occurs in cameras today, so as to change the focus *during exposure* in order to obtain a mixture of softness and definition in the different planes of the face. A similar method was used by the popular photographer of Victorian sentimentality, Mrs. Julia Margaret Cameron, in the 1870s to control the quality of the image.

The colouring of daguerreotypes by hand was widely practised from the early 1840s. Because of the fragile surfaces of those plates the tints were delicate and sparingly employed. Though colouring was believed to enhance the artistic effects of daguerreotypes, the images themselves were not significantly altered. But in the 1850s photographs on more resilient materials like paper were often painted so that a new, somewhat hybrid image emerged. By 1861, at a time when photographs on canvas were frequently used as grounds for painting, serious proposals were made not just for colouring photographic images, but for scumbling and otherwise giving to photographs the impasto surfaces intrinsic to paintings.

To impart to the photograph the signs of the hand several other methods were adopted in the 1860s and 1870s for simulating the sketchy and broken lines of drawings. In one of these a revolving disc in front of the subject was used to blur and soften the peripheral areas in the manner of artists' vignettes. Another, called the 'photo-crayon' process, devised by the Canadian-born theatrical photographer Napoleon Sarony (1821–96) in 1871, combined a positive on glass with a crayoned backing. By printing on rough drawing-paper, a practice known as early as 1868, the photograph could be made to simulate work by hand.

The craft and aesthetics of photography are bound up inextricably with those of painting. In the 19th c. photographic techniques were explored mainly with the idea of giving to the medium the manipulative latitude of painting. A high degree of inventiveness and skill was thus engendered. The photographic compositions of Oscar Gustave Rejlander (1813–75), a Swede working in Wolverhampton, are noteworthy examples. Significantly it took him six weeks to plan and produce his famous picture *The Two Ways of Life* (1857). The procedure was painstaking and exceedingly elaborate, requiring great skill. More than thirty negatives were separately exposed, the lighting, scale and contours of the images cunningly controlled to produce a visually cohesive and homogeneous composition.

Other methods employed in the last half of the 19th c. for assembling diverse images into one uniform picture include the so-called 'combination printing' technique of Henry Peach Robinson. Robinson describes the tools of the photographic craftsman: varnishes to control the tonal gradations, special vignetting glass, leather daubers, curved pieces of zinc or cardboard and cotton-wool. The retouching of photographic negatives, though not always an acceptable procedure, was used extensively in the last few decades of the 19th c. not merely to eliminate error but to embellish and enrich.

By substituting for the lens cardboard with slits Jacques Ducos du Hauron in the 1880s was able to compress or elongate the photographic image in the manner of distorting mirrors. He called his method 'transformism', the idea being that by judiciously arranging the slits the proportions of a face or figure might be altered in an advantageous way. This use of slits in place of the lens is known to have occurred in landscape photography during the 1890s. It produced striking effects of tonal patches, recalling the paintings of Cézanne and others.

One of the most startling innovations in photographic technique was announced *c.* 1897. Based on an earlier commercial method, it was now called the 'Gum-Bichromate' process or sometimes 'Photo-Aquatint', the latter designation not without meaning. Two of its strongest advocates were Alfred Maskell and Robert Demachy. For the first time the actual image on the print could be altered, not by the introduction of extraneous materials such as paint, but by working with water sprays, brush or other implements into the soft gelatine of the emulsion itself. The method lent itself to the widest variety of applications. Any type of paper, of any colour or texture, could be used according to the effects wanted. The pigment, or even a combination of pigments, used in the emulsion was entirely open to choice. Parts of the image could be recoated if desired and changes or additions made. The Gum-Bichromate process and others based on the same principles came closer to turning photography into a manual graphic technique than any other. It was very popular, was extensively used in the first two decades of this century and enjoyed a revival in the 1960s.

By *c.* 1890 the first positive signs had appeared that photographic techniques were being explored in a new way, for their own sake rather than in simulation of painting techniques. Ironically they occurred as recreational activities, as photographic pastimes, realizing, as one such book puts it, 'many novel and curious effects to be obtained with the aid of the camera'. Several of these 'curious effects', such as light drawings, leaf prints, floral vignettes, double-exposed, composite and stroboscopic photographs, were later, in the 20th c., to be exploited with much more serious ends in view.

Somewhere around 1920 a fundamental change began to occur in the conception of the character of photography. Essential to this change, though seldom at first verbalized, was the idea that there was no such thing as a 'wrong' or a 'bad' element of photographic form. All qualities in the photographic image, whether arrived at by accident or design, were potentially useful in a creative and expressive way. It can hardly be imagined that such a change could have come about independently of similar changes in all the other arts and in painting especially. Inevitably new pictorial freedoms were accompanied by a greater licence in techniques. The cumulative experience of the medium of photography must also be taken into account. By *c.* 1920 a sizeable array of both orthodox and unorthodox processes was available, as was knowledge of the skill in technique with which these could now be employed. Often, too, scientific photography helped to open the doors to new species of imagery and to new techniques.

The propensity of Surrealists for assaulting the consciousness with startling images, together with their desire to elevate the commonplace into the sphere of art, put them in a very special relationship to photography and the imaginative exploration of its imagery and techniques. Three photographic processes can be associated with the Surrealists Man Ray and Ubac (Raoul Michelet): the photogram, solarization and the relief image. The first two of these are essentially much older in origin, the photogram especially going back to the earliest leaf and lace prints. None of these techniques is dependent on a camera; they are purely dark-room procedures. The photogram, made by placing objects directly on sensitized paper and exposing to light, is entirely independent of the lens. The solarized image, in which striking reversals from positive to negative are obtained either in the negative or in the print, depends on a judicious exposure to bright light at a certain moment during the developing. To obtain the relief image prints are produced through a slightly displaced sandwich of a negative and positive transparency of the same subject. All three processes lend themselves to a wide range of modifications.

The consciously artful use of photomontage first occurs about 1915, though its antecedents may be found much earlier in popular arts and pastimes. As it is usually employed the technique is not strictly speaking a photographic one. It is neither directly dependent on a camera nor does it necessarily involve any dark-room procedures. It is essentially a means of piecing together diverse photographic images, either of related or of unrelated subjects, in either a homogeneous or a random way. If the photomontage image is to be uniform in subject and pictorially, much skill may be required. If, as in the photomontages of John Heartfield and Max Ernst, disparate images are united by homogeneous formal means, even greater skill is needed. Sometimes, to obtain mechanically smooth and impersonal tonal transitions between photographic fragments, the fine spray of an air brush is used.

Visually related to photomontage are techniques like multiple exposure and printing, in which both camera and dark room are used. The image is even more difficult to control with these methods than with photomontage.

An immense range of photographic materials, equipment and skills gives to photography its present highly articulate vocabulary. The diversification of techniques is incalculable. Photography is now as versatile a medium as painting and has developed its own craftsmanship and skills.

PHUR-BU. Tibetan Lamaist ritual dagger. It was wedge-shaped and the blade had a triple arris. The hilt was surmounted by a head or three heads of the horse-headed demon Hayagriva; between this and the blade might be a VAJRA or half-*vajra*. The *phur-bu* was made either of wood or of metal; in the latter case the hilt was usually of bronze and the blade of iron. The *phur-bu* might be the size of a hand-dagger or some 2 metres and set in a socket. Its function was to hold in subjection the noxious demons which were summoned up in the course of the Tantric ritual.

PHYFE, DUNCAN (1768–1854). The pre-eminent and most original United States cabinet-maker of the latter part of the 18th c. Of Scottish origin, he was brought up in Albany and settled in New York *c.* 1792, first in Broad Street and then in Partition Street from *c.* 1795 until his retirement. In 1837 the style of the business changed from his own name to Duncan Phyfe & Sons, and in 1840 to Duncan Phyfe & Son. He retired in 1847 a wealthy man. During his long career he interpreted a variety of European styles in a highly personal and original manner and he exercised an important influence in creating the FEDERAL style.

His early manner was largely based on designs of SHERATON. From *c.* 1810 he used features of the English REGENCY in conjunction with the French DIRECTOIRE and EMPIRE styles, becoming the leading exponent of the last-named style in America. The production of his last years was heavier, in the style known as American empire which was then in vogue, and he himself sometimes referred to it as 'butcher furniture'.

Among his favourite motifs was the lyre, which he used for chair- and sofa-backs, bench arms, etc. He also made much use of REEDING and characteristic of his style are bulbous turnings terminating in delicately reeded legs. Although comparatively little of the work coming from his large workshop can have been executed by him personally, it is noted for its consistently fine execution and the excellence of the carving. There are examples of his furniture in many museums, among them the Metropolitan Museum of Art, New York, the Boston Museum of Fine Arts and the Henry Ford Museum.

PICCININO, LUCIO (recorded *c.* 1578–95) of Milan. The last of the important Italian armour-embossers, he produced elaborate parade-armours decorated with designs and scenes in relief and DAMASCENED in gold and silver. Though his work is technically of high quality, his designs are over-crowded and lack the sculptural qualities of his great predecessor Filippo Negroli (see NEGROLI FAMILY). An armour made for Alessandro Farnese, Duke of Parma *c.* 1578–9 (Kunsthist. Mus., Vienna) has been ascribed to him with reasonable certainty, and this has provided the basis for attributing other pieces to him on stylistic grounds. Examples are in the Wallace Collection; Victoria and Albert Museum; Metropolitan Museum of Art, New York. See ARMS AND ARMOUR.

PICK. Weaver's term for a cycle of the weaving operation consisting of one weft thread, i.e. one revolution of the loom wheel.

PICKERING, WILLIAM (1796–1854). Publisher and designer of books, who set up in London as an antiquarian bookseller in 1821. A man of literary tastes, he began publishing the next year by issuing the first of his 'Diamond Classics', a series of beautifully printed miniature editions of English, Latin and Italian classics, to which he afterwards added Homer in Greek. In 1821 he first issued his books cased in stiff boards covered with coloured cloth, a practice adopted by nearly all British and American publishers since then. In 1829 he first employed the younger Charles Whittingham as printer, and the two became such close collaborators that Pickering said they were the two halves of a pair of scissors. Pickering and Whittingham were responsible for a great improvement in the style of book production. They simplified title-pages and revived the use of 18th-c. types. In 1844 Pickering reprinted the early Anglican prayer-books with wood-engraved decoration in 16th-c. style, drawn by Whittingham's daughter and skilfully engraved by Mary Byfield. These books were very influential in promoting printing in period style.

PICTURESQUE, THE. See LANDSCAPE GARDENING (ENGLAND).

PIECRUST. Raised scalloped edging which was used as ornamentation for small circular tea-tables in the 3rd quarter of the 18th c. A similar type of ornament is also found on silver dishes, etc.

PIER GLASS. See MIRRORS.

PIETRE DURE (Italian, 'hard stones'). Term for a particular kind of mosaic work in which coloured stones, such as LAPIS LAZULI, agate and porphyry, are used to imitate the effect of painting. The main centre of the art was Florence, where in 1588 the Grand Duke Ferdinand established a factory in the Uffizi which continued to work well into the 19th c. The productions of the workshop consisted mainly of table-tops and panels for cabinets, decorated with birds and flowers or landscapes, which were executed with a naturalism and polychromatic brilliance that made them celebrated all over Europe. A cabinet designed by Robert ADAM in the Victoria and Albert Museum is inset with landscapes signed by Baccio Cappelli, one of the Uffizi workmen active between 1621 and 1670. See also FURNITURE (EUROPEAN).

PIFFETTI, PIETRO (1700–77). Italian cabinet-maker and cabinet-maker to the Court at Turin. He was outstanding as a craftsman, delighting in highly original MARQUETRY and creating colourful effects by using TORTOISESHELL, MOTHER OF PEARL and IVORY combined with exotic woods and splendid ORMOLU MOUNTS. Some of his best works were designed by the Sicilian architect Filippo Juvarra (1678–1736). There are examples of his work in the Royal Palace, Turin, and the Quirinale Palace, Rome.

PILE. See WEAVING and CARPETS AND RUGS.

PILLEMENT, JEAN-BAPTISTE (1727–1808). French painter and designer. As a painter of decorative landscape his work was often derivative from that of BOUCHER. But he was an exquisite draughtsman and prints made from his drawings were popular throughout Europe, helping to spread the ROCOCO taste. They were published in England as well as France. He was particularly important in the spread of CHINOISERIE. As a painter he was one of the group of minor French artists who influenced the trend of 18th-c. painting in Portugal.

PINCHBECK. An alloy of copper and zinc, named after a London watch- and clock-maker, Christopher Pinchbeck, who was credited with its invention *c.* 1732. Pinchbeck can be made to resemble gold in colour and therefore has the advantage that when used as a basis for gilding the metal does not show a different colour when the gilding is worn. It was much used in the 18th c. and early 19th c. for watch cases and for cheap jewellery. The word came to have a pejorative sense as the type of anything spurious or counterfeit. But by the middle of the 20th c. pinchbeck jewellery had acquired the status of an 'antique'.

PINEAU, NICOLAS (1684–1754). French sculptor and decorator, son of JEAN-BAPTISTE Pineau (d. 1694) who was employed as a carver at Versailles and elsewhere from *c.* 1680. Nicolas went to Russia in 1716 with the architect Alexandre Le Blond and on the latter's death in 1719 was the leading French decorative artist at the Court of the Tsar. His masterpiece while in Russia was the carving of the cabinet of Peter the Great at Peterhof. He left Russia *c.* 1727 and from *c.* 1732 became with MEISSONNIER one of the leaders in the lighter style of ROCOCO decoration. He was associated with the architect Jean-Baptiste Leroux in many works and his decorations for the Hôtel Rouillé (*c.* 1732), the Hôtel de Villars (1732–3), the Hôtel de Roquelaure (1733), etc., had considerable influence in establishing the asymmetrical phase of Rococo known as the *genre* PITTORESQUE. In *The Creation of the Rococo* (1943) Fiske Kimball wrote that 'it was Pineau who was primarily responsible for the creation and adoption of the *genre pittoresque* in French interiors. Earlier than Meissonnier, he designed and executed rooms fully incorporating the crucial innovations. Far more than Meissonnier or any other, he fixed the character and type of detail destined to prevail in France. Among all the works, his own were to remain unsurpassed.'

PINTADO (Portuguese and Spanish: painted, coloured or spotted). See CHINTZ and COTTON AND COTTON PRINTING.

PIPE METAL. A low-grade alloy of PEWTER used for making organ pipes.

PIQUÉ (French). The art of encrusting or inlaying TORTOISESHELL with gold or silver wire or foil. Though practised in the 17th c. in Holland and England, the finest piqué work was done in Paris and in southern Italy (Naples) during the 18th c. It was applied to caskets, boxes, stick heads and a variety of small articles. Gold piqué with MOTHER OF PEARL and tortoiseshell was a combination eminently suited to the potentialities of ROCOCO art.

PISANELLO, properly ANTONIO PISANO (*c.* 1395–*c.* 1455). Italian painter who lived as a young man in Verona and may have been a pupil of Stefano da Zevio. He collaborated with Gentile da Fabriano in frescoes for the Doge's Palace at Venice (1415–20) and later completed Gentile's frescoes at the Lateran Basilica, Rome (1431–2). From this time he was in great demand and was probably regarded as the successor to Gentile in the International Gothic style. Of his paintings only two frescoes and four or five panels have survived. The frescoes are *The Annunciation* (S. Fermo, Verona, 1423–4) and *St. George and the Princess of Trebizond* (Sta. Anastasia, Verona, 1437–8). The smaller paintings include a portrait of Lionello d'Este (Bergamo, *c.* 1441) and one of a Princess (? Ginevra) of the House of Este (Louvre, *c.* 1443) and two pictures in the National Gallery, London —*Vision of St. Eustace* and *Virgin and Child with SS. Anthony and George*—attributed to him. He is considered the most brilliant Italian master of the International Gothic style, turning it to original uses and giving evidence of a keen and penetrating power of observation and a lively fantasy within the decorative scheme. At times he recalls more than any other major Italian painter the spirit of the *Très Riches Heures du Duc de Berry.* He was an accomplished draughtsman and more of his drawings survive than of any other Quattrocento artist except Jacopo Bellini. The fastidious and enchanting drawings of birds and hunting animals and costume confirm his keen and alert eye for natural detail. He was also pre-eminent in the art of portrait medals, beginning with the famous medallion of John VIII Paleologue (*c.* 1438). He travelled extensively and many of the heads of the city states of northern Italy commissioned him to make portrait medals. He made a set for Alfonso of Aragon, King of Naples (1448–9). The portrait medal was a conscious revival of the ancient Roman practice, which had begun a little before Pisanello's time. But his own medals are neither antique nor Gothic but set a standard of delicacy, precision and clarity which has not been surpassed. See MEDALS.

PISTRUCCI, BENEDETTO (1784–1855). Italian gem engraver and designer of MEDALS and COINS. Born in Rome, where for a time he worked for the gem engraver Morelli, he gained considerable reputation and was patronized by the wealthy and famous, including Napoleon's sister. In 1814 he went to Paris and in 1815 settled in London. There he was commissioned by Wellesley Pole, Master of the Mint, to execute the cameo of St. George and the Dragon which is familiar from its use on English coinage. He became Chief Engraver to the Mint and produced dies for the re-coinage and coronation medals of George IV in 1820 and of Queen Victoria in 1838.

PITTORESQUE. *Genre pittoresque* was the contemporary term applied to the final and most fanciful phase of the French ROCOCO style. Its most striking characteristics were exaggerated contrast and asymmetry of ornament. The genesis of the new phase was attributed by Jacques-François Blondel (1705–74) and by Charles-Nicolas Cochin (1715–90) to Nicolas PINEAU and Juste-Aurèle MEISSONNIER.

PLANETARY CLOCK (ASTRARIUM). See DONDI.

PLANTIN, CHRISTOPHE (*c.* 1520–89). Born near Tours, he served an apprenticeship to a printer and bookbinder at Caen. After a time in Paris he moved in 1549 to Antwerp and worked as a bookbinder. About that time he joined a Quietist and clandestine sect, the Family of Love, and it was probably with money lent him by the sectaries that he was able to engage in printing and publishing in 1555. The quality of his work and his employment of learned correctors won him custom from scholars and support from powerful patrons. From this beginning he built up the largest publishing and printing business of the 16th c. In 1566 Plantin proposed to the king of Spain the printing of a Polyglot Bible to be financed partly by a grant from the king. This masterpiece of 16th-c. printing occupied him in the years 1568–72. By 1574 he was printing with 16 presses, a number far greater than that of any other printer until the 19th c. He had an international trade in learned editions, breviaries, liturgical works, and bibles in Latin and Hebrew. His business was constantly interrupted by wars and civil commotion; and steering a devious course between hostile powers he had narrow escapes from being brought to book for treason or heresy.

Plantin printed in the pleasant French style of the period and formed a magnificent collection of matrices for casting the type faces cut by the best French and Flemish masters. These and much of the other equipment of his office and the furniture of his house may be seen in the place where he worked and lived, now the Museum Plantin-Moretus.

146, 865.

PLATEL, PIERRE. Huguenot goldsmith and silversmith who worked in London from *c.* 1687 to *c.* 1728. Paul de LAMERIE was apprenticed to him in 1705. He was succeeded by his son, of the same name.

PLAYING-CARDS. The origin of playing-cards is uncertain. They were not known to Greco-Roman antiquity. On the one hand it has been argued that they originated in the Far East and spread to Europe either through Arab traders or by the instrumentality of returning crusaders; on the other hand it has been thought that they originated in Europe and spread from there to the East. Both these theories may be wide of the mark. European and Asiatic playing-cards developed along such very different lines that it is difficult, and seems unnecessary, to assume a common origin for the two types. But whatever their origin, playing-cards have been in use in Europe since the 14th c. and in the East for at least as long. The first known reference to playing-cards in Europe dates from 1377. It was written by Johannes, a German monk living in a Swiss monastery, and he says: '. . . a certain game called the game of cards has come to us in this year.' From that time ever more frequent references to cards appear in manuscripts throughout Europe. Had the crusaders brought cards to Europe from the Holy Land, their use would have been established long before 1377. Similarly it seems likely that Arab traders would have brought cards from the Far East to Europe and North Africa before this date.

The earliest European cards were hand-painted. The few that survive have great artistic beauty, and it is therefore not surprising that playing-cards have a long history of beautiful design. Today, although the number of good card-makers is distressingly few, attractive new designs are still being produced.

Evolution is perhaps the keynote in the development of cards. Although from early times the European pack has always been divided into four suits, these themselves have had a great variety of names, patterns and designs. One of the oldest surviving German hand-painted packs, now in the Kunsthistorisches Museum, Vienna, was the work of Konrad WITZ. Its theme is hunting, and the four suits are Falcons, Hounds, Herons and Lures, which were used to recall the falcons. Each of the cards, painted *c.* 1440, is a fine example of Witz's work as an artist. In particular, the suit of herons shows the birds incorporated in landscape scenes that make them almost paintings in their own right.

Since cards drawn and painted individually were expensive they were the prerogative of the rich. It was the invention, also in Germany, of wood-block printing that led to the popularization of cards for the masses, for it was now possible to produce sheets of cards which could be hand-coloured and cut up to make packs. Some of the early wood-block packs show remarkable skill. The pack designed in 1588 by Jost AMMAN has suits of inking-pads, books, drinking-cups and curiously shaped glasses known as 'Cabbage Stalks'. Apart from the suit emblems the aces to nines have scenes of contemporary life, fables and other interesting vignettes. Oddly enough, four centuries later some packs from Germany, Austria and Czechoslovakia still retain on the pip-cards vignettes of their regional designs.

From the 14th c. the various suit systems were becoming established in different parts of Europe. In Italy the suits were cups or chalices, swords, money and clubs—genuine cudgels—or batons. It is claimed that the four suits represented the four classes of the populace—the Church, the military and aristocracy, the merchants and the peasantry respectively. Some people believe that the earliest cards came from Italy, and the tradition of four suits to the pack derives from these. In France the four suits, later adopted in Britain, were *cœurs* (hearts), *piques* (pikes), *carreaux* (literally, paving tiles) and *trèfles* (trefoils). Since the Italian word for sword is '*spada*' and since we use the name 'clubs' for what is obviously a leaf design, it seems likely that the British first used Italian-suited cards, and retained two Italian names when adopting the French suits. Elsewhere the Germans had suits of leaves, bells, acorns and hearts, and the Swiss had shields, bells, flowers and acorns. The now standard pack in Britain and America with spades, hearts, diamonds and clubs, was evolved from a 16th-c. design from Rouen.

If all packs had four suits, the number of cards per suit was not constant. Nor was the number of court cards. Some very early packs had 14 cards to the suit, with four courts. These were King, Queen, mounted Cavalier and Valet—or in Italian packs, Foot Soldier. Basically card games fall into two main types: those involving the collection of like cards or runs—rummy, for example—and those involving taking tricks, of which whist is the prime example. A pack with 14 four-card tricks soon showed its disadvantages, and to ensure at least one trick difference one card was dispensed with. The Italian, Swiss and Germans settled for a pack with three male courts, while the French and British retained the Queen and banished the horseman.

Cards have evolved according to the types of game for which they were used and as games cease to be played the cards needed for them cease to be made. Throughout the German-speaking parts of Europe the chief card game is skat, which uses a 32-card or 36-card pack. In these areas the old traditional patterns survive as deeply entrenched as ever. The Spanish game of ombre, with three players, requires a 48-card pack. Here the Spanish pack, with suits similar to the Italian, is also strongly established. Elsewhere some of the curious national and regional packs are losing ground to the spread of the universal games of poker, whist and bridge, for which the standard British pack is used. Soon they will be found only in antique shops and museums.

Whereas European and American cards all have four suits and are roughly similar in size and shape, the same cannot be said of Asiatic cards. Traditional Hindu cards are circular. They have either 8 or 10 suits with 12 cards in each suit. There is a King and a Vizier, and 10 pip-cards. The cards are heavily lacquered or enamelled and are hand-painted, often with great charm and beauty. The 8-suited packs, known as *Gandjifah*, represent the court-life of Indian princes. The 10-suited *Dasavatara* packs represent the 10 incarnations of Vishnu. In direct contrast are Korean playing cards, which are about 19·5 centimetres long and about 1·25 centimetres wide. These too have 8 suits with 10 cards a suit. Their curious shape is said to derive from the fact that they are based on the use of the arrow for divination, and an arrow-pattern appears on the back of some Korean packs. Chinese cards tend to be shorter, from 5 to 10 centimetres long and about 2 centimetres wide. They are derived from three sources. The first type is derived from paper money, which first appeared in the T'ang Dynasty (611–906). These packs consist of 120 cards, which are in four sets of 30 cards each. There are 3 suits: coins, strings of coins and myriads of strings of coins. The second type is derived from dominoes, which were used for fortune-telling in China. Domino cards have 4 suits of 21 cards each. The third type is derived from Chinese chess, which differs from the game played in Europe. This too has 4 suits with from 28 to 33 cards a suit, each of which is a different colour—red, white, yellow and green. Persian cards, which were roughly square in shape, were also beautifully lacquered and hand-painted. The pack consisted basically of 5 designs repeated 4 times. The number of cards could be added to according to the number wishing to play.

Elsewhere cards in use in Asia show the influence of the early Portuguese explorers and travellers, who brought with them the Spanish-suited pack. Native artists copied the designs

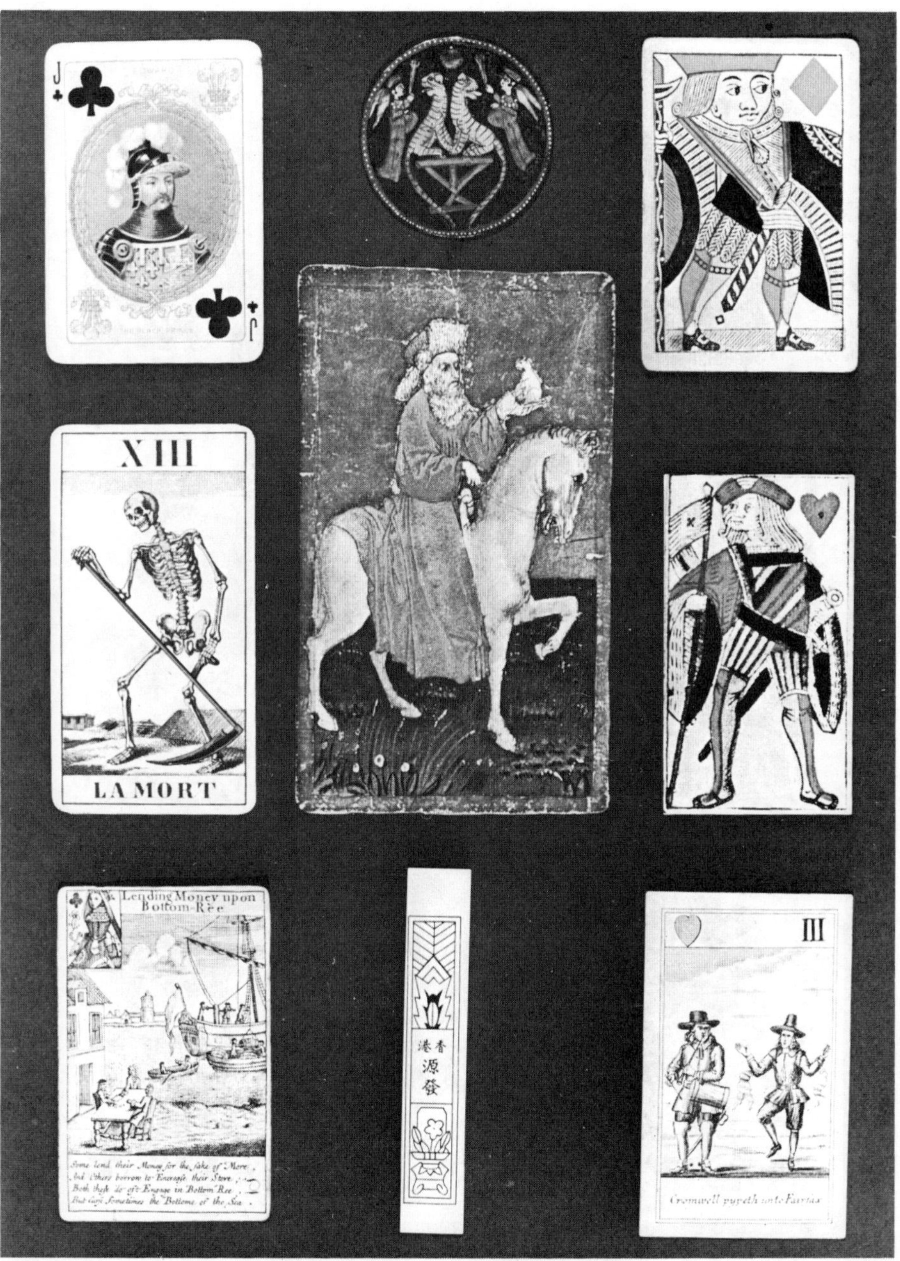

Top row. Card from the pack issued by Goodall, London, to mark Queen Victoria's Jubilee; court card from a hand-painted Indian pack of the 19th c.; 'full length' court card from a pack by Hunt & Co., London, *c.* 1850. *Centre row.* The 13th trump card from a Swiss tarot pack; King of Hounds from the Ambraser Hunting pack, *c.* 1440 (reprint); court card from a French pack from Lyon, 17th c. (reprint). *Bottom row.* Card from the satirical 'All the Bubbles' pack, 1720; card from a modern Chinese 'Money' pack; 'The Knavery of the Rump Parliament', a 17th-c. pack, reprinted in 1886

Top row. J. F. Kennedy, from a pack issued for the 1964 Presidential election; Queen from a Russian pack, which has been in production since pre-Soviet times; Churchill on a Belgian 'Victory' pack. *Centre row.* King of Spades from the Italian Trieste pattern; example of the decorative cards made around the turn of the 20th c. by the Frankfurt card-maker Dondorf; Ace of Bells from a Bavarian pack. *Bottom row.* Queen from a modern pack based on Pre-Columbian American art; card from an Icelandic mythological pack; Queen from a modern East German pack

on the cards, adding their own ethnic and cultural motifs to the designs. Nowhere do these cards survive in more interesting form than in Japan, where, as *Mekuri-fuda* or *Kabu-fuda*, they are used for gambling games. *Mekuri* packs have 48 cards made up of 4 different suits; *Kabu* packs have 40 or 48 cards, consisting of 1 suit (money or barons) repeated 3 times and the same suit repeated a fourth time with minor variations. *Mekuri* have 3 courts, *Kabu* only 1. There are several types of each pack, their design, clearly recognizable as based on the Spanish pack, varying from region to region. Another popular Japanese game has a distinct resemblance to playing-cards. *Hana-fuda*, or the Japanese Flower-Matching game, has 48 cards, 4 for each of the 12 months. Each month has its own flower or plant with 4 differing cards a set. They are delightful little packs, popular with collectors.

Clearly there is much room for research into the interrelated development of Asiatic and European cards. Africa and the Americas use cards introduced by the European colonizers. Latin America, for example, uses predominantly Spanish-suited packs.

Techniques in producing cards have changed over the centuries. Wood-blocks gave way to engraving, engraving to chromo-lithography and finally to web-offset. The method of colouring cards changed, too. Hand-colouring gave way to stencilling, which was used until comparatively recently. Colour printing has now developed to the point at which virtually any desired effect can be produced in card design. A knowledge of printing techniques is often a guide to dating older packs.

Alongside the evolving techniques came an evolution of the cards themselves. Until the early 19th c. British cards were all full-length portraits, and both court and pip-cards had no identifying number. During the middle part of the century double-headed cards gradually became the norm, but it was not until the closing years of the century that corner indices or numbers were in universal use. Until this time, too, the cards had square corners—a relic of the days when they were cut by hand from large sheets. Rounded corners were an innovation, and packs were advertised as such to enhance their sales. Square or round cornered, they were considerably wider than modern cards, the 'narrow' card being a 20th-c. refinement.

The card designer has often felt the urge to experiment. The standard designs of the day were often discarded in favour of courts depicting contemporary royalty, famous historical characters, national costume and a host of other subjects. Many of these packs display a high degree of artistry and can form the basis of a thematic collection. Two of the most beautiful modern packs have both been anniversary packs. In 1957 De La Rue marked 125 years of production with a special design by Jean Picart le Doux, better known as a TAPESTRY designer. Ten years later the Russians celebrated 150 years of playing-card manufacture with a pack designed by Palekh artists. They used Russian folk-lore and fairy-tale figures in bright colours and gold on a black background.

The educator soon found a painless way to impart knowledge, and packs to teach religion, geography, history, astronomy and the like have been frequent throughout the history of playing-cards. Even the satirist has made use of cards. In the 17th and 18th centuries many scurrilous political packs, attacking such topics as the Pretended Popish Plot, the knavery of the Rump Parliament and the South Sea Bubble, were produced. In post-war Europe political satire has been used in packs from Germany, Italy and France.

When South Africa became a Republic the occasion was marked by a special Boer pack. This had as its suits tent-pegs, powder-horns, boots and wagon-wheels. The courts represented Boer pioneers. This was not the first time a non-royal pack had been used. After the French Revolution all figures of royalty were banished from the cards. Either the original figures were used without their crowns or else completely new designs were introduced. Symbolic figures representing Liberty, Equality and Fraternity, or workers, peasants and others, were substituted. But with the restoration of the Emperor royalty gradually crept back into favour. The French have a further distinction in that they first used playing cards as money. In French colonial Canada at the end of the 17th c. there was such a shortage of money to pay the troops that cards were confiscated and reissued as money after suitable endorsement by the Governor.

One strange use to which playing-cards are put is divination or fortune-telling. While the ordinary 52-card pack can be, and is, used for fortune-telling, the most popular cards for this purpose are tarot cards. Originally these cards were intended for use in playing the game known in different parts of Europe as Tarot, Tarock or Tarocchino. The pack consists of 78 cards, 4 suits of 14 cards and 22 trump cards. They are usually numbered with Roman numerals, and have unusual named designs—The Emperor, Death, Judgement, Temperance and so on. It is hardly surprising that these trump cards, called the Major Arcana, have been eagerly adopted by fortune tellers. As is usual with playing-cards, all sorts of curious theories as to their origin are produced. It is claimed that they were brought to Europe by the gypsies but early tarot cards, produced before the arrival of the gypsies, discount this view. Tarot cards are still used in parts of Europe for their original purpose, but an esoteric cult employing them as the basis for divination has grown up in many places, especially in the U.S.A. See also TAROT.

Playing-cards as an art form provide considerable interest and much research remains to be done. 'The Playing Card Society' exists to further interest and research into the subject.

Important collections are housed in the British Museum, the Guildhall, London, the Bodleian Library, Oxford, the Bielefeld Museum, Germany, and in Cincinnati, U.S.A.

346, 567, 831, 832.

PLUMBATE WARE. Pottery made in Central America before the Conquest covered by greyish and lustrous vitrified slip. The name is derived from the leaden colour (Latin, *plumbum*: lead), but the colour did not result from the use of lead. The method was technically similar to that used for Greek black figured pottery.

POINT D'ANGLETERRE. A name under which BRUSSELS LACE was exported to many countries in Europe during the late 17th and 18th centuries. This lace was in much demand in England at the time of the Restoration and one theory to account for the misleading name is that it was given in response to restrictive legislation in England so that smuggled lace could be sold as if made in England.

POINTILLÉ BINDINGS. Bookbindings decorated with dotted instead of solid-outline TOOLS, a technique introduced in France during the 2nd quarter of the 17th c. A brilliant filigree effect was obtained by filling the spaces between the geometrical interlacings of FANFARE bindings with small tools of spirals, FLEURONS and leaf forms. Another design, frequently employed, substituted for the interlacings a large central MEDALLION or lozenge-shaped ornament of closely massed *pointillé* tooling. The best *pointillé* work, often erroneously attributed to the binder known as Le Gascon, was executed by Florimond BADIER and the MAGNUS family of Amsterdam.

POIRIER, SIMON-PHILIPPE. A Parisian *marchand-mercier* who supplied the French court in the 2nd half of the 18th c. and whose influence did much to establish the typical Louis XVI style. He provided furniture for Madame du Barry's famous pavilion at Louveciennes.

POKER-WORK. The art of decorating wood with patterns burnt into the surface with a hot metal tool and subsequently smoothed with sandpaper. This was practised as a home craft at least as early as the 18th c. and was popular through the Victorian period, receiving a fillip from the interest in home crafts which was encouraged by the ARTS AND CRAFTS MOVEMENT.

POMANDER. Container for sweet-smelling essences. It consisted of some half-dozen sections attached by hinges to a central core, so that it resembled an orange in construction. It developed out of the medieval musk-ball, a hollow ball of precious metal also shaped like an apple or orange, either carried in the hand or suspended from the neck or waist, as a preservative against infection. The earliest reference dates from the 12th c. but musk-balls were probably known earlier in the Orient. The pomander had less of a prophylactic role and was rather a portable scent-bottle than a prophylactic. Examples are of silver or gold, the former often decorated with NIELLO. They were fashionable chiefly in the 16th and 17th centuries, but have recently been revived as a novelty.

PORCELAIN. A white, highly vitrified and translucent pottery made from a body of kaolin (china clay), a highly refractory white clay, combined with a felspathic rock PETUNTSE or china stone. Porcelain was being made in China from T'ang times, although the exact time and place of its origin in China are uncertain. (See CHINA, CERAMICS.) The secret of its manufacture was not discovered in Europe until the 1st decade of the 18th c. Before that an imitation or 'soft-paste' porcelain was produced in Europe by mixing white clay with ground FRIT and other substances, such as steatite, and glazing with a modified lead glaze. (See also CERAMICS and POTTERY TECHNIQUES.) The true Chinese porcelain was called in contrast 'hard-paste'. (The terms 'hard' and 'soft' refer primarily to the temperatures of the firing rather than to the hardness of the product.)

The term 'porcelain' is of uncertain derivation. The Portuguese *porcelana*, from *porcela*, a diminutive of *porca*, pig, was locally current for cowrie shells which served as money in parts of southern Asia. Marco Polo (1254–1324) also applied it to ceramic wares whose manufacture he describes in the city of Tin-gui in the province of Fo-kien. It has been suggested that he applied the word *porcelana* to the pottery because of a resemblance of its glaze to the surface of the cowrie shell. The word did not come into general use in Europe until the 16th c., when it was applied to Ming wares, wares of the Sung and Yüan periods being then unknown apart from certain CELADONS.

The qualities of Chinese porcelain which excited the admiration and envy of the West were its whiteness, thinness of body and its translucency. The Chinese have laid emphasis rather on its power to emit a resonant note when struck and the general term in Chinese for porcelain, namely *tzŭ*, points to this property.

EUROPEAN HISTORY. At the time of the Renaissance porcelain was still a rare luxury in Europe. The Chinese wares occasionally brought from the Near East were greatly admired for their whiteness, hardness and translucency, but no comparable European ware was made until the 18th c. From the 16th c. onwards, however, the growth of direct trading with the East by the Portuguese and Dutch increased the knowledge of Chinese products in the West and provided a strong stimulus to experimentation, whereby some pleasing and practical substitutes were devised.

The earliest experiments were made in Florence, *c.* 1575, where the rare Medici porcelain—an artificial, or 'soft-paste' ware—was produced. But this expensive manufacture lasted barely 10 years and a century passed before the next successful venture, this time in France. The wares of Rouen (*c.* 1673) and St. Cloud (*c.* 1677) inaugurated a fine soft-paste tradition which included most of the best of SÈVRES, and remained dominant until *c.* 1770. Soft-pastes possess admirable properties of their own, not the least of which is a melting quality of the glaze which blends pleasingly with ENAMEL painting, providing much of the special charm of early French porcelain. The glazes generally contained lead, and were fired at a lower temperature than the BISCUIT. The softer pastes are often distinguishable by the eye or by scratching with a knife; also their broken edges are granular, not smooth and shell-like as in hard-pastes. Besides the French some Italian and nearly all English factories made various types of soft-paste.

Meanwhile a very different tradition arose in Germany, where *c.* 1708 a porcelain of 'hard-paste' type was invented at MEISSEN. This manufacture, which was to become the foremost in Europe, was shortly followed by factories in Vienna (1719) and Venice (Vezzi factory, 1720), aided by renegade Meissen workmen, and within 50 years factories in many countries were producing wares of similar type.

From the first porcelain was a luxury art, serving the dictates of princely fashion. It was both costly and difficult to make. Once established a factory might take many years to perfect its wares and the secrets of the 'ARCANIST', as he was called, who superintended its technicalities, were closely guarded. Much depended on the chief painter or designer and the chief modeller, who was responsible for the conception and realization of the factory style; and the renown of Meissen is due chiefly to the genius of Höroldt and KAENDLER in these posts. From early days porcelain was decorated with enamels in a technique akin to that of the miniaturist and one already practised on faience by the independent painters called HAUSMALER. Such coloured enamelling or gilding was painted over the glaze and separately fired in the low-temperature 'muffle kiln'. Another method was to paint the unglazed biscuit and then glaze it and fire it at full temperature; the familiar blue and white was made in this way. The elaborate 18th-c. styles offered great scope for relief-moulded or impressed decoration and applied features, setting a premium on ingenuity. The popular figurines were cast in sections, limb by limb, from a series of little moulds all prepared from the artist's original clay model, and the assembly of the pieces was in itself a highly skilled task. Many of the figure-modellers were men of artistic talent and their work reflects in miniature and with singular animation and charm the fancies and conceits of 18th-c. courtly life.

The porcelain mania which swept Europe was under way before the end of the 17th c. Some princes already devoted special rooms to the display of Oriental wares; during the 1720s Augustus the Strong of Saxony, the founder of Meissen, conceived a 'Japanese' palace to be furnished almost entirely with porcelain, which he ordered from Meissen, including some life-size figures of animals. Before long every prince of note was planning his *Porzellanzimmer*. It was Count Brühl, however, a minister under Augustus III, whose passion for the extravagantly decorated banquet table gave the greatest impetus to the porcelain figure, creating a fashion which came to embrace whole worlds of mythological and romantic imagination. '*Galanterien*'—SNUFF-BOXES, cane-handles and so on—and a whole range of articles from inkstands to chamber-pots were also made of porcelain, and domestic wares including fully appointed tea-sets, coffee-sets and dinner-services now competed with those of SILVER.

Until the middle of the 18th c. nearly all the factories making hard-paste porcelain which were later established in other countries borrowed heavily from Meissen's repertory of shapes, designs and figure models. At first the Oriental influence was strong but soon a number of quite original styles were developed, culminating from 1740 to *c.* 1755 in a ROCOCO style with a more and more flamboyant use of decorative scrollwork in asymmetrical compositions both moulded and painted, the colouring being softer than hitherto. Figure work was immeasurably advanced by the arrival at Meissen, in 1731, of J. J. Kaendler, the brilliant modeller whose fame inspired a host of gifted men at other factories.

In the second half of the century the lead passed to France, where at the royal factory of Sèvres greater emphasis was laid on enamelled decoration. Richly coloured grounds, elaborately patterned borders and chased gilding framed delicate flower, bird and landscape paintings. By 1760 the NEO-CLASSICAL style had come into its own in France and by 1775 a reaction against the extravagances of Rococo was spreading through Europe. But this more severe movement was not so sympathetic to the plastic qualities of porcelain. Typical of it was the 'Grecian Urn' vase with pedestal foot and fluted sides, frequently decorated with stiff friezes, floral swags and ribbons, and cameo scenes or portraits. More often than not antique severity was sweetened by a liberal flavouring of sentiment; and among the seemingly austere figures of 'biscuit' (unglazed) porcelain one frequently detects the touch of a BOUCHER or a Falconet. On many wares enamelling was heavy and ornate; and this tendency marks particularly the wares of the EMPIRE period (1804 to *c.* 1825), when textures of metal or marble were often simulated. Of later wares little need be said. The great age of porcelain was over—and indeed the truly creative period had scarcely extended beyond 1775. Nineteenth-c. production consisted chiefly of more or less debased revivals of former styles. After 1860 imitations and forgeries become numerous, and the unreliability of porcelain marks in general cannot therefore be too strongly stressed.

In England there were few patrons as wealthy as those on the Continent, and tablewares greatly predominate over ornamental productions. The attractive, well-finished wares of Derby and Worcester, which supplied a fairly wide public, seldom challenged prevailing Continental fashions; forms adapted from native pottery and silver traditions were decorated with flower, bird, landscape and figure painting derived from Meissen and Sèvres. The most outstanding English factory was CHELSEA, whose figures often surpass those of Bow and DERBY. Most of the English porcelain was soft-paste, but under Wm. Cookworthy's patent of 1768 competent hard-paste was made at Plymouth, Bristol (1770) and New Hall (1781). The introduction of bone ash into the 'body' at Bow led to the later development of bone china in the 19th c. by Spode and a host of other manufacturers. Copeland's invention *c.* 1846 of 'PARIAN', a type of hard-paste, was used chiefly for unglazed white figures.

Factories.

France. Rouen (*c.* 1673), St. Cloud (1678–1766), Chantilly (from 1725), Mennecy-Villeroy (1734–73), Vincennes (later Sèvres), Strasbourg (1753–79), Niderviller (from 1765), Luneville (1766 to *c.* 1777), Marseilles (1773–93), Paris (several factories which continued working in the 19th c.), Tournai (from 1751). All made soft-paste until hard-paste was introduced *c.* 1770.

Germany. Meissen, Höchst, Nymphenburg, Ludwigsburg, Fürstenberg, Berlin, Frankenthal, Ansbach (from 1758), Fulda (1764–90), Kloster-Veilsdorf. All made hard-paste wares.

Italy and Spain. Medici, Vezzi, Venice (*c.* 1720–7), Cozzi (1764–1812), Le Nove (1762–1825), Este (from 1781), Vinovo, near Turin (1776–1820). All made hard-paste wares. Doccia, near Florence (1735, still active), made a hybrid hard-paste, and Capo-di-Monte, Naples (1743–59) made soft-paste. Buen Retiro, near Madrid (1760–1808).

England. Chelsea, Bow, Derby, Lowestoft (1757–1802), Longton Hall (*c.* 1751–60) all made soft-paste modified by the use of bone ash. Bristol (Lund's factory, *c.* 1749–51), Worcester, Caughley, Salop (from 1772), Liverpool (various factories, from *c.* 1756) made soap-stone paste. Plymouth (1768–70), Bristol (1770 to *c.* 1783), New Hall, Shelton, Staffs. (from 1781) made hard-paste.

Other Countries. Copenhagen, Denmark; Marieburg, Sweden; Weesp, Oude Loosdrecht, Holland; Zürich, Switzerland; St. Petersburg, Moscow, Russia; are the most important centres of porcelain manufacture working from the 2nd half of the 18th c. onwards.

Notes on a few of these factories follow:

Berlin Porcelain. There were two factories. Wegely's (1752–7), patronized by Frederick the Great, followed Meissen without much distinction. Gotkowsky's, founded in 1761, became the Prussian Royal factory two years later and continued into modern times. It had the benefit of painters and a modeller (F. E. Meyer) from Meissen. The cold white paste which is typical was adopted *c.* 1765, and during the best period (until 1786) was decorated with the characteristic scale patterns and relief mouldings of 'Potsdam Rococo'. Mark: a sceptre (from 1763).

Bow Porcelain. The wares of this London factory (*c.* 1745 to *c.* 1775), contemporary with those of Chelsea, but seldom quite as polished, often possess great charm in modelling and colouring and include many attractive figures. Bow strengthened its soft-paste with bone ash, an innovation which strongly affected the subsequent history of English porcelain.

Chelsea Porcelain (*c.* 1745–84). An English soft-paste porcelain, which is at its best a fine white with brilliant, glassy glaze. The factory was managed during most of its career by Nicholas Sprimont, a Liège silversmith, and its earliest wares, marked with a triangle, often reproduce SILVER forms. About 1748–55 first the 'raised anchor' mark was used, and then the 'red anchor'. During these periods there was Meissen influence in the painting of flowers and landscapes and the popular KAKIEMON decoration, but also considerable individuality of treatment and discriminating use of colour. The 'red anchor' figures include mythological, pastoral and exotic subjects. 'Chelsea toys'—miniature scent-bottles, etc.—have a fanciful originality. The splendid 'gold anchor' wares (*c.* 1758–69) occasionally excel even Sèvres in the sumptuousness of their coloured grounds, Rococo scrollwork and chased gilding; and figure groups became larger and more elaborate. The factory failed in 1769, and Duesbury of Derby used its premises for some years. This period is known as 'Chelsea-Derby'.

Frankenthal Porcelain (1755–99). Paul-Antoine Hannong, an Alsatian, had been making porcelain at Strasbourg, but when Vincennes (Sèvres) obtained a monopoly he migrated to Frankenthal in the Palatinate and obtained a privilege from the Elector. The French influence persists in the tablewares; but some notably individual figures were modelled by J. W. Lanz, J. F. Lück, Konrad Linck and, from 1779, J. P. Melchior. Common Mark: CT monogram, from 1762.

Fürstenberg Porcelain. The Ducal manufacture of Brunswick, established in 1747 but scarcely active until 1753. In the period before 1768 it produced some remarkable figures from the Italian Comedy and figures of miners, modelled by Simon Feilner. The factory continued into modern times. Mark: commonly 'F' in underglaze blue.

Höchst Porcelain (1750–98). Patronized by the Elector of Mainz, the Höchst factory produced a distinctive porcelain with soft, milky-white glaze and fresh enamel painting in styles often resembling those of Meissen and Frankenthal. Distinguished early figure-modellers were Simon Feilner and L. Russinger; and even better known is J. P. Melchior (at Höchst 1767–79). Commonest Mark: a wheel.

Ludwigsburg Porcelain (1756–1824). Begun privately, the factory was taken over by Duke Carl Eugen of Württemberg in 1758, J. J. Ringler being appointed manager and G. F. Riedl chief designer. A smoky-toned paste is characteristic. Some of the models were by the Court sculptors, notably J. C. W. Beyer, and by J.-J. Louis. Common Mark: crossed Cs under a coronet.

Medici Porcelain. 'Soft-paste' porcelain wares, made in Florence for Francesco Maria de' Medici *c.* 1575–87. They appear to have been the first porcelain produced in Europe and are extremely rare. They are painted principally in underglaze blue, and show the influence of Chinese porcelain and Turkish pottery, as well as that of contemporary Italian MAIOLICA.

Nymphenburg Porcelain. One of the foremost German manufactories of porcelain, near Munich; first established at Neudeck in 1747, and transferred in 1761 to the grounds of the Nymphenburg Palace, where it still is. The wares of the early period are a flawless white, and include many adorned with lively Rococo mouldings and fine floral painting. The delightful Italian Comedy figures and groups of lovers by BUSTELLI, showing the influence of S. Gunther's wood-carvings, are modelled with subtlety of line and a lively sense of satire. But in 1767 a serious decline set in owing to financial difficulties. For a time the factory was owned by the Barvarian State, but since 1862 it has been in private hands. Mark: the *Rautenschild* of Bavaria.

St. Cloud Porcelain. A distinctive, creamy-toned soft-paste porcelain which was made at St. Cloud, near Paris, from the late 17th c. until 1766. The earlier shapes were borrowed from silver, and painted with 'lacework' borders in underglaze blue. The wares of *c.* 1725 onwards include some with moulded reliefs only, and others with enamelling based on the Chinese FAMILLE VERTE. Amusing Oriental figures, snuff-boxes, cane-handles, etc. were also made.

Swansea Porcelain (1814 to *c.* 1822). Superior soft-paste wares were made at Swansea according to W. Billingsley's formula following his short-lived venture at Nantgarw (1813). Strongly influenced in design by Sèvres, they exhibit much charming flower-painting by Welsh and London decorators.

Vienna Porcelain. A manufacture established in 1719 by Claude du Paquier, a court official. It was Meissen's first rival and produced wares of great distinction. The early paste was noticeably cream-toned, and certain characteristic Baroque features (e.g. scrollwork handles and applied masks) persisted over a long period. The painted decoration likewise has a distinct flavour, typified by scrollwork (*Laub- und Bandelwerk*) in red, black and gold. Many pieces were painted by HAUSMALER.

During the period 1744–84 when the factory belonged to the Austrian State its wares show influence from Rococo and other Sèvres styles. J. J. Niedermayer modelled many lively figures. Under K. von Sorgenthal's astute ownership (1784–1805) the severe Neo-Classical taste was adapted to a sumptuous style with minute cameo painting and rich gilding. The factory went out of business in 1864. Mark: the barred shield of Austria, used from 1744.

Worcester Porcelain. This factory was founded in 1751 with Dr. John Wall, a local physician, as a leading partner. It used a formula containing soap-stone, previously developed at Bristol, and produced serviceable, crisply potted, and pleasantly decorated wares which mostly conformed to current fashions. Effective use was made of coloured grounds, and TRANSFER PRINTING was popular. Few figures were made.

87, 137, 183, 262, 308, 309, 323, 401, 446, 448, 449, 519, 657, 673, 724, 740, 756, 773, 879, 894.

PORRON. Spanish GLASS drinking-vessel with a single spout from which wine is poured into the mouth in a thin stream without contact with the lips.

PORTLAND VASE. The most famous example of Roman GLASS in the CAMEO technique. It is made of a dark blue glass cased with opaque white. The outer layer is cut away or ground down to leave the dark background showing through in a design representing the story of the sea-goddess Thetis, mother of Achilles. The vase dates from the reign of Augustus (27 B.C.–A.D. 14). About the middle of the 17th c. it was in the Barbarini Palace at Rome; in 1783 it was bought by the Duchess of Portland and was loaned by her son, the third Duke of Portland, to Josiah WEDGWOOD, who used it as a model for his JASPER WARE. It was deposited in the British Museum in 1810 and was there broken into some 200 pieces by an eccentric in 1845, being reassembled from a Wedgwood copy. It was purchased by the British Museum in 1945. See GREEK AND ROMAN ANTIQUITY (GLASS).

POSTAL COMMUNICATIONS, PICTORIAL. Printed designs dating from the 15th c. with a picture of the Christ child and a simple message of goodwill can be seen in some museums, but whether they are greetings cards in the usual meaning of the word is debatable. They were probably used only within religious circles. The earliest form of greetings card used in the way it is used today seems to have been the visiting-card bearing a written message. About the middle of the 18th c. visiting-cards, at first plain and the size of a playing-card, were later printed and engraved in decorative style often with classical designs; sometimes with ancient ruins and buildings. These were the smallest pictures one could buy. They were valued as souvenirs of a Continental visit, and were Continental in origin. In some respects they served the same purpose as a picture postcard today.

British examples of a later date sometimes show a stately home or castle. It was a custom in several European countries when making a call on New Year's Day to leave one's card with a written message conveying the compliments of the season. About the 1760s, mainly in Germany and Austria, New Year cards were available with a printed message often in verse and romantic in style. The cards still conformed more or less to the size of a playing-card and would sometimes have an elegantly embossed design, with an almost cameo-like effect. From these emanated the *Freundschaftskarten* (Friendship, or Lovers' cards), which resembled the valentine cards of the next century. In Germany and also in Denmark extremely beautiful *Freundschaftskarten* of ingenious design were made, but the most beautiful—delicately coloured and sometimes ornamented against a background of gauze—were those published in Vienna and Prague. They displayed a high standard of craftsmanship and were designed by artists of repute, one of the foremost being Johann Endletzbergen. By this time too, the 1820s, valentines were much in vogue; but only in Britain and the U.S.A., the custom having lapsed in other countries on religious grounds.

Valentine's day takes its name from a Roman bishop, Valentinus, martyred on 14 February, the eve of the *Lupercalia*, who became the patron saint of lovers. In Chaucer's time it was a day for the exchange of lovers' vows and gifts. In the 16th c. an element of licentiousness and bawdiness had crept into the observances but by the middle of the 17th c. the day was observed with many quaint courtship customs and the presentation of a gift to one's 'valentine' (synonymous with 'sweetheart') was a recognized thing. Along with many other British customs this was introduced to the American Colonies by the early settlers.

By the latter part of the 18th c. handmade valentines, sometimes exquisite in design, were commonly used in Britain and the United States. They were generally large in format, and by the 1790s were being printed or engraved on quarto letter sheets, often delicately coloured. Some of these early valentines were engraved by Francesco Bartolozzi (1727–1815), and those done in copperplate by James Kendrew of York *c.* 1820 are highly prized by collectors. During the early part of the 19th c. valentines were published in Britain on the best quality embossed paper and by the 1830s on fine lace paper, the pioneers of this sort of work being Joseph Addenbrooke of London and the firm of Dobbs, well known as manufacturers of high-class fancy stationery; they were followed by countless other firms specializing in this sort of work. In the United States, too, beautiful valentines were drawn by hand, designed in the traditional 'True Love Knot' style, sometimes with an intricate puzzle motif. Exceptional examples are those decorated in the FRAKTUR style current among the Pennsylvania German settlers but used exceptionally by the English-speaking communities. Printed valentines made especially for the American market were exported from England, for it was not until the late 1840s that manufacture on a large scale began in the United States.

Along with the romantic and sentimental valentines were many that were rude, vulgar and cruel. It was not uncommon to send a particularly unpleasant valentine anonymously by post to spite a person against whom one had a grudge. Prominent among artists who designed humorous and satirical valentines were the Cruikshank brothers, Arthur Crowquill, Lewis Marks and Luke Limner—the pen-name of John Leighton—whilst George Corbould was responsible for several charming valentines of a sentimental sort. By the end of the 19th c. a tendency towards vulgarity in some of the cheaper cards caused a decline in the popularity of the valentine. But with the great increase in the popularity of picture postcards in the following century valentines also came back into fashion particularly in the United States, where romantic and tastefully designed valentines were imported from Germany.

The advent of the Uniform Penny Post system on 10 January 1840 was responsible for changing the writing habits of the British people. For the first time envelopes were available to the public, for letters were now rated by weight instead of by sheet of paper and by distance as formerly. Valentines, which before had been costly to send, were now used as never before. The innovation of envelopes was responsible for a new type of valentine smaller in size and convenient for envelopes, which was now either decorated or embossed. Nevertheless the larger, quarto valentines continued to be popular until well into the 1860s and were published in every conceivable style. Some of them were veritable works of art. Ornamented with coloured scraps and bearing tender messages of affection, they were often lavishly decorated with swan's down, MOTHER OF PEARL, cambric flowers and many other frivolities; and they would have cunning devices whereby a message could be concealed. The period from 1840 to 1860 has been called the golden age of the valentine.

The use of pictorial and decorated writing-paper began in Europe, mainly in France and Italy. Some of the earliest examples were headed by little views, sometimes printed from the same plates as pictorial visiting-cards. Later the entire upper portion of a letter sheet would be embellished with a finely engraved view of a city or resort. Such writing-sheets served the same purpose as picture postcards today. By this time, throughout Europe, beautifully decorated letter sheets, with ornamental borders, sometimes in colour, were commonly used for special occasions—for invitations and exchange of courtesies, or at Christmas and New Year. The usage came into vogue in Britain *c.* the 1830s and was stimulated by the institution of cheap postage.

Pennsylvania German. A fine example in *Fraktur* style, hand-coloured. This delightful love letter, written within eight hearts, with a puzzle message in the centre, is dated 1769. (Free Lib. of Philadelphia)

Engraved in sepia by Bartolozzi. With the motif of the Endless Knot of Love (*c.* 1800)

Visiting card used as a New Year's greetings card. Engraved in green (mid 18th c.)

The first envelopes issued by the Post Office at the prepaid one-penny rate depicted Britannia in the act of bestowing the benefits of cheap postage upon the public. They were designed by William Mulready, R.A. (1786–1863). The public did not take kindly to these new pictorial envelopes and hurled abuse and ridicule upon the design. From its inception in May 1840 imitations were published which burlesqued Mulready's drawing, and the gates were opened to a flood of caricatures lampooning the Mulready envelopes. The first to appear was an extremely clever effort drawn by John Leech (1817–64). Another by Hablot Knight Browne (Phiz) (1815–82) appeared soon after, and a brilliant series of 10 designs, which were also available hand-coloured, were drawn by the young Richard Doyle, only 15 years old, assisted by his brother James. Included in this series was a Christmas envelope, the first printed design for Christmas

Two-page letter sheet, quarto size, dated 1 January 1861, from Mannheim, Germany, addressed to Boston, Mass. With lithograph view of the Paradeplatz

Left. New Year's card dated 1871. German. Hand-coloured in green, pink and yellow with gilded ornaments. The message, printed in *Fraktur* on red silk, reads (in translation): 'May the Lord Pluto, god of silver and gold, / do you well and fill up your coffers. / May the god of love do you well / and give you a sweet little wife. / Enjoy her to your heart's content and be at peace'

Below. Early example of English pictorial headed writing paper. Dated 1832. Quarto size. South view of Worthing taken at sea. Printed in colour

Valentine envelope printed in sepia. Postmarked February 1863. The scene has implications from the American Civil War

intended for postal use. From these caricatures followed a spate of pictorial envelopes printed for all manner of purposes—propaganda (political and general), religious and humorous. In some cases writing-paper was printed pictorially to match the envelopes. These papers and envelopes are now avidly collected and command very high prices.

Cheap postage was also instrumental in promoting a new fashion—the greetings card—in Britain. In 1843, Henry Cole under the name of Felix Summerly published the first Christmas card, drawn by John C. Horsley, R.A. It was the size of a modern postcard and hand-coloured, showing a middle-class Victorian family sitting down to a Christmas dinner. Only 1,000 were issued and today fewer than 20 are known to exist. Another early effort was by W. M. Egley, probably in 1848; and although a few other early examples of Christmas cards have been seen, it was not until the early 1860s that Christmas and New Year cards were published in large numbers to satisfy a prodigiously growing demand. Thanks to the development of cheap colour printing these early cards were printed in colour and conformed to the usual size of a visiting-card. For the most part they were prettily designed, and were frequently embossed with an ornamental border. They were manufactured in much the same style as the smaller valentines, differing only in the text. Some of these early cards were printed in colour by the process invented by William Baxter. The demand for all manner of greetings cards, especially Christmas cards and valentines, brought about keen competition among the many publishing houses concerned. Firms such as Kershaw, Meek, Windsor and Mansell, to mention only a few, excelled in the quality and craftsmanship of the fancy paper they produced with an exquisite lacy

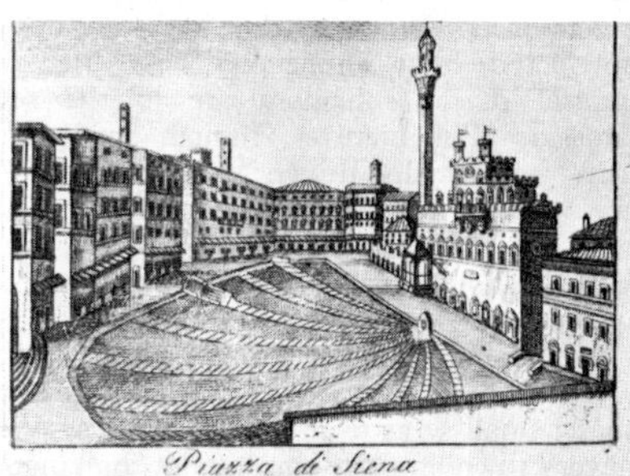

Pictorial writing cards showing views of Siena. Printed as heading to quarto writing paper. Postmarked from Siena in 1835

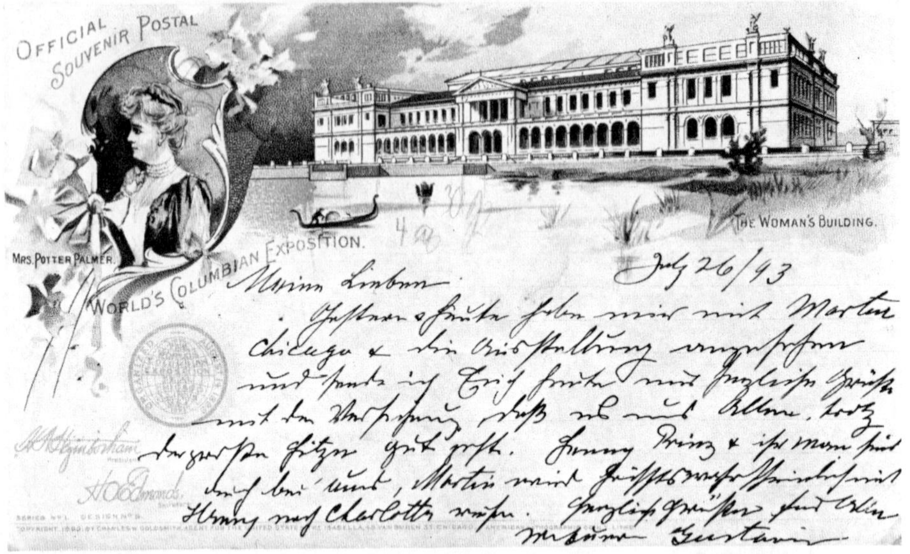

The first official picture postcards in the U.S.A., called 'postals', were issued by the Post Office in 1893 for the World's Columbian Exhibition at Chicago

effect and fine embossing. In the United States, too, similar tastes prevailed and greetings cards of every description were imported from Britain in large quantities.

It was in 1848 that a young lady named Esther Howland of Worcester, Massachusetts, tried her hand at making valentines. She assembled coloured scraps from Germany on to fancy paper imported from England and created a number of pretty valentines which she was able to market. The success of this venture resulted in her establishing herself in a business which came to be known as The New England Valentine Co. Employing young ladies in the work, she quickly made a name for herself as the leading manufacturer of high-class valentines and fancy stationery in the United States. Her initiative was soon copied by others, who eventually became successful in this field, and in this way the valentines industry was established in America. Pictorial writing-paper was popular in the United States as well as in Canada. This was published in quarto sets featuring every city and town of importance, and was often in colour. Foremost in this work was the publishing house of Charles Magnus of New York, which also published several sets of well designed envelopes with views of various towns and places of interest, many of them in colour. Propaganda and advertising on envelopes was widely used in the U.S.A., particularly propaganda for postal reform and for cheap ocean postage. The main advocate for this was an American philanthropist named Elihu Burritt. A series of events brought him to England, where he became actively occupied in philanthropic movements such as Universal Peace and Brotherhood, and Temperance. He undertook a vigorous campaign for an Ocean Penny Postage, for which he campaigned on both sides of the Atlantic, with his headquarters in London. He was responsible for numerous pictorial envelopes issued as propaganda in this and other causes. His pioneer work for cheap ocean postage, which he began in 1849, led the way to the formation of the Universal Postal Union in 1875. The American Civil War also resulted in the publication of pictorial envelopes with patriotic motifs in many cities of the United States both northern and southern. Many were sentimental, some were comic, some political, but the majority were patriotic, glamorizing generals and regiments and the bravery of the soldier. In many cases pictorial notepaper matched the envelopes. The Western Express companies too issued pictorial envelopes which today give nostalgic memories of the Wild West, depicting the romantic Pony Express riders and Wells Fargo stage-coaches, gold-mining and 'ghost towns'—features of a scene which no longer exists. From all this it can readily be appreciated how important these pieces of pictorial postal ephemera are to the social historian. The pictures, though small, show places not usually drawn; advertisements on envelopes are often of articles long since forgotten—farm machinery, clothing, appliances and household articles of a kind not generally remembered.

In Britain, too, pictorial notepaper was much in vogue, but after the 1850s the format was usually small so as to fit into envelopes. Views of every town and city throughout the kingdom were depicted on notepaper, showing a different aspect from the usual prints and engravings.

Numerous sets of comic notepaper came out, the comic seaside series in particular giving a revealing idea of English humour of those days. More serious were papers with a patriotic theme, showing the battlefields of the Crimea and typical soldiers and sailors. Pictorial notepaper served the same purpose as did picture postcards some 50 years later.

Postcards of a sort, handmade and bearing normal one-penny postage, had been in occasional use by private persons throughout the century. Lipman's Postal Card was registered in Philadelphia in 1861 and during the 1860s many business houses abroad, in Germany particularly, used cards with a printed message and sent them through the post. The idea of a simple 'open' card for a short communication and prepaid for postage had been suggested by Dr. Heinrich von Stephan at a meeting of German postal officials in 1865, but the plan was not taken up. The idea was again proposed a few years later in Vienna by Dr. Emanuel Herrmann, and was adopted by the Austrian Post Office. On 1 October 1869 the world's first postcard appeared, on sale at all Post Offices throughout the Austrian Empire. It was prepaid at a low rate of postage, and sufficient space allowed for a short message. Great Britain and Switzerland introduced postcards exactly one year later, and other countries followed. The creation of the postcard marked a new era in writing; messages were written in abbreviated style and were kept short.

At the time of the Franco-Prussian war a few pictorial postcards were printed, patriotically by the French and humorously by the Germans. Early in the 1870s Germany led the world by printing postcards with little views along the top, following the style of pictorial notepaper. Germany quickly became supreme in the publishing of picture postcards, which at first were printed in one colour. By the 1880s a two-colour process was tried and during the 1890s multicolour was used, commonly in chromolithography. Within an elaborate ornamental frame or entwined between clusters of flowers would be three or four little views with the words '*Gruss aus—*' ('Greetings from') followed by the name of the place or resort, but with space left for a short message to be written. The process of chromolithography was largely used for the printing of all manner of greetings cards, the 'golden era' being the 1870s and 1880s when firms such as Marcus Ward, De La Rue, Hildesheimer and Raphael Tuck became interested in the Christmas card market. Well known artists were employed such as H. Stacy Marks, R.A., Georgina Bowers, W. S. Coleman, Marcus Stone, R.A., Walter CRANE, and a host of others, including Kate Greenaway. Many of the charming illustrations made by Kate Greenaway in her children's books were reproduced as greetings cards, which today are popular among collectors.

In the United States during this period Louis Prang, an immigrant from Germany in 1850, started the production of Christmas cards near Boston, Massachusetts, and has come to be known as the father of the American Christmas card. Prang perfected a process of lithographic colour printing and had a high reputation for the quality of his work. Employing well known artists such as Rosina Emmett, Alexander Sandier, Elihu Vedder, Dora Wheeler, L. B. Humphrey, W. St. John Harper and Will H. Low, to mention only a few, he published many beautiful valentines and Christmas cards during the 1870s and 1880s. Picture postcards were not generally available in America until 1893, when on the occasion of the Chicago World's Fair the postal laws were eased and government-printed cards with coloured views of the exhibition were on sale along with those published privately. They were known as 'Postals' whereas the privately printed cards were called 'Private Mailing Cards', a distinction which has remained in force.

In Britain too because of Post Office restrictions picture postcards were not published commercially until 1894. They were small at first, having to conform to the size of the Post Office cards; but by the turn of the century they were allowed to be larger. By 1900 numerous firms were engaged in what had become a lucrative business of picture-postcard publishing; many, such as Valentine's of Dundee, were old-established. A newcomer was the firm of Raphael Tuck, who became the foremost publisher of postcards in the United Kingdom and by colour lithography produced the finest cards. Although designed in England, their early cards were mainly printed in Germany, which excelled in high-class colour printing and held the world's market in the publishing of postcards. The new century saw the biggest international collecting mania ever known for postcards, which were now available the world over, depicting every conceivable subject. By present standards many of these early cards are miniature works of art. Apart from the usual editions with views and 'Greetings from', cards were designed by artists who later became well known. Alphonse Mucha, famous in Paris for his poster work, designed many series of postcards in ART-NOUVEAU style, and some of his best work appeared as publicity on postcards for well known brands of champagne. Raphael Kirchner, who came to Paris from Vienna, gained a reputation for his delightful softly coloured studies of lightly clothed, simpering young ladies. The technique and craftsmanship of the Germans was ably copied in other countries, notably Switzerland, Austria and Italy. In Vienna the firm of M. Munk published numerous editions of artistic cards in *art-nouveau* style, as well as cards which admirably captured the spirit of Vienna. From Paris came several series of postcards delicately tinted as though hand-coloured, showing seductive ladies wearing large and beautiful hats and in all manner of alluring attitudes; some of the best known artists of these were G. Mouton, Vindier and Xavier Sager.

In Britain Harry Payne, commissioned by Raphael Tuck, was outstanding for his military and naval studies, whilst Tom Browne, the *Punch* artist, excelled with his comic postcards. Contrary to a belief held by some, Kate Greenaway was never commissioned to design picture postcards although reproductions of her work were made in Germany after her death. Most British artists were humorous—Lance Thackeray, John Hassall, Phil May, Hilda Cowham, A. Ludovici, Louis Wain, famous for his cats, and G. E. Studdy, famous for his comic dog, Bonzo. More recent was Donald McGill who made his name with his often vulgar but always funny comic cards.

With the relaxation of the postal laws in 1898 the publishing of picture postcards became general all over the United States and their popularity increased. A great many artists made their names as illustrators and others, already established, became better known by postcard reproductions of their art.

Charles Russell was famous for his Wild West subjects, as was Frederic Remington. Beautiful flower studies were done by Paul De Longpre and by Catherine Klein, whose cards are now cherished by collectors. Charles Dana Gibson immortalized a type of American girl as the 'Gibson girl'. Well known for their pretty ladies were also Philip Boileau and Harrison Fisher. Popular for studies of children were Frances Brundage and Ellen Clapsaddle, and Dr. Bernhardt Wall for his sun-bonnet children. There were many others besides whose cards are keenly sought after today.

In the England of King Edward VII the expression 'drop me a postcard' meant much the same as today when one says 'give me a ring', for postal collections and deliveries were made several times daily and a postcard mailed in the morning could be delivered by the afternoon. The postcard catered for all tastes. It depicted views and places of interest, historical and social events; it was important for propaganda, especially political propaganda, and it was used for advertising; it glamorized Royalty and the stage, and its humour was for everyone. There were novelties too of every description: cards that changed picture when held to the light, revolving discs showing a range of pictures, cards that squeaked when pressed or opened out and changed shape when a tag was pulled; cards made of leather, of tin, of peat; cards decorated with feathers, with hair, and with every kind of material. It can thus readily be understood how important is the postcard as a social document, for it records aspects of the times more vividly than any history book.

113, 377, 406, 510, 786, 787, 788.

POTTER'S WHEEL. A mechanical device which facilitates the fashioning of pottery vessels from clay. It was the pioneer among machines which turn out consumer goods by the application of rotary motion, and it is thought that whereas previously the making of pottery was a household task performed by the women of each family—as it still is in parts of Africa—with the introduction of the wheel and more efficient kilns it became a specialized craft. The wheel probably came into use *c.* the end of the 4th millennium B.C. From the marks on broken potsherds found in ancient dumps (called 'kitchen middens' among archaeologists) it is often possible to tell whether the vessels were moulded by hand or turned on a wheel. From this sort of evidence there is good reason to believe that the wheel was known in Mesopotamia by *c.* 3500 B.C. The earliest wheels were of wood and have not survived, but a clay wheel with a bitumen-lined pivot hole discovered at Ur is dated *c.* 3000 B.C. During the following millennium the use of the wheel spread and it seems to have been known in Egypt in the 2nd Dynasty *c.* 2750 B.C. Matched stone wheels and pivots similar to those depicted in an Egyptian mural from *c.* 1900 B.C. have been found in Palestine at Jericho, Megiddo and elsewhere and on the Syrian coast near Hama. During the same millennium much of the Nal river ware in western India was wheel-turned. Wheel-made pottery was discovered at the site of Troy from as early as *c.* 2500 B.C. and the technique seems to have reached Crete and China *c.* the end of the millennium. The earliest mention of the potter's wheel in literature is in Homer, *Iliad* xviii. 599–601. According to V. Gordon Child in *A History of Technology* (1954) the use of the potter's wheel spread to the mainland of Greece *c.* 1800 B.C., and to southern Italy *c.* 750 B.C., to the Danube–Rhine basins *c.* 400 B.C. and to southern England *c.* 50 B.C. It was not known in America before the Conquest.

The advantages of the wheel are that it frees both hands of the potter for shaping a vessel from clay, which spins round on a rotating disc, and that the rotary motion reduces the amount of muscular force necessary for moulding the clay with the hands. By the use of the wheel pots of regular shape could be produced many times more rapidly than by the older techniques of free-hand modelling or strip coiling. Furthermore the circular movement facilitates and indeed encourages the formation of symmetrical shapes about a vertical axis and symmetrical patterns of decoration.

The simplest form of potter's wheel was a disc of wood, stone or terracotta, perhaps about 60 cm in diameter, which revolved horizontally on a pivot or some sort of cup and spike bearing. It is important that the motion of the wheel shall be regular, without wobble or vibration, and that it shall spin for as long as possible at a reasonably steady or controlled speed. It has therefore been usual for wheels to be heavy and various systems of double bearings fixed to an axle have been devised. Again, the potter needs to get well above his clay and to have both hands free to work it. Therefore a helper was often employed to turn the wheel and keep it in motion, sometimes by hand and sometimes by means of a pole which fitted into a notch cut in the wheel. Sometimes the wheel was mounted in a shallow pit so that the potter could keep it in motion with his feet. As this made the clay rather low, such wheels often had a raised 'throwing' centre. ('Throwing' is the technical term for fashioning a clay object on a rotating wheel.) A more sophisticated type of wheel, used in Europe from the 16th c. onwards, had a double bearing supporting a vertical spindle to which was fixed a fly-wheel with a throwing head on top, while everything was mounted in a wooden frame with a bench or saddle for the potter to sit on. The potter operated the wheel by kicking the fly-wheel. This was the principle of the standard European kick-wheel in the 19th c. and it has become normal art-school equipment made of metal and with a stirrup crank so that a kick-bar is used instead of kicking the fly-wheel. The basic principle of the potter's wheel has continued unchanged from earliest antiquity and the only substantial modern advances are the use of an electric motor to turn the wheel and gearing systems to regulate speed. A more sophisticated form of electrical wheel using a D.C. motor with transformers makes possible electrical speed control as with D.C. current it is possible to reduce the current without drastically reducing the torque.

POTTERY TECHNIQUES. The making of pottery appears to have begun in response to the challenge of Neolithic living conditions. The fact that pre-farming communities in Denmark made excellent pottery whilst city dwellers in Jericho did not may be no more than an anomaly that tends to prove the rule. Clay had been used before more sedentary ways of life evolved; cave-dwellers modelled animals with it and baked them with fire. But the need, brought about by the demands of the earliest farming settlements, to contain and store food and liquid must have been the spur to the introduction of this, one of man's earliest technologies. Vessels were made of wood, stone and soft minerals such as steatite before and alongside early pottery; but clay has properties that make it both easier to manage and as aesthetically pleasing to use as those other more intractable materials.

1. CLAY. Clay is the product of the decomposition of the mineral felspar, and is the result of the continuous change taking place in the earth's crust. Felspar is the most abundant mineral found in crystalline rocks and early in the process of rock formation, as the molten magma begins to cool, most of the minerals, including the felspar, crystallize out. The felspar is first attacked by the hot residual gaseous constituents of the magma and later by hot aqueous solutions, which causes a major physical and chemical change resulting in the formation of the clay minerals. Although certain clays are thought to have been formed in this way, notably the china clay deposits in Cornwall, other clays have come into being by a milder and more gradual decomposition caused by carbonic acid and water percolating into the body of the rock, particularly when it was covered by marsh and swamps. The manner in which the parent material has been decomposed will result in clays of different characteristics. Clay is seldom pure; in addition to the clay mineral a number of accessory minerals such as QUARTZ, mica and iron oxide are present. The clay mineral is a plate-like substance that gives clay its recognizable physical qualities such as plasticity, shrinkage and air hardening. Kaolinite is the clay mineral present in all the potter's most useful clays and has the theoretical composition of 46·3% silica, 39·8% alumina and 13·9% water.

Clay which is still on or near the place where it was originally formed is called 'residual' or 'primary' clay. China clay is a very pure residual clay. If the clay is carried from its original source by streams, glaciers, etc., it is called 'sedimentary' or 'secondary' clay. Ball clays, fire clays and brick clays are of this type. Because of transportation the grain size of these clays tends to be much smaller and they also contain a greater number of impurities, a factor which makes for great variation in both their working and their fired properties. For example red firing clays contain a high percentage of iron oxide, which results in a low firing range but has the advantage of giving a fairly hard body at low temperature.

Early man, like primitive peoples today, used the ready-to-hand secondary clays contaminated with iron and other impurities. When clay is heated to approximately 600 °C. or more this iron content will give a colour range of warm pink through to red-brown to black, depending on the amount of iron, heat and air present at the time of firing. This clay would probably have been dug out from river banks or from pockets just beneath the top soil by the earliest cultivator-potters. The process of 'improving' the natural clay might have started by removing the large particles of grit, twigs and other impurities by hand; but as the shards found in the very earliest sites show, relatively soon more sophisticated methods were used to produce a clay body suitable to the needs of building forms by hand.

(i) *Clay preparation.* For example slip, a mixture of clay and water, can be passed through sieves of varying mesh to separate out the coarse, uneven and unwanted foreign matter usually present in freshly dug clay. Some refractory material of even grain, however, is desirable as a tempering agent, helping the clay to retain its shape whilst drying and firing. To this end potters have made use at various times of crushed rock and shells, sands and mica, and it is common practice to use the fired clay itself ground down to form potters' 'grog'. With one or other of these additions the clay is beaten and kneaded into a homogeneous mass ready for working.

Advances in technique must have been made

Building the pot body by the coil strip method

slowly over a long process of trial and error with many failures along the way. Indeed there is evidence in early Cyprus of abandoned attempts even to fire pottery successfully. When clay is well 'tempered' with some coarser material, however, and allowed to dry off to a malleable, not too sticky state, it is extremely well behaved as a shape-forming medium. Add to this its ability to retain that shape through fire and to emerge as a hard relatively permanent substance, and it can be seen why its use is so extensive. It is, moreover, distributed in its various forms widely over the world's surface. See also CLAY.

How the first pots were made can never be known, but certain well tried non-wheel forming methods must have been used.

(ii) *Methods of Shaping without the Wheel.* Preformed shapes such as baskets, stones or fired-clay forms themselves can be used to support the wet clay as it dries out so that it retains the contours of the inside or outside of the mould. The clay can be manipulated in small pieces or flat even sheets, then squeezed, pressed or beaten into shape. A ball of clay held in the hand can be pinched into a hollow form, whilst much larger pieces can be pulled and stroked upwards by the potter, either turning the work in a slow rotating action or moving round the pot himself. Rope-like coils of clay can be built up ring

POTTERY TECHNIQUES IN NIGERIA

Cleaning and smoothing the inside with a leaf

Pattern decorating the outside with a comb

upon ring to make shapes held upright by a judicious use of beaters to compress the surface; in larger work more coils are added only when the previous ones are firm enough to support the new work. Very high standards, both technical and artistic, can be achieved by such methods as these as is proved by Pre-Conquest American pottery, all of which was made without the use of the wheel.

For the technique of the wheel see POTTER'S WHEEL.

(iii) *Decoration.* Even from the earliest times man's innate desire to decorate showed in and on the forms he produced in clay; alongside the functional interest the decorative is found from the beginning. Although virtually all prehistoric pottery is porous, because it was unglazed and relatively low fired, some decorative methods seem to have evolved deliberately to circumvent this disadvantage.

If clay is compressed by being worked over with a hard tool perhaps of bone, wood, stone or metal, the surface becomes denser and much smoother, the coarser grains of the clay body having been driven deeper into the fabric of the work. This burnishing is both a decorative and a functional process. The contrasting smooth and rough textures are aesthetically pleasing whilst rendering the pot less porous than untreated ware. Decoration can take place at many stages of the pot's formation prior to BISCUIT. As it is being built it may receive a surface texture from incisions, which may be either left or inlaid with other clays or SLIPS, later to be pared away to reveal the line or area of the original marks. Coils, rolls or balls of clay can be added to the still soft pot. Probably the most common method of decoration is the use of slip which can be painted on or the vessel can be dipped in it or again the slip can be trailed as from a spouted vessel. Sometimes the slip coating is cut away to reveal the body underneath, which is the so-called *sgraffiato* (scratching or incising) method.

Slip was in fact the main decorative medium from Neolithic times up to the early 18th c. in Europe, in Pre-Columbian America and in many other areas. Such peasant traditions as remain today still employ it in one form or another.

(iv) *The Effects of Heat on Clay.* When clay has been fashioned and allowed to dry it can be subjected to heat. If the clay is the right type and the rise in temperature at the correct rate, then very great heat such as 1400 °C.–1500 °C., or more in some cases, can be applied without distortion or collapse of the clay form. Early man seems generally to have fired within the range of 800 °C.–1000 °C. though softer and harder baked shards have been found. Subjecting clay to heat brings about major physical and chemical changes. Before it is fired clay is sensitive to the action of water and can be moulded into shape, but once it is heated in excess of 500 °C.–600 °C. an irreversible change takes place and the clay cannot be reconstituted and used again. If the heating is continued, the clay will begin to fuse and viscous liquid will be formed from the free silica combining with the various impurities such as sodium, potassium and calcium oxides; this liquid begins to fill up the pore spaces in the clay, causing a decrease in volume with resulting shrinkage. Clay, if subjected to enough heat, will eventually melt and form a GLASS. The particular point in temperature at which this happens will depend on the type of clay. Some common red clays melt at *c.* 1250 °C. and can become the basis of a stoneware GLAZE. PORCELAIN represents a clay body at the transition point where the melt must be sufficient to give translucency but not so great as to cause the body to collapse. The viscosity of the fused glassy liquid is a great help in achieving the balance.

The first kilns make their appearance in the archaeological records towards the end of the 6th millennium B.C. Successful firing probably started much earlier, however, because an enclosed chamber is not really an essential requirement for taking clay through the firing cycle.

(v) *Bonfire Firing.* Primitive potters of central Africa and America still fire pots without a kiln, either singly or in quite large numbers, the fuel being whatever comes to hand—wood, grasses or even dung. The fuel and the pots must be quite dry. Sometimes the pots are pre-heated to ensure this. The pots are then carefully heaped on a bed of fuel with more fuel between them. The whole heap is covered with still more fuel, usually dry grass, and it is then set alight. Such firings may take as little as one to three hours according to the number of pots. The temperature achieved is probably 650 °C.–750 °C., sufficient to produce soft porous pottery.

The colour of the fired pots may be controlled by the method of firing and cooling. If the pots are allowed to cool in the air, being removed from the firing with sticks while still glowing hot, they will be the familiar buff or red terracotta colour, the iron impurity in the clay having become oxidized to the ferric (red) state. If on the contrary they are cooled while shut off from the air by being covered with ash, the iron will be reduced to the ferrous (black) form and some impregnation of the body with carbon is likely to take place. The pots will then be a rich black, and incidentally rather less porous. Such pottery has two great virtues in the context in which it is made and used: it is extremely resistant to thermal shock and can thus be placed straight on to an open fire; and its porosity when used for water storage causes slow evaporation through the pot walls, which has the effect of cooling the water. Temporary kilns such as these developed into the more sophisticated up-draught kilns as used in Roman Britain. These were semi-permanent structures in which a combustion chamber was constructed, the pots being placed on a grid above this out of contact with the fuel, while a dome of clay with an outlet for the smoke was built over all.

Pre-agricultural potters made use of all the basic techniques. The only two major discoveries not used by them were in fact those of glazing and the potter's wheel. These were introduced into the first civilizations at *c.* 4500 B.C. and 3500 B.C. respectively.

2. GLAZE. As it was first used, glaze seems not to have been so much applied to pots as part of their fabric. This is the so-called Egyptian faience or paste, used initially in Mesopotamia.

(i) *Egyptian paste.* This seems to have arisen from the observation that the sandstone rocks and saline muds grew a frost of soda crystals when dried. When heated the crystals turned into a glassy coating. Further to this an addition of a copper compound (probably MALACHITE, then used as a cosmetic) caused the glass to become a rich turquoise blue. Clay material and iron oxide tended to destroy this blue, turning it green, so the pastes were composed largely of iron-free sands. Such a paste is friable and difficult to form and was usually fashioned into tiles and jewellery by means of terracotta moulds. The inconvenience of the soda flux being soluble in water was later overcome by the invention of 'fritting', the beginning of true glass technology. In this process dry mixtures of glass ingredients —soda, lime and sand or quartz—were heated in a pan until molten. For glazing purposes this 'frit' would be cooled, ground into powder and applied to the ware with water. A proportion might also be added to the paste itself to render it more vitreous and durable.

By Assyrian times lead was being used as a flux and the two major European glaze-forming methods were known, although they were not used consistently throughout the ensuing centuries. Speaking generally it can be said that glazes are vitreous coatings fused on to the clay surface and although they are very similar to glass in their physical characteristics and chemical composition, they must be able to become fluid without running off the surface of the pot when fired to a given temperature.

(ii) *Glaze Composition.* The ability to form glass when subjected to heat is possessed by a small number of inorganic oxides, the most important being silica and borax. As the melting-point of silica is too high for normal pottery temperatures, other oxides have to be introduced to reduce the firing range and these in turn affect the quality and character of the glaze. These substances are sometimes referred to as basic oxides or 'fluxes'. The most common basic oxides used in the formation of glazes are soda, potash, lime and lead, but the use of lead is limited to the lower, EARTHENWARE temperatures. A further modification to glaze is provided by alumina, which acts as a stabilizer and prevents too much flow.

Metals, usually in oxide form, are the source of colour in glazes. Glaze composition and firing conditions can affect the colour drastically. Copper if added in small quantities will give a grass-green in a high lead glaze, turquoise in a high soda glaze and red if fired in a smoky, 'reduced' kiln. Iron gives colours ranging from yellow or brown to the soft grey-green or grey-blue of Chinese CELADONS and at the lower ENAMEL temperatures a bright red. Manganese gives brown to purple, while COBALT remains a remarkably stable blue. Tin oxide is responsible for the whiteness of delft and maiolica glazes.

Although glazing began at an early date, glazed pottery must have remained numerically much the smaller group compared with unglazed, burnished or slip-decorated pottery. Indeed the functional advantages of glazing seem not to have been appreciated until later Roman times, and a few hundred years before then the apogee of unglazed, wheel-made slip-painted pottery had been reached in the Attic red- and black-figure wares of the 5th c. B.C. See GREEK AND ROMAN ANTIQUITY (GREEK POTTERY).

3. THE GREEK METHOD. The classical Greek method of figure painting was based upon the use and intimate control of the fine iron-bearing clay common around the Mediterranean together with a few simple materials. First the clay for decoration was finely levigated, that is mixed with water and stirred; after the coarser particles had settled the finer ones were drawn off for use. This process could be repeated more than once until only the finest grained clay remained for use. To this was added a peptising potash, probably in the form of wood ash, to break down the aggregates of clay particles, and also a colloid, possibly sour wine or urine, to prevent the smaller particles released by the peptiser from coagulating again. This mixture formed the wash that covered the entire pot and then in a thicker state it was used to paint the central figures in the black-figure ware, or the background in the red-figure pieces. The rest was now in the hands of the kiln firer. The pots were first fired to *c.* 800 °C.–1000 °C. fully oxidized, a process which made the whole surface bright red in varying tones. Then a reducing flame was obtained, perhaps by wet wood, and the iron present throughout pot and decoration turned black, the ferric oxide changing to black ferrous oxide. Then the pots were subjected to a vigorous oxidizing atmosphere so that once again the oxygen penetrated the decoration, turning the areas of weaker mixture red but leaving the heavier painting unaffected. Observing the precise moment when black and red stood alongside each other, the potter would cut the firing and seal off the kiln.

4. ROMAN MOULDS. The Roman world, catering for more mass demand, standardized production by the introduction of throwing in moulds on the potter's wheel. The decoration on the inside surface of the mould was INTAGLIO, much use being made of the silversmiths' craft to divide the pot into horizontal lines with stamps to frame the impressed draped figures placed

around the ware. When this mould made of fired clay was centred on the potter's wheel, the clay could be pushed into the shallow decoration to be covered by the thrown clay lining. The rims were thrown in the normal way above the edge of the mould. As the pot dried it would shrink away from the biscuited clay mould and could be removed to have an added foot thrown on at this later stage, and whilst the clay was still in a 'leather' condition.

On the periphery of this world the Parthians were developing throwable quartz frit, whilst Byzantium and the Levant extended the use of lead-glazed ware. Both these types were to be further developed in the next great pottery era, that occasioned by the Islamic invasion. Henceforth the wares of the Far East and the techniques by which they were produced were to play an ever increasing role in the development of Middle Eastern and thence European pottery.

5. FAR EAST. Pottery making in the Far East went through tribulations similar to those it had undergone in the West in its earlier phases. The brilliant Neolithic age, from which the painted pottery of Kansu has rarely been rivalled, was followed by an equally brilliant Bronze Age. Soft unglazed, burnished and decorated pots were made and by Han times lead glazes were common. But even in the Shang Dynasty the Chinese potters had begun to show their genius for controlling high temperatures to produce hard, impervious wares. Indeed one has to be consciously reminded that in dealing with the main contribution coming from the Far Eastern potters, which was undoubtedly in this realm of the high fire, at no time did the other, the earthenware, tradition die out. Concurrently with the simple peasant unglazed and later lead-glazed ware—which reached great heights of aesthetic achievement during the T'ang period—was the mounting experience with high-fired stoneware culminating, again in the T'ang era, in the production of the first porcelain. See CHINA (CERAMICS).

Until Far Eastern products were known the West, with the one notable exception of German salt-glazed stoneware, produced earthenwares. It is not, however, only on technical considerations that the difference between East and West is based, and to illustrate this difference we may take the extreme example of Japanese pottery as a guide—an Attic amphora and a Bizen water jar must represent the polarities of the ceramic art. Japanese pottery itself divides into two distinct types: one symmetrical, refined, even miniature in feeling and execution; the other rough-hewn, asymmetrical and peasant in origin. It is this latter group, associated with Zen Buddhism, that seems to epitomize the furthest extreme of Far Eastern Art. It has its own methods of making and firing and much of its products are used in the tea ceremony, that catalyst of Japanese art in a period of intense nationalism. See JAPAN, CERAMICS.

Japanese BIZEN and RAKU have enjoyed a revival which has left its mark on the techniques of American and British artist potters.

When China and the main Asiatic continent emerged from Muslim (Yüan) domination the ceramics began to show a new feeling derived from the Islamic world. Porcelain was brought to new heights of refinement and enamel decoration was added to the repertory of decorative techniques.

6. ENAMELS. Enamel colours are applied on top of the glaze. They are made by mixing coloured oxides of metals such as iron (red) or copper (green) with frits of low softening temperature. The frits are ground glasses consisting of lead-borosilicates and potash or soda.

Today the powdered colours are mixed with oils and turpentine and either painted on to the ware with a brush or applied by TRANSFER-PRINTING processes such as engraving, lithography, silk-screen or ground-laying. The ware is then fired to between 600 °C. and 900 °C. First the oils are driven off, then the frits soften and envelop the metal oxide pigments and weld them firmly on to the glaze surface. This technique was common to both East and West during later Islamic times.

As soon as the Islamic world came into contact with the Far East during T'ang times cross-fertilization between the two civilizations went on apace. The trade in artefacts, the exchanges of ideas and eventually the exigencies of war were the main channels of contact. The role of the nomadic tribes of central Asia must not be overlooked in this process. By far the most important outcome for pottery was the introduction of fine hard white translucent porcelain to the West. Once seen this porcelain was to start a quest, first Islamic and later European, to wrest the secrets of its manufacture. (See PORCELAIN, EUROPEAN.) Islamic pottery generally can be seen as a struggle to lighten the body and to whiten the glaze in order to approximate to the valued Chinese product. Their materials and processes would never have allowed them to achieve their goal; but as in Europe, great advances were made in the course of the struggle.

7. ISLAMIC TECHNIQUES. Islamic potters followed up the Roman and Byzantine traditions of lead-glazed earthenware and took up the challenge to achieve the hardness and whiteness of Chinese stonewares and porcelain. The materials available to them were really unable to lead to high temperature wares, but instead they started many new kinds of fine earthenware and a tradition of pottery whose *raison d'être* lay as much in decoration and inscriptions as in the forms and functions of the pots.

The polychrome slipwares of Samarkand and Khurasan range from tribal pottery with animal and plant decoration and abstract ornament to wares inscribed with texts and aphorisms which remain amongst the most perfect SLIPWARES ever made. Beginning with directly applied slips and clear glazes, the technique came later to include incised and relief wares with many kinds of coloured glazes over the slips. About the 11th c. there developed in Syria earthenwares coated in a white over-all slip decorated with underglaze painting in cobalt blue, manganese and iron brown, black and copper green, a technique which soon spread to Egypt and was later used in the Sultanabad region of Persia. This was the technique which was used with variations under the Ottoman Turks in the pottery and tiles of Iznik, Damascus and Kütahya, with colours greatly enriched by the famous Armenian bole reds. Carved, moulded and pierced wares, often closely indebted to Oriental originals, were made in north-west Persia from the 11th c. onwards of white or buff clays covered with blue, turquoise, green, brown and opaque white lead and alkaline glazes.

Earthenware with opaque white tin glaze appears to have been developed around Baghdad by A.D. 800. Though it may have started as an attempt to imitate porcelain, it soon went its own way and was early painted with striking emblems in blue, brown and green, spread to Egypt and reached Morocco and Andalucia by *c.* A.D. 950. Painted iridescent lustres were being produced in Baghdad and Cairo from the 9th to the 10th centuries. The technique involved the reduction of silver and copper pigments on an already fused glaze, and was adapted from earlier glass techniques. The earliest wares were usually polychrome lustre with three or four different colours, but after *c.* A.D. 1000 single-colour lustres prevailed. Lustre technique was revived in Persia in the late 16th c. Applied to alkaline glazes over a hard white clay body, it led to intensely rich ruby and flame colours, very different from the early polychrome palette.

Under the Seljuks, Rayy and Kashan in north-west Persia became centres of an area producing finely potted and painted lustreware, usually on tin glaze, with the backs or insides of vessels glazed in clear deep blue. Elaborate pieces were painted with legends, scenes and inscriptions, and probably reflect collaboration between potters and scribes or manuscript painters. From *c.* A.D. 1200 this area produced large moulded and painted tiles, usually in lustre and blue, for mosques and palaces. The earliest enamel wares, known as *minai*, probably also began there in the late 12th c. Like lustre these were also painted on the already fired glaze. They have an affinity with book illumination, and were quite often gilded with gold leaf.

Islamic wares have mostly been fired in the temperature range 950 °C.–1050 °C. Compared with the high-temperature wares of the Far East the clay body was inevitably fragile and the glazes were liable to crazing, especially when alkaline fluxes were used. These difficulties were ingeniously overcome by the development of siliceous frit-pastes, which have been used from *c.* A.D. 1100 to the present day, especially for luxury pottery with decoration. The technical treatise of Abu'l Qasim of Kashan A.D. 1301 which describes the preparation of glazes, clays and pigments, gives the following frit-paste recipe: 10 parts powdered quartz; 1 part glass frit; 1 part white plastic clay. Various bodies of this type, white and dark-coloured, have been current in the Middle East for centuries. Some are translucent and are a simple form of soft-paste porcelain such as was developed in Europe centuries later, like so many other Islamic pottery methods. As a final example may be mentioned the use of tile murals and architectural ceramics current in Islam from the first centuries, as indeed was the whole concept of ceramics as potentially a noble art, a concept which had more far-reaching consequences in Europe than any single technique. See CERAMICS (ISLAMIC).

Through conquest and trade the Islamic potters introduced their wares into a Europe emerging from the Middle Ages. A lead-glazed, slip-decorated tradition with a Roman and north-European sense of form mingled with Middle Eastern tin-glazed oxide-painted styles. The older European tradition was to produce the English lead-glazed jugs and pitchers of the 12th and 13th centuries and evolve in Germany into the first salt-glaze stoneware of the Rhineland.

8. GLAZING. Glazing seems to have come about as a natural consequence of applying heat to clay, observing the tendency for glass to form on pottery surfaces under certain conditions, deducing the cause and then deliberately bringing about the effect more intensely and in a controlled way. Historically speaking glazing is conveniently divided into three kinds:

(*a*) *Evaporation Glazing*. The soluble alkalis are introduced into the body itself before shaping and migrate to the surface during the process of drying. There, under heat, they combine with silica in the body to form glassy alkaline silicates.

(*b*) *Vapour Glazing*. This comes about in the higher temperature range when alkali-containing ashes of the fuel vaporize and blow on to the ware, again causing glasses to form on the surface. The observation of this in Europe led to the deliberate introduction of alkali (salt) into the furnace so as greatly to intensify the effect. In this way the new technique of salt glazing was born.

(*c*) *Applied Glazing*. In the Middle East the first technique was developed by melting the alkali and silica into a glass frit which could be cooled, ground and applied to pottery surfaces and re-melted on them (or formed in the molten state to make glass objects).

In the Far East the second technique was at first developed by the deliberate application of wood ashes to the clay surfaces before firing and later by mixing the ashes with fusible rocks and clays to diversify and control the effect. A further discovery made in the Middle East was that lead compounds, not naturally associated with clay, would also form glassy silicates with clay.

Lead Glazing. During the medieval period lead glazing was introduced gradually. Fundamentally the process is no more than the application of a powdered lead compound, probably galena (lead ore), to the surface of the ware. Under heat the lead corrodes the surface of the pot, forming a lead glass with the silica and alumina of the body. In the early period this glaze was used purely as decoration, a few blobs, a 'bib' or a powdering of lead being applied to the still wet ware or some kind of adhesive being applied to hold the lead in place until it fused. There is documentary evidence that, presumably to overcome the corrosive effect on surface decoration, more particularly in tiles, a frit was prepared by melting a mixture of lead oxide and sand into a glass, cooling it and grinding it before application. Only by degrees did the glaze assume a functional purpose and begin to be applied to the inside and the whole outer surface of the pot.

Translucent Bodies. The intermingling of the two traditions led first to the painted maiolica of the Renaissance and eventually to the discovery by BÖTTGER in 1708 of the first true (hard-paste) porcelain made in the West. As usual hybrids were the outcome of this search. For example European attempts to achieve the translucency of Chinese porcelain also produced imitation or soft-paste porcelain, which is a mixture of ground glass and white clay, usually lead glazed. Fired unglazed to *c.* 1100 °C. to mature the body, the ware was then glaze-fired at a lower temperature. Kiln loss was high owing to distortion in the firing. Unlike true porcelain, the glaze was easily scratched. English bone china, which used calcined ox bones as the flux, was introduced by Spode as an improvement on soft-paste porcelain.

But by a typical irony of history at about the time that the first Continental porcelain factories were setting up Britain was beginning her Industrial Revolution. The rise of Staffordshire as the pottery centre saw certain technical innovations which, coupled with increased specialization and division of labour, culminated during the life of Josiah WEDGWOOD in the change from craft to industry. A century later the lead-glazed earthenware tradition had triumphed over tin glaze, salt glaze and most of the porcelain as well.

9. TECHNICAL DEVELOPMENTS IN THE EIGHTEENTH CENTURY. During the 18th c., important technical improvements were made, particularly in the quality of clay bodies. The whiteness of salt-glaze ware was first improved by coating the unfired clay with a white slip, but later China clay and ground, calcined flint were added to the natural stoneware clay to make a hard, dense and lighter body. Cream-coloured earthenware was similarly perfected by the blending of clays with non-plastic materials and this culminated in the superb 'Queen's Ware' body developed by Wedgwood. An outstanding example of this new sophistication in body construction was his vitreous Jasper body, which contained additions of barium sulphate, barium carbonate and felspar with various metallic oxides providing the colour. These dense bodies enabled the ware to be turned on a horizontal lathe while in the 'leather' hard state and made possible the fineness of potting associated with this period.

The development of wet glazing in contrast with the dust glazing of SLIPWARE meant that thin glaze application was possible, and with the introduction of biscuit firing even finer pots could be made. The ware could be supported during the high biscuit firing and so little distortion would take place in the lower temperature of the glaze kiln. This accounts for the strength yet softness of 18th-c. English earthenware.

Plaster of Paris was introduced from France during the middle of the century and this made possible comparatively cheap porous moulds, which encouraged the multiple techniques of slip casting and pressing. Mass production was carried a stage further with the invention by Sadler and Green of a method of transferring prints from copper plates to the surface of pottery. Metallic oxides mixed with oil were printed on to a prepared tissue-paper, allowed to dry and then rubbed firmly on to the biscuit pot. The tissue-paper was peeled away and the pot fired to a low temperature to burn out the oil, which otherwise would have resisted the glaze. See TRANSFER PRINTING.

At the Midland Institute in Birmingham in 1882 William MORRIS laid down the nine principles of pottery-making. These proved prophetic rather than immediate, for they summarized the way of working and thinking of the modern potter but hardly reflected the decorative style of his close friend de Morgan or similar work elsewhere such as that of Deck in France or Bindesbøll in Denmark. The Morris principles of pottery-making were in fact closer to the Japanese tea aesthetic than any pottery to be produced in Europe for the next forty years.

121, 128, 139, 163, 263, 506, 579, 631, 685.

POUNCE. (1) A fine powder such as pulverized sandarac, charcoal or pipeclay, which is used to prepare the surface of PARCHMENT for writing or such as is dusted over a perforated pattern sheet to transfer a design in EMBROIDERY, etc. The verb 'to pounce' means to transfer a design by dusting a perforated pattern with pounce.

(2) To emboss metalwork with raised patterns by striking the underside, as in EMBOSSED work.

PRAGUE COURT WORKSHOP. The Habsburg Emperor Rudolf II (1576–1612), one of the great art collectors, established in the Prague castle of the Hradschin (Hradčany) a group of artists and craftsmen to produce works of art of all kinds for his own collections and for presents to foreign princes. Rudolf's prevailing passion was for gemstones and his collection of vessels of ROCK-CRYSTAL and hard stones made by members of the Miseroni family and other craftsmen was unrivalled in Europe. Amongst the artists whom he brought to Prague were the goldsmiths Paul van VIANEN, Christoph JAMNITZER, the sculptor Adriaen de VRIES, the clock-maker Jost Burgi and the painters Joseph Heinz and Bartholomäus Spranger. Used descriptively the term 'Prague workshop' refers to the characteristic vessels of hardstone mounted in ENAMELLED gold, many of which, once in Rudolf's collection, survive in the Kunsthistorisches Museum, Vienna.

PRAYER-RUGS. Rugs on which devout Muslims kneel for their five daily sessions of prayer have designs which recall the prayer niche (MIHRAB) of the mosque and often include associated objects such as mosque lamps and ewers. They are made from central Asia to the Mediterranean coast, but the type of arch used in the representation of the niche often suffices to reveal the provenance. Multiple prayer-rugs, or saphs, with several niches side by side, belong usually to the Majar or Samarkand types. See also CARPETS AND RUGS.

PREHISTORIC TECHNOLOGY. Man is distinguished from his fellow creatures by, amongst other things, his ability to create and use tools, but our knowledge of this characteristic of early man is restricted by two major factors. In the first place only the most durable of materials have survived, so that one is apt to consider stone to have been man's initial tool-making material, and this may not have been the case; and secondly, one is unable to recognize a stone tool with certainty until a *tradition* of tool-making had developed. The majority of early stone tools, however, conform to a basic form that would allow them to have been used for a wide variety of functions such as cutting, scraping, digging and hammering. Tools of this kind were certainly being used by man a million years ago, at a time when he was living entirely by hunting large animals and gathering wild foodstuffs. Until *c.* 100,000 B.C. one can detect a very slow development towards diversification of tools, but they appear to share one feature in common in that they were designed primarily for the killing of game or for the preparation of food and skins, being largely knives, spearheads or scraping-tools.

It is not always appreciated that a million years ago man had also mastered another important technique: he was able to light and maintain fires. How this was achieved, and to what purposes the fires were put, are matters of speculation, but his ability to overcome his natural fear of fire and to control it must be seen as an important development which paved the way for many later technologies.

The period from *c.* 100,000 B.C. to 10,000 B.C., the last of the great ice ages, is one on which there is rather more information to be had, at least in Europe, as it was during this period that the limestone caves of northern Spain and southern France were extensively occupied. The tendency to make tools for a particular function continued to develop and one can recognize arrowheads, chisels or gravers, and awls as examples of this trend towards single-function tools. More important, however, is the fact that these tools were all made from identically shaped pieces of stone—thin, roughly rectangular 'blanks' which could be worked into a wide range of tools. Furthermore many of these tools were used to shape hunting equipment made of bone, antler and IVORY, much of which has survived. To what extent wood, skins or natural plant fibres were worked is an open question, but the presence of perforated bone needles suggests that netting or even textiles may well have been produced. The great series of cave paintings, whose purpose is totally obscure, required for their execution not only the grinding of pigments in a simple pestle and mortar, but also the manufacture of lamps, in this case shallow stone bowls.

The hunting equipment of the last ice age also shows that a number of important mechanical principles had been grasped by man. For example, the spear-thrower and the bow demonstrate that both the concept of leverage and the elasticity of some materials were being put to practical use. Even when one has allowed for the destruction of so much material with time, one comes to the view that the hunting economy of these people more or less enforced a use of animal by-products on the hunters, and that they seldom explored the possibility of materials outside this range.

In the eastern Mediterranean and the Middle East a fundamental change took place between the years 10,000 and 4000 B.C., for gradually mankind changed the nature of his basic economy from hunter to that of farmer. The development of crops and the domestication of animals brought with them many changes, but the most far-reaching was the need to construct settlements. Buildings in wood and stone, for which there is some evidence in the earlier periods, became more sophisticated; but the use of sun-dried mud-brick was an innovation. At first hand-modelled, bricks were at a surprisingly early date shaped in simple box-like moulds. The need to cook and to store foodstuffs brought with it many other uses of mud and CLAY. Storage pits were lined with clay; hearths and ovens were made of it; and, of prime importance, the manufacture of pottery was developed. In its shaping either ring-building or simple moulding processes were employed, while firing appears to have been done either in the domestic hearth or in a small bonfire. In the early phases decoration was rudimentary, being confined to designs scratched or impressed in the damp body. More commonly, however, pottery was left undecorated except for a fine surface burnish, presumably made to render it less porous. See also POTTERY TECHNIQUES.

Since much agricultural land had to be won from virgin forest, it is hardly surprising that wood-working crafts evolved more than during the earlier epoch. The stone-bladed axe and adze were developed, and wooden objects varying in size from bowls and platters to dug-out canoes were produced. Many of the developments of this period, however, relate directly to the newly progressing arts of farming, being little more than new applications of methods already known in the previous hunting age. Thus the stone-bladed sickle can be seen as an adaptation of the hunter's stone knife; the flat quern, used for grinding grain, was merely the palaeolithic artist's mortar enlarged and put to another use. Woollen textiles in plain weave are known from this period, as too are many different types of basket, both appearing to be technologically well developed, so that we may well be correct in our supposition that weaving techniques first developed in an earlier age, while the presence of spindle whorls suggests a considerable production of thread. The cultivation of flax in the Middle East area and COTTON in the Punjab during this epoch emphasizes this development, although no evidence of the type of loom used is known until the subsequent age. Presumably the common device was one in which the warp threads were supported a short distance above the ground, the so-called horizontal loom. See also TEXTILE MANUFACTURE IN ANTIQUITY.

In the two millennia following 4000 B.C. there was yet another major economic development in the eastern Mediterranean and the Middle East: slowly village life based on agriculture and stock-breeding gave way to a pattern of urban settlement, and it was from the towns and cities that the stimuli for further technological innovation were to stem. The next dramatic, although perhaps not the most significant, development was the appearance of primitive metallurgical techniques. Gold and copper, both of which could be found in limited quantities as native metals, were at first worked solely by hammering. But it was rapidly discovered that the hardness imparted to copper by hammering could be alleviated by heating (annealing); and that by heating to a still higher temperature the metal would become molten and could be shaped by casting into moulds. Meanwhile the bright blue and green ores of copper had attracted attention and were in use as pigments, and there followed the discovery that these same materials could be reduced to metallic copper in a furnace. Other innovations in this field followed quickly. Silver and lead were won from their ores, while the whole process of shaping metals became increasingly more sophisticated. Broadly speaking two schools of metal-working developed side by side. The first was based on the use of the hammer, sheet metal being produced and decorated by repoussé work either to form vessels such as bowls and jugs or as a cladding for a wooden carcase as, for example, in the production of statues or ornamental doors. The other tradition was that of shaping by casting. Moulds were at first either depressions cut in a suitable piece of stone or impressed in clay. The severe limitations of this kind of mould were soon overcome by the introduction of piece-moulds, usually of only two parts, and this type of mould was further adapted within the course of four centuries to include a false core of clay, so making possible the products of hollow castings. See also BRONZE AGE METALLURGY.

Parallel with the development of metal-working ran that of man's first truly synthetic material, euphemistically known as 'Egyptian faience', but in fact identical in composition with some European soft-paste bodies of the 18th c. This development embraces, in fact, two distinct discoveries. The first was that any quartz-bearing rock, in practice largely steatite, heated in contact with the ores of copper to a sufficient temperature, would develop a turquoise glaze on the surface; while the second discovery was that a fine quartz sand, if mixed with the natural mineral natron (impure sodium carbonate) and heated to similar temperatures, would fuse to form a white body. Glazed, carved steatite, and later moulded 'Egyptian faience' objects, were increasingly produced in Mesopotamia and Egypt prior to 3000 B.C., and were to lead ultimately to the development of glass wares and glazed ceramics. See GLASS and GREEK AND ROMAN ANTIQUITY (GLASS).

The manufacture of pottery during this period underwent a number of interrelated changes, perhaps as the result of the move from home to market production. Ring-building and moulding methods were largely replaced by shaping on a turn-table, in all probability not 'throwing' in the sense used by modern potters but rather a system in which one hand only was used to shape the vessel while the other turned the wheel. This method not only allowed the production of more delicate wares but also demanded the use of a fine body prepared by the levigation of the raw materials, while the finer body in turn demanded a less cavalier method of firing than the use of a bonfire. Furthermore, even before 4000 B.C. a new style of ceramic decoration had become popular in which different coloured SLIPS were applied to the surface; and since the designs were apt to become marred in a bonfire, there was a need to separate the wares from the fuel during firing. What emerged was a simple up-draught kiln with the fire set below a perforated clay floor, above which was the chamber in which the wares were set. See also CERAMICS, POTTER'S WHEEL and POTTERY TECHNIQUES.

It was probably improved methods of firing which also led to the introduction of fired brick as a building material, especially in Mesopotamia, although the high cost limited the application to buildings such as temples and palaces. Where suitable building stone was available, as in Egypt, it was used extensively. Quarrying was done largely by driving wooden wedges into a series of slots cut in the rock, but the tools used for shaping remained totally Neolithic in character, since the metals then available were quite unsuitable for the work. Broadly speaking, the shape, be it plain ashlar or sculpture or low relief, was roughed out with hand-held picks of a hard rock, and the final form was given to the work by rubbing down with blocks of sandstone. Other stone objects, largely vessels and seals used to impress damp clay, were made by similar means, while the faces of the seals were normally 'cut' by rubbing a fine point loaded with abrasive backwards and forwards to form an impression.

The introduction of metal tools appears to have made its greatest impact in the field of wood-working. Enormous strides were made in such diverse productions as shipbuilding, cart-wrighting and furniture making, and all the more common carpenter's joints known today came into use during this period. Shaping was carried out with axes, adzes and a saw shaped rather like a large butcher's knife with a serrated cutting edge but in which the teeth were not set to give a scarf wider than the blade. The bow-drill and mallet-struck chisel were used to prepare mortices and peg-holes, but the final surface, as in the case of stone objects, was produced by the use of sandstone rubbers. See also WOOD-WORKING.

Two other developments of this period ultimately were to assist the craftsman, the introduction of standardized systems of recording and of measurement. In Mesopotamia records were kept by impressing symbols on the surface of tablets of damp clay which were subsequently sun-dried, while in Egypt records were made with brush and ink on papyrus. The material was made by hammering overlapping strips of the papyrus reed until they became welded into a single sheet. Throughout the whole of the Middle East there developed a complex system of weight measurement based upon the unit of the grain of wheat and its multiples, while for linear measurement the digit, and its multiples the palm, foot and cubit, were generally adopted.

Towards the end of the third millennium B.C. further advances were made in the field of metallurgy. Copper began to be alloyed with small quantities of tin to provide bronze, and different forms of CUPELLATION began to be applied to the refining and the separation of SILVER from the ore of lead, galena. See also COPPER AND ITS ALLOYS.

The period from 2000 B.C. to 500 B.C. saw yet another major economic development in the Middle East. Even before 2000 B.C. urban development had advanced to such a point that individual rulers had found it profitable to control a number of adjacent cities, so building up small kingdoms, but as a general rule these domains were confined within the boundaries of natural geographic regions. From the beginning of the second millennium onwards, however, there was an ever-increasing tendency for rulers to extend their territory to embrace several geographically distinct regions. In so far as the craftsman was concerned these embryonic empires had two marked effects: trade and communications were greatly improved, with an increasing demand for consumer goods, while the craftsmen themselves became a valuable commodity and were often transferred over great distances, either as captives or as the result of financial inducement. Concomitant upon these changes was the development of cities that became renowned as the centres of specific crafts.

The period saw the introduction of two new materials, IRON and GLASS. The origins of iron-working are, even today, almost totally obscure, and all that can really be said is that throughout the second millennium B.C. small quantities of wrought iron were being made in, or finding their way into, the Middle East. It was, apparently, not until the very end of the second millennium that the processes of extraction and forging were brought under complete control, but when this was achieved the effect on other crafts was dynamic. The reason for this slow development possibly lay in the fact that the metal is more difficult to reduce from its ores than those previously worked, while without being reduced to the molten state it could only be shaped by forging at red heat.

The production of glasswares is more easily understood, for if 'Egyptian faience' became overheated, as it demonstrably was from time to time, a glass was automatically produced. During the period under review glass vessels were shaped by applying the molten glass metal to the surface of a sandy clay core which was later extracted, while decoration was restricted almost entirely to the addition of coloured filaments of glass to the surface. A considerable range of colours was produced: copper salts gave a turquoise in these alkaline glasses, but with the further addition of lead a leaf-green was produced; lead was also used with antimony to provide a deep yellow; manganese gave aubergine or, in large quantity, black; while white was made by overloading the glass with lime. Limited quantities of cobalt and chromium were used in the production of blues and greens.

The same range of colours was applied to the production of moulded objects of 'Egyptian faience', especially in Minoan Crete, in Egypt during the reign of Akhenaten, and rather later in the Levant and Mesopotamia. The technique was to reach its apogee in the glazed brick façades of Assyrian and Neo-Babylonian palaces, in which a layer of 'Egyptian faience' was applied to fired bricks to give elaborately coloured motifs. See also COLOURS AND COLOURANTS.

The techniques of working other metals also showed considerable improvements. The introduction of a simple form of bellows (rather than fanning the fire by lung-power through a hollow tube) allowed large quantities of BRONZE to be cast at a time. The use of the *cire-perdue* method of mould preparation, which included a core held in place by chaplets, permitted more complex and more economical castings to be made than was possible with the piece-moulds and false cores of earlier periods. Furthermore, by the addition of a certain quantity of lead to the bronze alloy a more fluid melt could be obtained, so allowing the production of sounder and more elaborate castings than was hitherto possible. In the shaping of gold more elaborate forms of jewellery were possible with the introduction of soldering techniques. These were not the solders we know today but a system in which an adhesive and a copper compound were mixed together and applied to the faces to be soldered. Held in position the work was then heated so that the copper salt was reduced to the metal, which then formed an alloy with the adjacent metal surfaces, so creating a bond.

From this period onwards a larger range of organic materials has survived, so that one can at last begin to assess the position of crafts such as weaving, leather and wood-working. On the whole the production of textiles seems rather disappointing. There appears to be no indication of any form of pattern weaving other than a simple twill; but this may be fortuitous since there is pictorial evidence of quite elaborate pattern weaving by Classical Greek times. It is probable, however, that energies were largely devoted to the production of light-weight cloths, confined to wool and linen, in the Middle East. Dye vats are known from this period, and a number of vegetable dyes, including indigo, madder and saffron, have been identified; but dyeing appears to have been carried out largely in the piece rather than in the hank. Equally there is considerable evidence for the whole process of TANNING, including plumping, puering and dehairing with lime, while the older processes of alum tawing and dressing with other natural preservations continued to be practised. See also WEAVING; GREEK AND ROMAN ANTIQUITY (TEXTILE MANUFACTURE) and (LEATHER); LEATHERCRAFT.

The introduction of iron tools was to make its major impact upon craftsmanship in the fields of wood-working and stone-working. As far as the carpenter was concerned the major innovation was the bow-saw, rapidly to evolve into the frame saw; but elsewhere pre-existing forms of bronze tools, largely chisels and augers, were copied in iron. The increased efficiency of these tools, however, is reflected in the added complexity and size of wooden structures, including ships. For the mason and sculptor, however, it was now possible to create a completely new toolkit—jads, bolsters, chisels, and claw-tools—and this happened with great rapidity and so effectively that the tools have changed little to this day. Without these tools Greek sculpture and architecture could never have evolved in the way they did in so short a period.

By the fifth century B.C. mankind had learned to extract, process or synthesize virtually all the raw materials to be employed by the craftsman for the subsequent two millennia. By 500 B.C. the silk-worm was being cultivated in China while cotton, long cultivated in India, was beginning to be grown in Mesopotamia. The more common dye-plants were similarly cultivated. Many more raw materials depended still upon growth in their natural habitat. Supplies of wood came from the seemingly boundless virgin forests, but already natural supply was beginning no longer to keep pace with demand, a situation to some extent rectified by improved methods of transport, particularly by sea. Some materials were used in prodigious quantities. African ivory, for example, used on a truly lavish scale for the manufacture of furniture, was a major item of early Arab commerce in the Indian Ocean; and it seems certain that in some parts of Africa the elephant had already become extinct by the later Roman period.

The last five centuries of the Pre-Christian era, however, are remarkable for the introduction of a large number of new devices and machines. Both the potter's kick-wheel and the lathe, used either for turning wood or for spinning sheet metal, appear for certainty in Ptolemaic Egypt, although almost certainly of Greek origin. The lapidary's wheel, presumably evolved from the lathe, appeared at much the same time. Blown glass, either freely formed or blown into a mould, seems to have been an innovation of the Levant. Screws, pulleys, and crown-wheel and pinion gearing, all of uncertain origin, were to ease the craftsman's burden considerably. The effects of other devices introduced during this period were not felt immediately by the craftsman. The water-wheel, for example, was used initially almost exclusively for grinding grain, and its application to other industries was a gradual process extending throughout much of the Middle Ages.

3, 158, 264, 318, 343, 351, 396, 544, 623, 624, 654, 769, 770, 845.

PRÉSENTOIR (French). A broad-bladed, blunt-ended knife on which the carver placed pieces of meat before offering them to guests. Surviving examples can be dated between the 14th and the early 18th centuries. See CUTLERY.

PRESS CUPBOARD. A large CUPBOARD, sometimes confused with a COURT CUPBOARD, which came into use in the latter half of the 16th c. and remained in fashion until the 18th c. It had the upper part recessed with contained cupboards and a shelf running in front of them. See FURNITURE (ENGLISH).

PRICE, UVEDALE (1747–1829). Wealthy Whig landowner and a leading exponent of the *Picturesque* school of thought, he was born in 1747 at Foxley, the family seat in Herefordshire. His father was Robert Price, a talented amateur artist and musician who claimed descent from a Tudor Ap Rhys. Robert's great-grandfather had come into the Foxley estate through marriage with an heiress, and here a new mansion was built *c.* 1717. Uvedale, christened after a grandfather, was the eldest of Robert's six sons and was only 14 when he succeeded to Foxley on his father's death, but he was to develop into one of those all-round characters in whom literary and artistic talents are combined with a strong sense of public duty and the interests of a country gentleman. Educated at Eton, he passed to Oxford, where he matriculated on 13 December 1761, but left without taking a degree. An early friendship with Charles James Fox led to their setting out together on a grand tour in 1767, visiting among other places Florence, Rome, Turin, Geneva and finally Ferney across the French border, where they met Voltaire. Fox subsequently returned to England while Price continued to Germany before returning home. Although he made several tours abroad in the ensuing years, the greater part of Price's time was spent at Foxley, where he continued the improvements to the grounds initiated by his father. On 28 April 1774 he married Lady Caroline Carpenter, youngest daughter of the Earl of Tyrconnel, a happy marriage which lasted for 52 years until her death in 1826.

Price's interest in picturesque aspects of the landscape was first inculcated at an early age by his father, but was developed through his own experiments on his estate and by discussion with the many friends who shared this interest, notably the Revd. William Gilpin, a parson-schoolmaster who was also a talented landscape artist and writer. Gilpin's theories led him to create the term 'Picturesque Beauty' for effects which were not only pleasing in themselves but had paintable qualities. His first publication, *Observations on the River Wye*, which appeared in 1782, had an undoubted influence on Price, whose interest was further stimulated by his neighbour, Richard Payne KNIGHT of Downton, and the latter's cousin, Thomas Johnes. From 1783 onwards Johnes's energies were concentrated on that embodiment of picturesque principles, Hafod in Cardiganshire. It was Hafod which so captivated Price and Lady Caroline in the course of a visit that they decided to build, a few years later, a retreat of their own on the coast at Aberystwyth, employing their host's architect, John Nash. Gainsborough and Reynolds, Wordsworth and George Beaumont were others in Price's circle who shared his intellectual pursuits.

In 1780 Price produced his first book, *Statues . . . in Greece translated from the Greek of Pausanias*. Later in that decade he began to assemble material intended for a publication which was to appear in 1794 under the title *An Essay on the Picturesque as compared with the Sublime and the Beautiful; and on the use of studying pictures for the purpose of improving real landscape*. Price's ideas in fact went beyond those of Gilpin in that he thought that the term 'picturesque' could be applied not only to subjects suitable for painting, but also to music and the other arts. As far as painting was concerned the characteristics of pictures should be 'roughness and sudden variation joined to irregularity'. Pictures which presented contrasts of light, rugged outlines or textures, rich colours and deep shadows, while they might not necessarily be beautiful or sublime, must be 'picturesque', and these were the attributes which he felt should also be applicable to LANDSCAPE GARDENING.

In the preface to his book Price explained the circumstances in which it followed by a month or two the publication of Payne Knight's didactic poem *The Landscape*, which had been dedicated to him. 'I did not intend publishing till it was more complete', Price wrote of his own work, 'and till I had endeavoured, at least, to render it more worthy the publication. I have, however, been induced to send it into the world earlier than I wished from the general curiosity which my friend Mr. Knight's poem has awakened on the subject . . . I had mentioned to Mr. Knight that I had written some papers on the present style of improvement, but that I despaired of ever getting them ready for the press; though I was very anxious that the absurdities of that style should be exposed. Upon this he conceived the idea of a poem on the same subject; and having all his materials arranged in his mind, from that activity and perseverance which so strongly mark his character, he never delayed or abandoned the execution till the whole was completed. When it was nearly finished he wrote to me to propose, what I consider as the highest possible compliment, and the strongest mark of confidence in my taste,—that my papers (when properly modelled) should be published with his poem, in the same manner as Sir Joshua Reynolds's notes were published with Mr. Mason's *Du Fresnoy*.'

As it transpired it was probably as well that their works appeared separately, for with the publication in 1801 of Price's *Dialogue on the Distinct Character of the Picturesque and the Beautiful* Knight took offence at a passage in which the author refuted a criticism of this argument which appeared in the second edition of *The Landscape*. The reason for Knight's pique now seems trivial enough, Price having set out his views in the form of a light-hearted and witty discussion between three travellers as they passed through a varied stretch of country-side; but the upshot was that Knight in turn ridiculed Price's arguments in his essay *An Analytical Enquiry into the Principles of Taste* (1805).

It is surprising that so mild a subject as the English landscape, whether portrayed in painting or emulated by garden enthusiasts, should have provoked such intense controversy between these authors and such bitter attacks on those of whom they disapproved, in particular Lancelot BROWN. In this Price, who had a broad and liberal outlook on most things, was on common ground with Knight, neither of them understanding that the compact plantations which they disliked in 'Capability's' landscapes were intended to be thinned out as these developed. It was Humphry REPTON's defence of the latter which was to draw him into the wordy battles of his two erstwhile friends.

Price's participation in controversies over the picturesque has tended to obscure his other activities. In 1793 he served as High Sheriff of Herefordshire and subsequently took a serious view of the threatened Napoleonic invasion and rumoured landings in Wales. This prompted the publication of his *Thoughts on the Defence of Property Addressed to the County of Herefordshire*, printed in 1797, and advising the formation of groups of yeoman cavalry, armed and united in 'their efforts in the cause of peace and security'. In spite of impaired eyesight through an accident in 1815, he continued in good health and Wordsworth during a visit in 1828 described him as 'all life and spirits, and as active in ranging about his woods as a setter dog'. In 1826 he contributed additions to a reissue of Gilpin's *Tour on the Wye*, and a year later published his *Essay on the Modern Pronunciation of the Greek and Latin Languages*. A baronetcy was conferred on him in 1828, but he was to enjoy it for only a few months. On his death at Foxley on 14 September 1829 he was succeeded by his only son Robert Price, M.P.

387, 428, 541, 628.

PRIE-DIEU. Name given in the early 17th c. to a small praying desk made in Germany, Austria, France and England from the 14th c. onwards until the 17th c. In essentials a prie-dieu is composed of a vertical member supporting a shelf serving as an arm-rest or a support for devotional books and a shelf near the floor upon which to kneel. Within the basic form the prie-dieu varied considerably from a simple article, such as was commonly found in Elizabethan bedrooms, to handsomely decorated examples. The upright was sometimes fitted with a shallow cupboard and one or two drawers might be included. In Italy in the 16th c. the prie-dieu combined with a chair was a notable article of furniture.

The prie-dieu was revived in England *c.* the middle of the 19th c. under the influence of the High Church movement.

PRIE-DIEU CHAIR. A high-backed armless chair with low seat popular in England in the middle of the 19th c. These chairs were both suitable for prayers and adapted to accommodate the crinoline which was then coming into fashion. A high-backed prie-dieu chair with BAROQUE styles and elaborately carved back panels was also made in the U.S.A. *c.* 1830–60 in the style contemporarily known as Elizabethan.

PRINTERS' MARKS. Ornamental devices and designs used by printers and publishers as personal marks to distinguish their books and usually inserted on the title-page or at the end of the colophon. Motifs for the designs were taken from many sources, including heraldry, monograms and initials, pictorial emblems, puns on the owner's name, mottoes, location signs, and merchants' marks used on bales of goods. The earliest example is the pair of shields suspended from a branch which appears in the Psalter (1457) and Bible (1462) printed at Mainz by Fust and Schoeffer. In England the earliest device is probably that of the St. Alban's press (1485), followed by Caxton's mark with his initials (1487).

194, 556.

PRISONER-OF-WAR CRAFTS. From the 17th c. at least it had become customary for prisoners to fill up their enforced leisure by creative work. A Dutch pamphleteer kidnapped by Louis XIV's agents because of his attacks on the Sun King, and shut up in a wooden cage on Mont St. Michel, carved the bars of his prison into beautiful figures of animals, birds and flowers with pieces of broken oyster shells. Macdonald of Keppoch, a Jacobite chief imprisoned in Carlisle Castle after the '45 rebellion, covered the walls of his cell with carvings of very plump nudes.

It was not till the Napoleonic wars, however, that large numbers of prisoners began to congregate in English gaols. Hitherto everyone in prison had been there on a temporary basis, either until he was tried or until he had discharged his debts. State prisoners were the only exception. When Napoleon refused to continue the 18th-c. practice of exchanging prisoners (unless he got 10 Frenchmen for every Englishman he released) the British Government reluctantly built the first prison camps at places like Dartmoor, Portchester, Forton, Norman Cross and Valleyfield. By the time the war of 1812 broke out the internment of prisoners of war had become such a normal course that the American prisoners were automatically sent to one or other of the camps. Although the British Government provided food, clothing, housing, and medical inspection, there were no luxuries such as gambling, grog or tobacco, for prisoners who had no money. Accordingly many American prisoners adopted the money-making practice, which had been begun by the French, of turning out luxuries and knick-knacks ('toys' as they were called in the 18th c.) for rich people, who were deprived of one of their sources of luxury goods—France—because of the blockade.

The types of craft work which prisoners produced have been itemized by Mrs. Jane Toller as 'Straw work, Bone work, Wood Work, Rolled and Cut Paper Work, Horn Work, Thread Lace, Hair Work, Bank Note Forging, Coining, and Indecent Toys'. However, Mrs. Toller omits one important item: pictures and drawings. These were turned out in large numbers by at least one French prisoner, Louis Garnier, one of whose pictures is preserved in the Royal Maritime Museum, Greenwich. Contrary to a suggestion made in the *Daily Telegraph Magazine* of 5 February 1971 that prison craftsmen were poorly paid, they were in reality often able to command high prices for their work. 'We walked to Norman Cross to see the barracks for

A model in bone of a French 120 gun ship, with marquetry stand. (Science Mus., London)

French prisoners', noted the Revd. Robert Forby in June 1807. 'Their dexterity in little handicraft nick-nacks, particularly in making toys of the bones of their meals, will put many pounds into the pockets of several of them. We were very credibly assured that there are some who will carry away with them £200 or £300.' One modeller called Garnier, from St. Malo (apparently no relative of the Garnier mentioned above) built a tiny vessel 5 cm long, with every part worked exactly to scale, and with microscopic brass guns which could be run out, and rigging made from human hair with working tackle for lowering the yards. This model took a year to build and was sold for £100. Another ship model, built by one Germain Lamy at Forton in 1811, which was made with the help of a friend in six months, sold for £40.

Ivory and bone models of ships commanded such high prices that it is not surprising that they were the objects on which the carver lavished the greatest care. He would begin by laying in a stock of bones. These, another American prisoner called 'The Greenhorn' tells us, had to be bought from the kitchen. The bones would then be sawn into strips, which would be divided into plates or planks, depending on how the model was to be made. They would then be drilled and pinned to a wooden model of the hull with fine brass wire. Thicker wire would be used to make the guns. Bone was used not because, as is sometimes suggested, it was the only material available to the prisoners, but because it was already in use in Dieppe, where Bernardin de St. Pierre had noticed great piles of beef bones in the studio of one carver called Le Flaman. Human hair too was used not because it was the only material which prisoners could obtain, but because it was an ideal cordage, having a finer count than could be obtained in thread. The museum of St. Malo, France, possesses a most interesting model ship, made by French prisoners of war and given to the famous French privateer Surcouf, which is rigged with hair from the heads of some English ladies who were captured aboard a ship. The gift was made in gratitude to the chivalrous Frenchman who ensured that not a hair of their heads was harmed during their captivity. Wood was also used and The Science Museum, London, and The Royal Maritime Museum, Greenwich, have a number of wooden model ships by prisoners of war.

Although much more is known about the work of American ship modellers than about the French, only two American models are identifiable. Both are in the Peabody Museum, Salem. One is of wood; the other, made from bone, is a model of an 80-gun ship apparently made by American prisoners at Dartmoor and presented to the museum by Commodore William Bainbridge in the 1820s. Nevertheless the Americans must have been very skilful modellers because their work has been eagerly sought for by collectors, who pay very high prices for them under the impression they are French.

Although the Americans achieved such distinction in ship-modelling, the ivory or bone model was introduced into the prison camps by Dieppe craftsmen, who must in turn have received it from 17th-c. Scandinavia, where the first examples are known. Bone or ivory models in the prison style, with marquetry stands, sometimes ornamented with straw mosaic, ivory and hair rigging, and ornamental balustrades, are to be found in the museum of Dieppe. Some of them were made by free craftsmen working in the town at the turn of the 18th and beginning of the 19th c. Napoleon bought one of these and another was presented to Josephine by the town. Other models of the same sort, made by prisoners in England, are to be found in the museum. Another bone ornament—a watch-holder with the lid surmounted by the lion and unicorn—bears witness to the connection between Dieppe and the camps.

The model ships have often been criticized because they are not always true to scale, and do not necessarily bear a resemblance to any particular ship. It must be remembered, however, that these models were not intended as meticulous blueprints of naval architecture but as toys for grown-up children (as can be seen from their movable guns and rigging). Although built by men whose only horizon was a prison wall, they will always convey that limitless sense of freedom conferred by a ship under full sail.

Next to model ships, straw work by prisoners, whether in plait, marquetry or mosaic, had an irresistible attraction for the British public. There was, however, an English straw-plaiting industry and its members complained so forcefully to the Government that from time to time the camps would be raided and contraband straw work burned. Paper, gilt and rolled into spills, was used to ornament pictures, fans and screens. Many prisoners did very creditable wood-carving, like one American who supplied the dealers in Portsmouth with 'Chinese' carvings which were eagerly bought by customers under the impression they had just arrived from the Indies.

Russian prisoners in England during the Crimean War made wooden toys and puzzles and during the war between the states, some prisoners in Confederate prison camps made SCRIMSHAW napkin rings from their beef-bones. With these exceptions no prison crafts of any interest survived the evacuation of Dartmoor and the other prisons after Waterloo.

836.

PRIVATE PRESS MOVEMENT. Though private presses have formed a part of the history of book production since printing was invented (see TYPOGRAPHY), the modern overtones of the phrase link them with a movement for reform in printing, allied to the larger ideal of the ARTS AND CRAFTS MOVEMENT, which developed towards the end of the 19th c. England was the home of this movement. English private presses had existed before this—Walpole's at Strawberry Hill in the late 18th c., and the Lee Priory Press under Sir Egerton Brydges in the early 19th c., for example; but these literary and dilettante performances expressed no printing purpose beyond the right to independence. The Daniel Press at Oxford in the fourth quarter of the 19th c., run by a Fellow of Worcester College with his wife and daughters, belongs in their tradition though it is also associated with the revived use of Fell types which had come to the University two centuries earlier by the gift and energy of Dr. Fell. The true pioneer of modern fine printing in the private press movement was William MORRIS.

Morris's achievement was astonishing in relation to the flourishing printing industry of late-Victorian England. His protest took the form of new example. The impulse, as with much of his work before this began, was a revolt against the products of industrialism and the boring conditions of work which industrialism involved. To the 'Arts and Crafts' rebels a new equation seemed manifest, that between the pleasure a man takes in his work and resultant beauty; but of these two pleasure in labour ('work-satisfaction' is the phrase now) came first. As ASHBEE put it, 'the standard of artistic excellence must depend ultimately upon the pleasure given, not to the consumer, but to the producer.'

Inspiration for the printing reforms came from the 15th c. by historical sympathy and a Pre-Raphaelite tradition which had become established over half a century. The phrase 'pre-Raphael' had once meant pre-academic, but its point of reference coincided with the first period of printing. Morris, a collector of early printed books and manuscripts, had studied letter forms for the manuscripts he liked to write and decorate. It is remarkable that most of the print reformers returned, following his example, to the ROMAN letter of Nicolas Jenson, a Frenchman who set up his presses and foundry in Venice in the late 15th c. However different from each other they may have been, we are generally told the types they designed were based upon Jenson: at least the homage, if not always the scholarship, was present. The writing encouraged at Tours by Alcuin of York in the time of Charlemagne stood as the spring of inspiration, but as Charles RICKETTS put it: 'At a charmed time in the development of man, in the Renaissance namely, the old vein was reopened.'

In 1888 Morris's friend Emery Walker lectured to the Arts and Crafts Exhibition Society on

15th-c. printing and illustrated his talk with slides. These pictures gave Morris the notion that by using enlarged letter forms, correcting and reducing them, he could attempt to design a type face based upon the early books he admired. It was characteristic of the Arts and Crafts printers that each would design a type, or have one made for his own use, and then grow so identified with it that the thought of other users seemed intolerable. In this way it became impossible, even if acceptable on other grounds, for direct influence from the private presses to be exerted upon later and more general practice in book design. The influence had to be a looser one, from standards and ideals rather than the shape of an alphabet. It is often recalled that DOVES PRESS types were thrown into the Thames by Cobden-Sanderson from Hammersmith Bridge; it is less well known that Ricketts had started the habit with smaller drama and guilt by ditching his VALE types in the river also, and that ERAGNY PRESS types lie under the English Channel.

The first KELMSCOTT book appeared in 1891. Morris had named his press (and his London home) after the Cotswold house he loved, and the printing was of course done in London. In the next seven years 52 titles were issued in 64 volumes, a remarkable achievement for this home industry which was far from full-time work for him though the decoration, method and energy depended upon him wholly. After his death in 1896 the trustees continued the life of the Press for two years, completing work which had been started and for which sufficient ground existed.

There can be no doubt that the influence of the Kelmscott Press dominated the private press movement, though later styles show great differences and a shift towards simplicity on the page. It would have been impossible to imitate the Kelmscott books intelligently, for they show Morris in his talented energy of decoration distilled from a knowledge of early printed books. But his concern for fine material and contempt for the shoddy persisted with his successors. Certain laws of margin and presswork, setting and solidity, also weighed with them.

The Kelmscott Press is best remembered for its Chaucer, work upon which he began in 1892 though it was not issued until 1896, in the summer before Morris died. Though most of his printing formed a preparation for this, each book was made with equal care and in great variety of format. The literary choice tended to follow CAXTON: the better known poets, and his own work, with charming excursions in his private taste among medieval romance and poetry. Three type faces were cut, known as 'Chaucer', 'Troy', and 'Golden' after the books for which they were intended; but as the first is only a reduced version of the second, only two kinds, a roman and BLACK LETTER served.

Each page of a Kelmscott book was completed, as we learn from Sydney Cockerell its secretary, as if it had been intended for separate issue as a fine print. Woodcuts from Morris's borders and initial letters generously decorate the books, and illustrations are cut on wood after designs by Burne-Jones. Kelmscott title-pages are often in a rich Victorian style of decoration which might properly be called Hammersmith–Venetian.

The successors of the Kelmscott Press were in sympathy with Morris's philosophy of craftsmanship and with the principle that each stage in the process of book production should be viewed as a problem in art. Ricketts showed the independence of an artist in his Vale Press (1894–1907), over which he presided with help from Charles Shannon. The types he designed for its use were again based upon 15th-c. models or earlier calligraphy. Many Vale books are printings—'editions' is not the word, for next to nothing editorial was attempted—of established literary classics: Shakespeare, Milton, Wordsworth, Keats, Shelley, Blake. All this met the motive of a private press which concerned itself with the form of statement rather than new or original information. 'The aim of the revival of printing', said Ricketts, 'is to give a permanent and beautiful form to that portion of our literature which is secure of permanence'. Ricketts printed in 39 volumes a complete Shakespeare, the only private press of that generation to do so. Several Shakespeare plays came from the Doves Press, with Cobden-Sanderson's emendations to text and punctuation, and a trial sheet for *Macbeth* exists from Kelmscott. But the most memorable aspect of Vale Press books was their woodcut illustration. For this and the sensitive line of his flower borders Ricketts has a special place in book history. Unlike Burne-Jones, he knew about engraving and prepared the entire work himself. Ricketts designed three type faces called 'Vale', 'Avon' (for the long Shakespeare) and 'King's' (for *The Kingis Quair* in 1903). The half-uncial King's type, an interesting and scholarly experiment, had small chance of popularity though it was his favourite. When sales and energy declined the Vale Press died, with the futile reason that 'the number of books which were suitable to the conditions of the firm have dwindled with time'.

The most admired among private presses for the quality of its illustration, Lucien Pissarro's Eragny Press, grew from the Vale and for a period shared the use of its type. Later Pissarro designed his own rather finely sculptured alphabet, called 'Brook' type after the name of his house. No major work came from the Eragny Press, but the elegance of its minor pieces is expressed in trellis borders and simple illustration, printed from wood-blocks and often in several colours, recalling without affectation the Normandy of Pissarro's childhood. In several instances a collaboration between father and son, when Camille Pissarro made the designs and Lucien translated them to woodcuts, lends particular attraction to Eragny books. Poems of

Ben Jonson, Browning and Christina Rossetti were among his successful work. *Some Old French and English Ballads* suited well most aspects of his abilities. The patterned-paper bindings which Lucien Pissarro designed, and Ricketts followed for many Vale books, produced an attractive though impermanent dress for Vale and Eragny books, in a department of life which had lacked inspiration before. Some skill in printed gold also characterized several of the later Eragny productions.

The life of the Doves Press spanned 19 years, from 1901 to 1920, and for the first eight Emery Walker shared responsibility as a formal partner. The spirit of the Press was Cobden-Sanderson's, already in his sixties when it began. This passionate man with a mystic gift, rescued from bored day-dreams by Richard Cobden's daughter, had turned from a dim legal practice to work with his hands to become a bookbinder. For several years he bound at home in his workshop, then limited himself to designing and founded the Doves Bindery. His friendship with Morris, his neighbour in Hammersmith, is sympathetically expressed in Kelmscott Press books bound at the Doves Bindery. His *Journals* trace a progress towards the printing of books, which represented for him a marriage between the temporal and eternal. This simple perception he expressed in remarkably long sentences with touching conviction. Emery Walker designed the type, modelled as usual upon Jenson's roman, which served in one size for large books and small to carry the profundity of his religious burden. He printed Shakespeare, Milton, Keats, Shelley, Wordsworth, Browning, the Bible and much of his own fractious ephemera also. His 5-volume folio Bible was the *magnum opus*, intended for church lecterns but removed by bibliophiles and librarians from any such use. The Doves Bible and Kelmscott Chaucer have held their foundation place in private press history. Cobden-Sanderson printed several works by Goethe, and his example had great influence upon the development of a comparable movement in Germany. This may be the place for a word about the German achievement.

Again it was Emery Walker whose message was received from England, and Count Harry Kessler who had with missionary singleness of mind invited it. Kessler, a complex character and half-Irish, introduced the theme first to the Insel Verlag in an admirable sequence of books before the First World War; then from his own Cranach Press at Weimar some of the most fastidious volumes in this half-century appeared. A perfectionist, he employed talented printers from England with artists whose work he admired—Eric Gill, Gordon Craig, Maillol. With these and with compositors bringing experience from Kelmscott and Doves presses he produced his two masterpieces, the *Eclogues of Vergil* and the *Hamlet*. Apart from such illustrated work, the German habit was to follow a more austere Doves Press tradition of unadorned text and fine press work. In this orthodox spirit no finer books spring from the revival of printing than a long line of steady excellence from the Bremer Presse, Janus Presse, Kleukens Presse, Ernst Ludwig Presse and Serpentis Presse. There were others, but these perhaps represented the movement most ably. Like their English models the owners of these presses tended to design their own type faces and to base them upon examples from the 15th c. The Bremer Presse perhaps possessed greatest self-assurance and fluency in type design, with large and smaller letters and an elegant Greek type for the 2-volume Homer. Among many splendours of the German movement might be mentioned especially the Bremer Presse folio Bible in 5 volumes, comparable with the Doves *Bible*, and their *De Civitate Dei* of St. Augustine, a magnificent instance of marathon control; the Serpentis Presse *Dante* with drawn initials, comparable with the Ashendene *Dante*; 7 Shakespeare volumes from the Ernst Ludwig Presse, greatly preferable to Doves Press excursions into Shakespeare; and of course the thoroughly imaginative *Hamlet* and *Eclogues* from Weimar. Apart from the last two all the books mentioned have simple text with only the initial letters, generally uncoloured, as decorative distraction.

In England ESSEX HOUSE completes the main story from this first period, with the ASHENDENE PRESS which continued its quiet way past them all and issued its final book in 1935. C. R. ASHBEE, moving from architecture and Cambridge to guild-socialism and the Mile End Road, gave practical example in his life as a follower of Ruskin. Essex House in London, later at Chipping Campden in the Cotswolds, became a co-operative workshop with much success in art and in life over two decades. One aspect of its achievement was the printing press imported from Kelmscott along with two of the compositors. The Essex House Press produced a long succession of books very competently, its range intelligently expressing Guild endeavour in Ashbee's writings or a choice of relevant literature and a series of home-decorated editions of poems on vellum. Ashbee made alphabets of woodcut initials and designed a type face, less derivative or 'scholarly' than other private-press founts, which has never been graciously received. The *magnum opus* of the press, in Ashbee's types, was the Prayer Book of King Edward the Seventh with its Guild binding of oak boards and niger back with silver clasps.

In many ways the Ashendene Press, run for pleasure by St. John Hornby at home with a merciful minimum of theory, achieved most in the art of printing allied to literate taste and calm of mind. During 40 years his books showed command of a great range in size and mood, from Christmas greetings and children's stories to his splendid folio editions of Dante, Boccaccio, Malory, Spenser and Cervantes. He straddles the whole movement, inspired very early by a visit to Morris's press and using Fell types provided by Hart at Oxford. When his last book appeared the standards he and his friends had wanted were already accepted, the models they admired were being imitated by type designers, the authority of the 15th c. was established. Walker and Cockerell had provided the type face associated especially with Ashendene books, a heavy roman letter closely copying the few works printed by Conrad Sweynheym and Arnold Pannartz at Subiaco outside Rome in the 1460s. To this equipment Hornby added another type before printing his *Don Quixote* folios, this time following the 1482 Ulm edition of Ptolemaeus. Most Ashendene books are printed in the black Subiaco or lighter 'Ptolemy' types, as Hornby varied their use according to literary character with flawless taste and skill. Graily Hewitt's initial letters, drawn or printed in several colours, give some gaiety to the Ashendene Press production.

Meanwhile the printing revival had its influence in America, but it took a different form there. After a period of instant imitation in which books of a Kelmscott sort abounded—not the kind of respect Morris would ever have wanted—the work of several scholar-designers took control with beautiful effect. Bruce ROGERS, D. B. UPDIKE, F. W. Goudy, C. P. Rollins as designers rather than proprietors of private presses lie outside the theme of the present article. Perhaps the most vigorous private-press contribution, apart from earlier and imitative work in the east, was from the GRABHORNS in California from 1920 and for as long a period as Hornby controlled the Ashendene Press. Enthusiasm, especially in California and New England, has grown so that it may become possible to view the American private presses of 1955–75 as a splendid episode in printing history, with focus upon the work of Victor HAMMER (Anvil Press), Henry Morris (Bird and Bull) and the ALLENS with their press in California. Though slight flamboyance may characterize type-design and format of American private-press work, Bruce Rogers stands as a giant internationally through the vital period of printing revival. Nothing was finer than his 3-volume Montaigne (Riverside Press, 1904) or the edition of T. E. Lawrence's translation of the *Odyssey*, which he and Emery Walker printed in 1932. Geofroy TORY was the influence upon Rogers, as Jenson upon Walker and Morris. One exception to this form of development in the United States, Dard Hunter's Mountain House press, which in 1917 moved to Chillicothe, Ohio, remains a monument to Arts and Crafts ideals and single-minded work. Whatever problem in definition the phrase offers, no press was ever more 'private' than this. His books were printed by him and his son on paper they themselves made, with type they designed, cut and cast. In 1915 he printed *The Etching of Figures* for the Chicago Society of Etchers and another book in 1917. During the 1920s his Press produced a series of books on the history of paper-making printed in his own type. His autobiographical work *My Life with Paper* (1958) tells the story of the birth of this type, the matrices, punches, moulds and tools for which were acquired by the Smithsonian Institution. Perhaps no other private press enthusiast made the production of a book so completely his own work as Hunter.

Between the two wars private presses in Britain tended to be somewhat less jealous of their privacy and readier to accept new methods so long as these did not conflict with their basic purpose. Though their influence was less vigorously exerted, they were responsible for much attractive production. In Wales the Gregynog Press was founded in 1919 by the wealthy sisters and art patrons Gwendoline and Margaret Davies as part of a wider project for fostering craftsmanship in ceramics, furniture, weaving, etc. under the general management of a young artist, R. A. Maynard. The first three books of the Gregynog Press were the *Poems* of George Herbert, the *Poems* of Henry Vaughan and a volume of Welsh poems entitled *Caneuon Ceiriog*, by John Ceriog Hughes. After these three the Press acquired a Monotype caster for the production of type for hand-setting.

The GOLDEN COCKEREL PRESS, starting in 1920, is chiefly remembered as patron of excellent woodcut illustration. In its finest hour under the artist-engraver Robert Gibbings (1889–1958) several major works appeared with woodcuts by Eric Gill, who also designed the 'Golden Cockerel' type. His *Four Gospels* is a landmark in the private press movement. NONESUCH and Shakespeare Head books, nearer generally to the world of commercial publishing, provided many splendours which cannot be mentioned in the space available here.

The private press movement, as deriving from William Morris, is primarily associated with printing reform. Missionary and literary presses and a legion of honourable home-printers do not belong within that circle. The Hogarth Press, in its early years private, stands outside the movement and the Ditchling Press has little affinity with it. The Cuala Press in Dublin is of interest in its relation to Yeats rather than printing, though Walker offered early advice about specimen pages.

The craft of BOOKBINDING developed with the private presses, in equal excitement and a similar spirit. Though Kelmscott and Doves books did not appear in fine bindings, owners might arrange to have them bound at the Doves Bindery or by one of several pupils and followers of Cobden-Sanderson. Cockerell, MacLeish and De Sauty had all worked for him. Several women continued in the high tradition, their bindings peculiarly appropriate upon books so carefully printed—Katherine Adams, Sarah Prideaux and Sybil Pye especially. In Germany a high standard of private-press binding under similar influence prevailed in such work as Frieda Thiersch's for Bremer Presse books and in binderies which worked in conjunction with the Ernst Ludwig and Kleukens presses.

Private-press enthusiasm continues, but a certain movement ran its course to completion in the half-century after Morris began.

39, 64, 131, 134, 226, 277, 517, 525, 526, 855.

PRUNT. A piece of ornamental glass which is applied to the body of a glass vessel for decoration.

PUGIN, AUGUSTUS WELBY NORTHMORE (1812–52). English architect, designer, writer and medievalist, who exercised an important influence on Victorian furniture design. He was the son of A. C. Pugin, a refugee from the French Revolution and a gifted artist who published two illustrated works on Gothic architecture. The young Pugin was a devotee of GOTHIC art and began designing in the Gothic style at the age of 15, in silver for Rundell & Bridge and in furniture for Morel & Seddon at Windsor Castle. After his conversion to Roman Catholicism in 1835 he devoted himself with furious energy to building churches and houses and designing over a very wide field. His ideas, based on a thorough mastery of medieval art, were promulgated in a number of publications, notably in his most influential book *The True Principles of Pointed or Christian Architecture*, 1841. He had already published *Gothic Furniture in the Style of the 15th Century* in 1835, while in 1849 his *Floriated Ornament*, based on an old botanical work of 1590, showed Gothic ornament derived from natural forms. Pugin's furniture designs marked a totally new approach and followed the two fundamental rules laid down in *The True Principles*: 'first that there should be no features . . . which are not necessary for convenience, construction and propriety; second, that all ornament should consist of enrichment of the essential construction.' The stress on rational structure and revealed construction was repeated by later reformist designers.

Pugin was in charge of the Medieval Court at the Great Exhibition, 1851, and was engaged on designing the interior of the new Houses of Parliament at the time of his death. A small collection of furniture designed by him, including a cabinet made by the firm of Crace for the 1851 Exhibition, is in the Victoria and Albert Museum.

Q

QUAICH. Scottish form of porringer with two lugs. See PEWTER (DOMESTIC).

QUARE, DANIEL (*c.* 1648–1724). British inventor and maker of fine WATCHES and LONG-CASE and BRACKET CLOCKS. He was admitted to the Clock-makers' Company in 1671 and was Master in 1708. He was the inventor (1680) of the repeating mechanism for watches in which a single push of the operating button causes the watch to sound both the hours and the quarters. He also probably devised the 'motion-work' used in both clocks and watches to the present day with which both hour- and minute-hands can be set together in a single operation.

40, 106, 154.

QUARTZ. A widely diffused mineral crystallizing in hexagonal prisms which includes many varieties of gemstones. It has a hardness index of 7 on the MOHS SCALE. Crystalline quartz includes ROCK-CRYSTAL, AMETHYST, the citrine and the cairngorm. Crypto-crystalline quartz is chalcedony and in modern lapidary work goes by the names of agate, onyx, cornelian, sardonyx, jasper, bloodstone, chrysoprase, crocidolite, etc. according to colour and structure.

Citrine is a glassy, greenish-yellow variety of quartz used as a gemstone in rings, etc. and is sometimes known as 'false topaz'. It can be produced by heat treatment from pale amethysts.

The *cairngorm*, a yellow or reddish variety, is found in Scotland, where it is fashionable for brooches and costume jewellery.

Agates are varieties of chalcedony in which the colours are patterned in bands or blended in clouds or swirling circles. *Onyx*, stratified with plane layers of different colours, is closely akin to agate. It is often black, banded with white. *Cornelian* is semi-transparent, glowing orange red, often used for beads. Agate, onyx and cornelian were all considered gemstones in antiquity and were used for cutting seals and for CAMEOS and INTAGLIOS.

Sardonyx is a type of onyx interspersed with strata of orange-red cornelian. *Jasper* (Greek *iaspis*) meant in antiquity any brightly coloured chalcedony except cornelian, the most prized being green. It is now used of any variety of opaque chalcedony adulterated with clayey substances. It is usually red, yellow or brown and there is a variety striped with dull green and maroon. *Bloodstone* is a dark green jasper with red spots. In antiquity the name *chrysoprase* was given to a golden green variety of BERYL. It is now an apple-green variety of chalcedony found mainly in Silesia. *Crocodilite*, known as 'tiger's eye', has a brilliant yellowish-brown lustre caused by inclusions of asbestos fibre.

QUEEN ANNE STYLE. Term for English styles of design and decoration identified with the reign of Queen Anne (1702–14). In metal-work, as in furniture, applied ornament was subordinated to good design and fine workmanship. In silver this style, with absence of EMBOSSED decoration, predominated from *c.* 1705 to *c.* 1720. In furniture the Dutch BAROQUE outlines introduced in the WILLIAM AND MARY period became less flamboyant and ornament more restrained. Comfort and elegance were the keynote and design depended on proportion and grace rather than on applied decoration. Distinctive of the period were the CABRIOLE leg and the upholstered 'love seat'. New social habits called for new furniture types: tea-drinking led to the use of numerous small tables, the vogue for collecting china led to the china cabinet, and so on.

In architecture the term 'Queen Anne' often covers the reign of William and Mary as well. In large building it is the period of English Baroque; in smaller, domestic architecture the Wren type of house persisted. The term 'Queen Anne' is also applied to a type of house popularized by Richard Norman Shaw (1831–1912) *c.* 1870 based on a combination of Dutch and William and Mary styles. See also FURNITURE (AMERICAN).

7, 86, 233, 305.

QUILTING. The word 'quilt' is derived from the Latin *culcita*, a stuffed bolster or cushion.

Sicilian quilted linen coverlet. (V. & A. Mus., *c.* 1400)

A piece of quilting consists of two layers of cloth stitched together and usually interlined with flock or down secured in place by lines of stitches. The stitching produced patterns, which were enhanced by alternation of stitched line and padded surface. In the form known as Italian quilting the padding is inserted between two parallel lines of stitching set close together and the design appears as linear relief. Sometimes, as particularly in early 18th-c. English quilting, the padding was omitted and the two pieces of material were simply stitched together. The basic stitches were the back stitch and the closely related running stitch. Each stitch had to be made individually as the needle must pass through all the layers of the quilt and expert craftsmanship was often displayed in executing the minute and varied stitchery which formed the intricate patterns used.

Many of the traditional pattern names have come down, such as Inch Square, Broken Plaid, Single Diamond and Hanging Diamond. Lines of stitchery were often curved into shells or scrolls and these were developed into more intricate designs known by such terms as Ocean Wave, Twisted Rope, True Lovers' Knot. Over-all patterns were made from a basic feather design and several patterns were sometimes worked on one quilt. Quilts were often ornamented in addition by EMBROIDERY or patchwork and surrounded by an elaborate border. APPLIQUÉ decoration was also used and was apparently popular in the splendid 16th-c. quilts which are now known only from inventories.

Patchwork decoration was popular mainly in quilts of the latter part of the 18th c. and early 19th c., though patchwork quilts are still in vogue in parts of America. The pieces of material used, often of some sentimental value, were collected over many years and finally incorporated into a quilt. By one method shaped patches were cut and mounted on calico or camlet with turnings which were folded under and hemmed down. In the alternative 'crazy' patchwork pieces of every size and shape were joined together and then mounted on a reasonably firm fabric. Another type of quilt was made from squares of unbleached calico and CHINTZ, the calico squares being decorated with embroidery before they were made up.

Quilting is an old traditional craft which can be traced back into the Middle Ages, the word itself dating at least from the 13th c. It was used for making coverlets and warm, light clothing. Sometimes quilted garments were worn under armour and sometimes thick quilting took the place of metal armour. Quilting was popular from an early date in most European countries and was also practised in the Far East and India. It was known in Persia, Turkestan, and in the Muslim regions of Africa. In England its popularity reached its peak in the early 17th c., when quilted satin doublets and breeches were worn. Towards the latter part of the century quilted satin petticoats, jackets and waistcoats were fashionable and richly ornamented quilted bed-covers were made. From medieval times elaborate quilts were often mentioned in inventories and quilts became family heirlooms.

Quilting has always been largely a folk art. It has persisted in many regions of Britain, notably in the north and in south Wales. The art was carried from Holland and England to America by early settlers in New Amsterdam, New England, Virginia and the Carolinas and later spread westwards to Kentucky and Tennessee. It is still carried on as a folk craft in some areas. Traditionally when a young woman was about to marry she would hold a quilting bee, usually before hay-making. A quilting frame with chintz or other material fixed to it was set up and layers of woollen cloth for underlining were prepared. Sewing materials were set ready and friends and neighbours would assemble from early morning with the object of completing the quilt before sunset.

156, 259, 334, 789, 863, 888.

R

RAKU. Japanese coarse-grained, low-fired pottery associated with the tea ceremony. With a plain, soft glaze, usually black, red or yellow, it favoured simple undecorated forms and refined rusticity. There were some 14 generations of Raku potters from the early 16th c. onwards. Raku is a hereditary craftsman's title and also the name used to describe a method of firing by which the biscuited ware, glazed, is placed in a kiln which has already attained its maximum temperature and the glaze-firing is completed in minutes. The immediacy and spontaneity of this technique had appeal for the artist-decorators of Japan, who were more painters than potters. The pots, mostly tea bowls, were largely hand-made by pinching or coiling, and an extreme economy of means produced deceptively simple forms of great sophistication. See JAPAN.

206, 704.

RANDOLPH, BENJAMIN (d. after 1792). American cabinet-maker and chair-maker. He was born in Monmouth County, New Jersey, and conducted business in Philadelphia from *c.* 1762 until his retirement in 1792. His work is notable for its robust design and opulent carving and he is considered to be one of the leading exponents of the PHILADELPHIA CHIPPENDALE style. The back legs of his pieces are usually made intentionally crude and without ornamentation. Chairs attributed to his hand are in the Philadelphia Museum of Art and the Boston Museum of Fine Arts. His work was commissioned by President Jefferson and the table on which the Declaration of Independence was drafted has been attributed to him.

67, 160, 220, 301, 645.

RASCH, ANTHONY. American silversmith of Philadelphia. Best known for his work in Philadelphia between *c.* 1807 and 1825, Rasch made some of the finest American silver known in the EMPIRE STYLE, work that required exceptional skill. A French emigré, his designs follow closely the style current in France. From *c.* 1812 to 1819 the Philadelphia directories list him in partnership with Simon Chaudron and their names appear together on silver during that time. After 1820 Rasch left Philadelphia for New Orleans, where he remained active until the middle of the century. The Metropolitan Museum owns a pair of sauce-boats by him of superb quality, but few examples of his work are known today.

454, 666, 683.

RAVENET, SIMON-FRANÇOIS (1706–74). Engraver, born in Paris and trained under J. P. Le Bas. He settled in England *c.* 1750, where he was employed by Sir Stephen Theodore Janssen in his enamels factory at York House. (See BATTERSEA ENAMELS.) He worked for Hogarth, engraving Plates IV and V of his series *Marriage à la Mode*, and later for the publisher John Boydell (1719–1804). After the closing of the Battersea Enamels factory at York House he went to the Bow china factory. Ravenet is sometimes credited with introducing the method of TRANSFER PRINTING. SIMON-FRANÇOIS (*c.* 1749–after 1814), son of the foregoing, was also an engraver. Born in London, he studied painting in Paris under BOUCHER, and then settled in Parma, Italy, where he undertook the task of engraving the complete *œuvre* of Correggio.

RAVENSCROFT, GEORGE (1618–81). Shipowner, merchant and amateur chemist who became interested in Venetian glass and set up as a glass-maker in England. In the course of experiments to cure the CRIZZLING of 'flint' glass he discovered in 1675 the new 'lead glass', in which lead was for the first time used as a principal ingredient. See GLASS (MATERIAL AND TECHNIQUES).

REEDING. Term in architecture and the decorative arts for an ornament which is the

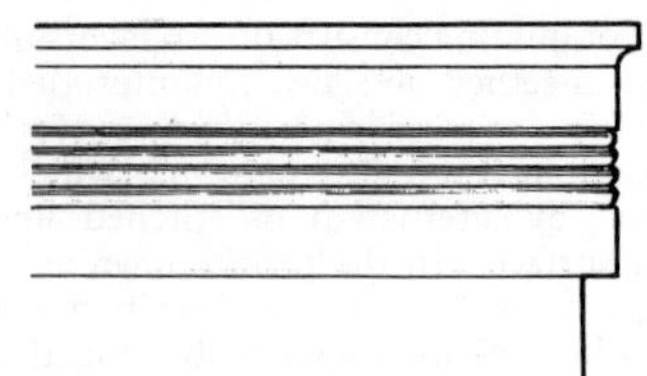

reverse of FLUTING, consisting of thin convex contiguous parallel MOULDINGS. A form of decoration stylized from long reed leaves, it was much used in metalwork during the latter part of the 17th c. and tended to succeed fluting in cabinet-work towards the end of the 18th c.

RÉGENCE. A transition style in French taste between that of Louis XIV and that of Louis XV. The name is taken from the regency of Philip of Orléans (1715–23) but as a stylistic term it applies to the years *c.* 1700 to 1720 or 1730, when the new and more fanciful types of ornament begun by BÉRAIN, Pierre Lepautre (1648–1716), Bernard Toro (1672–1731) and Claude Audran III (1658–1734) were being developed in the direction of the ROCOCO by such decorators as Robert de Cotte (1656–1735), Jacques Gabriel (1667–1742), Germain Boffrand (1667–1754) and Claude Gillot (1673–1722). In art history the term is more commonly applied to furniture and the decorative arts than to the arts of painting and sculpture. In furniture the name of the cabinet-maker and bronze-worker Charles CRESSENT (1685–1768) is closely identified with the *Régence* style. He was associated with the coming into fashion of such brilliantly coloured woods as amaranth and palisandre and for richly chased and gilded bronze appliqués and he was particularly noted for his bronze espagnolettes, which were inspired by the CHINOISERIES of Gillot and Watteau (1648–1721).

REGENCY. 1. INTRODUCTION. A descriptive term denoting the style and taste in architecture, decoration, furniture and design which prevailed during the years (1811–20) when George, Prince of Wales, was Regent for his father, George III. The style began, however, with a revolution in taste which took place during the last decades of the 18th c. and continued into the 1830s. Historically it may be regarded as the concluding phase of GEORGIAN. Otherwise it may be looked upon as the second phase of the Classical Revival (see NEO-CLASSICISM), which was paralleled in France by the DIRECTOIRE and the EMPIRE styles. It was incidental to a cult for Greek, Roman and Egyptian antiquity and to a more deliberately archaeological approach of which the French architects and designers Charles PERCIER (1764–1838) and Pierre-François FONTAINE (1762–1853) were typical. The new attitude to classical antiquity, sometimes referred to as the Greek Revival (see GREEK TASTE), owed much to the researches of James 'Athenian' Stuart (1713–88) and Nicholas Revett (1720–1804), the first volume of whose *Antiquities of Athens* appeared in 1762, a second in 1789 and a third in 1795. A similar interest inspired the work of the Society of Dilettanti and is reflected in the drawings of the sculptor John Flaxman (1755–1826) and the paintings and designs of Giovanni Battista Cipriani (1755–1826), who came to London in 1755 and was a foundation-member of the Royal Academy, and of Angelica Kauffmann (1740–1807).

A prominent inaugurator of the early phases of Regency was the architect Henry Holland (1745–1806), son-in-law of the landscape gardener Capability BROWN. Holland built Brook's Club, London (1776–8), enlarged Carlton House, London (1783–5) and built the Marine Pavilion, Brighton (1786–7), subsequently transformed by Nash into the Royal Pavilion. His designs for interior decoration combined Louis XVI motifs with French *Directoire* in a style of elegant simplicity. He was largely responsible for introducing Greek and Roman details from the *Directoire* into English decorative arts. An outstanding figure in promoting Regency taste in the early 19th c. was Thomas HOPE. In its final phases the style lost spontaneity and tended to become rigid and dogmatic, as represented in the architecture of George Basevi (1795–1845), who was a cousin of Disraeli and a pupil of Sir John Soane and who designed Belgrave Square, London (1825) and Pelham Crescent (1820–30) and was engaged on the Fitzwilliam Museum, Cambridge, at the time of his death. Springing from the Classical Revival at the close of the 18th c., Regency merged into the middle-class ostentation of Victorianism.

In art history the term 'Regency' is used in architecture and the decorative arts and in the field of taste and manners generally rather than in the fine arts of painting and sculpture or the literary arts. Despite its comparative brevity few periods have been more important for the development of taste in the practical sphere not only in England but also indirectly in America.

Among the most important general characteristics of the period was a merging of the various 'tastes' in the arts—Greek, Roman, Rococo, Chinese, Gothic, Egyptian, Oriental—into a fully self-conscious eclecticism informed by more accurate scholarship than had been the case in previous ages as a result of new archaeological discoveries at Herculaneum, Pompeii, Palmyra, Baalbek, Spalato, Egypt and Greece. The main trends of design resulted from the interaction between the Classical tradition and the cult of the PICTURESQUE, each imparting fresh variety and individuality to the other. Yet beneath particular manifestations one may discern a more general movement away from the ideals of simplicity, refinement and elegance which had characterized the preceding age of Robert ADAM in the direction of greater richness, opulence and exuberance of form, ornament and colour. This over-all change may have been to some extent due to a decline in taste among the new class of wealthy industrialists and merchants who now constituted the chief patrons of the arts, and partly the delight in richness and splendour may have been an expression of the sense of Britain's triumph in the Napoleonic wars.

2. INTERIOR DESIGN. Many of the features which are popular in modern houses had their origin or were developed during the Regency: central heating; open planning; large areas of window to admit the maximum of light and air; close identification of the interior with the garden and a fondness for indoor plants. Some features persisted from the days of Robert Adam: the semicircular window-bay with its enlarged French or 'Italian' windows; the corresponding semicircular interior apse, giving interest and beauty to the shape of a room; and open planning, in which two rooms could be separated not by a wall but with an open arch, sometimes having multiple folding doors which could be opened or closed to provide greater or less space. There was, however, a reaction, pioneered by Henry Holland and James Wyatt, against the Adam style of interior decoration with its fine and delicate stucco ornaments on wall-panels and ceilings. Adam's much-criticized 'effeminate' and 'finicky' 'sea-weed' ornament gave place between 1785 and 1800 to plain ceilings and wall-surfaces, as at Holland's Carlton House, London (1783–5), and Wyatt's Goodwood (1800), although at both houses some rooms still showed the surviving influence of the Adam style. With the enlargement of the windows came an increased liability to draughts and chill, which was mitigated by the use of voluminous window-draperies. Designs for these appeared frequently in magazines such as Ackermann's *Repository of Arts*. Close-fitted wall-to-wall carpeting was also now adopted instead of the polished boarded floors of early Georgian days and patent stoves came into use, such as those invented by Count Rumford. Jane Austen observed that at Northanger Abbey the fireplace was 'contracted to a Rumford'. Writing of Carlton House, the Prince of Wales's London establishment, Horace Walpole remarked: 'it is the august simplicity . . . the taste and propriety that strike', and the same comment might apply to Holland's rooms at Southill Park, Bedfordshire (*c.* 1791–1802), which had plain panelled ceilings and showed a strong French influence, deriving from his visit to Paris and his study of French architects, in the arrangement and design of MIRRORS and mouldings. The interiors and furniture designed by the wealthy connoisseur Thomas Hope for his house in Duchess Street, London, between 1799 and 1803, and later transferred in part to The Deepdene, Surrey, were described in his *Household Furniture and Interior Decoration* (1807). This work gave more precise indications than had appeared anywhere hitherto for the creation of interiors in the manner of ancient Rome, Greece and Egypt, and even of Turkey, India

and China. Following him in 1808 with *Designs for Household Furniture and Interior Decoration*, the cabinet-maker and upholsterer George Smith showed designs for rooms in Roman, Grecian, Pompeian, Gothic and Chinese taste, with furniture like the interiors obviously inspired by Hope's designs, although he illustrated also many of the more purely domestic types of furniture, such as beds, which Hope had not shown. After the fall of Napoleon French influences of the Louis XIV and Louis XV periods became increasingly evident, having been introduced by the architect B. J. Wyatt at Belvoir Castle, Crockford's Club, York (Lancaster) House, Londonderry House and Apsley House, *c.* 1825–8.

3. FURNITURE. In the early Regency years, *c.* 1780–1815, furniture tended to be simple and elegant in form, with little carving or applied ornament. Small, light articles were favoured, pieces which could be moved about a room as need prompted instead of being ranged stiffly against the walls. Jane Austen in *Persuasion* writes of the daughters at Uppercross creating 'the proper air of confusion with a grand pianoforte and a harp, flower-stands and little tables placed in every direction'. Thomas SHERATON's first design-book *The Cabinet-Maker's and Upholsterer's Drawing-Book* (1791–4) remained influential until the appearance of new trends in his *Cabinet Dictionary* (1803), in which some of Hope's classical innovations were featured. The ornament of chair and table supports now often consisted of REEDING, a form of moulding deriving from the Classical motif of a bundle of reeds, in place of the fluting of the Adam and HEPPLEWHITE period. A distinctive Regency invention was the sofa-table with its falling end-flaps, intended for use at a sofa for writing, games, needlework, etc. At first, *c.* 1800, plain, straight upright end-supports rested on claw feet; *c.* 1805 the supports were sometimes made in the form of classical lyres; but by 1812 a single central turned pedestal support had become general, usually rising from a 'tablet base' on small claw feet. The earlier simple decoration of a line of box-wood inlay in the mahogany or rosewood surface now gave place to brass inlay work deriving from Louis XIV BOULLE, now anglicized to 'buhl'. Brass inlay was simple at first, small Classical flower or star motifs being inlaid in detached fashion or in a string forming a border to a table or cabinet. From 1815 to 1820 the brass inlay became more elaborate, with flowering foliage patterns or over-all designs of ARABESQUES spreading over large areas of a piece, until it might—as in the hands of its chief practitioner, George Bullock (d. 1818)—come to present 'a brazen front' in the words of another designer, Richard Brown. In time the fondness for brass inlay on dark mahogany, rosewood, calamander, coromandel, snakewood, zebrawood or other dark exotic woods yielded to the use of light woods, often English, such as maple, yew, elm and oak, or light foreign woods such as amboyna. The tightly curled 'bird's eye' or burr-grain of such woods, cut near the root or from pollarded trees, was now relied upon (*c.* 1815–26) to give interest and beauty instead of elaborate inlays. An important feature of Hope's house was his furniture in the manner of the French *Directoire* and *Empire*, simple and rectilinear in form, with large, plain surfaces of red Spanish mahogany, and ornamented with Classical motifs in ORMOLU. The 'English Empire' aspect of Regency furniture received a strong impetus after the fall of Napoleon in 1815, when many English connoisseurs visited Paris. The productions of the craftsman Snell in Albemarle Street were remarked upon as being indistinguishable from the French.

The pursuit of 'Classical' taste involved the use of supports in animal form for chairs, sofas, tables, cabinets and *torchères*. Such animal-supports were usually the 'lion-monopodium', consisting of a stylized lion leg topped by a lion head. They derived from articles found at Pompeii. Both Hope and Smith made considerable use of them, as in a *torchère* by Hope at Buscot Park, a chair by George Smith, a gilt sofa by Gillow and a *torchère*, the last three in the Victoria and Albert Museum.

Especially characteristic of the Regency was the development of the chair. Classical forms exemplified in Hope's furniture were derived from vase-paintings, then called ETRUSCAN but now known to have been 5th-c. Greek. Such chairs had strongly curved arc-backs, curved side-rails and sweeping, pointed 'scimitar' legs. A modification with a scroll-back led to the 'Trafalgar' chair of 1805 incorporating the twisted 'cable moulding' that alluded to Britain's naval victories. This type of chair persisted, with modifications such as square or turned legs, until as late as 1850. Chairs in the severely antiquarian phase of the Classical taste with arc-backs and scimitar-legs or cross-framed supports from Hope's house are to be seen in the Victoria and Albert Museum and at Brighton Pavilion. Following Napoleon's expedition to Egypt in 1798 and the publication in 1802 of Denon's great work on Egyptian art, decorative motifs based on hieroglyphics, sphinxes, deities and canopic vases appeared in French furniture and were adopted in England after Nelson's victory of the Nile. A sofa and armchairs in the Egyptian taste from Hope's house are to be seen at Buscot Park, Berkshire. *Torchères*, a bronze clock and other articles from the room are at Brighton Pavilion, together with a 'crocodile sofa' which could have come from the drawing-room of the cottage described by Mary Russell Mitford in *Our Village* (1819) as 'swarming with sphinxes and crocodiles'. Public celebrations of naval triumphs called into being ceremonial furniture embodying marine emblems such as ropes, masts, sails, anchors and dolphins. Designs for 'Nelson chairs' appeared in Sheraton's *Cabinet Dictionary*, and an especially handsome example of the type may be seen in the famous 'Dolphin' suite presented to Greenwich Hospital in 1813, and now at Brighton Pavilion. The centre-piece incorporates the sphinxes and crocodiles of the Egyptian taste. Changes took place also in the form of the sideboard. The type of unit introduced by Adam consisting of a side-table flanked by separate pedestals and urns was transformed into a single piece in which the pedestals became cupboards supporting the table-top, upon which stood the urns. Various types of extending dining-tables supported on different forms of pedestal base were evolved, particularly by the firm Gillow of Lancaster. There were numerous characteristic types of beds. Tester-beds had posts carved with Classical ornament such as reeding and GADROONING instead of the FLUTING and leaf-carving of the Hepplewhite period. Many beds were on the French *Empire* model, made of mahogany and boat-shaped, standing lengthwise against a wall, sometimes with a small crown-shaped canopy above, hung with draperies. The revived interest in Louis XIV and Louis XV styles was indicated in design-books by Whitaker in 1825 and Smith in 1828, but the final stages of Regency taste expressed themselves in a heavy Classicism rather than Rococo, which in furniture, unlike Regency porcelain and silver, did not reach the height of its popularity until nearer the mid century. All the banalities of early- and mid-Victorian taste had been forecast in the later years of the Regency.

4. SILVER. The age begins with the chaste, elegant and refined shapes of the Adam period still in vogue—the tureens, sauce-boats, teapots, urns and vases, sometimes of ovoid form, often with their surfaces predominantly plain or thinly relieved with bands of garlands, swags or Classical border-patterns. New departures date from 1789, when King George III bestowed the office of Jewellers, Goldsmiths and Silversmiths to the Crown upon the then little known firm of Rundell & Bridge in Ludgate Hill, London. The Prince of Wales and other members of the Royal family conferred their own warrants upon the firm, which from then onwards rapidly increased its importance and influence. Fully modelled figures of Classical character became more and more prevalent, and the precise designs of Thomas Stothard (1775–1834) and John Flaxman (1755–1826) demanded more exacting standards of craftsmanship than had contented earlier craftsmen. At the height of the naval campaigns against Napoleon, from *c.* 1798 to 1805, there was a great demand for presentation cups in silver and silver-gilt. Their form still owed much to Robert Adam's designs, such as the Richmond Cup of 1770. Royal patronage caused Rundell & Bridge greatly to increase their stocks not only of contemporary English silver but also of earlier European silver brought to England by French emigrés. Handsome sets of plate became a necessary part of the equipment of British ambassadors and other representatives overseas, so that a young naval officer in the novel *Tom Cringle's Log* could speak of the West Indian Governor's dining-room as 'looking like the back parlour of Rundell's shop'. The ambassadorial silver, now to be seen at Brighton Pavilion, of Charles, 3rd Marquess of Londonderry, British Ambassador in Vienna at the time of the fateful Congresses, covers a wide range of Regency taste. In 1807 a large collection of silver made for the Royal family was exhibited in Rundell & Bridge's new showrooms, and formed the introduction of the new Regency style in silver to the fashionable world. The plate shown was almost entirely the work of the craftsmen Benjamin Smith, James Smith and Digby Scott. The work of the first is especially notable for the fine quality of the chasing, particularly in his wine-coasters and borders of trays and dishes, etc., with their ornament of grapes, vine-leaves and boys. In 1803 and 1805 two massive soup-tureens of Egyptian design had been made by Paul STORR, who later became the most outstanding silversmith of the Regency. These objects were the first articles of the Grand Service which the Prince Regent built up over his lifetime. During his early association with the firm Storr was engaged on the 'Nelson Plate' including sixty-six Trafalgar Vases made to the design of John Flaxman between 1804 and 1809, but from the latter date onwards it was Storr who was chiefly responsible for making articles for the Regent. After *c.* 1790 Egyptian motifs came to be used more frequently. Massiveness was a characteristic which became apparent during the middle years of the Regency. Forms were fulsome and exuberant, and ornament, though of Classical type, was bolder and heavier in scale than in earlier years. Storr made much use of fully modelled figures such as Classical nymphs and shepherds in naturalistic vein, and under French *Empire* influences of figures in a more formal style such as Grecian caryatids or figures of Victory or of the Graces. In the field of domestic silver style followed the examples set in the grander services, especially in small articles, although a number of small pieces such as tea-caddies and toasted-cheese dishes were of very severe, unornamented form. Branched candelabra became less popular after 1820, and by 1830 the single candlestick had generally gone out of fashion because of the increasingly widespread use of oil-lamps (the argand burner) and gas-light. Deriving their inspiration from French porcelain and silver, the silversmiths, like the potters, were quick to introduce Rococo forms and decoration into silverware some years before these features were adopted in furniture. It was in this phase that the late Regency tendency towards opulence of style in silverware became largely manifest.

5. POTTERY AND PORCELAIN. The ceramic productions of the Regency were esteemed during the Victorian period and up to modern times more highly than the furniture. The enormous quantities of brightly coloured wares found even in modest homes caused them to be regarded as

amongst the most characteristic and charming features of Regency life. Technical improvements in manufacture resulted in stronger and more colourful wares being available, and the export market embarked on a period of prosperity that lasted for over a century. Most of the existing factories continued to develop during the Regency. Among new potteries were the Herculaneum works (Liverpool), 1800; Ridgway, 1802; Rockingham, 1807; Nantgarw and Swansea, 1813; and Madeley, 1813. Many of the factories responded to the increasing demand for blue and white TRANSFER-PRINTED domestic wares. After 1810 improved printing and engraving methods brought about higher standards in the decoration of these wares. The resumed import of high quality COBALT from Saxony after the fall of Napoleon, *c.* 1816, enabled new blues of great variety and brilliance to be developed. In 1812 Samuel Walker's high-temperature enamelling kiln replaced earlier types of furnace. Wares could now be decorated in the factory instead of being sent out to an independent enameller. The cult of the Picturesque encouraged the use, especially by Spode, of English landscapes, castles, cathedrals, seaside resorts and other views, and by 1810 these had partly replaced *chinoiserie* designs. The *Empire* style was manifest especially after 1810, when Spode adopted such features as grounds of gold and deep green, plinth bases with lion-paw feet, and vase handles of Classical form. The Derby factory was strongly influenced by Continental design, which expressed itself in rich, often gilt ornament covering much of the surface of their pieces. Amongst many notable painters working at Derby were the several generations of the HANCOCK family. The porcelain figures of this factory continued to be produced but now in bone china instead of soft-paste porcelain. Pottery figures of popular characters produced by the numerous Staffordshire factories were found in the humblest homes. Obadiah Sherrott specialized in large and complicated chimney-piece ornaments such as 'Wombwell's Menagerie'. The general trend towards opulence and fulsomeness of design expressed itself, as with the silversmiths, in the revival of Rococo and this style, first adopted by the Coalport and Rockingham factories, was soon followed by Spode and others. The Madeley works produced, after 1825, an imitation of SÈVRES porcelain that is difficult to distinguish from the original, although the makers did not copy the French mark. In the later Regency years the Worcester firm of Barr, Flight & Barr up to 1813, and Flight, Barr & Barr until 1830, produced ornamental wares of remarkable quality and richness as well as domestic articles in refined taste, including pieces in the Etruscan and *Empire* styles. A large school of potters working in the WEDGWOOD tradition continued to make articles of high technical excellence and severe beauty of design in the Neo-Classical mode of Adam and Flaxman rather than that of the *Empire*.

6. TEXTILES. Coverings of domestic furniture in the early Regency were often of silk in French designs of the Neo-Classical or *Directoire* periods, sometimes of DAMASK in late 18th-c. designs. Later unpatterned silks and worsteds were used, their plainness relieved by coloured braids and fringes. A distinctive development was the continued and increased use of printed COTTONS, particularly coloured, glazed, block-printed CHINTZES, with designs influenced by Chinese and Indian originals. After Trafalgar nautical subjects became prevalent. Chintzes were used not only for curtains and bed-hangings but for covering upholstered furniture. TOILE DE JOUY fabrics continued to be made until 1810, especially with Dutch genre-subjects and landscapes as well as *chinoiseries*. An impetus was given to carpet-making by the increasing popularity of wall-to-wall carpeting. Hand-knotted Axminster pile-carpeting was adopted at Brighton Pavilion and came into common use. Improvements in machine-weaving brought the carpets of Wilton and Axminster into increased favour. These were of the Brussels type, with a looped pile, and were made in strips 67·5 to 90 cm wide with a repeating pattern which could be sewn together to cover the space required. Carpets with the looped-pile cut originated at Wilton and were later made at Axminster and elsewhere. Scottish carpets were usually of the woven, non-pile variety, and were often reversible. In the early years of the period the influence of the Adam school was still apparent, but later French *Empire* designs were widely used and after 1812 designs were of the exuberant, robustly Classical kind found in architectural ornament of the period.

7. GLASS. The main trend was again from elegance to massiveness and opulence. The tall narrow decanters of the late 18th c. with smooth slender necks and sloping shoulders gave place to squat, cylindrical or barrel forms with short necks encircled by rings to assist in holding. Stoppers were usually mushroom-shaped until 1820, when elaborate pinnacles became fashionable. Drinking-glasses developed from the trumpet shape on tall air-twist stems to stumpy bowl or bucket-like forms on a short, knopped stem and a broad base. Jugs also evolved from tall and elegant shapes to squat, low forms with large open necks. The Regency saw important developments in the highly elaborate cutting of glass, especially after the increased use of steam-driven cutting wheels after 1810. Production was greatly speeded up and extremely complex patterns became possible in the form of diamonds, step or prismatic cutting, fluting, lozenges, stars and geometrical motifs. In cheaper types of glass the vessels were blown into moulds and the cutting finished on the wheel. CHANDELIERS developed from the delicate late 18th-c. shapes of a central open stem, incorporating vase forms with a small number of widely spaced festoons, to a tent-like form completely enclosing the stem in a mass of closely set festoons and surrounded by a

number of nozzles and pans set in a ring. Irish glass was extensively used in England because it was not taxed until 1825 and thus could be sold much cheaper than English glass. The chief centres of glass production were London, Birmingham and Stourbridge. Coloured glass from Bristol was an important aspect of Regency glass production. Eventually it was made also at other centres: Stourbridge, Birmingham, Gateshead, Warrington and Sunderland. Of flint-metal, with added lead, Bristol glass was predominantly in the famous blue colour, but was also made in green, purple, amethyst, and after 1826 in ruby red. Nailsea coloured glass (from near Bristol) was a slightly inferior product of more popular appeal, being used considerably for souvenirs and other articles embodying an element of fun and fantasy, such as pipes, walking sticks, rolling-pins, even trumpets and swords, and the especially popular oval flasks often decorated with swirling ribbons of white glass embedded in the coloured shape. A more sophisticated form of ornamental glass was the 'CRYSTALLO-CERAMIE' of Apsley Pellatt, consisting of decanters, tumblers, mugs, sugar-basins, flasks, small bottles and wall-plaques. These were made of a brilliant glass enclosing portraits, coats-of-arms and other ornaments formed of a solid opaque paste set in the depths of the glass.

8. COSTUME. The interpenetration of Classical and Romantic ideas—formality and restraint on the one hand, naturalness and freedom on the other—was found in the sphere of ideas no less than in architecture. Under the influence of the Neo-Classical movement from *c.* 1770 onwards women's dress was becoming simpler in form. The hoops had been removed from panniered skirts, giving the softer outline seen in the portraits of Reynolds, Gainsborough and Romney. With the Revolution of 1789 an even severer Classical style was adopted from France, where ideas of 'Republican virtue' were cultivated in dress as in decoration and furniture. Following his first book, Thomas Hope published in 1809 a work *Costume of the Ancients*, which was welcomed as a practical fashion handbook as well as for its historical interest. Another volume, *Modern Costume* by Henry Moses, showed the same Classical dresses in domestic surroundings. This characteristic dress of the early Regency, with its straight vertical lines, high bodice and narrow skirt falling close to the figure in soft clinging muslins remained the standard until *c.* 1810, when Romantic influences brought in Spanish, Russian, Prussian and military features such as cloaks, mantles, braids and epaulettes in place of Grecian borders. Even 'Gothic' features began to appear. The skirt became gradually more *bouffant* from 1813 onwards and was emphasized by flounces at the hem. The waistline gradually fell and sleeves ballooned, the bodice developed a V-shaped line, until by 1830 the characteristic early Victorian outline had arrived. In men's dress even before the Revolution a simpler, plainer style had taken the place in daytime wear of the earlier full-skirted coats with satin breeches and silk stockings. By 1793 the close-fitting tail-coat with cutaway front, buckskin breeches and high boots had become the established vogue. Eventually breeches gave way from 1810 onwards to trousers, at first in the form of slim pantaloons strapped under the instep, and later, in the 1820s, to more voluminous garments, even of loose balloon-like shape, caught in at the ankle. In this manner did the pure classical severity of the early Regency give way to the typical exuberance and extravagance of the years at the threshold of the Victorian era.

7, 20, 233, 320, 349, 414, 618.

REJA (Spanish: 'grille'). The finest productions of the Spanish 16th-c. iron-workers were the great sanctuary and chapel grilles, constructed in two or more tiers and reaching as much as ten metres in height. At first the uprights were of square section but spindled balusters of hammered iron were made during the 16th c. The upper part of the screen was adorned with a CRESTING of foliage. Sometimes, as at Toledo, the balusters were heavily plated with silver. Wrought-iron grilles were also made for civic buildings, such as the House of the Shells at Salamanca. See also IRON AND STEEL (DECORATIVE WROUGHT IRONWORK).

RENIER (REGNIER, REINER) **OF HUY.** First of the great Mosan goldsmiths and bronze-founders, he was active at Liège in the first quarter of the 12th c. and is last mentioned in 1125. His only certain work is the bronze font made for Abbot Hellinus (1107–18), now in the church of St. Barthélemy, Liège. This work stands very much on its own; only a few Mosan IVORY-carvings of the late 11th and early 12th centuries are at all comparable in style and distinction. A few pieces have been attributed to Renier by analogy with the font, but only an exquisite small censer in the Lille Museum has been accepted generally as a work done under his close supervision.

REPTON, HUMPHRY (1752–1818). Remembered today as the third and last of the trio who led the English LANDSCAPE GARDEN movement during its heyday, Repton became the acknowledged successor to Capability BROWN, made his own particular contribution by developing a number of theories which he published, and became involved in the literary controversies on the subject of the *Picturesque* which followed the appearance in 1794 of Richard Payne KNIGHT's *The Landscape*, Uvedale PRICE's *Essay on the Picturesque*, and his own *Sketches & Hints*, published early in 1795.

Born at Bury St. Edmunds on 21 April 1752, Repton was intended for a mercantile career, to which end his father sent him to Holland at the age of 12 in order that he might learn the language.

On his return he joined a textile firm in Norwich, found the work uncongenial but endured it for seven years, which were made bearable by spending as much spare time as possible in pursuing his real interests of poetry, music and sketching. On 5 May 1773, he married Mary Clarke, by whom he had 16 children in the ensuing years, although only seven survived infancy. In 1778, having inherited a modest income on the death of his father, Repton forsook business and purchased a small estate at Sustead near Aylsham. Here he became absorbed in the practical aspects of husbandry and horticulture and made the acquaintance of two influential neighbours, Robert Marsham of Stratton Strawless, an authority on trees, and William Windham of Felbrigg. On the latter's appointment as Secretary to the Lord Lieutenant of Ireland in 1783 he invited Repton to accompany him as an assistant, but this employment lasted only a short time owing to Windham's illness. Repton returned to find that the expenses of a growing family were too heavy and therefore resolved to sell Sustead and move to a cottage at Hare Street in Essex, where he occupied himself for the next few years in writing art criticisms and a small book of essays entitled *Variety*.

Although he had long been interested in landscape gardening, it was not until 1788 that Repton had the idea of putting the practical experience gained at Sustead, and his natural gift of drawing, to use as a designer in this field, realizing that since the death of Brown five years earlier there had been no comparable expert. Commissions from various friends, notably Jeremiah Ives of Catton, Thomas Coke of Holkham, and Lady Salusbury of Brandesbury Park (now built over by part of Brondesbury, Middlesex), soon established him on what was to prove a highly successful practice. Repton's early works followed very much along the lines of Brown's designs, with serpentine water, sweeps of lawn and plantations on the higher ground; but the scale was usually smaller, the outlines more complex, and the plantations more prolific. In many cases he was called in to add further details to a lay-out of Brown's by way of more groups of trees, a 'pleasure garden', covered walk or greenhouse. Later on he began to advocate a return to some formality in the immediate surroundings of the house by way of terraces with steps and balustrading; also areas devoted to specific types—exotics, American trees, or even reconstructions of what he imagined to have been 'ancient' gardens.

An undoubted factor in Repton's success was the manner in which he presented designs to his clients, the text interspersed with watercolour drawings, many of which had movable flaps superimposed to show the effect before and after his proposals. He claimed to have prepared some 400 of these 'Red Books', which took their name from the red leather in which most of them were bound.

Not infrequently his commissions involved the alteration of an existing house or even the building of a new one. Like his predecessor Brown, Repton regarded architecture as an 'inseparable and indispensable auxiliary' to landscape gardening, but his own inexperience led him at first to seek collaboration with such professional friends as William Wilkins or Samuel Wyatt. Towards the end of 1795, however, he entered into a form of partnership with John Nash which, although it lasted for only a few years, produced some highly picturesque results, notably at Luscombe, Southgate Grove, Sundridge Park and the Casina at Dulwich. The financial arrangement was that Repton should recommend Nash for architectural work and that the latter should then pay him $2\frac{1}{2}\%$ on the cost, though this seems not to have been scrupulously observed by the architect. Their collaboration finally came to an end after a series of disagreements, although GEORGE STANLEY Repton, Humphry's second son, continued as an assistant in Nash's office for several more years. It was particularly ironic for Repton, who had introduced Nash to the Prince of Wales, that his own designs for altering the Brighton Pavilion should have been set aside while Nash sailed away to success as the Prince's architect and confidant.

At the turn of the century Repton's eldest son, JOHN ADEY, deaf from childhood but a fine draughtsman, became his father's architectural partner after serving for a short but not very happy period as an assistant in Nash's office. Together father and son undertook several important commissions, including Panshanger, Sheringham Bower, and extensive alterations to Cobham Hall, Kent.

From the earliest days of his practice Repton collected together his writings and early in 1795 published his first volume on the subject under the title of *Sketches and Hints on Landscape Gardening*. This was followed by the *Theory and Practice of Landscape Gardening* (1803), *Designs for the Brighton Pavilion* (1808) and finally *Fragments on the Theory and Practice of Landscape Gardening* (1816), all of them relying heavily on passages and quotations from the various Red Books, and containing engravings from his drawings.

The publication of the first of these books followed closely on those of his one-time friends, *The Landscape* by Richard Payne Knight, and the *Essay on the Picturesque* by Uvedale Price. There was just enough time between them, however, for him to insert in his own work a note refuting Knight's sarcastic lines on Repton's recommendation that the milestones at Tatton Park might bear their owner's heraldic device. Knight must, in fact, have seen the Tatton Red Book in the course of a visit to that house, and rather improperly used that proposal as a butt for one of his broadsides. In general, however, the comments of Price and Knight seem to have had little effect on Repton's reputation, and he continued to be busily employed until a carriage accident in 1811 disabled him for a long period. Thereafter he could undertake only a few works, and those with the help of his eldest son. He died at his cottage at Hare Street on 24 March 1818, but was taken to the parish church at Aylsham for burial in a grave near the south porch, the headstone of which has recently been restored and bears a poem of his own composition.

428, 430, 542, 628, 805.

RETICELLA. An early form of needlepoint LACE. It was a kind of NEEDLEWORK done on a foundation of woven linen which was almost completely cut away, and open-work patterns, usually geometrical in character, were worked with buttonhole stitching in the holes. Reticella work was practised chiefly in Italy during the

Reticella lace border. Italian. (V. & A. Mus., late 16th c.)

16th and early 17th centuries and was much used for ecclesiastical vestments and for civilian garments of an elaborate type. Such garments, decorated with reticella work, are frequently depicted in portraits of the time.

As time went on the stitchery became more elaborate and ornamental. Intricate cut-work was done on a frame to the back of which a panel of fine lawn was attached. On this the pattern was outlined in buttonhole stitch and the rest of the lawn cut away. Later the lawn was replaced by parchment, which was completely removed when the pattern was complete. The use of parchment led to freer patterns since the needleworker was no longer influenced by the rectilinear lines of warp and weft in woven linen.

REVERE, PAUL (1735–1818) of Boston. Son of Apollos Rivoire, of French Huguenot stock, who left France for Massachusetts in 1715 and set up *c.* 1729 as a silversmith in Boston, after serving an apprenticeship with John Coney. Paul Revere is best known as the American patriot who made his famous midnight ride on 18 April 1775, to warn of the British approach. He was an able silversmith. His best known pieces are a historic silver Liberty bowl and a group of presentation pitchers. He was skilled as an engraver of prints, book-plates and money. He engraved the earliest paper money of Massachusetts. He was also a merchant, and in 1801 he established a copper mill in Canton, Massachusetts. His portrait with a teapot in his hand, is in the Museum of Fine Arts, Boston.

150, 454, 666, 683.

RICKETTS, CHARLES (1866–1931). English painter, designer and writer on art. While a youth he met Charles Shannon (1863–1937), painter and editor of *The Dial*, and the two became lifelong friends. Ricketts founded the VALE PRESS in 1896 and was responsible for designing its type faces and decorations. But after 1904 he abandoned typography and turned to painting, sculpture and theatrical design. He was a notable connoisseur and collector. See ARTS AND CRAFTS MOVEMENT and PRIVATE PRESS MOVEMENT.

RIESENER, JEAN-HENRI (1734–1806). French cabinet-maker of German origin, born near Essen. He worked under OEBEN, whose widow he married in 1767. He was admitted as a master in 1768 and became the most celebrated exponent of the Louis XVI style. In 1774 he was made *ébéniste du Roi*. From 1774 to 1784 he was in high favour with the court, receiving commissions to the value of some 900,000 livres. Eventually his prices became too high and he lost the royal patronage. He stopped working soon after the Revolution. His first important task in 1769 was to finish the celebrated *Bureau du Roi* (now in the Louvre) begun by Oeben, and Riesener's name alone is stamped on it. He also finished the *Bureau du Roi Stanislas* (now in the Wallace Collection). This early work included elaborate pictorial MARQUETRY. By the mid 1770s this form of decoration was replaced by lattice-patterned designs enclosing water-lilies and finally, by the mid 1780s, Riesener was relying for the elegance of his cabinet-pieces upon simple veneers of plain mahogany.

509, 738.

RIETVELD, GERRIT (1888–1965). Dutch designer and member of the *de Stijl* group. His designs for furniture were in the Constructivist manner, displaying function and employing standard elements with rectangular cubic forms not joined but set together. His armchair, designed *c.* 1917 and illustrated in the magazine *de Stijl* in 1919, developed ideas derived from Frank Lloyd WRIGHT and anticipated the designs of Marcel BREUER. See FURNITURE (MODERN) and ART NOUVEAU.

347, 602, 662, 743.

RISEN BURGH (or RISENBOURGH), BERNARD VAN (d. *c.* 1767). French cabinet-maker of Dutch origin who signed his work with the initials B.V.R.B. He worked in the Louis XV ROCOCO manner, and specialized in LACQUER work and naturalistic flower decoration in MARQUETRY. There is a fine lacquer commode stamped with his initials in the Victoria and Albert Museum.

RITSUŌ (1637–1747). Celebrated Japanese lacquer craftsman, famous for his *inrō*. See JAPAN (INRŌ).

RITTENHOUSE, DAVID (1732–96). American clockmaker of Norristown, near Philadelphia. He was noted for his LONG CASE CLOCKS and afterwards for astronomical clocks. He was for a time Professor of Astronomy at the University of Pennsylvania, was secretary of the American Philosophical Society and was the first Master of the American Mint.

ROBBIA, DELLA. Family of Italian workers in maiolica. The most important members of the family were LUCA (1399–1482), his nephew ANDREA (1435–1525) and Andrea's five sons, the best-known of whom are GIOVANNI (1469–1529) and GIROLAMO (1488–1566). Luca was a sculptor who was regarded by his contemporaries as an innovator and modernist comparable with Donatello (1386–1466) and Ghiberti (1378–1455). His earliest recorded work is the *Cantoria* or Singing Gallery for Florence Cathedral (1431–8). He turned to ceramics primarily for practical reasons and *c.* 1430 founded the workshop business of modelling small figures in a characteristic style. The della Robbia style differed from that of other workers in maiolica in that the sculptural element predominates and the products are fully three-dimensional free-standing figures. Luca and Andrea used a white tin-glaze against a sky-blue background, but Giovanni approached nearer the conventional craftsman in maiolica by the use of a wider variety of colours. The della Robbia works were also distinctive for the non-vitreous character of their glaze, the opacity of their thickly applied colours and because they did not have recourse to the repertory of ornament used by other maiolica craftsmen. Girolamo della Robbia went to France, where he may have taught Masséot Abaquesne of Rouen, the first great French craftsman in faience. See also CERAMICS.

ROCAILLE. See ROCOCO.

ROCK-CRYSTAL. A colourless, transparent variety of QUARTZ, which takes a high polish but lacks the fire and brilliance of many gemstones. For this reason, and also because it is fairly abundant in a number of countries, it is not highly valued by jewellers. From early antiquity, however, it has been much prized for the production of small *objets d'art* and has been used for purposes similar to those for which GLASS was used. In many ways it was superior to glass. It is harder, and therefore retains its polish better and the cutting and faceting do not blur with time. It retains its clarity and does not cloud with age. And its colour is clearer than that of the early glass metals, so that indeed the clear Venetian glass and other similar glasses were named 'crystal' because of their likeness to it. Rock-crystal is cooler to the touch than glass.

Rock-crystal was much used in ancient Egypt, Crete and the Middle East for purposes of jewellery and for carving vessels and ornaments. It continued to be so used in Greek and Roman antiquity. It was carved by the Anglo-Saxons but was little used in Europe during the Middle Ages until the 16th c.—although the mace of the Lord Mayor of London is of rock-crystal and gold. Carving of rock-crystal became popular in Italy in the 16th c., where it was used among others by CELLINI, and later in Prague. Rock-crystal balls are commonly used by 'crystal gazers'.

Rock-crystal was much used in Islamic countries. See also GLASS (ISLAMIC GLASS AND ROCK-CRYSTAL). It is not known from where the Muslim crystal came. Literary documents speak of semi-legendary islands in the Indian Ocean, such as the Maldive and Laccadive islands and Madagascar, where crystal was said to have been sold. Nor is it always clear from the way they are described whether the objects the literature refers to were indeed in rock-crystal or in cut glass. Early Islamic rock-crystal objects—ewers, goblets, even chess pieces—are very similar in shape and decoration to their counterparts in blown and cut glass and stylistically do not belong to any specific region or time, even though a fair number of them obviously form a coherent group as far as their decoration goes.

Evidence points to Egypt as the birthplace of one such group under the brilliant dynasty of the Fatimid caliphs (A.D. 969–1171), which had amassed famous treasures apparently containing, amongst many other precious items, an enormous number of rock-crystal objects. The treasures of the Fatimids were dispersed between A.D. 1061 and 1069 and some of these pieces found their way to Europe, where they were highly sought after for a beauty and preciousness which were unparalleled in Europe at the time, so much so that some of these Islamic pieces were mounted in silver and gold and transformed into reliquaries. As such they found a place in collections as far apart as the Abbey of St. Denis in France, the treasury of San Marco in Venice and the Medici collection in Florence. These pieces are often the only ones to which one can ascribe an unquestionable latest date, since it is possible to refer to the entries in the inventories of the monasteries or princely collections.

Rock-crystal objects such as these were mostly decorated with a restrained type of arabesque as well as with heraldic birds and animals, singly or in groups. They were carved in relief with the details cut and engraved. Sometimes the name of the patron who commissioned them is included as part of their decoration, together with laudatory words in ornate calligraphy—the only other source of information as to their provenance.

Centuries later, in Mogul times in India, rock-crystal vessels were encrusted with jewels and decorated with typical Mogul flower motifs symmetrically repeated. They were similar in decoration and shape to those made out of JADE, which is even harder to carve than rock-crystal. It is therefore not surprising that the same Indian craftsmen are thought to have worked in both materials.

ROCKING-CHAIR. Chair with curved members, known as *bends*, connecting the front and back feet so that the chair may be rocked. Rocking-chairs were introduced in the 2nd half of the 18th c. and their invention has sometimes been attributed to Benjamin Franklin. They were very popular in the U.S.A., where they were principally developed. The earliest rocking-chairs were country-made WINDSOR chairs, ladder-backed or rush-bottomed chairs with bends added to the feet. In the early 19th c. a chair known as the 'Boston rocker' was first designed specially for rocking. The Boston rocker resembled a high-backed Windsor chair with the arms and back curved for greater comfort to match the curve of the bends. This became the standard type of rocking-chair in the U.S.A. Second in popularity to the Boston rocker was the Lincoln, which had an upholstered back continuous with the seat, and padded elbow rests. A simpler type of rocker, descended from the early ladder-back, was developed in the 2nd half of the 19th c. with rush bottom and caning in the back, and chairs of this type were exported to Britain. So-called 'American rockers' were produced by English chair-makers at High Wycombe and elsewhere, and these together with the American imports became a familiar article in the British home.

A different principle of rocking-chair, called the platform-rocker and in Britain the swing rocking-chair, was introduced in America *c.* 1870. The platform-rocker moved upon a stationary base instead of bends. A different type again was a rocking-chair in which the frame was made from bentwood or curved steel or brass strips so that the whole design of the chair expressed its function. The back and seat were either upholstered or caned. Rocking-chairs of this sort were made in the United States and also in Britain from the middle of the 19th c.

220.

ROCOCO. Stylistic term with both a historical and a descriptive connotation. Historically it refers to a style of European art which followed and to some extent emerged out of the BAROQUE and which was first developed in France during the first half of the 18th c. Although an accepted denomination in the history of the fine arts, it was primarily a system of decoration manifested in wall surfaces, furniture, plate, porcelain and ornament. Its influence on architecture, except in Germany, was slight. It was largely a protest against the intrusion of Classical principles of architecture inside the house and represented a movement towards freedom and informality, making use of Chinese motifs and GROTESQUES. In the days of Charles Lebrun (1619–90) the classical orders with their columns and massive entablatures had dominated interior decoration, creating a setting attuned to the ceremonious atmosphere of Louis XIV's court. But during the last years of the reign a revolt against strict etiquette on the one hand and against classical disciplines on the other began to gather force and triumphed during the rule of the Regent. The paintings of Watteau (1684–1721) reflect the tastes of the newly emancipated society—its sensuousness, elegance and informality, its cult of grace and lightness, its delight in the fanciful and the capricious. These qualities were also pervasive in the decorative arts. Heavy architectural features were banished from salon and boudoir and in their place sinuous linear curves in low relief, sometimes evocative of foliage, shells or other natural forms, sometimes echoing a classical motif and sometimes quite abstract, came into vogue for walls and furniture alike. Structural divisions were largely eliminated, the walls of a room merging gradually into the ceiling and the back, legs and arms of a chair being fused into one continuous all-embracing contour.

The characteristic ornament was a peculiar kind of shell-work called '*rocaille*' in France. A singularly abstract and formless motif that could be varied at will, it only resembled the natural object in its serrated edge and hollow, ribbed surface often pierced with a row of holes. After *c.* 1730, under the influence of designers such as PINEAU and MEISSONNIER, there was a marked tendency towards asymmetry, which may to some extent have been encouraged by the vogue for Chinese art. In furniture the dominant form was the cabriole leg or *pied de biche*, an S-shaped curve seen in the outline of commodes and the supports of chairs, tables, etc.

Between 1740 and 1760 the Rococo style was adopted by most European countries with characteristic national modifications. It was carried to extremes in Germany, where its influence was extended beyond the decorative arts to architecture. In England, however, the Palladian tradition of the 1730s and 1740s retarded the arrival and restricted the development of the style. Fashionable cabinet-makers such as CHIPPENDALE produced a certain amount of furniture 'in the French taste', but the convention never entirely dominated furniture design, still less the interior decoration of houses. A revolt against the extravagances of the Rococo and a movement in favour of classical discipline were simultaneously nurtured in France, England and Italy during the 1760s, leading in the next decade to the triumph of the NEO-CLASSICAL style.

ROENTGEN, ABRAHAM (1711–93). German cabinet-maker. After spending his early years as apprentice and journeyman in England and Holland he opened a workshop at Neuwied-am-Rhein in 1750, and built up a successful business in the German ROCOCO style of furniture. His son DAVID (d. 1807) worked in his father's business from 1761 and took over the management of it in 1772. He achieved international reputation and was one of the most sought after furniture-makers of the century. He had a branch in Paris, where he was made master of the guild in 1780. He was patronized by Marie-Antoinette and had contacts in Berlin and St. Petersburg. The workshop at Neuwied was brought to a standstill by the French occupation in 1795 but much of the stock was saved.

While his bronze MOUNTS lack the delicacy of those of CARLIN and RIESENER, Roentgen excelled in pictorial MARQUETRY. In this he combined delicacy with vivid colour and achieved new effects of light and shade by the skilful arrangement of small pieces of darker woods in the manner of PIETRE DURE mosaic. During part of his career he had as partner Peter Kinzing and towards the end of the 1770s they specialized in pieces of furniture equipped with elaborate built-in mechanisms. David Roentgen was the outstanding cabinet-maker of European status working in the NEO-CLASSICAL style.

Another member of the family, GEORG Roentgen, worked for a time in Copenhagen and was instrumental in introducing certain aspects of German Rococo taste into Denmark.

429, 509, 738.

ROGERS, BRUCE (1870–1957). Born in Indiana and educated at Purdue University, he was a TYPOGRAPHER and America's greatest book designer. From 1896 to 1911 he worked for the Houghton Mifflin Company's Riverside Press in Boston, heading a department for the production of limited editions. After a short visit to England he settled in New York and produced the Centaur typeface, one of the most successful modern adaptations of early ROMAN, based upon the type of Nicolas Jenson in his *Eusebius*. It was commissioned by the Metropolitan Museum of Art and first used for a book in 1915. From 1916 to 1918 he was adviser to the Cambridge University Press and from 1919 adviser to the Harvard University Press and at the same time worked with the New York printer William E. Rudge. He spent the years 1928 to 1932 again in England, where he produced works which are considered his greatest: the Oxford lectern *Bible*; T. E. Lawrence's translation of the *Odyssey*; and Stanley Morison's *Pacioli*. The last years of his life were passed in New Fairfield, Connecticut, where the books he designed included the Frick catalogue (begun by Porter Garnett), the *World Bible* and the Limited Editions Club Shakespeare.

517, 526.

ROMAN. A style of lettering combining capitals imitating ancient Roman inscriptions with small letters based on the Carolingian hand assimilated to the capitals in their formation. In printing it was the kind of type most commonly used for the Latin alphabet, distinguished from BLACK LETTER, and ITALIC script, and sans serif ('block letters'), by uprightness, rounded shapes, and serifs terminating the straight strokes. The immediate ancestor of roman type was the writing evolved by Italian humanists, chiefly for copying the Latin classics, which reached perfection soon after 1400 with the adoption of Roman inscriptional forms for the capitals. Of the early printers who adapted this script to typography Nicolas Jenson (Venice, 1470) and Aldus MANUTIUS (Venice, 1495) are outstanding for the beauty of their letters, and faithful reproductions of their types are in constant use now.

In subsequent times roman type has undergone many changes of fashion associated with the names of famous letter-cutters and designers, GARAMOND, the French Académie des Sciences, BASKERVILLE, BODONI, the family of Didot, generally tending towards greater delicacy and refinement of the thin strokes. Special varieties of it have been developed for newspapers and for display advertisements. The pale and over-refined book types of the 19th c. have given way, largely under the influence of William Pickering and William MORRIS, to reproductions of the bolder and more calligraphic romans of the 15th to 18th centuries. See TYPOGRAPHY.

ROMANESQUE. Term in art history for an international style manifested in the architecture and fine art of western Europe from *c.* the middle of the 11th c. to the close of the 12th c. Historically it is primarily an architectural term which has been extended to the other arts of the period.

ROMAYNE WORK. Contemporary term for a decorative motif consisting of small profile-heads in MEDALLIONS carved on furniture and panelling. This form of decoration was introduced into England from Italy in the time of Henry VIII and was often combined with Tudor roses and traditional GOTHIC tracery or LINEN-FOLD.

RONDE BOSSE. See ENAMEL.

ROSE CUT. Term used by jewellers and lapidaries for a style of cutting a gemstone so that it resembles a symmetrical rose. The base of the stone is a flat circular surface and the dome or CROWN is cut in rows of facets coming to a point and usually triangular in shape, the number of facets varying with the size of the stone. This cut has been much used for small DIAMONDS, especially for fragments resulting from sawing or cleaving operations on larger stones. It has also been commonly used for GARNETS and for pyrites (known as MARCASITES when so cut). But some historical diamonds have been rose-cut, notably the Great Mogul and the Orloff. See JEWELLERY.

ROSENBERG, CARL CHRISTIAN (1745–1844). Silhouettist of German birth who came to England in the retinue of Princess Charlotte of Mecklenburg in 1761. He was employed as King's Messenger by George III. He had a talent for profile drawing and after working at

Cheltenham and Ramsgate set up in Bath in 1787 with royal patronage. Here he prospered until 1799, when he seems to have been in difficult circumstances. In 1816 he moved to Windsor with the appointment of King's Messenger and retired in 1834 with a pension of £140 a year until his death. He worked mainly on glass and backed his glass paintings with a pink paper, which in most surviving examples has faded. He also did tiny profiles meticulously executed for setting in jewels, SNUFF-BOXES, etc.

ROSETTE. Ornamental motif of circular shape, radiating from a centre. It may be free ornament in high relief, as the ROMANESQUE and GOTHIC boss, or it may be painted, moulded or engraved on a flat surface. It may be naturalistic, composed of oak, sycamore or any other leaves, or it may be stylized or purely geometrical. It may have any number of divisions, but 3, 4, 5, 6, 8, 10, 12 or 16 are the most common.

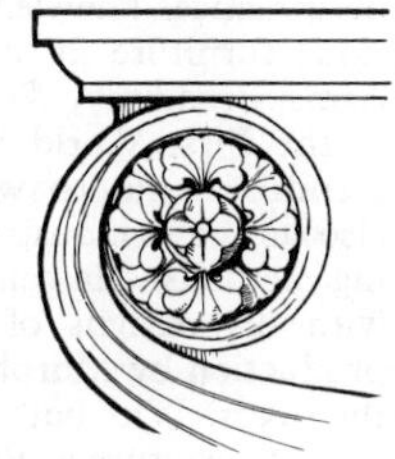

The rosette was used in ancient Egyptian ornament, chiefly in tomb-paintings. Different forms of rosette have been thought to be derived from the ovary stigma of the LOTUS, from the lotus flower with spread petals seen from above, and from a radiating group of lotus flowers or buds. It was an important feature of Babylonian and Assyrian decoration and became popular throughout the Middle East. It was very widely used in proto-Greek and Greek art for architectural, ceramic, mural and other ornamentation.

The rosette is one of the most widely disseminated of all decorative motifs. It is sometimes indistinguishable in appearance from the sun-disc and the wheel.

ROSE-WATER DISH. Term frequently applied to the silver basin over which guests washed their hands after dining. The basin was accompanied by a ewer but many more basins than ewers have survived, probably because when the practice of washing the hands at table after a meal was given up the basin could still be used as a dish whereas no useful function could be found for the ewer.

RUBY. A red variety of gem corundum closely akin to the SAPPHIRE. It is second to the DIAMOND in the scale of hardness and is the most prized gem after the diamond. The ruby is valued for clarity, transparency, intensity of colour and size. Large unflawed rubies are scarce in the extreme and may be more costly than diamonds. The most prized rubies are the dark crimson, almost purple, variety known as 'pigeon blood'. These, as with most of the finest rubies, come from Upper Burma. Other sources are Thailand and Ceylon.

The ruby has for centuries been particularly prized in India, where indeed all varieties of gem corundum were known as 'rubies'. In the past red SPINELS have often been confused with rubies and some of the famous historical rubies were in fact spinel. Synthetic rubies are made by the Verneuil process both for jewellery and for industrial purposes. They can be distinguished from natural stones by the fact that the colour distribution lies in curved instead of straight-edged bands.

RUGS. See CARPETS AND RUGS. In modern English usage the two terms are differentiated only in respect of size, 'carpet' referring to a larger and 'rug' to a smaller piece of fabric of the same type and serving a similar purpose.

RUGS, AMERICAN. North American rug-making began as a home craft with the practical object of providing some meagre measure of comfort amidst the privations of the early Colonial period. Woven carpets were virtually unknown before Independence. Floors were of sand or were covered by painted sailcloth and up to 1775 rag carpets were sometimes placed upon these for warmth and protection against draught. These were woven on hand-looms strung with stout linen warp, and were made from scraps and remnants of used textiles of all sorts which were cut into strips and sewn together. Pieces of carpet the width of the loom were sewn together to make a larger area.

Rugs too were made from scraps of worn clothing and other used textiles upon a foundation of coarse homespun or of burlap made from sugar and meal sacks. They were of three main types. (1) Patchwork rugs were made by sewing scraps of material on to the foundation. The best known of these are called 'tongue' rugs because the scraps were cut in tongue-shaped pieces, which were sewn on so as to overlap. (2) Braided, knitted or crocheted rugs were made from pieces of worn material which were cut into narrow strips and sewn together. For braided rugs three or more strips were braided together and then wound from the centre in a circular or oval shape and sewn at the edges. For knitted rugs balls of rags were knitted into strips about 15 cm wide and these were sewn together. Patterns were made by braiding dark and light colours together or by varying the knitted strips. Needletufts included candlewick, feathertuft (a delicate clipped tufting with a velvety finish) and unclipped rippletuft. Sometimes clipped and unclipped were used together in one rug to create a patterned surface.

(3) The third and best known type were the hooked rugs. Hooking is a very ancient technique, which was brought by the American settlers from their home countries. Loops of coloured material are pulled through the meshes of an open fabric to form a pile. The hooked rug developed, however, into a specifically American home craft. Few of those now in existence were

made before the 1850s and it is probable that few hooked rugs were made before 1700.

Worn-out materials were cut up into narrow strips and these were dyed and then hooked into a foundation of open-mesh burlap or home-woven flax. The hook, like a large crochet-hook, was often home-made from wood or bone or forged from a piece of old metal. The dyes used were also those to hand. Red was obtained from cranberries, beets, madder or logwood, crimson from pokeberry juice. A characteristic pink was made by powdering old bricks. Yellow was made by boiling onion skins with alum and for green the juice of goldenrod flowers was mixed with indigo. Blueberries and hickory bark were also used. Designs were very various, sometimes crude and sometimes more sophisticated. But crude or not they were almost invariably naturalistic in intention; there was no tradition of stylization as with many Oriental rugs. (See CARPETS AND RUGS.) Marine designs, popular among collectors, were often made by sailors—or by their wives. French settlers of Quebec and Nova Scotia specialized in elaborate floral designs. Animal designs were common and mottoes were often included. In the latter part of the 19th c. Edward Sands Frost, an invalided soldier and former tin-peddler, began the sale of patterns made from metal stencils to the women of New England and built up a business which flourished into the 20th c.

Among the North American Indians the Navajo rugs have been particularly fine. These were really blankets, made at first to be worn over the shoulders, though they have often been used as rugs. They were woven by a distinctive technique in which bast fibres, feathers, etc. were introduced into the foundation of warp threads. The early patterns were in dark and light stripes from natural, undyed wool. The stripes were then broken by zig-zag lines in what is known as the 'terrace' pattern. The famous 'bayeta' was made from red baize obtained from the Spanish and later combined with indigo and other dyes. The modern Navajo rugs are made in geometrical patterns of natural grey, white and black interspersed with patches of colour.

472, 705.

RUNNING DOG. See VITRUVIAN SCROLL.

RUSKIN, JOHN (1819–1900). English writer who combined art theory and criticism with social and economic theory and who in his day was considered the most important influence in this field. His views continued to influence the theory and practice of the ARTS AND CRAFTS MOVEMENT.

RUSSELL, SIR GORDON (1892–1980). English furniture designer and artist–craftsman. He was a self-taught craftsman, who acquired his practical knowledge through repairing antique furniture in his father's inn, the Lygon Arms, Broadway, Worcestershire. After service in the First World War he took to designing furniture in the COTSWOLD SCHOOL tradition, then also turned to industrial design and manufacturing methods. He gained a European reputation with his designs of radio cabinets for mass production by Murphy and other radio firms in the 1930s. With both hand and machine production of furniture at Broadway ('making the best modern furniture by hand [and] . . . the best-designed modern furniture by machine'—N. Pevsner, *Architectural Review*, cxxxii, 1962) he emerges with Sir Ambrose HEAL as pioneer of the Modern Movement in English furniture design. He was knighted in 1955. During his period as director of the Council of Industrial Design, 1947–59, the Design Centre was opened in 1956 in the Haymarket, London.

734.

RUSSIA

1. INTRODUCTION. In 988/9 Vladimir, Great Prince of Kiev, adopted Christianity as his country's official religion and decreed that all things pagan were to be destroyed. His order was obeyed with such thoroughness that few works of a pagan nature survived in his principality and it has therefore become customary to date the beginnings of Russia's arts to the time of the country's conversion to Christianity. By choosing to join the Orthodox Church rather than the Catholic Vladimir linked Russia's culture so firmly to the BYZANTINE that the association was not weakened when Byzantium succumbed to the Turks. Even when impaired by Peter the Great's Westernizing reforms it persisted in the religious arts until the outbreak of the Revolution. None the less even when still in its opening stage—that dating from its inauguration to the break in its development caused by the Mongol occupation (1237/40–1480)—this northern offshoot of Byzantine art quickly acquired its own very distinctive flavour.

2. WOODWORK. Although artistry as distinct from fine craftsmanship was not attained before the 11th c., excavations have shown that the crafts were well developed and fully established in most urban centres well before the end of the 10th c. There was hardly a Russian who did not excel at working wood, whether on a large or a small scale; metal-workers were producing a wide range of articles; potters were making use of the wheel, jewellers had acquired the art of fashioning silver. At the country's conversion

these craftsmen were therefore able quickly to adapt themselves to the needs of the Church and its congregations. The portrayal of the human figure in the round having been forbidden on the grounds of idolatry, carvers concentrated on the production of crosses, medallions, icons, reliquaries and the like in addition to that of the bowls, vessels, spoons, mugs, lamps and other domestic utensils which they had been in the habit of making. Oak being primarily reserved for the building of houses, bridges and pavements, carvers generally worked in pine, sometimes in maple. Many must also have carved the religious scenes depicted on small devotional objects made of bone, slate or stone in addition to providing the stone moulds used for casting metal articles of devotion and personal adornment. The basically Byzantine style of these small and delicate religious works varied from region to region, from workshop to workshop and from individual to individual. The variations represented the first efforts made by the Russians to mould the Christian art they had adopted to suit their own tastes. Details of pagan origin often infiltrated into these early Christian works and persisted in doing so in the remoter regions till relatively late times. The pagan motifs which survived the Mongol occupation were assimilated into folk art and since most of the later carvers were of peasant stock ancient designs of this type, such as the *sirin*—the fabulous woman-headed bird of Russian folklore which led travellers to their doom by the beauty of its singing—often figured in their carvings, whether of a religious or secular content.

The earliest small-scale religious carving to have survived is a small icon of SS. Boris and Gleb (1067–8), which was found in the Taman peninsula. A slightly later one is double-faced, presenting St. Demetrios of Salonica on one side and The Seven Sleepers of Ephesus on the other. These icons are surpassed in quality by two others both illustrating the Doubting Thomas, one presenting the scene with great restraint whilst the other stresses its emotional content.

Carving suffered a less severe setback under the Mongols than the other arts and many small carvings dating from the Mongol occupation depict complex scenes with a number of figures. Many were deeply undercut to produce both dark and light, and the lace-like effects so sought after by the Russians in their architecture. Much of the best work was, however, done in the unoccupied and prosperous Novgorod region. It is characterized by the predominance of curved lines and a profusion of detail. The fondness for curves dictated the curious shape of the extremely ornate Ludogoshchinsky cross, which was erected in 1359 in the Church of Florus and Laurus in Novgorod by the inhabitants of the Legoshchaya Street. The arms of the cross are outlined by circular incisions, each of which originally contained four small crosses to mark the circle's quarters; the semicircular sections protruding from near the ends of each arm provide them with cross-shaped terminals, whilst the entire body of the cross is studded with 18 carved roundels set against a background consisting of religious symbols, geometrical motifs and interlacing patterns of Norse origin. The rarity of Norse influence in Russian art of this period is surely an indication of the selectivity of the artists; for although the interlace occasionally figures in work of the pre-Mongol invasion period, more especially in calligraphy, on rarer occasions in sculpture and articles of personal adornment, it plays all in all a very small part in the country's arts.

In the 15th c. octagonal medallions carved in a style closely in accord with that of the period's religious paintings became popular. In the workshops of the Troitsky-Sergeeva Lavra (now Zagorsk) the carver Dionysios Amarosy was profoundly influenced by Andrey Rublev's pictorial style and was in his turn to influence others. In the 16th c. the proportions of the figures were elongated just as in the paintings of Dionysios and his followers. Although it includes some later work, the Kilikievsky cross from the Spasso-Belosersky Monastery near Vologda is a fine example of this early 16th-c. style.

The introduction of the wooden iconostasis towards the end of the 14th c. or during the opening decades of the 15th provided carvers with great scope for decoration. The earliest example of an ornate iconostasis to survive is the one which Archbishop Makariy commissioned in 1533 for the Cathedral of Sta Sophia at Novgorod. Like the Ludogoshchinsky cross, and in conformity with the carving style, the iconostasis was worked in a flat manner lacking the modelling of sculpture. The same approach is evident in the almost life-size figures of saints which were generally carved in remote, heavily wooded regions such as those of Vologda or Kaluga. Few of them were worked completely in the round, for mindful of the ancient prohibition on statues their makers preferred to leave a strip uncarved at the figure's back in order to fix it to a wall. Sometimes they were carved in very high relief to form the centre of a large panel; then roundels containing figures of Christ, the Virgin or a favourite saint were added to the background to increase the carving's resemblance to an icon. Although these works are often artless, they are so candid and expressive that they convey the deep sincerity and piety which animated their makers. Because of their function the Royal Doors of the iconostases received particular attention and were the first to be deeply undercut and floridly decorated. When these innovations were resorted to on the rest of the iconostasis such ancient pagan motifs as the *sirin*, the griffin and the lion often appeared amidst scrolls of vegetation and fruit. In the 17th c. the best carved and gilt work of this type was produced in the Tsar's workshops in the Palace of Arms at Moscow. The finest wood-workers were also employed there at making furniture and carriages in addition to church furnishings. When Peter the Great closed the Armoury workshops he transferred the best artists and craftsmen to St. Petersburg. By then their carvings were so deeply undercut and well modelled that they resembled sculptures and as such came to influence such eminent 18th-c. architects as Rastrelli and Ukhtomsky. Their descendants helped to provide the magnificent PARQUET floors required by architects for the imperial palaces and great private mansions.

In the pagan and early Christian periods men were in the habit of suspending bone combs from their belts. To help avoid the evil eye they often adorned the handles of these combs with horse-shaped terminals, emblems of the sun cult. Other amulets depicted the bear or combined the head of a creature resembling a Shaman idol with a Norse interlace. CHESS PIECES, on the other hand, were never decorated with anything more elaborate than geometrical or linear incisions. Domestic utensils retained their earlier shapes with the handles of spoons and other articles often ending in the bird or animal heads which had been popular since the 3rd millennium B.C., when a wooden prototype of a much later silver *kovsh* or scoop was being used by the Gorbunovskaya bog-dwellers. In the 17th and 18th centuries fishermen living on the shores of the White Sea, carvers of fish IVORY, began making elaborate caskets of Western shape. The peasants carved TOYS of wood and whalebone from a very early date. Excavations at Novgorod have shown that the wooden ones included hobby-horses and horse-drawn chariots—emblems of Apollo's carriage—decorated with painted emblems of the sun cult. When Peter the Great's Westernizing reforms relegated the carver's art to the position of a craft the peasants created for themselves a folk art of great richness and fascination.

3. METALWORK. Excavations have shown that the Slavs had worked precious metals such as silver in antiquity and that metallurgy became established in Rus several centuries prior to the country's conversion to Christianity. By the end of the 10th c. urban craftsmen were turning out a wide range of iron tools and implements, casting the majority from clay matrices. Contemporary jewellers excelled at delicate filigree work, fixing it to its base by a method of cold soldering that soon after became a forgotten technique. In the 11th and 12th centuries they made much use of granules and their skill at NIELLO and ENAMEL earned them the admiration of THEOPHILUS. Above all, however, jewellers were fond of EMBOSSING and CHASING their designs. In a country where the purchase of luxury wares of a secular character was largely confined to court circles and where the Church was a far more important patron than even the Great Prince, much of the jeweller's output was of a religious character; yet there were always some women who were able to buy such articles of personal adornment as half-moon shaped earrings with three filigree balls attached to their rounded ends, rings, necklaces, bracelets, belt buckles, even ball-shaped buttons covered with strands of filigree. There were also still many pagans secretly requiring amulets and belt buckles shaped like women but either having swan or bird attributes or assuming the shape of a stylized human head flanked either by two animals or by two animal attributes of Scythian character. Sometimes these pagan motifs were accompanied by an interlace of Norse origin. The Norse element is unusually strong in a 12th-c. bangle found on the site of the Mikhaylovsky Monastery at Kiev, where it is combined with motifs of a strongly Oriental character; but the number of objects representing this transitional phase in Russia's development remains extremely small. Two examples of 10th-c. secular art that do so were recovered from the Chornaya Mogila near Chernigov; although fragmentary and much damaged, they are of quite outstanding interest. Both formed part of the silver MOUNTS fitted round the tops of the two auroch horn oliphants which are now in the Historical Museum, Moscow. On both the decorations are executed in REPOUSSÉ work set against a POUNCED background. On one the design is confined to vegetation, but the other displays a hunting scene in which single or paired animals and birds not only retain a physical resemblance to those found in the art of the Eurasian nomads of the first millennium B.C., but also adhere to the ancient iconography. Thus two griffin-headed animals resembling horses are posed back to back on either side of an emblem derived from the ancient Tree of Life. Other creatures, including cocks, are ranged on either side of them in accordance with Achaemenid principles, while two hunters—one a bowman, the other a spearman—are seen on the extreme right. Norse influence is reflected in the tentative, almost uncomprehended use of interlace, logically interpreted here as a chain or rope linking the various animals rather than as a decorative device. The fragment is a well-nigh unique representative of the vigorous, secular type of art favoured by the few Slavs who were rich enough to satisfy their love of luxury at a time when the ancient culture was giving way to a newer, wholly different ideology.

Descriptions of the magnificences of Constantinople that reached Kiev, together with the visible beauty of Vladimir's new palace and the splendour of gold first seen on a large scale in the mosaic decorations of Kiev's Cathedral of Sta Sophia, made an instant and lasting impression on the Russians. From the 15th c. Muscovy was to express this taste for splendour by means of its gold domes; in the 18th c. the Empress Elizabeth did so by having the sculptures on the façades of her palaces and the statues ranged along their roofs gilded, while in the 19th and 20th centuries those in a position to do so adorned their tables with numerous gold objects.

In the 11th and 12th centuries, however, gold was so expensive and in such limited supply that burnished copper was often used instead for larger works. As in Constantinople so in Vladimir, the Golden Gate into the town was faced with copper, the floor of Suzdal's Cathedral of the Nativity was made of copper and its ambo and west and south doors were of DAMASCENED copper. The ambo has disappeared, but the two sets of doors survive to rank as extremely important examples of European art in the 13th c. They were made between 1230 and 1233. Originally each door contained 28 square damascened panels—14 to a side—with 7 narrow rectangular panels at the centre. The west door has lost 4 square and 3 rectangular panels, the south door only 4 square ones. The west doors are devoted to the Virgin, who was regarded as the guardian of the principality of Vladimir, and to the Evangelists, whilst the south doors feature the archangels, angels and saints most closely associated with the region's rulers. The titles of the various scenes are inscribed on each panel, the third narrow one on the west doors representing Bishop Mitrofan, who was to be burnt alive in this very cathedral in 1238 by the invading Mongols. Prior to the Mongol invasion damascene work of fine quality was also done on a small scale, chiefly on bangles and icon embellishments. The decorations on a 12th-c. half-moon plaque from an icon in the Dormition Cathedral at Vladimir, now to be found in the town's museum, consists of two birds placed back to back on either side of a Tree of Life with a leaf design framing the scene.

Kiev became the chief, possibly the only, centre for the manufacture in Russia of cloisonné enamels. The industry was established there almost with the adoption of Christianity and its output appears to have been of a uniformly high quality. Although most of the surviving examples are religious in character, consisting of medallions containing the busts of saints, small plaques depicting religious scenes and even smaller ones of a decorative type, some necklaces and earrings have also been found in Kiev. In both the religious and the secular enamels the colour range is made up of white, turquoise, dark blue and a distinctive pinkish-yellow. Although not quite so luminous as the colours found in Byzantine enamels, the Kievan examples fully justify the praise which Theophilus bestowed on them. The religious enamels conform closely to the Byzantine style. The secular give freer expression to the Russian love of imagery and decoration by featuring perky birds, gay geometrical motifs and either flower petals or lozenges. Stylish *sirin* birds adorn the finer pieces, their pear-shaped wings linking the world of the Scythian nomads to that of the Norsemen and their tails, counterparts of which appear in the early book illuminations, connecting them still more closely to Scandinavia.

Bronze was used for church bells; copper and iron for the cast crosses erected on the roofs of churches; bronze, copper or iron for knockers and the better lamps used in churches and private dwellings, while the cheapest lamps were of pottery. Church lamps followed the Byzantine pattern consisting of a hoop fitted with small oil containers made of metal or glass.

Necklace and two pendants of gold cloisonné enamel, together with coloured glass rings and a bracelet. (Russian State Mus., Leningrad, 11th–12th c.)

In the 12th c. quarrels over the succession weakened Kiev and whilst the principality of Vladimir became representative of the courtly arts, Novgorod consolidated its position as the fountain-head of the national style. Its Cathedral of Sta Sophia became the repository for some of the finest examples of silver dating from the 11th and 12th centuries. Between the 12th and 14th centuries the Small and Great Zions of silver made in the form of rotundas topped by crosses acquired great importance. They were used in religious services to symbolize the Church. Their domes and either the sections serving as drums or those forming their walls were often divided into niches by means of columns in order to contain figures of saints worked almost in the round. Equally characteristic of the region and period are the silver vessels which were used for the Eucharist. Shaped like mugs of wavy outline, they were fitted with two S-shaped cast handles ending in a flower head and thus resembling the handles on the Byzantine 11th-c. bowl in enamelled glass preserved in the Treasury of St. Mark's Cathedral, Venice. The decorations on these vessels combine relief work and engraving, with inscriptions contributing to the balance of the designs. The main inscription usually encircles the vessel's rim. Two examples preserved in the Museum at Novgorod include the names of the silversmiths who made them, the maker of one being Constantine Kosta, of the other Frolov.

As in earlier times, so both in the Novgorodian and the Muscovite periods, much attention was lavished on the decoration of Gospel covers, reliquaries and crosses. Among the finest of the earlier silver plaques pride of place must be given to a 12th-c. one of SS. Peter and Paul executed in repoussé work which is now preserved in the Historical Museum at Novgorod. The gold cover which was made in the 13th c. for the famous icon of the Virgin of Vladimir is preserved in the Palace of Arms, Moscow, and is a work of exceptional beauty. Also in the Palace of Arms is the helm which was made for Prince Yaroslav Vsevolodovich. A fine silver Gospel cover in the Lenin Library, dated 1392, has decorations embossed and chased on it in the customary manner. It was not unusual, however, for the subsidiary designs on objects of this type to be engraved or for jewels mounted in pearl circlets to figure among their decorations. At Novgorod the influence of the ROMANESQUE style of western Europe can sometimes be seen, though seldom as clearly as in the silver Panagiria made in 1435 by the silversmith Peter for the town's Cathedral of Sta Sophia on behalf of Bishop Euphymios. Peter concealed the vessel's stem by the figures of four angels worked almost in the round yet still with a touch of the flatness which characterizes carved works of a similar date. The angels stand on the backs of lions couchant, supporting in their raised hands a shallow dish the lid of which is decorated with the scene of the Annunciation.

By the 15th c. Moscow's position as the country's capital and leading cultural centre could no longer be challenged. Its rulers were once again in a position to exercise authority and to enjoy the wealth of kings. In 1449 Vasili the Blind was able to present the Troitsky-Sergeeva Lavra with a superb chalice made of red marble set in gold, one of the first truly sumptuous objects to have been produced since the Mongol invasion. In the country towns fine work was also devoted to the production of BOOK COVERS of a wholly decorative character and devoid of religious significance. Yet it was the silver, silver-gilt, and sometimes gold, icon covers that were in especially great demand. Their borders often contained the figures of saints and scenes were sometimes included in the central area, although that was generally covered either with rows of rosettes or with geometrical or floral motives. Book covers of a similar kind continued to be made throughout Russia until the Revolution.

The Church's need for vessels of various kinds grew apace after Constantinople's conquest by the Turks with Russia's new role as the chief representative of Orthodoxy. Then and in the following century censers were frequently given an architectural shape. Some reflected the influence of the Gothic West, but the majority reproduced such features of contemporary Russian architecture as the tent-shaped steeple or kokoshnik-shaped gable. A fine example of the former type in the Historical Museum at Moscow is dated to 1597, one of the latter type in the Kremlin's Armoury to 1578. Yet from *c.* the middle of the 15th c. the output of secular articles almost equalled that of the ecclesiastical and was soon to outstrip it. Every type of tableware was from then onwards produced in silver, sometimes in gold, with niello from the start contributing in no small measure to the decorations of the silver vessels. Perhaps as an indirect result of the establishment of a printing press by Ivan IV, the Terrible, inscriptions also played a prominent part in their decorations. A foremost place was from the start assigned to the silver *bratina* or loving cup, later used as a punch-bowl; but the *kovsh* or dipper became a Tsar's traditional gift to a courtier whom he wished to honour, whilst the *charka* or quaich was soon to be found in most households. All three retained the shapes of their wooden predecessors, but were covered with a profusion of floral or leaf scrolls. Only one attempt at portraiture survives from the Muscovite period. It takes the form of a silver full-length portrait of the Tsarevich Dmitri, which was made to lie on his coffin in 1630 by the Armoury silversmith Ovdokimov and four of his companions. The work is delicate, accomplished and extremely sensitive; the expression on the young prince's face clearly reflects the look of an indulged yet unhappy, perhaps ailing child. The cover has been moved from the Palace of Arms Museum to its original place above the child's coffin in the Cathedral of the Archangel Michael in the Kremlin.

Copper continued to be used in the Muscovite period for chandeliers, lamps, and even for table tops, when it was burnished to resemble gold. The ornate gates and their elaborate hinges made in 1625 for the Dormition Cathedral in Moscow are of gilt bronze and so are those in the Novodevichy Convent there. Following the conquest of Siberia in the mid 16th c., however, IRON started to reach Moscow in sufficient quantities to enable blacksmiths to produce the lace-like wrought-iron crosses which were to contribute so much to the beauty of Moscow's sky-line. In Rus iron had been used for implements, tools and amulets; henceforth its range was extended to include a wide variety of objects, many of which were in wrought iton. The Historical Museum at Moscow contains a very strange weather-cock in its iron collection. It is dated to the 17th or 18th c. and takes the form of a large-beaked, big-clawed bird, its hindquarters twisted upwards in the opposite direction to the rest of its body, its tail terminating in a half-crescent. The habit of inverting a section of a creature's body characterizes the Scythian type of art practiced by the Altaian nomads of

Belt buckle in the form of a woman with bird attributes from the district of Poltava. (The Historical Mus., Moscow, 7th c. A.D.)

Silver censer whose forms are reminiscent of the tent-shaped steeple and *kokoshnik* gables of contemporary architecture. (The Historical Mus., Moscow, 1579)

Copper candlesticks of the type popular in Moscow in the 17th c.

Seventeenth-century silver tableware. A. short-handled ladle or *kovsh*; B. quaich or *charka*; C. loving cup or *bratina*; D. ladle or *cherpak*; E. strainer or *sito*. (V. & A. Mus.)

Cut steel ornaments from the Tula works. (V. & A. Mus., latter half of 18th c.)

Pazyryk during the last half of the first millennium B.C. Its extraordinary reappearance in this weather-cock must surely be due to the influence exercised by one such work stolen during the reign of Peter the Great from a prehistoric Siberian burial and brought back to western Russia. See ANIMAL STYLE and ASIA, CENTRAL.

Delight in size for its own sake originated in mid Muscovite times. It expressed itself in the immense dimensions of the church bells cast at this period and induced Andrey Chokhov to cast the huge cannon which stands in the Kremlin and is, a trifle incongruously perhaps, edged at its muzzle with a band of rosettes. When Peter the Great's military requirements decreased he did not hesitate to employ the men working in his TULA munition works for making steel ornaments. The industry was expanded under Catherine II to include furniture and mantelpieces, and maintained till her death in 1796. It has been suggested that the technique used for the purpose may have been developed in the Matthew BOULTON works, but this seems unlikely both because of the early date of the works sponsored by Peter and also because the Russians cut the steel into many-faceted rosettes which they riveted to the framework according to a method which appears to have been unknown in Birmingham but which was used regularly in the Tula Arsenal.

The art of cloisonné enamelling was brought to an abrupt end by the Mongol invasion, but late in the 14th c. enamels were being made again, this time in Novgorod, where they consisted of a coating of a single colour applied to a slightly hollowed-out section of a silver or gold background. By the latter half of the 16th c. polychrome effects were once again being achieved. Two gold Gospel covers in the Museum at Novgorod, the one dated to 1554, the other to 1560, are adorned with brightly coloured flowers and foliage. The finest work of the period is to be seen in the adornments of Andrey Rublev's masterpiece, the icon of the Old Testament Trinity. Here the enamel was not placed in cavities but white, black, pale and dark blue particles were dropped on to the surface of the repoussé-worked flowers. This is early Muscovite enamelling seen at its most delicate. As Moscow's output grew so did the price of enamels fall, the range of colours widen and become brighter in tone. Polychrome all-over decorations made much use of the distinctive, essentially Russian shades of green, yellow and pink. They stood out with especial clarity when placed against a white ground on dishes, plates and quaiches decorated with bird, flower and fruit designs. Enamels featuring green, pale and dark blues and black started to be made at the time in the workshops set up by the Stroganovs at Solvychegodsk, which concentrated on producing crosses, buttons and ear-rings, which had a ready sale in many markets. By the 17th c. small icons made of painted enamels were in current production and the same technique came to be used to great advantage in St. Petersburg for SNUFF-BOXES and other small objects. Great Ustyug, lying as it does on the trade route linking Siberia to the White Sea, also became a thriving centre for the making of jewellery and enamels. It was there that in the 1730s the technique originated of covering copper objects with several coatings of fired enamel in order firmly to fix small silver plaques to the surface of the last coat. The technique was used for making boxes, trays, tea and coffee services, the earlier greenish-turquoise enamelled ground being replaced later in the century by either an opaque white one or a midnight blue. Catherine II often chose these enamels for prizes in the lotteries she liked to organize.

In the 18th c. goldsmiths and silversmiths produced a full range of tableware and a wide variety of articles in the styles prevailing at the time in western Europe whilst shaping and decorating them in accordance with Russian taste. Delicate jewellery combining several precious metals and stones became the fashion. The finest brooches, hair sprays, necklaces, rings and bangles were made in St. Petersburg. Flower motifs were especially popular during the reign of the Empress Elizabeth (1741–61), gold, silver, diamonds, emeralds, sapphires, spinels, pearls and enamels often being combined in a single article. During the reign of Catherine II (1761–96) bows and clusters tended to replace the sprays and black profiles or silhouettes set against a gold ground were favoured for rings. Technical and mining advances made it possible for urns, vases and similar marble objects set in ORMOLU to be made in increasing numbers. Their shapes were well suited to the severe EMPIRE style and satisfied the Russian preference for the large and massive; but the flower decorations, which had been popular first in Moscow and were then encouraged by the Empress Elizabeth, continued to appear. In the 19th c. jewellers sympathizing with the Slavophile movement often produced small objects or decorations reverting to the shapes and styles which had originated in medieval times. For example they made miniature replicas of oak settles to serve as salt cellars and inscribed proverbs or greetings on them in ancient lettering. FABERGÉ's work sharply contrasted with theirs, for although the flowers and animals which he fashioned in rare marbles and jewels were essentially naturalistic in style, his more elaborate works were attuned in spirit to the 18th c. and his more ingenious ones, notably the intricate Easter eggs which he devised for members of the imperial family, to that of the Baroque world. They were a swan song to an out-dated society.

4. CERAMICS. The history of ceramics is less glorious than that of the country's woodwork and metalwork, but it is just as long a one. Nor is it entirely lacking in distinction. The pottery which the pagan Slavs made between the 5th and 8th centuries showed a steady improvement, but the real advances were made between the 9th and the 13th centuries owing to the adoption of the wheel and the development of high-temperature firing. The earlier pottery vessels copied the shapes of the primitive wooden ones which they replaced, but new techniques led to the creation of new shapes, most of which were derived from Byzantine models. As a result a flat-bottomed, two-handled jug became available as well as a large assortment of ewers, bowls and dishes. Many were stamped either with the maker's or the purchaser's mark or monogram. Soon after many were being decorated with lines or inscriptions in the form of greetings, traced on them with a stick. The inscriptions were to become traditional in Muscovite times, when they were transferred to silver ware.

Glazed tiles dating from the 10th c. were found in the Gnezdovo burials. In the 11th c. those made in Kiev for flooring the finest churches were coated with yellow, white, blue and brown GLAZES. Tiles from the Taman peninsula display creatures of Sassanian origin such as the *semurv*, or two birds set back to back on either side of a Tree of Life, similar to designs appearing on Kiev's cloisonné enamel ear-rings and on Suzdal's damascene plaques. In contrast to these the tiles recovered from the site of the Great Princess Olga's palace and the Church of the Dime at Kiev are decorated with wavy lines, loops and circles. Similar tiles have been found in contemporary churches in Vladimir, Galich, Gorodetz, Ryazan, Polotsk, Smolensk and Chernigov, where they are executed in yellow on a brown ground. The earliest of these are dated to the 10th and 11th centuries, a period when pottery toys were being made in Novgorod. Those in the form of human or animal figurines were unglazed, but whistles were glazed. In the 16th c. potters diversified the figurines, adding those of musicians as well as bears with rings in their noses, bird-shaped whistles and riders seated on high-backed saddles on horses closely resembling those in icons of St. George. In the 19th c. the greatly sought after rattles and figurines made in Radonezh were coated with a red glaze and decorated with white patterns. Viatka became noted at the time for its comic figurines and Okhta for its satirical representations of St. Petersburg's middle-class inhabitants, personages paralleled in the writings of Griboedov and the paintings of Perov.

Elaborate vessels such as the amphora disappeared during the Mongol occupation, when only coarse, utilitarian wares were made. Early in the 15th c. the dawning revival was heralded by the introduction of the white clay which was to become characteristic of the finer 16th-c. wares. By the end of the 15th c. it was occasionally being covered with a yellow glaze. Before long potters were turning out aquamaniles and jugs of complicated shapes, some of which were inspired from Persian and Turkish metal models. They were covered with the black glaze which remained very popular throughout the 16th c. and were decorated with animal designs of Eastern origin. Potters also produced at this time flasks shaped like barrels but for the flat base at their centres and others with their sides flattened to resemble discs, with the spouts placed at their centres and their bases fitted with two pairs of tiny feet. The disc-shaped sides were generally decorated with animals of heraldic appearance.

Terracotta tiles were first made in the 15th c. They were often decorated with flowers or mythological creatures such as unicorns or with dolphins. They were then white-washed in order to resemble sculptures and used to form friezes on the façades of important buildings. In the 16th c. they were replaced by glazed tiles decorated with either religious or secular subjects. The earliest were given a green ground and their designs were carried out in yellow, ochre and blue. They were used for facing the large built-in stoves which were used for heating. Although they were first produced in Moscow and Ryazan, Yaroslavl quickly became the chief manufacturing centre. The output there was so large and varied and the quality so good that by the 17th c., possibly owing to Persian and Turkish influence, they were being used to decorate façades of buildings such as the Krutitsky Teremok in Moscow and to panel church interiors or even to cover their columns, capitals and cornices, as in the main churches of Yaroslavl. The colour range was widened to include white and turquoise, the subjects varied to extend to genre, mythological and battle scenes with their titles inscribed on them. In the latter part of the 17th c. excellent tiles were being made in the workshops which the Patriarch Nikon had attached to the New Jerusalem Monastery. A fascinating collection of tiles is on view in the Kolomenskoe Museum, in the suburbs of Moscow.

All the attempts which were made during Peter the Great's reign to learn the secret of manufacturing PORCELAIN failed and it was not until 1748 that as a result of trial and error a chemist called Vinogradov discovered it for himself. Within two years he was able to provide the Empress Elizabeth with a large dinner service, a year later he was turning out snuff-boxes of quality and in 1752 he began making figurines of the type which the MEISSEN factory had made universally popular. Vinogradov's workshop was reorganized in 1803 into the Imperial Porcelain Manufactory and it soon came to rank sixth in importance in Europe. It remains in existence today as the State Porcelain Manufactory. Throughout its history it supplied the court with most of the china which it needed. The first dinner service which Vinogradov made for the Empress Elizabeth took account of her love of flowers, for the joins in its basketwork

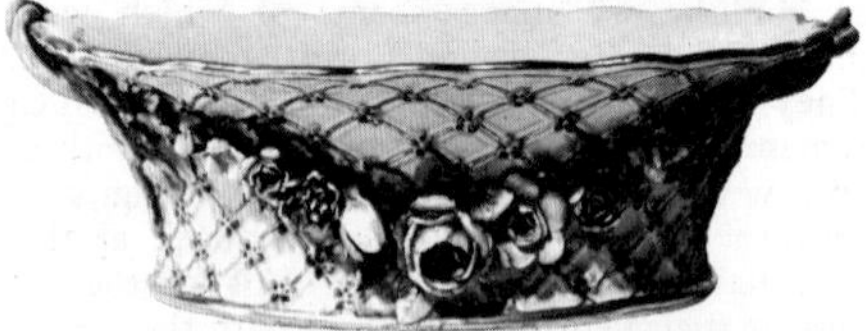

Bread basket from the Empress Elizabeth's porcelain dinner service. (Hermitage Mus., mid 18th c.)

design were marked by a rosette. Catherine II enlarged the factory and encouraged the production of figurines, especially those featuring regional costumes and occupations, rather than mythological characters and blackamoors. Alexander I preferred to have his services decorated with views, especially those including buildings, Nicholas I demanded military uniforms, whilst medieval Russian designs became popular during the reign of Alexander II.

The Imperial Porcelain Manufactory was not the only one in existence in the latter part of the 18th c. and the first half of the 19th c. Many of those founded at the time proved short-lived, but an exceedingly successful, privately owned one was established at Verbilki, near Moscow, in 1776 by Francis Gardner, a descendant of an Aberdonian who had emigrated to Russia in Cromwell's day. The excellent quality of his wares came to be quickly recognized and although he had to contend with many difficulties, he was able in 1777 to fulfil Catherine II's order for the 4 dinner services needed at the annual dinners given by the sovereign to the holders of the 4 main imperial orders, those of St. George, St. Andrew, St. Alexander Nevsky and St. Vladimir. Each piece in each of these sets displayed the appropriate decorations and symbols. Nicholas I arranged for replicas to be made by the Imperial Porcelain Manufactory for use at the annual banquets in place of the Gardner originals. Gardner's factory prospered till the 1880s, when it was bought by Kuznetzov and amalgamated with his own to become the largest porcelain works in Russia. The excellence of Kuznetzov's china and faience enabled him to capture the Afghan, Indian and Chinese markets, but he continued to use the Gardner mark on these exports till the first decade of the 20th c. Although the Gardner factory acquired a great reputation for its figurines, Kuznetzov ceased making them. In the 19th c. there were at least 20 factories producing excellent china. Of these the Yusupov Porcelain Factory (1814–31) at Arkhangelskoe, near Moscow, the Batenin (1812) which was bought up by Kornilov of St. Petersburg after it had been gutted by fire in 1839; the A. G. Popov (1806–75), near Moscow; the N. M. Sipiagin (1820) which was taken over in 1865 by Ikonnikov who ran it till 1875 and won much admiration for the figurines which he made from Popov moulds; the Kornilov Factory in St. Petersburg (1835–1917) and the A. T. Safronov Factory in Moscow (1830–51) were all especially admired. But it was the original A. G. Popov factory (1806–75) at Gorbunovo, near Moscow, which ranked as second in importance to the Imperial Manufactory during the greater part of its entire existence.

5. GLASS. During the Mongol occupation GLASS suffered the same setbacks as the other minor arts. The large number of beads recovered from burials dating from pagan times has led some authorities to believe that glass was being made in Rus before its conversion and the establishment of its links with Byzantium. It was certainly produced in Kiev in the 11th c. for excavations have uncovered the sites of workshops manufacturing glass mosaic cubes. Glass was in such plentiful supply at that time that bangles and rings made of it were very fashionable. The same pale and dark blue, green and yellow glass was used for them as for the vessels which were being made not only in Kiev, but also in Vladimir and Ryazan. But the Mongol invasion killed the industry and it did not revive till well into the 16th c., and then only in the Ukraine.

The first glass-works to become established in central Russia were founded at Dukhanino, near Moscow, in 1635 by a Swede who hoped to compete successfully with the glass being imported from abroad, chiefly from Germany. Soon afterwards Tsar Alexey founded the Izmailovsky factory near his country estate of Ismailovo, close to Moscow. He staffed it with three Russians and one foreigner. At much the same date he established another factory at Voskresensky, near Moscow, which, although he called it the Chernogolovsky, was generally called after that village. In 1691 Peter the Great established another factory in Moscow, close both to the Kremlin's Tainitsky Gate and to the river. There Ukraninian glass-blowers produced some good quality glass adorned with gold decorations. Peter also founded the Imperial Glass Manufactory on the Sparrow Hills, but in 1720 he merged it with the large works at Yamburg and transported both to St. Petersburg to become the new Imperial Manufactory. By the middle of the 18th c. it had acquired an experimental unit and a school of its own. It was quickly recognized as the best in the country. Much of its glass was intended for use at court and was therefore decorated with the sovereign's portrait, crest or monogram. Most of the fine

Lidded glass goblet made at the Imperial Glass Manufactory, St. Petersburg,? and engraved with the arms and monogram of the Empress Elizabeth (18th c.)

turquoise glass used for chandeliers and sconces of the best quality, as well as for dressing-table accessories, was also made there. Towards the middle of the 18th c. the physicist and grammarian Lomonosov had started making mosaic cubes for the purpose of reviving the art of mosaic. He established a factory for the purpose at Ust-Ruditsky, some 80 kilometres from St. Petersburg and he intended to immortalize Peter the Great's achievements by a series of mosaic panels. He personally designed and set the Tsar's portrait, but the only other panel to be completed was that of the Battle of Poltava and this was largely done by Lomonosov's pupil, Pyotr Druzhynin. At Lomonosov's death in 1765 his heirs sold the factory.

6. EMBROIDERY. Although there is indirect evidence that a great deal of fine needlework was done in Russia in pagan times, it was the acceptance of Byzantium's artistic traditions that transformed EMBROIDERY into an art. Worked in silk in a flat stitch it rapidly established itself and in the 11th c. the Yanchin Convent in Kiev already possessed its own school of weaving and embroidery, where the finest textiles were imported from both the Eastern and the Western worlds to serve as models. The chronicles contain a number of references to the embroideries which adorned the country's chief cathedrals. Those in the Dormition Cathedral at Vladimir must have been particularly fine for they receive special mention, but none survived the fire which destroyed the first structure in 1183. Nor does any of the embroidery done at Kiev survive. The contemporary textiles which have been preserved all consist of unpatterned woven stuffs, but some had had designs block-printed on them. The blocks and dyes used at the time were provided by icon painters, a practice which persisted until the 17th c. The blocks were generally made of pear or maple wood and measured some 30 by 40 centimetres. Their designs were often geometrical although some of the earliest included patterns of Byzantine and Persian origins, whilst later ones reproduced Italian, Persian and Turkish textile designs. The dyes were obtained from vegetables and had at first to be diluted with butter. Although several shades of ochre and red, including a very bright one, were available in addition to gold, silver, black, indigo and orange, it was unusual for more than two colours to be used for a block print. Favourite colour schemes consisted of red and black, and orange with natural shades. In the 17th c. the block-printing of plain textiles was done by the peasants and run as a cottage industry. In their hands colours became brighter and the designs increasingly elaborate. In the 18th c. metal sections were inserted into the carved blocks to help in obtaining tonal variations.

Until the 18th c. icon painters also furnished the embroiderers with their designs and dyes. Several examples of Novgorodian embroidery from the 12th c. have survived and serve to illustrate the period's religious style. Some are exhibited in the Historical Museum in Moscow and in the Novgorod Museum. An exhibit in the Historical Museum is perhaps the earliest of all. It is worked in a flat stitch on a fine 8th- to 9th-c. Byzantine textile displaying designs of

Sassanian origin; it presents a very linear rendering of the Crucifixion, showing two figures aligned on either side of the cross with four angels above them. The scene is enclosed in a border which is studded with 11 medallions containing the busts of Christ and some evangelists and apostles. The robes are worked in gold, the rest of the scene in silk. Although very Byzantine in character, the scene is infused with more emotion and movement than is usual in Constantinopolitan work of the same date.

The vestments of Barlam of Khutin (d. 1193) are preserved at Novgorod. They are worked in gold on a blue ground. The three main figures in the *deesis* scene have the sturdy, stolid bodies found in contemporary painting of Novgorod. They are placed in arches which together with their supporting capitals and columns recall the arches used by Bactrian silversmiths some 1,500 years earlier to contain nude women in works produced under Indian influence; these Bactrian works are in their turn related to decorations of a similar kind found on Sogdian ossuaries of much the same date, such as that of Bia Naiman. The scrolls which border the embroidery, however, recall the sculptured scrolls on the façades of the buildings which the Seljuks were erecting in Asia Minor and Anatolia at much the same time. The embroidered vestments of St. Anthony the Roman, who is said to have floated to Russia on a stone in the 12th c., are different again, their designs consisting of both circular and oval sections containing paired animals of Eastern appearance standing on either side of a Tree of Life. V. N. Lazarev believes that they derive from a Byzantine or Eastern stuff. The motifs undoubtedly originated in the ancient Orient, but the convolutions of the animals' tails and the length of their claws seem to resemble certain nomadic works rather than Persian ones.

No major examples of 13th-c. embroidery or textiles have been preserved, but the best Novgorod embroideries from the 14th and 15th centuries are finer than those which survive from the period before the Mongol invasion. Like the earlier panels they too follow the Byzantine tradition, but their style keeps step with that of the contemporary Russian school of religious painting. Flat stitches continued to be used as of old to the exclusion of raised work. To judge by the hangings which the Great Princess Maria, widow of Semyon the Proud, commissioned in 1389, the backgrounds also remained plain and empty. In this case the ivory ground has embroidered on it the Vernicle with the Virgin and St. John standing on each side of it to form the *deesis* scene. The work is carried out in violet, pale blue, raspberry red, pale brown and green silk with gold thread forming the haloes. The figures are well proportioned and elegant. The embroidered trimmings of much the same date worked on the cope of the Metropolitan Alexey are very different in conception; there the needlework sets out to simulate metalwork and makes use of metal plaques to assist in doing so. Photius, a native of the Peloponnese, became Metropolitan of Russia in 1410 and held that office till 1431. He wore a cope made of a woven Byzantine stuff and on several occasions sent to Byzantium for embroidered panels and epitaphies to serve as models for the Russian embroiderers whom he employed. Their influence proved limited and of short duration, for even their colour schemes failed to appeal to the Russians.

Until the 15th c. nuns were responsible for all the important religious panels embroidered in Russia and continued until the 18th c. to provide the greater part of what was needed. But in the 15th and 16th centuries many fine panels were also embroidered in the sewing rooms which the ladies of the ruling families established in their palaces. The list of these palace embroideries is headed by the fine altar-cloth worked under the direction of the Princess Agrafevna between 1409 and 1425 for the Cathedral of the Virgin's Birth at Suzdal. Christ appears on it twice, and each time his figure is worked in gold whilst the rest of the colour scheme is carried out in pale blue, violet, pale brown, green and raspberry silk.

By the 15th c. it was not unusual to place a life-sized portrait-icon of a saint beside his coffin. Following the death *c.* 1422 of the great prelate St. Sergius of Radonezh, founder and first abbot of the Troitsky-Sergeeva Lavra, the Great Princess of Moscow and her embroideresses worked a portrait shroud of St. Sergius to be placed over his coffin. Although its style is iconic and the saint's face ascetic, his mouth, pursed in pain, contains an element of true portraiture. That element is lacking in the slightly later version of the same shroud. A small number of shrouds of the same type were embroidered during the 15th and 16th centuries in several princely sewing rooms and similar ones, this time of notables rather than of saints, were also worked in Romania in the 16th c. Several of the Russian examples are to be found in the museum at Zagorsk.

Many of the finest large embroideries were produced between 1430 and 1453, when Archbishop Evfimy's workshop developed a style in which grace, sentiment and profound piety were expressed with great restraint and economy of detail. The style is admirably represented by a panel of a nine-figure *Deesis* in the Tretyakov Gallery in Moscow. Each personage stands beneath a slender, delicate arch of simple yet charming shape. The candour and purity of the rendering presents a striking contrast to the elaborate, very similar presentation of the Deesis adorning the vestment of Barlam of Khutin. Like so many 15th-c. panels this clearly reflects the influence which the painter Andrey Rublev exercised over his fellow artists, an influence which was later to be supplanted by that of the painter Dionysios.

In the latter part of the 15th c. Sophia Paleologina, the second wife of Ivan III, and Helen of Moldavia, wife of Ivan's son and heir, were often exceedingly jealous of each other. Their rivalry extended to their embroidery. It was Sophia, a Byzantine princess who had spent 20 years of her youth as a refugee in Rome, who was responsible for the cloth embroidered with religious scenes made for draping round Andrey Rublev's masterpiece, the icon of the Old Testament Trinity, painted 1422–5, in memory of St. Sergius of Radonezh, Rublev's first abbot. The stitch used for most of it is the flat Russian one, but Sophia had the trees, clothes and buildings which appear on it dotted with multicoloured speckles, a technique which was new to Russia but well known in Rome. Two other embroideries with similar speckles in the Zagorsk museum should also probably be ascribed to Sophia's workshop. In 1498 Helen of Moldavia must have undertaken the embroidering of a panel commemorating the Palm Sunday procession which was attended by Ivan III, Sophia, and his nephew Dmitri, all of whom appear on it. Their figures are devoid of any element of portraiture, but the embroidery is a splendid one. Helen was not content only to choose a Wallachian colour scheme for it but in order not to be outdone by her stepmother-in-law she had the border worked in a Wallachian stitch. Indeed, she may have embroidered that section of the panel herself.

In the 16th c. backgrounds became fuller and more use was made of gold and silver thread. As the metal was apt to tear the stuff it became customary to couch the thread along the fabric and to stitch it into place with coloured silks. Much work of this type was done in the palace sewing rooms as well as in those which had become established in the households of certain prominent boyars. Sometimes gems were added, in which case the embroidery attempted to simulate metal FILIGREE work. Pearl embroidery also became extremely popular at this date. Together with the gold and silver work it was especially admired by Boris Godunov. He commissioned several panels as gifts to the Troitsky-Sergeeva Lavra, where they are still preserved. Since woven patterned fabrics were still extremely expensive and in short supply, plain stuffs were often embroidered to simulate the imported ones. By the 17th c. much excellent embroidery was also being produced in the major regional capitals, but it was in the workshops which the Stroganovs established at Solvychegodsk that much of the best work was done. Among many notable panels pride of place must be given to the hanging in the form of a travelling iconostasis worked in 1592 for Tsar Fyodor and his wife Irina. It was used by Peter the Great when campaigning and suffered as a result, but the fragments preserved in the Russian Museum, Leningrad, testify to its beauty. The slightly later Sapieha standard was also made in the Stroganov sewing rooms. It is as notable for the quality of its design as for its workmanship and the delicacy of its colour scheme, where silver, gold, pale blue and lemon yellow are admirably attuned.

Embroidered chasuble. The yoke simulates the delicate metalwork of the period and the figural, geometrical and floral motifs of the robe include Turkish-looking tulips and embroidered inscriptions. (Palace of Arms, Moscow, 1587)

7. LACE. The Muscovy Company was the first to import gold and silver LACE to Moscow. Ivan IV, the Terrible, and Boris Godunov were quick to trim their finest robes with it in place of the locally produced braids and embroidery. Although the imports of lace of this type rapidly increased, within 25 years some was being made in the sewing rooms of the Palace of Arms in the Kremlin. By 1627 it was also being made in the Stroganov workshops and by the middle of the century so much was being produced that a cheaper type made of copper thread could be bought in the markets of Moscow. Often pearls, sequins and coloured stones were worked into it, heavier qualities being intended for use as bed-hangings and curtains, the more delicate as dress trimmings. At the same time lace-makers engaged in copying Flemish lace were producing floral designs which often featured tulips and carnations, whilst those who copied lace of the Italian type were creating geometrical patterns. In the Petrine age lace of various types and drawn-thread work had become very decorative while some lace-makers even succeeded admirably in reproducing the great spectacles, pageants, state functions, even the firework displays, of their day. In the 19th c. the Slavophile movement led to the revival of certain ancient motifs such as the cock, the Great Goddess of antiquity, the Tree of Life. They had never ceased to figure in the red cross-stitch embroideries with which peasant women were fond of adorning their household linen and furnishings, but these elaborate, extremely decorative creations belong to folk art rather than to the more pretentious luxury creations.

8. LACQUER WORK. The LACQUER boxes, brooches, trays and similar objects which are to be numbered with the finest decorative works produced today in the U.S.S.R. have a fairly long history. Although PAPIER MÂCHÉ was being

used in Russia for purposes of interior decoration, as a substitute for stucco, from the 16th c., it was not lacquered. When the distinguished traveller Pallas visited Siberia in 1770 he noted that lacquered objects were being produced by the Demidovs, a family of industrial magnates, on their Lower Tagil estates. At the time the technique was unknown in western Russia, although it was already being quite widely practised in other major European countries. At the end of the 18th c. a Russian merchant, Pyotr Korobov, whilst visiting Braunstein, Germany, was enthralled by the lacquer snuff-boxes which were being made there. After much effort he managed to bring 10 German lacquer-workers to Russia and in 1796 to establish a factory of his own on his estate of Danilovka, near the village of Fedoskino, in the district of Moscow. Within a few years he was able to replace the Germans by Russian workers and greatly to expand his works. After his death in 1819 the works continued to flourish till 1904 under the name of his son-in-law, Pyotr Lukutin. It was from Fedoskino that the icon painters living in the villages of Palech, Mstera and Kholui, where icon painting was a hereditary occupation, learnt to make equally fine lacquer work.

Korobov's rapid success was due initially to orders for the lacquered peaks fitted to military caps—a line which quickly went out of production because of the introduction of new uniforms. He had, however, also produced trays, and these had sold well. Lukutin acquired an international reputation for his snuff-boxes. By 1832, when he employed over 100 workers, his annual sales exceeded 65,000 roubles, individual snuff-boxes selling for 35 roubles. Lacquer objects were always included in the Russian sections of the great industrial exhibitions held in various European capitals in the latter part of the 19th c. In 1803 F. N. Vishnyakov set up as Lukutin's rival in Moscow and by the 1830s Bool, Petz and I. Mullert had all founded workshops in St. Petersburg which were admired for their goods. By the middle of the century the number had considerably increased.

The scenes depicted on the earlier objects were drawn from peasant life, but some private customers had their houses, parks and favourite landscapes pictured on the objects they ordered direct from the lacquer workshops. By the end of the century the range of objects and scenes had greatly increased. At Fedoskino a school-teacher, L. D. Derzhavina, kept the craft alive by founding in 1910 a craft centre in the village. The Soviet authorities have infused new life into the craft, encouraging its growth and sponsoring a very wide choice of illustrations. The best designs are signed by their makers and these objects rank as minor works of art in the U.S.S.R.; they deserve to be more widely recognized as such.

9, 41, 345, 546, 649, 701, 723, 724, 808.

RUTILE. A form of native titanium dioxide used *inter alia* as a colouring agent for GLASS and PORCELAIN and also rarely as a gemstone. Since 1948 synthetic rutile has been made by the Verneuil process which is superior to natural rutile for the purposes of jewellery. It has the fire and brilliance of a DIAMOND but lacks the hardness of diamond, having a hardness index of only 6·5 on the MOHS SCALE.

S

SADDLERY. See LEATHERCRAFT.

SADELER, EMMANUEL and DANIEL. See MUNICH SCHOOL.

SALOMON, BERNARD (1506–10?–*c.* 1561). Engraver and illustrator for the Lyon printers, especially Jean de Tournes. He belonged to the period of the Italianization of French culture. He is best known as an inventive engraver of ARABESQUE patterns. The Apocalypse designs for his *New Testament* (1541) are taken from Holbein and he was also indebted to Dürer. His two most celebrated works are *Quadrains historiques de la bible* (1553–4) and *La Métamorphose de l'Ovide figurée* (1557).

SAMBIN, HUGUES (*c.* 1515–*c.* 1601). French designer and wood-carver of Dijon. His published ornamental designs *Œuvre de la diversite des termes* (1572) made him famous. They were Mannerist in style and proved a rich source of ideas, particularly for the furniture-makers of the Dijon and Lyon areas of France, whose late 16th-c. cabinets were profusely carved with caryatids, figure subjects and interlacing strapwork.

SAMPLERS. A sampler was a piece of cloth worked with various stitches and designs in EMBROIDERY and serving originally the same sort of purpose as was served by pattern-books. The word 'sampler' derives ultimately from the Latin *exemplum* or *exemplar* in the sense of a 'model for imitation', and indeed by the 14th c. '*exemplar*' had already acquired the special meaning of an ornamental pattern or design.

Samplers were of various sorts. Professionally worked samplers were used to record and disseminate ornamental motifs in embroidery just as pattern-books were used in ornamental metalwork, furniture, interior decoration, etc. Embroidery fragments which may have been from samplers of this sort have been found in Egyptian burials from as early as the 4th c. A.D. and may have been used in the Near East even earlier than this. Samplers were also used to teach the elements of stitchery to beginners. As embroidery became a recognized accomplishment of young ladies the sewing of samplers came to be a regular feature of the schoolroom. There is evidence that early in the 17th c. samplers were even used for teaching children the alphabet as well as stitchery (an alphabet was included in Giovanni Ostau's pattern-book of 1561, but this may well have been intended as guidance for embroidering signatures or inscriptions), and in his *History of the Horn-book* (1827) A. W. Tuer was able to argue that the true function of the sampler coincided with that of the horn-book in that it taught letters and numerals as well as stitches. Dr. Johnson grumbled that: 'Our girls forsake their samplers to teach Kingdoms wisdom.'

There is no evidence that samplers were known or used in Europe until late in the 15th c. They seem to have become fashionable *c.* the middle of the 16th c. after the emergence of printed pattern-books, and motifs taken from the books can be found in early samplers. The fashion coincided with the rise of domestic embroidery and the idea that needlework belonged peculiarly to the province of women of leisure. From the tone of literary references, which are quite numerous, it would appear that samplers were often made as showpieces, examples of fine craftsmanship and virtuosity.

Printed pattern-books from which designs were introduced into samplers are known from Germany and Italy in the 1520s. *Esemplario di lavori* by Giovanni Andra Vavassorie was published in Venice in 1530 and *La Vera perfettione del designo* by Giovanni Ostau in 1561. French and English publications were later: *La Clef des Champs* by Jacques le Moyne in 1586 and a translation of *Les Singuliers et Nouveaux Pourtraits pour touttes sortes d'ouvrages di Lingerie* by Frederic di Vinciolo in 1591. A book of patterns by William Barley entitled *A Booke of Curious and Strange Inventions, called the first part of Needleworkes* appeared in 1596. Perhaps the most influential of all was Johann Sibmacher's *Schön Neues Mödelbuch* (1597), published in Nuremberg, motifs from which were reproduced in John Taylor, the Water poet's popular pattern-book, *The Needle's Excellency.*

The earliest known reference to English samplers occurs in the account books of Queen Elizabeth of York for the year 1502, in which it is recorded that a sum of viijd. was paid to a certain Thomas Fisshe for 'an elne of lynnyn cloth for a sampler for the Quene'. A reference to gold thread in connection with a sampler occurs in the Welsh poet Tudur Aled (d. *c.* 1520) and Thomas Skelton (1460–1529), tutor to Prince Henry (Henry VIII), spoke in the *Boke of Phyllyp Sparowe* of a child embroidering her dead sparrow into a sampler and again in *Garlande of Laurell* describes the sewing of the ladies of the household of the Countess of Surrey:

> With that the tappetis and carpettis were layde,
> Whereon theis ladys softly myght rest
> The sampler to sow on, the lacis to enbraid.

Sir Philip Sidney in Bk. II of *Arcadia* wrote: 'And then, O Love, why dost thou in thy beautiful sampler set such a work for my desire to take out?' And Shakespeare has two well-known allusions. In *Titus Andronicus* he makes Marcus recall to his niece Lavinia how Philomela, deprived of her tongue by Tereus, 'in a tedious sampler sew'd her mind'. And in *A Midsummer Night's Dream* Helena, pleading with Hermia, recalls how once they had 'with our needles created both one flower, / Both on one sampler, sitting on one cushion . . .' Actual samplers known to survive from the 16th c. number only seven: a German and an Italian example in the Victoria and Albert Museum are believed to be from the first half of the century. The five English examples include one worked in lace patterns, silk and metal threads on linen, with the Royal Arms of Queen Elizabeth I and beneath the signature Susan Nebabri. The earliest dated example, discovered in 1960, now in the Victoria and Albert Museum, was made by Jane Bostocke in 1598. Before this discovery the earliest known dated sampler was one of German origin signed 'Lucke Boten' and dated 1618. It may thus be said that the history of the sampler begins roughly with the 17th c. It extends to the middle of the 19th c.

The 17th c. was the great age of the sampler. Samplers were done both in embroidery and in cut-work (called *punto tagliato*) and the closely allied drawn-thread work until the diminution in the popularity of ruffs and other forms of lace adornment about the end of the century put the latter somewhat out of fashion. Samplers were worked on bleached or unbleached linen and their size and shape depended on the material available. In many of them the length was the woven width of the linen. The most popular type in the earlier and middle years of the century were long and narrow, up to 90 centimetres or more in length and from 16 to 30 centimetres wide, with decoration arranged in parallel bands. Another type, of which fewer examples are known, was squarer in shape and the motifs and devices were more or less regularly dispersed over the whole area. These are commonly referred to as 'spot' patterns. From *c.* 1630 samplers of the band type were usually

British sampler. Cross stitch in bright colours on white canvas. The sampler includes alphabets and numerals and the traditional Oriental theme of birds confronting a Tree of Life. (Embroiderers' Guild, 1866)

dated, but those with 'spot' patterns were very rarely dated or signed. The fashion in Elizabethan and Stuart embroidery for basing decorative motifs on flowers and fruit, animals, insects, fishes, as well as human figures, was reflected in the samplers. In doggerel verses introducing *The Needle's Excellency* John Taylor catalogues the variety of patterns as follows:

Flowers, Plants and Fishes
Beasts, Birds, Flyes, and Bees
Hills, Dales, Plains and Pastures
Skies, Seas, Rivers, Trees.
There's nothing near at hand or farthest sought
But with the needle may be shap'd and wrought.

An interesting book by Randal Holme entitled *The Academy of Armory* and printed in Chester in 1688, deals with needlework in Book III and referring to 'a sam-cloth vulgarly called a sampler', gives the following list of stitches: 'Plat stitch or single plat stitch which is good on one side; plat stitch or double plat stitch which is alike on both sides; Spanish stitch which is true on both sides; tent stitch on the finger, tent stitch in the tent, Irish stitch, back stitch, fore stitch, Queen stitch, gold stitch, satin stitch, tent stitch upon satin, fern stitch, finney, new, chain, bread, fisher, rosemary, bow, whip and cross stitches.' The different kinds of work were also listed: 'Raised-needlework, pearl, Geneva, Virgin's device, cutwork, laid stitch and thorough stitch, lapwork, rock, frost, net, purle, tent and fingerwork, all of which are several sorts and manners of work wrought by the needle with silk of all natures, purls, wyres, which cannot be described.'

As the century progressed lace patterns and the use of metallic threads and beads decreased, quality of needlework and stitchery deteriorated. As the sampler became more and more an educational device for the young, diversity of pattern and technique tended to give way to a sameness. Early

Instruct me, Lord, to lift my heart
To thee, in praise and prayer.
And love and gratitude impart
For every good I share.
Martha Price aged 11, 1841.

British sampler. Multi-coloured pattern in cross stitch on linen scrim. (Welsh Folk Mus., 1841)

in the 18th c. a notable change in the character of samplers took place. While the honeysuckle and carnation motifs remained established throughout the century, pattern changed to a more freehand style with the influence of imported Indian printed cottons on embroidery and on fashion generally. See COTTON AND COTTON PRINTING; INDIA (TEXTILES). Samplers were made rather as exhibition pieces to be framed and hung instead of being kept folded in the workbox or on wooden or ivory rollers for personal use. As their educational function became more and more pronounced alphabets and numerals were regularly included in the design. (John Brightland's *Grammar of the English Tongue*, published in 1711, contained a model 'Sampler Alphabet'.)

Mexican sampler. Shot pattern in silver-gilt thread and silk on linen. The initials surmounted by a crown probably stand for 'Maria Regina'. (V. & A. Mus., late 18th or early 19th c.)

Inscriptions grew in length and instead of the rather naïve personal records which had before been customary they now consisted of the moral precepts, prayers or edificatory verses from such books as Dr. Isaac Watts's *Divine Songs for Children* (1715), which the century thought suitable for the education of the very young. Where the personal note is there the child is obsessed with sentiments of death and duty.

The soul by blackning defiled
can never enter Heaven
Till god and it be reconciled
and all its sins forgiven.
Charlotte Robertson. Aged Six.
Time Flies. Death Approaches.

Another bears the inscription: 'Elizabeth Hide is my name, And with my needle I work the same, That all the worlde may plainly see, How Kind my parents have been to me, In the Year of Our Lord 1780.' Many of the designs too were of a religious character, among the most popular being the Fall of Man, the Sacrifice of Isaac, the Dove of Noah, and the Lily and the Celestial Crown. By the end of the century the sampler had almost completely lost its original function and come to be considered as primarily an appurtenance of the schoolroom and an educational exercise of the child. In Oliver Goldsmith's *She Stoops to Conquer* (1773) Hastings is given the words: 'For instance, miss there would be considered as a child, a mere maker of samplers.'

The 19th c. added nothing of importance to the history of the sampler. There was a marked deterioration in design and in variety. The cross stitch was ubiquitous and became known as the 'sampler stitch'. Patterns were stereotyped, favourite motifs being the strawberry border, stiff pots of flowers, rows of numbers and letters. By the middle of the century the sampler as a spontaneous craft was virtually dead.

Although the sampler flourished most abundantly in England, samplers were made also in Spain, Italy, Holland, Germany and France. French examples are mostly from the 19th c.; in general they are embroidered in a finer stitch than the English. In Germany squarish samplers with conventional designs were popular in the 17th c., the longer type with biblical scenes and sometimes with heraldic devices became more popular in the 18th c. The darning sampler was much used in Germany and may have been introduced from there into England. Dutch and Scandinavian samplers were similar in style to the German but often coarser in execution. In Sweden a special kind of sampler with coarse cut and drawn work was made by the peasants in

Danish sampler. Silver-gilt thread, silk and wool on linen with padded and couched work. (V. & A. Mus., 1751)

the 18th and early 19th centuries. Italian samplers from the 17th c. with cut-out work may have been the forerunners of the English type. Spanish samplers mostly of the late 17th and early 18th centuries are brilliantly coloured and highly decorative with large floral patterns round a central panel.

The art of the sampler was imported into America from England. An interesting example of how this happened is given by a drawn-work sampler, now in the Essex Institute, Salem, signed by Anne Gower, who married Governor Endicott and sailed for America in 1628, taking her sampler with her. Samplers became extremely popular in America and distinctively American styles developed. Few examples have survived from the 17th c. and it is to 18th-c. examples that one must look for the typically American trends. On the whole their originality consisted in pattern and design rather than in workmanship, though there are exceptions displaying craftsmanship to rival anything from other nationalities. The designs are in general more pictorial than the English counterparts, displaying a bold gift for anecdote. In many cases the whole background was covered with stitches. A special feature was the American genealogical sampler in which the ramifications of family relationships were recorded in meticulous detail.

22, 89, 157, 422, 456, 478.

SANG, JACOB. Dutch engraver on glass whose signature appears on pieces dated between 1752 and 1762. He may have been connected with a family of German engravers, A. F. Sang and J. H. B. Sang. He was the greatest virtuoso in the difficult art of wheel-engraving and also developed diamond-point stipple-engraving. See GLASS (NETHERLANDS).

SAPPHIRE. Nowadays 'sapphire' is a general term for all translucent gem corundums except the RUBY, with a hardness grade of 9 on the MOHS SCALE, second to the DIAMOND. The most prestigious sapphires are the blue and of these the most prized are the distinctive cornflower-blue known as 'Kashmir blue'. The gold, green and violet sapphires are sometimes known respectively as 'Oriental' topaz, emerald and amethyst, although their likeness to these stones is not close. The best sapphires come from the Mogok region of Upper Burma and from Kashmir. Thailand and Ceylon are also sources of good-quality stones.

Sapphires have the quality of changing their colour in different lights. A special variety known as 'star' sapphires have the property of ASTERISM: that is, when cut in the form of a high CABOCHON they show an elusive and evanescent six-pointed star. Such stones often have a misty appearance owing to the presence of minute massed rutilated needles called 'silk'. When asterism is combined with strong and definite colour these stones are greatly prized.

The sapphire was known as a gemstone from *c.* 800 B.C. and was much valued by the Romans, although the Greek word 'sappheiros' was applied to LAPIS LAZULI and the so-called sapphires of the ancients were in fact often lapis lazuli. Sapphires have always been talismanic stones. The sapphire was a favourite stone of necromancers and was also since the 7th c. the traditional stone of the episcopal ring.

Synthetic sapphires and rubies are made by the Verneuil process both as gemstones and for industrial purposes from powdered alumina and a colouring agent.

SARACENIC BRASSWORK. Modern term for the brassware encrusted with gold and silver produced in Venice by immigrant Oriental craftsmen in the 15th and 16th centuries. The earliest examples are decorated with inscriptions and signatures in Arabic, and only the European shape of the vessels distinguishes them as having been made in Venice. Gradually the Saracenic features became less marked until *c.* the middle of the 16th c., when Renaissance styles of ornament began to preponderate. The Italian craftsmen did not achieve the mastery of the Saracens in encrusting brass with precious metal and most of the later Italian examples are engraved, the DAMASCENING being only perfunctory. Vessels which had only engraving were gilt or sometimes enriched with coloured LACQUER (KALTEMAIL). The engraving, whether Saracenic or Renaissance in style, is usually of high quality. A restricted range of objects was made: basins and ewers, dishes, bowls, candlesticks, caskets and spherical perfume-burners.

SARDONYX. See QUARTZ.

SARMATIAN ARTS AND CRAFTSMANSHIP. See ASIA, CENTRAL and ANIMAL STYLE.

809.

SATIN. A type of weave; or a fabric, originally of silk, woven by this process. See WEAVING (FABRIC).

SATIN STITCH. See EMBROIDERY (STITCHES).

SAUNIER, CLAUDE-CHARLES (1735–1807). French cabinet-maker. He was made master of the guild in 1752 and took over his father's business in 1765. He was an expert in MARQUETRY and adopted classical features of the Louis XVI style before the accession of that monarch to the throne. His work illustrates the development of French taste from occasional classical features through close imitation of antiquity to the EMPIRE STYLE.

SAVERY, WILLIAM (1721–88). American cabinet-maker and carver of the Philadelphia School (see FURNITURE, AMERICAN) pre-eminent particularly for his HIGHBOYS. His carving was very elaborate in the CHIPPENDALE ROCOCO manner. The scroll-tops and bonnet-tops of his highboys were usually topped by a flamboyant central ornament. His work compares favourably with that of European craftsmen in the Chippendale style.

67.

SAVONNERIE CARPETS. A term often applied generically to all hand-knotted carpets of French origin, it denotes specifically those made by the French national carpet-manufactory established in 1626 at Chaillot (in a former soap-works) and transferred thence in 1826 to the GOBELINS, where the work still continues. Fine examples of its products, including small pieces such as chair-seats and screen panels as well as large carpets in all the main ornamental styles from the period of Louis XIV onward, are preserved at the Mobilier National and in public and private collections.

442.

SCARAB. A type of gem or amulet introduced by the Egyptians and popular from the end of the 3rd millennium B.C. One side of the scarab was made in the form of a sacred beetle, and the flat back opposite was engraved with hieroglyphics or charms. Scarabs were sometimes worn as amulets, sometimes mounted in a ring and used as a seal when required. Scarabs spread throughout the Near East and Mediterranean world during the 1st millennium B.C.

When reproduced in centres where the beetle had no religious or magical significance, the upper surface sometimes changed to CABOCHON form or the beetle was replaced by other subjects. Such scaraboids, with a design engraved underneath, continued to be used in early Greek and in Etruscan work and according to one view may have been the forerunners of the CAMEO.

SCENT-BOTTLES. Perfumes were enjoyed by the ancient Egyptians, and some of their pottery scent-containers survive from the 26th Dynasty (*c.* 600 B.C.). With the introduction of GLASS it became possible to make small bottles of more colourful patterns, which were the forerunners of many centuries of bottles in all kinds of materials and innumerable shapes.

Following the Dark Ages there was a revival of the use of perfumes, although at first they were usually carried in POMANDERS. These were supplanted during the 17th c. by bottles, which remain the most convenient for the purpose. As regards shape, that of a pear with flattened sides was universally popular, and was employed for those made of coloured and clear glass, enamelled copper and gold. Only a little less popular was a simple oblong with a short neck rising from the top, of which examples dating from the later 18th c. exist in all the aforementioned materials.

An English speciality was to make scent-bottles of porcelain, for which the anonymous craftsmen at the Chelsea 'Girl-in-Swing' manufactory were perhaps originally responsible from *c.* 1753. The porcelain bottles were modelled in many forms (see G. E. Bryant, *The Chelsea Porcelain Toys*, 1925): mythological and other figures, bunches of flowers, fruit, birds and animals, and so forth, many of them being embellished with gallant legends in misspelt French. The necks and tiny stoppers were mounted in gold, and sometimes also the bases, while some examples still retain the shagreen-covered boxes in which they were retailed. A number of German factories, including MEISSEN, made comparable porcelain bottles, and in some instances copied those of Chelsea. The latter have also been reproduced in modern times.

Many of the Chelsea models were imitated also in copper, rolled thinly and beaten into shape, covered with enamel and realistically coloured. The workers at Bilston and elsewhere in south Staffordshire and Birmingham ingeniously made small figures and other objects. In those places, as well as in France and Germany, simpler types, such as vase-shapes were produced in enamel.

About 1785 Josiah WEDGWOOD and his imitators produced some scent-bottles in blue jasperware with Neo-Classical designs in white relief. They were very neatly finished and provided with gilt metal screw caps.

Double-ended glass bottles, clear and coloured, were made in large numbers during the 19th c. and were fitted with embossed silver or silver-gilt caps. Some examples were intended to contain perfume at one end with the other for use as a vinaigrette. Glass was also employed for dressing-table scent-bottles in the middle years of the century, when at French and English factories coloured MILLEFIORI patterns of paperweight type were incorporated in their bases and stoppers. Later on similar pieces were made in the United States at the Millville, New Jersey, and other factories (see Evelyn Campbell Cloak, *Glass Paperweights*, 1969).

In the 20th c. the Paris perfumers market their products in attractively designed glass bottles, many of which are indebted for their inspiration to René LALIQUE, who pioneered 'chunky' forms with a matt finish.

273, 295.

SCHAPER, JOHANN (1621–70). Glass-maker of Nuremberg, who introduced the technique of SCHWARZLOT. He painted delicate landscapes and architecture, details being incised with a fine point through the black enamel pigment to the clear glass beneath.

SCHLEMMER, OSCAR (1888–1943). See BAUHAUS.

SCHMALCALDER, C. English instrument-maker who in 1806 patented an instrument for making SILHOUETTE portraits.

SCHMELZGLAS. See CALCEDONIO and GLASS.

SCHNELL, MARTIN (*c.* 1675–*c.* 1740). German cabinet-maker working between 1703 and 1710 in Berlin and then in Dresden. He specialized in making LACQUER furniture and while in Dresden also worked at the MEISSEN porcelain factory. He died in Warsaw.

SCHWANHARDT, GEORG (1601–67). German glass-maker who developed the art of glass-engraving at Nuremberg, which was at this time the leading glass-making centre of Germany. Although metal of the Venetian type was used, the Italianate decoration was abandoned in favour of severer forms such as tall, covered goblets on stems with spherical knops and discs and low cylindrical cups usually mounted on three ball-feet. The goblets were frequently engraved by artists of the school founded by Schwanhardt with town and country scenes and with fine calligraphy. Schwanhardt introduced polished engraving to contrast with the parts left mat by the coarser abrasives and supplemented his wheel-work with diamond-point engraving. His son HEINRICH is alleged to have been the first to use hydrofluoric acid for etching glass. See GLASS (BOHEMIA AND GERMANY).

SCHWARZLOT. A type of glass, chiefly small beakers, painted in black enamel pigment by a method borrowed from the painters of stained glass. (See also ENAMELLING ON GLASS.) The technique was introduced by a craftsman of

Nuremberg, Johann SCHAPER, *c.* the middle of the 17th c. See GLASS (BOHEMIA AND GERMANY).

SCHWARZLOTMALEREI. See ENAMELLING ON GLASS.

SCIENTIFIC TOYS.

1. INTRODUCTION. Education and amusement go closely together, particularly with children. It is not, therefore, surprising that the direct forerunner of the many toys and amusements based on scientific principles in the 19th c. was the extensive dissemination of scientific ideas in the 18th c. The new knowledge also enabled certain traditional toys to be seen in a fresh light.

On the Continent and in England groups of men learned in literature and in science came together during the early years of the 17th c., and as a consequence the great scientific academies in Italy, France and England were founded. The Royal Society was notable for setting up the post of Curator of Experiments, whose duty was to provide 'three or four considerable experiments each day the Society met'. Robert Hooke was the first Curator, having previously been assistant to Robert Boyle. Hooke knew and advised most of the instrument-makers in London, and his inventiveness and their skill helped to stimulate and provide for the new interest in natural philosophy. Hooke's work with the microscope and Newton's work on optics and astronomy encouraged the optical instrument trade to provide for the awakened imaginations of men at about the turn of the 17th c. Newton's studies of mechanics also had the result of creating a demand for demonstrations of elementary and complex effects.

In the 18th c. science became for the first time a subject of interest and study for the layman. Those who were wealthy enough formed their own collections of rarities, items of natural history and scientific instruments and apparatus. In England very large and remarkable collections were formed by King George III and the Earl of Bute. Scientific societies and learned institutions also acquired collections and some of these still exist, largely intact, in America, Holland, Germany and Great Britain. This interest extended into a great many homes, and it would be a poor household that did not have at least a microscope and a telescope. In order to learn how to use these strange devices people eagerly attended lecture-demonstrations. These were being given in London in the first decade of the 18th c., and soon itinerant lecturers spread the knowledge all over the country. It is hardly surprising that what was established by adults for their edification should subsequently have spread to their children. This is why so many types of toys may be traced to the topics dealt with in the lecture-demonstrations.

Scientific interest was also constantly stimulated by an apparently endless series of books on scientific recreations. These reproduced at popular level the well-established topics of the serious writers such as Desaguiliers and Musschenbroek. A pioneer in this education by way of recreation was Jacques Ozanam (d. 1717), and his work was continued by Montucla and translated into English by Hutton in 1803. The title-page of a little book produced anonymously in the early 19th c., and clearly derived from Hutton and similar authors, shows that science was by this time very much at home in the parlour: *Philosophical Recreations, or Winter Amusements: A Collection of Entertaining & Surprising Experiments*. This sort of book appealed to the family-life ideal of the Victorians, who believed that recreation should be improving and required it to cater for all ages.

The children's book came into its own in the 19th c., but again the Victorians preferred it to be improving, as was exemplified by such titles as *The Boy's Playbook of Science*, *The Fairyland of Science* and *Through Magic Glasses*, the last of which was devoted to prisms, the microscope, the telescope and the spectroscope.

The scientific categories used by the demonstration-lecturers included mechanics, hydrostatics, pneumatics, optics, magnetism and electricity. One can distinguish toys in all these groups. Chemistry was usually taught separately from the other, physical, topics and developed its own specialist suppliers of apparatus and materials. Chemistry sets for children were advertised in the 1840s and they have continued to be popular to the present day. The great private collections of natural history specimens—minerals, plants, seeds, shells—were reflected in the small chests containing sea-shells and polished stones that were made available for the delight and instruction of children. Some travelling lecturers made a speciality of astronomy and models of the solar system, usually going under the name of 'orrery', were in great demand. From the elaborate, expensive, clockwork-driven models, they ranged to the simple wooden variety with a crank handle to rotate the wire arms holding the representations of the planets.

2. MECHANICAL TOYS. The whip-top, the hoop and the yo-yo all have very ancient origins, and the first two are among the very few traditional boys' toys. All three can be categorized as inertial devices as their stability depends on conservation of momentum. In REGENCY times a yo-yo could be made of ivory, elaborately carved on an ornamental lathe, but the majority are made of wood. The name 'yo-yo' derives from the 1932 craze for this toy. Another inertial plaything was the diabolo, also called 'the devil on two sticks', already established by 1820, when it was described in a book of juvenile games. It consisted of a double cone that was rotated by a string held between two sticks, so that it might be regarded as a cross between a top and a yo-yo. During the later Victorian period the gyroscope became popular after its dynamics had been the subject of mathematical treatises.

The force of gravity is used in a number of toys to produce their various effects. One of the oldest balance toys is the tumbler, where the figure is heavily weighted in its rounded base so that it always rights itself after being pushed down; the effigy of a clown was popular. The figure of an acrobat could be balanced on a point because he carried a curved bar with counter-weights at the ends so as to bring the centre of gravity of the combination below the point of support. This achieved the figure's stability. Another trick for toy acrobats was for them to be attached by a wire to a rod which then rolled down parallel bars in a frame, the figures constantly rotating. Mercury, a heavy metal in liquid form, was used in a hollow body to cause a flexible acrobat to perform somersaults down a flight of steps. The mercury provided a mobile centre of gravity to the figure. The same effect was achieved by two acrobats holding a pair of hollow rods which contained the mercury. Another gravitational effect occurs when a figure with pivoted legs and leaded feet is placed on an inclined plane and performs a shuffling walk.

The principle of the lever is shown by the lazy tongs with a joker's head at the end or a parade of wooden soldiers fixed at the joints. Animation may be given to pecking birds, singly or in groups, by a pendulum weight below the base-board. A development from the large centrifugal machine of the lecture-demonstration was the ball rolling inside a circular track made of two wire hoops joined together and provided with a handle. When given a small circular motion the ball can acquire quite a high speed in the track and is held in place by centrifugal force.

3. MAGNETIC TOYS. The magnetic compass was introduced into the West by navigators in the 12th c., but the first scientific study of the subject of magnetic attraction was that published by William Gilbert in 1600. The loadstone had a practical use in making magnetic needles for compasses, but it also found a place as a curiosity because of its power to exert a mysterious force over distance. During the 18th c. artificial magnets were made either from powdered magnetite or from iron. In Victorian times not only was the horseshoe magnet a perennial toy, but circular artificial magnets with a hole in the middle were positioned on a peg and with the appropriate polar orientation could be made to levitate. One magnetic toy, which finds various expressions, involves a secreted magnet. In one of these there is a picture of an artist painting at an easel and a group of scenes is provided, each containing a magnet in a different position. When one of these scenes is placed under the picture a miniature of the scene appears on the artist's easel, having been brought into place by the attraction of another small magnet located in the rotating disc that carries the miniature scenes behind the picture of the artist. Instruction and amusement were combined in a magnetic toy for teaching the rules of grammar. Cardboard discs bearing printed questions and a secret magnetic bar were located at the centre of a dial ringed by the answers. By magnetic attraction a pointer moved to indicate the correct answer.

The production of static electricity by friction was an 18th-c. development and provided one of the most testing fields of investigation for natural philosophers. From 1800 on kits were made for domestic entertainment, and although father may have had to turn the handle of the glass friction machine, the effects produced were very much for the benefit of the children. These effects included dancing pith puppets and a model head with long hair which could be made to stand on end. There were also the electric chimes rung by electrified clappers.

The electric dynamo was invented and developed by Michael Faraday in the 1830s and, later, toy dynamos were made to be driven by model steam-engines, the small current generated causing an electric lamp to light up. During the 1890s electric motors were adapted to model trains, but the heyday of the electric toy train was reached *c.* 1930.

4. AIR AND HEAT TOYS. The force of the wind is common knowledge, and kites and propellers took advantage of this. The windmill for drainage and corn-grinding was important economically, and working models were made for serious instructional purposes. Subsequently simplified model mills reached the toy market and became a part of farmyard sets. A familiar sight in a large kitchen was the smoke-jack, a spit-turning device, which was operated by the up-draught of hot air from the fire. All manner of heat and air power was the subject of investigation and demonstration by lecturers, and some of their apparatus was modified into toys. The smoke-jack gave rise to a paddle wheel, turned by hot air from a gas jet, with a cranked axle activating little figures.

A great many experimental demonstrations turned on the use of the air-pump, first produced by Robert Hooke for Boyle's experiments with gases. Among the popular demonstrations were the breaking of evacuated glass bottles by air pressure, the expansion of a bladder in a vacuum and a water fountain produced in an evacuated bell-jar. Like the electrostatic machine the air-pump was also used in the home, but again father's expertise would have been necessary. Among the toys that could safely be put into the hands of young children, illustrating some of the principles of air pressure, are a ball balanced on a jet of air blown through a tube by the mouth, and the long bladder or paper tube which uncoils when inflated. Suction pads, operating by air pressure, were used for holding arrows and other toys on to vertical or horizontal surfaces.

The first effective steam-engine in the world was that built by Thomas Newcomen in 1712. Models of this engine were made for university and institutional use. When James Watt's improvements to the steam-engine caused it to be more generally used, especially for traction purposes, a wider range of models was made for educational purposes and naturally these soon found their way into the playroom. Later in the Victorian period clockwork took over from steam as the motive power for toy trains since it was less hazardous and cheaper, but the stationary engine for driving model machine-tools or dynamos continued to be steam-powered. Other working models of industrial processes could include toy breweries and threshing machines.

5. WATER TOYS. In the 17th and 18th centuries the grounds of great houses and public gardens were replete with fountains and model fountains based on Hero of Alexandria's pattern, which was self-contained and portable, were produced for amusement and instruction. To show the effect of buoyancy and specific gravity figures, usually imps, were blown of glass to have a specific gravity close to that of water. When placed in a jar of water with a membrane over the top the figure could be made to rise or sink by varying the pressure on the membrane with the fingers. Model water-mills could show the effect of over-shot and under-shot wheels, although for general sale the models did not use water. The Tantalus beaker continued to have an appeal from the early 18th c. to the 20th c. Here a figure of a man stood in a glass cup into which water was slowly poured. When the water reached the level of his mouth, the water in the cup slowly syphoned out by means of a tube secreted in his body. The increasing attention to personal hygiene during the Victorian period led to the provision of bathrooms and hence bath toys. Here, then, was scope for model marine divers and boats powered by camphor pellets, where the power was derived from the surface tension of the water–camphor solution.

6. OPTICAL TOYS. Sight is the prime sense of man and optics is the chief provider of illusions; it could, therefore, transmit effects that were thought to be magical. This is particularly evident with mirrors having various curved surfaces, including the anamorphoscopes, the 'magic' lantern and the *camera obscura* (a box with a pin-hole and a ground glass screen on to which the inverted image of the outside scene was projected by the hole; large versions employed a whole room with a lens in the window-shutter). Although the microscope and telescope were invented rather later than one might have expected, that is *c.* 1600, they immediately caught the imagination. Throughout the 18th c. they were nearly ubiquitous and in Victorian times, though the improved scientific telescope was very large and quite unsuitable for domestic use, the improved microscope was not, and it enjoyed an unrivalled place in the home. The microscope made it possible to look at all manner of common, but minute, objects: insects, seeds, hairs, plant organs. It also encouraged the systematic collection of material from ponds, rivers and hedgerows. By the 1860s there were instruments to suit every taste and pocket from the simplest penny microscope, consisting of a bead of Canada balsam in a piece of card, to the highest-powered research instruments costing over £100. Many books were produced aimed specifically at the young microscopist from the age of ten upwards.

For some reason, optical illusions attracted elaborate Greek names. The zograscope of the mid 18th c. consisted of a lens and mirror for looking at coloured engravings and set the fashion for peering at things. It continued in use, reduced from drawing-room to playroom dimensions, until at least 1870, but was joined by the stereoscope in the 1830s. This instrument was designed to give a vivid impression of three dimensions, an effect that was greatly assisted by the invention of the photographic camera in 1839. The kaleidoscope was a tube that enabled ever-changing symmetrical patterns of coloured light to be viewed. The simple thaumatrope of 1825, a cardboard disc spun between the fingers with, for example, a drawing of a bird one side and its cage on the other, engaged the persistence of vision effect in the eye and marked the beginning of the road that led to the cinema. Other milestones on this road were the phenakistoscope of 1832 and the zoetrope of 1860. In these a series of drawings was viewed through slits in a rotating disc and a rotating drum respectively, so giving the impression of movement. The praxinoscope of 1877 was an elaboration of the zoetrope which made use of mirrors. It could be arranged with a frame to give the impression of a theatrical performance. Muybridge was the first to analyse the movement of animals when with a battery of forty cameras he photographed a horse galloping. The prints from these photographs were arranged on a wheel, called a zoogyroscope, which when spun in a projector recreated the movement. Toy versions of these wheels were made during the 1880s for projection in the magic lantern. After the turn of the century, when cine-cameras had been produced, sets of prints were reproduced in small books whose pages were 'flipped' by the thumb, so giving an impression of movement. These flip books were cheap and had a considerable vogue.

SCISSORS. See CUTLERY.

SCONCE. An ornamental bracket fastened to a wall, holding one or more candles and often fitted with a mirror.

SCOTIA (Greek *skotia*: shadow). A concave MOULDING which casts a strong shadow. Often used between TORUS mouldings on the base of a column. Also called CASEMENT.

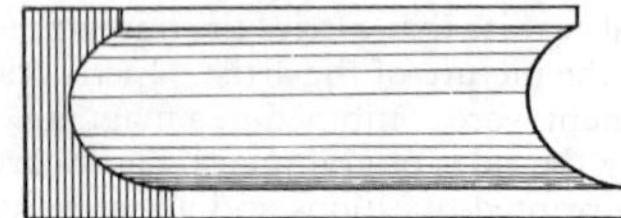

SCRAMASAX. See CUTLERY.

SCREEN. In church architecture, a partition of stone, wood or ironwork separating without wholly cutting off part of the church, e.g. dividing the nave or dividing the piers from the aisles or dividing the aisles to form chapels. Openwork iron screens were used to protect shrines or reliquaries while leaving them visible to worshippers. See IRON AND STEEL (DECORATIVE WROUGHT IRONWORK). See also REJA.

SCRIMSHAW. A term of American origin applied to any kind of craft work made on board ship, usually aboard a whaler, in a wide variety of substances, including marine ivory, whale jaw-pan, baleen, wood and decorative inlays such as silver. Although the last whaler sailed from Europe in 1969, a long time after whaling declined in America, scrimshaw is still carried on among seafarers who learned the art when they were boys. The only kind of scrimshaw which is still being made, however, is engraving on whale's teeth. Whale jaw-pan and whale bone are ground into chicken feed in the machinery of a modern whaling factory-ship, so they are no longer available for scrimshaw. Whale's teeth are in short supply, and once they too are no longer available it seems safe to assume that scrimshaw will disappear.

Marine ivory is obtained from the sperm whale, whose lower jaw may contain 40–50 teeth, some sharply pointed and curved, others ground down to a flat top. A coating of enamel, thicker at the top than the bottom, surrounds the ivory in the whale's teeth, and the surface is heavily ridged to enable the whale to tackle its enemy, the giant squid. In the 19th c. teeth 28 cm long and nearly 2 kg in weight were not unknown; nowadays the average weight is about 0·75 kg. Other marine mammals such as the smaller killer whale and elephant seals contributed teeth for scrimshaw. Walrus ivory too was often used for scrimshaw; it was traded by the Eskimos to the whalers in Alaskan waters or in the Arctic. Although the bones of the whale are osseous and spongy, the jaws can be sawn into slabs of white hard bone, rather like an inferior kind of ivory, flecked here and there with striations. When it was captured a sperm whale would have its lower jaw removed; the bone would then be stored for carving and the teeth pulled out with a tackle and stored in a brine cask.

From these materials, and the others mentioned, the crew, the deck officers and on occasion the captain's wife, would make a wide variety of articles. Useful carvings would include boxes, games-pieces, implements for embroidery and knitting, articles for the kitchen such as ladles, pastry crimps (called 'jagging wheels' in New England), rolling pins, and many other items. The most important functional piece of scrimshaw was the busk. This was a long oblong slip of whalebone, engraved all over with designs, and sometimes poetry as well, intended to be worn as part of a foundation garment. Busks were favourite presents to girls from their sailor sweethearts.

American scrimshaw. Engraved whales' teeth. The middle example is inscribed 'The General Merrion of New York'. (Scott Polar Research Institute, Cambridge)

Scrimshaw included, however, luxury and decorative items such as elaborate walking sticks and riding whips. The most familiar pieces of decorative scrimshaw were the whale's tooth and the walrus tusk or slab of whale's jaw-pan engraved with a black line picture.

Carved scrimshaw was made with files, jack-knives, chisels and sandpaper. Often a piece of sharkskin was used instead of sandpaper. Sometimes a scrimshaw artist would have special tools made for him by the cooper, at other times he would adapt existing ones. An English seaman who had been shanghaied aboard a New Bedford whaler remarked: 'The tools used are of the roughest. Some old files softened in the fire and filed into grooves something like saw teeth are most used, but old knives, sail-needles, and chisels are pressed into service.' (Frank Bullen in *The Cruise of the Cachalot*, 1898.) The finished scrimshaw would be polished with oil and whiting, pumice-powder or sailmaker's wax and canvas.

The 'graphic', as the engraved whale's tooth has been called, demanded a more elaborate technique. Most workers would start by grinding the ridges off the tooth with a file, grindstone or sandpaper. Then they would place a piece of transparent paper over the tooth, which would be covered with a cutting from some paper or magazine. The illustration would then be painstakingly pricked through the paper into the tooth, so that the picture would be outlined by a kind of POUNCING process. The holes would then be joined up by minute scratches, which would be filled with Indian ink. A pad of lampblack was sometimes used instead of Indian ink. The whole tooth would then be polished with china clay and whale oil.

The subjects for 'graphics' were often taken from illustrated papers. The more interesting ones, however, are free-hand drawings of whaling scenes. Writing in 1853 in his *Illustrated Natural History*, the naturalist John Wood remarked: 'In Europe the teeth of the Cachalot or Spermaceti Whale are of no great value, being considered merely as marine curiosities, and often carved with rude engravings representing the chase of the animal from which they were taken, together with a very precise account of the latitude and longitude, and a tolerably accurate view of the vessel.'

The olive branch design which appears on so much scrimshaw originates in Russian walrus-ivory boxes made at Archangel in the 17th c. Much of the decoration of scrimshaw is deliberately international in nature, consisting of flags of all nations or emblems such as the foul anchor, which were common to both Britain and America. Although it has often been supposed that scrimshaw was made merely as souvenirs to be given to the maker's family or friends, much of it was deliberately made for sale. 'Ninety per cent of the old "real" U.S.A. scrimshaw', a living exponent of the art told the writer, 'was sold to get home to Dundee, Whitby, or Lyme [Britain's three principal whaling ports]. Once made it stays in your pocket (in the leather bag you have made for it) until required for currency.' The Master at Arms, in Melville's *White Jacket* is presented with a piece of scrimshaw as a bribe.

None of the very earliest scrimshaw, which was made of wood, has survived. The first dated piece is from 1827, and thereafter the genius of the American whaleman was mainly exercised on 'graphics' in ivory or whalebone. The output was enormous, but still the quality was high. No greater testimony can be paid to American scrimshoners than the fact that their work was copied by their British colleagues, who were much fewer in number. The American Civil War brought great disruption to whaling, and the decline of the calling which followed the Second World War was accompanied by the decline of scrimshaw as a living art.

The writer discovered the earliest recorded dated scrimshaw in the shape of two tobacco boxes in the Museum of Fisheries in Hull. They were made of hard wood with sections of walrus ivory. One bore the date 1665, the other 1712.

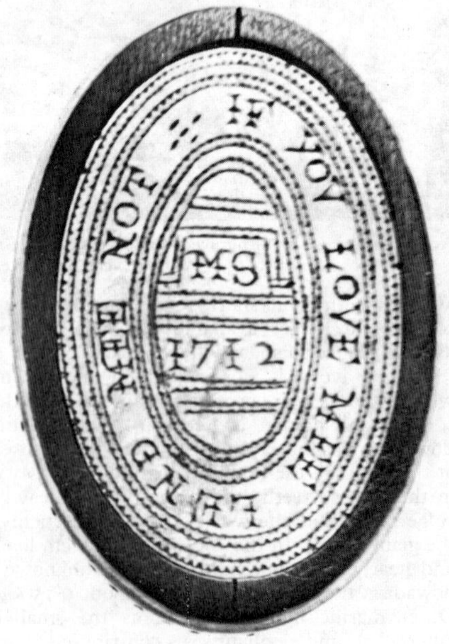

The earliest dated pieces of scrimshaw. (Mus. of Fisheries, Hull, 1665 and 1712)

St. John de Crevecoeur noticed wooden scrimshaw being made in Nantucket in 1782. But although the earliest dated examples have been preserved in England, this is not conclusive for the vexed question of its origin since it may well be that scrimshaw was being made before the examples that have survived.

711.

SCRUTOIRE (or SCRIPTOIRE). Contemporary term for a now obsolete form of cabinet with fall-front for writing. This type was introduced from France into England in the reign of Charles II and was superseded by the writing bureau in the second half of the 18th c. See FURNITURE (ENGLISH).

SCYTHIAN ARTS AND CRAFTSMANSHIP. See ASIA, CENTRAL and ANIMAL STYLE.

SEAWEED MARQUETRY (sometimes called ENDIVE). MARQUETRY patterns composed of very fine elements resembling seaweed or endive leaves. Employed with delicate scrollwork and sometimes with arabesques, it was in vogue in England during the last decade of the 17th c. and the early years of the 18th c. but went out of fashion in the GEORGIAN period. It may be regarded as a translation into woods (sycamore, holly, pear, etc. on walnut) of the metal and shell marquetry of BOULLE. Seaweed pattern was generally used on small panels in contrast with over-all arabesque marquetry.

SECRETARY. Term current in the 18th c. in the U.S.A. and also in Britain for a small writing desk fitted with drawers. The term was later replaced by 'secretaire'. See FURNITURE (AMERICAN).

SENÉ, JEAN-BAPTISTE-CLAUDE (1748–1803). French carver and chair-maker whose grandfather, father, and brother were all active and successful chair-makers. After Georges JACOB, he is the most important chair-maker of the Louis XVI period, receiving royal orders and providing fine seat-furniture for Marie-Antoinette. Like Jacob he sometimes worked in mahogany and adopted English lyre-back forms. He survived the Revolution and received commissions in 1794 and 1795 to make writing desks for Government use.

SENEFELDER, ALOIS (1771–1834). The inventor of lithography (1798). Born in Prague of German parents, he aspired to write plays and experimented with methods of printing them himself. In 1796 he printed successfully from stone etched so that the inked image stood in relief, a technique in which he had been anticipated by others. Two years later he discovered the process, since called 'lithography', of printing from flat stones, relying on the mutual repulsion of fatty ink and water. Soon afterwards he found out a method of transferring to the stone writing and drawing done on paper.

He was granted an exclusive privilege for his process in the kingdom of Bavaria in 1799, and he used it, chiefly for printing music, in partnership with publishers in Germany, England and Austria. He obtained a British patent in 1801. The application of the technique to reproducing works of fine art was first seen in *Specimens of Polyautography* produced in London in 1803, by a concessionaire of Senefelder's patent, from drawings on stone by Benjamin West, Henry Fuseli, and others.

Senefelder was unskilful and unfortunate in business. He first gained a substantial income when he was appointed to supervise the printing of a cadastral map of Bavaria at Munich in 1809. His treatise *Vollständiges Lehrbuch der Steindruckerey*, giving practical instruction in his methods and his account of his discovery, was published in 1818 and quickly translated into French and English. A year later he opened a lithographic establishment in Paris from which he drew an income enough to support him while he spent his remaining years in Munich experimenting with improvements to his process.

844.

SERICIN (also called GUM). A protein material which binds together the filaments of raw SILK and cements two filaments to form the BAVE. In the manufacture of nett as opposed to SPUN-SILK the sericin serves as a natural size.

SERVANDONI, JEAN NICOLAS (1695–1766). Architect, stage-designer and ornamentalist, born in Florence of a French father and Italian mother. He was trained as a painter under Panini (*c.* 1692–1765). After travelling to Grenoble, Portugal and England, he settled in Paris in 1728 and became *Décorateur-en-Chef* to the Opéra. As revealed by surviving models, his stage settings were ROCOCO in style. In 1732 he won a competition for the west façade of St. Sulpice and succeeded OPPENORD as architect of the church. This design has been described as one of the earliest manifestations of a classical reaction against the Rococo in architecture but it is likely that the original design, later modified, was far less severely classical than the finished work would suggest. Nor do his other architectural works present him as a pioneer of Classicism despite his support by the Comte Caylus. (Baldaquin in the Carthusian monastery at Lyon; baldaquin at Sens.) He returned to England in 1748 to supervise the illuminations for the peace of Aix-la-Chapelle. There he designed a gallery for the house of Thomas Wyndham at Hammersmith, originally built by Robert Morris (1701–54) for Lord Melcombe. An engraving of this gallery appeared in the fourth volume of *Vitruvius Britannicus* (1767).

SEUSENHOFER FAMILY. Important armourers working at Augsburg and Innsbruck during the 15th and 16th centuries. The most eminent members were KONRAD (1450/60–1517), his brother HANS (1470–1555) and the latter's son JÖRG (1500/5–1580), all of whom were successively armourers to the Imperial Court. Examples of their work are in the Kunsthistorisches Museum, Vienna; Musée de l'Armée, Paris; Metropolitan Museum, New York; Tower of London Armouries. See ARMS AND ARMOUR.

SÈVRES. The national porcelain manufactory of France, still active today, was begun in private hands at Vincennes *c.* 1738; but it soon came under the patronage of Louis XV, received a protective monopoly, and moved to Sèvres in 1756. The royal cipher of crossed 'L's' became the factory mark. During the Vincennes period the wares often bore 'Oriental' or ROCOCO decoration in the MEISSEN style, but their cream-white soft-paste material, their simple, graceful forms and their soft enamel colourings were already distinctively French. Some rare Vincennes figure models show off the *pâte tendre* (soft paste) to perfection, being as a rule uncoloured.

During the finest period, *c.* 1750–70, the characteristic ground colours, including the superb *gros bleu*, turquoise, yellow, and *rose Pompadour* set off by abundant rich gilding, framed paintings of birds, slight landscapes, and figures in the manner of BOUCHER. Specially fine work was done in monochrome blue or purple. The elaborate ornamental pieces often show a somewhat stronger Rococo flavour than the table services. Under Louis XVI the style became even more sumptuous: the grounds were minutely diapered and sometimes 'jewelling' in transparent ENAMEL completely covered the porcelain. A lighter manner persisted at the same time, with sprigs, garlands, stripes, and cameos sometimes relieving the rather mechanical forms of the NEO-CLASSICAL fashion. After hard-paste porcelain was introduced in 1769, this lighter manner was increasingly employed. See CERAMICS and PORCELAIN.

SEYMOUR, JOHN. American cabinet-maker, probably trained in England, who worked in Boston from *c.* 1794 and is considered to be the pre-eminent Boston designer and craftsman of furniture after the Revolution. Characteristic of his work is a robin's-egg blue paint, which he used on compartment interiors. Other characteristic features include inlaid pilaster forms, sliding tambour shutters, a lunette or half-ring inlay pattern on top edges and skirts and the use of a variety of secondary woods in a single piece. Together with his son THOMAS he continued to produce furniture of delicate design and fine workmanship into the 19th c.

SEZESSION (SECESSION). During the last decade of the 19th c. many of the more advanced German artists found themselves out of sympathy with the traditional schools and therefore 'seceded' and founded revolutionary associations and groups to organize exhibitions. Such a movement was called *Sezession.* The earliest of these groups came together in Munich in 1892, its leading members being Franz von Stuck (1863–1928) and Wilhelm Trübner (1851–1917). The *Sezession* was much influenced by ART-NOUVEAU ideas and the Belgian Henri van de VELDE was represented at its exhibition of 1899. In his book *Painting in the Twentieth Century* (Vol. 1, p. 55) Werner Haftmann wrote of their early groping towards abstract form: 'These ideas were first applied in the ornaments and abstract decorations of the Jugendstil. It was in the relatively sheltered domain of the decorative arts that the first but resolute steps were taken to drop natural appearances in favour of abstract signs derived from the world of human expression.' The Berlin *Sezession*, under the leadership of Max Liebermann (1847–1935), represented the revolt of the Germanic form of Impressionism and remained from 1899 until the First World War the main centre of Impressionism in Germany. When in 1910 young Expressionist painters, including members of *Die Brücke*, were rejected from this *Sezession* they founded their own *Neue Sezession.* The Vienna *Sezession*, formed by Gustav Klimt (1862–1918) in 1897, was during its earlier years almost as much concerned with architecture, interior decoration and the decorative arts as with easel painting and did much to further the late introduction of *art-nouveau* ideas in Austria.

SGRAFFIATO or SGRAFFITO (Italian: scratched). A method of decorating pottery by scratching or incising a design through a coating of slip so as to show the underlying body in the marks. The term is also used for ceramic works decorated in this way. See CERAMICS; POTTERY TECHNIQUES; SLIP.

SHAKER. An American religious sect consisting of mixed communities of men and women living in celibacy was established near Albany on the Hudson River in 1784, taking the name 'The Society of Believers in Christ's Second Appearing'. They were popularly known as 'Shakers'. Many of the men were wood-workers and they made furniture in a strong and simple style devoid of ornament. The type of furniture remained relatively unchanged until the 1860s. See FURNITURE (AMERICAN).

SHAWLS. The Persian '*shal*', from which the English word 'shawl' is derived, originally denoted a type of woven fabric rather than a garment. In Persia it was worn usually around the waist as a girdle, in India over the shoulders. It was worn mainly by men and the fineness of the fabric was a mark of nobility.

The home of the shawl was Kashmir and according to a local tradition the craft originated with Turkistan weavers introduced by Zain-ul-ʿAbidin (A.D. 1420–70). The shawls were woven from the fine fleece of wild mountain goats imported first from Tibet and in the 19th c. from the nomadic Kirghiz tribes by way of Yarkand and Khotan or later from Sinkiang. Sometimes also the wool of the wild Himalayan mountain sheep or ibex was used. The most highly prized wool was that from wild animals of the high altitudes since these grow a particularly fine fleece (known as *alsi tus*) as protection against the winter cold. It was shawls made from this material which in Mogul times were said to be so fine that they could be drawn through a thumb-ring. The method of weaving was akin to TAPESTRY weaving: the pattern was formed from the weft alone and the threads forming the design were not carried across the whole length of the loom but were woven into the woof threads only so far as each colour was required by the pattern. The work was highly skilled and a single shawl took as much as a year and a half to complete on one loom: during the 19th c. the practice grew up of dividing the patterned portion of a single shawl among a number of looms and then joining the pieces by needlework.

In the 19th c. another type of shawl called *amli* was also made, simulating the woven pattern by handwork EMBROIDERY on a plain woven ground. Shawls in which the pattern was loom-woven were known as *tilikar*.

The craft was divided among a large number of specialists ranging from the women who graded and spun the wool to the master weavers. The most highly paid were the pattern designers (*naqqāsh*). In Mogul times over 300 colours were in regular use, mainly vegetable dyes, though these were later reduced to 64. The borders were woven with silk warps sometimes patterned with silver and gold threads. The weavers were particularly badly paid and were taxed out of existence, a condition which was still further aggravated after Kashmir came under British rule in 1846, so that many fled to the Punjab, leaving their families behind, and set up in business there. The shawls produced in the Punjab were less highly valued, however, largely because there the craftsmen had not access to the finest fleeces.

The early shawls of Kashmir were decorated only on the end-borders, which were about 30 cm in width. Decoration consisted of floral motifs (called *buta*)—first a plant spray with roots, later a more formal vase of flowers—combining the Persian calligraphic floral tradition with the more naturalistic style of 17th-c. Mogul art. In the latter half of the 18th c. this motif was conventionalized into the so-called 'cone', which itself became increasingly rigid and formalized in the 19th c. until it was eventually transformed into a purely formal scroll-like element in an over-all pattern which had lost any suggestion of its floral origin. 'Cashmere' shawls came into fashion in the West from the 3rd quarter of the 18th c. and import trade increased during the 19th c., reaching a maximum in the 1860s. Considerable pressure was put upon the local craftsmen, particularly by French merchants from *c.* 1850, to adapt their patterns to European ideas of Oriental design and a 'mystique' was created which went some way towards corrupting the Kashmir tradition. From *c.* 1830 the embroidered shawls (*amli*) began to introduce figural designs illustrating Indo-Persian poetical romances. Shawls with DIAPERED background came into fashion and a square type of shawl known as 'moon shawl' (*chand-dar*) with a central medallion and a quarter-medallion in each corner was also introduced. An abrupt change of fashion in the 1860s together with the effects of the Franco-Prussian war (1870–1) brought about a collapse of the European market and the weakened industry was finally ruined by a famine in 1877–9.

The fashion for the Cashmere shawl as an article of costume was established in the 1770s and Cashmere-type shawls began to be manufactured in England, first at Norwich during the 1780s. Edinburgh, another centre of manufacture, was the first to imitate Kashmir patterns and Cashmere shawls continued to be made there by a brocade-weaving technique until 1847. In Norwich a new type of shawl with Cashmere patterns began to be made on harness looms from 1803. These shawls, called 'fillovers', established Norwich as the chief centre of British shawl weaving for 25 years. The Paisley shawl industry started as an offshoot from that of Edinburgh and at first pirated the Norwich patterns. They were ahead, however, in technique and were the first to use the JACQUARD loom.

The fashion for the shawl took root in France later than in England, being first known there as the 'English fashion'. But under the leadership of the Empress Josephine it rapidly established itself and Cashmere-type shawls were made in France from the early years of the 19th c. The original patterns of Kashmir had less appeal for the French than for the English, however, and during the first decades of the century the services of leading French designers were constantly called upon to modify the designs more into line with the national taste. From *c.* 1840 English manufacturers began to turn to these French designs rather than to the original Indian ones.

By means of a technical improvement known as the 'ten-box lay' introduced from Manchester in 1812, Paisley shawl-manufacturers were able to make exact reproductions of the patterns of shawls imported from India. By the 1820s these imitations were even being exported to Persia and Turkey. During the 1830s Paisley was the chief English centre for the manufacture of shawls; the Jacquard loom was introduced *c.* 1833 and was in general use by the mid 1840s. From then onwards the Paisley makers were reproducing the French modifications of Kashmir designs. But neither the French nor the English shawl-manufacturers could rival the quality of texture or the fineness of the genuine shawls of Kashmir. One of the more romantic stories of industrial enterprise is afforded by the repeated but always unsuccessful expeditions to Tibet, by French and English both, in the attempt to bring back and domesticate the Tibetan mountain goat which had supplied the Kashmiri industry. By the 1870s the shawl had been eclipsed as a luxury trade by new fashions and remained only as a popular industry for which quality did not matter. See INDIA (TEXTILES).

76, 432, 696, 794.

SHEFFIELD PLATE, OLD. 1. HISTORY. Exactly when the phrase 'Old Sheffield Plate' was first used is hard to say, presumably sometime in the very late years of the 19th c., or the early years of the 20th., when the styles of the NEO-CLASSICAL age of Robert ADAM, fashionable during the heyday of Sheffield Plate, once more enjoyed a vogue and 'Old' was added to differentiate the old from the new in the same styles. Certainly by the time Frederick Bradbury produced his mammoth work on the subject in 1912, 'Old Sheffield' or 'Old Sheffield Plate' was the term used to refer to the wares produced in Sheffield and to a lesser extent in Birmingham from the middle of the 18th c. to the middle of the 19th c. when this process was superseded by the cheaper method of electroplating.

The idea of covering a base metal with a thin coating of a precious metal was not new when Thomas BOULSOVER, a Sheffield cutler, invented his process of plating by fusing SILVER upon COPPER. From antiquity base metal had been covered in various ways with a precious metal; but this was never entirely satisfactory, for complete union was not obtained. Close plating, a process whereby a made-up article is covered with silver foil, tin being used as solder between the two metals, was difficult except for small objects and was completely superseded after Boulsover's invention until the early years of the 19th c., when it was once more found useful in the manufacture of dessert knives and forks, buckles, skewers and other small items.

Up to the time of Boulsover's invention Sheffield had been renowned for its steel and for CUTLERY, in which trade generation had followed generation from the 12th and 13th centuries. These goods had for the most part been produced in small workshops either above or below or alongside the living quarters of the cutler or 'Little Mester', as he was called locally. The Company of Cutlers in Hallamshire, now the only livery company still extant outside London, had been founded in 1624 to protect and discipline this trade. It is against this background that, it is said, Thomas Boulsover discovered, whilst repairing the haft of a knife, that silver fused with copper when heated and—most importantly—that the two metals expanded in unity together when rolled under pressure. It is thought that he applied a blowpipe to heat and stretch out the silver on a knife haft to hide the copper which was showing through. Shortly afterwards he was manufacturing small objects such as buttons and snuff-boxes by this technique. Bradbury quotes a letter by Horace Walpole, to Mr. Montagu, dated 1 September 1760, in which he says: 'As I went to Lord Strafford's I passed through Sheffield, which is one of the foulest towns in England, in the most charming situation, where there are 22,000 inhabitants making knives and scissors. They remit eleven thousand pounds a week to London. One man there has discovered the art of plating copper with silver. I bought a pair of candlesticks for two guineas, they are quite pretty.'

The commercial importance of Boulsover's discovery was more fully realized by a distant relative of his by marriage, Joseph HANCOCK, who became in 1765 Master of the Company of Cutlers in Hallamshire and a town trustee. It was Hancock's initiative which seems to have firmly launched the industry in the early 1750s according to an account by Charles Dixon (1776–1852), a candlestick-maker of Sheffield, in which he says: 'The first articles made by Mr. Hancock were saucepans plated inside . . . candlesticks were then made, and one, the Corinthian, was very neat, care being taken to preserve the order in its construction.' During the 1750s and 1760s the copper could only be plated on one side before being rolled into sheets and made up into objects. After *c.* 1770 copper plated on both sides was introduced.

Amongst the other platers of note was Thomas Law (1717–75), who was entered as an apprentice in the Cutler's Company books in 1730 and is recorded as having taken out his freedom in 1748, becoming Master Cutler in 1752. Henry Tudor and Thomas Leader, who had been apprenticed to London silversmiths, must have brought many new ideas and designs to the industry. They were backed by capital from a certain Dr. Sherburn, and this firm provided some of the best of the early Old Sheffield Plate. But it seems to have come to an end about the year 1803. Others to be mentioned are Thomas Bradbury of Thomas Bradbury & Sons, Samuel Roberts of Roberts, Eyre, Belson & Co., Thomas Nicholson of Gainsford & Nicholson, and Matthew BOULTON. Boulton was responsible for starting the new industry in Birmingham and the quality of the plated candlesticks, urns and other domestic objects produced at his 'Soho Manufactory' there was exceptionally good.

The industry grew and flourished until *c.* 1790, when the imposition of high tariffs in America followed by the French Revolution caused the export markets to decline considerably. Production never fully recovered from this setback. Design, however, was not affected by a slowly diminishing market and with the advent of the NEO-CLASSICAL style Old Sheffield Plate found its fullest flowering, the material itself being highly suitable for expression in Neo-Classical form. Indeed to some extent the designers of Old Sheffield Plate led the way instead of lagging behind the SILVER fashions. This situation

A

B

C

A. Snuff-box with pull-off cover chased in Rococo style (*c.* 1750–60)

B. Wine cooler. The badge is that of the Green Howards 19th Regiment of Foot (*c.* 1830)

C. Sugar-basin with inside fitted with a blue glass 'liner' (*c.* 1785–90)

D. Set of candlesticks thought to be from a design by Sir Francis Chantrey. (The Bowes Mus., *c.* 1805)

D

Candlestick. (Sheffield City Mus., *c.* 1755–60)

seems to have lasted until the early years of the 19th c., when a gradual decline and vulgarization of design overtook the industry. After *c.* 1815, although high standards were maintained in construction, ornamentation and form became ponderous and heavy until the whole industry was overcome by the advent of electroplating, which was initiated by a Rotherham engineer in 1844. This new process of plating a base metal with silver was commercially far cheaper so that by 1851 the industry was virtually dead. Epitomizing the change which took place in the design of Old Sheffield Plate soon after 1800 is a set of candlesticks thought to be from a design by Sir Francis Chantrey (1781–1841), a native of Sheffield, and probably made by Gainsford and Nicholson. They are derived directly from caryatid columns on the Erechtheum, Athens, and illustrate the interest in ancient Greek art and architecture which characterized the REGENCY period. But by about 1815 a return to the more exuberant styles of the Rococo period once more became fashionable, though the curving scroll-work now lacked the restraint of the earlier period. Thus the design of Sheffield Plate, like that of the other useful arts of the period, was influenced by fluctuations of taste and style. At the beginning (1750–70) Rococo designs with chased and embossed ornament; during the middle years (1770–1800) Neo-Classical and towards the end Neo-Greek influenced by the Adam Brothers and Flaxman. From *c.* 1800 onwards the elegant oval forms were replaced by heavier shapes and ornament consisting of coarsely designed applied reliefs stamped from thin silver filled with solder. Among the leading designers were Matthew Boulton himself, who is known to have spent time in the British Museum working up designs from the antique, and Samuel Roberts the Younger, of Roberts, Eyre, Belson & Co.

2. THE TECHNIQUES. Starting with a flat sheet of plated copper, the method adopted for shaping any article varied according to the size and form of the article itself. *Raising by hand* was used for such relatively simple vessels as bowls, dishes, urns and tureens. A flat sheet was gradually shaped over a steel stake, first by mallet and then by hammer. More complicated forms such as coffee-pots and jugs were made from a cylindrical shape by a soldered seam, and after further hammering to shape other fittings such as handle and spout would be added. The edges of plates, meat dishes and trays were shaped by *swaging*; the swages, or pair of hinged steel jaws, were gripped in a vice so that the edge of the dish could be passed between them and gently hammered to shape. In the later years of the industry round, hollow vessels such as bowls and basins were *spun* to shape by forcing a disc of plated metal against a shaped wooden block whilst revolved in a lathe. This process was first used in Sheffield *c.* 1825 and by 1840 had practically superseded hand-raising except for complicated forms.

The decoration of plated articles created difficulties unknown to silversmiths, for if the silver surface were broken the copper was revealed beneath. Moreover every cut edge exposed the copper, and it is by the solutions of these problems that the special skills peculiar to this industry are to be judged. As alternatives to engraving, techniques of *die-stamping* and *flat-chasing* were developed. Repoussé work, or CHASING in high relief, was frequently used up to *c.* 1780 and again after *c.* 1820. The face of the article was hammered while it was supported from the back by a steel rake of chosen shape and size. Pierced decoration, to give lightness and elegance to such things as cake baskets, could not be achieved by the fretsaw method of the silversmith, for every cut would have revealed the underlying copper. Instead the *fly punch* was adopted. A punch of the shape of the desired hole was precisely aligned over a similarly perforated steel plate. When the punch was driven through the plated metal into the steel plate beneath, it not only cut out the desired shape but dragged the silver through the hole, thus concealing the copper which would otherwise have been exposed. The exposed edges of articles were covered up to *c.* 1765 by silver solder or by turning them in some way. Later silvered copper wire or solid silver wire (plain, threaded or beaded) was soldered along the edge. About the year 1787 separate mounts began to be made for the decoration of the borders of dishes, trays, tureens, etc. These applied shapes, which became of increasingly ornate design, were made by striking strips of metal into dies and then filling the back with molten solder. As with silverware, customers frequently required initials, dates, crests or coats of arms to be inscribed on their purchases. Since this would normally be in the hands of the retailer who would not have access to a skilled chaser, an area was specially provided for this purpose. Until *c.* 1780 most makers cut out from the side of the tray or teapot an oval or other shape and then soldered on in its place a piece of silver or heavily plated fused plate, which could later be engraved. After *c.* 1810 this laborious process was replaced by burnishing-on a thin wafer of hot silver, the edges of which may still be discernible.

After all the processes of shaping and decorating the essential process of *finishing* remained, to give the plated article its final brilliance. Skilful *flat hammering* over large areas of smooth metal, such as on trays, salvers and dishes, gave an even and mirror-like surface. For teapots and coffee-pots, and for trays where the underside was not seen, single-sided plate was used and on completion the copper surface was protected by a covering of glue and whitening. The last step was *burnishing*, and after thorough scouring and washing the article was first burnished with a highly polished steel tool and then re-burnished with a softer stone tool. Finally the whole surface was polished by hand, using wet rouge.

95, 208, 419, 934.

SHELDON TAPESTRIES. These were produced during the reigns of Elizabeth I and James I in the private manufactory maintained by William Sheldon (d. 1570) and his descendants on their estate at Barcheston in Warwickshire. The work was directed first by Richard Hyckes (*c.* 1524–1621), who had learned his weaving in Holland, and later by his son Francis (*c.* 1566–1630).

The products of the Sheldon looms are mainly cushion-covers and other small pieces, numbers of which survive in museums and private collections. They are pleasant, unpretentious furnishings. The biblical scenes and allegorical figures which form their chief subjects are apt to be dull and conventional in treatment, but backgrounds and borders are enlivened with pleasant flowers.

Large hangings were rarely attempted. Those from Chastleton and at Sudeley Castle have, like the cushions, small panels with figures set against floral backgrounds; when a more ambitious type of composition was adopted, as in the set of four 'Seasons' at Hatfield after engravings by Martin de Vos, the result is more quaint than beautiful. Perhaps the most characteristic Sheldon weavings are the large tapestry maps of Warwickshire and the adjacent counties, which in their minute pictorial renderings of town and village, park and woodland, breathe the authentic charm of the Shakespearian countryside.

SHELL CAMEOS. Although gem CAMEOS, which are cut from different coloured layers of a precious stone such as those found in a banded agate, for example, are usually made for use as jewels, many shell cameos were made purely for ornament, not personal wear. The most striking instance of a shell cameo made purely for exhibition or display, is the masterpiece of the cameo carver Francesco Bruno, who was invited to Paris in 1902 for the celebration of the centenary of Victor Hugo. Bruno, a cameoist from Trapani in Sicily, reproduced part of the text of *Les Misérables* in an illumination composed of cameos, CORAL, various precious woods, IVORY and lithographic stone.

A large number of shells yield the banded layers of different colours which are necessary to produce cameos. In Renaissance times mussels of different sorts were used for this purpose. Modern cameos are cut from just a few shells, the most important of which are the Helmet shells, which include the Black Helmet (*Cassis madagascarensis*). In spite of its name this shell does not come from Madagascar but from the Caribbean. It has an outside-colour of chalky white, a middle-colour of white and a ground-colour of chocolate brown. The Bull Mouth Helmet (*Cassis rufa*) has a brown outside-colour, a white middle-colour and a tawny red ground-colour. The Horned Helmet (*Cassis cornuta*) has a white outside-colour, a white middle-colour and a

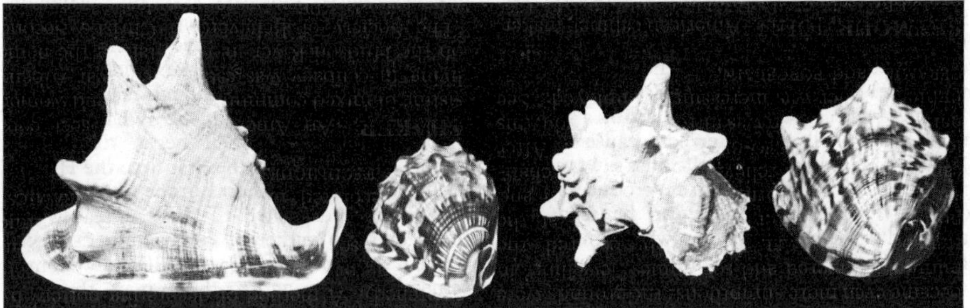

The principal cameo shells: Horned Helmet, Red Helmet, Queen Conch and King Helmet

orange ground-colour. But it has a bad reputation for 'doubling', i.e. the layers of the shell separate under the graver. The King Helmet (*Cassis tuberosa*) has a white outside-colour, a white middle and a brown ground-colour. It is used only as a substitute for the Black Helmet. Then come Conches, represented by but one variety, the Queen Conch (*Strombus gigas*), which has a yellow outside-colour, a white middle-colour and a pink ground-colour. Unfortunately the pink colour is not always quite distinct from the white, and it sometimes fades if exposed to light. Next follow the Cowries. The Tiger Cowrie (*Cypraea tigris*) has a brown spotted and white mottled outside-colour, a white middle-colour and a brown ground-colour. Like all the cowries the Tiger is much smaller than the Helmets or Conches. They are about 17 cm long, while this, the largest of the Cowries, is only 9 centimetres long. The Panther Cowrie (*Cypraea pantherina*) has a dark brown and white mottled exterior, a white middle-colour and a dark brown ground-colour. The Gold Ringer (*Cypraea anulus*) has a grey outside-colour, a grey middle-colour and a deep black to violet ground-colour. The Snake's Head (*Cypraea caput serpentis*) has a mottled brown and white outside-colour, a white middle-colour and a violet ground-colour. In spite of its name it does not look a bit like a snake's head. The Money Cowrie (*Cypraea moneta*), once used for currency and as counters for children in schools, has a golden yellow outside-colour, a matt white middle-colour and a violet ground-colour. Finally the Poached Egg (*Ovulo ovum*) has a shiny white glistening outside-colour, a matt white middle and a port wine ground-colour. This shell really does look like a poached egg.

Cameo shells are made of the same substances as MOTHER OF PEARL but in different proportions, so that they are harder than nacre. They appear so hard that many people are astonished to be told that it does not require a lapidary's wheel to cut them but that they can be carved with a steel tool.

It is a remarkable fact that although some of the best Helmet shells are to be found in the Caribbean, and all shells appear to pass through the London warehouses for sale, neither Britain nor the U.S.A. has ever produced cameo carvers in large numbers. Apart from a few who work in Paris, almost all cameoists live in Naples and they can sometimes be seen selling their wares under the arches of the Colosseum in Rome.

The cameo carver starts by selecting a suitable shell. Male shells are preferred because they are heavier and thicker. A shell must always have a good colour right through to produce a good cameo. Frequently cameos can be seen, still attached to the parent shell, in which the ground colour has petered out, making an unsatisfactory contrast. Usually, however, cameos are not attached to the shell while they are being carved. It is normal, nowadays at any rate, for the whole shell to be cut up with a lapidary's slitting disc into blanks of suitable size. These are then looked over for suitability by the carver, who selects one and attaches it with dop cement (a jeweller's compound of beeswax and resin) to a dopstick. He then holds it in one hand or immobilizes it in a vice or some other device, while tracing on it with a pencil the design he is going to carve. Some carvers, now and in the past, work from models made in white wax on a contrasting disc, and Archibald Billing, a Victorian amateur who studied cameo-carving as a hobby, suggests that the artist should learn to make his own models by making life studies and then sculpting them in wax before carving. Much cameo-carving, however, both now and in the past, is repetitive. There is a certain turn of the nose in profiles, which could be described as 'the Torre del Greco nose', which suggests that the cameoist is a product of the school of CORAL in Torre del Greco, Naples. It is therefore not surprising that through having carved the same cameo so often a carver, such as some of the Neapolitan workers in the 19th c., could sit down and without a model make a cameo completely finished in every detail.

Having drawn in the outline of the cameo, the carver proceeded to file away the part of the shell outside the profile until he had got down to the ground-colour. He then selected a scorper—a steel tool with a mushroom-shaped handle, which could be flat faced, rounded or three-cornered—and with one of these shapes, together with a double-edged pointed knife and a darning needle ground to any point he desired and fitted into a handle, he would outline the whole of the face in silhouette against the dark background and cut in its features. Often the part of the white middle layer which touched the ground-colour was 'melted' into it, that is cut so fine in parts as to be almost transparent and as it were swim upon the darker background. Many carvers, however, especially during the 19th c., preferred to do just the opposite, to undercut slightly the white design so that it would stand out starkly and boldly on the dark ground. What the cameo cutter was particularly afraid of doing was to cut into the ground-colour. He would then have been forced to level down the whole of the background once more. Cameos were polished fairly gingerly, lest the detail be obscured, with flour pumice applied on a shaped piece of limewood. Nowadays power tools have probably replaced much of the hand-carving of the old cameo craftsmen, though many modern cameos are advertised as 'made by hand'.

Cameo-carving in shell began during the Renaissance, when for the first time the Helmet shells became available in Europe as discoverers and traders penetrated the distant seas where they could be gathered. Benvenuto CELLINI's reference to the discovery of allegedly Roman cameos in tombs and to the opinion that they were intended by the ancients as AMULETS, to prevent men's minds from being swayed by

German cameos, signed 'F', showing scenes from the life of Christ and the Virgin. (V. & A. Mus., 1571)

excess of good or evil fortune, and his description of his own efforts at cameo-carving, may be the first important literary reference to the subject. Cameos have never really declined in popularity since, though they have had to stand a good deal of competition, first from Wedgwood's ceramic cameos and more recently from plastics. By the 18th c., at least, cameo-carving was established in Naples and Sicily. During the 19th c., as has been already said, many masters preferred to leave their cameos on the shell, or even decorate the whole shell with carving. Thus the master craftsman Giovanni Sabbato (1873–83) spent ten years in carving a Helmet shell with an allegory of England's Greatness at Sea. Although some carvers signed their work by scratching their names on the back of the cameo, not much is known about them unless their products have been preserved in museums or private collections.

At present cameo-carving is a languishing art. The products of Naples and Paris have become stereotyped and uninviting and the prices discourage prospective buyers.

709.

SHERATON, THOMAS (1751–1806). English cabinet-maker and furniture designer. Born at Stockton-on-Tees, he settled in London *c.* 1790. Although a trained cabinet-maker, he appears not to have owned a workshop and no furniture by his hand has been identified. His fame rests on his publications and through them his name has come to be identified with the fashions in MAHOGANY, satinwood and painted furniture which prevailed from *c.* 1790 to *c.* 1805. The most important of his books is *The Cabinet-Maker and Upholsterer's Drawing Book*, which was issued in four parts 1791–4. The first half of the book is devoted to treatises on architecture, perspective and drawing. Part III contains designs for furniture accompanied by technical and practical notes. Sheraton states: 'The design of this part of the book is intended to exhibit the present taste of furniture, and at the same time to give the workman some assistance in the manufacturing part of it.' The book is an excellent conspectus of the prevailing fashion in furniture during the last decade of the 18th c. The designs were extensively used by furniture-makers both in Britain and in America and were an important formative influence on REGENCY cabinet-making.

In 1803 Sheraton published *The Cabinet Dictionary, containing an explanation of all the terms used in the Cabinet, Chair and Upholstery Branches, with directions for varnishing, polishing and gilding*. It had 88 copper engravings and the designs show certain aspects of the French DIRECTOIRE style which were popular in England in the first decade of the 19th c. In 1805 he published the first part of an unfinished *The Cabinet-Maker, Upholsterer and General Artist's Encyclopaedia*. While the designs of his first book represent the later phase of the NEO-CLASSICAL movement in England, the later books reveal influences of the French Directoire and EMPIRE styles which were apparent in the development of the Regency. The terms 'Early' and 'Late' Sheraton are sometimes used to distinguish these phases. It does not appear, however, that Sheraton originated the styles which bear his name. See FURNITURE (ENGLISH) and (AMERICAN).

SHERATON STYLE. Term loosely applied to the style in fine MAHOGANY, satinwood and painted furniture which was in vogue in England from *c.* 1790 to *c.* 1805. The term 'Early Sheraton' is applied to the later NEO-CLASSICAL vogue in furniture style which prevailed in the last decade of the 18th c., influenced both by the ADAM brothers and by CHIPPENDALE. 'Late Sheraton' is applied to the style of the designs in the *Cabinet Dictionary* and *Encyclopaedia* which contained features of French DIRECTOIRE and EMPIRE styles. It is not now thought that the style which goes by his name was originated by SHERATON.

24, 251.

SHIBAYAMA (18th c.). Japanese family of *netsuke*-carvers, noted for a distinctive style of inlay work. See JAPAN (NETSUKE).

SHOAMI. Japanese family of armourers. See JAPAN (SWORDS AND SWORD FURNITURE).

SHŌSŌIN. A collection of Chinese T'ang objects of decorative art preserved at Nara, Japan. The collection was dedicated in A.D. 756 by the Empress Kōken, widow of the Emperor Shōmu, to the Buddha of Todaiji, Nara. They were placed in the treasury Shōsōin and have been preserved practically intact to this day. They represented the lifetime collection of the Emperor Shōmu and are today the richest depository of Chinese decorative art from this period. 'This remarkable collection contains furniture, musical instruments and gaming boards painted, lacquered, or inlaid with magnificant floral and animal designs in mother of pearl, tortoise-shell, gold and silver; there are glass vessels from the Arab world, silver platters, jugs and ewers, mirrors, silk brocades, weapons, pottery, maps, paintings and calligraphy. What is astonishing about this collection is the extent of the foreign influence present. This is particularly true of the arts of the goldsmith and silversmith which came into their own in the T'ang Dynasty.' (Michael Sullivan, *A Short History of Chinese Art*, 1967.)

SHŪZAN, YOSHIMURA. See JAPAN (NETSUKE).

SILHOUETTE. In classical antiquity the legendary origin of all figural painting, according to Pliny (A.D. 23/24–79), was ascribed to *skiagraphia*, tracing the outline of a shadow cast upon a wall. But silhouettes of hands, etc. in red pigment go back to Palaeolithic times and silhouette representations as pottery decoration are found as early as the 2nd millennium B.C. In the Middle Ages silhouette was the principle of the Islamic shadow plays and cut-paper silhouettes were popular in Turkey and the Middle East. But the heyday of the art of the silhouette was in the 18th and early 19th centuries.

The term 'silhouette' is derived from the name of Étienne de Silhouette (1709–67), French Finance Minister under Louis XV notorious for his economies in an extravagant age. Hence the phrase 'à la Silhouette' was used to denote parsimony and perhaps because de Silhouette took up paper cutting as a hobby in retirement, it came to be associated particularly with what we now call silhouettes as a cheaper substitute for portraiture. The term seems not to have been current with this sense in England before the early 19th c., where it was used for example in an instruction book *The Art of Cutting Out Designs in Black Paper* by Miss Barbara Anne Townshend, published in 1815. It occurs earlier in the title of an instruction book published by P. H. Perrenon of Münster, Germany, in 1780. Up to the end of the 18th c. silhouette portraits were commonly known in England as 'Shades' or 'Profiles'.

In England the fashion for silhouettes grew up in close association with portrait miniatures and the genre of paintings known as conversation pieces. In Germany the Swiss physiognomist Johann Kaspar Lavater was largely responsible for adding a scientific cachet to what was otherwise an amusing interest in the line of the traditional woodcut. In his *Essays on Physiognomy* (1775–8) Lavater set great store by the silhouette portrait in support of his theories; he travelled Germany with the draughtsman Georg Friedrich Schmoll, making portraits in profile of important personages for future publication. Among others the poet Goethe became an enthusiastic convert. In France the silhouette became fashionable chiefly in the EMPIRE period and primarily as a bibelot, in jewellery, VERRE ÉGLOMISÉ, and so on. Many French craftsmen in silhouette travelled or worked abroad, popularizing the fashion in Italy, Spain, Russia, the Netherlands and America. Francis Torond (1743–1812) worked in England and did much to popularize the silhouette 'conversation piece'. Augustin Amant Constant Fidèle EDOUART settled in England in 1814, spent part of the 1830s in Ireland and most of the 1840s in America. Johann Friedrich ANTHING, after touring the courts of Europe, ended up in Russia. Another traveller was François GONORD, who like Gilles-Louis CHRÉTIEN used the *physionotrace*, a somewhat cumbersome machine for tracing life-size silhouettes of the sitter, to be subsequently reduced to miniature size by a kind of pantograph. Gonord also cut free-hand silhouette portraits of French notabilities as they ascended the steps of the guillotine. F. G. Sideau was in Russia 1782–4 and made both ink and cut-out silhouette portraits of Catherine II and the Russian court. Four albums of these silhouettes are in the Hermitage Museum.

Silhouettes were made both by painting (or

ink) and by cutting out shapes. Silhouette painting was done on plaster, card, ivory, porcelain, glass (including *verre églomisé*) and rarely on enamel. Cut silhouettes were produced by either of two techniques. The shape might be cut out from the middle of a sheet of white paper and the resulting hole backed with black velvet giving the required silhouette; or on black-surfaced paper the surround might be cut away, leaving a silhouette that could be embellished with touches of gold or brown and mounted on white card. The former method was called 'hollow' cutting. Cutting was either free-hand or mechanically guided and a succession of more or less complicated contraptions were devised, and patented, for producing life-size silhouettes with mechanical accuracy and then reducing them to the required size. (Finished life-size portraits were comparatively rare.) An extremely complicated device was recommended by Lavater and something rather similar was described by Perrenon. The *physionotrace* used in various forms by Chrétien, Gonord, Charles Balthazar Julien Févret de Saint-Memin (1770–1852), who worked in America from 1795 to 1814, has been mentioned. The popular English silhouettist Mrs. HARRINGTON patented *c.* 1786 a 'new and curious method of taking and reducing shadows with appendages and apparatus never before known or used in the above art, for the purpose of taking likenesses, etc., in miniature . . .' In 1806 a maker of optical and mathematical instruments, C. Schmalcalder, patented a 'Delineator, Copier, Proportionometer for the use of Taking, Tracing and Cutting out Profiles . . .' It involved a telescopic rod which was passed over the features of the sitter and to which was attached either a cutter or a tracer. In America Moses Chapman (1783–1821), an itinerant artist of hollow-cut silhouettes, toured Massachusetts using a machine which he advertised as 'universally allowed by the best judges to be more correct than ever before invented'. Charles Willson Peale (1741–1827), born in Maryland, studied art in Boston, possibly under Copley, and came to London, where he was a pupil of Benjamin West 1767–9. He was fascinated by machine cutting of silhouettes while in London and when he established his own Museum and Art Gallery in Philadelphia he installed a silhouette-cutting machine. He later collaborated in the foundation of the Pennsylvania Academy of Fine Arts but remained faithful to his silhouettes. His eldest son, Rembrandt Peale (1778–1860), studied painting under Benjamin West, exhibited at the Royal Academy, London (1803), and established a museum at Baltimore. In an advertisement holding himself out as a painter of miniatures he added that he 'appropriates the afternoons to cutting profiles and the evenings to pencilling of them'. Most silhouette machines involved some variant of the Camera Obscura, some sort of device to enable the sitter to remain still, and a mechanical method of reducing the portrait to scale. In the most common method a carefully arranged and diffused candlelight threw the sitter's shadow upon a sheet of glass set vertically beside the chair; a sheet of oiled paper was fixed to the opposite side of the glass and the artist, standing behind the glass, outlined the shadow on to the paper. Methods of reducing the image to scale were based upon the principle of the pantograph, a mathematical copying instrument invented by the German astronomer Christoph Scheiner in 1603; its definitive form was described by a French instrument-maker, Claude Langlois, in 1743.

One of the most popular techniques in the 18th c., both in England and in Paris, was to paint the side view of the sitter on to a small medallion of plaster—or 'composition' as it was called—the dead matt white of the plaster admirably setting off the vivacity of the portrait. Most silhouettists also used card or occasionally small plaques of ivory. It was customary to paint the head and profile in unrelieved black while the hair and accessories were done in a smoky, half-transparent grey. Towards the end of the century it became fashionable to bring up the highlights by touches of gold or bronze. One of the finest as well as the most prolific practitioners was John MIERS of Leeds (some 40 of his silhouette portraits are in the Victoria and Albert Museum), who was ably supported by his assistant and successor John FIELD. J. Thomason, a follower of John Wesley, worked in London and the provinces in the late 1780s and was in Ireland from 1790 to 1792. He painted on both plaster and glass. A. Charles, an indifferent miniature artist, achieved great popularity as a silhouettist in the second half of the century, painting on plaster, card, ivory or even enamel. He was appointed 'Likeness Painter' to the Prince of Wales in 1793 and is said to have made over 13,000 miniatures and 'shades', after which he raised his prices from 10*s.* 6*d.* (52½p) to 13*s.* (65p) for silhouettes, charging 25 guineas (£26·25) for coloured miniatures. Fanny Burney speaks in her *Diary* of having had her 'shade' taken by him. Outstanding among painters of conversation pieces were the French emigré who used the name Francis Torond and William Wellings, who worked in black, grey and tones of brown between 1792 and 1795. Under the Regency profile-portraits were a fashion in the entourage of the Prince of Wales, Mrs. Fitzherbert being one of the earliest collectors. Later in the century full-length portraits came increasingly into vogue.

Glass painting was done on the underside of a sheet of glass, either flat or convex, and the painting was so framed that the light would project the painted silhouette—or 'shade'—on to the backing behind it so as to cause a true shadow. The glass and framing were often elaborately embellished. In size glass paintings varied from the large wall-pictures done mainly in Silesia and Nuremberg (examples in the Linz Museum) to the tiny, jewel-like portraits in *verre églomisé* at which the French were particularly expert.

The Birthday Party by F. Torond. (V. & A. Mus.)

The general run of glass-painted silhouettes were of the size of miniature paintings. Among the earliest practitioners in England were a bookseller's son, Joliffe, said in correspondence of the poet Thomas Gray to have been popular with members of White's, and Carl ROSENBERG, who came to England at the age of 14 in the suite of the Princess Charlotte of Mecklenburg-Strelitz. Both worked in the second half of the 18th c. Equally prominent with Rosenberg, and perhaps a better artist, was Mrs. BEETHAM, whose husband, Edward Beetham, in addition to inventing the roll-up theatre curtain and the modern type of clothes mangle, devised an improved method of glass gilding for frames and mounts. Mrs. Beetham also painted on card and took lessons from the miniaturist John Smart (1741–1811). Indeed all the leading silhouettists worked in more than one medium. The popular A. Charles, who has been mentioned as a painter on card, also advertised himself as 'the original miniaturist on glass, and the only one who can take them in whole length by a pantograph'. Thomason, who was a painter on plaster, changed from plaster to glass at the beginning of the 19th c. Similarly, a majority of the more proficient silhouettists worked with the techniques of both painting and cutting.

The use of the silhouette, both the silhouette portrait and other forms of silhouette, as pottery decoration was a natural development certainly encouraged by the fact that the great vogue of the

Two Ladies by William Wellings. (V. & A. Mus.)

silhouette coincided with the Classical Revival in the latter half of the 18th c. and the first quarter of the 19th c. For the silhouette fitted admirably into the pseudo-antique style which was then in vogue. Among the many factories which made use of the portrait silhouettes as decoration were Sèvres, Dresden, Royal Copenhagen, Royal Worcester, Bristol. The French Empire style spread to many Continental manufactories. At Dresden, for example, during the years 1796–1814 when Count Marcolini, Minister of the Elector Frederick Augustus, was director, classical ornament with medallions containing profile portraits took the place of ornate BAROQUE floral decoration. The new black-glaze style bordered in red outlines often contained a panel in gold with a black silhouette head. Silhouettes of royalties or notabilities were much used on presentation or commemorative china.

Silhouette portraits were also fashionable for the embellishment of personal jewellery, lockets and fine boxes. The custom of wearing small miniatures as costume jewellery in lockets, brooches, even rings, goes back to the beginning of the 16th c. With the rise of silhouette portraiture silhouette portraits on porcelain were used for similar purposes. They were also employed on mourning rings. Indeed all the leading silhouettists advertised their miniature portraits on porcelain or ivory to be set in rings, lockets, bracelets, brooches, etc. and undertook to preserve the likeness, however small. Their great popularity is attested by examples of PINCHBECK bracelets, etc. with silhouette portraits. Silhouettes also became fashionable to ornament SNUFF-BOXES, PATCH-BOXES, needle-work-boxes, cases for tooth-picks, for cards, for toilet accessories, and so on. The French were particularly skilled at adapting the silhouette portrait to expensive and exquisite bibelots. The Viennese silhouettist Karl Schmid (active 1795–1801), who worked on glass, and was for a time court silhouettist to the Schwarzenbergs, was also renowned for his exquisite jewellery with silhouette ornamentation. (Patch-box in the Metropolitan Museum, New York.)

The alternative technique of making silhouettes by cutting out has also a long history. The cut silhouette seems to have had a particular appeal for the amateur portraitist. As has been said, it was taken up by Étienne de Silhouette in retirement. An early example of an English amateur cut-out silhouette portrait was that of Sir John Wedderburn cut from brown paper and backed with black silk by the daughter of his gaoler on the night before his execution on 27 November 1746. Joseph Tussaud, elder son of Madame Tussaud, a worker in wax, also cut profiles during the 1820s with the help of an instrument. He advertised as follows: 'Son of the great Madame Tussaud Respectfully informs the nobility and gentry and the public in general that he has a machine by which he takes profile likenesses. Price 2*s.* to 7*s.* [10p–35p] according to style.' A cut-out portrait of J. M. W. Turner, R.A., by John Ruskin is illustrated in *British Silhouettes* by John Woodiwiss. Most of the professional silhouettists worked in cut paper as well as other techniques. Among the best of those who specialized in cuts were Frederick Frith of Dover and A. Edouart. Amateur and itinerant professional silhouette-cutters in

A

B

C

A. *Portrait of the artist in the act of cutting a silhouette* by A. Edouart. From F. Nevill Jackson, *Ancestors in Silhouette* (1921). B. *George IV, Prince of Wales, with the Duke of Mecklenburg-Strelitz* by Charles Rosenberg (silhouette painted on glass). (Royal Lib., Windsor.) Reproduced by gracious permission of H.M. the Queen. C. *Portrait of Sir Walter Scott* by A. Edouart. (Nat. Portrait Gal., London)

America worked chiefly in New England at the beginning of the 19th c. The names of some 60 American silhouettists and about 20 foreigners are known. Among the more talented amateurs were Eleanor Parke Custis (1779–1852), step-granddaughter of George Washington, who was adopted by the President on his marriage, and John André (1751–80), major in the British Army and aide-de-camp successively to General Grey and Sir Henry Clinton, who was hanged as a spy. Among professional silhouettists Moses Chapman and Charles Willson Peale have been mentioned. Others who are outstanding were Charles Peale Polk (1767–1822), a nephew of Charles Willson Peale, and William Henry Brown (1808–83) of Charleston, who cut his first portrait, of Lafayette, in Philadelphia at the age of 16. His memory was said to be so good that he could cut portraits of persons he had seen casually in the street even some hours later. In 1845 Brown published a collection of 27 of his most important portraits entitled *Portrait Gallery of Distinguished American Citizens with Biographical Sketches.* Examples of his work may be seen in Salem, Massachusetts. Brown also made large compositions commemorating events of historical interest.

The silhouette flourished as a cheaper substitute for the miniature portrait. Yet it was never a popular craft. The leading silhouettists were patronized by royalty and the nobility and examples of their work may be found in most of the great museums. Yet after enjoying a heyday of more than a century the vogue failed to survive the introduction of the DAGUERREOTYPE and more or less from the time when the copyright of photographs was secured by Act of Parliament in 1862 the craft of the silhouettist was fighting a losing battle in England as in other countries. It has survived as a stunt and a curiosity mainly at the popular watering-places, while examples from the great age of the silhouette have become collectors' pieces. Silhouettes do, of course, continue to be used as a graphic means among others for advertisements, containers, etc., although they are now usually photographically produced.

374, 434, 436, 514, 533, 582, 583, 587, 752, 926.

SILK. The story of silk, the most beautiful of textile fibres, is linked with power politics, the supernatural, and industrial espionage.

Silk may be of two kinds. What we call today 'wild' silk comes from the Indian states of Assam and Mysore and is the product of an indigenous Indian moth which produces several broods a year and feeds on the leaves of various species of tropical tree, a food which gives the silk a rather harsh texture and a brownish colour. This is the famous tussore silk, which forms only a small percentage of the world production. The account which follows deals with the other type of silk, produced by the larva of the moth *Bombyx mori*. This, as its name implies, feeds only on the young leaves of the white mulberry tree, which grows freely in China, the Levant, Italy and the south of France. Unlike the wild silks of Assam, that produced by *Bombyx mori* is the result of highly selective breeding and a complex technique of rearing and processing. The jealously guarded secret of silk lay not so much in the fact that it was the product of caterpillars as in the precise details of how they were reared and how the thread was prepared, i.e. the arts of sericulture, reeling and throwing.

All these were discovered by the Chinese, probably in the Neolithic age, and legend credits them to Lei-tsu, wife of the mythical emperor Huang-ti. Leaving the age of legend, we come to the well-documented Han Dynasty, whose sixth emperor, Wu-ti, *c.* 140 B.C. was troubled by incessant raids of the Huns, nomadic tribes from Mongolia. Therefore when he heard that in a country far to the east there was a breed of horses which sweated blood and were the progeny of supernatural stallions, swifter and more powerful than the Mongol ponies with which his cavalry was equipped, he sent a mission under Chang Chʿen to investigate and, if possible, to buy these animals. Among the gifts which he sent were rolls of silk fabric, the product of what had by this time become the greatest industry in China and already of superb technical and artistic quality.

The indomitable Chang Chʿen was setting out on what proved to be a 5,000 km journey which lasted thirteen years. Captured by the Huns he was kept in prison for ten years. But after escaping he continued on his way, over the Pamirs and the Roof of the World and through the deserts of central Asia until he came to Khotan in the vale of Fergana (Russian Uzbekistan) not far from the city of Samarkand. Here he found his horses, which did indeed sweat blood; for even to this day there is in Chinese Turkestan a parasite which penetrates the horse's hide, causing blisters which bleed. But the natives refused to sell, and Chang returned empty-handed. Wu-ti eventually secured the horses after a desperate military campaign and became interested in the report which his envoy brought back concerning a hitherto unknown people, rich and highly civilized and dwelling in a fertile country. These were the Parthians, who dwelt in what was then Persia and who were the bitter foes of a still greater and richer empire, Rome. Contact was made and thus the Persians became acquainted with silk thread and fabric. A vigorous trade in both soon developed, but China retained the secret of their origin. And so was established the China–Persia *rapprochement*, which lasted for centuries and established the Persians as middlemen when in course of time silk became known to the Romans. See also CHINA (TEXTILES).

We know precisely when, where, and how the Romans first saw silk. It was in the year 53 B.C. when Marcus Licinius Crassus was routed at Carrhae (modern Harran). Survivors told how at the moment when defeat turned to utter rout the charging Parthian horsemen unfurled terrible banners embroidered with designs of dragons totally unlike anything the Romans had ever seen before. Thus knowledge of silk came to Europe. The new and wonderful fabric made a strong appeal to the affluent society of the Roman Empire, ever hungry for novelties, and what had first been known as a symbol of enemy power became a prime luxury commodity. In the time of Augustus a special market existed for imported Chinese silk, which was split and rewoven in Syria to provide a gossamer material, 'clad in which', wrote Seneca, 'no woman can honestly say she is not naked'.

The intrinsically high cost of silk was enhanced by the long and difficult journey it had to make and by the avarice of the Persian middlemen, who successfully guarded the secret of its origin for nearly 500 years. It was literally worth its weight in gold; and so scarce was the thread that Roman women unravelled Persian and Chinese fabrics in order to obtain thread for their embroidery. Naturally the Romans were intensely curious about the source of silk. From the time of Augustus it was known to be a product of the Asiatic people (Chinese and Tibetans), whom they called by the Greek name 'Seres' when approached by the overland route ('Sinae' was the name for them when approached by sea from India). Therefore the Roman name for silk was *sericum* (the product of the Seres) and for silk fabrics and garments they used the plural *serica*. Not much was reliably known to them about the Chinese. According to the encyclopedist Pliny (A.D. 23/24–79), who recorded what information was currently available, they were a red-haired people with blue eyes and harsh voices, who combed the silk fibres from trees. They were said to be extremely taciturn, trading the silk for gold in silence. By Nero's time (A.D. 54–68), when other Chinese commodities besides silk were beginning to trickle into the Roman empire, the position of the Seres in relation to India was roughly understood. In A.D. 97 Kan Ying visited Antioch after Chinese conquests in central Asia and *c.* A.D. 120 agents of a certain Maes Titianus penetrated beyond Kashgar and Daraut Kurghan. The latter came into contact with the Chinese, learnt of cities which they called Daxata and Sera (possibly Singanfu and Loh Yang), gained some idea of Pamir, Tian Shan, and the Altay mountains, but knew nothing of the sea east of China. They were the first to know that silk is an animal product. In A.D. 166 a mission reached China from Marcus Aurelius and another in A.D. 284.

During this period silk was traded along the Imperial Highway, renamed in modern times 'The Silk Road', which started from Shanghai and ended at Antioch or Tyre; a distance of 6,500 km as the crow flies although the actual travelling distance was nearer 10,000 km. It was along this terrible road that silk caravans

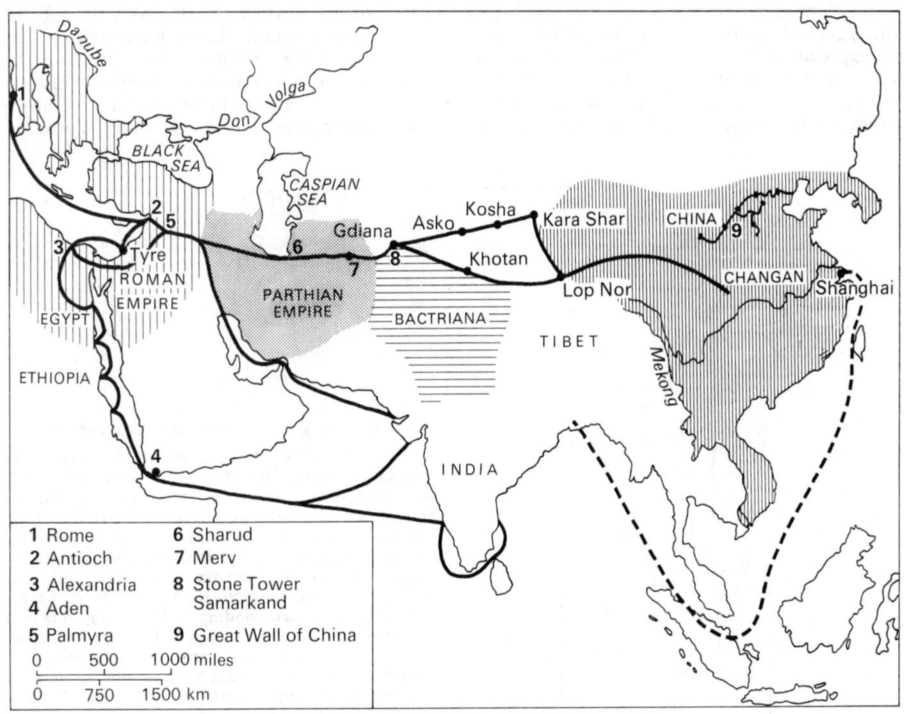

'The Silk Road'

wound their way in constant danger from hostile attack, sandstorms or death from thirst in the desert. About A.D. 100 the Han dynasty went through a political crisis and were no longer able to hold in check the brigands on their borders who infested the road. For a time supplies were cut off and Rome experienced a silk famine. About A.D. 100 too a sailor named Alexander discovered Cattigara, a port of southern China (perhaps the modern Canton), reaching it by sea from India. A sea route from India to Asia was also opened up by a certain Hippalus so that silk, having come down the Burma Road to Thailand, could be shipped across the Indian Ocean. But the Arabs were in control of the Red Sea and once more contact between Rome and China was frustrated.

What, then, was the nature of the secret so keenly desired by Rome and so jealously guarded by China and by the middlemen to whom the trade was so profitable? The fact that silk was the product of a caterpillar was of minor importance compared with the knowledge of how to rear a creature which generations of selective breeding had so debilitated that the females were completely immobile and the males only could walk, while both were so delicate that loud noises, strong smells or the threat of thunder might kill them and they needed a daily ration of freshly gathered and finely chopped mulberry leaves. The art of sericulture involves intensive toil and can only flourish where there is an abundance of female peasant labour. The life-cycle of the silkworm starts in the winter, when the eggs, laid during the previous autumn, must be exposed to dry cold conditions. When the mulberry trees begin to sprout the women carry the eggs about on their bodies, whose warmth promotes hatching. So small are the eggs that 25 g will produce 35,000 worms—which by the time they have reached maturity will have eaten a tonne of leaves. Four times during its life the worm will moult, and while it is casting its skin it becomes extremely vulnerable to adverse conditions. When it reaches maturity the worm spins, from a pair of glands in its head, a silk cocoon consisting of a continuous thread varying in length from around 500 to 1,000 metres and so fine that 3,000 km of it would only weigh a kilogramme. In order to encourage them to spin bowers of twigs are now provided and the worms are left in peace. As one Chinese poet says: 'The worker may now rest and play with her children.' But not for long, because if the chrysalis is left to hatch out, it will bite its way to freedom and so chop the continuous thread into short lengths. To prevent this the cocoons must either be steamed or given a chemical treatment, so that they may be reeled at leisure. This technique of stifling the worms was one of the most carefully guarded secrets.

The problem of unwinding the silk from the cocoon was both complex and delicate, the gossamer-fine thread (called 'bave') being laid in figure-of-eight loops bound together in a firm structure by a natural gum (sericin) with which it was coated and which solidified as soon as it came into contact with the air. It was necessary, therefore, to soften the gum and to provide a frictionless bearing on which the cocoon would revolve; and this took the form of a bowl of hot water, on the surface of which six or eight of them could unwind. There were two reasons for choosing this number. First because the resultant thread was the finest which was strong enough to withstand the strains of the subsequent textile processes; and secondly in order to

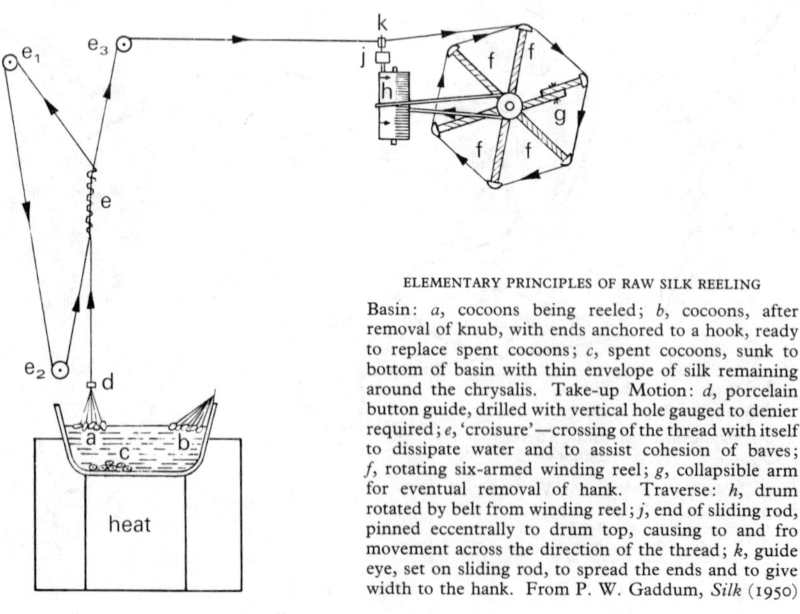

ELEMENTARY PRINCIPLES OF RAW SILK REELING

Basin: *a*, cocoons being reeled; *b*, cocoons, after removal of knub, with ends anchored to a hook, ready to replace spent cocoons; *c*, spent cocoons, sunk to bottom of basin with thin envelope of silk remaining around the chrysalis. Take-up Motion: *d*, porcelain button guide, drilled with vertical hole gauged to denier required; *e*, 'croisure'—crossing of the thread with itself to dissipate water and to assist cohesion of baves; *f*, rotating six-armed winding reel; *g*, collapsible arm for eventual removal of hank. Traverse: *h*, drum rotated by belt from winding reel; *j*, end of sliding rod, pinned eccentrally to drum top, causing to and fro movement across the direction of the thread; *k*, guide eye, set on sliding rod, to spread the ends and to give width to the hank. From P. W. Gaddum, *Silk* (1950)

give a thread of uniform diameter; because the thread spun by the worm tapers from one end to the other and so the reeler had to make sure that at any one moment all her cocoons were at different stages of exhaustion. An essential part of the reeling process was the *croissure*, a device whereby a group of filaments was consolidated in a circular section and made to cohere while the gum was still soft. At the same time it expressed the surplus water carried over from the bowl to the reel. The method was to pass the thread over two small pulleys so arranged that it turned back on itself and was then made to travel a second time parallel to its former path; but on this second passage the two threads were twined round one another before one of them went on to the reel. This created sufficient pressure to consolidate the thread without use of any mechanical device.

The original 25 g of eggs would yield about 5 kg of silk, and would need such a number of carefully tended mulberry trees that from a hectare of land only about 50 kg of silk could be expected. Bearing in mind these figures of productivity, we get some idea of the importance of silk in the ancient world. Pliny says that the annual drain on the gold reserves of the Empire amounted to 50 million sesterces and inventories of royal treasuries included, alongside gold and jewels, large numbers of rolls of silk cloth. We may ask what besides gold flowed eastwards to pay for all this silk, and the answer is Roman GLASS, especially beads, and Roman acrobats and jugglers, whose skill was greatly admired by the Chinese. But the balance of trade remained heavily against the Romans and this helped to aggravate the chronic inflation which eventually destroyed the Empire.

Not only did the peoples of western Asia exact a middleman's profit on the raw silk; they also developed a highly skilled and powerful WEAVING industry. Beautiful examples of Persian (Sassanian) work may be seen in museums, together with that of the Copts, who were noted for their skill both in weaving and in dyeing. When in A.D. 330 Byzantium became the centre of the empire a government monopoly of silk-weaving was established, and this school of design flourished for many centuries. Relationships between the empire and its eastern neighbours fluctuated with the changing balance of power; Persia, Khotan, Sogdiana (a vassal state of the Turks) and Kashan (Afghanistan and north India) each in turn dominated the situation, and silk played the part in ancient economy which oil does in the modern world.

Meanwhile Byzantium went through a chequered economic history. Sometimes it was strong enough to sign treaties with Persia, as in A.D. 297 when Diocletian agreed with Narses of Persia that Nisbis should be the official exchange point for imports and exports; at others it suffered famines of raw materials, as in A.D. 369 when according to Procopius the Persians drastically raised their prices. The weaving industry, hitherto in private hands, became a state monopoly and Justinian fell between the two stools of private avarice and a restrictive practice of price control. Having fixed the price of silk at the totally unrealistic figure of 8 chrysos per pound, he then allowed his wife Theodora to grant to her favourite Petros Barsayme a monopoly which enabled him to fix his selling price at 6 chrysos per ounce. The effect of this piece of royal chicanery was disastrous and many of the impoverished weavers took refuge in Persia, where their skill was highly welcome.

While the flow of East–West trade involved silk, gold, glass and acrobats, there was also a reverse flow of ideas, mainly religious and artistic, a story which is highly relevant to the history of silk and its entry into Europe. While the West declined into what has been called the Dark Ages two religious movements—Zoroastrianism and Nestorian Christianity—reached the powerful kingdom of Sogdiana, halfway across Asia and a clearing-house for both trade and ideas.

Frescoes discovered near Samarkand reveal Mediterranean types of art, including cherubs and people with distinctly European features. These are found alongside Zoroastrian designs, characteristic of Sassanid art, one of the commonest being a pair of fabulous beasts, usually griffins, chained on either side of an altar. Under the Sassanian dynasty (A.D. 226–641) the Persians developed a characteristic style of woven silk with boldly designed animals and hunting scenes in roundels, whose influence was felt even in China and persisted in Near Eastern and in European textiles down to the 13th c.

The stele of Hsi-an-fu, put up in A.D. 781, records how some years previously a Christian missionary had come from the West and had been honourably received by the Emperor T'ai-tsung, and allowed to preach his faith to the inhabitants. While this was indeed true, he was of the heretical Nestorian sect, a fact which caused considerable embarrassment to Marco Polo and his companions many years later. It was monks from this Nestorian church who came to Byzantium in A.D. 550/1 representing the kingdom of Serinda. Justinian was at this moment having conversations with Hellastheus, king of Ethiopia, and Esimiphaeus of the Himyarites, suggesting that these most Christian monarchs should form an anti-Persian alliance, the bribe offered to Ethiopia being that it should become the channel through which the silk from China would flow. The Nestorian monks were therefore welcomed as co-religionists and as potential military allies, but even more so because they said that in their country they had knowledge of the secrets of sericulture. Religious zeal, power politics, and private profit united to show Justinian the path of duty. The monks were promised rich rewards and sent back as industrial spies. In order to avoid the hostile Persians, whose counter-espionage organization was very powerful, they took a northern route via the Caucasus and two years later *c.* A.D. 550, returned with a supply of the precious eggs, and the even more valuable technology of silk reeling.

The delighted Justinian, having rewarded the monks (overlooking that they were Nestorian heretics) proceeded to prove the truth of that definition of a fool which describes him as 'a man who makes the same mistake twice' by making the cultivation of silk a state monopoly. What might have been a profitable industry only made modest growth; and although the cultivation of the silkworm has been carried on in the Levant down to modern times, it has only played a minor part in the silk industry of the world. As long as China was willing to sell silk she remained the main source of raw material for the weavers of Persia and Byzantium; but when she became more and more isolationist it was the Japanese who became the largest producers in the world.

The next chapter in the silk story began in A.D. 636 when the new and aggressive power of Islam captured Syria only four years after the death of Muhammad. A contemporary historian said: 'From A.D. 660 the Christians could not launch a plank upon the sea.' Persia soon fell under Muslim domination. In A.D. 751 Ziyad-ibn-Salih defeated the Chinese general Kao Hasiang at the battle of Tlass and as part of the spoils of war carried off a number of craftsmen, who were taken and settled in Iraq. During its early stages Islam was puritan in outlook and frowned on such luxuries as silk, although the Koran promised to the pure and just that they would be clad in brocade and satin when they reached paradise. Before long, however, the temptations of luxury proved too strong, and the *Thousand and One Nights* gives a vivid picture of Oriental splendour in which silk played a prominent part. Designs reflect the ideas of the two sects into which Islam split. The one forbade the use of natural forms, especially human or animal, and from this we get those designs which are commonly called ARABESQUES, while from the other came the animal and floral garden designs typical or many of the best Persian CARPETS.

For the next three centuries Europe drew most of its silk fabrics from the Middle East. In England there was a flourishing school of EMBROIDERY, and mention of the 'Silk Women' refers to those engaged in the production of *opus anglicanum*, in which silk threads were used. Among the treasures of Charlemagne was a silk cope, a gift from Haroun-al-Raschid; and the manuscript of Theodulf, written at the end of Charlemagne's reign, was interleaved with pages of silk, of which four were Chinese, six Arabian and three or four Greco-Syrian, reflecting a picture of the silk industry at the end of the 9th c.

Until near the end of the Middle Ages silk textiles remained rare and very costly articles in the West. The majority of existing specimens have survived as wrappings of holy relics or as the shrouds of dead princes. A few early silks dating from the 5th or 6th c. A.D. show two-colour designs of shepherds, animals or religious scenes, rather naturalistically conceived in a late antique spirit. Religious subjects recur in the superb Byzantine five-colour silk in the Vatican showing the Annunciation and the Nativity in roundels, which dates perhaps from the 8th or 9th c. But most later Byzantine weavings utilize the Oriental repertory of eagles, beasts and winged monsters ornamentally treated. Nor is this surprising when we consider that the majority of the silks which reached medieval Europe were woven in the Muslim factories of Asia, North Africa and Spain, and that the whole of this vast Islamic crescent was interlinked by common traditions of design, so that for instance a Spanish fabric might often be a reproduction of a Syrian or a Persian one. Woven silks were in fact a major vehicle in the international diffusion of ornamental ideas. They were the immediate inspiration of much of the strange fauna of ROMANESQUE art. At a later date we find a wave of Chinese motifs, carried westwards by the Mongol conquests, appearing first in the Near Eastern silks and subsequently in those of Italy. To the medieval eye the glamour of strange monsters and indecipherable Oriental scripts was inseparable from the luxury silks and such motifs recur constantly in European textiles down to the end of the Middle Ages.

The First Crusade (A.D. 1095) brought the West into closer contact with the East, and from then on the literature of chivalry abounds in detailed references to silken fabrics whose names indicate their Eastern origin. The Sicilian silk industry was thus established by captured Byzantine weavers who were set to work there by Roger II after his victories in Greece in 1147. After the death of Manfred in 1266 the remnants of this Sicilian industry transferred themselves to Lucca, which remained the most important centre of Italian silk-weaving throughout the 14th c. For this reason the large number of 14th-c. Italian silks preserved in church treasuries and museums are generally attributed to Lucchese weavers. Many of them are red or blue satins brocaded with gold. The same period saw a rapid increase in the importance of velvet-weaving, a technique which gives the cloth a silk pile by running extra warp threads over a series of wires so that when these are removed the extra threads form a large number of small up-standing loops which may be cut or left uncut as desired.

Though many other weaves were in use, velvets continued to be the characteristic products of Italian looms during the Renaissance, when the centre of gravity of the industry shifted to Venice and Florence. The splendour of these Renaissance stuffs with their monumental designs, freed at last from Oriental influence, generally in deep crimson and gold thread, is familiar from paintings of the period as well as from surviving specimens. They have been frequently imitated down to the present day. Italian 17th-c. velvets, generally attributed to Genoa, are of two kinds: one with large formal

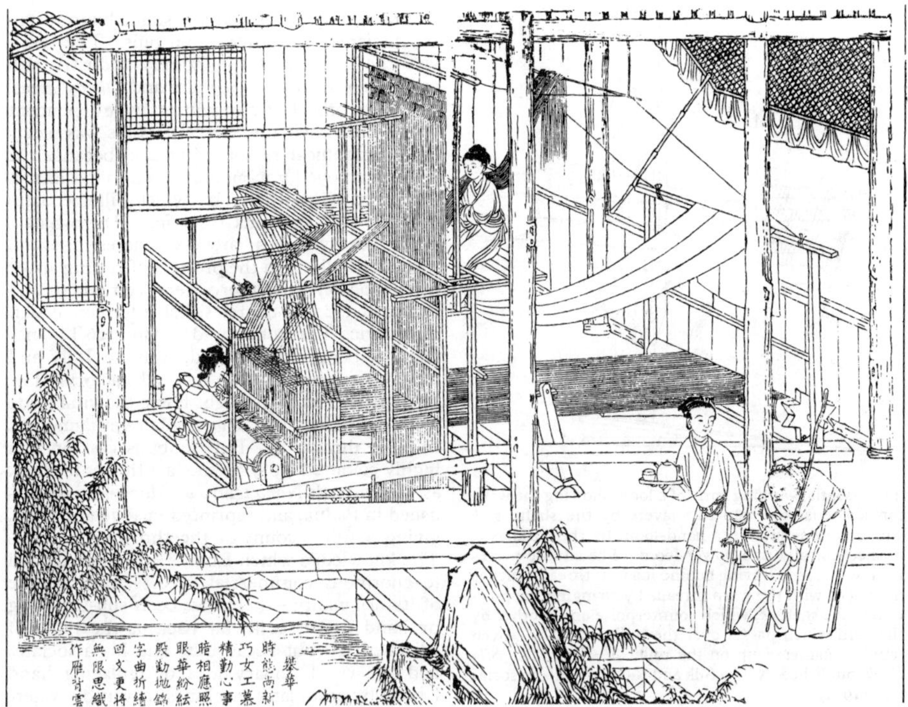

Weaving Figured Satins. From *Silk Culture and Manufacture* by Emperor Kang hi (1796)

patterns of flowers and foliage often in several colours, and used for furnishing; the other, for costume, with small, scattered motifs in DIAPER patterns.

Meanwhile the Arabs had established in Moorish Spain a strong silk-weaving industry. and it is said that in Seville alone there were 6,000 looms at work. Their products are easily identifiable on stylistic grounds. In 1149, when the Crusades were at their height, a commercial treaty was signed between the Muslim king of Valencia and the merchants of Genoa. Skill in all the crafts of processing silk combined with the enterprise of the Genoese merchants to give Italy a monopoly of the trade and once again a rich and powerful state, i.e. France, found its treasury being drained of gold. Louis XIV and Colbert, alarmed by the drain of between four and five hundred million gold *écus* a year, established a silk industry at Lyon, where there had long been a market to which the Genoese merchants had brought their goods. Here the northward progress of the art of rearing silkworms stops because only in Italy and southern France was the climate favourable. Thus when in the 17th c. James I tried to establish sericulture in England he was doomed to failure; partly for climatic reasons, but also because he planted *morus nigra* instead of *morus alba*, a botanical error soon detected by the discriminating palate of the silkworm.

Meanwhile silk-weaving continued to flourish in Asia. The Turkish lands wove silks and velvets of great magnificence though somewhat overshadowed by the contemporary production of Italy and Persia. The Persian silks and velvets of the Safavid period (1499–1736) were of unparalleled refinement in design and execution. They depict scenes of romance or of courtly life, or exquisitely delicate floral sprays. The Mogul conquest initiated a related style in India, but Indian weaving remains best known for its airy cottons and the woollen SHAWLS of Kashmir. In the Far East Chinese and Japanese silk-weavers continued their own splendid traditions down to comparatively recent times.

Although sericulture went no further than central France, the art of silk-working was developed in the Netherlands during the 15th c. Here there was already a prosperous textile industry in wool and linen and the city of Mons, capital of Hainault, became the silk centre of northern Europe. But once again the unfortunate silk-weavers became the victims of war and persecution as the majority of them were Protestants and when the Duke of Alva conquered the Low Countries he put to death a number of wealthy silk merchants who had financed the resistance movement. Driven from their homes the weavers took refuge in England and settled in cities such as Norwich in East Anglia. For the next three centuries this area became noted for the quality

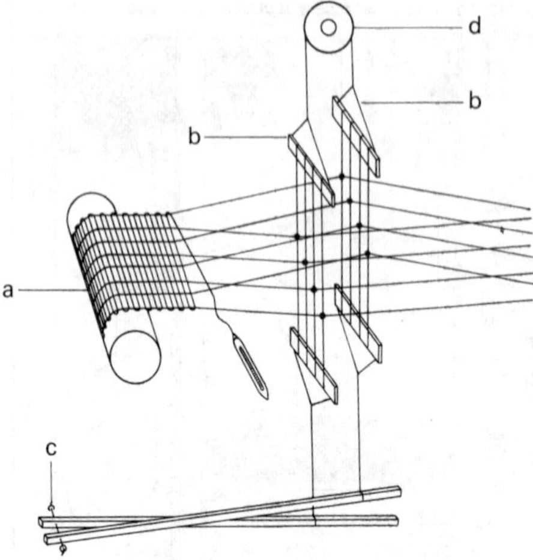

The essential working parts of a loom showing the warp threads separated into two layers by the shafts *b*, *b* which are operated in a hand-loom by the treadles *c*, or mechanically in a power-loom. The shuttle passes from side to side leaving behind it a weft thread which is interlaced with the warp threads by changing the position of the shafts *b*, which counterpoise one another by the cord which passes over the pulley *d*. The woven fabric is gathered up on the roller *a*. From *The Silk Book*, published by The Silk and Rayon User's Association (1951)

of its silk-weaving. The famous 'fillover' shawls were a mixture of silk and fine wool, and may be studied in museums as masterpieces of the weaver's art.

The Huguenots of St. Étienne, who had improved the machinery taken over originally from Italy and had proved themselves no less skilled craftsmen in silk techniques than in other fields, brought the crafts of ribbon-making and watch-making to Coventry, where these remained the chief trades until after the middle of the 19th c. Most of the broadloom weavers either settled in the Spitalfields district of London or went further north to Macclesfield.

Despite the loss of the Huguenot craftsmen, however, France remained prominent in silk-weaving as in so many other fields of taste during the 18th c. At Lyon men such as Jean Revel (1684–1751), Philippe de Lassalle (1733–1803), J. F. Bony (1754–1825) and a host of lesser designers interpreted the changing styles of Louis XIV, Louis XV, Louis XVI, the DIRECTOIRE and the EMPIRE with light touch and charming fantasy, rearranging with inexhaustible inventiveness their restricted repertory of flowers, twisted ribbons, stripes and NEO-CLASSICAL motifs.

The last chapter in the silk story is a strange mixture of enterprise and skill, tinged with sadness because it marks the beginning of the decline of this beautiful craft all over the world. In 1589 an impoverished clergyman Richard Lee had invented the stocking frame, remarkable because it sprang fully developed at a single bound from the ancient art of knitting on pins. The result was the growth of the hosiery industry still carried on in the Nottingham and Derby areas. For a long time the frame knitters were dependent on Italy for their raw material. This was partly for geographical reasons, but also because the Italians enjoyed a monopoly over a vital link in the chain of processes by which silk becomes fabric. This was silk-throwing (Anglo-Saxon *thraw*, to twist), a process whereby several strands of silk, each the product of reeling six or more cocoons together, were combined and strengthened to a degree suitable for conversion into fabric. The story is told that in 1716 Thomas Lombe, being unemployed, went to Italy and worked as a journeyman in a silk factory. The account of how he brought home the vital trade secrets is a cloak and dagger affair with amorous intrigue thrown in. But doubt is cast on this highly coloured story by the fact that as far back as 1607 a book *Novo teatro di Machine* was published in Padua, and reprinted in 1620 and 1668, giving a full account of the throwing process. The knowledge which Lombe brought back led to enormous commercial success, not because of its originality—there had been silk-throwing by hand processes as far back as the reign of Elizabeth I—but because he and his associates had the revolutionary idea of replacing hand labour by automatic machines driven by water-power. The Lombe mill became one of the wonders of the age and authors waxed lyrical about the fabulous number of wheels driven, they said, 'with the utmost conceivable velocity' by a water-wheel which only revolved three times a minute. The factory, which worked day and night, was said to be heated by a 'fire engine which conveyed warm air to all parts of the building'. A somewhat sour and jaundiced contemporary says, however, that the 'superb fire engine was nothing but a common stove, which only heated one corner of the building'. The result nevertheless was to cut prices far below those of the Italians and to establish a thriving silk-throwing industry in the Midlands in partnership with the even more prosperous hosiery trade.

Unfortunately we cannot end the silk story on this note of commercial triumph. The water-power which was turning Lombe's mill was to sweep away the silk industry in the tide of the Industrial Revolution. The mill at Derby has been called a landmark in industrial history. Within less than a century, and only a few miles from Derby, the great textile inventions of HARGREAVES, ARKWRIGHT, and Crompton changed textiles from what they had been for thousands of years, i.e. handicraft industries, into the pioneers of the new mechanical age. For technical reasons silk must involve a high degree of finger dexterity and personal judgement at every stage. The figures given above show that the small yield per hectare must make it an expensive commodity, and the rising population of the world and the increasing pressure on food resources means that there is an ever diminishing incentive to practise sericulture. This, coupled with the fact that it does not lend itself to being woven on high speed automatic looms, makes silk costly to fabricate. Cotton, wool and later man-made fibres were ideal for machine processes. So everywhere silk declined in importance and although it is still the most beautiful of all textile materials, it is now of little more than historical interest.

See also BYSSUS SILK; SPIDER SILK; TUSSORE (wild silk); CHINA (TEXTILES) and TEXTILE MANUFACTURE IN ANTIQUITY.

94, 282, 293, 767, 814.

SILVER

1. The material
2. Methods of working plate
3. Early history
4. Europe to the sixteenth century
5. Europe from the sixteenth century
6. Britain
7. The Americas

1. THE MATERIAL. GOLD AND SILVER were considered to be the only two precious metals until the discovery of palladium, platinum and other related metals in the 19th c. The permanent brilliance of gold and the pure whiteness of silver, their malleability, resistance to oxidation and above all their scarcity, ensured their constant employment for ornaments, jewellery and currency. Industrial demands, particularly during the last 100 years, while not appreciably affecting the amount of gold available, have drastically engulfed increasing quantities of silver even though the annual production of this metal amounts to ten times that of gold. In its pure state silver is harder than gold but softer than copper; it is also superior to gold and copper as a conductor of heat and electricity. Silver has a lower specific gravity than gold but is almost as malleable or ductile. To be put to any use as plate, jewellery or coinage it is too soft to be employed in its pure state and has therefore to be alloyed. This is usually done by adding a small proportion of copper, which also lowers the melting point. The metal will retain its brilliance until the alloy exceeds about a quarter, while gold retains most of its characteristics to well beyond this level. In unpolluted air pure silver will not oxidize but it will tarnish or turn black if exposed to any sulphur either in the atmosphere or in compound form, for example egg yolks. It will also react to chlorides, leaving a white or, later, a purplish stain.

(*a*) *Sources.* It is probable that no satisfactory results were achieved in the extraction of silver from ores until the 4th and 3rd millennia B.C., the principal silver mines being in Asia Minor and the Aegean Islands. Gold was more common than silver in Egypt until trade with the eastern Mediterranean opened up during the 18th Dynasty. Being scarce silver was used sparingly for jewellery and amulets as well as for objects with a mystical significance. It was likened to the moon, as was gold to the sun, and later it was given the name Luna by the alchemists.

Silver was derived at this time from gold-bearing ores as well as the more plentiful deposits of galena or lead sulphide, which can contain between 600 and 6,000 g of fine silver per tonne of lead. Native silver occurs only rarely, for example in Norway and parts of the major producing countries such as Canada, the United States and Australia. Other argentiferous ores, apart from gold, include copper and zinc although not in the same proportions as lead. The ancient Greeks used a natural alloy of gold and silver called ELECTRUM, in which the proportion of silver, according to Pliny, amounted to one-fifth. He adds that an artificial electrum was made by adding silver to gold. Today gold is alloyed with copper or silver according to the colour of metal required.

The Romans derived most of their silver from Spain, but during the medieval period mines in Austria and Germany supplied most European requirements. A growing scarcity was only relieved in the early 16th c. by the discovery of rich resources in the New World, particularly those at Potosí and elsewhere in the Viceroyalty of Peru, first worked in 1545. Shiploads of bullion began to arrive in Europe via Seville, resulting in an increase in production of plate and coinage. The mines of North and South America have continued to supply most of the world's needs in spite of a temporary lapse at the beginning of the 19th c. during the various Wars of Independence, when the older European mines in Germany, Austria and Spain were reopened and developed. Today Mexico and the United States between them produce more than a third of the world's output and the entire continent produces *c.* 65%.

Production of silver has risen from an estimated annual world total of 1,500,000 oz. troy in 1500 to over 10,000,000 in 1550, a total which remained almost static until the 18th c., by the end of which it had risen to *c.* 25,000,000 oz. This amount was almost halved during the politically disrupted period (1820–30) referred to above, but thereafter rose steadily until the 1870s. It was during this and the following decades that the most substantial discoveries of new deposits were made, principally in Nevada and Colorado in the U.S.A. and also in Australia and Asia. Annual output rose tenfold, from

22,000,000 oz. in 1872 to 230,000,000 oz. in 1912, followed by a slight decline at the time of the First World War. From a peak output of 263,000,000 oz. in 1929, silver has fluctuated considerably until in 1972 there was a continuing shortage.

The photographic industry, whose demands for silver nitrate rise annually, is attempting to find a substitute, since otherwise the world's supply of silver will be exhausted by the end of the present century. To keep down the price of the metal and satisfy present requirements, almost all of the world's silver currency has been withdrawn, notably in the United States, Canada, Britain and other Commonwealth countries.

(*b*) *The Economics of Silver*. The recently defunct 'pennyweight' (dwt.), of which there used to be 20 in each troy ounce, had its origins in the medieval silver penny derived from the Roman *denarius*. Its size then approximated to that of the former English sixpence. By the end of the 16th c., silversmiths were paying *c*. six shillings per ounce for their bullion, i.e. slightly more than the face value of coinage silver, with an excess added 'for fashion' depending on the degree of decoration on the article of plate being produced. Since the mid 1870s and the first effects of the new finds in Nevada and elsewhere, the price fell steadily from five shillings per ounce (1875) to just under two shillings during the First World War. This decline was also assisted by the abandoning of a fixed currency ratio between gold and silver and the adoption of a single gold standard by many countries. This lessened the demand for silver and reflected the much greater abundance of gold during this period. Silver then rose to a new peak of just over 4*s*. 11*d*. (24½p) per ounce in 1920, resulting in the debasement of the British silver coinage from the sterling standard of 0·925 to 0·500 fine. An increase in output during the 1920s, followed by a marked lack of demand in the early and depressed 1930s, brought the price down to its cheapest in modern times—a little over 1*s*. 2*d*. (6p) per ounce in 1931. The price had risen again to 4*s*. (20p) by 1946, when it was decided to debase the British silver coinage completely to a base-metal alloy of copper and nickel to assist repayments of large loans of bullion to the United States. Between 1951 and 1968, in which latter year a world shortage accompanied by the devaluation of the pound sterling brought about almost freak conditions, the price trebled from 6*s*. 5*d*. (32p) to 18*s*. 4*d*. (91½p) per ounce troy. The price levels of antique silver especially, as well as new plate, were not unnaturally badly distorted during the following period; but the price of silver had declined to 57p by February 1972, bringing with it more settled conditions. Smelting and other charges naturally add a little to this sum for the purposes of the manufacturing silversmith.

(*c*) *Assaying and Hallmarking*. The oldest method of testing silver objects to check the amount of pure metal present was by 'touch'. This involved the use of a set of 'touch-needles', each one of which was alloyed with a known proportion of base metal. These could be scratched on a 'touch stone' to compare with a mark made by any article under assay (or trial). It was more by the feel or sensation of the streak made by the metal than by its colour that the assayer could be sure of the standard used. A technique called CUPELLATION, which is of a more scientific nature, is in use by many present-day assay offices. Scrapings are taken from different parts of the object to be tested, carefully weighed, and then wrapped in a small lead sheet. Both the scrapings, called the 'diet', and the lead are then melted together in a porous bowl ('cupel') of bone-ash until both the lead and the copper alloy in the silver have oxidized. The oxides are absorbed by the bone-ash cupel, leaving a button of pure silver which is then weighed against the original scrapings. By subtraction the proportion of alloy is then deduced.

The earliest English statute governing the standard of silver used in plate dates from 1238, when the minimum coinage standard of 0·925 purity was laid down. The 'esterling' of sterling standard contains therefore 0·075 of copper alloyed with silver, and is more properly expressed as 11·1 ounces troy of silver alloyed with 0·9 ounce of copper in each troy pound. In an Act of Parliament of 1300 a leopard's-head punch was introduced to be applied after assay by the 'gardiens of the Craft' in London on every object submitted. After 1544 the significance of this mark changed to one symbolizing the authority of the Goldsmiths' Company and as such it was applied over a long period by some provincial assay offices in addition to their own town marks. The reason for this change was the introduction of a new standard mark in the form of a lion passant gardant, taken, like the leopard's head, from the Royal Arms of England. This was an added guarantee to the public that the bullion used for the wrought plate of the day had nothing to do with the drastically debased silver coinage which at that time was being issued by King Henry VIII. It should be remembered that coinage and plate were virtually interchangeable under normal circumstances, being made of the same standard of silver. From this date, therefore, the leopard's head began to take on the role of the London town mark and the lion passant that of the sterling mark. The latter had to be applied on all silver assayed in England. The maker's symbol or, later, his initials, had to be applied from 1363 onwards as a check in the assay office on the source of any sub-standard plate being submitted. The coding system of date letters, this time as a check on the Assay Master, who was becoming personally responsible for maintaining standards of assaying, was introduced again in London in 1478.

During the period 1697 to 1719 English silversmiths were compelled to adopt a higher standard of 0·958 fineness, known as the 'new Sterling' or

'Britannia' standard. This was a measure to assist the re-coinage of William III's reign, preventing the use of newly minted coin as bullion for the silversmith. Old clipped and hammered coin was being redeemed at this period at full face value, and the government wanted to attract as much old wrought plate to the mint as possible to help make up the deficit. The higher silver content of plate thus introduced, as well as the awkwardness of re-alloying old sterling silver, helped to make the re-coinage a success, assisted as it was by special mints set up in five provincial cities. Meanwhile new marks were introduced, consisting of a seated figure of 'Britannia' to replace the lion passant gardant and a leopard's head erased, i.e. in profile, to replace the normal full-face design. These marks were also introduced compulsorily at the five principal English assay offices from 1700/1 to 1719/20. The new measures were not popular in spite of the fact that this purer standard made the metal easier to work, if more expensive by weight, and they were eventually withdrawn by the Wrought Plate Act of 1719. The sterling standard was restored as from 1 June 1720, although any silversmith could, and still can, continue to use the higher Britannia standard, in which case his wares are hallmarked accordingly.

From 1784 to 1890 an additional puncheon containing the sovereign's head in profile was applied to indicate that a duty, normally of 6*d*. per ounce, had been paid to the government at the time of assay. Two later sovereign's marks have been used since: that of King George V and Queen Mary to celebrate the Silver Jubilee in 1935, and that of Queen Elizabeth II on her Coronation in 1953. A rare mark of Britannia shown standing up was used only for nine months from December 1784 to July 1785 on plate exported from England. All plate imported into the country, provided it is more than 100 years old, has to be tested and marked accordingly if it is going to be sold. An additional 'F' mark (for 'foreign') was introduced in 1867, but a new series of assay office marks was introduced early in the 20th c.

Scotland and Ireland have employed their own guilds and marking systems, but based fairly closely on the English procedure. Each country used to have many more smaller guilds than England, using their own particular marks but often without any dating system. At the present time there are only five active assay offices left in the entire British Isles: London; the two offices opened in 1773 at Birmingham and Sheffield; Edinburgh; and Dublin.

Standards on the Continent vary considerably. France was one of the earliest countries to introduce a hallmarking system *c*. 1275, but in recent times has also employed two standards of purity, 0·950 and 0·800, each with distinctive marks. The Netherlands also has two standards, 0·934 and 0·833; while Germany has kept to one of 0·800 fineness. The United States used also to employ 'Coin' or 'Dollar' silver of 0·900 purity, but more normally plate is marked with the word 'Sterling' when of, or above, the 0·925 standard.

2. METHODS OF WORKING PLATE. Hand-wrought silver has to be worked from the sheet, which was formerly hammered out from the ingot but is nowadays rolled by machine to the required thickness. Hollow wares or vessels can either be raised from a circular disc by a laborious process of concentric hammering until the required concave shape is achieved; or, if tall dimensions are needed, a rectangular sheet can be bent into a cylindrical shape and the seam soldered vertically. A modern technique called 'spinning' is also used for shallower vessels. A silver disc is pressed hard against a rotating, lathe-mounted chuck of the inside dimensions of the vessel; this acts as a die and the shape is achieved rather as a potter turns his clay on the POTTER'S WHEEL. See Illustration on p. 821.

With sheet silver of sufficiently thin gauge decoration can be EMBOSSED, that is punched into the silver from underneath, forcing out the metal into a rough relief design. Cruder wares may simply be punched with blunt chisels from the front or rear, resulting in a rough geometrical design; but repoussé or embossed work is normally more ambitious and can be used for figurative or pictorial decoration of a higher standard. Some surface-finishing with CHASING tools is required after the basic design has been shaped. These are small, more detailed punches, often bearing simple set patterns which are hammered into the metal. The vessel is normally reinforced at this stage by filling the inside with pitch. Matting and other surface textures can be achieved by this method, but no actual metal is removed by chasing. Other more mechanical techniques can be used for roughening or texturing the surface of silver, including engine-turning and acid-etching. Engraving, in which a sharper tool, a 'scorper' or 'graver', is used, involves the cutting and gouging out of the surface of the metal to achieve a finer line. This method is normally restricted to fine drawing involving cursive outlines and to hatching, inscriptions and armorial bearings. Engraving is sometimes confused with flat-chasing, which is likewise a purely surface-decoration; but chasing is coarser and consists only of repeated indentations which leave a blurred impression on the underside of the metal surface. The three basic techniques of embossing, chasing and engraving may often be seen decorating the same object.

Where decoration of a particularly bold or detailed relief style is required, or when the object itself is large or heavy, the silversmith will have to resort to casting. The spouts of teapots or the shafts and bases of candlesticks, where the thickness of the metal is of importance structurally, demand the use of this more irksome and expensive technique. After soldering the roughly cast components together, or perhaps to the hand-wrought vessel already prepared, the bubbly surface of the castings will still have to be thoroughly chased and polished. Today, with mass-production methods, many components required by the silversmith are not cast but die-stamped in large quantities and with considerable choice of design. Spoons and forks have been decorated by this method since the 17th c. and a number of steel dies originating from the early 19th c. are still used in the manufacture of table silver or flatware. In addition silver wires, tubes and other basic shapes can be obtained direct from specialist firms.

The working of silver by the hammer seriously disrupts and weakens the molecular structure of the metal. For this reason the silver being worked has to be annealed frequently, that is heated to a cherry-red colour and then quenched in an acid solution to dissolve any oxides thus formed on the surface. This essential process re-aligns the molecules and prevents the silver from becoming too brittle. The hammer marks themselves can be removed later by the application of a smooth, round-headed planishing hammer, after which the object can be buffed on an electrically powered wheel to give it a satin finish before a final polishing with jeweller's rouge, if required.

3. EARLY HISTORY.

(*a*) *Pre-Roman.* Knowledge of gold and silver plate manufactured before the pre-Christian era is mainly derived from the contents of burials and hoards excavated during the last 200 years. Among the earliest discoveries have been quantities of treasure from the site of the second city of Troy dating from not later than 2000 B.C. These have included gold pectorals, bracelets and rings consisting of thin wire made up into chains and coils supporting embossed foil pendants or rosettes. In general the jewellery from the Trojan region of the Aegean was only slightly more elaborate than that produced in Minoan Crete. Pre-Mycenean plate from the spectacular Treasure of Priam discovered at Troy is notable for the simple shapes of its vessels and the heavy loop-handles riveted to their bodies, which were often fitted with cupped ring-feet. Some have oval bowls in the Sumerian style, a symptom of the prevalent Asiatic influence on the design of plate as well as on pottery shapes of Helladic and Cycladic type.

Mainland tombs have yielded funerary furniture and masks of embossed gold similar in technique to contemporary EGYPTIAN work, together with more ordinary silver drinking-cups and jugs. Examples found at Mycenae, usually of plain or carinated shape, are not dissimilar to Trojan wares; other vessels in the Minoan tradition are embossed with vertical or horizontal bands of figurative and geometrical designs, the bodies usually conical and the handles consisting of flat plates riveted at one end and joined to the vessel by means of a cylindrical shaft at the other.

Inlay work in gold, silver and NIELLO has survived, decorating the blades of Mycenean and other weapons. This technique, which derived from Egypt, involved plating copper strips with the precious metal chosen before insetting them to the required linear or naturalistic design.

Between 1000 B.C. and 300 B.C. the Phoenicians produced much of the better quality plate in the Aegean region. Most of this was decorated, by embossing or engraving, in an Egyptian or Assyrian manner, although some shallow flower-bowls survive in the style of the first Hellenic period. The jewellery of the archaic Greek and Etruscan eras (*c.* 700–500 B.C.) was also greatly influenced by Oriental work. New forms included coiled bracelets with the ends formed of animal heads, masks and pendants. Granulated grounds were replaced in Grecian jewellery with filigree work while a revival of enamelling techniques took place during the 5th c. B.C.

Many of the technical achievements of the Mediterranean cultures had their counterparts in the less well documented plate of northern European peoples. One of the most spectacular single finds was the Gundestrup Cauldron discovered in north Jutland in 1891. Both inlayed and silver-gilt, this vessel dates from the late 2nd to 1st c. B.C. and is now in the National Museum, Copenhagen.

(*b*) *Roman and Early Christian.* Much of the plate of the Roman period was decorated with embossed designs of mythological, historical or mystical subjects. The silverware of Antioch and Alexandria, as well as that from the Greek mainland, remained popular in Rome throughout the periods of conquest and the later Empire. In the 2nd c. B.C. large quantities of bullion were brought from the eastern Mediterranean to be converted into ostentatious dishes and other ornamental vessels.

Most of the surviving Roman plate once formed part of hoards buried for safe-keeping during the break-up of the Empire. The principal treasures were found at BOSCOREALE in Italy (now mostly in the Louvre), at Hildesheim (Berlin), and at MILDENHALL (British Museum) and Traprain Law (National Museum of Antiquities of Scotland) and date predominantly from the 4th c. A.D. Plate of the Augustan style representative of the period was embossed with heavy architectural ornament, portrait-busts and figurative scenes, all in bold relief.

Roman jewellery made use of natural as well as simply cut stones, often in rough groupings, as well as gems cut as CAMEOS or INTAGLIOS. The metal-worker's skills continued to be restricted to filigree, granulation and ornamental borderings.

Late Roman plate is noted for its plainer surfaces, most of the ornament being confined to friezes, central medallions and formal borders. In early Christian work pagan subjects continued to provide decorative schemes, for example that

Gundestrup Cauldron. Inlaid and silver gilt. (Nat. Mus., Copenhagen, late 2nd–1st c. B.C.)

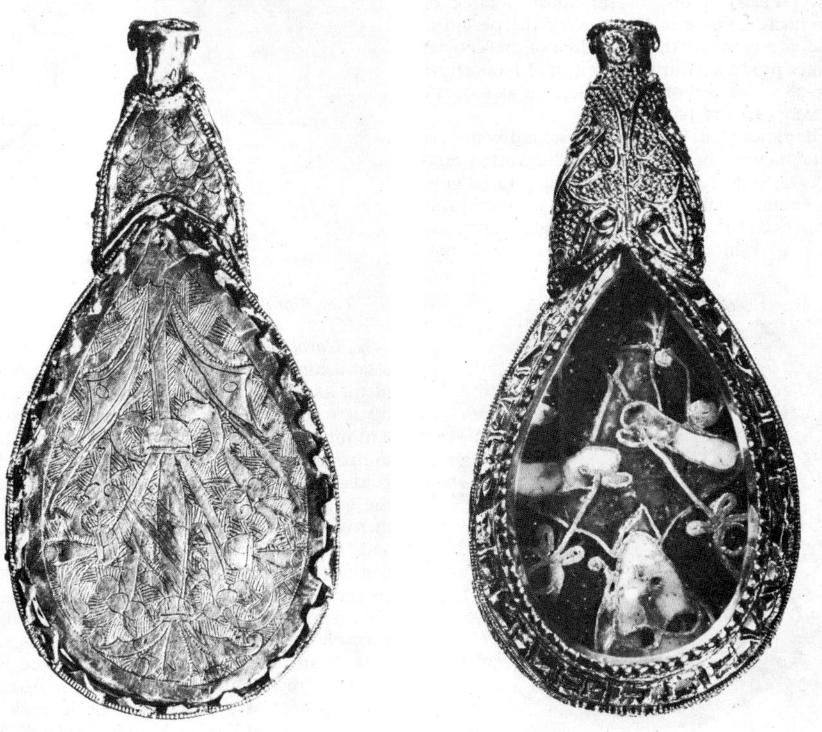

Alfred Jewel. Kentish craftsmanship. (Ashmolean Mus., Oxford, 9th c.)

Marriage Casket of Projecta. Esquiline Treasure. (B.M., late 4th c. A.D.)

of the silver and gilt marriage casket of Projecta in the Esquiline Treasure (British Museum), dating from the late 4th c. A.D. After this period a harder, more hieratic style began to dominate the plate of Antioch and BYZANTIUM together with an increasing amount of abstract patterning. Some plate, including bowls from the SUTTON HOO Treasure of the 7th c. A.D. (British Museum), has been found to bear Byzantine control-stamps as used during the 6th and 7th centuries, forerunners of modern hallmarks. Early Christian plate as such is best represented in France, Spain and Italy, consisting mainly of jewelled votive crowns, BOOK COVERS, baldachins as well as chalices decorated with enamelled work and precious stones. The Guarrazar Treasure (Musée Cluny, Paris) is one of the most notable of such hoards, while in Rome itself the period is well represented by the silver door of the Vatican Basilica produced during the reign of Honorius I (625–38). See also GREEK AND ROMAN ANTIQUITY (METALWORK and JEWELLERY).

The influential Anglo-Saxon school began its ascendancy in the 7th c. A.D. The Sutton Hoo Treasure is noted for the fine quality of its gold and enamel cloisonné jewellery of rectilinear abstract design. The slightly later Ormside Bowl (Yorkshire Museum) made of silver and copper gilt is ornamented with less austere cursive interlacings of a Celtic character. By the reign of Alfred the Great (849–901) Anglo-Saxon, and particularly Kentish, craftsmanship was well known throughout western Europe, one of the best examples being the Alfred Jewel (Ashmolean Museum, Oxford), again in gold and cloisonné enamel. In Ireland the Celtic art of the Hiberno-Saxon school began to excel that of the English by the 8th c. The Ardagh Chalice (9th c.) and the Tara Brooch (10th c.), both in the National Museum of Ireland, may be compared, for intricacy of ornament not without Oriental associations in its sources, with the Book of Kells or the Lindisfarne Gospels.

Ormside Bowl. Silver and copper gilt. (Yorkshire Mus., 7th–8th c.)

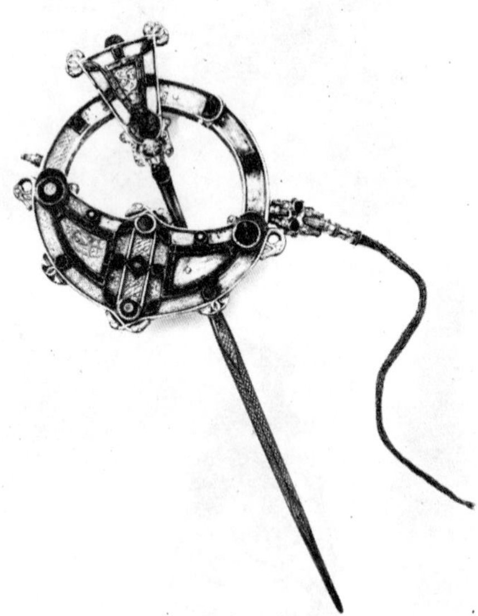

Tara Brooch. (Nat. Mus. of Ireland, 10th c.)

(c) *Carolingian to Romanesque.* Following the establishment of Charlemagne's court at Aachen in the early 9th c., a conscientious attempt was made to revive some of the grandeur of Roman antiquity in the form of a renewed interest in the human figure. Among the masterpieces of the goldsmith's craft produced during this period is the gold and silver-gilt altar of San Ambrogio in Milan of *c.* 838. Signed by one 'Wolvinius' and showing distinct northern characteristics, it consists of embossed figures with cloisonné enamel and filigree work. The Tassilo Chalice at Kremsmünster in Austria of A.D. 777 is decorated with chiselled-out animal-like interlacings, the only extant English equivalent being the much plainer Trewhiddle Bowl of *c.* 875. Although much altered at a later date, the famous *Pala d'Oro* in St. Mark's, Venice, ordered from Constantinople, still shows the hieratic figure style of Byzantine art at its finest.

By the 10th and 11th centuries a more rigid formality began to dominate European metalwork, especially north of the Alps. On the technique of silversmithing one of the first books of instruction, THEOPHILUS's *De Diversibus Artibus*, was also published during this period. This technical knowledge was put to good use by an increasing amount of church patronage, mainly during the 12th c., resulting in an increasing emphasis upon subject-matter and symbolism. Among the principal patrons were the Abbot Suger of St. Denis and Henry of Blois, Bishop of Winchester, but little of the splendour of their commissions has survived.

One of the centres of metal-working was the Meuse Valley in present-day Belgium, centred upon the city of Liège. The Mosan School became renowned for its use of champlevé enamelling, chiefly in gilt copper, which was perfected at the end of the 12th c. The Altar-tryptych at Klosterneuburg, near Vienna, by one of the principal craftsmen, NICOLAS OF VERDUN, is a *tour de force* of this technique in which enamels of different hues are pooled in gouged-out hollows. The same master executed the Shrine of the Virgin in Tournai Cathedral, an architectural structure including figures of the Virgin, the Three Kings, the six prophets and six apostles set altogether with 1,500 stones. The rhythmic draperies and sculptural assertiveness of figure styling at this date look forward to a new naturalism embodied in the nascent Gothic era.

4. EUROPE TO THE SIXTEENTH CENTURY.

During the Middle Ages in western Europe the Church was the main patron and much of the work was done in monasteries, where craftsmen could employ their skills free from commercial considerations. From the 13th c. two new features emerged into prominence. Domestic silver became more important and in many countries the guilds increased their strength, often obtaining legal recognition. The support given to the guilds depended in large part on their activities in protecting the public from fraud by ensuring that both the raw material and the workmanship were up to standard. Not only the various centres of silversmithing, but individual makers also, acquired their marks of identification and in many cases a letter or numerals indicated the year in which an article was assayed and passed. (See section on Assaying and Hallmarking.) Stamped on a piece such marks provided a guarantee of authenticity, reassuring for buyers, and ensured so far as possible that shoddy goods were neither made nor exposed for sale. Theoretically, therefore, the origin and date of most pieces of silver made subsequent to the 14th c. should be determinable, though in practice this by no means always obtains. Assaying added to the price of an article, and a purchaser might collaborate with a maker in evading the marking and its cost. Further marks were sometimes required to show that a government-levied duty had been paid, and in those cases there was a further inducement to malpractice. On occasion, too, industrious owners or their servants have polished their possessions so as to render the marks illegible and, finally, a proportion of the marks remains unidentifiable despite the researches of generations of collectors and students.

The Italian silversmiths in Tuscany were governed by rules enforced from 1231, which were applicable to craftsmen established in Pisa, Siena and Florence. In France the Provost of Paris drew up statutes for the guilds in 1260, and eight years later they were incorporated by Louis IX. Among their rules was one insisting on beginners serving an apprenticeship of ten years, whereas the Tuscans demanded only three years. The principal French towns each had a mark, and from at least 1355 so did every maker. Similar regulations became current in other countries.

The art of silversmithing had by this time been accorded a high status, and the craftsmen employed in it were treated with respect. In Florence Filippo Brunelleschi (1377–1446) was trained as a silversmith before turning to sculpture and architecture. Such versatility was not uncommon, with more than one man able to turn his talents to several art forms with equal success.

(i) *Italy*. Surviving examples testify to the competence of the craftsmen, who continued to supply ecclesiastical plate. Their work was frequently influenced by that of painters and sculptors, so that pieces from the different regions of the country can show characteristics as recognizable in silver and gold as they are in marble and pigment. In fact the most able silversmiths rivalled painters in their use of enamels and could produce free-standing figures and relief plaques comparable with those carved by sculptors.

An example of this is the reliquary in Orvieto Cathedral made to contain the blood-stained *corporale* of the Bolsena miracle of 1263. The reliquary was made about 70 years later in the workshop of Ugolino da Vieri, a Sienese goldsmith, and it has been accepted widely as the finest specimen of such work executed at the time. It is of architectural form in silver-gilt, inset with a series of enamel plaques depicting the story of the miracle and scenes from the life of Christ, while figures of the Virgin, St. John and others provide further ornamentation.

Florentine silversmiths provided a remarkable altar frontal and retable for the cathedral at Pistoia, and an altar frontal for San Giovanni, Florence. Among those employed on the latter were men of diverse talents, combining painting, sculpture and the art of the silversmith: Antonio Pollaiuolo (1433–98), Andrea Verrocchio (1436–88) and Michelozzo di Bartolommeo (1396–1472).

In numerous other cities and towns there remain examples of the work executed during the period. Some of the craftsmanship does not reach the high standard of execution of the above works and the artistic content is sometimes less satisfactory, but the skill and integrity of those employed in it was nevertheless of a high order.

(ii) *Germany*. Highly ornamented objects for ecclesiastical use continued to be made: silver, gold, precious stones and enamel were combined to form articles that were certainly decorative but were often impractical. Thus a late 13th-c. chalice (Nikolaikirche, Berlin) has a shallow bowl of which the lower portion is decorated, the stem has a broad central knop and the domed foot rests on a vertical rim pierced with arcading. The whole is heavily ornamented with figures and leaf patterns interspersed with stones, and only a comparatively slight depth of bowl remains for actual use.

Monstrances of the same date and later are topped by delicate pinnacles, while a reliquary of 1473 represents the bust of St. Peter, whose mitre and clothing are elaborately chased and inset with stones; the simulation of embroidery is a remarkable *tour de force*. The reliquary is signed by Hans von Dirmstein of Frankfurt, and its original cost is noted in the archives of the Collegiate Church, Aschaffenburg, where it is preserved.

Among early examples of secular wares were ceremonial drinking cups, which began to make an appearance in the 15th c. The cups usually had covers and bore ornament little less extravagant than that on ecclesiastical articles; appearance in both cases was considered to be of greater importance than functionalism. Most of the cups, which were known at the time as *hanaps* and later as *pokals*, were raised on tall stems and may properly be termed goblets. Their ornament sometimes included contemporaneous coins and medals applied to, or inset in, the silver (*Münzpokal*) so that the reliefs on them formed ready-made decoration. Others were given bowls and covers modelled with bosses or shaped so that they resemble a bunch of grapes (*Traubenpokal*), while another variety is known as a 'Columbine Cup' (*Akleibecher*) from its resemblance to that flower, also known as the *Aquilegia*. This last type was often the masterpiece demanded of a Nuremberg apprentice before he could be admitted as a master-craftsman.

Short, tumbler-like cups or beakers were also made, and two covered examples in the British Museum date from *c*. 1480–1500. The earlier of them has both bowl and cover ornamented with circular niello panels of playing children, the spreading foot modelled with bands of cusps and rope-work as well as with a broad border of birds on leafy branches, the whole resting on three small winged figures. The other, later, cup was made in Lübeck and is less rich in appearance; the body has two bands of engraved decoration divided by a removable ring in the form of a wreath of flowers.

(iii) *France*. French silver made prior to the early 19th c. is probably scarcer than that of any other European country. Successive wars were financed by melting down silver articles for conversion into coin, a process which reached its culmination during the Revolution. None the less documents record what was once in existence and sufficient wares remain to show that at all periods French silversmiths reached such standards as to make it a matter for regret that not more is extant.

Paris was the principal centre, with the goldsmiths located for security on one of the bridges over the Seine. Having been in existence since at least the 13th c., they were granted their own arms in 1330 and lists of the wardens of the guild go back almost as far. Provincial towns also had their groups of craftsmen, but as elsewhere the finest work usually came from the capital. Thus what has justifiably been called the finest surviving example of French work of the period is the Paris-made Royal Gold Cup of the late 14th c. The cup and cover are of gold, enamelled in *basse taille* with scenes from the legend of St. Agnes and with the symbols of the Evangelists. It was presented to Charles VI of France by his uncle in 1391, probably ten years after it had been made, and for some reason it was sent to England in 1434 to become the property of Henry VI. Later it went to Spain, returned to France and at last, in 1891, was bought for the British Museum.

The few surviving pieces of earlier date do not attain the excellence of the Royal Gold Cup, but demonstrate that French silversmiths had mastered all the techniques known at the time. A table ornament known as a *nef* was made in France, Germany and elsewhere, and was a small-scale model of a sailing-ship to serve as a salt, or as a container for a napkin or knife, fork and spoon, or simply as a centrepiece. The Burghley Nef (formerly at Burghley House, Northamptonshire, at the Victoria and Albert Museum since 1959) is of parcel-gilt silver with a nautilus shell forming the hull; on the deck sit a couple clasping hands while playing chess, and the whole bears the mark of the Paris maker Pierre le Flamand and the date 1482. The lovers have been identified as Tristan and Iseult, who were recorded as playing chess to relieve boredom when they journeyed from Ireland to Cornwall.

(iv) *Spain and Portugal*. In Spain and Portugal much ecclesiastical silver was produced and a remarkable quantity of it has been preserved in the cathedrals and churches of those countries, as well as in museums elsewhere. Examples of earlier date than the 13th c. are, however, just as scarce as in other lands. Advantage was taken of the immense quantity of silver reaching Spain from the New World, and as a result it often proved simpler and cheaper to use the ample supplies for making articles in a new fashion instead of following the usual practice of melting down the outmoded. Marking was general at a number of places in each of the Spanish provinces but was less well organized in Portugal,

The Burghley Nef, silver gilt with a nautilus-shell hull. By Pierre le Flamand. Paris. (V. & A. Mus., 1482)

where Lisbon and Oporto appear to have been the sole centres of the craft. An early 15th-c. standing pyx (Victoria and Albert Museum) bears the mark of Palma de Mallorca, and other pieces have been recorded from the same place.

Moorish influence is clearly discernible in a number of specimens embodying in their decoration the interlaced ribbons and the OGEES and curves commonly employed in Islamic decorative art. They are seen, for example, in the inside of a late 15th-c. casket from Granada (Victoria and Albert Museum). The Gothic style current elsewhere in Europe was more widely favoured, the silversmiths in each area adapting it and often elaborating it to suit local taste.

A silver-gilt processional cross made in Barcelona towards the end of the 15th c. (Victoria and Albert Museum) is typical of many other articles of that date and later. It is in the form of a double cross fleury, that is with the ends of the horizontal arms terminating in FLEURS-DE-LIS. All the outer edges are decorated with tiny crockets, the upright and arms are modelled with scrolling foliage interspersed with shaped plaques depicting religious scenes, while on the front and back are figures of Christ crucified and Christ in Majesty. The complexity of patterning is very striking, and when the plaques still retained the coloured enamel which has been lost the effect must have been even more remarkable.

The best known of Spanish silversmiths was Enrique de Arfe of León, whose son, Antonio, and grandson, Juan, followed the same craft. The latter wrote a book (*De varia conmensuración para la Esculptura y Architectura*, Seville, 1585) in which he advocates the Renaissance style and mentions numerous Spanish silversmiths and their work. Enrique de Arfe was trained at Cologne. In 1501 he was commissioned to make a *custodia* (monstrance) for León Cathedral, which was not finished until 21 years later. It stood nearly 2 metres in height, and went into the melting-pot in 1809 to help swell the military budget in the war against Napoleon. Another *custodia* and a processional cross from the same workshop are in the cathedral at Córdoba.

No less impressive is the Portuguese Belem monstrance (Museu de Arte Antiga, Lisbon), with its tall pinnacled Gothic towers above a group of kneeling apostles supported on a decorated stem and foot. The monstrance was made in 1506 from gold brought back from India by the navigator Vasco da Gama. Portuguese silversmiths were adept at embossed and chased work, and a number of surviving dishes with Lisbon and Oporto marks of the late 15th or early 16th centuries prove their mastery. Some show figures of men and monsters, but others are distinctively decorated with deep borders of small studs or with rows of studded bosses.

(v) Elsewhere in Europe silversmiths made their own adaptation of Italian and German prototypes, with rare excursions into originality. In all countries there was an admiration for the curious, man-made or natural, and suitable specimens were enhanced with mounts of silver or gold. Nautilus shells and ostrich eggs, coconuts, marbles and hardstones were coveted, and even greater regard was accorded such few examples of Chinese PORCELAIN as reached the Western world. The earliest of the porcelains is a vase of the Yüan Dynasty (1280–1367), which was given mounts of enamelled silver-gilt upon its arrival in Europe, so as to transform it into a ewer with curled handle and spout. The decoration included coats of arms, among which is that of Louis the Great of Hungary, who died in 1382. The piece had for long been known only from an 18th-c. drawing, but within recent years it has been rediscovered in the National Museum of Ireland.

Later, in the 16th c., there were several craftsmen who specialized in the mounting of ROCK-CRYSTAL and other hardstones in jewelled and enamelled gold. Members of the Sarachi family of Milan acquired renown for such work.

Silver-gilt processional cross. Barcelona. (V. & A. Mus., late 15th c.)

5. EUROPE FROM THE SIXTEENTH CENTURY.

(i) *Italy*. In 1509 the goldsmiths of Rome were reorganized and obtained permission from Pope Julius II to build a church in the Via Giulia. It was dedicated to their patron, St. Eligius, and in due course they were able to obtain from France a holy relic for it: an arm of the saint. As Rome was the seat of the Papal court, the important orders to be gained there attracted many of the best craftsmen from all over Italy.

The re-establishment of the Roman craftsmen coincided with the flowering of the Renaissance style and a general spread of luxury. Predictably, it was the silversmiths of Rome who produced great numbers of fine ecclesiastical pieces, while at the same time they supplied secular wares for their own countrymen as well as for visitors. The latter carried their purchases to all parts of the Continent, where the objects found their way into cathedrals and churches, palaces and less grand residences, where the styling and workmanship might exercise influence.

Without doubt the most celebrated of all Italian craftsmen was Benvenuto CELLINI, who was born in Florence and received training there and at Siena and Pisa before settling at Rome and working for a time in France. Most of Cellini's productions are known only from drawings and descriptions, and the sole surviving documented example of his skill as a goldsmith is the table salt in the Kunsthistorisches Museum, Vienna. This is modelled in gold, partly enamelled, and was made in *c.* 1540 for Francis I of France. On an oval base are seated figures of Neptune, designed to hold a ship to contain salt, and Amphitrite, beside whom is a temple for pepper. Cellini also worked for Popes Clement VII and Paul III, but the morse he made for the cope of the former, as well as other pieces from his workshop, no longer exist. With much else of equal magnificence they contributed to the indemnity of 30,000,000 francs demanded of the Vatican by Napoleon in 1797.

In Rome, as elsewhere, it was not uncommon for members of a family to succeed one another in business. Thus Corinzio Colleoni (1579–1656) was followed by his nephew Bartolomeo (1633–1708), and the latter by his nephew Agostino (1663–1746), all of whom supplied chalices to the Magistrato of Rome for presentation to various churches in the city. Giovanni Francisco Arrighi (1646–1730) and his two sons, Agostino (1682–1762) and Antonio (1687–1776), produced ecclesiastical pieces. Vincenzo Belli (1710–87) was succeeded by his son, grandson and great-grandson, whose total working lives spanned more than a hundred years during which they established a reputation for excellent wares. And Andrea Valadier (1695–1759), who was born in the south of France and came to Rome in 1720, was followed by two sons and a grandson, the last of whom, known for his work in the Neo-Classical style, died in 1839.

A number of articles became Italian specialities, although some were also made in other Roman Catholic countries. They included holy-water stoups, crucifixes and *cartagloria* frames. The last were intended for holding prayer-cards, although they were often subsequently converted into mirrors. Domestic articles of similar types to those made and used elsewhere in Europe occur in Italian silver, but with national characteristics. These usually emphasize the features of current styles: bold curves whenever curves were fashionable, and a liking for modelled ornament reflecting the Italian natural ability in sculpture.

The main centres in addition to Rome were Turin, Genoa, Venice and Naples. Each concentrated to some degree on articles of certain types and of distinctive patterns, with the Roman silversmiths usually in advance of their provincial colleagues in the matter of design. Many of the craftsmen went from one city to another in search of opportunity, so it is neither easy nor wise to base attributions of origin on style alone. The provincial cities lacked the large market available to silversmiths in Rome, but many of the craftsmen worked to high standards. As a result of the French occupation of the city from 1536 to 1552 and from 1640 to 1706 Turin was much influenced by French styles, and the hallmark with the arms of the House of Savoy is found on many articles that might otherwise be mistaken for French. This is exemplified in two pairs of silver-gilt candlesticks (Jones Collection, Victoria and Albert Museum) in the contemporaneous Paris taste; one of them is engraved '*Fait à Turin dans l'Atelier des Orpheureries Rojales 1783*', and the pair is said to have belonged to Louis XVI.

Genoa was famed for its work in filigree, at which the city's craftsmen were particularly skilled. The hallmark, a tower, rarely appears on examples because such delicate work would not withstand stamping. Small and large articles were constructed in the technique, including improbable objects such as sets of vases as much as 30 centimetres in height. Filigree was by no means the sole product and finely chased decorative objects could reach the standard of Roman work.

Venetian and Neapolitan silversmiths also had their specialities. The former were sometimes influenced by English styles for domestic ware, but conversely their ecclesiastical pieces were of extravagant design. Patterns embossed in notably high relief were employed for *cartagloria* frames and other objects. In Naples there was an output of all types of silverware, the 18th-c. craftsmen being noted for pairs of vases complete with flowers, all in silver or silver-gilt, which were used alike for the decoration of church altars and in the home.

(ii) *Germany*. Albrecht Dürer (1471–1528) was one of many artists who designed silver articles and the decoration for them. Others, remembered equally as painters and engravers, included Hans Burgkmair (1473–?1559), Heinrich Aldegrever (1502–58), Hans Holbein (1497–1543), Albrecht Altdorfer (1480–1538) and Virgil Solis (1514–62). The engraved designs of these men circulated widely but were used especially in Augsburg and Nuremberg, where large numbers of craftsmen had been established for a long time.

Gothic features persisted in much of the work until late in the 16th c., and traces can be seen even after that date. The wares made for secular use continued to include further types of drinking vessels, ranging from simple beakers to large and elaborate but impractical cups in the form of animals and birds with removable heads. The latter were made from *c.* 1575 for a period of about a hundred years, and like many other German show pieces were reproduced in quantity, although seldom in quality, in the second half of the 19th c. In place of the earlier nef, which gradually went out of use, table decoration took the form of elaborate centrepieces. Typical of these is the Merkel *Tafelaufsatz* (Rijksmuseum, Amsterdam) of silver, parcel gilt and enamelled, made by the eminent Nuremberg silversmith Wenzel JAMNITZER in 1549. The central feature is a female figure representing Mother Earth, who balances on her head a vase of flowers from which springs a large dish decorated with more flowers and centred in a vase, again of flowers. The whole object, which stands one metre in height, is a mixture of Gothic and Renaissance, not uncommon in Germany at the time.

From the 18th c. onwards German silver was less distinctive in design than it had been earlier. The influence of Versailles and its splendours inspired imitation at the numerous small princely courts, and many of them felt it imperative to own at least one suite of silver furniture. If not cast in solid metal, wholly or in part, it was of wood overlaid with repoussé plaques.

Equally luxurious was the work of Johann Melchior Dinglinger (1664–1731), who held the appointment at Dresden of goldsmith and jeweller to Augustus the Strong. His pieces are embodiments of the grotesque designs favoured at the time and seen in engravings after Jacques Callot (1592–1635) and Stefano della Bella (1610–64). Among Dinglinger's numerous extravagances preserved in the Grünes Gewölbe, Dresden, is a cup whose scallop-shaped bowl is of jasper, standing on a tall stem, mounted in enamelled and jewelled gold, hung about with cameos and surmounted by a miniature portait of Augustus as the 'Hercules of Saxony'.

Although much silverware was made successively in the BAROQUE, ROCOCO and NEO-CLASSICAL styles, little of great distinction was produced. An exception might be claimed for some of the Rococo pieces with their characteristic Germanic exuberance. The Augsburg silversmith Franz

Anton Gutwein was particularly adept at chasing asymmetrical arrangements of scrolls and other motifs to achieve an effect of movement, although he often lacks the flowing rhythm of the best Rococo work.

(iii) *France*. A very large proportion of French silverware made prior to the late 17th c. was consigned to the melting-pot to finance the wars and personal extravagances of Louis XIV. Some remains in being, however, and more is recorded, so that an idea can be obtained of what was once plentiful. Chance has certainly played a large part in the preservation of specimens, which cannot therefore be taken as truly representative.

A silver-gilt table salt of *c*. 1530 represents the best work of the time. It is a ceremonial object which was recorded as being in the possession of Henry VIII of England by 1550, was disposed of in 1649 following the execution of Charles I, and reappeared at a London auction sale in 1967. The salt has a hexagonal base set with small oval ivory carvings of heads, and rests on agate ball feet; the upper portion is inset with stones and enamelled, and the ornamentation includes Gothic gables intermixed with Renaissance motifs. It is the property of the Worshipful Company of Goldsmiths, London.

Clock-salt, silver gilt ornamented with carved agate heads, garnets and rock crystal. The figure at the top and the upper half of the sphere on which it stands are careful modern restorations replacing 18th-c. alterations. French. (Worshipful Company of Goldsmiths, London, *c*. 1530)

Contrasting in pattern is a simple cup with shallow bowl, baluster stem and domed foot, the stem and foot engraved and the whole parcel-gilt (Victoria and Albert Museum). It is provincial work, made at Orleans *c*. 1550, and bears a close resemblance to some glass drinking vessels of the period. Whereas the salt combines old and new in its decoration, the cup is fully Renaissance in style, with small panels of formal floral and other ornament on a matted ground within strapwork.

Parcel-gilt cup. Orleans. (V. & A. Mus., *c*. 1330)

It was the building and equipping of Versailles from *c*. 1660 that stimulated silversmiths to produce suites of solid silver furniture, as well as such prodigality as silver guard rails to protect the royal bed and throne. Some of these were the work of Pierre Germain (1645–84), the first of an important family of Parisian silversmiths to attain eminence. Comparable extravagance existed outside the Court, but almost all has long vanished and only the engraved designs by Jean Lepautre (1618–82) and others remain to convey an impression of what some pieces may have looked like.

An important survivor of the period is the Lennoxlove toilet-service, which was given to Frances Teresa, Duchess of Richmond and Lennox, by Charles II (Royal Scottish Museum, Edinburgh). The 15 pieces include covered boxes and vases, a mirror and other articles, some of which bear the Paris mark of *c.* 1670.

Marking was made more explicit by the imposition of a duty in 1672, which required the stamp of the tax-farmer (*poinçon de charge*) and another in 1681 denoting payment of the duty (*poinçon de décharge*). By the same date a number of articles had become peculiar to France and remained popular there for much of the ensuing century. Among them were the *écuelle*, a squat tureen usually with two horizontally placed flat handles, a cover and stand, and spice containers with two or three lidded compartments for use at the table.

Early in the 18th c. the RÉGENCE style held sway with its use of the cut-card technique for ornament combined with strength. The patterns employed for decoration at the time can be studied in the six sheets of engravings entitled *Nouveaux Desseins pour graver sur l'orfèvrerie, Inventés et gravés par le Sieur Masson.* They owned much to the work of Jean BÉRAIN, who held the appointment of *dessinateur de la chamber et du cabinet du Roi* and was in effect the 'oracle of taste'.

By the mid 1730s a violent change was beginning to take place, with the classicism of the Régence being supplanted by the asymmetry of Rococo. With regard to silverware, the moving spirit was Juste-Aurèle MEISSONNIER, born at Turin, who held Bérain's post of *dessinateur.* Meissonnier was not only a designer but a working silversmith, one of his first full Rococo productions being a table centrepiece and two tureens for an Englishman, the 2nd Duke of Kingston, which were made in 1735. The design for this suite was engraved, but the actual articles have eluded discovery since their appearance at a Paris auction sale in 1909. The son of Pierre Germain, Thomas (1673–1748), and his son, François-Thomas (1726–91), enjoyed Royal patronage until the Revolution. The work of the members of the family was of distinctive quality, and pieces made up to, say, the mid 1750s, were predictably of Rococo pattern. Later work, however, incorporated classical elements. Also working in the mid century were, among numerous others, Nicolas Besnier (active 1714–54) and Jacques Roëttiers (1707–84). The latter learned his craft under Germain and Besnier, and married Besnier's daughter.

When the country had begun to resettle after the Napoleonic upheavals the silversmiths set to work again to make good the enormous losses of ware sacrificed to the Exchequer. Those who achieved success in the new EMPIRE style included Martin-Guillaume Biennais (1764–1843), Jean-Baptiste-Claude Odiot (1763–1850) and Henry Auguste (1759–1816), who used the English version of his forename.

(iv) *Netherlands.* The silversmiths of the Netherlands were content to adapt German models until early in the 17th c. when there came to the fore a style invented by a Utrecht-born silversmith Paul van VIANEN. It is known in Dutch as *Kwabornament* (literally, 'lobed ornament') and as the AURICULAR or Cartilaginous style. Paul van Vianen's brother, Adam (*c.* 1565–1627), and the latter's son, Christaen (active *c.* 1628–66), developed the style effectively. The last was employed for a time by Charles I, and while in England he made a set of altar plate for St. George's Chapel, Windsor. This proved irresistible to Cromwell's troops, who sent it to be melted down in 1642.

Examples of the work of the van Vianen family and others in the *Kwabornament* style can be seen in Amsterdam (Rijksmuseum) and London (Victoria and Albert Museum). Some

Tazza in the *Kwabornament* style. By Adam van Vianen. Utrecht, 1628

of Adam van Vianen's designs for silverware were published in 1650 by his son under the title *Modelles Artificiels de divers Vaisseaux d'argent*, and a further set of engravings after Gerbrand van den Eeckhout (1621–74), *Veelderhande Niewe Compartemente*, showed how the fleshy components might be employed generally. Work in the same style as that of the van Vianens was produced by a few other silversmiths, notably Jan Lutma, the Elder (*c.* 1585–1669), of Amsterdam.

Dutch ware of more conventional pattern was also made at various towns, including some items that were specialities of the Netherlands. Among these were wager-cups formed as a woman with a capacious skirt holding aloft a swinging small-sized cup and others incorporating a windmill in their design (types made also in Germany); a brandy bowl, known as *Brandewijkom,* with flat handles, many of which were produced at Sneek, in Friesland; and a glass-holder in the shape of a tall stem with open grips at the top for taking a drinking glass, known as a *Bekershroef.*

Many late 17th-c. Dutch pieces were similar in style to those favoured at the time in England, the two countries temporarily sharing a monarch. Much of the coincidence in design was due to the published work of Daniel MAROT, who was born in France and fled to Holland to escape religious persecution. He came to England with William of Orange and styled himself Architect to William III.

During most of the 18th c. Dutch silversmiths adapted French styles to suit their taste, while their Neo-Classical pieces often resembled English prototypes.

(v) *Spain and Portugal.* In both countries ecclesiastical articles continued to be made and in both there was a gradual increase in the manufacture of wares for domestic use. Renaissance ornament was employed early in the 16th c., an example being the Shrine of San Froilán (León Cathedral) of 1525, which is attributed to Enrique de Arfe. Of the same year is a silver-gilt monstrance by an unidentified maker in Burgos; the piece is chased with flowers and foliage among Gothic pinnacles and cusps (Victoria and Albert Museum).

Almost all the objects in use elsewhere in Europe were copied or adapted, usually with sufficient variation to give them individuality. The treatment of the Rococo was unsympathetic, but late in the 18th c. better results were achieved in the Neo-Classical style.

Following Wellington's success in driving the French out of Portugal, it was decided that he should be presented with a worthy testimonial. It took the form of a silver-gilt dinner service of over 1,000 pieces, begun in 1811 and delivered five years later. The service was made at the Military Arsenal, Lisbon, and demonstrates that Portuguese skill in silversmithing remained at a high level. (Wellington Museum, Apsley House, London.)

(vi) *Scandinavia.* The lidded tankard with cylindrical body was a favourite in the 17th c. and has survived in quite large numbers, the greater quantity originating in Sweden. The tankards vary in details but are usually supported on three feet, ball-and-claw or a part-opened pomegranate being popular designs. Lids are frequently inset with a contemporary coin, and a figural thumbpiece is not uncommon. The so-called 'peg' tankard is similar in external appearance to others, but is fitted inside the body with a series of small pegs. The user was required to drink down to the first peg before passing on the vessel to his neighbour, over-drinking being subject to a forfeit.

A saucer-like two-handled bowl for drinking hot brandy was made in the 18th c. It was known in Norway as a *oreskaal*, in Denmark as a *orekovsken* and in Sweden as a *dopskal.*

Eighteenth-c. wares were pale imitations of French styles.

(vii) *Russia and other countries.* For their most important silverware the inhabitants of many countries followed the example of the Russians, who made their purchases in Paris. Catherine the Great had her toilet service made by François-Thomas Germain in 1765, and following Germain's bankruptcy in the same year went to Jacques-Nicolas Roëttiers in 1771 for a large dinner service. This comprised 842 pieces, and she gave it to her favourite, Count Orloff.

Silver-gilt tureen, cover and stand made for the Empress Elizabeth of Russia by François-Thomas Germain. Paris, 1758

Among articles made specifically for Russian use is the *kovsh*, which is a small boat-shaped ladle with a short handle; the *charka*, a small single-handled cup; and the *bratina*, a covered cup with a contracted lip. All these were made in silver and gold, often enamelled and set with gems. See also RUSSIA (METALWORK).

Table silver made in Russia mostly follows French styles. In other countries wares made for local use similarly imitated prevailing fashionable patterns, albeit later in date and with only partial success. This applied especially to the Baroque and Rococo, but the Neo-Classical, which was less demanding technically, is frequently comparable in design and execution with the productions of more sophisticated centres.

(viii) *Later Nineteenth Century.* A confusion of styles overtook European silver by the middle of the 19th c. Gothic, Rococo and other styles were revived, distorted and often intermixed. At the same time rapidly increasing mechanization dictated that design should be subservient to mass production, and the long-enduring craft of the silversmith declined in importance. In many instances the term became applied to one who did no more than retail machine-made goods.

At the numerous large-scale exhibitions held in London, Paris and other capital cities spectacular examples of silverware were displayed. They were shown to enhance national prestige, and cannot be looked on as representative of normal productions.

A reaction set in *c.* 1890, with the introduction and spread of ART NOUVEAU. By then a fresh generation of artist–craftsmen was arising and a great gap in quality of design and execution as well as price had become established between commercial, machine-made ware and the work of the artist–craftsman.

6. BRITAIN. It has been estimated by Gerald Taylor that less than 400 articles of plate, including spoons, survive from the medieval period up to 1525. Of these only a third consists of domestic plate. Not unnaturally a very low proportion of

this total includes Saxon or Norman pieces, but their scarcity is due to losses created by subsequent political and economic events. Chief among these were the subscription of large quantities of plate to pay the ransom of Richard I, borrowings of plate from the abbeys and cathedrals by Edward III, the Wars of the Roses and, most drastic of all, the Reformation and consequent calling in of all Mass plate for replacement. In the 17th c. the Civil War brought about a dearth of silver coin which was only partially met by the compulsory melting or conversion of plate. The heavy demands for plate following the Restoration, culminating in the Wrought Plate Act of 1697, also took their toll in drastic refashioning of old or worn plate. It should not be forgotten that before collecting as such became a significant private as well as public activity in the 19th and 20th centuries plate was regarded as little more than a readily negotiable asset rather than a relic of historical importance. Owners aware of fashion and wishing to keep up to date unhesitatingly provided old plate as 'bullion' for the use of their silversmiths in fulfilling new orders.

Contact with France and the growing impact of the French and northern European Gothic movement remained close from the Norman invasion of the 11th c. to the final loss of Calais, England's last possession in France, in 1556. The importance of English wool exports also led to cultural ties with Flanders and north Germany. As a result much foreign plate found its way into England, as is attested by inventories of the period. The Royal Gold Cup in the British Museum, finely decorated with champlevé enamel figure-groups, was made in France *c.* 1380, although added to in the early 16th c. A further example is the Founder's Cup of Oriel College, Oxford (one among the articles of University plate spared by Charles I in the Civil War for historical reasons), which bears a late-15th-c. French hallmark.

The character of some of the more impressive metalwork of the early Gothic period can be judged almost solely by the examination of important examples of bronze church plate such as the Gloucester Candlestick of *c.* 1150 (V. and A. Mus.). This is most notable for the tendril-like interlacings of its open-work, which are interspersed with small draped figures. The 13th c. is also almost totally devoid of any examples of plate which can confidently be described as English. Of the following century King John's Cup, belonging to West Norfolk District Council, is now thought to be English workmanship of *c.* 1320. It has a cursive bowl ornamented with figurative subjects in champlevé enamel, supported on a thin Early English column-stem. The Battersea Dish of *c.* 1325 (on loan to the V. and A. Mus.) is embellished with lobes emanating from a central boss engraved with a scene of the Annunciation, a form of decoration which remained popular until the beginning of the 16th c.

English church and secular plate of the 14th and 15th centuries generally employed ornament closely derived from contemporary architectural detail. A notable example is the boat-shaped Ramsey Abbey Censer of *c.* 1350 in the Victoria and Albert Museum and the Pastoral Staff of William of Wykeham (New Coll., Oxford) of *c.* 1379, which is decorated with figures in relief and enamelled panels within elaborate architectural settings of the English Decorated style. Of similar date is the more modest Studely Bowl in the Victoria and Albert Museum, engraved all over with the letters of the alphabet in Gothic script on a hatched ground. With the introduction of hallmarking, it becomes less difficult to classify spoons, which by 1475 had taken on a marked national character. This was typified by the use of a slender hexagonal stem tapering towards a finial in the form of a diamond, acorn or similar motif, of figures representing the Master or one of the twelve apostles. The stem itself widens soon after 1475, perhaps to facilitate receiving the additional maker's symbol. See also CUTLERY.

The shapes of drinking-vessels contract to a more modest 'font' shape by the opening of the 16th c., the very simply designed Campion Cup of 1500–1 (V. and A. Mus.) being typical of this group. Other drinking-bowls called 'mazers' (after the old English word for maple), made of

The Royal Gold Cup, enamelled gold embellished with pearls. The two decorated bands in the upper part of the stem are later additions, while the cover once had a rim garnished with pearls matching the rim at the foot and a finial set with rubies, sapphires and pearls. French. (B.M., *c.* 1380)

A B C

A. Founder's Cup. (Oriel College, Oxford, late 15th c.) B. King John's Cup. English workmanship. (West Norfolk District Council, *c.* 1320.) C. Pastoral staff of William of Wykeham, silver gilt. (New College, Oxford, 1379)

turned maple wood, survive in more profusion from this period probably on account of the low weight of their silver mounts. Similarly other substances, from Chinese CELADON to coconuts, are found mounted in silver on account of their scarcity and value.

The most important and expensive form of domestic plate in the Gothic and Renaissance periods was the standing salt container, of which any household might have owned eight or more of varying size and status. The 14th-c. examples described in inventories took the forms of animals supporting the salt container. Others of the Perpendicular period of English architecture were generally shaped like ornate hour-glasses.

The influence of the Renaissance did not affect the design of plate in England until the third decade of the 16th c. One of the most important surviving vessels of this type is the Howard Grace Cup (V. and A. Mus.) of 1525–6 which, although maintaining a font shape for its turned ivory bowl and employing some Gothic borderings, is mounted with a frieze of classical masks and surmounted by a baluster-shaped finial of Renaissance style, studded with jewels.

Henry VIII's natural extravagance, his rivalry with Francis I of France and his wish to be recognized as one of the most eligible princes of Europe helped to ensure a heavy expenditure on plate. Although unable to attract such a prodigious circle of Italian craftsmen and artists as Francis I, notable among these being Leonardo da Vinci and Benvenuto CELLINI, he obtained the services of the sculptor Pietro Torrigiano (1472–1528) to design the tombs of Henry VII and Margaret Beaufort for Westminster Abbey. Most of the craftsmen who came to work in England were from Flanders, Germany and France and there was a not unnatural decline in the attraction of Italian talent as Henry's religious policies began to take effect.

The greatest single influence on design was undoubtedly Hans Holbein the Younger, who arrived in England for his first visit in 1526. In addition to his many portrait drawings Holbein has left many designs for cups and jewellery, mostly of the enriched and detailed Northern Renaissance style, although no single surviving vessel can be credited to him. Many Gothic forms continued to be used, although after Holbein's arrival craftsmen began to rely heavily upon classically based sources. The Boleyn Cup of 1535 (Cirencester church) is for example still Gothic in its ribbed bowl and cover while its ornament consists of engraved foliage and applied acanthus leaves. The Goldsmiths' Company own the magnificent Bowes Cup of 1554, which consists of a ROCK-CRYSTAL bowl with cast and embossed ornament, including figures, almost of Italian quality. At this period ewers and cups began to assume a thistle shape, the bowls mounted by means of cast scroll-brackets upon baluster-shaped stems, the lids generally supporting a roughly cast figure-finial very much in the German manner. Most decorative schemes were adapted from the prolific pattern-books available through the 16th c. Notable among these were Geoffrey Whitney's *Emblems and Other Devices*, published at Leiden in 1586, or the earlier pattern-book by the Fleming Thomas

Geminus, illustrating examples of Moorish and other Islamic ornament, published in London in 1548.

Towards the end of the 16th c., plate was decorated in an increasingly plastic manner by means of embossing as well as chasing and engraving. Mannerist ornament derived from north European and Italian pattern-books, such as Vredeman de VRIES'S *Architectura* of 1577 and the engravings of Virgil Solis and Abraham Collaert, began to influence the decoration of some of the more important plate of the period. New shapes in the form of tankards and flagons were added to the traditional assemblage of salts, ewers and basins, standing dishes or TAZZAS and cups belonging to prosperous households. Almost every square inch of surface began to be covered with grotesque mask heads, sea monsters, scallop shells or flowers within flat bandings of strapwork. The new plate of the Church of England, necessarily more modest in both design and decoration, adopted the shapes and proportions of domestic plate to serve the greater demands of the Communion service.

There was no appreciable change in the style of English silver until well into the reign of James I (1603–27). The standing cup had already begun to adopt an oviform bowl-shape and more vertical proportions by the turn of the century, a distinctive new feature being the open-worked 'steeple' or pyramid surmounting the lid. During the 1620s and 1630s bullion became scarcer as the economic situation worsened. Less extravagance was called for, the use of gilding steadily declined mainly under Puritan influences, and a certain paucity of decoration, for example the crude punched-work ornamentation of thin shallow sweetmeat dishes, accompanied a tendency towards plain surfaces. Some Portuguese influences can be traced in the embossed and open-worked style used for some dishes and baskets during this period, but an increased reliance on plain shapes with the occasional use of matted rather than engraved surfaces established itself by the 1630s. A new type of 'Puritan' spoon with an oval bowl and a flat stem was introduced in Charles I's reign, gradually replacing the older type with its slightly flattened hexagonal stem.

The techniques of German silversmiths had been the chief influence on their English counterparts since the time of Holbein the Younger. Under the Stuarts this sometimes stiff style began to be replaced by a more naturalistic approach, principally through contact with the Netherlands. In the 1630s and 1640s the Utrecht silversmith Christaen van VIANEN took up residence in England and executed commissions notably for the Chapel of the Knights of the Garter, St. George's, Windsor. Few of his marked pieces survive, but the late Mannerist distortions of the AURICULAR or 'cartilagenous' style which he introduced continued to influence some English silversmiths until after the Restoration.

During the late Commonwealth and Protectorate period, from *c.* 1655 to 1660, plate began to assume a lively, naturalistically embossed character quite different from that of the abstract 'cartilaginous' style—designs of plants, animals and scroll work, mostly copied from Dutch and German sources—which was in common use before the Restoration. It is also very likely that the melting and refashioning of plain and modestly decorated Puritan pieces had also begun in earnest by 1660 although this process was naturally accelerated during Charles II's reign. It has often been wrongly assumed that the scarcity of English silver between *c.* 1649 and 1660 is due to a falling off of patronage during these unluxurious years. This is not borne out by the facts. Quantities of plate sent to assay remained fairly constant under the Commonwealth compared with the years of Charles I's reign. The answer most probably lies with the popular pastime of refashioning, or bringing the style of one's possessions—silver and furniture being the best examples—up to date without radically altering the over-all shape of the original. The association of modest or plainly decorated silver with an artistically restrictive period must have been very considerably felt and thus been responsible for the wholesale meltings and refashionings which were the cause of the present-day scarcity.

Not all plate of the post-Restoration period required elaborate decoration. Large quantities of bullion were employed for useful objects such as quart tankards, vehicles not only for ale but for the material wealth of the owner. The new-milled silver coinage introduced in 1662 became a reliable source of ready-alloyed sterling silver, causing eventual restrictions on the quantity and type of plate to be fashioned for utilitarian purposes. The extravagance of the period also made itself felt in the taste for silver furniture, reflecting a Continental appetite for BAROQUE interiors on the grand scale. Sheet silver was employed, usually heavily embossed, for covering tables, mirror frames and chimney-furniture. Chandeliers, toilet services and *garnitures de cheminée* consisting of sets of large vases and beakers, their shapes based upon Chinese PORCELAIN originals, were accompanied in the more affluent households by wine cisterns and coolers and pilgrim bottles of immense proportions. Their manufacture was, as usual, documented in terms of shillings per ounce and an additional proportion 'for fashion'.

The habit of commissioning silver furniture of large proportions reached a peak in the last quarter of the 17th c. This era also witnessed a distinct change in style from what may be termed Dutch Baroque to Louis XIV. In England this process was assisted by the increasing numbers of Huguenot refugees from France, who brought to friendly Protestant countries a new sophistication both in technique and in style. Basically the Louis XIV style was a severe and symmetrical prolongation of the Baroque with a strong emphasis upon classical niceties.

The embossed and chased acanthus-leaf frieze ornamenting the base and lid of a porringer may be cited as an early omen of the more precise and better finished metalwork which began to be produced in England from *c.* 1685 onwards. During this year Louis XIV finally revoked the Edict of Nantes. A large efflux resulted and during the last 15 years of the 17th c. English silversmiths felt increasingly obliged to accept the new standard of the immigrant craftsmen, although traditional embossed sheet silver with punched ornament continued to survive into Queen Anne's reign.

One of the principal protagonists of the new style was Pierre Harache the Elder, a first-generation Huguenot. His work and that of his contemporary immigrants, where known, exhibits casting and chasing skills of a high standard. Fluting, matting and engraving and also applied fretted silver layers ('cut-card' work) are among the techniques which received a much needed revitalizing and took on new dimensions with the heavier-gauge silver used by immigrant goldsmiths in the French manner. Pierre Platel and Simon Pantin can be named, although little is known about them outside their marked works, as being similarly influential. Many of their contemporaries, however, had to work in a humble capacity in large London silversmiths' workshops, where their fine craftsmanship was credited to their English employers and their works bore English makers' marks.

Much of the design of the more important silver and silver-gilt of the period 1685–1720 was influenced by engravings of Jean BÉRAIN and Jean Lepautre (1618–82) as well as Daniel MAROT. High standards of finish were reached, for example in an exceptional set of hexagonal salvers bearing Benjamin Pyne's mark in the Victoria and Albert Museum, hallmarked 1698–9. But the English taste generally tended in favour of French proportions and against elaborate decoration. The results culminated in the plain octagonal, circular and rectilinear objects of the reigns of Queen Anne and George I, whose undecorated surfaces won peculiar popularity in the functionalist atmosphere of the 1930s and 1940s.

A no less important revolution in English silversmithing occurred during the evolution of tea, coffee and chocolate drinking in western Europe. Vessels and other equipment had to be specially designed in precious metals as well as other media to meet these new and at first luxurious requirements, although some help was afforded by imported Chinese earthenwares and porcelains which often accompanied consignments of tea. A small Persian globular winepot was used as another early model for a teapot (*c.* 1685, V. and A. Mus.), while coffee and chocolate were accommodated in taller vessels (those beverages were relatively cheaper, and went further) based upon the larger form of flagon. At first the spout was set awkwardly, but by 1700 it had evolved into its standard form. An early feature was the setting of the handle, Continental style, at right angles to the spout, a convention which survived until *c.* 1725. Kettles with stands were also fashioned at this period as part of the silver tea equipment although the mahogany tripod table was later especially provided for the kettle and its supporting silver salver.

It was only during the latter half of the 17th c. that the basic eating implement of the English table, the spoon, began to be gradually supplemented by the fork. (See CUTLERY.) Surviving examples are very rare but those there are show the normal flat-stemmed proportions of the contemporary spoons, sets normally being provided in dozens. The Puritan period witnessed the end of the hexagonal stem and the introduction of a modestly shaped handle sometimes notched at the top ('slip-top' spoons). The stamping of the reverse of the bowl and front of the stem with elaborate scroll designs became common after the Restoration, the stem itself broadening out into a 'trifid end'.

The compulsory introduction of the Britannia Standard in 1696 radially changed certain silversmithing practices. The new 0·958 alloy was rightly claimed to be softer than the traditional sterling standard and therefore unsuitable for the usual degrees of strength and durability. As a result flatware assumed a more robust appearance as well as an increased relative weight, the cost of which was naturally passed on to the customer. The rounded cylindrical stem and a well accented 'rat-tail' back became features of this period and continued into the 1730s after the demise of the *compulsory* higher standard in 1719–20. Casting, particularly of candlesticks, handles and feet of vessels and applied ornament, may also to some extent have been encouraged by the need to strengthen plate, although older methods such as embossing and fluting continued to be used with traditional shapes.

During the second quarter of the 18th c., corresponding roughly with the reign of King George II, a further reaction took place both from the heaviness of Baroque and from the economy of the plain Queen Anne and George I style. From the heavy classicism of the influential Continental designer OPPENORD there emerged a lighter, airier use of scroll ornament in the RÉGENCE period in France, which had its effects in England during the reign of George I. The major revolution took place with the advent of the ROCOCO, one of whose chief protagonists was Juste-Aurèle MEISSONNIER. At first surface-decoration, and then shapes, took on a movement and asymmetry based not upon classical architectural detail but on naturalistic plant forms. Foliate and floral ornament, rock-work—to which the original French term 'rocaille' was applied—and the use of light spiral abstract forms produced in the character of most western European silver from 1735 to 1765 a sharp contrast with that of the previous generation.

Media such as gilt wood and plaster-work and,

in particular, porcelain were well fitted to the Rococo style. The malleability of silver afforded similar freedom to express movement and rippling brilliant surface-textures. Certain types of objects readily lent themselves to the new style. The rose-water ewer and basin, the milk-jug and tureen and the salvers were fashioned on occasion with casting, chasing and engraving ornamenting almost the entire surface. The two-handled cup and cover which had evolved by *c.* 1700 from the flat-bottomed cylindrical porringer also became a prestigious vehicle for the skills of such silversmiths as Paul de Lamerie, Frederick Kandler and George Wickes.

After attaining a peak of exuberance in the mid century with accompanying forays into the CHINESE, GOTHIC and rustic tastes, a more subdued transitional phase followed in which plain surfaces again began to gain popularity. The borderings of objects were contained within even and thin GADROON edges, a little like pie-crusting, and the use of heavy cast ornament fell out of favour to be succeeded by the less obtrusive media of embossing and chasing. The Rococo predilection for open-work, as in the fretted borders of CHIPPENDALE's furniture, also found more favour in the 1750s and 1760s.

Classical ornament, which had for a generation been forgotten by silversmiths, re-asserted itself first in an uneasy union with Rococo styling and then almost totally dominated the entire range of shapes and forms of objects from *c.* 1775 onwards. The painted interiors of Roman rooms had a profound effect on ADAM who, after a strongly three-dimensional early period, became more content to rely on decoration in very low relief, a tendency which can be seen in furniture and silver over the period 1765–85. Gadroon edges were replaced first by beading and then by simple reeded or thread-edges; cast and chased and embossed ornament alike were put aside in favour of engraved decoration preserving more rigidly the pure classical shapes of the objects involved.

The NEO-CLASSICAL style in England brought the different practical arts into much closer relation than before. For example WEDGWOOD based his stoneware shapes upon the classical urn and developed a form of relief decoration derived from GLASS and gem-cutting techniques. His two-colour jasperware medallions were imitated by Adam and Wyatt, among others, in their architectural interiors. Above all it was the mechanical accuracy of his output which influenced other crafts, silversmithing among them, as well as the high quality of the designs he employed. The shapes and proportions of silverware changed radically with the abandonment of the ROCOCO S-curve. The plan and elevation of vessels were made to conform to the classical urn, geometrical shapes such as the straight-sided cylindrical teapot of the 1780s were adopted in the purest practical form, and gradually even relief decoration, cast or embossed, came to seem obtrusive especially in the restrained style of the late 1780s and 1790s. The so-called Adam style was originally more robust especially as interpreted by such silversmiths as Andrew Fogelberg (who was the master of Paul STORR), Thomas Heming, the Crown Goldsmith, and John Schofield. Less prestigious wares, relying more upon engraving techniques for their decoration, were produced by members of the Hennell, Chawner and Bateman families.

This period saw a general increase in the output of plate in consequence of new industrial techniques. Milling, rolling and stamping sheet metal became possible with steam-power, processes which were equally adaptable to the most popular substitute for real silver, SHEFFIELD PLATE. Friezes, medallions, edge-ornaments and whole components could be mass-produced with the fly-press or rolling mill, which greatly reduced the cost of bullion needed for traditionally wrought metalwork and so increased the availability of silver to the new merchant classes. If prices of silver were still too high, silver-on-copper could be produced instead for about a third of the sterling price. The main centres of this production were the industrial towns of Sheffield and Birmingham, which in 1773 were eventually permitted to assay and mark their own plate, owing mainly to the efforts of the Birmingham manufacturer Matthew BOULTON. Only gradually were the new techniques assimilated by the London manufacturers, who were thus able to expand their middle and lower priced range of wares.

By the turn of the century the Adam style had become remote and had lost most of its impetus. Owing as much to the economic situation as to the precepts of fashion a high proportion of silver was either entirely plain or only modestly engraved and the metal itself was used only sparingly, reinforced by simple reeded edges. This economy of style had its counterpart in the 1790s in SHERATON's and Shearer's furniture designs, many of which relied upon lightness and an almost total lack of three-dimensional decoration. The design of flatware likewise tended towards modesty and lightness by the 1790s. The spoon lost its elongated oval shape at the mid century and by the early 1800s spoons were made with a pointed bowl reminiscent of the urn or the shield-back of the chair.

The REGENCY style in England and the EMPIRE style in France evolved more or less simultaneously. They were both re-assertions of the classical ideal based upon a more exact archaeological understanding of ancient, and in particular Greek, architecture. Both styles echoed, moreover, the heroic and portentous atmosphere of the era, favouring strong colours, heavy gilding and sheer physical massiveness in contrast to the undecided lameness of the troubled 1790s. Silver design, like that of furniture, found an added stimulus in the EGYPTIAN revival and it was the accuracy of the documents which followed Napoleon's expedition, together with their illustrations, which appealed to such silversmiths

Teapot, silver gilt, by Benjamin Pyne. (Carter Coll., Ashmolean Mus., Oxford, *c.* 1690)

Ewer by Paul de Lamerie. With arms of George Treby, who presented the set to his wife on the occasion of their wedding. (Farrer Coll., Ashmolean Mus., Oxford, 1724)

Two-handled cup and cover by Paul de Lamerie. With arms of Sir John Chardin.. (Farrer Coll., Ashmolean Mus., Oxford, 1730)

Teapot by Paul de Lamerie. Made from a tea-kettle into a teapot. (Farrer Coll., Ashmolean Mus., Oxford, 1735)

Tea-kettle and stand by Charles Kandler. (V. & A. Mus., 1727–37)

A

B

C

A. Candelabrum by Paul Storr. (Keble College, Oxford, 1823)

B. Goodwood Cup. Engraved: 'The Goodwood Cup, 1829, won by His Majesty's mare, Fleur de Lis, beating Mameluke, Varna, Lamplighter and Rough Robin', and also with garter and motto. The front of the stand is engraved: 'Goodwood 1829'. It is of silver gilt and the body is decorated with chariot races in antique style. (Royal Coll.) Reproduced by gracious permission of H.M. the Queen

C. Theocritus Cup, silver gilt, by Paul Storr after a design by John Flaxman. Engraved with the cypher of Queen Charlotte and the badge of George IV as Prince of Wales. The subjects shown in relief are taken from the description of the famous cup of the First *Idyll* of Theocritus. (Royal Coll., 1812–13.) Reproduced by gracious permission of H.M. the Queen

as Paul Storr, Digby Smith and Benjamin Scott and to their employers, the Crown Goldsmiths Rundell, Bridge and Rundell. T. H. Tatham, the furniture designer Thomas HOPE and such well-known sculptors as John Flaxman all contributed to moulding the Regency style into maturity, though not without considerable French influence. During the second decade of the 19th c., revivals of the Rococo and the Gothic, not to mention the Chinese, also distracted the silversmith, beginning a new wave of eclecticism.

The reigns of George IV and his brother William IV were marked by a new, mainly naturalistic extravagance in silver design, derived in the main from the French Rococo of the 18th c. but with a boldness of shape and contour in the Regency manner. Vessels tended to be lower and broader with distinct flanges or broad rims stressing horizontality. Heavily embossed decoration, often die-struck, continued on into Victorian plate, especially in the years before 1860. The Great Exhibition of 1851 did little to change the extravagance of a popular taste always searching for diversity and technical virtuosity. Such figures as Cole, RUSKIN and PUGIN abhorred the obvious effects of industrialization in metalwork as in almost every other field of the decorative arts and conscious attempts at reviving traditional techniques were encouraged. Pugin's own designs for plate were based upon medieval Gothic prototypes, principally of the 15th c. A similar but more exclusive market was served later by the architects Butterfield, Street and Burgess. By the time of the 1862 and 1871 exhibitions taste had generally returned to the Neo-Classical, and later to the Elizabethan. The opening up of trade with Japan brought an influx of Oriental designs towards the end of the 1870s. At the same period the designer Dr. Christopher Dresser produced some astonishingly functional formulae principally for the electro-plating industry. Economy of price and facility of production were his guiding principles, in marked contrast to the ambitious productions of the original patentees of electro-plated nickel silver, Elkington & Company of Birmingham. Apart from producing cheaper replicas of almost every form of solid silver object, their aspirations included electrotyping elaborate shields and other *tours de force* by leading sculptors of the day such as L. Morel Ladeuil. Similar prestige pieces, such as elaborate centrepieces and testimonials, many of them sculptural in character, had been produced throughout the mid 19th c. by Paul Storr's successors Hunt and Roskell, the Crown Goldsmiths Garrard & Co. and Messrs. Smith and Nicholson.

In the 1880s C. R. ASHBEE founded the Guild and School of Handicraft very much under the influence of William MORRIS and his followers. (See ARTS AND CRAFTS MOVEMENT.) The intention was to produce hand-wrought plate at reasonable cost by means of basic techniques such as the simple beating processes and the use of enamelling. The results, especially in the mid 1890s, show a cursive organic feeling for the quality of the metal not dissimilar from the ART-NOUVEAU plate being produced on the Continent at the same time, the vertical whip-lash line typical of this style being often combined with plain surfaces. The Guild was forced to liquidate in 1909, but its influence was widely felt especially with the larger manufacturers such as Liberty & Company and Messrs. Hutton of Sheffield. The younger generation of silversmiths, principally Omar Ramsden and Alwyn Carr, carried on the Guild's spirit well into the 20th c.

As the price of the metal and the costs of hand wroughting have increased, especially since the Second World War, individual craftsmen have become scarce. Much of their work has taken the form of institutional commissions for plate of a purely ceremonial character, but there have been instances of outstanding modern design based primarily on Scandinavian prototypes. The influence of stainless steel, the current substitute often for silver as well as for electroplate, has been noticeable in the sheer rigidity of post-war design. The malleability of the metal is rarely taken advantage of, owing principally to the influence of modern industrial techniques and the necessity of keeping down costs.

7. THE AMERICAS. Although a great deal has been written about silver of the Colonial period made in the eastern part of the U.S.A., little attention has been given to what was produced in Canada and to the south in Mexico and South America. Any discussion of Colonial American silver should cover the production of these areas and a great deal is known about both Mexican and Peruvian as well as Brazilian silver. Moreover our knowledge of silver made on the North Atlantic seaboard of the U.S.A. in the 19th and 20th centuries has increased to the point that we are now aware that the craft of hand-wrought silver did not cease with the close of the 18th c. but in fact continues (in spite of the introduction of mass-production techniques) until today.

In both North and South America the history of silver reflects the history of Colonial development generally. Almost without exception craftsmanship in silver remained under the influence of the mother countries—Spain, England, Holland, France—and the silver of the Americas was a provincial interpretation, with an inevitable time-lag, of the styles which were successively fashionable in Europe. Colonial Boston, for example, followed the British fashions; silver made in Mexico City followed the styles of Madrid, Seville, Salamanca, Burgos and Toledo; the silver of Montreal followed the styles of Paris; and so on.

(i) *Spanish Colonial silver*. The hope of finding new sources of gold and silver was one of the primary motives of the Spanish explorers who came to the New World. On 12 April 1519, Hernando Cortés landed at what is now Veracruz, Mexico, and found in the cities ruled by Montezuma an incredible wealth of gold and silver. Obtained from one of the great central plateaus of Mexico, these metals were taken casually by the natives and used by them for a number of everyday objects, including armour and clothing. It was silver, for example, not porcelain, that was used in the kitchen as well as the dining room.

The Colonial period of Peru, Chile and Bolivia lasted from the Conquest to the first quarter of the 19th c. In spite of the legal restriction that South American silversmithing be done only by immigrant Spaniards and by Creoles, native craftsmen continued to work in defiance of this law. In order to avoid the tax on silver Spanish, Creole and native workers in many cases did not mark their pieces. This makes it difficult to pinpoint particular makers and to determine the origin or dates, apart from quite general attributions. Even inscriptions with a date may have been added later. South American Colonial silver is interesting because of its combination of native and Spanish traditions. The forms are derived from Spanish prototypes, while the ornamentation was frequently of Indian inspiration. Spanish silver in turn showed Moorish and Dutch influences. A candelabra, which is one of a pair made *c*. 1650, is a distinguished example of Bolivian (then part of Peru) silver. The heart-shaped plaque attached to the shaft is the key feature of this piece, whose ecclesiastical use is seen in such details as the rosary-bead motif bordering the plaque and

Candlestick (one of a pair). Bolivia. (St. Louis Art Mus., *c.* 1650)

Detail of crozier. Chile. (St. Louis Art Mus., late 17th or early 18th c.)

repeated on the base and the crucifix below the heart. The letter 'A' on this candelabra probably stands for 'Agnus Dei, Lamb of God' and the 'I' on its pendant for 'Jesus'. The crozier made in Chile cannot be dated more specifically than the 17th or 18th c. The beautifully worked handle has motifs of lilies of the valley or tulips. The entire handle is detachable from its staff for travelling.

(ii) *The English and Dutch Colonies.* Spain's success in finding gold and silver in the New World in the 16th c. was an incentive to England's exploration and colonization efforts in the 17th c., the first enduring colony being founded at Jamestown in 1607. The hope of finding precious metals in Virginia was abandoned early, as no significant deposits were discovered in any of the settlements. In fact it was not until the 1850s that silver was found in the United States and this was in the western part of the country, particularly in Nevada.

Although the South American and Mexican silversmith had ready supplies of silver from deposits, the northern silversmiths had to rely on silver that was brought to them in the form of coins or actual silver objects which could be melted down and formed into a new object. A coffeepot or other object had the advantage of easy identification over coins as it could be engraved with the crests or initials of the owner. Colonial silver of the eastern seaboard was ordinarily made in New England and the middle Colonies. Virginia, with its plantation economic system was more likely to import furniture and silver from England or from the middle or New England Colonies, where there was a rich merchant class which demanded silver objects.

Unlike his European counterpart, the North American silversmith was not required by law to stamp his wares with marks indicating place and date of origin as well as the sterling content. He was not even required to stamp his own name or initials on his pieces, although this was the usual practice. Of the English Colonies Massachusetts Bay Colony was the most important in terms of silver-making and in particular the city of Boston. John Mansfield was the first recorded silversmith in this Colony (1634), and by 1680 Boston had at least 24 silversmiths, most of whom had received their training in London. But by this date some of them in turn had trained a number of native-born craftsmen, including Edward Winslow, who made the handsome trefoil salver *c.* 1705–15, whose form is derived from English silver design. As with most Colonial silver, it is simpler than its prototype

Salver by Edward Winslow. Boston. (The Art Institute of Chicago, early 18th c.)

and depends more upon its proportions, form and craftsmanship than on ornamentation.

The Dutch influence was slight in comparison to the English, Spanish and French. And New York was second to Boston in silver-making at the beginning of the Colonial period. The longevity of the Dutch influence is surprising, as the New Netherlands became an English Colony in 1664. The Dutch in this area were slow to mingle with the English, and Dutch institutions and traditions continued long into the 18th c. In parts of Rockland County a Dutch dialect was still spoken after 1900. New York silver is interesting because it combines English, Dutch and French influences. A fine early example of New York silver is the two-handled cup made by Cornelius Vander Burgh (1653–99) and stamped with his initials 'CVB' in a heart three times on the bottom. The arms of the Van Cortlandt family are engraved on the side. Particularly remarkable are the cast beaded

Two-handled cup by Cornelius Vander Burgh. New York. (The Art Institute of Chicago, 17th c.)

handles with BAROQUE caryatids and forked scrolls. The form is derived from English and Dutch prototypes.

Little if any of the Dutch influence is seen in the handsome ROCOCO coffeepot by one of New York's best and most prolific silversmiths, Myer MYERS. Its inverted pyriform is notable for its fine proportions. In contrast to the simplicity of the body is the rich ornamentation of the CHASED spout and handle, the bold GADROONING at the base and lid and the superbly executed FINIAL. Of Dutch Jewish origin, Myers was famous for the high quality of his work and in particular for pieces he made for synagogues in Newport and Philadelphia. In style, his work spans the Rococo and Federal periods.

(iii) *The French Colonies.* Although French settlements in the New World were behind those of Spain, Holland and England, French influence is seen in a number of French territories. Huguenot craftsmen were working in New York in the later 17th c. and the influx of French silversmiths after the Revolution influenced early 19th-c. American silver designs. In addition to the Gallic influence along the eastern sea-

Coffeepot by Myer Myers. New York. (St. Louis Art Mus., *c.* 1760)

board, French enclaves in Detroit, Mobile and New Orleans were also centres of importance. It was Canada, of course, where this influence was strongest, and where it still most importantly lingers. Specifically, the settled part of Colonial French Canada was composed of the long strip of land bordering both sides of the St. Lawrence River from Quebec on the east to Montreal on the west. Quebec, Trois Rivières and Montreal were the three principal cities. Of these Quebec was the chief silver-producing city and was the administrative and cultural centre of the Colony. Unlike the English Colonies Canada was dominated by one religion, which was the main influence on the silver that was produced. Therefore in contrast to the French Huguenot silversmiths working in New York in the late 17th c. and early 18th c., the French silversmith working in Quebec probably devoted his highest skills to the making of ecclesiastical silver. It was later that the English and Loyalist silversmiths were working in Canada, and became noted for their domestic silver. The processional crucifix was made by the Montreal silversmith Pierre Huguet called Latour (1749–1817). Because of the large amount of silver required and the workmanship involved, only the richest parishes could afford a processional cross such as this. The design in this example is simpler than its counterparts produced in France in the Louis XVI period. The tubular base originally fitted over a wooden staff. The corpus is a particularly fine casting, with carefully worked details. Another fine example of Canadian ecclesiastical silver is the ciborium made by the London

Processional crucifix by Pierre Huguet called Latour. Montreal. (St. Louis Art Mus., late 18th c.)

Ciborium by Robert Cruickshank. Montreal. (St. Louis Art Mus., late 18th c.)

silversmith Robert Cruickshank (1767–1809), who emigrated to Boston *c.* 1768 and fled to Montreal *c.* 1773. Although not an elaborate piece, its success depends upon its good proportions and fine workmanship seen in the finely cast cross at the top and the crimped edge at the base, lip and crest. Since French styles were sometimes used in Quebec before they were adopted in England, stylistically Canadian silver could be in advance of what was being done in the American Colonies whose dependency on English designs was so strong.

(iv) *United States silver: the 19th c.* During and immediately after the Revolution, the activity of American silversmiths had virtually come to a halt. By the early 1790s, however, economic conditions had improved and they continued to do so until the war of 1812, when conditions again were poor. In addition to Philadelphia, Boston and New York, Baltimore was rapidly expanding and became an important silver-making centre. The influence of English fashion continued in American silver after the Revolution, as is seen in a beautiful two-handled cup made by the Boston silversmith Benjamin Pierpont. The form was one used for church vessels, and this piece is inscribed 'The Gift of / Deacon Obadiah Dickinson / to / the Church of Christ in Hatfield. / 1788.' Dickinson

Two-handled cup by Benjamin Pierpont. Boston. (The Art Institute of Chicago, *c.* 1780)

lived in Hatfield, Massachusetts, and gave his church four such cups. Unlike Canadian silver, United States ecclesiastical silver, except for Anglican usage, closely followed the domestic forms; in fact, silver made for domestic use was often given to the church. Technical innovations introduced at the end of the 18th c. meant that this cup would not necessarily have been stretched and raised in the traditional manner but could have been made from a single sheet of metal. Its simple lines are in contrast to the Rococo form of Myers's coffeepot. A taste opposed to this restraint, characteristic of Boston, is reflected in a finely proportioned sugar urn made in Philadelphia *c.* 1800. This city, with New York and Boston, was an important silver-making centre from the 18th c. on, and was particularly known for its exuberant Rococo silver forms. This piece, made by Daniel Van Voohis, exhibits the pineapple finial usually associated with Philadelphia silver.

During the 2nd decade of the 19th c. the so-called Empire style, a later phase of the Classical Revival, emerged. A new group of French emigré silversmiths, having fled the French Revolution, were working in New York and Philadelphia, and these craftsmen brought with them the new French style as exemplified in a tea-caddy by Anthony RASCH, a French silversmith working in Philadelphia. The beading and bands of anthemia are typical of this style. Typically, too, the flower finial, the SWAGS and the ram's-head supports are cast. The classicism of this Empire piece is one of a number of revival styles to be seen throughout the 19th c. These revivals include the Greek, Egyptian, Rococo and Renaissance. Baltimore was especially known for its early repoussé work; particularly noteworthy is the firm of Samuel Kirk and Sons, who began work in the early part of the 19th c. Other companies which had their beginnings in the 19th c. and are still in business include the Gorham Co. of Providence, Rhode Island, and TIFFANY & Co. of New York.

Although a number of firms retained their high standards of design and workmanship, the encroachment of mass-production techniques led to poorly made pieces by many of the companies, which turned out cheap silver-plated wares in quantity, especially after 1850. Casting and stamping techniques encouraged even more elaborate designs. One company, however, to maintain a high level of craftsmanship was E. Jaccard of St. Louis. A water pitcher was made for that company *c.* the mid century. The inverted pyriform here is in the Rococo revival style and the body has been carefully raised through hammering. The fine repoussé work of leaves and flowers reflects the exquisite traditional hand-craftsmanship of Colonial silver. Although its form was derived from a Classical prototype, the decoration was inspired by the Rococo. Here both have been freely adapted in a design which is related to the form. Although revivalist silver tended to be excessively exuberant at times, this example, made for the Corwith family of St. Louis, displays unusual restraint and achieves harmony and balance. Jaccard's were retailers then, as today, and this piece is marked only by the firm, though some examples have both the retailer's and maker's stamp. Therefore this water pitcher was probably made for E. Jaccard by a craftsman whom they employed or whose products they bought.

Regional characteristics in 19th-c. silver were less apparent. Boston silver of this period, how-

Sugar urn by Daniel Van Voohis. Philadelphia. (The Art Institute of Chicago, 1785–90)

Tea-caddy by Anthony Rasch. Philadelphia. (St. Louis Art Mus., 1807–10)

Water-pitcher made for the E. Jaccard Jewellery Company of St. Louis, Miss. (Coll. David Dangler, Chicago, 1855–65)

ever, is characteristically restrained in contrast to the products of Philadelphia, New York and other cities.

Towards the end of the 19th c. Beaux-Arts and ART-NOUVEAU influences made themselves felt in American silver. Although *art nouveau* was not as widespread in America as in Europe, it is particularly associated with the Gorham Company of Providence, Rhode Island (*art-nouveau* silver designed by William Codman for this firm was called 'Martelé'). Also particularly popular were *art-nouveau* toilet sets, made by a number of companies. These sets included mirrors and brushes, whose forms incorporated long-haired ladies entwined with floral motifs.

(v) *United States silver: the 20th century.* Reform movements in the decorative arts had their origin in England with John Ruskin (1819–1900) and William MORRIS. The reform emphasized simplicity of form and a return to handicraft methods and encouraged modern guild systems when individual craftsmen could not be replaced by a machine. In the United States the ARTS AND CRAFTS MOVEMENT was particularly strong in Boston, Chicago, Detroit, Philadelphia and New York, and by the early part of the century a number of Arts and Crafts organizations had been formed in these cities. In Chicago the Kalo Shop, founded in 1901 by Clara B.

Water-pitcher by the Kalo Shop, Park Ridge, Ill. (Private Coll., Chicago, 1901–14)

Wells, was one of a number of craft shops which employed craftsmen and was at the same time a school for young ladies and others to learn handicraft techniques. Pieces made in the Kalo Shop were entirely hand-wrought, as was frequently indicated on the bottom, and were left in an unfinished state, showing the hammer marks rather than planishing them. This roughness emphasized the craft technique employed. Although some Arts and Crafts designs were inspired by medieval silver, the designs of Kalo were quite simple and reflected innovative English and European designs of the period as may be seen in a water-pitcher made between 1901 and 1914.

Although the zenith of the craft movement had passed by the beginning of the First World War, craft groups working in silver have continued. Throughout the 20th c., however, machine-made silver has been by far the most predominant. Most of the silver made in the United States which is for sale today is neither well designed nor well wrought. Contemporary machine-made silver is usually a cheap reproduction of traditional forms, frequently electroplated, reproducing the antique appearance that is associated by the public with silver. In some cases, however, followers of the BAUHAUS have succeeded in utilizing machine techniques in designs suitable to machine manufacture. And there is still a number of craft workshops producing hand-wrought silver of good design.

1, 3, 21, 29, 110, 116, 132, 150, 184, 202, 203, 208, 247, 264, 280, 286, 321, 360, 362, 386, 396, 418, 454, 497, 545, 571, 640, 641, 642, 643, 666, 668, 683, 722, 728, 802, 820, 821, 843, 919, 933.

SIMONIN, CLAUDE. French designer and engraver of decorations for firearms. In 1685 he published *Plusieurs pièces et ornaments d'arquebuzerie*, consisting of seven sheets of designs stated to be based on the work of the gunsmith Laurent de Languedoc. In 1693 he published, together with his son JACQUES, a second pattern-book, *Plusieurs pièces et autres ornements pour les arquebuziers*. These books of designs were the most widely disseminated of all French pattern-books for firearms and carried the influence of French gunsmiths and decorators in the Grand Manner of Louis XIV into every country of Europe. The former was reissued by Laurent de Languedoc under his own name in 1705 and four pirated editions appeared, two in Amsterdam and two in Nuremberg. The popularity of these pattern-books contributed to the prestige of French gun-making in the 17th and early 18th centuries.

SINGERIES. Motifs of monkeys aping human occupations and sports, a conceit which was particularly popular during the French RÉGENCE period both in painting and in the decorative arts.

SIT, VENTURA. A Catalan who set up the famous glass-house of La Granja de San Ildefonso, near Madrid, with the patronage of Queen Isabella and later of King Philip V (1683–1746). From 1740 Sit himself took charge of the manufacture there of plate and mirror GLASS, for which the factory was famous on account of the unusual size of the plates, some of which measured nearly 4 m by about 2·5 m. La Granja was also celebrated for the splendid CHANDELIERS which were produced there.

SKELETON CLOCKS. As their name implies, these CLOCKS have their framework reduced to a minimum of bars, straight or curved, and their dials are pierced so that the maximum amount of the mechanism is visible. They originated in France in the late 18th c., and the early examples were generally of high quality. Skeleton clocks came fully into fashion, however, mainly in England during the Gothic Revival in the 19th c., when their design tended to run riot and occasionally to take on fantastic forms.

SLIP. Term in pottery manufacture for a clay paste diluted to the consistency of cream. It may be the product of the final washing of the clay which is undertaken to remove impurities and render it suitable for use. In primitive pottery the shaped vessel after drying was often dipped in a bath of slip and then burnished to render it watertight.

Slip is used for decoration of pottery in three main techniques. (i) The design may be painted on the body of the vessel in slip of a different colour or the slip may be 'trailed' on to the body from a nozzle. This is called 'slip painting'. (ii) The whole or part of the body may be covered with slip and the design then drawn with a pointed tool in the liquid slip so that the different colour of the body shows through. This technique is known as 'SGRAFFIATO'. (iii) As with GLAZE, the design may be painted on the body in liquid wax which when dried and hardened 'resists' or repels the application of the slip, thus leaving 'negative' areas of design. The method is known as 'wax resist'.

Slip is also used for casting. A plaster-of-Paris mould is made from a master model and when this is assembled liquid slip is poured into it. The porous walls of the mould absorb liquid from the slip so that a layer of thicker consistency adheres to the inside walls of the mould while it is still full of liquid clay. When the desired thickness has been obtained the surplus slip is poured off and the cast is left to dry to leather hardness before the mould is removed. It is then trimmed for firing. This method is suitable for vessels with fine ornamental detail and thin walls. Alternatively in 'solid' casting the slip is allowed to remain in the mould until the whole cast is solid.

Special methods are in use for preparing slip to be used for casting because if liquid clay is fluid enough to be readily pourable, the solid content is insufficient to be effective. It is prepared by adding a deflocculant, such as sodium carbonate or sodium silicate, which renders a more sticky slip pourable.

In the 19th c. clay for EARTHENWARE was united with a creamy mixture of powdered flint and the mixture was technically known as 'slip'. The fluid mixture of clay and flint was subsequently reduced by a complicated process to the doughy consistency required by the potter.

See CERAMICS and POTTERY TECHNIQUES.

SLIPWARE. Pottery decorated by the use of SLIP. Slipware is known from many parts of the world. It was a very common form of decoration in the Pre-Columbian pottery of Central and Southern America. Both positive and negative slip decoration was used. Nazca pots were painted in as many as eight different colours on a background of slip. A slip is commonly applied in African domestic pottery and the Kabyles of north Africa use both a red and a white slip. From the 9th to the 11th centuries slip-painted pottery was produced in Iran, Turkestan and Afghanistan. Finds of this pottery, which was often decorated with inscriptions in Kufic script, have been associated with Nishapur and Samarkand. A similar type of slip-painted ware was made at Iznik in the 14th c. before the Ottoman rule. A second Iznik type, made from the latter part of the 14th c. to the end of the 15th c., sometimes called 'Miletus ware', is of red clay, painted in black, blue and green on a white ground slip under a clear GLAZE. In south-eastern England during the 14th and 15th centuries jugs were painted with a brushed slip and the black-glazed 'Cistercian' ware decorated with trailed white slip patterns foreshadowed the slipwares of the 17th c. made at Wrotham in Kent and Harlow in Essex. During the 17th c.

Staffordshire became the main centre of a widely disseminated manufacture of slipware, the most celebrated examples of which are large slip-trailed dishes associated with the name of Thomas Toft. In the 20th c. the tradition of slipware was revived by artist-potters both in England and in the U.S.A. In England the pioneers were Bernard Leach and his pupil Michael Cardew. In the United States Mary Louise McLaughlin with a group of amateur ceramic painters of Cincinnati developed a technique of underglaze painting in coloured slips; Maria Longworth Storer, also of Cincinnati, founded the Rookwood pottery in 1880 and much of the Rookwood wares were decorated with flowers in the Japanese style painted in coloured slips beneath the glaze. See CERAMICS and POTTERY TECHNIQUES.

SLODTZ. Family of French sculptors and designers originating from Antwerp. They were SÉBASTIEN (1655–1726) and his three sons: SÉBASTIEN-ANTOINE (1695–1754), PAUL-AMBROISE (1702–58) and RENÉ-MICHEL called Michel-Ange (1705–64). All three sons followed MEISSONNIER at the Menus-Plaisirs and all three were prominent as designers in the ROCOCO manner for furniture, ironwork, etc. Among their designs is one for the famous commode made by Jacques CAFFIERI in 1738 for the Chambre du Roi at Versailles and a medal cabinet now at the Bibliothèque nationale.

SMITH, GEORGE. English cabinet-maker, upholsterer and designer, established in business in Cavendish Square, London, *c.* 1804. He is best known for his book *A Collection of Designs for Household Furniture and Interior Decoration in the Most Approved and Elegant Taste*, which was issued in two parts each with 50 plates in 1805 and subsequently incorporated in a book of 158 plates published in 1808. He declares that he is guided by the finest specimens of ancient Roman, Greek and EGYPTIAN styles, though he also includes examples of the GOTHIC and CHINESE, and he says that for tasteful and picturesque design an exact examination of antique models is required, 'taking not so much the mere pattern or imitation but the spirit and principle on which the original was composed'. Unfortunately, unlike the work of Thomas HOPE, his designs betray no first-hand knowledge of antique examples. None the less Smith's designs had considerable influence on, and are interestingly revealing of, REGENCY taste. In 1812 he published *A Collection of Ornamental Designs after the Manner of the Ancients*. By the 1820s he had built up a flourishing business in Golden Square, London, describing himself as 'Upholsterer and Furniture Draughtsman to His Majesty and Principal of the Drawing Academy'. In 1826 he published *The Cabinet-Makers' and Upholsterers' Guide, Drawing Book and Repository of New and Original Designs for Household Furniture*. The plates illustrate the heavy and over-ornamented trends of style at the end of the GEORGIAN period and herald the transition to Victorianism. No furniture by Smith has been identified.

SMOCKING. A NEEDLEWORK technique used at least since the Middle Ages in dressmaking, embroidery, etc. It consists of an ornamental gathering of surplus material. The traditional patterns of the smock-frock worn in some parts of the English countryside down to the beginning of the 20th c. varied according to the locality and the trade of the wearer. See also EMBROIDERY.

SMYRNA CARPETS. See TURKISH RUGS.

SNAPHAUNCE (from Dutch or German *Schnapphahn*, snap cock). An alternative device to the wheel-lock for firing a hand gun without the use of a slow match. Whereas the wheel-lock produced sparks by the rotation of a wheel against iron pyrites, the principle of the snaphaunce was to produce sparks by striking a flint against steel. It therefore belonged to the general family of flintlocks, and in fact the word 'snaphaunce' was applied generally to all types of flintlock during the 17th c. and into the 18th c. Modern historians, however, tend to reserve 'flintlock' for the improved type of mechanism which was invented in France early in the 17th c. and to use 'snaphaunce' for models where the striking steel is separate from the pan cover.

The flint was held in a dog, called a 'cock', which was worked by a strong spring. The lock was set by bending back the cock with the thumb until it engaged with a horizontal sear, which held it in position. When this was released by pulling the trigger the spring brought down the cock sharply, striking the flint against a steel plate (the hammer) so positioned that a stream of sparks was directed into the priming pan. The earliest snaphaunces had an external mainspring and this continued to be used in the Spanish miquelet; but elsewhere by the latter part of the 16th c. the mainspring was usually inside the lock. The priming pan was provided with a cover for protection and to avoid the clumsy necessity of opening it manually the pan was connected by a lever with the cock so that it opened automatically when the cock descended and brought the flint against the hammer. One of the main characteristics of the 'true' flintlock was to combine pan cover and striking steel in one.

The snaphaunce had the advantage over the wheel-lock that it was simpler, cheaper to manufacture and on the whole more reliable in operation. The earliest known snaphaunces are Scandinavian, but it is thought that these were introduced from Germany or Holland and that the snaphaunce type of spark-firing gun was first made in Germany or Holland *c.* 1540. The earliest surviving German snaphaunces are from the 1570s. The snaphaunce was current in France during the last quarter of the 16th c.

A French snaphaunce musket from the 1570s with walnut stock inlaid with engraved horn is in the Pitt Rivers Museum, Oxford.

SNUFF-BOXES. Snuff reached the Western world from the North American Indians. Its introduction throughout Europe was due to the 16th-c. French Ambassador to Portugal, Jean Nicot, whose name is remembered in that of the herb *Nicotiana tabacum.* Its use quickly spread from one country to another, reaching England by way of Ireland and Scotland; a carved and painted wood figure of a costumed Highlander in the act of taking snuff was at one time the sign outside a snuff-seller's premises. By the 18th c. the habit was so much a part of daily life that boxes containing the powder were carried about the person. The man-in-the-street had boxes made of horn, copper or brass, wood, TORTOISE-SHELL and ENAMELLED copper; but the fashionable were content with nothing less than gem-encrusted gold, silver, ivory or something equally exotic. The snuff-box became a splendid object of male JEWELLERY and every device of the goldsmith and jeweller was employed in its adornment. It was said of a fastidious English nobleman, Lord Petersham (1753–1829), that he owned so many snuff-boxes he could select a different one on each day of the year, carefully choosing an example appropriate to the weather and the company he was likely to meet.

The Scots favoured containers known as 'mulls', which were made from the ends of cattle horns. For a formal dinner a table mull was sometimes provided and would be circulated in the manner of port. The more imposing of them are in the shape of a complete ram's head, the horn tips set with cairngorms, and in addition to one or more snuff-containers they are equipped with chained spoons, a small rake and a hare's foot.

The most elaborately designed boxes were made by the French in the reigns of Louis XV and Louis XVI, and Parisian pattern-books set the fashion elsewhere. The goldsmiths of Paris employed coloured gold, enamels and precious stones in some of the most costly extravagances, which rival the creations of jewellers. German goldsmiths joined forces with lapidaries to acquire a reputation for boxes carved skilfully from rare stones mounted in gold with jewels, and for others of gold patterned with specimen stones. London produced boxes of agate or bloodstone mounted in pierced or chiselled gold, and in most other European lands comparably luxurious boxes were made. At the close of the 18th c. Paris gave way to Geneva as the centre of the industry. Swiss craftsmen of the early 19th c. specialized in enamelled gold boxes fitted with watches, musical movements, and automata. The space remaining for holding snuff was negligible, and the designs no longer showed the fantasy of the mid 18th c.

Snuff-boxes were often decorated with an enamel miniature portrait. The French miniaturist J. Petitot produced large numbers of portraits of contemporary celebrities for this purpose, as did many other less well known artists. It was not unusual for a snuff-box to be equipped with a false lid concealing some erotic subject painted in enamels.

In the course of the 18th c. it became a practice for monarchs to present snuff-boxes as a mark of honour instead of a gold chain as before. Ambassadors were particularly singled out for such gifts, and following the Congress of Vienna in 1814–15 the senior British Plenipotentiary received enough boxes for the gold to be re-made into an inkstand. The custom of presenting snuff-boxes continued for some time after snuff-taking had ceased to be fashionable.

Also connected with the ritual of 'snuffing' were graters, with which the earlier devotees powdered their hard twists of tobacco leaf. Some French and Flemish examples of carved ivory have survived from the late 17th c. and early 18th centuries. An 18th-c. refinement was a tiny silver spoon for ladling the powder from box to hand, but genuine specimens of these are very scarce.

508, 547.

SOAP-STONE. Otherwise known as steatite, potstone, pagodite or algamatolite, soap-stone is a massive form of talc, and is a silicate of magnesium similar in chemical composition to JADE but differing from it in being the softest craft material in common use for carving. Soap-stone has a hardness of only 1 on the MOHS SCALE and can easily be scratched with a finger nail. It occurs in a wide variety of colours, some of which resemble those of jade and which include: white, grey, yellow, green, red, brown and black. It is often coloured in banded layers, which can be cut through to produce a contrasting pattern. Soap-stone is very widely distributed. A belt of deposits runs down North America between the Rocky Mountains and the eastern seaboard. It is found in many parts of the British Isles, such as Cornwall and Wales, and also in Scandinavia, France and Italy. Large deposits occur in Africa. It is present in China, India and the Arctic.

Soap-stone occupies a unique place among the minerals of the world because of its multifarious uses. It has been eaten by Indians in North America and by Africans in Senegal, used as soap by the Arabs, and made into sculptures and useful articles.

Objects made from soap-stone include cooking utensils and lamps, cylinder seals and stamp seals, statuettes, bottles and inkstands, and architectural units such as roof bosses, finials, balustrades, panels and lintels. It is a favourite stone for making images of deities because though soft, it will carve into the finest detail and polishes easily; indeed it is this which has earned it the name 'agalmatolite' (Greek: stone from which images are produced) and in China 'pagolite'. It will mark cloth, and the familiar 'tailor's chalk' is made from processed steatite. It has also been used for pencils in Burma. Whereas many minerals will splinter if exposed to heat, soap-stone can be made into stoves, lamps and cooking-pots (hence its name of 'potstone'). Supposedly the raw material is softer when just mined than after it has been exposed to the air for some time. Although it readily chips and scratches, and most old soap-stone carvings have been broken at least once, steatite needs little maintenance and it will retain a polish which has once been imparted to it. Because it is readily available in many localities, and because it is so easy to work, it has always had a double appeal: to the primitive craftsman, such as the Eskimo or Bantu, whose tools would not enable him to carve hard stone; and to more sophisticated artists who wanted to make a large number of fairly similar carvings in a hurry or carry out some very intricate carving which would not be possible in a harder material. Although palaces have been built with soap-stone in India, it is usually claimed that it will not stand weathering or any kind of out-of-doors conditions.

Carving methods have varied from the primitive to the elaborate. When the Eskimos began carving soap-stone for lamps and cooking-pots they used such tools as they had—flint knives in bone hafts. When in the 20th c., however, foreign patrons urged them to begin making aesthetic carvings and block prints, they brought modern tools with them in the aeroplanes or dog-sleighs which they used for their visits. Photographs of modern Eskimo carvers show them holding these tools, hacksaws for example. In India traditional carving methods have evolved since the first carvings began to be made 5000 years ago.

In the Indus Valley civilizations centred on Mohenjo-daro and Harappa stamp seals were engraved with figures of animals or mythological scenes and before use the carvings were heated to a hard, lustrous finish like enamel. Small sculptures were also made and pots, bowls and plates were carved and fired. Through the Middle Ages to our own day soap-stone carving has continued to be an important craft in India. It was used for fine decorative work, as on the Orissa temples, or for making small figures of deities such as those bought by pilgrims at Puri as a memento of their visit to the famous temple of Jaganath. Bowls made from soap-stone have always been popular with orthodox Brahmins in India as they can be re-used after a meal instead of being broken, like earthenware, which may only be employed once. Soap-stone has been turned on a lathe for balustrades, sawn into blocks, marked out with a bamboo in pigment and then carved by means of long, thin chisels with flat edges. A long, pointed chisel was used for the final dressing. Finally the soapstone was polished with steel powder (made by pulverizing a lump of steel with a hammer) and with a rubber, half a centimetre wide by 12·7 cm long, made from a heated mixture of sealing wax and *kurvundam* dust (a powdered silicate rock) in equal proportions. The final polish was given by steel powder applied with a lead brick. This turned the soap-stone black and very glossy. The hereditary castes of soap-stone carvers, such as the Asari class in Devanahali, Bangalore, acquired great skill and expedition through generations of practice. They could carve chains of linked rings, or turn out a bird, an ink-stand or some other quite elaborate trifle, in less than a forenoon's work. Sesame oil and human milk were smeared on some stones to expedite the work of carving, and they may have been employed on soap-stone as well.

In China the traditional home of soap-stone carving is Fukien province, particularly the cities such as Fuchow. Chekiang province was also an important centre. One of the most highly reputed branches of the art consisted in making stamp seals. An artist or calligrapher might use hundreds of these during his life time, yet each of them must give a calligraphically perfect print. It is known from literary sources that seals were carved with a knife. Other tools used can be deduced from the carvings themselves, which show marks of a saw, a drill, a straight-edged tool such as a graver, a knife and abrasives. The hollowed out parts of carvings have been made with a toothed scraper.

Soap-stone was used in Ming and Ching times, mainly for figures of deities, carvings for the study table, flower vases of all sorts and seals. Most of the Chinese carvings which have reached the West, often as sailors' souvenirs, are particularly hideous, but some of the best work shows real perception and finish, and has found its way into museums. The Chinese preferred red and white streaky stone, and a dark brown.

Some of the best soap-stone comes from Italy, and the town of Pleurs, near Lake Como, collapsed and was destroyed when the mine workings underneath it caved in in 1618. A soap-stone oven remained intact in the Valais for centuries, while for many years the monastery of St. Bernard had a stove made of soap-stone.

The most striking development in modern soapstone carving has been the Arctic Renaissance. Eskimos, inspired by social well-wishers, have begun to make toys, models and even stone block-prints. These carvings are a new development by a people who only used soap-stone for kitchen equipment in the past, and who have now been deprived of their traditional carving material, walrus IVORY. The work of artists uncontaminated by the art schools, these carvings display spontaneity and natural talent which has been recognized by connoisseurs.

712.

SOFT-PASTE. Term used for the imitation PORCELAIN manufactured from the end of the 16th c. in Italy and *c.* the middle of the 17th c. in France before the secret of true Chinese or 'hard-paste' porcelain was discovered. The term 'Chinese soft-paste', however, refers to a natural white-firing clay body, Hua-shih, from the province of Kiangsi, which came into use in the 18th c. See CHINA (CERAMICS); CERAMICS; POTTERY TECHNIQUES; PORCELAIN.

SOHO TAPESTRIES. It is common practice to ascribe all English tapestries of the 18th c. to Soho looms, though some of the smaller pieces, furniture-coverings and the like, were certainly made elsewhere, at establishments such as Le Blon's at Chelsea, inaugurated about 1723, and Parisot's at Fulham, which closed down in 1755.

It is, however, true that the more important workshops were situated in the Soho area. John Vanderbank, best known for sets of the Elements after Lebrun (1619–90), and for CHINOISERIE tapestries based on the designs of Oriental LACQUER work, was established in Great Queen Street from 1689; he died in 1727. Very elegant ARABESQUE tapestries, with vases of flowers and exotic birds, were produced by Joshua Morris, resident in Frith Street in 1726. Paul Saunders of Soho (d. 1770) wove romantic Oriental subjects after designs by Francesco Zuccarelli (1702–88), while subjects adapted from Watteau (1684–1721) were woven and signed by a certain Bradshaw, probably George Smith Bradshaw of Soho. The products of these Soho workshops, while hardly comparable with the best French tapestries of the period, are of good quality and excellent decorative effect.

SORG, JÖRG, the Younger (d. 1603). Armour-etcher of Augsburg, the son of JÖRG Sorg the Elder by his second wife, daughter of the distinguished armourer Kolman HELMSCHMIED. His work has been identified from an album of pen and wash drawings of forty-five armours he decorated between 1548 and 1563, now preserved in the State Library, Stuttgart. Like the similar *Jacobe Album* (see GREENWICH ARMOURY) this is concerned more with decoration than with form. On each drawing is written the name of the owner of the suit concerned and also that of the armourer responsible for making it. Most of the important Augsburg armourers of the period are included and distinguished owners both in and outside Germany. Armour etched by Sorg is in the Kunsthistorisches Museum, Vienna; Tower of London Armouries; Metropolitan Museum, New York. See ARMS AND ARMOUR.

SPANISH WORK. See EMBROIDERY (SPAIN AND PORTUGAL).

SPÄT, CASPAR. See MUNICH SCHOOL.

SPECULUM. See MIRRORS.

SPIDER SILK. In addition to moths, spiders also spin silk-like threads. Their extreme fineness (the diameter is $\frac{1}{40}$ that of a human hair) explains their only use by man: the forming of the cross-wires in optical instruments. Like real silk these threads are made from protein, and their molecular structure is similar to that of high-polymer man-made fibres. Most spiders have three pairs of spinnerettes connected to different kinds of gland. From these they are able to produce six different kinds of thread, each adapted to some special purpose. These include drag-line thread, by which the spider moves about like a rock climber who belays his rope; the frame and radial threads of the web, which have to be strong but not too elastic; the spiral thread, whose high elasticity helps to trap insects; cocoon thread formed from multi-strand crimped filaments with good heat-insulating properties and an effective barrier against predators; an attachment disc for anchoring the drag line; and finally a swathing band with which the spider binds its prey. A full account of this subject by F. Lucas is in *Discovery*, January 1964.

SPINDLER, JOHANN FRIEDRICH and HEINRICH WILHELM. Brothers, German cabinet-makers who after working for the court at Bayreuth came to Berlin in 1762 and made furniture for the palaces of Frederick the Great at Potsdam and Berlin. They worked in the ROCOCO style of NAHL and excelled in sumptuous polychromatic MARQUETRY.

SPINEL. One of a group of minerals which has had considerable importance as a gemstone. It has a hardness index of 8 on the MOHS SCALE, very slightly less than the SAPPHIRE and RUBY. Natural spinel occurs in brown, red, orange and pink as well as blue and violet. The most prized spinel is the clear crimson red, which under the name 'balas ruby' was formerly confused with the true ruby. Indeed many of the large historical 'rubies' have been spinels. The most celebrated source of spinel has been Badakhshan in central Asia; it also occurs in Burma, Thailand, India, Ceylon, Madagascar and Australia. Synthetic spinels, including yellow, green and colourless, are also made by the Verneuil process.

SPINNING. This process is described under WEAVING. See also TEXTILE MANUFACTURE IN ANTIQUITY (SPINNING).

SPOONS. See CUTLERY and SILVER.

SPUN-SILK. Spun-silk yarns are composed of silk filaments made by dressing and spinning processes from WASTE. They contrast with nett silk, which is reeled from the cocoon.

STEVENGRAPHS. Woven SILK pictures and portraits produced at Coventry from 1879. The name is derived from that of Thomas Stevens (1828–88), a silk-weaver of Coventry. He was trained in the ribbon industry and in 1854 opened his own business in which he attempted to adapt the Jacquard loom to WEAVING designs in colour, using perforated cards for the manipulation of the warp threads. By 1863 he had developed the process sufficiently to be able to offer for sale woven silk bookmarks with elaborate floral designs, texts, etc., of which he claimed to have produced 900. In 1875 he opened a factory under the name Stevengraph Works and from 1879 produced coloured silk pictures which were issued in cardboard mounts. The factory continued in operation until 1914. Over 200 different subjects have been recorded, including representations of famous Victorian politicians, sportsmen and other celebrites, historical scenes and contemporary events. These Stevengraphs are sought after by collectors of Victoriana on both sides of the Atlantic.

Stevengraphs were not the only or the first pictures woven in silk. The earliest one known was a portrait of J. M. Jacquard, the inventor of the Jacquard loom. It was done in 1839 by François Carquillat (1803–84), an artist-weaver of Lyon, and was based on a portrait of Jacquard by C. Bonnefond (Mus. Historique des Tissues, Lyon). An example of Carquillat's portrait of Jacquard is in the Victoria and Albert Museum. Carquillat also did a woven silk portrait of the German naturalist Baron Alexander von Humboldt.

A stimulus to ingenuity was given when the removal of the tariff on imported silk goods threatened decline to the ribbon industry in England. A consortium of Coventry manufacturers produced a specially designed and woven ribbon for the Great Exhibition of 1851 (V. and A. Mus. and Herbert Art Gall. and Mus., Coventry). Other makers of silk pictures were: John Caldicott; John & Joseph Cash, who in 1863 made a rosette for the wedding of Prince Edward; Dalton, Barton & Co. Ltd., who were noted for their woven silk portraits and bookmarks of members of the Royal Family; William Henry Grant, J.P., known for portraits of Gladstone and Queen Victoria; and J. Ratliff & Son, pre-eminent as weavers of wide decorative ribbons.

310, 523, 785.

STIEGEL, HENRY WILLIAM (1729–85). German immigrant who opened glass factories in Pennsylvania in 1763 and exercised an important influence on early United States glass manufacture. See GLASS (AMERICA).

STONE CHINA (also called IRONSTONE). Trade name for heavy English EARTHENWARE. See CERAMICS.

STONEWARE. Wares made from CLAYS fired at temperatures between *c.* 1200° C. and 1280° C. The body vitrifies and is impermeable to water. See CERAMICS.

STOOL. The oldest form of normally backless seat for a single person. Stools are recorded from ancient Egypt in the 3rd millennium B.C. and were a common article of furniture in antiquity. (See GREEK AND ROMAN ANTIQUITY, FURNITURE.) There have been many types of stools designed for specific purposes and known under particular names, as for example: the X-stool with an X-shaped structural frame, which was used in Egypt *c.* 1350 B.C. and several varieties of which were known to the Greco-Roman world; the medieval faldstool or folding stool often used in church; the Scottish cutty stool or 'creepie' also for use in church before pews were introduced in Scotland; the close stool or necessary stool; the gouty stool for the afflicted; the adjustable and revolving music stool; the three-legged milking stool; and so on.

In Africa low wooden stool seats are an important item of everyday and ceremonial furniture. In many tribes the stool denotes the office of chief or king as does the throne in some European countries. Thus the expression 'the Ashanti stool' carries a similar meaning to 'the English throne'. Traditional shapes and designs of stools serve specific functions and are the prerogative of particular ranks. Much religious symbolism is associated with the stool. The Golden Stool of the Ashanti has been believed to house the spirit of the tribe and ceremonially 'blackened' stools feature in the cult devoted to the spirits of ancestors. Some account of the ceremonial importance of the stool is given in *The Sacred Stools of the Akan* by the Revd. Dr. Peter Sarpong, Catholic Bishop of Kumasi, published by the Ghana Publishing Corporation in 1971.

According to Guaman Poma de Ayala, under the regime of the Inca in the Central Andes the height, material and decoration of ceremonial stools were determined in accordance with the ranks of officials.

STORR, PAUL (1771–1844). English silversmith. The son of a London silver chaser, who later turned licensed victualler, he was apprenticed in 1785 to an Anglo-Swedish plate-worker, Andrew Fogelberg. In 1792 he set up business in partnership with William Frisbee, dissolved the partnership and set up on his own in 1796 and in 1811 entered into partnership with the jeweller Philip Rundell, though continuing to use his own mark on silver made under his direction. In 1819 he left the firm of Rundells and from 1822 to 1838 worked in partnership with John Mortimer. He retired in 1839.

Storr was responsible for a very large output of utilitarian and decorative plate, from simple cutlery to elaborate centre-pieces and candelabra. His name, however, was made chiefly in the field of presentation silver such as the 'Battle of the Nile Cup' presented to Lord Nelson by the Governors and Company of the Merchants of England Trading in the Levant Seas and the 'Anglesey Victory Trophy' presented to Lieutenant-General Lord Paget. Storr worked in the NEO-CLASSICAL style and was skilled in adapting to the medium of silver designs by artists familiar with other media such as the sculptor Flaxman, the painter Stodhard and the sculptor-painter William Theed. He also produced work in a revival ROCOCO style inspired perhaps by silver brought over by French emigrés.

During the lifetime of Paul Storr the status of the goldsmith and silversmith changed from that of craftsman to manufacturer or merchant as the industrialization of the trade proceeded apace.

413, 659.

STRAPWORK. Type of ornamental pattern in architecture and the decorative arts consisting of interlacing bands or straps sometimes combined with foliage and resembling fretwork or cut leather. It was popular in northern Europe in the second half of the 16th and early 17th centuries, being generally used in ceilings, screens and funerary ornaments. It was common in Elizabethan England. Late BAROQUE decoration also included delicate foliated strapwork based on designs by Jean BÉRAIN. It formed part of the repertory of the CHIPPENDALE style of furniture. It is found in American furniture from the 17th c. onwards.

STUMPWORK. Modern name for relief embroidery in which human figures and other subjects are worked over shaped blocks of wood or padding. Embroidery of this kind was practised in Europe from the 15th c. onwards. It was a favourite technique of the Stuart embroiderers, who used it with great ingenuity for such articles as needlework pictures, miniature cabinets and mirror-frames. It was known at that time as 'raised work'. See EMBROIDERY.

SUMAK. Name given to a class of rugs made in the neighbourhood of Shemakha in the Caucasus, and to the technique by which they are made. This technique, used also in Persian and early Scandinavian weaving, is related to that of TAPESTRY, but the weft-threads, instead of passing over and under alternate warp-threads, travel forward over several (usually four) warp-threads and back under a smaller number (usually two) continuously. See also CARPETS AND RUGS.

SUTTON HOO. The site of some fifteen Anglo-Saxon burial mounds, outside the small town of Woodbridge, near Ipswich, in Suffolk. The largest of these mounds, a ship burial, was uncovered in 1939 and a report of the excavations by C. W. Phillips, who was in charge of the work, was published in *Antiquaries Journal*, xx (1940). On the evidence of a purse of thirty-seven miscellaneous gold coins found among the grave goods the burial is dated to the years following *c.* A.D. 625–30. No body was found in the grave. But the evidence points with some probability to its having been the burial of Raedwald (d. 624 or 625), Bretwalda or High King of East Anglia, who was converted to Christianity but subsequently relapsed. Less likely are considered to be Ecgric (d. 635/6) or Raedwald's son Eorpwald (d. 627/8 or 632/3).

The grave goods discovered in this barrow have been called 'the most marvellous find in the archaeological annals of England' and point to a level of craftsmanship not hitherto encountered. They revealed for the first time the standard of pagan Anglo-Saxon culture at the royal level.

The gold jewellery, more than twenty pieces, consists of buckles, clasps, ornamental studs, etc. and most of the pieces are jewelled with GARNETS set by a cloisonné technique. More than 4,000 individually cut garnets were used. Some of the pieces are also ornamented with MILLEFIORI glass. The most important item is a solid gold belt buckle weighing 414·62 g. It is decorated with interlacing animal patterns partly picked out in NIELLO in a style similar to that found in early Swedish boat-graves. Outstanding also are a purse-lid whose gold frame is spectacularly ornamented with garnets and millefiori glass and a sword with jewelled gold pommel, two filigree gold mounts on the hilt and gold quillon mounts. The craftsmanship is of a very high standard and the pieces appear to have come from one workshop. The sixteen pieces of silver, on the contrary, appear to have come from eastern Europe or the Near East. In craftsmanship they are inferior to the silver found in the MILDENHALL treasure. They include: a large dish (72·4 cm in diameter) dated by control stamps to the reign of Anastasius (A.D. 491–518) but with incised ornament in a style belonging to *c.* 100 years earlier; a set of ten shallow circular bowls and a large fluted bowl (*c.* 40 cm in diameter) ornamented with a profile female head in a clumsy classical manner; a long-handled ladle decorated with fine beading round the rim and with gilded triangles under the rim and on the faces of carinated moulding a third of the way up the body; and a pair of spoons engraved with the names Paulos and Saulos in Greek letters.

Among other objects of interest are the remains of a large circular shield, of a shattered iron helmet and of a musical instrument which has been reconstructed as a round Germanic lyre. There was also a group of crushed and partially disintegrated drinking vessels, six of which were of maplewood and two of large aurochs horns. The latter had silver-gilt mounts at the rim and bird's-head finials with silver-gilt foil patterns at their terminals.

599.

SWAG. See FESTOON.

SWASTIKA. A cross with four equal arms intersecting at right angles and limbs projecting at right angles from the end of each arm, all in the same direction. The word is derived from the Sanskrit *svasti*: well-being. The left-handed or anti-clockwise cross is known in India as *suavastika*.

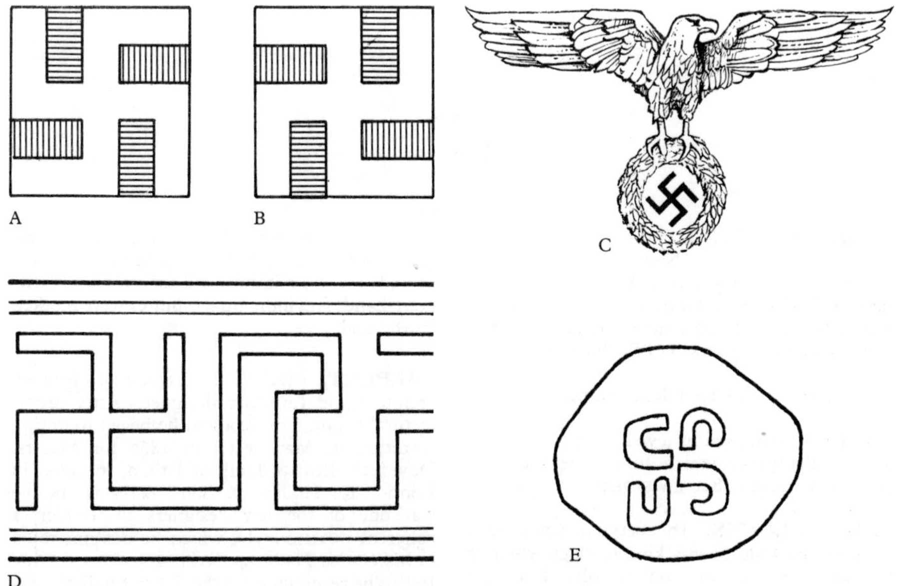

A. swastika; B. left-handed swastika or *suavastika*; C. Nazi emblem; D. swastika and meander from Greek vase; E. gammadion from Corinthian coin, *c.* 500 B.C.

The swastika is one of the oldest and most widely disseminated of all decorative symbols. It was used in the Mediterranean countries and the Near East from *c.* the 3rd millennium B.C. and remained one of the commonest decorative devices except possibly in Egypt, Babylon and Assyria. It occurs in the Minoan civilization of Crete, in the Mycenaean and in Greece, the Aegean Islands and Etruria. It is found in the catacombs and on Roman mosaics, and it was widely used in Gaul and western Europe. It is known from prehistoric times in central Asia, China and India and it was also familiar to Pre-Columbian America. As a black cross on a white disc the swastika in modern times was revived by Hitler as the emblem of Nazi Germany.

There has been much speculation about the significance of the swastika symbol. Some have argued that it represents the solar wheel with rays and feet at the extremities so as to symbolize the power and movement of the sun. This explanation was common in the Middle Ages. Some have thought that it symbolized the four cardinal directions. In Christian symbolism, as a form of the Cross, it appears to have stood for the resurrection or Second Coming. And generally it has had the implications of regeneration or revival—which appears to have been the significance attached to it by Hitler as a national emblem. There is no certainty, however, that the swastika bore the same significance wherever it was used or indeed that it was always more than a purely decorative motif. Nor is it unlikely that a form of swastika device may have arisen independently at different times in different parts of the world. In Greece it was closely associated with the *gammadion*, a form in which the arms do not intersect but which resembles four gammas in combination. It has also been associated with the Anglo-Saxon *fylfot* cross.

901, 922.

SWINGER. See HORSE-BRASSES.

T

TABER, ELNATHAN (1784–1854). American clock-maker born in New Bedford, Massachusetts, of Quaker parents. After being apprenticed to Simon WILLARD he set up in business at Roxbury as a maker of MANTEL CLOCKS. In 1839 he took over the goodwill of Willard's business.

TABERNACLE CLOCKS. See TABLE CLOCKS.

TABLE. Term used by jewellers and lapidaries for the flat plane which forms the top of a faceted gemstone. See JEWELLERY.

TABLE CLOCKS. In everyday language a table clock would be any kind of clock which is normally kept or used on a table. But as a technical descriptive term it is normally used to describe only the spring-driven clocks in gilt metal cases of the 16th and 17th centuries. The earliest of these, made by German and French craftsmen, were usually in the form of small drums, about 5 cm high and a few cm in diameter, with the dial on the upper face. They had a single hour-hand, and touch-pins were often placed outside the hour numerals to enable the time to be 'felt' at night. In some examples the curved surface of the drum was quite plain, in others finely engraved. Horizontal table clocks were also often made with square, hexagonal or octagonal cases. Some were quite elaborate, with astronomical indications of the position of the sun, moon and some stars on the main dial, and subsidiary dials giving calendar indications and showing the hour last struck by the striking mechanism. About the middle of the 16th c. clocks of upright form, with the dial on the side, began to appear in north France and Germany: these are generally referred to as 'tabernacle clocks'. The French examples were usually in the form of a small hexagonal two-storied tower, with the dial visible through a circular aperture. In Germany the usual form was a square tower surmounted by an open spire inside which the bell was supported, or by a pierced dome covering the bell. The sides of the tower were usually engraved with simple landscapes or allegorical figures and subjects. Many German tabernacle clocks were also provided with extra dials giving astronomical and calendrical information. Two especially fine examples are those made by Jeremias Metzker of Augsburg in 1563 and 1564.

The simpler tabernacle clocks were normally provided with only a single hour-hand, but from *c.* 1560 onwards occasional examples were given a separate small dial divided into quarter hours and a hand rotating once an hour. More rarely still the main dial, as in modern practice, was provided with a minute-hand concentric with the hour-hand, and individual minutes were marked on the dial.

TALBERT, BRUCE J. (1838–81). English architect and furniture designer. After architectural training in Scotland he began to design furniture in Manchester in 1862 for Messrs. Doveston, Bird & Hull, and then, in 1865, in London for Holland & Sons. Like PUGIN, he was one of the few designers to develop a coherent GOTHIC style, which he demonstrated in his *Gothic Forms applied to Furniture* (1867). In this he recommended the 'Early English' style for 'its great breadth and simplicity', with 'construction honestly shown'. In 1876 he published *Examples of Ancient and Modern Furniture*, in which he abandoned the Gothic for the Jacobean style. Talbert was one of the earliest professional furniture designers to become known internationally. Examples of his furniture, including the well known 'Pet Sideboard', made by GILLOW and exhibited in London in 1873, are in the Victoria and Albert Museum.

TALBOT, WILLIAM HENRY FOX (1800–77). English scientist and mathematician. For his attainments in the latter field he was elected Fellow of the Royal Society in 1831. He is now chiefly remembered for his work in developing the photographic process known as calotype (see PHOTOGRAPHY), which was the chief rival of the DAGUERREOTYPE. He patented the calotype process in England in 1841 and in America in 1847. The American rights were bought in 1849 by William and Frederick Langeheim, professional portrait daguerreotypists of Philadelphia, but the process did not find favour in the States and they were bankrupt in 1851. In June 1844 Talbot published *The Pencil of Nature*, the first photographically illustrated book in the world. In 1852 he developed steel plates for use in photomechanical reproduction.

TALLBOY. A high chest with seven or more drawers, divided into two sections by a cornice. The term came into use in the course of the 18th c. as an alternative for 'chest-on-chest', but the furniture type was introduced in the late 17th c. as a development from a high chest of drawers on a stand. In the United States of America the term 'HIGHBOY' is used.

TAMBOUR. (1) A circular frame consisting of one hoop fitting inside another, in which material is stretched for embroidery. See EMBROIDERY (TECHNIQUES).

(2) Cabinet-maker's term for a thin and flexible shutter or door running in guiding grooves, as for example the top of a roll-top desk. Tambour covers for writing-tables and desks were introduced into England from France in the late 18th c. and tambour doors for small articles of furniture were mentioned in SHERATON's *The Cabinet Dictionary* (1803).

TAMBOUR TABLE. Tambour writing-tables and sewing-tables were mentioned by SHERATON in *The Cabinet Dictionary* (1803), though he noted that the former had almost gone out of use as they were considered insecure and liable to injury. They were introduced into America during the Classical Revival period (1780–1810). See FURNITURE (AMERICAN).

TAPA. A general word which in many Polynesian languages has the meaning 'edge' or 'border'. In Samoa it was also used for the uncoloured border of a piece of decorated BARK CLOTH, there called *siapo*. In Hawaii bark cloth was called *kapa*, the Hawaiian variant of *tapa*, but in other Polynesian islands bark cloth had other names. It was owing to the white whalers that the term *tapa* came into general use in the course of the 19th c. as a technical term for bark cloth and has since been applied not only to Oceanic bark cloth but also to that from Africa and South America. An interesting account of techniques and patterns of Oceanic bark cloth will be found in the chapter '*Tapa* Techniques and *Tapa* Patterns in Polynesia: A Regional Differentiation' by Simon Kooijman in *Primitive Art and Society* (1973) edited by Anthony Forge.

TAPESTRY

1. Technique 2. History

1. TECHNIQUE. A tapestry is a decorative fabric made by weaving coloured weft threads alternatively over and under the warps to form a pictorial or ornamental design, and should not be confused with EMBROIDERY. The wefts do not pass from selvage to selvage, but only as far as their colour is required by the pattern. They are then battened firmly down so that eventually the warps are completely hidden. Tapestries were woven on either a high-warp or a low-warp loom. With the former, which stood upright, the warps were parted manually, while the latter was placed horizontally and the warps controlled by harnesses attached to treadles. The low-warp method was considerably faster and although it was considered inferior in the Middle Ages, it is virtually impossible to distinguish on which type of loom a tapestry was woven as the results appear identical. The weaver copied the design from a cartoon which in the case of high-warp weaving stood behind him. As he worked from the back of the tapestry mirrors were placed in front so that by looking through the warps he could see how his work was progressing. With the low-warp method the cartoon lay underneath the loom and so was less easily visible. Another disadvantage was that the weaver could not see his work until it was completed. A swinging loom was perfected by Vaucanson in 1757 that enabled the weaver to check the front of his work more easily. While the warps could be of wool, linen or hemp, the wefts were characteristically of wool, although SILKS and silver and gold threads were also used for richer effects. In the Middle Ages only 15 to 20 dyes were used, but this number steadily increased and in France by the end of the 18th c. some 400 to 500 colour tones were in use.

Each coloured yarn is carried on a separate bobbin and as the design is gradually built up the bobbin is passed over and under the warps until the pattern calls for a different colour. Then the old bobbin is left hanging and a new one is taken up. The pattern may be built up one line of weft at a time, the weaver dropping one bobbin and taking up the next as the design changes. Or one colour design may be completed before taking up the next. The latter technique requires the more skill as it is difficult to keep the weft lines even. It was used, among others, for the Chinese k'o-ssŭ. Tapestries may be made to be seen from one side only, as were the GOBELINS and most European tapestries, with the backs unfinished and the yarn ends hanging loose. Or—as the majority of the ancient Peruvian tapestries—the two sides may be identical in pattern and equally well finished, the ends of the yarns being hidden between the warps.

The fineness of a tapestry is judged by the number of wefts to the centimetre. The coarse Gobelins average eight and the finest European tapestries about 33. In ancient Peruvian tapestry weaving 80 wefts to the centimetre is not uncommon and one piece has been recorded with an average of 130 running up to 200 in parts of the design.

2. HISTORY. Little is known of the origins of European tapestry. Gallic weavers were referred to by the Romans (Pliny, *Nat. Hist.* viii) and it seems probable that they produced textiles woven with the tapestry technique. It has been suggested that tapestry weaving was introduced to southern Europe by the Arabs in the 8th c. The Crusades later did much to increase European contacts with the Middle East, where for several centuries weaving had been a thriving craft, and

St. Jean et le Fils de l'Homme from the *Apocalypse* series woven by Nicolas Bataille after designs by Jean de Bondol. (Mus. des Tapisseries, Angers, late 14th c.)

no doubt tapestries were numbered among the spoils of war brought back by crusading knights. In the colder climate of northern Europe, where there were ready supplies of wool, tapestry had particular appeal and from the later Middle Ages the art flourished.

(i) *Middle Ages.* As the Middle Ages progressed tapestries, like embroideries, served an increasing number of uses both domestic and ecclesiastical. They covered large expanses of bare wall and were draped over beds and tables, bringing colour and warmth to rooms that were otherwise sparsely furnished. The nobility travelled extensively and tapestries could be easily rolled up and transported from place to place; indeed they often accompanied kings and generals on military campaigns. Tapestries were displayed on ceremonial occasions as symbols of prestige, while in churches they were hung over altars and choir-stalls.

A tapestry from the church of St. Gereon (now divided between the Germanisches Mus., Nuremberg, the Mus. des Tissues, Lyon, and the V. & A. Mus., London) has decorative motifs in the BYZANTINE–Sassanian style and is thought to have been woven in the Rhineland during the late ROMANESQUE period. Of similar provenance is a group of tapestries woven *c.* 1200 and preserved in Halberstadt Cathedral; they include a representation of *Charlemagne among the Four Philosophers.* More or less contemporary with these is a fragment illustrating the months of April and May discovered at Baldishol in Norway. A number of German tapestries, probably woven in monastic workshops, survives from the 14th and 15th centuries depicting romantic love-scenes (*Minneteppiche*), allegories and wild men, as well as religious subjects. The most important centres of production were in the Middle Rhine, Switzerland, Alsace and Nuremberg. These early tapestries have considerable charm with their often naïve designs and vivid colours, but after the 15th c. the quality of German tapestry rapidly declined.

The great development of medieval tapestry took place in Paris and the Franco-Burgundian territories in the latter half of the 14th c. This was largely due to Charles V of France (1364), who with his brothers the Dukes of Anjou, Berry and Burgundy did much to encourage the industry. Nicolas Bataille emerges as the most distinguished weaver of this period and between 1387 and 1400 he sold some 250 tapestries to the royal household. In 1375–9 he produced a set of *Apocalypse* tapestries for the Duke of Anjou. These superb hangings were woven to the designs of the Flemish painter Jean de Bondol (also known as Jean de Bruges), who became Court Painter to Charles in 1368. Originally 152 metres long, about two-thirds of this tapestry, the oldest surviving medieval set, is in the Musée des Tapisseries, Angers. Another set, possibly woven in Bataille's workshop, is *The Nine Worthies* (Met. Mus., New York), a favourite theme of the Middle Ages, combining biblical, classical and contemporary heroes.

A mon seul désir from the *La Dame à la Licorne* series. Possibly woven in Brussels. (Mus. Cluny, late 15th c.)

The English occupation (1418–36) was the primary cause for the dispersal of the Parisian weavers, many of whom fled to ARRAS, where tapestry workshops had probably existed since the 13th c. Their reputation grew to such an extent that within a short time the very name of Arras became synonymous with tapestry in several European languages. Yet there is now only one surviving set known to have been executed there: *The Story of St. Piat and Eleuthère*, woven in 1402 (Tournai Cathedral). After the sack of the town in 1477 Arras never regained the supremacy enjoyed there in the 1st half of the century and her great rival Tournai became the chief centre of tapestry weaving. The close links between these two cities make it difficult to distinguish their tapestries but reasonable attributions to Tournai include *The Knight of the Swan* (Cracow), *The Story of Alexander* (Palazzo Doria, Rome) and the *Seven Sacraments* (Met. Mus., New York), all of which were associated with Pasquier Grenier, a leading Tournai weaver. War and an outbreak of the plague caused Tournai's decline during the 1st quarter of the 16th c. Tapestry weavers were also active in the Middle Ages at Avignon, FELLETIN, AUBUSSON, Reims and Lyon.

Authorities have long been disagreed about the circumstances of the production of a group of delightful tapestries dating from *c.* 1480 to *c.* 1520 and known as *milles-fleurs* because they depict hundreds of scattered flowers, sometimes as a background to courtly and pastoral scenes. One widely held theory is that they were made by itinerant weavers working in the region of the Loire valley, while some authorities have attributed certain hangings to Tournai or to weaving centres in the Marche. One of the most beautiful series in this group, *La Dame à la Licorne*, has been attributed to Brussels (P. S. Schneebalg-Perelman, *Gazette des Beaux-Arts*, lxx, 1967) and it would now seem likely that a number of high quality *milles-fleurs* tapestries were woven there.

(ii) *Flanders.* By the beginning of the 16th c. BRUSSELS had a rapidly developing tapestry industry soon to be unrivalled in Europe. At the same time the craft was growing in importance all over Flanders and among the many centres were OUDENARDE, Bruges, Ghent, Lille, Louvain and Valenciennes. The output from the looms of these towns was enormous and tapestries were exported to all parts of Europe. One of the greatest patrons of the period was the Emperor

Charles V (Charles I of Spain), who in 1519 became Holy Roman Emperor, inheriting Flanders and the kingdoms of Aragon and Castile. Indeed many of the finest Flemish tapestries are today preserved in the Habsburg collections of Spain. Other notable patrons included Leo X, the Doges of Venice and Francis I of France. But it would be a mistake to assume that tapestries were made only for the great ruling families of Europe, for hangings differing widely in quality and size were in demand from people at many social levels and especially from the increasingly prosperous merchants and burghers.

The wide variety of subjects depicted in tapestry reflected many facets of public life and were largely identified with the religious, political and intellectual feelings of the time. Biblical and classical themes continued to be much in demand. Ovid's *Metamorphoses* was a popular source for mythological subjects, for example *Vertumnus and Pomona* (Vienna, Lisbon, etc.), while allegories offered themes such as *The Triumphs* (V. & A. Mus., Hampton Court, Madrid, etc.). Kings continued to have their military victories commemorated in tapestries (*The Conquest of Tunis*, Madrid), as well as their courtly pursuits (*The Fêtes of Henry III*, Florence). Towards the middle of the 16th c. the tapestry border was developed into a more complex and individual feature with designs of fruit, flowers, cavorting *putti*, and sometimes complete pictorial scenes.

The influence of the Italian Renaissance brought about important stylistic changes in the 2nd quarter of the century. In 1515 Pieter Coecke van Aelst, who with Wilhelm Pannemaker and Frans Geubels was among the leading Brussels weavers, undertook a commission from Pope Leo X to weave a set of the *Acts of the Apostles* from cartoons by Raphael (V. & A. Mus.). The new monumental style seen in these tapestries was a considerable departure from the crowded

Falconry from the set of Chatsworth hunting tapestries. Probably woven in Tournai. (V. & A. Mus., 2nd quarter of 15th c.)

Suzannah and the Elders. Flemish. This tapestry has an unusually elaborate border for its period. (V. & A. Mus., *c.* 1500)

surfaces of the Gothic and was adopted with particular success by the Italian-trained painter Bernaert van Orley, who produced many important cartoons including those for the *Hunts of Maximilian* (Louvre) and *The Story of Abraham* (Hampton Court). It was followed by other Flemish artists such as Michel Coxcie and Jan Vermeyen.

In 1528 a decree was issued stipulating that all weavers must use the Brussels mark of a red shield flanked by two 'B's on any tapestry of more than six Flemish ells (1·20 m), and that each tapestry should bear the mark of the weaver or of the merchant who had commissioned the work. The most important market was Antwerp, where hangings from all over Flanders were bought and sold. Many heraldic tapestries were woven at Enghien while Oudenarde was noted for *verdures*, depicting leafy foliage often combined with birds and beasts. It is difficult to identify the countless tapestries woven in the workshops of less important towns and indeed in the minor workshops of Brussels itself, for little documentary evidence has survived.

The Return of Sarah by the Egyptians from the *Abraham* series after cartoons by Bernaert van Orley. Brussels. (Hampton Court, *c.* 1540.) By gracious permission of H.M. the Queen

The persecution of the Protestants by the Spanish rulers in the latter part of the 16th c. resulted in the emigration of many Flemish weavers to other European countries. Although there was a decline in the quality of Brussels tapestries at this period, the industry prospered in the following century when the most prominent influence was that of Rubens. His exuberant BAROQUE style was adopted by many other artists, the most notable of whom was Jacob Jordaens, and is illustrated in such sets as *The Story of Achilles* (Turin and Boston) and *The Story of Aurelian and Zenobia* (Mus. Royaux d'Art et d'Histoire, Brussels). Among the leading 17th-c. tapestry weavers were Jan Raes, Martin Reymbouts and the Leyniers family.

Tapestry weaving continued to thrive in Flanders during the 1st half of the 18th c. in spite of increasing competition from France. New designs were produced by such artists as Justus van Egmont, Jan van Orley and Ludwig van Schoor, who at the end of the 17th c. gave new importance to landscape backgrounds. But by far the most influential artist was David Teniers II, whose paintings of rural scenes were adapted by a number of designers for tapestry cartoons and were known as 'tenières'. At the same time mythological and biblical subjects continued to be woven. Technically the quality of Flemish tapestries was still good, but their importance in the 2nd half of the century steadily declined. One by one the workshops of the famous families of Brussels weavers, such as Le Clerc, van den Hecke and de Vos, shut down and with the closing of Jan van den Borght's shop in 1794, the great era of Brussels tapestry was at an end. The last productions of the Brussels workshops were the *Loves of Venus* by Jos de Vos, *Don Quixote* by Pieter van den Hecke and *Triumphs of the Gods* by D. Leyniers.

(iii) *France.* In France a workshop was founded by Francis I at Fontainebleau in 1540 but seems to have been only a temporary venture. The one set known to have come from this manufactory reproduces part of the decoration in the Grande Galerie at Fontainebleau by Rosso and Primaticcio (Kunsthist. Mus., Vienna). Another workshop was established in the Hôtel de la Trinité by Henri II soon after his succession in 1551 and placed under the direction of Maurice Dubourg. In 1608 Dubourg together with Girard Laurent became director of a new manufactory in the Louvre where other craftsmen were already working for the Crown. Henry IV, who came to the throne in 1589, encouraged foreign craftsmen to settle in France with the hope they would stimulate the French economy by establishing trades and industries. This was supported by a prohibition on the import of foreign tapestries. In 1607 he granted letters patent to two Flemish weavers, Marc Comans and François de la Planche, according them many privileges. They set up their workshop in the Faubourg St.-Marcel, agreeing to maintain 80 looms in Paris and the provinces, to instruct 25 apprentices and not to sell their products for more than the current selling price of Flemish tapestries. Among their early productions were *The Story of Coriolanus* and *The Story of Artemisia* (Mobilier National). The cartoons of the latter set have been attributed to Henri Lerambert (d. 1609), who was Painter of the Royal Tapestries. His successors included Laurent Guyot, Philippe de Champaigne and Eustache Le Sueur. Simon Vouet was one of the most distinguished artists to hold this position and his designs for *The Trials of Ulysses* (Château de Cheverny) and *Rinaldo and Armida* (Haras du Pin) are lively compositions surrounded by imaginative borders.

Septembre, Chambord. From *The Royal Residences* series after designs by Charles Lebrun. Gobelins. (Mobilier National, Paris, late 17th c.)

Towards the middle of the century the Parisian workshops declined as a result of the wars of the Frondes, but the industry was revived in 1658 when Fouquet, the King's Minister of Finance, founded a tapestry workshop at Maincy in order to furnish his splendid château Vaux-le-Vicomte. After Fouquet's fall from power his successor Colbert brought many of the Maincy weavers to the GOBELINS, which he founded in 1663. The Gobelins had two main purposes, to provide suitably magnificent furnishings for the king's palaces and to contribute on the cultural front to France's aspiring supremacy in Europe. Charles Lebrun, previously director at Maincy, was placed in charge of the Gobelins and it was to his ability both as designer and as administrator that the early success of the factory can be largely credited. Weaving began there with the completion of the portières *The Fames and Mars*, which had been started at Maincy. *The Acts of the Apostles* after Raphael, *The History of Alexander* (Louvre), *The Life of the King* (Mobilier National) and *The Royal Residences* (Mobilier National) soon followed, and like all the tapestries produced at the Gobelins were intended exclusively for the king's palaces and châteaux. Under the direction of Lebrun's elderly and less imaginative successor, Pierre Mignard, the factory produced tapestries mainly to old designs. Owing to France's military defeats and subsequent financial difficulties the Gobelins was forced to close between 1694 and 1699.

Colbert also established a Manufacture Royale at Beauvais in 1664, which had little commercial success until Philippe Behagle was made director 20 years later. A delightful series of grotesques designed by J. B. Monnoyer after BÉRAIN heralded 18th-c. ROCOCO. Workshops were also active at Felletin and Aubusson, where tapestries had probably been produced since the beginning of the 14th c., but at both these centres production remained small and provincial, consisting mainly of landscapes.

After the Gobelins reopened in 1699 the first set of tapestries to be woven was the portières of *The Gods* after Claude AUDRAN III. This set with others such as the *Grotesque Months* and *Don Quixote* were produced many times and illustrate the transformation in style that took place in France during the 1st quarter of the 18th c. There was a strong reaction against historical subjects and a marked leaning towards lighter and more decorative themes. Interest in the exotic and picturesque led to tapestries such as the *New Indies* (Mobilier National) after Desportes and *The Turkish Embassy* (Mobilier National) by Parrocel. From 1735 to 1747 Robert de Cotte, a pioneer of the Rococo style, was director of the Gobelins and in 1733 J.-B. OUDRY became artistic director. Oudry imposed a strict discipline on the weavers, insisting on the exact reproduction of the artist's cartoon. Previously the weavers had been allowed considerable latitude in their interpretation of colours and details and Oudry's policy gave rise to a bitter dispute. His superb designs for the *Hunts of Louis XV* (Compiègne and Pitti Palace, Florence) contain portraits of the King and his courtiers set in naturalistic landscapes. These tapestries mirror Oudry's cartoons and the illusion that they are paintings is completed by the imitation carved gilt frames.

Grotesque after a design by Jean Bérain. Beauvais. (V. & A. Mus., early 18th c.)

From 1726 Oudry was painter to the Beauvais factory, where he was appointed director in 1734. (See also BEAUVAIS TAPESTRIES.) He designed for Beauvais such sets as *Country Pleasures*, scenes from the Molière comedies and a *Don Quixote* after Charles Natoire. For the same manufactory François BOUCHER painted some 45 cartoons, including *chinoiseries* and subjects from opera, which are among the most characteristic and delightful examples of French art of the middle of the 18th c. Many of the series woven at Beauvais were also reproduced at Aubusson and both centres specialized in the production of furniture covers. Boucher followed Oudry at the Gobelins, becoming artistic director in 1752/3. He collaborated with Carle van Loo and others to produce designs for the popular *Loves of the Gods*. In the last quarter of the 18th c. a number of tapestry portraits were woven at the Gobelins. The Revolution forced the closure of the factory in 1794.

(iv) *England*. Itinerant weavers appear to have been active in England from the 14th c. During the Tudor period a number of emigré weavers are known to have settled in East Anglia, Sandwich, Canterbury and York. English weavers probably wove small armorials but seem to have been mainly employed on repair work. The great majority of tapestries were imported from Flanders and feature frequently in inventories of the time. Among the most enthusiastic patrons were Cardinal Wolsey and Henry VIII, who at one time owned more than 2,000 hangings.

The first English manufactory was established *c.* 1560 by a country squire named William SHELDON on his estates at Barcheston and Bordesley and placed under the direction of Richard Hyckes. When Sheldon died in 1570 production continued under the auspices of his son Ralph, but appears to have ceased after the latter's death in 1613. The Sheldon workshops produced mainly small hangings and pieces suitable for cushions and book covers. Perhaps the best known set is the *County Maps* (V. & A. Mus.) with the Sheldon arms, the names of Richard Hyckes and his son Francis and the date 1588. A set of the *Four Seasons* (Hatfield House) has been attributed to the Sheldon looms and shows an appealing if naïve attempt at figurative design. Although these tapestries possess great charm, the manufactory remained provincial and important commissions were still given to foreign weavers.

The MORTLAKE factory was founded in 1619 under very different circumstances. To begin with it had the royal patronage and financial backing of Charles I that were essential if the manufactory were to compete with European centres. It also had a shrewd director in the person of Sir Francis Crane, who recruited some 50 Flemish weavers, and Philip Maeght from the Comans's shop in Paris. *Vulcan and Venus* (V. & A. Mus. and St. James's Palace) was the first set woven at Mortlake and was followed by the *Twelve Months* (Royal Colls.) and *The Acts of the Apostles*. This last set was woven many times (Boughton House, Chatsworth, Forde Abbey, etc.) from the original Raphael cartoons (V. & A. Mus.) which had mysteriously appeared in Genoa, where they were purchased by Crane. In 1624 Francis Cleyn was appointed designer to Mortlake and made an important contribution with his cartoons for the series of *Hero and Leander* (Royal Coll., Stockholm, V. & A. Mus., etc.), *The Horses*, *The Five Senses* (Haddon Hall) and the popular *Playing Boys* adapted from designs by Giulio Romano. From 1620 to 1635 Mortlake was producing some of the finest tapestries in Europe, but after the death of Francis Crane in 1636 the manufactory suffered grave financial difficulties that were the main cause of its gradual decline. It was supported by the Cromwellians and a set of *The Triumphs of Caesar* (Buccleuch Coll.) after Mantegna was commissioned in 1657. Production struggled on until 1703, when Mortlake was finally closed down.

The history of tapestry weaving in England during the latter part of the 17th c. is confused, for a number of Mortlake weavers moved to the Great Wardrobe where tapestries were also being woven for the Royal Collection, while others, such as William Benood and Stephen de May, set up on their own account. Francis and Thomas Poyntz were distinguished weavers associated with the Great Wardrobe, which was situated first at Hatton Garden and then from 1786 in Great Queen Street. Francis Poyntz's signature appears on a large tapestry (Houghton) portraying Kings James I and Charles II, their queens and Christian II of Denmark, dated 1675, about three years before he was appointed chief 'Arras-Maker' to the King. From 1689 to 1727 this position was held by John Vanderbank, who is mainly remembered for his delightful *chinoiserie* subjects (The Vyne, V. & A. Mus., Belton House). The Wauters family, working in Antwerp, made tapestries especially designed for the English market, copying such series as *Hero and Leander*.

Although there was less demand for woven hangings in Georgian England and the majority were still imported from Flanders, there were several workshops in the 18th c. producing good quality tapestries. The style of Vanderbank's *chinoiseries* was adopted by other weavers, including Joshua Morris, who had a workshop in SOHO. He is chiefly known for his ARABESQUES with ornamental devices of vases, parrots, scrollwork, etc. (Hagley Park, Grimsthorpe). A workshop set up by two French weavers from Savonnerie later came under the direction of Pierre Parisot at Fulham, but did not survive beyond 1755. A tapestry depicting a hunting scene signed by Bradshaw and Stranover belongs to a group of similar subjects (e.g. Clandon Park) which have affinities with 18th-c. French designs. One of the last notable English weavers was Paul

The Miraculous Draught of Fishes from the *Acts of the Apostles* series after cartoons by Raphael. Mortlake. (V. & A. Mus., 2nd quarter of 17th c.) By kind permission of His Grace the Duke of Buccleuch

Tapestry Room at Osterley Park House, property of the National Trust. The tapestries were specially woven for the room by Jacques Neilson after designs by François Boucher. Gobelins

Saunders, who like Morris worked in Soho. He supplied tapestries for Holkham House and specialized in Oriental designs.

English tapestries were not suited to the Neo-Classical taste of the later 18th c. and at this period commissions were mostly given to the Gobelins. Here some sets with subjects after Boucher and with floral borders designed by Maurice Jacques were woven by Jacques Neilson to hang in special tapestry rooms such as can be seen at Osterley Park House and Newby Hall.

(v) *Italy*. Manufacture of tapestries in Italy began in the 15th c. when Flemish and French itinerant weavers worked there in various towns. The earliest workshop was organized *c.* 1445 by Lionello d'Este at Ferrara and continued to the middle of the 16th c., when it was operated by two Flemish emigrés, Hans and Nicolas Karcher. Among the hangings woven there were subjects from Ovid's *Metamorphoses* and the *Story of Hercules*. From 1539 to 1541 Nicolas Karcher lived in Mantua, where he worked for the Gonzaga family; a series of *Playing Boys* (Gulbenkian Foundation, Lisbon; Mus. Poldi Pezzoli, Milan) after designs by Giulio Romano are attributed to this workshop. He also helped Duke Cosimo I to establish tapestry workshops in Florence, where a *History of Joseph* (Palazzo Vecchio) was woven to the designs of the Medici court painter Bronzino. A plan to furnish the Palazzo Vecchio with tapestries extolling the virtues of the Medici was devised by Vasari and the weaver given the task was a Fleming, Jan van den Straecht (also known as Stradanus). The factory flourished for nearly 200 years, continuing predominant until *c.* 1630, when a private workshop was founded in Rome by Cardinal Francesco Barberini and placed under the direction of Jacob van den Vliete. The first tapestries produced there depicted famous European castles and lands belonging to the Barberini family. During the middle part of the century Pietro da Cortona and G. F. Romanelli were notable for their fine Baroque designs for such sets as *The Mysteries of the Life and Death of Christ* (St. John's Cathedral, New York) and *The Story of Constantine* (Mus. of Art, Philadelphia). The Barberini workshops seem to have languished after their patron's death and closed down towards the end of the century.

At the beginning of the 18th c. the Medici manufactory was producing mainly landscape subjects. The Rococo painter Giovanni Sagrestani did some cartoons of *The Four Quarters of the World* (Mus. Bardini, Florence), which were woven by Leonardo Bernini and Victor Demignot. In 1737 the Medici workshops closed and many of the weavers settled in

Naples, where weaving continued until the French conquest of 1799. Subjects included *The Elements* after Lebrun, *The Rape of Prosperine*, *Love and Chastity* and many others.

In Rome a manufactory was founded in 1710 by Clement XI at the Opitale San Michele. Signoret was appointed director and Andrea Procaccini chief designer. Production was extremely varied and included religious themes, portraits of popes, small decorative pieces and wooded landscapes with figures. In 1731 Demignot went to Turin, where he opened a low-warp workshop at the court of Savoy in 1737, while high-warp looms were placed under the direction of Antonio Dini. Claudio Beaumont was the most important designer, whose subjects were taken mainly from classical history, an unusual choice for this period. Demignot's son continued his work until 1784 while in 1760 Dini went to Venice, leaving his two daughters in charge until the manufactory closed in 1789.

(vi) *Germany*. A number of Flemish weavers emigrated to Germany, where by the end of the 17th c. workshops had sprung up in Frankenthal, Dresden, Hamburg, Cologne, Wismar, Lower Saxony, Lauingen, Lüneburg and Heidelberg. The possession of a tapestry workshop became a desirable status symbol for every German court and the most important was that established in Munich by Hans van Biest in 1604 for the Dukes of Bavaria. In the 18th c. weavers were also working in Berlin, Dresden and Würzburg.

(vii) *Holland*. At the end of the 16th c. Flemish weavers established workshops in various Dutch towns, including Amsterdam, The Hague, Rotterdam and Utrecht. One of the most distinguished was that founded in 1591 by Frans Spierinc at Delft, where he made tapestries for the Danish court and also a number for the English market, such as *The Story of Diana* (Knole). The shop continued to flourish under his sons until *c.* 1640, when it was superseded by Maximilian van der Gucht. But competition from the Gobelins increased during the second

The Ball Game from the *Playing Boys* series attributed to the workshop of Nicolas Karcher after cartoons by Guilio Romano. This later became a popular subject at Mortlake. (Calouste Gulbenkian Foundation Mus., Lisbon, *c.* 1540)

half of the century and Dutch tapestry died out with the end of the 17th c.

(viii) *Denmark.* In Denmark Flemish weavers worked in the service of Frederik II (1559–88) and Christian IV (1588–1648). Towards the end of the 17th c. Christian V brought weavers from Flanders and Aubusson to Copenhagen. Provincial workshops specialized in making furniture covers and were active well into the 18th c.

(ix) *Spain.* A small number of Flemish weavers were active in Spain in the 17th c. In 1720 Philip V opened a manufactory at Santa Barbara in Madrid, placing it under the direction of Jacob van der Goten. Many rustic and genre subjects were woven. The most important tapestries produced there were those designed by Goya. Production continued until 1808.

(x) *Russia.* Peter the Great of Russia set up a factory in St. Petersburg in 1716 with a team of French weavers under the direction of Philippe Behagle, son of the Beauvais director. The factory was organized in a similar way to the Gobelins and many portraits were produced as well as copies of paintings at the Hermitage. Production continued until 1858.

(xi) *19th and 20th centuries.* By the end of the 18th c. the demand for tapestries had greatly diminished and most tapestry workshops foundered. Nevertheless two important workshops were opened in England in the 2nd half of the 19th c. The first was that at Windsor, where some French weavers from Aubusson worked under the direction of M. Henri. A considerable number of tapestries were produced, including *A Tournement on London Bridge* and views of the Royal Residences.

In 1881 William MORRIS began tapestry weaving at Merton Abbey, where he made it his aim to recover the high quality of medieval craftsmanship. Sir Edward Burne-Jones, Walter CRANE and Philip Webb were among the artists who assisted Morris in producing designs for the factory. Many tapestries were woven, often with medieval or romantic themes such as *The Quest of the Holy Grail.*

Weaving was resumed at the Gobelins and Beauvais after the Revolution and many tapestries were woven to old cartoons. The concept of a tapestry as a woven reproduction of a picture was widely maintained throughout the 19th c. and for the first decades of the 20th c. The artist primarily responsible for initiating the modern movement in tapestry was Jean Lurçat, who from 1916 experimented with new and original ideas for cartoons. He reduced the colour scale to about 20 shades and advocated coarse textures such as had been used in the Middle Ages.

Owing to the initiative of Lurçat and Denise Majorel the most important artists interested in painting tapestry cartoons formed a group, and in 1944 held a successful exhibition at the Salon des Artistes Décorateurs. Among those who contributed to this and to successive exhibitions were Marc Saint-Saëns, Jean Picart Le Doux, Robert Vogenski, Jacques Lagrange and Dom. Robert. In 1947 the Association of Painters of

Où naissent les Étoiles after a design by Jean Lurçat inspired by a poem of Guillaume Apollinaire. Aubusson. (V. & A. Mus., 1965)

Tapestry-Cartoons was formed with Lurçat as president. Exhibitions were held in many countries, thus creating interest in tapestry weaving throughout the world. By the 1950s the art was thriving and tapestry had recovered a gratifying diversity of style and inspiration.

See also: ANTWERP TAPESTRIES; ARRAS TAPESTRIES; AUBUSSON TAPESTRIES; BEAUVAIS TAPESTRIES; BRUSSELS TAPESTRIES; FELLETIN TAPESTRIES; MORTLAKE; OUDENARDE TAPESTRIES; SHELDON TAPESTRIES; SOHO TAPESTRIES; VERDURE TAPESTRIES; AMERINDIANS (2) (TEXTILES).

36, 46, 149, 221, 257, 311, 365, 422, 442, 451, 491, 570, 702, 828, 829, 858, 884, 891.

TAROT. Though the tarot playing cards are thought to go back to the 12th c. in Europe, the earliest surviving set is from 1390. There are tarot cards in the Museo Correr, Venice, from *c.* 1445. The origin of the cards and of their symbolism is obscure and the many systems of occultist belief which have been occupied with them have advocated as many differing theories of their origin on no better evidence than the arcane meanings which they have read into the symbolism. They have been thought to encapsulate the secret lore of ancient Egypt and Chaldaea preserved and disseminated by the gypsies; the ancient lore of the Eleusinian mysteries; the secrets of the Gnostics, the Manichaeans, the Albigenses and the Kabalah. A particularly colourful theory is that which maintains that after the destruction of the library at Alexandria learned men foregathered at Fez and there devised the cards as a system of mystic symbols embodying universal learning. Modern interest in the tarot stems from the work of the French scholar Count Gébelin, who suggested their Egyptian origin and in *Le Monde primitif*, published in 1773, depicted the 'Marseilles' deck. Interest was revived by the publication in 1854 of Eliphas Levi's *Dogma and Ritual of Transcendental Magic*, in which he connected the Major Arcana of the tarot with the 22 letters of the Hebrew alphabet and made the tarot a basis of his occultist speculations. In 1886 the Hermetic Order of the Golden Dawn was founded in England and took up the interest in tarot symbolism. The leader of the Order, S. L. MacGregor Mathers, wrote a pamphlet entitled *The Tarot, Its Occult Signification, Use in Fortune-telling, and Method of Play, etc.*, and *The Tarot of the Bohemians* (1889) by Pappus (Dr. Gerard Encausse) was published with a preface by A. E. Waite, a member of the Order, who in 1910 also published his own *The Pictorial Key to the Tarot.* Waite also issued a new deck of tarot cards drawn by the artist Pamela Colman Smith after his own designs. In 1947 an American, Paul Foster Case, also a member of the Order, published *The Tarot, A Key to the Wisdom of the Ages* based upon the records and notes of the Golden Dawn. See also PLAYING CARDS.

TATTING. See NEEDLEWORK.

TATTOOING. The decoration of the human body with permanent patterns made by puncturing the skin and inserting pigment is a practice which has been very widespread among the peoples of the world. Tattooing has been found on Egyptian mummies as far back as *c.* 2000 B.C., and tattoo markings on Libyan figures represented in the tomb of Sety I (*c.* 1295 B.C.), which in a simplified form are still used in northern Africa, testify to an astonishing continuity of symbolism. In parts of China tattooing is known to have existed from *c.* 1100 B.C. and in Japan from the 5th or 6th c. B.C. From the mainland the practice may have spread to the islands of the Pacific in prehistoric times. In historical times anthropology records the practice among most peoples at a tribal level of culture from the Eskimos of Greenland to the South Sea Islands and the West Indies. At the time of the conquest of America tattooing was extensively practised by the Indians of North and Central America and by some peoples mainly in the tropical areas of South America. It was known to the ancient Greeks though not practised by them and its use was familiar to the contemporary peoples of Britain, Gaul and central Europe. Tattooing was used by the Romans for branding runaway slaves and criminals and in Japan condemned criminals were tattooed with devil markings in order that they should be recognized by the receivers of lost souls. Deserters from the British Army were formerly tattooed with a distinguishing mark, as were second-term convicts released from State prisons of Massachusetts and convicts in Siberian prisons. The abuse of tattooing in Nazi concentration camps is notorious.

Most ethnologists agree in treating tattooing among tribal peoples as a form of bodily adornment analogous to body painting, scarification, ear, nose and lip ornaments, head-dress, featherwork, costume and jewellery. Besides decoration, however, tattooing has been practised for a variety of other purposes by different peoples at different times. It may be interesting to mention some of the main functions it has been held to serve; examples are ubiquitous in the literature of ethnology and only a few typical ones will be given here. (1) Tattoo patterns have been endowed with prophylactic or talismanic powers against disease, accident or ill luck. (Métraux, *Handbook of South American Indians*, v. 581: 'The *Toba* specifically explained to me that the tattoo motifs on their limbs were talismans against disease.' Ackerknecht, ibid., p. 632: 'Tattooing as a prophylactic measure is reported from the *Chorotí*, *Guarayú* and *Tupinamba*, especially in mourning.' One may compare the once common belief among petty criminals that a religious device tattooed on the back would save them from the 'cat'.) (2) Tattooing has been very widely used for its supposed curative effects. For example, the Arabs of Tangiers and Morocco regard tattooing for embellishment as effeminate, but Arab men use tattooed devices to cure sprains, diseases of the eye, etc. (Richard Kanutz, *Tatuiermuster aus Tunis*, 1908; Winifred Smeaton, *Tattooing among the Arabs of Iraq*, 1937.) (3) Tattooing is often associated with puberty or maturity rites and as such acquires a ritualistic significance. Different patterns often have a practical function to indicate a man's tribe or clan, social status or even profession. In Sweden, France, Germany and Belgium (though rarely in England or America) workers and craftsmen were commonly tattooed with the symbol of their craft. (4) Among many peoples tattooing has been regarded as a sign of manliness and courage (North American Indians), while among others it is a mark of wealth and social prestige (Polynesians). But for all these different functions, and not confiicting with them, tattooing has most generally been regarded as an adornment and it is as a manifestation of that impulse to decoration which from the earliest times has gone hand in hand with craftsmanship that tattooing finds a place in this volume. So eminent a naturalist as Charles Darwin was keenly alive to the aesthetic effects of tattooing. Speaking of the Tahitians he says: 'Most of the men are tattooed, and the ornaments follow the curvature of the body so gracefully, that they have a very elegant effect. One common pattern, varying in its details, is somewhat like the crown of a palm-tree. It springs from the central line of the back, and gracefully curls round both sides. The simile may be a fanciful one, but I thought the body of a man thus ornamented was like the trunk of a noble tree embraced by a delicate creeper.' With the Maoris of New Zealand, by contrast, 'the extraordinary manner in which tattooing is here practised, gives a disagreeable expression to their countenances. The complicated but symmetrical figures covering the whole face puzzle and mislead an unaccustomed eye: it is moreover probable that the deep incisions, by destroying the play of the superficial muscles, give an air of rigid inflexibility.' (From *The Voyage of the Beagle*, 1839.) He mentions that when the wives of the missionaries tried to dissuade the young women from being tattooed, they replied: 'We really must just have a few lines in our lips; else when we grow old, our lips will shrivel, and we shall be so very ugly.' And he adds that tattooing 'is a badge of distinction between the chief and the slave'. Of the Trobrianders Malinowski writes: 'The body, as distinguished from the face, is very seldom painted, and no tattoo markings are ever visible. I am told that girls at the time of their first menstruation are tattooed round the vagina. This tattooing is called *ki 'uki'u* and is done, according to my informants, for aesthetic purposes.' (*The Sexual Life of Savages*, 1929.)

Tattooing was frowned on by the Christian Church. Facial tattooing was forbidden by the Emperor Constantine and all forms of tattooing were condemned by a Church Council in A.D. 787. Thus during the Middle Ages the practice was lost sight of in Europe or known only as an outlandish foible of the 'Moors'. It was rediscovered through the medium of travellers' tales and reports, as expanding exploration brought Europe again into contact with the world. Captain John Smith, who went with the Virginia colonists in 1606 and who wrote a *General History of Virginia, New England and the Summer Isles* (1624), mentioned tattooing and the water-colour drawings of John White, who was Governor of Virginia in 1587 and 1590, show some figures with tattoo decoration. White also made a drawing of a tattooed Eskimo woman who was brought back by Frobisher after his voyages in search of a north-west Passage. Not unnaturally tattooing, thus rediscovered, was regarded as an aberration of savage peoples and tattooed persons were treated until the 19th c. as freaks and curiosities to be exhibited at fairs and side-shows. The first of these to be shown publicly was 'Prince Jeoly', brought back from the South Seas by William Dampier in 1691. Even more famous was Omai, a South Sea Islander brought back to England by Captain Cook in 1774 and exhibited up and down the country. The word 'tattoo' is the anglicized version of the Polynesian *tatau*. 'Tataou' was first used by Louis-Antoine Bougainville in *Voyage autour du monde* (1771) and 'tattow' was probably first used by Captain Cook himself. It is this accident of the manner of rediscovery by Europe which has led to the false impression, favoured among others by the *Oxford English Dictionary*, that tattooing is a practice distinctive of 'tribes of a low civilisation'. In fact it was carried to its highest level of technical and artistic perfection in Japan. It was banned there in 1889 on the ground that the persons of all Japanese are the property of the Emperor, but the Japanese *horis*, or tattoo artists, continued to operate on foreigners, including many from the European aristocracy.

The tattooing of Europeans began as a feature of the show business and most of the more flamboyant freaks had stories, more imagination than credible, of their forcible tattooing while captured by savages. Among the earliest were a Frenchman Joseph Cabri, an English seaman John Rutherford, and an Albanian Alexandrinos, known in America as Prince Constantine. The first tattooed lady, La Belle Irène, appeared in 1890 and the first tattooed couple, the Americans Frank and Emma de Burgh, were on show in Berlin in 1893. The showman P. T. Barnum exhibited tattooed dwarfs, hunchbacks, fat ladies, knife throwers, etc., and tattooed Red Indians were an attraction at fairs and booths both in Europe and in the U.S.A. Lilly Barnum was 'tattooed with attar of roses and for ever sweet smelling'. But tattooing was by no means limited to the show-booth. By the middle of the 19th c. it had spread pretty widely among all classes and tattooists were established in the U.S.A. The first electric tattooing machine was patented by Tom Riley in 1891. Tattooing has been particularly popular among seafaring persons, among soldiers in wartime and among the criminal classes. But the impression that it has been in any way restricted to these classes of people has been a misapprehension resulting partly from the fact that most statistical investigations (e.g. Dr. A. Lacassagne, 1881) have been conducted in this sort of milieu. At the turn of the century tattooing even became a vogue in smart society led by such people as Lady Randolph Churchill, King Frederik of Denmark, Edward VII and later George V of England, Field Marshal Montgomery, and a number of American millionaires. Favourite tattooists visited by the nobility were the *hori* Chyo of Yokohama and a Mr. Sutherland Macdonald, who set up his studio, *The Hamman*, in Jermyn Street, London, and who specialized in drawings in the Japanese style and English sporting scenes.

Tattooing in English-speaking countries was in recession in the 1930s but came into fashion again together with decorative body painting among younger groups about the middle of the century.

336, 653.

TAZZA (Italian). Dish standing on a tall baluster foot. The form, based on an antique prototype, was reintroduced by the Renaissance goldsmiths. On the finer examples the foot and the inner surface of the bowl were both embossed with subjects drawn from classical mythology or the scriptures. Engraved tazzas were popular in Holland and Germany during the first half of the 17th c., some of the finest being decorated by J. T. de Bry. The German term, *Presentierschale*, suggests that these dishes were used for offering wine or sweetmeats, but their highly decorative character suggests that they were often intended as show-pieces. They went out of fashion on the Continent before the middle of the 17th c., but remained in use in England until well into the 18th c. See also PEWTER.

TERRY, ELI (1772–1852). American clockmaker. After being apprenticed to Daniel BURNAP in East Windsor, Connecticut, he started manufacturing brass-wheeled clocks. He is chiefly remembered, however, for having taken the first steps in the mass production of clocks by designing LONG-CASE wooden clocks with standardized and interchangeable parts. In 1811 he moved to Plymouth, New Hampshire, and manufactured a 30-hour MANTEL CLOCK, also of wood, which from *c.* 1817 led to the popular 'pillar and scroll' clock. From 1833 the business was carried on by his eldest son, ELI, Jr.

TEXTILE MANUFACTURE IN ANTIQUITY. The processes of textile manufacture in the ancient world can be considered under five headings: 1. Raw materials; 2. Preparation of fibres; 3. Spinning; 4. WEAVING; 5. Dyeing and finishing. Archaeological remains are the most important source of information, but written records (where they exist) also contribute. Study of technical practices in modern primitive communities can often be helpful.

1. RAW MATERIALS. The main textile fibres in antiquity were either of animal (sheep's wool, SILK) or of vegetable (linen, hemp, cotton) origin. In northern and western Europe wool takes first place from the Bronze Age onwards, while in the Near East linen and to a lesser extent cotton textiles predominate throughout antiquity.

The prehistoric sheep of Europe was a small goat-like animal closely resembling the modern Soay breed of St. Kilda in the Outer Hebrides. Its fleece was normally light or dark brown and contained kemps and hair in addition to wool. Selective breeding, which began before 1000 B.C., gradually improved the fleece, eliminated most of the kemps and banished the natural pigmentation. A fine-woolled sheep, probably white, had been developed in Asia Minor by A.D. 100. The average fleece-weight was about 1 kilogramme. The sheep was an ubiquitous domestic animal, providing meat and milk as well as wool in most peasant households. Large-scale ranching was already being practiced in Bronze-Age Crete, as the Linear B documents reveal.

Silk was a highly prized item of trade in prehistoric and classical times, and both wild (TUSSORE) and cultivated silk were known. The Greeks were familiar with the silkworms of Cos in the Aegean, which gave wild silk, but the true silkworm was not introduced into the Mediterranean world until A.D. 552. The silk garments often mentioned by classical writers were made from silk fabrics and yarns imported from China.

The flax plant (*Linum usitatissimum*) was widely cultivated for its fibre in the Near East. It was also grown, and its products worn, by the Neolithic communities of central Europe, but in general it played a minor role in the north, where it was less suitable for clothing. Great quantities of fine linen have been found by excavators in EGYPT preserved in the dry conditions of the area. Egyptian tomb-paintings and written sources indicate that flax cultivation was a major industry there from very early times.

The hemp plant (*Cannabis sativa*) yields a fibre similar in character to linen, but coarser. Its main use in antiquity was for cordage and sails, but clothing was also woven from it. It reached Europe from the Near East by 300 B.C., but never became of great economic importance.

COTTON growing is attested in the Nile Valley, on the island of Bahrein and in India. References in Greco-Roman papyri from Egypt suggest that it was a fairly common fibre there; but wherever it occurs in Europe it must be regarded as an exotic import. Aboriginal American cultivated cotton found in the pre-ceramic culture of Huaca Prieta (*c.* 2500 B.C.) at the mouth of the Chicama valley on the northern coast of Peru is believed by some botanists to be a hybrid between Asiatic cultivated and American wild cotton.

Lastly, several other fibres can be cited which were never widely used—rabbit and goat hair, pinna (the anchor-fibres of the mollusc *Pinna nobilis*), mallow, nettle and asbestos.

2. PREPARATION OF FIBRES. When man's metallurgical skill became equal to making shears sheep were shorn of their fleeces; but the more wasteful primitive method of plucking the wool still survived into the Roman period in wilder regions. The wool might be washed (before or after shearing), but this was not essential. It was regularly dyed in the fleece (see below). Carding with hand-cards was unknown in antiquity, but in some areas the wool was combed with iron wool-combs to separate short from long fibres when long-stapled wool was required. Burrs and dirt could be picked out by hand.

According to Aristotle the filament from Coan wild silk cocoons could be reeled off, presumably before the moth could bite its way out. Chinese artists show the reeling process.

Flax and hemp, harvested in the summer, were pulled by hand to obtain maximum length of fibre. Thereafter the separation of the useful bast fibres in the stem from the cellulose core and bark was a very laborious operation. We know from various sources that methods of preparing flax have changed remarkably little over the past 5000 years. The stalks were first steeped in water for two to three weeks to break down the structure of the cellulose (*retting*). Then, after drying, they were beaten with a wooden mallet to break up the woody core. *Scutching* followed, in which the bast fibres were further loosened from the bark with a wooden blade. In the final stage, *hackling*, the fibre-bundles were drawn across a board set with spikes to comb out the remnants of the bark and core. The fibres were then ready to spin.

When the cotton plant is ripe the cotton 'wool' spills from the seed capsule but remains attached to the seeds. Presumably the seeds had to be detached from the fibre-mass by hand in antiquity, but information on this is lacking.

3. SPINNING. In the era before the spinning wheel was invented the main implements used in spinning were the distaff and spindle. The distaff was a short stick carried in the left hand, to the top of which the prepared fibres were secured. The spindle was a short rod of wood or bone, on which a metal or pottery spindle-whorl was wedged to give it momentum when rotating. The skill of the spinner was paramount; for an experienced hand-spinner can produce yarn consistently as fine as a machine. The size and weight of the spindle varied according to the nature of the yarn and fibre.

The most sophisticated method of hand-spinning, with a free-rotating spindle ('suspended spindle spinning'), is well attested in antiquity; but in the Near East the spindle was often turned in the fingers. Similar methods of spinning were used in aboriginal Peru, where some of the finest and most even yarns were spun from cotton and from alpaca and vicuña wool. A forked stick was used for distaff together with a simple hand-spindle consisting of a straight stick with a whorl or disk on it to give it momentum. Today the drop-spindle is used for wool yarns while cotton is spun while seated, the spindle being whirled in a bowl or gourd. The principle behind spinning, however, was universal: a small quantity of the fibre fastened to the distaff was attached to the tip of the spindle and by simultaneously pulling and twisting the spinner converted it into a stable yarn.

Preference for either a right-hand (clockwise) or left-hand (anti-clockwise) spin direction is exhibited in certain areas at certain times. In prehistoric Scandinavia and early Egypt spinning with an anti-clockwise rotation was normal, while in India and the western Roman provinces clockwise rotation was regular.

4. WEAVING. The loom is the most important piece of apparatus required in textile production. There were many different types in use in the ancient world, but outside Egypt (where models and tomb-paintings are particularly informative) unequivocal evidence for their structure and manipulation is scanty.

In the most primitive loom, the *horizontal ground-loom* native to the Nile Valley, the warp was simply spanned between two beams, each supported on two pegs in the ground. The weaver crouched over his work. By *c.* 1500 B.C., however, the *two-beam vertical loom* came into use in Egypt. This had uprights to which the two beams were fixed and the weaver sat at his work, pushing the newly woven cloth downwards. Surviving textiles suggest that this loom was also known in Iron-Age Scandinavia and it is mentioned by Roman writers in the 1st c. A.D., i.e. comparatively late.

The *warp-weighted vertical loom*, the principal loom throughout Europe and parts of the Near East until late antiquity, is more complicated. The uprights carry a single cloth-beam which links them horizontally across the top, and the warp is secured to this by means of a narrow 'starting-border' created in a preliminary operation. The other end of the warp is fastened to a series of weights and the whole loom is propped at a sloping angle against a wall or roof-beam. The warp is more flexible than in the two-beam type and hence a broader web of cloth can be woven; for several weavers can pass the hank of weft from hand to outstretched hand through the wide shed.

The origin, date, and even the form of the earliest *raised horizontal loom*, are controversial. It was in existence by the 4th c. A.D. and probably developed in the Near East from a simple frameless loom in which the warp was attached at one end to the weaver's belt and at the other to a tree or other fixed object. It was the vehicle for technical experiments in weaving which eventually gave rise to DAMASK and related pattern-weaves.

Alongside the larger looms there were various types of small band-looms, on which long bands or strips of cloth could be woven, such as those used for wrapping mummies in Egypt. One of the most interesting band-looms was for tablet-weaving, whereby pattern effects are created in the warp by rotating in different directions three-hole or four-hole tablets, which resemble triangles or playing cards with holes in the corners. This art was popular in northern Europe.

Ancient weavers employed a series of characteristic small tools to help them in their work. The shuttle with rotating spool was unknown and a simple stick—or merely a hank of weft ('dolly')—sufficed. Weaving-combs and cigar-shaped pin-beaters helped to push into place the newly inserted weft.

Plain weave was common throughout the ancient world in all fibres; indeed for linen and hemp it was virtually the only weave. Two-over-two twill was widely used for woollen cloth in Bronze-Age and Iron-Age Europe, and herring-bone and diamond twill were known before the end of the Bronze Age. In the Eastern Mediterranean region and further east, by contrast, twill was rare; but two-over-one twill, which made reversed-colour cloth possible, may have developed there. From this the 4th-c. damask silks ultimately developed.

All manner of complex non-woven fabrics were made by prehistoric man. (See also BARK CLOTH.) Many forms of plaiting and knitting with one or two needles are recorded. (See NEEDLEWORK.) But the more widespread use of the loom in Greco-Roman times discouraged this kind of intricate work. EMBROIDERY, too, was commoner in an earlier period, as the textiles from the Swiss Neolithic lake-villages suggest.

5. DYEING AND FINISHING. Dyeing and finishing (fulling) demand special knowledge and skill and stand apart from the other textile manufacturing processes. At an early date they became independent crafts, and were industrialized in the Greco-Roman period.

Silk and wool were often dyed in antiquity (normally before spinning), but linen was more commonly bleached since it does not take dye-stuffs so readily. Evidence for prehistoric dyeing is slight, for no equipment has survived. But analysis of extant cloth remains shows that vegetable dyes predominated. On the Mediterranean coast certain shellfish, especially the *Murex brandaris*, yielded a dyestuff giving a range of blue-red-purple tones. Dyers' workshops with characteristic vats and boilers are found in Egyptian, Phoenician, Greek and Roman contexts. From Roman sources we learn of the practical talents of the dyers, their use of mordants to prepare the fibres to take the dye-stuffs and the recipes for the various colours and shades which could be achieved by vat-dyeing.

The fuller of antiquity acted both as a finisher of newly woven cloth and as laundry-man. The first stage in the fulling of wool cloth is to tread it out in a tub of water with a detergent such as fullers' earth or urine. This both cleans it and shrinks it into a compact fabric. The linguistic evidence indicates that the process is almost as old as weaving itself. The other treatments in which the fuller specialized involved the raising of the nap on cloth and the trimming (cropping) of projecting fibres to make a smooth surface. There is a hint that Bronze-Age fullers in Crete practised this technique and it was widespread in the Roman world.

See also GREEK AND ROMAN ANTIQUITY (TEXTILE MANUFACTURE); NEEDLEWORK; SILK; TAPESTRY; WEAVING.

TEXTILES, NON-WOVEN. See BARK CLOTH.

THANG-KA. Lamaist religious scroll painting. *Thang-kas* were hung in temples or on family altars, carried as banners in religious processions, or used for purposes of meditation. The iconography was often extremely complicated and in some cases required the help of an adept to explain. Some *thang-kas*, such as those containing a *mandala*, were thought to have quasi-magical powers and to be a means of conjuring up deities or supernatural beings.

Thang-kas were first made in the 10th c., but few of those now surviving are earlier than the 17th c. They were painted on canvas primed with a mixture of chalk and size. The skeleton of the complicated design was first POUNCED upon the smoothed surface, or even printed from wood blocks, and the outlines were gone over in red or black ink. The work of the colourist, not usually identical with the printer, then began. His skill consisted to a large extent in his knowledge of pigments and of their symbolical significance. The colourants used were water-soluble vegetable and mineral pigments prepared with size and they therefore combined with the size priming of the ground. A very complicated and beautiful method of gilding and gold painting was also used. Great store was set by rich and brilliant colours and these have often survived well despite the hard wear on the canvas. After the work of the colourist was finished a draughtsman would draw in with a thin brush the finer details, outlines of the figures, faces, eyes, etc. The painting was then ready for mounting.

The canvas might first be framed in a narrow border of silk, usually red and yellow to symbolize the power emanating from it. This was then enclosed in a much larger piece of embroidered or figured silk and hung from a bamboo stick. At the bottom was a double hem into which was inserted a heavier wooden stick, which served to hold the *thang-ka* taut when it was hung and round which it was rolled when not in use. About a third of the way down the silk frame a thin cord was threaded through and wound round the top stick in order that the *thang-ka* could be hung from it. In the lower border was usually inserted a panel of differently coloured

Mandala *thang-ka*. (Kemper Coll., early 19th c.)

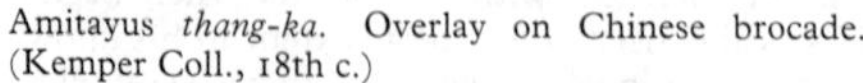

Amitayus *thang-ka*. Overlay on Chinese brocade. (Kemper Coll., 18th c.)

silk embroidered with lotus, dragon or serpent symbols; it was called the 'door' (*thang-gso*) or the 'root' (*rtsa-ba*). Finally a thin veil of silk gauze was hung from the top border, covering the whole *thang-ka*. When not in use *thang-ka* and veil were rolled up from the bottom over the heavy bottom pole.

Earlier *thang-kas* in good condition are now eagerly sought by museums and collectors. The later ones, some of which were painted in aniline colours, are less highly prized.

THEOPHILUS. The author of a treatise on medieval Christian arts and crafts entitled *De Diversis Artibus*. The work has been variously dated from the 9th to the 13th c. C. R. Dodwell, who translated and edited it in 1961, assigns it to a date between A.D. 1110 and 1140. Little or nothing is known with certainty about the writer, but internal evidence suggests that he was a German Benedictine monk and priest, an educated person conversant with scholastic philosophy and also a practising craftsman whose primary interest lay in metalwork. He has sometimes been identified with Roger of Helmarshausen.

Theophilus writes as a practical craftsman conversant with a large number of the techniques which he described. His interest in BYZANTINE crafts seems to reflect the increased contacts with Byzantium which resulted in the 12th c. from the First Crusade. Unlike other medieval technical handbooks, the *De Diversis Artibus* is not a mere compilation from traditional sources but 'represents the deliberate attempt by one person to give shape to his own personal knowledge and experience and present it in a rational and ordered way'. Dodwell gives the following general account of it: 'It has with some justification been described by three 19th-c. scholars (Guichard, Hendrie and Bourassé) as an encyclopedia of Christian art, for it embraces most of the medieval skills and crafts. What adds still more to its significance as a document of the arts is the fact that it describes art techniques of which no ROMANESQUE examples survive, such as oil-painting and painting on tin. It is also of great importance for medieval science. It contains, for example, what is perhaps the first direct reference to PAPER in the Latin West, the earliest medieval description of BELL FOUNDING and the most complete medieval account of the building of an organ; it discusses in detail metallurgical techniques such as CUPELLATION, refining, casting, and smelting and also describes the making of the crucible furnace and the bloomery hearth.'

THONET, MICHAEL (1796–1871). Austrian furniture designer from whose method of bending birch rods into curvilinear shapes the 'bentwood' furniture was evolved. His furniture was shipped in parts and screwed together. Considerable quantities were exported to America, where the style established itself. See FURNITURE (MODERN).

THROW. (1) Term in SILK production for processing raw silk threads into yarns suitable for knitting and WEAVING.

(2) Term in CERAMICS for moulding CLAY on a POTTER'S WHEEL.

TIBET. The idea of free artistic expression was foreign to the Lamaist culture of Tibet. Art and craft were united in the service of a religious system which permeated the whole of life so that even the most mundane and utilitarian objects held some religious import. Making things, anything at all, was an act of worship and therefore involved the subordination of the maker to an overriding tradition. This is why Tibetan arts and crafts were essentially anonymous: it is barely possible in Tibet, as with other artistic traditions, to trace periods and styles and fashions so as to be able to ascribe particular objects to an artist or a school. A conservatism of symbolism more rigid than the conservatism of China was imposed by a dogmatic theological control. Since everything that was made, whether it was made for purposes ancillary to religious ritual or for domestic uses, fell within the same all-embracing context of religious belief, everything had to be made worthily of its dignity. Religious motivation affected standards of production in such a way that all production was artistic. Native craftsmanship was always dominated by the idea of decoration. It was not, however, undisciplined ornamentation or artistic licence run riot in the interests of embellishment for its own sake, but a rigid and sacred use of all available space for the expression in recondite and traditional symbolism of a totally involved system of dogma. Outside influences followed the path of political and cultural penetration: Nepal, Kashmir, China, India and central Asia all contributed importantly at various times to the development of Tibetan arts and crafts. Yet all these influences were absorbed in a distinctive and highly idiosyncratic symbolic style.

Examples of utilitarian craftsmanship from Tibet are rare, partly because they were made of impermanent materials (wood, fabric, clay, etc.) and partly because they were never preserved in museums or collections as art objects but were replaced when their purpose was served. Ceremonial objects, appurtenances of public or private rituals, amulets, and so on, have survived in greater numbers. Both are of interest as the supreme example of a craftsmanship which developed almost into modern times under complete theocratic control.

1. CLAY. From *c.* the 5th c. A.D. clay began to be imported in large quantities from India for the manufacture of pots. Tibetan wood is for the most part hard to carve and is vulnerable to the harsh weather conditions which prevail; clay pots were better adapted for containing food and liquids and soon superseded the wooden bowl in certain contexts. But even in the attitude to clay the peculiarly religious Tibetan mentality made itself felt. Clay was regarded as a gift from Earth. Many designs found on clay vessels suggest that they were believed to have innate magical properties and that their use was reserved for certain substances only. The symbolic is more important than the ornamental function of decoration. Handles and other appendages were given therianthropic or divine forms, imbuing them with the mystical power of icons. Generally the over-all shape was simple and functional.

Votive tablets of clay mixed with incinerated human ashes, excreta, saliva, seeds and bits of sacred paper were used on shrines, to fill amulet boxes and in the construction of large figures of deities which adorned the numerous alcoves of the temples.

Clay was also used up to the 20th c. for moulds in the casting of bronze.

2. WOOD. Owing to the ravages of time, deterioration from moisture, insects, etc., not a great deal of Tibetan woodwork remains. As already mentioned, native Tibetan woods were very hard and difficult to carve. India again came to the rescue by providing fine-quality sandalwood, which was used mostly for the carving of sacred figures and for the interior decoration of temples. Window lintels of important houses had carved surfaces very similar to the exquisitely detailed engraving found on the sacred wooden BOOK COVERS.

Along with the almost Baroque exuberance of Tibetan ingenuity a certain sophisticated simplicity existed in the manufacture of furniture. An example of this is the folding table, usually carried by a wandering Lama, at which one squats to drink tea and participate in a ceremony. Three sides are hinged on wooden or metal pegs affixed to the outside of the table-top's frame so that the whole contrivance can be folded up into a flat and easily portable shape. The third side is open so that the person seated at it can get as close as possible to the objects placed on the top. On the whole, however, furniture was sparse. Corner cabinets rather similar to those of 17th-c. and 18th-c. Europe were occasionally to be seen in the homes of the rich, and elaborately carved altars were standard furniture in temples. Many architectural supports were richly carved with mythological motifs, but again owing to the appalling weather conditions these had very short lives.

Tibet had many carpenters or turners of wood who specialized in the manufacture of household utensils. A very high gloss called *phor-tse* was given to some wooden bowls and by the use of the seeds of a wild plant they were made heat-resistant. When *tsampa*, or buttered tea, was drunk from cups made of this material the taste was reputedly improved to a degree that bordered on ecstasy. The birch-tree knot was considered a great luxury, as precious as gold, and very fine and delicate tea-cups were made from this. Rosaries of 108 wooden beads were worn by most people round the neck and an occasional prayer-wheel has been found with its central cylinder made from imported bamboo.

3. TEXTILES. Fibres of grass, bark, wool, silk, cotton and goat and yak hair, together with metal threads, were woven by the Tibetans in a rich variety of processes which contrasted with the somewhat stereotyped techniques that prevailed in the other arts. In wealthy families the preparation and weaving of wool was usually the responsibility of servants. In poorer households the man would spin wool and hair while tending his sheep and yaks; the women would wash, brush and comb the fibres and weave them on simple wooden looms. Vegetable dyes were available in a wide variety of colours and were combined in strange and dazzling patterns. Appliqué needlework was a speciality for ritual and festive costumes, brocaded image covers, hats and even for THANG-KAS. About the 8th c. Tibetan needlework was so popular that it was traded into China, and even Japan, where it influenced local fashion.

Tailors in Tibet did not work in shops or factories but travelled with their equipment from house to house as their services were required and received room and board until the garments were completed. Tibetans had two styles of clothing, one for everyday wear and another for special occasions. Women wore richly coloured aprons either of wool or of cotton. Both men and women wore waist-length shirts made from cotton or silk, trousers of treated sheepskin or fox-skin and felt gowns tied at the waist with a plaited sash. The rich dressed in expensive brocaded silks and only in the late 19th c. started wearing underclothes and shoes of European style. Monks and other members of the ecclesiastical class wore saffron robes of silk or cotton varying in quality and design according to rank.

During the Chinese Ming era small quantities of carpets and rugs were bought from Chinese merchants by the monasteries and before long the nobility also began to use carpets in the homes. Skilled weavers imported from China and Iran brought with them their own designs and these were amalgamated with traditional Tibetan designs to form elaborately beautiful patterns with a distinctive ethnic character. The famous 'Peacock and Dragon' carpet design, obviously derived from both Arabic and Chinese sources, proved so popular that it was still being manufactured in the 20th c.

4. PAPER. The art of paper-making was introduced from China. A fine, strong paper produced from vegetable fibres superseded palm leaves imported from India and the birch bark from the sparse forests of Tibet. Books consisting of stacks of loose fibrous leaves between carved wooden covers were bound with woven cords and wrapped in exquisitely embroidered fabrics. In the 20th c., however, these beautifully made objects have virtually disappeared, craftsmanship being almost entirely displaced by machine manufacture.

5. METALWORK. Metal was the most important material of Tibetan craftsmanship both for religious and for domestic purposes and a wide variety of metals was worked. Newars from Nepal (metal-workers of the Banras class) brought their traditional skills to Tibet and the techniques were assimilated by the local craftsmen with consummate ability to produce some of the finest craftsmanship in metal that the world has known. Bronze and copper were considered to be as pure as gold and were used in the manufacture of images of the gods and of the Buddha. Most of the objects which have survived were ritualistic in character. Monks' staves and wands of office, VAJRAS (thunderbolts), PHUR-BUS (three-edged triangular daggers for exorcising evil spirits), *trisulas* (tridents) and many other items were embellished with chasing and inlay work of a very high order. Metal objects of gold, silver, brass, iron, tin and gilt bronze were made for religious and domestic ceremonials: teapots, shrine boxes, flageolets, telescopic trumpets, alms boxes, prayer wheels, reliquaries, roof ornaments for house or temple, dishes, water vessels and ornate stands for human skulls that held animal blood. The shapes (not the decoration) usually reflected the function of domestic articles. Decoration often astounds both by its quality and by its quantity, embodying almost always a ritualistic and symbolic connotation. Among the most common motifs are the LOTUS flower, *Makara* (elephant monsters), dragons and serpents, and the prayer *Om Mani Padme Hum* (Hail to the Jewel in the Lotus) written in ornate script. Other ornamental designs are a variety of sacred symbols, masses of complicated foliage and geometrical patterns formed by studding with gemstones such as TURQUOISE, EMERALDS, LAPIS LAZULI, ROCK-CRYSTAL, CORAL, etc. In the 19th and 20th centuries coloured glass of poor quality often took their place. Vessels often have intricately designed spouts in the form of fantastic heads of monsters springing from pot-bellied shapes. The jugs, teapots, ewers and other vessels are most typically Tibetan and can only amaze. Their extraordinary and sometimes horrific shapes speak of a culture clothed in mystery and magic. Effective use is made of the contrasting colours of gold, silver, copper and brass in perforated and open-work plaques riveted on to the body. Sometimes one comes across an exciting shape with poor ornamentation or vice versa,

Front and back of plaque with relief ornament of Garuda and mantras. (Kemper Coll., 18th c.)

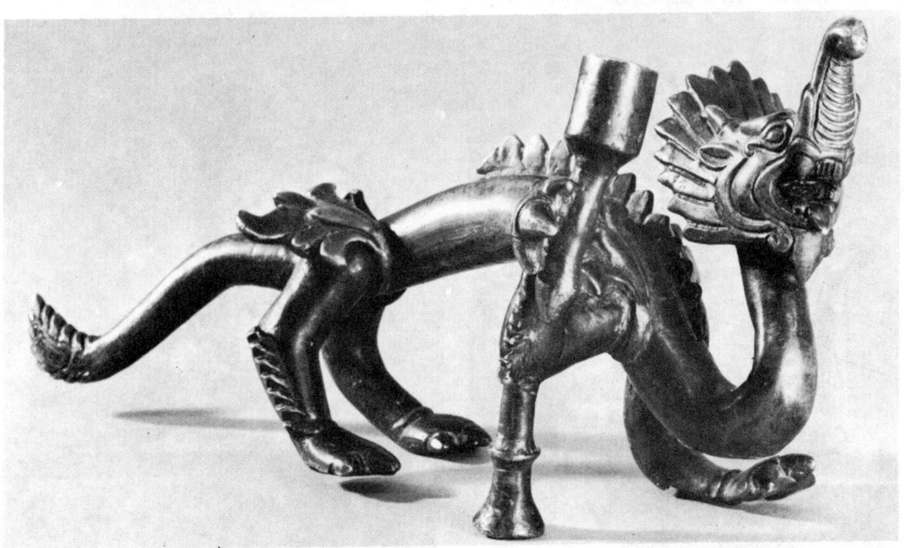

Bronze candle-holder in the form of a dragon. (Kemper Coll., 16th c.)

but in general design and ornament are matched while the craftsmanship is meticulous and superb. The religious outlook on manufacture of all kinds prohibited casual or slipshod workmanship.

Round his neck or attached to his ornate saddle the Tibetan wore his *gahu* (amulet shrine-box) made from a number of different metals ornamentally combined. The *gahu* contained prayers, seeds and metal images. *Gahus* were intricately engraved or beaten and many had elaborate filigree work. The finest examples are to be found on the monumental sculpture within the monasteries.

On the flat roofs of most temples and monasteries, at each of the four corners, were strange cone-shaped cylindrical constructions housing scrolls of hand-written prayers whose function was apotropaic. Their quality and workmanship depended on the wealth of the temple. Made of gilt bronze or copper, sometimes of gold, these large and ornate structures could be seen for miles.

The main centres of metalwork were Kham, Derge and Lhasa. Damascened ironwork from Derge is particularly rich in invention, especially in the popular crown-topped beer jugs. The rich embellishment of arabesque and foliage even on such everyday objects testifies to the ingrained Tibetan reverence for craftsmanship. The Tibetan metal-workers were adept at brazing, soldering, repoussé, damascening, piercing, chasing and engraving. Engraving in particular has a long and honoured tradition in Tibet, as is

Ceremonial apron made from human bones. (Kemper Coll., 19th c.)

Embossed bronze altar with Garuda decoration. (Kemper Coll., 18th c.)

Copper and silver ceremonial teapot. (Kemper Coll.)

Bronze figure of god Vajrapani. (Kemper Coll., 15th–16th c.)

shown by the few ancient works to be seen in museums and collections throughout the world. The engraving of convoluted dragons amid cloud formations, a popular theme, sounds typically Chinese; yet at the hands of the Tibetan craftsman it takes on a form which is unmistakably Tibetan.

6. JEWELLERY. Jewellery was an indispensable accessory for every Tibetan regardless of rank or station. At the ends of their plaits women wore medallions set with turquoise or perhaps an Indian rupee. Elongated gold or silver mounts framing turquoise or coral stones hung from locks of hair on either side of the forehead. Men and women wore many rings of silver or gold, their whole surface crammed with religious and prophylactic charms. Jewellery was both an adornment and a symbol of rank. A gold and turquoise hair-clip and a long cylindrical tear-drop ear-ring were part of a government official's regalia. Crowns of intricate filigree adorned men and images. Walls of jewelled mosaic reflected colours unknown outside Tibet. Although a certain sophistication may be lacking to Tibetan jewellery, the detailed workmanship was of such delicacy and elegance that comparison with anything else is virtually impossible.

7. MUSICAL INSTRUMENTS. The music of Tibet was as mysterious as its temples and monasteries. The great Tibetan trumpet has frequently been mentioned. Many Tibetan musical instruments were borrowed from India or China: flutes, trumpets, rattles, clappers, drums and bells

Silver shrine amulet box. (Alain Presencer Coll.)

Necklace amulet box. (Alain Presencer Coll.)

But bells of various kinds and clashing bronze discs became peculiarly Tibetan. All musical instruments were used both in religious services and in orchestras whose major functions were religious. Craftsmanship and skill were lavished upon them. Bells were particularly important both to punctuate religious ceremonial and as musical instruments, and the Tibetans excelled in casting them. Small ankle bells were worn by dancers and used as charms and clapper bells were hung from the necks of animals. A small tulip-shaped bell called *dril-bu* with the handle in the form of the head of *Pranjina Parainita* (symbol of wisdom) was held in the left hand of the Lama while he carried the Thunderbolt in his right hand. Much use was made of a wide range of flat metal discs and cymbals of various sizes. Small and large drums were often objects of exquisite craftsmanship. In the Victoria and Albert Museum there is a Lamaist drum with a beaten metal plate instead of a stretched membrane; the wooden frame is overlaid with brass and set with turquoises and corals. Flutes were made from human tibiae and drums from skulls.

BUTTER SCULPTURE. Butter has been moulded into fanciful shapes for centuries in Europe, but Tibet is perhaps the only country in which butter sculpture achieved the level of a minor art. The possibility of working in this medium was helped by the conditions. Yak butter contains many impurities, notably the hairs of the animal, and these help to bind it together. Ground pigment was added, turning it into a kind of putty and making it more malleable. The cold climate helped and made it possible to exhibit the finished work even in the open air without danger of melting. Bronze, calyx-shaped lamps filled with heaped-up butter and surmounted by a cotton wick were in common use for festive occasions and it has been suggested that the unmelted portion of the butter was shaped and thus gave rise to the practice of butter sculpture. However this may be, the practice was well established when it was first recorded by European observers. On the Feast of Flowers, which fell on the 15th day of the Tibetan year, 10 January on our reckoning, in 1845, two French missionaries, the Abbés Huc

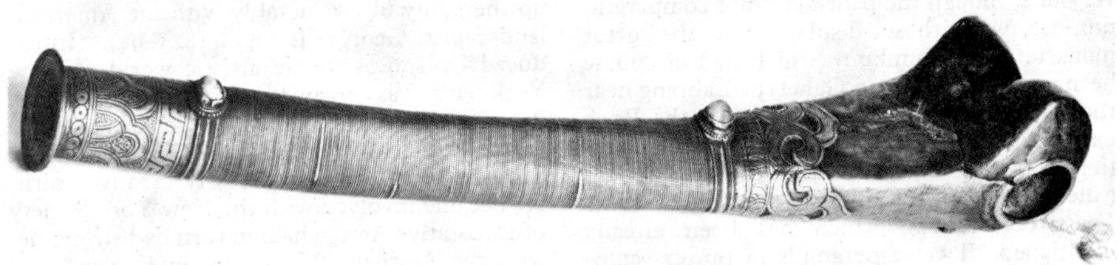

Trumpet from human femur. (Kemper Coll.)

and Gabet, visited the butter sculpture display at the monastery of Kumbum and left a graphic description of it. (See R. E. Huc, *Souvenirs d'un voyage dans le Thibet*.)

The exhibition was held for one night only before the various temples in the lamasery town. The exhibits were brilliantly lit by innumerable lamps disposed on scaffoldings and consisted of large low reliefs illustrating subjects drawn from Tibetan Buddhism. Framing the larger sculptures were panels of animals, birds and flowers, while lines of smaller panels flanked the paths which led from one temple display to another. The smaller reliefs showed battles, hunts, scenes from nomadic life and views of the most celebrated monasteries in Tibet and Tartary. Huc and his companion describe admiringly the faithfulness with which different racial types were portrayed and the technical skill with which the artists produced details such as the colour and texture of different types of fur. Before the principal temple there was a puppet theatre in which foot-high figures made of butter, and representing a procession of lamas going to prayer, were moved across the stage before coloured decorations also of butter.

The butter sculptures were known as 'flowers', and Huc describes how they were moulded by sculptors who kept plunging their hands in cold water lest they should become too warm and melt the butter. This, he adds, was a fearful ordeal in the climate of Tibet. The sculptures were made from fresh butter by a team of twenty selected lamas, who took three months over the task. They began by kneading the butter with their hands in water to harden it and then, working to an over-all design prepared by the leading artist, who was required to furnish a new scheme of decoration every year, they each executed different sections of the reliefs. Finally the completed sculptures were handed over to artists who coloured them, and after they had gone on exhibition for a single night they were broken up and thrown into a ravine, where the remains were eaten by birds.

An American expedition which visited Chomi monastery in the eastern provinces of China, bordering on Tibet, in 1925 was able to take pictures of butter sculptures on exhibition, which add significantly to our knowledge of the art. (Joseph F. Rock, 'Life among the Lamas of Chomi', *National Geographic Magazine*, liv, 1928, 569.) At Chomi the workmanship was very fine, though the panels did not compare in number with those displayed at the great monasteries of Kumbum (which had of course been visited by Huc and Gabet) or Labrang near the Koko Nor border. Members of the Rock expedition attended two butter sculpture exhibitions, one on the 25th day of the 10th moon, called the 'Feast of Lights', and the other on the Feast of Flowers, which has been already mentioned. Twelve pyramids of butter sculpture were arranged on either side of a central pagoda of butter. Dr. Rock discovered that the sculptors belonged to wandering fraternities of lamas who made the rounds of the monasteries in search of employment. Different lamaseries would compete for the service of a particularly gifted sculptor, and he would have the task of completing two or more panels of reliefs. Yak butter soared in price as the time for the festival drew near, and 1,000 catties (2,860 kilogrammes) might be consumed in a single festival. Once the reliefs had been moulded on to dark wood panels the panels themselves would be lashed on pyramidal frameworks, which in turn were supported by stout posts driven into the ground. A large panel looked like an inverted letter 'V'. It would have a cone-shaped sculpture at the top, two side panels representing the two arms of the letter, and three circular reliefs (the lowest of which might be replaced by a miniature shrine). The easel-like frameworks were arranged in groups of five. Smaller square reliefs, also on frames, ran along a balustrade in front of the main display.

Rock states categorically that the colours were not painted on to the butter, but mixed with it in powder form before it was shaped. Often as many as twenty shades might be employed in one picture, and the whole effect, as the sculptures stood out in the white glare from innumerable butter lamps, was one of dazzling magnificence.

TIFFANY AND COMPANY. It was natural that New York, which had become the artistic centre of the U.S.A. in the 19th c., should produce a number of outstanding silver companies, the most famous being the firm founded in 1837 by Charles L. Tiffany and John B. Young. The company became Tiffany & Co. in 1853, and continues today under this name.

TIFFANY, LOUIS COMFORT (1848–1933). American painter, decorator, architect, landscapist and mosaicist, and a leader in many spheres of American decorative arts in the later 19th c. He is best remembered today as one of the few American masters of the ART-NOUVEAU style. The glass production of his Tiffany Furnaces is internationally regarded as one of the finest achievements of *art-nouveau* craftsmanship.

The family was well established in New York through its celebrated store, Tiffany and Company. Young Louis did not show any talent for his father's business, however, and early took up the study of art, notably with the American landscapist George Inness (1825–94). Introduced by Inness to the artistic world of New York, he was encouraged to work abroad. A perceptive man, Tiffany was soon aware of the weaknesses in his painting and began to seek another outlet for his restlessly creative spirit. He became involved with the New York Society of Decorative Arts, which in turn had strong ties with the Aesthetic Movement in England and the work of William MORRIS, Edward Burne-Jones and Walter CRANE. Interest in the Society led him in 1881 to form Louis C. Tiffany and Associated Artists, a decorating firm which met with prompt success. Drawing on a variety of design sources, the company specialized in the conception of interior spaces and their decoration as integrated units rather than as a confusion of parts. Tiffany was asked to do interiors for many socially prominent New Yorkers as well as for clubs. One of his most important commissions was the redecoration of the White House in 1882–3.

Becoming more interested in his increasingly important experiments with glass, Tiffany withdrew from the associated artists of his original company and devoted himself to the development of an ornamental glass for coloured windows. These experiments drew upon his knowledge of Oriental and Egyptian art, producing a new gem-like treatment of the coloured window, which was widely admired. The manufacture of Tiffany's famed Favrile glass did not begin until 1893. It was not until after 1900 that the Tiffany name came to be more associated with decorative glass of an *art-nouveau* character than with stained glass or mosaic work.

Vase by Louis Comfort Tiffany. (The Art Institute of Chicago, 1901)

A brilliant and eclectic designer, Tiffany was able to draw upon elements from ancient Egyptian, Roman, Chinese, Japanese and Persian arts in his creations. These influences were combined into glass of sumptuous form and decoration, much of which was characterized by nacreous, iridescent surfaces. The brilliance of his designs was early recognized by the influential Parisian critic and dealer Samuel Bing, who won international acclaim for Favrile glass objects and encouraged Tiffany to continue, giving him an exhibition at his new Salon de l'Art Nouveau in 1895. Tiffany glass was characterized by its elegant form and finish and was also notable for its freedom of handling and the successful cultivation of accident or chance into the final design.

From 1903 on Tiffany devoted himself to the decoration of his fabulous estate, Laurelton Hall, on Long Island, which was the total expression of his aesthetic concepts. As his interest in the house and the Tiffany Foundation increased, he became less involved with the daily operations of the glass-works. In 1919 he turned over business operations to Douglas and Leslie Nash while providing financial support. But in 1928 he withdrew that support, and the Tiffany Furnaces closed shortly afterwards.

See ART NOUVEAU, and GLASS (AMERICA).

TIJOU, JEAN (active 1688–1712). Best known of the craftsmen in decorative wrought iron who worked in England. Before the 17th c. it is only rarely that the names of the great smiths were even recorded and Tijou is one of the first who emerges partially from obscurity. Nothing is certainly known of his origins or early life, but it is conjectured that he may have fled from France in consequence of the Revocation of the Edict of Nantes. He is first heard of as one of the skilled craftsmen employed in the spring of 1688 by William Cavendish, first Duke of Devonshire, at Chatsworth, where he worked until late in 1689 at the balustrade and balcony for the Great Staircase. From 1689 to 1699 he worked at Hampton Court, where he executed three gates for the garden front of the palace and staircase balustrades (1694), railings for the Fountain Garden (1699) and 12 ornamental panels and two small gates for the Fountain Garden. The last-mentioned, set up in 1690, is regarded as his masterpiece and is one of the outstanding masterpieces of BAROQUE ironwork in Europe. From 1695 to 1707 he was executing gates for the aisles and screens for the choir at St. Paul's. His screen for the organ case, now split up and repositioned, is known as the Golden Gates and the two great gates at the east end of the choir are known as the Candelabra Gates. About 1700 he began to work outside London again and made the entrance gates (Golden Gates) at Burleigh House, Stanford, while in 1706 he was working for Lord Ashburnham at Ampthill, Bedfordshire, where he made the staircase balustrade.

In 1693 he published a book of designs entitled *A New Booke of Drawings Invented and Designed by Jean Tijou . . . for the use of them that will work iron in perfection and with art*, which was the first book of designs for ironwork to appear in England. It is thought that some of the designs showed familiarity with the six plates of designs published by MAROT in Holland in 1690. His book of designs had considerable importance in disseminating the Baroque style in ironwork which Tijou had established in England. It was a more classical and dignified version of the Baroque style of Louis XIV in France. Tijou excelled as a repoussé smith, a technique which was based on the art of the silversmith and which had not been part of the English tradition of ironwork before his time and was little practised after he left the country in 1712. Although some English smiths made use of his designs, none equalled his mastery of repoussé work. Among Tijou's assistants may have been John Gardom, John (or Thomas) Warren, William Edney and Huntingdon Shaw.

Tijou evidently left England some time in 1712 for his wife, Anne, had a letter of attorney and was collecting moneys owing to her husband in November of that year. His destination is conjectured to have been Paris, for by 1723 Louis Fordrin the Younger had got hold of the copper plates of his 1693 pattern book and reissued them under the title *Nouveau livre de Serrurerie de composition anglaise*.

See also IRON AND STEEL (DECORATIVE WROUGHT IRONWORK).

TILLIARD, JEAN-BAPTISTE (1685–1766). French chair-maker who was providing seat furniture for the royal palaces from *c.* 1730. Between 1751 and 1756 he fulfilled orders from the Prince de Soubise to the value of some 6,000 livres. He handed over his workshop to his son, JEAN-BAPTISTE TILLIARD II in 1764, the same workshop stamp 'TILLIARD' being used by both father and son.

TOILES DE JOUY. '*Toiles de Jouy*' are the cotton prints produced by the factory operating at Jouy, near Versailles, from 1760 to 1843. The term is not infrequently extended, however, to all furnishing fabrics, irrespective of origin, which have figure scenes printed in monochrome (red, blue, violet, etc.) from engraved metal. Some of the earliest and best of these were in fact printed in England during the 3rd quarter of the 15th c., and in the later 18th and early 19th centuries, when they were extremely popular in France, Jouy was only one of many factories which produced them.

That the reputation of Jouy eclipsed that of its competitors was largely due to the acumen of C.-P. OBERKAMPF, who—under the favour of both Louis XVI and Napoleon I—laid the foundations of the factory's success by securing the services of J.-B. Huet as designer. The elegance and gay spontaneity with which Huet adapted the most diverse subjects to the exigencies of textile design make the Jouy prints one of the most charming expressions of the furnishing taste of the period, and they are repeatedly copied even today. Rather less happy were the designs contributed, after Huet's death in 1811, by Horace Vernet and Hippolyte Lebas.

These furnishing prints formed, at Jouy and elsewhere, only a small part of the total output. The prosperity of the business rested mainly on the enormous production of small floral patterns printed from wood-blocks or rollers and none the less attractive for being reproductions.

See COTTON AND COTTON PRINTING.

TOMIHARU. See JAPAN (NETSUKE).

TOMOTADA. See JAPAN (NETSUKE).

TOMPION, THOMAS (1639–1713). One of the greatest clock-makers of all times and all countries, his CLOCKS combining artistic design of the highest order with mechanical excellence. He was also a maker of watches of quality. He was born at Northill, Bedfordshire, the son of the local blacksmith and farrier. Nothing is known of his apprenticeship, but it is assumed that it lasted through the years 1653–60, and he appears to have returned to work in Northill in 1660. He probably went to London in 1664, and was admitted a Brother of the Clockmakers' Company in 1671, by which time he must have already acquired some reputation as a clock-maker. He became free of the Company, by purchase, in 1674, and was then living in Water Lane, Fleet Street. From 1701 to 1708 he was in partnership with his former apprentice Edward Banger, and from 1710 to 1713 with George GRAHAM, also a former apprentice. In 1676 he was chosen to make the two main clocks for the famous Octagon Room of the newly founded Royal Greenwich Observatory, whose pendulums were suspended above them in cavities in the walls of the room. His LONG-CASE CLOCKS include a great range of domestic designs of great style and beauty; and he also made outstanding larger clocks of 'Royal' class, including one for the bedchamber of William III at Hampton Court Palace (*c.* 1700) and one in 1703 for Prince George of Denmark, which is now in Buckingham Palace. This ran for a whole year at a single winding, as did a noteworthy spring-driven BRACKET CLOCK also made for William III. Near the end of his life he made an outstanding 'equation' clock for the Pump Room at Bath, where it still stands. Tompion pioneered the application of the spiral balance-spring to WATCHES in England, an invention due to Huygens, then in Paris, in 1675, and his firm made during his lifetime about 6,000 watches. He is buried in Westminster Abbey, beside his one-time apprentice and partner George Graham.

TONDER LACE. LACE made in southern Denmark. In the 17th and 18th centuries it resembled Flemish bobbin lace and in the 19th and 20th centuries the laces of LILLE and BUCKINGHAMSHIRE.

TOOL, TOOLING. Terms used in LEATHER-WORK and BOOKBINDING. Tooling consists of impressing designs with heated tools into the leather surface. The 'finishing tools' are small metal dies, usually of brass, engraved with an ornament and fitted with wooden handles; a 'roll' is a cylindrical tool with the design engraved on the periphery, enabling the binder to impress by rotation a continuous strip of repeating pattern. On 'fine' bindings many separate tools are combined with rolls and plain lines, or FILLETS, to produce elaborate designs. A similar effect may also be obtained by using a large panel-stamp of iron or brass, engraved with the complete design, which is impressed on the damped leather in a single operation by a hand-press. The terms 'tool' and 'stamp' are also used to signify the impressions made in the leather as well as the actual implements used.

'Gold tooling' is the technique of impressing heated tools into the leather through gold leaf previously laid on glair, a white-of-egg preparation; the glair, heated by the tools, causes the gold leaf to stick to the leather. When no gold is used tooling is described as 'blind'. A coloured effect may also be obtained by painting the leather or using other metals. Silver leaf is rarely used on account of tarnishing but in recent times binders have successfully experimented with aluminium and palladium.

TOPAZ. In classical antiquity 'topaz' was the name given to a yellow SAPPHIRE or PERIDOT and sometimes (e.g. by Pliny) to the type of corundum now called 'chrysolite'. In modern usage topaz is a transparent and lustrous fluosilicate of aluminium much prized as a gemstone. It has a hardness index of 8 on the MOHS SCALE. It occurs in yellow, white, pale blue and pale green. The most highly valued are the golden, sherry-yellow stones, most of which come from Duro Preto in Brazil. After the yellow the most prestigious topazes are the pale blue variety, which also come from Brazil and from the Urals and Nerchinsk in Siberia. Pink opals rarely occur in nature and most of those seen in jewellery are heat-treated yellow stones.

TOPINO, CHARLES. French cabinet-maker of whose life little is known. He became a master in 1773 and worked principally for other cabinet-makers who were also *marchands-merciers*. An original craftsman, whose reputation relies on his small pieces such as tables and *bonheurs-du-jour*, the MARQUETRY designs he favoured included somewhat stiffly arranged domestic utensils and vases in light woods set against a dark ground. He was not, however, a well organized business-man and was finally rendered bankrupt in 1789, after which no more is known of him.

TOROND, FRANCIS. See SILHOUETTE.

TORTOISESHELL. The horny substance known as tortoiseshell is not a shell and has had no association with tortoises since the early 19th c., when the whole carapace of a small tortoise used to be worked up into SNUFF-BOX lids. Tortoiseshell is a compound of keratin, hydrogen and hydroxyl, rather similar in nature to the horns and hooves of mammals. But it is much more tacky and tenacious to the edge of the tool than horn. It has a hardness of about 2 on the MOHS SCALE, is semi-translucent, and coloured brown, red or yellow. Only three species of marine turtles produce true tortoiseshell, of which the most important is the Hawksbill (*Chelone imbricata*) found in West Indian waters and off Brazil. This turtle, which is fished for by the inhabitants of the Antilles who are fast leaving the trade for better paid and safer jobs on the Florida coast and so causing a rise in price through scarcity, provides most of the shell used by American and European tortoiseshell workers. The plates on the back, or carapace, are a mottled dark brown, amber and red. The central or main plates are those which are preferred for good work, unless a blonde is required. This is found on the belly or plastron, where all the plates are yellow and smaller than those on the back. Blonde is preferred for combs, even in Japan, because of the contrast it offers to the hair of brunettes. It has been fashionable at least since the 19th c., when Spanish women wore back combs which were sometimes a foot in height, all of yellow shell. The plates vary in thickness and width according to the age of the turtle. A main plate (one from near the centre of the back) from an average reptile would be about six millimetres thick and weigh about 255 grammes. The Seychelles Hawksbill, a variety from the Indian Ocean, has a red belly. The Loggerhead turtle (*Thalassochelys caretta*) provides most of the shell used in the Far East, and it has been said that no finer tortoiseshell is to be found than that fished between Celebes and Borneo. Although in Japan blonde shell was always favoured for combs, the Chinese and Japanese seem to have preferred, for other work, a well mottled shell with the dark and blond colours lying close together. Some Loggerhead shell was brought to Europe and used amongst other things for BOULLE furniture. The Chinese caught Loggerheads by trailing a *remora* or sucker-fish on the end of a line. The *remora* would attach its mouth to a turtle's back; the amphibian would be inescapably caught and both would be hauled aboard together. The Green Turtle (*Chelone midas*) yields a second-rate shell which welds badly and has greenish reflections. It is more like horn than the shell of other turtles. While the shell is of little use except for veneering, the turtle itself provides turtle soup.

Tortoiseshell has been one of the most sought-after treasures of the sea for thousands of years. Besides its magnificent lustre and brilliant and unfading colours, half opaque and half translucent like a rock pool, it has sympathetic tactile qualities. These have made it a favourite material for objects which are to be handled every day, such as combs, hair brushes, items of feminine adornment, and musical instruments. Apart from its appeal to the user tortoiseshell is a material dear to the heart of the craftsman because it is easy to work and is very versatile. It comes into the tortoiseshell worker's hands already detached from the bony carapace of the turtle and sorted out into separate plates or 'flakes', so that he can select pieces of exactly the size and colour he wants. A piece too small to be used for a particular task can be welded to another, while scraps left over from cutting can be welded together so that nothing is wasted.

Even today no craftsman in tortoiseshell will discuss his working methods. They are cherished family secrets which have been handed down for generations in the same line of workers. Tortoiseshell craftsmen become fewer with each generation owing to the competition from plastics and the shortage of people who are prepared to pay a good price for the superior article, and unless amateurs take up tortoiseshell working it seems likely to disappear, at least from Europe.

The shell to be welded is boiled in water to which salt has been added in the proportion of a handful to every quart (litre) of water. Young turtles' shells should be boiled for a shorter time and with more salt in the water, but the usual time is an hour's boiling. The hydrogen in the water acts on the hydrogen and hydroxyl in the tortoiseshell to produce a hydrogen bond. But if too much salt is put in the water when boiling an old turtle's shell, it might replace some of the protein in the shell, which varies with the age of the animal. Once they have been boiled the two pieces of shell are pressed together and a weld takes place. Strips of shell can be welded end to end to produce hoops or rings. Shell can also be cut into veneer, which can be bent round a thin box or pressed into a mould. In the past and in some primitive societies today tortoiseshell was welded by enveloping the joint in wet linen rags and then nipping the bundle between red-hot iron pincers. Steam thus released welded the shell. Thin pieces of mother of pearl, gold or silver can also be pressed into the shell to decorate it. It has been suggested that tortoiseshell which has been welded together can be detected because the veins of colour, all of which radiate from a common centre, will not match in a welded plate. Genuine tortoiseshell should fluoresce yellow-brown under an ultra-violet lamp. When sawed or filed it will yield a very pungent and characteristic odour, rather like that of a horse's hoof when it is singed by the blacksmith. A strip of tortoiseshell can also be burned as a test and compared with a strip of imitation plastic tortoiseshell, and the shell can also be tested for hardness. Tortoiseshell can be bought in blocks of veneer. It is from these welded blocks that oculists cut the frames of spectacles. The bulk of commercial tortoiseshell nowadays is used for this and for the backs of hair brushes.

The technique of polishing tortoiseshell has been as closely guarded as every other part of the craft. Originally the shell was scraped down with a newly broken glass edge; now a metal tool is used. Sandpapering with very fine paper follows; no coarse papers must be used or else they produce ineradicable scratches. Finally the shell is polished with a cotton rag dipped in sweet oil (almond or olive oil) and spread with powdered rotten stone. The next stage is to polish with a rag dipped in crocus powder, keeping a sweet-oil polish for the final finish. Once applied, a polish should be so good that the craftsman can see his face in it.

Often shell which is 'scabby', that is flaking and splitting into different layers, can be split further and used as veneer. Several veneers can be sawn from a single plate, but this is an extremely specialized operation, like cutting the ivory veneers for piano-keys. Because thin veneers are likely to be very transparent, some craftsmen in the past used to underlay them with a painted background or silver foil. Research is going on at present into new ways of processing tortoiseshell. Welding has been tried by coating shell with a protective paint and then baking it in a kiln. Shell could also be welded in steam, such as that produced in a pressure cooker, or impregnated with ammonia in order to bend it. Moulding small pieces of tortoiseshell into a whole is an industrial rather than a craft technique.

Because tortoiseshell is generally thin, it has hardly ever been carved in low relief, although the Chinese have succeeded in making carved boxes from it for the European market. Generally speaking it has been used in the flat, either moulded or applied, with or without pressed decoration. Snuff-boxes, tobacco-boxes, watch-covers and card-cases, hairbrush backs, combs, veneers for furniture, musical instruments, cane-heads, jewellery and other articles have been made from it.

The shell was imported from the East in Roman times when it was used for inlay on expensive furniture. From the Renaissance onwards it was used for furniture inlay, particularly for cabinet work. Toilet articles, tea-caddies and fans were also made from it. In China it was also used for furniture inlay and was combined with ivory in figure sculpture, while in Japan it was moulded in wooden moulds into combs, lacquered, inlaid in a variety of articles (such as the delightful *oikimono* elephants) and made into NETSUKE.

TORUS. Term in architecture and the decorative arts for a large convex MOULDING of semi-circular section. It is found in architecture especially at the base of a column.

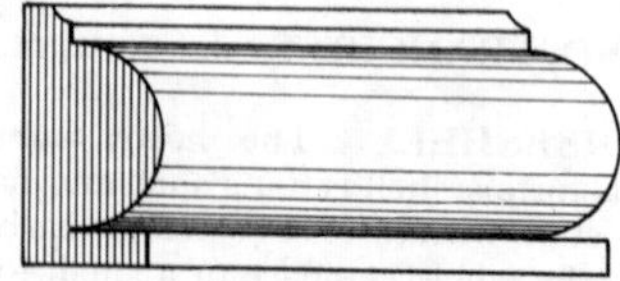

TORY, GEOFROY (*c.* 1480–1533). A native of Bourges, publisher, woodcut artist and grammarian, who played a leading part in introducing the French Renaissance style in book production. In early life, when he taught Latin grammar, he made two visits to Italy, and settling in Paris *c.* 1522 he published and ornamented in Italian style a series of Books of Hours which broke with tradition by being set in ROMAN type. He was the author of the *Champ fleury*, published in 1529, a discursive work devoted mainly to the proper design of the roman capital alphabet, relating it to the proportions of the human body and to classical myths and incidentally advocating an increased use of the French language for learned writing and reforms in its spelling. He illustrated the book with his own woodcuts.

About that time Tory began to print his publications and though he did not excel in this art, he was appointed *Imprimeur du roi* in 1531, probably as a recognition of his services as a reformer of decorative style. He printed a French translation from Eusebius by the king's command in 1532.

Some of Tory's engravings are signed with a Lorraine cross. Woodcuts with this mark occur in books printed in 1521–46, so that it is unlikely that he could have made all of them.

See TYPOGRAPHY.

60, 452, 453.

TOUDOUZE, ANAÏS (1822–99). One of the outstanding FASHION PLATE artists of the 2nd half of the 19th c. She designed plates for *Le Follet Courrier des Salons* in the 1850s and worked regularly for *Le Magazine des Demoiselles* and *La Mode Illustrée.* ISABELLA Toudouze, her daughter, designed plates for *The Queen.*

TOURMALINE (Sinhalese: *toramalli*). A borosilicate mineral, the black variety of which is also known as 'schorl'. In crystalline form it is pyro-electric, i.e. when heated one end of the crystal receives a positive and the other a negative charge, which are reversed on cooling. It is also piezo-electric, responding to changes of pressure, and has been used for depth-sounding. It was first found in Ceylon early in the 18th c.

Tourmaline is generally opaque and has a vitreous lustre. Its hardness index is 7 to 7·5 on the MOHS SCALE. Transparent or semi-transparent crystals are valued as gemstones. Precious tourmaline occurs in green (known sometimes as 'Brazilian emerald'), red ('rubellite'), pink and various shades of indigo and blue ('indicolite'). The yellow variety found in Ceylon was formerly mistaken for a ZIRCON and the greenish variety for a PERIDOT. There is a Californian variety which is green at the core with a red surround and a Brazilian variety with red core and green surround (sometimes known as 'water-melon' tourmalines). Besides Ceylon precious tourmalines are found in Madagascar, the Urals, Brazil and southern California.

TOUTIN, JEAN (1578–1644). Reputed originator of painting in enamel. See ENAMEL.

TOWNSEND. Quaker family of cabinet-makers established at Newport, Rhode Island, who with the Goddard family constituted one of the outstanding groups of American furniture-makers. during the 18th and early 19th centuries. (For the characteristics of the work of this group see GODDARD.) The founder of the family was SOLOMON Townsend. His sons JOB (1699–1765) and CHRISTOPHER (1701–73) were both cabinet-makers and are known to have been in business from at least 1738. They were the elders of the Newport group and John Goddard I was apprenticed to them as a young man. Job had five sons and Christopher two sons who were cabinet-makers. In the fourth generation there were still five members of the family in the same business.

There was a cabinet-maker Stephen Townsend working in Charleston 1760–71, who apparently was no connection of the Newport family.

TOYOMASA (1773–1856). See JAPAN (NETSUKE).

TOYS

1. Primitive and Ancient Egyptian
2. Greek and Roman antiquity
3. Early European
4. The eighteenth century
5. The nineteenth century
6. America
7. The Far East

1. PRIMITIVE AND ANCIENT EGYPTIAN. No recognizable examples of playthings have been discovered among the effects of cave-dwellers and other primitive men. Nevertheless it can be assumed that even in the most distant past young children used objects of one sort or another as toys, for play activity is essential in the development of those skills necessary for growth and survival. It seems probable, therefore, that archetypes of most toys can be found in nature: branches or sticks dragged along the ground or ridden astride served as pull-toys or hobby-horses; rounded stones or fruits as balls; pebbles as marbles and counters; a small animal or a younger child as a doll substitute—and so on.

It is only with the development of sophisticated arts and crafts that specially made toys appear. However, even during relatively late periods in the history of mankind they were rarer than was once commonly supposed. The ancient Egyptians were skilled makers of tomb models and miniatures of many kinds, but these were mainly scaled down representations of objects believed to be of use to the dead in after life. Nevertheless we can say with some certainty that these same craftsmen were among the first toy-makers. In Egypt a number of undoubted playthings have been discovered, including pull-toys in the form of animals, like the toy tiger from Thebes (*c.* 1000 B.C.) with a hinged mouth, balls of fabric, papyrus, leather or pottery of varying dates, glazed clay spinning tops and marbles, and even sets of what appear to be nine-pins. Board games were popular and some beautifully made examples have come to light, although these were almost certainly intended for adults rather than children.

2. GREEK AND ROMAN ANTIQUITY. The children of ancient Greece and Rome enjoyed a large variety of playthings. Many of their toys have been recovered from tombs, and others can be seen pictured on the sides of vases, urns or in frescoes. It is interesting to find that some of the more simple types are almost identical with folk-toys still being made today. There are fired clay whistling birds, rattles in the form of animals, miniature carts and dolls with jointed limbs. The ancient game of astragalus or knucklebones is pictured in a wall-painting in Pompeii, and it is thought that the yo-yo first made its appearance during Greek times. It was required of children that they should leave their playthings, when they had outgrown them, as offerings at the shrine of a suitable deity, and there are several references to this custom in the *Greek Anthology*:

'To Hermes this fair ball of pleasant sound
This boxen rattle fraught with lively noise,
These maddening dice, this top well whirling round,
Philocles has hung up his boyhood toys.'

See also GREEK AND ROMAN ANTIQUITY (TOYS AND GAMES).

3. EARLY EUROPEAN. With the collapse of the Roman Empire many traditions of learning and craftsmanship were broken, skills lost, and life became altogether briefer, harder and less luxurious. From *c.* the 5th c. A.D. until almost the beginning of the 16th c. children were put to work and expected to grow up at an early age: they had little time or use for playthings. Nevertheless in central Europe a cottage industry of toy-making developed from the Middle Ages onwards. Simple wooden toys, from designs that were to remain virtually unaltered until modern times, were made by peasants during periods of enforced leisure in the snow-bound winter months, and collected every spring by pedlars to be sold either from door to door or at the big seasonal fairs.

Pieter Brueghel's famous painting *Kinderspielen*, now in Vienna, depicts many 16th-c. toys and games. In that animated and crowded scene of childish activity can be seen whipping-tops, hobby-horses, hoops, hand-held windmills, dolls, skittles, marbles and knucklebones. These are all traditional toys, with pedigrees stretching back through the Dark Ages to Greek and Roman times. In Ben Jonson's comedy *Bartholomew Fair* (1614) are mentioned several playthings for sale on the stalls: hobby-horses, gilt gingerbreads, drums, fiddles, toy dogs and horses, dolls (known then as 'babies') and what he calls 'the device of Smiths'—presumably that push-me-pull-you toy on which a man and a bear strike an anvil turn and turn about.

Very soon toys began to be manufactured and distributed on a much larger scale. Factories were built, and the town of Nuremberg was established as a centre not only for children's playthings, but for small luxury articles for adults as well. It became fashionable to collect curiosities and examples of fine craftsmanship in miniature. Cabinets were constructed to hold these, and in many cases the shelves were divided into room-like compartments in which scaled-down furniture in silver, ivory or exotic woods could be set out. The first such baby-house on record was made for the Duke Albrecht of Saxony in 1558. Though originally they were no more than cabinets on stands with plain doors, later examples have elaborately carved and painted façades in imitation of real houses. Among outstanding baby-houses that have survived, there are three examples on display in the Rijksmuseum, Amsterdam (one with a contemporary oil painting showing how its rooms were originally furnished *c.* 1690); and another in the Germanisches Museum, Nuremberg, so perfect and so complete that when contemplating it one has the illusion of watching an actual establishment of 1639 seen small as through a reducing-glass. Roughly contemporary with these houses, and originating too in Germany or the Low Countries, are some equally well-equipped Nuremberg kitchens, whose purpose it was to instruct small girls in the domestic arts.

Dolls during the 16th and 17th centuries were almost always costumed as adults, though sometimes they were supplied with a baby's leading-strings attached to their shoulders. They were basically simple in construction, with wooden or wax heads and wooden or rag bodies, often legless but with a circle of wood under the hem of their skirts by way of stand. Portraits of the period show elaborately dressed examples held stiffly in their young owners' arms, and a much reproduced woodcut of 1540 tells us that they were sometimes supplied with their own cradles.

Meanwhile boys were playing with miniature weapons, soldiers, tops, hoops and equipment designed to develop their bodies and skills. Examples of primitive boat-shaped rocking-horses have been preserved, and we know that inflated footballs (though without a rubber lining) were used from Elizabethan times.

4. THE EIGHTEENTH CENTURY. Children in the 18th c. were dressed as little grown-ups and obliged to behave as such. Even those fortunate enough to be born into upper- or middle-class homes could hope to enjoy but a brief, severely disciplined childhood. Toys were few, and quickly cast aside. On the surface patterns of social behaviour seemed set and unalterable, especially where attitudes to the young were concerned. Nevertheless the century was one in which major changes were being brought about through industrial and technological development. These came at first slowly and then with gathering momentum. The development and exploitation of colonies overseas meant increased prosperity at home, a widespread rise in standards of living and more children receiving at least an elementary education. Simple teaching toys,

such as bone alphabet blocks and various similar devices for the learning of numbers were used extensively both in the home and in the proliferating dame-schools.

Many of the fine old baby-houses reflect the elegance and luxury of the period. In England a number have been preserved in public or private collections. Among the best known are the extraordinarily evocative Ann Sharp house, dating from the end of the 17th c., the cabinet-like Westbrook House (1705), the Nostell Priory House (*c.* 1740) designed by Robert ADAM with furniture that may be apprentice work of the young Thomas CHIPPENDALE, and the Tate baby-house (1760) with its superb outside staircase sweeping up to the front door and its carefully scaled furniture within.

In 1746 an astonishing craze swept through France for the *pantin*, or Jumping-Jack as it was known in England. These flat, marionette-like figures were operated by a single master string and though only capable of a limited range of movement, exerted a strange fascination on children and adults alike. The Duchess de Chartres commissioned BOUCHER to paint one for her; Voltaire's friend Jean d'Alembert condemned the habit of playing with what he called 'this ridiculous toy', and eventually the police banned Jumping-Jacks on the ground that women were in danger of bearing children with limbs twisted like *pantins*.

Paper toys were also popular, and could be bought in sheets for cutting out and assembly at home. A paper caravan is mentioned in the *Woodforde Diaries* of 1782, and the closely related 'Protean Figure', or paper doll with changes of costume, appears in an entry for 1787. The latter was apparently an English invention.

Flat filigree metal toys in slight relief called 'Nuremberg Figures' were exported in large quantities from Germany in the last decades of the century, the finest being made by the firm of Schweitzer in Bavaria. In soft alloys, these could be folded and clipped together to produce charming three-dimensional pieces: miniature furniture; park and garden components, including trees, houses, pergolas and urns of flowers; ships and carriages of many different designs. From 1775 the Hilpert family of tin-smiths in Nuremberg produced a long series of 'flat-back' soldiers inspired by Frederick the Great's army, and also many figures of a non-military nature.

The dolls of the 18th c. are especially attractive, being still formalized and unnaturalistic yet more sophisticated in workmanship than those of an earlier date. The so-called 'Queen Anne type' have wooden heads under a thin coat of gesso plaster, prominent, pug-dog-like glass eyes (usually brown and without pupils) and delicately painted complexions. A group of dolls of *c.* 1740 in the Victoria and Albert Museum, London, is typical of this genre. Many of these dolls have survived mainly by virtue of their clothes, which were treasured as samples of fine needlework: some were even supplied with whole trousseaux. In 1776 a Miss Delaney wrote about a doll she had dressed as a gift for a young friend: 'Miss Dolly's mode box just packed up containing a lady *à la mode* in accoutrements . . .' A similar doll with several outfits and a miniature fan can be seen in the collection of the Wiltshire and Blackmore Museum in America. This doll is reputed, though on what evidence is uncertain, to have been dressed by Marie-Antoinette while she was imprisoned in the Tuileries.

5. THE NINETEENTH CENTURY. The arbitrary division of time into parcels of a hundred years is at best an historian's cataloguing device. But as the 18th c. drew to a close every aspect of living and taste underwent a transformation. The collapse of the old aristocratic order in France during the Revolution consolidated the position of the middle classes as social arbiters both in that country and elsewhere; under their leadership a strengthened Puritan morality was applied not only in the sexual sphere but to all forms of pleasure, even of the most innocent kind. Jean-Jacques Rousseau's theories of education hardly affected the majority of parents, and children were if anything even more repressed than they had been before. Over a hundred years were still to elapse before any general and lasting improvement in their lot took place.

The new century was one of rapid expansion. Between 1801 and 1831 the population of England, Wales and Scotland rose from eleven to sixteen and a half millions. Taking the country as a whole, most people were enjoying a marginally higher standard of living and the market for all manner of goods was growing at an unprecedented rate. Moreover the drift away from the land meant that many things which before had been made at home were now manufactured in the towns for sale nationally and abroad. This development tended to standardize many consumer goods but a far greater choice was offered. The toys that came into the shops, though still partly hand-finished, were increasingly factory-produced: if they lost something of their old individuality, they gained in variety and also in cheapness. In many respects the decades between *c.* 1820 and 1860 can be considered a golden age of playthings.

Folk-toys, however, continued to be made by hand, often by the street traders who sold them for a living. In the anonymous *Letters Written from London* (1808) the author describes a crowded scene in Butcher Row in the Borough, where women traders sold from their baskets figures of Harlequins and Columbines, painted paper for making flags and windmills, and a disabled soldier offering his toys cried:

'Young lambs to sell! Young lambs to sell!
If I'd as much money as I could tell,
I never would cry, young lambs to sell!'

Faster and more reliable transport brought increasing numbers of goods from abroad to compete with those made in Britain. The journalist George Sala, writing in 1859, speaks of the Lowther Arcade, a contemporary mecca for children, as the toy-shop of Europe, and goes on to list all the main types of playthings that might be purchased under its light glass roof: cockhorses, toy carts of various kinds, mail phaetons, block-tin omnibuses, trains, monkeys on sticks, 'old gentlemen that swing from their own door-knockers', squeezeable comic masks and faces, gutta-percha snakes, pop-guns, Noah's arks, dolls' houses and India-rubber balls.

The serious-minded and self-improving nature of the period is reflected in its educational and SCIENTIFIC TOYS. At first these were almost exclusively didactic, though as time went on more entertainment jam was applied to coat the educational pill. Board-games, all deriving from the very ancient Game of Goose, were adapted to help in the learning of geography, history, elementary science or scripture. Questions on these subjects had to be correctly answered by players alighting on certain squares before proceeding, or a forfeit was demanded. Similarly packs of specially designed PLAYING-CARDS were brought out in which a great deal of general knowledge was required in order to win; some games were very stiff going indeed, and probably appealed more to the adult purchaser than to the children who were expected to benefit from the game.

The jig-saw puzzle was invented by a firm of cartographers, Messrs. Wallis and Son, between 1760 and 1770. They were first known as Dissected Maps, that is maps cut up into eccentric shapes. The idea was sound educationally, for a knowledgeable pupil had a distinct advantage over one whose geography was weak. In Jane Austen's *Mansfield Park* (1814) the heroine Fanny's cousins criticize her, observing that she 'cannot put the map of Europe together'. This casual reference indicates how widespread was the use of puzzles at the time. The jig-saw idea was next applied to history and scripture wall-sheets, and eventually picture puzzles with no educational bias appeared. Sometimes, however, even these had a map on the reverse side, perhaps designed to be pieced together first, before the puzzle was turned over to reveal the illustration by way of reward.

In his three-volume *Philosophy of Sport*, published in 1832, Dr. J. Paris writes recommending to his young readers certain 'philosophical' toys, whose educational value seems somewhat exaggerated today. These optical devices with outlandish names—the Thaumatrope (*c.* 1826), Zoetrope (1832), Phenakistoscope (also 1832) and Praxinoscope (1878)— all demonstrate the principle of persistence of vision, and are all direct ancestors of the cinema and television.

Magic lanterns, not only for adult use but in a simplified toy form, were also increasingly popular. A great variety of hand-painted glass slides could be bought for projection with subjects ranging from the purely educational to brightly-coloured illustrations of nursery rhymes and tales. Some slides even achieved a measure of simple animation by means of images painted on two sections of glass which could be moved in relation to one another: cats appeared to claw at birds in cages, negroes rolled their eyes, and so on. The workmanship of these rather expensive toys was extremely fine, often making use of turned and polished hardwoods and brass trim.

A cheaper form of home entertainment was offered by the toy theatre. In England this originated *c.* 1811 as a theatrical souvenir in the form of etchings, sold plain or hand-coloured, depicting actors and scenery from the shows of the day. The sheets were issued in series suitable for mounting on pasteboard, cutting out and displaying behind miniature proscenium stage fronts. With the help of a shortened version of the book of words the plays could be presented by those with sufficient self-confidence, dexterity and patience to mount a production. Robert Louis Stevenson confessed that he was not one of these in his essay *A Penny Plain Twopence Coloured*, but he remained a life-long toy-theatre enthusiast, and there is little doubt that the 'Juvenile Drama', as it was known, inspired him to write his *Treasure Island*. The earliest sheets were brought out by a jobbing printer, William West. Other publishers include J. H. Jameson, the Dyer family, Robert Lloyd, J. K. Green, Hodgson & Co., Orlando Hodgson, the Skelts, W. Webb, John Redington and Benjamin Pollock. The most famous toy theatre play was based on Pocock's *The Miller and his Men* (1813), and so great is its staying power that a version can still be bought today from the firm of Benjamin Pollock Ltd., in whose toy museum a representative collection of old theatres and sheets are on display alongside toys of all types.

A vast quantity and variety of dolls were produced during the 19th c. Most closely associated with the period are those made of poured wax, though in fact these were rare before the 1850s. The name this kind of doll immediately calls to mind is that of Montanari. Augusta Montanari received praise and a medal for her dolls when they were exhibited in the Great Exhibition of 1851, where examples illustrating all ages from infancy to womanhood were on display with elegant miniature furniture. Rival firms were those of Marsh (who was patronized by the Queen), Meech, Peck and, most famous of all, the Pierottis. The Pierotti family, like the Montanaris, were of Italian origin, and are known to have been making wax dolls as far back as the 1780s, when Domenico Pierotti first came to England on a visit. It is said he had such a bad channel crossing he could not face the return journey, and stayed on to found a firm that continued to supply the well known toy shop Hamley's until the 1930s. An alternative way of making wax-headed dolls was the wax over PAPIER MÂCHÉ method; but though cheaper to produce, the thin coating of wax on its painted foundation tended to crack. Another disadvantage was that the hair, instead of being set into the wax strand by strand, had to be applied in the form of a less natural-looking wig.

'Dutch' or 'peg' dolls were evolved, as their hair-styles suggest, during the late Georgian or REGENCY periods. Early examples have more delicate and elaborately painted *coiffures*, including grey kiss-curls; some were carved with projecting combs on the top of their heads. By the late 1840s and 1850s a centre parting was universally adopted, and the turning and finish of the bodies tended to be less fine.

During the whole of the century glazed china was used for dolls' heads, either in its 'hard-paste' or 'soft-paste' form. Most have painted dark hair, though occasionally some are bald (the BIEDERMEIER type) with a black spot on the crown to indicate where a wig should be glued. Unglazed china, including pure white PARIAN ware, was cast into heads in the potteries of Dresden and elsewhere from the 1850s. This hard, fine-textured paste lent itself to detailed work, and some of the earlier designs have elaborately modelled hair-styles.

By *c.* 1862 France had taken the lead in doll-making. Glazed china was largely superseded by matt china-bisque as a material for dolls' heads. The name of Jumeau is usually associated with these dolls. Large eyed, with extremely refined features, they are undoubtedly the aristocrats of their world. Their rivals from the firm of Bru, although beautifully made, lack something of the Jumeau elegance. About 1880 a sudden change of fashion produced a new style: instead of fine ladies, dolls now were made in the form of little chubby girls. In 1898 the firms of Jumeau and Bru amalgamated to form La Société Française de Fabrication des Bébés et Jouets. Towards the end of the century Germany began to dominate the market for toys of all kinds. With its greater organizational capacity it was able to compete successfully with the French and produce cheaper, though not always superior, dolls. The best known German manufacturers of the period were Simon & Halbig, Steiner, Handwerck and Armand Marseille.

Dolls' houses, made especially for children, appeared from *c.* 1800 onwards. Simpler and more homely than the adult baby-houses of the previous century, they were supplied with an enormous variety of furnishings and effects by competing toy-makers, mostly in Germany. Almost every kind of domestic appliance could be bought for a few pence from loaded toy-shop shelves to delight small girls engaged on fitting out their houses. Best of all was the imitation rosewood furniture made by an unknown manufacturer whom Mrs. Vivien Greene in her study on dolls' houses calls 'the dolls' Duncan PHYFE'. A room in the 'Princess May of Teck's' house in the London Museum is furnished almost entirely by this master of commercially produced miniatures.

In Nuremberg lead toy soldiers continued to be made for export all over the world. In 1848 the firm of Hienrichsen instituted the 30 mm standard. Hollow-cast figures were invented by the Englishman William Britain, a secret process which enabled him to compete both at home and abroad. But on the whole it was Germany which continued pre-eminent in the toy field, at least in Europe. Notable were their cheap ranges: tin penny-toys, clockwork figures and train-sets; and the wooden Noah's Arks, farmyards, soldiers and fair-ground toys made in the Erzgebirge.

No survey of toys, however brief, would be complete without mentioning two well-loved nursery characters: the black fabric gollywog (*c.* 1890) and the teddy-bear (*c.* 1903). Both came to Europe from America. The first was based on a character in a series of story-books by Florence and Bertha Upton; the second appears to have been inspired by a bear-cub, spared by President Teddy Roosevelt when hunting and pictured in a famous cartoon of the day.

Modern toys really fall into three categories: first the standard, mass-produced article, often making use of advanced production techniques and new materials such as vinyl plastic; secondly those made by craftsmen, partly by hand, for the discriminating parent or collector; and lastly traditional peasant toys, perhaps modified in design to meet the requirements of an international market.

It can justly be said that there is now a greater variety of type and quality in the toy-shops of Europe and America than ever before in the history of toy-making.

6. AMERICA. Our knowledge of the toys and recreational activities of children among the Amerindians before the Conquest is imperfect and patchy. The chroniclers from whom our literary evidence of Pre-Conquest America is derived have very little to say on the subject.

Ball games were the most widely distributed over the continent. Balls were made from maize leaves, rubber (solid or hollow) and stuffed animal skins. Dolls were also widely distributed. They were made of wood, bone, straw, clay, wax, gum and other materials. Dolls, sometimes dressed, have been recovered from Pre-Inca burial sites of coastal Peru; they were made by the Incas and continued to be made surreptitiously under the Spanish domination. Rattles and small whistles or ocarinas of ceramic in animal shapes have been found in some quantity in Mochica and Chimù burials. These and small animal figures in stone and ceramics from the Chancay area and from Inca times may or may not have been made for the amusement of children. Tops, which were spun by whipping, were common to the Andean area of South America and were fairly widely distributed east of the Andes. Bullroarers, buzzers, bean-shooters and corncob darts were also known. Stilts have been reported from the West Indian, central American, Amazonian, Guiana and Chaco areas; they were used by adults as well as children. Dexterity in hunting and military use of weapons was part of the initiation ceremonies of boys and training in these accomplishments took the part to a large extent of children's games.

In the Andean highlands the cult of the miniature was particularly associated with the good-luck deity Ekkekko. Annual fairs called *alacitas* are still held in the Bolivian towns of La Paz, Oruro and Cochabamba at which all things are sold in miniature. While these are patronized by adults, miniature objects are also cherished by children as toys.

The earliest travellers and settlers from Europe took children's toys with them to barter with the natives of the New World. Dolls are mentioned in 1585 as being among the trinkets brought to Roanoake Island by English colonists. Just over a hundred years later William Penn brought a doll across the Atlantic, and this famous example is still in the possession of the Historical Society of Pennsylvania. Several other dolls of almost the same date have survived, notably one ('Old Susan') in the Museum of the City of New York.

Most 17th-c. children in America had few playthings. As members of communities fighting for survival, they were obliged to work for their living from an early age. Nearly all household utensils had to be made by hand, for importations were expensive and difficult to come by. No doubt young people employed the skills they learned helping their elders to produce an occasional toy. Sometimes Indian models were copied, as in the making of corncob dolls and raw-hide balls.

The Puritans were hostile to the idea of play. In New England, for instance, the celebration of Christmas and May Day was forbidden. Yet it is in this area that light industries, including toy-making, were first established.

From the 18th c. onwards an altogether freer atmosphere began to prevail, and at least some children were allowed to play in their spare time. Many toys of the period have found their way into public and private collections. These include dolls, a dolls' bed of *c.* 1785 (now in the Museum of the City of New York), primitive boat-shaped rocking-horses, pierced coins adapted to act as 'buzzers' when pulled on a double string, and a German type horse-and-whistle wooden toy, which once belonged to Robert Livingston.

After the War of Independence home-based craftsmen, working part-time and in isolation, began increasingly to supplement the supplies of playthings imported from Europe. Two famous names of the early 1800s are Pennsylvania's famous carver of wooden animals Schimmel, and the Swiss Huegenin, whose toys are eagerly sought by collectors today.

During the first half of the 19th c. guild-like trade associations of toy-makers were established. About 1830 the long-lived Tower Toy Company of Massachusetts was formed. The founder, William S. Tower, has been called the father of the American toy industry. Products of this firm were exhibited in the Paris International Exhibition of 1878 in an attempt to exploit the European market, but they were too expensive to compete successfully with their European rivals.

After the Civil War many iron foundries turned from supplying the army to the making of pull-toys, stoves and mechanical banks. The firm of J. & E. Stevens was a noted manufacturer during the 1870s and 1880s, and many of these typical American toys were exported to Europe. Pennsylvania became a centre for tin-smiths, making gayly enamelled miniature cooking utensils, whistles and windmills.

Late 19th-c. companies such as Ives and Althof, and Bergman, brought out an enormous variety of ingenious and charming clockwork toys so robustly made that many have been found in perfect working order after almost a hundred years. Their tall funnelled trains and doll figures on clockwork tricycles are well known. Two famous firms belonged to distantly related members of the Crandall family. Jesse and Charles M. Crandall were highly inventive. Probably the most original and widely sold of their products were the famous Charles M. Crandall tongue-and-groove building blocks (1867) and Jesse's much imitated nursery blocks, which were decorated boxes without lids, graduated in size so that they could fit one inside another when not in use. Both were international best-sellers. A. Schoenut and Company, too, produced many toys for the world market, including a Humpty Dumpty Circus (1903) consisting of jointed clowns, animals and accessories, designed to arrange into circus tableaux.

Like their European counterparts, children's playing-cards issued in America early in the 1800s were often dauntingly educational. But at least one uninstructive game achieved popularity even in England—Miss Anne W. Abbott's *Doctor Busby*, a variant of *Happy Families*.

Modern American toys are notable for their originality. The revival of the adult doll, after half a century of almost exclusively baby dolls, can be traced back to 'Barbie', a sophisticated teenager who not only has an extensive selection of clothes, which can be bought piece by piece, but even a boy-friend, 'Ken'. And in the mid 1960s the firm of Hessenfeld Brothers adapted the idea of a male doll by bringing out the 'Action Man' figures for boys with a series of uniforms, weapons and space-age accessories.

Even by the outbreak of the First World War the United States had become one of the largest producers of toys, competing successfully with her main rivals, Germany and Japan. Today her products are exported to every corner of the world.

7. THE FAR EAST. As early as 206 B.C. the Chinese buried miniatures of cooking utensils

and other household objects in the tombs of their dead; but it is not known if the skills in making these were used also in the production of toys. At about the same date it is recorded that a General Han-Sin flew a kite to measure the distance between his army and the enemy. With the invention of PAPER kites could be made cheaply from the new material; their popularity increased, and today kite flying is a national pastime in both China and Japan. There is no record in what year, or by what route, kite-making was introduced into Europe, but a German manuscript of 1405 has an illustration representing a young man on horseback flying a dragon-shaped kite.

The paintings of Su Han Chʻen (A.D. 1115–70) depict pedlars of toys and many playthings, including masks, kites, dolls, paper-and-stick wind-toys, pull-along carts and whipping-tops.

The Japanese woman novelist Murasaki, writing about a hundred years before Su Han Chʻen, describes a game of football with an inflated ball and mentions *hina*-playing. The *hina*, or small paper dolls, were used in purification ceremonies. In time dolls made of more permanent materials were used, and these were kept instead of being cast into running water at the end of the rites. The Dolls' Festivals (of 3 March and 5 May) were instituted soon afterwards. It seems probable that the religious significance of dolls was not relinquished until much later for according to Gustav Schlegel in the 1850s little girls in neighbouring China were not allowed to play with anything in human form.

The natural genius of the Japanese for making miniatures was applied to the production of many types of folk toys. Each district produced its own speciality: snakes constructed of bamboo sections, softwood cockerels with proud tails, painted clay dogs, *Sinno-no-Tora* (tigers with moving heads), horses of rice straw, devils made of shells, embroidered balls, *Yumijishi* (lions' heads whose mouths open), fish and bird whistles, *Kokeshi* (a type of primitive doll), kites, hobby-horses and many other ingenious toys.

In the late 19th c. Japan started to make a great quantity of European style playthings for the world market. With the advantage of a low-paid labour force, she was able to compete successfully with Germany and America. Today one of her profitable side-lines is the making of reproductions of period toys for collectors.

See also GREEK AND ROMAN ANTIQUITY (TOYS AND GAMES); SCIENTIFIC TOYS.

84, 176, 235, 251, 278, 279, 319, 325, 326, 383, 548, 630, 680, 783, 819, 898, 899.

TRAILING. Term used in GLASS-making for a technique of ornament in which the vessel is decorated by winding or 'trailing' threads of glass 'metal' upon or round the surface. The term is also used of an analogous technique of decorating CERAMICS by 'trailing' SLIP.

TRANSFER PRINTING. Transfer printing is thought to have been first practised by Simon-François RAVENET and Robert HANCOCK at the York House enamel factory. (See BATTERSEA ENAMELS.) When that factory ceased production in 1756 the craft was taken by them to the china factory at Bow and subsequently by Hancock to Worcester and then to Caughley. After the technical difficulties of underglaze transfer printing had been mastered it became the basis of the English blue and white porcelain ware.

The method consists of taking a print on transfer paper from an engraved copper plate and then transferring the impression from the paper to the biscuit-fired CERAMIC body to be decorated. The plates had to be cut more deeply than usual because the porous biscuit surface of the ceramic is more absorbent of ink than is paper. After the print had been transferred to the earthenware it was fixed by heating in a muffle oven. The object was then covered with a protective glaze, which was fired in a glost oven. The method had obvious advantages over hand-painting both in speed and because the design engraved by an accomplished artist could be reproduced again and again on a variety of wares. There were, however, serious technical difficulties, which were overcome only after a period of experimentation and after improvements in porcelain manufacture. COBALT was at that time the only pigment which would withstand the heat of the glost firing without blurring; at the middle of the 18th c. it was imported mainly from Germany and the methods of processing it were imperfectly understood. More serious still, the paste used in most English factories at this time was not hard enough after biscuit-firing to stand up to transfer printing. In the early years transfers were printed after the glazing. The technique of underglaze transfer printing was not exploited before 1760. It was developed chiefly by Thomas Turner and Robert Hancock at the Salopian china factory at Caughley in Shropshire though at New Hall in Staffordshire a somewhat smudgy darkish blue effect was obtained with blue underglaze transfers. Other factories, such as Plymouth and Bristol were less successful.

During the 1780s underglaze printing techniques were being practised in Staffordshire by John Turner at Lane End, Joshua Heath at Hanley and Josiah Spode at Stoke. Before the end of the century other firms which had adopted the technique included Thomas Minton of Stoke, John Davenport of Longport, Staffordshire, the Castleford Pottery, the Leeds Pottery and the Don Pottery, all in Yorkshire, the Herculaneum Pottery at Liverpool and the Cambrian Pottery in Swansea. Early in the 19th c. an improvement in the technique of PAPER-making resulted in a better transfer paper which made it possible for engravers to use finer detail and to combine stipple with line-engraving.

In 1810 Peter Warburton of New Hall took out a patent for a method of transfer printing in gold. An important export trade in blue-printed transfer wares grew up after the Napoleonic Wars, with North America as the chief market, and lasted until *c.* 1830, when United States pottery production expanded.

43.

TRIER, TREASURE OF. A hoard of 3rd-c. and 4th-c. silver plate which was discovered on the property of the Jesuits and melted down for the value of the silver. An account of the discovery, published in the *Epitome annalium Treverensium* 1676, gives the following description of some of the pieces. 'Ten large silver dishes decorated in gold and antique emblematic figures; one larger than 24 lbs. showed a head of Caesar in the centre, another showed a hunt with figures of wild beasts around the margin, with the inscription *audentia nicetio*. A third had the joined heads of a man and woman in the middle, from which it is conjectured to have been a wedding present. A fourth had boxers in the centre and other heathen allegorical figures round the margin. Besides these ten, eight other dishes with poetic emblems within and extra ornaments outside. Then there were vessels embossed with gold figures of men and beasts, two dishes (*disci*) of more recent workmanship with engraved borders showing four opposed heads and the inscription *Petrus et Paulus : Justus et Hermes*. . . . The whole collection came to 250 lbs.'

TROPHY (Greek: *tropaion*). Originally a monument to commemorate a victory in battle, usually composed of arms captured from the enemy and set up on the site. Trophies were of two types, either a heaped-up tumulus of weapons and booty or a single panoply hung on a tree or stake. Under the Roman Empire the trophy often became the crowning ornament of a permanent stone memorial. In both Greek and Roman times trophies were represented on coins. By transference the term 'trophy' came to be used of any artistic representation of such a monument and later for an ornamental or symbolic group of objects as a decorative motif.

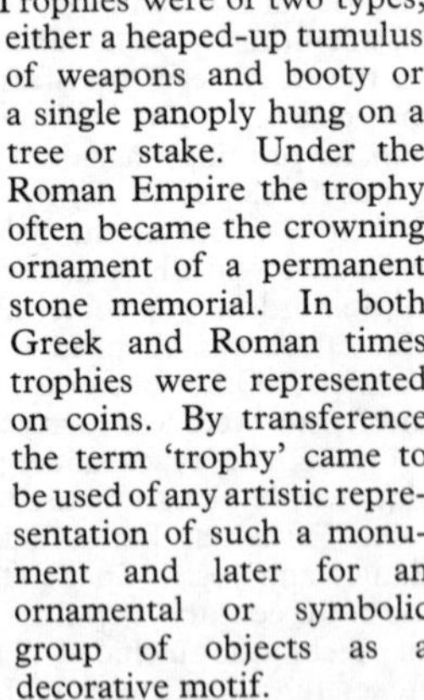

In Italy and other European countries the trophy was a familiar decorative convention from the early Renaissance onwards. In France under Charles Lebrun and his followers it became a major device of interior decoration and ornamental sculpture. (Lebrun's decorations of the *Escalier du Roi* at Versailles; the Porte Saint-Denis by Lebrun and Michel Anguier in collaboration with François Blondel; the Observatoire of Claude Perrault.) In his *Cours d'architecture* (1683) François Blondel described the practice as follows: 'In the Book of Albrecht Dürer there are drawings of Trophies made of rural domestic utensils and agricultural implements arranged with great art. . . . They are arranged in the form of festoons, not only Trophies of weapons of war but also Trophies of Peace: as Trophies of the Sciences or the Arts or amusements, arranging for example divers musical instruments; whatever serves the Sciences such as books, the sphere, globes, mathematical instruments; the principal ornaments of the Ball and the Comedy; hunting or fishing gear; and a thousand other things of this nature, whose beauty consists chiefly in the choice and disposition and in the relation which these ornaments ought to bear to the general design of the building.'

TROUBADOUR STYLE. A Gothic-Revival style in French furniture produced between 1830 and 1840. A typical example was the Princesse Marie d'Orléans's oratory in the Tuileries. See FURNITURE (EUROPEAN).

TS'AI LUN. Chinese court official who is traditionally credited with having originated the idea of making paper from wood in A.D. 105. See PAPIER MÂCHÉ.

TULA. The town of Tula, some 200 kilometres due south of Moscow, has given its name to a particular type of silverwork decorated with NIELLO and sometimes partly gilt, though such work was not in fact confined to Tula. The articles made there were mostly SNUFF-BOXES or small toilet-boxes, and the *niello* decoration took the form of figure subjects, floral or geometrical ornament, or even maps. Surviving examples are not earlier than the beginning of the 19th c. but *niello* certainly had a much longer history in Russia. In later examples the design is naïve and the workmanship coarse, seldom rising above the tourist-trade level.

Since the 16th c. Tula has been a centre of the iron and steel industry, and Peter the Great established a small-arms factory there in 1705. Production was at first confined to military arms, but from *c.* 1720 to *c.* 1790 elaborately decorated presentation fire-arms were also turned out. They were made by craftsmen specially recruited from Germany, Denmark and Sweden, while the decoration was largely based on designs from the pattern-book of Nicolas Guerard. During the reign of Catherine the Great the Tula factory began to manufacture domestic articles—tables, chairs, fireplace furniture and candlesticks—in cut and burnished steel encrusted according to a technique peculiar to Tula with gold, silver, platinum or copper. The style, a somewhat provincial version of the ADAM style, was derived from Birmingham cut-steel work and some Tula pieces have been mistaken for English work. Numerous examples made for Catherine the Great are in the Hermitage Museum at Leningrad.

See also RUSSIA.

TULA METAL. See NIELLO.

TUNG WANG KUNG. Taoist decorative motif. The god of the immortals, King of the East, who lived in a palace in the misty heavens, is in Taoist legend also the purest substance of the Eastern Air and sovereign of the active male, or *yang*, principle. He kept a register of the Immortals and was waited on by the immortal youth Hsien T'ung and the JADE maiden Yü-nü.

TURCOMAN RUGS. Often misnamed Bokhara rugs, these include floor-rugs and various kinds of tent-furnishings made by tribes who formerly led a nomadic pastoral existence in western Turkestan, but whose old way of life, together with its rug-making traditions, seems now to have practically disappeared.

These rugs, in which the pile is generally tied with the Sena knot, are mostly of excellent quality, but this cannot be said of the imitations of them made commercially in various parts of Asia. They have no ascertainable history and probably no existing specimen was made before the 19th c.

There is, however, an obvious kinship between the Holbein rugs of the 15th and 16th centuries and the neat ranks and files or complex octagons on quiet red grounds which form the favourite designs of the very finely knotted, short-piled rugs of the Salor, Tekke, Saryq and Pinde types, made in the region of Merv. Yomud and Chudur rugs, which originate farther to the north-west, in the coastlands east of the Caspian, are similar, but distinguishable by a taste for lozenge forms and an admixture of motifs derived from Caucasian types. A third group, made farther eastwards than the two preceding, is characterized by a longer, more coarsely knotted pile and by occasional departures from the principle of employing the characteristic Turcoman reds as the main ground colour. These rugs are the Afghans, with rows of bold simplified octagons, the Beluchis, very sombre in tone with much dark blue, and the Ersari or Beşiri rugs, from the Bukhara region.

A design peculiar to Turcoman rugs is that known as katchli, in which the field is divided into four rectangular panels recalling the form of a wooden door. Such rugs were used as doors for the tents and—sometimes with a diminutive arch added to the design—as prayer-rugs.

See also CARPETS AND RUGS.

TURKEY WORK. The name given between the 16th and the 18th centuries to the English knotted-pile fabrics made in the same technique as TURKISH RUGS. The technique was used principally for table-carpets, cushions and upholstery, with floral patterns resembling those of contemporary English EMBROIDERY.

TURKISH RUGS. Turkish rugs of recent times (for earlier types see CARPETS AND RUGS) fall into two main groups: the large, hard-wearing, coarsely knotted carpets made in factories, primarily for export, and the small rugs, many of them prayer-rugs, made on domestic looms. The carpets of the former group cannot usefully be described since their designs are entirely eclectic, deriving from Turkish, Caucasian, Persian and other sources; patterns and colours are often chosen with a view to market prospects in the West. Many of them are known by the collective name of Smyrna carpets, while others take their names from the places of manufacture: Akhisar, Demirçi, Ghiordes, Hereke, Kayseri, Konya, Sivas, Sparta and Uşak.

Of the domestic production most modern specimens are coarse in texture and crude in colour, but the older rugs are generally vivid and attractive compositions of angular floral ornament carried out in strong reds, blues, yellows and white. The pile is invariably tied with the Turkish or Ghiordes knot.

The town of Ghiordes has given its name not only to this knot but also to the best of the native Turkish rugs, distinguished by their soft, light tones and very refined designs, which retain echoes from the Ottoman court style of the 16th and 17th centuries. Kula rugs are readily recognized by their blunt drawing, many narrow borders, and predominant blues and yellows. Melas and Megri rugs display a highly conventionalised flora, often arranged in narrow panels. The bold angularities of Bergama rugs are worked out mainly in sober blues and reds. All these types are products of the west coast and its hinterland. A second group, in the interior of Anatolia, is distinguished by thin rectilinear drawing and the characteristic stepped form of the PRAYER-RUG arch. These are Lâdik, Konya, Majar and Kir Shahr rugs. Yuruk rugs, made by Kurdish mountaineers, approximate to Caucasian taste in their designs of lozenges fringed with hooks.

Large numbers of KILIMS are also made in Turkey.

TURQUOISE. A composite crystalline mineral, consisting of phosphate of aluminium and copper with some iron, which has been valued as a gemstone from the 5th or 6th millennium B.C. In colour it ranges from blue through green to greenish grey; the purest blue is most highly prized for jewellery and decorative work. It is opaque, with a faint waxy lustre and takes a medium polish. Its hardness on the MOHS SCALE is 5 to 6.

Turquoise has been used from very remote antiquity for beads, jewellery, amulets and for decorative inlay; it was often set in gold or silver throughout antiquity. Gold and turquoise bracelets found with the mummy of the Egyptian queen Zer are among the oldest fabricated jewellery known.

Turquoise was mined by the Egyptians on the Sinai peninsula along with MALACHITE, manganese and copper at least as far back as the fourth millennium B.C. The finest turquoise has come from Nishapur in the Khurasan province of Iran, where mines were worked in antiquity. The name, from the French *pierre turquois* (Turkish stone), derives from the fact that Persian turquoise was brought by way of Turkey into Europe. A fine light blue turquoise also comes from Mexico and the southern U.S.A., where it has been used for some centuries by the Navajo Indians as amulets and for decoration.

TURRET CLOCKS. The early iron CLOCKS which were set in the bell-towers of churches or civic buildings and sounded the hours.

TUSSORE (Hindi: *tasar*). A coarse brownish SILK obtained from the cocoon of several indigenous Indian species of multivoltine silk-producing moths, also called 'wild' silk. The 'Tussah' moth of Assam is the most important species and is closely related to the Tussah moth of Manchuria. Interest in this wild-silk production was stimulated at the middle of the 19th c. when supplies of mulberry silk were seriously reduced by a widespread silkworm disease. A multivoltine mulberry silk is also made in Bengal and another type in Mysore. See also TEXTILE MANUFACTURE IN ANTIQUITY.

TUTENAG (derived, perhaps through Portuguese, from Sanskrit *tuttha*, sulphate of copper, and *nāga*, tin or lead). The name under which commercial zinc or spelter was exported from China and the East Indies to Europe in the 18th c. Its export was prohibited by China *c.* 1780 because it was needed to form the brass alloy for Chinese copper coinage; but the trade continued clandestinely. Its import was prohibited except by the Government when a tariff was imposed on Chinese goods in 1858. Tutenag was used in the preparation of BRASS. Zinc was not smelted in the West until *c.* 1730 in England; the first Continental smelting works was at Liège in 1807. Before that the ore *lapis calaminaris* or calamine was also used in conjunction with copper to form the alloy brass. The varying colour of early brasswork is due to the fact that when the unsmelted ore was used it was not possible to regulate exactly the quantity of zinc in proportion to copper.

In the 19th c. the word 'tutenag' was sometimes used of articles made from the alloy PAKTONG.

TWILL. A method of weaving which causes a pattern of parallel diagonal ridges. Also the name of fabric so produced. See WEAVING (FABRIC).

TYPOGRAPHY. There are, broadly, three printing processes: relief, or letterpress, from a raised inked surface; intaglio, from a lowered surface, into which ink is forced and any surplus wiped off; and lithography, or planography, from a flat surface, in which ink is repelled from the moistened part of the surface of a lithographic stone or printing plate and adheres to the grease-treated image, a result of the antipathy of grease and water. Letterpress and intaglio printing are comparatively ancient processes, whose invention and development cannot be dated exactly; lithography was invented in the late 18th c. Letterpress was the commonly used process for the printing of textual matter until recently, when it has been largely superseded by offset lithography, so called because the image is first printed on to a rubber cylinder and thence transferred, or 'offset', to paper, metal or other surface; intaglio processes, which include line engraving, etching, mezzotint, aquatint, gravure and related methods, have generally been confined to the printing of mainly pictorial matter.

Printing from movable types first occurred in the West in the mid 15th c. There had been earlier printing in the Far East, from carved blocks and from movable types, but the available evidence indicates that Western printing, which required only the letters of the alphabet, numbers, and various conventional signs (unlike the thousands of complex ideographs required for some Oriental languages) did not derive from Eastern methods.

European printing came at a propitious time. There was a strong demand for books, a result of increased literacy, the secularization of the book trade and the new learning traditionally associated with the Renaissance. The new universities required text-books; the rising middle classes wanted books not only for religious instruction but for diversion and for education in the practical arts; both church and state would soon demand books for their work of conquering, colonizing and converting the New World. Moreover the materials for the mass production of books were available.

PAPER, the prime essential, was invented in China *c.* A.D. 105 and introduced by the Moors into Spain; it was being manufactured there by the 12th c. and soon spread to Italy and over the Continent. While VELLUM was plentiful enough to take care of the comparatively small needs of the manuscript trade, it could not have met the enormous demands of the printing industry. Printing on vellum produces superlatively handsome and durable results, but vellum is a far slower and more difficult printing surface than paper as well as a far more costly one.

The first presses were probably adapted from some kind of press used for wine, oil or cheese-making; heavy, viscous oil-bound inks, similar to painters' colours, were newly available; binding techniques were the same as those used for manuscripts. It was the invention of a method of manufacturing a large quantity of movable, replaceable, and re-usable individual characters which was the key to the production by printing of large editions of correct and identical texts. Manuscripts were not only costly but often incorrect, since texts were easily corrupted in copying.

The exact date, place and nature of the invention—even the name of the inventor—cannot be conclusively proved from documentary evidence. There is, however, a consensus among most informed scholars that Johann GUTENBERG, a goldsmith born in Mainz, devised a method of casting identical metal characters from a metal mould *c.* 1440. He was one of a number of men trying to find a way to reproduce books mechanically. His family's connection with the mint at Mainz provided him with the basic technique required: engraving punches which could be used to strike matrices of individual characters or frequently used combinations of letters, from which types could be cast. His invention probably consisted of the adjustable mould which could accommodate matrices of varying width, depending upon the width of the letter being cast. This made possible the creation of as many individual types as were required, cast, generally, from a mixture of lead, tin and antimony, which could be assembled into words and lines in a composing stick; these could be locked up into formes for printing and, after use, distributed for recombination into further text matter. After casting each letter had to be trimmed and finished to a uniform height so that a full forme of type would make a flat surface when laid on the press during printing.

By 1456 the process had been perfected to the point where a large, complex book was feasible; various small pieces had been printed before then. It is generally thought that the first book was a Latin Bible, containing some 42 lines per page; it was probably begun by Gutenberg and completed by his partner and backer, Johann Fust, a Mainz banker. Fust, impatient for a return on the considerable capital invested during the period of Gutenberg's experiments, apparently forced out the inventor and took over his equipment and shop. He took into partnership a local scribe, Peter Schoeffer, who later became his son-in-law. The first book which can be dated with certainty from internal evidence appeared under their imprint, a massive Psalter whose colophon declared that they were the printers and that it had been produced without the aid of a pen in Mainz in the year 1457. It contained large initial letters in red and blue—the first colour printing—which imitated the decorated letters commonly used in liturgical manuscripts. The problems of colour printing (particularly of achieving accurate register of several colours, each of which had to be printed separately) were apparently incapable of economical solution; for several decades printed books contained capitals, rubrics and decorations inserted by hand, probably by many of the scribes displaced by the new process.

The first printed books were stately and handsome volumes, carefully designed and printed, legible and accurate. They were careful copies of the best available manuscripts (it was several years before the printing of new texts began).

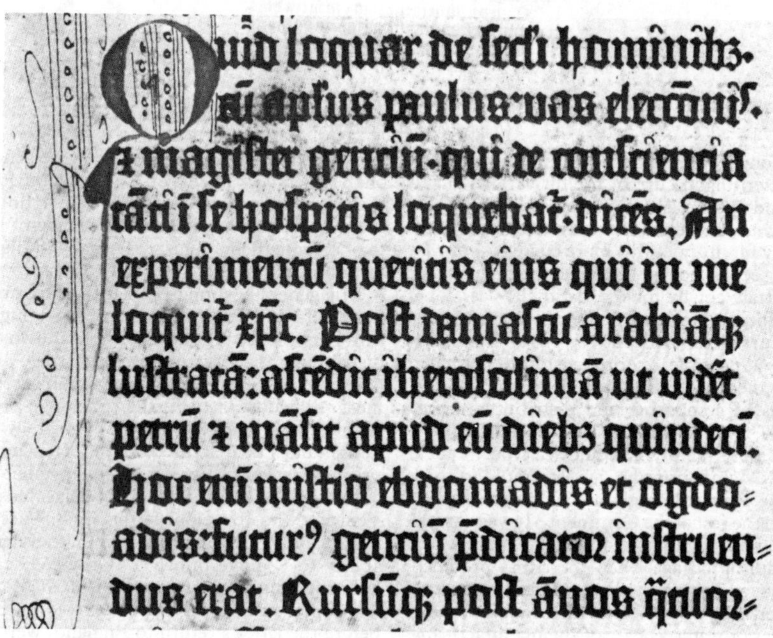
Quid loquar de ſecli hominibꝫ·
cũ apſus paulus:vas electõniſ·
⁊ magiſter gencium·qui de conſciencia
tanti i ſe hoſpitis loquebat·dicẽs. An
experimentu querit eius qui in me
loquit xpc. Poſt damaſcu arabiaq;
luſtratã:aſcẽdit iheroſolimã ut videt
petru ⁊ mãſit apud eu diebꝫ quindeci.
Hoc eni miſtio ebdomadis et ogdo=
adis:futur⁹ genciu pdicatoꝛ inſtruen=
dus erat. Rurſuq; poſt ãnos q̃tuoꝛ=

Type of the Forty-two-line Bible. Mainz (before August 1456). (*Reproduced actual size*)

Missale ad usum diocesis Leodiēsis.

Ad sacerdotes exhortatio.
Qui diuina cupit: summo libamina patri.
Donaque sublimi: mystica ferre deo.
Hec legat a tetra: purgata volumine labe.
Nam prestant faciles: ad pia sacra vias.
Horum presidio: mysteria sancta parabit.
Et celi domino: munera grata feret.

Liège Missal. Paris (1515). French type faces by Wolfgang Hopyl
(*Reproduced half actual size*)

Before long type was made reproducing the styles of writing in current use for various kinds of text and in different regions, roughly divisible into *textura*, the elaborate BLACK LETTER used especially for liturgies, the more current *bastarda* used for secular books, and the humanistic hand used in Italy chiefly for the Latin classics. The earliest founts included numerous contractions and ligatured letters in an attempt to approximate as closely as possible to scribal custom. Gradually most of these were abandoned to simplify the problems of composing and distributing type, since the fewer characters in the compositor's case the more rapidly he could set type.

From Mainz printing spread rapidly, first along the Rhine throughout Germany, then to Italy and the rest of the Continent. It was natural that the new industry should follow the water routes during an age when the rivers provided the fastest and cheapest means of transportation; moreover the paper mills, which required large quantities of water as part of the manufacturing process, were usually located near the rivers. Finally, the chief trading centres were generally on the rivers; few towns could absorb individually the large editions made possible by printing, and there had to be considerable exchange of books to distribute them. This was usually in the form of unbound sheets.

It is generally supposed that the first printers were self-sufficient, building and operating their own presses, cutting and casting their own types, distributing their own wares. This stage did not last long, and specialization soon took over. The most difficult part of the printing process, requiring the highest degree of skill, was the design and manufacture of type. It is not surprising that so many of the first printers were goldsmiths—Gutenberg and Nicolas Jenson of Venice, who developed the first successful ROMAN type, are examples—since they had the ability to engrave punches. Others, like Peter Schoeffer, Fust's partner, and Colard Mansion, who operated a press with CAXTON in Bruges before the latter's return to England, were calligraphers, who could supply models for the punch-cutter. By the late 16th c. type supply had become an independent industry.

Certainly by *c.* 1530 the work of cutting punches for type was concentrated in the hands of a very few craftsmen, of whom the best were in Paris. Prominent among them is Claude GARAMOND, who devoted himself wholly to this work and sold matrices struck with his punches which came to be widely distributed in France, the Low Countries and Germany. Many of Garamond's types appeared first in the productions of Robert ESTIENNE, the great scholar–printer, notably the Greek faces cut to the order of king Francis I, which set a fashion in Greek typography for two centuries. Another influential early French type-designer was Robert Granjon (1513–89), best known for his numerous ITALIC, greek and *civilité* faces; the last, a copy of the secretary hand, was widely used for the teaching of handwriting.

Garamond and Granjon not only designed types and engraved punches, they also sold strikes (unfinished matrices) to foundries and printers. Their types are found in the books of printers in France, Italy, Germany, Britain, and the Low Countries. A specimen showing one type face by Robert Granjon was issued in Antwerp in 1570. It offers strikes for sale and shows, in addition to letters, ARABESQUES and FLEURONS—simple decorative units which could be assembled to form borders and patterns; these were probably inspired by the TOOLS used by BOOKBINDERS to decorate their work. An earlier specimen showing the types stocked by Christopher PLANTIN was issued in Antwerp in 1567; it shows the characters of several designers.

By 1461 printing had been introduced into Italy at Subiaco, a Benedictine monastery near Rome; in 1470 the first French press had been established, at the Sorbonne; the first Spanish press began work in Valencia in 1474. William Caxton who had learned to print at Cologne and had conducted a press in Bruges, founded the first English printing-office, at Westminster, in 1476. Most of the early printers were Germans, invited to set up shops by local ecclesiastical or civil patrons.

The major early printing centres were towns which afforded a large market for books: university towns like Bologna, Strasbourg, Utrecht and Basle; ecclesiastical centres like Rome and Geneva; trading centres like Paris, London, Venice, Lyon and Frankfurt. The book trade was international even before the invention of printing. Monastic *scriptoria* produced manuscripts not only for their own libraries but for sale and exchange; secular ateliers in Paris, Bruges and Florence wrote and painted *de luxe* manuscripts for royal and noble patrons as well as for the wealthy bourgeoisie, especially Books of Hours, chivalric romances and classical texts. The stationers in university towns rented manuscripts to students for copying; their copies were sold when the students returned home and so became the originals for more copies.

This was essentially a bespoke industry, with copies produced to order. Publishing, with the rise of printing, became a speculative industry; the printer, whether working for himself or for a publisher or patron, produced as a rule an edition whose size was determined by his estimate of the capacity of the market. This tied up considerable capital in unsold books for a long time. There are few exact figures on the size of early editions, but they rarely seem to have been fewer than 200 copies during the 15th c. and editions of a thousand copies were not infrequent. These were mainly disposed of by exchange between publishers, often at the great trade fairs, particularly at Paris, Lyon and Frankfurt. Paris, Basle and Venice were not only great printing centres but the sites of a large and profitable wholesale book trade. Such men as Anton Koberger, of Nuremberg; the Alduses, of Venice; Froben and the Amerbachs, of Basle; and the Estiennes, of Paris and Geneva, had sizable stocks of books as well as large investments in type, presses and paper. To distribute these they set up branch offices and networks of distributors.

The fortunes of the various printing and publishing centres rose and declined in accordance with the political and economic importance of their primary market areas. Despite Germany's early ascendancy based upon the rapid spread of the industry through the country, it was soon supplanted by Italy as the major supplier of books. Venetian scholar–printers, merchants and shippers distributed Venetian books throughout Europe. With the decline of Venice's financial and military power came a corresponding decline in its importance as a publishing centre. France, especially Paris and Lyon, succeeded Italy in this role during the early 16th c., to be followed by the Low Countries during the next century.

The decline of Latin as a *lingua franca* and the increasing use of the vernaculars imposed barriers to the free exchange of books; each area began to publish primarily for its own linguistic community. In addition the religious wars led to an increase in nationalization of the book trade as a consequence of censorship and licensing. Fictitious imprints were devised to evade the censors, and stringent regulations were imposed almost everywhere as the civil and ecclesiastical authorities awoke to the dangers of freely circulating ideas. The Reformation and the Counter-Reformation did more than bring on a stricter regulation of the book trade; they also vastly increased the use of the press for polemics and propaganda. Germany, the Low Countries and Switzerland poured forth tens of thousands of broadsides, pamphlets and books on behalf of Luther and Calvin; Italy, France and Spain riposted for the Roman Church. Many printers went underground for their beliefs; some, like Étienne Dolet of Lyon, were martyred.

The technological changes during the first centuries of printing were few and slight. Intaglio printing was occasionally used in combination

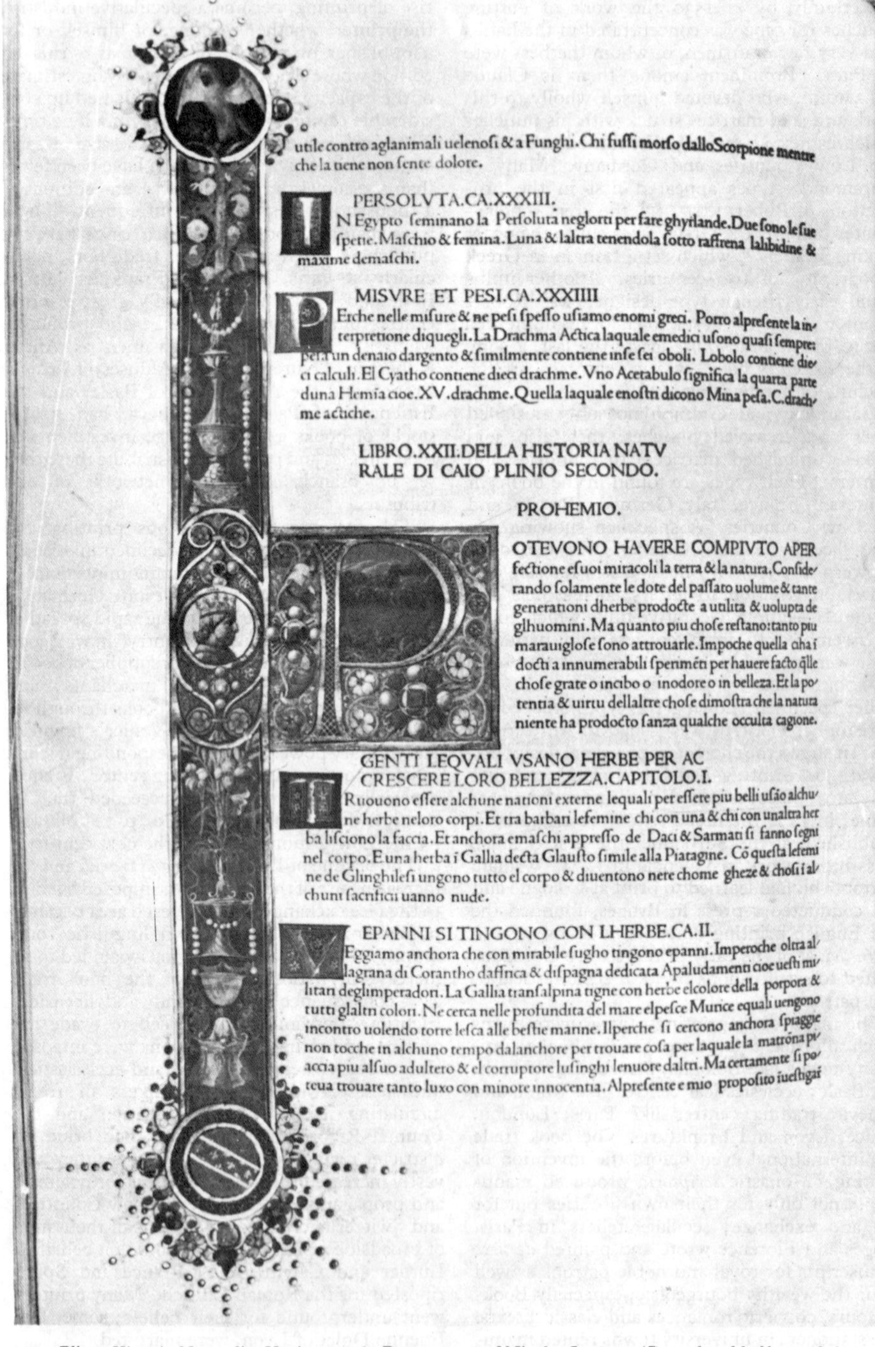

utile contro aglanimali uelenoſi & a Funghi. Chi fuſſi morſo dallo Scorpione mentre
che la tiene non ſente dolore.

IPERSOLVTA.CA.XXXIII.
IN Egypto ſeminano la Perſoluta neglorti per fare ghyrlande. Due ſono le ſue
ſpetie. Maſchio & femina. Luna & laltra tenendola ſotto raffrena lalibidine &
maxime demaſchi.

PMISVRE ET PESI.CA.XXXIIII
PErche nelle miſure & ne peſi ſpeſſo uſiamo enomi greci. Porro alpreſente la in-
terpretione diquegli. La Drachma Actica laquale emedici uſono quaſi ſempre:
peſa un denaio dargento & ſimilmente contiene inſe ſei oboli. Lobolo contiene dieci calculi. El Cyatho contiene dieci drachme. Vno Acetabulo ſignifica la quarta parte
duna Hemía cioe. XV. drachme. Quella laquale enoſtri dicono Mina peſa. C. drachme actiche.

LIBRO.XXII.DELLA HISTORIA NATV
RALE DI CAIO PLINIO SECONDO.

PROHEMIO.

POTEVONO HAVERE COMPIVTO APER
fectione eſuoi miracoli la terra & la natura. Conſide-
rando ſolamente le dote del paſſato uolume & tante
generationi dherbe prodocte a utilita & uolupta de
glhuomini. Ma quanto piu choſe reſtano: tanto piu
marauigloſe ſono attrouarle. Impoche quella cha ī
docti a innumerabili ſperimēti per hauere facto q̄lle
choſe grate o incibo o inodore o in belleza. Et la po-
tentia & uirtu dellaltre choſe dimoſtra che la natura
niente ha prodocto ſanza qualche occulta cagione.

GENTI LEQVALI VSANO HERBE PER AC
CRESCERE LORO BELLEZZA.CAPITOLO.I.
TRuouono eſſere alchune nationi externe lequali per eſſere piu belli uſāo alchune herbe neloro corpi. Et tra barbari lefemine chi con una & chi con unaltra herba liſciono la faccia. Et anchora emaſchi appreſſo de Daci & Sarmati ſi fanno ſegni
nel corpo. E una herba ī Gallia decta Glauſto ſimile alla Piatagine. Cō queſta lefemine de Glinghileſi ungono tutto el corpo & diuentono nere chome gheze & choſi ī al-
chuni ſacrificii uanno nude.

VEPANNI SI TINGONO CON LHERBE.CA.II.
VEggiamo anchora che con mirabile ſugho tingono epanni. Imperoche oltra al-
lagrana di Corantho daffrica & diſpagna dedicata Apaludamenti cioe ueſti militari deglimperadori. La Gallia tranſalpina tigne con herbe elcolore della porpora &
tutti glaltri colori. Ne cerca nelle profundita del mare elpeſce Murice equali uengono
incontro uolendo torre leſca alle beſtie marine. Ilperche ſi cercono anchora ſpiaggie
non tocche in alchuno tempo dalanchore per trouare coſa per laquale la matróna pi-
accia piu alſuo adultero & el corruptore luſinghi lenuore daltri. Ma certamente ſi po-
teua trouare tanto luxo con minore innocentia. Alpreſente e mio propoſito īueſtigaī

Pliny, *Historia Naturalis*. Venice, 1476. Roman type of Nicolas Jenson. (*Reproduced half actual size*)

ſieri poſſe uix puto : ſed plane quia ita de-
bemus inter nos : neq; enim arbitror cario
rem fuiſſe ulli quenquam ; q̃ tu ſis mihi.
Sed de his et diximus aliâs ſatis multa ; et
ſaepe dicemus: nũc autem ; quoniam iam
quotidie ferè accidit poſtea, q̃ e Sicilia ego,
et tu reuerſi ſumus ; ut de Aetnae incendi-
is interrogaremus ab iis, quibus notum
eſt illa nos ſatis diligenter perſpexiſſe ; ut
ea tandem moleſtia careremus; placuit mi
hi cum ſermonem conſcribere ; quem
cum Bernardo parente habui paucis poſt
diebus, q̃ rediiſſemus ; ad quem reiicien-
di eſſent ii, qui nos deinceps quippiam
de Aetna poſtularent. Itaq; confeci librũ;
quo uterq; noſtrum cõmuniter uteretur:
nã cum eſſemus in Noniano ; et pater ſe
(ut ſolebat) ante atrium in ripam Pluuici
contuliſſet ; acceſſi ad eũ progreſſo iam in
meridianas horas die: ubi ea, quae locuti
ſumꝰ inter nos, ferè iſta ſũt. Tibi uero nũc
orationẽ utriuſq; noſtrũ, tanq̃ habeatur,

A ii

Manutius' edition of Pietro Bembo, *De Aetna*. Venice, 1495. The roman type of Francesco Griffo da Bologna. (*Reproduced actual size*)

with letterpress in the 15th c., as in the edition of Dante which was published in Florence in 1481, which attempted to use engravings by Baldini after drawings by Botticelli. The problems of combining two different kinds of presswork proved so cumbrous and so uneconomical that only the first three cantos were so illustrated; the illustrations for the remainder were separately printed and were pasted on in the majority of copies.

During the 16th and 17th centuries this began to change. Books often contained engraved title-pages and decorations, despite the added cost, especially if they were destined for an upper-class audience or if they depended heavily upon a combination of text and illustration, as did the emblem books, which attained great popularity. Usually the engravings were the work of hacks, employed by the publishers, but occasionally first-rate artists were commissioned: Dürer and Holbein provided the models for woodcut illustrations and borders; Rubens designed plates for the Plantins in Antwerp; Poussin did a number of highly impressive title-pages for the Imprimerie Royale in Paris; Rembrandt did a few etchings for Dutch publishers; and a number of very skilled engravers, among them Crispin de Pas, Romain de Hooghe and Wenceslas Hollar, worked regularly for publishers. Eighteenth-c. books often contained not only engraved illustrations, title-pages and borders, but vignettes, head-pieces and tail-pieces, many of them minor works of art in their own right.

But it was the wood-block cutters who produced the most important book illustrations, particularly in the early period. Wood blocks, cut in relief, could be locked up and printed simultaneously with the type and were by far

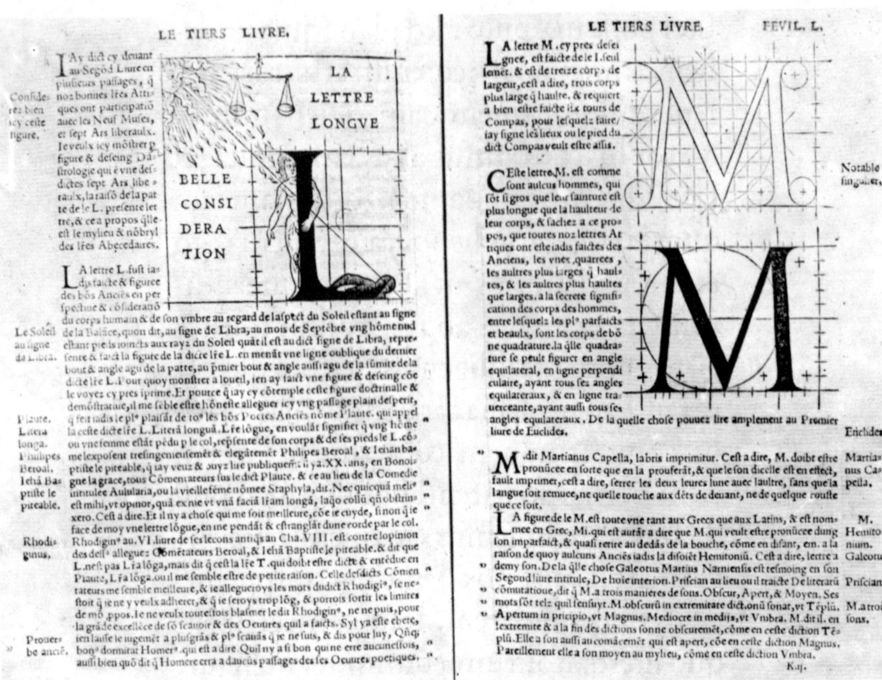

LE TIERS LIVRE.

LA LETTRE LONGVE

BELLE CONSIDERATION

IAy dict cy deuant au Segõd Liure en plusieurs passages, q̃ noz bonnes lr̃es Attiques ont participatiõ auec les Neuf Muses, et sept Ars liberaulx. Ie veulx icy mõstrer p figure & deseing Dastrologie qui e vne desdictes sept Ars liberaulx, la raisõ de la patte de le L. presente lettre, & ce a propos q̃lle est le mylieu & nõbryl des lr̃es Abecedaires.

Considerez bien icy ceste figure.

LA lettre L. fust iadis faicte & figuree des bõs Anciẽs en perspectiue & cõsideratiõ du corps humain & de son vmbre au regard de laspect du Soleil estant au signe de la Balãce, quon dit, au signe de Libra, au mois de Septẽbre vng hõme nud estant pieds ioincts aux rayz du Soleil quãt il est au dict signe de Libra, represente & faict la figure de la dicte lr̃e L. en menãt vne ligne oublique du dernier bout & angle agu de la patte, au p̃mier bout & angle aussi agu de la sũmite de la dicte lr̃e L. Pour quoy monstrer a loueil, ien ay faict vne figure & deseing cõe le voyez cy pres ip̃rime. Et pource q̃ iay cy cõtemple ceste figure doctrinalle & demõstratiue, il me sẽble estre hõneste alleguer icy vng passage plain desperit, q̃ feit iadis le pl⁹ plaisãt de to⁹ les bõs Poetes Anciẽs nõme Plaute. qui appella ceste dicte lr̃e L. Literã longuã. Lr̃e lõgue, en voulãt signifier q̃ vng hõme ou vne femme estãt pẽdu p le col, rep̃sente de son corps & de ses pieds le L. cõme lexposent tresingenieusemẽt & elegãtemẽt Philipes Beroal, & Iehan baptiste le piteable, q̃ iay veuz & ouyz lire publiquemẽt il y a. XX. ans, en Bonoigne la grace, tous Cõmentateurs sus le dict Plaute. & ce au lieu de la Comedie intitulee Aulularia, ou la vieille fẽme nõmee Staphyla, dit. Nec quicquã melius est mihi, vt opinor, quã ex me vt vnã faciã lr̃am longã, laq̃o collũ q̃n obstrinxero. Cest a dire. Et il ny a chose qui me soit meilleure, cõe ie cuyde, si non q̃ ie face de moy vne lettre lõgue, en me pendãt & estranglãt dune corde par le col. Rhodigin⁹ au. VI. liure de ses lecons antiq̃s au Cha. VIII. est contre lopinion des dess⁹ alleguez Cõmẽtateurs Beroal, & Iehã Baptiste le piteable. & dit que L. nest pas Lr̃a lõga, mais dit q̃ cest la lr̃e T. qui doibt estre dicte & entẽdue en Plaute, Lr̃a lõga. ou il me semble estre de petite raison. Celle desdicts Cõmentateurs me semble meilleure, & ie allegueroys les mots dudict Rhodigi⁹, se ne stoit q̃ ie ne y veulx adherer, & q̃ ie seroys trop lõg, & porrois sortir les limites de mõ ꝑpos. Ie ne veulx toutesfois blasmer le dit Rhodigin⁹, ne ne puis, pour la grãde excellẽce de sõ scauoir & des Oeuures quil a faicts. Syl y a este ebete, ien laisse le iugemẽt a plusgrãs & pl⁹ scauãs q̃ ie ne suis, & dis pour luy, Qñq; bon⁹ dormitat Homer⁹. qui est a dire. Quil ny a si bon qui ne erre aucunesfois, aussi bien quõ dit q̃ Homere erra a daucũs passages des ses Oeuures poetiques.

Le Soleil au signe de Libra.
Plaute.
Literã longã.
Philipes Beroal.
Iehã Baptiste le piteable.
Rhodiginus,
Prouerbe anciẽ.

LE TIERS LIVRE. FEVIL. L.

LA lettre M. cy pres deseignee, est faicte de le I. seulement. & est de treize corps de largeur, cest a dire, trois corps plus large q̃ haulte. & requiert a bien estre faicte six tours de Compas, pour lesquelz faire, iay signe les lieux ou le pied du dict Compas veult estre assis.

CEste lettre M. est comme sont aulcus hommes, qui sõt si gros que leur sainture est plus longue que la haulteur de leur corps, & sachez a ce propos, que toutes noz lettres Attiques ont este iadis faictes des Anciens, les vnes quarrees, les aultres plus larges q̃ haultes, & les aultres plus haultes que larges. a la secrete signification des corps des hommes, entre lesquelz les pl⁹ parfaicts et beaulx, sont les corps de bõne quadrature. la q̃lle quadrature se peult figurer en angle equilateral, en ligne perpendiculaire, ayant tous ses angles equilateraux, & en ligne trauerceante, ayant aussi tous ses angles equilateraux. De la quelle chose pouuez lire amplement au Premier liure de Euclides.

Notable singulier,
Euclides

M. dit Martianus Capella, labris imprimitur. Cest a dire, M. doibt estre pronũcee en sorte que en la prouferãt, & que le son dicelle est en effect, fault imprimer, cest a dire, serrer les deux leures lune auec laultre, sans que la langue soit remuee, ne quelle touche aux dẽts de deuant, ne de quelque couste que ce soit.

Martianus Capella.

LA figure de le M. est toute vne tant aux Grecs que aux Latins, & est nommee en Grec, Mi. qui est autãt a dire que M. qui veult estre pronũcee dung son imparfaict, & quasi retire au dedãs de la bouche, cõme en disant, em. a la raison de quoy aulcuns Anciẽs iadis la disoiẽt Hemitoniũ. Cest a dire, lettre a demy son. De la q̃lle chose Galeotus Martius Narniensis est tesmoing en son Segond liure intitule, De hoie interiori. Priscian au lieu ou il traicte De literarũ cõmutatioue, dit q̃ M. a trois manieres de sons. Obscur, Apert, & Moyen. Ses mots sõt telz quil sensuyt. M. obscurũ in extremitate dict. onũ sonat, vt Tẽplũ. Apertum in pricipio, vt Magnus. Mediocre in medijs, vt Vmbra. M. dit il. en lextremite & a la fin des dictions sonne obscuremẽt, cõme en ceste diction Tẽplũ. Elle a son aussi au comãcemẽt qui est apert, cõe en ceste diction Magnus. Pareillement elle a son moyen au mylieu, cõme en ceste diction Vmbra.

K.ij.

M. Hemitonium.
Galeotus
Priscian.
M. a trois sons.

Geofroy Tory, *Champ fleury*. Paris, 1529. (*Reproduced half actual size*)

Ad lectorem linguæ
GALLICAE STVDIOSVM.

L Ibros Galeni de vsu partium corporis humani quum ad Græcum exem
plar magna cura præcipuóque studio non modo recognouissem , sed
propemodũ nouos reddidissem, vigi
liis, curis, labore fractus, materiã disquisiui, in qua
ingenii vires longiore studio & grauiore fessas re-

Garamond's 'gros canon' and 'gros texte' romans in Jacques Du Bois, *In linguam gallicam isagoge*. R. Estienne. Paris, 1531. (*Reproduced actual size*)

DELLE EPIST. FAM. 110

*quale, hauendoti io ſcritto di Milone, meritamente ri=
deſti, ma alla Romana, come parlano gli huomini nõ inet
ti, che non è perſona, che di bontà, & di prudenza l'a=
uanzi. al che ſi aggiunge, che nelle ragioni ciuili egli è
dottiſſimo, & ha una memoria ſingulare. non doman
do, che tu lo faccia prefetto, ne Tribuno, ò gli dij qualche
altro grado: ſolamente domãdo, che tu l'ami, et uſi uerſo
lui la tua ſolita corteſia. ma nõ però mi fie diſcaro, ſe ti
piacerà anche di ornarlo di ſimili fregi di gloria. & final
mẽte togliẽdolo delle mie mani, põgolo, come ſi dice, nelle
tue mani uittorioſe, et fedeli. ſono forſe piu cerimonioſo
cõ teco, che non debbo: ma non lo fo forſe ſenza cauſa.
Attendi à ſtar ſano, & uoglimi bene, come uuoi.*

Cicerone à Trebatio.

*IO non ſcriuo mai à Ceſare, ne à Balbo ſenza rac=
commandarti loro: ne cio faccio con parole fredde ma tã
to calde, che danno grãdiſſimo indicio dell'amore, che ti
porto. ma di gratia laſcia andare queſte ſciocchezze, &
queſta fantaſia di ritornare à Roma: et cõ la diligẽza, &
col ualore intendi à conſeguir quello, che hai ſperato del=
l'andata tua. queſto coſi ti perdoneremo noi amici, come
perdonarono à Medea quelle matrone nobili, & ricche,
che habitauano nell'alta rocca di Corintho: alle quali ella
con ſue mani bianchiſſime perſuadette, che non la biaſi=
maſſero: perche uiueſſe lontana dalla patria ſua:
Peroche in ſtrani lidi
Molti auanzar lor ſorte,
Et di lor patria l'util procurorno.
Molti nel propio nido*

The italic of Aldus. Cicero, *Epistolas ad Familiares.* Venice, 1548
(*Reproduced actual size*)

Italique de la taille de Garamond / qui est sur le gros Romain.

Italique de Gros Romain

*Iuris præcepta ſunt hæc, Honeſtè viuere, alterum
non lædere, ſuum cuiq; tribuere. Huius ſtudij duæ
ſunt poſitiones, Publicum & priuatum. Publicum
ius eſt, quod ad ſtatum rei Romanæ ſpectat. Priua
tum, quod ad ſingulorum vtilitatem pertinet.
Dicendum eſt igitur de iure priuato, quòd triperti-
tum eſt: collectum eſt enim ex naturalibus præcep-
tis, aut gẽtium aut ciuilibus. Ius naturale eſt quòd*

The great primer italic of Garamond. (*Reproduced actual size*)

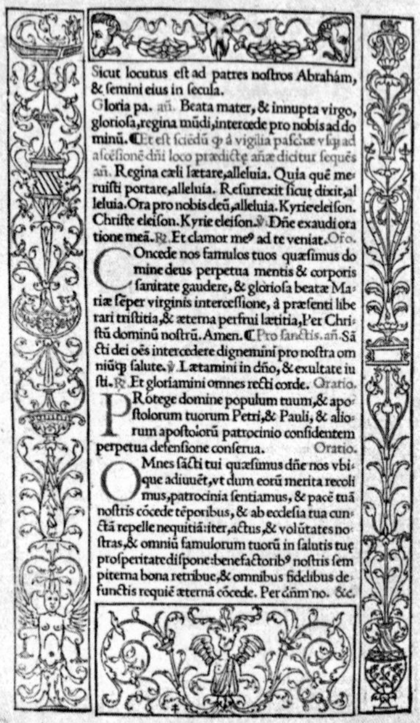

Sicut locutus eſt ad patres noſtros Abrahám, & ſemini eius in ſecula.
Gloria pa. añ. Beata mater, & innupta virgo, glorioſa, regina mũdi, intercede pro nobis ad dominũ. ℂ Et eſt ſciẽdũ ꝙ à vigilia paſchæ vſq; ad aſcẽſionẽ dñi loco prædictę añæ dicitur ſequẽs añ. Regina cæli lætare, alleluia. Quia quẽ meruiſti portare, alleluia. Reſurrexit ſicut dixit, alleluia. Ora pro nobis deũ, alleluia. Kyrie eleiſon. Chriſte eleiſon. Kyrie eleiſon. ℣. Dñe exaudi oratione meã. ℟. Et clamor me⁹ ad te veniat. Oro.
Concede nos famulos tuos quæſimus domine deus perpetua mentis & corporis ſanitate gaudere, & glorioſa beatæ Mariæ ſẽper virginis interceſſione, à præſenti liberari triſtitia, & æterna perfrui lætitia, Per Chriſtũ dominũ noſtrũ. Amen. ℂ Pro ſanctis. añ. Sãcti dei oẽs intercedere dignemini pro noſtra omniũq; ſalute. ℣. Lætamini in dño, & exultate iuſti. ℟. Et gloriamini omnes recti corde. Oratio.
Protege domine populum tuum, & apoſtolorum tuorum Petri, & Pauli, & aliorum apoſtolorũ patrocinio confidentem perpetua defenſione conſerua. Oratio.
Omnes ſãcti tui quæſimus dñe nos vbique adiuuẽt, vt dum eorũ merita recolimus, patrocinia ſentiamus, & pacẽ tuã noſtris cõcede tẽporibus, & ab eccleſia tua cunctã repelle nequitiã: iter, actus, & volũtates noſtras, & omniũ famulorum tuorũ in ſalutis tuę proſperitate diſpone: benefactorib⁹ noſtris ſempiterna bona retribue, & omnibus fidelibus defunctis requiẽ æternã cõcede. Per dñm no. &c.

Ad completorium Verſus.
Conuerte nos de⁹ ſalutaris noſter.
℟. Et auerte iram tuam à nobis.
℣. Deus in adiutoriũ meũ intẽde
℟. Dñe ad adiuuãdũ me feſtina.
Gloria patri, & filio. Sicut erat in principio, & nunc. &c. Alleluia. Pſalmus.

Geofroy Tory, *Heures à l'usage de Rome*. Paris, 1524. (*Reproduced half actual size*)

the commonest method of illustration except for maps (see CARTOGRAPHY) and smaller diagrams, which might be printed separately and bound in with the text. The block-cutters were remarkable craftsmen, whether cutting their own work or following the drawings of other artists. The illustrations to the *Hypnerotomachia Poliphili* (Venice, 1499), the *Theuerdank* (Nuremberg, 1517) or Geoffroy TORY's *Book of Hours* (Paris, 1525), while differing widely in style as one would expect from their various countries of origin and the content and format of their texts, are alike in the consummate skill of their execution and their appropriateness to the over-all design of the books in which they appear.

Equally impressive are the early technical illustrations: the first writing-books, of Arrighi, Tagliente and Palatino, issued in Italy in the 16th c.; the drawings of plants in the first herbals, like those for Leonard Fuchs's *De historia stirpium commentarii* (Basle, 1542); the maps in the early printed editions of Ptolemy's *Geographia* or in the first topographical guides to Rome; the illustrations to early editions of Vitruvius and Valturius; are all not only decorative but explicit in their interpretation of the text.

The changing appearance of the printed book gradually affected type-design. This can be seen particularly in French printing. The Imprimerie Royale was established in 1640, at the instigation of Cardinal Richelieu, with the deliberate intention of enhancing French prestige by the production of fine, often monumental books, an intention in which it succeeded admirably. It commissioned for its exclusive use a series of type faces, notably the *romains du roi*, designed to harmonize with the engraved illustrations and decorations which its directors and the court favoured. The task of design was assigned to the Académie Royale des Sciences, which in 1693 set up a committee under the chairmanship of Jacques Jaugeon; the type, designed according to mathematical principles, was the first which deliberately eschewed calligraphic models. It became the ancestor of many later modern type faces. The *romains du roi* employ a sharp contrast between thick and thin strokes, more typical of the engraver's burin than of the pen, and have a horizontal serif (finishing stroke), rather than the slanting one typical of pen-written letters. The punch-cutter Philippe Grandjean (1666–1714) considerably modified the designs, diluting their mathematical rigidity to achieve greater visual appeal; the final result is remarkable for its clarity and brilliance. The face is particularly effective in a large folio like the *Médailles sur les principaux événements du règne de Louis le Grand* (Paris, 1702), a sumptuous book combining engraved borders, decorations and illustrations to produce a suitably grandiose work.

The 18th c. saw a continuation in the refinement of type-design, particularly in England. Until the emergence of William CASLON and his successors the English trade depended mainly upon the Continent, especially France and Holland, for the supply of type. William Caslon, trained as an engraver of gun-locks and barrels, began to cut and found type in London in 1716; his models were mainly Dutch, and it was his version of the Dutch letter which dominated printing not only in England but in the English colonies during most of the 18th c. Printing had reached Spanish America early in the 16th c., when Juan Cromberger of Seville sent Juan Pablos to Mexico in 1539 to establish a branch; the first press in the English colonies was founded considerably later, at Cambridge, Massachusetts, in 1639. The first American printers imported most of their materials from the home country until well after the American Revolution. Isaiah Thomas, the most successful of the 18th-c. American printers, boasted on the title-page of his 1785 specimen book that the types displayed were those of Caslon. There was no successful type-foundry in the United States until 1809, when Binny and Ronaldson opened their shop in Philadelphia.

The greatest English type-designer of the century was John BASKERVILLE, a writing-master and stone-cutter, whose ambitions as a printer led to the design and production of his own types. In addition he experimented with new kinds of paper (his 1757 edition of Virgil was one of the first books to be printed on wove paper, whose smoother surface gave more brilliant impressions of his types, which were lighter and sharper in design than those of Caslon). Baskerville's books, sparing of ornament and relying primarily on careful workmanship and a nice sense of proportion for their effect, were highly influential in setting a new style; they prefigure those of BODONI and the DIDOTS, half a century later.

While there were considerable developments in typography and book design during the 17th and 18th centuries, there was still comparatively little technical advance. Minor improvements were made to the printing press, many of them by the Dutch printer W. J. Blaeu; in general, however, the press described and illustrated in Joseph Moxon's *Mechanick Exercises* (1683–4), the first comprehensive printer's manual, is not very different from that shown in 15th-c. and 16th-c. printing, the first since the original invention.

There is no satisfactory account of the invention of stereotyping, nor of the several people involved in its development. The first plates were apparently made by producing a plaster-of-Paris mould, baked before casting, from which printing plates could be cast. Since the mould had to be broken to extract the plate only one set could be made each time. PAPIER-MÂCHÉ moulds, developed later, could produce duplicate sets, useful when large editions were required

The punches of William Caslon the Elder for pica roman. (University Press, Oxford)

quickly; they also made possible the development of the curved printing surfaces essential for high-speed cylinder presses of the kind required for modern newspapers and other long-run jobs. First of those involved seems to have been Johann Müller (d. 1710), a Dutch minister who began experimenting with the production of small prayer-books from some form of stereotype plate *c.* 1701; later books produced by his method include Bibles and a Syriac lexicon. About 1727 a Scottish goldsmith, William Ged, developed an unsuccessful stereotyping process from cast plates. In France, later in the century, the Hoffman brothers developed a plaster method, which they called '*polytypage*', used for printing legal forms, pamphlets and a journal, among other matter. Stereotyping was first successfully carried on in England under the patronage of Lord Stanhope, who established the Stereotype Office in London in 1804. The use of papier-mâché (known as 'flong' in the printing trade) was introduced in France *c.* 1829; it is still commonly used since among other things its light weight makes easy and cheap shipment possible.

Lithography is one of the few printing processes whose invention and development can be described accurately, since its inventor, Alois SENEFELDER, a Bavarian, left a full account of his discovery, made by accident in 1796. An amateur printer, he bought a piece of local stone on which to grind ink. Needing to write a laundry list hurriedly, and having no paper, he wrote it on the stone. He had experimented with etching; this gave him the idea of trying the effect of acid on the stone before wiping off the ink, which was composed of wax, soap and lamp black. He covered the stone with a mixture of water and *aqua fortis* and found that the ink repelled the acid, which bit into the rest of the stone, leaving a raised printing surface. In later experiments he discovered that a raised printing surface was unnecessary; a water-soluble coating, such as gum, prevented ink from adhering to the stone. By using a greasy printing-ink, which was repelled by the water, and applying his designs with a greasy medium, either pencil or ink, he could print by wetting the stone and inking it with a roller. This is still the basic principle of lithography, although stones have been supplanted by plates made of metal and plastic, and images are now usually photographed upon the plate rather than drawn directly by the artist.

The Industrial Revolution hit the printing trade comparatively late; once started, however, its effects were both extraordinarily fast and extraordinarily complete. There had been few real changes, merely minor improvements, from the invention of printing until *c.* 1800. Each decade after that date saw enormous strides.

The basic stimulus was the rapid increase in the market for printing which resulted from the tremendous rise in literacy during the 19th c. An expanding middle class demanded not only novels but above all newspapers and periodicals, school books and reference works. As the century progressed the working class, taught in state schools, in private philanthropic institutions and in their own educational associations, further expanded this market. Huge editions resulted: the tracts of the S.P.C.K. and similar groups, Bibles and prayer-books, text-books and self-help manuals, the shilling shocker and the penny paper. In this new consumer-oriented market there was a constant pressure for more printed matter, produced more rapidly, at lower prices.

The rate of change was neither even nor smooth. Printing is a continuum, made up of many inseparable processes: paper supply, composition, presswork, distribution of type, folding and binding are but a few. Each time one step was speeded, a new bottleneck emerged. The inventors and engineers were rarely concerned with more than one element at a time.

The first, and constantly recurring, obstacle to mass printing was a shortage of paper. Originally all paper was made of waste rags, whose fibres provided a durable and printable surface; but there were never enough suitable rags for the purpose, and paper manufacturing countries often put embargoes on export to protect their supply. During the 18th c. critical shortages frequently occurred, and a search for substitute fibres began.

The newspaper industry, with its stress on speed, had most influence on the development of rapid printing presses and on mechanical type composition. *The Times* (London) was especially important both in supporting research and in installing new equipment. Friedrich Koenig, a German who settled in England and worked with various London printers, assisted by a fellow German, Andreas Bauer, developed in 1810 a steam-driven press which required manual labour only for feeding and removing the printed sheets. Thomas Bensley, one of the printers with whom Koenig worked, used this press for printing one sheet of the 1811 *Annual Register*. In 1812 Koenig patented an improved press which could print 800 sheets an hour. Two of these, installed in *The Times* office in 1814, produced 1,100 impressions per hour. In 1816 Koenig and Bauer devised the first press which could print on both sides of the sheet and work at about the same rate, thus effectively doubling speed as well as saving numerous other operations. The vertical rotary press, built by Augustus Applegath for *The Times* in 1848, averaged 12,000 impressions an hour, on one side only. A cylinder machine, it printed from type affixed to a rotary drum rather than from stereotype plates. William Bullock's American press of 1865 has been described as the first really automatic printing machine; it was fed by a continuous roll of paper, printed on both sides from curved stereo plates cast from papier-mâché moulds, and delivered 10,000 eight-page papers per hour. Other important 19th-c. press builders who made significant technical improvements included Robert Hoe of New York, whose machines were exported extensively, and Robert Miehle of Chicago. German manufacturers also made many improvements, especially in presses for book and jobbing work; the Heidelberg press is world famous for its engineering and the quality of its manufacture.

Higher speed in printing inevitably produced a demand for more rapid typesetting. Newspaper proprietors and editors wished to get the news out more quickly; moreover in order to sell the advertising which constituted the most profitable part of the paper, they had to increase the amount of surrounding text. Few readers will buy a publication consisting solely or mainly of advertising, despite the wish of publishers. In book printing text can be saved and reprinted if there is sufficient demand; there is little occasion to reprint dated news material, so that new composition is required constantly.

Even though over 1,500 patents on composing machines were issued in the United States alone during the 19th c., only two really successful machines for setting large bodies of textual material survived. These are now often being replaced by various photographic and electronic systems.

Among the earliest was a machine patented in 1822 by Dr. William Church of Vermont (during the 19th c. the lead in technology was increasingly taken by the United States). Part of a projected system which also included an improved press and a type-casting machine, there is no indication that it was ever built. It involved the storage of separate type sorts in inclined channels, from which they were to be released by a keyboard operator. Power was to be provided by a clockwork mechanism.

The earliest recorded composing machine actually to have been installed in a printing plant, *c.* 1840, was invented by James Young and Adrien Delcambre, assisted by Henry Bessemer; it incorporated many of Church's ideas. One of the longer-lived of the early machines was that of Robert Hattersley, introduced in 1857; a few were still in use as late as 1915. This had a more compact keyboard than its predecessors, delivered type in a form that could be spaced and justified into even lines in the machine, and could compose about 7,500 letters an hour. None of these machines gained wide acceptance, however, as did the Linotype and the Monotype.

The Linotype, as its name suggests, casts the words and spaces for a whole line in one piece (called by printers a 'slug') instead of a separate piece of type for each character and space. The machine is a composer, justifier and caster combined. The many matrices that it needs of each sort are stored in a magazine divided into channels from which they are released one at a time by impulses from the keyboard and to which they are returned by a mechanical distributor after each line has been cast. Justification of the lines of matrices to equal length is achieved mechanically by means of expanding spaces. The provision of the enormous number of matrices required was made possible by the invention by Lloyd B. Benton, an American, of a punch-cutting machine, which he patented in 1885.

The second successful composing machine was the Monotype, invented by Tolbert Lanston of Washington, D.C., in 1889. Unlike the Linotype it produces separate type and needs only one matrix for each character, and whereas the Linotype combines keyboard operation and casting in a single machine, the Monotype keyboard produces a perforated tape through which compressed air is directed, activating a separate casting machine. Justification of lines is effected by making the widths of characters and spaces multiples of a unit so that the operator can calculate for each line the width of the spaces needed to adjust it to the correct length. Virtually all texts in the Latin and exotic scripts are now set on composing machines, and handwork is confined to correcting, making up pages, adding finishing touches and imposing the pages to make formes. Now that they make their own type printers no longer distribute it back into cases to be used again, but melt it as soon as it has been printed. In the United States, Linotype has dominated both book and periodical composition. In England and Europe generally, Monotype has been far more extensively used for book work, where accuracy and ease of correction are most prized, while Linotype's greater speed and ease of make-up has made it the most commonly used composing machine for newspapers and magazines.

One reason for Monotype's success in book publishing is its highly successful programme of type-design, much of it performed under the direction of Stanley MORISON, who became typographical advisor to the Monotype Corporation in 1922. Under his direction a wide variety of historical typefaces was adapted for use on the machine. In addition a number of modern faces were designed specifically for it, notably the Sans Serif and Perpetua of Eric Gill and Morison's own Times roman; the latter was commissioned by *The Times* specifically for high-speed newspaper work and was adapted for Linotype as well. Linotype has also adapted many historical faces for machine use, and has commissioned new faces from such designers as W. A. DWIGGINS and Hermann Zapf.

There are three distinct methods of photomechanical reproduction (primarily of illustrations) in common use today, corresponding to the three major printing processes, letterpress, intaglio and lithography. While all share certain common features (the fixing of an image by photography on to a sensitized printing plate and the use of half-tone screens to achieve tonal gradation) each has involved its own technology and its own inventions. The question of the invention of PHOTOGRAPHY, like that of printing itself, is a highly complicated affair, involving numerous inventors, sometimes working independently, sometimes improving on the experiments of their predecessors. The first attempts at producing a photomechanical printing surface was made by Joseph Nicéphore Niepce, who is credited with being one of the inventors of photography. In 1815 he attempted, unsuccessfully, to fix a photographic image on to a sensitized stone. In 1826 he succeeded in producing a contact print on a sensitized pewter plate coated with a solution of asphalt dissolved in oil. The line engraving to be reproduced was oiled to make the paper translucent. When the plate was exposed, the black lines of the original print prevented light from reaching the asphalt; where light did come through, the asphalt softened and was soluble in a weak acid wash. The remaining hard black lines provided a printing surface. The plates were too soft to give many satisfactory impressions, and the process was not used widely. It became the basis, however, for the later development of photogravure. In 1841 L. H. Fitzeau succeeded in producing a printing surface from a photograph on copper which was far more durable. The development of steel plates, by W. H. Fox TALBOT in 1852, provided a still more satisfactory and durable printing surface.

Fox Talbot, who invented the negative/positive photographic process, in 1844–6 published a description of his invention, *The Pencil of Nature*, illustrated with actual photographs. His dissatisfaction with the cumbrousness of the procedure led to his experiments with photomechanical printing processes. His first process involved contact printing of actual objects—lace, leaves and similar materials—on to a metal plate coated with a potassium bichromate-sensitized gelatin which hardened and became insoluble when exposed to light. Subsequently he developed methods of reproducing gradations of tone by use of a screen which broke the image into small dots, each capable of holding ink; the size of these dots, and their closeness to one another, could produce varying depth of colour. The first screens were of fine gauze; later refinements, notably by Paul Pretsch, in 1854, and Karl Klič, *c.* 1860, led to the high-speed, cheap methods in use today.

The first successful attempts to produce relief-printing blocks photomechanically were made by Firmin Gillot, in Paris, *c.* 1850. They involved the transfer to zinc of a lithographed or engraved original and etching away with acid those parts not protected by the greasy lithographic ink. Pretsch's method of producing half-tones, involving a screen, was adapted to relief printing in 1854. It is the basis of today's commonly used method. In 1852 Lemercier, Lerebours, Barreswil and Davanne, in Paris, fixed photographic images on sensitized stones which could be printed on an ordinary lithographic press. This, however, was a slow and expensive process. The development of metal and later of plastic plates, which can be curved for use on a cylinder press, considerably lowered costs and increased speed of production. Offset lithography, which employs such plates, is most frequently used; it involves printing the image on to a rubber blanket, then transferring it, or offsetting it, on a paper, metal or other printing surface. As in gravure and relief printing, depth and gradation of tone are achieved by use of a screen. The finest tonal reproduction, however, is obtained by collotype, invented by Alphonse Louis Poitevin of Paris in 1855. This uses a plate coated with chromated gelatin on which a photographic image is fixed. Ink adheres to the exposed areas in proportion to the amount of light which has acted upon them; darker areas absorb more ink, and print more darkly. Collotype, while producing work of very high quality, is infrequently used because of its high cost; the plates are not suitable for long runs, and great skill is required in printing from them.

Colour printing, whether by relief, intaglio or lithographic processes, is fundamentally the same in principle: the combination of four basic colours, black, red, yellow and blue, each from a separate printing plate, achieves the effect of the various colours; the superimposition of the different coloured inks produces an optical illusion. The colours are separated during photography by the use of filters. Most colour work relies upon the four-colour process; really fine reproductions, as of works of art or maps, demanding high fidelity to the original, may call for half a dozen or more colours of ink.

The increased popularity of offset lithography from photographically produced plates led to experiments in composing type directly from film negatives, thus eliminating setting metal type and pulling proofs from them for photography on to the plates. The inhibiting factor which slowed down the development of photocomposition (or film-setting) was the difficulty of making corrections; it is far easier to correct a single letter or even a whole line cast in metal than to 'strip in' a tiny piece of film.

Experiments along these lines were begun as early as 1877, by Ottmar Mergenthaler among others, but the practical difficulties of making corrections on film negatives proved insuperable. One of the earliest film-setting machines was that of an Hungarian engineer Eugene Porzholt, who obtained a patent in 1896. Keyboard-operated, it photographed single letters on to a sensitized plate which advanced after each exposure and was developed after the whole plate had been exposed.

Numerous other machines have been patented during the present century, offering advantages besides the elimination of metal; for instance, a single alphabet can be photographically enlarged or reduced to provide a wide range of sizes, although considerable distortion may occur if the changes are too great. These have been most successful in setting display material (advertising, chapter-headings and the like); the difficulties of stripping in corrections, and the high cost of the equipment, have inhibited their complete acceptance for text setting. Even more highly sophisticated machines have recently been developed, involving the use of batteries of optical scanners capable of reading typed manuscripts, computers which transfer their product to magnetic tapes, and cathode tubes containing a fount of letters which are activated by these tapes and which produce images of single letters on paper or film. Computers can be used not only to set the type but to retain large quantities of material which requires frequent revision, making changes as needed; statistical tables, airline schedules, stock quotations, telephone directories and the like are particularly suitable for such work. However, the high cost not only of the machines but of programming them for a wide variety of uses has as yet confined them to the largest printing establishments; even there it is doubtful whether they are heavily used enough (their speed is such that they have an almost insatiable demand for copy) to be profitable.

Modern printing technology is changing so rapidly that it is impossible for the historian to keep abreast of it. The printer, indeed, whose continued existence depends upon his ability to do so, and to decide in which of the many new and expensive machines he will invest, finds the task a most vexatious one. Moreover, the competition with other media in the storage and dissemination of information and the provision of entertainment (television, particularly, has cut into newspaper and magazine audiences and drawn advertising from printing) has had considerable impact upon the printing industry in recent years, and has caused considerable speculation about the future of printing. The advantages of the printed text, however—its permanence, the ability of the reader to proceed at his own speed and to return to passages which he wishes to read again, the ability to treat abstract and difficult material and principles provided by the printed word—will undoubtedly ensure the survival of printing in some form, different though it be from that which we think of today.

17, 39, 45, 54, 60, 64, 71, 77, 129, 131, 134, 146, 175, 193, 194, 198, 204, 277, 291, 390, 505, 517, 526, 560, 562, 563, 603, 604, 605, 606, 610, 626, 679, 692, 848, 855, 865, 895, 912.

U

UMBRELLA. In the 16th c. the umbrella, or parasol, was still a fashionable novelty in Europe, used chiefly by Portuguese and Spanish ladies and in Italy. Catherine de Médicis brought a parasol to France in 1533 when she married the Duke of Orleans, and Henri's mistress, Diane de Poitiers, possessed a sunshade, parts of which have survived. Mary Queen of Scots in 1562 owned a sunshade or 'little canopy' of crimson satin decorated with fringes and tassels of gold and crimson silk. In 1578, however, in the satirical *Dialogues* of Henri Estienne, the carrying of a parasol is mentioned as a foreign custom in Italy and Spain, virtually unknown in France, and in the *Essais* of 1580 Montaigne speaks of it as an Italian habit prevalent there since the time of the ancient Romans. In England the earliest depiction of an umbrella is in a portrait of Sir Henry Unton, now in the National Portrait Gallery. An umbrella 'of perfumed leather with a gold fringe about it' was brought from Italy by Thomas Coryate in 1608 and was bequeathed in his will.

The word 'umbrella', taken from the Italian, appeared in John Florio's Italian–English dictionary of 1598: 'Ombrella, a fan, a canopie, also a testoon of cloth of state for a prince; also a kind of round fan or shadowing that they use to ride with in summer in Italy; a little shade.' It was used in a metaphorical sense by John Donne in a letter to Sir Henry Goodyer dated 1609 and in 1624 by Beaumont and Fletcher in *Rule a Wife and Have a Wife* (1624), Act III, sc. i. About the same period the word 'quitasol' or 'tiresol', taken from the Spanish, became current in a variety of spellings. It was generally associated with China. Before these innovations became established the umbrella was referred to in travel literature generally by the terms 'sombrero' or 'shadow' (Hakluyt, vol. iii, p. 299). The umbrella and the sunshade or parasol did not acquire distinct identity until *c.* 1800.

In the Netherlands the parasol began to make its appearance during the 1st half of the 17th c., particularly for ladies attending the hunt. A large, domed sunshade is depicted in Philips Wouwerman's painting *Departure for the Hunt* and a parasol of Oriental appearance features in Rembrandt's drawing *The Adoration of the Magi.* In France, Lebrun's painting of Pierre Séguier entering Rouen in 1640 shows him with two parasols held over his head by pages. In 1630 Louis XIII had a collection of 11 taffeta sunshades and three umbrellas of oiled cloth trimmed with silver and gold lace. In 1644 John Evelyn bought an umbrella in Marseilles and in 1644 he noted that the first paper 'umbrellas' from China had appeared in Paris. During the 2nd half of the century prints begin to show ladies carrying parasols and the *Dictionnaire* of César-Pierre Richelet in 1680 said that parasols were carried only by ladies and 'only in the spring, summer and autumn'. In England the umbrella took longer to establish itself. Catherine of Braganza brought with her a Portuguese umbrella as part of her trousseau on her marriage to

Charles II. But the umbrella or parasol did not find favour in Restoration times and two umbrellas presented to Prince Rupert in 1682 by the ambassadors of the King of Bantam remained a byword of ridicule. In the 1680s umbrellas in general were still regarded as curiosities and the word 'umbrello' was expounded as strange and unusual in Thomas Blount's *Glossographia*. The use of the waterproof umbrella by women as a protection against rain came in about the turn of the century and in the 1st quarter of the 18th c., but it was still regarded as effeminate for men. The 'umbrella in rainy weather' is mentioned in Swift's *A Tale of a Tub* (1696) and the word was defined in Kersey's *Dictionarium Anglo-Britannicum* (1708) as 'a kind of broad fan or skreen, commonly us'd by women to shelter them from rain'. In Swift's *Description of a City Shower* sempstresses hurry through the rain beneath an 'oil'd umbrella' and in Gay's *Trivia* (1712), Bk. I, lines 209–18, the use of the umbrella by housewives and maids against the rain is contrasted with the sunshade of tropical countries. The first umbrellas were kept in coffee-houses and clubs for the use of customers to protect them from the rain when walking from the door to their carriages.

In many parts of the world the umbrella has been an attribute of royal or divine status and an important item in ceremonial regalia. In Egypt by the 12th c. B.C. the royal umbrella symbolized the vault of heaven over a king and might be regarded as an extension of the power and protection of the king's shadow. In Assyria also it was the king's privilege to have an umbrella carried over his head by an attendant at ceremonial processions and at the hunt. In Greece at the women's festival of the Thesmophoria the participants carried umbrellas or had umbrellas held over them by attendants. (See Aristophanes, *Thesmophoriazusae* 830. In the *Birds*, 1550–1, Prometheus says humorously: 'Bring me an umbrella so that if Zeus should chance to see me from above, he will think I am an attendant of one of the celebrant women.') From a remark in the *Knights* ('Your ears unfurled themselves like an umbrella and folded up again', 1345) it appears that the Greek umbrella or parasol was designed to open and shut. Among the Romans the *umbracula* was used as a protection against the sun from *c.* the 3rd c. B.C. They were used in the amphitheatre and Ovid mentions the carrying of a woman's sunshade among the attentions of courtship (*Ars Amatoria* ii. 209). Their use by men was considered effeminate by Juvenal (*Satire* ix) but by the end of the 4th c. the fashion had become general, as indicated by Claudian. The umbrella appears to have had little religious or honorific significance among the Romans except perhaps in connection with the adoption of eastern cults as for example by the emperor Heliogabalus.

In Africa the ceremonial use of the umbrella has been prominent mainly in Ethiopia, Morocco and west Africa. In Ethiopia the use of the royal umbrella as a prerogative of kingship extends for some two and a half millennia up to the coronation of the emperor Haile Selassie in 1930. It also features in the religious ceremonial of the Abyssinian Church. In Morocco the tall, flat-topped umbrella has formed part of the royal regalia until modern times. The origin of the symbolic use of the umbrella in western Africa is uncertain, although it was widely established by the end of the 15th c., particularly among the Yoruba and in Dahomey and Ashanti. Its ceremonial use in Dahomey *c.* the middle of the 19th c. was of especial interest to Sir Richard Burton and a number of other travellers. At the defeat of the Ashanti by the British in 1874 and again in 1895 the king's umbrella was captured and sent to Queen Victoria.

In India and the Far East the umbrella has been a religious and honorific symbol for varying periods up to a couple of millennia. The sky god Varuna carried an umbrella (*abhoga*) made from the hood of a cobra and this attribute was transferred to Vishnu in certain incarnations. The umbrella played a prominent part in the iconography of Buddhism and the representation of the umbrella may often indicate the presence of the invisible Buddha. The umbrella is one of the Eight Treasures of the Buddha and the overshadowing umbrella gave its characteristic form to the Buddhist *stupa*. Many Indian monarchs adopted the umbrella as a symbol of sovereignty and it has been customary until the 20th c. for visiting dignitaries to be escorted under a ceremonial umbrella in honour of their rank. The royal or state umbrella has also been common in Nepal, Goa, Burma, Thailand, Cambodia, Laos and Vietnam. The religious use of the umbrella spread with the spread of Buddhism. In Tibet, for example, large silk umbrellas, called *gdugs*, were hung above the altars. In China the use of the umbrella goes back to very early times and an elaborate social etiquette was developed prescribing the number, type and colour of umbrellas a man might carry according to rank from the emperor downwards. The religious use of the umbrella, and perhaps also its extensive use in funeral ceremonial, probably dates from the introduction of Buddhism into China. In Japan umbrellas feature among the tomb sculptures or *haniwa* from the 5th c. and in the course of centuries the ceremonial umbrella for differentiation of rank and for use in pageantry developed on similar lines to China. The sunshade held a special place in Japanese art.

In Pre-Columbian America also the umbrella may have had an honorific significance since Guaman Poma speaks of the feather parasol among the insignia of the Inca monarch and represents the Coya, or Inca queen, attended by a parasol-bearing lady-in-waiting.

That the honorific significance of the umbrella was known to medieval Europe is evidenced *inter alia* by a representation in the Utrecht Psalter of King David with a crown on his head and behind him an angel holding over him an umbrella

Ceremonial use of umbrella by the Ashanti. Kumasi, 1973

Herod and Herodias. Mural from the Baptistry, Florence

(*Left*) The Coya Chuquillanto. The feather parasol is a symbol of rank. Guaman Poma de Ayala, *Nueva Coronica*, folio 142

as a symbol of royalty. But the umbrella was not generally used in this way in Europe, the one exception being its adoption among the regalia of the Church. A 12th-c. mural in the church of the Santi Quattro Coronati, Rome, representing the Donation of Constantine shows the Emperor Constantine presenting to Pope Sylvester I royal insignia among which is included a striped brown and white umbrella. Although the Donation is unhistorical, the umbrella was in fact included among the regalia of the Papacy and it was a custom for Church dignitaries to present elaborate models of an umbrella to high-ranking ecclesiastics and other dignitaries. In 1177 Pope Alexander III awarded the Doge of Venice the privilege of bearing an umbrella and until Venice fell to Napoleon in 1797 it was the custom for the Doge on ceremonial occasions to be escorted by a bearer of an elaborate state umbrella. In the course of the 13th c. the umbrella was to some extent superseded by the baldachinum, but it still continued to play a part in papal ceremony until the middle of the 19th c. Some time in the 1st half of the 15th c. it was adopted as a heraldic device of the Papal States and a fresco by Francesco Salviati in the Palazzo Farnese shows Pope Eugenius IV seated beneath the banner of the States on which is depicted an umbrella above crossed keys. In Vincencio Carducho's *Dream of Pope Honorius* (*c.* 1628) the Pope is shown seated under a tasselled and lappeted umbrella or *papilio*.

The commercial exploitation of the umbrella made some progress in Europe during the 1st half of the 18th c. first in Paris, whence the fashion spread to Germany and Britain. It was not, however, until about the end of the century that the umbrella and the parasol or sunshade achieved separate identities. In 1715 the *Frauenzimmerlexicon* defined 'parasol' as follows: 'Parasol really means a covering roof of oiled cloth supported on a small pole, which females carry over their heads to protect themselves from the heat of the sun. In this country, however, females use it when it rains. It can be opened and shut.' Mainly responsible for the introduction of the umbrella to Britain was the philanthropist and traveller Jonas Hanway (d. 1786), of whom it was written: 'When it rained, a small parapluie defended his face and wig; thus he was always prepared to enter into any company without impropriety or the appearance of negligence. And he was the first man who ventured to walk the streets of London with an umbrella over his head; after carrying one near thirty years, he saw them come into general use' (John Pugh, *Remarkable Occurrences in the Life of Jonas Hanway*, 1787). In America the umbrella established itself by the middle of the century despite some opposition from the Quakers, and imported umbrellas were to be seen in Baltimore and Philadelphia. In the 1760s the *Boston Evening Post* carried advertisements both for umbrellas and for frames to be covered by ladies 'whose Ingenuity, Leisure and Economy lead them to make their own'.

Throughout the 18th c. important strides were made, chiefly by Paris manufacturers, in the design of the umbrella for greater lightness and convenience. In 1776 a monopoly of the manufacture of umbrellas and parasols was given by edict to the *boursiers*, the makers of gloves and girdles. The *parasol à ressort* with telescoping stick was invented by Gosselin of Amiens *c.* 1785 and the same maker is said to have introduced the system of hinged ribs which could be folded into a third of their length. By the end of the century the sunshade or parasol had acquired a separate identity and was well on the way to becoming an article of feminine fashion. The umbrella in contrast remained a utility object and continued to attract satire and scorn as 'a bastard born of the walking-stick and the cabriolet'. In France Louis Philippe was caricatured for his untidy umbrella and the umbrella generally was regarded as bourgeois and inelegant. During the 2nd half of the 19th c., while the commonplace 'gamp' remained a symbol of vulgarity, more elegant and slimmer models began to creep into fashion. By the end of the century gentlemen were beginning to carry their 'city umbrella' and in the course of the 20th c. the tightly rolled silk umbrella became a symbol of the city man and the civil servant, until the notorious umbrella of Neville Chamberlain made history at Munich.

173.

UPDIKE, DANIEL BERKELEY (1860–1941). Born and educated in Providence, Rhode Island, after being employed by the Houghton Mifflin Company in Boston he founded the Merrymount Press in 1893 and is considered by many to have been America's greatest printer. His books, most of which he designed himself, were notable for their clarity of organization and their excellent workmanship. Starting as a disciple of William MORRIS, he later in the series 'The Humanist Library' grew interested in Renaissance book styles and as time went on became a connoisseur of historical type faces. He was lecturer on TYPOGRAPHY to the Harvard Business School from 1911 to 1916 and in 1922 published his scholarly study *Printing Types*.

URSO (or URSONI), FILIPPO. The author of an album of pen-and-ink designs for parade-armour, sword-hilts and horse-trappings in the Victoria and Albert Museum, which bears the date 1554. Nothing is known about him beyond the fact, given in the album, that he came from Mantua. See ARMS AND ARMOUR.

V

VAJRA. Originally the thunderbolt of the Indian god Indra, with which he dispersed the clouds of ignorance, the *vajra* became the symbol of the 'method' in the Tantric form of Buddhism which was introduced into TIBET by the teacher Padmasambhava. It was closely associated in Lamaist ritual with the prayer-bell or GHANTA, which symbolized the 'doctrine'. In form the *vajra* resembled two claws set opposite each other on a short rod; each claw had a central nail, which was straight, surrounded by four or eight others which curved in towards it.

The cruciform *vajra* was also a symbol in Chinese and Tibetan Lamaism, used on amulets and for magical purposes in the decorative arts.

VALENCIENNES LACE. Bobbin LACE was a traditional craft of Valenciennes, which in 1678 ceased to be Flemish and became French. The term 'Valenciennes lace' refers to a bobbin lace made here and elsewhere in France and Flanders during the 18th and 19th centuries. It lacks the heavier thread which in most bobbin lace outlines the pattern and its softness and delicacy made it a favourite trimming for personal linen and fine muslin. Because of the lack of a heavy outlining thread it was easily laundered. The ground and pattern were worked at the same time and although the floral patterns seemed modest, it was not inexpensive because of this; each of the fine threads in the solid parts of the pattern was continued to form the very regular ground-mesh (which was round in the 18th c., diamond-shaped in the 19th c.), a technique which demands great skill and deftness.

VALENTINES. See POSTAL COMMUNICATIONS, PICTORIAL.

510, 788.

VALE PRESS. A private printing press founded in 1896 by Charles RICKETTS in partnership with W. L. Hacon. The aim of the Press was to bring about a revival of printing based upon 15th-c. models and to this extent it followed the example of the KELMSCOTT PRESS of William MORRIS. Type face and decoration were designed by Ricketts, the books were printed at the commercial firm Ballantyne Press and were published by John Lane. The Press produced 46 titles, including a Shakespeare in 39 volumes. In 1903 after a disastrous fire at the Ballantyne Press Ricketts threw the punches and matrices of his types into the Thames and the Press was closed down. See PRIVATE PRESS MOVEMENT.

VANDERCRUSE, ROGER (1728–99). French cabinet-maker of Flemish origin, known as Lacroix (R.V.L.C.). Born in Paris, he was the son of a Flemish cabinet-maker, Franz van der Cruse. He was made master of the guild in 1755 and worked for Louis XV, Madame du Barry and the duc d'Orléans.

VARGUEÑO. Nineteenth-c. name for a highly original type of cabinet developed in the Spanish Renaissance from a type of chest used in church sacristies for keeping ecclesiastical vessels and ornaments. It consisted of a rectangular case divided into drawers, with a drop-leaf front and set upon an arcaded stand. While the exterior was usually fairly plain, the interior was highly decorated and enriched with MARQUETRY, carving and INLAY. The most typical *vargueños* are in the Mudejar style, decorated with ivory panels and gilding. The type was carried to the New World and in 1568 the guilds of Mexico required a cabinet-maker to be able to make a *vargueño* among other things as a condition of qualification. See FURNITURE (EUROPEAN).

VAUXHALL GLASS. See MIRRORS.

VELDE, HENRI VAN DE (1863–1957). Flemish architect and designer who was a leading apostle of functionalist aesthetics and an influential exponent of the modern movement in architecture. He first studied painting and from 1889 took part in the activities of the group known as *Les Vingt*. Coming under the influence of the English ARTS AND CRAFTS MOVEMENT and William MORRIS, he was largely instrumental in establishing ART-NOUVEAU style and philosophy in Belgium. In the 1890s he designed revolutionary layout, typography and woodcut illustrations for the journal *Van Nu en Straks* which contributed to a renaissance of book design in Belgium. From 1894 he experimented with the designing of FURNITURE. From 1895 he concentrated on architecture and his Maison Tassel, which he designed as a unity with furniture, glassware, carpets, silver, etc., is considered to be a seminal example of the new style. In 1896 he designed rooms for Bing's gallery L'Art Nouveau and his curvilinear furniture attracted attention at the Dresden Exhibition of Applied Arts in 1897. From *c.* 1900 his influence was mainly felt in Germany, where he propagated his artistic philosophy in a lecture tour 1900–1, designed the layout and decoration of the Folkwang Museum at Hagen in 1900–2 and designed a room for the Dresden Exhibition of Applied Arts in 1906, besides many private architectural commissions. From the early years of the century he began to repudiate his *art-nouveau* principles in favour of structuralism and a theory of functional form and artistic creativity. In 1906 he founded the Weimar School of Applied Arts, which was the forerunner of the BAUHAUS, and in 1907 he was associated with Hermann Muthesius (1861–1927) in the formation of the DEUTSCHER WERKBUND. In 1917 he moved to Switzerland, where he designed the Kröller-Müller museum which was ultimately built at Otterlo in 1937–54. Returning to Belgium in 1925, he founded and was Principal of the *Institut des Arts Décoratifs de la Cambre*, afterwards the *École Nationale Supérieure d'Architecture et des Arts Décoratifs*. He held the chair of Architecture in the University of Ghent from 1926 to 1936. See also ART NOUVEAU.

VELLUM and **PARCHMENT.** Untanned animal skins—chiefly sheep or calf, less frequently lamb, pig, goat and other animals—prepared for writing or for painting (e.g. miniature portraits). They were also occasionally used for printing or BOOKBINDING. The use of the two terms as synonymous is not strictly correct as 'parchment' is generally reserved for dressed sheepskins, etc. and 'vellum' was made mainly from unsplit skins of calves, lambs or kids. The skins were treated with lime, scraped with a knife to remove irregularities and finally polished with pumice stone. The use of animal skin as a writing material is mentioned by Herodotus v. 58 (*c.* 480–*c.* 425 B.C.) and by Pliny, *Nat. Hist.* xiii. 11 (*c.* A.D. 23–79).

VELVET. The special characteristic of velvet lies in the fact that in addition to the normal warp and weft there is a second set of warp threads, exceptionally rich and dense. This second or 'pile' warp, as it is called, weaves in two ways: first by interlocking itself with the ground fabric, and secondly by weaving over metal wires. At this stage the fabric looks somewhat like a corduroy, each cord being filled with a wire. Attached to the end of each wire is a sharp knife; when the wires are drawn out from the fabric the knife cuts through the pile threads, which thus become changed from loops into tufts. By the use of the JACQUARD machine pile may be formed in any desired part of the design, thus forming figured velvet. See WEAVING (PILE WEAVING).

VENEER. The application of thin sheets or strips of a decorative material to the surface of a piece of furniture or similar object. Veneering was known to ancient Egypt, usually in ebony or IVORY, and was sometimes used to hide inferior local woods; it was practised by ancient Greek and Roman craftsmen. It did not survive the break-up of the Roman Empire but was revived in association with the use of ebony by Dutch and Flemish craftsmen in the 17th c. Veneering with ebony and other exotic woods and with TORTOISE-SHELL or ivory both for decorative and for pictorial effects was a particular skill of the cabinet-makers of Antwerp, Amsterdam and The Hague. From the Netherlands the craft was carried to France about the middle of the century and together with MARQUETRY became the basis of ÉBÉNISME or skilled cabinet-making. In England the technique was introduced by Dutch and Huguenot craftsmen at the Restoration. Veneering is a technique which is basic to fine furniture-making and as an art it depends upon the selection and decorative use of ornamental woods and other materials. The art was popular throughout the 17th c. and was carried to the height of perfection, particularly by French craftsmen, in the 18th c. Veneering was adopted by American cabinet-makers of the FEDERAL period and particularly worthy of note is the case furniture of Philadelphia and Baltimore with large ovals of contrasting veneers.

The present pejorative sense arose in the 19th c. when veneering began to be used in order to conceal inferior material or shoddy workmanship in the body to which it was applied. See also WOOD-WORKING.

VENETIAN LACE. Though it remains uncertain whether lace-making techniques originated in Venice or were introduced there from the East, there is no doubt that both needlepoint and bobbin LACE were made there from the early 16th c. From Venice the technical knowledge spread rapidly throughout Europe, but for 100 years the floral scrolls and geometrical designs of the Venetian pattern-books so dominated the minds of lace-makers everywhere that it is no longer possible to distinguish Venetian work from that done in other countries. Certain needlepoint laces of the 17th c., however, are considered to be characteristically Venetian. The earliest of these Renaissance scrolls, whose linear character is slightly relieved by a heavier thread outlining the forms, carry naturalistic daisies. Floral ornament of a more flowing, BAROQUE character appears in the lace known as *point de Venise*: it was entirely without relief. Shortly after 1650 these types gave way to the spectacular *gros point de Venise*, whose conventional Baroque vegetation is so dense that the tie-bars or BRIDES linking the forms are frequently dispensed with and almost sculptural relief is obtained by the use of thick pads of threads worked over in buttonhole stitch. A more delicate variety is known as *rose point* from the little flower-like picots which ornament the brides. The very attenuated floral scrolls of another type have earned it the name *punto a vermicelli*.

VERDURE TAPESTRIES. Tapestries depicting a landscape or having a design composed of leaves, sometimes leaves of colossal size—so called large-leaf verdures. OUDENARDE in Belgium made a speciality of this type of tapestry, but they were also woven at many other European centres from the 15th to the 18th centuries. See TAPESTRY.

VERMICULATION. VERMICULATED. A form of ornament consisting of sinuous or wavy lines resembling the tracks of worms. In

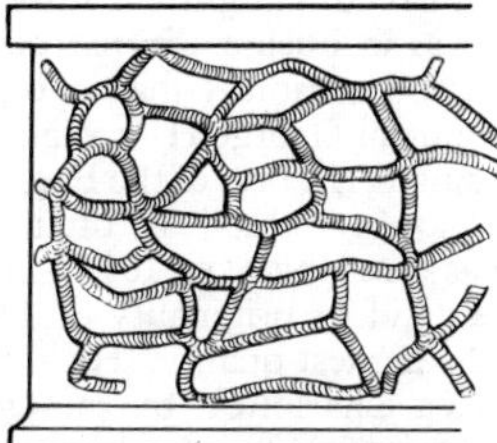

architecture the term is used of stonework or other surfaces carved or moulded in this way. The term is also used for a type of background ornament in metalwork and ENAMEL work.

VERNIS MARTIN. A name loosely used to describe the many forms of LACQUER produced in France during the 18th c. in imitation of Chinese and Japanese wares. The four brothers Martin—Guillaume, Étienne-Simon, Robert and Julien—from whom the name is taken, were celebrated for work of this kind from *c.* 1730 to 1770 and enjoyed the title of *vernisseurs du roi.* But they did not originate the process and did not have a monopoly of the goods, which ranged from SNUFF-BOXES to carriages. The basic ingredient of *vernis Martin* was usually copal varnish, not the true *Rhus vernicifera* used in Oriental lacquer. See also LACQUER and JAPANNING.

VERRE ÉGLOMISÉ. GLASS decorated with a layer of engraved gold. The term originated in the name of a French art dealer, Jean-Baptiste Glomy (d. 1786), who popularized the framing of prints within borders of black and gold applied to the backs of their protective glazing. His fellow traders referred to an example as an *églomisé,* which was rendered into Italian as *agglomizzato.* The name has further been used for many kinds of gold-engraved glass produced in classical times and later.

The technique was described by Cennino CENNINI in his manuscript treatise *Il libro dell'arte,* written in the 14th c. Gold leaf was affixed with glair to one side of a sheet of glass and the drawing executed on it with a fine needle, cutting right through the leaf for bold lines and pressing lightly to produce half-tones. Alternatively a pattern of dots would give a comparable shaded effect. A coating of coloured pigment, frequently black, caused the delicate pattern to stand out in contrast to the background metal and at the same time preserved the work. Among the earliest surviving examples are two bowls found at Canosa, southern Italy, and now in the British Museum. They date from the late 3rd c. B.C., and were probably made in Alexandria. To protect their decoration of stylized floral pattern each was carefully fitted by the maker within another bowl so that the gold is retained between the two layers of glass. The many surviving medallions (known as *fondi d'oro*), fragments of bowls and other vessels, which depict religious as well as secular subjects, were similarly encased. The backs of many of them are covered by a further layer of glass fused into place—a feat requiring considerable skill if the ornamentation was not to be ruined. A large number of these pieces, dating from the 3rd/4th c. A.D., have been found in the Roman catacombs, where they were embedded in the cement walls of the tombs. This was presumably done by mourners following a burial ceremony, but the presence of the glass in these circumstances has been the subject of several theories. Similar specimens have been excavated at burial sites in the Cologne area of Germany and in other countries.

The process was further used in Italy in the 14th c., and a few fine examples have been preserved (Mus. Civico, Turin, and other important museums). All depict biblical scenes, and scholars have attempted to classify them into schools using styles of manuscript illumination as guides. An increased use of colour in 15th-c. examples of *verre églomisé* reflects the influence of painting in oils, and soon afterwards the employment of the technique in Italy died out. It continued to be used in other countries, notably Germany, where plaques of the glass were inset into pieces of furniture. In England, France and the Netherlands in the late 17th and early 18th centuries it was used in lengths, often decorated with ARABESQUE patterns, to form the borders of large MIRRORS.

An ambitious variation of the process was practised at an undiscovered location in Bohemia —perhaps, it has been suggested, by a workshop connected with a monastery. The craftsmen concerned ornamented beakers and goblets with engraved gold, and to protect the work from damage they ingeniously enclosed it in a complex and close-fitting outer casing of glass. To minimize the risk of liquid penetrating the two layers of glass when the vessel was in use the join was made below the lip, where its presence is often unsuspected. To complete the whole a medallion was equally neatly inserted in the base. These glasses, known as ZWISCHENGOLDGLÄSER, were variously patterned; some with heraldic emblems but most of them with hunting scenes. They were produced during the 2nd quarter of the 18th c., and by *c.* 1755 it would appear that they were no longer being made.

In the 2nd half of the 18th c. and later *verre églomisé* was used for ornamenting buttons and other trifles. In Germany, England and elsewhere SILHOUETTISTS employed the process with good effect. The technique was also employed occasionally in England in the early years of the 19th c., when panels of *verre églomisé* formed the friezes of overmantel and other mirrors. It was also used for the tops of occasional tables and, more rarely, for the *surtout-de-table* which occupied the centre of a dining-table. In the latter breakages must have been a constant hazard, and examples have seldom survived in sound state.

An outstanding use was made of *verre églomisé* by a Dutch artist named Zeuner, whose Christian name has remained obstinately unknown. He painted landscapes and seascapes in Holland, England and Denmark, using engraved gold and silver foils backed with black paint. These he combined with skies rendered constrastingly in natural colours with ordinary oil-paints. The entire work was executed on the reverse of the glass, which in some instances is 75 centimetres wide. He is known to have exhibited in London in 1778, and usually signed his work 'Zeuner inv.'. Roughly contemporary with him, an Austrian, Johann Joseph Mildner (1763–1808) devised a modified *Zwischengoldglas* technique. His beakers were usually made for presentation and bear inscriptions as well as pictorial subjects. Mildner formed shaped glass roundels decorated on their inner sides with gold leaf and red LACQUER, which were then affixed to spaces hollowed precisely to fit them in the walls of the vessels. The result was a perfectly flush surface. He had his workshop at Gutenbrunn, and often signed and dated his productions.

410, 916.

VIANEN, VAN. Family of Dutch silversmiths from Utrecht. PAULUS (d. 1613) was employed by the court at Munich (1596–9) and afterwards worked for the Emperor Rudolf II at Prague. His development of the Nuremberg tradition of Wenzel JAMNITZER in low relief is illustrated by a ewer in the Rijksmuseum, Amsterdam, showing the punishment of Callisto. ADAM (d. 1627), brother of the foregoing, worked in Utrecht. Both elaborated the bulging BAROQUE cartouche and favoured the so-called 'AURICULAR' ('Knorpel') style, whose invention is credited to Paulus. A series of designs by Adam van Vianen, with the addition of some of his own, were published by his son CHRISTAEN *c.* 1652 under the title *Modelles Artificiels* and may have had some influence on the silverwork designs of Juste-Aurèle MEISSONNIER. Christaen van Vianen came to England *c.* 1630 and established residence at Westminster in 1634. He was commissioned to make a service of plate for St. George's Chapel, Windsor, which was, however, looted during the Civil War in 1641. He was working in Utrecht 1647–52 but was back in London in the early 1660s. He held the position of 'Silversmith in Ordinary' to the king, in which he was replaced by Jean-Gêrard Cockus (John Coque) in 1661. He is last heard of in 1666. An example of his work is a large laver signed and dated 1635 and decorated with water and dolphins in a style reminiscent of engravings by the Jan Lutmas, father (d. 1669) and son (1624–85/9). The publication of the designs of Adam van Vianen at the mid century may have had some influence in popularizing the 'auricular' style in English silver.

VILE, WILLIAM (d. 1767). One of the most highly regarded of English 18th-c. cabinet-makers, he was in business in partnership with John COBB and was cabinet-maker to the Crown at the beginning of George III's reign. His work qualifies as among the best of the English ROCOCO style (*c.* 1750–65) which is often popularly referred to as CHIPPENDALE. It is notable for its superb finish and its originality of design, with carving of the highest quality. His masterpieces include Queen Charlotte's bureau-cabinet and jewel cabinet (1761) and bookcase (1762), all still in the Royal possession, and George III's medal-cabinet (1761) now in the Victoria and Albert Museum.

VINOGRADOV, DMITRI (d. 1758). An originator of PORCELAIN manufacture in Russia. His factory became the Imperial Porcelain Manufactory in 1803. See RUSSIA.

VITRUVIAN SCROLL. Ornamental pattern used in a frieze or border. It is of Classical origin and consists of a sequence of convoluted scrolls. Also known as 'running dog'.

VOYSEY, CHARLES F. A. (1857–1941). English architect and furniture designer. He was trained by J. P. Seddon and set up practice in 1882. In 1884 he joined the Art Workers' Guild (ultimately becoming Master in 1924) and was thus linked to the ARTS AND CRAFTS MOVEMENT. He first exhibited furniture at the Arts and Crafts Exhibition, 1893. He was made a Fellow of the R.I.B.A. in 1929 and received the Institute's Gold Medal in 1940. Though he was the most widely imitated of English designers abroad, where he was regarded as the 'fountain-head' of ART NOUVEAU, Voysey had a decided insularity of outlook, unimpressed by Continental movements. He stressed tradition and his furniture was austere and straight-lined, sparingly ornamented in plain oak. He disliked historical revivals and pioneered simplicity in interior decoration, exemplified in the dining-room, The Orchard, Chorley Wood, 1900. He was also one of the first designers to appreciate the significance of industrial design.

VRIES, HANS VREDEMAN DE (1527–after 1604). Dutch painter, architect and decorative designer, born at Leeuwarden. Few of his paintings have survived and he is now chiefly remembered for the influence exerted by his pattern-books and books of decorative designs. Italian Renaissance and BAROQUE styles made their influence felt in the Low Countries during the 16th c. primarily in the field of ornament rather than structure and it was in this context that Vredeman de Vries came to the fore. Although his many books of designs carried Baroque fantasy to an extreme, they were in the mood of the place and time. His book on perspective, engravings of exaggeratedly ornate and fanciful Renaissance palaces, gardens and architectural details, remained for long a source-book for the school of artists who painted imaginary architectural scenes. His *Variae Architecturae Formae* (1601), a collection of fantastic and impossible architectural compositions, became nevertheless a source-book of ornamentation for Dutch Baroque and its influence was felt wherever the influence of Dutch Baroque extended outside the Netherlands. He was prolific of pattern-books of ornamental designs and motifs, which made a strong impact on the new style in FURNITURE, SILVER and the other decorative arts. Along with Cornelis Floris (1514–75) he introduced Italianate strapwork into northern decorative arts and together with Wendel Dietterlin (1550/1–1599) of Strasbourg and Lucas Kilian (1579–1637) of Augsburg he was one of the originators or popularizers of the AURICULAR STYLE.

WAINSCOT. Probably derived from Dutch or Low German *wagenschot*, the term originally referred to high-quality oak boards cut from the centre of the log, such as were used by wainwrights for wagon-building. Thus from the 14th c. to the early part of the 17th c. the word meant good-quality oak. During the 16th, 17th and 18th centuries the word was also used of any piece of furniture solidly constructed of oak boards. In the 17th c. it also came to be accepted as a general term for wood panelling, even if it was of deal. SHERATON in *The Cabinet Dictionary* (1803) describes wainscot as 'the wooden work which lines the walls of a room as high up as the surbase'.

WALDGLAS. A pale green utilitarian glass of inferior quality which in the late Middle Ages and afterwards was widely made throughout Bohemia and Germany. The name *Waldglas* ('forest glass') derives from the fact that after the break-up of the Roman Empire as a consequence of the Barbarian invasions the centralized glass industry of northern Europe was fragmented into a scattering of glass-houses isolated in the forests which supplied them with fuel and the wood-ash needed for manufacture. See GLASS (HISTORY, BOHEMIA AND GERMANY).

WALLPAPER. Wallpaper has a long and interesting history and its story is associated with many styles of interior decoration. It has always been looked upon as an acceptable substitute for costlier mural hangings and it has been made to resemble or imitate many different decorative fabrics. Its design, too, has followed many styles, notably those seen in woven, embroidered or printed textiles.

One of the most rewarding inquiries into the origin of wallpaper, though not the only one, is connected with the study of box- and cupboard-lining papers, examples of which are to be seen nowadays in museum collections. (See also PAPERS, DECORATIVE.) These were commonly produced by the early letterpress printers using techniques employed for book illustration, advertisements or proclamations, and the printing was done by wood-blocks, the sheet of paper often being no bigger than a foot square. Black printer's ink was generally used—on occasion red—and the most favoured designs were heraldic or floral; some of the more sophisticated sheets were printed with a design imitating the black-and-white stitchery of the Tudor period. These papers served very effectively as linings but were only used exceptionally as wallpaper. A number of the London leather gilders, makers of screens, hangings, etc., during the 17th c. turned over to making wallpaper when paper became available in suitable quantity and quality. But there are grounds for supposing that the first wallpapers, as we know them today, came into being at the end of the 17th c., for it was about this time that a few makers hit upon the idea of sticking the printed sheets together to form a roll—an advertisement issued during the reign of William and Mary mentions 'figured paperhangings in pieces of 12 yards long'.

A reference to wallpaper occurs in a trade journal of 1699 which plainly suggests the growing acceptance of patterned paper as a suitable and economical mural hanging: '. . . a great deal of Paper is nowadays printed to be pasted upon Walls to serve instead of Hangings; and truly if all parts of the sheet be well and close pasted on, it is very pritty, clean and will last with tolerable care a great while . . . there are some *done by rolls* in long sheets pasted together to be so long as the Height of a Room and they are managed like Woollen Hangings, and there is great Variety, with curious Cuts which are Cheap, and if kept from Wet, very lasting.'

By the middle of the 18th c. wallpaper was a viable commercial proposition and English manufacturers, mostly in London, besides developing a thriving industry at home, were exporting very considerable quantities to all parts of the world, including America.

But despite many and various attempts to mechanize production, printing processes remained for a long time much the same as those employed in calico printing before Thomas Bell and others perfected the machine towards the end of the century—a machine which wallpaper manufacturers adapted for their own purpose 50 years or so later. Of course from the outset wallpaper has been dependent on a regular and plentiful supply of paper. The 'flock' varieties, for example, demanded fine-quality paper to bear the weight of the wool and most wallpapers today are printed upon reliable stock. Fortunately this raw material has seldom been in short supply except perhaps during war time.

When during the early part of the 19th c. the paper-makers evolved the 'endless' sheet many problems of expansion were solved and from this time on the use of wallpaper increased enormously because even the poorest were able to afford it. The new wallpapers, somewhat ambiguously referred to as 'cylinder-printed by steam', were to be seen at the Great Exhibition of 1851 and were much admired, although the premier award in this section of the industrial arts was carried off by a French manufacturer evidently not yet convinced of the merits of machinery.

Nothing can be said in favour of the wallpaper designs at this time. Like those of the Axminster carpet they remained static and uninspired. William MORRIS, who made over 60 designs for wallpaper between 1862 and 1898, is said to have done so because of the poor quality of those he saw at the 1851 and also the 1862 International Exhibitions. Manufacturers both in England and on the Continent were more inclined to devote their energies to considerations of production than to standards of design and so, although the latter part of the 19th c. saw a steady rise in output year by year, it seems that this was only achieved at the cost of the quality of designs produced—a situation that persisted, particularly in England, hardly unchanged until after the Second World War, when new processes, including screen-printing, encouraged manufacturers and designers to set the stage for better things.

Modern methods of manufacture embrace a number of complex techniques some of which have been exclusively evolved on up-to-date scientific lines by wallpaper men themselves. The popular flock papers (known to the French, who claim a part in the invention of the process, as *papiers veloutés*) were first made by scattering wool shearings by hand on to a pattern that had previously been printed in a slow-drying adhesive. The result, difficult to distinguish from the genuine Italian cut-velvet hangings, no doubt justified the time and labour spent, but today the same result is achieved by machinery in half the time, the end-product being equally beautiful and, more important still, resistant to normal wear and tear. Similar improvements have been made in the production of block- and ordinary machine-printed papers, though the basic processes are superficially the same as those in force two or three centuries ago. Printing by block requires a somewhat special skill, and the preparation of the block itself is undertaken only by experienced craftsmen. The blocks are composed of three thicknesses of wood, the top layer generally being pear-tree because of its fine grain. It is this surface which is 'cut' to the outlines of the design by the operator, who must prepare in this way as many blocks as there are colours in the design. Many high-quality wallpapers are produced by these means, but most work of the kind described is now speeded up by automatic routers sometimes operated by an electronic eye. Screen-printing also plays a large part in wallpaper production at the present time.

Machine manufacture, developed since the early 19th c. when the first experiments were made to convert the calico-printing machine to wallpaper requirements, has also been brought to modern standards of efficiency. In this form of production the printing is done on a rotary machine which can print up to 20 colours at high speed. Care in the preparation of the various types of roller used is just as essential as in the case of the wood-block, for in both cases it is important that the feeling of the original design be preserved. It is interesting to observe that whereas in block-printing each colour has to be allowed to dry before the next is applied, the colours in machine-printing fall one on top of the other in rotation and are prevented from running by the introduction of fixatives and by precise roller cutting. Equally exacting treatment is accorded to the preparation of the design itself, and craftsmanship is required in 'putting on' the design (on the roller or block), in colour-mixing, grounding, embossing and even in the presentation of the wrapped finished product.

In appearance a roll of modern wallpaper has altered little from 250 years ago. Even the present length of 10 metres and the width of about 53 centimetres have not changed much, no doubt because a 10-metre roll permits the most economical coverage of a wall of average height. In recent years manufacturers have been obliged to improve the durability of their product and simplify the methods of application. The days of tedious and messy wall-stripping, selvedge trimming and pasting by hand have gone and these chores have been rendered so simple, if not removed entirely, as to make paper-hanging a pleasurable occupation. Today many wallpapers are 'pre-pasted', and the use of p.v.c. (poly-vinyl-chloride) has resulted in a vinyl range which, remarkably, is resistant to steam and even to scrubbing with soap and water. The difficult and laborious task of stripping a wall, especially in the case of coated papers, has been simplified by the recent appearance of a paper that can be easily peeled from a wall without using water or any stripping agent. The Do-It-Yourself movement in wallpaper owes its momentum to improvements of this kind, for it is now unusual to hear of any work other than contract work being done by the professional decorator. Certainly such improvements have much to do with the steady growth of the industry from the mid 20th c.

It has been mentioned that ever since its inception wallpaper has been accepted as a substitute for the more expensive materials available for interior decoration, but few realize the range of the imitations produced. For example wallpapers are obtainable which faithfully reproduce every variety of wood from walnut to tongue and groove, every type of marble and even animal and reptile skins. There are high- and low-relief papers, such as 'Anaglypta', a trade name now in common use as a descriptive word, and the embossed varieties that look like stone, brickwork, leather or tiles.

Wallpaper has not been entirely neglected by the art historian but has received serious attention since the middle of the 18th c., when J.-B. Michel Papillon published his book *Traité historique et pratique de la gravure en bois.* Papillon, though primarily a wood-engraver, was the son of a wallpaper-maker and the book, although mainly a history of wood-engraving, describes in some detail the methods employed in manufacturing wallpaper during his father's and his own lifetimes. One of the claims he makes is that as far back as 1688 his father invented a form of wallpaper whose pattern 'joined together' when pasted on the wall—a reference to the 'repeat' principle common to all wallpaper with the possible exception of the painted Chinese or the French 'scenic' types. Papillon also contributed a series of drawings illustrating wallpaper-making to the famous Diderot *Encyclopédie.*

Since that time there has been a growing literature on wallpaper in many languages. *Literary History of Wallpaper* by E. A. Entwisle lists almost every important publication on wallpaper from *c.* the beginning of the 18th c.

Progress in wallpaper production, except during the two world wars, has been continuous both in techniques and in output in most European countries, especially in Great Britain, Germany, France and Scandinavia.

In design Great Britain, Germany and Denmark have played important roles in the improvement of standards. English wallpapers, notably those of the Palladio range inaugurated a few years after the Festival of Britain (1951), were considered to be among the best. In Germany wallpapers after the Second World War derived some inspiration from the BAUHAUS which had been active in the 1930s.

239, 240, 807, 859.

WASTE. Term in SILK production for the by-products of processing raw silk, from the unreelable parts of the cocoons or from wild cocoons which are not reelable. Waste is the material from which spun-silk yarns are produced.

WATCHES. A watch is a time-keeping mechanism small enough to be carried about on the person, and the earliest watches were in fact hung from a chain draped round the neck rather than carried in a pocket. At the beginning of the 16th c. small drum-shaped metal-cased TABLE CLOCKS were being made, and the early watches developed from these. The earliest recorded with reasonable certainty were made by Peter Henlein, a locksmith of Nuremberg, *c.* 1510. These were probably spherical and were compared with 'musk-apples'. But most of the early German watches were of drum shape. A pierced cover was provided over the dial, and the decorative pattern of this and of the pierced sides of the drum was often of a high artistic standard. Many of these early watches were provided with striking mechanisms (then termed 'clock-watches') or alarms.

Shortly after 1600 the shape of the drum became oval instead of circular, and then *c.* 1630 the well known lens shape first appeared and later became the standard form of a watch. The dial was not at this period covered by glass, but some had dial covers of ROCK-CRYSTAL and more rarely the watch was enclosed in a case made mainly of rock-crystal instead of the more usual silver. During the 17th c. watch cases were created in a great variety of unusual forms, such as stars, skulls, crucifixes and shells. Watches of the more conventional lens shape were often provided with multiple cases, one within the other. Cases were engraved or ENAMELLED or decorated with gold filigree, TORTOISESHELL or with LEATHER and silver pinwork. Dials, at first engraved, were later enamelled, sometimes inset in a champlevé design.

The application of the balance-spring to the mechanism in 1675, though very important in improving the timekeeping, had little effect on the external form of the watch, as it took up so little space. The improved timekeeping, however, allowed a minute-hand to be usefully added to the former single hour-hand, and corresponding minute divisions, usually numbered every five, were added to the dial itself.

If we proceed now into the 18th c., GRAHAM's invention of the cylinder escapement *c.* 1725 enabled the watch to be made somewhat thinner, giving it a more delicate and refined appearance. The 18th c. was, in fact, a period of important advances in the timekeeping of watches rather

English Oval Verge Watch. (1st quarter of 17th c.) Verge escapement without balance-spring. Engraved silver dial with single blued steel hand. Engraved silver oval case

Edward East Watch. (2nd quarter of 17th c.) Verge escapement without balance spring. Engraved silver dial. Engraved silver case

Hubert Estienne Watch. (*c.* 1660.) Verge escapement without balance-spring. Engraved silver dial and steel hand. Engraved silver case

Daniel Quare Watch. (1713.) Verge escapement. Fusee with chain. Gold champlevé dial, blued steel tulip-type hour-hand and poker minute-hand

Breguet Perpetuelle Watch. (1787–94.) Self-winding quarter repeating watch. There is no provision for winding by hand but a mile or so of ordinary walking will wind it for 60 hours' operation. The sector on the left indicates the amount the watch is wound in hours. The aperture to the right shows the phases of the moon and its age

Breguet Quarter Repeating Watch. Typical quarter repeating watch with gold engine-turned case and silver engine-turned dial. Made in 1824 for the Minister of State

than bringing about any great change in appearance, though watches did tend to become simpler and less ornate. Improved escapements were invented in England by Mudge, ARNOLD and EARNSHAW and in France by Pierre Leroy, Berthoud, BREGUET and Robin. Furthermore, following the introduction of the marine CHRONOMETER late in the century, many of the features which contributed to its accuracy were incorporated in precision watches. Automatic winding was applied to some watches by Perrelet in Switzerland and by Breguet in Paris. The French and Swiss craftsmen succeeded in making the watch still thinner.

The main contribution of the 19th c. to watch-making was the replacement of the individual craftsman by mass-production methods, a process initiated by Roskopf in Switzerland in 1865 and immensely developed by the Waterbury Company in the U.S.A. from 1880 onwards.

40, 106, 154, 177, 440, 458.

WATER LEAF. Ornamental motif used in late 12th-c. capitals. The motif is a stylization of a broad, unribbed leaf curving outwards towards the corners of the abacus. The motif was much used in silverwork during the last quarter of the 18th c. until *c.* 1830.

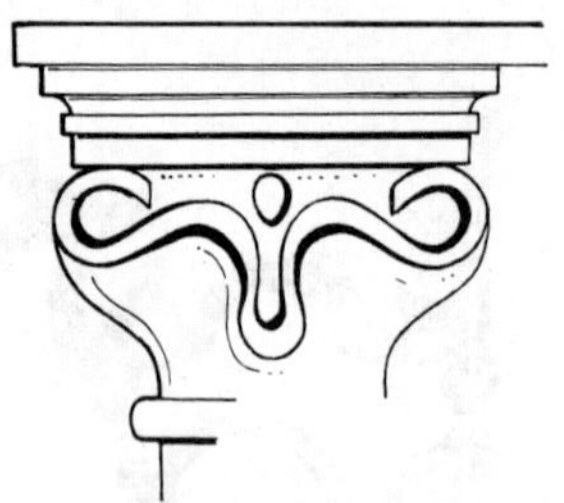

WATERMARKS. Transparent devices in paper formed during manufacture from the impression of designs in bent wire fastened into the paper mould. The first known watermarks appear in Italian paper in 1282 as a means of identifying the maker and his mill, or of denoting sizes and quality of paper. The designs are usually composed of religious emblems, animals or beasts, heraldic motifs, initials, monograms and personal marks. In addition to their use in dating, watermarks have a place in the history of design as a minor form of folk art. The naïve but often delicate distinction of the early watermarks made by anonymous craftsmen has attracted the attention in the 20th c. of professional artists, among them Maillol and Picasso, who have designed special watermarks for private press publications. See PAPER.

363, 371, 620.

WAVE. In architecture a compound moulding composed of a convex curve between two concave curves. It was typical of the English Decorated style. The term is also used in the decorative arts for an ornamental motif similar to the VITRUVIAN SCROLL. Sometimes called the 'evolute spiral band' it is an undulating moulding geometrical in character and somewhat resembling formalised waves. As a decorative motif it is used in wrought iron-work, cabinet-making, the borders of tapestry and embroidery, etc.

WEAPONS. See ARMS AND ARMOUR.

WEAVING

INTRODUCTION. Textile fabrics are the products of weaving, a process by which a set of threads (the warp) stretched in a frame, or loom, is bound together to form a coherent fabric by means of other threads (the weft) introduced at right angles to the warp threads and passing in a determinate order over and under them. The technique represents an advance over the kindred one of plaiting, as used for example in baskets and rush mats, in that it works not with the raw materials of nature but with subtle and refined products, such as wool, cotton, linen and silk, which require fairly elaborate preparation, called 'spinning'. We do not know when spinning and weaving first began to be practised. But they were certainly in use in Egypt and the Near East in the 9th millennium B.C. and there is evidence of silk weaving in China in the 2nd millennium. Woven fabrics have also been recovered from the lake-dwellings of Neolithic Switzerland. See also PREHISTORIC TECHNOLOGY and TEXTILE MANUFACTURE IN ANTIQUITY.

When the writer of Ecclesiastes said: 'A three-fold cord is not quickly broken', he was using an image which would be clear to his readers. It was also a sound piece of textile technology, because he might with equal truth have pointed out that it would be smoother, stronger and more uniform than a single strand. When telling the story of the evolution of the textile art we must study three strands which are inseparably intertwined. They are: (*a*) technology, or the art of discovering apparatus and processes; (*b*) man's desire to satisfy his need for physical comfort; and (*c*) his artistic craving for beauty of form and colour, both for their own sake and because they contribute to his self-esteem by denoting rank or social status or because they express deep religious emotions.

The history of textile technology starts in the late Paleolithic age, progresses rapidly in the Neolithic period, when nearly all the basic discoveries were made, and stretches right down to the present time with the introduction of new fibres and new techniques. In partnership with chemistry and physics textile technology has given us during the last 100 years the synthetic fibres, new dyes and machinery of great complexity. Yet when chemists recently produced the new carbon fibre, which bonded with plastic produces a material with the strength of steel combined with the lightness of aluminium, the baffling problem of how to spin a somewhat intractable fibre was solved in principle by an amateur, who used a spinning-wheel familiar to the people of India at least 3,000 years ago.

No other story has so many nameless heroes. By the time we read in Exodus 26 the astonishingly precise specifications of the textiles to be used in the furnishing of Solomon's temple, the spinning spindle, the shuttle and the reed had long since been invented. And in the illustration of the Cupbearer painted at Knossos in Crete *c.* 3000 B.C. we see a young man clad in a pair of shorts which have obviously been made from a finely woven cloth decorated with a neat pattern of white rosettes on a dark ground; and as there is no such thing as a white dye, we are justified in assuming that this is an example of resist dyeing, a process still in use today.

Nor do we know either the inventor or the place of origin of the draw-loom, which anticipates the computer in having a built-in memory system by means of which an unskilled operator can reproduce the most complex design as often as he wishes. It is wrong to assume that when the great age of mechanical invention dawned in the 18th and 19th centuries all hand-processes were instantly made obsolete. This was far from being the case. HARGREAVES's first spinning-jenny could only produce a limited range of counts; and these were only suitable for use as weft because they lacked the strength and uniformity needed for warp. Nor were the inventors of the spinning machinery used for linen quickly able to equal in fineness the hand-spun yarn made in Cambrai, from which the name 'cambric' was derived.

Among the notebooks left by Leonardo da Vinci is a set of drawings showing how this versatile genius approached the problems of spinning fibre into thread. There were three main problems and for each he produced a solution which showed his grasp of the scientific principles involved. The first was that of maintaining in a state of dynamic balance a spindle rotating at high speed but mounted in a bearing at only one end; this he did by using a flyer with two arms in the form of a U, which ensured that the forces tending to set up vibration were cancelled out. The second problem was to make the two operations of spinning and winding up continuous and simultaneous. This he also solved by the flyer, which rotated at a higher speed than the spindle but on a common axis. His third invention was to build up a yarn package on a flangeless bobbin by the use of a reciprocating thread guide which would lay the thread in a helical path. A simple illustration of this principle is the manner in which a boy winds up the string of his kite by making figure-of-eight loops on a rod. Leonardo's device consisted of a crown wheel, i.e. one on which teeth were arranged round the circumference like the figures on the dial of a clock but set in groups of four so arranged that diametrically opposite a group there would be a space. In contact with the crown wheel was a double-ended pinion so mounted that its top and bottom sets of teeth engaged alternately with the crown wheel and so made it rotate for a short distance clockwise and then anti-clockwise. Projecting from the side of the pinion was a forked arm which by its to-and-fro motion actuated the thread guide. Leonardo died in 1519 and 200 years elapsed before anyone gave any further thought to the matter. The reason for this will be discussed later when we come to consider the whole question of the history of textile invention.

The other two strands of our triple cord must be studied together because they involve the dual nature of man, who can be regarded as an automaton actuated by economic forces and self-interest only, a materialist whose ambition it is to build bigger, better and darker satanic mills, or as a sensitive creature with an awareness of beauty and a capacity for the joy in creation which the weaver–designer shares with poets, musicians and artists. Textiles are intimately connected with both sides of human nature. Protection of his body against cold may have been the first motive which drove man to invent cloth and perhaps the first market was the place where the weaver could exchange his surplus production for other things. But all the evidence goes to show that no sooner had man discovered how to make things than he felt an irresistible urge to decorate them and in so doing to give expression to such non-material values as the enjoyment of beauty for its own sake, the adornment of the body, the outward expression of rank and dignity and the expression of religious emotions by priestly vestments and TAPESTRY hangings. Everyone is familiar with the sumptuous garments in which divine and royal persons have always been portrayed; and the earliest examples of tapestry show sacred and secular designs. Nevertheless it comes as something of a shock to discover from Egypt of the 3rd c. A.D. a wall-hanging of arresting beauty which portrays a shoal of goldfish swimming in translucent green water (Louvre). Not only is each fish shown in fine detail, but each has a carefully observed shadow, which gives the picture a three-dimensional effect. It is interesting to note that the background scheme of cool greens is remarkably like the one used by Graham Sutherland in the Coventry Cathedral tapestry. But mankind cannot live on masterpieces. Men desire an abundance of good things at what they call a just price; and so the work of the weaver must abide by the judgement of the market-place as well as that of the salon. The notes which follow are an attempt to trace how over a period of probably ten centuries both objectives have been achieved.

1. MATERIALS. The development of weaving was greatly influenced by the availability of raw materials and this in turn depended on geography and climate. SILK weaving developed in those areas where the mulberry tree was abundant, i.e. China, the Levant and at a later period Italy and France. In tropical India, mainly in the province of Assam, we find species of multivoltine moths which produce 'wild' or TUSSORE silk. COTTON is the hairy coating of the seed pods of a shrub *Gosypium*, whose essential needs are a rich and fertile soil, a semi-tropical climate and a generous water-supply. It is indigenous to the Nile valley, the plains of India, the southern states of the U.S.A. and the coastal valleys of Peru. Wool and its allied fibres mohair, alpaca and vicuña are the protective coats of such animals as the sheep, the goat and the South American guanaco. The fleece-bearing sheep as we know it is very different from the wild mountain sheep from which it was evolved by selective breeding over long periods of time. It should also be understood that 'wool' is a generic term for a wide variety of yarns, each having its special properties of lustre, softness or resistance to abrasion. Linen is obtained from the stems of the flax plant, from which it is extracted by prolonged soaking, or retting. The flax plant needs a fertile soil and a moist climate such as is found in Northern Ireland, Belgium and parts of Russia. In ancient times it was grown in Egypt. The length and high tensile strength of its fibres made linen exceptionally suitable for use as warp as it gave extremely durable fabric, and it was therefore widely used to make garments for the common people. See also TEXTILE MANUFACTURE IN ANTIQUITY.

2. THREAD. Unlike all the other fibres, silk is spun by the worm in continuous lengths. But it is so fine—3,000 km would weigh less than a kilogramme—that after being reeled from the cocoon a number of these threads have to be twisted together in order to produce one strong enough to stand the strain of weaving.

Cotton, wool and flax are alike in consisting of fibres which vary in length from 1·75 cm to a few centimetres and also in that in their natural state they are a tangled mass. The first process is therefore to lay these fibres in parallel order, while at the same time removing foreign matter which may have become entangled with them. Brushing or, to give it its technical name, 'carding' is the first process. Formerly done by hand, the process was mechanized in the 18th c. by mounting the wire-bristled brushes on to a revolving cylinder. When yarn of exceptional fineness or superior quality was required it was then combed in order to remove the shorter fibres. The product of both these operations is a gossamer web, so tenuous as to be transparent but having virtually no tensile strength; yet because the fibres are in parallel order it is capable of being elongated by stretching. This web is gathered together to form a sliver—a bunch of fibres about as thick as a human finger—and this is drawn out by tension and made finer. Then by twisting the thread is made still finer and the fibres, being now compacted, cohere and gain greatly in strength. The tool used for this purpose was among the earliest human inventions and consisted of a slender wooden skewer wedged in a hole bored in a flat circular stone. These spindle whorls, as they are called, are found all over the world by archaeologists and were used by primitive peoples until quite recent times. The method of working was very simple, but called for the utmost delicacy of touch. The 'spinster', having

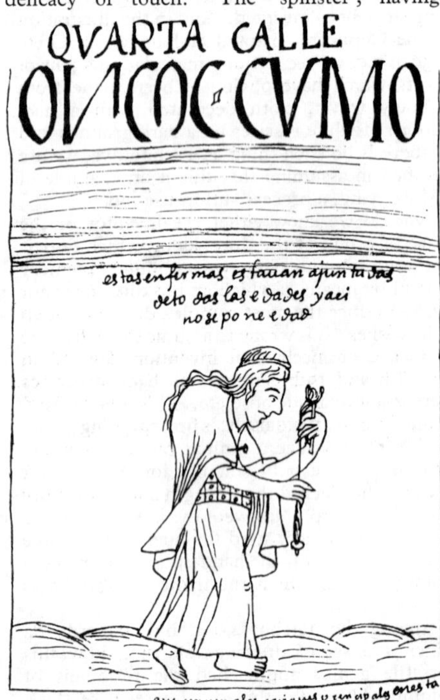

Under the Inca empire the aged and infirm engaged in spinning. Guaman Poma de Ayala, *Nueva Coronica*, fol. 221

mounted a bunch of the combed tow, pulled out a small tuft and wedged it under a tongue which was nicked in the side of the spindle, which she then set spinning by a twist of her finger and thumb. When the first few inches were spun she unhooked the thread from the notch and wound it up on the spindle. These three operations of drawing, twisting and winding are still the principles underlying modern spinning machinery.

It was the people of India who made the next step forward by using a driving wheel and belt to turn the spindle, and instead of hooking and unhooking the thread made the change from spinning to winding by changing the angle at which the thread was presented to the tip of the spindle. It was with this simple device that the yarn for the famous India muslins was spun. This type of wheel became known all over the world and was common in Ireland and Scotland. In 1530 Jurgens invented what became known as the Saxony wheel, which by a strange coincidence incorporated the flyer shown in Leonardo's design many years previously; there is no reason to think that Jurgens was influenced by this because he did not make use of the other part of Leonardo's design, the yarn-traversing mechanism. Instead he used a series of hooks fixed on the inner side of the flyer, leaving it to the spinner to move the thread progressively from hook to hook as the bobbin filled up. Thread wound in this way would not build a stable package; and so a flanged bobbin would have to be used.

All these spinning devices shared one common drawback: their productivity was low. One worker could only spin one thread at a time. In 1768 James HARGREAVES made the first of a group of associated inventions which revolutionized the art of spinning and paved the way for the Industrial Revolution. His famous spinning-jenny was in effect a ten-spindle machine with a three-phase working cycle; drawing, twisting and winding were three separate operations. Sir Richard ARKWRIGHT later adopted the flyer as used in the Saxony wheel and combined it with the draw rollers invented by Lewis Paul some 50 years earlier. This brilliant and simple idea was a mechanical solution of the essential operation of drawing out the fibres so as to make the sliver progressively finer. It consisted of two pairs of rollers, the second revolving faster than the first, the effect being to stretch the sliver by an amount proportional to the relative speeds of the rollers. This gave a high-speed, continuously acting machine; but the yarn it produced had technical weaknesses and could only be used for weft. When by the skill of the engineers these were overcome, the Arkwright frame evolved into the ring spinning-machine of today. In 1779 Samuel Crompton, stimulated by his failure to spin fine yarn on a Hargreaves jenny, invented the mule, so called because it combined the techniques of the jenny and Arkwright's throstle frame. As originally conceived the machine was changed by manual control through the threefold cycle of operations and it was not until 1830 that Richard Roberts (1789–1864), by designing one of the most brilliant examples of cam mechanism ever known, made it fully automatic. It was this machine which was the basis of the prosperous Victorian textile industry. With its aid it was at

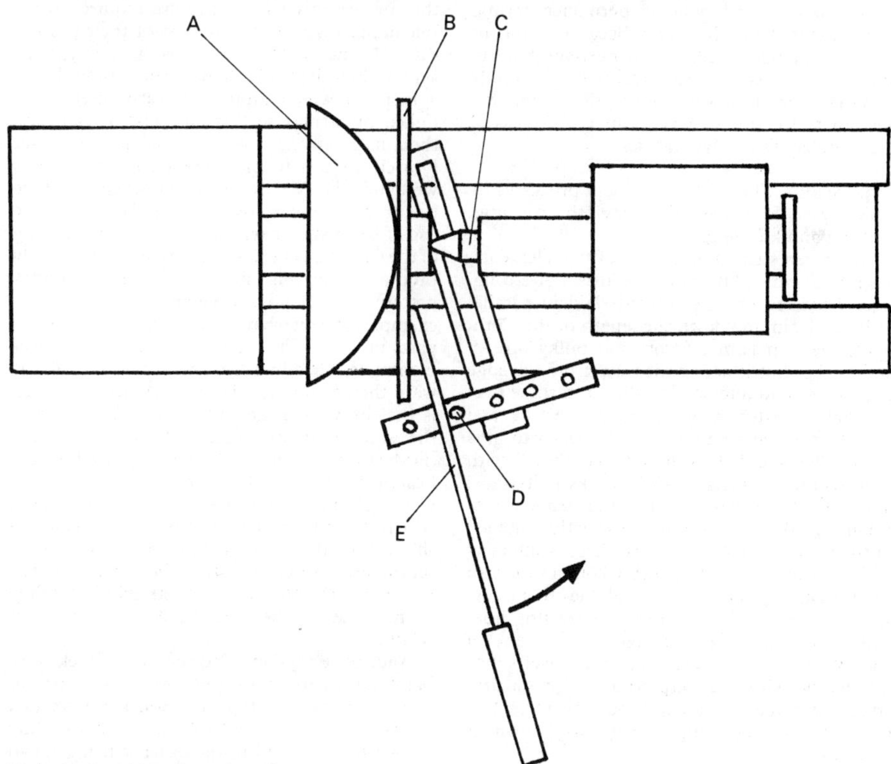

Methods of working silver plate. See p. 721.

Principles of spinning. A. Wooden former; B. Metal disc; C. Rotating centre; D. Metal peg; E. Spinning tool

last possible to spin by machine thread equal in fineness and uniformity to that of the old Indian workers.

Man-Made Fibres. The story of the making of thread comes full circle in the 20th c. with the evolution of man-made fibres, a triumph of chemical engineering and applied science but one which, by the adoption of the extrusion process, went back to the silk-worm for its basic technique. In his *Micrographia* (1664) Robert Hooke described how he thought that vegetable matter might be changed into a fluid and then extruded to form a thread similar to the silk produced by the silk-worm. But it was another 200 years before Chardonnet (an assistant of Louis Pasteur) succeeded in dissolving nitro-cellulose in an alcohol-ether mixture to make a substance from which thread could be spun. Several cellulose-based yarns were invented, the best known and commercially the most successful being 'Viscose', a Courtauld product.

In 1925 Duponts of America discovered Nylon, the first of a family of materials known as synthetic high polymers. Among some of the best known are Nylon, Terylene, Orlon and Courtelle. All these materials are part of the story of chemical invention and had little effect on the technique of weaving. But they had two exceptional properties. The first was their ability to take and retain a permanent crimp which made them bulky and, because of the air trapped among the filaments, pleasantly warm and soft as well as crease-resistant. Secondly they had very low water absorption compared with that of cotton or wool; this is the basis of the popular 'Drip-Dry' fabrics.

3. FABRIC. There are three main processes by which yarn is converted into cloth: weaving, knitting and knotting.

All woven structures consist of two elements, warp and weft. The former consists of strong, tightly twisted or sized threads laid in parallel order and running down the length of the cloth, while the weft is made from soft bulky thread, laid by the shuttle across the warp from selvedge to selvedge and intersecting with it in some predetermined order known as 'the weave'. Several colours may be combined in the warp to give stripe effects and these may be combined with multi-coloured wefts to give checks or tartans. The rule for tartans is that the sequence of colours in the warp should be exactly matched in the weft, so that when warp threads intersect with weft threads of their own colour a square of solid colour is produced, but at all the other intersections warp and weft are of contrasting hues and as the weave is a twill a rectangular panel of shot effects results. Again one of the wefts may interweave with the warp so as to give a firm structure while the others bind in a more free manner, forming complex patterns known as BROCADES.

A piece of hessian or sacking is a good example of the simplest, oldest and most widely used woven fabric. Known as the 'ground' or 'tabby' weave, it has all the utilitarian virtues. It calls only for the simplest type of loom and gives a cloth which, because warp and weft intersect in a '1–1' order, is firm and durable. A low-power magnifier will show that a wide range of fabrics are derived from this one simple weave: taffeta, lawn and cambric are this same weave, but made from softer and finer yarns and woven with much greater numbers of threads to the inch. A small square of this material can be produced by winding thread on a stiff card like the strings of a harp and then by means of a needle darning a weft thread over and under alternate warp ends. But if more than a few square inches of material is wanted, we must invent the loom, by means of which long strips of serviceable cloth can be made, each about a yard wide. The simplest form of loom must have a contrivance, necessary for all weaving, which will raise every alternate warp thread above the remainder of the warp in order to allow a weft thread to pass through, and then depress the same threads below the level of the rest of the warp for the next passage of the weft. But for all kinds of repeating patterns it is advantageous to be able to raise and depress various selected groups of warp threads in varying sequence in order that the threads forming the pattern shall appear on the surface only where they are required while remaining invisible for the rest of their passage through the cloth. This has generally been achieved by the use of some form of draw-loom, a loom in which groups of warp threads are linked by strings so that an assistant can raise them in prearranged sequence while the weaver himself attends to the insertion of the various weft threads. We do not know when or where the draw-loom was invented. But it was by the use of some such device that before the opening of the Christian era Chinese weavers were already producing woven silks with very complex patterns of clouds, dragons and horsemen, examples of which have been excavated in various parts of Asia. This tool has three basic movements: (i) shedding, or the separation of the warp threads into two layers; (ii) picking, which is the throwing either by hand or by power of the shuttle or weft-carrier across the warp; (iii) beating up, when the newly inserted weft is beaten firmly against the fell or the previously woven cloth. This is done by a comb or reed, which performs a double function: it regulates the uniform distribution of the warp all across the fabric and also ensures that the newly inserted weft is beaten into a perfectly straight line, while at the same time keeping the cloth to a constant width.

Ancient Egyptian pictures and Greek vase paintings clearly show the two main types of loom. In the one type the warp is stretched horizontally across a frame somewhat resembling a low bedstead, and in the other it hangs down like a curtain from an overhead beam. In both cases it is essential for the warp to be under

Young working woman under Inca empire making coarse weave material on a backstrap loom. Guaman Poma de Ayala, *Nueva Coronica*, fol. 215

Serving woman under Inca empire weaving fine material. Guaman Poma de Ayala, *Nueva Coronica*, fol. 217

tension. In the horizontal loom this is effected by pulling the threads against the friction of a band-brake; in the vertical loom the strands are gathered into bunches, to each of which is tied a pierced stone. If the loom perished by decay or, as so often happened, was destroyed by fire, these weights fell to the ground in a straight line and it is this clue which enables the archaeologist not only to state that weaving was being done but also to measure the size of the loom.

Old engravings show that at a very early stage the operation of shedding was controlled by treadles worked by the weaver's feet. But it was not until *c.* 1730 that Henry Kaye invented the fly-shuttle, which revolutionized the art of weaving. This simple device consisted of two hammer blocks mounted on either side of the loom and connected together by a cord which in turn was tied to a picking stick which the weaver could jerk from side to side with one hand, leaving the other hand free. The effect of this invention was startling: speeds were increased, fatigue was reduced, and breadths exceeding the arm span of a single weaver could be woven. Up to this moment the supply of thread produced on the old-fashioned devices such as the spindle or the wheel had been sufficient to keep the looms adequately supplied. But now a yarn famine was created almost overnight. And this provided the financial incentive to the inventors who worked on the problems of spinning later in the century, while it was the success of their efforts which in turn created such a problem of surplus yarn that a group of manufacturers from Manchester who were discussing the matter at Matlock were unanimous that the problem was insoluble. A clergyman who happened to be in their company contested this view and pointed out that there had already been on show in London an automaton which could play chess, and from this he advanced the proposition that if a machine could make the complicated moves of a game, then it ought to be possible to construct one which could weave. The clergyman's name was Edmund CARTWRIGHT, rector of Goadby Marwood in Leicestershire. In his own account of what followed he says: 'Some little time afterwards a particular circumstance recalling this conversation to my mind, it struck me that, as in plain weaving, according to the conception I then had of the business, there could only be three movements, which were to follow each other in succession, there would be little difficulty in producing and repeating them.' A carpenter and a blacksmith were employed, and 'to my great delight a piece of cloth, such as it was, was the produce'. Fortunately Cartwright could not foresee the dreary wasteland through which every inventor must toil. Nevertheless the idea was sound and the power loom was born.

In the old hand looms and in Cartwright's power loom the shed for plain cloth was formed by rods or staves to which were attached fine cords or leishes, each furnished with an eyelet through which a single warp thread passed. By pressing a treadle a stave could be raised, lifting with it all the attached warp ends. Given eight staves, it was possible to select any permutation which might be desired; and from this simple device all the great basic weaves were created. Twills and serges were made by lifting two or three threads together but on each successive PICK moving one place to right or left. The satin weave was made by lifting only one stave at a time but in a staggered order such as 1-2-4-7-5-8-3-6, the result of this arrangement being to flank each binding point by two long floats which close over and conceal it; the surface therefore appears to the eye smooth and grainless.

The earliest form of reed was the human finger-nail still used by Japanese *obi* weavers; but at an early stage the reed as we know it today was devised by making a comb from fine slips of bamboo bound at both ends to a pair of wooden rods and uniformly spaced by means of a fine cord wrapped round the rods and running between the bamboo slivers—the thickness of the cord governing the number of teeth per inch. Reeds as fine as 100 dents per in. (2·5 cm) were used, and by threading the warp at a uniform number of threads per dent uniform quality of cloth was ensured. Early Indian and Chinese drawings show the reed mounted on a horizontal wooden beam suspended by two rods so that it could swing like a pendulum.

A civil servant defined 'utility' cloth as 'maximum production from minimum resources' and if this were the end of human endeavour, the development of the weaver's art might well have stopped at this point. But just as the potter began to ornament his clay as soon as he had learnt how to manipulate it, so the weaver turned his attention to the problems of combining several weaves together and using colour as a pattern-making medium. There were two main lines of development, one leading to Oriental CARPETS AND RUGS and the other, generally worked in monochrome, associated with the city of Damascus, from which the name 'damask' is popularly derived. Paradoxically, it is the second type which displays the art of weaving in its highest form. This can best be illustrated by considering a ploughed field which, some would say, is brown, but to the more sensitive observer appears brown modified by the angle at which the furrows run relative to the eye, the angle of elevation of the sun and the angle at which the light strikes and is reflected. All of these factors may be further modified by the fact that there is no such thing as an absolutely flat field, so that what the eye actually sees is a complex geometrical pattern modified by being presented as a number of curved surfaces. If we examine a fabric through a magnifying glass, it will be seen to be three-dimensional, the surface being marked with grooves and ridges between which are deep shadows. Whereas the ploughman has no control over the pattern of his furrows, the weaver can so adjust matters that it is within his power to alter dramatically not only what the eye observes but also what the hand feels when the cloth is touched. If a piece of cloth is dipped in gum and then dried, it is easy to dissect the threads, which will be found to be crimped. But the depth and the shape of the curves will vary: sometimes the amount of crimp in warp and weft will be equal, but at others the difference will be marked. All this is the result of loom tuning, an art which is the true inner mystery of weaving. The relationship between the beating of the weft by the reed and the changing of the warp to close the old shed and to form a new one can be advanced or retarded; or by raising or lowering the back rail of the loom over which the warp enters and which forms the back end of the shed, the relative tensions of the upper and lower sets of threads can be altered. Also having selected threads of suitable thickness for the weight of cloth he wishes to make, the weaver can change the amount of twist and its direction; the choice of 'S' or 'Z' twist can radically alter the fabric. When we remember that all these changes may be combined or permuted the range of control in the power of the weaver is seen to be great. Nor are the effects purely optical; softness to the touch and the property of falling into graceful folds can be enhanced by a skilful weaver. Like tuning a violin these matters are easy to write about, but a lifetime may be spent in mastering the techniques. The sumptuous designs seen in damask fabric are entirely due to these optical effects especially in the satin weave, in which one face of the cloth is highly lustrous and has its grain running down the warp whereas the other is dull, being formed of the weft threads which are made from softer yarn and yarn having its grain running at right angles to the warp. By combining these two effects, using one for the pattern and the other for the ground, elaborate designs were produced.

4. PILE WEAVING is unique in having, in addition to the normal warp and weft, a third set of threads which project at right angles to the face of the cloth and from which the design is formed. As all fibres show their maximum resistance to abrasion when placed endwise, the practical value of pile weaving for carpets intended as floor coverings, prayer rugs or saddle-cloths, is obvious. Equally important is their property of reflecting light in a peculiar way. When it falls on the tips of the pile threads there is little reflection but considerable absorption among their roots; but if the pile is bent away from the observer, then there is strong reflection from the sides of the threads and being cylindrical in shape these exhibit characteristic highlights, making the colours seem luminous. In practice the pile will lie at every possible angle, and so these two effects will combine to produce subtle gradations of tone. This phenomenon of the play of light on fabrics was of particular interest to Vermeer, who portrays it with loving skill in many of his pictures. Oriental rugs used as

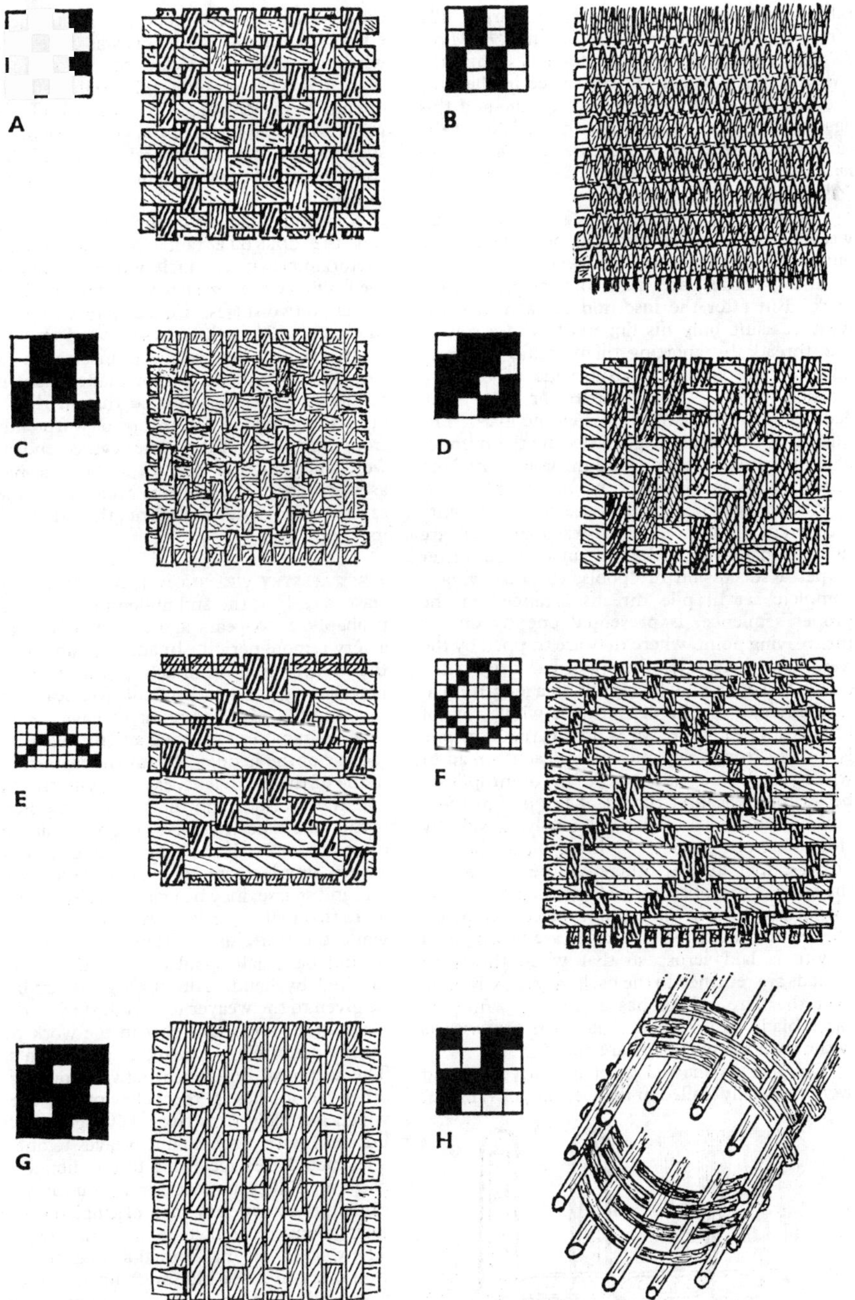

Weaves. A. Ground or tabby; B. Grogram; C. Basket weave or barathea; D. Plain twill; E. Herring-bone; F. Diamond pattern; G. Satin weave; H. Tubular weave

table-cloths are shown in *The Procuress*, *The Young Woman with the Water Jug* and *The Music Lesson*, while only taffeta could assume the sharp angular shapes which we see in the blue dress of the girl in *The Artist's Studio* and this again is in marked contrast with the folds of the satin fabric used for the dresses of *The Couple with the Wine-Glass* and *The Lady at the Virginals*.

The complexity of the designs used by rug weavers disguises the simplicity of the technique employed. Plain warp and weft, intersecting in a '1–1' order, are used to form the canvas back. But after the insertion of each pick the weaver, using only his fingers, ties in a row of pile threads by knotting them round a pair of adjacent warp threads, using one of the two classical knots, the Ghiordes or the Sena, according to the district in which he lives. The quality of the carpet is governed by the number of knots per square inch, and this may vary from as few as ten up to four or five hundred.

Modern machine carpets are made by quite a different method. Normal warp and weft are used to make the back. But in the Axminster carpet a succession of spools, each carrying a complete set of pile threads arranged in the proper sequence, is presented one by one at the weaving point, where they are trapped by the weft; and then, after the spool has been withdrawn to a distance which pulls off a length equal to the length of pile desired, the whole row of tufts is cut by a knife. In Wilton carpets the pile is formed from a separate warp, each thread of which might be said to be in quintuplicate because for the first thread of the design there will be the choice of five colours lying side by side. One of these will be lifted on to the face of the carpet and the others will be woven into the body of the fabric. The formation of a single row of pile tufts involves three successive picks. On the first the required threads are raised; then a wire is laid across so that when the warp threads are returned to the back they are wrapped over the wire, which has at its end a minute razor-blade so arranged that when the wire is withdrawn the pile loops are cut.

The Italians showed great inventiveness and were especially skilled in the weaving of VELVETS,

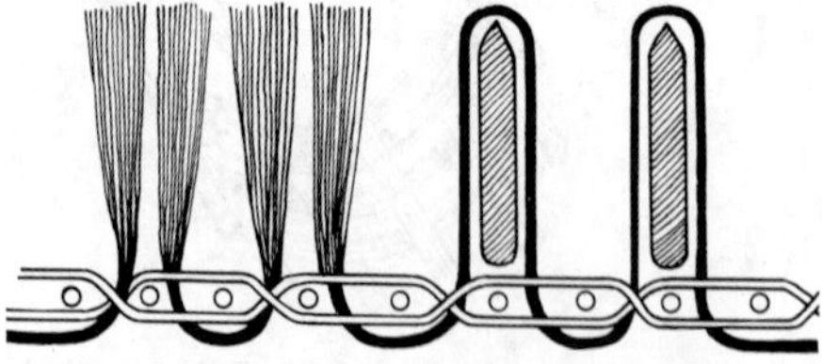

Velvet pile. The pile warp shown by the thick black line binds into the foundation fabric indicated by the light line, and passes over the wires, thus forming loops. When the wires are withdrawn and the loops are cut, tufts are left, and these packed together form the pile surface. From *The Silk Book*, published by The Silk and Rayon Users' Association (1951)

some of which were made to imitate the relief effects seen in CAMEOS. This was done by using wires of different thicknesses so as to form several heights of pile. The relief effect thus obtained was enhanced by the use of a warp made from two or three tints of the same colour so arranged that the different levels of the pile could be progressively lighter as they increased in height.

A curious offshoot of the art of pile weaving was the CHENILLE table-cloth, a hallmark of Victorian elegance, which derives its name from the French word for a hairy caterpillar. This was woven in two stages. First a warp was put on to the loom with its threads separated into groups so that when the weft was inserted a ladder formation was made. Razor-blades then slit the fabric into narrow strips so that in the centre of each was one of the groups of warp ends and from either side of these the severed ends of the weft stuck out like bristles or like the hairs of a caterpillar. These strips were then rewoven as the weft of a second fabric, the bristles forming a pile face.

5. TAPESTRY WEAVING was known in Egypt at least as early as the 2nd millennium B.C., in Peru probably 2000 years ago and in China also at a very remote period. In ancient America it was the weave used in much primitive weaving: Navaho rugs or blankets and Mexican serapes, for example. It is thought to have been older than loom pattern weaving and to have preceded the use of the heddle. It was the favourite technique of the Peruvians, especially in the Middle and Inca periods and the finest of the Peruvian textiles are tapestries. Although it is among the most ornate of all the fabrics, tapestry employs a very simple technique. The warp, which is fine and sparse, may be arranged either vertically or horizontally and is always of a neutral tint; while the weft, made from thick soft yarn, is wound on small spools or shuttles which are inserted by hand. Although great credit must be given to the weaver for his dexterity, the dyer plays an all-important part in the work by producing delicately graduated hues of each colour. The technical difference between tapestry and other fabrics lies in the behaviour of the weft, which normally runs from selvedge to selvedge but in tapestry each colour weaves to and fro in a restricted area according to the dictates of the pattern. This can most easily be understood by thinking of a tapestry map of England in which each county is shown in a distinctive colour. The weaver, having formed a shed in the warp, would lay in a sea-blue weft up to the coast of Cornwall, then the Cornish colour up to the Devon boundary and so on till the North Sea was reached. Then each weft would be worked backwards, and he would continue backwards and forwards till the required shapes had been built up. The result of this imaginary exercise would be a patchwork of rather monotonous colours which could be relieved by using a four-

ply weft blending two colours in varying proportions such as 4A/0B, 3A/1B, 2A/2B and so on, in exactly the same way that a painter blends his colours. An examination of the elaborate tapestries woven in the 14th and 15th centuries and those woven by the GOBELINS factories after 1662 shows how skilfully this method was employed to give the three-dimensional effect which characterizes all good tapestries.

This technique of weft inlay ornament, which in Europe took the form of pictorial story telling, was developed in other parts of the world in different styles. For example the Japanese *obi*, or ceremonial sash, is an example of this style of weaving done in silk of the finest quality; while in Mexico and Peru the natives evolved a characteristic style of their own. Pre-Columbian ceramic figures show that this art was fully developed as far back as 2000 B.C., characterized by the use of solid masses of colour in bold geometrical shapes. This American work is an interesting example of the effect of technique on design—for instance a Mexican swan is formed by an assembly of rhomboids; the diagonal lines of which were essential because, if the boundary between two adjacent colours occurs repeatedly on the same warp thread, a split will appear and therefore the weaver must move the joint one place to right or left; and so the diamond form arises automatically. In the case of European work this problem is solved by the use of a concealed stitching thread which draws the edges of the gap together. The Peruvians, making a virtue of necessity, evolved a type of design based on small squares of contrasting colours stacked in the form of stepped pyramids or diamonds. The split which formed along each vertical boundary formed an integral part of the design; but the stacking of the squares was arranged like the bonding joints of a brick wall, i.e. the verticals were staggered and so of limited length.

All the fabrics so far considered were produced on a very simple type of loom, complicated ornamentation being the result of finger dexterity, and as long as the basic weave remained a permutation of eight shafts or less, shedding by means of shafts was adequate. The problem was to invent a mechanism which would allow the weaver to select threads independently of one another. The solution was the 'draw-loom'. Where and by whom it was invented we do not know; but it was certainly known in ancient China and the Middle East and it was used in Italy and France. It was one of the skills brought by the Huguenots to Britain after the revocation of the Edict of Nantes. We may safely assume that all the elaborate patterns woven during or before the 18th c. were done on this machine. It consisted of a harness of strong but fine linen threads hanging down in a broad fan, each having near its lower end an eyelet through which was threaded a single warp end, and at the bottom a length of lead wire, called a lingo, the weight of which caused the leish to drop when the shed was closed. The selection of the lifting leishes was made by a series of nooses, each of which encircled one of the leishes it was desired to lift on any particular pick; and all these were knotted together and joined to a strong cord. All these cords were brought together in a frame and arranged like the strings of a harp so that if they were plucked in a sequence 1, 2, 3, 4 and so on, the whole design would be reproduced pick by pick. Once this system had been set up there was no limit to the number of times the pattern could be repeated. So great was the labour and skill involved in setting up this device that it was common for a pattern to remain on the loom for many years. The working of the draw mechanism required a second person, usually a child known as the 'draw-boy'. The similarity between this apparatus and a modern computer with its built-in memory bank is striking. In the year 1796 the Chinese Emperor Kang Hi caused a book to be written describing the Chinese silk industry in all its branches; and here we may see an exquisitely fine drawing of the loom as it was at that time. Not only was there an elaborate draw harness but also a twenty-shaft plain one, indicating a ground fabric of great richness and probably one combining several different weaves. The draw-loom was undoubtedly the most beautiful and complex mechanical device invented in what we often refer to as the pre-scientific age.

As long as the throwing of the shuttle was done by hand, there was no limit to the number of weft colours which could be used. When, however, Kaye invented the fly-shuttle in 1733 a retrograde step seemed to have been taken, because only a single shuttle could be used. But this drawback was overcome by the invention of the drop-box, which consisted of a small frame mounted at each end of the batten and carrying a series of slots in each of which a shuttle could be housed. By raising or lowering the boxes any desired shuttle could be brought in line with the striker; and the fact that the driving of the shuttle could be done with one hand only meant that the other one could be used to operate the drop-box mechanism.

6. LAPPET WEAVING. The elaborate designs now possible by the joint use of the draw-loom and the drop-box suffered from a serious defect. Because all the wefts had to run right across the fabric the resultant cloth was too heavy for many garments and also was very extravagant in the use of such costly materials as silk. What was needed was a mechanism which would allow decorative weft threads to work only in a restricted area. This was achieved by mounting a bar across the batten immediately in front of the reed and by hanging from it a series of brackets each carrying a small shuttle whose movement was limited to passing only from one bracket to the next. After the main shuttle had gone across to make one pick of the base cloth, a second shed would be formed in which groups of threads

corresponding in position with the spaces between the brackets would be lifted so as to bind the lappet thread only on the face of the cloth. As the lappet frame could be moved laterally, it was possible to space the motifs in any desired form. And this was the origin of the sprigged muslins once so popular.

7. THE JACQUARD LOOM. All the devices so far described suffered from one great drawback: their complexity made them laborious to use and made heavy demands on the skill of the weaver. Obviously the solution lay in what we today call automation, and this was achieved by the efforts of three men: Bonchon, Vaucanson and Jacquard, only the last of whom is now remembered although his contribution was rather that of the skilled mechanic who put the ideas of the other two into practical shape. It was Bonchon who in 1725 had the simple idea of punching holes in a card, which was pressed against the ends of a series of steel needles each of which could be made to control a single cord of the harness of a draw-loom; but it was Vaucanson who invented the square cylinder by which the cards, joined together in an endless band, were pressed against the needles which in turn selected a series of hooks which were actuated by a rising and falling frame known as a *griffe* that caused them to lift the desired leishes. It was not until 1801 that Jacquard showed at the Paris exhibition the perfected machine which bears his name.

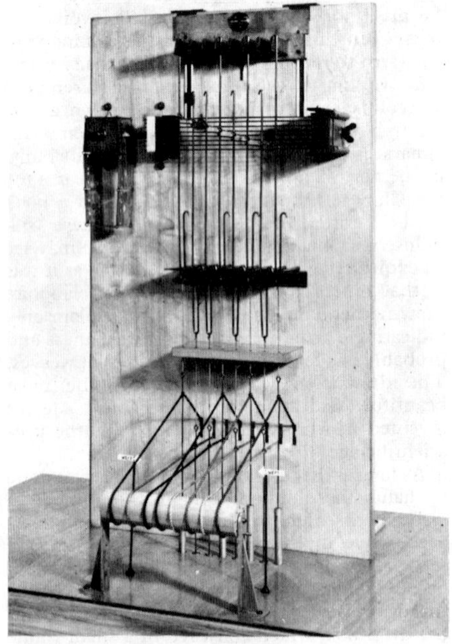

Model of Jacquard Loom. (Science Mus., London)

The results of this invention were threefold. The weavers of Lyon were so enraged that Jacquard went in peril of his life. The draw-boy was replaced by an automatic device so that costs were lowered. And the art of textile design became debased to an appalling degree. The new trade of the designer/card-cutter arose and it became only the work of a moment to change from one pattern to another. The Jacquard machine seems to have reached England about 1816 and created an inexhaustible demand for variety simply for its own sake. By the time of the Great Exhibition in 1851 matters had become so bad that the critics were as unanimous as they were scathing about what they described as a reckless display of vulgarity. It was left for William MORRIS and his friends to restore the textile trade to sanity.

149, 159, 400, 803, 890.

WEBB, PHILIP (1831–1915). English architect and furniture designer. While principal assistant to G. E. Street he met William MORRIS in 1856. He designed his first furniture for Morris in 1858–9, designed the Red House, Bexley Heath, for Morris (completed 1860) and after the formation of Morris & Co. in 1861 became the firm's chief designer in furniture, glass, metalwork, jewellery and embroideries. He was responsible for designing most of the firm's early furniture, mainly massive oak pieces with the structural elements strongly emphasized.

WEDGWOOD, JOSIAH (1730–95). English master potter, born at Burslem. In 1754 he entered into partnership with Thomas WHIELDON and in 1759 set up in business on his own. His organizing ability and flair for business were largely responsible for the successful expansion of the Staffordshire pottery industry. He established the taste for NEO-CLASSICAL designs in English ceramics. In 1774 he was commissioned to make for Catherine of Russia a service of more than 1,000 pieces enamelled in sepia. Among the wares for which he became best known were an unglazed black stoneware, which he called 'basaltes', a hard red stoneware, which he named '*rosso antico*', and his 'jasperware', a fine white stoneware capable of being coloured through the body by metallic oxides. See also CERAMICS.

WEISWEILER, ADAM. French cabinet-maker of German origin. He became a master in 1778 and achieved considerable popularity in his day, working among others for Marie-Antoinette at Saint-Cloud. He retired from business in 1809. He worked in the NEO-CLASSICAL manner and although he sometimes used LACQUER, his furniture is rarely decorated with MARQUETRY. He preferred plain woods, especially mahogany and ebony, and his style foreshadowed the DIRECTOIRE. A characteristic feature of his work were slender supports to his desks and tables in the form of gilt-bronze caryatids. In successfully surviving the Revolution, he enjoyed the patronage of the Napoleon family and in this period collaborated with the celebrated bronze-founder, Thomire.

WELLINGS, WILLIAM. See SILHOUETTE.

WHIELDON, THOMAS (1719–95). A prominent figure in the development of 18th-c. Staffordshire pottery, and for a time WEDGWOOD's partner. At Fenton Low (*c.* 1740–80) he manufactured all the chief types of the day, excelling particularly in the use of coloured glazes. See CERAMICS.

WHITEWORK. EMBROIDERY worked with a white thread on a white ground has been favoured since the Middle Ages for various articles of church use, and for personal and table linen and the like. Ayrshire whitework, a form of BRODERIE ANGLAISE, enjoyed considerable popularity in the 19th c.

WILLARD. American family of clock-makers. BENJAMIN (1740–1803) set up his workshop in Grafton, Massachusetts, *c.* 1764, moved to Lexingham in 1768 and again to Roxbury in 1771. He was known chiefly for his LONG-CASE CLOCKS with brass dials. SIMON (1753–*c.* 1845) was brother of the foregoing, to whom he was apprenticed. He set up in Roxbury *c.* 1788 and established a reputation for long-case clocks. He also patented a 'banjo'-shaped clock and a 'lighthouse' clock, which was enclosed within a glass bell standing on a pillar representing the tower of a lighthouse. Another brother, AARON (1757–1844), started business in Roxbury but moved to Boston in the 1790s, where he manufactured both long-case and MANTEL CLOCKS. He also made 'banjo' clocks. From 1823 the business was carried on by his son, AARON, who is credited with originating the 'lyre' clock. A fourth brother, EPHRAIM, also manufactured fine long-case clocks in Boston.

WILLIAM AND MARY STYLE. Style in English furniture, decoration, silverware, etc., which roughly coincided with the reign of William and Mary (1689–1702). The period was marked by increased Dutch influence. An influx of Dutch cabinet-makers brought about a revolution from the late Jacobean style. Queen Anne furniture marks a swing away from the excessive grandeur of the Restoration towards a simpler and more domestic style with emphasis on elegant design and finish. Walnut continued to be the predominant material. LACQUER and JAPANNING came into vogue, SEAWEED MARQUETRY was introduced and delicately finished VENEERS were emphasized by high polish. Chairs and sofas were comfortably upholstered and smaller rooms encouraged the use of lighter furniture generally.

In silver the term 'William and Mary' is applied to a style of EMBOSSED decoration composed of FLUTES, vertical, oblique or spiral, alternately concave and convex, and ending with a punched quatrefoil or similar motif. The style remained in vogue from *c.* 1685 to *c.* 1705.

WILLOW PATTERN. Term commonly applied to a wide range of CHINOISERIE designs used mainly on English blue and white TRANSFER PRINTED china of the 2nd half of the 18th and early 19th centuries. The origination of the pattern is traditionally attributed to Thomas Turner of Caughley and the earliest known *chinoiserie* design with a willow tree in a prominent position comes from the Caughley Pottery *c.* 1780. A copper engraving of the design exists with the initials T.T. in the margin. Thomas Minton, at that time an apprentice engraver at Caughley, has also been credited with the design, and as a number of copper plates were required in order to print a single service, more than one engraver may have had a hand in it.

The pattern was widely copied in many variants, among the earliest Staffordshire makers to use it being Josiah Spode and Joshua Heath. The romantic appeal of 'Cathay' to the popular imagination together with the use of the pattern on cheap mass-produced earthenware from the Staffordshire potteries in the 19th c. established this design and a legend was invented to 'explain'

the supposed story. As it became standardized *c.* 1830 the willow pattern has a pagoda standing on the edge of water, two birds in the sky, a boat being poled on the water, a fence in the foreground, a three-arched bridge across which walk three Chinese figures and a prominent willow tree overhanging the bridge.

WINDOW-GLASS. In early times windows were closed with shutters of mats or with stone or pottery lattices, mica slabs, oiled parchment, fish bladders, etc. The use of GLASS became popular in the villas of the rich and in the baths during the 2nd c. A.D. These early slabs were rarely more than about 30 cm by 60 cm and their use never became general in the Middle Ages. There is evidence of a demand for window-glass for churches in the 8th c. England was behind the Continent in the manufacture of glass during the Middle Ages and in 647 Benedict Bishop brought over Frankish craftsmen to make window-glass for the church of his monastery at Wearmouth. The foundation of the English glass-making industry is traditionally ascribed to a Norman, Laurence Vitrearius, who set up a glass-house *c.* 1226 near Chiddingfold in the Weald. His factory at first concentrated primarily on window-glass and in 1240 he was commissioned to make glass for the windows of Westminster Abbey. During the Middle Ages France was famous for stained and painted window-glass and in the 17th c. French glass-houses established a virtual monopoly for the manufacture both of mirror-glass and of window-glass in Europe. A new era in the production of window-glass was introduced by the discovery of the technique of casting, perfected by Louis Lucas in 1688, which made possible the production of large sheets of glass. The extended possibilities of glazing which resulted from this technique brought a revolution in the amenities of domestic life. Small leaded panes of thick, bottle-green glass have given way to the large, transparent and virtually colourless sheets with which we are now familiar in houses, shops and offices. The still more recent changes whereby glass virtually replaces the sustaining wall have been made possible by modern developments in architecture. See also GREEK AND ROMAN ANTIQUITY (GLASS).

WINDSOR CHAIR. Term describing a varied family of chairs of traditional design and construction which throughout the GEORGIAN period were the products of a widely disseminated village industry in Britain. Typically the seat is of solid wood and the legs consist of turned spindles socketed into the seat. The back is also made from turned spindles, called sticks, which are socketed into the seat and a top rail. This type of back is known as 'stick back' or 'spindle back'. The varied designs fall into a few main patterns. Windsor chairs may be armchairs or armless. There are high-back and low-back varieties. High-back Windsors may have a top rail curved like a bow or straight in the shape of a comb. These are known as 'hoop-back' and 'comb-back' respectively. The industry was particularly associated with High Wycombe in Buckinghamshire but many other regions developed their local fashions. Native woods were used (usually elm or yew for the seat, yew for the frame and beech or ash for the spindles). On the whole the traditional designs of the village craftsmen were little influenced by fashions of luxury furniture but some concessions were made, such as CABRIOLE legs and GOTHIC designs in the splats.

Windsor chairs were exported from England to the United States in the 1st half of the 18th c. and became indigenous there. They were used both in private houses and in public buildings such as inns and the State House of Pennsylvania. American craftsmen established their own traditions of design. The seat was saddle-shaped and generally thicker than the English pattern and the turned legs were set at a raked angle in it. Both hoop-back and comb-back patterns were used, in general lighter and with more delicate lines than the English. Characteristically American Windsor furniture was painted green or black. Philadelphia was the main centre for the production of Windsor furniture but it was made in other places as well. Mounted on bends, the Windsor chair gave rise to the popular Boston rocker. See ROCKING-CHAIR.

WINE LABELS. Wine labels, also called 'bottle tickets' or 'decanter labels', originated in England during the 18th c. It is impossible to pinpoint the exact year of their origin and the name of their originator is unknown; but since there are silver labels prior to 1739 bearing the lion HALLMARK and the marks of several silversmiths, it may be assumed that the wine label came into being *c.* 1730.

It may well have come into existence owing to a change in social conditions. During the austerities of the Commonwealth, when only ale and sack were in general consumption, the labelling of bottles was unnecessary. But with the greater luxury inaugurated by the Restoration more varieties of wine were imported and it became necessary to identify the coloured bottles by means of labels. At first these were quite plain, made of wood, bone or parchment and suspended from the necks of the bottles. But these early devices soon gave place to markers of greater elegance and the silversmiths began to make labels of silver. Judging by the numbers of labels which have survived 200 years and more, their use must certainly have become general at least by the middle of the century.

Enamel labels were also being produced by the middle of the century at Battersea and probably in the Midlands. Unfortunately these were more easily damaged in use and consequently comparatively few have survived, though those that remain are usually of fine quality. Later in the 18th c., in addition to silver and enamel, makers used SHEFFIELD PLATE, IVORY, bone, PORCELAIN; and in the 19th c. great quantities of silver-plated labels came into general use.

1. SILVER LABELS. Because of their quality, elegance of design and range, because also in most cases the age and maker can be determined, silver labels appeal most to the collector. The scope is enormous. A collector of different names of wines, spirits, cordials, toilet waters, medicines, sauces, etc. can expect to search for a lifetime and still fall short of the 1,800 or so names which have been recorded by J. F. Pidgeon for the Wine Label Circle. A collector may, on the other hand, be principally interested in different designs and types of decoration, and this field too is almost unlimited. Or he may concentrate on one or two of the principal makers, such as the Batemans, Phipps &

Top row: Lisbon by Louis Hamon, *c.* 1745; Sherry by T. and J. Phipps, London, 1817; Claret by Hester Bateman, London, *c.* 1780. *Second row*: Claret by Hester Bateman, London, *c.* 1780; Port by John Stoyte, Dublin, *c.* 1790; Hermitage by John Rich, London, 1800. *Third row*: Port by Crespin Fuller, London, 1813; Claret by R. Emes and E. Barnard, London, 1814; Port by J. Willmore, Birmingham, 1824. *Bottom row*: Claret by H. T. Irish, *c.* 1820; Madeira by W. K. Read, London, 1836; Barsac by M. and C. Reilly, London, 1826

Robinson, Susanna Barker or some of the more prolific Irish makers.

2. DATING. Until the Marking of Silver Plate Act of 1790 wine labels were exempt from hall-marking, and consequently from *c.* 1730 to 1790 one may find a label with a maker's mark only or a maker's mark and the lion passant. But few are fully marked. Incomplete marking obviously presents dating difficulties, but one can usually make a reasonably accurate approximation by examining the lion passant, taking account of the known working life of the maker, and also from the design. After 1790 most labels were fully marked (Irish labels after 1800), and with the aid of a list of British Silver Assay Marks the year of manufacture can be established. The makers' marks can usually be identified by referring to *English Goldsmiths and Their Marks* by Sir Charles J. Jackson.

3. METHODS OF MANUFACTURE. Early silver labels were made entirely by hand. Starting with a sheet of silver, the rough shape would be cut out with hand-cutters, the outline trimmed and finished with a file. Decoration was produced by engraving or CHASING or a combination of both. A hand-made label was obviously costly to produce, and towards the end of the 18th c. a cheaper and quicker method of manufacture was employed. This consisted of the preparation of steel-hardened dies which enabled labels to be stamped out from sheets of silver in great quantities. Some silversmiths such as Matthew LINWOOD and Matthew BOULTON produced die-stamped labels of intricate and fine detail. Die-stamping was also extensively used in making labels of Sheffield plate and electroplate. Labels were also cast by means of a mould by a technique somewhat similar to that used in the casting of MEDALS.

Although most labels were made of silver, some of the most attractive are to be found among the enamels, particularly those manufactured at the short-lived Battersea factory (see BATTERSEA ENAMELS) (1753–6), and the 18th-c. Staffordshire products. Basically all enamel labels are made in the same way. A thick layer of opaque white glass is fused on a very thin sheet of copper. After firing in a furnace a porcelain-like surface is produced, on to which some kind of decoration can be applied. The design may be painted with coloured enamels or added by means of a TRANSFER PRINT, after which a second firing takes place.

There are many different designs to be found on Battersea labels, usually in monochrome—red, brown, mauve or black—but occasionally additional colouring is added. The pictures generally depict some activity connected with wine or wine-making, the figures being little boys, black or white, fauns, satyrs, or cupids.

The most common enamel labels have a painted decoration of floral patterns and scrolls, and the earliest of these may be contemporary with the Battersea transfer prints. Enamellers were at work in London, Birmingham, Bilston and Wednesbury in the middle of the 18th c., and it is probable that some enamel labels were produced to match the popular silver labels. Dating such labels presents some difficulty, but in general it appears that the early labels were superior in quality of enamel and decoration to those made in the following century. One useful guide is that in the 18th c. and the very early 19th c., the eyelet holes of the labels, other than those of Battersea, were encircled with a blue ring.

The only other material for making labels worth mentioning is MOTHER OF PEARL. These are rather uncommon, but they are very attractive and delicately made in a variety of designs—rectangles, crescents, rings, ovals and escutcheons. They appear to have been made for about 100 years from *c.* 1750. Other materials such as bone, ivory, tortoiseshell, porcelain, have been used to a limited extent, but these products are somewhat undistinguished and not very attractive to collectors.

4. TYPES OF DESIGN. Attempts have been made, notably by Dr. Norman Penzer, to devise a comprehensive classification of the different types of silver labels. Design and decoration vary so enormously, however, that any such classification is really only of academic interest. Nevertheless a broad-based grouping is possible.

The commonest shape in the 100 years from 1750 is the rectangular label, which may have rounded or cut corners. We meet with a variety of simple decoration, usually on the edge; one or more lines forming a border (reeded), a feather edge, GADROONING, OVOLO, BRIGHT-CUT, beaded, etc. The wine names are usually scratched in with a lettering tool, but sometimes cut through the metal. Mostly these rectangular specimens are rather broad, but very narrow pieces were made fairly prolifically until early in the 19th c.

One of the earliest shapes is the escutcheon or shield. These escutcheons may be quite plain, or chased with grapes and vine leaves, or with edgings of various kinds. The design persisted until late in the 19th c. with each maker producing something just a little bit different.

An interesting form which lent itself to some very striking modifications is the crescent. This might be quite plain or with bright-cut or feather edges. But some elegant labels were made with festoons surrounding the basic shape, or with a shield, lozenge or goblet between the horns of the crescent. Nearly all were produced in the last 40 years of the 18th c.

The pecten shell, a handsome design but very rare, was made by English and Irish craftsmen in the early years of the 19th c. Die-stamped labels in silver are more usually from the Irish makers, and the silver-gilt cast pieces come from English workshops.

A great variety of attractive and elaborate designs which feature cupids, grapes and satyrs, appeared mostly *c.* 1790 to 1840 in both die-stamped and cast labels. The basic design seems to have been made quite early, *c.* 1745, by Sandylands Drinkwater, and then there were no further pieces until later in the century.

The single vine leaf, or group of two or more leaves, appeared from *c.* 1825 and sometimes grapes were included in the design. Mostly these labels are in silver, but occasionally they are to be found in silver-gilt.

The eye-shaped or oval varieties were popular from *c.* 1775 to 1820, and may be found with many types of edging—beaded, reeded, fretted, bright-cut. The Irish makers, notably John Stoyte and George Nangle, produced some very handsome and bold fretted and decorated eye shapes, with or without a ribbon motif imposed on the top edge of the label.

There are labels on which a crest is an outstanding feature, and these were usually made as a special order for a private individual or a regiment or a livery company. The crests, engraved on a lozenge or shield, are superimposed on the label or are incorporated into a popular design. They appear from *c.* the last quarter of the 18th c.

In addition to those already mentioned the designs include scrolls, kidney shapes, cut-out letters and cut-out words, neck rings—either as a loop of silver with label attached or as a collar with wine name engraved—vine and tendril with or without figures or masks, and a host of miscellaneous motifs such as guns, gauntlets, dragons, bats, birds, animals, barrels, etc.

5. PRINCIPAL MAKERS. More than 400 different makers of wine labels have been noted between 1740 and 1860. Surprisingly many of the famous silversmiths did not regard the humble wine label as beneath their dignity, and they applied their craft to the production of beautiful specimens. Among the more important of these, both for the quantity of their output and for quality and originality, were the Bateman family, the Phipps family, Paul STORR and Susanna Barker.

While Irish makers copied the popular English designs, they were not lacking in originality and the productions of some of the leading craftsmen will stand comparison with their English counterparts. The most prolific of the Irish makers was John Teare. Others lag behind in quantity but not in quality, for he had among his contemporaries, *c.* 1790, such fine craftsmen as John Stoyte, Benjamin Tait and George Nangle.

Surprisingly, there appear to have been few labels made in America, although Georgian labels were imported into the States in some quantity. Only one American-made label is in the possession of the Metropolitan Museum of Art in New York, and this is a *Madeira* made by Louis Boudo (1786–1827) of Charleston, S.C. There is one label in the Museum of Fine Arts, Boston, which may possibly have been made by Thomas Hammersley of New York, but this attribution is not certain. The 'Weed' collection of the New York Historical Society has 14 labels listed as American, 10 marked Sterling, and 4 marked with the name 'Tiffany'. A private collector of New Orleans has notified the Wine Label Circle that he has acquired two American labels.

As to labels from other countries, France in the 19th and early 20th centuries produced an abundance of enamel labels in the English style and some original designs, as well as porcelain labels; but no significant quantity of silver labels have been made elsewhere than in Britain. During the 19th c., however, English residents in India and China commissioned silver labels from local craftsmen, although these are usually of the curio variety.

658.

WISTAR, CASPAR. Immigrant German businessman who in 1739 opened the first colonial glass manufactory in southern New Jersey and inaugurated the glass style known as 'South Jersey'. See GLASS (AMERICA).

WOLFF, DAVID (1732–98). Dutch engraver on GLASS who excelled both in wheel and in diamond-point stipple engraving. He worked for the most part on glasses with faceted stems. Most of his signed work is dated between 1784 and 1795 but a number of unsigned pieces has been dubiously attributed to him.

WOOD-WORKING

1. Material
2. Properties of timber
3. Tools and techniques
4. Some main uses
5. Special techniques
6. Industrial production

1. MATERIAL. Wood is a material remarkable for the complexity of its structure and the variety of its qualities. It is one of the few natural materials that is found almost ready for working. In growth its contribution to the visual environment is matched only by its ecological importance, while after felling and conversion to usable dimensions it assumes a new purpose and reveals a new beauty. Ultimately its ability to decay, and so release its chemical constituents, prevents environmental pollution and ensures constant regeneration. The opportunity it affords for imaginative exploitation is in direct proportion to the challenge it constantly offers to the craftsman's skill and ingenuity.

Timbers are divided into two great classes, the softwoods and the hardwoods. The softwoods are almost all the product of cone-bearing trees, most of which, apart from such notable exceptions as the larch, have evergreen needles. The hardwoods are derived from the vast group of broad-leaved trees which provide the majority of the species found in the forests of the world.

Although the majority of softwoods are softer than the majority of hardwoods, there are exceptions and the terms should be thought of as broadly descriptive of the whole group rather than as specific to individual timbers. The basis of the division is, strictly, botanical; the softwoods are of a simpler primitive structure, whereas the hardwoods are complex and much more varied.

Timbers are distributed across the surface of the globe in broad bands of latitude, accounting even today for one-fifth of the total land surface. North and south of the equator are the vast tropical hardwood forests, from which come the MAHOGANIES, teak, afrormosia, the rosewoods, and other exotics such as tulipwood and zebrawood, and an abundance of lesser known varieties of great commercial importance. Further north and south come the temperate hardwoods, the oak, walnut, beech, chestnut, sycamore, elm, ash and birch, overlapping with the immense softwood forests which stretch, dense with pines and firs, still further towards the poles.

The distribution of timber is so wide and the working qualities of different woods are so varied that most communities have been able to rely on reasonably local supplies for their needs. At the turn of the 17th c. in western Europe, however, increasing travel, coupled with a surplus in the economy and the development of sophisticated tastes, led to the importation of timbers from the Far East and the New World to augment local supplies. Thus began a trade which has since assumed world-wide proportions. Although the bulk of this trade is concerned with softwoods for the PAPER industry as well as for building and general constructional work, the needs of the craftsman have usually been better satisfied by the hardwoods. Even so, of an estimated 40,000 different species of hardwood distributed throughout the world no more than 200 are currently listed as being of commercial importance in Europe.

Timber trees grow by the repeated division of a thin layer of cells, the *cambium*, situated directly under the bark. In temperate climates growth begins in the spring and continues until a few weeks before leaf-fall, during which time a complete layer of new wood is added to both trunk and branches. In many temperate hardwoods the early growth is rapid, resulting in an open, porous cell structure compared with the more dense and compact layer formed as the growth slows up in the summer. When the trunk is cut transversely the contrast between the spring-wood and summer-wood marks distinctly the extent of the annual growth rings. In timbers of more even growth the annual rings are less clearly visible, while in tropical hardwoods seasonal growth and annual growth do not always correspond. Once the tree has reached a certain age, varying with species, as each new layer is formed beneath the bark the oldest layer of sapwood within the trunk ceases to take any further active part in the life cycle and dies, forming heartwood. The cells harden and usually darken considerably as they become permeated with substances such as tannin and gum. Some timbers, of which ash, sycamore, beech and white spruce are well known examples, show no colour difference. For most purposes sapwood is removed and burnt as its high starch content makes it liable to attack by wood-boring insects and fungi.

The cells of which wood is composed are adapted to perform one of three functions: to conduct water and dissolved mineral salts from the roots to the leaves, to support the tree and to store food material in readiness for the spring growth. Softwood is made up of long thin cells, called *tracheids*, with rounded ends and thin points on their walls called pits. When they are arranged vertically, their ends overlapping and with pits corresponding, a means of communication for the distribution of watery solutions is created. This is the characteristic of typical softwood spring growth. The summer-wood structure of overlapping *tracheids* is similar, but the extra thickness of the cell walls, the smaller size of the pits and the smallness of the cavities all show that this zone is less concerned with food distribution than with support. Hardwoods are quite different, for they have specialized types of cell for water conduction and for support. Those concerned with conduction, the pores or vessels, are often relatively large and are arranged continuously one above the other. The supporting cells, known as fibres, resemble the summer-wood *tracheids* of softwood, being long, narrow and thick-walled. They are packed densely between the pores and form the bulk of the woody tissue. In different timbers the pores vary in size and in their distribution. When the pores of the spring-wood are large and form a distinct ring, as in oak, chestnut and ash, the timber is known as ring-porous; but when the pores are spread evenly throughout the spring-wood and summer-wood with no marked change in size, as in beech, sycamore and birch, it is known as diffuse-porous.

In both softwoods and hardwoods storage is effected by the *parenchyma* or soft tissue. This is composed of thin-walled, brick-like cells which occur both in vertical strands and in horizontal rays extending from the pith across the annual rings to the *cambium*. In certain hardwoods these medullary rays are clearly visible, but in softwoods and fine-grained hardwoods they can be seen only under magnification.

2. PROPERTIES OF TIMBER. In general timber structure determines working methods. Specifically it determines the characteristics of different timbers, their appearance, mechanical properties, individual working qualities and consequently their suitability for special purposes.

In timber with clearly marked annual growth-rings appearance depends considerably on the manner of its conversion into boards. This will be clear if the trunk is thought of as being made up of a series of concentric cylinders. When the sawcut is radial, from bark to pith, annual rings are cut at right angles and appear on the surface of the board as approximately parallel lines, that is as striped grain. Such radially sawn wood is usually referred to as 'quartered' or 'quarter-sawn'. The pronounced stripe associated with certain tropical hardwoods such as sapele, afrormosia, agba and Nigerian golden walnut is due rather to a peculiarity of growth which causes them to develop adjoining seasonal layers spirally, in opposite directions; when quartered the adjoining stripes consist of cells meeting the surface at an angle, but still in opposite directions, giving the appearance of a well mown lawn but presenting the craftsman with an enormous planing problem. When sawn tangentially, that is at right angles to a radius, the annual rings are cut, not square, but at an angle less than a right angle, dependent upon the distance of the cut from the centre. As the cut is seldom exactly parallel to the axis of the tree and as the annual rings are neither true circles in cross-section nor straight in their length, the consequent grain pattern is broad, irregular and wavy—and often very beautiful.

Timbers with clearly visible medullary rays are prized for their appearance when quarter-sawn, for then the flat rays are exposed on the surface of the board as bright flashes or flecks of texture superimposed on the normal straight grain. In oak, and sometimes in beech, this is called 'silver grain'; in English plane the effect is so dramatic that the quartered boards have been known since the 18th c. as 'lacewood'.

The mechanical properties of wood are determined largely by its fibrous nature, which is attributable to a definite orientation in the structural units of the walls of the individual cells, together with the fact that these cells are attached to each other more securely longitudinally than they are laterally. Thus the craftsman thinks of wood as being strong in the length but weak across the grain, without further definition of these terms. He must always be aware of grain direction when he is working, for it is easier and it demands a different technique to separate the fibres laterally with an edge tool than to cross-cut them.

Weight for weight, under certain conditions, wood will support twice the weight of steel. It also has the great advantage that after being bent it is sufficiently resilient to recover its original shape owing to the cells behaving like miniature springs.

As a consequence of its cellular structure a large proportion of the bulk of wood must consist of air, the proportion of wood substance to air varying from *c.* 7% in the case of balsa to 87% in *lignum vitae*. It is this characteristic that permits it to absorb paints, glues, polishes and preservatives, enables it to be compressed, steam-bent and laminated into curved forms, and to be worked so readily with hand-tools and machine-tools.

The choice of timber for a specific purpose is determined usually by the special properties it possesses by virtue of its structure. This may be illustrated by reference to the making of wooden tools, most of which require a dense, stable, even-wearing timber with considerable resistance to splitting. European wood-workers have been fortunate in having an abundant supply of beech, for this is a fairly dense, diffuse-porous hardwood, in which there is so little variation between spring-wood and summer-wood that the annual rings are scarcely visible. This gives it a particularly even-wearing quality, which makes it the obvious choice for plane stocks, gauges, work-benches and all purposes requiring a true, smooth and durable surface. More expensive substitutes for beech include hornbeam and *lignum vitae* for planes, rosewood for gauges and measuring devices, and boxwood for chisel handles. The springiness of European ash and of American hickory and their resistance to fracture across the grain account for their use, especially in their respective continents, for the handles of striking tools such as the hammer and the axe. Fruitwoods were often used when craftsmen made their own tool handles, apple being a particular favourite for saws, while Pliny refers to auger handles of olive, box, holm-oak, elm and ash—all timbers which would be resistant to shearing across grain under stress.

In the making of musical instruments the acoustic properties demanded of the woods can be especially exacting. Control begins with the growth of the tree, which must be at an appropriate rate to give the required number of evenly spaced annual rings for a specified increase in diameter; it extends to the conversion by methods which ensure exact quartering with no cross-cutting of the fibres, and to the seasoning, which is often closely supervised over several decades.

In such fine pieces of traditional design as the WINDSOR CHAIR and the farm waggon an absolute rightness in the choice of materials for the different parts is to be seen. For the chair, ash and fruitwoods were chosen for their ease of turning and beauty of grain, elm for its resistance to splitting when used for the seat, beech or yew for their ability to bend into the hoops. In the American version hickory and maple were commonly used to augment the fruitwoods. By taking advantage of their inherent structural characteristics it was possible to combine these disparate timbers into a single harmonious design, which at its best represents the finest achievement of the skill and craft tradition of the rural chair-maker. The use of material in the Wiltshire or Sussex waggon was based on similar principles, permitting the reduction of all members to cross-sectional dimensions, a thing which would not have been possible with less suitable timbers.

The choice of woods to be used for furniture

is related more to appearance than to strength or working qualities; hence the range is usually much wider and the decision more personal. Nevertheless, although the general requirements may be satisfied by any one of a number of timbers, the choice once made may have a considerable influence on the design, which should express something of the individual character of the timber, its coarseness or its fineness, its sturdiness or its delicacy.

The last, but one of the most important aspects of timber structure to be mentioned, is its hygroscopic nature. Newly felled timber may contain a greater weight of water than of dry wood substance and the majority of this must be removed during the seasoning process. Once the free water has been lost from the cell cavities, that contained in the cell walls begins to evaporate, causing extensive shrinkage. Seasoning is continued until the moisture content is in approximate equilibrium with the atmosphere; but even when well seasoned, timber retains the ability to absorb and give off moisture, expanding and contracting as it does so, in response to changing atmospheric humidity. Owing to cell structure movement is not equal in all directions, however. In the length it is so slight as to be negligible, whereas in the radial, and even more in the tangential, direction it is appreciable. Failure on the part of the craftsman to make allowance for this instability and uneven behaviour inevitably results in warping, twisting, splitting or similar deformation.

3. TOOLS AND TECHNIQUES. Wood-working tools have a continuous history of at least 10,000 years, but far from following an even pattern their development has taken place in bursts in response to changing needs and circumstances. The most obvious developments have come about as a result of new materials becoming available. The introduction of iron on a large scale for planes in Europe and the U.S.A. during the past 150 years, for example, has resulted in the complete re-design of the bodies of all types of plane, although in most instances the cutting action is essentially the same as in its wooden counterpart. Less obvious is the improvement in detail of a specific tool in order to enable it to perform the same task more efficiently; the introduction of the ratchet into the chuck mechanism of a brace is such an example. There is also a direct relationship between the craft skill demanded by a particular period or culture and the evolution of appropriately refined tools and methods of working. In Europe the Middle Ages and the 18th c. were periods when such demands were made, resulting in the invention of new tools as well as the adaptation of established tools to carry out new operations.

The evolution which most tools undergo usually results in increased specialization, but there are exceptions. The spokeshave, originally devised for the wheelwright to shape his spokes, is now used as a general shaping tool, while the metal shoulder plane is used for many operations quite unconnected with the planing of the shoulders of tenons, for which it was intended. It must also be accepted that changes in design do not necessarily result in improvements in all respects. For specific purposes the earlier types may be preferred with good reason so that change often results not so much in replacement as in an increase in range. The retention of certain wooden planes and of the wooden spokeshave may be accounted for in this way.

Once the basic function of a tool has been defined, it is remarkable how similar is the solution arrived at independently in different cultures and in different periods. Determining factors are an understanding of the working properties of wood, known by direct experience, and the application of elementary laws of mechanics, arrived at intuitively or discovered by trial and error. The earliest wood-working tool of all, the axe, essential as the means of felling the tree and so providing the raw material, is itself an interesting example of this. The modern felling axe, with its long handle to give considerable mechanical advantage and with its full weight concentrated on a narrow cutting edge in order to bite deep across the grain of the trunk, differs in only relatively minor details from the medieval forms represented so clearly in the BAYEUX TAPESTRY and in countless illustrations in manuscripts, stained glass, mosaics and relief carvings. But the medieval axes were, themselves, similar in design to Roman axes, to those used in northern Europe during the Iron Age and to the still earlier shaft-hole axes found in Crete, belonging to the early part of the 2nd c. B.C. It is only when we reach as far back as the Bronze Age in western Europe that we find a fundamental difference in design, namely in the inefficient method of attaching the axe-head to the bent shaft by means of a socket.

Methods of converting the felled log into usable dimensions have traditionally been of two kinds. Where the structure of the timber permits it there are advantages in riving or cleaving the log, by means of axe and wedges, down its length into half, quarters and then radially, along the lines of weakness caused by the medullary rays which radiate from the heart. It is economical in time, labour and material, it produces radially cut wood and it ensures a virtually weather-proof surface, as the grain of the wood is followed by the split instead of being crosscut and so exposing the severed ends of the pores to the atmosphere. Although this method of conversion is usually associated today with rural and coppice crafts, the oldest wooden building still standing, the Horiuji Pagoda in Japan of A.D. 607, was made from cypress wood split by wedges. The wooden shingles used in great quantities for roofing buildings in Scandinavia and North America are weather-proof only if cleft from the butt in this way, and one of the reasons for using oak or chestnut for barrels and casks is that they readily cleave into waterproof staves. We should not underestimate the skill required to produce, by this apparently simple means, pieces of material of even thickness, sufficiently straight and accurate to be used without further surface treatment in constructional work on a large scale in the past and quite extensively for small-scale rural purposes even today.

The second method of converting logs, namely by sawing, is a technique of great antiquity which, although laborious and to some extent wasteful, has the advantage of producing boards of greater accuracy and of larger dimensions than would be possible by cleaving. It is the only way of dealing with the many timbers which will not readily cleave. Most classical and medieval sources show the log supported at one end by means of a crotch or high trestle or else supported horizontally on a pair of trestles, while it is cut down the grain with a narrow-bladed saw stretched taut in a wooden frame and operated by one sawyer standing on the log and another below. Exactly the same equipment and methods are still to be found in use in parts of Europe as well as elsewhere in less technologically advanced countries.

A later development, apparently confined mainly to England and Denmark, was the use of a pit where a more permanent site for sawing was available, together with the introduction of the tapered pit saw without frame but with a removable box or handle at the lower end, which allowed the blade to be removed from the saw-kerf as it became necessary to move forward the supporting beams. For the professional sawyer the work must have been laborious indeed, yet even this was not without its skills and responsibilities. Apart from the obvious need to saw straight and true, it should be realized that a log is rarely circular in cross-section or straight, that the heart is seldom central and that each tree has its own structural peculiarities. The decision where to make the opening cut is crucial, affecting the quality and usefulness of all the boards; yet it must be made with a knowledge of the internal structure of the log which can be inferred only from an examination of the outside. Although the modern band-saw removes much of the monotonous labour, the need to treat each butt individually still remains.

The conversion of the round timber into boards of standard thickness is so readily effected today that timber is normally thought of as squared; indeed it is often imported ready machined in order to make maximum use of shipping space. Prior to mechanization, however, there was much greater use of small-section timber in the round, as in the sturdy stools, benches and trestle tables with roughly tapered legs driven into splayed auger holes, illustrated in 16th-c. and 17th-c. paintings of cottage and tavern scenes. The same simple method was used for the construction of the harvest cart shown so clearly in the Luttrell Psalter (*c.* 1340) at the British Museum, a cart almost identical with those in common use today in Catalonia and parts of southern and central Europe; it is also the construction employed in the long narrow farm waggons built on a central pole, many of which are still used, perhaps unexpectedly, in the Rift Valley and Black Forest regions of west Germany. The early incidence of turnery, made possible by the development of the primitive but surprisingly efficient pole lathe, was but a short step in the practice of working directly from the newly felled, round coppice timber. It made possible the evolution, from the crude examples quoted, of such refined products as chairs of the turned ash ladder-back and Windsor types, as well as the turned legs, pedestals and spindles which have been a constantly recurring feature of furniture design, both in Europe and in America.

For most purposes, nevertheless, timber has always been needed in a squared form. Once sawn into boards and seasoned, the sapwood has to be removed and a true edge worked. The early method, extending well into the 16th c., was to use a side axe, a tool quite different in design from the felling axe. It was broad-bladed, enabling a straight edge to be more readily obtained, with the shaft socket offset to permit one side to be perfectly flat. In skilled hands this method had much to recommend it, especially when dealing with thick timber. For thinner material sawing was more practical and no more laborious. In both cases, where a finer finish was required, the plane was used.

The adze is a variation of the axe in which the blade is set at right angles to the shaft, and like the axe it has always been made in both short-handled and long-handled forms. Together with the axe it was essential to the great constructional woodwork of the Middle Ages, but its ancestry extends into prehistory. It could be used for dressing the surface of timber, as is described in the *Odyssey*, but it was most efficient when used across grain to shape such curved members as the arch-braces of a timber roof or the ribs of a ship. Variations of the tool are associated with the special trades of shipbuilding, cartwrighting, wheelwrighting and coopering. As late as the end of the 19th c. tool-makers' catalogues in England listed 50 different types of axe and adze, described according to trade and locality, while in Europe in the 1960s adzes of different kinds have been seen in use by carpenters repairing the medieval roof-timbers at Carcassonne, by coopers in Spain, France and Dalmatia, and by shipwrights in Spain and Portugal.

A type of adze depicted in Egyptian wall-paintings and still sold today in country districts in Portugal consists of a flat heavy blade held to a short shaft by means of a metal collar and wooden wedge. It has been suggested that this may be one stage in the evolution of the plane, a tool which became essential as the trade of joiner, and later cabinet-maker, developed from that of the CARPENTER. Whether true or not, it does emphasize the point that a plane is essentially a metal wedge held in a stock at a fixed angle in such a way that it separates fibres from the surface of the wood in a controlled manner, ejecting them in the form of shavings. It can also be used to cut the fibres transversely provided that precautions are taken to prevent end-splitting.

Although so basically simple, the modern plane is one of the most highly developed of all tools, the product of long evolution from many early European types. While the design of wooden planes of all kinds was virtually complete by the end of the 18th c., the evolution of metal planes had scarcely progressed from the Roman and medieval patterns. During the 19th c. rapid developments were made as a result of experimental work by, among others, Stewart Spiers of Ayr, Norris of London and, on rather different lines, by Leonard Bailey of Boston, Mass., later in association with the firm of Stanley. To be effective the plane demands not only the greatest skill in design, manufacture, sharpening and setting, but above all in use. To produce a true surface, free from all tears and blemishes, on timber with a cross or transverse grain requires the use of several different types of plane, each serving a specific purpose and designed accordingly. For the craftsman the process is as much a matter of feeling as of seeing; indeed he must develop from his sensory experiences a complex kinaesthetic and tactile imagery. His contact with his material, through plane-stock and blade, is almost as direct and intimate as that of the potter with his clay. Besides its major functions in reducing timber to width and thickness, in preparing true surfaces and edges from which to set out dimensions and in producing in the final stages flat smooth surfaces of board and frame, the plane has always been subject to extensive and often complicated modifications to enable it to be used for moulding, rebating, grooving and other specific operations. More extreme variations include the compass plane used in curved work, the violin-maker's tiny planes, the spokeshave and—perhaps most unusual—the cooper's long wooden shooting plane mounted permanently in an inverted, sloping position, over which the edges of the barrel staves are passed in order to plane them true, out of twist and at precisely the correct angle to form moisture-proof joints.

In the development of the saw is seen, perhaps more clearly than with other tools, the extent to which progress was dependent upon the development of metal-working tools and metal technology. Because of the softness of the metal then available many early saws were designed to cut on the pull rather than the push stroke. The alternative method of preventing buckling by straining the blade in a wooden frame was certainly known to the Romans, who had, besides the pit saw already described, a number of small framed handsaws for working at the bench. Modern saws which use similar tensioned frames are the bow-saw, the Scandinavian and Canadian bushman's saws, the coping saw and the fret-saw, of which the last two cut on the pull stroke to compensate for the fineness of their blades and the comparative weakness of their frames. Until the middle of the 17th c. the only saw commonly found without a frame was the narrow, sword-like tool with round handle frequently shown in medieval illustrations. But developments in the application of water-power to the process of rolling strip steel now permitted the use of a wide blade of sufficient rigidity and spring to avoid buckling. To control this in use a wide flat handle was designed, into which the blade was slotted and riveted. Thus an entirely new type of saw was introduced, the precursor of all modern handsaws.

For the precise dimension-sawing and joint-cutting practised by the 18th-c. cabinet-maker a thinner blade combined with absolute rigidity was essential. To satisfy these apparently incompatible requirements the backed saws were developed. In such saws the fine blade was held true and straight by a heavy folded iron or brass back into which it was sprung so that the cutting edge was slightly in tension. These saws often took their names from the joints or constructions with which they were connected—dovetail, carcase and tenon—names which, together with their basic forms and dimensions, have remained essentially unchanged until the present.

With the evolution of many different types of saw there was a parallel development in the design both of the teeth and of the files and other tools necessary to cut, sharpen and set them. Developments in the mid 19th c. are associated with the names of Spear and Jackson in England and Henry Disston in America. One of the first requirements of a saw is that it shall move freely through the wood, to which end it must be designed to remove the waste from its kerf in the form of sawdust and to cut a kerf wider than the thickness of its own blade. The collection and ejection of the sawdust is normally effected by the gullet between the cutting edges of the teeth; but where this is inadequate, for example when wet or green timber has to be cut, various methods have been employed of arranging the teeth in groups separated by deeper gullets. The method of promoting lateral clearance by bending or setting adjoining teeth outwards in opposite directions is described in detail by Pliny and is an essential feature of all efficient saws. It has been assisted in modern handsaws by the sophisticated technique of taper-grinding the thickness of the blades so that the metal is of uniform thickness along the cutting edge and near the handle but is progressively thinner towards the far back edge.

Another aspect of saw design, the shape of the teeth, is dictated by the fibrous structure of the timber to be cut. Saws intended for ripping down the grain have to cut, transversely, those fibres immediately in front of each tooth and push the particles so produced forward and out of the kerf. Saws for cutting across the grain must sever the fibres cleanly on each side of the blade before scraping away the waste between the two rows of set teeth. To perform these quite different operations efficiently the teeth must be skilfully designed and precisely sharpened, a delicate task in the case of the modern dovetail saw with over 8 bevelled teeth to the centimetre.

One of the earliest methods of joining two pieces of wood together, by driving the smaller into a round hole bored in the larger, has already been referred to. A variation of this technique was to use a cleft oak peg, or tree nail, to join overlapping boards or crossed members, and to prevent the joints used in large constructional work from coming apart. The need for some means of boring holes for such purposes was satisfied by the early development of the auger, of which the basic shell or spoon type probably evolved from the awl. In spite of its apparent simplicity, its function is quite complex: to centre the hole, sever the fibres at the circumference both with and across the grain, remove waste material and guide the cutting end straight as it penetrates the wood. The tool was usually turned by means of a long handle attached to a tang or passed through an eye forged at the end of the shaft. The breast auger, usually shown in medieval illustrations in the hands of shipwrights, allowed additional pressure to be applied to the tool by the workman's body. An early variation of the spoon auger was the introduction of a twist into the blade to assist in pulling it into the wood. By the early 19th c. augers were available in which the shaft also had been twisted into an accurate spiral in order to lift the waste chips on the Archimedian principle. Modifications to the cutters produced an extremely efficient tool capable of cutting a straight accurate hole up to 7·5 centimetres in diameter, in end grain as well as side grain.

The development of the brace during the 18th and 19th centuries permitted continuous rotation for the first time and resulted in the gradual replacement of the auger by the removable bit for all but the heaviest work. Many types of bit were developed. Some, like the twist bit and spoon bit, were based on the auger, while others, like the hand-forged centre-bits, were intended for special tasks. The brace itself evolved slowly from the 15th-c. wooden type and in spite of modifications in Holland, Sweden and Germany, the 18th-c. versions are remarkably similar to that shown in the Merode Altarpiece by the Master of Flémalle, now in the Metropolitan Museum of Art, New York. Wooden braces by Marples, beautifully finished in rosewood and ebony reinforced with brass plates, were still being sold in England at the turn of the 19th c. The modern metal brace, together with its associated shell-type chuck with interlocking jaws and rachet, were all developed in America in the 1860s. For small holes the bradawl, with its cutting edge and parallel shank, is still quick to use and efficient, but the range of sizes available is limited. To remedy this deficiency metalworkers' twist drills are commonly used for boring timber today despite the fact that they are not designed to cut wood fibres and consequently do not leave a clean hole.

Of the fundamental tools the chisel is so adaptable in its simplest form that it can be used in widely different situations. Although potentially powerful, the forces acting on it being concentrated on an extremely narrow edge, it is also capable in sensitive hands of the most delicate work. One of its principal functions is in joint cutting, for which a number of different types have been evolved, such as the mortise chisel with blade thickened to withstand leverage and handle cushioned against mallet blows, the thin bevelled-edge chisel for removing waste between dovetails, and the long paring chisel for cutting housings across wide boards. The other main direction of development has been in the form of curved gouges, of which a considerable variety must have been available during the Middle Ages on the evidence of the superb quality of 14th-c. wood-carving.

Tools themselves can often be regarded as minor works of art, not in the sense that they are elaborately decorated—as was frequently the case with Continental wooden planes—but in their perfect adaptation for their special purposes. They invite handling, as does a piece of sculpture. There is a quality of balance in a well-made tool —axe, hammer, chisel or saw—which whether or not it is susceptible of scientific analysis, is certainly known to the craftsman. When tools were wholly or partly made by processes under the control of craftsmen they usually achieved a delicate refinement in the over-all length, the distribution of weight, and the precise set of the point of grip in relation to the cutting edge or striking surface, which makes them a delight to handle. They could even be modified to suit the exact needs or idiosyncrasies of the craftsman who would use them. Mass-produced tools, particularly when they are redesigned from first principles to suit the materials and methods used in their manufacture, occasionally achieve a comparable quality. See also GREEK AND ROMAN ANTIQUITY (WOOD-WORKING AND TOOLS).

4. SOME MAIN USES. It is scarcely surprising that a material so universally available as wood, so varied in its qualities and so readily worked, should have become one of the first and most important raw materials. Even today, with such a wide range of natural and synthetic materials to hand, the quantity of timber used throughout the world has never been exceeded, and new uses as well as new techniques are constantly being developed. Nevertheless in proportion to other materials the greatest use of timber in Europe occurred prior to large-scale industrialization. The period from the Middle Ages to the Industrial Revolution may therefore be used to illustrate the extent to which in one way or another wood served so many basic human needs and activities.

In many countries and districts wood was the

commonest building material, indeed distinct building styles such as those of Scandinavia, Switzerland, Austria and Slovenia, each with its local variations, were developed in order to exploit the abundant supply. This practice was followed later in North America to produce such superb wooden dwellings as those of Quebec, Salem and Nantucket. A similar development took place in South Africa. But even when stone and brick were used, whether from preference or from local shortage of timber, the carpenter was still responsible for floors and roofs and the joiner for interior fittings, staircases, doors and windows. Decay and fire have accounted for a great proportion of this woodwork and warfare has destroyed fine examples such as the Cloth Halls of the Low Countries with their high-pitched roofs, the magnificent ceilings of the Infantado Palace at Guadalajara, much of Nuremberg and the whole of medieval Frankfurt. Nevertheless, much remains in such medieval towns as Bruges and Ghent, Ulm and Augsburg, in the later half-timbered buildings of the English counties, particularly Cheshire, Shropshire and Suffolk, in the splendid panelled doors and shutters of Alsace and in the generous vernacular architecture of central Europe stretching from the Rhine to the Danube. Some of the best examples of the direct use of timber in building are to be seen in the great wooden farmhouses and barns of the Continent and in the earlier medieval tithe-barns of southern England. The importance of scaffolding and other falsework needed to provide initial support for arches and stone vaults is often forgotten as little evidence of these structures usually remains, but inside the tower of Lärbro in Gotland and inside the spire of Salisbury Cathedral the original falsework still exists as it was left by the carpenters in the 1st half of the 14th c. Salisbury also retains the wooden winding gear used for lifting the masons' materials to the great height of the spire, and a treadmill for a similar purpose is still in working order in the central tower of Beverley Minster.

Windmills, over 7,000 of which are recorded in England alone at the time of the Domesday Book, represent one of the earliest examples of the use of wood in power transmission, for the great gear wheels, cogs and pinions, as well as the elaborate mechanisms for controlling the rotation of the sails and turning them into the wind, were almost entirely wooden. For centuries the windmill must have been both a conspicuous landmark and an impressive source of power. Some may still be seen, often representative of quite different types—the few carefully preserved post and smock mills in Sweden, Denmark, Holland and England, the little white-washed mills with white triangular canvas sails which face the Atlantic winds from the hills around Lisbon or turn to the *meltémi* on the island of Mykonos, and the remains of those in the Alpilles of Provence and on the bleak plateau of La Mancha. Water was commonly used to provide power in the later development of wooden machinery for pumping the mines and quarries, fulling cloth, boring wooden water-pipes, rolling steel and a host of other purposes. Some water-mills were closely connected with the timber trade, notably those in Norway where in the Middle Ages nearly every farmhouse is reputed to have had its own simple sawmill, in Sweden where from the 16th c. large water-driven mills supplied the port of Göteborg, and in the Black Forest of Germany. An interesting use of water-mills may still be seen in Yugoslavia, on the broad River Sava, where they are mounted on large rafts moored in mid-stream to catch the slow-moving current. The extraordinary group of wooden Bosnian corn-mills, set among the cascades of the River Pliva at nearby Jajce, are said to be Turkish in origin and to date from the occupation.

Timber served transport on land through the work of the wainwright, wheelwright, cartwright, coach-builder and bridge-builder. On sea it was the universal material for vessels of all sizes and purposes from the early open clinker-built boats, similar to those found in the still earlier Viking sites at Gokstad and Oseberg, to the 18th-c. merchantmen and men-of-war. In agriculture wood was used to provide shelter, for making hurdles, gates and fences, for carts and waggons, for dairy equipment such as coopered milk-pails, butter-churns, barrels and tubs, and for implements of all kinds such as ploughs, harrows, ladders, hay-rakes, forks and flails.

In all these activities the craftsman was demonstrating his inventiveness, his ability to adapt the qualities of different timbers to his special needs and his readiness to devise new methods of working and assembly. He was often operating as a highly skilled structural or mechanical engineer. Although in woodwork the artistic side is often apparently subordinate to constructional and functional considerations, there is in almost every situation some opportunity for the exercise of choice or discrimination; it may even be argued that craftsmanship in its fullest sense always incorporates this aspect. But in at least two major areas, in medieval ecclesiastical woodwork and in domestic furniture from the mid 17th c. onwards, the imaginative and visual quality displayed far transcends mechanical or structural efficiency and removes the craftsman from the position of the engineer to that of the artist.

Only a small proportion of pre-Reformation woodwork remains, but what there is is still sufficient in quantity and diversity to show that in medieval church woodwork the skills of the carpenter, joiner and wood carver reached their culmination. In the choir-stalls, bench ends, screens, pulpits, lecterns and font covers may be seen principally the work of the joiner, enriched by the wood carver and originally in many cases also by the painter and gilder. To appreciate such woodwork it must be understood that the medieval craftsman was not concerned with that precision, exact repetition and symmetry which are characteristic of machine woodwork and are probably partly responsible for its lack of vitality. The carver was not mechanically copying a design; he was himself responsible for both design and execution. His bench ends, poppy heads and misericords, although they achieve unity by conforming to the over-all dimensions of the design and by the repetition of the main forms, invariably differ in their details, often revealing a continuous progression of ideas and always creating inexhaustible interest by their variety. Choir-stalls especially, whether in the northern styles of Halberstadt, Lübeck and Erfurt, in the more flamboyant manner of Barcelona Cathedral and the Convent of St. Thomas, Avila, or in the pure English style of Lincoln, Ripon and Beverley Minster, reveal a subtle balance between the intricate texture of the carving, the soft moulded edges and the plain surfaces, and an almost inevitable rightness in the placing of the decoration in relation to material, function and the visual requirements of the design. Rarely is there any attempt to obscure working methods or to disguise the spontaneity of the approach; tool-marks which, arising from unskilled or hesitant hands would be a clumsy blemish, are here a record of a confident and controlled movement of gouge or chisel and an unerring grasp of three-dimensional form.

The method of roofing was a major element affecting the whole design of the medieval church. The Continental preference was generally for stone vaults, most of which were surmounted by functional wooden framed roofs. Thus in spite of important exceptions, such as the complex panelled and coffered roof of the Basilica of St. Zeno, Verona, and those of the Florentine churches of San Miniato al Monte with painted tie-beams and rafters, and Santa Croce with simple low-pitched trusses in typical Franciscan style, the open timber roof belongs essentially to England and nowhere else were its possibilities developed to the same extent.

Roofing was principally the task of the carpenter. His usual method was to lay timbers called 'wall-plates' along the top of the side walls and to fix to these at close intervals inclined timbers called 'rafters', pitching against each other in pairs. The rafters were connected to each other at the apex by the ridge-pole and sometimes additionally at lower levels by means of widely spaced horizontal members called 'purlins'. Finally the rafters were covered with boarding to support the outer covering of lead, slates or tiles. Additional members were needed to resist wind pressure, to prevent the rafters from sagging under their immense load and either to tie their lower ends to prevent lateral thrust on the walls or, alternatively, to reduce such thrust by transmitting it lower down the walls. The method of joining these massive timbers was almost invariably by huge mortise and tenon joints, often cut by mortise axe and strengthened by oak pegs driven into auger holes bored across the joint.

No doubt it would have been possible to have designed a single utilitarian roof structure capable of application to almost all buildings, but the medieval carpenter reacted to the problem characteristically by producing a truly staggering range of solutions. Variations in structure, in the arrangements of the members to form trusses and frames and in the grouping of these units were sufficient to ensure that no two roofs were identical and an austere beauty was often achieved solely by rhythmic repetition combined with a fine sense of scale. But in addition the roof provided unusual opportunities for different decorative treatments, each of which produced its own strikingly individual effect. Mouldings were used to emphasize the linear quality of purlins and rafters, braces were arched to match the stone arcading of the nave, deep crestings and carved PATERAE enriched the beams, carved bosses stressed points of intersection between purlins and rafters, traceried panels filled the spaces between queen posts or between braces and beams, carved angels sprang from extended hammer beams, and to all was often added the brilliance of colour and gilding. But even in the richest roofs the purely decorative elements rarely hide the underlying structure, but rather they emphasize it.

The only rival of the English roof is to be found in the Mudejar work of Spain. The stucco ceilings, such as those of the Alhambra at Granada, hide the work of the carpenter on which they depend; but the coffered ceilings and *media naranja* cupolas of Seville's Alcazar often expose the surface of the cedar wood. ARTESONADO, or panelled ceilings composed of interlaced geometrical patterns of wonderful complexity may be seen in the chapter room of Toledo Cathedral and in convent churches in the old quarter of Seville, such as San Clemente and Santa Paula, as well as in the Alcazar. All these styles are essentially decorative and not constructional, the roof timbers proper being concealed. They rely for their effect on abstract surface decoration, deep texture and often on rich, sombre colours picked out with gold. The combination of these elements in the choir of the Convent of Santa Clara at Tordesillas can only be described as miraculous.

By the 16th c. the joiner had overcome many of the problems associated with working in solid wood. He had developed methods of joining together narrow members to form frames in which thin wooden PANELS were held flat but were able to expand and contract freely in their grooves. Such panelled frames could be assembled to form the basic construction of chests, chairs, tables, beds and cupboards of different kinds. Decoration included carving, turnery and inlay. The use of mouldings, scratched with simple tools or cut with special moulding planes, to soften the square edges of frames introduced considerable structural complications.

The sturdiness and spontaneity which were the great virtues of early ecclesiastical woodwork were less appropriate in FURNITURE. As living conditions became easier there was an increasing demand for furniture in greater quantity and of better quality, designed to satisfy a far wider range of activities. Improvements after the middle of the 17th c. resulted from growing specialization on the part of the craftsman, the introduction of new timbers from abroad, improvements in tools and techniques and the influence of informed taste and opinion. Furniture now satisfied more than the basic necessities of life; it was becoming part of the accoutrements of good living, prized for its own sake, as a source of beauty as well as for its function.

Although oak was the chief material of the medieval wood-worker, it was by no means his only timber. In *The Hous of Fame* Chaucer refers to a 'table of sicamour' and in *The Parlement of Foules* he lists a number of different woods and adds descriptive comments: 'the builder's oak, hardy ash, elm, box for pipes, holm oak, fir, cupress, the bowman's yew, aspen, the olive of peace, and the laurel'. As early as the mid 13th c. a thriving timber trade was established in Norway and in eastern Europe, centred on the Baltic ports of Danzig, Memel and Riga and dealing mainly in the finest quality oak, beech and softwoods from the great natural forests of Prussia and Poland. Transport, principally to the Low Countries and England, and later increasingly to the Mediterranean lands and even further afield, was readily accomplished by sea. In 1252 and again in 1260, the Pipe Rolls of Windsor Castle record the importation from the Baltic of a considerable quantity of Norway boards and of prime quarter-sawn oak boards, known as WAINSCOT, for tables and wall-panelling. It is evident that craftsmen were already demanding a higher quality timber for special purposes than could be provided from home sources.

The stylistic differences to be seen in early European furniture were certainly due in part to the preference for oak in the north and for walnut in the south. A consequence of Italian influence spreading northward during the Renaissance was the gradual replacement in popularity of oak by walnut, the warm beauty and unique working qualities of which contributed so much to furniture and interior design during the 17th c. Italian, French and English walnut are the same species, but differ in their colour and texture by reason of the different conditions under which they are grown. The walnut used extensively during the 19th c. in Europe, and following the Civil War in the eastern States of America, was the American species, grown principally in Indiana, Virginia and Tennessee. Often known as 'black walnut', this is a distinctly different timber, much larger and more uniform in its characteristics than the European variety, with a deep purplish-brown colour which fades to a soft golden brown with age. The Nigerian or 'golden' walnut which has enjoyed varying popularity in the 20th c. is quite unrelated botanically or indeed in any other way apart from a slight colour resemblance.

European walnut has never been plentiful and this fact, coupled with the appreciation of its rich colour and grain, led to the development of more economical methods of using it, in the form of VENEER. The need to conserve supplies became specially urgent after the severe winter of 1709, which killed most of the French trees and eventually led to the prohibition of further exports. This, together with the abolition in England in 1733 of the tax on imported timbers, encouraged the use for furniture of timbers from the West Indies and the South American seaboard, particularly of MAHOGANY. Known to Raleigh and used by him for ship repairs, these woods had formed part of the spoils of the Spanish Main since the 16th c. and with gold and silver had been lavished on the churches, monasteries and palaces of Spain and Portugal. Sometimes, as in the chapel of the Convent of Jesus at Aveiro, the woodwork of the ceiling, walls and altar was entirely covered with gold, but elsewhere the distinct qualities of the woods were valued for their own sakes. The furnishings of the library of the Escorial Palace, begun in 1584 and reputed to be the first example of the use of mahogany in Europe, the nuns' choir in the incomparable Convent of Santa Clara at Tordesillas and the imposing stalls and canopies in palisander and rosewood of the *coro alto* of Braga Cathedral, all demonstrate the early utilization of the new timbers and the exploitation of their decorative possibilities, although in an architectural rather than a domestic setting.

The true Cuban mahogany, also known as 'Spanish' and 'San Domingo', was extremely dense and strong, of a deep warm reddish-brown colour which deepened with age and with an elegant curl in the grain when specially sawn. It was this timber which dominated furniture design in England from the 1730s until nearly the end of the century and inspired as well as made possible the work of CHIPPENDALE and his contemporaries. It was introduced to Europe rather more slowly and although a considerable trade was established between the Danish West Indies and Schleswig, mahogany never achieved quite the same popularity on the Continent as it did in England. In Sweden it was regarded as suitable for only the most expensive furniture and even in France it was always in competition with a wide variety of other fine woods. Although it was used extensively in America after *c.* 1750, distinct mahogany styles developing in Boston, New York and Philadelphia, it by no means replaced entirely the cherrywood, maple and walnut in which much furniture reminiscent of the late GEORGIAN period was executed. During the FEDERAL period, however, San Domingo mahogany of a remarkably fine quality was used by the New York cabinet-maker, Duncan PHYFE. The milder, pale Honduras mahogany, usually called 'baywood', was imported in great quantities at the same time, but its inferiority to Cuban was such as to restrict its use to interior linings, drawer sides and bottoms, and groundwork for veneering. In the 19th c., however, it replaced the rapidly dwindling stocks of prime Cuban and provided the raw material for the ponderous mahogany styles, such as Victorian and BIEDERMEIER, which seemed to go hand in hand with early industrial development. During the 20th c. it has been replaced by the more abundant West African mahoganies, lagos, sapele and utile, none of which is a true mahogany.

The 2nd half of the 18th c. saw the use of an increasing range of decorative hardwoods, which were imported mainly from the East and West Indies, Brazil and India. Of these the satinwoods were probably the most important, followed during the 19th c. by the rosewoods and black walnut. Ebony, amboyna, bird's-eye maple, kingwood and other choice woods were used mainly in small quantities for their contrasting colours and grain patterns.

The special quality of the best 18th-c. furniture is attributable in no small measure to the splendid materials available, but these had to be matched by skill and craftsmanship of an order which had not been known before. Many of the new woods had structural characteristics and working qualities so different from European hardwoods that in order to be able to use them at all techniques had to be extensively refined, developed or even re-invented, having been forgotten since the decay of earlier civilizations. Some understanding of those techniques is necessary for the full enjoyment of different kinds of furniture.

5. SPECIAL TECHNIQUES

(*a*) *Veneering*, the craft of gluing thin sheets of wood, and occasionally other materials, on to a carefully prepared groundwork, is probably the most difficult of all decorative processes. Egyptian wall-paintings of 1500 B.C. illustrate the technique, which was also practised by the Greeks and Romans. Pliny in his *Natural History* (A.D. 77) advises: 'The best woods for cutting into layers and employing as a veneer for covering others are the citrus, terebinth, the different varieties of the maple, the box, the palm, the holly, the holm-oak, the wood of the elder, and the poplar.' Veneering was not practised in northern Europe until the 17th c., when it was re-developed from first principles, at first chiefly as a means of using newly arrived supplies of ebony. The parallel development of veneering and cabinet-making, originally in France, led to the use of the French word ÉBÉNISTE and its Anglicized form 'ebonist' to describe the cabinet-maker.

All veneers were originally cut by saw, a method which with skill could produce 2 or 3 sheets to the centimetre. The use of a frame saw by two workmen for this purpose is illustrated in Diderot's *Encyclopédie* of 1765. By the 19th c. special circular saws were available to cut as many as 6 sheets to the centimetre, but this technique has now been superseded by the less wasteful knife-cut methods for all but the most difficult timbers. The modern rotary-cut method, which unpeels the annual rings from the rotating log in a continuous sheet, is appropriate for plywood manufacture only, as the resulting grain pattern is singularly uninteresting.

The core on which a veneer is laid must be stable and true if the veneer is not to split or buckle. Whether flat or curved, it must have an unbroken surface, which entirely rules out the frame and panel construction. Most veneer was glued to oak or pine until the 2nd half of the 18th c. when mild Honduras mahogany was found to be specially suitable. Progress in veneering was assisted by the introduction soon after 1700 of efficient glue to replace the earlier curd or cheese glue, but great ingenuity was still demanded in the design of cauls and other cramping devices necessary to ensure a perfect bond between the two surfaces. The difficulty of gluing veneer to end grain required the development of advanced jointing techniques such as lap and secret dovetails, in which the joint is either partially or entirely enclosed.

Wood is used in the form of veneer for a number of reasons. It permits the most economical use of rare varieties of woods which are available only in very small sizes and of special samples of commoner woods which by some accident of growth possess such prized grain patterns as curl, feather, ripple or fiddleback. Woods which are particularly liable to twist or split because of their wild grain, or which have no strength in the solid because of their short grain or burr growth, could not be used successfully otherwise. It even enables thin cross-grain slices from the small trunks and branches of olive and laburnum to be assembled to produce the 'oyster-shell' effects (see OYSTERING) which were popular in England after the Restoration. Conversely, some of the best constructional timbers are so even in texture, so straight-grained and colourless, that they are far more suitable as a ground for veneered furniture than they would be if used alone.

The introduction of veneer opened up immense decorative possibilities and indeed required an entirely different approach from that appropriate to design in solid wood. Advantage was taken of the fact that almost the same grain pattern runs through a series of veneers cut from the same flitch, so that facing pairs could be opened out and joined together centrally to produce a number of identical symmetrical patterns for use on doors or drawer fronts. All kinds of shaped work which in the solid would have introduced the weakness of short grain, or the unsightliness of many surface joints, now became feasible. Not only was the underlying construction actually hidden, but the appearance of the veneered surface was often unrelated to any possible solid wood construction: large continuous surfaces, panel effects created by unlaid stringing or applied mouldings, cross-bandings on rails, drawer points and table-tops, were all artificial devices carefully calculated and introduced for their visual effect. Appearance was therefore much more under the control of the craftsman and became to a much smaller degree dependent on constructional necessities combined with the random grain pattern of the available solid timber.

(*b*) *Inlay* is a decorative technique which consists of inserting pieces of contrasting wood and other materials into a solid background. The usual method is to place the shaped inlay material in its final position on the surface, scribe round it accurately with a sharp, pointed knife and then cut a shallow recess, usually about 3 millimetres deep, into which the inlay may be glued. When wood is inlaid into wood the surface is usually finished flush, although not always so; other materials are frequently left slightly proud of the surface, thereby giving it life and texture.

Elaborate inlay was practised in the Far East at an early date. There is a beautiful inlaid cabinet of the late Ming Dynasty (1368–1628) in the Metropolitan Museum, New York, and Indo-Portuguese furniture of the 17th c. was often made of exotic woods inlaid with ivory, ebony and MOTHER OF PEARL, specially for the European market. Inlay was used extensively in Europe during the 16th and 17th centuries, when the panels of the framed oak furniture were often enriched with simple conventional floral and geometrical designs. White holly was commonly combined with the black fossil oak, which takes its name 'bog oak' from the peatbogs in which it is found, and coloured woods such as cherry, pear and yew were also used. One of the most splendid examples from the mid 16th c. is the Inlaid Room of Sizergh Castle, now preserved in the Victoria and Albert Museum, where fine panels of wainscot oak are inlaid with elaborate foliated arabesques and strapwork in bog oak and poplar, producing contrasting surfaces which are vibrant with soft glowing colour.

Almost by definition inlay requires a ground of solid timber into which it can be set. With the introduction of veneered furniture it was entirely practical for it to be replaced to a large extent by MARQUETRY. In at least one form, however, it could still be used with veneer—as narrow lines or strings of contrasting woods or silver wire, usually let into veneer and ground, either to trace linear designs over the surface or, more commonly, to produce panel effects and to emphasize carcase edges and the corners of square-sectioned legs. Being a delicate form of decoration it could be introduced most successfully into furniture of restrained classical style such as that produced for the court of the Emperor Joseph II in Vienna between 1780 and 1790. Elsewhere it belongs more to the later styles of SHERATON and HEPPLEWHITE, whether executed in Europe or, for example, by the younger TOWNSENDS and GODDARDS in their Newport, Rhode Island, workshops. In conjunction with veneer inlay enjoyed variable popularity during the 19th c. Mother of pearl became a favourite decorative medium in cultures as widely separated as those of Portuguese Brazil and Second Empire France, and it was also used on both sides of the Atlantic to provide an iridescent contrast to the rather dark, heavy surface of PAPIER-MÂCHÉ furniture. A number of pieces by Michael THONET of Vienna included in the Great Exhibition of 1851 were made of rosewood and walnut inlaid with metal and TORTOISESHELL as well as mother of pearl, and bold effects were achieved with inlay between 1900 and 1910 by two members of the Vienna SEZESSION: Koloman Moser, using rather traditional forms, and Josef HOFFMANN in an aggressively modern style.

Nevertheless wherever country-made furniture was produced on either side of the Atlantic during the 18th and 19th centuries, inlay continued to be used from time to time in the older manner. The revival *c.* 1900, under the influence of the ARTS AND CRAFTS MOVEMENT, of furniture made of solid wood in the vernacular tradition immediately provided the opportunity for exploiting the technique more fully. It was a favourite form of decoration of W. R. LETHABY, of C. R. ASHBEE's Guild of Handicraft and of K. P. C. de Brazil, the Dutch architect. But it was Ernest GIMSON who used inlay with the greatest exuberance during the first two decades of the 20th c. to give a rich, jewel-like quality to special pieces, such as branched candelabra, caskets and church furniture. His more intricate designs were based closely on observed natural forms and were inlaid, often boldly in ivory, bone, silver and mother of pearl on macassar ebony or rosewood, but sometimes with subtle judgement in less contrasting hardwoods on oak. The inlay, executed with great skill and a fine sense of two-dimensional design, was almost invariably left proud and slightly modelled. Magnificent examples of inlaid lecterns by Gimson and Waals may be seen at the Church of St. Andrew, Roker, and at Chalford Parish Church, while the Newarke Museum at Leicester has a number of fine inlaid caskets and cabinets.

(*c*) *Parquetry* is distinguished from other forms of decoration by its essentially geometrical nature. The effects can be created either by overlaid or by inlaid techniques. In its simplest form the pattern originates as two strips of veneer or blocks of wood, one light and one dark, which can be joined together, sliced up, and rejoined in many different ways, each producing a different kind of repeat. The chess-board is an obvious example of a parquetry design, based on light and dark squares, which could be developed from such simple origins and the same technique could be the means of producing a long string of tiny black-and-white rectangles for use as an inlaid border. When cut diagonally instead of at right angles, the resulting herring-bone, diamond or zig-zag repeat patterns can be combined to produce quite elaborate and powerful decorative effects.

Heavy inlaid parquetry banding in two colours was used on early oak and walnut furniture of both English and Continental origins. It was employed with increasing refinement during the latter part of the 18th c. as narrow stringing, the contrasting colours vibrating and emphasizing strongly the main proportions of the design. It was a favourite form of decoration on musical instruments, particularly early Italian stringed instruments, of which many superb examples may be seen in the collections in Naples, Geneva, Barcelona, Lisbon and London. Between 1800 and 1820 narrow chequered stringing featured on much of the mahogany furniture of REGENCY style which was produced in New England; and it was in this form, a century later, that parquetry had great appeal for the craftsmen of the COTSWOLD SCHOOL, who often left their elaborate inlaid strings standing above the surrounding surface, the edges rounded off to form cock beads. In a rather different context the French *ébéniste* Jacques-Émile Ruhlmann employed ivory and ebony inlays on the simple but sophisticated furniture he exhibited at the 1925 Paris Exhibition. The narrow inlaid lines of holly, rosewood and ebony, which have always been an important decorative element in the work of Edward BARNSLEY, are derived from the inlaid parquetry stringing of the previous generation.

Overlaid parquetry is really no more than a form of geometrical marquetry. By this technique elaborate panels in the style of Louis XIV were made in Genoa at the end of the 17th c. Lozenge and cube parquetry panels with chequered borders occur in furniture attributed to Jean-François OEBEN and Jean-Henri RIESENER, in the Swedish ROCOCO furniture of Gustaf Foltiern in the 1770s, in the work of Domingos Tenuta of Lisbon in 1790 and in the finely executed cabinet work produced between 1780 and 1830 for the Imperial Court of Vienna. Particularly rich effects with rare veneers were obtained in England during the Victorian period and experiments with panels consisting of opposed rectangles of PEWTER and ebony were carried out by Ambrose HEAL in 1900.

(*d*) INTARSIA is that branch of inlay in which different kinds of solid wood are inserted into a wooden ground, whereas marquetry is a branch of veneering in which the design is composed of pieces of thin veneer inserted into a base veneer to form a complete sheet, which is then overlaid on to the groundwork. The two techniques are frequently spoken of together and indeed are often confused, because they are both associated with the remarkable craft of picture-making in wood which assumed considerable importance in Italy between 1460 and 1510. In this situation the differences in technique are thought of, rightly, as subordinate to the purpose which they served.

The *intarsia* panels to be seen in choir-stalls and sacristry cupboards in the Church of Santa Maria dei Fiori in Venice, in the Upper Church at Assisi, in the Cathedrals of Parma, Modena and Padua and, most remarkable of all, in the *studiolo* of the Ducal Palace at Urbino, show that the exploration of perspective and the illusion of three-dimensional space was quite as advanced in this unexpected medium as it was in drawing and painting. The many delightful *trompe-l'œil* effects clearly anticipate still-life painting, even landscape painting to some extent, while it is possible to detect a striking similarity in the modes of perception revealed in the Urbino panels and in the contemporary paintings of Piero della Francesca displayed in the same building. Piero's influence, through his pupils the Lendinara brothers, is more certainly attributable in the large-scale work at Padua, however, while the credit for the designs of the Urbino masterpiece is sometimes given to Botticelli, whose mark, the silhouette of Minerva, is to be found on *intarsia* panelled doors elsewhere in the palace.

An unusually rich and florid style of picture-making developed in the 17th c. in Bohemia, centred on the town of Eger. This brought together the two crafts of *intarsia* and relief carving, each helping the other to produce an effect of vivid realism. In style this craft has the freedom and vitality which belongs essentially to the naturalistic tradition of central European wood-carving. It was used for altar panels as well as for domestic furniture and the lids of games boxes and caskets, and it was exported all over Europe. In the 19th c. another interesting, but equally local form of picture-making in wood grew up in England in the Tunbridge Wells area. Elaborate scenes involving landscapes and buildings of local interest, as well as abstract geometrical designs, were built up into thick blocks from tiny strips of veneer glued together vertically. These were then sliced across to form thin mosaic veneers composed of hundreds of pieces of coloured wood, for application to a host of boxes, caskets, tea-caddies and writing-cases. One of the best collections of Tunbridge ware outside of Tunbridge Wells is included in the Pinto Collection of Wooden Bygones, now housed in the Birmingham City Museum and Art Gallery. Although the geometrical style of this ware often resembles parquetry, it differs in its methods of production and in the direction of the grain of the tesserae.

(*e*) *Marquetry* developed from the older craft of *intarsia* following the invention in the 16th c. of the fine metal-framed fret-saw, which permitted base and inlay veneers to be sawn simultaneously. The resulting precision encouraged greater detail and elaboration, and the smaller scale of the work made it more suitable for application to domestic furniture. Although early examples of marquetry are displayed on the NONESUCH CHESTS made for Henry VIII, these are almost certainly not of English workmanship and full credit for the development of the technique must be accorded to Continental craftsmen, particularly to the Dutch. The 2nd half of the 17th c. saw the spread of the Dutch naturalistic style to the fashionable centres of Europe. It employed a considerable variety of coloured woods and often combined invention with superb decorative qualities. Rather more restrained but no less splendid was the SEAWEED MARQUETRY in which two veneers, one light and one dark, were cut together in continuous ACANTHUS or endive scrolls and then reassembled to make a pair of marquetry sheets with the figure and ground in counterchange. A similar technique, using TORTOISESHELL and thin sheets of copper or brass, was perfected by BOULLE and his pupils, and use with rich effect on pairs of tables, escritoires and cabinets. In England metal marquetry was practised by a craftsman of Flemish origin, Gerreit JENSEN, who is known to have set up workshops in London by 1680. Examples of superb marquetry and boulle work of this period are to be seen in the Rijksmuseum, Amsterdam, and in the Wallace Collection and the Victoria and Albert Museum, London.

During the 18th c. the finest marquetry continued to be made by Dutch craftsmen, one of the best known of whom, the younger Bernard van RISEN BURGH, worked in Paris. The German *ébénistes* Oeben and Riesener maintained the best traditions of the Boulle workshops, to which they in turn succeeded, while their compatriot David ROENTGEN settled at Neuwied in Westphalia and established a reputation throughout Europe both for the unrivalled quality and for the restraint of his later work. Craftsmen from Neuwied are known to have taken their skills as far afield as Poland and London. Elaborate marquetry decoration, often employing elaborate *trompe-l'œil* effects, was practised by Pietro PIFFETTI in Turin during the 2nd quarter of the century, but the best Italian work produced after 1770 is usually associated with the name of Guiseppe Maggiolini of Milan. Baltimore was one of the few American centres whose craftsmen specialized in marquetry to any extent, but they earned a considerable reputation for quality during the Federal period. Despite the work attributed to designers such as William VILE and John COBB, and the introduction by Robert ADAM and Thomas Sheraton of delicate·classical motifs to embellish panels, marquetry was never as popular in England as it was on the Continent.

In the early 19th c. mahogany furniture enriched with marquetry panels in pale birch was made in Denmark and Norway in a style derived from French EMPIRE, and the same combination of woods was used on a small scale in America. But although in France the unmatched technical virtuosity of the 18th-c. *ébénistes* persisted in many small workshops, possibly finding its final expression in the extravagant ROCOCO panels of Louis Gallé of NANCY in the 1880s, originality had begun to decline. The invention in 1780 of the marquetry cutter's donkey, a device for holding and sawing up to a dozen copies of the same design, had already increased the tendency towards repetition, even towards mass production; indeed by 1900 pictorial marquetry panels were being produced in the factory of Louis Majorelle, also of Nancy, by methods which were essentially industrial.

(*f*) *Painting* is probably the oldest of all methods of decorating wood, as any examination of Egyptian work will show. In conjunction with GILDING and carving, it contributed to the colourful splendour of the medieval scene. But at times it went much further than this. As easel painting had not yet been devised, there was no sharp distinction between painting as decoration and painting as fine art. Thus painted decoration intended as part of a decorative scheme might include the work of the most gifted artists of the period. Early religious panel paintings in national collections have often been removed from altar-pieces and from other religious furniture, as in the case of the Wilton Diptych in the National Gallery, the Berlinghieri Diptych in the Uffizi, Florence, and in an entirely different tradition the primitive but powerfully expressive Catalan paintings now displayed at Vich and Barcelona. One of the most exquisite specimens of medieval woodwork in which architecture, craftsmanship and painting merge, is the *Châsse* of St. Ursula, adorned with six miniature paintings by Memling of incidents in the life of the Saint, preserved in the Hospital of St. John, Bruges.

In order to provide a suitable surface to receive the paint and to fill the open grain of such hardwoods as oak, the wood was often given a number of coats of a mixture of whiting and size called 'gesso'. Normally these coats were carefully rubbed down to produce a smooth surface, but the material could also be textured and moulded. There is a delightful 14th-c. Florentine marriage chest, with painted panels of gesso on walnut, at the Victoria and Albert Museum and the Uccello painting *A Hunt in the Forest* in the Ashmolean Museum, Oxford, was almost certainly intended for the front panel of a similar chest. An Italian wooden CASSONE of *c.* 1500 with FLEUR-DE-LIS painted in a formal repeat pattern on gesso is in the Metropolitan Museum, New York.

If these examples represent art of a high order, the other extreme of charming but naïve decoration is to be found in the dower chests of Connecticut and Pennsylvania, dating from *c.* 1700 to the middle of the 19th c., which are descended from the virile folk tradition of southern Germany. The province of Dalarna in Sweden produced during the 17th c. a rather similar style of peasant art, usually in the form of painted friezes and including delightful figures in period dress. This unpretentious use of coloured decoration persisted until very recently in the long-boats of the English canals (see CANAL BOAT DECORATION IN ENGLAND), the covered gypsy carts and caravans of Europe and the elaborately painted Sicilian carts, their panels devoted equally to religious and operatic themes.

Painted furniture enjoyed particular favour in Italy during the 18th c. One of its main centres of manufacture was Venice, in whose products is often to be found a reflection of the decorative style of contemporary Venetian artists such as Tiepolo and Guardi. Elsewhere in Europe painting had been little used for decorating fashionable furniture since the 16th c., but the Italianate style slowly spread northward in the hands of such decorators as Angelica Kauffmann, Pergolesi and Cipriani, whose painted plaques were an important feature of the NEO-CLASSICAL styles of the last quarter of the 18th c. Paint was applied either directly on to dense timbers such as satinwood, or on to a prepared surface of hard white enamel. Delicate beech and satinwood chairs, bureaux and china-cabinets in the Hepplewhite and Sheraton styles were also painted with simple floral motifs, sometimes combined with gilding. A vogue for 'fancy' chairs, the best-known of which were produced by Lambert HITCHCOCK, grew up in the early years of the 19th c. in Baltimore and Connecticut. With many characteristics derived from Sheraton, these chairs were of light construction with caned seats and painted decoration, which often included panels with romantic landscape subjects. They were made by early mass-production methods, as was the painted cottage furniture of the mid century. This latter was attractively simple in design, usually of painted softwood. Furniture, elaborately painted in medieval style by Rossetti, Madox Brown, Burne-Jones, Poynter, Simeon Solomon and others, was designed in England in the 1860s by William MORRIS, Philip WEBB, J. D. Seddon and William Burges, but it represents little more than a temporary stylistic revival in response to pre-Raphaelite idealism. More forward-looking, although still produced under the influence of Morris, was the painted furniture of the Dutch designer, G. W. Dijselhof, dating from the early years of the 20th c., and the range of exquisite miniature cabinets by Sidney Barnsley, Ernest Gimson and Peter Waals, which, when opened, reveal contrasting interiors bright with intertwining floral tracery and tiny abstract patterns painted by Louise Powell.

The linear, two-dimensional qualities seen in Dijselhof's painted designs reflect the ART-NOUVEAU style which was already established in Europe, and particularly strong in the Low Countries at the beginning of the 20th c. Although the designs of the chairs published in 1899 by the Swedish artist Carl Larssen and intended for his own home were still in the classical tradition, they are nevertheless important because their white painted surfaces illustrate the new concern for light. By 1900 his fellow countryman Alf Wallender was producing simple white-painted furniture decorated with flowing motifs in Scandinavian *art-nouveau* style, and in the same year Charles Rennie MACKINTOSH showed his white tea-room at the VIIIth Exhibition of the Vienna Sezession. Perhaps the most fundamental use of colour was by the Dutch constructivist Gerrit RIETVELD, whose 'red-and-blue' armchair was made in 1918, and by the BAUHAUS designers Marcel BREUER and Peter Keler in the early 1920s. Keler's cradle, first shown in 1922, applied the colour theories of his colleague, the painter Kandinsky.

The popularity of painted furniture had already declined before the importation of the first Oriental LACQUER early in the 17th c. Great quantities of lacquered cabinets and screens, known as Coromandel screens, as well as lacquered boards for making up into furniture, were imported from China and Japan during the 17th and 18th centuries. The East India Company and the Portuguese were responsible for most of the early trade, but the latter were replaced during the mid 17th c. by the Dutch, who soon dominated the market and established standards which were seldom surpassed elsewhere in Europe. Japanese lacquer, often of superb quality, was used in moderation during the 18th c. by leading designers such as Riesener and Chippendale, and by the cabinet-makers of the Netherlands, who successfully combined and contrasted the Oriental panels with veneer and marquetry in the later Neo-Classical styles. Towards the end of the century lacquer in black and gold was a favourite medium of Adam WEISWEILER, whose Paris workshops supplied both the French and English Courts. A form of imitation lacquer, known as JAPANNING, was developed in England during the last quarter of the 17th c. and practised extensively in Europe and America from then on. Although using a different medium, some of the best 18th-c. work was comparable in quality with genuine Oriental lacquer; but the subsequent use of inferior materials and poor workmanship eventually gave it a bad name. Nevertheless japanning continued to be used in an unpretentious but often pleasing manner throughout the 19th c., applied both to lightly constructed wooden articles and to PAPIER-MÂCHÉ ware. Raised decoration in gold or silver on a coloured ground was usually Oriental in intent.

(*g*) *Gilding* has been one of the most popular methods of decorating wood, by reason both of the immutability of gold and of the strength of the bond which can be obtained between the two materials. The method of water gilding used on much of the best furniture was long and expensive, requiring the meticulous preparation of a gesso base on a suitable wood such as pine or lime. To this the gold film was attached with special size and brilliantly burnished. The less skilful process of oil burnishing produced an inferior flat appearance, while silvering, which was considerably cheaper, had the disadvantage of being liable to tarnish.

Although painting, lacquering and gilding all concealed the surface appearance of the wood, the underlying structure was by no means unimportant and it is a mistake to assume that inferior materials and unsatisfactory constructional methods could have been hidden for any length of time. While the production of a fine piece in any of these media demanded a high degree of collaboration between the different craftsmen involved and a deep-rooted understanding of the behaviour of the materials they were manipulating, it is also clear that the basic form, its suitability for its purpose, the balance, proportion and harmony of its parts, and its style, were all the prime responsibility of the craftsman in wood. Good form was quite as important as surface treatment.

The insensitive use of machine methods during the 19th c. and the growing separation of the architect and designer from those responsible for production, resulted in a decline in craftsmanship and design, which even the articulate and explosive William Morris could not entirely stem—for the lowest ebb was yet to be reached during the inter-war years. Nevertheless towards the end of the century there was a general revival of interest in craftsmanship and especially in the older tradition of joiner-made furniture, which had grown out of the Middle Ages and had been developed subsequently in country districts in Europe and America to satisfy local needs independent of the fine cabinet-making intended for fashionable society. Joinery techniques have to be applied when using solid timber because of the need to adapt to the essential instability of the material which results from its hygroscopic nature and which is rarely totally eliminated. Allowance has to be made at every point in the design for the possibility of expansion and contraction. This is far more than a mere technical consideration, for the manner whereby movement is allowed determines many of the design features peculiar to furniture made of solid wood. Different panelling techniques, each producing a different visual effect, the characteristic breaks between carcase and stand, or between drawer front and carcase edge, often stressed by bead, moulding or inlay, are all elements dictated first by practical considerations but exploited also for their decorative value and for the interest which they afford the user and the craftsman.

The example of door construction may be used to show the relationship, through the selection of appropriate material for the parts, between the structural and visual elements of design. Uneven shrinkage sets up stresses in timber during seasoning and this can cause a number of defects, of which warping is perhaps the most common. In quarter-sawn timber, however, the stresses either side of the board are equalized and maximal stability is achieved. It is appropriate, therefore, for two reasons, to use quartered timber for a door-frame: its natural stability prevents twisting and distortion, while its straight, parallel grain reduces the possibility of visual distortion and emphasizes the strong rectangular shape. The less stable, tangentially sawn material on the other hand is equally suitable for the panels, as the irregular wildness of its grain is desirable for its beauty, while its tendency to warp is controlled by reducing its thickness and so destroying its strength while it is held firmly in an adequately thick frame. In this and in many other such situations the needs of the design and the nature of the material are brought into relation.

The preference for through or open joints which is seen in much early hand-made modern furniture (see FURNITURE, MODERN) derived initially from a respect for direct, honest methods of assembly. The skill and technical excellence displayed is often superb, combining strength with delicacy and representing craftsmanship of a highly developed and advanced kind, quite distinct from dead mechanical precision. The decorative possibilities of exposed joints were quickly recognized, for the interlocking of the parts in rhythmic patterns emphasizes relationships and gives visual as well as physical strength to significant points in the design. It is also a source of satisfaction to the craftsman, an opportunity for him to exercise his skill, his imagination and his visual judgement.

Another main source of inspiration was the wood itself, for never previously had more conscious use been made of the natural beauty of hardwoods than in the work of the English Cotswold School. Although oak and walnut have a special place in this work, chestnut, yew, cherry and tropical hardwoods were freely used, as well as veneers when the occasion demanded. Decoration was often closely linked with construction or function and was used, not to obscure or to replace, but to display the qualities inherent in the timber. In the simplest pieces intended for use in country cottages, however plain and severe they may appear at first, there is rarely absent some small decorative feature which would give the craftsman pleasure to execute and raise the job above the mere utilitarian level. In the more elaborate pieces there is an exuberance and strength which make them a delight.

6. INDUSTRIAL PRODUCTION. One of the great charms of wood to the craftsman is its individuality. The most valued species are those in which some unpredictable quality of colour, grain or figure is most likely to occur. Industrial methods, on the contrary, require a uniform material, every piece of which has the same constant, stable and even characteristics. An early form of mass production, in which the division of labour was commonly practised, occurred in the making of Windsor chairs for which coppice timber provided a material of sufficiently uniform working characteristics and size, while steam-bending produced the curved hoops which could not be found in nature. In the mid 19th c.

steam-bent beech made possible industrial mass production of cheap, light and serviceable bentwood chairs, designed by Michael Thonet. Today curved members are usually produced by bending a number of thin wooden laminae and bonding them together under pressure, using either shaped formers or vacuum forming techniques. Early examples of the application of this method to chair-making were by Alvar AALTO and Marcel Breuer in the 1930s (see FURNITURE, MODERN). Where large surfaces are required plywood, blockboard and other manufactured boards satisfy the need, providing uniformity and stability, but only at the expense of those qualities which give wood its individuality and character. Indeed each of these techniques, although using natural wood as its raw material, produces a new material which in certain respects no longer behaves like wood. In some cases, prior to veneering, it does not even look like wood. Industrial veneering techniques themselves have little in common with traditional methods, for they require a minimum of skill in the actual application of the veneer to the artificial board—a process resembling mechanical wallpapering—and they produce an effect which, until closely examined, resembles solid wood, unlike traditional hand-veneering, which is always readily identifiable as such.

Mass-produced furniture must, therefore, be designed on different principles from those which belong to the craft traditions, and it must be judged according to its own standards. Skill is still needed but skill in the organization of the production line and in the design, manufacture and maintenance of the machines, rather than in the direct manipulation of the material. If the qualities inherent in solid wood are no longer valued, the designer has no special mandate to employ manufactured materials which are wood-based; his needs may be well satisfied by synthetic materials which have been evolved specially to suit mass-production methods.

The inevitable consequence is that the industrial product is impersonal, whatever values it may possess otherwise, and it is perhaps in this respect that it differs most from the product of hand craftsmanship. The modern craftsman in wood has made increasing use in recent years of machines of different kinds and of manufactured boards and laminated techniques, all of which increase the range of his work by suggesting new ways of using wood and by offering new opportunities for decorative treatment. But he has shown himself able to do this without loss of individuality because he uses the machine differently from the industrialist, not as a means of mass production but as an extension of his hands, as much under his immediate control as any other tool. Thus he pursues his independent course, taking advantage of the products of contemporary technology as far as they are useful to him, as he has always done, but still retaining in his work that personal, expressive element which justifies his claim to the titles both of designer–craftsman and of artist–craftsman.

318, 529.

WOTTON BINDINGS. Bindings made for Sir Thomas Wotton (1521–87), a book-collector sometimes known as the 'English GROLIER', on account of his use of the motto 'Thomas Wottoni et Amicorum'. He was father of Sir Henry Wotton, the poet–diplomat. Wotton's bindings were made in Paris or by Parisian craftsmen in London, or possibly at Canterbury near his estate at Boughton Malherbe. French decorative motifs are combined with two armorial stamps. The smaller stamp containing four quarterings, was used on a group of bindings made after 1551 in a style akin to that of Grolier with curvilinear interlacings and black-painted STRAPWORK. The Wotton armorial is one of a small number of early armorial bindings in which colour or metal is used, the stamp being impressed in silver and black.

WRIGGLE. Decoration in the form of a zig-zag pattern, used chiefly on pewter. It is executed by rocking a narrow, chisel-shaped tool from side to side as the design is traced out. See PEWTER (DOMESTIC).

WRIGHT, FRANK LLOYD (1869–1959). American architect and theorist. His views, particularly as expressed in his lecture *The Art and Craft of the Machine* (1901), had considerable influence on the ARTS AND CRAFTS MOVEMENT. For his influence on furniture design see FURNITURE (MODERN).

Y

YALE, LINUS, Sr. Born in Middletown, Connecticut, in 1797, he set up as a lock-maker *c.* 1840 and was responsible for the cylinder lock which represented the most important advance in security lock-making during the 19th c. His aims were improved security against lock-picking and a small and handy key. Operated by a round, fluted key, which acted upon a pin-tumbler mechanism, his lock embodied the principle of the ancient Egyptian peg system. His son, LINUS YALE, Jr. (1821–68), after beginning as an artist turned to lock-making and founded The Yale Lock Manufacturing Company. Like his father he gave much attention to designing security bank keys. His Yale Infallible Bank Lock (1852) operated with a changeable key, i.e. a key the parts of which could be separated and reassembled to change the combination. The Yale Magic Bank Lock was an elaboration of this, the key having a detachable pod. The Yale Double Treasury Bank Lock, a still more complicated design, represents the high-water mark of intricate bank locks before the advent of the keyless Dial or Combination lock, anticipated in the Yale Monitor Bank Lock (1862) and realized in the Yale Double Dial Bank Lock (1863), whose principles became standard for bank lock construction. Yale also adapted the pin-tumbler mechanism to the improvement of small security locks for general use. See also LOCKS AND KEYS.

939.

YAYOI. A style of Japanese wheel-turned pottery made from *c.* the 3rd c. B.C. to *c.* the 3rd c. A.D. It is smoother in finish but less imaginative in design than the earlier pottery and it bears geometrical incised ornament. The tradition was continued to *c.* A.D. 600 in the *haniwa*, originally hollow cylinders but later sculptured figures, erected on burial mounds. See JAPAN (POTTERY AND PORCELAIN).

Z

ZAFFRE. See COBALT.

ZESHIN, SHIBATA. See JAPAN (INRŌ).

ZIRCON. A mineral, zirconium silicate, certain crystalline varieties of which have been prized as gemstones since the 2nd millennium B.C. The word is derived from the Arabic *zargun* and the translucent, colourless or smoky-grey type of zircons from Ceylon are still known alternatively as *jargons* or *jargoons*. The transparent red, orange, yellow types are the *jacinth* (or *hyacinth*) of classical antiquity. When heat-treated the yellow-brown zircon can be changed to blue, as was done in Siam, or can be rendered colourless.

Gem varieties of zircon are found in Indo-China, Burma, Ceylon, Australia and New Zealand. The zircon has a hardness index of 7½ on the MOHS SCALE. It has an adamantine lustre, fire and brilliance of a DIAMOND and colourless zircons have in the past been confused with diamonds.

ZWISCHENGOLDGLAS (German, 'gold between glass'). A technique of decorative GLASS developed in Bohemia *c.* 1730. The outside surface of a glass vessel, often a small straight-sided beaker, was covered with gold leaf (or sometimes with silver leaf). Another glass was fitted round this to protect the design and the two were cemented together. The outer surface was often cut with narrow flutes running vertically and the designs took the form of hunting, domestic or commemorative scenes. Prominent among the craftsmen who used this technique was Johann Joseph MILDNER. See also VERRE ÉGLOMISÉ.

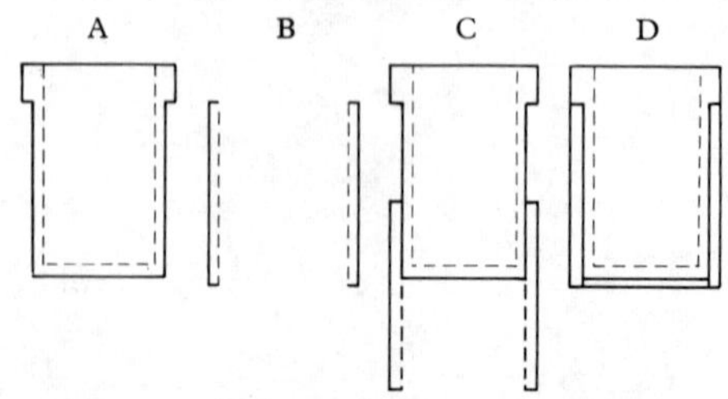

A. The inner glass with engraved gold foil on the outside; B. Outer casing; C. 'A' and 'B' partly assembled; D. The glass complete with the outer casing and the base medallion fixed in place with an adhesive

BIBLIOGRAPHY

(When no place of publication is given the book was published in London)

1. ABBEY, S., pseud. (BEVAN, W. N. STATON-). *The goldsmith's and silversmith's handbook*, 1968 (1952)
2. ABRAHAMS, E. B. *Greek dress*, 1908
3. AITCHISON, L. *A history of metals*, 2 vols., 1961
4. ALDRED, C. *Jewels of the pharaohs*, 1971
5. ALFORD, LADY M. M. *Needlework as art*, 1886
6. ALLEMAGNE, H.-R. D'. *Histoire des jouets*, Paris, 1903
7. ALLEN, B. S. *Tides in English taste, 1619–1800*, Cambridge, Mass., 1937
8. AMERICAN SOCIETY OF LANDSCAPE ARCHITECTS. *Landscape Architecture, Journal of the American Society of Landscape Architects*, 1910–
9. AMIRANASHVILI, S. *Medieval Georgian enamels of Russia*, New York, 1964
10. ANDERE, M. *Old needlework boxes and tools*, Newton Abbot, 1971
11. ANDREWS, F. H. 'Ancient Chinese figured silks, excavated by Sir Aurel Stein at ruined sites of Central Asia', *Burlington Magazine*, July–September 1920
12. ANGELOGLOU, M. *A history of make-up*, 1970
13. ANTAL, F. *Classicism and romanticism*, 1966
14. APPLETON, LEROY H. *American Indian design and decoration*, London and New York, 1971
15. ARIAS, P. A. *A history of French vase painting*, 1962
16. ARMSON, J. *The encyclopaedia of furniture*, 1966 (1938)
17. ARMSTRONG, A. E. *Robert Estienne, royal printer*, Cambridge, 1954
18. ARTAMANOV, M. I. *Treasures from Scythian tombs in the Hermitage Museum*, 1969
19. ARTS AND CRAFTS EXHIBITION SOCIETY, THE. *Arts and crafts essays*, by members of the Arts and Crafts Exhibition Society, 1893
20. ARTS COUNCIL OF GREAT BRITAIN, THE. *The age of neo-classicism*, 1970
21. ASH, D. *Dictionary of British antique silver*, 1972
22. ASHTON, SIR A. L. B. *Samplers*, 1926
23. — (ed.). *The art of India and Pakistan*, 1950
24. ASLIN, E. *Nineteenth century English furniture*, 1962
25. ASSER, J. *Historic hairdressing*, 1966
26. ATTWATER, W. A. *Leathercraft*, 1961
27. AUBOYER, J. *Daily life in ancient India*, 1965
28. AUGUSTI, S. *I colori pompeiani*, Rome, 1967
29. AVERY, C. L. *Early American silver*, New York, 1930
30. AYER, J. *Oriental costume*, 1973
31. AYERS, J. G. *The Seligman collection of oriental art, Chinese and Korean pottery and porcelain*, vol. 2, 1964
32. AYRTON, M. and SILCOCK, A. *Wrought iron and its decorative uses*, 1929
33. BABELON, J. F. L. *Great coins and medals*, 1959
34. *L'Orfèvrerie française*, Paris, 1946
35. BĀBUR, EMPEROR OF HINDUSTAN. *Memoirs of Zehīr-ed-Din Muhammad Bābur*. Trans. Leyden, J. and Erskine, W., 1921 (1826)
36. BADIN, J. *La Manufacture de tapisseries de Beauvais*, Paris, 1909
37. BAERWALD, M. and MAHONEY, T. *The story of jewelry*, London and New York, 1960
38. BAGROW, L. *History of cartography*. Revised and enlarged by R. A. Skelton, 1964
39. BAHR, L. F. (ed.). *Printing in privacy, a review of recent activity among American private presses*, Grosse Pointe Park, 1960
40. BAILLIE, G. H. *Watchmakers and clockmakers of the world*, 1951 (1929)
41. BAINBRIDGE, H. C. *Peter Carl Fabergé*, 1966
42. BAKER, H. S. *Furniture in the ancient world*, 1966
43. BALLANTYNE, A. R. *Robert Hancock and his works*, 1885
44. BALSDON, J. P. V. D. *Life and leisure in ancient Rome*, 1969
45. BARKER, N. *Stanley Morison*, 1972
46. BARNARD, E. A. B. and WACE, A. J. B. 'The Sheldon tapestry weavers and their work', *Archaeologia*, lxxviii, 1928
47. BARSALI, I. B. *European enamels*, London and New York, 1964
48. BASHAM, A. L. *The wonder that was India*, 1967 (1954)
49. BATTERSBY, M. *The decorative thirties*, 1972
50. — *The decorative twenties*, 1970
51. BAUER, J. and A. *A book of jewels*, 1966
52. BAYER, H., GROPIUS, W. H. and GROPIUS, I. (eds.). *Bauhaus, 1919–28*, Boston, 1952 (New York, 1938)
53. BEARD, G. W. *Modern glass*, 1968

54. BEAUJON, P. pseud. (WARDE, BEATRICE). 'The "Garamond" types, sixteenth and seventeenth century sources considered', *The Fleuron*, v, 1926
55. BECK, R. J. *New Zealand jade*, Wellington, 1970
56. BECKWITH, J. G. *The art of Constantinople*, 1968 (1961)
57. BEHN, F. *Musikleben im Altertum und frühen Mittelalter*, Stuttgart, 1954
58. BENNETT, W. C. *Ancient arts of the Andes*, New York, 1954
59. BENTLEY, K. W. *The natural pigments*, New York, 1960
60. BERNARD, A. *Geofroy Tory, peintre et graveur*, Paris, 1865 (1857). English trans. by G. B. Ives, Boston, Mass., 1909
61. BERTIN, J. *Sémiologie graphique*, Paris, 1967
62. BHUSHAN, J. B. *The costumes and textiles of India*, Bombay, 1958
63. BICKERTON, L. M. *Eighteenth-century English drinking glasses*, 1971
64. BIGMORE, E. C. and WYMAN, C. W. H. *A bibliography of printing*, New York, 1945
65. BILLING, A. *The science of gems, jewels, coins and medals*, 1875 (1867)
66. BIRD, J. B. and BENNET, W. C. *Andean culture history*, American Museum of Natural History, Handbook Series 15, 1960
67. BJERKOE, J. A. *The cabinetmakers of America*, New York, 1957
68. BLACKMORE, H. L. *Guns and rifles of the world*, 1965
69. — *Hunting weapons*, 1971
70. BLACKSHAW, H. and BRIGHTMAN, R. *Dictionary of dyeing and textile printing*, 1961
71. BLADES, W. *The biography and typography of William Caxton*, 1882 (1877)
72. BLAIR, C. *European and American arms*, 1962
73. — *European armour*, 1972 (1958)
74. — *Pistols of the world*, 1968
75. — *The silvered armour of Henry VIII in the Tower of London*, reprinted from *Archaeologia*, xcix, 1965
76. BLAIR, M. *The Paisley shawl*, Paisley, 1904
77. BLAKE, N. F. *Caxton and his world*, 1969
78. BOARDMAN, J. *Archaic Greek gems*, 1968
79. — *Engraved gems: the Ionides collection*, 1968
80. — *Greek gems and finger rings, early bronze age to late classical*, 1970
81. BOASE, T. S. R. *English art, 1800–1870*, Oxford, 1959
82. BOCCIA, L. G. and COELHO, E. T. *L'arte dell'armatura in Italia*, Milan, 1967
83. BODE, W. A. VON and KÜHNEL, E. *Antique rugs from the Near East*, 1958
84. BOEHN, M. U. VON. *Dolls and puppets*, New York, 1966
85. — *Modes and manners*, 5 vols., 1932
86. BOGER, L. A. *The complete guide to furniture styles*, 1961
87. — *A dictionary of world pottery and porcelain*, 1972
88. BOLLERT, M. *Lederschnittbände des XIV. Jahrhunderts*, Leipzig, 1925
89. BOLTON, E. S. and COE, E. J. *American samplers*, Boston, 1921
90. BONDY, S. S. *La cerámica peruana prehispánica*, Mexico, 1964
91. BONNIN, A. *Tutenag and paktong*, 1924
92. BORRADAILE, V. and R. *The student's Cennini*, Brighton, 1942
93. BOUCHER, F. *A history of costume in the West*, 1967
94. BOULNOIS, L. *The silk road*, 1966
95. BRADBURY, F. *History of old Sheffield plate*, 1912
96. BRADFIELD, N. *Costume in detail 1730–1930*, 1968
97. BRADFORD, E. D. S. *Four centuries of European jewellery*, Feltham, 1967 (1953)
98. BRAILSFORD, J. W. *The Mildenhall treasure*, 1955 (1947)
99. BRAIN, R. and POLLOCK, A. *Bangwa funerary sculpture*, 1971
100. BREPOHL, E. *Theorie und Praxis des Goldschmieds*, Leipzig, 1962
101. BRIGGS, A. (ed.). *William Morris, selected writings and designs*, 1973 (1962)
102. BRIGHAM, W. T. 'Ka Hana Kapa. The making of bark-cloth in Hawaii.' *Memoirs of the Bernice Pauahi Bishop Museum, Honolulu*, vol. III, 1911
103. BRIQUET, C. M. *Les Filigranes*, Amsterdam, 1968 (Paris, 1907)
104. BRITISH MUSEUM. *Guide to the exhibition illustrating Greek and Roman life*, 1929 (1920)
105. — *Treasures from Romania*, exhibition catalogue, 1971
106. BRITTEN, F. J. *Old clocks and watches and their makers*, 1956 (1894)
107. BROWN, L. A. *The story of maps*, Boston, 1949, London, 1951
108. BRUCE, D. *Sun Pictures: the Hill-Adamson calotypes*, London and New York, 1973
109. BRUHN, A. *Der Schwertfeger Gottfried Leygebe*, Copenhagen, 1945
110. BRUNNER, H. *Old table silver*, 1967
111. BUCHNER, A. *Mechanical musical instruments*, 1959
112. BUCK, A. M. *Victorian costume and costume accessories*, 1961
113. BUDAY, G. *The history of the Christmas card*, 1964 (1954)
114. BUECHNER, T. S. *Glass from the ancient world, the Ray Winfield Smith collection*, Corning Museum of Glass, New York, 1957
115. BÜHLER, A. Articles in *CIBA Review*, nos. 30 and 33, 1940
116. BULGARI, C. G. *Argentieri, gemmari e orafi d'Italia*, 2 vols., Rome, 1958–9
117. BURFORD, A. M. *Craftsmen in Greek and Roman society*, 1972
118. — *The Greek temple builders at Epidauros*, Liverpool, 1969
119. BUSHELL, S. W. *Chinese art*, 1909 (1904)

120. BUSHNELL, G. H. S. *Ancient arts of the Americans*, 1965
121. — and DIGBY, A. *Ancient American pottery*, 1955
122. CAMMANN, S. VAN R. *China's dragon robes*, New York, 1952
123. — *Archives of the Chinese Art Society of America*, vol. xvi, 1962
124. CAPART, J. *L'art égyptien, choix de documents*, vol. iv, Brussels, 1947
125. CAPON, E. and MACQUITTY, W. *Princes of jade*, 1973
126. CARLINE, R. *Pictures in the post*, 1971
127. CARSON, R. A. G. *Coins, ancient, medieval and modern*, 1962
128. CARSWELL, J. *Kühtuhya tiles*, Oxford, 1972
129. CARTER, H. G. *A view of early typography*, Oxford, 1969
130. CAVE, O. *English folk embroidery*, London 1965, New York, 1966
131. CAVE, R. *The private press*, 1971
132. CENNINI, CENNINO. *Il libro dell'arte* (*The craftsman's handbook*), ed. and trans. by D. V. Thompson, 2 vols. New Haven, 1932–3, London, 1933
133. CERAM, C. W. pseud. (MAREK, K. W.). *Archaeology of the cinema*, 1965
134. CHAMBERS, D. (ed.). *Private press books*, 1971
135. CHAPUIS, A. and others. *Histoire de la boîte à musique*, Lausanne, 1955
136. CHARBONNEAUX, J. *Greek bronzes*, 1962
137. CHARLES, R. *Continental porcelain*, 1964
138. CHARLESTON, R. J. 'Han damasks', *Oriental Art*, vol. I, no. 2, 1948
139. — *Roman pottery*, 1955
140. — (ed.). *World ceramics*, 1968
141. CHOTTO, K. *Handmade papers of Japan*, Tokyo, 1963
142. CHRISTIE, A. G. I. *English medieval embroidery*, Oxford, 1938
143. CHURCH, SIR A. H. *The chemistry of paints and painting*, 1915 (1890)
144. CHURCHILL, W. A. *Watermarks in paper in Holland, England, France, etc.*, Amsterdam, 1935
145. CIBA REVIEW. 'Japanese resist-dyeing techniques', articles by K. Tonomura and J. Langewis no. 4, 1967
146. CLAIR, C. *Christopher Plantin*, 1960
147. CLARK, H. F. *The English landscape garden*, 1948
148. CLARK, J. E. T. *Musical boxes, a history and an appreciation*, 1961 (1948)
149. CLARKE, L. J. *The craftsman in textiles*, 1968
150. CLAYTON, M. *The collector's dictionary of silver and gold of Great Britain and North America*, London and New York, 1971
151. CLEVELAND, H. W. S. *Landscape architecture as applied to the wants of the West*, Pittsburgh, 1965
152. CLIFFORD, A. *Cut-steel and Berlin iron jewellery*, 1971
153. CLOUGH, E. A. *Bookbinding for librarians*, 1957
154. CLUTTON, C. and DANIELS, G. *Watches*, 1965
155. COCHE DE LA FERTÉ, E. *Les Bijoux antiques*, Paris, 1956
156. COLBY, A. *Quilting*, 1968
157. — *Samplers*, 1964
158. COLES, J. M. and HIGGS, E. S. *The archaeology of early man*, 1969
159. COLLINGWOOD, P. *The techniques of rug weaving*, 1968
160. CONNOISSEUR PERIOD GUIDES, THE. *The Regency*, 1968
161. COOK, C. *The life and work of Robert Hancock, 18th century engraver, etc.*, 1948
162. — *The life and work of Robert Hancock: Supplement*, 1955
163. COOPER, E. *A history of pottery*, 1973
164. COPPER DEVELOPMENT ASSOCIATION. *Copper through the ages*, 1934
165. CORNELIUS, C. O. *Furniture masterpieces of Duncan Phyfe*, New York, 1922
166. COTTERELL, H. H. *Old pewter, its makers and marks*, 1963 (1929)
167. — *Pewter down the ages*, 1932
168. COUISSIN, P. *Les Armes romaines*, Paris, 1926
169. COX, J. S. *An illustrated dictionary of hairdressing and wigmaking*, 1966
170. COYSH, A. W. *Blue and white transfer ware 1780–1840*, Newton Abbot, 1970
171. CRANSTONE, B. A. L. *Melanesia, a short ethnography*, 1961
172. CRAUZAT, E. DE. *La Reliure française de 1900 à 1925*, vol. 1, 1932
173. CRAWFORD, T. S. *A history of the umbrella*, Newton Abbot, 1970
174. CRONE, G. R. *Maps and their makers*, 1968 (1953)
175. CROTCH, W. J. B. *The prologues and epilogues of Caxton*, 1928
176. CULFF, R. *The world of toys*, 1969
177. CUMHAILL, P. W. *Investing in clocks and watches*, 1967
178. CUNNINGTON, C. W. and P. *Handbook of English costume in the 19th century*, 1966 (1959)
179. — — and BEARD, C. *A dictionary of English costume, 900–1900*, 1960
180. CUNYNGHAME, E. H. H. S. *European enamels*, 1906
181. CUSHION, J. P. *Continental china*, 1970
182. — *Pottery and porcelain*, 1972
183. — and HONEY, W. B. *Handbook of pottery and porcelain marks*, 1956
184. CUZNER, B. *A silversmith's manual*, 1935
185. DALTON, O. M. *Byzantine art and archaeology*, Oxford, 1911
186. — *The treasure of the Oxus*, 1964 (1905)
187. DANIEL, D. *Cut and engraved glass, 1771–1905*, New York, 1950
188. DANKERMAN, C. C. *Sèvres*, London and New York, 1970

189. DARK, P. J. C. *Benin art and technology*, Oxford, 1973

190. DAUMAS, M. *Scientific instruments of the seventeenth and eighteenth centuries and their makers*, 1972

191. DAVENPORT, C. J. H. *Roger Payne*, Chicago, 1929

192. DAVENPORT, M. *The book of costume*, 2 vols., New York, 1948

193. DAVIES, D. W. *The world of the Elseviers, 1580–1712*, The Hague, 1954

194. DAVIES, H. W. *Devices of the early printers, 1457–1560*, 1935

195. DAVIS, F. *Continental glass. From Roman to modern times*, 1972

196. DAWSON, L. E. 'Slip casting: a ceramic technique invented in ancient Peru', *Nawpa Pacha* ii, Berkeley, Calif., 1964

197. DAY, F. H. CRIPPS- (ed.). *Fragmenta armentaria* 1, Frome, 1934–45

198. DAY, K. (ed.). *Book typography, 1815–1965*, 1966

199. DAY, L. F. *William Morris and his art, Art Journal*, extra number, 1899

200. DELDERFIELD, E. R. *British inn signs and their stories*, Dawlish, 1965

201. — *Introduction to inn signs*, Newton Abbot, 1969

202. DELIEB, E. *The great silver manufactory*, London and New York, 1972

203. DENNIS, F. *Three centuries of French domestic silver*, New York, 1960

204. DE VINNE, T. L. *The invention of printing*, London and New York, 1877

205. DEVOE, S. S. *English papier mâché of the Georgian and Victorian periods*, London and Middletown, Conn., 1971

206. DICKERSON, J. *Raku handbook*, London and New York, 1972

207. DICKIE, J. 'The Hispano-Arab garden: its philosophy and function', *Bulletin of the School of Oriental and African studies, University of London*, vol. xxxi, 1968

208. DICKINSON, H. W. *Matthew Boulton*, Cambridge, 1937

209. DICKINSON, J. Y. *The book of diamonds*, New York, 1965

210. DIGBY, A. *Maya jades*, British Museum Publication, 1964

211. DILBY, A. U. *Oriental rugs and carpets*, 1960 (1931)

212. DILLMONT, T. DE. *Encyclopedia of needlework*, Mulhouse, 1930 (Dornach, 1890)

213. DILLON, H. A. L., VISCOUNT (ed.). *An Almain armourer's album, selections from an original manuscript in the Victoria and Albert Museum*, 1905

214. DISSELHOFF, H.-D. *Ancient America*, 1961

215. DOESBURG, T. VAN. Principles of neo-plastic art, 1971 (1969)

216. DONNAN, C. B. 'Moche ceramic technology', *Nawpa Pacha* iii, Berkeley, Calif., 1965

217. DONNELLY, P. J. *Blanc de chine*, 1969

218. DORMOY, M. 'Les reliures de Legrain à la bibliothèque Jacques Doucet', *Le Portique* no. iii, 1946

219. DOWLE, A. and FINN, P. *Coins*, 1970

220. DOWNS, J. *American furniture*, New York, 1952

221. DRIVAL, E. VAN. *Les Tapisseries d'Arras*, 1878 (1864)

222. DUBOSC, J.-P. 'Contribution à l'étude des tapisseries d'époque Sung', *Artibus Asiae*, vol. xi, 1948

223. DUFF, E. G. 'The bindings of Thomas Wotton', *The Library*, third series, vol. i, 1910

224. EARLE, A. M. *Two centuries of costume in America 1620–1820*, 2 vols., New York, 1970 (1903)

225. EASBY, E. K. *Pre-Columbian jade from Costa Rica*, New York, 1968

226. EDE, C. (ed.). *The art of the book. Some records of work carried out in Europe and the U.S.A. 1939–1950*, London and New York, 1951

227. EDOUART, A. A. C. F. *A treatise on silhouette likenesses*, Cork, 1835

228. EDWARDS, A. C. *The Persian carpet*, 1953

229. EDWARDS, I. E. S. *Treasures of Tutankhamun*, 1972

230. EDWARDS, R. *The shorter dictionary of English furniture*, 1964

231. — and JOURDAIN, M. *Georgian cabinet-makers*, 1955 (1944)

232. — and MACQUOID, P. *The dictionary of English furniture*, 3 vols., 1954

233. — and RAMSEY, L. G. G. (eds.). *The connoisseur's complete period guides*, 1968

234. EGERTON, W. EARL. *A description of Indian and Oriental armour*, 1896

235. ELDERKIN, K. MCK. 'Jointed dolls in antiquity', *American Journal of Archaeology*, vol. xxxiv, 1930

236. ELIOSOFON, E. and FAGG, W. B. *The sculpture of Africa*, 1958

237. ENCYCLOPEDIA OF ISLAM, 1913–1939. Leiden and London, 1954

238. ENTHOVEN, J. *The stitches of creative embroidery*, New York, 1964

239. ENTWISLE, E. A. *The book of wallpaper*, Bath, 1970 (London, 1954)

240. — *A literary history of wallpaper*, 1960

241. ERAS, V. J. M. *Locks and keys throughout the ages*, Amsterdam, 1957

242. ERDMANN, K. *Oriental carpets, an account of their history*, 1961

243. — *Seven hundred years of Oriental carpets*, 1970

244. ERIKSEN, S. 'Lalive de Jully's furniture "à la grecque"', *Burlington Magazine*, 1961

245. EVANS, J. *English jewellery from the 5th century A.D. to 1800*, 1921

246. — *A history of jewellery, 1100–1870*, 1970 (1953)

247. — *Huguenot goldsmiths of England and Ireland*, 1933

248. EVANS, J. *Magical jewels of the Middle Ages and the Renaissance*, Oxford, 1922

249. — *Pattern in western Europe 1180–1900*, 2 vols., Oxford, 1931

250. FASTNEDGE, R. *English furniture styles, from 1500 to 1830*, 1962 (1955)

251. — *Sheraton furniture*, 1962

252. FAWCETT, C. H. *Dolls*, Boston, Mass., 1964

253. FEBVRE, L.-P.-V. and MARTIN, H.-J. *L'Apparition du livre*, Paris, 1958

254. FEDDERSEN, M. *Chinese decorative art*, 1961

255. — *Japanese decorative art*, 1962

256. FENAILLE, M. *État général des tapisseries de la Manufacture de Gobelins, 1600–1900*, 6 vols., Paris, 1903–23

257. FERNALD, H. E. *Chinese court costumes*, Royal Ontario Museum of Archaeology, Toronto, 1946

258. FFOULKES, J. C. *Decorative ironwork of XVIIth and XVIIIth centuries*, 1911

259. FINLEY, R. E. *Old patchwork quilts and the women who made them*, London and Philadelphia, 1929

260. FLETCHER, W. Y. *Foreign bookbindings in the British Museum*, 1896

261. FLOWER, M. *Victorian jewellery*, 1967

262. FOLNESICS, J. and BRAUN, E. W. *Geschichte der K.K. Wiener Porzellanmanufaktur*, Kaiserlich-Königlich Österreichisches Museum für Kunst und Industrie, Vienna, 1907

263. FOLSON, R. S. *Handbook of Greek pottery*, 1967

264. FORBES, R. J. *Metallurgy in antiquity*, Leiden, 1950

265. — *Studies in ancient technology*, vols. 1–9, Leiden, 1954–64

266. — *Studies in ancient technology*, vol. 3, Leiden, 1955

267. — *Studies in ancient technology*, vol. 4, Leiden, 1956

268. — *Studies in ancient technology*, vol. 5, Leiden, 1957

269. — *Studies in ancient technology*, vols. 7 and 8, Leiden, 1963 and 1964

270. FORMAN, W. and B., and DARK, P. *Benin art*, 1960

271. FOSHAG, W. F. *Mineralogical studies in Guatemalan jade*, Washington, 1957

272. FOSTER, G. M. 'The sociology of pottery: questions and hypotheses arising from contemporary Mexican work', in *Ceramics and man*, ed. F. R. Matson, Chicago, 1965, London, 1966

273. FOSTER, K. *Scent bottles*, 1966

274. FOUCHER, A. *L'Art gréco-bouddhique du Gandhâra*, 2 vols., Paris, 1905–41

275. FOX, H. M. *André Le Nôtre*, 1963

276. FRANK, E. B. *Old French ironwork*, Cambridge, Mass., 1950

277. FRANKLIN, C. *The private presses*, 1969

278. FRASER, LADY A. *Dolls*, 1963

279. — *A history of toys*, 1966

280. FREDERIKS, J. W. *Dutch silver*, 4 vols., The Hague, 1952–60

281. FRIEDBERG, R. *Gold coins of the world*, New York, 1958

282. GADDUM, P. W. *Silk*, Manchester, 1950

283. GAIBI, A. *Le armi da fuoco portatili italiane dalle origini al Risorgimento*, Milan, 1962

284. — 'Biografiske undersøgelser om familien Cominazzi', *Vaabenhistoriske Aarbøger* 11, Copenhagen, 1962–4

285. GALL, G. *Leder im europäischen Kunsthandwerk*, Brunswick, 1965

286. GANS, M. H. and KLINKHAMER, T. M. D. DE WIT-. *Dutch silver*, 1961

287. GARDNER, P. *Archaeology and the types of Greek coins*, Chicago, 1965

288. GARNER, SIR H. M. *Chinese and Japanese cloisonné enamels*, 1970 (1962)

289. — *Oriental blue and white*, 1970 (1954)

290. — and MEDLEY, M. *Chinese art in three-dimensional colour*, 1972

291. GASKELL, J. P. W. *John Baskerville, a bibliography*, Cambridge, 1959

292. GAUTHIER, M.-M.-S. *Émaux limousins champlevés des XIIe, XIIIe et XIVe siècles*, Paris, 1950

293. GEIJER, A. 'Chinese silks exported to Russia in the 17th century', *Bulletin of the Museum of Far Eastern Antiquities, Stockholm*, no. xxv, 1953

294. — *Oriental textiles in Sweden*, Copenhagen, 1951

295. GENDERS, R. *A history of scent*, 1972

296. GERE, C. *Victorian jewellery design*, 1972

297. GERNSHEIM, H. and A. *The history of photography*, 1969 (1955)

298. GETTENS, R. J. and STOUT, G. L. *Painting materials*, London and New York, 1942

299. GIAVANOLI, R. 'Provincial Roman wall painting investigated by electron microscopy', *Archaeometry*, ii, 1969

300. GIBBS-SMITH, C. H. *The Bayeux tapestry*, forthcoming

301. GILBORN, G. A. *American furniture 1660–1725*, 1970

302. GLAISTER, G. A. *Glossary of the book*, 1960

303. GLOAG, J. E. *English furniture*, 1965

304. — *The Englishman's chair*, 1964

305. — *Guide to furniture styles English and French, 1450 to 1830*, 1972

306. — *Mr. Loudon's England*, Newcastle, 1970

307. — *A short dictionary of furniture*, 1969 (1952)

308. GODDEN, G. A. *British pottery and porcelain, 1780–1850*, 1963

309. — *Encyclopaedia of British pottery and porcelain marks*, 1964

310. — *Stevengraphs and other Victorian silk pictures*, 1971

311. GOEBEL, H. *Wandteppiche*, 3 vols., Leipzig, 1923–34

312. — *Tapestries of the Lowlands* (English trans. of *Wandteppiche*, part 1), New York, 1924

313. GOLDSCHMIDT, E. P. *Gothic and Renaissance bookbindings*, Niewkoop, 1967 (London, 1928)
314. GOLISH, V. DE. *Primitive India*, 1954
315. GOMPERTZ, G. ST. G. M. *Chinese celadon wares*, 1958
316. — *Korean pottery and porcelain of the Yi period*, 1968
317. GOODISON, N. *Ormolu, the work of Matthew Boulton*, 1974
318. GOODMAN, W. L. *The history of woodworking tools*, 1964
319. GORDON, L. *Peepshow into paradise, a history of children's toys*, 1953
320. GRANDJEAN, S. *Empire furniture 1800–1825*, 1966
321. — *L'Orfèvrerie du xixe siècle en Europe*, Paris, 1962
322. GRANDO, M. G. *Jewelry, form and technique*, London and New York, 1969
323. GRAY, B. *Early Chinese pottery and porcelain*, 1953
324. GREEN, D. B. *Grinling Gibbons, his work as carver and statuary, 1648–1721*, 1964
325. GREENE, V. *English dolls' houses*, 1955
326. GRÖBER, K. *Children's toys of bygone days*, 1932 (1928)
327. GROENMAN-VAN WAATERINGE, W. *Romeins Lederwerk uit Valkenburg*, Groningen, 1967
328. GROUT, D. J. *A history of Western music*, 1962
329. GROVES, S. *The history of needlework tools and accessories*, 1966
330. GUIFFREY, J.-M.-J. *Les Caffieri*, Paris, 1877
331. HABERLAND, W. *North America*, 1964
332. HADFIELD, M. *Gardening in Britain*, 1960
333. HAEDEKE, H.-U. *Metalwork*, 1970
334. HAKE, E. F. *English quilting old and new*, 1937
335. HAMBLY, G. *Cities of Mughal India*, 1968
336. HAMBLY, W. D. *The history of tattooing and its significance*, 1925
337. HAMBRUCH, P. *Oceanische Rindenstoffe*, Oldenburg, 1926
338. HAMMOND, A. *The book of chessmen*, 1950
339. HANSEN, H. H. *Costume cavalcade*, 1972 (1956)
340. HANSFORD, S. H. *Chinese carved jades*, 1968
341. — *Chinese jade carving*, 1950
342. HANSON, T. W. 'Edwards of Halifax' in *Book handbook*, no. 6, 1948
343. HARDEN, D. B. 'Ancient glass', *Archaeological Journal*, cxxv, 1968 and cxxvi, 1969
344. — and others. *Masterpieces of glass* (British Museum, exhibition catalogue), 1968
345. HARE, R. G. *The art and artists of Russia*, 1965
346. HARGRAVE, C. P. *A history of playing cards and a bibliography of cards and gaming*, London and New York, 1966 (1930)
347. HARLING, R. (ed.). *Modern furniture and decoration*, 1971
348. HARRIS, E. *The furniture of Robert Adam*, 1963
349. HARRIS, J. 'Early neo-classical furniture', *Furniture History*, vol. II, 1966
350. — *English decorative ironwork, 1610–1836*, 1960
351. HARRIS, J. R. 'Technology and materials' in *The legacy of Egypt*, 2nd edition ed. J. R. Harris, Oxford, 1971
352. HARRISON, M. *The history of the hat*, 1960
353. HARTMAN, J. M. *Chinese jade of five centuries*, Rutland, Vt., and Tokyo, 1969
354. HAVARD, H. *Les Boulle*, Paris, 1893
355. HAYES, W. C. *Scepter of Egypt*, vols. I and II, New York, 1953 and 1968
356. HAYWARD, H. 'The drawings of John Linnell in the Victoria and Albert Museum', *Furniture History*, vol. V, 1969
357. — *Thomas Johnson and English rococo*, 1964
358. — (ed.). *World furniture*, 1965
359. HAYWARD, J. F. *The art of the gunmaker*, 2 vols., 1962–3
360. — *Huguenot silver in England 1688–1727*, 1959
361. HEAL, SIR A. *The London furniture makers, 1660–1840*, 1953
362. — *The London goldsmiths 1200–1800*, Cambridge, 1937
363. HEAWOOD, E. *Watermarks, mainly of the 17th and 18th centuries*, Hilversum, 1950
364. HEIDELOFF, N. I. W. C. VAN. *Gallery of fashion, 1790–1822, from plates by Heideloff and Ackermann*, 1949
365. HEINZ, D. *Medieval tapestries*, 1967
366. HENDERSON, P. P. *William Morris, his life, work and friends*, 1973 (1962)
367. — (ed.). *The letters of William Morris*, 1950
368. HENZE, W. *Ornament, Dekor und Zeichen*, Dresden, 1958
369. HERBERT, A. P. *Sundials old and new*, 1967
370. HERBERTS, K. *Oriental lacquer*, 1962
371. HERDEG, W. (ed.). *Art in the watermark*, Zürich, 1952
372. HEYDENRYK, H. *The art and history of frames*, New York, 1963, London, 1964
373. — *The right frame*, New York, 1964
374. HICKMAN, P. *Two centuries of silhouettes*, 1971
375. HIGGINS, R. A. *Greek and Roman jewellery*, 1961
376. — *Jewellery from classical lands*, 1965
377. HILL, C. W. *Discovering picture postcards*, Tring, 1970
378. HILL, G. F. *Renaissance medals from the Samuel H. Kress collection*, revised by Graham Pollard, 1967
379. HILL, M. H. and BUCKNELL, P. A. *The evolution of fashion, pattern and cut from 1066 to 1930*, London and New York, 1967
380. HILLIER, B. *Art deco of the 20s and 30s*, London and New York, 1968
381. — *The world of art deco* (exhibition catalogue), Institute of Arts, Minneapolis, 1971

382. HILLIER, J. *Japanese emblems and designs*, Zürich, 1970
383. HILLIER, M. *Dolls and doll-makers*, 1968
384. HIMSWORTH, J. B. *The story of cutlery*, 1953
385. HINCKLEY, F. L. *A directory of antique furniture*, New York, 1953
386. HIORT, E. *Modern Danish silver*, 1954
387. HIPPLE, W. J. *The beautiful, the sublime and the picturesque in eighteenth-century British aesthetic theory*, Carbondale, 1957
388. HIRSCH, O. *A display of decorated papers from the collection of Olga Hirsch*, Cambridge, 1955
389. HITTI, P. K. *History of the Arabs*, 1970 (1937)
390. HLAVSA, O. *A book of type and design*, 1960
391. HOBSON, B. *Historic gold coins of the world*, 1971
392. HOBSON, G. D. *English bindings, 1490–1940, in the library of J. R. Abbey*, 1940
393. — *Maioli, Canevari and others*, 1926
394. — *Les Reliures à la fanfare*, Amsterdam, (1935)
395. HODGES, H. *Artifacts*, 1964
396. — *Technology in the ancient world*, 1970
397. HOEVER, O. *An encyclopaedia of ironwork*, 1962
398. — *A handbook of wrought iron*, 1962
399. HOFF, A. *Feuerwaffen*, 2 vols., Brunswick, 1969
400. HOFFMANN, M. *The warp-weighted loom*, Oslo, 1964
401. HOFMANN, F. H. *Geschichte der Bayerischen Porzellan-Manufaktur Nymphenburg*, 3 vols., Leipzig, 1921–3
402. HOGARTH, M. *Modern embroidery*, London and New York, 1933
403. HOLAS, B. *Industries et cultures en Côte d'Ivoire*, Abidjan, 1965 (Paris, 1960)
404. HOLLAND, V. B. *Hand coloured fashion plates, 1770–1899*, 1955
405. HOLSTEIN, P. P. H. *Contribution à l'étude des armes orientales*, 2 vols., Paris, 1931
406. HOLT, T. and V. *Picture postcards of the golden age*, 1971
407. HONEY, W. B. *Dresden china*, 1954 (1934)
408. — *European ceramic art*, 1963 (1952)
409. — *Glass: a handbook*, Victoria and Albert Museum Publication, 1946
410. — 'Gold-engraving under glass', *The Connoisseur*, xcii, 1933
411. HONOUR, P. H. *Cabinet makers and furniture designers*, 1969
412. — *Chinoiserie: the vision of Cathay*, 1961
413. — *Goldsmiths and silversmiths*, 1971
414. — *Neo-classicism*, 1968
415. HOPKINS, A. A. *The lure of the lock, treatise on the John Mossman collection*, Museum of the General Society of Mechanics and Tradesmen, New York, 1928
416. HOWE, B. *Lady with the green fingers, the life of J. Loudon*, 1961
417. HUGHES, G. *Modern jewelry*, 1968 (1963)
418. HUGHES, G. *Modern silver throughout the world 1880–1967*, London and New York, 1967
419. HUGHES, G. BERNARD. *Antique Sheffield plate*, 1970
420. — *Horse brasses*, 1956
421. HUGHES, T. *English domestic needlework, 1680–1860*, 1961
422. HUISH, M. B. *Samplers and tapestry embroideries*, 1913 (1900)
423. HUMBERT, C. *Ornamental design*, 1970
424. HUNTER, D. *Old papermaking in China and Japan*, Chillicothe, 1932
425. — *Papermaking, the history and technique of an ancient craft*, 1947
426. — *Paper-making through 18 centuries*, New York, 1930
427. HUSSEY, C. E. C. *English gardens and landscapes, 1700–1750*, 1967
428. — *The picturesque*, 1967 (London and New York, 1927)
429. HUTH, H. *Abraham und David Roentgen und ihre Neuwieder Möbelwerkstatt*, Deutscher Verein für Kunstwissenschaft, Berlin, 1928
430. HYAMS, E. *Capability Brown and Humphry Repton*, 1971
431. INSTITUTE OF LANDSCAPE ARCHITECTS. *Journal*, 1934–
432. IRWIN, J. C. *Shawls, a study in Indo-European influences*, Victoria and Albert Museum Monograph, 1955
433. IRWIN, J. and HALL, M. *Indian painted and printed fabrics*, Ahmadabad, 1972
434. JACKSON, E. N. *Ancestors in silhouette*, London and New York, 1921
435. — *A history of hand-made lace*, 1900
436. — *Silhouette, notes and dictionary*, 1938
437. JACOBY, H. *How to know Oriental carpets and rugs*, 1962
438. JAHANGIR, EMPEROR. *The Tuzuk-I-Jahangir, Memoirs of Jahangir*, Delhi, 1968
439. JAHSS, M. and B. *Inro and other miniature forms of Japanese lacquer art*, 1972
440. JAQUET, E. and CHAPUIS, A. *Technique and history of the Swiss watch*, London and New York, 1970 (1953)
441. JARRY, M. *The carpets of Aubusson*, Leigh-on-Sea, 1969
442. — *The carpets of the Manufacture de la Savonnerie*, Leigh-on-Sea, 1966
443. — *La Tapisserie des origines à nos jours*, Paris, 1968
444. JENKINS, N. *Photo graphics*, London and New York, 1973
445. JENYNS, R. S. *Chinese art: the minor arts*, vol. II, 1965
446. — *Japanese porcelain*, 1965
447. — *Japanese pottery*, 1971
448. — *Later Chinese porcelain*, 1971 (1951)
449. — *Ming pottery and porcelain*, 1953
450. JETTMAR, K. *Art of the Steppes*, 1967
451. JOBÉ, J. (ed.). *The art of tapestry*, 1965
452. JOHNSON, A. F. 'Geofroy Tory', *The Fleuron*, vi, 1928

453. JOHNSON, A. F. *Type designers*, 1959 (1934)

454. JONES, E. A. *Old silver of Europe and America*, 1928

455. JONES, E. INGLIS-. *Peacocks in Paradise*, Shoreham-by-Sea, 1971 (London, 1950)

456. JONES, M. E. *British samplers*, Oxford, 1948

457. — *A history of western embroidery*, 1969

458. JORDAN, E. VON BASSERMAN-. *The book of old clocks and watches*, 1964

459. JOURDAIN, M. *The work of William Kent*, 1948

460. — and JENYNS, R. S. *Chinese export art in the eighteenth century*, Feltham, 1967 (London, 1950)

461. JOY, E. T. *The Country Life book of chairs*, 1967

462. — *The Country Life book of English furniture*, 1968

463. JUGAKU, B. *Paper-making by hand in Japan*, Tokyo, 1959

464. KAEMMERER, E. A. *Trades and crafts of old Japan*, Rutland, Vt., and Tokyo, 1961

465. KÄMPFER, F. and BEYER, K. G. *Glass. A world history*, London and New York, 1966

466. KAYSER, H. *Ägyptisches Kunsthandwerk*, Brunswick, 1969

467. KAYSER, W. *Das Groteske, seine Gestaltung in Malerei und Dichtung*, Oldenburg, 1957

468. KEIM, J. and KLUMBACH, H. *Der römische Schatzfund von Straubing*, Munich, 1951

469. KELLY, F. and SCHWABER, R. *A short history of costume and armour*, vol. i, *1066–1485*, 1968 (1931)

470. KENDRICK, A. F. *English needlework*, 1933

471. — and TATERSALL, C. E. C. *Hand-woven carpets, Oriental and European*, 1922

472. KENT, W. W. *Hooked rug*, New York, 1930

473. KENYON, G. H. *The glass industry of the world*, Leicester, 1967

474. KERFOOT, J. B. *American pewter*, Boston and New York, 1924, reprinted 1942

475. KERTÉZ, A. *Sixty years of photography*, London and New York, 1972

476. KEYNES, SIR G. L. *William Pickering, publisher. A memoir and a hand-list of his editions*, 1969 (1924)

477. KIMBALL, F. and DONNELL, E. 'The creators of the Chippendale style', *Metropolitan Museum of Art Studies*, vols. I and II, 1928–9 and 1929–30, New York

478. KING, D. *Samplers*, Victoria and Albert Museum, 1960

479. KINMOND, J. (ed.). *Anchor book of European embroidery*, Boston and London, 1964

480. KIPPENBERGER, A. *Die deutschen Meister des Eisengusses*, Marburg, 1931

481. KLEIN, A. E. *Child life in Greek art*, Oxford and New York, 1932

482. KNITTLE, R. M. *Early American glass*, London and New York, 1927

483. KOCH, R. *Louis C. Tiffany, rebel in glass*, New York, 1964

484. KOOILMAN, S. *Ornamented bark-cloth in Indonesia*, Leiden, 1963

485. KORNITZER, L. *Pearls and men*, 1935

486. KRAMISCH, S. *The art of India*, 1965 (1954)

487. KRIEGER, H. W. 'Design areas in Oceania', *Bulletin of U.S. Natural History Museum, Washington*, vol. 79, article 30, 1932

488. KUBLER, G. *The art and architecture of ancient America*, 1962

489. KÜHN, F. *Wrought iron*, 1965

490. KYBULOVÁ, L. and DARBOIS, D. *Carpets of the orient*, London and New York, 1969

491. LACROCQ, L. 'Chronique des tapisseries d'Aubusson et de Felletin', *Bulletin de la Société archéologique et historique du Limousin*, 1911–26

492. LANE, A. *Early Islamic pottery*, 1947

493. — *Greek pottery*, 1971 (1948)

494. — *Later Islamic pottery*, 1971 (1957)

495. — *Style in pottery*, 1948

496. LANG, D. M. *The Georgians*, 1966

497. LANGDON, J. E. *Canadian silversmiths, 1700–1900*, Toronto, 1966

498. LARSEN, S. and KYSTER, A. (eds.). *Danish 18th century bindings, 1730–1780*, Copenhagen and London, 1930

499. LARSON, K. *Rugs and carpets of the orient*, 1966

500. LAUDE, J. *The arts of black Africa*, California, 1971

501. LAUFER, B. *Paper and print in old China*, Chicago, 1931

502. LAUGHLIN, L. I. *Pewter in America. Its makers and their marks*, Boston, 1940

503. LAURIE, A. P. *Greek and Roman methods of painting*, Cambridge, 1910

504. LAVER, J. *Fashion and fashion plates 1800–1900*, London and New York, 1943

505. LE BÉ, G. *Sixteenth-century French type-founders: the Le Bé memorandum*, ed. H. Carter, Paris, 1967

506. LEACH, B. *A potter's book*, 1945 (1940)

507. LECOQ, R. *Les Bamiléké*, Paris, 1953

508. LE CORBEILLER, C. *European and American snuff boxes, 1730–1830*, 1966

509. LEDOUX-LEBARD, D. *Les Ébénistes parisiens, 1795–1830*, Paris, 1951

510. LEE, R. W. *A history of valentines*, 1953

511. — *Nineteenth-century art glass*, New York, 1952

512. — *Sandwich glass*, Northborough, Mass., 1947

513. — *Victorian glass*, Northborough, Mass., 1944

514. LEER CARRICK, A. VAN. *Shades of our ancestors: American profiles and profilists*, Boston, 1928

515. LEFUEL, H. *François-Honoré Jacob-Desmalter, ébéniste de Napoléon Ier et de Louis XVIII*, Paris, 1925

516. — *Georges Jacob, ébéniste du XVIIIe siècle*, Paris, 1923

517. LEHMANN-HAUPT, H. and others. *The book in America*, New York, 1951

518. LENK, T. R. *The flintlock*, 1965

519. LENZ, G. *Berliner Porzellan*, Berlin, 1913
520. LESPINASSE, R. DE. *Métiers et Corporations de la ville de Paris*, Paris, 1879
521. LETHABY, W. R. and others. *Ernest Gimson*, Stratford-on-Avon, 1924
522. LEUZINGER, E. *The arts of black Africa*, 1972
523. LEVAN BAKER, W. S. *The silk pictures of Thomas Stevens*, New York, 1957
524. LEWIS, C. FRANCIS-. *The art and craft of leatherwork*, 1928
525. LEWIS, J. *Anatomy of printing*, 1970
526. — *The twentieth century book*, London and New York, 1967
527. LEWIS, M. D. S. *Antique paste jewellery*, 1970
528. LIDDELL, D. M. *Chessmen*, 1938
529. LINCOLN, W. A. *The art and practice of marquetry*, 1971
530. LINDSAY, J. S. *An anatomy of English wrought iron*, 1964
531. LING, SHUN-SHENG. 'Decorative prints on bark cloth and the invention of printing', *Bulletin of the Institute of Ethnology, Academia Sinica, Republic of China*, no. 14, 1962
532. LISTER, R. *Decorative wrought iron work in Great Britain*, 1957
533. LISTER, R. G. *Silhouettes*, 1953
534. LIVERSIDGE, J. *Furniture in Roman Britain*, 1955
535. LLOYD, H. A. *The collector's dictionary of clocks*, 1964
536. LOCKWOOD, A. *Diagrams, a visual survey of graphs, maps, charts and diagrams*, 1969
537. LORING, R. B. *Decorated book papers*, Cambridge, Mass., 1952 (1942)
538. — *Marbled papers, an address delivered before the members of the Odd Volumes*, Boston, Mass., 1933
539. LOTHROP, S. K. and others. *Essays in pre-Columbian art and archaeology*, Cambridge, Mass., 1961
540. LOUBIER, H. *Der Bucheinband*, Leipzig, 1926
541. LOUDER, SIR T. D. (ed.). *Sir Uvedale Price on the picturesque*, Edinburgh, 1842
542. LOUDON, J. C. (ed.). *The landscape gardening and landscape architecture of the late H. Repton*, 1840
543. LOW-BEER, F. 'Chinese lacquer of the early 15th century' and 'Chinese lacquer of the middle and late Ming period', *Bulletin of the Museum of Far Eastern Antiquities, Stockholm*, nos. 22 and 24, 1950 and 1952
544. LUCAS, A. *Ancient Egyptian materials and techniques*, 1962 (1926)
545. LUDDINGTON, J. *Antique silver*, 1971
546. LUKOMSKII, G. M. *L'Art décoratif russe*, Paris, 1928
547. MCCAUSLAND, H. *Snuff and snuff-boxes*, 1951
548. MCCLINTOCK, I. and M. *Toys in America*, Washington, 1961
549. MCGRATH, R. and FROST, A. C. *Glass in architecture and decoration*, 1937
550. MCINTYRE, J. and RICHMOND, I. A. 'Tents of the Roman army and leather from Birdoswald', *Cumberland and Westmorland Antiquarian and Archaeological Society*, xxxiv (N.S.), 1934
551. MACKAIL, J. W. *The life of William Morris*, 1950 (1899)
552. MACKAY, J. A. *Commemorative medals*, 1970
553. — *Greek and Roman coins*, 1971
554. MCKEARIN, G. S. and H. *American glass*, New York, 1941
555. — — *Two hundred years of American blown glass*, New York, 1950
556. MCKERROW, R. B. *Printers' and publishers' devices in England and Scotland, 1485–1640*, 1913
557. MACKETT-BEESON, A. E. J. *Chessmen*, 1968
558. MACLAGAN, SIR E. R. D. *The Bayeux tapestry*, 1949 (1943)
559. MCLAUGHLIN, T. *The gilded lily*, 1972
560. MCLEAN, R. *Asymmetrical typography*, 1967
561. — *Modern book design*, 1958
562. — *Victorian book design and colour printing*, 1972 (1963)
563. MCMURTRIE, D. C. *The book*, London and New York, 1960 (1943)
564. MADSEN, S. T. *Art nouveau*, 1967
565. MAIRET, E. M. *Vegetable dyes*, 1938 (1916)
566. MALINS, E. *English landscaping and literature, 1660–1840*, 1966
567. MANN, S. *Collecting playing cards*, 1966
568. MANWARING, E. W. *Italian landscape in eighteenth century England*, New York and London, 1925
569. MARIACHER, G. *Italian blown glass*, 1961
570. MARILLIER, H. C. *English tapestries of the 18th century*, 1930
571. MARSHALL-JOHNSON, A. *Hispanic silverwork*, New York, 1944
572. MARYON, H. *Metalwork and enamelling*, London and New York, 1971 (1912)
573. MASATAKA, OGAWA. *Enduring crafts of Japan*, New York, 1968
574. MASON, J. A. *The ancient civilisations of Peru*, 1957
575. MASSÉ, H. J. L. J. *Chats on old pewter*, 1949
576. — *The pewter collector*, revised by R. F. Michaelis, 1971 (1921)
577. — *Pewter plate*, 1904
578. MASSON, V. M. and SARIANIDI, V. I. *Central Asia, Turkmenia before the Achaemenids*, 1972
579. MATSON, F. R. (ed.). *Ceramics and man*, Chicago, 1965, London, 1966
580. MATTINGLEY, H. *Roman coins*, 1960 (1928)
581. MAY, F. L. *Hispanic lace and lace making*, New York, 1939
582. MAY, L. M. *A master of silhouette, J. Miers*, 1938
583. MAYNE, A. *British profile miniaturists*, 1970
584. MAYOUX, J. J. *Richard Payne Knight et le pittoresque*, Paris, 1933

585. MEADMORE, C. *Modern chairs*, 1973
586. MEDLEY, M. *A handbook of Chinese art*, 1973 (1964)
587. MÉGROZ, R. L. *Profile art through the ages*, 1948
588. MENZEL, B. *Goldgewichte aus Ghana*, Berlin, 1968
589. MERCER, E. *Furniture 700–1700*, 1969
590. METROPOLITAN MUSEUM OF ART, NEW YORK. *Chess: East and West, past and present, a selection from the G. A. Pfeiffer collection* (Exhibition catalogue), New York, 1968
591. MEW, E. *Battersea enamels*, 1926
592. MICHAELIS, R. F. *Antique pewter of the British Isles*, 1955
593. — *British pewter*, 1969
594. MICHON, L.-M.-E.-J. *La Reliure française*, Paris, 1951
595. MIDDLETON, B. C. *A history of English craft bookbinding technique*, New York and London, 1963
596. MIHALIK, S. *Old Hungarian enamels*, Budapest, 1961
597. MINNICH, H. B. *Japanese costume*, Tokyo, 1963
598. MINTER, D. P. *Modern needlecraft*, 1932
599. MITFORD, R. L. S. BRUCE-. *The Sutton Hoo ship-burial* (British Museum Publication), 1972 (1947)
600. MOHOLY-NAGY, L. *Painting, photography, film*, London and Cambridge, Mass., 1969
601. MONKHOUSE, F. J. and WILKINSON, H. R. *Maps and diagrams*, 1971 (1952)
602. MOODY, E. *Modern furniture*, 1966
603. MORAN, J. *Stanley Morison, his typographic achievement*, 1971
604. MORISON, S. *On type designs past and present*, 1962 (1926)
605. — *Four centuries of fine printing*, 1949
606. — *Politics and script*, ed. N. Barker, 1972
607. MORRIS, B. J. *Victorian embroidery*, 1962
608. MORRIS, E. *The history and art of change ringing*, 1931
609. MORTON, P. *Contemporary jewelry*, London and New York, 1970
610. MOSLEY, J. 'The early career of William Caslon', *Journal of the Printing Historical Society*, no. iii, 1967
611. MUKDEN, MANCHUKUO NATIONAL MUSEUM. *Tapestries and embroideries of the Sung, Yüan, Ming and Chʻing dynasties*, Mukden, 1935
612. MUKHARJI, T. N. *Art-manufactures of India, specially compiled for the Glasgow International Exhibition*, Calcutta, 1888
613. MÜNSTERBERG, O. *Japanische Kunstgeschichte*, Brunswick, 1904–7
614. MURRAY, H. J. R. *A history of board games other than chess*, Oxford, 1952
615. — *A history of chess*, Oxford, 1962 (1913)
616. MURRAY, P. *Toys*, 1968
617. MUSGRAVE, C. *Adam and Hepplewhite and other neo-classical furniture*, 1966
618. MUSGRAVE, C. *Regency furniture, 1800 to 1830*, 1970 (1961)
619. NARBETH, C. *An introduction to coins and medals*, 1970
620. NARITA, KIYOFUSA. *Patterned paper, obōshō, and watermarked paper*, Tokyo, 1961
621. NAYLOR, G. *The Arts and Crafts Movement*, 1971
622. NEAL, W. K. and BACK, D. H. L. *The Mantons: gunmakers*, 1967
623. NEUBERG, F. *Ancient glass*, 1962
624. NEUBURGER, A. *The technical arts and sciences of the ancients*, 1930
625. NEW OXFORD HISTORY OF MUSIC, THE, 1957
626. NEWDIGATE, B. H. *The art of the book*, London and New York, 1938
627. NEWHALL, B. *The history of photography, from 1839 to the present day*, Museum of Modern Art, New York, 1964
628. NEWTON, N. T. *Design on the land, the development of landscape architecture*, Cambridge, Mass., and London, 1971
629. NIXON, H. M. *Broxbourne Library. Styles and designs of book-bindings*, 1956
630. NOBLE, J. *Dolls*, 1967
631. NOBLE, J. V. *The techniques of painted Attic pottery*, New York and London, 1966
632. NOMACHI, K. *Japanese textiles*, Leigh-on-Sea, 1958
633. NORDENSKIÖLD, N. E. H. *Comparative ethnographical studies, no. 3: The ethnography of South-America seen from Mojos in Bolivia*, Göteborg, 1924
634. NORMAN, A. V. B. *Arms and armour*, 1964
635. NOTT, S. C. *Chinese jade throughout the ages*, Rutland, Vt., and Tokyo, 1962
636. OAKESHOTT, R. E. *The archaeology of weapons*, 1960
637. OKADA, Y. *Japanese handicrafts*, Tokyo, 1956
638. OLIVER, P. (ed.). *Shelter in Africa*, 1971
639. OMAN, C. C. *Catalogue of wall-papers*, Victoria and Albert Museum, 1929
640. — *Caroline silver*, 1970
641. — *English domestic silver*, 1959 (1934)
642. — *English silversmiths' work, civil and domestic*, Victoria and Albert Museum, 1965
643. — *The golden age of Hispanic silver 1400–1665*, Victoria and Albert Museum, 1968
644. ORD-HUME, A. W. J. G. *Collecting musical boxes, and how to repair them*, 1967
645. ORMSBEE, T. H. *Early American furniture makers*, New York, 1930
646. — *The windsor chair*, New York, 1962
647. ORTMANN, E. *Tin soldier, tin sailor, the history of the tin figure*, London and New York, 1973
648. OVERBECK, J. A. *Pompeji*, Leipzig, 1884 (1856)
649. OVSYANIKOV, Y. *Russian folk arts and crafts*, Moscow, 1972

650. PAGÉ, C. *La Coutellerie depuis l'origine jusqu'à nos jours*, Châtellerault, 1896
651. PALLISER, B. *History of lace*, 1900
652. PALMER, J. P. *Jade*, 1967
653. PARRY, A. *Tattoo*, New York, 1933
654. PARTINGTON, J. R. *Origins and development of applied chemistry*, 1935
655. PAYNE, B. *History of costume*, New York, 1965
656. PEARSON, J. M. and D. T. *American cut glass for the discriminating collector*, New York, 1965
657. PENKALA, M. *European pottery*, Rutland, Vt., and Tokyo, 1968
658. PENZER, N. M. *Book of the wine-label*, 1947
659. — *Paul Storr*, 1971 (1954)
660. PERRY, J. *The paper industry*, New York and Toronto, 1946
661. PETERSON, H. L. (ed.). *Encyclopaedia of firearms*, 1964
662. PEVSNER, SIR N. B. L. *Pioneers of modern design*, 1960 (1936)
663. — 'Richard Payne Knight', *The Art Bulletin, U.S.A.*, vol. xxxi, no. 4, 1949
664. — *Studies in art, architecture and design*, vol. 2, *Victorian and after*, 1968
665. PHILLIPS, E. D. *The royal hordes*, 1965
666. PHILLIPS, J. M. *American silver*, New York, 1959
667. PHILLIPS, P. A. S. *John Obrisset*, 1931
668. — *Paul de Lamerie*, 1935
669. PLANCHÉ, J. R. *A cyclopaedia of costume or dictionary of dress*, 1876
670. POHL, H. *Gold*, Stuttgart, 1958
671. POLAK, A. B. *Modern glass*, 1962
672. POPE, A. U. *A survey of Persian art*, 1965 (1938–9)
673. POPE, J. A. *Chinese porcelains from the Ardebil shrine*, Washington, 1956
674. PORTALIS, R. and BÉRALDI, H. *Les Graveurs du XVIIIe siècle*, Paris, 1880–2
675. PORTEOUS, J. *Coins*, 1964
676. POWELL, T. G. E. *The Celts*, 1958
677. POWYS, M. *Lace and lace-making*, Boston, Mass., 1953
678. PRIEST, A. and SIMMONS, P. *Chinese textiles, occasioned by the exhibition of Chinese court robes*, Metropolitan Museum of Art, New York, 1931
679. PROCTOR, R. G. C. *The printing of Greek in the fifteenth century* (Bibliographical Society illustrated monographs), Oxford, 1900
680. RABECQ-MAILLARD, M.-M. *Histoire du jouet*, Paris, 1962
681. RACINET, A. *Le Costume historique*, 6 vols., 1876–88
682. RACKHAM, B. *Italian maiolica*, 1963
683. RAINWATER, D. *American silver manufacturers*, Hanover, Penn., 1966
684. RANSOM, C. L. *Studies in ancient furniture. Couches and beds of the Greeks, Etruscans and Romans*, Chicago, 1905
685. RAWSON, P. *Ceramics*, 1971
686. READE, B. E. *Regency antiques*, 1953
687. REECE, R. *Roman coins*, 1970
688. REED, T. B. *A history of the old English letter foundries*, A. F. Johnson (ed.), 1952 (1887)
689. REICHWEIN, A. *China and Europe*, 1968 (1925)
690. REIKICHI, UEDA. *The netsuke handbook, adapted from the Japanese by Raymond Bushell*, Tokyo and Rutland, Vt., 1961
691. REINFELD, F. *A catalogue of European coins*, 1961
692. RENOUARD, A.-A. *Annales de l'imprimerie des Alde*, Paris, 1834 (1803)
693. REVI, A. C. *American art nouveau glass*, Camden, N.J., 1968
694. — *American cut and engraved glass*, Camden, N.J., 1965
695. — *Nineteenth century glass; its genesis and development*, Camden, N.J., 1959
696. REY, J. *Études pour servir à l'histoire des châles*, Paris, 1823
697. RICE, D. TALBOT. *The art of Byzantium*, 1959
698. — *Art of the Byzantine era*, 1963
699. — *Byzantine art*, 1968 (1935)
700. RICE, T. TALBOT. *Ancient arts of Central Asia*, 1965
701. — *A concise history of Russian art*, 1963
702. — *The Scythians*, 1957
703. RICHTER, G. M. A. *The furniture of the Greeks, Etruscans and Romans*, 1966
704. RIEGGER, H. *Raku: art and technique*, London and New York, 1970
705. RIES, E. H. *American rugs*, New York, 1950
706. RINHART, F. and M. *American miniature case art*, South Brunswick, New York and London, 1969
707. RISLEY, C. *Creative embroidery*, London and New York, 1969
708. — *Machine embroidery*, 1973
709. RITCHIE, C. I. A. *Carving shells and cameos*, London, 1970, South Brunswick and New York, 1971
710. — *Modern ivory carving*, Cranbury, N.J., 1972
711. — *Scrimshaw*, New York and London, 1972
712. — *Soft stone carving*, 1971
713. ROBINSON, B. W. *Arms and armour of old Japan*, Victoria and Albert Museum, 1951
714. — *The arts of the Japanese sword*, 1970 (1961)
715. ROBINSON, H. R. *Oriental armour*, 1967
716. ROBINSON, S. *A history of dyed textiles*, 1969
717. ROBIQUET, J. *Gouthière*, Paris, 1912
718. ROCHE, S. *Mirrors*, 1957
719. ROEBUCK, C. (ed.). *The muses at work: arts, crafts and professions in ancient Greece and Rome*, 1969
720. RONDOT, N. *Bernard Salomon*, Lyon, 1897
721. ROOT, W. C. 'Metallurgy' in *Handbook of South American Indians*, vol. 5, Smithsonian Institution, Bureau of American Ethnology, *Bulletin* 143, 1949

722. ROSENBERG, M. *Jamnitzer*, Frankfurt, 1920
723. ROSS, C. M. and POST, M. M. *The art of Karl Fabergé and his contemporaries*, Norman, U.S.A., 1965
724. —— *Russian porcelains*, Norman, U.S.A., 1968
725. ROSTOVZEFF, M. I. *Iranians and Greeks in South Russia*, Oxford, 1922
726. ROTH, H. L. *The natives of Sarawak and British North Borneo*, vol. II, 1896
727. ROWAN, A. 'Downton Castle, Herefordshire' in *The country seat*, H. C. Colvin and J. Harris (eds.), 1970
728. ROWE, R. *Adam silver, 1765–1795*, 1965
729. RUDENKO, S. I. *Frozen tombs of Siberia, the Pazyric burials of Iron Age horsemen*, Berkeley, Calif., and London, 1970
730. RUFFLE, J. *Introduction to Egyptian archaeology*, 1974
731. RUPPEL, A. L. *Johannes Gutenberg*, Niewkoop, 1967 (Berlin, 1939)
732. RURAL INDUSTRIES BUREAU. *Wrought ironwork. A manual of instruction for rural craftsmen*, 1963 (1953)
733. RUSH, J. The ingenious Beilbys, 1973
734. RUSSELL, SIR G. *Designer's trade*, 1968
735. RYERSON, E. *The netsuke of Japan*, London and New York, 1968
736. SACHS, C. *The history of musical instruments*, New York, 1940, London, 1942
737. SAH, O. *The book of necklaces*, 1953
738. SALVERTE, F. DE. *Les Ébénistes du XVIIIe siècle*, Paris, 1934 (1923)
739. SARRE, F. P. T. and TRENKWALD, H. *Old Oriental carpets*, 1926
740. SAVAGE, G. *Porcelain through the ages*, 1969 (1954)
741. — *Glass*, 1965
742. SAWYER, A. R. *Mastercraftsmen of ancient Peru*, New York, 1968
743. SCHAEFER, H. *The roots of modern design*, 1970
744. SCHARF, A. *Creative photography*, New York and London, 1965
745. SCHEDELMANN, H. *Die grossen Büchsenmacher. Leben, Werke, Marken. Vom 15. bis 19. Jahrhundert*, Brunswick, 1972
746. SCHEIDIG, W. *Crafts of the Weimar Bauhaus*, 1907
747. SCHMIDT, R. *Das Glas*. Handbücher der Königlichen Museen zu Berlin, 1912
748. SCHMUTZLER, R. *Art nouveau*, 1964
749. SCHNEIDER, H. *Zinn*, Freiburg i.B., 1970
750. SCHNETTE, M. and MÜLLER-CHRISTENSEN, S. *The art of embroidery*, 1964
751. SCHUBRING, P. *Cassoni*, Leipzig, 1923 (1915)
752. SCHÜDDEKOPF, C. VON. 'Johann Friedrich Anthing' in *Collection de cent silhouettes*, Gesellschaft der Bibliophilen, Weimar, 1913
753. SCHULER, F. W. and L. *Glass forming*, 1971
754. SCHUNKE, I. *Leben und Werk Jacob Krauses*, Leipzig, 1943
755. SCHÜRMANN, U. *Caucasian rugs*, Brunswick, 1967
756. SCOTT, C. M. and G. R. *Antique porcelain digest*, 1961
757. SEGERSTAD, U. H. *Modern Scandinavian furniture*, 1963
758. SEITZ, H. *Blankwaffen*, 2 vols., Brunswick, 1965–8
759. SELTMAN, C. *Masterpieces of Greek coinage*, Oxford, 1949
760. SENTER, A. C. *Baroque and rococo art*, 1972
761. SERVEN, J. E. *Colt firearms 1836–1954*, Santa Ana, Calif., 1954
762. SEVENSMA, W. S. *Tapestries*, 1965
763. SHEPPARD, A. O. 'Rio Grande glaze-paint pottery' in *Ceramics and Man*, F. Matson (ed.), Chicago, 1965, London, 1966
764. SHEPPARD, L. A. 'A new light on Caxton and Colard Mansion', in *Signature*, N.S. XV (1952)
765. SHORT, G. J. HOLLISTER-. *Discovering wrought iron*, Tring, 1970
766. SIEBER, R. *African textiles and decorative arts*, New York, 1972
767. SIMMONS, P. *Chinese patterned silks*, Metropolitan Museum of Art, New York, 1948
768. — 'Some recent developments in Chinese textile studies', *Bulletin of the Museum of Far Eastern Antiquities, Stockholm*, vol. 28, 1956
769. SINGER, C., HOLMVALD, E. J., HALL, A. R., WILLIAMS, T. I. (eds.). *A history of technology*, vol. I, Oxford, 1954
770. — *A history of technology*, vol. II, Oxford, 1956
771. — *A history of technology*, vol. III, Oxford, 1957
772. — *A history of technology*, vol. V, Oxford, 1958
773. SITWELL, SIR S. *Theatrical figures in porcelain*, 1949
774. SKERTCHLY, S. B. J. *On the manufacture of gun flints*, Memoirs of the Geological Survey of the United Kingdom, 1879
775. SMITH, C. H. GIBBS-. *The fashionable lady in the 19th century*, Victoria and Albert Museum, 1960
776. SMITH, G. F. HERBERT. *Gemstones*, 1962 (1912)
777. SNODGRASS, A. M. *Arms and armour of the Greeks*, 1967
778. — *Early Greek armour and weapons*, Edinburgh, 1964
779. SNOOK, B. *The creative art of embroidery*, London and New York, 1972
780. SNOWMAN, A. K. *Eighteenth-century gold boxes of Europe*, 1966
781. SOUSBERGHE, L. DE. *L'Art Pende*, Brussels, 1959
782. SOUSTELLE, J. *Arts of ancient Mexico*, 1967
783. SPEAIGHT, G. *The history of the English toy theatre*, 1969
784. SPERISEN, F. J. *The art of the lapidary*, Milwaukee, 1953

785. SPRAKE, A. and DARBY, M. *Stevengraphs*, St. Peter Port, 1968
786. STAFF, F. W. *The penny post*, 1964
787. — *The picture postcard and its origins*, 1966
788. — *The valentine and its origins*, 1969
789. STAFFORD, C. L. and BISHOP, R. *America's quilts and coverlets*, London and New York, 1973
790. STALKER, J. and PARKER, G. *A treatise on japanning and varnishing*, 1688 (reprinted with introduction by Molesworth, H. D., 1960)
791. STENTON, SIR F. (ed.). *The Bayeux tapestry*, 1965 (1957)
792. STEVENS, R. T. *The art of paper-making in Japan*, New York, 1909
793. STEVENSON, R. L. 'A penny plain and twopence coloured', *Magazine of Art*, vol. VII, 1884
794. STEWART, A. M. *The history and romance of the Paisley shawl*, Paisley, 1946
795. STÖCKLEIN, H. *Meister des Eisenschnittes*, Esslingen, 1922
796. STONE, G. C. *A glossary of the construction, decoration and use of arms and armor*, Portland, Maine, 1934
797. STOPFORD, F. *The romance of the jewel*, 1920
798. STRANGE, E. F. *Catalogue of Japanese lacquer in the Victoria and Albert Museum*, 1924
799. — *Catalogue of Chinese lacquer in the Victoria and Albert Museum*, 1925
800. — *Chinese lacquer*, 1926
801. STRONG, D. E. *Catalogue of the carved amber in the department of Greek and Roman antiquities*, British Museum, 1966
802. — *Greek and Roman gold and silver plate*, 1966
803. STRONG, J. H. *Foundations of fabric structure*, 1953 (1946)
804. STROUD, D. *Capability Brown*, 1957 (1950)
805. — *Humphry Repton*, 1962
806. STUART, C. M. VILLIERS-. *Gardens of the great Mughals*, 1913
807. SUGDEN, A. V. and EDMONDSON, J. L. *A history of English wall-paper*, 1925
808. SULIMIRSKI, T. *Prehistoric Russia, an outline*, 1970
809. — *The Sarmatians*, 1970
810. SULLIVAN, M. *Chinese ceramics, bronzes and jades in the collection of Sir Alan and Lady Barlow*, 1963
811. SUMMERSON, SIR J. N. *John Nash*, 1949 (1935)
812. SUNG YING-HSING. *T'ien-kung k'ai-wu, Chinese technology in the seventeenth century*, Pennsylvania, 1966
813. SUTHERLAND, C. H. V. *Gold. Its beauty, power and allure*, 1959
814. SYLWAN, V. 'Silk from the Yin dynasty', *Bulletin of the Museum of Far Eastern Antiquities, Stockholm*, no. ix, 1937
815. SYMONDS, R. W. (ed.). *Chippendale furniture designs*, 1948
816. — and WHINERAY, B. B. *Victorian furniture*, 1962
817. TALLIS, D. *Musical boxes*, 1972
818. TARASSAK, L. *Antique European and American firearms at the Hermitage Museum*, Leningrad, 1972
819. TAYLOR, A. *Discovering model soldiers*, Tring, 1970
820. TAYLOR, G. *Continental gold and silver*, 1967
821. — *Silver*, 1963 (1956)
822. TESCIONI, G. *Il corallo nella storia e nell'arte*, Naples, 1965
823. THACHER, A. B. *Turkoman rugs*, New York, 1940
824. THOMAS, B. 'Die Münchner Harnischvorzeichnungen etc.', *Jahrbuch der kunsthistorischen Sammlungen in Wien*, nos. 55, 56, 58, 61; 1959, 1960, 1962, 1965
825. — and GAMBER, O. 'L'arte milanese dell'armatura', *Storia di Milano*, XI, Milan, 1958
826. THOMAS, M. *Mary Thomas's dictionary of embroidery stitches*, London, 1934, New York, 1935
827. THOMPSON, E. P. *William Morris, romantic to revolutionary*, 1955
828. THOMSON, W. G. *A history of tapestry*, 1930
829. — *Tapestry weaving in England*, 1915
830. THORPE, W. A. *English glass*, 1935
831. TILLEY, R. *A history of playing cards*, London and New York, 1973
832. — *Playing cards*, 1967
833. TINDALE, T. K. and H. R. *Handmade papers of Japan*, Rutland, Vt., and Tokyo, 1952
834. TISCHER, F. *Böhmischer Zinn*, Leipzig, 1928
835. TOKYO NATIONAL MUSEUM. *Pageant of Japanese art*, vol. v, *Lacquer art and Japanning*, Tokyo, 1954
836. TOLLER, J. *Prisoners-of-war work, 1756–1815*, Cambridge, 1965
837. TOOLEY, R. V. *Maps and map-makers*, 1970 (1949)
838. TOWER OF LONDON. *Catalogue of exhibition of armour made in the Royal Workshops at Greenwich*, 1951
839. TOYNBEE, J. M. C. *Art in Britain under the Romans*, Oxford, 1964
840. TREVER, K. V. *Excavations in northern Mongolia 1924/5*, Leningrad, 1932
841. TROWELL, K. M. *African design*, 1960
842. — and WACHSMANN, K. P. *Tribal crafts of Uganda*, 1953
843. TURNER, N. D. *American silver flatware 1837–1910*, New York, 1972
844. TWYMAN, M. *Lithography 1800–1850*, 1970
845. TYLECOTE, R. F. *Metallurgy in archaeology*, 1962
846. ULLMAN, B. L. *The origin and development of humanistic script*, Rome, 1960
847. ULLYETT, K. *In quest of clocks*, 1968 (1950)
848. UPDIKE, D. B. *Printing types, their history, forms and use*, 2 vols., Cambridge, Mass., and London, 1962

849. VASARI, G. *Vasari on technique*, trans. by L. S. Maclehose, 1907
850. VAUGHAN, A. J. *Modern bookbinding*, 1960 (1929)
851. VECELLI, C. *Costumes anciens et modernes*, 2 vols., Paris, 1859–63
852. VELDE, VAN DE. *Zum neuen Stil*, Munich, 1955
853. VERNEUIL, M. P. *Japanese textiles, woven and embroidered*, 1910
854. VERSTER, A. J. G. *Old European pewter*, 1958
855. VERVLIET, H. D. L. *The book through 5,000 years*, 1972
856. VETTER, R. M. and WACHA, G. *Linzer Zinngiesser*, Munich and Vienna, 1967
857. VEYRIN-FORRER, J. (ed.). *Campionari di caratteri nella tipografia del settecento*, Milan, 1963
858. VIALE FERRERO, M. *Tapestries*, 1969
859. VICTORIA AND ALBERT MUSEUM. *Catalogue of wall-papers*, 1942
860. — *English wrought-iron work*, 1950
861. — *European printed textiles*, 1949
862. — *Guide to the Japanese textiles and fabrics, Part II: Costume*, 1920
863. — *Notes on quilting*, 1960 (1932)
864. — *A short history of English furniture*, 1966
865. VOET, L. B. *The golden compasses, a history and evaluation of the printing and publishing activities at the Officina Plantiniana at Antwerp*, Amsterdam, London, New York, 1969
866. VOLBACH, F. *Early decorative textiles*, 1969
867. WALTERS, H. B. *Church bells of England*, 1912
868. WANSCHER, O. *The art of furniture*, 1968
869. WARD, F. A. B. *Timekeepers*, Science Museum, London, 1963
870. WARDLE, P. *Victorian lace*, 1968
871. WARNER, SIR F. *The silk industry of the United Kingdom*, 1921
872. WARREN, P. *Irish glass*, 1971
873. WATERER, J. W. 'Leather' in *A history of technology*, vol. II (see Bibliography 770)
874. — *Leather craftsmanship*, 1968
875. — *Leather in life, art and industry*, 1946
876. — *Spanish leather*, 1971
877. WATKINS, L. W. *Cambridge glass, 1818–1888, the story of the New England glass company*, Boston, 1930
878. WATKINSON, R. *William Morris as designer*, 1967
879. WATNEY, B. *English blue and white porcelain of the eighteenth century*, 1963
880. WATSON, F. J. B. *Louis XVI furniture*, 1960
881. WATSON, W. *An exhibition of archaeological finds of the People's Republic of China, 1973* (Catalogue of Royal Academy Exhibition)
882. WATT, A. *The art of leather manufacture*, 1906 (1885)
883. WAUGH, N. *The cut of women's clothes, 1600–1930*, 1968
884. WAUTERS, A. *Les Tapisseries bruxelloises*, Brussels, 1878
885. WEBB, G. *The cylinder musical box handbook*, 1968
886. WEBER, C. J. *A thousand and one fore-edge paintings*, Waterville, Maine, 1949
887. WEBSTER, G. *The Roman imperial army*, 1969
888. WEBSTER, M. D. *Quilts: their story and how to make them*, New York and London, 1916
889. WEBSTER, T. B. L. *Potter and patron in classical Athens*, 1972
890. WEIBEL, A. C. *Two thousand years of textiles*, New York, 1952
891. WEIGERT, R.-A. *La Tapisserie française*, Paris, 1956. London, 1962
892. WEINER, P. *Old pewter in Hungarian collections*, 1972
893. WEISS, G. *The book of glass*, 1971
894. — *The book of porcelain*, 1971
895. WELLS, J. M. *Book typography in the United States of America*, Chicago, 1966
896. WHEELER, C. T. *Development of embroidery in America*, New York, 1921
897. WHEELER, SIR R. E. M. *Early India and Pakistan*, 1968 (1959)
898. WHITE, G. *Antique toys and their background*, 1971
899. — *European and American dolls*, London and New York, 1966
900. WHITING, J. R. S. *Commemorative medals*, Newton Abbot, 1972
901. WHITTICK, J. A. *Symbols: signs and their meaning*, 1971 (1960)
902. WICHMANN, H. and S. *Schach, Ursprung und Wandlung der Spielfigur*, Munich, 1960, London and New York, 1964
903. WILBER, D. N. *Persian gardens and garden pavilions*, Rutland, Vt., 1962
904. WILCOX, R. T. *The dictionary of costume*, New York, 1970
905. — *The mode in footwear*, New York and London, 1948
906. — *The mode in hats and headdresses*, New York, 1946
907. WILD, J. P. *Textile manufacture in the northern Roman provinces*, Cambridge, 1970
908. WILKINSON, A. *Ancient Egyptian jewellery*, 1971
909. WILKINSON, C. K. *Iranian ceramics*. Catalogue of exhibition in Asia House, New York, 1963
910. WILKINSON, O. N. *Old glass*, 1968
911. WILKINSON, R. *The hallmarks of antique glass*, 1968
912. WILLEMS, A.-C.-J. *Les Elzevier, histoire et annales typographiques*, Brussels, 1880
913. WILLIAMSON, G. C. *The book of amber*, 1932
914. WILLS, G., pseud. (STAAL, C.). *The book of copper and brass*, 1968
915. — *English and Irish glass*, 1968
916. — *English looking-glasses*, 1965
917. — *Jade*, 1964

BIBLIOGRAPHY

918. WILSON, E. *A history of shoe fashions*, 1969

919. WILSON, H. *Silver work and jewellery*, 1966 (1912)

920. WILSON, J. L. and DU MONT, J. S. *Samuel Colt presents: a loan exhibition of presentation percussion Colt firearms*, Wadsworth Athenaeum exhibition catalogue, Hartford, Conn., 1961

921. WILSON, M. *Gems*, 1967

922. WILSON, T. *The Swastika*, Smithsonian Institution, Washington, 1896

923. WINGLER, H. M. (ed.). *The Bauhaus*, Cambridge, Mass., 1969

924. — (ed.). *Graphic work from the Bauhaus*, 1969

925. WIRGIN, J. *Sung ceramic designs*, Stockholm, 1970

926. WOODIWISS, J. C. *British silhouettes*, 1965

927. WORSHIPFUL COMPANY OF PEWTERERS, THE. *A short history of the worshipful company of pewterers and a catalogue of pewter ware in its possession*, 1968

928. WRIGHT, L. *Clockwork man*, 1968

929. WRIGHT, T. *The romance of the lace pillow*, Olney, 1919

930. WU, G. D. *Prehistoric pottery in China*, 1938

931. WULFF, H. E. *The traditional crafts of Persia*, Cambridge, Mass., 1966

932. WULHENAU, A. VON. *Pre-Columbian terracottas*, 1970

933. WYLER, S. B. *The book of old silver. English, American, foreign*, New York, 1937

934. WYLLIE, B. *Sheffield plate*, London and New York, 1935

935. YADIN, Y. *The art of warfare in biblical lands*, 1963

936. YAMADA, C. F. (ed.). *Decorative arts of Japan*, Tokyo and London, 1965

937. YAMANOBE, T. 'Textiles' (*Arts and crafts of Japan*, no. 2), Rutland, Vt., and Tokyo, 1957

938. ZARA, L. *Jade*, London and New York, 1969

939. — *Locks and keys*, New York, 1969

940. ZINELLI, U. and VERGERIO, G. *Decorative ironwork*, London and New York, 1966

CORRIGENDA

The bibliography for the article on Decorative Papers (pp. 601–3) is as follows:
141, 388, 424, 463, 464, 498, 501, 537, 538, 639, 792